"In American Samoa, where I live, South Pacific Handbook has scooped even the most inventive island travelers. The best guidebook this road junkie has seen anywhere."
—Robert Brock, THE COEVOLUTION QUARTERLY, Sausalito, California

"Stanley provides the reader with solid and up-to-date information on the geography, traditional and modern history, and contemporary trends of every part of the Pacific islands in which even the most avid travel buff is likely to find himself."
—Norman Douglas, PACIFIC ISLANDS MONTHLY, Fiji

"The book is worth reading for its historical perspective alone, for the author is unafraid to approach such 'delicate issues' as nuclear testing and 'culture clash'— topics one would not normally find in Fielding's or Birnbaum's."
—Georgia Lee, RAPA NUI JOURNAL, California

". . . the information source most often recommended by young budget travelers . . . the cheapest and most interesting means to visit over 500 South Sea islands . . . for the adventurous there are suggested mountain climbs, jungle walks, cave explorations, river trips, camping, bicycle routes, skin diving and snorkeling locations. Among the most valuable points are ideas on how to get around the islands on your own, from money-saving freighter travel to island transportation systems. The South Pacific Handbook by David Stanley is well worth the investment."
—Lucy Izon, TORONTO STAR

"Frankly, we at Pacific Magazine have to say we couldn't get along without this book as a principle reference source . . . travelers and adventurers going to the South Pacific will find this the only book they really need."
—Bud Bendix, PACIFIC MAGAZINE, Honolulu

"If you want to visit off-beat destinations and you only have a shoestring budget this softcover bible belongs in your backpack. The advice is specific and invaluable, the kind that takes the average traveler weeks to acquire."
—Ronn Ronck, STAR-BULLETIN & ADVERTISER, Honolulu

"This is not your usual travel guide . . . it is simply 'packed with information.' The compilers lace all the practical details (how to get there, where to stay, how much) with doses of well-reasoned opinion so that the book stands ahead of many travel guides in giving you a down-to-earth feeling for the places described."
—Phil Hanson, VANCOUVER SUN

P9-EDB-084

SOUTH PACIFIC HANDBOOK

DIANA LASICH HARPER

STORYTELLER

Hungry faces sit in a half moon,
listening to the storyteller
journeying the evening,
mixing laughter with fear.
Then the half moon gets smaller
and smaller,
until all the bodies touch, nesting
a pool of fear in childhood minds.
The storyteller exhausted
sleeps alone with a smile.

—MAKIUTI TONGIA,
COOK ISLANDS

SOUTH PACIFIC HANDBOOK

SEVENTH EDITION

DAVID STANLEY

MOON
TRAVEL
HANDBOOKS

SOUTH PACIFIC HANDBOOK
7TH EDITION

Published by
Avalon Travel Publishing
5855 Beaudry St.
Emeryville, California 94608, USA

Printed by
Colorcraft Ltd., Hong Kong

© Text, maps, illustrations, and photos copyright 2000
David Stanley. All rights reserved.

Some photographs and illustrations are used by permission
and are the property of the original copyright owners.

ISBN: 1-56691-172-9
ISSN: 1085-2700

Editor: Asha Johnson
Production & Design: Carey Wilson
Cartography: Allen Leech, Bob Race, Brian Bardwell, Chris Folks, Eric Green,
          Mark Stroud/Moon Street Cartography, Mike Morgenfeld
Index: Deana Shields

Front cover photo: Statues, Ahu A Kivi, the Seven Moai, Easter Island,
          © Jan Stromme/Picturesque, 2000.
          Background image courtesy of Tony Stone

Distributed in the United States and Canada by Publishers Group West

Printed in China

SUDSEE-HANDBUCH: A German translation of this book is published by Verlag Gisela E. Walther, Oppen-
heimerstrasse 26, D-28309 Bremen, Germany.

Please send all comments,
corrections, additions,
amendments, and critiques to:

**DAVID STANLEY
MOON TRAVEL HANDBOOKS
5855 BEAUDRY ST.
EMERYVILLE, CA 94608, USA
e-mail: travel@moon.com
www.moon.com**

Printing History
1st edition — 1979
7th edition — January 2000

All rights reserved. No part of this book may be translated or reproduced in any form, except brief extracts by a re-
viewer for the purposes of a review, without written permission of the copyright owner. In the case of photocopying
or other reprographic copying, a license can be obtained from CANCOPY (Canadian Copyright Licensing
Agency), One Yonge St., Suite 1900, Toronto, Ontario M5E 1E5, Canada (tel. 1-800/893-5777, fax 1-416/868-1621,
www.cancopy.com).

Although the publishers have made every effort to ensure the information was correct at the time of going to press,
the publishers do not assume and hereby disclaim any liability to any party for any loss or damage caused by errors, omissions, or any potential travel disruption due to labor or financial difficulty, whether such errors or omissions result from negligence, accident, or any other cause.

No subscription fees or payments in services have been received from any of the tourism operators included in
this book.

CONTENTS

INTRODUCTION

INTRODUCTION **25-73**
The Land 25
   Coral Reefs; Climate
Flora and Fauna 34
History 39
   The Era of Discovery and Settlement; European Contact and
   Exploration; Conversion, Colonialism, and War; Decolonization; The
   Pacific Today
Government 51
Economy 54
   Tourism
The People 61
   The Polynesians; The Melanesians; Religion; Language
Conduct and Customs 71

SPECIAL TOPICS
The Greenhouse Effect 29   *Museums of the Pacific* 65
The Law of the Sea 57   *The Pacific in Literature* 68-69

ON THE ROAD **74-126**
Highlights 74
Sports and Recreation 74
Entertainment 76
Holidays and Festivals 77
Arts and Crafts 78
Accommodations 79
Food and Drink 82
Getting There 84
   Air Services; Problems; By Boat; Organized Tours
Getting Around 104
   By Air; By Sea; By Sailing Yacht; Other Travel Options
Services and Information 109
   Visas and Officialdom; Money; Post and Telecommunications; Time;
   Weights and Measures; Media and Information
Health 116
What to Take 123
   Film and Photography

SPECIAL TOPICS
Ecotourism 80   *Philately* 112
Pioneers of Pacific Aviation 88

POLYNESIA

TAHITI-POLYNESIA 129-279

Introduction 129
The Land; History; Government; Economy; The People; Conduct and
Customs

On the Road 145
Accommodations and Food; Services and Information; Transportation

Tahiti 166
Papeete; Sights; Sports and Recreation; Mountain Climbing;
Accommodations; Food; Entertainment and Events; Shopping;
Services; Information; Health; Transportation; Around Tahiti;
Accommodations around Tahiti; Other Windward Islands

Moorea 196
Sights; Accommodations; Food; Entertainment; Services and
Information; Transportation

Huahine 211
Fare; Sights; Accommodations; Food and Entertainment; Services and
Information; Transportation; Maeva; Huahine-Iti

Raiatea 222
Uturoa; Practicalities; Transportation; Around Raiatea

Taha'a 230
Practicalities

Bora Bora 233
Sights; Accommodations; Food; Entertainment and Events; Shopping
and Services; Transportation

Maupiti 245
Other Leeward Islands 247
The Austral Islands 248
Rurutu; Tubuai; Other Austral Islands

The Tuamotu Islands 252
Rangiroa; Manihi; Other Islands and Atolls; The Nuclear Test Zone

The Gambier Islands 264
The Marquesas Islands 266
Nuku Hiva; Ua Pou; Ua Huka; Hiva Oa; Tahuata; Fatu Hiva; Other
Islands

SPECIAL TOPICS

Buying a Black Pearl 139   *Capsule Tahitian Vocabulary* 279
Paul Gauguin 166

PITCAIRN ISLANDS 280-288

Introduction 280
History; Pitcairn Today; Practicalities

The Pitcairn Islands 286
Norfolk Island

SPECIAL TOPIC

A Letter from John Adams 282

EASTER ISLAND. **289-303**
Introduction. 289
   History; Government; The People
On the Road 295
   Sights; Accommodations; Food and Entertainment; Other Practicalities;
   Transportation

COOK ISLANDS. **304-355**
Introduction. 304
   History and Government; Economy; The People
On the Road 312
   Services and Information; Transportation
Rarotonga. 318
   Sights; Accommodations; Food; Entertainment and Events; Shopping;
   Services and Information; Transportation
Aitutaki 337
   Accommodations; Food and Entertainment; Practicalities;
   Transportation
Atiu 344
   Sights; Practicalities
Mauke 348
Mangaia 350
Other Southern Islands 352
The Northern Group 353

NIUE **356-366**
Introduction. 356
On the Road 360
   Sights; Practicalities; Transportation

KINGDOM OF TONGA **367-429**
Introduction. 367
   History and Government; Economy; The People; Conduct and Customs
On the Road 378
   Highlights; Sports and Recreation; Public Holidays and Festivals; Arts
   and Crafts; Accommodations and Food; Services and Information;
   Transportation
Tongatapu 385
   Nuku'alofa; Sights; Accommodations; Food; Entertainment; Shopping;
   Services and Information; Transportation; Western Tongatapu;
   Southern Tongatapu; Eastern Tongatapu; Northeastern Tongatapu;
   Ha'amonga 'A Maui; Offshore Islands
'Eua Island 406
   Sights; Practicalities
The Ha'apai Group. 409
   Lifuka; Accommodations; Other Practicalities; Islands around Lifuka
The Vava'u Group 415
   Neiafu; Accommodations; Food; Entertainment; Services and
   Information; Transportation; South of Neiafu; West of Neiafu; Northeast
   of Neiafu; Offshore Islands

The Niuas 427
   Niuatoputapu; Tafahi Island; Niuafo'ou

SPECIAL TOPICS

The Tu'i Tongas 369   *Capsule Tongan Vocabulary* 429

AMERICAN SAMOA **430-456**
Introduction 430
On the Road 437
   Transportation
Tutuila 441
   Sights; Sports and Recreation; Accommodations; Food; Entertainment;
   Shopping; Services and Information; Getting Around
The Manu'a Group 454
   Ofu and Olosega; Ta'u; Coral Atolls

SAMOA **457-510**
Introduction 457
   History and Government; Economy; The People; Conduct and Customs
On the Road 468
   Accommodations and Food; Services and Information; Getting There;
   Airports
Upolu 475
   Apia and Environs; Accommodations; Food; Entertainment; Shopping;
   Services; Information; Health; Transportation
Around Upolu 494
   Sights and Recreation; Accommodations; Manono Island
Savai'i 501
   Sights and Recreation; Practicalities; Getting There; Getting Around

SPECIAL TOPIC

Capsule Samoan Vocabulary 510

TOKELAU **511-518**
Introduction 511
On the Road 515
The Tokelau Islands 517

SPECIAL TOPICS

The Riddle of the Joyita 513   *Tropical Cricket* 515

WALLIS AND FUTUNA **519-528**
Introduction 519
Wallis 522
   Sights; Practicalities; Transportation
Futuna and Alofi 527

TUVALU **529-544**
Introduction 529
On the Road 534
   Transportation

Funafuti 537
   Accommodations; Other Practicalities
Other Islands of Tuvalu 542
SPECIAL TOPICS
Capsule Tuvaluan Vocabulary 544

MELANESIA

FIJI ISLANDS **547-712**
Introduction 547
   History and Government; Economy
The People 564
   Language; Customs; Conduct
On the Road 571
   Highlights; Sports and Recreation; Entertainment; Public Holidays and
   Festivals; Arts and Crafts; Shopping; Accommodations; Food and Drink;
   Services and Information; Transportation; Airports
Nadi and the Mamanucas 590
   Nadi; South of Nadi; The Mamanuca Group
Southern Viti Levu 610
   Natadola and the Fijian; Sigatoka; Korotogo; Korolevu; Pacific Harbor;
   Navua and Vicinity; Offshore Islands
Suva and Vicinity 625
   Sights; Accommodations; Food; Entertainment and Events; Shopping;
   Services; Information; Health; Transportation; Nausori; Around Nausori
Northern Viti Levu 646
   Rakiraki; Nananu-I-Ra Island; Northwestern Viti Levu; Into the Interior
Lautoka and Vicinity 654
   Sights of Lautoka and Vicinity; Accommodations; Food; Entertainment;
   Other Practicalities
The Yasawa Islands 661
Kadavu 667
   Sights; Practicalities
The Lomaiviti Group 672
   Ovalau Island; Practicalities; Islands Off Ovalau; Other Islands of the
   Lomaiviti Group
Vanua Levu 682
   Labasa; Savusavu; Buca Bay
Taveuni 695
   Sights; Accommodations; Other Practicalities; Offshore Islands
The Lau Group 705
   Northern Lau; Southern Lau
Rotuma 709
SPECIAL TOPICS
Capsule Hindi Vocabulary 710   *Capsule Fijian Vocabulary* 711

NEW CALEDONIA **712-777**

Introduction. 712
History; Government; Economy; The People

On the Road 725
Transportation; Airports

Nouméa 731
Sights; Accommodations; Food; Entertainment; Shopping; Services and
Information; Transportation

Grande Terre 751
Yaté and the South; The Center; The Northeast Coast; Hienghène and
the North; The Northwest Coast

Isle of Pines 768
Sights; Practicalities

The Loyalty Islands 771
Ouvéa; Lifou; Maré

SPECIAL TOPIC

Capsule French Vocabulary 777

VANUATU **778-847**

Introduction. 778
History and Government; Economy; The People

On the Road 792
Accommodations and Food; Services and Information; Transportation

Efate 799
Port Vila; Sights; Sports and Recreation; Accommodations; Food;
Entertainment; Shopping; Services; Information; Transportation;
Around Efate

Tanna 818
Introduction; Sights; Practicalities; Other Tafea Islands

Malekula 825
Norsup/Lakatoro; North of Norsup

Espiritu Santo 829
Luganville; Sights; Accommodations; Other Practicalities;
Transportation; East Santo; Into the Interior; South Santo

The Eastern Chain 840
Paama and Lopevi; Ambrym; Pentecost; Ambae; Banks and Torres
Islands

SPECIAL TOPICS

Cargo Cults. 784   *Why Driving Is on the Right* 814
Women in Vanuatu. 791   *Capsule Bislama Vocabulary*. . . . 847

SOLOMON ISLANDS. **848-928**

Introduction. 848
History and Government; Economy; The People; Conduct and Customs

On the Road 862
Accommodations and Food; Services and Information; Health;
Transportation

Guadalcanal 871
   Honiara and Environs; Sights; Accommodations; Food; Entertainment;
   Shopping; Services; Information; Health; Transportation; West of
   Honiara; East of Honiara; Southeast Guadalcanal
Malaita Province 892
   Auki; Langa Langa Lagoon; Malu'u; Lau Lagoon; Southeast Malaita
Rennell and Bellona Province 898
Central Province 900
Western Province 903
   Munda and Vicinity; Kolombangara; Gizo; The Shortland Islands
Choiseul Province 918
Isabel Province 919
Makira/Ulawa Province 920
   Kirakira and Around
Temotu Province 922
   Santa Cruz; Other Islands; Tikopia and Anuta

SPECIAL TOPICS

Nguzunguzu 863   The Crawl 908
Traditional Currency   Capsule Solomon Islands
   in the Solomons 895   Pijin Vocabulary 928

RESOURCES **929-956**
Information Offices 929
Bibliography 931
Discography 942
The Internet 945
International Airport Codes 955
Alternative Place Names 956

GLOSSARY **957-961**
INDEX **962-976**

MAPS

INTRODUCTION
The Pacific. 26
Pacific and Indo-Australian Plates 27
Discovery and Settlement of the Pacific 42
Exclusive Economic Zones 50

ON THE ROAD
Pacific Air Routes 85

TAHITI-POLYNESIA
Tahiti-Polynesia 130
Tahiti 167
Vicinity of Papeete 170
Papeete. 174
Tetiaroa. 194
Moorea 196
Cook's Bay 204
Huahine. 212
Fare. 213
Maeva. 220
Raiatea and Taha'a 224
Bora Bora 234
Maupiti 246
Tubuai 250
Rangiroa 254
Gambier Islands 264
The Marquesas Islands 267
Nuku Hiva 269
Ua Pou 273
Hiva Oa 275

PITCAIRN ISLANDS
Pitcairn Island 281
The Pitcairn Islands 286
Oeno 287

EASTER ISLAND
Easter Island 291
Hanga Roa 298

COOK ISLANDS
The Cook Islands 305
Avarua 319
Rarotonga 320-321
Aitutaki Atoll 337
Arutanga 340
Atiu 344
Mauke. 348
Mangaia 350
Manihiki 354
Penrhyn. 355

NIUE
Niue. 357
Alofi 364

KINGDOM OF TONGA
Kingdom of Tonga 368
Tongatapu 386
Nuku'alofa 390
'Eua 407
The Ha'apai Group. 409
Vicinity of Lifuka 410
Pangai 412
The Vava'u Group 416
Neiafu 418
Niuatoputapu 427
Niuafo'ou 428

AMERICAN SAMOA
The Samoan Islands. 431
Tutuila and Aunu'u 442
Pago Pago Harbor Area 448
Ofu and Olosega 455
Ta'u 455

SAMOA
Apia and Environs 478
Central Apia 481
Upolu 496
Savai'i 501
Salelologa 505

TOKELAU
Atafu 517
Nukunonu 517
Fakaofo. 518

WALLIS AND FUTUNA
Wallis and Futuna 520
Wallis 523
Mata-Utu 524
Futuna and Alofi 527

TUVALU
Tuvalu 530
Funafuti 538
Around Vaiaku 539

FIJI ISLANDS
The Fiji Islands 548
Around Nadi 591
Central Nadi 594
The Mamanuca Group. 604

(continues on next page)

FIJI ISLANDS (continued)
Viti Levu 612-613
Sigatoka 614
Pacific Harbor 619
Around Suva 626
Colo-i-Suva Forest Park 629
Suva 631
Nananu-i-Ra 648
The Sigatoka River Trek 653
Lautoka 656
Yasawa Islands 664
Kadavu 668
Ovalau 673
Levuka 676
Gau 681
Vanua Levu and Taveuni 684
Labasa 685
Savusavu 688
Vanua Balavu 705
Rotuma 709

NEW CALEDONIA
New Caledonia 713
Nouméa and Vicinity 732
Nouméa 738
The Beach Area 740
Grande Terre 752
Isle of Pines 768
Ouvéa 772
Lifou 773
Maré 775

VANUATU
Vanuatu 780
Vila and Environs 800
Port Vila 804
Efate 816
Tanna 819
Erromango 824
Malekula 825
Luganville and Environs 829
Espiritu Santo 830
Luganville 833
Ambrym 841
Ambae 845

SOLOMON ISLANDS
Provinces of the Solomons 849
The Solomon Islands 852-853
Guadalcanal 872
Honiara 876
North Guadalcanal 889
North Malaita 893
Rennell and Bellona 898
Vicinity of Seghe Point 904
Vicinity of Munda 907
Ghizo Island 911
Gizo Town 912
Temotu Province 923

MAP SYMBOLS

═══════ Primary Road	⊛ Capital City	▲ Mountain
▬▬▬▬ Secondary Road	○ City	⎯⎯ Waterfall
├—┼—┤ Railroad	○ Town	Mangrove
·············· Ferry	• Accommodation	Reef
- - - - - - - Trail	▪ Sight	Water
✗ Airfield/Airstrip	⚑ Golf Course	

CHARTS

Accommodations Price Ranges 79
Apia's Climate 458
Atuona's Climate 132
Cook Islands at a Glance 305
Distances around Grande Terre 752
Easter Island Climate 290
European Contact Countdown 43
Fiji at a Glance 549
Largest Islands in the South Pacific 28
Longest Reefs in the World 30
Nadi's Climate 550
New Caledonia at a Glance 713
Nouméa's Climate 714
Oceania at a Glance 50
Pacific Chronology, A 46
Pacific Time 114
Pago Pago's Climate 431
Papeete's Climate 132
Polynesia at a Glance 131
Port Vila's Climate 779
Rarotonga's Climate 306
Samoa at a Glance 432
Solomons at a Glance, The 849
Suva's Climate 550
Tonga at a Glance 369
Tourist Arrivals 60
Trading Partners 54
Tulagi's Climate 850
Tuvalu at a Glance 530
Vanuatu at a Glance 781
Vava'u's Climate 368

ABBREVIATIONS

A$—Australian dollars
a/c—air-conditioned
ATM—automated teller machine
B.P.—*boîte postale*
C—Centigrade
C$—Canadian dollars
CDW—collision damage waiver
CFP—French Pacific Franc
EEZ—Exclusive Economic Zone
E.U.—European Union
F$—Fiji dollars
4WD—four-wheel drive
km—kilometer
kph—kilometers per hour

LDS—Latter-day Saints (Mormons)
LMS—London Missionary Society
MV—motor vessel
No.—number
N.Z.—New Zealand
NZ$—New Zealand dollars
PK—*pointe kilométrique*
P.N.G.—Papua New Guinea
pp—per person
P.W.D.—Public Works Department
S$—Samoan *tala*
SDA—Seventh-Day Adventist

SI$—Solomon Islands dollars
SPF—South Pacific Forum
STD—sexually transmitted disease
Sq.—square
tel.—telephone
T$—Tongan *pa'anga*
U.S.—United States
US$—U.S. dollars
Vt—Vanuatu *vatu*
WW II—World War Two
YHA—Youth Hostel Association
YWCA—Young Women's Christian Association

ACCOMMODATIONS PRICE RANGES

Throughout this book, accommodations are generally grouped in the price categories which follow. Of course, currency fluctuations and inflation can lead to slight variations.

Shoestring: less than US$15 double
Budget: US$15-35 double
Inexpensive: US$35-60 double
Moderate: US$60-85 double
Expensive: US$85-110 double
Premium: US$110-150 double
Luxury: more than US$150 double

ACKNOWLEDGMENTS

The nationalities of those listed below are identified by the following signs which follow their names: as (American Samoa), at (Austria), au (Australia), be (Belgium), ca (Canada), ch (Switzerland), ck (Cook Islands), de (Germany), dk (Denmark), es (Spain), fj (Fiji), fr (France), gb (Great Britain), hk (Hong Kong), it (Italy), nc (New Caledonia), nl (Netherlands), no (Norway), nu (Niue), nz (New Zealand), pf (Tahiti-Polynesia), pt (Portugal), sb (Solomon Islands), se (Sweden), to (Tonga), us (United States), vu (Vanuatu), ws (Samoa), and za (South Africa).

Some of the antique engravings by M.G.L. Domeny de Rienzi are from the classic three-volume work *Oceanie ou Cinquième Partie du Monde* (Paris: Firmin Didot Frères, 1836).

Chico artist Gordon Ohliger (us) used the drawings at the beginning of each chapter to set the theme: the rugged majesty of Fatu Hiva's Hanavave Bay, Marquesas Islands (Tahiti-Polynesia); the forbidding remoteness of Bounty Bay (Pitcairn Islands); lonely Ahu Akivi (Easter Island); Rarotonga's famous Betela Dance Troupe (Cook Islands); a tailed Niuean boy picking passion fruit (Niue); imposing Rainmaker Mountain, Tutuila Island (American Samoa); relaxed Samoan *fale* (Samoa); men unloading supplies at Nukunonu (Tokelau); haunting Lake Lalololo, Wallis Island (Wallis and Futuna); boys playing in the Nanumea lagoon (Tuvalu); a Fijian village (Fiji); the pine-fringed beauty of Anse de Kanumera, Isle of Pines (New Caledonia); Vanuatu's proverbial cattle beneath coconuts (Vanuatu); headhunters setting out (in times gone by) from New Georgia's Roviana Lagoon (Solomon Islands). When Gordy heard we weren't going to include his photo in the book, he decided to have the last word: that's him on the Tonga banner.

Special thanks to the South Pacific Creative Arts Society and Linda S. Crowl (fj) for permission to use Makiuti Tongia's poem "Storyteller," which originally appeared in *Mana* magazine, to Jack D. Haden (au) for checking Pacific radio frequencies, to Tatiana Blanc (nc) of the Secretariat of the Pacific Community and Chantale and Philippe (pf) of the Institut National de la Statistique for statistical support, to David Fanshawe (gb) and Ad Linkels (nl) for information on Pacific music, to Robert Rousseau (fr) for climate charts, to Armand Kuris (us) for correcting the section on coral reefs, to Antonio Trindade (pt) for surfing tips, to Gabriel Teoman (at) for his many candid reports on adventures around the Pacific, to Garry Hawkins (gb) for splendid letters from Niue, Tokelau, and most areas covered in this handbook, to Charlie Appleton (au) for photos and documentation of his return to Mt. Aorai, to Leslie Mc-Donald (us) for a frank report on Moorea, to Ylva Carosone (au) for Tahiti website reviews, to Dr. Georgia Lee (us) for help in updating Easter Island, to Stafford Guest (nu) for providing useful materials about Niue, to Ben Ponia (ck) for an update on the Cook Islands cultured pearl industry, to Warwick Latham (ck) for feedback from Penrhyn, to Peter McQuarrie (nz) for updating Tokelau, to Rowland Burley (hk) for a detailed report on Wallis and to Pierre Tchoubar (fr) for the same on Futuna, to James M. Conway (us), John J. Howe (tv), and Ludo Kuipers (au) for updating Tuvalu, and to Kirk W. Huffman (es) for inspiration, to Asha Johnson (us) for maintaining communications at the publishers, and to my wife Ria de Vos for her continuing assistance, suggestions, and support.

Thanks too to the following readers who took the trouble to write us letters about their trips:

Kilali Alailima (us), Danielle Alvey (gb), Else Baker (us), Lauren Baldoni (au), Klaus Bayer (de), Prof. Nan van der Bergh (za), Ann Bernsen (us), Inger Best (us), Kim Birkedahl (dk), Roberta Blackburn (us), Larry Bleidner (us), John Blyth (gb), Geoff Bourke (nz), Tracy Brassfield (us), Claire Brenn (ch), Carl P. Budrecki (us), Rowland Burley (hk), Thom Burns (us), T. Cardosa (us), Ms. T.J. Carlsen (gb), Peter Christensen (us), Gisela Comas Garcia (es), John Connell (au), Paul A. Cote (nz), Ron Crocombe (ck), Patrick Cuff (us), John Davies (gb), Francesco de Nardis (it), Stefen Deneberg (se), Marianne Denning (dk), Louie DeNolfo (nz), Kim Des Rochers (us), Bob Duchan (us), Tania Dunnette (us), Richard Eastwood (au), Ray Fielding (us), Lisa A. Fournier (us), Carol Gaskell (ca), Sandy Gaudette (us), Karin Gavin (us), Mary Graham (us), Caroline Green (gb), Linda Greenman (us), Pauline M. Grocki (us), André Gussekloo (nl), William F. Hachmeister (us), Daniel Haenggi (ch), Lisanne Bruno Hansen (dk), Morina Harder (us), Ed Hartz (nz), Garry Hawkins (gb), Danee Hazama (pf), Fredrik S. Heffermehl (no), Mark Henley (au), Roger Hill (gb), Martin J. Kahn (us), Pat Kirikiti (us), Fr. John Knoernschild (us), Christoph Kopke (gb), Sheena Leatham (us), Randoph W. Lenz (us), José Emilio Lorente (es), Louie the Fish (as), John Maidment (gb), Sue and Richard March (us), Allegra Marshall (au), Philip R. Marshall (us), Bogumil Matijaca (ca), Merritt Maxim (us), James K. McIntyre (us), Jim McLauchlin (us), John Metzger (us), Thierry

Minet *(be)*, Lynne Mitchell *(au)*, Joyce B. Moore *(us)*, Doug and Kristine Moser *(us)*, Manuel Müller-Fahrenholz *(de)*, Alessandro and Francesca Nardella *(it)*, Simone Neull *(gb)*, Erica Noorlander *(nl)*, Lorraine Oak *(us)*, B. Orenstein *(us)*, Yolanda Ortiz de Arri *(es)*, Marcia Ouellette *(us)*, John Penisten *(us)*, Leroy Lefty Pfistener *(us)*, Juan Rabasa *(us)*, Rick Range *(us)*, Steven A. Rasmussen *(us)*, Jonathan Reap *(us)*, Amanda J. Reidy *(gb)*, Paula Robertson *(us)*, Shawn Rohan *(us)*, Robert Rousseau *(fr)*, Francesc Rubio i Barceló *(es)*, Paul A. Runyon *(us)*, Bev Schmidt *(us)*, Barbara Schniter *(ch)*, Nan Schmitz *(us)*, Doug Schrader *(us)*, Bernhard Sengstschmid *(at)*, Rosie Simpson *(gb)*, Eugene L. Sly *(us)*, Mark Smaalders *(us)*, Chris Spoerri *(ch)*, Chad and Christina Stamford *(us)*, Stan Steele *(us)*, Robert Steffen *(ch)*, Bill Steinmetz *(us)*, Keoki Stender *(us)*, Carol Stetser *(us)*, Tae Sung *(us)*, Robert Takashi Imagire *(ck)*, Gabriel Teoman *(at)*, Antonio Trindade *(pt)*, Bjorn Wahlin *(se)*, Brent Webb *(us)*, C. Webb *(us)*, Hugh Williams *(us)*, J.R. Williams *(us)*, Otmar Witzko *(de)*, Sidsel Wold *(no)*, Anselm Zänkert *(de)*, and Arthur and Jane Zeeuw *(nl)*.

All their comments have been incorporated into the volume you're now holding. To have your own name included here next edition, write: David Stanley, c/o Moon Travel Handbooks, 5855 Beaudry St., Emeryville, CA 94608 U.S.A. (e-mail: travel@moon.com)

Attention Hotel Keepers, Tour Operators, and Divemasters
The best way to keep your listing in *South Pacific Handbook* up to date is to send us current information about your business. If you don't agree with what we've written, please tell us why—there's never any charge or obligation for a listing. Thanks to the many island tourism workers and government officials who *did* write in, but are far too numerous to list here.

From the Author
On my latest field research trip I was able to personally visit and inspect facilities on these islands: Aitutaki, Alu, Ambae, Ambrym, Atiu, Ballalae, Bora Bora, Choiseul, Efate, Espiritu Santo, Faisi, Ghizo, Grande Terre, Guadalcanal, Huahine, Makira, Malekula, Mana, Mauke, Mitiaro, Moorea, Nanuya Lailai, Nacula, New Georgia, Nila, Ovalau, Poporang, Raiatea, Rarotonga, Santa Cruz, Savai'i, Tahiti, Tanna, Taveuni, Tavewa, Tongatapu, Tutuila, Upolu, Vanua Levu, Vao, Vava'u, Viti Levu, Waya, and Wayasewa. In addition, Foa, Lifuka, Malaita, Manono, Nananu-i-Ra, and Norfolk were visited on my previous trip. Other islands

had to be updated through secondary sources (including direct reports from the correspondents listed above), and that information should be used with a bit more care. However, over the past 20 years I've visited almost every area included herein. This edition was actually written in Guelph, Ontario, Canada.

While out researching my books I find it cheaper to pay my own way, and you can rest assured that nothing in this book is designed to repay freebies from hotels, restaurants, tour operators, or airlines. I prefer to arrive unexpected and uninvited, and to experience things as they really are. On the road I seldom identify myself to anyone. Unlike many other travel writers I don't allow myself to be chaperoned by local tourist offices or omit necessary criticism just to boost book sales. The essential difference between this handbook and the myriad travel brochures free for the taking in airports and tourist offices all across the region is that this book represents you, the traveler, while the brochures represent the travel industry. The companies and organizations included herein are there for information purposes only, and a mention in no way implies an endorsement.

YOU WILL HAVE THE LAST WORD

Travel writing is among the least passive forms of journalism, and every time you use this book you become a participant. I've done my best to provide the sort of information I think will help make your trip a success, and now I'm asking for your help. If I led you astray or inconvenienced you, I want to know, and if you feel I've been unfair somewhere, don't hesitate to say. If you thought I sounded naive, starry-eyed, co-opted, servile, or unable to separate the good from the bad, tell me that too. Some things are bound to have changed by the time you get there, and if you write and tell me I'll correct the new edition, which is probably already in preparation even as you read this book.

Unlike many travel writers, this author doesn't accept "freebies" from tourism businesses or obtain VIP treatment by announcing who he is to one and all. At times that makes it difficult to audit the expensive or isolated resorts, thus I especially welcome comments from readers who stayed at the upmarket places, particularly when the facilities didn't match the rates. If you feel you've been badly treated by a hotel, restaurant, car rental agency, airline, tour company, dive shop, or whomever, please let me know, and if it concurs with other information on hand, your complaint certainly will have an impact. Of course, we also want to hear about the things you thought were great. Reader's letters are examined during the concluding stages of editing the book, so you really will have the final say.

When writing, please be as precise and accurate as you can. Notes made on the scene are far better than later recollections. Write comments in your copy of South Pacific Handbook as you go along, then send me a summary when you get home. If this book helped you, please help me make it even better. Address your feedback to:

David Stanley
Moon Travel Handbooks
5855 Beaudry St.
Emeryville, CA 94608 U.S.A.
e-mail: travel@moon.com

EXCHANGE RATES
(approximate figures for orientation only)

US$1 = CFP 105 (French Pacific francs)
US$1 = NZ$1.82 (New Zealand dollars)
US$1 = A$1.56 (Australian dollars)
US$1 = T$1.51 (Tongan *pa'anga*)
US$1 = S$2.99 (Samoan *tala*)
US$1 = F$1.94 (Fiji dollars)
US$1 = Vt129 (Vanuatu *vatu*)
US$1 = SI$4.88 (Solomon Islands dollars)

INTRODUCTION

DOROTHY J. HILL

The Pacific, greatest of oceans, has an area exceeding that of all dry land on the planet. Herman Melville called it "the tide-beating heart of earth." Covering more than a third of the planet's surface—as much as the Atlantic, Indian, and Arctic oceans combined—it's the largest geographical feature in the world. Its awesome 165,384,000 square km (up to 16,000 km wide and 11,000 km long) have an average depth of around 4,000 meters. You could drop the entire dry landmass of our planet into the Pacific and still have room for another continent the size of Asia. One theory claims the moon may have been flung from the Pacific while the world was still young.

The liquid continent of Oceania is divided between Melanesia, several chains of relatively large, mountainous land masses, and Polynesia, scattered groups of volcanic and coral islands. North of the equator are the coral and volcanic islands of Micronesia. It's believed that, in all, some 30,000 islands dot the Pacific basin—four times more than are found in all other oceans and seas combined. Of the 7,500 islands in the South Pacific, only 500 are inhabited. Something about those islands has always fascinated humans and made them want to learn what's there. Each one is a cosmos with a character of its own. This book is about some of those islands.

GORDON OHLIGER

INTRODUCTION

THE LAND

Plate Tectonics

Much of the western Pacific is shaken by the clash of tectonic plates (a phenomenon once referred to as continental drift), when one section of earth's drifting surface collides head-on with another. The northern and central Pacific rest on the Pacific Plate, while New Guinea, Australia, Fiji, New Caledonia, and part of New Zealand sit on the Indo-Australian Plate. The western edge of the Pacific Plate runs northeast from New Zealand up the eastern side of Tonga to Samoa, where it swings west and continues up the southwestern side of Vanuatu and the Solomons to New Britain. North of New Guinea the Pacific Plate faces the Eurasian Plate, with a series of ocean trenches defining the boundary. The greatest depths in any ocean are encountered in the western Pacific, reaching 10,924 meters in the Marianas Trench, the deepest point on earth.

The dividing line between the Pacific Plate and the plates to the west is known as the Andesite Line, part of the circum-Pacific "Ring of Fire." In the South Pacific much of the land west of this line remains from the submerged Australasian continent of 100 million B.C. East of the line, only volcanic and coralline islands exist. Three-quarters of the world's active volcanoes occur around the edge of the Pacific Plate, accounting for 85% of the world's annual release of seismic energy. As the thinner Pacific Plate pushes under the thicker Indo-Australian Plate at the Tonga Trench it melts; under tremendous pressure, some of the molten material escapes upward through fissures, causing volcanoes to erupt and atolls to tilt. Farther west the Indo-Australian Plate dives below the Pacific Plate, causing New Caledonia to slowly sink as parts of Vanuatu and the Solomons belch, quake, and heave. Fiji, between these two active areas, is strangely stable.

Darwin's Theory of Atoll Formation

The famous formulator of the theory of natural selection surmised that atolls form as high volcanic islands subside into lagoons. The original

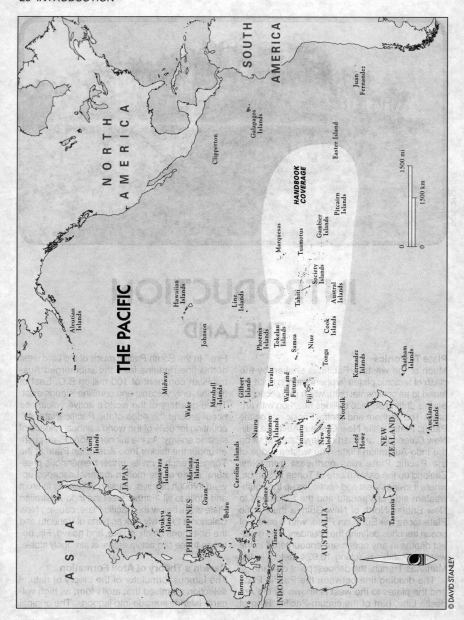

NORTH
AMERICA

SOUTH
AMERICA

THE PACIFIC

ASIA

JAPAN

PHILIPPINES

INDONESIA

AUSTRALIA

NEW
ZEALAND

Aleutian
Islands

Kuril
Islands

Ryukyu
Islands

Ogasawara
Islands

Mariana
Islands

Guam

Belau

Caroline Islands

New
Guinea

Timor

Borneo

Tasmania

Auckland
Islands

Chatham
Islands

Lord
Howe

Norfolk

Kermadec
Islands

New
Caledonia

Fiji

Vanuatu

Solomon
Islands

Nauru

Wallis and
Futuna

Tuvalu

Gilbert
Islands

Marshall
Islands

Wake

Midway

Johnson

Hawaiian
Islands

Line
Islands

Phoenix
Islands

Tokelau
Islands

Samoa

Tonga

Niue

Cook
Islands

Austral
Islands

Society
Islands

Tahiti

Marquesas

Tuamotus

Gambier
Islands

Pitcairn
Islands

Easter Island

Clipperton

Galapagos
Islands

Juan
Fernandez

HANDBOOK
COVERAGE

0   1500 km

0   1500 mi

© DAVID STANLEY

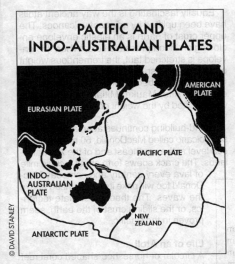

PACIFIC AND INDO-AUSTRALIAN PLATES

AMERICAN PLATE

EURASIAN PLATE

PACIFIC PLATE

INDO-AUSTRALIAN PLATE

NEW ZEALAND

ANTARCTIC PLATE

© DAVID STANLEY

island's fringing reef grows into a barrier reef as the volcanic portion sinks. When the last volcanic material finally disappears below sea level, the coral rim of the reef/atoll remains to indicate how big the island once was.

Of course, all this takes place over millions of years, but deep down below every atoll is the old volcanic core. Darwin's theory is well-illustrated at Bora Bora, where a high volcanic island remains inside the rim of Bora Bora's barrier reef; this island's volcanic core is still sinking imperceptibly at the rate of one centimeter a century. Return to Bora Bora in 25 million years and all you'll find will be a coral atoll like Rangiroa or Manihi.

Hot Spots

High or low, all of the islands have a volcanic origin best explained by the "Conveyor Belt Theory." A crack opens in the earth's mantle and volcanic magma escapes upward. A submarine volcano builds up slowly until the lava finally breaks the surface, becoming a volcanic island. The Pacific Plate moves northwest approximately 10 centimeters a year; thus, over geologic eons the volcano disconnects from the hot spot or crack from which it emerged. As the old volcanoes disconnect from the crack, new ones appear to the southeast, and the older islands are carried away from the cleft in earth's crust from which they were born.

The island then begins to sink under its own weight and erosion also cuts into the now-extinct volcano. In the warm, clear waters a living coral reef begins to grow along the shore. As the island subsides, the reef continues to grow upward. In this way a lagoon forms between the reef and the shoreline of the slowly sinking island. This barrier reef marks the old margin of the original island.

As the hot spot shifts southeast in an opposite direction from the sliding Pacific Plate (and shifting magnetic pole of the earth), the process is repeated, time and again, until whole chains of islands ride the blue Pacific. Weathering is most advanced on the composite islands and atolls at the northwest ends of the Society, Austral, Tuamotu, and Marquesas chains. Maupiti and Bora Bora, with their exposed volcanic cores, are the oldest of the larger Society Islands. The Tuamotus have eroded almost to sea level; the Gambier Islands originated out of the same hot

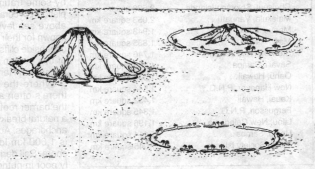

Darwin's theory of atoll formation: As the volcanic portion of the island subsides, the fringing reef is converted into a barrier reef. After the volcanic core has disappeared completely into the lagoon, the remaining reef island is called an atoll.

LOUISE FOOTE

spot and their volcanic peaks remain inside a giant atoll reef. In every case, the islands at the southeast end of the chains are the youngest.

By drilling into the Tuamotu atolls, scientists have proven their point conclusively: the coral formations are about 350 meters thick at the southeast end of the chain, 600 meters thick at Hao near the center, and 1,000 meters thick at Rangiroa near the northwest end of the Tuamotu Group. Clearly, Rangiroa, where the volcanic rock is now a kilometer below the surface, is many millions of years older than the Gambiers, where a volcanic peak still stands 482 meters above sea level.

Equally fascinating is the way ancient atolls have been uplifted by adjacent volcanoes. The upper crust of earth is an elastic envelope enclosing an incompressible fluid. When this envelope is stretched taut, the tremendous weight of a volcano is spread over a great area, deforming the seabed. In the Cook Islands, for example, Atiu, Mauke, Mitiaro, and Mangaia were uplifted by the weight of Aitutaki and Rarotonga.

Island-building continues at an active undersea volcano called MacDonald, 50 meters below sea level at the southeast end of the Austral Islands. The crack spews forth about a cubic mile of lava every century and someday Mac-Donald too will poke its smoky head above the waves. The theories of plate tectonics, or the sliding crust of the earth, seem proven in the Pacific.

Life of an Atoll

A circular or horseshoe-shaped coral reef bearing a necklace of sandy, slender islets *(motus)* of debris thrown up by storms, surf, and wind is known as an atoll. Atolls can be up to 100 km across, but the width of dry land is usually only 200-400 meters from inner to outer beach. The central lagoon can measure anywhere from one km to 50 km in diameter; huge Rangiroa Atoll is 77 km long. Entirely landlocked lagoons are rare; passages through the barrier reef are usually found on the leeward side. Most atolls are no higher than four to six meters.

A raised or elevated atoll is one that has been pushed above the ocean's surface by some trauma of nature to become a platform of coral rock rising up to 20 meters above sea level. Raised atolls are often known for their huge sea caves and steep oceanside cliffs. The largest coral platform of this kind in the South Pacific is 692-square-km Rennell in the Solomons.

Where the volcanic island remains there's often a deep passage between the barrier reef and shore; the reef forms a natural breakwater, which shelters good anchorages. Australia's Great Barrier Reef is 1,600 km long and 25 to 44 km offshore. Soil derived from coral is extremely poor in nutrients, while volcanic soil is

---

LARGEST ISLANDS IN THE SOUTH PACIFIC

New Guinea	820,033 square km
South Island, New Zealand	151,010 square km
North Island, New Zealand	114,051 square km
Tasmania, Australia	67,800 square km
New Britain, P.N.G.	37,736 square km
Grande Terre, New Caledonia	16,192 square km
Big Island, Hawaii	10,458 square km
Viti Levu, Fiji Islands	10,429 square km
Bougainville, P.N.G.	10,000 square km
New Ireland, P.N.G.	8,650 square km
Vanua Levu, Fiji Islands	5,556 square km
Guadalcanal, Solomon Islands	5,302 square km
Isabela, Galapagos Islands	4,588 square km
Isabel, Solomon Islands	4,014 square km
Espiritu Santo, Vanuatu	4,010 square km
Malaita, Solomon Islands	3,885 square km
New Georgia, Solomon Islands	3,365 square km
Makira, Solomon Islands	3,188 square km
Choiseul, Solomon Islands	2,538 square km
Malekula, Vanuatu	2,053 square km
Manus, P.N.G.	1,943 square km
Maui, Hawaii	1,885 square km
Stewart, New Zealand	1,746 square km
Savai'i, Samoa	1,709 square km
Oahu, Hawaii	1,572 square km
New Hanover, P.N.G.	1,544 square km
Kauai, Hawaii	1,432 square km
Fergusson, P.N.G.	1,345 square km
Lifou, New Caledonia	1,196 square km
Upolu, Samoa	1,114 square km
Tahiti, Society Islands	1,045 square km

THE GREENHOUSE EFFECT

The gravest danger facing the atolls of Oceania is the greenhouse effect, a gradual warming of Earth's environment due to fossil fuel combustion and the widespread clearing of forests. By the year 2030 the concentration of carbon dioxide in the atmosphere will have doubled from preindustrial levels. As infrared radiation from the sun is absorbed by the gas, the trapped heat melts mountain glaciers and the polar ice caps. In addition, seawater expands as it warms up, so water levels could rise almost a meter by the year 2100, destroying shorelines created 5,000 years ago.

A 1982 study demonstrated that sea levels had already risen 12 centimeters in the previous century; in 1995 2,500 scientists from 70 countries involved in an Intergovernmental Panel on Climate Change commissioned by the United Nations completed a two-year study with the warning that over the next century air temperatures may rise as much as 5° Celsius and sea levels could go up 95 centimeters. Not only will this reduce the growing area for food crops, but rising sea levels will mean salt water intrusion into groundwater supplies—a horrifying prospect if accompanied by the droughts that have been predicted. Coastal erosion will force governments to spend vast sums on road repairs and coastline stabilization.

Increasing temperatures may already be contributing to the dramatic jump in the number of hurricanes in the South Pacific. For example, Fiji experienced only 12 tropical hurricanes from 1941 to 1980 but 10 from 1981 to 1989. After a series of devastating hurricanes in Samoa, insurance companies announced in 1992 that they were withdrawing coverage from the country. In 1997 and 1998 the El Niño phenomenon brought with it another round of devastating hurricanes, many hitting Cook Islands and Tahiti-Polynesia, which are usually missed by such storms. The usual hurricane season is November to April but in June 1997 Hurricane

Keli struck Tuvalu—the first hurricane ever recorded in the South Pacific that month.

Coral bleaching occurs when an organism's symbiotic algae are expelled in response to environmental stresses, such as changes in water temperature, and widespread instances of bleaching and reefs being killed by rising sea temperatures have been confirmed in Tahiti-Polynesia and Cook Islands. To make matters worse, the coral-crunching crown-of-thorns starfish is again on the rise throughout the South Pacific (probably due to sewage and fertilizer runoff, which nurture the starfish larvae). Reef destruction will reduce coastal fish stocks and impact tourism.

As storm waves wash across the low-lying atolls, eating away the precious land, the entire populations of archipelagos such as Tokelau and Tuvalu may be forced to evacuate long before they're actually flooded. The construction of seawalls to keep out the rising seas would be prohibitively expensive and may even do more harm than good by interfering with natural water flows.

Unfortunately, those most responsible for the problem, the industrialized countries led by the United States (and including Australia) have strongly resisted taking any action to significantly cut greenhouse gas emissions, and new industrial polluters like India and China are sure to make matters much worse. And as if that weren't bad enough, the hydrofluorocarbons (HFCs) presently being developed by corporate giants like Du Pont to replace the ozone-destructive chlorofluorocarbons (CFCs) used in cooling systems are far more potent greenhouse gases than carbon dioxide. This is only one of many similar consumption-related problems, and it seems as if one section of humanity is hurtling down a suicidal slope, unable to resist the momentum, as the rest of our race watches the catastrophe approach in helpless horror. It will cost a lot to rewrite our collective ticket but there may not be any choice.

known for its fertility. Dark-colored beaches are formed from volcanic material; the white beaches of travel brochures are entirely coral-based. The black beaches are cooler and easier on the eyes, enabling plantlife to grow closer to the shore, providing patches of shade; the white beaches are generally safer for swimming, as visibility is better.

CORAL REEFS

To understand how a basalt volcano becomes a limestone atoll, it's necessary to know a little about the growth of coral. Coral reefs cover some 200,000 square km worldwide, between 35 degrees north and 32 degrees south latitude. A

LONGEST REEFS IN THE WORLD

Great Barrier Reef, Australia	1,600 km
Southwest Barrier Reef, New Caledonia	600 km
Northeast Barrier Reef, New Caledonia	540 km
Sabana-Camaguey Reef, Cuba	400 km
Great Sea Reef, Fiji Islands	260 km
Belize Reef, Central America	250 km
South Louisiade Archipelago Reef, P.N.G.	200 km

reef is created by the accumulation of millions of calcareous skeletons left by myriad generations of tiny coral polyps, some no bigger than a pinhead. Though the skeleton is usually white, the living polyps are of many different colors. The individual polyps on the surface often live a long time, continuously secreting layers to the skeletal mass beneath the tiny layer of flesh.

They thrive in clear salty water where the temperature never drops below 18° C. They must also have a base not more than 50 meters below the water's surface on which to form. The coral colony grows slowly upward on the consolidated skeletons of its ancestors until it reaches the low-tide mark, after which development extends outward on the edges of the reef. Sunlight is critical for coral growth. Colonies grow quickly on the ocean side due to clearer water and a greater abundance of food. A strong, healthy reef can grow four to five centimeters a year. Fresh or cloudy water inhibits coral growth, which is why villages and ports all across the Pacific are located at the reef-free mouths of rivers. Hurricanes can kill coral by covering the reef with sand, preventing light and nutrients from getting through. Erosion caused by logging or urban development can have the same effect.

Polyps extract calcium carbonate from the water and deposit it in their skeletons. All limy reef-building corals also contain microscopic algae within their cells. The algae, like all green plants, obtain energy from the sun and contribute this energy to the growth of the reef's skeleton. As a result, corals behave (and look) more like plants than animals, competing for sunlight just as terrestrial plants do. Many polyps are also carnivorous; with minute stinging tentacles they supplement their energy by capturing tiny planktonic animals and organic particles at night. A small piece of coral is a colony composed of large numbers of polyps.

Coral Types

Corals belong to a broad group of stinging creatures, which includes polyps, soft corals, stony corals, sea anemones, sea fans, and jellyfish. Only those types with hard skeletons and a single hollow cavity within the body are considered true corals. Stony corals such as brain, table, staghorn, and mushroom corals have external skeletons and are important reef builders. Soft corals, black corals, and sea fans have internal skeletons. The fire corals are recognized by their smooth, velvety surface and yellowish brown color. The stinging toxins of this last group can easily penetrate human skin and cause swelling and painful burning that can last up to an hour. The many varieties of soft, colorful anemones gently waving in the current might seem inviting to touch, but beware: many are also poisonous.

The corals, like most other forms of life in the Pacific, colonized the ocean from the fertile seas of Southeast Asia. Thus the number of species declines as you move east. More than 600 species of coral make their home in the Pacific, compared to only 48 in the Caribbean. The diversity of coral colors and forms is endlessly amazing. This is our most unspoiled environment, a world of almost indescribable beauty.

Exploring a Reef

Until you've explored a good coral reef, you haven't experienced one of the greatest joys of nature. While one cannot walk through pristine forests due to the lack of paths, it's quite possible to swim over untouched reefs. Coral reefs are the most densely populated living space on earth—the rainforests of the sea! It's wise to bring along a high quality mask that you've checked thoroughly beforehand, as there's nothing more disheartening than a leaky, ill-fitting mask. Otherwise dive shops throughout the region rent or sell snorkeling gear, so don't pass up the opportunity to get into the clear, warm waters around you.

CORALS OF THE PACIFIC

acropora

staghorn fire coral
(Millepora accicornis)

table coral

mushroom coral
(Fungia fungites)

elkhorn fire coral
(Millepora platyphylla)

brain coral
(Meandrina)

honeycomb coral (Favia matthaii)

DIANA LASICH HARPER

Conservation

Coral reefs are one of the most fragile and complex ecosystems on earth, providing food and shelter for countless species of fish, crustaceans (shrimps, crabs, and lobsters), mollusks (shells), and other animals. The coral reefs of the South Pacific protect shorelines during storms, supply sand to maintain the islands, furnish food for the local population, form a living laboratory for science, and are major tourist attractions. Without coral, the South Pacific would be immeasurably poorer.

Hard corals grow only about 10 to 25 millimeters a year and it can take 7,000 to 10,000 years for a coral reef to form. Though corals look solid they're easily broken; by standing on them, breaking off pieces, or carelessly dropping anchor you can destroy in a few minutes what took so long to form. Once a piece of coral breaks off it dies, and it may be years before the coral reestablishes itself and even longer before the broken piece is replaced. The "wound" may become infected by algae, which can multiply and kill the entire coral colony. When this happens over a wide area, the diversity of marinelife declines dramatically.

Swim beside or well above the coral. Avoid bumping the coral with your fins, gauges, or other equipment and don't dive during rough sea conditions. Proper buoyancy control is preferable to excessive weight belts. Snorkelers should check into taking along a float-coat, which will allow equipment adjustments without standing on coral.

We recommend that you not remove seashells, coral, plantlife, or marine animals from the sea. Doing so upsets the delicate balance of nature, and coral is much more beautiful underwater anyway! This is a particular problem along shorelines frequented by large numbers of tourists, who can completely strip a reef in very little time. If you'd like a souvenir, content yourself with what you find on the beach (although even a seemingly empty shell may be inhabited by a hermit crab). Also think twice about purchasing jewelry or souvenirs made from coral or seashells. Genuine traditional handicrafts that incorporate shells are one thing, but by purchasing unmounted seashells or mass-produced coral curios you are contributing to the destruction of the marine environment. The triton shell, for example, keeps in check the reef-destroying crown-of-thorns starfish.

The anchors and anchor chains of private yachts can do serious damage to coral reefs. Pronged anchors are more environmentally friendly than larger, heavier anchors, and plastic tubing over the end of the anchor chain helps minimize the damage. If at all possible, anchor in sand. A longer anchor chain makes this easier, and a good windlass is essential for larger boats. A recording depth sounder will help locate sandy areas when none are available in shallow water. If you don't have a depth sounder and can't see the bottom, lower the anchor until it just touches the bottom and feel the anchor line as the boat drifts. If it "grumbles" lift it up, drift a little, and try again. Later, if you notice your chain grumbling, motor over the anchor, lift it out of the coral and move. Not only do sand and mud hold better, but your anchor will be less likely to become fouled. Try to arrive before 1500 to be able to see clearly where you're anchoring—Polaroid sunglasses make it easier to distinguish corals. If you scuba dive with an operator who anchors incorrectly, let your concerns be known.

There's an urgent need for stricter government regulation of the marine environment, and in some places coral reefs are already protected. Appeals such as the one above have only limited impact—legislators must write stricter laws and impose fines. Unfortunately fishing with the help of dynamite, scuba gear, and poisons are all too common, almost entirely practiced by local residents. If you witness dumping or any other marine-related activity you think might be illegal, don't become directly involved but take a few notes and calmly report the incident to the local authorities or police at the first opportunity. You'll learn something about their approach to these matters and make them aware of your concerns.

Resort developers can minimize damage to their valuable reefs by providing public mooring buoys so yachts don't have to drop anchor and pontoons so snorkelers aren't tempted to stand on coral. Licensing authorities can make such amenities mandatory whenever appropriate, and in extreme cases, endangered coral gardens should be declared off limits to private boats. As consumerism spreads, once-remote areas become subject to the problems of pollution and overexploitation: the garbage is visibly piling up on many shores. As a visitor, don't hesitate to practice your conservationist attitudes, and leave a clean wake.

CLIMATE

The Pacific Ocean has a greater impact on the world's climate than any other geographical feature on earth. By taking heat away from the equator and toward the poles, it stretches the bounds of the area in which life can exist. Broad circular ocean currents flow from east to west across the tropical Pacific, clockwise in the North Pacific, counterclockwise in the South Pacific. North and south of the "horse latitudes" just outside the tropics the currents cool and swing east. The prevailing winds move the same way: the southeast trade winds south of the equator, the northeast trade winds north of the equator, and the low-pressure "doldrums" in between. Westerlies blow east above the cool currents north and south of the tropics. This natural air-conditioning system brings warm water to Australia and Japan, cooler water to Peru and California.

The climate of the high islands is closely related to these winds. As air is heated near the equator it rises and flows at high altitudes toward the poles. By the time it reaches about 30 degrees south latitude it will have cooled enough to cause it to fall and flow back toward the equator near sea level. In the southern hemisphere the rotation of the earth deflects the winds to the left to become the southeast trades. When these cool moist trade winds hit a high island, they are warmed by the sun and forced up. Above 500 meters elevation they begin to cool again and their moisture condenses into clouds. At night the winds do not capture much warmth and are more likely to discharge their moisture as rain. The windward slopes of the high islands catch the trades head-on and are usually wet, while those on the leeward side may be dry.

Rain falls abundantly and frequently in the islands during the southern summer months (Nov.-April). This is also the hurricane season south of the equator, a dangerous time for cruising yachts. However, New Zealand and southern Australia, outside the tropics, get their finest weather at this time; many boats head south to sit it out.

The southeast trade winds sweep the South Pacific from May-Oct., the cruising season. Cooler and drier, these are the ideal months for travel in insular Oceania, though the rainy season is only a slight inconvenience and the season shouldn't be a pivotal factor in deciding when to go.

Over the past few years climatic changes have turned weather patterns upside down, so don't be surprised if you get prolonged periods of rain and wind during the official "dry season" and drought when there should be rain. A recent analysis of data shows that in 1977 the belt of storms and winds abruptly shifted eastward, making Tonga and Melanesia drier and Tahiti-Polynesia wetter. Hurricanes are also striking farther east and El Niño is expected to recur more frequently.

Temperatures range from warm to hot year-round; however, the ever-present sea moderates the humidity by bringing continual cooling breezes. Countries nearer the equator (Samoa, Solomon Islands) are hotter than those farther south (Cook Islands, Tonga, New Caledonia). There's almost no twilight in the tropics, which makes Pacific sunsets brief. When the sun begins to go down, you have less than half an hour before darkness.

When to Go

Compared to parts of North America and Europe, the seasonal climatic variations in the South Pacific are not extreme. There is a hotter, more humid season from November to April and a cooler, drier time from May to October. These contrasts are more pronounced in countries closer to the equator such as Samoa and Solomon Islands and less noticeable in Cook Islands, Tonga, Fiji, and New Caledonia. Hurricanes can also come during the "rainy" season but they only last a few days a year. The sun sets around 1800 year-round and there aren't periods when the days are shorter or longer.

Seasonal differences in airfares are covered in the **Getting There** section that follows, and these should be more influential in deciding when to go. On Air New Zealand flights from North America to Fiji, Tonga, and Samoa the low season is mid-April to August, the prime time in those countries. To Tahiti, on the other hand, June to August is the high tourist season for airfares, festivals, and tourism in general.

French tourists are notorious for scheduling their trips in August, and both Australians and New Zealanders crowd into the islands in July and August to escape winter weather in their home countries. Christmas is also busy with islanders returning home. In February and March

many hotels stand half empty and special discounted rates are on offer.

In short, there isn't really any one season which is the "best" time to come. Go whenever you can, but book your airline seat well in advance as many flights from the U.S. run 90% full.

FLORA AND FAUNA

FLORA

The flora and fauna of Oceania originated in the Malaysian region; in the two regions, ecological niches are filled by similar plants. Yet one sees a steady decline in the variety of genera as one moves east: even in distant Hawaii very few native plants have an American origin. New Guinea has more than 5,000 vegetal species, New Caledonia 3,250, and Tahiti-Polynesia only 1,000. Some species such as casuarinas and coconuts were spread by means of floating seeds or fruit, and wind and birds were also effective in colonization. The microscopic spores of ferns can be carried vast distances by the wind. Yet how creatures like Fiji's crested iguana or the flightless megapode bird of Niuafo'ou and Savo could have reached the Pacific islands remains a mystery. Later, humans became the vehicle: the Polynesians introduced taro, yams, breadfruit, plantains, coconuts, sugarcane, kava, paper mulberry, and much more to the islands.

The high islands of the South Pacific support a great variety of plantlife, while the low islands

are restricted to a few hardy, drought-resistant species such as coconuts and pandanus. Rainforests fill the valleys and damp windward slopes of the high islands, while brush and thickets grow in more exposed locations. Hillsides in the drier areas are covered with coarse grasses. Yet even large islands such as Viti Levu have an extremely limited variety of plantlife when compared to Indonesia. The absence of leaf-eating animals allowed the vegetation to develop largely without the protective spines and thorns found elsewhere.

Distance, drought, and poor soil have made atoll vegetation among the most unvaried on earth. Though a tropical atoll might seem "lush," no more than 15 native species may be present! On the atolls, taro, a root vegetable with broad heart-shaped leaves, must be cultivated in deep organic pits. The vegetation of a raised atoll is apt to be far denser, with many more species, yet it's likely that fewer than half are native.

Mangroves can occasionally be found along some high island coastal lagoons. The cable roots of the saltwater-tolerant red mangrove anchor in the shallow upper layer of oxygenated mud, avoiding the layers of hydrogen sulfide below. The tree

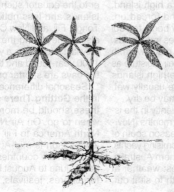

provides shade for tiny organisms dwelling in the tidal mudflats—a place for birds to nest and for fish or shellfish to feed and spawn. The mangroves also perform the same task as land-building coral colonies along the reefs. As sediments are trapped between the roots, the trees extend farther into the lagoon, creating a unique natural environment. The past decade has seen widespread destruction of the mangroves.

Sugarcane probably originated in the South Pacific. On

The cassava bush (Manihot esculenta) can grow over two meters high. The tuberous root, though less prized than yams, sweet potatoes, or breadfruit, is a common source of island food. A native of Brazil, cassava was transported to the Pacific in post-Columbian times. Other names for this plant include yuca, manioc, and tapioca.

DIANA LASICH HARPER

New Guinea the islanders have cultivated the plant for thousands of years, selecting vigorous varieties with the most colorful stems. The story goes that two Melanesian fishermen, To-Kabwana and To-Karavuvu, found a piece of sugarcane in their net one day. They threw it away, but after twice catching it again they decided to keep it and painted the stalk a bright color. Eventually the cane burst and a woman came forth. She cooked food for the men but hid herself at night. Finally she was captured and became the wife of one of the men. From their union sprang the whole human race.

Rainforests at Risk

In our day man has greatly altered the original vegetation by cutting the primary forests and introducing exotic species. For example, most of the plants now seen in the coastal areas of the main islands are introduced. The virgin rainforests of the world continue to disappear at the rate of 40 hectares a minute, causing erosion, silting, flooding, drought, climatic changes, and the extinction of countless life forms. The Solomon Islands and New Caledonia have been the hardest hit by commercial logging, but the forests of Vanuatu, Fiji, and Samoa are also suffering.

Locally operated portable sawmills have been promoted in Melanesia as an alternative to large-scale exploitation by foreign corporations. These low-tech sawmills can be operated by a couple of persons, and there's a ready market for the cut lumber. Logging roads and heavy equipment are not required, and nearly 100% of the income remains in the community. By providing villagers with a steady income from their forests, the *wokabout somils* make customary landowners far less ready to sign away timber rights to large companies that devastate the environment. It is becoming recognized that what's needed is sustainable development rather than short-term exploitation, the creation of forest reserves, and better management across the board.

FAUNA

As with the flora, the variety of animal and bird species encountered in Oceania declines as you move away from the Asian mainland. The Wallace Line between Indonesia's Bali and Lombok was once believed to separate the terrestrial fauna of Southeast Asia from that of Australia. Although it's now apparent that there's no such clear-cut division, it still provides a frame of reference. Many of the marsupials and monotremes of Australia are also native to Papua New Guinea. Sea cows (dugongs) are found in New Guinea, the Solomons, and Vanuatu. The fauna to the east of New Guinea is much sparser, with flying foxes and insect-eating bats the only mammals that spread to all of Oceania (except Eastern Polynesia) without the aid of man.

Birds

Island birdlife is far more abundant than land-based fauna but still reflects the decline in variety from west to east. Birdwatching is a highly recommended pursuit for the serious Pacific traveler; you'll find it opens unexpected doors. Good field guides are few (ask at local bookstores, museums, and cultural centers), but a determined interest will bring you into contact with fascinating people and lead to great adventures. The best time to observe forest birds is in the very early morning—they move around a lot less in the heat of the day.

Introduced Fauna

Ancient Polynesian navigators introduced pigs, dogs, and chickens; they also brought along rats (a few species of mice are native to Australia and New Guinea). Captain Cook contributed cattle, horses, and goats; Captain Wallis left behind cats. The mongoose was introduced to the region more than a century ago to combat rats. Giant African snails (*Achatina fulica*) were brought to the islands by gourmets fond of fancy French food. Some of the snails escaped, multiplied, and now crawl wild, destroying the vegetation. They now exist in the Samoas, New Caledonia, Tahiti-Polynesia, Vanuatu, and Wallis and Futuna.

Perhaps the most unfortunate newcomer of all is the hopping Indian mynah bird (*Acridotheres tristis*), introduced to many islands from Indonesia at the turn of the century to control insects, which were damaging the citrus and coconut plantations. The mynahs multiplied profusely and have become major pests, inflicting great harm on the very trees they were brought in to protect. Worse still, many indigenous birds are forced out of their habitat by these noisy, aggressive birds with yellow beaks and feet. This and rapid deforestation by man have made the South Pacific the region with the highest proportion of endangered endemic bird species on earth.

Fish

The South Pacific's richest store of life is found in the silent underwater world of the pelagic and lagoon fishes. It's estimated that half the fish remaining on our globe are swimming in this great ocean. Coral pinnacles on the lagoon floor provide a safe haven for angelfish, butterfly fish, damselfish, groupers, soldierfish, surgeonfish, triggerfish, trumpet fish, and countless more. These fish seldom venture more than a few meters away from the protective coral, but larger fish such as barracuda, jackfish, parrot fish, pike, stingrays, and small sharks range across lagoon waters that are seldom deeper than 30 meters. The external side of the reef is also home to many of the above, but the open ocean is reserved for bonito, mahimahi, swordfish, tuna, wrasses, and the larger sharks. Passes between ocean and lagoon can be crowded with fish in transit, offering a favorite hunting ground for predators.

In the open sea the food chain begins with phytoplankton, which flourish wherever ocean upwellings bring nutrients such as nitrates and phosphates to the surface. In the western Pacific this occurs near the equator, where massive currents draw water away toward Japan and Australia. Large schools of fast-moving tuna ply these waters feeding on smaller fish, which consume tiny phytoplankton drifting near the sunlit surface. The phytoplankton also exist in tropical lagoons where mangrove leaves, sea grasses, and other plant material are consumed by far more varied populations of reef fish, mollusks, and crustaceans.

It's believed that most Pacific marine organisms evolved in the triangular area bounded by New Guinea, the Philippines, and the Malay Peninsula. This "Cradle of Indo-Pacific Marinelife" includes a wide variety of habitats and has remained stable through several geological ages. From this cradle the rest of the Pacific was colonized.

Marine Mammals

While most people use the terms dolphin and porpoise interchangeably, a porpoise lacks the dolphin's beak (although many dolphins are also beakless). There are 62 species of dolphins, and only six species of porpoises. Dolphins leap from the water and many legends tell of their saving humans, especially children, from drowning (the most famous concerns Telemachus, son of Odysseus). Dolphins often try to race in front of ferries and large ships. The commercialization of dolphins in aquariums or enclosures for the amusement of humans is a questionable activity.

Whales generally visit the tropical South Pacific between July and October. Humpbacks arrive in Tonga about this time to give birth in the warm waters off Vava'u. Whales are also commonly seen in Cook Islands. As the weather grows warmer they return to the summer feeding areas around Antarctica. (Sadly, Japanese whalers continue to hunt the animals in Antarctica for "scientific purposes," and endangered fin and humpback whales are hidden among the 400 minke whale kills reported each year. Whale meat is openly available at Tokyo restaurants.)

Sharks

The danger from sharks has been greatly exaggerated. Of some 300 different species, only 28 are known to have attacked humans. Most dangerous are the white, tiger, and blue sharks. Fortunately, all of these inhabit deep water far from the coasts. An average of only 50 shark attacks a year occur worldwide, so considering the number of people who swim in the sea, your chances of being involved are about one in 10 million. In the South Pacific shark attacks on snorkelers or scuba divers are extremely rare and the tiny mosquito is a far more dangerous predator.

Sharks are not aggressive where food is abundant, but they can be very nasty far offshore. You're always safer if you keep your head underwater (with a mask and snorkel), and don't panic if you see a shark—you might attract it. Even if you do, they're usually only curious, so keep your eye on the shark and slowly back off. The swimming techniques of humans must seem very clumsy to fish, so it's not surprising if they want a closer look.

Sharks are attracted by shiny objects (a knife or jewelry), bright colors (especially yellow and red), urine, blood, spearfishing, and splashing (divers should ease themselves into the water). Sharks normally stay outside the reef, but get local advice. White beaches are safer than dark, and clear water safer than murky. Avoid swimming in places where sewage or edible wastes enter the water, or where fish have just been cleaned. You should also exercise care in places where local residents have been fishing with spears or even hook and line that day.

Never swim alone if you suspect the presence of sharks. If you see one, even a supposedly harmless nurse shark lying on the bottom, get out of the water calmly and quickly, and go elsewhere. Studies indicate that sharks, like most other creatures, have a "personal space" around them that they will defend. Thus an attack could be a shark's way of warning someone to keep his distance, and it's a fact that more than half the victims of these incidents are not eaten but merely bitten. Sharks are much less of a problem in the South Pacific than in colder waters because small marine mammals (commonly hunted by sharks) are rare here, so you won't be mistaken for a seal or an otter.

Let common sense be your guide, not irrational fear or carelessness. Many scuba divers come actually *looking* for sharks, and local divemasters seem able to swim among them with impunity. If you're in the market for some shark action, most dive shops can provide it. Just be aware that getting into the water with feeding sharks always entails some danger, and the divemaster who admits this and lays down some basic safety guidelines (such as keeping your hands clasped or arms folded) is probably a safer bet than the macho man who just says he's been doing it for years without incident.

Supplying food to any kind of wild creature destroys their natural feeding habits and handling marine life can have unpredictable consequences. Never snorkel on your own (without the services of an experienced guide) near a spot where shark feeding is practiced as you never know how the sharks will react to a surface swimmer without any food for them. More study is required to determine whether shark feeding by tourism operators tends to attract sharks to lagoons and beaches used for public recreation. Like all other wild animals, sharks deserve to be approached with respect.

Sea Urchins

Sea urchins (living pincushions) are common in tropical waters. The black variety is the most

dangerous: their long, sharp quills can go right through a snorkeler's fins. Even the small ones, which you can easily pick up in your hand, can pinch you if you're careless. They're found on rocky shores and reefs, never on clear, sandy beaches where the surf rolls in.

Most sea urchins are not poisonous, though quill punctures are painful and can become infected if not treated. The pain is caused by an injected protein, which you can eliminate by holding the injured area in a pail of very hot water for about 15 minutes. This will coagulate the protein, eliminating the pain for good. If you can't heat water, soak the area in vinegar or urine for a quarter hour. Remove the quills if possible, but being made of calcium, they'll decompose in a couple of weeks anyway—not much of a consolation as you limp along in the meantime. In some places sea urchins are considered a delicacy: the orange or yellow urchin gonads are delicious with lemon and salt.

Other Hazardous Creatures

Although jellyfish, stonefish, crown-of-thorns starfish, cone shells, eels, and poisonous sea snakes are dangerous, injuries resulting from any of these are rare. Gently apply methylated spirit, alcohol, or urine (but not water, kerosene, or gasoline) to areas stung by jellyfish. Inoffensive sea cucumbers (bêche-de-mer) punctuate the lagoon shallows. Stonefish also rest on the bottom and are hard to see due to camouflaging; if you happen to step on one, its dorsal fins inject a painful poison, which burns like fire in the blood. Fortunately, stonefish are not common.

It's worth knowing that the venom produced by most marine animals is destroyed by heat, so your first move should be to soak the injured part in very hot water for 30 minutes. (Also hold an opposite foot or hand in the same water to prevent scalding due to numbness.) Other authorities claim the best first aid is to squeeze blood from a sea cucumber scraped raw on coral directly onto the wound. If a hospital or clinic is nearby, go there immediately.

Never pick up a live cone shell; some varieties have a deadly stinger dart coming out from the pointed end. The tiny blue-ring octopus is only five centimeters long but packs a poison that can kill a human. Eels hide in reef crevices by day; most are harmful only if you inadvertently poke your hand or foot in at them. Of course, never tempt fate by approaching them (fun-loving divemasters sometimes feed the big ones by hand and stroke their backs).

Reptiles and Insects

Very few land snakes live in Oceania and the more common sea snakes are shy and inoffensive. This, and the relative absence of leeches, poisonous plants, thorns, and dangerous wild animals, makes the South Pacific a paradise for hikers. One creature to watch out for is the centipede, which often hides under stones or anything else lying around. It's a long, flat, fast-moving insect not to be confused with the round, slow, and harmless millipede. The centipede's bite, though painful, is not lethal to a normal adult.

Geckos and skinks are small lizards often seen on the islands. The skink hunts insects by day; its tail breaks off if you catch it, but a new one quickly grows. The gecko is nocturnal and has no eyelids. Adhesive toe pads enable it to pass along vertical surfaces, and it changes color to avoid detection. Unlike the skink, which avoids humans, geckos often live in people's homes, where they eat insects attracted by electric lights. Its loud clicking call may be a territorial warning to other geckos. Two species of geckos are asexual: in these, males do not exist and the unfertilized eggs hatch into females identical to the mother. Geckos are the highest members of the animal world where this phenomenon takes place. During the 1970s a sexual species of house gecko was introduced to

Samoa and Vanuatu, and in 1988 it arrived on Tahiti. These larger, more aggressive geckos have drastically reduced the population of the endemic asexual species.

Six of the seven species of sea turtles are present in the South Pacific (the flatback, green, hawksbill, leatherback, loggerhead, and olive ridley turtles). These magnificent creatures are sometimes erroneously referred to as "tortoises," which are land turtles. All species of sea turtles now face extinction due to ruthless hunting, egg harvesting, and beach destruction. Sea turtles come ashore Nov.-Feb. to lay their eggs on the beach from which they themselves originally hatched, but female turtles don't commence this activity until they are 20 years old. Thus a drop in numbers today has irreversible consequences a generation later, and it's estimated that breeding females already number in the hundreds or low thousands. Turtles are often choked by floating plastic bags they mistake for food, or they drown in fishing nets.

Importing any sea turtle product is prohibited in most developed countries, but protection is often inadequate in the South Pacific countries themselves. An amazing demonstration of the lack of regional consciousness of the plight of the turtle occurred at the 1996 South Pacific Forum meeting on Majuro in the Marshall Islands, where a large number of endangered sea turtles were slaughtered to feed the visiting heads of state. Ironically, the same leaders who dined on turtle steak had observed "The Year of the Turtle" in 1995!

Because it and its eggs are taken for human food, the green sea turtle (Chelonia mydas) *is in danger of extinction. Fortunately the shell is too thin to be made into jewelry.*

HISTORY

THE ERA OF DISCOVERY AND SETTLEMENT

Prehistory

Oceania is the site of many "lasts." It was the last area on earth to be settled by humans, the last to be discovered by Europeans, and the last to be both colonized and decolonized. It all began more than 50,000 years ago when Papuan-speaking Australoid migrants from Southeast Asia arrived in New Guinea and Australia, at a time when the two formed a single landmass. Buka Island in the North Solomons had already been settled by Papuans 30,000 years ago. During the Pleistocene (Ice Age), sea level was 150 meters lower and people could cross the narrow channels from Indonesia on primitive rafts more easily. Cut off by rising waters 10,000 years ago, the Australian Aboriginals maintained their Paleolithic (Old Stone Age) culture undisturbed until modern times.

Little is known about the prehistory of the Papuan peoples of New Guinea as their first

This lapita *pottery shard dated 500 B.C. was found on Watom Island off New Britain, Papua New Guinea.*

LOUISE FOOTE

coastal settlements are now covered by the sea, but they spoke non-Austronesian languages and were characterized by convex noses. Similar short, black peoples are found in various parts of Asia (the Philippine Negritos, for example). Some of the Dravidian peoples of southern India are also very short and dark, indicating the direction from which these migrations came. These pre-Austronesian societies were egalitarian, religious rites were performed communally, and a preference was shown for the curvilinear style in art.

The Austronesians

Next to arrive, after about 1600 B.C., were the broad-nosed, lighter-skinned Austronesians from Indonesia, the Philippines, or Taiwan. They settled in enclaves along the coast of New Guinea and gradually populated the islands of Melanesia as far as Fiji. They mixed with the Papuans to become the Melanesians of today; in the Western Solomons the blue-black-skinned inhabitants still speak Papuan languages. The Papuans evolved their Neolithic (New Stone Age) culture long before the Austronesians passed this way: the earliest confirmed date for agriculture in the Western Highlands of Papua New Guinea is 4000 B.C., proving that the shift away from hunting and gathering was much earlier.

The Austronesians almost certainly introduced pottery and had more advanced outrigger canoes. Distinctive *lapita* pottery, decorated in horizontal geometric bands and dated from 1500 to 500 B.C., has been found at sites ranging from New Britain to New Caledonia, Tonga, and Samoa. *Lapita* pottery has allowed archaeologists not only to study Melanesian prehistory, but also to trace the migrations of an Austronesian-speaking race, the Polynesians, with some precision. These *Lapita* people were great traders: obsidian from New Britain Island in Papua New Guinea was exported to Santa Cruz in the Solomons—some 1,700 km away. By A.D. 300 at the latest the Polynesians had ceased to make pottery.

It's interesting to note that the third to second millenniums B.C. saw continuous movement of peoples from Southeast Asia and southern China into Indonesia. All insular Southeast Asian peoples are Austronesian-speaking, and the Polynesians were the advance guard of this migration. These population movements continue today with contemporary Javanese colonization of West Papua and Polynesian migration to New Zealand, Hawaii, and the American continent. Recent comparisons of DNA samples have confirmed that the Polynesians traveled from Taiwan to the Philippines, Indonesia, New Guinea, Fiji, and Samoa.

The colorful theory that Oceania was colonized from the Americas is no longer seriously entertained. The Austronesian languages are today spoken from Madagascar through Indonesia all the way to Easter Island and Hawaii, half the circumference of the world! All of the introduced plants of old Polynesia, except the sweet potato, originated in Southeast Asia. The endemic diseases of Oceania, leprosy and the filaria parasite (elephantiasis), were unknown in the Americas. The amazing continuity of Polynesian culture is illustrated by motifs in contemporary tattooing and tapa, which are very similar to those on ancient *lapita* pottery.

The Colonization of Polynesia

Three thousand five hundred years ago the early Polynesians set out from Southeast Asia on a migratory trek that would lead them to make the "many islands" of Polynesia their home. Great voyagers, they sailed their huge double-hulled canoes far and wide, steering with huge paddles and pandanus sails. To navigate they read the sun, stars, currents, swells, winds, clouds, and birds. Sailing purposefully, against the prevailing winds and currents, the *Lapita* peoples reached the Bismarck Archipelago by 1500 B.C., Tonga (via Fiji) by 1300 B.C., and Samoa by 1000 B.C. Around the time of Christ they pushed out from this primeval area, remembered as Havaiki, into the eastern half of the Pacific.

Perhaps due to overpopulation in Samoa, some Polynesians pressed on to the Society Islands and the Marquesas by A.D. 300. About this time a backtracking movement settled the outliers of the Solomons, probably originating in Tuvalu or Futuna. Easter Island (A.D. 400), Hawaii (A.D. 500), and Mangareva (A.D. 900)

were all reached by Polynesians from the Marquesas. Migrants to the Tuamotus (A.D. 900), the Cook Islands (A.D. 900), and New Zealand (A.D. 1100) were from the Society Islands. The stone food pounders, carved figures, and tanged adzes of Eastern Polynesia are not found in Samoa and Tonga (Western Polynesia), indicating that they were later, local developments of Polynesian culture.

These were not chance landfalls but planned voyages of colonization: the Polynesians could (and often did) return the way they came. That one could deliberately sail such distances against the trade winds and currents without the help of modern navigational equipment was proved in 1976 when the *Hokule'a*, a reconstructed oceangoing canoe, sailed 5,000 km south from Hawaii to Tahiti. The expedition's Micronesian navigator, Mau Piailug, succeeded in setting a course by the ocean swells and relative positions of the stars alone, which guided them very precisely along their way. Other signs used to locate an island were clouds (which hang over peaks and remain stationary), seabirds (boobies fly up to 50 km offshore, frigate birds up to 80 km), and mysterious *te lapa* (underwater streaks of light radiating 120-150 km from an island, disappearing closer in).

Since 1976 the *Hokule'a* has made several additional return trips to Tahiti; during 1985-87 Hawaiian navigator Nainoa Thompson used traditional methods to guide the *Hokule'a* on a 27-month "Voyage of Rediscovery" that included a return west-east journey between Samoa and Tahiti. To date the vessel has logged more than 100,000 km using traditional methods, introducing Polynesian voyaging to countless thousands. In 1992 the canoe *Te Aurere* sailed from New Zealand to Rarotonga for the Festival of Pacific Arts—the first such voyage in 1,000 years—where it joined the *Hokule'a* and a fleet of other canoes in a dramatic demonstration of the current revival of traditional Polynesian navigation. In 1995 the *Hokule'a* led a three-canoe flotilla from Hawaii to Tahiti, returning in May with another three double-hulled canoes, which joined them in the Marquesas. A voyage from Hawaii to Easter Island is planned for the millennium. (For more information on the *Hokule'a*, click on http://leahi.kcc.hawaii.edu/org/pvs.)

The Polynesians were the real discoverers of the Pacific, completing all their major voyages long before Europeans even dreamed this ocean existed. In double canoes lashed together to form rafts, carrying their plants and animals with them, they penetrated as close to Antarctica as the South Island of New Zealand, as far north as Hawaii, and as far east as Easter Island—a full 13,000 km from where it's presumed they first entered the Pacific!

Neolithic Society

To some extent, the peoples of Polynesia, Micronesia, and Melanesia all kept gardens and a few domestic animals. Taro was cultivated on ingenious terraces or in organic pits; breadfruit was preserved by fermentation through burial (still a rare delicacy). Stone fishponds and fish traps were built in the lagoons. Pandanus and coconut fronds were woven into handicrafts. On the larger Polynesian islands these practices produced a surplus, which allowed the emergence of a powerful ruling class. The common people lived in fear of their gods and chiefs.

The Polynesians and Melanesians were cannibals, although the intensity of the practice varied from group to group: cannibalism was rife in the Marquesas but relatively rare on Tahiti. Early European explorers were occasionally met by natives who would kneel beside them on the shore, squeezing their legs and pinching their posteriors to ascertain how tasty and substantial these white people would be to eat. It was believed that the mana or spiritual power of an enemy would be transferred to the consumer; to eat the body of one who was greatly despised was the ultimate revenge. Some Melanesians perceived the pale-skinned newcomers with "odd heads and removable skin" (hats and clothes) as evil spirits, perhaps ancestors intent on punishing the tribe for some violation of custom.

Jean-Jacques Rousseau and the 18th-century French rationalists created the romantic image of the "noble savage." Their vision of an ideal state of existence in harmony with nature disregarded the inequalities, cannibalism, and warfare that were a central part of island life, just as much of today's travel literature ignores the poverty and political/economic exploitation many Pacific peoples now face. Still, the legend of the South Pacific maintains its magic hold.

EUROPEAN CONTACT AND EXPLORATION

Hispanic Exploration

The first Europeans on the scene were Spaniards and Portuguese. The former were interested in gold and silver, new territories and colonies, and conversion of the heathen, while the latter were concerned with finding passages from Europe to the Moluccas, fabled Spice Islands of the East. Vasco Núñez de Balboa became the first to set eyes on this great ocean when he crossed the Isthmus of Panama in 1513 to discover the Mar del Sur, or South Seas (as opposed to the Mar del Norte, or North Seas, the Caribbean). On 28 November 1520 Ferdinand Magellan's three ships entered the Pacific around the bottom of South America. Pointing the vessels northwest, their next landfall was Guam, two months later. Though Magellan himself was killed in the Philippines, his surviving crew made it back to Spain in September 1522. The first circumnavigation in history had taken three years!

In 1568 Álvaro de Mendaña sailed from Peru to the Solomon Islands in search of gold. On his second trip to the Solomons in 1595 Mendaña discovered the southern Marquesas Islands. The voyage of Mendaña's pilot, Pedro Fernandez de Quirós, from Espiritu Santo in what is now Vanuatu to Mexico in 1606, against contrary winds in rotten ships with a starving, dying company, must rank as one of the greatest feats of Pacific journeying. The 16th-century Spaniards defined the bounds of the Pacific and added whole clusters of islands to geographic knowledge.

Terra Australis Incognita

The systematic European exploration of the Pacific was actually a search for *terra australis incognita,* a great southern continent believed to balance the continents of the north. There were many daring voyages during this period. The 17th century was the age of the Dutch explorations in search of new markets and trade routes. The first Dutch ships followed the routes pioneered by the Spanish and made few discoveries of significance. However, Anthony van Diemen, the Dutch governor-general of Batavia (present-day Jakarta) and a man of vision and great purpose, pro-

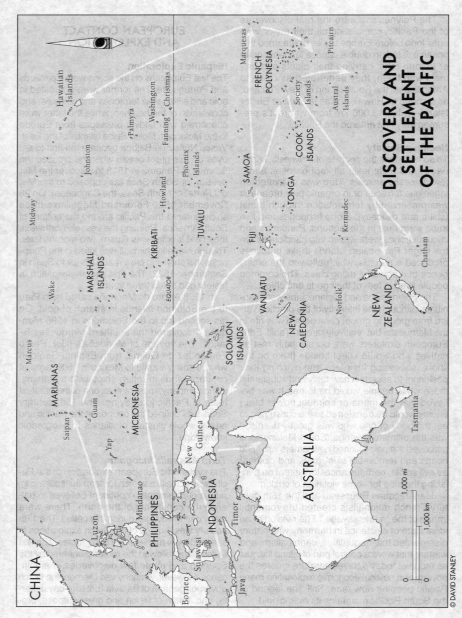

DISCOVERY AND SETTLEMENT OF THE PACIFIC

CHINA

PHILIPPINES
Luzon
Mindanao

INDONESIA
Borneo
Sulawesi
Java
Timor

New Guinea

AUSTRALIA

Tasmania

MARIANAS
Saipan
Guam
Yap

MICRONESIA

Marcus
Wake

MARSHALL
ISLANDS

KIRIBATI

EQUATOR

TUVALU

SOLOMON
ISLANDS

VANUATU

NEW
CALEDONIA

FIJI

TONGA

SAMOA

COOK
ISLANDS

Phoenix
Islands

Howland

Midway

Johnston

Hawaiian
Islands

Palmyra

Washington
Fanning · Christmas

Marquesas

FRENCH
POLYNESIA

Society
Islands

Austral
Islands

Pitcairn

Kermadec

Norfolk

NEW
ZEALAND

Chatham

EUROPEAN CONTACT

0   1,000 mi

0   1,000 km

© DAVID STANLEY

EUROPEAN CONTACT COUNTDOWN

DATE	EXPLORER AND NATIONALITY	LANDFALL
1513	Balboa, Spanish	Pacific Ocean
1521	Magellan, Spanish	Mariana Islands, Philippines
1526	Meneses, Portuguese	Irian Jaya
1527	Saavedra, Spanish	Marshall Islands
1543	Villalobos, Spanish	Caroline Islands
1545	Ortiz de Retes, Spanish	New Guinea
1568	Mendaña, Spanish	Tuvalu, Solomon Islands
1595	Mendaña, Spanish	Marquesas Islands
1606	Quirós, Spanish	Tuamotu Islands, Vanuatu
1606	Torres, Spanish	Australia
1616	Schouten/Le Maire, Dutch	Futuna
1642	Tasman, Dutch	Tasmania, New Zealand
1643	Tasman, Dutch	Tonga, Fiji
1722	Roggeveen, Dutch	Easter Island, Samoa
1765	Byron, English	Tokelau Islands
1767	Wallis, English	Tahiti, Wallis
1767	Carteret, English	Pitcairn
1769	Cook, English	Leeward Islands, Australs
1773	Cook, English	Cook Islands
1774	Cook, English	Niue, New Caledonia, Norfolk
1777	Cook, English	Christmas Island
1778	Cook, English	Hawaiian Islands
1781	Mourelle, Spanish	Vava'u
1791	Vancouver, English	Chatham Islands, Rapa
1798	Fearn, English	Nauru

titude. In 1745, the British Parliament passed an act promising £20,000 to the first British subject who could, in a British ship, discover and sail through a strait between Hudson's Bay and the South Seas. Thus many explorers were motivated to investigate the region. This route would have proven infinitely shorter than the one around Cape Horn, where the weather conditions were often foul and the ships sailed in perpetual danger; on Samuel Wallis's voyage of 1766-67, it took his two ships four months to round the chaotic Straits of Magellan. Captain John Byron (grandfather of the poet) ignored his orders to find a passage between the South Seas and Hudson's Bay; instead he sought the Solomons, discovered initially by Mendaña. His circumnavigation took only two years. The great ocean was becoming an explorer's lake.

Captain Cook

vided the backing for Abel Tasman's noteworthy voyage of 1642, which entered the Pacific from the west, rather than the east.

Tasman was instructed to find "the remaining unknown part of the terrestrial globe"—your basic Herculean task. Because of his meticulous and painstaking daily journals, Tasman is known as the historian of Pacific explorers. His observations proved invaluable to geographers, and he added Tasmania, New Zealand, Tonga, and parts of Fiji to Western knowledge. Tasman was the first to sail right around Australia. Jacob Roggeveen's voyage in 1722 also failed to discover the unknown continent, but he narrowed down the area of conjecture considerably.

The exploratory success of the 18th-century English was due to this 17th-century scientific labor. Although using 17th-century equipment, William Dampier explored with an 18th-century at-

The extraordinary achievements of James Cook (1728-79) on his three voyages in the ships *Endeavor, Resolution, Adventure,* and *Discovery* left his successors with little to do but marvel over them. A product of the Age of Enlightenment, Cook was a mathematician, astronomer, practical physician, and master navigator. Son of a Yorkshire laborer, he learned seamanship on small coastal traders plying England's east coast. He joined the British Navy in 1755 and soon made a name for himself in Canada where he surveyed the St. Lawrence River, greatly contributing to the capture of Quebec City in 1759. Later he charted the coast of Newfoundland. Chosen to command the *Endeavor* in 1768 though only a warrant officer, Cook was the first captain to eliminate scurvy from his crew (with sauerkraut).

The scientists of his time needed accurate

WILLIAM HODGES

Omai, a Polynesian from Huahine, accompanied Captain Cook to England and returned.

observations of the transit of Venus, for if the passage of Venus across the face of the sun were measured from points on opposite sides of the earth, then the size of the solar system could be determined for the first time. In turn, this would make possible accurate predictions of the movements of the planets, vital for navigation at sea. Thus Cook was dispatched to Tahiti, and Father Hell (a Viennese astronomer of Hungarian origin) to Vardo, Norway.

So as not to alarm the French and Spanish, the British admiralty claimed Cook's first voyage (1768-71) was primarily to take these measurements. His real purpose, however, was to further explore the region, in particular to find *terra australis incognita*. After three months on Tahiti, he sailed west and spent six months exploring and mapping New Zealand and the whole east coast of Australia, nearly tearing the bottom off his ship, the *Endeavor,* on the Great Barrier Reef in the process. Nine months after returning to England, Cook embarked on his second expedition

(1772-75), resolving to settle the matter of *terra australis incognita* conclusively. In the *Resolution* and *Adventure,* he sailed entirely around the bottom of the world, becoming the first to cross the Antarctic Circle and return to tell about it.

In 1773 John Harrison won the greater part of a £20,000 reward offered by Queen Anne in 1714 "for such Person or Persons as shall discover the Longitude at Sea." Harrison won it with the first marine chronometer (1759), which accompanied Cook on his second and third voyages. Also on these voyages was Omai, a native of Tahiti who sailed to England with Cook in 1774. Omai immediately became the talk of London, the epitome of the "noble savage," but to those who knew him he was simply a sophisticated man with a culture of his own.

In 1776 Cook set forth from England for a third voyage, supposedly to repatriate Omai but really to find a Northwest Passage from the Pacific to the Atlantic. He rounded the Cape of Good Hope and headed east to New Zealand, Tonga, and Tahiti. He then turned due north, discovering Kauai in what we now know as the Hawaiian Islands on 18 January 1778. After two weeks in Hawaii, Cook continued north via the west coast of North America but was forced back by ice in the Bering Strait. With winter coming, he returned to Hawaiian waters and located the two biggest islands of the group, Maui and Hawaii. On 14 February 1779, in a short, unexpected, petty skirmish with the Hawaiians, Cook was killed. Today he remains the giant of Pacific exploration. He'd dispelled the compelling, centuries-old hypothesis of an unknown continent, and his explorations ushered in the British era in the South Seas.

The Fatal Impact

Most early contacts with Europeans had a hugely disintegrating effect on native cultures. When introduced into the South Pacific, European sicknesses—mere discomforts to the white man—devastated whole populations. Measles, influenza, tuberculosis, dysentery, smallpox, typhus, typhoid, and whooping cough were deadly because the islanders had never developed resistance to them. The white man's alcohol, weapons, and venereal disease further accelerated the process.

CONVERSION, COLONIALISM, AND WAR

Conversion

The systematic explorations of the 18th century were stimulated by the need for raw materials and markets as the Industrial Revolution took hold in Europe. After the American Revolution, much of Britain's colonizing energy was deflected toward Africa, India, and the Pacific. This gave them an early lead, but France and the U.S. weren't far behind.

As trade with China developed in the late 18th and early 19th centuries, Europeans combed the Pacific for products to sell to the Chinese. A very profitable triangular pattern of trade developed, in which European ships traded the islanders cheap whiskey, muskets, and glass beads for sandalwood, bêche-de-mer (sea cucumbers), pearls, and turtle shell, which were then sold to the Chinese for silk, tea, and porcelain. Ruffian whalers, sealers, and individual beachcombers flooded in. Most were unsavory characters who acted as mercenaries or advisers to local chiefs, but two, William Mariner and Herman Melville, left valuable accounts of early Polynesia.

After the easily exploited resources were depleted, white traders and planters arrived to establish posts and to create copra and cotton plantations on the finest land. Missionaries came to "civilize" the natives by teaching that all their customs—cannibalism, warring with their neighbors, having more than one wife, wearing leaves instead of clothes, dancing, drinking kava, chewing betel nut, etc.—were wrong. They taught hard work, shame, thrift, abstention, and obedience. Tribespeople now had to wear sweaty, rainsoaked, germ-carrying garments of European design. Men dressed in singlets and trousers, and the women in Mother Hubbards, one-piece smocks trailing along the ground. To clothe themselves and build churches required money, obtained only by working as laborers on European plantations or producing a surplus of goods to sell to European traders. In many instances this austere, harsh Christianity was grafted onto the numerous taboo systems of the Pacific.

Members of the London Missionary Society arrived at Tahiti in 1797, though it was not until 1815 that they succeeded in converting the Tahitians. One famous LMS missionary, Rev. John Williams, spread Protestantism to the Cook Islands (1823) and Samoa (1830). Methodists were active in Tonga (1822) and Fiji (1835). The children of some of the European missionaries who "came to do good, stayed to do well" as merchants. Later, many islanders themselves became missionaries: some 1,200 of them left their homes to carry the word of God to other islands. The first Catholic priests arrived in Polynesia in 1834. They competed with the Protestants for influence and divided islands on religious grounds.

Due to the inhospitable environment and absence of a chiefly class, the conversion and commercialization of Melanesia was not carried out until several decades later. After the 1840s, islanders were kidnapped by "blackbirders," who sold them as slaves to planters in Fiji and Queensland. Worst were the Peruvians, who took 3,634 islanders to Peru in 1862 and 1863, of whom only 148 were returned.

Colonialism

The first European colonies in Oceania were Australia (1788) and New Zealand (1840). Soon after, the French seized Tahiti-Polynesia (1842) and New Caledonia (1853). A canal across Central America had already been proposed and Tahiti was seen as a potential port of call on the sea routes to Australia and New Zealand. New Caledonia was used first as a penal colony; nickel mining only began in the 1870s. The French annexed several other island groups near Tahiti in the 1880s.

Not wishing to be burdened with the expense of administering insignificant, far-flung colonies, Britain at first resisted pressure to officially annex other scattered South Pacific island groups, though Fiji was reluctantly taken in 1874 to establish law and order. In 1877 the Western Pacific High Commission was set up to protect British interests in the unclaimed islands.

Then the emergence of imperialist Germany and construction of the Panama Canal led to a sudden rush of annexations by Britain, France, Germany, and the U.S. between 1884 and 1900. In 1899 Samoa was partitioned between Germany and the U.S., with Tonga and the Solomon Islands added to the British sphere of influence as compensation. The last island group to be taken over was New Hebrides (Vanuatu), declared a "condominium" by Britain and France in

A PACIFIC CHRONOLOGY

50,000 B.C.—Papuans enter the Pacific
8000 B.C.—Papuans reach the Solomons
1600 B.C.—Polynesians enter the Pacific
1300 B.C.—Polynesians reach Tonga
1000 B.C.—Polynesians reach Samoa
A.D. 300—Polynesians reach Tahiti and the Marquesas
A.D. 500—Polynesians reach Hawaii and Easter Island
A.D. 900—Polynesians reach Cook Islands
A.D. 1100—Polynesians reach New Zealand
1521—Europeans enter the Pacific
1768—Captain Cook's first Pacific voyage
1779—Captain Cook killed by the Hawaiians
1788—Australia becomes a British colony
1789—the mutiny on the *Bounty*
1797—Protestant missionaries reach Tahiti
1815—Christianity accepted in Tahiti
1821—Protestant missionaries in Cook Islands
1830—Rev. John Williams arrives in Samoa
1836—Catholic missionaries reach Tahiti
1840—New Zealand becomes a British colony
1842—Tahiti becomes a French protectorate
1845—George Tupou I becomes king of Tonga
1847—Tongans invade eastern Fiji
1853—French annex New Caledonia
1874—Fiji becomes a British colony
1875—Tupou I signs Tongan constitution
1879—the first Indians arrive in Fiji
1880—Tahiti-Polynesia becomes a full French colony
1888—Cook Islands becomes a British protectorate
1888—Chile annexes Easter Island
1893—Solomon Islands becomes a British protectorate
1898—U.S. annexes Hawaii
1899—Germany and the U.S. partition Samoa
1906—Britain and France assume joint control of Vanuatu

1914—New Zealand takes Samoa from Germany
1942—Japanese invade Solomon Islands
1947—South Pacific Commission established
1959—Hawaii becomes the 50th state
1962—Samoa achieves independence
1965—Cook Islands becomes self-governing
1966—France begins nuclear testing at Moruroa
1968—University of the South Pacific founded
1970—Fiji and Tonga achieve independence
1971—South Pacific Forum established
1974—Niue becomes internally self-governing
1975—Papua New Guinea achieves independence
1978—Solomon Islands and Tuvalu achieve independence
1980—Vanuatu achieves independence
1985—French agents sink the *Rainbow Warrior*
1985—South Pacific Nuclear-free Zone Treaty signed
1987—two military coups in Fiji
1988—provincial autonomy granted in New Caledonia
1990—universal suffrage approved in Samoa
1992—France suspends nuclear testing in Polynesia
1994—Law of the Sea comes into force
1995—Chirac restarts French nuclear testing
1996—Chirac halts testing after worldwide protests
1997—constitutional democracy restored in Fiji
1998—Nouméa Accords signed in New Caledonia
2000—The Pacific heralds the new millennium

LOUISE FOOTE

Sea slug, sea cucumber, trepang, or bêche-de-mer. The rows of feet along the length of this echinoderm show its close relationship to the sea urchin and starfish. Food particles caught on the long sticky tentacles are licked off in the mouth. These creatures, obtained in the South Pacific by early traders, are eaten in China as an aphrodisiac, and in recent years they have been gathered almost to the point of extinction on many islands.

1906 to forestall German advances.

Around the time of WW I Britain transferred responsibility for many island groups to Australia and New Zealand. The struggle for hegemony in imperialist Europe in 1914-18 prompted Germany's colonies (New Guinea, Samoa, and Micronesia) to be taken by the British and Japanese empires. The South Pacific had become a British lake, economically dependent on Australia and New Zealand, a situation largely unchanged today.

By the late 19th century, the colonies' tropical produce (copra, sugar, vanilla, cacao, and fruits) had become more valuable and accessible; minerals—such as nickel and phosphates—and guano were also exploited. Total control of these resources passed to large European trading companies, which owned the plantations, ships, and retail stores. This colonial economy stimulated the immigration of Indian laborers to Fiji, the alienation of major tracts of native land in New Caledonia, and a drop in the indigenous populations in general by a third, not to mention the destruction of their cultures.

There were fundamental differences in approach between the British and French colonial administrations in the South Pacific. While the French system installed "direct rule" by French officials appointed by the French government, the British practiced "indirect rule" with the customary chiefs (Fiji) or royalty (Tonga) retaining most of their traditional powers. Not only was this form of government cheaper, but it fostered stability. British colonial officials had more decision-making authority than their French counterparts who had to adhere to instructions received from Paris. And while the French sought to undermine local traditions in the name of assimilation, the British defended the native land tenure on which traditional life was based.

War

World War II provided the U.S. with unparalleled opportunities to project power across the Pacific and grab territory. Although the U.S. had gained a toehold in the Pacific by annexing Hawaii and the Spanish colonies (Guam and the Philippines) in 1898, further expansion was frustrated by the British and Japanese. Japan had hoped to become the dominant force in Asia and the Pacific by establishing a "Greater East Asia Co-Prosperity Sphere." After the Japanese occupation of French Indochina in July 1941, an economic embargo on iron from the U.S. and oil from the Dutch East Indies presented the Japanese with a choice: strangulation, retreat, or war.

The history of the Pacific War can be found in many books. Half a million Japanese soldiers and civilians died far from their native shores. The only area covered in this handbook actually occupied by Japanese troops was the Solomon Islands; an account of the fighting there is included in that chapter's introduction. Large American staging and supply bases were created on Grande Terre, Espiritu Santo, Guadalcanal, and Bora Bora. The Americans built airfields on islands right across the South Pacific, while their ships controlled the southern supply routes to Australia and New Zealand.

DECOLONIZATION

In 1960 the United Nations issued a Declaration of Granting of Independence to Colonial Countries and Peoples, which encouraged the trend toward self-government, yet it was not until the independence of Samoa from New Zealand in 1962 that a worldwide wave of decolonization reached the region. During the 1960s and 1970s seven South Pacific countries (Fiji, Papua New Guinea, Solomon Islands, Tonga, Tuvalu, Vanuatu, and Samoa) became independent as Britain, Australia, and New Zealand dismantled their colonial systems.

Cook Islands and Niue have achieved de facto independence in association with New Zealand. The French territories, Tahiti-Polynesia, New Caledonia, and Wallis and Futuna, have varying degrees of internal autonomy, although great power continues to be wielded by appointed French officials who are not responsible to the local assemblies. Decolonization is a hot issue in these French colonies, where the South Pacific's only active independence movements are found (without forgetting the struggles for land and freedom in nearby Bougainville, West Papua, Timor, and Guam). American Samoa remains firmly tied to Washington by the subsidies it receives. Pitcairn is still a British colony, and New Zealand administers Tokelau, but this is at the request of the inhabitants. Easter Island is an old-fashioned colony of Chile.

The postwar period also witnessed the growth of regionalism. In 1947 the South Pacific Commission (now called the Secretariat of the Pacific Community) was established by Australia, Britain, France, the Netherlands, New Zealand, and the U.S. to maintain the status quo through coordination among the colonial powers, yet conferences organized by the SPC brought the islanders together for the first time. In 1971 the newly independent states formed the South Pacific Forum, a more vigorous regional body able to tackle political as well as social problems. In 1988 Papua New Guinea, the Solomon Islands, and Vanuatu formed the Melanesian Spearhead regional grouping, which Fiji also joined in 1996.

French Colonialism

New Caledonia, Tahiti-Polynesia, and Wallis and Futuna are part of a worldwide chain of French colonies also including Kerguelen, Guiana, Martinique, Guadeloupe, Mayotte, Reunion, and St. Pierre and Miquelon, under the DOM-TOM (Ministry of Overseas Departments and Territories). It costs France billions of francs a year to maintain this system, a clear indicator that it's something totally different from colonial empires of the past, which were based on economic exploitation, not subsidies. For more than 30 years France has been willing to spend vast sums to perpetuate its status as a medium-sized world power.

These conditions contradict what has happened elsewhere in the South Pacific. During the 1960s and 1970s, as Britain, Australia, and New Zealand voluntarily withdrew from their Pacific colonies, French pretensions to global status grew stronger. This digging in created the anachronism of a few highly visible bastions of white colonialism in the midst of a sea of English-speaking self-governing nations. When French officials summarily rejected all protests against their nuclear testing and suppression of independence movements, most Pacific islanders were outraged.

The final round of nuclear testing in the Tuamotu Islands in 1995 was a watershed as French national prestige had seldom sunk as low, both in the Pacific and around the world. Since that debacle, France has tried to mend fences by supplying economic aid to the independent states and granting enhanced autonomy to its colonies. As France becomes fully integrated into the new Europe, it's quite likely that the ability and desire to maintain remote colonies will decline, and the decolonization process will finally be concluded.

Nuclear Testing

No other area on earth was more directly affected by the nuclear arms race than the Pacific. From 6 August 1945 until 27 January 1996, scarcely a year passed without one nuclear power or another testing their weapons here. The U.S., Britain, and France exploded more than 250 nuclear bombs at Bikini, Enewetak, Christmas Island, Moruroa, and Fangataufa, an average of more than six a year for more than 40 years, more than half of them by France. The U.S. and British testing was only halted by the 1963 Partial Nuclear Test Ban Treaty with the Soviets, while the French tests continued until unprecedented worldwide protests made it clear that the Cold War really was over (as usual, France was a slow learner).

The British and American test sites in Micronesia are now part of independent countries, but the Marshallese still suffer radiation sickness from

U.S. testing in the 1940s and 1950s (some of it deliberately inflicted—the islanders were used as human guinea pigs), and the French are still covering up the consequences of their tests. The end result of nuclear testing in Micronesia and Polynesia is ticking away in the genes of thousands of servicemen and residents present in those areas during the tests, and at the fragile underground Tuamotu test site used by the French.

The fact that the nuclear age began in their backyard at Hiroshima and Nagasaki has not been lost on the islanders. They have always seen few benefits coming from nuclear power, only deadly dangers. On 6 August 1985 eight member states of the South Pacific Forum signed the South Pacific Nuclear-Free Zone Treaty, also known as the Treaty of Rarotonga, which bans nuclear testing, land-based nuclear weapon storage, and nuclear waste dumping on their territories. Each country may decide for itself if nuclear-armed warships and aircraft are to be allowed entry. Of the five nuclear powers, China and the USSR promptly signed the treaty, while the U.S., France, and Britain only signed in March 1996 when it became obvious they could no longer use the region as a nuclear playground.

THE PACIFIC TODAY

The modern world has transformed the Pacific. Outboards have replaced outriggers and Coca-Cola has been substituted for coconuts. Consumerism has caught on in the towns. As money becomes more important, the islanders learn the full meaning of urban unemployment, poverty, homelessness, inequality, and acculturation. Television is spreading, and attitudes are molded by the tens of thousands of VCRs that play pirated videotapes available at hundreds of corner stores. Villagers are trapped by material desires.

The diet is changing as imported processed foods take the place of fiber-rich fresh foods such as breadfruit, taro, and plantain. The ocean would seem a bountiful resource, but on many islands the reef waters are already overharvested, and the inhabitants often lack the ability to fish the open sea. Thus the bitter irony of Japanese canned mackerel.

Noncommunicable nutrition-related ailments such as heart disease, diabetes, and cancer now account for three-quarters of all deaths in urban Polynesia, but less than a quarter in predominantly rural Vanuatu and Solomon Islands, where infectious and parasitic diseases such as malaria, dengue fever, pneumonia, diarrhea, hepatitis, and tuberculosis prevail. Cigarette smoking is a major health problem; more than 50% of Pacific men are habitual smokers. Rural islanders tend to smoke more than those in the towns, and 88% of rural indigenous Fijian men are smokers.

Salaried employment leads inevitably to the replacement of the extended family by the nuclear family, and in Melanesia there's a growing gap between new middle classes with government jobs and the village-based populace. Western education has aroused expectations that the island economies cannot fulfill, and the influx to the capitals has strained social services to the breaking point, creating serious housing and employment problems, especially for the young. Populations are growing faster than the local economies—leading to declining living standards—and oversized bureaucracies stifle development. Melanesian women are victimized by domestic violence, economic burdens, and cultural change.

Subsistence agriculture continues to play an important role in the South Pacific, and most land is still held communally by extended families or clans; however, pressure is mounting from outside agencies such as the World Bank and the International Monetary Fund (IMF) to convert communal land into individual ownership under the guise of "economic development." Western economic models give importance only to commodity crops useful to industrialized countries as raw materials, discounting the stabilizing effect of subsistence. When the tiller of the soil is no longer able to eat his own produce, he becomes a consumer of processed foods marketed by food-exporting countries such as Australia and New Zealand, and the country loses a measure of its independence.

Individually registered land can be taxed and sold on the open market, and throughout the third world the privatization of land has inevitably led to control of the best tracts passing into the hands of transnational corporations, banks, and the government. Pressure from agencies such as the IMF to force local governments to register land and allow it to be used as loan collateral is

OCEANIA AT A GLANCE

Land areas and sea areas (the ocean area within the 200-nautical-mile Exclusive Economic Zone of each country, indicated on the map below) are expressed in square kilometers. The category "Political Status" gives the year in which the country became independent, or the territory/province/state fell under colonial rule by the power named. The sea areas (and various other figures) were taken from Selected Pacific Economies: A Statistical Summary, *published by the Secretariat of the Pacific Community, Nouméa.*

COUNTRY	POPULATION	LAND AREA	SEA AREA	CAPITAL	POLITICAL STATUS
Tahiti-Polynesia	219,521	3,543	5,030,000	Papeete	France 1842
Pitcairn Islands	65	47	800,000	Adamstown	Britain 1838
Easter Island	3,000	171	355,000	Hanga Roa	Chile 1888
Cook Islands	18,904	240	1,830,000	Avarua	N.Z. 1901
Niue	1,750	259	390,000	Alofi	N.Z. 1900
Tonga	97,446	691	700,000	Nuku'alofa	Ind. 1970
American Samoa	46,773	201	390,000	Utulei	U.S. 1900
Samoa	161,298	2,842	120,000	Apia	Ind. 1962
Tokelau	1,507	12	290,000	Fakaofo	N.Z. 1925
Wallis and Futuna	14,000	274	300,000	Mata-Utu	France 1887
Tuvalu	9,061	25	900,000	Funafuti	Ind. 1978
Total Polynesia	**573,325**	**8,305**	**11,105,000**		
Fiji	772,655	18,272	1,290,000	Suva	Ind. 1970
New Caledonia	196,836	18,576	1,740,000	Nouméa	France 1853
Vanuatu	180,000	12,189	680,000	Port Vila	Ind. 1980
Solomon Islands	348,922	27,556	1,340,000	Honiara	Ind. 1978
Total Melanesia	**1,498,413**	**76,593**	**5,050,000**		

EXCLUSIVE ECONOMIC ZONES (EEZ)

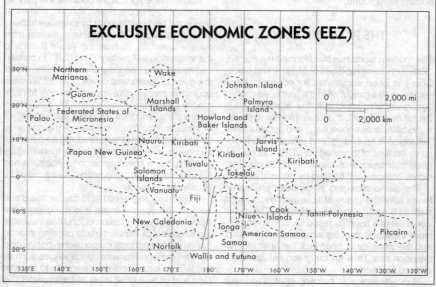

© DAVID STANLEY

part of a stratagem to dispossess the islanders of their land. Once their communal land is gone, people are no longer able to fall back on their own produce when economies deteriorate, and they find themselves forced to take any job they can find. Acutely aware of the fate of the Hawaiians and the New Zealand Maoris, the islanders are highly sensitive about land rights, yet these instincts are coming under increasing pressure as local governments have "land mobilizations" forced upon them by foreign capital.

All across the South Pacific, regional stability is eroded by class differences, government corruption, uneven development, industrial exploitation, and the declining terms of trade. By making the economies dependent on external markets, much current "economic development" destabilizes societies once secure in "primitive affluence," and virtually every Pacific entity is now subservient to some degree of neocolonial control. Local interests are sacrificed for the benefit of transnational corporations and industrialized states far across the sea.

GOVERNMENT

Generally, the South Pacific is governed on the basis of constitutional law, an independent judiciary, and regular elections, with some regional idiosyncrasies. In Samoa only *matai* (Samoan chiefs) may stand as candidates for 47 of the 49 parliamentary seats, although since 1991 all adults can vote. Fiji has a constitution that segregates voting for 46 of the 71 members of parliament along racial lines, while in Tonga only nine of the 30 members of parliament are elected directly by the people.

The two-party system is a relatively recent legacy of the last years of colonial rule. Traditionally, Melanesians governed themselves by consensus: those involved would sit down and discuss a problem until a compromise was reached, which everyone then accepted, and this bottom-up democracy still governs life throughout Melanesia. Governments in Melanesia today are typically weak coalitions of small parties dependent on skillful leaders to hold them together. There were no regional leaders or powerful chiefs in Melanesia before the arrival of Europeans. Polynesia, on the other hand, was governed by powerful hereditary chiefs and kings; the Fijian political system was strongly influenced by the Polynesians.

Although only six of the 15 political entities covered in this book are fully independent, most of the others are internally self-governing to some degree. Tokelau, a dependency of New Zealand, has resisted self-government out of fear that it might lead to a reduction in subsidies. The appointed French high commissioners in Tahiti-Polynesia, Wallis and Futuna, and New Caledonia wield considerable power in those territories, though locally elected assemblies have some control over economic and social matters.

Regional Organizations
The oldest and largest regional grouping is the **Secretariat of the Pacific Community** (B.P. D5, 98848 Nouméa Cedex, New Caledonia; tel. 687/26-20-00, fax 687/26-38-18, www.spc.org.nc, e-mail: spc@spc.org.nc), known as the South Pacific Commission until 1997. This technical assistance organization was established in 1947 to promote the economic and social well-being of the peoples of the South Pacific. Fields of activity include agriculture, fisheries, health, rural development, training, women's development, and statistical services. Twenty-two Pacific island countries and territories are members, together with Australia, Britain, France, New Zealand, and the United States. The Netherlands withdrew from the body in 1962 after Indonesia annexed eastern New Guinea. Since 1950 delegates from all 27 member governments have met at an annual conference every other October to discuss the Community's program and budget. About 90% of the PC's US$19 million budget comes out of grants from the four larger members; the island governments contribute only token amounts (the U.S. has arrears dating back to 1986).

The other main regional organization is the **South Pacific Forum** with 16 self-governing members (Australia, Cook Islands, Federated States of Micronesia, Fiji, Kiribati, Marshall Islands, Nauru, New Zealand, Niue, Palau, Papua New Guinea, Solomon Islands, Tonga, Tuvalu,

Vanuatu, and Samoa). Founded in 1971, the Forum grew out of dissatisfaction with the apolitical SPC, which was seen as a vestige of colonialism. Two-thirds of the Forum's US$6 million budget is provided by Australia and New Zealand. Each year the heads of government of the Forum countries meet for informal political discussions. (The 1996 Majuro Forum was marred by the turtle steak incident mentioned above.) In October 1994 the Forum's international influence was enhanced when the SPF was granted observer status at the United Nations (Fiji, Solomon Islands, Vanuatu, and Samoa were already U.N. members). Since 1995 a parallel forum of nongovernment organizations designed to press regional social and environmental issues has coincided with the official forum.

In 1972 the SPF established the **Forum Secretariat** (Box 856, Suva, Fiji Islands; tel. 679/312-600, fax 679/305-573, www.forumsec.org.fj, e-mail: info@forumsec.org.fj), called the South Pacific Bureau for Economic Cooperation until 1988, as its executive body. The SPF is engaged in fields such as sustainable development, investment, trade, and international affairs, and has set up a regional shipping line (the Pacific Forum Line). The **Forum Fisheries Agency** (Box 629, Honiara, Solomon Islands; tel. 677/21124, fax 677/23995, www.ffa.int, e-mail: ffa@ffa.int), formed in 1979, coordinates the fisheries policies of the island member states, negotiates licensing agreements with foreign countries and 1,400 foreign fishing boats, assists in surveillance and enforcement, carries out scientific and commercial studies of marine resources, and provides technical assistance to local fishing industries. In 1989 the FFA was instrumental in having long driftnets banned from the region and in 1993 a treaty on surveillance cooperation was signed.

The **South Pacific Regional Environment Program** (Box 240, Apia, Samoa; tel. 685/21-929, fax 685/20-231, www.sprep.org.ws, e-mail: sprep@sprep.org.ws), established in 1982 by the SPC, the SPF, and the United Nations, became an autonomous regional organization with 26 member countries in 1993. With a budget of US$7 million and a staff of more than 50, SPREP promotes sustainable development by creating programs in fields such as environmental management, global change, species conservation, nature reserves, and pollution management, and through education and international coordination.

Other Regional Institutions

The **University of the South Pacific** (Box 1168, Suva, Fiji Islands; tel. 679/313-900, fax 679/301-305, www.usp.ac.fj, e-mail: webmaster@usp.ac.fj) was organized in 1967 to serve the Cook Islands, Fiji, Kiribati, Marshall Islands, Nauru, Niue, Solomon Islands, Tokelau, Tonga, Tuvalu, Vanuatu, and Samoa—the widest catchment area covered by any university in the world. The initial campus was at Laucala, near Suva, and in 1977 the USP's School of Agriculture was established at Alafua, outside Apia, Samoa. The USP has six action-oriented institutes, such as the Institute of Marine Resources at Honiara. The major USP complex at Port Vila houses the Pacific Languages Unit and Law Department. The original aim of the USP was to facilitate the localization of posts held by expatriates until independence, but in recent years the emphasis has shifted from teacher training to business studies and technology. In 1998 the USP had about 4,400 students studying at the two main campuses, plus 5,400 taking degree courses at USP extension centers in all 12 member countries except Tokelau. Another 1,600 persons were enrolled in Continuing Education courses. The USP extension centers are well worth visiting to purchase the excellent, inexpensive books published by the university's Institute of Pacific Studies.

In 1987 the **Université française du Pacifique** (B.P. 4635, 98713 Papeete, Tahiti; tel. 689/42-16-80, fax 689/41-01-31) was established, with university centers at Tahiti and Nouméa specializing in law, humanities, social sciences, languages, and science. In 1994 this university had about 2,400 students.

One of the few regional grass roots coalitions is the **Nuclear-Free and Independent Pacific** (NFIP) movement, which organizes conferences periodically (Fiji 1975, Pohnpei 1978, Hawaii 1980, Vanuatu 1983, Manila 1987, New Zealand 1990, Fiji 1996) to allow activists from groups from all around the Pacific to get together and map out strategy and solidarity in the struggle against militarism and colonialism. The directing body of the NFIP movement is the **Pacific Concerns Resource Center** (Private Mail Bag,

Suva, Fiji Islands; tel. 679/304-649, fax 679/304-755, e-mail: pcrc@is.com.fj).

Other institutions fostering a feeling of regional unity include the **Festival of Pacific Arts** and the **South Pacific Games** (see **Holidays and Festivals** later in this introduction).

The United States

Washington has precipitously downgraded its presence in the South Pacific in the aftermath of the Cold War. In 1995 the regional office of U.S. Agency for International Development was closed, in 1996 the U.S. Information Agency disappeared, the American-funded Asia Foundation has gone, and the U.S. no longer promptly pays its assessed dues to regional organizations. It took personal intervention by the congressman from American Samoa to save the U.S. embassy in Apia; Fiji hosts the only other U.S. diplomatic mission in the region. Several Hawaii-based think tanks, including the East-West Center at the University of Hawaii and the Pacific Islands Development Program (PIDP), are reeling under the loss of U.S. government grants, and the Fulbright scholarship program has been scrapped. Even the Peace Corps is being cut back.

To many North Americans, "the Pacific" means essentially the Pacific Rim, and the South Pacific is Australia/New Zealand. To them, the hundreds of islands and cultures included in this handbook are only the hole in the donut. The sole exception to this neglect is Hawaii which has an airline, bank, and hotel chain doing brisk business south of the equator. Small wonder many island leaders feel a certain nostalgia for the days when they could easily get the U.S. government's attention by throwing a few fish to the Russian bear. It's an irony that's hard to miss.

The hermit crab (Pagurus) uses empty snail shells to protect its soft abdomen from predators. The crab hooks himself into the shell and would sooner be torn in two than let go. As these nocturnal scavengers grow, they must find larger shells to live in. Contrary to the name, the hermits are quite sociable and are often seen in groups searching for food or new shells.

LOUISE FOOTE

ECONOMY

Trade

Australia and New Zealand have huge trade surpluses with the Pacific islands. In 1995, for example, Australia sold them A$780 million in goods while purchasing only A$255 million worth. New Zealand sells nine times more than it buys. Ten South Pacific countries participate in the Pacific Forum Line, a shipping company set up by the South Pacific Forum to facilitate trade with Australia and New Zealand, but in practice, the Line's large container ships run full northbound and empty southbound. The trade deficits make the industrialized, exporting nations the main beneficiaries of the island economies. For Australia and New Zealand, the South Pacific market is not very important, but for every island nation this trade is vital to its interests.

The main products exported by the South Pacific countries are sugar (Fiji), fish and seafood (American Samoa, Fiji, New Caledonia, and Solomon Islands), clothing and footwear (Fiji), minerals (Fiji, New Caledonia, and Solomon Islands), timber (Fiji, Solomon Islands, and Vanuatu), and black pearls (Cook Islands and Tahiti-Polynesia). The United Kingdom and Japan are the only major powers that buy much more from the islands than they sell. The U.K. buys much of Fiji's sugar and fish while Japan purchases timber and fish from Solomon Islands and nickel ore from New Caledonia. In recent years Tonga has exported large quantities of squash (pumpkin) to Japan.

Products such as bananas, cacao, coconut oil, coffee, copra, palm oil, pineapples, sugar, taro, tea, and vanilla are subject to price fluctuations over which local governments have no control, plus low demand and strong competition from other third-world producers. Most of these commodities are processed and marketed outside the islands by transnationals. Even worse, efforts to increase the output of commodities such as these reduces local food production, leading to expensive imports of processed food. New Zealand meat exporters routinely ship low-quality "Pacific cuts" of fatty, frozen mutton flaps unsalable on world markets to countries like Tonga and Samoa. American companies dump junk foods such as "turkey tails" in the islands, and tinned mystery meats arrive from afar.

Aid, investment, remittances, and tourism help offset the trade imbalances, but this also fosters dependence. Trade between the various South Pacific countries is limited by a basic similarity of their products and shipping tariffs that encourage bulk trade with Australia and New Zealand rather than local interisland trade. In 1993 the three countries of the Melanesian Spearhead established free trade in beef from Vanuatu, canned tuna from Solomon Islands, and tea from Papua New Guinea, and more than 140 products are now covered by the Melanesian Trade Agreement. Fiji's decision to join the Spearhead in 1996 had a lot to do with a desire to gain access to this large market. Tonga and Fiji have a limited free-trade agreement and steps are being taken toward creating a larger regional free-trade area.

External Aid

An overwhelming proportion of aid money is given by the colonial powers to their colonies, past or present. In 1995 Australia provided A$238 million in aid to the South Pacific, of which A$198 million went to Papua New Guinea. Much of New Zealand's aid goes to Cook Is-

TRADING PARTNERS

(Figures are from 1995 and expressed in A$ million)

REGION	IMPORTS FROM	EXPORTS TO
Australia	780	255
New Zealand	431	49
South Pacific	59	59
France	1,140	271
United Kingdom	95	238
Other Europe	339	107
U.S.A.	370	186
Japan	220	438
Other Asia	244	222
Other countries	412	122
TOTAL	**4,090**	**1,947**

lands, while most U.S. aid is spent in American Samoa and the U.S.-related entities in Micronesia. France expends monumental amounts maintaining its three colonies though much of the money returns to France to pay for French imports.

Other European countries such as Britain and Germany channel most of their aid through the European Union, which is the region's second-most-important donor, providing soft loans, import quotas and subsidies, technical assistance, etc. Japan provides A\$138 million a year in bilateral aid to the independent countries and it's the region's largest donor, if you don't count the Australian money given to Papua New Guinea. Between 1987 and 1995, Japanese aid doubled. The Asian Development Bank, United Nations Development Program, and UNESCO are also significant.

Although the South Pacific absorbs the highest rate of aid per capita in the world, much aid is wasted on doing things for people instead of helping them do things for themselves. Aid that empowers people by increasing their capacity to identify, understand, and resolve problems is the exception, while prestige projects like huge airports, sophisticated communications networks, and fancy government buildings, which foster dependence on outsiders, are the rule. The U.S. paid for the new parliament building in Honiara and the Chinese government has bankrolled massive government complexes in Vanuatu and Samoa. In response, Taiwan has financed high profile buildings in Solomon Islands and Tonga.

Japanese aid is intended primarily to ensure easy access for its fishing fleet and to support Japanese business activities in the islands. Virtually all Japanese aid is "tied," with most of the benefit going to Japanese companies. In contrast, Australia and New Zealand are to be commended for taking the trouble to develop low-profile microprojects to assist individual communities. The closest the U.S. comes to this is the Peace Corps but its activities are presently being downsized to cut costs (in 1998 the Peace Corps pulled out of Tuvalu and Fiji).

Aid spent in the capitals prompts unproductive migrations to the towns. There's a growing imbalance between the cost of government in relation to locally generated revenues. Salaries for officials, consultants, and various other "experts" eat up much aid. The only country with a high per capita income that is not greatly dependent on aid is Fiji.

Aid to local communities is also provided by nongovernment organizations such as the Foundation for the Peoples of the South Pacific, a branch of **Counterpart** (1200 18th St. NW, Suite 1100, Washington, DC 20036, U.S.A.; tel. 202/296-9676, fax 202/296-9679, www.counterpart. org, e-mail: info@counterpart.org), a nonprofit voluntary organization 85% funded by the U.S. Agency for International Development. The FPSP has projects in Fiji, Samoa, Solomon Islands, Tonga, and Vanuatu that emphasize sustainable development, health and nutrition, income generation, and family food production.

Other groups of this kind include the **South Pacific Peoples Foundation of Canada** (1921 Fernwood Rd., Victoria, BC V8T 2Y6, Canada; tel. 250/381-4131, fax 250/388-5258, www.sppf.org, e-mail: sppf@sppf.org), the **Australian Foundation for the Peoples of Asia and the Pacific** (Box 12, Crows Nest, NSW 1585, Australia; tel. 61-2/9906-3792, fax 61-2/9436-4637, e-mail: afsp@mpx.com.au), the **United Kingdom Foundation for the South Pacific** (4A Newmills Rd., Dalkeith, Midlothia EH22 1DU, Scotland; tel. 44-131/663-7428, fax 44-131/663-7433, e-mail: ukfsp@cableinet.co.uk), and **Counterpart Deutschland e.V.** (Bonn Center H 1503, Bundeskanzlerplatz 2-10, D-53113 Bonn, Germany; tel. 49-228/22-43-71, fax 49-228/22-43-76).

Trade Agreements

The current trend toward "globalization" is not to the islands' advantage. Free trade forces Pacific countries to compete with low-wage producers in Asia and Latin America where human rights and the environment are of scant concern. The World Bank and other international banks aggressively market "project loans" to facilitate the production of goods for sale on world markets. The initial beneficiaries of these projects are the contractors, while the ability of transnational corporations to exploit the region's natural resources is enhanced. Subsistence food production is reduced and the recipient state is left with a debt burden it can only service through exports.

Should commodity exports fail, the International Monetary Fund steps in with emergency loans to make sure the foreign banks don't lose their money. Local governments are forced to accept "structural adjustment programs" dictated from Washington, and the well-paid Western bankers mandate that social spending be cut. Another favorite trick is persuade governments to shift the tax burden from rich to poor by replacing income and company taxes with a value-added tax. Tottering administrations are forced to clearcut their rainforests and sell their soil to meet financial obligations. This kind of chicanery has caused untold misery in Africa, Asia, and Latin America, often with the connivance of corrupt local officials.

A much fairer arrangement is the Lomé Convention, which provides for the preferential entry into the European Union at fixed prices of set quotas of agricultural commodities from 70 African, Caribbean, and Pacific countries. Many experts believe that trade subsidies of this kind are the most direct way of delivering aid to developing countries without the intervention of state bureaucracies. Indeed, this type of arrangement is crucial to countries that rely on a single export for much of their foreign exchange. In the year 2000 Lomé IV is due to expire, and if it's not renewed disastrous consequences await the eight Pacific countries involved (the bulk of Fiji's sugar crop enjoys free entry into the United Kingdom thanks to Lomé). If Lomé disappears it will largely be the work of the United States, which has lobbied vigorously in favor of "free trade" so American corporations can export to Europe tropical commodities produced cheaply in Latin America through the use of semislave labor.

Since 1980 New Zealand and Australia have tried to help the island countries balance their trade deficits by allowing most of the products of the South Pacific Forum countries unrestricted duty-free entry on a nonreciprocal basis, provided they have 50% local content. The only exceptions are sugar, steel, motor vehicles, and clothing, which are subject to quotas in Australia. The **South Pacific Regional Trade and Economic Cooperation Agreement** (SPARTECA) has allowed Tonga, Samoa, and others to set up Small Industries Centers producing manufactured goods for export south. A large Japanese-owned factory in Samoa exports automotive electrical parts to Australia. Garments are now Fiji's second-largest export, with A$192 mil-

lion sold in 1995. Low wages, inadequate labor legislation, and weak unions combine with tax concessions, exemption from customs duties, government subsidies in the form of infrastructure and training, and an open market in Australia and New Zealand to make Fiji attractive to foreign garment manufacturers. Women make up the vast majority of the workforce, earning less than a tenth as much as their counterparts in New Zealand, where working conditions are far better.

Critics of SPARTECA say the 50% local content rule discourages companies from operating efficiently by reducing local costs, and relegates them to the bottom end of the market since the raw materials required for quality products are not available in the islands. Now with universal trade barriers falling in the wake of the 1994 signing of the GATT, the value of selective trade agreements such as SPARTECA and Lomé is decreasing, and in the future it will be much more difficult for Pacific island industries to compete with cheap-labor areas in Asia. The 1994 Bogor Declaration reduces tariffs between the 19 members of the Asia Pacific Economic Cooperation (APEC) to 25% by 2000 and to zero by 2010, thereby eliminating the competitive advantage of SPARTECA by granting Asian producers similar access to Australia and New Zealand.

Business
Foreign investment in tourism, retailing, banking, construction, transportation, and mining is heavy. Foreign logging operations and local slash-and-burn agriculture threaten the rainforests of the high islands, and many governments lack the political will to enforce conservation. In Solomon Islands, Malaysian logging companies are cutting the forests at far beyond the sustainable rate while paying landowners a royalty of less than one percent of the value of the timber. An Australian study has shown how Vanuatu and Solomon Islands lost A$350 million in 1993 due to overcutting and underpaying by the Asian loggers. Payoffs to local officials allow this practice to continue. Despite these depredations, three-quarters of the old growth forest in these two countries is still intact and capable of being saved.

The Asian economic crisis of 1997-98 had an immediate impact in the South Pacific as Fiji and Solomon Islands were forced to sharply devalue their national currencies in order to remain competitive with Asian holiday destinations and exporters. One of the few beneficial side-effects of the crash was a drop in the value of tropical hardwoods on Asian markets, giving Pacific forests a respite.

The Asian crisis only exacerbated a process already underway in the islands as national banks approached collapse, government indebtedness soared, and official corruption ran rampant. Like their counterparts in Jakarta, Kuala Lumpur, and Bangkok, many island political leaders have become hooked on the joys of borrowing, burdening their countries with unrepayable debts. In 1995 Cook Islands was forced to withdraw the Cook Islands dollar from circulation after colossal governmental mismanagement, and official corruption has reached the highest levels in Samoa, Vanuatu, and Solomon Islands. The economic turmoil may make the islands cheaper for visitors than ever before, but the people are suffering.

Minerals

The most important minerals are nickel in New Caledonia and gold in Fiji. Extensive mineral exploration is being conducted in Solomon Islands, and there are potential oil basins around Tonga, Fiji, New Caledonia, Vanuatu, and the Solomons, though as yet no oil has been discovered.

More important are the undersea mineral nodules within the exclusive economic zones (EEZ) of Tahiti-Polynesia, Cook Islands, and Kiribati. Three known nodule deposits sit in more than 6,000 meters of water in the Pacific: one stretches from Mexico to a point southeast of Hawaii; another is between Hawaii and the Marshall Islands; a third is in Tahiti-Polynesia and Cook Islands. The potato-sized nodules contain manganese, cobalt, nickel, and copper; total deposits are valued at US$3 trillion, enough to supply the world for thousands of years. The **South Pacific Applied Geoscience Commission** (Private Mail Bag, Suva, Fiji Islands; tel. 679/381-377,

THE LAW OF THE SEA

This treaty has changed the face of the Pacific. States traditionally exercised sovereignty over a three-mile belt of territorial sea along their shores; the high seas beyond those limits could be freely used by anyone. Then on 28 September 1945, President Harry Truman declared U.S. sovereignty over the natural resources of the adjacent continental shelf. U.S. fishing boats soon became involved in an acrimonious dispute with several South American countries over their rich anchovy fishing grounds, and in 1952 Chile, Ecuador, and Peru declared a 200-nautical-mile exclusive economic zone along their shores. In 1958 the United Nations convened a Conference on the Law of the Sea at Geneva, which accepted national control over shelves up to 200 meters deep. Agreement could not be reached on extended territorial sea limits.

National claims multiplied so much that in 1974 another U.N. conference was convened, leading to the signing of the Law of the Sea convention at Jamaica in 1982 by 159 states and other entities. This complex agreement—200 pages, nine annexes, and 320 articles—extended national control over 40% of the world's oceans. The territorial sea was increased to 12 nautical miles and the

continental shelf was ambiguously defined as extending 200 nautical miles offshore. States were given full control over all resources, living or nonliving, within this belt. Fiji was the first country to ratify the 1982 convention, and by November 1994 a total of 60 countries had signed up, allowing the treaty to come into force for them.

Even before it became international law, many aspects of the Law of the Sea were accepted in practice. The EEZs mainly affect fisheries and seabed mineral exploitation; freedom of navigation within the zones is guaranteed. In 1976 the South Pacific Forum declared an EEZ for each member and decided to set up a fisheries agency soon after. The Law of the Sea increased immensely the territory of independent oceanic states, giving them real political weight for the first time. The land area of the 23 separate entities in Micronesia, Melanesia, and Polynesia (excluding Hawaii and New Zealand) total only 550,361 square km, while their EEZs total 29,878,000 square km! It's known that vast mineral deposits are scattered across this seabed, though the cost of extraction (estimated at US$1.5 billion) has prevented their exploitation to date.

fax 679/370-040, www.sopac.org.fj) or SOPAC, a regional body set up by the United Nations in 1972, is in charge of assessing the development of mineral resources in the EEZs of the Pacific countries, though actual mining is still decades away. Over the past decade Japan has spent US$100 million on seabed surveys in preparation for eventual mining.

This undersea wealth has made France unwilling to consider independence for its Pacific colonies and has convinced the U.S. Senate not to ratify the Law of the Sea. The original text of this treaty required transnational corporations to share the benefits of undersea mining with developing nations, but a compromise adopted by the United Nations General Assembly on 28 July 1994 watered down those provisions considerably and four months later the treaty came into force. The ocean bed in international waters has been divided among the U.S., Britain, France, Germany, South Korea, China, Japan, and others by the United Nations' International Seabed Authority.

Fisheries

Tuna is the second-largest commercial fishing industry in the world (after shrimp and prawns), and 55% of the world's catch is taken in the central and western Pacific. Most of the one million metric tonnes of tuna (worth US$1.5 billion) fished from the region each year is taken by about 1,200 foreign fishing boats, which pay a mere US$60 million in annual fees to work the EEZs of the island nations. The number of large purse seiners present in the region has increased from 14 in 1980 to around 147, of which 42 are Taiwanese, 35 Japanese, 33 American, 26 Korean, and 11 Filipino. Longliners make up the bulk of the remainder, including 700 Chinese and Taiwanese boats and 400 Japanese, but they account for only 12% of the catch as opposed to 79% for the purse seiners. Pole-and-line boats take another eight percent and just one percent is caught by trolling.

About 70% of the tuna pulled in are skipjack, 23% yellowfin, four percent albacore, and four percent bigeye. Due to the introduction of purse seiners, catches doubled in the 1980s and the bigeye is already being harvested at close to maximum sustainable rates. By the year 2020 the southern bluefin tuna is expected to be com-

pletely wiped out. Fears are growing that the entire resource could soon be ravaged as European high seas fleets are redeployed from oceans already stripped of fish. The huge Norwegian and Spanish factory ships that destroyed the North Atlantic fisheries are already plundering waters off South America and the Indian Ocean, and their entry into the South Pacific is awaited with trepidation. In June 1997 a Majuro conference of Asian, American, and Pacific fisheries officials agreed unanimously to create an agreement on tuna management and conservation in international waters within three years.

To collect fair compensation for the exploitation of their only renewable resource, the island governments have had to sail a stormy course right from the start. For many years the U.S. tuna fleet refused to pay licensing fees because the fish were deemed migratory. Then, after two unlicensed U.S. purse seiners were confiscated by Papua New Guinea and the Solomons in 1982 and 1984, and Kiribati signed a fishing agreement with the Soviets in 1985, the U.S. government finally got the message. In 1987 the U.S. agreed to a US$60-million aid package, which included five-year licensing fees for American tuna boats to work the EEZs of the 14 member states of the Forum Fisheries Agency. In 1990 the whole matter seemed settled when the U.S. Congress imposed management on tuna stocks in the U.S. EEZ. The "migratory" fish had finally found owners. In 1992 the U.S. agreed to pay another US$180 million to allow up to 58 American purse seiners access to FFA waters for 10 years. The money is divided up according to the quantity of fish caught in the waters of each member country.

The Forum Fisheries Agency, which negotiated the Tuna Treaty, now handles all fisheries agreements between the 14 FFA member states and the U.S., Korea, Japan, Taiwan, and the Philippines. The Koreans and Taiwanese have a reputation for massively under-reporting their catches to avoid paying proper access fees. The Japanese report their catches more honestly but Japan has steadfastly refused to sign a multilateral fisheries agreement with the FFA. Instead the Japanese prefer to drive a hard bargain with each Pacific country individually, using aid money as bait. Smaller Pacific countries are often unable to stand up to this bullying, and

Japanese fishing companies are not above paying bribes to island officials. In 1993 Australia donated 23 naval patrol boats to the island states to help police the island fisheries zones.

Some Pacific countries have established small pole-and-line fishing industries, but the capital-intensive, high-tech purse seiner operations carried out by the Americans and Japanese are beyond their means. A workable fishing fleet requires at least 10 boats plus large amounts of fresh water and electricity for processing. Also, U.S. customs regulations tax tuna heavily unless it's processed in an American territory, which is why the two canneries at Pago Pago, American Samoa, receive most of the purse seiner-caught fish. The other regional canneries at Levuka (Fiji) and Noro (Solomon Islands) benefit from a 24% duty advantage in the European Union thanks to the Lomé Convention. Without this they'd be unable to compete with low-wage canneries in Thailand and Indonesia. The longline vessels are used to supply the lucrative Japanese sashimi market with iced tuna, which is transshipped by air.

Various Moneymaking Scams

In 1971 the New Hebrides (now Vanuatu) became the first Pacific entity to offer offshore banking facilities to foreign corporations attempting to avoid taxation in their home countries. In 1982 Cook Islands also set up a tax haven, followed by Tonga in 1985 and Samoa in 1989. Niue has also entered the field. Almost 100 brass-plate banks and more than 1,000 dummy corporations now operate in Vanuatu with little or no staff, fixed assets, or capital. In 1990 Australia plugged the loopholes, which had been costing it millions of dollars a year in lost taxation, and most of the clients of the "financial centers" are now companies based in Asia.

Vanuatu also runs a "flag of convenience" shipping register that allows first-world shipping companies to evade Western safety, environmental, and labor regulations, while employing cheap third-world crews on their ships. Tonga sells its sovereignty to affluent foreigners in the form of dummy Tongan passports intended to be used to slip into third countries. A sizable Chinese transient population is in Nuku'alofa awaiting the chance to move on to greener pastures. Tuvalu and Niue have leased their international telephone circuits to the operators of sex-by-phone hot lines.

One of the largest sources of income for countries like Tonga, Samoa, and Cook Islands is remittances sent home by emigrants living in New Zealand and Australia. The Diaspora also provides the bulk of visitors to countries like Tonga.

TOURISM

Tourism is the world's largest and fastest-growing industry, growing 260% between 1970 and 1990. Some 593 million people traveled abroad in 1996 compared to only 25 million in 1950, and each year more than 25 million first-world tourists visit third-world countries, transferring an estimated US$25 billion from North to South. Tourism is the only industry that allows a net flow of wealth from richer to poorer countries, and in the islands it's one of the few avenues open for economic development, providing much-needed foreign exchange required to pay for imports. Unlike every other export, purchasers of tourism products pay their own transportation costs to the market.

Australia provided the largest percentage of the 932,016 South Pacific tourists in 1997, followed by New Zealand, the U.S., Japan, France, the United Kingdom, Germany, and Canada in that order. Australia is the main source of visitors to Fiji, Solomon Islands, and Vanuatu, while New Zealanders are the biggest group in Cook Islands, Niue, Tonga, and Samoa. Americans and French are the largest single groups in Tahiti-Polynesia, while the French and Japanese are tied in New Caledonia. On a per-capita basis, Cook Islands gets the most tourists and Solomon Islands the fewest. It's the number-one industry in Tahiti-Polynesia, Cook Islands, Tonga, Samoa, Fiji, and Vanuatu, and some 45,000 islanders now rely on tourism as a way of making a living. Yet tourism is relatively low key: overcrowded Hawaii gets 10 times as many annual visitors as the entire South Pacific combined. The "tyranny of distance" has thus far prevented the islands from being spoiled.

Arrival levels from Australia and New Zealand are expected to remain stable in coming years, and Japan, Europe, and North America are seen

TOURIST ARRIVALS (1997)

Fiji Islands	359,441
Tahiti-Polynesia	180,440
New Caledonia	105,137
Samoa	67,960
Papua New Guinea	66,143
Cook Islands	49,964
Vanuatu	49,605
American Samoa	39,802
Tonga	26,162
Solomon Islands	15,894
Easter Island	10,000
Niue	2,041
Tuvalu	1,029

as the main growth markets for South Pacific tourism. Japanese interest in the region increased dramatically in the late 1980s, and Japanese companies now own top hotels in Fiji, Tahiti-Polynesia, Vanuatu, Samoa, and the Solomon Islands. Yet the Japanese tend to go on short holidays and only those countries with direct flights from Japan (Fiji, New Caledonia, and Tahiti-Polynesia) receive sizable numbers of Japanese tourists. Increasing numbers of European and North American visitors can be expected if airfares remain low and the region's many advantages over competing Mediterranean and Caribbean destinations can be effectively marketed.

Only about 40% of the net earnings from tourism actually stays in the host country. The rest is "leaked" in repatriated profits, salaries for expatriates, commissions, imported goods, food, fuel, etc. Top management positions usually go to foreigners, with local residents offered low-paying service jobs. To encourage hotel construction, local governments must commit themselves to crippling tax concessions and large infrastructure investments for the benefit of hotel companies. The cost of airports, roads,

communications networks, power lines, sewers, and waste disposal can exceed the profits from tourism.

Tourism-related construction can cause unsightly beach erosion due to the clearing of vegetation and the extraction of sand. Resort sewage causes lagoon pollution, while the reefs are blasted to provide passes for tourist craft and stripped of corals or shells by visitors. Locally scarce water supplies are diverted to hotels, and foods such as fruit and fish can be priced beyond the reach of local residents. Access to the ocean can be blocked by wall-to-wall hotels.

Although tourism is often seen as a way of experiencing other cultures, it can undermine those same cultures. Traditional dances and ceremonies are shortened or changed to fit into tourist schedules, and mock celebrations are held out of season and context, and their significance is lost. Cheap mass-produced handicrafts are made to satisfy the expectations of visitors; thus, the New Guinea-style masks of Fiji, mock-Hawaiian tikis of Tonga, and Balinese carvings of Bora Bora. Authenticity is sacrificed for immediate profits. While travel cannot help but improve international understanding, the aura of glamour and prosperity surrounding tourist resorts can present a totally false image of a country's social and economic realities.

To date most attention has focused on luxury resorts and all-inclusive tours—the exotic rather than the authentic. Packaged holidays create the illusion of adventure while avoiding all risks and individualized variables, and on many tours the only islanders seen are maids and bartenders. This elitist tourism perpetuates the colonial master-servant relationship as condescending foreigners instill a feeling of inferiority in local residents and workers. Many island governments are publicly on record as favoring development based on local resources and island technology, yet inexplicably this concept is rarely applied to tourism. Without local participation, tourism can be the proverbial wolf in sheep's clothing.

THE PEOPLE

The aquatic continent of Oceania is divided into three great cultural areas: Polynesia and Melanesia lie mostly below the equator while Micronesia is above it. The name Polynesia comes from the Greek words *poly* (many) and *nesos* (islands). The Polynesian Triangle has Hawaii at its north apex, New Zealand 8,000 km to the southwest, and Easter Island an equal distance to the southeast. Melanesia gets its name from the Greek word *melas* (black), probably for the dark appearance of its inhabitants as seen by the early European navigators. Micronesia comes from the Greek word *mikros* (small), thus, the "small islands."

The term Polynesia was coined by Charles de Brosses in 1756 and applied to all the Pacific islands. The present restricted use was proposed by Dumont d'Urville during a famous lecture at the Geographical Society in Paris in 1831. At the same time he also proposed the terms Melanesia and Micronesia for the regions that still bear those names. The terms are not particularly good, considering that all three regions have "many islands" and "small islands"; in Melanesia it is not the islands, but the people, that are black.

The notion that the Pacific islands and their peoples are all similar—if you've seen one you've seen 'em all—is a total fallacy. No other group of six million people anywhere on earth comes from such a variety of cultures. The population is divided between Melanesians (80%), Polynesians (seven percent), Asians (six percent), Micronesians (five percent), and Europeans (two percent). Ninety percent of the people live on high islands, the rest on low islands and atolls. About a million reside in urban areas. The region's charming, gentle, graceful peoples are among its main attractions.

Population

The high birth rate (more than three percent a year in parts of Melanesia) and rapid urbanization severely tax the best efforts of governments with limited resources. The average population density across the region (excluding Papua New Guinea) is 27 persons per square kilometer, though some atolls can have more than 1,000 people per square kilometer. The most densely populated Pacific countries are the Polynesian islands of American Samoa, Tokelau, Tonga, and Tuvalu, while the larger Melanesian countries have far fewer people per square kilometer. Due to the absence of family planning, populations in Melanesia are doubling every 20 years and half the total population is under 18 years of age. Population growth rates vary from zero in Niue and Tokelau, where people are emigrating, to 3.4% per annum in Solomon Islands.

More developed countries like American Samoa, Cook Islands, Fiji, New Caledonia, and Tahiti-Polynesia are highly urbanized, with around half the population town dwellers. Samoa, Solomon Islands, and Vanuatu are the least urbanized, with about 85% still living in villages. The rapid growth of cities like Apia, Honiara, Nuku'alofa, Papeete, Port Vila, and Suva has led to high levels of unemployment and social problems such as alcoholism, petty crime, and domestic violence.

Emigration relieves the pressure a little and provides income in the form of remittances sent back. However, absenteeism also creates the problem of idled land and abandoned homes. Cook Islanders, Niueans, Tongans, and Samoans emigrate to New Zealand; American Samoans and Micronesians to the U.S.; Fiji Indians to Canada and Australia; people from the Australs, Tuamotus, and Marquesas to Tahiti; and Tahitians and Wallis Islanders to New Caledonia. In American Samoa, Cook Islands, Niue, Tokelau, and Wallis and Futuna, more islanders now live off their home islands than on them. About 175,000 insular Polynesians live in New Zealand, another 65,000 in the United States. Some 25,000 Fiji Indians are in Canada. In 1987 New Zealand withdrew visa-free entry facilities for Fijians, Tongans, and Samoans to limit the flow.

Pacific Women

Traditionally Pacific women were confined to the home, while the men would handle most matters outside the immediate family. The clear-cut roles of the woman as homemaker and the man as defender and decision-maker gave stability to village life. In Melanesia the woman was responsible for working the land and doing most of the housework, thereby increasing the status of the man as head of the family; life was similar for Polynesian women, though they had greater influence.

Western education has caused many Pacific women to question their subordinate position and the changing lifestyle has made the old relationship between the sexes outmoded. As paid employment expands and—thanks to family planning—women are able to hold their jobs, they demand equal treatment from society. Polynesian women are more emancipated than their sisters in Melanesia, though men continue to dominate public life throughout the region. Tradition is often manipulated to deny women the right to express themselves publicly on community matters.

Cultural barriers hinder women's access to education and employment, and the proportion of girls in school falls rapidly as the grade level increases. Female students are nudged into low-paying fields such as nursing or secretarial services; in Fiji and elsewhere, export-oriented garment factories exploit women workers with low wages and poor conditions. Levels of domestic violence vary greatly. In Fiji, for example, it's far less accepted among indigenous Fijians than it is among Fiji Indians, and in Fiji's Macuata Province women have a suicide rate seven times above the world average, with most of the victims being Indians. Those little signs on buses reading "real men don't hit women" suggest the problem. Travelers should take an interest in women's issues.

Traditional Customs

Although the South Pacific is a region of great variety, there are a number of rituals and ceremonies that many islands have in common. The most important of these is the kava ceremony found in Fiji, Samoa, Tonga, and Vanuatu. Kava (called *yaqona* in Fiji) is a drink made from the crushed root of the pepper plant. The powder or pulp is strained or mixed with water in a large wooden bowl and drunk from a coconut-shell cup. Elaborate protocols accompany formal kava ceremonies although kava is also a social drink consumed by ordinary people when they get together to relax and chat. See the introductions to the Fiji Islands and Vanuatu chapters for more information.

Another widespread feature of Pacific culture is the making of bark cloth called tapa (*masi* in Fijian) used for clothing or decoration. This felt-like cloth with stenciled or printed designs is described under **Arts and Crafts** in this introduction.

Other customs include firewalking (see **Customs** in Fiji Islands chapter), stone fishing (see **On the Road** in the Tahiti-Polynesia chapter), the use of an earth oven called an *umu* in Polynesia or a *lovo* in Fiji (see **Food and Drink** in this introduction), tattooing (see **People** in the Samoa chapter), land diving (see **Pentecost** in the Vanuatu chapter), shell money (see the **Solomon Islands** chapter), and the presentation of a whale's tooth called a *tabua* (see **Customs** in the Fiji Islands chapter). These unique traditions are a thread uniting the diverse peoples of the Pacific.

THE POLYNESIANS

The Polynesians, whom Robert Louis Stevenson called "God's best, at least God's sweetest work," are a tall, golden-skinned people with straight or wavy, but rarely fuzzy, hair. They have fine features, almost intimidating physiques, and a soft, flowing language. One theory holds that the Polynesians evolved their great bodily stature through a selective process on their long ocean voyages, as the larger individuals with more body fat were better able to resist the chill of evaporating sea spray on their bodies (polar animals are generally larger than equatorial animals of the same species for the same reason). Other authorities ascribe the Polynesian's huge body size to a high-carbohydrate vegetable diet.

The ancient Polynesians developed a rigid social system with hereditary chiefs; descent was usually through the father. In most of Polynesia there were only two classes, chiefs and commoners, but in Hawaii, Tahiti, and Tonga an intermediate class existed. Slaves were outside the class system entirely, but there were slaves only in New Zealand, the Cook Islands, and Mangareva. People lived in scattered dwellings rather than villages, although there were groupings around the major temples and chiefs' residences.

They lived from fishing and agriculture, using tools made from stone, bone, shell, and wood. The men were responsible for planting, har-

AUCKLAND INSTITUTE AND MUSEUM

moai *on the slopes of Rano Raraku, Easter Island*

vesting, fishing, cooking, house and canoe building; the women tended the fields and animals, gathered food and fuel, prepared food, and made clothes and household items. Both males and females worked together in family or community groups, not as individuals.

The Polynesians lost the art of pottery making during their long stay in Havaiki and had to cook their food in underground ovens *(umu)*. Breadfruit, taro, yams, sweet potatoes, bananas, and coconuts were cultivated (the Polynesians had no cereals). Pigs, chickens, and dogs were also kept for food, but the surrounding sea yielded the most important source of protein.

Numerous taboos regulated Polynesian life, such as prohibitions against taking certain plants or fish that were reserved for exploitation by the chiefs. Land was collectively owned by families and tribes, and there were nobles and commoners. Though the land was worked collectively by commoners, the chiefly families controlled and distributed its produce by well-defined customs. Large numbers of people could be mobilized for public works or war.

Two related forces governed Polynesian life: mana and *tapu*. Mana was a spiritual power of which the gods and high chiefs had the most and the commoners the least. In this rigid hierarchical system, marriage or even physical contact between persons of unequal mana was forbidden, and children resulting from sexual relations between the classes were killed. Our word "taboo" originated from the Polynesian *tapu*. Early missionaries would often publicly violate the taboos and smash the images of the gods to show that their mana had vanished.

Gods

The Polynesians worshipped a pantheon of gods, who had more mana than any human. The most important were Tangaroa (the creator and god of the oceans), and Oro, or Tu (the god of war), who demanded human sacrifices. The most fascinating figure in Polynesian mythology was Maui, a Krishna- or Prometheus-like figure who caught the sun with a cord to give its fire to the world. He lifted the firmament to prevent it from crushing mankind, fished the islands out of the ocean with a hook, and was killed trying to gain the prize of immortality for humanity. Also worth noting is Hina, the heroine who fled to the moon to avoid incest with her brother, and so the sound of her tapa beater wouldn't bother anyone. Tane (the god of light) and Rongo (the god of agriculture and peace) were other important gods. This polytheism, which may have disseminated from Raiatea in the Society Islands, was most important in Eastern Polynesia. The *Arioi* confraternity, centered in Raiatea and thought to be possessed by the gods, traveled about putting on dramatic representations of the myths.

The Eastern Polynesians were enthusiastic temple builders, evidenced today by widespread ruins. Known by the Polynesian name *marae,* these platform and courtyard structures of coral and basalt blocks often had low surrounding walls and internal arrangements of upright wooden slabs. Once temples for religious cults, they were used for seating the gods and for presenting fruits and other foods to them at ritual feasts. Sometimes, but rarely, human sacrifices took place on the *marae.* Religion in Western Polynesia was very low-key, with few priests or cult images. No temples have been found in Tonga and very few in Samoa. The gods of Eastern Polynesia were represented in human form. There was an undercurrent of ancestor worship, but this was nowhere as strong as in Melanesia. The ancestors were more important as a source of descent for social ranking, and genealogies were carefully preserved. Surviving elements of the old religion are the still-widespread belief in spirits *(aitu),* the continuing use of traditional medicine, and the influence of myth. More than 150 years after conversion by early missionaries, most Polynesians maintain their early Christian piety and fervid devotion.

man blong Vanuatu

Art

The Polynesians used no masks and few colors, usually leaving their works unpainted. Art forms were very traditional, and a defined class of artists produced works of remarkable delicacy and deftness. Three of the five great archaeological sites of Oceania are in Polynesia: Easter Island, Huahine, and Tongatapu (the other two are Pohnpei and Kosrae in Micronesia).

THE MELANESIANS

The Melanesians have features that resemble those of the Australian Aborigines and have tightly curled hair. Their skin color ranges from chocolate brown to deep blue-black, with the inhabitants of the Western Solomons the most heavily pigmented people in the world. Most Melanesians live on high, volcanic islands and great differences exist between the bush people of the interiors and the saltwater people of the coasts. There's also great variety among the tribes of the interior; for centuries they waged wars with each other. Some clans were matrilineal, others patrilineal.

This carving of a bonito from Santa Ana, Solomon Islands, was used to preserve the skull of an individual totemically related to the fish. The bones were stored in a model canoe.

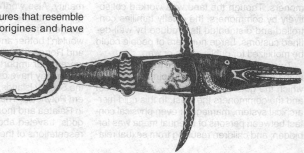

LOUISE FOOTE

Art and Society

The Melanesians have developed a startling variety of customs, traditions, and cultures. The tremendous array of art objects and styles was due to the vast number of microsocieties; there was little variation within a single clan. Art among the Melanesians was a rigidly traditional medium of expression. If an object didn't correspond precisely to an accepted form, it couldn't capture the magic and the spirits, and thus would be meaningless and useless.

Melanesian society was based on consensus, gift giving, exchange, and obligation. Although there were a headman and a few sorcerers in each village, these were either elected at village councils or they "bought" their way up in society by giving feasts and pigs. Unlike Polynesian life, there were no hereditary classes of rulers or priests and no political unions outside the clan unit (the social structures in Fiji were influenced by Polynesia).

Secret societies existed and needed objects for initiation ceremonies and feasts to mark a man's passage to a higher grade. Some objects ensured fertility for man and the soil; others celebrated the harvest. Totemic figures (animals believed to be related to the clan by blood) were common. Everyday objects were artistically made, and almost everything was brightly painted. Many figures and masks were made specifically for a single ceremony, then discarded or destroyed.

MUSEUMS OF THE PACIFIC

The most important South Pacific history or anthropology museums are at Punaauia (Tahiti), Rarotonga, Nuku'alofa, Pago Pago, Suva, Nouméa, Port Vila, and Honiara, but most of the objects in their collections are of relatively recent origin. To see Pacific artifacts dating from the period of first European contact you must visit museums outside the region. The Museum of Man (or British Museum) in London, for example, has a huge collection covering the entire region, gathered by British officials and missionaries, but most of it is locked in storage for lack of display space and funding. The warehouses of many other European museums are also bulging with Pacific art objects inaccessible to the public for the same reason, yet very few are willing to return their treasures to the islands where they originated.

Some of the 2,000 objects brought back from the Pacific by Captain Cook can be seen in the Institut für Volkskunde, Göttingen, Germany; the Hunterian Museum, Glasgow, Scotland; and the Museo Borbonico, Naples, Italy. Many British universities, such as those of Cambridge, Oxford, and Aberdeen, have impressive Pacific collections. The ethnographical museums of Budapest, St. Petersburg, and Vienna have Oceanic artifacts from former imperial collections. The vast collections of the ethnographical museums of Germany were gathered by scientific expeditions during the German colonial period before 1914. The collection of Berlin's Dahlem Museum is perhaps the best displayed, but those of Bremen, Cologne, Dresden, and Hamburg are also outstanding.

Many objects in New England museums were brought back by whalers, including the rich array of objects from Fiji and Tonga in the Peabody Museum, Salem, Massachusetts. The collections of the American Museum of Natural History, New York, and the University Museum of Philadelphia were gathered by systematic collectors at the turn of the century. The Field Museum of Natural History, Chicago, has more than 50,000 Melanesian art objects, assembled by A.B. Lewis 1909-1913. The Bernice Bishop Museum, Honolulu, has been adding to its Polynesian collection for more than a century.

Mention must also be made of the Melanesian art at Basel, plus the fine collections of the Royal Museum of Art and History, Brussels; the Museum of Man, Paris; the Musée Barbier-Muller, Geneva; the Asia and Pacific Museum, Warsaw; the Exeter City Museum; the Metropolitan Museum of Art, New York; the St. Louis Art Museum; and the de Young Memorial Museum, San Francisco. The museums of New Zealand, especially those of Auckland, Christchurch, Dunedin, and Wellington, hold a rich store of Pacific art, and a few have recently loaned objects for display at South Pacific museums such as the Museum of the Cook Islands on Rarotonga. The enormous wealth of Pacific art held by Australia's museums is mostly locked away in storerooms although the Australian Museum in Sydney occasionally mounts exhibitions.

More important than the social function of art was the religious function, especially in the cult of the dead. Ancestors were believed to remain in this world, and their advice and protection were often sought. The skull, considered the dwelling place of the soul, was often decorated and kept in the men's house. Sometimes carvings were made to provide a home for the spirits of the ancestors, or they were represented by posts or images. Masks were used to invoke the spirits in dance. The beauty of the objects was secondary; what the Melanesian artist sought was to create an embodied symbolism of the ancestors. In this rigid, ritual world the spirits of the dead possessed greater power than the living, and this power could be both harmful and beneficial.

Today we know little about the precise meaning of many Melanesian art objects, largely due to the haphazard, unscientific way in which they were collected many years ago. Yet we can appreciate and enjoy their beauty and power nonetheless, just as we may enjoy a song sung in a language we don't know.

RELIGION

Religion plays an important role in the lives of the Pacific islanders, holding communities together and defending moral values. No other non-European region of the world is as solidly Christian as the South Pacific, and unfortunately it sometimes seems to be one of the most uncritical, obedient, narrow-minded, and hypocritical strains of Christianity extant on the planet. The first missionaries to arrive were Protestants, and the Catholic fathers who landed almost 40 years later had to rely on French military backing to establish missions in Tahiti, the Marquesas, and New Caledonia. In Fiji 45% of the population is Hindu or Muslim due to the large Indian population.

Since the 1960s, the old rivalry between Protestant and Catholic has been largely replaced by an avalanche of well-financed American fundamentalist missionary groups that divide families and spread confusion in an area already strongly Christian. While the indigenous churches have long been localized, the new evangelical sects are dominated by foreign personnel, ideas, and money. American televangelists proselytize from TV screens clear across the South Pacific Bible Belt from Rarotonga to Fiji. The ultraconservative outlook of the new religious imperialists continues the tradition of allying Christianity with colonialism or neocolonialism.

The fundamentalists tend to portray God as a white man and discourage self-sufficiency by telling the islanders to await their reward in heaven. They stress passages in the Bible calling for obedience to authority and resignation, often providing the ideological justification for the repression of dissent, as happened after the military coups in Fiji. "Liberation theologists," on the other hand, whether Catholic or Protestant, try to apply the spirit of the Bible to everyday life by discussing social problems and protecting the human rights of all. The late Roman Catholic Bishop of Tonga, Patelisio Finau, was a good example of a church leader with the courage to identify social injustices and take an active role in correcting them.

The established Protestant denominations are the Evangelicals of Tahiti-Polynesia and New Caledonia, the Methodists of Tonga and Fiji, the Congregationalists of Samoa, the Presbyterians of Vanuatu, and the Anglicans of Solomon Islands. Catholics are present in every country. The ecumenical **Pacific Conference of Churches** (Box 208, Suva, Fiji Islands; tel. 679/311-277, fax 679/303-205) began in 1961 as an association of the mainstream Protestant churches, but since 1976 many Catholic dioceses have been included as well. Both the Pacific Theological College (founded in 1966) and the Pacific Regional Seminary (opened in 1972) are in southern Suva, and the South Pacific is one of the few areas of the world with a large surplus of ministers of religion.

Of course, the optimum way to experience religion in the South Pacific is to go to church on Sunday. Just be aware that the services can last 1.5 hours and will often be in the local language. If you decide to go, don't get up and walk out in the middle—see it through. You'll be rewarded by the joyous singing and fellowship, and you'll encounter the islanders on a different level. After church, people gather for a family meal or picnic and spend the rest of the day relaxing and socializing. If you're a guest in an island home you'll be invited to accompany them to church.

The Mormons

Mormon missionaries arrived on Tubuai in the Austral Islands as early as 1844, and today "Mormonia" covers much of the South Pacific. You don't have to travel far in the South Pacific to find the assembly-line Mormon chapels, schools, and sporting facilities, paid for by church members who are expected to tithe 10% of their incomes. The Mormon church spends more than US$500 million a year on foreign missions and sends out almost 50,000 missionaries, more than any other American church by far. Like Thor Heyerdahl, Mormons believe that Polynesia was settled by American Indians, who were themselves descendants of the 10 lost tribes of Israel, and that they must be reconverted to hasten the second coming of Christ. So the present church is willing to spend a lot of time and money spreading the word.

The Mormons are especially successful in countries like Tonga and Samoa, which are too poor to provide public education for all. Mormon fascination with genealogy parallels the importance of descent in Polynesian society where it often determines land rights. There's a strong link to Hawaii's Brigham Young University (www.byuh.edu), and many island students help pay for their schooling by representing their home country at the Mormon-owned Polynesian Cultural Center on Oahu. In Melanesia, Mormon missionary activity is a recent phenomenon, as prior to a "revelation" in 1978 blacks were barred from the Mormon priesthood. The pairs of clean-cut young Mormon "elders" seen on the outliers—each in shirt and tie, riding a bicycle or driving a minibus—are sent down from the States for two-year stays.

Other Religious Groups

More numerous than the Mormons are adherents of the **Seventh-Day Adventist Church,** a politically ultra-conservative group that grew out of the 19th-century American Baptist movement. This is the largest nonhistorical religious group in the South Pacific, holding the allegiance of 10% of the population of Solomon Islands, and with large followings in Tahiti-Polynesia, Tonga, Samoa, Fiji, and Vanuatu. The SDA Church teaches the imminent return of Christ, and Saturday (rather than Sunday) is observed as the Sabbath. SDAs regard the human body as the temple of the Holy Spirit, thus much attention is paid to health matters. Members are forbidden to partake of certain foods, alcohol, drugs, and tobacco, and the church expends considerable energy on the provision of medical and dental services. They're also active in education and local economic development. Like many of the fundamentalist sects, the SDAs tend to completely obliterate traditional cultures.

The **Assemblies of God** (AOG) is a Pentecostal sect founded in Arkansas in 1914 and presently headquartered in Springfield, Missouri. Although the AOG carries out some relief work, it opposes social reform in the belief that only God can solve humanity's problems. The sect is strongest in Fiji, where their numbers increased twelvefold between 1966 and 1992. A large AOG Bible College operates in Suva, and from Fiji the group has spread to other Pacific countries. Disgraced American tele-evangelists Jimmy Swaggart and Jim Bakker were both former AOG ministers.

The **Jehovah's Witnesses** originated in 19th-century America and since 1909 their headquarters has been in Brooklyn, from whence their worldwide operations are financed. Jehovah's Witnesses' teachings against military service and blood transfusions have often brought them into conflict with governments, and they in turn regard other churches, especially the Catholic Church, as instruments of the Devil. Members must spread the word by canvassing their neighborhood door-to-door, or by standing on street-corners offering copies of The Watchtower. This group focuses mostly on Christ's return, and since "the end of time" is fast approaching, Witnesses have little interest in relief work. They're most numerous in Tahiti-Polynesia, Fiji, New Caledonia, and Solomon Islands, but you'll find them in virtually every Pacific country.

LANGUAGE

Some 1,200 languages, a third of the world's total, are spoken in the Pacific islands, though most have very few speakers. The Austronesian language family includes more than 900 distinct languages spoken in an area stretching from Madagascar to Easter Island. Of all the Oceanic languages, only the Papuan languages

THE PACIFIC IN LITERATURE

Over the years a succession of European writers has traveled to the South Pacific in search of Bougainville's Nouvelle Cythère or Rousseau's noble savage. Brought to the stage and silver screen, their stories entered the popular imagination alongside Gauguin's rich images, creating the romantic myth of the South Seas paradise presently cultivated by the travel industry. Only since independence have indigenous writers such as Epeli Hau'ofa, Julian Maka'a, Fata Sano Malifa, Raymond Pillai, John Saunana, Subramani, and Albert Wendt come to the fore.

Herman Melville, author of the whaling classic *Moby Dick* (1851), deserted his New Bedford whaler at Nuku Hiva in 1842 and *Typee* (1846) describes his experiences there. An Australian whaling ship carried Melville on to Tahiti, but he joined a mutiny on board, which landed him in the Papeete *calabooza* (prison). His second Polynesian book, *Omoo* (1847), was a result. In both, Melville decries the ruin of Polynesian culture by Western influence.

Pierre Loti's *The Marriage of Loti* (1880) is a sentimental tale of the love of a young French midshipman for a Polynesian girl named Rarahu. Loti's naiveté is rather absurd, but his friendship with Queen Pomare IV and his fine imagery make the book worth reading. Loti's writings influenced Paul Gauguin to come to Tahiti.

In 1888-90 Robert Louis Stevenson, famous author of *Treasure Island* and *Kidnaped*, cruised the Pacific in his schooner, the *Casco*. His book *In the South Seas* describes his visits to the Marquesas and Tuamotus. In 1890 Stevenson and his family bought a large tract of land just outside Apia, Samoa, and built a large, framed house he called Vailima. In 1894 he was buried on Mt. Vaea, just above his home.

Jack London and his wife Charmian cruised the Pacific aboard their yacht, the *Snark*, in 1907-09. A longtime admirer of Melville, London found only a wretched swamp at Taipivai in the Marquesas. His *South Sea Tales* (1911) was the first of the 10 books that he wrote on the Pacific. London's story "The House of Mapuhi," about a Jewish pearl buyer, earned him a costly lawsuit. London was a product of his time, and the modern reader is often shocked by his insensitive portrayal of the islanders.

In 1913-14 the youthful poet Rupert Brooke visited Tahiti, where he fell in love with Mamua, a girl from Mataiea whom he immortalized in his poem "Tiare Tahiti." Later Brooke fought in WW I and wrote five famous war sonnets. He died of blood poisoning on a French hospital ship in the Mediterranean in 1915.

W. Somerset Maugham toured Polynesia in 1916-17 to research his novel, *The Moon and Sixpence* (1919), a fictional life of Paul Gauguin. Of the six short stories in *The Trembling of a Leaf* (1921), "Rain" casts strumpet Sadie Thompson against the Rev. Mr. Davidson during an enforced stay at Pago Pago, "marooned in a dilapidated lodging house, upon whose corrugated roof the heavy tropical rain beat incessantly." Three film versions of the story have appeared. Maugham's *A Writer's Notebook,* published in 1984, 19 years after his death, describes his travels in the Pacific.

American writers Charles Nordhoff and James Norman Hall came to Tahiti after WW I, married Tahitian women, and collaborated on 11 books. Their most famous was the *Bounty Trilogy* (1934), which tells of Fletcher Christian's *Mutiny on the Bounty*, the escape to Dutch Timor of Captain Bligh and his crew in *Men Against the Sea,* and the mutineer's fate in *Pitcairn's Island*. Three generations of filmmakers have selected this saga as their way of presenting paradise.

Hall remained on Tahiti until his death in 1951 and he was buried on the hill behind his home at Arue. His last book, *The Forgotten One,* is a collection of true stories about expatriate intellectuals and writers lost in the South Seas. Hall's account of the 28-year correspondence with his American friend Robert Dean Frisbie, who settled on Pukapuka in the Cook Islands, is touching.

James A. Michener joined the U.S. Navy in 1942 and ended up visiting around 50 South Sea islands, among them Bora Bora. His *Tales of the South Pacific* (1947) tells of the impact of WW II on the South Pacific and the Pacific's impact on those who served. It was later made into the long-running Broadway musical, *South Pacific*. Michener's *Return to Paradise* (1951) is a readable collection of essays and short stories.

The literary traditions of the Pacific islanders themselves were largely oral until 1967 when the University of the South Pacific was established at Suva, Fiji. The student newspaper *Unispac* began carrying fiction by Pacific writers in 1968, but it was the formation of the South Pacific Creative Arts Society and its magazine *Mana* in 1973 that really stimulated the creation of a Pacific literature distinct from the expatriate writings that had prevailed up until that time. The first Festival of Pacific Arts held at Suva in 1972 greatly encouraged the development of a unique South Pacific culture.

Whereas the main characters in the expatriate writings are Europeans with the islands and islanders treated only as exotic background, indigenous post-colonial writers deal with the real problems and concerns of the island people. The writings of outsiders such as Maugham and Michener often tell us more about the writers themselves than about the islands where their stories are set. In contrast to the Pacific paradise approach, island authors decry the impact of European colonialism and materialism on their traditional cultures and declare their own uniqueness.

The Pacific's most famous contemporary writer is Samoan novelist Albert Wendt. His novels, such as *Sons for the Return Home* (1973), *Flying Fox in a Freedom Tree* (1974), *Pouliuli* (1977), and *Leaves of the Banyan Tree* (1979) portray the manipulative nature and complex social organization of Samoan society. Wendt studied in New Zealand for 12 years before returning to teach in Samoa in 1965, and he is now a professor of English literature at Auckland University.

Tongan poet and short-story writer Epeli Hau'ofa satirizes the foreign aid business and other aspects of island life in his humorous book *Tales of the Tikongs*. His 1977 essay *Our Crowded Islands* deals with overpopulation in Tonga and the Westernization of Tongan life. *Kisses in the Nederends* and *Corned Beef and Tapioca* are among his other books. Other Pacific writers of note include Samoa's Fata Sano Malifa *(Alms for Oblivion)* and Sia Figiel *(Where We Once Belonged)*, Fiji's Sudesh Mishra *(Tandava)* and Raymond Pillai *(The Celebration)*, and Solomon Island's John Saunana *(The Alternative)*. See **Resources** at the end of this book for more detailed reviews of some of these titles and a list of booksellers and publishers.

Scottish author Robert Louis Stevenson spent his last years in Samoa.

HAWAII STATE ARCHIVES

spoken in New Guinea and the Solomons do not belong to this group. In all some 720 languages are spoken in Papua New Guinea, 105 in Vanuatu, and 87 in the Solomon Islands (the 250 languages spoken by the Australian Aborigines are unrelated to these). Many islanders are trilingual, equally fluent in the national lingua franca (pidgin), a local tribal tongue (or two), and an international language (either English or French). English is the predominant language of business and government in all but the French colonies.

Pidgin

Pidgin developed in Fiji and Queensland during the labor trade of the late 19th century. Because many separate local languages might be spoken on a single Melanesian island, often in villages only a few kilometers apart, the need for a common language arose when it became possible for people to travel beyond tribal boundaries. The three Pacific pidgins are Tok Pisin (P.N.G.), Pijin (Solomon Islands), and Bislama (Vanuatu). Solomons' Pidgin is the more Anglicized; the other two are surprisingly similar. Today pidgin is viewed as a pillar of a new Melanesian regional identity, although it's not spoken in Fiji or New Caledonia.

Pacific Pidgin, although less sophisticated than West African or China Coast Pidgin, is quite ingenious within its scope. Its vocabulary is limited, however, and pronouns, adverbs, and prepositions are lacking, but it has a bona fide Melanesian syntax. A very roundabout speech method is used to express things: "mine" and "yours" are *blong mifela* and *blong yufela*, and "we" becomes *yumi tufela*. Frenchman is *man wewi* (oui-oui), *meri* is woman, while *bulamakau* (bull and cow) means beef or cattle. Pidgin's internal logic is delightful.

Polynesian

The Polynesians speak about 21 closely related languages with local variations and consonantal changes. They're mutually unintelligible to those who haven't learned them, although they have many words in common. For instance, the word for land varies between *whenua, fenua, fanua, fonua, honua, vanua,* and *henua.* In the Polynesian languages the words are softened by the removal of certain consonants. Thus the Tagalog word for coconut, *niog,* became *niu, ni,* or *nu.* They're musical languages whose accent lies mostly on the vowels. Polynesian is rhetorical and poetical but not scientific, and to adapt to modern life many words have been borrowed from European languages; these too are infused with vowels to make them more melodious to the Polynesian ear. Thus in Tahitian governor becomes *tavana* and frying pan *faraipani.* Special vocabularies used to refer to or address royalty or the aristocracy also exist.

CONDUCT AND CUSTOMS

Foreign travel is an exceptional experience enjoyed by a privileged few. Too often, tourists try to transfer their lifestyles to tropical islands, thereby missing out on what is unique to the region. Travel can be a learning experience if approached openly and with a positive attitude, so read up on the local culture before you arrive and become aware of the social and environmental problems of the area. A wise traveler soon graduates from hearing and seeing to listening and observing. Speaking is good for the ego and listening is good for the soul.

The path is primed with packaged pleasures, but pierce the bubble of tourism and you'll encounter something far from the schedules and organized efficiency: a time to learn how other people live. Walk gently, for human qualities are as fragile and responsive to abuse as the brilliant reefs. The islanders are by nature soft-spoken and reserved. Often they won't show open disapproval if their social codes are broken, but don't underestimate them: they understand far more than you think. Consider that you're only one of thousands of visitors to their country, so don't expect to be treated better than anyone else. Respect is one of the most important things in life and humility is also greatly appreciated.

Don't try for a bargain if it means someone will be exploited. What enriches you may violate others. Be sensitive to the feelings of those you wish to "shoot" with your camera and ask their permission first. Don't promise things you can't or won't deliver. Keep your time values to yourself; the islanders lead an unstressful lifestyle and assume you are there to share it.

If you're alone you're lucky, for the single traveler is everyone's friend. Get away from other tourists and meet the people. There aren't many places on earth where you can still do this meaningfully, but the South Pacific is one. If you do meet people with similar interests, keep in touch by writing. This is no tourist's paradise, though, and local residents are not exhibits or paid performers. They have just as many problems as you, and if you see them as real people you're less likely to be viewed as a stereotypical tourist. You may have come to escape civilization, but keep in mind that you're just a guest.

Most important of all, try to see things their way. Take an interest in local customs, values, languages, challenges, and successes. If things work differently than they do back home, give thanks—that's why you've come. Reflect on what you've experienced and you'll return home with a better understanding of how much we all have in common, outwardly different as we may seem. Do that and your trip won't have been wasted.

The Pacific Way

A smile costs nothing but is priceless. Islanders smile at one another; tourists look the other way. In Western societies wealth is based on the accumulation of goods; in Pacific societies it's based on how much you can give away. Obligations define an individual's position in society, while sharing provides the security that holds a community together. If people are hospitable, look for some way of repaying their kindness and never exploit their goodwill. It's an island custom that a gift must be reciprocated, which is why tipping has never caught on.

Questions

The islanders are eager to please, so phrase your questions carefully. They'll answer yes or no according to what they think you want to hear—don't suggest the answer in your question. Test this by asking your informant to confirm something you know to be incorrect. Also don't ask negative questions, such as "you're not going to Suva, are you?" Invariably the answer will be "yes," meaning "yes, I'm not going to Suva." It also could work like this: "Don't you have anything cheaper?" "Yes." "What do you have that is cheaper?" "Nothing." Yes, he doesn't have anything cheaper. If you want to be sure of something, ask several people the same question in different ways.

Dress

It's important to know that the dress code in the islands is strict. Short shorts, halter tops, and bathing costumes in public are considered offensive: a *sulu* or pareu wrapped around you solves this one. Women should wear dresses that adequately cover their legs while seated. Nothing will mark you so quickly as a tourist nor make you more popular with street vendors than scanty dress. Of course, there *is* a place for it: on the beach in front of a resort hotel. In a society where even bathing suits are considered extremely risqué for local women, public nudity is unthinkable. Exceptions are Tahiti, Bora Bora, and Nouméa, where the French influence has led to topless beaches.

Women

In many traditional island cultures a woman seen wandering aimlessly along a remote beach or country road was thought to be in search of male companionship, and "no" meant "yes." Single women hiking, camping, sunbathing, and simply traveling alone may be seen in the same light, an impression strongly reinforced by the type of videos available in the islands. In some cultures local women rarely travel without men, and some day-hikes and interisland ship journeys mentioned in this book may be uncomfortable or even dangerous for women. Two women together will have less to worry about in most cases, especially if they're well covered and look purposeful.

Women traveling alone should avoid staying in isolated tourist bungalows by themselves—it's wise to team up with other travelers before heading to the outer islands. In many Polynesian cultures there's a custom known as "sleep crawling" in which a boy silently enters a girl's home at night and lies beside her to prove his bravery, and visiting women sometimes become objects of this type of unwanted attention even in well-known resorts like Bora Bora.

Annette Nyberg of Sweden sent us this:

The South Pacific is an easy place for a single woman, as long as she's not stupid. I'm talking about shorts, minitops, bikinis, etc., which place an unnecessary barrier between you and the local women. In the handbook a lot of traditional ceremonies are described, and I think it's important to point out that some of them (such as a traditional kava *party) are open to men only. On the other hand, as a woman I could sit down with the local women when they were weaving, cooking, etc. and get plenty of contact, something a man couldn't do. There's nothing like weaving a mat to make a Tongan woman more talkative! I've had "complicated" discussions I believe wouldn't have taken place if both of us hadn't been so occupied with those pandanus leaves! Don't attempt to be an "independent modern woman" trying to get a close look at every aspect of village life, but take advantage of those opportunities which come naturally from your being a woman.*

island-style dress at Gau Island, Fiji

DAVID STANLEY

Women planning a trip on their own can obtain useful general information on what to expect by visiting www.journeywoman.com.

Children
Karen Addison of Sussex, England, sent us the following:

Traveling with children can have its ups and downs, but in the Pacific it's definitely an up. Pacific islanders are warm, friendly people, but with children you see them at their best. Your children are automatically accepted, and you, as an extension of them, are as well. As the majority of the islands are free of any deadly bugs or diseases, acclimatizing to the water, food, and climate would be your paramount concern. Self-contained units, where you can do your own cooking, are easy to find and cheap; having set meals every day gives children a sense of security. Not having television as a distraction, I've attempted to teach my son the rudiments of reading and writing. As a single mother with a little boy, traveling with him opened my eyes to things I'd normally overlook and has been an education to us both.

ON THE ROAD

HIGHLIGHTS

Few areas of the world are as rewarding to visitors as the South Pacific. Life here is relaxed, and the tremendous variety of cultures and choice of things to see and do make this the sort of place you just keep coming back to. When you tire of beachlife you can go to the mountains; city and town visits can alternate with stays in rural areas. There's no overcrowding, and you don't have to hassle with vendors or be constantly on guard against thieves. Public transportation of all kinds is well developed, it's relatively inexpensive, and almost everywhere you can easily sidestep the tourist track and go native.

The South Pacific's distance from Europe and North America has saved it from becoming overrun, as Spain and the main Caribbean resorts are overrun. Only tiny New Zealand has the South Pacific in its backyard (Australians are more attracted to Bali and Thailand). Part of the higher amount you'll spend on airfare will come back to you in the form of lower everyday prices. The islanders themselves are the region's greatest attraction: you'll seldom make friends as fast as you do here.

Each Pacific country is unique. In Tahiti-Polynesia the spectacular scenery of Tahiti, Moorea, and Bora Bora compensates for the higher cost of living. Cook Islands has easygoing resort life on Rarotonga and Aitutaki and unspoiled outer-island life everywhere else. Each of the three main island groups of Tonga has its own distinct character and Vava'u is an undiscovered pearl of the South Seas. Sultry Samoa is notable for its intact traditional life. Everyone likes Fiji, both for its excellent facilities and the fascinating variety of cultures. New Caledonia is also a land of stirring contrasts. In Vanuatu alternate between the polished capital and unspoiled outer islands. Solomon Islands is perhaps the South Pacific's biggest surprise: friendly welcoming people, satisfactory transportation, reasonable prices, and lots of things to do.

In the "Highlights" sections of each chapter introduction we list a few sights you won't want to miss. Give yourself as much time in the islands as you can, and try to get to at least three different countries to be able to see things in perspective. No matter how hard you travel, there'll always be lots left over to see next time.

SPORTS AND RECREATION

Scuba Diving
Scuba diving is offered in resort areas throughout the South Pacific, with certification courses usually available. The waters are warm, varying less than one degree centigrade between the surface and 100 meters, so a wetsuit is not essential (although it will protect you from coral cuts). Lagoon diving is recommended for beginners; those with some experience will find the most beautiful coral along reef dropoffs and the most fish around passes into the lagoon.

Commercial scuba operators know their waters and will be able to show you the most amazing things in perfect safety. Dive centers at all

the main resorts operate year-round, with marinelife most profuse July to November. Before strapping on a tank and fins you'll have to show your scuba certification card, and occasionally divers are also asked to show a medical report from their doctor indicating that they are in good physical condition. Serious divers will bring along their own mask, buoyancy compensator, and regulator.

Prices differ slightly across the region: a one-tank dive with equipment will cost about US$35 in Cook Islands, American Samoa, and Vanuatu, US$50 in Tahiti-Polynesia, Fiji, and the Solomons, and US$55 and up in New Caledonia,

Samoa, and Tonga. Most dive shops tack on an extra US$10 or more for "equipment rental" (regulator, buoyancy compensator, and gauges) and frequent divers will save a lot by bringing their own. Precise information on scuba diving is provided throughout this handbook, immediately after the sightseeing sections.

Many of the scuba operators listed in this book offer introductory "resort courses" for those who only want a taste of scuba diving, and full CMAS, NAUI, or PADI open-water certification courses for those wishing to dive more than once or twice. Scuba training will enhance your understanding and enjoyment of the sea.

Snorkeling

Scuba diving can become expensive if you get addicted, but snorkeling is free—all you need is a mask and pipe. Be careful, however, and know the dangers. Practice snorkeling over a shallow sandy bottom and don't head into deep water or swim over coral until you're sure you've got the hang of it. Breathe easily; don't hyperventilate. When snorkeling on a fringing reef, beware of deadly currents and undertows in channels that drain tidal flows. Before going into the water, ask a local to point the channels out to you, and observe the direction the water is flowing before you swim into it. If you feel yourself being dragged out to sea through a reef passage, try swimming across the current rather than against it. If you can't resist the pull at all, it may be better to let yourself be carried out. Wait till the current diminishes, then swim along the outer reef face until you find somewhere to come back in. Or use your energy to attract the attention of someone onshore.

Snorkeling on the outer edge or drop-off of a reef is thrilling for the variety of fish and corals, but attempt it only on a very calm day. Even then it's wise to have someone stand onshore or paddle behind you in a canoe to watch for occasional big waves, which can take you by surprise and smash you into the rocks. Also, beware of unperceived currents outside the reef—you may not get a second chance. Many scuba operators will take snorkelers out on their regular trips for a third to a quarter the cost of diving. This is an easy way to reach some good snorkeling spots, just don't expect to be chaperoned for that price.

A far better idea is to limit your snorkeling to the protected inner reef and leave the open waters to the scuba diver. Yet while scuba diving quickly absorbs large amounts of money, snorkeling is free and you can do it as often as you like. You'll encounter the brightest colors in shallow waters anyway as beneath six meters the colors blue out as short wavelengths are lost. By diving with a tank you trade off the chance to observe shallow water species in order to gain access to the often larger deep water species. The best solution is to do a bit of both. In any case, avoid touching the reef or any of its creatures as the contact can be very harmful to both you and the reef. Take only pictures and leave only bubbles.

Ocean Kayaking

This is a viable sport best practiced in sheltered lagoons, such as those of Raiatea/Taha'a, Bora Bora, Aitutaki, Vava'u, and New Georgia, or among Fiji's Yasawa Islands. You can rent kayaks in some places, but it's better to bring your own folding kayak. See **Getting Around,** later in this chapter, for more information on kayaking.

Yachting

Cruising the South Pacific by yacht is also covered in **Getting Around,** and for those with less time there are several established yacht charter operations, the most important of which are based at Raiatea (Tahiti-Polynesia), Vava'u (Tonga), Malololailai (Fiji), and Nouméa (New Caledonia). Turn to Yacht Tours and Charters in **Getting There,** which follows, and check the introductions to the chapters mentioned above.

Hiking

Hiking is an excellent, inexpensive way to see the islands. A few of the outstanding treks covered in this handbook are Mt. Aorai on Tahiti, Vaiare to Paopao on Moorea, the Cross-island Track on Rarotonga, Mt. Matafao on Tutuila, Lake Lanoto'o on Upolu, the Sigatoka River Trek on Viti Levu, White Sands to Port Resolution on Tanna, and the Mataniko River on Guadalcanal. There are many others.

Surfing and Windsurfing

The South Pacific's most renowned surfing camps are Club Masa (Kulukulu), Frigate Surfriders (Yanuca Island), Seashell Cove (Momi Bay), and Tavarua and Namotu Islands (Mamanuca Group), all in Fiji, and the Ha'atafu Beach Resort on Tongatapu. Other famous surfing spots include Tahiti's Papara Beach, Huahine's Fare Reef, Laulii and Solosolo on Upolu, Salailua and Lano on Savai'i, Suva's Sandspit Lighthouse, Grande Terre's Po'e Beach, and Malu'u (Malaita). The top surfing season is generally July-Sept. when the trade winds push the Antarctic swells north. During the hurricane season Jan.-March tropical storms can generate some spectacular waves. Prime locales for windsurfing include Rarotonga's Muri Lagoon and many others. Pago Pago Harbor would be the windsurfing locale par excellence if the quality of the water weren't so poor.

Hunting and Fishing

There isn't much to hunt in the islands, and the wretches who shoot flying foxes and birds are worthy only of contempt. Sportfishing is also a questionable activity—especially spearfishing, which is sort of like shooting a cow with a handgun. An islander who spearfishes to feed his family is one thing, but the tourist who does it for fun is perhaps worthy of the attention of sharks. Deep-sea game fishing from gas-guzzling powerboats isn't much better, and it's painful to see noble fish slaughtered and strung up just to inflate someone's ego. That said, one

has to admit that taking fish from the sea one by one for sport is never going to endanger the stocks the way net fishing by huge trawlers does. It's a viable sport and we cover it throughout this book. On most big-game boats, the captain keeps the catch.

Golf

The former British and New Zealand administrators left behind an abundance of golf courses in the islands, and virtually all are open to visitors. Major international competitions are held at Fiji's Pacific Harbor Golf Course and Tahiti's Olivier Breaud Golf Course. Greens fees vary considerably: Olivier Breaud Golf Course, US$45; Rarotonga Golf Club, US$7; Tonga Golf Club, US$4; Tutuila's 'Ili'ili Golf Course, US$7; Apia's Royal Samoa Country Club, US$7; Nadi Airport Golf Course, US$10; Nadi's Denarau Golf Club, US$65; Pacific Harbor Golf Course, US$20; Suva's Fiji Golf Club, US$14; Nouméa's Tina de Golf, US$45; Port Vila's White Sands Country Club, US$22-44; Port Vila Golf and Country Club, US$15; Honiara Golf Club, US$7. Club and cart rentals are usually available for a bit less than the greens fees and most of the courses have clubhouses with pleasant colonial-style bars.

Package tours incorporating the activities just mentioned are described under **Getting There** in this introduction. For information on bicycling, see **Getting There,** which follows.

ENTERTAINMENT

Considering the strong Aussie presence and the temperature, it's not surprising that the South Seas has its fair share of colorful bars where canned or bottled beer is consumed cold in amazing quantities. These are good places to meet local characters at happy hour around 1700, and many bars become discos after 2200. Respectably attired visitors are welcome at the ex-colonial "clubs," where the beer prices are generally lower and the clientele more sedate. Barefoot (or flip-flop-shod) beachcombers in T-shirts and shorts may be refused entry, and you should take off your hat as you come in. Don't overlook the resort bars, where the swank surroundings cost only slightly more.

A small glass of draft beer at a normal bar will cost just over US$1 in Samoa, around US$2 in Cook Islands, Fiji, and Solomon Islands, less than US$2.50 in Tonga and Vanuatu, and US$3 or more in Tahiti-Polynesia, New Caledonia, and American Samoa. Needless to say, Apia is a beer drinkers paradise. Don't worry about the quality as it's excellent everywhere, in fact, despite the price, Samoa's Vailima beer may be the best and Fiji Bitter is a close second.

Many big hotels run "island nights," or feasts where you get to taste the local food and see traditional dancing. If you don't wish to splurge on the meal it's sometimes possible to witness the spectacle from the bar for the price of a drink.

These events are held weekly on certain days, so ask. On most islands Friday night is the time to let it all hang out; on Saturday many people are preparing for a family get-together or church on Sunday. Except in the French territories, everything grinds to a halt Saturday at midnight and Sunday is very quiet—a good day to go hiking or to the beach.

In the English-speaking countries it's cheap to go to the movies. Unfortunately it's usually romance, horror, or adventure, and as everywhere, good psychological films are the exception. In the French territories the films are just as bad, plus they're dubbed into French and admission is three times as high. Video fever is the latest island craze, and you often see throngs of locals crowded into someone's living room watching a violent and/or sexy tape rented from one of the ubiquitous video rental shops. Some guesthouses have video too, so make sure your room is well away from it.

Music and Dance

Traditional music and dance is alive and well in the South Pacific, be it the exciting *tamure* dancing of Tahiti-Polynesia and Cook Islands, the graceful *siva* of Samoa, the formalized *meke* of Fiji, or the *kastom* dances of Vanuatu. British ethnomusicologist David Fanshawe (see **Resources**) has suggested that the sitting dances common in Tonga, Fiji, and elsewhere may be related to the movements of the upper part of the body while paddling a canoe.

The slit-log gong (or *lali* in Fiji) beaten with a wooden stick is now a common instrument throughout Polynesia, even though the Eastern Polynesians originally had skin drums. The *to'ere* slit drum was only introduced to Tahiti from Western Polynesia after 1915, and it's marvelous the way the Tahitians have made it their own.

Melanesia has always excelled in the use of the flute, especially the panpipes of Solomon Islands. Flutes were known in Polynesia too, for example the nose flutes of Tonga and Tahiti. In the early 19th century, missionaries replaced the old chants of Polynesia with the harmonious gospel singing heard in the islands today, yet even the hymns were transformed into an original Oceanic medium. Contemporary Pacific music includes bamboo bands, brass bands, and localized Anglo-American pop. String bands have made European instruments such as the guitar and ukulele an integral part of Pacific music.

HOLIDAYS AND FESTIVALS

The special events of each island group are described in the respective chapters. Their dates often vary from year to year, so it's good to contact the local tourist information office soon after your arrival to learn just what will be happening during your stay.

The most important annual festivals are the Tapati Rapa Nui festival on Easter Island (late January or early February), American Samoa's Flag Day (17 April), the Independence Celebrations at Apia (first week of June), Nuku'alofa's Heilala Festival (first week in July), the Heiva i Tahiti at Papeete and Bora Bora (first two weeks of July), Solomon Islands Independence Day (7 July), Independence Day at Port Vila (30 July), the Constitution Celebrations on Rarotonga (early August), Suva's Hibiscus Festival (August), the Bourail Agricultural Show in New Caledonia in mid-August, and the Constitution Celebrations on Niue in mid-October. Catch as many as you can and try to participate in what's happening, rather than merely watching like a tourist.

Regional Events

The most important cultural event of the region is the **Festival of Pacific Arts,** held every four years (Suva, Fiji, 1972; Rotorua, N.Z., 1976; Port Moresby, P.N.G., 1980; Tahiti, 1985; Townsville, Australia, 1988; Rarotonga, 1992; Samoa, 1996). The next will be in New Caledonia in 2000. The festival gathers in one place the cultures and folklores of all of Oceania. The coordination of each festival is in the hands of the Council of Pacific Arts, founded at Nouméa in 1977 under the auspices of the Secretariat of the Pacific Community. The first **Melanesian Arts and Cultural Festival** of the five Melanesian Spearhead countries was held in Honiara in July 1998 (see it all happen again in Vanuatu in 2002). Since 1987 a **Marquesas Islands Fes-**

tival has been held about every four years (the last was in December 1999).

The **South Pacific Games,** the region's major sporting event, was created at the 1961 South Pacific Conference to promote friendship among the peoples of the Pacific and encourage the development of amateur sports. Since then the games have been held in Fiji (1963), New Caledonia (1966), P.N.G. (1969), Tahiti-Polynesia (1971), Guam (1975), Fiji (1979), Samoa (1983), New Caledonia (1987), P.N.G. (1991), Tahiti-Polynesia (1995), and Guam (1999) with the larger Pacific countries (New Caledonia, Fiji, P.N.G., and Tahiti-Polynesia) dominating. The next games will be in Fiji in 2003. Some 5,000 athletes from 22 countries gather for the games and, to give the smaller countries a better chance, Australia, Hawaii, and New Zealand don't participate. The five compulsory sports are athletics, basketball, soccer, swimming, and tennis, but almost any sport can be included if at least six teams approve it. The Mini South Pacific Games take place two years after the main games.

ARTS AND CRAFTS

The top countries in which to purchase handicrafts are Tonga, Samoa, Fiji, Vanuatu, and Solomon Islands. Not surprisingly, the traditional handicrafts that have survived best are the practical arts done by women (weaving, basketmaking, tapa). In cases where the items still perform their original function (such as the astoundingly intricate fine mats of Samoa—not for sale to tourists), they remain as vital as ever. A tourist will purchase whatever corresponds to his image of the producing community and is small enough to be accepted as airline luggage. Thus a visitor to Fiji may be looking for masks, figures with large penises, or carvings of pigs, even though none of these has any place in Fijian tradition. The mock-Hawaiian "tikis" of Tonga also have no precedents in traditional Tongan art.

Whenever possible buy handicrafts from local women's committee shops, church groups, local markets, or from the craftspeople themselves, but avoid objects made from turtle shell/leather, clam shell, or marine mammal ivory, which are prohibited entry into many countries under endangered species acts. Failure to declare such items to customs officers can lead to heavy fines. Also resist the temptation to purchase jewelry or other items made from seashells and coral, the collection of which damages the reefs. Souvenirs made from straw or seeds may be held for fumigation or confiscated upon arrival.

Weaving

Woven articles are the most widespread handicrafts, with examples in almost every South Seas country. Pandanus fiber is the most common, but coconut leaf and husk, vine tendril, banana stem, tree and shrub bark, the stems and leaves of water weeds, and the skin of the sago palm leaf are all used. On some islands the fibers are passed through a fire, boiled, then bleached in the sun. Vegetable dyes of very lovely mellow tones are sometimes used, but gaudier store dyes are much more prevalent. Shells are occasionally utilized to cut, curl, or make pliable the fibers. Polynesian woven arts are characterized by colorful, skillful patterns.

Tapa

To make tapa, the white inner bark of the tall, thin paper mulberry tree *(Broussonetia papyrifera)* is stripped and scraped with shells, rolled into a ball, and soaked in water. The sodden strips are then pounded with wooden mallets until they reach four or five times their original length and width. Next, several pieces are placed one on top of another, pressed and pounded, and joined with a manioc juice paste. Sheets of tapa feel like felt when finished.

In Tonga, tapa *(ngatu)* is decorated by stitching coconut fiber designs onto a woven pandanus base that is placed under the tapa, and the stain is rubbed on in the same manner one makes temple rubbings from a stone inscription. The artisan then fills in the patterns freehand. In Fiji, stencils are used to decorate tapa *(masi)*. Sunlight deepens and sets the copper brown colors.

Each island group has its characteristic colors and patterns, ranging from plantlike paintings to geometric designs. On some islands tapa is still used for clothing, bedding, and room dividers, and as ceremonial red carpets. Tablecloths, bedcovers, place mats, and wall hangings of tapa make handsome souvenirs.

Woodcarving

Melanesia is especially well known for its woodcarvings, with designs passed down from generation to generation. Though shells are sometimes used for polishing the finest artifacts, steel tools are employed for the most part these days. Melanesian woodcarvings often suggest the mystic feelings of their former religious beliefs, the somber spirits of the rainforests and swampy plains of Melanesia. Polynesia also produces fine woodcarvings (especially kava bowls and war clubs), and those of the Marquesas Group are outstanding in detail.

Other Products

Other handicrafts include polished shell, inlays of shell in ebony, spears with barbs of splintered bone, thorn spines or caudal spines, "bride money," shell necklaces, and anklets. Among the European-derived items are the patchwork quilts *(tifaifai)* of Tahiti and the Cooks, and the hand-painted and silk-screened dress fabrics of Fiji, Samoa, Cook Islands, and Tahiti.

ACCOMMODATIONS

Hotels

With the *South Pacific Handbook* in hand you're guaranteed a good, inexpensive place to stay on every island. To allow you the widest possible choice, all price categories are included in this handbook, and throughout we've tried to indicate which properties offer value for money. If you think we're wrong or you were badly treated, be sure to send a written complaint to the author. Equally important, let us know when you agree with what's here or if you think a place deserves a better rave. Your letter will have an impact!

We don't solicit freebies from the hotel chains; our only income derives from the price you paid for this book. So we don't mind telling you that, as

---

ACCOMMODATIONS PRICE RANGES

Throughout this book, accommodations are generally grouped in the price categories which follow. Of course, currency fluctuations and inflation can lead to slight variations.

Shoestring: less than US$15 double
Budget: US$15-35 double
Inexpensive: US$35-60 double
Moderate: US$60-85 double
Expensive: US$85-110 double
Premium: US$110-150 double
Luxury: more than US$150 double

---

usual, most of the luxury hotels are just not worth the exorbitant prices they charge. Many simply recreate Hawaii at twice the cost, offering far more luxury than you need. Even worse, they tend to isolate you in a French/American/Australian environment, away from the South Pacific you came to experience. Most are worth visiting as sightseeing attractions, watering holes, or sources of entertainment, but unless you're a millionaire, sleep elsewhere. There are always middle-level hotels that charge half what the top-end places ask, while providing adequate comfort. And if you really *can* afford US$400 a night and up, you might do better chartering a skippered or bareboat yacht!

Dormitory, "bunkroom," or backpacker accommodations are available on all of the main islands, with communal cooking facilities usually provided. If you're traveling alone these are excellent, since they're just the place to meet other travelers. Couples can usually get a double room for a price only slightly above two dorm beds. For the most part, the dormitories are safe and congenial for those who don't mind sacrificing their privacy to save money.

Throughout the South Pacific, double rooms with shared bath at budget guesthouses average US$20-40, dorm beds US$6-12 pp. Solomon Islands and Samoa have a selection of double rooms beginning at US$18, but in American Samoa, New Caledonia, and Tahiti-Polynesia very few rooms are as low as US$40 double. The cheapest dormitory beds are found in Fiji,

Tonga, and Samoa. Moving into the medium-price category, you'll be able to get a quality a/c room with all the facilities for US$75 double everywhere except in Tahiti-Polynesia and New Caledonia where you'll probably have to spend more than US$100.

Needless to say, always ask the price of your accommodations before accepting them. This especially applies in remote areas of Melanesia where local guesthouses may be required to charge high prices by travel agencies that would prefer that all bookings be channeled through them. In cases where there's a local and a tourist price, you'll always pay the higher tariff if you don't check beforehand. Asking first gives you the opportunity to bargain if someone quotes an absurdly high starting price, and by calling ahead you may be able to avoid a disastrous trip. Otherwise, hotel prices are usually fixed and bargaining isn't the normal way to go.

ECOTOURISM

Recently "ecotourism" has become the thing, and with increasing concern in Western countries over the damaging impact of solar radiation, more and more people are looking for land-based activities as an alternative to lying on the beach. This trend is also fueled by the "baby boomers" who hitchhiked around Europe in the 1970s. Today they're looking for more exotic locales in which to practice "soft adventure tourism" and they've got a lot more money to spend this time around. In the South Pacific the most widespread manifestation of the ecotourism/adventure phenomenon is the current scuba diving boom, and tours by chartered yacht, ocean kayak, surfboard, bicycle, or on foot are proliferating.

This presents both a danger and an opportunity. Income from visitors wishing to experience nature gives local residents and governments an incentive for preserving the environment, although tourism can quickly degrade that environment through littering, the collection of coral and shells, and the development of roads, docks, and resorts in natural areas. Means of access created for ecotourists often end up being used by local residents whose priority is not conservation. Perhaps the strongest argument in favor of the creation of national parks and reserves in the South Pacific is the ability of such parks to attract visitors from industrialized countries while at the same time creating a framework for the preservation of nature. For in the final analysis, it is governments that must enact regulations to protect the environment—market forces usually do the opposite.

Too often what is called ecotourism is actually packaged consumer tourism with a green coating, or just an excuse for high prices. Some four-wheel-drive jeep safaris, jet-boat excursions, and helicopter trips have more to do with ecoterrorism than ecotourism. In 1997 the Tourism Council of the South Pacific conferred its highest ecotourism award on a local guide on Niue who captured endangered coconut crabs for the amusement of tourists!

A genuine ecotourism resort will be built of local materials using natural ventilation. This means no air conditioning and only limited use of fans. The buildings will fit into the natural landscape and not restrict access to customary lands or the sea. Local fish and vegetables will have preference over imported meats on tourist tables, and wastes will be minimized. The use of aggressive motorized transport will be kept to an absolute minimum. Cultural sensitivity will be enhanced by profit sharing with the landowning clans and local participation in ownership. It's worth considering all of this as a flood of phony ecotourism facilities are popping up.

Through this handbook we've tried to encourage this type of people-oriented tourism, which we feel is more directly beneficial to the islanders themselves. Whenever possible we've featured smaller, family-operated, locally owned businesses. By patronizing these you'll not only get to meet the inhabitants on a person-to-person basis, but also contribute to local development. Guesthouse tourism offers excellent employment opportunities for island women as proprietors, *and* it's exactly what most visitors want. Appropriate tourism requires little investment, there's less disruption, and full control remains with the people themselves. The luxury a/c hotels are monotonously uniform around the world—the South Pacific's the place for something different. (For a more complete discussion of this topic than can be included here, click in www2.planeta.com/mader/ecotravel/etour.html).

Be aware that some of the low-budget places included in this book are a lot more basic than what are sometimes referred to as "budget" accommodations in the States. The standards of cleanliness in the common bathrooms may be lower than you expected, the furnishings "early attic," the beds uncomfortable, linens and towels skimpy, housekeeping nonexistent, and window screens lacking, but ask yourself, where in the U.S. are you going to find a room for a similar price? Luckily, good medium-priced accommodations are usually available for those of us unwilling to put up with Spartan conditions, and we include all of them in this book too.

When picking a hotel, keep in mind that although a thatched bungalow is cooler and infinitely more attractive than a concrete box, it's also more likely to have insect problems. If in doubt, check the window screens and carry mosquito coils and/or repellent. Hopefully there'll be a resident lizard or two to feed on the bugs. Always turn on a light before getting out of bed to use the facilities at night, as even the finest hotels in the tropics have cockroaches.

A room with cooking facilities can save you a lot on restaurant meals, and some moderately priced establishments have weekly rates. If you have to choose a meal plan, take only breakfast and dinner (Modified American Plan or "half pension") and have fruit for lunch. As you check into your room, note the nearest fire exits. And don't automatically take the first room offered; if you're paying good money look at several, then choose.

Reserving Ahead

Booking accommodations in advance usually works to your disadvantage as full-service travel agents will begin by trying to sell you their most expensive properties (which pay them the highest commissions) and work down from there. The quite adequate middle and budget places included in this handbook often aren't on their screens or are sold at highly inflated prices. Herein we provide the rates for direct local bookings, and if you book through a travel agent abroad you could end up paying considerably more as multiple commissions are tacked on. Thus we suggest you avoid making any hotel reservations at all before arriving in the South Pacific (unless you're coming for a major event).

We don't know of any island where it's to your advantage to book ahead in the medium to lower price range, but you can sometimes obtain substantial discounts at the luxury hotels by including them as part of a package tour. Even then, you'll almost always find medium-priced accommodations for less than the package price and your freedom of choice won't be impaired. If, however, you intend to spend most of your time at a specific first-class hotel, you'll benefit from bulk rates by taking a package tour instead of paying the higher "rack rate" the hotels charge to individuals who just walk in off the street. Call Air New Zealand's toll-free number and ask them to mail you their *Go As You Please* brochure, which lists deluxe hotel rooms in Fiji, Cook Islands, Tahiti, Tonga, Samoa, New Caledonia, and Vanuatu that can be booked on an individual basis at slightly reduced rates. Polynesian Airlines has a similar *Polypac Hotel Accommodation* brochure covering their destinations. Also call Discover Wholesale Travel and some of the other agents listed herein in **Getting There.**

Homestays

In some countries such as Tahiti-Polynesia there are bed and breakfast *(logement chez l'habitant)* programs, where you pay a set fee to stay with a local family in their own home. Meals may not be included in the price, but they're often available, tending toward your host family's fare of seafood and native vegetables. Ask about homestays at tourist information offices once you're in the islands.

A new development in Samoa is the appearance of basic beach resorts run by local families who supply meals, bedding, and *fale* (hut) accommodations at set rates. See the Samoa chapter for details. This is genuine ecotourism for you, and we hope people on some of the other islands catch on and start doing the same sort of thing.

Staying in Villages

If you're in the islands long and get off the beaten track, you'll eventually be invited to spend the night with a local family. There's a certain etiquette to follow and you'll be a lot more welcome if you observe the customs. For example, in Fiji the guest is expected to present a bundle of kava roots to the host. Although payment is rarely the islander's objective in inviting you, it's sort of expected that you'll somehow pay them back.

The peoples of the Pacific are so naturally hospitable that it sometimes works to their disadvantage. We recommend that you repay their kindness with either cash (US$10 pp a day is standard) or gifts. In places that obviously receive a regular flow of visitors, such as villages on trekking routes or surfing beaches, the villagers are probably used to receiving money. We're not suggesting that hospitality is a commodity to be bought and sold, but it's easy to see how the unscrupulous few can—and have—taken advantage of the situation. The offer of a little money to show your appreciation may not be accepted, but it won't cause offense when done properly and with sincerity.

Things to take with you as gifts include T-shirts, flashlights and batteries, a big jar of instant coffee, and marbles and balloons for the kids (not candy, which rots their teeth and attracts ants). You may also be able to buy a few things at village trade stores to leave as gifts, but don't count on it.

If you're headed to a really remote atoll for an extended stay, take with you all the food you'll need, plus gifts. Be friendly, patient, and courteous, and don't seem afraid. Respect the property and customs of your hosts, and do your best to leave a good impression. Once you get home, don't forget to mail prints of any photos you've taken. If you make friends on one island, ask them to write you a letter of introduction to their relatives on another.

If you're embarking on a trip that involves staying in villages, make sure everyone who's going agrees in advance on what you're going to do to compensate the islanders for their trouble. Of course, don't go to the opposite extreme and overpay. But if you really can't afford to contribute anything to your hosts, it's better to camp or sleep on the beach. Staying in villages is a great way to meet and communicate with the people, an act of good will with great reward. It's *not* a cheap way to travel.

Camping

Your number one home away from home is a tent. There are now organized campgrounds in Tahiti-Polynesia, Tonga, Samoa, Fiji, New Caledonia, and Vanuatu, and the only place where camping is totally forbidden is Cook Islands. Always get permission of the landowner; you'll rarely be refused in places off the beaten track. Set a good precedent by not leaving a mess or violating custom. If you pitch your tent near a village or on private property without asking permission, you're asking for problems. Otherwise, camp out in the bush well away from gardens and trails.

Make sure your tent is water- and mosquito-proof, and try to find a spot swept by the trades. Never camp under a coconut tree, as falling coconuts hurt (actually, coconuts have two eyes so they only strike the wicked). If you hear a hurricane warning, pack up your tent and take immediate cover with the locals.

FOOD AND DRINK

The traditional diet of the Pacific islanders consists of root crops and fruit, plus lagoon fish and the occasional pig. The vegetables include taro, yams, cassava (manioc), breadfruit, and sweet potatoes. The sweet potato *(kumara)* is something of an anomaly—it's the only Pacific food plant with a South American origin. How it got to the islands is not known.

Taro is an elephant-eared plant cultivated in freshwater swamps. Although yams are considered a prestige food, they're not as nutritious as breadfruit and taro. Yams can grow up to three meters long and weigh hundreds of kilos. Papaya (pawpaw) is nourishing: a third of a cup contains as much vitamin C as 18 apples. To ripen a green papaya overnight, puncture it a few times with a knife. Don't overeat papaya—unless you *need* an effective laxative.

Raw fish (*poisson cru* or sashimi) is an appetizing dish enjoyed in many Pacific countries. To prepare it, clean and skin the fish, then dice the fillet. Squeeze lemon or lime juice over it, and store in a cool place about 10 hours. When it's ready to serve, add chopped onions, garlic, green peppers, tomatoes, and coconut cream to taste. Local fishmongers know which species make the best raw fish, but know what you're doing before you join them—island stomachs are probably stronger than yours. Health experts recommend eating only well-cooked foods and peeling your own fruit, but the islanders swear by raw fish.

Lobsters have become almost an endangered species on some islands due to the high prices they fetch on restaurant tables. Countless more are airfreighted to Hawaii. Before asking for one of these creatures to be sacrificed for your dinner, consider that the world will be poorer for it. Coconut crabs are even more threatened and it's almost scandalous that local governments should allow them to be fed to tourists. Sea turtles and flying foxes are other delicacies to avoid, although these are seldom offered to tourists.

Never order mutton at a restaurant as the lowest quality New Zealand mutton flaps are exported to the South Pacific and you could get some very fatty pieces. Also beware of "exotic" meats like "lamb" and goat to which your stomach may not be accustomed. The turkey tails shipped in from the U.S. are solid chunks of fat. Chicken is safer provided it is freshly cooked. In general, the low-fat or diet foods popular in the States are unknown in the islands. Vegetarianism is only understood in Fiji where many Fiji Indians spurn meat.

Islanders in the towns now eat mostly imported foods, just as we Westerners often opt for fast foods instead of meals made from basic ingredients. The Seventh-Day Adventists don't smoke, chew betel nut, dance, eat pork or rabbit, or drink tea, coffee, or alcohol. If you're going to the outer islands, take as many edibles with you as you can; they're always more expensive there. And keep in mind that virtually every food plant you see growing on the islands is cultivated by someone. Even sea shells washed up on a beach, or fish in the lagoon near someone's home, may be considered private property.

Restaurants

Eating out is an adventure, and first-rate restaurants are found in all the main towns, so whenever your travels start to get to you and it's time for a lift, splurge on a good meal and then see how the world looks. Tahiti-Polynesia and New Caledonia have some of the finest restaurants in the region, with prices to match. Fiji is outstanding for the variety of cuisines you can sample, and prices are very reasonable. Nuku'alofa and Apia also offer an increasing number of good inexpensive places to eat.

You should be able to get a filling meal at a restaurant serving the local population for under US$3 in Fiji, Samoa, Solomon Islands, Tonga, and Vanuatu, for under US$5 in Cook Islands and American Samoa, and for about US$7.50 in Tahiti-Polynesia and New Caledonia. At a tourist restaurant expect to pay under US$12 in American Samoa, Samoa, Tonga, Solomon Islands, and Vanuatu, under US$15 in Cook Islands and Fiji, and under US$25 in Tahiti-Polynesia and New Caledonia. Unlike Australia and New Zealand, it's not customary to bring your own (BYO) booze into restaurants.

Cooking

The ancient Polynesians stopped making pottery over a millennium ago and instead developed an ingenious way of cooking in an underground earth oven known as an *umu, ahimaa,* or *lovo.* First a stack of dry coconut husks is burned in a pit. Once the fire is going well, coral stones are heaped on top, and when most of the husks have burnt away the food is wrapped in banana leaves and placed on the hot stones—fish and meat below, vegetables above. A whole pig may be cleaned, then stuffed with banana leaves and hot stones. This cooks the beast from inside out as well as outside in, and the leaves create steam. The food is then covered with more leaves and stones, and after a couple of hours everything is cooked.

Others

Betel chewing is a widespread practice among men, women, and children in the Western Pacific, as far southeast as Santa Cruz in the Solomons. First the unripe nut of the Areca palm is chewed, then the leaves of the fruit of the betel pepper. Lime from a gourd (made by burning coral or shells, or grinding limestone) is inserted into the mouth with a spatula, and the chewer's saliva turns bright red. It's said to relieve hunger and fatigue but also causes cancer of the mouth.

Kava drinking is easier to get into (see **Customs** in the Fiji chapter for a full description). While kava is extremely popular in Fiji and

Tonga, extremely potent in Vanuatu, and extremely dignified in Samoa, it's unknown in Tahiti, Hawaii, and New Zealand. Recently German pharmaceutical firms have discovered kava's usefulness in the manufacture of nonaddictive painkillers and antidepressants.

GETTING THERE

Preparations

First decide where and when you're going and how long you wish to stay. Some routes are more available or practical than others. The major transit points for visitors are Auckland, Brisbane, Honolulu, Nadi, Nouméa, Tahiti, and Sydney; you'll notice how feeder flights radiate from these hubs. Most North Americans and Europeans will pass through Los Angeles International Airport (code-named LAX) on their way to Polynesia or Fiji, and Fiji's Nadi Airport (NAN) is the gateway to the Melanesian countries.

Your plane ticket will be your biggest single expense, so spend some time considering the possibilities. Before going any further, read this entire chapter right through and check the **Transportation** sections in the various chapter introductions for more detailed information. If you're online, peruse the internet sites of the airlines that interest you, then call them up directly over their toll-free 800 numbers to get current information on fares. The following airlines have flights from the United States:

Air France (tel. 1-800/237-2747, www.airfrance.com, flies to Nouméa and Tahiti)

Air New Zealand (tel. 1-800/262-1234, www.airnz.co.nz, flies to Apia, Nadi, Nouméa, Rarotonga, Tahiti, and Tongatapu)

Air Pacific (tel. 1-800/227-4446, www.airpacific.com, flies to Apia, Nadi, Tongatapu, Port Vila, and Honiara)

Air Tahiti Nui (tel. 1-877/824-4846, e-mail: fly@airtahitinui.pf, flies to Tahiti)

AOM French Airlines (tel. 1-800/892-9136, www.flyaom.com, flies to Nouméa and Tahiti)

Canada 3000 (tel. 1-416/674-0257, www.canada3000.com, flies to Nadi and Rarotonga)

Corsair (tel. 1-800/677-0720, www.corsair-int.com, flies to Nouméa and Tahiti)

Hawaiian Airlines (tel. 1-800/367-5320, www.hawaiianair.com, flies to Pago Pago and Tahiti)

LanChile Airlines (tel. 1-800/735-5526, www.lanchile.com, flies to Easter Island and Tahiti)

Polynesian Airlines (tel. 1-800/644-7659, www.polynesianairlines.co.nz, flies to Apia, Nadi, Pago Pago, and Tongatapu)

Royal Tongan Airlines (tel. 1-800/486-6426, http://kalianet.candw.to/rta, flies to Apia, Nadi, Niue, and Tongatapu)

Sometimes Canada and parts of the U.S. have different toll-free numbers, so if the number given above doesn't work, dial 800 information at 1-800/555-1212 (all 800 and 888 numbers are free). In Canada, Air New Zealand's toll-free number is tel. 1-800/663-5494.

Call all of these carriers and say you want the *lowest possible fare*. Cheapest are the excursion fares but these often have limitations and restrictions, so be sure to ask. Some have an advance-purchase deadline, which means it's wise to begin shopping early. Also check the fare seasons.

If you're not happy with the answers you get the first time, call the number back later and try again. Many different agents take calls on these lines, and some are more knowledge-

GORDON OHLIGER

able than others. The numbers are often busy during peak business hours, so call first thing in the morning, after dinner, or on the weekend. *Be persistent.*

Other Airlines
The international airlines listed below don't fly directly between North America and the South Pacific, but they do service the islands, so you could end up using them at some point:

Aircalin (tel. 1-800/677-4277, www.aircalin.nc, flies from Nouméa to Nadi, Port Vila, Tahiti, and Wallis)

Air Nauru (tel. 1-800/677-4277, www.airnauru.com.au, flies from Nauru to Nadi)

Air Vanuatu (tel. 1-800/677-4277, flies from Port Vila to Nadi and Nouméa)

Continental Airlines (tel. 1-800/231-0856, www.flycontinental.com, flies from Guam to Nouméa)

Qantas Airways (tel. 1-800/227-4500, www.qantas.com.au, flies from Australia to Honiara, Nadi, Nouméa, Port Vila, and Tahiti)

Samoa Air (tel. 684/699-9106, flies from Pago Pago to Apia and Vava'u)

Solomon Airlines (tel. 1-800/677-4277, flies from Honiara to Nadi and Port Vila)

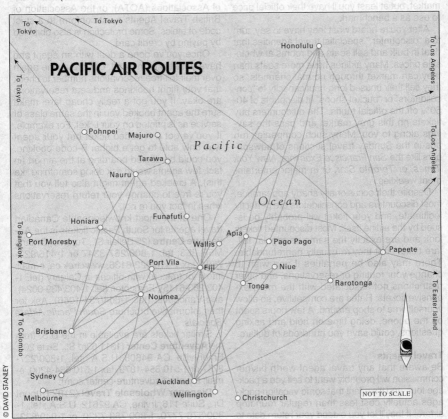

PACIFIC AIR ROUTES

To Tokyo

To Tokyo

To Tokyo

To Bangkok

To Colombo

To Los Angeles

To Los Angeles

To Easter Island

Pacific

Ocean

Honolulu

Pohnpei · Majuro · Tarawa · Nauru · Honiara · Port Moresby · Funafuti · Wallis · Apia · Pago Pago · Port Vila · Fiji · Niue · Papeete · Tonga · Rarotonga · Noumea · Brisbane · Sydney · Auckland · Melbourne · Wellington · Christchurch

NOT TO SCALE

© DAVID STANLEY

Cheaper Fares

Over the past few years South Pacific airfares have been deregulated and companies like Air New Zealand no longer publish set fare price lists. Their internet websites are also evasive, usually with tariff information kept secret (they might have prices for their all-inclusive package tours on the web but not air prices alone). Finding your way through this minefield can be the least enjoyable part of your before-trip planning, but you'll definitely pay a premium if you take the easy route and accept the first or second fare you're offered. With fares in flux, the airline employees you'll get at the numbers listed above probably won't quote you the lowest fare on the market, but at least you'll have their official price to use as a benchmark.

After you're heard what they have to say, turn to a "discounter," specialist travel agencies that deal in bulk and sell seats and rooms at wholesale prices. Many airlines have more seats than they can market through normal channels, so they sell their unused long-haul capacity to "consolidators" or "bucket shops" at discounts of 40-50% off the official tariffs. The discounters buy tickets on this gray market and pass the savings along to you. Many such companies run ads in the Sunday travel sections of newspapers like the *San Francisco Examiner, New York Times,* or *Toronto Star,* or in major entertainment weeklies.

Despite their occasionally shady appearance, most discounters and consolidators are perfectly legitimate, and your ticket will probably be issued by the airline itself. Most discounted tickets look and are exactly the same as regular full-fare tickets but they're usually nonrefundable. There may also be penalties if you wish to change your routing or reservations, and other restrictions not associated with the more expensive tickets. Rates are competitive, so allow yourself time to shop around. A few hours spent on the phone, doing time on hold and asking questions, could save you hundreds of dollars.

Travel Agents

Be aware that any travel agent worth his/her commission will probably want to sell you a package tour, and it's a fact that some vacation packages actually cost less than regular roundtrip airfare! If they'll let you extend your return date to give you some time to yourself this could be a good deal, especially with the hotel thrown in for "free." But check the restrictions.

Pick your agent carefully as many don't want to hear about discounts, cheap flights, or complicated routes, and will give wrong or misleading information in an offhand manner. They may try to sell you hotel rooms you could get locally for a fraction of the cost. Many agents depend on reservations systems like Auckland-oriented Sabre, Australia-biased Galileo, or Asia-focused Worldspan, which often come up with routings that are totally illogical for island travel. Agencies belonging to the American Society of Travel Agents (ASTA), the Alliance of Canadian Travel Associations (ACTA), or the Association of British Travel Agents must conform to a strict code of ethics. Some protection is also obtained by paying by credit card.

Once you've done a deal with an agent and have your ticket in hand, call the airline again over their toll-free reservations number to check that your flight bookings and seat reservations are okay. If you got a really cheap fare, make sure the agent booked you in the same class of service as is printed on your ticket. For example, if you've got a K-coded ticket but your agent was only able to get a higher B-code booking, you could be denied boarding at the airport (in fact, few agents would risk doing something like this). A crooked agent might also tell you that you're free to change your return reservations when in fact you're not.

One of the most knowledgeable Canadian travel agents for South Pacific tickets is the **Adventure Centre** (25 Bellair St., Toronto, Ontario M5R 3L3; tel. 1-800/267-3347 or 1-416/922-7584, fax 1-416/922-8136, www.trek.ca, e-mail: info@tor.trek.ca) with offices in Calgary (tel. 1-403/283-6115), Edmonton (tel. 1-403/439-0024), and Vancouver (tel. 1-604/734-1066). Ask for their informative brochure *South Pacific Airfare Specials.*

Similar tickets are available in the U.S. from the **Adventure Center** (1311 63rd St., Suite 200, Emeryville, CA 94608, U.S.A.; tel. 1-800/227-8747 or 1-510/654-1879, fax 1-510/654-4200, e-mail: tripinfo@adventure-center.com).

Discover Wholesale Travel (2192 Dupont Dr., Suite 116, Irvine, CA 92612, U.S.A.; tel. 1-800/576-7770, 1-800/759-7330, or 1-949/833-

1136, fax 1-949/833-1176, www.discovertravel. net, e-mail: info@discovertravel.net) sells discounted air tickets and offers rock-bottom rates on rooms at the top hotels. They sometimes have significantly lower fares for passengers booking within two weeks of departure ("distressed seats"). President Mary Anne Cook claims everyone on her staff has 10 years experience selling the South Pacific and "most importantly, we all love the area!"

Some of the cheapest return tickets to the South Pacific are sold by **Fiji Travel** (8885 Venice Blvd., Suite 202, Los Angeles, CA 90034, U.S.A.: tel. 1-800/500-3454 or 1-310/202-4220, fax 1-310/202-8233, www.fijitravel.com). They make their money through high volume, and to attract customers they keep their profit margins as low as possible. Thus you should absorb the airline's time with all your questions about fare seasons, schedules, etc., and only call companies like Fiji Travel and Discover Wholesale Travel after you know exactly what you want and how much everybody else is charging.

One U.S. agent willing to help you work out a personalized itinerary is Rob Jenneve of **Island Adventures** (574 Mills Way, Goleta, CA 93117, U.S.A.; tel. 1-800/289-4957 or 1-805/685-9230, fax 1-805/685-0960, e-mail: motuman@aol.com). Rob can put together flight and accommodation packages that are only slightly more expensive than the cheapest return airfare, and it's often possible to extend your return date to up to 30 days on the lowest fares or up to 90 days for a bit more. This option combines the benefits of packaged and independent travel, and you could end up spending a week at a medium-priced hotel with transfers for only US$50-100 more than you'd have to spend anyway just to get to the islands! Rob also books complex circle-Pacific routes and can steer you toward deluxe resorts that offer value for money.

Seasons
The month of outbound travel from the U.S. determines which seasonal fare you'll pay, and inquiring far in advance could allow you to reschedule your vacation slightly to take advantage of a lower fare.

Air New Zealand has their low (or "basic") season on flights to Cook Islands, Fiji, Samoa, and Tonga from mid-April to August, shoulder season Sept.-Nov. and in March, and high (or "peak") season Dec.-February. They've made April- Nov.—the top months in the South Pacific—their off-season because that's winter in Australia and New Zealand. If you're only going to the islands and can make it at that time, it certainly works to your advantage. Air Pacific's fare seasons to Fiji are the same.

However, if you're flying to Tahiti on one of the four French carriers, the high seasons are timed to correspond to holiday time in Europe: June to mid-September and December. This also applies on Air New Zealand if you're not going beyond Tahiti (if you're continuing to any of the other islands normal Air New Zealand seasons apply to the whole ticket). Air New Zealand's low season to Tahiti alone is January to May.

Current Trends
High operating costs have caused the larger airlines to switch to wide-bodied aircraft and long-haul routes with less frequent service and fewer stops. In the South Pacific this works to your disadvantage, as many islands get bypassed. Most airlines now charge extra for stopovers that once were free, or simply refuse to grant any stopovers at all on the cheapest fares.

Increasingly airlines are combining in global alliances to compete internationally. Thus Air Pacific is part of "Oneworld" (www.oneworldalliance.com) comprised of Qantas, American Airlines, Canadian Airlines, British Airways, Cathay Pacific, and Japan Airlines, while Air New Zealand has close links to the "Star Alliance" (www.star-alliance.com) of Ansett Australia, United Airlines, Air Canada, Lufthansa, SAS, Singapore Airlines, Varig, and others. Other groups less active in the South Pacific include "Wings" with KLM, Northwest, Continental, Malaysian, and Korean Air, and "Delta/Swissair" linked to Alitalia, Sabina, and Austrian. This trend is to your advantage as within the different blocks frequent flier programs and airport lounge privileges are often interchangeable, "seamless" booking becomes possible, flight schedules are coordinated, luggage handling is easier, and through fares exist. The alliances have special air passes and round-the-world deals combining the networks of a variety of affiliated carriers, several of which are discussed below. These passes are still developing and things could soon get much easier than they are today.

PIONEERS OF PACIFIC AVIATION

The first flight from the U.S. to Australia took place in 1928. Charles Kingsford-Smith and Charles Ulm flew their trimotor Fokker VII-3M, the *Southern Cross*, from Oakland to Brisbane (11,906 km) in 83 hours and 38 minutes, with intermediate stops in Hawaii and Fiji. The original aircraft is now on display outside the domestic terminal of Brisbane's Eagle Farm Airport. In 1937 Pan American Airways began commercial flights between the U.S. and New Zealand, with stops at Hawaii and American Samoa. The flying boat service was tragically interrupted on the third flight when the *Samoa Clipper* exploded just after leaving Pago Pago on 10 January 1938.

Within the South Pacific, many regional carriers have attempted to cut costs by pooling their services through "code sharing." This means that two or three different airlines will "own" seats on the same flight, which they sell under their own two-letter airline code. The weekly flight from Nadi to Honiara is designated both FJ (Air Pacific) and IE (Solomon Airlines). Similarly, two flights a week between Nadi and Tahiti are FJ (Air Pacific) and SB (Aircalin). The flights to Honolulu and Los Angeles sold by Polynesian Airlines and Royal Tongan Airlines are actually code shares operated by Air New Zealand. Most Qantas flights to Fiji are now operated by Air Pacific planes.

Interline Tickets

If you plan a wide-ranging trip with stops on several continents, the **Global Explorer** may be the ticket for you. This fare allows six free stops selected from more than 400 destinations on 28,500 miles of routes. You can use the services of any of these airlines: Air Liberté, Air Pacific, American Airlines, British Airways, Canadian Airlines, Deutsche Airlines, and Qantas. This costs US$3,089 in the U.S. or CDN$3,969 in Canada, and additional stops after the first six are US$100 each. You must purchase the pass a week in advance and it's valid one year. Date changes and the first rerouting are free (additional reroutings US$100). Ask Qantas about this ticket.

A similar fare available only in the South Pacific and Europe is the **World Navigator,** which encompasses the networks of Aircalin, Air New Zealand, Air UK, Ansett Australia, Emirates, KLM Royal Dutch Airlines, Northwest Airlines, Kenyan Airlines, and South African Airways. From London, the World Navigator costs £1,099/1,199/1,299 in the low/shoulder/peak seasons (the low season is April to June only). From Australia, it's A$2,569/2,779/2,979/3,189 according to season with the lowest seasons running from mid-January to February and October to mid-November.

In North America, Air New Zealand sells a **World Escapade** valid for a round-the-world journey on Air New Zealand, Ansett Australia, and Singapore Airlines. You're allowed 29,000 miles with unlimited stops at US$2,799. One transatlantic and one transpacific journey must be included, but the ticket is valid one year and backtracking is allowed.

Air New Zealand's **Pacific Escapade** allows a circle-Pacific trip on the same three airlines. With this one you get 22,000 miles at US$2,600 with all the stops you want (maximum of three each in Australia and New Zealand). You'll have to transit Singapore at least once and travel must begin in either Los Angeles or Vancouver (no add-ons). On both Escapades, should you go over the allowable mileage, 4,500 extra miles are US$300. Reservation changes are free the first time but extra after that.

Northwest Airlines in conjunction with Air New Zealand offers a **Circle-Pacific fare** of US$2,650 from Los Angeles with add-on airfares available from other North American cities. This ticket allows four free stopovers in Asia and the South Pacific, additional stops US$50 each. To reissue the ticket also costs US$50. It's valid for six months and date changes are free. You must travel in a continuous circle without any backtracking. Air Pacific also has a Circle-Pacific fare, so compare.

The packages described above may well have changed by the time you read this, but similar (and perhaps even better) things should be available. Alternative methods of flying around the region are explained in the **Getting Around By Air** section that follows. For example, you may be better off using a "Visit South Pacific Pass" or a "Polypass" from a gateway city such as Nadi or

Honolulu, accessible on cheap flights from cities worldwide.

Onward Tickets

All of the South Pacific countries require an onward ticket as a condition for entry. Although the immigration officials don't always check it, the airlines usually do. If you're planning a long trip including locally arranged sea travel between countries, this can be a nuisance. One way to satisfy the ticket-to-leave requirement is to purchase a full-fare one-way economy ticket out of the area from Air New Zealand (valid one year). As you're about to depart for the next country on your route have the airline reissue the ticket, so it's a ticket to leave from there. Otherwise buy a full-fare ticket across the Pacific with stops in all the countries you'll visit, then use it *only* to satisfy check-in staff and immigration. When you finally complete your trip return the ticket to the issuing office for a full refund. Remember that airline tickets are often refundable only in the place of purchase and that the sort of deals and discount airfares available elsewhere are not available in the South Pacific. Have your *real* means of departure planned.

Airport Taxes

When planning your route, keep airport departure taxes in mind, as they can add up fast on a trip with lots of stops. You needn't worry in Tahiti-Polynesia, where no tax is collected, or in American Samoa and New Caledonia where the tax is included in the ticket price, but in many places increasingly high airport taxes are collected on the spot. You'll pay about US$10 in Samoa and Solomon Islands, US$15 in Cook Islands, Fiji, Niue, and Tonga, and more than US$20 in Vanuatu and Tuvalu. New Zealand and Australia also have very high airport taxes (as do the U.S. and Canada, though it's usually included in the ticket price). You can often avoid paying the tax if you're in transit for less than 24 hours.

AIR SERVICES

From North America

Air France, Air New Zealand, Air Pacific, Air Tahiti Nui, AOM French Airlines, and Corsair are the major carriers serving the South Pacific out of

Los Angeles, although Air France, Air Tahiti Nui, AOM French Airlines, and Corsair only go as far as Tahiti. Corsair also flies Oakland-Tahiti. Fiji's **Air Pacific** has nonstop Boeing 747 service from Los Angeles to Nadi four times a week. From Los Angeles, a 30-day return ticket to Fiji is US$888/1,048/1,298 low/shoulder/high season. From Honolulu it's US$688/848/1,098. These are the midweek fares—weekend departures are US$60 more expensive. When booking check the times carefully as some flights are overnight while others arrive just before midnight. Flying with Air Pacific is like being in Fiji from the moment you board the plane.

The only U.S. airline serving the South Pacific is **Hawaiian Airlines**, which offers flights to Pago Pago and Tahiti via its base in Honolulu with connections to/from Las Vegas, Los Angeles, San Francisco, Portland, and Seattle. To Pago Pago the 30-day advance purchase fare is US$499 (plus US$29 tax) from Honolulu or US$799 from the U.S. west coast year-round. From the west coast to Tahiti a 14-day advance purchase roundtrip is US$690/890 low/high season plus tax. Fare seasons to Tahiti are complicated, so call well ahead. Date changes after ticketing are US$75. A free stop in Honolulu is available on these fares.

Other flights out of Honolulu include Air Pacific to Nadi, Polynesian Airlines to Apia, Royal Tongan Airlines to Tongatapu, and Air New Zealand to Rarotonga.

From Canada, **Canadian Airlines International** connects with Air Pacific in Honolulu for Nadi. **Canada 3000** has direct flights to Nadi and Rarotonga via Honolulu Nov.-April only (tickets on charter carriers like Canada 3000 embody numerous burdensome restrictions and should only be considered if the savings is very large). Air New Zealand passengers originating in Canada must change planes in Honolulu or Los Angeles.

Air New Zealand

In the 1950s Air New Zealand pioneered its "Coral Route" using Solent flying boats, and today the carrier has achieved a death grip over long-haul air routes into the region by allowing stopovers in Tahiti-Polynesia, Cook Islands, Fiji, Samoa, and Tonga as part of through services between North America and New Zealand. Smaller island-based carriers have difficulty competing due to Air New Zealand's lower operating costs and high capacity, and this advantage is backed up by self-serving government restrictions.

In past both Air New Zealand and Qantas have managed to squelch competition from up-starts like Air Pacific and Polynesian Airlines by restricting their ability to carry passengers between Australia and New Zealand, or beyond Australia to Asia. Air Pacific's North American operations are stymied by the New Zealand government's denial of permission to fly passengers beyond Fiji, although Air New Zealand is allowed to fly its passengers through Fiji to both Japan and North America. Long after Air New Zealand and Qantas were privatized, their governments continue to favor the home team.

Air New Zealand's first priority is to fly people to Auckland, and it's sometimes cheaper to buy a return ticket to Auckland with a couple of free stops in the islands than a roundtrip ticket from Los Angeles only as far as Tahiti-Rarotonga-Fiji. If you don't wish to visit New Zealand, you can transit Auckland the same day. Despite Air New Zealand's frequent services, travelers in Europe and North America often have difficulty booking stops in the islands on their way down under and it's advisable to reserve seats well ahead. Air New Zealand's near monopoly does have the advantage of allowing you to include a number of countries in a single ticket if you do some advance planning.

The cheapest tickets involve a number of restrictions. Air New Zealand's "Coral Experience" allows one stop plus your destination with additional stops available at US$145 each. Thus you can fly Los Angeles-Tahiti-Rarotonga-Fiji-Los Angeles for US$1,143/1,343/1,593 low/shoulder/high season if you leave at the beginning of the week for a trip of three months maximum. Add US$150 if wish to extend your period of stay to six months, plus another US$60 if you'd like to set out on Thursday, Friday, Saturday, or Sunday. Drop either Tahiti, Rarotonga, or Fiji from your itinerary and you'll save US$145. Other possible routings are Los Angeles-Fiji-Vanuatu-Los Angeles at US$1,108/1,398/1,648, or Los Angeles-Fiji-Honiara-Los Angeles at US$1,248/1,498/1,748. Trips originating in Honolulu are US$200 cheaper in all cases. Remember that the "Coral Experience" must be purchased 14 days in advance and

there's a US$75 penalty to change your flight dates. A 35% cancellation fee also applies after the 14-day ticket deadline.

For a more wide-ranging trip with fewer restrictions, ask for Air New Zealand's "Coral Explorer Airpass," which costs US$1,758/2,008/2,258 low/shoulder/high season. This worthwhile ticket allows you to fly Los Angeles-Tahiti-Rarotonga-Fiji-Auckland-Tongatapu-Apia-Honolulu-Los Angeles or vice versa. Extend the ticket to Australia for US$100 more; eliminate Auckland-Tongatapu-Apia and it's about US$100 less. Begin in Honolulu and it's US$200 less again. You can stay up to one year but rerouting costs US$75 (date changes are free). There's no advance purchase requirement and you can go any day. To follow the same routing minus two stops on a six-month "Coral Experience" with all its restrictions costs US$1,633/1,883/2,133.

Return tickets from Los Angeles to a single island are cheaper. For example, the "No Stop Apex" is US$888/1,048/1,298 at the beginning of the week to either Rarotonga and Fiji, or US$1,098/1,348/1,598 to Honiara, both from Los Angeles (US$200 cheaper from Honolulu). To set out on Thursday, Friday, Saturday or Sunday is US$60 more. The maximum stay is one month and you must pay at least 21 days before departure (50% cancellation penalty).

In Canada, Air New Zealand calls the same thing by different names: the "No Stop Apex" is the "Shotover Fare" while the "Coral Experience" is the "Bungy Fare" (the "Explorer" is still the "Explorer"). There's also a cheaper "Backpacker Downunder" fare that must be purchased 14 days in advance and does not cover hotel expenses due to flight misconnections.

On most tickets special "add-on" fares to Los Angeles or Vancouver are available from cities right across the U.S. and Canada. Also ask about Air New Zealand's "Pacifica Airpass," which covers side trips to destinations not directly on their Coral Route (details in **Getting Around**, which follows). One problem with Air New Zealand is its unfriendly schedules, which are built around Auckland and Los Angeles: they'll drop you off in the middle of the night if you get out almost anywhere else.

Air New Zealand's cabin service is professional, and you'll like the champagne breakfasts and outstanding food with complimentary beer and wine. Another plus are the relaxing seats with adjustable head rests and lots of leg room. The *Blue Pacific* videos about their destinations are entertaining the first time you see them, but after a while you get bored. The only reading material provided is the *Pacific Wave* inflight magazine, the *Skyshop* duty free catalog, and the *Primetime* entertainment magazine. These are unlikely to hold your attention for long, so bring along a book or magazine of your own (the daily newspaper is provided only to passengers in first class).

Tonga/Samoa

If Tonga and Samoa are as far as you wish to go, Air New Zealand offers Los Angeles-Apia-Auckland-Tongatapu-Los Angeles for US$1,343/ 1,593/1,843 low/shoulder/high as a six-month "Coral Experience" (same conditions as described above). Otherwise a "No Stop Apex" from Los Angeles to either Apia or Tongatapu is US$973 Jan.-April and Aug.-Nov. or US$1,231 other months (maximum stay one month, 21-day advance purchase, 50% cancellation fee). Also compare Polynesian Airlines and Royal Tongan Airlines, which could work out cheaper.

Air New Zealand flies between Apia and Tongatapu as part of their Los Angeles-Honolulu-Apia-Tongatapu-Auckland weekly service, but this leg is heavily booked and should be reserved as far in advance as possible. If you wait too long and can't obtain a seat for that sector, consider leaving it open and going Apia-Pago Pago-Vava'u-Ha'apai-Tongatapu. Air tickets Pago Pago-Vava'u can only be purchased in Samoa or Tonga, but you'll have no difficulty making bookings at the Samoa Air office in Apia and boats ply regularly from Apia to Pago Pago and Vava'u to Ha'apai and Tongatapu. Your unused Apia-Tongatapu coupon will probably be nonrefundable, so this side trip will cost extra, but you'll see a lot without having to backtrack. Further information is provided under **Transportation** in the American Samoa chapter.

French Charter Flights

The French tour company **Nouvelles Frontières** or "New Frontiers" handles weekly charter flights from Paris and Los Angeles/Oakland to Tahiti and from Paris to Nouméa on their own airline, **Corsair.** A round-the-world routing Los Angeles/Oakland-Tahiti-Nouméa-Bangkok-Paris-Los Angeles/Oakland is also possible on Corsair.

Seasons are based on the exact date of each flight with the low or "green" season Jan.-June and Sept.-November. There are many restrictions and penalties. On the cheapest tickets you must pay 50% of the price upon booking and the balance 21 days before departure. There are no refunds if you decide to cancel. To change the date of your return flight is US$100, provided you do so 15 days in advance. Corsair reserves the right to alter flight times up to 48 hours without compensation, but if you miss your flight you lose your money. Still, if you're sure when you'll be traveling, the Corsair fare of around US$600/ 700 low/high roundtrip plus tax is a couple of hundred dollars lower than anything offered by the scheduled airlines.

All told, Nouvelles Frontières (www.nouvelles-frontieres.fr) has 200 offices in France and 40 others around the world, including these: 12 East 33rd St., 10th floor, New York, NY 10016, U.S.A. (tel. 1-212/779-0600, fax 1-212/779-1007); Air Promotions Systems, 5757 West Century Blvd., Suite 660, Los Angeles, CA 90045-6407, U.S.A. (tel. 1-800/677-0720 or 1-310/670-7318, fax 1-310/338-0708, www.corsair-int.com, e-mail: webmaster@corsair-int.com); and 2/3 Woodstock St., London W1R 1HE, England (tel. 44-171/355-3952, fax 44-171/491-0684).

From Australia

Since the Australian government sold Qantas and deregulated airfares, the cost of flying out of Australia has dropped dramatically. Now you can often find deals much better than the published Apex fares, especially during off months. Air New Zealand is competing fiercely in the Australian market, and they offer competitive fares to many South Pacific points via Auckland. You can usually buy such tickets for a lower price than you'd pay at the airline office itself by working through an agent specializing in bargain airfares. Check the travel sections in the weekend papers and call Flight Centres International. For information on slightly reduced fares available from STA Travel contact them at 1-800/777-0112 or www.sta-travel.com.

The Circle-Pacific and round-the-world fares described above are also available here. Apex (advance purchase excursion) tickets must be bought 14 days in advance and heavy cancellation penalties apply. The low season ex-Australia is generally Feb.-May to Tahiti, and mid-January to June, mid-July to mid-September, and mid-October to November to Apia, but this varies. A return fare from Sydney to Apia via Auckland will cost A$1,167 in the low season.

Qantas flies to Honiara and Port Vila from Brisbane, to Nadi and Nouméa from Brisbane, Melbourne, and Sydney, and to Tahiti from Auckland and Sydney. There are also nonstop flights from Brisbane, Melbourne, and Sydney to Fiji on **Air Pacific,** to Nouméa on **Aircalin,** and to Port Vila on **Air Vanuatu. Polynesian Airlines** has direct flights to Apia from Melbourne and Sydney. **Royal Tongan Airlines** flies to Tongatapu from Sydney, and **Solomon Airlines** flies to Honiara from Brisbane. In late 1998 Air New Zealand's business partner, **Ansett Australia,** launched direct flights to Fiji.

From New Zealand

Unrestricted low airfares to the South Pacific are surprisingly hard to come by in New Zealand. Some tickets have advance purchase requirements, so start shopping well ahead. Ask around at a number of different travel agencies for special unadvertised or under-the-counter fares. Agents to call include STA Travel and Flight Centres International. Fares to Tahiti often allow a stop in the Cook Islands, but it's hard to get a seat on these fully booked planes.

Air New Zealand offers reduced excursion fares from Auckland to all the main South Pacific islands with a maximum stay of 45 days to Tahiti or 90 days to Fiji, Tonga, and Samoa. Fares depend on the season with the low season to Fiji Jan.-June and mid-October to mid-December, to Tonga and Samoa from January to mid-April and Oct.-Nov., and to Tahiti in February, March, October, and November. In the low/high seasons expect to pay NZ$822/983 to Fiji, NZ$979/1,169 to Tongatapu, NZ$1,202/1,392 to Apia, and NZ$1,211/1,417 to Tahiti. One-year, seven-day advance purchase fares to Rarotonga are NZ$1,056/1,296 low/high. It's often cheaper to buy a package tour to the islands with airfare, accommodations, and transfers included, but these are usually limited to seven nights on one island and you're stuck in a boring touristic environment. Ask if you'll be allowed to extend your return date and still get the low inclusive tour price.

Air New Zealand flies from their Auckland gateway to Apia, Nadi, Norfolk, Nouméa, Rarotonga, Tahiti, and Tongatapu. Other airlines with flights from Auckland include **Aircalin** to Nouméa, **Air Pacific** to Nadi (also from Christchurch and Wellington), **Air Vanuatu** to Port Vila, **Polynesian Airlines** to Tongatapu and Apia, **Royal Tongan Airlines** to Tongatapu and Niue, and **Solomon Airlines** to Honiara.

From South America

LanChile Airlines flies from Santiago to Tahiti via Easter Island three times a week, with additional flights during the high southern summer season. The regular one-way fare Santiago-Easter-Tahiti is US$1,133 economy class. Santiago-Easter Island is US$448 each way.

LanChile's 30-day roundtrip excursion fare between Tahiti and Santiago, with a stopover on Easter Island, costs US$1,200. If you only want to visit Easter Island, 30-day excursion tickets Tahiti-Easter Island-Tahiti are available in Papeete, but it's cheaper to buy a tour package from one of the agencies mentioned in this book's **Papeete** section (from Tahiti, low season fares are available March-November).

LanChile offers a variety of "Pacific Circuit Fares" including Miami/Los Angeles-Santiago-Easter Island-Tahiti-Honolulu-Los Angeles (US$1,645), New York-Santiago-Easter Island-Tahiti-Honolulu-Los Angeles (US$1,775), and Los Angeles-Santiago-Easter Island-Tahiti-Los Angeles (US$1,828), all valid one year. From Australia or New Zealand you can get Sydney/Melbourne/Brisbane-Auckland-Tahiti-Easter Island-Santiago-Los Angeles-Australia (US$2,091).

LanChile must rate as one of the most unreliable carriers flying to the South Pacific, and service irregularities are routine. The Santiago-Easter Island portion of their Tahiti service is often heavily booked, so try to reserve far in advance, although this can be hard to do.

From Europe

Since few European carriers reach the South Pacific, you may have to use a gateway city such as Singapore, Sydney, Honolulu, or Los Angeles. Air New Zealand offers nonstop flights London-Los Angeles five times a week and Frankfurt-Los Angeles three times a week, with connections in L.A. to their Coral Route. Air France, AOM French Airlines, and Corsair fly to Tahiti from Paris via Los Angeles or Oakland. AOM also flies from Paris-Orly to Nouméa via Sri Lanka and Sydney three times a week.

Air New Zealand reservations numbers around Europe are tel. 03/202-1355 (Belgium), tel. 0800/907-712 (France), tel. 01/3081-7778 (Germany), tel. 1678-76126 (Italy), tel. 08-002527 (Luxembourg), tel. 06/022-1016 (Netherlands), tel. 900/993241 (Spain), tel. 020/792-939 (Sweden), tel. 0800/557-778 (Switzerland), and tel. 44-181/741-2299 (United Kingdom). Call them up and ask about their Coral Route fares. Be aware that Air New Zealand flights from Europe are heavily booked and reservations should be made far in advance.

The British specialist in South Pacific itineraries is **Trailfinders** (44-50 Earls Court Rd., Kensington, London W8 6FT; tel. 44-171/938-3366, fax 44-171/937-9294), in business since 1970. They offer a variety of discounted round-the-world tickets through the South Pacific that are often much cheaper than the published fares. For example, a routing via Easter Island and Tahiti is £1,150. Call or write for a free copy of their magazine, *Trailfinder*, which appears in April, July, and December. **Bridge the World** (47 Chalk Farm Rd., Camden Town, London NW1 8AN; tel. 44-171/911-0900, fax 44-171/813-3350, e-mail: sales@bridge-the-world.co.uk) has a ticket that includes Fiji, Rarotonga, Tahiti, and a variety of stops in Asia for £935. Check the ads in the London entertainment magazines for other such companies.

In Holland **Pacific Island Travel** (Herengracht 495, 1017 BT Amsterdam, the Netherlands; tel. 31-20/626-1325, fax 31-20/623-0008, e-mail: pitnet @xs4all.nl) sells most of the air passes and long-distance tickets mentioned in this section, plus package tours. **Barron & De Keijzer Travel** (Herengracht 340, 1016 CG Amsterdam, the Netherlands; tel. 31-20/625-8600, fax 31-20/622-7559) sells Air New Zealand's Coral Route with travel via London. Also in Amsterdam, **Reisbureau Amber** (Da Costastraat 77, 1053 ZG Amsterdam, the Netherlands; tel. 31-20/685-1155, fax 31-20/689-0406) is one of the best places in Europe to pick up books on the South Pacific.

In Switzerland try **Globetrotter Travel Service** (Rennweg 35, CH-8023 Zürich, Switzerland; tel. 41-1/213-8080, fax 41-1/213-8088), with offices in Baden, Basel, Bern, Luzern, St. Gallen, Thun, Winterthur, Zug, and Zürich. Their quarterly newsletter, *Ticket-Info,* lists hundreds of cheap flights, including many through the South Pacific.

Bucket shops in Germany sell a "Pacific Airpass" on Air New Zealand from Frankfurt to the South Pacific that allows all the usual Coral Route stops and is valid six months. All flights must be booked prior to leaving Europe, and there's a charge to change the dates once the ticket has been issued. One agency selling such tickets is **Walther-Weltreisen** (Hirschberger Strasse 30, D-53119 Bonn; tel. 49-228/661-239, fax 49-228/661-181).

The **Pacific Travel House** (Bayerstrasse 95, D-80335 München; tel. 49-89/530-9293) offers a variety of package tours. **Schöner Tauchen** (Hastedter Heerstr. 211, D-28207 Bremen; tel. 49-421/450-010, fax 49-421/450-080, www.schoener-tauchen.com, e-mail: info@schoener-tauchen.com) specializes in dive tours to Fiji, Tonga, Solomon Islands, and Vanuatu.

Regional Airlines

Aside from the big international airlines described above, a number of island-based carriers fly around the South Pacific. These include the Fijian carrier **Air Pacific,** with flights from Fiji to Apia, Auckland, Brisbane, Christchurch, Honiara, Honolulu, Los Angeles, Melbourne, Port Vila, Sydney, Tokyo, Tongatapu, and Wellington. Samoa's **Polynesian Airlines** serves Auckland, Honolulu, Los Angeles, Melbourne, Nadi, Pago Pago, Sydney, Tonga, and Wellington from Apia. **Aircalin** flies from Nouméa to Auckland, Brisbane, Nadi, Port Vila, Sydney, Tahiti, and Wallis. From Fiji **Air Fiji** flies north to Funafuti (turn to the Tuvalu chapter for details). **Air Nauru** flies from Nadi to Nauru and Tarawa. Pago Pago-based **Samoa Air** services only Apia and Vava'u. **Royal Tongan Airlines** has flights from Tongatapu to Auckland, Honolulu, Nadi, Niue, and Sydney, and from Vava'u to Nadi. **Air Vanuatu** flies from Port Vila to Auckland, Brisbane, Honiara, Melbourne, Nadi, Nouméa, and Sydney. **Solomon Airlines** links Honiara to Auckland, Brisbane, Nadi, Port Moresby, and Port Vila. Details of these services are included in the relevant destination chapters of this book. Keep in mind that few regional flights operate daily and quite a few are only once or twice a week.

Important Note

Airfares, rules, and regulations tend to fluctuate a lot, so some of the information above may have changed. This is only a guide; we've included a few fares to give you a rough idea how much things might cost. Your travel agent will know what's available at the time you're ready to travel, but if you're not satisfied with his/her advice, keep shopping around. The biggest step is deciding to go—once you're over that, the rest is easy!

PROBLEMS

When planning your trip allow a minimum two-hour stopover between connecting flights at U.S. airports, although with airport delays on the increase even this may not be enough. In the islands allow at least a day between flights. In some airports, flights are not called over the public address system, so keep your eyes open. Whenever traveling, always have a paperback or two, some toiletries, and a change of underwear in your hand luggage.

If your flight is canceled due to a mechanical problem with the aircraft, the airline will cover your hotel bill and meals. If they reschedule the flight on short notice for reasons of their own or you're bumped off an overbooked flight, they should also pay. They may not feel obligated to pay, however, if the delay is due to weather conditions, a strike by another company, national emergencies, etc., although the best airlines still pick up the tab in these cases. Just don't expect much from local, "third-level" airlines on remote islands where such difficulties are routine.

It's an established practice among airlines to provide light refreshments to passengers delayed two hours after the scheduled departure time and a meal after four hours. Don't expect to get this on an outer island, but politely request it if you're at a gateway airport. If you are unexpectedly forced to spend the night somewhere, an airline employee may hand you a form on which they offer to telephone a friend or relative to inform them of the delay. Don't trust them to do this, however. Call your party yourself if you want to be sure they get the message.

Overbooking

To compensate for no-shows, most airlines overbook their flights. To avoid being bumped, ask for your seat assignment when booking, check in early, and go to the departure area well before flight time. Of course, if you *are* bumped by a reputable international airline at a major airport you'll be regaled with free meals and lodging and sometimes even free flight vouchers (don't expect anything like this from a domestic carrier on a remote Pacific island).

Whenever you break your journey for more than 72 hours, always reconfirm your onward reservations and check your seat assignment at the same time. Get the name of the person who takes your reconfirmation so they cannot later deny it. Failure to reconfirm could result in the cancellation of your complete remaining itinerary. This could also happen if you miss a flight for any reason. If you want special vegetarian or kosher food in-flight, request it when buying your ticket, booking, and reconfirming.

When you try to reconfirm your Air New Zealand flight the agent will tell you that this formality is no longer required. Theoretically this is true, but unless you request your seat assignment in advance, either at an Air New Zealand office or over the phone, you could be "bumped" from a full flight, reservation or no reservation. Air New Zealand's ticket cover bears this surprising message:

. . . no guarantee of a seat is indicated by the terms "reservation," "booking," "O.K." status, or the times associated therewith.

They do admit in the same notice that confirmed passengers denied seats may be eligible for compensation, so if you're not in a hurry, a night or two at an upmarket hotel with all meals courtesy of Air New Zealand may not be a hardship. Your best bet if you don't want to get "bumped" is to request seat assignments for your entire itinerary before you leave home, or at least at the first Air New Zealand office you pass during your travels. Any good travel agent selling tickets on Air New Zealand should know enough to automatically request your seat assignments as they make your bookings. In the islands Air New Zealand offices will still accept a local contact telephone number from you. Check Air New

Zealand's reconfirmation policy at one of their offices as it could change.

Baggage

International airlines allow economy-class passengers either 20 kilos of baggage or two pieces not more than 32 kilos each (ask which applies to you). Under the piece system, neither bag must have a combined length, width, and height of more than 158 centimeters (62 inches) and the two pieces together must not exceed 272 centimeters (107 inches). On most long-haul tickets to/from North America or Europe, the piece system applies to all sectors, but check this with the airline. The frequent flier programs of some major airlines allow participants to carry up to 10 kilos of excess baggage free of charge. Small commuter carriers sometimes restrict you to as little as 10 kilos total, so it's better to pack according to the lowest common denominator. Polynesian Airlines allows only five kilograms on its domestic flights!

Bicycles, folding kayaks, and surfboards can usually be checked as baggage (sometimes for an additional US$50-100 charge), but sailboards may have to be shipped airfreight. If you do travel with a sailboard, be sure to call it a surfboard at check-in.

Tag your bag with name, address, and phone number inside and out. Stow anything that could conceivably be considered a weapon (scissors, penknife, toy gun, mace, etc.) in your checked luggage. One reason for lost baggage is that some people fail to remove used baggage tags after they claim their luggage. Get into the habit of tearing off old baggage tags, unless you want your luggage to travel in the opposite direction! As you're checking in, look to see if the three-letter city codes on your baggage tag receipt and boarding pass are the same.

If your baggage is damaged or doesn't arrive at your destination, inform the airline officials *immediately* and have them fill out a written report; otherwise future claims for compensation will be compromised. Airlines usually reimburse out-of-pocket expenses if your baggage is lost or delayed more than 24 hours. The amount varies from US$25 to US$50. Your chances of getting it are better if you're polite but firm. Keep receipts for any money you're forced to spend to replace missing articles.

Claims for lost luggage can take weeks to process. Keep in touch with the airline to show your concern and hang on to your baggage tag until the matter is resolved. If you feel you did not receive the attention you deserved, write the airline an objective letter outlining the case. Get the names of the employees you're dealing with so you can mention them in the letter. Of course, don't expect any pocket money or compensation on a remote outer island. Report the loss, then wait till you get back to their main office. Whatever happens, try to avoid getting angry. The people you're dealing with don't want the problem any more than you do.

BY BOAT

Even as much Pacific shipping was being sunk during WW II, airstrips were springing up on all the main islands. This hastened the inevitable replacement of the old steamships with modern aircraft, and it's now extremely rare to arrive in the South Pacific by boat (private yachts excepted). Most islands export similar products and there's little interregional trade; large container ships headed for Australia, New Zealand, and Japan don't usually accept passengers.

Those bitten by nostalgia for the slower prewar ways may like to know that a couple of passenger-carrying freighters do still call at the islands, though their fares are much higher than those charged by the airlines. A specialized agency booking such passages is **TravLtips** (Box 188, Flushing, NY 11358, U.S.A.; tel. 1-800/872-8584 or 1-718/939-2400, fax 1-718/939-2047, www.TravLtips.com, e-mail: info@travltips.com). Also try **Freighter World Cruises** (180 South Lake Ave., Suite 335, Pasadena, CA 91101, U.S.A.; tel. 1-818/449-9200, fax 1-818/449-9573, www.gus.net/travel/fwc/fwc.html).

These companies can place you aboard a British-registered **Bank Line** container ship on its way around the world from Europe via the Panama Canal, Papeete, Nouméa, Suva, Lautoka, Port Vila, Santo, Honiara, and Papua New Guinea. A round-the-world ticket for the four-month journey is US$12,125, but segments are sold if space is available 30 days before sailing. Similarly, TravLtips books German-registered **Columbus Line** vessels, which make 45-day roundtrips between Los Angeles and Australia via Suva. These ships can accommodate only about a dozen passengers, so inquire well in advance. Also ask about passenger accommodation on cargo vessels of the **Blue Star Line,** which call at Suva and Nouméa between Los Angeles and Auckland.

Nature Expeditions International (6400 E. El Dorado Circle, Suite 210, Tucson, AZ 85715, U.S.A.; tel. 1-800/869-0639 or 1-520/721-6712, fax 1-520/721-6719, www.naturexp.com, e-mail: NaturExp@aol.com) books cruises to the farthest corners of Polynesia on the expedition ship *World Discoverer.* Passengers land on remote islands from Zodiacs and there are on-board lectures by world authorities. Twice a year there's an 18-day cruise from Easter Island to Tahiti via Pitcairn, Mangareva, and the Marquesas (from US$6,930 pp double occupancy, airfare extra). One-week trips from Tahiti to Rarotonga and island-hopping voyages from Tahiti to Apia or Fiji to Rarotonga are also offered. In addition, Nature Expeditions has very good two-week archaeology tours to Easter Island.

Quest Nature Tours (36 Finch Ave. West, Toronto, Ontario M2N 2G9, Canada; tel. 1-800/387-1483 or 1-416/221-3000, fax 1-416/221-5730, e-mail: travel@worldwidequest.com) books an annual 29-night cruise in April from Chile to Tahiti that visits such remote islands as Easter, Pitcairn, Mangareva, Rapa, Raivavae, and more. Cabins on the Russian mini-cruise ship begin at US$5,995 pp double occupancy, plus gratuities and US$595 port taxes, but including return airfare from Los Angeles. Other extended Quest cruises explore Polynesia and Melanesia.

Adventure cruises to the Marquesas Islands aboard the freighter *Aranui* are described in the Tahiti-Polynesia chapter. **Radisson Seven Seas Cruises** offers tourist trips around Tahiti-Polynesia on the huge cruise ship *Paul Gauguin* (details in the introduction to the Tahiti-Polynesia chapter). In Fiji, **Captain Cook Cruises** (Box 23, Nadi; tel. 701-823, fax 702-045, www.captcookcrus.com.au, e-mail: captcookcrus@is.com.fj) runs very popular deluxe cruises to the Yasawa Islands from Nadi. Blue Lagoon Cruises are similar. Turn to the Fiji chapter for details.

ORGANIZED TOURS

Packaged Holidays

While packaged travel certainly isn't for everyone, reduced group airfares and hotel rates make some tours worth considering. For two people with limited time and a desire to stay at a first-class hotel, this may be the cheapest way to go. The "wholesalers" who put these packages together get their rooms at rates far lower than individuals pay. Special-interest tours are very popular among sportspeople who want to be sure they'll get to participate in the various activities they enjoy. The main drawback to the tours is that you're on a fixed itinerary in a touristic environment, out of touch with local life. Singles pay a healthy supplement. Some of the companies mentioned below do not accept consumer inquiries and require you to work through a travel agent.

Specialists in tours (and all travel arrangements) to Tahiti-Polynesia include **Discover Wholesale Travel** (2192 Dupont Dr., Suite 116, Irvine, CA 92612, U.S.A.; tel. 1-800/576-7770, 1-800/759-7330, or 1-949/833-1136, fax 1-949/833-1176, www.discovertravel.net), **Iaora Tahiti Ecotours** (Frank Murphy, B.P. 6845, 98702 Faa'a, Tahiti; tel./fax 56-46-75, www.iaora.com), **Islands in the Sun** (2381 Rosecrans Ave. #325, El Segundo, CA 90245-4913, U.S.A.; tel. 1-800/828-6877, fax 1-310/536-6266), **Manuia Tours** (74 New Montgomery St., San Francisco, CA 94105, U.S.A.; tel. 1-415/495-4500, fax 1-415/495-2000), **Pleasant Holidays** (Box 5020, Westlake Village, CA 91359-5020, U.S.A.; tel. 1-800/644-3515, fax 1-619/283-3131, www.pleasantholidays.com), **Tahiti Legends** (Box 733, Corona del Mar, CA 92625, U.S.A.; tel. 1-800/200-1213 or 1-714/673-0816, fax 1-714/673-5397, www.tahitilegends.com, e-mail: info@tahitilegends.com), **Tahiti Nui's Island Dreams** (Box 9170, Seattle, WA 98109, U.S.A.; tel. 1-800/359-4359 or 1-206/216-2900, fax 1-206/216-2906), and **Tahiti Vacations** (9841 Airport Blvd., Suite 1124, Los Angeles, CA 90045, U.S.A.; tel. 1-800/553-3477 or 1-310/337-1040, fax 1-310/337-1126, www.tahitivacation.com). Check all of these companies for specials before booking a tour or cruise to Tahiti.

A company dealing with all aspects of travel to Fiji is **Fiji Reservations and Travel** (2439 S.

Kihei Rd., Suite 204A, Kihei, Maui, HI 96753, U.S.A.; tel. 1-800/588-3454 or 1-808/879-1598, fax 1-808/879-6274, www.fijireservations.com, e-mail: fiji@maui.net). Check their website for surfing, kayaking, and diving tours, plus discounted packages to all the top resorts. They also arrange house rentals and land purchases. Also try **Fiji Holidays** (8885 Venice Blvd., Suite 202, Los Angeles, CA 90034, U.S.A.; tel. 1-800/500-3454 or 1-310/202-4220, fax 1-310/202-8233, www.fijitravel.com). **Islands in the Sun** (address above) has a useful brochure describing many package tours to Fiji. In Canada the Fiji specialist is **Goway Travel** (3284 Yonge St., Suite 300, Toronto, Ontario M4N 3M7, Canada; tel. 1-800/387-8850, fax 1-416/322-1109, www.goway.com, e-mail: res@goway.com).

Sunspots International (1918 N.E. 181st, Portland, OR 97230, U.S.A.; tel. 1-800/334-5623 or 1-503/666-3893, fax 1-503/661-7771, www.sunspotsintl.com) has informative color brochures on Cook Islands, Fiji, and Samoa, plus a good website. **Sunmakers** (100 West Harrison, South Tower, Suite 350, Seattle, WA 98119, U.S.A.; tel. 1-800/359-4359 or 1-206/216-2900, fax 1-206/216-2906) books customized itineraries in Cook Islands, Fiji, Tahiti-Polynesia, and Samoa. The **Pacific Destination Center** (18685 Main St., A622, Huntington Beach, CA 92648, U.S.A. (tel. 1-800/227-5317 or 1-714/960-4011, fax 1-714/960-4678) specializes in Tonga and Samoa. **Travel Arrangements Ltd.** (1268 Broadway, Sonoma, CA 95476, U.S.A.; tel. 1-800/392-8213 or 1-707/938-1118, fax 1-707/938-1268) has individual color brochures depicting upmarket accommodations in Cook Islands, Tonga, Samoa, Fiji, New Caledonia, Norfolk Island, and Vanuatu.

Club Méditerranée (40 W. 57th St., New York, NY 10019, U.S.A.; tel. 1-800/147-1522 in the U.S. or 1-800/465-6633 in Canada, fax 1-212/750-1696) offers one-week packages to their resort villages on Bora Bora, Moorea, and New Caledonia. Package prices include room (double occupancy), food, land and water sports, evening entertainment, and transfers, but airfare and bicycle rentals are extra. Due to all the activities, Club Med's a good choice for singles and couples; families with small children should look elsewhere. Book a couple of months in advance, especially if you want to travel in July,

August, or December. For more information on *le Club*, see the Tahiti-Polynesia and New Caledonia chapters in this handbook.

From Australia and New Zealand
Hideaway Holidays (Val Gavriloff, Box 121, West Ryde, NSW 2114, Australia; tel. 61-2/9743-0253, fax 61-2/9743-3568, www.hideawayholidays.com.au, e-mail: sales@hideawayholidays.com.au) specializes in off-the-beaten-track packages to every part of the South Pacific and can organize complicated itineraries.

Coral Seas Travel (Suite 1405, 33 Bligh St., Sydney, NSW 2000, Australia; tel. 61-2/9231-2944, fax 61-2/9231-2029, e-mail: cst@acay.com.au) has attractive color brochures on most South Pacific countries that fully describe their upscale tour offerings.

Qantas Jetabout Holidays (Level 6, 141 Walker St., North Sydney, NSW 2060, Australia; tel. 1-300/360-347 or 61-2/9957-0538, fax 61-2/9957-0393, www.qantas.com.au) offers a variety of standard package tours to Fiji, Vanuatu, and Tahiti. In Europe these trips can be booked through Jetabout Holidays, Sovereign House, 361 King St., Hammersmith, London W6 9NJ, England (tel. 44-181/748-8676, fax 44-181/748-7236).

The **Pacific and International Travel Company** (Level 1, 91 York St., Sydney, NSW 2000, Australia; tel. 61-2/9244-1811, fax 61-2/9262-6318, www.pitc.com.au, e-mail: andrewc@pitc.com.au) books package tours to Fiji and Blue Lagoon Cruises. Also check **Adventure World** (Box 480, North Sydney, NSW 2059, Australia; tel. 61-2/9223-7966, fax 61-2/9956-7707, www.adventureworld.com.au, e-mail: syd@adventureworld.com.au).

From New Zealand **ASPAC Vacations Ltd.** (Box 4330, Auckland; tel. 64-9/623-0259, fax 64-9/623-0257, e-mail: southpacific@aspac-vacations.co.nz) has packaged tours and cruises to most of the areas covered in this book. **Travel Arrangements Ltd.** (Box 297, Auckland; tel. 64-9/379-5944, fax 64-9/373-2369, e-mail: tours@tal-tvl.co.nz) offers sailing holidays and package tours through the region (try them for Norfolk Island).

Scuba Tours
The South Pacific is one of the world's prime scuba locales, and most of the islands have ex-

cellent facilities for divers. Although it's not that difficult to make your own arrangements as you go, you should consider joining an organized scuba tour if you want to cram in as much diving as possible. To stay in business, the dive travel specialists mentioned below are forced to charge prices similar to what you'd pay on the beach, and the convenience of having everything prearranged is often worth it. Before booking, find out exactly where you'll be staying and ask if daily transfers and meals are provided. Of course, diver certification is mandatory.

Consider live-aboard dive boats such as the *Sere ni Wai, Nai'a, Princess II,* and *Aggressor* in Fiji, the *Miz Mae* in Vanuatu, and the *Solomon Sea, Spirit of the Solomons,* and *Bilikiki* in the Solomon Islands. Live-aboard catamarans in the Tuamotus and Marquesas also offer scuba tours. They're a bit more expensive than hotel-based diving, but you're offered up to five dives a day and a total experience. Some repeat divers won't go any other way.

One of the top American scuba wholesalers selling the South Pacific is **Poseidon Ventures Tours** (359 San Miguel Dr., Newport Beach, CA 92660, U.S.A.; tel. 1-800/854-9334 or 1-949/644-5344, fax 1-949/644-5392, www.poseidontours. com, e-mail: poseidon@fea.net; or 3724 FM 1960 West, Suite 114, Houston, TX 77068, U.S.A.; tel. 1-281/586-7800, fax 1-281/586-7870). They offer seven-night diving tours to Fiji beginning at US$2,129 including five days of two-tank diving, airfare from Los Angeles, double-occupancy hotel accommodations, meals, taxes, and transfers. They also sell live-aboard diving in Fiji and Solomon Islands.

Tropical Adventures Travel (Box 4337, Seattle, WA 98104-0337, U.S.A.; tel. 1-800/247-3483 or 1-206/441-3483, fax 1-206/441-5431, www. divetropical.com, e-mail: dive@divetropical.com) also specializes in booking live-aboard diving in Fiji and Solomon Islands. In the Solomons they favor the *Bilikiki,* while in Fiji there are three boats to choose from. Expect to pay about US$300 a night all-inclusive and singles are expected to share (no supplement). Airfare is extra. Ask for Tropical's South Pacific specialist, Geoff Hynes. More than 6,000 divers a year book through this company, which has been in business since 1973.

In 1998 the noted underwater photographer and author, Carl Roessler, closed down See &

Sea Travel Service, which he'd founded in 1966, and became an independent consultant providing advice on scuba facilities and sites worldwide. He makes his money out of "finder fees" paid by selected island suppliers, and his 35 years of experience leading dive tours around the Pacific costs nothing extra to you. Check out his website at www.divxprt.com/see&sea and if you like what you see get in touch with him at **Sea Images** (Box 471899, San Francisco, CA 94147, U.S.A.; tel. 1-415/922-5807, fax 1-415/922-5662, e-mail: divxprt@ix.netcom.com).

Island Dreams (8582 Katy Freeway, Suite 118, Houston, TX 77024, U.S.A.; tel. 1-800/346-6116 or 1-713/973-9300, fax 1-713/973-8585, www. islandream.com, e-mail: Ken@islandream.com) specializes in Fiji and the Solomons. Check their website for Ken Knezick's revealing resort reports in "Fiji on the Fly."

The Fiji specialist is **Aqua-Trek** (110 Sutter St., Suite 205, San Francisco, CA 94104, U.S.A.; tel. 1-800/541-4334 or 1-415/398-8990, fax 1-415/398-0479, www.aquatrek.com, e-mail: info@aquatrek. com). **Adventure Express** (650 5th St., Suite 505, San Francisco, CA 94107, U.S.A.; tel. 1-800/443-0799 or 1-415/442-0799, fax 1-415/442-0289, www.AdventureExpress.com) offers "shoestring" diving at Kadavu, Suva, or Taveuni from US$1,852 pp including return airfare from Los Angeles, transfers, double-occupancy accommodations, meals, and six days of diving. They also book the live-aboards and more upmarket land-based diving.

Jean-Michel Cousteau's **Project Ocean Search** offers all-inclusive two-week programs based at the Cousteau Fiji Islands Resort near Savusavu for serious scuba divers. For information contact **Cousteau Productions** (tel. 1-805/899-8899, fax 1-805/899-8898, e-mail: jmcousteau@aol.com) in Santa Barbara, California.

In Australia try **Dive Adventures** (Level 9, 32 York St., Sydney, NSW 2000; tel. 61-2/9299-4633, fax 61-2/9299-4644, www.diveadventures.com, e-mail: advnture@magna.com.au), a scuba wholesaler with packages to Fiji, New Caledonia, Solomon Islands, Tonga, and Vanuatu. **Allways Dive Expeditions** (168 High St., Ashburton, Melbourne, Victoria 3147, Australia; tel. 61-3/9885-8863, fax 61-3/9885-1164, www.allwaysdive.com. au, e-mail: allways@netlink.com.au) organizes PADI dive expeditions to all the Melanesian countries. **Diversion Dive Travel** (Box 7026, Cairns 4870, Australia; tel. 61-7/4039-0200, fax 61-7/4039-0300, www.diversionoz.com, e-mail: info@diversionoz.com) is the Solomon Islands specialist. Also check www.prodive.com.au for Solomon Islands.

Dive 'N Fishing Travel (15E Vega Pl., Mairangi Bay, Auckland 10, New Zealand; tel. 64-9/479-2210, fax 64-9/479-2214, e-mail: divefish@ihug.co.nz) arranges scuba and game fishing tours to Fiji, Solomon Islands, Tonga, and Vanuatu at competitive rates. They can book cruises in Tongan waters June-Oct. on humpback whale-watching expeditions, with cave, reef, and wreck diving thrown in! ("We have always seen humpbacks but only 70-80% of the time have the whales shown interest in us and allowed us to join them.")

Alternatively, you can make your own arrangements directly with island dive shops. Information about these operators is included under the heading **Sports and Recreation** in the respective destination chapters of this book.

Tours for Naturalists

Perhaps the most rewarding way to visit the South Seas is with **Earthwatch** (Box 9104, Watertown, MA 02471, U.S.A.; tel. 1-800/776-0188 or 1-617/926-8200, fax 1-617/926-8532, www.earthwatch.org, e-mail: info@earthwatch.org), a nonprofit organization founded in 1971 to serve as a bridge between the public and the scientific community. The programs vary from year to year, but in past they've sent teams to survey spinner dolphins at Moorea, examine the coral reefs of Fiji and Tonga, study the rainforests of Fiji, restore *marae* at Rarotonga, assist archaeologists on Easter Island, or save the giant clams of Tonga. These are not study tours but opportunities for amateurs to help out with serious work, a kind of short-term scientific Peace Corps. As a research volunteer, a team member's share of project costs is tax-deductible in the U.S. and some other countries. For more information contact Earthwatch at the address above, or 126 Bank St., South Melbourne, Victoria 3205, Australia (tel. 61-3/9682-6828, fax 61-3/9686-3652), or Belsyre Court, 57 Woodstock Rd., Oxford OX2 6HU, England (tel. 44-1865/311-600, fax 44-865/311-383), or Technova Inc., Imperial Tower, 13 F Uchisaiwai-Cho 1-1-1, Chiyoda-Ku, Tokyo 100-0011, Japan (tel. 81-3/3508-2280, fax 81-3/3508-7578).

The Australian branch of OXFAM International, Community Aid Abroad, runs **One World Tours** (Box 34, Rundle Mall, Adelaide, S.A. 5000, Australia; tel. 61-8/8232-2727, fax 61-8/8232-2808, www.caa.org.au/travel, e-mail: bwitty@ozemail.com.au), which is dedicated to promoting "responsible tourism." Four times a year they offer a 16-day ecotour to a remote hill village on Makira Island in the Solomon Islands. The trip involves a fairly strenuous hike through the rainforest with many opportunities for cultural interplay. It costs A$1,445 from Honiara and is highly recommended for anyone who wants to get well off the beaten tourist track and learn about local development issues.

Reef and Rainforest Adventure Travel (4000 Bridgeway, Suite 103, Sausalito, CA 94965-1444, U.S.A.; tel. 1-800/794-9767 or 1-415/289-1760, fax 1-415/289-1763, www.reefrainforest.com, e-mail: rnrtravel@aol.com) books diving, kayaking, whale or dolphin watching, and other adventure tours to five Pacific countries. Check their website for details.

From August to October, Joel Simon's **Sea for Yourself** (729 College Ave., Menlo Park, CA 94025, U.S.A.; tel. 1-650/322-1494, www.snorkeltours.com, e-mail: info@snorkeltours.com) offers snorkeling tours to Fiji and Tonga. A 10-day tour with whalewatching in Tonga and reef watching in Fiji costs US$3,750 excluding airfare to Fiji (the same to Fiji alone will run US$3,650 including airfare). Joel only takes a dozen people at a time, and he's usually sold out months in advance.

Tours for Seniors

Since 1989 the **Pacific Islands Institute** (Box 1926, Kailua, HI 96734, U.S.A.; tel. 1-808/262-8942, fax 1-808/263-0178, www.pac-island.com, e-mail: info@pac-island.com) has operated educational tours to most of the South Pacific countries in cooperation with Hawaii Pacific University. Their **Elderhostel** people-to-people study programs designed for those aged 55 or over (younger spouses welcome) last two or three weeks. For example, the 24-day tour of Fiji, Tonga, and Samoa offered about 10 times a year costs US$4,400 from Los Angeles or US$4,771 from Boston including airfares, meals, double-occupancy accommodations, transfers, excursions, admissions, tips, taxes, and excursion (singles pay US$435 extra). A 14-day tour to Rarotonga is US$3,056 from Honolulu, otherwise it's US$5,056 for 21 days to Rarotonga, Tahiti, Moorea, Huahine, and Aitutaki. These culturally responsible trips are highly recommended.

Tours for Veterans

Every August **Valor Tours Ltd.** (10 Liberty Ship Way, Suite 160, Sausalito, CA 94965, U.S.A.; tel. 1-800/842-4504 or 1-415/332-7850, fax 1-415/332-6971, www.valortours.com, e-mail: bobatsqv@msn.com) organizes a tour of WW II battlefields in the Solomons at US$2,900 including airfare. Most tours are personally led by Valor's president, Robert F. Reynolds, who was the moving force behind construction of the U.S. war memorial in Honiara.

Tours for Children

About the only packages to the South Pacific especially designed for families traveling with children are the "Rascals in Paradise" programs offered by **Adventure Express** (650 5th St., Suite 505, San Francisco, CA 94107, U.S.A.; tel. 1-800/872-7225 or 1-415/978-9800, fax 1-415/442-0289, www.AdventureExpress.com). Special "family week" group tours to Fiji's Matagi Island Resort are operated in late March. The price is based on two adults with one or two children aged 2-11, and international airfares and transfers to Vatulele are additional. A single parent with child would have to pay two adult fares. Adventure Express also books regular scuba diving tours and upmarket hotel rooms throughout the Pacific.

Hiking Tours

May-Oct. **Adventure Fiji,** a division of Rosie The Travel Service (Box 9268, Nadi Airport, Fiji Islands; tel. 679/722-935, fax 679/722-607, e-mail: rosiefiji@is.com.fj), runs adventuresome five-night hiking trips in the upper Wainibuka River area of central Viti Levu south of Rakiraki. Horses carry trekkers' backpacks, so the trips are feasible for almost anyone in good condition. The F$600 pp price includes transport to the trailhead, food and accommodations at a few of the 11 Fijian villages along the way, guides, and a bamboo raft ride on the Wainibuka River.

Trekkers only hike about five hours a day, allowing lots of time to get to know the village people. These tours begin from Nadi every Monday. In Australia bookings can be made through Rosie The Travel Service (Level 5, Suite 505, 9 Bronte Rd., Bondi Junction, Sydney, NSW 2022; tel. 61-2/9389-3666, fax 61-2/9369-1129).

Bicycle Tours

About the only North American company offering tours especially designed for cyclists is **Cyclevents** (Box 7491, Jackson, WY 83002-7491, U.S.A.; tel. 1-888/733-9615 or 1-307/733-9615, fax 1-307/734-8581, www.cyclevents.com, e-mail: biking@cyclevents.com). Five times a year there are 12-day cycle tours of Tahiti-Polynesia (US$1,750, double occupancy). Interisland travel between Tahiti, Moorea, Huahine, and Raiatea is included, as is accommodations, most food, and guides, but airfare is extra and you have to bring your own bicycle on the flight.

In New Zealand, **Fish-Eye & Associates** (Brian Fisher, www.cyclefiji.com, e-mail: info@cyclefiji.com) operates bicycle tours to Fiji's Vanua Levu and Taveuni. The nine-night trips operate July-Oct. at NZ$2,650 pp and you must also bring your own bicycle.

Surfing Tours

The largest operator of surfing tours to the South Pacific is **The Surf Travel Company** (Box 446, Cronulla, NSW 2230, Australia; tel. 61-2/9527-4722, fax 61-2/9527-4522, www.surftravel.com.au, e-mail: surftrav@ozemail.com.au) with packages to Moorea, Easter Island, Ha'atafu Beach (Tonga), Frigates Pass (Fiji), Seashell Cove (Fiji), and Upolu (Samoa). In New Zealand book through Mark Thompson (7 Danbury Dr., Torbay, Auckland; tel./fax 64-9/473-8388).

For information on tours to Tavarua Island and the famous Cloudbreak contact **Tavarua Island Tours** (Box 60159, Santa Barbara, CA 93160, U.S.A.; tel. 1-805/686-4551, fax 1-805/683-6696, e-mail: tavarua@is.com.fj). Tavarua's neighbor, **Namotu Island Resort** (Box 531, Nadi, Fiji; tel. 706-439, fax 706-039, e-mail: namotu@is.com.fj), is similar. Additional information on these is provided in the Fiji chapter.

One of the largest American companies offering surfing tours to Fiji, Samoa, Tahiti, and Tonga is **Waterways Travel** (15145 Califa St.,

Suite 1, Van Nuys, CA 91411, U.S.A.; tel. 1-800/928-3757 or 1-818/376-0341, fax 1-818/376-0353, www.waterwaystravel.com).

Kayak Tours

The **Friendly Islands Kayak Company** operates ocean kayaking tours through Tonga's Vava'u and Ha'apai groups from Vava'u's Tongan Beach Resort, at US$995/1,220 for 9/11-day packages (ground cost only). May-Dec. the Canadian managers, Doug and Sharon Spence, will be in Tonga (Private Bag, Neiafu, Vava'u, Tonga; tel./fax 676/70-173, www.fikco.com/kayaktonga, e-mail: kayaktonga@kalianet.to), but Jan.-April they should be contacted at their New Zealand address (Box 142, Waitati, Otago 9060; tel./fax 64-3/482-1202). In North America, kayaking tours to Tonga can be booked through **Ecosummer Expeditions** (5640 Hollybridge Way, No. 130, Richmond, BC V7C 4N3, Canada; tel. 1-604/214-7484, fax 1-604/214-7485, www.ecosummer.com, e-mail: trips@ecosummer.com). Call them toll-free at 1-800/465-8884 in Canada or 1-800/465-8884 in the United States.

Among the most exciting tours to the South Pacific are the nine- to 11-day kayaking expeditions to Fiji offered May-Nov. by **Southern Sea Ventures** (Suite 263, 184 Blues Point Rd., McMahons Point, NSW 2060, Australia; tel. 61-2/9460-3375, fax 61-2/9460-3376, www.evo.com.au/cventure, e-mail: cventure@tpg.com.au). Their groups of 12 persons maximum paddle stable two-person sea kayaks through the sheltered tropical waters of the Yasawa chain. Accommodations are tents on the beach, and participants must be in reasonable physical shape, as three or four hours a day are spent on the water. The price varies from A$1,400-2,700 and doesn't include airfare. In North America you can book through Quest Nature Tours (36 Finch Ave. West, Toronto, Ontario M2N 2G9, Canada; tel. 1-800/387-1483 or 1-416/221-3000, fax 1-416/221-5730, e-mail: travel@worldwidequest.com). In New Zealand contact Adventure South (Box 33-153, Christchurch; tel. 64-3/332-1222, fax 64-3/332-4030, e-mail: geoff@advsouth.co.nz).

Mountain Travel/Sobek Expeditions (6420 Fairmount Ave., El Cerrito, CA 94530, U.S.A.; tel. 1-800/227-2384 or 1-510/527-8100, fax 1-510/ 525-7710, www.mtsobek.com, e-mail: info@mtsobek.com) runs a 13-day combination hiking/sea kayaking tour to Fiji four times a year at US$1,990 plus airfare. Participants combine trekking through central Viti Levu with kayaking the Yasawas. They're usually sold out well ahead.

Deluxe kayak tours to Kadavu, Fiji, are offered May-Dec. by Michael and Melissa McCoy of **Kayak Kadavu** (www.fiji-kayak-kadavu.com). Their seven/nine-night trips are US$1,325/1,675 pp. An escort boat carries all the heavy gear, allowing participants the luxury of paddling a lightweight sit-on-top kayak around some really breathtaking locations. In North America book through Fiji Reservations and Travel (address above). Other kayaking trips to Ono and Kadavu are organized by **Tamarillo** (Box 9869, Wellington, New Zealand; tel. 64-4/239-9990, fax 64-4/239-9789, www.tamarillo.co.nz/tamarillo.html, e-mail: enquiries@tamarillo.co.nz). There are four one-week trips offered in August and September at NZ$1,735 from Nadi or NZ$2,590 from Auckland.

In New Caledonia, **Terra Incognita** (B.P. 18, 98830 Dumbéa; tel./fax 687/41-61-19) offers kayak trips on a different river, lake, or bay every weekend, and they also rent canoes and kayaks. Special kayak expeditions can be organized for groups of eight or more. Their specialty is whitewater kayaking on wild and scenic rivers, one of the few places in the South Pacific where this is offered.

Kayak Solomons (Box 84 HP, Hermit Park, Queensland 4812, Australia; tel./fax 61-7/4775-1323, www.kayaksolomons.com, e-mail: uepi@ultra.net.au) offers kayaking on Solomon Island's Marovo Lagoon. The packages cost A$1,033 to A$1,805 for 6-10 days, including three nights at Uepi Island Resort, leaf house accommodations at eco-lodges around the lagoon, meals, kayaks, guides, and transfers, but cultural activities and airfare are extra.

Yacht Tours and Charters

If you were planning on spending a substantial amount to stay at a luxury resort, consider chartering a yacht instead! Divided up among the members of your party the per-person charter price will be about the same, but you'll experience much more of the Pacific's beauty on a boat than you would staying in a hotel room. All charterers visit remote islands accessible only by small boat and thus receive special insights into

island life unspoiled by normal tourist trappings. Of course, activities such as sailing, snorkeling, and general exploring by sea and land are included in the price.

Yacht charters are available either "bareboat" (for those with the skill to sail on their own) or "crewed" (in which case charterers pay a daily fee for a skipper plus his/her provisions). On a "flotilla" charter a group of bareboats follow an experienced lead yacht.

One of the finest companies arranging such charters is **Ocean Voyages Inc.** (1709 Bridgeway, Sausalito, CA 94965, U.S.A.; tel. 1-800/299-4444 or 1-415/332-4681, fax 1-415/332-7460, www.crowleys.com/ocean.htm, e-mail: sail@oceanvoyages.com). Unlike their competitors, Ocean Voyages organizes "shareboat" charters in which singles and couples book a cabin on yachts sailing to the remotest corners of the South Pacific. Ask about shareboat yacht cruises on fixed itineraries of anywhere from one week to two months. Shorter trips are usually around the Society Islands, Fiji, and Vanuatu while longer journeys encompassing several island groups are possible in Tonga, Fiji, Vanuatu, Solomon Islands, and New Caledonia. Individuals are welcome and there are about 50 departures a year on a range of vessels. Prices average from US$100-250 pp a day, and scuba diving is possible at extra cost on some boats (ask). This is perfect if you're alone or in a party of two and can't afford to charter an entire bareboat yacht. Most vessels take only four to eight passengers but the brigantine *Soren Larsen* can accommodate up to 22. For groups of four or six they can help select the right charter yacht for a dream vacation.

Other outstanding Ocean Voyages offerings include the voyages from Tahiti or Mangareva to Pitcairn, charter programs out of Port Vila, Santo, Raiatea, Vava'u, Suva, Lautoka, and Taveuni, and extended tours of the entire South Pacific by classic square-rigger sailing boats. They've also developed one-week catamaran cruises especially designed for individual scuba divers to the remote islands of the Marquesas (US$2,450 pp)—the *crème de la crème* of Polynesian dive experiences. These prices are all-inclusive, covering everything but air transportation and liquor. All trips should be booked and paid for at least 60 days in advance. Ocean Voyages caters to a very select, professional clientele, and their crews are carefully chosen. More than 35% of the participants are repeaters—the foremost recommendation there is.

One of the classic "tall ships" cruising the South Pacific is the two-masted brigantine *Soren Larsen,* built in 1949. May-Nov. this 42-meter square rig vessel operates 10-19 day voyages to Tonga, Fiji, Vanuatu, and New Caledonia costing NZ$2,500-3,680. The 12-member professional crew is actively assisted by 22 voyage participants. For information contact **Square Sail Pacific** (Box 310, Kumeu, Auckland 1250, New Zealand; tel. 64-9/411-8755, fax 64-9/411-8484). Ocean Voyages handles bookings in North America. In the U.K. contact **Explore Worldwide** (1 Frederick St., Aldershot, Hants GU11 1LQ, United Kingdom; tel. 44-1252/319-448, fax 44-1251/343170, www.explore.co.uk).

The Moorings (4th floor, 19345 U.S. 19 North, Clearwater, FL 34624, U.S.A.; tel. 1-800/535-7289, fax 1-813/530-9747, www.moorings.com, e-mail: yacht@moorings.com) offers bareboat and crewed yacht charters from their own bases at Raiatea and Vava'u. At Raiatea (Tahiti-Polynesia), prices range from US$430-1,030 a day; charters out of Vava'u (Tonga) are US$300-720 a day. The low season is November to mid-March at Raiatea and January to mid-March at Tonga. Prices are for the entire boat, but extras are airfare, food (US$32 pp daily), skipper (US$100-140 daily plus food, if required), and cook (US$80-120 plus food, if desired). They check you out to make sure you're really capable of handling their vessels. Other obligatory extras are security insurance (US$25 a day), cancellation insurance (US$75 pp), and local tax (three percent in Tahiti-Polynesia, 7.5% in Tonga). Always ask about "specials," such as nine days for the price of seven (reservations clerks often don't volunteer this information). The Mooring's New Zealand agent, **Club Seafarer** (Box 90413, Auckland,

New Zealand; tel. 64-9/377-4840, fax 64-9/377-4820, e-mail: info@clubseafarer.co.nz), also handles charters in Fiji.

The Moorings' Raiatea competitors, Tahiti Yacht Charters and Stardust Marine, are represented by **Tahiti Nui Travel** (B.P. 718, 98713 Papeete; tel. 54-02-00, fax 42-74-35, www.tahiti-nui.com, e-mail: info@tahitinuitravel.pf). It's always wise to compare prices before booking.

A few private brokers arranging bareboat or crewed yacht charters at Raiatea, Vava'u, and Nouméa are **Sun Yacht Charters** (Box 737, Camden, ME 04843, U.S.A.; tel. 1-800/772-3500, fax 1-207/236-3972, www.sunyachts.com), **Paradise Adventures & Cruises** (Box 121, West Ryde, NSW 2114, Australia; tel. 61-2/9743-0253, fax 61-2/9743-3568, www.paradiseadventures.

com.au, e-mail: sales@paradiseadventures.com.au), **Charter World Pty. Ltd.** (23 Passchendaele St., Hampton, Melbourne 3188, Australia; tel. 61-3/9521-0033, fax 61-3/9521-0081), **Sail Connections Ltd.** (Box 3234, Auckland 1015, New Zealand; tel. 64-9/358-0556, fax 64-9/358-4341, e-mail: jeni@sailconnections.co.nz), **Yachting Partners International** (28-29 Richmond Pl., Brighton, Sussex, BN2 2NA, United Kingdom; tel. 44-1273/571-722, fax 44-1273/571-720, e-mail: ypi@ypi.co.uk), and **Crestar Yachts Ltd.** (125 Sloane St., London SW1X 9AU, United Kingdom; tel. 44-171/730-9962, fax 44-171/824-8691). As the brokers don't own their own boats (as The Moorings does), they'll be more inclined to fit you to the particular boat that suits your individual needs.

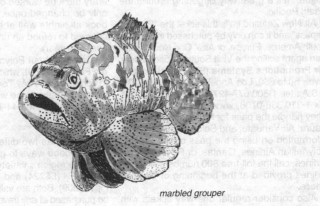

marbled grouper

GETTING AROUND

BY AIR

In 1995 the Association of South Pacific Airlines introduced a **Visit South Pacific Pass** to coincide with "Visit South Pacific Year" and the pass has been so successful that the Association decided to extend it indefinitely. This pass allows travelers to include the services of 10 regional carriers in a single ticket. The initial two-leg air pass has to be purchased in conjunction with an international ticket into the region, but additional legs up to eight maximum can be purchased after arrival. Only the first sector has to be booked ahead.

The flights are priced at three different levels. For US$175 per sector you can go Fiji-Apia/Nauru/Tongatapu/Port Vila/Vava'u/Funafuti, Apia-Tongatapu, Nouméa-Port Vila, Nauru-Pohnpei/Tarawa, Niue-Tongatapu, or Funafuti-Tarawa. For US$220 you have a choice of Honiara-Nadi/Port Vila/Port Moresby, Nouméa/Tahiti-Nadi, Funafuti-Majuro, Fiji-Tarawa, or a variety of flights from Australia and New Zealand to the islands. For US$320 there's Honiara-Auckland, Tahiti-Nouméa, Sydney-Tongatapu, and Fiji-Majuro. It's a great way of getting around the South Pacific.

Air New Zealand calls this ticket the "Pacifica Airpass" and it can only be purchased in North or South America, Europe, or Asia. One North American agent selling the Visit South Pacific Pass is **Air Promotions Systems** (5757 West Century Blvd., Suite 660, Los Angeles, CA 90045-6407, U.S.A.; tel. 1-800/677-4277 or 1-310/670-7302; fax 1-310/338-0708, www.pacificislands.com). They handle the pass for flights on Aircalin, Air Nauru, Air Vanuatu, and Solomon Airlines. For information on using the pass on Air Pacific, Polynesian Airlines, Qantas, or Royal Tongan Airlines, call the toll-free 800 numbers of those airlines provided at the beginning of **Getting There.**

Also consider regular one-way tickets with stopovers as a way of island hopping around the South Pacific, linking flights together with a free stop in the home country of the airline. For example, buy Auckland-Port Vila or Sydney-Fiji with a free stop in Nouméa from Aircalin, Port Vila-Port Moresby or Brisbane-Fiji with a free stop in Honiara from Solomon Airlines, Port Vila-Apia or Honiara-Nuku'alofa with a free stop in Fiji from Air Pacific, Apia-Auckland or Niue-Fiji with a free stop in Nuku'alofa from Royal Tongan Airlines, etc. You may have to buy these tickets directly from the airlines themselves as travel agents will want to add up all the sector fares, but full-fare tickets like these are valid one year and have virtually no restrictions. Compare prices and be creative.

Polynesian Airlines

Polynesian Airlines flies to Apia, Auckland, Honolulu, Los Angeles, Melbourne, Nadi, Pago Pago, Sydney, Tongatapu, and Wellington, and if you've got a month and a half to see a slice of the South Pacific, their **Polypass** may be for you. This allows 45 days unlimited travel between Nadi, Tongatapu, Apia, and Pago Pago, plus one roundtrip from Sydney, Melbourne, Auckland, or Wellington for US$999. From Honolulu the pass costs US$1,149, from Los Angeles US$1,399. Restrictions are that your itinerary must be worked out in advance and can only be changed once. Thus it's important to book all flights well ahead. A 20% penalty is charged to refund an unused ticket (no refund after one year).

Also ask about Polynesian's **Pacific Triangle Fare** (US$450), which allows one a full year to complete the Apia-Tongatapu-Nadi loop. For more information, see www.polynesianairlines. co.nz or call 1-800/644-7659.

Air Pacific

Air Pacific has two different **Pacific Triangle Fares**—good ways to get around and experience the region's variety of cultures: Fiji-Apia-Tonga-Fiji (F$724) and Fiji-Nouméa-Port Vila-Fiji (F$809). Both are valid for one year and can be purchased at any travel agency in Fiji or direct from the airline. They're usually only good for journeys commencing in Fiji. Flight dates can be changed at no charge. When booking these circular tickets, be aware that it's much better to go Fiji-Apia-Tonga-Fiji than vice versa, because the flights between Apia and Fiji are often fully booked while it's easy to get on between Tonga and Fiji. Also obtainable locally are Air Pacific's special 28-day roundtrip excursion fares from Fiji to Apia (F$561), Tonga (F$469), Port Vila (F$579), and Honiara (F$1045). Some of these fares have seasonal variations.

A **Pacific Air Pass** allows 30 days travel (on Air Pacific flights only) from Fiji to Apia, Tonga, and Port Vila (US$462). This pass can only be purchased from Qantas Airways offices in North America and Europe, or from Air Pacific's U.S. office, Suite 475, 841 Apollo St., El Segundo, CA 90245-4741 (tel. 1-800/227-4446 or 1-310/524-9350, fax 1-310/524-9356, www.airpacific.com). Available in North America only is the **Fiji/Vanuatu/Solomons Triangle Fare,** which gives you 60 days to go around this circuit at US$617. The 30-day Nadi-Honiara excursion fare is US$514 if purchased in North America, but a Visit South Pacific Pass would work out cheaper here.

Solomon Airlines

The 30-day **Discover Solomons Pass** allows four domestic flights within the Solomons for US$249 (additional coupons US$50 to a maximum of eight). On this one you only have to book your first flight at the time of ticketing; the other flights can be booked upon arrival in the Solomons. To reissue the ticket costs US$50. It must be purchased prior to arrival in the South Pacific through Air Promotions Systems in Los Angeles (see above).

Domestic Air Services

Nearly every Pacific country has its local airline servicing the outer islands. These flights, described in the destination chapters of this guide, can be booked upon arrival. The most important local carriers are Air Calédonie (New Caledonia), Air Fiji (Fiji), Air Tahiti (Tahiti-Polynesia), Air Rarotonga (Cook Islands), Polynesian Airlines (Samoa), Royal Tongan Airlines (Tonga), Samoa Air (American Samoa), Solomon Airlines (Solomon Islands), Sunflower Airlines (Fiji), Vanair (Vanuatu), and Western Pacific Airline (Solomon Islands). Most fly small aircraft, so only 10 kilograms free baggage may be allowed. A typical interisland flight will cost around US$45 in the Samoas, US$50 in Tonga, US$60 in Fiji, Solomon Islands, and New Caledonia, US$75 in Cook Islands and Vanuatu, and US$90 in Tahiti-Polynesia.

BY SEA

Ninety-nine percent of international travel around the South Pacific is by air. With few exceptions travel by boat is a thing of the past, and about the only regular international service is Apia to Pago Pago. Local boats to the outer islands within a single country are available everywhere, however. Among the local trips you can easily do by regularly scheduled boat are Tahiti-Moorea, Tahiti-Bora Bora, Tongatapu-Vava'u, Tongatapu-'Eua, Upolu-Savai'i, Suva-Kadavu, Suva-Taveuni, Nabouwalu-Natovi, Natovi-Ovalau, Nouméa-Loyalty Islands, Honiara-Malaita, and Honiara-Gizo. Details of these and other shipping possibilities are explored in the different destination chapters of this book.

BY SAILING YACHT

Getting Aboard

Hitch rides into the Pacific on yachts from California, Panama, New Zealand, and Australia, or around the yachting triangle Papeete-Suva-Honolulu. At home, scrutinize the classified listings of yachts seeking crews, yachts to be delivered, etc., in magazines like *Yachting, Cruising World, Sail,* and *Latitude 38.* You can even advertise yourself for about US$25 (plan to have the ad appear three months before the beginning of the season). Check the bulletin boards at yacht clubs, and explore the links at www.cruisingworld.com and www.latsandatts.com. The **Seven Seas Cruising Association** (1525 South Andrews Ave., Suite 217, Fort Lauderdale, FL 33316, U.S.A.; tel. 1-954/463-2431, fax 1-954/463-7183, www.ssca.org, e-mail: SSCA1@ibm.net) is in touch with yachties all around the Pacific, and the classified section "Crew Exchange" in their monthly *Commodores' Bulletin* contains ads from captains in search of crew.

Cruising yachts are recognizable by their foreign flags, wind-vane steering gear, sturdy appearance, and laundry hung out to dry. Put up notices on yacht club and marine bulletin boards, and meet people in bars. When a boat is hauled out, you can find work scraping and repainting the bottom, varnishing, and doing minor repairs. It's much easier, however, to crew on yachts already in the islands. In Tahiti, for example, after a month on the open sea, some of the original crew may have flown home or onward, opening a place for you. Pago Pago, Vava'u, Suva, Musket Cove, and Port Vila are other places to look for a boat.

If you've never crewed before, it's better to try for a short passage the first time. Once at sea on the way to Tahiti, there's no way they'll turn around to take a seasick crew member back to Hawaii. Good captains evaluate crew on personality, attitude, and a willingness to learn more than experience, so don't lie. Be honest and open when interviewing with a skipper—a deception will soon become apparent.

It's also good to know what a captain's *really* like before you commit yourself to an isolated month with her/him. To determine what might happen should the electronic gadgetry break down, find out if there's a sextant aboard and whether he/she knows how to use it. A rundown-looking boat may often be mechanically unsound too. Also be concerned about a skipper who doesn't do a careful safety briefing early on, or who seems to have a hard time hanging onto crew. If the previous crew have left the boat at an unlikely place such as the Marquesas, there must have been a reason. Once you're on a boat and part of the yachtie community, things are easy. (P.S. from veteran yachtie Peter Moree: "We do need more ladies out here—adventurous types naturally.")

Time of Year

The weather and seasons play a deciding role in any South Pacific trip by sailboat and you'll have to pull out of many beautiful places, or be unable to stop there, because of bad weather. The favorite season for rides in the South Pacific is May-Oct.; sometimes you'll even have to turn one down. Around August or September start looking for a ride from the South Pacific to Hawaii or New Zealand.

Be aware of the hurricane season: Nov.-March in the South Pacific, July-Dec. in the northwest

Pacific (near Guam), and June-Oct. in the area between Mexico and Hawaii. Few yachts will be cruising those areas at these times. A few yachts spend the winter at Pago Pago and Vava'u (the main "hurricane holes"), but most South Pacific cruisers will have left for hurricane-free New Zealand by October.

Also, know which way the winds are blowing; the prevailing trade winds in the tropics are from the northeast north of the equator, from the southeast south of the equator. North of the tropic of Cancer and south of the tropic of Capricorn the winds are out of the west. Due to the action of prevailing southeast trade winds, boat trips are smoother from east to west than west to east throughout the South Pacific, so that's the way to go.

Yachting Routes

The South Pacific is good for sailing; there's not too much traffic and no piracy like you'd find in the Mediterranean or in Indonesian waters. The common yachting route or "Coconut Milk Run" across the South Pacific utilizes the northeast and southeast trades: from California to Tahiti via the Marquesas or Hawaii, then Rarotonga, Niue, Vava'u, Suva, and New Zealand. Some yachts continue west from Fiji to Port Vila. In the other direction, you'll sail on the westerlies from New Zealand to a point south of the Australs, then north on the trades to Tahiti.

Some 300 yachts leave the U.S. west coast for Tahiti every year, almost always crewed by couples or men only. Most stay in the South Seas about a year before returning to North America, while a few continue around the world. About 60-80 cross the Indian Ocean every year (look for rides from Sydney in May, Cairns or Darwin from June to August, Bali from August to October, Singapore from October to December); around 700 yachts sail from Europe to the Caribbean (from Gibraltar and Gran Canaria Oct.-December).

Cruising yachts average about 150 km a day, so it takes about a month to get from the U.S. west coast to Hawaii, then another month from Hawaii to Tahiti. To enjoy the finest weather conditions many yachts clear the Panama Canal or depart California in February to arrive in the Marquesas in March. From Hawaii, yachts often leave for Tahiti in April or May. Many stay on for the *Heiva i Tahiti* festival, which ends on 14 July, at which time they sail west to Vava'u or Suva, where you'll find them in July and August. In mid-September the yachting season culminates with a race by about 40 boats from Musket Cove on Fiji's Malololailai Island to Port Vila (it's very easy to hitch a ride at this time). By late October the bulk of the yachting community is sailing south via New Caledonia to New Zealand or Australia to spend the southern summer there. In April or May on alternate years (1995, 1997, etc.) there's a yacht race from Auckland and Sydney to Suva, timed to coincide with the cruisers' return after the hurricane season.

Blue Water Rallies (Peter Seymour, Windsor Cottage, Chedworth, Cheltenham, Gloucestershire GL54 4AA, United Kingdom; tel./fax 44-1285/720-904) organizes annual round-the-world yachting rallies, departing Europe each October. Inquiries from both owners and potential crew members are welcome for these 20-month circumnavigations that visit Galapagos, the Marquesas, Tahiti, Tonga, and Fiji. Blue Water's professional support services will help make that "voyage of a lifetime" a reality! Similar events are organized by Jimmy Cornell's **World Cruising** (Box 165, London WC1B 3XA, United Kingdom; tel. 44-171/405-9905, fax 44-171/831-0161), departing Fort Lauderdale, Florida, in February.

Be aware that a law enacted in New Zealand in 1995 requires foreign yachts departing New Zealand to obtain a "Certificate of Inspection" from the New Zealand Yachting Federation prior to customs clearance. This regulation has led to a 30% decline in the number of yachts visiting New Zealand, and it's wise to consider alternative summer anchorages before sailing into a situation where some clerk may force you to spend of thousands of dollars upgrading safety standards on your boat before you'll be permitted to leave.

Life Aboard

To crew on a yacht you must be willing to wash and iron clothes, cook, steer, keep watch at night, and help with engine work. Other jobs might include changing and resetting sails, cleaning the boat, scraping the bottom, pulling up the anchor, and climbing the main mast to watch for reefs. Do more than is expected of you. A safety harness must be worn in rough weather.

As a guest in someone else's home you'll want to wash your dishes promptly after use and put them, and all other gear, back where you found them. Tampons must not be thrown in the toilet bowl. Smoking is usually prohibited as a safety hazard.

You'll be a lot more useful if you know how to tie knots like the clove hitch, rolling hitch, sheet bend, double sheet bend, reef knot, square knot, figure eight, and bowline. Check your local library for books on sailing or write away for the comprehensive free catalog of nautical books available from International Marine Publishing, Box 548, Black Lick, OH 43004, U.S.A. (tel. 1-800/262-4729, fax 1-614/759-3641, www.pbg.mcgraw-hill.com/im).

Anybody who wants to get on well under sail must be flexible and tolerant, both physically and emotionally. Expense-sharing crew members pay US$10 a day or more per person. After 30 days you'll be happy to hit land for a fresh-water shower. Give adequate notice when you're ready to leave the boat, but *do* disembark when your journey's up. Boat people have few enough opportunities for privacy as it is. If you've had a good trip, ask the captain to write you a letter of recommendation; it'll help you hitch another ride.

Food for Thought

When you consider the big investment, depreciation, cost of maintenance, operating expenses, and considerable risk (most cruising yachts are not insured), travel by sailing yacht is quite a luxury. The huge cost can be surmised from charter fees (US$500 a day and up for a 10-meter yacht). International law makes a clear distinction between passengers and crew. Crew members paying only for their own food, cooking gas, and part of the diesel are very different from charterers who do nothing and pay full costs. The crew is there to help operate the boat, adding safety, but like passengers, they're very much under the control of the captain. Crew has no say in where the yacht will go.

The skipper is personally responsible for crew coming into foreign ports: he's entitled to hold their passports and to see that they have onward tickets and sufficient funds for further traveling. Otherwise the skipper might have to pay their hotel bills and even return airfares to the crew's country of origin. Crew may be asked to pay a share of third-party liability insurance. Possession of dope can result in seizure of the yacht. Because of such considerations, skippers often hesitate to accept crew. Crew members should remember that at no cost to themselves they can learn a bit of sailing and visit places nearly inaccessible by other means. Although not for everyone, it's *the* way to see the real South Pacific, and folks who arrive by *vaka* (sailing canoe) are treated differently than other tourists.

OTHER TRAVEL OPTIONS

By Bus

Almost all of the islands have highly developed bus systems serving mostly local people. In this handbook, we cover them all. Bus services are especially good in Fiji with all of the main centers connected by frequent services at very reasonable prices. Buses are also a good and inexpensive way to get around Tahiti, Rarotonga, Tongatapu, Tutuila, Upolu, and Guadalcanal. There's a good city bus service in Port Vila, but other than that, buses are few and far between in Vanuatu. A local bus ride will cost less than US$0.25 in Tonga and both Samoas, about US$0.50 in Fiji and Solomon Islands, less than a dollar in Vanuatu, and more than a dollar in Tahiti-Polynesia, Cook Islands, and New Caledonia.

By Car

A rental car with unlimited mileage will generally cost around US$40 a day in Cook Islands, Samoa, and Tonga, US$50 in American Samoa and Solomon Islands, US$60 in Fiji, Vanuatu, and New Caledonia, and US$70 in Tahiti-Polynesia. The price of a liter of gasoline also varies considerably: American Samoa US$0.37, Samoa US$0.39, Solomon Islands US$0.48, Tonga US$0.55, Fiji US$0.64, Cook Islands US$0.79, Vanuatu US$0.82, New Caledonia US$0.94, Tahiti-Polynesia US$1.12. To determine the price of an American gallon, multiply any of these by 3.8.

Due to the alternative means of travel available, the only places where you really need to consider renting a car are in New Caledonia (Grande Terre), Tahiti-Polynesia, and Vanuatu (Efate), and perhaps also on Upolu in Samoa

and Guadalcanal in the Solomons. Renting a car is an unnecessary luxury in American Samoa and Fiji due to the excellent public transportation in those countries. In Cook Islands and Tonga one must pay a stiff fee for a local driver's license (international driver's license not recognized) and it's better to tour those countries by rented bicycle anyway. Bicycle is also the way to see Bora Bora.

The car rental business is very competitive and it's possible to shop around for a good deal upon arrival. Although the locally operated companies may offer cheaper rates than the international franchises, it's also true that the agents of Avis, Budget, Europcar, and Hertz are required to maintain recognized standards of service and they have regional offices where you can complain if anything goes seriously wrong. Always find out if insurance, mileage, and tax are included, and check for restrictions on where you'll be allowed to take the car. If in doubt, ask to see a copy of their standard rental contract before making reservations.

Driving is on the right (as in continental Europe and North America) in American Samoa, New Caledonia, Tahiti-Polynesia, Vanuatu, and Samoa, and on the left (as in Britain, New Zealand, and Japan) in Cook Islands, Fiji, Solomon Islands, and Tonga. If you do rent a car, remember those sudden tropical downpours and don't leave the windows open. Also avoid parking under coconut trees (a falling nut might break the window), and never go off and leave the keys in the ignition.

By Bicycle

Bicycling in the South Pacific? Sure, why not? It's cheap, convenient, healthy, quick, environmentally sound, safe, and above all, *fun.* You'll be able to go where and when you please, stop easily and often to meet people and take photos, save money on taxi fares—really *see* the countries. Cycling every day can be fatiguing, however, so it's smart to have bicycle-touring experience beforehand. Most roads are flat along the coast, but be careful on coral roads, especially inclines: if you slip and fall you could hurt yourself badly. On the high islands, interior roads tend to be very steep. Never ride your bike through mud.

A sturdy, single-speed mountain bike with wide wheels, safety chain, and good brakes might be ideal. Thick tires and a plastic liner between tube and tire will reduce punctures. Know how to fix your own bike. Take along a good repair kit (pump, puncture kit, freewheel tool, spare spokes, cables, chain links, assorted nuts and bolts, etc.) and a repair manual; bicycle shops are poor to nonexistent in the islands. Don't try riding with a backpack: sturdy, waterproof panniers (bike bags) are required; you'll also want a good lock. Refuse to lend your bike to *anyone*.

Most international airlines will carry a bicycle as checked luggage, usually free but sometimes at the standard overweight charge or for a flat US$50 fee. The charter carriers are the more likely to charge extra, but verify the airline's policy when booking. Take off the pedals and panniers, turn the handlebars sideways and tie them down, deflate the tires, and clean off the dirt before checking in (or use a special bike-carrying bag) and arrive at the airport early. The commuter airlines usually won't accept bikes on their small planes. Interisland boats sometimes charge a token amount to carry a bike; other times it's free. If you'd just like to rent a bicycle locally, you'll have the most opportunities to do so at the lowest prices in Cook Islands and Tonga.

By Ocean Kayak
Ocean kayaking is experiencing a boom in Hawaii, but the South Pacific is still largely virgin territory. Virtually every island has a sheltered lagoon ready-made for the excitement of kayak touring, but this effortless transportation mode hasn't yet arrived, so you can be a real independent 20th-century explorer! Many international airlines accept folding kayaks as checked baggage at no charge.

For a better introduction to ocean kayaking than is possible here, check at your local public library for sea kayaking manuals. Noted author Paul Theroux toured the entire South Pacific by kayak, and his experiences are recounted in *The Happy Isles of Oceania: Paddling the Pacific* (London: Hamish Hamilton, 1992).

By Canoe
If you get off the beaten track, it's more than likely that a local friend will offer to take you out in his outrigger canoe. Never attempt to take a dugout canoe through even light surf: you'll be swamped. Don't try to pull or lift a canoe by its outrigger—it will break. Drag the canoe by holding the solid main body. A bailer is *essential* equipment.

SERVICES AND INFORMATION

VISAS AND OFFICIALDOM

If you're from an English-speaking country or Western Europe you won't need a visa to visit most of the South Pacific countries as a tourist. The only exception is Easter Island, where New Zealanders still need one. Unlike the U.S., which is very sticky about visas, American Samoa does not require a visa of most tourists.

Australia requires a visa of everyone except New Zealanders. This is free if obtained "electronically" by your travel agent at the time you buy your air ticket, but could cost A$50 if obtained in person at a high commission or consulate in the islands.

Other Requirements
Everyone must have a passport, sufficient funds, and a ticket to leave. Your passport should be valid six months beyond your departure date. Some officials object to tourists who intend to camp or stay with friends, so write the name of a likely hotel on your arrival card (don't leave that space blank).

Immigration officials will often insist on seeing an air ticket back to your home country, no matter how much money you're able to show them. The easy way to get around this if you're on an open-ended holiday or traveling by yacht is to purchase a regular one-way ticket to Hawaii or Los Angeles from Air New Zealand. This will be accepted without question, and Air New Zealand offices throughout the Pacific will reissue the ticket, so you'll always have a ticket to leave from the next country on your itinerary. When you finally get home, you can turn in the unused coupons for a full refund. (See **Getting There** later in this chapter.)

The easiest way to obtain a residence permit in a South Pacific country is to invest money in a small business. Almost every country and territory has a special government department intended to facilitate investment and the local tourist office will be able to tell you who to contact. As little as US$50,000 capital may be required and lots of low-tech opportunities exist in the tourist industry. Drawbacks are that you may be obliged to accept a local partner, your residence permit will end as soon as you cease to be actively involved in the business, and you'll be subject to immediate deportation if you get on the wrong side of local politicians. Unconditional permanent residence and citizenship are rarely granted to persons of ethnic origins other than those prevailing in the countries.

Diplomatic Missions

The country with the widest representation in the South Pacific is New Zealand, which has high commissions in Apia, Honiara, Nuku'alofa, Port Vila, and Rarotonga, an embassy in Suva, a consulate in Nouméa, and an honorary consul in Papeete. Australia has exactly the same level of diplomatic representation as New Zealand except that they lack an office on Rarotonga. Britain has high commissions in Honiara, Nuku'alofa, and Port Vila, an embassy in Suva, and an honorary consul in Papeete. Canada has no diplomatic offices of its own, but in 1986 Canada and Australia signed a reciprocal agreement extending full consular service to Canadians at Australian missions throughout the region. The United States is very poorly represented with embassies only in Apia and Suva.

France has embassies in Port Vila and Suva, high commissions in Nouméa and Papeete, and honorary consuls in Nuku'alofa and Rarotonga. China has embassies in Apia, Nuku'alofa, Port Vila, and Suva, while Taiwan has an embassy in Honiara. Japan has embassies in Honiara and Suva and a consulate in Nouméa. South Korea has an embassy in Suva, a consulate in Pago Pago, and honorary consuls in Apia, Nuku'alofa, and Papeete. Papua New Guinea has an embassy in Suva, a high commission in Honiara, and an honorary consul in Port Vila.

Numerous member countries of the European Union have consulates or honorary consuls in Nouméa and Papeete, and these are listed in the respective chapters. Other honorary consuls include those of Germany in Apia, Nuku'alofa, and Papeete; of Sweden in Apia, Nuku'alofa, Papeete, and Port Vila; of Switzerland in Nouméa and Papeete; of Spain in Nuku'alofa; of Chile in Papeete; and of Indonesia and Vanuatu in Nouméa.

Customs

Agricultural regulations in most Pacific countries prohibit the import of fresh fruit, vegetables, flowers, seeds, honey, eggs, milk products, meat (including sausage), live animals and plants, as well as any old artifacts that might harbor pests. If in doubt, ask about having your souvenirs fumigated by the local agricultural authorities and a certificate issued prior to departure. Processed food or beverages, biscuits, confectionery, sugar, rice, seafood, dried flowers, mounted insects, mats, baskets, and tapa cloth are usually okay. If you've been on a farm, wash your clothes and shoes before going to the airport, and if you've been camping, make sure your tent is free of soil.

MONEY

All prices quoted herein are in the local currency unless otherwise stated. Each Monday the *Wall Street Journal* runs a "World Value of the Dollar" column that lists the current exchange rates of all Pacific currencies. If you have access to the internet you'll find most of the rates at www.oanda.com. There's strong opposition in the three French territories to the replacement of the Pacific franc (CFP) by the Euro, thereby bringing them under the jurisdiction of the European Central Bank in economic matters, and the Maastricht Treaty specifically exempts them from this fate.

Most South Pacific airports have banks changing money at normal rates (check the **Airport** listing at the end of each chapter introduction) and the most convenient currencies to carry are Australian, N.Z., and U.S. dollars. If you'll be visiting American Samoa or the U.S., be sure to have enough U.S. dollar traveler's checks to see you through, as foreign currencies are little known in the States and whopping commissions are charged. French francs in cash are the best currency to carry to Tahiti-Polynesia and New Caledonia as they're changed into CFP at a fixed rate without any commission.

The bulk of your travel funds should be in traveler's checks, preferably American Express, although that company's representation in the region is dwindling. American Express has travel service offices in Papeete, Rarotonga, Suva, Nadi, and Nouméa, but the American Express agencies in Pago Pago and Apia have closed and the company has no representation in Tonga, Vanuatu, and Solomon Islands. Thomas Cook has large offices in Nadi and Suva, Fiji. To claim a refund for lost or stolen American Express traveler's checks call the local office (listed in the respective chapter) or their Sydney office collect (tel. 61-2/9886-0689). They'll also cancel lost credit cards, provided you know the numbers. The banks best represented in this part of the world are the ANZ Bank, the Bank of Hawaii, and the Westpac Bank, so if you need to have money sent, you'll want to work through one of them.

If you want to use a credit card, always ask beforehand, even if a business has a sign or brochure that says it's possible. Visa and MasterCard can be used to obtain cash advances at banks in most countries, but remember that cash advances accrue interest from the moment you receive the money—ask your bank if they have a debit card that allows charges to be deducted from your checking account automatically. The use of bank cards such as Visa and MasterCard is expensive in Samoa and Solomon Islands because those currencies aren't recognized internationally. Thus the charge must first be converted into N.Z. or Australian dollars, then into your own currency, and you'll lose on the exchange several times. American Express is probably the best card to use as they don't go through third currencies (this could vary—ask).

When you rent a car the agency will probably ask you to sign a blank credit card charge slip as security on the vehicle. As you do so, be sure to count the number of pages in the slip, and if you later pay cash and the blank slip is returned to you, make you sure you get all the pages back. Otherwise a dishonest operator could already have removed the page to be sent to the credit card company and processed the charge "by accident." Also retain the blank slip as proof that it was returned when you paid cash, but be sure to write Void across it in case it's stolen or lost. Also keep your signed cash receipt, and don't let your credit card out of sight, even for a moment. Credit card fraud is not common in the South

Pacific, but cases have occurred (including a fraudulent US$440 Visa charge against the author of this book during his last visit to Nouméa).

Many banks now have automated teller machines (ATMs) outside their offices and these provide local currency against checking account Visa and MasterCard at good rates without commission. Occasionally the machines don't work due to problems with the software, in which case you'll almost always be able to get a cash advance at the counter inside. To avoid emergencies (such as if a machine were to "eat" your card), it's smart not to be too dependent on ATMs. Ask your bank what fee they'll charge if you use an ATM abroad and find out if you need a special personal identification number (PIN).

Cost-wise, you'll find Cook Islands, Fiji, Tonga, Samoa, and Solomon Islands to be the least expensive South Pacific countries, with Tahiti-Polynesia and New Caledonia consistently dearer. The lack of budget accommodations makes the price of a visit to American Samoa stiff, while in Vanuatu it's the cost of interisland transportation that breaks your budget. Inflation is consistently low in New Caledonia and Tahiti-Polynesia but high in Solomon Islands, Tonga, and Samoa, something to keep in mind when looking at the prices in this book.

Upon departure avoid getting stuck with leftover local banknotes, as currencies such as the Fiji dollar, Pacific franc, Solomon Islands dollar, Vanuatu *vatu,* Samoan *tala,* and Tongan *pa'anga* are difficult to change and heavily discounted even in neighboring countries. Change whatever you have left over into the currency of the next country on your itinerary, but don't wait to do it at the airport. The Thomas Cook office in central Nadi, Fiji, buys and sells all Pacific currencies.

Don't show everyone how much money you have in your wallet, as this causes resentment and invites theft. Bargaining is not common: the first price you're quoted is usually it. Tipping is *not* customary in the South Pacific and often generates more embarrassment than gratitude.

POST AND TELECOMMUNICATIONS

Postal Services
Always use airmail when posting letters from the South Pacific. Airmail takes two weeks to

PHILATELY

Postage stamps of the South Pacific are highly valued by collectors around the world, and many smaller Commonwealth countries such as the Cook Islands, Kiribati, Niue, Norfolk Island, Pitcairn, Samoa, Tokelau, Tonga, and Tuvalu earn a substantial portion of government revenue from the sale of stamps. In order to generate more revenue, the Cook Islands issues separate stamps for Penrhyn and Aitutaki, and Tonga has Niuafo'ou stamps. Some countries also try to boost income by increasing the number of annual issues, a practice that can cost them collectors. Bad actors in this regard are Cook Islands, Niue, and Tuvalu. Most of the stamps are printed in Britain, where the highest technical standards are employed.

Popular themes include birds, seashells, coral, maps, atoll scenes, fishing, dancing, musical instruments, and headdresses. As the bicentenaries of his voyages of discovery rolled around during the 1970s, Captain Cook was the subject of stamp issues by many of the islands he discovered. Easily obtained, inexpensive postage stamps and first-day covers make memorable souvenirs. Local post offices usually have a few colorful ones, or write for information in advance. The only address you need is Philatelic Bureau, the name of the country, and South Pacific Ocean. A dealer specializing in the region is Pacific Stamps (Box 816, Tewantin, QLD 4565, Australia; tel. 61-7/5474-0799, fax 61-7/5474-0757). *Pacifica,* the quarterly journal of the Pacific Islands Study Circle (c/o John Ray, 24 Woodvale Ave., London SE25 4AE, England; http://dspace.dial.pipex.com/jray/pisc. html, e-mail: jray@dial.pipex.com), contains a wealth of very useful information on collecting Pacific stamps.

reach North America and Europe, surface mail takes up to six months. Postage rates to the U.S. are very low from Fiji, Solomon Islands, and American Samoa, a wee bit more from Tonga and Samoa, medium-priced from Cook Islands and Vanuatu, and very expensive from Tahiti-Polynesia and New Caledonia. Plan your postcard writing accordingly.

When writing to South Pacific individuals or businesses, include the post office box number (or *Boîte Postale* in the French territories), as mail delivery is rare. If it's a remote island or small village you're writing to, the person's name will be sufficient. Sending a picture postcard to an islander is a very nice way of saying thank you.

When collecting mail at poste restante (general delivery), be sure to check under the initials of your first and second names, plus any initial that is similar. Have your correspondents print and underline your last name.

Telephone Services

Cook Islands, Fiji, New Caledonia, Solomon Islands, Tahiti-Polynesia, and Vanuatu all have card telephones and these are very handy. If you'll be staying in a country more than a few days and intend to make your own arrangements, it's wise to purchase a local telephone card at a post office right away. In this handbook we provide all the numbers you'll need to make hotel reservations, check restaurant hours, find out about cultural shows, and compare car rental rates, saving you a lot of time and inconvenience.

By using a telephone card to call long distance you limit the amount the call can possibly cost and won't end up overspending should you forget to keep track of the time. On short calls you avoid three-minute minimum charges. International telephone calls placed from hotel rooms are always much more expensive than the same calls made from public phones using telephone cards. What you sacrifice is your privacy as anyone can stand around and listen to your call, as often happens. Card phones are usually found outside post offices or telephone centers. Check that the phone actually works before bothering to arrange your numbers and notes, as they're often out of service.

Unfortunately, Tonga and Samoa still don't have card (or coin) telephones, and to place local calls you must go to a telephone center and book the call through a clerk at the desk. This situation is the result of the stranglehold that inefficient state monopolies have over the local telephone systems. Card phones for international calls only have recently been installed in Tonga and hopefully they will be available for domestic calls soon. Samoa's telephone system is easily the most primitive in the Pacific.

A local telephone call will cost less than US$0.20 in all countries except Tahiti-Polynesia and New Caledonia where they cost more than US$0.50. A three-minute station-to-station call to the U.S. will cost less than US$7 from Tahiti-Polynesia, Fiji, and both Samoas, less than US$8 from Tonga and Solomon Islands, less than US$10 from New Caledonia, less than US$12 from Cook Islands, and around US$13.50 from Vanuatu. These differences make it well worth waiting to call home from a cheaper country.

Calling from the U.S. to the South Pacific is cheaper than going in the other direction, so if you want to talk to someone periodically, leave a list of your travel dates and hotel telephone numbers (provided in this book) where friends and relatives can try to get hold of you. All the main islands (except Samoa) have direct dialing via satellite. One reader on a wide-ranging trip said he found it very effective to leave an extra copy of this book with his family. Not only were they able to follow his travels around the Pacific, but they had all the telephone and fax numbers needed to contact him.

To place a call to a Pacific island from outside the region, first dial the international access code (check your phone book), then the country code, then the number. The country codes are:

American Samoa	684
Cook Islands	682
Easter Island	56-32
Fiji	679
New Caledonia	687
Niue	683
Papua New Guinea	675
Pitcairn Islands	872
Samoa	685
Solomon Islands	677
Tahiti-Polynesia	689
Tokelau	690
Tonga	676
Tuvalu	688
Vanuatu	678
Wallis	681

None of the Pacific countries have local area codes, but local telephone numbers have varying

numbers of digits: four digits in Niue and Tokelau; five digits in Cook Islands, Tonga, Samoa, Tuvalu, Vanuatu, and Solomon Islands; six digits in Tahiti-Polynesia, Easter Island, Wallis and Futuna, Fiji, and New Caledonia; and seven digits in American Samoa.

If a fax you are trying to send to the South Pacific doesn't go through smoothly on the first or second try, wait and try again at another time of day. If it doesn't work then, stop trying as the fax machine at the other end may not be able to read your signal, and your telephone company will levy a minimum charge for each attempt. Call the international operator to ask what is going wrong.

Electronic Mail

An increasing number of tourism-related businesses in the South Pacific have e-mail addresses, which makes communicating with them from abroad a lot cheaper and easier. To allow ourselves the flexibility of updating our listings more frequently, we have committed most e-mail and website addresses to this book's backmatter (some overseas addresses meant to be used prior to arrival are embedded in the introductions). If you use the web, have a look at that part of the appendix now, if you haven't already done so.

Websites and e-mail addresses based in the islands are recognizable by their country codes: American Samoa (as), Cook Islands (ck), Fiji (fj), New Caledonia (nc), Niue (nu), Samoa (ws), Solomon Islands (sb), Tahiti-Polynesia (pf), Tokelau (tk), Tonga (to), Tuvalu (tv), Vanuatu (vu), and Wallis and Futuna (wf). Some countries have made a profitable business out of selling website domain names using these codes.

When sending e-mail to the islands never include a large attached file with your message unless it has been specifically requested as the recipient may have to pay US$1 a minute in long distance telephone charges to download it. This is a serious breach of etiquette and not the best way to win friends or influence people.

TIME

The international date line generally follows 180 degrees longitude and creates a difference of

---

PACIFIC TIME

	Hours from GMT	Standard Time at 1200 GMT
Chile	-4	0800
Easter Island	-6	0600
California	-8	0400
Pitcairn	-8.5	0330
Marquesas Islands	-9.5	0230
Hawaii, Tahiti	-10	0200
Cook Islands	-10	0200
Niue, Samoa	-11	0100

(International Date Line)

yesterday

↑

today

↓

Tonga	+13	0100
Fiji, Tuvalu	+12	2400
New Zealand	+12	2400
New Caledonia	+11	2300
Vanuatu, Solomons	+11	2300
NSW, Queensland	+10	2200
Japan	+9	2100

Note: *Chile, Easter Island, Fiji, and New Zealand adopt daylight saving time from October to February, while California does so from April to October. The others do not. GMT is Greenwich Mean Time, the time at London, England.*

---

24 hours in time between the two sides. It swings east at Tuvalu to avoid slicing Fiji in two. This can be confusing, as Tonga, which chooses to observe the same day as neighboring Fiji and New Zealand, has the same clock time as Samoa but is a day ahead! Everything in the Eastern Hemisphere west of the date line is a day later, everything in the Western Hemisphere east of the line is a day earlier (or behind). Air travelers lose a day when they fly west across the date line and gain it back when they return. Keep track of things by repeating to yourself, "If it's Sunday in Samoa, it's Monday in Melbourne."

You're better off calling from North America to the South Pacific in the evening as it will be mid-af-ternoon in the islands (plus you'll probably benefit from off-peak telephone rates). From Europe, call very late at night. In the other direction, if you're calling from the islands to North America or Europe, do so in the early morning as it will already be afternoon in North America and evening in Europe. The local time at almost any point worldwide is available at www.isbister.com/worldtime.

In this book all clock times are rendered according to the 24-hour airline timetable system, i.e. 0100 is 1:00 a.m., 1300 is 1:00 p.m., 2330 is 11:30 p.m. The islanders operate on "coconut time"—the nut will fall when it is ripe. In the languid air of the South Seas punctuality takes on a new meaning. Appointments are approximate and service relaxed. Even the seasons are fuzzy: sometimes wetter, sometimes drier, but almost always hot. Slow down to the island pace and get in step with where you are. You may not get as much done, but you'll enjoy life a lot more. Daylight hours in the tropics run 0600-1800 with few seasonal variations.

WEIGHTS AND MEASURES

The metric system is used everywhere except in American Samoa. Study the conversion table in the back of this handbook if you're not used to thinking metric. Most distances herein are quoted in kilometers—they become easy to comprehend when you know than one km is the distance an average person walks in 10 minutes. A meter is slightly more than a yard and a liter is just over a quart.

Unless otherwise indicated, north is at the top of all maps in this handbook. When using official topographical maps you can determine the scale by taking the representative fraction (RF) and dividing by 100. This will give the number of meters represented by one centimeter. For example, a map with an RF of 1:10,000 would represent 100 meters for every centimeter on the map.

Electric Currents

If you're taking along a plug-in razor, radio, computer, electric immersion coil, or other electrical appliance, be aware that two different voltages are used in the South Pacific. American Samoa uses 110 volts AC, while the rest of the region uses

220-240 volts AC. Take care, however, as some luxury hotel rooms have 110-volt outlets as a convenience to North American visitors. A 220-volt appliance will only run too slowly in a 110-volt outlet, but a 110-volt appliance will quickly burn out and be destroyed in a 220-volt outlet.

Most appliances require a converter to change from one voltage to another. You'll also need an adapter to cope with different socket types, which vary between flat two-pronged plugs in American Samoa, round two-pronged plugs in the French territories, and three-pronged plugs with the two on top at angles almost everywhere else. Pick up both items before you leave home, as they're hard to find in the islands. Some sockets have a switch that must be turned on. Remember voltages if you buy duty-free appliances: dual voltage (110/220 V) items are best.

Videos
Commercial travel videotapes make nice souvenirs, but always keep in mind that there are three incompatible video formats loose in the world: NTSC (used in North America, American Samoa, and Tonga), PAL (used in Britain, Germany, Australia, New Zealand, Cook Islands, and Samoa), and SECAM (used in France, Tahiti-Polynesia, New Caledonia, and Russia). Don't buy prerecorded tapes abroad unless they're of the system used in your country.

MEDIA AND INFORMATION

Daily newspapers are published in Tahiti-Polynesia (*La Dépêche de Tahiti* and *Les Nouvelles de Tahiti*), Cook Islands (*Cook Islands News*), American Samoa (*The Samoa News*), Samoa (*The Samoa Observer*), Fiji (*The Fiji Times* and *The Daily Post*), New Caledonia (*Les Nouvelles Calédoniennes*), and Solomon Islands (*The Solomon Star*). Weekly or twice-weekly papers of note include the *Tahiti Beach Press, Cook Islands Press, The Tonga Chronicle, The Trading Post, The Vanuatu Weekly*, and *The Solomons Voice*.

The leading regional news magazines are *Islands Business Pacific* and *Pacific Islands Monthly*, both published in Fiji, and *Pacific Magazine* from Honolulu. Copies of these are well worth picking up during your trip, and a sub-

scription will help you keep in touch. Turn to Resources at the end of this book for more Pacific-oriented publications.

The **Pacific Islands News Association** (Private Mail Bag, Suva, Fiji; tel. 679/303-623, fax 679/303-943, e-mail: pina@is.com.fj), based in Suva, Fiji, holds an annual conference of regional editors to discuss media issues. PINA is usually seen as representing editorial interests, while the **Pacific Journalists' Association** is composed of working journalists. The regional news service **PacNews** (16 Ma'afu St., Suva, Fiji; tel. 679/315-732, fax 679/315-379, e-mail: pacnews@is.com.fj) was founded in 1987 with the assistance of the Friedrich Ebert Stiftung of Germany.

Radio
A great way to keep in touch with world and local affairs is to take along a small AM/FM shortwave portable radio. Your only expense will be the radio itself and batteries. Throughout this handbook we provide the names and frequencies of local stations, so set your tuning buttons to these as soon as you arrive. At least once a day the major local stations rebroadcast news reports from the BBC World Service, Radio Australia, and Radio New Zealand International, and we've tried to provide the times.

You can also try picking up the BBC World Service (www.bbc.co.uk/worldservice) directly on your shortwave receiver at 5.98, 7.15, 9.66, 9.74, 11.77, 11.96, 12.08, or 15.36 MHz (15.36 MHz generally works best). For Radio Australia try 6.08, 7.24, 9.66, 11.88, 12.08, 15.51, and 17.71 MHz. Look for Radio New Zealand International at 6.10, 6.14, 9.87, 11.69, 11.73, and 17.67 MHz. These frequencies vary according to the time of day and work best at night. (Unfortunately both RNZI and Radio Australia have recently faced cutbacks that could impact their services.) In the Western Pacific, check Radio Vanuatu at 3945 MHz and the Solomon Islands Broadcasting Corporation at 5020 MHz (a strong signal heard as far away as Australia and Fiji). None of the other countries have shortwave frequencies.

Information Offices
All the main countries have official tourist information offices. Their main branches in the cap-

itals open during normal business hours but the information desks at the airports open only for the arrival of international flights, if then. Always visit the local tourist office to pick up brochures and ask questions. Their overseas offices, listed in this handbook's appendix, often mail out useful information on their country and most of them have internet websites.

Be aware, however, that some information on the internet is old or misleading, and mali- cious individuals occasionally use the web to publish inaccurate reports on resorts and dive shops as a "payback" for a perceived grievance. Things change and absolutes are rare in life, and we welcome feedback from readers and is- land suppliers to ensure that what appears in this handbook is as close to reality as possible. No comment will be disregarded. For more de- tailed information, see our *Fiji Handbook, Tonga-Samoa Handbook,* and *Tahiti Handbook.*

HEALTH

For a tropical area, the South Pacific's a healthy place. The sea and air are clear and usually pol- lution-free. The humidity nourishes the skin and the local fruit is brimming with vitamins. If you take a few precautions, you'll never have a sick day. The information provided below is intended to make you knowledgeable, not fearful. If you have access to the internet, check www.cdc.gov/ travel/index.htm for the most up-to-the-minute information.

The government-run medical facilities men- tioned in this book typically provide free med- ical treatment to local residents but have special rates for foreigners. It's usually no more expen- sive to visit a private doctor or clinic, and often it's actually cheaper (in Nouméa, for example, the government hospital charges three times more than local doctors for consultations). Private doc- tors can afford to provide faster service since everyone is paying, and we've tried to list local doctors and dentists throughout the handbook. In emergencies and outside clinic hours, you can al- ways turn to the government-run facilities. Un- fortunately, very few facilities are provided for travelers with disabilties.

American-made medications may by unob- tainable in the islands, so along bring a supply of whatever you think you'll need. If you need to replace anything, quote the generic name at the drug store rather than the brand name. Other- wise go to any Chinese general store and ask the owner to recommend a good Chinese patent medicine for what ails you. The cost will be a third of what European medicines or herbs cost, and the Chinese medicine is often as effective or more so. Antibiotics should only be used to treat serious wounds, and only after medical advice.

Travel Insurance

The sale of travel insurance is big business but the value of the policies themselves is often questionable. If your regular group health insur- ance also covers you while you're traveling abroad it's probably enough as medical costs in the South Pacific are generally low. Most poli- cies only pay the amount above and beyond what your national or group health insurance will pay and are invalid if you don't have any health insurance at all. You may also be cov- ered by your credit card company if you paid for your plane ticket with the card. Buying extra trav- el insurance is about the same as buying a lottery ticket: there's always the chance it will pay off, but it's usually money down the drain.

If you do opt for the security of travel insur- ance, make sure emergency medical evacua- tions are covered. Some policies are invalid if you engage in any "dangerous activities," such as scuba diving, parasailing, surfing, or even riding a motor scooter, so be sure to read the fine print. Scuba divers should be aware that the only re- compression chambers in the South Pacific are at Papeete (Tahiti) and Suva (Fiji). Elsewhere you'll need an emergency medical evacuation to Aus- tralia or New Zealand and there isn't any point buying a policy that doesn't cover it. Medical in- surance especially designed for scuba divers is available from **Divers Alert Network** (6 West Colony Pl., Durham, NC 27705, U.S.A.; tel. 1- 800/446-2671 or 1-919/684-2948, fax 1-919/490- 6630, www.diversalertnetwork.org). In Australia, New Zealand, or the South Pacific, write Box 134, Carnegie, Victoria 3163, Australia (tel. 61-3/9563- 1151, fax 61-3/9563-1139).

Some companies will pay your bills directly

while others require you to pay and collect receipts that may be reimbursed later. Ask if travel delays, lost baggage, and theft are included. In practice, your airline probably already covers the first two adequately and claiming something extra from your insurance company could be more trouble than it's worth. Theft insurance never covers items left on the beach while you're in swimming. All this said, you should weigh the advantages and decide for yourself if you want a policy. Just don't be influenced by what your travel agent says as they'll only want to sell you coverage in order to earn another commission.

Acclimatizing

Don't go from winter weather into the steaming tropics without a rest before and after. Minimize jet lag by setting your watch to local time at your destination as soon as you board the flight. Westbound flights into the South Pacific from North America or Europe are less jolting since you follow the sun and your body gets a few hours extra sleep. On the way home you're moving against the sun and the hours of sleep your body loses cause jet lag. Airplane cabins have low humidity, so drink lots of juice or water instead of carbonated drinks, and don't overeat in-flight. It's also wise to forgo coffee, as it will only keep you awake, and alcohol, which will dehydrate you.

Scuba diving on departure day can give you a severe case of the bends. Before flying there should be a minimum of 12 hours surface interval after a nondecompression dive and a minimum of 24 hours after a decompression dive. Factors contributing to decompression sickness include a lack of sleep and/or the excessive consumption of alcohol before diving.

If you start feeling seasick onboard a ship, stare at the horizon, which is always steady, and stop thinking about it. Anti-motion-sickness pills are useful to have along; otherwise, ginger helps alleviate seasickness. Travel stores sell acubands that find a pressure point on the wrist and create a stable flow of blood to the head, thus miraculously preventing seasickness!

Frequently the feeling of thirst is false and only due to mucous membrane dryness. Gargling or taking two or three gulps of warm water should be enough. Keep moisture in your body by having a hot drink like tea or black coffee, or any kind of slightly salted or sour drink in small quantities. Salt in fresh lime juice is remarkably refreshing.

The tap water is safe to drink in the main towns, but ask first elsewhere. If in doubt, boil it or use purification pills. Tap water that is uncomfortably hot to touch is usually safe. Allow it to cool in a clean container. Don't forget that if the tap water is contaminated, the local ice will be too. Avoid brushing your teeth with water unfit to drink, and wash or peel fruit and vegetables if you can. Cooked food is less subject to contamination than raw.

Sunburn

Though you may think a tan will make you look healthier and more attractive, it's actually very damaging to the skin, which becomes dry, rigid, and prematurely old and wrinkled, especially on the face. Begin with short exposures to the sun, perhaps half an hour at a time, followed by an equal time in the shade. Drink plenty of liquids to keep your pores open and avoid the sun 1000-1500, the most dangerous time. Clouds and beach umbrellas will not protect you fully. Wear a T-shirt while snorkeling to protect your back. Sunbathing is the main cause of cataracts to the eyes, so wear sunglasses and a wide-brimmed hat, and beware of reflected sunlight.

Use a sunscreen lotion containing PABA rather than oil, and don't forget to apply it to your nose, lips, forehead, neck, hands, and feet. Sunscreens protect you from ultraviolet rays (a leading cause of cancer), while oils magnify the sun's effect. A 15-factor sunscreen provides 93% protection (a more expensive 30-factor sunscreen is only slightly better at 97% protection). Apply the lotion *before* going to the beach to avoid being burned on the way, and reapply every couple of hours to replace sunscreen washed away by perspiration. Swimming also washes away your protection. After sunbathing take a tepid shower rather than a hot one, which would wash away your natural skin oils. Stay moist and use a vitamin E evening cream to preserve the youth of your skin. Calamine ointment soothes skin already burned, as does coconut oil. Pharmacists recommend Solarcaine to soothe burned skin. Rinsing off with a vinegar solution reduces peeling, and aspirin relieves some of the pain and irritation. Vitamin A and calcium counteract overdoses of vitamin D received from the sun. The fairer your skin, the more essential it is to take care.

As earth's ozone layer is depleted due to the commercial use of chlorofluorocarbons (CFCs) and other factors, the need to protect oneself from ultraviolet radiation is becoming more urgent. In 1990 the U.S. Centers for Disease Control and Prevention in Atlanta reported that deaths from skin cancer increased 26% between 1973 and 1985. Previously the cancers didn't develop until age 50 or 60, but now much younger people are affected.

Ailments
Cuts and scratches infect easily in the tropics and take a long time to heal. Prevent infection from coral cuts by immediately washing wounds with soap and fresh water, then rubbing in vinegar or alcohol (whiskey will do)—painful but effective. Use an antiseptic like hydrogen peroxide and an antibacterial ointment such as neosporin, if you have them. Islanders usually dab coral cuts with lime juice. All cuts turn septic quickly in the tropics, so try to keep them clean and covered.

For bites, burns, and cuts, an antiseptic such as Solarcaine speeds healing and helps prevent infection. Pure aloe vera is good for sunburn, scratches, and even coral cuts. Bites by *no-no* sandflies itch for days and can become infected if scratched. Not everyone is affected by insect bites in the same way. Some people are practically immune to insects, while traveling companions experiencing exactly the same conditions are soon covered with bites. You'll soon know which type you are.

Prickly heat, an intensely irritating rash, is caused by wearing heavy clothing that is inappropriate for the climate. When the glands are blocked and the sweat is unable to evaporate, the skin becomes soggy and small red blisters appear. Synthetic fabrics like nylon are especially bad in this regard. Take a cold shower, apply calamine lotion, dust with talcum powder, and take off those clothes! Until things improve, avoid alcohol, tea, coffee, and any physical activity that makes you sweat. If you're sweating profusely, increase your intake of salt slightly to avoid fatigue, but not without concurrently drinking more water.

Use antidiarrheal medications such as Lomotil or Imodium sparingly. Rather than take drugs to plug yourself up, drink plenty of unsweetened liquids like green coconut or fresh fruit juice to help flush yourself out. Egg yolk mixed with nutmeg helps diarrhea, or have a rice and tea day. Avoid dairy products. Most cases of diarrhea are self-limiting and require only simple replacement of the fluids and salts lost in diarrheal stools. If the diarrhea is persistent or you experience high fever, drowsiness, or blood in the stool, stop traveling, rest, and consider seeing a doctor. For constipation eat pineapple or any peeled fruit.

If you're sleeping in villages or with the locals you may pick up head or body lice. Pharmacists and general stores usually have a remedy that will eliminate the problem in minutes (pack a bottle with you if you're uptight). You'll know you're lousy when you start to scratch: pick out the little varmints and snap them between your thumbnails for fun. The villagers pluck the creatures out of each other's hair one by one, a way of confirming friendships and showing affection. Intestinal parasites (worms) are also widespread. The hookworm bores its way through the soles of your feet, and if you go barefoot through moist gardens and plantations you may pick up something.

Malaria
Malaria is the most serious regional health hazard, but it's restricted to Vanuatu, Solomon Islands, and Papua New Guinea *only*. Guadalcanal now ranks as one of the most malarial areas in the world, and Chloroquine-resistant *falciparum* malaria is widespread in all three countries. Read the relevant references in the introductions to the Vanuatu and Solomon Islands chapters a couple of weeks before you embark for those islands. If you're only going to Fiji or the Polynesian countries, forget malaria entirely as it's unknown there.

Malaria *can* be avoided, and even if you're unlucky, it won't kill you so long as you're taking prophylactics. So don't become alarmed or let fear of malaria prevent you from visiting Melanesia. Symptoms of malaria are chills, aches in the back, head, and joints, plus a high periodic fever. Doctors outside the area often misdiagnose these symptoms (which may not begin until months after you leave the area) as common flu. Yet once identified through a blood test, malaria can usually be cured.

The *Anopheles* carrier mosquitoes are most active from dusk to dawn, so try to avoid getting bitten at this time. Wear long shirts and pants, sleep in a screened room, burn a mosquito coil, and use an insect repellent containing a high concentration of N,N diethylmetatoluamide (deet). For some reason people taking vitamin B-1 aren't as attractive to mosquitoes. On the other hand perfumes, colognes, and scented soaps do attract them.

Begin taking an antimalarial drug a week before you arrive in Vanuatu or the Solomons and continue for four weeks after you leave. Malaria pills are a bit cheaper in the South Pacific than in North America or Australia, so you only need the minimum number required to get you started.

An often-recommended drug effective against *falciparum* malaria is Lariam, also known as Mefloquine, and the usual dose is one 250-mg tablet a week (these pills cost about US$5 each). Lariam is a good choice if you're going to Solomon Islands or northern Vanuatu but would probably be overkill if you were only headed for Port Vila and southern Vanuatu where the risk is less. In southern Vanuatu, Paludrine or Chloroquine might be sufficient but you should always take something. Paludrine can cause nausea if taken on an empty stomach, so take it after dinner. Chloroquine can affect the eyes, but only if you take it continuously for eight years!

Some people also carry a three-tablet dose of the drug Fansidar to be used for self-treatment in case of fever. If you take Fansidar, discontinue use if you experience adverse skin reactions. Fansidar must not be taken by pregnant women or anyone allergic to sulfa drugs.

There's still no successful vaccination against malaria and none of the various pills are 100% effective. It's something of a scandal in the medical profession that while hundreds of millions of dollars are spent annually on research into the lifestyle diseases of the affluent, such as cancer and heart disease, comparatively little is allocated to the tropical and parasitic diseases of the third world. Vaccines only account for one percent of the profits of the big pharmaceutical companies, and just three percent of their research budgets are devoted to tropical diseases, largely because there's little money to be made from them.

AIDS

In 1981 scientists in the United States and France first recognized the Acquired Immune Deficiency Syndrome (AIDS), which was later discovered to be caused by a virus called the Human Immuno-deficiency Virus (HIV). HIV breaks down the body's immunity to infections leading to AIDS. The virus can lie hidden in the body for up to 10 years without producing any obvious symptoms or before developing into the AIDS disease and in the meantime the person can unknowingly infect others.

HIV lives in white blood cells and is present in the sexual fluids of humans. It's difficult to catch and is spread mostly through sexual intercourse, by needle or syringe sharing among intravenous drug users, in blood transfusions, and during pregnancy and birth (if the mother is infected). Using another person's razor blade or having your body pierced or tattooed are also risky, but the HIV virus cannot be transmitted by shaking hands, kissing, cuddling, fondling, sneezing, cooking food, or sharing eating or drinking utensils. One cannot be infected by saliva, sweat, tears, urine, or feces; toilet seats, telephones,

swimming pools, or mosquito bites do not cause AIDS. Ostracizing a known AIDS victim is not only immoral but also absurd.

Most blood banks now screen their products for HIV, and you can protect yourself against dirty needles by only allowing an injection if you see the syringe taken out of a fresh unopened pack. The simplest safeguard during sex is the proper use of a latex condom. Unroll the condom onto the erect penis; while withdrawing after ejaculation, hold onto the condom as you come out. Never try to recycle a condom, and pack a supply with you as it's a nuisance trying to buy them locally.

HIV is spread more often through anal than vaginal sex because the lining of the rectum is much weaker than that of the vagina, and ordinary condoms sometimes tear when used in anal sex. If you have anal sex, only use extra-strong condoms and special water-based lubricants since oil, Vaseline, and cream weaken the rubber. During oral sex you must make sure you don't get any semen or menstrual blood in your mouth. A woman runs 10 times the risk of contracting AIDS from a man than the other way around, and the threat is always greater when another sexually transmitted disease (STD) is present.

The very existence of AIDS calls for a basic change in human behavior. No vaccine or drug exists that can prevent or cure AIDS, and because the virus mutates frequently, no remedy may ever be totally effective. Other STDs such as syphilis, gonorrhea, chlamydia, hepatitis B, and herpes are far more common than AIDS and can lead to serious complications such as infertility, but at least they can usually be cured.

The euphoria of travel can make it easier to fall in love or have sex with a stranger, so travelers must be informed of these dangers. As a tourist you should always practice safe sex to prevent AIDS and other STDs. You never know who is infected or even if you yourself have become infected. It's important to bring the subject up *before* you start to make love. Make a joke out of it by pulling out a condom and asking your new partner, "Say, do you know what this is?" Or perhaps, "Your condom or mine?" Far from being unromantic or embarrassing, you'll both feel more relaxed with the subject off your minds and it's much better than worrying afterwards if

you might have been infected. The golden rule is safe sex or no sex.

By 1999 an estimated 33 million people worldwide were HIV carriers, and 14 million had already died of AIDS (mostly in Africa). In the South Pacific, the number of cases is still extremely small compared to the 650,000 confirmed HIV infections in the United States. Tahiti-Polynesia, New Caledonia, Papua New Guinea, and Guam are the most affected countries, yet it's worth noting that other STDs have already reached epidemic proportions in the urban areas of Fiji, Vanuatu, and Solomon Islands, demonstrating that the type of behavior leading to the rapid spread of AIDS is present.

An HIV infection can be detected through a blood test because the antibodies created by the body to fight off the virus can be seen under a microscope. It takes at least three weeks for the antibodies to be produced and in some cases as long as six months before they can be picked up during a screening test. If you think you may have run a risk, you should discuss the appropriateness of a test with your doctor. It's always better to know if you are infected so as to be able to avoid infecting others, to obtain early treatment of symptoms, and to make realistic plans. If you know someone with AIDS you should give them all the support you can (there's no danger in such contact unless blood is present).

Toxic Fish

More than 400 species of tropical reef fish, including wrasses, snappers, groupers, jacks, moray eels, surgeonfish, shellfish, and especially barracudas are known to cause seafood poisoning (ciguatera). There's no way to tell if a fish will cause ciguatera: a species can be poisonous on one side of the island, but not on the other.

In 1976 French and Japanese scientists working in the Gambier Islands determined that a one-celled dinoflagellate algae or plankton called *Gambierdiscus toxicus* was the cause. Normally these microalgae are found only in the ocean depths, but when a reef ecosystem is disturbed by natural or human causes they can multiply dramatically in a lagoon. The dinoflagellates are consumed by tiny herbivorous fish and the toxin passes up through the food chain to larger fish where it becomes concentrated in the head and guts. The toxins have no effect on the fish that feed on them.

Tahiti-Polynesia's 700-800 cases of ciguatera a year are more than in the rest of the South Pacific combined, leading to suspicions that the former French nuclear testing program is responsible. Ciguatera didn't exist on Hao atoll in the Tuamotus until military dredging for a 3,500-meter runway began in 1965. By mid-1968 43% of the population had been affected. Between 1971 and 1980 more than 30% of the population of Mangareva near the Moruroa nuclear test site suffered from seafood poisoning. Yet ciguatera has been around for a long time, having been reported in New Caledonia by Captain Cook.

The symptoms (numbness and tingling around the mouth and extremities, reversal of hot/cold sensations, prickling, itching, nausea, vomiting, erratic heartbeat, joint and muscle pains) usually subside in a few days. Induce vomiting, take castor oil as a laxative, and avoid alcohol if you're unlucky. Symptoms can recur for up to a year, and victims may become allergic to all seafoods. In the Marshall Islands, an injected drug called Manitol has been effective in treating ciguatera, but as yet little is known about it.

Avoid biointoxication by cleaning fish as soon as they're caught, discarding the head and organs, and taking special care with oversized fish caught in shallow water. Small fish are generally safer. Whether the fish is consumed cooked or raw has no bearing on this problem. Local residents often know from experience which species may be eaten. Information on the new ciguatera test kit is available at www.cigua.com.

Other Diseases

Infectious hepatitis A (jaundice) is a liver ailment transmitted person to person or through unboiled water, uncooked vegetables, or other foods contaminated during handling. The risk of infection is highest among those who eat village food, so if you'll be spending much time in rural areas, consider getting an immune globulin shot, which provides six months protection. Better is a vaccine called Havrix, which provides up to 10 years protection (given in two doses two weeks apart, then a third dose six months later). If you've ever had hepatitis A in your life you are already immune. Otherwise, you'll know you've got the hep when your eyeballs and urine turn yellow. Time

and rest are the only cure. Viral hepatitis B is spread through sexual or blood contact.

Cholera is rare in the South Pacific but there have been sporadic outbreaks in Micronesia. Cholera is acquired via contaminated food or water, so avoid uncooked foods, peel your own fruit, and drink bottled drinks if you happen to arrive in an infected area. Typhoid fever is also caused by contaminated food or water, while tetanus (lockjaw) occurs when cuts or bites become infected. Horrible disfiguring diseases such as leprosy and elephantiasis are hard to catch, so it's unlikely you'll be visited by one of these nightmares of the flesh.

More of a problem is dengue fever, a mosquito-transmitted disease that appeared in the South Pacific in the 1970s. In early 1998 a major outbreak in Fiji resulted in an estimated 25,000 cases and 11 deaths. Tonga, Cook Islands, and Vanuatu have also experienced dengue fever epidemics recently, and the disease is now spreading to new areas due to global warming. Signs are headaches, sore throat, pain in the joints, fever, chills, nausea, and rash. This painful illness also known as "breakbone fever" can last anywhere from five to 15 days. Although you can relieve the symptoms somewhat, the only real cure is to stay in bed, drink lots of water, and wait it out. Avoid aspirin as this can lead to complications. A new vaccine developed in Thailand is still in the testing stages, so meanwhile just try to avoid getting bitten (the *Aedes aegypti* mosquito bites only during the day). Dengue fever can kill infants so extra care must be taken to protect them if an outbreak is in progress.

Vaccinations

Most visitors are not required to get any vaccinations at all before coming to the South Pacific. Tetanus, diphtheria, and typhoid fever shots are not required, but they're worth considering if you're going off the beaten track. Tetanus and diphtheria shots are given together, and a booster is required every 10 years. The typhoid fever shot is every three years. Polio is believed to have been eradicated from the region.

The cholera vaccine is only 50% effective and valid just six months, and bad reactions are common, which is why most doctors in developed countries won't administer it. Forget it unless you're sure you're headed for an infected area. If you'll be visiting Tuvalu, Nauru, Kiribati, or anywhere in Micronesia before Fiji, ask Air Marshall Islands or Air Nauru if a cholera vaccination is required. In that case you'll be able to obtain it locally without difficulty.

A yellow-fever vaccination is required if you've been in an infected area within the six days prior to arrival. Yellow fever is a mosquito-borne disease that only occurs in Central Africa and northern South America (excluding Chile), places you're not likely to have been just before arriving

in the South Pacific. Since the vaccination is valid 10 years, get one if you're an inveterate globe-trotter.

Immune globulin (IG) and the Havrix vaccine aren't 100% effective against hepatitis A, but they do increase your general resistance to infections. IG prophylaxis must be repeated every five months. Hepatitis B vaccination involves three doses over a six-month period (duration of protection unknown) and is recommended mostly for people planning extended stays in the region.

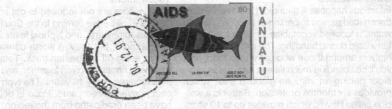

WHAT TO TAKE

Packing

Assemble everything you simply must take and cannot live without—then cut the pile in half. If you're still left with more than will fit into a medium-size suitcase or backpack, continue eliminating. You have to be tough on yourself and just limit what you take. Now put it all into your bag. If the total (bag and contents) weighs more than 16 kg, you'll sacrifice much of your mobility. If you can keep it down to 10 kg, you're traveling *light*. Categorize, separate, and pack all your things into clear plastic bags or stuff sacks for convenience and protection from moisture. Items that might leak should be in resealable bags. In addition to your principal bag, you'll want a day pack or flight bag. When checking in for flights, carry anything that cannot be replaced in your hand luggage.

Your Luggage

A soft medium-size backpack with a lightweight internal frame is best. Big external-frame packs are fine for mountain climbing but get caught in airport conveyor belts and are very inconvenient on public transport. The best packs have a zippered compartment in back where you can tuck in the hip belt and straps before turning your pack over to an airline or bus. This type of pack has the flexibility of allowing you to simply walk when motorized transport is unavailable or unacceptable; and with the straps zipped in it looks like a regular suitcase, should you wish to go upmarket for a while.

Make sure your pack allows you to carry the weight on your hips, has a cushion for spine support, and doesn't pull backwards. The pack should strap snugly to your body but also allow ventilation to your back. It should be made of a water-resistant material such as nylon and have a Fastex buckle.

Look for a pack with double, two-way zipper compartments and pockets you can lock with miniature padlocks. They might not *stop* a thief, but they will deter the casual pilferer. A 60-cm length of lightweight chain and another padlock will allow you to fasten your pack to something. Keep valuables locked in your bag, out of sight, as even upmarket hotel rooms aren't 100% safe.

Clothing and Camping Equipment

Take loose-fitting washable cotton clothing, light in color and weight. Synthetic fabrics are hot and sticky, and most of the things you wear at home are too heavy for the tropics—be prepared for the humidity. Dress is casual, with slacks and a sports shirt okay for men even at dinner parties. Local women often wear long colorful dresses in the evening, but respectable shorts are okay in daytime. If in doubt, bring the minimum with you and buy tropical garb upon arrival. Stick to clothes you can rinse in your room sink. In midwinter (July and August) it can be cool at night in the Cooks, Tonga, New Caledonia, and even Moorea, so a light sweater or windbreaker may come in handy. (Reader Claire Brenn writes: "If you have some good but unfashionable clothes you don't want to take home, just leave them behind in your hotel room with a small thank you note. The locals will gladly have them but to offer them directly might be embarrassing.")

The *lavalava, sulu,* or *pareu* (pronounced "par-RAY-o") is a bright two-meter piece of cloth both men and women wrap about themselves as an all-purpose garment. Any islander can show you how to wear it. Missionaries taught the South Sea island women to drape their attributes in long, flowing gowns, called muumuus in Hawaii. In the South Pacific, the dress is better known as a Mother Hubbard for the muumuu-attired nursery rhyme character who "went to the cupboard to fetch her poor dog a bone."

Take comfortable shoes that have been broken in. Running shoes and rubber thongs (flip-flops) are handy for day use but will bar you from nightspots with strict dress codes. Scuba divers' wetsuit booties are lightweight and perfect for both crossing rivers and lagoon walking, though an old pair of sneakers may be just as good (never use the booties to walk on breakable coral).

A small nylon tent guarantees backpackers a place to sleep every night, but it *must* be mosquito- and waterproof. Get one with a tent fly, then waterproof both tent and fly with a can of waterproofing spray. You'll seldom need a sleeping bag in the tropics, so that's one item you can easily cut. A youth hostel sleeping sheet is ideal—all HI handbooks give instructions on how to make your own or buy one at your local hostel. You don't really need to carry a bulky foam pad, as the ground is seldom cold.

Below we've provided a few checklists to help you assemble your gear. The listed items combined weigh well over 16 kg, so eliminate what doesn't suit you:

- pack with internal frame
- day pack or airline bag
- sun hat or visor
- essential clothing only
- bathing suit
- sturdy walking shoes
- rubber thongs
- rubber booties
- nylon tent and fly
- tent-patching tape
- mosquito net
- sleeping sheet

Accessories

Bring some reading material, as good books can be hard to find in some countries. A mask and snorkel are essential equipment—you'll be missing half of the Pacific's beauty without them. Scuba divers will bring their own regulator, buoyancy compensator, and gauges to avoid rental fees and to eliminate the possibility of catching a transmissible disease from rental equipment. A lightweight three-mm Lycra wetsuit will provide protection against marine stings and coral.

Neutral gray eyeglasses protect your eyes from the sun and give the least color distortion. Take an extra pair (if you wear them). Keep your laundry soap inside a couple of layers of plastic bags.

Also take along postcards of your hometown and snapshots of your house, family, workplace, etc; islanders love to see these. Always keep a promise to mail islanders the photos you take of them.

- portable shortwave radio
- camera and 10 rolls of film
- compass
- pocket flashlight
- extra batteries
- candle
- pocket alarm calculator
- extra pair of eyeglasses

- sunglasses
- mask and snorkel
- padlock and lightweight chain
- collapsible umbrella
- string for a clothesline
- powdered laundry soap
- universal sink plug
- minitowel
- silicon glue
- sewing kit
- miniscissors
- nail clippers
- fishing line for sewing gear
- plastic cup and plate
- can and bottle opener
- corkscrew
- penknife
- spoon
- water bottle
- matches
- tea bags

Toiletries and Medical Kit

Since everyone has his/her own medical requirements and brand names vary from country to country, there's no point going into detail here. Note, however, that even the basics (such as aspirin) are unavailable on some outer islands, so be prepared. Bring medicated powder for prickly heat rash. Charcoal tablets are useful for diarrhea and poisoning (they absorb the irritants). Bring an adequate supply of any personal medications, plus your prescriptions (in generic terminology).

High humidity causes curly hair to swell and bush, straight hair to droop. If it's curly have it cut short or keep it long in a ponytail or bun. A good cut is essential with straight hair. Water-based makeup is preferable, as the heat and humidity cause oil glands to work overtime. High-quality locally made shampoo, body oils, and insect repellent are sold on all the islands, and the bottles are conveniently smaller than those sold in Western countries. See **Health** for more ideas.

- wax earplugs
- soap in plastic container
- soft toothbrush
- toothpaste
- roll-on deodorant
- shampoo
- comb and brush

- skin creams
- makeup
- tampons or napkins
- toilet paper
- vitamin/mineral supplement
- insect repellent
- PABA sunscreen
- Chap Stick
- a motion-sickness remedy
- contraceptives
- iodine
- water-purification pills
- delousing powder
- a diarrhea remedy
- Tiger Balm
- a cold remedy
- Alka-Seltzer
- aspirin
- antihistamine
- antifungal
- Calmitol ointment
- antibacterial ointment
- antiseptic cream
- disinfectant
- simple dressings
- adhesive bandages (like Band-Aids)
- painkiller
- prescription medicines

Money and Documents

Most post offices have passport applications. If you lose your passport you should report the matter to the local police at once, obtain a certificate or receipt, then proceed to your consulate (if any!) for a replacement. If you have your birth certificate with you it expedites things considerably. Don't bother getting an international driver's license as your regular license is all you need to drive here (except in Cook Islands and Tonga where you'll be required to buy a local license).

Traveler's checks in U.S. dollars are recommended, and in the South Pacific, American Express is the most efficient company when it comes to providing refunds for lost checks. Bring along a small supply of US$1 and US$5 bills to use if you don't manage to change money immediately upon arrival or if you run out of local currency and can't get to a bank. In the French territories French francs in cash are best currency to have by far as they're exchanged at a fixed rate without commission.

Carry your valuables in a money belt worn around your waist or neck under your clothing; most camping stores have these. Make several photocopies of the information page of your passport, personal identification, driver's license, scuba certification card, credit cards, airline tickets, receipts for purchase of traveler's checks, etc.—you should be able to get them all on one page. On the other side, write the phone numbers you'd need to call to report lost documents. A brief medical history with your blood type, allergies, chronic or special health problems, eyeglass and medical prescriptions, etc., might also come in handy. Put these inside plastic bags to protect them from moisture, then carry the lists in different places, and leave one at home.

How much money you'll need depends on your lifestyle, but time is also a factor. The longer you stay, the cheaper it gets. Suppose you have to lay out US$1,000 on airfare and have (for example) US$50 a day left over for expenses. If you stay 15 days, you'll average US$117 a day ($50 times 15 plus $1,000, divided by 15). If you stay 30 days, you'll average US$83 a day. If you stay 90 days, the per-day cost drops to US$61. If you stay a year it'll cost only US$53 a day. Some countries are more expensive than others: while you'll certainly want to experience the spectacular scenery of Tahiti, spend those extra days lounging in the sun in budget-priced Fiji, Tonga, Samoa, or the Solomons.

- passport
- airline tickets
- scuba certification card
- driver's license
- traveler's checks
- some U.S. cash
- credit card
- photocopies of documents
- money belt
- address book
- notebook
- envelopes
- extra ballpoints

FILM AND PHOTOGRAPHY

Scan the ads in photographic magazines for deals on mail-order cameras and film, or buy at a discount shop in any large city. Run a roll of film through your camera to be sure it's in good working order; clean the lens with lens-cleaning tissue and check the batteries. Remove the batteries from your camera when storing it at home for long periods. Register valuable cameras or electronic equipment with customs before you leave home so there won't be any argument over where you bought the items when you return, or at least carry a copy of the original bill of sale.

The type of camera you choose could depend on the way you travel. If you'll be staying mostly in one place, a heavy single-lens reflex (SLR) camera with spare lenses and other equipment won't trouble you. If you'll be moving around a lot for a considerable length of time, a 35-mm automatic compact camera will be better. The compacts are mostly useful for close-up shots; landscapes will seem spread out and far away. A wide-angle lens gives excellent depth of field, but hold the camera upright to avoid converging verticals. A polarizing filter prevents reflections from glass windows and water, and makes the sky bluer.

Take double the amount of film and mailers you think you'll need: only in American Samoa, Fiji, and Vanuatu is film cheap and readily available, and even then you never know if it's been spoiled by an airport X-ray on the way there. On a long trip mailers are essential as exposed film shouldn't be held for long periods. Choose 36-exposure film over 24-exposure to save on the number of rolls you have to carry. In Tahiti-Polynesia and New Caledonia camera film costs more than double what you'd pay in the U.S., but you can import 10 rolls duty free. When purchasing film in the islands take care to check the expiration date. Specialty films like black-and-white or color slides are available only in main centers like Nadi or Suva; standard color print film will be about all you'll find in most places.

Films are rated by their speed and sensitivity to light, using ISO numbers from 25 to 1600. The higher the number, the greater the film's sensitivity to light. Slower films with lower ISOs (like 100-200) produce sharp images in bright sunlight. Faster films with higher ISOs (like 400) stop action and work well in low-light situations, such as in dark rainforests or at sunset. If you have a manual SLR you can avoid overexposure at midday by reducing the exposure half a stop, but *do* overexpose when photographing dark-skinned Melanesians. From 1000 to 1600 the light is often too bright to take good photos, and panoramas usually come out best early or late in the day.

Keep your photos simple with one main subject and an uncomplicated background. Get as close to your subjects as you can and lower or raise the camera to their level. Include people in the foreground of scenic shots to add interest and perspective. Outdoors a flash can fill in unflattering facial shadows caused by high sun or backlit conditions. Most of all, be creative. Look for interesting details and compose the photo before you push the trigger. Instead of taking a head-on photo of a group of people, step to one side and ask them to face you. The angle improves the photo. Photograph subjects coming toward you rather than passing by. Ask permission before photographing people. If you're asked for money (rare) you can always walk away—give your subjects the same choice.

When packing, protect your camera against vibration. Checked baggage is scanned by powerful airport X-ray monitors, so carry both camera and film aboard the plane in a clear plastic bag and ask security for a visual inspection. Some airports will refuse to do this, however. A good alternative is to use a lead-laminated pouch. The old high-dose X-ray units are seldom seen these days but even low-dose inspection units can ruin fast film (400 ASA and above). Beware of the cumulative effect of X-ray machines.

Keep your camera in a plastic bag during rain and while traveling in motorized canoes, etc. In the tropics the humidity can cause film to stick to itself; silica-gel crystals in the bag will protect film from humidity and mold growth. Protect camera and film from direct sunlight and load the film in the shade. When loading, check that the takeup spool revolves. Never leave camera or film in a hot place like a car floor, glove compartment, or trunk.

POLYNESIA

Tahiti-Polynesia, Pitcairn Islands,
Easter Island, Cook Islands,
Niue, Kingdom of Tonga,
American Samoa, Samoa, Tokelau,
Wallis and Futuna, Tuvalu

JOHN WEBBER

THE POLYNESIAN TRIANGLE *between Hawaii, New Zealand, and Easter Island stretches 8,000 km across the central Pacific Ocean—a fifth of the earth's surface. Since the late 18th century, when Captain Cook first revealed Polynesia to European eyes, artists and writers have sung the praises of the graceful golden-skinned peoples of the "many islands." While there's certainly homogeneity in Polynesia, there are also striking contrasts resulting from a history of American, French, and New Zealand colonial rule. Hawaii and New Zealand are parts of Polynesia not covered herein because most visitors carry separate guidebooks to them.*

Polynesia consists of boundless ocean and little land. This vast region is divided into two cultural areas, Western Polynesia (Tonga and Samoa) and Eastern Polynesia (Hawaii, Tahiti-Polynesia, Cook Islands, and New Zealand). Of the three countries and eight territories included in this section, only Tahiti-Polynesia and Samoa are larger than 1,000 square km, though both Cook Islands and Tahiti-Polynesia control sea areas well above a million square km.

Only Tahiti-Polynesia, Tonga, and Samoa have populations of more than 100,000; American Samoa has 50,000 while all the rest have less than 20,000 inhabitants. The mainly subsistence economies have inspired many Polynesians to emigrate to the Pacific rim: there are now more Samoans in the U.S. than in American Samoa itself and more Cook Islanders in New Zealand than in their homeland. Only three Polynesian states are completely independent: Tonga, Samoa, and Tuvalu. All the rest still have legal ties to some outside power.

TAHITI-POLYNESIA

INTRODUCTION

Legendary Tahiti, isle of love, has long been the vision of "la Nouvelle Cythère," the earthly paradise. Explorers Wallis, Bougainville, and Cook all told of a land of spellbinding beauty and enchantment, where the climate was delightful, hazardous insects and diseases unknown, and the islanders, especially the women, among the handsomest ever seen. Rousseau's "noble savage" had been found! A few years later, Fletcher Christian and Captain Bligh acted out their drama of sin and retribution here.

The list of famous authors who came and wrote about these islands reads like a high-school literature course: Herman Melville, Robert Louis Stevenson, Pierre Loti, Rupert Brooke, Jack London, W. Somerset Maugham, Charles Nordhoff and James Norman Hall (the Americans who wrote *Mutiny on the Bounty*), among others. Exotic images of uninhibited dancers, fragrant flowers, and pagan gods fill the pages. Here, at least, life was meant to be enjoyed.

The most unlikely PR man of them all was a once-obscure French painter named Paul Gauguin, who transformed the primitive color of Tahiti and the Marquesas into powerful visual images seen around the world. When WW II shook the Pacific from Pearl Harbor to Guadalcanal, rather than bloodcurdling banzais and saturation bombings, Polynesia got a U.S. serviceman named James A. Michener, who added Bora Bora to the legend. Marlon Brando arrived in 1961 on one of the first jets to land in Polynesia and, along with thousands of tourists and adventurers, has been coming back ever since.

THE LAND

Tahiti-Polynesia (or Te Ao Maohi as it is known to the Polynesians themselves) consists of five great archipelagos, the Society, Austral, Tuamotu, Gambier, and Marquesas Islands, arrayed in chains running from northwest to southeast. The Society Islands are subdivided into the Windwards, or *Îles du Vent* (Tahiti, Moorea, Maiao, Tetiaroa, and Mehetia), and the Leewards, or *Îles Sous-le-Vent* (Huahine, Raiatea, Taha'a, Bora Bora, Maupiti, Tupai, Maupihaa/Mopelia, Manuae/Scilly, and Motu One/Bellingshausen).

Together the 35 islands and 83 atolls of Tahiti-Polynesia total only 3,543 square km in land area, yet they're scattered over a vast area of the southeastern Pacific Ocean, between 7° and 28° south latitude and 131° and 156° west longitude. Papeete (149° west longitude) is actually eight degrees *east* of Honolulu (157° west

longitude). Though Tahiti-Polynesia is only half the size of Corsica in land area, if Papeete were Paris then the Gambiers would be in Romania and the Marquesas near Stockholm. At 5,030,000 square km the territory's 200-nautical-mile exclusive economic zone is by far the largest in the Pacific islands.

There's a wonderful geological diversity to these islands midway between Australia and South America—from the dramatic, jagged volcanic outlines of the Society and Marquesas islands, to the 400-meter-high hills of the Australs

TAHITI-POLYNESIA

SOUTH

PACIFIC

OCEAN

Coral Is.
Hatutu
Eiao
Motu Iti
Nuku Hiva
Ua Huku
Ua Pou
Fatu Huku
Hiva Oa
Marquesas
Tahuata
Motane
Islands
Fatu Hiva

Manihi Takaroa
Tepoto
Napuka
Ahe
Rangiroa
Mataiva
Arutua
Takapoto
Tikei
Tuamotu
Bellingshausen
Motu-Iti
Tikehau
Puka Puka
Scilly
Bora-Bora
Makatea
Apataki
Aratika
Takume
Fangatau
Islands
Maupiti
Kaukura
Toau
Raraka
Taenga
Tahaa
Niau
Katiu
Makemo
Raroia
Fakahina
Mopelia
Raiatea
Huahine
Fakarava
Faaite
Hiti
Nihiru
Society Islands
Maiao
Moorea
Tetiaroa
Tahanea
Motutunga
Tatakoto
Anaa
North Marutea
Rekareka
Tahiti
Hararaiki
Hikueru
Tauere
Pukaroa
Mehetia
Reitoru
Amanu
Marokau
Hao
Aki-Aki
Reao
Ravahere
Manuhangi
Vahitahi
Hereheretue
Nengonengo
Paraoa
Nukutavake
Manuhangi
Vairaatea
Pinaki
Nukutipipi
Ahunui
Tureia
Vanavana
Tenararo
Maria
Tematangi
Moruroa
Maturei-
Marutea
Rururu
Fangataufa
Vavao
Maria
Rimatara
Morane
Temoe
Tubuai
Mangareva
Gambier
Raivavae
Islands

Austral

Islands

Rapa Iti

0 ___ 250 mi

0 ___ 250 km

POLYNESIA AT A GLANCE

ISLAND	POPULATION (1996)	AREA (hectares)
WINDWARD ISLANDS	162,686	118,580
Tahiti	150,721	104,510
Moorea	11,682	12,520
LEEWARD ISLANDS	26,838	38,750
Huahine	5,411	7,480
Raiatea	10,063	17,140
Taha'a	4,470	9,020
Bora Bora	5,767	2,930
Maupiti	1,127	1,140
AUSTRAL ISLANDS	6,563	14,784
Rurutu	2,015	3,235
Tubuai	2,049	4,500
TUAMOTU ISLANDS	14,283	72,646
Rangiroa	1,913	7,900
Manihi	769	1,300
GAMBIER ISLANDS	1,087	4,597
MARQUESAS ISLANDS	8,064	104,930
Nuku Hiva	2,375	33,950
Hiva Oa	1,837	31,550
TAHITI-POLYNESIA	219,521	354,287

and Gambiers, to the low coral atolls of the Tuamotus. All of the Marquesas are volcanic islands, while the Tuamotus are all coral islands or atolls. The Societies and Gambiers include both volcanic and coral types.

Tahiti, around 4,000 km from both Auckland and Honolulu or 6,000 km from Los Angeles and Sydney, is not only the best known and most populous of the islands, but also the largest (1,045 square km) and highest (2,241 meters). Bora Bora and Maupiti are noted for their combination of high volcanic peaks within low coral rings. Rangiroa is one of the world's largest coral atolls while Makatea is an uplifted atoll. In the Marquesas, precipitous and sharply crenellated mountains rise hundreds of meters, with craggy peaks, razorback ridges, plummeting waterfalls, deep, fertile valleys, and dark broken coastlines pounded by surf. Compare them to the pencil-thin strips of yellow reefs, green vegetation, and white beaches enclosing the transparent Tuamotu lagoons. In all, Tahiti-Polynesia offers some of the most varied and spectacular scenery in the entire South Pacific.

Climate

The hot and humid summer season runs Nov.-April. The rest of the year the climate is somewhat cooler and drier. The refreshing southeast trade winds blow consistently May-Aug., varying to easterlies Sept.-December. The northeast trades Jan.-April coincide with the hurricane season. The trade winds cool the islands and offer clear sailing for mariners, making May-Oct. the most favorable season to visit. (In fact, there can be long periods of fine, sunny weather anytime of year and these seasonal variations should not be a pivotal factor in deciding when to come.)

Hurricanes are relatively rare, although they do hit the Tuamotus and occasionally Tahiti (but almost never the Marquesas). From November 1980 to May 1983 an unusual wave of eight hurricanes and two tropical storms battered the islands due to the El Niño phenomenon. The next hurricane occurred in December 1991. In November 1997 two hurricanes struck Maupiti and neighboring isles, one passed over the Tuamotus in February 1998, and another hit Huahine in April 1998, again the fault of El Niño. A hurricane would merely inconvenience a visitor staying at a hotel, though campers and yachties might get blown into oblivion. The days immediately following a hurricane are clear and dry.

Rainfall is greatest in the mountains and along the windward shores of the high islands. The Societies are far damper than the Marquesas. In fact, the climate of the Marquesas is erratic: some years the group experiences serious drought, other years it could rain the whole time you're there. The low-lying Tuamotus get the least rainfall of all. Tahiti-Polynesia encompasses such a vast area that latitude is an important factor: at 27° south latitude Rapa is far cooler than Nuku Hiva (9° south).

Winds from the southeast (maraamu) are generally drier than those from the northeast or north. The northeast winds often bring rain: Papenoo on the northeast side of Tahiti is twice as wet as rain-shadowed Punaauia. The annual rainfall is extremely variable, but the humidity is generally high, reaching 98%. In the evening

ATUONA'S CLIMATE

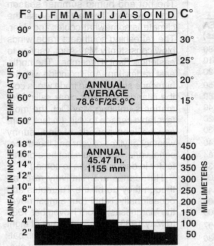

PAPEETE'S CLIMATE

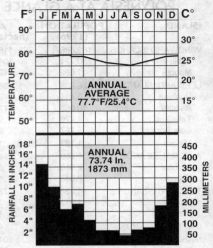

the heat of the Tahiti afternoons is replaced by soft, fragrant mountain breezes called *hupe,* which drift down to the sea.

Tahiti and Moorea have a solar (rather than a lunar) tide, which means that the low tides are at sunrise and sunset, high tides at noon and midnight. Because of this, snorkeling in or near a reef passage will be safest in the morning as the water flows in. Shallow waters are best traversed by yachts around noon when the water is high and slack, and visibility is at its peak.

Flowers and Birds

The national flower, the delicate, heavy-scented *tiare Tahiti (Gardenia tahitiensis),* can have anywhere from six to nine white petals. It blooms year-round, but especially Sept.-April. In his *Plants and Flowers of Tahiti* Jean-Claude Belhay writes: "The tiare is to Polynesia what the lotus is to India: a veritable symbol." Follow local custom by wearing this blossom or a hibiscus behind your left ear if you're happily taken, behind your right ear if you're still available.

Of the 90 species of birds in Tahiti-Polynesia, 59 are found in the Society Islands, of which 33 are native. Among the seabirds are the white-tailed tropic birds, brown and black noddies, white and crested terns, petrels, and boobies.

The hopping Indian mynah bird *(Acridotheres tristis)* with its yellow beak and feet was introduced from Indonesia at the turn of the century to control insects. Today these noisy, aggressive birds are ubiquitous—feeding on fruit trees and forcing the native finches and blue-tinged doves out of their habitat.

HISTORY

Discovery and Settlement

The eastern Polynesian islands, including those of Tahiti-Polynesia, were colonized at uncertain dates during the 1st millennium A.D. It's thought that about A.D. 300 the Polynesians reached the Marquesas from Samoa, and sometime around A.D. 500 they sailed on from the Marquesas to Hawaii and Easter Island. They were on the Society Islands by 800 and sailed from there to the Cooks and New Zealand around 1000, completing the occupation of the Polynesian triangle. On these planned voyages of colonization they carried all the plants and animals needed to continue their way of life.

Prior to European contact three hereditary classes structured the Society Islands: high chiefs *(ari'i),* lesser chiefs *(raatira),* and commoners *(manahune)*. A small slave class *(titi)* also existed. The various *ari'i* tribes controlled wedge-shaped valleys, and their authority was balanced. None managed to gain permanent supremacy over the rest.

Religion centered around an open-air temple, called a *marae,* with a stone altar. Here priests prayed to the ancestors or gods and conducted all the significant ceremonies of Polynesian life. An individual's social position was determined by his or her family connections, and the recitation of one's genealogy confirmed it. Human sacrifices took place on important occasions on a high chief's *marae.* Cannibalism was rife in the Marquesas and was also practiced in the Tuamotus.

The museums of the world possess many fine stone and wood tikis in human form from the Marquesas Islands, where the decorative sense was highly developed. Sculpture in the Australs was more naturalistic, and only here were female tikis common. The Tahitians showed less interest in the plastic arts but excelled in the social arts of poetry, oratory, theater, music, song, and dance. Life on the Tuamotus was a struggle for existence, and objects had utilitarian functions. Countless Polynesian cult objects were destroyed in the early 19th century by overzealous missionaries.

European Exploration

While the Polynesian history of the islands goes back at least 1,700 years, the European period only began in the 16th century when the Magellan expedition sailed past the Tuamotus and Mendaña visited the Marquesas. The Spaniard Quirós saw the Tuamotus in 1606, as did the Dutchmen Le Maire and Schouten in 1616, the Dutchman Roggeveen in 1722, and the Englishman Byron in 1765. But it was not until 18 June 1767 that Capt. Samuel Wallis on the HMS *Dolphin* happened upon Tahiti. He and most of his contemporary explorers were in search of *terra australis incognita,* a mythical southern landmass thought to balance the Northern Hemisphere.

At first the Tahitians attacked the ship, but after experiencing European gunfire they decided to be friendly. Eager to trade, they loaded the Englishmen down with pigs, fowl, and fruit. Iron was in the highest demand, and Tahitian women lured the sailors to exchange nails for love. Consequently, to prevent the ship's timbers from being torn asunder for the nails, no man was allowed onshore except in parties strictly for food and water. Wallis sent ashore a landing party, which named Tahiti "King George III Island," turned some sod, and hoisted the Union Jack. A year later the French explorer Louis-Antoine de Bougainville arrived on the east coast, unaware of Wallis's discovery, and claimed Tahiti for the king of France.

Wallis and Bougainville only visited briefly, leaving it to Capt. James Cook to really describe Polynesia to Europeans. Cook visited "Otaheite" four times, in 1769, 1773, 1774, and 1777. His first three-month visit was to observe the transit of the planet Venus across the face of the sun. The second and third were in search of the southern continent, while the fourth was to locate a northwest passage between the Pacific and Atlantic oceans. Some of the finest artists and scientists of the day accompanied Captain Cook. Their explorations added the Leeward Islands, two Austral islands, and a dozen Tuamotu islands to European knowledge. On Tahiti Cook met a high priest from Raiatea named Tupaia, who had an astonishing knowledge of the Pacific and could name dozens of islands. He drew Cook a map that included the Cook Islands, the Marquesas, and perhaps also some Samoan islands!

In 1788 Tahiti was visited for five months by HMS *Bounty* commanded by Lt. William Bligh with orders to collect young breadfruit plants for transportation to the West Indies. However, the famous mutiny did not take place at Tahiti but in Tongan waters, and from there Bligh and loyal members of his crew managed to escape by navigating an open boat 6,500 km to Dutch Timor. In 1791, the HMS *Pandora* came to Tahiti in search of the *Bounty* mutineers, intending to take them to England for trial. They captured 14 survivors of the 16 who had elected to stay on Tahiti when Fletcher Christian and eight others left for Pitcairn. Although glamorized by Hollywood, the mutineers helped destroy traditional Tahitian society by acting as mercenaries for rival chiefs. In 1792 Bligh returned to Tahiti in another ship and completed his original mission.

By the early 19th century, ruffian British and American whalers were fanning out over the Pacific. Other ships traded with the islanders for sandalwood, bêche-de-mer, and mother-of-pearl, as well as the usual supplies. They brought with them smallpox, measles, influenza, tuberculosis, scarlet fever, and venereal diseases, which devastated the unprepared Polynesians. Slave raids, alcohol, and European firearms did the rest.

Kings and Missionaries

In March 1797 the ship *Duff* dropped off on Tahiti 18 Protestant missionaries and their wives after a 207-day journey from England. By this time Pomare, chief of the area adjoining Matavai Bay, had become powerful through the use of European tools, firearms, and mercenaries. He welcomed the missionaries but would not be converted; infanticide, sexual freedom, and human sacrifices continued. By 1800 all but five of the original 18 had left Tahiti disappointed.

In 1803 Pomare I died and his despotic son, Pomare II, attempted to conquer the entire island. After initial success he was forced to flee to Moorea in 1808. Missionary Henry Nott went with him, and in 1812 Pomare II turned to him for help in regaining his lost power. Though the missionaries refused to baptize Pomare II himself because of his deeply ingrained heathen and drunken habits, his subjects on Moorea became nominal Christians. In 1815 this "Christian king" managed to regain Tahiti and overthrow paganism. Instead of being punished, the defeated clans were forgiven and allowed to convert to Christianity The persistent missionaries then enforced the Ten Commandments and dressed the Tahitian women in "Mother Hubbard" costumes—dresses that covered their bodies from head to toe. Henceforth the singing of anything but hymns was banned, dancing proscribed, and all customs that offended puritanical sensibilities wiped away. Morality police terrorized the confused Tahitians in an eternal crusade against sin. Even the wearing of flowers in the hair was prohibited.

Queen Pomare IV

The Rape of Polynesia

Upon Pomare II's death from drink at age 40 in 1821, the crown passed to his infant son, Pomare III, but he passed away in 1827. At this juncture the most remarkable Tahitian of the 19th century, Aimata, half-sister of Pomare II, became Queen Pomare Vahine IV. She was to rule Tahiti, Moorea, and part of the Austral and Tuamotu groups for half a century until her death in 1877, a barefoot Tahitian Queen Victoria. She allied herself closely with the London Missionary Society (LMS), and when two French-Catholic priests, Honoré Laval and François Caret, arrived on Tahiti in 1836 from their stronghold at Mangareva (Gambier Islands), she expelled them promptly.

This affront brought a French frigate to Papeete in 1838, demanding $2,000 compensation and a salute to the French flag. Although the conditions were met, the queen and her chiefs wrote to England appealing for help, but none came. A Belgian named Moerenhout who had formerly served at the U.S. consul was appointed French consul to Queen Pomare in 1838, and soon after a second French gunboat returned in 1839 and threatened to bombard Tahiti unless 2,000 Spanish dollars were paid and Catholic missionaries given free entry. Back in Mangareva, Laval pushed forward a grandiose building program, which wiped out 80% of the population of the Gambiers from overwork.

In September 1842, while the queen and George Pritchard, the English consul, were away, he tricked four local chiefs into signing a petition asking to be brought under French "protection." This demand was immediately accepted by French Admiral Abel Dupetit-Thouars, who was in league with Moerenhout, and on 9 September 1842 they forced Queen Pomare to accept a French protectorate. When the queen tried to maintain her power and keep her red-and-white royal flag, Dupetit-Thouars deposed the queen on

8 November 1843 and occupied her kingdom, an arbitrary act that was rejected by the French king, who reestablished the protectorate in 1844. Queen Pomare fled to Raiatea and Pritchard was deported to England in March 1844, bringing Britain and France to the brink of war. The Tahitians resisted for three years: old French forts and war memorials recall the struggle.

A French Protectorate

At the beginning of 1847, when Queen Pomare realized that no British assistance was forthcoming, she and her people reluctantly accepted the French protectorate. As a compromise, the British elicited a promise from the French not to annex the Leeward Islands, so Huahine, Raiatea, and Bora Bora remained independent until 1887. The French had taken possession of the Marquesas in 1842, even before imposing a protectorate on Tahiti. The Austral Islands were added in 1900 and only prior British action prevented the annexation of the Cook Islands. French missionaries attempted to convert the Tahitians to Catholicism, but only in the Marquesas were they fully successful.

Queen Pomare tried to defend the interests of her people as best she could, but much of her nation was dying: between the 18th century and 1926 the population of the Marquesas fell from 80,000 to only 2,000. In April 1774 Captain Cook had tried to estimate the population of Tahiti by counting the number of men he saw in a fleet of war canoes and ascribing three members to each one's family. Cook's figure was 204,000, but according to anthropologist Bengt Danielsson, the correct number at the time of discovery was about 150,000. By 1829 it had dropped to 8,568, and a low of 7,169 was reached in 1865. The name "Pomare" means "night cough," from po, night, plus mare, cough, because Pomare I's infant daughter died of tuberculosis in 1792.

Pomare V, the final, degenerate member of the line, was more interested in earthly pleasures than the traditions upheld by his mother. In 1880, with French interests at work on the Panama Canal, a smart colonial administrator convinced him to sign away his kingdom for a 5,000-franc-a-month pension. Thus, on 29 June 1880 the protectorate became the full French colony it is today, the "Etablissements français de l'Océanie." In 1957 the name was changed to "Polynésie française." Right up until the 1970s the colony was run by governors appointed in Paris who implemented the policies of the French government. There was no system of indirect rule through local chiefs as was the case in the British colonies: here French officials decided everything and their authority could not be questioned. Even the 18-member Conseil Générale created in 1885 to oversee certain financial matters had its powers reduced in 1899, and was replaced in 1903 by an impotent advisory council composed of French civil servants. The only elected official with any authority (and a budget) was the mayor of Papeete.

The most earthshaking event between 1880 and 1960 was a visit by two German cruisers, the Scharnhorst and Gneisenau, which shelled Papeete, destroying the marketplace on 22 September 1914. (Two months later both were sunk by the British at the Battle of the Falkland Islands.) A thousand Tahitian volunteers subsequently served in Europe, 300 of them becoming casualties. On 2 September 1940 the colony declared its support for the Free French, and soon after Pearl Harbor the Americans arrived to establish a base on Bora Bora. Polynesia remained cut off from occupied metropolitan France until the end of the war, although several hundred Tahitians served with the Pacific battalion in North Africa and Italy. In 1946 the colony was made an overseas territory or territoire d'outre-mer (TOM) endowed with an elected territorial assembly. Representation in the French parliament was also granted.

The economy of the early colonial period had been based on cotton growing (1865-1900), vanilla cultivation (1870-1960), pearl shell collecting (1870-1960), copra making, and phosphate mining (1908-1966). These were to be replaced by nuclear testing (1963-1996), tourism (1961-present), and cultured pearls (1968-present).

The Nuclear Era

The early 1960s were momentous times for Polynesia. Within a few years, MGM filmed Mutiny on the Bounty, an international airport opened on Tahiti, and the French began testing their atomic bombs. After Algeria became independent in July 1962 the French decided to move their Sahara nuclear testing facilities to Moruroa Atoll in the Tuamotu Islands, 1,200 km southeast of

Tahiti. In 1963, when all local political parties protested the invasion of Polynesia by thousands of French troops and technicians sent to establish a nuclear testing center, President Charles de Gaulle simply outlawed political parties. The French set off their first atmospheric nuclear explosion at Moruroa on 2 July 1966, spreading contamination as far as Peru and New Zealand. In 1974 international protests forced the French to switch to the underground tests that continued until 1996. During those three decades of infamy 181 nuclear explosions, 41 of them in the atmosphere, rocked the Tuamotus.

In the 1960s-70s, as independence blossomed across the South Pacific, France tightened its strategic grip on Tahiti-Polynesia. The spirit of the time is best summed up in the life of one man, Pouvanaa a Oopa, an outspoken WW I hero from Huahine. In 1949 he became the first Polynesian to occupy a seat in the French Chamber of Deputies. His party gained control of the territorial assembly in 1953 and in 1957 he was elected vice-president of the newly formed Government Council. In 1958 Pouvanaa campaigned for independence in a referendum vote, but when this failed due to a controversy over the imposition of an income tax, the French government reestablished central control and had Pouvanaa arrested on trumped-up charges of arson. He was eventually sentenced to an eight-year prison term, and exiled to France for 15 years. De Gaulle wanted Pouvanaa out of the way until French nuclear testing facilities could be established in Polynesia, and he was not freed until 1968. In 1971 he won the "French" Polynesian seat in the French Senate, a post he held until his death in early 1977. Tahitians refer to the man as *metua* (father), and his statue stands in front of Papeete's Territorial Assembly.

Pouvanaa's successors, John Teariki and Francis Sanford, were also defenders of Polynesian autonomy and opponents of nuclear testing. Their combined efforts convinced the French government to grant Polynesia a new statute with a slightly increased autonomy in 1977. In 1982 the neo-Gaullist Tahoeraa Huiraatira (Popular Union) won the territorial elections, and the pronuclear, anti-independence mayor of Pirae, Gaston Flosse, became head of the local government. To stem growing support for independence, Flosse negotiated enhanced autonomy

for the territory in 1984 and 1996. The leading pro-independence party is the Tavini Huiraatira, the Polynesian Liberation Front, formed in 1978 by Faa'a mayor Oscar Temaru.

The independence cause was given impetus by a heavy-handed last fling at nuclear testing by the French government. In April 1992, President Mitterrand halted the testing program at Moruroa, but in June 1995, newly elected President Jacques Chirac ordered a resumption of underground nuclear testing in the Tuamotus, and despite worldwide protests the first test was carried out on 5 September 1995. Early the next morning nonviolent demonstrators blocked the runway of Faa'a Airport because they believed Gaston Flosse was attempting to escape on a flight to France. When the police charged the protesters to clear the runway, the demonstration turned into an ugly riot in which the airport and Papeete were ransacked.

Meanwhile at the Moruroa test site, two large Greenpeace protest vessels had been boarded by tear gas-firing French commandos and impounded (the ships were only released six months later). With the local opposition crushed, the rest of the Chirac tests went ahead without incident. However, worldwide condemnation of the series reached unprecedented levels, and in January 1996 the French announced that the testing had been completed. The facilities on Moruroa have since been decommissioned and it's almost inconceivable that the testing could ever resume, yet deadly radiation may already be leaking into the sea through cracks in the atoll's porous coral cap. A mantle of secrecy continues to hang over the France's former nuclear playground in the South Pacific and the credibility of official French sources on this subject is almost nil. (For more information, turn to **The Nuclear Test Zone** in this book's Tuamotu Islands section.)

GOVERNMENT

In 1885 an organic decree created the colonial system of government, which remained in effect until the proclamation of a new statute in 1958. In 1977 the French granted the territory partial internal self-government, and Francis Sanford was elected premier of "autonomous"

Polynesia. A new local-government statute, passed by the French parliament and promulgated on 6 September 1984, gave slightly more powers to the Polynesians, and in 1996 additional powers were transferred to the territory to slow the momentum toward full independence. Yet the constitution of the Republic of France remains the supreme law of the land. Territorial laws can be overridden by the French Parliament or the Constitutional Commission, and administrative decisions by territorial officials can be overturned by French judges.

A Territorial Assembly elects the president of the government, who chooses 15 cabinet ministers. The 41 assembly members are elected every five years from separate districts, with 22 seats from Tahiti/Moorea, eight from the Leeward Islands, five from the Tuamotus and Gambiers, three from the Australs, and three from the Marquesas. The territory is represented in Paris by two elected deputies, a senator, and a social and economic counselor. The French government, through its high commissioner (called governor until 1977), retains control over foreign relations, immigration, defense, justice, the police, the municipalities, higher education, TV and radio, property rights, and the currency.

Tahiti-Polynesia is divided into 48 communes, each with an elected Municipal Council, which chooses a mayor from its ranks. Every main town on an island will have its *mairie* (town hall). These elected municipal bodies, however, are controlled by appointed French civil servants, who run the five administrative subdivisions. The administrators of the Windward, Tuamotu-Gambier, and Austral subdivisions are based at Papeete, while the headquarters of the Leeward Islands administration is at Uturoa (Raiatea), and that of the Marquesas Islands is at Taiohae (Nuku Hiva).

The territorial flag consists of horizontal red, white, and red bands with a double-hulled Polynesian sailing canoe superimposed on the white band. On the canoe are five figures representing the five archipelagos.

ECONOMY

Government Spending

Tahiti-Polynesia has the highest per capita gross domestic product (GDP) in the South Pacific, about US$15,500 pp or seven times as much as Fiji. Paris contributes little to the territorial budget, but it finances the many departments and services under the direct control of the high commissioner, spending an average of US$1 billion a year in the territory or almost a third of the GDP. Most of it goes to the military and to the 2,200 expatriate French civil servants who earn salaries 84% higher than those doing the same work in France. Of the total workforce of 45,000, about 16,500 work for some level of government while the other 28,500 are privately employed.

The inflow of people and money since the early 1960s has substituted consumerism for subsistence, and except for tourism and cultured pearls, the economy of Tahiti-Polynesia is now totally dominated by French government spending. The nuclear testing program provoked an influx of 30,000 French settlers, plus a massive infusion of capital, which distorted the formerly self-supporting economy into one totally dependent on France. In the early 1960s, many Polynesians left their homes for construction jobs with the *Centre d'Expérimentations du Pacifique* (CEP), the government, and the hotel chains. Now that the volume of this work is decreasing, most of them subsist in precarious circumstances on Tahiti, dependent on government spending.

In 1994 the territorial government introduced an income tax of two percent on earnings over CFP 150,000 a month where none had previously existed, plus new taxes on gasoline, wine, telecommunications, and unearned income. The conclusion of nuclear testing in 1996 meant that 1,000 local workers had to be laid off and tax revenues on military imports suddenly dropped. To compensate for this and to shore up the political fortunes of their local allies, the French government agreed to a "Pacte de Progrès" which will provide the territory with an additional subsidy of US$200 million a year until 2005.

Trade

Prior to the start of nuclear testing, trade was balanced. Only 30 years later, 1996 imports stood at CFP 89,388 million while exports amounted to just CFP 15,452 million, one of the highest disparities in the world. Much of the imbalance is consumed by the French administration itself, and 17% of imports are related to military activities. Foreign currency spent by tourists on imported goods and services also helps steady the situation. A plan exists to lift income from exports and tourism to 50% of the value of imports by the year 2003.

Nearly half the imports come from France, which has imposed a series of self-favoring restrictions. Imports include food, fuel, building material, consumer goods, and automobiles. The main agricultural export from the outer islands is copra; production has been heavily subsidized by the government since 1967 to discourage migration to Tahiti. The copra is crushed into coconut oil and animal feed at the Papeete mill, while cultured pearls from farms in the Tuamotus are the biggest export by far. Perfume, vanilla, and monoï oil are also exported.

Indirect taxes, such as licensing fees and customs duties of 20-200%, have long accounted for more than half of territorial government revenue, and the price of many imported goods is more than doubled by taxation. There's also a flat 35% levy on businesses, which is simply passed along to consumers. In late 1998 it was announced that customs duties were to be phased out and replaced by a taxe sur la valeur ajoutée (TVA) or value-added tax (VAT). Since 1 January 1998 a three percent TVA has been added to the price of most goods and services, and this is to be increased to 15% over five years.

Agriculture

Labor recruiting for the nuclear testing program caused local agriculture to collapse in the mid-'60s. Between 1962 and 1988 the percentage of the workforce employed in agriculture and fishing dropped from 46% to 10%, and since then the proportion has declined even further. Exports of coffee and vanilla had ceased completely by 1965 and coconut products dropped 40% despite massive subsidies. Vanilla, copra, and coconut oil combined now comprise only four percent of exports. South Korean companies pay US$1.5 million a year in licensing fees to fish the territory's exclusive economic zone.

About 80% of all food consumed locally is imported. Tahiti-Polynesia does manage, however, to cover three-quarters of its own fruit requirements, and most of the local pineapple and grapefruit crop goes to the fruit-juice factory on Moorea. In the 1880s-90s four million oranges a

year were exported to Australia, New Zealand, and California. The industry was wiped out by a blight at the turn of the century, and now only a few trees grow wild.

Local vegetables supply half of local needs, while Tahitian coffee covers 20% of consumption. Considerable livestock is kept in the Marquesas. Large areas have been planted in Caribbean pine to provide for future timber needs. Aquaculture, with tanks for freshwater shrimp, prawns, live bait, and green mussels, is being developed. Most industry is related to food processing (fruit-juice factory, brewery, soft drinks, etc.) or coconut products. It's rumored that marijuana (pakalolo) is now the leading cash crop, though you won't be aware of it.

Cultured Pearls

Tahiti-Polynesia's cultured-pearl industry, now second only to tourism as a money earner, originated in 1963 when an experimental farm was established on Hikueru atoll in the Tuamotus. The first commercial farm opened on Manihi in 1968, but the real boom only began in the late 1980s and today hundreds of cooperative and private pearl farms operate on 26 atolls, employing thousands of people. Fourteen large companies account for half of production with the rest coming from 50 smaller companies and 450 family operations. The industry is drawing many Tahitians back to ancestral islands they abandoned after devastating hurricanes in 1983. Pearl farming is ecologically benign, relieving pressure on natural stocks and creating a need to protect marine environments. Pollution from fertilizer runoff or sewage can make a lagoon unsuitable for pearl farming, which is why the farms are concentrated on lightly populated atolls where other forms of agriculture are scarcely practiced.

Unlike the Japanese cultured white pearl, the Polynesian black pearl is created only by the giant blacklipped oyster (Pinctada margaritifera), which thrives in the Tuamotu lagoons. Beginning in the 19th century the oysters were collected by Polynesian divers who could dive up to 40 meters. The shell was made into mother-of-pearl buttons; finding a pearl this way was pure chance. By the middle of this century overharvesting had depleted the slow-growing oyster beds and today live oysters are collected only to supply cultured-pearl farms. The shell is now a mere by-product, made into decorative items or exported. The strings of oysters must be monitored constantly and lowered or raised if there are variations in water temperature.

It takes around three years for a pearl to form in a seeded oyster. A spherical pearl is formed when a Mississippi River mussel graft is introduced inside the coat; the oyster only creates a hemispherical half pearl if the graft goes between the coat and the shell. Half pearls are much cheaper than whole pearls and make outstanding rings and pendants. Some of the grafts used are surprisingly large and the layer of nacre

---

BUYING A BLACK PEARL

The relative newness of this gemstone is reflected in varying prices. A radiant, perfectly round, smooth, and flawless pearl with a good depth of metallic green/blue can sell for many times more than a similar pearl with only one or two defects. The luster is more important than the color. Size can vary from eight millimeters to 20 millimeters with the larger pearls that much more expensive. Black pearls are now in fashion in Paris, so don't expect any bargains. A first class necklace can cost as much as US$50,000 and individual pearls of high quality cost US$1000 and up, but slightly flawed pearls are much cheaper (beginning at US$100). The "baroque" pearls still make exquisite jewelry when mounted in gold and platinum.

Consider purchasing a loose pearl and having it mounted back home. If you think you might do this, check with your local jeweler before leaving for Tahiti. Half the fun is in the shopping, so be in no hurry to decide and don't let yourself be influenced by a driver or guide who may only be after a commission. If no guide is involved the shop may even pay the commission to you in the form of a discount (ask). It's preferable to buy pearls at a specialized shop rather than somewhere which also sells pareus and souvenirs (and never buy a pearl from a person on the street). A reputable dealer will always give you an invoice or certificate verifying the authenticity of your pearl. If you've made an expensive choice ask the dealer to make a fresh X-ray right in front of you in order to be sure of the quality.

---

around such pearls may be relatively thin, but only an X-ray can tell. Thin coating on a pearl greatly reduces its value.

The cooperatives sell their production at Papeete auctions in April and October. The pearls are usually offered to bidders in unmixed batches. Local jewelers vie with Japanese buyers at these events, with some 65,000 black pearls changing hands for about US$5 million. Private producers sell their pearls through independent dealers or plush retail outlets in Papeete. Every year about a million black pearls worth US$150 million are exported to Japan, Hong Kong, Singapore, and the U.S., making the territory the world's second-largest source of loose pearls (after Australia which produces the smaller yellow pearls). By comparison, the combined export value of coconut oil, copra, mother of pearl shells, vanilla, fruit, and vegetables is paltry at around US$8 million.

Tourism

Tourism only got underway with the opening of Faa'a Airport in 1961 and today Tahiti-Polynesia is second only to Fiji as a South Pacific tourist center, with 180,440 visitors in 1997, a quarter of them from France and another quarter from the United States. Japan, New Zealand, Germany, Italy, Britain, Canada, and New Caledonia also account for significant numbers. Even though flying from Los Angeles to Tahiti takes only three hours longer than flying to Honolulu, tourism is far less developed here than it is in Hawaii. A single Waikiki hotel could have more rooms than the entire island of Tahiti; Hawaii gets more visitors in 10 days than Tahiti-Polynesia gets in a year.

Miscalculations of distance and reports of high prices have kept Tahiti out of the American mass market, and high local labor costs have hampered development (the minimum wage is CFP 505 an hour). Now tourism by high-budget Japanese (especially honeymooners) is being vigorously promoted and the number of European visitors is growing quickly. The US$360 million a year generated by tourism covers 28% of Tahiti-Polynesia's import bill and provides thousands of jobs, but 80% of the things tourists buy are also imported.

Transnational corporations, either hotel chains, tour companies, or airlines, dominate the tourist industry. Top management of the big hotels is invariably French or foreign, as ownership rests with Japanese (Beachcomber Parkroyal, Bora Bora Lagoon, Kia Ora Village), French (Sofitel/Accor, Club Med, Méridien), and American (Bali Hai and Outrigger) corporations. Air New Zealand promotes Tahiti only as a stopover on the way to Auckland, limiting many tourists to a few nights in Papeete.

Many Polynesians are rather nervous about this transnational tourism development, and in June 1991 Moorea voters decided against a US$93.4 million Sheraton hotel and Arnold Palmer championship golf course that Japanese investors had wanted to build on their island. In May 1990 the traditional owners of Tupai, just north of Bora Bora, blocked the atoll's sale to a Japanese corporation that had intended to build a major resort there. On Tahiti, protest occupations by hundreds of Tahitians from April 1992 to January 1996 tried unsuccessfully to halt construction of Hôtel Le Méridien near the Museum of Tahiti in Punaauia. Tourism from Japan almost dried up during the 1995 nuclear testing but visitor levels are growing again.

THE PEOPLE

The 1996 population of 219,521 is around 68% Polynesian, 11% European, 12% Polynesian/European, five percent Chinese, and three percent Polynesian/Chinese. All are French citizens. About 69% of the total population lives on Tahiti (compared to only 25% before the nuclear-testing boom began in the 1960s), but a total of 65 far-flung islands are inhabited.

The indigenous people of Tahiti-Polynesia are the Maohi or Eastern Polynesians (as opposed to the Western Polynesians in Samoa and Tonga), and some local nationalists refer to their country as Te Ao Maohi. The word *colon* formerly applied to Frenchmen who arrived long before the bomb and made a living as planters or traders, and practically all of them married Polynesian women. Most of these *colons* have already passed away and their descendants are termed *demis,* or *afa.* The present Europeans are mostly recently arrived metropolitan French *(faranis).* Most *faranis* live in urban areas or are involved in the administration or military. Their numbers increased dramatically in the 1960s

and 1970s. In contrast, very few Polynesians have migrated to France although 7,000 reside in New Caledonia.

Local Chinese *(tinito)* dominate the retail trade throughout the territory. In Papeete and Uturoa entire streets are lined with Chinese stores, and individual Chinese merchants are found on almost every island. During the American Civil War, when the supply of cotton to Europe was disrupted, Scotsman William Stewart decided to set up a cotton plantation on the south side of Tahiti. Unable to convince Tahitians to accept the heavy work, Stewart brought in a contingent of 1,010 Chinese laborers from Canton in 1865-66. When the war ended the enterprise went bankrupt, but many of the Chinese managed to stay on as market gardeners, hawkers, and opium dealers. Although all Tahitians became French citizens right after WW II, this status was granted to the territory's Chinese only in 1964.

From 1976 to 1983 some 18,000 people migrated to the territory, 77% of them from France and another 13% from New Caledonia. Nearly 1,000 new settlers a year continue to arrive. Some 40,000 Europeans are now present in the territory, plus 8,000 soldiers, policemen, and

a Polynesian woman

transient officials. Most Tahitians would like to see this immigration restricted, as it is in virtually every other Pacific state.

There's an undercurrent of anti-French sentiment; English speakers are better liked by the Tahitians. Yet inevitably the newcomers get caught up in the Polynesian openness and friendliness—even the surliest Parisian. In fact, the Gallic charm you'll experience even in government offices is a delight. Tahiti-Polynesia really is a friendly place.

Tahitian Life

For the French, lunch is the main meal of the day, followed by a siesta. Dinner may consist of leftovers from lunch. Tahitians traditionally eat their main meal of fish and native vegetables in the evening, when the day's work is over. People at home often take a shower before or after a meal and put flowers in their hair. If folks are in a good mood, a guitar or ukulele might appear.

Tahitians often observe with amusement or disdain the efforts of individuals to rise above the group. In a society where sharing and reciprocal generosity have traditionally been important qualities, the deliberate accumulation of personal wealth was always viewed as a vice. Now with the influx of government and tourist money, Tahitian life is changing, quickly in Papeete, more slowly in the outer islands. To prevent the Polynesians from being made paupers in their own country, foreigners other than French are not usually permitted to purchase land here and 85% of the land is still owned by the Polynesians. A new impoverished class is forming among those who have sold their ancestral lands to recent French immigrants.

The educational curriculum is entirely French. Children enter school at age three and for 12 years study the French language, literature, culture, history, and geography, but not much about Polynesia. Although 80% of the population speaks Tahitian at home there is little formal training in it (teaching in Tahitian has only been allowed since 1984). The failure rate ranges 40-60%, and most of the rest of the children are behind schedule. The brightest students are given scholarships to continue studying, while many of the dropouts become delinquents. About a quarter of the schools are privately run by the churches, but

festival fun, Papeete

TAHITI TOURISME

these must teach exactly the same curriculum or lose their subsidies. The whole aim is to transform the Polynesians into Pacific French. In 1987 the Université française du Pacifique (B.P. 4635, 98713 Papeete; tel. 42-16-80, fax 41-01-31) opened on Tahiti, specializing in law, humanities, social sciences, languages, and science.

Most Tahitians live along the coast because the interior is too rugged and possibly inhabited by *tupapau* (ghosts). Some people leave a light on all night in their home for the latter reason. A traditional Tahitian residence consists of several separate buildings: the *fare tutu* (kitchen), the *fare tamaa* (dining area), the *fare taoto* (bedrooms), plus bathing and sanitary outhouses. Often several generations live together, and young children are sent to live with their grandparents. Adoption is commonplace and family relationships complex. Young Tahitians generally go out as groups, rather than on individual "dates."

The lifestyle may be summed up in the words *aita e peapea* (no problem) and *fiu* (fed up, bored). About the only time the normally languid Tahitians go really wild is when they're dancing or behind the wheel of a car.

Sex

Since the days of Wallis and Bougainville, Tahitian women have had a reputation for promiscuity. Well, for better or worse, this is largely a thing of the past, if it ever existed at all. As a short-term visitor your liaisons with Tahitians are likely to remain polite. Westerners' obsession with the sexuality of Polynesians usually reflects their own frustrations, and the view that Tahitian morality is loose is rather ironic considering that Polynesians have always shared whatever they have, cared for their old and young, and refrained from ostracizing unwed mothers or attaching stigma to their offspring. The good Christian Tahitians of today are highly moral and compassionate.

Polynesia's *mahus* or "third sex" bear little of the stigma attached to female impersonators in the West. A young boy may adopt the female role by his own choice or that of his parents, performing female tasks at home and eventually finding a job usually performed by women, such as serving in a restaurant or hotel. Generally only one *mahu* exists in each village or community, proof that this type of individual serves a certain sociological function. George Mortimer of the British ship *Mercury* recorded an encounter with a *mahu* in 1789. Though Tahitians may poke fun at a *mahu*, they're fully accepted in society, seen teaching Sunday school, etc. Many, but not all, *mahus* are also homosexuals. Today, with money all-important, some transvestites have involved themselves in male prostitution and the term *raerae* has been coined for this category. Now there are even Miss Tane (Miss Male) beauty contests! All this may be seen as the degradation of a phenomenon that has always been a part of Polynesian life.

Religion

Though the old Polynesian religion died out in the early 19th century, the Tahitians are still a strongly religious people. Protestant missionaries arrived on Tahiti 39 years before the Catholics and 47 years before the Mormons, so almost half of the Polynesians now belong to the Evangelical Church, which is strongest in the Austral and Leeward Islands. Until the middle of the 20th century this church was one of the only democratic institutions in the colony and it continues to exert strong influence on social matters (for example, it resolutely opposed nuclear testing).

Of the 35% of the total population who are Catholic, half are Polynesians from the Tuamotus and Marquesas, and the other half are French. Another eight percent are Seventh-Day Adventists and seven percent are Mormons. A Mormon group called Sanitos, which rejects Brigham Young as a second prophet, has had a strong following in the Tuamotus since the 19th century. Several other Christian sects are also represented, and some Chinese are Buddhists. It's not unusual to see two or three different churches in a village of 100 people. All the main denominations operate their own schools. Local ministers and priests are powerful figures in the outer-island communities. One vestige of the pre-Christian religion is a widespread belief in ghosts *(tupapau)*.

Protestant church services are conducted mostly in Tahitian, Catholic services are in French. Sitting through one (one to two hours) is often worthwhile just to hear the singing and to observe the women's hats. Never wear a pareu to church—you'll be asked to leave. Young missionaries from the Church of Latter-day Saints (Mormons) continue to flock to Polynesia from the U.S. for two-year stays. They wear short-sleeved white shirts with ties and travel in pairs—you may spot a couple.

Language

French is spoken throughout the territory, and visitors will sometimes have difficulty making themselves understood in English, although most of those involved in the tourist industry speak some English. Large Chinese stores often have someone who speaks English, though members of the Chinese community use Hakka among themselves. Young Polynesians often become curious and friendly when they hear you speaking English. Still, unless you're on a package tour everything will be a lot easier if you know at least a little French. Check out some French language recordings from your local public library to brush up your high school French before you arrive. The **Capsule French Vocabulary** at the end of the New Caledonia chapter may also help you get by. (It's often the recently arrived French immigrants who are the most arrogant, a reflection of the way monolingual English-speakers are treated in France itself.)

Tahitian has been recognized as an official language alongside French only since 1980. Contemporary Tahitian is the chiefly or royal dialect used in the translation of the Bible by early Protestant missionaries, and today, as communications improve, the outer-island dialects are becoming mingled with the predominant Tahitian. Tahitian or Maohi is one of a family of Austronesian languages spoken from Madagascar through Indonesia, all the way to Easter Island and Hawaii. The related languages of Eastern Polynesia (Hawaiian, Tahitian, Tuamotuan, Mangarevan, Marquesan, Rarotongan, Maori) are quite different from those of Western Polynesia (Samoan, Tongan). Among the Polynesian languages the consonants did the changing rather than the vowels. The *k* and *l* in Hawaiian are generally rendered as a *t* and *r* in Tahitian.

Instead of attempting to speak French to the Tahitians—a foreign language for you both—turn to the Tahitian vocabulary at the end of this chapter and give it a try. Remember to pronounce each vowel separately, *a* as the *ah* in "far," *e* as the *ai* in "day," *i* as the *ee* in "see," *o* as the *oh* in "go," and *u* as the *oo* in "lulu"—the same as in Latin or Spanish. Written Tahitian has only eight consonants: *f, h, m, n, p, r, t, v.* Two consonants never follow one another, and all words end in a vowel. No silent letters exist in Tahitian, but there is a glottal stop, often marked with an apostrophe. A slight variation in pronunciation or vowel length can change the meaning of a word completely, so don't be surprised if your efforts produce some unexpected results!

CONDUCT AND CUSTOMS

The dress code in Tahiti-Polynesia is very casual—you can even go around barefoot. Cleanliness *is* important, however. Formal wear or jacket and tie are unnecessary (unless you're to be received by the high commissioner!). One exception is downtown Papeete, where scanty dress would be out of place. For clothing tips, see **What to Take** in the On the Road chapter.

People usually shake hands when meeting; visitors are expected to shake hands with every-

one present. If a Polynesian man's hand is dirty he'll extend his wrist or elbow. Women kiss each other on the cheeks. When entering a private residence it's polite to remove your shoes.

All the beaches of Tahiti-Polynesia are public to one meter above the high-tide mark, although some watchdogs don't recognize this. Topless sunbathing is completely legal in Tahiti-Polynesia and commonly practiced at the resorts by European tourists, though total nudity is only practiced on offshore *motus* and floating pontoons.

Despite the apparent laissez-faire attitude promoted in the travel brochures and this book, female travelers should take care: there have been sexual assaults by Polynesian men on foreign women. Peeping toms can be a nuisance both in budget accommodations and on beaches away from the main resorts, and women should avoid staying alone in isolated tourist bungalows or camping outside organized campgrounds. A California reader who was there in September 1998 sent us this:

My friend and I must have been unusual looking travelers. Though we dressed in pants and baggy clothes when we had to go to town, our age (we're both 26) and not unattractive appearance drew some very undesirable attention. Video rental stores are a common sight here and the local men seem to have developed ideas about what white women are after from watching blue movies. So we found ourselves being threatened time and again by aggressive local men. On Bora Bora we took an all-day outrigger trip and found ourselves left alone with the guides in the afternoon. We didn't know how to cancel at that point, so we were taken to a motu *for lunch. The two male guides extended our time on the* motu *so long that we were both sunburnt despite 45 block and entirely missed the afternoon activities we had paid for. At 1530 we had to insist they bring us back to shore. We didn't panic on the* motu *and escaped unhurt, but I think it is essential that you include a caution for all single women traveling in Tahiti to make sure there are other guests, including couples* or men, on these day-trips before putting themselves in the hands of strangers. We had to forego any future island trips, including safaris, for fear of the guides themselves. Based on our experience I would say that for women, even in pairs, things like hiking, hitchhiking, or walking along the road should not be taken lightly. The harassment continued even in very rural parts of the islands and we had to learn to be very unfriendly, even rude, to keep men from aggressively entering our space/lives. Our joke came to be, "women wandering alone?—must be looking for sex," as this was definitely the local male mindset and it was evidenced by the fact that young Tahitian women were never seen walking around away from their parent's homes, but young men were everywhere. Even at the main resorts we had problems with the entertainment staff hitting on us every time we went to a show. On Moorea we'd booked a charming beach fare and spent a positively terrible first night there. The locks on our unit were unreliable and we were soon discovered by the local men, several of whom began to slink around quietly behind our bungalow or watch us from the shadows at the corner of the beach. As it got dark, we kept hearing people standing directly outside our bungalow or darting past our windows. It was terrifying and we slept in shifts, barricading the door and arming ourselves as best we could. It wasn't until 0400 that the bastards finally left the area. There was no other reason they should have been there— a wall was directly behind the place and only other guests slept nearby. I'm sure we were targeted for more than theft. The next morning we insisted on having our deposit back and moved to the Sofitel Ia Ora where we felt safe, although the motu guides still did their best to get us into their boats (we began to call that the motu scam). I think women visitors are best not even saying hello to men who approach them here—rudeness seems to be the only reaction that does not signal the wrong thing. Don't think we were unable see the humor in some of this and make the most of our stay—but it would have been helpful if we'd known about it beforehand from your book.

In addition to the situation outlined above, we've heard of cases of laundry being stolen from the line, hotel and car break-ins, park muggings, and even mass holdups at knifepoint, but luckily such things are still the exception here and it's highly unlikely you'll become a victim of armed robbery. Do keep an eye on your valuables, however.

ON THE ROAD

Highlights

Tahiti-Polynesia abounds in things to see and do, including many in the "not to be missed" category. Papeete's colorful morning market and captivating waterfront welcome you to Polynesia. Travelers should not pass up the opportunity to take the ferry ride to Moorea and see the island's stunning Opunohu Valley, replete with splendid scenery, lush vegetation, and fascinating archaeological sites. Farther afield, an even greater concentration of old Polynesian *marae* (temples) awaits visitors to Maeva on the enchanting island of Huahine. The natural wonders of Bora Bora have been applauded many times, but neighboring Maupiti offers more of the same, though its pleasures are less well known. Polynesia's most spectacular atoll may be Rangiroa, where the Avatoru and Tiputa passes offer exciting snorkel rides on the tide flows. The shark feeding and manta ray viewing on Rangiroa, Bora Bora, and other islands, and dolphin encounters on Moorea, are memorable experiences.

Sports and Recreation

As elsewhere in the South Pacific, **scuba diving** is the most popular sport among visitors, and well-established dive shops exist on Tahiti, Moorea, Huahine, Raiatea, Bora Bora, Rangiroa, Manihi, Tikehau, Fakarava, and Nuku Hiva. The best coral and marinelife viewing by far is available in the Tuamotus and serious divers won't go wrong by choosing Rangiroa, the shark-viewing capital of Polynesia. In the warm waters of Polynesia wetsuits are not required. If you take a scuba certification course make sure it's PADI accredited as the French CMAS certification may not be recognized elsewhere.

There's good **surfing** around Tahiti, Moorea, Huahine, and Raiatea, usually hurricane swells on the north shores Oct.-March (summer) and Antarctic swells on the south shores April-Sept. (winter). The summer swells are the same ones that hit Hawaii three or four days earlier and the reef breaks off the north shore of Moorea work better than Tahiti's beach breaks. The most powerful, hollow waves are in winter. The reef breaks in the passes are a lot longer paddle than those off the beach (where you can expect lots of company).

Excellent, easily accessible **hiking** areas exist on Tahiti, Moorea, and Nuku Hiva. **Horseback riding** is readily available on Moorea, Huahine, Raiatea, and in the Marquesas with the Huahine and Raiatea operations especially recommended. **Golfers** will certainly want to complete all 18 holes at the International Golf Course Olivier Breaud on Tahiti, the territory's only major course. The Society Islands are a sailor's paradise with numerous protected anchorages and excellent **sailing** weather, which is why most of Tahiti-Polynesia's charter yacht operations are concentrated on Raiatea.

Entertainment

The big hotels on Tahiti, Moorea, Huahine, and Bora Bora offer exciting dance shows several nights a week. They're usually accompanied by a barbecue or traditional feast, but if the price

asked for the meal is too steep, settle for a drink at the bar and enjoy the show (no cover charge). Many of the regular performances are listed in this book, but be sure to call the hotel to confirm the time and date as these do change to accommodate tour groups.

On Friday and Saturday nights discos crank up in most towns and these are good places to meet the locals. The nonhotel bar scene is limited mostly to Papeete and Uturoa. The drinking age in Tahiti-Polynesia is officially 18, but it's not strictly enforced.

Music and Dance
Though the missionaries banned dancing completely in the 1820s and the 19th-century French colonial administration only allowed performances that didn't disturb Victorian decorum, traditional Tahitian dancing experienced a revival in the 1950s with the formation of Madeleine Moua's Pupu Heiva dance troupe, followed in the 1960s by Coco Hotahota's Temaeva and Gilles Hollande's Ora Tahiti. These groups rediscovered the near-forgotten myths of old Polynesia and popularized them with exciting music, dance, song, and costumes. During major festivals several dozen troupes consisting of 20-50 dancers and 6-10 musicians participate in thrilling competitions.

The Tahitian *tamure* or *'ori Tahiti* is a fast, provocative, erotic dance done by rapidly shifting the weight from one foot to the other. The rubber-legged men are almost acrobatic, though their movements tend to follow those of the women closely. The tossing, shell-decorated fiber skirts *(mores)*, the hand-held pandanus wands, and the tall headdresses add to the drama.

Dances such as the *aparima, 'ote'a,* and *hivinau* reenact Polynesian legends, and each movement tells part of a story. The *aparima* is a dance resembling the Hawaiian hula or Samoan siva executed mainly with the hands in a standing or sitting position. The hand movements repeat the story told in the accompanying song. The *'ote'a* is a theme dance executed to the accompaniment of drums with great precision and admirable timing by a group of men and/or women arrayed in two lines. The *ute* is a restrained dance based on ancient refrains.

Listen to the staccato beat of the *to'ere,* a slit rosewood drum, each slightly different in size and pitch, hit with a stick. A split-bamboo drum *(ofe)* hit against the ground often provides a contrasting sound. The *pahu* is a more conventional bass drum made from a hollowed coconut tree trunk with a sharkskin cover. Its sound resembles the human heartbeat. The smallest *pahu* is the *fa'atete,* which is hit with sticks. Another traditional Polynesian musical instrument is the bamboo nose flute *(vivo),* which sounds rather like the call of a bird, though today guitars and ukuleles are more often seen. The ukulele was originally the *braguinha,* brought to Hawaii by Portuguese immigrants a century ago. Homemade ukuleles with the half-shells of coconuts as sound boxes emit pleasant tones, while those sporting empty tins give a more metallic sound. The hollow, piercing note produced by the conch shell or *pu* once accompanied pagan ceremonies on the *marae.*

Traditional Tahitian vocal music was limited to polyphonic chants conveying oral history and customs, and the contrapuntal *himene* or "hymn" sung by large choirs today is based on those ancient chants. The spiritual quality of the *himene* can be electrifying, so for the musical experience of a lifetime, attend church any Sunday.

Public Holidays and Festivals
Public holidays in Tahiti-Polynesia include New Year's Day (1 January), Gospel Day (5 March), Good Friday and Easter Monday (March/April), Labor Day (1 May), Victory Day (8 May), Ascension Day (May), Pentecost or Whitmonday (May/June), Internal Autonomy Day (29 June), Bastille Day (14 July), Assumption Day (15 August), All Saints' Day (1 November), Armistice Day (11 November), and Christmas Day (25 December). Ironically, Internal Autonomy Day really commemorates 29 June 1880 when King Pomare V was deposed and Tahiti-Polynesia became a full French colony, not 6 September 1984 when the territory achieved a degree of internal autonomy. *Everything* will be closed on these holidays (and maybe also the days before and after—ask).

The big event of the year is the two-week-long **Heiva i Tahiti,** which runs from the end of June to Bastille Day (14 July). Formerly known as La Fête du Juillet or the Tiurai Festival (the Tahitian word *tiurai* comes from the English July), the Heiva originated way back in 1882. Today it brings contestants and participants to Tahiti from all over the territory to take part in elaborate processions, competitive dancing and singing, feasting, and partying. There are bicycle, car, horse, and outrigger-canoe races, *pétanque,* archery, and javelin-throwing contests, fire walking, sidewalk bazaars, arts and crafts exhibitions, tattooing, games, and joyous carnivals. **Bastille Day** itself, which marks the fall of the Bastille in Paris on 14 July 1789 at the height of the French Revolution, features a military parade in the capital. Ask at the Papeete tourist office about when to see the historical reenactments at Marae Arahurahu, the canoe race along Papeete waterfront, horse racing at the Pirae track, and the traditional dance competitions at the Moorea ferry landing. Tickets to most Heiva events are sold at the Cultural Center in Papeete or at the door. As happens during carnival in Rio de Janeiro, you must pay to sit in the stands and watch the best performances, but acceptable seats begin at just CFP 500 and you get four hours or more of unforgettable nonstop entertainment.

The race of the banana bearers is part of July's Tiurai Festival.

TAHITI TOURISME

The July celebrations on Bora Bora are as good as those on Tahiti, and festivals are also held on Raiatea and Taha'a at that time. Note that all ships, planes, and hotels are fully booked around 14 July, so be in the right place beforehand or get firm reservations, especially if you want to be on Bora Bora that day.

Chinese New Year in January or February is celebrated with dances and fireworks. **World Environment Day** (5 June) is marked by guided excursions to Tahiti's interior and on the following weekend special activities are arranged at tourist sites around the island. The **Agricultural Fair** on Tahiti in mid-August involves the construction of a Tahitian village. The **Carnival** parade through Papeete is held at the end of October. On **All Saints' Day** (1 November) when the locals illuminate the cemeteries at Papeete, Arue, Punaauia, and elsewhere with candles. On **New Year's Eve** the Papeete waterfront is beautifully illuminated and there's a seven-km foot race. For advance information on special events and sporting competitions contact **Tahiti Manava** (B.P. 1710, 98713 Papeete; tel. 50-57-12, fax 45-16-78).

Major Sporting Events

The **Moorea Blue Marathon** has been held every February since 1988 (in 1997 Patrick Muturi of Kenya set the record time of two hours and 21.5 minutes). A traditional Maohi sports festival in late April features javelin throwing, rock lifting, coconut tree climbing, coconut husking, races while carrying loads of fruit, etc. Triathlons involving swimming, bicycling, and running are held on Moorea in April and May. The **Tahiti Open** at the Atimaono golf course on Tahiti is in July. The **Te Aito** individual outrigger canoe race is held on Tahiti around the end of July. The **Hawaiki Nui Va'a** outrigger canoe race in early November is a stirring three-day event with canoe teams crossing from Huahine to Raiatea the first day, Raiatea to Taha'a the second, and Taha'a to Bora Bora the third.

Shopping

Most local souvenir shops sell Marquesas-style wooden "tikis" carved from wood or stone. The original Tiki was a god of fertility, and really old tikis are still shrouded in superstition. Today they're viewed mainly as good luck charms and often come decorated with mother-of-pearl. Other items carved from wood include mallets (to beat tapa cloth), *umete* bowls, and slit *to'ere* drums. Carefully woven pandanus hats and mats come from the Australs. Other curios to buy include hand-carved mother-of-pearl shell, sharks'-tooth pendants, hematite (black stone) carvings, and bamboo fishhooks.

Black-pearl jewelry is widely available throughout Tahiti-Polynesia. The color, shape, weight, and size of the pearl are important. The darkest pearls are the most valuable. Prices vary considerably, so shop around before purchasing pearls.

As this is a French colony, it's not surprising that many of the best buys are related to fashion. A tropical shirt, sundress, or T-shirt is a purchase of immediate usefulness. The pareu is a typically Tahitian leisure garment consisting of a brightly colored hand-blocked or painted local fabric about two meters long and a meter wide. There are dozens of ways both men and women can wear a pareu and it's the most common apparel for local women throughout the territory, including Papeete, so pick one up! Local cosmetics like Monoï Tiare Tahiti, a fragrant coconut-oil skin moisturizer, and coconut-oil soap will put you in form. Jasmine shampoo, cologne, and perfume are also made locally from the tiare Tahiti flower. Vanilla is used to flavor coffee.

Early missionaries introduced the Tahitians to quilting, and two-layer patchwork *tifaifai* have now taken the place of tapa (bark cloth). Used as bed covers and pillows by tourists, *tifaifai* is still used by Tahitians to cloak newlyweds and to cover coffins. To be wrapped in a *tifaifai* is the highest honor. Each woman has individual quilt patterns that are her trademarks and bold floral designs are popular, with contrasting colors drawn from nature. A good *tifaifai* can take up to six months to complete and cost US$1,000. The French artist Henri Matisse, who in 1930 spent several weeks at the now-demolished Hôtel Stuart on Papeete's boulevard Pomare, was so impressed by the Tahitian *tifaifai* that he applied the same technique and adopted many designs for his *"gouaches découpees."*

Those who have been thrilled by hypnotic Tahitian music and dance will want to take some Polynesian music home with them on cassette (CFP 2,000) or compact disc (CFP 3,000), available at hotels and souvenir shops throughout the islands. The largest local company producing these CDs is Editions Manuiti or Tamure Records (B.P. 755, 98713 Papeete; tel. 42-82-39, fax 43-27-24). Among the well-known local singers and musicians appearing on Manuiti are Bimbo, Charley Mauu, Guy Roche, Yves Roche, Emma Terangi, Andy Tupaia, and Henriette Winkler. Small Tahitian groups like the Moorea Lagon Kaina Boys, the Barefoot Boys, and Tamarii Punaruu, and large folkloric ensembles such as Maeva Tahiti, Tiare Tahiti, and Coco's Temaeva (often recorded at major festivals) are also well represented. The Tahitian recordings of the Hawaiian artist Bobby Holcomb are highly recommended. Turn to **Resources** at the end of this book for specific CD listings.

Hustling and bargaining are not practiced in Tahiti-Polynesia: it's expensive for everyone. Haggling may even be considered insulting, so just pay the price asked or keep looking. Many local food prices are subsidized by the government. You can sometimes avoid whopping markups and taxes by purchasing food and handicrafts from the producers themselves at markets or roadside stalls.

ACCOMMODATIONS AND FOOD

Accommodations

A wise government regulation prohibiting buildings higher than a coconut tree outside Papeete means that most of the hotels are low-rise or consist of small Tahitian *fares.* As the lagoon waters off the northwest corner of Tahiti become increasingly polluted with raw sewage, hotels like the Beachcomber and Maeva Beach fall back on their swimming pools. On most of the outer islands open to foreign tourists, the water is so clear it makes pools superfluous.

Hotel prices range from CFP 800 for a dormitory bed all the way up to CFP 70,000 single or double without meals, plus tax. Price wars often erupt between rival hotels, and at times you're charged less than the prices quoted herein! When things are really slow even the luxury hotels sometimes discount their rooms. If your hotel can't provide running water, electricity, air-conditioning, or something similar because of a hurricane or otherwise, ask for a price reduction. You'll often get 10% off.

The budget places often provide cooking facilities; this allows you to save a lot on food.

An eight percent room tax used to finance tourism promotion is added to the room rates at the hotels (never included in the quoted price), but it doesn't apply to pensions and family-operated accommodations. Some islands such as Moorea and Bora Bora add a room tax of CFP 150 pp per day to accommodation bills to cover municipal services. Many small hotels add a surcharge to your bill if you stay only one night and some charge a supplement during the high seasons (July, August, and around Christmas). Discounts may be offered during the low months of February, March, September, and October.

A tent saves the budget traveler a lot of money and proves very convenient to fall back on. The Polynesians don't usually mind if you camp, and quite a few French locals also have tents. Regular campgrounds exist on Moorea, Huahine, Raiatea, and Bora Bora, catering to the growing number of camper-tourists. On Rangiroa it's possible to camp at certain small hotels (listed herein). On the outer islands camping should be no problem, but ask permission of the landowner, or pitch your tent well out of sight of the road. Please ensure this same hospitality for the next traveler by not leaving a mess. Make sure your tent is water- and mosquito-proof, and never pitch a tent directly below coconuts hanging from a tree or a precariously leaning trunk.

Paying Guests

A unique accommodations option worth looking into is the well-organized homestay program, in which you get a private room or bungalow with a local family. *Logement chez l'habitant* is available on all the outer islands, and even in Papeete itself; the tourist office supplies printed lists. Many travel agents abroad won't book the cheaper hotels or lodgings with the inhabitants because no commissions are paid, but you can make reservations directly with the owners themselves either by mail or phone. Letters are usually not answered, so calling ahead from Papeete is best; things change fast and the printed listings are often out of date. One Papeete travel agency specializing in such bookings is **Tekura Tahiti Travel** (B.P. 2971, 98713 Papeete; tel. 43-12-00, fax 42-84-60, e-mail: go@tahiti-tekuratravel.com) in Papeete's Vaima Center, although they tend to work with the more upmarket places. Most pensions don't accept credit cards, and English may not be spoken.

These private guesthouses can be hard to locate. There's usually no sign outside, and some don't cater to walk-in clients who show up unexpectedly. Also, the limited number of beds in each may all be taken. Sometimes you'll get airport transfers at no additional charge if you book ahead. Don't expect hot water in the shower or a lot of privacy. Blankets and especially towels may not be provided. Often meals are included (typically seafood), which can make these places quite expensive. If you're on a budget, ask for a place with cooking facilities and prepare your own food. The family may loan you a bicycle and can be generally helpful in arranging tours, etc. It's a great way to meet the people while finding a place to stay.

Food and Drink

The restaurants are often exorbitant, but you can bring the price way down by ordering only a single main dish. Fresh bread and cold water come with the meal. Avoid appetizers, alcohol, and desserts. No service charges are tacked on, and tipping is unnecessary. So it's really not as expensive as it looks! US$15 will usually see you through an excellent no-frills lunch of fried fish at a small French restaurant. The same thing in a deluxe hotel dining room will be about 50% more. Even the finest places are affordable if you order this way.

Most restaurants post their menu in the window. If not, have a look at it before sitting down. Check the main plates, as that's all you'll need to take. If the price is right, the ambience congenial, and local French are at the tables, sit right down. Sure, food at a snack bar would be half as much, but your Coke will be extra, and in the end it's smart to pay a little more to enjoy excellent cuisine once in a while. Steer clear of restaurants where you see a big plastic bottle of mineral water on every table, as this will add a couple of hundred francs to your bill. Also beware of set meals designed for tourists, as these usually cost double the average entree. If you can't order à la carte walk back out the door.

Local restaurants offer French, Chinese, Vietnamese, Italian, and, of course, Tahitian dishes. The *nouvelle cuisine Tahitienne* is a combination of European and Asian recipes, with local seafoods and vegetables, plus the classic *maa tahiti* (Tahitian food). The French are famous for their sauces, so try something exotic. Lunch is the main meal of the day in Tahiti-Polynesia, and many restaurants offer a *plat du jour* designed for regular customers. This is often displayed on a blackboard near the entrance and is usually good value. Most restaurants stop serving lunch at 1400, dinner at 2200. Don't expect snappy service: what's the rush, anyway?

If it's all too expensive, groceries are a good alternative. There are lots of nice places to picnic, and at CFP 40 a loaf, that crisp French white bread is incredibly cheap and good. French baguettes are subsidized by the government, unlike that awful sliced white bread in a plastic package, which is CFP 250 a loaf! Cheap red wines like Selection Faragui are imported from France in bulk and bottled locally in plastic bottles. Add a nice piece of French cheese to the above and you're ready for a budget traveler's banquet. *Casse-croûtes* are big healthy sandwiches made with those long French baguettes at about CFP 250—a bargain.

There's also Martinique rum and Hinano beer (CFP 140 in grocery stores), brewed locally by the Brasserie de Tahiti. Founded in 1914, this company's first beer was called Aorai and today they produce Heineken as well as Hinano. Remember the deposit on Hinano beer bottles (CFP 30/60 on small/large bottles), which makes beer cheap to buy cold and carry out. Supermarkets aren't allowed to sell alcohol after 1700 daily or on Sunday or holidays (stock your fridge in the morning).

Moorea's famous Rotui fruit drinks are sold in tall liter containers in a variety of types. The tastiest is perhaps *pamplemousse* (grapefruit), produced from local Moorea fruit, but the pineapple juice is also outstanding. At about CFP 250 a carton, they're excellent value. At CFP 100, bottled Eau Royale mineral water is also quite cheap.

Tahitian Food

If you can spare the cash, attend a Tahitian *tamaaraa* (feast) at a big hotel and try some Polynesian dishes roasted in an *ahimaa* (underground oven). Basalt stones are preheated with a wood fire in a meter-deep pit, then covered with leaves. Each type of food is wrapped separately in banana leaves to retain its own flavor and lowered in. The oven is covered with more banana leaves, wet sacking, and sand, and left one to three hours to bake: suckling pig, mahimahi, taro, *umara* (sweet potato), *uru* (breadfruit), and *fafa,* a spinachlike cooked vegetable made from taro tops.

Also sample the gamy flavor of *fei,* the red cooking banana that flourishes in Tahiti's uninhabited interior. The Tahitian chestnut tree *(mape)* grows near streams and the delicious cooked nuts can often be purchased at markets. *Miti hue* is a coconut-milk sauce fermented with the juice of river shrimp. Traditionally *ma'a Tahiti* is eaten with the fingers.

Poisson cru (ia ota), small pieces of raw bonito (skipjack) or yellowfin marinated with lime juice and soaked in coconut milk, is enjoyable, as is *fafaru* ("smelly fish"), prepared by marinating pieces of fish in seawater in an airtight coconut-shell container. As with the durian, although the smell is repugnant, the first bite can be addicting. Other typical Tahitian plates are chicken and pork casserole with *fafa,* pork and cabbage casserole *(pua'a chou),* and goat cooked in ginger.

Po'e is a sticky sweet pudding made of starchy banana, papaya, taro, or pumpkin flour, flavored with vanilla, and topped with coconut-milk sauce. Many varieties of this treat are made throughout Polynesia. *Faraoa ipo* is Tuamotu coconut bread. The local coffee is flavored with vanilla bean and served with sugar and coconut cream.

SERVICES AND INFORMATION

Visas and Officialdom

Everyone other than French citizens needs a passport. French are admitted freely for an unlimited stay, and citizens of the European Union (E.U.) countries, Australia, Norway, and Switzerland, get three months without a visa. Citizens of the United States, Canada, New Zealand, Japan, and 13 other countries can obtain a one-month stay free upon arrival at Papeete. If you do require a visa, make sure the words *valable pour la Polynésie Française* are endorsed on the visa as visas for France are not accepted.

Extensions of stay are possible after you arrive, but they cost CFP 3,000 and you'll have to go to the post office to buy a stamp. You'll also need to show "sufficient funds" and your ticket to leave Tahiti-Polynesia and provide one photo. North Americans are limited to three months total; if you know you'll be staying over a month, it's better to get a three-month visa at a French consulate prior to arrival, making this formality unnecessary.

Tahiti-Polynesia requires a ticket to leave of everyone (including nonresident French citizens). If you arrive without one, you'll be refused entry or required to post a cash bond equivalent to the value of a full-fare ticket back to your home country.

Yacht Entry

The main port of entry for cruising yachts is Papeete. Upon application to the local *gendarmerie*, entry may also be allowed at Moorea, Huahine, Raiatea, Bora Bora, Rurutu, Tubuai, Raivavae, Rangiroa, Mangareva, Nuku Hiva, Hiva Oa, and Ua Pou. Have an accurate inventory list for your vessel ready. Even after clearance, you must continue to report your arrival at each respective office every time you visit any of those islands (locations and phone numbers are provided throughout this chapter). The *gendarmes* are usually friendly and courteous, if you are. Boats arriving from Tonga, Fiji, and the Samoas must be fumigated (also those that have called at ports in Central or South America during the previous 21 days).

Anyone arriving by yacht without an onward ticket must post a bond or *caution* at a local bank equivalent to the airfare back to their country of origin. In Taiohae the bond is US$1,200 pp, but in Papeete it's only US$600 (for Americans). This is refundable upon departure at any branch of the same bank, less a three percent administrative fee. Make sure the receipt shows the currency in which the original deposit was made and get an assurance that it will be refunded in kind. To reclaim the bond you'll also need a letter from Immigration verifying that you've been officially checked out. If any individual on the yacht doesn't have the bond money, the captain is responsible.

Once the bond is posted, a "temporary" three-month visa (CFP 3,000) is issued, which means you have three months to get to Papeete where an additional three months (another CFP 3,000)

may be granted. After that you have to leave although boats can be left at Raiatea Carenage another six months. Yachts staying longer than one year are charged full customs duty on the vessel. Actually, the rules are not hard-and-fast, and everyone has a different experience. Crew changes should be made at Papeete. Visiting yachts cannot be chartered to third parties without permission.

After clearing customs in Papeete, outbound yachts may spend the duration of their period of stay cruising the outer islands. Make sure every island where you *might* stop is listed on your clearance. Duty-free fuel may be purchased immediately after clearance. The officials want all transient boats out of the country by 31 October, the onset of the hurricane season.

Money

The French Pacific franc or *Cour de Franc Pacifique* (CFP) is legal tender in Tahiti-Polynesia, Wallis and Futuna, and New Caledonia (there is no difference between the banknotes circulating in those territories). There are beautifully colored big banknotes of CFP 500, 1,000, 5,000, and 10,000, and coins of CFP 1, 2, 5, 10, 20, 50, and 100.

The CFP is fixed at one French franc (FF) to 18.18 Pacific francs (or one Euro to CFP 119.25), so you can determine how many CFP you'll get for your dollar or pound by finding out how many FF you get, then multiplying by 18.18. Or to put it another way, 5.5 FF equals CFP 100, so divide the number of FF you get by 5.5 and multiply by 100. A rough way to convert CFP into U.S. dollars is simply to divide by 100, so CFP 1,000 is US$10, etc.

All banks levy a stiff commission on foreign currency transactions. The Banque Socredo and the Banque de Polynésie deduct CFP 400 commission, the Banque de Tahiti CFP 500. Traveler's checks attract a rate of exchange about 1.5% higher than cash, but a passport is required for identification (photocopy sometimes accepted). The easiest way to avoid the high commissions and long bank lines is to change enough to cover your entire stay on the first occasion, then guard all that cash with your life (keep it in a moneybelt strapped to your body while you're awake and under the middle of the mattress at night). If changing a large amount it might be worth it to compare the rates at all four banks as they do differ slightly.

The number-one currency to have with you is French francs *in cash* as these are converted back and forth at the fixed rate of CFP 18.18 to one FF without any commission charge (traveler's checks in FF *are* subject to commission). However, it certainly isn't worth buying FF with dollars before leaving home for this purpose alone. If prior to departure you find you've changed too much and want your FF back, don't wait to do it at the airport as that branch may refuse and even the Papeete branches may be reluctant to carry out an operation on which they won't earn their blessed commission. How the introduction of the Euro in France will affect all of this was still unclear at press time. If you're from the States, you might also bring a few U.S. dollars in small bills to cover emergency expenses.

Credit cards are accepted in many places on the main islands, but Pacific francs in cash are easier to use at restaurants, shops, etc. If you wish to use a credit card at a restaurant, ask first. Visa and MasterCard credit cards are universally accepted in the Society Islands, but American Express is not. The American Express representative on Tahiti is Tahiti Tours (B.P. 627, 98713 Papeete, tel. 54-02-50) at 15 rue Jeanne d'Arc near the Vaima Center in Papeete. Most banks will give cash advances on credit cards, but it's still wise to bring enough traveler's checks to cover all your out-of-pocket expenses, and then some.

An alternative are the ATM machines outside Banque Socredo offices throughout the territory (including at Faa'a airport). These give a rate slightly better than traveler's checks without commission, however checking account ATM cards may not work despite advertised links to international services like Cirrus. Credit card withdrawals work better, but keep in mind that a high rate of interest is charged from the moment you receive the money (avoid this by leaving a balance with your credit card company). Some readers have reported problems with ATMs that gave "amount too high" messages instead of banknotes. This situation should improve as the banks upgrade their computer systems.

On most outer islands credit cards, traveler's checks, and foreign banknotes won't be accepted, so it's essential to change enough money before leaving Papeete. Apart from Tahiti, there are banks on Bora Bora, Huahine, Hiva Oa, Moorea, Nuku Hiva, Raiatea, Rangiroa, Rurutu, Taha'a, Tubuai, and Ua Pou. All of these islands have Banque Socredo branches, and the Banque de Tahiti (86% of which is owned by the Bank of Hawaii) is represented on six of them. Bora Bora, Moorea, and Raiatea each have four different banks. If you're headed for any island other than these, take along enough CFP in cash to see you through.

Costs

Although Tahiti is easily the most expensive corner of the South Pacific, it also has the lowest inflation rate in the region (only 1.5% in 1996, compared to 10% and up in many neighboring countries). Fortunately, facilities for budget travelers are now highly developed throughout the Society Islands, often with cooking facilities which allow you to save a lot on meals. Bread (and indirectly the ubiquitous baguette sandwiches) are heavily subsidized and a real bargain. Beer, fruit juice, and mineral water from grocery stores are reasonable. Cheap transportation is available by interisland boat, and on Tahiti there's *le truck*. Bicycles can be hired in many places.

On 1 January 1998 a value-added tax (VAT) or *taxe sur la valeur ajoutée* (TVA) came into effect at the rate of one percent on accommodations and prepaid meals, two percent on store purchases, and three percent on restaurants, bars, car rentals, and excursions. This tax is usually included in the basic price and it's expected to rise in future years.

Time is what you need the most of to see Tahiti-Polynesia on the cheap, and the wisdom to avoid trying to see and do too much. There are countless organized tours and activities designed to separate you and your money, but none are really essential and the beautiful scenery, spectacular beaches, challenging hikes, and exotic atmosphere are free. Bargaining is not common in Tahiti-Polynesia, and no one will try to cheat you (with the exception of the odd taxi driver). There's *no tipping*.

Post

The 34 regular post offices and 58 authorized agencies throughout Tahiti-Polynesia are open weekdays 0700-1500. Main branches sell ready-made padded envelopes and boxes. Parcels with an aggregate length, width, and height of more than 90 cm or weighing more than 20 kg cannot be mailed. Rolls (posters, calendars, etc.) longer than 90 cm are also not accepted. Letters cannot weigh more than two kg and when mailing parcels it's much cheaper to keep the weight under two kilograms. Registration *(recommandation)* is CFP 500 extra and insurance *(envois avec valeur déclarée)* is also possible. Always use airmail *(poste aérienne)* when posting a letter; surface mail takes months to arrive. Postcards can still take up to two weeks to reach the United States. Though twice as expensive as Cook Islands or Fiji, the service is quite reliable.

To pick up poste restante (general delivery) mail, you must show your passport and pay CFP 55 per piece. If you're going to an outer island and are worried about your letters being returned to sender after 30 days (at Nuku Hiva after 15 days), pay CFP 2,000 per month for a *garde de courrier,* which obliges the post office to hold all letters for at least two months. If one of your letters has "please hold" marked on it, the local postmaster may decide to hold all your mail for two months, but you'll have to pay the CFP 2,000 to collect it. Packages may be returned after one month in any case. For a flat fee of CFP 2,000 you can have your mail forwarded for one year. Ask for an *"Ordre de Réexpédition Temporaire."*

There's no residential mail delivery in Tahiti-Polynesia and what appear to be mail boxes along rural roads are actually bread delivery boxes! Almost everybody has a post office box, rendered B.P. *(Boîte Postale)* in this chapter. Since there are usually no street addresses, always include the B.P. and postal code when writing to a local address, plus the name of the commune or village and the island. The postal authorities recognize "French Polynesia" as the official name of this country, and it's better to add "South Pacific" to that for good measure. Tahiti-Polynesia issues its own colorful postage stamps—available at local post offices. They make excellent souvenirs.

Telecommunications

Local telephone calls are CFP 50, and the pay phones usually work! A flashing light means you're about to be cut off, so have another coin ready. However, most public telephones now accept local telephone cards only (no coins). All calls within a single island are considered local calls, except on Tahiti, which is divided into two zones. Long-distance calls are best placed at post offices, which also handle fax *(télécopier)* services. Calls made from hotel rooms are charged double or triple—you could be presented with a truly astronomical bill. Collect calls overseas are possible to Australia, Canada, France, Mexico, New Zealand, and the U.S. (but not to the U.K.): dial 19 and say you want a *conversation payable a l'arrivée.* For information (in French), dial 12; to get the operator, dial 19.

Anyone planning on using the phone should pick up a local telephone card *(télécarte),* sold at all post offices. They're valid for both local and overseas calls, and are available in denominations of 30 units (CFP 1,000), 60 units (CFP 2,000), and 150 units (CFP 5,000). It's cheaper than paying cash for long distance and you don't get hit with stiff three-minute minimum charges for operator-assisted calls (CFP 1,056 to the U.S.). North American AT&T, HTC, and Teleglobe Canada telephone cards can be used in Tahiti-Polynesia.

To dial overseas direct from Tahiti, listen for the dial tone, then push 00 (Tahiti's international access code). When you hear another dial tone, press the country code of your party (Canada and the U.S. are both 1), the city or area code, and the number. The procedure is clearly explained in notices in English in the phone booths. If calling from abroad, Tahiti-Polynesia's telephone code is 689.

The cost of placing international calls was sharply reduced in 1997, and with a card the cost per minute is now CFP 180 to Australia, New Zealand, and Hawaii, CFP 200 to the U.S. and Canada, and CFP 300 to Britain and Germany. Calls to any of these countries (except Germany and the UK) are half price from midnight to 0600. To call Tahiti-Polynesia direct from the U.S. or Canada, one must dial 011-689 and the six-digit telephone number. International access codes do vary, so always check in the front of your local telephone book. If you need to consult the Tahiti-Polynesia phone book, ask to see the *annuaire* at any post office.

Throughout this chapter we've tried to supply the local telephone numbers you'll need. Most tourist-oriented businesses will have someone handy who speaks English, so don't hesitate to call ahead. You'll get current information, be able to check prices and perhaps make a reservation, and often save yourself a lot of time and worry.

Electronic mail is still in its infancy here but those e-mail addresses that do exist should be listed at www.tahiti.com/directories/zframes/yellow-pages.htm. A selection of Tahiti-related websites and e-mail addresses are included in this book's appendix.

Business Hours

Businesses open early in Tahiti-Polynesia and often close for a two-hour siesta at midday. Normal office hours are weekdays 0730-1130/1330-1630. Many shops keep the same schedule but remain open until 1730 and Saturday 0730-1200. A few shops remain open at lunchtime and small convenience stores are often open Saturday afternoon until 1800 and Sunday 0600-0800. Banking hours are variable, either 0800-1530 or 0800-1100/1400-1700 weekdays. A few banks in Papeete open Saturday morning (check the sign on the door).

Media

Two French-owned morning papers appear daily except Sunday. *Les Nouvelles de Tahiti* (B.P. 1757, 98713 Papeete; tel. 43-44-45, fax 42-18-00) was founded in 1961 and currently has a circulation of 6,700 copies. In 1964 *La Dépêche de Tahiti* (B.P. 50, 98713 Papeete; tel. 46-43-43, fax 46-43-50) merged with an existing paper and 14,000 copies a day are presently sold. In 1989 the previously locally owned *Les Nouvelles* was purchased by the Hersant publishing empire, which also owns *La Dépêche*. *La Dépêche* provides more international news, but both papers run a constant barrage of stories emphasizing the economic dangers of independence.

The free weekly *Tahiti Beach Press* (B.P. 887, 98713 Papeete; tel. 42-68-50, fax 42-33-56), edited by Jan Prince, includes tourist information and is well worth perusing to find out which local companies are interested in your business. The same folks put out the monthly newspaper *Tahiti Today* with more in-depth articles (to subscribe mail a check for US$34 to the address above). If you read French, the monthly magazine *Tahiti Pacifique* (www.tahitiweb.com/f/info) is a lively

observer of political and economic affairs (single copies CFP 500, airmail subscription US$100).

Television was introduced to Tahiti in 1965 and state-owned Radio-Télévision Française d'Outre-Mer (www.rfo.fr) broadcasts on two channels in French and (occasionally) Tahitian. (After the 1996 election a Court of Appeal found that RFO's coverage was biased in favor of the ruling party, and for this and other reasons, fresh elections were ordered in 11 ridings.) A private commercial television station, Canal Polynésie, and two cable companies (Téléfenua and Canal +) also operate. There are nine private radio stations and it's fun to listen to the Tahitian-language stations, which play more local music than the French stations. The Tahitian call-in shows with messages to families on outer islands are a delightful slice of real life.

Among the FM radio stations you can receive around Papeete is **Radio Tahiti** (RFO), a government-run station picked up at 89.0 or 91.8 MHz. Their main news of the day (in French) is at 0630 but it's mostly official propaganda. **Radio 1** (98.7, 100.0, and 103.8 MHz) gives a more independent news report at 0630, but it's better known as Tahiti's rock music station. More rock and rap can be heard on **NRJ** (88.6 and 103.0 MHz). **Radio Bleue** (88.2, 88.5, 93.3, 96.0, 97.0, and 100.3 MHz) presents a mix of Tahitian, French, and Anglo-American music. For more local music, tune in **Radio Tiare** (104.2 and 105.9 MHz), Radio 1's sister station. **Radio Te Reo o Tefana** (92.8 and 94.4 MHz) is a pro-independence station based at Faa'a which features Tahitian talk shows and local music. Outside Tahiti the frequencies used by these stations varies (Radio Tahiti is on 89.0 MHz at Taravao and 738 kHz AM elsewhere. Radio 1 uses 90.9 MHz at Taravao and 100.9 MHz at Raiatea, while Radio Tiare is at 98.3 MHz at Taravao.) None of the local AM/FM stations broadcast in English.

Information

Tahiti-Polynesia has one of the best-equipped tourist offices in the South Pacific, Tahiti Tourisme (B.P. 65, 98713 Papeete; tel. 50-57-00, fax 43-66-19, www.tahiti-tourisme.com, e-mail: tahiti-tourisme@mail.pf). For a list of their overseas offices, turn to the Information Offices appendix at the back of this book. Within Tahiti-Polynesia the same organization calls itself the

Tahiti Manava Visitors Bureau and operates tourist information offices on Tahiti, Moorea, Huahine, Raiatea, Bora Bora, and Hiva Oa. These offices can provide free brochures and answer questions, but they're not travel agencies, so you must make your own hotel and transportation bookings. Ask for their current information sheets on the islands you intend to visit.

Moon Travel Handbook's *Tahiti Handbook* covers off-the-beaten track islands that cannot be included here due to space considerations.

Health

Public hospitals are found in Papeete (Tahiti), Taravao (Tahiti), Afareaitu (Moorea), Uturoa (Raiatea), Mataura (Tubuai), Taiohae (Nuku Hiva), and Atuona (Hiva Oa). Most other islands have only infirmaries or dispensaries. Medical treatment is not free and in non-life-threatening situations it's better to see a private doctor or dentist whose attention will cost you no more but whose services are generally more convenient. Private clinics are found throughout the Society Islands but there are none on the eastern outer islands (there, ask for the *infirmerie*). Papeete's Mamao Hospital (tel. 46-62-62) has one of only two recompression chambers in the South Pacific.

TRANSPORTATION

Getting There

Aircalin, Air France, Air New Zealand, Air Tahiti Nui, AOM French Airlines, Corsair, Hawaiian Airlines, Lan Chile Airlines, and Qantas Airways all have flights to Papeete. For more information on these, turn to the **Introduction** to this book.

In 1990 France's state-owned national airline, **Air France** (tel. 800/237-2747), bought out privately owned UTA French Airlines to become *the* international carrier to the French colonies in the South Pacific. Both Air France and **AOM French Airlines** (9841 Airport Blvd., Suite 1120, Los Angeles, CA 90045, U.S.A.; tel. 800/892-9136) fly four times a week from Paris to Papeete via Los Angeles. Air France also flies nonstop between Tokyo and Papeete once a week. AOM (Air Outre-Mer), owned by the French bank Crédit Lyonnais, has a policy of consistently set-

ting their fares slightly below those of Air France while offering comparable service.

The charter airline **Corsair,** owned by the French tour operator Nouvelles Frontières (APS, Inc., 5757 West Century Blvd., Suite 660, Los Angeles, CA 90045-6407, U.S.A.; tel. 800/677-0720 or 310/670-7318, fax 310/338-0708, www.nouvelles-frontieres.fr, e-mail: webmaster@corsair-int.com), also has scheduled Paris-Los Angeles-Papeete flights twice a week, plus Paris-Oakland-Papeete weekly.

A new, locally owned airline, **Air Tahiti Nui** (B.P. 1673, 98713 Papeete; tel. 1-877/824-4846, e-mail: fly@airtahitinui.pf), began service from Papeete in November 1998. Their 286-passenger Airbus flies to Los Angeles three times a week, and to Tokyo twice a week.

Air New Zealand (tel. 800/262-1234 or 800/663-5494) has eight-hour flights from Los Angeles to Papeete twice a week, with connections to/from many points in North America and Western Europe. These flights continue southwest to Auckland with one calling at Rarotonga and Fiji. **Qantas** (tel. 800/227-4500) flies from Melbourne to Papeete via Auckland with connections for six other Australian cities. **Hawaiian Airlines** (tel. 800/367-5320) offers weekly nonstop service to Papeete from Honolulu with connections from Los Angeles, Las Vegas, San Francisco, Portland, and Seattle.

Aircalin (tel. 1-310/670-7302) has flights from Nouméa to Papeete via Wallis Island or Nadi. These services also have connections to/from Australia.

Lan Chile Airlines (tel. 800/735-5526) runs their Boeing 767 service from Santiago to Tahiti via Easter Island three times a week.

A new, locally owned airline, **Air Tahiti Nui** (B.P. 1673, 98713 Papeete; tel. 46-02-02, fax 46-02-90, e-mail: fly@airtahitinui.pf), began service from Papeete in November 1998. Their 286-seat Airbus files to Los Angeles three times a week, and to Tokyo twice a week.

By Boat

The only scheduled international passenger-carrying freighter service to Tahiti is the monthly Bank Line service from Le Havre (France) to Auckland via the Panama Canal. The local agent is **Agence Maritime de Fare Ute** (B.P. 9003, 98715 Papeete; tel. 42-55-61, fax 42-86-08).

Getting Around by Air

The domestic carrier, **Air Tahiti** (B.P. 314, 98713 Papeete; tel. 86-42-42, fax 86-40-69, e-mail: rtahitim@mail.pf), flies to 37 airstrips in every corner of Tahiti-Polynesia, with important hubs at Papeete (Windward Islands), Bora Bora (Leeward Islands), Rangiroa (western Tuamotus), Hao (eastern Tuamotus), and Nuku Hiva (Marquesas). Their fleet consists of three 66-seat ATR 72s, three 48-seat ATR 42s, and two 19-seat Dornier 228s. The Italian-made ATRs are economical in fuel consumption and maintenance requirements, and perform well under island conditions. The high-winged design makes them perfect for aerial sightseeing along the way.

Air Tahiti doesn't allow stopovers on their tickets, so if you're flying roundtrip from Tahiti to Bora Bora and want to stop at Raiatea on the way out and Huahine on the way back, you'll have to purchase four separate tickets (total CFP 30,500). Ask about their "Pass Bleu," which allows you to visit these islands plus Moorea for CFP 20,000 (certain restrictions apply). An "Excursion Bleue" allows a 30% reduction on a roundtrip to any island in the Society or North Tuamotu groups provided you fly on off-peak "blue" flights.

No student discounts are available, but persons under 25 and over 60 can get discounts of up to 50% on certain flights by paying CFP 1,000 for a discount card *(carte de réduction)*. Family reduction cards (CFP 2,000) provide a potential 50% reduction for the parents and 75% off for children 16 and under. Identification and one photo are required, and application must be made at least three working days before you wish to travel.

Better than point-to-point fares are the six Air Tahiti **Air Passes.** These are valid 28 days, but only one stopover can be made on each island included in the package. For example, you can go Papeete-Moorea-Huahine-Raiatea-Maupiti-Bora Bora-Papeete for CFP 30,500. Otherwise pay CFP 45,500 for Papeete-Moorea-Huahine-Raiatea-Bora Bora-Rangiroa-Manihi-Papeete. This compares with an individual ticket price of CFP 41,400 to do the first circuit, CFP 69,800 for the second, which makes the air passes good value. Air Passes that include the Austral Islands are CFP 50,500 (compared to CFP 81,400 on an individual basis); with the Tuamotu and Marquesas islands they're CFP 87,000 (compared to CFP 116,000). All flights must be booked in advance but date changes are possible. Air Tahiti's agent in North America (tel. 800/553-3477) will have current information. The passes are nonrefundable once travel has begun.

Air Tahiti's "Decouverte Marquises" fare allows you to fly from Papeete to Nuku Hiva for CFP 49,900 return; to Atuona, Ua Pou, or Ua Huka it's CFP 54,900 return. This is for a stay of between seven and 15 days with only one reservation change allowed. There's a 25% cancellation penalty and you can only fly on low-load "blue" flights (not valid around Christmas or Easter or in July and August). This ticket is only available in Papeete.

Air Tahiti also offers packages to almost all their destinations including airfare, transfers, hotel rooms (double occupancy), and the occasional breakfast or excursion. Of course, they only use the more upmarket hotels, but if you were planning to stay in one of them anyway, Air Tahiti's packages are cheaper than what you'd pay directly. Cruise packages are also offered. All the possibilities are clearly outlined (in French) with exact prices given in Air Tahiti's well-designed timetable.

Air Tahiti tickets are refundable at the place of purchase, but you must cancel your reservations at least two hours before flight time to avoid a CFP 1,000 penalty. Do this in person and have your flight coupon amended as no-shows are charged 25% of the value of the ticket to make a new reservation (all existing reservations will be automatically canceled). If you're told a flight you want is full, keep checking back as local passengers often change their minds and seats may become available (except around major public holidays). It's not necessary to reconfirm reservations for flights between Tahiti, Moorea, Huahine, Raiatea, Bora Bora, Rangiroa, and Manihi, but elsewhere it's essential to reconfirm. (If your bookings were made from abroad do reconfirm *everything* upon arrival in Papeete as mix-ups in communications between foreign travel agencies and Air Tahiti are routine.) Beware of planes leaving 20 minutes early.

If you buy your ticket locally, the baggage allowance on domestic flights is 10 kg, but if your Air Tahiti flight tickets were purchased seven days prior to your arrival in Tahiti-Polynesia, the allowance is 20 kg. All baggage above those limits is charged at the rate of the full fare for that sector divided by 80 per kilogram (surfboards more than 1.8 meters long are not accepted). If you don't already have a plane ticket, are traveling only within the Society Islands, and are carrying baggage above Air Tahiti's absurd 10-kg limit, you should seriously consider taking the jet cruiser *Ono-Ono,* discussed below, which allows any reasonable amount of luggage and is cheaper to boot. Fresh fruit and vegetables cannot be carried from Tahiti to the Austral, Tuamotu, Gambier, or Marquesas islands.

On Bora Bora, Maupiti, and Mangareva passengers are transferred from the airport to town by boat. This ride is included in the airfare at Bora Bora but costs extra at Maupiti (CFP 400) and Mangareva (CFP 500). Smoking aboard the aircraft is prohibited and all flights are free seating.

The main Air Tahiti office in Papeete is upstairs in Fare Tony, the commercial center off boulevard Pomare just west of rue Georges Lagarde. They're closed on weekends. Check carefully to make sure all the flights listed in their published timetable are actually operating! Any travel agency in Papeete can book Air Tahiti flights for the same price as the Air Tahiti office, and the service tends to be better.

An Air Tahiti subsidiary, **Air Moorea** (B.P. 6019, 98702 Faa'a; tel. 86-41-41, fax 86-42-69), has hourly flights between Tahiti and Moorea (CFP 2,700 one-way) leaving Papeete daily every half hour 0600-0900, hourly 0900-1600, and half hourly 1600-1800. Reservations are not necessary on this commuter service: just show up 15 minutes before the flight you wish to take. The Air Moorea terminal is in a separate building at the east end of Faa'a Airport. However, flying between Tahiti and Moorea is not recommended because going over by ferry is a big part of the experience and there's no bus service to/from Moorea Airport. A cramped, stuffy plane ride at three times the cost of the relaxing 30-minute ferry is to be avoided.

Air Tahiti Services

Air Tahiti flies from Papeete to Huahine (CFP 8,800), Raiatea (CFP 10,100), and Bora Bora (CFP 12,400) several times a day. Every day there's an expensive direct connection from Moorea to Huahine (CFP 11,000); Raiatea to Maupiti (CFP 5,600) is three times a week. The three weekly transversal flights from Bora Bora to Rangiroa and Manihi (CFP 20,700) eliminate the need to backtrack to Papeete.

Flights between Papeete and Rangiroa (CFP 13,600) operate daily, continuing from Rangiroa to Manihi (CFP 8,800) five times a week. Air Tahiti also has flights to the East Tuamotu atolls and Mangareva. Many flights between outer islands of the Tuamotus operate in one direction only.

Flights bound for the Marquesas are the longest and most expensive of Air Tahiti's services. Five times a week there's an ATR service from Papeete to Nuku Hiva (CFP 28,700). Once or twice a week these flights call at Hiva Oa on their way to or from Nuku Hiva, and one weekly ATR flight calls at Rangiroa and Manihi. In addition, there's a heavily booked Dornier 228 flight from Rangiroa to Hiva Oa once a week calling at Pukapuka or Napuka along the way. At Nuku Hiva one of the Papeete flights connects for Ua Pou (CFP 5,100), Hiva Oa (CFP 8,800), and Ua Huka (CFP 5,100). If you know you'll be going on to Hiva Oa, Ua Huka, or Ua Pou, get a through ticket from Papeete; the fare is only CFP 1,300 more than a ticket as far as Nuku Hiva.

The Austral group is better connected to Papeete, with flights to Rurutu (CFP 17,700) and Tubuai (CFP 19,800) four days a week with alternating Papeete-Rurutu-Tubuai-Papeete or Papeete-Tubuai-Rurutu-Papeete routings. The Tubuai-Rurutu leg costs CFP 8,300.

During July and August, the peak holiday season, extra flights are scheduled. Air Tahiti is fairly reliable; still, you should never schedule a flight back to Papeete on the same day that your international flight leaves Tahiti. It's always wise to allow a couple of days' leeway in case there's a problem with the air service. Save your trip around Tahiti until the end.

Getting Around by Sea

To save money, most budget travelers tour Tahiti-Polynesia by boat. There's a certain romance and adventure to taking an interisland freighter and you can go anywhere by copra boat, including islands without airstrips and resorts. Ships leave Papeete regularly for the different island groups. You'll meet local people and fellow travelers and receive a gentle introduction to the island of your choice. Problems about overweight baggage, tight reservations, and airport transport are eliminated, and thanks to government subsidies travel by ferry or passenger-carrying freighter is four times cheaper than the plane. Seasickness, cockroaches, diesel fumes, and the heavy scent of copra are all part of the experience.

Below you'll find specific information on the main interisland boats; the tourist office in Papeete also has lists. Prices and schedules have been fairly stable over the past few years, and new services are being added all the time. Lots of visitors travel this way to Moorea and Bora Bora, so don't feel intimidated if you've never done it before.

For the cheapest ride and the most local color, travel deck class. There's usually an awning in case of rain, and you'll be surrounded by Tahitians, but don't count on getting a lot of sleep if you go this way—probably no problem for one night, right? Lay your mat pointed to one side of the boat because if you lie parallel to the length of the boat you'll roll from side to side. Don't step over other peoples' mats, but if you must, first remove your shoes and excuse yourself. Otherwise take a cabin, which you'll share with three or four other passengers, still cheaper than an airplane seat. Food is only included on really long trips (ask), but snacks may be sold on board. On a long trip you're better off taking all your own food than buying a meal plan.

For any boat trip farther than Moorea check the schedule and pick up tickets the day before at the company office listed below. If you're headed for a remote island outside the Societies or want cabin class, visit the office as far in advance as possible. Take along your passport as they may insist on checking the expiration date of your visa before selling you a ticket to a point outside the Society Islands. Except on the tourist-class Aranui, it's not possible (nor recommended) to book your passage before arriving on Tahiti. If you really want to go, there'll be something leaving around the date you want. On an outer island, be wary when someone, even a member of the crew, tells you the departure time of a ship: they're as apt to leave early as late.

Boat trips are always smoother northwestbound than southeast-bound because you go with the prevailing winds. Take this into consideration if you plan to fly one way, in which case it would be better to come back by air. *Bon voyage.*

Ferry to Moorea

Two types of ferries travel to Moorea: two fast 320-passenger catamarans carrying walk-on commuters only (30 minutes), and two large car ferries with a capacity for 400 foot-passengers and 80 vehicles (one hour). Departure times are posted at the ferry landing on the Papeete waterfront (punctual) and reservations are not required: you buy your ticket just before you board. Stroll around the open upper deck and enjoy the scenic one-hour crossing.

The high-speed catamarans *Aremiti III* (B.P. 9254, 98715 Papeete; tel. 42-88-88, fax 42-83-83) and *Tamahine Moorea* (B.P. 3917, 98713 Papeete; tel. 43-76-50, fax 42-10-49) make five or six trips a day between Tahiti and Moorea at CFP 900 pp. The ultimate in speed is the *Tamarii Moorea VIII,* a very fast Corsaire 6000 ferry brought into service in June 1996. On the Moorea cats you're allowed to sit or stand outside on the roof and get an all-round view, which makes them fun and well worth taking at least once.

The car ferries *Tamarii Moorea* and *Aremiti Ferry* shuttle four or five times a day between Papeete and Vaiare Wharf on Moorea (CFP 800 one-way, students and children under 13 CFP 400, car CFP 2,000, scooter CFP 500, bicycle free).

A bus meets all ferries on the Moorea side and will take you anywhere on that island for CFP 200. Just don't be too slow boarding the bus or it could be full. The Moorea ferries carry more than a million passengers a year making Papeete the third-largest port under the French flag (after Calais and Cherbourg) as far as passenger movements go.

Jet Cruiser to the Leeward Islands

In 1994 the high-speed monohull *Ono-Ono* (Société Polynesienne d'Investissement Maritime, B.P. 16, 98713 Papeete; tel. 45-35-35, fax 43-83-45, e-mail: onoono@mail.pf) began whisking passengers from Papeete to Huahine, Raiatea, Taha'a, and Bora Bora. This Australian-built, 48-meter jet boat carries 450 passengers at speeds of up to 35 knots, cutting traveling times from Papeete to Huahine to just 3.5 hours (CFP

4,944), to Raiatea 4.5 hours (CFP 5,499), to Taha'a 5.5 hours (CFP 6,055), and to Bora Bora eight hours (CFP 6,610). Children under 12 years of age pay half price on tickets to/from Papeete. Bicycles are CFP 1,200, surfboards CFP 650.

The *Ono-Ono* departs Papeete's Moorea ferry wharf Monday and Wednesday at 0900, Friday at 1630, departing Bora Bora for the return trip on Tuesday and Thursday at 0700, Sunday at 1200. On Saturday there's a shorter interisland run within the Leeward Islands only (about CFP 1,778 a hop). *Ono-Ono* is seldom full and tickets can be purchased an hour before departure (for insurance purposes, the booking agent will need to know the name and age of each passenger). To refund a ticket is CFP 1,000. The *Ono-Ono* ticket cover instructs you to check in at the harbor 45 minutes before the scheduled departure time and you should do so as they often leave half an hour early! Canceled services with little notice are also quite routine.

Place your luggage in a special baggage container near the gangway (there are none of the worries about overweight luggage you might have on Air Tahiti). Another big advantage that this ferry has over the plane is that on Tahiti, Huahine, Raiatea, and Taha'a you'll arrive right in the center of town, eliminating the need for airport transfers. Seating is 10 or 12 abreast in rows of airplane-style seats on two enclosed decks, plus on a covered deck at back where you can sit outside. Though more than twice as expensive as the cargo boats or ferry, it's half the price of going by air and certainly makes getting around these enchanting islands a lot easier.

Ferry to the Leeward Islands

The **Compagnie Maritime Raromatai Nui** (B.P. 50712, 98716 Pirae; tel. 43-19-88, fax 43-19-99), with an office in a red-and-white kiosk at the Moorea ferry wharf in Papeete, handles the car-carrying, 400-passenger *Raromatai Ferry,* which departs Papeete to Huahine, Raiatea, Taha'a, and Bora Bora on Tuesday and Friday afternoons. This ship uses a landing behind the tourist office in downtown Papeete, not the wharf at Motu Uta where *Taporo VI* and the *Vaeanu* dock. Tickets for walk-on passengers are usually available just prior to departure. Prices from Papeete to Bora Bora are CFP 3,200 for a seat in

the salon, CFP 5,000 pp in a four-berth cabin, CFP 10,000 for a car, CFP 500 for a bicycle. A double "cruise cabin" is CFP 20,000 for two people. There are discounts for students and those 18 and under.

The *Raromatai Ferry* salon is a spacious sitting room with aircraft-style Pullman seats, but French TV shows blast at you nonstop and the powerful air-conditioning means you freeze at night unless you've got a sleeping bag. The *Raromatai Ferry* rolls a lot in rough weather. Between the Leeward Islands the *Raromatai Ferry* is a good deal (CFP 1,000 salon interisland) for these daylight crossings (southbound), with an excellent open promenade deck on top. Unfortunately this ship is often out of service for one reason or another.

Cargo Ships to the Leeward Islands

The cargo ship MV *Taporo VI* departs Papeete's Motu Uta wharf every Monday, Wednesday, and Friday afternoon around 1600. *Taporo VI* calls at Huahine at 0200, Raiatea at 0530, and Taha'a at 0700, reaching Bora Bora at 1000 Tuesday, Thursday, and Saturday. It departs Bora Bora for Papeete once again Tuesday, Thursday, and Saturday at 1130, calling at Raiatea at 1400 and Huahine at 1700, reaching Papeete early Wednesday, Friday, and Sunday morning (you can stay on board till dawn).

Northbound the MV *Vaeanu* leaves Papeete Monday, Wednesday, and Friday at 1700; southbound it leaves Bora Bora Tuesday at 1030, Thursday at noon, and Sunday at 0900.

The timings are more civilized if you stay on the boat right through to Bora Bora northbound: you get to see the sunset over Moorea, go to bed, and when you awake you'll be treated to a scenic cruise past Taha'a and into the Bora Bora lagoon. Getting off at Huahine at 0200 is no fun (although there is a good shelter on the wharf where you can spend the rest of the night for free). Southbound between Bora Bora, Raiatea, and Huahine you travel during daylight hours which makes it easy to island hop back (you'll save a day by taking the *Ono-Ono* between Bora Bora and Taha'a/Raiatea). The only fly in the ointment is that southbound you must board at Huahine just before dark and all of the sheltered places in which to stretch your mat may be taken. However, there's usually ample sleeping space

left on the *Vaeanu* and there will be no disturbances before Tahiti. If the risk of being forced to
sleep on deck under the stars (and possibly the
rain) intimidates you, there's always the option of
finally splurging on the high-speed ferry *Ono-
Ono* straight back to Papeete.

Although the ships do make an effort to stick to
their timetables, the times are approximate—
ask at the company offices. They're more likely
to be running late on the return trip from Bora
Bora to Tahiti (unlike the *Ono-Ono,* which tends
to run a little early). Expect variations if there's a
public holiday that week. Also beware of voyages marked "carburant" on the schedules because when fuel *(combustible)* is being carried,
only cabin passengers are allowed aboard (this
often happens on the Wednesday departures
from Papeete). Northbound you won't get much
sleep due to noise and commotion during the
early-morning stops. No mattresses or bedding
are provided for deck passengers. In Papeete,
board the ship two hours prior to departure to
be sure of a reasonable place on deck to sleep
(mark your place with a beach mat). Luckily
these ships aren't promoted in the Australian
guidebooks, so they aren't overwhelmed by
tourists. If you've got some time to kill before
your ship leaves Papeete, have a look around
the coconut-oil mill next to the wharf.

On *Taporo VI* the deck fare from Papeete to
any of the Leeward Islands is CFP 1,709. However, they only accept a limited number of deck
passengers (who sleep on pallets in three large
open containers on the upper rear deck), so it's
important to book ahead at the **Compagnie
Française Maritime de Tahiti** (B.P. 368, 98713
Papeete; tel. 42-63-93, fax 42-06-17; open weekdays 0730-1100/1330-1700, Saturday 0730-
1100) in Fare Ute. The two four-bed cabins are
CFP 20,000 each (seldom full). If you're only
traveling between the islands of Huahine, Raiatea, Taha'a, and Bora Bora, the interisland
deck fares are under CFP 1,000 each trip. If you
jump off for a quick look around while the ship is
in port, you may be asked to buy another ticket
when you reboard. A bicycle is about CFP 600
extra. No meals are included, so take food and
water with you.

The *Vaeanu* carries a much larger number of
deck and cabin passengers, and you can usually
buy a ticket at their office (B.P. 9062, 98715 Pa-

peete; tel. 41-25-35, fax 41-24-34) facing the
wharf at Motu Uta a few hours prior to departure (except on holidays). Do buy your ticket before boarding, however, as there can be problems for anyone trying to pay once the ship is underway. In the Leeward Islands buy a ticket from
the agent on the wharf as soon as the boat arrives. The *Vaeanu* offers mats in the spacious
hold down below or floor space on the enclosed
upper rear deck (with the lights on all night).
Most travelers prefer the *Vaeanu* as there's a
lot more elbowroom and shade than on *Taporo
VI.* The passengers and crew on both boats are
mostly Tahitian as tourists and French usually
take the *Ono-Ono,* but *Vaeanu* and *Taporo VI*
are excellent options for the adventurous traveler.

The Compagnie Française Maritime de Tahiti also runs a supply ship from Papeete to Maiao
occasionally, so ask. (The CFMT itself has a
place in local history, having been founded
around 1890 by Sir James Donald, who had the
contract to supply limes to the British Pacific
fleet. At the turn of the century Donald's
schooner, the *Tiare Taporo,* was the fastest in
Polynesia, and the CFMT is still the Lloyd's of
London agent.)

Barge to Maupiti

The government supply barges *Meherio* or
Maupiti Tou Ai's leave Papeete for Maupiti
Wednesday at 1900 (20 hours) calling at Raiatea on the way. Tickets to Maupiti are available from the **Direction de l'Equipment** (weekdays 0730-1500; B.P. 85, 98713 Papeete; tel.
42-44-92, fax 43-32-69) at Motu Uta, costing
CFP 2,221 from Papeete or CFP 1,058 from
Raiatea.

Ships to the Austral Islands

The **Service de Navigation des Australes** (B.P.
1890, 98713 Papeete; tel. 42-93-67, fax 42-06-
09), at the Motu Uta interisland wharf on the
west side of the copra sheds in Papeete, runs the
Tuhaa Pae II to the Austral Islands two or three
times a month: CFP 12,500 a day including
meals cabin class for the 10-day roundtrip. One-
way deck/cabin fares from Papeete at CFP
3,799/6,649 to Rurutu, Rimatara, or Tubuai, CFP
5,475/9,582 to Raivavae, CFP 7,486/13,101 to
Rapa. Between Rurutu and Tubuai it's CFP
1,780 deck. No meals are included, but food

can be ordered at CFP 2,300 pp a day extra (take your own). Some of the cabins are below the waterline and very hot. The rear deck has a diesely romantic feel, for a day or two. For sanitary reasons the seats have been removed from the ship's toilets (squat). The *Tuhaa Pae II* calls at Rimatara, Rurutu, Tubuai, Raivavae, and about once a month Rapa Iti. Maria Atoll is visited annually. Their schedule changes at a moment's notice, so actually going with them requires persistence. Consider going out by boat and returning on the plane.

Ships to the Tuamotus and Gambiers
The motor vessel *Dory* (B.P. 9274, 98715 Papeete; tel. 42-30-55, fax 42-06-15) leaves from Motu Uta every Monday at 1300 for Tikehau (Tuesday 0600), Rangiroa (Tuesday 1200), Arutua (Wednesday 0600), and Kaukura (Wednesday 1400), arriving back in Papeete Thursday at 0800. This routing means it takes only 23 hours to go from Papeete to Rangiroa but 44 hours to return. There are five double and two triple cabins, and cabin/deck fares are CFP 3,535/5,050 each way. Meals are not included. This small 26-meter vessel tosses a lot in rough weather as it visits the islands to pick up fish and deliver frozen bread, chicken, and ice cream. Their Papeete office is across the hall from the *Aranui* office at Motu Uta. Foreign visitors use this boat regularly, so it's a good bet. The same company runs the *Cobia II* to the Tuamotus, departing Monday at 1200 for Kaukura (Tuesday 0800), Arutua (Tuesday 1300), Apataki (Tuesday 1630), Aratika (Wednesday 0700), and Toau (Wednesday 1330), returning to Papeete Friday at 1000 (also CFP 2,500 one-way). No cabins are available and you must take all your own food.

The *Vai-Aito* (tel. 43-99-96, fax 43-53-04) departs Motu Uta every other Saturday morning for Rangiroa (CFP 4,000 deck from Papeete), Kaukura (CFP 4,500), Apataki (CFP 5,000), Ahe (CFP 5,400), Manihi (CFP 5,800), Aratika (CFP 6,300), Kauehi (CFP 6,600), Raraka (CFP 7,100), and Fakarava (CFP 7,600). A complete roundtrip costs CFP 15,000.

The 48-meter cargo boat *Manava II* (B.P. 1816, 98713 Papeete; tel. 43-83-84, fax 42-25-57) runs to the northern Tuamotus (Rangiroa, Tikehau, Mataiva, Ahe, Manihi, Takaroa, Takapoto, Aratika, Kauehi, Fakarava, Toau, Apataki, Arutua,

and Kaukura) once or twice a month. There are no cabins: the deck passage to Rangiroa is CFP 4,000 (meals CFP 1,800 a day extra).

Many smaller copra boats, such as the *Au' Ura Nui III, Hotu Maru, Kauaroa Nui, Kura Ora II, Mareva Nui, Nuku Hau, Rairoa Nui, Ruahatu, Saint Xavier Maris Stella,* and *Vai Aito* also service the Tuamotus. For the Gambiers, it's the monthly *Manava IV* (B.P. 1291, 98713 Papeete; tel. 43-32-65, fax 41-31-65) which does an 18-day roundtrip to Rikitea and the southern Tuamotus. Ask about ships of this kind at the large workshops west of Papeete's Motu Uta interisland wharf.

Ships to the Marquesas
Every two weeks the 75-meter cargo ship *Taporo IV* departs Papeete Thursday at 1700 for Takapoto, Tahuata, Hiva Oa, Nuku Hiva, and Ua Pou, charging passengers CFP 20,200 deck or CFP 30,300 cabin one-way from Papeete to any port in the Marquesas. It takes 3.5 days on the open sea to reach the first Marquesan island, so you should certainly try for a cabin. Otherwise you can do the whole eight-day roundtrip for CFP 40,400 deck or CFP 60,600 cabin, but only three to eight hours are spent at each port so you should plan on getting off somewhere and flying back. The *Taporo IV* has two four-berth cabins and 12 seats on deck. Food is included but it's marginal, so take extras and bring your own bowl. Meals are served at 0600, 1030, and 1730. No pillows or towels are supplied in the cabins and the shower is only open three hours a day. The agent is **Compagnie Française Maritime de Tahiti** (B.P. 368, 98713 Papeete; tel. 42-63-93, fax 42-06-17) at Fare Ute. At island stops *Taporo IV* lowers a container that it uses as an office onto the wharfs.

The *Tamarii Tuamotu II* also departs for the Marquesas monthly with only deck passage available (no cabins). Passage is cheaper at CFP 7,500 each way, plus CFP 2,000 a day for meals, but this ship visits various Tuamotu atolls in each direction, so it takes a lot longer to get to the Marquesas and is only for the very hardy. It calls at every inhabited bay in the Marquesas (this alone takes 12 days). Check at their city office, the Bureau Tamarii Tuamotu (Jacques Wong, B.P. 2606, 98713 Papeete; tel./fax 42-95-07), 43 avenue du Prince Hinoï, corner of rue des

Remparts (next to the Europcar office on the east side of the street). It may be out of service.

The *Aranui*

The *Aranui*, a passenger-carrying freighter revamped for tourism, cruises 15 times a year between Papeete and the Marquesas. The ship calls at most of the inhabited Marquesas Islands, plus a couple of the Tuamotus. The routing might be Papeete-Takapoto-Ua Pou-Nuku Hiva-Hiva Oa-Fatu Hiva-Hiva Oa-Ua Huka-Nuku Hiva-Ua Pou-Rangiroa-Papeete. A vigorous daily program with fairly strenuous but optional hikes is included in the tour price. The only docks in the Marquesas are at Taiohae, Vaipaee, Hakahau, and Atuona; elsewhere everyone goes ashore in whale boats, a potential problem for passengers with mobility limitations. Still, the *Aranui* is fine for the adventuresome visitor who wants to see a lot in a short time.

This modern 105-meter freighter had its inaugural sailing in 1990, replacing a smaller German-built boat that had served the Marquesas since 1981. It's clean and pleasant compared to the other ships, but far more expensive. A hundred passengers are accommodated in 40 a/c double cabins or given mattresses on the bridge deck. The cheapest cabin with shared bath for a 15-day, eight-island cruise to the Tuamotus and Marquesas is CFP 304,868 pp roundtrip (double occupancy), all meals included. Cabins with private bath start at CFP 350,632 pp. Single occupancy costs 50% more. There's also an a/c dormitory with upper and lower berths that works out a third cheaper and, of course, doesn't involve a single supplement. A US$75 port tax is extra. Less expensive one-way deck fares are supposed to be for local residents only but it's sometimes possible for tourists to go one way on deck. You can also travel interisland within the Marquesas on deck (about CFP 2,000 a hop), but it's highly unlikely you'd be permitted to do a roundtrip that way. In any case, deck passage can be hot, noisy, and tiring on such a long trip. If traveling one way, pick Nuku Hiva as your destination as you'll save on the exorbitant airport transfers of that island.

Despite the fares charged, don't expect cruise-ship comforts on the *Aranui*. Accommodations are spartan (but adequate), and meals are served in two shifts due to lack of space in the dining area. Aside from three classes of cabins (the cheaper ones are cramped), there's a large covered area where the deck passengers sleep. The roster of American/French/German passengers is congenial.

The *Aranui*'s Papeete office (**Compagnie Polynésienne de Transport Maritime,** B.P. 220, 98713 Papeete; tel. 42-62-40, fax 43-48-89) is at the interisland wharf at Motu Uta. The CPTM's U.S. office is at 2028 El Camino Real South, Suite B, San Mateo, CA 94403, U.S.A. (tel. 800/972-7268 or 1-650/574-2575, fax 1-650/574-6881, e-mail: cptm@aranui.com). In the U.S. advance bookings can be made through Tahiti Vacations (tel. 800/553-3477, www.tahitivacation.com) or any of the agents listed at www.aranui.com. One Australian reader wrote: "The trip is fantastic and I hope to do it again soon." (The *Aranui* recently costarred with Warren Beatty and Annette Bening in the Warner Brothers film *Love Affair*.)

Tourist Cruises

In 1998 the tall-masted cruise ships *Wind Song* and *Club Med 2* were withdrawn from Tahiti and replaced by the conventional, 320-passenger *Paul Gauguin*, built at St. Nazaire, France, in 1997 and presently operated by Radisson Seven Seas Cruises (600 Corporate Dr., Suite 410, Fort Lauderdale, FL 33334, U.S.A.; tel. 1-800/477-7500 or 1-800/333-3333, www.rssc.com). This ship does seven-night cruises from Papeete to Rangiroa, Bora Bora, Raiatea, and Moorea year-round, beginning at US$3,195 pp a week double-occupancy for one of the 14 cabins on the bottom deck including airfare from Los Angeles (US$189 port charges are extra). Upper deck cabins with balconies start at US$4,295 pp. There's a spa and fitness center, watersports platform, and lecture program.

Beginning in late 1999 Renaissance Cruises (www.renaissancecruises.com) will operate 10-night cruises from Papeete to the Leeward Islands on the 690-passenger Liberian cruise ship *R3*. The 15 inside cabins on the lowest deck begin at US$2,699 pp double occupancy, plus US$99 port fees, roundtrip airfare from Los Angeles included. Cabins with balconies start at US$3,499 pp (these sale prices could rise). The main market for both of these vessels is the U.S. west coast, which is almost as close to Tahiti as it is to the better-known cruising grounds in the Caribbean.

Since early 1998 the 34-meter mini-cruiseship *Haumana* has done luxury cruises around Raiatea, Taha'a, and Bora Bora. The 21 cabins are US$1,215/1,630 pp double occupancy (plus US$45 port fees) for a three/four-day cruise including excursions. It's run by **Bora Bora Pearl Cruises** (B.P. 9274, 98715 Papeete; tel. 43-43-03, fax 43-17-86). Tour operators such as Tahiti Vacations can book yacht tours in the same area for less money, such as six days on the *Danae III* at US$985 pp. They also offer yacht cruises of the Marquesas Islands.

Also consider **Archipels Croisieres** (B.P. 1160, 98729 Papetoai, Moorea; tel. 56-36-39, fax 56-35-87, www.archipels.com, e-mail: archimoo @mail.pf), which operates all-inclusive cruises on 17-meter, eight-passenger catamarans. There are three possibilities: a six-night tour of the Leeward Islands is US$1,880 pp, two/three nights cruising the Rangiroa lagoon is US$790/1,030 pp, and seven nights touring five islands in the Marquesas Islands is US$2,050 pp (all double occupancy). Shore excursions and almost everything other than interisland airfare and alcohol is included. A five percent discount is allowed if you book two of the three options back to back. If you don't require the glamour (and large crowds) of large cruise ship, these trips bring you a lot closer to the islands and departures are guaranteed even if only two people reserve. For couples it's much cheaper than chartering a yacht and your experienced crew does all the work. In North America, Tahiti Vacations (tel. 1-800/553-3477, www.tahitivacation.com) can handle reservations.

Yacht Charters

Yachts are for rent from **Tahiti Yacht Charter** (B.P. 608, 98713 Papeete; tel. 45-04-00, fax 42-76-00, e-mail: tyc@mail.pf) with a base on the Papeete waterfront almost opposite Air France. Their Leeward Island base (tel. 66-28-86, fax 66-28-85) at the Marina Apooiti, one km west of Raiatea Airport, has 10 charter yachts available. Prices begin at CFP 245,000 a week for a six-person Oceanis 350 and increase to CFP 574,000 for a 10-person Kennex 445 catamaran with a supplement in July and August. Charters longer than a week are discounted. A skipper will be CFP 12,000 a day, a cook CFP 10,000.

The South Pacific's largest bareboat yacht charter operation is **The Moorings Ltd.** (B.P. 165, 98735 Uturoa; tel. 66-35-93, fax 66-20-94, e-mail: moorings@mail.pf), a Florida company with 30 yachts based at Raiatea's Marina Apooiti. Bareboat prices begin at US$3,000 a week for a yacht accommodating six and go up to US$6,000 for an eight-person catamaran. Prices are higher during the April-Oct. high season. Provisioning is US$32 pp a day (plus US$120 a day for a cook, if required). If you're new to sailing, a skipper must be hired at US$140 a day and the charterer is responsible for the skipper/cook's provisions. Local tax is three percent, security insurance is US$25 a day, and the starter kit is US$87 and up. This may seem like a lot, but split among a nautical-minded group it's comparable to a deluxe hotel room. Charterers are given a complete briefing on channels and anchorages, and provided with a detailed set of charts. All boats are radio-equipped, and a voice from the Moorings is available to talk nervous skippers in and out. Travel by night is forbidden, but by day it's easy sailing. All charters are from noon to noon. Book through The Moorings Ltd., 19345 US 19 North, Suite 402, Clearwater, FL 34624-3147, U.S.A. (tel. 1-800/535-7289, fax 1-813/530-9747, www.moorings.com, e-mail: yacht@moorings.com). Ask about "specials" when calling.

A third yacht charter operation, French-operated **Stardust Marine** (B.P. 331, 98735 Uturoa; tel. 66-23-18, fax 66-23-19), is based at Raiatea's Faaroa Bay. A four-person bareboat yacht is US$337/442/503 in the low/intermediate/high season with substantial reductions for periods more than eight or 15 days. Their top-of-the-line eight-passenger deluxe catamaran is US$669/ 882/951 and there are eight other categories in between. The high season is July and August, intermediate April- June and Sept.-November. If you can schedule a 15-day trip between January and March you can have a bareboat yacht for as little as US$242 a day! Those without the required sailing skills will have to hire a skipper at US$140 a day.

Bookings for all three companies above can be made through **Tahiti Nui Travel** (B.P. 718, 98713 Papeete; tel. 54-02-00, fax 42-74-35, e-mail: info@tahitinuitravel.pf) in Papeete's Vaima Center. Check their internet website at www.tahiti-nui.com for the current prices of all boats.

Le Truck

Polynesia's folkloric *le truck* provides an entertaining unscheduled passenger service on Tahiti, Huahine, and Raiatea. Passengers sit on long wooden benches in back and there's no problem with luggage. Fares are fairly low and often posted on the side of the vehicle. You pay through the window on the right side of the cab. Drivers are generally friendly and will stop to pick you up anywhere if you wave—they're all self-employed, so there's no way they'd miss a fare! On Tahiti the larger *trucks* leave Papeete for the outlying districts periodically throughout the day until 1700; they continue running to Faa'a Airport and the Maeva Beach Hôtel until around 2200. On Huahine and Raiatea service is usually limited to a trip into the main town in the morning and a return to the villages in the afternoon. On Moorea and Bora Bora buses or *trucks* meet the boats from Papeete. No public transportation is available on the roads of the Austral, Tuamotu, Gambier, or Marquesas islands.

Car Rentals

Car rentals are available at most of the airports served by Air Tahiti and they're more expensive on the Leeward Islands than on Tahiti or Moorea due to a lack of competition. On Tahiti there's sometimes a mileage charge, whereas on Moorea, Huahine, Raiatea, and Bora Bora all rentals come with unlimited mileage. Public liability insurance is included by law, but collision damage waiver (CDW) insurance is extra. The insurance policies don't cover flat tire repair, stolen radios or accessories, broken keys, or towing charges if the renter is found to be responsible. If you can get a small group together, consider renting a minibus for a do-it-yourself island tour. Unless you have a major credit card you'll have to put a cash deposit down on the car. Your home driver's license will be accepted, although you must have had your driver's license for at least a year. Some companies rent to persons aged 18-24, but those under 25 must show a major credit card and the deductible amount not covered by the CDW insurance will be much higher.

Except on Tahiti, rental scooters are usually available and a strictly enforced local regulation requires you to wear a helmet *(casque)* at all times (CFP 5,000 fine for failure to comply). On some outer islands you car rent an open two-seater "fun car" slightly bigger than a golf cart and no helmet or driver's license is required for these. These and bicycles carry no insurance.

One major hassle with renting cars on the outer islands is that they usually give you a car with the fuel tank only a quarter full, so immediately after renting you must go to a gas station and tank up. Try to avoid putting in more gas than you can use by calculating how many km you might drive, then dividing that by 10 for the number of liters of gasoline you might use. Don't put in more than CFP 2,000 (about 20 liters) in any case or you'll be giving a nice gift to the rental agency (which, of course, is their hope in giving you a car that's not full). Gas stations are usually only in the main towns and open only weekdays during business hours, plus perhaps a couple of hours on weekend mornings. Expect to pay around CFP 112 a liter for gas, which works out to just over US$4 per American gallon—the South Pacific's highest priced gasoline to drive the most region's expensive rental cars.

Two traffic signs to know: a white line across a red background indicates a one-way street, while a slanting blue line on a white background means no parking. At unmarked intersections in Papeete, the driver on the right has priority. As in continental Europe and North America, driving is on the right-hand side of the road. The seldom-observed speed limit is 40 kph in Papeete, 60 kph around the island, and 90 kph on the RDO expressway. Drive with extreme care in congested areas—traffic accidents are frequent.

A good alternative to renting a car are the 4WD jeep safaris offered on Tahiti, Moorea, Huahine, Raiatea, and Bora Bora. These take you along rough interior roads inaccessible to most rental vehicles and the guides know all the superlative spots. Prices vary CFP 3,500-7,000 pp depending on how far you go.

Others

Taxis are a rip-off throughout Tahiti-Polynesia and are best avoided. If you must take one, always verify the fare before getting in. The hitching is still fairly good in Polynesia, although local residents along the north side of Moorea are fed up with it and don't stop. Hitching around Tahiti is only a matter of time.

Bicycling on the island of Tahiti is risky due to wild devil-may-care motorists, but most of the outer islands (Moorea included) have excellent, uncrowded roads. It's wiser to use *le truck* on Tahiti, though a bike would come in handy on the other islands where *le truck* is rare. The distances are just made for cycling!

International Airport

Faa'a Airport (PPT), 5.5 km southwest of Papeete, handles around 32,000 domestic, 2,300 international, and 1,000 military flights a year. The runway was created in 1959-61, using material dredged from the lagoon or trucked in from the Punaruu Valley. A taxi into town is CFP 1,500, or CFP 2,500 after 2000. *Le truck* up on the main highway will take you to the same place for only CFP 120 (CFP 200 at night) and starts running around 0530.

Many flights to Tahiti arrive in the middle of the night, but you can stretch out on the plastic benches inside the terminal (open 24 hours a day). Be aware that the persons who seem to be staffing the tourist information counter at the airport during the night may in fact be taxi drivers who will say anything to get a fare. We've received complaints from readers who were driven all over town from one closed hostel to another, only to be presented with a tremendous bill (you have been warned). Unless you're willing to spend a lot of money for the possibility of a few hours sleep it's better to wait in the terminal until dawn.

The airport bank (tel. 82-44-24), to the left as you come out of customs, opens weekdays 0730-1200/1245-1600, and one hour before and after the arrival and departure of all international flights. They charge commission CFP 450 on all traveler's checks (but no commission on French francs in cash). For other currencies, their rate is one percent better for traveler's checks than it is for cash. There's also a Banque Socredo branch (tel. 83-86-95) next to the Air Tahiti ticket office facing the parking lot at the far right (west) end of the airport. This office is not easily visible from inside the terminal, so search. It's open weekdays 0800-1200/1400-1700 (no exchanges after 1630) and an adjacent ATM machine is accessible 24 hours.

The airport luggage-storage counter is open weekdays 0700-1800, weekends 0700-1200/1400-1830, and two hours before and after international departures. They charge CFP 180 per day for a handbag, CFP 360 for a suitcase, backpack, or golf bags, CFP 600 for a bicycle, and CFP 1,000 for surfboards. If they're closed when you arrive, ask at the nearby snack bar. The left-luggage counter is poorly marked; it's to the right as you come out of customs and just outside the main terminal in an adjacent building.

Air Tahiti has a ticket office in the terminal open daily 0530-1730. These car rental companies have counters at the airport: Avis, Daniel, Europcar, Hertz, and Pierrot et Jacqueline. The airport post office is open weekdays 0600-1000/1300-1600, weekends 0600-1000. Several coin and card phones available at airport. The snack bar at the airport is open 24 hours (CFP 200 for cafe au lait). Public toilets are located near the snack bar and upstairs from the bank. The airport information number is tel. 86-60-61.

You can spend your leftover Pacific francs at the duty-free shops in the departure lounge, but don't expect any bargains. The Fare Hei, just outside the terminal, sells shell and flower leis for presentation to arriving or departing passengers.

All passengers arriving from Samoa or Fiji must have their baggage fumigated upon arrival, a process that takes about two hours (don't laugh if you're told this is to prevent the introduction of the "rhinoceros" into Polynesia—they mean the rhinoceros *beetle*). Fresh fruits, vegetables, and flowers are prohibited entry. Free luggage carts are supplied. There's no airport tax.

TAHITI

Tahiti, largest of the Societies, is an island of legend and song lying in the eye of Polynesia. Though only one of 118, this lush island of around 150,000 inhabitants is paradise itself to most people. Here you'll find an exciting city, big hotels, restaurants, nightclubs, things to see and do, valleys, mountains, reefs, trails, and history, plus transportation to everywhere. Since the days of Wallis, Bougainville, Cook, and Bligh, Tahiti has been the eastern gateway to the South Pacific.

Legends created by the early explorers, amplified in Jean-Jacques Rousseau's "noble savage" and taken up by the travel industry, make it difficult to write objectively about Tahiti. Though the Lafayette Nightclub is gone from Arue and Quinn's Tahitian Hut no longer graces Papeete's waterfront, Tahiti remains a delightful, enchanting place. In the late afternoon, as Tahitian crews practice canoe racing in the lagoon and Moorea gains a pink hue, the romance resurfaces. If you steer clear of the traffic jams and congestion in commercial Papeete and avoid the tourist ghettos west of the city, you can get a taste of the magic Paul Gauguin encountered in 1891. But whether you love or hate the capital, it's only on the outer islands of Polynesia, away from the motorists and the military complexes, that the full flavor lingers.

The Land

The island of Tahiti (1,045 square km) accounts for almost a third of the land area of Tahiti-Polynesia. Like Hawaii's Maui, Tahiti was formed more than a million years ago by two or three shield volcanoes joined at the isthmus of Taravao. These peaks once stood 3,000 meters above the sea, or 12,700 meters high counting from the seabed. Today the rounded, verdant summits of Orohena (2,241 meters) and Aorai (2,066 meters) rise in the center of Tahiti-nui and deep valleys radiate in all directions from these central peaks. Steep slopes drop abruptly from the high plateaus to coastal plains. The northeast coast is rugged and rocky, without a barrier reef, and thus exposed to intense, pounding surf; villages lie on a narrow strip between mountains and ocean. The south coast is broad and gentle with large gardens and coconut groves; a barrier reef shields it from the sea's fury.

CARLSBERG GLYPTOTEK, COPENHAGEN

PAUL GAUGUIN

Paul Gauguin's *Girl with a Flower,* pictured here, is now in the Carlsberg Glyptotek, Copenhagen. Gauguin was one of the first patrons of the French impressionists. Before he turned professional painter, Gauguin was a successful broker who worked at the Paris exchange. He went further than most of his contemporaries to search out the exotic, to paint in strong flat color, and to employ broad, bold decorative patterns made popular in France by the widespread distribution of Japanese wood block prints. Whereas later painters borrowed from African masks and carvings, Gauguin himself traveled directly to the source of his inspiration, arriving in Tahiti on 9 June 1891.

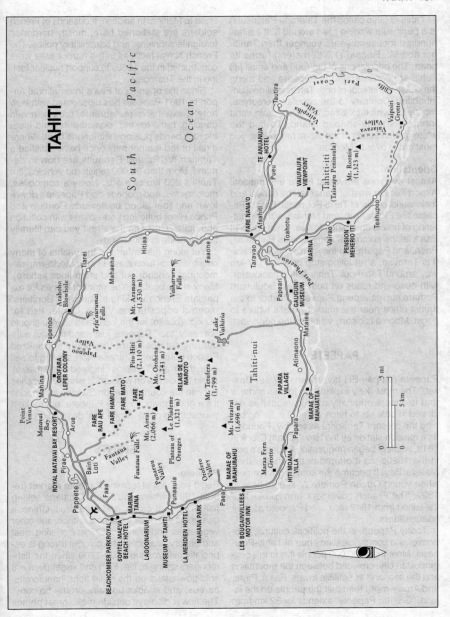

TAHITI

Pacific Ocean

South Pacific Ocean

Pari Coast

Tautira

Vaipori Grotto

Vairaava Valley

Vairapepa Valley

TE ANUANUA HOTEL

Pueu

Afaahiti

FARE NANA'O

Toahotu

Teahupoo

VAUFAUFA VIEWPOINT

Tahiti-iti (Taiarapu Peninsula)

▲ Mt. Roonui (1,323 m)

MARINA

PENSION MEHERIO ITI

Vairao

Toahotu

Hitiaa

Faaone

Mahaena

Tiarei

Arahoho Blowhole

Papenoo

Tefaauruamai Falls

Vaiharuru Falls

Taravao

Port Phaeton

Papeari

Papeari

GAUGUIN MUSEUM

Mataiea

Atimaono

PAPARA VILLAGE

MARAE OF MAHAIATEA

Papara

Marea Fern Grotto

HITI MOANA VILLA

▲ Mt. Aramaoro (1,530 m)

Paopoo Valley

Pito Hiti (2,110 m) ▲

▲ Mt. Orohena (2,241 m)

RELAIS DE LA MAROTO

Lake Vaihiria

▲ Mt. Tetufera (1,799 m)

Tahiti-nui

▲ Mt. Ivirairai (1,696 m)

MARAE OF ARAHURAHU

Paea

LES BOUGAINVILLEES MOTOR INN

Mahina

OROFARA LEPER COLONY

Papenoo

Point Venus

Matavai Bay

Arue

Pirae

ROYAL MATAVAI BAY RESORT

FARE RAU APE

FARE HAMUTA

FARE MATO

FARE ATA

Fautaua Valley

Fautaua Falls

Punaruu Valley

▲ Mt. Aorai (2,066 m)

Plateau of Oranges

Le Diademe (1,321 m)

Orofero Valley

Faaa

Papeete

Bain Loti

MARINA TAINA

SOFITEL MAEVA BEACH HOTEL

BEACHCOMBER PARKROYAL

LAGOONARIUM

MUSEUM OF TAHITI

LA MERIDIEN HOTEL

MAHANA PARK

Punaauia

5 mi

5 km

Tahiti-iti (also called the Taiarapu Peninsula) is a peninsula with no road around it. It's a few hundred thousand years younger than Tahiti-nui and Mt. Rooniu (1,323 meters) forms its heart. The populations of big *(nui)* and small *(iti)* Tahiti are concentrated in Papeete and along the coast; the interior of both Tahitis is almost un-inhabited. Contrary to the popular stereotype, mostly brown/black beaches of volcanic sand fringe this turtle-shaped island. To find the white/golden sands of the travel brochures, you must cross over to Moorea.

Orientation

Almost everyone arrives at Faa'a International Airport five km west of Papeete, the capital and main tourist center of Tahiti-Polynesia. East of Papeete are Pirae, Arue, and Mahina, with a smattering of hotels and things to see, while south of Faa'a lie the commuter communities Punaauia, Paea, and Papara. On the narrow neck of Tahiti is Taravao, a refueling stop on your 117-km way around Tahiti-nui. Tahiti-iti is a backwater, with dead-end roads on both sides. Boulevard Pomare curves around Papeete's harbor to the tourist office near the market—that's where to begin. Moorea is clearly visible to the northwest.

PAPEETE

Papeete (pa-pay-EH-tay) means "Water Basket." The most likely explanation for this name is that islanders originally used calabashes enclosed in baskets to fetch water at a spring behind the present Territorial Assembly. Founded as a mission station by the Rev. William Crook in 1818, whalers began frequenting Papeete's port in the 1820s, as it offered better shelter than Matavai Bay. It became the seat of government when young Queen Pomare IV settled here in 1827. The French governors who "protected" the island from 1842 also used Papeete as their headquarters.

Today Papeete is the political, cultural, economic, and communications hub of Tahiti-Polynesia. More than 100,000 people live in this cosmopolitan city, crowded between the mountains and the sea, and its satellite towns, Faa'a, Pirae, and Arue—more than half the people on the island. "Greater Papeete" extends for 32 km from

Paea to Mahina. In addition, thousands of French soldiers are stationed here, mostly hardened foreign legionnaires and paramilitary police. The French Naval facilities in the harbor area were constructed in the 1960s to support nuclear testing in the Tuamotus.

Since the opening of Faa'a International Airport in 1961 Papeete has blossomed with new hotels, expensive restaurants, bars with wild dancing, radio towers, skyscrapers, and electric rock bands pulsing their jet-age beat. Where a nail or red feather may once have satisfied a Tahitian, VCRs and Renaults are now in demand. More than 35,000 registered vehicles jam Tahiti's 200 km of roads. Noisy automobiles, motorcycles, and mopeds clog Papeete's downtown and roar along boulevards Pomare and Prince Hinoï buffeting pedestrians with pollution and noise. Crossing the street you can literally take your life in your hands.

Yet along the waterfront the yachts of many countries rock luxuriously in their Mediterranean moorings (anchor out and stern lines ashore). Many of the boats are permanent homes for expatriate French working in the city. "Bonitiers" moored opposite the Vaima Center fish for *auhopu* (bonito) for the local market. You should not really "tour" Papeete, just wander about without any set goal. Visit the highly specialized French boutiques, Chinese stores trying to sell everything, and Tahitians clustered in the market. Avoid the capital on weekends when life washes out into the countryside; on Sunday afternoons it's a ghost town. Explore Papeete, but make it your starting point—not a final destination.

SIGHTS

Papeete

Begin your visit at teeming **Papeete market** (rebuilt 1987) where you'll see Tahitians selling fish, fruit, root crops, and breadfruit; Chinese gardeners with their tomatoes, lettuce, and other vegetables; and French or Chinese offering meat and bakery products. The colorful throng is especially picturesque 1600-1700 when the fishmongers spring to life. Fish and vegetables are sold downstairs on the main floor, handicrafts, pareus, and snacks upstairs on the balcony. The flower displays outside make great photos and the vendors are quite friendly. The biggest market of the week begins around 0500 Sunday morning and is over by 0730.

The streets to the north of the market are lined with two-story Chinese stores built after the great fire of 1884. The US$14.5-million **Town Hall** on rue Paul Gauguin was inaugurated in 1990 on the site of a smaller colonial building demolished to make way. The architect designed the three-story building to resemble the palace of Queen Pomare that once stood on Place Tarahoi near the present post office. The Town Hall gardens are a nice place to sit.

Notre Dame Catholic Cathedral (1875) is on rue du Général de Gaulle, a block and a half southeast of the market. Notice the Polynesian faces and the melange of Tahitian and Roman dress on the striking series of paintings of the crucifixion inside. Diagonally across the street is the **Vaima Center,** Papeete's finest window shopping venue, erected in 1977.

Farther down on rue de Gaulle is Place Tarahoi. The **Territorial Assembly** on the left occupies the site of the former royal palace, demolished in 1966. The adjacent residence of the French high commissioner is private, but the assembly building and its lovely gardens are worth a brief visit. In front of the entrance gate is a monument erected in 1982 to **Pouvanaa a Oopa** (1895-1977), a Tahitian WW I hero who struggled all his life for the independence of his country. The plaque on the monument says nothing about Pouvanaa's fight for independence and against the bomb! In July 1995 nearly a third of the adult population of Tahiti gathered here to protest French nuclear testing in the Tuamotus.

Beside the post office across the busy avenue from Place Tarahoi is **Parc Bougainville** with its garden café. A monument to Bougainville himself, who sailed around the world in 1766-69, is flanked by two old naval guns. One, stamped "Fried Krupp 1899," is from Count Felix von Luckner's famous raider *Seeadler,* which ended up on the Maupihaa reef in 1917; the other is off the French gunboat *Zélée,* sunk in Papeete harbor by German cruisers in 1914.

Much of the bureaucracy works along avenue Bruat just west, a gracious tree-lined French provincial avenue. The protectorate's first governor, Admiral Armand Bruat, set up a military camp here in 1843. You may observe French justice in action at the **Palais de Justice** (weekdays 0800-1100). The public gallery is up the stairway and straight ahead. Opposite the police station farther up avenue Bruat is the War Memorial.

Back on the waterfront just before the Protestant church is the **Tahiti Perles Center** (B.P. 850, 98713 Papeete; tel. 50-53-10). A black pearl museum (weekdays 0800-1200 and 1400-1730, Saturday 0900-1200; admission free) and aquarium are the main attractions, but look around the showroom where the famous black pearls are sold. A 20-minute video presentation shown on request explains how cultured black pearls are "farmed" in the Gambier Islands. The center is owned by a pioneer of the black pearl industry, Robert Wan, whose nine farms in the Gambier and Tuamotu groups are linked to Tahiti by his own charter airline Wanair.

Next to the pearl museum is the headquarters of the **Evangelical Church** in Tahiti-Polynesia, with a church dating from 1875 but rebuilt in 1981, a girls' hostel, public cafeteria, and health clinic. It was here that the London Missionary Society established Paofai Mission in 1818. The British consulate occupied the hostel site from 1837 to 1958 and George Pritchard had his office here.

Continue west along the bay past the outrigger racing canoes to the "neo-Polynesian" **Cultural Center** (1973) or Te Fare Tahiti Nui, which houses a public library, notice boards, and auditoriums set among pleasant grounds. This complex is run by the Office Territorial d'Action Culturelle (OTAC), which organizes the annual Heiva Festival and many other events. The municipal swimming pool is beyond (go upstairs to the restaurant for a view). Return to the center of town along the waterfront.

Fautaua Valley

If you'd like to make a short trip out of the city, go to the Hôtel de Ville and take a Mamao-Titioro *truck* to the **Bain Loti,** three km up the Fautaua Valley from the Mormon Temple. A bust of writer Pierre Loti marks the spot where he had the love affair described in *The Marriage of Loti.* Today the local kids swim in a pool in the river here.

A dirt road continues three km farther up the Fautaua Valley but because it's part of a water catchment, private cars are prohibited, so you

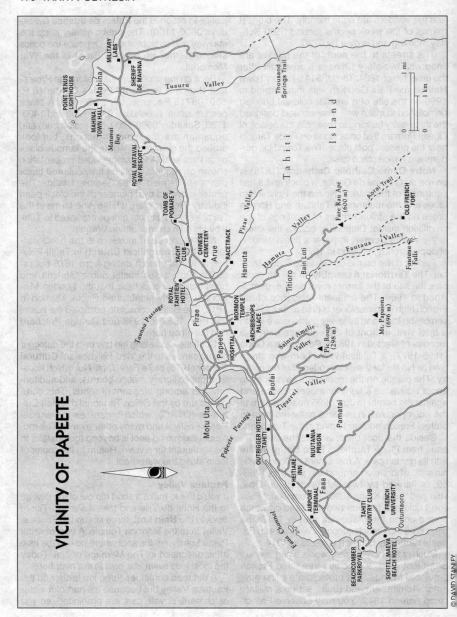

VICINITY OF PAPEETE

MILITARY LABS

SHERIFF
DE MAHINA

POINT VENUS
LIGHTHOUSE

Mahina

Tuauru Valley

Thousand
Springs Trail

MAHINA
TOWN HALL

Matavai
Bay

ROYAL MATAVAI
BAY RESORT

TOMB OF
POMARE V

Pirae Valley

Tahiti Island

Fare Rau Ape
(600 m)

Aorai Trail

OLD FRENCH
FORT

Pirae Valley

CHINESE
CEMETERY

Arue

RACETRACK

YACHT
CLUB

Hamuta

Titioro

Fautaua Valley

Fautaua
Falls

ROYAL
TAHITIEN
HOTEL

Pirae

MORMON
TEMPLE

ARCHBISHOPS
PALACE

Papeete

HOSPITAL

Sainte Amelie
Valley

Mt. Papaiona
(696 m)

Taunoa Passage

Motu Uta

Paofai
Valley

Pic Rouge
(298 m)

Tipaerui Valley

Pamatai

Papeete Passage

OUTRIGGER
HOTEL
TAHITI

HEITIARE
INN

NUUTANIA
PRISON

AIRPORT
TERMINAL

Faaa

Faaa Channel

TAHITI
COUNTRY CLUB

FRENCH
UNIVERSITY

Outumaoro

BEACHCOMBER
PARKROYAL

SOFITEL MAEVA
BEACH HOTEL

0   1 mi

0   1 km

© DAVID STANLEY

must walk. From the end of the road, a trail straight ahead leads directly to **Fautaua Falls** (30 minutes) with several river crossings. Back a bit on the left, just before the end of the road, is a wooden footbridge across the river. Here begins a steep one-hour trail up to a 19th-century French fort at the top of the falls. The fort controlled the main trail into Tahiti's interior, and it's still an excellent hiking area. There's a CFP 600 pp charge to go up the valley, and it's only open on weekdays. Go early and make a day of it.

Back on avenue Georges Clemenceau near the Mormon Temple is the impressive **Kanti Chinese Temple,** built in 1987, which is usually open mornings until noon.

East of Papeete

Arue (a-roo-AY) and Point Venus can be done easily as a half-day side trip from Papeete by *le truck* (12 km each way). Begin by taking a Mahina *truck* from near the tourist office to the **tomb of King Pomare V** at PK 4.7 Arue, five km outside the city. The mausoleum surmounted by a Grecian urn was built in 1879 for Queen Pomare IV, but her remains were subsequently removed to make room for her son, Pomare V, who died of drink in 1891 at the age of 52 (Paul Gauguin witnessed the funeral). Irreverent tour guides often remark that the urn resembles a bottle of Benedictine, Pomare V's favorite liqueur. A century earlier, on 13 February 1791, his grandfather, Pomare II, then nine, was made first king of Tahiti on the great *marae* that once stood on this spot. Pomare II became the first Christian convert and built a 215-meter-long version of King Solomon's Temple here, but nothing remains of either temple. The colonial-style **Mairie de Arue** (1892) is at PK 5.6.

The **Royal Matavai Bay Resort Hôtel** (PK 8.1) on One Tree Hill, a couple of km east, was built in 1968 on a spectacular series of terraces down the hillside to conform to a local regulation that no building should be more than two-thirds the height of a coconut tree. There's a superb view of Point Venus, Tahiti, and Moorea from the Governor's Bench on the knoll beyond the swimming pool above the hotel entrance. In Matavai Bay below the resort, Capt. Samuel Wallis anchored in 1767, after having "discovered" Tahiti. There's good swimming off the black beach below the hotel.

Catch another *truck* or walk on to **Point Venus** (PK 10). Captain Cook camped on this point between the river and the lagoon during his visit to observe the transit of the planet Venus across the sun on 3 June 1769. Captain Bligh also occupied Point Venus for two months in 1788 while collecting breadfruit shoots for transportation to the West Indies. On 5 March 1797, the first members of the London Missionary Society landed here, as a monument recalls. From Tahiti, Protestantism spread throughout Polynesia and as far as Vanuatu.

Today there's a park on the point, with a 25-meter-high lighthouse (1867) among the palms and ironwood trees. The view of Tahiti across Matavai Bay is superb, and twin-humped Orohena, highest peak on the island, is in view (you can't see it from Papeete itself). Topless sunbathing is common on the wide dark sands along the bay and you can see pareus being made in the handicraft center in the park. Weekdays, Point Venus is a peaceful place, the perfect choice if you'd like to get away from the rat race in Papeete and spend some time at the beach (weekends it gets crowded).

SPORTS AND RECREATION

Information on the **International Golf Course Olivier Breaud,** on the south coast at Atimaono, can be found later in this chapter.

Tahiti Plongée (B.P. 2192, 98713 Papeete; tel./fax 41-00-62), also known as "Club Corail Sub," offers scuba diving several times daily from its base at the Hôtel Te Puna Bel Air, Punaauia. The charge is CFP 4,000 per dive all-inclusive, or CFP 19,000 for a five-dive card, CFP 30,000 for 10 dives. You can ocean dive Tues.-Sun. at 0800 and on Wednesday and Saturday at 1400; lagoon diving is daily at 1000 and weekdays at 1400 (no diving on Monday). Divemaster Henri Pouliquen was one of the first to teach scuba diving to children. The youngest person Henri has taken down was aged two years, six months—the oldest was a woman of 72 on her first dive. Since 1979 Tahiti Plongée has arranged more than 10,000 dives with children, certainly a unique achievement. Another specialty is diving for people with disabilities.

Diving is also offered by a new scuba operation at the **Sofitel Maeva Beach** (B.P. 6008, 98702 Faa'a; tel. 42-80-42, fax 43-84-70) and by **Eleuthera Plongée** (tel. 42-49-29) at the Marina Taina in Punaauia.

On the other side of Papeete, you can dive with Pascal Le Cointre of the **Yacht Club of Tahiti** (B.P. 51167, 98716 Pirae; tel. 42-23-55, fax 43-64-36) at PK 4, Arue. Outings are offered at 0900 and 1400 daily except Sunday afternoon and Monday. It's CFP 5,000 for one dive or CFP 22,500 for five dives. A certification course costs the same as five dives, plus CFP 2,200/2,500 for CMAS/PADI registration (log book CFP 1,600 extra)—good value.

International Tahiti Immersions (Joël Roussel, tel./fax 57-77-93), at the Marina Puunui on the southeast side of the island, does scuba diving at CFP 5,000 a dive.

If you want to set out on your own, **Nauti-Sport** (B.P. 62, 98713 Papeete; tel. 50-59-59, fax 42-17-75; weekdays 0800-1145/1315-1700, Saturday 0730-1130) in Fare Ute sells every type of scuba gear and also rents tanks (CFP 2,500). The **Centre de Plongée Dolphin Sub** (B.P. 5213, 98716 Pirae; tel. 45-21-98, fax 43-39-49) behind Nauti-Sport offers scuba trips at 0845 and 1400 daily at competitive prices and has information on diving all around Polynesia.

Most diving is on the Punaauia reef. Other favorite scuba locales include a scuttled Pan Am Catalina PBY seaplane near the airport, its upper wing 12 meters down; and a schooner wreck, 10 meters down, about 45 meters from the breakwater at the entrance to the harbor.

The **Ski Nautique Club de Tahiti** (tel. 77-22-62; Tues.-Fri. 1200-1800, weekends 0900-1800) on the waterfront at the Hôtel Te Puna Bel Air, Punaauia, offers water skiing at CFP 2,300 or CFP 20,000 for 10 sessions.

The **Tura'i Mata'are Surfing School** (B.P. 4232, 98713 Papeete; tel./fax 41-91-37), at Kelly Surf Boutique in the Fare Tony Commercial Center on boulevard Pomare, Papeete, teaches surfing and body surfing to persons from the age of eight and up. Their half-day introduction to surfing is CFP 4,000, and courses with five three-hour lessons (CFP 18,000) or 10 lessons (CFP 25,000) are offered. Boards and transportation are supplied and a certificate is issued.

Papeete's **municipal swimming pool** (tel. 42-89-24) is open to the public Tues.-Fri. 1145-

1600, Saturday and Sunday 0730-1700 (CFP 350). Most evenings after 1800 **soccer** is practiced in the sports field opposite the municipal swimming pool.

MOUNTAIN CLIMBING

Tahiti's finest climb is to the summit of **Aorai** (2,066 meters), second-ranking peak on the island. (Some guides claim 2,110-meter Piti Hiti is the second-highest peak on Tahiti but it's actually a shoulder of Orohena.) A beaten 10-km track all the way to the top of Aorai makes a guide unnecessary, but food, water, flashlight, and long pants *are* required, plus a sleeping bag and warm sweater if you plan to spend the night up there. At last report the refuges at Fare Mato (1,400 meters) and Fare Ata (1,800 meters) were in good shape with drinking water available and splendid sunset views. Each refuge sleeps about 10 persons on the floor at no charge.

The trailhead is at Fare Rau Ape (600 meters) near **Le Belvédère** (tel. 42-73-44), a fancy French restaurant seven km up a rough, pot-holed road from Pirae. Taxis want CFP 5,000 for the trip from Papeete and few people live up there, so hitching would be a case of finding tourists headed for the restaurant, and weekends are best for this. You could rent a small car at the kilometer rate but parking near the restaurant is limited.

The restaurant does provide their clients with free *truck* transportation from most Papeete hotels and this the easiest way to get there. You can reserve the Belvédère *truck* at the Hôtel Royal Papeete reception or at Tahiti Nui Travel in the Vaima Center. Of course, in order to use it you'll be required to take a complete meal including salad, dessert, coffee, and wine at CFP 4,500. The specialty is fondue bourguignone, a meat fondue, but you can substitute mahi mahi, steak, or shish kebab. The *truck* departs most Papeete hotels at 1130 and 1630, leaving the restaurant for the return trip to Papeete at 1430 and 1930.

To make a day of it, catch the 1130 *truck* up to the restaurant on the understanding that you'll be eating dinner and returning to town on the 1930 *truck* (make sure all of this is clearly understood before you pay—Tina Brichet at Le Belvédère

The track to the top of Aorai runs along this razor-back ridge.

DAVID STANLEY

speaks good English). This would give you all afternoon to cover part of the trail, although it's unlikely you'd have time to reach the top (even if you only get as far as Fare Mato it's still well worth the effort). Take a sandwich along for lunch. You should be able to leave some clean clothes at the restaurant to change into for dinner, and be sure to bring your bathing suit and a towel in case you have time to use their swimming pool. If you can get in all of this, the CFP 4,500 pp price becomes quite reasonable.

A large signboard outside the restaurant maps out the hike. Just above the restaurant is the French Army's Centre d'Instruction de Montagne, where you can sign a register. From Fare Rau Ape to the summit takes seven hours: 1.5 hours to Hamuta, another two to Fare Mato (good view of Le Diadème, not visible from Papeete), then 2.5 hours to Fare Ata, where most hikers spend the first night in order to cover the last 40 minutes to the summit the following morning. The hut at Fare Ata is in a low depression 100 meters beyond an open shelter.

The view from Aorai is magnificent, with Papeete and many of the empty interior valleys in full view. To the north is Tetiaroa atoll, while Moorea's jagged outline fills the west. Even on a cloudy day the massive green hulk of neighboring Orohena (2,241 meters) often towers above the clouds like Mt. Olympus. A bonus is the chance to see some of the original native vegetation of Tahiti, which survives better at high altitudes and in isolated gullies. In good weather

Aorai is exhausting but superb; in the rain it's a disaster.

Mt. Marau

The road inland from directly opposite Faa'a Airport goes under the RDO bypass road and up the side of the island to an excellent viewpoint over northwestern Tahiti. It's a rough 10 km drive which should only be attempted in dry weather. From the TV tower at the end of the track it's only 30 minutes on foot to the summit of Mt. Marau (1,493 meters). From here you'll get another incredible view down into the Plateau of Oranges to the south, up the Fautaua Valley to the north, and along the ridge to Le Diadème and Aorai to the east.

ACCOMMODATIONS

Most of the places to stay are in the congested Punaauia-to-Mahina strip engulfing Faa'a International Airport and Papeete and they tend to offer much poorer value for many than comparable accommodations on Moorea, which is only a short ferry ride away. With the closure of the Hiti Mahana Beach Club near Point Venus in 1995 there are no longer any regular campgrounds on Tahiti. Recently several new medium-priced places to stay have sprung up on the Tahiti-iti peninsula and south side of Tahiti, offering the chance to break your trip around the island. These (and the selections in Punaauia

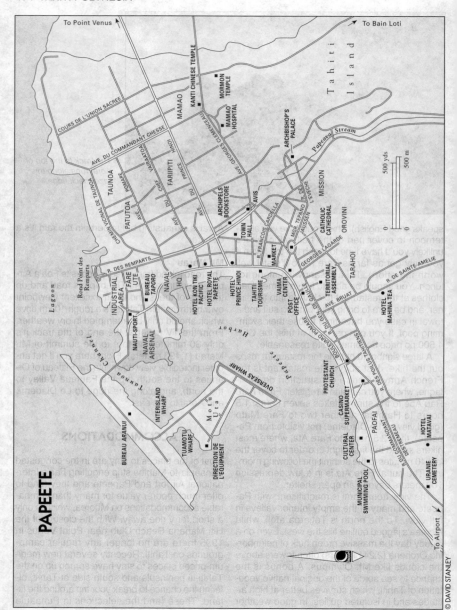

To Point Venus

To Bain Loti

Tahiti Island

Pahaeau Stream

COURS DE L'UNION SACREE

AVE. DU COMMANDANT CHESSE

MAMAO

KANTI CHINESE TEMPLE

MORMON TEMPLE

MAMAO HOSPITAL

ARCHBISHOP'S PALACE

MISSION

TAUNOA

PATUTOA

TAUNOA

POMAPE

FARIIPITI

CHEF

DU PRINCE

VAIRAATOA

AVE. GEORGES CLEMENCEAU

HINOI

ARCHIPELS' BOOKSTORE

AVIS

CATHOLIC CATHEDRAL

OROVINI

TARAHOI

Rond Point des Remparts

R. DES REMPARTS

FARE UTE

BUREAU TAPORO

NAVAL HQ

TOWN HALL

MARKET

MGR. TEPANO JAUSSEN

R. FRANÇOIS CARDELLA

GEORGES LAGARDE

TERRITORIAL ASSEMBLY

R. DE SAINTE-AMELIE

INDUSTRIAL AREA

Lagoon

HOTEL KON TIKI PACIFIC

HOTEL ROYAL PAPEETE

HOTEL PRINCE HINOI

TAHITI TOURISME

VAIMA CENTER

POST OFFICE

AVE. BRUAT

HOTEL MAHINA TEA

NAUTI-SPORT

NAVAL ARSENAL

Tipaeru Channel

Harbor

BOULEVARD POMARE

AVE. DU GEN. DE GAULLE

PROTESTANT CHURCH

R. DES POILUS TAHITIENS

Papeete Harbor

INTERISLAND WHARF

Motu Uta

OVERSEAS WHARF

CASINO SUPERMARKET

PAOFAI

BUREAU ARANUI

TUAMOTU WHARF

DIRECTION DE L'EQUIPMENT

CULTURAL CENTER

AVE. DU COMMANDANT DESTREMEAU

HOTEL MATAVAI

PAPEETE

MUNICIPAL SWIMMING POOL

URANIE CEMETERY

To Airport

500 yds

500 m

© DAVID STANLEY

within commuting distance of Papeete) are covered later in this chapter.

Budget

Many backpackers head straight for **Hostel Teamo** (B.P. 2407, 98713 Papeete; tel. 42-47-26, fax 43-56-95), 8 rue du Pont Neuf, Quartier Mission, a century-old house in an attractive neighborhood near the Archbishop's Palace, just a short walk east of downtown. To get there from the market head inland on rue François Cardella. It's a little hard to find the first time, but convenient once you know it. Shared dormitory-style accommodations with variable cooking facilities are CFP 1,200 pp in a nine-bed dorm or CFP 1,500 pp in a better six-bed dorm. Private rooms are CFP 3,500 double with shared bath, CFP 4,000 double with private bath (bring your own towel). There's a nice veranda with French TV, but the managers can be temperamental and theft is not unknown (even food left in the fridge may not be considered sacred). Checkout time is 1000, but you can stay until 1900 for an additional CFP 800 pp fee (otherwise, you must leave). The receptionist will hold your luggage at CFP 150 a day and will provide free transportation to the airport if you're catching a late flight. Their minibus also meets international flights at the airport and provides free transfers to the hostel. It's all rather basic (and we've received letters from several readers who thought it was *awful*) but Teamo remains the choice of those looking for the cheapest possible place.

Nearby on busy rue du Frère Alain is the **Tahiti Budget Lodge** (B.P. 237, 98713 Papeete; tel. 42-66-82, fax 43-06-79), a quiet white wooden house with green trim, straight back on rue Édouard Ahnne from the market. The 11 four-bed rooms are CFP 1,900 pp, CFP 3,900 double with shared bath, CFP 4,800 double with private bath. Some rooms don't have locks on the doors. Communal cooking facilities are provided (but screens on the windows are not). They charge CFP 500 pp to leave your luggage until 2000, or CFP 1,000 per piece to leave items for one week. Although not without problems (or mosquitos), it's better kept and less crowded than Teamo for only a little more money. Just don't show up in the middle of the night expecting to get a room as you'll be most unwelcome.

Instead wait in the airport until *le truck* begins running at daybreak.

Inexpensive

On the mountain side of the highway at PK 8.3, Punaauia, not far from the Centre Commercial Moana Nui, is a five-bed dormitory run by **Moana Surf Tours** (Moana David, B.P. 6734, 98702 Faa'a; tel./fax 43-70-70). A place here is CFP 10,300 a day including breakfast, dinner, and unlimited surf transfers to breaks off Tahiti and Moorea. Reductions are possible for long stays.

In a pinch, **Pension Dahl Fifi** (Joséphine Dahl, tel. 82-63-30), directly across the street from the airport terminal (the second house on the left up the hill beside Blanchisserie Pressing Mea Ma), has three rooms with bath at CFP 3,500/6,000 single/double, breakfast included. Communal cooking facilities are available, but the location is noisy due to the nearby industrial laundry and airport.

The **Hôtel Shogun** (Bruno Gatto, B.P. 2880, 98713 Papeete; tel. 43-13-93, fax 43-27-28), 10 rue du Commandant Destremeau, Papeete, has seven a/c rooms with bath facing the noisy road at CFP 6,000 single or double, or CFP 6,500 single or double on the back side. A monthly rate of CFP 90,000 double is available.

The **Hôtel Mahina Tea** (B.P. 17, 98713 Papeete; tel. 42-00-97), up rue Sainte-Amélie from avenue Bruat, is about the only regular economy-priced hotel in the city. The 16 rooms are CFP 4,000 single or double, reduced to CFP 3,400/3,700 single/double if you stay three or more nights. A room with twin beds instead of a double bed is CFP 500 more. Six small studios with cooking facilities cost CFP 90,000 a month double. All rooms have private bath with hot water. No cooking facilities are provided in the daily rental rooms but you may use the shared fridge downstairs. The Mahina Tea does occasionally get some village-style noise from the surrounding houses. This family-operated place has been around for many years but it's not overrun by the backpack brigade. An easy walk from town, the Mahina Tea is excellent value for Papeete.

Expensive

The high-rise **Hôtel Prince Hinoï** (B.P. 4545, 98713 Papeete; tel. 42-32-77, fax 42-33-66), avenue du Prince Hinoï at boulevard Pomare, has 72 small a/c rooms at CFP 10,260 single or double plus tax but including breakfast. The New Diamond Casino is on the 2nd floor of this six-story hotel.

The venerable **Hôtel Royal Papeete** (B.P. 919, 98713 Papeete; tel. 42-01-29, fax 43-79-09), downtown on boulevard Pomare opposite the Moorea ferry landing, has 78 large a/c rooms beginning at CFP 9,000/10,500/12,000 single/double/triple plus tax. The Royal Papeete should be your choice if you want to stay right in the belly of Papeete's nightlife quarter. The hotel's two lively nightclubs downstairs offer free admission to guests and the Royal Casino is open nightly. Just make sure you don't get a room directly above the clubs unless you like being rocked to sleep by a disco beat. There's a Hertz desk at the Royal Papeete.

Hôtel Kon Tiki Pacific (B.P. 111, 98713 Papeete; tel. 43-72-82, fax 42-11-66), nearby at 271 boulevard Pomare, has long been popular among French military personnel in transit and its high-rise building opposite the Moorea ferry wharf offers excellent views into the nearby French naval base. The 44 spacious a/c rooms begin at CFP 8,500/9,900/11,900 single/double/triple plus tax. Don't accept one of the noisy rooms near the elevator, which are always offered first. Instead, get one with a balcony on the front side of the building and immerse yourself in the intrigue.

Premium

The six-story **Hôtel Tiare Tahiti** (B.P. 2359, 98713 Papeete; tel. 43-68-48, fax 43-68-47), at 417 boulevard Pomare on the waterfront next to the post office, has 38 a/c rooms beginning at CFP 12,000/14,000 double/triple plus tax (the first child under 12 free). Ask for an upstairs room with a balcony facing the harbor. Opened in December 1996, the Tiare Tahiti is not worth 50% more than the three places listed under "Expensive" above.

The **Hôtel Le Mandarin** (B.P. 302, 98713 Papeete; tel. 42-16-33, fax 42-16-32), 51 rue Colette, is a modern hotel with an Asian flair built in 1988. The 37 a/c rooms here are also overpriced at CFP 12,500/14,000/16,000 single/double/triple (children under 12 free). One British reader reported that her room was grubby and in poor repair, the walls not soundproof,

the charges for laundry and drinks excessive, and the service lacking.

Luxury

The French-owned **Sofitel Maeva Beach** (B.P. 6008, 98702 Faa'a; tel. 42-80-42, fax 43-84-70) at PK 7.5, Punaauia, was built by UTA French Airlines in the late 1960s. The 224 a/c rooms in this pyramidal high-rise cost CFP 20,000 single or double garden view, CFP 23,000 lagoon view, CFP 25,000 panoramic view plus tax (children under 12 free). The seven-story Maeva Beach faces a man-made white beach but with pollution on the increase in the adjacent Punaauia Lagoon, most swimmers stick to the hotel pool. Tennis courts are available and scuba diving is offered. For CFP 700 pp roundtrip the hotel's recreation people will shuttle you out to their offshore sunbathing pontoon anchored above a snorkeling locale (no lifeguard or shade). Numerous cruising yachts anchor offshore and use the resort's wharf to tie up their dinghies. Europcar has a desk here.

The Japanese-owned **Tahiti Beachcomber Parkroyal** (B.P. 6014, 98702 Faa'a; tel. 86-51-10, fax 86-51-30), at PK 7, Faa'a, is a former Travelodge built in 1974. It's the first place west of the airport, and a smart international hotel. The 180 a/c rooms in the main building begin at CFP 29,300 single or double; for one of the 32 overwater bungalows add 50% again. Children under 14 sharing the room with their parents stay for free. A breakfast and dinner meal plan is CFP 6,500 pp extra. Tahitian dancing and crafts demonstrations are regular features. The hotel pool is reserved for guests and the beach is artificial, but the attendants in the water sports kiosk on the beach will gladly ferry you out to the nudist pontoons anchored in mid-lagoon for CFP 800 roundtrip. Other paid activities include water-skiing, kayaking, winsurfing, and scuba diving. The Automatic Currency Exchange machine in the lobby of this hotel changes the banknotes of nine countries for CFP 400 commission. Europcar and Hertz have desks here.

The **Outrigger Hôtel Tahiti** (B.P. 416, 98713 Papeete; tel. 53-23-77, fax 53-28-77), at PK 2.6 between Papeete and the airport, reopened in mid-1999 after being completely redeveloped by Outrigger Hotels of Hawaii. This site was once the residence of Princess Pomare, daughter of the last king of Tahiti, and from 1961 to 1996 a historic colonial-style hotel stood there. The 163 a/c rooms with fridge are divided between a large three-story building and garden and lagoon front bungalows. Rates begin at CFP 27,500 and increase to CFP 50,000 for the best suite. There's a swimming pool, 300-seat conference room, and an overwater restaurant with splendid sunset views of Moorea. It's the closest luxury hotel to central Papeete.

The **Royal Matavai Bay Resort Hôtel** (B.P. 14700, 98701 Arue; tel. 46-12-34, fax 48-25-44) at PK 8, Mahina, was built by Pan American Airways in 1968. Formerly known as the Tahara'a Hôtel, and a Hyatt Regency from 1988 to 1997, it's owned by Réginald Flosse, son of the territory's president, Gaston Flosse. Fully renovated in 1998, the 190 spacious a/c rooms begin at CFP 27,000 single or double, CFP 32,000 triple (children under 18 free). For breakfast and dinner, add CFP 5,500 pp. Happy hour at the hotel bar is 1730-1830. Built on a hillside overlooking Matavai Bay, this is one of the few hotels in the world where you take an elevator *down* to your room. The views from the balconies are superb and a black-sand beach is at the foot of the hill. The Royal Matavai Bay provides a shuttle service to and from Papeete for guests. Europcar has a desk here.

FOOD

Food Trailers

In the early evening take a stroll along the Papeete waterfront near the Moorea ferry landing, past the dozens of gaily lit vans known as *les roulottes* which form a colorful night market. Here you'll find everything from couscous, pizza, waffles, crêpes, and *brouchettes* (shish kebab) to steak with real *pommes frites*. There's no better place to try *poisson cru*. As the city lights wink gently across the harbor, sailors promenade with their *vahines,* adding a touch of romance and glamour. The food and atmosphere are excellent, and even if you're not dining, it's a scene not to miss. The most crowded *roulottes* generally have the best food but you may have to wait as lots of people bring large bowls to be filled and taken home. No alcohol is available.

Self-Service

Poly-Self Restaurant (tel. 43-75-32), 8 rue Gauguin behind the Banque de Polynésie, dispenses filling Chinese-style lunches at about CFP 800. It's unpretentious but a little overpriced.

The **Foyer de Jeunes Filles de Paofai** (tel. 46-06-80) opposite the Protestant church has a good modern self-service cafeteria open weekdays for lunch 1130-1300. Alcohol is not available here.

Snack Bars

To sample the cuisine of the people, check out the Chinese/Tahitian eateries on rue Cardella right beside the market. Try *ma'a tinito,* a mélange of red beans, pork, macaroni, and vegetables on rice (CFP 750). A large Hinano beer at these places is around CFP 350.

Acajou (tel. 43-19-22), 7 rue Cardella by the market, half a block from the tourist office, serves a large coffee with fresh buttered bread which makes an excellent CFP 250 breakfast or mid-morning snack.

Some of the cheapest and freshest baguette sandwiches in town are sold over the counter at **Boulangerie L'Epi d'Or** (tel. 43-07-13), 26 rue du Maréchal Foch near the market.

Inexpensive grilled meat and fish dishes are the specialty at **Snack Paofai** (tel. 42-95-76; Mon.-Sat. 0500-1400) near Clinique Paofai. A complete meal chosen from among the specials listed on the blackboard and consumed on their airy terrace will run CFP 750, but arrive before 1300 or you'll find little left. On Thursday they prepare a special couscous dish. It's among the best values in town, as you'll gather from all the Tahitians eating there.

If you're catching the interisland boats *Vaeanu* or *Taporo VI* from Motu Uta, check out the **Restaurant Motu Uta** behind the *Vaeanu* office near the wharf. They offer takeaway lunches and big bottles of cold beer. Also check the food trailers at the south end of the parking lot near the tall blue port administration building, 75 meters from Motu Uta wharf.

Asian

The most popular Chinese restaurant in Papeete may be the **Waikiki Restaurant** (tel. 42-95-27; open daily 1100-1300 and 1800-2100, closed

Sunday lunch and Monday dinner), rue Leboucher 20, near the market.

The inexpensive **Cathay Restaurant** (tel. 42-99-67), 28 rue du Maréchal Foch, also near the market, serves large portions of dishes *maa tinito* and steak frites, accompanied by large Hinano beers.

Papeete's finest Cantonese restaurant is **Restaurant Le Plazza** (tel. 42-16-33) at the Hôtel Mandarin, 26 rue des Écoles. Their specialty is Chinese fondue at CFP 3,300 pp for four to seven persons, CFP 3,100 pp for eight or more. You must reserve 24 hours in advance.

Restaurant La Saigonnaise (tel. 42-05-35; closed Sunday) on avenue du Prince Hinoï has moderately expensive Vietnamese food. Saigonese soup makes a good lunch.

Italian

For a taste of the Mediterranean, **La Pizzeria** (tel. 42-98-30; open Mon.-Sat. 1130-2200), on boulevard Pomare near the Tahiti Pearl Center, prepares real pizza in a brick oven. The prices are reasonable for the waterfront location—they're all spelled out in a big blackboard menu.

Pizzeria Lou Pescadou (tel. 43-74-26; open Mon.-Sat. 1100-1430 and 1630-2300), on rue Anne-Marie Javouhey a long block back from the Vaima Center, is friendly, unpretentious, breezy, inexpensive, and fun. Their pizza pescatore (CFP 650) makes a good lunch, and a big pitcher of ice water is included in the price. Owner Mario Vitulli may be from Marseilles, but you won't complain about his spaghetti—a huge meal for about CFP 700. And where else will you get unpitted olives on a pizza? Nonalcoholic drinks are on the house while you stand and wait for a table. The service is lively, and Lou Pescadou is very popular among local French, a high recommendation.

More good pizza in the CFP 700-1,000 range is baked at **Don Camillo** (tel. 42-80-96), 14 rue des Écoles, next to the Piano Bar.

Other Restaurants

The *plat du jour* at **Big Burger** (tel. 43-01-98; closed Sunday), opposite MacDonald's, is often big value (CFP 1,400), and it's not fast food as the name implies. All of their one-person pizzas are CFP 800.

Restaurant La Madona (tel. 45-16-52; open Mon.-Sat. 1130-1400, Friday and Saturday 1900-2200), below Hôtel Shogun, specializes in seafood such as *poisson cru* (CFP 1,100), sashimi (CFP 1,200), mahimahi (CFP 1,600), and shrimps (CFP 1,700-2,300). **Salvani's Snack Express** (tel. 45-16-52) next door has inexpensive sandwiches and *plats du jour* at lunchtime.

Cafes

Le Retro (tel. 42-86-83) on the boulevard Pomare side of the Vaima Center is *the* place to sit and sip a drink while watching the passing parade. The fruit-flavored ice cream is intense and for yachties a banana split after a long sailing trip can be heavenly. The atmosphere here is thoroughly Côte d'Azur.

L'Oasis du Vaima (tel. 45-45-01), on the back side of the Vaima Center in front of the Air New Zealand office, is another scene in which to be seen, especially by the trendy youths who drop by in the late afternoon.

The Papeete equivalent of a Hard Rock Cafe is **Morrison's Café** (tel. 42-78-61; weekdays 1100-0100, Saturday 1600-0100), upstairs in the Vaima Center, which offers a full pub menu (not cheap), and a swimming pool. Here MTV-deprived local youths mix with island-hopping yachties on an airy terrace with a view of Tahiti.

On boulevard Pomare across the park from the Moorea ferry landing is a row of sidewalk cafes frequented by French servicemen, hookers, gays, and assorted groupies. Some establishments even have a happy hour. This is a good place to sit and take in the local color of every shade and hue.

When the heat gets to you, **Pâtisserie La Marquisienne** (tel. 42-83-52), 29 rue Colette, offers coffee and pastries in a/c comfort. It's popular among French expats.

Groceries

Downtown there's **Casino** (tel. 43-70-40; open Mon.-Sat. 0630-1900, Sunday 0630-1200), a large supermarket on rue du Commandant Destremeau. Get whole barbecued chickens and chow mein in the deli section.

At PK 8.3 Punaauia, just south of the junction of the auto route to Papeete, is the **Centre Commercial Moana Nui,** Tahiti's first enclosed shopping mall which opened in 1986. Some of the cheapest groceries on the island are available at the large adjoining supermarket, **Continent** (tel. 43-25-32; Mon.-Sat. 0800-2000, Sunday 0800-1200). The deli section has a good selection of takeaway meals including barbecued chickens, and there's also a snack bar on the mall. Continent doesn't only sell groceries but also clothing and souvenirs at the best prices you'll find around here.

Other big supermarkets around the island include a second **Continent** (tel. 45-42-22) at PK 4.5, Arue, **Supermarche Venustar** (tel. 48-10-13; Mon.-Sat. 0600-1930, Sunday 0600-1200) at the turnoff to Point Venus on the circle island highway (PK 10), and **Casino** in Taravao. All of these are good places to pick up picnic supplies.

ENTERTAINMENT AND EVENTS

Five Papeete cinemas show B-grade films dubbed into French (admission CFP 800). The Concorde is in the Vaima Center; Hollywood I and II are on rue Lagarde beside the Vaima Center; Liberty Cinema is on rue du Maréchal Foch near the market; and the Mamao Palace is near Mamao Hospital.

All three entertainment district hotels—the Prince Hinoï, Royal Papeete, and Kon Tiki—have gambling casinos where local residents unload excess cash.

Ask for the monthly program of activities at the Departement Fêtes et Manifestations in the **Cultural Center** (B.P. 1709, 98713 Papeete; tel. 54-45-44, fax 42-85-69) at Te Fare Tahiti Nui on the waterfront.

Nightlife

After dark when the tourists have returned to their swank beach hotels, local carousers and French sailors take over the little bars crowding the streets around rue des Écoles. The places with live music or a show generally impose a CFP 1,000-1,500 cover charge, which includes one drink. Nothing much gets going before 2200, and by 0100 everything is very informal for the last hour before closing. For the glitzy capital of a leading French resort, the nightlife is unexpectedly downmarket.

The **Piano Bar** (tel. 42-88-24), beside Hôtel Prince Hinoï on rue des Écoles, is the most no-

fire dancers at a Papeete resort

torious of Papeete's *mahu* (transvestite) discos. It's open daily 1500-0300 with a special show at 0130. **Le Club 5** nearby features female stripping. The CFP 1,500 cover charge on Friday and Saturday includes one drink; during the week there's no cover but it's obligatory to have a drink and a dress code is in effect. Young French servicemen are in their element in these places.

Café des Sports on the corner across the street from the Piano Bar has beer on tap and usually no cover. More locals than tourists patronize this colorful establishment, where a good Tahitian band plays on weekends. Just don't believe the low drink prices advertised outside.

French soldiers and sailors out of uniform patronize the bars along boulevard Pomare opposite the Moorea ferry landing, such as **La Cave** (tel. 42-01-29) inside the Hôtel Royal Papeete (entry through the lobby), which has live Tahitian music for dancing on Friday and Saturday 2200-0300 (CFP 1,000 cover charge, free for Royal Papeete guests). Male visitors should ensure they've got their steps right before inviting any local ladies onto the floor—or face immediate

TAHITI TOURISME

rejection. **Le Tamure Hut** (tel. 42-01-29), also at the Royal Papeete, is one of the few downtown Papeete clubs that caters to visitors. Through the music and decor they've attempted to recapture the nightlife milieu of a decade or more ago, before Quinn's Tahitian Hut closed in 1973. It's open Friday and Saturday 2100-0300, cover charge CFP 1,000 (includes one drink).

Paradise Night Club (tel. 42-73-05; open nightly 1900-0100, weekends until 0200), next to Hôtel Kon Tiki opposite the Moorea ferries, has an island night every Thursday at 1900 with Polynesian karaoke. Other nights it's West African and reggae music. Monday to Thursday admission is CFP 1,500 pp including one drink, or CFP 2,000 on weekends. Popular French singers perform here on Friday and Saturday nights, and a dress code applies. Their restaurant serves dinners with meat dishes or seafood in the CFP 1,400-2,800 range. **Chaplin's Cafe** next door is a popular hangout for French sailors.

The **Tiki d'Or Bar Américain,** 26 rue Georges Lagarde near the Vaima Center, gets lively around happy hour. You'll locate it by the ukuleles and impromptu singing.

Le Rolls Club Discotheque (tel. 43-41-42) in the Vaima Center (opposite Big Burger) is Papeete's top youth disco and sharp dress is in order (open Thurs.-Sat. nights, admission CFP 1,500).

Cultural Shows for Visitors

A Tahitian dance show takes place in the Bougainville Restaurant, downstairs at the **Hôtel Maeva Beach** (tel. 42-80-42), Friday and Saturday at 2000. If you're not interested in having dinner, a drink at the Bar Moorea by the pool will put you in position to see the action (no cover charge). Sunday this hotel presents a full Tahitian feast at 1200, complete with earth oven (*ahimaa*) and dancing at 1300.

The **Beachcomber Parkroyal Hôtel** (tel. 86-51-10) stages one of the top Tahitian dance shows on the island; attend for the price of a drink at the bar near the pool (no cover charge). Tahiti's top dance troupe, Coco's Temaeva, often performs here (check). The dancers' starting time tends to vary (officially Wednesday, Friday, and Sunday at 2000), so arrive early and be prepared to wait. For something special try the Tahitian feast on Sunday—CFP 4,850. The

seafood dinner show on Friday is CFP 6,250.

At the **Royal Matavai Bay Resort Hôtel** (tel. 46-12-34) the Tahitian dancing is Friday and Saturday at 2000 and Sunday at 1300.

There's often Tahitian dancing in the **Captain Bligh Restaurant** (tel. 43-62-90) at the Punaauia Lagoonarium (PK 11.4) on Friday and Saturday nights at 2100 (call ahead to check). The buffet here is CFP 3,500.

SHOPPING

Normal shopping hours in Papeete are weekdays 0730-1130 and 1330-1730, Saturday 0730-1200. Papeete's largest shopping complex is the **Vaima Center,** where numerous shops sell black pearls, designer clothes, souvenirs, and books. It's certainly worth a look; then branch out into the surrounding streets. **Galerie Winkler** (tel. 42-81-77), 17 rue Jeanne d'Arc beside American Express, sells contemporary paintings of Polynesia.

Galerie d'Art Reva Reva (tel. 43-32-67, fax 58-46-78), 36 rue Lagarde, displays the works of Moorea artist François Ravello and other local painters. They also may have copies of an illustrated book on Bobby Holcomb called *Bobby: Polynesian Visions* with reproductions of many of his paintings.

O.P.E.C. (tel. 45-36-26), 20 rue Gauguin (upstairs), and **Tahiti Pearl Dream** (tel. 43-43-68), rue Leboucher 10 (upstairs), are black-pearl sales rooms a block from the market. They'll show you a free video about the pearls if they think you're a potential buyer. Several dozen other jewelers around Papeete, including **Vaima Perles** (tel. 42-55-57) and **Maison Sibani** (tel. 54-24-24) in the Vaima Center, also sell pearls and it's wise to visit several before making such an important purchase.

For reproductions of authentic Marquesan woodcarvings, have a look in **Manuia Curios** (tel. 42-04-94) on the east side of the cathedral. Upstairs in the market is another good place to buy handicrafts, or just a pareu. Surprisingly, handicrafts are often cheaper in Papeete than on their island of origin.

Don't overlook the local fashions. **Marie Ah You** (tel. 42-05-56) on the waterfront between the Vaima Center and the tourist office sells very chic island clothing—at prices to match. Several shops along rue Paul Gauguin flog slightly cheaper tropical garb.

The **Music Shop** (tel. 42-85-63), 13 rue du General de Gaulle, opposite Concorde Cinema behind the Vaima Center, has a large selection of compact discs of Tahitian music. You can use headphones to listen to the music.

If you're a surfer, check **Shop Tahiti** (tel. 42-66-51), 10 rue Édouard Ahnne near the market, for boards, plus all attendant gear. **Caroline** (tel. 42-98-86), 41 rue Colette, and **Waikiki Beach** (tel. 42-34-97), 9 rue Jeanne d'Arc, also sell surfing gear.

Nauti-Sport (tel. 50-59-59) in Fare Ute carries a good selection of quality snorkeling/dive masks at reasonable prices.

The **Philatelic Bureau** (tel. 41-43-35, fax 45-25-86) at the main post office sells the stamps and first-day covers of all the French Pacific territories. Some are quite beautiful and inexpensive. (To get on their mailing list write: Centre philatélique, 8 rue de la Reine Pomare IV, 98714 Papeete.)

SERVICES

Money
A good place to change is the Banque de Polynesie (tel. 46-66-74; Mon.-Thurs. 0745-1530, Friday 0745-1430, Saturday 0800-1130), boulevard Pomare 355, directly across from the tourist office. They take CFP 400 commission. The Banque de Tahiti (tel. 41-70-14; weekdays 0800-1145/1330-1630, Saturday 0800-1130) in the Vaima Center charges CFP 500 commission.

Several banks around town have automatic tellers where you can get cash advances on credit cards. For example, Banque Socredo (tel. 45-31-83), boulevard Pomare 411, on the waterfront just east of the post office, has an ATM outside accessible 24 hours a day. Adjacent is a nifty Automatic Currency Exchange machine that changes the banknotes of nine countries for CFP 400 commission (an identical machine is at the Beachcomber Parkroyal Hôtel).

Post and Telecommunications
The main post office (weekdays 0700-1800, Saturday 0800-1100) is on boulevard Pomare across from the yacht anchorage. Pick up poste restante (general delivery) mail downstairs (CFP 55 per piece). The public fax number at Papeete's main post office is fax 689/43-68-68, and you'll pay CFP 250 a page to pick up faxes sent to this number. The post office is also a place to make a long-distance telephone call, but there's a stiff three-minute minimum for operator-assisted calls and it's cheaper to use a telephone card for such calls.

Around Tahiti, small branch post offices with public telephones are found in Arue, Faa'a Airport, Mahina, Mataiea, Paea, Papara, Papeari, Pirae, Punaauia, and Taravao.

If you have an American Express card you can have your mail sent c/o Tahiti Tours, B.P. 627, 98713 Papeete. Their office (tel. 54-02-50) is at 15 rue Jeanne d'Arc next to the Vaima Center.

Immigration Office
If you arrived by air, visa extensions are handled by the Direction du Contrôle de l'Immigration (DCILEC, B.P. 6362, 98702 Faa'a; tel. 82-10-10, fax 86-60-20; open weekdays 0800-1200/1400-1700) at the airport (up the stairs beside the snack bar). Yachties are handled by the immigration office (tel. 42-40-74; Mon.-Thurs. 0730-1100/1330-1530, Friday 0730-1100/1330-1500) next to a small Banque Socredo branch on the waterfront behind Tahiti Tourisme in the center of town. Be patient and courteous with the officials if you want good service.

For those uninitiated into the French administrative system, the police station (in emergencies tel. 17) opposite the War Memorial on avenue Bruat deals with Papeete matters, while the *gendarmerie* (tel. 46-73-73) at the head of avenue Bruat is concerned with the rest of the island. The locally recruited Papeete police wear blue uniforms, while the paramilitary French-import *gendarmes* are dressed in khaki.

Consulates
The honorary consul of Australia (tel. 43-88-38), at the Qantas office in the Vaima Center, can issue Australian visas. In case of need, Canadians should turn to the Australian consul for emergency assistance. The honorary consul of New Zealand (tel. 54-07-40; weekdays 0900-1500) is upstairs in the Air New Zealand office,

also in the Vaima Center. The honorary British consul is Transpolynésie (tel. 85-58-75) opposite the Outrigger Hôtel Tahiti in Faa'a. The honorary consul of Germany is Claude-Eliane Weinmann (tel. 42-99-94), on rue Tihoni Te Faatau, the road off avenue du Prince Hinoï next to the Lycée Hôtelier Paaone in Afareru on the far east side of the city. Other countries with honorary consuls at Papeete are Austria (tel. 43-91-14), Belgium (tel. 82-54-44), Chile (tel. 43-89-19), Denmark (tel. 54-04-54), Finland (tel. 43-60-67), Holland (tel. 42-49-37), Italy (tel. 43-45-01), Norway (tel. 43-79-72), South Korea (tel. 43-64-75), and Sweden (tel. 42-73-93). There's no U.S. diplomatic post in Tahiti-Polynesia. All visa applications and requests for replacement of lost passports must be sent to the U.S. Embassy (tel. 679/314-466) in Suva, Fiji. Japan is also *not* represented.

Laundromats
Central Pressing (tel. 42-08-74), 72 rue Albert Leboucher, offers a special service to visitors: for CFP 580 they'll wash, dry, and fold one kg of laundry. It's on the street behind the Hôtel Royal Papeete.

Laverie Gauguin Pressing Lavomatic (tel. 43-71-59; Mon.-Sat. 0630-1200/1330-1730), rue Gauguin 64, charges CFP 700 to wash six kg, another CFP 700 to dry, and CFP 100 for soap.

Laverie Automatique "Lavex ça m'plein" (tel. 41-26-65; Mon.-Sat. 0600-2000, Sunday 0800-1200), 301 boulevard Pomare opposite the Moorea ferry wharf, is CFP 700 to wash up to seven kilograms, plus CFP 800 to dry same.

Public Toilets
Public toilets are found next to the immigration office near the small Banque Socredo behind Tahiti Tourisme, at the bus stop opposite Hôtel Le Mandarin beside the Hôtel de Ville, and on the waterfront opposite Air France. The ones near immigration are the most likely to be open regularly, so locate them early in your stay.

Yachting Facilities
Yachts must report their arrival to the port authorities over VHF channel 12 before entering the pass. The yacht master, customs, and immigration are all in the building next to Banque Socredo behind Tahiti Tourisme. A one-time entry

fee and optional daily electricity and water hookup are charged. Yachts pay a daily fee based on the length of the vessel to moor Mediterranean-style (stern-to, bow anchor out) along the quay on boulevard Pomare. For half price you can anchor farther west along the boulevard at Hokulea Beach. It's also possible to anchor at the Hôtel Maeva Beach or to dock at the Marina Taina (tel. 41-02-25) in Punaauia, both accessible via the Faa'a Channel without exiting the lagoon. Visiting boats can use one of the anchor buoys at the **Yacht Club of Tahiti** (B.P. 1456, 98713 Papeete; tel. 42-78-03) at PK 4, Arue, for a monthly charge. Tahiti's sunny west and south coasts are excellent cruising grounds, while there are few good anchorages on the windward, rainy, and often dangerous east and north coasts.

INFORMATION

Tahiti Tourisme (B.P. 65, 98713 Papeete; tel. 50-57-00, fax 43-66-19) at Fare Manihini, a neo-Polynesian building on the waterfront not far from the market, can answer questions and supply a free map of Papeete. Ask for their lists of "small hotel" accommodations on virtually all of the islands, and inquire about special events and boats to the outer islands. The office is open weekdays 0730-1700, Saturday 0800-1200. The CFP 100 cold drink machine outside their office is also notable.

Bookstores
You'll find Papeete's biggest selection of books in English at Libraire Archipels (B.P. 20676, 98713 Papeete; tel. 42-47-30, fax 45-10-27), 68 rue des Remparts. Ask for the *Tahiti Handbook* from Moon Travel Handbooks.

The Libraire du Vaima/Hachette (B.P. 2399, 98713 Papeete; tel. 45-57-44, fax 45-53-45), in the Vaima Center, and Polygraph (B.P. 707, 98713 Papeete; tel. 42-80-47, fax 43-97-89), 12 avenue Bruat, are Papeete's largest French bookstores (and most of their titles are in French). Libraire Le Petit Prince (B.P. 13080, 98717 Punaauia; tel. 43-26-24) in the Centre Commercial Moana Nui, Punaauia, has a few international newspapers and magazines in English.

There's a newsstand (tel. 41-02-89) with magazines in English in front of the Vaima Center by the taxi stand on boulevard Pomare.

Maps

Topographical maps (CFP 1,500 a sheet) of some islands are available from the Section Topographie of the Service de l'Urbanisme (B.P. 866, 98713 Papeete; tel. 46-81-67, fax 43-49-83), 4th floor, Administrative Building, 11 rue du Commandant Destremeau.

La Boutique Klima (B.P. 31, 98713 Papeete; tel. 42-00-63, fax 43-28-24), 13 rue Jaussen behind the cathedral, sells nautical charts (CFP 2,600) and many interesting French books on Polynesia.

Nauti-Sport (tel. 50-59-59) in Fare Ute also retails French nautical charts of Polynesia at CFP 3,000 a sheet, and Marine Corail (tel. 42-82-22) nearby has more of the same (compare).

Libraries

A public library (tel. 54-45-44; open Mon.-Thurs. 0800-1700, Friday 0800-1600) is located in the Cultural Center. To take three books out for 15 days you must buy an annual card for CFP 4,000. The padded chairs in their air-conditioned reading room are great for relaxing.

The Université Française du Pacifique Bibliothèque (B.P. 4532, 98713 Papeete; tel. 45-01-65, fax 41-34-25; Mon.-Fri. 0800-1800, Saturday 0830-1200), is on the top floor at 21 rue Cook, between Commandant Destremeau and boulevard Pomare, Paofai (entry from the back of the building).

Travel Agencies

One of Papeete's most reliable regular travel agencies is Tahiti Tours (B.P. 627, 98713 Papeete; tel. 54-02-50), 15 rue Jeanne d'Arc next to the Vaima Center.

Tahiti Nui Travel (B.P. 718, 98713 Papeete; tel. 54-02-00, fax 42-74-35) in the Vaima Center often has cheap package tours to Easter Island (check the vouchers carefully). Vahini Tahiti Travel (tel. 42-44-38) next to Tahiti Nui Travel also has three-night packages to Easter Island costing about US$660 all inclusive. Before booking one of these, check the price of a return air ticket alone at the LanChile office in the same center (low off-season fares available March-

Nov.). It's sometimes cheaper to make a side trip to Easter Island from Tahiti than to go to the Marquesas! New Zealanders require a Chilean visa to visit Easter Island but most other nationalities need only a passport.

Airline Offices

Reconfirm your international flight at your airline's Papeete office. Most of the airline offices are in the Vaima Center: Air New Zealand (tel. 54-07-47), Hawaiian Airlines (tel. 42-15-00), LanChile (tel. 42-64-55), and Qantas (tel. 43-06-65). AOM French Airlines (tel. 54-25-25) is at 90 rue des Remparts. Corsair (tel. 42-28-28) is at boulevard Pomare 297 next to the Hôtel Royal Papeete. Air France (tel. 42-22-22), which also represents Aircalin, is on boulevard Pomare near avenue Bruat.

HEALTH

Mamao Territorial Hospital (tel. 46-62-62) is always crowded with locals awaiting free treatment, so unless you've been taken to the recompression chamber there, you're better off attending a private clinic. The Clinique Paofai (B.P. 545, 98713 Papeete; tel. 43-02-02) on boulevard Pomare accepts outpatients weekdays 0630-1700, Saturday 0730-1130, emergencies anytime. The facilities and attention are excellent, but be prepared for fees of around CFP 3,000.

Dr. Bernard Bensaid and Dr. Bruno Voron operate a Cabinet Médical (tel. 43-10-43; open weekdays 0700-1330/1500-1800, Saturday 0700-1200, Sunday 0730-1000) in the building above the pharmacy opposite the Catholic cathedral.

In case of emergencies around Papeete call S.O.S. Médecins at tel. 42-34-56. To call an ambulance dial 15.

Two dentists, Dr. Michel Ligerot and Dr. Valérie Galano-Serra (tel. 43-32-24), are on the second floor of the building next to the Hôtel Tiare Tahiti at boulevard Pomare 415.

The Pharmacie de la Cathedrale (tel. 42-02-24) across the street from the Catholic cathedral opens weekdays 0730-1800, Saturday 0730-1200. There are many other pharmacies around Papeete.

TRANSPORTATION

For information on air and sea services from Tahiti to other Polynesian islands, see the **Transportation** section in the introduction to this chapter.

Le Truck

You can go almost anywhere on Tahiti by *les trucks,* converted cargo vehicles with long benches in back. *Trucks* marked Outumaoro run from Papeete to Faa'a International Airport and the Maeva Beach Hôtel every few minutes during the day, with sporadic service after dark until 2000 daily, then again in the morning from 0500 on. On Sunday long-distance *trucks* run only in the very early morning and evening; weekdays the last trip to Mahina, Paea, and points beyond is around 1700.

Trucks to Arue, Mahina, Papenoo, Taravao, and Tautira leave from boulevard Pomare across the street from Tahiti Tourisme. Those to the airport, Outumaoro, Punaauia, Paea, and Papara are found on rue du Maréchal Foch near the market. Local services to Motu Uta, Mission, Mamao, Titioro, and Tipaeriu depart from rue Colette near the Hôtel de Ville.

Destinations and fares are posted on the side of the vehicle: CFP 120 to the airport, CFP 140 to Punaauia, CFP 160 to Mahina, CFP 170 to Paea, CFP 190 to Papara, CFP 200 to Mataiea, CFP 240 to Papeari, CFP 300 to Taravao, CFP 330 to

Pueu, and CFP 350 to Teahupoo or Tautira. After dark all *truck* fares increase. Outside Papeete you don't have to be at a stop: *trucks* stop anywhere if you wave. Luggage rides for free.

Taxis

Taxis in Papeete are expensive, and it's important not to get in unless there's a meter that works or you've agreed to a flat fare beforehand. The minimum fare is CFP 800 during the day or CFP 1,200 at night (2000-0600 daily). Add to this the per kilometer charge of CFP 120 by day or CFP 240 at night. The flat rate per hour is CFP 4,000 during the day or CFP 6,000 at night. Waiting time is CFP 2,000 an hour by day, CFP 3,000 at night. Baggage is CFP 100 per piece at night only. Expect to pay at least CFP 800 for a short trip within Papeete, CFP 1,500 to the airport, or CFP 1,800 to the Royal Matavai Bay Resort Hôtel or Maeva Beach. Taxi stands are found at the Vaima Center (tel. 42-33-60) and the airport (tel. 83-30-07). If you feel cheated by a taxi driver, take down the license number and complain to the tourist office, although what you consider a ripoff may be the correct amount. We have received many complaints about Papeete taxi drivers and they're best avoided if at all possible.

Car Rentals

Check the car as carefully as they check you; be sure to comment on dents, scratches, flat tires, etc. All the car rental agencies include third-party public liability insurance in the basic price,

Not many public transport systems are as much fun as Tahiti's le truck.

DAVID STANLEY

but collision damage waiver (CDW) varies from CFP 700 to CFP 2,000 extra per day with CFP 20,000 and up deductible (called the *franchise* in French). Most agencies charge the client for damage to the tires and stolen accessories, insurance or no insurance, and Tahiti insurance isn't valid if you take the car across to Moorea. You'll also pay for towing if you are judged responsible. On Tahiti the car comes full of gas, and you'll see Mobil and Total gas stations all around the island. As yet it's still free to park on the street anywhere in Papeete, which helps explain the heavy traffic. European-style parking fee machines are sure to make their debut on street-corners before long!

If you want to whiz the island and pack in as many side trips as you can in one day, an unlimited-mileage rental is for you, and with a few people sharing it's not a bad deal. You should only consider renting on a per-kilometer basis if you plan to keep the car for at least three days and intend to use it only for short hops. Most agencies impose a 50-km daily minimum on their per-km rentals to prevent you from traveling *too* slowly; most rentals are for a minimum of 24 hours. Many car rental companies have kiosks inside Faa'a Airport, and most offer clients a free pickup and drop-off service to the hotels and airport.

Avis/Pacificar (B.P. 4466, 98713 Papeete; tel. 41-93-93, fax 42-19-11), 56 rue des Remparts at pont de l'Est, at the east end of rue Paul Gauguin, is open 24 hours a day. If the main office is closed, the guard in the parking lot can give you a car. They also have a kiosk facing the Moorea ferry wharf, a desk at the airport, and an office next to the military barracks in Taravao. Avis/Pacificar has unlimited km cars from CFP 8,000/13,000/18,800 for one/two/three days, plus CFP 1,200 a day insurance.

Also open 24 hours is **Europcar** (tel. 45-24-24, fax 41-93-41, www.europcar.com), at the corner of avenue du Prince Hinoï and rue des Remparts, two blocks back from Moorea ferry wharf, at the Moorea ferry wharf, the airport, and several hotels. Their Fiat Pandas are CFP 1,700, plus CFP 36 a kilometer. With unlimited kilometers and insurance it's CFP 7,600/13,000/18,000 for one/two/three days. Europcar also has a depot at Taravao (tel. 57-01-11). Their minimum age is only 18 but the insurance coverage is limited for those under 25.

Hertz (tel. 42-04-71, fax 42-48-62), at Paradise Tours, on Vicinal de Tipaerui opposite Hôtel Matavai, has cars from CFP 2,350 a day, plus CFP 36 a kilometer, plus CPF 1,250 insurance. Otherwise it's CFP 7,750/18,800/36,800 for one/three/seven days with unlimited mileage and insurance.

A good place to try for a per-km rental is **Robert Rent-a-Car** (B.P. 1047, 98713 Papeete; tel. 42-97-20) on rue du Commandant Destremeau (from CFP 1,200 daily, plus CFP 35 a kilometer, plus CFP 700 insurance). Robert's unlimited km rentals begin at CFP 5,600 including insurance. They may offer you an upgrade at no charge.

The least expensive Citroën available from **Location de Voitures Pierrot et Jacqueline** (B.P. 1855, 98713 Papeete; tel. 42-74-49 or 81-94-00, fax 81-07-77) is CFP 1,700 a day, plus CFP 30 a kilometer and CFP 1,000 insurance. With unlimited kilometers it's CFP 10,000/15,000/30,000 for two/three/seven days, insurance included. They'll allow you to take their car to Moorea if you ask before, but the insurance won't be valid over there. The minimum age to rent is 18. This friendly, efficient company has an office near the Total oil tanks and Mobil service station at Fare Ute (open weekdays 0730-1100/1400-1730, Saturday 0730-1100), and another at the airport.

Bicycle Rentals

Unfortunately the fast and furious traffic on Tahiti's main highways makes cycling dangerous and unpleasant, and motor scooter rentals have been discontinued after fatal accidents. Nevertheless, **Rando Cycles** (tel./fax 41-22-08; weekdays 0800-1200/1400-1700, Saturday 0800-1200), at PK 20.2, Paea, rents bicycles at CFP 1,500/9,000 a day/week, or CFP 2,500 a weekend (Saturday morning to Monday before 0900).

Garage Bambou (B.P. 5592, 98716 Pirae; tel. 42-80-09), on avenue Georges Clemenceau near the Chinese temple, sells new Peugot bicycles from CFP 35,000 and does repairs.

Local Tours

William Leeteg of **Adventure Eagle Tours** (B.P. 6719, 98702 Faa'a; tel. 41-37-63 or 77-20-03) takes visitors on a full-day tour around the island at CFP 4,000 (admissions and lunch not included). William speaks good English and will do special guided tours for groups of up to seven.

Patrice Bordes of **Tahiti Safari Expédition** (B.P. 14445, 98701 Arue; tel. 42-14-15, fax 42-10-07) and several other companies offer 4WD jeep tours to Mt. Marau, the Papenoo Valley, and Lake Vaihiria.

Marama Tours (B.P. 6266, 98702 Faa'a; tel. 83-96-50, fax 82-16-75), at the airport and several deluxe hotels, does six-hour circle-island tours at CFP 4,000 and a 4WD island crossing via Lake Vaihiria at CFP 7,000. They also have a circle-Moorea tour from Tahiti at CFP 9,000 including the ferry. Also offered are day tours by air to Tetiaroa (CFP 24,500) and Bora Bora (CFP 26,900). **Tahiti Nui Travel** (tel. 54-02-00) at the Vaima Center and various hotels offers much the same.

Day Cruises

Many of the yachts and catamarans tied up along the waterfront opposite the Vaima Center offer excursions to Tetiaroa, deep-sea fishing, scuba diving, yacht charters, etc. Departures are often announced on notice boards and a stroll along there will yield current information. **Archipels Croisières** (tel. 56-36-39) operates a day cruise around Moorea on a 34-meter classic schooner departing from the Punaauia resorts. It's around CFP 11,000 pp including a buffet lunch.

Getting Away

The **Air Tahiti** booking office (tel. 43-39-39, weekdays 0730-1200/1300-1630) is upstairs in Fare Tony off boulevard Pomare between the post office and Vaima Center. **Air Moorea** (tel. 86-41-41) is at Faa'a International Airport. Interisland services by air and sea are covered in the **Transportation** section of the introduction to this chapter.

The ferries to Moorea depart from the landing just behind the tourist office downtown. The *Raromatai Ferry* and *Ono-Ono* to the Leeward Islands also leave from there, as do cruise ships and a few other small boats. All other interisland ships, including the cargo vessels *Taporo VI* and *Vaeanu,* leave from the Tuamotu wharf or Quai des Caboteurs in Motu Uta, across the harbor from downtown Papeete. You can catch *le truck* directly to Motu Uta from the Hôtel de Ville. The ticket offices of some of the vessels are in Fare Ute just north of downtown, while others are at Motu Uta (addresses given in the **Transportation** section in the introduction to this chapter).

AROUND TAHITI

A 117-km Route de Ceinture (Belt Road) runs right around Tahiti-nui, the larger part of this hourglass-shaped island. Construction began in the 1820s as a form of punishment. For orientation you'll see red-and-white kilometer stones, called PK *(pointe kilométrique),* along the inland side of the road. These are numbered in each direction from the Catholic cathedral in Papeete, meeting at Taravao.

Go clockwise to get over the most difficult stretch first; also, you'll be riding on the inside lane of traffic and less likely to go off a cliff in case of an accident (an average of 55 people a year are killed and 700 injured in accidents on this island). Southern Tahiti is much quieter than the northwest, whereas from Paea to Mahina it's hard to even slow down as tailgating motorists roar behind you.

If you're a bit adventurous it's quite possible to do a circle-island tour on *le truck,* provided you get an early start and go clockwise with no stop until Taravao. *Trucks* don't run right around the island, although some go as far as Tautira and Teahupoo on Tahiti-iti. *Trucks* and buses to Tautira leave from boulevard Pomare opposite the tourist office about six times a day with the first around 0830. Some *trucks* to Tautira go via the south coast, so if you want to be sure you'll be able to do a full circle trip, ask for one going via Papenoo. If you're told none are available or it looks like they won't be going for quite a while, switch to asking for a *truck* to Papenoo itself, then hitch from the end of its line or wait there for an onward *truck.*

Once at Taravao, walk across the peninsula (15 minutes) and look for another *truck* coming from Teahupoo or elsewhere to take you back to Papeete along the south coast. They stop running in the early afternoon, but if you get stuck, it's comforting to know that hitchhiking *(l'autostop)* is fairly easy and relatively safe on Tahiti. The local people are quite receptive to foreign visitors, so you'll improve your chances if it's obvious you're not French. For instance, try using a destination sign (never used by locals).

There's lots of traffic along the straight south coast highway all day and it's almost certain you'll get a ride eventually. However you travel around Tahiti, it's customary to smile and wave to the Tahitians you see (outside Papeete).

The Northeast Coast

The coast is very rugged all along the northeast side of the island with no barrier reef from Port Venus to Mahaena. The **leper colony** at Orofara (PK 13.2) was founded in 1914. Previously the colony was on Reao atoll in the Tuamotus, but this proved too remote to service. Although leprosy is a thing of the past, about 50 of the former patients' children who grew up there and have nowhere else to go remain at Orofara today. They make money by selling cheap woodcarvings.

From November to March surfers ride the waves at Chinaman's Bay, Papenoo (PK 16), one of the best rivermouth beach breaks on the north side of the island. The bridge over the broad **Papenoo River** (PK 17.9) allows a view up the largest valley on Tahiti. A paved road leads a kilometer up the valley to the rough track across the island via the Relais de la Maroto (18 km) and Lake Vaihiria (25 km). You wouldn't get far in an ordinary car and even a 4WD jeep could get stuck. (See **Lake Vaihiria.**)

At the **Arahoho Blowhole** (PK 22), jets of water shoot up through holes in the lava rock beside the highway at high tide. It's dangerous to get too close to the blowhole as a sudden surge could toss you out to sea! Carefully lock your car here. Just a little beyond the blowhole, a road to the right leads 1.3 km up to the three **Tefa'aurumai Waterfalls** (admission free), also known as the Faarumai Falls. Vaimahuta Falls is accessible on foot in five minutes along the easy path to the right across the bridge. The 30-minute trail to the left leads to two more waterfalls, Haamaremare Iti and Haamaremare Rahi. The farthest falls has a pool deep enough for swimming. Bring insect repellent and beware of theft if you park a rental car at these falls.

At **Mahaena** (PK 32.5) is the battleground where 441 well-armed French troops defeated a dug-in Tahitian force twice their size on 17 April 1844 in the last fixed confrontation of the French-Tahitian War. The Tahitians carried on a guerrilla campaign another two years until the French captured their main mountain stronghold. No monument commemorates the 100 Tahitians who died combating the foreign invaders here.

The French ships *La Boudeuse* and *L'Étoile,* carrying explorer Louis-Antoine de Bougainville, anchored by the southernmost of two islets off **Hitiaa** (PK 37.6) on 6 April 1768. Unaware that an Englishman had visited Tahiti a year before, Bougainville christened the island "New Cythera," after the Greek isle where love goddess Aphrodite rose from the sea. A plaque near the bridge recalls the event. The clever Tahitians recognized a member of Bougainville's crew as a woman disguised as a man, and an embarrassed Jeanne Baret entered history as the first woman to sail around the world. (Bougainville lost six large anchors during his nine days at this dangerous windward anchorage.)

From the bridge over the Faatautia River at PK 41.8 **Vaiharuru Falls** are visible in the distance. The American filmmaker John Huston intended to make a movie of Herman Melville's *Typee* here in 1957, but when Huston's other Melville film, *Moby Dick,* became a box-office flop, the idea was dropped.

Tahiti-iti

At Taravao (PK 53), on the strategic isthmus joining the two Tahitis where the PKs meet, is an **old fort** built by the French in 1844 to cut off the Tahitians who had retreated to Tahiti-iti after the battle mentioned above. Germans were interned here during WW II, and the fort is still occupied today by the 1st Company of the Régiment d'Infanterie de Marine du Pacifique.

The small assortment of grocery stores, banks, post office, gasoline stations, and restaurants at Taravao make it a good place to break your trip around the island. Lunch is served at **Restaurant Chez Guilloux** (closed Monday; tel. 57-12-91), opposite Casino supermarket, 100 meters down the road to Tautira from the bank in Taravao. They have large bottles of Hinano (CFP 400) and sandwiches (CFP 350), plus more formal dishes such as steak (CFP 1,450), mahimahi (CFP 1,500), and Chinese food (CFP 1,000). It's popular among French locals. Another excellent choice is **Restaurant Chez Jeannine** (tel. 57-29-82; closed Wednesday), on the main highway next to Europcar, which specializes in seafoods and Vietnamese dishes.

If you have your own transportation, three roads are explorable on rugged Tahiti-iti. If you're hitching or traveling by *le truck,* choose the excellent 18-km highway that runs east from Taravao to quaint little **Tautira.** Two Spanish priests from Peru attempted to establish a Catholic mission at Tautira in 1774 but it lasted for only one year. Scottish author Robert Louis Stevenson stayed at Tautira for two months in 1888 and called it "the most beautiful spot, and its people the most amiable, I have ever found." The road peters out a few km beyond Tautira but you can continue walking 12 km southeast to the Vaiote River where there are petroglyphs, sacred rocks, and *marae.* These are difficult to find without a guide, and a few km beyond are the high cliffs that make it impractical to try hiking around the Pari Coast to Teahupoo.

Another paved nine-km road climbs straight up the Taravao Plateau from just before the hospital in Taravao, 600 meters down the Tautira road from Casino supermarket. If you have a car or scooter and only time to take in one of Tahiti-iti's three roads, this one should be your choice. At the 600-meter level on top is the **Vaiufaufa Viewpoint,** with a breathtaking view of both Tahitis. No one lives up here: in good weather it would be possible to pitch a tent on the grassy hill above the reservoir at the end of the road (or sleep in your car if it's cold and raining). You'll witness spectacular sunsets from here and the herds of cows grazing peacefully among the grassy meadows give this upland an almost Swiss air. A rough side road near the viewpoint cuts down to rejoin the Tautira road.

The third road on Tahiti-iti runs 18 km along the south coast to Teahupoo. Seven km east of Taravao is a **marina** with an artificial beach (PK 7). American pulp Western writer Zane Grey had his fishing camp near here in the 1930s. Just east of the marina is **Toouo Beach,** a long stretch of natural white sand beside the road where you'll see fishermen spearing by torchlight on the opposite reef in the evening. In the afternoon it's a great picnic spot. The two huge moorings near the shore were used by ocean liners before Papeete harbor was developed in the 1960s as this is the finest natural deep-water harbor on Tahiti. Some of Tahiti's finest reef break surfing is possible out there in the Tapuaeraha Pass, but you'll need a boat.

Worth seeking out is **Marae Nu'utere,** 500 meters up a side road on the west side of the École Maternelle Tefaao at Vairao, PK 9.5 east of Taravao on the Teahupoo road. This large stone platform with a huge *ora* (banyan tree) growing in the center belonged to the female chief of the district. It was restored in 1994 and an explanatory board has been posted. Yachts can tie up to a pier near the *mairie* in Vairoa. An oceanographic research station studying shrimp breeding is nearby.

The **Teahupoo** road ends abruptly at a river crossed by a narrow footbridge. There's an excellent mountain view from this bridge, but walk east along the beach to get a glimpse of Polynesian village life. After a couple of kilometers the going becomes difficult due to yelping dogs, seawalls built into the lagoon, fences, fallen trees, and *tapu* signs. Beyond is the onetime domain of the "nature men" who tried to escape civilization by living alone with nature more than half a century ago.

Three hours on foot from the end of the road is **Vaipoiri Grotto,** a large water-filled cave best reached by boat. Try hiring a motorized canoe or hitch a ride with someone at the end of the road. Beyond this the 350-meter-high cliffs of the Pari Coast terminate all foot traffic along the shore; the only way to pass is by boat. All the land east of Teahupoo is well fenced off, so finding a campsite would involve getting someone's permission. It's probably easier to look elsewhere.

One option is **Le Bon Jouir** (Annick Paofai, B.P. 9171, 98715 Papeete; tel. 57-02-15, fax 43-69-70) beyond the end of the road on Pari Coast. The three bungalows start at CFP 4,000 double, otherwise a mattress in a large dorm is CFRP 2,000. You can cook for yourself or order breakfast and dinner at CFP 3,500 pp a day. Return boat transfers are CFP 2,000 pp and it costs CFP 500 a day for parking in Teahupoo. It's in a verdant location backed by hills. Inexpensive.

Gauguin Museum

Port Phaeton on the southwest side of the Taravao Isthmus is a natural "hurricane hole" with excellent holding for yachts in the muddy bottom and easy access to Taravao from the head of the bay. (The entire south coast of Tahiti is a paradise for yachties with many fine protected anchorages.) Timeless oral traditions tell that the first Polynesians to reach Tahiti settled at Papeari (PK 56—measured now from the west). In precontact times the chiefly family of this district was among the most prestigious on the island.

The **Gauguin Museum** (B.P. 7029, 98719 Taravao; tel. 57-10-58; open daily 0900-1700, CFP 500 admission) is at PK 51.7 in Papeari District. Opened in 1965 thanks to grant from the Singer Foundation of sewing machine fame, the museum tells the painter's tormented life story and shows the present locations of his works throughout the world. Strangely, Gauguin's Tahitian mistresses get little attention in the museum. Twenty-five of his minor works are exhibited. Most of the photos of his paintings are numbered and you may be able to borrow a catalog (from the gift shop, go around clockwise). The two-meterish, two-ton stone tiki on the museum grounds is said to be imbued with a sacred *tapu* spell. Tahitians believe this tiki, carved on the island of Raivavae hundreds of years ago, still lives. The three Tahitians who moved the statue here from Papeete in 1965 all died mysterious deaths within a few weeks. A curse is still said to befall all who touch the tiki.

A **botanical garden** rich in exotic species is part of the Gauguin Museum complex (CFP 400 additional admission). This 137-hectare garden was created in 1919-21 by the American botanist Harrison Smith (1872-1947), who introduced more than 200 new species to the island, among them the sweet grapefruit (pomelo), mangosteen, rambutan, and durian. A large Galapagos tortoise traipses through the east side of the gardens, the last of several such animals given to the children of writer Charles Nordhoff way back in the 1930s. Yachts can enter the lagoon through Temarau Pass and anchor just west of the point here.

The attractive **Gauguin Museum Restaurant** (tel. 57-13-80), a kilometer west of the museum, hosts circle-island tour groups for lunch. Even without the food it's worth a stop to see the fish swimming in the enclosure around the wharf and to take in the view.

At PK 49 is the **Jardin Public Vaipahi** with a lovely waterfall minutes from the road (admission free). It's a good substitute if you missed the botanical garden. A few hundred meters west of Vaipahi is the **Bain du Vaima,** a strong freshwater spring with several deep swimming pools.

This is one of the favorite free picnic spots on the island and on weekends it's crowded with locals. Yachts can anchor offshore.

Lake Vaihiria

The unmarked road to Lake Vaihiria begins at PK 47.6 between a housing settlement and a Mormon church (Église de Jesus-Christ des Saints des Derniers Jours), just before the bridge over the Vairaharaha River, as you travel west. The rough track leads 12 km up to Lake Vaihiria, Tahiti's only lake, following the Vaihiria River, which has been harnessed for hydroelectricity. Two km up the road you'll encounter a white hydro substation and the first of a series of Piste Privée signs advising motorists that the road is closed to rental cars *(vehicles de location),* though open to pedestrians. For those who don't mind taking risks, in dry weather a rental car could continue another five km to a dam and the lower power station, provided the chain across the road isn't locked.

A kilometer beyond is an archaeological site with restored *marae.* Three km beyond this (11 km from the main road) is a second dam and an upper (larger) power station. Beyond this point only a 4WD vehicle could proceed, passing prominent Danger signs, another km up a concrete track with a 37-degree incline to Lake Vaihiria itself.

Sheer cliffs and spectacular waterfalls squeeze in around the spring-fed lake, and the shore would make a fine campsite (though overrun by mosquitoes). Native floppy-eared eels known as *puhi taria,* up to 1.8 meters long, live in these cold waters, as do prawns and trout. With its luxuriant vegetation this rain-drenched 473-meter-high spot is one of the most evocative on the island.

The track proceeds up to the 780-meter level and through the 110-meter Urufau Tunnel (opened in 1989) and over to the Papenoo Valley, the caldera of Tahiti-nui's great extinct volcano. The ancient Tahitians considered this the realm of the gods and the **Marae Farehape** is near the Relais de la Maroto. Another large dam, the Barage Tahinu, is a couple of km west of the Relais. Developed since 1980, these facilities now supply more than a third of Tahiti's electric requirements. On the slopes of Orohena, eight km north of the Relais and 10 km short of Papenoo, is the access to the **Parc naturel Te Faaiti,** Tahiti's first (and as yet undeveloped) territorial park. On the east side of the Papenoo Valley stands Mt. Aramaoro (1,530 meters).

From coast to coast it's a four-hour, 40-km trip by 4WD jeep, or two days on foot. You must wade through the rivers about 20 times. The easiest way to do this trip is seated in a chauffeur-driven 4WD jeep booked through any the tour companies that leave their brochures at Tahiti Tourisme. Expect to pay CFP 9,500 pp including lunch and drinks or CFP 7,000 without lunch (four-person minimum participation). These trips don't usually operate during the rainy season (Nov.-March).

The 12-room **Relais de la Maroto** (B.P. 20687, 98713 Papeete; tel. 57-90-29, fax 57-90-30) is at the junction of the Vaituoru and Vainavenave rivers in the upper Papenoo Valley, about five km north of the tunnel. The only access is by 4WD, helicopter, or foot (the Papenoo River must be forded 10 times between here and the north coast highway). This cluster of solid concrete buildings was built to house workers during construction of the hydroelectric installations here, and rooms with bath start at CFP 8,800 single or double. Add CFP 5,000 pp for breakfast and dinner, plus CFP 14,500 pp for return transfers from Papeete. Local French often come here for the weekend and the flashy restaurant, wine cellar, and disco are designed to cater to them. Despite this, the Relais does provide a good base for exploring the many water-falls and archaeological remains in this area if your budget is generous enough. Expensive.

The South Coast

Tahiti-Polynesia's only golf course, the **International Golf Course Olivier Breaud** (B.P. 12017, 98712 Papara; tel. 57-43-41; open daily 0800-1700) at PK 41, Atimaono, stretches up to the mountainside on the site of Terre Eugenie, a cotton and sugar plantation established by Scotsman William Stewart at the time of the U.S. Civil War (1863). Many of today's Tahitian Chinese are descended from Chinese laborers imported to do the work, and a novel by A. T'Serstevens, *The Great Plantation,* was set here. The present 5,405-meter, 18-hole course was laid out by Californian Bob Baldock in 1970 with a par 72 for men, par 73 for women. If you'd like to do a round, the greens fees are CFP 4,500, and clubs and cart rent for another CFP 3,000. Since 1981 the Tahiti Open in July has attracted golf professionals from around the Pacific. The course restaurant is said to be good.

The **Marae of Mahaiatea** (PK 39.2) at Papara was once the most hallowed temple on Tahiti, dedicated to the sea god Ruahatu. After a visit in 1769 Captain Cook's botanist Joseph Banks wrote, "It is almost beyond belief that Indians could raise so large a structure without the assistance of iron tools." Less than a century later planter William Stewart raided the *marae* for building materials, and storms did the rest. All that's left of the 11-story pyramid today is a rough

Mahaiatea Marae at Papara on the south coast of Tahiti: This 11-step pyramid was once the largest pagan temple on the island, but time, nature, and the depredations of man have taken their toll.

M.G.I. DOMENY DE RIENZI

heap of stones, but still worth visiting for its aura and setting. You could swim and snorkel off the beach next to the *marae,* but watch the currents. The unmarked turnoff to the *marae* is 100 meters west of Beach Burger, then straight down to the beach. April-Oct. surfers often take the waves at black-colored **Papara Beach** on nearby Popoti Bay (PK 38.5), one of the top beach break sites on southern Tahiti.

By the church at **Papara** (PK 36) is the grave of Dorence Atwater (1845-1910), U.S. consul to Tahiti 1871-88. Atwater's claim to fame dates back to the American Civil War, when he record-ed the names of 13,000 dead Union prisoners at Andersonville Prison, Georgia, from lists the Confederates had been withholding. Himself a Union prisoner, Atwater escaped with his list in March 1865. Atwater's tombstone provides de-tails. Across the street from the church is a Cen-tre Artisanal selling handicrafts, and a Sea Shell Museum. A commercial bird park and green-house called **Mataoa Gardens** is at PK 34.5.

Maraa Fern Grotto (PK 28.5) is by the road just across the Paea border. An optical illusion, the grotto at first appears small but is quite deep, and some Tahitians believe *varua ino* (evil spir-its) lurk in the shadowy depths. Others say that if you follow an underground river back from the grotto you'll emerge at a wonderful valley in the spirit world. Paul Gauguin wrote of a swim he took across the small lake in the cave; you're also welcome to jump in the blue-gray water. You can fill your water bottle with fresh mineral water from eight spouts next to the parking lot. Maraa Pass is almost opposite the grotto and yachts can anchor in the bay.

The Southwest Coast

The **Marae Arahurahu** at PK 22.5, Paea, is up the road inland from Magasin Laut—take care, the sign faces Papeete, so it's not visible if you're traveling clockwise. This temple, lying in a tran-quil, verdant spot under high cliffs, is perhaps Tahiti's only remaining pagan mystery. The an-cient open altars built from thousands of cut stones were completely restored in 1954 (open daily, admission free). Historical pageants (CFP 1,500 admission) recreating pagan rites are per-formed here on Saturday from July to September.

You get a good view of Moorea from **Mahana Park** (admission free) at PK 18.3, Papehue. This

Early tourists ride in style in this 1910 photo taken at Punaauia.

AUCKLAND INSTITUTE AND MUSEUM

is a public beach park with a restaurant (tel. 48-19-99) and cafe. Pedal boats and kayaks are for rent.

The West Coast

Paea and Punaauia are Tahiti's sheltered "Gold Coast," with old colonial homes hidden behind trees along the lagoonside and *nouveau riche* villas dotting the hillside above. **Hôtel Le Méridien** at PK 15, Punaauia, opened in 1998 amid con-siderable local controversy as Tahitian protesters had been occupying the site for nearly four years to protect an ancient Moahi burial ground and to defend one of the last remaining customary ac-cesses to the sea. In January 1996 French *gen-darmes* were called in to evict the demonstrators and construction went ahead under tight security.

At Fishermen's Point, Punaauia, is the **Mu-seum of Tahiti and the Islands** (B.P. 6272, 98702 Faa'a; tel. 58-34-76; open Tues.-Sun. 0930-1730; admission CFP 500), which opened in 1977. Located in a large, modern complex on Punaauia Bay, about a kilometer down a narrow road from PK 14.8, this worthwhile museum has four halls devoted to the natural environment, the origins of the Polynesians, Polynesian culture, and the history of Polynesia. Outside is a huge double-hulled canoe and Captain Cook's anchor from Tautira. Most of the captions are in French, Tahitian, and English (photography allowed).

When the waves are right, you can sit on the seawall behind the museum and watch the Tahitian surfers bob and ride, with the outline of Moorea beyond. It's a nice picnic spot. On your way back to the main highway from the museum, look up to the top of the hill at an **old fort** used by the French to subjugate the Tahitians in the 1840s. The crown-shaped pinnacles of **Le Diadème** (1,321 meters) are also visible from this road.

From 1896 to 1901 Gauguin had his studio at PK 12.6 Punaauia, but nothing remains of it; his *Two Tahitian Women* was painted here. The **Lagoonarium** (B.P. 2381, 98713 Papeete; tel. 43-62-90; closed Monday), below the lagoon behind Captain Bligh Restaurant at PK 11.4, Punaauia, provides a vision of the underwater marinelife of Polynesia safely behind glass. The big tank full of black-tip sharks is a feature. Entry is CFP 500 pp, open daily, free for restaurant customers, and CFP 300 for children under 12. The shark feeding takes place around noon. Straight out from the Lagoonarium is the Passe de Taapuna, southern entrance to the Punaauia Lagoon and another popular surfing venue.

At PK 8, Outumaoro, is the turnoff for the RDO bypass to Papeete, Tahiti's only superhighway! Follow the Université signs from here up to the ultramodern campus of the **French University of the Pacific** (tel. 80-38-03) with its fantastic hilltop view of Moorea.

On the old airport road just north are Tahiti's biggest hotels: the **Sofitel Maeva Beach** (PK 7.5) and **Beachcomber Parkroyal** (PK 7), each worth a stop—though their beaches are polluted. From the point where the Beachcomber Parkroyal is today, the souls of deceased Tahitians once leapt on their journey to the spirit world. A sunset from either of these hotels, behind Moorea's jagged peaks across the Sea of the Moon, would be a spectacular finale to a circle-island tour.

The **Mairie de Faa'a** (PK 5) was erected in the traditional Maohi style in 1989 (Faa'a mayor Oscar Temaru is the territory's leading independence advocate). As you reenter Papeete, **Uranie Cemetery** (PK 1.5) is on your right.

The west coast of Tahiti can also be visited as a day-trip from Papeete; start by taking *le truck* to the Fern Grotto at Paea, then work your way back. *Trucks* back to Papeete from the vicinity of the Maeva Beach Hôtel run late into the night, but the last one from the Museum of Tahiti is around 1630.

ACCOMMODATIONS AROUND TAHITI

Accommodations near Taravao

Fare Nana'o (B.P. 7193, 98719 Taravao; tel. 57-18-14, fax 57-76-10), operated by sculptor Jean-Claude Michel and his wife Monique Meriaux, is an unusual place to stay. It's beside the lagoon in a colorful compound overflowing with vegetation and fragments of sculpture, very near the PK 52 marker a kilometer north of the old French fort at Taravao. The six thatched *fares* vary in price, from CFP 5,000 double for the treehouse (you climb up a tree), CFP 5,500 double for an overwater *fare* on stilts (you must wade through the lagoon), CFP 6,500 double for one of the two units with cooking facilities, to CFP 8,500 double for the only room with private bath and hot water. A third person is CFP 1,000 extra in all these, and the weekly discount is 10% (no credit cards). Although unique and wonderful, Fare Nana'o is not for everyone: the walls are constructed of tree trunks and branches left partially open, there's no hot water, flashlights are required to reach the shared toilet and shower at night, and you may be visited in the night by crabs, spiders, lizards, and a marauding cat. This Robinson Crusoe-style place has had TV exposure in Los Angeles, so advance reservations are necessary, especially on weekends. Inexpensive.

A good sightseeing base is **Chez Jeannine** (Jeannine Letivier, B.P. 7310, 98719 Taravao; tel./fax 57-07-49), also known as "L'Eurasienne," on the Route de Plateau five km above Taravao. You'll need a rental car to stay here as it's way up on the road to the Vaiufaufa Viewpoint and *le truck* doesn't pass anywhere nearby.

The four two-story bungalows with cooking facilities and wicker furniture are CFP 6,000/30,000/80,000 double a day/week/month, while the five rooms above the restaurant are CFP 4,000/20,000/50,000. Chez Jeannine only opened in 1997 and the cool breezes and good views are complemented by a swimming pool. Information is available at Restaurant Chez Jeannine (closed Wednesday) next to Europcar in Taravao. Inexpensive.

The **Te Anuanua Hôtel** (Hilda Lehartel, B.P. 1553, 98713 Papeete; tel./fax 57-12-54), just east of the church in Pueu at PK 10, Tahiti-iti, has four duplex bungalows. Garden bungalows here are CFP 5,500/6,500 single/double plus tax but including breakfast; the lagoonfront bungalows are CFP 1,000 more. Check the rooms before checking in, as some lack window screens, fans, or functioning plumbing. On weekends the disco pulses 2200-0300. A nice seafood restaurant faces the lagoon, making the Te Anuanua worth a stop as you travel around the island. This hotel doesn't have a beach, but there's a pool and the crystal clear water off their wharf invites one to jump in. Moderate.

The backpackers best bet is probably **Chez Mado** (tel. 57-32-77 or 57-00-57), the snack bar on the east beach at the end of the road in Tautira. The friendly folks running the restaurant accommodate visitors in their own home at CFP 3,000 pp including all meals. The snack bar is usually closed on Monday and Tuesday, so it would be best to call ahead those days (a good idea anytime). Tautira makes a good base for hikers and it would be fun to spend a couple of nights in this attractive village. Budget.

On the opposite side of the Tahiti-iti peninsula is **Pension Meherio Iti** (Maria Maitere, B.P. 3695, 98713 Papeete; tel. 57-74-31 or 77-22-73), at PK 11.9 in Vairao district on the road to Teahupoo. Four rooms are available in a house next to the main road at CFP 3,500/4,000/4,500 single or double depending on whether the room has cooking facilities or private bath. There are also three newer bungalows with cooking facilities down near the lagoon, 400 meters off the road. These cost CFP 6,000 double in the garden or CFP 7,000 on the beach (extra person CFP 700). This place is usually fully booked by local French families on weekends but a possibility during the week. Inexpensive.

Southwest Side of Tahiti

Hiti Moana Villa (Steve Brotherson, B.P. 10865, 98711 Paea; tel. 57-93-93, fax 57-94-44), at PK 32, is an attractive small resort right on the lagoon between Papara and Paea. The eight deluxe apartments each have a kitchen, living room, TV, terrace, and private bath at CFP 8,000 single or double, or CFP 12,500 for four persons (minimum stay three nights). There's a swimming pool and pontoon, and the manager will loan a boat and motor free (you pay the gas). This place is usually full—especially on weekends—and advance bookings are recommended. Moderate.

Les Bougainvillées Motor Inn (B.P. 63, 98713 Papeete; tel. 53-28-02, fax 43-77-11) is at PK 22, Paea (lagoon side). The eight apartments with kitchen, living room, TV, terrace, and private bath in a four-story building facing the swimming pool are CFP 8,000 for two people, or CFP 12,000 for up to four people. The minimum stay is three nights and reduced rates are offered for long stays. It's a cozy arrangement with access to the beach via the owners' driveway, but call ahead for reservations as it's often full. Moderate.

Pension Te Miti (Frédéric Cella, B.P. 130088, 98717 Punaauia; tel./fax 58-48-61) at PK 18.5, Paea, is in Papehue village, 450 meters up off the main road. Five rooms in two adjacent houses cost CFP 4,500 double in a small room, or CFP 6,000 double in a large room. Backpackers and surfers often stay in the four-mattress dormitory at CFP 1,500 pp. There's a communal fridge but no cooking facilities. Breakfast is CFP 250, dinner CFP 1,200. Use of the washing machine is CFP 500. It's run by a young French couple named Frederick and Crystal and their future plans include a campground across the road. Airport transfers are CFP 2,000 pp but it's easy to get here on *le truck*. Inexpensive.

Chez Armelle (Armelle Faille, B.P. 388640, 98718 Punaauia; tel. 58-42-43, fax 58-42-81), at PK 15.5 in Punaauia (almost opposite a large Mobil service station), has eight rooms at CFP 4,500/6,000 single/double. A bed in a six-bed dorm is CFP 2,000. Some of the rooms have private bath, and communal cooking facilities are provided. Dinner is available at CFP 1,000 pp and breakfast is included in all rates. It's right on the beach (though the rooms are not), but this pension caters more to French migrants planning long stays: you get seven nights for the price of six, and one month is CFP 120,000 double. There's a two-night minimum stay and the managers can be rather abrupt with English speakers. Snorkeling gear, surfboards, canoes, and bicycles are loaned free. Airport transfers are CFP 1,000 pp return. Inexpensive.

In June 1998 the **Hôtel Le Méridien** (B.P. 380595, 98718 Punaauia; tel. 47-07-07, fax 47-07-08) opened at PK 15, Punaauia, about nine km southwest of the airport. The 138 a/c rooms in the four-story main building begin at CFP 34,650 single or double, CFP 41,650 triple, while the 12 overwater bungalows are CFP 48,300 single or double, CFP 55,300 triple, plus tax. A huge sand-bottomed swimming pool linked to the beach and a 500-seat conference center are on the premises. The waters off their sandy beach are pollution-free, the Museum of Tahiti and the Islands is just a 15-minute walk away, and the sunsets over Moorea are superb. Luxury.

OTHER WINDWARD ISLANDS

Maiao

Maiao, or Tapuaemanu, 70 km southwest of Moorea, is a low coral island with an elongated, 180-meter-high hill at the center. On each side of this hill is a large greenish blue lake. Around Maiao is a barrier reef with a pass on the south side accessible only to small boats. Some 250 people live in a small village on the southeast side of 8.3-square-km Maiao, all of them Polynesians. Problems with an Englishman, Eric Trower, who attempted to gain control of Maiao for phosphate mining in the 1930s, have resulted in a ban on Europeans and Chinese residing on the island. Most of the thatch used in touristic constructions on Moorea and Tahiti originates on Maiao.

There are no tourist accommodations on Maiao and an invitation from a resident is required to stay. There's no airstrip. For information on the monthly supply ship from Papeete, contact the **Compagnie Française Maritime de Tahiti** (B.P. 368, 98713 Papeete; tel. 42-63-93) at Fare Ute. A roundtrip voyage on this ship would at least give you a glimpse of Maiao.

Mehetia

Mehetia is an uninhabited volcanic island about 100 km east of Tahiti. Although Mehetia is less than two km across, Mt. Fareura reaches 435 meters. There's no lagoon and anchorage is untenable. Landing is possible on a black beach on the northwest side of the island but it's difficult. Anglers from the south coast of Tahiti visit occasionally.

Tetiaroa

Tetiaroa, 42 km north of Tahiti, is a low coral atoll with a turquoise lagoon and 13 deep-green coconut-covered islets totaling 490 hectares. Only small boats can enter the lagoon. Tahuna Iti has been designated a seabird refuge (fenced off), the lagoon a marine reserve. Three-km-long Rimatuu islet served as a retreat for Tahitian royalty and the remains of Polynesian *marae* and giant *tuu* trees may be seen.

In 1904 the Pomare family gave Tetiaroa, once a Tahitian royal retreat, to a Canadian dentist named Walter J. Williams to pay their bills. Dr. Williams, who served as British consul from 1916 until his death in 1937, had a daughter who sold Tetiaroa to actor Marlon Brando in 1966. Brando came to Tahiti in 1960 to play Fletcher Christian in the MGM film *Mutiny on the Bounty* and ended up marrying his leading lady, Tarita Teriipaia (who played Mameetee, the chief's daughter). She and her family still run the small tourist resort

TETIAROA

Auroa
Oroatera
Tauini Hira
Anae
Tiaraunu
Motu Aie
Honuea   Lagoon
AIRSTRIP HOTEL
Onetahi   Rimatuu
Tahuna Iti
Tahuna
Rahi
0   2 mi
0   2 km   Reiono

on Motu Onetahi. Tarita and Marlon had two children, son Teihotu, born in 1965, and daughter Cheyenne, born in 1970.

The gunshot death of Dag Drollet, Cheyenne's ex-boyfriend and father of her son Tuki, at the Brando residence in Los Angeles in 1990, resulted in a 10-year prison sentence for Cheyenne's half-brother, Christian Brando, on a plea bargain. On Easter Sunday 1995 Cheyenne committed suicide and was buried next to Dag in the Drollet family crypt on Tahiti. These tragedies continue to haunt the Brando family, and the resort on Tetiaroa has been seriously neglected as a result. Brando is seldom present on Tetiaroa these days, and when he's on the atoll it's closed to tourists.

Getting to Tetiaroa

A reservation office (B.P. 2418, 98713 Papeete; tel. 82-63-03, fax 85-00-51) in the Air Moorea terminal at Faa'a International Airport arranges flights to Tetiaroa. A seven-hour day-trip including airfare, bird island tour, and lunch is CFP 23,800 pp. If you arrange this trip through your hotel, their commission will inflate the price. To stay in a rustic bungalow at the **Tetiaroa Village Hôtel** costs CFP 31,000/56,000/72,000 single/double/triple for a one-night package, or CFP 41,900/77,800/107,700 for a two-night package, air ticket, bungalow, meals, and excursion included. If you arrive in the morning you must also leave in the morning. To be frank, this hotel is in need of major renovations and you'll be shocked to see the traces of past glory being slowly eaten away by termites. So—though the price may suggest it—don't come expecting anything resembling a luxury resort, and be prepared to rough it. Luxury.

Aremiti Pacific Cruises (tel. 42-88-88) at the Moorea ferry wharf has tours to Tetiaroa on Wednesday and Sunday at CFP 14,000 pp including lunch and a guided tour of bird island. Other yachts and catamarans tied up opposite the Vaima Center offer day-trips to Tetiaroa and their departure times and rates are posted. Prices vary according to whether lunch is included and the quality of the boat, and you can sometimes go for as little as CFP 7,000 (meals not included). On all of the boat trips to Tetiaroa, be aware that up to three hours will be spent traveling each way and on a day-trip you'll only have about four hours on the atoll. The boat trip tends to be rough and many people throw up their fancy lunch on the way back to Papeete. (In mid-1995 Marlon Brando won a lawsuit to prohibit "floating hotels" in the Tetiaroa lagoon, so overnight trips many now only be possible for those staying at the Tetiaroa Village Hôtel.)

Cruising yachts with careless captains occasionally find their journey coming to a sudden end at low-lying Tetiaroa as it's directly on the approach to Papeete from Hawaii. Several good boats have ended their days here.

MOOREA

Moorea, Tahiti's heart-shaped sister island, is clearly visible across the Sea of the Moon, just 16 km northwest of Papeete. This enticing island offers the white-sand beaches rare on Tahiti, plus long, deep bays, lush volcanic peaks, and a broad blue-green lagoon. Much more than Tahiti, Moorea is the laid-back South Sea isle of the travel brochures. And while Bora Bora has a reputation as Polynesia's most beautiful island, easily accessible Moorea seems to merit the distinction more (and it's a lot less expensive too). As soon as Papeete starts to get to you, Moorea is only a hop away.

With a population of just 12,000, Moorea lives a quiet, relaxed lifestyle; coconut, pineapple, and vanilla plantations alternate with pleasant resorts and the vegetation-draped dwellings of the inhabitants. Tourism is concentrated along the north coast around Paopao and Club Med; many of the locals live in the more spacious south. Yet like Bora Bora, Moorea is in danger of becoming overdeveloped, and heavy traffic already roars along the north coastal road all day. The choicest sections of shoreline have been barricaded by luxury resorts. On the plus side, most of the hotels are clusters of thatched bungalows, and you won't find many of the monstrous steel, glass, and cement edifices the scream at you in Hawaii. The accommodations are plentiful and good, and weekly and monthly apartment rentals make even extended stays possible. Don't try to see Moorea as a day-trip from Tahiti: this is a place to relax!

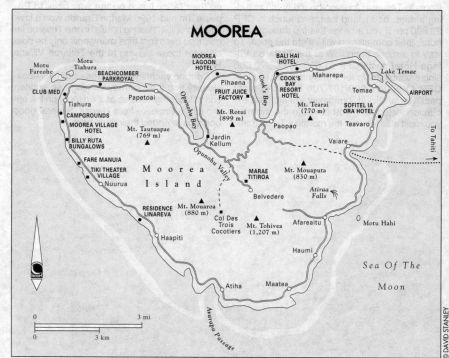

© DAVID STANLEY

The Land

This triangular, 125-square-km island is actually the surviving southern rim of a shield volcano once 3,000 meters high. Moorea is twice as old as its Windward partner, Tahiti, and weathering is noticeably advanced. The two spectacular bays cutting into the north coast flank Mt. Rotui (899 meters), once Moorea's core. The crescent of jagged peaks facing these long northern bays is scenically superb.

Shark-tooth-shaped Mouaroa (880 meters) is a visual triumph, but Mt. Tohivea (1,207 meters) is higher. Polynesian chiefs were once buried in caves along the cliffs. Moorea's peaks protect the north and northwest coasts from the rain-bearing southeast trades; the drier climate and scenic beauty explain the profusion of hotels along this side of the island. Moorea is surrounded by a coral ring with several passes into the lagoon. Three *motus* enhance the lagoon, one off Afareaitu and two off Club Med.

History

Legend claims that Aimeho (or "Eimeo," as Captain Cook spelled it) was formed from the second dorsal fin of the fish that became Tahiti. The present name, Moorea, means "offshoot." It has also been called Fe'e or "octopus" for the eight ridges that divide the island into eight segments. A hole right through the summit of Mt. Mouaputa (830 meters) is said to have been made by the spear of the demigod Pai, who tossed it across from Tahiti to prevent Mt. Rotui from being carried off to Raiatea by Hiro, the god of thieves.

Captain Cook anchored in Opunohu Bay for one week in 1777, but he never visited the bay that today bears his name! His visit was uncharacteristically brutal, as he smashed the islanders' canoes and burned their homes when they refused to return a stolen goat.

In 1792 Pomare I conquered Moorea using arms obtained from the *Bounty* mutineers. Moorea had long been a traditional place of refuge for defeated Tahitian warriors, thus in 1808 Pomare II fled into exile here after his bid to bring all Tahiti under his control failed. A party of English missionaries established themselves at Papetoai in 1811, and Moorea soon earned a special place in the history of Christianity: here in 1812 the missionaries finally managed to convert Pomare II after 15 years of trying. On 14 February 1815, Patii, high priest of Oro, publicly accepted Protestantism and burned the old heathen idols at Papetoai, where the octagonal church is today. Shortly afterward the whole population followed Patii's example. The *marae* of Moorea were then abandoned and the Opunohu Valley depopulated.

After Pomare II finally managed to reconquer Tahiti in 1815 with missionary help (the main reason for his "conversion"), Moorea again became a backwater. American novelist Herman Melville visited Moorea in 1842 and worked with other beachcombers on a sweet-potato farm in Maatea. His book *Omoo* contains a marvelous description of his tour of the island. Cotton and coconut plantations were created on Moorea in the 19th century, followed by vanilla and coffee in the 20th, but only with the advent of the travel industry has Moorea become more than a beautiful backdrop for Tahiti.

Orientation

If you arrive by ferry you'll get off at Vaiare, four km south of Temae Airport. Your hotel may be at Maharepa (Hôtel Bali Hai), Paopao (Bali Hai Club, Motel Albert), Pihaena (Moorea Lagoon Hôtel), or Tiahura (Club Med, the campgrounds, Moorea Village Hôtel), all on the north coast. The Paopao hotels enjoy better scenery, but the beach is far superior at Tiahura. Add a CFP 150 pp per day municipal services tax to the accommodations prices quoted below.

The PKs (kilometer stones) on Moorea are measured in both directions from PK 0 at the access road to Temae Airport. They're numbered up to PK 35 along the north coast via Club Med and up to PK 24 along the south coast via Afareaitu, meeting at Haapiti halfway around the island. Our circle-island tour and the accommodations and restaurant listings below begin at Vaiare Wharf and go counterclockwise around the island in each category.

SIGHTS

Northeast Moorea

You'll probably arrive on Moorea at **Vaiare Wharf,** which is officially PK 4 on the 59-km road around the island. To the north is the **Sofitel Ia Ora** (PK 1.3), built in the mid-1970s. If you have your own transport, stop here for a look around the resort and a swim. It's also enjoyable to walk north along the beach from this hotel or even to go snorkeling. At PK 1 on the main road, high above the Ia Ora, is a fine **lookout** over the deep passage, romantically named the Sea of the Moon, between Tahiti and Moorea.

One of the only public beach parks on Moorea is at **Temae,** about a kilometer down a gravel road to the right a bit before you reach the airport access road. Watch out for black spiny sea urchins here. The Temae area is a former *motu* now linked to the main island and surfers will find an excellent long right wave around the point next to the airstrip.

Around Cook's Bay

On the grounds of the American-owned **Hôtel Bali Hai** at PK 5.3 are replicas of historic anchors lost by captains Bougainville and Cook in the 18th century. Just past the Bali Hai on the mountain side of the road is the "White House," the stately mansion of a former vanilla plantation, now used as a pareu salesroom.

At the entrance to Cook's Bay (PK 7) is the **Galerie Aad Van der Heyde** (tel. 56-14-22), as much a museum as a gallery. Aad's paintings hang outside in the flower-filled courtyard; inside are his black-pearl jewelry, a large collection of Marquesan sculpture, and more paintings.

Teva Yrondi's **Aquarium de Moorea** (B.P. 483, 98728 Maharepa; tel. 56-24-00, fax 56-30-00; Tues.-Sun. 0930-1200/1430-1730), just south of the Cooks Bay Resort, displays turtles, crabs, coral, seashells, pearls, and jewelry in tanks that had once held tropical fish. Out back is a garden with a large travelers tree in the middle. Dozens of birds are attracted by feeders near the beach and you can see fish in an enclosure by their dock. Although the intention is to sell you a black pearl, the aquarium is worth treating as a museum and admission is free.

Also as good as a museum is the **Galerie Baie de Cook** (B.P. 103, 98728 Maharepa; tel. 56-25-67; open daily 0900-1700; admission free), opposite Club Bali Hai. Here you can inspect paintings by local artists, several huge Polynesian canoes, and a good collection of old artifacts. **Paopao Market** is almost defunct but it's still worth stopping to admire the large mural of a market scene by Temae artist François Ravello.

Cook's Bay, Moorea

A rough four-km dirt road up to the paved Belvédère viewpoint road begins just west of the bridge at Paopao (PK 9), and it's nice to hike up it past the pineapple plantations. This is a good shortcut to the Opunohu Valley.

On the west side of Cook's Bay, a kilometer farther along the north-coast highway, is a new **Catholic church** (PK 10). In the older St. Joseph's Church next door is an interesting altar painting with Polynesian angels done by the Swedish artist Peter Heyman in 1948. Unfortunately this building is not being maintained and is presently closed (although you may still be able to peek at the painting through the windows).

It's possible to visit the sales room (but not the production facilities) of the Distillerie de Moorea **fruit-juice factory** (B.P. 23, 98728 Temae; tel. 56-11-33, fax 56-21-52, daily 0800-1600), up off the main road at PK 12. Aside from the excellent papaya, grapefruit, and pineapple juices made from local fruits, the factory produces apple, orange, and passion fruit juices from imported concentrate, with no preservatives added. They also make 40-proof brandies (carambola or "star fruit," ginger, grapefruit, mango, orange, and pineapple flavors) and 25-proof liqueurs (coconut, ginger, and pineapple varieties). These are for sale and if they think you might buy a bottle they'll invite you to sample the brews (no free samples for obvious backpackers).

Opunohu Bay to Le Belvédère

The Moorea Lagoon Hôtel at PK 14 is the only large hotel between Paopao and Tiahura. At PK 17.5 is the **Jardin Kellum Stop** (tel. 56-18-52) a tropical garden along Opunohu Bay with a colonial-style house built in 1920. Marie Kellum is an amateur archaeologist whose personal collection is full of interest and she can tell you anything you need to know about Tahitian medicinal plants. Until 1962 the Kellum family owned most of the Opunohu Valley. The garden is open Wed.-Sat. mornings until noon. Ring the cow bell on the gate—it's CFP 300 pp admission. A famous yacht anchorage called Robinson's Cove is just offshore. From the unspoiled surroundings it's easy to understand why the 1984 remake of *The Bounty* was filmed here.

Shrimp are bred in large basins at the head of Opunohu Bay (PK 18). From here a paved five-km side road runs up the largely uninhabited **Opunohu Valley** to the Belvédère viewpoint. After two km you reach the junction with the dirt connecting road from Cook's Bay previously mentioned, then another km up and on the right is the **Lycée Professionnel Agricole,** Moorea's agricultural high school. This worthy institution, with students from all the islands of Tahiti-Polynesia, has hundreds of hectares planted in pineapples, vanilla, coffee, fruit trees, decorative flowers, and native vegetables on land seized from a German company in 1914. (In 1991 Moorea voters rejected a proposal to build a Sheraton resort and Arnold Palmer golf course in this area.)

Another km above this is **Marae Titiroa,** largest of a group of Polynesian temples restored in 1969 by Prof. Y.H. Sinoto of Honolulu. The small platform or *ahu* at the end of this *marae* was a sacred area reserved for the gods, and stone backrests for chiefs and priests are also seen. Here the people offered gifts of tubers, fish, dogs, and pigs, and prayed to their gods, many of whom were deified ancestors. Near the water tanks just 50 meters northwest of Marae Titiroa is a long council platform, and 50 meters farther are two smaller *marae* surround-ed by towering Tahitian chestnut trees *(mape).* The most evocative of the group is four-tiered **Marae Ahu o Mahine,** about 250 meters down the trail.

Continue up the main road from Marae Titiroa about 200 meters and watch for some stone **archery platforms** on the left. Here kneeling nobles once competed to see who could shoot an arrow the farthest. The bows and arrows employed in these contests were never used in warfare. Just up on the left is access to another archery platform and **Marae Afareaito.** The stone slabs you see sticking up in the middle of the *marae* were backrests for participants of honor.

From the archaeological area the winding road climbs steeply another km to the **Belvédère,** or Roto Nui, a viewpoint high up near the geographical center of the island. Much of northern Moorea is visible from here and it's easy to visualize the great volcano that once existed. Mt. Rotui (899 meters) in front of you was once the central core of an island more than three times as high as the present. The north part is now missing, but the semicircular arch of the southern half is plain to see. (An ice cream from the *roulotte* in the parking lot may be a welcome treat.)

Papetoai to Club Med

Return to the main circuminsular highway and continue west. The octagonal **Protestant church,** behind the post office at Papetoai (PK 22), was built on the site of the temple of the god Oro in 1822. Despite having been rebuilt several times, the church is known as "the oldest European building still in use in the South Pacific."

As the road begins to curve around the northwest corner of Moorea, you pass a number of large resort hotels, including the **Beachcomber Parkroyal** (PK 24.5), **Club Med** (PK 26.5), and the **Moorea Village Hôtel** (PK 27); only Club Med forbids you to walk through their grounds to the beach (there are no public beaches anywhere along here). It's possible to snorkel out to Tarahu and Tiahuru *motus* from this beach; recreation people at the Beachcomber Parkroyal and Moorea Beach Hôtel could also ferry you over. Try feeding bread to the fish. There's excellent reef break surfing in Taotai Pass off the Parkroyal.

Patrice Bredel's **Galerie Api** (tel. 56-13-57, fax 56-28-27; Mon.-Sat. 0930-1200/1430-1730), on the beach northeast of Club Med, displays the works of local artist François Ravello who paints in a Gauguin-like style. Bredel's personal collection of old Pacific artifacts is fascinating. In **Le Petit Village** shopping mall, across the street from Club Med, are a tourist information kiosk, bank, grocery store, snack bar, gas station, and many tourist shops.

Southern Moorea

The south coast of Moorea is much quieter than the north. You'll drive for kilometers through the open coconut plantations past unspoiled villages and scenic vistas. At PK 31 is **Tiki Village Theater,** described below under **Entertainment,** the only one of its kind in the territory. Just past the Fire Department at PK 31.5 Haapiti is **Marae Nuurua,** on the beach across the soccer field. This three-tiered *marae* restored in 1991 bears a petroglyph of a turtle, and beyond is the much higher rubble heap of an unrestored *marae.*

At PK 33 you can have your photo taken in front of a huge fiberglass Tahitian warrior! It's also fun to stop for an upmarket lunch or a drink at **Résidence Linareva** (PK 34). Linareva's upscale floating seafood restaurant, the *Tamarii Moorea I,* is an old ferryboat that once plied between Moorea and Tahiti. Colorful reef fish swim around the dock, which also affords an excellent mountain view. Drop into **Pai Moana Pearls** (tel. 56-25-25) next to the hotel driveway and ask for a free copy of owner Rick Steger's excellent brochure on pricing pearls.

At PK 35/24, Haapiti, the kilometer numbering begins its descent to Temae Airport. The twin-towered **Église de la Sainte Famille** (1891) at Haapiti was once the head church of the Catholic mission on the island. There's good anchorage here for yachts entering Matauvau Pass and a tall left-hander for surfers out there (Tubb's Pub offers surf shuttles).

Tiny Motu Hahi lies just off **Afareaitu** (PK 9), the administrative center of Moorea. After Papetoai this was the second center of missionary activity on Moorea, and on 30 June 1817, at the printing works at Afareaitu, King Pomare II ceremonially printed the first page of the first book ever published on a South Pacific island, a Tahitian translation of the Gospel of St. Luke. Before the press was moved to Huahine a year later, more than 9,000 books totaling more than half a

million pages had been printed at Afareaitu! After 1821 the London Missionary Society established its Academy of the South Seas here to instruct the children of the missionaries and the Tahitian chiefs. The old Protestant church (1912) in Afareaitu remains as a reminder.

You get a good view of Mt. Mouaputa, the peak pierced by Pai's spear, from the hospital just north of Afareaitu. The access road to **Atiraa Falls** is a little beyond the hospital. Admission is CFP 200 pp, but it's a 30-minute hike from the parking area.

Across the Island

An excellent day hike involves taking a morning bus to Vaiare Wharf, then hiking over the mountains to Paopao. From there you can catch another bus back to your accommodations, or try hitching. The shaded three-hour trail, partly marked by red, white, and green paint dabbed on tree and rock, does demand attention and perseverance, however. There are a few steep ascents and descents, and after rains it can be muddy and slippery.

Take the road inland beside Magasin Chez Meno, about 50 meters south of the first bridge south of the Vaiare ferry wharf. As you follow the dirt road up the valley, you'll take two forks to the right. Don't cross the stream after the second fork but go left and walk past some houses, just beyond which is an old Polynesian *marae* on the left. Further along you cross the stream and continue past a number of local gardens. The trail to Paopao leads off to the left near the last garden, and once you're on it it's fairly easy to follow if you keep your eyes open. When you see an old stone stairway on the left five minutes after leaving the gardens you'll know you're on the correct trail. All of the locals know about this trail and if you say "Paopao?" to them in a questioning way, they'll point you in the right direction. (It's hard to understand why Tahiti Tourisme, which has millions to spend on lavish overseas promotions, can't spare a few francs to erect proper trail markers here.)

When you reach the divide, go a short distance south along the ridge to a super viewpoint. On a clear day the rounded double peak of Orohena, Tahiti's highest, will be visible, plus the whole interior of Moorea. On the way down the other side avoid taking the wrong turn at a bamboo grove. You'll come out among the pineapple plantations of central Moorea behind Paopao. It's not possible to do this hike eastbound from Paopao to Vaiare without a guide, but westbound an experienced hiker should have no difficulty, and it's worth going simply to see a good cross section of the vegetation. Don't miss it, but do take water and wear sturdy shoes.

Sports and Recreation

M.U.S.T. Plongée Scuba Diving, or Moorea Underwater Scuba-diving Tahiti (B.P. 336, 98728 Paopao; tel. 56-17-32, fax 56-15-83), has their base on the dock behind the Cook's Bay Resort Hôtel. They offer diving daily except Monday at 0900 and 1400 for CFP 5,000 for one dive, CFP 22,500 for five dives. If you pay by credit card there's a three percent surcharge. Divemaster Philippe Molle, author of a well-known French book on scuba diving, knows 20 different spots in and outside the reef.

Moorea's only female divemaster, Ms. Pascale Souquieres, runs **Moorea Fun Dive** (B.P. 737, 98728 Maharepa; tel. 56-40-38, fax 56-40-74) at the Moorea Lagoon Hôtel. It's CFP 4,800 a dive or CFP 4,500 a dive for five dives or more including all gear (except a wetsuit, which is CFP 300 extra). Hotel pickups are offered twice a day for almost anywhere on northern Moorea. This is a professional yet laid-back operation we can recommend.

Bernard and Collette Begliomini's **Bathy's Club** (B.P. 1247, 98729 Papetoai; tel. 56-31-44, fax 56-38-10), at the Beachcomber Parkroyal, offers scuba diving for CFP 5,000, diving with dolphins CFP 13,000. This is the only PADI five-star facility in the territory. Bathy's and M.U.S.T. do underwater fish, eel, and shark feeding. Sometimes the swarm of fish becomes so thick the guide is lost from sight, yet as the resident shark scatters the mass of fish to steal the bait, the divemaster is seen again patting *le requin* as it passes. (It's still unknown if this activity will eventually attract sharks into the Moorea lagoon, but to date no incidents have been reported.)

Marc Quattrini's **Scubapiti** (B.P. 58H, 98729 Haapiti, Moorea; tel. 56-12-67, fax 56-20-38), at Résidence Les Tipaniers, offers scuba diving daily at 0900 and 1430 (CFP 5,500). Instead of putting on a show, Marc keeps things natural

on his cave, canyon, and drift dives. He also offers PADI or CMAS scuba certification courses and free hotel transfers from anywhere in northwestern Moorea.

The "Activities Nautiques" kiosk on the wharf at the **Beachcomber Parkroyal** (tel. 55-19-19) rents jet skis at CFP 6,500 for half an hour, CFP 10,000 for one hour, or try your hand at parasailing (CFP 5,000).

Surfing is possible in most of the passes around the island or off the beach next to the airstrip, but it's not quite as good as on Tahiti or Huahine. A boat or a long paddle is required to reach the reef breaks.

For horseback riding try **Rupe-Rupe Ranch** (tel. 56-26-52), or the "Crazy Horse Corral," at PK 2 between Vaiare Wharf and the Sofitel la Ora. To take one of their 12 horses along the beach for an hour is CFP 3,000. Group rides commence at 0830, 1400, and 1600, but it's best to call ahead.

Tiahura Ranch (tel. 56-28-55) across the highway from the Moorea Village Hôtel offers horseback riding at 0900 and 1615 daily except Monday (CFP 3,000 for 1.5 hours). You must reserve at least an hour in advance.

ACCOMMODATIONS

Camping

One of the South Pacific's nicest campgrounds is **Camping Chez Nelson** (Nelson and Josiane Flohr, tel. 56-15-18), beside the Hôtel Hibiscus, just south of Club Med (PK 27, Tiahura). It's beautifully set in a coconut grove right on the same beach tourists at the fancy resorts are paying hundreds of dollars a day to enjoy. The camping charge is CFP 700 pp, with toilets, showers, refrigerator, and good communal cooking facilities provided. No tents are for rent, but the 10 two-bed "dormitory" rooms go for CFP 1,000 pp (CFP 1,500 for one night). The five beach cabins with shared bath are CFP 2,200 single or double (CFP 2,500 for one night); four larger *fares* near the office are CFP 2,500 single or double (CFP 3,000 for one night). They also have three larger bungalows with kitchen and private bath at CFP 6,000 double. For CFP 300 pp (minimum of seven) they'll ferry you across to a *motu* for snorkeling. The campground office is open only during normal business hours. Josiane is a little eccentric and can be rather reserved at first, but she has a heart of gold. The place is clean, quiet, breezy, spacious, and well equipped, but unfortunately, however, there have been reports of theft here, so don't leave valuables unattended or within reach of an open window at night.

A second, smaller campground is just a little south of Chez Nelson, near the Moorea Village Hôtel. Friendly **Moorea Camping** (tel. 56-14-47, fax 56-30-22), also known as "Chez Viri et Claude," faces the same white-sand beach and has nine four-bed dorms at CFP 800 pp (CFP 1,000 for one night), plus another nine double rooms in a long building at CFP 2,000 single or double (CFP 3,000 for one night). The five beachfront bungalows with fridge are CFP 4,000 single or double (CFP 5,000 for one night). Camping is CFP 700 pp (CFP 800 for one night). The reception is open 0800-1200/1330-1700 only (closed Sunday afternoon). Communal kitchen and washing facilities are provided, and they'll loan you snorkeling gear and perhaps even a canoe. Bus trips around the island are CFP 1,000 pp if at least six people sign up and they can also take you to a *motu*. The activities manager, Coco (one of the nicest Tahitians you'll ever meet), will be able fill you in on all the cheapest deals around Moorea. He'll also help you book trips even if you're not staying here. But as at Chez Nelson, we've heard of things going missing from the dorms, so chain your pack to something solid and keep the top locked. Break-ins often occur when everybody is at a party on the veranda and the campground is empty. Despite the insecurity, both campgrounds are great for young low-budget travelers and other adventurers—you'll meet some wonderful people. Two grocery stores (with cold beer) are between the two camping grounds.

Budget

Motel Albert (Iris Haring, tel./fax 56-12-76), opposite Club Bali Hai at Paopao (PK 8.5), catches splendid views across Cook's Bay. The four older apartments with one double bed, kitchen, and private bath are CFP 3,500 single or double, while four larger apartments with two double beds, kitchen, and private bath are CFP 4,500 double or triple (two-night minimum

stay). The 10 two-bedroom bungalows with kitchen and private bath are CFP 7,000 for up to four persons. The cheaper apartments are often taken by monthly rentals at CFP 80,000 or 90,000. Each unit has cooking facilities, fridge, and hot water in a garden setting on spacious grounds. Several stores are nearby and the Mobil service station next door sells bread and groceries. Bicycles are for rent at CFP 1,200 a day. It's excellent value and often full (try to make reservations).

Inexpensive

Chez Dina (Dina Dhieux, B.P. 512, 98728 Maharepa; tel. 56-10-39) is behind Magasin Vairagi Pihaena at PK 13, Pihaena, a kilometer east of the Moorea Lagoon Hôtel. The three thatched bungalows are CFP 4,500 triple, CFP 5,000 for up to five (reductions on a weekly basis). Cooking facilities are provided, and the bathroom is communal.

Billy Ruta Bungalows (tel. 56-12-54) is right on the beach at PK 28.3, Tiahura. The 12 thatched A-frame bungalows begin at CFP 4,000 double without kitchenette, CFP 5,000 double with kitchenette. Another eight rooms in a long block with shared bath are CFP 3,000 single or double, and they sometimes allow camping at CFP 500 pp. There's occasionally disco dancing here on weekends. Billy drives the local school and church *truck* and is a very friendly guy.

Chez Pauline (Jean-Pierre Bouvier, tel. 56-11-26) at PK 9, Afareaitu, is between the two stores near the church. It's a lovely old colonial house with three rooms with double beds and shared bath at CFP 4,000/5,000 single/double including breakfast. One larger room sleeping five is CFP 10,000. A picturesque restaurant with tikis on display rounds out this establishment, which has great atmosphere. Dinner here is around CFP 3,000 (fish and Tahitian vegetables) and it must be ordered in advance.

Moderate

The **Cook's Bay Resort Hôtel** (Béatrice and François Michel, B.P. 30, 98728 Temae; tel. 56-10-50, fax 56-29-18) is beside the highway at the entrance to Cook's Bay (PK 7.2). You can't miss this mock-colonial edifice constructed in 1985, with its false-front Waikiki feel. The 76 rooms cost CFP 6,500 single or double with fan,

CFP 8,500 with a/c, plus tax. The accommodations are rather small and spartan with old furniture, but at least they're clean and each room has a fridge. Don't bother taking the a/c as it probably won't work anyway. The resort also has 24 wooden bungalows opposite the wharf at CFP 8,500 single or double in the garden or CFP 9,500 facing the water. Discounts are sometimes offered. The breakfast and dinner plan here is CFP 3,800 pp, but plenty of better restaurants are nearby. You can swim or snorkel off the pier in front of the restaurant and there's a swimming pool. Moorea's top dive shop is on the premises, and all the usual resort activities and entertainment are available. The Cook's Bay caters mostly to people on cheap Hawaii-style packages, and this captured clientele helps explain the variable service. Many readers liked this resort, but a few did not. The views of the bay are stunning. (A late report indicates that the main building has closed for renovations, and guests are now accommodated only in the wooden bungalow section known as Hôtel Kaveka.)

Moorea Fare Auti'ura (Viri Pere, tel. 56-14-47, fax 56-30-22), opposite Moorea Camping at PK 27.5, Tiahura, has six thatched bungalows on elevated concrete platforms at CFP 6,000 single or double (minimum stay two nights). Cooking facilities are provided. It's run by Moorea Camping, so check there if nobody seems to be around.

Fare Mato Tea (Iris Cabral, B.P. 1111, 98729 Papetoai; tel. 56-14-36), on the beach just south of Billy Ruta (PK 29, Tiahura), is okay if you're a family or group: CFP 8,500 for four, CFP 10,500 for six (minimum stay two nights). All eight large thatched *fares* on the spacious grounds have full cooking facilities and private bath. It's a do-your-own-thing type of place.

Near the south end of the west coast strip (PK 30) is **Fare Manuia** (Jeanne Salmon, tel. 56-26-17) with six *fares* with cooking facilities at CFP 8,000 for up to four people, CFP 10,000 for up to six people, or CFP 12,000 on the beach.

Résidence Linareva (B.P. 1, 98729 Haapiti; tel. 56-15-35, fax 56-25-25) sits amid splendid mountain scenery at PK 34 on the wild side of the island. Prices begin at CFP 7,200/8,200/9,900 single/double/triple, with 20% weekly discounts. Each of the seven units is unique, with TV, fan, and full cooking facilities. Bicycles and an outrigger canoe are loaned free.

Expensive

Résidence Les Tipaniers (B.P. 1002, 9827 Papetoai; tel. 56-12-67, fax 56-29-25) at PK 25.9, Tiahura, is cramped around the reception, but better as you approach the beach. The 22 bungalows start at CFP 8,500/10,200 single/double (those with kitchen are a few thousand francs extra). The hotel also has five self-catering lagoonside bungalows at PK 21 on Opunohu Bay costing CFP 7,500 plus tax for up to four persons with weekly rates available. Les Tipaniers' well known restaurant offers Italian dishes. They'll shuttle you over to a nearby *motu* for snorkeling or loan you a bicycle or outrigger canoe at no charge. This hotel has a good reputation and a resident divemaster.

The **Hôtel Hibiscus** (B.P. 1009, 98729 Papetoai; tel. 56-12-20, fax 56-20-69), on beach right next to Club Med (PK 27), offers 29 thatched bungalows beneath the coconut palms at CFP 11,000 triple in the garden or CFP 13,000 on the beach, plus tax. A fourth person is CFP 1,000 extra. There's a 20% discount on a weekly basis. The breakfast and dinner plan is CFP 3,900 pp, but all units have kitchenettes so this is a good choice for families. You don't get a lot of mosquitoes here because Club Med fumigates their adjacent property daily (you do get occasional disco noise from the same source).

The **Moorea Village Hôtel** (B.P. 1008, 98729 Papetoai; tel. 56-10-02, fax 56-22-11), also called "Fare Gendron," at PK 27.9, Tiahura, offers 70 fan-cooled thatched bungalows beginning at CFP 8,000/9,000 single/double plus tax, or CFP 11,500 for up to four people. To be on the beach is another CFP 2,500. The 10 new units with kitchen are double price; all units have fridges. The breakfast and dinner plan costs CFP 3,900 pp. Saturday at 1900 there's a barbecue; the Tahitian feast with Polynesian dancing is Sunday at noon. There are lots of free activities, such as the canoe trip to the *motu,* outrigger canoes, tennis, snorkeling, and swimming pool. Though on the package tour circuit, this place is also somewhat of a hangout for local Tahitians, and the management leaves a lot to be desired.

Premium

The 63-room **Hôtel Bali Hai** (B.P. 26, 98728 Temae; tel. 56-13-52, fax 56-19-22) at PK 5.3, Maharepa, caters mainly to American tour groups staying three, four, or seven nights. If you go for stuff like that you'll love the Bali Hai (although the staff become less friendly as soon as they find out you're not a guest). Standard rooms are CFP 11,500 single or double, bungalows from CFP 14,000 (children under 12 free). The cheaper rooms are rather gloomy and it's better to go for a bungalow if you stay here. For breakfast and dinner add CFP 4,500 pp extra. Rides on the Bali Hai's thatched catamaran *Liki Tiki* are CFP 2,000 and up. Happy hour

here is daily 1700-1900 with live music and popcorn, and Wednesday there's a dance show. The Bali Hai was founded by the so-called Bali Hai Boys, ex-Californians Hugh, Jay, and Muk, who arrived on Moorea in 1959 to take over a vanilla plantation but ended up inventing the overwater bungalow right here in 1961.

Club Bali Hai (B.P. 8, 98728 Maharepa; tel. 56-13-68, fax 56-13-27) at PK 8.5, Paopao, has 20 rooms in the main two-story building starting at CFP 12,000 single or double, and 19 beachfront or overwater bungalows at CFP 18,000 or 24,000. Slightly reduced room rates are available to walk in guests. Only the bungalows include cooking facilities, but most rooms have a spectacular view of Cook's Bay. There's a swimming pool by the bay. Many units have been sold to affluent Americans on a time-share basis, with each owner getting two weeks a year at the Club. Enjoy reduced-price drinks, free popcorn, and Tahitian trio music during happy hour at the lagoonside bar Tuesday and Friday 1800-1900—a Moorea institution. The snack bar serves a wicked hot dog at lunchtime. We've heard Club Bali Hai welcomes visiting yachties warmly.

Luxury

The **Sofitel la Ora** (B.P. 28, 98728 Temae; tel. 56-12-90, fax 56-12-91), at PK 1.3 between Vaiare and the airport, sits on one of the finest beaches on the island with a splendid view of Tahiti. The 110 thatched bungalows begin at CFP 23,200 single or double, plus tax (children under 12 free). Upgrade to a/c if possible. Breakfast and dinner are CFP 5,600 pp extra together. The meals here are often not up to scratch (the Molokai Restaurant has better food and service than La Pérouse), and because the Sofitel is rather isolated some of the Paopao restaurants won't pick up diners here (Le Pêcheur might). Unfortunately, the service deteriorates fast when large groups are present and some of the local staff are rude and unhelpful (several complaints have been received). We've heard of local children with improper toilet training being allowed in the hotel pool, so use the beach. There's a Europcar desk in the lobby.

The 147-room **Moorea Beachcomber Parkroyal** (B.P. 1019, 98729 Papetoai; tel. 55-19-19, fax 55-19-55) at PK 24.5, was erected on an artificial beach in 1987 and purchased in

COOK'S BAY

Avaroa Pass

Cook's Bay

Moorea Island

BANKS AND POST OFFICE

PHARMACIE FARE RAAU

LE PECHEUR RESTAURANT

To Vaiare Wharf

GALERIE VAN DER HEYDE

COOK'S BAY RESORT HOTEL

AQUARIUM DE MOOREA

ALLO PIZZA

GENDARMERIE

To Club Med

SUPERMARCHE PAOPAO

RESTAURANT CAPRICE DES ILES

CLUB BALI HAI

MOTEL ALBERT

CATHOLIC CHURCH

MOBIL SERVICE STATION

ALFREDO'S RESTAURANT

RESTAURANT CHEZ JEAN PIERRE

FISH MARKET

Paopao

SUPERMARCHE ARE

MAGASIN LEE HEN

MAIRIE DE PAOPAO

Paopao Valley

0   500 yds

0   500 m

To Opunohu Valley

© DAVID STANLEY

1989 by Japanese interests. It's Moorea's top hotel. The 49 standard a/c rooms in the main building start are CFP 28,800 single or double plus tax, but it's better value to pay CFP 30,900 for a garden bungalow. Beach bungalows are CFP 35,000. For one of the 50 overwater bungalows, have your CFP 39,100 ready (50% less than you'd pay for the same thing on Bora Bora). Third persons are CFP 6,000, but children under 16 are free. The breakfast and dinner plan is CFP 6,500 pp (alternative eateries are quite a walk away). There's a pool and the full spectrum of paid sporting activities is available (only daytime tennis, snorkeling gear, and canoeing are free for guests). The hotel's dolphins are a big attraction and you'll see them standing on their heads and roughhousing at all hours day and night. Europcar has a desk here.

Club Méditerranée (B.P. 1010, 98729 Papetoai; tel. 55-00-00, fax 55-00-10) at PK 26.5, Tiahura, has 350 simple fan-cooled bungalows. You can reserve one by paying CFP 14,000 pp a day (double occupancy) at the Club Med office in the Vaima Center, Papeete (B.P. 575, 98713 Papeete; tel. 42-96-99, fax 42-16-83). Children under 12 are CFP 7,000, under four CFP 1,400. The price includes buffet breakfast, lunch, and dinner, and a wide range of regimented activities (including one scuba dive a day), but no airport transfers. Unlimited beer and wine come with lunch and dinner, but other drinks are expensive and laundry charges will knock your socks off! The PADI scuba diving center here is for guests only. Sunbathing in the raw is permitted on the small *motu* just offshore (the tiniest of bottoms is required in front of the resort). Club Med's for you if nonstop activity is a high priority, otherwise all the canned entertainment can be to the detriment of peace at night, and occasional helicopter landings beside the restaurant often interrupt afternoon naps. Clocks inside the village are set ahead to give guests an extra hour in the sun. Club Med's G.O.s *(gentils organisateurs)* tend to resist the unusual or nonroutine (such as requesting a specific room or not sitting where you're told in the restaurant), so try to "go with the flow" (i.e., conform). Nonguests can purchase a CFP 5,500 day pass valid for lunch and some sporting activities. Don't attempt to trespass as these guys are security freaks. The Moorea Club Med has been around for quite a while and it can't compare to the newer, smaller, and smarter Club Med on Bora Bora.

FOOD

Aside from the hotel restaurants, table hoppers are catered to by a mixed bag of eateries along the east side of Cook's Bay. **Restaurant Le Mahogany** (tel. 56-39-73; closed Wednesday), at PK 4, Maharepa, is a new place offering French and Chinese dishes. A bit west is the popular **Le Cocotier Restaurant** (tel. 56-12-10; Mon.-Sat. 1100-1430/1730-2100) meat dishes priced CFP 1,400-1,650 and fish at CFP 1,350-2,400. There's a menu at the entrance.

Snack Le Sylésie (tel. 56-15-88), next to the post office at PK 5.5, Maharepa, has a nice terrace and fast service—perfect for breakfast. It's also good for pastries, sandwiches, and crepes, and try the coconut ice cream. Of course, the coffee here is *magnifique!*

Le Pêcheur Restaurant (tel. 56-36-12; closed Sunday), also at Maharepa (PK 6), near the pharmacy at the east entrance to Cook's Bay, has an excellent reputation for its seafood dishes, which begin around CFP 1,500. The service is also good and on Saturday night there's local entertainment. If you lack transport, they'll come and pick you up.

The overwater **Fishermen's Wharf Restaurant** (tel. 56-15-56; Tues.-Sat. 1130-1400/1700-2100) near the Cook's Bay Resort Hôtel also serves seafood in the CFP 1,500-1,900 range. Readers report that while the view from their terrace is superb, the food is variable.

Cook's Pizza (tel. 56-10-50), across the street from the Cook's Bay Resort Hôtel (PK 7.2), has small/large thick or thin crust pizzas beginning at CFP 900/1,300—not bad for Moorea. **Allo Pizza** (tel. 56-18-22; daily except Tuesday 1100-2100), opposite the *gendarmerie* in Paopao (PK 7.8), dispenses large takeaway pizzas costing CFP 900-1,300, which you must consume picnic-style somewhere.

Restaurant Caprice des Îles (tel. 56-44-24; closed Tuesday), occupies a thatched pavilion next to Supermarché Paopao on the mountain side of the road, 150 meters north of Club Bali Hai. They offer Italian pastas (CFP 800-1,400), Chinese dishes (CFP 900-1,900), Tahitian dishes (CFP 1,000-1,900), and French dishes (CFP 1,300-2,400)—more expensive than other places along this way. We've heard rave reviews of their seafood but the pastas can be rather heavy in such a warm climate.

Restaurant Chez Jean Pierre (tel. 56-18-51; closed Wednesday), close to the market, is reasonable and has roast suckling pig in coconut milk on Saturday night. Cheaper is the outdoor snack bar at Paopao Market, which is only open in the evening (a huge swordfish steak for CFP 900).

Alfredo's Restaurante Italiano (tel. 56-17-71; open daily), on the inland side of the road a few hundred meters south of Club Bali Hai, has some of the island's top pizza and pasta, plus a few reasonably priced fish and meat dishes. The piña coladas aren't bad either. It's owned by an American named Syd Pollock who has been running hotels and restaurants around Polynesia for years. He's an interesting guy to chat with and he does hotel pickups on request. Recommended.

Also check **Chez Michèle** (tel. 56-34-80), by the river at the head of Cooks Bay, which lists its menu on a blackboard facing the terrace.

Restaurants near Club Med

Le Garden (tel. 56-47-00), in Le Petit Village shopping mall opposite Club Med, has ice-cream sundaes at CFP 650, and it's also a good place for breakfast (omelettes CFP 300-500, served 0900-1430). The continental breakfast is served 0800-1100 only.

Nearby is **Restaurant L'Aventure** (tel. 56-23-36; Tuesday 1830-2100, Wed.-Sun. 1200-1400/1830-2100) with salads (CFP 400-900), pastas (CFP 800-1,600), and meat and fish dishes (CFP 1,000-1,800). Specials are advertised on a blackboard menu.

Good pizza and ocean views are available at beachfront **Le Sunset Pizzeria** (tel. 56-26-00) at the Hôtel Hibiscus (but avoid the salads). **Pâtisserie Le Sylésie II** (tel. 56-20-45) is nearby.

Groceries

If you've got access to cooking facilities, shop at one of the many grocery stores spread around Moorea. The largest and cheapest is **Toa Moorea** (tel. 56-18-89; Mon.-Thurs. 0800-1900, Friday and Saturday 0800-2000, Sunday 0600-1200), a kilometer south of the Vaiare ferry wharf.

Libre Service Maharepa (tel. 56-35-90), at PK 5.5, is almost opposite the Banque de Tahiti. **Supermarché Pao Pao** (tel. 56-17-34), 150 meters north of Club Bali Hai, opens Mon.-Sat. 0530-1200/1400-1800, Sunday 0500-1000. At the head of Cook's Bay you have a choice of **Magasin Lee Hen** (tel. 56-15-02; daily 0600-1200/1400-1830) or **Supermarché Are** (tel. 56-10-28) just west of the bridge nearby.

The nearest grocery store to the three small hotels near Faimano Village is **Magasin Vairagi Pihaena,** a kilometer east of the Moorea Lagoon Hôtel. The supermarket in Le Petit Village opposite Club Med opens Monday, Friday, and Saturday 0830-1800, Tues.-Thurs. 0830-1230/1430-1830, and Sunday 0800-1200.

All you're likely to find at the **municipal market** at Paopao is a limited selection of fish. Fresh produce is much harder to obtain on Moorea than it is on Tahiti, so buy things when you see them and plan your grocery shopping carefully. Ask the stores what time the bread arrives, then be there promptly. The hybrid lime-grapefruit grown on Moorea has a thick green skin and a really unique taste.

ENTERTAINMENT

Disco

The disco at **Billy Ruta Bungalows** (tel. 56-12-54), at PK 28.3, Tiahura, is a nice, very Polynesian scene with a good music mix of Tahitian, French, American, reggae, etc. It's a fun place that gets very busy with some very talented dancers (Friday and Saturday from 2230). Otherwise there's a show and disco at **Club Med** (tel. 55-00-00) Friday and Saturday nights at 2130 (CFP 2,500 cover charge includes CFP 1,800 in drinks).

Cultural Shows for Visitors

See Tahitian dancing in the Sofitel Ia Ora's **La Pérouse Restaurant** (tel. 56-17-61) on Tuesday, Thursday, and Saturday at 2000. At **Hôtel Bali Hai** (tel. 56-13-59) there's Polynesian dancing Wednesday and Saturday at 1800, Sunday at 1200. The **Cook's Bay Resort Hôtel** (tel. 56-10-50) has Tahitian dancing Tuesday, Thursday, and Saturday after 1900. The **Moorea Village Hôtel** (tel. 56-10-02) presents Polynesian dancing Sunday at lunchtime. The Tahitian show at the **Moorea Beachcomber Parkroyal** (tel. 55-19-19) is on Wednesday and Saturday nights after 2000. **Club Med** (tel. 55-00-00) presents Tahitian dancing on Thursday (CFP 5,500 admission includes the buffet at 1930). These times often change, so check. The Tahitian feasts that come with the shows cost CFP 4,000 and up, but you can often observe the action from the bar for the price of a drink. It's well worth going.

Since 1986 Moorea has had its own instant culture village, the **Tiki Village Theater** (Olivier Briac, B.P. 1016, 98729 Papetoai; tel. 56-18-97, fax 56-10-86) at PK 31, Haapiti. The doors are open Tues.-Sat. 1100-1500, with a charge of CFP 2,000 to visit the village and see the small dance show at 1300, plus CFP 500 if you want to visit the demonstration black-pearl farm (or CFP 5,500 including the tour, lunch, and transfers). The guided tour of the recreated Tahitian village is informative and the 30 dancers and other staff members who live in the village year-round are enthusiastic, but sometimes they're a little disorganized so you might obtain some details about the show time before parting with your francs. Lunch is available in the à la carte restaurant. Line fishing from a *pirogue* is CFP 1,500 extra. Four or five nights a week at 1800 there's a big sunset show with a *tamaaraa* buffet and open bar (CFP 7,300, reservations required). It's possible to pay CFP 2,500 for the show alone at 2045 (plus CFP 1,000 for hotel transfers, if required). If you've got CFP 130,000 to spare, a "royal" Tahitian wedding can be arranged at the village (bring your own husband/wife). The ceremony lasts two hours, from 1600 to sunset. The bridegroom arrives by canoe and the newlyweds are carried around in procession by four "warriors." Otherwise there's the less extravagant "princely" wedding for CFP 99,000, photos included. Yes, it's kinda tacky, but that's show biz! (Such weddings are not legally binding.) Most readers say they really enjoyed Tiki Village.

SERVICES AND INFORMATION

Services

The Banque Socredo, Banque de Polynésie, and Banque de Tahiti are near the Hôtel Bali Hai at Maharepa. Another bank is in Le Petit Village shopping mall opposite Club Med. None of these banks are open on Saturday but Banque Socredo has an ATM outside.

The main post office (Mon.-Thurs. 0700-1500, Friday 0700-1400) is near the banks at Maharepa. Branch post offices are found at Afareaitu and Papetoai. The *gendarmerie* (tel. 56-13-44) is at PK 7.8, Paopao, just south of the Aquarium de Moorea.

The Tahiti Parfum shop (tel. 56-16-87; daily 0900-1300) in Le Petit Village will wash and dry six kg of laundry for CFP 1,600 (same-day service if you get your wash in early). Look for the Lav'matic sign.

Information

The Moorea Visitors Bureau (B.P. 1121, 98729 Papetoai; tel./fax 56-29-09; closed Sunday) has a poorly marked but helpful kiosk next to the gas station in front of Le Petit Village. Activities and tours can be booked here, including day-trips to Tetiaroa.

There's also a tourist information counter at Vaiare ferry wharf but don't stop to visit them when you first arrive or you'll miss the bus to your hotel. (Why don't they relocate this office to the *Papeete* ferry wharf?)

The boutique at the Hôtel Bali Hai offers a book-exchange service (on the top shelf above the new books).

Kina Maharepa (tel. 56-22-44), next to the post office at PK 5.5, Maharepa, sells books and magazines. There's also a newsstand in Le Petit Village opposite Club Med.

Health

The island's hospital (tel. 56-23-23) is at Afareaitu, on the opposite side of the island from most of the resorts, and it's much easier to see a private doctor or dentist in case of need.

The nearest to Cook's Bay is the Gabinet Medical (tel. 56-32-32) behind the Banque de Polynésie at PK 5.5, Maharepa, not far from the Hôtel Bali Hai. General practitioners Dr. Christian Jonville and Dr. Jean-Pierre Senechal share this clinic, which is open weekdays 0700-1200/1400-1800. Dr. Jonville is fluent in English. In the same building is the Cabinet Dentaire (tel. 56-32-44) of Dr. Jean-Marc Thurillet and Dr. Nadine Tremoulet, open weekdays 0800-1130/1500-1800.

General practitioner Dr. Hervé Paulus (tel. 56-10-09, in emergencies tel. 56-10-25) is conveniently located at Le Petit Village near Club Med. Dr. Dominique Barraille (tel. 56-27-07) has an office between Hôtel Hibiscus and Camping Chez Nelson. Also near Camping Chez Nelson and opposite Magasin Rene Junior at PK 27, Tiahura, is the joint office of Dr. Bernard Sztejnman (tel. 56-47-51; closed Thursday), a dentist, and Dr. Brigitte Busseuil (tel. 56-26-19, residence tel. 56-13-98), a medical doctor.

Pharmacie Fare Raau (tel. 56-10-51; weekdays 0730-1200/1400-1730, Saturday 0800-1200/1530-1800, Sunday 0800-1100) is at PK 6.5 between Maharepa and Paopao. There's a second branch of Pharmacie Fare Raau (tel. 56-38-37; Mon.-Sat. 0830-1200/1530-1830, Sunday 0900-1100) at PK 30.5, Haapiti, near Tiki Village Theater.

TRANSPORTATION

Air Moorea and **Air Tahiti** (both tel. 56-10-34) are based at Moorea Temae Airport. Details of the air and ferry services from Tahiti are given in the introduction to this chapter.

Buses of 28 or 45 seats meet the ferries at Vaiare Wharf five times a day, charging CFP 100/200 child/adult to anywhere on the island. Although they don't go right around the island, the northern and southern routes meet at Le Petit Village opposite Club Med, so you could theoretically effect a circumnavigation by changing there, provided you caught the last bus back to Vaiare at 1545 from Le Petit Village.

Buses leave Le Petit Village for the ferry weekdays at 0445, 0545, 0645, 0945, 1145, 1345, 1445, and 1545, Saturday at 0445, 0545, 0645, 0845, 0945, 1130, 1345, 1445, and 1545, and Sunday at 0445, 0645, 1245, 1345, 1445, and 1645. If you have to catch a bus somewhere along its route, add the appropriate traveling time and ask advice of anyone you can. Some of the buses run 30 minutes early.

A taxi on Moorea is actually a minibus with a white letter **T** inside a red circle. In past, the taxi drivers have occasionally employed heavy-handed tactics to discourage visitors from using other means of transportation such as rental cars and the bus. A regular bus service along the north coast was launched in mid-1994 but the active opposition of taxi drivers managed to scuttle the service a year later. Some hotel staff will claim not to know about the ferry buses, and we've even heard of rental car tires being slashed! You should have no problem catching a bus when you arrive on Moorea from Tahiti by ferry, but be quick to jump aboard. Hitching is wearing thin with Moorea motorists, although it's still possible. If you really need the ride you'll probably get it; just be prepared to do some walking.

Car Rentals
Europcar (tel. 56-34-00, fax 56-35-05), with a main office opposite Club Med and branches at five other locations around the island plus various hotel desks, almost has the car rental business on Moorea wrapped up, and their dominant position is reflected in their lofty prices. Europcar's unlimited-mileage cars begin at CFP 5,000/6,000/7,000 for four/eight/24 hours. A weekend rate of CFP 13,000 is also offered. Scooters are CFP 4,500/5,000/5,500, bicycles CFP 1,200/1,500/2,000 (a ripoff).

Avis (tel. 56-12-58) at the ferry terminal and the airport has cars from CFP 7,400/13,100/19,200 for one/two/three days including kilometers and insurance. If you have limited time it's best to reserve an Avis or Europcar vehicle a day or two ahead at one of their offices in Papeete as all cars on Moorea are sometimes taken.

Rental cars and bicycles are also obtained at **Albert Activities Center** (B.P. 77, 98728 Temae; tel. 56-13-53, tel./fax 56-10-42), with locations opposite the Hôtel Bali Hai, Club Bali Hai, and Club Med. Unlimited-mileage cars begin at CFP 6,000/6,500/12,000 for eight/24/48 hours, including insurance. Some of their vehicles are of the "rent a wreck" variety, so before signing the credit card voucher look the car over and insist on a replacement or a discount if it's a high-mileage bomb. Otherwise, take your business elsewhere or just skip renting a car. Bicycles cost about CFP 800/1,200 for a half/full day.

There are five gasoline stations around Moorea: Mobil a kilometer south of Vaiare Wharf, Shell opposite Vaiare Wharf, Total at the airport access road, another Mobil near Motel Albert at Paopao, and another Total opposite Club Med. The maximum speed limit is 60 kph.

Local Tours
Daily at 0900 **Albert Activities** (tel. 56-13-53) does a three-hour circle-island bus tour, including a visit to the Belvédère, for CFP 2,000 (lunch not included). Albert's five-hour 4WD jeep safari is CFP 3,500 pp (do it in the morning). Several other companies such as **Ben Tours** (Benjamin Teraiharoa, tel. 56-26-50), **Moorea Transports** (Greg Hardy, tel. 56-12-86), and **Inner Island Photo Tours** (tel. 56-20-09) offer the same.

Ron's Adventure Tours (Ronald Sage, B.P. 1097, 98729 Papetoai; tel. 56-42-43) specializes in hiking tours and mountain climbing, such as an ascent of Mt. Mouaputa at CFP 3,000 pp. Ron also does bicycle (CFP 2,500) and 4WD jeep (CFP 4,500) tours. Contact him through the Moorea Visitors Bureau kiosk in front of Le Petit Village. **Derek Grell** (tel. 56-41-24) at Paopao also leads climbs up Mt. Rotui and to the Col des Trois Cocotiers.

Alexandre Haamaterii's **Inner Island Safari Tours** (tel. 56-20-09, fax 56-34-43) also offers an exhilarating 4WD tour to various viewpoints and around Moorea for CFP 4,500 pp.

Day Cruises
Albert Activities (tel. 56-13-53) runs a five-hour motorized aluminum canoe ride right around Moorea with a stop for snorkeling (gear provided), departing the Hôtel Bali Hai dock every Monday, Wednesday, and Friday at 0930 (CFP 4,000 pp, minimum of four). For a free pickup, inquire at one of the three Albert Activities centers around Moorea. You could see dolphins, whales, and human surfers on this trip. Others such as Hiro Kelley (tel. 56-13-59) also operate circle-island tours, so compare.

At 0930 and 1400 daily the **Moorea Beachcomber Parkroyal** (tel. 55-19-19) offers a three-hour cruise on the catamaran *Manu* at CFP 5,000 pp. The 1.5-hour sunset cruise is CFP 2,500 including drinks. You can take a one-hour ride in a glass-bottom motorboat called the *Aquascope* at CFP 2,500 pp and they'll go anytime between 0900 and 1500 even for only one person (the catamaran has a six-person minimum).

Other companies like **Moorea Transport** (tel. 56-12-87) run a variety of trips such as a *motu* excursion by outrigger (CFP 2,500) or a *motu* picnic party (CFP 4,800) but the canoes are usually without radios, life jackets, or flotation devices and they can be frightening if you're not a good swimmer. The snorkeling itself is great.

Archipels Croisières (tel. 56-36-39) offers a day cruise around Moorea on a 34-meter classic schooner with various snorkeling and sightseeing stops, plus a buffet lunch (CFP 11,000 pp). They visit "Le Monde de Mu," an underwater sculpture garden in the lagoon off Papetoai with 10 large tikis created in 1998 by the renowned Tahitian stone carver Tihoti.

Dolphin Watching
The trendiest thing on Moorea these days is **Dolphin Quest,** at the Moorea Beachcomber Parkroyal (B.P. 1021, 98729 Papetoai; tel. 55-19-48, fax 56-16-67). Here tourists pay CFP 8,500 a head to spend 30 minutes wading around a shallow lagoon enclosure at the hotel with rough-toothed and bottlenose dolphins, and touching is allowed. These activities begin at 0930, 1330, and 1430. At 1030 and 1530 it's possible to don a mask and snorkel and actually swim with dolphins in a deeper part of the enclosure at CFP 9,500 for 30 minutes (the Parkroyal may tack on a CFP 1,000 surcharge in either case if you're not a hotel guest). Dolphin Quest's brochure claims that part of the proceeds "helps fund education, research, and conservation programs around the world," but it looks a lot more like a case of somebody making lot of money by exploiting captive animals as a tourist attraction.

A quite different type of dolphin encounter is offered by Dr. Michael Poole of **Dolphin Watch** (B.P. 1013, 98729 Papetoai; tel. 56-28-44, 56-14-70, or 56-13-45, fax 56-28-15). Here small groups are taken out in speedboats to see acrobatic spinner dolphins—the only dolphins to spin vertically in the air like tops or ballerinas—in the wild. You may also observe dolphins surfing (!) and July-Oct. humpback whales are often seen. These 3.5-hour trips go out early on Wednesday, Thursday, and Sunday mornings, and again on Wednesday and Sunday afternoons, costing CFP 4,650 pp with reductions for children 12 and under. Included in the price are boat pickups at all hotels between the Bali Hai and Les Tipaniers (bus transfers arranged from the Sofitel). Space is quite limited, so reserve well ahead through one of the Moorea activities offices (but not Albert), a hotel tour desk, or by calling the numbers above. Be sure to state clearly that you want "Dr. Poole's boat" as several unscientific imitators are trying to do the same thing with varying success.

Moorea Airport
Moorea Temae Airport (MOZ) is at the northeast corner of the island. No buses service the airport, so unless you rent a car you'll be stuck with a rip-off taxi fare in addition to the airfare: CFP 1,000 to Vaiare Wharf, CFP 1,150 to the Hôtel Bali Hai, CFP 2,100 to the Moorea Lagoon Hôtel, or CFP 3,500 to Club Med. Thanks to intimidation from the taxi drivers, none of the hotels are allowed to offer airport pickups and even the major tour companies are only authorized to carry tourists who have pre-booked. (All

of this is specifically aimed at foreign visitors: Moorea residents can obtain a card that provides them with ground transfers anywhere on Moorea for CFP 500 and flights for as little as CFP 1,000.) This considered, we suggest you give Air Moorea a miss and take the ferry to/from Moorea. At a third the price of the plane (CFP 800 compared to CFP 2,700), the scenic 30-minute catamaran ride to/from Tahiti may end up being one of the highlights of your visit.

If you do fly, be sure to sit on the left side of the aircraft on the way to Moorea and on the right on the way to Papeete. Avis and Europcar have counters at the airport but it's essential to reserve, otherwise they may not have a car for you and you'll be subjected to the scam described above.

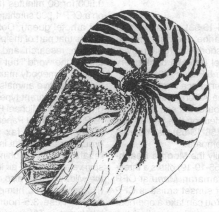

The chambered nautilus (Nautilis pompilius) *uses the variable bouyancy of its shell to lift itself off of the ocean bed and jet-like squirts of water to propel itself along.*

LOUISE FOOTE

HUAHINE

Huahine, the first Leeward island encountered on the ferry ride from Tahiti, is a friendly, inviting island, 170 km northwest of Papeete. In many ways, lush, mountainous Huahine (74 square km) has more to offer than overcrowded Bora Bora. The variety of scenery, splendid beaches, deep bays, lush vegetation, archaeological remains, and charming main town all invite you to visit. Huahine is a well-known surfing locale, with consistently excellent lefts and rights in the two passes off Fare. Schools of dolphins often greet ships arriving through Avapeihi Pass.

It's claimed the island got its name because, when viewed from the sea, Huahine has the shape of a reclining woman—very appropriate for such a fertile, enchanting place. *Hua* means "phallus" (from a rock on Huahine-iti) while *hine* comes from *vahine* (woman). A narrow channel crossed by a concrete bridge slices Huahine into Huahine-nui and Huahine-iti (Great and Little Huahine, respectively). The story goes that the demigod Hiro's canoe cut this strait.

The almost entirely Polynesian population numbers 5,500, yet some of the greatest leaders in the struggle for the independence of Polynesia, Pouvanaa a Oopa among them, have come from this idyllic spot. The artist Bobby Holcomb and poet Henri Hiro are also well remembered.

In recent years Huahine has been discovered by international tourism, and deluxe hotels and bungalow-style developments are now operating on the island. Luckily Huahine has been able to absorb these new properties fairly painlessly, as it's a much larger island than Bora Bora and the resorts are well scattered and tastefully constructed in the traditional Tahitian style. It's an oasis of peace after Papeete or Bora Bora. The island has also become a major port of call for the yachts that anchor off the Hôtel Bali Hai. Backpackers pioneered Huahine in the mid-1980s, and good facilities still exist for them.

Archaeology

Archaeologists have found that human habitation goes back 1,300 years on Huahine; Maeva village was occupied as early as A.D. 850. In 1925 Dr. Kenneth P. Emory of Hawaii's Bishop Museum recorded 54 *marae* on Huahine, most of them built after the 16th century. In 1968 Prof. Yosihiko H. Sinoto found another 40. Huahine-nui was divided into 10 districts, with Huahine-iti as a dependency. As a centralized government complex for a whole island, Maeva, on the south shore of Lake Fauna Nui, is unique in Tahiti-Polynesia. The great communal *marae* at Maeva and Parea have two-stepped platforms *(ahu)* that served as raised seats for the gods. Since 1967 about 16 *marae* have been restored, and they can be easily visited today. Like those of Raiatea and Bora Bora, the Huahine *marae* are constructed of large stone slabs, whereas comparable structures on Tahiti and Moorea are made of round stones. During construction of the Hôtel Bali Hai just north of Fare in 1972 a *patu* hand club was uncovered, proving that New Zealand's Maoris originated in this area.

History of the Leeward Islands

Huahine was settled by Polynesians around 850. Roggeveen, coming from Makatea in the Tuamotus, sighted (but did not land on) Bora Bora and Maupiti on 6 June 1722. Captain Cook "discovered" the other Leeward Islands in July 1769, which was quite easy since the Tahitians knew them all. In fact, Cook had the Raiatean priest Tupaia on board the *Endeavour* as a pilot. Cook wrote: "To these six islands, as they lie contiguous to each other, I gave the names of Society Islands." Later the name was extended to the Windward Islands. In 1773 a man named Omai from Huahine sailed to England with Cook's colleague, Captain Furneaux, aboard the *Adventure;* he returned to Fare with Cook in 1777.

During the 19th century, American whalers spent their winters away from the Antarctic in places like Huahine, refurbishing their supplies with local products such as sugar, vegetables, oranges, salted pork, and *aito,* or ironwood. These visits enriched the island economy, and the New England sailors presented the islanders with foreign plants as tokens of appreciation for the hospitality received. English missionaries arrived in 1808 and later Pomare II extended his power to Huahine, abolishing the traditional religion. In

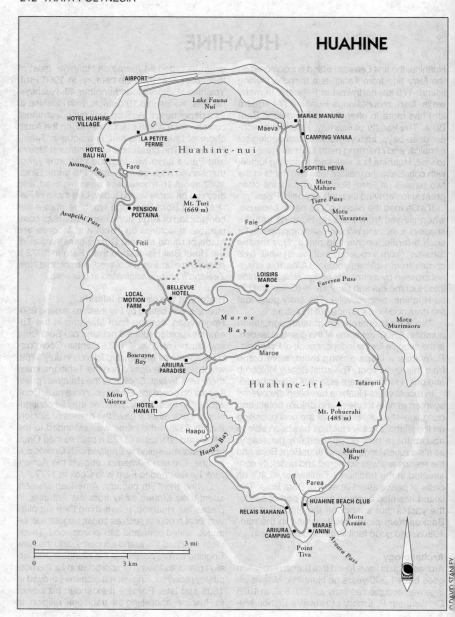

HUAHINE

AIRPORT

Lake Fauna Nui

HOTEL HUAHINE VILLAGE

LA PETITE FERME

Huahine-nui

HOTEL BALI HAI

Fare

Avamoa Pass

Avapeihi Pass

PENSION POETAINA

▲ Mt. Turi (669 m)

Fitii

LOCAL MOTION FARM

BELLEVUE HOTEL

Bourayne Bay

ARIIURA PARADISE

Motu Vaiorea

HOTEL HANA ITI

Haapu

Haapu Bay

MARAE MANUNU

Maeva

CAMPING VANAA

SOFITEL HEIVA

Motu Mahare

Tiare Pass

Motu Vavaratea

Faie

LOISIRS MAROE

Farerea Pass

Maroe Bay

Maroe

Motu Murimaora

Huahine-iti

Tefarerii

▲ Mt. Pohuerahi (485 m)

Mahuti Bay

Parea

HUAHINE BEACH CLUB

RELAIS MAHANA

Motu Araaara

ARIIURA CAMPING

MARAE ANINI

Point Tiva

Araara Pass

0 _____ 3 mi

0 _____ 3 km

© DAVID STANLEY

1822 missionary law was imposed. Among the missionaries was William Ellis whose book, *Polynesian Researches,* published in London in 1829, has left us a detailed picture of the island at that time.

Though Tahiti and Moorea fell under French control in 1842, the Leeward Islands remained a British protectorate until 1887 when these islands were traded for fishing rights off Newfoundland and a British interest in what was then New Hebrides (today Vanuatu). Marines from the French warship *Uranie* had attacked Huahine in 1846, but they were defeated at Maeva. A year later France promised Britain that it would not annex the Leeward Islands, yet in 1887 it proceeded to do so. The local chiefs refused to sign the annexation treaty until 1895, and resistance to France, especially on Raiatea, was only overcome by force in 1897. The French then expelled the English missionary group that had been there 88 years; nonetheless, today 80% of the population of the Leewards remains Protestant.

In 1918 a Spanish influenza epidemic wiped out a fifth of the population including the last queen, Tehaapapa III. Only in 1945 was missionary law finally abolished and French citizenship extended to the inhabitants. In the 1958 referendum, 76% of the population of Huahine voted in favor of independence. Tourism began in 1973 with the building of the airstrip and the Hôtel Bali Hai.

FARE

The unsophisticated little town of Fare, with its tree-lined boulevard along the quay, is joyfully

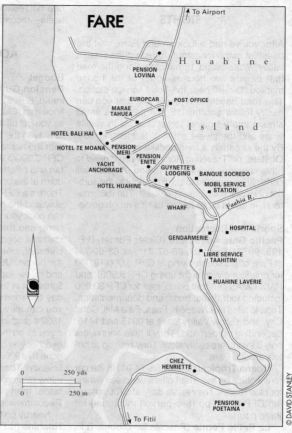

FARE

To Airport
Huahine
PENSION LOVINA
EUROPCAR
POST OFFICE
MARAE TAHUEA
Island
HOTEL BALI HAI
HOTEL TE MOANA
PENSION MERI
PENSION ENITE
YACHT ANCHORAGE
GUYNETTE'S LODGING
BANQUE SOCREDO
HOTEL HUAHINE
MOBIL SERVICE STATION
WHARF
Faahia R.
HOSPITAL
GENDARMERIE
LIBRE SERVICE TAAHITINI
HUAHINE LAVERIE
CHEZ HENRIETTE
0   250 yds
0   250 m
PENSION POETAINA
To Fitii

© DAVID STANLEY

peaceful after the roar of Papeete. A beach runs right along the west side of the main street and local life unfolds without being overwhelmed by tourism. Local men play *pétanque* on the Fare waterfront around sunset. From here Bora Bora is visible in the distance to the left while the small twin peaks of Taha'a are to the right. The seven other villages on Huahine are linked to Fare by winding, picturesque roads. Despite the easygoing atmosphere it's unwise to leave valuables unattended on the beach anywhere between town and the Bali Hai (and beware of unperceived currents).

SIGHTS

After you've had a look around Fare, visit the beautiful *mape* (chestnut) forest up the Faahia valley. Walk inland 15 minutes along the road that begins two houses south of the house marked "Oliveti" near the Total service station. This road becomes a jungle trail that you can easily follow another 15 minutes up a small stream into a tropical forest laced with vanilla vines and the sweet smell of fermenting fruit. By the stream is a long bedlike rock known as Ofaitere, or "Traveling Rock," but you'd need to have someone point it out to you. A guide will certainly be required to continue right to the summit of Huahine's highest peak, Mt. Turi (669 meters), in about three hours, but it's rough going.

Sports and Recreation

Pacific Blue Adventure (Didier Forget, B.P. 193, 98731 Fare; tel. 68-87-21, fax 68-80-71) at Fare offers scuba diving at CFP 5,000/18,000 for one/four dives (night diving CFP 6,500), and PADI/CMAS certification courses for CFP 30,000 including four dives, texts, and documentation. Trips to sites like Avapeihi Pass, Fa'a Miti, Coral City, and Yellow Valley leave at 0915 and 1415, depending on demand. They'll take snorkelers only if things are really slow. They pick up at hotels around Fare.

    Moana Tropical (tel./fax 68-74-01) in the car rental office on the wharf offers deep-sea fishing for blue marlin. They leave daily at 0700, charging CFP 8,500 pp (two-person minimum) for three hours.

    La Petite Ferme (Pascale Le Diouris, B.P. 12, 98731 Fare; tel./fax 68-82-98), between Fare and the airport, offers riding with Pascale, Yvon, and their 16 small, robust Marquesan horses. A two-hour ride along the beach is CFP 3,500 pp, and they also offer a two-day ride and campout in the mountains or on the beach for CFP 17,500 pp, meals included. Call the day before to let them know you're coming. If riding is your main interest, it's possible to stay in their on-site guesthouse at CFP 3,600 double or CFP 1,500 pp dormitory (six beds), breakfast included. They also have a self-catering bungalow at CFP 5,000/7,500/9,500 single/double/triple (CFP 500 supplement for one night). This is the number-one horseback-riding operation in Tahiti-Polynesia—recommended.

ACCOMMODATIONS

Budget

Pension Guynette (Alain and Hélène Guerineau, B.P. 87, 98731 Fare; tel. 68-83-75), also known as "Club Bed," on the waterfront to the left as you get off the boat, is one of the nicest places to stay in the territory. The seven rooms, each with the name of a different Society island, are CFP 3,300/3,900/4,500 single/double/triple with fan and private bath (cold water). The eight-bed dorm at the back of the building is CFP 1,400 pp. There's a CFP 300 pp surcharge for a one-night stay and the maximum stay is one month. You can cook your own food in the communal kitchen here, and the meals prepared by the friendly staff are good value (order before 1400). It's a pleasant, clean place; no shoes are allowed in the house. Upon arrival peruse the list of rules and rates—applied rigorously (for example, it's lights out in the kitchen at 2200). On departure day the rooms must be vacated by 1000, but you can leave your bags at the reception until 1830 if catching a late boat. They don't mind at all if you sit on their terrace all afternoon and they'll even let you cook your dinner so long as you're gone by 1900. Most readers say they liked the efficiency. Thankfully, the management doesn't allow overcrowding and will turn people away rather than pack them in for short-term gain. Recommended.

    Nearby on the waterfront is three-story **Hôtel Huahine** (B.P. 220, 98731 Fare; tel. 68-82-69), at CFP 3,500 single or double, CFP 4,500 triple, or CFP 1,200 in a dorm. The 10 bare rooms are large with their own toilet and shower, and there's no surcharge for a one-night stay (but no cooking facilities). Fish dishes on the menu are in the CFP 850-1,200 range. You may sit in the restaurant and watch TV for the price of a beer. Stalwart surfers who don't care for the house rules at Pension Guynette often stay here. Love it or leave it.

    Two more good budget places to stay are between Fare and the airport just beyond the Bali Hai, about 800 meters north of the wharf. **Pension Lovina** (Lovina Richmond, B.P. 173, 98731

Fare; tel./fax 68-88-06) has five small *fares* with TV and shared bath at CFP 3,000/5,000 single/double. For families and groups, there are four oversized thatched bungalows with cooking and bathing facilities at CFP 5,000/6,000/8,000 single/double/triple, CFP 12,000 for up to five persons, CFP 13,000 for seven people. Dormitory accommodations are CFP 1,500 pp, and camping is CFP 1,000 pp. All guests have access to communal cooking facilities (and mosquitoes). The minimum stay is two nights, and discounts may be negotiable. Airport pickups cost CFP 1,000 pp return; from the harbor it's CFP 500 pp.

In the same area is **Pension Vaihonu** (Etienne Faaeva, B.P. 302, 98731 Fare; tel./fax 68-87-33) with three *fares* at CFP 2,000/3,000 single/double and a six-bed dorm at CFP 1,200. A larger cottage with private bath, kitchen, and TV is CFP 6,500/10,000 double/quad. Camping is CFP 1,000 per person. There's an open communal kitchen in the small compound jammed with potted flowers. Unfortunately access to the nearby beach has recently been blocked by residential construction and you have to go back toward Fare to find a place to swim.

Inexpensive

Pension Enite (Enite Temaiana, B.P. 37, 98731 Fare; tel./fax 68-82-37) is an eight-room boardinghouse at the west end of the waterfront beyond the snack bar. Rooms with shared bath are CFP 6,000 pp with half board (two-night minimum stay, no room rentals without meals). Enite also serves meals to guests in a thatched cookhouse on the beach and the food is good. In the event of a shortened stay, the pension will bill for the number of nights originally reserved. Middle-of-the-night arrivals mustn't knock on the door before 0700. French expats often stay here.

Just north of Fare is **Pension Meri** (Milton Brotherson, B.P. 35, 98731 Fare; tel./fax 68-82-44), past two doctors' offices down the road toward the lagoon from opposite the large Mormon church. Meri has two rooms with private bath and cooking facilities at CFP 5,500 single or double, CFP 6,500 for three or four (minimum stay three nights). There's direct access to the beach.

Chez Ella (Ella Mervin, B.P. 71, 98731 Fare; tel. 68-73-07), next to Motel Vanille at the airport turnoff, has three bungalows with kitchen, fridge, and TV at CFP 6,000 single or double, plus CFP 1,000 per additional person. You can ask to use the washing machine.

Moderate

Hôtel Te Moana (Moana Baumgartner, B.P. 195, 98731 Fare; tel. 68-88-63, fax 68-71-74), on the beach right beside Hôtel Bali Hai north of Fare, has five thatched bungalows with private bath and coral floors at CFP 5,500/6,500 single/double (minimum stay two nights). The large family bungalow capable of sleeping four is CFP 13,000 and only this unit has cooking facilities. The breakfast and dinner plan is CFP 3,000 pp. Mosquitos can be a problem here.

Fare Tehani (Frédéric Girard, B.P. 335, 98731 Fare; tel./fax 68-71-00) is on the beach down the road from the back entrance to Pension Lovina previously mentioned, between Fare and the airport. The two *fares* with kitchen and fridge are CFP 10,000/12,000 double/quad (expensive). Weekly and monthly rates are available. Ask about this place at the *Ono-Ono* office at the harbor. Nearby an American named Rande Vetterli (tel. 68-86-27) has a couple of self-catering units right on the beach at CFP 6,000 double (or CFP 4,000 if you stay a month). It's one heck of a deal.

In 1997 **Motel Vanille** (B.P. 381, 98731 Fare; tel./fax 68-71-77) opened on the corner of the airport access road and the Fare-Maeva highway. Their six thatched bungalows positioned around the swimming pool are CFP 13,000 double with breakfast, dinner, bicycles, and airport transfers included (credit cards not accepted). The meals are served at the host's table and it's all rather informal, but a kilometer from the beach.

Premium

The American-owned **Hôtel Bali Hai** (B.P. 341, 98731 Fare; tel. 68-84-77, fax 68-82-77), just north of Fare, is tastefully placed between a lake and the beach. The 10 rooms in the main building begin at CFP 11,500 single or double plus tax; the 34 bungalows cost CFP 13,500-15,500 in the garden, CFP 19,900 facing the beach. Some of the rooms could use a facelift, but prices are much lower than those at comparable accommodations on Bora Bora and the staff is helpful. Cooking facilities are not provided, but the restaurant serves excellent food and the largely French crowd is chic. The hotel restaurant (open daily 0700-0930/1200-1400/1900-2100) is reasonable for such a deluxe place, and you can get a breakfast and dinner plan at CFP 4,500 pp. A showcase in the lobby displays artifacts found here by Prof. Yosihiko H. Sinoto of the Bishop Museum, Hawaii, who excavated the site during construction of the hotel in 1973-75. Marae Tahuea has been reconstructed on the grounds. The snorkeling off the resort's beach is great although questions have been raised about their sewage disposal system. Airport transfers are CFP 1,200 pp return.

FOOD AND ENTERTAINMENT

Food Trailers

Food trailers congregate at Fare Wharf selling spring rolls, pastries, and long French sandwiches. Coffee and bread is CFP 200. At night you can get steak frites, chicken and chips, and *poisson cru* for CFP 700. Look for the trailer that parks next to a row of telephone booths as it has excellent fish brochettes for CFP 150.

Restaurants

Snack Temarara (tel. 68-86-61; closed Sunday) at the west end of the waterfront has a nice terrace built over the lagoon, fine for a sunset beer. During happy hour Friday 1600-1800 the place is crowded with Polynesians enjoying *kaina* (folkloric) music. It's quite elegant, with fish dishes costing CFP 950-1,400, meat dishes CFP 1,100-1,400. One reader's comment: "Overpriced food that is really lacking in quality."

The **Restaurant Bar Orio** (tel. 68-83-03; lunch 1100-1430, dinner 1830-2130), at the opposite end of the Fare waterfront, also has a terrace overlooking the lagoon but it has less class than Temarara. Fish dishes are in the CFP 1,000-1,600 range, lobster CFP 2,500-2,800, Chinese dishes CFP 900-1,200.

Opposite the car rental offices on the waterfront is **Restaurant Te Vaipuna** (tel. 68-70-45; Mon.-Sat. 1100-1430/1800-2130) with Chinese and French dishes. A cheaper snack bar is next door.

Pension Guynette (tel. 68-83-75) serves an inexpensive breakfast and lunch on its water-front terrace, and this is also a good choice for only coffee and a snack.

The **Tiare Tipanier Restaurant** (tel. 68-80-52; Monday 1800-2045, Tues.-Sat. 1130-1345/1800-2045), next to the *mairie* at the north entrance to Fare from the Bali Hai, is a typical French rural restaurant without the tourist touches of some of the others. They serve meat and fish dishes in the CFP 1,150-1,600 range, fondue bourguignone at CFP 1,500 (two-person minimum), and a set menu for CFP 1,900 including wine. A large Hinano is CFP 480.

Also check thatched **Restaurant Te Moana** (tel. 68-88-63), facing the beach next to Hôtel Bali Hai. Complete meals (without drinks) are CFP 2,500, 3,000, and 3,800.

Groceries

Super Fare-Nui (tel. 68-84-68; weekdays 0600-1200/1300-1800, Saturday 0600-1200, Sunday 0600-1100), on the Fare waterfront, sells groceries and cold beer. An alternative place to shop is **Libre Service Taahitini** (tel. 68-89-42; weekdays 0600-1200/1330-1900, Saturday 0600-1200/1600-1900, Sunday 0600-1100/1700-1900), just beyond the *gendarmerie* south of town. **Magasin Matehau** at Fitii also has groceries.

If you see a cruise ship tied up at Fare one morning, pop into the supermarket quickly to buy your daily bread before the ship's cook comes ashore to snap up the day's entire supply, leaving the townspeople to eat cake (a classic example of how tourism exploits small island communities).

The tap water on Huahine can be clouded after heavy rains.

Cultural Shows for Visitors

If you're staying in budget accommodations around Fare, you'll be able to witness the Polynesian dancing at the **Hôtel Bali Hai** (tel. 68-84-77) on Friday evening at 2000 for the price of a drink from the bar, although the regular dinner menu isn't outrageous (CFP 1,100-1,700 entrees). Drop by beforehand to check the program.

There's also traditional dancing at the **Sofitel Heiva Huahine** (tel. 68-88-88) at Maeva on Monday, Thursday, and Saturday nights, but you'll need motorized transportation to get there.

SERVICES AND INFORMATION

Services

ATM machines are outside the Banque de Tahiti (tel. 68-82-46; weekdays 0745-1145/1330-1630), facing the Fare waterfront, and the Banque Socredo (tel. 68-82-71; weekdays 0730-1130/1330-1600), on the first street back from the waterfront.

The post office (Mon.-Thurs. 0700-1500, Friday 0700-1400), opposite the access road to the Hôtel Bali Hai, has a convenient Coca-Cola vending machine. The *gendarmerie* (tel. 68-82-61) is opposite the hospital over the bridge at the south end of town.

The laundromat (no phone) just south of Fare charges CFP 750 to wash and CFP 750 to dry (Mon.-Thurs. 0730-1600, Friday 0730-1500).

Public toilets and washbasins are in one of the yellow buildings on the waterfront (if open).

Information

The Comité du Tourisme information office (B.P. 54, 98731 Fare; tel./fax 68-89-49; weekdays 0800-1500) shares a pavilion on the waterfront with Europcar, Pacifique Car Rental, the *Ono-Ono* office, and Pacific Blue Adventure.

Health

A Gabinet Medical-Dentaire (tel. 68-82-20) is next to the Mobil service station on the next street back from the wharf. Dr. Hervé Carbonnier and Dr. Pascal Matyka, general practitioners, see patients 0730-1200/1400-1600.

Dr. Caroline Veyssiere and Dr. Isabelle Damery-Beylier (tel. 68-70-70; weekdays 0700-1200/1330-1700, Saturday 0800-1200), have small offices opposite the large Mormon church just north of Fare.

La Pharmacie de Huahine (tel. 68-80-90; weekdays 0730-1130/1400-1700, Saturday 0730-1130), is behind the yellow warehouse facing the waterfront.

TRANSPORTATION

Getting There

The **Air Tahiti** agent (tel. 68-82-65) is at the airport. For information on flights to Huahine from Papeete, Moorea, Raiatea, and Bora Bora see the introduction to this chapter. Air Tahiti's direct flight between Huahine and Moorea would be great if it didn't cost CFP 11,000 when the flight to Papeete is only CFP 8,800.

The jet cruiser *Ono-Ono* departs Huahine for Raiatea (45 minutes, CFP 1,778), Taha'a (two hours, CFP 2,111), and Bora Bora (3.5 hours, CFP 3,111) Monday and Wednesday at 1245, Friday at 2000, and Saturday at 1500. To Papeete (3.5 hours, CFP 4,895) it leaves Huahine Tuesday and Thursday at 1015, Sunday at 1515. The Tuesday and Thursday services connect to the Moorea ferries at Papeete.

The Papeete cargo ships tie up to the wharf in the middle of town. If you arrive in the middle of the night you can sleep in a large open pavilion until dawn. *Taporo VI* arrives from Papeete bound for Raiatea, Taha'a, and Bora Bora around 0200 on Tuesday, Thursday, and Saturday, returning from Raiatea on its way to Papeete Tuesday, Thursday, and Saturday evenings. Northbound, the *Vaeanu* calls at Huahine on Tuesday, Thursday, and Saturday at 0230; southbound on Tuesday and Sunday at 1700 and Thursday at 1800. The *Raromatai Ferry* arrives from Papeete very early Wednesday and Saturday mornings, departing for Papeete again on Wednesday at 1530 and Sunday at 2000 (nine hours, CFP 3,200 deck). You can also take this ship to Raiatea, Taha'a, and Bora Bora (all CFP 1,000) Wednesday and Saturday in the very early morning.

Tickets for *Vaeanu* go on sale at their office adjoining the yellow warehouse on the wharf four hours before sailing or you can buy one as the ship is loading. Tickets for the *Taporo VI* are sold on board upon arrival. The office of the *Raromatai Ferry* is next to the public washrooms on the mountain side of the yellow warehouse on the wharf. The *Ono-Ono* office (tel./fax 68-85-85) is next to Pacifique Car Rental on the wharf.

Getting Around

Getting around Huahine is not easy. Only one *truck* a day runs to Maeva, leaving Fare weekdays at 0900 (CFP 150). However, it's fairly easy to hitch back to Fare from Maeva. The bus to Parea leaves Fare on weekdays at 1100, returning from Parea to Fare at 0500 and 1400 (CFP 250 one-way). Other *trucks* run to Haapu and Tefarerii.

Car Rentals
Pacifique Car Rental/Hertz (tel./fax 68-73-37; daily 0800-1200/1400-1800) on the wharf has Peugeot cars from CFP 4,600/6,000/6,900 for five/10/24 hours with unlimited kilometers. Insurance with CFP 50,000 deductible is included and the deductible can be waved for CFP 1,000 a day. The minimum age is 18. The manager Serge is very helpful.

Avis (tel. 68-73-34, fax 68-73-35) is at the Mobil service station a street back from the waterfront. Their cars start at CFP 7,300/13,600/18,900 for one/two/three days all inclusive.

Europcar (tel. 68-82-59, fax 68-80-69) is beside the entrance to the Hôtel Bali Hai. The smaller Europcar office on the wharf is often closed. Their smallest car is CFP 2,000 a day plus CFP 44 a kilometer plus CFP 700 insurance, or CFP 7,000/13,000 for one/two days with unlimited kilometers (insurance extra). Their older cars have transmission problems.

Tropic 2000 Rent a Car (tel. 68-70-84, fax 68-70-96), between La Petite Ferme and Motel Vanille north of town, has slightly cheaper rates than Avis and Europcar with CFP 30,000 deductible insurance included. You must be 24 or over to rent from them.

Huahine has only two gas stations, both in Fare: Mobil (tel. 68-81-41) is open weekdays 0630-1745, Saturday 0700-1100, Sunday 0630-0930, while Total (tel. 68-71-25) is open weekdays 0630-1700, Saturday 0630-1100, Sunday 0630-0930.

Huahine Lagoon (tel. 68-70-00), next to Snack Bar Te Marara at the north end of the Fare waterfront, rents small aluminum boats with outboard motor for CFP 3,000/5,000/8,000 for two/four/eight hours (gas not included). Masks, snorkels, life jackets, anchor, and oars come with the boat. Bicycles are for rent here at CFP 1,200 a day.

Boutique Photo Jojo (tel. 68-89-16), next to Pension Guynette, also has bicycles but they're more expensive because they charge the full Europcar tariff.

Local Tours
Jacques and Sylvie at **Huahine Land** (B.P. 140, 98731 Fare; tel. 68-89-21, fax 68-86-84) offer 3.5-hour 4WD safaris at CFP 4,000 pp, which is a good alternative to renting a car (and the

guides are highly knowledgeable). **Piteta Tour** (tel. 68-82-31 or 68-87-00) at the Hôtel Huahine Village offers the same.

Félix Tours (tel. 68-81-69) does a three-hour morning archaeological tour at CFP 3,000 daily except Sunday.

Héli-Inter Polynésie (tel. 68-86-86) at the Sofitel Heiva offers 20-minute helicopter tours of Huahine-nui at CFP 15,000 pp (minimum of four).

Boutique Photo Jojo (tel. 68-89-16) runs a seven-hour boat trip Mon.-Sat. at 1000 for CFP 5,000 pp including lunch.

Airport
The airport (HUH) is three km north of Fare. Make arrangements for the regular airport minibus (CFP 500 pp) at Pension Enite. Avis, Europcar, and Pacifique Car Rental have counters at the airport.

MAEVA

At Maeva, six km east of Fare, you encounter that rare combination of an easily accessible archaeological site in a spectacular setting. Here each of the 10 district chiefs of Huahine-nui had his own *marae,* and huge stone walls were erected to defend Maeva against invaders from Bora Bora (and later France). The plentiful small fish in Lake Fauna Nui supported large chiefly and priestly classes (ancient stone fish traps can still be seen near the bridge at the east end of the village). In the 1970s Prof. Y.H. Sinoto of Hawaii restored many of the structures strewn along the lakeshore and in the nearby hills. Once a day Maeva is accessible by *le truck* from Fare (CFP 150), and there are two small stores in the village where you can get cold drinks.

On the shores of the lake is round-ended **Fare Pote'e** (1974), a replica of an old communal meetinghouse. This now contains an **Eco-Museum** operated by the Opu Nui Association, B.P. 150, 98731 Fare. Half the museum consists of historical explanations through texts, old photos, and replicas of traditional paddles, fish hooks, adzes, stilts, and tapa cloth. The other part is a shop selling quality handicrafts such as *tifaifai* quilts, pottery, woven hats and bags, and pareus. Prices are clearly marked and all income goes to supporting the museum. You can also buy music cassettes and compact discs, cards, books, and T-shirts. The reproductions of paintings by Bobby Holcomb (CFP 1,200) are excellent. Changing exhibitions of artifacts from other Pacific countries are presented regularly. The museum is open weekdays 0900-1500 and Saturday 0900-1200. Admission is free but there's a donation box at the door. This is a visit not to miss. Guided 1.5-hour tours of the ruins and gardens of Maeva leave here weekdays at 1000 and 1300, Saturday at 1000 (CFP 1,200 pp). **Marae Rauhuru** next to Fare Pote'e bears petroglyphs of turtles.

From Fare Pote'e, walk back along the road toward Fare about 100 meters, to a **fortification wall** on the left, built in 1846 with stones from the *marae* to defend the area against the French. Follow this inland to an ancient well at the foot of the hill, then turn right and continue around the base of the hill until you find the trail up onto Matairea Hill (opposite a stone platform). Twenty meters beyond a second, older fortification wall along the hillside is the access to **Marae Te Ana** on the right. The terraces of this residential area for chiefly families, excavated in 1986, mount the hillside.

Return to the main trail and continue up to the ruins of **Marae Tefano,** which are engulfed by an immense banyan tree. **Marae Matairea Rahi,** to the left, was the most sacred place on Huahine, dedicated to Tane, god of light. The backrests of Huahine's principal chiefs are in the southernmost compound of the *marae,* where the most important religious ceremonies took place. Backtrack a bit and keep straight, then head up the fern-covered hill to the right to **Marae Paepae Ofata,** which gives a magnificent view over the whole northeast coast of Huahine.

Continue southeast on the main trail past several more *marae* and you'll eventually cross another fortification wall and meet a dirt road down to the main highway near **Marae Te Ava.** Throughout this easy two-hour hike, watch for stakes planted with vanilla by the present villagers (please don't touch).

When you get back down to the main road, walk south a bit to see photogenic **Marae Fare Miro,** then backtrack to the bridge, across which is a **monument** guarded by seven cannon. Be-neath it are buried French troops killed in the Battle of Maeva (1846), when the islanders successfully defended their independence against marauding French marines sent to annex the island.

Seven hundred meters farther along toward the ocean and to the left is two-tiered **Marae Manunu,** the community *marae* of Huahine-nui, dedicated to the gods Oro and Tane. According to a local legend, Princess Hutuhiva arrived at this spot from Raiatea hidden in a drum. In the base of the *marae* is the grave of Raiti, the last great priest of Huahine. When he died in 1915 a huge stone fell from the *marae.* The coral road passing Marae Manunu runs another six km along the elevated barrier reef north of Lake Fauna Nui directly to Huahine Airport, an alternative route back to Fare. White beaches line this cantaloupe- and watermel-on-rich north shore.

Faie

Below the bridge in the center of Faie, five km south of Maeva on a good paved road, is a river populated by sacred blue-eyed eels. Legend holds that it was the eels who brought fresh water to the village. You can buy fish to feed them at the red kiosk for CFP 100. From Faie the very steep Route Traversiere crosses the mountains to Maroe Bay (2.5 km), making a complete circuit of Huahine-nui possible. Two hundred meters up this road from the bridge is **Faie Glaces** (tel. 68-87-95; closed weekends), which manufactures ice cream from natural ingredients. If continuing south by bicycle don't begin coasting too fast on the other side as you may not be able to stop.

Accommodations

On the road to the Sofitel Heiva Huahine, a kilometer from the bridge at Maeva, is **Camping Vanaa** (Vanaa Delord, tel. 68-89-51) with 13 small thatched *fares* on the beach at CFP 5,000 double including breakfast. Camping is CFP 1,000 pp. Meals in the restaurant are in the CFP 1,300-2,000 range. It's a shady spot, conveniently located for exploring the *marae.* The huts are a bit better than those at Ariiura Camping (see below) but the beach isn't as good as the one at Parea. Loud music is broadcast from the bar all afternoon. Inexpensive.

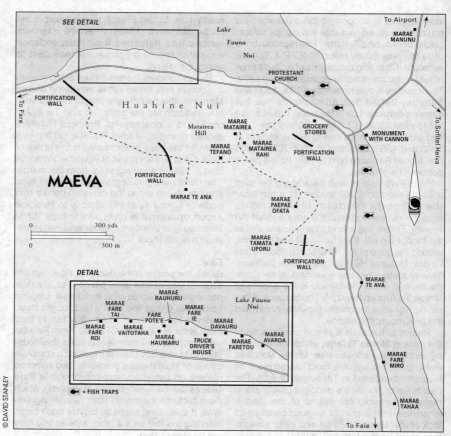

To Airport

MARAE MANUNU

SEE DETAIL

Lake Fauna Nui

PROTESTANT CHURCH

To Fare

Huahine Nui

FORTIFICATION WALL

Matairea Hill

MARAE MATAIREA

MARAE TEFANO

MARAE MATAIREA RAHI

GROCERY STORES

MONUMENT WITH CANNON

To Sofitel Heiva

MAEVA

FORTIFICATION WALL

FORTIFICATION WALL

MARAE TE ANA

MARAE PAEPAE OFATA

0   300 yds

0   300 m

MARAE TAMATA UPORU

FORTIFICATION WALL

DETAIL

MARAE TE AVA

MARAE RAUHURU

MARAE FARE TAI

FARE POTE'E

MARAE FARE IE

Lake Fauna Nui

MARAE FARE ROI

MARAE VAITOTAHA

MARAE OAVAURU

MARAE HAUMARU

TRUCK DRIVER'S HOUSE

MARAE FARETOU

MARAE AVAROA

MARAE FARE MIRO

= FISH TRAPS

MARAE TAHAA

© DAVID STANLEY

To Faie

In 1989 the exclusive **Sofitel Heiva Huahine** (B.P. 38, 98731 Fare; tel. 68-86-86, fax 68-85-25), part of the French-owned Accor chain, opened in a coconut grove on a *motu* two km southeast of Maeva along a rough road. The 24 rooms in long blocks are CFP 22,500 single or double, the 12 thatched garden bungalows CFP 32,000, the 18 beach bungalows CFP 48,000 plus tax. Six overwater suites are CFP 60,000 single or double. For a third person add CFP 4,500 (children under 12 free). Some of the more expensive bungalows are exposed to the southeast trades and can be dark and unpleasant in windy weather when you're forced to

keep the windows shut. The breakfast and dinner plan is CFP 5,600 pp and it's prudent to be punctual at mealtime as the staff will refuse service to latecomers. Happy hour at the Manuia Bar is 1700-1800 (drinks two for one). The architecture is impressive and one of the best Polynesian cultural shows you'll ever see usually takes place here on Monday, Thursday, and Saturday nights at 2000, complete with fire dancing, acrobatics, and coconut tree climbing. Evocative neo-Polynesian paintings by the late artist/singer Bobby Holcomb highlight the decor in the public areas, and ancient *marae* are preserved in the gardens. Unspoiled white beaches stretch all along this section of the lagoon and there's passable snorkeling off the oceanside beach. A swimming pool is available. The hotel tacks a hefty surcharge on any tours or activities arranged through their reception but the Maeva archaeological area is only a 30-minute walk away. Europcar has a desk at this hotel. Return airport transfers are CFP 1,800 pp extra. Luxury.

HUAHINE-ITI

Though the concrete "July Bridge" joins the two islands, Huahine-iti is far less accessible than Huahine-nui. Le truck only runs to **Parea** village once a day (CFP 250), so you'll have to stay the night unless you rent a bicycle or car. The 24 km from Fare to Parea via Haapu are paved, but only four of the 16 km from Parea back to the bridge via Maroe are paved: a kilometer or so around Tefarerii, then the two km from Maroe to the bridge.

Haapu village was originally built entirely over the water, for lack of sufficient shoreline to house it. The only grocery store on Huahine-iti is at Haapu, otherwise three grocery trucks circle the island several times daily; the locals will know when to expect them. There's a wide white beach along Avea Bay with good swimming right beside the road as you approach the southern end of the island. Yachts can follow a protected channel inside the barrier reef down the west coast of Huahine to the wonderful (if occasionally rough) anchorage at Avea Bay but shallows at Point Tiva force sailboats to return to Fare.

On another white beach on the east side of Point Tiva, one km south of Parea, is **Marae Anini**, the community *marae* of Huahine-iti. It was built toward the end of the 18th century by Ta'aroari, son of grand chief Mahine. Look for petroglyphs on this two-tiered structure, dedicated to the god of war Oro, where human sacrifices once took place. The *marae* is unmarked and hard to find. Go down the track without a bread delivery box, 900 meters north of Ariiura Camping or 500 meters south of the Huahine

Beach Club. After 200 meters this track reaches the beach, which you follow 100 meters to the right (south) to the huge stones of the *marae*. Surfing is possible in Araara Pass, beside the *motu* just off Marae Anini. If snorkeling here, beware of an outbound current in the pass.

Accommodations

The only low-cost place to stay on Huahine-iti is **Ariiura Camping** (Hubert Bremond, B.P. 145, 98731 Fare; tel. 68-83-78 or 68-85-20), 22 km south of Fare via the paved road. It's 1,400 meters from the upmarket Hôtel Huahine at Parea and shares the same lovely white beach with Relais Mahana, 800 meters northwest. There are 12 small open *fares*, each with a double bed, at CFP 2,000/3,500 single/double. Camping is CFP 1,200 pp a day, and a communal kitchen and pleasant eating area overlooks the turquoise lagoon. Bring food as no grocery stores are nearby, although grocery trucks pass daily, once in the morning and twice in the afternoon Mon.-Sat. and twice in the morning on Sunday. Also bring insect repellent and coils. An outrigger canoe is available, and you may be able to rent bicycles at Relais Mahana. The snorkeling here is superb. The owner will pick you up at the airport or wharf if you stay three nights or more; watch for his pickup truck on the wharf if you arrive by boat from Papeete. Otherwise take *le truck* that leaves Fare at 1030 Mon.-Sat. (CFP 250 pp). Budget.

If Ariiura Camping is too primitive for you, the only other choice apart from the luxury hotels is **Pension Mauarii** (Marcelle Flohr, tel. 68-86-49), 20 km south of Fare. It's on the same long white beach as the upscale Relais Mahana but a bit back toward Fare. Rooms in the main building are CFP 6,500/7,500 single/double, or CFP 9,000 in the mezzanine. The three garden bungalows are CFP 9,000/10,000 single/double, or CFP 15,000 for four persons. A beach bungalow is CFP 35,000, while the 10-mattress dormitory is CFP 2,400 pp. No cooking facilities are provided and the breakfast/dinner plan is CFP 3,000 pp. Every Friday 1900-2300 there's a buffet dinner (CFP 2,500 pp) with local music. Moderate to expensive.

RAIATEA

At 171 square km, Raiatea is the second-largest island of Tahiti-Polynesia. Its main town and port, Uturoa, is the business, educational, and administrative center of the Leeward Islands or Îles Sous-le-Vent (islands under the wind). The balance of Raiatea's population of about 10,000 lives in eight flower-filled villages around the island: Avera, Opoa, Puohine, Fetuna, Vaiaau, Tehurui, Tevaitoa, and Tuu Fenua. The west coast of Raiatea south of Tevaitoa is old Polynesia through and through.

Raiatea is traditionally the ancient Havai'i, the "sacred isle" from which all of eastern Polynesia was colonized. It may at one time have been reached by migrants from the west as the ancient name for Taha'a, Uporu, corresponds to Upolu, just as Havai'i relates to Savai'i, the largest islands of the Samoan chain. A legend tells how Raiatea's first king, Hiro, built a great canoe he used to sail to Rarotonga. Today Raiatea and Taha'a are mostly worth visiting if you want to get off the beaten tourist track. Though public transportation is scarce, the island offers good possibilities for scuba diving, charter yachting, and hiking, and the varied scenery is worth a stop.

The Land

Raiatea, 220 km northwest of Tahiti and 45 km west of Huahine, shares a protected lagoon with Taha'a three km away. Legends tell how the two islands were cut apart by a mythical eel. About 30 km of steel-blue sea separates Raiatea from both Huahine and Bora Bora. Mount Temehani on mountainous Raiatea rises to 772 meters, and some of the coastlines are rugged and narrow. The highest mountain is Toomaru (1,017 meters). All of the people live on a coastal plain planted in coconuts, where cattle also graze.

No beaches are found on big, hulking Raiatea itself. Instead, picnickers are taken to picture-postcard *motus* in the lagoon. Surfing is possible at the 10 passes that open onto the Raiatea/Taha'a lagoon, and windsurfers are active. The Leeward Islands are the most popular sailing area in Tahiti-Polynesia, and most of the charter boats are based at Raiatea.

History

Originally called Havai'i, legend holds that the island was rechristened by Queen Rainuiatea in honor of her parents, Rai, a warrior from Tahiti, and Atea, queen of Opoa. Before European encroachment, Raiatea was the religious, cultural, and political center of Tahiti-Polynesia. Tradition holds that the great Polynesian voyages to Hawaii and New Zealand departed from these shores.

Raiatea was Captain Cook's favorite island; he visited three times. During his first voyage in 1769 he called first at Opoa from 20 to 24 July. After having surveyed Bora Bora from the sea, he anchored for a week in the Rautoanui Pass on the northwest coast of Raiatea, near the village of Tuu Fenua. During his second voyage Cook lay at anchor twice, first from 8 to 17 September 1773 and again from 25 May to 4 June 1774, both times at Rautoanui. His third visit was from 3 November to 7 December 1777, again at Rautoanui. It can therefore be said that Rautoanui (which he calls "Haarnanino Harbour" in his journals) was one of Cook's favorite anchorages.

These islands accepted Christianity soon after the Tahitians were converted and the noted Protestant missionary John Williams arrived in 1818, as a monument in the form of a black basalt pillar standing in front of the Protestant church just north of Uturoa recalls. From Raiatea, Williams carried the gospel to Rarotonga in 1823 and Samoa in 1830. Later Queen Pomare IV spent the years 1844-1847 in exile on Raiatea. When France annexed the island in 1887 Chief Teraupoo launched a resistance campaign that lasted until 1897, when French troops and warships conquered the island. Teraupoo was captured after six weeks of fighting and deported to New Caledonia where he remained until 1905. The Queen of Raiatea and 136 of her followers were exiled to remote Eiao Island in the Marquesas.

UTUROA

Uturoa (pop. 3,500) is an easy place to find your way around. The double row of Chinese stores along the main drag opens onto a colorful market built in 1946 (the Sunday market is over by 0800). Beyond the market is the harbor, with a pleasant park alongside. All of the ferries plying between Tahiti and Bora Bora call here and there's a frequent shuttle to Taha'a. The island's airport is three km west of town with the main yacht charter base, Marina Apooiti, a kilometer beyond that. This is the territory's second city and the first stop on any exploration of the island.

Sights

For a view of four islands, climb **Tapioi Hill** (294 meters), the peak topped by a TV antenna behind Uturoa—one of the easiest and most satisfying climbs in Tahiti-Polynesia. Take the road beside the *gendarmerie* up past the Propriété Privé sign (don't worry, visitors are allowed). This is private property, and although the owners allow visitors to climb the hill on foot, they've posted a sign just before the cattle grid at the bottom of the hill asking that private cars not be used, and this request should be respected. The fastest time on record for climbing Tapioi is 17 minutes, but it's best to allow two or three hours to hike up and down.

Sports and Recreation

The coral life at Raiatea is rather poor, but there's ample marinelife, including gray sharks, moray eels, barracudas, manta rays, and countless tropical fish. Experienced divers will appreciate the shark action in Teavarua Pass, while beginners and others will enjoy diving near Motu Taoru. South of Uturoa is the century-old wreck of a 50-meter Dutch coal boat, the top of which is 18 meters down.

Hémisphère Sub (Hubert Clot, B.P. 985, 98735 Uturoa; tel. 66-12-49, fax 66-28-63, VHF channel 68), at the Marina Apooiti, offers scuba diving at CFP 5,000 per dive. The second to fifth dives are CFP 4,500 each, the sixth to 10th CFP 4,300. Night dives cost CFP 5,500. They go out daily at 0830 and 1430 and offer free pickups. A five-dive CMAS certification course is CFP 30,000 but to enroll you'll need a medical certificate, which can be obtained locally for CFP 3,000.

Raiatea Plongée (B.P. 272, 98735 Uturoa; tel. 66-37-10, fax 66-26-25, VHF channel 18) is run by Patrice Philip, husband of the Marie-France mentioned under **Accommodations,** below. He also charges CFP 5,000 for a one-tank dive. A trip right around Taha'a by motorized canoe with visits to two *motus* is CFP 5,500 (eight-person minimum), snorkeling in a pass is CFP 3,500. PADI scuba certification (four dives) is CFP 50,000. A swimming pool on the premises is used for the lessons. We've had varying reports about Patrice's operation.

Nauti-Sport (tel./fax 66-35-83), next to the Kuomintang building at the south end of Uturoa, sells quality snorkeling gear.

There's good swimming in a large pool open to the sea at the **Centre Nautique** *("la piscine")* on the coast just north of Uturoa, beyond the new yacht harbor. The local Polynesians keep their long racing canoes here.

The **Kaoha Nui Ranch** (Patrick Marinthe, B.P. 568, 98735 Uturoa; tel. 66-25-46) at PK 6, Avera, a few hundred meters north of Pension Manava, charges CFP 3,500 for horseback riding (an hour and a half). You must reserve 24 hours in advance, and there's a two-person minimum.

Turn to **Transportation** in the chapter introduction for information on yacht charters.

PRACTICALITIES

Accommodations

Most of the places to stay are on the northeast side of Raiatea and we've arranged them here from north to south. The proprietors often pick up guests who call ahead for reservations at the airport or harbor. The transfers are usually free, but ask.

The friendly **Sunset Beach Motel Apooiti** (Moana Boubée, B.P. 397, 98735 Uturoa; tel. 66-33-47, fax 66-33-08) is in a coconut grove by the beach, five km west of Uturoa. It's on the point across the bay from Marina Apooiti, about 2.5 km west of the airport. The 22 comfortable, well-spaced bungalows with cooking facilities and private bath (hot water) are CFP 7,000/8,000/9,000 single/double/triple—good value for families. Camping is CFP 1,100 pp here, and there's a large communal kitchen. Discounts of 10% a fortnight and 20% a month are available, but there's a CFP 1,000 surcharge if you stay only one night. Bicycles are for rent and hitching

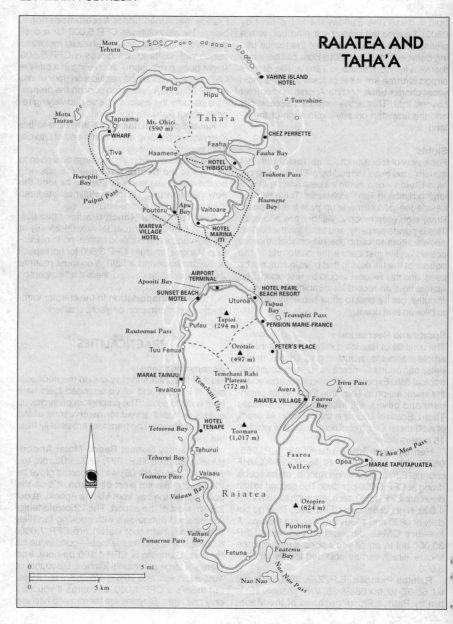

RAIATEA AND TAHA'A

Motu Tehutu

VAHINE ISLAND HOTEL

Patio   Hipu

Tuuvahine

Taha'a

Motu Tautau

Tapuamu

WHARF

Mt. Ohiri (590 m)

CHEZ PERRETTE

Tiva   Haamene   Faaha   Faaha Bay

HOTEL L'HIBISCUS

Hurepiti Bay

Toahotu Pass

Paipai Pass

Haamene Bay

Poutoru   Apu Bay   Vaitoare

MAREVA VILLAGE HOTEL

HOTEL MARINA ITI

AIRPORT TERMINAL

Apooiti Bay

HOTEL PEARL BEACH RESORT

SUNSET BEACH MOTEL

Uturoa   Tupua Bay   Teavapiti Pass

Tapioi (294 m)

PENSION MARIE-FRANCE

Rautoanui Pass   Pufau

Tuu Fenua   Orotaio (497 m)   PETER'S PLACE

MARAE TAINUU

Temehani Rahi Plateau (772 m)

Iriru Pass

Tevaitoa

Temehani Ute

Avera

RAIATEA VILLAGE

Faaroa Bay

Tetooroa Bay   HOTEL TENAPE

Toomaru (1,017 m)

Tehurui

Te Ava Moa Pass

Tehurui Bay

Faaroa Valley

Opoa   MARAE TAPUTAPUATEA

Toamaro Pass   Vaiaau

Vaiaau Bay   Raiatea

Oropiro (824 m)

Vaihuti Bay

Puohine

Punaeroa Pass

Fetuna   Faatemu Bay

Nao Nao Pass

Nao Nao

0   5 mi
0   5 km

into Uturoa is easy. It's one of the nicest places to stay in the islands. Budget to moderate.

Europcar (Raiatea Location, tel. 66-34-06, fax 66-16-06) has four small bungalows with private bath for rent behind their office between the airport and Uturoa. It's CFP 4,500 single or double, or pay CFP 9,000 for a bungalow and an unlimited mileage car. It's a deal worth checking out if you were planning to rent a car anyway (but cooking facilities are not provided). Inexpensive.

The **Hôtel Hinano** (Georges Moulon, B.P. 196, 98735 Uturoa; tel. 66-13-13; fax 66-14-14), conveniently located on the main street in the center of Uturoa, has 10 rooms at CFP 4,500/5,500 single/double (CFP 1,000 extra for one of the four a/c rooms). Cooking facilities are not available. The Hinano would be a good choice if you were interested in Uturoa's bar/disco scene or only wanted to spend one night here between boats. Inexpensive.

Pension Marie-France (Patrice and Marie-France Philip, B.P. 272, 98735 Uturoa; tel. 66-37-10, fax 66-26-25), by the lagoon just beyond Magasin Andre Chinese store, 2.5 km south of Uturoa (yellow sign), caters to scuba divers and misplaced backpackers. The four rooms with shared bath are CFP 4,000 single or double in back, or CFP 4,500 single or double facing the lagoon. Five bungalows with kitchen and TV facing the lagoon are CFP 7,000/8,000/9,000 single/double/triple. There's also a six-bed dormitory with cooking facilities at CFP 1,200 pp (sheets provided on request). A supplement of up to CFP 1,000 is charged if you stay only one night. Bicycles (CFP 1,000 daily) and a washing machine are for rent, and there's sometimes hot water. The lagoon off Pension Marie-France is good for windsurfing and there's surfing off Taoru Island in nearby Teavapiti Pass. Unfortunately they're a little pushy in the way they try to convince you to sign up for the half-day minibus tour of the island (CFP 4,000), so don't come expecting to rest. As soon as Marie-France senses that you're not interested in taking any of her trips, she becomes rather abrupt. The food in the restaurant is satisfactory and the accommodations okay, but Marie-France's unhelpful management style means bad vibes all around. Airport transfers are CFP 600 pp each way (nothing is free here). Inexpensive to moderate.

Three of the best value places to stay on Raiatea are close together six km south of Uturoa, a CFP 1,500 taxi ride from Uturoa. **Kaoha Nui Ranch** (B.P. 568, 98735 Uturoa; tel./fax 66-25-46) has two rooms with private bath at CFP 5,500 single or double, CFP 6,500 triple. Otherwise there are four double "dormitory" rooms with shared bath at CFP 1,800 per bed (plus CFP 500 for one-night stays). Communal cooking facilities are provided. It's the obvious selection if you have an interest in riding. Airport transfers are free. Inexpensive.

Pension Manava (B.P. 559, 98735 Uturoa; tel. 66-28-26, fax 66-16-66), right next door to Kaoha Nui Ranch at PK 6, Avera, is run by Andrew and Roselyne Brotherson. This warm, sympathetic couple has four Polynesian-style bungalows with cooking facilities and private bath at CFP 4,500 or CFP 5,500 single or double, depending on the unit. Two rooms in a separate building are CFP 3,500 single or double with shared kitchen and bath. A half-day boat trip to southern Raiatea is CFP 2,500 pp, and they also do a full-day boat trip right around Taha'a at CFP 3,750 including lunch (five-person minimum)—these trips are also open to nonguests. Bicycles are CFP 1,000. Inexpensive.

The backpacker's number-one choice on Raiatea is **Peter's Place** (Peter Brotherson, tel. 66-20-01) at Hamoa, six km south of Uturoa and just beyond Pension Manava. The eight neat double rooms in a long block are CFP 1,400 pp, or you can pitch a tent in the large grassy area facing the rooms at CFP 700 pp. A large open pavilion is used for communal cooking but there are no grocery stores nearby, so bring food. The pavilion doubles as a traveler's library with good lighting and it's very pleasant to sit there on a rainy night as torrents of water beat on the tin roof. Bicycles rent for CFP 800 a day. Peter is the progeny of a Danish sea captain named Brotherson who left hundreds of descendants on Raiatea. He or his son Frame take guests on a hike up the valley to a picturesque waterfall with swimming in the river, fish feeding, and a tour of a vanilla plantation included at CFP 3,000 per group. They can also guide you directly to the Temehani Plateau, taking about three hours up and two hours down (CFP 5,000 per group). Peter's boat trips cost around CFP 1,000 pp when a few people are interested, and he'll also loan you a dugout canoe free to paddle yourself around the lagoon. Budget.

Pension Yolande Roopinia (Yolande Roopinia, B.P. 298, 98735 Uturoa; tel. 66-35-28) is in an attractive location facing the lagoon at PK 10, Avera. The four rooms are CFP 5,000 single or double (private bath). Cooking facilities are provided, but you may be asked to take half pension (CFP 7,000/13,000 single/double). You'll like the family atmosphere. Inexpensive.

On a hillside facing Faaroa Bay (PK 11) is **La Croix du Sud** (Annette and Eric Germa, B.P. 769, 98735 Uturoa; tel./fax 66-27-55). The three rooms with bath are CFP 6,350/9,090 single/double including breakfast and dinner (no cooking facilities). Facilities include a swimming pool, bicycles, and free airport pickups. Expensive.

Luxury

The 32-unit **Hôtel Raiatea Pearl Beach Resort** (B.P. 43, 98735 Uturoa; tel. 66-20-23, fax 66-20-20), 1.5 km south of Uturoa, is Raiatea's only luxury hotel. This is the former Raiatea Bali Hai, destroyed by a kitchen fire in 1992 and completely rebuilt in 1994 as the Hôtel Hawaiki Nui. In 1998 it became the Pearl Beach Resort, changing CFP 17,000 single or double for one of the eight thatched garden bungalows, CFP 21,000 for the 12 lagoonside bungalows, or CFP 29,000 for the 12 overwater bungalows, plus tax. The layout is attractive with a swimming pool overlooking the lagoon. A Europcar desk is here. Airport transfers are CFP 1,400 pp.

Food

To escape the tourist scene, try **Bar Restaurant Maraamu,** also known as Chez Remy, in what appears to be an old Chinese store between the market and the wharf. The few minutes it takes to locate the place will net you the lowest prices in town. Coffee and omelettes (CFP 600) are served in the morning, while the lunch menu tilts toward Chinese food. There's also excellent *poisson cru* (CFP 350, sold out by 1400) and a good selection of other dishes. Hinano beer is on tap.

Snack Moemoea (tel. 66-39-84; weekdays 0600-1700, Saturday 0600-1300, closed Sunday), on the harbor, serves hamburgers plus a range of French and Chinese dishes on their terrace. Despite the name it's rather upmarket.

Le Quai des Pécheurs (tel. 66-36-83), closer to the wharf, offers a view of the port.

Unpretentious **Restaurant Michele** (tel. 66-14-66; weekdays 0500-1530/1800-2100, Saturday 0500-1530) below Hôtel Hinano (rear side of the building) is a good place for breakfast with coffee, bread, and butter at CFP 250. Chinese meals are around CFP 800, otherwise take one of the French dishes costing CFP 1,000-1,200 listed on the blackboard at the door. Their *poisson cru* is CFP 400, a small glass of beer CFP 250.

A more upmarket choice would be the **Jade Garden Restaurant** (tel. 66-34-40; open Wed.-Sat. 1100-1300/1830-2100) on the main street, offering some of the tastiest Chinese dishes this side of Papeete.

The upstairs dining room at **Restaurant Moana** (tel. 66-27-49; open Tues.-Sun. 1030-1330/1830-2130) opposite Uturoa Market also serves Chinese dishes. Weekdays the lunch specials are listed on a blackboard downstairs, costing around CFP 1,000 including a beer. If you have a late dinner on weekends and wish to stay for the disco you won't have to pay the CFP 1,000 cover charge provided you don't go out.

The largest supermarket is **Champion** facing the small boat harbor, open weekdays 0700-1200/1330-1830, Saturday 0700-1200/1430-1800. Whole barbecued chickens are CFP 700. All of the stores in Uturoa close for lunch 1200-1330.

Entertainment

Friday, Saturday, and Sunday at 2200 Restaurant Moana (tel. 66-27-49) opposite Uturoa Market becomes **Discothèque Le Zénith.** They begin collecting a CFP 1,000 cover charge at 2200, but if you arrive around 2100 and have a few drinks at the bar you won't have to pay it.

The nicest place for a drink is Le Quai des Pécheurs, which transforms itself into **Disco Quaidep** on Friday and Saturday from 2200 (CFP 1,000 cover).

Services and Information

None of Uturoa's four banks open on Saturday but ATMs accessible 24 hours are outside the market and in front of the Banque de Tahiti.

The large modern post office (Mon.-Thurs. 0730-1500, Friday 0700-1400, Saturday 0800-

1000) is opposite the new hospital just north of town, with the *gendarmerie* (tel. 66-31-07) about 50 meters beyond on the left.

There are free public toilets *(sanitaires publics)* on the wharf behind Le Quai des Pêcheurs.

A kilometer west of the Sunset Beach Motel is Raiatea Carenage Services (B.P. 165, 98735 Uturoa; tel. 66-22-96), a repair facility often used by cruising yachts. The only easily accessible slip facilities in Tahiti-Polynesia are here (maximum 22 tons).

Beside the souvenir stalls opposite the wharf is a tourist information stand (B.P. 707, 98735 Uturoa; tel. 66-23-33), open Mon.-Fri. 0800-1130/1330-1600. They can supply a few brochures but are not very helpful.

Health

Uturoa's public hospital (tel. 66-35-03) is on the north side of town.

Dr. Patrick Lazarini (tel. 66-23-01), general practitioner, and Dr. Françis Falieu (tel. 66-35-95), dentist, have adjacent offices above La Palme d'Or in the center of Uturoa. Both are open weekdays 0730-1145/1330-1700, Saturday 0800-1130.

Several private doctors and dentists have offices above the pharmacy opposite the Catholic church in central Uturoa. Among them are Dr. Alain Repiton-Préneuf and Dr. Bruno Bataillon, general practitioners, and Dr. Frederic Koutzevol (tel. 66-31-31; weekdays 0730-1130/1400-1700, Saturday 0730-1000), a dentist.

The Pharmacy (tel. 66-35-48), opposite the Catholic church, is open weekdays 0730-1130/1400-1730, Saturday 0730-1130, Sunday 0930-1030.

TRANSPORTATION

Getting There and Away

The **Air Tahiti** office (tel. 66-32-50) is at the airport. Flights from Raiatea to Maupiti (CFP 5,600) operate three times a week. For information on flights from Papeete, Huahine, and Bora Bora see the introduction to this chapter.

The jet cruiser *Ono-Ono* departs Raiatea for Taha'a (45 minutes hours, CFP 667) and Bora Bora (2.5 hours, CFP 1,778) Monday and Wednesday at 1400, Friday at 2100, and Satur-

day at 1615. To Huahine (one hour, CFP 1,778) and Papeete (4.5 hours, CFP 5,499) it leaves Tuesday and Thursday at 0900, Sunday at 1430. There's an extra trip to Huahine Saturday at 1000. Check the departure information carefully as they often leave earlier than the time printed in their timetable. The *Ono-Ono* office (tel. 66-24-25, fax 66-39-83; open Mon.-Sat. 0630-1730, Sunday 0900-1400) is on waterfront between Snack Moemoe and Champion Supermarket. A Europcar desk is in the same office.

You can catch the *Vaeanu, Taporo VI,* and *Raromatai Ferry* to Taha'a, Bora Bora, Huahine, and Papeete twice weekly. Consult the schedule in the introduction to this chapter. Tickets for the *Vaeanu, Taporo VI,* and *Raromatai Ferry* are sold when the ships arrive.

A government supply barge, the *Meherio III,* shuttles twice a month between Raiatea and Maupiti, usually departing Raiatea on Thursday (CFP 1,058 deck). The exact time varies, so check with the Capitainerie Port d'Uturoa (tel. 66-31-52) on the wharf.

The yellow-and-blue *Maupiti Express,* a fast ferry with 62 airline type seats, charges CFP 2,500 each way between Raiatea and Bora Bora, departing Uturoa for Bora Bora Wednesday and Friday afternoons. Inquire at Agence Blue Lagoon (tel. 66-17-74) next to Snack Moemoe on the waterfront.

Blue Lagoon should also have information about **Les Navettes des Îles** (B.P. 158, 98735 Uturoa; tel. 65-67-10, fax 65-67-11), which shuttle between Raiatea and Taha'a at CFP 750 pp each way (bicycles CFP 500). The fleet consists of two 57-seat ferries painted yellow and blue. The *Uporu* serves Taha'a's west coast (Marina Iti, Poutoru, Patii, Tiva, Tapuamu) while the *Iripau* serves the east coast (Haamene, Faaha Quai Amaru). Both leave Uturoa three times daily on weekdays, but one of the *Uporu's* trips terminates at Marina Iti. On Monday, Wednesday, and Friday one of the *Iripau* trips has a bus connection between Faaha Quai Amaru and Patio. On Saturday only the west coast service operates—once. There's no schedule at all on Sunday and holidays.

Getting Around

Getting around Raiatea by *le truck* isn't practical as they only leave Uturoa in the afternoon (except Sunday) to go to Fetuna, Vaiaau, and Opoa. You might be able to use them to get into town in the morning, however, and the people where you're staying will know at what time you have to be waiting. In Uturoa the *trucks* usually park in front of Restaurant Michele and the drivers themselves are the only reliable source of departure information.

Raiatea Location Europcar (tel. 66-34-06, fax 66-16-06), between the airport and Uturoa, is the main car rental operator on Raiatea. Their cars begin around CFP 7,000 a day, including mileage and insurance (minimum age 18). Ask about the package that gives you a small car and a bungalow behind their main office between Uturoa and the airport at CFP 9,000. Bicycles are CFP 1,200/1,500/2,000 for four/eight/24 hours (expensive). Apart from cars and bikes, Raiatea Location rents a four-meter boat with a six-horsepower motor at CFP 6,000/8,000 a four/eight hours. Scooter rentals are generally unavailable.

Avis (tel. 66-15-59) is at the airport only. Their cars start at CFP 6,900/12,500/16,900 for one/two/three days all inclusive.

Many of the hotels and pensions run circle-island bus tours and boat trips to a *motu* or Taha'a. **Raiatea Safari Tours** (tel. 66-37-10) and **Raiatea 4X4** (tel. 66-24-16) offer 4WD excursions into the interior, which you can't do on your own by rental car at CFP 4,000 and up. **Almost Paradise Tours** (tel. 66-23-64), run by Faaroa Bay resident Bill Kolans, offers a very good three-hour minibus tour in American English for CFP 3,000.

Airport

The airport (RFP) is three km northwest of Uturoa. A taxi from the Uturoa market taxi stand to the airport is CFP 800 (double tariff late at night). Most of the hotels pick up clients at the airport free of charge upon request. Avis and Europcar both have car rental desks inside the terminal. The Air Tahiti reservations office is in a separate building adjacent to the main terminal. The friendly but unknowledgeable Tourist Board information kiosk at the airport is open at flight times only. The airport restaurant offers a good *plat du jour* at lunchtime.

AROUND RAIATEA

It takes 5-10 hours to ride a bicycle the 97 km around Raiatea, depending on how fast you go; by car you can take anywhere from a couple of hours to a leisurely day. The road down the east coast is paved to the head of Faaroa Bay, then the paved road cuts directly across the island to the south coast. Down the west coast, the road is paved as far as Tehurui. The bottom half of the circuminsular road is unpaved, but no problem for a car.

The road down the east coast circles fjordlike **Faaroa Bay,** associated with the legends of Polynesian migration. Stardust Marine has a yacht charter base on the north side of the bay, and from the anchorage there's a fine view of Toomaru, highest peak in the Leeward Islands. The Apoomau River drains the Faaroa Valley. (The boat trips occasionally offered up this river are not recommended, as the boat can only proceed a couple of hundred meters. However, if you're off a yacht you could explore it with your dingy.)

Instead of crossing the island on the paved road, keep left and follow the coast around to a point of land just beyond Opoa, 32 km from Uturoa. Here stands **Marae Taputapuatea,** one of the largest and best preserved in Polynesia, its mighty *ahu* measuring 43 meters long, 7.3 meters wide, and between two and three meters high. Before it is a rectangular courtyard paved with black volcanic rocks. A small platform in the middle of the *ahu* once bore the image of Oro, god of fertility and war (now represented by a reproduction); backrests still mark the seats of high chiefs on the courtyard. Marae Taputapuatea is directly opposite Te Ava Moa Pass, and fires on the *marae* may once have been beacons to ancient navigators. Human sacrifices and firewalking once took place on the *marae.* In 1995 a fleet of traditional Polynesian voyaging canoes, including three from Hawaii and two each from Cook Islands and Tahiti, plus an Easter Island raft, gathered at Taputapuatea to lift a 650-year-old curse and rededicate the *marae.* The seven canoes then left for the Marquesas, navigating by the stars and swells. Some carried on to Hawaii and the west coast of the U.S. in an amazing demonstration of the current revival of this aspect of traditional culture.

The only places to buy food in the southern part of Raiatea are the two Chinese grocery stores at **Fetuna** and another at **Vaiaau,** on the west side of Raiatea. Vaiaau Bay marks the end of the protected inner channel from Uturoa around Raiatea clockwise and yachts must exit the lagoon through Toamaro Pass in order to continue northward. At Rautoanui Pass sailboats can come back in behind the barrier reef to continue the circumnavigation, with the possibility of a side trip south to Tevaitoa.

Behind Tevaitoa church is **Marae Tainuu,** dedicated to the ancient god Taaroa. Petroglyphs on a broken stone by the road at the entrance to the church show a turtle and some other indistinguishable figure. At Tevaitoa Chief Teraupo and his people fought their last battles against the French invaders in early 1897.

The territory's largest yacht charter base is the **Marina Apooiti,** which opened in 1982 one km west of the airport. Aside from The Moorings and Tahiti Yacht Charter, there's a large restaurant here, a dive shop, and the **Musée de la Mer** (tel. 66-27-00; closed Sunday), whose collection you can peruse for CFP 500. Otherwise check out the polished seashells in their souvenir shop for free.

Hiking

According to Polynesian mythology the god Oro was born from the molten rage of **Mt. Temehani** (772 meters), the cloud-covered plateau that dominates the northern end of the island. *Tiare apetahi,* a sacred white flower that exists nowhere else on earth and resists transplantation, grows above the 400-meter level on the slopes around the summit. The fragile one-sided blossom represents the five fingers of a beautiful Polynesian girl who fell in love with the handsome son of a high chief, but was unable to marry him due to her lowly birth. The petals pop open forcefully enough at dawn to make a sound,

and local residents sometimes spend the night on the mountain to be there to hear it. These flowers are protected and there's a minimum CFP 50,000 fine for picking one. Small pink orchids also grow here.

Temehani can be climbed from Pufau, the second bay south of Marina Apooiti. Note a series of old concrete benches by the road as you come around the north side of the bay (which offers good anchorage for yachts). The track inland begins at a locked gate, 700 meters south of the bridge, beyond the concrete benches. It's private property, so ask permission to proceed of anyone you meet. You hike straight up through an area reforested in pine until you have a clear view of Temehani Rahi and Temehani Ute, divided by a deep gorge. Descend to the right and continue up the track you see on the hillside opposite. It takes about three hours to go from the main road to the Temehani Rahi Plateau. Friday and Saturday are the best days to go, and long pants and sturdy shoes are required. A guide up Temehani should charge about CFP 5,000 for the group.

Reader Will Paine of Maidstone, England, sent us this:

The through hike from Pufau to Uturoa takes five or six hours on foot with beautiful views from high vantage points where the difficultly manageable jeep track becomes a path. The same trail is shared by the Temehani route until it splits up shortly after the ford/bathing pool on the higher reaches. Here take the left branch. Follow it down across a water catchment and up to a ridge. The Orotaio cone will come into view to the east and the path drops to a better four-wheel-drive track. From here it's just under two hours down to a gas station on the coastal road a few km south of Uturoa.

TAHA'A

Raiatea's 90-square-km lagoonmate Taha'a is shaped like a hibiscus flower with four long bays cutting into its rugged south side. Mount Ohiri (590 meters), highest point on the island, got its name from Hiro, god of thieves, who was born here. Taha'a is known as the "vanilla island" for its plantations, which produce 70% of the territory's "black gold." The Taha'a Festival in late October includes stone fishing, with a line of canoes herding the fish into a cove by beating stones on the surface of the lagoon. In November the Hawaiki Nui Outrigger Canoe Race passes Taha'a on its way from Huahine to Bora Bora.

It's a quiet island, with little traffic and few tourists. Most families use speedboats to commute to their gardens on the reef islets or to fishing spots, or to zip over to Raiatea on shopping trips, so they don't really need cars. Beaches are scarce on the main island but the string of *motus* off the northeast side of Taha'a have fine white-sand beaches. The pension owners and tour operators arrange picnics on a few of these, such as Tautau off Tapuamu, and pearl farms have been established on some. This is the only Society island you can sail a yacht right around inside the barrier reef, and the many anchorages and central location between Raiatea, Huahine, and Bora Bora make Taha'a a favorite of both cruisers and charterers.

There aren't many specific attractions on Taha'a, and the dearth of inexpensive places to stay and lack of public transportation has kept this island off the beaten track. The easy way to visit Taha'a is still an all-day outrigger canoe tour from Raiatea. This could change but meanwhile the isolation has made the 4,500 Taha'a islanders rather wary of outsiders.

Orientation

The administrative center is at Patio (or Iripau) on the north coast, where the post office, *mairie*, and *gendarmerie* (tel. 65-64-07) share one compound. A second post office is at Haamene where four roads meet. The ship from Papeete ties up to a wharf at Tapuamu, and there's a large covered area at the terminal where you could spread a sleeping bag in a pinch. The

Banque Socredo branch is also at Tapuamu.

The 70-km coral road around the main part of the island passes six of the eight villages; the other two are south of Haamene. Only the scenic road over the 141-meter Col Taira between Haamene and Tiva, and a stretch around Patio, are paved. There are ferries from Raiatea to Tapuamu and Haamene but no regular public transportation.

Sights

The mountain pass between Haamene and Tiva offers excellent views of Hurepiti and Haamene Bays, two of the four deep fjords cutting into the southern side of the island. You could also follow the rough track from Haamene up to the Col Vaitoetoe for an even better view. This track continues north, coming out near the hospital in Patio.

Rarahu, the girl immortalized in Pierre Loti's 1880 novel *The Marriage of Loti*, is buried near Vaitoare village at the south end of Taha'a, east of the Marina Iti.

PRACTICALITIES

Accommodations

Unfortunately, there aren't any budget accommodations on Taha'a. The most convenient and least expensive place is **Chez Pascal** (Pascal Tamaehu, tel. 65-60-42). From the Tapuamu ferry wharf you'll see a small bridge at the head of the bay. Turn left as you leave the dock and head for this. Chez Pascal is the first house north of the bridge on the inland side. The rate is CFP 5,000 pp for bed, breakfast, and dinner, or CFP 3,000 pp with breakfast only. Boat trips to a *motu* are CFP 4,000 pp, and the loan of the family bicycle is possible. Inexpensive.

The **Mareva Village Hôtel** (B.P. 214, 98734 Haamene; tel. 65-61-61, fax 65-68-67) on Apu Bay is easily accessible weekdays on the ferry *Uporu* to Poutoru. Standing in a row between the road and the lagoon are six large bungalows with kitchen, bath, TV, and porch at CFP 7,000 single or double, CFP 8,500 triple, CFP

10,000 quad. The cooking facilities allow you to avoid the expensive meals you're forced to take in some of the other hotels, but bring groceries from Raiatea. Moderate.

The **Hôtel Marina Iti** (B.P. 888, 98735 Uturoa, Raiatea; tel. 65-01-01, fax 65-63-87, VHF channel 12) sits at the isolated south tip of Taha'a, opposite Raiatea on Taha'a's only sandy beach. The five clean, pleasant bungalows by the lagoon are CFP 16,000 double, or pay CFP 12,000 for a room in a duplex garden bungalow. Third persons pay CFP 2,000. Cooking facilities are not provided and meals are CFP 5,000 pp extra for breakfast and dinner. Use of bicycles, canoe, and snorkeling gear is included, and scuba diving is available. As you'll have guessed, the Marina Iti caters to an upmarket crowd on yacht charters from Raiatea, and numerous cruising yachts anchor in the calm waters offshore. The ferry *Uporu* from Raiatea stops here. (In 1998 the Marina Iti changed hands for just over a million dollars.) Premium.

The **Hôtel L'Hibiscus** (B.P. 184, 98734 Haamene; tel. 65-61-06, fax 65-65-65, VHF channel 68), also know as the Hôtel Taha'a Lagon, is run by Léo and Lolita on the northeast side of windy Haamene Bay. L'Hibiscus has two classes of accommodations: two plain rooms with shared bath at CFP 5,750 for up to three people, and four small bungalows with private bath at CFP 8,000/9,350 double/triple. Virtually everything you consume here—even the water you drink—is charged extra at resort prices. Common drinking water is not available at L'Hibiscus; bottled water must be purchased. The prices of the meals are fixed at CFP 3,500 pp half pension, CFP 5,500 full pension (not possible to order à la carte). Don't accept a "free welcome drink" unless you don't mind having it added to your bill ("misunderstandings" about prices are routine here). There are no cooking facilities, and the nearest store is three km away in Haamene (bring food and bottled water). L'Hibiscus has 10 yacht moorings that are "free" to those who patronize the restaurant and bar. However, Haamene Bay catches the full force of the southeast trades and there's far better anchorage off the Marina Iti. The ferry *Iripau* will drop you at Faaha Quai Amaru near here. We have received several convincing complaints about this place. Moderate.

Chez Perrette (Perrette Tehuitua, tel. 65-65-78) is in an isolated location at Faaopore, 10 km east of Haamene. At CFP 2,500 for a mattress in an eight-bed dorm or CFP 15,000 double with breakfast and dinner in a self-catering bungalow, it's not worth the trip. Premium.

In 1998 the **Tupena Village** pension opened at Patio. It offers three rooms downstairs and two upstairs with plans for four bungalows, but prices were still unknown.

Food

Village stores are at Tapuamu, Tiva, Haamene, and Patio. A grocery truck passes L'Hibiscus around 1000 on Monday, Tuesday, Thursday, and Saturday; the same truck calls at the Marina Iti about noon daily except Sunday. The only nonhotel restaurant on Taha'a is at **Magasin Tissan** (tel. 65-64-15) in Patio.

Health

There's a medical center (tel. 65-63-31) at Patio and a dispensary (tel. 65-61-03) at Haamene. Dr. Marc Chabanne (tel. 65-60-60) is also at Haamene.

Transportation

There's no airport on Taha'a. The **Le Navette des Îles** shuttles between Raiatea and Taha'a three times daily on weekdays and once on Saturday (CFP 750 pp each way, bicycles CFP 500). Make sure your boat is going exactly where you want to go. For more information see **Raiatea** above.

Large ships and ferries call at Tapuamu Wharf on the west side of Taha'a just behind the Total service station. There's a telephone booth on the wharf that you could use to call your hotel to have them pick you up. The *Ono-Ono* leaves Taha'a for Bora Bora (CFP 1,333) Monday and Wednesday at 1445 and Saturday at 1700. To Raiatea (CFP 667), Huahine (CFP 2,111), and Papeete (CFP 6,050) it leaves Tuesday and Thursday at 0815, Saturday at 0915, and Sunday at 1315.

Taporo VI arrives from Papeete, Huahine, and Raiatea Tuesday, Thursday, and Saturday at 0700, and continues on to Bora Bora (southbound it doesn't stop at Taha'a). The *Vaeanu* departs Taha'a for Raiatea, Huahine, and Papeete Tuesday and Sunday at noon;

Saturday at 0800 it goes to Bora Bora. The *Raromatai Ferry* visits Taha'a on Wednesday and Saturday mornings northbound, and Sunday afternoon southbound. The *Maupiti Express* leaves Taha'a for Bora Bora Wednesday and Friday at 1615.

Trucks on Taha'a are for transporting schoolchildren only, so you may have to hitch to get around. It's not that hard to hitch a ride down the west coast from Patio to Haamene, but there's almost no traffic along the east coast.

Rental cars are available from **Europcar** (tel. 65-67-00, fax 65-68-08) at the Total station next to Tapuamu Wharf, **Taha'a Transport Services** (tel. 65-67-10) at the Marina Iti, and **Monique Location/Avis** (tel. 65-62-48) at Haamene Wharf. Marina Iti also rents bicycles. Avis charges CFP 7,900 a day with 100 kilometers (extra kilometers CFP 40 each); Europcar is CFP 7,000 a day with unlimited kilometers and insurance. It's smart to book ahead if you want to be sure of a car.

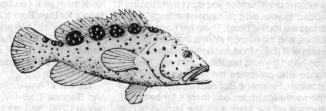

sea bass (Cephalopholis catesi)

BORA BORA

Bora Bora, 260 km northwest of Papeete, is everyone's idea of a South Pacific island. Dramatic basalt peaks soar 700 meters above a gorgeous, multicolored lagoon. Slopes and valleys blossom with hibiscus. Some of the most perfect beaches you'll ever see are here, complete with topless sunbathers. Not only are the beaches good but there's plenty to see and do. The local population of 6,000 includes many skilled dancers. To see them practicing in the evening, follow the beat of village drums back to their source.

Bora Bora is the only island of Tahiti-Polynesia that can be said to have reached a tourist glut. The relentless stream of cars, pickups, hotel *trucks,* and scooters up and down the main road from Vaitape to Matira Point approaches Tahitian intensity at times. The uncontrolled expansion of tourism continues as luxury resorts are thrown up around the island, creating the illusion of being in Hawaii or some West Indies hot spot. Yet many of the US$500-a-night hotels stand almost empty. Related problems for Bora Bora include an upsurge of petty theft from visitors and improper garbage disposal by almost everyone. You may also find the swarms of young honeymooners from Chicago milling around Matira rather anticlimactic.

The Land

Seven-million-year-old Bora Bora (29 square km) is made up of a 10-km-long main island, a few smaller high islands in the lagoon, and a long ring of *motus* on the barrier reef. Pofai Bay marks the center of the island's collapsed crater with Toopua and Toopuaiti as its eroded west wall. Mount Pahia's gray basalt mass rises 649 meters behind Vaitape, and above it soar the sheer cliffs of Otemanu's mighty volcanic plug (727 meters). The wide-angle scenery of the main island is complemented by the surrounding coral reef and numerous *motus,* one of which bears the airport. Motu Tapu of the travel brochures was featured in F.W. Murnau's classic 1931 silent movie *Tabu* about two young lovers who escape to this tiny island. Te Ava Nui Pass is the only entry through the barrier reef. Watch for dolphins near this channel as your ship enters Bora Bora's lagoon; whole colonies sometimes race the boats. However these days you're more likely to be met by a line of tourists on jet skis following their guide.

History

The letter *b* doesn't exist in Tahitian, so Bora Bora is actually Pora Pora, meaning "first born" since this was the first island created after Raiatea. The island's traditional name, Vava'u, suggests Tongan voyagers may have reached here centuries ago. It's believed Bora Bora has been inhabited since the year 900, and 42 *marae* ruins can still be found around the island. The Bora Borans of yesteryear were indomitable warriors who often raided Maupiti, Taha'a, and Raiatea.

"Discovered" by Roggeveen in 1722, Bora Bora was visited by Capt. James Cook in 1769 and 1777. The first European to live on the island was James O'Connor, a survivor of the British whaler *Matilda* wrecked at Moruroa atoll in 1793. O'Connor made his way to Tahiti where he married into the Pomare family, and eventually ended up living in a little grass shack on "Matilda Point," later corrupted to Matira Point. In 1895 the island was annexed by France.

In February 1942 the Americans hastily set up a refueling and regrouping base, code-named "Bobcat," on the island to serve shipping between the U.S. west coast or Panama Canal and Australia/New Zealand. You can still see remains from this time, including eight huge naval guns placed here to defend the island against a surprise Japanese attack that never materialized. The big lagoon with only one pass offered secure anchorage for as many as 100 U.S. Navy transports at a time. A road was built around the island and by April 1943 the present airfield on Motu Mute had been constructed. The 4,400 American army troops also left behind 130 half-caste babies, 40% of whom died of starvation when the base closed in June 1946 and the abandoned infants were forced to switch from their accustomed American baby formulas to island food. The survivors are now approaching ripe middle age. Novelist James A. Michener, a young naval officer at the time, left perhaps the most enduring legacy by modeling his Bali Hai on this "enchanted island," Bora Bora.

Orientation

You can arrive at Motu Mute airport and be carried to Vaitape Wharf by catamaran, or disembark from a ship at Farepiti Wharf, three km north of Vaitape. Most of the stores, banks, and offices are near Vaitape Wharf. The finest beaches are at Matira Point at the island's southern tip.

SIGHTS

Vaitape

Behind the Banque de Tahiti at Vaitape Wharf is the **monument to Alain Gerbault,** who sailed his yacht, the *Firecrest,* solo around the world from 1923 to 1929—the first Frenchman to do so. Gerbault's first visit to Bora Bora was from 25 May to 12 June 1926. He returned to Polynesia in 1933 and stayed until 1940. A supporter of

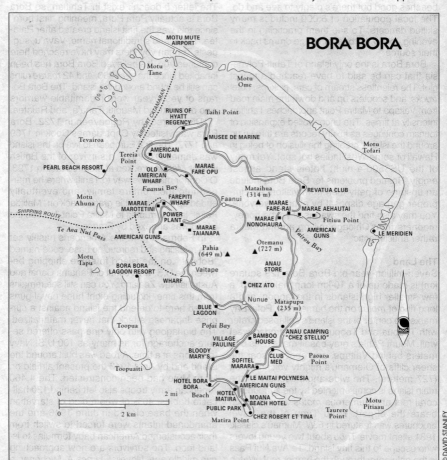

BORA BORA

© DAVID STANLEY

the Pétian regime, he left Bora Bora when the colony declared its support for General de Gaulle and died at Timor a year later while trying to return to Vichy France.

To get an idea of how the Bora Borans live, take a stroll through Vaitape village: go up the road that begins beside the Banque Socredo.

Around the Island

The largely paved and level 32-km road around the island makes it easy to see Bora Bora by rented bicycle (it's unnecessary to rent a car). At the head of **Pofai Bay** notice the odd assortment of looted war wreckage across the road from Alain Linda Galerie d'Art. Surrounded by a barbed wire fence are a seven-inch American gun dragged here from Tereia Point in 1982 and two huge anchors. On the hillside above is an abandoned A-frame museum, which didn't prove as profitable as its promoters had hoped. The locations of seven other MK II naval guns that have thus far escaped desecration are given below.

Stop at **Bloody Mary's Restaurant** to scan the goofy displays outside their gate, but more importantly to get the classic view of the island's soaring peaks across Pofai Bay as it appears in countless brochures. For an even better view go inland on the unmarked road that begins at a double electricity pole 100 meters north of Bloody Mary's. This leads to a jeep route with two concrete tracks up the 139-meter-high hill to a **radio tower**, a 10-minute hike. From the tower you get a superb view of the south end of the island.

The finest beach on the island stretches east from **Hôtel Bora Bora** to Matira Point. Some of the best snorkeling on the island, with a varied multitude of colorful tropical fish, is off the small point at Hôtel Bora Bora. Enter from east of the hotel grounds (such as via the Bora Diving Center or the beach beyond) and let the current pull you toward the hotel jetty, as the hotel staff don't appreciate strangers who stroll through their lobby to get to the beach. From the way they approach you, the small fish quite obviously accustomed to being fed here, and for a more natural scene you could snorkel due south to the northern edge of the barrier reef. Just beware of getting run over by a glass-bottom boat! If you stay on the east side of the point, the hotel employees will leave you alone.

Two **naval guns** sit on the ridge above Hôtel Matira. Take the track on the mountain side of the road that winds around behind the bungalows from the east end of the property and keep straight ahead on a trail to the top of the ridge (10 minutes).

Bora Bora's most popular public beach is **Matira Beach Park** directly across the street from the Moana Beach Hôtel on Matira Point. At low tide you can wade from the end of Matira Point right out to the reef. These same shallows prevent yachts from sailing around the island inside the barrier reef.

Proceed north to the **Sofitel Marara**, a good place for a leisurely beer. Visitors are unwelcome at the new Club Med, which the road climbs over a hill to avoid. The two general stores at **Anau** can supply a cold drink or a snack.

On the north side of Vairou Bay the road begins to climb over a ridge. Halfway up the slope, look down to the right and by the shore you'll see the *ahu* of **Marae Aehautai,** the most intact of the three *marae* in this area. From the *marae* there's a stupendous view of Otemanu and you should be able to pick out Te Ana Opea cave far up on the side of the mountain. To visit the two American **seven-inch guns** on Fitiuu Point, follow the rough jeep track to the right at the top of the ridge a few hundred meters east (on foot) to a huge black rock from which you can see the guns. The steep unpaved slope on the other side of this ridge can be dangerous on a bicycle, so slow down or get off and walk. There's a municipal dump in this area and you could catch the stench of burning garbage.

Just before Taihi Point at the north end of the main island is a **Musée de Marine** (tel. 67-75-24, donations accepted) on the right, which is usually closed. Just beyond Taihi Point you'll notice a concrete trestle running right up the side of the hill from the ruins of a group of platforms meant to be the overwater bungalows. This is all that remains an undercapitalized **Hyatt Regency hotel** project that went broke in the early 1980s.

One American **naval gun** remains on the hillside above the rectangular concrete water tank with a transformer pole alongside at Tereia Point. The housing of a second gun, vandalized in 1982, is nearby. The remains of several American concrete wharves can be seen along the north shore of **Faanui Bay.** Most of the wartime

American occupation force was billeted around here and a few Quonset huts linger in the bush. Just beyond the small boat harbor (a wartime American submarine base) and the Service de l'Equipment is **Marae Fare Opu,** notable for the petroglyphs of turtles carved into the stones of the *ahu*. Turtles, a favorite food of the gods, were often offered to them on the *marae*. (Mindless guides sometimes highlight the turtles in chalk for the benefit of tourist cameras.)

Between Faanui and Farepiti Wharf, just east of the Brasserie de Tahiti depot and the electricity-generating plant, is **Marae Taianapa;** its long *ahu*, restored in 1963, is clearly visible on the hillside from the road. The most important *marae* on Bora Bora was **Marae Marotetini,** on the point near Farepiti Wharf—west of the wharf and accessible along the shore at low tide. The great stone *ahu*, 25 meters long and up to 1.5 meters high, was restored by Professor Sinoto in 1968 and is visible from approaching ships.

The last two **American guns** are a 10-minute scramble up the ridge from the main road between Farepiti Wharf and Vaitape. Go straight up the concrete road a bit before you reach Otemanu Tours (where you see several *trucks* parked). At the end of the ridge there's a good view of Te Ava Nui Pass, which the guns were meant to defend, and Maupiti is farther out on the horizon. This is private property so ask permission to proceed of anyone you meet.

Sports and Recreation

The **Bora Diving Center** (Anne and Michel Condesse, B.P. 182, 98730 Nunue; tel. 67-71-84, fax 67-74-83, VHF channel 8), just east of Hôtel Bora Bora, offers scuba diving daily at 0830, 1330, 1930. Prices are CFP 5,500/9,000 for one/two tanks, CFP 25,000 for a five-dive package, or CFP 6,500 for night dives, plus three percent tax. Snorkelers are welcome to tag along for CFP 1,500. Both PADI and CMAS openwater certification courses are offered at CFP 35,000 (three days). Otherwise try a one-tank initiation shore dive at CFP 5,500 (no experience required). Gear is included. Ten different sites are visited (those around Toopua Island are recommended for snorkelers). They also have a new activity called "Aqua Safari" in which participants put on a funny yellow diving helmet and walk along the lagoon floor (no experience

required), also CFP 5,500. Bookings for any of this can be made through their dive shop on Matira Beach (which is closed while their five boats are out but usually staffed at 1030 and 1530), or at Aqua Safari inside the Bora Bora Beach Club. If you book through your hotel reception, a surcharge may be added. Hotel pickups are available to divers who have booked ahead.

Scuba diving can also be arranged through Ben Heriteau's **Nemo World Diving** (B.P. 503, 98730 Vaitape; tel. 67-63-00, fax 67-63-33) near the Sofitel Marara. They charge CFP 6,000/ 11,000/26,250 for one/two/five dives, gear included, and go out daily at 0900 and 1400 (hotel pickups available). Snorkelers can go along at CFP 2,000 pp. Nemo's specialty is diving with manta rays (worth doing to see the mantas, though you won't see much else in that area as the coral is all dead and the waters fished out). Since it's a long way around to the single pass, most scuba diving at Bora Bora is within the lagoon and visibility is sometimes limited.

Sportfishing from a luxury catamaran is a Bora Bora eccentricity invented by ex-Californian Richard Postma of **Island Sport Charters** (B.P. 186, 98730 Vaitape; tel./fax 67-77-79). His 15-meter *Tara Vana* based at Hôtel Bora Bora is fitted with a flybridge and two fighting chairs, and the sails and multihull stability make for a smooth, quiet ride. Any doubts you may have about fishing from a sailboat can be laid aside as this prototype vessel ranks among the best. A half-day fishing charter is CFP 60,000 for up to 10 people.

Horseback riding is available at **Ranch Reva Reva** (Olivier Ringeard, B.P. 117, 98730 Vaitape; tel. 67-63-63) on Motu Pitiaau, the long coral island east of Matira Point. Organized riding is four times a day at CFP 5,500 for 1.5 hours. Book through Miki Miki Jet Ski (tel. 67-76-44) at Matira, which arranges free transfers to the *motu*.

ACCOMMODATIONS

There's an abundance of accommodations on Bora Bora and, except at holiday times (especially during the July festivities), it's not necessary to book a room in advance. When things are slow, the hotel owners meet the interisland boats in search of guests. If someone from the hotel of your choice isn't at the dock when you arrive, get on the blue *truck* marked Vaitape-Anau and ask to be taken there. This should cost CFP 500 pp from Farepiti Wharf, CFP 300 pp from Vaitape Wharf, plus CFP 100 for luggage. However, if you're staying at a luxury resort you could be charged CFP 1,800 pp return for airport transfers. A daily CFP 150 pp municipal services tax is collected at all accommodations.

The luxury hotels add an eight percent tax to their room rates (often not included in the quoted price) but most of the budget places include the tax in their price. Be aware that the hotels frequently tack a CFP 1,000 commission onto rental cars, lagoon excursions, and scuba diving booked through their front desks. Bora Bora suffers from serious water shortages, so use it sparingly, and protect yourself against theft from the room by locking up when you go out.

Budget

Backpackers often stay at **Chez Stellio** (B.P. 267, 98730 Vaitape; tel. 67-71-32), also known as "Camping Chez Henriette," at Anau on the east side of the island. The nine shared-bath rooms in a long lime-roofed block at CFP 4,000 double and two smaller rooms in a separate unit in the garden are CFP 5,000. A room with private bath is CFP 8,000. There's a refundable CFP 2,000 key deposit. To stay in a 10-bed dormitory next to the lagoon is CFP 1,500 pp, but a majority of guests pay CFP 1,000 pp to camp. Communal cooking facilities are provided (shortage of utensils). The nearest grocery stores are 2.5 km north (the second store you reach is the better) or opposite Motel Bora Bora at Matira. Although Chez Stellio is not on a natural beach it is right beside the lagoon and the kitchen and picnic area are at the waterside. It's nice and breezy when the southeast trades are blowing. Stellio owns land on idyllic Motu Vaivahia and he's planning to build another 10 thatched bungalows over there, so ask. In any case, you can go over for the day by paying CFP 500 pp each way for boat transfers. Stellio has also built a Seventh-Day Adventist Church in the campground and interminable sermons are presented most evenings (no problem if you're sitting down by the shore). Yelping dogs take over at night followed by roosters in the morning, each adding their own flavor. Bring mosquito repellent. A neighbor rents bicycles at CFP 500 per half day (reserve ahead if possible). Stellio's own *le truck* runs from the campground into Vaitape twice a day, but let the staff know in advance if you're going as they often leave ahead of the scheduled departure time. It's a free ride for Stellio's guests. It's also possible to hike straight across the island to Pofai Bay. Go up the overgrown dirt road directly across the street from Stellio's. As you approach the ridge you'll see a Private Property sign and a house ahead on the left. Here cut straight up the hill to the right toward a radio transmitter from which a concrete road runs down to the west coast. As you disembark on Bora Bora look for Stellio's blue Vaitape-Anau *truck* with "Vaiho" on the door at the wharf or a green Land Rover marked Bora Safari Land. They'll give you a free ride to the camping ground when you first arrive, although upon departure everyone must pay CFP 300 pp for the transfer back to the wharf.

Inexpensive

Pension Au Lait de Coco (B.P. 626, 98730 Vaitape; tel. 67-61-48, fax 45-37-15) is between Magasin Chin Lee and the Total station on the north side of Vaitape, a 10-minute walk from the ferry wharf. It's in the village on the mountain side of the road near the landing for the Bora Bora Lagoon Resort. The two rooms with shared bath in this pleasant local house are CFP 6,000 single or double. The one room with private bath is CFP 7,500. Cooking facilities are provided, and there's a shaded porch and lounge in which to sit. The son of the family, Hinano, guides visitors up Mt. Pahia at CFP 4,000 pp (minimum of two).

At Nunue, right up below Otemanu's soaring peak is **Pension Chez Ato** (B.P. 49, 98730 Vaitape; tel. 67-77-27), a secluded little hideaway with five rooms at CFP 4,000 double. You can use a small kitchen to cook and Ato can arrange guides for mountain hikes at CFP 4,000 pp. Ato is a member of the environmental group *atu atu te natura* and he takes the concept of ecotourism seriously. He's also a defender of Polynesian tradition, and in 1987 and 1994 he organized firewalking rituals here, the first time this had happened in decades. Staying with Ato is a good way to experience a slice of old Tahitian life, so long as you don't mind being away from the beach. Look for a paved road running inland from opposite a large stone engraved Bora 2000 at the head of Pofai Bay and follow it right up to the end past a water pumping station (there's no sign).

Chez Rosina (B.P. 51, 98730 Vaitape; tel./fax 67-70-91), next to Honeymoon Boutique a few hundred meters north of Village Pauline on Pofai Bay, has four rooms at CFP 4,500/6,000 single/double with private bath and shared cooking facilities. Breakfast and transfers are included. Rosina is friendly and her place is less crowded and less touristy than Pauline's but there's no beach.

In 1997 **Village Pauline** (Pauline Youssef, B.P. 215, 98730 Vaitape; tel. 67-72-16, fax 67-78-14) moved from the white beach where the Hôtel Le Maitai Polynesia now stands to a hot interior location (no breeze, many mosquitos) on Pofai Bay. Despite the downgrade, prices went up and you'll now pay CFP 1,800 pp to camp (own tent), CFP 2,500 in the eight-bed dormitory, or CFP 6,000 single or double for a room with shared bath. The thatched bungalows are CFP 9,000. Children under 11 are free. Communal cooking facilities are provided for campers but don't leave too much in their fridge as things tend to disappear. Bicycles rent for CFP 500/800/1,000 for two/four/eight hours. These accommodations are grossly overpriced and not recommended.

On the Matira Point peninsula are two excellent alternatives to the upmarket hotels. **Chez Nono** (Noël Leverd, B.P. 282, 98730 Vaitape; tel. 67-71-38, fax 67-74-27) faces the beach across from the Moana Beach Hôtel. They have one large bungalow with cooking facilities (CFP 10,000), two smaller bungalows with private bath (CFP 8,000), and a six-bedroom thatched guesthouse with shared kitchen at CFP 5,000/6,000 single/double per room. Ventilation spaces between the ceilings and walls mean you hear *everything* in the other rooms, but the atmosphere is amiable and all guests soon become good friends. Tahitians from other islands and local French often stay here. Their garden is a pleasant place to sit, but the bungalows occasionally experience a lot of noise from beach parties. The solar hot water heating only works when the sun is shining. Their boat tour around the island 0930-1600 includes shark feeding and an excellent fish lunch (CFP 5,000 including lunch).

Also good is **Chez Robert et Tina** (tel. 67-72-92), two European-style houses with cooking facilities down the road from Chez Nono at the tip of Matira Point (CFP 4,000/6,000 single/double). Robert offers excellent low-key lagoon trips at CFP 4,000 pp without lunch (the savings are passed on to you). You'll enjoy it more if you know a little French.

On the beach near the Moana Beach Parkroyal and just north of the junction to Matira Point is **Chez Maeva Masson** (Rosine Temauri-Masson, B.P. 33, 98730 Vaitape; tel. 67-72-04). There's no sign, but this large house has four rooms with shared bath at CFP 6,000 double, plus dorm beds at CFP 2,500 pp (CFP 1,000 pp surcharge for stays of only one night). Communal cooking facilities are provided and there's a picturesque lounge decorated with bright paintings by Rosine's late husband, the noted artist Jean Masson. It's one of the most colorful places to stay on the island, if you don't mind sharing the facilities.

Moderate

In Anau village to the north of Club Med is **Pension Chez Teipo** (B.P. 270, 98730 Vaitape; tel. 67-78-17, fax 67-73-24), also known as Pension Anau, with three neat little thatched bungalows by the lagoon at CFP 6,000/7,000/8,000 single/double/triple (children under 12 free). Cooking facilities are provided and it's a step up from Chez Stellio, a stone's throw away in the same village. There's no sign, so ask. Transfers are free.

Expensive

The **Yacht Club de Bora Bora** (B.P. 17, 98730 Vaitape; tel. 67-70-69), near Farepiti Wharf and opposite Te Ava Nui Pass, has two garden bungalows at CFP 9,000 for up to four persons and three overwater bungalows at CFP 10,000 double. No cooking facilities are provided and there's no beach. During the night you could be visited by mosquitoes and burglars. Cruising yachties may use the moorings, and fresh water and showers are provided. These services are free to cruisers who splash out in the outstanding seafood restaurant, otherwise they're CFP 2,500 per day per group, plus CFP 300 per shower (drinks at the bar are not good enough for free mooring). Yachties are asked not to carry bicycles through the restaurant. Beware of theft off yachts anywhere around this island.

Premium

Hôtel Matira (B.P. 31, 98730 Vaitape; tel. 67-70-51, fax 67-77-02) near Matira Point is one of the few medium-priced places offering cooking facilities. Their nine thatched bungalows with kitchenettes on the mountain side of the road are CFP 12,960/17,280 double/triple. The 16 deluxe thatched bungalows without kitchenettes in the annex right facing the lagoon at the neck of Matira Point peninsula are CFP 20,520/24,840 and up. The Matira's Chinese restaurant (closed Monday) is reasonable, and the beach is excellent. Airport transfers are CFP 1,000 pp return.

Motel Bora Bora (Jean Vanfau, B.P. 180, 98730 Vaitape; tel. 67-78-21, fax 67-77-57), on the main hotel strip across the street from Vairupe Villas, shares a white beach with the Sofitel Marara at Matira. Their four studios with bedroom, living room, dining room, kitchen, and fridge are CFP 13,000 double, while the three slightly larger apartments are CFP 17,000 double, extra persons CFP 3,000 each (children under 13 years CFP 1,500, under age six free). You'll probably have a great ocean view from your deck. These units built in 1991 are comfortable and spacious, a good compromise if you want to go upmarket while controlling expenditure. The cooking facilities make the motel ideal for families and there's a minimarket across the street. Transfers are CFP 1,500 pp return. Unfortunately mosquitos can be a real nuisance.

Luxury

Hôtel Bora Bora (B.P. 1, 98730 Vaitape; tel. 60-44-60, fax 60-44-66), which opened on a spectacular point in 1961, was the island's first large hotel. At CFP 70,000 single or double without meals for a deluxe overwater bungalow, it's one of the most exclusive millionaire's playgrounds in the South Pacific. Garden rooms in this ostentatious 55-unit resort begin at CFP 39,500 single or double, CFP 47,000 triple. Rather than pay CFP 65,000 for a rather poorly situated overwater bungalow, for the same price take one of the eight deluxe bungalows each with its own private swimming pool, but beware of noisy rooms near the road. Breakfast and dinner are CFP 7,200 pp

extra. Their beach is superb and the hotel restaurant's cuisine exceptional.

Japanese-owned **Hôtel Moana Beach Parkroyal** (B.P. 156, 98730 Vaitape; tel. 60-49-00, fax 60-49-99), on a superb white-sand beach at Matira Point, opened in 1987. One of the 10 beachfront bungalows here will set you back CFP 49,800 single or double plus tax; the 41 posh overwater bungalows are CFP 63,800 (children under 14 free). It's CFP 6,800 pp extra for breakfast and dinner. We've had reports of unpleasant sewer smells around the overwater bungalows.

Hôtel Le Maitai Polynesia (B.P. 505, 98730 Vaitape; tel. 60-30-00, fax 67-66-03) is on the site of the former Camping Chez Pauline at Matira. In 1997 the backpackers were bumped from this piece of prime real estate and in 1998 a new three-story hotel was opened. The 28 a/c rooms in the main complex are CFP 21,900 single or double, CFP 27,990 triple, plus tax (children under 12 free). The six beach bungalows go for CFP 31,620, while the 11 overwater bungalows are CFP 39,180. Although the prices indicate otherwise, this place still has a budget feel. A hundred meters north and on the inland side of the road is **Vairupe Villas**, which is under the same management. The 10 spacious thatched villas with kitchen and TV are CFP 29,460 for up to four people. Although the cooking facilities are useful, the villas are not on the beach and seem rather exorbitant compared to the places in the premium category above.

Somehow the **Hôtel Sofitel Marara** (B.P. 6, 98730 Vaitape; tel. 67-70-46, fax 67-74-03) is less pretentious than most of the other luxury places. The Sofitel Marara (the name means "Flying Fish") was built in 1978 to house the crew filming Dino de Laurentiis's *Hurricane* (based on a novel by Nordhoff and Hall); the film flopped but the hotel has been going strong ever since. The 32 garden bungalows are CFP 30,000 single or double plus tax, the 11 beach bungalows CFP 39,000, and the 21 larger overwater units, arranged along the shore rather than far out in the lagoon, are CFP 50,000. This is less than what some of the other top-end hotels charge and you shouldn't expect quite the same degree of opulence. Still, it's open and informal, and instead of the Americans you hear at Hôtel Bora Bora and the Japanese you see at the Moana Beach, the Marara caters to an international mix of tourists. The beach doesn't have the policed feel of the Bora Bora's, and this is the only hotel on the main island with a swimming pool. The Marara's bar is fairly reasonable for such a swank place but the restaurant isn't highly rated (and the service is incredibly slow). Luckily there are lots of other restaurants nearby.

In late 1993 a 150-bungalow **Club Méditerranée** (B.P. 34, 98730 Vaitape; tel. 60-46-04, fax 60-46-11) opened on the southeast side of Bora Bora to replace an earlier Club Med north of Vaitape. The circuminsular road had to be rerouted around this US$30-million enclave just north of the Sofitel, and as usual, security is tight. You can't just stroll in and rent a room at Club Med, as only prepackaged guests are allowed to set foot on these sanctified premises, so book in advance at the Club Med office in Papeete's Vaima Center (tel. 42-96-99) or at any travel agency (two-night minimum stay). The Bora Bora Club Med is more chic than the larger Club Med on Moorea, and as usual, lavish buffet meals and a range of nonmotorized nautical activities are included in the basic price. The gaudy orange and yellow bungalows go for CFP 19,000 pp in the garden or CFP 22,800 pp on the beach, double occupancy (singles can be matched with other same-sex singles). Some of the "oceanview" units are far from the water. Club Med is good value for Bora Bora when you consider how much you save on food. There's a dazzling beach and a canoe shuttle out to a fabulous snorkeling spot. Plenty of "animation" is laid on by the staff and the eclectic clientele can be fun, if you're sociable. Club's disco is the wildest nightspot on the island. For just a taste of paradise, the CFP 5,500 day pass includes a splendid lunch with drinks plus unlimited sporting activities and *motu* transfers. Unfortunately, bicycles are not available (Boutique Hibiscus on the hill behind the resort rents them).

Several of the *motus* bear outlandishly expensive tourist resorts, such as the Hôtel Bora Bora Pearl Beach Resort on Teveiroa Island between the airport and Vaitape, the Bora Bora Lagoon Resort on Toopua Island opposite Vaitape, and Le Méridien Bora Bora on a 10-km-long *motu* opposite Fitiuu Point. As if to disprove the theory that Bora Bora is already overbuilt, Outrigger Hotels of Hawaii is to erect a 79-unit hotel with hillside and overwater bungalows on the site of the old Club Méditerranée near Vaitape.

FOOD

Vaitape
Pâtisserie-Bar Le Vaitape, across the street from the Banque de Polynésie in Vaitape, has reasonable beer prices and the *poisson cru* (CFP 700) is excellent, but they don't have it every day (ask). Their coffee is terrible.

Snack Michel (no phone; weekdays 0630-1600, Sunday 0730-1500, closed Saturday), opposite the college just north of Magasin Chin Lee, serves filling meals for CFP 700 (but no alcohol). Try the *ma'a tinito*. You eat at picnic tables behind a thatched roof. This good local place is a little hard to find as the sign is not visible from the street.

The **Restaurant Manuia** at the Collège de Bora Bora (tel. 67-71-47), just north of Magasin Chin Lee in Vaitape, is used to train students for employment at the large hotels. Since their aim is not profit, you can get a three-course meal for CFP 1,200 here, but only on Wednesday and Friday 1130-1330 during the school year (mid-January to June and August to mid-December). It's a nice change of pace and excellent value.

Cold Hinano beer is available for a reasonable price at the **Jeu Association Amical Tahitien Club** (tel. 43-48-63) next to Farepiti Wharf. You must consume your beer at one of their picnic tables as they don't want to lose any bottles. It's a good stop on your way around the island and the perfect place to sit and wait for your boat.

Pofai Bay
Bloody Mary's (closed Sunday; tel. 67-72-86) on Pofai Bay is the longest established nonhotel restaurant on the island with a tradition dating back to 1979. A board outside lists "famous guests," including Jane Fonda and Baron George Von Dangel. Other than pizza, the lunch menu (available 1100-1500) includes fish and chips (CFP 900) and *poisson cru* (CFP 1,000). Upmarket seafood is served at dinner (1830-2100). For ambience, menu, service, and staff it's

hard to beat. Free hotel pickups for diners are available at 1830 if you call ahead.

The **Bamboo House Restaurant** (tel. 67-76-24), next to Le Jardin Gauguin nearby, tries to challenge Bloody Mary's famous seafood but doesn't quite succeed. In the South Pacific, one should get a slab of mahimahi, not cubes—those could be anything. It's also a bit cramped.

The **Blue Lagoon Restaurant** (tel. 67-65-64; daily 1000-0200), south of Vaitape by the lagoon at the entrance to Pofai Bay, offers things like pizza (CFP 1,000) and lobster (from CFP 1,500). Free hotel pickups are available.

Matira

Facing the beach just east of Hôtel Bora Bora are two reasonable places to eat. **Ben's Snack** (tel. 67-74-54) manages to turn out surprisingly good home-cooked pizza (CFP 1,000), lasagna, pasta, and omelettes, and the colorful American-Tahitian owners, Robin and Ben, add a Bohemian air to the place. Lunch here would be a great change of pace if you're staying at one of the fancy resorts. **Snack Matira** (tel. 67-77-32; closed Monday), across the street and a bit east, offers hamburgers and *poisson cru* for slightly lower prices.

Snack-Restaurant Le Temanuata (tel. 67-75-61), near the turnoff to the Moana Beach Parkroyal, offers meats, seafood, fish, and Chinese dishes. The dinner menu is expensive so you might come for lunch (1200-1430).

Snack Kaina Beach serves hamburgers and various types of fish including *poisson cru* in their garden between the Moana Beach and Sofitel (daily until 2200).

In 1995 **Restaurant Le Tiare** (tel. 67-61-39) opened across the street from the Bora Bora Motel. In the evening the tables are all taken, which perhaps says something about the restaurants in the nearby Bora Bora Beach Club and Sofitel Marara. You've a choice of pasta, meat, fish, lobster, and other seafood.

Groceries

Bora Bora's largest supermarket is **Magasin Chin Lee** (tel. 67-63-07; open Mon.-Sat. 0500-1800), opposite the island's Mobil gas station north of Vaitape Wharf. Takeaway meals at the checkout counters are CFP 500. It and another well-stocked grocery store in Vaitape are open

Mon.-Sat. 0500-1800. The Total service station is farther north.

Tiare Market (tel. 67-61-38; daily 0630-1300/1500-1830), opposite Motel Bora Bora at Matira, is very well stocked with a good wine section and even some fresh vegetables. It's always crowded with tourists from the upmarket hotels.

Other places to buy groceries are the two general stores (closed Sunday) at Anau, halfway around the island, and a small grocery store at the head of Pofai Bay. A grocery truck passes Matira between 1000 and 1100 daily except Sunday.

The **Pofai Shoppe** on the road near Hôtel Bora Bora sells cold fruit drinks and takeaway beer at normal prices (open daily).

ENTERTAINMENT AND EVENTS

Disco

Le Récife Bar (B.P. 278, 98730 Vaitape; tel. 67-73-87), between Vaitape and Farepiti Wharf, is Bora Bora's after-hours club, open Friday and Saturday from 2230. Disco dancing continues almost until dawn, but expect loud, heavy-on-the-beat music with few patrons. Steer clear of the local drunks hanging around outside who can't afford the CFP 500 cover charge.

Cultural Shows for Visitors

To see Polynesian dancing on the beach at **Hôtel Bora Bora** (tel. 60-44-60) grab a barside seat before it starts at 2030 on Wednesday and Sunday nights (buffet CFP 5,500).

Additional Tahitian dancing occurs after dinner Tuesday, Thursday, and Saturday nights at 2030 at the **Moana Beach Parkroyal** (tel. 60-49-00).

Another Tahitian dance show takes place at the **Hôtel Sofitel Marara** (tel. 67-74-01) every Tuesday, Friday, and Saturday night at 2030; see it all for the price of a draft beer. On Saturday at 1830 they open the earth oven and a Tahitian feast begins.

Events

The **Fêtes de Juillet** are celebrated at Bora Bora with special fervor. The canoe and bicycle races, javelin throwing, flower cars, singing, and dancing competitions run until 0300 nightly.

A public ball goes till dawn on the Saturday closest to 14 July. Try to participate in the 10-km foot race to prove that all tourists aren't lazy, but don't take the prizes away from the locals. If you win, be sure to give the money back to them for partying. You'll make good friends that way and have more fun dancing in the evening. The stands are beautiful because the top decorations win prizes, too.

SHOPPING AND SERVICES

Shopping

Plenty of small boutiques around Vaitape sell black coral jewelry, pearls, pareus, T-shirts, designer beachwear, etc. The **Centre Artisanal** near Vaitape Wharf is a good place to buy a shell necklace or a pareu directly from the locals.

A cluster of shops on Pofai Bay offers some of Bora Bora's best tourist shopping. **Boutique Gauguin** (tel. 67-76-67) has tropical clothing, T-shirts, souvenirs, and jewelry. Next door is an upmarket black pearl showroom called **O.P.E.C.** (tel. 67-61-62) where numbered black pearls complete with X-ray and certificate go for US$400-900. The pearls can be set in gold as earrings or necklaces in one day. A full pearl necklace will cost US$12,000—the gift of a lifetime. Alongside O.P.E.C. is **Art du Pacifique** (tel. 67-63-85) with a display of woodcarvings from the Marquesas Islands, and behind it is another shop selling shell jewelry and photographic supplies. These shops surround a small garden called *Le Jardin Gauguin* with a series of tacky plaster sculptures of scenes from Gauguin's paintings. A few hundred meters south of here is **Honeymoon Boutique** (tel. 67-78-19) with more clothing, jewelry, and souvenirs.

At photographer Erwin Christian's **Moana Art Boutique** (tel. 67-70-33) just north of Hôtel Bora Bora you can buy striking postcards and other souvenirs. **Martine's Créations** (tel. 67-70-79) east of Hôtel Bora Bora has finely crafted black-pearl jewelry and designer beachwear.

Services and Information

The four main banks all have offices near Vaitape Wharf, but none are open on Saturday (open weekdays 0730-1130/1330-1600). Many yachties "check out" of Tahiti-Polynesia at Bora Bora and reclaim their bond or *caution* at these banks. It's wise to check a few days ahead to make sure they'll have your cash or traveler's checks ready.

The post office (Monday 0800-1500, Tues.-Fri. 0730-1500, Saturday 0800-1000), *gendarmerie* (tel. 67-70-58), and health clinic *(Santé Publique)* are within a stone's throw of the wharf.

The helpful tourist information office (B.P. 144, 98730 Vaitape; tel./fax 67-76-36; weekdays 0730-1200, Saturday 0800-1130) and public toilets are in the Centre Artisanal next to Vaitape Wharf. The Air Tahiti office (tel. 67-70-35) is beside the Banque de Tahiti on Vaitape Wharf.

Health

The private Cabinet Médical (tel. 67-70-62) behind the Banque de Polynésie is open weekdays 0700-1200 and 1500-1800, Saturday 0700-1200.

Dr. François Macouin's Cabinet Dentaire (tel. 67-70-55; weekdays 0730-01130/1600-1800, Saturday 0730-1130) is in the Centre Commercial Le Pahia opposite Magasin Chin Lee and the large Protestant church.

Pharmacie Fare Ra'au (tel. 67-70-30; weekdays 0800-1200/1530-1800, Saturday 0800-1200/1700-1800, Sunday 0900-0930) is north of the wharf.

TRANSPORTATION

Getting There

Air Tahiti (tel. 67-70-35) has a useful transversal flight direct from Bora Bora to Rangiroa (CFP 20,700) and Manihi (CFP 23,400) three times a week. For information on flights to Bora Bora from Papeete, Huahine, and Raiatea, see the introduction to this chapter.

The high-speed cruiser *Ono-Ono* (tel./fax 68-85-85), with an office at Farepiti Wharf, departs Bora Bora for Taha'a (one hour, CFP 1,333), Raiatea (two hours, CFP 1,778), Huahine (3.5 hours, CFP 3,111), and Papeete (seven hours, CFP 6,610) on Tuesday and Thursday at 0700, Sunday at 1200. On Saturday there's a trip to Taha'a, Raiatea, and Huahine alone at 0800. Consider calling to check the schedule the afternoon before, as departures are often abruptly canceled.

Ships from Raiatea and Papeete tie up at Farepiti Wharf, three km north of Vaitape. The shipping companies have no representatives on Bora Bora, so for departure times just keep asking. Drivers of the *trucks* are the most likely to know. You buy your ticket when the ship arrives. Officially the *Taporo VI* leaves for Raiatea, Huahine, and Papeete on Tuesday, Thursday, and Saturday at 1130. The *Vaeanu* departs Bora Bora for Raiatea, Huahine, and Papeete Tuesday at 1030, Thursday at noon, and Sunday at 0900. The *Raromatai Ferry* leaves for Taha'a, Raiatea, Huahine, and Papeete Wednesday at 1000 and Sunday at 1400. Beware of ships leaving early.

A fast yellow-and-blue passenger ferry, the *Maupiti Express* (tel./fax 67-66-69), departs Vaitape Wharf for Maupiti, Taha'a, and Raiatea. It leaves for Maupiti on Thursday and Saturday at 0830 (CFP 3,000), for Taha'a and Raiatea on Wednesday and Friday at 0700 (CFP 2,500). Tickets are sold on board.

Getting Around

Getting around is a bit of a headache, as *le truck* service is irregular and at lunchtime everything stops. Public *trucks* usually meet the boats, but many of the *trucks* you see around town are strictly for guests of the luxury hotels. If you do find one willing to take you, fares between Vaitape and Matira vary from CFP 300-500, plus CFP 100 for luggage. Taxi fares are high, so check before getting in. If you rent a bicycle, keep an eye on it when you stop to visit sights.

Farepiti Rentacar (B.P. 53, 98730 Vaitape; tel. 67-71-58, fax 67-65-29), opposite Farepiti Wharf, has cars from CFP 4,500/5,500/6,500/7,500 for two/four/eight/24 hours with unlimited kilometers. Scooters are CFP 2,500/3,500/4,500/5,000 (CFP 3,000 deposit—no license required). Bicycles cost CFP 500/800/1,000/1,500. Third party insurance is included with the cars but collision insurance is not available. They can deliver cars to any hotel.

Europcar (tel. 67-70-15, fax 67-79-95; daily 0730-1800), next to the *gendarmerie* opposite Vaitape Wharf and with desks at 15 hotels around the island, has Fiats at CFP 6,000 for a 0800-1700 day, CFP 7,000 for 24 hours. The price includes insurance and unlimited kilometers; a valid driver's license is required. They

also have motor scooters for CFP 5,000 0800-1700 or CFP 5,500 for 24 hours (license required). Two-seater "fun cars" are CFP 4,500 for four hours and no helmet or driver's licence is required.

Avis (B.P. 99, 98730 Vaitape; tel. 67-70-31, fax 67-62-07), on the inland side of the road south of Vaitape (where you see a lot of long blue trucks parked), is also known as Fredo Rent a Car. Cars/scooters/bicycles are available at CFP 6,800/5,500/1,500 for eight hours.

Mataura Rent-A-Bike (tel. 67-73-16) just south of Vaitape rents bicycles (if you can find anyone around). At **Chez Pauline** bicycles are CFP 800 half day, CFP 1,000 full day.

Taahana Tourisme (tel. 67-64-04, fax 67-64-44), almost opposite the Sofitel Marara, rents scooters at CFP 2,500/3,500/4,500/5,000 for two/four/eight/24 hours and bicycles at CFP 500/800/1,000 two/four/eight hours. They also have jet skis, motor boats, and pedal boats.

Boutique Hibiscus (tel. 67-72-43), on the hill behind Club Med, rents well-maintained bicycles with baskets at CFP 400/600/800/1,000 for two/four/eight/24 hours. (Their T-shirts and pareus are also good value.)

If you rent a car and drive at night, watch out for scooters and bicycles without lights. However, to better enjoy the scenery and avoid disturbing the environment, we suggest you dispense with motorized transport here. Little Bora Bora is perfect for cycling as there's an excellent paved road right around the island (with only one unpaved stretch on the incline at Fitiuu Point), almost no hills, and lots of scenic bays to shelter you from the wind. Do exercise caution with fast-moving vehicles between Vaitape and Matira Point, however.

Land Tours

Otemanu Tours (tel. 67-70-49), just north of Vaitape, offers a 2.5-hour minibus tour around Bora Bora daily except Sunday at 1400 (CFP 2,000). **Jeep Safaris** (tel. 67-70-34) and **Tupuna 4WD Expeditions** (tel. 67-75-06) offer Land Rover tours up a steep ridge opposite Otemanu at CFP 5,500. You can book these and many other activities through **Taahana Tourisme** (tel. 67-64-04, fax 67-64-44), almost opposite the Sofitel Marara.

Day Cruises

Like Aitutaki in the Cook Islands, Bora Bora is famous for its lagoon trips. Prices vary depending on whether lunch is included, the length of the trip, the luxury of boat, etc., so check around. A seafood picnic lunch on a *motu*, reef walking, and snorkeling gear are usually included, and you get a chance to see giant clams, manta rays, and shark feeding. For the latter you don a mask and snorkel, jump into the shark-infested waters, and grasp a line as your guide shoves chunks of fish at a school of generally innocuous reef sharks in feeding frenzy. It's an encounter with the wild you'll never forget. See the Chez Nono and Chez Robert accommodations listings for two possibilities. Motorized canoe trips right around Bora Bora are also offered. An excursion of this kind is an essential part of the Bora Bora experience, so splurge on this one. (Several readers have written in to say they agree completely.)

Taahana Tourisme (tel. 67-64-04, fax 67-64-44), almost opposite the Sofitel Marara, operates a circle-island boat tour lasting 0900-1630 daily. The CFP 5,300 price includes a barbecue lunch, snorkeling with sting rays, and shark feeding. Half day boat trips are CFP 3,500. The same company also organizes catamaran cruises, one-day yacht charters, and deep-sea fishing.

Three-hour tours to the so-called **Bora Lagoonarium** (B.P. 56, 98730 Vaitape; tel. 67-71-34, fax 67-60-29) on a *motu* off the main island occur daily except Saturday at 0900 or 1400 (CFP 4,000). You'll see more colorful fish than you ever thought existed. Call for a free hotel pickup.

The activities people at the Sofitel Marara will ferry nonguests over to a *motu* for a day of snorkeling at CFP 1,500 return (take food, water, and sunscreen).

René et Maguy Boat Rental (B.P. 196, 98730 Vaitape; tel. 67-60-61, fax 67-61-01), next to Le Tiare Restaurant at Matira, rents small boats with motor at CFP 4,500/5,500/6,500/9,500 two hours/three hours/half day/full day. Pedal boats are CFP 3,500 for two hours, plus CFP 1,500 each for additional hours. *Motu* transfers are CFP 1,500 pp roundtrip. Free hotel pickups are available if you call.

Airport

Bora Bora's vast airfield (BOB) on Motu Mute north of the main island was built by the Americans during WW II. The first commercial flight from Paris to Tahiti-Polynesia landed here in October 1958, and until March 1961 all international flights used this airstrip; passengers were then transferred to Papeete by Catalina amphibious or Bermuda flying boat seaplanes. Today, a 25-minute catamaran ride brings arriving air passengers to Vaitape Wharf (included in the plane ticket).

When the catamaran from the airport arrives at Vaitape Wharf, all of the luxury hotels will have guest transportation waiting, but the budget places don't always meet the flights (the deluxe places don't bother meeting the interisland boats). As you arrive at the wharf, shout out the name of your hotel and you'll be directed to the right *truck* (they don't have destination signs).

The airport cafe serves a very good cup of coffee.

If you're flying to Bora Bora from Papeete go early in the morning and sit on the left side of the aircraft for spectacular views—it's only from the air that Bora Bora is the most beautiful island in the world!

MAUPITI

Majestic Maupiti (Maurua), 44 km west of Bora Bora, is the least known of the accessible Society Islands. Maupiti's mighty volcanic plug soars above a sapphire lagoon, and the vegetation-draped cliffs complement the magnificent *motu* beaches. Almost every bit of level land on the main island is taken up by fruit trees, while watermelons thrive on the surrounding *motus*. Maupiti abounds in native seabirds, including frigate birds, terns, and others. The absence of Indian mynahs allows you to see native land birds that are almost extinct elsewhere.

The 1,125 people live in the adjacent villages of Vai'ea, Farauru, and Pauma. Tourism is not promoted because there aren't any regular hotels, which is a big advantage! It's sort of like Bora Bora was 25 years ago before being "discovered" by the world of package tourism. Maupiti was once famous for its black basalt stone pounders and fishhooks made from the seven local varieties of mother-of-pearl shell. In late November 1997 Hurricane Oséa devastated Maupiti.

Sights

It takes only three hours to walk right around this 11-square-km island. The nine-km crushed-coral road, lined with breadfruit, mango, banana, and hibiscus, passes crumbling *marae*, freshwater springs, and a beach.

Marae Vaiahu, by the shore a few hundred meters beyond Hotuparaoa Massif, is the largest *marae*. Once a royal landing place opposite the pass into the lagoon, the *marae* still bears the king's throne and ancient burials. Nearby is the sorcerers' rock: light a fire beside this rock and you will die. Above the road are a few smaller *marae*.

Terei'a Beach, at the west tip of Maupiti, is the only good beach on the main island. At low tide you can wade across from Terei'a to Motu Auira in waist-deep water. **Marae Vaiorie** is a double *marae* with freshwater springs in between. As many as two dozen large *marae* are hidden in Maupiti's mountainous interior, and the island is known for its ghosts.

It's possible to climb to the 380-meter summit of Maupiti from the 42-meter-high saddle where the road cuts across Terei'a Point. You follow the ridge all the way to the top and the whole trip shouldn't take more than three hours roundtrip.

Accommodations

Several of the inhabitants take paying guests, and they usually meet the flights and boats in search of clients. The absence of a regular hotel on Maupiti throws together an odd mix of vacationing French couples, backpackers, and "adventuresome" tourists in the guesthouses (none of which have signs). Agree on the price beforehand and check your bill when you leave. You could camp on the white sands of Terei'a Beach, but water and *no-nos* (insects) would be a problem. If you're set on camping, get across to the airport *motu,* hike south, and look for a campsite there—you'll have to befriend someone to obtain water. Otherwise check with Pension Auira, which allows camping on their grounds. Like Bora Bora, Maupiti experiences serious water shortages during the dry season.

Chez Mareta (Mareta and Anua Tinorua, tel. 67-80-25), in the center of Vai'ea village, is the house with the sloping blue roof a few minutes' walk from the *mairie*. They offer mattresses on the floor in the upstairs double rooms for CFP 1,000 pp. You can cook your own food or pay CFP 3,000 pp for breakfast and dinner. An agreeable sitting room faces the lagoon downstairs. Upon request, they'll drop you on a *motu* for the day (beware of sunburn). Chez Mareta is okay for a couple of days, but not an extended stay. The church choir in the next building practices their singing quite loudly each night. Budget.

Next door to Chez Mareta is **Chez Floriette Tuheiava** (B.P. 43, 98732 Maupiti; tel. 67-80-85), an island-style house with four pleasant shared-bath rooms at CFP 5,000/7,800 single/double including breakfast, dinner, activities, and airport transfers. Moderate. Other places of the same type include **Pension Eri** (Eri Mohi, tel. 67-81-29), south of Chez Floriette, with four rooms in a separate house at CFP 4,500 pp with breakfast and dinner, and **Pension Marau** (Tino and Marau Tehahe, tel. 67-81-19), on the hillside north of the *mairie,* with three rooms at CFP 4,500 pp including half board and transfers. Moderate.

Pension Tamati (Ferdinand and Etu Tapuhiro, tel. 67-80-10), a two-story building at the south end of Vai'ea, rents eight bleak rooms at CFP 2,000 pp with breakfast or CFP 4,000 pp with half board. Unfortunately, tourists are usually given the inside rooms without proper ventilation, but communal cooking facilities are available. Moderate.

Fare Pae'ao (Janine Tavaearii, B.P. 33, 98732 Maupiti; tel./fax 67-81-01) on Motu Pae'ao is quiet

and offers a superb white beach with some of the finest snorkeling on Maupiti. The three thatched bungalows with bath are CFP 6,000 single or double, CFP 7,500 triple. Meals cost CFP 3,000/5,000 pp for two/three meals (children under 13 half price). Reservations are required to ensure an airport pickup (CFP 1,000 pp roundtrip for everyone over the age of three). (In 1962 Kenneth Emory and Yosihiko Sinoto excavated a prehistoric cemetery on Pae'ao and found 15 adzes of six different types, providing valuable evidence for the study of Polynesian migrations.) Moderate.

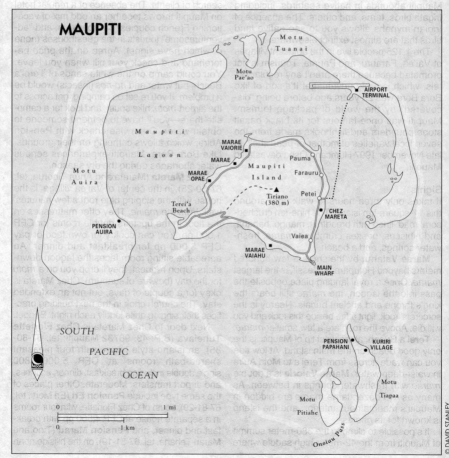

Pension Auira (Edna Terai and Richard Tefaatau, B.P. 2, 98732 Maupiti; tel./fax 67-80-26) on Motu Auira, the *motu* opposite Terei'a Beach, has seven thatched bungalows with private bath. The garden variety are CFP 6,000 pp a day including breakfast and dinner; the better quality beach bungalows are CFP 7,000 pp. At those prices you'd expect fans in the rooms, reading lights, beach furniture, and nautical activities, but no such luck. Camping is CFP 1,000 pp. The food is good but the beach could use a cleaning. Boat transfers from the airport are CFP 2,000 pp return. In sum, Pension Auira is a wonderful experience, but not for everyone. Premium.

In addition, there are two small resorts on Motu Tiapa'a, one of the islands framing Onoiau Pass. **Pension Papahani** (Vilna Tuheiava, B.P. 1, 98732 Maupiti; tel. 67-81-58, fax 67-80-11) has a four-room house with shared bath at CFP 5,000 pp and two thatched bungalows with private bath at CFP 6,500 pp, both including breakfast and dinner. Excursions and return airport transfers are CFP 2,000 pp. Expensive. The four *fares* with bath at the **Kuriri Village** (Gérard Bede, B.P. 23, 98732 Maupiti; no phone; fax 67-82-00), also on Tiapa'a, are Maupiti's most expensive at CFP 10,000/12,000 pp with half/full board, transfers included. Luxury.

Services
Banque Socredo (tel. 67-81-95) has a branch on Maupiti, but it's not always operating, so change beforehand and don't count on using your credit cards. The post office and *mairie* are nearby. The bakery is in the power plant on the edge of town. It's important to check when the baguettes come out of the oven and to be punctual, as they sell out fast. The island youths come here an hour before and hang around waiting. Not all stores sell beer and the island's supply does run out at times.

Getting There
Like that of Bora Bora, Maupiti's airport (MAU) is on a small *motu* and you must take a launch to the main island (CFP 400 pp). **Air Tahiti** has flights to Maupiti from Raiatea (CFP 5,600 one-way) and Papeete (CFP 12,700) three times a week, from Bora Bora twice a week (CFP 5,300). Reconfirm with the Air Tahiti agent (tel. 67-80-20) near the *mairie*.

The 62-seat fast ferry *Maupiti Express* arrives from Bora Bora (CFP 3,000 each way) on Thursday and Saturday mornings, returning to Bora Bora the same afternoon.

The government supply barges *Meherio III* or *Maupiti Tou Ai'a* depart Papeete for Raiatea and Maupiti Wednesday at 1900, departing Maupiti for the return Friday at 0800. Deck fares from Maupiti are CFP 1,058/2,221 to Raiatea/Papeete. See the chapter introduction for more information.

Ships must enter the channel during daylight, thus the compulsory morning arrival, and the boat usually returns to Raiatea from Maupiti on the afternoon of the same day. Onoiau Pass into Maupiti is narrow, and when there's a strong southerly wind it can be dangerous—boats have had to turn back. At low tide a strong current flows out through this pass and the optimum time for a yacht to enter is around noon.

OTHER LEEWARD ISLANDS

Tupai
Tupai or Motu Iti (Small Island), 13 km north of Bora Bora, is a tiny coral atoll measuring 1,100 hectares. The facing horseshoe-shaped *motus* enclose a lagoon that small boats can enter through a pass on the east side. A small airstrip is in the northwest corner of the atoll. In 1860 the king of Bora Bora gave the atoll to a planter named Stackett and for decades a few dozen people were employed to make copra from coconuts off the 155,000 trees on Tupai. In 1997 the territorial government bought Tupai from its last owner, a Mr. Lejeune, for US$8 million with an eye to resort development. Although there are no permanent inhabitants at the moment, the 1,000 traditional landowners are contesting the title.

Maupihaa
Tiny 360-hectare Maupihaa (Mopelia), 185 km southeast of Maupiti, is the only Society Islands atoll that can be entered by yachts, but to at-

tempt to do so in stormy weather is dangerous. Narrow, unmarked Taihaaru Vahine Pass on Maupihaa's northwest side can only be found by searching for the strong outflow of lagoon water at low tide. Despite this, cruising yachts traveling between Bora Bora and Cook Islands or Samoa often anchor in the atoll's lagoon. About 50 people from Maupiti live on Maupihaa.

In July 1917 the notorious German raider *Seeadler* was wrecked at Maupihaa after capturing 15 Allied ships. The three-masted schooner was too large to enter lagoon, and while being careened outside the pass, a freak tsunami picked the vessel up and threw it onto the reef. Eventually the ship's chivalrous captain, Count Felix von Luckner, was able to carry on to Fiji in a small boat, where he was captured at Wakaya Island. Count von Luckner's journal, *The Sea Devil,* became a best-seller after the war.

Sea turtles come to Maupihaa to lay their eggs only to be illegally butchered for their flesh by poachers. Large numbers of terns, boobies, and frigate birds nest on the small *motus* and seabird fledglings are slaughtered for their meager meat or the unhatched eggs collected according to need. All this is supposed to be prohibited but it's hard to control what goes on in such an isolated place. (In August 1996, the municipal boat *Maupiti Tou Ai'a* was seized with a cargo of 1,500 kilos of turtle meat on board. At the trial 10 months later, the captain and 30 others were fined and each given a one-month suspended sentence over the affair.)

Manuae

Manuae (Scilly), 75 km northwest of Maupihaa, is the westernmost of the Society Islands. This atoll is 15 km in diameter but totals only 400 hectares. Pearl divers once visited Manuae. In 1855 the three-masted schooner *Julia Ann* sank on the Manuae reef. It took the survivors two months to build a small boat, which carried them to safety at Raiatea.

Motu One

Motu One (Bellingshausen), 65 km north of Manuae, got its second name from the Russian explorer Thadeus von Bellingshausen who visited Tahiti in 1820. Tiny 280-hectare Motu One is circled by a guano-bearing reef, with no pass into the lagoon. Of the 10 persons present on Motu One when Hurricane Martin swept through in November 1997, the sole survivor was a woman named Alice Haano who tied herself to a coconut tree.

THE AUSTRAL ISLANDS

The inhabited volcanic islands of Rimatara, Rurutu, Tubuai, Raivavae, and Rapa, plus uninhabited Maria (or Hull) atoll, make up the Austral group. This southernmost island chain in the South Pacific is a 1,280-km extension of the same submerged mountain range as the southern Cook Islands, 900 km northwest. The islands of the Australs seldom exceed 300 meters, except Rapa, which soars to 650 meters. The southerly location makes these islands notably cooler and drier than Tahiti. Collectively the Australs are known as Tuhaa Pae, the "Fifth Part" or fifth administrative subdivision of Tahiti-Polynesia. It's still a world apart from tourism.

History

Excavations carried out on the northwest coast of Rurutu uncovered 60 round-ended houses arranged in parallel rows, with 14 *marae* scattered among them, demonstrating the presence of humans here as early as A.D. 900. Ruins of *marae* can also be seen on Rimatara, Tubuai, and Raivavae. Huge stone tikis once graced Raivavae, but most have since been destroyed or removed. The terraced mountain fortifications, or *pa,* on Rapa are unique.

Rurutu was spotted by Capt. James Cook in 1769; he found Tubuai in 1777. In 1789 Fletcher Christian and the *Bounty* mutineers attempted to establish a settlement at the northeast corner of Tubuai. They left after only three months, following battles with the islanders in which 66 Polynesians died. The European discoverer of Rapa was Capt. George Vancouver in 1791. Rimatara wasn't contacted until 1813, by the Australian captain Michael Fodger.

English missionaries converted most of the people to Protestantism in the early 19th century. Whalers and sandalwood ships introduced diseases and firearms, which decimated the Austral islanders. The French didn't complete their annexation of the group until 1901. Since then the Australs have gone their sleepy way. Today the 6,500 mostly Polynesian inhabitants are fishermen and farmers who live in attractive villages with homes and churches built of coral limestone. Many people from the Australs live in Papeete.

Getting There

Air Tahiti has four flights a week to Rurutu and Tubuai, the only islands with airports. Two operate Papeete-Tubuai-Rurutu-Papeete, the other two Papeete-Rurutu-Tubuai-Papeete. One-way fares from Tahiti are CFP 17,700 to Rurutu and CFP 19,800 to Tubuai. Rurutu-Tubuai is CFP 8,300.

All the other Austral Islands are accessible only by boat. For information on the twice-monthly sailings of the *Tuhaa Pae II* from Papeete, see the introduction to Tahiti-Polynesia.

RURUTU

This island, 572 km south of Tahiti, is shaped like a miniature replica of the African continent. For the hiker, 32-square-km Rurutu is a more varied island to visit than Tubuai. Grassy, fern-covered Taatioe (389 meters) and Manureva (384 meters) are the highest peaks and coastal cliffs on the southeast side of the island drop 60 meters to the sea. A narrow fringing reef surrounds Rurutu, but there's no lagoon. The climate of this northernmost Austral island is temperate and dry. The recent history of Rurutu revolves around four important dates: 1821, when the gospel arrived on the island; 1889, when France declared a protectorate over the island; 1970, when Cyclone Emma devastated the three villages; and 1975, when the airport opened.

In January and July Rurutuans practice the ancient art of stone lifting or *amoraa ofai*. Men get three tries to hoist a 150-kg boulder coated with *monoï* (coconut oil) up onto their shoulders, while women attempt a 60-kg stone. Dancing and feasting follow the event. The women of Rurutu weave fine pandanus hats, bags, baskets, fans, lamp shades, and mats. A fine handicraft display is laid out for departing passengers. Rurutu's famous Manureva (Soaring Bird) Dance Group has performed around the world. The main evening entertainment is watching dancers practice in the villages.

Orientation

The pleasant main village, **Moerai,** boasts a post office, medical center, four small stores, two bakeries, and a bank. Two other villages, Avera and Hauti, bring the total island population to about 2,000. Neat fences and flower gardens surround the coral limestone houses. This is the Polynesia of 50 years ago: though snack bars have appeared and electricity functions 24 hours a day, there's almost none of the tourism development you see in the Society Islands nor the pearl farms common in the Tuamotus.

Public transportation is also lacking on the 36-km road around Rurutu, and even by bicycle it can be quite an effort to circle the island as the route climbs away from the coast on four occasions to avoid high cliffs. South of Avera the road reaches 190 meters, dropping back down to sea level at the southern tip, then rising again to 124 meters on the way up to Hauti. The direct road from Moerai to Avera also climbs to 168 meters. For hikers a three-km foot trail across the center of the island between Avera and Hauti makes a variety of itineraries possible. Beaches, waterfalls, valleys, bluffs, and limestone caves beckon the undaunted explorer.

One of the nicest spots is near **Toataratara Point** where a side road cuts back up the east coast to a *marae* and a few small beaches. It's quite easy to hike to the TV tower on the summit of **Manureva** from either the 200-meter-high Tetuanui Plateau toward the airport or the saddle of the Moerai-Avera road. Rurutu's highest peak, Taatioe, is nearby.

Accommodations

The **Hôtel Rurutu Village** (B.P. 22, 98753 Moerai; tel. 94-03-92, fax 94-05-01), on a beach a kilometer west of the airport, is the only regular hotel in the Austral Islands. The eight tin-roofed bungalows with bath go for CFP 3,500/4,500 single/double, plus CFP 500 for breakfast and CFP 2,500 each for lunch and dinner (if required). Facilities encompass a restaurant, bar, and swimming pool. Inexpensive.

Pension Catherine (B.P. 11, 98753 Moerai; tel. 94-02-43, fax 94-06-99), in a concrete building behind Moerai's Protestant church, has 10 rooms with bath at CFP 3,000/4,000 single/double, plus CFP 2,500/4,000 pp for half/full board (monthly rates available). Car rentals, scuba diving, and deep-sea fishing can be arranged. Airport transfers are free. Inexpensive.

Services and Transportation
Banque Socredo (tel. 94-04-75) and the post office are at Moerai. The *gendarmerie* (tel. 94-03-61) is at the east end of Moerai.

Unaa Airport (RUR) is at the north tip of Rurutu, four km from Moerai. **Air Tahiti** can be reached at tel. 94-03-57. The supply ship from Papeete ties up at Moerai.

TUBUAI

Ten-km-long by five-km-wide Tubuai, largest of the Australs, is 670 km south of Tahiti. Hills on the east and west sides of this oval 45-square-km island are joined by lowland in the middle; when seen from the sea Tubuai looks like two islands. Mount Taitaa (422 meters) is its highest point. Tubuai is surrounded by a barrier reef; a pass on the north side gives access to a wide turquoise lagoon bordered by brilliant white-sand beaches. Picnics are often arranged on the small reef *motus,* amid superb snorkeling grounds, and surfers are just discovering Tubuai's possibilities.

Tubuai has a mean annual temperature 3° C lower than Tahiti and it's at its driest and sunniest Sept.-November. The brisk climate permits the cultivation of potatoes, carrots, oranges, and coffee, but other vegetation is sparse. Several *marae* are on Tubuai, but they're in extremely bad condition, with potatoes growing on the sites. The *Bounty* mutineers attempted unsuccessfully to settle on Tubuai in 1789 (though nothing remains of their Fort George, southeast of Taahuaia). Mormon missionaries arrived as early as 1844, and today there are active branches of the Church of Latter-day Saints in all the villages. The islanders weave fine pandanus hats, and some woodcarving is done at Mahu.

Most of the 2,050 inhabitants live in Mataura and Taahuaia villages on the north coast, though

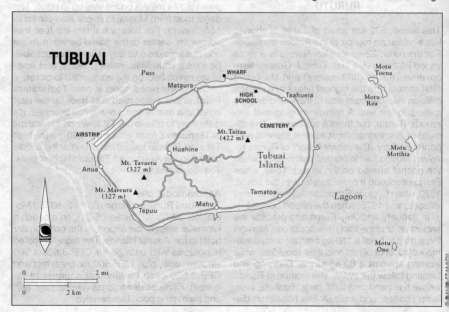

TUBUAI

Pass
Mataura — WHARF
HIGH SCHOOL
Taahueia
Motu Toena
Motu Roa
AIRSTRIP
CEMETERY
Mt. Taitaa (422 m) ▲
Huahine
Motu Motihia
Anua
Mt. Tavaetu (327 m) ▲
Tubuai Island
Mt. Mareura (327 m) ▲
Tamatoa
Lagoon
Tepuu
Mahu
Motu One

MOON

0   2 mi
0   2 km

houses and hamlets are found all along the level 24-km road around the island. An eight-km road cuts right across the middle of Tubuai to Mahu village on the south coast, but even this presents no challenges for bicyclists (it's an easy hike to the summit of Mt. Taitaa from this road). Mataura is the administrative center of the Austral Islands, and the post office, hospital, dental clinic, *gendarmerie* (tel. 95-03-33), and the branches of two banks are here. The two stores at Mataura bake bread. There's no public transportation so plan on doing a lot of walking.

Accommodations and Food

Pension Vaiteanui (Mélinda Bodin, B.P. 141, 98754 Mataura; tel./fax 95-04-19), near a small beach between the airstrip and Mataura, has five rooms with bath in a long block at CFP 2,500/4,000 single/double, plus CFP 2,500 pp for half board (no cooking facilities). Inexpensive.

Nearby is **Chez Sam et Yolande** (Yolande Tahuhuterani, B.P. 77, 98754 Mataura; tel./fax 95-05-52) with five rooms at CFP 2,500/4,000 single/double and you can cook. Inexpensive.

Also in Mataura, **Chez Doudou** (B.P. 64, 98754 Mataura; tel. 95-06-71) has 20 rooms with bath in a long two-story building at CFP 3,000/4,500 single/double. Cooking facilities are not provided, and breakfast and dinner are CFP 2,300 pp extra. Inexpensive.

Getting There

Tubuai Airport (TUB), in the northwest corner of the island, opened in 1972. The best beach on the main island is beside the five-km road from the airport to Mataura. **Air Tahiti** (tel. 95-04-76) arrives from Rurutu and Papeete several times a week. Ships enter the lagoon through a passage in the barrier reef on the north side and proceed to the wharf a kilometer east of Mataura. Otherwise, the lagoon is too shallow for navigation.

OTHER AUSTRAL ISLANDS

Rimatara

Without airport, harbor, wharf, hotels, restaurants, bars, and taxis, Rimatara is a place to escape the world. Only a narrow fringing reef hugs Rimatara's lagoonless shore; arriving passengers are landed at Amaru or Mutua Ura by whale-boat. This smallest (nine square km) and lowest (84 meters) of the Australs is home to fewer than 1,000 people. Dirt roads lead from Amaru, the main village, to Anapoto and Mutua Ura.

Uninhabited Maria (or Hull) is a four-islet atoll 192 km northwest of Rimatara, visited once or twice a year by men from Rimatara or Rurutu for fishing and copra making. They stay on the atoll two or three months, among seabirds and giant lobsters.

Raivavae

This appealing, nine-km-long and two-km-wide island is just south of the tropic of Capricorn, and thus outside the tropics. It's the third most southerly island in the South Pacific (only Rapa and Easter Island are farther south). Fern-covered Mt. Hiro (437 meters) is the highest point on 18-square-km Raivavae. A barrier reef encloses an emerald lagoon, but the 20 small coral *motus* are all located on the southern and eastern portions of the reef.

A malignant fever epidemic in 1826 reduced the people of Raivavae from 3,000 to 120. The present population of around 1,050 lives in four coastal villages, Rairua, Mahanatoa, Anatonu, and Vaiuru, linked by a dirt road. A shortcut route direct from Rairua to Vaiuru crosses a 119-meter saddle, with splendid views of the island.

Different teams led by Frank Stimson, Don Marshall, and Thor Heyerdahl have explored the ancient temples and taro terraces of Raivavae. Many two- to three-meter-high stone statues once stood on the island, but most have since been destroyed, and two were removed to Tahiti where they can be seen on the grounds of the Gauguin Museum. One big tiki is still standing by the road between Rairua and Mahanatoa villages.

The inhabitants of Raivavae have decided they don't want an airport. If you'll be taking a boat to the Australs anyway, you may as well go to Raivavae, where airborne tourists can't follow! Ships enter the lagoon through a pass on the north side and tie up to the pier at Rairua. A boat calls at the island about every 10-14 days. Several people rent rooms.

Rapa

At 27°38' south latitude, Rapa is the southernmost island in the South Pacific, and one of the most isolated and spectacular. Its nearest neighbor is Raivavae, 600 km away, and Tahiti is 1,300 km north. It's sometimes called Rapa Iti (Little Rapa) to distinguish it from Rapa Nui (Easter Island). Soaring peaks reaching 650 meters surround magnificent Haurei Bay, Rapa's crater harbor, the western portion of a drowned volcano. This is only one of 12 deeply indented bays around the island; the absence of reefs allows the sea to cut into the 40-square-km island's outer coasts. Offshore are several sugarloaf-shaped islets. The east slopes of the mountains are bare, while large fern forests are found on the west. Coconut trees cannot grow in the foggy, temperate climate. Instead coffee and taro are the main crops.

A timeworn **Polynesian fortress** with terraces is situated on the crest of a ridge at Morongo Uta, commanding a wide outlook over the steep, rugged hills. Morongo Uta was cleared of vegetation by a party of archaeologists led by William Mulloy in 1956 and is still easily visitable. Half a dozen of these *pa* (fortresses) are found above the bay, built to defend the territories of the different tribes of overpopulated ancient Rapa. Today the young men of Rapa organize eight-day bivouacs to hunt wild goats, which range across the island.

During the two decades following the arrival of missionaries in 1826, Rapa's population dropped from 2,000 to 300 due to the introduction of European diseases. By 1851 it was down to just 70, and after smallpox arrived on a Peruvian ship in 1863 it was a miracle that anyone survived at all. The present population of about 550 lives at Area and Haurei villages on the north and south sides of Rapa's great open bay, connected only by boat. A number of local residents rent rooms in their homes at CFP 4,500 pp including meals. The *Tuhaa Pae II* calls at Rapa every four to six weeks, so that's how long you'll be there.

Marotiri, or the "Bass Rocks," are 10 uninhabited islets totaling just four hectares, 74 km southeast of Rapa. Amazingly enough, some of these pinnacles are crowned with man-made stone platforms and round "towers." One 105-meter-high pinnacle is visible from Rapa in very clear weather. Landing is difficult.

THE TUAMOTU ISLANDS

Arrayed in two parallel northwest-southeast chains scattered across an area of ocean 600 km wide and 1,500 km long, the Tuamotus are the largest group of coral atolls in the world. Of the 78 atolls in the group, 21 have one entrance (pass), 10 have two passes, and 47 have no pass at all. A total of around 14,500 people live on the 48 inhabited islands. Although the land area of the Tuamotus is only 726 square km, the lagoons of the atolls total some 6,000 square km of sheltered water. All are atolls: some have an unbroken ring of reef around the lagoon, while others appear as a necklace of islets separated by channels.

Variable currents, sudden storms, and poor charts make cruising this group by yacht extremely hazardous—in fact, the Tuamotus are popularly known as the Dangerous Archipelago, or the Labyrinth. Wrecks litter the reefs of many atolls. The breakers only become visible when one is within eight km of the reef, and once in, a yacht must carry on through the group. The usual route is to sail either between Rangiroa and Arutua after a stop at Ahe, or through the Passe de Fakarava between Toau and Fakarava. Winds are generally from the east, varying to northeast Nov.-May and southeast June-October. A series of hurricanes devastated these islands between 1980 and 1983.

The resourceful Tuamotu people have always lived from seafood, pandanus nuts, and coconuts. They once dove to depths of 30 meters and more, wearing only tiny goggles, to collect mother-of-pearl shells. This activity has largely ceased as overharvesting has made the oysters rare. Cultured black pearls *(Pinctada margaritifera)* from the Tuamotus and Gambiers are world famous and cultured-pearl farms operate on many of the atolls. The pearl industry has reversed the depopulation of the atolls and spread prosperity through this remote region.

The scarcity of land and fresh water has always been a major problem. Many of these dry, coconut-covered atolls have only a few hundred inhabitants. Although airstrips exist on 26 islands, the isolation has led many Tuamotuans to

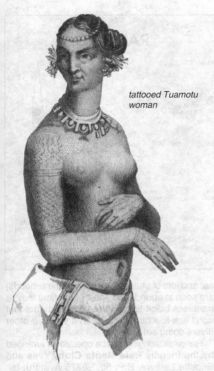

tattooed Tuamotu woman

RANGIROA

Rangiroa, 350 km northeast of Papeete, is the Tuamotus' most populous atoll and the largest in Polynesia (although Ontong Java in the Solomons is bigger). Its 1,020-square-km aquamarine lagoon is 78 km long, 24 km wide (too far to see), and 225 km around—the island of Tahiti would fit inside its reef. The name Rangiroa means "extended sky." Some 240 *motus* sit on this reef.

Two deep passages through the north side of the atoll's coral ring allow a constant exchange of water between the open sea and the lagoon, creating a most fertile habitat. While lagoons in the Society Islands are often murky due to runoff from the main volcanic islands and pollution from coastal communities, the waters of the Tuamotus are clean and fresh, with some of the best swimming, snorkeling, and scuba diving in the South Pacific. You've never seen so many fish! However in May 1998 it was revealed that 80% of the reefs at Rangiroa had suffered bleaching due to the El Niño phenomenon, completing the destruction wrought earlier by hurricanes. What draws people to Rangi (as everyone calls it) is the marinelife in the lagoon, not the coral. For this one of the prime shark-viewing locales of the world.

Orientation

Rangiroa's twin villages, each facing a pass 500 meters wide into the lagoon, house 2,700 people. Avatoru village on Avatoru Pass is at the west end of the airport island, about six km from the airport itself. A paved 10-km road runs east from Avatoru past the airport and the Kia Ora Village Hôtel to Tiputa Pass. Tiputa village is just across the water. The accommodations listings below are arranged by category from west to east along this road.

Both villages have small stores; the town hall, *gendarmerie* (tel. 96-03-61), and hotel school are at Tiputa, and the medical center, college, and marine research center are at Avatoru. Avatoru has better commercial facilities, but Tiputa is less touristed and offers the chance to escape by simply walking and wading southeast. **Gauguin's Pearl** (tel. 96-05-39; Mon.-Sat. 0830-1400), a pearl farm between Avatoru and the airport, can be visited at no charge. There are no

migrate to Papeete. The only regular hotels are on Rangiroa and Manihi but homestay accommodations are available on most of the atolls and Tahiti Tourisme in Papeete will have details. Beware of eating poisonous fish all across this archipelago.

Getting There

Air Tahiti has flights to Apataki, Arutua, Fakarava, Kaukura, Manihi, Mataiva, Rangiroa, Takapoto, Takaroa, and Tikehau in the northern Tuamotus, and Anaa, Faaite, Fakahina, Fangatau, Hao, Makemo, Mangareva, Napuka, Nukutavake, Pukapuka, Pukarua, Reao, Takume, Tatakoto, Tureia, and Vahitahi in the south.

Interisland boats call at most of the Tuamotu atolls about once a week, bringing foods and other goods and returning to Papeete with fish. Information on the cargo boats from Papeete is given in the introduction to Tahiti-Polynesia.

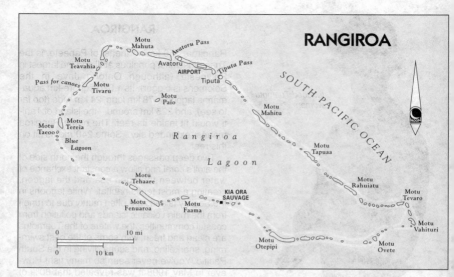

real restaurants outside the hotels and unless you get a place with cooking facilities it's better to take half board. Lunch can be obtained at one of the small snack bars or you can buy picnic fare.

Most of the accommodations face on the tranquil lagoon rather than the windy sea and large ships can enter the lagoon through either pass. For yachts, the sheltered anchorage by the Kia Ora Village Hôtel near Tiputa Pass is recommended (as opposed to the Avatoru anchorage, which is exposed to swells and chop). Far less English is spoken on Rangiroa than in the Society Islands.

Sports and Recreation

The strong tidal currents *(opape)* through Avatoru and Tiputa passes generate flows of three to six knots. It's exciting to shoot these 30-meter-deep passes on an incoming tide, and the three dive shops offer this activity using small motorboats or Zodiacs. Some of the dives tend to be longer and deeper than the norm. The Tiputa Pass current dive begins 27.5 meters down and is only for advanced divers; even the Tiputa Pass right side dive to 18 meters calls for some experience. Beginners should ask for the Motu Nuhi Nuhi dive. On all, the marinelife is fantastic, and humphead wrasses, manta rays, barracud-

as, and lots of sharks (including hammerheads) are seen in abundance. Most of the time they're harmless black-tip or white-tip reef sharks (but don't risk touching them even if you see other divers doing so).

Rangiroa's original scuba operator is arranged by the friendly **Raie Manta Club** (Yves and Brigette Lefèvre, B.P. 55, 98775 Avatoru; tel. 96-84-80, fax 96-85-60), with three branches at Rangiroa: near Rangiroa Lodge in Avatoru village, next to Pension Teina et Marie on Tiputa Pass, and at the Kia Ora Village Hôtel. Diving costs CFP 5,500 pp for one tank, including a float through the pass (night diving CFP 6,000). For the more enthusiastic, a 10-dive package is CFP 49,500. Every dive is different (falling, pass, cave, undulating bottom, hollow, and night). Snorkelers can go along when practical, otherwise an introductory dive is CFP 6,000. PADI and CMAS certification courses are offered at CFP 35,000 (five days, medical examination required). Divers come from all parts of the world to dive with Yves and his highly professional seven-instructor team.

Rangiroa Paradive (Bernard Blanc, B.P. 75, 98775 Avatoru; tel. 96-05-55, fax 96-05-50) is next to Chez Glorine at Tiputa Pass. It's CFP 5,500/10,000 for a one/two-tank dive; the package prices are CFP 26,500/50,000 for five/10 dives. Night dives are CFP 2,000 extra (minimum of four). Bernard isn't as aggressive about shark feeding as Yves but he does explore the shark caves and you'll see legions of sharks on his drift dives. He's obliging, hospitable, and one of the most highly qualified instructors in Polynesia. Both PADI and CMAS certification courses are offered at CFP 40,000 (three days, medical examination not necessary). There's no provision for snorkelers here and divers must show their cards. Without a card you could still do an introductory dive for CFP 6,000.

The Six Passengers (Frédéric Aragones, B.P. 128, 98775 Avatoru; tel./fax 96-02-60), in a hut between Chez Glorine and the Kia Ora, is Rangiroa's newest dive shop. Frédéric charges about the same as Yves and Bernard. Diving from a Zodiac is CFP 5,500/11,000/50,000 for one/two/10 tanks, night dives CFP 7,500, gear and pickups included. An all-day boat trip with two dives at the far end of the lagoon costs CFP 16,000 pp (minimum of six passengers). Snorkelers are not accepted, but a five-day CMAS certification course is offered at CFP 38,000.

Popular lagoon excursions include picnics to the slightly overrated **Blue Lagoon,** a fish-filled pool at Motu Taeoo (CFP 7,000 pp), to the **Île aux Récifs,** a number of uplifted coral formations on the south side of the lagoon (CFP 6,500), to the **Sables Roses,** a stretch of pink sand at the southeast end of the lagoon (CFP 9,000), and to tiny **Motu Paio,** a mid-lagoon bird sanctuary. Several companies offer a snorkel through the pass at CFP 4,000 (or do it in a glass-bottom boat for CFP 2,000). **Sharky Parc Excursions** (tel. 96-84-73), at Chez Punua et Moana in Avatoru, organizes some better value trips starting at CFP 2,500.

Budget Accommodations

Chez Nanua (Nanua and Marie Tamaehu, B.P. 54, 98775 Avatoru; tel. 96-83-88), between the airport and Avatoru village, is an old favorite of budget travelers who are allowed to pitch their tents here at CFP 1,000 pp (CFP 2,000 pp with two meals). The four simple thatched bungalows with shared/private bath are CFP 3,000/4,000 including two meals. The six-bed dorm is CFP 3,000 pp including food. You eat with the owners—a little fish and rice every

meal. There's no electricity, communal cooking, or running water, but you're right on the beach. Ask about bicycle and scooter rentals at Carole Pareo nearby.

Inexpensive

Chez Henriette (Henriette Tamaehu, tel. 96-85-85), by the lagoon in Avatoru village, is a four-bungalow place charging CFP 2,500 pp for a bed, CFP 5,000 with half pension, CFP 6,000 full pension. It can be a little noisy here but the food is excellent (especially the banana crêpes) and it's possible stop by for lunch even if you're staying elsewhere. They organize their own Blue Lagoon excursions.

Rangiroa Lodge (Jacques and Rofina Ly, tel. 96-82-13) in Avatoru has four rooms at CFP 4,000 double with shared bath or CFP 5,000 with private bath (plus CFP 200 for a fan, if desired). A place in the six-bed dorm is CFP 1,500 pp. This is one of the few places with communal cooking facilities, though the proprietors also prepare meals upon request. The snorkeling just off the lodge is outstanding and they'll loan you gear if you need it. Divers from the adjacent Raie Manta Club often stay here.

Moderate

The son and daughter-in-law of the folks mentioned at Chez Nanua above operate **Chez Punua et Moana** (Punua and Moana Tamaehu, B.P. 54, 98775 Avatoru; tel. 96-84-73) in Avatoru village. The four thatched bungalows with shared bath are CFP 3,500 pp with breakfast, or CFP 4,500 pp with half board. Camping is CFP 1,500 pp. It's right by the road and can be a little noisy due to the activities of the surrounding village. Watch your gear here. For those who really want to get away, Punua can arrange overnight stays on Motu Teavahia. Otherwise all are welcome on the daily lagoon tours and "Sharky Parc" excursions costing CFP 2,500 pp. Airport transfers are CFP 500 pp.

On the lagoon between the airport and Avatoru is **Pension Cécile** (Alban and Cécile Sun, B.P. 98, 98775 Avatoru; tel./fax 96-05-06) where the four bungalows are CFP 4,000 pp, plus CFP 2,000 pp for half board (no cooking). (Reader Rowland Burley writes that "this was the friendliest accommodation I found in Tahiti-Polynesia. Cécile speaks excellent English, the units are spotlessly clean, and dinner is superb.") Alban does lagoon tours in his boat upon request at CFP 6,000 pp.

The **Turiroa Village** (Olga Niva, B.P. 26, 98775 Avatoru; tel./fax 96-04-27), less than a kilometer west of the airport terminal, has four bungalows with cooking facilities at CFP 8,000 for up to four persons. If required, half/full board is CFP 3,000/3,500 pp.

A five-minute walk west of the airport terminal is **Pension Félix** (Félix and Judith Tetua, B.P. 18, 98775 Avatoru; tel. 96-04-41) with six bungalows with bath at CFP 2,500 pp, plus another CFP 3,000 pp for breakfast and dinner.

Pension Martine (Martine and Corinne Tetua, B.P. 68, 98775 Avatoru; tel. 96-02-53, fax 96-02-51), by the lagoon near the airport terminal, has four fan-cooled bungalows with private bath and terrace (but no cooking) at CFP 3,000 pp, plus another CFP 2,500 pp for half board (lots of fresh fish). There's no single supplement if you're alone, and it's friendly, clean, and relaxed. Ask Corinne to show you around the family pearl farm.

A sister of the Henriette mentioned previously runs the popular **Chez Glorine** (Glorine To'i, tel. 96-04-05, fax 95-03-58) at Tiputa Pass, four km from the airport. The six thatched bungalows with private bath (cold water) are CFP 5,500/6,500 pp including two/three meals (specialty fresh lagoon fish). Children under 13 are half price and bicycle rentals are available. Airport transfers are CFP 800 pp. Nonguests can order meals here.

Expensive

The **Miki Miki Village** (B.P. 5, 98775 Avatoru; tel./fax 96-83-83), also known as the Rangiroa Village, is an 11-bungalow resort near Avatoru: CFP 8,000/14,000 single/double, including breakfast and dinner. Reader comment about this place has been favorable. Lagoon tours are offered and it's possible to stop by for lunch or drinks.

Premium

The **Raira Lagon** (Maxime Boetsch, B.P. 87, 98775 Avatoru; tel. 96-04-23, fax 96-05-86), a bit more than a kilometer west of the airport terminal, offers 10 thatched bungalows with private bath and fridge (but no cooking facilities or hot water) at CFP 8,000/10,000 pp with half/full

board. A few well-used bicycles are loaned free and it's right on the beach. Their beachfront restaurant is open to the public.

Just west of the airport is the friendly 20-unit **Rangiroa Beach Club** (B.P. 17, 98775 Avatoru; tel. 96-03-34, fax 96-02-90), next to the Raira Lagoon. A thatched garden bungalow will set you back CFP 13,000 single, double, or triple plus tax, and for CFP 2,000 more you can have a beach bungalow. Children under 12 sharing a room with their parents are free. Additional units were being added in late 1998 and most guests arrived on prepaid packages. The restaurant serves excellent food (compulsory CFP 4,700 pp breakfast and dinner plan). The beach here is poor, so protective footwear should be used. Snorkeling and fishing gear are loaned free, and all land and water tours are arranged.

Luxury

Rangiroa's top resort is the snobbish **Kia Ora Village** (B.P. 1, 98776 Tiputa; tel. 96-03-84, fax 96-02-20), established in 1973 near Tiputa Pass, a bit more than two km east of the airport by road. The 30 beach bungalows and five larger garden bungalows are CFP 32,000/36,500 double/triple plus tax, while the 10 overwater units go for CFP 49,000 single or double, plus another CFP 5,500 pp for breakfast and dinner. Yachties anchored offshore are certainly not welcome to dingy in and use the facilities but the pricey seafood restaurant is open to all. A wide range of lagoon excursions and activities are offered at higher than usual prices. In 1991 the Kia Ora Village began offering accommodation in five thatched bungalows at "Kia Ora Sauvage" on Motu Avaerahi on the far south side of the lagoon. It's CFP 32,000 single or double plus a compulsory three-meal plan at CFP 7,000 pp, plus CFP 7,500 pp for return boat transfers (two-night minimum stay). The boat leaves at 0900 daily so you'll probably have to wait one night to go. Both Kia Ora's cater mostly to the package-tour market.

Services

The Banque de Tahiti (tel. 96-85-52) has a branch at Avatoru, while Banque Socredo (tel. 96-85-63) has branches at the *mairies* in both Avatoru and Tiputa. All branches are open limited hours according to a variable timetable (in Tiputa only on Monday, Tuesday, and Thursday).

Post offices are found in Avatoru, Tiputa, and the airport. There's a medical center (tel. 96-03-75) two km east of Avatoru and an infirmary (tel. 96-73-96) at Tiputa. It's prudent to drink bottled water on Rangiroa.

Getting There

Air Tahiti (tel. 96-03-41) flies Tahiti-Rangiroa daily (CFP 13,600 one-way). Three times a week a flight arrives direct from Bora Bora (CFP 20,700), but from Rangiroa to Bora Bora there's only a weekly flight. There's service five times a week from Rangiroa to Manihi (CFP 8,800). From Rangiroa to the Marquesas (CFP 24,500), there's a weekly ATR 42 flight (48 passengers) to Nuku Hiva and a weekly Dornier 228 flight (19 passengers) to Hiva Oa. Seats on flights to the Marquesas should be booked well in advance.

Schooners *(goélettes)* from Papeete take 23 hours to get there from Tahiti, but 72 hours to return (not direct). One cargo boat, the *Dory,* departs Papeete for Rangiroa every Monday at 1300 (CFP 2,500), the most regular connection. To return, ask about the copra boat *Rairoa Nui,* which is supposed to leave Rangiroa Wednesday at 0230 and arrive at Papeete Thursday at 0500 (CFP 3,000 including meals and a bunk—men only). The *Manava II, Saint Xavier Maris Stella,* and *Vai Aito* also call here regularly. They may dock at either Avatoru or Tiputa. The *Aranui* stops at Rangiroa on the way back to Papeete from the Marquesas and you could disembark here. For more information on transport to the Tuamotus, see the introduction to Tahiti-Polynesia.

Archipels Croisieres (B.P. 1160, 98729 Papetoai, Moorea; tel. 56-36-39, fax 56-35-87) offers two/three-night cruises around the Rangiroa lagoon on the 18-meter, eight-passenger catamaran *Motu Iti* at US$790/1,030 pp double occupancy (excluding airfare). It's a great way to explore the atoll and they'll go even if only two people reserve. When you consider that all meals and activities are included, it's no more expensive than staying at the Kia Ora. The entire vessel can be chartered at CFP 250,000 a day including meals. Tahiti Vacations handles North American bookings.

Getting Around

There's no public transportation on Rangiroa although the scuba operators offer shuttles to their clients. To reach Tiputa village across Tiputa Pass from the airport island wait for a lift on the dock next to Chez Glorine (watch for dolphins in the pass).

Europcar (tel./fax 96-03-28) with an office near Avatoru and a desk at the Kia Ora Village has cars beginning at CFP 5,500/6,500/7,500 for four/eight/24 hours, scooters at CFP 4,000/5,000/5,500, bicycles CFP 800/1,200/1500. Two-person "fun cars" are slightly cheaper than regular cars.

Arenahio Locations (tel./fax 96-82-85), at Carole Pareo between the airport and Avatoru village, rents bicycles at CFP 500/1,000 a half/full day and scooters at CFP 3,000/4,000. Many of the pensions also rent bicycles.

Airport

The airstrip (RGI) is about six km from Avatoru village by road, accessible to Tiputa village by boat. Most of the Avatoru pensions offer free airport transfers to those who have booked ahead (ask).

MANIHI

Manihi, 175 km northeast of Rangiroa, is the other Tuamotu atoll on the package tour circuit with visions of white-sand beaches and cultured black pearls radiating from its glossy brochures. You can see right around Manihi's six-by-30-km lagoon and the 50,000 resident oysters on the 60 commercial pearl farms outnumber the 1,000 human inhabitants 50 to one. Due to the pearl industry the people of Manihi have become more affluent than those on some of the other Tuamotu islands.

Turipaoa (or Paeua) village and its 50 houses shaded by flowers and trees face Tairapa Pass at the west end of a sandy strip just over a kilometer long. The airport island and main resort are just across the pass from Turipaoa, and many of the other *motus* are also inhabited.

Scuba Diving

Gilles Pétré of **Manihi Blue Nui** (B.P. 2460, 98713 Papeete; tel./fax 96-42-17) at the Manihi Pearl Beach Resort offers year-round scuba diving on the outer reef walls. A one-tank dive is CFP 6,000 (plus CFP 7,000 for night diving).

Five/10-dive packages are CFP 27,500/50,000. Rental of a wetsuit or waterproof light is CFP 500. Gilles will also take snorkelers on the boat at CFP 1,500 pp including mask and snorkel. Both PADI and CMAS certification courses are offered, otherwise a one-dive resort course is CFP 7,000.

It's exciting to shoot Tairapa Pass on the incoming tide, and since it's shallower than the passes at Rangiroa, you see more. Reef sharks are less common here but manta rays are often seen, as are countless Moorish idols. Just inside the lagoon at the mouth of the pass is a site called "The Circus" frequented by huge, science fiction-like rays with enormous socket eyes, and it's a fantastic experience to swim near them (also possible at Rangiroa).

The ocean drop-off abounds in gray sharks, Napoleon fish, giant jack fish, and huge schools of snappers, barracudas, and tuna. Each year, around late June or early July, thousands of groupers gather here to breed in one of the most fascinating underwater events in the world. Among Gilles' other favorite spots are "West Point" with fire, antler, and flower-petal coral in 65-meter visibility, and "The Break" where he feeds black-tip, white tip, gray, and occasionally hammerhead sharks.

Accommodations

Air Tahiti owns and heavily promotes the **Manihi Pearl Beach Resort** (B.P. 2460, 98713 Papeete; tel. 96-42-73, fax 96-42-72), by the lagoon near the airport. This place was known as the Kaina Village until a hurricane blew it away in 1993. Now rebuilt, the eight beach bungalows are CFP 26,000 single or double, while the 22 overwater bungalows go for CFP 46,000 plus tax. Add CFP 5,950 pp for breakfast and dinner, or CFP 8,250 full board. Roundtrip airport transfers are a ripoff at CFP 1,200 pp. Almost all guests arrive on prepaid packages. There's a beachfront saltwater swimming pool and floodlit tennis courts at the Manihi Pearl. Luxury.

Nine km northeast of the airport by road is **Chez Jeanne** (Jeanne Huerta, tel. 96-42-90, fax 96-42-91), formerly known as Le Keshi, at Motu Taugaraufara. The two self-catering beach bungalows here are CFP 8,000 for up to three people, while the overwater unit is CFP 12,000 double (minimum stay two nights). Food, water, and excursions are extra. Moderate.

The **Vainui Pearls Resort Lodge** (Edmond and Vaiana Buniet, B.P. 10, 98771 Manihi; tel. 96-42-89, fax 96-42-00) is across the lagoon on Motu Marakorako. The three rooms with shared bath in the main house and the one beach bungalow go for CFP 7,000 pp a day including airport transfers, activities, and all meals. A free tour of the owner's pearl farm is offered and it's the place to stay if your main interest is pearls. Reservations are recommended. Moderate.

In Turipaoa village you can rent a *fare* from Madame Puahea Teiva (no phone), but they're decrepit and remarkably overpriced at CFP 3,500 pp with two miserable meals. Itinerant pearl industry workers are the target clientele. Moderate.

Getting There

Manihi airport (XMH) is 2.5 km north of Turipaoa village by boat. Most Air Tahiti (tel. 96-43-34) flights to Manihi from Papeete (CFP 17,100) or Bora Bora (CFP 23,400) are via Rangiroa. Flights between Manihi and Rangiroa are also expensive at CFP 8,800. Boats from Papeete enter the lagoon and tie up to a wharf at Turipaoa.

OTHER ISLANDS AND ATOLLS

Ahe

Ahe, 13 km west of Manihi, is often visited by cruising yachts, which are able to enter the 16-km-long lagoon through Tiarero Pass on the northwest side of the atoll. Tenukupara village is south across the lagoon. Facilities include two tiny stores, a post office, and a community center where everyone meets at night. Despite the steady stream of sailing boats, the 400 people are very friendly. As well as producing pearls, Ahe supplies oysters to the pearl farms on Manihi. In March 1998 an airport constructed by the Foreign Legion opened on Ahe.

Fakarava

Fakarava is the second-largest Tuamotu atoll, about 250 km southeast of Rangiroa and 450 km northeast of Tahiti. A pass gives access to each end of this rectangular 60-by-25-km lagoon, which is dotted and flanked by 80 coconut-covered *motus*. There's spectacular snorkeling and drift diving in the passes or along the vertical dropoffs. Passe Garuae on the north is one km wide, nine meters deep, and the haunt of countless sharks, dolphins, barracuda, and rays.

French colonial administration for the Tuamotus moved here from Anaa in 1878 and Fakarava's Catholic church is one of the oldest in the group. Robert Louis Stevenson visited Fakarava aboard the yacht *Casco* in 1888 and spent two weeks living in a house near the church in the center of the village, Rotoava. The present airstrip, eight km from village, only opened in 1995. About 500 people live on the atoll and a number of pearl farms have been established around the lagoon.

The least expensive place to stay is the **Relais Marama** (Marama Teanuanua, tel. 98-42-25), in Rotoava village, four km from the airstrip. The three rooms with shared bath in the main house are CFP 2,500/4,000 single/double, otherwise it's CFP 5,000 double for the garden bungalow. Cooking facilities are available. Inexpensive.

The **Kiritia Village** (Marcelline Kachler, tel. 98-42-37), also in Rotoava, offers two bungalows and four *fare* with shared bath at CFP 8,500/15,000 single/double including all meals and transfers. Bicycles are for rent. Premium.

Marc-Antoine Baudart runs a scuba diving operation called **Club Aventure** or **CPSM Rotoava** (B.P. 330002, 98711 Paea, Tahiti; fax 43-07-54) next to the Kiritia Village. Diving is CFP 6,000 a tank day or night, or CFP 27,000 for five dives, gear included. He also takes snorkelers out at CFP 3,800 pp (black pearl farm visits possible). Otherwise sign up for his four-day CMAS certification course at CFP 20,000 (medical certificate required). An excursion to uninhabited Toau Atoll is CFP 5,000 pp (five person minimum), plus the diving or snorkeling charges. Don't bother asking about shark feeding as that's not his thing.

Air Tahiti flies from Papeete to Fakarava (CFP 14,700) twice a week with one flight going on to Rangiroa (CFP 4,400).

Hao

Hao Atoll was visited by the Spaniard Quirós in 1606. Kaki Pass gives access to the 50-km-long lagoon from the north. The pass has been dredged to a depth of seven meters and medium-sized ships can enter and proceed eight km to the anchorage off Otepa village on the northeast side of the atoll.

From 1966 to 1996 the giant French air base on Hao (population 1,400) served as the main support base for nuclear testing on Moruroa, 500 km southeast, allowing the French military to fly materials directly into the area without passing through Faa'a Airport. The formidable airstrip on Hao is more than three km long, big enough to be considered a possible emergency landing site for NASA space shuttles.

Hao is strategically situated in the heart of Tahiti-Polynesia, equidistant from Tahiti, Mangareva, and the Marquesas, and despite the windup of nuclear testing on Moruroa in 1996, France continues to project its military power from Hao, current home of the 5th Foreign Legion Regiment. There are no tourist accommodations on Hao and prior to 1996 non-French visitors were forbidden to even transit the atoll. Most Air Tahiti flights to Mangareva and the southern Tuamotus are via Hao, and it might be worth inquiring about the current situation before making too many plans.

Makatea

Unlike the low coral atolls of the Tuamotus, Makatea, 200 km northeast of Tahiti, is an uplifted limestone block with a lunar surface eight km long and 110 meters high. Gray cliffs plunge 50 meters to the sea. Phosphate was dug up here by workers with shovels from 1908 to 1966 and exported to Japan and New Zealand by the Compagnie française des Phosphates de l'Océanie. At one time 2,000 workers were present but fewer than 100 people are there today. Even though the mining has been abandoned, many buildings and a railway remain. Numerous archaeological remains were found during the mining. There are no flights to Makatea.

Tikehau

Rangiroa's smaller and less commercialized neighbor, Tikehau (400 inhabitants), is an almost circular atoll 26 km across with the shallow Passe de Tuheiava on its west side. Tuherahera village and the airstrip share an island in the southwest corner of the atoll. Five pearl farms operate on Tikehau. Plans exist to build a five-star resort called "Eden Beach" on Tikehau but the project has been delayed due to a lack of funds.

A variety of places to stay are found on Tikehau, beginning with the **Panau Lagon** (Arai and

Lorina Natua, tel./fax 96-22-99) on a white beach a few minutes walk from the airport. The six simple bungalows with bath are CFP 2,500 pp, plus CFP 3,000 pp for breakfast and dinner. Camping is possible. Inexpensive.

Also in the direction away from the village and a few minutes beyond Panau Lagoon is **Chez Justine** (Justine and Laroche Tetua, tel. 96-22-37, fax 96-22-26) with two *fares* at CFP 5,000 pp with half board. Expensive. **Pension Kahaia** (Merline Natua, tel. 96-22-77), on an adjacent *motu,* has three *fares* at CFP 5,000 pp with half board. Expensive. The **Tikehau Village** (Caroline and Pa'ea Tefaiao, tel. 96-22-86, fax 96-22-91), on the beach between the airstrip and the village, has eight *fares* at CFP 7,000 pp including all meals. Premium.

All of the other accommodations are in Tuherahera village, a bit more than one km from the airstrip. At these you'll usually get a room with shared bath in a family home at CFP 2,000-2,500 pp for the room only or CFP 4,000 pp and up with two meals. Among the people offering this are Isidore and Nini Hoiore (tel. 96-22-89), Colette Huri (tel. 96-22-47), Maxime Metua (tel. 96-22-38), and Hélène Teakura (tel. 96-22-52). Some places such as Chez Maxime or Chez Colette may allow you to cook your own food (ask). Inexpensive.

All of these organize boat trips to bird islands such as Puarua, picnics on a *motu,* snorkeling in the pass, visits to Eden Point, etc, costing CFP 3,000-6,000 pp. Scuba diving is available with the **Raie Manta Club** (Alex Vaure, B.P. 9, 98778 Tikehau; tel. 96-22-53, fax 96-85-60) in Tuherahera. Alex will show you huge manta rays, sea turtles, shark-infested caves, great schools of barracuda, and fabulous red reefs.

Air Tahiti flies from Papeete to Tikehau (CFP 13,600) four times a week and from Rangiroa (CFP 4,400) twice a week. The supply boat *Dory* sails direct from Papeete to Tikehau (CFP 2,500) once a week.

THE NUCLEAR TEST ZONE

The former French nuclear test site operated by the Centre d'Expérimentations du Pacifique until 1996 is at the southeastern end of the Tuamotu group, 1,200 km from Tahiti. The main site was 30-km-long Moruroa atoll, but Fangataufa atoll 37 km south of Moruroa was also used. In 1962 the French nuclear testing facilities in the Algerian Sahara had to be abandoned after that country won its independence, so in 1963 French president Charles de Gaulle officially announced that France was shifting the program to Moruroa and Fangataufa. Between 1966 and 1996 a confirmed 181 nuclear bombs, reaching up to 200 kilotons, were set off in the Tuamotus at the rate of six a year. By 1974 the French had conducted 41 *atmospheric* tests, 36 over or near Moruroa and five over Fangataufa. Five of these were megaton hydrogen bombs.

Way back in 1963, the U.S., Britain, and the USSR agreed in the Partial Test Ban Treaty to halt nuclear tests in the atmosphere. France chose not to sign. On 23 June 1973, the World Court urged France to discontinue the nuclear tests, which might drop radioactive material on surrounding territories. When the French government refused to recognize the court's jurisdiction in this matter, New Zealand Prime Minister Norman Kirk ordered the New Zealand frigate *Otago* to enter the danger zone off Moruroa, and on 23 July Peru broke diplomatic relations with France. On 15 August French commandos boarded the protest vessels *Fri* and *Greenpeace III,* attacking and arresting the crews.

In 1974, with opposition mounting in the Territorial Assembly and growing world indignation, French President Giscard D'Estaing ordered a switch to *underground* tests. Eighteen years and 134 tests later, as the Greenpeace *Rainbow Warrior II* confronted French commandos off Moruroa, French prime minister Pierre Bérégovoy suddenly announced on 8 April 1992 that nuclear testing was being suspended. President Boris Yeltsin had already halted Russian nuclear testing in October 1991, and in October 1992 U.S. president George Bush followed suit by halting underground testing in Nevada. Despite the French moratorium, the testing facilities in the Tuamotus were maintained at great expense, and in June 1995 newly elected President Jacques Chirac ordered the testing to resume without bothering to consult the Polynesians.

On 31 August 1995, with the first test imminent, the Greenpeace ship *Rainbow Warrior II* reached Moruroa just over 10 years after its predecessor had been sunk by French terrorists at

Auckland, New Zealand. As the ship crossed the 12-mile limit and launched six Zodiacs toward the French drilling rigs in the lagoon, the *Rainbow Warrior* was boarded by French commandos who fired tear gas at the unresisting crew and smashed computers, generators, and the ship's engine. The MV *Greenpeace* was nearby in international waters at the time, and the French seized it too on the pretext that it had launched a helicopter that crossed the territorial limit. With the main protest vessels impounded and their crews deported, the French hoped they could carry on with the tests without further interference.

So on 5 September 1995, despite opposition from 63% of the French public and a large majority of Polynesians, the French military exploded the first of a planned series of eight bombs under Moruroa. This led to the worst rioting ever seen in Polynesia as thousands of enraged Tahitians ran amok, ransacking Faa'a Airport and much of Papeete. The independence leader Oscar Temaru managed to calm the crowd, and the French brought in additional riot police to guard the capital. After a second blast on 2 October the South Pacific Forum carried out its threat to suspend France as a "dialogue partner."

In an attempt to deflect mounting worldwide condemnation, Chirac announced that the number of tests would be reduced from eight to six. For over a decade the U.S. and Britain had quietly backed the French testing, refusing to sign the protocols of the 1985 South Pacific Nuclear-Free Zone Treaty. By now it had become obvious that the Pacific could no longer be used as a nuclear playground, and in March 1996, Britain and the U.S. joined France in signing the treaty. The sixth and last test was carried out below Fangataufa atoll on 27 January 1996. Since then the facilities on Moruroa have been demolished and it's very unlikely there will ever be another nuclear test in this area.

Moruroa

Obviously, an atoll, with its porous coral cap sitting on a narrow basalt base, is the most dangerous place in the world to stage underground nuclear explosions. It's doubtful this was ever considered. Moruroa was chosen for its isolated location, far from major population centers that might be affected by fallout. By 1974, when atmospheric testing had to cease, the French military had a huge investment in the area. So rather than move to a more secure location in France or elsewhere, they decided to take a chance. Underground testing was to be carried out in Moruroa's basalt core, 500-1,200 meters below the surface of the atoll. Eventually 130 bombs were exploded below Moruroa and 10 below Fangataufa, making France the only nuclear state that conducted tests *under* a Pacific island.

On 10 September 1966 President Charles de Gaulle was present at Moruroa to witness the atmospheric test of a bomb suspended from a balloon. Weather conditions caused the test to be postponed, and the following day conditions were still unsuitable, as the wind was blowing in the direction of inhabited islands to the west instead of toward uninhabited Antarctica to the south. De Gaulle complained that he was a busy man and could afford to wait no longer, so the test went ahead, spreading radioactive fallout across the Cook Islands, Niue, Tonga, Samoa, Fiji, and Tuvalu. Tahiti itself was the most directly affected island, but the French authorities have never acknowledged this fact.

Archive documentation published by the French weekly *Nouvel Observateur* in February 1998 has confirmed that French defense officials knew very well that nearby islands such as Mangareva, Pukarua, Reao, and Tureia were receiving high doses of radiation during the 1966 tests, even as spokespersons publicly described the tests as "innocuous." France's radiological security service recommended at the time that the four islands be evacuated, but the newly discovered documents only note that "the hypothesis of an evacuation was excluded for political and psychological reasons."

A serious accident occurred on 25 July 1979 when a nuclear device became stuck halfway down an 800-meter shaft. Since army engineers were unable to move the device, they exploded it where it was, causing a massive chunk of the outer slope of the atoll to break loose. This generated a huge tsunami, which hit Moruroa, overturning cars and injuring seven workers. After the blast, a crack 40 cm wide and two km long appeared on the surface of the island. As a precaution against further tsunamis and hurricanes, refuge platforms were built at intervals around the atoll. For an hour before and after each test all personnel had to climb up on these platforms.

By 1981 Moruroa was as punctured as a Swiss cheese and sinking two centimeters after every test, or a meter and a half between 1976 and 1981. In 1981, with the atoll's 60-km coral rim dangerously fractured by drilling shafts, the French switched to underwater testing in the Moruroa lagoon, in order to be closer to the center of the island's core. In 1987 the famous French underwater explorer Jacques Cousteau filmed spectacular cracks and fissures in the atoll as well as submarine slides and subsidence, and described the impact of testing on the atoll as creating "premature and accelerated aging." By 1988 even French officials were acknowledging that the 108 underground blasts had severely weakened the geological formations beneath Moruroa, and it was announced that, despite the additional cost involved, the largest underground tests would take place henceforth on nearby Fangataufa atoll. The military base remained on Moruroa, and small groups of workers and technicians were sent over to Fangataufa every time a test was made there.

The French government always claimed that it owned Moruroa and Fangataufa because in 1964 a standing committee of the Territorial Assembly voted three to two to cede the atolls to France for an indefinite period. This was never ratified by the full assembly, and French troops had occupied the islands before the vote was taken anyway. The traditional owners of Moruroa, the people of Tureia atoll, 115 km north, were not consulted and have never been compensated.

Impact

In 1983 the French government invited a delegation of scientists from Australia, New Zealand, and Papua New Guinea to visit Moruroa. Significantly, they were not permitted to take samples from the northern or western areas of the atoll, nor of lagoon sediments. The scientists reported that "if fracturing of the volcanics accompanied a test and allowed a vertical release of radioactivity to the limestones, specific contaminants would, in this worst case, enter the biosphere within five years."

On 21 June 1987 Jacques Cousteau was present for a test at Moruroa and the next day he took water samples in the lagoon, the first time such independent tests had been allowed. Two samples collected by Cousteau nine km apart contained traces of cesium-134, an isotope with a half-life of two years. Though French officials claimed the cesium-134 remained from atmospheric testing before 1975, a 1990 study by American radiologist Norm Buske proved that this is not scientifically feasible, and that leakage from underground testing is the only possible explanation. In 1990 a computer model of Moruroa developed by New Zealand scientists indicated that radioactive groundwater with a half-life of several thousand years may be seeping through fractures in the atoll at the rate of 100 meters a year and, according to Prof. Manfred Hochstein, head of Auckland University's Geothermal Institute, "in about 30 years the disaster will hit us." In December 1990 Buske found traces of cesium-134 in plankton collected in the open ocean, outside the 12-mile exclusion zone. Buske's findings indicate that the release of contamination into the Pacific from the numerous cracks and fissures has already started.

Unlike the U.S., which has paid millions of dollars in compensation money to the Marshallese victims of its nuclear testing program, the French government has refused to even acknowledge the already-apparent effects of its 41 atmospheric nuclear tests. From 1963 to 1983, no public health statistics were published in the colony. Now the rates of thyroid cancer, leukemia, brain tumors, and stillbirths are on the upswing in Tahiti-Polynesia, and the problem of seafood poisoning (ciguatera) in the nearby Gambier Islands is clearly related. Before being employed at the base, all workers at Moruroa had to sign contracts binding them to eternal silence and waiving access to their own medical records or to any right to compensation for future health problems. Surveys conducted by the Tahitian NGO Hiti Tau among 737 of the 12,000 Polynesians who worked at Moruroa between 1966 and 1996 have demonstrated that many have experienced adverse health effects, yet no official studies of this impact have been carried out.

In July 1998 the pro-nuclear International Atomic Energy Agency issued a report commissioned by the French government that claims there has been no adverse effect on human health or the environment that can be attributed to radiation from radioactive residue. The study only dealt with the 1995 test series and made no attempt to investigate the previous testing. The report does admit that about eight kilograms of plutonium and other dangerous elements still rest in sediments in the Moruroa and Fangataufa lagoons as a result of the atmospheric testing and plutonium safety trials. More worrisome are the tritium levels in the Moruroa lagoon, which are 10 times higher than those of the surrounding sea, a result of leakage from cavities created by the underground tests. A detailed geological examination of Moruroa's fragile basalt base was not carried out, yet the IAEA report concludes that "no remedial action is needed" and "no further environmental monitoring" is required for purposes of radiological study.

A detachment of 30 foreign legionnaires now keeps watch over the abandoned wharf, airstrip, and concrete bunkers at the dismantled Moruroa test site (Fangataufa has been abandoned). No one is allowed in without official approval. One can only hope the IAEA is right and that there's nothing to worry about, although based on the experience of previous official pronouncements on Moruroa, the credibility of this French-funded study is open to question. Without ongoing monitoring Moruroa remains wrapped in the same sinister mystery that has dogged it since 1966. Nothing will ever change the fact that even with the testing over, French radioactivity will remain in the Tuamotus for thousands of years, and the unknown future consequences of the tests remain as uncertain as ever. The story definitely isn't over yet.

traveler's tree

THE GAMBIER ISLANDS

The Gambier (or Mangareva) Islands are just north of the tropic of Capricorn, 1,650 km southeast of Tahiti. The southerly location means a cooler climate. The archipelago, contrasting sharply with the atolls of the Tuamotus, consists of 10 rocky islands enclosed on three sides by a semicircular barrier reef 65 km long. In all, there are 46 square km of dry land. The Polynesian inhabitants named the main and largest island Mangareva, or "Floating Mountain," for 482-meter-high Mt. Duff. Unlike the Marquesas, where the mountains are entirely jungle-clad, the Gambiers have hilltops covered with tall *aeho* grass. Black pearls are cultured on numerous platforms on both sides of the Mangareva lagoon. A local seabird, the *karako,* crows at dawn like a rooster.

History

Mangareva, which was originally settled from the Marquesas Islands around A.D. 1100, was shortly afterwards the jumping-off place for small groups that discovered and occupied Pitcairn and Henderson islands. In 1797 Capt. James Wilson of the London Missionary Society's ship *Duff* named the group for English Admiral James Gambier (1756-1833), a hero of the Napoleonic wars who had helped organize the expedition. France made the Gambiers a protectorate in 1871 and annexed the group in 1881.

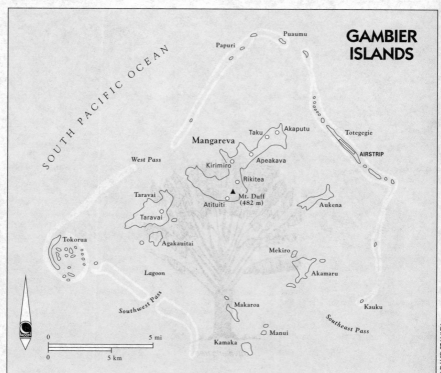

GAMBIER ISLANDS

SOUTH PACIFIC OCEAN

Puaumu
Papuri

Taku Akaputu Totegegie
Mangareva AIRSTRIP
West Pass Kirimiro Apeakava
Rikitea
Taravai Mt. Duff (482 m)
Atituiti Aukena
Taravai
Tokorua Agakauitai
Mekiro
Akamaru
Lagoon
Southwest Pass Makaroa Kauku
Southeast Pass
Manui
Kamaka

0   5 mi
0   5 km

© DAVID STANLEY

19th-century sailors being attacked by islanders at Mangareva, Gambier Islands

Mangareva was the area of operations for a fanatical French priest, Father Honoré Laval of the Congregation for the Sacred Hearts. Upon hearing whalers' tales of rampant cannibalism and marvelous pearls, Laval left his monastery in Chile and with another priest reached the Gambiers in 1834. An old Mangarevan prophecy had foretold the coming of two magicians whose god was all-powerful and Laval himself toppled the dreaded stone effigy of the god Tu on the island's sacred *marae*. He then single-handedly imposed a ruthless and inflexible moral code on the islanders, recruiting them as virtual slaves to build a 1,200-seat cathedral, convents, and triumphal arches—116 stone buildings in all—with the result that he utterly destroyed this once vigorous island culture and practically wiped out its people. During Laval's 37-year reign the population dropped from 9,000 to 500. You can still see his architectural masterpiece—the Cathedral of St. Michael with its twin towers of white coral rock from Kamaka and altar shining with polished mother-of-pearl—a monument to horror and yet another lost culture. The cathedral was built between 1839 and 1848 on the *ahu* of the island's principal *marae,* and Laval's colleague, Father François Caret, who died in 1844, lies buried in a crypt before the altar. In 1871 Laval was removed from Mangareva by a French warship, tried for murder on Tahiti, and declared insane.

Orientation

Most of the current 1,100 inhabitants of the Gambiers live on eight-by-1.5-km Mangareva, of which Rikitea is the main village. A post office, seven small shops, a *gendarmerie* (tel. 97-82-68), an infirmary, schools, and a cathedral three times as big as the one in Papeete make up the infrastructure of this administrative backwater.

Sights

The tomb of Grégoire Maputeoa, the 35th and last king of Mangareva (died 1868), is in a small chapel behind the cathedral. Follow the path behind the church to the top of the hill and through the gate on the left (close it after you as dogs dig up the graves). Among the walled ruins of Rouru convent in Rikitea one can pick out the chapel, refectory, infirmary, and a dormitory for 60 local nuns. On the opposite side of Rikitea is a huge nuclear-fallout shelter built during the French atmospheric testing at Moruroa.

A 28-km road runs around Mangareva offering ever-changing views. At the north end of the island it passes St. Joseph's Chapel (1836) at Taku, place of worship of the Mangarevan royal family. The south coast of Mangareva is one of the most beautiful in Polynesia, with a tremendous variety of landscapes, plants, trees, smells, and colors.

The white sands of **Aukena** make a good day-trip destination by boat. The Church of St. Raphael here is the oldest in the Gambier Islands and to the south are the ruins of the Rehe Seminary (1840). The Church of Notre-Dame-de-la-Paix (1844) on abandoned **Akamaru** has twin towers added in 1862. Solitary **Makaroa** is a barren, rugged 136-meter-high island.

St. Gabriel Church (1868) on **Taravai** has a neo-Gothic facade decorated with seashells. In a cliffside cave on the uninhabited island of **Agakauitai** the mummies of 35 generations of cannibal kings are interred.

Budget Accommodations
Although it costs an arm and a leg to fly here, staying is inexpensive. The four guesthouses on Mangareva each charge around CFP 2,000/3,000/3,500 single/double/triple for a room with shared bath. Cooking facilities are provided, or you can order food at CFP 2,000/4,000 pp for half/full board. Be aware of ciguatera (seafood poisoning) in the Gambiers. All offer boat transfers from the airport at CFP 1,000 pp return and children under 13 are half price for all services.

    Chez Bianca et Benoit (B.P. 19, 98755 Rikitea; tel. 97-83-76) is a modern two-story house with three rooms. It's just above Rikitea and the view across to Aukena is lovely.

    Chez Pierre et Mariette (B.P. 28, 98755 Rikitea; tel. 97-82-87), near the wharf, also has

three rooms. **Chez Terii et Hélène** (tel. 97-82-80) nearby has two rooms.

    Farther north is **Chez Jojo** (Jocelyne Mamatui, B.P. 1, 98755 Rikitea; tel. 97-82-61) with two rooms. Camping space here is CFP 1,000 pp.

Transportation
The airstrip (GMR) is on Totegegie, a long coral island eight km northeast of Rikitea. Arriving passengers pay CFP 500 pp each way for the boat ride to the village. The Air Tahiti flights from Papeete (CFP 30,000 one-way) are either nonstop or via Hao. The monthly supply ship from Papeete, the *Manava IV,* also travels via Hao. The one-way fare from Papeete is CFP 7,500/13,101 deck/couchette (no cabins), plus CFP 2,575 a day for three meals. Large vessels can enter the lagoon through passes on the west, southwest, and southeast. Mr. Jean Anania (nicknamed "Siki") offers speedboat charters and fishing trips.

THE MARQUESAS ISLANDS

The Marquesas Islands are the farthest north of the high islands of the South Pacific, on the same latitude as the Solomons. Though the group was known as Te Henua Enata (The Land of Men) by the Polynesian inhabitants, depopulation during the 19th and 20th centuries has left many of the valleys empty. Ten main islands form a line 300 km long, roughly 1,400 km northeast of Tahiti, but only six are inhabited today: Nuku Hiva, Ua Pou, and Ua Huka in a cluster to the northwest, and Hiva Oa, Tahuata, and Fatu Hiva to the southeast. The administrative centers, Atuona (Hiva Oa), Hakahau (Ua Pou), and Taiohae (Nuku Hiva), are the only places with post offices, banks, *gendarmes,* etc.

    The expense and difficulty in getting there has kept many potential visitors away. Budget accommodations are scarce and public transport is nonexistent, which makes getting around a major expense unless you're really prepared to rough it. Of the main islands, getting to and from Hiva Oa airport is easier, but Nuku Hiva has more variety. Cruising yachts from California often call at the Marquesas on their way to Papeete, and yachties should also steer for Hiva Oa first to enjoy the smoothest possible sailing

through the rest of the group. For hikers, the Marquesas are paradise. Multitudes of waterfalls tumble down the slopes, and eerie overgrown archaeological remains tell of a golden era long gone. The Marquesas have been left behind by their remoteness.

The Land
These wild, rugged islands feature steep cliffs and valleys leading up to high central ridges, sectioning the islands off into a cartwheel of segments, which creates major transportation difficulties. Large reefs don't form due to the cold south equatorial current though there are isolated stretches of coral. The absence of protective reefs has prevented the creation of coastal plains, so no roads go around any of the islands. Most of the people live in the narrow, fertile river valleys. The interiors are inhabited only by hundreds of wild horses, cattle, and goats, which have destroyed much of the original vegetation. A Catholic bishop introduced the horses from Chile in 1856, and today they're almost a symbol of the Marquesas. Birdlife is rich, and the waters around the Marquesas teem with lobster, fish, and sharks.

The subtropical climate is hotter and drier than that of Tahiti. July and August are the coolest months. The deep bays on the west sides of the islands are better sheltered for shipping, and the humidity is lower there than on the east sides, which catch the trade winds. The precipitation is uneven, with drought some years, heavy rainfall the others. The southern islands of the Marquesas (Hiva Oa, Tahuata, Fatu Hiva) are green and humid; the northern islands (Nuku Hiva, Ua Huka, Ua Pou) are brown and dry.

Pre-European Society

Marquesan houses were built on high platforms *(paepae)* scattered through the valleys (still fairly easy to find). Each valley had a rectangular ceremonial area *(tohua)* where important festivals took place. Archaeologists have been able to trace stone temples (*me'ae,* called *marae* elsewhere in Tahiti-Polynesia), agricultural terraces, and earthen fortifications *(akaua)* half hidden in the jungle, evocative reminders of a vanished civilization. Then as now, the valleys were isolated from one another by high ridges and turbulent seas, yet warfare was vicious and cannibalism an important incentive. An able warrior

could attain great power. Local hereditary chiefs exercised authority over commoners.

The Marquesans' artistic style was one of the most powerful and refined in the Pacific. The ironwood war club was their most distinctive symbol, but there were also finely carved wooden bowls, fan handles, and tikis of stone and wood, both miniature and massive. The carvings are noted for the faces: the mouth with lips parted and the bespectacled eyes. Both men and women wore carved ivory earplugs. Men's entire bodies were covered with bold and striking tattoos, a practice banned by the Catholic missionaries. Stilts were used by boys for racing and mock fighting. This was about the only part of Polynesia where polyandry was common. There was a strong cult of the dead: the bodies or skulls of ancestors were carefully preserved. Both Easter Island (around A.D. 500) and Hawaii (around A.D. 700) were colonized from here.

European Contact

The existence of these islands was long concealed from the world by the Spanish, to prevent the English from taking possession of them. The southern group was found by Álvaro de Mendaña in July 1595 during his second voyage of exploration from Peru. He named them Las Marquesas de Mendoza after his benefactor, the Spanish viceroy. Mendaña's men were brutal, shooting natives on sight, and in one instance hanging three bodies in the shore camp on Santa Cristina (Tahuata) as a warning. They left behind three large crosses, the date cut in a tree, and more than 200 dead Polynesians. When Captain Cook arrived at Tahuata in 1774 it soon became obvious that knowledge of the earlier Spanish visit had remained alive in oral traditions, and Cook and his crew were shunned.

The northern Marquesas Islands were "discovered" by Joseph Ingraham of the American trading vessel *Hope* on 19 April 1791. After that, blackbirders, firearms, disease, and alcohol reduced the population. American whalers called frequently from 1800 onwards. Although France took possession of the group in 1842, Peruvian slavers kidnapped some Marquesans to South America in 1863 to work the plantations and mines. Those few able to return thanks to diplomatic lobbying by their French protectors brought a catastrophic smallpox epidemic. The Marque-

Hatutu

Eiao

THE MARQUESAS ISLANDS

Nuku Hiva

Ua Huka

Hane

Taiohae Taipivai Vaipaee

Ua Pou Hakahau

Fatu Huku

Hiva Oa

Puamau

Vaitahu Atuona

Tahuata Mohotani

Fatu Hiva

Hanavave

Omoa

0   50 mi

0   50 km

© DAVID STANLEY

sans clung to their warlike, cannibalistic ways until 95% of their number had died—the remainder adopted Catholicism. (The Marquesas today is the only island group of Tahiti-Polynesia with a Catholic majority.) From 80,000 at the beginning of the 19th century, the population fell to about 15,000 by 1842, when the French "protectors" arrived, and to a devastated 2,000 by 1926. Even today the total population is just 8,000.

The Marquesan language, divided into north and south dialects, is only about 50% comprehensible to a Tahitian and is actually a bit closer to Rarotongan and Hawaiian. There's a small separatist movement here

the priest Taawattaa as seen by American explorer Capt. David Porter at Nuku Hiva in 1812

that believes the Marquesas will receive more benefits as a distinct colony of France, or failing that, as a country independent of Tahiti. And just to complicate matters, twice as many Marquesans live in Papeete as in the Marquesas itself.

Events

The Marquesas Islands Festival or *Matava'a o te Henua Enata* is a major cultural event celebrated every few years in December with dancing, singing, drumming, and sports, plus handicraft displays and feasts. Aside from strengthening and reviving traditional knowledge and skills, numerous archaeological sites have been restored or rebuilt in preparation for these events. Previous festivals have been at Ua Pou (1987), Nuku Hiva (1989), Hiva Oa (1991), and Ua Pou (1995), and the next was to be on Nuku Hiva again in 1999, just in time for the millennium.

Transportation

A visit to the Marquesas requires either lots of money or lots of time, or both. An **Air Tahiti** ATR flies from Papeete to Nuku Hiva five times a week (three hours, CFP 28,700). One of these ATR flights is via Manihi and Rangiroa. There's also a weekly Dornier 228 flight from Rangiroa to Hiva Oa via Napuka or Pukapuka (CFP 24,500), but the plane is always full. Ask about Air Tahiti's "Decouverte Marquises" ticket, which allows a re-

turn flight from Papeete to Nuku Hiva for CFP 49,900, to Atuona, Ua Pou, or Ua Huka for CFP 54,900. It's valid for a stay of 7-15 days and you may only use off-peak "blue" flights (not available in March, July, August, or around Christmas).

Dornier flights between Nuku Hiva and Ua Huka and Ua Pou operate weekly, connecting with one of the ATR flights from Papeete. Fares from Nuku Hiva are CFP 5,100 to Ua Pou, CFP 5,100 to Ua Huka, and CFP 8,800 to Atuona. No flight goes straight from Ua Pou to Ua Huka—you must backtrack to Nuku Hiva. Get a through ticket to your final destination, as flights to Hiva Oa, Ua Pou, and Ua Huka are all the same price from Papeete (Nuku Hiva is CFP 1,300 cheaper). Tahuata and Fatu Hiva are without air service. All flights are heavily booked. Coming or going, remember the 30-minute time difference between Tahiti and the Marquesas.

Three ships, the *Aranui, Tamarii Tuamotu,* and *Taporo IV,* sail monthly from Papeete, calling at all six inhabited Marquesas Islands. The *Aranui* and *Taporo IV* are the easiest to use, as they follow a regular schedule. For more information turn the chapter introduction.

The freighter Aranui is the more convenient and comfortable, if you can afford it. The round-trip voyages designed for tourists flown in from Europe and the U.S. cost cruise-ship prices (from US$3,000 pp return). See the introduction to Tahiti-Polynesia for details. The other main interisland boat, Taporo IV, is cheaper at CFP 20,000/30,000 deck/cabin one-way from Papeete to any Marquesan port, but it's basic. Food is included in the passages and it's not necessary to reserve deck passage on these boats. The ships tie up to the wharves at Taiohae, Atuona, Vaipae'e, and Hakahau; at Tahauta and Fatu Hiva, passengers must go ashore by whaleboat. In stormy weather, the landings can be dangerous.

Archipels Croisieres (B.P. 1160, Papetoai, Moorea; tel. 56-36-39, fax 56-35-87) offers seven-night catamaran cruises around the Marquesas at US$2,050 pp double occupancy, airfare not included. The eight passengers sleep in four cabins and visit five of the six inhabited islands with shore excursions and airport transfers included. Departures are guaranteed even if only two people book. In the U.S. and Canada, Tahiti Vacations handles bookings for both Archipels and the *Aranui*.

To island hop within the Marquesas you could try using any of the three ships mentioned above, if they happen to be going where you want to go, or ask at local town halls about the government boat *Ka'oha Nui*, which circulates among the islands on official business. Private boats run from Taiohae to Ua Pou fairly frequently, and there are municipal boats from Atuona to Tahuata and Fatu Hiva at least once a week. Chartering boats interisland is extremely expensive, and to join a regular trip you just have to be lucky, persistent, and prepared to wait. You can also island-hop by helicopter if you've got tons of money to throw around.

Getting around the individual islands can be a challenge as there's no organized public trans-portation other than expensive airport transfers, and due to the condition of the roads, rental cars are limited to a few pricey vehicles at Taiohae and Atuona. It's fairly easy to hire a chauffeur-driven vehicle on Hiva Oa, Nuku Hiva, Ua Huka, and Ua Pou, but expect to pay CFP 15,000 a day and up. Since this amount can be shared among as many people as can fit inside, you'll want to join or form a group. While making your inquiries, keep your ears open for any mention of boat tours as these are often no more expensive than land tours. Low-budget travelers with plenty of time could consider walking from place to place.

NUKU HIVA

Nuku Hiva is the largest (339 square km) and most populous (2,375 inhabitants) of the Marquesas. Taiohae (population 1,700) on the south coast is the administrative and economic center of the Marquesas. It's a modern little town with

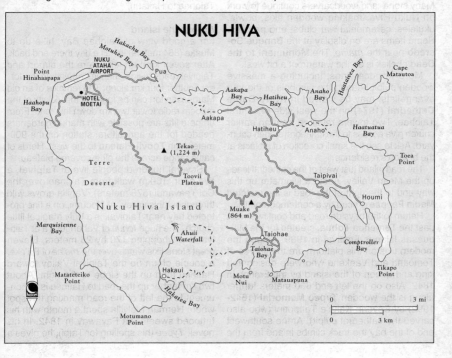

NUKU HIVA

Point Hinahaapapa
Haahopu Bay
NUKU ATAHA AIRPORT
Motuhee Bay
Hakaehu Bay
Pua
HOTEL MOETAI
Aakapa Bay
Aakapa
Hatiheu Bay
Hatiheu
Anaho Bay
Anaho
Haatuivea Bay
Cape Matautoa
Haatuatua Bay
▲ Tekao (1,224 m)
Terre Deserte
Toovii Plateau
Toea Point
Taipivai
Nuku Hiva Island
▲ Muake (864 m)
Houmi
Marquisienne Bay
Ahuii Waterfall
Taiohae
Taiohae Bay
Comptroller Bay
Matateteiko Point
Hakaui
Motu Nui
Matauapuna
Tikapo Point
Hakatea Bay
Motumano Point

0   3 mi
0   3 km

post office, a hospital, a town hall, a bank, five grocery stores, street lighting, and several hotels. Radio Meitai broadcasts over 101.3 MHz. Winding mountain roads lead northeast from Taiohae to Taipivai and Hatiheu villages or northwest toward the airport. In the center of the island Mt. Tekao (1,224 meters) rises above the vast, empty Toovii Plateau.

Taiohae Bay is a flooded volcanic crater guarded by two tiny islands called The Sentinels. Though open to the south, Taiohae's deep harbor offers excellent anchorage. Cruising yachts toss in the hock on the west side of the bay below the Keikahanui Inn, while the *Aranui* and *Taporo* tie up to a wharf at the southeast end of town. Take care with the drinking water at Taiohae. Unfortunately, many beaches around Nuku Hiva are infested with sandflies called *no-nos* that give nasty bites (the bugs disappear after dark).

Sights of Taiohae

Many stone- and woodcarvers continue to work on Nuku Hiva, making wooden tikis, bowls, ukuleles, ceremonial war clubs, and paddles. Some items are on display at the **Banque So-credo** near the *mairie*. The **Monument to the Dead** obelisk is on the waterfront a bit west.

More woodcarvings, including a massive wooden pulpit bearing the symbols of the four evangelists, may be viewed in **Notre-Dame Cathedral** (1974) on the west side of central Taiohae. Two towers retained from an earlier church give access to the cathedral's open courtyard. Ask to see the small collection of artifacts at the bishop's residence.

The road inland just west of the cathedral leads up the Meau Valley. About a kilometer up this way and to the right of the road is the restored **Mauia Paepae** graced by a contemporary tiki.

Return to the bayside road and continue west past the **Temehea Tohua,** created for the Marquesas Islands Festival in 1989. Among the modern tikis on this platform are the figures of Temoana and Vaekehu who were designated king and queen of the island by the French in 1842. Also on the left and 600 meters further along is the wooden **Typee Memorial** (1842-1992) by Séverin Kahe'e Taupotini (who also carved the cathedral pulpit). At the southwest end of the bay the track climbs inland from the Nuku Hiva Village Hôtel and continues two km over the ridge to secluded **Haaotupa Bay,** a nice picnic spot.

West of Taiohae

At Hakaui, 15 km west of Taiohae, a river runs down a narrow steep-sided valley. Fantastic 350-meter **Ahuii Waterfall,** highest in the territory, drops from the plateau at the far end of the valley, four km from the coast. It's a two-hour walk from Hakaui to the waterfall with a few thigh-high river crossings after rains (guide not required). The trail passes many crumbling platforms, indicating that the valley was once well populated. If you swim in the pool at the falls beware of falling pebbles. A boat from Taiohae to Hakaui would cost CFP 12,500 and up return, but an overgrown 12-km switchback trail also crosses the 535-meter ridge from above Haaotupa Bay to uninhabited Hakaui. You'll need to be adventurous and good at finding your own way to follow it (allow four hours each way between Taiohae to Hakaui).

Across the Island

For a good view of Taiohae Bay, hike up to **Muake** (864 meters) in half a day there and back. After seven km turn left where the airport and Taipivai roads divide, then left again into the forest another four km along. The remains of an old Marquesan fort can be found in the vicinity of the modern radio tower two km down this road. From up here lifts are possible with market gardeners headed for the agricultural station on the 900-meter-high **Toovii Plateau** to the west. Herds of cattle range across the pine-covered plateau.

Several hundred people live at **Taipivai,** a five-hour, 16-km walk from Taiohae over the Col Teavanui (576 meters). Vanilla grows wild throughout this valley. At Hooumi, on a fine protected bay near Taipivai, is a truly magical little church. The huge *tohua* of Vahangeku'a at Taipivai is a whopping 170 by 25 meters. Eleven great stone tikis watch over the *me'ae* of Pa'eke, a couple of km up the Taipivai Valley toward Hatiheu then up the slope to the right. About two km farther up the road to Hatiheu is a monument to the left of the road marking the spot where Herman Melville spent a month with his tattooed sweetheart Fayaway in 1842. In his novel, *Typee* (his spelling for Taipi), he gives a delightful account of the life of the great-grand-parents of the present forlorn and decultured inhabitants.

From Taipivai it's another 12 km via the Col Teavaitapuhiva (443 meters) to **Hatiheu** on the north coast. Some spectacular falls are seen in the distance to the left of the road near the mountain pass. A statue of the Virgin Mary stands on a green peak 300 meters above Hatiheu Bay and its black-sand beach. (Yachties are better off anchoring in protected Anaho Bay than here.) Hatiheu was destroyed by a tsunami in 1946 but 350 people still live there today. The restored Hikoku'a Tohua is a bit more than a kilometer from Hatiheu back toward Taipivai. Several of the tikis on the structure were added during the 1989 Marquesas Islands Festival while others are old (notice the phallic fertility statue on the left). In the jungle a kilometer farther up the valley and across the road is the Te l'ipoka Me'ae where many human sacrifices were made to the goddess Te Vana'uau'a. The victims were kept in a pit beneath a huge sacred banyan tree until their turn to be consumed at cannibal feasts arrived. Up the steep wooded slope from here is the overgrown Kamuihei Tohua with petroglyphs.

Anaho is two km east of Hatiheu over a 217-meter pass. It's one of the most beautiful of Nuku Hiva's bays, with a fine white beach and some of the finest snorkeling in the Marquesas (lovely coral and the possibility of seeing turtles or reef sharks). Even better white-sand beaches face Ha'atuatua and Haataivea bays beyond Anaho. No one lives there, though wild horses are seen.

Sports and Recreation

Scuba diving is offered by Xavier Curvat's **Centre Plongée Marquises** (B.P. 100, 98742 Taiohae; tel./fax 92-00-88) at the old marina in Taiohae. A 10-dive package is CFP 45,000 including gear. Snorkelers are welcome and scuba certification is offered. Xavier has explored the archipelago thoroughly during his 20 years in the Marquesas and his local knowledge is unequaled. There's not much coral to be seen here but the underwater caves and spectacular schools of hammerhead sharks or pygmy orcas compensate. Dive trips to Ua Pou are offered weekly.

Horseback riding is offered by Sabine Teikiteetini (B.P. 171, 98742 Taiohae), who can be

contacted through the *mairie* in Taiohae. Rides from Taiohae to Taipivai are possible.

Accommodations in Taiohae

The least expensive place to stay is **Chez Fetu** (Cyprien Peterano, B.P. 22, 98742 Taiohae; tel. 92-03-66), on a hill behind Magasin Kamake, an eight-minute walk from the wharf in Taiohae. The four rooms with shared bath in the family residence and one bungalow are CFP 2,000/4,000/6,000 single/double/triple, or CFP 50,000 a month. Communal cooking facilities are available and there's a terrace, but the children can be loud. Inexpensive.

Andy's Dream (André Teeikiteetini, B.P. 111, 98742 Taiohae; tel. 92-00-80, fax 92-04-05) is at Hoata about a kilometer from the wharf. A room with breakfast in an island house is CFP 3,000 pp and you may be able to cook. Inexpensive.

The friendly, two-story **Hôtel Moana Nui** (Charles Mombaerts, B.P. 33, 98742 Taiohae; tel. 92-03-30, fax 92-00-02), on the waterfront in the middle of Taiohae, has seven clean rooms with private bath (hot water) above their popular restaurant/bar. Bed and breakfast is CFP 4,000/4,500 single/double, other meals CFP 2,500 each. The Moana Nui is famous for its pizza. Mosquitos and bar noise are drawbacks, the excellent views from the terrace a plus. Cars are for rent at CFP 8,000 a day and boat excursions can be arranged. Inexpensive.

In 1993 the **Nuku Hiva Village Hôtel** (Bruno and Gloria Gendron, B.P. 82, 98742 Taiohae; tel. 92-01-94, fax 92-05-97) opened in Taiohae village with 15 thatched *fares* with private bath arrayed along the west side of Taiohae Bay opposite the yacht anchorage. The rates are CFP 6,500/7,500/8,500 single/double/triple, plus CFP 3,500 pp a day for breakfast and dinner. A local band plays in the restaurant Saturday nights. Excursions by 4WD, horseback riding, and scuba diving can be arranged. Moderate.

The **Keikahanui Inn** (B.P. 21, 98742 Taiohae; tel. 92-03-82, fax 92-00-74), just up the hill from the Nuku Hiva Village, is named after a tattooed chief but owned by ex-American yachtie Rose Corser (ask to see Maurice McKittrick's logbooks). They have five screened Polynesian bungalows with private bath: CFP 8,500/12,000/14,000 single/double/triple plus tax. In early 1999 it was reported that the Inn was being completely rebuilt as "Pearl

Lodge" with a swimming pool and 20 new a/c bungalows costing CFP 18,000-22,000 double plus tax. Cooking facilities are not provided, so for breakfast and dinner add CFP 5,300 pp. Rose's restaurant/bar is Nuku Hiva's unofficial yacht club (rinse the sand off your feet before entering). You can buy Fatu Hiva tapa at the inn. Premium to luxury.

Accommodations around the Island

The **Hôtel Moetai Village** (Guy Millon, tel. 92-04-91), a five-minute walk from Nuku Ataha Airport, has five bungalows with private bath (cold water): CFP 2,500/3,500/4,500 single/double/triple for bed and breakfast, other meals CFP 2,500. Budget.

At Taipivai village, **Chez Martine Haiti** (B.P. 60, 98742 Taiohae; tel. 92-01-19, fax 92-05-34) has two bungalows at CFP 2,000/3,500 single/double. You can cook for yourself or order dinner at CFP 2,000 pp. It's also possible to camp on Taipivai's football field (ask). Inexpensive.

In Hatiheu village, **Chez Yvonne Katupa** (B.P. 199, 98742 Taiohae; tel. 92-02-97, fax 92-01-28) offers five pleasant bungalows without cooking facilities or hot water at CFP 2,500/4,800 single/double, breakfast included. The bungalows are set in their own garden with views of Hatiheu Bay. A small restaurant nearby serves fried fish and lobster. Ask to see Yvonne's collection of artifacts from Ha'atuatua. It's possible to hire horses here. Inexpensive.

You can also stay on the white-sand beach at Anaho Bay, two km east of Hatiheu, accessible on horse or foot. **Te Pua Hinako** (Juliette and André Vaianui, B.P. 202, 98742 Taiohae; tel. 92-04-14), also known as Chez Juliette, has two rooms with shared bath at CFP 2,000 pp with breakfast, or CFP 5,000 pp with all meals. Yachties often come ashore to buy fresh vegetables from Teiki Vaianui's garden. Inexpensive.

In 1998 a new place opened at Anaho Bay, the **Kaoha Tiare** (Raymond Vaianui, B.P. 290, 98742 Taiohae; tel. 92-00-08 or 92-02-66). The five bungalows with bath are CFP 3,000/4,000 single/double, plus CFP 3,000 pp for all meals.

Services and Information

Central Taiohae boasts a Banque Socredo branch (tel. 92-03-63). The post office on the east side of town sells telephone cards that you can use at the public phone outside and several other locations around the island. The *gendarmerie* (tel. 92-03-61) is just up the road to the left of the post office, while the public hospital (tel. 92-03-75) is to the right. A private dentist, Dr. Jean-Michel Segur (tel. 92-00-83), is in the *mairie*. Tourist information is available from Déborah Kimitete's Nuku Hiva Visitors Bureau (tel. 92-03-73) in the old jail between the *mairie* and the post office. Air Tahiti (tel. 92-01-45) is next to the *mairie*.

Don't have your mail sent c/o poste restante at the local post office as it will be returned via surface after 15 days. Instead have it addressed c/o the Keikahanui Inn, B.P. 21, 98742 Taiohae, Nuku Hiva. You can also receive telephone calls and faxes through the inn (tel. 92-03-82, fax 92-00-74) 1600-1800, but remember that Rose Corser is running a restaurant and your patronage will be appreciated.

Getting Around

There's no public transportation from Taiohae to other parts of the island, though it's possible to hike across the island if you're fit. From Taiohae you could walk to Taipivai and Hatiheu in two days, camping or staying at local pensions along the way. The helicopter to the airport will pick up prebooked passengers at Hatiheu for the usual CFP 6,900, so it's not necessary to return to Taiohae. Check with Héli-Inter Marquises (tel. 92-02-17) at the Air Tahiti office in Taiohae. Also ask about the new road from Hatiheu to the airport via Aakapa and Pua, which may be open by the time you get there.

Island tours by Land Rover or speedboat can be arranged, but get ready for some astronomical charges (for example, CFP 15,000 for a visit to Hatiheu). Most car rentals are with driver only and thus cost taxi prices. To rent a car without driver for something approaching normal prices, ask at the **Hôtel Moana Nui** (tel. 92-03-30) or check with Alain Bigot (B.P. 51, 98742 Taiohae; tel. 92-04-34, fax 92-02-27) who has a store on the road inland from the beach. **Teiki Transports** (Mr. Teikivaini Puhetini, tel. 92-03-47) arranges chauffeur-driven cars.

Airport

Nuku Ataha Airport (NHV) is in the arid Terre Déserte at the northwest corner of Nuku Hiva, 32 km from Taiohae along a twisting dirt road over the Toovii Plateau. Upon arrival from Papeete or Rangiroa turn your watch ahead 30 minutes. A restaurant and hotel are near the terminal. The main drawback to flying into Nuku Hiva is the cost of airport transfers, which run CFP 3,500 each way by 4WD Toyota Landcruiser by day (CFP 5,000 pp by night), or CFP 6,900 pp each way by helicopter. Air Tahiti weight limits also apply on the 10-minute helicopter ride, so the 2.5-hour drive should be your choice if you're not traveling light. When shopping for woodcarvings during your stay on Nuku Hiva keep in mind the problem of getting the stuff back to Papeete.

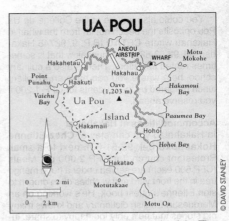

© DAVID STANLEY

UA POU

This spectacular, diamond-shaped island lies about 40 km south of Nuku Hiva. Several jagged volcanic plugs loom behind Hakahau, the main village on the northeast coast of 105-square-km Ua Pou, the third-largest Marquesan island. One of these sugarloaf-shaped mountains inspired Jacques Brel's song "La Cathédrale" and the name Ua Pou itself means "the pillars." Mount Oave (1,203 meters), highest point on Ua Pou, is often cloud-covered. The population of 2,000 plus is larger than Hiva Oa's. In 1988, 500 French foreign legionnaires rebuilt the breakwater at Hakahau, and the *Aranui* can now tie up to the concrete pier.

Sights
The first stone church in the Marquesas was erected at Hakahau in 1859, and the present **Church of Saint-Etienne** (1981) has a pulpit shaped like a boat carved from a single stump. The **Tenai Paepae** in the center of the village was restored for the 1995 Marquesas Islands Festival, the same occasion that saw the inauguration of the small **museum** at the south end of Hakahau.

Anahoa Beach is a scenic 30-minute walk east of the marina, and from the ridge halfway there you can climb up to the cross overlooking Hakahau for a superlative bird's-eye view.

A road leads south from Hakahau to a beach beyond Hohoi. Three km along this road turn left and halfway down the track to **Hakamoui**

Bay you'll find several *paepae* on the right. The stones bear carvings of faces and a tiki are nearby. On 88-meter-high **Motu Oa** off the south coast, millions of seabirds nest. The villages of Hakatao and Hakamaii on the west coast are only accessible by foot, hoof, or sea.

Accommodations in Hakahau
Right beside the post office and just back from the beach is **Chez Marguerite Dordillon** (B.P. 87, 98745 Hakahau; tel. 92-51-36). Here guests are accommodated in a modern two-room house with cooking facilities at CFP 2,000/3,500 single/double (CFP 500 surcharge for one or two nights). Marguerite herself lives in the southern part of town up the hill from the museum. Budget.

Pension Pukuéé (Hélène and Doudou Kautai, B.P. 31, Hakahau; tel./fax 92-50-83) is on a hill overlooking the village, just a few minutes walk from the wharf on the road to Anahoa Beach. The six shared-bath rooms are CFP 3,000 pp with breakfast, plus CFP 1,000/2,000 for lunch/dinner. Yachties often order seafood meals here. Inexpensive.

Chez Sam Teikiehuupoko (Samuel and Jeanne-Marie Teikiehuupoko, B.P. 19, 98745 Hakahau; tel. 92-53-16), opposite the Air Tahiti agent in the center of the village, has a pair of two-room houses with cooking facilities at CFP 2,500 pp with reductions for stays of three days or more. Inexpensive.

You could also inquire at the Collège de Ua Pou opposite the beach not far from the wharf in Hakahau where **CETAD** (B.P. 9, 98745 Hakahau; tel. 92-53-83) has a bungalow that is sometimes rented to visitors. There's also a culinary school here where you can have an excellent lunch prepared by the students for CFP 1,200 if you reserve ahead.

Accommodations at Hakahetau

In Hakahetau you can stay at **Chez Étienne Hokaupoko** (tel. 92-51-03), next to a small Protestant church, for CFP 2,000 pp. Meals (CFP 600 each) are served under a huge mango tree in the front yard and yachties often drop in to sign Étienne's guest book. He's working on an Marquesan-English dictionary and knows many old stories that he's only too happy to share. Inexpensive.

Shopping

A craft shop near the wharf at Hakahau sells local carvings, goatskin ukuleles, and beautiful hand-painted pareus. Four woodcarvers work in Hakahau village—just ask for *les sculpteurs.* If you're buying, shop around at the beginning of your stay, as many items are unfinished and there'll be time to have something completed for you.

Services

The Banque Socredo (tel. 92-53-63), *mairie,* and a post office are all adjacent opposite the market and not far from the beach. The *gendarmerie* (tel. 92-53-61) is a bit south. Infirmaries are in Hakahau, Hakatao, and Hakamaii. Six or seven stores are to be found in Hakahau.

Getting There

Ua Pou's Aneou airstrip (UAP) is on the north coast, 10 km west of Hakahau on a rough road over a ridge. The pensions in Hakahau offer airport transfers for CFP 1,000 pp return. You can reach **Air Tahiti** in Hakahau at tel. 92-53-41.

Xavier Curvat's Centre Plongée Marquises (tel./fax 92-00-88) in Taiohae generally has a launch from Nuku Hiva to Hakahau Friday at 0700, departing Hakahau for the return to Taiohae the same afternoon at 1600 (1.5 hours each way, CFP 4,000 one-way or CFP 6,000 for a roundtrip the same day). It's better to check on this a few days before.

UA HUKA

Ua Huka lies 35 km east of Nuku Hiva and 56 km northeast of Ua Pou. Crescent-shaped Ua Huka is the surviving northern half of an ancient volcano and the 575 inhabitants reside in the truncated crater in the south. Goats and wild horses range across this arid, 83-square-km island, while the tiny islands of Teuaua and Hemeni, off the southwest tip of Ua Huka, are a breeding ground for millions of *kaveka* (sooty terns). Sadly, local residents use these islands as a source of eggs. Mount Hitikau (884 meters) rises northeast of Hane village. Vaipae'e is the main village of the island, although the clinic is at Hane.

Archaeological excavations by Prof. Y.H. Sinoto in 1965 dated a coastal site on Ua Huka to A.D. 300, which makes it the oldest in Tahiti-Polynesia; two pottery fragments found here suggest that the island was probably a major dispersal point for the ancient Polynesians. Sinoto believes the migratory paths of Ua Huka's terns may have led the ancient Polynesians on their way to new discoveries.

Three small tikis cut from red rock may be visited in the valley behind Hane. Between Hane and Vaipae'e is a plantation that has been converted into a botanical garden complete with an aviary (open weekday mornings). Near the post office in Vaipae'e is a small but admirable **Musée Communal** of local artifacts and seashells, and replicas made by local artist Joseph Tehau Va'atete. Many other woodcarvers are active here.

Accommodations

Chez Alexis (Alexis Scallamera, tel. 92-60-19) in Vaipae'e village, six km from the airport, is a two-room house with shared bath at CFP 1,500 pp, or CFP 5,000 with full board. You're welcome to cook your own food. Alexis can arrange horseback riding and boat excursions. Budget.

Also in Vaipae'e is **Chez Christelle** (Christelle Fournier, tel. 92-60-85), a four-room house with shared bath at CFP 2,000 pp with breakfast, plus CFP 1,000/2,000 for lunch/dinner. It's run by the Air Tahiti agent. Inexpensive.

In Hane village, the **Auberge Hitikau** (Céline and Jean Fournier, tel. 92-60-68) offers four rooms with shared bath in a concrete building at CFP 2,000/3,500 single/double with breakfast.

Lobster is served in their restaurant at CFP 2,000. Jean has a car and boat for rent. Inexpensive.

Getting There

The airstrip (UAH) is on a hilltop between Hane and Vaipae'e, slightly closer to the latter. The Vaipae'a pensions generally provide free airport transfers, while those at Hane and beyond want CFP 2,000-3,000 for the car. The Air Tahiti number is tel. 92-60-85. The *Aranui* enters the narrow fjord at Vaipae'e and ties up to a wharf. It's quite a show watching the ship trying to turn around.

HIVA OA

Measuring 40 by 19 km, 315-square-km Hiva Oa (population 1,900) is the second largest of the Marquesas and main center of the southern cluster of islands. Mount Temetiu (1,276 meters) towers above Atuona to the west. Steep ridges falling to the coast separate lush valleys on the long crescent-shaped island. Ta'aoa, or "Traitors'," Bay is a flooded crater presently missing its eastern wall, while Puama'u sits in a younger secondary crater. The administrative headquarters for the Marquesas group has switched back and forth several times: Taiohae was the center until 1904, then it was Atuona until 1944, when Taiohae took over once more.

Sights of Atuona

Along with exhibits on the life of Atuona's most famous resident, the **Musée Ségelin-Gauguin** (admission CFP 400) in central Atuona is dedicated to the life of French writer Victor Ségelin who visited Atuona just after Gauguin's death. In 1991 Gauguin's thatched "Maison du Jouir" (House of Pleasure) was reconstructed next to the museum and it's presently used as a place for local artists to display their works. Jacques Brel's aircraft is on display here. The *paepae* platforms near the museum were also built for the Marquesas Islands Festival in December 1991.

Back on the main street is **Magasin Pierre Shan** where Gauguin left an unpaid wine bill when he died. Go up the hill from just past the nearby *gendarmerie* and take the first fork in the road to the left to reach **Calvary Cemetery,** which hosts the graves of Brel and Gauguin. The views of Atuona from here are excellent.

The beach at Atuona is poor and for better swimming, take the road six km southwest along the bay to the black beach at **Ta'aoa.** A big restored *tohua* with several *me'ae* platforms and a basalt tiki is found a bit more than a kilometer up the river from there.

Puama'u

A second village, Puama'u, is on the northeast coast, 30 km from Atuona over a winding mountain road. It's a good eight-hour walk from Atuona

HIVA OA

Matatepai Point

Hanaui Bay

Hanaiapa

Hiva Oa Island

Hanapaaoa

Ootua (924 m)

Nahoe

Cape Matafenua

Natue Bay

Kiukiu Point Hanamenu

Efeani (1,126 m)

AIRPORT

Puama'u

Temetiu (1,276 m)

Atuona

Traitors Bay

Ta'aoa

Point Teachoa

Bordelais Channel

0   3 mi

0   3 km

to Puama'u, up and down all the way. A few descendants of Gauguin are among the 300 people who live there today. Aside from the village's golden beach, the main reason for coming is to see the the five huge stone tikis on the Te I'ipona Me'ae in the valley behind Puama'u, a 15-minute walk from the village soccer field. One stands almost three meters high—the largest old stone statue in Polynesia outside of Easter Island. Notice the statue of the priestess who died in childbirth and the sculpted heads of victims of human sacrifice. The site was restored in 1991 and an admission of CFP 300 is charged (previous thefts from the site have necessitated the presence of a custodian).

Accommodations and Food

The **Mairie de Atuona** (B.P. 18, 98741 Atuona; tel. 92-73-32, fax 92-74-95) rents five well-equipped bungalows behind the town hall and post office at CFP 2,500/3,000 single/double. These have cooking facilities and private bath but can only be booked directly at the *mairie* during business hours. Budget.

Pension Gauguin (André Teissier, B.P. 34, 98741 Atuona; tel./fax 92-73-51), a bit east of the post office and up, has four rooms with shared bath at CFP 5,500/10,000 single/double with half board. It may be possible to get a room without meals at CFP 3,000 pp, and a kitchen and common room are provided. Deep-sea fishing and excursions can be arranged. Moderate.

Chez Ozanne (Ozanne and Marie Rohi, B.P. 43, 98741 Atuona; tel./fax 92-73-43), up the hill from Pension Gauguin, offers two rooms with shared bath at CFP 1,500/2,500 single/double. There's also a two-story bungalow in the yard at CFP 2,000/3,500. Cooking facilities are provided in the bungalow, or you can order breakfast/dinner at CFP 500/2,000. Ozanne has a 12-meter boat he uses for excursions and trips to Tahuata. He also organizes garden parties for yachties at CFP 1,000 pp, which includes transportation from the harbor and plenty of good local food (bring your own drinks). Ask to see Ozanne's log books, which date back to the 1970s and contain dozens of entries by cruisers who have passed this way over the years. Budget.

Overlooking Tahauku Bay is the **Temetiu Village** (Gabriel Heitaa, B.P. 52, 98741 Atuona; tel. 92-73-02), a kilometer east of Atuona on the way to the airport, then up the hill. The three bungalows with bath (cold water) are CFP 5,500/10,000 single/double with half pension (no cooking facilities). Nonguests are welcome at their terrace restaurant. Gabriel also has an eight-passenger boat for rent. Moderate.

Atuona's upmarket place, the **Hôtel Hanakéé** (Serge Lecordier, B.P. 57, 98741 Atuona; tel. 92-71-62, fax 92-72-51), has five stylish A-frame bungalows on the hillside above Tahauku wharf, two km east of the center. Accommodations run CFP 12,000/18,000/20,000 single/double/triple plus tax. Breakfast and dinner are CFP 3,360 pp extra, airport transfers CFP 3,600 pp return. Each bungalow contains a TV, VCR, washing machine, kitchen, fridge, and bathtub. A path behind the hotel leads up to the Jacques Brel Memorial on the spot where the singer had wished to build his home. There's a splendid view from there. Luxury.

In Puama'u village on northeastern Hiva Oa, you can stay at **Chez Heitaa** (Bernard and Marie-Antoinette Heitaa, tel. 92-72-27). The two rooms with cooking facilities and shared bath are CFP 3,000 pp including half board (or CFP 1,000 pp without meals). Airport transfers are CFP 20,000 for up to four people. Horses are for hire. Inexpensive.

For a juicy hamburger, *poisson cru,* or grilled fish with a cold beer try **Snack Make Make** (tel. 92-74-26), 100 meters east of the post office and on the opposite side of the street.

Services and Information

Banque Socredo (tel. 92-73-54) is next to the Air Tahiti office opposite the museum. The post office, town hall, dental center, and hospital (tel. 92-73-75) are two blocks east with the *gendarmerie* (tel. 92-73-61) diagonally opposite.

The Hiva Oa Comité du Tourisme (B.P. 62, 98741 Atuona; tel./fax 92-75-10) is in the craft shop at the museum.

Transportation

Yachts anchor behind the breakwater in Tahauku harbor, two km east of the center of town. Copra boats and the *Aranui* also tie up here. A lighthouse on the point between Tahauku and Atuona looks across the bay.

Location David (Augustine Kaimuko, tel. 92-72-87), next to Magasin Chanson up from the museum, rents cars at around CFP 10,000 a day all inclusive. To hire a four-passenger Land Rover with driver from Atuona to Puama'u will run you CFP 20,000 for the vehicle.

Airport

The airstrip (AUQ) is on a 441-meter-high plateau, eight km northeast of Atuona. In 1991 the runway was upgraded to allow it to receive direct ATR 42 flights from Papeete (via Nuku Hiva). Weekly flights by the smaller Dornier 228 aircraft continue to arrive from Rangiroa. **Air Tahiti** is at tel. 92-73-41.

It's a two-hour downhill walk from the airport to Atuona. The normal taxi fare from the airport to Atuona is CFP 1,800 pp each way, but the actual amount collected by the various hotels seems to vary, so check when booking.

TAHUATA

Tahuata (population about 650) is just six km south of Hiva Oa across Bordelais Channel. Fifteen km long by nine km wide, 69-square-km Tahuata is the smallest of the six inhabited islands of the Marquesas. A 17-km track crosses the island from Motopu to Vaitahu.

On the west coast is the main village, Vaitahu, where a new Catholic church was completed in 1988 to mark the 150th anniversary of the arrival here of Catholic missionaries. Mendaña anchored in Vaitahu Bay in 1595, followed by Captain Cook in 1774. Here too, Admiral Abel Dupetit-Thouars took possession of the Marquesas in 1842 and established a fort, despite strong resistance led by Chief Iotete. The anchorage at Hana Moe Noa north of Vaitahu is protected from the ocean swells. There's a lovely white beach and the water here is clear, as no rivers run into this bay.

Hapatoni village, farther south, is picturesque, with a century-old *tamanu*-bordered road and petroglyphs in the Hanatahau Valley behind. Coral gardens are found offshore and white-sand beaches skirt the north side of the island.

Accommodations

The only official place to stay is **Chez Naani** (François and Lucie Barsinas, tel. 92-92-26) in Vaitahu village. A room in this four-room concrete house with communal cooking facilities is CFP 1,500 pp (or CFP 4,850 pp with full board). Budget.

Getting There

There's no airport on Tahuata. To charter a six-passenger boat to/from Atuona is CFP 15,000-25,000 (one hour). Small boats leave Hiva Oa for Tahuata almost daily, so ask around at the harbor on Takauku Bay near Atuona.

The launch *Te Pua O Mioi,* belonging to the Commune of Tahautu (tel. 92-92-19), shuttles between Atuona and Vaitahu on Tuesday and Thursday (one hour, CFP 1,000 pp each way). It leaves Tahuatu around dawn, departing Hiva Oa for the return at noon. Southbound, take groceries with you.

FATU HIVA

Fatu Hiva is the southernmost (and youngest) of the Marquesas Islands, 56 km southeast of Tahuata. It was the first of the Marquesas to be seen by Europeans (Mendaña passed by in 1595). None landed until 1825 and Catholic missionaries couldn't convert the inhabitants until 1877. In 1937-38 Thor Heyerdahl spent one year on this island with his young bride Liv and wrote a book called *Fatu Hiva,* describing their far from successful attempt "to return to a simple, natural life." Fatu Hiva (84 square km) is far wetter than the northern islands, and the vegetation is lush. Mount Tauaouoho (960 meters) is the highest point.

This is the most remote of the Marquesas, and no French officials are present. With 650 inhabitants, Fatu Hiva has only two villages, Omoa and Hanavave, in the former crater on the western side of the island. It takes about five hours to walk the 17-km track linking the two, up and down over the mountains amid breath-taking scenery. Surfing onto the rocky beach at Omoa can be pretty exciting! Hanavave on the Bay of Virgins offers one of the most fantastic scenic spectacles in all of Polynesia, with tiki-shaped cliffs dotted with goats. Yachts usually anchor here. Horses and canoes are for hire in both villages.

Today a revival of the old crafts is taking place in Fatu Hiva, and it's again possible to buy not only wooden sculptures but painted tapa cloth.

Hats and mats are woven from pandanus. *Monoï* oils are made from coconut oil, gardenia, jasmine, and sandalwood. Yachties trade perfume, lipstick, and cosmetics for the huge Fatu Hiva grapefruits. Fatu Hiva doesn't have any *no-nos,* but lots of mosquitoes. If you plan on staying more than four months, get some free anti-elephantiasis pills such as Notézine at any clinic. Several families in Omoa village take paying guests.

Getting There

There's no airstrip on Fatu Hiva but the Mairie de Fatu Hiva (tel. 92-80-23) operates the 30-passenger catamaran *Atuona II,* once a week between Atuona and Omoa. It usually leaves Atuona Tuesday or Friday at 1400 (ask) and on the return trip they may agree to drop you on Tahuata. The trip takes just over three hours and costs CFP 4,000 pp each way.

OTHER ISLANDS

Motane (Mohotani) is an eight-km-long island rising to 520 meters about 18 km southeast of Hiva Oa. The depredations of wild sheep on Motane turned the island into a treeless desert. When the Spaniards "discovered" it in 1595, Motane was well-wooded and populated, but today it's uninhabited.

Uninhabited Eiao and Hatutu islands, 85 km northwest of Nuku Hiva, are the remotest (and oldest) of the Marquesas. Eiao is a 40-square-km island, 10 km long and 576 meters high, with rather difficult landings on the northwest and west sides. The French once used Eiao as a site of deportation for criminals or "rebellious" natives. The Queen of Raiatea and 136 Raiateans who had fought against the French were interned here 1897-1900. In 1972 the French Army drilled holes 1,000 meters down into Eiao to check the island's suitability for underground nuclear testing but deemed the basalt rock too fragile for such use. Wild cattle, sheep, pigs, and donkeys forage across Eiao, ravaging the vegetation and suffering from droughts. In contrast, the profusion of fishlife off Eiao is incredible.

Hatutu, the northernmost of the Marquesas, measures 7.5 square km. Thousands of birds nest here.

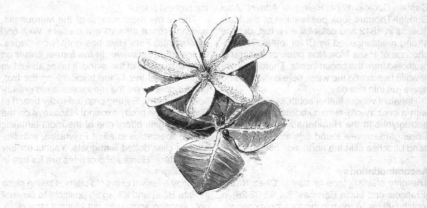

CAPSULE TAHITIAN VOCABULARY

ahiahi—evening
ahimaa—earth oven
aita—no
aita e peapea—no problem
aita maitai—no good
aito—ironwood
amu—eat
ananahi—tomorrow
arearea—fun, to have fun
atea—far away
atua—god
avae—moon, month
avatea—midday (1000-1500)

e—yes, also *oia*
Eaha te huru?—How are you?
E haere oe ihea?—Where are you going?
e hia?—how much?

faraoa—bread
fare—house
fare iti—toilet
fare moni—bank
fare niau—thatched house
fare punu—tin-roofed house
fare pure—church
fare rata—post office
fare toa—shop
fenua—land
fetii—parent, family
fiu—fed up, bored

haari—coconut
haere—goodbye (to a person leaving)
haere mai io nei—come here
haere maru—go easy, take it easy
hauti—play, make love
hei—flower garland, lei
here hoe—number-one sweetheart
himene—song, from the English "hymn"
hoa—friend

ia orana—good day, may you live, prosper
i nanahi—yesterday
ino—bad
inu—drink
ioa—name
ite—know

ma'a—food
maeva—welcome
mahana—sun, light, day
mahanahana—warm
maitai—good, I'm fine; also a cocktail
maitai roa—very good
manava—conscience
manu—bird
manuia—to your health!
manureva—airplane
mao—shark
mauruuru—thank you
mauruuru roa—thank you very much
miti—salt water
moana—deep ocean
moemoea—dream
moni—money

nana—goodbye
naonao—mosquito
nehenehe—beautiful
niau—coconut-palm frond

oa oa—happy
ohipa—work
ora—life, health
ori—dance
oromatua—the spirits of the dead
otaa—bundle, luggage
oti—finished

pahi—boat, ship
painapo—pineapple
pape—water, juice
parahi—goodbye (to a person staying)
pareu—sarong
pia—beer
pohe—death
poipoi—morning
popaa—foreigner, European
poti'i—teenage girl, young woman
raerae—effeminate
roto—lake
taapapu—understand
taata—human being, man
tabu—forbidden
tahatai—beach
tama'a—lunch
tama'a maitai—bon appetit

tamaaraa—Tahitian feast
tamarii—child
tane—man, husband
taofe—coffee
taote—doctor
taravana—crazy
tiare—flower
to'e to'e—cold
tupapau—ghost

ua—rain
uaina—wine
uteute—red

vahine—woman, wife
vai—fresh water
veavea—hot

NUMBERS

hoe—1
piti—2
toru—3
maha—4
pae—5
ono—6
hitu—7
vau—8
iva—9
ahuru—10
ahuru ma hoe—11
ahuru ma piti—12
ahuru ma toru—13
ahuru ma maha—14
ahuru ma pae—15
ahuru ma ono—16
ahuru ma hitu—17
ahuru ma vau—18
ahuru ma iva—19
piti ahuru—20
piti ahuru ma hoe—21
piti ahuru ma piti—22
piti ahuru ma toru—23
toru ahuru—30
maha ahuru—40
pae ahuru—50
ono ahuru—60
hitu ahuru—70
vau ahuru—80
iva ahuru—90
hanere—100
tauatini—1,000
ahuru tauatini—10,000
mirioni—1,000,000

PITCAIRN ISLANDS
INTRODUCTION

Legendary Pitcairn, last refuge of HMS *Bounty*'s mutinous crew, is the remotest populated place in the Pacific. This tiny colony, founded in 1790 by nine fugitive Englishmen and 19 Polynesians, is presently more than 200 years old. It's one of the ironies of history that Pitcairn, born out of treason to the British crown, was the first Pacific island to become a British colony (in 1838) and remains today the last remnant of that empire in the South Pacific.

The Land
Pitcairn Island, poking out of the sea more than 2,200 km southeast of Tahiti, sits alone between Peru and New Zealand at 25° south latitude and 130° west longitude. Its nearest inhabited neighbor is Mangareva, a small island in Tahiti-Polynesia 490 km to the northwest. Easter Island lies 1,900 km to the east. A high volcanic island, Pitcairn reaches 347 meters at the Pawala Ridge and is bounded by rocks and

high cliffs on all sides. There's no coral reef, and breakers roll right in to shore. The island is only 4.5 square km, almost half of which is fertile ground and well suited for human habitation. The uninhabited islands of Henderson, Ducie, and Oeno, belonging to Pitcairn, are described individually below. The tiny colony controls an exclusive economic zone of 800,000 square kilometers, an important reason why Britain is in no hurry to leave.

Climate
Pitcairn enjoys an equitable climate, with mean monthly temperatures varying from 19° C in August to 24° C in February. Daily temperatures can vary from 13° C to 33° C. The 2,000 mm of annual rainfall is unevenly distributed, and prolonged rainy periods alternate with droughts. Moderate easterly winds predominate with short east-to-southeast gales occurring between April and September.

HISTORY

The Lost Civilization

Although Pitcairn was uninhabited when the nine *Bounty* mutineers arrived in 1790, the remains of a vanished civilization were clearly evident. The sailors found four platforms with roughly hewn stone statues, somewhat like smaller, simpler versions of those on Easter Island. Being good Christians, the Pitcairners destroyed these platforms and threw the images into the sea. Unfortunately, almost nothing remains of them today. The only surviving piece of sculpture resides in Dunedin's Otago Museum in New Zealand. Sporadic visits by European archaeologists have uncovered traces of ancient burials and stone axes, and 22 petroglyphs are to be seen below "Down Rope." This evidence indicates that Pitcairn was occupied for a considerable period in the past, but where these ancient people came from and where they went are still mysteries.

European Discovery

Pitcairn was discovered in 1767 by Captain Carteret, on the HMS *Swallow*. The island was named for the son of Major Pitcairn of the marines, the first to sight it.

In 1788 the HMS *Bounty* sailed from England for the Pacific to collect breadfruit plants to supplement the diet of slaves in the West Indies. Because the *Bounty* arrived in Tahiti at the wrong time of year, it was necessary to spend a long five months there collecting samples, and during this time, part of the crew became overly attached to that isle of pleasure. On 28 April 1789, in Tongan waters, they mutinied against Lt. William Bligh under 24-year-old Master's Mate Fletcher Christian. Bligh was set adrift in an open boat with the 18 men who chose to go with him. He then performed the amazing feat of sailing 3,618 nautical miles in 41 days, reaching Dutch Timor to give the story to the world.

After the mutiny, the *Bounty* sailed back to Tahiti. An attempt to colonize Tubuai in the Austral Islands failed, and Fletcher Christian set out with eight mutineers, 18 Polynesians—men, women, and one small girl—to find a new home where they would be safe from capture. In 1791 the crew members who elected to remain on Tahiti were picked up by the HMS *Pandora* and returned to England for trial. Three were executed. The *Bounty* sailed through the Cook Is-

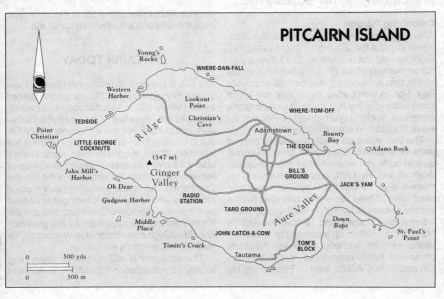

PITCAIRN ISLAND

A LETTER FROM JOHN ADAMS

John Adams was the only mutineer to survive the bloodshed of the first years on Pitcairn. In 1819, 10 years prior to his death, he wrote these words to his brother in England:

I have now lived on this island 30 years, and have a wife and four children, and considering the occasion which brought me here it is not likely I shall ever leave this place. I enjoy good health and except the wound which I received from one of the Otaheiteans when they quarreled with us, I have not had a day's sickness. . . . I can only say that I have done everything in my power in instructing them in the path of Heaven, and thank God we are comfortable and happy, and not a single quarrel has taken place these 18 years.

M.G.L. DOMENY DE RIENZI

lands, Tonga, and Fiji, until Christian remembered Carteret's discovery. They changed course for Pitcairn and arrived on 15 January 1790.

Colonizing Pitcairn

After removing everything of value, the mutineers burned the *Bounty* to avoid detection. Right up until the present, each 23 January on the anniversary of the *Bounty*'s demise, a model of the ship is launched and burned at Bounty Bay. For 18 years after the mutiny, the world knew nothing of the fate of the *Bounty,* until the American sealer *Topaz* called at Pitcairn for water in 1808 and solved the mystery.

The first years on Pitcairn were an orgy of jealousy, treachery, and murder, resulting from a lack of sufficient women after the accidental death of one. By 1794, only four mutineers remained alive, and all the Polynesian men had been killed. Three more men had died from a variety of causes by 1800, leaving only John Adams, nine women, and 19 children. Adams brought the children up according to strict Puritanical morality, and later the British Admiralty chose—all things considered—not to take action against him. Adams lived on Pitcairn until his

death in 1829 at the age of 65; of the mutineers, he is the only one with a known burial site.

PITCAIRN TODAY

The British Dependent Territory of Pitcairn, Henderson, Ducie, and Oeno Islands is administered by the Pitcairn Island Administration in Auckland, New Zealand, on behalf of the South Pacific Department of the Foreign and Commonwealth Office in London. The highest resident official is the island magistrate, elected for three years. There's also a 10-member Island Council, made up of the island magistrate, the chairman of the Internal Committee, the island secretary, four elected members, and one advisory member appointed by the elected members. One voting and one advisory member are appointed by the governor (the British high commissioner in Wellington). Island Council elections are annual.

The economy is self-sufficient, depending largely on subsistence agriculture, investment returns, and postage stamp sales. Collectors value Pitcairn stamps due to the history depicted on the limited issues (fewer than 500 Pitcairn stamps have come out since 1940). British government aid is available for major capital expenditures from time to time. All the men work for the administration, mostly part-time. The fertile soil supports a variety of fruits and vegetables for local consumption, with three crops of sweet potatoes grown a year. The only domestic animals are goats, chickens, cats, and dogs. The islanders make baskets, small wooden carved sharks, and tiny models of the *Bounty*.

There are 6.5 km of dirt roads on Pitcairn (muddy after rains), and the islanders ride around on three- and four-wheeled Honda motorcycles. There are also tractors, microwaves, freezers, and VCRs; electricity is on 0900-1200 and 1600-2200. The quaint Pitcairn wheelbarrows are a thing of the past. The modern conveniences have brightened the lives of the islanders, reduced the number of people required to sustain the community, and convinced more of the young to stay.

Even so, a fifth of the present population is older than 59, double the regional norm, and the median age of 35 is 10 years above the next oldest Pacific country. It takes at least four men to operate one of the longboats used to ferry passengers and goods from ship to shore and only eight working men remain on the island. Some Pitcairners feel that construction of an airstrip is the only way to avoid an eventual evacuation but Britain has refused to finance such a project. An air service could only be made viable through the development of tourism via Mangareva and the cost would be considerable. A realistic picture of life on Pitcairn today is provided in Dea Birkett's *Serpent in Paradise* (see **Resources**).

In 1998, with Hong Kong off its hands, the British government conferred full citizenship on residents of all its remaining colonies, including Pitcairn.

The People

Of the 65 permanent inhabitants of Pitcairn, 47 are direct descendants of the mutineers and their Tahitian wives. In 1831, there was an attempt to resettle them on Tahiti, out of fear of drought, but the Pitcairners returned to their island the same year. In 1856, all 194 islanders were forcibly taken by the British to Norfolk Island, between New Zealand and New Caledonia, where many of their descendants live today. Two families returned to Pitcairn in 1858, followed by four more in 1864. The present population is descended from those six families. Nearly half the people bear the surname Christian; all of the others are Warrens, Browns, and Youngs. The population peaked at 233 in 1937.

The Pitcairners speak a local patois of English and Tahitian. For example, rough seas is *illi illi* from "hilly" plus Tahitian repetitive emphasis. There's a primary school with a N.Z. teacher who also assists the post-primary students with

an early 19th-century view of Adamstown, Pitcairn Island

their N.Z. correspondence-school lessons. Scholarships are made available by the Island Council for older postprimary students wishing to further their education in New Zealand.

In 1967 David Silverman wrote in his book *Pitcairn Island* that there were around 1,500 true Pitcairners: 45 on Pitcairn, 150 in Tahiti-Polynesia, 160 in New Zealand, 400 in Australia, and most of the rest on Norfolk Island.

PRACTICALITIES

Accommodations and Food
No hotels or guesthouses exist on Pitcairn, and the two government hostels are reserved for official use. The island magistrate can organize paying guest accommodation with local families (around NZ$175 pp a week), but such arrangements must be made prior to arrival.

Visiting yachties are welcomed into the Pitcairners' homes. If you're headed for Pitcairn, take along a good supply of canned foods and butter, plus worthwhile books for the library, to repay the hospitality you'll receive. An American Seventh-Day Adventist missionary converted the Pitcairners in 1887, so pork, cigarettes, drugs, and alcohol are banned.

The Cooperative Store opens for a few hours three times a week. Canned foods are usually obtainable, but flour, eggs, meat, and butter must be ordered from New Zealand several months in advance. Since no freight is charged to Pitcairn for foodstuffs, prices are about the same as in New Zealand, with a markup of 20% to cover losses.

Visas
No visa is required of passengers and crew who visit while their vessel is at Pitcairn. Anyone wishing to stay on Pitcairn after the ship has left requires a residence permit issued by the Commissioner for Pitcairn Islands, Pitcairn Island Administration, Private Box 105696, Auckland, New Zealand (tel. 64-9/366-0186, fax 64-9/366-0187, e-mail: pitcairn@iconz.co.nz). If you're in Auckland you can visit them at Level 12, Patent House, 57 Fort Street. Applications must be approved by the Island Council and the governor, and a processing fee of NZ$10 is payable in advance (plus another NZ$30 if communicating by fax). If granted, a "li-

cense to land and reside" on Pitcairn for up to six months costs NZ$150. You'll be asked to provide a specific reason for wanting to go (researchers and writers are not welcome). Detailed information is provided on the Pitcairn Island Government Web Page (http://users.iconz.co.nz/pitcairn).

Money
New Zealand currency is used, with local Pitcairn coins. No bank exists on Pitcairn, but the island secretary will change foreign cash and traveler's checks.

Telecommunications
In 1992 an Inmarsat A Satellite Communications System was installed on Pitcairn and it's now possible to contact the island directly at tel. 872/144-5372 or fax 872/144-5373. Incoming calls are answered by an operator at 0900 (1830 GMT), 1200 (2030 GMT), 1600 (0030 GMT), and 2100 (0530 GMT). At other times an answering machine is used, although 2100-0900 (0530-1730 GMT) the whole system is switched off because the main power supply closes down at night. However, before dialing Pitcairn, check the cost with your long-distance operator as Inmarsat calls are extremely expensive (around US$10 a minute). If you know who you want, try calling person-to-person. Some Pitcairn locals are also not very happy with this high-tech replacement of the much cheaper radio telephone link with New Zealand that went before. A dozen Pitcairners are licensed ham radio operators, the highest proportion of amateur radio operators per capita in the world.

Media and Information
The *Pitcairn Miscellany* is a delightful monthly newsletter sponsored by the Pitcairn Island School. One may become a subscriber by sending US$10 cash or an undated check to: *Pitcairn Miscellany*, Pitcairn Island, via New Zealand. Allow several months for your letter to reach Pitcairn.

The **Pitcairn Islands Study Group** publishes *The Pitcairn Log* quarterly (US$15 a year). It contains much interesting material on the people of Pitcairn, as well as the collecting of Pitcairn postage stamps. For more information write: Mr. William Volk, 2184 6th Ave., Yuma, AZ 85364, U.S.A. (www.visi.com/~pjlareau/pisg.html).

Getting There

Talk of building an airstrip on Pitcairn has gone on for decades, and in early 1998 it was announced that the residents had finally agreed to surrender a good part of their farmland for this purpose. Whether construction will actually go ahead remains to be seen but such a facility would change the island forever.

There's no harbor on Pitcairn. All shipping anchors in the lee, moving around when the wind shifts. This is why most passing ships don't drop anchor but only pause an hour or so to pick up and deliver mail. The islanders come out to meet boats anchored in Bounty Bay and ferry visitors ashore.

There are two open anchorages: Bounty Bay is best when winds are blowing from the southwest, west, and northwest; Western Harbor should be used when there's an east wind. Both have landings, but Bounty Bay is tricky to negotiate through the surf, and Western Harbor is far from the village. A jetty was constructed at Bounty Bay by the Royal Engineers in 1976. The anchorage at Down Rope could be used in case of north or northeast winds, but there's no way up the cliff except the proverbial rope. Dangerous rocks lie off the south coast. The wind is irregular, so yachts must leave someone aboard in case it shifts.

The Pitcairn Island Administration in Auckland, New Zealand, will have information on container vessels that call at Pitcairn between New Zealand and the Panama Canal three or four times a year. Other ships occasionally stop at the discretion of the captain. Passage on these ships costs around US$800 one-way. Return passage is usually a matter of chance, and it may be necessary to wait several months for the next ship.

Tours

Unless you own a yacht, the only practical way of visiting Pitcairn is a yacht tour arranged by **Ocean Voyages Inc.** (1709 Bridgeway, Sausalito, CA 94965, U.S.A.; tel. 1-415/332-4681, fax 1-415/332-7460, www.crowleys.com/ocean.htm). These occur about once a year, usually involving a flight from Tahiti to Mangareva in the Gambier group, then a two-day sail to Pitcairn aboard a chartered yacht. One or two weeks are spent ashore as guests of the Pitcairners, and rather than lie idle, the yacht often does a wood run to Henderson and a fishing trip to Oeno during this period. Group members are invited to participate in the sailing of the yacht, if they wish. In recent years the trip has taken place between April and June. Prices range from US$3,250 to US$5,850 pp including the boat trip, lodging, and all meals on Pitcairn. Add US$600 for the return flight from Papeete to Mangareva and the cost of small gifts for the Pitcairners. Ocean Voyages has operated trips like this since 1980 and they're a once-in-a-lifetime opportunity for most of us, so if you have the time and money, just go.

Luxury cruise ships also visit Pitcairn occasionally, but they spend only a few hours ashore and are unable to land at all in bad weather. Check the listings for Nature Expeditions International and Quest Nature Tours in the introductory **Getting There** chapter.

If you can organize a small group, Ocean Voyages or any of the yacht charter brokers listed in the main introduction to this book can book crewed Tahiti-based yachts for trips to Pitcairn via Mangareva anytime. The cost will be US$8,000 a week for six persons, and three weeks must be allowed for the roundtrip sea journey alone, with the possibility of stops at the Tuamotus.

THE PITCAIRN ISLANDS

Pitcairn Island

Scattered along a plateau 120 meters above the landing at Bounty Bay is Adamstown, the only settlement. At the top of the hill over the bay is The Edge, a restful spot with benches, shady trees, and a great view of everything. The original Bible from the *Bounty* is showcased in the church at Adamstown. The Bible, sold in 1839, was eventually acquired by the Connecticut Historical Society, which returned it to Pitcairn in 1949. The four-meter anchor of the *Bounty,* salvaged in 1957, is now mounted in the square outside the courthouse. Pitcairn postage stamps may be purchased at the post office between the courthouse and church. The library is adjacent. A bell on the square is used to announce church services and the arrival of ships. The graves of John Adams, his wife Teio, and daughter Hannah are also visited.

On the ridge west of Adamstown is a cave in which Fletcher Christian stayed during the period of strife on the island. He was finally killed by two Tahitians.

Oeno and Ducie

Grouped together with Pitcairn under the same administration are the uninhabited islands of Oeno, Henderson, and Ducie, annexed by Britain in 1902. The four islands together total 47.4 square km. Unlike Pitcairn and Henderson, both Ducie and Oeno have central lagoons inaccessible to shipping. Passing Japanese freighters often dump garbage in these waters and tankers illegally flush their holds, as the trash and tar littering the beaches of these remote atolls clearly proves.

Oeno, a tiny 5.1-square-km atoll 128 km northwest of Pitcairn, is visited by the Pitcairners from time to time to collect shells, coral, and pandanus leaves to use in their handicrafts. Small boats can enter the shallow lagoon through a passage on the north side. In 1969-70 Oeno was used by the U.S. Air Force as a satellite observation post.

Ducie atoll (6.4 square km) is 472 km east of Pitcairn. The poor soil and lack of fresh water account for the sparse vegetation. Large whirlpools in the Ducie lagoon are caused by tunnels that drain the lagoon to the sea. Due to its inaccessibility Ducie is rarely approached, and tens of thousands of petrels and other seabirds nest here.

Henderson

Henderson, a 31-square-km elevated atoll 169 km east-northeast of Pitcairn, is the largest of the Pitcairn Islands. The island measures five km by 10 km and is flanked by 15-meter-high coral cliffs on the west, south, and east sides. Henderson is surrounded by a fringing reef with only two narrow passages: one on the north, the other on the northwest coast. The passages lead to a sandy beach on the island's north shore. The interior of the island is a flat coral

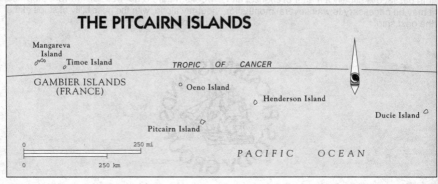

THE PITCAIRN ISLANDS

Mangareva Island

Timoe Island

GAMBIER ISLANDS (FRANCE)

TROPIC   OF   CANCER

Oeno Island

Henderson Island

Ducie Island

Pitcairn Island

PACIFIC   OCEAN

0   250 mi

0   250 km

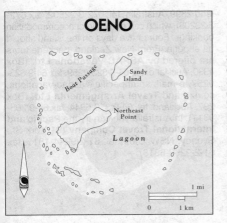

OENO

Boat Passage

Sandy Island

Northeast Point

Lagoon

0   1 mi

0   1 km

plateau about 33 meters high, but the dense undergrowth, prickly vines, and sharp coral rock make it almost impenetrable. There's said to be a freshwater spring visible only at low tide at the north end of the island, but this is doubtful, and no other source of water on the island is known.

There are two unique species of land birds on the island: a black flightless rail (Henderson chicken) and a green fruit pigeon. Fish and lobster are numerous, as are Polynesian rats. The Pitcairners visit Henderson to collect *miro* wood, which is excellent for carving. The last human inhabitant was an American, Robert Tomarchin, who was dropped off on Henderson in 1957 with his chimpanzee, Moko. Tomarchin lasted only three weeks before being rescued by a passing ship. In 1983 an American coal-mining millionaire named Smiley Ratliff offered to build airstrips on Pitcairn and Henderson, and to donate three small planes and about a million dollars for development projects if the British government would give him title to the latter. Luckily, he was turned down. There was also talk of constructing an emergency runway on Henderson to support air services between South America and the South Pacific but this was also rejected, and in 1988 the island was declared a World Heritage Site, the first South Pacific locale to be added to UNESCO's prestigious list. From January 1991 a Cambridge University team studied the flora and fauna of Henderson continuously for a 15-month period.

NORFOLK ISLAND

Norfolk Island, 1,120 km northwest of Auckland, 800 km south of Nouméa, and 1,400 km east of Brisbane, measures eight km by five km and is 3,455 hectares in area. When Captain Cook discovered this uninhabited island in 1774 it was tightly packed with tall, straight pine trees which he incorrectly judged would make fine masts for sailing ships. In 1788 the British government set up a penal colony here, but the island was abandoned in 1814. Fears that Norfolk might be occupied by a rival power led the British to reestablish their penal colony in 1825, but this facility gained notoriety through reports of wanton cruelty, and in 1855 the remaining prisoners were transferred to Tasmania, Australia.

In 1856 the existing prison infrastructure of staff quarters and farms was used to resettle the Pitcairn Islanders, and today a third of the 1,800 inhabitants have Pitcairn names. The Melanesian Mission established its headquarters on Norfolk in 1866, and until 1921 it had a college there used to train Solomon Islanders and others as pastors. The mission church and burial ground remain. Whaling was practiced by the islanders from the 1850s until 1962, but the event that changed Norfolk forever was the building of a wartime airport in 1944.

Today the island is a favorite vacation spot for middle-aged or retired Australians and New Zealanders who come for a quiet holiday. A small national park with hiking trails, the convict settlement, and lovely coastal scenery are the main attractions. The Pitcairn connection is heavily exploited by the local tourist industry, and there are Pitcairn museums, shows, film evenings, tours, and souvenirs.

Norfolk Island is a self-governing territory under Australian authority. Those making a return visit from Auckland or Nouméa do not require a visa for a stay of 30 days, but an Australian tourist visa is required of those continuing on to Australia (obtain beforehand). There are scheduled flights to Norfolk Island from Auckland, Brisbane, Lord Howe Island, and Sydney, and charters from Nouméa. An A$25 airport tax is collected upon departure.

Tourism is tightly controlled by the **Norfolk Island Government Tourist Bureau** (Box 211,

Norfolk Island 2899, Australia; tel. 672-3/22147, fax 672-3/23109, e-mail: info@nigtb.gov.nf) and only persons with prepaid accommodations are allowed entry. Camping, youth hostels, and most other forms of independent budget travel are strictly prohibited. There are more than 40 official places to stay on the island and prices are reasonable for a couple of nights, just be sure to get something with cooking facilities and perhaps a rental car included.

If your air ticket allows a stopover on Norfolk Island between New Zealand and Australia, contact **The Travel Center** (Box 172, Norfolk Island 2899, Australia; tel. 672-3/22502, fax 672-3/23205), which can make direct accommodation bookings. Four or five days on the island should be enough. From New Zealand, package tours are offered by **ASPAC Vacations Ltd.** (Box 4330, Auckland; tel. 64-9/623-0259, fax 64-9/623-0257, e-mail: southpacific@aspac-vacations.co.nz), and **Travel Arrangements Ltd.** (Box 297, Auckland; tel. 64-9/379-5944, fax 64-9/308-9311). In Australia you can try the **Pacific and International Travel Company** (91 York St., Sydney, NSW 2000; tel. 61-2/9244-1811, fax 61-2/9262-6318).

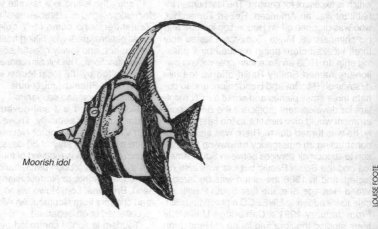

Moorish idol

LOUISE FOOTE

GORDON OHLIGER

EASTER ISLAND
INTRODUCTION

The mystery of Easter Island (Isla de Pascua) and its indigenous inhabitants, the Rapanui, has intrigued travelers and archaeologists for many years. Where did these ancient people come from? How did they transport almost 1,000 giant statues from the quarry to their platforms? What cataclysmic event caused them to overthrow all they had erected with so much effort? And most importantly, what does it all mean? With the opening of Mataveri airport in 1967, Easter Island became more easily accessible, and many visitors now take the opportunity to pause and ponder the largest and most awesome collection of prehistoric monuments in the Pacific. This is one of the most evocative places you will ever visit.

The Land
Barren and detached, Easter Island lies midway between Tahiti and Chile, 4,000 km from the former and 3,700 km from the latter. Pitcairn Island, 1,900 km west, is the nearest inhabited land. No other populated island on earth is as

isolated as this. At 109°26' west longitude and 27°9' south latitude, it's the easternmost and almost the southernmost island of the South Pacific (Rapa in Tahiti-Polynesia is a bit farther south). Easter Island is triangular, with an extinct volcano at each corner. It measures 23 by 11 km, totaling 171 square km.

The interior consists of high plateaus and craters surrounded by coastal bluffs. Ancient lava flows from Maunga Terevaka (507 meters), the highest peak, covered the island, creating a rough, broken surface. Maunga Pukatikei and Rano Kau (to the east and south respectively) are nearly 400 meters high. Many parasitic craters exist on the southern and southeast flanks of Maunga Terevaka. Three of these, Rano Aroi, Rano Raraku, and Rano Kau, contain crater lakes, with the largest (in Rano Kau) more than a kilometer across. Since 1935 about 42% of the island, including the area around Rano Kau and much of the island's shoreline, has been set aside as **Parque Nacional Rapa Nui** administered by the Corporación Nacional Fore-

EASTER I. CLIMATE

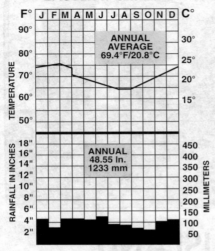

Climate
The climate is moderated by the cool Humboldt current and the annual average temperature is 20.3° C. The hottest month is February; the coolest are July and August. Winds can make the island feel much cooler. The climate is moist and some rain falls 200 days a year. March to June are the rainiest months; July to October are generally the driest and coolest, although heavy rains are possible year-round. Drizzles and mist are common, and a heavy dew forms overnight. Snow and frost are unknown, however. The porous volcanic rock dries out quickly, so the dampness need not deter the well-prepared hiker/camper.

HISTORY

Polynesian Genesis
It's believed that Easter Island was colonized around A.D. 400 by Polynesians from the Marquesas Islands, as part of an eastward migratory trend that originated in Southeast Asia around 1500 B.C. Here they developed one of the most remarkable cultures in all of Polynesia.

Long platforms or *ahu* bearing slender statues known as *moai* were built near the coasts, with long retaining walls facing the sea. Each *ahu* carried four to six *moai* towering four to eight meters high. These statues, or *aringa ora* (living faces), looked inland towards the villages, to project the mana (protective power) of the *aku-aku* (ancestral spirits) they represented.

The *moai* were all cut from the same quarry at Rano Raraku, the yellowish volcanic tuff shaped by stone tools. Some writers have theorized that the statues were "walked" to their platforms by a couple of dozen men using ropes to lean the upright figures from side to side while moving forward; others claim they were pulled along on a sledge or log rollers. Some statues bore a large cylindrical topknot *(pukao)* carved from the reddish stone of Punapau. Eyes of cut coral were fitted into the faces.

Other unique features of Easter Island are the strange canoe-shaped house foundations with holes for wall supports, and the incised wooden tablets *(rongorongo),* the only ancient form of writing known in Oceania. Only 25 examples survive, and Dr. Steven Roger Fischer,

stal (CONAF). In 1995 the park was added to UNESCO's World Heritage List, the first place in Chile to be so honored.

The forests of Easter Island were wiped out by the indigenous inhabitants long ago, and during the 19th century sheep finished off most of the remaining native vegetation. The last indigenous *toromiro* tree died in the 1960s and attempts have been made to reintroduce the species from overseas botanical gardens without success. Grasslands now envelop the green, windswept landscape; few endemic plants and no native land birds survive. The lakes feature thick, floating bogs of peat; *totora* reeds related to South American species surround and completely cover their surfaces. Pollen studies have determined that these reeds have existed here for at least 30,000 years. Large tracts of eucalyptus have been planted in recent years.

Small coral formations occur along the shoreline, but the lack of any continuous reef has allowed the sea to cut cliffs around much of the island. These bluffs are high where the waves encountered ashy material, low where they beat upon lava flows. Lava tubes and volcanic caves are other peculiarities of the coastline. The only sandy beaches are at Ovahe and Anakena, on the northeast coast.

Director of the Institute of Polynesian Languages and Literatures in Auckland, has shown how the neat rows of symbols on the boards record pro-creation chants.

In 1774 Captain Cook reported internecine fighting among the islanders, with statues toppled and their platforms damaged, and by 1840 all of the *moai* had been thrown off their *ahu,* either by earthquakes or rival tribes.

Fantasy and Fact

The first comprehensive explorations of Easter Island were carried out by Katherine Routledge in 1914-15, Alfred Metraux in 1934, and Thor Heyerdahl in 1955-56. Earlier, in 1947, Heyerdahl had achieved notoriety by sailing some 6,500 km from South America to the Tuamotu Islands in a balsa raft, the *Kon Tiki.* His 1955 Norwegian Archaeological Expedition was intended to uncover proof that Polynesia was populated from South America, and Heyerdahl developed a romantic legend that still excites the popular imagination today.

Heyerdahl postulated that Easter Island's first inhabitants (the "long ears") arrived from South America around A.D. 380. They dug a three-km-long defensive trench isolating the Poike Peninsula and built elevated platforms of perfectly fitted basalt blocks. Heyerdahl noted a second wave of immigrants, also from South America, who destroyed the structures of the first group and replaced them with the *moai-*bearing *ahu* mentioned above. Heyerdahl theorizes that the toppling of the *moai* was a result of the arrival of Polynesian invaders (the "short ears") who arrived from the Marquesas and conquered the original inhabitants in 1680. According to Heyerdahl, the birdman cult, centering on the sacred village of Orongo, was initiated by the victors.

Modern archaeologists discount the South American theory and see the statues as having developed from the typical backrests of Polynesian *marae.* The civil war would have resulted from over-exploitation of the island's environment, leading to starvation, cannibalism, and

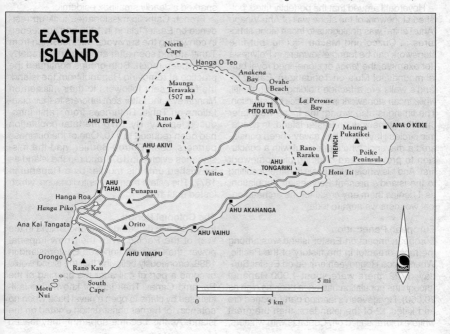

A rongorongo *tablet of incised driftwood, figures darkened. These boards were used as prompters by priests reciting procreation chants. The hieroglyphic* rongorongo *are the only known examples of writing in ancient Polynesia. Since every other line is upside down, a reader would have had to rotate the board continually.*

the collapse of the old order. Previous destruction of the forests would have deprived the inhabitants of the means of building canoes to sail off in search of other islands. The Poike trench was only a series of discontinuous ditches dug to grow crops, probably taro. Despite decades of study by some of the world's top archaeologists, no South American artifacts have ever been excavated on the island.

Heyerdahl argued that the perfectly fitted, polished stonework of the stone wall of Ahu Vinapu (Ahu Tahira) was analogous to Incan stone structures in Cuzco and Machu Picchu, but fine stonework can be found elsewhere in Polynesia (for example, the *langi*, or stone-lined royal burial mounds, of Mu'a on Tongatapu). Easter Island's walls are a facade holding in rubble fill, while Incan stonework is solid block construction. The timing is also wrong: the Incas were later than the stonework on Easter Island. In academic circles Heyerdahl has always been considered a maverick who started out with a conclusion to prove instead of doing his homework first. And his whole hypothesis is rather insulting to the island's present Polynesian population, as it denies them any credit for the archaeological wonders we admire today.

European Penetration

European impact on Easter Island was among the most dreadful in the history of the Pacific. When Jacob Roggeveen arrived on Easter Sunday, 1722, there were about 4,000 Rapanui (though the population had once been as high as 20,000). Roggeveen's landing party opened fire and killed 12 of the islanders; then the great white explorer sailed off. Contacts with whalers, sealers, and slavers were sporadic until 1862 when a fleet of Peruvian blackbirders kidnapped some 1,400 Rapanui to work in the coastal sugar plantations of Peru and dig guano on the offshore islands. Among those taken were the last king and the entire learned class. Missionaries and diplomats in Lima protested to the Peruvian government, and eventually 15 surviving islanders made it back to their homes, where they sparked a deadly smallpox epidemic.

French Catholic missionaries took up residence on Easter Island in 1865 and succeeded in converting the survivors; businessmen from Tahiti arrived soon after and acquired property for a sheep ranch. Both groups continued the practice of removing Rapanui from the island: the former sent followers to their mission on Mangareva, the latter sent laborers to their plantations on Tahiti. Returnees from Tahiti introduced leprosy. By 1870 the total population had been reduced to 110. One of the business partners, Jean Dutrou-Bornier, had the missionaries evicted in 1871 and ran the island as he wished until his murder by a Rapanui in 1877. The estate then went into litigation, which lasted until 1893.

The Colonial Period

In 1883 Chile defeated Peru and Bolivia in the War of the Pacific. With their new imperial power, the Chileans annexed Easter Island in 1888, erroneously believing that the island would become a port of call after the opening of the Panama Canal. Their lack of knowledge is illustrated by plans to open a naval base when no potential for harbor construction existed on the island. As this became apparent, they leased most of it to a British wool operation, which ran the island as a company estate until the lease was revoked in 1953. The tens of thousands of sheep devastated the vegetation, causing soil erosion, and stones were torn from the archaeological sites to build walls and piers. During this long period, the Rapanui were forbidden to go beyond the Hanga Roa boundary wall without company permission, to deter them from stealing the sheep.

In 1953 the Chilean Navy took over and continued the same style of paternal rule. After local protests, the moderate Christian Democratic government of Chile permitted the election of a local mayor and council in 1965. Elections were terminated by Pinochet's 1973 military coup, and Easter Island, along with the rest of Chile, suffered autocratic rule until the restoration of democracy in 1990. In 1984 archaeologist Sergio Rapu became the first Rapanui governor of Easter Island.

GOVERNMENT

Easter Island is part of the Fifth Region of Chile, with Valparaíso (Chile) as capital. The Chilean government names the governor; the appointed mayor and council have little power. Many local leaders would like to see Easter Island made a separate region of Chile, a change that would greatly increase local autonomy. Chile heavily subsidizes services on the island, and a large military and official staff are present, mostly *continentales* (mainlanders). A five-member Comisión de Desarrollo (development committee) representing the 800 ethnic Rapanui was established in 1994 under Chile's Indigenous Law.

Politics

After the return to democracy in Chile an indigenous rights group, the Consejo de Ancianos (Council of Elders), was formed to represent the island's 36 original families. They called for the creation of a new electoral district giving Easter Island its own representative in the Chilean Congress. In 1994 the Consejo split into two rival factions over the question of land rights, the original Consejo No. 1 led by former Mayor Alberto Hotus and a radical Consejo No. 2 without any legal authority but representing a growing body of opinion. The second group has posted banners outside the church demanding the return of lands and has tried to collect "cultural taxes" from off-island filmmakers and archaeologists. There have even been attempts to "tax" tourists! The clash of the long ears and short ears is reenacted here.

Today most of Easter Island's land is held by the Chilean State but any local will be able to tell which part of the island originally belonged to his/her original clan. On several occasions Chilean governments have tried to give the Rapanui clear title to rocky, eucalyptus-covered areas unsuitable for agriculture or cattle grazing, but these offers have been refused. Only about 10% of the island has ever been offered, and the Rapanui want much more than that. Protesters from Consejo No. 2 demand that the government turn over most of the island, despite the very negative effect this would have on the environment. At the moment Hanga Roa is the only permanent settlement, but many locals wish to colonize other areas. Unserviced squatter shacks are already springing up around the island and fields are being plowed without any archaeological impact studies being carried out. In Hanga Roa, houses have even been constructed right on top of ancient *ahu* platforms. The national park authorities are very upset about all this, but hesitate to expel anyone out of fear of provoking major unrest.

At times officials in far-off Chile have come up with reckless development plans of their own, such as projects for a "monumental" lighthouse on a hill overlooking the airport flight path, a naval base to proclaim Chilean sovereignty, a huge container port at La Pérouse Bay to service shipping across the Pacific, and a new airport on the north side of the island to support a massive increase in tourism. The Sociedad Agrícola y Servicios Ltda. (SASIPA), which provides water and electricity to the island and operates a cattle ranch at Vaitea, has come up with crazy ideas, such as an elitist golf course, resort, and botanical garden at Vaitea (the island's richest agricultural land). As yet, none of these wild plans have been implemented, but "progress" is catching up with this remote island. Sadly, there is no coherent management plan for Easter Island as a whole, no long pants in Paradise. It's just one interest group clawing against another, the world on a small scale.

THE PEOPLE

The original name of Easter Island was Te Pito o Te Henua, "navel of the world." The Rapanui believe they are descended from Hotu Matua, who arrived by canoe at Anakena Beach from Te Hiva, the ancestral homeland. The statues were raised by magic. The original inhabitants wore tapa clothing and were tattooed like Marquesans; in fact, there's little doubt their forebears arrived from Eastern Polynesia. The language of the Rapanui is Austronesian, closely related to all the other languages of Polynesia, with no South American elements.

The Rapanui have interbred liberally with visitors for more than a century, but the Polynesian element is still strong. Three-quarters of the almost 3,000 people on Easter Island are Rapanui or Rapanui-related. Since 1966 the Rapanui have been Chilean citizens, and many have emigrated to the mainland where about 1,000 Rapanui presently live. In turn, about 1,000 continentales live on Easter Island, most of them government employees and newly arrived small shopkeepers. The island around receives 10,000 tourists a year from Europe, Chile, the U.S., and Japan in that order.

Many of the local Rapanui made money during the 1993 filming of Kevin Costner's US$20 million epic Rapa Nui, and almost all of them bought a car. There's now one car for every two Rapanui and the newly paved streets of Hanga Roa are often jammed! Cars have replaced horses as status symbols and people cruise around town to show off. The sweet potato gardens around Hanga Roa have been abandoned, and frozen chickens, vegetables, and TV dinners are imported from Santiago in increasing quantities. Many people earn money from tourism as innkeepers, guides, and craftspeople, and lots more are employed by the Chilean government.

The locals generally speak Rapanui in private, Spanish in public, French if they've been to Tahiti, and English almost not at all. Spanish is gradually supplanting Rapanui among the young, and it's feared the language will go out of everyday use within a generation or two. Television is diluting the local culture. In general, the Rapanui are honest and quite friendly toward visitors.

Public Holidays and Festivals

Public holidays in Chile include New Year's Day (1 January), Easter Friday (March or April), Labor Day (1 May), Battle of Iquique Day (21 May), San Pedro and San Pablo Day (29 June), Assumption Day (15 August), Policarpo Toro Day (9 September), Military Coup Day (11 September), Independence Day (18 September), Army Day (19 September), Columbus Day (12 October), All Saints' Day (1 November), Conception Day (8 December), and Christmas Day (25 December). Policarpo Toro Day recalls the Chilean captain who annexed the island for Chile in 1888.

In late January or early February is the carnival-like **Tapati Rapa Nui** festival, with traditional dancing, sporting events, canoe races, a horse race, art shows, statue-carving contest, shell-necklace-stringing competition, body-painting contest, kai-kai (string figure) performances, mock battles, and the election of Queen Rapa Nui (who is dramatically crowned on a spotlit Ahu Tahai). A unique triathlon at Rano Raraku involves male contestants in body paint who paddle tiny reed craft across the lake, pick up bunches of bananas on poles and run around the crater and up the hill, where they grab big bundles of totora reeds to carry down and around the lake before a final swim across. There's also haka pei, which involves young men sliding down a grassy mountainside on banana-trunk sleds at great speed. Colored lights are strung up along the main street. Since 1994 Tapati Rapa Nui parades have displayed strong Hollywood influences in the floats and costumes, and you may even see topless young women riding on floats through Hanga Roa, just as they appeared in Kevin Costner's movie Rapa Nui! Needless to say, all flights immediately before and after the festival are fully booked far in advance.

Chilean Independence Day (18 September) is celebrated with parades and a fonda (carnival). Everybody takes three days off for this big fiesta. On the day of their patron saint, the main families stage a traditional feast (curanto), complete with an earth oven.

ON THE ROAD

SIGHTS

Vicinity of Hanga Roa

The **Catholic church** in the center of town is notable for its woodcarvings. Buried next to the church is Father Sebastian Englert, who founded the one-room **Museo Antropólogico** (tel. 100-296, closed Sunday afternoon and all day Monday; US$1 admission) on the north side of Hanga Roa. Inside is kept the white coral and red scoria eye of the *moai* found at Anakena in 1978. The William Mulloy Research Library (e-mail: BiMulloy@entelchile.net), presently at the Museo Fonck in Viña del Mar, Chile, is to be relocated here when funding allows.

Nearby at **Ahu Tahai,** just outside the town, are three *ahu,* one bearing five restored *moai* and a large restored statue complete with a red 10-ton topknot reerected by the late Dr. William Mulloy in 1967. The statue's "eyes" are crude copies recently cemented in place for the bene-

When La Pérouse visited Easter Island in 1786, the stone statues were still erect on their stepped platforms, topknots still in place. Notice the islander behind the statue attempting to steal an article of clothing from the explorers.

ATLAS DU VOYAGE DE LA PÉROUSE (1791)

fit of tourists. The islanders launched their canoes from the ramp leading down to the water between the *ahu.*

Five km north along the rough coastal road is unrestored **Ahu Tepeu,** with the foundations of canoe-shaped and round houses nearby. Inland via a little-used track and 10 km from Hanga Roa is **Ahu Akivi** (Siete Moai), with seven statues restored in 1960 by Dr. Mulloy. The seven *moai* that once overlooked a village are visible from afar.

On the way back to Hanga Roa climb **Punapau,** where the topknots were quarried. About 25 red topknots are in or near Punapau, the largest weighing 11 tons. **Maunga Orito,** south of Punapau, contains black obsidian, which the islanders used for weapons and tools.

Five km from Hanga Roa via the road along the north side of the airstrip are the fine Inca-like stone walls of the two *ahu* at **Ahu Vinapu** (Ahu Tahira). According to Heyerdahl, the perfectly fitted stonework of one dates from the earliest period and is due to contact with South America. Most authorities dispute this claim and suggest it was a later development by the skilled Polynesian stonemasons.

Rano Kau and Orongo

From Hanga Roa, the brisk six-km uphill hike south to Orongo and the vast crater of Rano Kau (316 meters) is easily done in a morning, but take along a lunch and make a day of it if you have the time. On the way, just past the west end of the airstrip, at the foot of the cliff near the water, is **Ana Kai Tangata,** the Cannibal Cave. Paintings of birds grace the ceiling of this cave.

The road, which swings around and up the side of Rano Kau to Orongo, offers an exciting panorama of cliffs, crater lake, and offshore islands. An admission of US$10 is charged by the national park ranger, who also sells a few interesting publications about the island and an excellent map. The entry fee may seem stiff, but all the other sites on the island are free, and CONAF is desperately short of funds needed to protect and maintain Easter Island's monuments. Save your receipt if you plan a repeat visit up this way.

(Beware of paying the money to unauthorized persons—check at the CONAF office if in doubt.)

At Orongo, the main ceremonial center on the island, are many high-relief carvings of bird-headed men on the rock outcrops. The 40 cave-like dwellings here (restored by Dr. Mulloy in 1974) were used by island chiefs and participants during the birdman festival. Each year a race was staged to the farthest offshore island, **Motu Nui,** to find the first egg of a species of migratory sooty tern *(manutara).* The winning swimmer was proclaimed birdman *(tangata manu)* and thought to have supernatural powers. You can hike right around the rim of Rano Kau. On the way back to town, it's possible to cut back toward Ahu Vinapu along the south side of the airstrip.

Around the Island

Although many of the enigmatic statues *(moai)* are concentrated at moss-covered Rano Raraku (the statue quarry), they are also found along the coast around the island. The stone walls seen at various places date from the English sheep ranch. Take the road along the south coast toward Rano Raraku, 18 km from Hanga Roa. Eight fallen *moai* lie facedown at **Ahu Vaihu.** The first king of the island, Hotu Matua, is buried at **Ahu Akahanga,** where four toppled statues are seen.

Work on the statues ended suddenly, and many were abandoned en route to their *ahu.* About 300 are still in the quarry at **Rano Raraku** in various stages of completion, allowing one to study the process; one unfinished giant measures 21 meters long. Others, visible from the top of Rano Raraku, lie scattered along the roadway to the coast. Some 70 statues stand on the slopes or inside the volcano; another 30 lie facedown on the ground. The kneeling statue, called Tukuturi, on the west side of Rano Raraku is unusual. A park ranger is posted in this area.

After climbing Rano Raraku, circle around to **Ahu Tongariki** at Hotu Iti, destroyed in 1960 by a huge tsunami that tossed the 15 statues around like cordwood. Between 1992 and 1994 Japanese archaeologists reconstructed the *ahu* and reerected the *moai* using an enormous crane donated by the Japanese crane manufacturer Tadano. Some extraordinary petroglyphs are at Tongariki, very close to the road.

Continue up along the ancient trench, which still isolates the **Poike Peninsula.** Legends maintain that the "long ears" filled the trench with wood to create a burning barrier between them and their "short-eared" adversaries, but were annihilated in the end. Heyerdahl claimed to have found a thick layer of red ash in the trench, but more recent excavations here have found no evidence of any battle.

The tallest *moai* ever to stand on Easter Island is at **Ahu Te Pito Kura** on the north coast by La Pérouse Bay. The toppled 10-meter-long statue lies facedown beside the *ahu,* awaiting restoration.

The inviting white sands of palm-fringed **Anakena Beach** are 20 km northeast of Hanga Roa via the paved central highway or 30 km via Rano Raraku. The National Parks Department has set up picnic tables, barbecue pits, toilets, and a campground here, and many locals come to swim or fish on Sunday (an easy time to hitch a ride). Anakena is the traditional disembarkation point of Hotu Matua, the legendary founder of the island. The one *moai* on **Ahu Ature Huki** here was reerected by Thor Heyerdahl in 1955, as is indicated on a bronze plaque—the first statue to be restored on the island. **Ahu Naunau** at Anakena bears seven *moai,* four with topknots. During the restoration of this *ahu* in 1978, archaeologist Sergio Rapu discovered the famous white coral eyes of the statues. Unfortunately this area is threatened by plans for a new major new port and fish-freezing plant with all its attendant industrial development.

Sports and Recreation

The scuba diving off Easter Island is not for beginners as one must dive in the open sea and the water is cool (Nov.-April is warmest). On the plus side are the unique caves, walls, corals, and fish. Michel García's **Orca Diving Center** (tel. 100-375, fax 100-448) offers diving, but certification is mandatory.

Surfers will find a couple of consistent waves adjacent to town, such as the rights at Ahu Tahai and Hanga Roa Bay and the left at Hanga Mataveri Otai. On the south side of the island a powerful right plows into the lava at Hanga Poukura. Some of the highest walls are a couple of kilometers east at Cabo Koe Koe. Summer is the best season on the north coast, winter on the south (especially March-Sept.). Ask for Carlos Lara, the local surf guide, who can provide vehicles and support.

Horseback riding is fun, and at about US$20/30 a half/full day, it's inexpensive. Guys on the street around Hanga Roa rent horses for less, but both animal and saddle may, sadly, be the worse for wear. Many of the island's hoofed animals look like the traditional woodcarvings of emaciated ancestor figures *(moai kavakava)* with their ribs sticking out. Anakena is a little far to go by horse and return in a day anyway, so look upon riding more as a change of pace than as a way of getting around. The area north of Hanga Roa can be explored by horse.

You can hike 60 km clockwise right around the island in three or four days, but take all the food and water you'll need. Camping is allowed at the national park attendant's post at Rano Raraku, and there's a regular campsite at Anakena. The park rangers may deign to replenish your water supply, but on very dry years no water is available for campers, so ask. If you camp elsewhere, try to stay out of sight of motorized transport. This is not an easy trip, so only consider it if you're in top physical shape. Good boots and a wide-brimmed hat are musts, as the terrain is rough and there's absolutely no shade. There are no snakes but watch out for scorpions and black widow spiders.

ACCOMMODATIONS

The median price for guesthouse accommodation is US$35/50/75 single/double/triple with private bath—expensive for Chile. The rooms are clean and simple, often facing a garden, but the cheaper places don't always have hot water (ask if it's included). All rates include a light breakfast, but for a full English breakfast you'll have to add US$5-10 pp. Beware if something extra is "offered," as you could end up paying US$40 more for one small frozen lobster. If you're asked to choose a meal plan, take only breakfast and dinner as it's a nuisance to have to come back for lunch. Picnic fare can be purchased at local stores. Unfortunately few places offer cooking facilities.

Room prices do fluctuate according to supply and demand, and when things are slow bargaining is possible everywhere except at the most upmarket places. Foreign tourists paying for rooms at the top hotels in U.S. dollars (cash or traveler's checks) rather than with pesos or by credit card may be exempt from the 18% value-added tax, something to ask about. If you're on a very low budget, ask about camping at a *residencial*. The only organized campsite is the one left by the Norwegian archaeological expedition at Anakena Beach, and you'll need to carry all your own food and water if you go there.

If you haven't booked a package, accommodations are easily arranged upon arrival, as many of the *residencial* (guesthouse) owners meet the flights. Only members of the tourist association representing the more expensive hotels are allowed inside the arrivals area at the airport. Outside the terminal you'll find several people offering less-expensive accommodations, and you'll save money by waiting to deal with them. Try to speak to the owner in person rather than a tout who will take a commission. Once it's all arranged they'll give you a free lift to their place. Don't promise to stay more than one night until you've seen the place and are happy.

The peak season with the highest visitor levels is Dec.-Feb.; June is the slackest month. Rooms are always available and advance bookings are not required, except perhaps during the Tapati Rapa Nui festival. The oldest and most reliable travel agency on Easter Island itself is **Mahinatur** (Benito Rapahango, tel. 100-220, fax 100-420, e-mail: mahina@entelchile.net) on Ave. Policarpo Toro near the airport. They can book hotel accommodations, excursions, and rental vehicles in advance, and their services are used by most overseas tour operators. Otherwise most of the properties listed below (or anybody on the island) can be faxed at 56-32/100-105, the Entel telephone office, which will call the hotel and ask them to come and get their fax.

If you do have reservations, beware of touts who may come up to you as you're leaving the baggage area claiming that the hotel you booked is full and that your reservation has been transferred to another hotel. If you get this story insist on checking directly with the original hotel, otherwise you could end up with a worse room for a higher price. Japanese tourists who don't speak English or Spanish are often targeted in this way.

The listings that follow are not exhaustive because almost every family on the island is in-

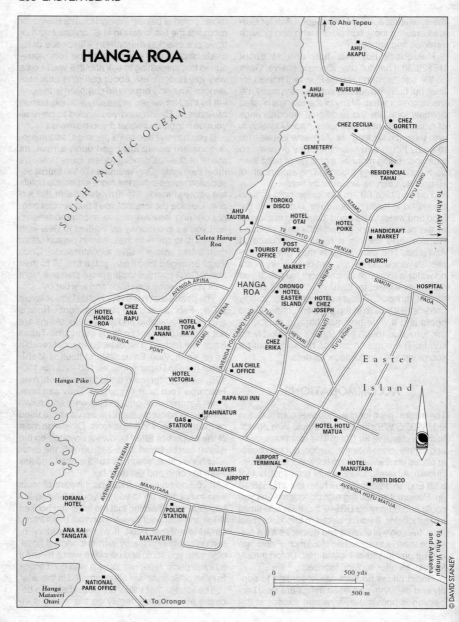

HANGA ROA

SOUTH PACIFIC OCEAN

To Ahu Tepeu

AHU AKAPU

AHU TAHAI

MUSEUM

CHEZ CECILIA

CHEZ GORETTI

CEMETERY

RESIDENCIAL TAHAI

To Ahu Akivi

TOROKO DISCO

HOTEL OTAI

HOTEL POIKE

HANDICRAFT MARKET

AHU TAUTIRA

POST OFFICE

TOURIST OFFICE

MARKET

CHURCH

Caleta Hanga Roa

HANGA ROA

ORONGO HOTEL EASTER ISLAND

HOTEL CHEZ JOSEPH

HOSPITAL

AVENIDA APINA

Easter

Island

HOTEL HANGA ROA

CHEZ ANA RAPU

TIARE ANANI

HOTEL TOPA RA'A

CHEZ ERIKA

AVENIDA PONT

Hanga Piko

HOTEL VICTORIA

LAN CHILE OFFICE

RAPA NUI INN

MAHINATUR

GAS STATION

HOTEL HOTU MATUA

AIRPORT TERMINAL

HOTEL MANUTARA

PIRITI DISCO

MATAVERI AIRPORT

AVENIDA HOTU MATUA

AVENIDA ATAMU TEKENA

MANUTARA

IORANA HOTEL

POLICE STATION

MATAVERI

ANA KAI TANGATA

To Ahu Vinapu and Anakena

Hanga Mataveri Otari

NATIONAL PARK OFFICE

To Orongo

0   500 yds

0   500 m

© DAVID STANLEY

volved in tourism in some way. The prices given are those charged in the low season (May-Nov.), and one should expect basic conditions at the cheapest places and less than might be hoped for at the more expensive ones. All of the 10 hotels and 30 *residenciales* are in Hanga Roa, arranged here beginning with those closest to the airport.

Budget

Residencial Anna Rapu Briones (tel. 100-540), near Hotel Hanga Roa on Ave. Apina, offers eight rooms at US$30 double with shared bath, US$35 with private bath, or US$5 pp to camp in the garden. You can also wash clothes here and cook your own food. Ask for Anna at the airport.

Residencial Tekena Inn (tel. 100-289), on Policarpo Toro in the center of town, is US$30 double, plus US$10 pp for dinner.

Residencial Maorí (tel. 100-497), Calle Te Pito o Te Henua, is also US$30 double.

Inexpensive

One of the island's best established guesthouses is the **Rapa Nui Inn** (tel. 100-228), Ave. Policarpo Toro at Ave. Hotu Matua near the airport. The 10 spacious rooms with bath begin at US$30/45 single/double.

Martín and Anita Hereveri (tel. 100-593), on Simón Paoa opposite the hospital just east of the church, offer 10 double rooms at US$20 pp with shared bath, US$30 pp with private bath. Another US$10 pp nets you an ample three-course dinner. Camping on their lawn is also possible. Martin picks up guests at the airport and he's very helpful.

One of the least expensive hotels easily booked from abroad through Chile Hotels is **Cabañas Vai Moana** (tel. 100-626) on Policarpo Toro just north of the center. The 10 large tin-roofed bungalows are US$40/60/90 single/double/triple, plus US$15 for a romantic dinner by candlelight. If you book locally upon arrival you'll probably pay US$25 pp (ask for Edgar inside the airport terminal). He rents bicycles, scooters, and jeeps at reasonable rates and is very helpful.

Residencial Chez Cecilia (tel. 100-499), also off Ave. Policarpo Toro north of center near Ahu Tahai, charges US$35/50/75 single/double/triple plus US$15 pp for dinner. Camping may be possible here. Cecilia is a good cook and there's

hot water. A city tour is also included. Nearby on Pasaje Reimiro in this same quiet area a bit north of town is **Residencial Tahai** (tel. 100-395) at (US$30/50 single/double).

Lucía Riroroko de Haoa runs **Mahina Taka Taka Georgia** (tel. 100-452, fax 100-282), near the museum and Ahu Tahai. The four clean, quiet rooms with private bath are US$25 pp (plus US$20 for dinner). Sliding doors lead out to the garden and you're really made to feel like part of the family.

Moderate

The friendly, 18-room **Hotel Topa Ra'a** (tel. 100-225), Calle Hetereki at Atamu Tekena, is conveniently located right in town. It's US$45/78/90 single/double/triple with a good view from the patio. Ask to see the room before accepting. This place belongs to archaeologist and ex-governor Sergio Rapu, who also owns the Tumu Kai shopping mall and supermarket on Ave. Policarpo Toro.

The **Hotel Orongo Easter Island** (Juan Chávez, tel. 100-294), formerly the Hotel Easter Island International, is on Ave. Policarpo Toro in the center of town. The 12 rooms with private bath are US$60/80/100 single/double/triple, breakfast and dinner included.

Hotel Chez Maria Goretti (tel./fax 100-459), on the north side of town near near Ahu Tahai, has 13 large rooms at US$50/70/90 single/double/triple, plus US$10 pp for dinner.

Expensive

Hotel Chez Joseph (tel. 100-281), on Calle Avareipua in the center of town, charges US$65/90/105 single/double/triple with breakfast and dinner for the 12 rooms with bath.

Hotel O'tai (Nico and Rosita Haoa, tel. 100-250, fax 100-482), also known as "Rosita's Pension," is on Calle Te Pito o Te Henua across from the post office. In 1993 the movers and shakers in Kevin Costner's team stayed here during the filming of *Rapa Nui,* and with her profits Rosita has increased the number of rooms to 31 (all with private bath). These cost US$68/104/134 single/double/triple with reductions April-September. The new swimming pool and jacuzzi also came out of movie money, and there's a nice garden. Unfortunately it's just around the corner from the noisy Toroko Disco.

Luxury

The **Hotel Hanga Roa** (tel. 100-299, fax 100-426), overlooking the bay at the west end of Ave. Pont, was occupied by Hollywood moviemakers for six months in 1993, and they really tore the place apart. A year later the Hanga Roa was taken over by the Panamericana hotel chain, which added 10 large bungalows, nine of them containing three a/c rooms with marble bathrooms and fake thatched roofs at US$180/200 single/double. The 10th unit is a deluxe suite at US$350. Lunch or dinner is US$25. The 60 older rooms with bath in the prefabricated main building are still US$90/110/130, but plans call for this section to be demolished and placed by additional bungalows, a shopping complex, oceanfront restaurant/bar, tennis courts, and a second swimming pool.

Top of the line on Easter Island is the **Hotel Hotu Matua** (tel. 100-444, fax 100-445), at the east end of Ave. Pont near the airport. The 57 rooms with private bath and mini-fridge are US$129/169 single/double including a buffet breakfast. This single-story, motel-style complex angles around a half-moon freshwater swimming pool, and there's a bar. The Hotua Matua is owned by local businessman Orlando Paoa who also owns the supply ship *Piloto Pardo*.

FOOD AND ENTERTAINMENT

Food

Although three supermarkets sell basic foodstuffs, a limited selection of postcards, Chilean newspapers a week or two old, and expensive recordings of local music, bring with you everything you're likely to need during your stay, especially film, PABA sunscreen, a canteen, and sturdy shoes. Supply ships only arrive every couple of months, meaning high prices and limited selection, so canned or snack foods might also be a good idea if you can spare the weight. It's prohibited to bring in fresh fruit and vegetables however, so get these at the *feria municipal* (market) held on Ave. Policarpo Toro (largest early Tuesday and Saturday mornings). **Tumu Kai Supermarket** on Ave. Policarpo Toro stays open all day (you can pay in dollars here, but will get your change in pesos). Fresh fish is available from fishermen who land their catch at the

caleta. Watch for tasty local pastries called *empanadas*.

A growing number of snack bars and restaurants exist along Calle Te Pito o Te Henua and Ave. Policarpo Toro. For seafood try the restaurants down by the *caleta*. Insist on a menu with prices clearly listed, otherwise you'll be charged absurdly high tourist rates. The local lobsters *(langostas)* are becoming very scarce due to overharvesting. Many visitors take meals at their lodgings for a fixed price. The local water piped down from Rano Kao has a high magnesium content and is a little brown, but it's safe to drink.

Entertainment

The discos, **Toroko** in town and **PiRiTi** near the airport, crank up on Thursday, Friday, and Saturday nights: US$6 for a Coke. They open around 2200, but nothing much happens before midnight. Avoid taking a room near either of these or you'll be blasted until 0600 (numerous requests to have the Toroko moved out of earshot of the sleepless citizenry to a new location have been ignored because the mayor gets a piece of the action).

Ask at the tourist office and the Hotel Hanga Roa about Polynesian dancing. Sunday there's church singing at 0900 and soccer in the afternoon. Otherwise it's pretty dead at night, with lots of private *pisco* (brandy) drinking by the locals (no problem). Expect everything except church to start late.

OTHER PRACTICALITIES

Shopping

Aside from shell necklaces, the main things offered to shoppers are *moai kavakava* (woodcarvings of emaciated ancestor figures), dance paddles, miniature stone *moai,* and imitation *rongorongo* tablets. The obsidian jewelry sold locally is imported from mainland Chile. The handicraft market near the church in Hanga Roa has overpriced woodcarvings, and this is one of the only places in Polynesia where bargaining is expected.

A commercial art gallery, the **Galería Aukara** on Ave. Pont off Policarpo Toro, sells woodcarvings by Bene Tuki Aukara and paintings by Amaya.

Money

The local currency is the Chilean peso (approximately US$1 = 475 pesos), which comes in notes of 500, 1,000, and 10,000 pesos. Chilean currency is almost worthless outside Chile itself, so only change what you're sure you'll need, and get rid of the remainder before you leave. The shops at the airport will often sell you dollars.

The Banco del Estado, beside the tourist office in Hanga Roa, charges a rip-off 10% commission to change traveler's checks, so bring U.S. dollars in cash, which are accepted as payment at all tourist-oriented establishments (though not always at good rates). If coming from Santiago, bring an adequate supply of pesos. The Sunoco gas station west of the airport gives good rates for U.S. cash (posted in the office) and the Tumu Kai Supermarket gives a better rate for traveler's checks than the local bank. Currencies other than U.S. dollars can be difficult to exchange, and credit cards are rarely usable as those accepting them have to wait a long time to be paid.

Except for the most basic things, it's often hard to determine exactly what a service will cost and some islanders have an inflated idea of value. To avoid shocks, it's wise to make sure prices are clearly understood beforehand.

Post and Telecommunications

All mail is routed through Chile and Chilean postage stamps are used. The Entel telephone center (fax 56-32/100-105) is opposite the tourist office and bank. When calling Easter Island from abroad, dial your international access code plus 56 for Chile, 32 for Easter Island, and the six-digit local number (which always begins with 100).

Visas and Officialdom

Most visitors require only a passport valid three months ahead to visit Chile. Visas are not necessary for North Americans, Australians, and most Europeans, but New Zealanders do need a visa (NZ$90), which must be obtained beforehand. Check with any LanChile Airlines office, the Chilean Consulate in Papeete, or the Chilean Embassy in New Zealand (12/1 Willeston St., Wellington; tel. 64-4/471-6270, fax 64-4/472-5324). No vaccinations are required, and malaria is not present anywhere in Chile.

Yachting Facilities

Some 40 cruising yachts a year visit Easter Island between Galapagos or South America and Pitcairn/Tahiti. Due to Rapa Nui's remoteness, the boats will have been at sea two to four weeks before landfall. As Easter is well outside the South Pacific hurricane zone, they usually call between January and March, so as to time their arrival in Tahiti-Polynesia for the beginning of the prime sailing season there. The southeast trades extend south to Easter Island most reliably Dec.-May, allowing for the easiest entry/exit. The rest of the year, winds are westerly and variable.

Anchorages include Hanga Roa, Vinapu, Hotu Iti, and Anakena/Ovahi, and a watch must be maintained over yachts at anchor at all times as the winds can shift quickly in stormy weather. The anchorages are deep with many rocks to foul the anchor and little sand. Landing can be difficult through the surf. The frequent moves necessitated by changing winds can be quite exhausting, and crews often have only one or two days a week ashore. Luckily the things to see are quite close to these anchorages.

A pilot is required to enter the small boat harbor at Hanga Piko and US$100 is asked. Entry through the breakers and rocks is only possible in calm weather. Mooring to the concrete wharf here is stern to as at Tahiti (no charge), but there's little space and this is only supposed to be done by boats in need of repairs. The harbor has 2.8 meters of water at low tide.

Information

There's a Sernatur tourist office (tel. 100-255; open weekday mornings) on Calle Tuu Maheke a few doors west of the bank. Their airport branch opens only for flights.

A very good 1:30,000 topographical map of Easter Island printed in Spain is sold locally at souvenir shops, such as Hotu Matua's Favorite Shoppe on Ave. Policarpo Toro. The CONAF office on the road to Orongo sells an even better map coated with rainproof plastic.

No newspapers or magazines are published on Easter Island, so the easiest way to keep in touch with what's happening is to subscribe to Georgia Lee's *Rapa Nui Journal* (Easter Island Foundation, Box 6774, Los Osos, CA 93412-6774, U.S.A.; tel. 1-805/528-6279, fax 1-805/534-

9301, www.netaxs.com/~trance/rapanui.html). The *Journal* comes out four times a year, and contains an interesting mix of scientific studies, announcements, and local gossip—well worth the US$30 annual subscription price (US$40 airmail outside Canada and the U.S.).

The most useful travel guides to the island are *An Uncommon Guide to Easter Island* by Georgia Lee (available through the Easter Island Foundation) and Alan Drake's *The Ceremonial Center of Orongo*. Both are the sort of books you can pick up and read from cover to cover without getting bored.

A quarterly newspaper called *Te Rapa Nui* contains articles in English and Spanish. Radio Manukena broadcasts locally over 580 kHz AM and 101.7 MHz FM, whereas the Chilean Navy station uses 98.5 MHz FM.

TRANSPORTATION

Getting There

LanChile Airlines (www.lanchile.com) flies a Boeing 767 to Easter Island from Tahiti and Santiago three times a week, with an additional weekly flight between Easter Island and Santiago operating Nov.-March (summer holiday time for Chilean students). For North America and Europe, LanChile has direct flights to Santiago from Los Angeles, Miami, New York, Madrid, and Frankfurt. See the main introduction to this book for sample fares and special deals (such as the "Pacific Circuit Fares"). Occasionally LanChile won't honor their own announced fares. In North America, call LanChile toll-free at 1-800/735-5526 for information.

In Santiago, check carefully which terminal you'll be using, as flights that turn around at Easter Island and return to Santiago are classified "domestic" and leave from the old terminal, whereas flights continuing to Tahiti are "international" and use the new terminal. Occasionally you'll be sent to the wrong terminal, so allow a little extra time. The "international" flights are often inconveniently timed, with late-night arrivals common at all three points.

LanChile has a history of changing schedules or canceling flights at a moment's notice. Book and reconfirm your onward flight well ahead, as the plane is often overbooked between Easter Island and Santiago—a week is enough time to see everything. You'll occasionally witness heated arguments at Mataveri Airport as people who were careless with their bookings try desperately to get off Easter Island, and there have even been cases when the police had to intervene to restore order! Foreigners pay higher fares than local residents, so it's usually the locals who get bumped. The local LanChile office (tel. 100-279), on Ave. Pont at Policarpo Toro, is open mornings.

Package Tours

Nature Expeditions International (6400 East El Dorado Circle, Suite 210, Tucson, AZ 85715, U.S.A.; tel. 1-800/869-0639 or 1-520/721-6712, fax 1-520/721-6719, www.naturexp.com, e-mail: Naturexp@aol.com) runs a comprehensive archaeology tour of Easter Island every other month (US$2,490 double occupancy, airfare extra). The groups spend seven of the tour's 15 days exploring Easter Island under the guidance of local archaeologists.

Far Horizons Trips (Box 91900, Albuquerque, NM 87199-1900, U.S.A.; tel. 1-800/552-4575 or 1-505/343-9400, fax 1-505/343-8076, www.farhorizon.com, e-mail: journey@farhorizon. com) organizes a 10-day tour to coincide with the Tapati Rapa Nui festival in early February (US$3,095 pp double occupancy, airfare extra). A noted archaeologist or scholar escorts the group. They also offer trips to the Marquesas.

Travel agencies around Papeete's Vaima Center offer cheap package tours from Tahiti to Easter Island, some of which are discussed in this book's Papeete section. The largest such agency is Tahiti Nui (www.tahiti-nui.com). In the U.S., Tahiti Vacations (tel. 1-800/553-3477, www.tahitivacation.com) can add Easter Island extensions to all of their Tahiti tours at US$799. From Tahiti, low season fares apply March-November.

The Surf Travel Company (Box 446, Cronulla, NSW 2230, Australia; tel. 61-2/9527-4722, fax 61-2/9527-4522, www.surftravel.com.au, e-mail: surftrav@ozemail.com.au) offers seven-night surfing tours to Easter Island, available year-round whenever at least three bookings come in.

Getting Around

There's no public transport but the locals are pretty good about giving lifts (a knowledge of Spanish is a big help here). On Sunday there's often a beach bus to Anakena from the vicinity of the church (ask). Several dozen taxis are available, charging the locals a bit more than a dollar for a ride around town or US$15-25 to Anakena. Tourists are expected to pay more and bargaining may be required.

A daylong minibus tour around the island is US$25-50 pp—beware of two-hour "half day" tours. Boat tours to the *motus* off the southwestern tip of the island cost about US$30 pp a half day.

The top hotels rent vehicles at US$50 a half day, US$100 a full day, but you can usually get one for less than that. Lots of cars are available and to find one all you need to do is stroll down the main street watching for the signs. Do ask around, as prices vary (bargaining possible in the off season), and check to make sure the car has a spare tire *(neumático)* and a jack *(gata)*. We've received complaints about the condition of many of the cars. Sometimes the agency will throw in a driver for "free." Insurance is not available but gasoline is cheaper than on the mainland and the distances are small. An international driver's license is required. Scooters can be hired at US$30-45 a day, but a motorcycle license is mandatory. The gas tanks on some of the scooters are too small to visit both Rano Raraku and Anakena. The island's red cinder roads are gradually being paved and speeding on the central highway to Anakena has led to serious accidents. The improved roads have made bicycling a lot more practical and you should be able to rent a bike for no more than US$15 a day.

Airport

Mataveri Airport (IPC) is within half an hour on foot of most of the places to stay in Hanga Roa. Ask for the free map and hotel list at the tourist office to the right past customs. The departure tax is US$18 to Tahiti or US$6 to Santiago (check the amount when you reconfirm and have exactly that ready, otherwise you'll get your change in pesos). If you're headed for Tahiti, don't bother taking any fresh fruit as it will be confiscated at Papeete.

parrotfish

GORDON OHLIGER

COOK ISLANDS
INTRODUCTION

The Cook Islands lie in the center of the Polynesian triangle about 4,500 km south of Hawaii. They range from towering Rarotonga, the country's largest island, to the low oval islands of the south and the solitary atolls of the north. Visitors are rewarded with natural beauty and colorful attractions at every turn. There is motion and excitement on Rarotonga and Aitutaki, peaceful village life on the rest. Since few tourists get beyond the two main islands, a trip to Atiu, Mangaia, or Mauke can be a fascinating experience. After Tahiti, Cook Islands is inexpensive, and the local tourist industry is efficient and competitive. It's a safe, quiet place to relax and you feel right at home. The local greeting is *kia orana* (may you live on). Other words to know are *meitaki* (thank you), *aere ra* (goodbye), and *kia manuia!* (cheers!).

The Land
These 15 islands and atolls, with a land area of only 240 square km, are scattered over 1.83 million square km of the Pacific, leaving a lot of empty ocean in between. It's 1,433 km from Penrhyn to Mangaia. The nine islands in the southern group are a continuation of the Austral Islands of Tahiti-Polynesia, formed as volcanic material escaped from a southeast/northwest fracture in the earth's crust. Five of the northern islands stand on the 3,000-meter-deep Manihiki Plateau, while Penrhyn rises directly out of seas 5,000 meters deep.

Practically every different type of oceanic island can be found in the Cooks. Rarotonga is the only high volcanic island of the Tahiti type. Aitutaki, like Bora Bora, consists of a middle-aged volcanic island surrounded by an atoll-like barrier reef, with many tiny islets defining its lagoon. Atiu, Mangaia, Mauke, and Mitiaro are raised atolls with a high cave-studded outer coral ring *(makatea)* enclosing volcanic soil at the center. It's believed these islands were uplifted during the past two million years due to the weight of Rarotonga on the earth's crust. There are low rolling hills in the interiors of both Atiu and Mangaia, while Mauke and Mitiaro are flat. The swimming and snorkeling possibilities at Atiu, Mangaia, Mauke, and Mitiaro are limited, as there's only a fringing reef with small tidal pools. Aitutaki and Rarotonga have protected lagoons where snorkeling is relatively safe. The rich, fertile southern islands account for 89% of the Cooks' land area and population.

Manihiki, Manuae, Palmerston, Penrhyn, Pukapuka, Rakahanga, and Suwarrow are typical lagoon atolls, while tiny Takutea and Nassau are sand cays without lagoons. All of the northern atolls are so low that waves roll right across them during hurricanes, and you have to be within 20 km to see them. This great variety makes Cook Islands a geologist's paradise.

Climate
The main Cook Islands are about the same distance from the equator as Hawaii and have a similarly pleasant tropical climate. Rain clouds hang over Rarotonga's interior much of the year, but the coast is often sunny, and the rain often comes in brief, heavy downpours. The other islands are drier and can even experience severe water shortages. Winter evenings June- Aug. can be cool. On both Rarotonga and Aitutaki,

the best combination of prolonged hours of sunshine, fresh temperatures, and minimal rainfall runs July-September.

May-Oct. the trade winds blow from the southeast in the southern Cooks and from the east in the more humid northern Cooks; the rest of the year winds are generally from the southwest or west. November-April is the summer hurricane season, with an average of one every other year, coming from the direction of Samoa. If you happen to coincide with one, you're in for a unique experience!

For weather information call the Meteorological Office (tel. 20-603) near Rarotonga Airport.

Fauna
The only native mammals are bats and rats. The mynah is the bird most often seen, an aggressive introduced species that drives native birds up into the mountains and damages fruit trees. By 1989 only about 29 examples of the Rarotonga flycatcher or kakerori remained due to attacks on the birds' nests by ship rats. Fortunately a local landowners group, the Takitumu Conservation Area, took an interest in the kakerori's survival and began laying rat poison in the nesting areas

THE COOK ISLANDS

Penrhyn •

Rakahanga •
                  ° Manihiki
◦ Pukapuka
• Nassau
                  Northern Group

Suwarrow ◊

Palmerston •   Southern Group

              Aitutaki •
              Manuae •
              Takutea •   • Mitiaro
                Atiu   • Mauke

0   250 mi
|——————————| Rarotonga •
0   250 km
                        Mangaia °

COOK ISLANDS AT A GLANCE

	AREA (hectares)	POPULATION (1996)
Rarotonga	6,718	11,100
Mangaia	5,180	1,104
Atiu	2,693	960
Mitiaro	2,228	319
Mauke	1,842	646
Aitutaki	1,805	2,332
Penrhyn	984	600
Manuae	617	0
Manihiki	544	662
Pukapuka	506	780
Rakahanga	405	249
Palmerston	202	49
Takutea	122	0
Nassau	121	99
Suwarrow	40	4
COOK ISLANDS	24,007	18,904

RAROTONGA'S CLIMATE

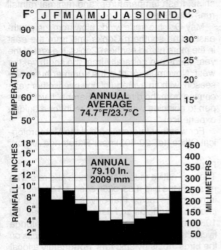

during the breeding season. By 1996 the number of *kakerori* had been raised to 134. More common native birds are the Cook Islands fruit dove *(kukupa),* the Rarotonga starling *('i'oi),* and the Cook Islands warbler *(kererako).*

The most interesting aspect of the natural environment is found among the fish and corals of the lagoons and reefs. Reef walks on Rarotonga and lagoon trips on Aitutaki display this colorful world to visitors. Humpback whales can sometimes be seen cruising along the shorelines July-Sept., having migrated 5,000 km north from Antarctica to bear their young. Pilot whales (up to six meters) are in the Cooks year-round.

HISTORY AND GOVERNMENT

Discovery

One of several legends holds that Rarotonga was settled about A.D. 1200 by two great warriors, Karika from Samoa and Tangiia-nui from Tahiti. The story goes that Karika and Tangiia-nui met on the high seas but decided not to fight because there would be no one to proclaim the victor. Instead they carried on to Rarotonga together and divided the island among themselves by sailing their canoes around it in opposite di-

rections, with a line between their starting and meeting points becoming the boundary. Even today, tribes in the Cooks refer to themselves as *vaka* (canoes), and many can trace their ancestry back to these chiefs.

Archaeologists believe Rarotonga was reached much earlier, probably around A.D. 800 from Raiatea or the Marquesas. The mythical chief Toi who built the Ara Metua on Rarotonga is associated with this earlier migration. Recent excavations of a *marae* on a *motu* in the Muri Lagoon point to an even earlier date, perhaps A.D. 500. Atiu was a chiefly island that dominated Mauke, Mitiaro, Takutea, and sometimes Manuae.

The Spanish explorer Mendaña sighted Pukapuka in 1595, and his pilot, Quirós, visited Rakahanga in 1606. Then the islands were lost again to Europeans until the 1770s when Captain Cook contacted Atiu, Mangaia, Manuae, Palmerston, and Takutea—"detached parts of the earth." *He* named Manuae the Hervey Islands, a name others applied to the whole group; it was not until 1824 that the Russian cartographer, Johann von Krusenstern, labeled the southern group the Cook Islands. Cook never saw Rarotonga, and the Pitcairn-bound *Bounty* is thought to be its first European visitor (in 1789). The mutineers gave the inhabitants the seeds for their first or-

Sir Nathaniel Dance's 1776 portrait of Captain Cook

ange trees. Aitutaki was discovered by Captain Bligh just before the famous mutiny. Mauke and Mitiaro were reached in 1823 by John Williams of the London Missionary Society.

European Penetration

Williams stopped at Aitutaki in 1821 and dropped off two Tahitian teachers. Returning two years later, he found that one, Papeiha, had done particularly well. Williams took him to Rarotonga and left him there for four years. When he returned in 1827, Williams was welcomed by Papeiha's many converts. The missionaries taught an austere, puritanical morality and believed the white man's diseases such as dysentery, measles, smallpox, and influenza, which killed two-thirds of the population, were the punishment of God descending on the sinful islanders. The missionaries became a law unto themselves; today, the ubiquitous churches full to overflowing on Sunday are their legacy. (The missionaries arrived from Australia, and since they weren't aware of the idea of an international date line, they held Sunday service on the wrong day for the first 60 years of their presence!) About 63% of the population now belongs to the Cook Islands Christian Church (CICC), founded by the London Missionary Society. Takamoa College, the Bible school they established at Avarua in 1837, still exists.

Reports that the French were about to annex the Cooks led the British to declare a protectorate over the southern group in 1888. The French warship approaching Manihiki to claim the islands turned back when it saw a hastily sewn Union Jack flying and in 1889 the northern atolls were added to the protectorate. The local chiefs, well aware of how their counterparts on Tahiti had been marginalized by the French, petitioned the British to have their islands annexed to the British Crown, a position strongly endorsed by the missionaries. Thus on 11 June 1901 both the northern and southern groups were included in the boundaries of New Zealand. During WW II, the U.S. built air bases on Aitutaki and Penrhyn.

A legislative council was established in 1946, followed by an assembly with greater powers in 1957. After decolonizing pressure from the United Nations, a new constitution was granted in 1964 and the Cook Islands was made an internally self-governing state in free association with

HUNGARIAN ETHNOGRAPHICAL MUSEUM, BUDAPEST

daughter of the ex-queen of Manikiki, turn of the century, Cook Islands

New Zealand on 4 August 1965. New Zealand has no veto over local laws; the Cook Islands also runs its own external affairs and operates as an independent country. The paper connection with New Zealand deprives the country of a seat at the U.N. but brings in millions of dollars in financial and technical assistance from Wellington that might otherwise be withheld. New Zealand citizenship, which the Cook Islanders hold, is greatly valued.

Government

Cook Islands' 25-member Parliament operates on the Westminster system, with a prime minister as the head of government. The cabinet consists of seven ministers. While almost all members of parliament are men, most of the chiefly titles are held by women who are also the main landowners. In theory, the 15-member House of Ariki (chiefs) should be consulted on custom and land issues, but in practice this seldom happens.

On all the outer islands there's an appointed chief administrative officer (CAO), formerly known as the resident agent. Although each island also has an elected Island Council, the CAO runs the local administration on behalf of the local and central governments.

Politics

Party politics, often based on personalities, is vicious. The most dramatic event in the last few decades was the removal of Premier Albert Henry and the Cook Islands Party from office in 1978 by the chief justice of the High Court when it was proven that Henry had misused government funds to fly in his voters from New Zealand during the preceding election. Then, Queen Elizabeth II stripped Sir Albert of his knighthood. This was the first time in Commonwealth history that a court ruling had changed a government; the shock waves are still being felt in Rarotonga. Albert Henry died in 1981, it's said of a broken heart.

Albert Henry's successor, Sir Tom Davis of the Democratic Party, served as prime minister from 1978 until July 1987, when he was ousted by a vote of no confidence. The Cook Islands Party, led by Sir Geoffrey Henry, a cousin of Albert, won the 1989 and 1994 elections. The opposition is split between the Democratic Alliance, led by outspoken Atiu politician Norman George, and the New Alliance Party.

ECONOMY

Cook Islanders live beyond their means. Imports outweigh exports by 11 times, and food imports alone are nearly three times all exports. Tourism makes up for some of this, but without New Zealand aid (about NZ$12 million a year) Cook Islands would be bankrupt. The largest exports are cultured pearls, fish and seafood, fruits and vegetables (papaya, bananas, beans, taro), and clothing, in that order. Fresh fruit production is hindered by the small volume, uneven quality, inadequate shipping, poor marketing, and the unreliability of island producers.

The economy's small size is illustrated by the importance of the post office's Philatelic Bureau. Money remitted by Cook Islanders resident in N.Z. contributes about NZ$3 million a year to the local economy, and licensing fees from South Korean and other foreign fishing companies to exploit the exclusive economic zone bring in additional income. A number of small clothing factories in Avarua supply tropical beachware to the local and tourist markets and exports are picking up. Subsistence fishing and agriculture are important on the outer islands.

Finance

Since 1984 Cook Islands has operated as an "international finance center" providing offshore banking facilities to foreign corporations and individuals attempting to avoid taxation and regulation in their home countries. In contrast to local businesses, which are heavily taxed, some 3,000 Asian companies that don't operate in the Cooks are now registered in the Rarotonga "tax haven," bringing in more than NZ$5 million a year in banking and licensing fees. Offshore "banks" can be owned by a single person and it's believed that millions of illicit dollars have been laundered through Rarotonga.

In 1987 the director of the Cook Islands Office of Audit and Inquiry was sacked after he warned the New Zealand and Australian governments that large corporations based in their countries were illegally evading taxation through the use of false tax withholding certificates issued by Cook Islands for a fraction their face value. The bogus certificates allowed the companies to claim deductions for overseas taxation; several large Japanese banks were also involved. In 1991 Australia and New Zealand revised their tax laws to restrict the use of tax havens by their citizens (penalties of up to 125% of the tax due and five years in prison).

In early 1995 *Islands Business* magazine reported that the Cook Islands government had guaranteed 12 letters of credit worth a total of US$1.2 billion in a scheme that Prime Minister Sir Geoffrey Henry had hoped would earn US$10 million in commissions. The worthless guarantees were quickly withdrawn when they came under scrutiny by the Reserve Bank of New Zealand.

The country has a NZ$200 million national debt, most of it incurred by tourism-related developments such as the Sheraton Hotel project, the National Cultural Center, power generation, and telecommunications since 1989 when Sir Geoffrey's administration took over. Much of the money is owed to the governments of Italy and Nauru, which foolishly guaranteed huge unsecured loans to this tiny country, but NZ$23 million of it came from the Asian Development Bank, which has had to intervene several times to save Cook Islands from bankruptcy. About NZ$9 million is owned to the New Zealand Government Superannuation Fund.

In mid-1994 local branches of the ANZ and Westpac banks began to severely restrict private credit after the government proved unable to service its heavy debt load. A few months later the banks stopped clearing checks drawn in Cook Islands dollars through the New Zealand banking system and announced that these would have to be collected locally. Local businesses moved money offshore, and in late 1994 the Reserve Bank of New Zealand confirmed that it no longer guaranteed the convertibility of the Cook Islands dollar. The threat of imminent financial collapse forced the government to withdraw the currency from circulation in 1995. New Zealand banknotes are presently used.

Until 1996 Cook Islands had a bloated public service of 3,600 persons or 60% of the workforce. Then, after the Westpac Bank bounced official salary checks due to a US$5 million dollar overdraft in the government's current account, civil servants were forced to accept a 15% across the board pay cut. As interest on the unpaid government loans continued to mount, it became clear that harsher measures were required. Thus it was announced that government employee numbers would be reduced to 1,200 and the pay cut increased to 65%. From 1996 to 1998 some 6,000 Cook Islanders (30% of the population) voted with their feet and left for greener pastures in Australia and New Zealand. State assets (including four hotels and the telephone company) were hurriedly sold off, and the number of government departments cut in half. Sir Geoffrey accurately concluded that by abruptly imposing a harsh structural adjustment program three years in advance of the next election, the worst of it would be over before he had to face the voters again and many of those most affected would already have left the country.

Cook Islands runs a discount "flag of convenience" ship registry that allows foreign shipping companies to avoid the more stringent safety and labor regulations of industrialized countries. Ominously, one of the first ships to sign up, the freighter *Celtic Kiwi,* sank off New Zealand in October 1991. After further sinkings and reports of gun running, most insurance companies won't touch ships registered in the Cooks.

The newest hustle is cyber-gambling over the internet with the world's fifth-largest online casino, Casinos of the South Pacific (www.cosp.com), based here since 1997. Blackjack, draw poker, roulette, and slots are all offered. The company operates under Rarotonga's financial center legislation, which means that taxation and regulation are minimal, but local punters are blocked from accessing the site and cosp.com's Avarua headquarters is unmarked. Of course, none of the profits go to charity.

Tourism

Since the opening of the international airport in 1973, tourism has been important, and directly or indirectly, it now employs a quarter of the workforce and accounts for more than half the gross national product. Cook Islands has the highest tourist density in the South Pacific with three tourists a year for every local resident, compared to two Fijians, three Samoans, and four Tongans for every tourist visiting those countries. At times Rarotonga (with five tourists a year per Cook Islander) really has the feel of a little Hawaii.

About a third of the 50,000-odd arriving tourists are New Zealanders who spend all their time at resorts on Rarotonga and Aitutaki on prepaid packaged holidays. The rest are fairly evenly divided between Americans, Australians, Canadians, and Europeans. Few Asian tourists make it this far. Although arrival levels have stagnated since 1994, overdevelopment has led to ominous sewage disposal and water supply problems on Rarotonga.

The Rarotongan Resort Hotel was built in 1977 by the Cook Islands government, the Tourist Hotel Corporation of N.Z., and Air New Zealand, with each owning a third. In 1982, after the hotel proved to be a consistent money-loser, the Cook Islands government had to buy out its two partners to prevent closure. When the poorly planned Aitutaki Lagoon Hotel tottered on bankruptcy in 1989, the government was forced to take it over too. In the two decades to 1997 the Rarotongan Resort Hotel lost millions of dollars, but that year it was privatized in a sweetheart deal that handed the property interest-free for 10 years to local businessman Tata Crocombe despite a better offer from an Australian company. A major refurbishment has now put the Rarotongan back on its feet.

In 1984 "experts" from the United Nations Development Program advised that the way to make tourism more "profitable" was to allow more large hotels and stop construction of the smaller, family-owned motels. Finding itself unable to attract the required foreign investment, the government itself decided to bankroll construction of a new four-star luxury hotel, and in 1987 NZ$52 million was borrowed from an Italian bank. A year later the Democratic Party government collapsed and in 1989 Sir Geoffrey Henry's Cook Islands Party was voted in after promising to stop the project. Once in office, however, Sir Geoffrey did an about-face and announced that he now backed the hotel. A management contract was signed with the Sheraton chain and in May 1990, despite many objections from local residents, construction began on the south side of Rarotonga using Italian building materials and contractors.

The 204-room Cook Islands Sheraton Resort was conceived as a cluster of two-story buildings, similar to the Fiji Sheraton, with the inevitable 18-hole golf course. The project suffered repeated delays, and then it was announced that the Italian construction company had gone broke after spending NZ$30 million of the government's loan money without getting much done. A second Italian construction company (Stephany SpA) was brought in, and the government borrowed another NZ$20 million so work could resume. In mid-1993 the Italian government began its "clean hands" crackdown on Mafia activities, and several people involved in the Sheraton project were arrested in Italy, causing the Italian insurers to freeze coverage on the loans, and work on the Sheraton stopped again.

For five years, the empty structure of the unfinished Sheraton (also known as the "Vaimaanga Hotel") faced an uncertain future, and the full story of what went on behind the scenes has yet to be told. The government has NZ$90 million and rising in accumulated Sheraton debts to repay, and it's estimated that at least another NZ$20 million will be required to finish the hotel, plus about NZ$5 million for the golf course. In late 1998 things began moving forward again as the government let its lease on the property lapse, al-lowing the landowners to make a new deal with Japanese investors and the Castle Group of Hawaii to complete the project without further participation by the Italians. So there's a good chance the "Sheraton" may be up and running under a new name by the time you get there! (Sheraton has had nothing to do with the construction scandal.)

Pearls

In 1982 research began at Manihiki into the possibility of creating a cultured-pearl industry similar to that of Tahiti-Polynesia. The first commercial farms were set up on Manihiki in 1989 and some 800,000 cultured oysters are presently held there. It's believed the Manihiki lagoon is approaching its maximum sustainable holding capacity, and in 1994 farms began to be established on Penrhyn. These presently have 150,000 oysters and the Penrhyn hatchery is expected to increase these numbers considerably. Rakahanga and Suwarrow are now under consideration as prospective pearl-farming areas. Fluctuations in water temperature and overstocking can affect the amount of plankton available to the oysters and reduce the quality of the pearls. Rising temperatures can have an immediate impact.

To establish a farm, an investment of NZ$5,000 is required, and no return will be forthcoming for five years. In 1998 there were 300 farms with just 20% of them accounting for 80% of the oysters. The oysters are seeded once or twice a year by Japanese, Chinese, and Cook Islands experts screened by the Ministry of Marine Resources. Annual production is around 200 kilograms, with Japanese and Chinese dealers the big buyers. Black pearls are now Cook Islands' largest export, bringing in US$4 million a year and employing 700 people. Fortunately a major hurricane at Manihiki in November 1997 did little harm to the underwater oysters, although surface facilities were destroyed.

THE PEOPLE

About 84% of the people are Polynesian Cook Island Maoris, most of whom also have some other ancestry. They're related to the Maoris of New Zealand and the Tahitians, although the

Pukapukans are unique in that they are closer to the Samoans. Almost everyone on Rarotonga and most people on the outer islands speak flawless English while their mother tongue will be a form of Maori. Rarotongan and its dialects are spoken throughout the southern group. Penrhyn is closely related to Rarotongan, Rakahanga-Manihiki is more distantly related, and Pukapukan is related to Samoan.

More than half the population resides on Rarotonga; only 13% live in the northern group. Cook Islanders reside near the seashore, except on Atiu and Mauke, where they are interior dwellers. The old-style thatched *kikau* houses have almost disappeared from the Cook Islands, even though they're cooler, more esthetic, and much cheaper to build than modern housing. A thatched pandanus roof can last 15 years.

While 18,904 (1996) Cook Islanders live in their home islands, some 40,000 reside in New Zealand and another 20,000 in Australia. Emigration to N.Z. increased greatly after the airport opened in 1973 but New Zealanders do not have the reciprocal right to reside permanently in Cook Islands. During the 1980s the migratory patterns reversed and many ex-islanders returned from New Zealand to set up tourism-related businesses, but the steady flow of people to New Zealand and Australia has now resumed due to Cook Island's recent economic crisis. The loss of many teachers and students forced schools and classes to be amalgamated and led to an increase in the dropout rate among teenagers. Education is compulsory until the age of 15.

Almost no Chinese live in the Cooks due to a deliberate policy of discrimination initiated in 1901 by N.Z. Prime Minister Richard Seddon, although many islanders have some Chinese blood resulting from the presence of Chinese traders in the 19th century. About 14% of the population was born outside the South Pacific and the proportion of Americans, New Zealanders, Australians, and others is gradually increasing as expatriates arrive to set up businesses while Cook Island migrants move in the opposite direction.

Under the British and N.Z. regimes, the right of the Maori people to their land was protected, and no land was sold to outsiders. These policies continue today, although foreigners can lease land for up to 60 years. The fragmentation of inherited landholdings into scattered miniholdings hampers agriculture and many fine turn-of-the-century stone buildings have fallen into ruins because of ownership disputes.

The powerful *ariki*, or chiefly class, that ruled in pre-European times is still influential today. The *ariki* were the first to adopt Christianity, instructing their subjects to follow suit and filling leadership posts in the church. British and N.Z. colonial rule was established with the approval of the *ariki*. Now materialism, party politics, and emigration to N.Z. are eroding the authority of the *ariki*. Until self-government, Cook Islanders were only allowed to consume alcohol if they had a permit; now it's a serious social problem.

Dangers and Annoyances

There's been an increase in rape cases lately. Women should keep this in mind when stepping out at night and when choosing a place to stay. There's safety in numbers. Scanty dress outside the resorts will cause offense and maybe trouble. To go to church, women should wear a dress with long sleeves and a hat, while men need long trousers. Be aware of petty theft, particularly if you're staying somewhere with young children running loose. Don't go off and leave things on the clothesline or beach. Never purchase pearls from people on the street and be wary of such vendors as black pearls have been used as a ruse to establish contact with visitors whose hotel rooms were later burglarized. Try to avoid being bitten by mosquitoes, as these are sometimes carriers of dengue fever (see **Health** in the main introduction). Of the 15 islands of the Cooks, Rarotonga is the most affected by this painful disease and a serious epidemic occurred in April 1997.

ON THE ROAD

Highlights

Everyone will arrive on Rarotonga and the short-list of "musts" includes an island night dance show, a bicycle ride around the island, a swim in the Muri Lagoon, and a hike up to the Needle. The snorkeling at Aitutaki is even better and it's another nice place to hang loose. However, to get a real feel for the group, you must get beyond this rather touristy pair to an outer island like Mangaia, Mauke, or Atiu. All three have regular flights from Rarotonga and a few small hotels although other visitor facilities are scanty—they're that unspoiled.

Sports and Recreation

Most organized sporting activities are on Raro-tonga and Aitutaki. Several professional scuba diving companies are based on these islands, and there are many snorkeling possibilities. Both islands offer lagoon tours by boat, with those at Aitutaki by far the better.

Several firms based on Rarotonga's Muri Beach rent water-sports equipment, including surfboards, sailboats, and kayaks, with training in their use available. The surfing possibilities are very limited in Cook Islands—windsurfing's the thing to do. Horseback riding and deep-sea fishing are other popular activities.

Most of the best hiking possibilities are on mountainous Rarotonga, but uplifted islands such as Atiu, Mauke, and Mangaia are also fascinating places to wander around, with many interesting hidden features. The nine-hole golf courses on Aitutaki and Rarotonga aren't too challenging, but greens fees are low and the atmospheres amicable. Tournaments are held at both in September.

The spectator sports are cricket Dec.-March, with matches every Saturday afternoon, and rugby June-August. Rugby is the main team sport played in the Cooks; soccer is a more recent introduction. On Rarotonga, ask about rugby matches at Tereora National Stadium (built for the 1985 South Pacific Mini Games), on the inland side of the airport, and in the sports ground opposite the National Cultural Center in Avarua.

Music and Dance

Among main genres of Cook Islands music and dance are drum dancing ('ura pa'u), choreographed group dancing (kaparima) to string band music, dance dramas (peu tupuna) based on island legends, religious pageants (nuku), formal chants (pe'e), celebratory song/chants ('ute), and polyphonic choral music ('imene tapu) or hymns.

Among the drums used are the small pate or to'ere slit drum used guide the dancers, the pa'u, a double-headed bass drum that provides the beat, and the upright pa'u mango that accompanies the pa'u. The larger ka'ara slit drum and the conch shell accompany chanting. Tahitian drummers have often copied Cook Island rhythms. String band music is based on the ukulele although guitars are also used.

The top traditional dancing is seen during annual events on Rarotonga when the outer islanders arrive to compete. The drum dancing at hotel shows features the sensuous side-to-side hip movements of the women (differing somewhat from the circular movements seen on Tahiti) and the robust knee snapping of the men. In the hura (equivalent of the Hawaiian hula) the female dancers must keep their feet flat on the ground and shoulders steady as they sway in a stunning display.

Public Holidays and Festivals

Public holidays include New Year's Day (1 January), ANZAC Day (25 April), Good Friday, Easter Monday (March/April), Queen Elizabeth's Birthday (first Monday in June), Constitution Day (4 August), Gospel Day (26 October), Christmas Day (25 December), and Boxing Day (26 December). On Rarotonga, Gospel Day is celebrated on 26 July; elsewhere it's 26 October.

Cultural Festival Week, with arts and crafts displays, takes place in mid-February. The Dancer of the Year Competition is in late April. The 10-day **Constitution Celebration,** beginning on the Friday before 4 August, is the big event of the year. There are parades, dancing and singing contests, sporting events, and an agricultural fair. The Round Raro Run is a 31-km marathon held on the first Saturday of October (the record time is 98 minutes set by Kevin Ryan in 1979). Gospel Day (26 October) recalls 26 October 1821, when Rev. John Williams landed on Aitutaki. Ask about itinerant religious plays *(nuku)* on that day. On All Souls Day (November 1st) Catholics visit the cemeteries to place candles and flowers on the graves of family members. The third or fourth week in November is Tiare Festival Week, with flower shows and floral parades. A food festival is also held in late November. On Takitumu Day (3 December), visits are made to historic *marae*.

Accommodations

There's an abundance of accommodations in all price categories on Rarotonga and Aitutaki, and many outer islands also have one or two regular places to stay. Local regulations prohibit visitors from staying in private homes, camping, living in rental cars, or sleeping on the beach, so have the name of a licensed hotel ready upon arrival.

As you come out of the airport terminal, someone may ask you at which hotel you plan to stay and will direct you to the representative of that establishment (if he/she happens to be present). Repeat the name of the licensed accommodations you wrote on your arrival card, then go over and talk to the representative of that establishment if he/she is pointed out to you. It used to be necessary to make a hotel booking before you were allowed entry to Cook Islands, but this regulation is no longer enforced and you're now only required to stay at a licensed hotel, motel, or hostel.

In order to have the best choice of places to stay and maximum flexibility in your plans, it's better not to prepay any hotel accommodations at all. The backpacker places always have empty beds, but accommodation is sometimes tight in the medium-price range. If you're sure you want to stay at a particular place and wish to play it safe, you can make an advance hotel booking through Air New Zealand offices in the South Pacific (but not overseas), the Cook Islands Tourism Corporation in Avarua (fax 21-435, e-mail: tourism@cookislands.gov.ck), or directly to the hostel or hotel. This service costs nothing extra and you can pay upon arrival. If you end up with something you don't like, it's always possi-

ble to move somewhere else later (although most places have a two-night minimum stay). If you do have a reservation, a representative of your hotel will be at the airport to take you to your assigned room for a fee of about NZ$20 roundtrip.

You'll save money and get closer to the people by staying at the smaller, locally owned "self-catering" motels and guesthouses. The fewer the rooms the motel has, the better. A "motel" in the Cooks is styled on the New Zealand type of motel, which means a fully equipped kitchen is built into each unit. Some of them are quite attractive, nothing like the dreary roadside motels of the United States. The motels generally offer rooms with private bath and hot water, but some guesthouses and hostels do not, although communal cooking facilities are usually available. At the big resorts you not only pay a much higher price, but you're forced to eat in fancy dining rooms and restaurants.

Hotel prices tend to fluctuate in Cook Islands and when things are slow some places cut their rates to attract guests, so in some cases you could end up paying less than the prices quoted herein. Outer islands without licensed accommodations, or where such accommodations are full, may be effectively closed to visitors. Ask Air Rarotonga about this before heading too far off the beaten track.

Booking Agencies

Three times a week **Stars Travel** (Box 75, Rarotonga; tel. 23-669; fax 21-569, e-mail: holidays@starstravel.co.ck), near the ANZ Bank in Avarua, has a seven-night package tour from Rarotonga to Atiu, Mitiaro, and Mauke for NZ$739 for one person, NZ$662 pp for two, NZ$615 pp for three, including airfare, accommodations (double occupancy), meals on Mitiaro, transfers, tax, and a full lei greeting on each island. These packages are for local sale on Rarotonga only. Other Stars Travel packages offer two nights on Aitutaki, Atiu, or Mauke. Stars Travel can also reserve rooms alone at any hotel or guesthouse in the Cook Islands. They also book entire houses on Aitutaki at NZ$200 a week.

Island Hopper Vacations (Box 240, Rarotonga; tel. 22-026, fax 22-036, e-mail: travel@islandhopper.co.ck), next to the Banana Court in Avarua, offers similar deals and arranges airport transfers to outer island flights. Other agencies specialized in booking rooms from overseas are **Hugh Henry & Associates** (Box 440, Rarotonga; tel. 25-320, fax 25-420, e-mail: hhenry@gatepoly.co.ck) and **Tipani Tours** (Box 4, Rarotonga; tel. 25-266, fax 23-266, e-mail: tours@tipani.co.ck), owned by the Tahitian tour company Tahiti Nui Travel. It's usually cheaper, however, to make your own arrangements.

Food and Drink
The Rarotonga restaurant scene has improved in recent years and you now have a good choice. A few restaurants are found on Aitutaki, but none exist on the outer islands. When ordering, keep in mind that an "entree" is actually an appetizer and not a main dish.

By law all bars are required to close at midnight, except Friday night when they can stay open until 0200. On Sunday no alcohol may be sold at grocery stores, and even restaurants are only allowed to serve alcohol with a meal that day, although this rule is not always followed. Wine is expensive at restaurants, due to high import duties, and drinking alcoholic beverages on the street is prohibited. You'll save a lot on meals if you stay at one of the many motels and guesthouses that offer cooking facilities.

Rukau is Cook Islands *palusami,* made from spinachlike young taro leaves cooked in coconut cream. *Ika mata* is marinated raw fish with coconut sauce. Locals insist that slippery foods such as bananas lead to forgetfulness, while gluey foods like taro help one to remember. Dogs are sometimes eaten by young men on drinking sprees. Turn to the Atiu section for information on "bush beer" (called "home-brewed" on Rarotonga and Aitutaki).

SERVICES AND INFORMATION

Visas and Officialdom
No visa is required for a stay of up to 31 days, but you must show an onward ticket. For NZ$70 you can get extensions up to six months in the Cooks. Apply at the Immigration office on the top floor of the Government Office Building behind the post office. Actually, one week is plenty of time to see Rarotonga and 31 days is sufficient to visit all of the southern Cook Islands.

If you're thinking of taking a boat trip to the northern group, be sure to get a visa extension before you leave Rarotonga. Otherwise you could have problems with Immigration if your entry permit has expired by the time you get back. Any non-Maori running afoul of government ministers is subject to fast deportation regardless of how long they've been there, how much money they have invested, or whether they have a local family.

Rarotonga, Aitutaki, and Penrhyn are ports of entry for cruising yachts; the only harbors for yachts are at Aitutaki, Penrhyn, Suwarrow, and Rarotonga.

Money
The currency is the New Zealand dollar. After a financial crisis in 1995 the Cook Islands dollar, which had circulated at par with the New Zealand dollar since 1987, was withdrawn. Cook Islands coins are still in use, however, although these are worthless outside Cook Islands. The Cook Islands dollar coin bearing an image of the god Tangaroa makes an offbeat souvenir.

Traveler's checks are worth about three percent more than cash at the banks. Changing money on an outer island is difficult or impossible—do it before you leave Rarotonga. The upmarket hotels and restaurants accept the main credit cards, and the banks will give cash advances. The local American Express representative is Stars Travel (tel. 23-669). Unless otherwise indicated, all prices this chapter are in N.Z. dollars, currently worth about half as much

as U.S. dollars, which makes the Cook Islands inexpensive.

A 12.5% value-added tax (VAT) is added to all sales, services, activities, and rentals. Most places include it in the price, but some charge it extra, so ask. Bargaining has never been a part of the local culture and some locals find it offensive when tourists try to beat prices down. The way to do it is to ask for "specials." Thankfully tipping is still not widespread in the Cooks.

Telecommunications
Telecom Cook Islands (Box 106, Avarua; tel. 29-680, fax 26-174) charges a flat rate for international telephone calls with no off-hours discounts. Three-minute operator-assisted calls cost NZ$7.60 to New Zealand, NZ$10.90 to Australia, and NZ$18.50 to most other countries— very expensive. Person-to-person calls attract an additional two-minute charge.

It's a bit cheaper to use a local telephone card for international calls, and there's no three-minute minimum with a card (dial the international access code 00, the country code, the area code, and the number). More importantly, with a card you can't lose track of the time and end up being presented with a tremendous bill. The cards come in denominations of NZ$10, NZ$20, and NZ$50 and are good for all domestic and international calls. Calls to outer islands within Cook Islands cost NZ$1.20 a minute with a card. You'll probably also need a card to make local calls as very few coin phones remain on Rarotonga.

Collect calls can be placed to Australia, Canada, Fiji, Hong Kong, India, Netherlands, New Zealand, Niue, Sweden, Tahiti-Polynesia, Tonga, the United Kingdom, the U.S.A., and Vanuatu only. To call collect, dial the international/outer island operator at tel. 015. Directory assistance numbers within Cook Islands are tel. 010, international tel. 017. The country code of Cook Islands is 682.

For calls to the U.S., AT&T's "USADirect" service is more expensive than using a local telephone card, but perhaps useful in emergencies. To be connected to this service dial 09111 from any phone in the Cook Islands. The Telecom "New Zealand Direct" number is tel. 0964-09682.

Many local businesses now have e-mail and both www.ck and www.oyster.net.ck include directories of them. Gatepoly provides e-mail services only, while Telecom Cook Islands' more expensive Oyster service hosts both websites and e-mail.

Measurements and Time
The electric voltage is 240 volts DC, 50 cycles, the same as in New Zealand and Australia. American appliances will require a converter. The type of plug varies, but bring a three-pin adaptor. On outer islands other than Aitutaki electricity is provided only a few hours a day. Faxes to Atiu, Mauke, and some other outer islands don't go through between midnight and 0500 local time because the central electricity supply is switched off during that time.

The time is the same as in Hawaii and Tahiti, two hours behind California and 22 hours behind New Zealand. "Cook Islands time" also runs a bit behind "Western tourist's time," so relax and let things happen. All travel agencies, banks, and offices are closed on Saturday, although most shops and restaurants are open until noon. In recent years regulations have been relaxed and many small shops on Rarotonga are now open early Sunday morning (until 0900) and again on Sunday evening (after 1700). The car rental places also open on Sunday.

Media
Be sure to pick up a copy of the *Cook Islands News* (Phil Evans, Box 15, Rarotonga; tel. 22-999, fax 25-303, www.cinews.co.ck), published daily except Sunday (70 cents). Its reporting on island affairs really gives you a feel for where you are, and local happenings are listed.

The *Cook Islands Press* (Jason Brown, Box 741, Rarotonga; tel. 24-865, fax 24-866), published weekly (NZ$2), provides outstanding coverage of domestic political issues. Unfortunately, the paper is facing financial difficulties. The *Cook Islands Sun* is a free tourist newspaper.

On Rarotonga, Radio Ikurangi KC-FM (tel. 23-203), a private commercial station, broadcasts over 103.3 MHz 0530-2400 with overseas news at 0600 and 0700. Radio New Zealand International news is rebroadcast over this station at 0800, 0900, and 1200. The FM station can be difficult to pick up on the south side of Rarotonga, but Radio Cook Islands at 630 kHz AM can be heard anywhere on the island (and even on nearby islands like Mauke in the evening).

In the northern Cooks, KC-FM uses a Penrhyn relay at 95.3 MHz.

Information

For advance information about the country, write to one of the branches of the government-operated Cook Islands Tourism Corporation listed in the appendix, or to their head office at Box 14, Rarotonga (tel. 29-435, fax 21-435, www.cook-islands.com, e-mail: tourism@cook-islands.gov.ck). Ask for their free magazine, *What's On In The Cook Islands,* and the color map *Jasons Passport Cook Islands.* Websites with useful information are listed in the appendix.

Elliot Smith's *Cook Islands Companion* is recommended for those who want more detailed information on the country than can be included here. Smith's book has much more of a "hands-on" feel than some other guides to the Cooks, and it's possible to purchase a personally autographed copy directly from the author at Shangri-La Beach Cottages on Muri Beach. Also ask for the *Tahiti Handbook* from Moon Travel Handbooks, which has detailed sections on Easter Island and the Cooks.

TRANSPORTATION

Getting There

Air New Zealand (tel. 26-300), with an office at the airport, has direct services to Rarotonga from Auckland, Honolulu, Nadi, Papeete, and Los Angeles. Air services into Rarotonga are heavily booked, so reserve your inward and outward flights as far ahead as possible. If you try to change your outbound flight after arrival you could be put on standby.

In November 1998 the charter carrier **Canada 3000** began weekly service between Vancouver and Rarotonga via Honolulu with connections to/from Toronto. Like Canada 3000's flights to Fiji, these flights operate only during the Nov.-April winter season in Canada. Polynesian Airlines has announced that it hopes to launch a weekly Apia-Rarotonga-Papeete service but these flights were still not operating at press time, so check.

Getting Around by Air

All of the main islands of the southern Cooks and a few of the northern group have regular air service from Rarotonga, but keep in mind that no flights operate on Sunday. **Air Rarotonga** (Box 79, Rarotonga; tel. 22-888, fax 23-288, e-mail: bookings@airraro.co.ck) serves Aitutaki (NZ$272 roundtrip) three times a day except Sunday. The "super saver" roundtrip excursion fare to Aitutaki is NZ$218 return provided you fly northbound on the afternoon flight and southbound on the morning flight for any length of time. There's no advance purchase requirement but seats cannot be booked more than 14 days in advance. This pass is not available outside Cook Islands or in December and January (homecoming time for overseas Cook Islanders when many flights run full). Air Rarotonga runs day trips to Aitutaki from Rarotonga, but these are expensive and rushed at NZ$329 including air tickets, transfers, a lagoon tour, lunch, and drinks. Northbound sit on the left side of the aircraft for the best views.

Every weekday Air Rarotonga flies to Atiu (NZ$244 roundtrip), Mangaia (NZ$244 roundtrip), and Mauke (NZ$272 roundtrip). Mitiaro (NZ$272 roundtrip) is served three times a week. The interisland connection Atiu-Mitiaro-Mauke only works twice a week and interisland flights Atiu-Mitiaro and Mitiaro-Mauke are NZ$110 each. There's no flight Atiu-Mauke and you must stop over on Mitiaro en route to make the connection.

Manihiki (NZ$1,092 roundtrip) and Penrhyn (NZ$1,210 roundtrip) receive Air Rarotonga flights weekly. Manihiki-Penrhyn costs NZ$160. Only charter flights operate to Pukapuka and the plane can't land at Rakahanga. Sitting in an 18-seat Bandierante for four hours from Rarotonga to Manihiki or Penrhyn can be quite an experience!

Children under 12 pay half price. Air Rarotonga's 30-day "Paradise Island Pass" allows unlimited flights in the southern group only at NZ$110 per sector but you must visit at least two islands. Advance reservations are required, as space is limited. Try to reconfirm your return flight, and beware of planes leaving early! Avoid scheduling your flight back to Rarotonga for the same day you're supposed to catch your international flight.

The baggage allowance is 16 kilos, though you can sometimes get by with more. On flights to Manihiki and Penrhyn the limit is 10 kilos.

Overweight is not expensive, but if the plane is full and too heavy for the short outer-island runways they'll refuse excess baggage from all passengers. Thus it pays to stay below the limit.

Air Rarotonga offers 20-minute scenic flights (NZ$55 pp) around Rarotonga out of their hangar, 500 meters west of the main terminal. You can often arrange this on the spur of the moment if a pilot and plane are available.

Getting Around by Ship
Taio Shipping Ltd. (Teremoana Taio, Box 2001, Rarotonga; tel. 24-905, fax 24-906), in the Ports Authority Building on Rarotonga's Avatiu Harbor, operates the interisland vessels *Te Koumaru,* the former *Yrjar* from Trondheim, Norway, and the smaller *Maungaroa,* the former *Frida* from Svolver, Norway. Taio tries to run a ship around the southern group once a week, around the northern group fortnightly. The schedule varies according to the amount of cargo waiting to move and the only way to find out is to ask at the office. Also ask about special trips to Apia in Samoa.

To do a four- to five-day roundtrip to the southern group costs NZ$90 deck, NZ$185-225 cabin. To sail around the northern group for 12-13 days costs NZ$600 deck, NZ$800-850 cabin. On a one-way basis it's NZ$50 deck or NZ$100-125 cabin from Rarotonga to any of the islands of the southern group, or NZ$20 deck between Atiu, Mauke, and Mitiaro only. One-way fares to the northern group are around NZ$280 deck or NZ$380-450 cabin.

Cabin prices include meals for the first two days but from the third day onwards cabin passengers must pay NZ$15 per day for meals. Deck passengers must bring their own food. The cheaper cabins are in a 10-berth dormitory cabin and it's better to try for one of the few double cabins that have private facilities. Deck passengers to the northern group must pay NZ$7 a day for tea/coffee and one meal, and considering the small price difference and long sailing times cabin passage is a much better deal.

Be forewarned that accommodations on this sort of ship are often next to noisy, hot engine rooms and are often cluttered with crates. Deck passengers sleep under a canvas awning, and although it may be a little crowded, the islanders are friendly and easy to get along with. On the

outer islands, check with the radio operator in the post office to find out when a ship from Rarotonga might be due in. Delays of a few days are routine. In July 1998 the Taio vessel *Aroa Nui* was wrecked on the reef at Atiu.

Airport
Rarotonga International Airport (RAR) is 2.4 km west of Avarua. Immigration will stamp a 31-day entry permit onto your passport. Be sure to enter the name of a hotel in the relevant space on your arrivals card—to leave blank that space will prompt the Immigration clerk to ask you where you plan to stay.

As you come out of customs you'll find representatives from most of the backpacker's hostels waiting to the left, at a counter marked "budget accommodations." State the name of the establishment you think best suits your needs and their representative will inform you whether they have vacant rooms. Have a second choice ready in case your first choice is fully occupied. This will make it easier to deal with the drivers eagerly jostling for your business. Most offer a free transfer to their lodging on the understanding that you'll stay with them at least two nights. A taxi to Avarua will cost around NZ$5.

Hugh Henry Travel, Stars Travel, Cook Islands Tours, Island Hopper Vacations, Budget Rent-a-Car, and Avis all have offices outside arrivals at the airport. There's only a card telephone at Rarotonga Airport but you can use the public phone at the RSA Club across the street for 20 cents. If you're stuck here waiting for a flight the RSA Club is a much better place to relax than the dreary airport terminal.

The Westpac Bank at the airport charges NZ$2.50 commission per transaction. Cook Islands Tours & Travel (tel. 28-270) at the airport will store excess luggage at NZ$2 per piece per day. Clarify their hours to make sure they'll be there when you want to collect your bags. Several duty-free shops open for international arrivals and departures, and arriving passengers are allowed to duck into the duty-free liquor shop (tel. 29-322) to the right before clearing customs.

A NZ$25 departure tax is charged for international flights (children aged 2-11 pay NZ$10, and transit passengers staying fewer than 24 hours are exempt).

RAROTONGA

The name Rarotonga means "in the direction of the prevailing wind, south," the place where the chief of Atiu promised early explorers they would find an island. It's fairly small, just 31 km around. Twisting valleys lead up to steep ridges covered with luxuriant green vegetation and towering mountains crowned in clouds. Yet, Te Manga (653 meters) is only a fraction of the height Rarotonga reached before the last volcanic eruption took place, more than two million years ago.

Though Rarotonga is younger than the other Cook islands, continuous erosion has cut into the island, washing away the softer material and leaving the hard volcanic cones naked. The mountains are arrayed in a U-shaped arch, starting at the airport and then swinging south around to Club Raro, with Maungatea plopped down in the middle. Together they form the surviving southern half of the great broken volcanic caldera that became Rarotonga.

The reef circling the island defines a lagoon that is broad and sandy to the south, and narrow and rocky on the north and east. The finest beaches are on the southeast side near the Muri Lagoon, with crystal-clear water and a sandy bottom, but the best snorkeling is at Titikaveka. Elsewhere the water can be cloudy, with a lot of coral and shells that make wading difficult. Take care everywhere, as several snorkelers have drowned after being sucked out through the passes where a lot of water moves due to surf and tidal swings. Scuba diving on Rarotonga features coral dropoffs, canyons, caves, walls, sharks, wrecks, and swim throughs. All beaches on the island are public.

In recent years Rarotonga has become New Zealand's answer to Honolulu with 50,000 visitors to an island of 10,000 inhabitants, the same five-to-one visitor/resident ratio experienced in Hawaii. To find that "last heaven on earth" promised in the brochures you must escape to an outer island. Yet Raro remains one of the most beautiful islands in Polynesia, somewhat reminiscent of Moorea (though only half as big). If you enjoy the excitement of big tourist resorts with plenty of opportunities for shopping and eating out, you'll like Rarotonga.

SIGHTS

Avarua

This attractive town of around 5,000 inhabitants is strung along the north coast beneath the green, misty slopes of Maungatea. Somehow Avarua retains the air of a 19th-century South Seas trading post, and offshore in Avarua Harbor lies the boiler of the Union Steam Ship SS *Maitai*, wrecked in 1916. Near the bridge over Takuvaine Stream is the **Seven-in-One Coconut Tree** planted in 1906. In May 1992 a devastating fire swept through the old colonial buildings of the government complex south of the tree, badly damaging the post office, telephone exchange, and courthouse, all of which have since been demolished.

Just inland from the new post office is the privately owned **Rarotonga Brewery** (Box 814, Rarotonga; tel. 21-083, fax 21-089), which offers a free guided tour weekdays at 1400, during which participants get to taste the 4.5 percent alcohol draft beer (bottled beer is six percent alcohol). The Cooks Lager T-shirts sold at the brewery souvenir counter are hot items.

Inland again and a block south of the brewery is the stone on which in 1823 Papeiha preached the first Christian sermon on Rarotonga. It's set up on a pedestal in the middle of the crossing with the Ara Metua, Rarotonga's old interior road. Turn left and follow the Ara Metua 150 meters east to a small bridge and a gate leading into the original missionary compound, now **Takamoa Theological College.** You pass a row of student residences, and at the next crossroad you'll find a monument to the missionaries of the London Missionary Society who have served in the Cook Islands. Across the street is an impressive monument to Polynesian missionaries from the college who carried the Gospel to other Pacific islands. In 1837 the third LMS missionary, Rev. Aaron Buzacott, erected the two-story **Takamoa Mission House** facing the monuments. It's now a government office. The adjacent lecture hall dates from 1890.

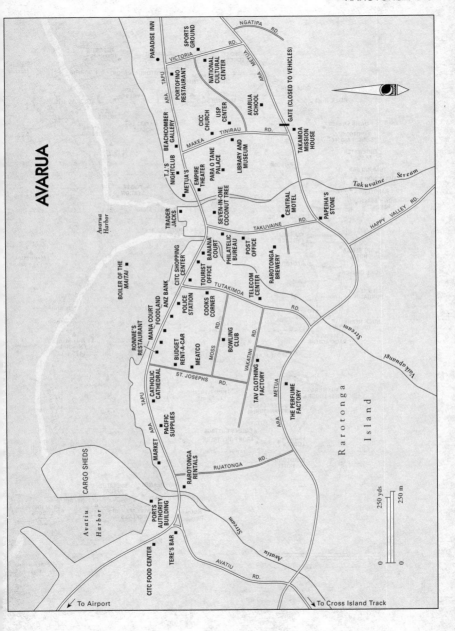

AVARUA

Avarua Harbor

To Airport

To Cross Island Track

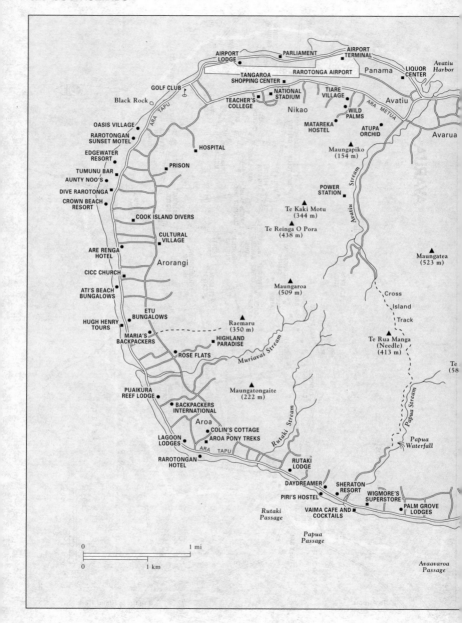

RAROTONGA

PARADISE INN

DENTAL CLINIC

GAME FISHING CLUB

CLUB RARO

KIIKII MOTEL

Avarua

Pue

ARA

TAPU

ARA

METUA

Pue Stream

ARIANA BUNGALOWS MOTEL

MARAE ARAI-TE-TONGA

Matavera

CICC CHURCH

Ikurangi (485 m)

Oroenga (292 m)

Tapapa Stream

Matavera Stream

POKATA MARAE

Te Manga (653 m)

Te Vaakauta (450 m)

Turangi Stream

Te Atukura (638 m)

SUNRISE BEACH MOTEL

Ngatangiia

AVANA MARINA CONDOS

CICC CHURCH

Avana Stream

Ngatangiia Bay

VAKA VILLAGE

Motutapu

AROKO BUNGALOWS

Arore (198 m)

SOKALA VILLAS

PACIFIC DIVERS

FLAME TREE

Oneroa

Muri

PACIFIC RESORT

Koromiri

RAROTONGA SAILING CLUB

Toroume (329 m)

Akapuao Stream

VARA'S LODGE

MURI BEACHCOMBER

VARA'S BEACH HOUSE

SHANGRI-LA

ARA METUA

ARA TAPU

QUEEN'S REPRESENTATIVE

AREMANGO GUESTHOUSE

Taakoka

CICC CHURCH

Titikaveka

FRUITS OF RAROTONGA

RAINA BEACH APARTMENTS

MOANA SANDS RESORT

LITTLE POLYNESIAN MOTEL

© DAVID STANLEY

Follow the road north between the monuments and you'll reach the **Library and Museum of the Cook Islands** (Box 71, Rarotonga; tel. 20-748; open Mon.-Sat. 0900-1300, Tuesday also 1600-2000, NZ$2 admission) with assorted artifacts, many of them on loan from museums in New Zealand. Across the street from the museum is the **Cook Islands Center** (tel. 29-415) of the University of the South Pacific, which is worth entering for the interesting books in the showcase on the right.

The massive white walls and roof of the **Cook Islands Christian Church** (1853) are visible from here. Check out the massive wooden balcony inside. It's worth being here Sunday morning at 1000, if only to see the women arrive in their Sunday best and to stand outside and listen to the wonderful singing (only go inside and sit down if you're prepared to stay for the entire service). Near the front of the church is the tomb of Albert Henry (1907-81), topped by a lifelike statue of the man. American writer Robert Dean Frisbie (1895-1948), author of *The Book of Pukapuka* and *The Island of Desire,* is buried in the southwest corner of the cemetery.

Across the road, beyond some old graves, is the **Para O Tane Palace** of the Makea Takau Ariki, high chief of the landowning clan of most of the Avarua town area. **Marae Taputaputea** and a basalt investiture pillar are on the palace grounds.

Backtrack to the University Center and turn left along a wide road to the massive green and white **Are-Karioi-Nui National Auditorium** with 2,000 seats. The four huge buildings to the left of this road are hostels used to house outer islanders when they visit Rarotonga. The auditorium forms part of the **National Cultural Center**, erected for the sixth Festival of Pacific Arts in 1992. The two yellow buildings beyond the auditorium contain the **National Library** (tel. 20-725; Monday and Wednesday 0900-2000, Tuesday, Thursday, and Friday 0900-1600) in the building to the right, and the **National Museum** (tel. 20-725; weekdays 0800-1600) in the one on the left. The museum has a collection of model canoes and modern replicas of South Pacific artifacts. This outlandish complex was one of the pet projects of the Honorable Sir Geoffrey Henry who put his country NZ$11.6 million in debt to finance construction of the island's second museum and library.

The Ara Metua

Two roads circle Rarotonga: the new coastal road (the Ara Tapu) and an old inner road (the Ara Metua). The main sights are arranged below for a counterclockwise tour of the island on the Ara Tapu with the distances from Avarua shown in parentheses. On a scooter you should be able to do it in four hours with stops; by bicycle give yourself a leisurely day.

On your second time around try using the scenic Ara Metua, passable much of the way. You'll encounter lush gardens, orchards, and good viewpoints. This inner road is said to be the oldest in Polynesia, the coral-block foundation laid some 1,000 years ago by chief Toi. Up until the mid-19th century, when the missionaries concentrated the population around their churches on the coast, most of the people lived on the inland side of this road. During WW II the road was resurfaced and much of it is now paved. There's very little traffic, which makes it perfect for cycling.

Around the Island

A little less than one km west of Rarotonga airport is the **Parliament of the Cook Islands** in a building originally used to house workers during construction of the airport in 1973. Parliament meets Feb.-March and July-Sept., and if you're properly dressed (no shorts or jeans), you can observe the proceedings from the public gallery (Monday, Tuesday, and Thursday 1300-1700, Wednesday and Friday 0900-1300). Call 26-500 for information. Notice how all the important positions here are occupied by men.

Across the street from the Golf Club (see **Sports and Recreation,** below) west of the airport is a beach park with toilets and outdoor showers. From here it's not far to **Black Rock** (6 km), standing alone in a coral lagoon (good snorkeling at high tide). This rock marks the spot where the spirits of deceased Rarotongan Polynesians pass on their way back to the legendary homeland, Avaiki. The Tahitian missionary Papeiha is said to have swum ashore here, holding a Bible above his head (in fact, he landed in a small boat).

Arorangi (8.5 km) was established by the Rev. Aaron Buzacott (who served in the Cooks 1828-57) as a model village, and Papeiha is buried in the historic white cemetery at the old

CICC church (1849). It was the LMS missionaries who resettled the people near the coast and built the **Tinomana Palace** by the church for the last native ruler of this district. **Mount Raemaru** (350 meters tall) rising up behind Arorangi has a flattened top—a local legend tells how Aitutaki warriors carried off the missing upper part.

Monday, Wednesday, and Friday at 1000 the **Cultural Village** (Box 320, tel. 21-314, fax 25-557; admission NZ$39), on the back road in Arorangi, enthusiastically demonstrates Cook Islands history, medicine, cooking, arts, crafts, dances, and traditions during an informative three-hour program, which includes a lunch of local foods. Advance reservations through a hotel, travel agency, or directly by phone are required. Several readers have written in strongly endorsing the Cultural Village.

Takitumu

The southeast side of Rarotonga is known as Takitumu. The ironic **Sheraton Resort** symbolizes the financial calamities that gripped these islands in the 1990s. At press time moves were underway to finally complete the hotel, which will probably have a new name by the time you get there. The building with the flagpole a couple of kilometers east is the residence of the representative of Queen Elizabeth II (his NZ$120,000 annual salary comes out of local taxes). East again and on the corner before Kent Hall in **Titikaveka** is Te Pou Toru Marae. Beyond this another fine coral-block CICC church (1841) stands beside the road, 19 km from Avarua counterclockwise or 14 km clockwise.

Some of the finest **snorkeling** on Rarotonga is off the beach opposite Raina Beach Apartments, behind the cemetery with the radio mast next to TM Motors. There's not a lot of coral but plenty of small fish. Some of the scuba operators bring their clients here for diving.

Turn in at the Rarotonga Sailing Club, four km northeast, to see the lovely **Muri Lagoon,** with the nicest swimming and windsurfing area on the island. At low tide you can wade across to uninhabited **Koromiri Island,** where hermit crabs forage as bathers enjoy the oceanside beach. Full nautical gear is for rent at the club (open daily) and the restaurant serves a good lunch.

The road up the **Avana Valley** begins near the bridge over Avana Stream and runs along the south bank. You can cycle halfway up, then continue on foot.

On the right just beyond the Avana Stream bridge is **Vaka Village** with a monument marking the historic gathering of ocean voyaging and war canoes here during the 1992 Festival of Pacific Arts. Local fishing boats anchor on the spot today. A little beyond is another old white **CICC church** on the left, once the seat of the Rev. Charles Pitman who translated many works into Maori during his stay here 1827-54. Across the street from the church is a small park with a good view of the tiny islands or *motus* in the Muri Lagoon and **Ngatangiia Harbor.** Legend claims seven canoes departed from here in A.D. 1350 on a daring voyage to N.Z., and the names of the canoes are inscribed on a monument. Cruising yachts sometimes anchor here, though it's rather exposed to the southeast trades.

Back near the bridge is a road in to the **Ara Metua.** On the right a short distance along this road is an old burial ground with a Polynesian *marae* among the trees on a hillock behind. Many other similar *marae* are in the vicinity.

Continue along the Ara Metua and turn left up the road alongside Turangi Stream, on the far side of a small bridge. The **Turangi Valley** is larger and more impressive than Avana, and swamp taro is grown in irrigated paddies. Once again, you cycle halfway up and continue on foot.

Matavera

At Matavera there's yet another lovely CICC church (1865) beside the road. Farther along, just a few km before Avarua, watch for a signboard on Maotangi Road pointing the way in to **Marae Arai-te-tonga,** on the Ara Metua. Marae Arai-te-tonga, the most sacred on the island, was a *koutu,* or place where the ta'unga (priest) invested and anointed the high chiefs *(ariki)* of the island. The route of the ancient Ara Metua is quite evident here, and there are other stone constructions 100 meters along it to the east.

The Cross-Island Track

From Avarua walk three km up the Avatiu Valley. Just beyond the power station you get your first view of Te Rua Manga, **the Needle** (413 meters). In another 10 minutes the road ends at a concrete water intake; you continue up a footpath for 15 minutes until you reach a huge boulder.

Pass it and head up the steep forested incline. This climb is the hardest part of the trip, but when you reach the top, the Needle towers majestically above you (the hike from the end of the road to the top takes less than an hour).

There's a fork at the top of the ridge: the Needle on your right, the trail down to the south coast on the left. After scrambling around the Needle, start down the trail to the south coast, past the giant ferns along the side of Papua Stream. On this part of the trek you really get to see Rarotonga's interior rainforest. The road out begins at **Papua Waterfall** at the bottom of the hill. The stream above Papua is a drinking water source, so save your swimming for the pool below the falls (often it will be dry unless there have been rains recently). The Sheraton Resort is to your right just before you reach the main road.

Though sometimes slippery, the cross-island track can be covered in all weather and even if it has been raining, you can still do the trip the next day. Parts of the track are badly eroded, so it might not be a good idea to go alone. Allow 45 minutes to walk up Avatiu Road, then an hour and a quarter to climb to the Needle. The descent down the Papua Valley takes two hours, and it's easier to do a roundtrip to the Needle from the end of the road on the Avatiu side, allowing a return to a parked vehicle. If you'll be hiking right across it's best to go during the week as onward bus service on the other side will be limited or nonexistent on weekends. Several companies offer guided cross-island treks Mon.-Sat. at 0930 if the weather is okay, but lots of visitors do this hike on their own and you don't really need a guide.

Sports and Recreation

Dive Rarotonga (Barry and Shirley Hill, Box 38, Rarotonga; tel. 21-873, fax 21-878) offers scuba trips every afternoon at 1300 (including Sunday!). A one-tank dive is NZ$55 (NZ$45 if you have your own equipment), while two different dives at 0900 and 1300 on the same day are NZ$90 (or NZ$80 with your own equipment). Snorkelers can go along for NZ$20 pp (rental of snorkeling gear extra).

Scuba diving is also offered by Greg Wilson's **Cook Island Divers** (Box 1002, Rarotonga; tel. 22-483, fax 22-484), just up the road. Dive Rarotonga is a bit cheaper but if the weather looks at all bad they'll cancel that day's diving, whereas Cook Islands Divers tries to go out in almost any weather. Greg does two trips a day, at 0800 and 1300, and he runs a highly professional show. His four-day NAUI or PADI scuba certification course is NZ$425—what better place to learn?

Pacific Divers (Graham McDonald, Box 110, Rarotonga; tel./fax 22-450), also known as "Scuba Divers," opposite the Flame Tree Restaurant at Muri Beach, offers dives on the nearby Titikaveka Reef at 0800 and 1300 daily (at 1300 only on Sunday). It's NZ$60/100 for one/two tanks and two people together get a NZ$10 discount. A PADI open-water certification course (four days) will run NZ$425. All three scuba operators offer discounts for three or more dives.

The **Aqua Sports Centre** (Junior Ioaba, Box 67, Rarotonga; tel. 27-350, fax 20-932) at the Rarotonga Sailing Club on Muri Beach rents kayaks (NZ$8 an hour), windsurfers (NZ$10 an hour), sailboats (NZ$20 an hour), and snorkeling gear (NZ$7 a half day). Lessons in windsurfing (NZ$20) and sailing (NZ$20) are given. A five-hour sailing course is NZ$130. Mornings 0900-1300 they'll ferry you over to an uninhabited offshore island for NZ$5 return. Daily at 1100 Aqua Sports runs a glass-bottom coral reef boat tour costing NZ$15; combined with an afternoon lagoon cruise and barbecue lunch it's NZ$35 in total (on Sunday the glass-bottom boat trip is at 1330). Equipment rental is possible every day.

Captain Tama's Water Sportz World (Tamaiva Tuavera, tel. 20-810) at the Pacific Resort, Muri, rents out the same sort of gear and also does lagoon cruises in a boat with a thatched sunroof. Wednesday at 1100 Captain Tama does a special backpacker's cruise at NZ$20 including lunch.

Reef Runner (tel. 26-780, closed Sunday), at the south end of Muri Beach, rents small glass-bottomed boats with outboard motors that you can use to explore the lagoon (NZ$35 first hour, NZ$25 second hour).

For kayaking call **Kayak Adventure Tours** (tel. 25-359, fax 29-223) based in a yellow and red building opposite Puaikura Community Services in Arorangi. A full day of paddling right around Rarotonga is NZ$90 pp plus tax. Call ahead for reservations.

The **Reef-Sub** (tel. 25-837) at Avatiu Harbor is a sort of glass-bottom boat with an underwater viewing deck (it's not a real submarine). The 90-minute trips Mon.-Sat. at 1000 and 1400 cost NZ$35/20 for adults/children.

Pacific Marine Charters (Box 770, Rarotonga; tel. 21-237, fax 27-237) at Avatiu Harbor offers deep-sea fishing from its fast yellow cruiser. Also at Avatiu is the larger 10-meter *Seafari* of **Seafari Charters** (Elgin Tetachuk, Box 148, Rarotonga; tel./fax 20-328). Four hours of fishing costs about NZ$100 pp (NZ$60 pp for nonfishing passengers), a light lunch included. Both boats depart weekdays at 0900 and the fishing takes place right off Rarotonga, so you get very good views of the island and don't waste time commuting. On both of these, the captain gets to keep the fish, but Brent Fisher of **Fisher's Fishing Tours** (Box 880, Rarotonga; tel. 23-356, fax 23-354) might let you keep your catch or even take you home for a barbecue. His catamaran, the *Corey-Anne,* goes out at 0800 or 1300 (NZ$60 pp). Another catamaran, the *Tangaroa III,* is similar.

For horseback riding it's **Aroa Pony Treks** (tel. 21-415), up the road from Kaena Restaurant near the Rarotongan Resort Hotel. They offer two-hour rides to Papua Waterfall, returning along the beach, weekdays at 1000 and 1500 (NZ$30 pp).

Try your swing at the nine-hole **Rarotonga Golf Club** (tel. 27-360; closed Sunday), under the radio towers near the end of the airstrip. Greens fees and club rentals are NZ$12 each. If you hit a mast, wire, or stay during your round, there's a compulsory replay; balls have been known to bounce back at players. There's an annual tournament here in late September and the club has a very pleasant colonial-style bar perfect for a cold beer (visitors are always welcome).

The bar at the **Rarotonga Bowling Club** (tel. 26-277) on Moss Rd., Avarua, opens at 1600 weekdays, at 1000 on Saturday. If you've never tried lawn bowling before, do so—it's only NZ$1 greens fees plus NZ$1 bowls hire (a white outfit is required on Saturday).

The **Rarotonga Squash Club** (tel. 21-056; daily 0900-2000), directly behind the Catholic cathedral, charges NZ$5 a session.

Both the Edgewater Resort and Rarotongan Resort Hotel have tennis courts open to the public, and the Edgewater also has squash courts.

Monday at 1730 you can jog with the **Hash House Harriers.** For the venue, call David Lobb at tel. 22-055 during business hours, check the notice outside the Westpac Bank, or scrutinize the back page of the Monday edition of the *Cook Islands News*. It's good fun and a nice way of meeting people. Similarly, the **Frangi Road Race** begins across the street from Frangi Dairy near Parliament every Thursday at 1700.

ACCOMMODATIONS

There's such a glut of accommodations on Rarotonga that you'd have to be very unlucky to arrive on a day when everything was full, and you can take advantage of competitive rates by not booking ahead from overseas. Bargaining for rooms isn't done but it's okay to ask if they have any specials on. If saving money is a concern, get a place with cooking facilities as restaurant meals can add up. All of the budget and medium-priced hotels are self-catering, but many of the upmarket resorts are not. When choosing, keep in mind that the west coast is drier and gets beautiful sunsets, while the finest snorkeling is at windy Titikaveka in the south and the top beach faces the gorgeous Muri Lagoon in the east. The places near Avarua are best for those more into shopping, sightseeing, and entertainment than beachlife.

Most places include the 12.5% VAT in the quoted rate but some charge it extra. Check out time at the motels is 1000.

In past most of the budget hotels have provided free or inexpensive airport transfers to those who booked direct (there's pressure from the tour companies to change this). Even if you do get a free ride there, you'll probably be charged something for the ride back to the airport. The listings below are arranged counterclockwise around the island in each price category.

Shoestring

Aunty Noo's Beach Lodge (Box 196, Rarotonga; tel. 21-253, fax 22-275), halfway down to the beach behind Sunbird Laundry in Arorangi, offers the cheapest accommodations on Rarotonga and is thus the choice of backpackers on the barest of budgets. Beds in the four-bed dormitory and two double rooms are NZ$10-15 pp (depending on what the competition is charging), or you can camp in the back yard for NZ$7 pp. Rudimentary cooking facilities are provided and many guests sit and play cards at the picnic tables in the lounge all day. A party ensues whenever a duty-free bottle appears. It's basic but a good place to meet other budget travelers (mostly male) and a nice beach is just half a minute away.

Maria's Backpackers Accommodations (Exham and Maria Wichman, Box 777, Rarotonga; tel. 21-180) is just off the Ara Metua in Arorangi, up near the trailhead of the Raemaru trek. From main road in Arorangi turn inland opposite Bunny's Restaurant. There are two self-catering rooms at NZ$15/25 single/double. This is a place for people who like peace and quiet; those interested in meeting other travelers should head elsewhere.

Piri's Coconut Beach Hostel (Box 624, Rarotonga; tel. 20-309), on the beach just west of the Sheraton, offers 16 mattresses in an open dorm at NZ$12.50 or beds in a basic room at NZ$14 pp. There are communal cooking facilities but it's all really scruffy and to be avoided. The manager, Piri Puruto III, puts on a tacky coconut tree climbing show for tourists here Thursday at 1700 and Sunday at 1400. Watch out for him at the airport as he tends to pounce on fresh arrivals (we've received several complaints). On the plus side, the beach here is great, but when snorkeling beware of dangerous currents in passes draining the lagoon.

Budget

The first budget place to the west of town is **Atupa Orchid Units** (Box 64, Rarotonga; tel. 28-543, fax 28-546), run by a German woman named Ingrid Caffery who has been in the Cooks since 1970. There are 10 rooms in four screened houses, each house with its own cooking facilities and hot water. Prices vary from NZ$25/48/68 single/double/triple in a budget room to NZ$45/65/80 in a more private flat. It's excellent value and discounts are available when things are slow. Rental bicycles are NZ$8. Quiet and comfortable, central Avarua is just a 10-minute walk away. The transfer from the airport is free but everybody pays NZ$4 pp to return to the airport.

Hugh Baker's **Matareka Hostel** (Box 587, Rarotonga; tel. 23-670, fax 23-672), on the hillside facing the far side of the airport, is Rarotonga's original budget hostel, founded in 1980. There are three breezy three-bed dormitories on the hilltop at NZ$15 pp, plus three rooms behind the owner's home below at NZ$25/40 single/double. The weekly rate is NZ$85 pp. A communal kitchen, laundry, and lounge area are available, and the washing machine is NZ$3 a load. In season, Hugh will give you all the fresh fruit you desire, and he rents some of the cheapest bicycles (NZ$5) and scooters (NZ$12) on Rarotonga. People who want a restful, do-your-own-thing type of holiday rather than 24-hour partying will like it here.

At the bottom of the hill below Hugh Baker's are the A-frame chalets and guesthouse of the popular **Tiare Village Dive Hostel** (Mary Pernetta, Box 719, Rarotonga; tel. 23-466, fax 23-969). This friendly establishment has three fan-cooled, self-contained chalets, each with two singles and one double at NZ$20 pp and three triples in the main house at NZ$18 pp to share. In addition, six new self-catering units beside the swimming pool cost NS$25 pp. Tiare's guests share the communal cooking facilities, lounge, and hot water showers in a family-style environment, and the tropical garden is bursting with fruit there for the picking. Free luggage storage is available. It's only a 30-minute walk from town (and provides a convenient base for hiking to the Needle). Ask for their free airport pickup.

The **Are Renga Motel** (Box 223, Rarotonga; tel. 20-050, fax 29-223) at Arorangi has 20 simple thin-walled units with well-equipped kitchens at NZ$25/40/55 single/double/triple. The quality varies, so ask to see another room if the first one you're shown isn't to your liking. Beware of rooms with open ventilation spaces near the ceiling, as these let in every sound from adjacent rooms. The Are Renga offers a reduced "backpacker's rate" of NZ$15 per bed in a couple of shared double rooms. The location is good with a store and other facilities nearby, and a lending library is available in the office. Use of their washing machine costs NZ$5, but there's no drier. In season you may harvest fruit from the large orchard behind the property. Airport transfers are also free.

Backpackers International Hostel (Bill Bates, Box 878, Rarotonga; tel./fax 21-847) is in the southwest corner of the island, only 150 meters from a grocery store, the Island Bus, and the beach. They offer six rooms with double beds and another 12 rooms with twin beds at NZ$34 double. In addition, there are six singles at NZ$22 and 21 dorm beds in rooms of three to eight at NZ16 pp. A common TV lounge and cooking area are provided, and Bill will probably give you some free fruit. It's convivial, and on Saturday night the managers prepare a special buffet dinner at NZ$15 pp (NZ$18 for nonguests). Just ask Bill if you need to send an e-mail.

The **Aremango Guesthouse** (Box 714, Rarotonga; tel. 24-362, fax 24-363) is just 50 meters from Muri Beach, south of the Muri Beachcomber. The 10 spacious fan-cooled rooms with shared bath are NZ$17 pp plus tax (airport transfers NZ$5 pp). Singles must be prepared to share or pay for both beds. Communal cooking facilities are available, and lockable cupboards for groceries are provided. Peace and quiet will be up to your fellow guests.

Vara's Beach House & Lodge (Vara Hunter, Box 434, Rarotonga; tel. 23-156, fax 22-619), on the south side of the Muri Beachcomber, consists of two distinct sections. The "beach house" right on Muri Beach has double rooms and a four-bed dorm, while the two large two-story "cottages" sleeping four or five are 400 meters up the hillside. The "lodge" is up above the cottages. At NZ$18 pp in a dorm, NZ$42 double with shared bath, or NZ$60 double with private bath, beds in both sections cost the same with discounts for stays of more than a week. The accommodations on the hillside are of higher quality while those at the beach have the water only a few meters away. All guests have access to communal cooking facilities, fans, free laundry facilities, canoe rentals, and free airport pickups (NZ$6 to return to the airport). At Vara's you get to enjoy the same beach as guests at the adjacent Muri Beachcomber for a tenth the price.

The **Ariana Bungalows Motel** (Box 925, Rarotonga; tel./fax 20-521), also known as Ariana Backpackers Accommodation or the Ariana Hostel, a couple of km east of Avarua, offers quite a range of accommodations. The seven self-catering duplex bungalows are NZ$65 single, double, or triple with bath, whereas the six shared doubles are NZ$30/40 single/double with specials sometimes offered. The two segregated dormitories are NZ$18 pp (six beds for men, nine beds for women)—one of the only Rarotonga hostels with separate dorms for male and female. On a weekly basis it's 10% off. The pleasant grounds are peaceful and spacious, but it's 500 meters in off the main road and quite a distance from town or the beach. On the plus side, this is one of the only budget properties with a swimming pool. Ariana is an excellent base from which to climb Ikurangi. Bicycles and scooters are for rent, and a few basic groceries are sold at the office for normal prices. Ariana is run by an American named Bob Healey who also heads the Cook Islands Budget Accommodation Council. Ask for Bob's free airport pickup.

Rarotonga's latest low-budget hostel is **Lovely Planet Backpackers** (Box 711, Rarotonga; tel./fax 25-100), opposite the Outpatients Medical Clinic at Tupapa, a kilometer east of central Avarua. The five triple-bunk rooms start at NZ$20 pp. A shared kitchen, refrigerator, and laundry room are provided, and bicycles are for rent. Despite the name, this colonial-style home hostel with a spacious porch is run by Papa Ross Grant and has no connection with a certain Australian mass-market guidebook publisher.

Inexpensive

Ati's Beach Bungalows (Jim and Ati Robertson, Box 693, Rarotonga; tel. 21-546, fax 25-546), on the beach a little south of the church in Arorangi, offers nine self-contained units with cooking facilities and hot water showers. It's NZ$80/100 double/triple for one of the five garden bungalows or NZ$120/150 for one of the four deluxe beach bungalows. There's a communal TV lounge/bar, and you should try to get a room well away from both it and the office as the walls don't keep out the sound. The flagpole outside bears the flags of all the countries currently represented there. Ati's caters to mature crowd and more youthful travelers may feel out of place. Airport transfers are NZ$10 pp return.

Daniel Roro's **Aroko Bungalows** (Box 850, Rarotonga; tel. 23-625, fax 24-625), at Ngatangiia facing Muri Beach, has five individual bungalows with basic cooking facilities at NZ$80 single or double roadside, NZ$90 beachside.

The **Sunrise Beach Motel** (Depot 8, Raro-tonga; tel. 20-417, fax 22-991) at Ngatangiia has four beachfront bungalows at NZ$125 single or double, while the two garden units are NZ$95. Two rooms in a duplex block are cheaper and the rates are reduced when things are slow. All have cooking facilities and are excellent value. The beach here is poor but it's peaceful and a store is nearby. Some lovely nature hikes are available in the nearby valleys and it's an easy walk to Muri Beach.

The clean, pleasant **Kiikii Motel** (Box 68, Rarotonga; tel. 21-937, fax 22-937), a 30-minute walk west of Avarua, has an attractive swim-ming pool overlooking a rocky beach. Rooms in this solid two-story motel begin at NZ$54/67/113 single/double/triple, and even the four older "budget rooms" are quite adequate. The eight standard rooms in the west wing are 20% more expensive but they're large enough to accom-modate a family of five. The six deluxe and six premier rooms (overlooking the sea) are 20% higher again. All 24 rooms have good cooking facilities, and the efficient staff is helpful in as-sisting with any special arrangements. Kiikii pro-vides a good combination of proximity to town and beachside atmosphere, and several good bars and entertainment possibilities are near-by. Club Raro and its nightlife is only a stroll away (although you won't be bothered by the noise when you want to sleep). It's probably the closest you'll come to a U.S.-style motel, al-though much nicer. Airport transfers are NZ$7 each way.

A good bet very near Avarua's shopping, en-tertainment, and sightseeing possibilities is the **Paradise Inn** (Dianne Haworth, Box 674, Raro-tonga; tel. 20-544, fax 22-544), just east of Portofi-no Restaurant. In a former existence "the Par-adise" was the Maruaiai Dancehall, but it has been completely refurbished into a cozy little 16-room motel. The fan-cooled split-level rooms are NZ$72/80/93 single/double/triple, and there are two smaller budget singles that are a third cheap-er. Cooking facilities are provided, and there's a large lounge and a nice terrace overlooking the ocean where you can sit and have a drink. Children under 12 are not accommodated.

The only hotel right in Avarua itself is the **Cen-tral Motel** (Box 183, Rarotonga; tel. 25-735, fax 25-740), opposite the entrance to Rarotonga

Breweries. The 14 units in this two-story con-crete block edifice are NZ$95 single or double. No real cooking facilities are provided but a toast-er, kettle, cups and plates have been added as an afterthought for making snacks. It's clean and convenient and might be okay if you were there on business.

Moderate

Puaikura Reef Lodges (Box 397, Rarotonga; tel. 23-537, fax 21-537) on the southwest side of the island offers 12 self-catering rooms in three single-story motel wings arranged around a cloudy swimming pool at NZ$126 single or dou-ble. A grocery store is adjacent, and the beach is just across the road with no houses blocking ac-cess to the sea. A paperback library is available for guests. The motel office is only open week-days 0900-1600, Saturday 0900-1200, and the no-nonsense manager would rather you booked from overseas through Air New Zealand instead of just showing up unannounced on his doorstep.

Lagoon Lodges (Box 45, Rarotonga; tel. 22-020, fax 22-021), on spacious grounds near the Rarotongan Resort Hotel, has 15 attractive self-catering units of varying descriptions beginning at NZ$140 single, double, or triple. There's a swimming pool, terrace café, and NZ$23 Sunday night barbecue for in-house guests only. It's a good choice for families with small children. La-goon Lodges is run by Des Eggelton who ar-rived on Raro to help build the airport in 1973 and just couldn't bring himself to leave.

Travel writer Elliot Smith operates **Shangri-La Beach Cottages** (Box 146, Rarotonga; tel. 22-779, fax 22-775) on the beach south of the Muri Beachcomber Motel. The two comfortable a/c cottages are NZ$145 single or double with jacuzzi, microwave, fridge, and lounge (four more units are planned). After serving as a Cal-ifornia judge for many years, Elliot dropped out of the legal profession and became a South Sea islander, sort of. His *Cook Islands Com-panion* is a best-seller on Rarotonga and he'll be able to tell you on anything you want to know about Cook Islands.

Club Raro (Box 483, Rarotonga; tel. 22-415, fax 24-415) is a medium-sized resort just two km east of Avarua. The 39 fan-cooled rooms are NZ$120/165 double/triple standard, NZ$160/225 superior, including breakfast (no cooking facilities). Their all-inclusive meal and tour plan costs NZ$95 pp extra and twice a week the evening meal is off-site at a local restaurant. In 1995 an artificial beach was constructed and there's also a swimming pool. It's walking distance from town and might be a good choice for those interested in activities and having fun. Traditional dancing is staged Wednesday and Friday in their adjacent entertainment center.

Expensive

The **Rarotongan Sunset Motel** (Box 377, Rarotonga; tel. 28-028, fax 28-026), on the beach a bit south of Black Rock, has 20 self-catering units in long blocks of four or five units at NZ$175 single, double, or triple in the garden or NZ$195 beachfront. These prices may be heavily discounted if you book direct on arrival and not through a travel agent. There's a swimming pool. It's popular and often full.

If your flight is delayed, Air New Zealand may accommodate you at the **Edgewater Resort** (Box 121, Rarotonga; tel. 25-435, fax 25-475), a crowded, impersonal cluster of two-story blocks, service buildings, and tennis courts facing a mediocre beach. This is Raro's largest hotel, with 182 a/c rooms beginning at NZ$200 single or double for those in the most unfavorable locations and rising to NZ$390 for an executive suite. Third persons are NZ$50 extra. No cooking facilities are provided but there's traditional dancing twice a week.

Near the south end of Muri Beach is the **Muri Beachcomber Motel** (Box 379, Rarotonga; tel. 21-022, fax 21-323) with 16 self-catering seaview units in eight duplex blocks at NZ$150/175/215 single/double/triple. Children under 12 are only accepted in two larger garden units facing the pool, which cost NZ$215 for up to four. Three "watergarden" units back near the road cost NZ$200/225/285.

Premium

The **Rarotongan Resort Hotel** (Box 103, Rarotonga; tel. 25-800, fax 25-799), in the southwest corner of Rarotonga, has been the island's premier hotel since its opening in 1977. In 1997 the complex was fully renovated and made wheelchair accessible, one of the few South Pacific resorts where this is so. The 151 a/c rooms in nine one- and two-story blocks begin at NZ$240 single or double, NZ$300 triple, breakfast included (no cooking facilities). Children under 16 sleep free and some water sports are also included. The beach and swimming pool are fine, and island nights with traditional dancing are held twice a week.

The **Pacific Resort** (Box 790, Rarotonga; tel. 20-427, fax 21-427) at Muri offers 54 self-catering rooms beginning at NZ$270 single or double, NZ$310 triple. The sandy beach is okay for swimming but not for snorkeling. A swimming pool, water-sports facility, and evening entertainment are part of this well-rounded resort. Their Barefoot Bar is fine for a hamburger-and-beer lunch but skip the stingy NZ$12 breakfast in their Sandals Restaurant.

House Rentals

Renting a entire house by the week or month can be excellent value, and with hundreds of islanders moving to New Zealand each month, there are lots of places are available. Advertisements for furnished houses are often published in the classified section of the *Cook Islands News,* otherwise watch for signs around the island or ask at the Cook Islands Tourism Corporation. Prices being as low as NZ$100 a week plus utilities.

Upon arrival at Rarotonga Airport, ask for Nan Noovao of Cook Islands Tours and Travel (Box 611, Rarotonga; tel. 20-270, fax 27-270) who has eight furnished houses for rent at NZ$350/450 a week for a one/two-bedroom. Transfers are NZ$10 per person.

Kiikii Motel (Box 68, Rarotonga; tel. 21-937, fax 22-937) rents four fully equipped two-bedroom cottages near the Rarotongan Resort Hotel in Arorangi. These cost NZ$316 a week, plus about NZ$20 for electricity.

FOOD

Some upmarket restaurants don't include the value-added tax in their menu prices, and if in doubt, ask when booking rather than get a 12.5% surprise on the bill. Most of the budget eateries popular among local residents are in Avarua, but fancy tourist restaurants are found all around the island with a cluster near the Edgewater Hotel.

Budget Eateries

The cheapest meals are dispensed from food trailers at the market and there are covered picnic tables at which to eat.

Mama's Cafe (tel. 23-379; weekdays 0800-1630, Saturday 0800-1200), beside Foodland in Avarua, offers an interesting combination of healthy sandwiches and fattening desserts. The ice-cream cones here are great! It's always crowded with locals.

The outdoor lunch counter at the **Cooks Corner Cafe** (tel. 22-345; open weekdays 0700-1500, Saturday 0700-1200) beside the Island Bus stop is also popular and specials are posted on blackboards.

Opposite Empire Theater is **Metua's Cafe** (tel. 20-850; open 0730-2200, closed Sunday) with lunch specials at NZ$6.50, dinner specials for NZ$11.90, all listed on a blackboard (large portions). It's good for a coffee or draft beer anytime.

In Arorangi **Flamboyant Takeaway** (tel. 23-958; open 0800-0100 daily including Sunday), opposite Dive Rarotonga, serves inexpensive meals at their picnic tables. Friday at 1600 there's a special NZ$5 barbecue dish here. They also have good ice-cream cones.

Avarua

Ronnie's Bar and Restaurant (Ronnie Siulepa, tel. 20-823; closed Sunday), on the Avarua waterfront, serves medium-priced lunches and dinners, and beside the restaurant bar is a pleasant, shady patio for cool drinks and conversation. Their *ika mata* (marinated raw fish) is excellent. It's okay to bring your own bottle of wine to dinner.

Much celebrated **Trader Jacks** (tel. 26-464) on the waterfront is a better venue for drinking or consuming *kati kati* (bar snacks) than ordering a full meal (although one reader recommended the seafood). It's one of the only places away from the resorts where you can get a beer on Sunday, and weekdays at happy hour you may meet some very senior, very drunk members of the local administration. It's lots of fun when the crew off one of the longliners working out of Avatiu Harbor rolls in.

The **Portofino Restaurant** (tel. 26-480), on the east side of town, specializes in Italian dishes such as pizza, pasta, and steaks. It opens for dinner at 1830 but is closed on Sunday. It gets good reviews from readers ("good food, lots of it, and well prepared") and could be crowded, so try to reserve. Just be aware that the menu in the window is the takeaway menu—the regular restaurant menu you'll be handed inside is much more expensive (tricky, tricky).

Arorangi

Alberto's Steakhouse (tel. 23-597; open Mon.-Sat. 1800-2100), near the Rarotongan Sunset Motel, offers steaks from NZ$17.50 to NZ$24.50 or pastas in the NZ$13-19 range. The cook is Swiss.

PJ's Sports Cafe (tel. 20-367; Mon.-Fri. 1200-1400/1800-2200, Saturday 1800-2200 only), 50 meters south of Alberto's and across the street, has less expensive burgers, chicken, fish and chips, and Chinese dishes you can carry out and consume at their roadside picnic tables. They also offer a more upmarket Chinese dinner menu served in the main dining room and provide free transportation from most west coast hotels.

Seafood, steaks, and chicken are available nightly 1800-2130 at the **Tumunu Tropical Garden Bar and Restaurant** (tel. 20-501), near the Edgewater Resort. This spacious bar opened in 1979 and the bartender, Eric, offers sightseers a popular guided tour of his picturesque establishment for a NZ$1 tip. Ask the waitress if you can see Eric's scrapbooks of life on Raro in the early 1970s.

Titikaveka to Muri

The **Vaima Cafe and Cocktails** (tel. 26-123), on the south coast just east of the Sheraton, offers a reasonable lunch menu 1100-1500 and more upmarket dinner fare 1800-2200 every day. Friday to Monday nights, there's live music.

Under the same management as the Portofino in Avarua is the famous **Flame Tree Restaurant** (tel. 25-123), near Sokala Villas at Muri Beach, the island's top restaurant since it opened in 1988. Every day they offer a different set three-course menu for NZ$25, otherwise the seafood platter is NZ$30. À la carte starters are in the NZ$10-15 range and main plates run NZ$25-30. Owner Sue Carruthers was brought up in Kenya and some surprisingly exotic choices are on the menu (and in her two published cookbooks). This is one of the few restaurants on Rarotonga that doesn't allow smoking at the tables (only at the bar). It opens at 1830 daily and reservations are recommended.

Cafes

The **Blue Note Café** (tel. 23-236; daily 0800-1500, weekdays also 1800-2200), next to Banana Court, has the best coffee in town (NZ$3.50) and there's a stack of New Zealand newspapers on the counter for free reading. Check out the adjacent art gallery.

Fruits of Rarotonga (tel. 21-509; weekdays 0730-1700, Saturday 0900-1700), by the road in the southeast corner of the island, sells a variety of jams, chutneys, pickles, sauces, and dried fruits made on the premises. It's a great place to stop for coffee and muffins on your way around the island, and you can snorkel right off their beach.

Sunday Barbecues

Several of the hotels prepare a special Sunday barbecue dinner or "roast" open to everyone. The favorite of those in the know takes place at 1900 at Ati's Beach Bungalows (tel. 21-546), a bit south of the church in Arorangi (NZ$17.50 pp, reservations required). Return minibus transfers from anywhere on the island can be arranged at NZ$5 pp.

At the main hotels, there's one at the Rarotongan Sunset Motel (tel. 28-028) at 1730 (NZ$20 pp), at the Edgewater Resort (tel. 25-435) at 1830 (NZ$27.50), and at the Pacific Resort's Barefoot Bar (tel. 20-427) at 1900 (NZ$33). Call ahead to check times, prices, transportation arrangements, and bookings. Other possibilities may be advertised in the local paper.

Groceries

Every budget hotel provides kitchen facilities, so Rarotonga is perfect for those who enjoy preparing their own food. At the supermarkets, newcomers to the South Pacific will be surprised to find the milk and juice in boxes on the shelves and long loaves of unwrapped bread in barrels near the check-out. Unfortunately it's almost impossible to buy fresh fish at Avarua market or elsewhere because the lagoons have been fished out and anything that's caught goes straight to the hotel kitchens.

CITC Food Center (tel. 27-000; Mon.-Thurs. 0800-1700, Friday 0800-1800, Saturday 0800-1300), next to Tere's Bar opposite Avatiu Harbor, is generally cheaper than Foodland Supermarket

in town. **Meatco** (tel. 27-652), just down from Budget Rent-a-Car in town, usually has the least expensive vegetables and the best meat (except pork). The **Real Butcher** (tel. 27-418) opposite Metua's Cafe also sells quality meats.

Fresh milk and fruit juices are sold at **Frangi Dairy** (tel. 22-153), beside Parliament. You can also buy imported frozen meat and vegetables here, and super ice-cream cones.

For beer or liquor, go to the **Liquor Center** (tel. 27-351; weekdays 1000-1630, Saturday 0900-1200) at Avatiu on the way to the airport.

On the south side of the island you can usually get everything you need at **Wigmore's Super Store** (tel. 20-206; Mon.-Sat. 0600-2100, Sunday 0600-0900/1400-2100) between the Sheraton and Palm Grove Lodges.

The water on Rarotonga is safe to drink.

ENTERTAINMENT AND EVENTS

The **Empire Theater** (tel. 23-189) in Avarua projects feature films in two separate halls nightly except Sunday at 1930 and 2130 (NZ$4). On Saturday there's a matinee at 1000. It's almost worth going just to experience the enthusiasm of the local audience!

The most popular watering hole on the island used to be the historic **Banana Court** (Robert Ioaba, tel. 27-797) in central Avarua in what was once a hostel for expatriate workers. Since 1994 the place has been in a state of limbo due to land disputes but it still opens on Friday nights with a live pop band for disco-style dancing. It's a genuine local scene.

The local teen spot is the **First Club,** behind Ronnie's Bar and Restaurant in Avarua, which opens from 1830 on Friday (NZ$2 admission).

T.J.'s Maruaiai Club (tel. 24-722), next to BECO Hardware Store just east of Metua's Cafe, opens Friday and Saturday around 1930. There's karaoke singing on Friday and a disco on Saturday. It's popular with the local teenagers, and dress regulations are in force to maintain standards.

Bars

Tere's Bar (tel. 20-352; closed Sunday), across the street from Avarua Harbor, is a breezy hangout with mugs of cold beer and occasional live music.

It's the sort of place where you might expect to meet a former prime minister and other colorful local characters. Mention of "golden oldies" on the blackboard outside probably announces a dancing competition for senior citizens rather than Chubby Checkers or The Rondelles.

Another good drinking place is the **Cook Islands Game Fishing Club** (tel. 21-419; weekdays 1600-midnight, Saturday 1400-midnight) near Club Raro east of town. There's a terrace out back with picnic tables overlooking the beach and a large paperback library inside. This is a private club but a little tact and charm will see you through. Other agreeable bars include those at the **Rarotonga Bowling Club** (tel. 26-277; opens at 1600 weekdays) in Avarua and at the **Rarotonga Golf Club** (tel. 27-360) west of the airport. Both are closed on Sunday.

The **Returned Services Association Club** or "RSA" (tel. 20-590; weekdays 1200-2400, Saturday 1100-2400, public holidays 1300-2400, closed Sunday), directly across the street from the airport terminal, is a good place for a beer while you're waiting for a flight. They also have two pool tables, but food service is erratic. Tom Neale, who wrote a well-known book about his experiences living alone on Suwarrow atoll in the northern Cooks, is buried in the cemetery next to the club.

Cultural Shows for Visitors

Rarotonga is one place where the dance shows put on for tourists are worth seeing. Cook Islands dancers are renowned and "island night" performances are staged regularly at the hotels and restaurants. A buffet of traditional Cook Island food (umukai) is laid out and those ordering the meal can watch the show for free, otherwise there's usually a cover charge (around NZ$5-10). Things change, so call the hotels to check. Best of all, try to attend a show related to some special local event when the islanders themselves participate (look in the newspaper for listings).

Club Raro (tel. 22-415) does its island nights Wednesday at 2000 and Friday at 2100 (NZ$35 with dinner, otherwise NZ$5 cover). The Orama Dance Troupe, winner of many awards, often performs at Club Raro on Friday (Tuesday it's Awaiki Nui). The **Edgewater Resort** (tel. 25-435) has island nights Tuesday and Saturday at 2030, costing NZ$35 for the buffet or NZ$10 cover if you don't take dinner. The Taakoka Troupe often performs at the Edgewater on Tuesday with Orama on Saturday (ask). The **Rarotongan Resort Hotel** (tel. 25-800) usually has shows Wednesday and Saturday at 2030 (NZ$35 buffet or NZ$10 cover). The **Pacific Resort** (tel. 20-427) at Muri has an island night with children dancing Friday at 1900 (no cover change).

SHOPPING

Shopping hours in Avarua are weekdays 0800-1600, Saturday 0800-1200. Supermarkets in Avarua stay open about an hour longer, and

musicians at
island night

small general stores around the island are open as late as 2000 weekdays and also on weekends. The **Dive Shop** (tel. 26-675) in Mana Court in Avarua sells quality snorkeling gear.

Raro Records (tel. 25-927), next to Empire Theater, sells Tahitian compact discs and cassettes a third cheaper than what you'd pay in Tahiti! **CITC Shopping Center** (tel. 22-000) nearby has more recordings of Cook Islands music.

The **Philatelic Bureau** (Box 13, Rarotonga; tel. 29-334, fax 22-428) next to the post office has colorful stamps, first-day covers, and mint sets of local coins, which make good souvenirs. In addition to the Cook Islands issues, they also sell stamps of Aitutaki and Penrhyn (only valid for postage on those islands). A crisp, new Cook Islands $3 bill costs NZ$7 here.

Crafts

Check out **Rosie's Are Crafts** (tel. 28-370), at the Avatiu Market, which carries grass skirts, baskets, dancing shakers, pandanus *rito* hats, and hat bands. *Tivaevae* quilts are available on request, NZ$200 and up for a medium-size one. This is the only shop where you can be sure that anything you buy is a genuine locally made handicraft. Also peruse the other handicraft stands in the market.

More commercial but also recommended is **Island Craft** (Box 28, Rarotonga; tel. 22-009), selling teak or *tamanu* (mahogany) carvings of Tangaroa, the fisherman's god (a fertility symbol), white woven hats from Penrhyn, mother-of-pearl jewelry, and good, strong bags. Other popular items include handbags, fans, tapa cloth from Atiu, replicas of staff gods, wooden bowls, food pounders, pearl jewelry, seats *(no'oanga),* headrests, slit gongs *(tokere),* and fishhooks. They've also got a branch at the airport that opens for international departures, but the selection in town is much better.

fisherman's god, Tangaroa

Pearls and Souvenirs

The black pearls of Manihiki may be inspected at the **Pearl Shop** (tel. 21-902, fax 21-903) at Cooks Corner. They provide certificates of authenticity, essential when you're spending hundreds of dollars for a single one! Cheaper, slightly imperfect gold-set pearls (with imperfections only obvious to an expert) are also available. Unfortunately, prices are not marked.

The **Beachcomber Gallery** (tel. 21-939; weekdays 1000-1630, Saturday 1000-1230), at the corner of the Ara Tapu and Makea Tinirau Rd., is housed in a former London Missionary Society school building (1843). It's well worth entering this museum-like gallery to peruse the lovely pearl jewelry and other artworks on sale. Here all prices are clearly marked.

The **Perfume Factory** (tel. 22-690), on the Ara Metua behind town, sells a variety of coconut oil-based lotions and soaps produced on the premises. They also have the distinctive Tangaroa coconut coffee liqueur sold in souvenir ceramic Tangaroa bottles at NZ$40 for a large 500-ml bottle or NZ$20 for a 100-ml bottle. A regular 750-ml glass bottle of the same is NZ$30. Strangely, these items are not available at the airport.

Clothing

Visit the **Tav's Clothing Factory** (Elena Tavioni, tel. 23-202) on Vakatini Rd. for the attractive lightweight tropical clothing and swimsuits screenprinted and sewn on the premises. Special-size items can be made to measure. Tav's designer garments are presently in fashion in Australia.

Get into style with some bright tropical apparel from **Joyce Peyroux Garments** (tel. 20-205) in the same mall as the ANZ Bank in Avarua and opposite the Are Renga Motel in Arorangi. Joyce Peyroux and other retailers carry beautiful selections of hand-printed dresses, pareus, tie-dyed T-shirts, bikinis, etc.—all locally made.

SERVICES AND INFORMATION

Money

Two banks serve Rarotonga, the Westpac Bank and the ANZ Bank, both open weekdays 0900-1500. Both change traveler's checks and give cash advances on Visa and MasterCard. The Westpac branch at the airport charges NZ$2.50

commission on traveler's checks, while the branch of the same bank in Avarua charges no commission. The ANZ Bank in Avarua charges NZ$2 commission on traveler's checks. If you're changing much, check both banks as their rates do vary slightly.

Post and Telecommunications

The post office in Avarua holds general delivery mail 28 days and there's no charge to pick up letters.

Telecom Cook Islands (Box 106, Rarotonga; tel. 29-680, fax 26-174) at the Earth Station Complex on Tutakimoa Rd., Avarua, is open 24 hours a day for overseas telephone calls and telegrams. If you want to receive a fax here, the public fax number for Rarotonga is fax 682/26-174 and it costs NZ$2.20 to receive the first page, plus 50 cents per additional page.

Most public telephones around town are card phones but the Blue Note Café has a public telephone that accepts 20-cent coins.

Internet Access

If you'd like to catch up on your e-mail, Telecom Cook Islands (e-mail: info@oyster.net.ck) at the Earth Station Complex in Avarua has a "cyberbooth" available 24 hours a day at NZ$1.75 per five minutes. If you have a computer and are staying a while, you can get connected to the internet here for NZ$25 registration plus NZ$20 a month, which includes the first three hours (additional hours NZ$15 each). Of course, you'll need access to a phone line.

Visas and Officialdom

For an extension of stay go to the Immigration office (tel. 29-347) on the top floor of the Government Office Building behind the post office. Visa extensions cost NZ$70 to extend your initial 31 days to three months, then it's another NZ$70 to bring your total up to five months. Otherwise you can pay NZ$120 and get a five-month extension on the spot. The maximum stay is six months. If you lose your passport, report to the Ministry of Foreign Affairs in the same building.

The Honorary Consul of Germany is Dr. Wolfgang Losacker (tel. 23-304) near the tourist office in Avarua. The New Zealand High Commission (tel. 22-201; weekdays 1030-1430) is next to the Philatelic Bureau.

Other Services

Snowbird Laundromat (tel. 20-952), next to the Tumunu Restaurant in Arorangi, will do your wash for NZ$9 a load including washing, drying, and folding.

There are public toilets at Cooks Corner and at the Avatiu Market.

Yachting Facilities

Yachts pay a fee to anchor Mediterranean-style at Avatiu Harbor and are subject to the NZ$25 pp departure tax. The harbor is overcrowded and it's wise to do exactly what the harbormaster (tel. 28-814) asks as he's been around for a while. If you're trying to hitch a ride on a yacht to Aitutaki, Suwarrow, or points west, the harbormaster would be a good person to ask. There's a freshwater tap on the wharf, plus cold showers on the ground floor of the Ports Authority building. During occasional northerly winds Nov.-March, this harbor becomes dangerous, and it would be a death trap for a small boat during a hurricane. Westbound from Rarotonga, consider stopping at unspoiled little Niue on the way to Vava'u.

Information

The government-run Cook Islands Tourism Corporation Visitor Center (Box 14, Rarotonga; tel. 29-435, fax 21-435; open weekdays 0800-1600), has brochures and information sheets giving current times and prices. Ask for a free copy of *What's On in the Cook Islands,* which contains a wealth of useful information.

The Statistics Office (Box 41, Rarotonga; tel. 29-390, fax 21-511), on the 2nd floor of the Government Office Building behind the post office, sells the informative *Annual Statistic Bulletin* (NZ$10).

The Bounty Bookshop (tel. 26-660), next to the ANZ Bank in Avarua, carries books on the Cook Islands, the latest regional newsmagazines, and the *Cook Islands News.* Ask if they have Moon Travel Handbook's *Tahiti Handbook,* which also covers the Cooks. Pacific Supplies (tel. 27-770), next to South Seas International on the waterfront, also has the latest international newspapers and magazines. Good cultural books can be purchased at the Cook Islands Library and Museum and the University of the South Pacific Center.

The Postshop (tel. 29-992), in the mall opposite Dive Rarotonga, sells books on the Cook Islands, stationery, and postage stamps.

Panama Mini Mart (tel. 25-531), between the airport terminal and town, has a used paperback book exchange (NZ$1 to exchange, NZ$2 to buy).

Visitors can become temporary members of the Cook Islands Library (tel. 20-748; open Mon.-Sat. 0900-1300, Tuesday also 1600-2000) for an annual fee of NZ$25, of which NZ$10 is refunded upon departure.

Stars Travel (tel. 23-669) near the ANZ Bank is Rarotonga's most efficient and reliable travel agency. This agency and Island Hopper Vacations (tel. 22-026) next to the Banana Court arrange package tours to the outer islands with flights and accommodations included. Tipani Tours (tel. 25-266) is just west of the airport terminal.

Health

Rarotonga's main hospital (tel. 22-664), on a hill between the airport and Arorangi, is open for emergencies 24 hours a day. To call an ambulance dial 998.

The Outpatients Medical Clinic (tel. 20-066) at Tupapa, a kilometer east of town, is open weekdays 0800-1600, Saturday 0800-1100. In the same building is the Central Dental Clinic (tel. 29-312), open weekdays 0800-1200 and 1300-1600.

With the Ministry of Health still reeling after massive budget cutbacks in 1996, you'll receive better service from a private practitioner, such as Dr. Robert Woonton (tel. 23-680; weekdays 0900-1400, Saturday 0900-1100), upstairs in Ingram House opposite Avatiu Harbor. He also has a clinic next to the Rarotongan Sunset Motel in Arorangi. Dr. Terepai Tairea has a Private Dental Surgery (tel. 25-210; weekdays 0800-1600) next to Dr. Woonton upstairs in Ingram House.

You could also turn to Dr. Teariki Noovao (tel. 20-835), between the Teachers College and the Golf Club opposite Avatea School on the Ara Metua. His medical clinic is open weekdays 1630-2030, Saturday 0900-1200. A private Dental Surgery (tel. 20-169; weekdays 0800-1600) is a few hundred meters east along the same road back toward town.

Dr. Wolfgang Losacker (tel. 23-304; weekdays 1000-1300), operates a medical clinic and photo gallery between the Banana Court and the tourist office in Avarua. He's a specialist in internal and tropical medicine, cardiology, and parasitology, and at his office he sells his own Cook Islands photo book (NZ$66) and quality postcards (NZ$1 each).

The CITC Pharmacy (tel. 29-292; weekdays 0800-1630, Saturday 0800-1200) is in central Avarua at CITC Shopping Center.

TRANSPORTATION

For information on air and sea service from Rarotonga to other Cook islands turn to the introduction to this chapter.

By Road

The **Cook's Island Bus Passenger Transport Ltd.** (Box 613, Rarotonga; tel./fax 25-512) operates a round-the-island bus service leaving Cooks Corner every half hour weekdays 0700-1600, Saturday 0800-1300. These yellow, 32-seat buses alternate in traveling clockwise (leaving on the hour) and counterclockwise (leaving on the half hour), stopping anywhere (no counterclockwise service on Saturday). The night bus leaves town Mon.-Sat. at 1800, 1900, 2100, and 2200, plus midnight and 0130 on Friday, and 2300 on Saturday. The current schedule is published in *What's On in the Cook Islands*. Fares are NZ$2 one-way, NZ$3 return, NZ$4 return at night, or NZ$5 for an all-day pass (NZ$12 for families). There's also a NZ$15 10-ride ticket that can be shared. Tourists are the main users of this excellent, privately run service and the drivers make a point of being helpful.

Taxi rates are negotiable, but the service is slightly erratic. Ask the fare before getting in and clarify whether it's per person or for the whole car. Some drivers will drive you the long way around the island to your destination. In Avarua the taxi stand is at the hut marked Are Tapaeanga across the street from the police station. Beware of prebooking taxis to the airport over the phone, as they often don't turn up, especially at odd hours. Service is generally 0600-2200 only. Hitchhiking is not understood here.

Rentals

A Cook Islands Driver's License (NZ$15 and one photo) is required to operate motorized rental vehicles. This can be obtained in a few minutes at the police station (tel. 22-499) in the center of Avarua any weekday 0800-1500, Saturday 0800-1200, upon presentation of your home driver's license (minimum age 21 years). This whole exercise is purely a moneymaking operation and the International Driver's License is not accepted.

If you wish to operate a scooter they'll require you to show something that states explicitly that you're licensed to drive a motorcycle, otherwise you may have to pass a test (NZ$5 extra) that involves riding one up and down the street without falling off. Bring your own scooter and keep in mind that if you fail the test you won't be allowed to ride any further and that day's scooter rental must still be paid. (In theory the person giving the driving tests takes lunch 1200-1300 and knocks off at 1500.) Without a license, the insurance on the vehicle will not be valid and you'll be liable for a stiff fine if caught. No license is required to ride a bicycle.

You're supposed to wear a helmet while operating a motorbike. Although it's unlikely you'll ever see anybody wearing one, and the local tourism brochures carry photos of girls on scooters with little more than flowers in their hair, an anti-tourist cop could always bring it up. Drive slowly, as local children tend to run onto the road unexpectedly, and beware of free-roaming dogs that often cause accidents by suddenly giving chase at night. Take special care on Friday and Saturday nights, when there are more drunks on the road than sober drivers. The speed limit is 40 km per hour in Avarua, 50 km per hour on the open road, and driving is on the left.

Car rental agencies on Rarotonga include Budget/Polynesian, Avis, Rarotonga Rentals, Tipani Rentals, T.P.A. Rental Cars, and others. Rates include unlimited km, and the seventh consecutive day is usually free. Some places quote prices including the 12.5% government tax, others without the tax. Check all the agencies for special deals—most are also open on Sunday. Most cars and scooters rent for 24 hours, so you can use them for a sober evening on the town.

Many smaller companies rent motor scooters for NZ$15-20 a day, NZ$75-100 a week, and bicycles at NZ$8-10 daily—ask your hotel for the nearest. **Hogan Rentals** (Box 100, Rarotonga; tel./fax 22-632), 250 meters north of the Are Renga Motel in Arorangi, rents cars at NZ$55 a day, tax, insurance, and kilometers included. Hogan's 12-speed mountain bikes are NZ$8 daily or NZ$48 weekly (NZ$20 deposit). The bicycles have baskets on the front and are fairly sturdy, but there are no lamps for night riding. **BT Bike Hire** (tel. 23-586), right next to the Are Renga Motel, also has bicycles and scooters.

There aren't enough women's bicycles to go around, but men's cycles are easy to rent. The main advantage to renting a bicycle for the week is that you have it when you want it. Rarotonga is small enough to be easily seen by bicycle, which makes renting a car or scooter an unnecessary expense—you also avoid the compulsory local driver's license rip-off. Bicycles are also quiet, easy on the environment, healthy, safe, and great fun. One of the nicest things to do on a sleepy Rarotonga Sunday is to slowly circle the island by bicycle.

Tours

The **Takitumu Conservation Area** project (Box 817, Rarotonga; tel./fax 29-906) operates four-hour guided hikes into the bush up Avana Stream. You'll be shown the colorful *neinei* flower and the unique Rarotonga orchid, and hopefully catch a glimpse of the endangered *kakerori* or Rarotonga flycatcher, which the group is working to save. A large colony of flying foxes may also be visited. At NZ$30 pp including light refreshments, it's good value and you'll be contributing to a worthy cause. Visit their office behind the post office in Avarua where distinctive T-shirts and posters are sold.

Pa's Nature Walk (tel. 21-079) is another good way to get acquainted with the natural history of the island. The four-hour hike through the bush behind Matavera includes a light lunch; both it and Pa's guided cross-island hike are NZ$35 pp with hotel transfers included. With his blond Rastafarian good looks, Pa is quite a character and it's worth signing up just to hear his spiel. You don't get the change to go on a hike with an internationally known guide like Pa every day!

One reader wrote in recommending the 3.5-hour, NZ$25 circle-island tour offered weekdays by **Hugh Henry** (Box 440, Rarotonga; tel. 25-320, fax 25-420) in Arorangi. Call ahead and they'll pick you up at your hotel. The **Cultural Village** (tel. 21-314) offers a full-day combined circle-island tour and cultural show for NZ$60 including lunch.

AITUTAKI

Aitutaki, 259 km north of Rarotonga, is the second-most-visited Cook Island and the scenery of this oversold "dream island" is quite lovely. The low rolling hills are flanked by banana plantations, taro fields, and coconut groves. Atiu-type coffee is grown here. A triangular barrier reef 45 km around catches Aitutaki's turquoise lagoon like a fishhook. The maximum depth of this lagoon is 10.5 meters but most of it is less than five meters deep. The 15 small islets or *motus* and many sandbars on the eastern barrier reef all have picture-postcard white sands and aquamarine water.

The main island is volcanic: its highest hill, Maungapu (124 meters), is said to be the top of Rarotonga's Raemaru, chopped off and brought back by victorious Aitutaki warriors. All of the *motus* are coralline except for Rapota and Moturakau, which contain some volcanic rock. Legend holds that just as the warriors were arriving back with their stolen mountain they clashed with pursuing Rarotongans and pieces of Maungapu fell off creating Moturakau and Rapota. Moturakau served as a leper colony from the 1930s to 1967. Motikitiu at the south end of the lagoon is the nesting area of many of the Aitutaki's native birds as mynahs have taken over the main island. Be on the lookout for the blue lorikeet *(kuramo'o)* with its white bib and orange beak and legs.

The 2,300 people live in villages strung out along the roads on both sides of the main island and generally travel about on motor scooters. The roads are red-brown in the center of the island, coral white around the edge. The administration and most of the local businesses are clustered near the wharf at Arutanga. The *motus* are uninhabited, and there aren't any dogs at all on Aitutaki.

Aitutaki is the only Cook island other than Rarotonga where there's a good choice of places to stay, entertainment, and organized activities. One way to go is to catch a Thursday or Friday flight up from Rarotonga so as to be on hand for "island night" at the Rapae Hotel or Ralphie's that evening. Book a lagoon trip for Saturday and you'll still have Sunday to scooter around the island or laze on the

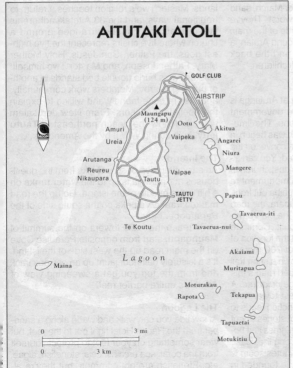

AITUTAKI ATOLL

GOLF CLUB

AIRSTRIP

Maungapu (124 m)

Amuri

Ootu

Akitua

Ureia

Vaipeka

Angarei

Arutanga

Niura

Reureu
Nikaupara

Vaipae

Mangere

Tautu

TAUTU JETTY

Papau

Te Koutu

Tavaerua-iti

Tavaerua-nui

Lagoon

Akaiami

Maina

Muritapua

Moturakau

Tekapua

Rapota

Tapuaetai

Motukitiu

0   3 mi

0   3 km

This is how they looked on Aitutaki in 1903.

AUCKLAND INSTITUTE AND MUSEUM

beach. Fly back on Monday or Tuesday, having sidestepped Rarotonga's dull Sunday. This is probably too short a stay, however, and a week on the island would be much better.

Aitutaki is north of Rarotonga and therefore warmer. During the hot season Dec.-March, sand flies and mosquitoes are at their worst. They're more of a nuisance on the north side of the main island, far less so on the *motus*. Around Arutanga beware of theft from the beach and the back yards of the guesthouses by small children.

Sights

Opposite the Administration Center at Arutanga is the colonial-style residence of the government representative set in lovely gardens. The limestone **CICC church** just to the south was begun in 1828, only a few years after Papeiha converted the islanders, but it's usually solidly locked. You can always peek in the windows of this oldest church in the Cook Islands and admire the monument to missionaries John Williams and Papeiha out front.

South of Arutanga beyond Nikaupara, the road turns inland at a dry stream where the old **Vainamu Washing Pool** has been rebuilt. Continue east along this road, turning right at the junction of the road to Te Koutu Point. About 700 meters south is **Marae Te Poaki O Rae,** down a short trail to the left. A signpost east of the road marks this double row of stones beneath a huge *puka* tree. A more overgrown road running west toward the beach from the Te Poaki O Rae junction leads to **Marae Arangirea.** Look for a line of stones about 150 meters down on the left, in high grass just before you enter the chestnut forest along the coast.

At Te Koutu Point another 10 minutes south is **New Jerusalem,** a religious village founded in 1990 by the followers of Master Two. In 1986 this leader established the cult on Rarotonga and it's presently based in a thatched compound there known as the "Land of Life," by the shore 100 meters east of the Parliament of the Cook Islands. Master Two's religion teaches a return to traditional ways, and the 33 Aitutaki adherents live in thatched houses arranged around a church where five chairs represent the five highest gods: the Father, Son Jesus, Holy Mother Mary, Father Joseph, and Master Two himself! Master Two's huge double bed stands in another building nearby. Members work communally, and they're quite friendly and willing to explain their beliefs to visitors. From New Jerusalem you can follow the beach northeast to **Tautu jetty,** built during WW II by the Americans.

The Interior

An easy afternoon or sunset hike from the guesthouses at Arutanga is up to the **water tanks** on a hill in the middle of the island. Go up the road marked Pirake/Vaipeka on the south side of the Paratrooper Motel.

To reach the radio towers on the summit of **Maungapu,** start from opposite Paradise Cove on the main road up the west side of the island. It's a leisurely half-hour jaunt up an obvious track and from the top you get a sweeping view of Aitutaki's entire barrier reef.

The Lagoon

At low tide you can walk and wade along a sandbar from the Rapae Hotel right out to the reef, but wear something on your feet to protect yourself from the coral, sea urchins, eels, stonefish, algae, etc. Stonefish are not common, but they're almost impossible to spot until it's too late. At high tide snorkel out from the black rocks on the beach just north of the Rapae. Snorkelers and paddlers must keep at least 200 meters inside the main reef entrance at Arutanga, due to the strong outgoing current.

The finest snorkeling off the main island is at the far west end of the airstrip and to the south. Beware of dangerous currents in the passes near the edge of the reef here. Elsewhere on the main island the snorkeling is poor.

Wave-shelled giant clams *(pahua)* intended to restock the Aitutaki lagoon are reared at the **Araura Marine Research Station** established with Australian aid money just north of the west end of Aitutaki's airstrip. One tank contains an assortment of adult clams, baby sea turtles, sea slugs, sea urchins, and colorful fish. Weekdays you can take a tour and see a video for NZ$2.

The top beach on the main island is at the southeast end of the airstrip near the bridge to the Aitutaki Lagoon Resort Hotel. It's fine to swim here, but snorkelers won't see many fish or corals.

Sports and Recreation

Neil Mitchell's **Aitutaki Scuba** (Box 40, Aitutaki; tel. 31-103, fax 31-310) offers diving at the drop-off once or twice a day (except Sunday). If you have your own equipment, diving is NZ$60 for one dive or NZ$55 each for two or more dives (NZ$10 extra if you need gear). Snorkelers are welcome to go along at NZ$20 pp when space is available. No reservations are required, but bring your own mask; wetsuits are handy June-December. The diving here is better March-November. Aitutaki is great place to learn to dive and Neil does four-day NAUI certification courses for NZ$490 (minimum of two persons). You'll find Neil about 100 meters down the side road that branches off the main road at Sunny Beach Lodge. Aitutaki is not an easy dive destination. The lagoon may be great for snorkeling, but it's too shallow for serious diving and the dropoff outside the reef is very steep (not for beginners).

Aitutaki Sea Charters (Box 43, Aitutaki; tel. 31-281) offers deep-sea fishing off the 10-meter cruiser *Foxy Lady*. A special "backpackers rate" of NZ$50 pp applies when you book direct (2-8 persons). You'll often find Captain Jason or his father Don Watts at the Game Fishing Club around happy hour. Skipjack tuna, giant trevally,

mahimahi, and barracuda are caught year-round off Aitutaki. The billfish (marlin) season is Nov.-March, while in August and September wahoo are frequently caught.

The **Aitutaki Golf Club** (Box 98, Aitutaki; no phone) beside the airport welcomes visitors. Greens fees are NZ$5 but there are no club rentals. If your ball falls on the airstrip, it's considered out of bounds. The Aitutaki Open Golf Tournament is in mid-October.

ACCOMMODATIONS

Budget

The pleasant **Tiare Maori Guest House** (Box 16, Aitutaki; tel. 31-119), formerly known as Mama Tunui's, in Ureia village, has seven rooms at NZ$32/42 single/double. Mama serves an all-you-can-eat dinner (NZ$15) including clams, chicken, and island vegetables. You can also use her stove, and watch the family television. She'll even give you a flower *ai* to wear to island night at the Rapae.

Josie's Lodge (Josie and David Sadaraka, tel. 31-111, fax 31-518), an older island house next door to the Tiare Maori, has four double and two single rooms with shared bath at NZ$26/36/45 single/double/triple. The rooms are screened to keep out insects, and communal cooking facilities are provided.

Tom's Beach Cottage (Box 51, Aitutaki; tel. 31-051, tel. 31-121 at home, fax 31-409) is a large island-style house (no sign) right on the beach just north of Rino's Bungalows. It's a favorite backpacker's hangout and also gets a lot of people who've booked budget packages through travel agents. The seven rooms with old fashioned brass beds and mosquito nets are NZ$32/48/58 single/double/triple but the two facing the street get considerable traffic noise. A nicer thatched "honeymoon" bungalow a bit closer to the beach is NZ$76/86 single/double. When things are slow these rates are reduced. A communal kitchen is available (beware of mice), plus a sitting room with photos of the family and a lounge with a pool table. Local calls on the house phone are 20 cents each. Tom will ferry you to Ootu Beach for kayak rentals.

The **Paratrooper Motel** (Box 73, Aitutaki; tel. 31-563 or 31-523), in Amuri almost opposite Swiss Rentals, consists of four wooden buildings in a crowded compound a block back from the beach. It's run by a laid-back ex-New Zealand paratrooper named Geoffrey Roi and his wife Maine who are shaking up the local tourist establishment by offering discount prices. Geoffrey's official rates are NZ$57 single or double for their two one-bedroom apartments with full cooking facilities, reduced to NZ$31 if you stay eight nights or more. The three two-bedroom family units come down to NZ$74 if you stay six nights. All rates are negotiable—this is one place where you can bargain when things are slow. It's more of a place for an extended stay than only one or two nights, and despite the name, there's no strict military discipline here.

Vaikoa Units (Box 71, Aitutaki; tel. 31-145), a kilometer north of the Rapae Hotel, offers six self-catering units in parallel wooden blocks at NZ$30/40 single/double. The nearest grocery

store is a 15-minute walk away. It's right on one of the best snorkeling beaches on the main island and dugout canoes are loaned free. This attractive place is highly recommended.

Junior Maoate's **Paradise Cove Guesthouse** (Box 64, Aitutaki; tel. 31-218, fax 31-456) is at Anaunga, between the airstrip and the Rapae Hotel. Spacious grounds lead down to a white-sand beach with excellent snorkeling just offshore. The five rooms in the main house are NZ$30/40 single/double, while the six thatched Polynesian beach huts with fridge and shared bath are NZ$40/60. Junior provides good communal cooking facilities and sometimes offeres special reduced rates.

Inexpensive

On the beach almost opposite Josie's Lodge is **Rino's Beach Bungalows** (Box 140, Aitutaki; tel.

31-197, fax 31-559) with four hotplate-equipped units in a two-story roadside block at NZ$55/85/95 single/double/triple. Four new beachfront duplex apartments are NZ$134 single or double complete with fridge, stove, washing machine, and terrace overlooking the lagoon. Rino's also has an older three-bedroom house across the street that is rented out at NZ$250 a week (up to six persons). This well-managed hotel also rents bicycles, scooters, and cars.

For years there's been talk of replacing the government-owned **Rapae Hotel** (Box 4, Aitutaki; tel. 31-320, fax 31-321), just north of Arutanga, with a flash resort on the same site, but as yet nothing has materialized. If it's still open, the 12 duplex rooms will cost about NZ$80 single or double, but the only one with cooking facilities is number 13 (about NZ$20 extra). Be aware that on Friday disco dancing continues half the night (other nights it's peaceful). Only minimal maintenance is being done on the bungalows at the moment and discounts are possible.

Moderate

In 1995 the **Maina Sunset Motel** (Box 34, Aitutaki; tel. 31-511, fax 31-611) opened in Nikaupara district, a

20-minute walk south of Arutanga. The 12 self-contained units are arranged in a U-shape around a freshwater swimming pool that faces the lagoon (poor beach). The eight rooms without cooking are NZ$145 double, while the four with cooking are NZ$175. It's peaceful as you don't get a lot of traffic noise down here. Scooter hire is available. Their speedboat anchors at the landing directly in front of the motel and they'll shuttle you over to the fantastic snorkeling spots near Maina Island at NZ$30 pp with sandwiches and fresh fruit for lunch.

Premium

The isolated **Aitutaki Lagoon Resort Hotel** (Box 99, Aitutaki; tel. 31-201, fax 31-202), on Akitua Island near Ootu Beach at the east end of the airstrip, is connected to the main island by a small wooden bridge. The 16 a/c garden bungalows with private bath and fridge are overpriced at NZ$286 single or double, the nine lagoon bungalows NZ$427, and the five beachfront bungalows NZ$550. The plumbing fixtures are poorly maintained and cooking facilities are not provided. All rates include a buffet breakfast but no meal plan is available. Ordering à la carte in the restaurant is very expensive and you can't just walk across the street to a grocery store (the nearest is on the other side of Aitutaki). The Wednesday night seafood buffet is NZ$39, the Saturday island night NZ$30, both with traditional dancing. You get the feeling they're out to fleece you: a Coke from the minibar in your room will be NZ$4.50 and it's NZ$8 to leave valuables in the office safe. No environmentally friendly bicycles are for hire, only noisy motor scooters. Checkout time is 1030. There's a small swimming pool and the beach is lovely but the water offshore is murky and there's nothing much to see with a mask. Unfortunately the resort is also infested with tiny mosquitoes (bring a net to hang over your bed).

FOOD AND ENTERTAINMENT

Food

In 1995 the **Orongo Center** (closed Sunday) opened in the former banana packing house near the wharf. A small **vegetable market** here operates 0800-1500 during the week, offering lots of bananas, cabbage, coconuts, green peppers, oranges, papaya, tomatoes, and watermelon. Several handicraft stalls sell bright pareus and beachware, and the **Seabreeze Cafe** (tel. 31-573; Mon.-Sat. 0800-1330/1730-2100) beyond them serves fish and chips (NZ$7.50) to be consumed at picnic tables overlooking the lagoon. The public toilets behind the cafe are often handy.

Donald's CITC Branch (tel. 31-055; weekdays 0800-2000, Saturday 1700-2000) is one of several grocery stores near the wharf. **Maina Traders Ltd.** (tel. 31-219; Mon.-Sat. 0700-2000), between Tom's Cottage and the wharf, offers a good selection of groceries, fresh vegetables, and drinks.

Kuramoo Takeaways (Mon.-Sat. 1100-2100) serves a variety of seafood including parrot fish and octopus on their outdoor terrace near Maina Traders.

Tip Top Store, a few hundred meters north of Rino's, scoops out ice-cream cones as well as selling fresh vegetables.

Ralphie's Bar & Grill (tel. 31-418; daily 1000-1400/1800-2130), across the street from the Rapae Hotel, dispenses cheeseburger (NZ$4.50) or fish and chip (NZ$10.50) lunches that you can eat at the picnic tables outside. Dinner (F$16.50) is served in an a/c room and the food is good. They're open daily, but on Sunday only dinner is served. Free hotel pickups are available for diners.

The **Crusher Bar & Restaurant** (tel. 31-283; closed Friday), near Paradise Cove on the way to the airport, is a funky open-air bar with picnic tables under a tin roof. Monday to Wednesday from 1800 you can get a grilled steak or fish dinner with salad bar for NZ$15.50. Thursday night is island night with a Polynesian buffet (NZ$26 pp) followed by an excellent show by the dance group "Tiare Aitutaki." Saturday night is "backpackers nite" with main course and dessert at NZ$10.50. The Sunday night roast or fish of the day is NZ$16.50 with dessert. Nightly animation is provided by the infamous lady killer Ricky de Von (also an excellent cook). Call ahead for bookings and free hotel pickups.

Ask the people where you're staying if the water is safe to drink. It's always good to boil it and store it in your fridge, if you can.

Entertainment

Aside from the Thursday night show at the Crusher Bar, two Polynesian dance shows take place on Friday night. Most people start the evening with island night at the **Rapae Hotel**

(tel. 31-320) where the buffet (NZ$30) begins at 1930, followed by the show at 2100. As soon as the one at Rapae finishes, almost everyone crosses the street to **Ralphie's Bar** (tel. 31-418) where the action starts at 2200 (be fast to get a reasonable seat). Neither place has a cover charge and a few drinks from the bar are all you need. The atmosphere at both places is excellent with as many locals present as tourists.

The **Aitutaki Game Fishing Club** (tel. 31-379, VHF channel 16; daily except Sunday from 1600), in a container behind the Ports Authority on the way to the harbor, has cheap beer and is a good place to meet people at happy hour.

PRACTICALITIES

Services

Traveler's checks can be cashed at the hotels but it's smarter to change your money on Rarotonga beforehand as the rates here are lousy. Trying to use one of the small banking agencies on Aitutaki can be a real pain.

The post office (weekdays 0800-1600) in the Administration Center opposite the wharf sells local telephone cards (NZ$10, NZ$20, and NZ$50), which can be used for international calls at the public telephone outside (dial 00 for international access). If you need to receive a fax here, the number is fax 682/31-683.

Outpatients are accepted at the hospital (tel. 31-002) Mon.-Fri. 0830-1200/1300-1600, Saturday 0830-1200, emergencies anytime. Some of the equipment here (such as the X-ray machine) seems to have been left behind by the U.S. military in 1945, so grab a flight back to Raro fast if anything serious goes wrong.

TRANSPORTATION

Because Aitutaki's small population doesn't justify a regular ferry service from Rarotonga, getting here is much more expensive than visiting similar outer islands in Tahiti-Polynesia, Tonga, and Fiji, and almost always involves a stiff plane ticket. For flight and boat information see the chapter introduction. **Air Rarotonga** (tel. 31-888, fax 31-414; weekdays 0800-1600, Saturday 0800-1200) has an office at Ureia.

The shipping companies have no local agent, but the people at the Ports Authority (tel. 31-050) near the wharf will know when a ship is due in. Dangerous coral heads and currents make passage through Aitutaki's barrier reef hazardous, so passengers and cargo on the interisland ships must be transferred to the wharf by lighters. The Americans built Arutanga Wharf during WW II. They had planned to dredge the anchorage and widen the pass, but the war ended before they got around to it. Blasting by the N.Z. military in 1986 improved Arutanga Passage somewhat, but it's still narrow, with a six-knot current draining water blown into the lagoon from the south. The depth in the pass is limited to two meters at high tide, but reader C. Webb reports that "the bottom of the pass is sand, so it's a good place to be somewhat aggressive." Once inside, the anchorage off Arutanga is safe and commodious for yachts. This is an official port of entry to the Cooks and the local customs officials readily approve visa extensions for yacht crews. "Having fun" is sufficient reason.

No taxis or buses operate on Aitutaki but there's considerable scooter and pickup traffic along the west coast. Mike Henry (tel. 31-379) does airport transfers at NZ$6 pp.

Rentals

Cook Islands driver's licenses can be obtained at the police office behind the Administration Center in Arutanga for NZ$2.50 and no photo is required (they're also valid on Rarotonga).

The T & M Ltd. gasoline station next to the Ports Authority at the wharf opens weekdays 0730-1630, Saturday 0730-1200.

Rino's Rentals (tel. 31-197, fax 31-559), near Tom's Cottage, and **Swiss Rentals** (tel. 31-600 or 31-223, fax 31-329) both have Suzuki jeeps (NZ$70 for 24 hours), Subaru cars (from NZ$40 daily), motor scooters (from NZ$20 the first day, NZ$15 subsequent days), and pushbikes (from NZ$8 daily). Rino's has a NZ$100 weekly rate for Honda 50s.

Aremati Bicycle Rentals, between Vaikoa Units and the Rapae Hotel, has mountain bikes at NZ$7 a day. Some of the guesthouses and hotels also rent bicycles—all you really need.

The **Samade Shop** (tel. 31-526) at Ootu Beach, not far from the Aitutaki Lagoon Resort Hotel, rents two-person canoe/kayaks at NZ$10 for four hours. They also serve drinks on their white-sand terrace (when open). Call ahead if you want a kayak. From Ootu by kayak you can reach Angarei in 15 minutes, Papua in an hour, and Akaiami in 2.5 hours.

Lagoon Tours

Several companies offer boat trips to uninhabited *motus* around the Aitutaki Lagoon, such as Akaiami or Tapuaetai (One Foot Island) where you can swim in the clear deep-green water, although the snorkeling there is mediocre. Unfortunately the very popularity of these trips has become their undoing as "desert islands" like Tapuaetai can get rather overcrowded when all of the tourist boats arrive!

Some trips also go to Maina, or "Bird Island," at the southwest corner of the lagoon. Only a few tropicbirds still nest on a sandbar called "Honeymoon Island" next to Maina—most have been scared off by marauding tourists and their guides. There's good snorkeling at Honeymoon Island as the fish are fed here. But when the wind whips up the sea it gets hard to snorkel and you miss out on half the fun.

Different tour operators concentrate on varying aspects and the smaller independent operators tend to serve you a bigger and better lunch for a lower price. If snorkeling is your main interest you should find out if they plan to spend all afternoon eating and drinking at Tapuaetai (also great fun). Bishop's Cruises is the most reliable company and they try to run on a schedule. This may be what you want if you have only one chance to get it right, but they're inevitably touristy and the amateur operators you learn about by word of mouth or from notices taped on the walls of the backpackers hostels are far more personal (and less dependable). It's also possible to arrange to be dropped off for the day on Akaiami or Maina for NZ$20-30 pp.

Bishop's Lagoon Cruises (Teina Bishop, Box 53, Aitutaki; tel. 31-009, fax 31-493), inland from Arutanga Wharf, offers lagoon trips daily except Sunday. One trip goes to Maina, another to Akaiami, and both continue to Moturakau and Tapuaetai. The Maina trip is the better, and to get it you must specifically request a visit to Maina when booking, otherwise they'll only take you to Akaiami and Tapuaetai. Either way, the price is NZ$50 including lunch. **Paradise Islands Cruises** (Box 98, Aitutaki; tel. 31-248) operates the Aitutaki day tour cruises from Rarotonga, and both they and Bishop's are rather commercialized and jaded. Often the cooks can be rather miserly rationing out the fried fish in order to have an ample supply left over for themselves and the boat crews. You'll probably be whisked back to the main island earlier that you would have liked so the day-trippers from Rarotonga can catch their flight.

Tautu resident Mr. Tetonga Kepopua (tel. 31-264), better known as "Tu" and the leader of the local dance group "Tiare Aitutaki," takes visitors to Tapuaetai for a huge fish lunch Mon.-Sat. at 1000 (NZ$40 pp). He also does *motu* dropoffs at NZ$20 pp. **Vaipae Canoe Sailing** (tel. 31-207) offers *motu* trips at NZ$30 pp and exactly which island you'll visit depends on the wind. And if you're on a really low budget you can get comparable snorkeling right off the west end of the airstrip for free. Whatever you decide, take sunscreen and insect repellent.

Reef Tours

Sonja and Tauono (Box 1, Aitutaki; tel. 31-562), who live between Paradise Cove and Vaikoa Units, offer unique reef tours in a traditional outrigger sailing canoe. The NZ$25 pp fee (NZ$35 if you go out alone) includes a light lunch, and they'll prepare any of the fish you catch for an additional fee of NZ$10-25 depending on what you want. You may also take your fish back to your guesthouse and cook them yourself. If you'd like to do any reef walking or fishing with a bamboo rod you must go at low tide; the swimming and snorkeling are better at high tide. Tauono is a sensitive guide more than willing to explain Aitutaki's delicate reef ecology during the four hours the trips usually last. Call the night before to arrange a time. Tauono and Sonja keep the only organic garden on Aitutaki and it's always worth stopping by to pick up some vegetables, herbs, cakes, and fresh fish.

ATIU

The old name of Atiu, third-largest of the Cook Islands, was Enuamanu, which means "land of birds." These days native birds are found mostly around the coast as the interior has been taken over by an influx of mynahs. Unlike neighboring Mauke and Mitiaro, which are flat, Atiu has a high central plateau (71 meters) surrounded by low swamps and an old raised coral reef known as a *makatea*. This is 20 meters high and covered with dense tropical jungle. Taro is Atiu's main cash crop, grown in swamps along the inner edge of the *makatea*. Arabica coffee is grown, processed, roasted, packaged, and marketed as "Kaope Atiu."

Atiu is one of the only islands in Polynesia where the people prefer the center to the shore, and cooling ocean breezes blow across Atiu's plain. Once fierce warriors who made cannibal raids on Mauke and Mitiaro, the islanders became Christians after missionary John Williams converted high chief Rongomatane in 1823. Today the 1,000 Atiuans live peacefully in five villages on the high central plain. The villages radiate out from an administrative center where

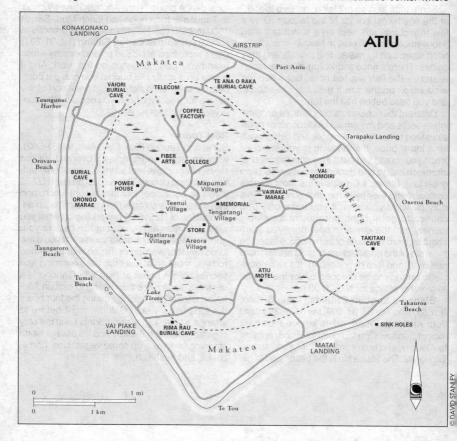

ATIU

KONAKONAKO LANDING

AIRSTRIP

Makatea

Pari Aniu

VAIORI BURIAL CAVE

TELECOM

TE ANA O RAKA BURIAL CAVE

Taunganui Harbor

COFFEE FACTORY

FIBER ARTS

Tarapaku Landing

Orovaru Beach

COLLEGE

BURIAL CAVE

POWER HOUSE

Mapumai Village

VAI MOMOIRI

ORONGO MARAE

Teenui Village

VAIRAKAI MARAE

Oneroa Beach

MEMORIAL

Tengatangi Village

Taungaroro Beach

Ngatiarua Village

STORE

Areora Village

TAKITAKI CAVE

Tumai Beach

ATIU MOTEL

Lake Tiroto

Takauroa Beach

VAI PIAKE LANDING

RIMA RAU BURIAL CAVE

SINK HOLES

Makatea

MATAI LANDING

0   1 mi

0   1 km

Te Tou

© DAVID STANLEY

A fragment from one of Atiu's caves marks the spot adjoining Marae Teapiripiri where John Williams preached in 1823.

the main churches, hospital, PWD workshops, stores, and government offices are all found. The women of Atiu meet throughout the week to work on handicrafts in their community halls. Pigs outnumber people on Atiu two to one.

The good beaches, varied scenery, and geological curiosities combine with satisfactory accommodations and enjoyable activities to make a visit well worthwhile. Atiu will appeal to hikers who want to explore the island's lonely roads, to adventurers who enjoy looking for caves and archaeological remains hidden in the bush, or to anyone in search of a restful holiday and a chance to spend some time on an unspoiled island without sacrificing creature comforts. Atiu has little to offer those interested in scuba diving, fancy resorts, or lagoon trips.

SIGHTS

The massive white walls of the **CICC church** dominate the center of Teenui village. Just south

a road leads east toward Tengatangi village from almost opposite the Atiu Administration Building. On the right just beyond the house behind the tennis court is a stalagmite with twin inscribed stones in front. This marks the spot where John Williams preached in 1823. Next to the monument a row of huge stalagmites or stalactites indicates the rectangular site of **Teapiripiri Marae.** Further south on the main road south into Areora village is the picturesque **Catholic mission.**

The East Coast

The 20-km road around Atiu is best covered in stages. From the motel it's a 15-minute walk down to **Matai Landing** and its white-sand beach. You can swim only if the sea is fairly calm but it's a nice picnic spot anytime. About 800 meters east of Matai Landing you'll come into a partly cleared area where pigs have been kept. Here search for a small trail out to the coast, where two **sinkholes** drain the reef. The lagoon along the south coast is a meter above sea level and when no waves are crashing over the reef sending water into the lagoon the whole lagoon drains through these sinkholes. With nowhere else to go, all of the lagoon fish congregate in the sinkholes, which become natural aquariums accessible to snorkelers. Due to the currents, it's only safe to swim here when the sea is very calm, and even then it's wise to remain on guard for changing or unexpected conditions.

A stretch of reefless shoreline on the northeast coast lets breakers roll right in to the cliffs. Look for the high white sands of **Oneroa Beach** and continue to **Tarapaku Landing** where the islanders keep their dugout canoes. There's a ladder down to the water here. From the landing take the Tengatangi road inland through the *makatea* watching for **Vai Momoiri,** a large water-filled cave that tunnels under the track then opens up on both sides. The route crosses a taro swamp passing **Vairakaia Marae,** a wall of upright stones right beside the road, and Vai Inano pool where the legendary chief Rongomatane's 12 wives used to bathe. (Rongomatane later adopted Christianity and forsook all of his wives except the youngest.)

The West Coast

The coastal road up the west shore of the island runs through a beautiful shady forest. A few really huge *puka* trees sport low bird's-nest ferns to create a dense green cover. These leaves are used to wrap fish for cooking in the *umu*. **Taungaroro** is the nicest beach on Atiu, and one of the finest in the Cooks, with white sands descending far into the quiet blue-green lagoon, protected from ocean breakers by the surrounding reef. The cliffs of the *makatea* frame this scenic masterpiece.

Orovaru Beach, where Captain Cook arrived on 3 April 1777, is easily identified by a large coral rock that sits 15 meters out in the lagoon. On the island side of the road opposite Orovaru is a stone trail once used by Cook's crew to reach the main settlement of that time named **Orongo Marae,** the most important *marae* on Atiu. Once you're on the trail it's fairly easy to follow, bending right toward the end and terminating at a pig farm on an interior road. This interesting hike offers a chance to view the vegetation on the *makatea* up close. Beyond the pigs, turn right and go about 100 meters south on the road to a track on the right toward a huge Barringtonia or *utu* tree. Orongo Marae is just behind the tree—one of the best-preserved archaeological sites in Cook Islands. Cut coral slabs and giant stalagmites form the walls of several rectangular structures here.

Farther north is **Taunganui Harbor** with a striking zigzag configuration, constructed in 1975. Barges can dock here in all weather but large ships must anchor offshore. The swimming and snorkeling in the deep, clear harbor water is good, and if you're here at 1500 you may be able to purchase fresh fish from returning fishermen.

Lake Tiroto

According to legend, the eel Rauou dug Lake Tiroto and, when he was finished, traveled to Mitiaro to dig the lakes there. A tunnel runs under the *makatea* from the lake right through to the seashore and you can enter it with a lamp and guide if you're willing to wade through the muddy water. Wear old shoes and clothes, plus an old hat to protect your head from bumping against the cave's sharp roof. Retired schoolteacher Vaine Moeroa Koronui (tel. 33-046) takes advantage of the visits to catch eels by organizing teams that herd the creatures up dead-end tunnels—a rare experience. Be sure to sign his Cave of Lake Tiroto visitors book.

Takitaki Cave

This cave is one of the few in the Cooks inhabited by birds: little *kopekas,* a type of swiftlet, nest in the roof. Their huge saucerlike eyes help them catch insects on the wing. They never land nor make a sound while outside the cave; inside, they make a cackling, clicking sound, the echoes of which help them find their way through the dank dark. Fewer than 200 pairs of this bird remain and their nesting success is poor. Visitors to the cave should keep at least two meters away from bird nests and discourage their guide from catching the tiny creatures.

Takitaki is in the middle of the *makatea,* east of the motel, a taxing 40-minute hike in from the road. A guide (NZ$15 plus NZ$5 pp) is required. The main part of the cave is large and dry, and

An eel trap. Eels are found in the swamps and lakes of Atiu, Mitiaro, and Mangaia; the locals catch them in traps or with hooks. The eel traps (inaki) are made of bush vines woven in long, basketlike form, which the eel can easily enter but cannot get out of. Pieces of chicken, crab, or bee's wax are used as bait.

you can walk in for quite a distance. Many stalactites, broken off by previous visitors, lie scattered about the floor. The story goes that Ake, wife of the hero Rangi, lived many years alone in this cave before being found by her husband, led to the spot by a *ngotare* (kingfisher) bird.

Keep an eye out for *unga* (coconut crabs) while exploring the *makatea,* and wear boots or sturdy shoes as the coral is razor-sharp. Go slowly and take care, as a fall could lead to a very nasty wound.

PRACTICALITIES

Accommodations

The **Atiu Motel** (Roger and Kura Malcolm, Box 7, Atiu; tel. 33-777, fax 33-775), eight km south of the airstrip, offers four comfortable self-catering chalets with fridge, each capable of accommodating four persons, at NZ$90/100/110 single/double/triple. There's also a six-bed family unit at NZ$110 single, plus NZ$10 per additional guest. The minimum stay is two nights. There's hot water but the electricity is off midnight-0500. These A-frame units are constructed of natural materials with beams of coconut-palm trunks. The motel doesn't have bicycles, but Roger can arrange rentals. Due to the ups and downs of Atiu's roads, motor scooters are more practical than bicycles as a means of getting around and Tauu Porio (tel. 33-050) rents Yamaha 50s at NZ$25. Inexpensive.

A less-expensive place to stay is the **Are Manuiri Guest House** (Box 13, Atiu; tel. 33-031, fax 33-032) opposite the bakery in Areora village, 300 meters south of ADC/ANZ Store and on the left. This three-room family house with shared cooking and bathing facilities is NZ$25 pp in a shared room, NZ$50 single or double in a private room, or NZ$66 for a larger family room. There's a lounge and veranda. It's run by Andrea Eimke who arrived on Atiu in 1986 where she operates a small art studio and cafe. Her husband Juergen runs the local coffee factory and tours can be arranged (NZ$10 pp). They hire 18-speed mountain bikes at NZ$10, and return airport transfers are also NZ$10 pp. Budget.

Food

There are three main shops on Atiu, and two bakers make bread weekdays and Sunday. Andrea Eimke's **Tivaevae Café** (tel. 33-027; weekdays 0800-1600, Saturday 0800-1300), at the north end of Teenui village, serves excellent cups of Atiu coffee (NZ$2) with homemade cakes. It's pleasant to sit and chat with Andrea, and her **Atiu Fiber Arts Studio** here has women's jackets, dresses, and vests, plus wall hangings in the *tivaevae* quilt style.

Bush Beer

Venerable institutions worthy of note are the bush beer schools, of which there are nine on Atiu. Bush beer is a local moonshine made from imported yeast, malt, hops, and sugar. The concoction is fermented in a *tumunu,* a hollowed-out coconut tree stump about a meter high. Orange-flavored "jungle juice" is also made. The mixing usually begins on Wednesday, and the resulting brew ferments for two days and is ready to drink on the weekend. A single batch will last three or four nights; the longer it's kept, the stronger it gets.

Gatherings at a school resemble the kava ceremonies of Fiji and the practice clearly dates back to the days before early missionaries banned kava drinking. Only the barman is permitted to ladle bush beer out of the *tumunu* in a half-coconut-shell cup and the potent contents of the cup must be swallowed in one hearty gulp. Those who've developed a taste for the stuff usually refer to regular beer as "lemonade." The village men come together at dusk, and after a few rounds, the barman calls them to order by tapping a cup on the side of the *tumunu.* A hymn is sung and a prayer said. Announcements are made by various members, and work details assigned to earn money to buy the ingredients for the next brew. After the announcements, guitars and ukuleles appear, and the group resumes drinking, dancing, and singing for as long as they can. The barman, responsible for maintaining order, controls how much brew each participant gets.

Nonmembers visiting a school are expected to bring along a kilo of sugar, or to put NZ$5 pp on the table, as their contribution (enough for the whole week). Guests may also be asked to work in the taro patches the next day.

Airport

A new airstrip (AIU) was built on Atiu's north

side in 1983, after the old airstrip on the plateau, built only in 1977, was found to be too small. Roger Malcolm from the Atiu Motel is often there to meet flights (transfers NZ$8 pp each way). He'll give you a bit of an island tour on your way to the motel.

MAUKE

Mauke, the easternmost of the Cooks, is a flat raised atoll. It and neighboring Mitiaro and Atiu are collectively known as Ngaputoru, "The Three Roots." As on its neighbors, the crops grow in the center of Mauke; the *makatea* ringing the island is infertile and rocky. Both the *makatea* and the central area are low, and you barely notice the transition as you walk along the road inland from the coast to the taro swamps and manioc plantations. Pigs and chickens run wild on the island, and many goats can be seen. Thankfully dogs are banned from Mauke.

The men fish for tuna just offshore in small outrigger canoes, and the women weave fine pandanus mats with brilliant borders of blue, red, yellow, and orange. There are also wide-rimmed pandanus hats and *kete* baskets of sturdy pandanus with colorful geometric designs. The men carve the attractive white-and-black *tou* or red-and-brown *miro* wood into large bowls shaped like breadfruit leaves. They also carve large spoons and forks, miniature models of chiefs' seats, and small replicas of the canoe of Uke, legendary founder of Mauke, who gave the island its name.

Mauke has the best beaches of the three neighboring islands, but it's too shallow for snorkeling. Coral overhangs provide shade at many of the beaches and in August and September whales are often seen off Mauke. It's a very friendly island to poke around for a few days and a good choice for a prolonged stay.

Sights

The harbor, market, Catholic mission, government residen-

cy, and administration building are all at **Taunganui Landing.** The area behind the administration building is known as **Te Marae O Rongo** with a stone circle and a large boulder once used as a seat by the chief. Inland at Makatea village, opposite a store with massive masonry walls, is the two-story concrete palace of the last queen of Mauke who died in 1982. Unfortunately the building is falling into ruins due to squabbles among her descendants. At one end of the taro swamp in the valley behind the palace is **Koenga Well,** a source of fresh drinking water in years gone by.

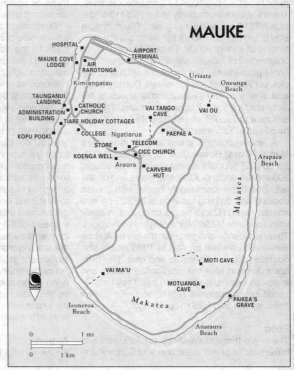

The **CICC church** (1882) at the hub of the island has an almost Islamic flavor, with its long rectangular courtyard, tall gateways, perpendicular alignment, and interior decoration of crescents and interlocking arches. Due to an old dispute between Areora and Ngatiarua villages, the church was divided across the center and each side was decorated differently. The dividing partition has been removed, but dual gateways lead to dual doors, one for each village. The soft pastels (green, pink, yellow, and blue) harmonize the contrasting designs, and the pulpit in the middle unifies the two. Inset into the railing in front of the pulpit are nine old Chilean pesos. Look carefully at the different aspects of this building; it's one of the most fascinating in the Cook Islands.

Vai Tango Cave is fairly easy to find. From the Telecom office, go 500 meters northeast through Ngatiarua village and turn left after the last house. The cave is 500 meters northwest of the main road, at the end of a trail along a row of hibiscus trees. A large circular depression with Barringtonia trees growing inside, Vai Tango has a clear freshwater pool under the overhanging stalactites. The locals swim and bathe here. There are large rooms farther back in the cave but you'd need scuba gear and lamps to reach them.

A *marae* called **Paepae A,** 50 meters beyond the Vai Tango turnoff, was reconstructed from scratch in 1997. The stalagmites standing on the *marae* platform are two pieces of a single pillar once carried by the legendary chief Kai Moko (Eater of Lizards). On the ground behind Paepae A are four huge stones remaining from Marae Terongo. The origin of these volcanic rocks, unique on this coral island, is lost in time.

Back in Areora village, visit the woodcarvers who work in the house next to the Catholic church. One of their fine breadfruit-shaped bowls would make a unique souvenir.

Around the Island

It's only 18 km around Mauke, and no one lives on the south or east sides of the island, so the secluded beaches there are ideal for those who want to be completely alone. There's good reef walking at low tide on the west side of Mauke, but ocean swimming is difficult everywhere. A coral trail just south of Tiare Cottages gives access to a small beach, and south around the point from this beach is a sea cave known as **Kopu Pooki** ("stomach rock"). It's about two meters deep and small fish congregate there.

About 450 meters southeast of Tukune junction, just past the second rock quarry, a trail leads 150 meters inland between the Barringtonia or *utu* trees to **Vai Ma'u,** a deep water-filled crack in the *makatea* with a tall coconut tree growing out. The water is very clear but the opening is narrow and steep.

The finest beaches on Mauke are on the south side of the island and the white sands of **Ieoneroa** are just 500 meters southeast of Vai Ma'u. Also most inviting is the beach at **Anaraura,** where a long stretch of clean white sand borders a green lagoon. This piece of paradise is flanked by rugged limestone cliffs and backed by palm, pine, and pandanus. A short track leads down to the beach.

Two upright stone slabs to the right of the road about a kilometer beyond Anaraura mark the site of **Paikea's grave.** A secluded white beach is just behind. Yet another good beach is found at **Arapaea,** three km north of Paikea's Grave.

At Oneunga, just under two km northwest of Arapaea, two huge stones thrown up between the shore and the road have trees growing out of them. Directly opposite these two rocks is a trail leading across the *makatea* to **Vai Ou,** a series of three caves. You can swim in the first cave's pool, about 800 meters in from the coastal road. A five-minute scramble beyond Vai Ou is **Vai Moraro,** and beyond that **Vai Tunamea.** The coastal road meets the road to the interior villages and the airstrip less than a kilometer west of Oneunga.

Accommodations and Food

There are two excellent, inexpensive places to stay on Mauke, both offering some degree of privacy. **Tiare Holiday Cottages** (tel./fax 35-102), a few hundred meters south of Taunganui Landing, offers a duplex unit with two single rooms, two larger cottages with double beds, and one deluxe cottage with double beds. All units have their own fridge, but only the deluxe unit has a private bathroom and shower. There's no hot water. Accommodations are NZ$25/35 single/double with the deluxe unit NZ$5 more expensive. If you stay a week the seventh night is free. A separate communal kitchen and dining area sits in the center of the compound. If you don't wish to cook, filling meals are served at reasonable prices, and tea, coffee, and tropical fruit are supplied free. Scooters (NZ$20) and bicycles (NZ$10) are for rent. Your hosts, Tautara and Kura Purea, are very helpful and make you feel like one of the family. This peaceful place with lovely sea views has been in business for more than 20 years and it's easily one of the nicest low-budget places to stay in the South Pacific.

Archie and Kura Guinea run **Mauke Cove Lodge** (Box 24, Mauke; tel. 35-888, fax 35-094), near the sea on the northwest side of the island.

Archie's a semiretired Scottish doctor who settled here in 1983; Kura is a Maukean. They offer three rooms with private bath in a one-story coral house with a large covered porch at NZ$39/57/77 single/double/triple. No food is provided, but there's a communal kitchen and lounge. A coral pathway leads down to the lagoon. This attractive European-style house built in 1912 offers a rather romantic style of island living.

MANGAIA

Mangaia is pronounced "mahng-ah-ee-ah," not "man-gaia," as there's no "g" sound in the Polynesian languages. It's 204 km southeast of Rarotonga and just north of the tropic of Capricorn, a position that makes it the southernmost and coolest of the Cook Islands. South of here you don't strike land again until Antarctica. With an area of 52 square km, it's also the country's second-largest island, just a bit smaller than Rarotonga. Without soaring peaks or an azure lagoon, Mangaia doesn't fit the tropical island stereotype and it remains an undiscovered tourist destination.

One of the major geological curiosities of the South Pacific, Mangaia is similar to Atiu and Mauke but much more dramatic. A *makatea* or raised coral reef forms a 60-meter-high ring around the island with sheer cliffs towering as high as 80 meters on the inland side. Lifted from the sea in stages over the past two million years, this outer limestone rim has eroded into quite remarkable rock formations with numerous caves hundreds of meters in length, some of them below sea level.

The volcanic earth inside the *makatea* is the only fertile soil on the island; this rises in rolling hills to slopes once planted with pineapples. At 169 meters elevation, Rangimotia is the island's highest point. Forested ridges radiate from this hill with the valleys between them used for farming. Near the inner edge of the *makatea,* where water is caught between the coral cliffs and the hills, low taro swamps are flanked by banana fields and miscellaneous crops. Nothing but bush and coconut palms grow on the *makatea* itself, and pigs are kept there in makeshift pens.

Legend tells how Rongo rose from the deep with his three sons to colonize the island. Captain

Cook "discovered" Mangaia in 1777 and Polynesian missionaries followed in 1826. Mangaia was the last Cook island to accept Christianity, and traditionally, the 1,100 Mangaians have a reputation for being a cautious lot, but you'll probably find them quite friendly when you get to know them. They live in three scattered coastal villages, Oneroa, Tamarua, and Ivirua. The population is static, with some continuing to migrate to New Zealand as others return. The Mangaians speak a language similar to that of Rarotonga, part of the great Austronesian family.

Sights
A 30-km road along the coastal strip rings most of the island. It's 10 km from the airstrip to **Oneroa,** the main village, where a monument in front of the church recalls Mangaian church ministers and missionaries (such as Rev. Wyatt Gill who served

in the Cooks 1852-83). If the church is open, enter to see the sennit rope bindings in the roof. On a large stone near Avarua landing are the footprints of the legendary giant, Mokea, and his son; both jumped across the island in a race to this spot. The huge stones on the reef to the north were thrown there by Mokea, to prevent a hostile canoe from landing. The queen of Mangaia still has a large flag given to her grandfather by Queen Victoria.

George Tuara (tel. 34-105) will guide you through **Teruarere Cave** for NZ$20 pp. Used as a burial ground in the distant past, the cave has old skeletons that add a skin-crawling touch of reality. The opening is small and you have to crawl in, but the cave goes on for a great distance. A lamp is necessary. Below Teruarere on the cliff is **Touri Cave.** Use indicators to find your way back out—be careful not to get lost inside! There are two streams in this cave: one freshwater, the other salty.

An impressive cut leads up through the *makatea* from Oneroa. Follow a jeep track up to the flat summit of Rangimotia for varied views. From the plateau you can follow a footpath back down to Ivirua and return to Oneroa via **Tamarua,** a rather longish day-hike. The church at Tamarua has a sennit-bound roof.

A water-filled cave at **Lake Tiriara** is the legendary hiding place of the island hero Tangiia. Water from the lake runs through the cave under the *makatea* to the sea, and rises and falls with the tide. **Tuatini Cave** near Tamarua village has a huge gaping entrance, but gets narrower toward the back. There's really nowhere safe to swim on the island.

Accommodations

Babe's Place (Box 6, Mangaia; tel. 34-092, fax 34-078), just south of Oneroa, has six rooms with bath, fridge, fan, and TV at NZ$75/120/150 single/double/triple including all meals (cooking facilities not provided). Four of the rooms are in a long block, the other two in a family house. The bar here gets lively during the Friday and Saturday night dances. Island tours are NZ$40 pp, otherwise it's NZ$20 for an inflatable boat ride on Lake Tiriara. Bicycles can be arranged.

In 1997 **Ara Moana Bungalows** (tel. 34-278, fax 34-279) opened on the coast just southeast of Ivirua village, about five km from the airport. It's run by a Swede named Jan Kristensson and his local wife Tu. There are four tiny thatched cabins with shared bath at NZ$40/55 single/double, and two larger units with private bath at NZ$60/75. Airport transfers are included but add NZ$30-45 pp a day for meals (self-catering facilities are not available). Kawasaki 100 cc motor bikes are rented at NZ$30 a day, while an island tour by jeep or truck is NZ$35 pp with lunch. Bareback horses can also be hired. A nice beach is not far from Ara Moana.

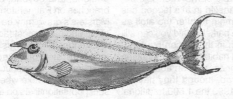

unicornfish

OTHER SOUTHERN ISLANDS

Mitiaro

Mitiaro, formerly known as Nukuroa, is a low island with two lakes and vast areas of swampland. Of the lakes, Rotonui is much longer and broader than Rotoiti. This surprisingly large lake is surrounded by an unlikely combination of pine trees and coconut palms. Before the arrival of Europeans, the people occupied the center of the island near their gardens. Today they all live in one long village on the west coast. Four different sections of the village maintain the names of the four original villages, and each has a garden area inland bearing the same name.

It's 20 km around Mitiaro but the road across the center of the island offers more variety than the coastal road (no shade on either road, so be prepared). A number of caves, *marae,* rock pools, and small golden beaches await visitors. Small, edible black tilapia are abundant in the lakes, providing food for the common black eels (*'itiki*). About 600 meters north of the Lake Rotonui road on the east side of the island is the access road to **Vai Nauri,** a cool, crystal-clear freshwater cave pool. A stairway leads down to the water's edge, and on a hot afternoon a swim here is almost divine.

Mitiaro receives fewer than 50 tourists a year and there are no motels or tourist cottages. Instead, several families take paying guests. The Rarotonga travel agencies and Air Rarotonga collect around NZ$65 pp a night including three meals for these arrangements, which makes Mitiaro a rather expensive island to visit, and two nights here are quite enough.

Manuae

This small island consists of two islets, Manuae and Te Au O Tu, inside a barrier reef. The unspoiled wealth of marinelife in this lagoon has prompted the government to offer the atoll as an international marine park. It's said you can still catch large parrot fish in the lagoon by hand. There's no permanent habitation. Copra-cutting parties from Aitutaki once used an abandoned airstrip to come and go, though they haven't done so for years. In 1990 the 1,600 traditional Aitutaki-origin owners of Manuae rejected a government proposal to lease the island to an Australian company for tourism development. Captain Cook gave Manuae its other, fortunately rarely used, name, Hervey Island.

Takutea

Clearly visible 16 km off the northwest side of Atiu, to whose people it belongs, Takutea is in no place more than six meters high. The island's other name, Enuaiti, means "Small Island." Until 1959 the people of Atiu called here to collect copra, but Takutea gets few visitors now. There are a few abandoned shelters and a freshwater collection tank. The waters along the reef abound with fish; many red-tailed tropic birds and red-footed boobies nest on the land. Permission of the Atiu Island Council is required for visits.

Palmerston

Palmerston, 367 km northwest of Aitutaki, is an atoll 11 km across at its widest point. Some 35 tiny islands dot its pear-shaped barrier reef, which encloses the lagoon completely at low tide. Although Polynesians had once lived on what they called Ava Rua ("two hundred channels"), Palmerston was uninhabited when Captain Cook arrived in 1774.

William Marsters, legendary prolific settler, arrived here to set up a coconut plantation in 1863. He brought with him from Penrhyn his Polynesian wife and her sister, who were soon joined by another sister. Marsters married all three, and by the time he died in 1899 at the ripe age of 78 he had begotten 21 children. Thousands of his descendants are now scattered around the Cook Islands, throughout New Zealand, and beyond, but the three Marsters branches on Palmerston are down to about 50. Marsters's grave may be seen near the remains of his original homestead.

Like lonely Pitcairn Island where the inhabitants are also of mixed British descent, on Palmerston the first language is English, the only island in the Cooks where this is so. The present population lives on tiny Home Island on the west side of the atoll, and as in any small, isolated community there's some tension between the three families. In 1995 officials from Rarotonga arrived on Palmerston and by playing one group off against another succeeded in undermining the authority of the island council and imposing centralized rule on the islanders.

Fish are caught at Palmerston using a circular net called a *rau* made of coconut fronds. People beat the water's surface with sticks to drive the fish into the net, which then closes upon them. Ships visit Palmerston three or four times a year to bring ordered supplies and to take away parrot fish and copra. Although unable to enter the lagoon, ships can anchor offshore.

THE NORTHERN GROUP

The northern Cooks are far more traditional than the southern Cooks. All of the northern atolls except Penrhyn sit on the 3,000-meter-deep Manihiki Plateau; the sea around Penrhyn is 5,000 meters deep. These low-lying coral rings are the very image of the romantic South Seas, but life for the inhabitants can be hard and many have left for New Zealand. Reef fish and coconuts are abundant, but fresh water and everything else is limited. Now a commercial cultured pearl industry is bringing prosperity to several of the atolls.

All of the scattered atolls of the northern Cooks except Nassau have central lagoons. Only the Penrhyn lagoon is easily accessible to shipping, although yachts can anchor in the pass at Suwarrow. Until recently these isolated islands were served only by infrequent ships from Rarotonga, and tourist visits were limited to the ship's brief stop, as to disembark would have meant a stay of several weeks or even months. Now Air Rarotonga has flights to Manihiki and Penrhyn, taking 4.5 hours each way.

Suwarrow

In 1814 the Russian explorer Mikhail Lazarev discovered an uninhabited atoll, which he named for his ship, the *Suvarov*. A mysterious box containing US$15,000 was dug up in 1855, probably left by the crew of a wrecked Spanish galleon in 1742. Later an additional US$2,400 was found. Early this century, Lever Brothers unsuccessfully attempted to introduce to the lagoon gold-lipped pearl oysters from Australia's Torres Straits. In the 1920s and 1930s A.B. Donald Ltd. ran Suwarrow as a copra estate, until the island became infested with termites and the export of copra was prohibited. During WW II New Zealand coastwatchers were stationed here—the few decrepit buildings on Anchorage Island date from that time.

At various times from 1952 onward, New Zealander Tom Neale lived alone on Suwarrow and wrote a book about his experiences titled, not surprisingly, *An Island to Oneself.* Tom never found the buried treasure he was searching for on Suwarrow, and in 1977 he died of cancer on Rarotonga. Today coconut-watchers serve on Suwarrow to ensure that none of the termite-infested nuts are removed. Officially Suwarrow is a Marine Park, and the caretakers live in Tom Neale's house. A government meteorologist may also be present, and pearl divers from Manihiki and Penrhyn visit occasionally.

Yachts often call on their way from Rarotonga or Bora Bora to Samoa. The wide, easy lagoon entrance is just east of Anchorage Island on the northeast side of the atoll and a 40-meter-long coral rock jetty points to the deep anchorage. There's good holding, but in stormy weather the lagoon waters can become very rough. Though Suwarrow is not an official port of entry, yachts often stop without clearing in at Rarotonga or Aitutaki. Passports must be taken to the caretakers in Tom's house, who also accept outgoing mail (yachties often volunteer to carry mail to/from Rarotonga). The table and chairs outside the caretaker family's home provide welcome neutral ground for whiling away the time.

Of the 25 *motus*, only five are sizable. The snorkeling in the lagoon is fantastic, with lots of shark action—they won't usually bother you unless you're spearfishing. Scuba diving is not allowed. In the past, hurricanes have washed four-meter waves across the island and during one storm in 1942 those present survived by tying themselves to a large tree (see *The Island of Desire,* by Robert Dean Frisbie). Thousands of seabirds, turtles, and coconut crabs nest on this historically strange and still mysterious island.

Nassau

Egg-shaped Nassau is the only northern island without an inner lagoon; instead, taro grows in gardens at the center of the island. The American whaler *Nassau* called in 1835. Europeans ran a coconut plantation here until l945, when the government bought the island for £2,000 in order to get it back for the Pukapukans. In 1951, the chiefs of Pukapuka, 89 km to the northwest, purchased it from the government for the same amount and they've owned it ever since. There's no safe anchorage here.

Pukapuka

An island sits at each corner of this unusual triangular atoll. Because of its treacherous reef, where no anchorage is possible, Pukapuka was formerly known as "Danger Island." Discovered by Mendaña in 1595 and rediscovered by Byron in 1765, Pukapuka was outrageously victimized during a Peruvian slave raid in 1863. Captain Gibson of HMS *Curacao* annexed the island in 1892.

Pukapuka is closer to Samoa than to Rarotonga, so the people differ in language and custom from other Cook Islanders. Three villages on Wale (pronounced "wah-lay") island have co-existed since precontact times, each with its own island council. They compete enthusiastically with each other in singing, dancing, contests, and cricket.

An airstrip was constructed on Pukapuka in 1994 but Air Rarotonga only calls if there's sufficient demand. Their Rarotonga office should know about this and any accommodation options.

Manihiki

One of the Pacific's most beautiful atolls, Manihiki's reef bears 39 coral islets, enclosing a closed lagoon four km wide that's thick with sharks. The dark green *motus* are clearly visible across the blue waters. Until 1852, Manihiki was owned by the people of Rakahanga, who commuted the 44 km between the two islands in outrigger canoes, with great loss of life. In that year the missionaries convinced the islanders to divide themselves between the two islands and give up the hazardous voyages. In 1889 some disenchanted Manihiki islanders invited the French to annex their island. When a French warship arrived to consummate the act, anxious missionaries speedily hoisted the Union Jack, so the French sailed off. The same August Britain officially declared a protectorate over the island.

Mother-of-pearl shell was once taken from the lagoon by island divers who plunged effortlessly to depths of 25-30 meters. Today, more than 100 farms on Manihiki produce cultured pearls from the 800,000 oysters hanging on racks below the surface of the lagoon. It's believed that with the growth in pearl farming over the past decade, the Manihiki lagoon has already reached its maximum carrying capacity of oysters, and further development here would be disastrous. Unfortunately the money flowing in from this multi-million-dollar industry has eroded the authority of the *ariki* and led to drinking problems.

Manihiki is famous for its handsome people. The administrative center is Tauhunu, and there is a second village at Tukao. Permission of the chief of Tauhunu is required to dive in the lagoon. There's no safe anchorage for visiting ships but with the pearl boom in full swing, Air Rarotonga now flies here twice a week from Rarotonga (1,204 km) and two rooms are now available at **Danny's Bungalow** at NZ$45/75 single/double including meals.

Rakahanga

Two opposing horseshoe-shaped islands almost completely encircle the lagoon of this rectangular atoll. Still lacking the pearl wealth of

Manihiki, this is a much quieter island. There are several small *motus* that can be reached on foot at low tide. An airstrip in the middle of the west side of the atoll was destroyed by Hurricane Wasa in December 1991 and has not been repaired.

Penrhyn

Penrhyn's turquoise 280-square-km lagoon is so wide that you can just see the roof of the church at Tautua from Omoka, the administrative center. The *motus* at the far end of the lagoon are too far away to be seen. The lagoon is thick with sharks, mostly innocuous black-tips; only the black shark is dangerous. The islanders ignore them as they dive for oysters. Now pearl farming is developing with 150,000 cultured oysters already hanging on racks in the lagoon and an oyster hatchery near Omoka is adding to their numbers every day.

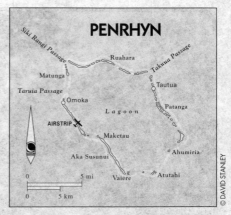

Penrhyn was named for the British ship *Lady Penrhyn,* which arrived in 1788, although one of the Polynesian names is Tongareva. The legendary hero Vatea fished Penrhyn up from the sea using a hook baited with a piece of flesh from his own thigh. In 1863 four native missionaries on Penrhyn were tricked into recruiting their congregation for Peruvian slavers at $5 a head and sailed with them to Callao as overseers for $100 a month in the hope of obtaining enough money to build a new church! The blackbirders dubbed Penrhyn the "Island of the Four Evangelists" in gratitude. This tragedy wiped out the chiefly line and Penrhyn is today the only Cook Island without an *ariki.* Remnants of old graves and villages abandoned after the raid can still be seen on the *motus,* and the ruins of an unfinished church crumble away at Akasusu.

The island has a good natural harbor, one of the few in the Cook Islands, and vessels can enter the lagoon through Taruia Passage, just above Omoka, to tie up at Omoka wharf. Fine pandanus *rito* hats and mother-of-pearl shell jewelry are made on Penrhyn and visiting yachties can trade kitchen- and tableware, dry cell batteries, rope, and small anchors for crafts and pearls.

American forces occupied Penrhyn during 1942-46 and built a giant airfield at the south end of Omoka about five km from the present village. Concrete building foundations from the war and from a base camp that supported British and American atmospheric nuclear tests on Christmas Island in the early 1960s can be seen. The waters around the atoll are a rich fishing ground, and Penrhyn is used as a base for patrol boats and planes monitoring the activities of foreign fishing fleets.

Air Rarotonga flies once a week from Rarotonga (1,365 km) to this most northerly Cook island. The airfare (NZ$1,210 return from Rarotonga) is high due in part to an exorbitant landing fee levied by the island council. Soa Tini operates the **Tarakore Guest House** (tel. 42-018 or 42-087, fax 42-015) out of his own home at the center of Omoka village, charging NZ$55 pp including meals. As well, other families take guests and the local Air Rarotonga agent Warwick Latham (e-mail: penrhyn@airraro.co.ck) has a house for rent. Electricity is only available 0600-1200 and 1800-2400.

NIUE
INTRODUCTION

A single 259-square-km island, Niue is one of the world's smallest self-governing states (in free association with New Zealand). It stands alone 560 km southeast of Samoa, 386 km east of Vava'u, and 2,400 km northeast of New Zealand. The name comes from *niu* (coconut tree) and *e* (behold). This little-known island boasts some of the finest coastal limestone crevices and chasms in the South Pacific, all open to visitors and freely accessible. Each is unique—you'll need at least a week to do them justice.

Niue is for the explorer who likes to get out and make discoveries on his or her own, for the skin diver in search of clean clear water brimming with coral, fish, and sea snakes, and for those who want to relax in a peaceful, uncommercialized environment among charming, friendly people, without sacrificing creature comforts. Niue is perhaps the most unspoiled main island in the Pacific—it's an island of adventure.

The Land
Niue is an elevated atoll shaped like a two-tiered

wedding cake with two terraces rising from the sea. It's one of the largest coral islands in the world (though 692-square-km Rennell Island in the Solomons is much bigger). The lower terrace rises sharply, creating the 20-meter coastal cliffs that virtually surround the island. Inland, the second terrace rises abruptly from this coastal belt to a central plateau some 60 meters above the ocean. A fringing reef borders much of the coast, but in places the ocean breakers smash directly into the precipitous cliffs. Faulting during the island's uplifting has created the chasms and crevices that are Niue's greatest attractions. Water dripping from their ceilings has added a touch of the surreal in the form of stalactites and stalagmites.

Climate
December-March are the hurricane months, with average temperatures of 27° C. The southeast trades blow April-Nov. and temperatures average 24° C. The 2,047 mm of annual rainfall is fairly well distributed throughout the year, with a slight

peak during the hot southern summer. There is good anchorage at Alofi, except during strong westerly winds.

Flora and Fauna

The waters off Niue are clear as can be, with countless species of colorful fish. There are also many varieties of sea snakes—though they're poisonous, their mouths are too tiny to bite, and divers handle them with impunity. On most dives underwater sightseers also spot white-tip reef sharks, but they aren't dangerous and add to the thrill.

Butterflies are everywhere, as are orchids, hibiscus, frangipani, and bougainvillea. One-fifth of the island's surface is covered by undisturbed primary forest, much of the rest by secondary growth. A profusion of huge "crow's nest" *(nidum)* and other ferns, rhododendron, and poinsettia grow wild, and there are ancient ebony trees.

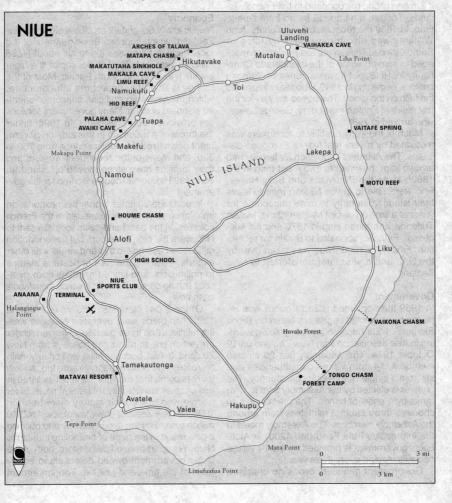

The birdlife is rich; white long-tailed terns, weka, swamp hens, and parakeets abound.

History

Niue was colonized by Samoans in the 9th or 10th century A.D., then Tongans invaded in the 16th century, and the present Niuean language is related to both. Captain Cook made three landings in 1774, but he got a hostile reception from warriors with red-painted teeth! Cook called it Savage Island (as opposed to the Friendly Islands, Tonga), a name still heard from time to time. In 1830 the redoubtable missionary John Williams was also thrown back by force. A Samoa-trained Niuean named Peniamina managed to convert some of the islanders to Christianity in 1846, but it was a series of Samoan pastors, beginning in 1849, who really implanted the faith on the island. This paved the way for the first resident English missionary, George Lawes, who arrived in 1861.

Much of the early hostility to foreigners was motivated by a very real fear of European diseases. The islanders' reputation for ferocity had always kept the whalers away, but then in the 1860s came the Peruvians and Bully Hayes, who were able to entice Niuean men to leave their island voluntarily to mine phosphate for years at a time on distant Malden Island. Mataio Tuitonga was made king in 1876 and his successor, Fataaiki, appealed to Britain for protection. Finally, in 1900, Niue was taken over by the U.K. and a year later transferred to New Zealand.

Government

In 1959 the appointed Island Council was replaced by an elected Legislative Assembly (Fono Ekepule). Niue became internally self-governing in free association with New Zealand on 19 October 1974. The Assembly has 20 elected members, 14 from village constituencies and six from a single island-wide constituency. The premier is elected by the Assembly from its own ranks by a show of hands. The premier in turn chooses three cabinet ministers from among the Assembly members. The Assembly meets in the impressive Fale Fono (tel. 4200) in Alofi. Local government is provided by the 14 village councils elected every three years.

Government ministers brook no criticism.

When the editor of the local newspaper became overly annoying to the powers that be, her expatriate husband suddenly had visa problems. In early 1995 an Australian Catholic priest with years of service on Niue was subjected to deportation proceedings after he dared comment publicly on nepotism in the allocation of government scholarships. In a small community like Niue's one has to take care not to step on the wrong toes.

Economy

Niue is totally dependent on official aid from New Zealand, which supplies three-quarters of the local budget. Overseas aid totals about NZ$6 million a year, or NZ$3,158 per capita, the highest such level in the South Pacific. Most of the money is used to support the infrastructure, which maintains an artificial, consumer-oriented standard of living. Many government services are provided free to residents. In 1996, under the threat of a reduction in this aid, the government downsized the public service from 750 to 320, and many of the redundant workers and their families have since moved off island. In early 1999 some 430 people worked for the government.

Imports are 20 times higher than exports, an imbalance of trade only exceeded in the French colonies. In the past hand-sewn footballs sent to N.Z. were the biggest export, but transportation difficulties have halted this and virtually all other exports. Tourism, the sale of postage stamps to philatelists, and limited royalties from overseas fishing companies help balance the island's cash flow.

Of the 2,041 "tourists" who visited Niue in 1997, two-thirds were overseas Niueans visiting relatives and three-quarters of the remainder arrived on cheap packaged holidays from New Zealand. In fact, because Niue isn't on any main air routes and is an expensive side trip, so few tourists come that many of the facilities listed in this chapter are actually retirement projects for people who made their money elsewhere. In 1996 the New Zealand government spent NZ$10 million extending the airport runway and building a new resort in the hope of promoting tourism to Niue. Yet apart from official visitors, both of the larger government-owned hotels stand empty most of the time and just two Tongan aircraft touch down on the shiny new airstrip each week.

In 1993 Niue set up a "financial center" similar to those of Vanuatu and Cook Islands to support overseas firms trying to avoid taxation in their actual places of business. Although this scam brings in NZ$400,000 in licensing fees each year from the 200 companies involved, the Audit Office of New Zealand is unhappy about being refused access to the records and official aid has been cut back. In 1996 Niue was earning US$50,000 a month by leasing its international telephone circuits to route overseas sex calls to "phone girls" in New Zealand, but in 1997 Niue's prime minister canceled the arrangement after complaints from local residents who were being accidentally connected to phone-sex clients in the U.S., Britain, and Japan.

Niue has also profited from the sale of its internet ending .nu, which has been marketed worldwide by local entrepreneur Stafford Guest via http://something.really.nu. At just US$25, top level dot nu domain names are among the cheapest on the web and thousands have been sold.

The People

Niueans are related to Tongans and Samoans rather than to Tahitians. The population is about 1,750 and falling (down from 4,000 at self-government in 1974). Another 14,400 Niueans reside in New Zealand (all Niueans are N.Z. citizens), and every year more people leave "the Rock" (Niue) to seek employment and opportunity abroad. Many of the landowners have left—you'll never see as many empty houses and near-ghost towns as you see here. The villages on the east coast give an idea of how Europe must have looked in the Middle Ages after a plague, as direct flights to Auckland have drained the population. Remittances from Niueans in New Zealand are important sources of income.

The inhabitants live in small villages scattered along the coast, with a slight concentration near the administrative center, Alofi. After disastrous hurricanes in 1959 and 1960, the New Zealand government replaced the traditional lime-plastered, thatched-roofed houses of the people with tin-roofed "hurricane-resistant" concrete-block dwellings. Niue has the lowest population density of any Pacific country (excluding Papua New Guinea). At 15 per 1,000, Niue's birth rate is the lowest in the Pacific, and the life expectancy is the lowest in Polynesia at 60 for men and 65 for women.

All land is held by families. Three-quarters belong to the Ekalesia Nieue, founded by the London Missionary Society. Other churches such as the Catholics and Mormons have only a few hundred members. There are no longer any chiefs, and lineage means little. Since the 1950s education has been free and compulsory until the age of 14 and literacy is almost 100%. Two Polynesian dialects are spoken: Motu in the north and Tafiti in the south. Everyone on the island knows one another.

A major event for a teenage boy is his haircutting ceremony, when the long tail of hair he has kept since childhood is removed. Guests invited to the concurrent feast each contribute hundreds of dollars to a fund that goes to the boy after celebration expenses are paid. For girls there's a similar ear-piercing ceremony. These gatherings are usually held on a Saturday in private homes; you may be allowed to observe if you know someone.

Public Holidays and Festivals

Public holidays include New Year's Day, Commission Day (2 January), Waitangi Day (6 February), Good Friday, Easter Monday (March/April), ANZAC Day (25 April), White Sunday (second Sunday in May), Queen Elizabeth's Birthday (a Monday in early June), Constitution Days (19 and 20 October), Peniamina Day (fourth Monday in October), and Christmas Days (25 and 26 December).

Prayer Week and Takai Week are both held during the first week of January. The main event of the year is the Constitution Celebrations, which last three days around 19 October. There are traditional dancing and singing, parades, sports, and a display of produce and handicrafts at the high school grounds two km inland from Alofi. A highlight is the exciting outrigger canoe race off Alofi wharf. Peniamina Day falls on the Monday during the Constitution Celebrations.

ON THE ROAD

SIGHTS

Exploring Niue

Virtually all of Niue's scenic attractions are within earshot of the sea, but while sites on the west coast are easily accessible in a few minutes from the road, those on the east coast are only reached over slippery rough trails requiring hikes of up to 40 minutes. Some of these trails, such as those through the fantastic petrified coral forests at Vaikona and Tongo, are not well marked. Sturdy shoes are required to go almost anywhere off the road on Niue.

If you're a good walker, you could visit the sites south of Alofi on foot in less than a day. Those to the north can be covered by a combination of walking, hitching, and good luck, but to get to the places on the northeast and southeast coasts and return to Alofi the same day, you'll need your own transport. Alternatively, camp in one of the east coast villages and visit the area more at your leisure. Take your own food with you, as little is available in the villages. The Huvalu Forest Camp near Hakupu village described below is ideal for hikers interested in spending time in this unspoiled area.

Photographers should note that conditions on the east coast are best in the morning, on the west coast in the afternoon. Vaikona and Tongo are definitely not afternoon trips, as the declining light in the forest makes the trails hard to discern. Also, limestone makes for slow walking.

Near Alofi

The **Huanaki Museum and Cultural Center** (tel. 4011, open weekdays 0800-1500, free) is next to the hospital near the junction of the airport and coastal roads in Alofi. According to popular tradition, Captain Cook landed at **Opaahi Reef** opposite the Mormon church in Alofi. It's a scenic spot, well worth the short detour.

Two kings of Niue, Mataio Tuitonga (reigned 1876-87) and Fataaiki (reigned 1888-96), are buried in front of the **LMS Church** opposite Alofi's post office. Nearby, adjoining the war memorial, are two stone backrests used by these kings. The last king of Niue, Togia (died 1917), ceded his kingdom to Britain on 21 April 1900, just four days after the Americans annexed Eastern Samoa. He's buried in front of the church at Tuapa.

It's fascinating to walk on the reef southwest of Alofi wharf at low tide. Crevices, cliffs, and coral abound, and there are natural pools on the reef where you can swim safely. Beware of waves heralding the incoming tide, however.

This impressive stairway at Motu is used to lower dugouts to the reef.

North of Alofi
Houme Chasm at Alofi North, about four km from the hotel, is behind the house across the street and slightly north of the Catholic Mission. A flashlight is required to reach the pool.

Avaiki Sea Cave is another six km north and an easy five minutes from the road. The pool in the main cave just north of the landing contains a variety of marinelife and is a great place to swim, but this is often prohibited. The limestone formations are outstanding. Just 200 meters north of the Avaiki sign is the trail down to **Palaha Cave,** with stalagmites and stalactites. **Hio Reef,** a little more than a kilometer farther north, just before the point where the road divides, is a nice secluded sandy beach best for swimming at high tide.

Farther north again, just beyond Namukulu, is the trail to **Limu Reef,** a perfect snorkeling locale with colorful coral and fish. A natural stone bridge over the lagoon is just a little north of here across the rocks. The trail to **Makalea Cave** is 200 meters north of the Limu signboard. Near the road just opposite the southernmost house in Hikutavake is **Makatutaha,** a large pothole containing a pool connected to the sea.

Two of Niue's highlights are **Matapa Chasm** and the **Arches of Talava,** reached along an extension of the coastal road just north of Hikutavake. Follow the road straight down to Matapa, a wide, sunken chasm that was once the bathing place of Niuean royalty—very good swimming and snorkeling. The Arches of Talava are harder to find. The trail branches off the Matapa track to the right just before the beginning of the descent. Keep straight on the trail about 15 minutes, then watch for yellow marks on the trees, which indicate the branch trail on the left to Talava. The site itself is entered through a cave. A great series of stone arches above the sea complement side caves with red and green stalactites and stalagmites in fantastic flowing formations. Behind the outermost arch is a large cave best entered at low tide with a flashlight. The constant roar of the surf adds to the overwhelming impression the place makes.

The Southeast Coast
Niue's wild east coast has some of the most fantastic limestone features in the entire South Pacific, though finding your way around without a guide requires intuition and caution. About four km northeast of Hakupu, the second-largest village on the island, is the unmarked trail to **Tongo Chasm.** After a 20-minute walk you reach a wasteland of coral pinnacles much like the interior of Nauru Island. The path leads down to a wide chasm with coconut trees growing on the sandy bottom. Climb down the ladder to the sand, and swim in the pools at each end of the chasm. The green of the coconut trees combined with the golden sand contrasts sharply with the rocky wasteland, creating an almost North African effect—until you hear the ocean crashing into the cliffs just meters away: one of the scenic wonders of the Pacific.

From the Tongo trailhead, travel northeast another four km through the **Huvalu Forest,** with its many species of banyan, Tahitian chestnut, and *kafika* trees, to the Vaikona trailhead. The trail to **Vaikona Chasm** is partially marked with red paint, but careful attention is required, as there is a good chance of getting lost. This trip is for experienced hikers only, unless you come with a guide. As you approach the coast through pandanus brush covering the jagged limestone, you pass a sudden opening straight down into the chasm. Wind your way around the back of the opening and drop into a deep cave, grasping the stout orange rope provided for the purpose. You enter the chasm over huge rocks from the cave. There are two crystal clear pools to swim in, one at each end of Vaikona; tiny freshwater crayfish and black carp live here.

The Northeast Coast
The trail to **Motu Reef** is about a kilometer south of Lakepa. There's a wide wooden stairway down to the reef from the cave where canoes are stored. It's a 25-minute walk along an easy-to-follow trail from the trailhead to **Vaitafe Spring,** a couple of km north of Lakepa. Fresh water from a crevice at the foot of a sheer cliff bubbles into a pool where you can swim, but the area is accessible only at low tide. You can reef walk here.

At the north end of the island, opposite the church in **Mutalau** village, is a monument commemorating the arrival of the first Christian missionaries; the first Niuean convert, Peniamina (1846); and Paulo (1849), the first Samoan teacher. A jeep track across from the monument leads down to Uluvehi Landing, an easy five-minute walk. This was the main landing on the island in the early days; the islanders' sleek outrigger canoes are still stored in caves in the cliffs. To reach **Vaihakea Cave,** look for an overgrown trail just 100 meters inland from the streetlight at Uluvehi on the east side of the track. Once you get on the trail, it's only a five-minute walk to this fantastic submerged cave full of fish and coral, but you must climb down a sharp limestone cliff near the trail end. There's excellent swimming and snorkeling at low tide.

The sites mentioned above are only the *highlights* of Niue; there are many other caves for the avid spelunker to explore.

Sports and Recreation

Kevin Fawcett of **Niue Dive** (Box 140, Alofi; tel. 4311 or 3483, fax 4028, www.dive.nu), behind the hospital, offers scuba diving at NZ$50/175/350/475 for one/three/six/eight-dive packages with a mix of shore and inflatable boat dives. Gear rental (if required) is NZ$15 per dive. Kevin is a professional and his equipment is first class. A certification card is required, otherwise a PADI open-water course will be NZ$500 pp (minimum of two). Featured are dives through caves to drop-offs, and Niue's small, timid sea snakes. If you're very lucky, you may be able to dive with dolphins or migrating whales (June-Nov.). Due to the absence of rivers, the water is unbelievably clear—worth every penny. Niue Dive also arranges snorkeling, whalewatching or coastal sightseeing trips at NZ$30 pp.

Game fishing is available on an eight-meter *alia* catamaran operated by Paul Pasisi's **Horizon Charter** (tel. 4067). More of the same is offered by **Wahoo Fishing Charters** (Box 112, Alofi; tel./fax 4345), which has a six-meter aluminum tri-hull fishing boat available at NZ$220/360 for four/eight hours (up to four anglers). Fish caught belong to the boat. Wahoo's Graham Marsh has been fishing Niue's waters since 1983. The main season for wahoo is July-Nov.; marlin, sailfish, tuna, and mahi mahi are taken Nov.-April. Fishing on Sunday is taboo.

Visitors are welcome at the nine-hole **golf course** (tel. 4292) near the airport. An annual tournament is in November.

Sporting events such as soccer (March-June), rugby (June-Aug.), and netball (June-Aug.t) take place on the high school grounds. Cricket (Dec.-Feb.) and softball matches are usually held in the villages on alternating Saturday. The locals will know what is happening.

PRACTICALITIES

Budget Accommodations

The **Waimanu Guest House** (Asu and Mine Pulu, tel. 4366, fax 4225), next to the public works depot at Amanau southwest of Alofi, has two singles at NZ$40, two doubles with shared bath at NZ$55, one double with private bath at NZ$66, and two self-catering suites at NZ$80. A communal kitchen is available to all. It's good value for scuba divers or anglers.

Peleni's Guest House (Fita and Toke Talagi, Box 11, Alofi; tel. 4135, fax 4322) is in a former family house near the Handicraft Center in central Alofi. The three very homey bedrooms with shared bath and cooking facilities are NZ$35/40 single/double. A three-bed family room costs NZ$50. Prepared meals are available at reasonable cost and everything is clean and well maintained. It's handy to great swimming spots at Utuko and the wharf. They rent cars to guests only at NZ$25 a day. Airport transfers are free.

Kololi's Guest House (Box 177, Alofi; tel. 4171), near the Commercial Center in central Alofi, charges NZ$35 single or double for the three standard rooms and NZ$50 for the family room upstairs. Your hosts Neil and Opo Morrisey provide convenient communal cooking and laundry facilities in this stylishly designed guesthouse.

Right above the Avaiki Caves a bit north of Makefu is the **Anaiki Motel** (Moka and Ataloma Mitihepi, Box 183, Alofi; tel. 4321, fax 4320) with five units in a long block at NZ$50 single or double, NZ$65 triple, tropical breakfast included. A hot plate is provided for heating up simple meals. It's a nice place from which to see the sunset and watch the local fishermen launching their canoes on the evening tide. Your kind hosts will be happy to show you around the village.

Moderate

The two-story **Niue Hotel** (Box 80, Alofi; tel. 4092, fax 4310), on the coast between the airport and Alofi, was originally built by the government in 1975. The charge is NZ$109/125 single/double for one of the 32 fan-cooled rooms with fridge, private bath, transfers, and breakfast. An ocean-view executive suite is NZ$135/160 single/double, while a family suite sleeping six is NZ$175. Cooking facilities are not available but the hotel has a 100-seat dining room, plus bar, gift shop, and swimming pool.

The **Coral Gardens Motel** (Box 91, Alofi; tel. 4235, fax 4222), at Makapu Point four km north of Alofi, has five wooden clifftop bungalows with cooking facilities and excellent views at NZ$120/150 single/double including breakfast. Sails Restaurant is on the premises, and there's an excellent swimming hole at the foot of the cliff. Managers Stafford and Salome Guest are very helpful and can make any arrangements you may require.

Namukulu Motel (Robyn and Joe Wright, Box 171, Alofi; tel. 4052, fax 3001), at Namukulu nine km north of Alofi, offers three self-catering bungalows with fridge and TV at NZ$105/130/155/180 single/double/triple/quad. There's a swimming pool and three of Niue's finest reef swimming pools are nearby. Ten-speed bicycles are loaned free. Airport pickups are complimentary.

Expensive

The upscale **Matavai Resort** (Box 133, Alofi; tel. 4360, fax 4361), perched on a cliff at the south end of Tamakautonga village, was built in 1996 with NZ$2.4 in New Zealand aid money and the government retains 51% ownership. Radio Sunshine general manager Hima Douglas and K-Mart owner Russell Kars are partners. The 24 rooms with fridge and TV in two-story blocks begin at NZ$150/170 single/double, continental breakfast included (no cooking facilities). Specials may be available when business is slow. The dramatic location has made the managers reluctant to accept children under 12 who might be endangered, and parents or guardians may be required to sign a release. The resort features a restaurant, bar, two swimming pools, tennis courts, and a huge terrace from which you may spot dolphins, turtles, or humpback whales. The Niue Island Sport Fishing Club is based at the resort. Several nights a week local cultural groups provide entertainment here.

Others

For a longer stay, ask around about renting a house by the week or month. There are usually plenty available. Unexpected complications can arise, however, as the house may have hundreds of owners, and visiting relatives might throw you out! Camping would be possible on the east coast, but get permission or keep out of sight. For indoor camping, unfurnished houses without hot water in Hakupu village start at NZ$50 a week.

A better bet is the **Huvalu Forest Camp**, about 200 meters south of the trail to Tongo Chasm (or three km northeast of Hakupu and eight km southwest of Liku). There's a bunkhouse where you'll pay NZ$15 pp for a dorm bed and ample camping space at NZ$10 per tent. Communal toilets, showers, and cooking facilities are available in separate buildings. Information is available from Afele and Pati Paea (Box 130, Alofi; tel. 4244) who live at Namoui between Alofi and Makefu. The Forest Camp makes a great base for exploring the most beautiful part of the island, so long as you're prepared to rough it a bit. It's beautiful in the moonlight: wonderfully silent except for the sounds of the forest (and occasional mosquito). Ask for Robert Jackson at the bakery in Hakupu who rents mountain bikes at NZ$5/30 a day/week.

Food and Entertainment

The dining room at the **Niue Hotel** (tel. 4092) serves lunch 1200-1300 sharp (open daily). Check to see if they're still serving endangered species like the *unga* (coconut crab), fruit bat, and native pigeon to tourists. Thursday or Sunday at 1900 (check to find out which day) the hotel has a tropical smorgasbord, sometimes followed by disco dancing to recorded music. The hotel bar picks up in the afternoon as people get off work, but they close early if nobody's around, even on Friday night.

Light snacks are served at **Mitaki's Cafe** (tel. 4084) south of Alofi, at the **Huanaki Snack Bar** (tel. 4071) at the Cultural Center, and at the **Tavana Cafe** (tel. 4334) in the Commercial Center in Alofi. The **Ciao Cafe** (tel. 4316) near the Mormon Church offers cappuccino, pizza, lasagna, spaghetti, and gelato. Up on the road toward the airport is **Tapeu Fisheries** (tel. 4106) with super seafood. **Island Style Restaurant** (tel. 3707) is at Talamaitonga near Avatele.

Gabes Food Bar (tel. 4379) in Alofi lays on an "island night buffet" featuring Polynesian vegetables and seafoods at NZ$15 pp. Included is a cultural show and live music—ask about this as dates vary.

Sails Restaurant (tel. 4235), at the Coral Gardens Motel north of town, serves good food at prices lower than those asked at the Niue Hotel. Their patio is a great place for a drink around sunset, and a live band plays on Friday night (closed Sunday and Monday). Ask about their weekly barbecue.

The **Niue Sports Club** (tel. 4292), better known as the Top Club, at the nine-hole golf course near the airport, is nominally private, but visitors are welcome and bar prices low. Village dances take place on Friday and Saturday nights. The **Pacific Way Bar,** near the Niue Hotel southwest of Alofi, has the local Fia Fia beer on tap.

The tap water is safe to drink on Niue.

Shopping

Imported goods are fairly expensive. The largest supermarkets are Niue Trading (tel. 4080), Rex's Store (tel. 4027), and Jessop's (tel. 4306), all in Alofi. Check their snack bars. They close at 1600

weekdays and don't open at all weekends. There's only a market once a week, held early Friday morning beside Rex's Store. Buy a bottle of Niue honey, if you can.

A **Commercial Center** in Alofi houses the bank, telephone center, butcher shop, gift shop, stationery store, art gallery, and several handicraft shops. The **Philatelic Bureau** (Box 73, Alofi; tel. 4371, fax 4386) in this center sells a variety of beautiful stamps, which make excellent souvenirs.

The people produce very fine, firmly woven baskets of pandanus wound over a coconut-fiber core—among the sturdiest in Polynesia. Fine pandanus and coconut leaf bud hats are also made. Visit the **Niue Handicraft Shop** (tel. 4144) in Alofi and **Hinapoto Handicrafts** (tel. 4340) at the Cultural Center. Coral and valuable shells cannot be exported from Niue.

Services

The administration buildings in Alofi contain the post office and Treasury Department. Change

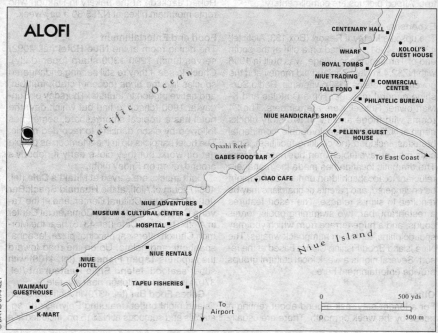

ALOFI

CENTENARY HALL

KOLOLI'S GUEST HOUSE

WHARF

ROYAL TOMBS

NIUE TRADING

COMMERCIAL CENTER

FALE FONO

PHILATELIC BUREAU

Pacific Ocean

NIUE HANDICRAFT SHOP

PELENI'S GUEST HOUSE

Opaahi Reef

GABES FOOD BAR

To East Coast

CIAO CAFE

Niue Island

NIUE ADVENTURES

MUSEUM & CULTURAL CENTER

HOSPITAL

NIUE RENTALS

NIUE HOTEL

WAIMANU GUESTHOUSE

TAPEU FISHERIES

K-MART

To Airport

0   500 yds

0   500 m

© DAVID STANLEY

money at the Westpac Bank branch (tel. 4221, weekdays 0900-1500). New Zealand currency is used. Many hotels and restaurants accept credit cards, but ask first.

Telecom Niue (tel. 4000, open 24 hours) next to the satellite dish in Alofi handles overseas calls and wires. You can send a fax to anyone on the island at fax 4010 and they'll be called and asked to pick it up here. Niue's telephone code is 683.

Doctors and dentists are available at Lord Liverpool Hospital (tel. 4100; weekdays 0730-1500).

Yachting Facilities

Yachts anchor in about 15 meters (good holding) in an open roadstead off Alofi and are well protected except for winds from the west. The **Niue Island Yacht Club** (Box 129, Alofi) provides 18 secure moorings in Alofi Bay that can be used for a NZ$5-a-day charge. Water, toilets, and showers are available at the wharf, but it's necessary to have a bridle arrangement on the dingy to allow it to be lifted out of the water using an electronic winch. Yachts must call "Niue Radio" on VHF channels 10 or 16 for clearance before coming ashore, and Customs and Immigration (tel. 4122, fax 4150) are closed on weekends (exceptions are occasionally made). The NZ$20 pp departure tax also applies to yachties. An annual yacht race is held around the end of August if enough boats are in the bay. Niue makes an excellent stop for yachts sailing between Rarotonga/Aitutaki and Vava'u.

Information

The Tourism Office (Box 42, Alofi; tel. 4224, fax 4225, www.niueisland.com, e-mail: niuetourism @mail.gov.nu) in Alofi's Commercial Center can answer most questions about the island and books activities. Every Wednesday night they organize a *fia fia* at Hakupu village at NZ$35 pp for transportation, a village tour, island food, and entertainment. It's well worth going.

The *Niue Star* (Box 84, Alofi; tel. 4207) is an independent weekly newspaper published in English and Niuean on Friday (circulation around 600). An airmailed subscription to Stafford Guest's informative monthly *Niue Economic Review* (Box 91, Alofi; tel. 4235) is NZ$60 a year.

The Broadcasting Corporation of Niue (Box 68, Alofi; tel. 4026) provides television service

1800-2300 daily and Radio Sunshine broadcasts over 594 kHz AM and 91.0 MHz FM 0600-2130, but both are off the air on Sunday. Most TV programs are supplied by Television New Zealand.

TRANSPORTATION

Getting There

Royal Tongan Airlines flies a Boeing 737 to Niue from Auckland once a week, returning to New Zealand via Tonga. Royal Tongan also has a second weekly flight to Niue from Nuku'alofa using a propeller-driven, 40-seat Hawker-Siddley 748, connecting with flights to/from Auckland in Tonga. These services are only viable due to subsidies from the Niue government, which has designated Royal Tongan as Niue's national carrier. Rumor has it that Polynesian Airlines may take over from Royal Tongan and recommence service to Apia and Rarotonga, and that might lead to service to/from Tonga being canceled, so check. Also ask about direct flights from Niue to Vava'u.

Meanwhile it's T$217/434 one-way/roundtrip from Nuku'alofa, with a 28-day excursion fare of T$340 available year-round. From Auckland the 90-day excursion fare is NZ$1,185/1,381 low/high season (the high season is June-Oct. and December). Avoid Christmas when the flights will be full of islanders returning home. Flying from Auckland or Nuku'alofa to Niue you arrive a day earlier because you cross the international date line, so check your flight dates carefully (Niue and Samoa share the same day).

Go International Travel (Box 9144, Auckland, New Zealand; tel. 64-9/914-4700, fax 64-9/307-3235), **Go Pacific Holidays** (tel. 64-9/379-5520, fax 64-9/377-0111), and **ASPAC Vacations Ltd.** (Box 4330, Auckland, New Zealand; tel. 64-9/623-0259, fax 64-9/623-0257, e-mail: southpacific@aspac-vacations.co.nz) offer well-planned package tours to Niue from Auckland. These trips start at NZ$959, which is less than a regular roundtrip ticket, and yet airfare, seven nights double-occupancy lodging, and transfers are included! In Australia contact **Hideaway Holidays** (Val Gavriloff, 994 Victoria Rd., West Ryde, NSW 2114; tel. 61-2/9807-4222, fax 61-2/9808-2260, www.hideawayholidays.com.au).

Reconfirm your flight reservations well ahead at **Peleni's Travel Agency** (tel. 4317, fax 4322) in Alofi, the Royal Tongan Airlines agent. The same office should have information about the monthly Cook Islands National Line supply ship *Ngamaru III* to Rarotonga (cabin passage is NZ$100 a day). Ask at Niue Trading Store (tel. 4080) in Alofi about occasional boats to Tonga (NZ$50 one-way). Large ships must anchor offshore; their cargo is transferred by lighters.

Getting Around

There's no bus service on Niue, but taxi services are available from Cedric's (tel. 4245) and Mitaki's (tel. 4084). Hitching is easy along the west coast, but you could get stranded on the east. Don't underestimate the size of the island: it's a long, long way to walk. The road around the island is 64 km and the pavement doesn't extend beyond the west coast.

Four car and scooter rental companies operate on Niue. Car rentals include kilometers and insurance but you're still responsible for the first NZ$1,000 in "excess" damages in case of an accident. Before heading around the island on a scooter make sure the tank is full and ask the renter if you can make it on one tank. All rental vehicles are in short supply, so don't wait until the last minute. A Niue driver's license (NZ$5) must be obtained at the police station opposite the Commercial Center (no test required if you have any other license). Driving is on the left and speed limits are 40 kph in the villages or 60 kph on the open road. The penalty for being caught inebriated at a roadside breath analyzer test is NZ$1,500.

Helen's Niue Tours (Helen Sipeli, Box 81, Alofi; tel. 4054, fax 4167) next to the Niue Hotel offers a variety of trips, including tours to Vaikona Chasm, a breakfast bush walk, a "behind the hedges" tour, a circle-island tour, and a Huvalu Forest and Tongo tour. Ask about the Saturday afternoon *fia fia* feast tour with *umu* food and Niuean dancing.

Tali Magatogia of **Tali's Tours** (tel. 3505) can take you to hard-to-reach attractions such as Tongo Chasm, Vaikona Chasm, Ulupaka Cave, and Anatoloa Cave. Ulupaka (near Lakepa) is more than a kilometer long and coated with dirty black fungus. At NZ$20 pp including transportation, sandwiches, and lamps, Tali's cave tours are highly recommended unless you're claustrophobic, just be prepared to get a little dirty. Misa Kulatea (tel. 4101) also offers three-hour forest walks at NZ$25 pp.

Airport

Hanan International Airport (IUE) is three km southeast of Alofi. Some accommodations offer free airport transfers while others charge NZ$5 each way. Otherwise it's fairly easy to hitch a ride into town. Though you'll need a passport and onward ticket, no visa is required for a stay of up to 30 days. There's no bank or duty-free shop. The airport departure tax is NZ$20.

KINGDOM OF TONGA
INTRODUCTION

The ancient Kingdom of Tonga, oldest and last remaining Polynesian monarchy, is the only Pacific nation never brought under foreign rule. Though sprinkled over 700,000 square km of ocean from Niuafo'ou, between Fiji and Samoa, to the Minerva Reef 290 km southwest of Ata, the total land area of the kingdom is only 691 square km.

Tonga is divided into four main parts: the Tongatapu Group in the south, with the capital, Nuku'alofa; the Ha'apai Group, a far-flung archipelago of low coral islands and soaring volcanoes in the center; the Vava'u Group, with its immense landlocked harbor; and in the north, the isolated, volcanic Niuas. The four groups are pleasingly diverse, each with interesting aspects to enjoy: no other Pacific country is made up of components as scenically varied as these.

More than 100 km of open sea separate Tongatapu and Ha'apai, then another 100 between Ha'apai and Vava'u, then it's another 300 km north to remote Niuafo'ou and Niuatoputapu. In all, Tonga comprises 170 islands, 42 of them

inhabited. Even though they're some of the most densely populated in the Pacific, the Tongan islands are set quite apart from the 20th century. Due to the position just west of the international date line, the Tonga Visitors Bureau uses the marketing slogan "where time begins," but they could just as well use "where time stands still."

The Land
Tonga sits on the eastern edge of the Indo-Australian Plate, which is forced up as the Pacific Plate pushes under it at the Tonga Trench. This long oceanic valley running 2,000 km from Tonga to New Zealand is one of the lowest segments of the ocean floor, in places more than 10 km deep. Tonga is on the circum-Pacific Ring of Fire, which extends from New Zealand to Samoa, then jogs over to Vanuatu and the Solomons. Where Tongatapu (a raised atoll), Lifuka (a low coral island), and Vava'u (another uplifted atoll) are today, towering volcanoes once belched fire and brimstone. When they sank, coral polyps gradually built up the islands.

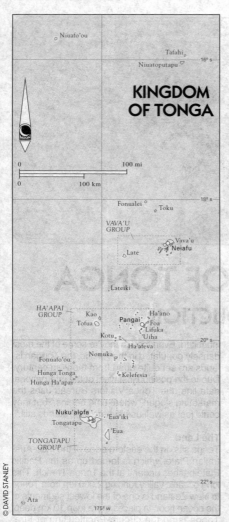

© DAVID STANLEY

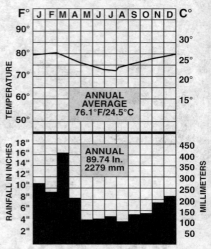

VAVA'U'S CLIMATE

ANNUAL AVERAGE 76.1°F/24.5°C

ANNUAL 89.74 In. 2279 mm

Tongatapu, tilted toward the center, creating cliffs on their outer edges and half-submerged islands facing in. Tonga is moving east-southeast at the rate of 20 millimeters a year and the crack in the earth's crust that originally built Tonga has shifted northwest. Thus, the active volcanoes of today are in a line 50 km west of Ha'apai-Vava'u: Fonuafo'ou, Tofua, Lateiki, Late, Fonualei, and Niuafo'ou have all erupted during the last 200 years.

Climate

The name Tonga means south; it's refreshingly cooler and less humid here than on islands closer to the equator (such as sultry Samoa). December-April is the hot, rainy season, with especially high humidity Jan.-March. June-Aug. can be cool enough to occasionally necessitate a sweater

Tonga gets an average of two tropical hurricanes a year, usually between November and April, although they can occur as late as May. Rainfall, temperatures, and the probability of hurricanes increase the farther north you go. The southeast trade winds prevail from May to November, and easterlies the rest of the year; in Tonga, west and northwest winds herald bad weather. In February and March north winds bring heat waves and heavy rains.

Study the map of Tonga and you'll distinguish four great atolls in a line 350 km long. The two central atolls (Ha'apai) are now largely submerged, with Lifuka and Nomuka the largest remaining islands of each. As Ha'apai sank under the weight of new volcanoes such as Kao and Tofua, the outermost groups, Vava'u and

TONGA AT A GLANCE

ISLAND	POPULATION (1996)	AREA (sq. km)
'Eua	4,924	87
Tongatapu	66,577	259
Ha'apai Group	8,148	109
Vava'u Group	15,779	119
Niuas*	2,018	72
TONGA	**97,446**	**646****

* Niuafo'ou, Niuatoputapu, Tafahi
** inhabited islands only

HISTORY AND GOVERNMENT

Prehistory

According to myth, the demigod Maui acquired a fishhook from Samoa that he used to yank the Tonga Islands out of the sea. He then stamped on the islands to make them flat and suitable for gardening. The historic Polynesians reached Tonga from Fiji more than 3,000 years ago. These early arrivers made incised *lapita* pottery, though the art was lost around A.D. 200. The first hereditary king, or Tu'i Tonga, ruled perhaps around A.D. 950, initiating the "classical era" in Tongan history, which continued until about 1600. Many of the great monuments of Tongatapu were built during this period, which gradually ended after European contact.

THE TU'I TONGAS

The Tu'i Tongas (hereditary kings of Tonga) were considered to be of divine origin. The creator god Tanaloa descended from the sky and had a son, 'Aho'eitu, by a beautiful Tongan girl named Va'epopua, The child became the first of the line, perhaps about A.D. 950. These absolute monarchs were the only Tongan males who were not tattooed or circumcised; there was an elaborate etiquette to be observed in all contacts with their subjects.

Fierce Tongan warriors traveled throughout Western Polynesia in large double-hulled canoes *(kalia),* each capable of carrying up to 200 people. In the 13th century the domain of the Tu'i Tonga extended all the way from Rotuma in the west through part of the Lau Group, Wallis and Futuna, Samoa, and Tokelau, to Niue in the east. The eventual collapse of this empire led to civil and spiritual unrest and a series of Tu'i Tonga assassinations, so in 1470 the 24th Tu'i Tonga delegated much of his political power to a brother, the *hau* or temporal ruler, while retaining the spiritual authority. Later the power of the *hau* was divided between the Tu'i Ha'atakalaua and Tu'i Kanokupolu, resulting in three distinct lines.

European Contact

Although the Dutchmen Schouten and Le Maire sighted the Niuas in 1616, another Dutchman, Abel Tasman, was the first European to visit Tongatapu and Ha'apai. Arriving on 19 January 1643, as Tongans approached his ship in narrow canoes, Tasman fired a gun—terrifying the chief. A trumpet, violin, and flute were then played in succession to this chief's further astonishment. Tasman received sorely needed food and water to carry on with his journey. At one point he escaped disaster by charging full-tilt over the

JOHN WEBBER

Fatafehi Paulaho, the 36th Tu'i Tonga, who hosted Captain Cook at Tongatapu in 1777

Nanuku Reef, which was luckily covered with sufficient water to be traversed.

When Captain Cook visited Tonga in 1773, 1774, and 1777, he and his men were received with lavish friendliness—pyramids of food were offered them, and dances and boxing matches in which little girls and women took part were staged in their honor. (The skillful Tongan pugilists made short work of Cook's crew in a competition.) Some say the islanders intended to roast and eat Cook and his men as part of the feast, but Cook's profuse thanks at his reception prompted them to change their minds. Ever since Cook's visit, Tonga has been known as "The Friendly Islands." Cook never visited Vava'u, which was only "discovered" in 1781 by the Spaniard Antonio Mourelle.

The Formation of a Nation
European contact led to a decline in population as warring chiefs turned newly acquired muskets and cannons on each other. The new armaments also allowed Tongan warriors to conquer the Lau Group of Fiji about this time. Members of the London Missionary Society arrived in 1797, in the middle of these civil wars, but were unable to attract a following, and by 1804 all had left.

A British Wesleyan (Methodist) missionary, Rev. William Lawry, arrived in 1822. He and his associates built the first school in Tonga in 1829, and in 1831 printed the first book, the Bible of course. Their most noteworthy convert (in 1831) was Taufa'ahau, chief of Ha'apai, who defeated two rival dynasties with the missionaries' help and in 1845 became King George Tupou I, ruler of a united Tonga. In 1862 he freed the Tongan people from forced labor on the estates of the chiefs while making hereditary nobles of the chiefs. Tupou I decreed that each of his subjects be allotted a *tax'api* consisting of a town lot and 3.34 hectares of farmland for only T$3.20 annual rental. At the same time, the king established constitutional government, with a Privy Council of his choice and representation for both nobles and commoners in a Legislative Assembly.

This system, institutionalized in the Tongan Constitution of 4 November 1875, remains in force today. A year later Germany concluded a Treaty of Friendship, which recognized Tongan independence and the sovereignty of the king.

King George Tupou I. In 1831 this young chief of Ha'apai was baptized by Wesleyan missionaries. With their help he supplanted the Tu'i Tonga on Tongatapu and in 1845 was proclaimed king, taking the name of England's monarch. The present royal line is descended from him. In 1862 George I freed the Tongan slave class and in 1875 he gave his country the constitution that is in effect today.

Similar treaties were signed with England (1879) and the U.S. (1888). The king's closest adviser in all of this was a Wesleyan missionary, Rev. Shirley Baker, who served as premier during the 1880s. Tupou I died in 1893 at 97 years of age, the creator of a unified Christian Tonga and one of the most remarkable men of the 19th century. The pervasive influence of the missionaries, who dominated Tonga from the early 19th century onward, can still be experienced any Sunday.

The Twentieth Century
Tonga (along with Japan, Thailand, Nepal, and a few Middle Eastern states) is one of the few countries in the world that has never been colonized by a European power. Germany had strong influence in Tonga during the late 19th century

and wanted to include it in its colonial empire but bowed out to the British in exchange for a free hand in Samoa. In 1900 Tupou I's grandson, King George Tupou II (ruled 1893-1918), signed a new Treaty of Friendship with Britain, which gave the latter control of Tonga's foreign affairs as a means of forestalling encroachments by other colonial powers. The British protection remained in effect until 1970, but the rule of the royal family continued unbroken.

Magnificent, much-loved Queen Salote Tupou III ruled Tonga from 1918 until her death in 1965. Her achievements included the reunification of part of the Wesleyan church and the development of public health and education services. In 1953, she won the hearts of millions by riding through London in an open coach, despite tor-

This magnificent bronze statue of High Majesty King Taufa'ahau Tupou IV can be seen at the Taliai Military Camp near Fua'amotu International Airport.

rential rain, at Queen Elizabeth's coronation. In fact, she was only observing the Tongan custom of showing respect for royalty by appearing before them unprotected in bad weather.

Although just short of his mother's two-meter height, H.R.H. King Taufa'ahau Tupou IV, the present monarch, looks every bit the Polynesian king he is. As crown prince during WW II, he studied at the University of Sydney, becoming the first Tongan to earn a university degree. He served as prime minister from 1949 until his coronation in 1967. Tupou IV initiated a cautious modernization program, opening Tonga to the world by having the airport upgraded for jet aircraft and approving the construction of the first large hotels. On 4 June 1970 he reestablished Tonga's full sovereignty, which allowed Tonga to receive aid money from other countries.

Government

Tonga is a constitutional monarchy in which the king rules absolutely. He appoints the 12 members of the Cabinet, including the governors of Ha'apai and Vava'u, who retain their posts for life. They sit in the 30-seat Legislative Assembly or Parliament, along with nine members who represent the 33 Nobles of the Realm, and another nine elected every three years to represent Tonga's 100,000 commoners. The king appoints one of the nobles as speaker of parliament (the king also decides who will hold the 33 noble titles). The king can dissolve parliament, dismiss ministers, veto legislation, suspend habeas corpus, and proclaim martial law at will.

The king's younger brother, Prince Fatafehi Tu'ipelehake, served as prime minister for 26 years until his retirement in 1991. Until May 1998, the king's eldest son and heir, Crown Prince Tupouto'a, was minister of foreign affairs and defense. He resigned on his 50th birthday to devote himself to business activities and the king appointed his youngest son, Prince 'Ulukalala Lavaka Ata, to replace him. It's rumored that the crown prince may soon be appointed prime minister. There are no municipal councils; Nuku'alofa is administered directly by the central government. Though appointed by the king, the judiciary is independent, with the highest court of appeal consisting of three judges from other Commonwealth countries. Tonga faces no external threat but the country still maintains a 200-person defense force, with facilities behind the royal palace, at the airport, and near Queen Salote Wharf (the only other South Pacific countries with armies are Fiji and Papua New Guinea). Much of the press and radio are government-owned, and formal criticism of the king is prohibited.

Yet as educational levels increase and Tongan commoners become economically independent, the power of the privileged few is being called into question. There have been allegations of corruption, and church leaders have backed increased democracy. The 1990 elections gave candidates advocating an increase in the number of people's representatives five of the nine commoner seats, and in August 1992 four of them banded together to form the Tonga Pro-democracy Movement (TPDM). Constitutional reform was discussed at a landmark November 1992 convention, which foreigners and overseas Tongans with foreign passports were prevented by the government from attending.

In subsequent elections the pro-democracy members have been reelected with those from Tongatapu and Ha'apai winning by large margins. Tongatapu representative 'Akilisi Pohiva is the best known spokesman for the TPDM, but unfortunately several attempts to create a viable people's party have degenerated into factional squabbles. In late 1998, the TPDM was reorganized as the Tonga Human Rights and Democracy Movement, in a move intended to put constitutional reform squarely on the national agenda. The old guard has attempted to intimidate the elected members through legal action, and journalists have been imprisoned for reporting events. No one questions the continued existence of the monarchy, and King Tupou IV is dearly loved by most of his subjects, but the intermediate noble class is declining in both economic and political influence.

In a way, Tonga's current political problems are a direct result of the absence of colonization, because a European system of representative government was not instituted in Tonga as part of a normal decolonization process, as happened in virtually every other island state. The world has changed beyond recognition since 1875, yet Tonga's missionary-inspired constitution remains the law of the land. This cannot last forever, and the future of the monarchy may well depend on its ability to adapt to the times and accept a fully elected parliament.

ECONOMY

Agriculture and Land

In Tonga's feudal system, all land is property of the crown but administered by nobles who allot it to the common people. The king and nobles retain 27% of the land for their own use, while the government owns another 18%. Although Tongan commoners still have a right to the 3.34-hectare *tax'api* granted them by King George Tupou I, there's no longer enough land to go around. This system has not been altered substantially since 1862, and a 1976 parliamentary law intended to redistribute unused land was vetoed by the king. Frustrations with the system are relieved by migration to New Zealand, Australia, and the United States. If those avenues were to close, Tonga would face serious unrest. Foreigners cannot purchase land, and even leasing requires Cabinet approval.

Only half the population is involved in the cash economy; the rest live from subsistence agriculture, fishing, and collecting. The production of food, housing, and handicrafts used by the producer is higher than the value of all goods sold for cash, a situation rarely reflected in official statistics. The staples are yams, taro, manioc, and sweet potato. Crops are rotated, and up to two-thirds of a garden is left fallow at any time. In many localities, humans are outnumbered by domestic pigs, which range freely across the islands.

The biggest cash crop is pumpkins (squash), and since its introduction in 1987, this vegetable has become Tonga's biggest export by far, shipped mostly to Japan by air and worth T$11 million a year. More than 13,000 tonnes of Tongan pumpkins supply about half Japan's requirements for November and December, a "niche market" producers in other parts of the world can't cover for climatic reasons. Some 700 small farmers grow pumpkins July-Dec., and overproduction has led to soil degradation, groundwater pollution, deforestation, and an increase in pests. Much of the income has gone into cars, and throughout the day there's now bumper-to-bumper traffic on Nuku'alofa's Taufa'ahau Road as nouveau riche Tongans drive up and down to show off. Tonga's growing dependence on this monoculture carries with it the risk of economic collapse should the Japanese market evaporate due to competition from producers in Vanuatu and New Caledonia, a fall in yields caused by depleted soils, plant disease, or any other cause. In 1998 the harvest was 50% lower than usual due to drought. Vanilla is seen as an alternative, and the production, though still small, fetches top prices on world markets.

Trade and Development

Tonga's main exports in order of importance are pumpkins, vanilla, tuna, leather goods, clothing, coconut oil, and taro. Although it had a favorable trade balance prior to 1960, Tonga now imports seven times as much as it exports, with food imports alone exceeding all exports. Australia and New Zealand profit most from the trade imbalance, selling food, machinery, fuels, and manufactured goods to Tonga. Japan, Australia, the European Union, New Zealand, the United Nations Development Program, and the Utah-based Church of Latter-day Saints are Tonga's largest aid donors, and total aid compensates for a third of the trade deficit.

In 1980 the government created a Small Industries Center (SIC) in the eastern section of Nuku'alofa for companies producing consumer goods for export to Australia and New Zealand under the regional free-trade agreement, SPARTECA, which was designed to correct the imbalance. In recent years the value of SPARTECA had declined due to "globalization," a worldwide liberalization of trade, and Tongan exports of knitwear, leather jackets, and footballs have been pushed off Australasian markets by competitors in Asia. Today companies in the SIC produce mostly for a tariff-sheltered local market. Traditional agricultural exports to New Zealand such as bananas were wiped out by transnational producers and strict quarantine requirements. The replanting of Tonga's aging coconut plantations has been inadequate and copra exports have dwindled to almost nothing in recent years. The Tonga Commodities Board coconut products plant outside Nuku'alofa closed in 1996. Commercial fishing is on the increase with longline vessels supplying tuna to the Pago Pago canneries and quality fish like red snapper to restaurants in Honolulu and Tokyo by air freight.

Tonga has thus far avoided the financial crises that have gripped Samoa in recent years, but both countries are still very much part of the third world. The T$50 million a year remitted by Tongans living abroad, the country's largest single source of income, is crucial to maintaining the balance of payments, covering more than half Tonga's import bill. In future years these amounts could decline as emigrants lose touch with relatives and friends back home. Meanwhile rural areas are neglected as government facilities and light industry gravitate toward Nuku'alofa. A quarter of all Tongans now live in the capital, and hundreds more commute daily from outlying villages. Shantytowns have sprung up in the suburbs of Nuku'alofa, and there's a growing gap between the haves and have-nots. In 1986 the income tax was slashed from 40% to a flat 10% and company taxes were greatly reduced; the lost revenue was made up by a five percent sales tax, an unprecedented shift in taxation from rich to poor. Labor unions are banned.

The royal family itself has used its unquestioned political clout to assemble extensive business interests. Crown Prince Tupouto'a is a major shareholder in Royal Beer Company, MBf Bank Ltd., and Sea Star Fishing Co., plus electricity generation, an insurance company, computer technology, and real estate developments, while Princess Pilolevu Tuita is involved in the airport duty-free trade and satellite communications. According to New Zealand journalist Michael Field, the crown prince and princess have squabbled recently over control of Tonga's lucrative satellite slots.

Communications

In 1989 Tonga scored a coup by claiming six satellite orbital slots, which it registered with the International Telecommunications Union over the objections of most large satellite communications companies. One condition was that the slots had actually to be used within 10 years, so a company called Tongasat was formed with Princess Pilolevu as 60% shareholder. Thanks to American telecommunications experts who arranged the leasing of Tonga's valuable slots, Tongasat managed to get two satellites into orbit launched from Kazakhstan and several more have been sub-let to Asian companies. Tongasat and the government have split income from this arrangement: *Forbes Magazine* reports that Princess P herself has pocketed a cool US$25 million.

A lot of complicated maneuvering has gone on behind the scenes. In 1995 the scheme's Malaysian financiers filed suit when the U.S. partner declared bankruptcy after being paid US$38 million by the Malaysians. The transnational Intelsat has claimed that the scheme violates international agreements which declare that geostationary arcs are common property and not meant to be claimed by countries with the intention of leasing them to third parties. In 1993 an Indonesian company muscled into one of Tonga's slots, and in 1995 they started radio-jamming Tonga's other satellites to warn the Tongans to back off. To remain a commercial satellite superpower, Tonga has had to take on the big boys.

A similar scheme involves the marketing of Tonga's internet code ".to" for use in registering desirable domain names already occupied under the ".com" ending. In its first year, Tonic (www.tonic.to), a join venture between Crown Prince Tupouto'a and a couple of California computer bugs, sold 7,000 domain names at US$50 each. This is a lot cheaper than the US$1,000 a name being charged for Tuvalu's catchier ".tv" ending! (Despite all the high tech dabbling, Tonga's domestic telephone network is unchanged since the early 1950s.)

Sale of Passports

In recent years Tonga has peddled its nationality directly by selling Tongan passports to Hong Kong Chinese and others in need of an alternative nationality. In 1983 Tonga began selling "Tongan Protected Persons" passports to all comers at US$10,000 a shot. As the bearers still required a visa to enter Tonga, many countries, including Australia and New Zealand, refused to recognize them. Thus in 1984 legislation was passed allowing ordinary Tongan passports and naturalization certificates to be issued to anyone willing to pay US$20,000—among the takers were Imelda Marcos and her children. This was questioned by commoner members of the Tongan parliament, who pointed out that the five-year residency requirement was being ig-

nored, so in 1988 the previous legislation was repealed, but the sales strangely continued.

In all, some 450 ordinary passports and another 2,570 "special" passports were sold between 1983 and 1991. The passport scheme has brought in an estimated US$25 million, and the sales may be continuing (although the government periodically denies this). Many countries, including Australia, New Zealand, and Fiji, do not recognize these mail-order passports, and even genuine Tongans traveling on bona fide Tongan passports occasionally face unexpected immigration hassles abroad as a result of this scam. The number of Chinese-operated hotels and restaurants in Nuku'alofa indicates where many of the buyers ended up.

Tourism

Earnings from tourism are higher than all exports combined, and a larger proportion of the tourist dollar remains in Tonga than is the case elsewhere in the Pacific because of the high proportion of small, locally owned guesthouses and motels. Tonga is off the beaten track and is seldom overrun by tourists (Fiji gets 14 times as many visitors). About 26,000 tourists a year visit Tonga, coming from New Zealand, the U.S., Australia, Germany, and Fiji, in that order. Nearly half are overseas Tongans visiting friends and relatives.

Vava'u is being developed as Tonga's main international tourist center, and the European Union has provided funds to upgrade Vava'u's airport to allow direct flights from Fiji. One of the South Pacific's most important yacht charter operations has been based at Vava'u for years, and since 1995 whalewatching has been developed. Scuba diving, kayaking, fishing, and cultural tourism are all on the upswing at Vava'u.

THE PEOPLE

For visitors, Tonga is its culture and people. The Tongans are exceptionally warm, relaxed, impassive toward delays, etc., and with the world's lowest death rate, it seems Tongans even pass away slowly. They have a lot of fun and tease each other and sympathetic visitors constantly. The very happy, contented lifestyle is summed up in expressions like *mo'ui fiemalie* (a contented life), *mo'ui nonga* (a peaceful life), *nofo fiefia* (living happily), and *nofo fakalata* (making others feel at home). It's also said that if a Tongan loses his identity, he will slowly become cold and die.

Tonga is typical of developing countries, with its large families and young population. Tongans reside in small villages near their bush gardens, and except in the Europeanized areas, isolated houses along the roads are rare. Most Tongans live in tin-roofed wooden or cement block houses with electricity and running water, and only 12% still live in traditional thatched *fales*. With 150 people per square kilometer, Tonga is one of the most densely populated countries in the Pacific (twice as dense as the Cooks, three times as dense as Fiji). Yet despite a high birth rate, emigration has kept population figures stable since the 1970s. Around 3,000 Tongans a year leave the country, many for good, and some 24,000 now live in New Zealand, 11,000 in the U.S., and 4,500 in Australia.

In Tonga women have traditionally enjoyed a higher social status than in some other parts of Polynesia due to the *fahu* system, which gives Tongan women certain authority over male family members. The eldest sister is the family matriarch, exercising considerable control over younger brothers, nephews, and nieces. Public life in Tonga, however, is almost completely dominated by men due to sexist succession and land ownership laws, as well as cultural norms.

The missionaries increased the importance of the family unit. Each family member has a role, with the older persons commanding the most respect. Children may reside with an aunt or uncle just as easily as with their parents and are taught obedience from an early age, which is why they are so much better behaved than Samoan children. The most important occasions in Tongan life are first and twenty-first birthdays, marriages, and funerals. Tonga has the lowest infant mortality rate and one of the highest levels of school enrollment in the South Pacific, and 99.6% of Tongans are literate.

Tongans have a long traditional history, and many can name up to 39 generations by heart. There is little social mobility: a commoner can never become a noble, though a noble or a member of the royal family can be stripped of his title. Commoners have been appointed Cabinet ministers through education and ability, how-

ever, and may be elevated to the rank of *mata-pule* (talking chief), a spokesperson for the king or a noble. Ordinary Tongans must use a special dialect quite different from everyday Tongan when speaking to a noble or member of the royal family. An equivalent English example for "eating heartily" might go as follows: commoners *gorge,* the nobles *feed,* and the king *dines.*

To a Tongan, great physical size is the measure of beauty—Tongan women begin increasing prodigiously in beauty from age 15 onward.

Traditional Dress

The *ta'ovala* is the distinctive Tongan traditional skirt. The custom may have originated when Tongan mariners used canoe sails to cloak their nakedness. Made of a finely woven pandanus-leaf mat, the *ta'ovala* is worn around the waist. The men secure it with a coconut-fiber cord, while the women wear a *kiekie* waistband. The sight of a group of Tongan women on the road, each with a huge pandanus mat tied around herself, is truly striking. Worn especially on formal occasions, these mats are often prized heirlooms. Tongans dress in black and wear huge *ta'ovalas* when mourning. The king and queen wear European dress to a European function but dress in their plaited *ta'ovala,* tied around the waist over the *vala* (skirt or kilt), and wear sandals or go barefoot to a Tongan ceremony or entertainment.

Religion

The bold red cross in the upper left corner of the royal red Tongan flag symbolize the facts of life in this country. The Tongan Constitution (drafted by Methodist missionary Shirley Baker) declares the Sabbath day forever sacred: it's unlawful to work, hold sporting events, or trade on Sunday. Contracts signed that day are void. Most tours are also canceled, though picnic trips do run to the small islands off Nuku'alofa. All shops and most restaurants are closed on Sunday. The Sabbath is so strong that even the Seventh-Day Adventists here observe Sunday as the Lord's Day (not Saturday). They claim this is permissible because of the "bend" in the international date line, but it would be intolerable to have two Sunday in Tonga!

Tongans are great churchgoers—a third of all Tongans and most of the noble class are members of the mainstream Free Wesleyan Church. Three other branches of Methodism also have large followings in Tonga: the Free Church of Tonga (9,250 members), the Church of Tonga (6,250 members), and the Tokaikolo Christian Fellowship (2,600 members). In addition, there are 14,200 Mormons, 13,500 Roman Catholics, and 5,000 Seventh-Day Adventists. Smaller groups include the Anglicans, Assemblies of God, and Baha'is. In all, 16 official churches are active in the country, and missionaries from new groups are arriving all the time. Between 1966 and 1992 affiliation in the new religious groups increased from 9.7% to 29.5% of Tongans as all four Methodist churches declined.

Attend the service at Centenary Church (Free Wesleyan) in Nuku'alofa Sunday at 1000 to hear the magnificent church choir and perhaps catch a glimpse of the royal family. Gentlemen are expected to wear coats and ties (although tourists are usually admitted without). After church, the rest of the day is spent relaxing, strolling, and visiting friends—what Tongans like to do anyway, so it wasn't hard for the missionaries to convince them to set aside a whole day for it.

The Mormons

Mormons account for around 15% of the population of Tonga, the highest such ratio in the world. The Church of Latter-day Saints has become the largest private employer in the kingdom, spending more on construction than even the government, and the American church sends far more financial aid to its Tongan flock than the U.S. government provides to Tonga as a whole. Mormon missionary efforts in Tonga are aimed at making this the first country on earth with a Mormon majority.

Assembly line Mormon churches (with their inevitable basketball courts) are popping up in villages all over Tonga as the children of Israel convert in droves to be eligible for the free buildings, schools, sporting facilities, and children's lunches. Many Tongans become "school Mormons," joining as their children approach high school age and dropping out as they complete college in Hawaii. Unlike Cook Islanders and American Samoans, Tongans don't have the free right of entry to a larger country, so church help in gaining a toehold in Honolulu or Salt Lake City is highly valued.

Mormonism still has a lower profile in Nuku'alofa, however, as the king, a Wesleyan, is reputed to be uncomfortable with the new fast-faith religion. A building behind the International Dateline Hotel was a Mormon church until it was judged too close to the palace for comfort. The present Nuku'alofa Tonga Temple, the largest building in Tonga, is beside Mormon-operated Liahona High School near Houma on the opposite side of the island. Recently the king has been refusing to renew any Mormon land leases. Yet the Church of Jesus Christ of Latter-day Saints is a bastion of conservatism and a strong supporter of the political status quo (which is rather ironic in view of American posturing on democracy and human rights in other parts of the world).

CONDUCT AND CUSTOMS

The key to getting things done in Tonga is knowing how to find the right person. Tongans hate to say no to requests, and if you ask people to do things which really aren't their responsibility, they may give the impression of agreeing to do them, but in fact nothing will happen. Tongans in official positions may seem sluggish and could keep you waiting while they finish chatting with friends over the phone. Just keep smiling and be patient: they'll notice that and will usually go out of their way to be helpful once they get around to you. Impatiently demanding service will have the opposite effect (it's illegal to anger or threaten a civil servant in Tonga).

Both men and women appearing in public topless are punished with a T$20 fine. Of course, this doesn't apply to men at the beach. Like Victorian English, Tongans often go swimming fully dressed—most of them don't even have bathing suits. For a Tongan woman to appear in a halter top and miniskirt is almost unthinkable, and female travelers too will feel more accepted in skirts or long pants than in shorts. A woman in a bathing suit on a beach anywhere other than in front of a resort will attract unwelcome attention, and it would be prudent to keep a T-shirt on at all times and to cover your legs with a *lavalava* while out of the water. It's also considered bad form to kiss or even hold hands in public. (Despite all the strident public morality, in private

Tongans are often sexually permissive, and it's commonplace for married men to have affairs.)

In Tonga the possession of dope is a serious offense, and the word soon gets around. Customs watches for yachts with drugs aboard. If you're busted, they'll toss you in a tiny flea-ridden cell and throw away the key. Make no mistake—they mean business.

Be careful too with your gear in Tonga, as there have been reports of thefts—don't tempt people by leaving valuables unattended. Even hotel rooms are unsafe. It's said that a Tongan will never buy anything if he thinks he can borrow or steal it. Thus, *everything* left unattended will be pilfered, especially if it's out where anyone could have taken it. This also applies to food and drink

left in the communal fridge at a hotel or guesthouse which also has Tongan guests. It's safe to invite one or two Tongans to your home or room, but with three or more things will disappear. Items left on the beach while you're in swimming will have vanished by the time you come out of the water. Armed robbery, on the other hand, is almost unheard of.

Dogs can be a nuisance in Tonga, chasing cyclists and barking through the night. They can be especially aggressive as you approach a private residence, but pretending to pick up a stone will usually be enough to scare them away. (Looking at it the other way, you'll see some of the most wretched, abused dogs in the world in Tonga, and it's not surprising that they bite.)

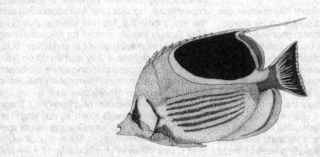

saddleback

ON THE ROAD

HIGHLIGHTS

Tonga stands out for its living Polynesian culture, which can be traced from the Ha'amonga trilithon on northeastern Tongatapu through the ancient *langi* or royal tombs of Mu'a to the gingerbread Royal Palace in downtown Nuku'alofa. Traditional arts and crafts are nurtured and preserved at the Tonga National Center just south of town. The country's most charming town, however, is Neiafu, which faces Vava'u's magnificent Port of Refuge Harbor. In fact, along with Levuka in Fiji and Gizo in the Solomons, Neiafu is one of the three most picturesque towns in the South Pacific.

Tonga's foremost natural feature is probably its coastal cliffs, especially the striking limestone formations at Keleti Beach Resort on Tongatapu, the east coast of 'Eua Island, and the north coast of Vava'u. Lovers of wildlife will not wish to miss the flying foxes of Kolovai on Tongatapu. Humpback whales come to Ha'apai and Vava'u to mate and calve July-Oct., and there are whale-watching cruises from Neiafu at this time. You're even allowed to snorkel with the whales, if conditions allow.

SPORTS AND RECREATION

Although Tonga's preeminent hiking areas are on 'Eua and its only golf course is on Tongatapu, it is Vava'u that has the most to offer water sports enthusiasts. Vava'u is a famous sailing locale with one of the South Pacific's largest yacht charter operations. It's also perfect for ocean kayaking with lots of lovely protected waterways; a kayak touring company operates in this area. Deep-sea anglers too will find Tonga's top charter fishing boats based here. There's also undeveloped potential for windsurfing at Vava'u, but the mecca for regular reef-break surfers is Ha'atafu Beach on Tongatapu. In Samoa the surfing waves tend to be far offshore (boat required), while in Tonga you can often swim out from shore. It's no place for beginners, however. Southern swells arrive May-Sept., northern swells Dec.-February.

Scuba divers are well catered for by professional dive shops in Nuku'alofa, Lifuka, and Neiafu, with many outstanding diving possibilities. Snorkelers have even more options, beginning with the island resorts off Nuku'alofa, all of which operate day-trips by boat. The finest snorkeling off Tongatapu itself is reputed to be at Ha'atafu Beach. At Ha'apai there's excellent snorkeling at the Captain Cook Beach Resort on Uoleva Island. At Vava'u, visitors can get in some excellent snorkeling by taking a day excursion from Neiafu by boat.

PUBLIC HOLIDAYS AND FESTIVALS

Public holidays include New Year's Day, Good Friday, Easter Monday (March/April), ANZAC Day (25 April), Crown Prince's Birthday (4 May), Emancipation Day (4 June), King's Birthday (4 July), Constitution Day (4 November), King Tupou I Day (4 December), and Christmas Days (25 and 26 December).

The **Vava'u Festival** during the first week of May features all sorts of sporting, cultural, and social events to mark Crown Prince Tupouto'a's birthday on 4 May. The **Ha'apai Festival** coincides with Emancipation Day in early June. Nuku'alofa's **Heilala Festival,** with brass band and dancing contests, parades, and sporting competitions, occupies the week coinciding with the king's birthday, the first week in July. The Miss Galaxy beauty contest for *fakaleitis* (men dressed as women) is great fun and always sold-out. On the night of 4 July and again on New Year's Eve, Tongans standing along the beach light palm-leaf torches, illuminating the entire coast in rite called *tupakapakanava.*

Agricultural shows are held throughout Tonga during September and October, with the king in attendance at each. The ferry *Olovaha* makes special trips at these times, so ask and book early. Red Cross Week in May is marked by several fund-raising activities, including a grand ball. During the National Music Association Festival in late June and early July you can hear string bands, brass bands, electric bands, and singers.

A military parade in Nuku'alofa marks the closing of parliament in late October. The Tonga Visitors Bureau should know what's happening.

ARTS AND CRAFTS

Most of the traditional handicrafts here are made by women: woven baskets, mats, and tapa cloth. The weaving is mostly of tan, brown, black, and white pandanus leaves. The large sturdy baskets are constructed of pandanus wrapped around coconut-leaf midribs. A big one-meter-high laundry basket makes an excellent container to fill with other smaller purchases for shipment home. (Remember, however, that the post office will not accept articles more than a meter long or weighing more than 10 kilograms by airmail or 20 kilograms by surface mail, though this does vary according to destination.) The soft, fine white mats from the Niuas, often decorated with colored wool, are outstanding but seldom sold.

Tonga's tapa cloth originates mostly on Tongatapu, where the paper mulberry tree (Broussonetia papyrifera) grows best. When the tree is about four meters high the bark is stripped and beaten into pieces up to 20 meters long, then hand-painted with natural brown and tan dyes. The cloth itself is called tapa but the painted product is known as ngatu. Big pieces of ngatu make excellent wall hangings or ceiling covers. In the villages, listen for the rhythmic pounding of tapa cloth mallets. The women are always happy to let you watch the process, and you may be able to buy something directly from them. Smaller pieces made for sale to tourists are often sloppily painted in a hurried fashion, and serving trays, fans, and purses made from tapa are often in poor taste.

Unfortunately too, Tongan woodcarving is now oriented toward producing imitation Hawaiian or Maori "tikis" for sale to tourists. Some shops will tell you the figures represent traditional Tongan gods, which is nonsense. Buy them if you wish, but know that they're not traditionally Tongan. The beautiful war clubs one sees in museums are rarely made today, perhaps out of fear they might be used! Tongan kava bowls are also vastly inferior to those made in Samoa and Fiji.

FIELD MUSEUM OF NATURAL HISTORY, CHICAGO

Miniature wooden statues of this kind were the only graven images made in Tonga. In 1830 the missionary John Williams witnessed the desecration of five of these at Ha'apai by hanging.

a stylized turtle on a piece of Tongan tapa

Many handicraft shops in Tonga sell items made from turtle shell, whale bone, ivory, black coral, seeds, and other materials that are prohibited entry into the U.S., New Zealand, and many other countries, so be careful. Triton shells, conch shells, giant helmet shells, giant clam shells, winged oyster pearl shells, trochus shells, green snail shells, and other sea shells may also be banned. It's one of the negative aspects of tourism that such a catalog of endangered species should be so widely sold.

ACCOMMODATIONS AND FOOD

All middle and upmarket hotels add five percent sales tax to their rates, plus a further five percent room tax which covers the salaries of the staff at the Tonga Visitors Bureau—money well spent, right? This 10% tax usually won't be included in the amount you're quoted when you ask the price of a room but will be added when the time arrives to pay. We also do not include tax in the Tonga accommodation prices listed in this book.

Inexpensive accommodations are readily available, but upmarket places are less common, and even in the select few, the service is often lacking. Be aware that some of the shoestring and budget lodgings listed herein are extremely basic. Two organized campgrounds are just outside Nuku'alofa and some of the budget beach resorts will also allow you to pitch your own tent on their grounds. Camping was recently banned in Ha'apai, so if you were thinking of unrolling the tent, don't stop there. Unlike in Fiji and Samoa (but as in the Cook Islands), you'll rarely be invited to spend the night in a local home. It's not forbidden to stay with the locals (as it is on Rarotonga), it's just that the Tongans prefer to keep a certain distance between themselves and *palangi* tourists. On the plus side, you won't be expected to conform to as many complex social mores here as you would in Samoa, and people tend to leave you alone.

Self-catering accommodations are harder to find than in Cook Islands or Fiji, and only a few of the guesthouses in Nuku'alofa have cooking facilities. At Ha'apai most accommodations do allow cooking, but grudgingly, and they levy a T$2 pp charge for gas and electricity. Several places at Vava'u allow you to cook. Neiafu and Nuku'alofa have good public markets. Some stores sell horrendous fatty New Zealand mutton flaps called *sipi*, which unfortunately constitute the diet of many Tongans. Canned corned beef and salty luncheon meat are also popular. Restaurant meals are inexpensive, and Tonga is an ice cream lover's paradise with huge, inexpensive cones easy to find in Nuku'alofa. *Ota* is raw fish marinated in lime juice and coconut cream.

The tap water is chlorinated and it won't bother you if you have a strong stomach, otherwise boil it or drink something else. Several readers have reported that the water made them sick. Unfortunately beer is expensive in Tonga because it only comes in little 330-ml bottles, not the big 750-ml bottles used in most other Pacific countries.

SERVICES AND INFORMATION

Visas and Officialdom
Visitors in possession of a passport and onward ticket do not require a visa for a stay of one

month. Extensions of up to six months are possible at T$25 each (although the actual length of the extension is entirely up to the officers).

Government authorization is required to do any sort of scientific research in Tonga, including archaeological excavations and sociological studies. The application fee of T$1,000 is refundable if your project is approved. Clearly, officialdom wants to control just who is poking around. Recently one researcher studying alcoholism had his application rejected. No drinking problems in Tonga, was the reply!

Ports of entry for cruising yachts are Niuafo'ou, Niuatoputapu, Vava'u, Lifuka, and Nuku'alofa. Yachts arriving from the east should call at Vava'u before Nuku'alofa (and Samoa before Tonga), as the prevailing winds make it much easier to sail from Vava'u to Nuku'alofa than vice versa and there are fewer hazardous reefs between Nuku'alofa and Fiji than between Vava'u and Fiji. Customs and immigration are closed on weekends, and even on weekdays once can expect long waits at Vava'u before the officials come aboard to clear you in.

Money

The Tongan *pa'anga* (divided into 100 *seniti*) is worth about the same as the Australian dollar (around US$1 = T$1.65), although the actual value fluctuates slightly. From 1976 to 1991 the *pa'anga* was actually tied to the Australian dollar, but it's now based on a basket of the Australian, New Zealand, and U.S. dollars. There are notes of one, two, five, 10, 20, and 50 *pa'anga,* and coins of one, two, five, 10, 20, and 50 *seniti.* Try to keep a supply of small coins in your pocket if you don't want petty expenditures to be rounded up to your disadvantage. Tongan banknotes are

difficult to exchange outside Tonga, so get rid of them before you leave.

The Bank of Tonga is 40% government-owned, with the Bank of Hawaii and the Westpac Bank of Australia each holding another 30%. Change money at the bank branches in Nuku'alofa, 'Ononua ('Eua), Pangai (Lifuka), and Neiafu (Vava'u). The banks are very crowded on Friday (pay day) but a few branches in Nuku'alofa and Neiafu are open Saturday mornings. Foreign banknotes are changed at a rate about four percent lower than traveler's checks. The banks will give cash advances on credit cards for a T$6 commission. Cash advances through hotels cost about 10% commission and many businesses add 4.5% to all charges paid by credit card. Thus it's probably better to carry the bulk of your travel funds in traveler's checks. There's no American Express representative in Tonga.

Tipping and bargaining are not customary here, although monetary gifts *(fakapale)* are often given to performers at cultural events (Tongans stick small bills onto the well-oiled arms and shoulders of the dancers during the performance). A five percent sales tax is added to all goods and services. It's often hard to tell if this tax is included in the sticker price. Many stores include it, but some (such as Morris Hedstrom Supermarket) add it on at the cash register. At hotels and restaurants, you really never know and the only way to be sure is to ask first.

Post and Telecommunications

The government-owned Tonga Telecommunications Commission (Box 46, Nuku'alofa; tel. 24-255, fax 24-800) runs the domestic telephone service within Tonga, while the British company Cable & Wireless (Private Mailbag 4, Nuku'alofa; tel. 23-499, fax 22-970, www.candw.to) operates the international service. Guess which one is more efficient.

As in Samoa, the local telephone system is hasn't changed much since it was installed in the 1950s, and there are no public card or coin telephones for domestic calls. To place a local call, you must use your

hotel phone or go to a central telephone office and have the clerk dial the number for you. When your party answers, the clerk will direct you to a booth and what you pay will depend on how long you spoke. This procedure must be repeated for each individual call you wish to make. Everyone in the office will hear everything you say as you'll have to shout to be heard at the other end. The upside is that it's cheap: long-distance interisland calls within Tonga are only T$1 for three minutes. Urgent telegrams within Tonga cost 10 cents a word.

In 1995 card telephones were introduced on Tongatapu, but only for international calls. You cannot use these phones to call another island or even the number across the street. International telephone cards are available in denominations of T$5, T$10, and T$20. Not only do they make calling easier and more private but they're also cheaper since three-minute minimums don't apply with the cards. As with all direct-dial telephones in Tonga, the international access code is 00.

Three-minute calls cost T$5 to Australia or New Zealand, or T$9.50 to Canada, the U.S., or Europe. Person-to-person calls are T$2.50 extra. Collect calls are possible to Australia, New Zealand, the U.S., and the U.K. (but not to Canada or Germany). Internationally, faxing is a good inexpensive alternative to telephoning.

The telephone exchanges where you can make phone calls are listed in the travel sections of this chapter. Calls placed from hotel rooms are much more expensive. Directory assistance is 919, the interisland operator 910, the international operator 913. The Telecom "New Zealand Direct" number is tel. 080-0646. Tonga's telephone code is 676.

Cable and Wireless operates Tonga's kalianet.to e-mail service, named for the double-hulled Tongan war canoe called the *kalia*. If any of the e-mail addresses in this book don't work, try substituting candw.to for kalianet.to or vice versa, and consult the e-mail directory at www.candw.to. Nuku'alofa's cybercafe is listed in the Nuku'alofa section.

Business Hours and Time

Normal business hours are weekdays 0800-1300/1400-1700, Saturday 0800-1200. Government working hours are weekdays 0830-1230 and 1330-1630. Banking hours are weekdays 0900-1530. Post offices are open weekdays 0830-1600. Almost everything is closed on Sunday.

Due to its position just west of the international date line, Tonga is the first country in the world to usher in each new day. In fact, the date line seems to have so confused the local roosters that they crow constantly just to be safe. Tonga shares its day with Fiji, New Zealand, and Australia, but is one day ahead of Samoa, Niue, Tahiti, and Hawaii. The time is the same as in Samoa, but one hour behind Hawaii and one ahead of Fiji and New Zealand.

Tonga's sacred Sunday adds to the fun of the date line confusion. Commercial flights (and most other transport) are banned in the kingdom that day. Don't get worried if you suddenly realize that it's Sunday on a flight to Tonga from Honolulu or Samoa—you'll land on Monday. Just keep repeating: "If it's Sunday for the Samoans, it's Monday for the monarch."

Friday is a much bigger party night than Saturday because most Tongans get paid on Friday, so there's money to spend and it doesn't all have to stop at midnight. Only holy rolling is allowed on Sunday, but some bars, discos, and cinemas reopen a few minutes after midnight on Monday morning and try to make up for the time lost on the sabbath.

Electricity

The electric voltage is 240 volts, 50 cycles, with a three-pronged plug used, as in Australia and New Zealand.

Media

The government-owned *Tonga Chronicle* (Box 197, Nuku'alofa; tel. 23-302, fax 23-336, e-mail: chroni@kalianet.to) comes out every Thursday and you can usually pick up a copy at the Friendly Islands Bookshop in Nuku'alofa. The English edition is less extensive than the one in Tongan.

Taimi 'o Tonga (Times of Tonga, Box 880, Nuku'alofa; tel./fax 23-177, www.tongatimes.com, e-mail: times@kalianet.to), is a privately operated Tongan-language weekly paper with a circulation of 6,100.

Also watch for the monthly newsletter *Kele'a* (Box 1567, Nuku'alofa), published by 'Akilisi Pohiva, leader of the democratic reform movement in parliament. The newsletter's attempts to expose corruption among the old guard have made it the object of libel suits involving awards of thousands of *pa'anga* in damages.

The worldwide subscription rate to the bimonthly national news magazine *Matangi Tonga* (Box 427, Nuku'alofa; tel. 25-779, fax 24-749, e-mail: vapress@kalianet.to) is US$25 (airmail)—a practical way to keep in touch. The same company publishes a free bimonthly tourist newspaper called *'Eva.*

Radio
The government-run Tonga Broadcasting Commission (Box 36, Nuku'alofa; tel. 23-555, fax 24-417) transmits in Tongan and English over 1017 kHz AM Mon.-Sat. 0600-2400 and Sunday 1600-2300. FM 97 at 97.2 MHz broadcasts in English only Mon.-Sat. 0630-2300 and Sunday 1600-2300. On both stations you can hear the BBC news at 0700 and Radio Australia news at 0800, followed by a weather report. The FM station presents the news in brief at 1100 and 1700, and major news bulletins at 0900, 1300, and 1900, while the AM station has the Radio Australia news at 2000. An hour of classical music is broadcast over the AM station Sunday at 1630. The TBC transmitter at Vava'u was destroyed during a hurricane and you can only receive the AM station there very weakly. The AM is much stronger at Ha'apai and you should be able to receive both stations clearly on Tongatapu and 'Eua. On shortwave, you'll find them at 5030 MHz.

A private commercial station called The New Millennium Radio A3V (tel. 25-891, e-mail: vearw@alaska.net) at FM 89.1 MHz broadcasts no news but plays the best selection of pop music you'll hear anywhere in the South Pacific. It's part of the empire of the Vea brothers, Ron, Phil, and Sam, who also own Loni's Cinema and the adjacent video rental shop in Nuku'alofa. Ron has lived in Alaska since 1970 and tapes a show there, while Sam actually runs the station and Phil takes his turn as DJ. Christian programming is available at 93.1 MHz FM.

Vavau's local station, FM1, is a private commercial operator broadcasting over 89.3 MHz 24 hours a day.

Information
The Tonga Visitors Bureau (Box 37, Nuku'alofa; tel. 21-733, fax 23-507, www.vacations.tvb.gov.to, e-mail: tvb@kalianet.to) has information offices in Nuku'alofa, Lifuka, and Neiafu. Drop in or write for a supply of free brochures. These offices are good places to ask about events and much useful data is posted on their information boards. Moon Travel Handbooks publishes a *Tonga-Samoa Handbook,* which includes more detail on Tonga, the Samoas, and Niue than can be included here.

TRANSPORTATION

Getting There
Tonga's government-owned flag carrier, **Royal Tongan Airlines** (Private Mail Bag 9, Nuku'alofa; tel. 23-414, fax 24-056, e-mail: rtamktng@kalianet.to), has flights to Tongatapu from Sydney via Auckland twice a week, from Nadi three times a week, and from Auckland four times a week. Weekly flights operate between Apia and Tongatapu (T$303 one-way or T$320 for a one-month excursion return), between Niue and Tongatapu (T$228/357 one-way/roundtrip), and between Nadi and Vava'u (T$265/399 one-way/roundtrip). Royal Tongan also controls seats on one of Air New Zealand's flights to Honolulu with connections to Los Angeles under a code sharing arrangement. In the U.S., call tel. 1-800/486-6426 for information about Royal Tongan, and check their useful internet website (www.candw.to/rta), which explains some of their air passes and provides schedules.

Samoa's **Polynesian Airlines** (tel. 21-566) arrives from Apia, Auckland, and Sydney twice a week. The Fijian airline, **Air Pacific** (tel. 23-423), has service to Tongatapu from Nadi three times a week. Around Christmas all flights are fully booked six months in advance by Tongans returning home.

Air New Zealand (tel. 23-828) has direct weekly flights from Apia, Honolulu, and Los Angeles with connections from London. Their flights between Tonga and Auckland operate three times a week. This Coral Route connection is discussed under **Getting There** in the main introduction.

Samoa Air (tel. 70-644) has services twice a week from Pago Pago to Vava'u (US$235/424 one-way/roundtrip), a useful backdoor route. Their Tonga agents are S.F. Paea & Sons in Neiafu and Teta Tours in Nuku'alofa.

Getting Around by Air

In 1991 **Royal Tongan Airlines** (tel. 23-414) replaced Friendly Islands Airways as Tonga's national carrier. Royal Tongan has Twin Otter flights from Tongatapu to 'Eua (T$19), Ha'apai (T$67), Vava'u (T$129), Niuatoputapu (T$227), and Niuafo'ou (T$279), but never on Sunday. The flights to 'Eua and Ha'apai operate daily, to Vava'u twice a day, to the Niuas every other week. Book a northbound Friday or Saturday flight from Nuku'alofa to escape a depressing Sunday in the capital. Ask about special packages from Nuku'alofa to Vava'u including airfare, transfers, accommodations, breakfast, and some meals. A 30-day "Kingdom Pass" allowing flights from Tongatapu to 'Eua, Ha'apai, and Vava'u is available at T$250 (a 20% savings over regular fares), but it must be purchased beforehand in Europe or North America. The baggage allowance is only 10 kilos, but if your Royal Tongan domestic flights were booked from abroad as part of an international ticket the baggage allowance is 20 kilos. Overweight baggage is 45 cents a kilogram. Always reconfirm your onward flights a few days in advance. "No shows" are liable for a penalty of 50% of the ticket price if they fail to use confirmed space.

Getting Around by Ship

The government-owned **Shipping Corporation of Polynesia** (Box 453, Nuku'alofa; tel. 21-699, fax 22-617), at Queen Salote Wharf, Nuku'alofa, offers reliable boat service among the Tonga Islands. Their large car ferry, the MV *Olovaha*, departs Nuku'alofa every Tuesday at 1730, arriving at Pangai (T$28 deck) very early Wednesday morning and Vava'u (T$42 deck) on Wednesday afternoon. It leaves Vava'u again Thursday afternoon, calling at Pangai in the middle of the night and arriving back in Nuku'alofa Friday afternoon. In Ha'apai the ship calls at both Ha'afeva and Pangai. It's usually punctual.

Deck travel is sometimes very crowded but when the ship isn't too full you can stretch out on the plastic benches or the floor in a clean, protected room. No meals are included. Cabins cost four times the deck fare, as you must book an entire twin room (T$120 double to Ha'apai, T$170 double to Vava'u). There are only four such cabins, and they can be just as noisy as deck, though more comfortable. The Shipping

Corporation runs a boat from Vava'u to Niuatoputapu (T$50) and Niuafo'ou (T$60) about once a month.

The private **Uata Shipping Lines** ('Uliti Uata, Box 100, Nuku'alofa; tel. 23-855, fax 23-860), also known as the Walter Shipping Lines, has four red-and-white ships, the MV *Loto Ha'angana*, the MV *Tautahi*, the MV *'Ikale*, and the MV *Pulupaki*. The 32-meter *Loto Ha'angana*, an old Japanese ferry, is larger and faster than the *Olovaha*, but it does toss a bit more. The *Loto Ha'angana* or *Tautahi* leaves Nuku'alofa Monday at 1700, reaching Pangai in the middle of the night and Vava'u Tuesday afternoon. It departs Vava'u for Ha'apai and Nuku'alofa Wednesday at 1400, stopping at Pangai late that night and reaching Nuku'alofa Thursday morning. No cabins are available. Take food, water, and antiseasickness pills. The *Loto Ha'angana* has lots of long padded benches on which you can stretch out and try to get some sleep if it's not too crowded (as is usually the case between Ha'apai and Vava'u). The loud music broadcast over the ship's public address system all night is a disadvantage.

Other small ships serving Ha'apai irregularly include the wooden *Langi Fo'ou* which leaves Nuku'alofa's Faua Jetty for Nomuka Wednesday mornings, an eight-hour trip.

Several boats shuttle back and forth between Nuku'alofa and 'Eua (2.5 hours, T$6). The blue-and-white *Alai Moana* departs Faua Jetty daily except Sunday at 1300, leaving 'Eua for the return around 0600 in the morning. You pay onboard. It's a safe metal ferry with rows of plastic seats. The 24-meter MV *Pulupaki*, smallest of the Uata Shipping Lines ferries, and the 220-passenger *'Ikale*, also travel between Nuku'alofa and 'Eua. One or the other is supposed to leave Faua Jetty Mon.-Fri. at 1230, returning in the early morning, but the trip is canceled in choppy weather. However you go, be prepared for an extremely rough four-hour eastbound trip and a smoother, faster westbound voyage.

Note that all of the above information is only an indication of what might or should happen in ideal weather—the reality is often quite different. Make careful inquiries upon arrival and be prepared for a few delays. It's all part of the fun. (For information on yacht charters, turn to the **Vava'u** section.)

Airport

Fua'amotu International Airport (TBU) is 21 km southeast of Nuku'alofa. The new terminal building was constructed with Japanese aid money in 1991. The airport is closed on Sunday.

The airport bus (T$6 pp) operates four times a day. If there are two or more of you, the T$12 taxi fare to town is just as good or better. Be sure to check the fare before getting into the taxi, and don't let the driver steer you to some hotel you never intended to stay at just so he can collect a commission. Often they will tell you the hotel you requested is closed only in order to trick you into going where *they* want. Hope that your flight doesn't arrive in Tonga late at night as the taxis demand as much as T$30 then. Avis and E.M. Jones Travel have car rental offices at the airport.

Airport-bound, the International Dateline and Pacific Royale hotels have buses directly to the terminal costing T$6 pp, but they're only worth taking if you're alone. If you're on the lowest of budgets you could also take the infrequent Fua'amotu bus (70 cents) right to the airport access road, or any Mu'a bus to the crossroads at Malapo, then hitch the last six km.

The Tonga Visitors Bureau counter and the MBf Bank exchange office are to the right as you come out of arrivals. The MBf Bank at the airport changes traveler's checks at a rate similar to the banks in town, less their standard T$3 commission. The snack bar at the airport is reasonable and offers a good selection, and across the parking lot is a small farmers market with coconuts, pineapples, bananas, peanuts, etc. The duty-free shop in the departure lounge is also reasonably priced. The departure tax on international flights is T$20 (passengers in transit for less than 24 hours and children under 12 are exempt).

TONGATAPU

Tongatapu's 259 square km are just over a third of the kingdom's surface area, yet two-thirds of Tonga's population lives here. Of coral origin, Tongatapu is flat with a slight tilt—from 18.2-meter cliffs south of the airport to partly submerged islands and reefs to the north. Some 20,000 years ago Tongatapu was blanketed with volcanic ash from the explosion of Tofua Island, creating the rich soil that today supports intensive agriculture.

Tongatapu, or "Sacred Tonga," is the heartland of Tongan culture, history, and political power. Here Captain James Cook conferred with Tu'i Tonga, and the island is still the seat of Tongan royalty. The Tonga National Center outside the capital, Nuku'alofa, showcases Tongan culture, and compelling megalith monuments and royal tombs testify to Tongatapu's historical weight. Vying for visitor attention are noisy colonies of sacred flying foxes, an admirable bird park, breathtaking beaches, remarkable coastlines, tapping tapa mallets, and evocative archaeological remains. And unlike Samoa, no "custom fees" are collected from visitors out to see the island's sights. Captain Cook was enthralled by Tongatapu, and you will be too.

NUKU'ALOFA

Nuku'alofa (population 22,000) is just north of the azure Fanga'uta Lagoon, now sterile after sewage from adjacent Vaiola Hospital eliminated the fish and other marinelife. It's a dusty, ramshackle little place. Tourism, industry, commerce, and government are all concentrated in the town, which retains its slow-paced South Seas atmosphere. You'll find a good selection of places to stay, eat, and drink, reasonable entertainment (except on Sunday), a well-developed transportation network, and many reminders of Tonga's Victorian past and present. The name means "Abode of Love." A few days poking around here are certainly well spent, but this should not be the beginning and end of your Tongan trip as the other islands have even more to offer.

SIGHTS

Begin your visit at **Vuna Wharf,** the main port of entry to Tonga from 1906 until construction of Queen Salote Wharf in 1967. The **Treasury Building** (1928), opposite the wharf, was once

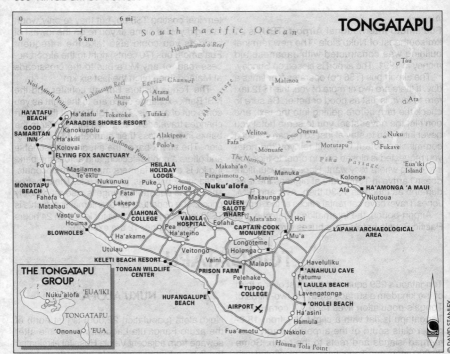

TONGATAPU

South Pacific Ocean

Hakaumama'o Reef

Nui Aunofo Point

Egeria Channel

Hakautapu Reef

Maria Bay

Atata Island

Tufaka

Toketoke

Ha'atafu

Lahi Passage

Malinoa

Tau

Ata

Atā

HA'ATAFU BEACH
PARADISE SHORES RESORT
Kanokupolu
GOOD SAMARITAN INN
Ha'akili
Kolovai
FLYING FOX SANCTUARY
Fo'ui

Alakipeau
Polo'a
Fafa
Velitoa
Onevai
Monuafe
Motutapu

Nuku
Fukave

'Eua'iki Island

HEILALA HOLIDAY LODGE
Masilamea
Te'ekiu
Nukunuku
Puke
Hofoa
Makaha'a
Pangaimotu
Manima
Manuka
Kolonga

Nuku'alofa
HA'AMONGA 'A MAUI
Afa
Niutoua

MONOTAPU BEACH
Fahefa
Matahau
Vaotu'u
Houma
BLOWHOLES
Fatai
Lakepa
LIAHONA COLLEGE
Ha'akame
Pea
VAIOLA HOSPITAL
Ha'ateiho
QUEEN SALOTE WHARF
Eofaha
Mata'aho
Hoi
CAPTAIN COOK MONUMENT
Mu'a

Makaunga

LAPAHA ARCHAEOLOGICAL AREA

Utulau
KELETI BEACH RESORT
TONGAN WILDLIFE CENTER
Veitongo
Holonga
Longoteme
Malapo
Pelehake
Vaini
PRISON FARM
Haveluliku
Fatumu
'ANAHULU CAVE
LAULEA BEACH
Lavengatonga
'OHOLEI BEACH
Ha'asini
Hamula
Nakolo

HUFANGALUPE BEACH
TUPOU COLLEGE
AIRPORT
Fua'amotu

Houma Tola Point

THE TONGATAPU GROUP
Nuku'alofa   'EUA'IKI
TONGATAPU
'Ononua   'EUA

Nuku'alofa's main post office. Nearby on Railway Rd. (named for a former line that once carried copra to the wharf and still Nuku'alofa's only one-way street) is the **House of Parliament,** a small wooden building prefabricated in New Zealand and reassembled here in 1894. The 30 members of parliament deliberate May-Oct. (no visitors). Walk through the park across the street from the parliament building, passing the **Tongan War Memorial,** and turn left on Taufa'ahau Road to the century-old **prime minister's office,** with its central tower.

Continue west across the soccer field beside the Bank of Tonga to the Victorian **Royal Palace,** closed to the public but easily viewed from outside the grounds. This gingerbread palace was also prefabricated in New Zealand for reassembly here in 1867. The second-story veranda was added in 1882. The gables and scalloped eaves of this white frame building are crowned by a red roof and surrounded by Norfolk pines. (The

king and queen no longer live here but in the Fua'amotu Palace south of the airport. The stately villa of the crown prince is at Pea, on the airport road, and across the street from it is the residence of another prince with a pair of white Bengali tigers guarding the gate.)

Many old colonial-style residences line Vuna Road west of the palace, including the **British High Commissioner's residence,** with a flagpole surrounded by cannon from the privateer *Port-au-Prince,* sacked at Ha'apai in 1806. South of the residence is **Mt. Zion,** site of an 18th-century Tongan fortress and, in 1830, the first missionary chapel. This hill is now crowned by several communications towers.

Centenary Church (1952), south of Mt. Zion, is the principle house of worship of the Free Wesleyan Church, the largest of Tonga's three Methodist denominations. Some 2,000 persons can be seated here, and most Sunday mornings the king and queen are among them for the 1000 service. The church's president lives in the impressive mansion (1871) on the west side of the church, a former residence of 19th-century missionary and Tongan premier Rev. Shirley Baker.

East on the south side of Laifone Rd. are the **Royal Tombs,** where Tongan royalty has been buried since 1893. Across Laifone Rd. from the Royal Tombs is another important Free Wesleyan church, which was only completed in 1985. The striking **Basilica of St. Anthony of Padua** (1980), back on Taufa'ahau Rd., is worth visiting for its soaring interior.

Cultural Center

Don't miss the **Tonga National Center** (Box 2598, Nuku'alofa; tel. 23-022), a complex of Polynesian-style buildings built in 1988 beside the Fanga'uta Lagoon opposite Vaiola Hospital using Japanese aid money. Here you'll see handicraft demonstrations (tapa and canoe making, woodcarving, basket making, mat weaving), contemporary art, and historical displays. The Center's impressive Exhibition Hall contains historic photos of Tonga and Samoa, a collection of war clubs and other carvings, and model canoes. The hall is open weekdays 0900-1600, admission T$2.

Weekdays at 1230 the Center prepares a barbecue lunch and traditional fashion show (T$12), and at 1400 the excellent two-hour guided cultural tour begins, featuring a kava ceremony, the telling of ancient legends and myths, and traditional Tongan dancing in the 450-seat amphitheater (T$8). The handicraft workshops will be operating at this time, and craft items may be purchased directly from the artisans. Some of the activities are curtailed or canceled when not enough visitors are on hand, so you might check that there really will be a performance in the amphitheater that day. Tuesday and Thursday are the usually the best days to come; otherwise just visit the museum and craft shop and come back for the evening performance another day.

Not to be missed is the dinner show put on every Tuesday and Thursday at 1900 (T$20). The package includes a visit to the exhibition hall, string band entertainment, kava drinking, an all-you-can-eat buffet dinner of authentic Tongan cuisine, and some very good traditional dancing (take small banknotes to give to the dancers). A small additional charge is collected for minibus hotel transfers. Advance reservations are required if you want to take lunch or dinner. Reserve the evening shows before 1630 at either the Tonga Visitors Bureau or directly by phone. Admission for children under 12 is half price to all of the above events.

Sports and Recreation

Since 1984 Bob and Sioa Holcomb of **Coralhead Diving Ltd.** (Box 211, Nuku'alofa; tel. 22-176) have offered scuba diving using the dive boat *African Queen*. A two-tank boat dive will cost T$95 pp, plus five percent tax. Lunch at Pangaimotu Island is T$10 extra. They depart Mon.-

the Royal Palace at Nuku'alofa

Island athletes play with a passion. Here Tonga meets Samoa at the annual Three-Nations Tournament in Suva, Fiji.

TONGA CHRONICLE

Sat. at 1000. Coralhead also does one-week PADI certification courses (T$400 pp), an excellent opportunity to learn diving. They will rent or repair equipment and fill tanks, and they specialize in underwater photography and night dives. Drop into their office on the back street behind Davina's Restaurant near Faua Jetty for information.

Tonga's newest scuba operation, the **Deep Blue Dive Center** (Box 913, Nuku'alofa; tel. 25-392, fax 29-647, e-mail: deepblue@kalianet.to), on Wellington Rd. near Fakalato Chinese Restaurant, is under German management. In 1999 they bought out another local scuba operator, and while much of Coralhead's trade comes from government and business contracts, Deep Blue caters almost exclusively to the tourist market. A full-day package, including two dives and lunch, is T$105/120 without/with equipment. Reductions are available for five or 10 dives, and snorkelers can go along for T$35. Their open-water certification course is T$400. Their 15-meter dive boat *Deep Blue* is always accompanied by a speedboat for fast pickups and deliveries. Visibility ranges from 15 meters within the Tongatapu Lagoon to 50 meters on the barrier reefs. A wetsuit is recommended during the cooler months, April-August.

The nine-hole **Tonga Golf Club** (no phone; closed Sunday) is opposite the indoor stadium at Alele near Veitongo on the road to the airport. Greens fees are only T$5 but club hire is not available. Saturday 1130-2100, the club bar is

worth a stop. The Heilala Classic Golf Tournament is at the beginning of July. The club is easily accessible on the Folaha, Malapo, Vaini, or Veitongo buses.

Friday or Saturday at 1500 (April-June) catch a game of rugby at the Teufaiva Stadium. During the soccer season (May-July) you can watch the teams compete at the Pangai Soccer Field on the waterfront next to the Bank of Tonga Saturday at 1500. Joggers meet in front of the Bank of Tonga every Monday at 1700 for a recreational run. It's a good way to meet local expats.

ACCOMMODATIONS

The accommodations listings below are arranged beginning with those closest to Queen Salote Wharf and Faua Jetty, then southwest through town. The only places with satisfactory communal cooking facilities are Kulukulu Backpackers, Toni's Guest House, Sela's Guest House, Breeze Inn, Angela Motel, Winnies Guesthouse, Heilala Holiday Lodge, Friendly Islander Hotel, and Captain Cook Apartments, although not all rooms at these have access. Unless otherwise stated, add 10% tax to all accommodation rates quoted below.

Shoestring
The **Kulukulu Backpackers and Tentsite** (Box 1682, Nuku'alofa; tel. 22-412, fax 24-113), next

door to the Friendly Islander Hotel, is three km east of town. The road next to Flemming Engineering leads directly back to the shady campsite where you'll pay T$6 pp to pitch your own tent. There's also an unusual domed dormitory with rooms of three and four beds at T$9 pp. Otherwise take one of the four beds on the second floor of the wooden building opposite the waterfront at T$12 pp. Communal cooking and fridge facilities are provided in both dorms and picnic tables are available for campers. Bring groceries as no stores are nearby. The Octopusy Bar adjacent to the campground has another bizarre dome which conveys whispers from one side of the room to the other. This eccentric place is the creation of a Danish woman named Brida Hou—a memorable place to stay. Although a little far from town, it's quite convenient to Queen Salote Wharf and Faua Jetty (take the Va'epoua bus from opposite the Tonga Visitors Bureau).

Kimiko's Guest House (Box 1323, Nuku'alofa; tel. 22-170), next to the Chinese Embassy on Vuna Rd., has nine bare but clean rooms with shared bath at T$10 pp (discounts for long stays). Empty beds in the double rooms are filled up as new guests arrive—singles must share or pay for both beds. There are no cooking facilities in this old wooden house (where the author stayed on his first visit to Tonga in 1978) but their agreeable Chinese restaurant is one of the few places open on Sunday. The fresh sea breeze is another plus (though no fans are in the rooms).

Toni's Guest House (Toni, Kesi, and Vili, Box 3084, Nuku'alofa; tel. 21-049, fax 22-970), on Mateialona Rd. near Queen Salote Memorial Hall, has eight clean rooms with shared bath at T$10 pp (bring mosquito coils). It's a good place to meet other travelers as guests swap stories around the kava bowl every evening. There's a pleasant lounge, but Toni's biggest advantage are the cooking facilities, which are the best you'll find in the shoestring range. Kesi's full day minibus tour is a bargain at T$15 pp (T$20 for nonguests), otherwise the Mu'a and Hihifo buses stop right across the street from the guesthouse if you'd rather go on your own. Toni's rents bicycles to guests only (T$5-10 a day), and snorkeling gear is free. Some travelers find Toni's English reserve and Kesi's forthright enthusiasm a bit odd, but you'll enjoy being with them if you accept them as they are. Toni charges T$6 pp for airport transfers. Don't believe airport taxi drivers who tell you this place is closed or full: they only want to take you elsewhere in order to collect a commission—insist on being driven straight to Toni's.

Though a bit out of the way, **Sela's Guest House** (Box 24, Nuku'alofa; tel. 21-430, fax 22-755), south of town, has been a favorite of overseas volunteers working in Tonga since the mid-1970s. There are nine clean rooms with shared facilities at T$15/24 single/double, plus a T$8 eight-bed dormitory. The six rooms with private bath and hot shower are T$30/36 double/triple. Discounts are available for long stays. Cooking

kava session at Toni's Guest House, Nuku'alofa

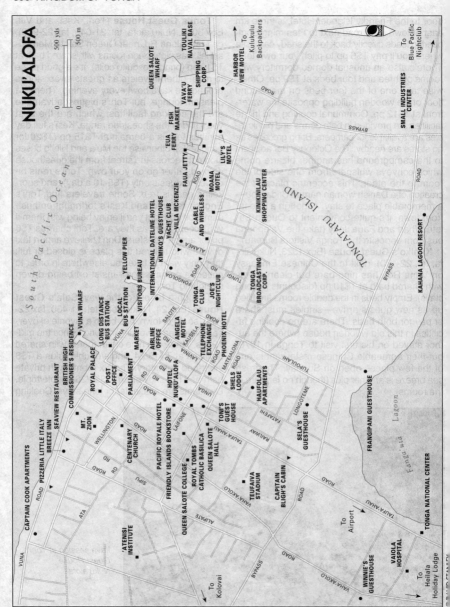

facilities for guests are provided, or you can order a full breakfast for T$4.50 and a large dinner for T$10. Sela serves the best home-cooked meals you'll receive at any guesthouse in Nuku'alofa (which perhaps accounts for the many repeat visitors). If noise bothers you, however, ask for a room away from the VCR and dining room. On the positive side, you can sit and watch videos or CNN to your heart's content. It's a good family-style place to relax and local meet people, and it's seldom full. The Halaleva bus from opposite the Tonga Visitors Bureau will bring you to within a block and a half of the guesthouse (ask).

Budget

The **Harbor View Motel** (Box 83, Nuku'alofa; tel. 25-488, fax 25-490), next to the Fakafanua Center opposite Queen Salote Wharf, has 12 clean rooms with private bath in a modern three-story building. Prices range from budget rooms downstairs with shared bath at T$35/50 single/double, to standard a/c rooms on the middle floor with private bath at T$60 single or double, and deluxe rooms on the top floor with fridge at S$120 single or double. No cooking facilities are available but a buffet breakfast is included. It's a good medium-priced choice near the interisland ferries and some colorful eating and drinking places.

The five-room **Fasi-moe-Afi Guest House** (Box 1392, Nuku'alofa; tel. 22-289, fax 23-313), next to the Visitors Bureau on Vuna Rd., is T$15 pp, including a good breakfast. The lighting in the rooms could be better—ask for one on the outside. The adjacent cafe/pizzeria is great for cappuccino and a sandwich on the terrace. The Fasi-moe-Afi is something of a hangout for Italian backpackers, and a live band plays in the back yard until well after midnight on Thursday and Friday nights.

The **Breeze Inn** (Box 2739, Nuku'alofa; tel. 23-947, fax 22-970), next to the Seaview Restaurant west of the palace on Vuna Rd., has seven spacious rooms with private bath (hot water) at T$30/40 single/double. Communal cooking facilities are available. This place is run by a very helpful Japanese woman who keeps everything spotlessly clean, so make it your choice if you're the fussy type.

Two-story **Angela Motel** (Box 1617, Nuku'alofa; tel. 23-930, fax 22-149), on Wellington Rd. in the center of town, has eight small, clean rooms with private bath at T$20/30/45 single/double/triple. The Taiwanese managers provide guests with a common kitchen and fridge. It's convenient enough for a couple of nights.

Winnies Guesthouse (Box 3049, Nuku'alofa; tel./fax 25-215), on Vaka'akolo Rd. near Vaiola hospital, two km south of the center, tries to recapture the atmosphere of an old South Seas guesthouse. The four rooms with shared bath are T$25 pp including a fruit and toast breakfast, and good communal cooking facilities are available. It's comfortable, with a plush sitting room where videos are shown nightly, and Winnie Santos and her son Marc are very helpful. The Vaiola bus stops at their door.

A variety of accommodations are available at **Heilala Holiday Lodge** (Box 1698, Nuku'alofa; tel. 29-910, fax 29-410), in a pleasant rural setting at Tofoa, three km south of town (off the road to the airport). The four fan-cooled rooms upstairs in the main two-story house are T$24/28 single/double, and there's also a larger family room at T$32 for up to three. Bathrooms are shared (hot water and *very* clean) and communal cooking facilities are provided. Out back in the garden are two thatched *fales* with bath costing T$45 single or double. The six new a/c deluxe bungalows with fridge and TV are T$60. In addition, Heilala offers Tonga's number one **camping facilities** across the street at T$6 pp. There's a rain shelter, picnic tables, and adjacent toilets/showers, and you can make tea from the lemongrass growing in the garden or feed on the papayas and bananas. If you don't have a tent, they'll rent you one at T$2 a night. When enough guests are present, an *umu* lunch is prepared at the campground at T$8 pp. A portable swimming pool and restaurant are on the premises. The whole place runs efficiently under the firm hand of a German woman named Waltraud Quick (or Maria as the Tongans call her) and her more laid-back son Sven. They arrange six-hour island tours with German-speaking guides at T$35 pp (minimum of four); one day they cover the west side of the island, another day the east side. Two weeks free luggage storage if offered against a T$20 deposit that can be applied to future accommodation charges (after two weeks the deposit is nonrefundable). Many of the guests are German or Swiss, which surprisingly seems to put off the

Germans as much as it does some of the other nationalities. Airport transfers are usually free (T$3 pp for campers)—ask for Sven at the airport. Heilala is easily accessible to town by bus or taxi, and bicycles are available at T$5 a day.

Inexpensive

The 31-room **Friendly Islander Hotel** (Box 142, Nuku'alofa; tel. 23-810, fax 24-199), on Vuna Rd. 500 meters beyond the Shell oil storage tanks three km east of town, has long been a favorite medium-priced place to stay. The 12 older fan-cooled apartments with cooking facilities and balcony in a two-story building near the main road are T$50/60 single/double for a one-bedroom or T$60/70 for a two-bedroom. The eight smaller bungalows without cooking facilities across the lane are T$65/75, while the six larger a/c units (also without cooking facilities) are T$85 for the first person, then T$10 for each additional person. All units have a fridge. In the hotel's rear garden is the Culture Bar, dedicated to the concept of "ecotourism," with a small botanical garden, a woodcarvers workshop currently run by master carver Steven Fehoko, a kava drinking hall, and a regular bar. Campers are allowed to pitch their own tents in this garden and a cultural show with *umu* cooking is organized for groups. A restaurant, swimming pool, and the 'Ofa Atu Night Club round out the facilities. The Friendly Islander is run by Papiloa Foliaki, a former elected member of parliament and current head of the local transvestite association—an interesting person to meet! The hotel is easily accessible on the Va'epopua bus from opposite the Tonga Visitors Bureau.

Captain Cook Vacation Apartments (Phillip Vea, Box 1959, Nuku'alofa; tel. 23-615, fax 25-600), on Vuna Rd. facing the lagoon a kilometer west of the Royal Palace, offers four two-bedroom apartments accommodating up to four persons at T$55/65/75/85 single/double/triple/quad. Each apartment has a kitchen, living room, and private bath. It's an excellent choice for two couples traveling together, but book ahead.

The German-owned **Hotel Nuku'alofa** (Uthana Sanft Taumoepeau, Box 32, Nuku'alofa; tel. 24-244, fax 23-154), above the MBf Bank on Taufa'ahua Rd., has 14 spacious a/c rooms with private bath and fridge at T$60/75/90 single/double/triple. There's a restaurant and bar.

Moderate

Anne and Milton McKenzie's **Villa McKenzie** (Box 1892, Nuku'alofa; tel./fax 24-998), on Vuna Rd. near the Yacht Club, offers four comfortable rooms with bath in a colonial-style house at T$85/115 single/double including tax and full breakfast. There's a spacious lounge, but no cooking facilities for guests (dinner is T$15 pp extra). Although expensive for what is offered, it's a good alternative to the Dateline and Pacific Royale, with a lot more South Seas atmosphere.

The three-story, government-owned **International Dateline Hotel** (Box 39, Nuku'alofa; tel. 23-411, fax 23-410) on Vuna Rd. was originally built in 1967 to accommodate guests at the coronation of King Taufa'ahau Tupou IV. The 76 a/c rooms with private bath and fridge begin at T$81/94/105 single/double/triple in the old wing along Vuna Road. The rooms in the adjacent new wing on Tupoulahi Rd. are better at T$109/120/130. Renovations and extensions are planned for the millennium celebrations. The Dateline has a pleasant resort feeling and the location is excellent. Their reasonably priced restaurant is one of the few open to the public on Sunday, and Polynesian dance shows are staged here Wednesday and Saturday nights at 2030. If you pay T$18 for the buffet (Wednesday) or the set three-course menu (Saturday), there's no cover charge. Otherwise T$5 is collected at the door. Despite the flip-flop-shod waiters, persons dressed in shorts, T-shirts, or sandals are not admitted to the dining room. A cold beer by the Dateline's pool is the perfect way to top off an afternoon and nonguests are allowed to swim upon payment of a T$2 fee (remember this if you're stuck in town on Sunday). Excursions to the islands just off Nuku'alofa can be booked at the hotel's tours and information desk, and transportation to the wharf is included.

The more commercial **Pacific Royale Hotel** (Box 74, Nuku'alofa; tel. 23-344, fax 23-833) on Taufa'ahau Rd. is owned by the Ramanlal brothers, sons of a Fiji Indian father and Tongan mother. The 15 standard rooms are T$70/85/95 single/double/triple, the 45 superior rooms T$99/115/125. All 60 rooms have private bath, fridge, and noisy air-conditioners, but they're dimly lit and rather overpriced. Back from the flashy reception area, just past the restaurant, is a tiny garden and swimming pool. Although the service is good here, the Dateline is a more memorable place to stay.

Long Stays
The information board at the Tonga Visitors Bureau lists furnished houses for rent at T$300-500 a month. You could also talk to Jimmy Matthews at the **House Rental Agency** (Box 134, Nuku'alofa; tel. 22-011, fax 22-970; weekdays 0930-1200) in the Tungi Arcade.

Also consider Dr. Mumui Tatola's **Olo Resort** (Box 2834, Nuku'alofa; tel. 29-945), beside the Fanga'uta Lagoon, four km south of town on the airport road. The eight smaller *fales* with private bath and cooking facilities are T$150 a month, while two larger houses are T$500 a month. Beds and cooking utensils are provided, but you have to pay for your own gas, water, and electricity, and supply your own sheets. The units are in a garden setting, some near the road, others pleasantly located on a slope overlooking the lagoon. Inquire at Olota'ane Store which is accessible on the Vaiola bus.

FOOD

Budget
'Ahopanilolo's Training Restaurant (tel. 25-091), down the street beside St. Mary's Catholic Cathedral opposite Queen Salote Wharf, serves a "pot luck" lunch at T$3-6 on Tuesday, Wednesday, and Friday 1200-1400. It's open only during the school year, March-Nov., but is always fun.

John's Place Takeaway (tel. 21-246), on Taufa'ahau Rd. in the center of town and opposite Vaiola Hospital (close to the Tonga National Center), dishes out hamburgers, grilled chicken and chips, and cassava and curry. It's okay for a quick snack, but with a little effort you'll do better elsewhere for the same money. They're open until midnight, but closed Sunday. **Angela Restaurant** (tel. 23-341; closed Sunday), next door to John's Taufa'ahau Rd. location, is similar but better.

Akiko's Restaurant (tel. 25-339; open Mon.-Fri. 1130-1400 and 1830-2000), in the basement of the Catholic basilica on Taufa'ahau Rd., has long been a budget standby. The lunch special is good, and there's a more extensive menu at dinner (but no alcohol).

Captain Bligh's Cabin (tel. 23-841), on Taufa'ahau Rd. next to Asco Motors south of the center, has a nice terrace where you can enjoy lunch specials at around T$4. Beer is sold.

Chinese
One of the best value Chinese places is **Kimiko Restaurant** (tel. 22-170) on Vuna Rd. facing the waterfront: try the wonton soup (T$2). Kimiko's is one of the few places open on Sunday.

The attractive **Fakalato Chinese Restaurant** (tel. 24-044, closed Sunday), above a supermarket on Wellington Rd., serves medium-priced Cantonese dishes of the type familiar to North Americans, so there will be no difficulty ordering. (While you're there, check out the Italian ice cream place nearby on the corner of Taufa'ahau Road.)

Italian
The **Italian Garden Restaurant** (tel. 23-313), at the Fasi-moe-Afi Guest House near the Tonga Visitors Bureau on Vuna Rd., serves pizzas big enough for two or three people. The appealing garden atmosphere compensates for the slow service, so long as you're not in a hurry. It's one of the few places in Nuku'alofa that's open for dinner on Sunday (1800-2300).

Pizzeria Little Italy (tel. 21-563; Mon.-Sat. 1200-1400/1830-2300), west on the waterfront beyond the Seaview Restaurant, serves some of the tastiest pizza and pasta in Tonga.

Upscale Restaurants
Several seafood restaurants are opposite the fish market at Faua Jetty, including **Davina's Restaurant** (tel. 23-385; closed Sunday), the **Waterfront Grill** (tel. 24-692), and **Lily's Chinese Restaurant** (tel. 24-226). Davina's has an elegant indoor dining room with a piano. The **Billfish Bar and Restaurant** (tel. 24-084, closed Sunday), opposite Queen Salote Wharf, has Italian dishes.

Nuku'alofa's finest place to eat is the **Seaview Restaurant** (tel. 23-709; weekdays 1800-2200, closed Saturday and Sunday), in a colonial-style house on Vuna Rd. west of the palace. The German chefs, Lothar and Martina, ensure that the food and atmosphere are excellent. Red snapper is around T$20, lobster or steak T$25, and tropical fruit appears in some dishes. They're open for dinner 1800-2200 (reservations recommended), and if you've got anything to celebrate or just want to treat yourself right, this should be your choice.

Groceries

Talamahu Market (closed Sunday) has all the fruit and vegetables you'd expect, and most prices are posted (beware of overcharging if they're not). Unexpectedly, you're not allowed to eat in the market, as the police may advise you if you do.

The large **Morris Hedstrom Supermarket** (tel. 23-355), opposite the market on Salote Rd., opens weekdays 0800-1800, Saturday 0800-1900.

Nuku'alofa's largest supermarket is the **Kinikinilau Shopping Center** (tel. 24-044; Mon.-Thurs. 0730-1800, Friday 0730-2100, Saturday 0730-1300) on Salote Rd. toward Faua Jetty. The adjacent bottle shop is called the Supa-Kava Market.

The **Tonga Cooperative Federation Store** (tel. 23-777), on Taufa'ahau Rd. opposite Tungi Arcade, is often cheaper than the others.

If you'll be spending a Sunday in Nuku'alofa, buy a few snacks on Saturday to tide you over as the whole town will be dead.

ENTERTAINMENT

Nuku'alofa's only movie house is **Loni's Cinema** (tel. 23-621), also known as Finau Theater Twin. Films begin Mon.-Sat. at 2000, with additional showings at 1300, 1500, 2200, and midnight on certain days. The Sunday midnight showing gets around Tonga's notorious blue laws, but all films are heavily censored. Expect the movie to start 20 minutes late if they think they can sell a few more tickets (admission T$3).

Friday is the big night at Nuku'alofa's discos because on Saturday they must be firmly shut by midnight. Amusingly, many of them reopen a few seconds after midnight on Sunday, and there's dancing until sunrise Monday morning. Such is the way of The Lord! At most of the places mentioned below, men must wear long pants and a shirt with a collar if they want to be admitted. These rules are for the convenience of doormen trying to keep out troublemakers, but there may be no exceptions. A $100 silk Gucci T-shirt won't do if it doesn't have a collar.

The trendiest disco is currently Italian-operated **Ambassador Night Club** (tel. 23-338), just beyond the Tonga National Center south of town. The location is nice next to Fanga'uta Lagoon and you can even get a table right beside the water. It's open Mon.-Sat. from 2000 (no cover Monday, Tuesday, Wednesday, and sometimes Saturday)—take a taxi to get there.

Also very popular is the **Blue Pacific International Night Club** (tel. 25-994), at Maufanga on the Bypass Rd. four km southeast of town (take a taxi). They're open Thursday, Friday, and Saturday nights, playing rock music and reggae. When you tire of dancing inside, you can sit out on the terrace and chat. It's safe, and large crowds turn out for the various beauty pageants, including one for cross dressers.

The downmarket disco at the **Phoenix Hotel** (tel. 23-270) has live music Mon.-Sat. from 2000. Occasional fistfights break out here among the local Tongans.

Joe's Tropicana Top Club (tel. 21-544), on Salote Rd., offers rock music by Pacific Comets and the Barbarians. Watch your drinks when you get up to dance. Right next door is the even rougher **Jungle Niteclub.** These places are okay for single males but not recommended for women or couples.

Bars

Friday nights Wanda's Bar at the **Pacific Royale Hotel** has a happy hour from 1800 to closing with T$2 Royal beer and T$1.50 wine.

The **Yacht Club** (tel. 21-840) on Vuna Rd. is a good place for a beer, but sandals and shorts are not acceptable dress. Despite the name, this club is not involved in any yachting activities but foreign visitors are welcome. It's one of few bars open on Sunday (1100-2300)!

Drink with the local elite at the **Tonga Club** (tel. 22-710). You're supposed to be a member, but you'll be welcome if you look all right. They're open daily until 2300 (on Sunday enter through the side door).

The quaint, old **Nuku'alofa Club** (tel. 21-160), on Salote Rd. near the Royal Palace, has been a hangout for local male expats since 1914, and they're a bit selective about who they let in: poorly dressed men and females of all descriptions are most unwelcome. Before you'll be served, the bartender will have to find someone to sign you in, and you'll probably be asked where you're staying (don't say the Pacific Royale unless it's true as the manager is a regular here). Watch the reaction if you mention a backpacker hostel.

The **Utulea Club** on Unga Rd., a block and a half up from the market, is a local kava drinking bar (T$1.50 a bowl).

Cultural Shows for Visitors

Traditional Tongan dancing can be witnessed at Fafa Island Resort on Monday nights, at the Tonga National Center on Tuesday and Thursday nights, at the International Dateline Hotel on Wednesday and Saturday nights, and at the Good SamariTAN Inn on Friday nights. Package tours with dinner and transfers are available to all of the above.

Intellectual Activities

The privately run **'Atenisi Institute** (Box 90, Nuku'alofa; tel. 25-034 or 24-819, fax 24-819, http://kalianet.candw.to/atenisi), in the western part of the city, began as an evening high school in 1963 but now offers university-level courses right up to Ph.Ds. It has an international reputation for its classical school of thought—a bastion of critical mindedness and creative thinking in the devout/happy-go-lucky South Pacific! During the school year (Feb.-Oct.) there's a free public lecture at the Institute every Monday at 2000. It's a good opportunity to meet a few of the students over coffee, but you might call ahead or visit beforehand to check the subject and to make sure there really will be a lecture that week. The traditional graduation ceremonies in November are not to be missed if you happen to be there at the

time. (The Institute receives no government or church funding, and is in urgent need of overseas assistance. Unfortunately, the Tongan Government has attempted to cripple this unique institution it doesn't control by insisting that all foreign funding proposals go through official channels, then deliberately holding up the paperwork until the application deadlines have passed.)

SHOPPING

Handicraft prices in Tonga have increased sharply in recent years but you can still find bargains if you shop around. Baskets, mats, and occasionally tapa are reasonable buys, and there's no hard sell anywhere, so you can browse at leisure. A good place to begin is **Langafonua,** the Tongan Women's Association Handicraft Center (tel. 21-014) on Taufa'ahau Rd. in the center of town. Also try the **Friendly Islands Marketing Cooperative Handicraft Shop** (Box 523, Nuku'alofa; tel. 23-155), otherwise known as "FIMCO" or "Kalia Handicrafts," opposite the Tungi Arcade. A fishing goods shore behind FIMCO sells snorkeling gear.

Also check upstairs at **Talamahu Market,** where you can buy directly from the craftspeople, but avoid buying anything at the market on a cruise-ship day when prices are jacked up. Tapa is best purchased directly from the producers—just listen for the sound of the beating while you're touring the island. In the market tapa sells for T$10 a "lane" or line.

The handicraft shop at the **Tonga National Center** is more expensive, and their woodcarvings are mostly nontraditional masks and tikis. The whalebone carvings sold here are prohibited entry into most countries under endangered species legislation, as is the black coral jewelry. It's a shame the center sells this type of tacky tourist art.

Ginette at **Tapa Craft** (no phone; weekdays 1200-1600), next to the Baha'i Temple on Lavina Rd., makes small tapa souvenirs and dolls which are excellent souvenirs. She also sells used paperbacks at T$1 apiece, and trades two of your books for one of hers. (If you love cats, drop in to visit Ginette's large family.)

The **Philatelic Bureau** (Box 164, Nuku'alofa; tel. 22-238), above the post office, sells beautiful stamps and first-day covers from Tonga and Niuafo'ou.

Bring with you all the film you'll need as it's rather expensive in Tonga.

SERVICES AND INFORMATION

Money

The Bank of Tonga (tel. 23-933; weekdays 0900-1530, Saturday 0830-1130), on Taufa'ahau Rd., and the ANZ Bank (tel. 24-332; Mon.-Fri. 0900-1600, Saturday 0830-1130), diagonally opposite the police station, change traveler's checks without commission (except Saturday when a 50-cent charge applies). The Malaysian-owned MBf Bank (tel. 24-600), below Hotel Nuku'alofa, charges T$2 commission all the time. Outside banking hours the Dateline Hotel will change money for about two percent less than the banks. You must show your passport.

The Bank of Tonga gives cash advances on MasterCard and Visa for T$6 commission, and they'll store valuables for you in their vault at T$5 per sealed envelope. American Express is not represented here.

Post and Telecommunications

Postage in Tonga is inexpensive compared to other countries, but if you plan on making any heavy purchases it's a good idea to drop in at the post office (tel. 21-700) beforehand to check on the rules and rates. It should be possible to mail parcels up to 20 kilograms by surface mail, although this does vary according to the destination country. Poste restante mail is held "one year," or until they get tired of seeing the letter, at which time it's sent back. If you're expecting a parcel, ask them to check that too. The DHL Worldwide Express agent (tel. 23-617) is next to Loni's Cinema on Wellington Road.

To make a domestic long-distance telephone call to 'Eua, Ha'apai, Vava'u, or anywhere else in Tonga you must go to the Telecom Telephone Exchange on Unga Rd. (open 24 hours daily).

The Cable and Wireless office (tel. 23-499) on Salote Rd. is open for international telephone calls, faxes, and telegrams Mon.-Fri. 0600-2400, Saturday 0700-2400, Sunday 1600-2400. You can receive faxes sent to fax 676/22-970 here at 50 cents a page.

Card telephones for international calls only are outside the main post office, at the Cable and Wireless office on Salote Rd., at the airport, and at a few other locations around Nuku'alofa. The post office sells the cards.

Internet Access

The Kalia Cafe (tel./fax 25-733, http://invited.to/kaliacafe, e-mail: kaliacafe@invited.to; open weekdays 0800-1800), on the top floor of the Tonga Cooperative Federation Building on Taufa'ahau Rd. opposite Tungi Arcade, offers casual walk-in internet access at T$16 an hour, broken down into four 15-minute blocks. They're helpful in setting up a "free" e-mail address—the world at your fingertips. Breakfast is served 0800-1000, coffee anytime.

Visas and Officialdom

You can get an extension of stay for T$25 from the Immigration Office (tel. 23-222; Monday, Tuesday, and Thursday 0900-1200 and 1400-1600, Wednesday and Friday 0900-1200) at the central police station on Salote Road.

The countries with diplomatic representatives in Nuku'alofa are France (tel. 21-831), on Taufa'ahau Rd., Germany (tel. 23-477), on Taufa'ahau Rd. between the Pacific Royale Hotel and Air Pacific, Korea (tel. 24-044), on Salote Rd., New Zealand (tel. 23-122), on Salote Rd. opposite the post office, Sweden (tel. 22-855), on Salote Rd. opposite the Reserve Bank of Tonga, China (tel. 21-766), on Vuna Rd., and the United Kingdom (tel. 24-285), on Vuna Rd. west of the Royal Palace.

The European Union (tel. 23-820) has an office on Taufa'ahau Rd. near Asco Motors. The Australian High Commission (tel. 23-244; weekdays 0900-1100), on Salote Rd. behind the International Dateline Hotel, also represents Canadians. The U.S. is not represented in Tonga, and U.S. citizens in need of assistance must contact the embassy in Suva, Fiji (tel. 679/314-466, fax 679/300-081).

Cleaning and Cutting

Savoy Dry Cleaners (tel. 23-314; Mon.-Fri. 0800-1800, Saturday 0800-1400), on Fatafehi Rd. south of the center, washes and dries laundry at T$1.20 a kilo. Unfortunately there have been reports of items going missing here.

Baby Blue Beauty Salon (tel. 22-349), next to the Baha'i Temple on Lavina Rd., is an upscale hairdresser charging T$7/10 for men's/women's haircuts.

Yachting Facilities

Cruising yachts can tie up to the seawall in the small boat harbor beside Queen Salote Wharf three km east of Nuku'alofa, though the channel is only two and a half meters deep in the center. Customs is on the wharf, but immigration is at the police station in town. Keep valuables carefully stowed, as there have been many thefts from boats here.

Information

The Tonga Visitors Bureau (open Mon.-Fri. 0830-1630, Saturday 0830-1230; tel. 21-733) on Vuna Rd. is usually helpful (if disorganized) and has lots of free brochures. Peruse their notice boards for all the latest tourist news. They will also help you make your accommodation or tour bookings.

Maps

Get good maps from the Lands and Survey Department (tel. 23-611) in the back yard of the Ministry Block.

Navigational charts (T$14 each) of Tonga, Samoa, and New Zealand are available at the Hydrographic Office (tel. 24-696; weekdays 0800-1600) at Touliki Naval Base, just east of Queen Salote Wharf. The hassle here is that you must first go the base to select your charts and get an invoice, then you must visit military headquarters near Centenary Church in town to pay, then return to the base with the stamped invoice to pick up the charts. The Dateline Bookshop (Box 1291, Nuku'alofa; tel. 24-049), opposite Loni's Cinema on Wellington Rd., sells some of the same nautical charts at T$16 each without all the running around.

Bookstores and Libraries

The Friendly Islands Bookshop (tel. 23-787, fax 23-631, e-mail: fibs@kalianet.to), below Tungi Arcade, is great for browsing. Ask for books by local authors 'Epeli Hau'ofa, Pesi Fonua, Konai Helu Thaman, and Tupou Posesi Fanua. They also carry Tongan music cassettes and compact discs, topographical maps of Tonga, and the *Tonga-Samoa Handbook,* which also covers

Niue. For a mail-order list of books on Tonga write: Friendly Islands Bookshop, Box 124, Nuku'alofa. Manager David May and his staff have built this bookshop into one of the best in the South Pacific.

The 'Utue'a Public Library (Box 1, Nuku'alofa; tel. 21-831; open Mon.-Fri. 1500-2100, Saturday 1000-1500), below the Catholic basilica on Taufa'ahau Rd., charges T$5 annual membership. There's also a good library in the **University of the South Pacific, Tonga Campus** (tel. 29-055) near the Golf Club at Ha'ateiho, out on the road to the airport. Ask to see their collection of antique Tongan war clubs.

Travel Offices

The Air New Zealand office (tel. 23-828) is in the Tungi Arcade. The Air Pacific agent is E.M. Jones Ltd. (tel. 23-423) on Taufa'ahau Road. The Royal Tongan Airlines office (tel. 23-414) is in the Royco Building on Fatafehi Road. Polynesian Airlines (tel. 21-566) is at the corner of Fatafehi and Salote Roads.

If you need a travel agent, Vital Travel (Box 838, Nuku'alofa; tel. 23-617) next to Loni's Cinema on Wellington Rd. is recommended.

Health

Medical and dental consultations are available at Vaiola Hospital (tel. 23-200), just outside town on the way to the airport.

Unless you have unlimited time and are on the barest of budgets, it's better to attend the German Clinic (Dr. Heinz Betz, tel. 22-736, after hours tel. 24-625), adjacent to the International Pharmacy on Wellington Rd., a block east of the cinema. Clinic hours are weekdays 0930-1230/1500-1900, but make an appointment. Next door is Dr. Lee Saafi's Town Clinic (tel. 24-784 or 23-695).

A recommended dentist is Dr. Sione Ui Kilisimasi (tel. 24-780), beside Fasi Pharmacy Clinic on Salote Rd. near the Australian High Commission.

TRANSPORTATION

For information on air and sea services from Tongatapu to the other Tongan islands, see the chapter introduction.

Ferries to 'Eua leave from Faua Jetty, but all ships to Ha'apai and Vava'u depart the adjoining Queen Salote Wharf. The office of **Uata Shipping** (tel. 23-855) is upstairs in the building at the corner of Taufa'ahau and Wellington Roads. The **Shipping Corporation of Polynesia** office (tel. 21-699) is at the entrance to Queen Salote Wharf.

By Bus

A local bus station opposite the Tonga Visitors Bureau has buses to Halaleva, Ma'ufanga, Va'epopua, and Vaiola. The Halalevu bus goes south to Fanga'uta Lagoon, then east to Queen Salote Wharf. The Va'epopua bus travels east to Queen Salote Wharf and the Friendly Islander Hotel. The Vaiola bus goes south to the hospital.

Opposite the Ministry Block farther west on the waterfront is another station with long-distance buses to marked Fahefa or Ha'akame to the Houma blowholes, marked Hihifo or Masilamea to the Kolovai flying foxes and Ha'atafu Beach, marked Veitongo, Folaha, or Vaini to the golf course or Tongan Wildlife Center, marked Malapo, Lapaha, or Mu'a to the Lapaha archaeological area, and marked Niutoua to the Ha'amonga trilithon. Fares are 50 cents to the blowholes, 60 cents to the Lapaha tombs, 70 cents to Ha'atafu Beach, and T$1 to the Ha'amonga trilithon. Visitors often use these buses.

The bus to the airport (70 cents) from opposite the Ministry Block might be labeled Halaliku or Fua'amotu. Some (but not all) of the larger Liahona buses also pass the airport, as does the large green-and-yellow Malolelei Transport bus. It's unusual for a tourist to take one of these buses to the airport as the entire tourism establishment assumes you'll want to take a special airport bus or a taxi.

The last bus back to Nuku'alofa from Kolovai and Ha'amonga is at 1500. The buses stop running around 1700 and don't run at all on Sunday. They're inexpensive and relatively efficient, and a great way to observe Tongan life.

Taxis

Throughout Tonga, registered taxis have a "T" on their license plate. Meterless taxis at the market are T$1 for a trip in town, T$2 and up for a longer trip in the vicinity, T$12 to the airport. Always ask the price beforehand. Taxis must purchase a special police permit to work on Sunday, so you won't see many around that day, and if you want one then, arrange it with a driver on Saturday and expect to pay a higher fare. Also, only telephone for a taxi at the exact moment you need it. If you call and ask them to come in 30 minutes they'll probably forget and not come at all. City Taxi (tel. 24-666) has a stand near Teta Tours.

Some taxi drivers double as tour guides, and an island tour with them will run T$6-80 for up to four people (check the price beforehand). There have been reports of thefts in taxis, involving drivers who removed objects from handbags left in the car while visitors got out to take photos, etc., so be forewarned.

Car Rentals

Foreign and international driver's licenses are not accepted in Tonga, so before renting a car you must first visit the Traffic Department at the Central Police Station (tel. 23-222) on Salote Rd. (weekdays 0830-1230 and 1330-1630) to purchase a Tongan driver's license (T$10). You must queue up several times—once to get the form, another time to pay, then again to get a stamp—so allow at least an hour. This is strictly a revenue generating excercise and no practical test is required.

The speed limit is 40 kph in town and 65 kph on the open road. Speed limits are strictly enforced on Tongatapu by police with hand-held radar, and on-the-spot T$50 fines are routine. Avoid hitting a pig, as heavy compensation will have to be paid. Also beware of getting hit from behind when you stop. Never drive a car in Tonga unless you're sure the insurance is valid, otherwise you'll have big problems in case of an accident. Driving is on the left.

The main car rental Agencies in Nuku'alofa are **Avis** (Box 74, Nuku'alofa; tel. 23-344, fax 23-833), at the Pacific Royale Hotel, **E.M. Jones Travel** (tel. 23-423), Taufa'ahau and Wellington roads, **Sisifa Rental Cars** (tel./fax 24-823), at Kiwi Tonga Garage on Salote Rd. behind the Chinese Embassy, and **Budget Rent a Car** (Box 51, Nuku'alofa; tel. 23-510, fax 24-059), on Taufa'ahau Rd. next to Asco Motors south of town.

By Bicycle

Rather than going to all the trouble and expense of renting a car, see Tongatapu by bicycle. From

Nuku'alofa you can easily reach all the main sights in two days, visiting the east and west sides of the island on alternate days. The main roads are excellent without too much traffic, and steep hills don't exist. The open landscape invites you to look around at leisure and there are lots of small villages. Abundant road signs make it very easy to find your own way, but don't trust the indicated distances. Cycling can be tiring and dusty, but the friendly islanders are quick to smile and wave at a pedaling visitor. And if you happen to see a long dark limousine with a police escort coming your way, pull over and let them pass: you're about to see the king and queen!

Quality 15-speed mountain bikes are for rent at **Niko Bicycle Rental** on the waterfront opposite the Dateline Hotel. They charge T$8/18 for one/three days. Many guesthouses also rent bicycles. A bicycle tour is a good way to liven up a dull Tongan Sunday, provided you've reserved your bike by Saturday morning.

Local Tours

The easy way to see Tongatapu is on a bus tour with **Teta Tours** (Box 215, Nuku'alofa; tel. 21-688, fax 23-238, e-mail: tetatour@kalianet.to), at Railway and Wellington Roads. Three-hour sightseeing tours to western and eastern Tongatapu are T$15 pp each, and they also book day cruises to Fafa Island Resort at T$35 including lunch. If you're interested, check well ahead, as they need a certain number of people to run a tour and don't go every day. The friendly, helpful staff can also book hotel rooms anywhere around Tonga.

Kingdom Tours (tel. 25-200, fax 23-447), in the Tungi Arcade next to Air New Zealand, also offers a variety of tours and cruises at slightly higher prices. The Tonga Visitors Bureau can also help arrange sightseeing tours. Few of the road tours operate on Sunday and it's more common to do a boat trip to one of the islands off Nuku'alofa that day (see **Getting There** in the Offshore Islands section that follows).

The 12-meter motor catamaran *Hakula* (Stuart and Francis Bollam, Box 1969, Nuku'alofa; fax 23-759), based at Faua Jetty, does day charters out to uninhabited islands like Malinoa and Nuku off northern Tongatapu at T$250 for up to seven people (bring your own lunch). They also offer extended charters to the idyllic atolls of the Ha'apai Group at T$500 a day for the boat, comfortable sleeping arrangements for up to six included. Catering on the overnight trips is T$25 pp for three meals. They'll do fun fishing along the way, but game fishing is not their specialty. Stuart and Francis are friendly, down-to-earth hosts who will do their best to make your trip a success without adding a lot of unnecessary frills.

Pacific Island Seaplanes (Box 1675, Nuku'alofa; tel. 25-177, fax 25-165, e-mail: pacisair@kalianet.to) uses a six-seater Canadian Beaver seaplane based on the Fanga'uta Lagoon next to the Tonga National Center for flightseeing trips all around Tonga. A scenic flight around Tongatapu costs T$85 pp (minimum of four), but their most unique offering takes you to the volcanic island of Tofua in the Ha'apai Group (T$250 pp, minimum of four). You land on a freshwater crater lake and hike across the active, smoking volcano. For an extra T$50 pp, this trip can be extended with flightseeing down the eastern Ha'apai chain.

WESTERN TONGATAPU

Take the Hihifo bus (70 cents) or ride a bicycle to Kolovai to see the **Flying Fox Sanctuary,** where countless thousands of the animals *(Pteropus tonganus)* hang in casuarina trees for about a kilometer along the road. Flying foxes are actually bats (the only mammals that can fly) with foxlike heads and wingspans of up to a meter across. Nocturnal creatures, they cruise after dark in search of food and hang upside down during the day. Legend says the bats were a gift from a Samoan maiden to an ancient Tongan navigator. Considered sacred, they may only be hunted by members of the royal family.

Just beyond Kolovai is the turnoff for the **Good SamariTAN Inn,** 1.5 km off the main road. Farther west, behind the primary school at **Kanokupolu,** is the *langi,* or stone-lined burial mound of the Tu'i Kanokupolu, an ancestor of the present royal family. The stones to built this tomb were quarried at nearby **Ha'atafu Beach,** and a few partially cut slabs are still anchored to the bedrock at the water's edge, just where the access road meets the beach. The marinelife at Ha'atafu is good because it's a designated "reef reserve" and there's a T$200 fine for fishing.

Ha'atafu is a *palangi* beach, which means there's no hassle about swimming on Sunday, but if you come for a picnic or a swim don't leave any rubbish or you'll also be liable for the fine. There's excellent snorkeling, especially at high tide—see dozens of species of fish. Just watch out for an east-to-west current. Some of the best reef-break surfing in Tonga is here, also at high tide, but even then it's challenging due to the shallow water, and a protective wetsuit is almost essential equipment. On the plus side, the waves are only 100 meters offshore. The Paradise Shores Resort at Ha'atafu Beach serves reasonably priced food and drink to nonguests.

Hihifo buses from Ha'atafu head straight back to town, but there's no bus from Fo'ui to Fahefa. If you want to go on to the blowholes discussed below, you'll find it a pleasant five-km walk (or hitch).

Accommodations

The **Good SamariTAN Inn** (Box 214, Nuku'alofa; tel. 41-022, fax 41-095) on Kolovai Beach, 18 km west of Nuku'alofa, is not such a great choice. Although prices have crept up here in recent years, the rooms are as basic as ever. The nine older bungalows with shared bath are T$35/50 single/double, while three newer bungalows with private bath are T$45/60/75 single/double/triple. One deluxe two-bedroom bungalow with private bath and cooking facilities is T$50/70/85. All prices include breakfast, and weekly rates are available. You can pitch your tent on the grounds for T$10 pp. No cooking facilities are provided, so you must use the Inn's expensive and variable restaurant/bar which sits on a large concrete terrace overlooking the rocky shore. Friday night there's a buffet dinner accompanied by Polynesian dancing (T$20 pp,

plus T$5 pp for return bus transfers from Nuku'alofa, if required). On Sunday they prepare an *umu* lunch (T$15). On cruise-ship days the Inn overflows with day-tripping passengers (fortunately, they're not that frequent). Take the Hihifo bus to Kolovai, then walk 1.5 km to the Inn. A taxi from Nuku'alofa will cost T$12, from the airport T$20. Budget to inexpensive.

If you came to Tonga for the sand, tan, and salt, you'll find it at **Paradise Shores Resort** (Box 976, Nuku'alofa; tel./fax 41-158), in a coconut grove on Ha'atafu Beach, near the end of the road, three km north of Kolovai. In July 1997 an Arizonan named Dave Bergeron opened this place with nine simple thatched *fales* at T$35 single or double. There are also a few set tents and a long thatched dormitory *fale*, all T$10 pp. Camping with your own gear is T$10 per tent. Dave's guests share common toilets, showers, and cooking facilities (outside alcoholic drinks are not allowed on the premises). The resort bar is reasonable, and the restaurant serves steaks or pan fried fish at around T$13. Less expensive sandwiches are also available and you get a great ocean view from the restaurant terrace. The large Elvis photo over the bar explains Dave's hairdo (ask him to do an impersonation, if you get him going). Paradise Shores experiences water shortages, but it's on a better beach than the Good SamariTAN with great snorkeling. It's a nice relaxed place to stay—a mecca for surfers and backpackers. There's even a jacuzzi and satellite TV! Bicycles are for rent. This resort is just a five-minute stroll from the Hihifo bus stop. It often fills up on Saturday night, so check to see if any rooms are available before heading out for the weekend. Budget.

For many years Tonga's premier surfing resort has been the **Ha'atafu Beach Motel** (Box 490,

Nuku'alofa; tel. 41-088, fax 22-970). No sign advertises this motel, but it's just 20 meters down the road opposite Paradise Shores. The Ha'atafu Beach is run by Australian surfer Steve Burling, who first came to Tongatapu in 1977, and whose son Michael is Tonga's national surfing champion. Unlike his neighbor, Steve doesn't cater to day-trippers who only drop in for lunch or drinks. The eight thatched *fales* with shared facilities are T$90/130 single/double including breakfast, buffet dinner, and nonmotorized sporting equipment. Shared rooms are T$70 pp. These prices only apply if you book directly; through a travel agent it's about 20% more. Call ahead if you don't have a booking, as they only take 15 guests at a time and are often full. There's a 10% discount if you stay a month (many do). The dining room, lounge, and public toilets have electricity, but kerosene lamp lighting is used in the *fales*. The meals are ample and excellent, and videos are shown every evening. When enough people are interested, Steve organizes boat trips for snorkeling, fishing, or surfing on outlying reefs (T$10 pp). The peak surfing season here is June, July, and August with five great left-handers within a 10-minute walk of the motel, as southern swells generated around New Zealand crash into the Ha'atafu coast. From January to March you have a choice of four right-handers and one left nearby, but at this time it's usually better to take a boat around to the reefs on the northwest side of Tongatapu, which catch waves rolling down from Hawaii. Steve knows all the better waves and his motel is *the* place for serious surfers (you must bring your own board). Inexpensive.

SOUTHERN TONGATAPU

Surf forced through naturally formed air vents creates spectacular **blowholes** on the rocky, terraced southwest coast near Houma, 15 km from Nuku'alofa. From the end of the road, walk along the path to the right. Waves batter the coral cliffs and spout water up to 30 meters in the air through eroded tunnels. These impressive blowholes number in the hundreds—come at high tide on a windy day! Bus service from Nuku'alofa to Houma is fairly frequent and continues west to Fahefa.

Just east of Utulau a dirt road branches off the paved highway (and bus route) between Houma and Nuku'alofa via Pea and runs along the south coast. Three km along this dirt road is **Keleti Beach Resort,** with more blowholes and several small but strikingly beautiful beaches and pools protected from the open sea by unusual coral terraces. Keleti is down a road to the right, distinguishable from other similar roads by the electricity lines. As previously mentioned, there's no bus service east of the Utulau-Pea road, so you're better off coming by bicycle.

The **Tongan Wildlife Center** (tel./fax 29-449), also known as the Veitongo Bird Park, is near the coast, a short distance east of Keleti on the south coast road. If you want to come by bus you'll have to walk about 2.5 km south from the main highway at Veitongo (a taxi from the corner will only be T$2). The Center is unique in Tonga for its small bird park and botanical garden. Examples of most native Tongan land birds are kept in aviaries brimming with vegetation—take the time to wait for them to appear. The small botanical garden displays all of the common Polynesian food plants, and at the entrance is an informative photo display on Tongan birds and reptiles. The Center is open Mon.-Sat. 0900-1600, Sunday and holidays 0900-1800. It's run by a nonprofit organization working to save endangered species of Tongan birds, so your T$3 admission fee goes to a good cause.

Also on the south coast is **Hufangalupe** ("Pigeon's Doorway"), a huge natural coral bridge with a sandy cove flanked by towering cliffs, six km east of the bird park and four km from Vaini, the closest bus stop. Make your way down the inside of the fault from the back to see the bridge and sea before you. As you return to the main south coast road, watch for a path on the left at the bottom of a slight dip, which leads down to a lovely white beach (beware of theft while you're swimming).

Accommodations

Secluded **Keleti Beach Resort** (Box 3116, Nuku'alofa; tel./fax 24-654), on the south coast 10 km from Nuku'alofa, has four individual *fales* with private bath and cold showers at T$30/40 single/double. Four duplex *fales* with shared facilities are T$30/40 single/double, and families can rent an entire duplex unit for T$60 and comfortably accommodate two adults and two children. Weekly rates with full board are available. No cooking facilities are provided, but meals prepared by an Italian chef are served Western style in a restaurant overlooking the sea. The accommodations are better than those at the other three beach resorts on Tongatapu, and if you don't mind paying T$25-40 pp a day for meals, Keleti is an excellent choice. The coast here is strikingly beautiful with several small beaches, blowholes, and coral terraces—in fact, this is Keleti's main attraction. Several golden sandy beaches are at your disposal, and one can snorkel among the brightly colored tropical fish in the large tidal pools at the foot of the resort, just be aware of the currents. Otherwise just sit on the rocks watching the waves crash onto the reef. The Tongan Wildlife Center is only a short walk away. This is the least crowded of the Tongatapu beach resorts, and in the off season (Dec.-April) you could have the place to yourself. It's isolated here, so be aware of theft. You should also know that the Italian owners tend to ignore their guests unless they speak Italian and the place is often empty. To get there from Nuku'alofa take the Folaha, Malapo, Vaini, or Veitongo buses to the turnoff, then a taxi three km down to the resort for T$2. A taxi straight from Nuku'alofa or the airport shouldn't be more than T$10. Budget.

EASTERN TONGATAPU

Tupou College (tel. 32-240) at Tuloa is three km off the airport road. No bus service reaches the college, but you can take a Malapo, Lapaha, or Mu'a bus to Malapo, then walk south on the road beside the Mormon church. Tupou College is the oldest secondary school in the South Pacific, established by the Free Wesleyan Church in 1866, and it's believed that the first royal capital of Tonga was near here. The college has a small museum of dusty local relics, crafts, and artifacts. There are no fixed hours, but someone will let you in if you ask at the school office.

The main reason to come is the **Tuloa Rainforest Reserve,** the last six hectares of natural forest remaining on Tongatapu. Most of the forest was cut down during the building of Fua'amotu Airport in 1940, and this remaining fragment is just 900 meters southeast of the college administration building. Take the road south beside a deep pit behind the library, and turn left onto a dirt road after 300 meters, then right to an old information shelter. Although the reserve is not as well cared for as might be desired, many of the trees are labeled, and colorful butterflies flutter across the trails. More importantly, Tuloa shelters a large colony of flying foxes, and it's much more intriguing to observe them here in their natural habitat than along the main road at Kolovai.

NORTHEASTERN TONGATAPU

Across the lagoon from Nuku'alofa, just southwest of Mu'a is a monument marking the spot where in 1777 Captain Cook landed from his ship the *Endeavor* and rested under a banyan tree (which has since disappeared). He then continued into Lapaha, the capital of Tonga at the time, to visit Pau, the Tu'i Tonga. Retrace Cook's footsteps into this richest archaeological area in western Polynesia.

For more than 600 years beginning around A.D. 1200, **Lapaha** (Mu'a) was the seat of the Tu'i Tonga dynasty. Nothing remains of the royal residence today, but some 28 *langi* (burial mounds of ancient royalty) have been located in or near Mu'a. Due to local objections, none have yet been excavated. Several of these great rectangular platforms with recessed tiers of coralline limestone are clearly visible from the main road, including the *langi* of the last Tu'i Tonga (1865), a Catholic, which has a cross on top.

The finest of the terraced tombs, rather hidden down a side road, is the **Paepae 'o Tele'a,** built during the early 17th century for the 29th Tu'i Tonga. Notice in particular the gigantic L-shaped monoliths at the corners, the slanting upper surfaces, and the feet that extend underground. In its context, this mighty monument has all the power and emotional impact of a classical Greek temple. Adjacent to the Paepae 'o Tele'a is the **Namoala,** a three-tiered pyramid with the stone burial vault still intact on top. The **Hehea mound** opposite Namoala bears another two vaults.

The *langi* of Lapaha are the most imposing ancient tombs in the South Pacific and rank with the *moai* of Easter Island and Huahine's Maeva ruins as major archaeological sites. The beating of tapa mallets from houses all around the *langi* adds an otherworldliness to this magical place. Bus service from Nuku'alofa to Mu'a (20 km) is frequent throughout the day, making it easy to visit.

HA'AMONGA 'A MAUI

Catch the Niutoua bus (T$1) to this famous trilithon, Tonga's most engaging relic, 32 km east of Nuku'alofa. The structure consists of an arch made from three huge rectangular blocks of nonstratified limestone. Two upright pillars of coral, each about five meters high, support a central lintel that is 5.8 meters long and weighs 816 kilos. The name means "The Burden of the God Maui" because, according to myth, the hero Maui brought the trilithon here on his shoulders all the way from Wallis Island using the connecting stone as his carrying pole.

Various other theories have been advanced to explain the origin of this massive 12-metric-ton stone archway. Some believe it was the gateway to Heketa, the old royal compound of Tonga. Others have called it Tonga's Stonehenge and assert that grooves incised on the upper side of the lintel could have been used in determining the seasons. To emphasize this concept, three tracks have been cut from the trilithon to the coast, the better to observe sunrise on the equinox, as well as the summer and winter solstices. This would have been useful to determine the planting and harvesting periods for yams or the sailing seasons. Most scholars believe, however, that the grooves were cut long after the trilithon was built and discount their utility as an astronomical calendar.

Since few archaeological excavations of ancient monuments have been conducted in Tonga, it's not known for sure when or why the Ha'amonga 'a Maui was built. Local tradition attributes it to the 11th Tu'i Tonga, Tu'itatui, who reigned around A.D. 1200. Evidently this king feared that his two sons would quarrel after his death, so he had the trilithon erected to symbolize the bond of brotherhood uniting them. As long as the monument stood, its magic would uphold social harmony.

Nearby is a 2.7-meter-tall slab called the **'Esi Makafaakinanga** against which, it's said, this king would lean while addressing his people, a precaution to prevent anyone from spearing him in the back. His name means "the king who hits the knees" because Tu'itatui would administer a sharp slap with his staff to anyone who came too close to his regal person. The area between this slab and the Ha'amonga was the meeting place or *mala'e* where the king would receive tribute from Samoa, Futuna, Wallis, Rotuma, and Niue, all of which were subservient to Tonga at that time.

Beyond the slab is three-tiered *Langi Heketa,* believed to be the oldest of Tongatapu's *langi* and the prototype of those at Mu'a. It's believed that either Tu'itatui or a female member of his family is buried here. It was Tu'itatui's son Tal'atama who moved the capital to Mu'a, which offered far better anchorage for their large seagoing canoes. In the bush behind Langi Heketa are a number of large platforms or *paepae* on which the royal residences would have stood.

Bus service to the trilithon is about hourly until 1700, and the trilithon is just beside the road. If you have time, follow one of the tracks down to the rocky coast. Actually, you'll need more than an hour to visit this interesting area and read all the posted explanations. When you've seen enough, just start walking back along the road and flag down the first bus that passes.

OFFSHORE ISLANDS

Some of the many small islands off Tongatapu's north coast bear small tourist resorts that are favorite day-trip destinations for tourists staying in Nuku'alofa, especially on Sunday. Pangaimotu Island and Makaha'a Island tend to cater to budget or independent travelers, while Fafa Island is more upmarket, and Atata Island is set up for packaged tourists from New Zealand. Scuba diving is possible upon prior arrangement, but these are mostly picnic places where you go to get some sun and have a day at the beach.

Accommodations

Pangaimotu Island Resort (Box 740, Nuku'alofa; tel. 22-588, fax 23-759), also known as "Tongan Beachcomber Island Village," is the closest island resort to Nuku'alofa. It's owned by the royal family and the name means "royal island." The four simple *fales* are T$45/60 single/double, while the six-bed dorm is T$20 pp and camping is T$15 pp. No cooking facilities are provided, and meals at their restaurant are medium priced: fish and chips lunch T$8, dinner T$15. The tap water is saline. The reef around the island is good, and there's even a half-sunken ship, the *Marner,* sticking up out of the water for snorkelers to explore. If you're a yachtie you'll want to know that Pangaimotu has excellent anchorage (all the other offshore islands are surrounded by treacherous reefs). Boat transfers are T$10 pp return. It's a day-trip island and somewhat of a local hangout. On Sunday many local expats come over to booze, and while it's not officially banned to bring over your own lunch, you'll be more comfortable having your picnic well away from the resort and other tourists. Budget.

Sun Island Resort (Private Bag 44, Nuku'alofa; tel. 23-335, fax 22-915), on Makaha'a Island just beyond Pangaimotu, is smaller, quieter, and less expensive than the other resorts. It's owned by Princess Pilolevu, but locally managed and a bit rundown with poor service—a do-your-own-thing type of place. There are just three *fales:* one double right on the beach at T$60 single or double, another double a bit back from the beach at T$45, and a triple a bit away from the beach at T$60 for up to three. Overnight campers pay T$10 pp. No cooking facilities are provided, but the restaurant/bar charges just T$5/7.50/10 for breakfast/lunch/dinner—less than at the other places. A range of water sports is available. Though the beach isn't as good as at Pangaimotu, the nearby reef features huge coral formations alive with baby fish (T$5 extra charge for boat shuttles to the reef). Their boat leaves Faua Jetty weekdays at 1000, weekends at 1000, 1100, and 1200 (T$10 roundtrip). Budget.

Fafa Island Resort (Box 1444, Nuku'alofa; tel. 22-800, fax 23-592), quite a distance farther out than Pangaimotu, is very professionally managed by Rainer Urtel. The eight standard *fales* with private bath (T$75/85/100 single/double/triple) are rustic but adequate, while the eight superior beachside *fales* (T$150 single or double, T$190 triple) are larger and more luxurious with open shower, sun deck, and garden. The marvelous meals in their pleasant thatched restaurant/bar are T$50/60 pp for two/three (no cooking facilities for guests). A full range of nonmotorized sporting activities is offered in the sapphire blue lagoon surrounding this delightful palm-covered, seven-hectare island. Snorkeling gear is loaned free but windsurfing and Hobie cat riding are T$20 an hour. The initial 30-minute boat ride is T$16 pp roundtrip, but once you're staying they'll ferry you into town and back as often as you like at no extra cost. Their shuttle boat leaves the island at 0900 and 1630, leaves Faua Jetty at 1100 and 1730, so you can easily spend the day in town. Fafa can be a little quiet at times, and would not be a good choice if you were out for aggressive motorized watersports, sightseeing, or socializing. Inexpensive to moderate.

The New Zealander-oriented **Royal Sunset Island Resort** (Box 960, Nuku'alofa; tel./fax 21-254), on Atata Island 11 km northwest of town, is the most remote of the small island hotels off Tongatapu. The entire island is owned by the king's third son, Prince Lavaka, and most of Royal Sunset's local employees are from the 233-person Tongan village on the island. The 26 units with private bath, fridge, kitchenette, and overhead fan are T$110/120/160/185 single/double/triple/quad for an eastern unit or T$116/135/180/205 on the western side. If you book through a travel agent abroad you could pay considerably more. Their three-meal plan is T$64 pp, and opinions about the food vary. Drinks at the bar are on the expensive side, so take along a couple of bottles of duty-free booze if somebody booked you in here. There's a swimming pool, and free activities for guests include tennis, Hobie cat sailing, paddleboarding, windsurfing, rowboating, and snorkeling. Scuba diving is T$70 for two tanks with equipment rental available at an additional charge. The resort is right on a broad white-sand beach, and the snorkeling along Egeria Channel is great. Deep-sea fishing is T$60 an hour (minimum of four hours) and up to six people can go for that price. Island transfers from Nuku'alofa on their large catamaran *Manutahi II* are T$34 pp roundtrip. Royal Sunset is the place to go if you want lots of sporting activities and organized entertainment. Moderate.

Getting There

While the cost of scuba diving in Tonga is high, the various day-trips to offshore islands are cheap and a leisurely boat trip to one of the island resorts described above is recommended. The Pangaimotu Island boat leaves daily at 1000 and 1100, with extra trips at 1200 and 1300 on Sunday (T$10 for transfers only). Children under 12 pay half price. Sun Island charges T$10 for roundtrip transfers Mon.-Sat. at 1000, Sunday at 1000, 1100, and 1200. Fafa Island also does excellent day-trips daily at 1100 (T$30 including a good lunch). On Monday, Fafa Island Resort offers a romantic dinner cruise with a Polynesian floor show departing Nuku'alofa at 1730

(T$40). Royal Sunset's day-trip departs Sunday at 1000 (T$30 including a barbecue lunch). All these leave from Faua Jetty near Nuku'alofa's fish market, and bookings can be made at Teta Tours or at the International Dateline Hotel tour desk (no booking required for the Pangaimotu and Sun Island shuttles). Provided the weather cooperates, they're an excellent way to pass Nuku'alofa's pious Sunday, and you'll have a better chance of meeting interesting people if you go that day.

TONGA
THE FRIENDLY ISLANDS

Protect
the Whales

Postage
64s

HUMPBACK WHALE
Megaptera novaeangliae

'EUA ISLAND

A rough 40-km boat ride from Nuku'alofa, 'Eua is a good place to go for the weekend. Since tourist facilities are undeveloped you won't feel as oppressed as you might on a Nuku'alofa Sunday, and you'll have to entertain yourself here anyway. Bony bareback horses can be hired, but all spots on the island are within walking distance.

'Eua's hills are a contrast to flat Tongatapu. The thickly forested spine down the east side of 'Eua drops to perpendicular cliffs, while the west half is largely taken up by plantations and villages. At 87 square km, it's Tonga's third-largest island.

Facilities on 'Eua are extremely basic; this is a chance to get off the beaten tourist track and see real Tongan life. It's a rather scrubby, depressing place, indicative of why so many Tongans live in Auckland. Three full days are enough to get the feel of the island.

SIGHTS

Matalanga 'a Maui

Legend tells how the demigod Maui thrust his digging stick into 'Eua and pulled it back and forth in anger at his mother, threatening thereby to upset the island. To visit the great pothole that remains from this event, head south of the sawmill and Ha'atua Mormon Church, take the second bush road on the left, and walk inland about 10 minutes. You'll need intuition or a guide to locate the pit hidden in the middle of a plantation on the right, although the lower level of the trees growing in it is an indicator. Holding onto vines, you can get right down into Matalanga 'a Maui itself for an eerie view of jungle-clad walls towering around you.

Southern 'Eua

Most of the families in Pangai and farther south were relocated from Niuafo'ou Island after a devastating volcanic eruption there in 1946. The road south from the wharf terminates after 10 km at **Ha'aluma Beach.** The deserted beach is a weathered reef with sandy pools to swim in, but it's only safe as long as you hug the shore. There

are some small blowholes and a view of Kalau Island.

Just before the descent to the beach, take the road to the left and keep straight one hour almost to the south tip of the island. Here a track veers left through high grass and starts going north up the east coast past a gate. The first cliff you come to across the field from the track is **Lakufa'anga,** where Tongans once called turtles from the sea. So many have been slaughtered that none appear anymore. Look down on the grassy ledges below the cliffs and you'll spot the nesting places of seabirds.

Continue north on the track a short distance, watching on the left for a huge depression partly visible through the trees. This is **Li'angahuo 'a Maui,** a tremendous natural stone bridge by the

Legend tells how Li'angahuo 'a Maui on 'Eua Island was formed when the demigod Maui hurled his spear across the island.

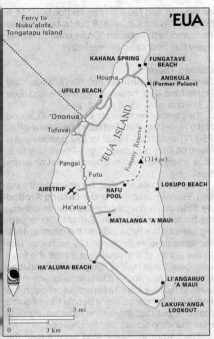

'EUA

Ferry to
Nuku'alofa,
Tongatapu Island

KAHANA SPRING · FUNGATAVE BEACH

Houma

ANOKULA (Former Palace)

UFILEI BEACH

'Ononua

Tufuvai

'EUA ISLAND

Forestry Reserve

(314 m)

Pangai

Futu

AIRSTRIP

HAFU POOL

LOKUPO BEACH

Ha'atua

MATALANGA 'A MAUI

HA'ALUMA BEACH

LI'ANGAHUO 'A MAUI

LAKUFA'ANGA LOOKOUT

0   3 mi

0   3 km

sea, which you can pass right over without realizing if you're not paying attention. Work your way around the side of the pothole for a clear view of the bridge. The story goes that after creating Matalanga, Maui threw his digging stick across 'Eua. It pierced the cliffs at this point and dove into the sea to carve out the Tonga Deep. After this impressive sight, continue up the coast a short distance to see more cliffs, which explain why the east side of 'Eua is uninhabited.

Northern 'Eua
Tufuvai village, two km south of 'Ononua wharf, is attractive but the undertow is deadly on an outgoing tide. Both this and **Ufilei Beach**, just two km north of the wharf across Tonga's only river bridge, are fine for a sunset stroll.

Tonga's most spectacular scenic viewpoint is just northeast of Houma village at **Anokula**, where in 1983 the king built himself a palace of which only the concrete foundations now remain. The soaring cliffs drop 120 meters straight

into the coastal strip, creating an unsurpassed panorama of power and beauty.

After this visual blast look for a trail north up the coast to another access road that leads down to **Kahana Spring**, which supplies 'Eua with Tonga's purest water. Just beyond the spring is a second magnificent viewpoint over the east coast, directly above **Fungatave Beach.**

The Interior
Tonga's finest tropical forest is on the slopes just above Futu. Take the road inland a little south of Haukinima Motel toward the Forestry Experimental Farm. Continue east along the main road about 30 minutes till you reach the nursery. **Hafu Pool** is near the office, down a trail that continues straight ahead from the road on the right, but it's hardly worth the effort.

The forest, on the other hand, is well worth exploring for the many exotic species planted by the Ministry of Agriculture and Forestry (pine, red cedar, tree ferns) and the abundant birdlife, especially Pacific pigeons, crimson-crowned fruit doves, white-collared kingfishers, blue-crowned lorikeets, and red-breasted musk parrots. Now both forests and birds of 'Eua are threatened by villagers who burn the trees for land on which to plant their sweet potatoes and yams. After a few years the soil is depleted and the farmers move on, while the loss of trees lowers 'Eua's water table, threatening the island with drought.

The road on the left at the nursery leads through the forest reserve to Topuva'e 'a Maui (312 meters), the highest point on the island, where there's the simple grave of a New Zealand soldier who died here during WW II. A track leads down to Lokupo Beach from just north of the grave.

PRACTICALITIES

Accommodations
The two guesthouses on 'Eua are about 200 meters apart on or near the main road down the middle of the island, a five-minute walk north of the airstrip (T$2-3 by taxi from the wharf). Your best bet is **Setaita Guest House** (Setaita Archibald, tel. 50-124), 400 meters north of the airport and three km south of the wharf. The three rooms in this two-story building are T$25/27 single/double. Camping in the yard is T$5. You

can pay a small fee for gas and cook for yourself or order meals from the family. Bicycle rental is T$10 a day. Budget.

The **Haukinima Motel** (Sione Manukia, tel. 50-088) nearby has eight rooms with shared bath are T$17/22 single/double. Grubby communal cooking facilities are provided (watch your food!) and simple but filling Tongan meals are served. Royal Tongan beer is available at the bar on the premises, which is where the problem lies. Unless you're stone deaf, don't expect to get any sleep until they close (ask Sione what time that might be). Shoestring.

Some of those who camped on the beach on the inhabited west side of the island have become victims of theft, and if you're interested in camping wild, a much better plan would be to trek around to the southeast side beyond Li'angahuo 'a Maui. Carry all the food and water you'll need.

Entertainment

The optimum time to come to 'Eua is late August or early September during the 'Eua Agricultural Show. The show grounds are right by the hospital at Futu.

If the nightlife at the Haukinima Motel doesn't satisfy you, there's **Maxi Disco Hall** across the street. A live band plays Friday and Saturday at 2000 and possibly a couple of other nights too. The hall is run by Taina, who named it after her cat, Maxi. On dance nights the place is packed.

Services

What facilities 'Eua offers are near 'Ononua wharf, including the Bank of Tonga (tel. 50-145), post office (tel. 50-066), Telecom center (tel. 50-115), Friendly Islands Bookshop (tel. 50-167), and TCFS Supermarket (tel. 50-120). Kaufana Airport and both guesthouses are in the center of the island, three km south. Here too are the Forestry Division (tel. 50-116), with a good map

on the wall, and Niu'eiki Hospital (tel. 50-111), a bit back toward 'Ononua. A public bus shuttles back and forth between 'Ononua and Ha'atua every half hour or so on weekdays.

Getting There

Royal Tongan Airlines (tel. 50-188) has daily flights Mon.-Sat. between Nuku'alofa and 'Eua (T$19 one-way, T$36 roundtrip).

To charter an aircraft between 'Eua and Nuku'alofa from **Pacific Island Seaplanes** (tel. 25-177) would cost T$360 for four persons (maximum 64 kilos of luggage total). They'll only fly to 'Eua when the wind is from the east or northeast.

The two boats shuttling between Nuku'alofa and 'Eua are described under **Getting Around by Ship** in the chapter introduction. In general the boats leave 'Eua Mon.-Sat. at 0630, departing Nuku'alofa's Faua Jetty for the return at 1300 the same days. Both charge T$6 each way. Due to the action of the southeast trades the four-hour boat trip is far less rough westbound than eastbound, so if you're a terrible sailor you might want to fly over from Nuku'alofa and catch the boat back. In fact, so many people have figured that one out that the airline folks have made their roundtrip tickets slightly cheaper!

The harbor at 'Eua is less secure than the one at Nuku'alofa, so if strong winds are blowing or a hurricane warning has been issued for anywhere within 1,000 km, that day's ferry trip will be canceled and the boat will remain tied up at Faua Jetty in Nuku'alofa. Of course, this happens more frequently during the southern summer (Dec.-April), but one should always be prepared to spend a day or two longer on 'Eua than planned or be prepared to fly back. The Saturday trip from Nuku'alofa is the most likely to be canceled in bad weather, so it's safer to go over on Friday and not count on being able to come back on Monday. When the boat is canceled, Royal Tongan schedules additional flights.

THE HA'APAI GROUP

This great group of 51 low coral islands and two volcanoes between Nuku'alofa and Vava'u is a beachcomber's paradise. Perfect white powdery beaches run right around the mostly uninhabited islands, but treacherous shoals keep cruising yachts away. There are two clusters: Nomuka is the largest of the seldom-visited southern islands, while Lifuka is at the center of a string of islands to the north. Some 8,000 people live on 16 of the islands. Ha'apai is mostly for beach people; if you're not a beach lover you'll soon get bored. Snorkelers and scuba divers have 150 km of untouched barrier reef, vast banks of soft and hard coral, and 1,600 species of tropical fish to keep them busy. Humpback whales (July-Oct.), spinner dolphins, and sea turtles add to the fun.

The first European to visit Ha'apai was Abel Tasman who called at Nomuka in 1643. Captain Cook made prolonged stops on the same island in 1774 and 1777; on a visit to Lifuka in 1777 he coined the term "Friendly Islands," unaware of a plot by the Tongans to murder him. Later, off Tofua on 28 April 1789, Fletcher Christian and his mutineers lowered Captain William Bligh and 18 loyal members of his crew into a whaleboat, beginning one of the longest voyages in an open boat in maritime history, from Tongan waters to Timor in the Dutch East Indies (6,500 km)—a fantastic accomplishment of endurance and seamanship. Bligh's group suffered its only casualty of the trip, John Norton, quartermaster of the *Bounty,* when they landed on the southwest side of Tofua just after the 1789 mutiny and clashed with Tongans.

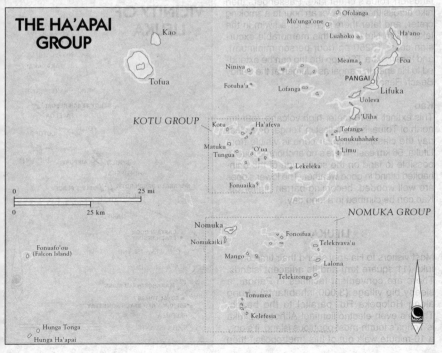

THE HA'APAI GROUP

Tofua

Tofua (56 square km) is a flat-topped volcanic island about 505 meters high with a steep and rocky shoreline all the way around the island. The 10 abandoned houses and three churches at Hokula near the north coast, and Manaka, a tiny settlement on the east coast, are used by villagers from Kotu Island, who come to harvest Tofua's potent kava. It takes about an hour to climb up to Tofua's rim from Hokula. The large steep-sided, four-km-wide caldera in the interior is occupied by a freshwater crater lake 30 meters above sea level and 250 meters deep. Tofua is still active: steam and gases issue from a volcanic cone on the north side of the lake, and a hot pool is on the east side. Passing ships can see flames at night.

Larry Simon and John Way of **Pacific Island Seaplanes** (tel. 25-177, fax 25-165) run charter flights to Tofua from Nuku'alofa. The Beaver seaplane makes a photo pass over Kao and lands on Tofua's crater lake. Passengers then hike across the caldera for an hour to a smoking crater, and later there's time for a swim in the lake. From Nuku'alofa this memorable excursion costs T$250 pp (four-person minimum), and for an extra T$50 pp the trip can be extended to Ha'apai. In Pangai ask Jürgen at the Sandy Beach Resort.

Kao

This extinct 1,046-meter-high volcano, four km north of Tofua, is the tallest in Tonga; on a clear day the classic triangular cone is visible from Lifuka, 56 km east. There's no anchorage, but it's possible to land on the south side of the uninhabited island in good weather. The lower slopes are well wooded, becoming barren higher up. Kao can be climbed in a long day.

LIFUKA

Most visitors to Ha'apai spend their time on Lifuka (11 square km) and its adjacent islands. There are convenient facilities in Pangai, a sleepy big village (3,000 inhabitants) strung along Holopeka Rd. parallel to the beach. There's even electric lighting! Although Lifuka is Tonga's fourth-most-populous island, it's only a 10-minute walk out of this "metropolis;" then you're all alone among the coconut palms or strolling along an endless deserted beach. The most convenient and enjoyable way to explore Lifuka and Foa is by rented bicycle.

It was near the north end of Lifuka that Captain Cook was so well received in 1777 that he called these the Friendly Islands. On the same spot in 1806, the crew of the British privateer *Port-au-Prince* received a different welcome when Tongan warriors stormed aboard and murdered most of the crew. The captain's clerk, William Mariner, age 15, was spared and taken under the protection of Chief Finau II. Mariner remained in Tonga four years, participating in Finau's conquest of Tongatapu using cannon taken from the ship. Eventually a passing ship carried him back to England where he spent the rest of his life as a stockbroker, accidentally drowning in the Thames in 1853. In 1816 Mariner published *An Account of the Natives of the Tongan Islands*

VICINITY OF LIFUKA

MUITOA
HA'ANO
HA'ANO ISLAND
FAKAKAKAI
NUKUNAMO ISLAND
SANDY BEACH RESORT
FALELOA
FOTUA
LOTOFOA
FOA ISLAND
KOULO · ✕ AIRPORT
HOLOPEKA
NIU'AKALO BEACH HOTEL · BILLY'S PLACE
PANGAI
LIFUKA ISLAND
HIHIFO
CAPTAIN COOK BEACH RESORT
UOLEVA ISLAND
TATAFA ISLAND
'UIHA · **MAKAHOKOVALU RUINS**
ROYAL TOMBS
'ESI-'O-MA'AFU BEACH HOMESTAY
FELEMEA
'UIHA ISLAND

0   5 mi
0   5 km

in the South Pacific Ocean, the classic narration of pre-Christian Tonga.

Sights

On Holopeka Rd. at the south end of town is the **King's Palace,** with many fine old trees bordering the compound. The king comes every September for the agricultural fair, which is held in the field across the street.

Just north of the palace and inland a block on Faifekau Rd. is the Free Wesleyan Church, where a **miraculous cross** appeared in 1975. The spot is now outlined in cement on the grass outside the church. Palasi Rd., the next street north, runs right across the island to the long, lonely **beach** of high golden sands extending down the east side of Lifuka, only a 10-minute walk from town. Unfortunately the locals have adversely affected the beauty of this beach by mining it for sand.

Just north of Pangai is the grave and monument of Wesleyan missionary **Reverend Shirley Baker** (1836-1903), an adviser to King George Tupou I, who helped frame the Emancipation Edict of 1862 and the 1875 constitution. In 1880 Baker resigned his ministry and governed Tonga in the name of the elderly king. To increase his power he persuaded King George to break with Wesleyan headquarters in Australia and establish the independent Free Wesleyan Church. Baker's persecution of Tongan Wesleyans still loyal to the Australian church and his dictatorial rule prompted the British High Commissioner in Fiji to send a warship to collect him in 1890. Baker was later allowed to retire to Ha'apai and his children erected this monument after his death.

Sports and Recreation

One of the main reasons to visit Ha'apai is the diving, and **Watersports Ha'apai** (Box 65, Pangai; tel./fax 60-097) based at the Niu'akalo Beach Hotel can show you some pretty incredible things with the help of a snorkel or tank. It's run by a German named Roland Schwara who charges T$50/80 for one/two tanks, plus T$15 for gear. His scuba resort course is T$75 (no certificate), and he'll happily take you snorkeling at T$16/25 a half/full day including a mask and snorkel. A guided day-trip in a sea kayak is T$48 including lunch (kayak rentals without lunch or guide are T$25 a day). If a group of six can be found,

Roland will run a speedboat trip to the volcano on Tofua, costing T$150 pp for the boat, plus T$60 pp a day for guides and meals. Overnight trips almost anywhere in Ha'apai are possible. If countless colorful fish swimming above unbroken coral in crystal clear water is your idea of paradise, you'll find it here (plus a shark or two).

ACCOMMODATIONS

Pangai

All of the guesthouses in Pangai itself allow guests to cook their own food, but a small additional charge for cooking gas is levied to use the communal kitchen. Of course, they'd rather do the cooking for you at T$4-6 for breakfast and T$8-12 for dinner, but you must order in advance. Their food is good and the portions are gargantuan (as you'd expect in Tonga), but at those prices it gets expensive. If you really do want to cook for yourself, check out the kitchen as soon as you arrive and ask about extra charges for gas and electricity if you use it. Expect to have to share the facilities with the managers, who will be cooking for other guests. In addition to the places listed below, the **Government Rest House** (tel. 60-100), behind the Tonga Visitors Bureau, sometimes accepts tourists at T$10 pp.

Fifita's Guest House (Fifita Vi, tel. 60-213), near the center of the village, offers eight comfortable rooms in a two-story building at T$15/22 single/double. You can cook your own food for a daily T$2 fee (or Fifita will happily do it for you). Bicycle rentals are T$5 and boat trips to Uoleva Island can be arranged at T$40 for up to four persons. Airport transfers are free upon request. Shoestring.

Evaloni Guest House (Mrs. Sitali Hu'akau, Box 56, Pangai; tel. 60-029), back behind the Visitors Bureau in Pangai, has eight basic rooms for T$18/25/30 single/double/triple. Meals are available at T$5 for breakfast or lunch, T$12 for dinner. It costs T$2 pp a day to use the cooking facilities. They're seldom full. Budget.

The friendly, nine-room **Fonongava'inga Guest House** (Mrs. Langilangi Vi, Box 14, Pangai; tel. 60-038) nearby has five small rooms in the main building at T$10/15 single/double and four larger rooms in the new wing at T$15/22/30

PANGAI

MARKET
TAUFA'AHAU WHARF
SHELL SERVICE STATION
VELATA NAVAL BASE
FRIENDLY ISLANDS BOOKSHOP
VELITOA RD
MORMON CHURCH
To
Niu'akalo Beach
Hotel and Airport
FAU
BANK OF TONGA
FIFITA'S GUEST HOUSE
TU'IFUA VAIKONA'S STORE
TONGA COOPERATIVE WHOLESALE STORE
CHURCH OF TONGA
To
Beach
PALASI
POST OFFICE
TONGA VISITORS BUREAU
EVALONI GUEST HOUSE
POLICE STATION
KAO JETTY
TELECOM TELEPHONE EXCHANGE
FONONGAVA'INGA GUEST HOUSE
MIRACULOUS CROSS
FREE WESLEYAN CHURCH
KING'S PALACE
PILOLEVU COLLEGE
CATHOLIC CHURCH
AGRICULTURAL FAIRGROUNDS
To
Hospital
MATEIALONA RD
HOLOPEKA
FAIFEKAU
ROAD
HAUFOLAU
TUAKOLO
LOTOKOLO
To
Lindsay Guest House

0   100 yds
0   100 m

© DAVID STANLEY

single/double/triple. The bathroom facilities are communal in all cases but only the new rooms have access to hot water. You can cook your own food in the owners' house next door at T$2 pp a week, or order excellent meals at T$3 for breakfast or lunch, T$8 for dinner. The atmosphere here is pleasant, with a large living room and front porch available to travelers. Bicycles are for hire at T$7. Langilangi is very kind and helpful. Shoestring.

In the southern section of Pangai is **Lindsay Guest House** (tel. 60-107), Pangai's newest place to stay, with six shared-bath rooms at T$15/25 single/double. Meals are served or you

can cook, and a small grocery store and bakery are on the premises. Bicycles are T$5 a day. Budget.

North of Town

The quiet **Niu'akalo Beach Hotel** (Box 18, Pangai; tel. 60-028), north of town between Pangai and Holopeka, offers 12 neat little rooms on landscaped grounds facing a long, sandy beach only good for swimming at high tide. A small room with shared bath in a four-room standard unit is T$16.50/22 single/double, while rooms with private bath in the duplex deluxe units are T$27.50/32 single/double, or T$60 for a complete unit (up to six persons). Each cluster has a common living room shared by all guests, but here's only cold water. The biggest drawback is the price of the meals in the restaurant/bar, and no cooking facilities are available for guests. Friday at 1900 there's a beach barbecue or a full Tongan feast, depending on how many guests are present. Rental snorkels, boats, and bicycles (T$10) are available. Your charming hosts, Mrs. Seletute Falevai, her husband, son, and two daughters, are very helpful. Shoestring to budget.

Billy's Place (Box 66, Pangai; tel./fax 60-058), also known as Evaloni Beach Fales, is run by Viliami Hu'akau and his American wife Sandy with a bit of help from Milika. Unlike the places in Pangai that are serenaded all night by barking dogs and rocked by legions of church bells at the crack of dawn, Billy's is in a coconut plantation on a long, deserted beach, 1.5 km north of town. It's on the breezy ocean side of the island, across narrow Lifuka from the Niu'akalo Beach Hotel. Watch for flying foxes headed north in the morning, south in the evening. Billy's five *fales* with lockable doors are T$35/55 single/double, a free breakfast, bicycle, and snorkeling gear included. Guests and nonguests alike can order surprisingly good burritos, fish, pizza, and pasta to be consumed on their pleasant patio (lunch is no problem, but order dinner in advance). One Swiss reader said she liked the cozy atmosphere and thought it was loads of fun. Airport transfers are free. Budget.

Telefoni Sunset Beachhouse (tel. 60-044) is farther north, beside the lagoon between the wharf and the airport. The three rooms in this family dwelling are T$15/28 single/double and all guests share the bathroom, kitchen, and lounge. Bicycles rent for T$10. Budget.

The **Mele Tonga Guest House** (tel. 60-042) is on a reasonable beach at Holopeka about 500 meters south of the airstrip. At T$15/20 single/double with breakfast, there are two double rooms and a single in the main house, plus another double in an adjacent *fale,* and a communal kitchen in a separate building. For T$7 you can rent a bicycle. It's run by a local schoolteacher named Letty, and if she's not around when you arrive, ask at the small store beyond the church next to the guesthouse. Shoestring.

OTHER PRACTICALITIES

Food and Entertainment
Pangai has several adequate stores opposite the Bank of Tonga and a small market on the north side of town. **Meloise Restaurant** is also near the Bank of Tonga. Ask around for dances in church halls on Friday and Saturday nights. You can drink kava all evening at several saloons around Pangai for a flat fee.

Services and Information
The Bank of Tonga (tel. 60-933) changes traveler's checks weekdays 0930-1230 and 1330-1530. The **Telecom telephone exchange** (tel. 60-255), where you can place long-distance calls, is on the small street behind the Visitors Bureau. If you want to fax anyone on Lifuka, or receive a fax yourself, direct those messages to fax 60-200 (the clerk will call whoever is named on the fax and ask them to come and pick it up). Yachties should report their arrival at the post office even if they've already checked in at Vava'u.

The Tonga Visitors Bureau (Mele Likiliki, tel./fax 60-733) has an office on Holopeka Rd. in the center of Pangai that can provide brochures and good local advice.

Niu'ui Hospital (tel. 60-201) is two kilometers south of the wharf.

Getting There
Royal Tongan Airlines (tel. 60-566), next to the post office, flies from Tongatapu to Ha'apai (T$67) daily except Sunday, and from Ha'apai to Vava'u (T$67) twice a week. Pilolevu Airport (HPA) is at Koulo, five km north of Pangai. Most of the places to stay offer free transfers, otherwise a taxi will be around T$3 for the car.

Ferries between Nuku'alofa and Vava'u call regularly at Pangai, northbound very early Tuesday and Wednesday mornings, southbound in the middle of the night on Wednesday and Thursday. The *Loto Ha'angana* or *Tautahi* runs a day before the *Olovaha* in both directions. The *Olovaha* office (tel. 60-699) is inside the red container on Taufa'ahau Wharf. The office of the *Loto Ha'angana* and *Tautahi* (tel. 60-855) is in the adjacent cream-colored container (open only on ship days). Deck fares from Pangai are T$28 to Nuku'alofa and T$21 to Vava'u. Ships tie up to

Taufa'ahau Wharf near the center of Pangai; turn right as you disembark. There's a large passenger shelter on the wharf where you can wait until dawn if you happen to arrive in the middle of the night (as is usually the case). When there are strong westerly winds, the ships may not risk landing at Pangai.

ISLANDS AROUND LIFUKA

Foa
A causeway links Lifuka and Foa (population 1,439). Weekdays from early morning until around 1600, and also on Saturday morning, buses leaves intermittently from Pangai for **Faleloa,** Foa's northernmost village. Continue 20 minutes on foot to Foa's northern tip to look across to **Nukunamo Island,** owned by the king. The beach is beautiful here and the snorkeling is fine at slack tide.

Outboard motorboats bring villagers from **Ha'ano Island** to the wharf at Faleloa, and you can go back with them most afternoons for about T$1 one-way.

The **Sandy Beach Resort** (Box 61, Pangai; tel./fax 60-600) opened in 1995 near the north end of Foa Island, 1.5 km from Faleloa. The 12 well-constructed beachfront bungalows with ceiling fan, fridge, 24-hour electricity, porch, and private bath cost T$140 single or double (third persons T$27). Cooking facilities are not provided for guests and children are not accepted. Like the accommodations, the fancy food in the restaurant is geared to a more upscale clientele than the backpacker places on Lifuka (T$45 for breakfast and dinner). The swimming and snorkeling are fine, even at low tide, and snorkeling gear, bicycles, and an outrigger canoe are loaned free. Dolphins swim offshore. Paid activities include bareback horse riding, boat trips, amphibian excursions, and ocean kayaking. German instructor Monika Rahimi handles scuba diving. All facilities (including the restaurant) are for resort guests only. The Sandy Beach is run by a German couple named Jürgen and Sigi Stavenow, former managers of the Seaview Restaurant in Nuku'alofa, and before you leave you'll know all there is to know about them. The weekly Tongan cultural show is good too. Airport transfers are free. Moderate.

Uoleva
From the south end of Lifuka, 3.5 km from town, you can wade across the reef at low tide to sparsely populated Uoleva Island, which has super snorkeling off its southwest end. Check tide times at the Visitors Bureau in Pangai and don't set out if the tide is about to come in as it takes at least 30 minutes to cross. Rubber booties or reef shoes will be required to protect your feet. Sunday is a good day to go as you won't meet any copra cutters.

The **Captain Cook Beach Resort** (Soni Kaifoto, Box 49, Pangai; tel. 60-014), on the northwest side of Uoleva, offers a real South Seas experience. The four rooms in two basic duplex units cost T$15/20 single/double, plus T$10 pp for breakfast and dinner. If you were thinking of camping here, check beforehand that it will be allowed. You should also carry some food with you as nothing can be purchased on the island although water is supplied. The long white beach is fabulous and you'll share this sizable, coconut-covered island with only your fellow guests, the occasional local who comes to work his/her garden, and free-ranging cows, goats, and pigs. It's restful, just don't expect luxuries like electricity and running water. Enjoy the sunsets off their beach, the stars in the sky, and the utter tranquility. One male reader wrote: "I fell in love with this place the minute I arrived." Unfortunately some female readers have had a different experience, and the Captain Cook can only be recommended to couples and men alone. Shoestring.

At low tide Uoleva can be reached on foot from Lifuka, but it would take several hours to walk/wade from Pangai to the Captain Cook Resort and it might be very dangerous to try to do so laden with a backpack when a current was running (carry a pole for balance). A much better idea is to come/go by boat and transfers from Pangai cost about T$8 pp each way. Try contacting the owner, Soni Kaifoto, at his home on Haufolau Rd. in Pangai, or if you're staying at Fifita Guest House, ask Fifita as Soni is her uncle. Otherwise the people in the shop on the Pangai waterfront can help you organize transfers for the same price.

'Uiha
'Uiha Island (population 756), south of Lifuka, is more slow moving than Pangai, but there are

things to see, an agreeable place to stay, and fairly regular access by boat. The burial ground of the Tongan royal family was on 'Uiha until the move to Nuku'alofa. Also to be seen in front of the church in the middle of 'Uiha village is a cannon from the Peruvian slave ship *Margarita*, which was sacked off 'Uiha in 1863. A second cannon inside the church serves as a baptismal font. Also visit the Makahokovalu, an ancient monument composed of eight connecting stones at the north end of 'Uiha Island. Uninhabited Tatafa Island between 'Uiha and Uoleva can be reached from near here on foot at low tide. The beach and snorkeling are good, and a colony of flying foxes can be seen.

The only place to stay is **'Esi-'O-Ma'afu Beach Homestay** (no phone), run by Hesekaia and Kaloni 'Aholelei. It's on the beach at Felemea vil-lage, a 15-minute walk south of the boat landing at 'Uiha village. The three Tongan *fales* with shared bath are T$12/18 single/double. Breakfast is T$4, dinner T$6 (or T$8 if lobster), or you can cook for yourself. An outrigger canoe can be borrowed. One reader's comments: "Wonderful family . . . we really participated in village life . . . our best ex-perience in the South Pacific." Shoestring.

'Uiha is fairly easy to get to on small boats departing the beach at Pangai, but at best the service is only once a day, so you'll have to spend the night. The regular trip is about T$10 pp each way. The people at Tu'ifua Vaikona's store (tel. 60-605) on the Pangai waterfront can take you over to 'Uiha Island for a few hours sight-seeing and bring you back at around T$80 for the boat—worth considering if you can get a small group together.

THE VAVA'U GROUP

Vava'u is Tonga's most scenic region. It's an uplifted limestone cluster that tilts to cliffs in the north and submerges in a myriad of small is-lands to the south. A labyrinth of waterways winds between plateaus thrust up by subter-ranean muscle-flexing. In Vava'u one superb scenic vista succeeds another, all so varied you're continually consulting your map to dis-cover just what you're seeing. Only Port Vila (Vanuatu) is comparable.

The Vava'u Group measures about 21 km east to west and 25 km north to south, and of the 34 elevated, thickly forested islands, 21 are in-habited. At 90 square km, the main island of Vava'u is Tonga's second largest. Ships ap-proach Vava'u up fjordlike Ava Pulepulekai chan-nel, which leads 11 km to picturesque, land-locked Port of Refuge Harbor, one of the finest in the South Pacific. The appealing main town of Neiafu, 275 km north of Nuku'alofa, looks out onto Puerto del Refugio, christened by Captain Francisco Antonio Mourelle, whose Spanish ves-sel chanced upon Vava'u in 1781 while en route from Manila to Mexico, making Vava'u one of the last South Pacific islands to be contacted by Europeans.

The many protected anchorages make Vava'u a favorite of cruising yachties, and it's also a prime place to launch an ocean kayak. Waters on the west side of the archipelago are generally deeper and better protected than those on the east. Beaches can be hard to find on the shores of the main island but there are many on the islets to the south. Vava'u is an economic backwater with industry limited to a giant-clam breeding project at Falevai on Kapa Island, and pearl-clam farming near Utulei in Port of Refuge Harbor and at three other loca-tions. Three-quarters of Tonga's vanilla is pro-duced here on plantations covering more than 500 hectares, and Vava'u vanilla is among the best in the world.

Tourism is growing with direct flights from Fiji and Pago Pago, and one of the South Pacific's two most important yacht charter operations is based here (the other is on Raiatea in Tahiti-Polynesia). Places to stay abound, both in town and on the outer islands, the entertainment is varied, and watersports such as kayaking, sail-ing, scuba diving, and fishing are well devel-oped. July-Oct., this is the South Pacific's main whalewatching venue. May-Oct. is the prime time for yachting, and if you arrive in the off sea-son, Nov.-April, you could have the place al-most to yourself. Vava'u is one Pacific island group you can't afford to miss.

THE VAVA'U GROUP

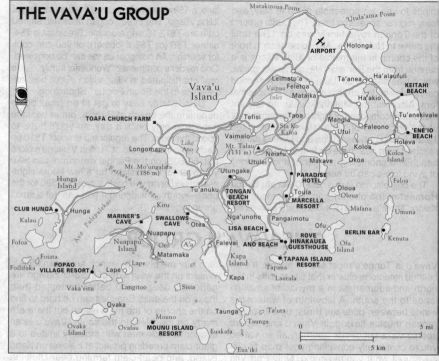

NEIAFU

Neiafu is Tonga's second "city" but it's still a sleepy little town of just 6,000 inhabitants. It's a great place to explore on foot, visiting the market or local attractions, shopping for handicrafts or groceries, dropping into a cafe or bar to hear yachties chatter, visiting travel offices to organize excursions, or simply hiking out into the unspoiled countryside all around. Neiafu is a much more colorful, attractive, appealing, and restful town than Nuku'alofa. The longer you stay, the more you'll like it, and the better you'll become attuned to the town's relaxed pace of life. You get the impression that this is a place where everyone knows one another, and where things can be arranged on short notice. The only drawback is that no swimmable beaches exist near town.

Be aware that nearly all shops, bars, and restaurants in Neiafu are closed on Sunday (except those at the Paradise Hotel). The only people you're likely to meet on the street on Sunday are those coming or going to church. Sunday nights a church service consisting mostly of hymns accompanied by rock music is broadcast across Neiafu on loudspeakers. This really is an unusual place.

Sights

One of the overgrown burials in the **cemetery** between the Bank of Tonga and Mormon church is of the ancient *langi* type, and it's believed that a daughter of the 35th Tu'i Tonga is buried here. Also resting in this cemetery is the Rev. Francis Wilson, who established the first seminary in Tonga and died here in 1846. The nameless tombstone right next to Wilson's is that of early Methodist missionary David Cargill, who rendered the Tongan and Fijian languages into writing.

The old fig tree in front of Neiafu's red-and-white colonial-style **post office** is a local meeting place. Notice the Spanish monument across the street. The **Vava'u Club** up the hill is the former German Club, founded by trader Hermann Karl Guttenbeil in 1875. The old German cemetery is just a bit farther up the hill, past the club and on the left.

For a splendid view of Port of Refuge and much of the archipelago, climb **Mt. Talau** (131 meters), the flat-top hill that dominates Neiafu to the west. Take the road between the police station and the market and follow it west for 25 minutes high above the shoreline. Where the road begins to descend and you reach an isolated house on the left, look for a trail up the hill on the right just beyond. Turn right at the top of the hill. This is an easy trip from town.

East of town is Neiafu's old harbor, which was used in the days of sail when it was more convenient to land on the beach. With the advent of steamships, interest shifted to the deeper Port of Refuge Harbor. There's another excellent walk at low tide along the shore from the old harbor to **Makave;** you pass a freshwater spring.

At **Toula** village, a half-hour walk south of Neiafu beyond the hotel, is a large cave called Ve'emumuni near the shore with a freshwater pool where the locals swim. To get there, turn left just beyond the Mormon church and go through the village, continuing up the hill past a cemetery to the cave. At low tide you can walk back to the old harbor along the beach in about an hour.

Sports and Recreation

Beluga Diving (Sybil and Huib Kuilboer, tel. 70-327), on the wharf below the Paradise Hotel, offers two-tank boat dives at T$80/95 without/with equipment. They also fill tanks at T$6, and their open-water certification course is T$350.

Dolphin Pacific Diving (Box 131, Neiafu; tel. 70-160, fax 70-292, VHF channel 71), based at the Tongan Beach Resort at 'Utungake, has a five-day PADI open-water scuba certification course, as well as diving.

Scuba divers frequent the wreck of the 123-meter-long *Clan McWilliam,* a copra steamer that burned and sank in Port of Refuge Harbor in 1927. Huge fish and clams hang around the wreck 20 meters down, marked by a buoy just out past the yacht anchorage. Many other good

dive sites are only 30 minutes by speedboat from Neiafu. Most diving is drift diving and there aren't many spots where dive boats can anchor, so it's important to note the current.

The **Friendly Islands Kayak Company** (Private Bag 10, Neiafu; tel./fax 70-173, www.fikco.com/kayaktonga, e-mail: kayaktonga@kalianet.to), based at the Tongan Beach Resort, runs guided kayaking trips of six to eight days at T$100 a day including meals, tents, and snorkeling gear (minimum two nights). The Canadian operators, Doug and Sharon Spence, also offer day-trips at T$50 pp including lunch. These prices only apply to local bookings on a space-available basis, and the operation closes down for holidays in March and April.

Year-round Jim McMahon's **Hook-Up Vava'u** (tel. 70-541) offers sportfishing "island style," which means fishing for big game from a small boat. Jim takes clients out in a five-meter, twin-engined fiberglass boat, equipped with professional fishing gear, swivel seats, radio, etc. It's T$95/130 a half day (five hours) for one/two anglers, T$160/200 a full day, and you're welcome to bring along a nonfishing child or spouse and still pay the one-angler rate. Jim also charters his four-passenger boat for sightseeing, snorkeling, and scuba diving. Reserve through the Paradise Hotel reception.

Two larger powerboats offering game fishing at Vava'u are Henk and Sandra Gros's eight-meter *Target One* (tel./fax 70-647), and Pat and Keith McKee's 10-meter *Kiwi Magic* (Box 153, Neiafu; tel./fax 70-441). Fishing from *Target One* costs T$150 pp a day (minimum of three). The McKee's, who are based at the Vava'u Guest House, charge T$300/600 for a half/full day (up to four anglers). While more expensive than Jim's boat, these two are faster and have better electronic and fishing gear (as well as toilets!). They also offer some shelter in case the weather turns bad.

Delray Charters (Box 104, Neiafu; tel./fax 70-380), at the Tongan Beach Resort, offers deep-sea game fishing. New Zealander John Going and his 14-meter cruiser *Delray* are based here June-Oct. only. Marlin, mahimahi, spearfish, and tuna are caught along the dropoffs below 200-meter cliffs on the northwest side of the island.

See rugby Saturday afternoons (April- June) on the Fangatongo Rugby Ground, just off the road to Mt. Talau.

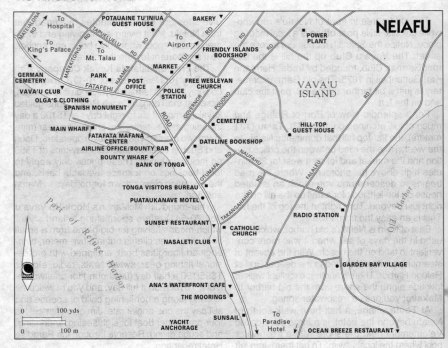

ACCOMMODATIONS

Shoestring
The **Potauaine Tu'iniua Guest House** (Box 65, Neiafu; tel. 70-479), also known as "Port Wine Guest House," a block west of the market, has four rooms with shared bath at T$10/18 single/double. This comfortable wooden house with a large lounge and communal cooking facilities and fridge is very central, and well worth checking out if you're looking for the least expensive accommodations.

Budget
The friendly **Hamana Lake Guest House** (Box 152, Neiafu; tel. 70-507), just west of the King's Palace, has a panoramic location on the hillside overlooking Port of Refuge. The six smallish rooms are T$20/30 single/double with shared bath (T$25/35 with a view), tax included. There's a communal kitchen.

The clean and attractive **Hill-Top Guest House** (tel. 70-209, fax 70-522) offers even more spectacular views of Neiafu and the harbor. The 10 rooms vary in price from T$13/23 single/double for a small, stuffy room with no view, to T$20/27 or T$28/35 for a large, airy room with a view, and T$45/55 for a four-person apartment with kitchen and private bath. They sometimes have water problems but there's a swimming pool. The excellent communal cooking facilities allow you to save a lot of money on restaurant meals. Standard precautions against theft should be taken here; for example, don't leave money and valuables in the room when you go out, and make sure nothing is within reach of an open window at night. If you wish, the manager provides safe-deposit boxes. If you leave food or beer in their common fridge, conceal it in a plastic bag or expect it to disappear. Noisy parties can also be a problem if the wrong crowd is present, and some of the long-term residents dampen the atmosphere. The Hill-Top offers scooter rentals at T$20 a day.

On the old harbor is the 13-room **Garden Bay Village** (Box 102, Neiafu; tel. 70-025, fax 70-200). The four duplex units (eight rooms) in the front row are T$20/35 single/double with private bath, while the two-room Princess Fale is T$48 for up to six persons (it's called that because one of the king's daughters once stayed there on a visit to Vava'u). Camping may be possible here. Continental breakfast is included, and if you ask, they'll allow you to use the restaurant kitchen to cook your own food when things aren't too busy. Two units with kitchen and fridge at the back of the property are rented out at T$250 a month for an entire unit, great if you can get one. Manager Marlene Moa arranges island tours. Loud music blares from the Garden Bay's nightclub on Wednesday, Friday, and Saturday nights (free admission for hotel guests).

Mikio Filitonga's **Vava'u Guest House** (Box 148, Neiafu; tel. 70-300, fax 70-441), right across the street from the Paradise Hotel, has a laid-back atmosphere. The five basic rooms with shared bath in an old stone building are T$9/14 single/double, while the five spacious bungalows with private bath, fan, and a table and chairs are T$20/25/30 single/double/triple. Unfortunately no cooking facilities are provided. The bountiful family-style dinners (T$11) served in the restaurant are quite good, although the service is extremely slow. Nonguests are welcome to eat here, and when there's sufficient demand Mikio stages a Sunday barbecue at 1700 (T$10 pp)—reserve directly by Friday.

Inexpensive

The **Paradise Hotel** (Box 11, Neiafu; tel. 70-211, fax 70-184), on a hill overlooking Port of Refuge Harbor near Neiafu, was purchased in 1981 by Kentucky millionaire Carter Johnson, who has done his best to keep the place up through the lean years of few tourists (the hotel is presently for sale at US$2.3 million). The 43 rooms with private bath start at T$47/52/62 single/double/triple for a fan-cooled budget room and go up to T$100/110/122 single/double/triple for a deluxe a/c harbor-view room—good value. The economy rooms have older furnishings and cold showers only, but they're clean with lots of towels and satisfactory beds. It's certainly Tonga's finest large hotel, and unlike some resorts in this category, the Paradise doesn't mind nonguests wandering in to use the restaurant, bar, and even the swimming pool (T$2 fee), and the atmosphere is friendly, relaxed, and welcoming. The bar at the Paradise is a good place to meet yachties and other visitors (try the ice cream), but skip the overpriced, poorly served meals in the restaurant. There's disco dancing to live music on Friday and Saturday nights; things pick up after 2200. Video films (T$2) are shown nightly at 2030; if you're a hotel guest ask to see the movie list and request a favorite. A book exchange is available at the reception. Not only does the hotel have a large pool. but there's good ocean swimming off their wharf. Fiberglass kayaks are for rent at T$10/20 a half/full day (pay and pick up the paddles at the bar). Airport transfers are free for guests.

FOOD

Tavake Refreshments (tel. 70-651), facing the main wharf behind Olga's Clothing, serves a good T$2 fish lunch weekdays until 1500.

The **Bounty Bar** (tel./fax 70-493; closed weekends), across from the banks in the center of town, serves breakfast, lunch, and dinner on weekdays. The menu includes five kinds of burgers, fried rice, and sandwiches. It's a real yachtie hangout and you get a great view of everything (including sunsets) from the back porch, though it's often hard to find a table. Live entertainment is often offered on Friday nights during the high May-Oct. season.

Ana's Waterfront Cafe (tel. 70-664; closed Sunday), directly below The Moorings, serves breakfast and lunch, and is a good place to come at happy hour (weekdays 1700-1800). The waterside location facing a dingy dock makes it another yachtie hangout. It's in a sort of cave, or 'ana in Tongan—there's no person called Ana here (The Moorings owns the place).

Francesco and Sonia Donati's **Sunset Restaurant** (tel. 70-397; closed Sunday), opposite the prominent Catholic church in Neiafu, serves Pisa-style Italian dishes and pizza on their harborfront terrace. Yachties can tie their dinghies to the Sunset's dock.

Neiafu's top place to eat may be the **Ocean Breeze Restaurant** (tel. 70-582, VHF channel 74), on the old harbor southeast of Neiafu.

Yachties anchored off Makave in the old harbor often use the Ocean Breeze's stone jetty to come for dinner. They specialize in seafood such as lobster, but also have steak, lamb, and chicken. You'll like the large portions, wine list, outstanding service, and excellent views. It's open daily 1800-2100 with reservations required on Sunday. One reader called it "an immaculate oasis of civilization." (Whenever at least three people want to go, English restaurateur John Dale runs day tours to outlying islands in his fiberglass speedboat. Ask to be shown the flying foxes.)

Groceries

Sailoame Market at Neiafu is crowded with people selling bananas, cabbage, carrots, Chinese lettuce, coconuts, green beans, lettuce, manioc, onions, papaya, tomatoes, taro, yams, zucchini, and oranges. Everything is about T$1 a bunch, and you're only assured a fair selection of fresh vegetables if you arrive early. You can also have lunch here for about T$2. The largest market is on Saturday and, if you come early enough, you'll hear street evangelists preach to the crowd outside as a policeman directs traffic.

Neiafu's two largest supermarkets, the **Tonga Cooperative Federation** (tel. 70-224), beside the MBf Bank, and the **Fatafata Mafana Center** (tel. 70-500), across the street, close weekdays at 1600, Saturday 1200, so shop early. Buy fish directly from locals at the harbor (no fish poisoning problems here).

ENTERTAINMENT

The **Neiafu Club** (tel. 70-566), near the Paradise Hotel, has a nice mix of tourists and locals. Once you sign the guest book, the bartender will remember your name next time you come in. It opens around 1500 daily (including Sunday) with happy hour starting at 1800.

The **Vava'u Club,** up the hill from the post office, has a great view but is more of a men's drinking place. They have two enormous pool tables where snooker and other such games are played; the bartender keeps sets of balls for eight-ball (hi-lo) and 15-ball pool. Beware of "mosquitoes" who will want you to buy them drinks. These characters are not allowed in the Neiafu Club.

From 2000 on Thursday, Friday, and Saturday nights a live dance band plays at the flashy **Puataukanave Disco** (tel. 70-644), below S.F. Paea & Sons opposite the Tonga Visitors Bureau (cover charge T$2/3 for women/men). A slightly older crowd frequents the nightclub at the **Garden Bay Village** (tel. 70-025) which cranks up on Wednesday, Friday, and Saturday nights.

For real earthy interplay, visit the **Nasaleti Club,** opposite the Catholic church. Here you can drink watery *kavatonga* all evening for a T$2.50 flat fee (open Mon.-Sat. 1930-2400).

Cultural Shows for Visitors

Several "feasts" are organized weekly for both land-based and water-bound visitors. For a set fee of around T$20 (half price for children under 10) you get a buffet-style meal of island foods such as roast suckling pig, octopus, fish, clams, lobster, crayfish, and taro, all baked in an *umu* (earth oven). Cooked papaya with coconut cream in the middle is served in half-coconut shells, and lots of watermelon is eaten while sitting on mats on the ground. Have a swim as soon as you arrive, then enjoy a drink (extra charge) to the strains of guitar music. Traditional dancing is performed later, and handicrafts are available for sale.

All of the feasts take place on outlying beaches; clients of The Moorings and Sunsail and other yachties are the biggest customers. Free minibus transfers are provided for visitors staying in Neiafu. Mr. 'Aisea Sikaleti of **Lisa Beach** and Matoto Latavao at **Ano Beach** always stage an island feast on Saturday afternoon, and sometimes also on Wednesday if demand warrants. John and Neti Tongia prepare a "gigantic roast" with traditional dancing and a kava ceremony at **Rove Hinakauea Beach** adjacent to Ano Beach on Thursday—good reports.

Book your spot for the feasts at the Paradise Hotel (tel. 70-211), the Bounty Bar (tel. 70-493), The Moorings, or Teta Tours. Often the feasts are canceled if not enough people sign up. Ask other visitors for their recommendations, as conditions do vary.

Events

The consummate time to be in Vava'u is the first week of May for the **Vava'u Festival** marking the crown prince's birthday on 4 May. There will be a display of handicrafts, sporting events, a game fishing tournament, a yacht regatta, boat parades, the Vava'u Marathon, island nights, concerts, dances, feasts, art exhibitions, church choir meetings, traditional Tongan games, a baby show, and a grand ball with the crowning of Miss Vava'u. Hotel rooms should be booked ahead at this time, as they should during the **Agricultural Show** in September when the king will be present.

Sunday morning the singing at the Free Wesleyan Church on Tui Rd. opposite the market is almost worth the plane fare to Vava'u.

Shopping

Handicrafts can be purchased at the **Langafonua Shop** (tel. 70-356), next to the Tonga Visitors Bureau, at the **FIMCO Handicraft Shop** (tel. 70-614), across the street, and at the **Vava'u Handicraft Shop**, in front of the post office.

Fa Sea Jewelry, opposite the yacht charter offices, also has crafts, some of them made from endangered species.

With enough lead time **Olga's Clothing** (tel. 70-064), between the post office and the Vava'u Club, makes clothes to order.

SERVICES AND INFORMATION

Money

The Bank of Tonga (tel. 70-068), near the Tonga Visitors Bureau, changes traveler's checks without commission, while the MBf Bank deducts T$2 commission. On the positive side, the MBf is open Saturday 0900-1130, when the Bank of Tonga is not. The ANZ Bank is next to the Fatafata Mafana Center. When the banks are closed the Paradise Hotel changes money for a small commission, but only for hotel guests.

Post and Telecommunications

Vava'u poste restante holds mail for two months. You can place local and long-distance telephone calls at the Telecom Telephone Exchange (tel. 70-255; open 24 hours) behind the post office. If you wish to receive a fax at Vava'u, you can have it sent here via fax 70-200 (T$1 a page to receive). Yachts, restaurants, and the police generally use VHF channel 16 to communicate.

Visas

Officially, extensions of stay up to six months are available for T$25 at the immigration office in the police station near the market. In practice, however, it's entirely up to the officers how long you'll get, and your attitude could have a lot to do with it.

Information

The Tonga Visitors Bureau (tel. 70-115, fax 70-630; closed Saturday afternoon and Sunday) in Neiafu has the usual brochures and can answer questions. Take the time to peruse their information boards to find out what's on around Vava'u. Teta Tours and the Paradise Hotel also have notice boards well worth checking. The Bounty Bar has a VHF radio that can be used to contact yachts at Vava'u.

The Friendly Islands Bookshop (tel. 70-153), diagonally opposite the Bank of Tonga and just up from the market, has postcards and a few good books about the islands.

The Dateline Bookshop (tel. 70-213), a bit up the side street from the Bank of Tonga, sells marine charts at T$18 and carries foreign newspapers.

The Moorings (tel. 70-016) produces a 32-page *Cruising Guide,* which comes with a chart indicating their 42 designated anchorages around Vava'u. The Friendly Islands Bookshop may sell a reproduction of their chart.

Teta Tours (tel. 70-488), next to the Bounty Bar, is a travel agency booking most activities and accommodations around Vava'u. They're usually very helpful.

Health

Ngu Hospital (tel. 70-201), on the northwest side of town, opened in 1981. You'll get better attention for T$25 at Dr. Alfredo Carafa's Italian Clinic (tel. 70-607; weekdays 0900-1400), behind the Bank of Tonga.

TRANSPORTATION

By Air

Royal Tongan Airlines (tel. 70-253) flies to Vava'u twice a week from Ha'apai (T$67) and fortnightly from Niuafo'ou (T$170) and Niuatoputapu (T$114). Service from Nuku'alofa (T$129) is twice daily except Sunday. The flights are often heavily booked, and cancellations occur without warning, so reconfirm early. Royal Tongan operates direct weekly flights between Vava'u and Nadi, Fiji (T$265/399 one-way/roundtrip).

Samoa Air (tel. 70-644, e-mail: tfpel-vv@kalianet.to), at S.F. Paea & Sons opposite the Tonga Visitors Bureau, sells tickets for the twice-weekly flight from Vava'u to Pago Pago (T$235/424 one-way/roundtrip). In past this flight has been on Wednesday and Saturday.

Lupepau'u Airport (VAV) is nine km north of Neiafu. The Paradise Hotel bus is T$4 pp (free for hotel guests) and a taxi is T$8 for the car (T$12 to the Tongan Beach Resort). Local buses (40 cents) run to/from Leimatu'a village, two km south of the airport, sporadically on weekdays and Saturday mornings; otherwise, it's easy to hitch from the airport into town (offer the driver a couple of *pa'anga*). There's no bank at the airport.

By Ship

Ships tie up to the wharf. The **Uata Shipping Lines** ferries *Loto Ha'angana* or *Tautahi* leave Neiafu for Ha'apai (T$21) and Nuku'alofa (T$42) Wednesday at 1400, whereas the **Shipping Corporation of Polynesia** ferry *Olovaha* leaves Thursday at 1600. Departures to the Niuas are about once a month. The office of the Shipping Corporation (tel. 70-128) is in the red container on the main wharf. The Uata Shipping office (tel. 70-490) is in the nearby white kiosk. See the chapter introduction for more information.

By Yacht

To crew on a cruising yacht, put up notices at the Paradise Hotel, the Bounty Bar, and Ana's Waterfront Cafe, and ask around the bar at the Neiafu Club and at the hotel. The yachting season is March-October. Until September try for a watery ride to Fiji; later most boats will be thinking of a run south to New Zealand.

Getting Around

Getting around Vava'u by public transport isn't really practical, although passenger trucks and minibuses departing Neiafu market do cover most of the roads on an unscheduled basis. Leimatu'a is fairly well serviced, as is Tu'anekivale. If you want to go to Holonga, you must take a bus as far as Mataika or Ha'alaufuli, then walk. Hitching is easy, but offer to pay if it looks like a passenger truck. They'll seldom ask more than T$1. Taxis charge about T$1.50 for the first kilometer, 50 cents each additional km. Waiting time is T$2.25 an hour. Check the price beforehand.

You can rent a car from **Teta Tours** (tel. 70-488), next to the Bounty Bar, at T$30/60 a half/full day. **Liviela Taxi** (tel. 70-240), opposite the Fatafata Mafana Center, charges T$70 a day. The adjacent **Vava'u Law Office** (tel. 70-549) asks T$50-60 a day. Before you taking a car, you'll have to obtain a Tongan driver's license (T$8) at the police station around the corner (bring your home driver's license). Insurance is not available and serious problems can arise in the event of an accident, so take care (ask how much extra they'll charge to supply a driver with the car). The speed limit is 40 kph in town or 60 kph on the open road.

Hill-Top Guest House (tel. 70-209 or 70-522) rents scooters at T$15/20/120 a half day/full day/week for a one-seater, or T$20/25/150 for a two-seater (Tongan license required).

Though Vava'u is a lot hillier than Tongatapu, a bicycle is still a good way to get around, and these can be rented from David Lavakeiaho (tel. 70-274), who lives between Chanel College and the Neiafu Club almost opposite the Paradise Hotel.

Local Tours

Minibus tours of Vava'u are offered by **Soane's Scenic Tours** (tel. 70-211) at T$35 pp without lunch (minimum of three persons). Book through the reception at the Paradise Hotel or Teta Tours.

Yacht Charters

Vava'u is one of the Pacific's top cruising grounds with more than 50 "world class" anchorages. Florida-based **The Moorings** (Box 119, Neiafu; tel. 70-016, fax 70-428, VHF channel 72, www.moorings.com, e-mail: moorings.tonga@kalianet.to) has a variety of charter yachts based here, beginning at US$370 a day for a two-couple Moorings 365 and increasing to US$720 daily for a 10-person Moorings 510. Add US$32 pp daily for provisioning, US$25 daily insurance, and 7.5% tax. If you're new to sailing (they check you out) it's another US$100 a day for a skipper. Additional crew might include a cook (US$80 daily) and a guide (US$60 daily). These charges soon add up—a party of four can expect to spend around US$4,000 a week to rent an uncrewed bareboat Beneteau yacht, meals included.

A 20% discount and security insurance waiver are possible if you book in person through the Vava'u office instead of booking ahead, although of course, there'd be no guarantee they'd have a yacht available for you if you followed that route. More information on The Moorings is provided under **Getting There** in the main introduction.

Sunsail (Private Bag, Neiafu; tel./fax 70-646), down by the water on the east side of The Moorings, has five charter yachts based here in the off season (Jan.-March), a dozen in the full season (April-Dec.). It's a bit cheaper than The Moorings because their prices are based on New Zealand dollars (from NZ$360/460 daily off/full season, plus tax). For more information contact Sunsail (Box 33729, Takapuna, Auckland, New Zealand; tel. 64-9/307-7077, fax 64-9/307-7177, www.sunsail.co.nz, e-mail: res.v@sunsail.co.nz). One-day trips around Vava'u by yacht are covered under Day Cruises, below.

Sailing Safaris (Box 153, Neiafu; tel./fax 70-650) is an independent yacht charter company based at Toula village. Some of their yachts are smaller than those offered by The Moorings and Sunsail, allowing couples to experience bareboat chartering without the high costs related to larger charter yachts. Prices range from T$225 a day for a 7.5-meter sloop accommodating two people to T$600 for an eight-person, 11-meter catamaran (plus T$115 for a skipper, if required). The minimum bareboat charter is three days. Aside from bareboat and skippered chartering, they also do day excursions and whalewatching at T$60 pp (lunch additional).

Day Cruises

A much more economical way to enjoy some sailing than chartering a yacht is to go out on Verne Kirk's 13-meter trimaran *Orion*. Verne offers a cruise to Swallows Cave and other sites daily 1000-1630 at T$35 pp (T$95 minimum). Verne is to be found near the swimming pool at the Paradise Hotel most afternoons at 1700. Similar is the 15-meter ketch *Melinda* owned by Christy Butterfield (tel. 70-861).

If the *Orion* and *Melinda* have sailed away by the time you get there, ask around for something similar. Small local operators like these know their waters and will take you on the South Seas adventure of your dreams.

Whalewatching

Each winter, July-Oct., more than 100 humpback whales come to Vava'u to bear their young before returning to the colder Antarctic waters for the southern summer. They generally stay on the western side of the group, in the lee of the prevailing trade winds. Lots of tour and fishing boats around Vava'u do whalewatching trips, and you'll easily see eight whales on a good day.

Whale Watch Vava'u (tel./fax 70-493) is the main operator with a specially designed boat including a proper viewing platform and a hydrophone that allows the mating songs of the males to be broadcast over speakers on board. Whale Watch offers full-day trips during the season, departing the Bounty Bar wharf at 0930 (T$65 pp, minimum of six). Lunch is T$10 extra. Under ideal conditions it's sometimes possible to swim with the whales, and snorkeling gear is provided. These trips can be booked at the Bounty Bar.

Whalewatching on the 10-meter fishing boat *Kiwi Magic* is T$55 pp with a minimum rate of T$120. Ask for Pat or Keith McKee (tel./fax 70-441) at the Vava'u Guest House.

SOUTH OF NEIAFU

The road south from Neiafu crosses two causeways before reaching **Nga'unoho** village (10 km), which has a lovely, clean beach. You can also swim at the Tongan Beach Resort at 'Utungake, and at Lisa and Ano Beaches south of Pangaimotu, although the snorkeling at all four is only fair. By bicycle, you'll find this is the hilliest part of Vava'u.

Accommodations

The **Tongan Beach Resort** (Box 104, Neiafu; tel./fax 70-380, VHF channel 71) is at 'Utungake village, about nine km from Neiafu. The beach here is fairly good and the 12 duplex bungalows (T$108/120/144 single/double/triple, tax included) are comfortable, although the six triples are nicer than the six doubles. The two overwater bungalows are T$220 double. There's a three-day minimum stay, and children 12 and under are half price. Rooms booked from abroad must be paid in full prior to arrival and will be more expensive. Scuba diving, game fishing, kayaking, and yacht charters are offered. One drawback is the cost of eating in their fancy thatched restaurant—it'll take some effort not to run up a daily food bill equal to the cost of your room (T$66 pp meal package available). Drinks at the bar are also expensive, so bring something along to put in your fridge (day-trippers from Neiafu are welcome to use the resort beach if they buy a few drinks). Actually, this resort suffers from its isolation without achieving the exotic effect of an outer-island hideaway (it faces the main shipping channel and is surrounded by a small Tongan village). Return airport transfers will be T$33 pp if arranged by the hotel, but you can get a taxi from Neiafu at T$7 for the car. Moderate.

The **Matamoana Tourist Court** (Toimoana and Kafoatu Taufaeteau, tel. 70-068, fax 70-332), right next to the Tongan Beach Resort, has four self-catering units with fan and fridge in two duplex blocks at T$42/48/53 single/double/triple—excellent value compared to the resort. It faces a beach only slightly worse than that of the resort itself. Budget.

The Tongia family operates **Rove Hinakauea Guesthouse** (VHF channel 16), on a lovely stretch of sand adjacent to Ano Beach at the south end of Pangaimotu Island. The four simple concrete bungalows with bath are T$20/35 single/double, and a T$6 pp dorm may also be available. The meals served here are expensive, but you may be able to do your own cooking (bring food). One the other hand, the T$20 feasts here on Thursday and Saturday evenings are good value. Ask about this place at the Tonga Visitors Bureau in Neiafu. A taxi from Neiafu will be around T$6.

WEST OF NEIAFU

From the Seventh-Day Adventist church on Tui Rd. in Neiafu a new highway leads west across the Vaipua Inlet causeway to western Vava'u. Beyond the causeway is a long steep incline at the top of which is a hill on the left called **Sia Ko Kafoa.** The track up the hill is on the left near the point where the road begins to descend again. Sia Ko Kafoa is an ancient burial mound built by the legendary chiefs Kafoa and Talau. It's an eerie, evocative spot with a good view of much of the island.

Keep straight (or left) at Tefisi and follow the rough track along the north side of **Lake Ano,** the still, fresh waters of which are easily accessible at one point. At Longomapu turn right and climb a long hill to **Toafa Church Farm** (Box 313, Neiafu; tel. 70-269) at the west end of the island, where there's a splendid view of the cliffs of

looking east along Vava'u's wild north coast from 'Utula'aina Point near Holonga

Hunga and many small islands trailing southward. If you have binoculars, you may see whales off Hunga July-October. A two-bedroom house with cooking facilities is sometimes for rent at the farm, but call ahead to make sure it's available and bring all of your own food. The Longomapu truck will drop you at the access road.

NORTHEAST OF NEIAFU

At **Feletoa** village, ask to see the burial place of Finau 'Ulukalala II behind the house opposite the primary school. The large rectangular *langi* is surrounded by big stone slabs. It was Finau's father, 'Ulukalala I, who had ordered the sacking of the British privateer *Port-au-Prince* at Ha'apai and who later adopted Will Mariner into his family. With the help of cannon from the ship and military advice from the survivors, 'Ulukalala II conquered Vava'u in 1808, and in 1810 he allowed Mariner to return to England. The dynasty came to an end when 'Ulukalala III's young son was deposed by King George Tupou I. Two centuries ago Feletoa was the center of power on Vava'u, and a Polynesian fortress was built here in 1808, but little remains today.

For a splendid view of the north coast, travel due north from Neiafu to Holonga. About two km beyond the village, turn left when the trail begins to descend to the beach, then right some 500 meters farther along. With a little luck you'll come out on **'Utula'aina Point,** a sheer cliff a couple of hundred meters above the sea. The quiet beach here is fine for relaxing but the water is too shallow for swimming. You could spend a whole day exploring this area.

OFFSHORE ISLANDS

The classic day tour at Vava'u encompasses Mariner's Cave, Swallows Cave, and Nuku Island. **Mariner's Cave** is a hollow in Nuapapu Island, southwest of Neiafu. You can approach it through an underwater tunnel in the island's stone face. The story goes that a young noble, fearing a despotic king might kill his sweetheart, hid her in this secret cave, coming back each night with food and water. Finally the young man and his friends built an oceangoing canoe and

spirited the girl away to safety in Fiji. The cave gets its name from William Mariner, who told the story to the world.

To find it, go west along the cliff about 300 meters from the northeast tip of Nuapapu, watching for a patch of dark, deep water. White calcium deposits speckle the rocks to the right of the underwater opening; a single coconut tree standing high above also marks the place. Snorkeling gear is recommended for entry, though a strong swimmer could go in without. The opening is about one meter below sea level at low tide, and you have to swim about four meters underwater to get through (it's comparable to diving under a yacht). The water is illuminated by sunlight, but come up slowly to avoid banging your head on a ledge. Swimming into Mariner's Cave is a bit like doing a bungee jump: it's certainly not for everyone and claustrophobic souls should give it a miss.

Swallows Cave on Kapa Island is far more obvious, and a small boat can motor right inside. Inside Swallows Cave is a rock that rings like a bell when struck, and in front of the entrance to another cave next to Swallows is a huge round coral that looks like an underwater elephant. There are also sea snakes here and an exciting vertical drop-off. All these caves face west, so the best conditions for photography are in the afternoon. Day-trips to these spots usually include a picnic on **Nuku Island** where the snorkeling may be good. One of the customary owners of Nuku may show up to collect a T$1 pp fee, one of the few places in Tonga where this happens.

Boat trips to the caves cost T$20-35 pp, depending on where you book, how many people are going, and whether lunch is included. **Soki Island Tours** (Sione Katalau) is a good company to go with, and all the guesthouse owners know about it. There's also Orion Charters and a few others. Soki Island Tours usually includes snorkeling on the Mala Island reef and along the dropoff at A'a Island in the Mariner's Cave trip (T$25 pp). Soki departs from the Bounty Wharf daily except Sunday at 1000, so long as four people book.

Vili Helu at the Island Gas Station (tel. 70-491), just below the ANZ Bank on the road to the wharf, runs all day boat trips at T$20 per head for four or more people, T$25 per head for three (bring your own lunch).

If you enjoyed the Mariner's Cave tour and are staying longer, consider going on the eastern islands tour (T$25) with **Lekeleka Tours** (Siaosi Maeakafa, tel. 70-101). Siaosi takes you from Neiafu's Old Harbor to Umuna Island (interesting cave), Kenutu Island (sea cliffs with huge breakers), and Ofu Island (nice beach). It's also possible to spend a few days at Siaosi's house in Ofu village.

The two tourist cafes, the Bounty Bar and Ana's Waterfront Cafe, are all good sources of information about all tours and activities around Vava'u, and can quickly put you in touch. The guesthouse managers too are very knowledgeable about such things, and Teta Tours can make the bookings. These trips are among the least expensive all-day boat excursions in the South Pacific.

Accommodations

A number of small resorts and restaurants exist on small islands south of Neiafu, and the easiest way to obtain current information on these is to check the information boards at the Bounty Bar, Tonga Visitors Bureau, Teta Tours, and the Paradise Hotel.

Tapana Island Resort (tel. 70-115), on a small island with seven beaches off Ano Beach, has three beach *fales* at T$10/12 single/double, plus camping space at T$3.50 pp. Meals are served at reasonable prices. It's run by a Tongan woman named Salote and her family, and information about this place is available at Teta Tours or at the Bounty Bar. Shoestring.

For four years a German named Joanna and her Tongan husband Moses ran a rustic restaurant and hideaway resort called the Berlin Bar on Kenutu Island, off the east side of Vava'u. In 1998 their lease expired so they moved over to anchorage number 28 on Ofu Island where **Mahina Lodge** now operates. The reefhouse with its private kitchen goes for T$40/75 single/double, while an a/c room in the main house is T$30/45, plus tax. Camping here is T$10/15 pp in your/their tent. Ask if you still need to bring (and cook) all your own food. Moses operates several boat tours, including a T$30 reef discovery tour. The shuttle boat leaves Neiafu's old harbor daily at 1000 May-Oct. (T$20 pp), provided someone has reserved. Bookings can be made from the Bounty Bar over VHF channel 16 or through Hilltop Guest House. Inexpensive.

Whale Watch Vava'u operates **Mounu Island Resort** (Allan and Lyn Bowe, tel. 70-576, fax 70-493, VHF channel 77), on a tiny island southeast of Vaka'eitu, with three *fales* are T$125 single or double (minimum stay three nights, children under 12 not accommodated). The three-meal plan is T$60 pp, return airport transfers T$30 pp. Whale-watching trips cost T$55 per head. Information is available at the Bounty Bar. Moderate.

Hans and Mele Schmeisser operate a small resort on otherwise uninhabited Vaka'eitu Island, near the southwest end of the Vava'u Group. **Popao Village Eco Resort** (tel. 70-308, fax 70-522) tries to recapture the lifestyle of an old Tongan village of thatched *fales* decorated with tapa wall hangings. The complex is set in natural surroundings on a low hill with grand views. The upper village has four deluxe *fales* with double beds, private bath, and wooden floors at T$50 double, and two traditional *fales* each with two single beds, shared bath, and gravel/mat floors at T$38. In the lower village are three standard *fales* at T$22/28 single/double. Discounts are available for those who stay 14 nights or more. There's no camping, electricity, generator, or traffic noise. Bucket showers are provided in a central bathhouse—you really experience everyday Tongan life as it was several decades ago. Breakfast, afternoon coffee and cake, and dinner are T$17 pp (T$7 extra for lunch, if required), and only fresh local foods are served. Guests are welcome to help with the cooking, which is done in the traditional way over an open fire or in a lava-stone *umu*. Fresh bread and rolls are baked in a firewood stone oven. Yachties anchored offshore can also eat in the Lighthouse Cafe if they announce their arrival over VHF channel 16 (and bring a flashlight). The snorkeling off the north end of Vaka'eitu is fantastic and small outrigger canoes are provided free. Fishing trips are organized using traditional methods such as the long spear and round throwing net *(kupenga)*. You can also try octopus fishing. Popao organizes yacht charters for whalewatching or visits to remote villages at T$29 pp (minimum for four), and boat trips to the southernmost Vava'u islands not visited by the tour boats from Neiafu are possible. Boat transfers from Neiafu to Popao cost T$29 pp each way (T$17 if you stay over a week). Popao is highly recommended as a totally unique Tongan experience, provided you don't mind roughing it a bit. Budget.

THE NIUAS 427

THE NIUAS

The isolated volcanic islands of Niuatoputapu, Tafahi, and Niuafo'ou sit midway between Vava'u and Samoa, and often share the devastating hurricanes common to the latter. Two owe their names to their ubiquitous coconut trees *(niu)*. Surprisingly, these were the first Tongan Islands to be seen by Europeans (by Schouten and Le Maire in 1616). The number of visitors to the Niuas today is negligible, but the islands have a lot to offer and are well worth including in your trip, if you can afford the extra airfare (and if the air service is operating).

NIUATOPUTAPU

Niuatoputapu Island, 300 km north of Vava'u, is a triangular island of 18 square km with a long central ridge 150 meters high. You can climb this ridge from Vaipoa village in the north and explore the many bush trails, which lead to small garden patches on top. A plain surrounds the ridge like the rim of a hat, and lovely white sandy beaches fringe the island, with a sheltered lagoon on the north side and pounding surf on the south. Much of the island is taken up by gardens producing copra and exquisite limes, but some fast-disappearing native forest remains in the south.

Niuatoputapu is a traditional island, where horse-drawn carts are still widely used and fine pandanus mats are made. All 1,300 inhabitants live in the three villages along the north coast. Hihifo, the administrative center, is about three km north of the airstrip. The wharf at Falehau offers good anchorage for yachties, good swimming for everyone.

The finest beaches are on **Hunganga Island,** accessible by wading at low tide. The channel between Hihifo and Hunganga is strikingly beautiful, with clean white sands set against curving palms, the majestic cone of Tafahi Island looming in the distance. The waterways south of the village are not only scenic but also idyllic swimming areas. Within Hihifo itself is **Niutoua Spring,** a long freshwater pool in a crevice—perfect for an afternoon swim. Countless pigs forage on the beach at Hihifo.

Practicalities
The only place to stay is **Kalolaine's Guest House** (tel. 85-021) in Hihifo, with five rooms at T$18/22 single/double (shared facilities). Meals can be ordered here. Shoestring.

The Produce Board maintains an adequate general store at Hihifo, and traveler's checks can be cashed at the post office. There's a bakery near the Mormon church at Vaipoa.

The top time to come is mid- to late August, when the king arrives for the annual Agricultural Show.

Getting There
Royal Tongan Airlines has fortnightly flights to Niuatoputapu (NTT) from Nuku'alofa (T$227) and Vava'u (T$114). Unfortunately there are no scheduled interisland flights between the Niuas and you must return to Vava'u to reach the other.

The supply ship from Nuku'alofa and Vava'u arrives about every month. Niuatoputapu is a port of entry and clearance for cruising yachts, most of which call on their way from Samoa to Vava'u between June and September.

TAFAHI ISLAND

Fertile, cone-shaped Tafahi Island, 3.4 square km in size and nine km north of the Niuatoputapu wharf, produces some of the highest quality

NIUATOPUTAPU

kava and vanilla in the South Pacific. Some 500 people live on the island and the only access is by small boat at high tide from Niuatoputapu. There are 154 concrete steps from the landing to clusters of houses on Tafahi's north slope.

The climb to the summit (555 meters) of extinct Tafahi volcano takes only three hours—get fresh water from bamboo stalks on top. On a clear day Samoa is visible from up there! You can also walk around the island in half a day, using the beach as your trail.

NIUAFO'OU

Niuafo'ou is Tonga's northernmost island, 574 km from Nuku'alofa and equidistant from Savai'i (Samoa), Taveuni (Fiji), and Vava'u. Despite the airstrip that opened in 1983, Niuafo'ou remains one of the most remot islands in the world. The supply ship calls about once a month, but there's no wharf on the island. Landings take place at Futu on the west side of the island.

For many years Niuafo'ou received its mail in oil-cloth-wrapped kerosene tins dropped from a passing freighter to waiting swimmers or canoeists, giving Tin Can Island its other name. In bad weather, rockets were used to shoot the mail from ship to shore. Early trader Walter George Quensell doubled as postmaster and brought fame to Niuafo'ou by stamping the mail with colorful postmarks.

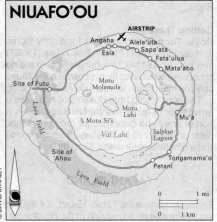

Special Niuafo'ou postage stamps, first issued in 1983, are prized by collectors.

The Land

Niuafo'ou (50 square km) is a collapsed volcanic cone once 1,300 meters high. Today the north rim of the caldera reaches 210 meters. The center of the island is occupied by a crater lake, **Vai Lahi,** nearly five km wide and 84 meters deep, lying 21 meters above sea level. From this lake rise small islands with crater lakes of their own—lakes within islands within a lake within an island. Grayish *lapila* fish live in these sulfurous waters.

Presently Niuafo'ou is dormant, but the southern and western sides of the island are covered by bare black **lava fields** from the many eruptions earlier this century. Lava flows emanating from fissures on the outer slopes of the caldera destroyed the villages of 'Ahau in 1853 and Futu in 1929. After Angaha disappeared under lava in 1946, the government evacuated the 1,300 inhabitants to 'Eua Island, where many live today. In 1958 some 200 refugees returned to Niuafo'ou, and by 1976 there were 678 people on the island once more (in 1996 735 people were present). Signs of the 1946 eruption are apparent in the vicinity of the airstrip.

Apart from the lava fields, the island is well forested. Incubator or megapode birds (*malau* in Tongan) lay eggs one-fifth the size of a grown bird in burrows two meters deep in the warm sands of the hot springs by the lake. Natural heating from magma close to the surface incubates the eggs, and after 50 days the megapode chicks emerge fully feathered and ready to fend for themselves. Unfortunately those *malau* eggs that aren't collected by the islanders for food are dug up by free-ranging pigs and the birds are facing extinction. Many tracks lead to the lake from all directions.

Facilities

Most government offices on Niuafo'ou are at Esia, but the Telecom office and Civil Aviation offices are at Sapa'ata. There are no official accommodations on Niuafo'ou, though some of the locals will accept paying guests. The Royal Tongan Airlines agent on Niuafo'ou should be able to arrange accommodation, and the airline office in Vava'u will radio ahead to let them know you're coming.

Getting There

Niuafo'ou (NFO) is theoretically accessible twice a month on the **Royal Tongan Airlines** flights from Nuku'alofa (T$279) and Vava'u (T$170). In practice the plane has a 50-50 chance of landing, as Niuafo'ou's airstrip is placed in such a way that dangerously strong winds whip across it. When that happens, the plane has to fly all the way back to Vava'u, and the people on the island see their long-awaited cargo go back where it came from for another two weeks. No scheduled flights go to Niuatoputapu.

CAPSULE TONGAN VOCABULARY

Although Tongans generally have a much better knowledge of English than do Samoans, a few words of Tongan will enrich your stay. Listen for the many glottal stops (marked below by apostrophes), which sound something like co'n (for cotton) in American English. In Tongan, "ng" is pronounced as in longing, not as in longer, making it Tong-a, rather than Tong-ga. The vowels sound as they do in Spanish or Italian.

afe to'ohema—turn left
afe to'omata'u—turn right
aha—no
alu—go (singular)
'alu a e—goodbye (to person going)
'alu hangatonu—go straight
amo—yes

baro—maybe
bimi—later

fakaleiti—transvestite
fakamolemole—please (polite form)
fale—house
fe'unga—that's enough
fefe hake?—how are you?
fefine—woman

ha'u—come (singular)
hena—there (by you)
heni—here (beside me)

'i fe?—where?
ika—fish
'ikai—no
'ikai ha taha—none, nothing
'io—yes

kataki—please (common form)
kaukau—bath
kaume'a—friend
koau—I
ko e ha?—what?
ko e me'a 'e fiha?—how many?

Ko fe 'a e fale malolo?—Where is the toilet?
kohai ia?—who is it?
ko koe—you
ko moutolu—you (plural)
kovi—bad

lahi—big, much

ma'ama'a—cheap
makona—full (of food)
malo—thank you
malo 'aupito—thank you very much
malo e lelei—hello
malohi—strong
malo pe—no thank you (at meals)
mamafa—expensive
mohe—sleep
mou nofo a e—goodbye (to several staying)
mou o a e—goodbye (to several going)

niu mata—drinking nut
niu motu'u—mature coconut
nofo a e—goodbye (to person staying)

o—go (plural)
'ofa—love
'oku fiha?—how much?
'oku mau—we
'oku nau—they
'Oku ou fieinua.—I'm thirsty.

'Oku ou fiekaia.—I'm hungry.
omai—come (plural)

palangi—foreigner

sai—good
sai pe—just fine
si'i—small

ta'ahine—girl
talitali fiefia—welcome
tamasi'i—boy
tangata—man
tulou—excuse me
tu'u—stop

NUMBERS

taha—1
ua—2
tolu—3
fa—4
nima—5
ono—6
fitu—7
valu—8
hiva—9
tahanoa—10
tahataha—11
uanoa—20
uanima—25
teau—100
tahaafe—1,000
tahamano—10,000

AMERICAN SAMOA
INTRODUCTION

American, or Eastern, Samoa, 4,000 km southwest of Hawaii, is the only U.S. territory south of the equator. Elbow-shaped Pago Pago Harbor (pronounced "Pahngo Pahngo"), made famous in Somerset Maugham's *Rain,* is one of the finest in the South Pacific, a natural hurricane shelter for shipping. It was this feature that attracted American attention in the late 19th century, as Germany built a vast commercial empire based around the coconut plantations of neighboring Upolu.

Until 1951 American Samoa was run as a naval base, but with advances in U.S. military technology it became obsolete, and control was turned over to civilian colonial administrators who created the welfare state of today. To replace lost income from the base closure, U.S. companies were encouraged to build tuna canneries in the territory. Today traffic constantly winds along Tutuila's narrow south coast highway, and American-style cops prowl in big black-and-white cruisers. Shopping centers and department stores have spread from the head of

Pago Pago Harbor out into suburbia beyond the airport.

American Samoa is a fascinating demonstration of the impact of American materialism on a communal island society. Although the Samoans have eagerly accepted the conveniences of modern life, the *fa'a Samoa,* or Samoan way, remains an important part of their lives. Thus far the Samoans have obtained many advantages from the U.S. connection, without the loss of lands and influx of aliens that have overwhelmed the Hawaiians. While this part of Samoa will always be American, the Samoans are determined to prevent it from going the way of Hawaii.

The Land
American Samoa is composed of seven main islands. Tutuila, Aunu'u, and the Manu'a Group (Ofu, Olosega, Ta'u) are high volcanic islands; Rose and Swains are small coral atolls. Tutuila is about midway between the far larger island of Upolu and the smaller Manu'a Group.

Tutuila is by far the largest island, with a steep

north coast cut by long ridges and open bays. The entire eastern half of Tutuila is crowded with rugged jungle-clad mountains, continuing west as a high broken plateau pitted with verdant craters of extinct volcanoes. The only substantial flat area is in the wide southern plain between Leone and the airport. Fjordlike Pago Pago Harbor, which almost bisects Tutuila, is a submerged crater, the south wall of which collapsed millions of years ago. Despite the natural beauty, recent studies have shown that the harbor is dying biologically as a result of pollutants dumped by the two tuna canneries and local villagers, and the culminating effect of oil and ammunition spills by the U.S. Navy decades ago. The marinelife of inner Pago Pago harbor is poisonously contaminated by heavy metals and unsafe for human consumption.

Climate

Although the climate is hot and humid year-round, it's hotter and rainier Nov.-April (the hurricane season). The frequency of hurricanes has increased dramatically in recent years. Many believe this is related to rising ocean temperatures caused by the greenhouse effect—and things could get worse in the future. Most hurricanes move into the area from the north but they can also come from east or west.

Temperatures are usually steady, but the stronger winds from May to October ventilate

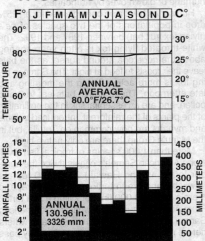

PAGO PAGO'S CLIMATE

the islands. The prevailing trade winds are from the east or southeast, with west or northwest winds and long periods of calm during the wetter season.

As warm easterlies are forced up and over Tutuila's Rainmaker Mountain, clouds form that drop their moisture on the harbor just to the west. Apia receives only half the annual rainfall of Pago Pago. From December to March the rain can continue for days, while the rest of the year it often comes in heavy downpours. The exact amount of rain in any given month varies greatly from year to year, and much of it falls at night. Actually, the weather can change from bright sunshine to heavy rain within five or 10 minutes at any time of year.

You can hear a recorded weather report along with tide times by calling tel. 699-9333. Dial 633-4949 and you'll be told the date, time, and temperature.

Fauna

The rarest of the territory's birds is the *manu-ma* (many-colored fruit dove), with only about 50 birds left in the wild. The only food the *manu-ma* has ever been observed to eat is the fruit of the *aoa* (banyan) tree, and the bird is now facing extinction largely due to the disappearance of

THE SAMOA ISLANDS

the *aoa,* many of which have been cut down by humans or blown over by hurricanes.

Hurricanes have also been blamed for an 85% drop in populations of the two species of *pe'a* (flying fox fruit bat) between 1987 and 1992. The white-throated flying fox is often seen soaring above the ridgetops around sunset as the bats leave their roosts to feed at night. The Samoan flying fox is more active during the morning and late afternoon. These native bats eat fruit and pollen, and are an essential link in the pollination of the plants of the rainforest. Introduced bulbuls and mynahs are now common on Tutuila, but in the Manu'a Group there are only native birds.

More than 1,000 species of tropical fish dwell along American Samoa's coasts (twice the number found around Hawaii). Only 120 female hawksbill and green turtles still nest here, and there's a US$10,000 fine for killing a sea turtle. From Aug.-Oct. humpback whales visit American Samoa to bear their young in these warm waters before returning to Antarctica, where they pass the southern summer. Sperm whales also call occasionally.

Two land snakes exist, neither poisonous. The blind potted soil snake, which looks rather like a plump earthworm, was introduced to Tutuila accidentally. The two-meter-long Pacific boa of Ta'u is found on islands from Indonesia to Samoa. Both are extremely rare and it's highly unlikely you'll ever see one.

History

The Polynesians emerged in Samoa some 3,000 years ago. By 600 B.C. they'd established a settlement on Tutuila at Tula. This nucleus (or a similar one in the Manu'a Group) may have been the jumping-off point for colonizing Eastern Polynesia (Tahiti and the Marquesas) about A.D. 300. The Samoans maintained regular contact by canoe with the other island groups of Western Polynesia, Tonga, and Fiji. Both Samoas belong to a single cultural area: the chiefs of Tutuila were subordinate to those of Upolu.

The first European in Samoa was the Dutchman Jacob Roggeveen, who visited the Manu'a Group in 1722. In 1786 Antoine de Bougainville, who was French, christened Samoa the "Navigator Islands" for the islanders in canoes he observed chasing schools of tuna far offshore. Another Frenchman, La Pérouse, called in 1787 and had a bloody encounter with the islanders. The Samoans nicknamed these early visitors *papalagi,* or "sky bursters," shortened today to *palagi* and applied to all whites.

Protestant missionary John Williams arrived in 1832 with eight Tahitians and influenza. His son, John Williams, Jr., became one of the first European traders. Nearly 40 years later, American businessmen chose Pago Pago Harbor as an ideal coaling station for their new steamship service from San Francisco to Australia. In 1872 the U.S. Navy sent a ship to negotiate a treaty with local chiefs. Though never ratified by the U.S. Senate, this agreement kept the other powers out of Tutuila. By the treaty of 7 November 1899, Germany and the U.S. partitioned Samoa between themselves, with British interests recognized in Tonga. In

SAMOA AT A GLANCE

POPULATION	AREA (sq. km)	HIGHEST POINT (meters)
Savai'i . . . . . . 45,050 (1991) 1,709 1,858		
Apolima . . . . 63 (1991) 1 168		
Manono . . . . . . 1,064 (1991) 3 107		
Upolu . . . . . 115,121 (1991) 1,114 1,100		
SAMOA . . . . . **161,298 (1991)** **2,842***		
Tutuila . . . . . . 44,643 (1990) 137 652		
Aunuu . . . . 400 (1990) 2 88		
Ofu . . . . 353 (1990) 7 494		
Olosega . . . . 225 (1990) 5 639		
Ta'u . . . . 1,136 (1990) 46 965		
Rose . . . . nil 1 5		
Swains . . . . 16 (1990) 3 5		
AMERICAN SAMOA . . . . **46,773 (1990)** **201**		

*The uninhabited islands of Nu'usafe'e, Nu'utele, Nu'ulua, Namu'a, and Fanuatapu are included in this total.

The Tu'i Manu'a, highest ranking chief of Eastern Samoa, was the last to sign a cession agreement with the U.S. (in 1904, four years after the chiefs of Tutuila signed). Before he died he willed that his title die with him, and to this day there has not been another Tu'i Manu'a. This photo was taken at Ta'u circa 1904.

iting the U.S.-administered Trust Territory of the Pacific Islands in Micronesia, north of the equator, leveled criticism at Washington for its "benign neglect." In 1961, with neighboring Western Samoa on the verge of independence and U.S. "colonialism" in Samoa becoming an issue, President Kennedy appointed Governor H. Rex Lee, a Mormon, to dispense a giant infusion of federal funds. A massive public works program financed construction of roads, schools, housing, port facilities, electrification, a new hospital, a tuna cannery, a modern hotel, and an international airport. Lee's most publicized innovation was educational television, introduced in 1964; by the mid-'70s, however, the emphasis of the broadcasts had shifted to the usual commercial programming.

This excessive government spending has created an artificial American standard of living. The Samoans became so dependent that three times they voted down proposals to increase home rule for fear it would mean fewer subsidies from Uncle Sam. Only in 1976, after a short tenure by unpopular Gov. Earl B. Ruth, did they finally agree in a referendum to elect their own governor. Even today, American Samoans receive more than US$5 million a year in food stamps, and lobbying for more money from Washington is the favorite occupation of local politicians.

Government

While Samoa received independence from New Zealand in 1962, American Samoa remains an "unincorporated" territory of the United States, meaning the U.S. Constitution and certain other laws don't apply. The Samoans have no desire to be brought under the jurisdiction of the U.S. Constitution, as this would mean an end to their system of chiefs and family-held lands, and would open the territory to uncontrolled migration and business competition from the U.S. mainland. Neither are they interested in independence so long as Washington is holding the purse strings and a majority of their people reside in the U.S. itself.

The territory is also defined as "unorganized," because it doesn't have a constitution sanctioned by the U.S. Congress. In 1966 federal officials authorized a Samoan constitution that included a bill of rights and gave legislative au-

1900 the U.S. annexed Tutuila and Aunu'u, adding the Manu'a Group in 1904. This act was not formally ratified by the U.S. Congress until 1929.

From 1900 to 1951 American Samoa was under the jurisdiction of the Navy Dept.; since then it has been the responsibility of the Department of the Interior. Thousands of U.S. Marines were trained on Tutuila during WW II, and concrete pillboxes built at that time still punctuate much of the island's coastline. The only wartime action the island experienced, however, was being hit by a few shells lobbed from a Japanese sub on 11 January 1942, which, ironically, damaged the store of one of Tutuila's few Japanese residents, Frank Shimasaki.

The Americanization of Samoa

Outside the war years, little happened to alter the centuries-old lifestyle of the Samoans until the early 1960s, when a United Nations mission vis-

thority to the Fono, a body composed of 20 representatives (two-year term) elected by the public at large and 18 senators (four-year term) chosen by the customary Samoan *matai* (chiefs). American Samoa's own colony, Swains Island, has a nonvoting representative. None of this has yet been made U.S. law by Congress.

The powers of the Fono increased during the 1970s; it now exercises considerable control over budget appropriations and executive appointments, though the Secretary of the Interior in Washington retains the right to cancel any law passed by the Fono, remove elected officials, and even cancel self-government itself without reference to the Samoans. The Secretary of the Interior appoints the Chief Justice of the High Court.

Every four years since 1977, American Samoans have elected their own governor and lieutenant governor. The governor can veto legislation passed by the Fono. Local political parties don't exist, although candidates often identify themselves with the U.S. Democratic or Republican parties. Since 1981 the territory has been represented in Washington by a nonvoting congressman elected every two years. Representative Eni F.H. Faleomavaega, a Democrat, was first elected in 1988 and has been reelected ever since.

Local government is conducted by three district governors, 15 county chiefs, and 55 *pulenu'u* (village mayors), all under the Secretary of Samoan Affairs, a leading *matai* himself.

Economy

Government, the largest employer, accounts for about a third of the workforce, followed by the tuna canneries with another third. The Government of American Samoa receives an annual US$72 million in subsidies and grants from Washington, half of its income. In fact, the territory gets more money in U.S. aid than the entire budget of independent Samoa, although American Samoa has one-third the population. This, and diverging living standards, ensure that the two Samoas will never be reunited. Residents of the territory pay exactly the same level of income tax as stateside taxpayers, and all such revenue is retained by the Government of American Samoa. Yet despite U.S. largess, the local government faces multimillion-dollar budgetary deficits every year, due largely to debts resulting

from overstaffing and the provision of free health and education services. Three-quarters of the local budget is spent on paying the salaries of the 4,000 government employees. American Samoans receive a total of US$18 million a year in federal social security payments.

American Samoa's primary industry is tuna processing by the Samoa Packing Co., user of the "Chicken of the Sea" label, and StarKist Samoa, a subsidiary of H.J. Heinz. The first cannery opened in 1954, and American Samoa today is the world's fourth-largest tuna processor and the most important commercial fishing port under the U.S. flag (Dutch Harbor, Alaska, is a distant second). Canned fish, canned pet food (from the blood meat), and fish meal (from the skin, guts, and bones) now account for the bulk of the territory's industrial output. Wastes from the canneries are barged out and dumped into the ocean.

Canneries thrive in this tiny U.S. territory because they allow Asian fishing companies to avoid U.S. import tariffs of up to 35% on processed fish. Goods have duty- and quota-free entry to the U.S. if 30% of their value is added in the territory. Federal law prohibits foreign commercial fishing boats from offloading tuna at U.S. ports; however, American Samoa is exempted. Thus the greater part of the South Pacific tuna catch is landed here, supplying the U.S. with about half its canned tuna, worth US$300 million a year. Even with this trade, imports into American Samoa are double exports (manufactured goods, food, and fuel are the biggest imports).

Both canneries pay virtually nothing in taxes to the local government and employ 4,000 cheap nonunion workers from western Samoa who put in two shifts. American Samoans themselves aren't at all interested in cleaning fish for US$3.10 an hour and instead work in business or government. Though they make millions on their tuna operations, the canneries have threatened to relocate if the minimum wage is raised or if the workers became unionized (cannery workers fearful of losing their jobs have several times voted against becoming members of the International Brotherhood of Teamsters). American Samoa and the Northern Mariana Islands are the only U.S. jurisdictions where federal minimum wage legislation doesn't apply.

The trend now is away from rust-eaten Korean

and Taiwanese longline tuna boats, toward large California purse seiners worth a couple of million dollars apiece. StarKist has 35 purse seiners under contract, Samoa Packing about 10. A total of 82 Korean and 36 Taiwanese longline boats also work out of Pago Pago. Most of the fish are taken in Papua New Guinea and Federated States of Micronesia waters (the Samoa canneries don't can fish caught by setting nets around dolphins). In aggregate, the canneries contribute about US$25 million a year to the local economy in wages, and spend another US$40 million on support services, fuel, and provisioning.

The Marine Railway near the canneries can dry-dock vessels up to 3,500 tons. In recent years harbor facilities have been upgraded through government investment as part of a scheme to make Pago Pago a transshipment center for surrounding countries, although not much has come of these plans.

The local government has recently established an industrial park at Tafuna near the airport where companies can lease land on which to build factories. Here manufacturers can exploit the territory's low minimum wages and duty- and quota-free tariff relationship with the United States. However, the first such company, Bao California Textile Corporation, announced in late 1998 that it was closing its new plant due to competition from low-cost producers in Asia.

Tourism development has been hampered by an unstable air connection to Honolulu, a reputation for unsuitable accommodations, environment degradation, and the incompetence of the local tourism authorities. Of the 39,802 arrivals in 1997, only about 10% were actual tourists. The rest came on business, to visit relatives, for employment, or in transit. Most were from the other Samoa, with U.S. citizens a distant second. The government-owned Rainmaker Hotel has only made a profit during two years of its three decades of operations and repeated attempts to sell the hotel have failed. It's now hoped that the creation of National Park of American Samoa will stimulate tourism.

The People

Between 1980 and 1998 the population of American Samoa almost doubled, from 32,297 to 61,600, an average increase of 3.7% a year. This is the fastest growth rate in the South Pacific, and at 308 persons per square kilometer, American Samoa is the second most densely populated South Pacific entity (after Tuvalu). All of this growth was on Tutuila; the population of the Manu'a Group declined slightly. The population of the harbor area is growing 8.2% a year.

American Samoans are U.S. "nationals," not citizens, the main difference being that nationals can't vote in U.S. presidential elections nor be drafted. American Samoans have free entry to the U.S., and some 65,000 of them now live in California and Washington State, and another 20,000 are in Hawaii, most in the lower income bracket. Nearly 70% of high school graduates leave within a year of graduation, many of them to voluntarily join the Armed Forces. About 1,175 students attend the American Samoa Community College at Mapusaga, a two-year institution established in 1970.

The people of the two Samoan groups are homogeneous in blood, speech, and traditions, and as fast as American Samoans leave for the States, people from the other Samoa migrate from west to east. Much intermarriage has occurred, and about 20,000 western Samoans now live in American Samoa. Some 1,750 Tongans and 900 Caucasians are also present, and only 41% of residents aged 15 years and over were actually born in the territory.

Although the young have largely forgotten their own culture in their haste to embrace that of the U.S., the *fa'a Samoa* is tenaciously defended by those who choose to remain in their home villages. For a complete description of the *fa'a Samoa,* see the Samoa **Introduction.** Under treaties signed with the Samoan chiefs in 1900 and 1904, the U.S. government undertook to retain the *matai* system and protect Samoan land rights. To its credit, it has done just that. In addition, the innate strength and flexibility of "the Samoan way" has permitted its survival in the face of German, New Zealand, and American colonialism.

On Tutuila the people live in 60 villages along the coast. After a hurricane in 1966, the U.S. government provided funds to rebuild the thatched Samoan *fales* in plywood and tin, resulting in the hot, stuffy dwellings one sees today. The most farsighted act of the former naval administration was to forbid the sale of Samoan land to outsiders. Except for a small area owned by the government and the two percent freehold land alienated before 1900, 90% of all land in the territory is communally owned by Samoan extended families *(aiga),* who even bury relatives in the yards in front of their homes to reinforce their titles. The family *matai* assigns use of communal land to different members of the *aiga.* If American citizens were allowed to buy land, the Samoans would undoubtedly be exploited as they have little knowledge of property values. Non-Samoans can lease Samoan land for up to 55 years, however.

American Samoa's largest churches are the Congregational Christian Church (20,680 adherents), the Catholic Church (8,500 adherents), the Church of Jesus Christ of Latter-day Saints (4,950 adherents), the Methodist Church (3,900

adherents), the Assemblies of God (2,700 adherents), and the Seventh-Day Adventists (1,700 adherents).

Away from Pago Pago Harbor, if there's a village behind a beach, you're expected to ask permission before swimming. Never swim anywhere near a church on Sunday, and be aware that most Samoans don't wear bathing suits—they swim in shorts and T-shirts. Foreigners in swimsuits on a village beach could give offense, hence the necessity of asking permission first.

During *sa* every afternoon around 1830 villagers pause in whatever they're doing for a brief prayer. If you hear a village bell around this time, stop walking, running, or riding to avoid raising the Samoans' ire. Some remote villages also have a 2200 curfew.

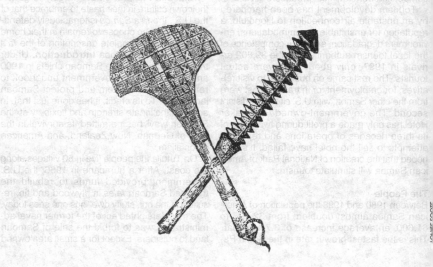

ON THE ROAD

Highlights

American Samoa's throbbing heart is Fagatogo Market, where buses unload passengers from both ends of Tutuila. Mount Alava, the canneries, Rainmaker Mountain, and Pago Pago Harbor are all visible from the market. Mount Alava itself may be the island's second-best sight, accessible on foot from the Fagasa road. A colorful island tour is easily arranged by boarding a bus to Tula or Leone. Those with more time, perseverance, and funds can catch a flight to the twin islands of Ofu and Olosega with their spectacular beaches and cliffs. A week is ample time to see Tutuila, and with two weeks you could do all of the above, if you can manage to get on the flight.

National Park

In 1988 the U.S. Congress authorized the creation the National Park of American Samoa, comprising 32 square km of tropical rainforest, coastal cliffs, and coral reef on Tutuila, Ofu, and Ta'u, and in 1993 nine villages signed 50-year leases involving annual fees of US$370,000 in total (this is the only U.S. national park in which the federal government leases the land).

On Tutuila the park stretches from Fagasa Bay to Afono Bay, encompassing everything north of the knifelike ridge. Countless seabirds nest on Pola Island. The largest unit is on Ta'u with Mt. Lata and the entire southeast corner of the island, including coastal, lowland, montane, and cloud forest communities. Ta'u's soaring cliffs and Laufuti Falls are spectacular. On Ofu the lovely southeastern beach and coral reef are included. Two endangered species of *pe'a* (flying fox), pollinators of the rainforest, are protected in the park.

This splendid national park, which ranks with Yellowstone and the Grand Canyon in majesty, seems destined to become American Samoa's biggest tourist attraction if an appropriate infrastructure for visitors can be put in place. Current information is available from the park visitor center (tel. 633-7082, fax 633-7085) in Suite 114 of the Pago Plaza at Pago Pago.

Public Holidays and Festivals

All standard U.S. public holidays are observed in American Samoa: New Year's Day (1 January), Martin Luther King Day (third Monday in January), Presidents' Day (third Monday in February), Flag Day (17 April), Good Friday (March/April), Memorial Day (last Monday in May), Independence Day (4 July), Labor Day (first Monday in September), Veteran's Day (11 November), Thanksgiving (fourth Thursday in November), and Christmas Day (25 December).

During Samoa Days in early April, schoolchildren perform traditional dances. American Samoa's **Flag Day,** 17 April, commemorates the first flying of the Stars and Stripes in 1900. This enthusiastic two-day celebration features *fautasi* (longboat) racing plus song and dance competitions in Fagatogo. Tourism Week in early July sees barbecues, canoe races, cultural demonstrations, fireworks, music, a parade, and the crowning of Miss American Samoa at Utulei Beach. (An invitation has been extended to the President of the United States to visit American Samoa for the centenary celebrations on 17 April 2000, possibly on his way to the Sydney Olympics.) Manu'a Cession Day is 16 July.

The second Sunday in October is White Sunday, when children dress in snow-white clothes and walk to church in procession, singing as they go. The children take the seats of honor and lead the service. After church there are family feasts, and gifts are given to the kids. Although European explorers didn't find Samoa until 230 years after Christopher got to America, Columbus or "Discoverer's" Day (second Monday in October) is also a public holiday. In fact, it's one of the biggest holidays of the year because it happens to coincide with White Sunday.

The **Moso'oi Tourism Festival** in mid-October is the occasion for sporting events, *fautasi* races, cultural performances, food and flower shows, a beauty pageant, and musical competitions. Most events are held at the Lee Auditorium.

Another important event is the rising of the *palolo* (coral worms) in late October or early November. When the moon and tide are just right and the *palolo* emerge to propagate, Samoans are waiting with nets and lanterns to scoop up this cherished delicacy, the caviar of the Pacific.

Visas and Officialdom

No visa is required for a stay of 30 days. An onward ticket is required of U.S. citizens and foreign nationals alike. Everyone except Americans requires a passport for entry. Americans can enter by showing a certified birth certificate, though a passport will be necessary to visit the other Samoa. Due to previous abuse of subsidized medical facilities, "alien" women more than six months pregnant are refused entry to American Samoa. Entry requirements are set by the Government of American Samoa—the U.S. Immigration and Naturalization Service does not exercise jurisdiction here.

Visa extensions are difficult to obtain (US$25 a month up to 90 days total) and work permits almost impossible unless you have a special skill somebody needs, in which case your sponsor will have to post a bond. For more information write: Chief Immigration Officer, Box 7, Pago Pago, American Samoa 96799 (tel. 633-4203). Their office is in the Executive Office Building in Utulei. If you're proceeding to Hawaii from Pago Pago and need a U.S. visa, be sure to pick it up at the U.S. Embassy in Apia or elsewhere as there's no visa-issuing office here.

Before departing Hawaii for American Samoa, cruising yachts must obtain a U.S. Customs clearance. Pago Pago is the only port of entry for cruising yachts and few try to fight their way back to Ofu and Ta'u against the wind. At Pago Pago, US$25 clearance fees are charged, plus an additional US$25 departure fee. On both occasions you must take your boat to the customs dock, where the waves bang it against the rough concrete. Tutuila is infested with the giant African snail. Customs officials in neighboring countries know this and carefully inspect baggage and shipping originating in Pago Pago.

Money

U.S. dollars are used, and to avoid big problems and exorbitant commissions when changing money, non-U.S. residents should bring traveler's checks expressed in American currency. Samoan currency is exchangeable in American Samoa but at a poor rate. If you lose your traveler's checks or credit cards, you can report American Express cards and checks at the Amerika Samoa Bank, and Visa at the Bank of Hawaii.

North American tourism has introduced tipping to the upmarket restaurants of the territory. The local saying goes, "it's not only accepted, it's expected." There's no bargaining in markets or shops.

Post and Telecommunications

Because U.S. postal rates apply, American Samoa is a cheap place for airmailing parcels to the U.S. (sea mail takes about 30 days to reach Oakland, California, by container). The mail service is reported to be erratic, so mark all mail to or from Pago Pago "priority post." The U.S. postal code is 96799, and regular U.S. postage stamps are used.

Long-distance telephone calls to the U.S. are unexpectedly more expensive than from Apia. A three-minute call costs US$5.70 to New Zealand or Australia, US$6 to the U.S., US$8 to Britain or Canada. Evenings and weekends you'll be eligible for a discount amounting to a few pennies on overtime charges to the U.S. but not elsewhere. Collect calls can be made to the U.S. only. More expensive but also available is AT&T's "USADirect" service at tel. 633-2771 (www.att.com/traveler).

Local telephone calls from public telephones anywhere in American Samoa cost only 10 cents each and the phones do work—get back into the habit of using them. Yes, it's only 10 cents to call the Manu'a Group from Tutuila. Local calls from private residences are free.

Local directory assistance is tel. 411. For the international operator, dial 0. American Samoa's telephone code is 684.

Media

The privately owned *Samoa News* (Box 909, Pago Pago 96799; tel. 633-5599, fax 633-4864, e-mail: samoanews@samoatelco.com), published weekdays, has been around since the 1960s. Special deals on accommodations and airfares are sometimes advertised in the *News*, and you get local insights.

Channel 2 at government-operated KVZK-TV (tel. 633-4191) broadcasts PBS, CNN, and a couple of hours of local programming 0600-2400 daily (local programs are on in the evening).

Catch CNN Headline News weekdays at 0800 and 1000, and KVZK local news weekdays at 1730. Commercial channel 4 has ABC/CBS/NBC programs 1500-2400 weekdays, 1200-2400 weekends. You can see the ABC world news weekdays at 1700, and the NBC nightly news weekdays at 1800. The tapes are broadcast with Hawaiian advertising. In 1995 satellite-generated cable television was introduced to the territory by two private companies, and although these cost about US$360 a year, dozens of channels are accessible 24 hours a day.

Privately operated Radio Samoa WVUV (tel. 688-7397, fax 688-1545) broadcasts 24 hours a day over 648 kHz AM. The music is a mix of Samoan, country, and adult contemporary, but there's no news.

KSBS-FM (Box 793, Pago Pago 96799; tel. 633-7000, fax 622-7839, www.samoanet.com/ksbsfm), at 92.1 MHz, broadcasts daily 0600-midnight, and you can pick it up everywhere on Tutuila. Throughout the day they play mostly island music and oldies, while in the evening there are also some top 40s for youthful listeners. KSBS rebroadcasts AP network news on the hour with live news in the morning.

Information Offices

The inefficient American Samoa Office of Tourism (Box 1147, Pago Pago, AS 96799, U.S.A.; tel. 633-1091, fax 633-1094, www.samoanet.com/americansamoa, e-mail: samoa@samoatelco.com), run by the Department of Commerce, occasionally mails out brochures upon request.

In the U.S. you can put your questions to American Samoa's congressman in Washington, the Hon. Eni F.H. Faleomavaega (tel. 1-202/225-8577, fax 1-202/225-8757, www.house.gov/faleomavaega).

Moon Travel Handbooks publishes a *Tonga-Samoa Handbook* with detailed travel information on Tonga, the Samoas, and Niue.

TRANSPORTATION

Getting There

Hawaiian Airlines (tel. 699-1875, fax 699-1282) links Pago Pago to Honolulu twice a week, with connections in Honolulu to/from Los Angeles, Las Vegas, Portland, San Francisco, and Seat-tle. Pago Pago-Honolulu costs US$728 roundtrip; Pago Pago-Los Angeles is US$1,028 roundtrip. Thirty-day advance purchase return fares are US$200 lower, but you must be physically there to buy such a ticket. One-way fares from Pago Pago are US$420 to Honolulu or US$600 to Los Angeles. Don't forget to reconfirm your onward flight if you don't want to get bumped. Since Hawaiian got rid of their ancient DC-8 and began using a wide-body, 230-seat DC-10 on this route, the service has improved.

Privately owned **Samoa Air** (Box 280, Pago Pago 96799; tel. 699-9106, fax 699-9751, e-mail: samoaair@samoatelco.com) has flights to Apia (US$69/93 one-way/roundtrip) four times a day or more, and to Maota on Savai'i (US$81/120) four times a week. Add US$8 tax to these fares. Most Samoa Air flights to Apia land at Fagali'i Airstrip and only those connecting with Air New Zealand go to Faleolo International Airport. When booking always check carefully which airport you'll be using.

Polynesian Airlines (tel. 699-9126) also has flights to Pago Pago from Apia six times a day, one landing at Faleolo International Airport and the other five at Fagali'i Airstrip. Polynesian charges fares one or two dollars lower than Samoa Air, and due to currency differences, tickets for the Pago Pago-Apia flight are much cheaper when purchased in Apia than in American Samoa or elsewhere. Most of the Apia flights on both airlines are on 19-seater Twin Otter aircraft. Beware of baggage handling irregularities on the flights of both companies, as damaged, delayed, or lost luggage is routine here—carry anything irreplaceable in your hand luggage.

Polynesian Airlines has connections in Apia to/from Australia and New Zealand on their own aircraft, to/from Honolulu and Los Angeles on Air New Zealand, and to/from Fiji on Air Pacific. Polynesian's 45-day Polypass (US$999) is valid for travel between the Samoas, Tonga, Australia, and New Zealand. For US$150 extra you can begin in Honolulu and for US$400 extra it's good from Los Angeles.

For those interested in a quick prearranged side trip from independent Samoa, **Oceania Tours** (tel. 685/24-443, fax 685/22-255), near the Kitano Tusitala Hotel in Apia, offers overnight fly/drive packages to Pago Pago. Beginning at US$159/250 single/double plus various taxes, these include return airfare, one night at the Api-olefaga Inn, and a car for 24 hours. They can also organize guided day-trips from Apia.

To/From Vava'u

Samoa Air's nonstop flight to Vava'u, Tonga (US$178/325 one-way/roundtrip), operates twice a week (currently on Tuesday and Friday) using a twin-engined, nine-seater Beechcraft King Air 100 plane. This is a useful connection, allowing you to visit Pago Pago, Vava'u, and Ha'apai for about the same price it might cost to fly straight from Apia to Nuku'alofa. The trouble is, such a routing is very difficult to arrange.

Since 98% of Samoa Air's customers are Tongans or Samoans, they couldn't be bothered going after international business, thus their fares aren't computerized in universal booking systems, and outside of Samoa or Tonga it's almost impossible to buy one of their tickets. This is a real problem since you need a ticket to leave American Samoa or Tonga before you'll be allowed entry, yet the Pago Pago-Vava'u ticket is very hard to obtain.

To order tickets directly from Samoa Air, you must call their office in Pago Pago to determine the exact price including the cost of shipping the tickets to you, then mail them an international money order expressed in U.S. dollars for that amount (credit cards are not accepted). Flight bookings can be made at the same time you check the ticket price, and you can always change them later.

Rather than get tied up in a clumsy, unreliable procedure such as this, you're better off having a Pago Pago, Apia, or Nuku'alofa travel agency handle your arrangements. Three well established companies to try are Royal Samoa Travel (Box 3483, Pago Pago, AS 96799, U.S.A.; tel. 684/633-5884, fax 684/633-1311), Oceania Travel (Box 9339, Apia, Samoa; tel. 685/24-443, fax 685/22-255), and Teta Tours (Box 215, Nuku'alofa, Tonga; tel. 676/21-688, fax 676/23-238, e-mail: tetatour@kalianet.to).

Hopefully by the time you read this, Samoa Air will have gotten its act together and you'll be able to purchase tickets at any travel agency worldwide, but don't count on it.

Local Flights

Samoa Air (tel. 699-9106) has two flights a day from Pago Pago to Ofu and Ta'u, leaving Pago Pago at 0600 and 1500 (US$44/86 one-way/roundtrip). The interisland flight *between* Ofu and Ta'u is US$22 and it's only guaranteed on Wednesday. Special fares are sometimes advertised in the local newspapers. The nine seats on these flights are often fully booked a week ahead, so inquire early and try making a telephoned reservation well in advance, if you're sure you want to go. Carefully reconfirm your Samoa Air flights every step of the way as this is a rather eccentric airline. The baggage limit on flights to Manu'a is 20 kilograms.

By Ship

The Samoa Shipping Corporation's ferry *Queen Salamasina* leaves Pago Pago for Apia Thursday at 1600 (eight hours, US$30/50 one-way/roundtrip). On major public holidays the ship makes two weekly trips, departing Pago Pago at 1600 on Wednesday and Friday. Safety regulations limit the number of passengers aboard to 206, and when that number of tickets have been sold, the ship is "full." Thus it's wise to book before noon a day ahead (take your passport). If you have to buy your ticket at the wharf, you'll be the last person allowed aboard and you won't find a proper place to sleep. The booking agent is **Polynesia Shipping** (Box 1478, Pago Pago 96799; tel. 633-1211), across from Sadie's Restaurant. Make sure your name is added to the passenger list or you won't be allowed on board. As your departure date approaches, keep in close touch with the agent as the schedule is subject to frequent change.

Boat fares are lower in the other Samoa, thus it's cheaper to buy only a one-way ticket to Apia and purchase your return portion there, although the Samoan ticket-to-leave requirement makes it difficult to take advantage of this savings. Coming from Apia, get a roundtrip ticket if you intend to return. Go aboard early to get a wooden bunk. The action of the southeast trade winds makes this a smoother trip westbound toward Apia than vice versa (but it can be rough anytime). Even veteran backpackers consider this a rough trip. Immigration formalities at both ends are chaotic because everyone pushes to be the first person off.

We don't know of any scheduled passenger boats from Pago Pago to Tonga, the Cook Islands, or Fiji. The main season for hitching rides to Tonga or Fiji on private yachts is mid-April to

October. Somebody at the Utulei Yacht Club may be able to advise.

The Port Administration, **Water Transportation Department** (tel. 633-5532), across the street from the Samoa News Building, runs a landing craft-type supply vessel, the *Manu'a Tele III*, to the Manu'a Group, an eight-hour trip. The boat leaves every two weeks on "pay week" when government employees get their checks, usually on a Wednesday, and it's US$20 each way to Ofu or Ta'u (or US$10 between these two islands).

Airport

Pago Pago International Airport (PPG) is built over the lagoon at Tafuna, 11 km southwest of Fagatoga. Transport to town is 75 cents by public bus or US$10-15 by taxi (agree on the price before and be sure you have exact change—the drivers *never* do). Public buses stop fairly frequently in front of the terminal (except on Sunday or after dark). Most of the car rental booths in the terminal open only for flights from Hawaii, although Avis stays open all day.

There's no tourist information desk or bank at the airport. The shops in front of the airline offices at the airport sell handicrafts, ice-cream cones, and snacks. The duty-free shop in the departure lounge is generally more expensive than these and is often closed. The restaurant (tel. 699-6070) around the corner behind the check-in counters serves filling American-style meals at reasonable prices. Watch your tickets and baggage tags carefully when you check in here, as the agents will happily book you through to wherever or strand you. The US$3 airport tax and US$5 "entry declaration fee" are included in the ticket price.

TUTUILA

The main island of American Samoa, Tutuila, is shaped like a Chinese dragon, 32 km long, anywhere from one to 10 km wide. Alone it accounts for 68% of American Samoa's surface area and more than 95% of its population. Surprisingly, this is one of the most varied and beautiful islands in the South Pacific. Its long mountainous spine twists from east to west with wild coastlines and cliffs on the north side, gentler landscapes and plains on the south. There are lots of good beaches scattered around, but for a variety of reasons, finding a good place to swim takes some doing. When it's calm the snorkeling is fine off the empty golden beaches all along the north coast, and the reef-break surfing along the south coast is especially good Dec.-March.

Fagatogo, the largest town, looks out onto elbowlike Pago Pago Harbor, while government is centered at Utulei, just east of Fagatogo. Despite the oil slicks and continual flood of pollution from canneries, shipping, yachts, and residents, this harbor is dramatically scenic with many fine hikes in the surrounding hills. Among the seemingly incompatible elements thrown together here are slow-moving Samoan villagers, immigrant cannery workers, taciturn Asian fishermen, carefree yachties, and colorful American expatriates—only tourists are missing. It's an unusual, unpretentious place to poke around for a few days.

SIGHTS

Utulei

At **Blunt's Point,** overlooking the mouth of Pago Pago Harbor, are two huge six-inch naval guns emplaced in 1941. To reach them from Utulei, start walking southeast on the main road past the oil tanks and keep watching on the right for a small pump house with two large metal pipes coming out of the wall. This pump is across the highway from a small beach, almost opposite two houses on the bay side of the road. The overgrown track up the hill begins behind the pump house. If arriving by bus from the west, get out as soon as you see the oil tanks and walk back. The lower gun is directly above a large green water tank, while the second is about 200 meters farther up the ridge. Concrete stairways lead to both guns but they're completely covered by vegetation, so be prepared.

After visiting the guns, walk back toward town as far as the Yacht Club where you see three long *fautasi* longboats, then turn left to the US$10-million **Executive Office Building** erect-

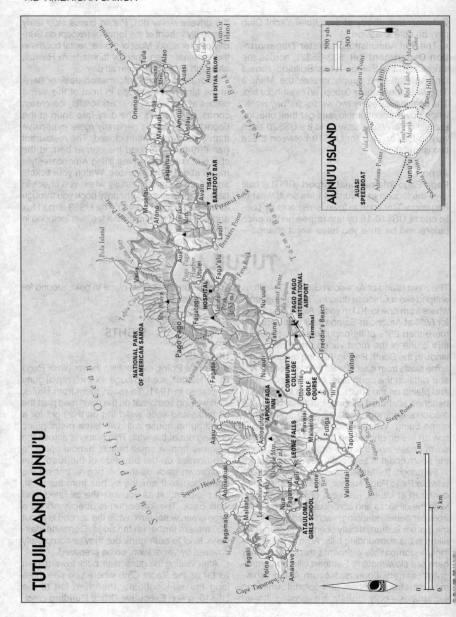

TUTUILA AND AUNU'U

AUNU'U ISLAND

500 yds
500 m

Ma Tama'a Cove
Aggaoleatu Point
Pola Hill
Red Lake
Pigatia Hill
Faaitafakaia Marsh
Pala Lake
Aloñsau Point
Aunu'u
Saiñuloñlu Point
AUASI SPEEDBOAT

Aunu'u Island
Red Lake
SEE DETAIL BELOW

Cape Matatula

Tula
Alao
Onenoa
Auasi
Ada
Amaua
Amouli
Afono
Masefau
Masausi
Alofau
Aoa
Fagaitua
Afono
Rainmaker Mtn.
Avalo
TISA'S BAREFOOT BAR
Pyramid Rock
Laulii
Breakers Point
Faga'alu
Fau Rock

Pola Island
Vatia
Craggy Point

Taema Bank
Nafanua Bank

HOSPITAL
Pago Pago
Fagasa
Mt. Alava
Utulei
Pago Pago Harbor
Matafao (653 m)
Fagatogo
NATIONAL PARK OF AMERICAN SAMOA

Nu'uuli
Coconut Point
Pala Lagoon
PAGO PAGO INTERNATIONAL AIRPORT
Terminal
Freddie's Beach
Fagalii Bay

South Pacific Ocean

Tafuna Cape

Aasu
Fagasa

COMMUNITY COLLEGE
Nu'uuli
Ottoville
Vaitogi
Laufou'ia
'APIOLEFAGA INN
Aoloaufou
Olotele Mtn. (491 m)
LEONE FALLS
Leafulalavao Mtn. (554 m)
Asili
Leone
Leone Bay
Pavaiai
Malaeloa
Futiga
Taputimu
Larsen Bay
Steps Point
Fagatele Bay

Square Head

Aoloautuai
Fagamutu
Nua
ATAULOMA GIRLS SCHOOL
Vailoatai
Siliaga

Fagamalo
Maloata
Matautu Bay
Malota Bay

Fagalii
Poloa
Amanave
Cape Taputapu

5 mi
5 km

ed in 1991 at Utulei. It's well worth going in to catch a glimpse of the territory's formidable bureaucracy. Behind this building is the new **Feleti Barstow Library** (1998), and beyond it a paved road winds up to the former **cable-car terminal** on Solo Hill. Here a monument recalls a 1980 air disaster in which a U.S. Navy plane hit the cables and crashed into the Rainmaker Hotel, killing the six servicemen aboard and two tourists at the hotel. The hotel manager refused to allow the memorial to be erected on the hotel grounds.

The cableway, one of the longest single-span aerial tramways in the world, was built in 1965 to transport TV technicians to the transmitters atop Mt. Alava (491 meters). The car would sway for a kilometer and a half over Pago Pago Harbor, with mountains such as rugged Rainmaker (524 meters) in full view, making this the most spectacular aerial ride in the Pacific. In 1992 Hurricane Val knocked the cableway out of service, but in early 1998 it was announced that a US$3 million federal grant would allow the cableway to be repaired in time for American Samoa's centenary in the year 2000. If so, the facility will allow easy access to the National Park facilities on Mt. Alava. Whatever happens, it's worth visiting the Utulei terminal for the excellent view of Rainmaker Mountain from the viewpoint.

Also in Utulei is the **Lee Auditorium** (1962) and American Samoa's **television studios,** which may be visited weekdays around 1030. In 1964 American Samoa became the first Pacific country to receive television, and although the original educational use has disappeared, KVZK-TV continues to broadcast commercially over two channels. Channel 2 is semi-educational, while Channel 4 is strictly commercial television. Channel 5 was blown off the air by Hurricane Val in 1992 and its equipment cannibalized to keep the other two channels going.

Fagatogo

The **Governor's Mansion,** on a hilltop just west of the Rainmaker Hotel, was built in 1903 during the naval administration as the Commandant's Residence, becoming Government House in 1951. A large sign requests the public not to enter the grounds. The **Jean P. Haydon Museum** (tel. 633-4347; open weekdays 1000-1500, admission free), farther west, was erected in 1917 as a naval commissary and served as the island's post office 1950-1971. The museum features exhibits on natural history, tapa making, and tattooing, plus a collection of war clubs, kava bowls, model canoes, and old photos.

Facing the Malae-O-Le-Talu field, where local chiefs ceded the island to the U.S. in 1900, is the **Fono Building** (1973), in which the territory's legislature convenes for 45-day sessions twice a year. The **police station,** across the field from the Fono, was originally the barracks of the Fitafita Guard, the former Samoan militia. Next to the police station is the **old jail** (1911), now the archives office.

Pago Pago Harbor as it looked in 1939 before roadbuilders broke out of the Bay Area

NATIONAL ARCHIVES, WASHINGTON, D.C.

Farther west just before the market is the old **courthouse** (1904), built in the U.S. Deep-South style. The **Fagatogo Public Market** is busiest early Saturday morning, when screaming red-faced evangelists backed up by ear-splitting gospel music harangue vendors selling tropical fruits and vegetables. Just inside the **Department of Marine and Wildlife Resources** office facing the bus station next to the market is a very good display of fish and birdlife of Samoa.

West of here is the former guesthouse where Somerset Maugham stayed in 1916, now **Sadie's Restaurant.** Today Maugham's tale of hooker Sadie Thompson and the repressed missionary, set here, is discussed over upscale seafood.

Pago Pago

Continue west to a sign reading National Park Visitor Center 1/4 Mile, where a road runs up the hill into Happy Valley. On this side road you pass six WW II ammunition bunkers on the left before reaching a dirt road, also on the left, which leads to a large **concrete bunker** used during WW II as a naval communications headquarters. Many of these military structures are now inhabited, and you'll need to ask permission before approaching the bunker, which is in a backyard.

The **National Park Visitor Center** (weekdays 0800-1600, Saturday 0800-1200, admission free), in Room 114 at Pago Shopping Plaza, contains a small collection of Samoan artifacts, seashells, coral, maps of American Samoa, and photos of the park. You can ask to see a brief video and the friendly staff will answer questions.

At the west end of the harbor is Pago Pago village, this area's namesake, and around on the north side of the harbor is the **Marine Railway,** which provides maintenance and repair facilities to the fishing fleet. The tuna canneries are nearby. To visit the **Samoa Packing Plant** (formerly owned by Van Camp) call the personnel office beforehand at tel. 644-5273 and make an appointment. You could also try asking at the gate. They'll want to know who you are, where you work, why you wish to visit, etc., and only persons wearing shoes and long pants are allowed inside the plant. StarKist (H.J. Heinz) is less amenable to visitors.

High on the reef just east of the canneries are eight Taiwanese and Korean fishing boats thrown up by Hurricane Val in 1992.

The North Coast

The easiest way to escape the congested Pago Pago harbor area is to jump on a bus to **Vatia** on Tutuila's north coast. Three buses (US$1.50) shuttle back and forth via Aua and Afono all day, so getting there is easy. Vatia is a picturesque village with a nice beach, and the scenery around here is superb with jungle-covered peaks surrounding the village on all sides. Look across to unforgettable Pola Island (also known as the "Cockscomb") with its sheer 100-meter cliffs and wheeling seabirds. Vatia is in the center of the Tutuila section of National Park of American Samoa, and if you're interested in some organized hiking or boating while at Vatia, call local resident Roy West (tel. 644-1416) who offers boat trips at US$25 pp and who can arrange hiking guides at the same rate.

The East End

Two more six-inch WW II guns are on the hillside near **Breakers Point.** Walk up past Mr. Paleafei's house, the large two-story dwelling at the high point in the road. The hill directly opposite the guns bears a small lighthouse with a view, while by the water at the bottom of the hill on the bay side is a concrete ammunition bunker now used for dynamite storage.

Eastern Tutuila is easily accessible on the frequent Tula buses that wind along the southeast coast through the day. At **Alao** and **Tula** are wide sandy beaches, but beware of the undertow. Unfortunately empty milk cartons and other trash from the nearby elementary school litter the area. From Tula (the end of the bus route), the road continues around to the north side of Tutuila as far as Onenoa.

Aunu'u Island

There's a single village on Aunu'u Island off the southeast end of Tutuila, but no cars. Motorboats shuttle across to Aunu'u constantly from the small boat harbor at Auasi, taking passengers at US$2 pp each way or US$10 one-way for a charter trip. Go over first thing in the morning and you shouldn't have any trouble getting back. Don't come on a Sunday though, as the locals don't appreciate *palagi* picnickers that day.

Aunu'u's eel-infested **Red Lake,** nested in the sprawling crater, is difficult to approach.

the monument to John Williams at Leone on Tutuila

Cliffs along the south coast and thick bushes make hiking around the island heavy going. Aunu'u's notorious stretch of red **quicksand** at Pala Lake is fairly close to the village, but you may have to wade through a swamp to get to it. The **taro swamps** just behind the village are easier to see, and a walk around to the new elementary school reveals an appealing slice of island life. At **Ma'ama'a Cove** on the east side of the island waves rush into "the teacup" with much spashing. It's picturesque, but don't swim here.

Around Leone

The Leone bus will drop you at **Leala Sliding Rock,** between Vailoatai and Taputimu, where the local kids take a running slide down the large, flat rocks covered by slimy algae. It's dangerous to imitate unless you know exactly how. From here you can hike east along the lovely coast toward Fagatele Point, but only in dry weather at low tide as the rocks become extremely slippery and dangerous when it rains. There are several clear tidal pools here where you can swim at low tide and even a blowhole.

Fagatele Bay, a drowned volcanic crater now a designated National Marine Sanctuary, cannot be reached from this side due to high cliffs.

From Sliding Rock it's a pleasant two km walk (or another bus) northwest to Leone village. Just before you reach the intersection with the main south coast road, ask someone to direct you to the former **Fagalele Boys School,** on the coast behind a row of large banyan trees. Built in the mid-19th century, this is the oldest European-style building on the island, unfortunately destroyed by Hurricane Val in 1992.

Leone was the ancient capital of Tutuila and when Samoa's first missionary, John Williams, visited on 18 October 1832, it was here that he landed. A monument to Williams is in front of **Zion Church** (1900) at Leone and the church itself is worth entering for its finely carved wooden ceiling. Until steamships were invented, Leone was the preferred anchorage of sailing ships unwilling to risk entering Pago Pago Harbor, and much of the early contact between Samoans and Europeans took place here. Two km up the road beginning beside the nearby Catholic church is **Leone Falls** (closed Sunday), where there's freshwater swimming.

Both Fagalele and Zion were built by the London Missionary Society, and a couple of kilometers west of Leone is the former **Atauloma Girls School** (1900), a third relic of LMS activity. Today the school building is owned by the territory and used as government housing for *palagis*—Samoans refuse to live there out of fear that it's haunted. When the sea is calm you can snorkel on the reef in front of Atauloma Girls School, and since there isn't a church is this village, it's usually okay to swim there even on Sunday. There's also surfing off the beaches at Atauloma and nearby Fagamutu.

Cape Taputapu

There's beautiful scenery along the road west of Leone. Get off the bus just beyond Amanave where the road swings north to Poloa. At low tide you can hike along the south coast from Amanave to Cape Taputapu in about 30 minutes, passing several lovely isolated beaches and rocky offshore islets. At high tide look for the slippery, muddy trail that cuts behind several of the more difficult stretches. There's a lovely white-sand beach at uninhabited Loa Cove

the Monument at Aasu to La Pérouse's
massacred crew members

DAVID STANLEY

halfway to the cape. The cape itself is magnificent, and it's exciting to stand on the rocky westernmost headland and watch the ocean rise and fall before you as it crashes into the shore.

The Northwest Coast

Buses run fairly frequently between Pavaiai and Aoloaufou, high in the center of the island. It's a short walk up a paved road from Aoloaufou to the radio towers on **Mt. Olotele** (493 meters) for the view.

From beyond Aoloaufou, a muddy, slippery trail leads down to Aasu village on **Massacre Bay,** about an hour each way. Only one family still lives here and in front of one of the houses is a monument erected in 1883 and surmounted by a cross. This memorializes 11 French sailors from the ships *Astrolabe* and *Boussole* of the ill-fated La Pérouse expedition, who were killed here in an encounter with the Samoans on 11 December 1787. Ask someone at Aasu to indicate the way to the waterfalls (and remember that this whole area is private property).

SPORTS AND RECREATION

Hiking

One of Tutuila's easiest and most rewarding hikes is through **National Park of American Samoa** to the TV towers on **Mt. Alava** (491 meters). The hourly Fagasa bus (50 cents) from Fagatogo Market runs up to the trailhead at the pass, but ask someone at the bus station where you should be waiting as the vehicle bears no destination sign. Don't worry if you have to sit there a while, as it's fun to observe the colorful locals coming and going, and on the way back to town it's easy to walk down through the village.

The TV towers on the summit are a two-hour walk northeast along a five-km jeep track from the Fagasa road (no chance of getting lost). A spectacular view of Pago Pago Harbor and Rainmaker Mountain is obtained from Mt. Alava, and if you're patient you may see an occasional flying fox glide silently by, even at midday. An overgrown trail down to Vatia on the north coast begins at the circular observation pavilion on the very top of the hill. Follow the ridge about 30 minutes east until you see power lines, which you follow down to Vatia. This trail is steep and should only be attempted in dry weather. Good boots and a some hiking experience are essential. Hopefully, the park authorities will upgrade this trail to make it accessible to everyone.

Mt. Matafao (653 meters), Tutuila's highest peak, can be climbed in half a day via a trail that begins directly opposite the beginning of the Mt. Alava track on the pass just mentioned. Climb the white metal ladder up onto the ridge south of the road; the trail is fairly obvious on top. It'll take about three hours up through a beautiful rainforest—stay on the ridge all the way. No special gear is required for this climb and you could even go alone, but avoid rainy weather when it gets slippery. In clear weather the view is one of the finest in the South Pacific.

Scuba Diving

Scuba diving is organized by the **Tutuila Dive Shop** (Box 5137, Pago Pago 96799; tel./fax 699-2842), under the big banyan tree in the center of Vaitogi village. It's run by John and Pisita Harrison: John has been diving Tutuila since 1986, Pisita runs the store and also dives. They charge US$65 for a two-tank dive including gear and a refreshment, and they rent tanks at US$7 a day, plus US$4 for a fill. A PADI open-water certification course is US$300.

Chuck Brugman's **Dive Samoa** (Box 3927, Pago Pago 96799; tel. 699-4980) operates out of Safety Systems (tel. 633-1701) in Faga'alu. You can also contact him through the Yacht Club. Chuck runs scuba trips at US$25 pp (minimum of two) for one tank, US$45 pp for two tanks, night dives US$35 (all gear is extra). Snorkelers can go along for US$10 pp, and sightseeing boat rides are US$10 pp (minimum of four persons). Most of Chuck's clients are local divers, and there's almost always a trip on Saturday. Unfortunately fish populations have been decimated by Samoans spearfishing with the help of scuba gear, and large areas of flat coral have been pulverized by fishermen standing on them or breaking off pieces to extract marinelife. On the up side, the currents aren't bad if the sea is flat.

Windsurfing

The windsurfing in Pago Pago Harbor is good year-round, although there's more wind June-October. The main drawback is the harbor's pollution. If you'd like some specific information, contact Bill Hyman at the Island Business Center (tel. 633-7457), behind the courthouse in Fagatogo.

Fishing

Captain Timothy D. Jones Sr. (Box 1413, Pago Pago 96799; tel. 633-2190) has a fishing boat called the *Miss Mihi,* which he charters at US$200 a half day (0630-1230) or US$300 a whole day. Up to four people can go for that price. If the fish are biting, Tim won't insist on returning to port or charge you extra, even if you only booked half a day. To motor out to the banks (50 km each way) where fish are guaranteed costs US$25 pp an hour (minimum of three people).

Golf and Tennis

Visitors are welcome at the 18-hole **'Ili'ili Golf Course** (tel. 699-2995 or 699-1762; open daily), maintained by the Department of Parks and Recreation at 'Ili'ili. You'll enjoy good views of the mountains and sea from the fairways, and inexpensive food and drink are available at the adjacent Country Club (tel. 688-2440). Greens fees are US$3/5 weekdays, US$4/7 weekends and holidays, for the nine/18 holes (or US$30 a month). Cart hire is US$7/14, plus US$10 for clubs (bring your own balls and tees). It's not necessary to book starting times, but clubs and carts should be reserved as they're in limited supply. The public tennis courts at Pago Pago and Tafuna are free.

ACCOMMODATIONS

Budget

Whether you love or hate Tutuila may well depend on the type of accommodations you get. Several good medium-priced places to stay do exist, but you should still expect to pay more than you would for similar accommodations elsewhere in the South Pacific. Knowing this in advance, it won't come as quite as much of a shock, and many other things such as food, drinks, groceries, toiletries, clothes, transportation, admissions, and telephone calls are relatively cheap, so it sort of averages out.

About the closest you'll come to backpackers' accommodations on Tutuila is offered by **Roy West** (Box 3412, Pago Pago 96799; tel. 644-1416), who lives in Vatia village on the north coast. He arranges places to stay with his extended Samoan family in the village at US$10 pp, and also has a secluded cabin at Amalau Bay, off the road to Vatia, which he rents at US$10 pp. Several beach *fales* are also here at US$5 pp, but you'd need a mosquito net. (The Amalau valley is a prime bird- and bat-watching area.) In addition, Roy has a plantation shack and accommodation in tent sites at Tafeu Bay, west of Vatia, accessible by trail in three hours or by boat in 10 minutes, plus 20 minutes on foot. Roy is probably your best bet for low-budget accommodations on Tutuila, so call him up as soon as you arrive. If you get his answering machine and don't have a number to leave, just say you're on your way and catch a bus over to Vatia (Roy says this system works fine). Other residents of Vatia also offer accommodations, if you don't manage to connect with Roy.

Another good choice for backpackers is **Tisa's Barefoot Bar** (Box 3576, Pago Pago 96799; tel. 622-7447), at Alega Beach on the southeast coast between Lauli'i and Avaio vil-

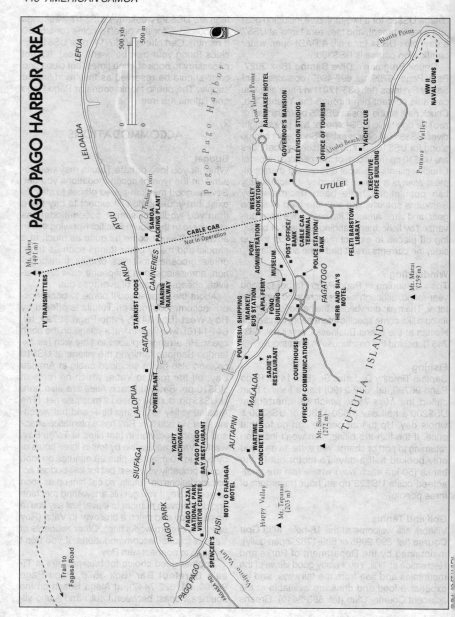

PAGO PAGO HARBOR AREA

lages. Tisa has two small *fales* right on the beach at US$25 for the entire *fale* (up to four people) with pillows, mosquito nets, and mats provided. If there are only one or two of you, they'll throw in breakfast. Running water is available, and Tisa's is in a secluded location away from the village. The bus service is cheaper and more frequent than to/from Vatia, but call ahead to check availability and prices.

Inexpensive

Herb and Sia's Motel (Box 430, Pago Pago 96799; tel. 633-5413), in the heart of Fagatogo, has gone downhill in recent years, although the prices haven't followed. The rooms, six with shared bath and three with private bath, all cost US$40/45 single/double. There's no hot water or cooking facilities, the air-conditioning and fridges may be out of order, and to be frank, the whole place is a dump. Avoid rooms five and six, which are without outside windows, and lock your door securely when you go out to the toilet. Be prepared for the sound of midnight "action" in adjacent rooms—women traveling alone shouldn't stay here.

Duke and Evalani's flashy **Motu O Fiafiaga Motel** (Box 1554, Pago Pago 96799; tel. 633-7777, fax 633-4767) is a big step up from Herb and Sia's for only a few dollars more. The 12 a/c rooms with TV and shared bath are US$60 single or double if you stay only one night, US$50 for two or more nights, breakfast included. This well-maintained two-story building overlooks a noisy highway, so ask for one of the five rooms on the back side if traffic bothers you, and while you're at it, try to get one end of the building away from the cabaret. House guests have access to an exercise room and sauna. The adjacent restaurant/bar under the same friendly management serves excellent and inexpensive American and Mexican food.

The top accommodation value in this category is without doubt **Barry's Bed & Breakfast** (Box 5572, Pago Pago 96799; tel. 688-2488, fax 633-9111), in a quiet residential area near the waterfalls at Leone. The four rooms in Barry's comfortable and solidly built two-story house go for US$35/40/50 single/double/triple including a large breakfast. There are full cooking facilities, hot water showers, a washing machine, TV, and a large tropical garden at your disposal. You can even borrow Barry's set of golf clubs. Local telephone calls are free. Barry Willis, a fifth generation part-Samoan, will make you feel right at home. Although it may at first appear out of the way, it's actually a bit closer to the airport than Fagatogo. Barry's makes a great base for seeing western Tutuila and is easily accessible on public transport with buses every 10 minutes throughout the day. Just be sure to catch the last bus back from town at 1700 and plan on spending Sunday around Leone. The bus rides back and forth from Fagatogo will be a memorable part of your visit.

Moderate

Tutuila's only big hotel is the 182-room **Rainmaker Hotel** (Box 996, Pago Pago 96799; tel. 633-4241, fax 633-5959), erected in the mid-'60s by Pan American Airways but now government-owned. The oval neo-Samoan architecture echoes Rainmaker Mountain across the bay. Rates start at US$60 single or double standard, US$72 beachfront, US$85 deluxe (with TV). More expensive *fales* and suites are also available. Third persons pay US$15, but children under 12 are free. Unfortunately it's rather run-down, so if the first room they give you is in bad condition, go back and ask for another. Request an upstairs room facing the beach. The Rainmaker features the usual bars, restaurants, gift shops, swimming pool, car rental offices, and landscaped grounds. The location is convenient and it should be your choice if you like Holiday Inn or TraveLodge type of places.

FOOD

Fast Food

An excellent selection of inexpensive eateries awaits you, although fried, high-sodium, and high-cholesterol foods are the norm at these. Most places provide the standard "bottomless" cup of coffee dear to American hearts. **Teo's Kitchen** (tel. 633-2250; open Saturday until 1600), beside Fagatogo Market, offers filling US$2 lunch specials, and it's always full of locals watching TV.

Da Maks Island Style Restaurant (tel. 633-5838; open weekdays 0700-1630), harborside behind the market, is more expensive with breakfast and "ono" lunch specials from US$5 a plate. You'll like Mel and Gretchen's mix of Samoan, Chinese, and Hawaiian foods, and the terrace just above the water is also nice.

Alamoana Fast Food (tel. 633-1854; weekdays 0700-1700, Saturday 0700-1500), next to the Record Store behind the Office of Communications, serves a hearty US$2 lunch. You point to what you want in a warmer at the counter.

Pinoy's Fast Foods, near the Samoa News Building between the Rainmaker and town, serves tasty Filipino dishes beginning at 0800 daily except Sunday and continuing until the food runs out. The portions are huge and prices excellent. Longshoremen and sailors are the clientele.

Krystal's Burger (tel. 688-2335), with four locations around Tutuila, puts McDonald's to shame with their tasty hot dogs, hamburgers, Mexican food, combo plates, and ice cream. They're open from 1000 until well after midnight (on Sunday from 1430). Look for them opposite the bus station in Fagatogo, and at Nu'uuli, Leone, and the airport.

Better Restaurants
The dining room at the **Rainmaker Hotel** (tel. 633-4241) offers a Samoan buffet lunch Friday 1130-1330 (US$9). Also try breakfast (0630-1100) or fish and chips (US$5.75) in the surprisingly good hotel coffee shop (open daily until 1800).

Vegetarians will have no trouble ordering at **Signore Paisano's Pizzeria** (tel. 633-2837; closed Sunday) in the Samoa News Building. Owner Jimmy Stevens, an animated New Jersey Italian, is kept hopping feeding homesick crews off the big purse seiners based nearby. Paisano's bakes some of the best pizza west of Santa Monica, plus huge submarine sandwiches jam-packed with corned beef, pastrami, and Italian sausage. Real mozzarella cheese is used.

Tutuila's top place to eat is **Sadie's Restaurant** (tel. 633-5981; closed Sunday), just west of the market. Despite the Maugham theme, Sadie's is as unpretentious as everything else on Tutuila and the American expats you see enjoying themselves at the tables are putting on no act. Dinner will set you back a lot farther than lunch, but the tuna dishes are said to be worth it.

The upmarket menu at the **Pago Bay Restaurant** (tel. 633-4197) in Pago Pago goes from hamburgers to Chinese food, with fresh seafood and U.S.-quality steak somewhere in between. Their fish and chips are worth asking for (here too, lunch is much less expensive than dinner).

Evie's Cantina (tel. 633-7777; lunch 1100-1400, dinner 1800-2200), at the Motu O Fiafiaga Motel in Pago Pago, dishes out some of the tastiest Mexican food in the South Pacific, plus karaoke nightly and a feature film with Sunday dinner. Need we say more?

Nu'uuli
Rubbles Tavern (tel. 699-4403; Mon.-Sat. 1100-midnight), in the Nu'uuli Shopping Center next to Transpac, is an a/c American-style diner with a smart bar. Steaks, fish, and pasta dishes are on the medium-priced menu.

A & A Pizza Drive-Thru (tel. 699-9428), at Malaeimi, a bit east of the Community College on the main road, is the favorite pizza place outside the bay area.

ENTERTAINMENT

The **Wallace Theaters** (tel. 699-9334), a.k.a. Nu'uuli Place Cinemas, in Nu'uuli, screens recent Hollywood films in two halls. All shows before 1800 weekdays and before 1300 weekends cost US$3.50 admission.

Bingo is now played (nightly except Sunday from 2000) in the former bowling alley across from Spencer's in Pago Pago.

Evalani's Cabaret Lounge (tel. 633-4776), at the Motu O Fiafiaga Motel in Pago Pago, has a spacious dance floor (dancing 2100 to closing), karaoke videos, and a nice local crowd. Co-owner Duke Wellington plays Tutuila's only grand piano during happy hours (1800-2100). The purse seiner guys tend to stand at the bar and cause trouble among themselves under the watchful eye of the mountainous bouncer.

Happy hours at the **Pago Bay Restaurant** (tel. 633-4197) in Pago Pago are a yachtie institution with free *pupus* (snacks) and US$2 drinks, weekdays 1700-1900. **Sadie's Restaurant** (tel. 633-5981) has happy hours weekdays 1630-1830 with the beer reduced from US$3 to US$2 (great with sashimi).

The Sadie Thompson Lounge off the main dining room at the **Rainmaker Hotel** has a consistently good happy hour band weekdays 1630-1830 (a favorite hangout of local politicians). Come early or you won't find a table. Shorts and bare feet are not permitted in the lounge after 1600; in fact, all of the places mentioned above except the bingo hall have strict dress codes in the evening. The drinking age in American Samoa is 21.

On Alega Beach between Lauli'i and Avaio villages is **Tisa's Barefoot Bar** (tel. 622-7447), subject of a number of magazine articles about a certain fertility tattoo on the proprietress. Tisa's is open on Sunday and you can swim here—a good place to go that day. Call to find out if they'll be serving the traditional Sunday *umu* lunch. "Tisa's jungle hop," a three-hour guided hike through the bush behind the bar, is US$10 pp including a snack.

Cultural Show for Visitors

A Polynesian variety show accompanies the Friday night Fia Fia buffet in the dining room at the Rainmaker Hotel (tel. 633-4241). Dinner is from 1830 and the show starts at 2000 (US$15 pp, reservations recommended). The food is excellent (prime rib, great salads), and you'll witness Maori war dances, Hawaiian hulas, and even a tropical version of "My Way!" The only other chance to see Samoan dancing is when a cruise ship arrives or leaves (which happens about four times a year), or on a local holiday.

SHOPPING

American Samoa is a poor place to shop for handicrafts and many of the items sold at the airport shops and elsewhere are imported from Tonga. About the easiest places to pick up souvenirs are the shops facing the airline offices at the airport (not the duty free shop in the departure lounge).

Clothing is a good buy here, and those long *puletasi* dresses make unique souvenirs. **Forsgren's** (tel. 633-5431) in Fagatogo has nice Samoan T-shirts and cut-rate clothes at some of the best prices in town. It's always crowded with nonresident Samoans who make the long pilgrimage from Apia just to shop here. **TK's Clothing** (tel. 633-2173), near Forsgren's, is another place to shop for cheap tropical garb and

lavalavas. **Spencer's** (tel. 633-4631) in Pago Pago also carries inexpensive clothing and shoes.

The **Transpac Corporation** (tel. 699-9589), in the Nu'uuli Shopping Center and below Sadie's Restaurant, has a good selection of imported goods. **The Record Store** (tel. 699-1283) sells cassette tapes of Samoan pop at two locations: Nu'uuli and Fagatogo. **Tropik-Traders** (tel. 699-5077), near Transpac in Nu'uuli, is the place to pick up magazines, compact discs, and gifts. Downtown closing time is inconveniently early at 1630 weekdays and 1200 on Saturday. You can buy tents at the hardware store across the street from Laufou Shopping Center in Nu'uuli.

In general, American Samoa is a cheap place to shop for consumer items because importers pay only three percent duty and there's no sales tax. Neighboring Samoa has a 10% sales tax and double-digit duties.

SERVICES AND INFORMATION

Money

The only place on the island which will change foreign currency is the Bank of Hawaii (tel. 633-4226, fax 633-2918; weekdays 0900-1500), beside the post office in Fagatogo and at Pava'ia'i out toward Leone. Brace yourself for a US$7.50 commission (no commission on U.S.-dollar traveler's checks). An ATM stands outside the Bank of Hawaii.

The locally owned Amerika Samoa Bank (tel. 633-1151) has branches next to the police station in Fagatogo and at Tafuna, both open Mon.-Fri. 0830-1500, Saturday 0900-1200. They won't touch foreign currencies but will cash U.S.-dollar American Express traveler's checks without commission (as will most other businesses in the territory). The Amerika Samoa Bank charges one percent commission on Visa traveler's checks (and other types are not accepted), so go to the Bank of Hawaii in you have anything other than American Express.

American Express itself is not represented in American Samoa.

Post and Telecommunications

The main post office (Monday and Friday 0900-1630, Tues.-Thurs. 0900-1500, Saturday 0900-

1300) is in Fagatogo with a contract station at Leone. There is no residential mail delivery but around 5,000 post office boxes are in use at the main post office. Mail addressed to General Delivery, Pago Pago, American Samoa, U.S.A. 96799, can be picked up at the main office Mon.-Fri. 0930-1100 and 1300-1500, Saturday 1030-1130 (mail is held 30 days). If you're a yachtie, ask the clerk to also check under the name of your boat.

Place long-distance telephone calls at the Office of Communications (tel. 633-1126; open 24 hours), diagonally across from the Fono Building in Fagatogo. Go at odd hours as this office is jammed around mid-afternoon. You can receive faxes addressed to fax 633-9111 here at a cost of US$3 for the first page, US$1 additional pages.

Laundromats and Toilets

Malia's Laundromat (tel. 633-5980; open daily until midnight), up the street opposite Fagatogo Market, charges 75 cents to wash or dry. You'll save 25 cents on the washing by going to Mary's Laundromat (closed Sunday), opposite Herb and Sia's Motel in Fagatogo, and there are many other laundromats around the island (ask the locals where they are).

The nameless laundromat next to The Tool Shop (tel. 633-7025), opposite the fisheries dock in Malaloa, has public showers (US$1) as well as washing machines.

Public toilets are next to the Jean P. Haydon Museum and near Da Maks Restaurant at the market.

Yachting Facilities

Harbormaster permitting, anchor your vessel as far away from the noise and smell of the canneries and power plant as you can. When all is calm, the stench can be almost unbearable and you feel this really is the armpit of the Pacific. There's bad holding in the harbor because the soft oozy bottom is covered with plastic bags. Lock your dinghy when you go ashore.

The Pago Pago Yacht Club (tel. 633-2465; Mon.-Thurs. 1130-2000, Fri.-Sun. 1130-2100) at Utulei is a friendly place worth frequenting in the late afternoon if you're looking to hitch a ride to Apia, Fiji, Wallis, Vava'u, or wherever. They can call any yachts in the vicinity over VHF channel 16. Check their notice board, or borrow a book

from their exchange. Friday 1600-1800 the whole yachting community converges here for happy hour-priced drinks and free *pupus* (snacks). That's also the time when local club members break out their longboats *(fautasi)* for a row around the harbor. The weekday luncheon menu is also good and visitors are always most welcome (ignore the Members Only sign on the door).

Pago Pago is a good place for cruising yachts to provision—ask about case discounts. For example, Tom Ho Ching Inc. (tel. 633-2430; open daily 0530-2300), in Faga'alu, has good case-lot prices on a variety of U.S. products. An even better place is Cost-U-Less (tel. 699-5975; Mon.-Fri. 0800-2000, Saturday 0800-1900, Sunday 1000-1800), a warehouse-style bulk store in Tafuna on the road from 'Ili'ili to the airport. Manager Jim Lutgen swears he won't be undersold. It's also easy to order yacht supplies from the U.S. mainland, and they're imported duty-free.

Tom French of Safety Systems (tel. 633-1701) opposite Matafao Elementary School at Faga'alu can repair life rafts and fire prevention systems for yachts. They also fill air tanks for scuba divers.

Information Offices

The rather muddled Office of Tourism (weekdays 0730-1600; tel. 633-1091), in the back of an old wooden building by the shore between the Rainmaker Hotel and the Yacht Club, can supply the usual brochures and answer simple questions. (This office has moved half a dozen times in as many years, so don't be surprised if they've moved again.)

The Department of Commerce (tel. 633-5155), in the Executive Office Building in Utulei, sells the *American Samoa Statistical Digest* (US$7.50).

The Wesley Bookshop (Box 4105, Pago Pago 96799; tel. 633-2201) at Fagatogo carries books by Samoan novelist Albert Wendt, which are hard to find in Apia. Ask if they have the *Tonga-Samoa Handbook* from Moon Travel Handbooks.

There's good reading at the Feleti Barstow Library (tel. 633-1182; weekdays 0730-1200 and 1300-1530), behind the Executive Office Building in Utulei. The Community College between Utulei and Leone also has a library (tel. 699-1151), which is open weekdays 0730-1600.

Hawaiian Airlines (tel. 699-1875), Polynesian Airlines (tel. 699-9126), and Samoa Air (tel. 699-

9106) all have their offices at the airport. Samoa Air represents Air New Zealand. If possible, reconfirm your flight out as soon as you arrive. The travel agencies directly above the post office in Fagatogo sell air tickets for the same price as the airlines, and they are usually less crowded and more helpful.

Health

The 140-bed LBJ Tropical Medical Center (tel. 633-1222, fax 633-1869) in Faga'alu has doctors on call 24 hours a day in the Outpatients Department (US$2 fee). A dental checkup is also US$2 (appointment required). Inpatient rates at the hospital are US$60 a day. Prescription drugs are US$3 per item, but no malaria pills are available.

Several private medical clinics are at Nu'uuli, including Anesi Medical Clinic (tel. 699-1276; open 1630-2030 weekdays), 50 meters east of Laufou Shopping Center, and F & P Clinic (tel. 699-5118; weekdays 1600-2100), in a corner of Laufou Shopping Center.

Dr. Isara T. Tago's private Family Dental Practice (tel. 699-9812), near Krystal's Burger at Nu'uuli, is open weekdays 0800-1600.

The Drug Store (tel. 633-4630) has branches in Laufou Shopping Center at Nu'uuli and on the road to the hospital.

GETTING AROUND

For an American territory, bus services on Tutuila are extremely good. Family-owned *aiga* buses offer unscheduled service from Fagatogo to all of the outlying villages. You can flag them down anywhere along their routes, and you bang on the roof when you want to get off. Not all the buses are marked with a destination, however; also, there's no service after 1600 on Saturday, and very little on Sunday or after dark any day. Bus service begins at 0400 to get workers to the first shift at the canneries—useful if you have to catch an early flight. No standing is allowed, so the rides are usually a lot of fun. Most buses play blaring music.

Bus fares are very reasonable. You pay as you leave and it's smart to carry small change: ask someone how much the fare should be before you get on and just pay the exact amount. A trip anywhere in the congested zone from the canneries to the hospital is 25 cents. Westbound to the airport intersection is 50 cents, US$1 to Leone and Amanave, US$1.25 to Fagamalo; eastbound it's 50 cents to Lauli'i, 75 cents to Avaio or Fagasa, US$1 to Aoloaufou or Tula. Service from Fagatogo to Leone is fairly frequent, and you can change buses at Leone for points west. Change at Pavaiai for Aoloaufou. The bus across the island to Vatia leaves from in front of Da Mak Restaurant at Fagatogo market about once an hour (US$1.50).

Taxis are expensive and it's important to agree on the price before getting into a meterless taxi anywhere on Tutuila. Expect to pay at least US$1 a mile. You'll find taxi stands at the market and airport (tel. 699-1179), otherwise call **Pago Cab Service** (tel. 633-5545) or **Samoa Cab Service** (tel. 633-5870), both next to the market, or **Island Taxi** (tel. 633-5645), near the Office of Communications.

Car Rentals

Bus service to the north coast villages of Fagamalo, Fagasa, Masefau, Aoa, and Onenoa is infrequent, so to reach them easily you'll need to rent a car. The main car rental companies have counters at the airport. If no one is present, use the nearby public telephones to call around, checking current prices and requesting a car delivery to the airport.

The most professional car rental company on Tutuila is **Avis** (tel. 699-4409 at the main office at Pavaiai, tel. 699-2746 at the airport, fax 699-4305). They charge US$45 a day, plus US$8 insurance (US$500 deductible), for their cheapest car.

Royal Samoa Car Rental (tel. 633-4545 at the Rainmaker Hotel) only staffs their airport counter for Hawaiian Airlines flights. They charge US$45 daily for a non-a/c car, plus US$5 for third-party liability insurance (US$500 deductible).

Pavitts U-Drive (tel. 699-1456 during business hours, tel. 699-2628 after hours) usually has a representative at the airport during the day and also for all Hawaiian Airlines flights. Pavitts charges US$50 a day but it's not possible to buy collision insurance coverage on their cars.

Collins Rental Agency (tel. 633-2652, fax 633-2654), above the post office in Fagatogo, rents cars at US$40 a day including insurance.

All rates include unlimited mileage and all vehicles must have public liability insurance. Most of the agencies only rent to persons over the age of 25 and your home driver's license is honored here for 30 days. Lock your car and don't leave valuables in sight. One of the biggest problems with driving on Tutuila is the lack of places to pull over and get out. Most villages have open *fales* facing the beach, so you'll often feel like an intruder.

Driving is on the right and the speed limit is 48 kph (30 mph) unless otherwise posted. You must stop if you see a yellow school bus loading or unloading, unless the driver signals you to proceed. Transporting open alcoholic beverage containers is illegal. On the other hand, seat belts and child restraints are not mandatory, you may drive a car barefoot or while listening to music with headsets, and it's okay to transport passengers in the back of an open pickup truck

(verify these points with the rental agency—the rules may have changed). Motorcyclists must wear helmets.

Local Tours
Roy West of **North Shore Tours** (Box 3412, Pago Pago 96799; tel. 644-1416) offers a wide range of hiking, mountain climbing, birdwatching, snorkeling, and boat trips at very reasonable prices. Roy's ecotours cost US$25-35 pp for a full day, plus US$5 for lunch (if required). If you want to hike Tutuila's rugged north coast, climb Rainmaker Mountain, or get dropped off at an inaccessible bay for a few days of real Robinson Crusoe living, Roy is the guy to call. He also has a good knowledge of Samoan plants. His base is at Vatia, so many of the trips leave from there.

Royal Samoa Travel (tel. 633-2017), next to the Fale Fono at Fagatogo, offers three-hour sightseeing tours of either the east or west sides of Tutuila at US$30 pp (two-person minimum).

THE MANU'A GROUP

The three small islands of the Manu'a Group, 100 km east of Tutuila, offer spellbinding scenery in a quiet village environment. Ta'u is the territory's most traditional island, but the beaches are far better and more numerous on Ofu and Olosega. All three islands feature stimulating hiking possibilities and an opportunity for the adventurer to escape the rat race on Tutuila. The biggest hassle is canine: a real or pretended stone will keep the dogs at bay.

Although a couple of small guesthouses are available, few tourists make it to Manu'a. Regular air service from Tutuila has now made these islands more accessible, but book early as local commuters fill the flights. Remember that telephone calls from Tutuila to the Manu'a Group cost only 10 cents each, so don't hesitate to call ahead to check on accommodations.

OFU AND OLOSEGA

Ofu and Olosega appear to be the remaining northern portions of a massive volcano whose southern side disintegrated into the sea. Some of the best snorkeling is around the concrete bridge

that links these soaring volcanic islands; just be aware of currents. The strong current between Ofu and Nuutele islands makes snorkeling off Alaufau or Ofu villages risky, though the small-boat harbor just north of Alaufau is better protected than the one on Ta'u. The airstrip is by a long white beach on the south side of Ofu, about an hour's walk from Olosega village, and it's still possible to have to yourself this quintessential Polynesian paradise of swaying palms, magnificent reef, and mountains rising out of the sea. The beach and reef between Papaloloa Point and the bridge are now part of National Park of American Samoa. Bring your own snorkeling gear as none is available locally.

To climb to the television tower atop Ofu's **Tumu Mountain** (494 meters), take the five-km jeep track up the hill from near the wharf at Alaufau village and continue up to the ridge top, then over the mountain to a spectacular lookout on Leolo Ridge (458 meters) above the airstrip. Notice how the vegetation changes as you rise.

Accommodations and Food
Most visitors stay at **Vaoto Lodge** (Box 1809, Pago Pago 96799; tel. 655-1120 or 699-9628),

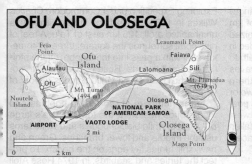

OFU AND OLOSEGA

(map labels) Leaumasili Point, Feia Point, Ofu Island, Faiava, Alaufau, Lalomoana, Sili, Ofu, Mt. Piumafua (639 m), Mt. Tumu (494 m), Nuutele Island, Olosega, NATIONAL PARK OF AMERICAN SAMOA, AIRPORT, VAOTO LODGE, Olosega Island, Maga Point, 0 2 mi, 0 2 km

near the beach beside the airstrip on Ofu. The 10 fan-cooled rooms with private bath are US$35/40/50 single/double/triple. Cooking facilities are not available but hosts Tito, Marty, and Marge Malae prepare good local meals at US$15 for all three. They'll make you feel like one of the family; ask Tito to tell you a ghost story. Inexpensive.

Don and Ilaisa's Motel (Box 932, Pago Pago 96799; tel. 655-1212) in Olosega village has five rooms at US$25/35 single/double. Some rooms have private bath, some shared, and all guests have access to a common kitchen and fridge. There's a small store in the village where you can get basic supplies. Often the whole building is rented out to contract workers for extended periods, so be sure to call ahead to check availability. Budget.

Prior to arrival, you could also try calling Faufano Autele (tel. 655-1123), who can sometimes arrange budget accommodations on Ofu. Ta'auau Peau (tel. 655-1110) in Ofu village rents rooms and provides meals at the same rate as Vaoto Lodge.

Rather than camp along Ofu's beautiful south coast beach, which is now part of the national park, keep east toward the bridge, then just before you reach the bridge cut down to the deserted beach on the north side of the island. You'll be less likely to have visitors here than you would by the road, but bring all the food and water you'll need.

TA'U

Ta'u is a rectangular island 10 km long and five km wide. It's only 11 km southeast of Olosega,

with a submarine volcano between the two. Eons ago the south side of Ta'u collapsed, leaving dramatic 500-meter-high cliffs that rise directly from the southern sea. Five smaller craters dot the steep northern slopes of Lata Mountain (995 meters), the highest peak in American Samoa.

The entire southeast corner of Ta'u is included in National Park of American Samoa, the largest of the park's three units. Craters punctuate the island's wild, thickly forested interior, known for its steep slopes and gullies. Terrain and bush can change suddenly from easy hiking to difficult, and most of the upland area is inaccessible.

From Ta'u the Tui Manu'a ruled the entire group. In 1925, as a young woman of 24, Margaret Mead researched her book, *Coming of Age in Samoa,* at Luma village on Ta'u. The present inhabitants of Ta'u live in villages at the northeast and northwest corners of the island. Small-boat harbors are at Luma and Faleasao, with the most sheltered anchorage for yachts at Faleasao. The reef pass is very narrow, and Luma harbor is used mostly by local fishing boats (not recommended for yachts). The airstrip is at Fitiuta in the northeast corner of the island.

Sights
At Luma village, see the tomb of the Tui Manu'a and other chiefly burials near the **Sacred Water,** or "royal pool" (dry). Also of interest is the **cave of Ma'ava,** the legendary giant. There's a nice beach at **Fagamalo Cove,** halfway down the west coast south of Fusi.

From Fitiuta it's possible to hike south along the coast into American Samoa's extraordinary

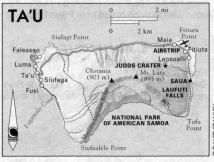

TA'U

(map labels) 0 2 mi, 0 2 km, Siulagi Point, Maia, Fitiuta Point, Faleasao, Leosoalii, AIRSTRIP, Fitiuta, Luma, Olotania (903 m), JUDDS CRATER, Ta'u, Siufaga, Mt. Lata (995 m), SAUA, Fusi, LAUFUTI FALLS, Maaloasaaman Ridge, Fagamalo Cove, NATIONAL PARK OF AMERICAN SAMOA, Tufu Point, Siufaalele Point, © DAVID STANLEY

national park. Legend tells how the god Tanga-loa created humans at Saua, a couple of km south of Fitiuata, and from here they colonized Polynesia. Everything south of here is included in the national park. The track continues south to Tufu Point, around which are views of waves crashing into Ta'u's rocky, volcanic southern coast, where sheer volcanic cliffs soar in two or three steps to cloud-covered Mt. Lata. It's possible to follow the shoreline a couple of km west to 450-meter-high **Laufuti Falls,** although fallen trees and huge rocks block the way in places. Beyond Laufuti, one must bushwhack.

Accommodations and Food

The most convenient place to stay is **Fitiuta Lodge** (Box 1858, Pago Pago 96799; tel. 677-3501 or 677-3411), in Fitiuta village a short walk from the airstrip. The eight rooms with shared bath are US$25/45 single/double and cooking facilities are provided. Inexpensive.

The **Ta'u Motel** (Box 637, Pago Pago 96799; tel. 677-3467 or 677-3504) is near the small-boat harbor in Luma village, on the opposite side of the island from the airstrip. It has nine clean rooms with bath and fridge at US$25/40 single/double, and you can cook your own food. Discounts are possible for long stays and often the entire motel is booked out by local contractors for extended periods, so call ahead (ask for Niumata Mailo). He can pick you up at the airport at between US$10-20 for the trip (not pp), depending on whether he has to go anyway. Inexpensive.

No restaurants are to be found on Ta'u, only small village stores. If your baggage isn't overweight, bring some food with you on the plane from Tutuila. There's no bakery on Ta'u so it's a good idea to bring bread from Pago Pago.

CORAL ATOLLS

Rose Atoll

Discovered by French navigator Louis de Frey-cinet in 1819, Rose Atoll was visited by the U.S. Exploring Expedition under Commodore Charles Wilkes in 1839. In 1921 the U.S. claimed this uninhabited atoll, 125 km east of Ta'u. A reef of pink coral surrounds the square, three-by-three-km atoll with a pass into the lagoon. Of the atoll's two small islands, Rose is covered with coconut and other trees, while Sand is devoid of vegetation.

Large numbers of red-footed boobies and frigate birds nest near the top of Rose's large *buka* trees, while black noddies and white terns use the middle and lower branches. Green and hawksbill turtles lay eggs on the beach. To protect the turtles and seabirds, in 1974 Rose Atoll was included in the **Pacific Islands National Wildlife Refuges,** administered by the U.S. Fish and Wildlife Service (Box 50167, Honolulu, HI 96850, U.S.A.; tel. 1-808/541-1201, fax 1-808/1216, www.fws.gov). Special permission is required to land.

Swains Island

Swains Island, 340 km northwest of Tutuila, is a circular coral atoll about two km across and 13 km around the fringing reef. There's a large lagoon in the center not connected to the sea. Swains is far closer to Tokelau than to the rest of Samoa. In fact, its customary owners were the Tokelauans of Fakaofo, who knew it as Olohega. In 1856 a New England whaling captain, Eli Jennings, arrived to set up a coconut plantation with the help of Polynesian labor; his descendants still run it as a private estate today. At present about a dozen people live on Swains.

Olohega was included in the Union Group (Tokelau), which Britain incorporated into the Gilbert and Ellice Islands Colony in 1916. In 1925, when Britain transferred Tokelau to N.Z. administration, the U.S. took advantage of the opportunity to annex Swains to American Samoa. Finally, in 1980 the U.S. government forced the Tokelauans to sign a treaty recognizing American sovereignty over Swains as a condition for the withdrawal of U.S. "claims" to the entire Tokelau Group and recognition of Tokelau's 200-nautical-mile fisheries zone.

SAMOA
INTRODUCTION

The sultry, verdant isles of Samoa, two-thirds of the way between Hawaii and New Zealand, lie in the very heart of the South Pacific. Independent since 1962 and called Western Samoa until 1997, this is the larger portion of an archipelago split apart by colonialism in 1899. Although both Samoa and American Samoa sprang from the same roots, differing patterns of development are reflected in contrasting lifestyles—this highlights the impact of Westernization on a Pacific people. Yet on both sides of the 100-km strait separating Upolu from Tutuila, Samoans have retained their ancient customs as nowhere else in Polynesia, and the *fa'a Samoa,* or Samoan way, continues to flourish.

Travelers inbound from a dreary industrial world may be forgiven if they imagine they've arrived in the garden of Eden, but there's more to it. In a series of provocative novels, Samoan author Albert Wendt has portrayed the conflicting pressures of *palagi* (foreign) life on his people. The protagonist in *Sons for the Return Home*

finds he can no longer accept the *fa'a*-sanctioned authority of his mother, while *Leaves of the Banyan Tree* explores the universal themes of a changing Samoan society. In *Pouliuli,* the complex social relationships of village life unravel in a drama of compelling force. Wendt's books bring us closer to the complexity of a third-world Samoa shaken by economic crises, incompetence, and corruption, and searching desperately for a formula to reconcile timeworn traditions and contemporary consumer needs. "Gauguin is dead! There is no paradise!" shouts a character in Sia Figiel's recent novel *Where We Once Belonged.*

Paradoxically, although your status as a foreigner will never be in doubt, you'll find the Samoans to be among the South Pacific's most approachable peoples. You'll sight some really striking physical types and meet a few unforgettable characters. Some visitors find it too intense, but almost everyone will leave with a story to tell about Samoa. Alongside the human element, an outstanding variety of landscapes and attractions are packed into a small area made all the more accessible because this is one of the least expensive countries in the region. Everything is vividly colorful and well-groomed, and it's still undiscovered by mass tourism. Add it all up and you'll recognize Samoa as one of the world's top travel destinations and an essential stop on any South Pacific trip.

The Land

Samoa is made up of four inhabited and five uninhabited islands totaling 2,842 square km, a bit bigger than the American state of Rhode Island. Unlike most Pacific countries, which are scattered across vast areas, all of these islands are in one main cluster, which makes getting around fairly easy. Upolu is the more developed and populous, containing the capital, Apia; Savai'i is a much broader island. Together these two account for 96% of Samoa's land area and 99% of the population. Between them sit populated Apolima and Manono, while the five islets off southeast Upolu shelter only seabirds. The fringing reefs around the two big islands protect soft, radiantly calm coastlines.

Samoa's lush volcanic islands increase in age from west to east. Savai'i, though dormant, spewed lava this century; the now-extinct cones of western Upolu erupted much more recently than those farther east. Well-weathered Tutuila and Manu'a in American Samoa are older yet, while 10-million-year-old Rose Island is a classic atoll.

Savai'i is a massive shield-type island formed by fast-flowing lava building up in layers over a long period. The low coast gradually slopes upward to a broad, 1,858-meter center of several parallel chains. Upolu's elongated 1,100-meter dorsal spine of extinct shield volcanoes slopes more steeply on the south than on the north. The eastern part of the island is rough and broken, while broad plains are found in the west.

Climate

Samoa is closer to the equator than Fiji, Tonga, or Rarotonga, thus it's noticeably hotter and more humid year-round. May-Oct. (winter) the days are cooled by the southeast trades; winds vary from west to north in the rainy season, Nov.-April (summer). Practically speaking, the seasonal variations are not great, and long periods

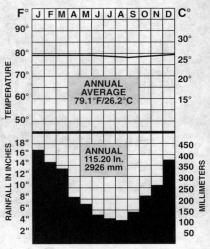

of sun are common even during the "rainy" months. Southern Upolu gets more rain than northern, but much of it falls at night. The rainfall feeds Samoa's many spectacular waterfalls and supports the luxuriant vegetation.

December to March is hurricane time; ships at Apia should put to sea at the first warning as the harbor is unsafe when a storm blows out of the north. In recent years, Samoa has suffered an increasing number of devastating hurricanes partially due to the greenhouse effect as the surrounding seas warm up.

Flora and Fauna

Rainforests thrive in the mountain areas, where heavy rainfall nurtures huge tree ferns and slow-growing, moss-laden hardwoods. The vegetation is sparse in the intermediate zones, where more recent lava flows fail to hold moisture or soil. The richer coastal strip is well planted in vegetable gardens and coconut plantations. The national flower is the *teuila* or red ginger *(Alpinia purpurata),* an elongated stalk with many waxy red petals.

Although Upolu is smaller than Savai'i, its rich volcanic soil supports 72% of the population of Samoa; much of Savai'i is barren due to recent lava flows and the porousness of the soil, which allows rapid runoff of moisture. The rainforests of Samoa are threatened by exploitive logging operations for short-sighted economic gain and already 80% of the lowland tropical rainforests have been replaced by plantations or logged. On a square kilometer basis, deforestation is occurring much faster than in the Amazon. Replanting is usually done in teak and mahogany, which native birds cannot use.

About 16 of 34 land bird species are unique to Samoa. One such species, the toothbilled pigeon or manumea (Didunculus strigirostris), is thought to be a living link with toothbilled birds of fossil times. Due to overhunting and habitat destruction, all native species of pigeons and doves are approaching extinction. Parliament has banned all hunting of fruit bats (flying foxes) and Pacific pigeons, but this is not enforced and the populations have not recovered from the carnage on the 1980s. From 1981 to 1986 more than 30,000 flying foxes were exported from Samoa to Guam for gastronomical purposes, a trade that ended only in 1989 when the bats were added to the endangered species list. No snakes live on Upolu, although two harmless species are found on Savai'i. Attack dogs are a nuisance throughout Samoa, but unless you've actually entered someone's yard, they'll soon retreat when they see you reaching down to pick up a stone.

HISTORY AND GOVERNMENT

Prehistory

Samoa was named for the sacred (sa) chickens (moa) of Lu, son of Tagaloa, the god of creation. Samoan tradition asserts that Savai'i was Hawaiki, the legendary Polynesian homeland where the Samoans originated. Archaeologists confirm that the Polynesians had settled in Samoa by 1000 B.C. and here evolved their distinctive culture. It was a beautiful, comfortable, productive place to live. Their vegetables thrived in the rich volcanic soil, and the lagoon provided ample fish. They had found their true home; not for another millennium did small groups push farther east from this "cradle of Polynesia" to colonize Tahiti and the Marquesas.

The ancient Samoans maintained regular contact with Fiji and Tonga; Tongan invaders ruled Samoa from A.D. 950 to 1250 and the oral traditions of Samoa date back to the expulsion of the Tongans. This feat was accomplished by the first holder of what is still the highest chiefly title, Malietoa, meaning brave (malie) warrior (toa). The legendary 15th-century queen, Salamasina, became the only Samoan ruler ever to unite the four chiefly titles into one, and for 60 years Samoa enjoyed peace. The matai, or chiefly system, was well developed for almost 1,000 years before Europeans arrived in the late 18th century. Religion was less developed, and the chiefs were elected from high-ranking lineages: everywhere else in Polynesia they were hereditary.

Christianity and Commercialization

Although several Dutch and French explorers had sighted Samoa during the 18th century, none had any impact until the Rev. John Williams of the London Missionary Society called at Savai'i aboard the Messenger of Peace in 1830. The ruling chief, Malietoa Vainu'upo, welcomed Williams, and by 1840 most Samoans had been converted to Protestantism. The missionaries taught the need for clothing, and white traders were soon arriving to sell the required cotton cloth. The first copra trader in Samoa was John Williams Jr., son of the missionary, who exported six tons in 1842. In 1844 Malua College was established on Upolu by the church. In true Samoan fashion, Malietoa's rival Mata'afa losefo converted to Catholicism in 1845.

In 1856 the German trading firm Johann Godeffroy and Son opened a store at Apia, and within a few years more than 100 Europeans resided in the new town, which soon became one of the main trading centers of the South Pacific. The first central government was formed by a group of district chiefs at Mulinu'u in 1868. During the 1870s German businessmen purchased large tracts of family land from individual chiefs for the establishment of coconut plantations using Chinese and Melanesian labor. Germany, Britain, and the U.S. soon appointed consuls.

In 1873 an American, Col. A.B. Steinberger, assisted the Samoan chiefs in creating a constitution; two years later he had himself appointed premier. His role was not supported by the U.S., however, although he was an official State Department agent. After five months in the premiership, Steinberger was arrested and taken to Fiji by the captain of a British warship who suspected him of German sympathies. He never returned.

Instability and Intrigue

The new Samoan government fumbled on and signed treaties of friendship with the U.S. and Germany. An intermittent civil war between the chiefly orator groups Pule and Tumua over the four highest ceremonial titles dragged on through most of the late 19th century. Rival Europeans sided with the different factions, but no one was able to establish a single, stable government. In 1879 the European residents of Apia took advantage of the situation to enact a municipal convention, which put control of the town in their hands.

In 1887 the German company Deutsche Handels-und Plantagen-Gesellshaft (successor to Godeffroy), tiring of the vicissitudes of native government in an area where they controlled 80% of the business, staged an unofficial coup. The nominal king, Malietoa Laupepa, was forced to flee, and the Germans installed a puppet in his place. The German regime, supported by German naval units but not sanctioned by Berlin, soon alienated Samoans, British, and Americans.

In March 1889 an armed Samoan rebellion brought the warships of Germany, Britain, and the U.S. to Apia's port in a major international confrontation. This came to a ludicrous pass when the seven men-of-war refused to abandon Apia Harbor in the face of a hurricane, for fear of leaving the field to the opposing Great Powers. This colonial stupidity and arrogance caused the wreck of four ships; two others were beached and damaged; 92 German and 54 American lives were lost. The German ship *Adler* was thrown up onto the reef, and only the British *Calliope* escaped to the open sea. The Samoans saw it as an act of God.

After this disaster the military posturing abated, and in June 1889 a Tripartite Treaty was signed in Berlin under which the three powers agreed to the formation of a neutral government led by Malietoa Laupepa with the three consuls controlling Apia. Yet instability and open factional warfare alternated with ineffectual government until 1899 when new treaties were drawn up partitioning Samoa between Germany and the U.S. (see **American Samoa**). Britain, distracted at the time by the Boer War in South Africa, withdrew completely in exchange for German concessions in Tonga and the Solomons.

The Colonial Period

On 1 March 1900 the German flag was raised over Samoa. Under Governors Wilhelm Solf (1900-1912) and Erich Schultz (1912-1914), the Germans created the first public school system, built and staffed a hospital, and constructed the only roads that existed right up until 1942. Though both Solf and Schultz tried to work according to the principle that the Samoans could be guided but not forced, they deported Samoan resisters to the Mariana Islands in 1909. The Germans carefully studied traditional Samoan culture in order to play rival factions off against each other. From Berlin, Samoa was seen as the brightest jewel of Germany's colonial empire.

On 29 August 1914, at the beginning of WW I, the last German governor surrendered without a fight to a New Zealand Expeditionary Force. The vast German plantations seized at the time are still held by the government-owned Samoa Land Corporation. Most of the 2,000 Chinese the Germans had brought from southern China to work the plantations were repatriated.

The new N.Z. administrators were real bunglers compared to the Germans. In November 1918, they allowed the SS *Talune* to introduce influenza to the territory, and 8,000 Samoans—22% of the population—died; a stricter quarantine kept the epidemic out of American Samoa and Fiji. This awkward administration revived a strong opposition movement, the Mau, which had existed during German times. The Mau not only rejected colonial authority but turned away from Western development and culture. Boycotts of imported goods were organized. In 1929 New Zealand crushed the Mau by military force, although the movement continued to enjoy the support of most of the villages, chiefs, and part-Samoan businessmen.

Only in 1947 was there a concrete step toward independence when a legislative assembly was created with some members elected from among the *matai* (chiefs). In 1960 a constitution was adopted; a year later both constitution and independence were approved in a plebiscite by universal ballot. And finally in 1962, with a Labor government in power in N.Z., Samoa became the first Polynesian nation to reestablish its independence in the 20th century. In 1976 Samoa joined the United Nations.

Government

Samoa has a parliamentary system with a prime minister elected by Parliament from its ranks. The prime minister chooses a 12-member Cabinet, also from among Parliament. Since independence, His Highness Malietoa Tanumafili II, Paramount Chief of Samoa, has been the ceremonial head of state, a position he may hold for life. The next head of state will be chosen by Parliament for a five-year term from among the four *tama aiga* or paramount chiefs (Malietoa, Mata'afa, Tuimalealiifano, and Tupua Tamasese).

Until recently, 47 of the 49 members of parliament were elected every five years by the 20,000 registered chiefs or *matai* (most of them men) on a constituency basis, and only two by non-Samoan residents on the Individual Voters Roll. In 1990 all citizens aged 21 and over were allowed to vote in a referendum that approved universal suffrage and an extension of the term of office from three to four years. The old system of only allowing *matai* to run for the 47 Samoan seats was retained, however. An untitled person *(tautau)* can only be elected to parliament after he/she first becomes a *matai,* a situation that helps preserve traditional Samoan culture.

There are two main political parties, the Human Rights Protection Party and the Samoa National Development Party. As elsewhere in Anglophone Oceania, political parties revolve more around personalities than policies. Campaign funds are used to "buy" votes and official corruption is rampant. A traditional coalition of orators and chiefs, the Tumua, Pule, and Aiga, has staged mass demonstrations in Apia against high taxes and government financial mismanagement.

The 11 administrative districts (A'ana, Aiga-i-le-Tai, Atua, Fa'asaleleaga, Gaga'emauga, Gagaifomauga, Palauli, Satupa'itea, Tuamasaga, Va'a-o-Fonoti, and Vaisigano) are used only for the organization of government services, and district officers don't exist. Samoa has no army and very few police: those responsibilities are assumed by the *matai.* The only police station on Upolu is the one in Apia; elsewhere the authority of village law prevails.

ECONOMY

In recent years Samoa's economy has been battered by hurricanes, agricultural decline, and government mismanagement. Despite all the revenue collected from the 10% value-added tax (VAGST) imposed in 1994, the foreign debt has remained high at around S$400 million, owed mostly to international agencies such as the Asian Development Bank and the World Bank for infrastructure and agricultural loans. In 1993-94 tens of millions went down the drain to support a reckless expansion program by Polynesian Airlines, and vast sums have been squandered on flashy new office buildings and a hilltop prayer house in Apia.

In 1994 Samoa's chief auditor submitted a report alleging high-level corruption and nepotism, but this was successfully swept under the carpet, and the chief auditor himself was given the boot. Many government departments keep no accurate financial records and no serious audits are carried out. Foreign business has been impacted by the incompetence: in 1998 the Samoan government inexplicably canceled the import permits of British Petroleum and handed Mobil Oil a monopoly. Tourism has been stifled by customary landowners who have demanded exhorbitant land-use fees for areas slated for resort development. When the an attempt was made to locate the resorts on government lands, the chiefs laid claim to those lands too. Major chains like Intercontinental and Marriott have withdrawn after seeing their costs spiral before they'd even turned any sod.

Samoa's per-capita gross domestic product is A$1,288 (1995) compared to A$6,660 (1985) in nearby American Samoa. Thus many Samoans migrate to Pago Pago to seek employment in the tuna canneries where the starting rate is US$3.10 an hour (in independent Samoa the private-sector statutory minimum wage is S$1.25 an hour). Tens of thousands of Samoans now live in American Samoa, the U.S., New Zealand, and Australia, and the S$100 million a year in private remittances they send home accounts for about half the country's gross domestic product.

Two-thirds of the workforce is engaged in subsistence agriculture, and fisheries and agriculture make up more than a third of the gross domestic product, the highest such proportion in the Pacific excluding Solomon Islands. Since the opening of a freezer plant in Apia in 1997, longline fishing for tuna from aluminum *alia* catamaran boats has experienced a boom. Only 27% of Samoans have nonagricultural employment, the lowest such percentage of any Polynesian country. Samoans have to hustle to obtain cash money, one reason why they look leaner and meaner than American Samoans (only those who have been to Tutuila will understand this comment).

In 1988 Samoa launched an off-shore banking center similar to that of Vanuatu and Cook Islands. Foreign companies can pay a one-time registration fee that allows them to undertake tax-evasion operations for 20 years (local companies are barred from participating and face strict bureaucratic regulation). Around 5,000 dummy and real companies from Hong Kong, South Korea, Indonesia, and Eastern Europe especially, download their profits here. In 1997 a new scam was uncovered when it was revealed that regular Samoan passports were being sold under the counter to Chinese businessmen at US$26,000 apiece. A good part of Samoa's immigration department was implicated in the scandal.

Samoa gets around 65,000 overseas tourists a year, 35% of them from American Samoa, 30% from New Zealand, and about 10% each from Australia, the U.S., and Europe. Well over half of these arrivals are expatriate Samoans visiting relatives and friends, and less than a third declare their purpose as tourism. About the only occasions on which Apia sees large numbers of tourists is during brief cruise-ship dockings, and these doesn't happen very often. Recently "ecotourism" has been embraced as the way forward for Samoan tourism, and at times it seems that almost everything is eco this or that: there are even aerial ecotours by helicopter! Business interests often exploit the term to justify eco-prices, but real ecotourism is alive and well out in the villages—the way to go in Samoa.

Industry

To stimulate light industry the government has established a "small industries center" at Vaitele, on the airport highway five km west of Apia,

where investing companies can obtain long-term leases at low rentals. Cheap labor and 15-year tax holidays are the main incentives to investing here. Most Samoan products have duty-free access to Australia and New Zealand under SPARTECA, to Europe under the Lomé Convention, and to the U.S., Canada, and Japan under the Generalized System of Preferences (GSP) scheme. Unfortunately these competitive advantages are declining as free trade expands worldwide.

The copra-crushing mill at Vaitele has experienced a turnaround since being privatized in 1993, and it now processes all local copra into coconut oil. To full utilize the installed capacity, additional copra is imported from Cook Islands and Tonga. The nearby government-owned Samoa Breweries has been highly successful with its excellent Vailima beer, and the Rothmans factory at Vaitele produces 50,000 cartons of cigarettes a month from raw materials imported from New Zealand.

In 1991 the Japanese corporation Yazaki transferred its automobile electrical wiring systems assembly plant from Melbourne to Vaitele, and Yazaki now exports A$75 million in automotive products to Australia each year. Since Yazaki pays low wages to its 2,000 mostly female local employees, gets the factory rent-free from the government, and pays no company taxes or duties, its real value to the Samoan economy is negligible. All of the materials used at Yazaki's Vaitele plant are imported tax free. A garment factory is also planned for Vaitele.

Trade

Imports run seven times higher than exports; food imports alone exceed all exports. Bony junk food not sold in its place of origin is dumped in Samoa: chicken backs and turkey tails from the U.S., mutton flaps and fatty canned corned beef from New Zealand. In 1996 even McDonald's got into the act. The main export items are automotive electrical systems, fresh fish, coconut oil, coconut cream, beer, kava, and cocoa.

During the 1950s Samoa exported 1.2 million cases of bananas a year to New Zealand, but shipping problems, hurricanes, disease, and inefficiency cost them this market, which is now supplied by Ecuador. Cacao continues to decline, and taro shipments to the Polynesian community in N.Z. were halted in 1994 due to an outbreak of taro leaf blight. A blight-resistent variety is now being developed. Infestations by rhinoceros beetles and giant African snails have hurt Samoan agriculture, and some 7,000 hectares of prime real estate is held by inept government agencies.

Japan, the U.S., and New Zealand profit most from the trade imbalance—a classic case of economic neocolonialism. New Zealand exports 10 times more to Samoa than it buys, the U.S. 20 times more, Japan 2,404 times more! An exception is Australia, which buys more than it sells due to the Yazaki operation previously mentioned. Foreign aid covers about 27% of the trade imbalance with the main donors being China, the Asian Development Bank, Japan, Australia, New Zealand, the European Union, and the United Nations Development Program, in about that order of importance. Taiwan has funded the opposition in Samoa in an attempt to break this country's close relationship with mainland China. American aid is negligible.

THE PEOPLE

Samoans are the second-largest group of full-blooded Polynesians in the world, behind the Maoris. About 89% of the population is Samoan and another 10% is part-Samoan (afakasi) with some European or Chinese blood. Although half of Samoa's people live in the northwest corner of Upolu, from Apia to the airport, only 21% live in the capital itself. Due to large-scale emigration to New Zealand and the U.S., the population growth rate is very low, averaging only 0.5% a year. In all, 85,000 Samoans live in N.Z. and 50,000 in the U.S. (compared to around 175,000 in Samoa itself).

While almost everyone in Apia speaks good English, the same is not always true in the villages. The Samoan language has similarities to Tongan, but the k sound in Tongan is replaced in Samoan by a glottal stop (rather like the English sound oh-oh). It's among the most sweetly flowing of Polynesian languages, and an entire special vocabulary exists for formal or polite discourse among the various levels of society.

The Samoan approach to life is almost the opposite of the European: property, wealth, and success are all thought of in communal or family rather than individual terms. Eighty percent of the country's land is owned communally by family groups (aiga) and cannot be sold or mortgaged. The matai work to increase the prosperity and prestige of their aiga.

Samoans are very conservative and resist outside interference in village affairs. The Samoans have an almost feudal concern for protocol, rank, and etiquette. They lead a highly complex, stylized, and polished way of life. Today, however, they are being forced to reconcile the fa'a Samoa with the competitive demands of Western society, where private property and the individual come first. The greatest burden of adjustment is on the young; between 1982 and 1992, Samoa experienced 230 suicides plus an equal number of unsuccessful attempt, 70% of them involving males aged 15-24, the highest suicide rate in the world.

Social Structure

Since ancient times, Samoan society has been based on the aiga, a large extended family group with a matai as its head, who is elected by consensus of the clan. The matai is responsible for the aiga's lands, assets, and distribution. He ensures that no relative is ever in need, settles disputes, sees to the clan's social obligations, and is the aiga's representative on the district or village council (fono). A pulenu'u (village mayor) appointed by the government presides over the fono. Around 85% of the total population lives under the direct authority (pule) of a matai (only residents of Apia are largely exempt from this). The 80% of Samoa's surface area that is customary land is under matai control (another 10% of the land is freehold and the government owns the balance).

The weight of traditional village law is enshrined in the Samoan constitution, and judges in the regular courts can take into account village fines or whether the offender has performed the traditional apology (ifoga) when passing sentence. A villager who chooses to ignore the rulings of his village fono faces ostracism, banishment, and worse. In exceptional cases, stoning, arson, and even murder have resulted.

Blood relationships count to a large extent in the elections of the matai, but even untitled persons can be elected on merit. (Foreigners can also be granted honorary *matai* titles, but these carry no social or legal weight.) In this formalized, ritualized society the only way a person can achieve place is to become a *matai*. This semi-democracy gives Samoan society its enduring strength.

A number of *aiga* comprise a village *(nu'u)* under an orator or talking chief *(tulafale)* and a titular or high chief *(ali'i)*. The high chiefs are considered too grand to speak for themselves at ceremonies, thus the need for orators. The *tulafale* conduct eloquent debates, give ceremonial speeches, and are the real sources of authority in the community. Direct conflicts are avoided through consensus decision-making. The villages are largely autonomous, and family welfare comes before individual rights—pure preindustrial socialism.

Villages

Samoans live in 362 villages near the seashore. Families share their work and food, and everyone has a place to live and a sense of belonging. It's difficult for individuals to get ahead in this communal society because as soon as anyone obtains a bit of money they're expected to spread it around among relatives and neighbors. Each immediate family has its own residence, called a *fale* (pronounced "fah-lay"), which may be round or oval. Without walls, it's the least private dwelling on earth. The only furniture may be a large trunk or dresser. A *fale* is built on a stone platform, with mats covering the pebble floor. Mats or blinds are let down to shelter and shield the *fale* from storms—a very cool, clean, fresh place to live.

Most food is grown in village gardens, and cooking is done in an earth oven *(umu)*. Families are large, eight children being "about right." The men wear a vivid wraparound skirt known as a *lavalava*. The women of the village are often seen working together in the women's committee *fale*, making traditional handicrafts. The *fono* meets in the *fale taimalo*. Also a part of each village is the cricket pitch—looking like an isolated stretch of sidewalk. Notice too the *tia*, stone burial mounds with several stepped layers under which old chiefs are buried.

Kava and Tattoos

Unlike Fiji and Tonga, the Samoan kava ceremony is an exceptional occurrence held at im-portant gatherings of *matai*, seldom witnessed by visitors. A *taupou* prepares the drink in a traditional wooden bowl; in the old days she was the fiercely guarded virgin daughter of a village high chief, a ceremonial princess. Chanting and dancing usually accompany this serving ceremony.

Tattooing is one of the few Polynesian cultural attributes adopted by Western civilization, and although missionaries 100 years ago predicted its demise, it's still widespread among Samoan men. The navel-to-knees tattoos are a visual badge of courage, as 16 or more highly painful sessions are required to apply a full *pe'a* using purple candlenut dyes. Once the tattooing begins it cannot end until completed, or the subject will be permanently marked with dishonor. Until recently a full body tattoo could only be applied to a talking chief as a mark of his rank, but today anyone who can stand the pain is eligible. The designs originally represented a large fruit bat, although this is only recognizable today in the lines of the upper wings above the waist. This art dates back to ancient times, and contemporary Samoan tattoo designs are strikingly similar to incised decorations on *lapita* pottery thousands of years old.

Religion

Ever since Rev. John Williams landed in 1830, the Samoans have taken Christianity very seriously and Samoan missionaries have gone on to convert the residents of many other island groups (Tuvalu, the Solomons, and New Guinea). Every Samoan banknote bears a radiant cross and the slogan *Fa'avae i le Atua Samoa* (Samoa is founded on God). Yet while the Samoans have embraced the rituals of Christianity, concepts such as individual sin are less accepted.

About 43% of the population belong to the Congregational Christian Church, 21% are Catholic, 17% Methodist, and 10% Mormon. The numbers of Mormons, Seventh-Day Adventists, and Assemblies of God are growing fast as the Congregational Christian Church declines. During the 19th century the main rivalry was between the British-connected Congregationals from the London Missionary Society active in Tahiti and Cook Islands and the Australian-based Methodists or Wesleyans who dominated the Tongan and Fijian missionary fields. Although the Methodists landed in Samoa first, they later withdrew until 1857 at the behest of the church authorities in England.

Today each village has one or more churches, and the pastor's house is often the largest residence. Minister of religion is usually the best-paying job in the village and many pastors enjoy an affluent lifestyle at the expense of their congregations (often the pastor will be the only one in the village who owns a car). There's continuous pressure on villagers to contribute money to the church and much of it goes into outlandishly huge and luxurious churches, which is rather scandalous in such a poor country. Some villages have regulations that *require* villagers to attend church as many as three times on Sunday and choir practice weekly. Public education is neither free nor compulsory and many of the schools are church-operated.

There's a daily vespers called *sa* around 1800 for family prayers. All movement is supposed to cease at this time; some villages are rather paranoid about it and levy fines on offenders. It only lasts about 10 minutes, so sit quietly under a tree or on the beach until you hear a gong, bell, or somebody beating a pan to signal "all's clear." Even if you're in a car on the main road at vespers, some remote villages may not allow you to continue driving through the village, although most will. If you do get stopped by white-shirted morality police, just wait patiently in the car until you get an all clear signal after about 10 minutes (don't get out). Many villages also have a 2200 curfew.

CONDUCT AND CUSTOMS

Custom Fees

In many parts of Samoa it's an established village law that outsiders pay a set fee to swim at the local beach or waterhole, or to visit a cave, lava tube, waterfall, etc. Sometimes the amount is posted on a sign and collected at a regular booth, but other times it's not. It's usually S$1 to S$5 either per person or per vehicle. In a few places, such as Falealupo on Savai'i, separate fees are charged for each individual thing you wish to see or do in the village. Although it may seem to Westerners that the Samoans have no *right* to charge for these things, the way the Samoans look at it, visitors have no right to enjoy them

free of charge. The best solution, if you don't wish to pay, is to just carry on quietly to some other beach or waterhole that is free or where no one's around. Complaining will get you nowhere.

Be aware, however, that a few ripoffs have become associated with this—sometimes an unauthorized person will demand payment, and you can't really tell if it's for real. We recommend that you only pay customary fees of this kind if there's a sign clearly stating the amount or someone asks for the money *beforehand*, thus giving you the choice of going in or not. Resist paying anything if someone tries to collect as you're leaving (unless there's a sign), and *never* give the money to children. If there's a dispute or you're in doubt about the authenticity of a customary fee, politely say you want to give the money directly to the *pulenu'u*. He will straighten things out quickly. Keep your cool in all of this—Samoans respect courtesy far more than anger or threats. To give you the opportunity to decide beforehand whether you feel a visit is still worth it, all customary fees we know about are listed in this book. Please let us know if we missed any.

Culture Shock

This can work two ways in Samoa, both you being intimidated by the unfamiliar surroundings and the Samoans being put off by your seeming affluence and intrusiveness. Because Samoan culture is a group culture, people can be over-friendly and unwilling to leave you alone. Of course, this doesn't apply in Apia, but in remote villages you may be viewed with suspicion, especially if you arrive in a taxi or rental car, the daily hire of which costs more than an average Samoan villager might earn in a month. You can easily smooth the situation over by smiling, waving, and saying *talofa* to those you meet. Be the first to say hello and everyone will feel a lot more comfortable.

Requests

Samoan culture is extremely manipulative, and there's a saying that you can buy anything with a *fa'amolemole* (please). Samoans are constantly asking each other for things; it's not just a game they play with foreigners. If you're staying in a village for long, somebody from another household may eventually come and ask you for money or something you're carrying. It's important that you be firm with them. Explain that you're sharing what you have with your hosts, and you simply don't have money to give out. If you "loan" money, consider it a gift, for if you insist on being repaid you will only make an enemy without collecting anything. Samoans will often invite you home for a meal, or ask you to accompany them on an excursion, and they're usually sincere and only wish to share some time with you. Occasionally, however, it will be someone who only wants to get something out of you, to have you pay their expenses at a restaurant, bar, nightclub, or whatever. You have to form appropriate defenses in Samoa.

Theft and Violence

Nobody means any harm, and violent crime is almost unknown, but be careful: the concept of individual ownership is not entirely accepted by the Samoans. Don't leave valuables unattended. Someone might even steal your laundry off the line, so it's better to hang it up in your room. Theft from hotel rooms and even beach *fales* in remote areas is also not unusual. The banks will keep a sealed envelope containing unneeded tickets, documents, and checks in their vault for a nominal fee—a good precaution if you'll be staying long.

The wisest policy when visiting Samoa is to remain low-key. Don't put yourself in high-risk situations, and if you ever have to defend yourself, it's always better to try to run away. If confronted by a belligerent drunk (quite possible in the evening), humble yourself, apologize even if you did nothing wrong, and ease yourself out of the confrontation. If it ends in violence, you'll always lose, because the culture pressures relatives and friends to join in the attack even if their side is clearly wrong. Loyalty is priority number one, and proving that is a lifelong obligation.

Getting Stoned

Some Samoans in remote areas resent sightseers who drive through their village in a rented automobile, especially if they're thought to be going a little fast. Cases of local children shouting insults, baring their bottoms, and even stoning motorists are not unknown. Sometimes *palagis* on buses, cycling, or even walking get this reaction if they're thought to be intruding. (Though the kids know how to throw stones with deadly accuracy, they seldom actually hit tourists.) Try to smile and keep your cool.

Children

At times village children can be a bit of a nuisance, calling to you and crowding around in an almost mocking way. You can forestall much of this by smiling and saying *talofa* (hello) as soon as you see them. Just keep smiling, keep going, and you'll soon leave them behind. It's important not to show any anger or irritation at their behavior, as this will only delight them and make them all the more unmannered with the next visitor who happens by.

If you're resting somewhere and don't really want to move on, the only way to get rid of annoying children is to complain very politely to their parents or to a local *matai*. Beware of ordering them away yourself as tourists who thought they could do whatever they liked have been stoned by local children many times. As always, a kind smile is your best defense. Occasionally you'll be accosted by groups of children who have been given money by tourists, and if they think you might do the same they'll stick to you like glue.

Love and Marriage

After a few days in the country it'll become fairly obvious to male visitors that Samoan women like to marry Western men. Age is not an important factor here: teenagers smile invitingly at middle-aged bachelors, and obesity is viewed as a sign of wealth. Samoans associate Europeans with the sort of affluence they see on television, and when a girl marries a *palagi* her economic situation, and that of her entire *aiga*, suddenly improves, or so they think.

If you're really smitten with a Samoan, you'll be expected to satisfy much more than just her needs. Be aware too that Samoan women are expert at stopping just short of lovemaking before they're married, and their brothers can be very hard on an insincere man who thinks he can play the game to his own advantage. Note too that marriage to a Samoan woman does not imply any legal right to stay in Samoa; in fact, the idea is that you take the woman *and* her family back and support them in your own home country. Somerset Maugham's story, "The Pool," in *The Trembling of a Leaf* deals with this subject.

Fa'a Samoa

It's considered impolite to eat while walking through a village, or to talk or eat while standing in a *fale*. Sit down cross-legged on a mat, *then* talk and eat. Don't stretch out your legs when sitting: it's bad form to point your feet at anyone or prop them up, and also a discourtesy to turn your back on a *matai*. Swaying from side to side indicates anger or contempt, and gesturing with the hands is considered bad taste.

If you arrive at a house during the family prayer session, wait outside until they're finished. A sign that you are invited to enter is the laying out of mats for you to sit on. Walk around the mats, rather than over them. Shoes should be removed and left outside. Your host will give a short speech of welcome, to which you should reply by giving your impressions of the village and explaining your reason for coming, beginning with the words *susu mai* (listen). If you are offered food, try to eat a small amount even if you're not hungry.

Some villages object to the use of their beach on Sunday, and some object anytime. If someone's around, ask, or find a beach that's se-

cluded. Public nudism is prohibited; cover up as you walk through a village. Women receive more respect when dressed in a *puletasi* (long dress) or *lavalava*, and not slacks or shorts. It's inappropriate to wear flowers or bright clothing to church.

This said, don't be intimidated by Samoan customs. Do your best to respect tradition, but rest assured that the Samoans are indulgent with foreigners who make an honest blunder. Samoans are fiercely proud of the *fa'a Samoa* and will be honored to explain it to you. It's all part of the Samoan experience, not an inconvenience at all.

In fact, the *fa'a Samoa* is open to interpretation, and even "world authorities" such as Margaret Mead and Derek Freeman can create diametrically opposed theories as to just what Samoan customs were or are. Mead's version of happy, uninhibited sexuality presented in *Coming of Age in Samoa* has been challenged by Freeman's description of a violent, competitive society that prizes virginity and forbids premarital sex (see **Resources**). Albert Wendt's 1979 novel, *Pouliuli*, is a superb analysis of that "laboratory of contradictions" that is Samoa.

ON THE ROAD

Highlights

Your most long-lasting impression of Samoa may be of people living in harmony with nature, and there's no better way to experience it than by sleeping in a Samoan *fale* at any of the growing number of beach *fale* resorts around the country. The bus rides from Apia to Aleipata and Lepa are also superb introductions to this exotic environment.

Samoa's most unforgettable sights draw their beauty from their natural surroundings, from the tomb of Robert Louis Stevenson on Mt. Vaea, to the Piula Cave Pool, the waterfall and pyramid at Savai'i's Letolo Plantation, and the nearby Taga blowholes. O Le Pupu-Pu'e National Park on Upolu's south side is Samoa's largest. You also won't want to miss the Cindy Show at Margrey-Ta's Beer Garden in Apia.

Sports and Recreation

Samoa has fewer organized recreational possibilities than some other Pacific countries, but there are unlimited opportunities to do your own thing. **Hiking** trails quickly become overgrown, which often makes local guides a good idea. Experienced hikers should be able to do the Lake Lanoto'o trip on their own.

The only **scuba diving** companies are in Apia and at Coconuts Beach Resort (scuba diving is not offered on Savai'i). A reasonable **snorkeling** locale, the Palolo Deep, is right in Apia, but Savai'i's Faga Beach is better. There are fewer options elsewhere, due in part to narrow fringing reefs, deadly currents, hurricane-impacted corals, and fishing with dynamite. Samoa Marine in Apia offers deep-sea **fishing.**

Samoa is a **surfing** paradise and the top waves are off the north-facing coasts in summer, off the south-facing coasts in winter. Thus optimum conditions are encountered at Lauli'i, Faleapuna, and Lano Dec.-March, and at Aufaga, Salani, Tafatafa, and Salailua May-August.

If you bring your own **bicycle** on the flight, many wonderful opportunities to use it will present themselves here. Both main islands have excellent paved roads and there isn't much traffic except on northern Upolu. The only real hazard is sudden chases by dogs, but one must also be prepared for the heat. Allow a week or more to cycle around each island, staying at village *fale* resorts along the way. The 176-km road around Savai'i is flat, except for the stretch between Asau and Sasina, which at 229 meters elevation is still lower than the passes on Upolu. (If you stop to talk to an adult on the road, be sure to get right off your bicycle, otherwise you might be seen as speaking down at a *matai*.)

Golfers will enjoy the 18-hole course at Apia.

Public Holidays and Festivals

Public holidays include New Year's Days (1, 2 January), Head of State's Birthday (first Monday in January), Good Friday, Easter Monday (March/April), ANZAC Day (25 April), Mothers of Samoa Day (a Monday in mid-May), Independence Days (1, 2, 3 June), Labor Day (a Monday in early August), White Monday (the Monday after the second Sunday in October), Arbor Day (the first Friday in November), and Christmas Days (25, 26 December).

Don't expect to get any official business done during the three-week period beginning a week before Christmas and ending a week after New Year's as most government employees knock off for extended holidays around then and many offices will be closed. Even basic public facilities such as the post office shut down for a week at a time! Also beware of Independence Days since the three public holidays in a row mean that all banks, offices, and most stores will be closed for five consecutive days, at least. Easter is also a bad time to come if you have anything specific to do.

Many Western countries celebrate Mother's Day and Father's Day, but only Samoa has made Children's Day (White Monday, the day after White Sunday) a public holiday. On White Sunday, children dressed in white parade to church; after the service, they take the places of honor and eat first at family feasts.

The big event of the year is the **Independence Days** celebrations during the first week of June with dancing, feasting, speeches by *tulafale* (talking chiefs), horse races, and other sporting events. A highlight is the *fautasi* race on the Saturday closest to Independence Days, with teams of dozens of men rowing great long-boat canoes. Though Samoa actually attained independence on 1 January 1962, the celebrations are held in June to avoid total paralysis around Christmas (which usually occurs anyway, however).

The **Teuila Tourism Festival** in early September is also a good time to be there. Among the many cultural activities are church choir competitions, dance and beauty contests, squash and cricket finals, *fautasi* (long-boat) races, traditional games, talent shows, etc.

Once a year the *palolo* reef worm *(Eunice viridis)* rises from the coral before dawn according to a lunar cycle (October on Upolu, November on Savai'i). The Samoans wait with lanterns and nets to catch this prized delicacy, the "caviar of the Pacific." This remarkable event takes place in Samoa, Fiji, and some other islands, but never in Hawaii.

Dance

The *sasa* is a synchronized group dance in which the rhythm is maintained by clapping or by beating on a rolled mat or drum. The *siva* is a graceful, flowing dance in which the individual is allowed to express him/herself as he/she sees fit. The *fa'ataupati* or slap dance employs body percussion. Knife-fire dances are done solo or in small groups, and they can be dangerous to the performers. Tradition holds that only men who are afraid will be burned during the fire dance. The waving of flaming weapons was originally done in times of war, to warn a tribe of approaching enemies.

Arts and Crafts

The Samoan love of elaborate ceremony is illustrated in the fine mat *(ie toga)*. Exquisitely and tightly plaited from finely split pandanus leaves, a good example might take a woman a year of her spare time to complete. Fine mats are prized family heirlooms used as dowries, etc., and they acquire value as they're passed from person to person at ceremonial exchanges *(lafo)*. Mats of this kind cannot be purchased.

Samoan tapa cloth *(siapo)* is decorated by rubbing the tapa over an inked board bearing the desired pattern in relief. In Samoa the designs are usually geometric but with a symbolism based on natural objects.

Traditional woodcarving includes kava bowls, drums, orator's staffs, and war clubs. In Tonga and Fiji, kava bowls have only four circular legs, while Samoan bowls are usually circular with a dozen or more round legs. A large kava bowl is an impressive object to carry home if you have six or seven kilograms to spare in your baggage allowance. Paradoxically, although carved from endangered trees such as the *ifilele,* the local production of kava bowls actually helps protect the rainforests as it greatly increases the value of the trees in the eyes of local villagers who become far less willing to sign away their timber rights for a pittance. A tree used to make handicrafts could be worth S$2,000 while a logging company would only pay about S$30 to cut it down.

It's also interesting to note that the tikis you see here are mock Maori or Hawaiian, not Samoan—don't buy the grotesque, grimacing little devils. Also beware of imitation tapa crafts in the Tongan style imported from Pago Pago, New Guinea-style masks, and turtle-shell jewelry, which is prohibited entry into many countries. If what you see in the craft shops of Samoa seems less impressive than what you might encounter in some other Pacific countries, remember that oratory and tattooing were the maximum expressions of Samoan culture, followed by the kava ceremony itself.

ACCOMMODATIONS AND FOOD

Accommodations

The higher-priced hotels usually quote their rates in U.S. dollars to make them seem lower, but in this book we've converted all prices into *tala* to make them easier to compare. Whenever a hotel mentions dollars when you ask the price of the room, be sure to clarify how they wish to be paid. If the amount has to be converted into *tala,* whether you're paying in *tala* cash or by credit card, your bill could be inflated about 15% due to the exchange rates used. You can sometimes avoid this by paying in U.S. dollars, cash or traveler's checks, otherwise ask them to quote a price in *tala* as that could work out cheaper. In all cases, a 10% value-added tax is charged and you should also ask if it's included. Failure to pay attention to these details could well result in a bill 25% higher than you'd expected!

Most of the regular hotels and guesthouses are in Apia, but an increasing number of places to stay are found on Savai'i and around Upolu. In the past few years numerous locally operated low-impact ecotourism resorts have opened on outlying beaches. These offer mattresses, blankets, and mats in Samoan *fales* right on the beach, with local meals provided at reasonable cost. Virtually all are run by the villagers themselves, and they're an excellent way to combine hiking, snorkeling, swimming, surfing, and just plain relaxing with a sampling of Samoan life. They're covered in the **Around Upolu** and **Savai'i** sections of this chapter and are highly recommended.

Food

Try *palusami*—thick coconut cream, onions, canned corned beef *(pisupo),* and young taro leaves wrapped in a breadfruit leaf, then baked on hot stones and served on slices of baked taro—a very tasty dish when well prepared. Other traditional Samoan specialties include *taofolo* (kneaded breadfruit and sweet coconut cream wrapped in taro leaves and baked), *fa'ausi* (pudding made of grated taro and coconut cream), *lua'u* (taro leaves cooked in coconut cream), *suafa'i* (ripe bananas with coconut cream), *faia'ife'e* (octopus in coconut cream), *faiaipusi* (sea eel in coconut cream), and *oka* (marinated raw fish).

If you spend a night in a village or *fale* resort, notice how almost everything you eat is locally grown. Taro and breadfruit are the staples, but there's also pork, fish, chicken, *ta'amu* (a large root vegetable like taro), and bananas. If you're a strict vegetarian, mention it at the outset, although this concept is often not understood in Samoa. In the villages food is normally eaten with the hands (no cutlery). After a meal with a family linger a while; it's considered rude for a guest to get up and abruptly leave. Don't continue to

occupy the table if others are awaiting their turn to eat, however. Samoans are big people. Most of us eat till we're full, but Samoans eat till they're tired.

SERVICES AND INFORMATION

Visas and Officialdom

No visa is required for a stay of up to 30 days, although you must have a ticket to leave (this ticket might not be looked at by the officials upon arrival at Apia airport, but it certainly will be requested by the airline staff when you're checking in for your flight to Samoa). Samoan immigration will stamp your passport to the date of your flight out, but you can get the 30 days without a struggle.

Apia is the only port of entry for cruising yachts and arriving boats can call customs over VHF channel 16. Clearance is done at the main wharf, then yachts anchor in the harbor off Aggie Grey's Hotel. Yachts may stop at Savai'i after checking out at Apia, provided they get prior permission.

Money

The Samoan *tala* is divided into 100 *sene*. There are coins of one, two, five, 10, 20, and 50 *sene* and one *tala,* and banknotes of two, five, 10, 20, 50, and 100 *tala.* The plastic S$2 banknotes make nice souvenirs. Samoans often speak of dollars when they mean *tala,* and many tourism-related businesses add to the confusion by quoting prices in U.S. dollars. Always note the currency carefully as the difference is around three to one! For consistency, we've quoted most prices in Samoan currency (S$).

Both banks charge 50 cents stamp duty per traveler's check, but only the Pacific Commercial

Bank charges S$3 commission (no commission at the ANZ Bank). Traveler's checks attract an exchange rate about four percent higher than cash, but it's always good to have some U.S. currency in small bills in case you happen to run out of *tala*, as everyone will gladly accept it (though at a low rate). If you plan to go upmarket, also have an adequate supply of U.S. dollar traveler's checks in small denominations (see below).

Upmarket facilities that quote prices in dollars are often cheaper if you pay them the exact amount in U.S. dollars, cash or traveler's checks. If you pay by credit card you risk having the charge inflated 15% because the dollar amount must be converted into *tala*, then the bank converts the *tala* into New Zealand dollars because all credit card charges are cleared through New Zealand, then the NZ$ are converted into your own home currency, all at rates unfavorable to you. This situation definitely applies to bank cards such as Visa and MasterCard, however it may be possible to be charged the exact amount in U.S. dollars if you use a private card such as American Express (ask the merchant/hotel).

Tala are heavily discounted outside Samoa, so change only what you think you'll need. If you overestimate, excess *tala* can be changed back into U.S. dollars at the airport bank without question. As you're doing so, try to pick up some Tongan or Fijian banknotes, if that's where you're headed.

Camera film is expensive here and the selection is poor, so bring a good supply. When buying drinks at a grocery store, be aware that there's a 30-cent deposit on large beer or soft drink bottles, 10 cents on small bottles, although many stores refuse to refund the deposit. Although annual inflation averages 10%, Samoa is still a very inexpensive country. Tipping is discouraged, and avoid giving money to children as this only creates a nuisance. There's a 10% sales tax.

Post and Telecommunications

Express Mail Service (EMS) is available from Apia to Australia, Fiji, Hong Kong, New Zealand, Papua New Guinea, Vanuatu, and the U.S.A. The charge to the U.S. is S$40 for the first 500 grams, then another S$8 for each additional 500 grams up to 20 kilos maximum. Delivery is guaranteed within less than one week. Small packets less than one kg benefit from a special reduced rate by regular mail.

Samoa is one of the few Pacific countries without card telephones (or any public telephones at all, for that matter). As in Tonga, the domestic telephone service is controlled by an inefficient state monopoly, which explains the appalling service. About the only easy way to make even a local call is to do so from your hotel, but you should ask how much you'll be charged beforehand. Turn to the **Apia** section for the price of calls made from the main telephone company office.

If you do manage to get access to a phone, make an operator-assisted domestic call by dialing 920. For the international operator, dial 900. If you have access to a direct-dial phone, the international access code is 0. For domestic directory assistance, dial 933; for international numbers, dial 910.

The country code for American Samoa is 684; for Samoa it's 685.

Business Hours and Time

Business hours are weekdays 0800-1200 and 1330-1630, Saturday 0800-1200, with government offices closed on Saturday. Banks open weekdays 0900-1500, the post office 0900-1630 weekdays. Expect most businesses to be closed on Sunday, although Samoa's Sunday closing laws are much more lenient than those of Tonga. Grocery stores aren't supposed to sell beer on Sunday (but some will if nobody's watching).

Both Samoas share the same hour, and since the international date line is just west of here, this is where the world's day really comes to an end. Tonga and Samoa are on the same hour but Samoa is 24 hours behind Tonga. The Samoas are three hours behind California time, 21 hours behind eastern Australian time.

Weights and Measures

In American Samoa Imperial measurements (yards, miles) are used, while in Samoa it's all metric (meters, kilometers). Unlike American Samoa, where the electric voltage is 110 volts, in Samoa it's 240 volts AC, 50 cycles. However, if you plan to plug in an appliance (such as a hair drier or electric razor) at a deluxe hotel in Samoa, check the voltage carefully as some supply 110 volts instead of the usual 240 volts.

Print Media

The main English-language newspaper is the *Samoa Observer* (Box 1572, Apia; tel. 21-099, fax 21-195), which appears daily except Monday and Saturday. Founded in 1979 by the acclaimed poet and novelist Sano Malifa, the *Observer* has faced constant government harassment and even mysterious arson attacks due its exposures of official corruption. Of course, this situation makes the *Observer* all the more worth reading (provided it's still publishing when you get there).

Newsline (Box 2441, Apia; tel. 24-216, fax 23-623), published on Wednesday and Sunday, carries general interest wire service news and a local gossip column titled "Rant Rave." **Savali** is an irregular government-run newspaper of little value.

Radio

The government-operated Broadcasting Department (Box 1868, Apia; tel. 21-420, fax 21-072) transmits over two AM radio frequencies. Radio 2AP at 540 kHz airs bilingual programs (English and Samoan) Mon.-Sat. 0600-1900. Their local news is at 0700 and 1200, the international news at 0800 and 0900 (rebroadcast from Australia or New Zealand). Radio 2AP's programming Mon.-Sat. 1900-2300 is in Samoan only, and Sunday 1100-2200 you'll hear nonstop Samoan hymns. Sunday 0800-1600 switch to 747 kHz AM for varied music introduced in English. For more than a decade, a directive from the "Human Rights Protection Party" leadership has prevented this station from airing interviews with opposition politicians.

A private commercial station, Magik 98 FM (Box 762, Apia; tel. 25-149, fax 25-147; e-mail: magic98fm@samoa.net), broadcasts over 98.1 MHz to points west of Apia and over 99.9 MHz east of Apia. They're on the air 060-midnight weekdays and Saturday 0800-midnight. Magik 98 rebroadcasts the Radio New Zealand International news at 0700 and 0800 weekdays, and on Saturday at 0800 only. Local news comes right after the 0700 international news weekdays, then again at noon, 1700, and 1900. On Saturday there's local news at 0700 and 1200. For Gospel music and inspirational programs, there's Radio Graceland at 90.1 and 106.1 MHz FM.

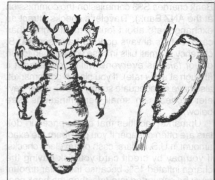

LICE FACTS

The louse *(Pediculus capitis)* is a small, wingless insect that can infest the hairy areas of all warm-blooded beasts. The parasite attaches its egg securely to the side of hair shafts. It's untrue that personal cleanliness prevents lice— anyone can get them, whether clean or dirty. By applying a solution available at any drugstore, you can zap the varmints in minutes.

Health

Although no vaccinations are required (except yellow fever or cholera in the unlikely case that you're arriving directly from an infected area), it may be worthwhile to get immunized against hepatitis A, typhoid fever, and tetanus (in case a dog bites you). Details of these are provided in the main introduction. Body lice and intestinal parasites are widespread among Samoan villagers; any pharmacy will have a remedy for the former. Check the expiration date before buying any medicines in Samoa. And take care with the tap water in Apia— boiled water or beer is safer.

In case of need, you'll receive faster attention from any of the private doctors and dentists listed in this book's **Apia** section than you would at a government hospital or clinic.

GETTING THERE

By Air

Polynesian Airlines (Box 599, Apia; tel. 685/21-261, fax 685/20-023, e-mail: enquiries@

polynesianairlines.co.nz), Samoa's government-owned flag carrier, connects Apia to Auckland, Melbourne, Pago Pago, Sydney, Tongatapu, and Wellington. Their schedules to Honolulu and Los Angeles are code shares with Air New Zealand, to Nadi with Air Pacific. Their Polypass allows 45 days unlimited travel over Polynesian's modest South Pacific network (a roundtrip to/from Australia and New Zealand included) for a flat US$999. From Honolulu/Los Angeles, the Polypass costs US$1,149/1,399. Details of this and their triangle fares are provided under **Getting Around** in the main introduction to this book. Also check their useful internet website (www.polynesianairlines.co.nz), which contains information about the Polypass. Polynesian's Los Angeles office can be reached at tel. 1-310/830-7363, fax 1-310/830-7782.

Air Pacific (tel. 22-693) has flights to Apia from Nadi and Suva (often full) with connections in Fiji to/from Japan. **Royal Tongan Airlines** (tel. 22-901) has a weekly flight to/from Tongatapu. **Air New Zealand** (tel. 20-825) arrives from Auckland, Tongatapu, and Honolulu with immediate connections in Honolulu to/from Los Angeles. See **Getting Around** in the main introduction for information on circular tickets between Fiji, Apia, and Tonga.

Both Polynesian Airlines and **Samoa Air** (tel. 22-901) operate shuttles between Pago Pago and Apia six or seven times a day. For the Pago Pago flights, check carefully which airport you'll be using as they alternate between Faleolo and Fagali'i and the ticket may only say "Apia." Both airlines charge identical fares from Apia to Pago Pago (S$120/189 one-way/roundtrip), and it's cheaper to buy your ticket in Samoa than elsewhere due to currency differences. Samoa Air also has direct flights between Pago Pago and Maota airstrip on Savai'i (S$145/244 one-way/roundtrip). Samoa Air offers through an excursion fare from Apia to Vava'u via Pago Pago that is the equivalent of the fare to Pago Pago plus US$178/365 one-way/roundtrip. American Samoan airport and customs taxes of US$8 must be added to these prices.

On both airlines, when the flight to/from Pago Pago is full all baggage may be bumped due to the limited carrying capacity of the aircraft (all passengers must be weighed and the average weight of Samoans is substantial). When the baggage does arrive on a later flight, you'll have to go back to the airport and clear it personally through customs. Don't expect compensation for any of this, and be aware that the check-in staff probably won't inform you about what's going on until they're just about to close the aircraft door. If the flight is full and you see people with mountains of excess luggage, expect this to happen. In any case, carry everything you can't afford to lose or might need during the first few days in your hand luggage.

In January 1997, a Polynesian Airlines Twin Otter aircraft arriving from Pago Pago crashed into a hillside near Upolu's Faleolo Airport in circumstances that have still not been adequately explained (pilot error and poor maintenance have been alleged). Three of the five persons on board, including the New Zealander pilot himself, were killed.

By Ship
The **Samoa Shipping Corporation** (Private Bag, Apia; tel. 20-935, fax 22-352) runs the car ferry Queen Salamasina from Apia to Pago Pago Wednesday at 2200 (nine hours, S$40/60 one-way/roundtrip). Buy your ticket before 1200 on Tuesday at their Vaea Street office and have your passport ready. If you wait to buy your ticket at the wharf you won't be allowed aboard until the last minute and all of the good places to sleep on deck will have been taken (it's an overnight trip). Expect basic conditions on the ship: bring a mat, take seasickness precautions, etc. During holiday periods the ship makes two trips, leaving Apia at 2200 on Tuesday and Thursday, and at these times it's often fully booked. If you'll be returning to Apia, be sure to get a roundtrip ticket, as the fare charged in Pago Pago is much higher. But if you won't be returning, change excess tala back into dollars at the bank the day before as there are no facilities on the wharf. Going by sea you save the S$20 airport departure tax paid by air travelers (although the US$5 American Samoan "entry declaration fee" must still be paid).

In early 1999 a new ferry, the 220-passenger Lady Naomi, was brought into service between Apia and Pago Pago. Unlike the Queen Salamasina, this ship offers berths at S$60 each way, while seats are S$40.

For information on the supply ship to the Tokelau Islands, contact the transport manager at the **Tokelau Apia Liaison Office** (Box 865, Apia; tel. 20-822, fax 21-761). There's about one a month, and a cabin would run NZ$528 roundtrip. Turn to the Tokelau chapter for more information.

The **Pacific Forum Line** (Box 655, Apia; tel. 20-345, fax 22-179), at the entrance to the main wharf, will know the departure dates of container ships to Tonga and elsewhere. Passage is sometimes possible but to arrange this you must see the captain when the ship arrives.

AIRPORTS

Faleolo International Airport
Faleolo Airport (APW), Samoa's main international airport, is 35 km west of Apia. All flights to points outside the Samoas, as well as some services to Pago Pago, depart from here. The airport bus (tel. 23-014; S$6) will take you right to your hotel, or you can wait on the highway for a public bus, which is only S$1.50, but very scarce after 1600 and on Sunday. Airport-bound, the airport bus departs Apia two hours before international flights. It picks up passengers in front of the Hotel Insel Fehmarn, then at Aggie Grey's Hotel, and finally at the Kitano Tusitala.

The airport taxi drivers often try to overcharge incoming foreign tourists, so take the bus if you can. A taxi from the airport to Apia should cost S$30 (30 *tala*) for the car but they will often insist on being paid US$30 in American currency, so be careful. It's a bit safer taking a taxi back to the airport as they'll know you're already familiar with Samoan currency and probably won't try this trick.

The Pacific Commercial Bank (S$3 commission) and the ANZ Bank (50 cents commission) in the arrivals area open for international flights

(excluding those from Pago Pago) and change traveler's checks for similar rates. For changing excess *tala* back, both banks in the departures hall at the airport are open for all international departures *except* those to Pago Pago. There's no left luggage room. In a pinch you can sleep on the floor upstairs in the terminal.

The airport post office (weekdays 0900-1530) sells philatelic stamps, a good way to unload excess *tala*. The duty-free shop in the departure lounge sells only expensive luxury goods and imported alcohol, so don't wait to do your shopping there. In general, alcohol and beer are relatively cheap in Samoa anyway.

The international departure tax is S$20 (children aged 5-9 pay S$10). You don't have to pay the tax if you stay less than 24 hours (transit), and if you'll be departing Samoa twice within any 30-day period, so keep your tax receipt to avoid paying the tax a second time.

Fagali'i Airport
Fagali'i Airport (FGI) is near the golf course on the east side of Apia, just five km from the center of town. All Polynesian Airlines flights to Savai'i leave from here. Some flights to Pago Pago use Fagali'i, others Faleolo, so check carefully to avoid disastrous mistakes. The local Fagali'i-uta bus should pass Fagali'i Airport Mon.-Sat. but service is irregular and not all of the Fagali'i buses come up here. However, just 200 meters west of the airport is a junction where the more frequent Vaivase or Moata'a buses pass. Taxi drivers charge US$5 from Fagali'i to Apia but only S$5 from Apia to Fagali'i. If you're unwilling to pay this arbitrary premium, try bargaining or just walk off and look for a bus. The Pacific Commercial Bank has a branch at Fagali'i Airport and there's a duty-free shop. The usual international departure tax applies.

UPOLU

Although much smaller than Savai'i, Upolu is Samoa's chief island with its stirring capital, international airport, industry, business, attractions, visitor facilities, and 71% of the total population. Physically, it's rather like Tahiti on a smaller scale with high verdant mountains in the background of Apia and a seaside boulevard encircling the harbor. The villages along the north coast also remind one of Tahitian villages, as do the valleys and black beaches. But Upolu is much wilder and more traditional, and less impacted by international tourism.

Even though Savai'i commands a faraway mystique, Upolu is a much more beautiful and varied island, especially the eastern half. Roads wind around the coast and across the center of the island. Some of the South Pacific's finest beaches are at Lepa and Aleipata with suitable facilities for budget travelers. Waterfalls cascade from the luxuriant green hillsides and there are countless places to swim. Hikers will feel rather like Tarzans and Janes cutting paths through exuberant jungles, and travelers will be enchanted by the easygoing Polynesian lifestyle. Upolu is an insular uncut jewel.

APIA AND ENVIRONS

Central Apia has been transformed in recent years, with enormous government buildings overshadowing the older churches and trading companies that still line the waterfront in the traditional South Seas movie-set manner. Yet away from the center this city of 35,000 is only a cluster of villages. Iin Apia Harbor, where the Vaisigano River has cut an opening in Upolu's protective reef, rock a motley assortment of interisland ferries, container ships, fishing boats, and cruising yachts. As at Papeete, you'll see teams of men paddling outrigger racing canoes around the harbor at sunset, about the only two towns in the South Pacific where this is still so. Yet the languid inertia of Apia is pervasive.

Apia makes a good base from which to explore northern Upolu, and there's lots of accommodation in all price brackets. The food and

entertainment possibilities are also very good, so give yourself a break and see the city one step at a time. Get into the culture and prepare yourself for that big trip around Savai'i. Samoa is Polynesia's heart and Apia is the bright light around which the country revolves.

Central Apia

By the harbor side where Falealili St. meets Beach Rd. is the **John Williams Memorial,** dedicated to the missionary who implanted Protestantism in Samoa in 1830. Nine years later Williams was killed and eaten by cannibals on Erromango Island in the New Hebrides (presently Vanuatu). Later his remains were returned to Samoa and buried beneath the porch of the old **Congregational Christian Church** (1898) across the street.

A block west on Beach Rd. is the historic wooden **Courthouse** dating from German times,

Apia's Catholic cathedral on Beach Road

DAVID STANLEY

which served as government headquarters until 1994. On Black Saturday, 29 December 1929, Tupua Tamasese Lealofi III, leader of the Mau Movement, was shot in the back by the N.Z. Constabulary while trying to calm his people during a demonstration against the colonial regime in front of this building. Eight other Samoans were also killed and five years of severe repression followed, only ending with a change of government in New Zealand.

West again is imposing **Mulivai Catholic Cathedral** (1885-1905), formerly a landmark for ships entering the harbor, and **Matafele Methodist Church,** a fine building where marvelous singing may be heard during Sunday services. Across the street is the gigantic eight-story **Government Building,** erected in 1994 with a S$35-million interest-free loan from the People's Republic of China. It and the neighboring seven-story **Central Bank of Samoa** wouldn't be out of place in Abu Dhabi, Dubai, or Kuwait, and stand as stunning examples of third-world megalomania. Earthquakes are common at Apia and both of these massive buildings stand on unstable reclaimed land, which tends to magnify the impact of quakes, so you could be looking at ancient ruins in the making. The police band marches from their barracks near the Courthouse and plays the national anthem at the raising of the flag here at 0750 on weekday mornings.

Nearby is the **Chief Post Office** with the modern headquarters of the **ANZ Bank** opposite. A block west in the center of the traffic circle where Vaea St. meets Beach Rd. is a **Clock Tower** built as a WW I memorial. On opposite corners of Vaea St. and Beach Rd. are the former Burns Philp store, now Chan Mow Supermarket, the **National Provident Fund** building housing the agency that administers the country's pension fund, and the **Nelson Memorial Public Library,** named for Olaf Nelson (1883-1944), a leader of the Mau Movement.

Farther west facing a small harbor is the **Fish Market.** The numerous locally owned longline fishing boats here have made fish a leading export during the past few years, but safety standards are minimal and several boats and crews are lost each year. The **Flea Market** nearby was Apia's main vegetable market until 1995 when it was moved three blocks inland. You can shop for handicrafts and clothing here, and cheap food stalls are along the side closest to the harbor. One of Apia's two bus stations is also here, and just beyond is the flashy new **Women's Center,** built with another Chinese loan. The large wooden building almost across the street is the headquarters of the **Samoa Trust Estates Corporation.** These were once the premises of the German trading companies whose assets were seized when New Zealand invaded in 1914.

Mulinu'u Peninsula

Just northwest of the old market is the **Kitano Tusitala Hotel,** which is well worth entering to appreciate the great hand-tied roofs of the main *fale*-like neo-Samoan buildings erected in 1974.

Continue northwest on Mulinu'u Street, past two monuments on the left commemorating the disastrous 1889 naval debacle when the German cruiser *Adler* and several other ships sank during a hurricane. There's also a monument on the right that recalls the raising of the German flag on 1 March 1900 *(die deutsche Flagge gehisst).*

The large beehive-style building farther along on the left is the neo-Samoan **Parliament of Samoa** (1972). The smaller old Fono House nearby now houses the office of the Ombudsman. Across the field is the **Independence Memorial** (1962), which declares, "The Holy Ghost, Council of all Mankind, led Samoa to Destiny," and behind it is the **Lands and Titles Court,** which reviews village council decisions, disagreements over customary lands, and *matai* title disputes.

At the end of the Mulinu'u Peninsula is the **Apia Observatory,** founded by the Germans in 1902. After the unexpected hurricane of 1889, the Germans weren't taking any more chances. Note the many impressive royal tombs of former paramount chiefs both here and down the road to the left. Mulinu'u is the heartland of modern Samoan history.

Vailima

In 1889 Robert Louis Stevenson, Scottish author of the adventure classic *Treasure Island,* purchased approximately 162 hectares of bushland at the foot of Mt. Vaea, 3.5 km inland from Apia and high above the sea, for US$4,000. Stevenson named the place Vailima, meaning "five waters," for the small streams that ran across the property, and here he built his home and spent the last five years of his life.

Fanny Osborne and Robert Louis Stevenson with friends at Vailima

During a power struggle between rival Samoan factions, some chiefs were imprisoned at Mulin-u'u. Stevenson visited them in confinement, and to show their gratitude, these chiefs built him a road up to Vailima when they were released. The Samoans called Stevenson Tusitala, or "Teller of Tales." On 3 December 1894, at the age of 44, Stevenson suffered a fatal brain hemorrhage while helping his wife Fanny fix dinner. He's buried just below the summit of Mt. Vaea, overlooking Vailima, as he'd requested.

The stately mansion with its beautiful tropical gardens was first sold to a retired German businessman, then bought by the German government to serve as the official residence of their governor. Of the present complex, Stevenson had the central building erected in 1890, and in 1891-92 the east wing was added to provide proper quarters for his mother. The Germans built the westernmost wing in 1897. The N.Z. regime took it over when they assumed power in 1914, and until recently Villa Vailima was Government House, official residence of Samoa's head of state.

In early 1992, after Hurricane Val did serious damage to Vailima, Mormon businessmen from Utah and Arizona obtained a 60-year lease on the property with the intention of creating a museum. The complex was largely rebuilt, and in 1994 the **Robert Louis Stevenson Museum** (tel. 20-798) opened on the centenary of the writer's death. You'll be led through a series of bedrooms dedicated to various members of the Stevenson family, but all of the furniture and heirlooms on display are replicas except for three chairs and a few books. Temporary exhibits are housed in a gallery upstairs in the west wing and you may visit these on your own after the tour. There's a marvelous view from the breezy upper veranda.

A bit east of the Stevenson mansion is a smaller red-roofed house once occupied by a son of the head of state but now empty. Outside this building is an old-fashioned mahogany steering wheel inscribed "Fear God and Honor the King, Samoa 1889." This is from the British ship *Calliope,* the only one to survive the naval debacle of that year. Britain donated the wheel to Samoa when the ship was broken up after WW II.

Entry to the museum grounds is free with admission to the house S$15 for adults and S$5 for children under 12. It's open Mon.-Fri. 0900-1530, Saturday 0900-1200, with the last tour commencing 30 minutes before closing.

In 1978 a **Botanical Garden Reserve** with a loop trail was established at the bottom of the hill adjoining Vailima. Adjacent is a pool for swimming and a small waterfall (dry except during the rainy months). The hiking trail up to Stevenson's grave on Mt. Vaea begins here, and both it and the gardens are open 24 hours, admission free. A map of area is just down the road to the grave to the right of museum gate. The Avele or Vaoala buses (80 cents) will bring you directly here from the markets, otherwise a taxi should cost around S$6.

Mount Vaea

An almost obligatory pilgrimage for all visitors to Samoa is the 45-minute climb along a winding trail to the tomb of Robert Louis Stevenson, just below the 475-meter summit of Mt. Vaea. After the small bridge turn left. Five hundred meters up, the trail divides with a shorter, steeper way to the right and a much longer less-used trail to the left. A good plan is to go up by the short trail

and come back down the longer way. After rains, the trail can get muddy.

The path to the top was cut by 200 sorrowful Samoans as they carried the famous writer's body up to its final resting place in 1894. From the tomb there's a sweeping panorama of the verdant valley to the east with the misty mountains of Upolu beyond, and in the distance the white line of surf breaking endlessly on the reef. The red roof of Vailima directly below is clearly visible. It's utterly still—a peaceful, poignant, lonely place. Stevenson's requiem reads:

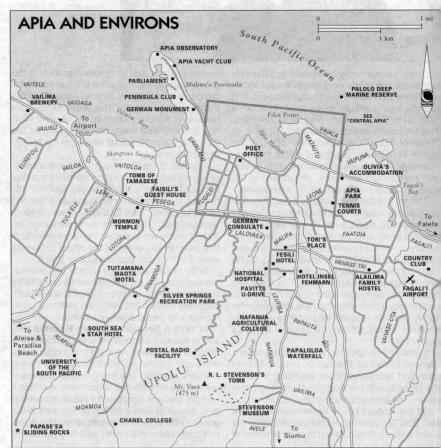

APIA AND ENVIRONS

South Pacific Ocean

0   1 mi
0   1 km

APIA OBSERVATORY
APIA YACHT CLUB
PARLIAMENT   Mulinu'u Peninsula
PENINSULA CLUB
GERMAN MONUMENT
VAITELE
VAILIMA BREWERY   VAIGAGA
To Airport
VAIUSU
Vaisu Bay
ELISEFOU
VAILOA
Mangrove Swamp
VAITOLOA
TOMB OF TAMASESE
FAISILI'S GUEST HOUSE
PESEGA
LEPEA
River
TULA'ELE
LOTOPA
MORMON TEMPLE
TUITAMANA MAOTA MOTEL
SINAMOGA
Falunima
SILVER SPRINGS RECREATION PARK
To Aleisa & Paradise Beach
ALAFUA
SOUTH SEA STAR HOTEL
UNIVERSITY OF THE SOUTH PACIFIC
POSTAL RADIO FACILITY
MOAMOA
PAPASE'EA SLIDING ROCKS
CHANEL COLLEGE

PALOLO DEEP MARINE RESERVE
SEE "CENTRAL APIA"
Pilot Point
VAIALA
Apia Harbor
MATAUTU
POST OFFICE
VAIPUNA
OLIVIA'S ACCOMMODATION
SAVALALO
FUGALEI
LEONE
APIA PARK
TENNIS COURTS
Fagali'i Bay
To Falefa
GERMAN CONSULATE
LALOVAEA
MALIFA
FAATOIA
FAGALI'I
TORI'S PLACE
FESILI HOTEL
VAIVASE-TAI
COUNTRY CLUB
NATIONAL HOSPITAL
PAVITTS U-DRIVE
LEUPISA
HOTEL INSEL FEHMANN
ALAILIMA FAMILY HOSTEL
FAGALI'I AIRPORT
NAFANUA AGRICULTURAL COLLEGE
PAPAUTA
PAPALOLOA WATERFALL
VAIVASE-UTA
Stream
UPOLU ISLAND
Mulivai
NAFANUA
R. L. STEVENSON'S TOMB
Mt. Vaea (475 m)
STEVENSON MUSEUM
VAILIMA
AVELE
To Siumu
Vaivase-Uta

Under the wide and starry sky,
Dig the grave and let me lie.
Glad did I live and gladly die,
And I laid me down with a will.

This be the verse you grave for me:
Here he lies where he longed to be;
Home is the sailor, home from the sea,
And the hunter home from the hill.

Stevenson's wife Fanny died in California in 1914 and a year later her ashes were brought back to Samoa and buried at the foot of her husband's grave. The bronze plaque bears her Samoan name, Aolele, and the words of Stevenson:

Teacher, tender comrade, wife,
A fellow-farer true through life
Heart-whole and soul free,
The August Father gave to me.

Side-Trip East

Buses marked Falefa, Falevao, and Lufilufi depart the Apia markets every hour or so for Falefa, 29 km east (you can also pick up these buses on Matautu Street). You'll get many fine views of Upolu's north coast as you pass along Upolu's finest summer surfing beach, Lauli'i, a long right point break (beware of undertow). No barrier reef breaks the waves that crash onto these black sandy shores. Change rooms and showers (S$1 pp) are provided at **Saoluafata Beach,** but no visitors are allowed on Sunday.

A kilometer east of Saoluafata Beach is Piula Theological College with the superb **Piula Cave Pool,** a natural freshwater pool fed by a spring directly below a large Methodist church. The water is unusually clear, despite all the carefree locals soaping up and washing clothes in it. Swim into the cave below the church. This is connected to a second cave by a small underwater opening on the left near the back. The second cave is long, dark, and deep, but can be explored with a mask and snorkel. The pool is open Mon.-Sat. 0800-1630, admission S$1, and there are changing rooms. If you leave Apia in the morning you'll have time for a swim in the pool before catching a midday bus to the beach *fales* at Lalomanu or Lepa (ask).

Falefa Falls, two km east of Piula through Falefa village, is impressive during the rainy season and it's freely visible beside the road. The Falefa bus turns around here.

Side-Trip Southwest

Catch a Seesee, Siusega, or Tafaigata bus at the markets and ask the driver to drop you at the closest point to **Papase'ea Sliding Rocks.** You can also come on the Alafua bus to the university (see below), but this will add about 15 minutes to your walking time. Even from the closest bus stop you'll still have to hike uphill two km and pay S$2 admission (don't give the money to children—only to the adult at the entrance). You slide down three rocks into freshwater pools—don't forget your bathing suit. It's open daily (Sunday included!).

At Alafua, below and to the east of this area, is the 30-hectare Samoan campus of the **University of the South Pacific** (the main campus is in Fiji). In 1977 the university's School of Agriculture was established here, with assistance from New Zealand. To the left of the main gate is an agricultural training center funded by the European Union. The university's two semesters run from February to the end of June and late July to mid-November. The university library (tel. 21-671) is open weekdays 0800-1200/1300-1600.

On the way back to Apia notice the **Apia Samoa Temple** (1983) on the airport highway. The golden angel Moroni trumpets The Word from above, but only Mormons are allowed inside. The Church of Jesus Christ of Latter-day Saints established its Samoan headquarters here in 1902.

Central Upolu

For an area of heavy hiking, catch a Mulivai, Salani, Sapunaoa, Siumu, or Vaovai bus up the Cross Island Highway to an unmarked turnoff on the right for **Lake Lanoto'o,** otherwise known as "Goldfish Lake," high in the center of Upolu at 590 meters above sea level. Walk straight west on the dirt access road for just under an hour until you see the power lines end abruptly at a transformer on a pole, plus several radio towers down a road to the left. Continue straight ahead another 500 meters to a point where the access road turns left (south). Walk 400 meters south on this road until the radio towers are visible again on the left. On the right directly opposite here an overgrown trail runs due west to the lake, another one-hour walk. When you arrive at a destroyed microwave reflector on top of a hill, the lake is just below you to the left.

The unmarked way takes a bit of intuition to find and some of the locals living on the main road to the trail ask exorbitant fees such as S$40 to act as guides. There's no admission fee to the lake, so just take your time and follow the instructions provided above and you'll be okay. The route to the lake is very muddy following heavy rains, so only go after a couple of days of sunny weather. Expect fallen trees across the route and some confusion toward the end. This is a *very* strenuous hike, so be prepared.

The opaque green waters of this seldom-visited crater lake are surrounded by a mossy green bush dripping from the mist. Swimming in the lake is an eerie experience. To add to the otherworldliness of the place, Lake Lanoto'o is full of goldfish, but you'll have to wait patiently if you want to see any from shore (bread crumbs might help). This hike is ideal for seeing Upolu's high-altitude vegetation without going too far from town, but sturdy shoes and long pants are essential.

On your way back to Apia stop to visit the **Baha'i House of Worship** (1984), Mother Temple to all Baha'is in the region. The temple is at Tiapapata, eight km from Apia and a 30-minute walk down the highway from the Lanoto'o turnoff. The monumental dome soars 30 meters above the surrounding area and has nine sides, symbolizing the unity of the nine major religions of the world. Inside, the latticework of ribs forms a nine-pointed star at the apex of the dome. The seating is arranged facing the Holy Land (Israel) because this is the final resting place of Baha 'Ullah (1817-92), Prophet-Founder of the Baha'i Faith. This majestic building, funded by Baha'is around the world, is open to all for prayer and meditation daily 0900-1700. Also visit the information center (tel. 24-192), to the left as you approach the temple. The Vaoala bus comes to within a 30-minute walk of the temple.

Palolo Deep

One of Apia's nicest attractions is the **Palolo Deep Marine Reserve** (daily 0800-1800, admission S$2), a natural reef aquarium operated by the Division of Environment and Conservation. The signposted entrance to the reserve is near the main wharf at Matautu, in fact, the Deep's main draw is its convenience to Apia. You can easily wade out to the Deep at low tide if you have something to protect your feet, and although the reef has been heavily damaged by hurricanes, much of the coral has regenerated and there are plenty of colorful fish (bring along bread to feed to them). Even if you don't intend to swim, the reserve garden is a very nice place to sit and read with lots of benches and relaxing lagoon views. This place is so peaceful it's hard to believe you're just a five-minute walk from the center of a capital city. The helpful staff do their best to serve visitors, but they also let you relax in privacy. Facilities include toilets, showers, and changing rooms. You can rent snorkeling gear (S$10) and buy cold soft drinks (no beer). The Deep is a perfect escape on Sunday—make an afternoon of it.

Scuba Diving

Sqvama Divers (Box 843, Apia; tel./fax 24-858), upstairs at Pasefika Inn, charges S$120/210 for one/two tank dives. Their open-water certification course is S$1,050. To dive at Aleipata or in the Apolima crater they require a minimum of six divers at S$390 each for two tanks including lunch.

Scuba diving is also available at the **Samoan Outrigger Hotel** (tel. 20-042) costing S$130 for a one-tank shore dive, or S$150/200 for a one/two tank boat dive at Lalomanu (two-person minimum). The hotel's Danish dive instructor, Claus, also does open-water certification courses at S$880 for hotel guests only.

Pacific Quest Divers (Gayle and Roger Christman, Box 9390, Apia; tel. 23-914, fax 24-728, VHF channel 16 or 68), based at Coconuts Beach Club, offers scuba diving at S$150 including gear. If you just want a taste of scuba, a no-experience-required resort dive is S$135. They also do PADI certification courses at S$1,155.

Other Sports and Recreation

Samoa Marine (Box 4700, Apia; tel. 22-721, fax 20-087), near the Seaside Inn, offers deep sea fishing for marlin, mahimahi, wahoo, yellowfin, skipjack, and dog tooth tuna at S$1,050/2,100 a half/full day (up to five anglers, gear included). You supply the beer and they'll supply the snacks. This firm isn't there only for tourists: if nobody charters their powerboat, the *Ole Pe'a,* they'll often go out anyway in the hope of catching enough fish for sale on the local market to make it worth their while. Their guarantee is "no fish, no pay!"

The 18-hole golf course of the **Royal Samoa Country Club** (tel. 20-120) is just beyond Fagali'i Airport east of Apia (Fagali'i-uta bus). The clubhouse bar has a pleasant balcony overlooking the course and the sea—recommended for an afternoon drink. The course is open to nonmembers daily except Saturday (open to all on Sunday). Tuesday is Ladies Day with tee-off at 1330 and 1430. Greens fees are S$20. The big tournaments of the year are the Head of State Tournament in early January and the Samoa Open in June.

Saturday afternoons see exciting rugby or soccer from the grandstand at **Apia Park** (tel. 21-400). The main rugby season is February for "sevens" and July-Nov. for league rugby. You shouldn't miss a chance to see a game by the famous national team, Manu Samoa. The gymnasium at Apia Park (a gift of the People's Republic of China for the 1983 South Pacific Games) hosts basketball (Tuesday and Thursday at 1700), badminton (Wednesday and Friday at 1900), and volleyball (Saturday from May to July) in the gym.

The **tennis courts** behind Apia Park are open to the public daily (nightly until 2200; S$5 pp an hour, plus S$10 an hour for night lights). The **Apia Squash Center** (tel. 20-554) is next to the Seaside Inn.

Kirikiti (cricket) is played mostly in rural villages at 1400 on Saturday throughout the year with the competition season July-September. Other traditional sports include *igavea* (hide and seek), *lape* (handball), *sioga afi* (fire making), and *oagapopo* (coconut husking).

ACCOMMODATIONS

Shoestring

Betty Moors Accommodation (Box 18, Apia; tel. 21-085), just before the Mobil station on Matautu St., has 13 cell-like cubicles with shared

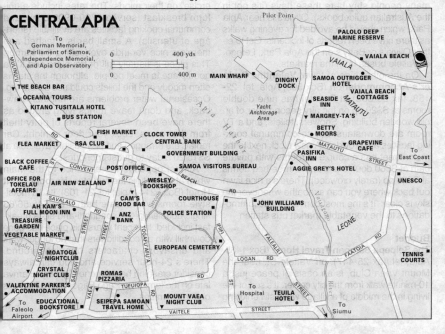

CENTRAL APIA

bath at S$20 pp (you'll almost certainly get one to yourself). Ask about the better room behind the main building. Out of safety considerations, no cooking facilities are provided in this wooden building (also no breakfast, towels, or hot water), and on weekends loud music spills over from nearby nightclubs. If you come back on foot at night, beware of a sudden attack by dogs from the adjacent laundromat (have a few stones ready). Betty will hold excess luggage while you're off touring Savai'i or south Upolu.

Farther along in the same direction, behind the gasoline station beyond the bank, is **Olivia's Accommodation** (Box 4089, Apia; tel./fax 23-465). There are eight three-bed rooms with shared bath in the main building at S$20 per bed in a shared room. Be sure to get a room with a fan. A large communal kitchen and lounge are provided. Peace and quiet at night depend on who your neighbors are, and Olivia's roosters and pigs will wish you a good morning. For more privacy ask for one of the two self-catering units in a three-unit block at back that cost S$44/55 double/triple. The family atmosphere is nice, but at times you may get lonely at Olivia's as not many people stay here these days (it's not in the Australian guidebooks). Olivia's is near Apia Park, which should be avoided for evening walks as there have been reports of incidents. Get to either Olivia's or Betty's on the Apia Park, Letogo, or Vailele buses from the markets.

On the other side of town, **Valentine Parker's Accommodation** (Box 395, Apia; tel. 22-158, fax 20-886) at Fugalei has nine double rooms at S$20 pp on the airy second floor of an old wooden building. Showers, toilets, and a TV room are downstairs, but no communal cooking facilities are provided. A new block next to the main street has a couple of rooms with private bath at S$60 double and some three-bed dorms at S$20 pp (rarely crowded). There's a nice lawn out back where you can sunbathe whenever the sky is clear. It's the most convenient accommodations to the vegetable market bus station.

Budget

The **Seipepa Samoan Travel Home** (Box 1465, Apia; tel./fax 25-447), off Vaitele St. near the Mount Vaea Club, is an oasis of peace just a 10-minute walk from the city center. It's sort of like living in the middle of a village while still enjoying some privacy. There are four fan-cooled rooms with shared bath in a European-style house and a few Samoan *fales* in the garden, one of them with an upper and lower floor! The overnight charge is whatever you wish to pay (offer at least S$25 pp) and includes a large tropical breakfast served Samoan style. Singles must be prepared to share. Cooking facilities are provided and at lunchtime on Sunday a traditional *umu* feast is prepared for guests at S$10 pp (S$15 for nonguests). Run by a Swede named Mats and his Samoan wife Sia, this place is highly recommended—so good all 16 beds are often full.

The **Seaside Inn** (Box 3019, Apia; tel. 22-578, fax 22-918), near the main wharf at Matautu, has a good location near the Palolo Deep and is also convenient to town. Several of Apia's top bars are only a few minutes walk away. The three rooms with shared bath are S$45/55 single/double, or S$28 pp if rented out as three-bed dorms. The 11 rooms with private bath are S$50/60/72 single/double/triple, and there's also a larger unit with fridge in the rear garden at S$60/72/88. The rooms aren't entirely soundproof and they're sometimes rented out to couples with "night exercise" on their minds. The rates include a uniform breakfast (served 0700-0900 only), and communal cooking facilities are available (shortage of utensils). A small bar is attached and there's a nice veranda overlooking the harbor. This place is usually full of travelers and it's a good place to meet people, although the staff is often moody and the toilets could use a cleaning. Occasional water problems are another drawback, and don't leave things lying around as there have been several reports of petty theft from the rooms. Lock your door at night. Car rentals are arranged and bicycles are available at S$15/20 a day to guests/nonguests.

Almost opposite the entrance to the main wharf at Matautu is the two-story **Harbour Light Hotel** (Box 5214, Apia; tel. 21-103). Its 18 motel-style rooms with private bath are S$45/56/68 single/double/triple, a spaghetti-and-eggs breakfast included. In recent years this place has gone downhill with air conditioners that no longer work and unsavory characters hanging around. There's 24-hour service and you can always consider crashing here for one night if you arrive late on the ferry from Pago Pago. A small store is on the premises.

Facing breezy Vaiala Beach, along in the opposite direction from town, is the **Samoan Outrigger Hotel** (Box 4074, Apia; tel./fax 20-042), a six-minute walk from the main wharf. It occupies a stately old mansion built in 1894 for Jonas Coe, the American consul of the time, and since 1994 it has been one of the finest backpackers' hostels in the South Pacific (no connection with the Hawaii-based Outrigger hotel chain). Rooms are S$44/55 single/double with shared bath, S$66/88 with private bath, or S$28 pp in the dorm, breakfast and tax included. Facilities include a communal kitchen and fridge, lounge, bar, and a washing machine (S$6 a load). An outrigger canoe is for rent at S$10. The presence of resident Danish dive instructor (and manager) Claus makes the Outrigger an ideal place to stay for scuba freaks, and a variety of sightseeing tours are offered in the hotel minibus. The lagoon views from the front lounge are very nice, and you'll enjoy sitting on the steps in the evening chatting with other guests. It's clean and pleasant, or sterile and business-like, depending on your tastes. You won't get bored here. Ask for their minibus at the airport.

Inexpensive

Ah Kam's Full Moon Inn (Box 1299, Apia; tel. 20-782, fax 20-782), on Savalalo Rd. in downtown Apia, has 10 fan-cooled rooms with fridge at S$99/132/165 single/double/triple. An a/c room will be about S$30 more. This two-story motel has a nice little bar in the courtyard—drop in for a drink at happy hour (1630-1900) even if you're not staying there.

The **Pasefika Inn** (Box 4213, Apia; tel. 20-971, fax 23-303), on Matautu St., has 26 rooms in a three-story building above the Peace Corps office. These begin at S$122/149/176 single/double/triple, plus S$27 extra if you want a balcony. Most rooms are a/c with a fridge and access to common cooking facilities, but seven budget rooms without a/c are S$81/95 single/double. There's also an eight-bed dorm at S$41 pp. Breakfast is included in all rates, but to be frank, this place is overpriced.

Rainforest Ecolodge (Ava and Steve Brown, Box 4609, Matautu-uta; tel. 22-144, fax 26-941) at Vailele-uta, five km east of town, caters mostly to people who book from overseas through Eco-Tour Samoa. The two guest

rooms with shared bath in a modern two-storey cement house are S$120 per room, including breakfast. Lunch (S$15) and dinner (S$30) can be supplied. Numerous hiking possibilities are available in the area, including a trail to a waterfall on the Letogo River. Frequent buses pass on the main road about 700 meters below the Ecolodge.

Moderate

The **Vaiala Beach Cottages** (Box 2025, Apia; tel. 22-202), facing the lagoon at Vaiala, offers seven pleasant, fan-cooled bungalows with cooking facilities and fridge at S$175/200/230 single/double/triple, plus 10% tax. Children 12 and under are free. Discounts are possible for long stays if you book directly, but bookings made through a travel agent or airline are 10% higher. The aggressive guard dogs of this neighborhood make it unwise to walk back here from town late at night, so take a taxi.

The three-story **Hotel Insel Fehmarn** (Box 3272, Apia; tel. 23-301, fax 22-204), up Falealili St. in Moto'otua, has 54 functional rooms at S$195/225/255 single/double/triple plus 10% tax. Each a/c unit has a fridge, full cooking facilities, video/TV, balcony, and private bath. The Insel Fehmarn caters to business travelers: typing, photocopying, and fax services are available. A swimming pool, tennis courts, guest laundromat, restaurant, and bar are on the premises. Apia's top pizzeria is right across the street and there are several car rental agencies nearby offering good rates. This unpretentious, well-managed hotel is a good alternative to Aggie's and the Tusitala for those who want value for money. Ask for a room on the top floor for panoramic views.

Expensive

Apia's premier tourist hotel, **Aggie Grey's** (Box 67, Apia; tel. 22-880, fax 23-626), on the east side of the harbor, originated in March 1942 as a hamburger stand catering to U.S. servicemen stationed in the area. Aggie's son Alan has continued the tradition of catering to American tastes, although the hotel lost much of its original South Seas atmosphere when the main waterfront building was reconstructed in mock-colonial style in 1989. The 154 rooms now begin at S$285/300/315 single/double/triple in the old section around the pool. Bungalows are about

S$60 more, rooms in the main lobby wing 50% more, suites 100% more. The cheaper rooms are rather shabby and stuffy, but the expensive ones facing the harbor are quite luxurious. Children under 16 are not allowed in the new wing or suites, but a fourth person in the old wing is S$15 regardless of age. Add 10% tax to these prices, and if you pay by credit card expect to have your bill inflated slightly due to the exchange rate scam discussed previously. Meals are S$150 pp extra. Weekly events include the barbecue on Sunday night and the Samoan feast on Wednesday. Aggie's is often full of dull business guests and rather bored conference participants, but the bar is nice and there's even an island in the large swimming pool!

The Japanese-owned **Kitano Tusitala Hotel** (Box 101, Apia; tel. 21-122, fax 23-652), at the beginning of the Mulinu'u Peninsula, is a complex of two-story blocks containing 96 a/c rooms with private bath beginning at S$225/255/285 single/double/triple, plus 10% tax, with children under 12 free. The open *fale* architecture of the main buildings is pleasant, and perhaps because it's a little disorganized, the atmosphere is surprisingly relaxed. Mosquitoes permitting, the poolside bar is a pleasant place to visit in the afternoon or early evening, and the snack bar serves good food at reasonable prices. Expect the waiters to try to shortchange you or to ask for a "loan" or a free trip to America. There's more local flavor than at Aggie's, just don't expect everything to work perfectly. For example, don't count on receiving your telephone messages or having your faxes go out. Occasionally overseas Samoans throw all-night parties in the rooms and the night manager may be unwilling to try to control these regular customers just to please a one-time tourist like you.

Beach *Fales* East of Apia

The closest village-run beach resort to Apia is **Saoluafata Beach Fales** (Box 820, Apia; tel. 40-216) on a nice beach near the Piula Cave Pool, 26 km east of Apia. To sleep in one of the three *fales* here costs S$16 pp, plus S$10 per meal. Picnickers pay S$2 pp. It's a good choice for a taste of this lifestyle without the long trip to Aleipata. Surfers come in summer (Dec.-March) for the reef break right-hander, 90 meters off nearby Faleapuna. Shoestring.

FOOD

Budget

The food stalls at Apia's vegetable and flea markets are the cheapest places to eat (S$3-5), and it's hard to beat a breakfast of hot chocolate with buttered bread, or a large bowl of cocoa and rice. Surprisingly, there's quite a bit here for vegetarians, including *palusami* and roasted breadfruit.

Many of Apia's cheapest eateries are near the corner of Vaea and Convent Streets, most of them open only until 1600 weekdays and 1300 Saturday. Here you'll find **Betty's Restaurant,** which dishes out huge lunches to huge Samoans, but you'll need a strong stomach to join them. **Pinati's** (tel. 26-395), next to Betty's, has no sign outside and no menu inside, but the large crowd of locals tells you it's something good. There are only a few choices, including curry, chop suey, fish, and chicken, all around S$3 a big plate. **Nana's Restaurant** (tel. 25-578), a few doors east on Convent St., is better than Betty's and the stuff in the warmer is only S$2 a scoop. Another choice is **Amani's Takeaway** (tel. 25-363), next to Retzlaff's Travel on Vaea St., with inexpensive chop suey, curries, and fish and chips.

A step up is the **Gourmet Seafood and Grill** (tel. 24-625; closed Sunday), on Convent St. a block back from the Chief Post Office, with lunch specials, sashimi, fried fish, and steaks. While the food certainly isn't "gourmet," the nautical decor is rather pleasant and their burgers are said to be the best in town (certainly more appealing than the predictable products doled out at the nearby McDonald's). You must pay a cashier first and get a number.

More Samoan-style fast food is scooped out at **Cam's Food Bar** (tel. 22-629; Mon.-Sat. 0800-2100), a block and a half behind the Chief Post Office (check the map). Cam's is great for lunch, passable at breakfast, but overpriced at dinner.

Pele Rose Mini Market (tel. 24-062), opposite the Samoa Visitors Bureau, has coffee, sandwiches, and other takeaway foods, and they're open 0500-2130 seven days a week.

Barbecues

For S$5 you can get a huge barbecue lunch at the **Maua Barbecue** (daily except Sunday until

1630) in the two-story stone building at the corner of Convent and Fugalei Streets. Watch for the smoke rising from the outdoor grill on Fugalei St. (the dining room is inside). Be sure to order chicken and not the tough, fatty mutton flaps or turkey tails.

More S$5 takeaway barbecue meals are available at the store in front of Crystal Night Club at Fugalei, south of the vegetable market. Try their *oka* (raw fish). Just down the road is **Frosty Boy** where obese passengers tumble out of taxis and order five soft-serve ice-cream cones at a time.

If mystery meats are not for you, **The Steak House** (tel. 22-962; closed Monday), in the same block as the ANZ Bank Saleufi Agency on Vaea St., grills quality cuts fresh from the adjacent butcher shop at fair prices.

Pub Food
For Mexican food and cold beer it's the **Grapevine Cafe and Vineyard Bar** (tel. 25-612; open Mon.-Sat. 0800-2200, Sunday 1200-2100), on Matautu St. just east of the Mormon church. Yachties often drop in for a cold one at happy hour (weekdays 1600-1800) and the management caters to this market with a paperback exchange and free showers in the adjacent fitness center. The Grapevine has one of the few compact disc jukeboxes in Apia (S$1 for three plays), and although owner Kasimani Lautusi looks as mellow as the Buddha, be aware that he's got a black belt in karate and runs his own private security firm. This is a great place to begin a pub crawl.

Another Apia institution is **Maua's Store** (tel. 23-942), next to Margrey-Ta's Beer Garden. It's open on Sunday and when the beer garden's open you can consume your takeaway food in there. The *oka* (raw fish) is a great bargain at S$2.50.

Jean's Blue Marlin Restaurant & Bar (tel. 24-065), next to Sails Restaurant on Beach Rd., has hamburgers and there's sometimes live music.

Chinese
Apia insiders reckon that finest Chinese food in town is served at the **Hua Mei Restaurant** (tel. 25-598; closed Sunday), upstairs in the Lotemau Center behind Air New Zealand. The lunch specials are inexpensive and there's a good medium-priced dinner menu.

Substantial Chinese meals are served at the **Treasure Garden Restaurant** (tel. 22-586; weekdays 1100-1400/1700-2200, Saturday 1700-2200) on Fugalei St. near the vegetable market. Although the food is good the noisy TV set in the dining room is jarring and the air conditioning may give you a chill. On Sunday (0930-1200) all you can get is takeaways from the counter outside (always a good option if you've rented a car and want to carry a cheap dinner back to your hotel).

For many years **Wong Kee's Restaurant** (tel. 26-778), in a ramshackle building behind Otto's Reef, was the "in" place to eat in Apia, and despite a recent change of ownership you'll still get some very good Chinese food here. It's not a bad plan to order extra rice and share one main dish between two people. The *aiga* lunch served weekdays is much less expensive than dinner. ("The routine of a friendly Samoan waitress translating my American English into Samoan English for the benefit of the Chinese-speaking cook was Monty Pythonesque.")

The **Canton Restaurant** (tel. 22-818), on Matautu St. near Betty Moors, gets varied reports, but it's one of the few places that opens for dinner on Sunday (1730-2100). Try the saltwater crabs.

Italian
Romas Pizzeria (tel. 25-948; daily until 2200, no lunch on Tuesday and Sunday), on Vaea St. a couple of blocks south of the clock tower, serves huge American-style pizzas (the large S$29 size is enough for three normal people). You can order a beer and have your pizza here, or take it away for the same price.

Giordano's Pizzeria (tel. 25-985; closed Monday), near the Hotel Insel Fehmarn on the road connecting the National Hospital to the Cross Island Rd., has richer pizza than Romas but it's a bit more expensive and the portions are smaller. Those who know say it's the best pizza in town and the candlelit courtyard dining area is agreeable.

Fine Dining
Apia cognoscenti say the number-one place in town is **Sails Restaurant and Bar** (tel. 20-628),

above Fale Tifaga Tauese Mini Cinemas on Beach Road. Their airy terrace provides pleasing harbor views to complement the fancy seafood, steaks, pastas, and sashimi, just count on paying at least S$20/40 pp for lunch/dinner here. Proprietors Ian and Livia Black managed top hotels in Tahiti and Fiji before settling in Apia. Thanks to Samoa's location next to the international date line, Sails can claim to be the last restaurant in the world to close every day. The wooden restaurant building itself was built by trader Harry Moors, and Robert Louis Stevenson himself stayed here before Vailima was built.

Sunday

Sunday brunch (S$22.50), either Western or Japanese style, is served 1030-1430 at the **Hotel Kitano Tusitala.**

A better bet might be the *to'onai* served around noon on Sunday at the **Pasefika Inn.** For S$30 you can eat as much *umu*-baked Samoan specialties as you wish.

For Sunday night dinner consider the poolside barbecue at **Aggie Grey's Hotel,** which offers a good selection of Samoan dishes for S$35. There's no traditional dancing but a corny hotel band is on the stage.

Cafes

The **Black Coffee Cafe** (tel. 26-528), on Convent St., opens for breakfast at 0630 Mon.-Sat., and has a choice of teas, coffees, spicy snacks, and healthy main courses all day.

Le Moana Cafe (tel. 24-828), in the Lotemau Center off Convent St. behind Air New Zealand, prepares good medium-priced meals and is also nice for a coffee. They also open for breakfast 0900-1300 on Sunday.

Gensil's Ice Cream Parlor, on the back side of the Lotemau Center off Vaea St., has real two-scoop cones for S$2.50, plus milk shakes, sundaes, and banana splits.

The **Rainforest Cafe** (tel. 25-030), next to Kava & Kavings on Beach Rd., really lives up to its name with the wood shavings on the floor and potted plants. It's run by a German couple named Barbara and Christian. They usually open weekdays only, serving breakfast and lunch 0900-1700, dinner from 1800 until late. You can also get handicrafts, postcards, and local guidebooks here.

ENTERTAINMENT

Fale Tifaga Tauese Nos. 1 & 2 mini-cinemas on Beach Rd. next to Don't Drink The Water shows the type of adventure and romance movies popular around the world.

Midcity Cinema on Vaea St. runs similar downmarket videos at 1400, 2000, and 2200 (no program Monday and Saturday nights, admission S$2.50).

Weekday mornings at 0750 the police band marches up Beach Rd. to the new Government Building for the flag-raising ceremony at 0800, and all traffic is stopped. Church choirs are worth a listen on Sunday morning (dress neatly and avoid bright clothing or shorts).

Nightclubs

Not to be missed is the Cindy Show Thursday at 2130 (S$7 cover) at **Margrey-Ta's Beer Garden** (tel. 25-395), near the Seaside Inn on Beach Road. It's great fun to watch the talented *fa'afafine* (female impersonators) do take offs on Tina Turner hits, and the fire dancing is spectacular. The audience will be mostly Samoan (this is definitely no tourist thing) and it's necessary to arrive half an hour early to get a good seat as the place will be packed. It's probably the number-one cabaret show in the South Pacific, but if you're a single male, be prepared to be approached after the show by entertainers interested in drinks, meals, and more (clear out as soon as it's over if you might find this offensive). Margrey-Ta's is open Mon.-Sat. 1000-midnight—always rowdy and fun.

Evening Shades (tel. 23-906), corner of Beach Rd. and Matautu St. not far from Margrey-Ta's, is the current "in" disco where Apia's trendy youth congregate on Saturday nights (S$3 cover).

Rougher is the **Mount Vaea Nightclub** (tel. 21-627; Mon.-Sat. 1900-midnight) on Vaitele St., Apia's meet market since 1968. It's fast and loud with the best band in town, and there are lots of boys/girls. Things don't get going until late, and drunks often spin into squabbles, so stay out of the middle and be really polite to everyone. The trouble is usually between local Samoans, rarely tourists.

The **Moatoga Nightclub** (no phone), opposite the Apia vegetable market, is a large Samoan dancehall with live music nightly except Sunday from 2200 (no cover). Take the same precautions you would at the Mount Vaea.

Crystal Night Club (tel. 22-155), south on Fugalei St. from the vegetable market, opens Wed.-Sat. 1830-midnight with live music from 2000. Friday is the best night to come with happy hour drink discounts 1700-1930 and free snacks including morsels of roast pig. Ask about fund-raising benefits here (the admission fee usually includes stacks of local food). Crystal offers a good mix of people, no rowdies, and no trouble.

After midnight the police begin making the rounds of the clubs and bars closing everything down, and by 0100 the city is dead. Everything except the hotel bars is tightly shut on Sunday and that day you're supposed to be a hotel guest to be drinking there. Persons under the age of 21 aren't supposed to be drinking at all.

Bars

Apia's favorite drinking place is the **RSA Club** (tel. 20-171; Mon.-Sat. 0900-midnight) on Beach Rd. in the center of Apia. Happy hour is 1600-2100 with free *pupus* (snacks) Friday at 1800. Whenever there's music here it's *loud*. Foreign visitors are welcome.

Otto's Reef (tel. 22-691) on Beach Rd. is a safe, casual place to drink or play pool. Check out their Samoan *oka* (spicy raw fish) served after 1600 (S$2.70). **Don't Drink the Water** (tel. 20-093), next to Kava & Kavings, is a no-smoking bar famous for its pitchers of piña colada and chocolate cake.

Apia's most atmospheric drinking place is hidden down the road beside the oil tanks directly opposite the German Flag Monument on the Mulinu'u Peninsula. The **Peninsula Club** (tel. 24-375; open Mon.-Sat. 1000-midnight), has open-air seating below three immense banyan trees and a main room with live music by Samoa's original pop band, Penina o le Tiafau, nightly except Sunday at 2000.

At the **Apia Yacht Club** (tel. 21-313), also out on the Mulinu'u Peninsula, you can get a great cheeseburger and a drink on Friday night, a barbecue on Sunday 1100-1600. All visitors are welcome *with* a member; polite, nicely dressed visitors *without* a member are usually invited in too.

Friday nights a rock band shakes **The Beach Bar** (tel. 25-956), just up the Mulinu'u Peninsula from the Kitano Tusitala. It's frequented by a congenial expatriate crowd.

Another safe Friday event is happy hour 1700-2000 at the bar of the **Insel Fehmarn Hotel** in Moto'otua with half-price drinks and free *pupus* (snacks). There's live music.

Cultural Shows for Visitors

An essential part of any visit to Samoa is attendance at a *fia fia* where the Polynesian dancing on stage comes with a buffet dinner of local foods (look over the whole spread before getting in line). There's usually a *fia fia* at **Aggie Grey's Hotel** on Wednesday and at the **Kitano Tusitala** on Thursday. The show at the Kitano Tusitala includes dances from several Pacific countries, while the "We Are Samoa" program put on by the hotel staff at Aggie Grey's is strictly Samoan and usually includes an appearance by a female member of the Grey clan, carrying on a tradition established by the late Aggie Grey herself. Another tacky touch at Aggie's is the Robert Louis Stevenson requiem set to music and sung in English and Samoan.

At Aggie's the show is before dinner at 1830, while at the Tusitala it's after dinner at 2000 (check these times). Admission for the show and the buffet is around S$45, otherwise there's a S$11 cover charge for the show alone. Patrons wearing T-shirts or shorts are not allowed in. Don't forget the Cindy Show at Margrey-Ta's Beer Garden on Thursday, which would be preferable to the Tusitala *fia fia*.

SHOPPING

Apia's colorful **vegetable market** or *maketi fou,* three blocks inland on Fugalei or Saleufi Streets, throbs with activity 24 hours a day—families spend the night here rather than abandon their places. You'll see a marvelous array of local produce, all with prices clearly marked, plus an eating area and a great assortment of classic Polynesian types.

Go native in Samoa by changing into some colorful, eye-catching clothing. Female travelers especially will enhance their appearance and acceptance by wearing a long *mu'umu'u* gown, a two-piece *puletasi,* or a simple wraparound *lavalava* available at the **Flea Market** on the waterfront. This is also a good place to shop for handicrafts.

Kava & Kaving Handicrafts (Box 853, Apia; tel. 24-145), on Beach Rd., has war clubs, kava bowls, baskets, fly whisks, tapa cloth, model canoes, slit drums, shell necklaces, and coconut shell jewelry. They carry mostly authentic traditional handicrafts at good prices. Handicrafts are also available at **Aggie's Gift Shop** (tel. 22-880), next to Aggie Grey's Hotel, **Chan Mow Supermarket** (tel. 22-615), opposite the Clock Tower, and **Perenise Handicrafts** (tel. 26-261), in the Lotemau Center behind Air New Zealand. Most shops are closed Saturday afternoon and Sunday.

The Samoa **Philatelic Bureau** (tel. 20-720) is in the Chief Post Office and at the airport—beautiful stamps at face value.

SERVICES

Money

The ANZ Bank gives cash advances on Visa credit cards, while the Pacific Commercial Bank (a joint venture of the Bank of Hawaii and the Westpac Bank) takes MasterCard. Obtaining money this way is expensive as you'll lose about 15% on the exchange, and interest is charged from the moment you collect the money.

The main branch of the ANZ Bank opposite the Chief Post Office changes traveler's checks weekdays 0900-1500, Saturday 0830-1130. Several small agencies of the ANZ Bank around

Apia will also change traveler's checks at the same rate. The ANZ Bank charges 50 cents commission on traveler's checks, whereas the Pacific Commercial Bank deducts S$3.

The locally owned National Bank of Samoa in the NPF Building behind Polynesian Airlines and at the vegetable market charges 50 cents commission. Their market branch also changes traveler's checks Saturday 0830-1230.

The rate of exchange for traveler's checks is considerably better than that for cash. Changing foreign currency outside Apia can be a nuisance, so do it here. On Saturday afternoon and Sunday, Aggie Grey's Hotel will change traveler's checks for a rate a bit lower than the bank. Allow extra time in any case as anything associated with bureaucracy moves slowly in Samoa.

There is no American Express representative in Apia.

Post and Telecommunications

The Chief Post Office in central Apia is open weekdays 0900-1630. Poste restante mail is held two months at a counter in the room with the post office boxes. Branch post offices exist at Matautu, Pesega, and Faleolo Airport.

Make long-distance telephone calls from the International Telephone Bureau (daily 0700-2200), inside the Chief Post Office. Three-minute station-to-station calls are S$7.50 to American Samoa, S$9 to Australia or New Zealand, S$13.50 to North America, and S$18 to Europe. Person to person service is only S$3 extra. These prices are about the lowest in the South Pacific. If you wish to receive a fax at this office, have it sent to fax 685/25-617. Public telephones for local calls are also available here, but you must ask at the counter (no public phone booths are available anywhere in Samoa). If you arrive to find a huge crowd of people waiting on lines of benches to place telephone calls, be aware that they're probably waiting to place overseas calls *collect.* If you're willing to pay for your call, you'll get priority and can go straight to the counter without waiting.

In late 1997 Pacific Internet Services, private operator of the talofa.net, was taken over by Computer Services Limited's samoa.net (try substituting this new stem to any old talofa.net addresses you may come across). They operate a cybercafe (tel. 20-926; e-mail: cafe@samoa.net) in the Lotemau Center behind Air New Zealand.

Immigration Office

For a visa extension, go to Immigration (tel. 20-291) in the Government Building (access from the parking lot at rear) with S$50, two photos, your onward ticket, sufficient funds, proof that you're staying at a hotel, and a good reason. You may also be asked to obtain a local sponsor who'll accept responsibility for you.

Embassies

The Australian High Commission (tel. 23-411; Mon.-Thurs. 0830-1600, Friday 0830-1200), next to The Rainforest Cafe on Beach Rd., issues tourist visas mandatory for everyone other than New Zealanders. Australia also represents Canada in Samoa.

Three countries have diplomatic missions in the John Williams Building on Beach Rd.: The Netherlands (tel. 24-337), 4th floor, the European Union (tel. 20-070), 4th floor, and the United States (tel. 21-631 or 22-696; weekdays 0930-1230), 5th floor. The New Zealand High Commission (tel. 21-711) is nearby on Beach Rd. opposite the John Williams Memorial (the a/c reading room here is an attraction in itself).

The British consul is Bob Barlow (tel. 21-406), a solicitor with an office on the 2nd floor of the NPF Building above Polynesian Airlines. France is represented by Norman Paul (tel. 20469), upstairs in the Gold Star Building opposite the RSA Club.

The Swedish Consulate (tel. 20-345) is at the Pacific Forum Line at the entrance to the main wharf. The German consul (tel. 24-981) is at the Rosenberg Clinic on the road up to the National Hospital. The Chinese Embassy (tel. 22-474) is at Vailima, a bit below the Robert Louis Stevenson Museum, down the road opposite the Carmelite Monastery.

Laundromats and Public Toilets

Cleanmaid Laundrette (tel. 21-934; Mon.-Sat. 0700-1900, Sunday 0700-1630), on Matautu St. between Betty Moors and the harbor, charges S$2.50 to wash, S$4 to dry. Bring your own laundry soap. At night, beware of vicious dogs here that often attack pedestrians headed for the guesthouses down the road.

Near the vegetable market is Homestyle Laundromat (tel. 21-551; closed Saturday), hidden behind A & S Hunt Service Center on Fugalei

Street. Laundrette Sil, across the street, is open on Saturday.

Public toilets are behind the clock tower in the center of town.

INFORMATION

Samoa Visitors Bureau

The government-run Samoa Visitors Bureau (Box 2272, Apia; tel. 26-500, fax 20-886, www.samoa.co.nz; weekdays 0800-1630, Saturday 0800-1200) is in a *fale* on Beach Rd. between the Government Building and the Catholic cathedral. A large part of the job training of the people behind the counter involves memorizing their own brochures, and they'll repeat information printed there even if it's out of date or incorrect.

Statistics and Maps

The **Department of Statistics** (Box 1151, Apia; tel. 21-371, fax 24-675), 1st floor, Government Buildings, sells the *Annual Statistical Abstract* and *Quarterly Statistical Bulletin* (S$5 each).

Get large topographical maps of Apia and Samoa for S$7 each at the Lands, Survey, and Environment Department (tel. 22-481) in the building marked "Matagaluega o Eleele, Faugafanua & Siosiomaga" next to the New Zealand High Commission on Beach Road. The *Samoa* map published by Hema Maps (S$12) is excellent and it's available both here and at Aggie's Gift Shop.

Books and Periodicals

The Wesley Bookshop (tel. 24-231) on Beach Rd. has a reasonable Samoa and Pacific section but the proprietors have long refused to sell the works of Samoa's leading novelist, Albert Wendt, which are too critical for their taste. For Wendt's novels you could try the Educational Bookstore (tel. 20-817), at the south end of Vaea St., although they're often out of stock. Ask for the *Tonga-Samoa Handbook* from Moon Travel Handbooks, which includes detailed coverage of Tonga, the Samoas, and Niue.

The place to buy Australian and New Zealand newspapers and magazines is Le Moana Cafe (tel. 24-828), in the Lotemau Center off Convent St. behind Air New Zealand.

P. Ah Him Co. General Merchants (tel. 24-559), on Saleufi St. near the vegetable market, has a good selection of used paperbacks for sale at the back of the store.

The Nelson Memorial Public Library (Box 598, Apia; tel. 20-118; Mon.-Thurs. 0900-1630, Friday 0800-1600, Saturday 0830-1200) is opposite the Clock Tower on Beach Road. Special permission of the librarian is required to enter the Pacific Room.

Environmental Information

Samoa's environmental group, the Siosiomaga Society (Box 5774, Matautu-uta, Upolu; tel./fax 21-993), in the office building above the Educational Bookstore at the south end of Vaea St., has a large library of environmentally oriented videos, which you can view at their office weekdays 0800-1630 or rent for 50 cents a day.

The South Pacific Regional Environmental Program (Box 240, Apia; tel. 21-929, fax 20-231, www.sprep.org.ws), opposite the Yazaki Samoa plant near the Vailima Brewery at Vaitele, sells many specialized publications on the South Pacific environment. (This office is to move to a new site near the Robert Louis Stevenson Museum in late 1999—ask before making the long trip out to Vaitele.)

Travel Information

Island Hopper Vacations (Box 2271, Apia; tel. 26-940, fax 26-941), in the Lotemau Center behind Air New Zealand, is an inbound tour operator that handles bookings from overseas.

Apia's airline offices are Air New Zealand (tel. 20-825), corner of Convent and Vaea Streets, Samoa Air (tel. 22-901), next to Molesi Supermarket on Beach Rd., and Polynesian Airlines (tel. 21-261), opposite the clock tower. Polynesian represents Air Pacific> (tel. 22-693) while Samoa Air is the Royal Tongan Airlines agent.

HEALTH

You can see a doctor for S$20 anytime at the National Hospital (tel. 21-212), in Moto'otua south of the center, but bring along a thick book to read while you're waiting. You can call an ambulance at tel. 996. The Moto'otua bus passes the hospital.

One of Apia's preeminent private doctors is Dr. John Atherton of Soifue Manuia Clinic (tel. 26-113), next to UNESCO above the post office at Matautu-uta. Call ahead for an appointment, if possible. Most private doctors charge S$30 for a nonresident consultation.

Dr. A.P. Leavai (tel. 20-172) operates a dental surgery above Business Systems Ltd. at the south end of Vaea Street.

Samoa Pharmacy (tel. 22-595) is next to the Pacific Commercial Bank on Beach Road. Both of the chemists (pharmacies) on Beach Rd. are only open Mon.-Fri. 0830-1630, Saturday 0830-1230.

TRANSPORTATION

By Bus

Local buses for Apia and vicinity, and long-distance buses for points all around Upolu, leave from the bus stations adjacent to the two Apia markets: the Flea Market on the waterfront and the vegetable market three blocks inland. The bus station at the Flea Market has separate areas marked Falelatai, Falealili, Taulaga, and Aleipata, but in practice these divisions are not followed.

The police do not allow buses to stand for long periods waiting for passengers at the vegetable market, so the buses make a loop between the two markets every 10 minutes or so until they're full. Long-distance buses have been known to drive around town for an hour looking for passengers. There are no set schedules but you can find a bus to virtually anywhere if you're there by 1000 Mon.-Saturday.

There are buses to the Robert Louis Stevenson Museum (marked Avele or Vaoala), the Papase'ea Sliding Rocks (Seesee, Siusega, or Tafaigata), the University of the South Pacific (Alafua), the main wharf (Matautu-tai), Fagali'i Airport (Fagali'i-uta or Vaivase), the National Hospital (Moto'otua), Piula Cave Pool (Falefa, Falevao, or Lufilufi), O Le Pupu-Pu'e National Park (Salani, Sapunaoa, or Vaovai), Faleolo Airport and the Savai'i ferry wharf (Falelatai, Manono, Mulifanua, Samatau, or Pasi Ole Va'a), and Manono Island (Falelatai, Manono, or Samatau).

Long-distance buses run to Lalomanu, Lepa, Safata, Sataoa, Siumu, and Lefaga. Buses to the Savai'i ferry wharf at Mulifanua begin their trips at the vegetable market, whereas all of the other buses begin from the Flea Market and only visit the vegetable market to pick up additional passengers. Buses to Mulifanua leave the vegetable market two hours before the scheduled departure times of the ferries to Savai'i (if you board this particular bus at the Flea Market, you won't get a good seat).

On Friday afternoon all buses departing Apia tend to be crowded with workers headed home. Saturday morning is a good time for buses, but on Saturday afternoon, Sunday, and evenings, service is very limited. It's not possible to make a day-trip to Aleipata or Lepa from Apia by bus—you must spend the night there.

In outlying villages only bus drivers are reliable sources of information about bus departure times. Others may give misleading information, so ask three or four people. On weekdays buses to Apia often leave villages in south and east Upolu at 0500, and then again at 1130. They often set out from Apia to return to their villages at 1100 and 1600.

Most of these colorful homemade wooden buses are village-owned and trying to use them to go right around Upolu is very difficult, as they serve remote villages by different routes that don't link up. The Lalomanu bus goes via Falevao and Amaile, while the Lepa bus goes via Lotofaga to Saleapaga.

The Salani, Sapunaoa, and Vaovai buses follow the Cross Island Highway to Siumu, then run along the south coast via Poutasi toward Salani. Four buses serve this route, but they all seem to run about the same time, making three or four trips a day. The last bus back to Apia from Salani is at 1400 (important to know if you're making a day-trip to O Le Pupu-Pu'e National Park).

There are good paved roads from Mafa Pass to Amaile and Lepa. The road along the south coast is paved from Siumu to Salani, but at Salani a river blocks eastbound vehicular traffic and cars must make a loop up and around via Sopo'anga Falls (no bus service). There's very little traffic along the south coast of Upolu if you intended to hitch.

Bus service is also very limited west of Siumu on the south coast. The Lefaga and Safata buses follow the north coast west to Leulumoega, then drive south through Tanumalamala to Matautu (Paradise Beach) or Tafitoala. There's no road between Lefaga and Falelatai. The only convenient way to go right around Upolu is to rent a car.

The buses are without cushions, but they do have destination signs and their fares are the lowest in the South Pacific. Buses around Apia cost 50 *sene;* S$1.50 to the Savai'i ferry wharf or Falefa; S$2 to Lefaga or Mafa Pass; S$2.50 to Siumu; S$3 to Lalomanu or Saleapaga. The bus fare from Apia to Lalomanu is supposed to be S$3, but some drivers ask S$5. On local buses around Apia, you pay as you get off. On long-distance buses, tell the driver where you're going as you board. You'll make a better impression on everyone if you have small change to pay your fare. Standing isn't allowed, so once a bus is full, extra passengers must sit on the knees of existing passengers! (Half of all traffic convictions in Samoa are for overloading vehicles.) The stereo music is a bus plus.

Taxis

Taxis have license plates bearing the prefix "T." Taxis parked outside the two airports and at the upmarket hotels tend to be a rip-off, while those waiting at taxi stands used mostly by local people are usually okay. Average taxi prices from the taxi stand adjacent to the Flea Market bus station are S$3 to the main wharf, S$5 to Fagali'i Airport, S$6 to the Robert Louis Stevenson Museum, S$30 to Faleolo Airport, or S$35 to Coconuts Beach Club.

Since the taxis don't have meters, always agree on the price before you get in and make sure you're both talking Samoan *tala,* otherwise the driver could insist on the same amount in U.S. dollars (a favorite trick). If you intend to get out and have the driver wait awhile, ask the price of that too. Failure to do so will lead to unpleasant demands for extra money at the end of the trip and ugly threats if you resist. To hire a taxi should cost S$25 an hour around town or S$30 into the countryside. There should be no additional charge for luggage, and tipping is unnecessary.

Beware of the taxis parked in front of Aggie Grey's Hotel, as these drivers are some of the most seasoned hustlers you'll ever meet. If you're staying at Aggie's and want a taxi, turn right as you come out the door, cross the bridge, and about 100 meters in front you'll see a regular taxi stand. In general, taxis are abundant in Apia.

Car Rentals

The international driver's license isn't recognized in Samoa. Officially you're supposed to get a local driver's license at the licensing office (open weekdays 0930-1200/1300-1500) opposite the main police station in Apia. A temporary 30-day driving permit costs S$10 with no photos required, while a regular Samoan license valid one year is S$30 and two photos. Some car rental agencies require the Samoan driver's license, while others don't. According to the Samoa Visitors Bureau, it's actually up to the agency!

Many side roads are too rough for a car and most agencies will tell you the insurance isn't valid if you drive on them. Make reservations well ahead if you want a jeep. A few of the car rental agencies are evasive about what is and isn't covered by the optional collision insurance, and some rental cars don't carry any collision insurance at all. Even with collision insurance you're still responsible for the "excess" or minimum deductible amount. Check the car *very carefully* before you drive off, and don't under any circumstances leave your passport as security on a car rental. Be suspicious, as we get more than the usual number of complaints about car rentals at Apia (if you get the feeling that a company is unreliable, trust that impression and don't do business with them). On the positive side, car rental rates in Samoa are the lowest in the South Pacific. Despite occasional shortages, gasoline prices in Samoa and American Samoa are also the best in the region.

As in American Samoa, driving is on the right. Speed limits are 40 kph around Apia or 56 kph on the open road. Drive very slowly and avoid hitting any people or animals—it can be as bad as in Mexico. Many drivers resist using their headlights after dark, and outside Apia pedestrians dominate the roadways. You'll often see people walking along a paved highway oblivious to approaching traffic, especially in the late afternoon. If you're forced to swerve dangerously to miss them or have to stop to avoid hitting another car, they'll just laugh. If you do hit something valuable like a large pig, drive back to Apia and turn yourself in to the police (tel. 22-222). If you stop you could be stoned, and heaven help you if you hit a Samoan! One Apia car rental company has this line in their brochure: "Stopping to verify the extend (sic) of possible injuries sustained to a third party could prove fatal to yourself." If you do become involved in a roadside dispute, don't react to excited bystanders—ask to speak to the *pulenu'u* right away. Occasionally Samoan children throw stones at cars they think are driving through their village too quickly and the rental agency may hold you responsible for the broken windshield. If you park a rental car in a village, you risk having it vandalized.

Except for two gas stations near Fasito'outa out toward Faleolo Airport, fuel isn't usually available outside Apia, so plan ahead. Ask the car rental company which gas station they recommend, as some stations have tanks that let rainwater leak in. If you want to take the car to Savai'i make sure it's allowed before signing the rental contract (most agencies won't allow you to do this). You can reserve a car space on the ferry at the office of the Samoa Shipping Corporation (tel. 20-935) on Vaea St. in Apia. However taking a rental car from Upolu to Savai'i is always risky because if there's any problem with the car you'll be responsible for getting it back to Upolu.

Budget Rent-a-Car (tel. 20-561, fax 22-284), between Polynesian Airlines and the Pacific Commercial Bank in the center of town, has Samurai jeeps at S$110/100/90 per day for one/three/seven days all inclusive. Sidekick jeeps are S$132/120/110. The deductible insurance "excess" for which you are responsible is S$675 and you cannot take the vehicle to Savai'i.

Avis Rent-a-Car (tel. 20-486, fax 26-069), behind the taxi stand at Beach Rd. and Matautu St., charges S$175 for their cheapest car with unlimited mileage (US$500 deposit). Avis cars also cannot be taken to Savai'i.

Pacific Helicopters Ltd. (tel. 20-047), opposite Aggie Grey's Hotel, rents Suzuki jeeps at S$130 a day including tax and mileage, but there's no insurance.

G & J Transport (Box 1707, Apia; tel. 21-078, fax 21-078), next to Kava & Kavings on Beach Rd., has cars at S$110. Unlimited mileage and S$500 deductible collision insurance are included and it's okay to take the car to Savai'i.

P & K Filo Car Rentals (Box 4310, Matautu; tel. 26-797, fax 25-574), in the mall behind Air New Zealand, has cars at S$110 a day for one or two days, including tax, mileage, and insurance (S$600 deductible). If you rent for six days the seventh is free. You must leave S$100 deposit and you may take the car to Savai'i.

Apia Rentals (Box 173, Apia; tel. 24-244, fax 26-193), on Vaea St., has Samurais at S$110 a day and Sidekicks at S$132 all inclusive (S$1,000 deductible insurance, S$200 deposit).

Billie's Car Rentals (Box 1863, Apia; tel. 25-363, fax 23-038), inside Amani's Takeaways on Vaea St., has cars which may be taken to Savai'i by ferry. This company is owned by Retzlaff Travel. We've received complaints about the condition of Billie's cars.

Another local company with a good reputation is **Pavitt's-U-Drive** (tel. 21-766, fax 24-667), between the National Hospital and Insel Fehmarn Hotel, with Suzuki jeeps beginning at S$100 one day or S$80 a day for two or more days. Also try **Hibiscus Rentals** (tel. 24-342, fax 20-162), opposite the Hotel Insel Fehmarn, and **Le Car Rentals** (Box 3669, Apia; tel./fax 22-754) on Fugalei St. near the vegetable market.

Scooter and Bicycle Rentals

The agencies renting motorbikes and bicycles change all the time, so ask at the Visitors Bureau for current locations. With scooters the insurance is usually included, but the gas is extra. A cash deposit will be required.

Local Tours

Several companies offer organized day tours of Upolu from Apia. Prices vary according to the number of participants, whether you travel by private car or minibus, if lunch is included, etc. Don't expect much "narration" from the guide—it's mainly a way of getting around. The tours don't operate unless at least eight people sign up, so ask about that, and if it looks questionable, check elsewhere. Even if organized sightsee-

ing isn't your usual thing, the convenience and price makes it worth considering here.

Samoa Scenic Tours (tel. 22-880, fax 23-626), next to Aggie Grey's Hotel, charges S$38 pp for an afternoon tour around town or a morning trip to the Piula Cave Pool. Full-day trips including lunch cost S$70 pp to Lefaga's Paradise Beach (Tuesday and Friday) or Aleipata (Wednesday and Saturday). Their full-day Manono Island excursion on Monday and Thursday is S$78 pp, lunch included.

Jane's Tours (Box 70, Apia; tel. 20-954, fax 22-680) on Vaea St. offers full-day trips to Aleipata on Wednesday and Saturday, and Paradise Beach on Thursday, both S$65 pp including lunch. The Manono trip on Tuesday is S$75 (half price for children under 12).

Cheaper are the minibus tours offered by **Outrigger Adventure Tours** (tel. 20-042), based at the Samoan Outrigger Hotel. The Aleipata beach tour on Sunday is S$40, the Manono Island tour on Tuesday S$60, and the Paradise and Matareva beaches/Togitogiga Waterfall tour on Wednesday S$40, a Samoan lunch included in all. A minimum of six persons is required to operate a tour and you must book by 1500 the day before.

Oceania Tours (tel. 24-443, fax 22-255), near the Kitano Tusitala Hotel, has a variety of overnight tours to Savai'i. These trips are reasonable value for those with limited time, but compare prices and book ahead.

Eco-Tour Samoa Ltd. (Steve Brown, Box 4609, Matautu-uta; tel. 22-144, fax 26-941), based at Rainforest Ecolodge at Vailele-uta, five km east of Apia, offers seven-day Samoan safaris, plus sea kayaking trips of two, four, and six days. They cater mostly to people who book from abroad, and prices are steep at S$450 pp per day and up all inclusive.

AROUND UPOLU

Like most other South Pacific "Bible Belt" towns, Apia is pretty dead on Saturday afternoon and Sunday. Luckily a number of *fale* resorts have opened on beaches around Upolu and Savai'i in recent years, giving visitors the option of evacuating Apia on Saturday morning. There are basically in two resort areas on Upolu, Aleipata/Lepa in the southeast corner of the island and Lefaga/Safata in the southwest. These also get quite a few Samoan day-trippers on the weekends, so be prepared.

There's no bus service right around Upolu, and if you want to do a circle trip without renting a car or returning to Apia, you'll need several days and a willingness to walk for long stretches. If you must choose only one destination, Saleapaga is a good bet.

SIGHTS AND RECREATION

Northeastern Upolu
The bridge above Falefa Falls previously mentioned gives access to a little-traveled seven-km road east along Upolu's north coast to **Sauago** and **Saletele** villages, an unspoiled corner of old Samoa worth exploring if you have your own transport. After the twin village, the onward track to **Fagaloa Bay** becomes much worse and only passable in a vehicle with high clearance. Fagaloa Bay's flooded volcanic crater is more easily reached via a steep side road off the paved road to Aleipata, a bit north of Mafa Pass. A road continues along Fagaloa Bay's south side to remote **Uafato** village, 14 km east of the turnoff. At Uafato one finds waterfalls, rainforests, flying foxes, and legendary sites associated with the demigod Moso, plus village *fale* accommodations (ask for Sulia) and a daily bus to/from Apia. It's possible to hike east along the coast to Ti'avea.

Eastern Upolu
Some eight km south of Falefa Falls, the road works its way over **Mafa Pass** (276 meters), beyond which is a junction, with Aleipata to the left and Lepa to the right. If you take the left-hand highway or "Richardson Road" toward Amaile (Lalomanu bus) you'll pass alongside the **Afulilo Reservoir** where Afulilo Falls above Fagaloa Bay were harnessed in 1993 in a US$33-million, four-megawatt hydroelectric development. More than half of Upolu's electricity comes from this and other hydroelectric projects.

Aleipata and **Lepa** districts feature many excellent and unspoiled white-sand beaches with good swimming but only average snorkeling. The authentic ecotourism resorts of this area are covered below, and a stay at one of them would allow the time to explore this attractive area. Visit the beautiful offshore islands at high tide with fishermen from Lalomanu. **Nu'utele Island,** a leper colony from 1916 to 1918, is now uninhabited, and two beautiful beaches flank the steep forested slopes. Hiring a boat out to Nu'utele would run about S$50 roundtrip (ask at Ulutogia village just north of Lalomanu). A trail to the volcanic crater behind Lalomanu begins behind the hospital in Lalomanu. A large colony of flying foxes lives here and a guide would be useful.

From Lalomanu it's seven km along the south coast to Saleapaga. The Lepa bus runs from Apia to Saleapaga via Mafa Pass and Lotofaga. Five km south of the pass, deep in the interior, are **Fuipisia Falls** (S$3 admission), signposted on the west side of the road. Just a 300-meter walk inland from the road, the falls plunge 56 meters down into a fern-filled valley of which you can get a good view from on top.

Three km south of Fuipisia, the same river plummets over 53-meter-high **Sopo'aga Falls** (admission S$3 per car, S$6 per bus). The signposted viewpoint is just a few hundred meters south of the junction with the westbound road to O Le Pupu-Pu'e National Park. A trail heads down to the falls from the viewpoint.

If you don't have your own transportation, you'll probably have to walk the four km from Sopo'aga Falls to the Salani turnoff. Buses run along the south coast from Salani to the National Park and Apia, but they're infrequent, and there's next to no traffic, so you're not likely to hitch a ride. The south coast of Upolu is more traditional than the north, and the people take pride in keeping their villages clean and attractively decorated with flowers.

O Le Pupu-Pu'e National Park

This 2,850-hectare national park (tel. 24-294), created in 1978, stretches along the insular divide from the summits of Mt. Le Pu'e (840 meters), the double-cratered peak east of Afiamalu, and Mt. Fito (1,100 meters), highest point on Upolu, right down to the lava fields of O Le Pupu and the south coast. The park is intended to provide a habitat for the endangered Tongan fruit bat, or flying fox *(Pteropus tonganus).* In past these giant bats with 1.5-meter wingspans would soar above the treetops at dusk, but illegal hunting has sharply reduced their numbers.

At Togitogiga, 28 km south of Apia via the Cross Island Highway, five km east of Siumu junction and just a short walk from the main road, are beautiful **Togitogiga Falls,** good for swimming, wading, and diving (middle pool). There are toilets, change rooms, and shelters at the falls. After heavy rains Togitogiga Falls becomes a raging torrent. It's crowded with Samoan picnickers on weekends (admission is free). With permission of the park staff, you may camp free near the falls for two nights maximum.

An overgrown trail from the falls leads up to **Peapea Cave,** three hours roundtrip on foot. It's hard to find the way on your own, so consider hiring a guide at the house on the right just beyond a gate a few hundred meters up the track (S$10/20 a half/full day). Beyond the cave, a trail continues north up the stream another four km to a waterfall where you could camp.

A rough four-km road begins two km west of the falls and leads across the lava fields to the black coastal cliffs in the southern section of the park. It probably isn't worthwhile to hike all the way down on foot and the road is too rough for a normal car, but you could do it in a jeep for fun. The **O Le Pupu Trail** follows the coast east from the end of the road, and the spent shotgun shells seen along the way are disheartening.

It's possible to do O Le Pupu-Pu'e National Park as a day-trip by catching a Salani, Sapunaoa, or Vaovai bus from the markets in Apia, but you'll probably only have an hour or two at Togitogiga Falls. Ask the driver what time he'll be returning to Apia, or better, get together with other travelers from your hotel and rent a vehicle for the day.

Southwest Upolu

The Cross Island Highway runs 23 km south from Apia to Siumu. To the right near the road, three km south of the Lake Lanoto'o turnoff (and 13.5 km from Apia), are **Papapapai-tai Falls,** also known as Tiavi Falls. The unmarked viewpoint (free) is near a store beside the road. It's only worth stopping if you have your own transportation.

From Siumu the South Coast Road continues west, reaching Sinalei Reef Resort and Coconuts Beach Club after one or two km, Salamumu Beach after 11 km, and Return to Paradise Beach after 13 km. Catching a bus along this way would be pure chance. One interesting south coast attraction is the **Sa'anapu-Sataoa Mangrove Forest,** accessible from either Sa'anapu or Sataoa villages. Each village has an information *fale* where you can pay S$1 pp to visit the mangroves on foot (only at low tide), or S$20 pp for an outrigger canoe tour (best at high tide). You'll see two types of mangroves here, the red mangrove with stilt roots and the oriental mangrove with buttress roots of knee-like extensions. Birds include the grey duck and reef heron. Both villages have guest *fales* where you can spend the night at S$20 pp.

The paved Lefaga/Safata road follows an inland course a few km from the coast and you must pay fees to visit the beaches. **Return to Paradise Beach,** named for a 1952 Gary Cooper film based on a James Michener novel of the same name, is accessible via a rocky two-km side road (S$5 per car, S$3 per motorbike, or S$1 per pedestrian).

ACCOMMODATIONS

Beach *Fales* at Aleipata and Lepa

During the past few years more than a dozen basic ecotourism resorts have sprung up at Lalomanu (Aleipata), on the golden sands facing Nu'utele Island, and on a less-frequented beach at Saleapaga (Lepa). These clusters of small two-person beach *fales* are simple, and amenities like electricity, toilets, and running water are provided at some but not at others. As well as being great shoestring places to stay, they're a wonderful introduction to Samoan culture.

For S$15-20 pp you'll get *fale* accommodation with a mat, pillow, and mosquito net but no bed.

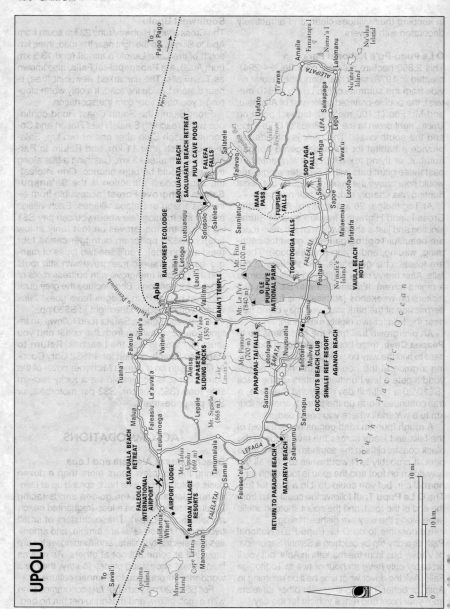

UPOLU

Food prices vary, costing anywhere from S$5 pp for one meal to S$26 pp for all three. Of course, these are open thatched *fales* with no walls or doors, so keep valuables well stowed at night, and if you go off during the day, it's wise to pack your bags and leave them with your hosts. Hurricanes tend to wipe these places out, but they're quickly rebuilt. There's always lots of space for visitors who show up unannounced (most don't have phones anyway).

At Saleapaga and Lalomanu the bus drops you right at the gates of the resorts, while at Lefaga in southwest Upolu you'll have a long hike down to the beach (which does enhance privacy). Picnickers pay S$2 pp or S$10 per car to use the facilities for the day (if you're just walking along the road and stop to sit down in an empty beach *fale* for a rest, someone will soon appear with a mat and the expectation of receiving the standard fee). Most day-trippers arrive on weekends, so during the week you could have the entire beach to yourself. It's lovely—the perfect antidote to Apia.

Lalomanu

As you come down from Lalomanu village and go west along the coast you'll pass Lusi and Gata's, Litia Sini's, Taufua's, Sieni & Ropert's, Romeo's, and Malo, in that order. Taufua's, Sieni and Ropert's, and Romeo's are used mostly by day-trippers and not recommended for an overnight stay.

Your best bet may be the one you reach first, **Lusi and Gata's Beach Fales,** which has a secluded beach all to itself, whereas all the other resorts share the same long beach. Lusi and Gata charge S$15 pp to sleep, plus S$5 per meal. The friendly demeanor, private beach, and low price recommend this place, but be prepared for some rather primitive toilets and showers.

Litia Sini's Beach Fales is better developed with 16 *fales* in a long row closed to the road but open to the sea (S$20 to sleep, plus S$10 a meal). **Taufua's Beach Fales** (Box 4802, Apia; tel. 20-180) has a bar you may visit but their beach is usually crowded with Samoan day-trippers and not recommended. **Sieni & Ropert's Beach Fales,** right next to Tuafua's, is also noisy and has poor security. **Romeo's** (tel. 20-878) is part of the same strip.

Half a kilometer west of Romeo's is **Malo Beach Fales,** which is much better protected from the road and picnickers. The 15 thatched *fales* here are S$20 pp to sleep, plus S$10 a meal. Their slogan is "my home your paradise." You're paying a bit extra here for the privacy, security, and a degree of comfort. Several unnamed collections of beach *fales* between Romeo's and Malo are cheaper and more basic.

Saleapaga

Whereas Lalomanu wins in the scenery category with its spectacular views of Nu'utele, Saleapaga offers a better choice of places to stay, fewer day-trippers, and good hiking possibilities in the hills overlooking the village. You may also find it quieter, friendlier, and safer—the whole South Seas dream.

Facing the white sands of Saleapaga Beach, seven km west of Lalomanu, are Lalopapa, Boomerang Creek, Tauiai, Gogosiva, Tila's Tropical Fales, Vaotea, Le Ta'alo, Faofao, Tagiilima, Tama o Le Aufuaina, Malaefono, Niusilani, Manusina, and Saleapaga Ocean View, cited here from east to west. All of the *fale* resorts charge S$15 pp to sleep and S$5 for breakfast, but at some it's S$10 each for lunch and dinner while at others it's only S$5 per meal. No alcohol is allowed at Saleapaga village.

Lalopapa Beach Fales is nicely isolated a few hundred meters east of Boomerang Creek (meals S$5 each).

Boomerang Creek Tourist Accommodation (Box 3680, Apia; tel. 40-358) is different from all the other places in that the *fales* are up on the hillside rather than on the beach. It's run by an Australian named Steve Harrison who charges S$40 pp including all meals. The communal toilets are clean, there's a small restaurant with a mini-library, and the security is good, although it's not quite the full Samoan experience of the others. It might be a good choice if you intended to stay longer than just one or two nights.

Gogosiva Beach Fales offers five thatched *fales* right on the beach at S$15 pp, meals S$5 each. Electricity and running water are available, and the family that runs the place is very helpful. Though open to the road, Gogosiva has one of the finest views of the crashing surf, the sound of which will lull you to sleep.

Vaotea Beach Fales (tel. 41-155) is sheltered from the road by trees and flowers, and it offers a bit more space. They charge S$15 pp to sleep, plus S$5 per meal.

Le Ta'alo Beach Fales is protected from the road by bushes and a fence, as is Tapu Legalo's **Faofao Beach Fales** (Box 2272, Apia; tel. 41-067). These neighboring places are run by related families and both charge S$30 pp with breakfast and dinner. Backpackers often stay here.

Buses leave Apia for Saleapaga Mon.-Sat. at 1000, and again at 1600 weekdays and Sunday. The return trip from Saleapaga to Apia is Mon.-Sat. at 0530, and again at 1200 weekdays and Sunday. There's no need to rent a car to come to Saleapaga or Lalomanu—just catch a bus.

Beach *Fales* at Falealili

The **Salani Surf Resort** (George Danellis, Box 6089, Pesega; tel./fax 41-069), at the end of the paved road in Salani village, is right beside the Salani River and near the beach. The 10 fan-cooled thatched *fales* have electric lighting but the toilets and showers are outside. The S$243 pp per day price is inclusive of room and board, airport transfers, surf guiding, kayaking, local tours, hammocks, and evening entertainment. No surfing is allowed on Sunday, so they usually take guests to the national park that day. It's used almost exclusively by surfers who book through Waterways Travel, 15145 Califa St., Suite 1, Van Nuys, CA 91411, U.S.A. (tel. 1-800/928-3757 or 1-818/376-0341, fax 1-818/376-0353, www.waterwaystravel.com). There's a long left-hander out in the channel, and when the surf is down on this side of the island they'll drive you across to the north. Other activities include canoeing in the mangroves or up the jade-green river to a waterfall, crab fishing, using the nearby village bathing pool, and exploring the south coast.

Backpackers and anyone interested in finding a quiet little hideaway are welcome at **Vaiula Beach** (Box 189, Apia; no phone), 1.5 km off the main highway at Tafatafa, nine km east of the junction of the Cross Island and South Coast Highways. There are five open *fales* at S$15 pp. You can use a communal kitchen and there are shared toilets and showers. Camping is S$5

pp (in your own tent) and picnic tables, toilets, and shelters are provided. The place fills up with picnickers on Saturday and Sunday (S$5 per car) but during the week it's usually empty. The snorkeling off their beach is only mediocre, but there's the possibility of surfing the hollow, fast right-hander out on the reef (boat required). Owner David Petersen is the grandson of a Danish sea captain and a bit of a character. Vaiula Beach makes a good base from which to explore O Le Pupu-Pu'e National Park and it's an okay stop on your way around the island.

Beach *Fales* in Southwestern Upolu

Another assortment of beach *fales* is found in Lefaga district, but these are quite a hike down from the main highway if you arrive on the Lefaga or Safata buses. It's possible to camp or sleep in a *fale* for S$10 pp at famous **Return to Paradise Beach**, two km off the main road, but obtaining drinking water is sometimes a problem.

Matareva Beach Fales at Lefaga charges only S$10 per carload or group of pedestrians to camp or stay overnight in one of their beach *fales*. Day use of the beach is S$5 per car or S$2 pp for pedestrians. Although there's a small store it's better to bring your own food from Apia. The money is collected up at main road, then it's a three km hike down to the beach. The swimming is better here than at Paradise Beach as there are no rocks and the location is nicely secluded.

More *fales* are available at **Salamumu Beach,** a few km east of Matareva, and showers are provided. Picnickers pay S$5 per car. The money is collected up at the main road, then it's five km to the beach. The new **Samoana Resort** here with four guest *fales* and a large restaurant/bar caters mostly to water sports enthusiasts. Beach hikes from Salamumu are possible to Matareva (30 minutes) and Nuu-o-Vasa (one hour).

Anapu Resort at Nuu-o-Vasa Beach near Sa'anapu-tai is also five km off the main road via a very rough track best covered in a pickup or by 4WD. The small *fales* stand along a lovely white beach flanked by black lava rock. A perfect small island is easily accessible just offshore and the snorkeling is good. At last report this resort was closed.

Sa'anapu

There are three places to stay at Sa'anapu-tai between Lefaga and Siumu. The first you reach is the **Manuia Wetland Holiday Retreat** (Ray Hepehi, Box 900, Apia; tel. 26-225) with three self-catering bungalows at S$80/120/150/170 single/double/triple/quad. To sleep in an open Samoan *fale* on their white beach is S$20 pp including bedding and a mosquito net. There's a bar and lots of free parking for overnight guests. Day visitors pay S$10 per car, plus another S$10 if the group wants a *fale* for the day, S$5 to use a barbecue, and S$20 to rent an outrigger canoe. It's a good bet if you want quality without the pricing of Coconuts and Sinalei.

Lagoon Lodges (Box 1319, Apia; tel. 20-196 or 20-965, fax 22-714), also known as Sa'anapu Beach Resort, right on the same lovely white beach, has five budget cottages with private bath, fridge, and stove at S$44/88 single/double. One larger five-person unit is also S$88, and if you stay three nights the price drops to S$66 double. The resort has a bar and outside alcohol is discouraged—if you do bring your own supply be prepared to pay S$20 "corkage" per cooler. Picnickers are welcome at S$5 pp per car, but there are no Samoan beach *fales* for overnighting. For that walk 100 meters farther west along the beach to a secluded spot where a family rents *fales* at S$10 pp a night.

Around Faleolo Airport

O Le Satapuala Beach Retreat (Box 1539, Apia; tel. 42-212, fax 42-386), on Fusive'a Beach near Satapuala village, is a 15-minute walk or a S$6 taxi ride east of the airport. Three fan-cooled bungalows with private bath and fridge cost S$65/85/100 single/double/triple, and for shoestringers there's an open Samoan *fale* costing S$22 pp a night. Camping is S$10 pp (own tent). Resort owner High Chief To'alepaialii Siueva or his wife Teri can arrange for you to stay in the local village, if you'd like. The adjacent restaurant specializes in local dishes, and there's also a seaside bar with live music on Friday and Saturday nights. On Sunday an *umu* is prepared (S$25 pp). Despite the proximity to the airport, it's peaceful and there's a good view of Savai'i from the beach. Since it's right on the main road to Apia, getting around is easy, and it's also a good choice if you're only in transit through Samoa

and don't want to go into Apia from the airport. A drawback is that the reef is far away and you have to swim quite a distance from shore to reach deep water. Windsurfing is a possible activity. Some 800 giant clams are being farmed offshore.

Airport Lodge (Box 498, Apia; tel. 45-583, fax 45-584), two km southwest of the Mulifanua ferry wharf or six km from the airport, opened 1997. The eight pleasant oval bungalows with fridge, fan, and private bath are S$77 single or double including breakfast. Communal cooking facilities are next to the bar, and a grocery store is only a short walk away. You get a nice view of Manono, Apolima, and Savai'i from their beach *fales* and there's safe swimming for children in the shallow water just off their beach (although no fish or corals to see). It's an agreeable budget place to relax after visiting Savai'i if you don't wish to head straight back to Apia, and convenient to the ferries to Savai'i and Manono. A taxi from Mulifanua wharf will be about S$3.

Manono Island View Cottages (tel. 23-259, fax 23-287), on Cape Tulivae a bit south of Manono-uta village, has three budget cottages with bath at S$50 single or double. There's a large restaurant on the premises. If nobody's around, ask at the house by the shore a bit back towards Apia.

Expensive Beach Resorts

American-operated **Coconuts Beach Club** (Jennifer and Barry Rose, Box 3684, Apia; tel. 24-849, fax 20-071) opened in 1992 at Maninoa on the south side of Upolu, a kilometer west of Siumu. Coconuts offers six categories of nicely appointed accommodations from standard courtyard rooms at S$255/285 single/double to a deluxe beach villa with kitchen at S$825/975 (plus 10% tax). The spacious treehouse rooms are cleverly designed with good ventilation and large covered balconies and Tahitian-style overwater bungalows were added in 1997. Some of the cheaper rooms at the rear of the complex are rather dark, and children are not allowed in the frontside deluxe units. Rates include a full cooked breakfast and the minimum stay is three nights. Snorkeling gear is loaned free. Gayle and Roger at the water sports hut (known variously as "Coconuts Watersports" or "Pacific Quest Divers") offer scuba diving at S$150 (snorkeling S$54), one/two-person kayak rentals at S$15/30 an hour, and a jungle boat cruise to a nearby mangrove swamp at S$50 pp (no charge for mosquitoes). Roger is friendly but he'll often cancel a scheduled trip if fewer than six people sign up. Jeeps are for rent at S$190 a day (free if you're staying in one of their deluxe units). On Saturday night, Coconuts has a *fia fia* on the beach under the stars (free admission to nonguests who order something at the restaurant or bar). Day visitors who patronize their beach-side bar and seafood restaurant are welcome to use the facilities, otherwise they'll be asked to leave. Day-trippers certainly aren't allowed to bring their own food or drink into the resort. For picnics, the adjacent village beach is available at S$5 per car. Coconuts has a more funky personal character than the slick Sinalei Reef Resort next door, and a more interesting mix of guests, but it's also less exclusive and the sight of a throng of Samoan kids splashing in the gecko-shaped swimming pool may discourage you from using it. Past readers have commented on "a certain edgy, underlying tension" at Coconuts, although efficiency has improved since Ned Brown took over as manager. Airport transfers are free.

The **Sinalei Reef Resort** (Box 1510, Apia; tel. 25-191, fax 20-285), next to Coconuts at Siumu, opened in 1996. This attractive international resort owned by Apia businessman Joe Annandale and family is a good choice if price is no concern of yours. The 16 a/c bungalows begin at S$480 single or double, S$570 triple (S$90 extra for ocean view), and there are four oceanside suites at S$780 single or double, S$945 triple (plus 10% tax). The neat rectangular bungalows have open bathrooms for showering under the stars, and the reception, restaurant, and bar are in the traditional Samoan style. Friday nights at 1900 a fire-knife act is performed, followed by a barbecue dinner (S$40). Sunday lunch (S$33) is an *umu* affair. The swimming pool is spectacular since the water is constantly replaced by a natural spring and it's strictly for house guests only. A 70-seat meeting room, nine-hole golf course, and two tennis courts are on the premises. For scuba diving and some other activities you must go to Coconuts, and rental cars must be ordered from Apia. Airport transfers are S$54 pp each way (otherwise take the airport bus to Apia for S$6, then a taxi direct to the hotel at S$35 for the car). Luxury.

MANONO ISLAND

Three-km-square Manono Island, four km off the west end of Upolu, is sheltered within the larger island's protective reef. Four villages are on Manono (Faleu, Lepuia'i, Apai, and Salua) but cars, dogs, and hotels aren't present, which makes it a delightful place (horses and bicycles are also banned). Electricity was installed on Manono in 1995, but as yet there are only a few small village stores, which are closed most of the time.

The trail around the island can be covered on foot in a little more than an hour. Near the landing at Faleu is a monument commemorating the arrival of the first European Methodist missionary to Samoa, Rev. Peter Turner, who landed here on 18 June 1835. A five-minute walk west of the missionary monument is the **Grave of 99 Stones** (Pa Le Soo) at Lepuia'i, with one stone for each of the wives of the chief buried here. On a hill in the center of the island is an ancient **star mound** (Mauga Fetu), but a guide will be necessary to find it. Manono has a few nice beaches, and the tour groups use one on the less-populated northern side of the island facing Apolima.

As yet the only place to stay is **Vaotu'ua Beach Fales** (tel. 46-077) run by Uili and Tauvela Vaotu'ua who live in the large white house in Faleu village. They charge S$45 pp to sleep in one of their two large *fales* including three meals and an island tour, perhaps less without lunch and the tour. It's a pleasant place and the Samoan food they serve is among the best. Hopefully more places like this will soon open as Manono is a great place to hang loose.

Getting There

Village boats to Manono depart from a landing just south of the Samoa Village Resorts at the west tip of Upolu. The Falelatai, Manono, and Samatau buses from Apia will bring you to the landing, and the boat leaves soon after the bus arrives, provided there are enough passengers. The boat operators always try to charge tourists ridiculous fares like "only 10 *tala*," but arrive early and show no impatience. Once they realize you're not about to pay these prices, they'll tell everyone to get aboard and leave (have small bills ready so there's no argument over change). The Samoan passengers pay only S$1 each, so if you give S$2 pp you'll already be paying double.

There are two landings on Manono, at Faleu on the south side of the island and at Salua on the northeast side. Get off at the first stop they visit, and when you want to return to Upolu, go back to the landing (before 1600) and wait patiently. When the boat finally arrives just get on with the others and pay the same exact fare when you reach the other side.

Some travel agencies in Apia offer full-day tours to Manono at S$78 pp, lunch included. Rather than taking the tour, get a small group together and charter a boat to Manono from the landing at S$20 each way for the whole boat. Pack a picnic lunch as little is available on the island. You could also visit nearby Apolima Island, in the strait between Upolu and Savai'i, this way by paying S$50 return to charter a boat. It takes about two hours to hike right around Apolima but you're supposed to be invited before you go.

SAVAI'I

Savai'i is just 20 km northwest of Upolu across the Apolima Strait. Although 50% larger and higher than its neighbor, Savai'i has less than two-fifths as many people. This unspoiled big island offers ancient Polynesian ruins, waterfalls, clear freshwater pools, white beaches, vast black lava fields, massive volcanoes, innumerable churches, and traditional Samoan life. Robert Flaherty's classic, *Moana of the South Seas* (1926), was filmed on Savai'i. Most of the villages are by the seashore, strung along the

fully paved circuminsular highway, and they're a pleasure to stroll through when the kids decide to leave you alone. Yet for an island, a visit to Savai'i is not sea-oriented since many of the attractions are away from the coast.

Savai'i is the largest island in Polynesia (outside of Hawaii and New Zealand). Though about the same length as Upolu, it's 50% wider with broad lava plateaus in the interior. Most of the northeast side of this high volcanic island was transformed in the great eruptions of Mt. Matavanu between 1905

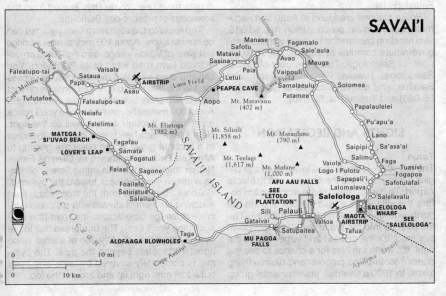

and 1911, which buried much fertile land and sent refugees streaming across to Upolu. Vast tracts of virgin rainforest survive despite agricultural clearings and heavy logging, but in 1998 large areas in the west were destroyed by forest fires facilitated by the drought associated with El Niño. Coral reefs are present along the east coast from Salelologa to Pu'apu'a, on the north coast from Saleaula to Sasina, then from Asau to Vaisala, and on the south coast at Palauli. Expect to pay a custom fee of anywhere from S$2 pp to S$10 per car to a responsible adult (not a child or teenager) to use a village beach.

Orientation

Other than Salelologa, there's nothing that could be called a town on Savai'i; it's just one village after another around the coast, with large gaps on all sides. In recent years Salelologa has developed into a busy little town with a market, stores, laundromat, several small restaurants and takeaways, and a couple of places to stay. The market and bus station are less than a kilometer north of where the Upolu ferry lands.

Actually, Salelologa is a dismal, uninteresting place best avoided by jumping directly on a bus to Lalomalava, Manase, Satuiatua, or Falealupo-tai.

Police stations are found at Asau and Fagamalo, but the main police station (tel. 53-515; also handling immigration matters) is in the small government complex at Tuasivi, about 10 km north of Salelologa. There are post offices at Salelologa, Tuasivi, Fagamalo, Asau, and Salailua, and district hospitals at Sataua (tel. 58-086) and Tuasivi (tel. 53-510).

SIGHTS AND RECREATION

Tafua

The paved six-km side road to Tafua village begins directly opposite the access road to Maota Airport. To the left (east) of the road, two km before the village, is a grassy track around the north side of Tafua Crater (560 meters). The footpath up into the crater is 500 meters down this road: it's the second and larger trail to the right. It's worth the hike for a chance to see the crater's tooth-billed pigeons and diurnal flying foxes. In 1990 a Swedish environmental group and the Tafua villagers signed a covenant in which the villagers agreed to protect their forests from logging and other misuse for 50 years in exchange for Swedish financial aid to local health and education. Tafua village itself is just above the beach, and one can walk east along the coast to black cliffs where lava flows from the volcano entered the sea. A S$2 pp entry fee to the Tafua Rainforest Reserve is collected at Maota at the start of the Tafua road. To stay in the village ask for Ulu or Anita.

Letolo Plantation

Catch a bus from the Salelologa ferry wharf to Letolo Plantation, eight km west in Palauli District. The largest remaining prehistoric monument in Polynesia is here, as well as an idyllic waterfall and pool. The huge **Pulemelei stone pyramid** *(tia)*, on a slope about two km from the main circuminsular highway, was concealed by thick undergrowth until the 1960s. This immense stone platform on a hillside in the middle of the coconut plantation is 73 meters long, 60 meters wide, and 15 meters high, and stones used in religious ceremonies are scattered around it. The structure is similar to some of the stone temple mounds of Tahiti and is possibly their predecessor, though its origins have been completely erased from the memories of present-day Samoans.

The route to the still-overgrown pyramid can be hard to follow. About 100 meters after a bridge just west of Vailoa village, turn right onto an unmarked farm road into Letolo Plantation. You can only drive a car 200 meters down the access road to the first river crossing. Continue on foot past a two-story concrete house on the right. About 200 meters beyond the house you'll notice an entrance through a stone wall on the right. Here a faint track heads east between the trees of a coconut grove where cows are grazing to **Afu Aau Falls** (also known as Olemoe Falls). Rather than visit the falls immediately, continue north on the main track toward the pyramid.

About 20 minutes from the main road, start watching for a small stream with a sizable concrete drainage pipe across the road (the only such pipe you'll see). The unmarked trail to the pyramid is on the left at the top of a small slope about 100 meters beyond the pipe. The pyramid is completely covered by ferns and bush but a trail runs right up and around the top.

After exploring the pyramid return to the falls for a well-deserved swim. The edge of the ravine is 400 meters straight east through the coconut plantation, and the steep path down to the pool is fairly obvious. The crystal-clear waters of Faleata Stream running down the east side of the plantation plunge over a cliff into a large, deep pool into which you can dive from the sides. Brown prawns live in the pool: drop in bread crumbs and wait for them to appear.

During your visit here, keep in mind that you're on private property, courtesy of the Nelson family. Politely ask permission to proceed of any people you meet along the way. Admission should be free.

The Southwest Coast

Eight km west of Letolo Plantation at the east entrance to Gautavai village is the **Mu Pagoa Waterfall** where the Vaiola River—Samoa's largest—tumbles over black cliffs into the sea just below the highway bridge. The best view is from the west side (free).

The **Alofaaga Blowholes** are along the coast near Cape Asuisui, 16.5 km west of the Mu Pagoa bridge and 40 km from Salelologa wharf. Just a short walk from Taga village, this series of rather spectacular blowholes *(pupu)* are at their best at high tide. Throw in a coconut and watch the roaring jet propel it skyward. (If you allow a boy to perform this trick for you he'll want a substantial tip.) Avoid getting too close to the blowholes as cases have occurred of people being dragged by the surge across the sharp rocks to their deaths. A S$1 pp admission fee is collected at the turnoff.

There's good **surfing** in winter (June-Sept.) at high tide just off the point at Salailua, 13 km northwest of Taga. At Fagafau, 11.5 km northwest of Satuiatua Beach Resort, the sheer cliffs of **Lovers' Leap** drop precipitously to the sea (S$2 pp fee if you stop by the road to peer down the cliffs). The story goes that due to family problems, an elderly blind woman and her only child jumped from the cliff. The woman turned into a turtle while the child became a shark. It's said that a certain magic chant can still bring the turtle and shark back to these shores.

Matega i Si'uvao Beach (S$2 pp admission, plus S$5 for video cameras) is four km northwest of Lovers' Leap. Waves crash into the black rocky coast right next to the road, 600 meters beyond the Si'uvao Beach turnoff, and you can stop and look for free.

Falealupo

From Falealupo-uta on the circuminsular highway it's nine km down a paved road to Falealupo-tai which stretches 1.5 km along a white sandy beach. A unique attraction of this area is the **Rain Forest Canopy Walkway,** two km up the Falealupo-tai access road. The stories of stairways ascend a Garuga floribunda tree to a suspension bridge spanning a 30-meter gap to a large banyan tree. Then the stairways climb another five stories to a large platform high above the rainforest canopy. Built in 1997 by the Seacology Foundation of Utah (www.seacology.org), it's part of a conservation project intended to provide local villagers with a financial incentive to preserve their lowland forests. At S$20 pp, admission to the walkway may seem expensive, but the money goes to supporting conservation efforts throughout this area. It's also possible to sleep on the uppermost platform at S$50 pp including dinner and breakfast.

Four km beyond the Canopy Walkway is **Moso's Footprint,** on the right beside the road. Three meters long, it's said to have been left when the war god Moso leaped from Samoa to Fiji. You'll pay S$5 per group to stop and admire the print.

Another designated tourist attraction is the **House of Rocks,** in the bush 300 meters behind the ruined Methodist church at Falealupo-tai, three km beyond Moso's Footprint. Here your guide will point out a row of stone seats, the largest belonging to Maleatoa, in a lava tube with a hole in its roof. You'll pay either S$5 per person or per group (make sure the price is understood).

Falealupo-tai village was devastated by Hurricane Val in 1991 and the picturesque thatched *fales* of before have now been replaced by modern housing. To use the beach at Falealupo-tai is S$5 per car. If you're staying at one of the *fale* resorts of this area, a good day hike is east along the coast to sandy Fagalele Bay and the lava cliffs of Cape Puava.

Three km southwest of Falealupo-tai is palm-covered **Cape Mulinu'u,** shaped like an arrow aimed against Asia and the spirit land of Pulotu.

This lovely white beach is Samoa's westernmost tip and the place where the world's day comes to an end. Dubbed Sunset Beach for tourists, it's controlled by Tufutafoe village and entry is S$10 per car. The rough track continues past Tufutafoe, 1.5 km southeast of the cape, to Neiafu on the main highway, a couple of hours walk.

As you may have gathered by now, the Falealupo/Tufutafoe locals are quite adept at collecting multiple customary fees from foreigners and it's one of their few sources of income. If you're driving you can usually get everyone in your vehicle in for the basic amount (or just drive on), but individuals roughing it on public transport may have to pay the same fees per person (or bargain). Unless you have your own transport, getting to Falealupo is difficult—there's only one bus a day, which leaves the village for Salelologa wharf at 0500 every morning, although it's usually possible to hitch a ride in a pickup. There's no store in Falealupo-tai village.

The North Coast

The road around the island continues past **Asau,** the main supply center on the north side of Savai'i. There's good holding for yachts in the well-protected small boat harbor in Asau Bay, but the channel is subject to silting, so seek local advice before attempting to enter. Asau wharf is seldom used but there's a large sawmill belonging to Samoa Forest Products and an airstrip with direct Polynesian Airlines flights from Apia's Fagali'i Airport (see **Getting There,** below).

From Asau, the newly paved road turns inland and climbs around a lava flow dating from an eruption in 1760. Very serious hikers can ascend **Mt. Silisili** (1,858 meters), Samoa's highest peak, from Aopo, 24 km east of Asau. The trail begins on the east side of the village. The charge for the three-day trip will be S$30 pp a day without a guide (not recommended) or S$50 pp a day with a guide. A tent and warm clothing will be required. To hike to the Aopo lava tube cave from the village is S$5 pp (two hours). Accommodations in the village are easily arranged. **Peapea Cave,** a lava tube that runs under the highway five km northeast of Aopo, is S$3 pp admission. Numerous white swiftlets live in the cave.

Soon after you rejoin the coast, you reach Matavai, 9.5 km northeast of Peapea Cave. The **Matavai Pool** here is fed by a strong freshwater spring *(mata ole alelo)* and you can swim for S$1 pp or S$5 per car. A *fale* is provided for resting. Ask a local to tell you the legend of "Sina and the spirit eel" associated with the pool.

You'll find more freshwater pools *(vaisafe'e)* at **Safotu** village, three km east of Matavai. Three huge churches stand in a row in Safotu: Catholic, Congregational, and Methodist. A picturesque beach lined with small dugout fishing canoes is opposite the Catholic church.

Three km south of Safotu is **Paia** village with a lava tube *(nu'uletau),* the "short people's cave," three km farther inland. You'll need guides and kerosene lamp to visit it (S$20 fee per group, plus S$5 for a lamp). Meter-high midgets are said to live inside.

A grassy road beginning beside the Mormon church in Paia leads eight km south to the crater of **Mt. Matavanu** (402 meters), which the locals call *mata ole afi* (eye of the fire). This was the source of the 1905-11 volcanic outbreak that covered much of northeast Savai'i with black lava. You don't really need a guide to find the crater—just look for a trail to the left where the road dips, about 2.5 hours out of Paia. Beware of deep crevices and crumbling edges as you near the crater; they have claimed at least one life. There's no charge to come up here. If you're a really intrepid explorer you could hike northeast down the lava field from Mount Matavanu and turn north on any road you meet, which should bring you through Vaipouli to the coast. You'll be on your own if anything goes wrong and a guide would be advisable unless you're a very experienced hiker.

The main north coast tourist resorts, Stevenson's and Tanu Beach, are only four km east of the turnoff to Paia at Safotu. May-Oct. a safe, though exposed, yacht anchorage is found at Matautu Bay, two km farther east.

The Lava Field

The road south of Saleaula runs across a wide, barren lava flow. A large stone Methodist church, nearly engulfed by the lava at the beginning of the century, is on the northeast side of the road under a large tree about 100 meters off the road near the flow's northern edge. The so-called **Virgin's Grave** is about 150 meters east of the church near a mango tree. Look for a rectangular depression about two meters deep in the lava; the grave is clearly visible at the bottom. Someone will collect S$2 pp admission at this managed tourist site signposted "Saleaula village lava ruins (1905-1911)."

As the fast-flowing *pahoehoe* lava approached the coast here in the early years of this century, it built up behind the reef and spread out in both directions. The highway now runs across it for eight km. It's intriguing to stop anywhere and go for a walk on the lava to get a feel for this awesome geological event. Maunga village, 3.5 km southeast of the Virgin's Grave, is built around a circular crater.

The East Coast

Picturesque villages and intermittent white beaches run all along the route south from Pu'apu'a to the wharf. **Lano** is a favorite surfing beach in summer (Dec.-March), and there's good snorkeling at **Faga.** In front of the large Congregational Christian Church at **Sapapali'i,** eight km north of Salelologa wharf, is a stone monument to John Williams. This marks the site where the missionary arrived in 1830 and converted the local chiefs to Christianity in a couple of days. Several hotels are found around here.

PRACTICALITIES

Salelologa

A few minutes walk from the ferry wharf is the **Savai'i Ocean View Motel** (Tui and Maselina Retzlaff, tel. 51-258), with two self-contained rooms with fridge in a large *fale* at S$77/99 single/double. Unfortunately loud music from the adjacent Le La-Oso Nite Club erases peace and quiet here Wed.-Saturday.

Next door to the Ocean View is Manumalo Baptist Church where Rev. Seumanu Alofa operates **Rita's Accommodation** (Box 5066, Salelologa, Savai'i; tel. 51-236) with one two-room *fale* at S$15/25 single/double. Reverend Seumanu also organizes circle island tours in his car or taxi at S$150 for one or two people, S$200 for three. This place makes a good base for visiting the island thanks to the radiating bus services.

A little farther up the road from Rita's, before the market, is **Taffy's Paradise Inn** (tel. 51-544) with five rooms with shared bath in an airy Eu-

ropean-style house overlooking the lagoon at S$33 pp. This place would be noisy if full, but it seldom is. The people in the store upstairs in the ferry terminal will know about this place (same ownership).

The restaurant (tel. 51-354) upstairs in the ferry terminal at Salelologa serves basic meals. It's closed on Sunday but the small shop here remains open. The store opposite the Ocean View Motel at Salelologa serves a good plate lunch weekdays for about S$6. You can also get lunch at the food stalls in the market but there's nowhere to order dinner as the market and most shops close down by 1600.

Le La-Oso Nite Club, a large bar 150 meters up from the Salelologa ferry, is open Wed.-Sat. 1000-midnight. On Friday and Saturday from 2000 the vicinity is serenaded by Le La-Oso Band (S$4 cover): the name means "sunrise."

The ANZ Bank (tel. 51-213) is next to the market, and the Pacific Commercial Bank (tel. 51-208) is farther up the same way, near the T-junction with the circuminsular road. (A second Pacific Commercial Bank branch is at Vaisala near Asau, two km from the Vaisala Hotel.)

Eastern Savai'i

The **Safua Hotel** (Private Mail Bag, Salelologa; tel. 51-271, fax 51-272), in a garden setting at Lalomalava, six km north of the wharf, was the

SALELOLOGA

© DAVID STANLEY

first hotel on Savai'i. The 12 rustic Samoan *fales* with private facilities and fan are S$77/88/99 single/double/triple. Rooms here are twice as expensive if booked through a travel agent overseas and one shouldn't expect luxury. Mammoth meals cost S$12/12/27 for breakfast/lunch/dinner if paid directly. Campers may pitch their own tents in the garden at S$10 pp on the understanding that they'll take dinner. The owner/hostess Moelagi Jackson and her family eat with guests at a long table, and Sunday lunch is a special treat. Moelagi, one of the very few female *failauga* in Samoa, is an expert on tapa making, and she usually keeps a few high-quality pieces on hand to sell. Island tours by minibus are arranged, or just ask to be shown around the family plantation. The Safua is not on the beach but an informal bar faces a shady garden, and there's a large library. You'll enjoy sitting in the lounge chatting with the other guests. Budget.

The **Savaiian Hotel** (Roger and Ama Gidlow, Box 5082, Salelologa; tel. 51-206, fax 51-291), behind the Mobil service station just south of the Safua at Lalomalava, has less Samoan atmosphere but more creature comforts. Built in 1992, it's on a rocky shore but is spacious and clean. The six a/c duplex units with cooking facilities, fridge, and private bath (hot water) are S$95/115/135 single/double/triple. Four thatched *fales* at the back of the yard are S$35 single, or S$25 pp for two, three, or four. These have a toilet, fan, and four beds but no cooking facilities. The hotel band plays soft Samoan pop music in the restaurant until midnight on Friday and Saturday nights. Free transfers to the airport or wharf are offered. Budget to inexpensive.

If you want to be at the beach, pick the **Siufaga Beach Resort** (Box 8002, Tuasivi; tel. 53-518, fax 53-535), also known as the Caffarelli Hotel, just a kilometer north of the new hospital at Tuasivi and about six km north of Lalomalava. Created by an Italian doctor and his Samoan family, the resort has a large green lawn that faces lovely Faga Beach, one of the top swimming/snorkeling locales in Samoa. It's in something of a rain shadow so it's drier than Salelologa. The six attractive *fales* with private bath, kitchenette, and local Samoan decor go for S$108/122/135 single/double/triple, and campers are also welcome to pitch their tents in the shade

of a big banyan tree for S$27. There's a good grocery store opposite the post office, a 10-minute walk south of the resort, but no cooking facilities for campers. Dr. Peter Caffarelli is an interesting character who enjoys chatting with guests on his veranda. The Puapua bus (S$1) will bring you here from Salelologa wharf, otherwise a taxi from the wharf will run S$15. Inexpensive.

Northeastern Savai'i

Tanu Beach Fales (Taito Muese Tanu, c/o Fagamalo Post Office; tel. 54-050) sits on a nice beach at Manase village, a couple of km west of Fagamalo and 45 km northwest of Salelologa. There are 16 open Samoan *fales* and one three-bedroom wooden house at S$50 pp including breakfast and dinner. Camping with your own tent will shave S$10-15 off the price. Drinking water, bananas, and nippy showers are free, and their store sells beer and cold drinks. The meals are served at a long common table and are variable. Evening entertainment features amplified music. The managers arrange half day tours covering most sites between here and the Taga blowholes at S$40 pp if six people go. It makes a good base for visiting Mt. Matavanu and is a safe, convenient place to stop and unwind on your way around the island. Many backpackers stay here (and most readers said they liked it). Budget.

Stevenson's at Manase (Box 210, Apia; tel. 58-219, fax 54-100), right next to Tanu Beach Fales, is more upmarket with 18 small a/c rooms in a long prefabricated block at S$172 single or double, plus five a/c villas with fridge and TV at S$300, plus tax. These prices are sharply reduced when things are slow. Get a room away from the noisy generator. Stevenson's caters to backpackers with six beach *fales* at S$30 pp, but there are no cooking facilities and meals in the hotel restaurant are expensive but good. The beach is also nice, but on nighttime strolls watch out for soft sand around a small spring. Outrigger canoes are S$11 a day. They organize full-day circle-island tours and half-day excursions, otherwise rental cars are S$120 a day. Transfers from Maota Airport or Salelologa Wharf are S$60 pp return. Stevenson's is often almost empty due to the unpopular food prices, so check that they're still operating. Budget to inexpensive.

Southwestern Savai'i
You can sleep in one of five *fales* at dark **Ananoa Beach** near Faaala in Palauli for S$10 pp, otherwise it's S$5 per car to use the beach. There's surfing here.

Savai'i's original backpackers camp is **Satuiatua Beach Resort** (Box 5623, Salailua; tel. 56-026) at Satuiatua, 55 km west of Salelologa wharf. For S$50 pp you get a mattress in an open Samoan beach *fale* with electric lighting, plus breakfast and dinner. The meals are huge with the emphasis on Samoan cuisine. Their small store across the road sells cold beer at normal prices (when available). The white beach is protected by a long lava ledge, making it safe for children, and you can snorkel. One of Samoa's best left-handers is nearby, and during the surfing season Satuiatua can get crowded. Tiny biting sand flies can be a problem. The whole complex is nestled in a row of huge *pulu* (banyan) trees. If you've got a couple of hours to spare, ask the staff to guide you to a lava tube up in the bush behind the resort. Otherwise hike west along the coast. A pickup truck is available for tours to Falealupo at S$25 pp (minimum of three). Guests must present themselves at church on Sunday morning. The Fagafau bus, which meets all ferries from Upolu, will bring you directly here for S$2.50. Budget.

In winter many surfers stay with the Methodist pastor at Salailua.

At Faiaai village, six km northwest of Satuiatua, you'll find a few *fales* by the highway where you can stay for S$15 pp, plus another S$15 for meals. There's a lovely beach at the bottom of the cliff below the village and you might be able to camp there for a similar price. For information about this place, call 56-023.

Western Savai'i
Right in the center of Falealupo-tai village, **Utusou Beach Fales** offers three *fales* with stone floors at S$30 pp a night including meals. The beach is lovely.

Tanumatiu Beach Fales, 800 meters southwest of Falealupo-tai, is on an even more spectacular beach with more privacy. The six *fales* with mats on the floors are also S$30 pp with meals, or S$5 per car if you're just picnicking. It's run by the Gisa Seumanutafa family; they can supply buckets of water from their home a few hundred meters away.

The only regular hotel on northwestern Savai'i is the **Vaisala Hotel** (Box 570, Apia; tel. 58-016, fax 58-017), four km west of Asau on the north coast. The 40 rooms in a cluster of European-style buildings overlooking a nice beach go for S$89/95/110 single/double/triple (sometimes they offer specials). Ask for a room with a balcony overlooking the beach. Although the accommodations are good, with private bath, coffee-making facilities, and fridge (but no cooking), meals in the restaurant are pricey at S$13.20 for breakfast and S$27.50 for dinner. You can rent the hotel outrigger canoe at S$35 a day. An Aussie named Keith Martin works out of the hotel as a surf guide and he has a boat to take you on "surfaris" to the offshore waves. The Vaisala makes a convenient base for exploring the northwest coast by rental car. Transfers from Asau Airport (six km) are S$7 pp each way. Budget.

GETTING THERE

By Air
For those who turn deep green at the thought of an 1.5-hour ferry ride, Polynesian Airlines (tel. 21-261) operates flights to Savai'i from Fagali'i Airport (FGI), five km east of Apia. There are three 10-minute flights a day to Maota airstrip, a few km west of Salelologa, costing S$34/60 one-way/roundtrip. Polynesian also has a daily flight to Asau airstrip at S$55/100 one-way/roundtrip. Only five kilograms of checked baggage are allowed on this eight-passenger Islander aircraft, but overweight luggage is just 40 cents a kilo (make sure it goes with you). If you fly you'll have to pay a taxi fare upon arrival at Maota, costing S$7 to Salelologa, S$15 to Lalomalava, or S$20 to Faga. If flying into Asau, arrange to be picked up by the Vaisala Hotel's car.

The Polynesian Airlines agent is Savai'i Tours and Travel (tel. 51-206) opposite the Pacific Commercial Bank in Salelologa. The Polynesian Airlines agent at Asau is T & M Vaai & Sons Ltd.

Samoa Air has flights from Maota direct to Pago Pago four times a week at S$145/244 one-way/roundtrip. These should be booked before leaving Apia.

By Boat

The **Samoa Shipping Corporation** (tel. 51-477) operates the car ferry MV *Lady Samoa II* between the wharfs at Mulifanua (Upolu) and Salelologa (Savai'i), departing each end two or three times daily. The ferry leaves Mulifanua Mon.-Sat. at 0800, 1200, and 1600, and Sunday at 1200 and 1600. Departure times from Salelologa are Mon.-Sat. at 0600, 1000, and 1400, Sunday at 1000 and 1400. Passenger fares are S$6 pp each way (children under 11 S$3); bicycles and motorcycles are S$5, cars S$30. Reservations are recommended for vehicles (and sometimes even foot passengers have to fight to get a ticket). To ensure that you'll get on the boat, buy a ticket as soon as your bus arrives at the dock and queue up when you see the others doing so—this may be the only time you'll ever see Samoans in a hurry. The trip takes an hour and a half. On the way across, you get a good view of Apolima Island's single village cradled in the island's classic volcanic crater, and flying fish and dolphins are often spotted.

In early 1999, the 220-passenger ferry *Lady Naomi* was brought into service between Apia and Salelologa, leaving Apia for Savai'i Tuesday at 0800 and returning in the afternoon (this introductory schedule should be checked well ahead). The 2.5 hour trip costs S$10.

GETTING AROUND

Travel around Savai'i is easy thanks to the broad paved highway that encircles the island, and bus service from the wharf is good. Yet all public transportation on Savai'i is a bit irregular, so don't plan itineraries or count on being able to get back to Upolu to catch an international flight the same day. If a storm came up and the ferries were canceled, you'd be as stranded as anyone else.

By Bus

Bus service on Savai'i focuses on the wharf at Salelologa, with departures to almost any point on the island immediately after a ferry comes in. More than a dozen buses will be revving up as the ferry arrives from Upolu, and they fill up fast, so quickly jump on the bus of your choice. They'll be marked Pu'apu'a or Tuasivi for the east coast,

Letui, Paia, Sasina, or Safotu for the north coast, Gataivai or Sili for the south coast, or Asau or Fagafau for the west coast. Fares from Salelologa average 50 *sene* to Lalomalava or Palauli, S$1 to Faga, S$2 to Sasina or Taga, S$2.50 to Satuiatua, and S$5 to Falealupo or Asau.

The buses pull out as soon as they're full, and you'll see as many as five buses racing along the same way, one right after another, then none until another ferry comes in. Buses that leave the wharf fully loaded won't stop to pick up additional passengers along the way, which can make it hard to carry on from places halfway around the island. If a ferry service is canceled, so will be the buses. Going back toward the ferry is much more inconvenient as early morning departures from villages in the northwest corner of Savai'i are a way of life. The last bus leaving Asau for the wharf via the west coast departs at 0600 and some buses leave Asau at 0300 and 0500!

Some of the Asau buses follow the north coast while others go via the south coast. The Tufutafoe bus generally uses the south road, while the Neiafu bus runs along the north coast (ask to be sure). Therefore, to go right around the island by bus, you could take the Tufutafoe bus from Salelologa to Falealupo, then after a couple of days at the beach *fales* there, try to get the Neiafu bus along the north coast as far as Manase where you could also stop. Getting back to the wharf from Manase is no problem. If you don't manage to catch the north coast bus in the very early morning, you could try hitching from Asau to Manase or go on the Forestry truck around 1300 weekdays (see below). Keep in mind that the Asau buses may not stop to pick up passengers in the middle of their runs (Manase or Satuiatua), so the only way to be sure of reaching Falealupotai without a tremendous struggle is to go directly there from the wharf and visit the midway points on the way back to Salelologa. The Tuasivi bus runs up and down the east coast fairly frequently throughout the day.

Hitchhiking

Hitchhiking is an option on Savai'i as most vehicles will stop, and the completion of paving right around the island has seen an increase in traffic. It's always good to offer the equivalent of the bus fare, although most drivers will refuse payment from *palagis*. Traffic diminishes greatly after 1400.

One useful thing to know about is the flatbed truck jammed with plantation laborers, which leaves the Forestry Office near Asau Post Office for Safotu weekdays at 1300. The driver is usually willing to give travelers a lift, in which case a pack of cigarettes would be welcome.

Others

Taxis are expensive on Savai'i, so be sure to settle the price before setting out. A full-day trip right around Savai'i by taxi will cost S$300 (or S$200 after bargaining) for the whole car.

Rental vehicles are scarce on Savai'i, and some of the car rental agencies in Apia won't allow you to bring their vehicles over on the ferry (be sure to ask, otherwise the insurance won't be valid). It would be risky to do so anyway as you'd be fully responsible for getting the vehicle back to Apia in case of trouble.

West End Co. (tel. 51-415, fax 51-603), opposite the ANZ Bank in Salelologa, has Suzuki jeeps at S$100 a day, plus S$10 for insurance (S$250 deductible). Motor scooters are S$50 a day. This company is unreliable and some of their vehicles are in bad shape.

Savai'i Car Rental (tel. 51-206, fax 51-291), opposite the Pacific Commercial Bank in Salelologa, is more reputable but slightly more expensive at S$120 for a Samurai jeep or S$132 for a Sidekick, insurance included (S$1,000 deductible). It's run by Savai'i Tours and Travel and you should call ahead from Apia to reserve. Neither of the Salelologa car rental companies will pick up at the wharf but their offices are only a 10-minute walk away.

Victor's Rentals (Box 1016, Asau; tel. 58-066, fax 58-114), at T & M Vaai & Sons Ltd. in Asau, rents Samurai vehicles at S$80 and up. It's just three km east of the Vaisala Hotel but they charge S$20 for delivery (if required). To deliver to Asau Airport (3.5 km) is S$15.

While driving through villages on Savai'i go very slowly as the local kids often use passing cars as moving targets and the rental agency will hold you responsible if a stone goes through the windshield. By going slowly your chances of seeing trouble ahead increase and you can defuse the situation by reducing your speed to dead slow.

Beware of traffic cops around Tuasivi and Salelologa who will pull you over in the hope of receiving a bribe if you don't use your turn signal, fail to stop at a crosswalk, or commit any of the other minor infractions that 90% of Samoan motorists do with impunity all the time. Gas stations are found at Salelologa, Vaisala, Asau, Manase, and Lalomalava.

The easiest and safest way to get around is on an organized sightseeing tour conducted by retired geologist Warren Jopling from the Safua Hotel. Warren has achieved a measure of notoriety from descriptions in the Australian guidebooks, which, depending on his mood, he finds complimentary or an annoyance. He does informative trips north across the lava fields to Mt. Matavanu and "short people's cave," and southwest to the Pulemelei stone pyramid and Taga blowholes, but only if four or five people sign up. The cost is around S$67 pp for a half day, S$112 a full day (including lunch and custom fees). If only two people sign up, the full day tour is S$125 pp.

CAPSULE SAMOAN VOCABULARY

Although you can get by with English in both Samoas, knowing a few words of the Samoan language will make things more enjoyable. Written Samoan has only 14 letters. Always pronounce *g* as "ng," and *t* may be pronounced "k." Every letter is pronounced, with the vowels sounding as they do in Spanish. An apostrophe indicates a glottal stop between syllables.

afakasi—half-caste
afio mai—a Samoan greeting
afu—waterfall
'ai—eat
aiga—extended family
aitu—ghost, spirit
alia—catamaran fishing boat
ali'i—high chief
alofa—love
alu—go
Alu i fea?—Where are you going?
'ata—laugh

fa'afafine—transvestite
fa'afetai—thank you
fa'afetai tele—thank you very much
fa'amafu—home-brewed beer
fa'amolemole—please
Fa'apefea mai oe?—How are you?
fa'a Samoa—the Samoan way
fa'a se'e—surfing
fafine—woman
fa'i—banana
faia—sacred
faife'au—an ordained church minister
failauga—orator
Fai se miti lelei.—Have a nice dream.
fale—house
faleoloa—store
fautasi—a Samoan longboat
fia fia—happy; a Samoan feast
fono—council
fou—new

i—to, toward
i'a—fish
ietoga—fine mat
inu—drink
ioe—yes

lafo—a ceremonial exchange of gifts
lali—a large wooden drum
lavalava—traditional men's skirt
le—the
leai—no
leaga—bad
lelei—good
lelei tele—very good
le tau—the cost, price
lotu—religion

maamusa—girlfriend
malae—meeting ground
malaga—journey
malo—hi
malo lava—response to *malo*
manogi—smell
manuia!—cheers!
manuia le po—good night
matafaga—beach
matai—head of an *aiga*
mau—opposition
mea alofa—gift
moe—sleep
motu—small island
musu—to be sullen

niu—coconut
nofo—sit
nu'u—village

oi fea—where is
Ou te alofa ia te oe.—I love you.
Ou te toe sau.—I shall return.

paepae—the stone foundation of a *fale*
palagi—a non-Samoan; also *papalagi*
paopao—canoe
pe fia?—how much?
pisupo—canned corned beef
Poo fea a alu iai?—Where are you going?

pule—authority, power
pulenu'u—village mayor
puletasi—traditional women's dress
pupu—blowhole

sa—taboo, sacred
sau—come
savali—walk
sene—a cent
siapo—tapa cloth
sili—best
siva—dance
soifua—good luck
sua—an important ceremonial presentation

taamu—giant taro
taavale—car
tai—sea, toward the coast
tala—dollar
talofa—hello
talofa lava—hello to you
tama—a boy
tamaloa—a man
tamo'e—run
tanoa—kava bowl
tauealea—untitled man
taupou—ceremonial virgin
tautau—untitled people, commoners
tele—much
tofa—goodbye
tofa soifua—fare thee well
tuai—old
tulafale—talking chief, orator

uku—head lice
ula—lei (flower necklace)
uma—finished
umu—earth oven
uta—inland

va'a—boat

TOKELAU
INTRODUCTION

Tokelau, a dependent territory of New Zealand, consists of three atolls 500 km north of Samoa (Tokelau means "north"). In British colonial times it was known as the Union Group. The central atoll, Nukunonu, is 92 km from Atafu and 64 km from Fakaofo. Swains Island (Olohega), 200 km south of Fakaofo, traditionally belongs to Tokelau but it is now part of American Samoa.

Each atoll consists of a ribbon of coral *motus* (islets), 90 meters to six km long and up to 200 meters wide, enclosing a broad lagoon. At no point does the land rise more than five meters above the sea, which makes the territory vulnerable to rising sea levels caused by the greenhouse effect. Together Atafu (3.5 square km), Fakaofo (four square km), and Nukunonu (4.7 square km) total only 12.2 square km of dry land, but they also include 165 square km of enclosed lagoons and 290,000 square km of territorial sea.

Life is relaxed in Tokelau. There are no large stores, hotels, restaurants, or bars, just plenty of coconuts, sand, and sun, and a happy, friendly people. This is outer-island Polynesia at its best.

Climate
There's little variation from the 28° C annual average temperature. Rainfall is irregular but heavy (2,900 mm annually at Atafu); downpours of up to 80 mm in a single day are possible anytime. Tokelau is at the north edge of the main hurricane belt, but tropical storms sometimes sweep through between November and February. Since 1846 Tokelau had only experienced three recorded hurricanes; then in February 1990 waves from Hurricane Ofa broke across the atolls, washing topsoil away and contaminating the freshwater lens. Residual salt prevented new plant growth for months. The recent increase in such storms seems related to global warming.

History
Legend tells how the Maui brothers pulled three islands out of the ocean while fishing far from shore. Later the Polynesians arrived with taro, which supplemented the abundance of fish and coconuts. The warriors of Fakaofo brought the other atolls under the rule of the Tui Tokelau.

The first European on the scene was Captain John Byron of HMS *Dolphin,* who saw Atafu in 1765. Ethnologist Horatio Hale of the U.S. Exploring Expedition of 1841 spent several days at Fakaofo and wrote an account of the inhabitants. Catholic and Protestant missionaries arrived between 1845 and 1863. In 1863 Peruvian slavers kidnapped several hundred Tokelauans, including nearly all of the able-bodied men, for forced labor in South America. Those who resisted were killed. A terrible dysentery epidemic from Samoa hit Tokelau the same year, reducing the total population to only 200.

The British belatedly extended official protection in 1877, but not until 1889, when it was decided that Tokelau might be of use in laying a transpacific cable, did Commander Oldham of the *Egeria* arrive to declare a formal protectorate. The British annexed their protectorate in 1916 and joined it to the Gilbert and Ellice Islands Colony. This distant arrangement ended in 1925, when New Zealand, which ruled Samoa at that time, became the administering power. With the Tokelau Islands Act of 1948, N.Z. assumed full sovereignty, and the islanders became N.Z. citizens. A N.Z. proposal for Tokelau to unite with either Samoa or Cook Islands was rejected by the Tokelauans in 1964. In 1974 responsibility for Tokelau was transferred from New Zealand's Department of Maori and Island Affairs to the Ministry of Foreign Affairs. In a 1980 treaty signed with N.Z., the U.S. government formally renounced claims to the group dating back to 1856. However, Tokelau's fourth atoll, Olohega (Swains Island), was retained by the U.S.

Government

New Zealand policy has been to disturb traditional institutions as little as possible. The administrator of Tokelau is appointed by the N.Z. Ministry of Foreign Affairs and Trade (Private Bag 18-901, Wellington, New Zealand; tel. 64-4/494-8500, fax 64-4/494-8514) and resides in Wellington. He works through the Office for Tokelau Affairs or "Tokalani," a liaison office in Apia, Samoa. The administrator is represented on each island by a *faipule* (headman), who is elected locally every three years.

weaving preparation

reef fishing

canoe making

a kitchen

THE RIDDLE OF THE *JOYITA*

One of the strangest episodes in recent Pacific history is indirectly related to Tokelau. On 10 November 1955, the crew of the trading ship *Tuvalu* sighted the drifting, half-sunken shape of the 70-ton MV *Joyita*, which had left Apia on 3 October bound for Fakaofo, carrying seven Europeans and 18 Polynesians. The *Joyita* had been chartered by Tokelau's district officer to take badly needed supplies to the atolls and pick up their copra, which was rotting on the beach. When the vessel was reported overdue, a fruitless aerial search began, which only ended with the chance discovery by the *Tuvalu* some 150 km north of Fiji. There was no sign of the 25 persons aboard, and sacks of flour, rice, and sugar had been removed from the ship. Also missing were 40 drums of kerosene, seven cases of aluminum strips, and the three life rafts.

The ghost ship was towed to Fiji and beached. Investigators found that the rudder had been jammed, the radio equipment wrecked, and the engines flooded due to a broken pipe in the saltwater cooling system. The navigation lights and galley stove were switched on. The *Joyita* hadn't sunk because the holds were lined with eight centimeters of cork. Though several books and countless newspaper and magazine articles have been written about the *Joyita* mystery, it has never been learned what really happened, nor have any of the missing persons ever been seen again.

All three atolls have a *pulenuku* (mayor), also elected for a three-year term, who directs *nuku* (village) activities. Each island has a *taupulega* (island council) comprised of village elders or heads of families. Each *taupulega* chooses six delegates to the 18-member General Fono, which meets twice a year (April and October) on alternate islands and has almost complete control over local matters. In 1993 Tokelau received an added degree of self-government when a Council of Faipule was created to act on behalf of the General Fono between sessions. The new position of *Ulu o Tokelau* (titular leader) is rotated annually among the Council's three members, all of whom act as government ministers. In 1994 the powers of the Administrator were delegated to the General Fono and the Council of Faipule, giving Tokelau de facto internal self-government and the right to impose taxes. In 1996 the Parliament of New Zealand amended the Tokelau Islands Act of 1948 to make this system official.

Rumors about the Office for Tokelau Affairs moving from Apia to one of the atolls have circulated for years, with the sticking point being disagreement over which atoll should become the host. Although Fakaofo seems the likely choice, there is great rivalry between the three and little "national" feeling. New Zealand would be quite happy to give Tokelau full independence, but without a source of income the prospect seems unlikely; free association with N.Z. on the Niue model seems more probable.

Economy

Tokelau receives more than NZ$6 million a year in N.Z. budgetary support and project assistance, NZ$3,805 per capita. This subsidy is nine times greater than all locally raised revenue, and exports of handicrafts are negligible (copra exports have ceased). In addition, the U.N. Development Program contributed just over US$1 million in 1992-96, mostly for telecommunications development.

Tokelau earns several hundred thousand dollars a year from the sale of postage stamps and coins, but a more important source of revenue is licensing fees from American purse seiners, which pull tuna from Tokelau's 200-nautical-mile exclusive economic zone (EEZ). Inshore waters within 40 km of the reef are reserved for local fishing. New Zealand has declared that all income from the EEZ will go to Tokelau (about NZ$1 million a year).

The 178 government jobs funded by New Zealand are about the only regular source of monetary income in Tokelau today. Nearly all of these jobs are held by Tokelauans—there are few resident expatriates—and to avoid the formation of a privileged class, nearly half are temporary or casual positions that are rotated among the community. The Community Services Levy of 6-12% collected from wage earners is used to subsidize copra and handicraft production, further distributing the wealth. The *fakaTokelau* (Tokelauan way of life) requires families to provide for their old and disabled.

Yet, limited resources have prompted many islanders to emigrate to New Zealand. Tokelauans are not eligible for N.Z. welfare payments unless they live in New Zealand and pay taxes there. However, they may now receive 50% of their pensions in Tokelau and this has stimulated some return migration.

The Changing Village

To be in the lee of the southeast trades, the villages sit on the west side of each atoll. The sandy soil and meager vegetation (only 61 species) force the Tokelauans to depend on the sea for protein. Coconut palms grow abundantly on the *motus:* what isn't consumed is dried and exported as copra. The islands are gradually being replanted with a high-yield coconut species from Rotuma. *Pulaka* (swamp taro) is cultivated in man-made pits up to two meters deep. Breadfruit is harvested Nov.-March, and some bananas and papayas are also grown. Pandanus is used for making mats and other handicrafts or for thatching roofs; pandanus fruit is also edible. Pigs, chickens, and ducks are kept, and crabs are captured for food (but there are no dogs). Most land is held by family groups *(kaiga)* and cannot be sold to outsiders.

Now, as Tokelau enters a cash economy, imported canned and frozen foods are gaining importance. Aluminum motorboats are replacing dugout sailing canoes, and when gasoline is scarce the islanders cannot travel to the *motus* to collect their subsistence foodstuffs. European-style concrete housing is now common, and 93% of households now depend on water channeled into storage tanks from the tin roofs. Some 39% of houses have flush toilets. Most cooking is done on kerosene stoves, and appliances such as washing machines, electric irons, freezers, and VCRs are widespread. Trousers are gaining preference over the traditional *kie* (loincloth).

The changing values have also meant a decline in the traditional sharing system *(inati)*. Outboard motors and electricity cost money: the rising standard of living has paralleled an increasing dependency on aid and remittances from relatives in New Zealand. Three-quarters of the adult population smokes. Imported foods and the changing lifestyle are largely to blame for the rapid increase in noncommunicable diseases such as hypertension, diabetes, heart disease, and gout. An average of one kilogram of sugar per person is consumed weekly, an 800% increase over the past 30 years. Dengue fever, influenza, and hepatitis are endemic in the population.

The People

The Tokelauans are closely related to the people of Tuvalu. In 1996, there were 499 people on Atafu, 578 on Fakaofo, and 430 on Nukunonu, totalling 1,507. Another 4,000 Tokelauans live "beyond the reef" in New Zealand (mainly around Wellington), the result of a migration that began in 1963, following overpopulation in Tokelau itself. A good many of the present islanders have been to New Zealand and the island population is actually declining due as many working age adults join this migration.

Due to the work of early missionaries, Atafu is Congregationalist (LMS), Nukunonu Catholic, and Fakaofo a combination of the two. Since the Samoan Bible is used, all adults understand Samoan. Young people learn English at school, but everyone speaks Tokelauan at home. In Tokelau, authority is based on age, rather than lineage. Arguably, nowhere else in the world are senior citizens as respected. Traditionally the women controlled family resources, but in recent years monetarism has led to this role being appropriated by men.

Conduct and Customs

In Tokelau, as elsewhere, proper conduct is mostly common sense. Take care not to expect better conditions than anyone else and avoid causing a disturbance. Keep in mind that you're a guest in someone's home. Step aside for the elders and *never* tell them what to do. When passing in front of another person, bow slightly and say *tulou*.

If people invite you into a house for a cup of coffee or a meal, politely refuse, saying that you have just finished eating. Such invitations are usually only a form of greeting, and they may not even have what is offered. If they insist a second or third time, or it's someone you know quite well, then they probably mean it. Sit on the mat with your legs crossed or folded, not stretched out.

Village men work together a day or two a week on communal projects. If you can manage to join in with the group (known as the *aumaga*) you'll fit into the community better. You should also accompany your hosts to church on Sunday. Over flirtations with members of the opposite sex are frowned upon. If you feel an attraction, simply mention it to one of his/her friends, and the word will be passed on. The women are crazy about bingo and stay up half the night playing it. You'll

have to learn how to count (*helu, tahi, lua, tolu, fa, lima, ono, fitu, valu, iva*) if you want to join them (two *sene* a game). The men may offer to take you line fishing, rod fishing, spearfishing, net fishing, trolling (for bonito), etc.

ON THE ROAD

Arts and Crafts

Some of the finest traditional handicrafts in the Pacific are made in the Tokelau Islands, especially high-quality coconut-fiber hats and handbags, fans, and exquisite model canoes. Some of the handbags have a solid coconut-shell liner—handy for female self-defense. The coconut-shell water bottles are authentic and unique. The most distinctive article on display is the *tuluma,* a watertight wooden box used to carry valuables on canoe journeys; its buoyancy also makes it an ideal lifesaver. Unfortunately, very little is produced these days.

Accommodations

Nukunonu has a small hotel but on Fakaofo and Atafu you'll have to stay with a local family. This should be arranged in advance through the **Office for Tokelau Affairs** (Box 865, Apia, Samoa; tel. 685/20-822, fax 685/21-761). They'll forward your request to the respective island council and you'll pay about NZ$10 pp a day for food and accommodations. You could also write in advance to the *faipule* or *pulenuku* of the island of your choice to let them know your intentions—having a contact or local friend makes everything easier. Once your stay has been approved, the Office for Tokelau Affairs will give you a visa application to complete and collect a NZ$20 processing fee.

When you go, take along a bottle of spirits for whoever made the arrangements, as well as gifts for the family. Suggested items are rubber thongs, housewares, tools, fishing gear (stainless steel fishhooks, fishing line, swivels, sinkers, lures, mask and snorkel, and spear-gun rubbers), and perhaps a rugby ball or volleyball. The women will appreciate perfumes, deodorants, cosmetics, printed cloth, and dyes. Kitchen knives and enamel mugs are always welcome.

You'll probably have to sleep on the floor and use communal toilets over the lagoon—there'll

be little or no privacy. Still, the facilities are of a much higher standard than in comparable Samoan villages. Most families own land on one of the *motus,* so you could spend a few days camping on your own if you have a tent and a large enough water container. Before you leave an atoll where you have stayed between ships, you could receive a "summons" from the council of elders at which you'll be asked to explain the purpose of your visit. If you give the right answers you could be honored with a traditional gift.

Food

There's only one cooperative store on each atoll, selling rice, flour, sugar, canned fish and meat,

---

TROPICAL CRICKET

Cricket is the most popular team sport in Tokelau, involving teams of 55 players or more. On Fakaofo the men and women play together, while on Atafu they play separately. Batters stand at each end of a concrete pitch holding heavy Samoan hardwood bats that appear to be a cross between an American baseball bat and a Fijian war club. The bowler attempts to hit a wicket made from a wooden plank with overarm bowling mandatory on Atafu (on Fakaofo an underarm technique is used to bowl to ladies). The batters (one at each end) must hit the ball as far and fast as possible, and injuries often occur because the rubber ball is softer than an English cricket ball and travels much faster. The Fakaofo teams have special "runners" ready to run back and forth as soon as the ball is hit, while on Atafu the batters must run themselves. There are two innings per team per game, and the games can last anywhere from a few hours to three days. On Fakaofo the teams often take time off to go fishing in the middle of a game and the number of fish caught are added to each team's score.

spaghetti, gasoline, etc. Take as much food as you can—bags of taro, a sack of bananas, fruit such as pineapples and mangoes, garlic, instant coffee, and tea. Ask at the Office for Tokelau Affairs about agricultural import restrictions. Camera film is not available.

All three coops sell imported liquor although the supply is often exhausted soon after the ship has left. Previously the locals made sour toddy, obtained by cutting the flower stem of a coconut tree and collecting the sap in a half-coconut container. The whitish fluid (kaleve) had many uses. It could be drunk fresh, or boiled and stored in a fridge. If kept in a container at room temperature for two days, it ferments into sour toddy beer. Boil fresh kaleve to a brown molasses for use in cooking or as a sauce. A tablespoon of boiled kaleve in a cup of hot water makes an island tea. You can even make bread out of it by adding saltwater, flour, and fat, as all Tokelauan women know. Unfortunately kaleve is now banned on all three atolls as it was used mostly to make alcohol, leading to drinking problems.

Services and Information
The New Zealand dollar is the currency used on the islands. You can change money at the Finance Department in the Administration Center on each island.

In 1997 Tokelau became the last country in the world to be connected to the rest of the planet by satellite telephone. Each of the atolls now has two card telephones deducting per minute charges of NZ$0.80 to numbers in Tokelau, NZ$2.50 to Australia, New Zealand, or Samoa, and US$4 to all other locations. Tokelau's telephone code is 690.

If you wish to send a fax to anyone in Tokelau, the public fax numbers are: Atafu fax 690/2108, Falaofo fax 690/3108, and Nukunonu fax 690/ 4108. Just put the person's name at the top and the clerk will deliver it for a small fee.

Stamp collectors can order Tokelau postage stamps from the Tokelau Philatelic Bureau, Box 68, Wellington, New Zealand. When writing to Tokelau, include the words "via Samoa" in the address.

There's a hospital on each of the three atolls, and treatment in them is free. Take a remedy for diarrhea.

Getting There
The seaplane service to Tokelau was suspended in 1983, but there's talk of building an airstrip on Fenuafala (Fakaofo). Meanwhile the only way to go is on the 1,100-tonne vessel Forum Tolelau chartered by the **Office for Tokelau Affairs,** leaving Apia, Samoa, for the three atolls about once a month. It takes just under two days to reach the first island and 7-9 days to complete the roundtrip. Cabin class is NZ$528 roundtrip, deck class NZ$286 roundtrip, including meals. Deck passengers can take cabin-class meals for a little extra (recommended), though those prone to seasickness won't be eating much. The ship often runs out of food on the way back to Apia, so carry a reserve supply.

This is not a trip for the squeamish or faint-hearted. The Forum Tokelau has two double cabins and one four-bed cabin, but most passengers travel deck, and every available space on deck will be packed with the Tokelauans and their belongings. The cabins are without ventilation, and washing facilities are minimal. As demand requires, the Office for Tokelau Affairs also runs the catamaran Tutolu between Apia and Tokelau. It has two double cabins and goes every couple of weeks. Pray that you travel with the wind because against the wind it's extremely rough and the smell of diesel pervades the air. The Samoan ferry Queen Salamasina, the Tuvaluan boat Nivagi II, and other ships are used from time to time. There's merry feasting when the boat arrives, and usually time for snorkeling and picnicking on the motus. The passengers are an interesting mix.

Tokelauans and officials get first priority on these trips, and tourists are only taken if there happens to be space left over. Advance reservations are not accepted, and cabins will be confirmed only a week prior to sailing. Check with the Office for Tokelau Affairs when you reach Apia—you may be lucky. Tokelauans pay only NZ$35 return on deck but this price is heavily subsidized and NZ$286 is considered to be the real cost without any profit element built in. You pass Samoan Immigration on the wharf in Apia, a unique way of renewing your Samoan tourist visa.

Internal Transport
Passages wide enough for small boats have been blasted through the reefs, but the ships

must stand offshore. Passengers and cargo are transferred to the landings in aluminum whaleboats, which roar through the narrow passes on the crest of a wave. In offshore winds there's poor anchorage at Fakaofo and Nukunonu, and none at all off Atafu. For safety's sake, interatoll voyages by outrigger canoe are prohibited, and the 19-meter, 50-passenger catamaran *Tutolu,* especially built for this purpose, entered service in 1992. Interisland fares are NZ$15 Fakaofo-Atafu, NZ$8 Fakaofo-Nukunonu, NZ$10 Nukunonu-Atafu. There are no cars or trucks in Tokelau, but most canoes are now fitted with outboards.

THE TOKELAU ISLANDS

Atafu

The smallest of the atolls, Atafu's lagoon totals only 17 square km (compared to 50 square km on Fakaofo and 98 square km at Nukunonu). It's claimed you can walk around the atoll in a day. This is the most traditional of the islands, the only one where dugout canoes are still made. The village is at the northwest corner of the atoll. There's a ceramic history of Tokelau on the side wall of Matauala Public School. The Office of the Council of Faipule (tel. 2133) is on Atafu. Be prepared for a NZ$50 fine if you get caught partaking of the local homebrew of yeast and sugar.

Nukunonu

This largest atoll in both land and lagoon area sits in the center of the group. A New Zealand reader reported that he hiked right around the atoll in

NUKUNONU

© DAVID STANLEY

2.5 days. One reef crossing lasted four hours but was possible. Since Nukunonu is Catholic (see the large whitewashed stone church), life is less restricted than on the Congregationalist islands. The village is divided into two parts by a reef pass spanned by a bridge. No dugout canoes are left on Nukunonu; everyone has switched to aluminum outboards. The rhinoceros beetle, a pest that attacks coconut trees, has established itself here.

Mr. Luhi'ano Perez, headmaster of the local school, and his wife Juliana operate the **Luanaliki Hotel** (tel. 690/4140, fax 690/4108) near the school and a four-minute walk from the store. This solid, lilac-colored concrete building contains nine double rooms. They charge NZ$25 pp a night including all meals. Luhi'ano can answer any questions about the atoll. Shoestring.

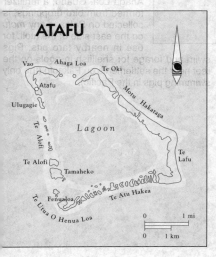

ATAFU

FAKAOFO

Mulifenua Island

Lalo Island

Matagi Island

Te Lafu

Ahaga Loa

Palea

Lagoon

Te Tu Fa

Motu Akea

Fenuafala

Fale

Te Atu Motu

Nukumatau

Pataliga

Te Papaloa

Akegamutu

Nukulakia

Te Loto

Fenua Loa

Te Atu Hakea

© DAVID STANLEY

0   2 mi

0   2 km

Fakaofo

Some 400 people live on tiny 4.5-hectare Fale Island, which is well shaded by breadfruit trees. Fale resident Vaopuka Mativa (Bob) is knowledgeable about Polynesian history and language links to other islands. A two-story administration building on Fale housing the health clinic, police station, post office, and village store was completed in 1989. In 1960, a second village was established on the larger island of Fenuafala, about three km northwest, to relieve the overcrowding. At low tide you can walk across the reef between the two. The school, hospital, and the Teletok (telephone company) headquarters are now on Fenuafala.

An ancient coral slab erected to the Tui Tokelau stands in the meetinghouse at Fale. This stone may once have exercised supernatural power, but the head on it today is a recent addition. On the lagoonside beach opposite the *hakava* (family meeting place) is a huge rock once used to crush wrongdoers; it takes a dozen men to lift it.

The freighter *Ai Sokula* can be seen wrecked on the reef at Ahaga Loa. Guano, a fertilizer formed from bird droppings, is collected on Palea, a tiny *motu* on the east side of the atoll, for use in nearby taro pits. Pigs swim and forage for shellfish in pools on the reef near the settlements on Fakaofo (the only swimming pigs in the Pacific).

WALLIS AND FUTUNA
INTRODUCTION

This little-known corner of Polynesia lies between Fiji and Samoa, with Futuna almost as close to Vanua Levu as it is to Wallis. Smallest of France's three South Pacific territories, Wallis and Futuna (Uvéa mo Futuna) is isolated from its neighbors geographically, culturally, and politically. All the marks of French colonialism are here, from overpaid European officials controlling functionless staff to little French *gendarmes* in round caps and shorts.

Although weekly flights and a monthly shipping service make the islands accessible from Nouméa, Fiji, and Tahiti, absurdly high airfares and the lack of moderately priced accommodations limits visitors to French officials, the eccentric, the adventuresome, and yachts' crews. Wallis and Futuna is still well off the beaten track.

The Land
The islands of Wallis and Futuna, 250 km apart, are quite dissimilar. Wallis (159 square km including adjacent islands) is fairly flat, with verdant volcanic hillsides rising gently to Mt. Lulu Faka-

hega (145 meters). There are freshwater crater lakes (Lalolalo, Kikila, and Lanutavake). The main island, Uvéa, and 10 other volcanic islands in the eastern half of the lagoon are surrounded by a barrier reef bearing 12 smaller coral islands, many with fine beaches. Five passes breach this reef but large ships bound for Mata-Utu wharf enter the lagoon through Honikulu Pass, the southernmost.

Futuna and Alofi, together totaling 115 square km, are mountainous, with Mt. Puke on Futuna reaching 524 meters. Futuna is near a fracture close to where the Pacific Plate pushes under the Indo-Australian Plate and the last major earthquake was in 1993. Though there are many freshwater springs on Futuna, Alofi two km to the southeast is now uninhabited, due to a lack of water. A reef fringes the north coast of Alofi; the south coast features high cliffs. Futuna has no lagoon.

Climate
As in neighboring Samoa, the climate is hot and humid year-round with an annual average tem-

WALLIS AND FUTUNA

Rotuma

Wallis

Futuna

Alofi

Samoa
Islands

Fiji Islands

Niuafo'ou

Niuatoputapu

Lau
Group

Vava'u

Niue

Tonga
Islands

0   250 mi

0   250 km

© DAVID STANLEY

perature of 27° C. Rainfall is heavy at more than 3,000 mm a year, usually falling in the late afternoon or night. The hurricane season in the islands is Nov.-March, and many storms form in the area between Wallis and Samoa. During the drier season, May-Oct., the islands are cooled somewhat by the refreshing southeast trades.

Fauna
Archaeologists have found pig bones associated with *lapita* pottery dating from 1400 B.C., proving that these animals were introduced by the first people, and Wallis and Futuna today is one of the few countries of the world where humans are outnumbered by swine. Some 11,000 hogs have free run of Wallis and another 6,000 are on Futuna; they're often seen foraging for shellfish on the beaches. In the early evening they are called back for feeding and penning: one can hear bells ringing, people shouting, the beating of drums, gongs, etc., as the owners utilize different methods of calling home *les cochones.* A fantastic array of sounds!

Beware of "electric" ants when hiking or camping on either Wallis or Futuna as these one-mm-long brown ants deliver a painful bite. Wallis is also overrun by African snails, although they won't harm you.

History
Legend tells how the Polynesian god of creation Tangaloa was out fishing one night when he caught a big fish in his net. He rushed home to

get a knife, and only when he returned did he realize how huge the fish really was, so he decided to wait until morning to pull it in and kill it. Some smaller fish were also in the net, and when Tangaloa returned he found that the larger fish had turned into an island called Uvéa and the smaller fish had become smaller islands with the net a coral reef.

Although these islands were discovered by the Polynesians more than 3,000 years ago, not until 28 April 1616 did the Dutch navigators Schouten and Le Maire arrive at Futuna and Alofi. They named Futuna Hoorn after their home port of Hoorn on the IJsselmeer, 42 km north of Amsterdam. The name of Cape Horn, in South America, is derived from the same old port. Captain Samuel Wallis of HMS *Dolphin* was the first European to contact Wallis (on 16 August 1767). American whalers began to visit from 1820 onward.

Marist missionaries arrived on both Futuna and Wallis in 1837, and from Wallis Bishop Pierre Bataillon directed Catholic missionary efforts in Fiji, Samoa, and Tonga. Wallis and Futuna was declared a French protectorate in 1887. In 1924 the protectorate officially became a colony. This was the only French colony in the Pacific to remain loyal to the collaborating government in Vichy France until after Pearl Harbor. From 1942 to 1944, Wallis was an important American military base, with as many as 6,000 U.S. troops on the island. Hihifo airport dates from the war, as does an abandoned airstrip just south of Lake Kikila. In a 1959 referendum, the populace voted to upgrade Wallis and Futuna's status to that of an overseas territory, and this status was granted by the French Parliament in 1961.

Government
The French High Commissioner in Nouméa selects a senior administrator to control the local bureaucracy from Mata-Utu on Wallis. An elected Territorial Assembly with 20 members (13 from Wallis and seven from Futuna) has limited legislative powers over local matters. The policy-making Territorial Council is composed of the Lavelua (king) of Wallis, two kings of Futuna (the Tuisigave of Sigave and the Tuiagaifo of Alo), and three members appointed by the French administrator, who presides. The three kings retain considerable influence and every French administrator who has tried to challenge

them has had to leave. The territory elects a deputy and a senator to the French Parliament in Paris. The traditional Polynesian monarchy and the Catholic Church continue to be powerful forces in the islands.

Economy

The only exports are taro to New Caledonia and a few tonnes of trochus shells. Most of the people employed on the island work for the French government, and what they produce is perhaps the most invisible export of all—the illusion of colonial glory. The strategic position of Wallis and Futuna in the heart of the South Pacific indicates its continuing importance in France's global empire.

The US$25 million annual budget mostly comes out of the pockets of French taxpayers, although some revenue is collected in customs duties. French civil servants on Wallis make three times as much as their counterparts in France, plus a respectable lump sum upon completion of their three-year contract. All prices on Wallis are set accordingly. The locals get free medical and dental care, and free education (in French) up to university level: with such French largess, independence is unthinkable. Considerable money also arrives in the form of remittances from Wallisian emigrants in New Caledonia.

The locals grow most of their own food in the rich volcanic soils. Taro, yam, manioc, breadfruit, and banana plantations are everywhere. All of the coconuts are used to feed the pigs. The coconut plantations on Wallis were destroyed by the rhinoceros beetle in the 1930s, but this pest has now been brought under control. The plantations of Futuna were saved, but they only produce a couple of hundred tons of copra a year (also fed to pigs). No effort is made to encourage tourism.

The People

The 9,000 people on Wallis and 5,000 on Futuna are Polynesian: the Wallisians or Uvéans descended from Tongans, the Futunans from Samoans. The Wallis Islanders are physically huge, bigger than Tongans. There's little mixing between the two groups and only about 100 Uvéans and Futunans live on the other island. Some 500 French expats reside on Wallis, but only 60 on Futuna. They have a small subdivision on Wallis named Afala on a hill just north of Mata-Utu.

Another 20,000 people from both islands live and work 2,500 km away in Nouméa, New Caledonia. Young Uvéans and Futunans often stay in New Caledonia after completing their compulsory military service, and many obtain employment in nickel mining or the construction industry. The many partially constructed or uninhabited dwellings on Wallis are a result of the migrations. Many residents still live in roundended thatched *fales*. One compromise with the 20th century is the electric line entering through the peak of the roof.

Very little English is spoken on Wallis, and even less on Futuna, so a knowledge of French, Tongan, or Samoan makes life a lot easier. Wallisian and Futunan are distinct: welcome is *malo te kataki/malo le ma'uli* in Wallisian/Futunan. Similarly, farewell said to someone leaving is *alu la/ano la.* Farewell said to someone staying is *nofo la* in both dialects.

Public Holidays and Festivals

Public holidays include New Year's Day, Easter Monday (March/April), Labor Day (1 May), Ascension Day, Pentecost, Assumption Day (15 August), All Saints' Day (1 November), Armistice Day (11 November), and Christmas Day. The biggest celebrations of the year center around St. Pierre Chanel Day (28 April) and Bastille Day (14 July). Territory Day (29 July) is also marked by traditional dancing and canoe races. Each of the three Wallis parishes has its own holiday: 14 May at Mu'a, 29 June at Hihifo (Vaitupu), and 15 August at Hahake (Mata-Utu). The Uvéans are expert sword dancers.

WALLIS

Situated almost exactly midway between Tahiti and Nouméa, Wallis sits on the threshold of Polynesia and Melanesia. Around the year 1400, warriors sent by the Tu'i Tonga conquered the island and installed the first member of Uvéa's current ruling dynasty. Several forts built to enforce Tongan domination of Wallis have recently been excavated. Samuel Wallis anchored off the island for two days in 1767, but he didn't disembark. Whalers began calling in 1825, and in 1832 they established a base on Nukuatea. Catholic missionaries arrived in 1837 and within five years the entire population had been converted. The missionaries protected the islanders from the excesses of other Europeans and controlled all aspects of society in congruence with the king. Massive stone churches were erected at Mata-Utu, Mu'a, and Vaitupu; the interior decoration of the one at Vaitupu is the best. Even today the bishop and king together carry more weight than the French prefect.

SIGHTS

Near Town

Mata-Utu resembles a village, except for a massive **cathedral** of hand-cut blue volcanic stone with two blocklike towers overlooking the wharf.

Sunday mass is quite a colorful spectacle, but sit near a door or window, as it gets very hot and congested inside. The **king's palace,** large but not ostentatious, is beside Mata-Utu Cathedral. On the waterfront opposite it is the **Fale Fono,** the main meeting place of the island's chiefs.

A track up to the tiny ruined chapel atop **Mt. Lulu Fakahega** (145 meters) brings you to the island's highest point. Take the road west from Mata-Utu to the main north-south road in the center of the island: the track is on the left about 500 meters north of the crossroads. From the summit the jungle-clad crater is fairly obvious, and you can descend to the taro plantation below along an easy trail. The view of Uvéa's rich red soil cloaked in greenery from Mt. Lulu Fakahega is quite good.

Farther Afield

Lake Lalolalo on the far west side of Wallis is spectacular: it's circular, with vertical red walls 30 meters high, which make the pea-green water almost inaccessible. Flying foxes *(peka)* swoop over Lake Lalolalo from their perches on overhanging trees in the late afternoon, and there are blind eels in the lake. Another of the crater lakes, **Lake Lanutavake,** is less impressive, but you can swim (approach it from the west side). The Americans dumped their war equipment into the lakes just before they left.

The massive hulk of Mata Utu Cathedral is a very visible bulwark of Gaulish Catholicism.

WALLIS

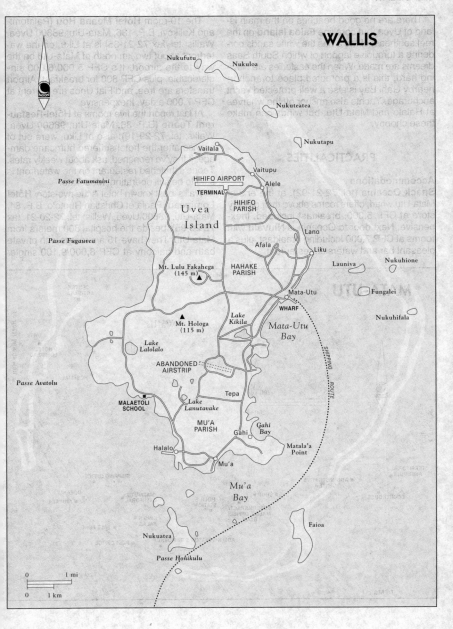

Nukufutu

Nukuloa

Nukuteatea

Nukutapu

Vailala

Passe Fatumanini

Vaitupu
Alele

HIHIFO AIRPORT
TERMINAL

**Uvea
Island**

**HIHIFO
PARISH**

Lano

Liku

Passe Fugauvea

Afala

Launiva

Nukuhione

Fungalei

Mt. Lulu Fakahega
(145 m) ▲

**HAHAKE
PARISH**

Mata-Utu

WHARF

Nukuhifala

▲ Mt. Hologa
(115 m)

Lake
Kikila

*Mata-Utu
Bay*

Passe Avatolu

Lake
Lalolalo

**ABANDONED
AIRSTRIP**

Tepa

S
H
I
P
P
I
N
G

R
O
U
T
E

■ **MALAETOLI
SCHOOL**

Lake
Lanutavake

**MU'A
PARISH**

Gahi

Gahi
Bay

Matala'a
Point

Halalo

Mu'a

*Mu'a
Bay*

Faioa

Nukuatea

Passe Honikulu

0 _____ 1 mi

0 _____ 1 km

There are no good beaches on the main island of Uvéa, but coralline **Faioa Island** on the reef southeast of Mu'a has the white sands bordering a turquoise lagoon of which South Seas dreams are made. When the easterlies are blowing hard, this is a protected place to anchor; nearby Gahi Bay is also a well-protected yacht anchorage. Yachts also anchor off the wharves at Halalo and Mata-Utu, but winds can make these choppy.

PRACTICALITIES

Accommodations
Snack Oceania (tel. 72-21-92), at the end of Mata-Utu wharf, offers rooms above their grocery store at CFP 5,000, breakfast included. Inexpensive. Next door to Oceania is **Niuvalu** with rooms at CFP 7,000 including breakfast, plus a pleasant bar and waterside restaurant.

The 10-room **Hôtel Moana Hou** (Palatomiano Kulikovi, B.P. 136, Mata-Utu, 98600 Uvéa, Wallis; tel./fax 72-21-35) is at Liku, on the waterfront about two km north of Mata-Utu on the way to the airport. It's CFP 5,000/6,000 single/double, plus CFP 800 for breakfast. Airport transfers are free, and Fiat Unos are for rent at CFP 7,000 a day. Inexpensive.

At last report the five rooms at **Hôtel-Restaurant Teone** (B.P. 36, Mata-Utu, 98600 Uvéa, Wallis; tel. 72-29-19), also at Liku, were out of service after the hotel suffered hurricane damage. If they've reopened, ask about weekly rates. Teone's thatched restaurant on the waterfront is said to be still operating. Moderate.

Wallis' best known hotel is the two-story **Hôtel Lomipeau** (Paola et Christian Ruotolo, B.P. 84, Mata-Utu, 98600 Uvéa, Wallis; tel. 72-20-21, fax 72-26-95), beside the hospital 800 meters from Mata-Utu. They have 15 a/c rooms with private bath and balcony at CFP 8,600/9,100 single/

MATA-UTU

To Afala

Wallis

Island

CENTRE ARTISANAL

To Airport

To Hotel Moana Hou

HOTEL LOMIPEAU

HOSPITAL

To Mt. Lulu / Fakaheqa

0   200 yds
0   200 m

TERRITORIAL ASSEMBLY

ADMINISTRATIVE CENTER

COURTHOUSE

UVEA SHOP

SUPERMARKET/ AIRLINE OFFICE/ BANK

POLICE STATION

SHIPPING OFFICE

MATA-UTU CATHEDRAL

OCEANIA

NIUVALA

KING'S PALAC

ADMINISTRATOR'S RESIDENCE

FALE FONO

POST OFFICE

WHARF

Lagoon

To Mu'a

double, slightly reduced if you stay a week. Meals at the hotel restaurant are pricey. The Lomipeau arranges lagoon excursions and car rentals. Airport transfers are free for guests. Expensive.

A retired French pilot named Jacques Bilco and his Wallisian wife operate **Hôtel Albatros** (B.P. 421, Mata-Utu, 98600 Uvéa, Wallis; tel./fax 72-18-27), 200 meters from the airport terminal. The four a/c rooms with fridge in the main building are CFP 10,000 single or double, while the three neat little bungalows around the pool are CFP 15,000 for up to three people. Breakfast is included. Expensive.

About the only alternative is to camp in the interior; the Uvéans are hospitable, and a request for permission to camp sometimes leads to an invitation to stay in their homes.

Food and Shopping

The Mata-Utu supermarkets, Au Bon Marché and Oceania, offer a reasonable selection of goods but there is no fresh produce market. Fresh meat is flown in from Nouméa weekly.

Boutique Tropical across from the bank has nice clothing and perfume. Owner Michel Goeppert speaks acceptable English and is a good contact. The **Philatelic Bureau** (tel. 72-21-21) adjoining Mata-Utu Post Office sells first-day covers. Wallis and Futuna issues its own colorful postage stamps. Ask at the **Uvéa Shop** in Mata-Utu for cassettes of the music of the well-known Wallisian singer/composer Palisio Tuauli or the band Talamohe.

Palme d'Or (tel. 72-27-05), opposite the Hôtel Lomipeau, sells postcards and the excellent IGN topographical maps of Wallis and Futuna (CFP 1,700 each).

Visas

Entry requirements are the same as those of New Caledonia and Tahiti-Polynesia. If you arrive by ship, go straight to the *gendarmerie* in Mata-Utu (tel. 72-29-17; weekdays 0700-1130 and 1500-1700) for a passport stamp. If you're going on to Futuna, return here for a *sortie* stamp, otherwise you could have trouble when you apply for an *entrée* stamp on Futuna.

Services

The Banque de Wallis et Futuna (tel. 72-21-24; Monday, Tuesday, Thursday, and Friday 0900-1200 and 1300-1500), opposite Super Wallis supermarket in Mata-Utu, is affiliated with the Banque Nationale de Paris. They charge CFP 750 commission on exchanges. In a pinch, the Trésor Public (tel. 72-29-29) at the Administrative Center will change French francs in cash into CFP. Credit cards are seldom accepted on Wallis, so bring sufficient traveler's checks or French francs in cash. If you'll be visiting Tahiti or New Caledonia before going to Wallis and Futuna, buy your Pacific francs there, as exactly the same currency is used in all three French territories. Though expensive, Wallis and Futuna has the lowest inflation rate in the South Pacific.

Card telephones are available at the post office near Mata-Utu wharf, the postal agencies at Mu'a and Vaitupu, the airport, and the Lycée. Wallis and Futuna's telephone code is 681.

There's no tourist information, but the Affaires Culturelles office (B.P. 131, Mata-Utu, 98600 Uvéa, Wallis; tel. 72-26-67, fax 72-25-63; weekdays 0730-1330) in the Administrative Center handles general inquiries.

The weekly newspaper, *Te Fenua Fo'ou* (B.P. 435, Mata-Utu, 98600 Uvéa, Wallis; tel./fax 72-17-46, e-mail: tff@wallis.co.nc), is mostly in French with a couple of pages in Wallisian and Futunan. New Caledonian newspapers are also distributed on Wallis.

The government-operated radio station RFO (tel. 72-20-20, www.rfo.fr) broadcasts over FM 100 MHz and AM 1188 kHz from Uvéa, FM 91 MHz from Alo, and 90.5 MHz and 89 MHz from Sigave.

Mata-Utu hospital (tel. 72-25-15) offers free consultations weekdays 0800-1000 and 1500-1600.

TRANSPORTATION

By Air

The New Caledonian carrier **Aircalin** (B.P. 49, Mata-Utu, 98600 Uvéa, Wallis; tel. 72-28-80, fax 72-27-11) flies to **Hihifo Airport** (WLS) on Wallis twice a week from Nouméa, weekly from Nadi and Papeete. The Fiji service should be verified in advance, as it has been canceled and reinstated several times in the past. Air tickets to Wallis work out noticeably cheaper when purchased in a French territory rather than in dollar areas. (Though the territory is actually east of the 180th meridian, in 1926 the international date line was moved east so Wallis and Futuna could share New Caledonia's day. Thus it's the same day here as in Nouméa or Nadi, but one day later than in Papeete.)

Aircalin also flies five times a week between Wallis and Futuna (CFP 17,800 return). Only 10 kilos of baggage are allowed on the 20-passenger Twin Otter turboprop that does the Wallis-Futuna run, and it's often full.

By Ship

Private yachts sometimes visit Wallis' sheltered lagoon between Pago Pago and Fiji. Otherwise, the only way to visit Wallis and Futuna by boat is on the MV *Moana III* of the **Compagnie Moana de Navigation** (tel. 72-26-15). This passenger-carrying freighter departs Nouméa monthly for Wallis via Futuna, with occasional stops at Suva, Fiji. Fares are CFP 30,000/37,000 dorm/cabin for

the five-day Nouméa-Wallis trip. Passage between Futuna and Wallis is CFP 6,000/8,700 (14-16 hours). Meals are included and, as they're prepared on a French ship, they're good. In the six-bed dormitory you sleep on a steel bunk on the upper deck, which makes a cabin better value. The *Moana III* is empty between Nouméa and Wallis, but fills up on the return trip. The ship's agent in Nouméa is Somacal (5 rue d'Austerlitz; tel. 687/27-38-98, fax 687/25-93-15); in Suva it's Carpenters Shipping.

Getting Around

Most of the villages are on Wallis' east coast from Halalo to Vailala, which has a paved road along its length. No bus service is available on Wallis but hitching is very easy.

Some of the hotels rent cars, otherwise there's **Pacific Dinh Motoka** (François Dinh, B.P. 153, Mata-Utu, 98600 Uvéa, Wallis; tel./fax 72-26-57) at Liku, which has Peugeot 205s at CFP 6,400 a day including kilometers.

FUTUNA AND ALOFI

Futuna (not to be confused with an island of the same name in Vanuatu) is a volcanic island five km wide by 20 km long (64 square km). The narrow southwestern coastal strip is 200 meters wide at most. Gardens are planted on the mountainside, which rises abruptly from the sea, and the terraced taro fields are quite ingenious. High cliffs on the northeast side of Futuna delayed completion of the road around the island until 1992, and the steep, narrow road from Ono to the airstrip and beyond is quite a feat of engineering. This side of Futuna receives the heaviest rainfall.

Kava drinking has died out on Wallis (people would rather watch videos) but on Futuna the men imbibe large quantities nightly at the *tau'asu*

(kava meetinghouse) found in each village. The Sunday meal is usually prepared in an *umu* (earth oven). The Futunans have also preserved their traditional handicrafts, such as tapa painted with a black dye made from cashew nut or a brown stain from the seed of a red fruit. Pandanus mats, kava bowls *(tanoa),* war clubs, and outrigger canoes are also made.

Around 2,000 people live in Sigave Kingdom, which has the only anchorage for ships at Leava. Ono, between Leava and the airport, is the main village of Alo Kingdom with about 3,000 inhabitants. A few small hotels have opened recently and the regular air service from Wallis makes a visit practical. Provided you know a little French and are willing to pay the price, it's a fascinating

FUTUNA AND ALOFI

North Point
Somaloma Rocks
Tavai
Tautafa
Sigave Kingdom
▲ Mt. Matsi
Fiua
▲ Mt. Puke (524 m)
Nuku
Tamana
Leava
Futuna
Poi
Taoa
Alo Kingdom
Ono
Kolia
AIRSTRIP
Vele Point
Pyramid Point

Salonga
Alofitai
Alofi
Volta Point
▲ Mt. Kolofau (417 m)
VAIKA BEACH

0   3 mi
0   3 km

St. Pierre Chanel, Polynesia's only Catholic saint

opportunity to see a part of the Pacific few English speakers even realize exists.

Sights

Both Nuku and Alo have old Catholic churches. At **Poi,** on the eastern coast, a peculiar church with a stepped tower has been erected to honor Pierre Chanel, Polynesia's first and only Catholic saint (canonized 1954). Relics of the saint, including some of his bodily remains, clothes, and the war club that killed him, are kept in a room near the chapel after being returned from France in 1976. King Niuliki, who feared the missionary was usurping his position, had Chanel martyred in 1841, four years after he had arrived on the island.

While on the northeast coast, ask about the "blue holes" where you can swim. Otherwise, about the only place on Futuna to swim is off the beach next to Vele Airport, but beware of the currents as there's no lagoon.

With the help of a guide, it's possible to climb **Mt. Puke** (524 meters) from Taoa in a about five hours return.

Alofi

Alofi (51 square km) is under the control of the King of Alo. People from Futuna travel to their gardens on Alofi in small boats kept on the beach near Vele Airstrip, leaving around 0600. They spend the week tending their gardens and come back to Futuna on Sunday for church. The shallow lagoon at Alofitai offers corals and colorful fish to snorkelers. Loka Cave is a couple of hours east of the landing on foot. Large ships can pass between Futuna and Alofi, so long as they keep to the middle of the two-km-wide passage.

Accommodations

The Aircalin agent at Leava operates Futuna's only organized accommodations, the **Motel du Motu** (B.P. 50, Sigave, 98620 Futuna; tel. 72-32-04, fax 72-34-39).

Patrick Tortey at Nuku just west of Leava operates **Motel Fia Fia** (tel. 72-32-45) with a/c rooms at around CFP 6,000 double. A lounge with cooking facilities and TV are provided. A meal at Patrick's restaurant is CFP 3,000. Inexpensive.

Snack Chez Marie Jo (Fabrice Fulilagi, B.P. 44, Sigave, 98620 Futuna; tel. 72-36-12), near the College de Saalauniu at Nuku, has two rooms at CFP 3,500. Budget.

Practicalities

A few shops and the bank (tel. 72-36-40) are opposite Leava wharf; the *gendarmerie* (tel. 72-32-17) is just outside Leava on the road to Ono. Card telephones are found at Leava and Ono post offices. The hospital (tel. 72-33-29) is at Taoa. The Aircalin office (tel. 72-32-04) is at Leava.

One of the largest of all insects, the rhinoceros beetle (Dynasinae) menaces the coconut plantations of the South Pacific.

DIANA LASICH HARPER

TUVALU
INTRODUCTION

Tuvalu is one of the world's smallest and most isolated independent nations. During British colonial times the group was known as the Ellice Islands, and while the current name Tuvalu means "cluster of eight," there are actually nine islands in all. The explanation lies with the smallest island, Niulakita, which was only resettled by people from Niutao in 1949. Internationally, Tuvalu is best known for its colorful postage stamps and internet address dot tv.

Due to high airfares, this remote group of low coral atolls gets only a few hundred tourists a year and most of those never go beyond the crowded little government center on Funafuti. This makes the almost inaccessible outer islands one of the most idyllic and unspoiled corners of the Pacific, particularly Nanumea, Vaitupu, and Nukulaelae. On these, time seems to stand still on, yet rising sea levels due to greenhouse gas emissions may soon bring the world to them. For the average traveler, Tuvalu is just a rather expensive stepping stone between Fiji and Micronesia.

The Land

Legend tells how an eel *(te Pusi)* and a flatfish *(te Ali)* were carrying home a heavy rock and began to quarrel. The eel killed the flatfish and fed on his body, just as the tall coconut trees still feed on the round, flat islands. Then *te Pusi* broke the rock into eight pieces and disappeared into the sea.

The nine atolls that make up Tuvalu together total only 25 square km in land area, curving northwest-southeast in a chain 676 km long on the outer western edge of Polynesia. Funafuti, the administrative center, is more than 1,000 km north of Suva, Fiji. Funafuti, Nanumea, Nui, Nukufetau, and Nukulaelae are true atolls, with multiple islets less than four meters high and central lagoons, while Nanumaga, Niulakita, and Niutao are single table-reef islands, with small landlocked interior lakes. Vaitupu is also closer to the table-reef type, though its interior lake or lagoon is connected to the sea. In all, the nine islands are composed of 129 islets, of which Fu-

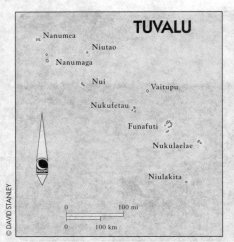

nafuti accounts for 34 and Nukufetau 37. Ships can enter the lagoons at Nukufetau and Funafuti; elsewhere they must stand offshore.

It's feared that within a century rising ocean levels will inundate these low-lying atolls and Tuvalu will cease to exist. Coastal erosion is already eating into shorelines, and seawater has seeped into the groundwater, killing coconut trees and flooding the taro pits. Sea walls may slow the erosion, but as ocean levels continue to rise, the entire population of Tuvalu may eventually have to evacuate, third-world victims of first-world affluence.

Climate
The climate is generally warm and pleasant. The mean annual temperature is 29° C and the average annual rainfall 3,000 mm (the southernmost atolls are somewhat wetter). Rain falls on more than half the days of the year, usually heavy downpours followed by sunny skies. The trade winds blow from the east much of the year. Strong west winds and somewhat more rain come Oct.-March, the hurricane season. Tuvalu is near the zone of hurricane formation, and these storms can appear with little warning and cause considerable damage. Otherwise, few seasonal variations disturb the humid, tropical weather. The waters lapping these shores are among the warmest in the world, and those of the interior lagoons are several degrees warmer again.

History
The Polynesians colonized Tuvalu some 2,000 years ago; Samoans occupied the southern atolls, while Tongans were more active in the north. Groups of warriors also arrived from Kiribati— their language is still spoken on Nui. Polynesian migrants reached the outliers of the Solomons and the Carolines from bases in Tuvalu.

Although the Spaniard Mendaña reportedly saw some of the islands in the 16th century, regular European contact did not occur until the 19th century. Slavers kidnapped 450 people from Funafuti, Nanumea, and Nukulaelae in 1863 to dig guano on the islands off Peru—none returned. In 1861 a Cook Islands castaway named Elekana was washed up on Nukulaelae. He taught Christianity to the islanders, and after reporting back to Protestant missionaries in Samoa, returned in 1865 with Rev. A.W. Murray and an organized LMS missionary party. Soon, most Tuvaluans were converted, and they remained under the spiritual guidance of Samoan pastors right up to 1969. The LMS-descended Ekalesia Kelisiano Tuvalu retains the loyalty of 92% of the population today.

To keep out American traders, Britain declared a protectorate over Tuvalu in 1892, upgrading it to colonial status in 1916. The ensuing period was fairly uneventful, except for the American military bases established at Funafuti, Nukufetau, and Nanumea during WW II. Funafuti was home to B-24 Liberator bombers of the U.S. Seventh Air Force, which launched raids against Japanese bases in the Gilberts and Marshalls. Warplanes en route from Wallis Is-

ISLAND	POPULATION (1996)	AREA (hectares)
Nanumea	818	361
Nanumaga	644	310
Niutao	749	226
Nui	608	337
Vaitupu	1,205	509
Nukufetau	756	307
Funafuti	3,836	254
Nukulaelae	370	166
Niulakita	75	41
TUVALU	**9,061**	**2,511**

TUVALU AT A GLANCE

This Tuvaluan, strips of pandanus around head and waist, came aboard a ship of the U.S. Exploring Expedition, which visited Nukufetau in 1841.

land to the Gilberts were refueled here. Japanese planes did manage to drop a few bombs in return, but Tuvalu was spared the trauma of a Japanese invasion.

The U.S. built its airfield across the most fertile land on Funafuti, reducing the area planted in coconuts and *pulaka* (swamp taro) by a third. The enduring impact of this loss is reflected in the fact that *pulaka* is no longer a staple food of the Tuvaluans on Funafuti. The Americans left behind a few wrecked cranes and huge "borrow" pits where they extracted (borrowed) coral. Today garbage is dumped into the stagnant lakes in the American pits, forming perfect breeding grounds for mosquitoes and rats. A plan to fill the pits and reclaim the land has been under discussion for decades.

Until 1975, Tuvalu was part of the Gilbert and Ellice Islands Colony. In the early 1970s the Polynesian Ellice Islanders expressed their de-

sire to separate from the Micronesian Gilbertese and proceed toward true independence. In a 1974 referendum, the Tuvaluans voted overwhelmingly to become a separate unit. Britain acceded to the wish in 1975, and on 1 October 1978, after only five months of full internal self-government, Tuvalu became a fully independent nation.

Political independence has greatly benefitted Tuvalu, as it would have received much less attention and economic aid as an outer-island group of Kiribati. In 1995 politicians removed the Union Jack from the country's flag in a bid to establish a republic and out of dissatisfaction with the amount of financial aid the country was receiving from Britain. Two years later there was a change of government and the old flag was brought back. Tuvalu is a member of the South Pacific Forum but not the United Nations.

Government

Tuvalu has an elected 12-member parliament headed by a prime minister chosen from its ranks. The five cabinet ministers and the speaker of the house must also be elected members of parliament. There are no political parties, instead prominent families control politics and virtually all leading officials are men. A Tuvaluan governor-general represents the British Crown. Decisions of the High Court of Tuvalu may be appealed to the Fiji Court of Appeal and finally to the Privy Council in London.

Since 1966 elected island councils *(kaupule)* have provided local government on each outer island; in 1977 a town council replaced the island council on Funafuti. Previously the heads of families had met in *maneapa* or *falekaupule* (community halls) to discuss island affairs. Moves are underway to strengthen outer island local government by providing the councils with centrally funded budgets that they can spend as they see fit.

Economy

Tuvalu's gross domestic product (A$15.7 million in 1995) is the smallest of any independent state. Only limited quantities of locally made clothing are exported, whereas most food, fuel, and manufactured goods are imported. In 1995 imports cost A$12.5 million while exports were

typical house, Tuvalu

limited to small quantities of fish and copra. Despite this, Tuvalu has no foreign debts and is financially sound due to fiscal prudence and a series of unique monetary arrangements.

The Tuvalu Trust Fund, created in 1987 with grants of A$27.1 million (worth A$60 million in late 1998) from the governments of Australia, N.Z., and the U.K., provides Tuvalu with a regular income of A$7 million a year. The sale of postage stamps to collectors provides further government revenue, and remittances from Tuvaluans overseas, such as the 400 young men working as crew on foreign ships, bring in another A$2 million a year. Taiwan sharply increased its aid to Tuvalu in late 1998, after Tonga switched recognition to Beijing, and a massive new government office building is to be erected on Funafuti with Taiwanese money. The first permanent diplomatic mission to be established in Tuvalu may be that of Taiwan.

In 1998 American, Korean, and Taiwanese tuna-fishing boats paid US$5.5 million in licensing fees to exploit Tuvalu's 900,000-square-km exclusive economic zone. Japan has also donated six 10-meter fishing boats to Tuvalu, and these supply the local fish market. Tourism has long been hampered by stiff air fares which effectively eliminate all but the most determined travelers. Of the 1,029 overseas visitors to Tuvalu in 1997, only 253 declared their purpose as tourism and not more than a handful of those got beyond Funafuti.

In 1996 each of the outer islands received a

solar-powered satellite telecommunications receiver system courtesy of Australian aid. At a cost of half a million dollars apiece, the systems make it possible for the islanders to pick up MTV, CNN, Discovery Channel, and other important programming. An earth station was installed on Funafuti and the fancy new gadgetry created excess international telephone service capacity that could be sold to the operators of sex chat lines in Japan, the U.S., and Britain. In 1996 "live one to one" telephone sex advertisements bearing Tuvalu's international telephone access code 688 began appearing in pornographic magazines. In 1998 the arrangement earned Tuvalu A$1.2 million and 10% of the country's budget is now covered by income from the telephone sex. This service cannot be accessed from Tuvalu itself since the national motto is "Tuvalu for God," and the calls are routed to "horny" operators in Auckland, New Zealand.

In 1998 Tuvalu's internet address dot tv began to be marketed by The .TV Corporation (www.internet.tv or www.information.ca), a Toronto company run by a Canadian named Jason Chapnick. It costs US$1,000 to register a domain name for the first year, then US$500 to renew, and television companies are the target market. At the time, officials on Funafuti provided ludicrous estimates of the tens of million of dollars in revenue the scheme was supposed to bring in. A year later when the promised instant riches failed to materialize, the same officials began making noises about pulling the plug on Jason.

Returning to earth, you can also pick up a Tuvaluan passport at US$11,000 for individuals or US$22,000 for a family of four. Although citizenship is not included, holders are allowed to reside in Tuvalu. Chinese nationals are the main clients of this scam, which is run out of the Tuvalu Trade Mission in Hong Kong. Tuvalu also barters ambassadorships for favors, and in 1996 an Italian restaurateur snapped up the post of Ambassador to the Vatican, even though Tuvalu has less than 100 Catholics and no diplomatic relations with the Holy See (Vatican-accredited diplomats enjoy a special tax status that allows them to make huge profits on business dealings in Italy).

The People

All nine atolls are inhabited, with one or two villages on each. The villages are often divided into two "sides" to foster competition. More than 70% of the people on the outer islands still live in traditional-style housing. The life of the people is hard—only coconuts and pandanus grow naturally, though bananas, papayas, and breadfruit are cultivated. A variety of taro (pulaka) has to be grown in pits excavated from coral rock. Reef fish and tuna are the main protein components in the diet. Chicken, both local and imported, is eaten quite regularly on Funafuti; pork is served on special occasions.

Tuvalu's population density (more than 400 persons per square km) is the highest in the South Pacific and one of the highest in the world. Since 1985 the number of persons per square km has doubled on Funafuti and nearly half the country's population now lives on this one atoll. Room to breathe is rapidly disappearing as additional people arrive continuously in search of government jobs. About 75% of the food consumed on Funafuti is now imported, and diet-related diseases such as diabetes, hypertension, and vitamin deficiency are on the increase.

The infant mortality rate of 51 per 1,000 is the highest in the South Pacific (excluding Papua New Guinea).

While some 10,000 people live in Tuvalu, another 2,000 Tuvaluans reside abroad. After the separation from the Gilbert Islands in 1975, many Tuvaluans who had previously held government jobs on Tarawa or worked at the phosphate mine on Banaba returned home. A second influx is presently underway as phosphate mining winds down on Nauru and the 750 Tuvaluans employed there are repatriated. This migration is causing major disruptions as overcrowded Funafuti tries to cope.

Mostly Polynesian, related to the Samoans and Tongans, the Tuvaluans' ancestry is evident in their language, architecture, customs, and tuu mo aganu Tuvalu (Tuvaluan way of life). Nui Island is an exception, with some Micronesian influence. Before independence, many Tuvaluans working on Tarawa took an I-Kiribati husband or wife, and there's now a large Gilbertese community on Funafuti. The Tuvaluan language is almost identical to that spoken in neighboring Tokelau, Wallis and Futuna, and Tikopia in the Solomons.

Conduct and Customs

If you're planning to stop at an outer island, take along things like sticks of tobacco, matches, chewing gum, volleyballs, fishhooks, T-shirts, cloth, and cosmetics to give as gifts. Don't hand them out at random like Santa Claus—give them to people you know as a form of reciprocation. It's the custom.

Scanty dress is considered offensive everywhere, so carry a sulu to wrap around you. Women should cover their legs when seated and their thighs at all times. Never stand upright before seated people, and try to enter a house or falekaupule shoeless, and from the lagoon side rather than the ocean side.

ON THE ROAD

Entertainment

Tuvaluans love dancing, be it their traditional *fatele,* more energetic than Gilbertese dancing, or the predictable twist. Traditional dancing is performed on special occasions, such as when opening a building, greeting special visitors, or celebrating holidays. Get in on the singing, dancing, and general frivolity taking place at the *falekaupule* almost every night. On Funafuti, migrants from each outer island have their own *falekaupule,* so ask around to find out if anything is on. Or just listen for the rhythmic sounds and head that way. Sometimes the local I-Kiribati do Gilbertese dances. On festive occasions many people wear flower garlands called *fou* (rhymes with Joe) in their hair. Each island has its own style.

Ask where you can watch *te ano* (the ball), the national game. Two teams line up facing one another and competition begins with one member throwing the heavy ball toward the other team, who must hit it back with their hands. Points are scored if the opposite team lets the ball fall and the first team to reach 10 wins. Obviously, weak players are targeted and the matches can be fierce (but usually friendly). The game ends with the losers performing a funny song and dance routine intended to bring the winners back to earth.

Public Holidays and Festivals

Public holidays include New Year's Day, Commonwealth Day (second Monday in March), Good Friday, Easter Monday (March/April), Gospel Day (second Monday in May), the Queen's Birthday (June), National Children's Day (August), Tuvalu National Days (1 and 2 October), Prince Charles' Birthday (November), Christmas (25 December), and Boxing Day (28 December). The period 25-28 December is the Christmas-Boxing Day Break.

Local Funafuti holidays include Bomb Day, which commemorates 23 April 1943, when a Japanese bomb fell through Funafuti's church roof and destroyed the interior. An American corporal had shooed 680 villagers out of the building only 10 minutes before, thus averting a major tragedy. Children's Day features kids' sports and crafts; dancing and a parade on Funafuti airstrip mark Independence Day (1 October). On 21 October, Hurricane Day, Tuvaluans recall 1972's terrible Hurricane Bebe. All of the outer atolls have a special holiday of their own, and that day everyone from that island gets the day off, even if they work on Funafuti.

Accommodations

One upmarket hotel and nearly a dozen small private guesthouses exist on Funafuti, but camping is not allowed. A 10% government room tax is added to all accommodations charges. Credit cards are not accepted—everyone expects to be paid in cash.

All of the outer islands except Niulakita and Nukufetau have guesthouses run by the island councils, where you can stay for A$5-15 pp, or A$20-35 including meals. The guesthouse attendants will do laundry for an additional charge. It's *essential* to announce your arrival by contacting the particular island council. This can be done either from the Telecom Center opposite the post office in Vaiaku or at the Department of Rural Development (tel. 20177) in the Ministry of Natural Resources and Environment building just south of the main government building next to the lagoon. Vaitupu has a small privately run guesthouse, the first outside Funafuti. Otherwise, it's possible to arrange accommodations with local outer-island families, but be prepared to renounce all privacy. Don't count on being able to buy *any* imported goods on the outer islands: take with you all you'll need.

Food

Pulaka (swamp taro) is eaten boiled or roasted or is made into pudding. Breadfruit, a staple, is boiled with coconut cream, baked, or fried in oil as chips. Plantain (cooking bananas) may also be boiled or chipped. Sweet potatoes, though becoming popular, are still only served on special occasions. Fish is eaten every day, both whitefish and tuna; pork, chicken, and eggs add a little variety. Reddish-colored fish caught in the lagoons may be poisonous. If you're interested in fishing, make it known and someone will take you out in their canoe. Imported foods such as rice, corned beef, sugar, and a variety of canned foods are used in vast amounts.

When eating on the outer islands, ask for some of the local dishes such as *laulu* or *lolo* (a taro leaf in coconut cream, not unlike spinach and delicious), *palusami* (*laulu*, onions, and fish, usually wrapped in banana leaves), *uu* (coconut crab, only readily available on Nukulaelae and Nukufetau), and *ula* (crayfish). Quench your thirst with *pi* (drinking coconut), *kaleve* (sweet coconut toddy, generally extracted morning and night), or supersweet coffee and tea. *Kao* is sour toddy produced by fermenting *kaleve* two or three days. Take care, as *kao* can quickly render you senseless and produces a vicious hangover. Drinking alcohol in public is prohibited.

Visas and Officialdom
Funafuti is the only port of entry. There are no visa requirements for any nationality, but make sure you have a passport valid for another six months and an onward ticket. Those arriving/departing by boat also require an air ticket to leave. Upon arrival by boat, immigration will inform you that it's prohibited to stay with the locals or to leave Funafuti. Diplomacy can usually overcome both obstacles.

The maximum stay is four months, but visitors are usually given only the time until their onward flight or 28 days. Sometimes you only get a week on arrival, with an extension to one month available for A$10 at the Immigration office (tel. 20706, fax 20241) in the government stores building near the library. Two additional months cost A$10 each (return ticket essential). Further extensions require government approval.

Most government offices are open Mon.-Thurs. 0800-1615, Friday 0800-1245.

Money
Australian currency is used, with Tuvaluan coins (about US$1 = A$1.65). The Tuvaluan one-dollar coin is of the same size and edging as the Australian 50-cent piece. It pays to be alert when handling these coins, or face a 50% devaluation. Kiribati coins are not accepted even though both countries use Australian banknotes.

An office upstairs at the National Bank of Tuvalu (tel. 20803, fax 20802; open Mon.-Thurs.

1000-1400, Friday 0900-1300) next to the airport at Funafuti will change traveler's checks. Credit cards aren't accepted anywhere in Tuvalu, although the Philatelic Bureau might help if you're desperate.

Tuvaluans do not expect to be tipped.

Media
The free monthly national newspaper, *Tuvalu Echoes,* is available at the Broadcasting and Information Office (tel. 20731, fax 20732) opposite the Vaiaku Lagi Hotel.

Radio Tuvalu (tel. 20138, fax 20732) broadcasts in English and Tuvaluan seven hours a day over 621 kHz AM and 100.1 MHz FM from Funafuti. The news in English is at 0700 and 1900. When the local station isn't on the air, the BBC World Service is broadcast over these frequencies.

Health
Princess Margaret Hospital (tel. 20481) on Funafuti has a pharmacist and dentist, but on the outer islands there are only "dressers." Hepatitis, cholera, dengue fever, and tuberculosis are occasional problems (the last major cholera outbreak was in 1990). Cuts can turn septic quickly, so one should pack and use an antiseptic such as hydrogen peroxide. Water should be considered suspect and boiled.

Recommended (but not compulsory) vaccinations for those who will be spending much time here include typhoid fever and immune globulin or the hepatitis A vaccine. The cholera vaccination is only 50% effective but you may be required to prove you've had it if you're arriving from an infected area. During outbreaks passengers are sometimes refused permission to board Fiji-bound flights at Funafuti unless they can show a cholera vaccination certificate not more than six months old. If need be, vaccinations and certificates can be obtained at the hospital. Ask about this when reconfirming your flight.

What to Take
Bring plenty of film, as what is sold locally is often expired. Only color print film is available (no black-and-white or color slides). Snorkelers should arrive with their own gear. Bring coffee too—it's priced out of reach here. Tampons can also be a problem. On the outer islands even

staples such as rice, flour, and sugar can be sold out.

TRANSPORTATION

Getting There

In March 1999 Air Marshall Islands (e-mail: amisales@ntamar.com) terminated the air service they had operated between Fiji, Tuvalu, Kiribati, and Marshall Islands for 15 years. The Fijian domestic carrier, **Air Fiji** (www.airfiji.net, e-mail: airfiji@is.com.fj), quickly took over the Suva-Funafuti route, but at press time no flights were operating north to Tarawa. Air Marshall Islands had long been notorious for its exorbitant airfares, and Air Fiji has driven them even higher: A$510 or F$650 each way between Fiji and Funafuti. At last report, no discounts were available and the Visit South Pacific Pass formerly accepted by Air Marshall Islands is no longer honored. Return flights operate on Wednesday, Thursday, and Sunday, and they're are often heavily booked by people on some sort of official business.

Tuvalu collects an A$20 departure tax, which yachties and boat passengers must also pay

By Boat

About four times a year the government-owned ship *Nivaga II* travels Suva-Funafuti (1,020 km). One-way fares are F$70 deck, F$124 second class, F$139 first class without meals, or F$200 second class, F$215 first class including meals. For information in Fiji, inquire at the Tuvalu Embassy (16 Gorrie St., Suva; tel. 679/301-355, fax 679/301-023), although they won't know anything until just a week before the sailing. In Funafuti, ask about ships at the Travel Office (tel. 20737) beside the post office in Vaiaku. The *Nivaga II* also makes occasional trips to Nauru (1,400 km), Tarawa, Tokelau, and Apia (1,000 km), carrying both passengers and cargo.

A more regular service from Fiji is offered by **Williams & Gosling Ltd. Ships Agency** (Box 79, Suva; tel. 312-633, fax 307-358), 80 Harris Rd. near Suva bus station. They book passage on the Kiribati Shipping Services vessel *Nei Matangare*, which leaves Suva for Funafuti and Tarawa about once a month. The three-day trip to Funafuti costs A$99/190 deck/cabin one-way, meals in-

cluded. The ship spends a week at Tarawa before returning to Fiji, so on a single roundtrip journey you'd have two weeks at Funafuti, provided everything went according to plan.

Reader Garry Hawkins of Northampton, England, sent us this:

I arrived in Apia on the Nivaga II *from Tokelau and assumed continuing to Tuvalu would only involve getting the captain's permission and paying when we reached Funafuti. The captain agreed I could stay on board, provided I got permission from a man named Paeli with the Marine Department in Tuvalu. It took three phone calls via New Zealand to get hold of the fellow, and he said okay. Up to this point no one had informed me that the boat had been chartered by the Office for Tokelau Affairs, so here I am sitting on deck when suddenly all the Samoa and Tokelau immigration people show up. When I asked what was going on they informed me that I should have bought a ticket from the Office for Tokelau Affairs. After much deliberation, the* Nivaga*'s administrative officer and the Tokelau Affairs woman agreed that my palagi price to Funafuti would be NZ$110 deck including meals. But, then I had to satisfy the Tuvalu immigration requirements regarding a ticket to leave. So the administrative officer sold me another one-way ticket from Tuvalu to Nauru at A$75 deck without meals. Unfortunately after all that I didn't have enough time to pick up any food in Apia for the 3.5-day voyage to Funafuti. This left me at the mercy of the* Nivaga*'s deck class meals, which were Lee's Cabin Biscuits alone for breakfast, canned corn beef with white rice for lunch, and a can of mackerel with white rice for dinner. Drinks consisted of hot water or milk diluted with hot water. Needless to say, I lost weight on that voyage. Upon arrival in Tuvalu I had to buy an Air Nauru ticket from Nauru to Fiji, or else. Before going to Nauru, the* Nivaga *made three trips to the outer Tuvalu atolls and I was able to go along on all three for A$130 total deck class. I managed to see all nine islands, though traveling on a boat that leaves several hours after it arrives makes you feel a bit like the Great White Hunter who arrives, says hello, and leaves. I hope you know what I mean! In the end, the boat trip to Nauru was canceled and I was given the choice of sailing back to Tokelau or buying yet another air ticket straight to Fiji. I did manage to get my A$75 back through sheer persistence, and together with the Air Nauru fare it about paid for my new ticket.*

Getting Around

There are no internal flights. In 1988 the British government donated the 58-meter interisland ship *Nivaga II* to mark Tuvalu's 10 years of independence. This ship makes the rounds of the outer islands roughly every fortnight stopping at each atoll for about an hour, depending on the tides. The southern trip to Nukulaelae and Niulakita takes three days; the northern trip visits about three of the six islands up that way in four days. If you decide to stop off at one of the islands, you could be there two weeks or more before the ship returns. Distances from Funafuti are 112 km to Nukulaelae, 221 km to Niulakita, 102 km to Nukufetau, 118 km to Vaitupu, 242 km to Nui, 301 km to Niutao, 352 km to Nanumaga, and 400 km to Nanumea.

There are three twin first-class cabins with private bath and eight second-class cabins with shared facilities. The 120 deck passengers must bring their own mats, eating utensils, and food (unless meals have been ordered beforehand). No booze is sold aboard, though it's okay to bring your own (no refrigerators available). Don't offer alcohol to the crew, however, as disciplinary action would be taken against them if they imbibed. If you must drink, do it in your cabin.

Roundtrip fares from Funafuti to the central islands of Vaitupu, Nui, and Nukufetau are A$94/154/184 deck/second/first class. Otherwise it's A$115/194/234 to the northern islands of Nanumaga, Nanumea, and Niutao. Meals are charged extra. Tuvaluans pay cheaper fares, so make sure you're being quoted the right amount. In busy periods women have a slightly better chance of getting cabin space on the *Nivaga II* than men, but even if you've booked and paid for a cabin you're not safe until the ship has actually sailed, since a VIP such as the prime minister or a member of parliament can requisition your cabin on short notice, and all the kicking and screaming in the world won't help a bit. The schedule is erratic and unreliable, so you really have to be lucky to be able to go!

FUNAFUTI

Captain Arent De Peyster "discovered" Funafuti in 1819 and named it Ellice, for Edward Ellice, the British member of parliament who owned the cargo that his ship, the *Rebecca,* was carrying. In 1841 Charles Wilkes, commander of the United States Exploring Expedition, applied the name to the entire Tuvalu group. Author James A. Michener, who visited Funafuti during WW II, called it "a truly dismal island."

The government offices are at Vaiaku, 50 meters west of the airstrip, the Funafuti Fusi cooperative supermarket is a kilometer northeast, and the deepwater wharf (built with Australian aid in 1981) is a little more than a kilometer beyond that. A Japanese fishing boat wrecked during a hurricane in 1972 is in the lagoon just north of the wharf. Most of the homes on Funafuti are prefabs put up after this same storm, which also left a beach of coral boulders along the island's east side.

The area between Vaiaku and the wharf has developed into a busy little township with street lighting installed by New Zealand in 1990, the roads paved by the U.S. in 1991, the airstrip sealed by the European Union in 1992, and a new airport terminal erected by Australia in 1993. Heavy motorcycle traffic circulates on the one potholed main street, and the litter is piling up along the lagoon as consumerism dampens the South Seas dream. Drunks and empty beer cans are proliferating. The unsupervised men in blue loincloths seen sweeping the streets and gardening around Vaiaku are doing community service as inmates from a prison across the airstrip.

Sights

Sights around Vaiaku include the open-sided government *falekaupule* next to the airport building and the former lighthouse next to the governor-general's residence. In the northeastern part of the Fongafale village directly across from the Nanumaga *falekaupule*, not far from the hospital, is a borehole known as **David's Drill**. In 1896-98 scientists sent by the Royal Society of London conducted experimental drilling at Funafuti to test Darwin's theory of atoll formation. The deepest bore (340 meters) failed to reach Funafuti's volcanic base. A second attempt in 1911 was also unsuccessful.

At the north end of Funafuti Island, 10 km from Vaiaku, is a white sandy beach on the lagoon side and a wartime bunker. Farther north is the **Tuvalu Maritime Training School** (tel. 20849) on Amatuku, which prepares young Tuvaluans for employment on oceangoing ships. Since the school opened in 1979, several hundred young Tuvaluans have completed 12-month courses here. At low tide you can walk across the reef to Amatuku (although you're expected to request advance permission before going).

Some of the top snorkeling on Funafuti can be found in the huge oceanside pits blasted by the Americans during the war. At low tide the pits are like immense swimming pools trapping thousands of fish until high tide returns. Otherwise one should use extreme caution when swimming on the ocean side of the atoll due to the big surf, currents, coral heads, etc. Lagoon beaches in the populated areas are often used as toilets by the locals, which makes swimming (or simply walking along the shore) hazardous.

Of the outlying *motus* on the atoll's coral ring, Funafala, Amatuku, and Fualefeke are inhabited. You can stay in a small guesthouse on the beach at Funafala; local families also take guests. This little tropical paradise only an hour away by boat is a perfect escape from town. Some of the guesthouse managers may be able to help with the arrangements. A maritime park is being established on the western side of the lagoon. A wartime bunker can be seen on Tepuka, which tourism planners dream of converting into a beach resort.

FUNAFUTI

Fualefeke Island

Te Ava I De Lape

Amatuku Island

Tepuka Island

Tengako

Fualopa Island

WHARF

Funafuti Island

Fuafatu Island

Lagoon

Fongafale

AIRPORT

Vaiaku

Te Ava Fuagea

Papaelise Island

Faatato Island

Te Puapua

Funamanu Island

Fuangea Island

Falefatu Island

Tefala Island

Mateika Island

Luamotu Island

Tutanga Island

Funafala Island

Telele Island

Motuloa Island

0   2 mi

0   2 km

© DAVID STANLEY

ACCOMMODATIONS

Budget

Solomai Guest House (Tetagisi Titivalu, tel. 20811), on the main road 150 meters from the airport, has three rooms at A$33/55 single/double. The self-catering flat upstairs is much better than the rooms with shared bath below.

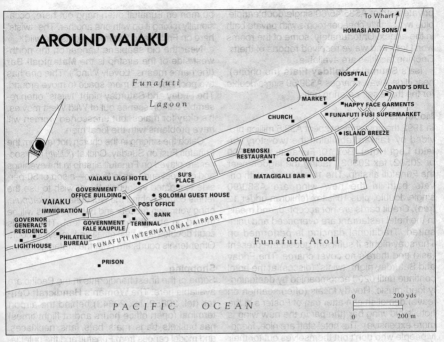

AROUND VAIAKU

Funafuti Lagoon

To Wharf

HOMASI AND SONS ■

HOSPITAL ■

DAVID'S DRILL ■

MARKET ■

HAPPY FACE GARMENTS ■

CHURCH ■

FUNAFUTI FUSI SUPERMARKET ■

ISLAND BREEZE ■

BEMOSKI RESTAURANT ■

COCONUT LODGE ■

MATAGIGALI BAR ■

VAIAKU LAGI HOTEL ■

SU'S PLACE ■

GOVERNMENT OFFICE BUILDING ■

SOLOMAI GUEST HOUSE ■

POST OFFICE ■

VAIAKU

IMMIGRATION ■

BANK ■

GOVERNOR GENERAL'S RESIDENCE ■

GOVERNMENT FALE KAUPULE ■

TERMINAL ■

FUNAFUTI INTERNATIONAL AIRPORT

PHILATELIC BUREAU ■

LIGHTHOUSE ■

Funafuti Atoll

■ PRISON

PACIFIC OCEAN

0 ————— 200 yds

0 ————— 200 m

Su's Place (Susana Tafaaki, tel./fax 20612), 250 meters northeast of Vaiaku post office up the main road, has four fan-cooled rooms with shared bath at A$30/48 single/double. One self-catering a/c apartment in a different location one km north goes for A$66. A small truck (A$2.50 a km) and a boat (A$120 a day) are for rent. A restaurant/bar is on the premises.

Bemoski Restaurant (tel. 20564), 700 meters north of the airport, offers two shared bath rooms upstairs at A$25 double (no cooking). A hundred meters beyond is **Coconut Lodge** (Funa Solomona, tel. 20911), on the main road near the turnoff to the Matagigali Bar. The four rooms with shared bath are overpriced at A$45 double (some rooms have only a curtain for a door). **Island Restaurant** (tel. 20474), 100 meters farther north, has three shoestring-priced upstairs rooms at A$17 each. Cooking facilities aren't provided, but the meals downstairs are reasonable.

Melemele Guest House (tel. 20493), on the lagoon not far from the 538Fusi, has two rooms with shared bath at A$39 double, one with private

bath at A$50, and a five-bed dorm at A$18 pp.

The **Island Breeze Motel** (Mr. Fononga Isala, tel. 20606), in the center of the village, 100 meters east of the Funafuti Fusi, is a bit of a misnomer as a hurricane would have to be raging for any breeze to reach there. Perhaps they're referring to the fans in the rooms! To call this place a motel is another a joke. The four rooms are poor value at A$33/55 single/double (no hot water).

Drum Guest House (tel. 20856), 200 meters south of the wharf, has five rooms with shared bath at A$17/28 single/double. It's run by a guy named Telaki who opened this place in 1997. A common kitchen is provided and the porch offers a fine lagoon view.

German expat Rolf Köpke and his Tuvaluan wife Emily operate **Hide-Away Guest House** (Box 59, Funafuti; tel. 20365, fax 20835), a two-story European-style house in spacious surroundings about five km north of Vaiaku. Take a bus to the deepwater wharf, then walk along the lagoon 30 minutes (some buses continue this far). Rolf offers a self-catering apartment with private bath at A$35/45/60 single/double/triple, plus two slightly cheaper rooms with private bath in the annex. Unfortunately, some of the rooms won't lock and we've received reports of thefts. Cooking facilities are available.

Isa's **Saumalei Holiday Flats** (no phone), near Hide-Away, charges A$39/50 single/double for the three self-catering units.

Moderate
In 1992 the government spent A$2.5 million provided by Taiwan rebuilding the two-story **Vaiaku Lagi Hotel** (Box 10, Funafuti; tel. 20500 or 20502, fax 20503), facing the lagoon near the Funafuti airstrip. The 16 a/c rooms with private bath in the new wing are A$80/90 single/double, plus 10% tax (children under 12 free). Credit cards are not accepted, and meals in the hotel restaurant are overpriced and uninspired. Traditional dancing is performed on Thursday nights if sufficient guests are present (ask) and there's no cover charge. The Friday and Saturday night "twists" (discos) at the hotel continue until 0200 accompanied by deafeningly loud music. Rowdy locals (often seamen on leave) demolish can after can of Foster's in the hotel's old wing bar (the bar in the new wing is more expensive). The hotel staff are nice, friendly people who don't put themselves out for their guests in any way. You must make all your own transportation or tour arrangements.

OTHER PRACTICALITIES

Food
Su's Restaurant (tel. 20612) at Su's Place serves the best meals you'll find around here, when she's cooking. Reservations are required at Su's (she might not bother opening otherwise). The economical Island and Bemoski Restaurants farther north offer substantial Chinese dishes but slow service. Lunch at the Vaiaku Lagi Hotel is A$4.50, and on Friday and Saturday they often have a A$3 lunch special. The snack bar at the airport has a cordial made from *kaleve* and water.

Entertainment
The **V.K. Public Bar**, 500 meters south of the wharf, is an open-walled establishment serving mostly beer. There's a small pool table, and Vaitu-pu men on Funafuti often hang out here, occasionally mixing it up with one another. The "twists" here on Friday and Saturday nights are wild.

Near the old seaplane hangar on the northwest side of the airstrip is the **Matagigali Bar** (the name means "Lovely Wind"). This one has two pool tables and more space to move around. The Friday and Saturday night "twists" often resemble saloon scenes out of Wild West movies. It's okay for males, but unescorted women will have problems with the local men.

Catch the singing in the church not far from the Funafuti Fusi on Sunday. Cricket *(kilikiti)* and soccer are played on Funafuti airstrip in the evenings and on weekends, as is *te ano*—a sort of 50-per-side elongated volleyball. If you wish to use the tennis courts behind the Nukufetau *falekaupule,* bring your own rackets and ball (the lights will be turned on at night for a small fee). This tennis court doubles as a basketball and volleyball court. Other tennis courts are near the Matagigali Bar.

Shopping
Some of the finest handicrafts in the Pacific are available here. The **Women's Handicraft Center** (tel. 20852, fax 20643) behind the airport terminal (open office hours and at flight times) has baskets, bags, mats, hats, fans, necklaces, and model canoes from Funafuti and the outer islands. Occasionally they're sold out of all items. Women sell crafts from private stalls at the airport on flight days. A fisherman's watertight wooden box *(tuluma)* is a unique souvenir. A booklet on Tuvaluan handicrafts is available at A$5.

The **Funafuti Fusi** (tel. 20867), halfway between Vaiaku and the deepwater wharf, is the biggest self-service supermarket on Funafuti. The small municipal market across the street is open daily except Sunday. Bread is available after 1600, fresh fish in the early morning and 1630-1700. A limited selection of food and merchandise is also available from stores owned by the various outer-island communities on Funafuti, most of them along the lagoonside road between the Funafuti Fusi and the wharf. The new **Island Supermarket,** 500 meters north of the Fusi, is as good as any.

Happy Face Garments (tel. 20622), between the Funafuti Fusi and the hospital, sells colorful T-shirts, shirts, shorts, towels, and *sulus* at reasonable prices. Ask the manager, Melina, to custom print you a Tuvalu T-shirt of your own design.

Post and Telecommunications

When writing, address your letter: Funafuti, Tuvalu, Central Pacific (via Fiji Islands). The post office sells very attractive Tuvalu aerogrammes, though Tuvalu's mail service is chaotic. Local acquaintances may ask you to carry letters to Fiji to mail for them. The **Philatelic Bureau** (Box 24, Funafuti; tel. 20224, fax 20712), a few doors southwest of the library, offers a vast selection of Tuvalu stamps produced since independence.

Normal telephone, fax, and telex facilities are provided by satellite from the Telecom Center (tel. 20846; daily 0730-midnight) opposite the post office. Local calls are 10 cents each. Long-distance calls are 80 cents a minute to other atolls of Tuvalu, A$1.70 a minute to Australia, A$2.20 a minute to Fiji, or A$4.20 a minute to North America or Europe (three-minute minimum). Calls made using telephone cards (available in denominations of A$2, A$5, A$10, and A$20) are not subject to minimum charges and work out 10% cheaper. Collect calls are not possible. Faxes can be sent for A$4 for the first page and 50 cents for each additional page, plus the regular telephone charge.

If you have access to a direct-dial telephone, you'll need to know the international access code is 00. For the local operator dial 010, for the international operator 012. Tuvalu's telephone code is 688. Try again if you don't get through the first time, as the operators go off duty at midnight.

Yachting Facilities

Te Ava Fuagea is the deepest (13 meters) of the three passes into the 14-by-18-km Funafuti lagoon; the others are only about eight meters deep. Yachties beware: Funafuti is probably the most poorly beaconed port of entry in the Pacific. At last report all the navigation buoys had disappeared from Te Ava Fuagea, making it an eyeball entrance. Navigation within the lagoon is also dangerous as it's studded with unmarked shoals, so yachts should proceed carefully along the marked channel to the anchorage off the main wharf to clear customs. From October to March, westerly winds can make this anchorage risky.

If you're a yachtie, buy your diesel oil at BP just north of the main wharf, as depot prices are 35% less than those charged at the Funafuti Fusi supermarket. Sammy's Service Station next to the Fusi and Mama's Petrol at the south end of the airstrip also sell gasoline and diesel.

Information

The Ministry of Tourism, Trade, and Commerce (Private Mail Bag, Funafuti; tel. 20184, fax 20829), in the same building as the immigration office, 150 meters south of the airport at Vaiaku, sells postcards at 50 cents each. Other postcards are available at Broadcasting House, the Funafuti Fusi, and the post office.

Excellent maps of each of the atolls are available from the Lands & Survey Department (tel. 20170), just north of the Library and Archives building fronting the lagoon.

The USP Extension Center (tel. 20811, fax 20704) near the hospital sells books on Tuvalu and the region. The excellent Tuvalu-English dictionary (A$8) produced by the Jehovah's Witnesses is available at the National Bank, the USP Center, and the Fusi. Niu Store (Box 76, Funafuti; tel. 20623) sells the regional news magazines.

A good National Library (tel. 20711; weekdays 0800-1230/1330-1600, Saturday 1000-1200) is near the government offices in Vaiaku (the USP also has a library).

Reconfirm your flight reservations not less than 72 hours in advance at the computerized Travel Office (tel. 20737) beside the post office in Vaiaku. There can be long waiting lists, and you'll be bumped if you fail to reconfirm.

Getting Around

Privately owned 26-seater buses run hourly between the Government Center at Vaiaku and the deepwater wharf on Funafuti 0700-2100 daily (40 cents). The buses marked "Vao" continue to the north end of the island, usually in the morning and late afternoon. There are no bus stops—you just wave the buses down.

Asivai Motorcycle Hire (Sio Patiale, tel./fax 20053), on the main road near the hospital, rents scooters at A$12 a day. **Sapea Motorcycle Hire** (tel./fax 20666), run by Sakaio Sualau who lives in the village, also rents small motorbikes at A$15 a day, plus bicycles. Several places rent pick-up trucks. **Sunrise Shop** has bicycles at A$3 a day. At night bicycles and motorcycles must carry a light; a flashlight in hand will do—this regulation *is* enforced. Driving is on the left.

The **Fisheries Department** (tel. 20742) near the main wharf has the only compressor on the island for filling scuba tanks. Government fishing boats are available for outer-island charters at A$1,000 per day including meals (deck accommodation only). Contact the Ministry of Natural Resources (tel. 20827) or phone the Fisheries Department direct. Also ask for Nuvali Kolone (tel. 20625, fax 20707) who arranges game fishing (A\$70) and scuba diving.

Luapou Lagoon Transport (Tailoa Kofe, tel. 20991, fax 20528) has a catamaran capable of carrying 25 adults available at A\$120 a day for the boat. On Monday and Thursday there is a regular trip to Funafala Island (locals A\$6 pp each way, tourists A\$20 pp each way). Many other private boats are available for rent.

OTHER ISLANDS OF TUVALU

Nanumaga

Nanumaga is a single island with only a narrow fringing reef. The main village is divided into the Tokelau (north) and Tonga (south) quarters, representing the island's two social groups. The Nanumaga people are conservative, but those few visitors who happen to call are warmly welcomed. If you visit, pay a courtesy call on the island chief, who belongs to the Mouhala clan. Fishing is prohibited on Tuesday and Wednesday.

Stay at the guesthouse for A\$6 pp, plus A\$13.50 for all meals. Shoestring.

Nanumea

Nanumea is the northwesternmost of the Tuvalu group, and its lagoon is considered by many to be the most beautiful. The two islands here are about five km apart. On Lakena Island is a small freshwater lake surrounded by palm and pandanus. American Passage, just west of Lolua village on Nanumea Island, was cut through the reef for 500 meters by the U.S. Army to allow small boats to enter the lagoon. It's said that yachts can reach an anchorage through this pass. A U.S. landing craft still sits wrecked on the reef as a reminder of the wartime U.S. base here and aircraft wreckage (mainly B-24s) is strewn around the atoll. If you have a head for heights, climb the pointed spire of the church—the view is worth it—but get permission from the pastor first. This German-style tower is one of the highest in the South Pacific, not at all what you'd expect to find on such a remote island.

The Nanumea island council guesthouse costs A\$15 pp without meals. Guests may cook for themselves, otherwise the attendant will prepare meals for an additional charge. Budget.

Niulakita

The southernmost, smallest, and least inhabited of the Tuvalu group, Niulakita is only a tiny coral dot just over a kilometer long. Niulakita sits up slightly higher than the other atolls, and the vegetation is lush. During the 19th century, the island was exploited by miners digging guano left by countless generations of seabirds. In 1926 the trading company Burns Philp set up a copra plantation here, which was sold to the British government in 1944. In 1946 the government ceded Niulakita to the people of Niutao, who have kept rotating groups here since 1949 (there never was any permanent population). They now live here making copra in shifts of a couple

The tower of the church on Nanumea is one of the tallest in the South Pacific.

of years each. There's no guesthouse here but you can stay with local families. In June 1997 Hurricane Keli struck Niulakita with 180 kph winds, the first hurricane ever recorded in the South Pacific in June.

Niutao

Legend has it that Pai and Vau, the two women who created Nanumea, also made Niutao, a tiny rectangular island about two km long with a small brackish lake. The people were converted by Protestant missionaries who arrived in 1870, and in 1991 a sturdy new church was completed, yet many traditional beliefs survive. Niutao is known for its decorative and durable pandanus floor mats.

Room and board at the island council guest-house costs A$20 pp. Budget.

Nui

A string of coconut-covered islands surrounds the closed Nui lagoon on the northern, eastern, and southern sides. This six-km-long oval body of water is flanked by lovely white beaches. Teriki-ai islet is especially beautiful. Nui was the first of the Tuvalu islands to be spotted by Europeans (Mendaña in 1568). Though the Nui people are known to be of Micronesian origin and still speak Gilbertese, today their culture is thoroughly Tuvaluan. The main, or "old," village (Tekawa Nikawai in Gilbertese) has recently been joined by Fakaifou, which means "new village" in Tuvaluan. The village houses sit in orderly rows.

The island council guesthouse is A$26 pp including meals or A$6.50 only to sleep. There's also a guesthouse without toilet facilities on Terikiai islet, which is usually only for locals (A$1.50 pp), but special permission may be granted to stay there. Shoestring.

Nukufetau

Nukufetau is the closest outer atoll to Funafuti (102 km) and the second largest after Funafuti in lagoon area. Unlike Funafuti's, the lagoon at Nukufetau is relatively safe for navigation and offers some protection from the westerlies. During WW II, the Americans constructed a wharf and an X-shaped airfield on Motolalo Island, eight km east of the present village across the lagoon. Quite a bit of debris remains. Seabird colonies occupy some of the easternmost islands.

There's no island council guesthouse on this island, but you can stay with the pastor for a similar price. If outer island tourism is ever to be developed in Tuvalu, Nukufetau would be the logical choice for a resort.

Nukulaelae

Nukulaelae is the easternmost of Tuvalu's nine islands, only a half degree west of the 180th meridian and the international date line, its 10-km-long lagoon partly surrounded by long, sandy islands. There is no passage for ships. Today climatic change threatens this isolated atoll and flooding has become a problem. Though the European Union has funded a seawall to slow the increasing erosion, salt water has already seeped into the large taro pits in the center of the main island. Pig pens stand on the mounds created when the pits were dug. The Nukulaelae people are renowned dancers.

It was here in 1861 that a Cook Islander named Elekana made an unscheduled landfall after drifting west in his canoe from the Cook Islands. Elekana introduced Tuvalu to Christianity, as a monument on Nukulaelae now records, and it was here too that the first organized missionary party from Samoa landed in 1865.

In 1863 visitors of a different kind called, as three Peruvian ships appeared off the atoll. An old man came ashore to tell the islanders they were mission ships and everyone was invited aboard for religious services. The trusting Polynesians accepted, and after all the men were aboard and locked in the hold, the same rascal returned to the beach to say that the men had asked that the women and children join them. The ships then sailed off with 250 of Nukulaelae's 300 inhabitants to be used as slave labor in the mines of Peru. Only two men, who managed to jump overboard and swim 10 km back, ever returned.

The island council guesthouse is A$5 pp to stay, plus another A$25 pp for three meals and morning and afternoon tea. Unless you're really big on food, ask if they can cut some of those meals from your bill. This island is dry, so don't carry any alcohol with you if you go ashore here. Shoestring.

Vaitupu

Vaitupu is the largest of the nine Tuvalu atolls in land area and, after Funafuti, the most Euro-

CAPSULE TUVALUAN VOCABULARY

ao—yes

Ea koe?—How are you?
e fia?—how much? how many?

fafine—women
fakafetai—thank you
fakafetai lasi—thank you very much
fakamolemole—please, sorry
fakatali—wait
fale—house
falefoliki—toilet
fesoasoani—help
fiafia—happy
foliki—small

gali—nice, good

igoa—name
ika—fish
ikai—no
inu—drink

kai—to eat
Koe e fano ki fea?—Where are you going?
Koi tou igoa?—What is your name?
kou kou—to wash, bathe

lasi—big, large
lei—fine, well

makalili—cold
makona—full
Malosi fakafetai.—I am well, thank you.
masaki—sick
masei—bad
mataku—afraid
meakai—food
meakaigali—good food
mea pusi—cigarettes
moa—chicken
moe—sleep

niu—coconut

palagi—non-Tuvaluan
pi—drinking coconut
poo—night

seai—none, none left
Seiloa ne au.—I don't know.
sene—cent

taala—dollar
tagata—man
tai—salt water
taimi—time
talofa—hello
tamaliki—child
tapu—forbidden
ti—tea
tofaa—goodbye
Toku igoa ko . . . — My name is . . .

vai—fresh water
vaka—boat, canoe
vakalele—airplane
vela—hot

---

peanized. The house of Herr Nitz, representative on Vaitupu of the German trading company J.C. Godeffroy for a quarter century in the late 19th century, still stands. In 1905 the London Missionary Society opened a primary school at Motufoua on Vaitupu to prepare young men for entry into the seminary in Samoa. Over the years this has developed into the large church/government secondary school, the only one in Tuvalu. There are a few expatriates, primarily teachers at the secondary school. In 1946 the *matai* (chiefs) of Vaitupu purchased Kioa Island in Fiji, where some 300 Vaitupu people now live. A new fisheries harbor built with Japanese aid money opened on Vaitupu in 1997.

The island council guesthouse is a wooden ex-missionary building costing A$10 pp to stay. At

mealtimes each guest is given a tray laden with corned beef, fish, chicken, pork, rice, taro, breadfruit, bread, biscuits, and cake, plus enormous pots of tea. This costs A$8.50/15.50 pp for breakfast/dinner and is far too much to finish, so tell them beforehand that you don't want lunch. As soon as you stop eating, the trays will be carried out to the veranda where a small crowd of women and children will finish everything off. There's a kitchen in the guesthouse but no cooking utensils. Budget.

A local school teacher named Faleefa occasionally accepts paying guests in her own home. A new place to stay on Vaitupu, the four-room **Aliki Guest House** (Box 27, Funafuti) is run by Fanonga Isala. For information, ask at the Island Breeze Motel on Funafuti.

MELANESIA

FIJI ISLANDS, NEW CALEDONIA, VANUATU, SOLOMON ISLANDS

Named for its "black" inhabitants, Melanesia encompasses the hulking island chains of the Western Pacific from Fiji to New Guinea. A tremendous variety of cultures, peoples, languages, and attractions make up this relatively large region of mountainous islands. Prior to European colonization in the late 19th century, the 900 linguistic groups of Melanesia had little contact with one another, and unlike Polynesia, this was a largely classless society. Today parts of New Caledonia are as cosmopolitan as southern France, but on the outer islands of Vanuatu and Solomon Islands people cling to their traditional ways. Custom and land ownership are intense issues everywhere.

Compared to Polynesia, the population and islands are large. Densely populated Fiji is equal in inhabitants to New Caledonia, Vanuatu, and Solomon Islands combined, yet in land area both New Caledonia and Solomon Islands are bigger than Fiji. In Vanuatu and Solomon Islands, Melanesians still comprise the overwhelming majority of the population and few foreigners are seen outside the capitals, but in Fiji and New Caledonia, British and French colonialism introduced new ethnic groups leading to political instability. During WW II northern Melanesia became a pivotal battlefield. Today all of the countries of Melanesia except New Caledonia are independent. We don't include Papua New Guinea herein because its extensive area merits a separate guidebook. For North Americans and Europeans, Fiji is the gateway to this exciting area.

FIJI ISLANDS
INTRODUCTION

Once notorious as the "Cannibal Isles," Fiji is now the colorful crossroads of the South Pacific. Of the 322 islands that make up the Fiji Group, more than 100 are inhabited by a rich mixture of vibrant, exuberant Melanesians, East Indians, Polynesians, Micronesians, Chinese, and Europeans, each with a cuisine and culture of their own. Here Melanesia mixes with Polynesia, ancient India with the Pacific, and tradition with the modern world in a unique blend.

Fiji preserves an amazing variety of traditional customs and crafts such as kava or *yaqona* (pronounced "yanggona") drinking, the presentation of the whale's tooth, firewalking, fish driving, turtle calling, tapa beating, and pottery making. Alongside this fascinating human history is a dramatic diversity of landforms and seascapes, all concentrated in a relatively small area. Fiji's sun-drenched beaches, blue lagoons, panoramic open hillsides, lush rainforests, and dazzling reefs are truly magnificent. Africa also

has such diversity, but there you'd have to travel weeks or months to see what you can see in Fiji in days.

Fiji offers posh resorts, good food and accommodations, nightlife, historic sites, outer-island living, hiking, kayaking, camping, surfing, snorkeling, and scuba diving. Traveling is easy by small plane, interisland ferry, copra boat, outboard canoe, open-sided bus, and air-conditioned coach. Even with a month at your disposal you'd barely scratch the surface of all there is to see and do.

Best of all, Fiji is a hassle-free country with uncrowded, inexpensive facilities available almost everywhere. You'll love these super-friendly people whose knowledge of English makes communicating a breeze. In a word, Fiji is a traveler's country *par excellence,* and whatever your budget, Fiji gives you good value for your money and plenty of ways to spend it. *Bula,* welcome to Fiji, everyone's favorite South Pacific country.

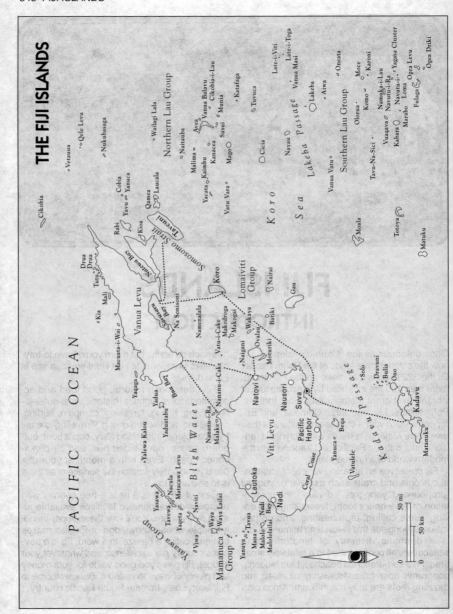

THE FIJI ISLANDS

Important Note

When early British missionaries created a system of written Fijian they established a unique set of orthographic rules followed to this day. In an attempt to represent the sounds of spoken Fijian more precisely, they rendered "mb" as **b**, "nd" as **d**, "ng" as **g**, "ngg" as **q**, and "th" as **c**. Thus Beqa is pronounced Mbengga, Nadi is Nandi, Sigatoka is Singatoka, Cicia is Thithia, etc. In order to become better to able pronounce Fijian names and words correctly, visitors must take a few minutes to learn these pronunciation rules. Turn to **Language,** which follows, for more information.

The Land

Fiji lies 5,100 km southwest of Hawaii and 3,150 km northeast of Sydney, astride the main air route between North America and Australia. Nadi is the hub of Pacific air routes, while Suva is a regional shipping center. The 180th meridian cuts through Fiji, but the international date line swings east so the entire group can share the same day.

The name Fiji is a Tongan corruption of the indigenous name "Viti." The Fiji Islands are arrayed in a horseshoe configuration with Viti Levu (great Fiji) and adjacent islands on the west, Vanua Levu (great land) and Taveuni to the north, and the Lau Group on the east. This upside-down-U-shaped archipelago encloses the Koro Sea, which is relatively shallow and sprinkled with the Lomaiviti, or central Fiji, group of islands. Together the Fiji Islands are scattered over 1,290,000 square km of the South Pacific Ocean.

If every single island were counted, the isles of the Fiji archipelago would number in the thousands. However, a mere 322 are judged large enough for human habitation and of these only 106 are inhabited. That leaves 216 uninhabited islands, most of them prohibitively isolated or lacking fresh water.

Most of the Fiji Islands are volcanic, remnants of a sunken continent that stretched through Australia. This origin accounts for the mineral deposits on the main islands. None of Fiji's volcanoes are presently active, though there are a few small hot springs. The two largest islands, Viti Levu and

FIJI AT A GLANCE

DIVISION/ PROVINCE	HEADQUARTERS	AREA (sq km)	POPULATION (1996)	PERCENT FIJIAN
Central Division	Suva	4,293	297,255	59.5
Naitasiri	Vunidawa	1,666	126,441	56.1
Namosi	Navua	570	5,893	91.4
Rewa	Nabalili	272	101,193	58.6
Serua	Navua	830	15,495	55.1
Tailevu	Nausori	955	48,233	67.7
Western Division	Lautoka	6,360	295,891	39.4
Ba	Lautoka	2,634	211,080	33.2
Nadroga	Sigatoka	2,385	54,049	52.5
Ra	Nanukuloa	1,341	30,762	59.4
Northern Division	Labasa	6,198	138,754	46.9
Macuata	Labasa	2,004	80,151	28.2
Bua	Nabouwalu	1,378	14,977	73.6
Cakaudrove	Savusavu	2,816	43,626	72.0
Eastern Division	Levuka	1,422	40,755	89.4
Kadavu	Vunisea	478	9,539	99.2
Lau	Lakeba	487	12,203	98.6
Lomaiviti	Levuka	411	16,203	91.2
Rotuma	Ahau	46	2,810	5.8
TOTAL FIJI	**Suva**	**18,272**	**772,655**	**51.1**

SUVA'S CLIMATE

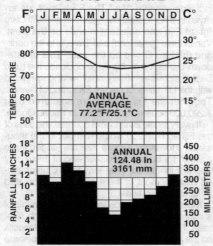

NADI'S CLIMATE

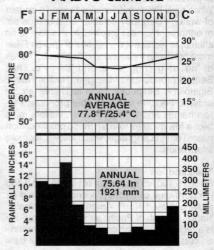

Vanua Levu, together account for 87% of Fiji's 18,272 square km of land. Viti Levu has 57% of the land area and 75% of the people, while Vanua Levu, with 30% of the land, has 18% of the population. Viti Levu alone is bigger than all five archipelagos of Tahiti-Polynesia; in fact, Fiji has more land and people than all of Polynesia combined.

The 1,000-meter-high Nadrau Plateau in central Viti Levu is cradled between Tomanivi (1,323 meters) on the north and Monavatu (1,131 meters) on the south. On different sides of this elevated divide are the Colo-East Plateau drained by the Rewa River, the Navosa Plateau drained by the Ba, the Colo-West Plateau drained by the Sigatoka, and the Navua Plateau drained by the Navua. Some 29 well-defined peaks rise above Viti Levu's interior; most of the people live in the river valleys or along the coast.

The Nadi River slices across the Nausori Highlands, with the Mt. Evans Range (1,195 meters) towering above Lautoka. Other highland areas of Viti Levu are cut by great rivers like the Sigatoka, the Navua, the Rewa, and the Ba, navigable far inland by outboard canoe or kayak. Whitewater rafters shoot down the Navua and occasionally the Ba, while the lower Sigatoka flows gently through Fiji's market garden "salad bowl." Fiji's largest river, the Rewa, pours into the Pacific

through a wide delta just below Nausori. After a hurricane the Rewa becomes a dark torrent worth a special visit to Nausori just to see. Sharks have been known to enter both the Rewa and the Sigatoka and swim far upstream.

Vanua Levu has a peculiar shape, with two long peninsulas pointing northeastward. A mountain range between Labasa and Savusavu reaches 1,032 meters at Nasorolevu. Navotuvotu (842 meters), east of Bua Bay, is Fiji's best example of a broad shield volcano, with lava flows built up in layers. The mountains are closer to the southeast coast, and a broad lowland belt runs along the northwest. Of the rivers only the Dreketi, flowing west across northern Vanua Levu, is large; navigation on the Labasa is restricted to small boats. The interior of Vanua Levu is lower and drier than Viti Levu, yet scenically superb: the road from Labasa to Savusavu is a visual feast.

Vanua Levu's bullet-shaped neighbor Taveuni soars to 1,241 meters, its rugged east coast battered by the southeast trades. Taveuni and Kadavu are known as the finest islands in Fiji for their scenic beauty and agricultural potential. Geologically, the uplifted limestone islands of the Lau Group have more in common with Tonga than with the rest of Fiji. Northwest of Viti Levu is the rugged limestone Yasawa Group.

Fringing reefs are common along most of the coastlines, and Fiji is outstanding for its many barrier reefs. The Great Sea Reef off the north coast of Vanua Levu is the fourth-longest in the world, and the Astrolabe Reef north of Kadavu is one of the most colorful. Countless other unexplored barrier reefs are found off northern Viti Levu and elsewhere. The many cracks, crevices, walls, and caves along Fiji's reefs are guaranteed to delight the scuba diver.

Climate
Along the coast the weather is warm and pleasant, without great variations in temperature. The southeast trades prevail from June to October, the best months to visit. In February and March the wind often comes directly out of the east. These winds dump 3,000 mm of annual rainfall on the humid southeast coasts of the big islands, increasing to 5,000 mm inland. The drier northwest coasts, in the lee, get only 1,500 to 2,000 mm. Yet even during the rainy months (Dec.-April), bright sun often follows the rains.

The official dry season (June-Oct.) is not always dry at Suva, although much of the rain falls at night. In addition, Fiji's winter (May-Nov.) is cooler and less humid, the preferred months for mountain trekking. During the drier season the reef waters are clearest for the scuba diver. Summer (Dec.-April) is hurricane season, with Fiji, Samoa, and Tonga receiving up to five tropical storms annually. Yet even in summer the refreshing trade winds relieve the high humidity.

In Fiji you can obtain prerecorded weather information by dialing 301-642.

Flora
More than 3,000 species of plants grow in Fiji, a third of them endemic. Patterns of rainfall are in large part responsible for the wide variety of vegetation here. The wetter sides of the high islands are heavily forested, with occasional thickets of bamboo and scrub. Coconut groves spread across the coastal plains. On the drier sides open savanna or *talasiga* of coarse grasses predominates where the original vegetation has been destroyed by slash-and-burn agriculture. Sugarcane is now cultivated in the lowlands here, and Caribbean pine has been planted in many dry hilly areas, giving them a Scandinavian appearance.

Fauna
The only native mammals are the monkey-faced fruit bat or flying fox, called *beka* by the Fijians, and the smaller, insect-eating bat. Two species of snakes inhabit Fiji: the very rare, poisonous *bolo loa,* and the harmless Pacific boa, which can grow up to two meters long. Venomous sea snakes are common on some coasts, but they're docile and easily handled. Fijians call the common banded black-and-white sea snake the *dadakulaci*.

One of the more unusual creatures found in Fiji and Tonga is the banded iguana, a lizard that lives in trees and can grow up to 70 centimeters long (two-thirds of which is tail). The iguanas are emerald green, and the male is easily distinguished from the female by his bluish-gray cross stripes. Banded iguanas change color to control their internal temperature, becoming darker when in the direct sun. Their nearest relatives are found in Central America, and how they reached Fiji remains a mystery. In 1979 a new species, the crested iguana, was discovered on Yaduataba, a small island off the west coast of Vanua Levu.

The Indian mongoose was introduced by planters in the 1880s to combat rats, which were damaging the plantations. Unfortunately, no one

banded iguana

DOUG HANKIN

realized at the time that the mongoose hunts by day, whereas the rats are nocturnal; thus, the two seldom meet. Today, the mongoose is the scourge of chickens, native ground birds, iguanas, and other animals, though Kadavu, Koro, Gau, Ovalau, and Taveuni are mongoose-free (and thus the finest islands for birdwatching).

Some Fijian clans have totemic relationships with eels, prawns, turtles, and sharks, and are able to summon these creatures with special chants. Red prawns are called on Vanua Vatu in Southern Lau, on a tiny island off Naweni in southern Vanua Levu, and on Vatulele Island. The Nasaqalau people of Lakeba in southern Lau call sharks, and villagers of Korolevu in central Viti Levu call eels. The women of Namuana on Kadavu summon giant sea turtles with their chants. Turtle calling is also practiced at Nacamaki village, in the northeast corner of Koro. Unfortunately sea turtles are becoming so rare that the turtle callers are having less and less success each year.

HISTORY AND GOVERNMENT

The Pre-European Period

The first people to arrive in Fiji were of a broad-nosed, light-skinned Austronesian-speaking race, probably the Polynesians. They originated in insular Southeast Asia and gradually migrated east past the already occupied islands of Melanesia. Distinctive *lapita* pottery, decorated in horizontal geometric bands and dated from 1290 B.C., has been found in the sand dunes near Sigatoka, indicating these people had reached here by 1500 B.C. or earlier. Much later, about 500 B.C., Melanesian people arrived, bringing with them their own distinct pottery traditions. From the fusion of these primordial peoples the Fijian race was born.

The hierarchical social structure of the early Fijians originated with the Polynesians. Status and descent passed through the male line, and power was embodied in the *turaga* (chief). The hereditary chiefs possessed the mana of an ancestral spirit or *vu*. Yet under the *vasu* system a chiefly woman's son could lay claim to the property of his mother's brothers, and such relationships combined with polygamy kept society in a state of constant strife. This feudal aristocracy

combined in confederacies, or *vanua,* which extended their influence through war. Treachery and cannibalism were an intrinsic part of these struggles; women were taken as prizes or traded to form alliances. For defense, villages were fortified with ring ditches, or built along ridges or terraced hillsides.

The native aristocracy practiced customs that today seem barbarous and particularly cruel. The skull cap of a defeated enemy might be polished and used as a *yaqona* (kava) cup to humiliate the foe. Some chiefs even took delight in cooking and consuming body parts as their agonized victims looked on. Men were buried alive to hold up the posts of new houses, war canoes were launched over the living bodies of young girls, and the widows of chiefs were strangled to keep their husbands company in the spirit world. The farewells of some of these women are remembered today in dances and songs known as *meke.*

These feudal islanders were, on the other hand, guardians of one of the highest material cultures of the Pacific. They built great ocean-going double canoes *(drua)* up to 30 meters long, constructed and adorned large solid thatched houses *(bures),* performed marvelous song-dances called *meke,* made tapa, pottery, and sennit (coconut cordage), and skillfully plaited mats. For centuries the Tongans came to Fiji to obtain great logs for canoe-making and sandalwood for carving.

European Exploration

In 1643 Abel Tasman became the European discoverer of Fiji when he sighted Taveuni, although he didn't land. In 1774, Captain Cook anchored off Vatoa (which he named Turtle Island) in southern Lau. Like Tasman he failed to proceed farther or land, and it was left to Capt. William Bligh to give Europeans an accurate picture of Fiji for the first time. After the *Bounty* mutiny in May 1789, Bligh and his companions were chased by canoe-loads of Fijian warriors just north of the Yasawa Islands as they rowed through on their escape route to Timor. Some serious paddling, a timely squall, and a lucky gap in the Great Sea Reef saved the Englishmen from ending up as the main course at a cannibal feast. The section of sea where this happened is known as Bligh Water today. Bligh cut directly

*Rotuma islanders
signaling to European
vessel*

across the center of Fiji between the two main islands, and his careful observations made him the first real European explorer of Fiji, albeit an unwilling one. Bligh returned to Fiji in 1792, but once again he stayed aboard his ship.

Beachcombers and Chiefs

All of these early explorers stressed the perilous nature of Fiji's reefs. This, combined with tales told by the Tongans of cannibalism and warlike Fijian natives, caused most travelers to shun the area. Then in 1800 a survivor from the shipwrecked American schooner *Argo* brought word that sandalwood grew abundantly along the Bua coast of Vanua Levu. This precipitated a rush of traders and beachcombers to the islands. A cargo of sandalwood bought from the islanders for $50 worth of trinkets could be sold to the Chinese at Canton for $20,000. By 1814 the forests had been stripped to provide joss sticks and incense, and the trade collapsed.

During this period Fiji was divided among warring chieftains. The first Europeans to actually mix with the Fijians were escaped convicts from Australia, who instructed the natives in the use of European muskets and were thus well received. White beachcombers such as the Swedish adventurer Charles Savage and the German Martin Bushart acted as middlemen between traders and Fijians and took sides in local conflicts. In one skirmish Savage was separated from his fellows, captured, and eaten. With help from the likes of Savage, Naulivou, the cannibal chief of

tiny Bau Island just off eastern Viti Levu, and his brother Tanoa extended their influence over much of western Fiji.

From 1820 to 1850 European traders collected bêche-de-mer, a sea cucumber which, when smoked and dried, also brought a good price in China. While the sandalwood traders only stayed long enough to take on a load, the bêche-de-mer collectors set up shore facilities where the slugs were processed. Many traders such as David Whippy followed the example of the beachcombers and took local wives, establishing the part-Fijian community of today. By monopolizing the bêche-de-mer trade and constantly warring, Chief Tanoa's son and successor, Ratu Seru Cakobau (pronounced Thakombau), became extremely powerful in the 1840s, proclaiming himself Tui Viti, or king of Fiji.

The beginnings of organized trade brought a second wave of official explorers to Fiji. In 1827 Dumont d'Urville landed on Bau Island and met Tanoa. The Frenchmen caused consternation and confusion by refusing to drink *yaqona* (kava), preferring their own wine. The American Exploring Expedition of 1840, led by Commodore Charles Wilkes, produced the first recognizable map of Fiji. When two Americans, including a nephew of Wilkes, were speared in a misunderstanding on a beach at Malolo Island, Wilkes ordered the offending fortified village stormed and 87 Fijians were killed. The survivors were made to water and provision Wilkes's ships as tribute. Captain H.M. Denham of the HMS *Herald* prepared accurate navigational charts of the island group in 1855-56, making regular commerce possible.

European and Tongan Penetration

As early as the 1830s an assortment of European and American beachcombers had formed a small settlement at Levuka on the east coast of Ovalau Island just northeast of Bau, which whalers and traders used as a supply base. In 1846 John Brown Williams was appointed American commercial agent. On 4 July 1849 Williams's home on Nukulau Island near present-day Suva burned down. Though the conflagration was caused by the explosion of a cannon during Williams's own fervent celebration of his national holiday, he objected to the way Fijian onlookers carried off items they rescued from the flames. A shameless swindler, Williams had purchased Nukulau for only $30, yet he blamed the Tui Viti for his losses and sent Cakobau a $5,001.38 bill. American claims for damages eventually rose to $45,000, and in 1851 and 1855 American gunboats called and ordered Cakobau to pay up. This threat hung over Cakobau's head for many years, the 19th-century equivalent of 20th-century third-world debt. Increasing American involvement in Fiji

Cakobau of Fiji: A drawing from a photo taken in 1877, now in the possession of the Museum of Archaeology and Ethnology, Cambridge, England

led the British to appoint a consul, W.T. Pritchard, who arrived in 1858.

The early 1830s also saw the arrival from Tonga of the first missionaries. Though Tahitian pastors were sent by the London Missionary Society to Oneata in southern Lau as early as 1830, it was the Methodists based at Lakeba after 1835 who made the most lasting impression by rendering the Fijian language into writing. At first Christianity made little headway among these fierce, idolatrous people, and only after converting the powerful chiefs were the missionaries successful. Methodist missionaries Cargill and Cross were appalled by what they saw during a visit to Bau in 1838. A white missionary, Rev. Thomas Baker, was clubbed and eaten in central Viti Levu by the *kai colo* (hill people) as late as 1867.

In 1847 Enele Ma'afu, a member of the Tongan royal family, arrived in Lau and began building a personal empire under the pretense of defending Christianity. In 1853 King George of Tonga made Ma'afu governor of all Tongans resident in Lau. Meanwhile, there was continuing resistance from the warlords of the Rewa River area to Cakobau's dominance. In addition the Europeans at Levuka suspected Cakobau of twice ordering their town set afire and were directing trade away from Bau. With his power in decline, in 1854 Cakobau accepted Christianity in exchange for an alliance with King George, and in 1855, with the help of 2,000 Tongans led by King George himself, Cakobau was able to put down the Rewa revolt at the Battle of Kaba. In the process, however, Ma'afu became the dominant force in Lau, Taveuni, and Vanua Levu.

During the early 1860s, as Americans fought their Civil War, the world price of cotton soared, and large numbers of Europeans arrived in Fiji hoping to establish cotton plantations. In 1867 the USS *Tuscaroga* called at Levuka and threatened to bombard the town unless the still-outstanding American debt was paid. The next year an enterprising Australian firm, the Polynesia Company, paid off the Americans in exchange for a grant from Cakobau of 80,000 hectares of choice land, including the site of modern Suva. The British government later refused to recognize this grant, though they refunded the money paid to the Americans and accepted the claims of settlers who had purchased land from the company. Settlers soon numbered around 2,000 and Levuka boomed.

It was a lawless era and a need was felt for a central government. An attempt at national rule by a confederacy of chiefs lasted two years until failing in 1867, then three regional governments were set up in Bau (western), Lau (eastern), and Bua (northern), but these were only partly successful. With prices for Fiji's "Sea Island" cotton collapsing as the American South resumed production, a national administration under Cakobau and planter John Thurston was established at Levuka in 1871.

However, Cakobau was never strong enough to impose his authority over the whole country, so with growing disorder in western Fiji, infighting between Europeans and Fijian chiefs, and a lack of cooperation from Ma'afu's rival confederacy of chiefs in eastern Fiji, Cakobau decided he should cede his kingdom to Great Britain. The British had refused an invitation to annex Fiji in 1862, but this time they accepted rather than risk seeing the group fall into the hands of another power, and on 10 October 1874 Fiji became a British colony. A punitive expedition into central Viti Levu in 1876 brought the hill tribes *(kai colo)* under British rule. In 1877 the Western Pacific High Commission was set up to protect British interests in the surrounding unclaimed island groups as well. In 1881 Rotuma was annexed to Fiji. At first Levuka was the colony's capital, but in 1882 the government moved to a more spacious site at Suva.

The Making of a Nation

The first British governor, Sir Arthur Gordon, and his colonial secretary and successor, Sir John Thurston, created modern Fiji almost single-handedly. They realized that the easiest way to rule was indirectly, through the existing Fijian chiefs. To protect the communal lands on which the chieftain system was based, they ordered that native land could not be sold, only leased. Not wishing to disturb native society, Gordon and Thurston ruled that Fijians could not be required to work on European plantations. Meanwhile the blackbirding of Melanesian laborers from the Solomons and New Hebrides had been restricted by the Polynesian Islanders Protection Act of 1872.

By this time sugar had taken the place of cotton and there was a tremendous labor shortage on the plantations. Gordon, who had previously served in Trinidad and Mauritius, saw indentured Indian workers as a solution. The first arrived in 1879, and by 1916, when Indian immigration ended, there were 63,000 present. To come to Fiji the Indians had to sign a labor contract *(girmit)* in which they agreed to cut sugarcane for their masters for five years. During the next five years they were allowed to lease small plots of their own from the Fijians and plant cane or raise livestock. More than half the Indians decided to remain in Fiji as free settlers after their 10-year contracts expired, and today their descendants form nearly half the population, many of them still working small leased plots.

Though this combination of European capital, Fijian land, and Indian labor did help preserve traditional Fijian culture, it also kept the Fijians backward—envious onlookers passed over by European and (later) Indian prosperity. The separate administration and special rights for indigenous Fijians installed by the British over a century ago continue in force today. In early 1875 Cakobau and two of his sons returned from a visit to Australia infected with measles. Though they themselves survived, the resulting epidemic wiped out a third of the Fijian population. As a response to this and other public health problems the Fiji School of Medicine was founded in 1885. At the beginning of European colonization there were about 200,000 Fijians, approximately 114,748 in 1881, and just 84,000 by 1921.

The Colonial Period

In 1912 a Gujerati lawyer, D.M. Manilal, arrived in Fiji from Mauritius to fight for Indian rights, just as his contemporary Mahatma Gandhi was doing in South Africa. Several prominent Anglican and Methodist missionaries also lobbied actively against the system. Indentured Indians continued to arrive in Fiji until 1916, but the protests led to the termination of the indenture system throughout the empire in 1920 (Manilal was deported from Fiji after a strike that year).

Although Fiji was a political colony of Britain, it was always an economic colony of Australia: the big Australian trading companies Burns Philp and W.R. Carpenters dominated business. (The ubiquitous Morris Hedstrom is a subsidiary of Carpenters.) Most of the Indians were brought to Fiji to work for the Australian-owned Colonial

Sugar Refining Company, which controlled the sugar industry from 1881 right up until 1973, when it was purchased by the Fiji government for $14 million. After 1935, Fiji's gold fields were also exploited by Australians.

Under the British colonial system the Governor of Fiji had far greater decision-making authority than his counterparts in the French Pacific colonies. Whereas the French administrators were required to closely follow policies dictated from Paris, the governors of the British colonies had only to refer to the Colonial Office in London on special matters such as finance and foreign affairs. Otherwise they had great freedom to make policy decisions.

No representative government existed in Fiji until 1904, when a Legislative Council was formed with six elected Europeans and two Fijians nominated by the Great Council of Chiefs (Bose Levu Vakaturaga), itself an instrument of colonial rule. In 1916 the governor appointed an Indian member to the council. A 1929 reform granted five seats to each of the three communities: three elected and two appointed Europeans and Indians, and five nominated Fijians. The council was only an advisory body and the governor remained in complete control. The Europeans generally sided with the Fijians against any demands for equality from the Indians—typical colonial divide and rule.

Fijians were outstanding combat troops on the Allied side in the Solomon Islands campaign during WW II, and again in 1952-56 suppressing Malaya's national liberation struggle. So skilled were the Fijians at jungle warfare against the Japanese that it was never appropriate to list a Fijian as "missing in action"—the phrase used was "not yet arrived." The war years saw the development of Nadi Airport. Until 1952, Suva, the present Fijian capital, was headquarters for the entire British Imperial Administration in the South Pacific.

In 1963 the Legislative Council was expanded but still divided along racial lines; women and indigenous Fijians got the vote for the first time. Wishing to be rid of the British, whom they blamed for their second-class position, the Indians pushed for independence, but the Fijians had come to view the British as protectors and were somewhat reluctant. A Constitutional Convention was held in London in 1965 to move Fiji

toward self-government, and after much discussion a constitution was adopted in 1970. Some legislature members were to be elected from a common roll (voting by all races), as the Indians desired, while other seats remained ethnic (voting in racial constituencies) to protect the Fijians. On 10 October 1970 Fiji became a fully independent nation and the first Fijian governor-general was appointed in 1973—none other than Ratu Sir George Cakobau, great-grandson of the chief who had ceded Fiji to Queen Victoria 99 years previously.

Political Development

During the 1940s Ratu Sir Lala Sukuna, paramount chief of Lau, played a key role in the creation of a separate administration for indigenous Fijians, with native land (83% of Fiji) under its jurisdiction. In 1954 he formed the Fijian Association to support the British governor against Indian demands for equal representation. In 1960 the National Federation Party (NFP) was formed to represent Indian cane farmers.

In 1966 the Alliance Party, a coalition of the Fijian Association, the General Electors' Association (representing Europeans, part-Fijians, and Chinese), and the Fiji Indian Alliance (a minority Indian group) won the legislative assembly elections. In 1970 Alliance Party leader Ratu Sir Kamisese Mara led Fiji into independence and in 1972 his party won Fiji's first post-independence elections. Ratu Mara served as prime minister almost continuously until the 1987 elections.

The formation of the Fiji Labor Party (FLP), headed by Dr. Timoci Bavadra, in July 1985 dramatically altered the political landscape. Fiji's previously nonpolitical trade unions had finally come behind a party that campaigned on bread-and-butter issues rather than race. Late in 1986 Labor and the NFP formed a coalition with the aim of defeating the Alliance in the next election. In the 12 April 1987 elections the Coalition won 28 of 52 House of Representatives seats; 19 of the 28 elected Coalition members were Indians. What swung the election away from Alliance was not a change in Indian voting patterns but support for Labor from urban Fijians and part-Fijians, which cost Alliance four previously "safe" seats around Suva.

The Coalition cabinet had a majority of Indian members, but all positions of vital Fijian interest (Lands, Fijian Affairs, Labor and Immigration, Education, Agriculture and Rural Development) went to indigenous Fijian legislators, though none of them was a traditional chief. Coalition's progressive policies marked quite a switch from the conservatism of the Alliance—a new generation of political leadership dedicated to tackling the day-to-day problems of people of all races rather than perpetuating the privileges of the old chiefly oligarchy.

The First Coup

After the election the extremist Fiji-for-Fijians Taukei (landowners) movement launched a destabilization campaign by throwing barricades across highways, organizing protest rallies and marches, and carrying out firebombings. On 24 April 1987 Senator Inoke Tabua and former Alliance cabinet minister Apisai Tora organized a march of 5,000 Fijians through Suva to protest "Indian domination" of the new government. Mr. Tora told a preparatory meeting for the demonstration that Fijians must "act now" to avoid ending up as "deprived as Australia's aborigines." (In fact, under the 1970 constitution the Coalition government would have had no way of changing Fiji's land laws without indigenous Fijian consent.) During the following weeks five gasoline bombs were thrown against government offices, though no one was injured. On 13 May 1987 Alliance Senator Jona Qio was arrested for arson.

At 1000 on Thursday 14 May 1987 Lt. Col. Sitiveni Rabuka (pronounced Rambuka), an ambitious officer whose career was stalled at number three in the Fiji army, and 10 heavily armed soldiers dressed in fatigues, their faces covered by gas masks, entered the House of Parliament in Suva. Rabuka ordered Dr. Bavadra and the Coalition members to follow a soldier out of the building, and when Dr. Bavadra hesitated the soldiers raised their guns. The legislators were loaded into army trucks and taken to Royal Fiji Military Forces headquarters. There was no bloodshed, though Rabuka later confirmed that his troops would have opened fire had there been any resistance. At a press conference five hours after the coup, Rabuka claimed he had acted to prevent violence and had no political ambitions of his own.

Australia and New Zealand promptly denounced the region's first military coup. Governor-General Ratu Sir Penaia Ganilau attempted to reverse the situation by declaring a state of emergency and ordering the mutineers to return to their barracks. They refused to obey. The next day the *Fiji Sun* ran a black-bordered editorial that declared, "Democracy died in Fiji yesterday. What right has a third-ranking officer to attack the sacred institutions of Parliament? What right has he to presume he knows best how this country shall be governed? The answer is none." Soon after, Rabuka's troops descended on both daily papers and ordered publication suspended. Journalists were evicted from the buildings.

Later that day Rabuka named a 15-member Council of Ministers, chaired by himself, to govern Fiji, with former Alliance prime minister Ratu Mara as foreign minister. Significantly, Rabuka was the only military officer on the council; most of the others were members of Ratu Mara's defeated administration. Rabuka claimed he had acted to "safeguard the Fijian land issue and the Fijian way of life."

On 19 May Dr. Bavadra and the other kidnapped members of his government were released after the governor-general announced a deal negotiated with Rabuka to avoid the possibility of foreign intervention. Rabuka's Council of Ministers was replaced by a 19-member caretaker Advisory Council appointed by the Great Council of Chiefs, which would govern until new elections could take place. The council would be headed by Ratu Ganilau, with Rabuka in charge of Home Affairs and the security forces. Only two seats were offered to Dr. Bavadra's government and they were refused.

Until the coup the most important mission of the Royal Fiji Defense Force was service in South Lebanon and the Sinai with peacekeeping operations. Half of the 2,600-member Fiji army was on rotating duty there, the Sinai force financed by the U.S., the troops in Lebanon by the United Nations. During WW II Fiji Indians refused to join the army unless they received the same pay as European recruits; indigenous Fijians had no such reservations and the force has been 95% Fijian ever since. Service in the strife-torn Middle East gave the Fiji military a unique preparation for its destabilizing role in Fiji itself. (Not many people outside Fiji realize that, after Australia and New Zealand, Lebanon is the foreign country indigenous Fijians know best.)

The Second Coup

In July and August 1987 a committee set up by Governor-General Ganilau studied proposals for constitutional reform, and on 4 September talks began at Government House in Suva between Alliance and Coalition leaders under the chairmanship of Ratu Ganilau. With no hope of a consensus on a revised constitution the talks were aimed at preparing for new elections.

Then, on Friday, 26 September 1987, Rabuka struck again, just hours before the governor-general was to announce a government of national unity to rule Fiji until new elections could be held. The plan, arduously developed over four months and finally approved by veteran political leaders on all sides, would probably have resulted in Rabuka being sacked. Rabuka quickly threw out the 1970 constitution and pronounced himself "head of state." Some 300 prominent community leaders were arrested and Ratu Ganilau was confined to Government House. Newspapers were shut down, trade unions repressed, the judiciary suspended, the public service purged, the activities of political opponents restricted, a curfew imposed, and the first cases of torture reported.

At midnight on 7 October 1987 Rabuka declared Fiji a republic. Rabuka's new Council of Ministers included Taukei extremists Apisai Tora and Filipe Bole, Fijian Nationalist Party leader Sakeasi Butadroka, and other marginal figures. Rabuka appeared to have backing in the Great Council of Chiefs, which wanted a return to the style of customary rule threatened by the Indian presence and Western democracy. On 16 October Ratu Ganilau resigned as governor-general and two days later Fiji was expelled from the British Commonwealth. On 6 November Rabuka allowed *The Fiji Times* to resume publication after it pledged self-censorship, but the more independent *Fiji Sun* has never appeared again.

The Republic of Fiji

Realizing that Taukei/military rule was a recipe for disaster, on 5 December 1987 Rabuka appointed Ratu Ganilau president and Ratu Mara prime minister of his new republic. The 21-member cabinet included 10 members of Rabuka's military regime, four of them army officers. Rabuka himself (now a self-styled brigadier) was once

again Minister of Home Affairs. This interim government set itself a deadline of two years to frame a new constitution and return Fiji to freely elected representative government. By mid-1988 the army had been expanded into a highly disciplined 6,000-member force loyal to Brigadier Rabuka, who left no doubt he would intervene a third time if his agenda was not followed. The Great Council of Chiefs was to decide on Fiji's republican constitution.

The coups transformed the Fijian economy. In 1987 Fiji experienced 11% negative growth in the gross domestic product. To slow the flight of capital the Fiji dollar was devalued 17.75% on 30 June 1987 and 15.25% on 7 October, and inflation, which had been less than two percent before the coups, was up to 11.9% by the end of 1988. At the same time the public service (half the workforce) had to accept a 25% wage cut as government spending was slashed. Food prices skyrocketed, causing serious problems for many families. At the end of 1987 the per capita average income was 11% *below* what it had been in 1980. Between 1986 and 1996 some 58,300 Indians left Fiji for Australia, Canada, New Zealand, and the United States. Nearly three-quarters of Fiji's administrators and managers, and a quarter of all professional, technical, and clerical workers departed taking tens of millions of dollars with them, a crippling loss for a country with a total population of less than 750,000.

On the other hand, the devaluations and wage-cutting measures, combined with the creation of a tax-free exporting sector and the encouragement of foreign investment, brought about an economic recovery by 1990. At the expense of democracy, social justice, and racial harmony, Fiji embarked on a standard IMF/World Bank-style structural readjustment program. In 1992 the imposition of a 10% value-added tax (VAT) shifted the burden of taxation from rich to poor, standard IMF dogma.

Interim Government

In May 1989 the interim government eased Sunday restrictions on work, trading, and sports. The nominal head of the unelected interim government, Ratu Mara, considered Rabuka an unpredictable upstart and insisted that he choose between politics or military service. Thus in late 1989, the general and two army colonels were

dropped from the cabinet, though Rabuka kept his post as army commander.

On 25 July 1990 President Ganilau promulgated a new constitution approved by the Great Council of Chiefs, which gave the chiefs the right to appoint the president and 24 of the 34 members of the Senate. The president had executive authority and appointed the prime minister from among the ethnic Fijian members of the House of Representatives. Under this constitution the 70-member House of Representatives was elected directly, with voting racially segregated. Ethnic Fijians were granted 37 seats from constituencies gerrymandered to ensure the dominance of the eastern chiefs. The constitution explicitly reserved the posts of president, prime minister, and army chief for ethnic Fijians. Christianity was made the official religion and Rabuka's troops were granted amnesty for any crimes committed during the 1987 coups. The Coalition promptly rejected this supremacist constitution as undemocratic and racist.

Not satisfied with control of the Senate, in early 1991 the Great Council of Chiefs decided to project their power into the lower house through the formation of the Soqosoqo ni Vakavulewa ni Taukei (SVT), commonly called the Fijian Political Party. Meanwhile Fiji's multiethnic unions continued to rebuild their strength by organizing garment workers and leading strikes in the mining and sugar industries.

In June 1991 Major-General Rabuka rejected an offer from Ratu Mara to join the cabinet as Minister of Home Affairs and co-deputy prime minister, since it would have meant giving up his military power base. Instead Rabuka attempted to widen his political appeal by making public statements in support of striking gold miners and cane farmers, and even threatening a third coup.

By now Rabuka's ambition to become prime minister was obvious, and his new role as a populist rabble-rouser seemed designed to outflank both the Labor Party and the chiefs (Rabuka himself is a commoner). President Ganilau (Rabuka's paramount chief) quickly applied pressure, and in July the volatile general reversed himself and accepted the cabinet posts he had so recently refused. As a condition for reentering the government, Rabuka was forced to resign as army commander and the president's son, Major-General Epeli Ganilau, was appointed his successor. With Rabuka out of the army everyone breathed a little easier, and the chiefs decided to co-opt a potential troublemaker by electing Rabuka president of the SVT.

Return to Democracy

The long-awaited parliamentary elections took place in late May 1992, and the SVT captured 30 of the 37 indigenous Fijian seats. Another five went to Fijian nationalists while the 27 Indian seats were split between the NFP with 14 and the FLP with 13. The five other races' seats went to the General Voters Party (GVP).

Just prior to the election, Ratu Mara retired from party politics and was named vice-president of Fiji by the Great Council of Chiefs. An intense power struggle then developed in the SVT between Ratu Mara's chosen successor as prime minister, former finance minister Josevata Kamikamica, and ex-general Rabuka. Since the SVT lacked a clear majority in the 70-seat house, coalition partners had to be sought, and in a remarkable turn of events populist Rabuka gained the support of the FLP by offering concessions to the trade unions and a promise to review the constitution and land leases. Thus Sitiveni Rabuka became prime minister thanks to the very party he had ousted from power at gunpoint exactly five years before!

The SVP formed a coalition with the GVP, but in November 1993 the Rabuka government was defeated in a parliamentary vote of no confidence over the budget, leading to fresh elections in February 1994. In these, Rabuka's SVT increased its representation to 31 seats. Many Indians had felt betrayed by FLP backing of Rabuka's prime ministership in 1992, and FLP representation dropped to seven seats, compared to 20 for the NFP.

Ratu Ganilau died of leukemia in December 1993, and Ratu Mara was sworn in as president in January 1994. Meanwhile, Rabuka cultivated a pragmatic image to facilitate his international acceptance in the South Pacific, and within Fiji itself he demonstrated his political prowess by holding out a hand of reconciliation to the Indian community. The 1990 constitution had called for a constitutional review before 1997, and in 1995 a three-member commission was appointed led by Sir Paul Reeves, a former governor-general of New Zealand, together with Mr. Tomasi Vakatora representing the Rabuka government and Mr. Brij Lal for the opposition.

The report of the commission titled *Towards a United Future* was submitted in September 1996. It recommended a return to the voting system outlined in the 1970 constitution with some members of parliament elected from racially divided communal constituencies and others from open ridings with racially mixed electorates. The commissioners suggested that the post of prime minister no longer be explicitly reserved for an indigenous Fijian but simply for the leader of the largest grouping in parliament of whatever race.

The report was passed to a parliamentary committee for study, and in May 1997 all sides agreed to a power-sharing formula to resolve Fiji's constitutional impasse. The number of guaranteed seats for indigenous Fijians in the lower house was reduced from 37 to 23, and voting across racial lines was instituted in another third of the seats. The prime minister was to be required to form a cabinet composed of ministers from all parties in proportion to their representation in parliament—a form of power sharing unique in modern democracy. Nearly half the members of the senate and the country's president would continue to be appointed by the Great Council of Chiefs. Human rights guarantees were included. The Constitution Amendment Bill passed both houses of parliament unanimously, and was promulgated into law by President Mara on 25 July 1997. In July 1998 the new constitution formally took effect. In recognition of the rare national consensus that had been achieved, Fiji was welcomed back into the British Commonwealth in October 1997.

In May 1999, 400,000 Fijians voted in the first election under the 1998 constitution. Although Rabuka himself won a seat, his SVT Party won only eight of the 71 parliamentary seats. The National Federation Party, which had allied itself with Rabuka, was wiped out by the Labor Party, which took 37 seats. Labor leader Mahendra Chaudhry was appointed prime minister—the first Fiji Indian ever to occupy the post. Among the seven women elected to parliament were the widow of ex-prime minister Timoci Bavadra and the daughter of President Mara. Also elected (for Labor) was a Fiji Indian named Anjad Ali who hijacked an Air New Zealand jumbo jet to protest the 1987 coup. The changes that this remarkable political turnabout will bring to Fiji remain to be seen.

Government

Fiji's constitution provides for a parliamentary system of government with a 71-seat House of Representatives or "lower house" consisting of 46 members from communal ridings and 25 from multiracial ridings with elections every five years. Twenty-three communal seats are reserved for indigenous Fijians, 19 for Fiji Indians, three for general electors (part-Fijians, Europeans, Chinese, etc.), and one for Rotumans. Voting is compulsory (F$50 fine for failing to vote). The 32-member "upper house" or Senate has 14 members appointed by the Great Council of Chiefs, nine by the prime minister, eight by the leader of the opposition, and one by the Council of Rotuma. Any legislation effecting the rights of indigenous Fijians must be approved by nine of the 14 senators appointed by the chiefs.

Aside from the national government, there's a well-developed system of local government. On the Fijian side, the basic unit is the village *(koro)* represented by a village herald *(turaga-ni-koro)* chosen by consensus. The 1,169 villages and 483 settlements are grouped into 189 districts *(tikina),* the districts into 14 provinces *(yasana),* the provinces into four administrative divisions: central, eastern, northern, and western. The executive head of a provincial council is known as a *roko tui,* and each division except eastern is headed by a commissioner assisted by a number of district officers. The Micronesians of Rabi and Polynesians of Rotuma govern themselves through island councils of their own. Ten city and town councils also function.

ECONOMY

Fiji has a diversified economy based on tourism, sugar production, garment manufacturing, gold mining, timber, commercial fishing, and coconut products. Although eastern Viti Levu and the Lau Group have long dominated the country politically, western Viti Levu remains Fiji's economic powerhouse, with sugar, tourism, timber, and gold mining all concentrated there.

Sugar

Almost all of Fiji's sugar is produced by small independent Indian farmers on contract to the government-owned Fiji Sugar Corporation, which took over from the Australian-owned Colonial Sugar Refining Company in 1973. Some 23,000 farmers cultivate cane on holdings averaging 4.5 hectares leased from indigenous Fijians. The corporation owns 595 km of 0.610-meter narrow-gauge railway, which it uses to carry the cane to the mills at Lautoka, Ba, Rakiraki, and Labasa. Nearly half a million metric tonnes of sugar are exported annually to Britain, Malaysia, Japan, and other countries, providing direct employment for 26,000 people and indirectly for another 30,000. Workers cutting cane earn F$6 a day and two meals. A distillery at Lautoka produces rum and other liquors from the by-products of sugar. Over the next few years the viability of Fiji's sugar industry may be badly shaken as European Union import quotas are phased out (under the Lomé Convention, 163,000 metric tonnes of Fijian sugar are sold to the E.U. each year at fixed prices far above world market levels). If lease payments were concurrently increased, thousands of Fiji's cane growers would face bankruptcy. In 1998 the drought associated with El Niño cut Fiji's sugar harvest to a third its normal size.

Timber

Timber is increasingly important as tens of thousands of hectares of softwood planted in western Viti Levu and Vanua Levu by the Fiji Pine Commission and private landowners in the late 1970s reach maturity. In addition, around 30,000 hectares of hardwood (74% of it mahogany) planted in southeastern Viti Levu after 1952 by the British is almost ready for harvesting (another 20,000 hectares in central Vanua Levu will be mature in a decade). Fiji exports about F$40 million a year in sawed lumber and wood chips (the export of raw logs was banned in 1987). The pine and mahogany projects have had the corollary benefit of reducing pressure on the natural forests to supply Fiji's timber needs.

Fishing

Commercial fishing is important, with a government-subsidized tuna cannery at Levuka supplied in part by Fiji's own fleet of 17 longline vessels. The 15,000 metric tonnes of canned skipjack and albacore tuna produced each year comprise Fiji's fifth-largest export, shipped mostly to Britain and Canada (see **Ovalau** for more information). In addition, 3,000 tonnes of chilled yellowfin tuna is air freighted to Hawaii and Japan to serve the sashimi market.

Mining

Mining activity centers on gold from Vatukoula on northern Viti Levu and from Mt. Kasi on Vanua Levu with other gold fields awaiting development (in 1998 Mt. Kasi closed due to low world prices). Since 1984 Placer Pacific has spent US$10 million exploring the extensive low-grade copper deposits at Namosi, 30 km northwest of Suva, but in 1997, despite offers of near tax-free status from the government, the company put the US$1-billion project on hold as uneconomic.

Rice and Copra

Fiji now grows almost half the rice it needs and is trying to become self-sufficient. Much of the rice is grown around Nausori and Navua and on Vanua Levu. Most of Fiji's copra is produced in Lau, Lomaiviti, Taveuni, and Vanua Levu, half by European or part-Fijian planters and the rest by indigenous Fijian villagers. Copra production has slipped from 40,000 tonnes a year in the 1950s to about 10,000 tonnes today due to the low prices paid to producers.

Garment Industry

The garment industry employs 15,000, with female workers earning an average of F$30 a week. At peak periods the factories operate three shifts, seven days a week. Women working in the industry have complained of body searches and sexual harassment, with those who protest or organize industrial action fired and blacklisted. About 1,000 recently arrived Asian workers are also employed in the factories. The clothing produced by the 68 companies in the sector is exported mostly to Australia and New Zealand, where partial duty- and quota-free entry is allowed under the South Pacific Regional Trade and Economic Cooperation Agreement (SPARTECA) for products with at least 50% local content, and some manufacturers in those countries have moved their factories to Fiji to take advantage of the low labor costs. SPARTECA rules prevent local manufacturers from importing quality fabrics from outside the region, limiting them to the bottom end of the market.

Other Manufacturing

Food processors and furniture and toy makers are also prominent in the tax-free exporting sector. Until recently it was believed that manufacturing would eventually overtake both sugar and tourism as the main source of income for the country, but the "globalization" of trade and progressive reduction of tariffs worldwide is cutting into Fiji's competitiveness. SPARTECA's local-content rule discourages local companies from reducing costs by introducing labor-saving technology, condemning them to obsolescence in the long term.

Agriculture

Aside from this cash economy, subsistence agriculture makes an important contribution to the life of indigenous Fijians in rural areas. Most are involved in subsistence agriculture, with manioc, taro, yams, sweet potato, and corn the principal subsistence crops. Kava is the fastest growing agricultural crop and in 1996 F$2.5 million worth of the roots was exported to Germany, the U.S., and other countries where they're used by major pharmaceutical firms to make antidepressants and muscle-relaxing drugs. Large European, American, and Japanese corporations have filed multiple patents in an attempt to monopolize the many uses of the plant. It's believed that kava could eventually overtake sugar as a moneymaker unless new plantations in Hawaii, Australia, and Mexico steal the market.

Economic Problems

Yet, in spite of all this potential, unemployment is a major social problem as four times more young

people leave school than there are new jobs to take them. Immediately after the 1987 coups Fiji's currency was devalued 33% and in January 1998 the Fiji dollar was devalued another 20%. These moves increased the country's competitiveness by giving exporters more Fiji dollars for their products and encouraged tourism while lowering the real incomes of ordinary Fijians. To stimulate industry, firms that export 95% of their production are granted 13-year tax holidays, the duty-free import of materials, and freedom to repatriate capital and profits.

Trade and Aid

Fiji's balance of trade has improved in recent years, and although the country still imports 30% more than it exports, much of the imbalance is resold to tourists and foreign airlines who pay in foreign exchange. Raw sugar is the nation's largest visible export earner, followed by garments, unrefined gold, canned fish, wood chips, molasses, sawed timber, and ginger, in that order. Yet trade imbalances still exist with Australia, Japan, and New Zealand.

Mineral fuels used to eat up much of Fiji's import budget, but this declined when the Monasavu Hydroelectric Project and other self-sufficiency measures came on-line in the 1980s. Manufactured goods, motor vehicles, food, petroleum products, and chemicals account for most of the import bill.

Fiji is the least dependent South Pacific nation. Overseas aid totals only US$50 million a year or about US$65 per capita (as compared to several thousand dollars per capita in Tahiti-Polynesia). Development aid is well diversified among more than a dozen donors; the largest amounts come from the European Union (US$20.5 million), Australia (US$16.8 million), New Zealand (US$4.6 million), and Japan (US$3.8 million). Canadian and U.S. aid to Fiji is negligible. The New Zealand Government deserves a lot of credit for devoting much of its limited aid budget to the creation of national parks and reserves. Aside from conventional aid, in 1996 Fiji earned F$11.4 million from United Nations peacekeeping duties while the army's role in other multinational forces brought in further F$5.8 million (to date about 20 Fijian soldiers have been killed in Lebanon). Some 3,650 people serve in Fiji's military (800 of them overseas) costing the country more than F$40 million a year.

In 1995 Fiji's financial standing was severely shaken when it was announced that the government-owned National Bank of Fiji was holding hundreds of millions of dollars in bad debts resulting from politically motivated loans to indigenous Fijian and Rotuman politicians and businesspeople. The subsequent run on deposits cost the bank another F$20 million, and the government was forced to step in to save the bank and cover its losses. In 1996 F$80 million was spent on the bailout and in 1997 another F$133 million (or 12% of the 1997 budget) was diverted from development projects to cover it. Rising public indebtedness and deficit spending are discouraging foreign investment, and Fiji's Customs and Excise Department is said to be riddled with corruption. By late 1998, government debt stood at F$1,424 million, 82% of it from local sources. The 1999 elections will bring in Fiji's first democratic government in a dozen years and it will have its hands full putting the country back on course.

Tourism

Tourism has been the leading money-maker since 1989, earning more than F$500 million a year—more than sugar and gold combined. Tourism surpassed sugar in 1989, and in the five years that followed, its contribution to the gross domestic product increased from 28% to 32%. In 1998 some 371,342 tourists visited Fiji—more than twice as many as visited Tahiti and 15 times as many as visited Tonga. Things appear in better perspective, however, when Fiji is compared to Hawaii, which is about the same size in surface area. Overpacked Hawaii gets nearly seven million tourists, more than 20 times as many as Fiji.

Gross receipts figures from tourism are often misleading, as 56 cents on every dollar is repatriated overseas by foreign investors or used to pay for tourism-related imports. In real terms, sugar is far more profitable for Fiji. In 1997 paid employment in the hotel industry totaled 6,511 (5,358 full-time and 1,153 part-time employees) with an estimated 40,000 jobs in all sectors related to tourism. Management of the top end hotels is usually expatriate, with Fiji Indians filling technical positions such as maintenance, cooking, accounting, etc., and indigenous Fijians working the high-profile positions such as receptionists, waiters, guides, and housekeepers. Fiji has 220 licensed hotels with a total of 5,861 rooms, more than a third of the South Pacific's tourist beds. Most of the large resort hotels in Fiji are foreign owned (although the Tanoa and Cathay hotel chains are local Fiji-based enterprises). The Fiji Government is doing all it can to promote luxury hotel development by offering 20-year tax holidays on new projects.

The main tourist resorts are centered along the Coral Coast of Viti Levu and in the Mamanuca Islands off Nadi/Lautoka. For years the Fiji government declared there would never be any hotel development in the Yasawa and Lau groups, but several resorts exist there now (including one owned by the president). Investment by the U.S. hotel chains is on the increase as Japanese firms pull out. In 1996 ITT-Sheraton bought two luxury hotels on Nadi's Denarau Island from a group of Japanese banks, and Hyatt and Hilton have announced multimillion-dollar investments in new hotels. Outrigger Hotels of Hawaii is building a major resort on the Coral Coast. About 23% of Fiji's tourists come from Australia, 19% from New Zealand, 13% from Japan, 11% from the U.S., nine percent from continental Europe, eight percent from Britain, and four percent from Canada. The vast majority of visitors arrive in Fiji to/from Auckland, Sydney, Tokyo, Honolulu, Los Angeles, and Vancouver.

THE PEOPLE

The Fijians

Fiji is a transitional zone between Polynesia and Melanesia. The Fijians bear a physical resemblance to the Melanesians, but like the Polynesians, they have hereditary chiefs, patrilineal descent, a love of elaborate ceremonies, and a fairly homogeneous language and culture. Fijians have interbred with Polynesians to the extent that they have lighter skin and larger stature than other Melanesians. In the interior and west of Viti Levu where the contact was less, the people tend to be somewhat darker and smaller than the easterners. Yet Fijians still have Melanesian frizzy hair, while most—but not all—Polynesians have straight hair.

The Fijians live in villages along the rivers or coast, with anywhere from 50 to 400 people led by a hereditary chief. To see a Fijian family living in an isolated house in a rural area is uncommon. The traditional thatched *bure* is fast disappearing

Fijian boys, Singatoka Valley

DAVID STANLEY

from Fiji as villagers rebuild in tin and panel (often following destructive cyclones). Grass is not as accessible as cement, takes more time to repair, and is less permanent.

Away from the three largest islands the population is almost totally Fijian. *Mataqali* (clans) are grouped into *yavusa* of varying rank and function. Several *yavusa* form a *vanua*, a number of which make up a *matanitu*. Chiefs of the most important *vanua* are known as high chiefs. In western Viti Levu the groups are smaller, and outstanding commoners can always rise to positions of power and prestige reserved for high chiefs in the east.

Fijians work communal land individually, not as a group. Each Fijian is assigned a piece of native land. They grow most of their own food in village gardens, and only a few staples such as tea, sugar, flour, etc., are imported from Suva and sold in local coop stores. A visit to one of these stores will demonstrate just how little they import and how self-sufficient they are. Fishing, village maintenance work, and ceremonial presentations are done together. While village life provides a form of collective security, individuals are discouraged from rising above the group. Fijians who attempt to set up a business are often stifled by the demands of relatives and friends. The Fijian custom of claiming favors from members of one's own group is known as *kerekere*. This pattern makes it difficult for Fijians to compete with Indians, for whom life has always been a struggle. A Fijian will stand and wait his turn while an Indian will crowd and fight to be first.

The Indians

Most of the Indians now in Fiji are descended from indentured laborers recruited in Bengal and Bihar a century ago. In the first year of the system (1879) some 450 Indians arrived in Fiji to work in the cane fields. By 1883 the total had risen to 2,300 and in 1916, when the last indentured laborers arrived, 63,000 Indians were present in the colony. In 1920 the indenture system was finally terminated, the cane fields were divided into four-hectare plots, and the Indian workers became tenant farmers on land owned by Fijians. Indians continued to arrive until 1931, though many of these later arrivals were Gujerati or Sikh businesspeople.

In 1940 the Indian population stood at 98,000, still below the Fijian total of 105,000, but by the 1946 census Indians had outstripped Fijians 120,000 to 117,000—making Fijians a minority in their own home. In the wake of the coups the relative proportions changed as thousands of Indians emigrated to North America and Australia, and by early 1989 indigenous Fijians once again outnumbered Fiji Indians. The 1996 census reported that Fiji's total population was 772,655, of which 51.1% were Fijian while 43.6% were Indian (at the 1986 census 46% were Fijian and 48.7% Indian). Between 1986 and 1996 the number of Indians in Fiji actually decreased by 12,125 with the heaviest falls in rural areas. Aside from emigration, the more widespread use of contraceptives by Indian women has led to a lower fertility rate. The crude birth rate per 1,000 population is 28.4 for Fijians and 21.0 for Fiji Indians.

Unlike the village-based Fijians, a majority of Indians are concentrated in the cane-growing areas and live in isolated farmhouses, small settlements, or towns. Many Indians also live in Suva, as do an increasing number of Fijians. Within the Fiji Indian community there are divisions of Hindu (80%) versus Muslim (20%), north Indian versus south Indian, and Gujerati versus the rest. The Sikhs and Gujeratis have always been somewhat of an elite as they immigrated freely to Fiji outside the indenture system.

The different groups have kept alive their ancient religious beliefs and rituals. Hindus tend to marry within their caste, although the restrictions on behavior, which characterize the caste system in India, have disappeared. Indian marriages are often arranged by the parents, while Fijians generally choose their own partners. Rural Indians still associate most closely with other members of their extended patrilineal family group, and Hindu and Muslim religious beliefs still restrict Indian women to a position subservient to men.

It's often said that Indians concentrate on accumulation while Fijians emphasize distribution. Yet Fiji's laws themselves encourage Indians to invest their savings in business by preventing them or anyone else from purchasing native communal land. High-profile Indian dominance of the retail sector has distorted the picture and the reality is that the per-capita incomes of ordinary indigenous Fijians and Fiji Indians are not that different. The Fijians are not "poor" because they are exploited by Indians; the two groups simply amass their wealth in different ways. In large measure, Fiji's excellent service and retail industries exist thanks to the thrift and efficiency of the Indians. When you consider their position in a land where most have lived four generations and where they form almost half the population, where many laws are slanted against them, and where all natural resources are in the hands of others, their industriousness and patience are admirable.

Other Groups

The 5,000 Fiji-born Europeans or *Kai Vavalagi* are descendants of Australians and New Zealanders who came to create cotton, sugar, or copra plantations in the 19th century. Many married Fijian women, and the 13,000 part-Fijians or *Kai Loma* of today are the result. There is almost no intermarriage between Fijians *(Kai Viti)* and Fiji Indians *(Kai India)*. Many other Europeans are present in Fiji on temporary contracts or as tourists.

Most of the 5,000 Chinese in Fiji are descended from free settlers who came to set up small businesses a century ago, although since 1987 there has been an influx of Chinese from mainland China who were originally admitted to operate market gardens but who have since moved into the towns. Fiji Chinese tend to intermarry freely with the other racial groups.

The people of Rotuma, a majority of whom now live in Suva, are Polynesians. On neighboring islands off Vanua Levu are the Micronesians of Rabi (from Kiribati) and the Polynesians of Kioa (from Tuvalu). The descendants of Solomon Islanders blackbirded during the 19th century still live in communities near Suva, Levuka, and Labasa. The Tongans in Lau and other Pacific islanders who have immigrated to Fiji make this an ethnic crossroads of the Pacific.

Social Conditions

Some 98% of the country's population was born in Fiji. The partial breakdown in race relations after the Rabuka coups was a tragedy for Fiji, though racial antagonism has been exaggerated and the different ethnic groups have always gotten along remarkably well together, with little animosity. You may hear individuals make disparaging remarks about the other group, but it's highly unlikely you'll witness any real confrontations.

As important as race are the variations between rich and poor, or urban (46%) and rural (54%). Avenues for future economic growth are limited, and there's chronic unemployment. The lack of work is reflected in an increasing crime rate. Two-thirds of the rural population is without electricity. Although Fiji's economy grew by 25% between 1977 and 1991, the number of people living in poverty increased by two-thirds over the same period. The imposition in 1992 of a 10% value-added tax combined with reductions in income tax and import duties shifted the burden of taxation from the haves to the have nots. A quarter of the population now lives in poverty, and contrary to the myth of Indian economic domination, Fiji Indians are more likely to be facing poverty than members of other groups, as the beggars on the streets of Nadi and Suva attest. Single-parent urban families cut off from the extended-family social safety net are the group most affected, especially women trying to raise families on their own. As a Fijian woman on Taveuni told the author: "Life is easy in Fiji, only money is a problem."

Literacy is high at 87%. Primary education is compulsory for all children aged 6-13 but many schools are still racially segregated. More than 100 church-operated schools receive government subsidies. The Fiji Institute of Technology was founded at Suva in 1963, followed by the University of the South Pacific in 1968. The university serves the 12 Pacific countries that contribute to its costs. Medical services in Fiji are heavily subsidized. The main hospitals are at Labasa, Lautoka, and Suva, though smaller hospitals, health centers, and nursing stations are scattered around the country. The most common infectious diseases are influenza, gonorrhea, and syphilis. At birth male citizens of Fiji have a life expectancy of 72 years, the longest in the South Pacific, and women average 75 years.

Land Rights

When Fiji became a British colony in 1874, the land was divided between white settlers who had bought plantations and the *taukei ni gele,* the Fijian "owners of the soil." The government assumed title to the balance. Today the alienated (privately owned) plantation lands are known as "freehold" land—about 10% of the total. Another seven percent is Crown land and the remaining 83% is inalienable Fijian communal land, which can be leased (about 30% is) but may never be sold. Compare this 83% (much of it not arable) with only three percent Maori land in New Zealand and almost zero native Hawaiian land. Land ownership has provided the Fijians with a security that allows them to preserve their traditional culture, unlike indigenous peoples in most other countries.

Communal land is administered on behalf of some 6,600 clan groups *(mataqali)* by the Native Land Trust Board, a government agency established in 1940. The NLTB retains 25% of the lease money to cover administration, and a further 10% is paid directly to regional hereditary chiefs. In 1966 the Agricultural Landlord and Tenant Act (ALTA) increased the period for which native land can be leased from 10 to 30 years. The 30-year leases began coming up for renewal in 1997, and from 2000 to 2005 28% of the leases will expire (another 19% will expire from 2006 to 2010). Many Fijian clans say they want their land back so they can farm it themselves, and Fiji's 23,000 Indian sugarcane farmers are becoming highly apprehensive. If rents are greatly increased or the leases terminated, Fiji's sugar industry could be badly damaged and an explosive social situation created. This whole question has become the single most important issue in Fiji politics and in late 1997 a Joint Parliamentary Select Committee began looking into ALTA and the possible resettlement of Indian farmers whose leases cannot be extended.

At the First Constitutional Conference in 1965, Indian rights were promulgated, and the 1970 independence constitution asserted that everyone born in Fiji would be a citizen with equal rights. These rights are reaffirmed in the 1997 constitution. But land laws, right up to the present, have very much favored "Fiji for the Fijians." Fiji Indians have always accepted Fijian ownership of the land, provided they are granted satisfactory leases. Now that the leases seem endangered, many Indians fear they will be driven from the only land they've ever known. The stifling of land development may keep Fiji quaint for tourists, but it also condemns a large portion of the population of both races to backwardness and poverty.

Religion

The main religious groups in Fiji are Hindus (290,000), Methodists (265,000), Catholics (70,000), Muslims (62,000), Assemblies of God (33,000), and Seventh-Day Adventists (20,000). About 78% of indigenous Fijians are Methodist, 8.5% Catholic. Only two percent of Indians have converted to Christianity despite Methodist missionary efforts dating back to 1884.

Membership in the Assemblies of God and some other new Christian sects is growing quickly at the expense of the Methodists. Due to a change in government policies, the number of Mormon missionaries granted Fijian visas has increased tenfold since 1987, and 90% of the money used to support Mormon activities in Fiji comes from the church headquarters in Utah. The Seventh-Day Adventist Church operates the Fulton Teacher Training College at Nakalawaca just south of Korovou in Tailevu Province.

LANGUAGE

Fijian, a member of the Austronesian family of languages spoken from Easter Island to Madagascar, has more speakers than any other indigenous Pacific language. Fijian vowels are pronounced as in Latin or Spanish, while the consonants are similar to those of English. Syllables end in a vowel, and the next-to-last syllable is usually the one emphasized. Where two vowels appear together they are sounded separately. In 1835 two Methodist missionaries, David Cargill and William Cross, devised the form of written Fijian used in Fiji today. Since all consonants in Fijian are separated by vowels, they spelled *mb* as *b*, *nd* as *d*, *ng* as *g*, *ngg* as *q*, and *th* as *c*.

Though Cargill and Cross worked at Lakeba in the Lau Group, the political importance of tiny Bau Island just off Viti Levu caused the Bauan dialect of Fijian to be selected as the "official" version of the language, and in 1850 a dictionary and grammar were published. When the Bible was translated into Bauan that dialect's dominance was assured, and it is today's spoken and written Fijian. From 1920 to 1970 the use of Fijian was discouraged in favor of English, but since independence there has been a revival.

Hindustani or Hindi is the household tongue of most Fiji Indians. Fiji Hindi has diverged from that spoken in India with the adoption of many words from English and other Indian languages such as Urdu. Though a quarter of Fiji Indians are descended from immigrants from southern India where Tamil and Telegu are spoken, few use those languages today, even at home. Fiji Muslims speak Hindi out of practical considerations, though they might consider Urdu their mother tongue. In their spoken forms, Hindi and Urdu are very similar. English is the second official language in Fiji and is understood by almost everyone. All schools teach exclusively in English after the fourth grade. Fiji Indians and indigenous Fijians usually communicate with one another in English. Gilbertese is spoken by the Banabans of Rabi.

See the **Capsule Fijian Vocabulary** and the **Capsule Hindi Vocabulary** for some useful words and phrases.

CUSTOMS

Fijians and Fiji Indians are very tradition-oriented peoples who have retained a surprising number of their ancestral customs despite the flood of conflicting influences that have swept the Pacific over the past century. Rather than a melting pot where one group assimilated another, Fiji is a patchwork of varied traditions.

The obligations and responsibilities of Fijian village life include not only the erection and upkeep of certain buildings, but personal participation in the many ceremonies that give their lives meaning. Hindu Indians, on the other hand, practice firewalking and observe festivals such as Holi and Diwali, just as their forebears in India did for thousands of years.

Fijian Firewalking

In Fiji, both Fijians and Indians practice firewalking, with the difference being that the Fijians walk on heated stones instead of hot embers. Legends tell how the ability to walk on fire was first given to a warrior named Tui-na-viqalita from Beqa Island, just off the south coast of Viti Levu,

LOUISE FOOTE

a tanoa carved from a single block of vesi wood

who had spared the life of a spirit god he caught while fishing for eels. The freed spirit gave to Tui-na-viqalita the gift of immunity to fire. Today his descendants act as *bete* (high priests) of the rite of *vilavilairevo* (jumping into the oven). Only members of his tribe, the Sawau, perform the ceremony. The Tui Sawau lives at Dakuibeqa village on Beqa, but firewalking is now only performed at the resort hotels on Viti Levu.

Fijian firewalkers (men only) are not permitted to have sex or to eat any coconut for two weeks prior to a performance. A man whose wife is pregnant is also barred. In a circular pit about four meters across, hundreds of large stones are first heated by a wood fire until they're white-hot. If you throw a handkerchief on the stones, it will burst into flames. Much ceremony and chanting accompanies certain phases of the ritual, such as the moment when the wood is removed to leave just the white-hot stones. The men psych themselves up in a nearby hut, then emerge, enter the pit, and walk briskly once around it. Bundles of leaves and grass are then thrown on the stones and the men stand inside the steaming pit again to chant a final song. They seem to have complete immunity to pain and there's no trace of injury. The men appear to fortify themselves with the heat, to gain some psychic power from the ritual.

Indian Firewalking

By an extraordinary coincidence, Fiji Indians brought with them the ancient practice of religious firewalking. In southern India, firewalking occurs in the pre-monsoon season as a call to the goddess Kali (Durga) for rain. Fiji Indian firewalking is an act of purification, or fulfillment of a vow to thank the god for help in a difficult situation.

In Fiji firewalking is performed in most Hindu temples once a year, at full moon sometime between May and September according to the Hindu calendar. The actual event takes place on a Sunday at 1600 on the Suva side of Viti Levu, and at 0400 on the Nadi/Lautoka side. In August firewalking takes place at the Sangam Temple on Howell Rd., Suva. During the 10 festival days preceding the walk, participants remain in isolation, eat only unspiced vegetarian food, and spiritually prepare themselves. There are prayers at the temple in the early morning and group singing of religious stories evenings from Monday through Thursday. The yellow-clad devotees, their faces painted bright yellow and red, often pierce their cheeks or other bodily parts with spikes or three-pronged forks as part of the purification rites. Their faith is so strong they feel no pain.

The event is extremely colorful; drumming and chanting accompany the visual spectacle. Visitors are welcome to observe the firewalking, but since the exact date varies from temple to temple according to the phases of the moon (among other factors), you just have to keep asking to find out where and when it will take place. To enter the temple you must remove your shoes and any leather clothing.

The *Yaqona* Ceremony

Yaqona (kava), a tranquilizing, nonalcoholic drink that numbs the tongue and lips, comes from the *waka* (dried root) of the pepper plant *(Macropiper methysticum)*. This ceremonial preparation is the most honored feature of the formal life of Fijians, Tongans, and Samoans. It is performed with the utmost gravity according to a sacramental ritual to mark births, marriages, deaths, official visits, the installation of a new chief, etc.

New mats are first spread on the floor, on which is placed a handcarved *tanoa* (wooden bowl) nearly a meter wide. A long fiber cord decorated with cowry shells leads from the bowl to the guests of honor. At the end of the cord is a white cowry, which symbolizes a link to ancestral spirits. As many as 70 men take their places before the bowl. The officiants are adorned with tapa, fiber, and croton leaves, their torsos smeared with glistening coconut oil, their faces usually blackened.

The guests present a bundle of *waka* to the hosts, along with a short speech explaining their visit, a custom known as a *sevusevu*. The *sevusevu* is received by the hosts and acknowledged with a short speech of acceptance. The *waka* are then scraped clean and pounded in a *tabili* (mortar). Formerly they were chewed. Nowadays the pulp is put in a cloth sack and mixed with water in the *tanoa*. In the chiefly ceremony the *yaqona* is kneaded and strained through *vau* (hibiscus) fibers.

Kava drinking is an important form of Fijian entertainment and a way of structuring friendships and community relations. Even in government offices a bowl of grog is kept for the staff to take as a refreshment at *yaqona* breaks. Some say the Fijians have *yaqona* rather than blood in their veins. Excessive kava drinking over a long period can make the skin scaly and rough, a condition known as *kanikani*.

Visitors are often invited to participate in informal kava ceremonies. Clap once when the cupbearer offers you the *bilo* (cup), then take it in both hands and say *"bula"* just before the cup meets your lips. Clap three times after you drink. Even though you may not like the appearance or taste of the drink, do try to finish at least the first cup. Tip the cup to show you're done.

In formal situations, it's considered extremely bad manners to turn your back on a chief during a kava ceremony, to walk in front of the circle of people when entering or leaving, or to step over the long cord attached to the *tanoa*. Remember, you're a participant, not an onlooking tourist, so don't take photos if the ceremony is rather formal.

Presentation of the *Tabua*

The *tabua* is a tooth of the sperm whale. It was once presented when chiefs exchanged delegates at confederacy meetings and before conferences on peace or war. In recent times, the *tabua* is presented during chiefly *yaqona* ceremonies as a symbolic welcome for a respected visitor or guest or as a prelude to public business or modern-day official functions. On the village level, *tabuas* are still commonly presented to arrange marriages, to show sympathy at funerals, to request favors, to settle disputes, or simply to show respect.

Old *tabuas* are highly polished from continuous handling. The larger the tooth, the greater its ceremonial value. *Tabuas* are prized cultural property and may not be exported from Fiji. Endangered species laws prohibit their entry into the United States, Australia, and many other countries.

The Rising of the *Balolo*

Among all the Pacific island groups, this event takes place only in Samoa and Fiji. The *balolo* (*Eunice viridis*) is a segmented worm of the Coelomate order, considered a culinary delicacy throughout these islands—the caviar of the Pacific. It's about 45 cm long and lives deep in the fissures of coral reefs. Twice a year it releases an unusual "tail" that contains its eggs or sperm. The worm itself returns to the coral to regenerate a new reproductive tail. The rising of the *balolo* is a natural almanac that keeps both lunar and solar times and has a fixed day of appearance—even if a hurricane is raging—one night in the last quarter of the moon in October, and the corresponding night in November. It has never failed to appear on time for more than 100 years now, and you can even check your calendar by it.

Because this rising occurs with such mathematical certainty, Fijians are waiting in their boats to scoop the millions of writhing, reddish brown (male) and moss green (female) spawn from the water when they rise to the surface before dawn. Within an hour after the rising, the eggs and sperm are released to spawn the next generation of *balolo*. The free-swimming larvae seek a suitable coral patch to begin the cycle again. This is one of the most bizarre curiosities in the natural history of the South Pacific, and the southeast coast of Ovalau is a good place to observe it.

CONDUCT

It's a Fijian custom to smile when you meet a stranger and say something like "Good morning," or at least "Hello." Of course, you needn't do this in large towns, but you should almost everywhere else. If you meet someone you know, stop for a moment to exchange a few words. Men should always wear a shirt in town, and women should forgo halter tops, see-through dresses, and short shorts. Scanty dress in public shows a lack of respect; notice how the locals are dressed. Shorts are not proper dress for women in villages, so carry a *sulu* to cover up. Topless sunbathing by women is not allowed in Fiji.

Fijian villages are private property and it's important to get permission before entering one. Of course it's okay to continue along a road that passes through a village, but do ask before leaving the road. It's good manners to take off your hat while walking through a village, where only the chief is permitted to wear a hat. Some villagers also object to sunglasses. Objects such as backpacks, handbags, and cameras are better carried in your hands rather than slung over your shoulders. Alcohol is usually forbidden. Don't point at people in villages.

If you wish to surf off a village, picnic on their beach, or fish in their lagoon, you should also ask permission. You'll almost always be made most welcome and granted any favors you request if you present a *sevusevu* of kava roots to the village headman or chief. If you approach the Fijians with respect you're sure to be so treated in return.

Take off your shoes before entering a *bure* and stoop as you walk around inside. Clap three times when you join people already seated on mats on the floor. Men should sit cross-legged, women with their legs to the side. Sitting with your legs stretched out in front is insulting. Fijian villagers consider it offensive to walk in front of a person seated on the floor (pass behind) or to fail to say *tulou* (excuse me) as you go by. Don't stand up during a *sevusevu* to village elders. When you give a gift hold it out with both hands, not one hand. Never place your hand on another's head and don't sit in doorways.

Fijian children are very well behaved. There's no running or shouting when you arrive in a village, and they leave you alone if you wish. The Fijians love children, so don't hesitate to bring your own. You'll never have to worry about finding a baby-sitter. Just make sure your children understand the importance of being on their best behavior in the village. Do you notice how Fijians rarely shout? In Fiji, raising your voice is a sign of anger.

Dangers and Annoyances

In Suva, beware of the seemingly friendly Fijian men (usually with a small package or canvas bag in their hands) who will greet you on the street with a hearty *Bula!* These are "sword sellers" who will ask your name, quickly carve it on a mask, and then demand F$20 for a set that you could buy at a Nadi curio shop for F$5. Other times they'll try to engage you in conversation and may offer a "gift." Just say "thank you very much" and walk away from them quickly without accepting anything, as they can suddenly become unpleasant and aggressive. Their grotesque swords and masks themselves have nothing to do with Fiji.

Similarly, overly sociable people at bars may expect you to buy them drinks. In the main tourist centers such as Nadi and Suva, take care if a local invites you to visit their home as you may be seen mainly as a source of beer and other goods.

Although *The Fiji Times* is usually full of stories of violent crimes including assaults, robberies, and burglaries, it's partly the very novelty of these events that makes them worth reporting. Fiji is still a much safer country than the U.S. and tourists are not specifically targeted for attack, but normal precautions should still be taken. Keep to well-lit streets at night, take a taxi if you've had more than one drink, and steer clear of robust, poorly dressed Fijian men who may accost you on the street for no reason. Don't react if offered drugs. It's wise to keep valuables locked in your bag in hotel rooms.

Women should have few real problems traveling around Fiji on their own, so long as they're prepared to cope with frequent offers of marriage. Although a female tourist shouldn't have to face sexist violence the way a local woman might, it's smart to be defensive and to lie about where you're staying. If you want to be left alone, conservative dress and purposeful behavior will work to your advantage. In village situations seek the company of local women.

Littering is punished by a minimum F$40 fine and breaking bottles in public can earn six months in jail (unfortunately seldom enforced).

ON THE ROAD

HIGHLIGHTS

Fiji's many attractions are hard to shortlist but two outstanding natural features on the south side of Viti Levu are the Sigatoka Sand Dunes and the Navua River with its cliff-hugging rapids. Tavewa and Wayasewa in the Yasawa Group combine natural beauty with budget accommodations. Fiji's finest bus rides take you through open rolling countryside from Lautoka to Rakiraki, or across the mountains of Vanua Levu from Savusavu to Labasa. Without doubt, the most picturesque town is the old capital Levuka and Suva has some of the South Pacific's top nightlife. There are many candidates for best beach, reef, and outer island: all are tops. Two weeks is the absolute minimum amount of time required to get a feel for Fiji, and one month is much better.

Parks and Reserves

The **National Trust for Fiji** (Box 2089, Government Buildings, Suva; tel. 301-807, fax 305-092) administers eight national parks and historic sites. Of these the Sigatoka Sand Dunes National Park and the Waisali Nature Reserve near Savusavu both have visitor centers easily accessible by public bus. Koroyanitu National Park, inland from Lautoka, is also easily reached and has accommodations for hikers. Although not an official reserve, the forested area around Nadarivatu in central Viti Levu is similar. The nature reserves at Bouma and Lavena on the northeastern side of Taveuni feature unspoiled rainforests and waterfalls reached along hiking trails. Colo-i-Suva Forest Park behind Suva also beckons the ecotourist with quiet walks through a mahogany forest. Further information on all of these is provided later in this chapter.

SPORTS AND RECREATION

Hiking

All of the high islands offer hiking possibilities and many remote villages are linked by well-used trails. The most important hike described in this chapter is the two-day Sigatoka River Trek down the Sigatoka River from Nadarivatu. Levuka makes an excellent base with the trail to The Peak beginning right behind the town, and a challenging cross-island trail to Lovoni is nearby. More arduous is the all-day climb to Lake Tagimaucia on Taveuni. For some outer-island hiking, you can walk right around Nananu-i-Ra in less than a day, or across Waya or Wayasewa. Kadavu offers many hiking possibilities.

Surfing

A growing number of surfing camps are off southern and western Viti Levu. The most famous is Tavarua Island in the Mamanuca Group, accessible only to American surfers on packaged tours from the States. Other mortals can also use speedboats from Seashell Cove Resort to surf nearby reef breaks at far less expense, or stay at the new top-end surf resort on Namotu Island right next to Tavarua. Beachbreak surfing is possible at Club Masa near Sigatoka, and budget surfing camps have been built on Yanuca and Kadavu islands. Surfing is also possible at Suva and from the Waidroka Bay Resort on the Coral Coast. Few of Fiji's waves are for the beginner, especially the reef breaks, and of course, you must bring your own board(s). There's surf throughout the year with the best swells out of the south March-October.

Fijian clans control the fishing rights on their reefs, and on many islands they also claim to own the surfing rights. This can also apply at breaks off uninhabited islands and even ocean reefs. In past upmarket surfing camps like Tavarua, Marlin Bay, and Namotu have paid big bucks to try to corner the right to surf famous waves like Cloudbreak and Frigates, and they often attempt to keep surfers from rival resorts away. On Yanuca Island a couple of Americans put a lot of time and money into building a surf camp, only to have the waves pulled out from under them when the moneymaking potential of the activity became apparent. Although none of this is enshrined in law, it's wise to check whether you'll actually be allowed to surf the environs before booking into a surfing resort in Fiji as things change fast. Once there, you'll soon become acquainted with the current situation. When surfing in a remote area without facilities it's important to present a *sevusevu* to the local chief and be on your best behavior.

Windsurfing

Windsurfing is possible at a much wider range of locales, and many upmarket beach hotels off southern and western Viti Levu include equipment in their rates. Windsurfing is possible at most of the Mamanuca resorts, including Castaway, Musket Cove, Naitasi Resort, Navini Island, Plantation Island, Tokoriki, and Treasure Island. Other offshore resorts around Fiji offering windsurfing are Kaimbu Island, Matana Resort, Naigani Island, Qamea Beach, Toberua Island, Turtle Island, and Vatulele. Almost all of the surfing camps also offer windsurfing. For those on a budget, check out the windsurfing at Nadi's Club Fiji.

Boating

Exciting **whitewater rafting** on the Upper Navua River is offered. In central Viti Levu, villagers will pole you through the Waiqa Gorge on a bamboo raft from Naitauvoli to Naivucini villages.

In the past, organized **ocean kayaking** expeditions have been offered among the Yasawa Islands, around Kadavu, and in Vanua Levu's Natewa Bay. Those who only want to dabble can hire kayaks at Kadavu, Taveuni, and Savusavu. Several upmarket Mamanuca Resorts loan kayaks to their guests.

Get in some **sailing** by taking one of the day cruises by yacht offered from Nadi. Yacht charters are offered at Musket Cove Resort in the Mamanuca Group.

Golf

Golfers are well catered to in Fiji. The two most famous courses are the Denarau Golf Club, next to the two Sheratons at Nadi, and the Pacific Harbor Country Club, one of the finest courses in the Pacific. Many tourist hotels have golf courses, including the Mocambo at Nadi; the Fijian Resort Hotel, Outrigger Reef Resort, and Naviti Beach Resort on the south side of Viti Levu; Naigani Island Resort and Wakaya Club in Lomaiviti; and Taveuni Estates on Taveuni. More locally oriented are the city golf courses at Nadi Airport, Lautoka, and in Suva, and the company-run courses near Rakiraki and Labasa sugar mills and at the Vatukoula gold mine, all built to serve former expatriate staffs. All are open to the public and only the Sheraton course could be considered expensive.

Team Sports

The soccer season in Fiji is Feb.-Nov., while rugby is played almost year-round. The main rugby season is June-Nov. when there are 15 players on each side. November-March it's "sevens" with seven team members to a side. (The Fijians are champion sevens players, "wild, intuitive, and artistic," and in 1997 they defeated South Africa to take the Rugby World Cup Sevens in Hong Kong.) Rugby is played only by Fijians, while soccer teams are both Fijian and Indian. Cricket is played Nov.-March, mostly in rural areas. Lawn bowling is also popular. Saturday is the big day for team sports.

Scuba Diving and Snorkeling

Fiji has been called "the soft coral capital of the world" and few experienced divers will deny that Fiji has some of the finest diving in the South Pacific, with top facilities at the best prices. If in doubt, you won't go wrong choosing Fiji. The worst underwater visibility conditions here are the equivalent of the finest off Florida. In the Gulf of Mexico you've about reached the limit if you can see for 15 meters; in Fiji visibility begins at 15 meters and increases to 45 meters in some places.

Diving is possible year-round in Fiji, with the marinelife most profuse July-November. Water temperatures vary from 24° C in June, July, and August to 30° C in December, January, and February. Many fantastic dives are just 10 or 15 minutes away from the resorts by boat (whereas at Australia's Great Barrier Reef the speedboats often have to travel more than 60 km to get to the dive sites). Fiji is a relatively safe place to dive since one of the only recompression chambers in the South Pacific is at Suva (tel. 305-154 in Suva or 850-630 in Savusavu). A nationwide Medevac service is on 24-hour standby at tel. 362-172.

Facilities for scuba diving exist at most of the resorts in the Mamanuca Group, along Viti Levu's Coral Coast and at Pacific Harbor, on Kadavu, Leleuvia, Beqa, Nananu-i-Ra, Tavewa, and Wayasewa, at Nadi, Lautoka, and

Savusavu, and on Taveuni and adjacent islands. Low-budget divers should turn to the Kadavu, Leleuvia, Taveuni, Tavewa, and Wayasewa sections in this book and read. Specialized nonhotel dive shops are found at Nadi, Pacific Harbor, Lautoka, Savusavu, and on Taveuni. If you've never dived before, Fiji is an excellent place to learn, and the Kadavu, Leleuvia, Nadi, Nananu-i-Ra, Pacific Harbor, Taveuni, Tavewa, and Wayasewa scuba operators offer certification courses taking four or five days from budget accommodations. For information live-aboard dive boats see **Scuba Cruises,** which follows.

Even if you aren't willing to put the necessary money and effort into scuba diving, you'd be foolish not to check out the many snorkeling possibilities. Some dive shops take snorkelers out in their boats for a nominal rate, but there are countless places around Fiji where you can snorkel straight out to the reef for free, mostly on smaller outer islands. The beach snorkeling off Viti Levu and Vanua Levu is usually poor and a complete waste of time around Nadi, Lautoka, Pacific Harbor, Suva, and Labasa. The snorkeling along the Coral Coast is fair but only at high tide. Around Savusavu sharp rocks make it hard to get into the water at all (the top beaches are private). On the other hand, you'll have no trouble finding fabulous reefs in the Mamanuca Group, the Yasawas, off Nananu-i-Ra, Kadavu, Ono, and Taveuni, and at the small resort islands near Ovalau.

ENTERTAINMENT

There are cinemas in towns such as Labasa, Lautoka, Ba, Nadi, Nausori, and Suva showing adventure and romance films for low admissions. These same towns have local nightclubs where you can enjoy as much drinking and dancing as you like without spending an arm and a leg. When there's live music, a cover charge is collected. Many bars and clubs in Fiji refuse entry to persons dressed in flip-flops, boots, rugby jerseys, shorts, singlets, or T-shirts, and one must remove one's hat at the door.

Fiji's one unique spectacle is the **Fijian firewalking** performed several times a week at the large hotels along the southwest side of Viti Levu: Sheraton Royal (Wednesday), Sheraton-

Fiji (Thursday), Fijian Resort Hotel (Friday), Outrigger Reef Resort (Friday), The Naviti (Wednesday), the Warwick (Friday), and Pacific Harbor (Tuesday and Saturday). A fixed admission price is charged but it's well worth going at least once. For more information on firewalking, see the Fiji Islands introduction. The same hotels that present firewalking usually stage a Fijian *meke* (described below) on an alternate night.

Fijian Dancing *(Meke)*
The term *meke* describes the combination of dance, song, and theater performed at feasts and on special occasions. Brandishing spears, their faces painted with charcoal, the men wear frangipani leis and skirts of shredded leaves. The war club dance reenacts heroic events of the past. Both men and women perform the *vaka-malolo,* a sitting dance, while the *seasea* is danced by women flourishing fans. The *tralala,* in which visitors may be asked to join, is a simple two-step shuffle danced side-by-side (early missionaries forbade the Fijians from dancing face-to-face). As elsewhere in the Pacific the dances tell a story, though the music now is strongly influenced by Christian hymns and contemporary pop. Less sensual than Polynesian dancing, the rousing Fijian dancing evokes the country's violent past. Fijian *meke* are often part of a *magiti* or feast performed at hotels. The Dance Theater of Fiji at Pacific Harbor is well regarded.

PUBLIC HOLIDAYS AND FESTIVALS

Public holidays in Fiji include New Year's Day (1 January), National Youth Day (a Friday in early March), Good Friday and Easter Monday (March/April), Ratu Sukuna Day (a Monday or Friday around 29 May), Queen Elizabeth's Birthday (a Monday or Friday around 14 June), Constitution Day (sometime around 27 July), Prophet Mohammed's Birthday (anytime from July to December), Fiji Day (a Monday around 10 October), Diwali (October or November), and Christmas Days (25 and 26 December).

Check with the Fiji Visitors Bureau to see if any festivals are scheduled during your visit. The best known are the Bula Festival in Nadi (July), the Hibiscus Festival in Suva (August), the Sugar Festival in Lautoka (September), and the Back

To Levuka Festival (early October). Around the end of June there's the President's Cup yacht race at Nadi. Before Diwali, the Hindu festival of lights, Hindus clean their homes, then light lamps or candles to mark the arrival of spring. Fruit and sweets are offered to Lakshmi, goddess of wealth. Holi is an Indian spring festival in February or March.

One of the main sporting events of the year is the **International Bula Marathon** held in June. The main event involves a 42-km run from Lautoka to the Sheraton at Nadi.

ARTS AND CRAFTS

The traditional art of Fiji is closely related to that of Tonga. Fijian canoes, too, were patterned after the more advanced Polynesian type, although the Fijians were timid sailors. War clubs, food bowls, *tanoas* (kava bowls), eating utensils, clay pots, and tapa cloth *(masi)* are considered Fiji's finest artifacts.

There are two kinds of woodcarvings: the ones made from *vesi (Intsia bijuga)*—ironwood in English—or *nawanawa (Cordia subcordata)* wood are superior to those of the lighter, highly breakable *vau (Hibiscus tiliaceus)*. In times past it often took years to make a Fijian war club, as the carving was done in the living tree and left to grow into the desired shape. The top *tanoas* are carved in the Lau Group.

Though many crafts are alive and well, some Fijians have taken to carving "tikis" or mock New Guinea masks smeared with black shoe polish to look like ebony for sale to tourists. Also avoid crafts made from endangered species such as sea turtles (tortoise shell) and marine mammals (whales' teeth, etc.). Prohibited entry into most countries, they will be confiscated by customs if found.

Tapa Cloth

This is Fiji's most characteristic traditional product. Tapa is light, portable, and inexpensive, and a piece makes an excellent souvenir to brighten up a room back home. It's made by women on Vatulele Island off Viti Levu and on certain islands of the Lau Group.

To make tapa, the inner, water-soaked bark of the paper mulberry *(Broussonetia papyrifera)* is stripped from the tree and steeped in water. Then it's scraped with shells and pounded into a thin sheet with wooden mallets. Four of these sheets are applied one over another and pounded together, then left to dry in the sun.

While Tongan tapa is decorated by holding a relief pattern under the tapa and overpainting the lines, Fijian tapa *(masi kesa)* is distinctive for its rhythmic geometric designs applied with stencils made from green pandanus and banana leaves. The stain is rubbed on in the same manner in which temple rubbings are made from a stone inscription.

The only colors used are red, from red clay, and a black pigment obtained by burning candlenuts. Both powders are mixed with boiled gums made from scraped roots. Sunlight deepens and sets the colors. Each island group had its characteristic colors and patterns, ranging from plantlike paintings to geometric designs. Sheets of tapa feel like felt when finished.

SHOPPING

Most large shops in Fiji close at 1300 on Saturday but smaller grocery stores are often open on Sunday. Fiji Indians dominate the retail trade. If you're buying from an Indian merchant, always bargain hard and consider all sales final. Indigenous Fijians usually begin by asking a much lower starting price, in which case bargaining isn't so important. When bargaining for handicrafts at a market remember that an Indian seller's starting price could be 10 times the real price and that it will be hard to disengage once the bargaining has begun. Avoid the hassle by going straight to the Fijian sellers.

Fiji's "duty-free" shops such as Prouds or Tappoo are not really duty-free, as all goods are subject to various fiscal duties plus the 10% value-added tax. Bargaining is the order of the day, but to be frank, Americans can usually buy the sort of Japanese electrical merchandise sold "duty-free" in Fiji cheaper in the States, where they'll get more recent models. If you do buy something, get an itemized receipt and international guarantee, and watch that they don't switch packages and unload a demo on you. Once purchased, items cannot be returned, so don't let yourself be talked into anything. Camera film is

a Fijian woman wrapped in a tapa blanket

inexpensive, however, and the selection good—stock up.

If you'd like to do some shopping in Fiji, locally made handicrafts such as tapa cloth, mats, kava bowls, war clubs, woodcarvings, etc., are a much better investment. The four-pronged cannibal forks available everywhere make unique souvenirs, but avoid the masks, which are made only for sale to tourists and have nothing to do with Fiji. If you're spending serious money for top-quality work, visit the Fiji Museum and the Government Handicraft Center in Suva beforehand to see what is authentic.

To learn what's available on the tourist market and to become familiar with prices, browse one of the half dozen outlets of **Jacks Handicrafts** around Viti Levu. You'll find them in downtown Nadi, Sigatoka, and Suva, and at the Sheraton-Fiji, Fiji Mocambo, and Warwick hotels. If the sales person is overenthusiastic and begins following you around too closely, just stop and say you're only looking today and they'll probably leave you alone.

You can often purchase your souvenirs directly from the Fijian producers at markets, etc.

Just beware of aggressive indigenous Fijian "sword sellers" on the streets of Suva, Nadi, and Lautoka who peddle fake handicrafts at high prices, high-pressure duty-free touts who may try to pull you into their shops, and self-appointed guides who offer to help you find the "best price." If you get the feeling you're being hustled, walk away.

ACCOMMODATIONS

A 10% government tax is added to all accommodations prices. Most hotels include the tax in their quoted rates, but some don't. You can often tell whether tax is included by looking at the amount: if it's F$33 tax is probably included, whereas if it's F$30 it may not be. When things are slow, specials are offered and some prices become negotiable, and occasionally you'll pay less than the prices quoted in this book. This is most likely to happen in February and March, the lowest tourist season. For economy and flexibility, avoid prepaying hotel accommodations from home.

Fiji offers a wide variety of places to stay, from low-budget to world-class. Standard big-city international hotels are found in Nadi and Suva, while many of the upmarket beach resorts are on small islands in the Mamanuca Group off Nadi and along the Coral Coast on Viti Levu's sunny south side. The Mamanuca resorts are secluded, with fan-cooled *bure* accommodations, while at the Coral Coast hotels you often get an a/c room in a main building. The Coral Coast has more to offer in the way of land tours, shopping, and entertainment/eating options, while the offshore resorts are preferable if you want a rest or are into water sports. The Coral Coast beaches are only good at high tide and the reefs degraded, while on the outer islands the reefs are usually pristine.

In recent years smaller boutique resorts have multiplied in remote locations, from the guest-accepting plantations near Savusavu and on Taveuni to luxury beach resorts on outlying islands such as Kaimbu, Kadavu (Matana), Laucala, Matangi, Beqa, Naigani, Namenalala, Nukubati, Qamea, Toberua, Turtle, Vatulele, Wakaya, and Yasawa. Prices at these begin at several hundred dollars a day and rise to four figures, so some care should be taken in selecting the right one. A few such as Beqa, Matana, and Matangi are marketed almost exclusively to scuba divers, and Namenalala is a good ecotourism choice. If you delight in glamorous socializing with other mixed couples, Turtle and Vatulele are for you. Families are welcome at Castaway, Matangi, Naigani, and Toberua, but children are generally not accepted at Kaimbu, Matamanoa, Nukubati, Qamea, Turtle, Vatulele, Wakaya, and Yasawa. The very wealthy will feel at home on Kaimbu, Laucala, and Wakaya, whereas many of the Mamanuca resorts are designed for larger numbers of guests interested in intensive sporting and social activities.

However, unless you're feeling charitable to the transnational conglomerates that control many of the top hotels, you'll do better by focusing on the middle and bottom ends of the market, while using the big resorts as sources of entertainment or sightseeing attractions. Like such places around the world, many of the deluxe hotels are boring, sterile enclaves of affluence carefully shielded from any type of spontaneity. They cater mostly to people on packaged holidays who book through travel agents abroad, while the budget places covered in this book are not in most agents computers and cater to a younger crowd who decide where they'll stay after reaching Fiji.

Low-budget accommodations are spread out, with concentrations in Korotogo, Nadi, Lautoka, Levuka, Suva, and Savusavu, and on Taveuni. Low-cost outer island beach resorts exist on Kadavu, Leleuvia, Mana, Nananu-i-Ra, Ono, Tavewa, Thaqalai, Waya, and Wayasewa. The largest budget chain in Fiji is Cathay Hotels with properties in Suva, Lautoka, and on the Coral Coast (visit their Fiji For Less website at www. fiji4less.com). At all of these, the easiest way to check on the availability of rooms is to call them up after you get to Fiji.

A few of the cheapies in Suva and Lautoka double as whorehouses, making them cheap in both senses of the word. Many hotels, both in cities and at the beach, offer dormitory beds as well as individual rooms. Most of the dorms are mixed. Women can sometimes request a women-only dorm when things are slow, but it's usually not guaranteed. Some city hotels lock their front doors at 2300, so ask first if you're planning a night on the town. Several islands with air service from Suva, including Koro, Moala,

Gau, and Cicia, have no regular accommodations for visitors at all, so it's good to know someone before heading their way.

Camping

Camping facilities (bring your own tent) are found at backpacker resorts on Kadavu, Leleuvia, Mana, Ono, Ovalau, Rotuma, Taveuni, Tavewa, Caqalai, Waya, Wayasewa, and Yanuca Lailai Islands. A few shoestring hostels in Nadi and Savusavu also allow it, as do Viti Levu beach resorts like Seashell Surf and Dive, The Beachouse, and the Coral Coast Christian Camp. On Vanua Levu, you can camp at Mumu Resort and at Buca Bay. Nature reserves where camping is possible include Colo-i-Suva Forest Park, Nukulau Island off Suva, and at Nadarivatu.

Elsewhere, get permission before pitching your tent as all land is owned by someone and land rights are sensitive issues in Fiji. Some freelance campers on beaches such as Natadola near Nadi have had their possessions stolen, so take care.

In Fijian villages don't ask a Fijian friend for permission to camp beside his house. Although he may feel obligated to grant the request of a guest, you'll be proclaiming to everyone that his home isn't entirely to your liking. If all you really want is to camp, make that clear from the start and get permission to do so on a beach or by a river, but *not* in the village. A *sevusevu* should always be presented in this case. There's really nowhere to camp totally for free.

Staying in Villages

The most direct way to meet the Fijian people and learn a little about their culture is to stay in a village for a few nights. A number of hiking tours offer overnighting in remote villages, and it's also possible to arrange it for yourself. If you befriend someone from an outlying island, ask them to write you a letter of introduction to their relatives back in the village. Mail a copy of it ahead with a polite letter introducing yourself, then start slowly heading that way.

In places well off the beaten track where there are no regular tourist accommodations, you could just show up in a village and ask permission of the *turaga-ni-koro* (village herald) to spend the night. Similarly, both Fiji Indians and native Fijians will spontaneously invite you in.

The Fijians' innate dignity and kindness should not be taken for granted, however.

All across the Pacific it's customary to reciprocate when someone gives you a gift—if not now, then sometime in the future. Visitors who accept gifts (such as meals and accommodations) from islanders and do not reciprocate are undermining traditional culture and causing resentment, often without realizing it. It's sometimes hard to know how to repay hospitality, but Fijian culture has a solution: the *sevusevu*. This can be money, but it's usually a 500-gram "pyramid" of kava roots *(waka)*, which can be easily purchased at any Fijian market for about F$13. *Sevusevus* are more often performed between families or couples about to be married, or at births or christenings, but the custom is certainly a perfect way for visitors to show their appreciation.

We recommend that travelers donate around F$20 pp per night to village hosts (carry sufficient cash in small denominations). The *waka* bundle is additional, and anyone traveling in remote areas of Fiji should pack some (take whole roots, not powdered kava). If you give the money up front together with the *waka* as a *sevusevu*, they'll know you're not a freeloader and you'll get VIP treatment, though in all cases it's absolutely essential to contribute something.

The *sevusevu* should be placed before (not handed to) the *turaga-ni-koro* or village herald so he can accept or refuse. If he accepts (by touching the package), your welcome is confirmed and you may spend the night in the village. It's also nice to give some money to the lady of the house upon departure, with your thanks. Just say it's your goodbye *sevusevu* and watch the smile. A Fijian may refuse the money, but he/she will not be offended by the offer if it is done properly. Of course, developing interpersonal relationships with your hosts is more important than money, and mere cash or gifts is no substitute for making friends. One thing *not* to give is alcohol, which is always sure to offend somebody.

Once you're staying with one family avoid moving to the home of another family in the same village as this would probably be seen as a slight to the first. Be wary of readily accepting invitations to meals with villagers other than your hosts as the offer may only be meant as a courtesy. Don't overly admire any of the possessions of your hosts or they may feel obligated to give

preparing a lovo (earthen pit oven) at Korovou on the Wainimata River, Viti Levu, to celebrate the opening of the primary school

DAVID STANLEY

them to you. Never arrive in a village on a Sunday, and don't overstay your welcome.

Village Life

When you enter a Fijian village, people will usually want to be helpful and will direct or accompany you to the person or place you seek. If you show genuine interest in something and ask to see how it is done, you'll usually be treated with respect and asked if there's anything else you'd like to know. Initially, Fijians may hesitate to welcome you into their homes because they may fear you will not wish to sit on a mat and eat native foods with your fingers. Once you show them this isn't true, you'll receive the full hospitality treatment.

Consider participating in the daily activities of the family, such as weaving, cooking, gardening, and fishing. Your hosts will probably try to dissuade you from "working," but if you persist you'll become accepted. Staying in a village is definitely not for everyone. Many houses contain no electricity, running water, toilet, furniture, etc., and only native food will be available. Water and your left hand serve as toilet paper.

You should also expect to sacrifice most of your privacy, to stay up late drinking grog, and to sit in the house and socialize when you could be out exploring. On Sunday you'll have to stay put the whole day. The constant attention and lack of sanitary conditions may become tiresome, but it would be considered rude to attempt to be alone or refuse the food or grog.

With the proliferation of backpackers resorts around Fiji, staying in villages has become much less a part of visits to remote parts of Fiji than it was a decade ago, and relatively few travelers do it today. The Australian guidebooks also discourage going off the beaten travelers track. However, so long as you're prepared to accept all of the above and know beforehand that this is not a cheap way to travel, a couple of nights in a remote village could easily be the highlight of your trip.

FOOD AND DRINK

Unlike some other South Pacific nations, Fiji has many good, inexpensive eateries. The ubiquitous Chinese restaurants are probably your best bet for dinner and you can almost always get alcohol with the meal. At lunchtime look for an Indian place. Indian dishes are spicy, often curries with rice and *dhal* (lentil soup), but orthodox Hindus don't consume beef and Muslims forgo pork. Instead of bread Indians eat *roti,* a flat, tortilla-like pancake. *Puri* are small, deep-fried *rotis.* Baked in a stone oven *roti* becomes *naan,* a Punjabi specialty similar to pita bread. *Palau* is a main plate of rice and vegetables always including peas. *Samosas* are lumps of potato and other vegetables wrapped in dough and deep-fried. *Pakoras* are deep-fried chunks of dough spiced with chili and often served with a pickle chutney. Yogurt mixed with water makes a refreshing drink called *lassi.* If you have the chance, try South Indian vegetarian dishes like *iddili* (little white rice cakes served with *dhal*) and *masala dosai* (a rice potato-filled pancake served with a watery curry sauce called *sambar*).

Fijian food is usually steamed or boiled instead of fried, and dishes such as baked fish *(ika)* in coconut cream *(lolo)* with cassava *(tapioca),* taro *(dalo),* breadfruit *(uto),* and sweet potato *(kumala)* take a long time to prepare and must be served fresh, which makes it difficult to offer them in a restaurant. Don't miss an opportunity to try *duruka* (young sugar cane) or *vakalolo* (fish and prawns), both baked in *lolo. Kokoda* is an appetizing dish made of diced raw fish marinated in coconut cream and lime juice, while smoked octopus is *kuita.* Taro leaves are used to make a spinach called *palusami* (often stuffed with corned beef), which is known as *rourou* when soaked in coconut cream. Taro stems are cut into a marinated salad called *baba.* Seasoned "bird meat" (chicken) is wrapped and steamed in banana leaves to produce *kovu. Miti* is a sauce made of coconut cream, oranges, and chilies.

A good opportunity to taste authentic Fijian food and see traditional dancing is at a *lovo* or underground oven feast staged weekly at one of the large hotels around Nadi or on the Coral Coast for about F$40. These are usually accompanied by a Fijian *meke* or song and dance performance in which legends, love stories, and historical events are told in song and gesture. Alternatively, firewalking may be presented.

Many restaurants are closed on Sunday, and a 10% tax is added to the bill at some upmarket restaurants although it's usually included in the menu price. Fijians have their own pace and trying to make them do things more quickly is often counterproductive. Their charm and the friendly personal attention you receive more than make up for the occasionally slow service at restaurants.

The Hot Bread Kitchen chain of bakeries around Fiji serves fresh fruit loaves, cheese and onion loaves, muffins, and other assorted breads. The Morris Hedstrom supermarket chain is about the cheapest, and many have milk bars with ice cream and sweets.

The famous Fiji Bitter beer is brewed by Australian-owned Carlton Brewery Ltd., with breweries in Suva and Lautoka. South Pacific Distilleries Ltd. in Lautoka produces brandy, gin, rum, vodka, and whisky under a variety of brand names. What could be better than a vodka and tonic in the midday heat or a rum and coke at sunset? Supermarkets in Fiji usually only sell beer and other alcohol weekdays 0800-1800, Saturday

0800-1300. Licensed restaurants can only serve alcohol to those who order meals. Drinking alcoholic beverages on the street is prohibited.

SERVICES AND INFORMATION

Visas and Officialdom

Everyone needs a passport valid at least three months beyond the date of entry. No visa is required of visitors from 101 countries (including Western Europe, North America, Japan, Israel, most Commonwealth countries, and more) for stays of four months. Tickets to leave Fiji are officially required but usually not checked. The required vaccination against yellow fever or cholera only applies if you're arriving directly from an infected area, such as the Amazon jungles or the banks of the Ganges River.

Fiji has established diplomatic missions in Brussels, Canberra, Kuala Lumpur, London, New York, Port Moresby, Seoul, Tokyo, Washington, and Wellington.

Extensions of stay are given out by the immigration offices at Lautoka, Nadi Airport, Savusavu, and Suva. You must apply before your current permit expires. After the first four months, you can get another two months to bring your total stay up to six months by paying a F$55 fee. Bring your passport, onward or return ticket, and proof of sufficient funds. After six months you must leave but you can return the next day and start on another four months.

Fiji has four ports of entry for yachts: Lautoka, Levuka, Savusavu, and Suva. Calling at an outer island before clearing customs is prohibited. Levuka is the easiest place to check in or out, as all of the officials have offices right on the main wharf, and Savusavu is also convenient. To visit the outer islands, yachts require a letter of authorization from the Secretary for Fijian Affairs in Suva, or the commissioner (at Labasa, Lautoka, or Nausori) of the division they wish to visit. Yacht permits to visit the Lau Group must be obtained from the president's office (tel. 314-244) in Suva and they're hard to get due to a yacht drug bust in 1993.

Money

The currency is the Fiji dollar, which is almost two to one to the U.S. dollar in value (about US$1 =

F$2). In January 1998 Fiji devalued its dollar 20% and in the months that followed it dropped another 10%. Despite this, tourism operators announced they would try to maintain their 1997 pricing through 1998, but substantial increases are to be expected in 1999. Thus you may pay considerably more in Fiji dollars than the prices quoted herein, but still less than you would have paid in U.S. dollar terms in 1997.

The first Fijian coins were minted in London in 1934, but Fiji continued to deal in British pounds, shillings, and pence until 1969 when dollars and cents were introduced (at the rate of two Fiji dollars to one pound). There are coins of one, two, five, 10, 20, and 50 cents and one dollar, and bills of F$1, F$2, F$5, F$10, F$20, and F$50 (the F$5 and F$50 notes have confusingly similar colors and designs).

Banking hours are Mon.-Thurs. 0930-1500, Friday 0930-1600. Commercial banks operating in Fiji include the ANZ Bank, Indian-owned Bank of Baroda, Pakistani-owned Habib Bank, Bank of Hawaii, Merchant Bank, National Bank of Fiji, and Westpac Banking Corporation. There are bank branches in all the main towns, but it's usually not possible to change traveler's checks or foreign banknotes in rural areas or on outer islands. Take care when changing at the luxury hotels as they often give a rate much lower than the banks. Recent cases of stolen traveler's checks being changed in Fiji has caused many hotels and restaurants to begin refusing them. Thus it's a good idea to plan ahead and change enough at a bank to keep you going over weekends. Credit cards are strictly for the cities and resorts (the most useful cards to bring are American Express, Diners Club, JCB International, MasterCard, and Visa). The Westpac Bank gives cash advances on MasterCard and Visa, the ANZ Bank on JCB International. Many tourist facilities levy a five percent surcharge on credit card payments.

The import of foreign currency is unrestricted, but only F$100 in Fijian banknotes may be exported. Avoid taking any Fijian banknotes out of the country at all, as Fijian dollars are difficult to change and heavily discounted outside Fiji. The Thomas Cook offices in Suva and Nadi will change whatever you have left into the currency of the next country on your itinerary (don't forget to keep enough local currency to pay your airport departure tax at the check-in counter).

For security, the bulk of your travel funds should be in traveler's checks. American Express is probably the best kind to have, as they're represented by Tapa International in Suva (4th floor, ANZ House, 25 Victoria Parade; tel. 302-333, fax 302-048) and Nadi (Nadi Airport Concourse; tel. 722-325). If your American Express checks are lost or stolen, contact either of these. Thomas Cook has offices at 21 Thomson St., Suva (tel. 301-603, fax 300-304), and in Nadi (tel. 703-110).

If you need money sent, have your banker make a telegraphic transfer to any Westpac Bank branch in Fiji. Many banks will hold a sealed envelope for you in their vault for a nominal fee—a good way to avoid carrying unneeded valuables with you all around Fiji.

In 1992 Fiji introduced a 10% value-added tax (VAT), which is usually (but not always) included in quoted prices. Among the few items exempt from the tax are unprocessed local foods and bus fares. Despite VAT, Fiji is one of the least expensive countries in the South Pacific, especially since the devaluation. Tipping isn't customary in Fiji, although some resorts do have a staff Christmas fund, to which contributions are welcome.

Post

Post offices are generally open weekdays 0800-1600 and they hold general delivery mail two months. Fiji's postal workers are amazingly polite and efficient, and postage is inexpensive, so mail all of your postcards from here! Consider using air mail for parcels, however, as surface mail takes up to six months. If time isn't important, however, most surface parcels do eventually arrive and small packets weighing less that one kilogram benefit from an especially low tariff. The weight limit for overseas parcels is 10 kilograms. Post Fiji's *fast* POST service guarantees that your letter or parcel will get on the first international airline connection to your destination for a small surcharge. Express mail service (EMS) is more expensive but faster and up to 20 kilograms may be sent (available to 28 countries). Post offices all around Fiji accept EMS mail. When writing to Fiji, use the words "Fiji Islands" in the address (otherwise the letter might go to Fuji, Japan) and underline Fiji (so it doesn't end up in Iceland).

Aside from EMS, the other major courier services active in Fiji are CDP (tel. 313-077) at Labasa, Lautoka, Ba, Nadi, Sigatoka, and Suva, DHL (tel. 313-166) with offices at Labasa, Lautoka, Levuka, Nadi, Savusavu, and Suva, TNT (tel. 384-677) at Lautoka, Nadi, and Suva, and UPS (tel. 312-697) at Lautoka, Nadi, and Suva. To Europe or North America, DHL charges F$110 for a small box up to 10 kilograms or F$195 for a big box up to 25 kilograms, less than you would pay by EMS.

Telecommunications

Coin phones have been largely replaced on street corners by phones requiring magnetic cards sold at all post offices and many shops in denominations of F$3, F$5, F$10, and F$20 (foreign phone cards cannot be used in Fiji). Public telephones are easy to find, although it seems that more than half the 500 card phones in Fiji are out of order at any given time. There's no privacy since fully enclosed booths are rare and out of curiosity passersby will shamelessly stop and listen to your call. Nevertheless, a telephone card is still a smart investment, allowing you to save time and avoid frustration by calling ahead for current information. It's wiser to get a F$3 or F$5 card rather than one of the higher values in case you happen to leave it behind in the phone (easy to do). Since telephone rates are low in Fiji, even the F$3 card lasts ages (local calls are 20 cents each). Long-distance domestic calls from public telephones are half price 1800-0600, and all day on Saturday, Sunday, and public holidays. Fiji domestic directory assistance is 011, international directory assistance 022, the domestic operator 010, the international operator 012. In emergencies, dial 000.

Fiji's international access code from public telephones is 05, so insert your card, dial 05, the country code, the area code, and the number. To call overseas collect (billed to your party at the higher person-to-person rate), dial 031, the country code, the area code, and the number. If calling Fiji from abroad, dial your own international access code, Fiji's telephone code 679, and the local six-digit number listed in this book (there are no area codes in Fiji). If the line is inaudible, hang up immediately and try again.

The basic long-distance charge for three minutes is F$5.28 to Australia or New Zealand,

F$8.91 to North America, Europe, or Japan. All operator-assisted international calls have a three-minute minimum charge and additional time is charged per minute, whereas international calls made using telephone cards have no minimum and the charges are broken down into flat six-second units (telephone cards with less than F$3 credit on them cannot be used for international calls). Calls to Australia and New Zealand are 25% cheaper 2300-0600. International calls placed from hotel rooms are always much more expensive (ask the receptionist for the location of the nearest card phone).

Faxes can be sent from the post offices in Labasa, Lautoka, Ba, Nadi, Sigatoka, and Suva. Outgoing faxes cost F$5.50 a page to regional countries, F$7.70 to other countries, both plus a F$3.30 handing fee. You can also receive faxes at these post offices for F$1.10 a page. The numbers you'll probably use are fax 702-467 at Nadi Airport Post Office, fax 702-166 at Nadi Town Post Office, and fax 302-666 at Suva General Post Office.

Public internet access is offered by Telecom Fiji opposite the post office in Suva, a chance to catch up on your e-mail. Fiji's first internet cafe opened in Lautoka in 1998 at The Last Call Italian Restaurant, 21 Tui Street. If an e-mail address provided in this chapter doesn't work, check www.is.com.fj or www.bulafiji.com for an update.

Time

Fiji shares a time zone with New Zealand, 12 hours ahead of Greenwich Mean Time. In order to be able to greet the new millennium an hour earlier than competing sites in New Zealand and at the same time as those in Tonga, Fiji officially adopted daylight saving time in November 1998. Henceforth Fijian clocks will be turned an hour forward from 1 Nov. to 1 February.

Print Media

The *Fiji Times* (G.P.O. Box 1167, Suva; tel. 304-111, fax 302-011), "the first newspaper published in the world today," was founded at Levuka in 1869 but is now owned by publishing mogul Rupert Murdoch's estate. The *Daily Post* (Box 7010, Valelevu, Nasinu; tel. 313-342, fax 313-363) is a morning newspaper mostly owned by Colonial Mutual Insurance and the government-run Fiji Development Bank. The *Times* has a daily print run of 37,000, the *Post* about 10,000.

Two excellent regional newsmagazines are published in Suva: *Pacific Islands Monthly* (tel. 304-111, fax 303-809), also part of the Murdoch empire, and *Islands Business* (Box 12718, Suva; tel. 303-108, fax 301-423), owned by local European businessmen. As well, there's a monthly Fijian business magazine called *The Review* (Box 12095, Suva; tel. 305-700, fax 301-930), owned by Fiji journalist Yashwant Gaunder.

TV and Radio

Television broadcasting began in Fiji only in 1991, and Fiji TV is on the air Mon.-Sat. 1400-2300 and Sunday 1000-2300 with one free and two paid channels. The Fiji Government owns 65% of the company and another 15% is owned by TV New Zealand, which manages the station.

The quasi-official Island Network Ltd. (Box 334, Suva; tel. 314-333, fax 301-643) operates five AM/FM radio stations: Radio Fiji Gold (RFG) in English, RF1 in Fijian for older listeners, Bula FM in Fijian for younger listeners, RF2 in Hindi for older listeners, and 98 FM in Hindi for younger listeners.

Privately owned Communications Fiji Ltd. (Private Mail Bag, Suva; tel. 314-766, fax 303-748) operates three commercial FM stations, which broadcast around the clock: FM 96 in English, Viti FM in Fijian, and Radio Navtarang in Hindi.

At Suva you can pick up the local stations at the following frequencies: RFG at 100.4 MHz, FM 96 at 96.0 MHz, RF1 at 107.6 MHz FM or at 558 kHz AM, Bula FM at 102.0 MHz, Viti FM at 102.8 MHz, RF2 at 105.2 MHz FM or at 774 kHz AM, 98 FM at 98.0 MHz, and Navtarang at 98.8 MHz. The university station, Radio Pasifik, is at 88.8 MHz.

At Nadi and Lautoka check the following frequencies: RFG at 94.2 MHz, FM 96 at 95.4 MHz, RF1 at 639 kHz AM, Bula FM at 91.0 MHz, Viti FM at 99.6 MHz, RF2 at 891 kHz AM, 98 FM at 88.6 MHz, and Navtarang at 97.4 MHz.

On the Coral Coast it's FM 96 at 99.0 MHz, RFG at 100.6 MHz, Navtarang at 102.2 MHz, Bula FM at 103.0 MHz, and Viti FM at 107.8 MHz. At Levuka pick up RFG at 90.6 MHz. Around Rakiraki look for RF1 at 1152 kHz AM, RF2 at 1467 kHz AM, and FM 96 at 98.8 MHz. Elsewhere in northern Viti Levu, you can get RFG at 94.6 MHz, FM 96 at 99.2 MHz, Navtarang at 101.6 MHz, and Viti FM at 103.2 MHz in Tavua and Ba.

On Vanua Levu, check the following frequencies at Labasa: RFG at 90.6 MHz, FM 96 at 95.4 MHz, RF1 at 684 kHz AM, Viti FM at 99.6 MHz, RF2 at 810 kHz AM, and Navtarang at 97.4 MHz. At Savusavu it's RF1 at 684 kHz AM and RF2 at 810 kHz AM. Reception of any station is difficult at Taveuni.

The local stations broadcast mostly pop music and repetitive advertising with very little news or commentary (the presenters sometimes get things hilariously mixed up). Radio Fiji Gold broadcasts local news and a weather report on the hour weekdays 0600-2200 (weekends every other hour) with a special news of the day report at 1745 followed by the BBC world news just after 1800. The BBC news is also broadcast on RFG at 1900 and 2100. Radio FM 96 broadcasts news and weather on the hour weekdays 0600-1800, Saturday at 0700, 1000, 1300, and 1800, Sunday at 0800, 1300, 1800.

There's no shortwave broadcasting from Fiji but you can pick up the SW broadcasts of the BBC and Radio Australia almost everywhere. Communications Fiji Ltd. rebroadcasts the BBC World Service over 106.8 MHz FM 24 hours a day (available around Suva only).

Information

The government-funded Fiji Visitors Bureau (Box 92, Suva; tel. 302-433, fax 300-970, www. bulafiji.com) mails out general brochures and a list of hotels with current prices free upon request. In Fiji they have walk-in offices at Nadi Airport and in Suva. For a list of their overseas offices see **Resources** at the end of this book. In Fiji, the FVB maintains a toll-free information number at tel. 0800-721-721.

The free *Fiji Magic* magazine (Box 12095, Suva; tel. 305-916, fax 301-930) is very useful to get an idea of what's on during your visit.

Also browse the local bookstores, Desai Bookshops, Zenon Bookshops, and Sigatoka Stationery Supplies, with branches all over Fiji. Ask for the *Fiji Handbook* from Moon Travel Handbooks, which provides more detailed coverage of the country than can be included herein.

Health

Fiji's climate is a healthy one, and the main causes of death are noncommunicable diseases such as heart disease, diabetes, and cancer. There's no malaria here, but a mosquito-transmitted disease known as dengue fever is endemic and major epidemics occurred in Fiji in 1990 and 1998. AIDS is now present in Fiji, and sexually transmitted diseases such as syphilis, gonorrhea, and herpes have reached almost epidemic proportions in urban areas. Turn to the section on AIDS in this book's main introduction for more information.

The tap water in Fiji is usually drinkable except immediately after a cyclone or during droughts, when care should be taken. Health care is good, with an abundance of hospitals, health centers, and nursing stations scattered around the country. The largest hospitals are in Labasa, Lautoka, Levuka, Ba, Savusavu, Sigatoka, Suva, and Taveuni. These have special rates for foreigners, and it's no more expensive to visit a private doctor or dentist than to wait for hours at a public hospital crowded with locals eligible for free treatment.

To call an ambulance dial 000. In case of scuba diving accidents, an operating dive recompression chamber (tel. 305-154 in Suva or 850-630 in Savusavu) is available at the Gordon Street Medical Center in Suva. The 24-hour recompression medical evacuation number is tel. 362-172.

TRANSPORTATION

Getting There

Fiji's geographic position makes it the hub of transport for the entire South Pacific, and **Nadi Airport** is the region's most important international airport, with long-haul services to points all around the Pacific Rim. Ten international airlines fly into Nadi: Aircalin, Air Nauru, Air New Zealand, Air Pacific, Air Vanuatu, Canada 3000, Polynesian Airlines, Qantas Airways, Royal Tongan Airlines, and Solomon Airlines. Air Pacific also uses Suva's Nausori Airport. When booking, ask for a flight that arrives at Nadi in the early morning to avoid the expensive hassle of arriving late at night.

The national airline of Fiji, **Air Pacific** (www. airpacific.com), was founded in 1951 as Fiji Airways by Harold Gatty, a famous Australian aviator who had set a record in 1931 by flying around the world in eight days with American Willy Post.

In 1972 the airline was reorganized as a regional carrier and the name changed to Air Pacific. Thanks to careful management, the Nadi-based company has made a profit every year since 1985. The carrier arrives at Nadi from Apia, Auckland, Brisbane, Christchurch, Honiara, Honolulu, Los Angeles, Melbourne, Port Vila, Sydney, Tokyo, Tongatapu, and Wellington, and at Suva from Apia, Auckland, and Sydney. Qantas owns 46% of Air Pacific (the Fiji government owns the rest) and most Qantas flights to Fiji are actually code shares with the Fijian carrier. Thus you may fly Air Pacific even if you thought you had booked on Qantas. To Honiara Air Pacific code shares with Solomon Airlines, to Papeete with Aircalin. Air Pacific's U.S. office is at Suite 475, 841 Apollo St., El Segundo, CA 90245, U.S.A. (tel. 800/227-4446, fax 310/524-9356). Qantas is Air Pacific's general sales agent in Europe, North America, and Australia. Flying Air Pacific means you enjoy the friendly flavor of Fiji from the moment you leave the ground.

From North America, Air Pacific flies to Nadi nonstop from Los Angeles four times a week and from Honolulu weekly. If you have to fly via Hawaii on Air New Zealand, it's a 5.5-hour flight from California to Honolulu, then another 6.5 hours from Honolulu to Fiji. The four nonstop Air Pacific flights from Los Angeles take only 10 hours as you save all the time Air New Zealand spends on the ground in Hawaii.

Air New Zealand arrives direct from Honolulu, Los Angeles, Papeete, and Rarotonga. In April 1998 Air New Zealand launched their own weekly nonstop flight between Nadi and Los Angeles, allowing European passengers to fly to Fiji from Frankfurt or London with only one change of aircraft at Los Angeles. November-May **Canada 3000** operates direct weekly charter flights from Vancouver via Honolulu with connections to/from Toronto. **Canadian Airlines International** and Air Pacific operate a code-share service between Vancouver/Toronto and Fiji via Honolulu.

From Australia, you can fly to Nadi on Air Pacific and Qantas, both of which arrive from Brisbane, Melbourne, and Sydney. From Sydney Air Pacific also has direct flights to Suva. From New Zealand, both Air New Zealand and Air Pacific fly to Nadi from Auckland, and Air Pacific

also flies from Christchurch and Wellington to Nadi and Auckland to Suva. In November 1998 Ansett Australia also began twice-weekly service to Fiji with an introductory advance purchase fare of A$725 roundtrip from Sydney. From Japan, Air Pacific arrives from Tokyo and Air New Zealand from Nagoya.

Air Nauru (tel. 312-377), Ratu Sakuna House, Macarthur St., Suva, flag carrier of the tiny phosphate-rich Republic of Nauru in Micronesia, has flights from Nadi to Nauru (A$486) twice a week, to Tarawa weekly. From Nauru there are onward connections to Pohnpei (A$499), Guam (A$585), and Manila (A$941) twice a week. Cheaper 28-day roundtrip excursion fares are available from Fiji. Their "Pacific Explorer Pass" allows you to do a Fiji-Tarawa-Nauru-Fiji circle trip for US$450 (available from Air Promotions Systems, 5757 West Century Blvd., Suite 660, Los Angeles, CA 90045, U.S.A.; tel. 800/677-4277 or 310/670-7302, fax 310/338-0708, www.pacificislands.com).

Other regional carriers landing at Nadi include Aircalin (from Nouméa, Wallis, and Papeete), Air Vanuatu (from Port Vila), Polynesian Airlines (from Apia), Royal Tongan Airlines (from Nuku'alofa and Vava'u), and Solomon Airlines (from Honiara and Port Vila).

Air Pacific offers direct flights to Suva from Apia, Auckland, and Sydney.

For special airfares from Fiji to other South Pacific countries, see **Getting Around** in the main introduction.

Getting Around by Air

While most international flights are focused on Nadi, Fiji's domestic air service radiates from Suva and two local airlines compete fiercely. **Air Fiji** (Box 1259, Suva; tel. 313-666, fax 300-771) flies fast Brazilian-made Bandeirantes (15 seats), sturdy Canadian-made Twin Otters, pocket-size Britten Norman Islanders, and exotic Chinese-made Y12 Harbins from Suva's Nausori Airport six times a day to Labasa (F$138) and Nadi (F$114), twice a day to Kadavu (F$92), Levuka (F$54), Savusavu (F$118), and Taveuni (F$150), five times a week to Gau (F$76), four times a week to Koro (F$104) and Moala (F$136), three times a week to Lakeba (F$150) and Vanua Balavu (F$150), and twice a week to Cicia (F$138). Savusavu to Taveuni (F$82) is twice daily (all fares one-way). The 30-day "Discover Fiji Air Pass" (US$236) must be purchased prior to arrival in Fiji and it's only valid on flights to Kadavu, Nadi, Savusavu, Suva, and Taveuni.

Sunflower Airlines (Box 9452, Nadi Airport; tel. 723-016, fax 723-611) bases much of its domestic network at Nadi, with four flights a day to Labasa (F$180), three a day to Suva (F$120) and Taveuni (F$222), two a day to Savusavu (F$180), and daily to Kadavu (F$126). From Suva, Sunflower has flights to Labasa (twice daily, F$148), Nadi (three daily, F$120), and Rotuma (twice weekly, F$376). From Taveuni, they go to Savusavu (twice daily, F$82) and Labasa (three weekly, F$82). Flying in their 10-seat Britten Norman Islanders, versatile, 20-seat Twin Otters, or the coffin-like, 35-seat Short 330 is sort of fun.

From Nadi, the busy little resort island of Malololailai gets 10 flights a day by Sunflower Airlines and six by Air Fiji (F$54). Mana Island is visited eight times a day by Sunflower and four times by Air Fiji (F$66).

Turtle Airways Ltd. (Private Mail Bag, NAP 0355, Nadi Airport, Nadi; tel. 722-988, fax 720-346) flies five Cessna floatplanes three times a day from Nadi to Castaway and Mana Islands (F$95 one-way, F$190 roundtrip).

Because only Nadi and Nausori airports have electric lighting on their runways all flights are during daylight hours. Always reconfirm your return flight immediately upon arrival at an outer island, as the reservation lists are sometimes not sent out from Suva. Failure to do so could mean you'll be "bumped" without compensation. Student discounts are for local students only and there are no standby fares. Children aged 12 and under pay 50%, infants two and under carried in arms 10%. Sunflower Airlines and Air Fiji allow 20 kilograms of baggage, but only 15 kilograms is allowed on Turtle Airways (overweight costs one percent of the full one-way fare per kilogram with a F$5 minimum).

Getting Around by Boat

Since most shipping operates out of Suva, passenger services by sea both within Fiji and to neighboring countries are listed in the Suva section. Ferries to the Mamanuca Group are covered under Nadi, those to the Yasawas under Lautoka, those between Vanua Levu and Taveuni under Buca Bay and Taveuni.

The largest company is **Patterson Brothers Shipping,** set up by Levuka copra planter Reg Patterson and his brother just after WW I. Patterson's Japanese-built car ferries, the *Ovalau* and *Princess Ashika,* are usually used on the Tues.-Sat. Buresala-Natovi-Nabouwalu-Ellington Wharf run. The barge *Yaubula* shuttles between Natuvu and Taveuni. Delays due to mechanical failures on Patterson's aging fleet are routine.

Consort Shipping Line runs the large car ferry *Spirit of Free Enterprise* from Suva to Koro, Savusavu, and Taveuni twice a week. The ferry *Adi Savusavu* of **Beachcomber Cruises** also visits Savusavu and Taveuni from Suva two or three times a week.

Other regular boat trips originating in Suva include the competing Patterson Brothers and Emosi Ferry Services shuttles to Levuka and the weekly ferries to Kadavu.

By Bus

Scheduled bus service is available all over Fiji, and fares are low. If you're from the States you'll be amazed how accessible, inexpensive, and convenient the bus service is. Most long-distance bus services operate several times a day and bus stations are usually adjacent to local markets. Buses with a signboard in the window reading Via Highway are local "stage" buses that will stop anywhere along their routes and can be excruciatingly slow on a long trip. Express buses are much faster but they'll only stop in a few towns and won't let you off at resorts along the way. Unfortunately the times of local buses are not posted at the bus stations and it's often hard to find anyone to ask about buses to remote locations. The people most likely to know are other bus drivers but you'll often receive misleading or incorrect information about local buses. Express bus times *are* posted at the stations and it's often possible to pick up printed express bus timetables at tourist offices.

On Viti Levu, the most important routes are between Lautoka and Suva, the biggest cities. If you follow the southern route via Sigatoka you'll be on Queens Road, the smoother and faster of the two. Kings Road via Tavua is longer and can be rough and dusty, but you get to see a little of the interior. Fares from Suva are F$2.12 to Pacific Harbor, F$5.30 to Sigatoka, F$7.77 to Nadi, F$8.12 to Nadi Airport, F$8.95 to Lautoka, and F$10.36 to Ba. Fares average about F$2 for each hour of travel. Express buses are 22 cents extra and to reserve a seat on a bus costs another 50 cents (usually unnecessary).

Pacific Transport Ltd. (G.P.O. Box 1266, Suva; tel. 304-366) has 11 buses a day along Queens Road, with expresses leaving Suva for Lautoka at 0645, 0830, 0930, 1210, 1500, and 1730 (five hours). Eastbound, the expresses leave Lautoka for Suva at 0630, 0700, 1210, 1550, and 1730. An additional Suva-bound express leaves Nadi at 0900. These buses stop at Navua, Pacific Harbor, Sigatoka (coffee break), Nadi, and Nadi Airport *only*. The 1500 bus from Suva continues to Ba. If you want off at a Coral Coast resort or some other smaller place, you must take one of the five local "stage" buses, which take six hours to reach Lautoka via Queens Road. The daily **Sunset Express** (tel. 322-811) leaves Suva for Sigatoka, Nadi, and Lautoka at 0845 and 1600 (four hours).

Sunbeam Transport Ltd. (tel. 382-122) services the northern Kings Road from Suva to Lautoka four or five times a day, with expresses leaving Suva at 0645, 1200, 1330, and 1715 (six hours). Another local Sunbeam bus leaves Suva for Vatukoula via Tavua daily at 0730 (seven hours). From Lautoka, they depart at 0615, 0630, 0815, 1215, and 1630. A Sunbeam express bus along Kings Road is a comfortable way to see Viti Levu's picturesque back side. These expresses only stop at Nausori, Korovou, Vaileka (Rakiraki), Tavua, and Ba. If you want anywhere else you must take one of the two local buses, which take nine fun-filled hours to reach Lautoka via Kings Road. **Reliance Transport** (tel. 382-296) also services Kings Road.

K.R. Latchan's Ltd. (tel. 477-268) also runs express buses around Viti Levu. Their buses often run about 30 minutes ahead of the scheduled Sunbeam or Pacific Transport services and scoop all their passengers.

There are many other local buses, especially closer to Suva or Lautoka. The a/c tourist expresses such as UTC's "Fiji Express" cost twice as much as the services just described and are not as much fun as the ordinary expresses, whose big open windows with roll-down canvas covers give you a panoramic view of Viti Levu. Bus service on Vanua Levu and Taveuni is also good. Local buses often show up late, but the long-distance buses are usually right on time. Passenger trucks serving as "carriers" charge set rates to and from interior villages.

Shared "running" taxis and minibuses also shuttle back and forth between Suva, Nadi, and Lautoka, leaving when full and charging only a little more than the bus. Look for them in the markets around the bus stations. They'll often drop you exactly where you want to go; drawbacks include the less safe driving and lack of insurance coverage (in 1997 three Japanese tourists were killed in a collision caused by a speeding minibus). In a speeding minibus you also miss out on much of the scenery. It's possible to hire a complete taxi from Nadi Airport to Suva for about F$50 for the car, with brief stops along the way for photos, resort visits, etc.

Often the drivers of private or company cars and vans try to earn a little money on the side by stopping to offer lifts to persons waiting for buses beside the highway. They ask the same as you'd pay on the bus but are much faster and will probably drop you off exactly where you want to go. Many locals don't really understand hitchhiking, and it's probably only worth doing on remote roads where bus service is inadequate. In such places almost everyone will stop. Be aware that truck drivers who give you a lift may also expect the equivalent of bus fare; locals pay this without question. It's always appropriate to offer the bus fare and let the driver decide.

Taxis

Fijian taxis are plentiful and among the cheapest in the South Pacific, usable even by low-budget backpackers. Only in Suva do the taxis have meters but everywhere it's usually easier to ask the driver for a flat rate before you get in. If the first price you're quoted is too high you can often bargain (although bargaining is much more accepted by Fiji Indian than by ethnic Fijian drivers). A short ride across town can cost F$1-2, a longer trip into a nearby suburb about F$3. Taxis parked in front of luxury hotels will expect much more than this and it may be worth walking a short distance and flagging one down on the street. Taxis returning to their stand after a trip will pick up passengers at bus stops and charge the regular bus fare (ask if it's the "returning fare").

Don't tip your driver; tips are neither expected nor necessary. And don't invite your driver for a drink or become overly familiar with him as he may abuse your trust. If you're a woman taking a cab alone in the Nadi area, don't let your driver think there is any "hope" for him, or you could have problems (videos often portray Western women as promiscuous, which leads to mistaken expectations).

Car Rentals

Rental cars are expensive in Fiji, due in part to high import duties on cars and a 10% government tax, so with public transportation as good as it is here, you should think twice before renting a car. By law, third-party public liability insurance is compulsory for rental vehicles and is included in the basic rate, but collision damage waiver (CDW) insurance is F$12-20 per day extra. Even with CDW, you're often still responsible for a "nonwaivable excess," which can be as high as the first F$2,000 in damage to the car! Many cars on the road have no insurance, so you could end up paying even if you're not responsible for the accident.

Your home driver's license is recognized for your first six months in Fiji, and driving is on the left (as in Britain and Japan). Get an automatic if you don't care to have to shift gears with your left hand. Seat belts must be worn in the front seat and the police are empowered to give roadside breath-analyzer tests. The police around Viti Levu occasionally employ hand-held radar. Speed limits are 50 kph in towns, 80 kph on the highway. Pedestrians have the right of way at crosswalks.

Unpaved roads can be very slippery, especially on inclines. Fast-moving vehicles on the gravel roads throw up small stones that can smash your front window (and you'll have to pay the damages). As you pass oncoming cars, hold your hand against the windshield just in case. When approaching a Fijian village, slow right down as there may be poorly marked speed humps in the road. Also beware of narrow bridges, and take care with local motorists, who sometimes stop in the middle of the road, pass on blind curves, and drive at high speeds. Driving can be an especially risky business at night. Many of the roads are atrocious (check the spare tire), although the 486-km road around Viti Levu is now fully paved except for a 62-km stretch on the northeast side which is easily passable if you go slowly. Luckily, there isn't a lot of traffic.

If you plan to use a rental car to explore the rough country roads in Viti Levu's mountainous interior, think twice before announcing your plans to the agency, as they may suddenly decline your business. The rental contracts all contain clauses stating that the insurance coverage is not valid under such conditions. However, some companies offer four-wheel-drive Suzukis just made for mountain roads. Tank up on Saturday, as many gas stations are closed on Sunday, and always keep the tank more than half full. If you run out of gas in a rural area, small village stores sometimes sell fuel from drums.

Several international car rental chains are represented in Fiji, including Avis, Budget, Hertz, and Thrifty. Local companies like Bula Rental Cars, Central Rent-a-Car, Dove Rent-a-Car, Kenns Rent-a-Car, Khan's Rental Cars, Roxy Rentals, Satellite Rentals, Sharmas Rent-a-Car, and Tanoa Rent-a-Car are often cheaper, but check around as prices vary. The international companies rent only new cars, while the less-expensive local companies may offer secondhand vehicles. If in doubt, check the vehicle carefully before driving off. The international franchises generally provide better support should anything go wrong. Budget, Central, and Khan's won't rent to persons under age 25, while most of the others will so long as you're over 21.

A dozen companies have offices in the arrivals concourse at Nadi Airport and three are also at Nausori Airport. Agencies with town offices in Suva include Avis, Budget, Central, Dove, Hertz, and Thrifty. In Lautoka you'll find Budget and Central. Avis and Thrifty also have desks in many resort hotels on Viti Levu. On Vanua Levu, Avis and Budget are at Savusavu and Labasa. The other islands, including Taveuni, do not have rental cars.

Both unlimited-kilometer and per-kilometer rates are available. **Thrifty** (tel. 722-935), run by Rosie The Travel Service, offers unlimited-kilometer prices from F$95/570 daily/weekly, which include CDW (F$700 nonwaivable) and tax, but there's a 150-km limit on one-day rentals. **Budget** (tel. 722-636) charges F$69/414 for their cheapest mini but F$18 a day insurance (F$500 nonwaivable). **Avis** begins at F$88/462 plus $20 a day insurance (F$500 nonwaivable). Hertz is a lot more expensive. Prices with Avis and

Budget may be lower if you book ahead from the U.S. The insurance plans used by all of the local companies have nonwaivable excess fees of F$1,500-2,000 which makes renting from them more risky. Also beware of companies like Central whose brochures advertise their off-season rates in large typeface (period not specified), or Satellite and Tanoa, which add the 10% tax later (most of the others include it in the quoted price). Of the local companies, **Sharmas Rental Cars** (tel. 701-055), at Nadi Airport and near the ANZ Bank in Nadi town, offers unlimited-kilometer rates of F$385 a week or F$1209 for 31 days, plus F$12.50 a day insurance. On a per-kilometer basis, **Khan's Rental Cars** (tel. 701-009) in Nadi charges F$15 a day plus 17 cents per kilometer and F$16 CDW (F$2,000 nonwaivable). **Roxy Rentals** (tel. 722-763) is similar.

Many of the local car rental agencies at Nadi Airport offer substantial discounts on their brochure prices for weekly rentals, and you can often get a car for F$350-400 a week with kilometers, tax, and insurance included. Ask how many kilometers are on the speedometer and beware of vehicles with more than 50,000 as they may be unreliable. On a per-kilometer basis, you'll only want to use the car in the local area. Some companies advertise low prices with the qualification in fine print that these apply only to rentals of three days or more. Most companies charge a F$30 delivery fee if you don't return the vehicle to the office where you rented it. If you want the cheapest economy subcompact, reserve ahead.

Tourist Cruises
Blue Lagoon Cruises Ltd. (Box 130, Lautoka; tel. 661-622, fax 664-098) has been offering upmarket minicruises from Lautoka to the Yasawa Islands since its founding in 1950 by Captain Trevor Withers. The three-night trips (from F$957) leave daily, while the six-night cruise (from F$1,716) is weekly. Four and seven-night cruises are also possible. Prices are per person, double occupancy, and include meals (excluding alcohol), entertainment, shore excursions, and tax (no additional "port charges" and no tipping). "A" deck is about 15% more expensive than "B" deck but you have the railing right outside your cabin door instead of a locked porthole window. On the three-night cruises they

use older three-deck, 40-passenger vessels, while larger four-deck, 60-passenger mini-cruise ships are used on the six-night (and some of the three-night) voyages. In 1996 the 72-passenger, US$8-million luxury cruiser *Mystique Princess* began operating three-night trips from F$1,419. The meals are often beach barbecue affairs, with Fijian dancing. You'll have plenty of opportunities to snorkel in the calm, crystal-clear waters (bring your own gear). Though a bit expensive, these trips have a good reputation. There are daily departures, but reservations are essential, as they're usually booked solid months ahead. (We've heard recently that Blue Lagoon has been having problems with the Yasawas chiefs who figured they were being taken for granted and that a few shore excursions have been stopped. Ask if they're still going to the Sawa-i-Lau cave, for example.)

Captain Cook Cruises (Box 23, Nadi; tel. 701-823, fax 702-045), on Narewa Rd. near the bridge into Nadi town, is an Australian company whose Fiji operation is 50% owned by Qantas Airways. Like Blue Lagoon Cruises they offer unpretentious three/four-night cruises to the Yasawa Islands aboard the 68-meter MV *Reef Escape*, departing Nadi Tuesday and Saturday. The 60 double-occupancy cabins begin at F$979/1,315 pp twin with bunk beds or F$1,216/1,623 with normal beds. The two itineraries vary somewhat and there's a discount if you do both in succession. Until recently used for cruises along Australia's Great Barrier Reef, the *Reef Escape* is the largest cruise ship based in Fiji and worth considering as a change of pace. The food is good, cabins bright, activities and entertainment fun, and there's even a miniature swimming pool and spa! Most of your fellow passengers will be Australians, which can be stimulating if you're from somewhere else, and the Fijian staff will spoil you silly.

In addition, Captain Cook operates two/three-night cruises to the southern Yasawas on the square-rigged brigantine *Ra Marama*—a more romantic choice than the mini-cruise ships. These trips depart Nadi every Monday and Thursday morning and cost F$475/595 pp (children under 12 not accepted). You sleep ashore in double *bures,* the food is good with lots of fresh vegetables and salads, and the staff friendly and well organized. Your biggest disappointment will probably be that they have the diesel engine on all the time, and they don't bother trying to use the sails. Still, the 34-meter *Ra Marama* is a fine vessel built for a former governor-general of Fiji of teak planks at Singapore in 1957. These trips can be booked through most travel agents in Fiji or call the number above; readers who've gone report having a great time.

Scuba Cruises

Four **live-aboard dive boats** ply Fiji waters. A seven-night stay on one of these vessels could run as high as F$5,000 pp (airfare, alcohol, and tax extra), but the boat anchors right above the dive sites, so no time is wasted commuting back and forth. All meals are included and the diving is unlimited. Singles are usually allowed to share a cabin with another diver to avoid a single supplement. Bookings can be made through scuba wholesalers worldwide.

The five-stateroom *Sere Ni Wai* (or "song of the sea") is a 30-meter boat based at Suva and operating around Beqa, Kadavu, Lomaiviti, and northern Lau. Captain Greg Lawlor's family has been in Fiji for four generations but his boat is new, launched in 1995. If you're already in Fiji, try calling **Mollie Dean Cruises** (Box 3256, Lami; tel. 361-174, fax 361-137, www.sere.com.fj), which books divers on the *Sere Ni Wai* locally.

Another famous boat is the 34-meter, eight-cabin *Nai'a,* which does seven-day scuba cruises to Lomaiviti and northern Lau at F$3,460, or 10 days for F$4,950, tax included. Captain Bob Barrel has a longstanding interest in dolphins and whales, and whalewatching expeditions to Tonga are organized annually in August or September. Local bookings are accepted when space is available and you might even be able to swing a discount. Call **Nai'a Cruises** (Box 332, Pacific Harbor, Fiji; tel. 450-382, fax 450-566, www.naia.com.fj).

In 1998 the American-owned, 32-meter dive boat *Fiji Aggressor* (tel. 361-382, fax 362-930, www.pac-aggressor.com) was deployed to the Cousteau Fiji Islands Resort near Savusavu. The *Aggressor's* jet-driven launch zips divers to scuba sites at 30 knots, providing unlimited diving for 16 divers flown in on packages from the States. Unlike the eco-friendly *Nai'a* that uses sails to cruise at night, this powerful catamaran projects an image of brute force.

The *Matangi Princess II,* a 26-meter cruise vessel with six a/c cabins, operates around Taveuni from its base at Maravu Plantation (Tropical Dive, tel./fax 880-660). In North America, information on the *Matangi Princess II* can be obtained by calling 888/234-5447 (www.Tropicalinspirations.com). We've heard this boat doesn't quite match the standards of the other three.

Yacht Charters

Due to the risks involved in navigating Fiji's poorly marked reefs yacht charters aren't as common in Fiji as they are on Vava'u, Tonga, or Raiatea in Tahiti-Polynesia. All charter boats are required by law to carry a Fijian guide.

Musket Cove Yacht Charters (Private Mail Bag NAP 0352, Nadi Airport; tel./fax 666-710) offers bareboat yacht charters among the Mamanuca and Yasawa islands from their base at the Musket Cove Marina on Malololailai Island in the Mamanuca Group. Some are exclusive crewed charters, others bareboat with the mandatory Fijian guide, others surfing charters. Chartering isn't for everyone, though two couples considering a stay together at a luxury resort may find prices comparable and the experience more rewarding.

Larger groups could consider the 27-meter ketch *Tau* at the Raffles Tradewinds Hotel, Suva, which costs F$2,550/16,500 a day/week plus 10% tax for up to six persons, including all meals, drinks, and a full crew (scuba diving is extra). It's available year-round. For full information contact Bilo Ltd., Box 3084, Lami, Fiji Islands; tel. 361-057, fax 362-177.

AIRPORTS

Nadi International Airport

Nadi Airport (NAN) is between Lautoka and Nadi, 22 km south of the former and eight km north of the latter. Frequent buses run to these towns until around 2200. To catch a bus to Nadi (54 cents), cross the highway; buses to Lautoka (F$1.18) stop on the airport side of the road. A few express buses drop passengers right outside the international departures hall. A taxi from the airport should be F$6 to downtown Nadi or F$20 to Lautoka. Taxi fares to all Nadi area hotels are posted behind the immigration counters at the airport.

As you come out of customs, a uniformed representative of the Fiji Visitors Bureau will ask you where you intend to stay in order to be helpful and to direct you to a driver from that hotel. Most Nadi hotels offer free transfers (ask) but you ought to change a bit of money before going. Agents of other hotels will also accost you and try to sign you up for the commission they'll earn. Be polite but defensive in dealing with them. The people selling stays at the outer island backpacker resorts can be especially aggressive. Most of the resorts have offices in the airport concourse in front of you—the upmarket places downstairs, the backpacker camps upstairs—and it's better to head straight for them rather than to deal with intermediaries.

The actual office of the Fiji Visitors Bureau (tel. 722-433) is beside the bank to the left as you come out of customs. They open for all international arrivals and can advise you on accommodations (and tell you if your resort of choice has an office at the airport). Pick up their brochures, hotel lists, and free tourist magazines (especially *Fiji Magic*).

There's a 24-hour ANZ Bank (F$2 commission) beside the Visitors Bureau and another bank in the departure lounge. Their rates are about one percent worse than the banks in town. The airport banks don't stock Tongan *pa'anga*, Samoan *tala*, French Pacific francs, or other regional currencies, so buy these at Thomas Cook in Nadi or Suva before coming to the airport.

Many travel agencies and car rental companies are also located in the arrivals arcade. The rent-a-car companies you'll find here are Avis, Budget, Central, Hertz, Kenns, Khan's, Roxy, Satellite, Sharmas, Tanoa, and Thrifty. All of the international airlines flying into Nadi have offices in this same arcade (Air Fiji represents Air Vanuatu).

The post office is across the parking lot from the arrivals hall (ask). The airport cafe just before the security check at departures serves inexpensive light meals. The luggage storage service, near the snack bar in the domestic departures area, is open 24 hours (bicycles or surfboards F$6 a day, bags larger than 75 by 50 centimeters F$4 a day, other luggage F$3 a day). Most hotels around Nadi will also store luggage. There's zero tolerance for drugs in Fiji

and a three-dog sniffer unit checks all baggage passing through NAN. One reader said the airport security officers allowed him to pitch his tent in the airport parking lot.

Duty-free shops are found in both the departure lounge and in the arrivals area just before the baggage claim area. If you're arriving for a prebooked stay at a deluxe resort, grab a bottle or two of cheap Fiji rum as drink prices at the resort bars are high (you can usually get mix at the hotel shops). You can use leftover Fijian currency to stock up on cheap film and cigarettes just before you leave (film prices here are the lowest in the South Pacific). Prices vary slightly at the different duty-free shops and it's worth comparing before buying.

A departure tax of F$20 in cash Fijian currency is payable on all international flights, but transit passengers connecting within 12 hours and children under the age of 16 are exempt (no airport tax on domestic flights). Take time to have a look at the museum exhibits near the departures gates upstairs as you're waiting for your flight. The airport never closes. NAN's 24-hour flight arrival and departure information number is 722-076.

Nausori Airport

Nausori Airport (SUV) is on the plain of the Rewa River delta, 23 km northeast of downtown Suva. After Hurricane Kina in January 1993 the whole terminal was flooded by Rewa water for several days. There's no special airport bus and a taxi direct to/from Suva will run about F$20. You can save money by taking a taxi from the airport only as far as Nausori (four km, F$3), then a local bus to Suva from there (19 km, with services every 10 minutes until 2100 for 90 cents). Airport-bound, catch a local bus from Suva to Nausori, then a taxi to the airport (only F$2 in this direction). It's also possible to catch a local bus to Nausori from the highway opposite the airport about every 15 minutes (40 cents).

Avis, Budget, and Hertz all have car rental offices in the terminal, and a lunch counter provides light snacks. You're not allowed to sleep overnight at this airport. The departure tax is F$20 on all international flights, but no tax is levied on domestic flights. The airport information number is tel. 478-799.

NADI AND THE MAMANUCAS

At 10,429 square km, Viti Levu is the eighth-largest island in the South Pacific, only a shade smaller than the Big Island of Hawaii. This 1,323-meter-high island accounts for more than half of Fiji's land area and dominates the country in almost every respect. Nadi International Airport facing Nadi Bay on the west side of Viti Levu has long been the main gateway to the Fiji Islands and the South Pacific. The airport itself sits in the center of an ancient volcano, the west side of which has fallen away.

A small airstrip existed at Nadi even before WW II, and after Pearl Harbor the Royal New Zealand Air Force began converting it into a fighter strip. Before long the U.S. military was there, building a major air base with paved runways for bombers and transport aircraft serving Australia and New Zealand. In the early 1960s, Nadi Airport was expanded to accommodate jet aircraft, and today the largest jumbo jets can land here. This activity has made Nadi what it is today.

All around Nadi are cane fields worked by the predominantly Indian population. There aren't many sandy, palm-fringed beaches on the western side of Viti Levu—for that you have to go to the nearby Mamanuca Group where a string of sun-drenched "Robinson Crusoe" resorts soak up vacationers in search of a place to relax. The long gray mainland beaches near Nadi face shallow murky waters devoid of snorkeling possibilities but fine for windsurfing and water-skiing. Fiji's tropical rainforests are on the other side of Viti Levu as this is the dry side of the island.

NADI

In recent years Nadi (pronounced "Nandi") has grown into Fiji's third-largest town with a mixed population of 32,000. The town center's main feature is a kilometer of restaurants and shops with high-pressure sales staffs peddling mass-produced souvenirs. It's easily the most touristy place in Fiji, yet there's also a surprisingly colorful market (especially on Saturday morning) and the road out to the airport is flanked by a multi-tude of places to stay. Still, if you're not that exhausted after your transpacific flight you'd do better to head for Lautoka. All of the hotels around Nadi tend to experience quite a bit of aircraft/traffic/disco noise, while those at Lautoka are out of range.

Sights

Nadi's only substantial sight is the **Sri Siva Subrahmaniya Swami Temple** at the south entrance to town, erected by local Hindus in 1994 after the lease on their former temple property expired. This colorful South Indian-style temple, built by craftspeople flown in from India itself, is the largest and finest of its kind in the South Pacific. Sober visitors may enter the temple, but shoes must be removed at the entrance, and smoking and photography are prohibited inside the compound (open daily 0500-1330/1530-2000, admission free).

Sports and Recreation

Aqua-Trek (Dave Dickinson, Box 10215, Nadi Airport; tel. 702-413, fax 702-412), located at 465 Queens Rd., opposite the Mobil station in Nadi town, is the only full-service dive shop in western Fiji. They also run a dive shop on Mana Island. Aqua-Trek charges F$80/160 for one/two boat dives with gear or F$520 for PADI open-water certification (medical examination required). Shark feeding is offered.

Dive Tropex (Eddie Jennings, Box 10522, Nadi Airport; tel. 703-944, fax 703-955), in the beach hut at the Sheraton, offers scuba diving at F$99/141/462 one/two/eight tanks including gear. When space is available snorkelers can go along for F$40. A four-day PADI certification course is F$614 for one to three students, or F$404 pp for four students or more. For an introductory dive it's F$135. Several Japanese instructors are on the staff.

Much less expensive diving is offered by **Inner Space Adventures** (Box 9535, Nadi Airport; tel./fax 723-883), between the Horizon and Travellers beach resorts at Wailoaloa Beach. They go out daily at 0900, charging F$60/77/105 for one/two/three tanks, equipment and pickup any-

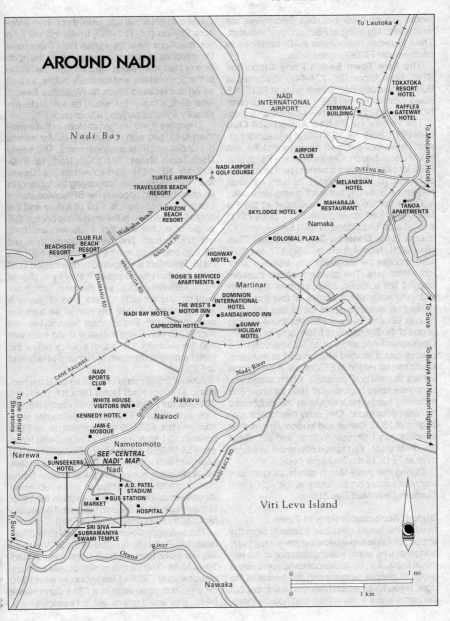

AROUND NADI

Nadi Bay

To Lautoka

NADI INTERNATIONAL AIRPORT

TERMINAL BUILDING

TOKATOKA RESORT HOTEL

RAFFLES GATEWAY HOTEL

To Mocambo Hotel

AIRPORT CLUB

QUEENS RD.

NADI AIRPORT GOLF COURSE

TURTLE AIRWAYS

MELANESIAN HOTEL

TRAVELLERS BEACH RESORT

MAHARAJA RESTAURANT

TANOA APARTMENTS

HORIZON BEACH RESORT

SKYLODGE HOTEL

Namaka

CLUB FIJI BEACH RESORT

COLONIAL PLAZA

BEACHSIDE RESORT

HIGHWAY MOTEL

ENAMANU RD.

WAILOALOA BEACH

WAILOALOA RD.

NADI BAY RD.

ROSIE'S SERVICED APARTMENTS

Martinar

DOMINION INTERNATIONAL HOTEL

To Suva

THE WEST'S MOTOR INN

NADI BAY MOTEL

SANDALWOOD INN

CAPRICORN HOTEL

SUNNY HOLIDAY MOTEL

To Bukuya and Nausori Highlands

CANE RAILWAY

NADI SPORTS CLUB

Nadi River

To the Denarau Sheratons

WHITE HOUSE VISITORS INN

QUEENS RD.

Nakavu

KENNEDY HOTEL

Navoci

JAM-E MOSQUE

Namotomoto

SUNSEEKERS HOTEL

SEE "CENTRAL NADI" MAP

Nadi

Narewa

A.D. PATEL STADIUM

MARKET

BUS STATION

HOSPITAL

Viti Levu Island

NADI BACK RD.

To Suva

SRI SIVA SUBRAMANIYA SWAMI TEMPLE

Otuna River

Nawaka

1 mi

1 km

where around Nadi included. Snorkelers are welcome to tag along at F$25 pp, gear included. Their four-day open-water PADI certification course costs F$320—good value.

The **New Town Beach Pony Club** (Box 9299, Nadi Airport; tel. 724-449) at Wailoaloa Beach offers one-hour beach rides at F$15, 1.5 hours crosscountry at F$20, or a two-hour combination at F$25. Longer rides can be arranged.

The 18-hole, par-71 **Nadi Airport Golf Club** (Box 9015, Nadi; tel. 722-148) is pleasantly situated between the airport runways and the sea at Wailoaloa Beach. Greens fees are F$15, plus F$20 for clubs. There's a bar and pool table in the clubhouse (tourists welcome). It's busy with local players on Saturday but quiet during the week.

Other golf courses are available at the Fiji Mocambo Hotel (greens fees F$11, clubs F$11) and at the Sheratons. The 18-hole, par-72 course at the **Denarau Golf & Racquet Club** (Box 9081, Nadi Airport; tel. 750-477, fax 750-484) opposite the Sheratons was designed by Ei-ichi Motohashi. The course features bunkers shaped like a marlin, crab, starfish, and octopus, and water shots across all four par-three holes (the average golfer loses four balls per round). Greens fees are F$85 for those staying at one of the Sheratons or F$94 for other mortals. Golfers are not allowed to walk around the course and a shared electric cart is included. Clubs can be rented at F$30 a set. A better deal is their "sunset golf" package, which allows you to do nine holes beginning at 1600 for only F$38 including happy hour drinks at the clubhouse bar after your round. On Friday this "chook run" begins at 1500. Call ahead to reconfirm as their specials vary from time to time, and ask about the dress code. Ten tennis courts are available here at F$12/18 day/night per hour.

During the June-March sports season, see rugby or soccer on Saturday at the A.D. Patel Stadium, near Nadi Bus Station.

Budget Accommodations in Town

Most of the hotels offer free transport from the airport, which is lucky because there aren't any budget places within walking distance of the terminal itself. As you leave customs you'll see a group of people representing the hotels to the right. If you know which hotel you want, call out the name and if a driver from that hotel is there,

you should get a free ride (ask). If not, the Fiji Visitors Bureau (tel. 722-433) to the left will help you telephone them for a small fee. (There have been reports of nocturnal muggings on the north side of Nadi town along the road from the bridge to the Sunseekers and Kennedy hotels, as well as on the isolated roads to Wailoaloa Beach. After dark, a bus or taxi would be advisable, especially if you're carrying a backpack.)

There are three budget choices in the downtown area, two with confusingly similar names but under separate managements. The seedy **Nadi Town Motel** (Box 1326, Nadi; tel. 700-600, fax 701-541), also known as the "Downtown Backpackers Inn," occupying the top floor of an office building opposite the BP service station in the center of Nadi, is a bit of a dive and the only attraction here is the shoestring price: F$20 single or double with fan, F$35 with a/c, both with private bath. The five-bed dormitory is just F$5 pp and basic rooms with shared bath are F$15. Breakfast is supposed to be included in all rates but don't be surprised if they try to charge extra. Definitely ask to see the room before accepting, expect dirty sheets, and, if you're a woman, don't tolerate any nonsense from the male motel staff. The adjacent Seventh Heaven Night Club sends out a steady disco beat well into the morning. The travel agency below the motel arranges transport to Nananu-i-Ra Island at F$20 pp.

Around the corner on Koroivolu St. is the two-story, 31-room **Nadi Hotel** (Box 91, Nadi; tel. 700-000, fax 700-280). Spacious rooms with private bath begin at F$22/28 single/double standard with fan, F$33/39 superior with a/c, or F$10 pp in an 10-bed dorm. Deluxe rooms with fridge are F$44/50/60 single/double/triple. The neat courtyard with a swimming pool out back makes this a pleasant, convenient place to stay. Some rooms are also subjected to nightclub noise though, so ask for a superior room in the block farthest away from Seventh Heaven. The restaurant has three-course meals at F$10.

The two-story **Coconut Inn Hotel** (Box 2756, Nadi; tel. 701-169, fax 700-616), 37 Vunavau St., is a block from the Nadi Hotel and the Nadi Town Motel. The 22 rooms with private bath upstairs begin at F$33/43 single/double (plus F$10 for a/c), and downstairs is a F$11 dorm (three beds). Beware of rooms without windows.

On Narewa Rd. at the north edge of Nadi town is the **Sunseekers Hotel** (Box 100, Nadi; tel. 700-400, fax 702-047). The 20 rooms here are F$50 double with fan but shared bath, F$55 with a/c and private bath, or F$11 for a bunk in the nine-bed dorm (F$16 in the six-bed dorm). There's a bar on the large deck out back, which overlooks the swimming pool (often dry) and surrounding countryside. Bicycle rentals are F$3.50 an hour or F$11 a day (0800-1600). Despite the sign, this is not an approved Hosteling International associate. Airport pickups are free but to return to the airport you must take a taxi (F$6).

Better is the two-story **White House Visitors Inn** (Box 2150, Nadi; tel. 700-022, fax 702-822), at 40 Kennedy Ave., up Ray Prasad Rd. just off Queens Rd., a 10-minute walk north of central Nadi. The 12 fan-equipped rooms are F$27 double with shared bath, F$33/38 single/double with private bath, or F$12 pp in the dorm. Rooms with a/c cost F$8 extra. The beds are comfortable, and a weight-watchers' toast-and-coffee breakfast is included in the price. You can cook your own meals in the communal kitchen, and there's a grocery store across the street. This small hotel is a fairly peaceful place to stay with a small swimming pool, video lounge, and free airport pickups. Baggage storage is F$1 per day (but only if you make your outer-island bookings through them). Though you'll hear a bit of traffic and animal noise, you won't be bothered by disco music. It's very popular and might be full.

Half a block up Kennedy Ave. from the White House is the three-story **Kennedy Hotel** (Box 9045, Nadi Airport; tel. 702-360, fax 702-218), the highest-priced hotel in this category. The 16 a/c rooms with private bath, TV, and coffee-making facilities are F$47 single or double without fridge, F$57 with fridge, tax included. Beds in the four fan-cooled, four-bed dormitory blocks cost F$11 pp, or F$15 for a bed in the eight-bed a/c dorm. Deluxe two-bedroom apartments with cooking facilities are F$95. A plus are the spacious gardenlike grounds with a large swimming pool, and there's a restaurant/bar on the premises. The Kennedy is quite popular and but some of the rooms are rather small and shabby so have a look before committing yourself.

Budget Airport Hotels

The listings below are arranged from the airport into town. The Chinese-operated **Westgarden Hotel** (Box 9968, Nadi Airport; tel. 721-788, fax 721-790), on the 3rd floor above Chopsticks Restaurant at Namaka, has nine a/c rooms with bath at F$50 single or double, F$55 triple, F$60 family.

The **Melanesian Hotel** (Box 10410, Nadi Airport; tel. 722-438, fax 720-425), near the Westgarden but a bit farther off the road, has 16 rooms with bath beginning at F$38/45 single/double, F$10 extra for a/c. A mixed five-bed dorm (F$15 pp) is also available. Ask about youth hostel discounts. The new management has picked the Melanesian up and it's now a pleasant place to stop, with a swimming pool, bar, and restaurant.

Across the street from the Shell service station in Martintar is **Mountainview Apartments** (Box 1476, Nadi; tel. 721-880, fax 721-800), above the Bounty Restaurant and near the Dominion International Hotel, with 10 fan-cooled rooms with bath at F$30/33 single/double. The one a/c room is F$39 single or double, and if you want cooking facilities it's an extra F$5 a day for the stove and gas tank.

The two-story **Sandalwood Inn** (John and Ana Birch, Box 9454, Nadi Airport; tel. 722-044, fax 720-103), on Ragg St. beside the Dominion International Hotel, is F$27/33/38 single/double/triple plus tax for one of the five rooms with shared bath in the old wing, or F$32/34/40 for one of the seven standard rooms with fridge and private bath in the new wing (the 13 a/c rooms are F$51/58/60). The atmosphere is pleasant and the layout attractive with a pool, a bar, and a medium-priced restaurant serving authentic Fijian dishes! A cooked breakfast and three-course dinner are F$24 plus tax. Avoid the rooms facing the swimming pool if you plan to go to bed early. Two hundred meters inland from the Inn is the two-story **Sandalwood Lodge** (same management) with 24 a/c rooms with bath, fridge, and cooking facilities in two blocks facing a swimming pool at F$64/71/76. Add 10% tax to all prices.

Close by is the 14-room **Sunny Holiday Motel** (Box 1326, Nadi Airport; tel. 722-158, fax 701-541), on Northern Press Rd. behind Hamacho Japanese Restaurant—the cheapest place to stay around Nadi. It's F$15/20 single/double with shared bath, F$22/27 with private bath, or

F$6 in the four-bed dorm. Self-contained apartments with cooking facilities are F$35. Inveterate campers may like to know that this is about the only place in this area where you're allowed to unroll your tent (F$2.50 pp). There's a pool table, TV room, bar, and luggage storage. It's all a little run-down, but friendly, uncrowded, and fine for those on shoestring budgets. They book the daily shuttle to Nananu-i-Ra Island (F$22 one-way).

A few hundred meters down Wailoaloa Beach Rd. off the main highway, in the opposite direction from the Sunny Holiday, is the **Nadi Bay Motel** (Bryan and Victoria Curran, Private Mail Bag, NAP 0359, Nadi; tel. 723-599, fax 720-092), a two-story concrete edifice enclosing a swimming pool. The 25 rooms are F$27/37 single/double with fan, F$8 extra for private bath, F$17 extra for private bath and a/c. An apartment with cooking facilities is F$53/63 single/double. There's also a F$10 dorm. Washing machines are available, plus a congenial bar, inexpensive restaurant, and luggage room. The airport flight path passes right above the Nadi Bay and the roar of jets on the adjacent runway can be jarring. If you take any scuba lessons in the motel swimming pool, be prepared for a steady stream of wisecracks from the jerks lounging by the pool.

Budget Beach Hotels

There are half a dozen budget or inexpensive places to stay on Wailoaloa Beach, also known as Newtown Beach, on the opposite side of the airport runway from the main highway. The first four places are near the seaplane base and golf club, a dusty three-km hike from the Nadi Bay Motel, so ask for their free shuttle buses at the airport or take a taxi (F$6). The Wailoaloa Newtown bus from Nadi market also passes nearby four

times a day. These places are probably your best bet on the weekend, and sporting types can play a round of golf on the public course or go jogging along the beach (the swimming in the knee-deep water isn't great). The main base of Inner Space Adventures is here, with scuba diving and horseback riding on offer.

The most popular of the lot is the **Horizon Beach Resort** (Box 1401, Nadi; tel. 722-832, fax 720-662), a large wooden two-story house just across a field from the beach. The 14 rooms with shared bath begin at F$30 single or double with fan, F$38 with a/c. Horizon's 10-bed dormitory is F$6 pp (F$8 pp in the five-bed room). No cooking facilities are provided but there's a medium-priced restaurant/bar. To use the washer/drier is F$10 a load.

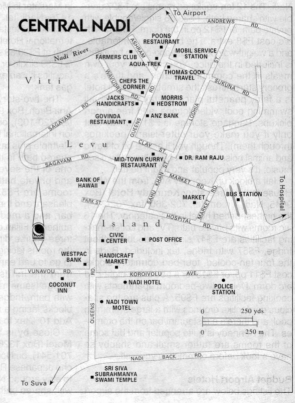

CENTRAL NADI

To Airport
ANDREWS RD.
Nadi River
Viti
POONS RESTAURANT
ASHRAM ST.
FARMERS CLUB
MOBIL SERVICE STATION
AQUA-TREK
WAQADRA RD.
CHEFS THE CORNER
THOMAS COOK TRAVEL
SUKUNA RD.
JACKS HANDICRAFTS
MORRIS HEDSTROM
QUEENS RD.
LODHA ST.
GOVINDA RESTAURANT
ANZ BANK
SAGAYAM RD.
Levu
CLAY ST.
SAGAYAM RD.
MID-TOWN CURRY RESTAURANT
DR. RAM RAJU
BANK OF HAWAII
SAHU KHAN LANE
MARKET RD.
PARK ST.
MARKET
BUS STATION
To Hospital
HOSPITAL RD.
Island
CIVIC CENTER
POST OFFICE
WESTPAC BANK
HANDICRAFT MARKET
VUNAVOU RD.
KOROIVOLU AVE.
COCONUT INN
NADI HOTEL
POLICE STATION
QUEENS RD.
NADI TOWN MOTEL
0   250 yds
0   250 m
NADI   BACK   RD.
SRI SIVA SUBRAHMANYA SWAMI TEMPLE
To Suva
Moon

A hundred meters inland from the Horizon is the friendly two-story **Newtown Beach Motel** (Box 787, Nadi; tel. 723-339, fax 720-087). The seven clean rooms with fan are F$33 single or double (or F$11 pp in the five-bed dorm). There's no cooking, but a huge dinner is offered for F$7.

A hundred meters along the beach from the Horizon is **Travelers Beach Resort** (Box 700, Nadi; tel. 723-322, fax 720-026). The 12 standard rooms with private bath are F$33/39 single/double, the eight a/c rooms F$39/50, the two a/c beachfront rooms F$55 single or double, and the 13 villas with kitchenette F$66/77/88 single/double/triple. Four four-bed dorms are provided at F$11 pp. The villas are tightly packed in a compound a block back from the beach. There's an expensive restaurant/bar and a swimming pool, but many of the other facilities listed in their brochure seem to have vanished. The management style leaves a lot to be desired, and several complaints have been received.

Ratu Kini Boko has a large modern house at Wailoaloa Beach opposite the Travelers Beach Resort villas called **Mana Rose Apartments** (tel. 723-333) where he puts up guests in transit to his backpacker resort on Mana Island. The three four-bed dorms are F$15 pp including breakfast, double rooms are F$40, and there's a plush lounge where you can relax.

Also on Wailoaloa Beach, a kilometer southwest of the places just mentioned and three km off Queens Rd. from McDonald's Restaurant (F$3 one-way by taxi), is **Club Fiji Beach Resort** (John and Elly Bullock, Box 9619, Nadi Airport; tel. 720-150, fax 720-350). The 24 thatched duplex bungalows, all with veranda, private bath, solar hot water, and fridge, are priced according to location: F$60 single or double for a garden unit, F$78 oceanview. The eight a/c beachfront suites in a two-story building are F$110/123 double/triple. One duplex has been converted into a pair of six-bunk, 12-person dormitories at F$10 pp, with a small discount if you have a youth hostel card. Add 10% tax to all rates. Club Fiji's staff does its utmost to keep the accommodations and grounds spotless. The atmosphere is friendly and relaxed, and you'll meet other travelers at the bar. Tea- and coffee-making facilities are provided but there's no cooking. The Club's restaurant serves authentic Fijian food and a variety of dishes (F$35 breakfast and dinner plan).

Special evening events include the *lovo* on Thursday and the beach barbecue on Saturday night. Horseback riding is F$15 an hour, the Hobie cat F$15 an hour, and windsurfing and paddle boats complimentary. A two-hour snorkeling trip by boat is F$20 pp. The day tour to Natadola Beach and the two-island boat trip each cost F$50 with lunch. At low tide the beach resembles a tidal flat, but there's a small clean swimming pool, and the location is lovely—the equivalent of the Sheratons at a fifth the price and without the stuffy upmarket atmosphere. Club Fiji is recommended as your top choice in this price range, but call ahead as they're often full.

Also good is the **Beachside Resort** (Box 9883, Nadi Airport; tel. 703-488, fax 703-688), next to Club Fiji at Wailoaloa Beach. The five a/c rooms on the ground floor of the main building are F$68/78 double/triple, while the 10 rooms on the second and third floors are F$88/98 (reduced rates often available). These rooms have fridges but no cooking facilities. However, seven new *bures* adjacent to the main building do have kitchens and run F$600 double a week. A three-course dinner at the resort's thatched restaurant is F$17.50. Despite the name, the Beachside isn't right on the beach although it does have a swimming pool. A timeshare condo development called "Fantasy Beach Estate" is going up just beyond the Beachside and beach access should be possible through the Fantasy complex. There will also be a yacht marina. Although the accommodations are of a high standard there's less atmosphere here than at Club Fiji, which makes it very much a second choice.

Inexpensive

The three medium-priced selections that follow are highly competitive and often run specials that reduce the quoted rates. **Rosie's Deluxe Serviced Apartments** (Box 9268, Nadi Airport; tel. 722-755, fax 722-607), in Martintar near Ed's Bar, offers studio apartments accommodating four at F$60, one-bedrooms for up to five at F$80, and two-bedrooms for up to seven at F$106. All eight a/c units have cooking facilities, fridge, and private balcony. The walls are not completely soundproof and the units facing the highway get considerable traffic noise, but they're still good value. You may use the communal washer and drier free. Rosie The Travel Service office at the airport is the place to check current prices and availability. Free airport transfers are provided in both directions, even in the middle of the night.

The **West's Motor Inn** (Peter Beer, Box 10097, Nadi Airport; tel. 720-044, fax 720-071) is next to the Dominion International, not far from Rosie's Apartments. The 62 a/c rooms with private bath and fridge begin at F$88 single or double standard (or F$99 for a larger deluxe room). Their 50% day-use rate can extend your occupancy from 1030 until 1800 if you have a late flight. The name really doesn't do justice to this pleasant two-story hotel with its courtyard swimming pool, piano bar, restaurant, conference room, secretarial services, and Rosie tour desk.

The **Capricorn International Hotel** (Box 9043, Nadi Airport; tel. 720-088, fax 720-522), between The West's Motor Inn and Hamacho Japanese Restaurant, consists of two-story blocks surrounding a swimming pool. The 62 small a/c rooms with fridge begin at F$75 single or double. Cooking facilities are not provided, but there's a restaurant/bar on the premises. Dove Rent-a-Car has a desk here.

Moderate

The two-story, colonial-style **Raffles Gateway Hotel** (Box 9891, Nadi Airport; tel. 722-444, fax 720-620) is just across the highway from the airport terminal, within easy walking distance. Its 92 a/c rooms begin at F$105 single or double. Happy hour at the poolside bar is 1800-1900 (half-price drinks)—worth checking out if you're stuck at the airport waiting for a flight.

Several km southwest of the airport is the **Skylodge Hotel** (Box 9222, Nadi Airport; tel. 722-200, fax 724-330), which was constructed in the early 1960s as Nadi Airport was being expanded to take jet aircraft. Airline crews on layovers originally stayed here, and business travelers still make up 50% of the clientele. The 53 a/c units begin at F$114 single or double; children under 16 are free, provided the bed configurations aren't changed. It's better to pay F$32 more here and get a room with cooking facilities in one of the four-unit clusters well-spaced among the greenery, rather than a smaller room in the main building or near the busy highway. If you're catching a flight in the middle of the night there's a F$66 "day use" rate valid until 2300. Pitch-and-putt golf, half-size tennis facilities, and a swimming pool are on the premises. Airport transfers are free.

The **Dominion International Hotel** (Box 9178, Nadi Airport; tel. 722-255, fax 720-187), halfway between the airport and town, is one of Nadi's nicest top end hotels. This appealing three-story building was built in 1973, and they've done their best to keep the place up. The 85 a/c rooms with balcony or terrace are F$110/115/125 single/double/triple, plus F$20 extra if you want a "deluxe" with a TV and a bath tub instead of a shower. Their 60% "extended stay rate" allows you to keep your room until 2200. If you stay six nights, the seventh is free. Lots of well-shaded tables and chairs surround the swimming pool, and the nearby hotel bar has a happy hour 1800-1900 daily. On Saturday night you'll be treated to a *meke.* There's a Rosie The Travel Service desk in the Dominion and a barber shop/beauty salon. The hotel bottle shop facing the highway is open Mon.-Fri. 1100-2100, Saturday 1100-1400/1600-2100, should you wish to stock your fridge. The tennis court is free for guests (day use only). It's all very relaxed and not at all pretentious.

Premium

People on brief prepaid stopovers in Fiji are often accommodated at one of the hotels off Votualevu Rd., a couple of km inland from the airport (take a taxi). For instance, the Malaysian-owned **Fiji Mocambo Hotel** (Box 9195, Nadi Airport; tel. 722-000, fax 720-324) is a sprawling two-story hotel with mountain views from the spacious grounds. The 128 a/c rooms with patio or balcony and fridge begin at F$213/225/265 single/double/triple including breakfast. Secretarial services can be arranged for businesspeople, conference facilities and a swimming pool are available, and there's a par-27, nine-hole executive golf course on the adjacent slope (free for guests). Lots of in-house entertainment is laid on, including a *meke* once a week. A live band plays in the Vale ni Marau Lounge Thursday, Friday, and Saturday 2100-0100.

Across the street from the Fiji Mocambo is the two-story **Tanoa International Hotel** (Box 9203, Nadi Airport; tel. 720-277, fax 720-191), formerly the Nadi Travelodge Hotel and now owned by local businessman Yanktesh Permal Reddy. The 133 superior a/c rooms with fridge are F$180 single or double, F$220 suite, and children under 16 may stay free. They have a half-price day-use rate, which gives you a room from noon until midnight if you're leaving in the middle of the night (airport transfers free). The hotel coffee shop is open 24 hours a day, and a swimming pool, fitness center, and floodlit tennis courts are on the premises.

Luxury

Nadi's two big transnational hotels, the Sheraton Royal and the Sheraton Fiji, are on Denarau Beach opposite Yakuilau Island, seven km west of the bridge on the north side of Nadi town and a 15-minute drive from the airport. These are Nadi's only upmarket hotels right on the beach, although the gray sands here can't match those of the Mamanuca Islands. The murky waters lapping Sheraton shores are okay for swimming, and two pontoons are anchored in deeper water, but there'd be no point in snorkeling here. Windsurfing, water-skiing, and sailboating are more practicable activities.

Sidestepping the Waikiki syndrome, neither hotel is taller than the surrounding palms, though the manicured affluence has a dull Hawaiian neighbor-island feel. In 1993 a F$15-million championship golf course opened on the site of a former mangrove swamp adjacent to the resort. In 1996 ITT-Sheraton bought both resorts from the Japanese interests that had controlled them since 1988. Two-thirds of the hotel staff and all of the taxi drivers based here belong to the landowning clan.

Almost all the tourists staying at these places are on package tours and they pay only a fraction of the rack rates quoted below. If you call direct upon arrival in Fiji (instead of booking through a travel agent abroad) you may be offered a 50% discount on the published rates. Ask if there are any "specials" going. Both hotels are rather isolated, and restaurant-hopping possibilities are restricted to the pricey hotel restaurants, so you should take the meal package if you intend to spend most of your time here. Also bring insect repellent unless you yourself want to be on the menu!

The pretentious **Sheraton Royal Denarau Resort** (Box 9081, Nadi Airport; tel. 750-000, fax 750-259) opened in 1975 as The Regent of Fiji. This sprawling series of two-story clusters with traditional touches between the golf course and the beach contains 285 spacious a/c rooms

beginning at F$345 single or double plus tax. Facilities include an impressive lobby with shops to one side, a thatched pool bar you can swim right up to, and 10 floodlit tennis courts.

The Sheraton Royal's neighbor, the modern-style **Sheraton Fiji Resort** (Box 9761, Nadi Airport; tel. 750-777, fax 750-818), has 300 a/c rooms that begin at F$448 single or double plus tax but including a buffet breakfast. This $60-million two-story hotel complex opened in 1987, complete with a 16-shop arcade and an 800-seat ballroom.

There's no bus service to either Sheraton. A taxi to/from Nadi town should be around F$6, though the cabs parked in front of the hotels will expect much more—perhaps as much as F$20 to the airport. Avis Rent A Car has a desk in each of the hotels. If your travel agent booked you into either of these, you'll only be exposed to Fiji on the short walk from the plane to your a/c car before being wrapped in North American safety again (the Mamanuca resorts like Naitasi are better value).

Downtown Restaurants

Several excellent places to eat are opposite the Mobil service station on Queens Rd. at the north end of Nadi town. For Cantonese and European food try the upstairs dining room at **Poon's Restaurant** (tel. 700-896; Mon.-Sat. 1000-2200, Sunday 1200-1400/1800-2200), which is recommended for its filling meals at reasonable prices, pleasant atmosphere, and friendly service. **Mama's Pizza Inn** (tel. 700-221), just up the road from Poon's, serves pizzas big enough for two or three people for F$8-23. Mama's has a second location in Colonial Plaza halfway out toward the airport. A number of other pricey Asian restaurants are between Mama's and the bridge.

The package tour buses often park in front of **Chefs The Corner** (tel. 703-131), Sangayam and Queens Roads opposite Morris Hedstrom. This rather expensive self-service restaurant does have some of the favorite ice cream in town (F$2-4). Just down Sangayam Rd. are **The Edge Cafe** and **Chefs Restaurant,** both very upmarket and also run by two former Sheraton chefs, Josef and Eugene. All are closed on Sunday.

Fewer tourists stray into **Govinda Vegetarian Restaurant and Coffee Lounge** (tel. 702-445; Mon.-Fri. 0800-1900, Saturday 0800-1700), on

Queens Rd. almost opposite the ANZ Bank. It's the equivalent of the famous Hare Krishna Restaurant in Suva with only pure vegetarian food on offer. Govinda's set Indian meal of two *rotis*, rice, two vegetable curries, *dhal, papadam, samosa,* and chutney is F$4.50. They also have ice cream for half the price of Chefs just up the street.

Probably the number-one low-budget eatery in Nadi is the basic **Mid-Town Curry Restaurant** (tel. 700-536; closed Sunday), around the corner from Govinda on Clay Street. They serve real Fiji Indian dishes instead of the usual tourist fare, which means *very spicy.* Come early as they close at 1800.

Chopsticks Restaurant (tel. 700-178), upstairs from the Bank of Baroda on the main street, offers Chinese dishes, curries, and seafood.

About the top place to try real Fijian dishes like *palusami* and *kokoda* is at the seafood buffet served daily 1200-1400 (F$7) at the **Coconut Tree Restaurant** (tel. 701-169) below the Coconut Inn Hotel, 37 Vunavau St., down the side street opposite the Nadi Handicraft Market.

Be aware that the sidewalk terrace restaurants near the Tourist Information Center on the main street in the center of Nadi are strictly for tourists not familiar with the local price structure.

Restaurants toward the Airport

Luigi and Carla operate **The Only Italian Restaurant** (tel. 724-590), next to the Shell service station in Martintar almost opposite the Dominion International Hotel. Their excellent pizzas average F$16, or you can take spaghetti for about F$12. Otherwise there are a few special meat and fish dishes. It's open for dinner only from about 1800. The **Bounty Restaurant** (tel. 720-840) across the street has Chinese dishes and hamburgers for lunch, steaks and seafood for dinner, all at reasonable prices. There's also a good bar here is you only want a drink.

RJ's for Ribs (tel. 722-900), directly behind Ed's Bar at Martintar, has a sister establishment in Beverly Hills, California. Pork or beef ribs run F$12, filet mignon F$18, a skewer of prawns F$22. RJ's is the perfect complement to happy hour (1730-2000) at Ed's, and a tasty way to polish off those leftover Fiji dollars if you're flying out the next day.

The **Maharaja Restaurant** (tel. 722-962), out near the Skylodge Hotel is popular with flight crews who come for the spicy Indian curries, tandoori dishes, and fresh local seafood. It's open daily but on Sunday for dinner only—a bit expensive but very good.

Entertainment

There are two movie houses in Nadi: **Jupiter Cinema** (tel. 703-950), next to the Coconut Inn on Vunavau St., and **Novelty Cinema** (tel. 700-155), upstairs from the mall next to the Nadi Civic Center, not far from the post office. Both show an eclectic mix of Hollywood and Indian films.

Seventh Heaven Night Club (tel. 703-188), next to the Nadi Hotel, has a live rock band 2100-0100 on Friday and Saturday nights. Locals call it "the zoo."

Bars and Clubs

The **Nadi Farmers Club** (tel. 700-415), just up Ashram Rd. from the Mobil station in Nadi town, is a good local drinking place.

The **Nadi Sports Club** (tel. 700-239) is a kilometer north of town, back on the road beside Jame Mosque, then right and past a garment factory. Aside from the bar (open Mon.-Thurs. 1600-2200, Friday 1600-2300, Saturday 1200-2300, Sunday 1200-2100) this very smart club has squash and tennis courts, lawn bowling, and a swimming pool. If you wish to play squash or tennis you must bring your own rackets as there are no rentals. To use the competition swimming pool is F$3.30 a day, the same fee which applies to the other facilities.

Your best bet out on the hotel strip toward the airport is **Ed's Bar** (tel. 720-373), a little north of the Dominion International Hotel. Happy hour is 1730-2000 daily with live music Friday and Saturday nights. It's a safe local place not only for tourists, with a friendly young staff.

The **Airport Club** (Mon.-Thurs. 1100-2300, Friday and Saturday 1100-0200), in the Airport Housing Area down the road past Namaka Police Station and almost underneath the airport control tower, is an old-fashioned colonial club with tables overlooking the runways. It's an interesting place to sit and drink draft beer as the planes soar above the swimming pool.

Cultural Shows for Visitors

The **Sheraton Fiji** (tel. 750-777) has a free *meke* Tuesday and Saturday at 2100. Thursday at

1900 Fijian firewalking comes with the *meke* and a F$11 fee is charged. The *meke* and *magiti* (feast) at the **Sheraton Royal** (tel. 750-000) happen Monday and Friday at 2000 (F$45).

You can also enjoy a *lovo* feast and *meke* at the **Fiji Mocambo Hotel** (tel. 722-828) on Monday (F$25), at the **Tokatoka Resort Hotel** (tel. 720-222) on Friday (F$24), and at the **Dominion International Hotel** (tel. 722-255) on Saturday.

Shopping

The **Nadi Handicraft Market,** opposite the Nadi Hotel just off Queens Rd., is worth a look. Before going there, have a look around **Jack's Handicrafts** (tel. 700-744), opposite Morris Hedstrom on the main street, to get an idea what's available and how much things should cost. Just beware the friendly handshake in Nadi, for you may find yourself buying something you neither care for nor desire.

Services

The Westpac Bank opposite the Nadi Handicraft Market, the ANZ Bank near Morris Hedstrom, and the Bank of Hawaii between these two, change traveler's checks without commission. They're open Mon.-Thurs. 0930-1500, Friday 0930-1600. The Bank of Hawaii has a Visa ATM.

Money Exchange (tel. 703-366; Mon.-Fri. 0830-1700, Saturday 0830-1600), between the ANZ Bank and Morris Hedstrom, changes cash and traveler's checks without commission at a rate just slightly lower than the banks.

Thomas Cook Travel (tel. 703-110; Mon.-Fri. 0830-1700, Saturday 0830-1200), across from the Mobil station on Queens Rd., is a good source of the banknotes of other Pacific countries—very convenient if you'll be flying to Australia, New Caledonia, New Zealand, Samoa, Solomon Islands, Tonga, or Vanuatu and don't want the hassle of having to change money at a strange airport upon arrival. They'll also change the banknotes of these countries into Fijian.

Tapa International (tel. 722-325), in the concourse at Nadi Airport, is the American Express representative. If you buy traveler's checks from them using a personal check and your American Express card, you'll have to actually pick up the checks at the ANZ Bank in Nadi town, so go early.

There are two large post offices, one next to the market in central Nadi, and another between the cargo warehouses directly across the park in front of the arrivals hall at Nadi Airport. Check both if you're expecting general delivery mail. Nadi Town Post Office near the market receives faxes sent to fax 702-166. At the Nadi Airport Post Office the public fax number is fax 720-467. Both post offices are open weekdays 0800-1700, Saturday 0800-1100.

The Canadian Consul can be reached at tel./fax 721-936. For the Italian Honorary Consul call Mediterranean Villas (tel. 664-011).

Public toilets are at the corner of Nadi Market closest to the post office, at the bus station, and in the Nadi Civic Center.

Information

The Fiji Visitors Bureau office (Box 9217, Nadi Airport; tel. 722-433, fax 720-141) is in the arrivals concourse at the airport. Ask for a copy of their budget guidebook, *Affordable Fiji.* There is no tourist information office in downtown Nadi although a certain travel agency masquerades as such.

The Nadi Town Council Library (Box 241, Nadi; tel. 700-606; weekdays 0900-1700, Saturday 0900-1300) is in the shopping mall at the Nadi Civic Center on Queens Road.

Travel Agents

The deceptively named Tourist Information Center (Victor M. Ali, Box 251, Nadi; tel. 700-243 or 721-295, fax 702-746; daily 0730-1830, Sunday 0930-1500), with offices in central Nadi, opposite the Dominion International Hotel, and in Suite 32 upstairs at the airport, is a commercial travel agency run by Victory Inland Safaris. Also known as "Fiji Island Adventures," they offer a variety of 4WD, trekking, and birdwatching excursions into the Nausori Highlands and book low-budget beach resorts on Mana, Malolo, Tavewa, Waya, Leleuvia, and Kadavu islands. They offer an e-mail service at 35 cents a minute.

PVV Tours (tel. 700-600) at the Nadi Town Motel is similar (their specialty is Nananu-i-Ra bookings and transfers).

Tourist Travel and Tours Fiji (tel. 700-199), in the courtyard between R.B. Patel Supermarket and Thomas Cook, makes the same sort of bookings as the Tourist Information Center. Many others are around town, including the Swiss Tourist Center (tel./fax 703-930) and

Bayrisches Tourist (tel./fax 703-922), both near the bridge into Nadi.

Out at the airport there's Rabua's Travel Agency (Box 10385, Nadi Airport; tel./fax 724-364), Office No. 23, situated upstairs in the arcade at international arrivals. The manager, Ulaiasi "Rambo" Rabua, books Dive Trek on Wayasewa (his home island) and most other offshore resorts. He shares an office with Eco-touring Fiji Ltd. (Box 2212, Nadi; tel./fax 724-364), which takes bookings of this kind from abroad. Margaret Travel Service (Box 9831, Nadi Airport; tel. 721-988, fax 721-992), upstairs in the airport arcade, also does outer island bookings. We've received several complaints about a company called Fiji Holiday Connections, also at the airport.

Rosie The Travel Service (tel. 722-935), at Nadi Airport and opposite the Nadi Handicraft Market in town, is a conventional travel agency that books somewhat more upmarket tours, activities, and accommodations.

There's little or no government regulation of the Nadi travel agencies, and some are quite unreliable. To increase their business they often promise things the managers of the resorts may be unwilling or unable to supply. Cases of travelers who reserved and prepaid a double room ending up in the dormitory are not unknown. Other times you'll be assured that the boat of one resort will drop you off at another, only to have the boatkeeper refuse to do so. If you prepay the return boat trip, the resort people won't have much incentive to bring you back to Nadi or Lautoka exactly on schedule.

For this reason it's better to avoid prepaying too much at the travel agencies, so as to retain some bargaining leverage. This is especially true when planning an itinerary that involves staying at more than one resort. If you can manage to pay the boat fare one-way only (instead of roundtrip) it'll be a lot easier to switch resorts, or just to walk out if the place you booked in Nadi isn't as nice as they said it would be. These agents take as much as 30% commission from the resorts and you can often get a better deal by booking direct (the Nadi agents are unable to give you discounts, no matter what they say). Most of the necessary phone numbers are provided in this book and a telephone card is all you need to get in touch.

Airline Offices

Reconfirm your flight, request a seat assignment, and check the departure time by calling your airline: Aircalin (tel. 722-145), Air Nauru (tel. 722-795), Air New Zealand (tel. 722-955), Air Pacific (tel. 720-888), Air Vanuatu (tel. 722-521), Qantas Airways (tel. 722-880), Royal Tongan Airlines (tel. 724-355), and Solomon Airlines (tel. 722-831). All these offices are at the airport.

Health

The outpatient department at Nadi District Hospital (tel. 701-128), inland from Nadi Bus Station, is open Mon.-Thurs. 0800-1630, Friday 0800-1600, Saturday 0800-1200.

You'll save time by visiting Dr. Ram Raju (tel. 701-375; weekdays 0830-1630, weekends 0900-1230), Lodhia and Clay Streets, a family doctor specializing in travel health. Dr. Adbul Gani (tel. 703-776; Mon.-Fri. 0800-1700, Saturday 0800-1300) has his dental surgery nearby on Lodhia Street.

Dr. Uma D. Sharma (tel. 700-718; Mon.-Fri. 0800-1700, Saturday 0800-1300) operates a dental clinic in the mall at the Nadi Civic Center near the post office. Two medical doctors have a clinic with similar hours a few shops away in the same mall.

Dr. A. Narayan runs the Namaka Medical Center (tel. 722-288) on Queens Rd., about two km from Nadi Airport on the way into town. After hours press the bell for service.

Transportation

See the chapter introduction for information on regular Air Fiji and Sunflower Airlines flights to Malololailai and Mana islands and other parts of Fiji.

Turtle Airways (Private Mail Bag NAP 0355, Nadi Airport; tel. 722-988, fax 720-346), next to the golf course at Wailoaloa Beach, runs a seaplane shuttle to the offshore resorts at F$95 one-way, F$190 roundtrip (baggage limited to one 15-kg suitcase plus one carry-on). Scenic flights with Turtle are F$55 pp for 10 minutes, F$120 for 30 minutes (minimum of three persons).

New Zealand-owned **South Sea Cruises** (Box 718, Nadi; tel. 722-988, fax 720-346) operates a catamaran shuttle to the offshore island resorts on the 25-meter, 300-passenger *Island Express*. The boat leaves from Nadi's Port

Denarau daily at 0900 and 1330 for Malololailai (F$33 each way), Malolo (F$36), Castaway (F$40), and Mana (F$40). With a connection to Matamanoa or Tokoriki, it's F$67. Interisland hops between the resorts themselves are F$30 each. Be prepared to wade on and off the boat at all islands except Mana. If all you want is a glimpse of the lovely Mamanuca Group, a four-island, four-hour, nonstop roundtrip cruise is F$35. Catamaran bookings can be made at any travel agency around Nadi, and transfers from the main Nadi hotels to the wharf are free.

Pacific Transport (tel. 701-386) has express buses to Suva via Queens Road daily at 0720, 0750, 0900, 1300, 1640, and 1820 (four hours, F$8). The 0900 bus is the most convenient, as it begins its run at Nadi (the others all arrive from Lautoka). Five other "stage" buses also operate daily to Suva (five hours). The daily **Sunset Express** (tel. 720-266) leaves Nadi for Sigatoka and Suva at 1010 and 1555. Nadi's bus station adjoining the market is an active place.

Local buses to Lautoka, the airport, and everywhere in between pick up passengers at the bus stop on Queens Road opposite Morris Hedstrom.

You can bargain for fares with the collective taxis cruising the highway from the airport into Nadi. They'll usually take what you'd pay on a bus, but ask first. Collective taxis and minibuses parked in a corner of the bus station take passengers nonstop from Nadi to Suva in three hours for F$10 pp.

For information on car rentals, turn to this chapter's introduction.

Local Tours

Many day cruises and bus tours that operate in the Nadi area are listed in the free tourist magazine *Fiji Magic*. Reservations can be made through hotel reception desks or at Rosie The Travel Service, with several offices around Nadi. Bus transfers to/from your hotel are included in the price, though some trips are arbitrarily canceled when not enough people sign up.

The "road tours" offered by **Rosie The Travel Service** (tel. 722-935), at Nadi Airport and opposite the Nadi Handicraft Market in town, are cheaper than those of other companies because lunch isn't included (lunch is included on all the cruises and river trips). Their day-trips to

Suva (F$46) involve too much time on the bus, so instead go for the Sigatoka Valley/Tavuni Hill Fort (F$45 including entry fees) or Emperor Gold Mine (F$44) full-day tours. If you're looking for a morning tour around Nadi, sign up for the four-hour Vuda Lookout/Viseisei Village/Garden of the Sleeping Giant tour, which costs F$45 pp, including admission to the garden; other than Viseisei, these places are not accessible on public transport. These trips only operate Mon.-Sat., but on Sunday Rosie offers a half-day drive to the Vuda Lookout and Lautoka for F$33 pp. Also ask about the full-day hiking tours to the Nausori Highlands (daily except Sunday, F$58), the easiest way to see this beautiful area.

The **United Touring Company** (Box 9172, Nadi Airport; tel. 722-811, fax 720-107), or UTC, offers the same kind of day tours as Rosie at higher prices with lunch included.

Peni's Waterfall Tours (Box 1842, Nadi; tel. 703-801), in the Westpoint Arcade off Queens Rd. in central Nadi, promises three nights of "genuine Fijian lifestyle" at Bukuya, a mountain village in the Nausori Highlands, for F$160 pp including meals, activities, and *bure* accommodations. The **Tourist Information Center** (tel. 700-243) offers "Sleeping Giant Safari Treks" with stays at different villages at F$169/190/210 for two/three/four night, plus tax. Hiking trips offered by Adventure Fiji, a division of Rosie The Travel Service, are more expensive than these but the quality is more consistent (see **Hiking Tours** in the main introduction).

Should you not wish to join an organized bus tour from Nadi, you can easily organize your own day tour by taking a local bus (not an express) to the Sigatoka Sand Dunes National Park visitor center on Queens Road. After a hike over the dunes, catch another bus to Sigatoka town for lunch at the Sigatoka Club, some shopping and sightseeing, and perhaps a taxi visit to the Tavuni Hill Fort. Plenty of buses run back to Nadi from Sigatoka until late. All this will cost you far less than the cheapest half-day tour and you'll be able to mix freely with the locals.

Day Cruises

Food and accommodations at the Mamanuca island resorts are expensive, and a much cheaper way to enjoy the islands—for a day at least—is by booking a full-day cruise to Plantation

(F$66), Castaway (F$70), or Mana (F$79) on the catamaran *Island Express,* operated by **South Sea Cruises** (tel. 722-988). The price includes transfers from most Nadi hotels, the boat trip, a buffet lunch on the island of your choice, nonmotorized sporting activities, and a day at the beach. Bookings can be made through Rosie The Travel Service or any other Nadi travel agent.

South Sea Cruises also has day-trips to Plantation Island Resort on the two-masted schooner *Seaspray* (F$66 including lunch). A "combo cruise" to Plantation has you going out on the *Island Express* and returning on the *Seaspray* or *Stardust II* (F$63 with lunch). By taking this option you see a few more resorts and experience another boat, but have less time on Plantation. By flying to Malololailai from Nadi Airport you can have the most time at Plantation for the lowest price (F$50 day return), but lunch won't be included.

Captain Cook Cruises (tel. 701-823) runs day cruises to Tivua Island aboard the MV *Lady Geraldine* for F$73 including a picnic lunch. Starlight dinner cruises on a tall ship are F$75 (dinner served at a restaurant ashore).

The **Oceanic Schooner Co.** (Box 9625, Nadi Airport; tel. 722-455, fax 720-134) does more upscale cruises on the 30-meter schooner *Whale's Tale,* built at Suva's Whippy Shipyard in 1985. You get a champagne breakfast and gourmet lunch served aboard ship, an open bar, and sunset cocktails in the company of a limited number of fellow passengers for F$160 pp.

Guests staying at one of the Sheratons can take the **Bounty Island Day Cruise** (tel./fax 650-200) to tiny Bounty Island on the MV *TJ Blue* (F$39/66 for a half/full day). Other companies offer day cruises to imaginatively named specks of sand such as Aqualand (tel. 722-988), Daydream Island (tel. 724-597), Fantasy Island (tel. 723-314), and Malamala Island (tel. 702-443), costing F$55-69, always including lunch and Nadi hotel pickups, and sometimes drinks and nonmotorized sporting activities as well. These are fine if all you want is a day at the beach, otherwise you'll find them a colossal bore. Any hotel tour desk can book them.

Younger travelers will enjoy a day cruise to **Beachcomber Island** (tel. 661-500), Fiji's unofficial Club Med for the under 35 set. Operating daily, the F$60 pp fare includes bus transfers from Nadi hotels, the return boat ride via Lautoka, and a buffet lunch. Large families especially should consider Beachcomber because after two full adult fares are paid, the first child under 16 is half price and additional children are quarter price. Infants under two are free.

Thirty-minute jet boat rides around the mouth of the Nadi River are offered by **Shotover Jet** (Box 1932, Nadi; tel. 750-400, fax 750-666) about every half hour from Port Denarau (adults F$59, children under 16 years F$29). It's fairly certain the birds and fish of this mangrove area are less thrilled by these gas-guzzling, high-impact craft than the tourists seated therein.

SOUTH OF NADI

Momi Bay
On a hilltop overlooking Momi Bay, 28 km from Nadi, are two **British six-inch guns,** one named Queen Victoria (1900), the other Edward VIII (1901). Both were recycled from the Boer War and set up here by the New Zealand army's 30th Battalion in 1941 to defend the southern approach to Nadi Bay. The only shots fired in anger during the war were across the bow of a Royal New Zealand Navy ship that forgot to make the correct signals as it entered the passage. It quickly turned around, made the correct signals, and reentered quietly. To get reach the battery, take a bus along the old highway to Momi, then walk three km west. The Nabilla village bus runs directly there from Nadi four times a day. This historic site is managed by the National Trust for Fiji and open daily 0800-1700 (admission F$2).

Seashell Cove
Seashell Cove Surf and Dive Resort (Box 9530, Nadi Airport; tel. 706-100, fax 706-094), on Momi Bay, 37 km southwest of Nadi, is a laid-back surfing/diving backpacker camp with hotel facilities. They have 11 duplex *bures* with fan, fridge, and cooking facilities at F$90 single or double, and 16 clean rooms with lumpy beds and shared bath in the lodge at F$45 single or double. Larger units are available for families at F$110 for up to six, and baby-sitters are provided. The big 25-bed dormitory above the bar is divided into five-bed compartments for F$15 pp.

Otherwise, pitch your own tent beside the volleyball court for F$8 per tent. Cooking facilities are not provided for campers, lodge, or dormitory guests, although a good-value meal plan is offered at F$30 pp and there's a small grocery store just outside the camp. A *meke* and Fijian feast (F$16) occurs on Friday. Seashell's coffee shop is open until midnight, with a pool table and table tennis. Some surfers stay up all night drinking kava with the friendly staff, a great opportunity to get to know them. Baggage storage is available free of charge.

The beach here isn't exciting and at low tide it's a 10-minute trudge across the mudflats to the water. Amenities and activities include a swimming pool, day-trips to Natadola Beach (F$28 including lunch), tennis (free), and volleyball (free). There's a horse used to walk kids under 10 around the resort, but skip the kayaks as they leak and become unstable after 20 minutes.

At F$25 pp, Seashell has two boats to shuttle surfers out to the reliable left at Namotu Island breakers or long hollow right at Wilkes Passage; the famous Cloudbreak left-hander at Navula Reef (F$35 pp) is between Wilkes and Seashell. (Recently only Seashell Cove and Tavarua Island were permitted to surf Cloudbreak through an exclusive arrangement with the traditional Fijian owners of the surf. Even then, expect crowds of 25 guys in the water—all other spots are uncrowded.) There's also an offshore right at the Momi Bay Lighthouse. This type of reef break surfing can be dangerous for the inexperienced.

In 1995 the well-organized scuba diving operation, **Scuba Bula,** run by Steve and Nicky Henderson, was upgraded with new equipment and a new boat but the cost is still reasonable at F$60/100 for one/two tanks plus F$10 for gear and F$440 for a PADI certification course. Seashell divers experience lots of fish/shark action at Navula Lighthouse, and there's great drift diving at Canyons (the guides really know their spots). When there's space, snorkelers are welcome to go along at F$15 pp.

Airport transfers are F$10 pp each way. Dominion Transport (tel. 701-505) has buses directly to Seashell from Nadi bus station at 0745, 1215, 1430, and 1600, and there are good onward connections from the resort by public bus to Sigatoka weekdays. A taxi from Nadi town might cost F$20.

THE MAMANUCA GROUP

The Mamanuca Group is a paradise of eye-popping reefs and sand-fringed isles shared by traditional Fijian villages and jet-age resorts. The white coral beaches and super snorkeling grounds attract visitors aplenty; boats and planes arrive constantly, bringing folks in from nearby Nadi or Lautoka. These islands are in the lee of big Viti Levu, which means you'll get about as much sun here as anywhere in Fiji. Some of the South Pacific's finest skin diving, surfing, game fishing, and yachting await you, and many nautical activities are included in the basic rates. The Mamanucas are fine for a little time in the sun, though much of it is a tourist scene irrelevant to the rest of Fiji.

Almost all of the regular tourist resorts described below are in the luxury price category, with Plantation Island Resort offering the least expensive regular rooms and Beachcomber Island providing dormitories with meals included in the rates. Among the top resorts, self-catering facilities are only provided at Musket Cove and Naitasi. Low-budget backpacker accommodations are on Mana and Malolo, the only islands permanently inhabited by Fijian villagers. If the beach and beyond are your main focus of interest you won't mind staying on a tiny coral speck like Tavarua, Namotu, Navini, Matamanoa, Beachcomber, and Treasure, but if hiking and land-based exploring are on your agenda pick a bigger island such as Malololailai, Malolo, Castaway, Mana, or Tokoriki.

Malololailai Island

Malololailai, or "Little Malolo," 22 km west of Nadi, is the first of the Mamanuca Group. It's a 216-hectare island eight km around (a nice walk). In 1880 an American sailor named Louis Armstrong bought Malololailai from the Fijians for one musket; in 1964 Dick Smith purchased it for many muskets. You can still be alone at the beaches on the far side of the island, but with two growing resorts, a marina, and projects for a golf course and lots more time-share condominiums in the pipeline it's becoming overdeveloped. An airstrip across the island's waist separates its two resorts; inland are rounded, grassy hills.

Plantation Island Resort (Box 9176, Nadi Airport; tel. 669-333, fax 669-200), on the southwest side of Malololailai, is one of the largest of the resorts off Nadi. The 110 rooms (beginning at F$190 single or double plus tax but including breakfast) are divided between 40 a/c hotel rooms in a two-story building and 70 individual *bures*. Add F$37 pp for lunch and dinner, as no cooking facilities are provided. Snorkeling gear, rowboats, and windsurfing are free, but boat trips cost extra. Coral viewing on Plantation's 30-passenger, glass-bottom "yellow submarine" is F$12 (free for guests). Plantation is a popular day-trip destination from Nadi. Expensive.

Also on Malololailai Island is **Musket Cove Resort** (Dick and Carol Smith, Private Mail Bag NAP 0352, Nadi Airport; tel. 662-215, fax 662-633), which opened in 1977. The eight seaview *bures* and four garden *bures,* all with kitchenettes, are F$260 single or double. Cooking facilities

are also provided in the six villas at F$395 single or double, plus F$15 per extra adult to a maximum of six. However, the 12 two-story beachfront *bures* and six lagoon *bures* at F$320 single or double only have a breakfast bar. A well-stocked grocery store selling fresh fruit and vegetables is on the premises. Dick's Place Restaurant and Bar by the pool has a F$55 pp three meal plan available. Entertainment is provided at the Thursday night pig roast. All drinks are F$2 at the bar on Ratu Nemani Island, a tiny coral islet connected to the marina by a floating bridge. Yachties are the main customers. Premium.

Activities at Musket Cove such as snorkeling, windsurfing, water-skiing, line fishing, and village boat trips are free for guests. Paid activities include the Hobie cats (F$25 an hour), kayaks (F$25 a half day), and mountain bikes (F$5 an hour). The launch *Anthony Star* is available for deep-sea game-fishing charters at F$50 pp for

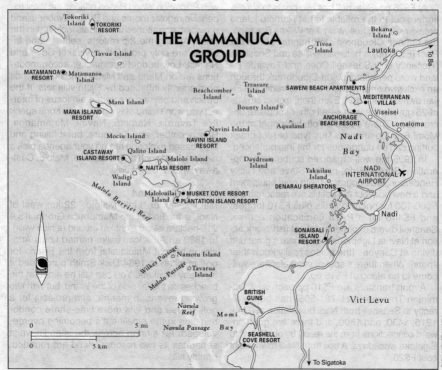

THE MAMANUCA GROUP

four hours with a four-person minimum (the catch belongs to the boat). The 10-meter cruiser *Dolphin Star* can be chartered for longer fishing trips at F$100 an hour. The 17-meter ketch *Dulcinea* does cruises for snorkeling (F$35 pp without lunch), dolphin watching (F$32 pp), and sunset viewing (F$22 pp). "Discover Sailing" lessons are F$100 pp.

Scuba diving with **Mamanuca Diving** (tel. 650-926, fax 662-633) at the marina costs F$75/105 one/two tanks including equipment, shark encounters cost F$85, or pay F$400 for the four-day PADI certification course (minimum of two persons). They operate daily trips to Sunflower Reef and The Three Sisters. **Musket Cove Yacht Charters** (tel./fax 666-710) has a small fleet of charter yachts stationed at Musket Cove. The compulsory Fijian guide is included in all charter rates.

Malololailai is a favorite stopover for cruising yachts with water and clean showers at the marina (mooring is F$5/30/100 a day/week/month). Fuel and groceries are also available. The marked anchorage is protected and 15 meters deep, with good holding. Most of the boats in the Auckland to Fiji yacht race in June end up here, and in mid-September there's a yachting regatta at Musket Cove, culminating in a 965-km yacht race from Fiji to Port Vila timed for the boats' annual departure east, prior to the onset of the hurricane season. If you're on a boat in Fiji at this time, Musket Cove is *the* place to be, and if you're trying to hitch a ride as crew you can't go wrong. There are even stories of people being *paid* to serve as crew for the race!

Malololailai's grass-and-gravel airstrip is the busiest in the Mamanuca Group and serves as a distribution point for the other resorts. You can fly to Malololailai from Nadi Airport 10 times a day on Sunflower Airlines and six times a day on Air Fiji (F$54 one-way). The F$75 day return fare includes lunch at Musket Cove. Otherwise take the twice-daily catamaran *Island Express* from Nadi's Port Denarau for F$33 each way; call 722-988 for free pickup. The *Malolo Cat* runs three times a day at F$60 return (45 minutes each way).

Malolo Island

At low tide you can wade from Malololailai to nearby Malolo Island, largest of the Mamanuca

Group. Solevu, one of the two Fijian villages on Malolo, is known to tourists as "shell village" for what the locals offer for sale (F$2 pp admission fee to the village). A couple of *bures* in the village have been erected to accommodate low-budget travelers at F$66 double, plus a 12-bed dorm at F$25 pp and camping at F$18 pp, all including meals. Transfers from Nadi are F$30/41 each way in a small/large boat. Add 10% tax to all charges. Bookings can be made through the Tourist Information Center in central Nadi. A stay here can be combined with a sojourn at the backpacker places on Mana Island, but only prepay your boat fare one-way in this case (they'll want you to pay for the roundtrip). A boat between Malolo and Mana costs F$15 pp each way. Budget.

The **Naitasi Resort** (Box 10044, Nadi Airport; tel. 669-178, fax 669-197), at Malolo's western tip, offers 28 one-bedroom bungalows with fan at F$295 for up to three adults, and 10 two-bedroom family villas at F$425 for up to six. Naitasi Resort's Nadi airport office offers special reduced rates when things are slow. The family units are privately owned by 10 individuals, and each is decorated differently. The Island Store sells basic groceries that allow you to make use of the cooking facilities provided, but you should also bring a few things with you. The Terrace Restaurant does its utmost to serve local produce, such as five types of edible seaweeds and six different salads. Saturday is the *lovo* and *meke* night. Baby-sitting is F$3.50 an hour. Luxury.

Naitasi Resort has a freshwater swimming pool, and nonmotorized water sports are free; scuba diving costs extra. Instructors will teach you how to windsurf, and this is the only resort offering ocean kayaking and horseback riding on a regular basis. Self-guided trail brochures are available to those who would like to discover Malolo's unique plant- and birdlife, so it's a good choice for hikers.

Get there on the twice-daily *Island Express* catamaran from the Nadi's Port Denarau for F$36 one-way, F$72 roundtrip. Otherwise fly Sunflower Airlines or Air Fiji to Malololailai (F$54), then catch a connecting speedboat straight to the resort at F$15 pp each way. The Turtle Airways seaplane from Nadi is F$95 one-way.

A timeshare operation called the **Lako Mai Resort** (Private Mail Bag, Nadi Airport; tel. 706-101, fax 706-017) operates on Malolo about three km from the Naitasi Resort. There are 12 *bures* and four Lockwood houses but these are owner-occupied and not open to casual tourists.

Tavarua Island

Tavarua Island Resort (Jon Roseman and Richard Isbell, Box 1419, Nadi; tel. 706-513, fax 706-395), just south of Malololailai, operates as a surfing base camp with surf rights to famous waves like Cloudbreak and Restaurants. The guests are accommodated in 12 beach *bures,* and Tavarua caters to older, more affluent surfers than places like Seashell Surf and Dive on Viti Levu. A one/two week package from Los Angeles could cost US$2,151/3,240 including airfare, plus US$20 for transfers. Though the price may suggest it, one should not expect luxurious facilities here. Rather, it's the exclusivity you pay for, as Tavarua has negotiated sole access to some of Fiji's finest waves. There are both lefts and rights in Malolo Passage at Tavarua, although the emphasis is usually on the lefts. When the swell is high enough you'll have some of the best surfing anywhere. On the off days you can get in some deep-sea fishing, windsurfing, snorkeling, or scuba diving (extra charge). Surfing guests are expected to have had at least three years experience in a variety of conditions. Bookings must be made in advance through Tavarua Island Tours (Box 60159, Santa Barbara, CA 93160, U.S.A.; tel. 805/686-4551, fax 805/683-6696)—local bookings from within Fiji are not accepted. They're usually sold out, especially in June, July, and August (US$250 deposit to get on the waiting list). Luxury.

Namotu Island

Just across Malolo Passage from Tavarua Island on tiny Namotu Island is **Namotu Island Resort** (Box 531, Nadi; tel. 706-439, fax 706-039), a "Blue Water Sports Camp" for surfers. They have four beach *bures* at F$500 pp, plus two deluxe *bures* at F$1,250 double, 10% tax additional. The dormitory has closed and children under 12 are not accepted but meals are included. The minimum stay is three nights and boat transfers are free if you stay more than a week. Otherwise it's F$80 pp return (the boat leaves Namotu at 1000 sharp). You must bring your own surfboards and sailboards as none are available here (currents in the channel often carry lost boards far out to sea). Fishing is free for the first hour, F$30 pp per additional hour. Scuba diving is F$75 and up (all motorized activities cost extra). As at Tavarua, Namotu's market is mostly upmarket American surfers and sailors who fly down from Hawaii to ride Fiji's spectacular waves. The famous Namotu Left peels off directly in front of their bar, and from your stool you can look across the channel to the more challenging Wilkes Right. Swimming Pools (a right) is off the southeastern corner of Namotu. Luxury.

Castaway Island

Castaway Island Resort (Private Mail Bag 0358, Nadi Airport; tel. 661-233, fax 665-753), on 174-hectare Qalito Island just west of Malolo and 15 km from Nadi, was built by Dick Smith in 1966 as Fiji's first outer-island resort. The 66 tastefully decorated thatched *bures* sleep four—F$410 and up including a buffet breakfast. No cooking facilities are provided but the all-meal plan is F$50 pp. The *lovo* and *meke* are on Monday night, the beach barbecue on Saturday. Among the free water sports are sailing, windsurfing, paddle boats, tennis, and snorkeling, but game fishing and scuba diving are extra. One/two tank dives with shark feeding are F$70/110, plus F$20 for gear. Their PADI certification course is F$600 for one or F$450 pp for two or more, and several other courses are also available. A swimming pool is available. Many Australian holidaymakers return to Castaway year after year; families with small children are welcome. A free "kids club" operates 0900-1600 and 1900-2100 daily with lots of fun activities for those aged three and over, while mom and dad have some time to themselves. There's the daily catamaran *Island Express* from Nadi's Port Denarau (F$40 one-way, F$70 roundtrip), and Turtle Airways has three seaplane flights a day from Nadi for F$95. Castaway has a booking office opposite the Capricorn International Hotel in Nadi. Luxury.

Navini Island

Navini Island Resort (Box 9445, Nadi Airport; tel. 662-188, fax 665-566) is the smallest of Mamanuca resorts, a tiny coral isle with only nine thatched *bures.* Rates vary from F$320 double for a fan-cooled beachfront unit to F$460 for the honeymoon *bure* with spa and enclosed courtyard. Discounts are available for stays of more than a week. The two/three meal package is F$57/65 pp a day (no cooking facilities). Everyone gets to know one another by eating at a long table (private dining is also possible). Complimentary morning boat trips are offered, as are snorkeling gear, windsurfers, and kayaks. Car/boat transfers from Nadi via the Vuda Point Marina are arranged anytime upon request (F$120 return). Only overnight guests are accepted. Luxury.

Mana Island

Mana Island, 32 km northwest of Nadi, is well known for its scuba diving facilities and jumbo luxury resort, but in recent years a whole slew of backpackers hostels have sprouted in the Fijian village on the eastern side of the island. There's much bad blood between the Japanese investors who run the resort and the Fijian villagers who accommodate the backpackers, and a high fence has been erected down the middle of the island to separate the two ends of the market. Uniformed security guards patrol the perimeter and shoestring travelers are most unwelcome anywhere in the resort, including the restaurants, bars, and watersports huts. Even the scuba diving facilities are segregated.

Although this situation does poison the atmosphere on Mana Island slightly, there are lots of lovely beaches all around the island, most of them empty because the packaged tourists seldom stray far from their resort. The long white beach on the northeast side of the island is deserted. At the resort, the snorkeling is better off South Beach at low tide, off North Beach at high tide, but the nicest beach is Sunset Beach at the western end of the island. There's a great view of the Mamanucas and southern Yasawas from the highest point on Mana, a 15-minute hike from the backpacker camps, and splendid snorkeling on the reef. The Mana Main Reef is famous for its drop-offs with visibility never less than 25 meters, and you'll see turtles, fish of all descriptions, and the occasional crayfish.

The presence of the resort supports the frequent air and sea connections from Nadi, and the budget places allow you to enjoy Mana's stunning beauty at a fraction of the price tourists at the Japanese resort are paying. But to be frank, some of the backpacker camps on Mana are rather squalid and the places on Tavewa Island in the Yasawas offer better accommodations for only a bit more money.

Right up against the security fence near an enclosed sentry box is **Mereani's Backpackers Inn** (Box 10486, Nadi Airport; tel. 663-099, fax 702-840), a large house with dormitories of four, six, and eight bunks at F$30 pp, and four double rooms at F$35 pp. When the main hostel fills up they open a 12-bed overflow dormitory next to the staff quarters, but this arrangement should be avoided. All rates include three generous meals served to your table (breakfast is a buffet). It's possible to knock about F$11 pp off the price by cooking your own food in their kitchen, but only very basic tinned foods are available on Mana so it's better to take the meal plan unless saving a few dollars is crucial. You can get drinks at their bar all day. Activities include deep-sea fishing trips (F$20 an hour) and a four-island boat excursions (F$20). Those staying two weeks get an extra night free and several complimentary trips. To book call 703-466 in Nadi, at which time launch transfers on the Shining Princess, also known as the Adi Neinoka, will be organized. Budget.

Ratu Kini Boko's Village Hostel or "Mana Backpackers" (Box 5818, Lautoka; tel. 669-143) has a dining area alongside the resort fence right next to Mereani's Inn but the large accommodations building is 100 meters back in the village. The concrete main house has one big 20-bunk dorm, another four-bunk dorm in the corridor, and two thatched dormitory bures with seven and 14 bunks in the back yard, all at F$30 pp including buffet-style meals. The main house also contains two double rooms with shared bath at F$66 double, and two better rooms with private bath and outside entrance at F$100 double, buffet meals included. One other large thatched bure in the back yard is F$77 double or F$100 for four. A full day boat trip to other resort islands is F$25 pp, snorkeling on the reef F$15. For current information, call their Lautoka office (tel. 723-333) or the hostel. People on their way to Ratu Kini's often stay at Mana Rose Apartments near Travelers Beach Resort at Wailoaloa Beach in Nadi. Both Ratu Kini's and Mereani's have generators that only work at lunchtime and from 1700 until after midnight, at which time the fans go off. Expect water shortages, overcrowding, rather messy conditions, and a total lack of privacy in the mixed dorms of both hostels. Budget.

Ratu Kini Boko is a colorful character. He's the chief of 20 islands in the Mamanuca Group, but years ago he leased the western half of Mana Island to an Australian company, which sublet their property to the Japanese who now run Mana Island Resort. The resort's founder, Errol Fifer, still has a house at Sunset Beach, in case you bump into him. Mereani's is run by another branch of Ratu Kini's family and they compete fiercely.

In 1997 a new backpacker hostel called **Dream Beach** (tel. 931-022) opened on a splendid beach on the north side of Mana Island, across the hill from Ratu Kini's. Two seven-bunk and one eight-bunk houses cost F$30 pp including meals. One private room with bath is available at F$77 double. If you have your own tent you can pitch it right on their beach at F$27 pp including three meals. There's a five percent discount if you stay four nights. Dream Beach is operated by Pastor Aisake Kabu and it's certainly your best bet at the moment, nicely secluded from the village and resort. Because of this, it could be full and you should book ahead either by calling them directly or through Cecilia Travel Services (Box 10725, Nadi Airport; tel. 724-033), upstairs in the airport arcade at arrivals. If you're willing to camp (own tent), just show up. Inexpensive.

Juxtaposed against the backpacker camps is **Mana Island Resort** (Box 610, Lautoka; tel. 661-455, fax 661-562), by far the biggest of the tourist resorts off Nadi. This opulent establishment boasts 128 tin-roofed bungalows clustered between the island's grassy rounded hilltops, white sandy beaches, and crystal-clear waters, and 32 hotel rooms in a pair of two-story blocks facing North Beach. The 90 standard bungalows are F$235 single or double, F$275 triple, while the 32 deluxe beachfront bungalows are F$380 single or double, F$425 triple. The six executive bungalows cost F$450 single or double, and the hotel rooms are F$350, breakfast included in all rates but add tax. Cooking facilities are not provided, so you'll have to patronize either the Mamanuca Restaurant, the North Beach Barbecue Buffet, or the South Beach A La Carte Restaurant (entrees F$20-31). Live entertainment is presented nightly, and three nights a week there's a Fijian or Polynesian floor show. The room rates include nonmotorized water sports, although water-skiing, para-flying, water scooters, game fishing, scuba diving, and the 45-minute semisubmersible rides (F$33 pp) are extra. Premium.

Resort guests may patronize **Aqua-Trek** (tel. 669-309), which offers boat dives at F$60 for one tank plus F$20 for equipment or F$330 for a six-dive package. Night dives are F$90. This five-star PADI facility runs a variety of dive courses, beginning with a four-day open-water certification course (F$520). Divemaster Apisi Bati specializes in underwater shark feeding.

Aqua Trek doesn't accept divers from the backpacker camps, who must dive with **Indigenous Scuba Service** (Mr. Valu Tamanivalu, Box 1809, Nadi Airport; tel. 997-795, fax 702-336) in a dive shop adjacent to Mereani's Inn. Their prices are a bit lower than those of Aqua-Trek at F$50 a dive plus F$20 for gear, F$270 for six dives, or F$450 for PADI open-water certification (four days). If you'd just like to try scuba, ask for a F$80 resort course. They'll take you out snorkeling for F$10 including mask and snorkel.

In 1995 an airstrip opened on Mana, and Sunflower Airlines now has eight flights a day from Nadi; Air Fiji has four flights (F$66 each way). The terminal is a seven-minute walk west of the resort (to get to the backpacker camps head for the wharf from which the security fence is visible). If you're already staying in Nadi it's just as easy to arrive on the twice-daily *Island Express* catamaran from Port Denarau (F$40 each way including Nadi hotel pickups). The *Island Express* ties up to the wharf at South Beach and Mana is the only Mamanuca island with a wharf, so you don't need to take off your shoes.

Any Nadi travel agency or hotel can book these transfers but only buy a one-way ticket so you'll have the freedom to return by another means (a roundtrip is no cheaper anyway). By taking the *Island Express* or plane to Mana you won't have to commit yourself to one backpacker hostel or another and can size up the situation when you get there. Ratu Kini's and Mereani's also have their own shuttle boats, which cost F$30 each way including bus transfers from Nadi hotels.

Beachcomber Island

Beachcomber Island (Dan Costello, Box 364, Lautoka; tel. 661-500, fax 664-496), 18 km west of Lautoka, is Club Med at a fraction of the price. Since the 1960s this famous resort has received many thousands of young travelers, and it's still a super place to meet the opposite sex. You'll like the informal atmosphere and late-night parties; there's a sand-floor bar, dancing, and floor shows four nights a week. The island is so small you can stroll around it in 10 minutes, but there's a white sandy beach and buildings nestled among coconut trees and tropical vegetation. This is one of the few places in Fiji where both sexes might be able to sunbathe topless. A beautiful coral reef extends far out on all sides and scuba diving is available with Subsurface Fiji (F$70/130 for one/two tanks, PADI certification F$495). A full range of other sporting activities is also available at an additional charge (parasailing F$48, windsurfing F$20 an hour, water-skiing F$28, jet skis F$40 for 15 minutes).

Accommodations include all meals served buffet style. Most people opt for the big, open mixed dormitory where the 42 double-decker bunks (84 beds) cost F$69 each a night, but you can also get one of 20 thatched beachfront *bures* with ceiling fan and private facilities for F$250/300/369 single/double/triple. Small families should ask for a *bure* as children 6-15 are half price, under six free. The 14 lodge rooms with shared bath at F$165/220 single/double (fridge and fan provided) are a good compromise for the budget-conscious traveler. Former water problems have been solved by laying pipes from the mainland and installing solar water heating. Premium.

Of course, there's also the F$60 roundtrip boat ride from Lautoka to consider, but that includes lunch on arrival day. You can make a day-trip to Beachcomber for the same price if you only want a few hours in the sun. There's a free shuttle bus from all Lautoka/Nadi hotels to the wharf; the connecting three-master ferry *Tui Tai* leaves daily at 1000. Faster access is possible on the twin-hulled *Drodolagi* from Port Denarau at 0900. Beachcomber has been doing

it right since the 1960s, and the biggest drawback is its very popularity, which makes it crowded and busy. Reserve well ahead at their Lautoka or Nadi Airport offices, or at any travel agency.

Treasure Island Resort

Beachcomber's little neighbor, **Treasure Island** (Box 2210, Lautoka; tel. 661-599, fax 663-577), caters to couples and families less interested in an intense singles' social scene. It's extremely popular among New Zealand and Australian holidaymakers and occupancy levels seldom drop below 80%. The resort is half owned by the Tokatoka Nakelo land-owning clan, which also supplies most of the workers, although the management is European. At Treasure, instead of helping yourself at a buffet and eating at a long communal picnic table as you would at Beachcomber, you'll be fed regular meals in a restaurant (meal plan F$57 pp daily). Cooking facilities are not provided. The 67 units, each with three single beds (F$350 single or double), are contained in 34 functional duplex bungalows packed into the greenery behind the island's white sands. Some nautical activities such as windsurfing, sailing, canoes, and spy board, which cost extra on Beachcomber, are free on Treasure Island. Several Dive Tropex personnel are based on Treasure Island, offering diving at F$70/125 including gear for one/two-tank boat dives. Unlike Beachcomber, Treasure doesn't accept any day-trippers (although the hawksbill turtles that arrive to lay their eggs around Christmas are welcome). Guests arrive on the shuttle boat *Stardust II,* which departs Nadi's Port Denarau daily at 0945 and 1400 (F$30 each way, half price under age 16). There's no wharf here, so be prepared to wade ashore. Luxury.

SOUTHERN VITI LEVU

The southwest side of Viti Levu along the Queens Road is known as the Coral Coast for the fringing reef along this shore. Sigatoka and Navua are the main towns in this area with most accommodations between them at Korotogo and Korolevu. This shoreline is heavily promoted as one of the top resort areas in Fiji, probably because of its convenient location along the busy highway between Nadi and Suva, but to be frank, the beaches here are second rate, with good swimming and snorkeling conditions only at high tide. Much of the coral has been destroyed by hurricanes. To compensate, most of the hotels have swimming pools and in some places you can go reef walking at low tide. Top sights include the Sigatoka sand dunes and the impressive gorge of the Navua River. The possibility of rainfall and lushness of the vegetation increases as you move east.

Scuba Diving

Sea Sports Ltd. (Denis Beckmann, Box 688, Sigatoka; tel. 500-225, fax 520-239) offers scuba diving from its well established base at Shangri-La's Fijian Resort. Its free red-and-blue minibus picks up clients at some other Coral Coast resorts just after 0700 (just after 0900 on Sunday). The charge is F$68 for one tank, F$99 for two tanks (both on the same morning), plus equipment. Night dives are possible. A 10-dive package is F$435. Sea Sports runs four-day PADI/NAUI open-water certification courses (F$485, medical examination required). Otherwise an introductory dive is F$104. Most dive sites are within 15 minutes of The Fijian, so you don't waste much time commuting. Snorkelers can go along when things are slow at F$10 pp including a mask and snorkel.

Getting Around

An easy way to get between the Coral Coast resorts and Nadi/Suva is on the a/c **Fiji Express** shuttle bus run by United Touring Company (tel. 722-811). The bus leaves the Travelodge, Berjaya Inn and other top hotels in Suva (F$27) at 0800 and calls at the Centra Resort Pacific Harbor (F$24), Warwick Hotel (F$19), Naviti Resort, Hideaway, Tabua Sands, Reef Resort (F$18), Fijian Hotel (F$15), most Nadi hotels, and the Sheratons (F$6), arriving at Nadi Airport at 1230 (quoted fares are to the airport). It leaves Nadi Airport at 1330 and returns along the same route, reaching Suva at 1800. Bookings can be made at the UTC office in the airport arrival concourse or at hotel tour desks.

Also ask about the a/c **Queen's Deluxe Coach**, which runs in the opposite direction, leaving The Fijian Hotel for Suva at 0910, the Warwick and Naviti at 1030, and Pacific Harbor at 1100. The return trip departs the Suva Travelodge around 1600.

Many less-expensive non-a/c buses pass on the highway, but make sure you're waiting somewhere they'll stop. Pacific Transport's "stage" or "highway" buses between Lautoka/Nadi and Suva will stop at any of the Coral Coast resorts, but the express buses call only at Sigatoka, Pacific Harbor, and Navua. If you're on an eastbound express, get a ticket to Sigatoka and look for a local bus (or taxi) from there.

Coral Coast Tours (Box 367, Sigatoka; tel. 500-314 or 500-646, fax 520-688) offers four-hour morning and afternoon Sigatoka Valley tours to the Tavuni Hill Fort at F$33. Pickups are offered at all hotels between The Warwick and Shangri-La's Fijian Resort. Their 11-hour around-the-island tour is F$120 including breakfast and lunch. There's also a 4WD highlands tour to Bukuya at F$94 including lunch. These trips offer a good introduction to Fiji if you've only limited time at your disposal.

NATADOLA AND THE FIJIAN

Natadola Beach

The long, white sandy beach here is the best on Viti Levu and a popular picnic spot with daytrippers arriving on the sugar train from The Fijian Hotel on the Coral Coast. The small left point break at Natadola is good for beginning surfers but one must always be aware of the currents and undertow. Plans to erect three or four luxury hotels here have been stalled by limited water supplies at the site. At the moment, very few facilities are available here, although the local villagers offer horseback riding. In past travelers have camped freelance on Natadola Beach, but theft is a problem here. Don't leave valuables unattended. It may be possible to rent a *bure* in Sanasana village at the south end of the beach at F$25 pp including meals.

The luxury-category **Natadola Beach Resort** (Box 10123, Nadi Airport; tel./fax 721-000) offers one block of three rooms, another block of four rooms, and two individual units at F$250 single or double (minimum stay three nights). Children under 16 are not accepted. Each of the nine fan-cooled units has a fridge but no cooking facilities are provided so you must use their restaurant. Day-trippers cannot order drinks here without having lunch. The long swimming pool winds between the palms.

Paradise Transport (tel. 500-028 or 500-011) has six buses a day on weekdays from Sigatoka to Vusama village about three km from the beach (call for times). Otherwise get off any Nadi bus at the Maro School stop on Queens Road and hitch 10 km to the beach. It's also possible to hike to Natadola in three hours along the coastal railway line from opposite Shangri-La's Fijian Resort Hotel. The train route passes Malomalo village where a six-story, 350-room Hilton Hotel is to be erected.

The Fijian

Shangri-La's Fijian Resort (Private Mail Bag NAPO 353, Nadi Airport; tel. 520-155, fax 500-402) occupies all 40 hectares of Yanuca Island, not to be confused with another island of the same name west of Beqa. This Yanuca Island is connected to the main island by a causeway 10 km west of Sigatoka and 61 km southeast of Nadi Airport. President Mara's wife is the main landowner of the island although the resort is Malaysian owned. Opened in 1967, the 436-room complex of three-story Hawaiian-style buildings was Fiji's first large resort and is still Fiji's biggest hotel, catering to a predominantly Japanese clientele. The a/c rooms begin at F$295 single or double, or F$865 for a deluxe beach *bure,* plus tax. There's no charge for two children 15 or under sharing their parents' room so this resort is a good choice for families. The Fijian offers a nine-hole golf course (par 31),

five tennis courts, four restaurants and five bars, two swimming pools, and a white sandy beach. Weekly events include a *meke* on Tuesday and Saturday (F$38 including the feast), and firewalking on Friday night. Three of the resort bars have a happy hour. The main Sea Sports Limited dive shop is at The Fijian, and Avis Rent A Car has a desk here. Luxury.

A local attraction is the Fijian Princess, a restored narrow-gauge railway originally built to haul sugarcane but that now runs 16-km daytrips to Natadola Beach daily at 1000. The train station is on the highway opposite the access road to The Fijian Hotel, and the ride costs F$59 pp including a barbecue lunch. For information call the **Coral Coast Railway Co.** (Box 571, Sigatoka; tel. 520-434).

Sigatoka Sand Dunes

From the mouth of the Sigatoka River westward, five kilometers of incredible 20-meter-high sand dunes separate the cane fields from the beach, formed over millennia as the southeast trade winds blew sediments brought down by the river back up onto the shore. The winds sometimes uncover human bones from old burials, and potsherds lie scattered along the seashore—these fragments have been carbon dated at up to 3,000 years old. Giant sea turtles come ashore here now and then to lay their eggs. It's a fascinating, evocative place, protected since 1989 as a national park through the efforts of the National Trust for Fiji. The **Visitors Center** (tel. 520-343; admission F$5 pp) is on Queens Road, about four km west of Sigatoka. Exhibits outline the ecology of the park, and park wardens lead visitors along a footpath over the dunes that reach as high as 50 meters in this area. It's well worth a visit to experience this unique environment. Any local bus between Nadi and Sigatoka will drop you at the Sand Dunes Visitors Center on the main highway (the express buses won't stop here).

SIGATOKA

Sigatoka (pronounced "Singatoka") is the main center for the Coral Coast tourist district and headquarters of Nadroga/Navosa Province with a racially mixed population of 8,000. A new

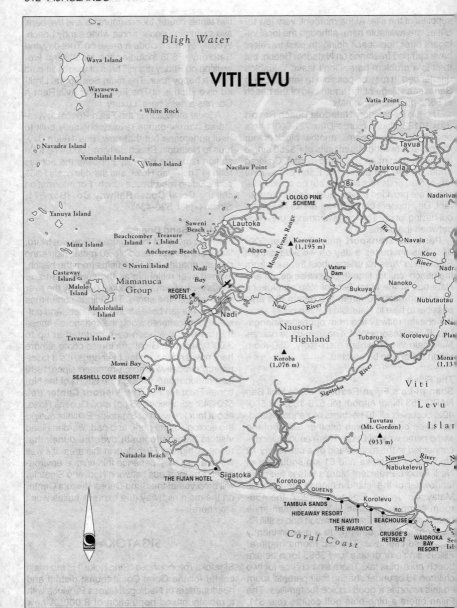

Bligh Water

Waya Island

Wayasewa
Island

White Rock

VITI LEVU

Vatia Point

Navadra Island

Vomolailai Island

Vomo Island

Nacilau Point

Tavua

Vatukoula

Ba

Nadariva

Yanuya Island

LOLOLO PINE
SCHEME

Mount Evans Range

Saweni
Beach

Lautoka

Koroyanitu
(1,195 m)

Abaca

Navala

Navala

Koro
River

Beachcomber Treasure
Island   Island

Anchorage Beach

Mana Island

Vaturu
Dam

Nadr

Navini Island

Nadi
Bay

Nanoko

Castaway
Island

Malolo
Island

Mamanuca
Group

REGENT
HOTEL

Nadi

Bukuya

Nubutautau

Malololailai
Island

Nadi   River

Na

Tavarua Island

Nausori
Highland

Tubarua

Korolevu

Plat

Momi Bay

Koroba
(1,076 m)

Mona
(1,13

SEASHELL COVE RESORT

Tau

Sigatoka   River

Viti

Levu

Tuvutau
(Mt. Gordon)
(933 m)

Islar

Natadola Beach

Navua   River

Nabukelevu

N

THE FIJIAN HOTEL

Sigatoka

Korotogo

QUEENS

Korolevu

RD.

TAMBUA SANDS

HIDEAWAY RESORT

THE NAVITI

THE WARWICK

BEACHOUSE

CRUSOE'S
RETREAT

WAIDROKA
BAY
RESORT

Se
Isl

Coral   Coast

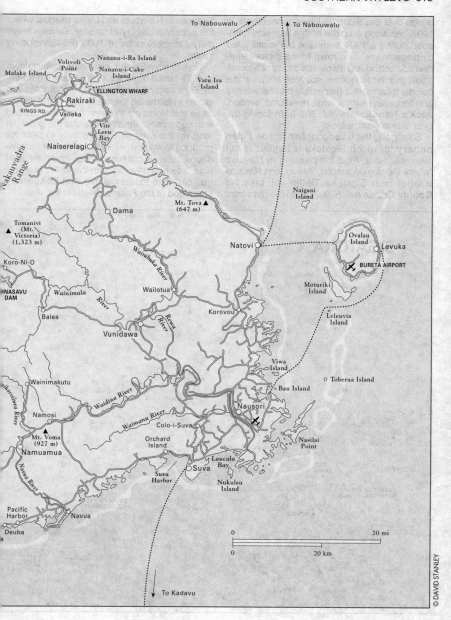

To Nabouwalu

To Nabouwalu

Volivoli Point

Nananu-i-Ra Island

Nananu-i-Cake Island

Malake Island

Vatu Ira Island

ELLINGTON WHARF

Rakiraki

KINGS RD.

Vaileka

Viti Levu Bay

Naiserelagi

Naigani Island

Nakauvadra Range

Mt. Tova (647 m)

Dama

Tomanivi (Mt. Victoria) (1,323 m)

Natovi

Ovalau Island

Levuka

Koro-Ni-O

BURETA AIRPORT

NASAVU DAM

Wainimala River

Wainibuka River

Moturiki Island

Wailotua

River

Balea

Rewa River

Korovou

Leleuvia Island

Vunidawa

Waidina River

Viwa Island

Wainimakutu

Toberua Island

Waimanu River

Bau Island

Namosi

Nausori

Mt. Voma (927 m)

Colo-i-Suva

Namuamua

Orchard Island

Nasilai Point

Navua River

Laucala Bay

Suva

Suva Harbor

Nukulau Island

Pacific Harbor

Deuba

Navua

0   20 mi

0   20 km

To Kadavu

© DAVID STANLEY

bridge over the Sigatoka River opened here in 1997, replacing an older bridge that was damaged during a 1994 hurricane but is still used by pedestrians. The town has a picturesque riverside setting and it's pleasant to stroll around. You'll find the ubiquitous souvenir shops and a colorful local market (especially on Wednesday and Saturday) with a large handicraft section. **Jack's Handicrafts** (tel. 500-810) facing the river is also worth a look.

Strangely, the traditional handmade **Fijian pottery** for which Sigatoka is famous is not available here. Find it by asking in Nayawa (where the clay originates), Yavulo, and Nasama villages near Sigatoka. Better yet, take the **Bounty Cruise** (tel. 500-963) up the river from Sigatoka to Nakabuta and Lawai villages, where the pottery is displayed for sale. Cruises leave daily except Sunday at 1000 (F$48 including lunch).

Upriver from Sigatoka is a wide valley known as Fiji's "salad bowl" for its rich market gardens by Fiji's second-largest river. Vegetables are grown in farms on the west side of the valley, while the lands on the east bank are planted with sugarcane. Small trucks use the good dirt road up the west side of the river to take the produce to market, while a network of narrow-gauge railways collects the cane from the east side. You can drive right up the valley in a normal car. The locals believe that Dakuwaqa, shark god of the Fijians, dwells in the river.

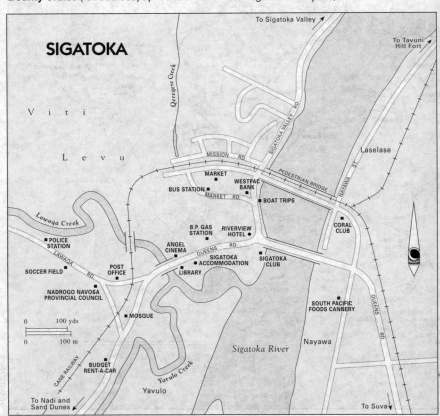

SIGATOKA

The valley also supplies a fruit juice cannery at Sigatoka that processes bananas, pineapples, mangos, guava, papayas, oranges, and tomatoes purchased from villagers who harvest fruit growing wild on their land (the creation of large plantations is inhibited by the threat of hurricanes). South Pacific Foods Ltd. sells mostly to the U.S. where their canned juice and pulp has secured a niche in the organic food market. Owned by the French transnational Pernod Ricard, the company's entire production is usually secured by advance orders a year ahead.

Also near Sigatoka, five km up the left (east) bank of the river from the bridge, is the **Tavuni Hill Fort** on a bluff at Naroro village. The fort was established by the 18th-century Tongan chief Maile Latemai and destroyed by native troops under British control in 1876. An interpretive center and walkways have been established, and admission is F$6 for adults or F$3 for children (closed Sunday). There's a good view of the river and surrounding countryside from here. Those without transport could take a taxi from Sigatoka to the reception area (about F$5), then walk back to town in an hour or so. Otherwise the Mavua bus will bring you here from Sigatoka.

Accommodations

The budget-priced **Riverview Hotel** (Box 22, Sigatoka; tel. 520-544, fax 520-200), above a restaurant facing the bridge in town, has seven rooms with bath and balcony at F$40/45 single/double.

The **Sigatoka Club** (Box 38, Sigatoka; tel./fax 500-026), across the traffic circle from the Riverview, has three fan-cooled rooms with private bath at F$28/38 single/double and a five-bed dorm at F$15 pp. Check that there's water before checking in and bring mosquito coils. The rooms are often full but the Club's bar is always perfect for a beer or a game of pool (three tables). The bar is open Mon.-Sat. 1000-2200, Sunday 1000-2100. Meals at the Club are good. Budget.

The basic **Sigatoka Accommodations** (Box 35, Sigatoka; tel. 520-965), opposite the BP service station on Queens Rd., has three shoestring rooms with bath at F$25 single or double. Camping on the back lawn is possible.

Food

The **Oriental Pacific Restaurant** (tel. 520-275) in front of the bus station dispenses greasy fast food to bus passengers during their 15-minute stop here.

The **Rattan Restaurant** (tel. 500-818), further along the row of shops beside the market, has inexpensive chicken, fish, sausage, and chip meals in the warmer behind the front counter. More expensive à la carte dishes are served in the dark dining room in back.

If you have the time, it's better to head over to the **Sigatoka Club** near the new bridge where meals average F$4 at lunchtime (listed on a blackboard) but are much more expensive at dinner (printed menu). The **Sea Palace Restaurant** (tel. 500-648), near Jack's Handicrafts, is a bit more upmarket. One reader recommended **Le Cafe** (tel. 520-877), up the riverside road from the old bridge.

Services and Transportation

Of the four banks in Sigatoka, the Westpac is the most convenient since they have a separate overseas section at the back and you don't have to join the long queue of local customers.

The District Hospital (tel. 500-455) is just southwest of Sigatoka, out on the road to Nadi.

Pacific Transport (tel. 500-676) express buses leave Sigatoka for Suva at 0845, 0910, 1025, 1425, 1800, and 1945 (3.5 hours, F$6), for Nadi Airport at 0935, 1115, 1220, 1500, 1800, and 2020 (1.5 hours, F$3.23). The daily **Sunset Express** leaves for Suva at 1120 and 1705, for Nadi and Lautoka at 1110 and 1825. Many additional local services also operate to/from Nadi. (Beware of taxi drivers hustling for passengers in the bus station who may claim there's no bus going where you want to go.)

Weekdays the 0900 bus operated by **Paradise Transport** (tel. 500-028 or 500-011) up the west side of the Sigatoka Valley to Tubarua offers a 4.5-hour roundtrip valley tour for F$5.40. Carriers to places far up the valley like Korolevu (F$6) and Namoli (F$7) leave weekdays just after noon.

Kulukulu

Fiji's superlative surfing beach is near Kulukulu village, five km south of Sigatoka, where the Sigatoka River breaks through Viti Levu's fringing reef to form the Sigatoka Sand Dunes. The surf is primarily a rivermouth point break with numerous beach breaks down the beach. It's one of the only places for beach-break surfing on Viti Levu, and unlike most other surfing locales around Fiji, no boat is required here. The windsurfing in this area is fantastic, as you can either sail "flat water" across the rivermouth or do "wave jumping" in the sea (all-sand bottom and big rollers with high wind). The surfing is good all the time, but if you want to combine it with windsurfing, it's good planning to surf in the morning and windsurf in afternoon when the wind comes up. Be prepared, however, as these waters are treacherous for novices. You can also bodysurf here. There's a nice place nearby where you can swim in the river and avoid the currents in the sea.

American surfer Marcus Oliver runs a small budget resort behind the dunes called **Club Masa** (Box 710, Sigatoka; no telephone), also known as Oasis Budget Lodge, "a licensed private hotel for nomads of the winds and surf." The rates including two good meals are F$40 pp in the 10-bed dormitory or F$50 pp in the two double rooms and two four-bed rooms (two-night minimum stay). Camping is not allowed. There's no electricity, but the layout is attractive and the location excellent. Have a beer on their pleasant open porch. Food and drinks are unavailable during the day, so you should bring something for snacks. Sporting equipment is not provided, and ask what time they plan to lock the gate before going out for an evening stroll. When Marcus is away (which is often) the Club is managed by his father Gordon Oliver and it's important to make a good impression when you first arrive as he doesn't accept just anybody as a guest. It's a good base from which to surf this coast (although many surfers find it more amenable to stay with the locals in nearby houses).

Sunbeam Transport (tel. 500-168) has buses from Sigatoka to Kulukulu village seven times a day on Wednesday and Saturday, five times on other weekdays, but none on Sunday and holidays. Taxi fare to Club Masa should be around F$4, and later you may only have to pay 50 cents for a seat in an empty taxi returning to Sigatoka.

KOROTOGO

A cluster of self-catering budget places is at Korotogo, eight km east of Sigatoka, with only the Outrigger Reef Resort and Tubakula Beach Resort right on the beach itself. Most of the places farther east at Korolevu are quite upmarket. East of Korotogo the sugar fields of western Viti Levu are replaced by coconut plantations merging into rainforests on the green slopes behind.

A road through the Reef Resort Golf Course near the Outrigger Reef Resort leads to a commercial bird park called **Kula Eco Park** (tel. 500-505; open daily 1000-1630, admission F$12, children under 12 half price).

Independent Tours (Box 1147, Sigatoka; tel./fax 520-678) at Tom's Restaurant in Korotogo rents mountain bikes at F$8/15 for a half/full day. They also offer a variety of bicycle tours costing F$79 for one day or F$299 for three days and two nights (minimum of two persons).

Accommodations

The **Crow's Nest Motor Lodge** (Charlie Wang, Box 270, Sigatoka; tel. 500-513, fax 520-354), at the east end of the Korotogo strip, offers 18 split-level duplex bungalows with cooking facilities and veranda at F$75/99 single/double. The Crow's Nest Dormitory at the bottom of the hill is F$11 pp for the 10 beds. The nautical touches in the excellent moderately priced restaurant behind the swimming pool spill over into the rooms. The nicely landscaped grounds are just across the highway from the beach and good views over the lagoon are obtained from the Crow's Nest's elevated perch. Unfortunately the new management seems to be letting maintenance slide. There's an Avis Rent A Car desk here. Moderate.

The **Vakaviti Motel and Dorm** (Arthur Jennings, Box 5, Sigatoka; tel. 500-526, fax 520-424), next to the Crow's Nest, has three self-catering units at F$45/55 single/double, and a five-bed family *bure* at F$65 double, plus F$6 per additional person. There are two six-bed dormitories, one with a nice ocean view at F$15 pp and another with no fan at F$12 pp. Facilities include a swimming pool and a large lending library/book exchange at the reception. The manager's half dozen dogs greet newcomers enthusiastically. It's often full. Budget to inexpensive.

The **Casablanca Hotel** (tel. 520-600, fax 520-616), next door to Vakaviti, is a two-story hillside building on the inland side of Queens Road. Its eight a/c rooms with cooking facilities and arched balconies begin at F$45/55 single/double. Inexpensive.

A more upmarket place to stay is **Bedarra House** (Box 1213, Sigatoka; tel. 500-476, fax 520-116), with four bath-equipped rooms facing the spacious restaurant/bar on the main floor and a *bure* out back for honeymooners, each F$132 double. A new two-story block with 10 additional rooms is planned. It's all tastefully decorated but cooking facilities are not provided in all rooms. This spacious two-story hotel prides itself on the personalized service, and a swimming pool, video room, and upstairs lounge round out their facilities. Expensive.

Just a few hundred meters east near the Reef Resort is **Waratah Lodge** (Box 86, Sigatoka; tel. 500-278, fax 520-616), with three large A-frame bungalows at F$44 double, plus F$5 per additional person up to six maximum. The two rooms below the reception in the main building are F$33/44 single/double. Cooking facilities are available and a grocery store is right next door. The swimming pool and charming management add to the allure. It's good value and recommended. Budget.

The **Outrigger Reef Resort** (Box 173, Sigatoka; tel. 500-044, fax 520-074) faces a white sandy beach about a kilometer east of the Crow's Nest. In April 1999, Outrigger Hotels of Hawaii (www.outrigger.com/pacific) began construction of a 208-room complex with five terraced buildings and 47 *bures*. The old Reef Resort offered tennis courts, a golf course, horseback riding, Fijian feasts, firewalking, and dancing, and all of this is likely to continue. Due to reopen in 2000, prices were still unknown at press time, but they'll probably be luxury level.

East of the Outrigger is **Tubakula Beach Resort** (Box 2, Sigatoka; tel. 500-097, fax 500-201). The 23 pleasant A-frame bungalows with fan, cooking facilities, and private bath, each capable of sleeping three, vary in price from F$50 in the garden to F$68 facing the beach. Superior bungalows are F$70 poolside or F$86 beachfront. One bungalow has three rooms with shared bath at F$30/36/39 single/double/triple. Their "Beach Club" dormitory consists of eight rooms, each with three or four beds at F$14 a bed. Small discounts are available to youth hostel, VIP, and Nomads card holders, and if you stay a week you'll get 10% off. Late readers will like the good lighting. A communal kitchen is available to all, plus a swimming pool, games

room, nightly videos, minimarket, and open-plan restaurant. If you'd like to scuba dive, arrange a pick-up by Sea Sports at The Fijian. Basically, Tubakula is a quiet, do-your-own-thing kind of place for people who don't need lots of organized activities. It's one of the most popular backpacker's resorts in Fiji and well worth a couple of nights. Budget.

Food
Those staying at the Outrigger Reef Resort can walk 800 meters west to the **Crow's Nest Restaurant** (tel. 500-230) for a change of pace. Better yet, check out the inexpensive terrace restaurant at the Tubakula Beach Resort on the Suva side of the Outrigger.

Tom's Restaurant (Tom Jacksam, tel. 520-238; open Mon.-Sat. 1200-1500/1800-2200, Sunday 1800-2200), at the west entrance to Korotogo, specializes in Chinese dishes, but there are several vegetarian items on the menu and grilled choices such as steaks. To date all reviews have been good.

KOROLEVU

At Korolevu, east of Korotogo, the accommodations cater to a more upscale crowd, and cooking facilities are not provided for guests. Places like Tambua Sands Beach Resort, Hideaway Resort, The Naviti Resort, and The Warwick Fiji are intended primarily for people on package holidays who intend to spend most of their time unwinding on the beach. Distances between the resorts are great, so for sightseeing you'll be dependent on your hotel's tour desk. An exception is the celebrated Beachouse, which only opened in 1996. The Coral Village Resort and Waidroka Bay Resort farther east also accommodate budget travelers, but they're both far off the highway.

Accommodations
One of the South Pacific's best budget resorts, **The Beachouse** (Box 68, Korolevu; tel. 530-500, fax 530-400; beachouse@is.com.fj), is on a very nice palm-fringed white beach just off Queens Rd., between Navola and Namatakula villages, about five km east of The Warwick. It's 35 km east of Sigatoka and 43 km west of Pacific Har-

bor—keep in mind that only local buses will stop here. Their slogan is "low cost luxury on the beach" and the whole project was specially designed to serve the needs of backpackers (and not as an upmarket hotel with a dormitory tacked on as an afterthought). The two wooden accommodation blocks each have four four-bunk dorms downstairs (F$17 pp) and four double fan-cooled loft rooms upstairs (F$39 double). When all of the dorms are full, an overflow cabin with four bunks and six mattresses on the floor is opened (also F$17 pp—call ahead to find out if you'll have to stay there). Campers are allowed to pitch their tents on the wide lawn between the rooms and the beach at F$9 pp. Separate toilet/shower facilities for men and women are just behind the main buildings, and nearby is a communal kitchen and dining area. It's all very clean and pleasant. Breakfast in their beachfront lounge consists of all the tea, bread, and jam you want for F$3. Fish and chips or lasagna for lunch costs around F$8, and there's also a dinner menu. If you wish to cook for yourself you should bring food as the closest grocery store is in Korolevu (there's only a tiny cooperative store in Namatakula). Not only is the ocean swimming good at high tide (unlike the situation at many other Coral Coast hotels where you end up using the pool) but they'll take you out to the nearby reef in their launch for snorkeling at F$3 pp. Ask about currents before going far off on your own. Other trips include a minibus tour to Vasevu Falls (F$2 for transportation, plus F$5 admission to the falls) and a shopping/shuttle to Suva on Tuesday (F$10 return). Canoes, surf-skis, and bicycles are loaned for free, and there's a bush track up into the hills behind the resort. The lending library serves those who only came to relax. Budget.

Crusoe's Retreat (Box 20, Korolevu; tel. 500-185, fax 520-666), formerly known as Man Friday Resort, is right by the beach, six km off Queens Rd. at Naboutini—the most secluded place to stay on the Coral Coast. The 27 large thatched *bures* are F$160 double including all meals served at a common table. The name alludes to Daniel Defoe's novel *Robinson Crusoe*, and the footprint-shaped freshwater swimming pool symbolizes Man Friday. This resort is reputed to be gay and lesbian friendly. Premium.

Coral Village Resort (Margaret and Tony Davon, Box 104, Korolevu; tel. 500-807, fax 308-383), previously known as Gaia Beach Resort, is on a lovely beach 4.5 km off Queens Rd. down the same access road as Crusoe's Retreat. The eight fan-cooled bungalows are F$65/75/85 single/double/triple with fridge, and there are three six-bed dorms at F$33 pp including two meals. Cooking your own food is impossible, so you must patronize their restaurant (F$26 pp meal plan). Scuba diving is offered. This secluded, peaceful place in harmony with nature is a good spot to relax. If you call ahead they'll pick you up from the bus stop on Queens Road. Inexpensive.

The **Waidroka Bay Resort** (Box 323, Pacific Harbor; tel. 304-605, fax 304-383) is up the road leading to the Dogowale Radio Tower between Korovisilou and Talenaua, four km off Queens Road. Accommodations range from a 12-bed dormitory at F$12 pp, three lodge rooms at F$48 for up to four, and four neat little oceanfront bungalows with bath and fan at F$75/110 double/triple. The meal plan is F$30 pp a day (cooking facilities not provided). Waidroka caters mostly to the scuba/surfing crowd, and diving is F$50/95 for one/two tanks, plus F$15 for equipment. There are three surf breaks just a five-minute boat ride from the resort, and they'll ferry you out at F$10 pp for two hours. Snorkeling trips cost the same. To surf on Frigate Passage is F$35 pp with a F$135 minimum charge for the boat. Call ahead and they'll pick you up from the bus stop and Queens Road. Budget.

PACIFIC HARBOR

Southeastern Viti Levu from Deuba to Suva is wetter and greener than the coast to the west, and the emphasis changes from beach life to cultural and natural attractions. Pacific Harbor satisfies both sporting types and culture vultures, while Fiji's finest river trips begin at Navua. Here scattered Fiji Indian dwellings join the Fijian villages that predominate farther west. All of the places listed below are easily accessible on the fairly frequent Galoa bus from Suva market.

Pacific Harbor is a sprawling, misplaced south Florida-style condo development and instant culture village, 152 km east of Nadi Airport and 44 km west of Suva. It was begun in the early 1970s by Canadian developer David Gilmour (the current owner of Wakaya Island) and his

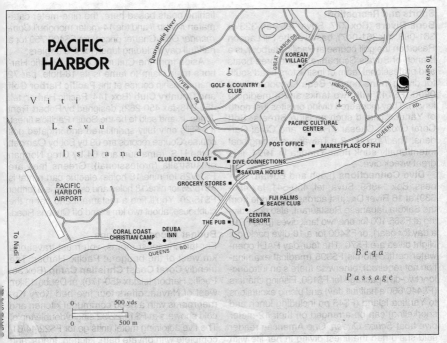

father Peter Munk, and good paved roads meander between the landscaped lots with curving canals to drain what was once a swamp. If it weren't for the backdrop of deep green hills you'd almost think you were in some Miami suburb. In 1988 a Japanese corporation purchased Pacific Harbor, and many of the 180 individual villas are owned by Australian or Hong Kong investors.

Sights

Pacific Harbor's imposing **Cultural Center** (Box 74, Pacific Harbor; tel. 450-177, fax 450-083) offers the chance to experience some freeze-dried Fijian culture. This recreated Fijian village on a small "sacred island" is complete with a 20-meter-tall temple and natives attired in jungle garb. Visitors tour the island hourly, seated in a double-hulled *drua* with a tour guide "warrior" carrying a spear, and at various stops village occupations such as canoe making, weaving, tapa, and pottery are demonstrated for the canoe-bound guests. At 1100 there are one-hour performances by the Dance Theater of Fiji (Monday, Wednesday, Thursday, and Friday) and Fijian firewalking (Tuesday and Saturday), and if you want to see one of the shows it's best to arrive with the tour buses in the morning. Admission is F$18 pp for the village tour (Mon.-Sat. 0900-1500), then another F$18 to see the dancing or firewalking, or F$33 for village tour and show combined. Rosie The Travel Service runs full-day bus tours to the Cultural Center from Nadi at F$73 pp including the tour and show but not lunch. The Dance Theater has an international reputation, with several successful North American tours to their credit.

Entry to the Waikiki-style **Marketplace of Fiji** at the Cultural Center, made up of mock-colonial boutiques and assorted historical displays, is free of charge. If you arrive here after 1500, all of the tourist buses will have left, and you'll be able to see quite a bit of the Cultural Center for nothing from the Flame Tree Restaurant. The main Pacific Harbor post office is next to the Cultural Center.

Sports and Recreation

Beqa Divers (Box 777, Suva; tel. 450-323 or 361-088, fax 361-047), based at the Fiji Lagoon Resort on the golf course at Pacific Harbour, is a branch of Suva's Scubahire. Their three boats and professional team of instructors head south for diving in the nearby Beqa Lagoon daily at 0900 (F$143 with two tanks and a mediocre lunch). They pioneered diving on sites just north of Yanuca Island such as Side Streets, Soft Coral Grotto, Caesar's Rocks, and Coral Gardens. The *Tasu No. 2,* a Taiwanese fishing boat intentionally sunk near Yanuca in 1994, is a great wreck dive.

Dive Connections (Leyh and Edward Harness, Box 14869, Suva; tel. 450-541, fax 450-539) at 16 River Dr., just across the bridge from the Sakura Japanese Restaurant, also does diving at F$65/100 for one/two tank dives (plus F$15 a day for gear), or F$400 for a 10-dive package. Night dives are F$70. The four-day PADI open-water certification is F$395 (medical examination not required), otherwise there's an introductory two-dive package for F$130. Fishing charters (F$440/660 a half/full day) and picnic excursions to Yanuca Island (F$45 pp including lunch and snorkeling) can be arranged on their 12-meter dive boat *Scuba Queen.* One American reader said she'd had the finest diving in her life with them. They'll pick up anywhere within eight kilometers of the Pacific Harbor bridge.

In early 1999 the American scuba wholesaler **Aqua-Trek** set up a new dive base at the Centra Resort Pacific Harbor's marina. They cater mostly to divers on pre-paid packages and individuals may be better off with the other operators.

Serious divers also have at their disposal the 18-meter live-aboard *Beqa Princess,* based at The Pub across the river from the Centra Resort Pacific Harbor. The *Beqa Princess* specializes in three-night scuba cruises to the islands south of Viti Levu and day-trips to the Beqa Lagoon. Two-tank day trips are F$100 including lunch or the boat may be chartered. Call **Tropical Expeditions** (Box 271, Pacific Harbor; tel. 450-767, fax 450-757) for the scoop on scuba or snorkeling day trips on the *Beqa Princess.* This boat can also be chartered for surfing trips to Frigate Pass.

Baywater Charters (Box 137, Pacific Harbor; tel. 450-235, fax 450-606) has two game-fishing boats based here, the nine-meter catamaran *Marau II* and the 14-meter monohull *Commander One.* Charter prices are F$400/750 for a half/full day including lunch for 4-6 anglers.

Aside from the Cultural Center, Pacific Harbor's main claim to fame is its 18-hole, par-72 championship course at the **Pacific Harbor Golf and Country Club** (Box 144, Pacific Harbor; tel. 450-048, fax 450-262), designed by Robert Trent Jones Jr. and said to be the South Pacific's finest. It's Fiji's only fully sprinklered and irrigated golf course. Course records are 69 by Bobby Clampett of the U.S. (amateur) and 64 by Greg Norman of Australia (professional). Greens fees are F$15/25 for nine/18 holes; electric cart rental is F$15/25 for nine/18 holes and club hire is a further F$15/20. You'll find a restaurant and bar in the clubhouse, about two km inland off Queens Road.

Budget Accommodations

For the cheapest rooms, you must travel one km west of the bridge at Pacific Harbor. The friendly **Coral Coast Christian Camp** (Box 36, Pacific Harbor; tel./fax 450-178), at Deuba 13 km west of Navua, offers four five-bed Kozy Korner rooms with a good communal kitchen and cold showers at F$14/22/32 single/double/triple. The five adjoining motel units go for F$22/44/61, complete with private bath, kitchen, fridge, and fan. Camping costs F$6 pp. A good selection of groceries is sold at the office. No dancing or alcoholic beverages are permitted on the premises; on Sunday at 1930 you're invited to the Fellowship Meeting in the manager's flat. The Camp is just across the highway from long golden Loloma Beach, the closest public beach to Suva, but watch your valuables if you swim here. Guests can obtain vouchers from the manager that allow a 20% discount on Cultural Center tours. The Christian Camp is also useful as a base for trips up the Navua River, and the managers will help organize the contacts. You might meet other travelers with whom to share the hire of a boat. It's also a good place to spend the night while arranging to get out to the surfers' camps on Yanuca Island. Just avoid arriving on a weekend as it's often fully booked by church groups from Friday afternoon until Monday morning.

Right next door to the Christian Camp is the **Deuba Inn** (Loraini Jones, Box 132, Pacific Harbor; tel. 450-544, fax 450-818), which opened in 1994. They have 10 rooms with shared bath at F$22/32/38 single/double/triple and five self-catering units at F$40/60/65/70 single/double/triple/quad. Camping is F$8 pp. The Inn's main drawback is that you can't cook your own food in the cheaper rooms and meals at the restaurant add up. However, inexpensive snacks are available at the takeaway counter at lunchtime and the Inn is a useful backup if you happen to arrive on a day when the Camp is full. Their bar is also handy if you're staying at the "dry" Christian Camp (happy hour 1700-1900).

Upscale Accommodations

The 84 a/c rooms at the three-story **Centra Resort Pacific Harbor** (Box 144, Pacific Harbor; tel. 450-022, fax 450-262) are F$160/180/200 single/double/triple plus tax. Built in 1972 and formerly known as the Pacific Harbor International Hotel, the Centra Resort is now Japanese-owned. It's at the mouth of the Qaraniqio River, between Queens Road and a long sandy beach, on attractive grounds and with a nice deep swimming pool. Floodlit tennis courts are provided. There's a *lovo* (F$33) with island entertainment here every Friday night. Premium.

The advantage of the **Fiji Palms Beach Club Resort** (Box 6, Pacific Harbor; tel. 450-050, fax 450-025), right next to the Centra Resort Pacific Harbor, is that the 14 two-bedroom apartments have cooking facilities, which allows you to skip the many expensive restaurants in these parts. The first night is F$150 for up to six people, but the second night is F$135, and a week costs F$900 for the unit. Many of the apartments have been sold as part of a timeshare scheme. Expensive.

Club Coral Coast (Tak Hasegawa, Box 303, Pacific Harbor; tel. 450-421, fax 450-900) offers quality rooms with shared cooking facilities and fridge in large modern villas at Pacific Harbor. It's on Belo Circle near Dive Connections, across the small bridge from Sakura House Restaurant and left. There are four a/c rooms with bath in one villa and two in another at F$70/80/90 single/double/triple. Budget accommodation with shared bath is F$25/35 single/double. Facilities include a 20-meter swimming pool, jacuzzi, tennis, and many other sporting facilities. Inexpensive.

Food

Kumarans Restaurant (tel. 450-294; daily until 2000), across the highway from the Centra Resort Pacific Harbor, has some cheap curries at lunchtime, but the dinner menu is pricey.

The **Oasis Restaurant** (tel. 450-617), in the Marketplace of Fiji, has a fairly reasonable sandwich, salad, and burger menu at lunchtime and more substantial blackboard specials for dinner. A pot of coffee is F$3.

Three small grocery stores are beside Kumarans by the bridge at Pacific Harbor, and the self-service Trading Post Supermarket at the Marketplace of Fiji has a good selection. For fruit and vegetables you must go to Navua.

Transportation

Only charter flights from Nadi Airport land at Pacific Harbor's airstrip, but all of the Queens Road express buses stop here. If coming to Pacific Harbor from Suva by express bus, you'll be dropped near the Centra Resort Pacific Harbor, a kilometer from the Cultural Center. The slower Galoa buses will stop right in front of the Cultural Center itself (advise the driver beforehand).

The a/c Queens Deluxe Coach leaves from the front door of the Centra Resort Pacific Harbor for Suva (F$12) at 1100, for Nadi at 1700 (F$25). The a/c Fiji Express leaves the resort for Nadi at 0900 and for Suva at 1700. Much cheaper and just as fast are the regular Pacific Transport express buses that stop on the highway: to Nadi Airport at 0750, 0930, 1035, 1315, 1605, and 1835 (three hours, F$7); to Suva at 1015, 1100, 1155, 1555, 1930, 2115 (one hour, F$2.50). **Rosie The Travel Service** (tel. 450-655) in the Marketplace of Fiji can make any required hotel or tour bookings.

NAVUA AND VICINITY

The bustling river town of Navua (pop. 4,500), 39 km west of Suva, is the market center of the mostly Indian-inhabited rice-growing delta area near the mouth of the Navua River. It's also the headquarters of Serua and Namosi Provinces. If low-grade copper deposits totaling 900 million metric tonnes located just inland at Namosi are ever developed, Navua will become a major mining port, passed by four-lane highways, ore conveyors, and a huge drain pipe for copper tailings. For at least 30 years millions of tonnes of waste material a year will be dumped into the ocean by an operation consuming more fossil fuel energy than the rest of the country combined. The present quiet road between Navua and Suva will bustle with new housing estates and heavy traffic, Fiji's social and environmental balance will be turned on its head, and the change from today will be total!

Transportation

All of the express buses between Suva and Nadi stop at Navua. Village boats leave from the wharf beside Navua market for Beqa Island south of Viti Levu daily except Sunday, but more depart on Saturday. Flat-bottomed punts to **Namuamua** village, 25 km up the Navua River, depart on Thursday, Friday, and Saturday afternoons, but almost anytime you can charter an outboard from Navua wharf to Namuamua at F$50 for the boat roundtrip. The hour-long ride takes you between high canyon walls and over boiling rapids with waterfalls on each side. Above Namuamua is the fabulous **Upper Navua,** accessible only to intrepid river-runners in rubber rafts. It's also possible to reach the river by road at Nabukelevu.

River Tours

An easy way to experience the picturesque lower Navua is with **Wilderness Ethnic Adventure Fiji** (Box 1389, Suva; tel. 315-730, fax 300-584), which runs full-day motorized boat trips 20 km up the river from Navua to Nukusere village, where lunch is taken and visitors get an introduction to Fijian culture. Any travel agent in Suva can make the bookings (adults F$54, children F$33). The same company also has more canoe and rubber raft trips down the same river at F$59. In Nadi, book through Rosie The Travel Service.

Discover Fiji Tours (Box 171, Navua; tel. 450-180, fax 450-549) also offers trips up the Navua River, leaving Navua at 1030 daily and returning at 1630. They take you upriver to a waterfall by motorized canoe. After a swim you go to Nakavu village where there's a welcoming kava ceremony and you have lunch. In the afternoon you float down the river on a bamboo raft (on Sunday the village visit is replaced by a riverside picnic). The cost is F$55 pp from Pacific Harbor or F$65 from Suva (minimum of two). Call to book.

Mr. Sakiusa Naivalu (tel. 460-641) of Navua also organizes upriver boat trips to Namuamua at F$50 with the possibility of spending the night there.

The brochures of some of the Navua River tour companies promise a kava ceremony and other events, but these are only organized for groups. If only a couple of you are going that day, nothing much of the kind is going to happen. Ask when booking, otherwise just relax and enjoy the boat ride and scenery, and wait to see your dancing at the Cultural Center. (If saving money is a priority and you can get a small group together, it's much cheaper to go to Navua by public bus and hire a market boat from there.)

Exciting whitewater rafting trips on the Upper Navua River west of Namuamua are offered by **Rivers Fiji** (Box 307, Pacific Harbor; tel. 450-147, fax 450-148). You're driven over the mountains to a remote spot where you get in a rubber raft and shoot through a narrow gorge inaccessible by motorized boat. Due to the class III rapids involved, children under 12 are not accepted, but for others it's F$250 including lunch. Rivers Fiji also does a less strenuous run down the Luva River north of Namuamua on which it's possible to paddle your own inflatable kayak. This costs F$168 for children 7-11 and F$216 for others. On both trips you finish the day by boarding a motorized punt at Namuamua and cruising down the main river to Nakavu village where you reboard the van to your hotel. Prices include pickups at Coral Coast and Suva hotels (F$15 extra for Nadi pickups). If you're really keen, ask about overnight camping expeditions even farther up the Navua where class IV whitewater is found.

OFFSHORE ISLANDS

Vatulele Island

This small island, 32 km south of Viti Levu, reaches a height of only 34 meters on its north end; there are steep bluffs on the west coast and gentle slopes facing a wide lagoon on the east. Both passes into the lagoon are from its north end. Five different levels of erosion are visible on the cliffs from which the uplifted limestone was undercut. There are also rock paintings, but no one knows when they were executed. Other unique features of 31-square-km Vatulele are the sacred **red prawns,** which are found in tidal pools at Korolamalama Cave at the foot of a cliff near the island's rocky north coast, and tapa cloth.

The 950 inhabitants live in four villages on the east side of Vatulele. Village boats from Viti Levu leave Paradise Point near Korolevu Post Office on Tuesday, Thursday, and Saturday if the weather is good. Sunflower Airlines flies to Vatulele from Nadi daily (F$616 pp return). The island's small private airstrip is near the villages, six km from the resort described below, to which tourists are transferred by bus.

In 1990 Vatulele got its own luxury resort, the **Vatulele Island Resort** (Box 9936, Nadi Airport; tel. 550-300, fax 550-062) on Vatulele's west side. The 12 futuristic villas in a hybrid Fijian/New Mexico style sit about 50 meters apart on a magnificent white-sand beach facing a protected lagoon. The emphasis is on luxurious exclusivity: villas cost F$1,342/1,936 single/double, including all meals and tax. The minimum stay is four nights, and children are only accepted at certain times of the year. To preserve the natural environment, motorized water sports are not offered, but there's lots to do, including sailing, snorkeling, windsurfing, paddling, tennis, and hiking, with guides and gear provided at no additional cost. The only thing you'll be charged extra for is scuba diving (F$132 a tank). This world-class resort is a creation of Australian TV producer Henry Crawford and local promoter Martin Livingston, a former manager of Turtle Island Resort in the Yasawas. Luxury.

Yanuca Island

In 1994 a surfers' camp opened on a splendid beach on little Yanuca Island, to the west of Beqa (not to be confused with the Yanuca Island on which The Fijian Resort Hotel is found). **Frigate Surfriders** (Ratu Penaia Drekeni, Box 39, Pacific Harbor; tel. 450-801) offers cots in two four-person dormitory *bures* and five double tents at F$65 pp for surfers, F$30 pp for nonsurfers, plus tax. Included are accommodations and all meals, windsurfing, surfing, and sportfishing. For information ask at the video rental shop in the Marketplace of Fiji at Pacific Harbor. Boat transfers are F$20 pp return. Inexpensive.

A 10-minute walk from Frigate Surfriders is a second surfing camp called **Batiluva Beach**

Resort (Box 149, Pacific Harbor; tel. 450-019 or 450-202, fax 450-067), which offers dormitory accommodations at F$75 pp, including meals, surfing, snorkeling, and fishing (transfers F$40 return). It's run by an American and information should be available from Rosie Delai at Alamanda Tours (Box 111, Pacific Harbor; tel. 450-330) opposite the Marketplace of Fiji video rental shop. Moderate.

The left-hander in Frigate Passage southwest of Yanuca has been called the most underrated wave in Fiji: "fast, hollow, consistent, and deserted." The Frigate Surfriders leaflet describes it thus:

Frigate Passage, out on the western edge of the Beqa Barrier Reef, is a sucking, often barreling photocopy of Cloudbreak near Nadi. The wave comprises three sections that often join up. The outside section presents a very steep take-off as the swell begins to draw over the reef. The wave then starts to bend and you enter a long walled speed section with stand-up tubes. This leads to a pitching inside section that breaks onto the reef, and if your timing is right you can backdoor this part and kick out safely in deep water.

Just be aware that there's an ongoing dispute over who holds the "rights" to surf here, so check the current situation before booking or you could get caught up in their squabbles. All surfing is banned on Sunday. Yet even without the surfing, Yanuca is still worth a visit (great beach-based snorkeling). As at neighboring Beqa, Fijian firewalking is a tradition here. Village boats to the one Fijian village on Yanuca depart on Tuesday and Saturday afternoons from the bridge near the Centra Resort Pacific Harbor.

Beqa Island

Beqa (pronounced "Mbengga") is the home of the famous Fijian firewalkers; Rukua, Naceva, and Dakuibeqa are firewalking villages. Nowadays, however, they only perform at the hotels on Viti Levu. At low tide you can hike the 27 km around the island: the road only goes from Waisomo to Dakuni. Malumu Bay, between the two branches of the island, is thought to be a drowned crater. Climb Korolevu (439 meters), the highest peak, from Waisomo or Lalati.

Mikaele Funaki's **Island and Village Concept Tours** (Box 14328, Suva; tel. 307-951) organizes three-night homestays at Naceva or another village at F$98 pp including food and shared accommodations, local sightseeing and snorkeling tours, and return boat transfers from Navua. The packages begin every Tuesday and Friday. Call for information.

The **Marlin Bay Resort** (Box 112, Deuba; tel. 304-042, fax 304-028) opened in 1991 on a golden beach between Raviravi and Rukua villages on the west side of Beqa. It's expensive because all prices are based on U.S. dollars. The 16 luxurious *bures* go for F$360 single or double, F$395 triple. The five-star meal plan is F$110 pp a day (no cooking facilities). Most guests are scuba divers who come to dive on spots like

Soft Coral Plateau, Fan Reef, and Joe's Best. It's F$160 for a two-tank boat dive (plus F$60 for equipment, if required), and unlimited shore diving is free. There's a swimming pool and surfing runs to Frigate Pass are arranged at F$100 pp for two sessions. Boat pickups for the Marlin Bay Resort take place at The Pub Restaurant, Pacific Harbor, and cost F$100 return.

The 65 km of barrier reef around the 390-square-km Beqa Lagoon features multicolored soft corals and fabulous sea fans at Side Streets, and an exciting wall and big fish at Cutter Passage. Aside from its surfing potential, **Frigate Passage** on the west side of the barrier reef is one of the top scuba diving sites near Suva. A vigorous tidal flow washes in and out of the passage, which attracts large schools of fish, and there are large coral heads. **Sulfur Passage** on the east side of Beqa is equally good.

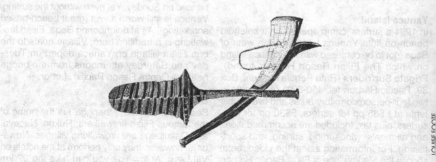

SUVA AND VICINITY

The pulsing heart of the South Pacific, Suva is the largest and most cosmopolitan city in Oceania. The port is always jammed with ships bringing goods and passengers from far and wide, and busloads of commuters and enthusiastic visitors constantly stream through the busy market bus station. In the business center are Indian women in saris, large sturdy chocolate-skinned Fijians, expat Australians and New Zealanders in shorts and knee socks, and wavy-haired Polynesians from Rotuma and Tonga.

Suva squats on a hilly peninsula between Laucala Bay and Suva Harbor in the southeast corner of Viti Levu. The verdant mountains north and west catch the southeast trades, producing damp conditions year-round. Visitors sporting a sunburn from Fiji's western sunbelt resorts may appreciate Suva's warm tropical rains (most of which fall at night). In 1870 the Polynesia Company sent Australian settlers to camp along mosquito-infested Nubukalou Creek on land obtained from High Chief Cakobau. When efforts to grow sugarcane in the area failed, the company convinced the British to move their headquarters here, and since 1882 Suva has been the capital of Fiji.

Today this exciting multiracial city of 170,000—nearly a fifth of Fiji's total population and half the urban population—is also about the only place in Fiji where you'll see a building taller than a palm tree. High-rise office buildings and hotels overlook the compact downtown area. The British left behind imposing colonial buildings, wide avenues, and manicured parks as evidence of their rule. The Fiji School of Medicine, the University of the South Pacific, the Fiji Institute of Technology, the Pacific Theological College, the Pacific Regional Seminary, and the headquarters of many regional organizations and diplomatic missions have been established here. In addition, the city offers some of the most brilliant nightlife between Kings Cross (Sydney) and North Beach (San Francisco), plus shopping, sightseeing, and many good-value places to stay and eat.

Keep in mind that on Sunday most shops will be closed, restaurants keep reduced hours, and fewer taxis or buses will be on the road. In short, the city will be quiet—a good time to wander around in relative peace. If you decide to catch the Friday or Saturday bus/boat service to Leleuvia or Levuka and spend the weekend there, book your ticket a day or two in advance. Otherwise, it's worth dressing up and attending church to hear the marvelous choral singing. Most churches have services in English, but none compare with the 1000 Fijian service at Centenary Methodist Church on Stewart Street.

The lovely *Isa Lei,* a Fijian song of farewell, tells of a youth whose love sails off and leaves him alone in Suva, smitten with longing.

SIGHTS

Central Suva

Suva's colorful **municipal market,** the largest retail produce market in the Pacific, is a good place to dabble (but beware of pickpockets). If you're a yachtie or backpacker, you'll be happy to know that the market overflows with fresh produce of every kind. It's worth some time looking around, and consider having kava at the *yaqona* dens upstairs in the market for about F$1 a bowl (share the excess with those present). Fijian women outside sell fresh pineapple and guava juice from glass "fish tank" containers.

From the market, walk south on Scott Street, past the colorful old Metropole Hotel, to the **Fiji Visitors Bureau** in a former customs house (1912) opposite Suva's General Post Office. At the corner of Thomson and Pier Streets opposite the visitors bureau is the onetime **Garrick Hotel** (1914) with a Sichuan Chinese restaurant behind the wrought-iron balconies upstairs. Go east on Thomson to Morris Hedstrom Supermarket and the picturesque colonial-style arcade (1919) along **Nubukalou Creek,** a campsite of Suva's first European settlers. You'll get good photos from the little park just across the bridge.

Cumming Street, Suva's main shopping area, runs east from the park on the site of Suva's original vegetable market before it moved to its

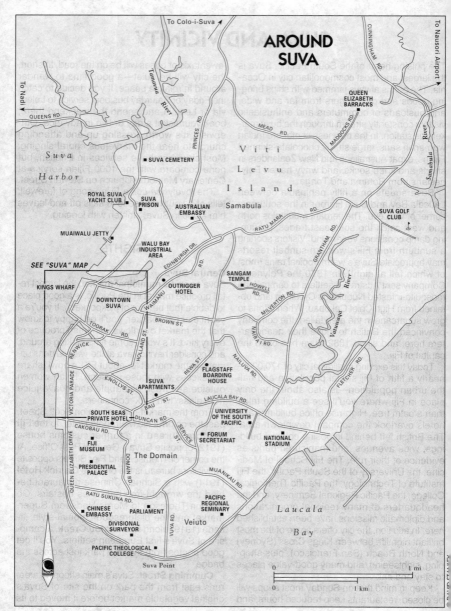

AROUND SUVA

To Colo-i-Suva

To Nausori Airport

To Nadi

QUEENS RD.

Tamavua River

PRINCES RD.

CUNNINGHAM RD.

QUEEN ELIZABETH BARRACKS

MEAD RD.

MACDONALD RD.

MADDOCKS RD.

Samabula River

Suva Harbor

SUVA CEMETERY

ROYAL SUVA YACHT CLUB

SUVA PRISON

AUSTRALIAN EMBASSY

Viti Levu Island

Samabula

RATU MARA RD.

SUVA GOLF CLUB

MUAIWALU JETTY

WALU BAY INDUSTRIAL AREA

EDINBURGH DR.

GRANTHAM RD.

SANGAM TEMPLE

HOWELL RD.

MILVERTON RD.

Vanuaqua River

SEE "SUVA" MAP

KINGS WHARF

DOWNTOWN SUVA

OUTRIGGER HOTEL

WAIMANU RD.

BROWN ST.

NAIRAI RD.

FLETCHER RD.

TOORAK RD.

RENWICK RD.

HOLLAND ST.

REWA ST.

FLAGSTAFF BOARDING HOUSE

NAILUVA RD.

KNOLLYS ST.

SUVA APARTMENTS

BAU ST.

LAUCALA BAY RD.

UNIVERSITY OF THE SOUTH PACIFIC

VICTORIA PARADE

SOUTH SEAS PRIVATE HOTEL

DUNCAN RD.

SERVICE ST.

FORUM SECRETARIAT

NATIONAL STADIUM

CAKOBAU RD.

FIJI MUSEUM

QUEEN ELIZABETH DRIVE

PRESIDENTIAL PALACE

DOMAIN RD.

The Domain

MUANIKAU RD.

RATU SUKUNA RD.

PACIFIC REGIONAL SEMINARY

CHINESE EMBASSY

PARLIAMENT

Veiuto

Laucala Bay

DIVISIONAL SURVEYOR

VUYA RD.

PACIFIC THEOLOGICAL COLLEGE

Suva Point

0   1 mi

0   1 km

present location just prior to WW II. During the war the street became a market of a different sort as Allied troops flocked here in search of evening entertainment, and since the early 1960s Cumming has served tourists and locals alike in its present form. To continue your walk, turn right on Renwick Road and head back into the center of town.

At the junction of Thomson Street, Renwick Road, and Victoria Parade is a small park known as **The Triangle** with five concrete benches and a white obelisk bearing four inscriptions: "Cross and Cargill first missionaries arrived 14th October 1835; Fiji British Crown Colony 10th October 1874; Public Land Sales on this spot 1880; Suva proclaimed capital 1882." Inland a block on Pratt St. is the **Catholic cathedral** (1902) built of sandstone imported from Sydney, Australia. Between The Triangle and the cathedral is the towering **Reserve Bank of Fiji** (1984), which is worth entering to see the currency exhibition.

Return to Suva's main avenue, Victoria Parade, and walk south past **Sukuna Park,** site of public protests in 1990 against the military-imposed constitution of the time. Farther along are the colonial-style **Fintel Building** (1926), nerve center of Fiji's international telecommunications links, the picturesque **Queen Victoria Memorial Hall** (1904), later Suva Town Hall and now the Ming Palace restaurant, and the **City Library** (1909), which opened in 1909 thanks to a grant from American philanthropist Andrew Carnegie (one of 2,509 public library buildings Carnegie gave to communities in the English-speaking world). All of these sights are on your right.

South Suva

Continue south on Victoria Parade past the somber headquarters of the **Native Land Trust Board,** which administers much of Fiji's land on behalf of indigenous landowners. Just beyond and across the street from the Centra Suva Hotel is Suva's largest edifice, the imposing **Government Buildings** (1939), once the headquarters of the British colonial establishment in the South Pacific. A statue of Chief Cakobau stares thoughtfully at the building. Here on 14 May 1987 Col. Sitiveni Rabuka carried out the South Pacific's first military coup, and for the next five years Fiji had no representative government. The chamber from which armed soldiers ab-

ducted the parliamentarians is now used by the supreme court, accessible from the parking lot behind the building. Prime Minister Timoci Bavadra and the others were led out through the doors below the building's clock tower (now closed) and forced into the back of army trucks waiting on Gladstone Road.

The main facade of the Government Buildings faces **Albert Park,** where aviator Charles Kingsford Smith landed his trimotor Fokker VII-3M on 6 June 1928 after arriving from Hawaii on the first-ever flight from California to Australia. (The first commercial flight to Fiji was a Pan Am flying boat, which landed in Suva Harbor in October 1941.) Facing the west side of the park is the elegant, Edwardian-style **Grand Pacific Hotel,** built by the Union Steamship Company in 1914 to accommodate its transpacific passengers. The 75 rooms were designed to appear as shipboard staterooms, with upstairs passageways surveying the harbor, like the promenade deck of a ship. For decades the Grand Pacific was the social center of the city, but it has been closed since 1992. The building is owned by the phosphate-rich Republic of Nauru, and in 1998 Outrigger Hotels of Hawaii announced that the Grand Pacific would be renovated and expanded into a 136-room luxury hotel, opening in late 1999.

South of Albert Park are the pleasant **Thurston Botanical Gardens,** opened in 1913, where tropical flowers such as cannas and plumbagos blossom. The original Fijian village of Suva once stood on this site. (It's fun to observe the young Indian couples enjoying brief moments away from the watchful eyes of their families.) On the grounds of the gardens is a clock tower dating from 1918 and the **Fiji Museum** (Box 2023, Government Buildings, Suva; tel. 315-944, fax 305-143), founded in 1904 and the oldest in the South Pacific. The first hall deals in archaeology, with much information about Fiji's unique pottery. Centerpiece of the adjacent maritime exhibit is a double-hulled canoe made in 1913, plus five huge *drua* steering oars each originally held by four men, several large sail booms, and a bamboo house raft *(bilibili).* The cannibal forks near the entrance are fascinating, as are the whale tooth necklaces and the large collection of Fijian war clubs and spears. The history gallery beyond the museum shop has a rich collection of 19th-century exhibits with items connected with the many peoples who have come to Fiji, including Tongans, Europeans, Solomon Islanders, and Indians. Notice the rudder from HMS *Bounty*. An a/c room upstairs contains a display of tapa cloth. You can ask to watch a video on Pacific themes in the museum theater. The museum shop sells an illustrated catalog titled *Yalo i Viti* and copies of the museum journal, *Domodomo*, plus other interesting books. Visiting hours are Mon.-Fri. 0930-1600, Saturday and Sunday 1300-1630, admission F$3.30. Plans exist for a National Center for Culture and the Arts to be built adjacent to the existing museum.

South of the gardens is **Presidential Palace,** formerly called Government House, the residence of the British governors of Fiji. The original building, erected in 1882, burned after being hit by lightning in 1921. The present edifice, which dates from 1928, is a replica of the former British governor's residence in Colombo, Sri Lanka. The grounds cannot be visited but you're welcome to take a photo of the sentry on ceremonial guard duty in his belted red tunic and immaculate white *sulu* (kilt). The changing of the guard takes place daily at noon with an especially elaborate ceremony the first Friday of every month to the accompaniment of the military band.

From the seawall south of Government House you get a good view across Suva Harbor to Beqa Island (to the left) and the dark, green mountains of eastern Viti Levu punctuated by Joske's Thumb, a high volcanic plug (to the right). Follow the seawall south past a few old colonial buildings, and turn left onto Ratu Sukuna Road, the first street after the Police Academy.

About 500 meters up this road is the **Parliament of Fiji** (1992), an impressive, traditional-style building with an orange pyramid-shaped roof. The main entrance is around the corner off Battery Road. If you want a complete tour, call the parliamentary library the day before at tel. 305-811, otherwise ask the librarians if they can admit you to the main chamber (weekdays only). When parliament is in session you may enter the public gallery. The top time to be there is for the debate on the budget in November, but you might need to arrive at 0800 to get a seat that day. Other sittings are poorly attended by both the public and members. Thirteen huge tapa banners hang from the walls, and skillfully plaited coconut fiber ropes from the Lau Group and a pair of *tabuas* complete the decor. The location is spectacular with scenic sea and mountain views.

From Parliament it's a good idea to catch a taxi to the University of the South Pacific. The Nasese bus does a scenic loop through the beautiful garden suburbs of South Suva: just flag it down if you need a ride back to the market. Both Protestants and Catholics have their most important regional training facilities for ministers and priests in South Suva.

University of the South Pacific

A frequent bus from near the Bank of Hawaii on Victoria Parade will bring you direct to the University of the South Pacific (ask the driver to let you know where to get out). Founded in 1968, this beautiful 72.8-hectare campus on a hilltop overlooking Laucala Bay is jointly owned by 12 Pacific countries. Although more than 70% of the almost 2,000 full-time and more than 600 part-time students are from Fiji, the rest are on scholarships from every corner of the Pacific.

The site of the USP's Laucala Campus was a Royal New Zealand Air Force seaplane base before the land was turned over to USP. As you enter from Laucala Bay Road you'll pass the Botanical Garden (1988) on the right, then the British-built Administration Building on the left. Next comes the $3.5-million university library (1988), erected with Australian aid. The design of the Student Union Building (1975), just across a wooden bridge from the library, was influenced by traditional Pacific building motifs of interlocking circles. Look for the pleasant canteen in the Student Union (open Mon.-Sat. 0800-2030 during the school year). There's a choice of Indian or island food.

Several buildings south of this, past the university bookstore and a traditional Fijian *bure,* is the **Institute of Pacific Studies** (Box 1168, Suva; tel. 313-632), housed in the former RNZAF officers' mess. Every available space on the walls of the IPS building has been covered with murals by Pacific painters. This Institute is a leading publisher of insightful books written by Pacific islanders; these books may be perused and purchased at the bookroom inside the building.

Students from outside the Pacific islands pay about F$8,200 a year tuition to study at USP.

Room and board are available at around F$3,162 and books will run another F$400. There are academic minimum-entry requirements and applications must be received by 31 December for the following term. The two semesters are late February to the end of June, and late July until the end of November. Many courses in the social sciences have a high level of content pertaining to Pacific culture, and postgraduate studies in a growing number of areas are available. To obtain a calendar (F$20), send a Visa or MasterCard authorization to: The Manager, Book Center, University of the South Pacific, Box 1168, Suva, Fiji Islands (tel. 313-900, fax 303-265).

The USP is always in need of qualified staff, so if you're from a university milieu and looking for a chance to live in the South Seas, this could be it. If your credentials are impeccable you should write to the registrar from home. On the spot it's better to talk to a department head about his/her needs before going to see the registrar.

Northwest of Suva

The part of Suva north of Walu Bay accommodates much of Suva's shipping and industry. Carlton Brewery on Foster Road cannot be visited. About 600 meters beyond the brewery is the vintage **Suva Prison** (1913), a fascinating colonial structure with high walls and barbed wire. Opposite is the **Royal Suva Yacht Club,** where you can sign in and buy a drink, meet some yachties, and maybe find a boat to crew on. In the picturesque **Suva Cemetery,** just to the north, the Fijian graves are wrapped in colorful *sulus* and tapa cloth, and make good subjects for photographers.

Catch one of the frequent Shore, Lami, or Galoa buses west on Queens Road, past **Suvavou** village, home of the Suva area's original Fijian inhabitants, and past Lami town to the **Raffles Tradewinds Hotel,** seven km from the market. Many cruising yachts tie up here, and the view of the Bay of Islands from the hotel is good.

Colo-i-Suva Forest Park

This lovely park, at an altitude of 122-183 meters, offers 6.5 km of trails through the lush forest flanking the upper drainage area of Waisila Creek. The mahogany trees you see here are natives of Central America and were planted

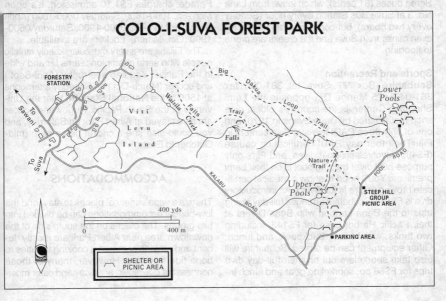

after the area was logged in the 1950s. Enter from the Forestry Station along the Falls Trail. A half-km nature trail begins near the Upper Pools, and aside from waterfalls and natural swimming pools there are thatched pavilions with tables at which to picnic. With the lovely green forests behind Suva in full view, this is one of the most breathtaking places in all of Fiji and you may spot a few native butterflies, birds, reptiles, and frogs. The park is so unspoiled it's hard to imagine you're only 11 km from Suva.

When the park first opened in 1973, camping was allowed near the upper and lower pools. Then in the mid-1980s the rangers were forced to prohibit camping due to thefts from both campers and swimmers. Recently security patrols have been stepped up and camping is once again allowed, but someone must still keep watch over the campsite at all times, especially on weekends. You must also keep an eye on your gear if you go swimming (valuables can be left at the visitors center). The park (tel. 361-128) is open daily 0800-1600, and there's a F$5 pp entry fee (under age 12 F$1, under six free) to cover park maintenance and management. Get there on the Sawani or Serea buses (61 cents), which leave from Lane No. 3 at Suva Bus Station every hour (Sunday every two hours), but come on a dry day as it's even rainier than Suva and the creeks are prone to flooding.

Sports and Recreation

Scubahire (Box 777, Suva; tel. 361-088, fax 361-047), 75 Marine Dr., opposite the Lami Shopping Center, is the country's oldest dive shop (established by Dave Evans in 1970) and one of only three PADI five-star dive centers in Fiji. Their four-day PADI certification course (F$495) involves six boat dives, and Fiji's only purpose-built diver training pool is on their Lami premises. You'll need to show a medical certificate proving you're fit for diving. An introductory dive is F$154. Scubahire arranges full-day diving trips to the Beqa Lagoon with Beqa Divers at their Pacific Harbor base for F$143, including two tanks, weight belt, backpack, and lunch. Other equipment can be rented. Scubahire will also take snorkelers out on their full-day dive trips for F$66 pp, snorkeling gear and lunch in-

cluded. When things are slow they may offer a "special" reduced rate for the all-day scuba trip, if you ask. All diving is out of Pacific Harbor—the Suva office only takes bookings, does certification courses, and sells equipment.

Dive Center Ltd. (Box 3066, Lami; tel. 300-599, fax 302-639), 4 Matua St., Walu Bay (opposite Carlton Brewery), also rents and sells scuba gear at daily and weekly rates, and fills tanks.

Surfers should call Matthew Light (tel. 361-560 or 998-830), who runs a shuttle out to Sandspit Lighthouse where there's good surfing on a southwest swell at high tide (F$15 pp roundtrip). He picks up at the Raffles Tradewinds Hotel in Lami.

At the 18-hole, par-72 **Fiji Golf Club** (tel. 382-872), 15 Rifle Range Rd., Vatuwaqa, the course record is 65. Greens fees are F$15/20 for nine/18 holes, club hire F$10/20 for a half/full set, plus trolley hire at F$3. Call ahead to ask if any competitions are scheduled as the course may be closed to the public at those times. (Prime Minister Rabuka and President Mara are regulars).

The **Olympic Swimming Pool,** 224 Victoria Parade, charges F$1.10 admission. It's open Mon.-Fri. 1000-1800, Saturday 0800-1800 (April-Sept.), or Mon.-Fri. 0900-1900, Saturday 0600-1900 (Oct.-March). Lockers are available.

The Fijians are a very muscular, keenly athletic people who send champion teams far and wide in the Pacific. You can see rugby (April-Sept.) and soccer (March-Oct.) on Saturday afternoons at 1500 at the **National Stadium** near the University of the South Pacific. Rugby and soccer are also played at Albert Park on Saturday, and you could also see a cricket game here (mid-October to Easter).

ACCOMMODATIONS

There's a wide variety of places to stay, and the low-budget accommodations can be divided into two groups. The places on the south side of the downtown area near Albert Park are mostly decent and provide communal cooking facilities to bona fide travelers. However, many of those northeast of downtown are dicey and cater most-

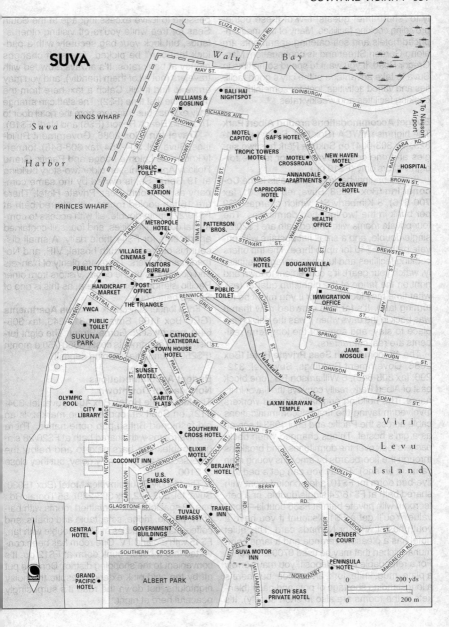

SUVA

Suva Harbor

KINGS WHARF

PRINCES WHARF

- BALI HAI NIGHTSPOT
- WILLIAMS & GOSLING
- MOTEL CAPITOL
- SAF'S HOTEL
- TROPIC TOWERS MOTEL
- MOTEL CROSSROAD
- NEW HAVEN MOTEL
- HOSPITAL
- PUBLIC TOILET
- BUS STATION
- ANNANDALE APARTMENTS
- OCEANVIEW HOTEL
- CAPRICORN HOTEL
- MARKET
- METROPOLE HOTEL
- PATTERSON BROS.
- HEALTH OFFICE
- VILLAGE 6 CINEMAS
- VISITORS BUREAU
- KINGS HOTEL
- BOUGAINVILLEA MOTEL
- PUBLIC TOILET
- HANDICRAFT MARKET
- POST OFFICE
- PUBLIC TOILET
- THE TRIANGLE
- YWCA
- IMMIGRATION OFFICE
- PUBLIC TOILET
- SUKUNA PARK
- CATHOLIC CATHEDRAL
- TOWN HOUSE HOTEL
- JAME MOSQUE
- SUNSET MOTEL
- SARITA FLATS
- OLYMPIC POOL
- CITY LIBRARY
- LAXMI NARAYAN TEMPLE
- SOUTHERN CROSS HOTEL
- ELIXIR MOTEL
- COCONUT INN
- BERJAYA HOTEL
- U.S. EMBASSY
- CENTRA HOTEL
- TUVALU EMBASSY
- TRAVEL INN
- GOVERNMENT BUILDINGS
- PENDER COURT
- SUVA MOTOR INN
- GRAND PACIFIC HOTEL
- PENINSULA HOTEL
- ALBERT PARK
- SOUTH SEAS PRIVATE HOTEL

Walu Bay

ELIZA ST.
FOSTER RD.
MAY ST.
EDINBURGH DR.
To Nausori Airport
RATA MARA RD.
BROWN ST.
RICHARDS AVE.
RENOWN
RODWELL
HARRIS RD.
ESCOTT
JELLICOE
STRUAN ST.
ROBERTSON RD.
DAVEY ST.
FORT ST.
STEWART ST.
BREWSTER ST.
MARKS ST.
CUMMING ST.
RENWICK
GREIG
ELLERY
THOMPSON
EDWARD ST.
CENTRAL ST.
STINSON
PARADE
SCOTT ST.
NINA ST.
USHER
WAIMANU RD.
RAQIBHA ST.
PATEL ST.
SUVA ST.
HIGH ST.
TOORAK RD.
AMY ST.
SPRING ST.
HUON ST.
JOHNSON ST.
EDEN ST.
Nubukalou Creek
JOSKE
GORDON
MURRAY ST.
PRATT ST.
FORSTER ST.
BUTT ST.
TOWER
HERCULES
SELBORNE
HOLLAND ST.
Viti Levu Island
MacARTHUR ST.
KIMBERLY ST.
GOODENOUGH ST.
MALCOLM ST.
DESVOEUX RD.
DISRAELI RD.
KNOLLYS ST.
VICTORIA PARADE
LOFTUS ST.
CARNARVON ST.
THURSTON ST.
GLADSTONE RD.
GORRIE ST.
GORDON ST.
BERRY RD.
MARION ST.
PENDER RD.
MacGREGOR RD.
MITCHELL ST.
SOUTHERN CROSS RD.
WILLIAMSON RD.
NORMANBY RD.

0   200 yds
0   200 m

Moon

ly to "short-time" guests; few of these bother providing cooking facilities. Many of the medium-priced hotels and self-catering apartments are along Gordon Street and its continuation, Mac-Gregor Road. If you want to spend some time in Suva to take advantage of the city's good facilities and varied activities, look for something with cooking facilities and weekly rates.

Budget Accommodations around Albert Park

The high-rise **YWCA** (Box 534, Suva; tel. 304-829, fax 303-004) on Sukuna Park has two singles and one double available for female foreign visitors only (F$10 pp).

Suva's original backpacker's oasis is the **Coconut Inn** (Box 14598, Suva; tel. 305-881, fax 700-616), 8 Kimberly St., which charges F$9 per bunk in the two four-bed dormitories. The four private rooms with shared bath are F$20/25 single/double, and a small flat upstairs with private bath is F$40 for up to three. The Inn offers cooking facilities and luggage storage (definitely, watch your gear). It's convenient to town and right on the fringe of the nightclub quarter (ask what time they lock the door if you might be returning late). It's far less crowded now than it was back in the days when it was the only cheap place to stay, and some of the long-term residents are real characters.

The 42-room **South Seas Private Hotel** (Box 2086, Government Buildings, Suva; tel. 312-296, fax 308-646), 6 Williamson Rd., one block east of Albert Park, really conveys the flavor in its name. The building originally housed workers involved in laying the first telecommunications cable across the Pacific and until 1983 it served as a girl's hostel. Things changed when backpackers took over the dormitories (and break-ins through the floorboards by amorous young men came to an end). Today you can get a bed in a five-bed dorm for F$10, a fan-cooled room with shared bath at F$16/24 single/double, or a better room with private bath at F$36 double—good value. You'll get a F$1 discount if you have a youth hostel, VIP, or Nomads card. This quiet hotel has a pleasant veranda and a large communal kitchen that may be used 0700-2000 only. For a refundable F$10 deposit, you may borrow a plate, mug, knife, fork, and spoon, but there's a longstanding shortage of pots and pans (blankets in the rooms are also in short supply). It's

possible to leave excess luggage at the South Seas for free while you're off visiting other islands, but lock your bag securely with a padlock that can't be picked. The staff changes money at bank rates. It's always crowded with travelers (not all of them friendly), and you may arrive to find it full. Catch a taxi here from the market the first time (F$2). The staff can arrange daily express bus transfers from the hotel door to Tubakula Beach Resort (F$6) and Nadi (F$10).

Travel Inn (Box 2086, Government Buildings, Suva; tel. 304-254, fax 308-646), formerly known as Loloma Lodge and Pacific Grand Holiday Apartments, an older two-story building at 19 Gorrie St., is owned by the same company as the South Seas Private Hotel. There are 16 fan-cooled rooms with shared bath at F$19/27 single/double, all with access to communal cooking facilities, and four self-contained apartments for F$44 triple daily. A small discount is offered to youth hostel, VIP, and Nomads card holders. There are plenty of blankets and good locks on the doors. Visitors from other Pacific islands often stay here, as this is one of Suva's better buys.

For a longer stay check **Nukurua Apartments** (GPO Box 1109, Suva; tel. 312-343, fax 305-644), nearby at 25 Gorrie Street. The eight furnished a/c apartments cost F$650-750 a month (F$250 refundable cleaning deposit).

Budget Accommodations Northeast of Downtown

The **Metropole Hotel** (Box 404, Suva; tel. 304-112), on Scott St. opposite the market, is an old-fashioned British pub gone native. There are five rooms with shared bath at F$20/28 single/double. The bars next to and below the hotel section are extremely noisy, but they close at 2100.

The friendly **Bougainvillea Motel** (Box 15030, Suva; tel. 303-522, fax 303-289), 55 Toorak Rd., has 12 spacious self-contained rooms with balcony, phone, fridge, sofa, table and chairs, and coffee-making facilities at F$35 double with fan, F$45 with a/c and TV. One room has been converted into a seven-bunk dorm at F$12 pp. It's convenient to the shopping district. Don't be put off by the acid pink exterior: despite the noisy nightclubs just down the road it's surprisingly peaceful here at night.

The colorful, 44-room **Oceanview Hotel** (Box 16037, Suva; tel. 312-129), 270 Waimanu Rd., has two singles at F$20, 33 doubles at F$25, and nine four-person family rooms at F$35. It has a pleasant hillside location, but avoid the noisy rooms over the reception area and bar. The new management has tried to clean the place up, and security has improved. It's one of the only "lowlife" hotels in this area with any atmosphere.

Apartment Hotels

Several apartment hotels behind the Central Police Station are worth a try. The congenial **Town House Apartment Hotel** (Box 485, Suva; tel. 300-055, fax 303-446), 3 Forster St., is a five-story building with panoramic views from the rooftop bar (happy hour 1700-1900). The 28 a/c units with cooking facilities and fridge are good value at F$47/64/80 single/double/triple and up. Inexpensive.

Nearby and under the same ownership is the four-story **Sunset Apartment Motel** (Box 485, Suva; tel. 301-799, fax 303-446), corner of Gordon and Murray Streets. Avoid the four rooms without cooking facilities that go for F$42/46 single/double, and ask for one of the 10 two-bedroom apartments with kitchens and fridge at F$50/64, or the deluxe apartment at F$77. The two-bedroom apartments cost F$70/88/99 for three/four/five persons. A place in their 12-bed dorm is F$9 (no cooking). Some of the cheaper rooms are noisy and have uncomfortably soft beds. Weekly rates are available. The friendly manager, Violet, owns a fleet of taxis. Budget to inexpensive.

The Town House reception also handles bookings at **Sarita Flats** (tel. 300-084), nearby at 39 Gordon St., where a bed-sitting room apartment with cooking facilities will be F$55 single or double. This two-story building lacks the balconies and good views of the Town House. Inexpensive.

Four-story **Elixir Motel Apartments** (Box 2347, Government Buildings, Suva; tel. 303-288, fax 303-383), on the corner of Gordon and Malcolm Streets, has 14 two-bedroom apartments with cooking facilities and private bath at F$55 without a/c for up to three people, F$66 with a/c. Weekly and monthly rates are 10% lower. Inexpensive.

The **Suva Motor Inn** (Box 2500, Government Buildings, Suva; tel. 313-973, fax 300-381), a three-story complex near Albert Park, corner of Mitchell and Gorrie Streets, has 37 a/c studio apartments with kitchenette at F$99 single or double, F$119 triple (25% discount by the week). The seven two-bedroom apartments capable of accommodating five persons are F$154 for the first two, plus F$20 for each extra person. A courtyard swimming pool with waterslide and cascade faces the restaurant/bar. This new building is generally more luxurious and expensive than the others in this category, but well worth considering by families who want a bit of comfort. Moderate.

Cheaper are the apartments with fan at **Pender Court** (GPO Box 14590, Suva; tel. 314-992, fax 387-840), 31 Pender Street. The 13 studios with kitchenettes begin at F$40 single or double (10% reduction by the week), and there are also six one-bedroom apartments with kitchens for F$50 (reduced rates possible). It's sometimes a little noisy but good value. Budget.

Eleven better self-catering units owned by the National Olympic Committee are available at **Suva Apartments** (Box 12488, Suva; tel. 304-280, fax 301-647), 17 Bau St., a block or two east of Pender Court. They're F$30/35/47 single/double/triple daily, with 10% off on weekly rentals. Be prepared for traffic noise. Budget.

Up in the Waimanu Road area, the **Capricorn Apartment Hotel** (Box 1261, Suva; tel. 303-732, fax 303-069), 7 St. Fort St., has 34 spacious a/c units with cooking facilities, fridge, and TV beginning at F$85 single or double, F$95 triple, plus tax. The three- and four-story apartment blocks edge the swimming pool, and there are good views of the harbor from the individual balconies. Inexpensive.

Tropic Towers Apartment Motel (Box 1347, Suva; tel. 304-470, fax 304-169), 86 Robertson Rd., has 34 a/c apartments with cooking facilities in a four-story building starting at F$61/72/83 single/double/triple. Ask about the 13 "budget" units in the annex, which are F$33/44 single/double with shared bath. Washing machines (F$9) and a swimming pool are available for guests; screened windows or mosquito nets are not. This and the Capricorn are good choices for families. Budget to inexpensive.

One of the best deals up this way is the **Annandale Apartments** (Box 12818, Suva; tel. 311-

054), 265 Waimanu Rd. opposite the Oceanview Hotel. The 12 spacious two-bedroom apartments are F$45/200/600 a day/week/month for up to three or four people. A fridge, kitchen, sitting room, and balcony are provided in each. Budget.

Upmarket Hotels

Suva's largest hotel is the **Centra Suva** (Box 1357, Suva; tel. 301-600, fax 300-251), formerly the Travelodge, on the waterfront opposite the Government Buildings. It's a big American-style place with 130 a/c rooms with fridge and TV beginning at F$135 single or double plus tax. The swimming pool behind the two-story buildings compensates for the lack of a beach. Special events here include "island night" on Wednesday with a *meke* at 2000, and the Sunday poolside barbecue lunch. Expensive.

Your best bet if you want to go upmarket are the Southern Cross, Berjaya, and Peninsula International hotels, all within minutes of one another along Gordon Street. You can save money by calling ahead to all three to inquire about that day's "local rate," then take a taxi to the place of your choice. When things are slow, the receptionist may also agree to upgrade you to deluxe at no additional charge if you agree to stay for a few days. Of course, these deals don't apply to overseas bookings.

The **Southern Cross Hotel** (Box 1076, Suva; tel. 314-233, fax 302-901) is a high-rise concrete building at 63 Gordon Street. The 35 a/c rooms cost F$69/79/88 single/double/triple. Beware of rooms on the lower floors, which are blasted by band music six nights a week. The hotel restaurant on the 6th floor serves delicious Fijian and Korean dishes. Inexpensive.

The nine-story **Berjaya Hotel** (Box 112, Suva; tel. 312-300, fax 301-300), part of the Best Western chain, at the corner of Malcolm and Gordon Streets, is the tallest hotel in Fiji. The 48 a/c rooms with fridge and TV all face the harbor. It's F$134 single or double on the lower floors or F$146 on the upper floors and on those days when they're giving the reduced "local rate" the Berjaya becomes the best value top end hotel in Suva. This Malaysian-owned hotel hosts Suva's only Malaysian restaurant. Moderate to expensive.

The **Peninsula International Hotel** (Box 888, Suva; tel. 313-711, fax 314-473), at the corner of MacGregor Rd. and Pender St., is a stylish four-floor building with swimming pool. The 39 a/c rooms begin at F$55/72 single/double, while the eight suites with kitchenettes run F$72/89. Inexpensive.

FOOD

Downtown Eateries

One of the few places serving a regular cooked breakfast is the **Palm Court Bistro** (tel. 304-662; Mon.-Fri. 0700-1700, Saturday 0700-1430) in the Queensland Insurance Arcade behind Air New Zealand on Victoria Parade. Their burgers and sandwiches are good at lunchtime.

Judes (tel. 315-461; closed Sunday), in the arcade opposite Sukuna Park, also has good sandwiches at lunchtime and reasonable coffee. An inexpensive snack bar with concrete outdoor picnic tables is at the back side of the Handicraft Market facing the harbor (the "long soup" is a bargain).

Economical snacks are also served at **Donald's Kitchen** (tel. 315-587), 103 Cumming Street. One block over on Marks Street are cheaper Chinese restaurants, such as **Kim's Cafe** (tel. 313-252), 128 Marks St., where you can get a toasted egg sandwich and coffee for about a dollar fifty. There are scores more cheap milk bars around Suva, and you'll find them for yourself as you stroll around town.

Fijian

A popular place to sample Fijian food is the **Old Mill Cottage Cafe** (tel. 312-134; closed Sunday and evenings), 49 Carnarvon St.—the street behind the Golden Dragon nightclub. Government employees from nearby offices descend on this place at lunchtime for the inexpensive curried freshwater mussels, curried chicken livers, fresh seaweed in coconut milk, taro leaves creamed in coconut milk, and fish cooked in coconut milk. It's great, but don't come for coffee as it's cold and overpriced.

Indian

The **Hare Krishna Vegetarian Restaurant** (tel. 314-154; closed Sunday), at the corner of Pratt and Joske Streets, serves ice cream (12 flavors), sweets, and snacks downstairs, main meals upstairs (available Mon.-Sat. 1100-1430,

pick of the produce at Suva's colorful market

Friday also 1900-2100). If you want the all-you-can-eat vegetarian *thali* (F$6.50), just sit down and they'll bring it to you. But if you're not that starved, go up to the self-service counter and pick up a couple of vegetable dishes, which you can have with one or two *rotis.* This will cost about half as much as the full meal, though ordering individual dishes can be unexpectedly expensive, so unless you want the full meal it's better to look elsewhere. No smoking or alcohol are allowed.

Another laudable Indian place is the **Curry House** (tel. 313-000 or 313-756; closed Sunday) at two locations: 87 Cumming St., and next to the Ming Palace in the old town hall on Victoria Parade. Their special vegetarian *thali* (F$3) is an exceptional lunch and they also have quality meat curries from F$5. Try the takeaway *rotis.*

The **Top Taste Cafe de Curry** (Mon.-Sat. 0830-1730), just across Nubukalou Creek from Morris Hedstrom Supermarket, around the corner from Cumming Street, has a large selection of Indian curry dishes and a nice covered terrace on which to eat them.

Chinese

Not many Indian restaurants in Suva are open at night or on Sunday, so this is when you should turn to the many excellent, inexpensive Chinese restaurants. Most serve beer while the Indian restaurants are usually "dry."

The **Diamond Palace Restaurant** (tel. 303-848), upstairs at 30 Cumming St., serves generous portions, and the staff and surroundings are pleasant. **Geralyne's Restaurant** (tel. 311-037; closed Sunday), 160 Renwick Rd., is similar.

Also try the good-value **Lantern Palace Restaurant** (tel. 314-633) at 10 Pratt St. near Hare Krishna. The **Guang Wha Restaurant** next door to the Lantern Palace is cheaper and more likely to be open on holidays.

The more expensive **Sichuan Pavilion Restaurant** (tel. 315-194), upstairs in the old Garrick Hotel building at 6 Thomson St., is perhaps Suva's finest Asian restaurant. Employees of the Chinese Embassy frequent it for the spicy-hot Chinese dishes (though not as hot as Sichuan food elsewhere). Weather permitting, sit outside on the balcony and watch all Suva go by.

The **Phoenix Restaurant** (tel. 311-889), 165 Victoria Parade, has inexpensive Chinese dishes like red pork with fried rice (F$6) and big bottles of beer. Just ignore the horrific green painted walls and the odd cockroach running around.

The popular **Peking Restaurant** (tel. 312-714; daily 1130-2230), 195 Victoria Parade, is only a bit more expensive than the Chinese places with their dishes in warmers at the entrance but the atmosphere is nicer and the meals are individually prepared. Small parties of four or more can order set dinner menus served in the traditional Chinese banquet manner (F$8.50 pp and up). To sample all the specialties of the house, eight hours advance notice and a group of at least six is required (F$18 pp).

Suva's most imposing Chinese restaurant by far is the 250-seat **Ming Palace** (tel. 315-111) in the old town hall next to the public library on Victoria Parade.

Fong Lee Seafood Restaurant, 293 Victoria Parade, is more expensive than the Peking Restaurant and the dining area isn't as agreeable but the food is said to be the tastiest in Suva (notice the many affluent local Chinese having dinner there). Lunch is cheaper than dinner at the Fong Lee, or you can eat at the **Zifu Restaurant**

(tel. 313-988) next door for a third the price (the Zifu is highly recommended for lunch).

Better Restaurants

Tiko's Floating Restaurant (tel. 313-626; dinner only) is housed in the MV *Lycianda,* an ex-Blue Lagoon cruise ship launched at Suva in 1970 and now anchored off Stinson Parade behind Sukuna Park. Their steaks and seafood are good for a splurge and there's a bar called the Engineroom.

Cardo's Chargrill (tel. 314-330), in Regal Lane around behind the Qantas and Air Pacific offices, is run by descendants of Espero Cardo, an Argentine gaucho said to have arrived on a Koro Sea cruise in the early 1800s only to have his cattle rustled from belowdecks by Fijian warriors. What's known for sure is that today you can sit at a table with a view of Suva Harbor and consume steaks of 250, 300, or 450 grams priced from F$13-25. Fancier dishes on the main menu cater to other tastes.

JJ's Bar & Grill (tel. 305-005), at 10 Gordon St. just up from Sukuna Park, is a smart yuppie place with daily specials listed on blackboards. Soups, salads, and sandwiches are available at lunch, and if you don't want any of the main courses it's just as good to order a couple of appetizer dishes (the calamari friti come recommended).

ENTERTAINMENT AND EVENTS

In 1996 **Village Six Cinemas** (tel. 306-006) opened on Scott St. and you now have a choice of six Hollywood films several times a day. Regular admission is F$4, reduced to F$3 on Tuesday. The air conditioning is a relief on a hot day. Most of Suva's other cinemas show Asian karate films or Indian movies in Hindi, and it's much easier to check their listings in the *Fiji Times* than to make the rounds in person. The films change every three days at downmarket cinemas like the **Century** (tel. 311-641), 67 Marks St., Lilac (tel. 311-411), 10 Waimanu Rd., and the **Phoenix** (tel. 300-094), 192 Rodwell Rd. north of the bus station. Admission there is F$2 for a hard seat or F$3 for a soft seat.

The only regular cultural show in Suva is "island night" at the Centra Suva (tel. 301-600)

Wednesday at 1900, which features Polynesian dancing at 2000.

The **Fiji Indian Cultural Center** (tel. 300-050), 271 Toorak Rd., offers classes in Indian music, dancing, art, etc. It's well worth calling to find out if any public performances are scheduled during your visit.

The top time to be in Suva is in August during the **Hibiscus Festival** fills Albert Park with stalls, games, and carnival revelers.

Nightclubs

There are many nightclubs, all of which have nominal weekend cover charges and require neat dress, although nothing much happens until after 2200, and women shouldn't enter alone. Late at night, it's wise to take a taxi back to your hotel. Suva is still a very safe city, but nasty, violent robberies do occur.

Gays will feel comfortable at **Lucky Eddie's** (tel. 312-884; daily after 2000), 217 Victoria Parade, but it's not really a gay bar, as the Fijian women present try to prove.

Signals Night Club (tel. 313-590; Mon.-Sat. 1800-0100), at 255 Victoria Parade opposite the Suva City Library, charges F$3 cover after 2000 Thurs.-Sat. only.

A shade rougher but also very popular is the **Golden Dragon** (tel. 311-018; open Mon.-Sat. 1930-0100), 379 Victoria Parade.

Birdland Jazz Club (tel. 303-833), 6 Carnarvon St., back behind the Shell service station on Victoria Parade, is open Tues.-Sun. from 1800 with outstanding live rhythm and blues from 2230 on Thursday, Saturday, and Sunday (F$3 cover). Other nights there's recorded jazz. It's a late night place where people come after they've been to the others. **Bojangles Night Club,** adjacent to Birdland, is a disco open nightly from 1800 (F$3 cover after 2200).

The Barn (tel. 307-845), 54 Carnarvon St., is a popular country-and-western club open Mon.-Thurs. 1900-0100, Friday 1800-0100, Saturday 1930-0100 (live entertainment and a F$5 cover from 2100).

The most interracial of the clubs is **Chequers Nightspot** (tel. 313-563), 27 Waimanu Rd., which has live music nightly except Sunday. Hang onto your wallet here.

For real earthy atmosphere try the **Bali Hai** (tel. 315-868), at 194 Rodwell Rd., the roughest club in Suva. Friday and Saturday nights the place is packed with Fijians (no Indians) and tourists are rare, so beware. If you're looking for action, you'll be able to pick a partner within minutes, but take care with aggressive males. The dance hall on the top floor is the swingingest, with body-to-body jive—the Bali Hai will rock you.

Bars

O'Reilly's Pub (tel. 312-968), 5 MacArthur St., just around the corner from Lucky Eddie's, has a happy hour with local beer at F$1 a mug weekdays 1700-1945, Saturday 1800-1945. It's a nice relaxed way to kick off a night on the town, and with the big sports screen and canned music it's super. They're open Sunday from 1800.

The **Bad Dog Cafe**, next door to O'Reilly's, is a trendy wine bar with a whimsical name serving margaritas, sangria, and a dozen imported beers. Mexican dishes are on the food menu and for F$6 corkage you may BYO bottle of wine from the adjacent Victoria Wines shop. A back door from Bad Dog leads into the **Wolfhound Bar,** Suva's second mock Irish pub.

This Fijian breastplate of sperm whale ivory bears a pearl-shell plaque with perforated star and birds.

Traps Bar (tel. 312-922; Mon.-Sat. from 1800), at 305 Victoria Parade next to the Shell service station, is a groupie Suva social scene with a happy hour until 2000 (drunks are unwelcome here). There's live music on Wednesday.

Shooters Bar, at 58 Carnarvon St. next to The Barn, has a happy hour Mon.-Sat. 1700-2000. They play harder rock music than the others and the atmosphere is somewhere between O'Reilly's and Traps.

The bar at the **Suva Lawn Bowling Club** (tel. 302-394), facing the lagoon opposite Thurston Botanical Gardens and just off Albert Park, is a very convenient place to down a large bottle of Fiji Bitter—the perfect place for a cold one after visiting the museum. You can sit and watch the bowling, or see the sun set over Viti Levu. Foreign tourists are welcome.

Those in search of more subdued drinking should try the **Piano Bar** at the Centra Suva, which often presents rather good jazz singers, or the **Rooftop Garden Bar** at the Town House Motel (tel. 300-055), which has a happy hour 1700-1900.

SHOPPING

The **Government Handicraft Center** (tel. 211-306) behind Ratu Sukuna House, MacArthur and Carnarvon Streets, is a low-pressure place to familiarize yourself with what is authentic, though prices are high here, making it better to do your buying elsewhere. **Jacks Handicrafts,** Renwick Rd. and Pier St., has a representative selection of Fijian crafts with prices clearly marked.

The large **Curio and Handicraft Market** (Mon.-Sat. 0800-1700) on the waterfront behind the post office is a good place to haggle over crafts, so long as you know what is really Fijian (avoid masks and "tikis"). Unfortunately many of the vendors are rather aggressive and it's not possible to shop around in peace. Never come here on the day when a cruise ship is in port—prices shoot up. And watch out for the annoying "sword sellers" mentioned in the chapter introduction as they could accost you anywhere in Suva.

For clothing see the fashionable hand-printed shirts and dresses at **Tiki Togs** (tel. 304-381), 38 Thomson St. across from the General Post Office, and at 199 Victoria Parade next to Pizza Hut. You could come out looking like a real South Seas character at a reasonable price. Also check **Sogo Fiji** (tel. 315-007), on Cumming Street and on Victoria Parade next to the Bank of Hawaii.

Cumming Street is Suva's busiest shopping street. Expect to receive a 10-40% discount at the "duty-free" shops by bargaining, but *shop around* before you buy. Be especially wary when purchasing gold jewelry, as it might be fake. And watch out for hustlers who will try to show you around and get you a "good price." The large

Morris Hedstrom store across Nubukalou Creek from Cumming Street has a good selection of sunscreens.

Sumit Cycles (tel. 300-135), 41 Toorak Rd., sells new and used bicycles and does repairs.

The **Philatelic Bureau** (Box 100, Suva; tel. 312-928) at the General Post Office sells the stamps of Niue, Pitcairn, Samoa, Solomon Islands, Tuvalu, and Vanuatu, as well as those of Fiji. To place a standing order from overseas, send a credit card authorization for F$30 deposit.

SERVICES

Money

Rates at the banks vary slightly and you might get a dollar or two more on a large exchange by checking the Westpac Bank, ANZ Bank, and Bank of Hawaii before signing your checks. All of them have branches on Victoria Parade near The Triangle (several have ATMs).

Thomas Cook Travel (tel. 301-603), opposite the General Post Office, changes foreign currency Mon.-Fri. 0830-1700, Saturday 0830-1200, at competitive rates, and sells the banknotes of neighboring countries like New Caledonia, Samoa, Solomon Islands, Tonga, and Vanuatu—convenient if you're headed for any of them.

On Sunday and holidays changing money is a problem (try your hotel if you get stuck).

Telecommunications

Fintel, the Fiji International Telecommunications office (tel. 312-933, fax 301-025), 158 Victoria Parade, is open Mon.-Sat. 0800-2000 for long-distance calls and telegrams. The six private card phone booths here are the most convenient place in Suva to place either local or international calls. The basic charge for three minutes is F$4.74 to Australia or New Zealand, F$8.01 to North America and Europe (no minimum when using card phones). There's a 25% discount on international calls from card phones daily 2200-0600 and all day on weekends.

The public fax at Suva General Post Office is fax 302-666 should you need to receive a fax from anyone.

Internet access is available at the Telecom Fiji Customer Care Center (tel. 311-342; www.is.com.fj; weekdays 0800-1630), opposite the General Post Office and Fiji Visitors Bureau. The charge is F$3.30 for the first 15 minutes, then 22 cents each additional minute, and it's possible to book ready access at a set time by calling ahead or dropping in.

Immigration

The Immigration Office (tel. 312-622; Mon.-Fri. 0830-1300/1400-1500) for extensions of stay, etc., is at the corner of Toorak Rd. and Suva Street.

Cruising yachts wishing to visit the outer islands must first obtain a free permit from the Provincial Development Unit at the Ministry for Fijian Affairs (Box 2100, Government Buildings, Suva; tel. 304-200), 61 Carnarvon Street. They'll want to see the customs papers for the boat and all passports but the procedure is fast and friendly. (Yachties anchoring off a Fijian village should present a *sevusevu* of kava to the chief.)

Consulates

The following countries have diplomatic missions in Suva: China (tel. 300-215), 147 Queen Elizabeth Dr., Suva Point; Chile (tel. 300-433), Asgar & Co., Queensland Insurance Arcade behind Air New Zealand, Victoria Parade; European Union (tel. 313-633), 4th floor, Development Bank Center, 360 Victoria Parade; Federated States of Micronesia (tel. 304-566), 37 Loftus St.; France (tel. 312-233), 1st floor, Dominion House, Scott St.; Germany (tel. 315-000), 4th floor, Dominion House, Scott St.; Japan (tel. 304-633), 2nd floor, Dominion House, Scott St.; Korea (tel. 300-977), Vanua House, Victoria Parade; Malaysia (tel. 312-166), 5th floor, Pacific House, Butt and MacArthur Streets; Marshall Islands (tel. 387-899), 41 Borron Rd., Samabula; Nauru (tel. 313-566), 7th floor, Ratu Sukuna House, Victoria Parade and MacArthur; New Zealand (tel. 311-422), 10th floor, Reserve Bank Building, Pratt St.; Papua New Guinea (tel. 304-244), 3rd floor, Credit Corporation Building, Gordon and Malcolm Streets; Taiwan (tel. 315-922), 6th floor, Pacific House, Butt and MacArthur Streets; Tuvalu (tel. 301-355), 16 Gorrie St.; United Kingdom (tel. 311-033), 47 Gladstone Rd.; and the U.S.A. (tel. 314-466, fax 300-081), 31 Loftus Street. Canada and Italy have honorary consuls at Nadi.

Everyone other than New Zealanders requires a visa to visit Australia, and these are readily available free of charge at the Australian Embassy (Box 214, Suva; tel. 382-219; weekdays 0830-1200), 10 Reservoir Rd., off Princes Rd., Samabula. You can also sit and read week-old Australian newspapers here. To get there it's probably easier to take a taxi, then return to town on the Samabula bus.

Public Toilets

Public toilets are just outside the Handicraft Market on the side of the building facing the harbor; beside Nubukalou Creek off Renwick Rd.; and between the vegetable market and the bus station. Some are free, others charge five cents a visit. The public toilets in Sukuna Park are 24 cents.

Yachting Facilities

The Royal Suva Yacht Club (Box 335, Suva; tel. 312-921, fax 304-433, channel 16), on Foster Rd. between Suva and Lami, offers visiting yachts such amenities as mooring privileges, warm showers, laundry facilities, cheap drinks, and the full use of club services by the whole crew for F$30 a week. Tuesday and Friday nights there are barbecues (F$6.50). There have been reports of thefts from boats anchored here, so watch out. Many yachts anchor off the Raffles Tradewinds Hotel on the Bay of Islands, a recognized hurricane anchorage.

INFORMATION

The Fiji Visitors Bureau (tel. 302-433; Mon.-Fri. 0800-1630, Saturday 0800-1200) is on Thomson Street across from the General Post Office.

The Tourism Council of the South Pacific (tel. 304-177, fax 301-995), FNPF Plaza, 3rd floor, 343-359 Victoria Parade at Loftus St., provides general brochures on the entire South Pacific. Ask for a copy of their free guidebook *The South Pacific Islands Travel Planner*.

The Bureau of Statistics (Box 2221, Suva; tel. 315-144, fax 303-656), 4th floor, Ratu Sukuna House, Victoria Parade and MacArthur, has many interesting technical publications on the country and a library where you may browse.

The Maps and Plans Room (tel. 211-395; Mon.-Thurs. 0900-1300/1400-1530, Friday 0900-1300/1400-1500) of the Lands and Survey Department, Ground Floor, Government Buildings, sells excellent topographical maps of Fiji.

Carpenters Shipping (tel. 312-244), 4th floor, Neptune House, Tofua Street, Walu Bay, sells British navigational charts (F$43 each). Nearby is the Fiji Hydrographic Office (tel. 315-457; weekdays 0830-1300 and 1400-1600), Top Floor, Freeston Rd., Walu Bay, with local navigational charts at F$16.50 a sheet.

Bookstores

Suva's number one bookstore is the USP Book Center (tel. 313-900, fax 303-265; Mon.-Thurs. 0830-1615, Friday 0830-1545) at the Laucala Bay university campus. Not only do they have one of the finest Pacific sections in the region, but they stock the publications of some 20 occasional publishers affiliated with the university and you can turn up some intriguing items. Also visit the Book Display Room in the Institute of Pacific Studies building, not far from the Book Center. They sell assorted books by local authors published by the IPS itself.

The Methodist Book Center (tel. 311-466), 11 Stewart St. adjacent to Centenary Methodist Church, has a good selection of local books on Fiji and the Pacific.

The Desai Bookshop (tel. 314-088), on Thomson Street opposite the General Post Office, has a shelf of books on Fiji. Ask if they carry Moon Travel Handbook's *Fiji Handbook*, which includes much more detailed information than can be included here. The Fiji Museum shop sells a few excellent books at reasonable prices.

Missions to Seamen (tel. 300-911; weekdays 0900-1300/1330-1600), on the main wharf (inside—go through the security gate and ask), trades used paperback books one for one.

Libraries

The Suva City Library (Box 176, Suva; tel. 313-433, extension 241; Monday, Tuesday, Thursday, Friday 0930-1800, Wednesday 1200-1800, Saturday 0900-1300), at 196 Victoria Parade, allows visitors to take out four books upon payment of a refundable F$20 deposit. Ask if they have any old paperbacks for sale.

The library at the Laucala Campus of the University of the South Pacific (tel. 212-402) is open weekdays 0800-1600 year-round. During semesters they also open Saturday, Sunday afternoons, and in the evening. A library tour is offered Friday at 0900. You'll find the reading room with international newspapers downstairs.

The Alliance Française (Box 14548, Suva; tel. 313-802, fax 313-803), 77 Cakobau Rd., has an excellent selection of French books, magazines, and newspapers. You're welcome to peruse materials in the reading room weekdays 0830-1200 and 1300-1700. Ask about their video and film evenings.

Ecology Groups
The Greenpeace Pacific Campaign headquarters (tel. 312-784, fax 312-861) is above the Ming Paiace Restaurant in the old town hall on Victoria Parade.

The Pacific Concerns Resource Center (tel. 304-649, fax 304-755), 83 Amy St. off Toorak Rd. (enter from the rear of the building), sells a number of issue-related books and booklets on social and political questions in the South Pacific.

The South Pacific Action Committee for Human Ecology and Environment or SPACHEE (Box 16737, Suva; tel. 312-371, fax 303-053; weekdays 0830-1630) has a resource center at the junction of Ratu Cakobau, Domain, and Denison Roads, a block back from the South Seas Private Hotel.

HEALTH

Suva's Colonial War Memorial Hospital (tel. 313-444), on Waimanu Rd. about a kilometer northeast of the center, is available 24 hours a day in emergencies. The hospital charges commercial rates to nonresidents so in non-life-threatening situations you're better off seeing a private doctor.

The poorly marked Health Office (tel. 314-988; open weekdays 0800-1630), on Davey Ave. off Waimanu Rd. near the YMCA, gives tetanus, polio, and yellow fever vaccinations Tuesday and Friday 0800-1000. They're free, except yellow fever, which costs F$16.

You'll receive good attention at the Gordon St. Medical Center (tel. 313-355, fax 302-423), Gordon and Thurston Streets (basic consultations F$15). There's a female doctor there. The Fiji Recompression Chamber Facility (tel. 305-154 or 850-630) is adjacent to this clinic (donated by the Cousteau Society in 1992).

Two dentists are Dr. David M. Charya (tel. 302-160), The Dental Center, 59 Cumming Street; and Dr. Abdul S. Haroon (tel. 313-870), Suite 12, Epworth House off Nina Street (just down the hall from Patterson Brothers). Dr. Haroon has treated many visitors, including me.

TRANSPORTATION

Although nearly all international flights to Fiji arrive at Nadi, Suva is still the most important transportation center in the country. Interisland shipping crowds the harbor, and if you can't find a ship going precisely your way at the time you want to travel, Air Fiji and Sunflower Airlines fly to all the major Fiji islands, while Air Pacific serves New Zealand, Tonga, and Samoa—all from Nausori Airport. Make the rounds of the shipping offices listed below, then head over to Walu Bay to check the information. Compare the price of a cabin and deck passage, and ask if meals are included. Start checking early, as many domestic services within Fiji are only once a week and trips to other countries are far less frequent.

A solid block of buses awaits your patronage at the market bus station near the harbor, with continuous local service, and frequent long-distance departures to Nadi and Lautoka. Many of the points of interest around Suva are accessible on foot, but if you wander too far, jump on any bus headed in the right direction and you'll end up back in the market. Taxis are also easy to find and relatively cheap.

Suva's bus station can be a little confusing as there are many different companies, and time tables are not posted. Most drivers know where a certain bus will park, so just ask. For information on bus services around Viti Levu and domestic flights from Nausori Airport, see the Fiji Islands' introduction. Shipping services from Suva are covered below.

Ships to Other Countries
The Wednesday issue of the Fiji Times carries a special section on international shipping, though most are container ships that don't accept passengers. Most shipping is headed for Tonga and Samoa—there's not much going westward, and actually getting on any of the ships mentioned below requires considerable persistence. It's

often easier to sign on as crew on a yacht. Try both yacht anchorages in Suva: put up a notice, ask around, etc.

Carpenters Shipping (tel. 312-244, fax 301-572), 4th floor, Neptune House, Tofua St., Walu Bay, is an agent for the *Moana III*, which sails occasionally from Suva to Wallis and Futuna, then on to Nouméa. This ship *does* accept passengers, although Carpenters may advise otherwise. If you get this story just find out when the ship will arrive at Suva, then go and see the captain. This is a beautiful trip, not at all crowded between Fiji and Wallis. Book a cabin, however, if you're going right through to Nouméa.

Carpenters is also an agent for the monthly **Bank Line** service to Lautoka, Port Vila, Luganville, Honiara, Papua New Guinea, and on to Great Britain. Again, they cannot sell you a passenger ticket and will only tell you when the ship is due in port and where it's headed. It's up to you to make arrangements personally with the captain, and the fare won't be cheap.

The **Pacific Forum Line** (tel. 315-444, fax 302-754), 187 Rodwell Rd., will know about container ships from Suva to Apia, Pago Pago, and Nuku'alofa, such as the Samoan government-owned *Forum Samoa* (every three weeks) and the Tongan government-owned *Fua Kavenga* (monthly service). The office doesn't sell passenger tickets, so just ask when these ships will be in port, then go and talk to the captain, who is the only one who can decide if you'll be able to go.

The **Tuvalu Embassy** (Box 14449, Suva; tel. 301-355, fax 301-023), 16 Gorrie St., runs the *Nivaga II* to Funafuti about four times a year, but the dates are variable. Tickets are F$124 without meals or F$200 with meals second class, F$139 without meals or F$215 with meals first class, F$70 deck. They only know about a week beforehand approximately when the ship may sail. After reaching Funafuti, the ship cruises the Tuvalu Group.

Williams & Gosling Ltd. Ships Agency (Box 79, Suva; tel. 312-633, fax 307-358), 80 Harris Rd. near the market bus station, books passengers on the Kiribati Shipping Services vessel *Nei Matangare,* which leaves Suva for Funafuti and Tarawa about once a month. The three-day trip to Funafuti costs A$99/190 deck/cabin one-way, otherwise the seven-day journey Suva-Tarawa with a day at Funafuti is A$184/368,

meals included. The ship spends a week at Tarawa before returning to Fiji, so on a single roundtrip journey you could either have a week at Tarawa or two weeks at Funafuti.

Ferries to Ovalau Island

Air Fiji flies from Suva to Levuka (F$54) two or three times a day, but the most popular ways to go are the bus/launch/bus combinations via Natovi or Bau Landing. Two different companies operate these trips, which take four or five hours right through. Reservations are recommended on Saturday and public holidays.

The **Patterson Brothers** service (book at their Suva office mentioned below) leaves from the Western Bus Stand in Suva Mon.-Sat. at 1400 (F$24). This express bus goes from Suva to Natovi (67 km), where it drives onto a ferry to Buresala on Ovalau, then continues to Levuka, where it arrives around 1745. For the return journey you leave the Patterson Brothers office in Levuka Mon.-Sat. at 0500, arriving in Suva at 0800. Bus tickets must be purchased in advance at the office—no exceptions. Bicycles are carried free on the ferry.

The second option is the *Emosi Express,* departing Suva Monday, Wednesday, and Friday at 1200 for Bau Landing, where you board a speedboat powered by two 40-horsepower Yamaha engines to Leleuvia Island and Levuka (four hours, F$21.50 one-way). A free stopover on Leleuvia is possible. To book this, go to Emosi's Ferry Service (tel. 313-366), 35 Gordon Street. There's a two-room dormitory at the Gordon St. office where backpackers headed for Leleuvia can spend the night at F$5 pp (the cheapest beds in Fiji).

For variety and the most convenient timings, we recommend traveling with Patterson northbound and Emosi southbound. In good weather Emosi's boat is a lot more fun and follows a much more scenic route, with a cruise past Bau and a stop at Leleuvia. It's also slightly cheaper going with Emosi, but he only uses a small 15-person launch with a roof, so on a stormy day the much larger Patterson Brothers car ferry would be preferable. It's a beautiful circle trip, not to be missed.

Ships to Northern Fiji

Quite a few ships leave Suva on Saturday, but none depart on Sunday. **Patterson Brothers**

Shipping (Private Mail Bag, Suva; tel. 315-644, fax 301-652), Suite 1, 1st floor, Epworth Arcade off Nina St., takes obligatory reservations for the Suva-Natovi-Nabouwalu-Labasa "Sea-Road" ferry/bus combination, which departs Suva's Western Bus Stand Tues.-Sat. at 0500. Fares from Suva are F$39 to Nabouwalu or F$43 right through to Labasa, an excellent 10-hour trip. There are special trips to Savusavu on holidays. Forthcoming departures are listed on a blackboard in their Suva office and the schedule varies slightly each week. Patterson Brothers also has offices in Labasa, Lautoka, Levuka, Savusavu, and Taveuni.

Taina's Travel Services (tel. 307-889, fax 306-189), upstairs in Epworth House opposite Patterson Brothers, handles bookings on the 65-meter MV *Adi Savusavu*, a former Swedish Scarlett Line ferry used on the Landskrona-Copenhagen run. Now operated by **Beachcomber Cruises,** this ferry generally leaves Suva northbound for Savusavu and Taveuni Tuesday at 1000; Thursday at 1800 the ship goes only to Savusavu; Saturday at 1100 a special bus departs Suva for Natovi where it connects with the *Adi Savusavu* to Savusavu at 1400. Fares from Walu Bay, Suva, are F$34/42 economy/first class to Savusavu or F$38/44 to Taveuni. A bus connection from Savusavu to Labasa is an extra F$5. The a/c first-class lounge contains 30 airline-style seats, plus six long tables with chairs. If you're fast it's possible to rent a mattress in first class at F$5 pp for the trip. Downstairs in economy are another 246 padded seats and space in which to spread a mat. The *Adi Savusavu* also carries 12 cars and 15 trucks.

Consort Shipping Line (Box 152, Suva; tel. 313-344, fax 303-389), in the Dominion House arcade on Thomson St., operates the MV *Spirit of Free Enterprise* (popularly known as the *"Sofe"*), an old 450-passenger car ferry that formerly shuttled between the north and south islands of New Zealand. The *Sofe* leaves Suva on Tuesday at 2100 for Koro (nine hours, F$25), Savusavu (14 hours, F$32), and Taveuni (23 hours, F$34/70 deck/cabin). On Saturday night there's a trip from Suva to Koro and Savusavu only. The Tuesday northbound voyage spends all day Wednesday tied up at Savusavu and Taveuni passengers can get off and walk around. The two-berth cabins of the *Sofe* are quite comfortable and excellent value at F$55 pp to Savusavu or F$66 pp to Taveuni. For a refundable F$20 deposit the purser will give you the key to your cabin, allowing you to wander around the ship without worrying about your luggage. Another advantage of taking a cabin is that you're able to order meals in the pleasant first-class restaurant. Only cabin passengers may do this and the meals are excellent value at F$3. If you're traveling deck, take along something to eat as the snack bar on board is unreliable. Readers have questioned safety standards on the *Sofe* and you use it at your own risk.

Ships to Kadavu

Whippys Shipping Co. (Box 9, Suva; tel. 311-507 or 340-015, fax 302-545), in an unmarked office hidden behind Galilee Church at Miller's Wharf, Muaiwalu, Walu Bay, operates the MV *Gurawa* to Kadavu weekly. They depart late Friday at 0600 for northern Kadavu (Jona's, Nukubalavu, Albert's), charging F$37 to Jona's, F$40 to Albert's, or F$42 to Matana Resort. Every two weeks they go as far as Great Astrolabe Hideaway Resort (ask). The return to Suva from Kadavu is on Saturday morning. Monday at 2200 the *Gurawa* leaves Suva for Gau (F$40) and Nairai (F$40). This 15-meter cruiser accommodates 43 passengers on long padded benches (no cabins). Check with them the day before to find out which wharf the boat will be using (it's usually Miller's Wharf).

Kadavu Shipping Co. (tel. 311-766, fax 312-987), in the Ports Authority office building, Rona St., Walu Bay, runs the MV *Bulou-ni-ceva* to Kadavu once or twice a week. The boat should leave Suva Monday and Thursday at midnight, with the Monday trip going to Vunisea and not calling at Jona's, Albert's, or Nukubalavu. The Thursday boat reaches Albert's Place around 1400. Saturday around 1000 they pick up passengers to return to Suva, arriving at 1700. Both trips call at Matana Resort. Fares are F$39/50 deck/cabin, but only the cabin fare includes meals. There are only two four-berth cabins, so early booking is advised. Otherwise you could ask for a place in the salon, which costs F$45 to/from Kadavu including meals. Deck passengers can stretch out on long benches on the middle deck when it isn't crowded. Once a month this ship sails to Rotuma, a two-day journey costing F$90/140 deck/cabin. The *Bulou-ni-ceva* is a former Chinese riverboat now owned by Kadavu Province (the entire crew is from Kadavu).

Ships to Other Islands

Ask on the smaller vessels tied up at Muaiwalu Jetty, Walu Bay, for passage to Nairai, Gau, Koro, Lau, etc. Don't believe the first person who tells you there's no boat going where you want—*ask around*. Food is included in the price and on the outward journey it will probably be okay, but on the return don't expect much more than rice and tea. If you're planning a long voyage by interisland ship, a big bundle of kava roots to captain and crew as a token of appreciation for their hospitality works wonders.

Keep in mind that all of the ferry departure times mentioned above and elsewhere in this book are only indications of what was true in past. It's essential to check with the company office for current departure times during the week you wish to travel.

Taxis

Taxi meters are set at level one 0600-2200 daily with 50 cents charged at flagfall and about 50 cents a kilometer. From 2200 to 0600 the flagfall is F$1 plus 50 cents a kilometer. You have to insist that they use their meter and it's a good idea if you'll be going far and aren't sure of the fare. Otherwise, just ask for a flat rate, which shouldn't be more than F$2 in the city center or F$3 to the suburbs.

Car Rentals

Car rentals are available in Suva from **Avis** (tel. 313-833) behind Asco Motors, Foster Rd., Walu Bay, **Budget** (tel. 315-899), 123 Forster Rd., Walu Bay, **Central** (tel. 311-866), 293 Victoria Parade, **Dove** (tel. 311-755), Harifam Center, Greig Street, **Hertz** (tel. 302-186), 173 Victoria Parade, and **Thrifty** (tel. 314-436), 46 Gordon Street.

Tours

For information on day-trips from Suva offered by **Wilderness Ethnic Adventure Fiji** (Box 1389, Suva; tel. 315-730, fax 300-584), turn to the Navua and Nausori sections in this chapter. Wilderness also runs two-hour city sightseeing tours three times a day (adults F$30, children

under 12 years F$15). These trips can be booked through any travel agency in Suva.

Ask **Air Fiji** (tel. 313-666), 185 Victoria Parade, about day tours to Levuka, which include airfare from Nausori to Ovalau, ground transfers to/from Levuka, sightseeing tours, and breakfast, lunch, and afternoon tea at F$149 for adults, F$114 for children 12 and under. It's possible to spend the night in Levuka for an additional F$25 pp.

Travel Agents

Hunts Travel (Box 686, Suva; tel. 315-288, fax 302-212), in the Dominion House arcade behind the Fiji Visitors Bureau, is the place to pick up air tickets. They often know more about Air Pacific flights than the Air Pacific employees themselves!

Also compare **Travelworld Services** (tel. 315-870, fax 303-729), 18 Waimanu Rd., which gives five percent discounts on plane tickets to other Pacific countries.

Rosie The Travel Service (tel. 314-436), 46 Gordon St., books tours and accommodations all around Fiji.

Airline Offices

Reconfirm your onward flight reservations at your airlines' Suva office: **Aircalin** (tel. 302-133), Provident Plaza One, Ellery St.; **Air Fiji** (tel. 313-666), 185 Victoria Parade (also represents Air Vanuatu and Polynesian Airlines); **Air Nauru** (tel. 312-377), Ratu Sukuna House, 249 Victoria Parade; **Air New Zealand** (tel. 313-100), Queensland Insurance Center, Victoria Parade; **Air Pacific** (tel. 304-388), CML Building, Victoria Parade; **Qantas Airways** (tel. 311-833), CML Building, Victoria Parade; **Solomon Airlines** (tel. 315-889), Global Air Service, 3 Ellery St., and **Sunflower Airlines** (tel. 315-755), Honson Arcade on Thompson St. opposite the Fiji Visitors Bureau (also represents Royal Tongan Airlines). While you're there, check your seat assignment.

NAUSORI

In 1881 the Rewa River town of Nausori, 19 km northeast of Suva, was chosen as the site of Fiji's first large sugar mill, which operated until 1959. In those early days it was incorrectly believed that sugarcane grew better on the wetter eastern side of the island. Today cane is grown only on the drier, sunnier western sides of Viti Levu and Vanua Levu. The old sugar mill is now a rice mill and storage depot, as the Rewa Valley has become a major rice-producing area.

Nausori is Fiji's fifth-largest town (population 22,000) and the headquarters of Central Division and Tailevu Province. The Rewa is Fiji's largest river and the nine-span bridge here was erected in 1937. The town is better known for its large international airport three km southeast, built as a fighter strip to defend Fiji's capital during WW II. There are several banks in Nausori. The population is predominantly Indian.

Accommodations and Food

The budget-priced **Kings Nausori Hotel** (tel./fax 478-833), 99 Kings Rd., beside the chickenfeed mill, has three grubby rooms with private bath and hot water at F$25/30 single/double. The rooms are attached to the noisy bar and are rented mostly for "short times"—only of interest to people on the make. Due to licensing restrictions, women are not admitted to the hotel bar.

A far nicer drinking place is the **Whistling Duck Pub**, a block from the bus station in the center of town (ask directions). Upstairs in the adjacent building is **Prasad's Wine and Dine** restaurant where you can get cold beer with your inexpensive curries.

From Nausori

Local buses to the airport (40 cents) and Suva (90 cents) are fairly frequent, but the last bus to Suva is at 2100. You can also catch Sunbeam Transport express buses to Lautoka from Nausori at 0715, 1240, 1400, and 1745 (5.5 hours).

AROUND NAUSORI

Rewa Delta

Take a bus from Nausori to Nakelo Landing to explore the heavily populated Rewa River Delta. Many outboards leave from Nakelo to take villagers to their riverside homes, and passenger fares are less than a dollar for short trips. Larger boats leave sporadically from Nakelo for Levuka, Gau, and Koro, but finding one would be pure chance. Some also depart from nearby Wainibokasi Landing.

At **Naililili** in the delta, French Catholic missionaries built St. Joseph's Church of limestone in 1905 complete with stained-glass windows. **Wilderness Ethnic Adventure Fiji** (Box 1389, Suva; tel. 315-730, fax 300-584) runs half-day boat tours of the Rewa Delta, with stops at Naililili, and at Nasilai village, where Fijian pottery is still made. The tour leaves twice daily at 0930 and 1300, and the F$35 pp price includes minibus transfers from Suva hotels (it only operates if at least four people sign up). A full-day delta trip with lunch at Nasilai village is F$49 (F$25 for children). This is a refreshing change of pace.

Bau Island

Bau, a tiny, eight-hectare island just east of Viti Levu, has a special place in Fiji's history as this was the seat of High Chief Cakobau, who used European cannons and muskets to subdue most of western Fiji in the 1850s. At its pinnacle Bau had a population of 3,000, hundreds of war canoes guarded its waters, and more than 20 temples stood on the island's central plain. After the Battle of Verata on Viti Levu in 1839, Cakobau and his father, Tanoa, presented 260 bodies of men, women, and children to their closest friends and allied chiefs for gastronomical purposes. Fifteen years after this slaughter, Cakobau converted to Christianity and prohibited cannibalism on Bau. In 1867 he became a sovereign, crowned by European traders and planters desiring a stable government in Fiji to protect their interests.

Sights of Bau

The great stone slabs that form docks and seawalls around much of the island once accommodated Bau's fleet of war canoes. The graves of the Cakobau family and many of the old chiefs lie on the hilltop behind the school. The large, sturdy stone church located near the provincial offices was the first Christian church in Fiji. Inside its nearly one-meter-thick walls, just in front of the altar, is the old sacrificial stone once used for human sacrifices, today the baptismal font. Now painted white, this font was once known as King Cakobau's "skull crusher" and it's said a thousand brains were splattered against it. Across from the church are huge ancient trees and the thatched Council House on the site of the onetime temple of the war god Cagawalu. The family of the late Sir George Cakobau, governor-general of Fiji 1973-82, has a large traditional-style home on the island. You can see everything on the island in an hour or so.

Getting There

Take the Bau bus (five daily, 50 cents) from Nausori to Bau Landing where outboards cross over to the island. Be aware that Bau is not considered a tourist attraction, and from time to time visitors are prevented from going to the island. It's important to get someone to invite you across, which they'll do if you show a genuine interest in Fijian history. Like most Fijians, the inhabitants of Bau are friendly people. Bring a big bundle of *waka* for the *turaga-ni-koro,* and ask permission very politely to be shown around. There could be some confusion about who's to receive the *sevusevu,* however, as everyone is Bau's a chief! The more respectable your dress and demeanor, the better your chances of success. If you're told to contact the Ministry of Fijian Affairs in Suva, just depart gracefully as that's only their way of saying no. After all, it's up to them. Alternatively, you get a good close look at Bau from the *Emosi Express* ferry service to/from Levuka via Leleuvia.

Viwa Island

Before Cakobau adopted Christianity in 1854, Methodist missionaries working for this effect resided on Viwa Island, just across the water from Bau. Here the first Fijian New Testament was printed in 1847; Rev. John Hunt, who did the translation, lies buried in the graveyard beside the church that bears his name.

Viwa is a good alternative if you aren't invited to visit Bau itself. To reach the island, hire an outboard at Bau Landing. If you're lucky, you'll be able to join some locals who are going. A single Fijian village stands on the island.

Toberua Island

Toberua Island Resort (Michael Dennis, Box 567, Suva; tel. 479-177 or 302-356, fax 302-215), on a tiny reef island off the east tip of Viti Levu, caters to upmarket honeymooners, families, and professionals (George Harrison of the Beatles was there recently). Built in 1968, this was one of Fiji's first luxury outer-island resorts. The 14 thatched *bures* are designed in the purest Fijian style, yet it's all very luxurious and the small size means peace and quiet. The tariff is F$344/373/416 single/double/triple plus F$87 pp for three gourmet meals and F$55 for boat transfers. Two children under 16 sharing with adults are accommodated free and they're fed for half price or less. Baby-sitters are F$24 a day or F$9 an evening. Toberua is out of eastern Viti Levu's wet belt, so it doesn't get a lot of rain like nearby Suva, and weather permitting, all meals are served outdoors.

Don't expect tennis courts or a golf course at Toberua, though believe it or not, there's tropical golfing on the reef at low tide! (Nine holes from 90-180 meters, course par 27, clubs and balls provided free.) Deep-sea fishing is F$50 an hour and scuba diving F$70 a dive. All other activities are free, including snorkeling, sailing, windsurfing, and boat trips to a bird sanctuary or mangrove forest. Launch transfers are from Nakelo landing. Luxury.

NORTHERN VITI LEVU

Northern Viti Levu has far more spectacular landscapes than the southern side of the island does, and if you can only travel one way by road between Suva and Nadi, you're better off taking the northern route. Kings Road is now paved from Suva north to Korovou, then again from Dama to Lautoka, and between Korovou and Dama the 62-km gravel road is smooth. Since Kings Road follows the Wainibuka River from Wailotua village almost all the way to Viti Levu Bay, you get a good glimpse of the island's lush interior, and the north coast west of Rakiraki is breathtaking. Many visitors stop for a few days at Nananu-i-Ra Island off Rakiraki, and intrepid hikers can trek south down the Sigatoka River from the hill station of Nadarivatu.

Korovou and Beyond

A good paved highway runs 31 km north from Nausori to Korovou, a small town of around 350 souls on the east side of Viti Levu at the junction of Kings Road and the road to Natovi, terminus of the Ovalau and Vanua Levu ferries. Its crossroads position in the heart of Tailevu Province makes Korovou an important stop for buses plying the northern route around the island. Sunbeam Transport express buses leave Korovou for Lautoka at 0800, 1325, 1500, and 1830 (five hours), with local buses departing at 0920, 0950, and 1015 (7.5 hours). (Be aware that because "korovou" means "new village," there are many places called that in Fiji—don't mix them up.)

The **Tailevu Hotel** (Box 189, Korovou; tel. 430-028, fax 430-244), on a hill overlooking the river just across the bridge from Korovou, has 10 rooms with bath and fridge at F$25/38/45 single/double/triple including breakfast, plus four cottages with cooking facilities at F$40 for up to four persons. Cheaper backpacker accommodation may be available if you call and ask, otherwise camping or a place in the five-bed dorm is F$8 a night. All three meals are F$14 pp. This colonial-style hotel features a large bar and restaurant, and a dance band plays on Friday and Saturday nights. The Tailevu makes a good base for visiting the surrounding area, and horse riding, river canoeing, and bush walks can be arranged. Budget.

The large dairy farms along the highway just west of Korovou were set up after WW I. **Dorothy's Waterfall** on the Waimaro River, a kilometer east of Dakuivuna village, is 10 km west of Korovou. Uru's Snack Bar overlooks the falls and it's a nice picnic spot if you have your own transportation. At Wailotua No. 1, 20 km west of Korovou, is a large **snake cave** right beside the village and easily accessible from the road. One stalactite in the cave is shaped like a six-headed snake (admission F$5). At Dama the paved road starts again and continues 45 km northwest to Rakiraki. (As you drive along this road you may be flagged down by Fijians emphatically inviting you to visit their village. At the end of the tour you'll be asked to sign the visitors book and make a financial contribution. If you decide to stop, don't bother trying to present anyone with kava roots as hard cash is all they're after.)

Ra Province

The old Catholic Church of St. Francis Xavier at **Naiserelagi,** on a hilltop above Navunibitu Catholic School, on Kings Rd. about 25 km southeast of Rakiraki, was beautifully decorated with frescoes by Jean Charlot in 1962-63. Typical Fijian motifs such as the *tabua, tanoa,* and *yaqona* blend in the powerful composition behind the altar. Father Pierre Chanel, who was martyred on Futuna Island between Fiji and Samoa in 1841, appears on the left holding the weapon that killed him, a war club. Christ and the Madonna are portrayed in black. The church is worth stopping to see, and provided it's not too late in the day, you'll find an onward bus. Flying Prince Transport (tel. 694-346) runs buses between Naiserelagi and Vaileka five times a day (F$1.50), otherwise all of the local Suva buses stop there. At **Nanukuloa** village just north of here is the headquarters of Ra Province.

RAKIRAKI

This part of northern Viti Levu is known as Rakiraki but the main town is called **Vaileka** (population 5,000). The Penang Sugar Mill was erected here in 1881. The mill is about a kilometer from the main business section of Vaileka. The sugar is loaded aboard ships at Ellington Wharf, connected to the mill by an 11-km cane railway. There are three banks and a large produce market in Vaileka, but most visitors simply pass through on their way to Nananu-i-Ra Island. A taxi from Vaileka to Ellington Wharf where the resort launches pick up guests will run F$8. Otherwise take a local bus east on Kings Road to the turnoff and walk two km down to the wharf. The express buses don't stop at the turnoff, but all buses from Lautoka (F$4) and Suva (F$7) stop in Vaileka.

Accommodations and Food

The **Rakiraki Hotel** (Box 31, Rakiraki; tel. 694-101, fax 694-545), on Kings Rd. a couple of kilometers north of Vaileka, has 36 a/c rooms with fridge and private bath at F$99 single or double, F$123 triple, and 10 fan-cooled rooms at F$35/40/48 single/double/triple. Reduced rates are sometimes offered. There are no communal cooking facilities. The reception area and restaurant occupy the core of the original hotel dating back to 1945; the two-story accommodations blocks were added much later. Extensive gardens surround the hotel and the Rakiraki's outdoor bowling green draws middle-aged lawn bowling enthusiasts from Australia and New Zealand, and those folks like old-fashioned "colonial" touches like the typed daily menu featuring British-Indian curry dishes, and gin and tonic in the afternoon. Ask the manager if he can arrange a round for you at the nearby golf course owned by the Fiji Sugar Corporation. Only the local or "stage" buses will drop you off on Kings Road right in front of the hotel (the express buses will take you to Vaileka). Budget to inexpensive.

The upmarket **Wananavu Beach Resort** (John Gray, Box 305, Rakiraki; tel. 694-433, fax 694-499), on Volivoli Point facing Nananu-i-Ra Island, four km off Kings Rd., is at Viti Levu's northernmost tip. There are 15 self-contained bungalows beginning at F$195 single or double, tropical breakfast included. No cooking facilities are provided, but each room does have a fridge. Stay four nights and the fifth is free. Ra Divers offers scuba diving from the resort, and a variety of other water sports are available. The resort has a swimming pool and tennis court, and the snorkeling off their beach is wonderful. Expensive.

A number of restaurants near the bus station at Vaileka serve Chinese meals, including Gafoor & Sons, Vaileka Restaurant, and Rakiraki Lodge. The "wine and dine" sections at Gafoor & Sons and Rakiraki Lodge are your best bets if you have time on your hands. The **Cosmopolitan Club** (tel. 694-330), a block from Vaileka bus station, is the local drinking place.

West of Rakiraki

Right beside Kings Rd., just 100 meters west of the turnoff to Vaileka, is the grave of **Ratu Udreudre**, the cannibal king of this region who is alleged to have consumed 872 corpses. **Navatu Rock**, a few kilometers west of Vaileka, was the jumping-off point for the disembodied spirits of the ancient Fijians. A fortified village once stood on its summit. Navatu's triangular shape is duplicated by a small island just offshore.

The **Nakauvadra Range**, towering south of Rakiraki, is the traditional home of the Fijian serpent-god Degei, who is said to dwell in a cave on the summit of Mt. Uluda (866 meters). This "cave" is little more than a cleft in the rock. To climb the Nakauvadra Range, which the local Fijians look upon as their primeval homeland, permission must be obtained from the chief of Vatukacevaceva village who will provide guides. A *sevusevu* should be presented.

NANANU-I-RA ISLAND

This small 355-hectare island, three km off the northernmost tip of Viti Levu, is a good place to spend some time amid tranquility and beauty. The climate is dry and sunny, and there are great beaches, reefs, snorkeling, walks, sunsets, and moonrises over the water—only roads are missing. Seven or eight separate white sandy beaches lie scattered around the island, and it's big enough that you won't feel confined. In the early 19th century Nananu-i-Ra's original Fijian inhabitants were wiped out by disease and tribal warfare, and an heir sold the island to the Europeans whose descendants now operate small family-style resorts and a 219-hectare plantation on the island.

The northern two-thirds of Nananu-i-Ra Island, including all of the land around Kontiki Island Lodge, is owned by Mrs. Louise Harper of southern California, who bought it for a mere US$200,000 in 1966 (she also owns a sizable chunk of Proctor & Gamble back in the States). Today some 22 head of Harper cattle graze beneath coconuts on the Harper Plantation, and the plantation management actively discourages trespassing by tourists. The manager lives in a house adjoining Kontiki, and it's common courtesy to ask his permission before climbing the hill behind the lodge.

To hike right around Nananu-i-Ra on the beach takes about four hours of steady going, or all day if you stop for picnicking and snorkeling. The thickest section of mangroves is between Kontiki and Mokusigas Island Resort, on the west side of the island, and this stretch should be covered at low tide. However you do it, at some point you'll probably have to take off your shoes and wade through water just over your ankles or scramble over slippery rocks, but it's still a very nice walk. The entire coastline is public, but only as far as two meters above the high tide line. Avoid becoming stranded by high tide and forced to cut across Harper land.

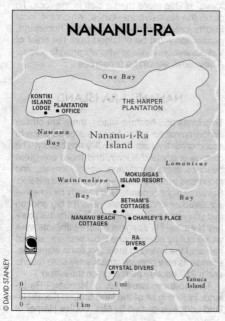

Scuba Diving

Ra Divers (Papu Pangalu, Box 417, Rakiraki; tel. 694-511, fax 694-611), based on Nananu-i-Ra, offers scuba diving at F$65/120 for one/two tanks plus F$15 for gear. A 10-dive package is F$525, night diving F$85. If you need equipment, it's $75 for five days. Snorkelers can go along for F$20, if space is available (mask and snorkel supplied). Ra Diver's resort course costs F$120; full four-day PADI or NAUI certification is F$450 if you're alone or F$390 pp for two or more. They pick up clients regularly from all of the resorts. Some of Papu's favorite sites are Breathtaker, Dreammaker, Pinnacles, and Maze.

In 1998 Dan Grenier, formerly of the Lomaloma Resort on Vanua Balavu, opened a new dive shop at the south end of Nananu-i-Ra called **Crystal Divers** (Box 705, Rakiraki; tel./fax 694-747). Many of Dan's clients book from overseas via his internet site, paying F$70/130/650 for one/two/12 tank dives, plus F$29 for full gear (if required). Snorkelers can go along for F$20 if space is available (bring your own mask). His five-day PADI or NAUI certification course is F$495, otherwise an introductory dive is F$130. Dan frequents extraordinary Bligh Water sites like Neptune Rhapsody, Never Ending Story, and Water Colors, and his personal service is a definite plus. Crystal Divers closes for annual leave in January and February.

Accommodations

Accommodation prices on Nananu-i-Ra have increased in recent years and the number of beds is limited. With the island's popularity still growing it's essential to call ahead to one of the resorts and arrange to be picked up at Ellington Wharf. None of the innkeepers will accept additional guests when they're fully booked and camping is not allowed. There's no public telephone at Ellington Wharf.

If you want an individual room or *bure* make 100% sure one is available, otherwise you could end up spending quite a few nights in the dormitory waiting for one to become free. All the budget places have cooking facilities, but you should take most of your own supplies, as shopping possibilities on the island are limited. There's a large market and several supermarkets in Vaileka where you can buy all the supplies you need. If you run out, groceries can be ordered from Vaileka for a small service charge, and Betham's Bungalows runs a minimarket with a reasonable selection of groceries (including beer). They also serve hot dogs and other snacks. Also bring enough cash, as only the Mokusigas Island Resort accepts credit cards.

Of all the places on Nananu-i-Ra, **Kontiki Island Lodge** (Box 87, Rakiraki; tel. 694-290) has more of the feeling of a low-budget resort, with ample opportunity for group activities. Because they cater mostly to backpackers, the dormitory guests are treated the same as everyone else, and the atmosphere is congenial. It's also ideal if you want to do your own thing, as the long deserted beach facing One Bay is just a 20-minute walk away. Kontiki is at the unspoiled north end of the island, with no other resorts or houses (except the Harper caretaker) nearby. It's quite popular and on Saturday night they're always full. Reservations are essential, and call again the morning before you'll arrive to make sure they haven't forgotten you.

Kontiki offers three modern self-catering bungalows, each with two double rooms at F$35 double and four dorm beds at F$16.50 pp plus tax. If you want privacy ask for one of the four rooms in the two thatched duplex *bures,* which are F$48 double. Check your mosquito net for holes when you arrive. All guests have access to fridges and cooking facilities, but take groceries as only a few very basic supplies are sold, including cold beer. In the evening the generator runs until 2200. (We've received some rather mixed feedback about Kontiki recently.) Budget.

At the other end of Nananu-i-Ra, a one-hour walk along the beach at low tide, are three other inexpensive places to stay, all offering cooking facilities. They experience more speedboat noise than Kontiki but are less crowded and perhaps preferable for a restful holiday. They almost always have a few free beds in the dorms but advance bookings are strongly recommended.

MacDonald's Nananu Beach Cottages (Box 140, Rakiraki; tel. 694-633) offers three individual houses with fridge at F$61 single or double, plus F$9 pp for additional persons, rooms with shared bath at F$44 double, and two five-bunk dormitory rooms at F$17 pp. Cooking facilities are provided in the dorm and a three-meal package is available at F$25 pp. Their snack bar sells sandwiches and pizzas as well as groceries, and a Fijian *lovo* feast is arranged once a week. It's peaceful and attractive with a private wharf and pontoon off their beach. Budget to inexpensive.

Right next to MacDonald's is friendly **Betham's Beach Cottages** (Peggy and Oscar Betham, Box 5, Rakiraki; tel. 694-132, fax 694-132) with four cement-block duplex houses at F$70 single or double, F$79 triple, plus two mixed dormitories, one with 10 beds and another with eight beds, at F$17 pp. It can get a bit crowded but cooking facilities and a fridge are provided. Budget to inexpensive.

Sharing the same high sandy beach with MacDonald's and Betham's is **Charley's Place** (Charley and Louise Anthony, Box 407, Rakiraki; tel. 694-676) run by a delightful, friendly family. The dormitory building has six beds (F$22 each) in the same room as the cooking facilities, plus one double room (F$45). The adjacent bungalow can sleep up to six people at F$60 for two, plus F$9 for each additional person. Both buildings are on a hill and you can watch the sunrise on one side and the sunset on the other. Charley's also rents two other houses farther down the beach, each F$50 double. Budget.

The **Mokusigas Island Resort** (Box 268, Rakiraki; tel. 694-449, fax 694-404) opened on Nananu-i-Ra in 1991. The 20 comfortable bungalows with fridge are the same and each accommodates three adults. The price varies according to the location with the ocean panorama units costing F$270 while lagoon vista units are F$250 with continental breakfast included in these. The four "economy" bungalows up on the hill near the restaurant/bar are only F$200, but no breakfast is included. Add 10% tax to all rates. Cooking facilities are not provided and but you can buy a F$52 pp meal plan. The resort's dive shop offers scuba diving at F$55 from a boat or F$36 from shore. A five-day PADI certification course costs F$440. To create a diving attraction, the 43-meter *Papuan Explorer* was scuttled in 25 meters of water, 60 meters off the 189-meter Mokusigas jetty, which curves out into the sheltered lagoon. The snorkeling off the wharf is good, especially at low tide, with lots of coral and fish. Don't be disappointed by the skimpy little beach facing a mudflat you see when you first arrive: the mile-long picture-postcard beach in their brochure is a few minutes away over the hill on the other side of the island. All the resort facilities, including the restaurant, bar, and dive shop, are strictly for house guests only. Luxury.

Getting There
Boat transfers from Ellington Wharf to Nananu-i-Ra are about F$18 pp return (20 minutes), though the resorts may levy a surcharge for one person alone. Check prices when you call to make your accommodation booking. A taxi to Ellington Wharf from the express bus stop in Vaileka is F$8 for the car. Several budget hotels in Nadi (including the Nadi Town Motel, Sunny Holiday Motel, and Kon Tiki Private Hotel) arrange minibus rides from Nadi direct to Ellington Wharf at F$20-25 pp, though it's cheaper to take an express bus from Lautoka to Vaileka, then a taxi to the landing. Coming from Nadi, you will have to change buses in Lautoka.

As you return to Ellington Wharf from Nananu-i-Ra, taxis will be waiting to whisk you to Vaileka where you'll connect with the express buses (share the F$8 taxi fare with other travelers to cut costs). You could also hike two km out to the main highway and try to flag down a bus, but only local buses will stop at this junction.

Patterson Brothers operates a car ferry service between Ellington Wharf and Nabouwalu on Tuesday, Thursday, and Saturday, a great shortcut to/from Vanua Levu (F$33 one-way). The ferry leaves Ellington Wharf at the difficult hour of 0630, so it's more useful as a way of coming here from Vanua Levu since it departs Nabouwalu at 1030. There's a connecting bus to/from Labasa (112 km). Often you'll be allowed to spend the night on the boat at Ellington Wharf.

NORTHWESTERN VITI LEVU

Tavua
West of Rakiraki, Kings Road passes the government-run Yaqara Cattle Ranch where Fijian cowboys keep 5,500 head of cattle and 200 horses on a 7,000-hectare spread enclosed by an 80-km fence. At Tavua (population 2,500), an important junction on the north coast, buses on the north coast highway meet the daily service to Nadarivatu. Catching a bus from Tavua to Vaileka, Vatukoula, or Lautoka is no problem, but the green Tavua General Transport bus from

Tavua to Nadrau (F$3.50) via Nadarivatu (F$2) leaves only Mon.-Sat. at 1500. There are three banks in Tavua.

The two-story **Tavua Hotel** (Box 81, Tavua; tel. 680-522, fax 680-390), an old wooden colonial-style building on a hill, a five-minute walk from the bus stop, has 11 rooms with bath at F$33/44 single/double (the one a/c room is F$66). The seven-bed dorm is F$11 pp. Meals are about F$7 here. This hotel looks like it's going to be noisy due to the large bar downstairs, but all is silent after the bar and restaurant close at 2100. It's a bit rundown but okay for one night and a good base from which to explore Vatukoula. Budget.

The **Golden Eagle Restaurant** (tel. 680-635) on Kings Rd. in Tavua serves standard Indian curries. Socialize at the **Tavua Farmers Club** (tel. 680-236) on Kings Rd. toward Ba, or the more elitist **Tavua Club** (tel. 680-265) on Nasivi Street.

Vatukoula
In 1932 an old Australian prospector named Bill Borthwick discovered gold at Vatukoula, eight km south of Tavua. Two years later Borthwick and his partner, Peter Costello, sold their stake to an Australian company, and in 1935 the **Emperor Gold Mine** opened. In 1977 there was a major industrial action at the mine and the government had to step in to prevent it from closing. In 1983 the Western Mining Corporation of Australia bought a 20% share and took over management. Western modernized the facilities and greatly increased production, but after another bitter strike in 1991 they sold out and the mine is now operated by the Emperor Gold Mining Company once again. The 700 miners who walked out in 1991 have been replaced by nonunion labor.

The ore comes up from the underground area through the Smith Shaft near "Top Gate." It's washed, crushed, and roasted, then fed into a flotation process where gold and silver are separated from the ore. Counting both underground operations and an open pit, the mine presently extracts 125,000 ounces of gold annually from 600,000 metric tonnes of ore. A tonne of silver is also produced each year and waste rock is crushed into gravel and sold. Proven recoverable ore reserves at Vatukoula are sufficient for another decade of mining, and in 1985 additional deposits were discovered at nearby Nasomo, where extraction began in 1988. Since 1935 the Emperor has produced five million ounces of gold worth more than a billion U.S. dollars at today's prices. Low world gold prices in the late 1990s have forced the mine to cut costs.

Vatukoula is a typical company town of 7,000 inhabitants, with education and social services under the jurisdiction of the mine. The 1,650 miners employed here, most of them indigenous Fijians, live in WW II-style Quonset huts in racially segregated ghettos. In contrast, tradespeople and supervisors, usually Rotumans and part-Fijians, enjoy much better living conditions, and senior staff and management live in colonial-style comfort. Sensitive to profitability, the Emperor has tenaciously resisted the unionization of its workforce. Women are forbidden by law from working underground.

To arrange a guided tour of the mine you must contact the Public Relations Officer, Emperor Gold Mining Co. Ltd. (tel. 680-477, fax 680-779), at least one week in advance (although at last report the tours were suspended). It's not possible to just show up and be admitted. There's bus service from Tavua to Vatukoula every half hour, and even if you don't get off, it's well worth making the roundtrip to "Bottom Gate" to see the varying classes of company housing, to catch a glimpse of the golf course and open pit, and to enjoy the lovely scenery. Rosie The Travel Service in Nadi runs gold mine tours (F$44 without lunch), but these do not enter the mine itself and you can see almost as much from the regular bus for 50 cents each way. Cold beer is available at the **Bowling Club** (weekdays 1600-2300, Saturday 1000-2300, Sunday 1600-2100) near Bottom Gate, where meals are served Mon.-Sat. 1600-2100.

Ba

The large Indian town of Ba (population 15,000) on the Ba River is seldom visited by tourists. As the attractive mosque in the center of town indicates, nearly half of Fiji's Muslims live in Ba Province. Small fishing boats depart from behind the Shell service station opposite the mosque, and it's fairly easy to arrange to go along on all-night trips. A wide belt of mangroves

covers much of the river's delta. Ba is better known for the large Rarawai Sugar Mill, opened by the Colonial Sugar Refining Co. in 1886.

The **Ba Hotel** (Box 29, Ba; tel. 674-000, fax 670-559), 110 Bank St., has 13 a/c rooms with bath at F$45/57 single/double—very pleasant with a functioning swimming pool, bar, and restaurant. Inexpensive.

Of the many places along Kings Rd. serving Indian and Chinese meals your best choice is probably **Chand's Restaurant** (tel. 670-822), near the ANZ Bank and a bit toward the mosque, which has a proper dining room upstairs and a fast-food center downstairs. **Vikan's Upper Restaurant** (tel. 674-426), Kings Rd. at Veitau St., has cheaper Indian food.

If you're spending the night here check out **Venus Cinema** beside the Ba Hotel, and the **Civic Cinema** on Tabua Place just up the hill. For drinks it's the **Farmers Club,** between Venus Cinema and the Ba Hotel, or the **Central Club** (tel. 674-348) on Tabua Place. Four banks have branches in Ba.

Important express buses leaving Ba daily are the Pacific Transport bus to Suva via Sigatoka at 0615 (six hours, F$10.30), and the Sunbeam Transport buses to Suva via Tavua at 0655, 0715, 0915, 1300, and 1715 (five hours). Local buses to Tavua and Lautoka are frequent. Buses to Navala and Bukuya are at 1200, 1635, and 1715 (except Sunday).

INTO THE INTERIOR

Nausori Highlands

A rough unpaved road runs 25 km southeast from Ba to Navala, a large traditional village on the sloping right bank of the Ba River. It then climbs another 20 km south to Bukuya village in the Nausori Highlands, from whence other gravel roads continue south into the Sigatoka Valley and 40 km due west to Nadi. The Nadi road passes the Vaturu Dam, which supplies Nadi with fresh water. Gold strikes near Vaturu may herald a mining future for this area. The powerful open scenery of the highlands makes a visit well worthwhile.

Navala is one of the last fully thatched villages remaining on Viti Levu, its *bures* standing picturesquely against the surrounding hills. When water levels are right, whitewater rafters shoot the rapids through the scenic Ba River Gorge near here, and guided hiking or horseback riding can also be arranged. Sightseers are welcome, and it's possible to spend the night in the village for a reasonable amount, but one must take along a *sevusevu* for the *turaga-ni-koro* and pay a F$10 pp admission/photography fee toward village development. Access is fairly easy on the three buses a day that arrive from Ba.

Nadarivatu

An important forestry station is at Nadarivatu, a small settlement above Tavua. Its 900-meter altitude means a cool climate and a fantastic panorama of the north coast from the ridge. Beside the road right in front of the Forestry Training Center is **The Stone Bowl,** official source of the Sigatoka River, and a five-minute walk from the Center is the **Governor General's Swimming Pool** where a small creek has been dammed. Go up the creek a short distance to the main pool, though it's dry much of the year and the area has not been maintained. The trail to the fire tower atop **Mt. Lomalagi** (Mt. Heaven) begins nearby, a one-hour hike each way. The tower itself has collapsed and is no longer climbable, but the forest is lovely and you may see and hear many native birds. Pine forests cover the land.

In its heyday Nadarivatu was a summer retreat for expatriates from the nearby Emperor Gold Mine at Vatukoula, and their large bungalow still serves as a **Mine Resthouse.** The resthouse is only rented out to the public in exceptional circumstances and there's a charge of F$100 a night for the whole house (up to 10 people). For information contact the Public Relations Officer (tel. 680-477, fax 680-779) at Vatukoula. Visitors with tents are allowed to camp at the Forestry Training Center. Ask permission at the Ministry of Forests office as soon as you arrive. Some canned foods are available at the canteen opposite the Mine Resthouse, but bring food from Tavua. Cabin crackers are handy.

Only one bus a day (excluding Sunday) runs between Tavua and Nadarivatu, leaving Tavua at 1500, Nadarivatu at 0700—a spectacular 1.5-hour bus ride (F$2). Arrive at the stop in Tavua at least 30 minutes ahead, as this bus does fill up. It originates/terminates in Nadrau village where

you might also be able to stay (take along a *sevusevu* if you're thinking of this). It's also quite easy to hitch.

Mount Victoria

The two great rivers of Fiji, the Rewa and the Sigatoka, originate on the slopes of Mt. Victoria (Tomanivi), highest mountain in the country (1,323 meters). The climb begins near the bridge at Navai, 10 km southeast of Nadarivatu. Turn right up the hillside a few hundred meters down the jeep track, then climb up through native bush on the main path all the way to the top. Beware of misleading signboards. There are three small streams to cross; no water after the third. On your way down, stop for a swim in the largest stream. There's a flat area on top where you could camp—if you're willing to take your chances with Buli, the devil king of the mountain. Local guides (F$10) are available, but allow about six hours for the roundtrip. Bright red epiphytic orchids *(Dendrobium moh-li-anum)* are sometimes in full bloom. Mount Victoria is on the divide between the wet and dry sides of Viti Levu, and from the summit you should be able to distinguish the contrasting vegetation in these zones.

Monasavu Hydroelectric Project

The largest development project ever undertaken in Fiji, this massive F$300 million scheme at Monasavu, on the Nadrau Plateau near the center of Viti Levu, took 1,500 men and six years to complete. An earthen dam, 82 meters high, was built across the Nanuku River to supply water to the four 20-megawatt generating turbines at the Wailoa Power Station on the Wailoa River, 625 meters below. The dam forms a lake 17 km long, and the water drops through a 5.4-km tunnel at a 45-degree angle, one of the steepest engineered dips in the world. Overhead transmission lines carry power from Wailoa to Suva and Lautoka. At present Monasavu is filling 95% of Viti Levu's needs, representing huge savings on imported diesel oil, but by the year 2000 the project will have reached maximum capacity.

The Cross-Island Highway that passes the site was built to serve the dam project. Bus service ended when the project was completed and the construction camps closed in 1985. Traffic of all kinds was halted in 1993 when a hurricane took out the bridge at Lutu, although 4WD vehicles can still ford the river when water levels are low. At the present time buses only go from Tavua to Nadrau and from Suva to Naivucini, although occasional carriers go farther. In June 1998 there were tense scenes near the dam as landowners set up roadblocks to press claims of F$35 million for land flooded in the early 1980s.

The Sigatoka River Trek

One of the most rewarding trips you can make on Viti Levu is the three-day hike south across the center of the island from Nadarivatu to Korolevu on the Sigatoka River. Northbound the way is much harder to find. There are many superb campsites along the trail, and luckily this trek is not included in the Australian guidebooks, so the area isn't overrun by tourists. Have a generous bundle of *waka* ready in case you're invited to stay overnight in a village. (Kava for presentations on subsequent days can be purchased at villages along the way.) Set out from Nadarivatu early in the week, so you won't suffer the embarrassment of arriving in a village on Sunday. Excellent topographical maps of the entire route can be purchased at the Lands and Survey Department in Suva and Lautoka.

Follow the dirt road south from Nadarivatu to Nagatagata where you should fill your canteen as the trail ahead is rigorous and there's no water to be found. From Nagatagata walk south about one hour. When you reach the electric high-power line, where the road turns right and begins to descend toward Koro, look for the well-worn footpath ahead. The trail winds along the ridge, and you can see as far as Ba. The primeval forests that once covered this part of Fiji were destroyed long ago by the slash-and-burn agricultural techniques of the Fijians.

When you reach the pine trees the path divides, with Nanoko to the right and Nubutautau down to the left. During the rainy season it's better to turn right and head to Nanoko, where you may be able to find a carrier to Bukuya or all the way to Nadi. Buses run between Bukuya and Ba three times a day (except Sunday). If you do decide to make for Nanoko, beware of a very roundabout loop road on the left. Another option is to skip all of the above by staying in the bus from Tavua right to the end of the line at Nadrau, from whence your hike would then begin.

Reverend Thomas Baker, the last missionary to be clubbed and devoured in Fiji (in 1867), met his fate at **Nubutautau.** Jack London wrote a story, "The Whale Tooth," about the death of the missionary, and the ax that brought about Reverend Baker's demise is still kept in the village. You should be able to stay in the community center in Nubutautau. The Nubutautau-Korolevu section of the trek involves 22 crossings of the Sigatoka River, which is easy enough in the dry season (cut a bamboo staff for balance), but almost impossible in the wet (Dec.-April). Hiking boots will be useless in the river, so wear a pair of old running shoes.

It's a fantastic trip down the river to **Korolevu** if you can make it. The Korolevu villagers can call large eels up from a nearby pool with a certain chant. A few hours' walk away are the pottery villages, Draubuta and Nakoro, where traditional, long Fijian pots are still made. From Korolevu you can take a carrier to Tubarua, where there are two buses a day to Sigatoka. A carrier leaves Korolevu direct to Sigatoka every morning except Sunday, departing Sigatoka for the return around 1400 (if you want to do this trip in reverse). Reader Bruce French of Edgewood, Kentucky, wrote that "this trek was a big highlight of my South Pacific experience."

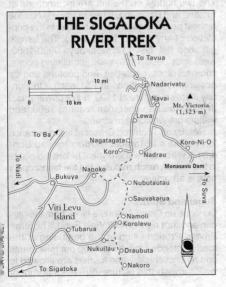

THE SIGATOKA RIVER TREK

LAUTOKA AND VICINITY

Fiji's second city, Lautoka (population 45,000), is the focus of the country's sugar and timber industries, a major port, and the Western Division and Ba Province headquarters. It's a likable place with a row of towering royal palms along the main street. Though Lautoka grew up around the Fijian village of Namoli, the temples and mosques standing prominently in the center of the city reflect the large Indian population. In recent years things have changed somewhat with many Indians abandoning Fiji as indigenous Fijians move in to take their place, and Lautoka's population is now almost evenly balanced between the groups. Yet in the countryside Indians still comprise a large majority.

Shuttle boats to Beachcomber and Treasure islands depart from Lautoka, and this is the gateway to the Yasawa Islands with everything from Blue Lagoon cruises to backpacker resort shuttles and village boats. Yet because Lautoka doesn't depend only on tourism, you get a truer picture of ordinary life, and the city has a rambunctious nightlife. There's some duty-free shopping, but mainly this is just a nice place to wander around. Unless you're hooked on tourist-oriented activities, Lautoka is a good alternative to Nadi.

SIGHTS OF LAUTOKA AND VICINITY

South of the Center
Begin next to the bus station at Lautoka's big, colorful **market,** which is busiest on Saturday (open Mon.-Fri. 0700-1730, Saturday 0530-1600). From here, walk south on Yasawa Street to the photogenic **Jame Mosque.** Five times a day local male Muslims direct prayers toward a small niche known as a *mihrab,* where the prayers fuse and fly to the *Kabba* in Mecca, thence to Allah. During the crushing season (June-Nov.) narrow-gauge trains rattle past the mosque along a line parallel to Vitogo Parade, bringing cane to Lautoka's large sugar mill.

Follow the line east a bit to the **Sikh Temple,** rebuilt after a smaller temple burned down in 1989. To enter you must wash your hands and cover your head (kerchiefs are provided at the door), and cigarettes and liquor are forbidden inside the compound. The teachings of the 10 Sikh gurus are contained in the Granth, a holy book prominently displayed in the temple. Sikhism began in the Punjab region of northwest India in the 16th century as a reformed branch of Hinduism much influenced by Islam: for example, Sikhs reject the caste system and idolatry. The Sikhs are easily recognized by their beards and turbans.

Follow your map west along Drasa Avenue to the **Sri Krishna Kaliya Temple** on Tavewa Ave., the most prominent Krishna temple in the South Pacific (open daily until 2030). The images inside are Radha and Krishna on the right, while the central figure is Krishna dancing on the snake Kaliya to show his mastery over the reptile. The story goes that Krishna chastised Kaliya and exiled him to the island of Ramanik Deep, which Fiji Indians believe to be Fiji. (Curiously, the indigenous Fijian people have also long believed in a serpent-god, named Degei, who lived in a cave in the Nakauvadra Range.) The two figures on the left are incarnations of Krishna and Balarama. Interestingly, Fiji has the highest percentage of Hare Krishnas in the population of any country in the world. The temple gift shop (tel. 664-112; weekdays 0900-1600, weekends 0900-1400) sells stimulating books, compact discs, cassettes, and posters, and it's possible to rent videos at F$1 each. On Sunday there's a lecture at 1100, *arti* or prayer *(puja)* at 1230, and a vegetarian feast at 1300, and visitors are welcome to attend.

Nearby off Thomson Crescent is the entrance to Lautoka's **botanical garden** (closed Sunday). It will be a few more years before the plants in the garden reach maturity, but the landscaping here is attractive.

Sugar and Spirits
Continue up Drasa Avenue a block from the garden and turn right on Mill View Road. The large Private Property sign at the beginning of the road is intended mostly to keep out miscreants and heavy vehicles, and tourists are allowed to walk through this picturesque neighborhood,

past the colonial-era residences of sugar industry executives and century-old banyan trees. Just beyond the Fiji Sugar Corporation offices is the **Lautoka Sugar Mill,** one of the largest in the Southern Hemisphere. The mill was founded in 1903. Although mill tours are not offered, you can see quite a lot of the operation (busiest June-Nov.) as you walk down Mill View Road toward the main gate.

Continue straight ahead on Navutu Road (the dirt road beside the railway line) to **South Pacific Distilleries** (Box 1128, Lautoka; tel. 662-088, fax 664-361), where free plant tours can be arranged on the spot weekdays during business hours. This government-owned plant bottles rum, whisky, vodka, and gin under a variety of labels and, of course, molasses from the sugar mill is the distillery's main raw material. The **fertilizer factory** across the highway uses mill mud from the sugar-making process.

The Waterfront

Backtrack to the sugar mill and turn left toward **Fisheries Wharf,** from which you'll have a fine view of the huge sugar storage sheds next to the mill and many colorful fishing boats. If you were thinking of visiting the Yasawa Islands, this is where you'll board your boat.

To the north, just beyond the conveyor belts used to load raw sugar onto the ships, is a veritable mountain of **pine chips** ready for export to Japan where they are used to make paper. Forestry is becoming more important as Fiji attempts to diversify its economy away from sugar. The **Main Wharf** behind the chips is the departure point for the famous Blue Lagoon Cruises to the Yasawa Islands, plus the 39-meter Beachcomber Island shuttle boat *Tui Tai.* As you return to central Lautoka, turn left onto **Marine Drive** for its view of the harbor, especially enchanting at sunset.

South of Lautoka

A popular legend invented in 1893 holds that **Viseisei village,** on the old road between Lautoka and Nadi, is the oldest settlement in Fiji. It's told how the first Fijians, led by Chiefs Lutunasobasoba and Degei, came from the west, landing their great canoe, the *Kaunitoni,* at Vuda Point, where the oil tanks are now. A Centennial Memorial (1835-1935) in front of the church commemorates the arrival of the first Methodist missionaries in Fiji, and opposite the memorial is a traditional Fijian *bure*—the residence of the present Tui Vuda.

Near the back of the church is another monument topped by a giant war club, the burial place of the village's chiefly family. The late Dr. Timoci Bavadra, the former prime minister of Fiji who was deposed by the Rabuka coup in 1987, hailed from Viseisei and is interred here. Dr. Bavadra's traditional-style home faces the main road near the church. His son presently lives there, and with his permission you'll be allowed to enter to see the photos hanging from the walls.

All this is only a few minutes' walk from the bus stop, but you're expected to have someone accompany you through the village. Ask permission of anyone you meet at the bus stop and they will send a child with you. As you part, you could give the child a pack of chewing gum (give something else if your escort is an adult). Nearby is a **Memorial Cultural Center,** where souvenirs are sold to passengers on the bus tours that often stop here. There's a fine view of Nadi Bay from the Center. It's better not to come on a Sunday. A new bypass on Queens Road avoids Viseisei and only local buses between Lautoka and Nadi take the old road past the village.

A couple of kilometers from the village on the airport side of Viseisei, just above Lomolomo Public School, are two **British six-inch guns** set up here during WW II to defend the north side of Nadi Bay. It's a fairly easy climb from the main highway, and you get an excellent view from the top.

Abaca

An ecotourism project supported by New Zealand aid money has been established at Abaca (pronounced "Ambatha") village directly below the Mt. Evans or Koroyanitu Range, 15 km east of Lautoka. **Koroyanitu National Heritage Park** is intended to support the preservation of Fiji's only unlogged cloud forest by creating a small tourism business for the locals. The village carrier used to transport visitors also carries the local kids to and from school. Four waterfalls are near the village, and Table Mountain, with sweeping views of the coast and Yasawas, is only an hour away. More ambitious hikes to higher peaks are

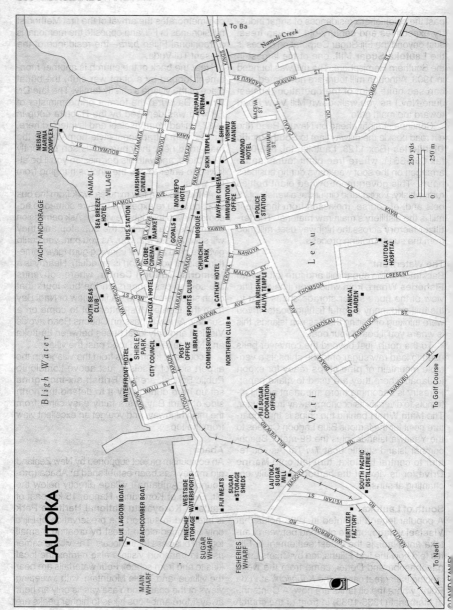

LAUTOKA

To Ba

Namoli Creek

KINGS RD.

YAVAVU ST.

DRAVUNI ST.

VOMO ST.

NACEVA ST.

CAVAU ST.

WAINUMU ST.

BOUWALU ST.

SACITAMATA ST.

BAVUQUQ ST.

NASAKI ST.

NAVA ST.

PARADE

ANUPAM CINEMA

SIKH TEMPLE

SHRI VISHNU MANDIR

DIAMOND HOTEL

NEISAU MARINA COMPLEX

NAMOLI ST.

NAMOLI VILLAGE

KARISHMA CINEMA

SEA BREEZE HOTEL

NAMOLI AVE.

MONI REPO HOTEL

MAYFAIR CINEMA

IMMIGRATION OFFICE

POLICE STATION

YAWINI ST.

VAVA ST.

YACHT ANCHORAGE

BUS STATION

BILA VEYE ST.

MARKET

TUKANI ST.

GLOBE CINEMA

NAVITI ST.

GOPALS

VITOGO

MOSQUE

CHURCHILL PARK

NANUYA ST.

VERONA ST.

MALOLO ST.

NANUYA ST.

LAUTOKA HOSPITAL

CRESENT

Levu

SOUTH SEAS CLUB

WATERFRONT RD.

LAUTOKA HOTEL

NEDE ST.

NARARA

PARADE

VIDILO ST.

SPORTS CLUB

CATHAY HOTEL

SRI KRISHNA KALIYA TEMPLE

TAVEWA AVE.

THOMSON ST.

NAMOSAU ST.

BOTANICAL GARDEN

TAGIMAUCIA ST.

Bligh Water

WATERFRONT HOTEL

SHIRLEY PARK

CITY COUNCIL

MARINE DR.

PARADE

WALU ST.

VITOGO

POST OFFICE

LIBRARY

COMMISSIONER

NORTHERN CLUB

DRASA ST.

Viti

To Golf Course

FIJI SUGAR CORPORATION OFFICE

MILL VIEW RD.

TAVAKUBU RD.

BLUE LAGOON BOATS

BEACHCOMBER BOAT

PINECHIP STORAGE

WESTSIDE WATERSPORTS

FIJI MEATS

SUGAR STORAGE SHEDS

LAUTOKA SUGAR MILL

NADOVU ST.

SOUTH PACIFIC DISTILLERIES

FERTILIZER FACTORY

VEITARI ST.

WATERFRONT RD.

NAVITU ST.

MAIN WHARF

SUGAR WHARF

FISHERIES WHARF

To Nadi

0   250 yds

0   250 m

250   250

© DAVID STANLEY

possible. The landscape of wide green valleys set against steep slopes is superb.

The **Nase Forest Lodge,** 500 meters from the village, is a six-bunk guesthouse with cooking facilities at F$15 pp (take food as there's no shop). Camping by the lodge is F$10 per tent. Otherwise you can sleep on a mat in a village home at F$30 pp including meals. The park entry fee is F$5 pp. Guided hiking trips include a two-hour walk to Savione Falls at F$5 pp or a full-day hike to Batilamu at F$10 pp. Three-day, two-night treks to Navilawa via Batilamu can be arranged for small groups but arrangements should be made in advance. Sweeping views of the Yasawas and western side of Viti Levu are obtained from Batilamu and various archaeological sites are seen.

You can call Abaca directly by radio telephone at tel. 666-644 (wait for two beeps, then dial 1234). You may get an answering machine and they sometimes don't check for messages for a week at a time, in which case the receptionists at the Cathay or Lautoka hotels in Lautoka may be able to help you. You can get there on an official village carrier, which leaves these hotels weekdays around 0900, charging F$8 pp. The closest public bus stop is Abaca Junction on the Tavakuba bus route, but it's 10 km from the village. It's also possible to hire a carrier direct to Abaca from Lautoka for Yasawa St. next to Lautoka market at about F$20 each way for the vehicle. Otherwise, the Lautoka hotels run daytrips at F$43 pp including lunch and the guided hike to the waterfall. It's an outstanding opportunity to see a bit of this spectacular area, just don't arrive on a Sunday, the traditional day of worship and rest.

Sports and Recreation

Westside Watersports (Lance Millar, Box 7136, Lautoka; tel./fax 661-462), on Wharf Rd., organizes scuba diving trips, fills tanks, and does Yasawa island transfers. Diving is F$88/132/450 for one/two/10 tanks including gear, night diving F$110. PADI open-water certification is F$430 (five days), an introductory dive F$110. They'll take snorkelers out in the boat for F$10 if space is available. Westside operates a dive shop on Tavewa Island.

Subsurface Fiji (Tony Cottrell, Box 1626, Lautoka; tel. 666-738, fax 669-955), at the corner of Nede and Naviti Streets near the Lautoka Hotel, also arranges scuba diving at F$77/140/320 for one/two/six tanks, plus F$11 for equipment. They'll sometimes takes snorkelers along for F$25. A four-day PADI certification course is F$495, otherwise an introductory dive is F$105. Divers should call for a free hotel pickup. Tank air fills at offshore islands can also be arranged. Subsurface handles all scuba diving at Beachcomber Island.

The **Lautoka Golf Club** (tel. 661-384), a nine-hole course, charges F$15 greens fees plus F$20 club rentals. A taxi from the market should cost around F$2.50.

All day Saturday you can catch exciting rugby (April-Sept.) or soccer (Sept.-May) games at the stadium in Churchill Park (admission is F$3-5). Information on upcoming games should be available to the adjacent Lautoka Sports and Social Club. Ask about league games.

ACCOMMODATIONS

Budget

A good choice is the clean, quiet, three-story **Sea Breeze Hotel** (Box 152, Lautoka; tel. 660-717, fax 666-080), at 5 Bekana Ln. on the waterfront near the bus station. They have 26 rooms with private bath from F$25/35 single/double (rooms with a/c F$30/42). A larger family room accommodating four adults is F$50. A good breakfast is F$3-6 extra. A very pleasant lounge has a color TV and a swimming pool overlooking the lagoon. Few backpackers stay here for some reason.

To be closer to the action, stay at the 38-room **Lautoka Hotel** (Box 51, Lautoka; tel. 660-388, fax 660-201), 2 Naviti St., which has a good restaurant and nightclub on the premises. There's also a nice swimming pool. Room prices vary from F$25/30 single/double for a spacious fan-cooled room with shared bath to F$46 single or double for a/c and private bath, F$70 for a/c, private bath, fridge, and waterbed, or F$10 pp in the dorm.

Also good are the 40 rooms at the friendly **Cathay Hotel** (Box 239, Lautoka; tel. 660-566, fax 660-136) on Tavewa Ave., which features a swimming pool, TV room, and bar. The charge is F$29/39 single/double with fan and private bath, F$40/47 with a/c. Some of the rooms in less desirable locations have been divided into dormitories with two to five beds or bunks. Each dorm has its own toilet and shower at F$10 pp (F$1 discount for youth hostel, VIP, or Nomads card holders). The dorms here are the best deal in the city, otherwise take one of the superior a/c rooms upstairs. The Cathay offers free luggage storage for guests and the notice board at the reception often has useful information on travel to Fijian villages and the outer islands. Beer is available at the hotel bar, and there's also the Sportsman's Bar outside and adjacent to the hotel.

Saweni Beach Apartments (Box 239, Lautoka; tel. 661-777, fax 660-136), a kilometer off the main highway south of Lautoka, offers a row of 12 self-catering apartments with fan and hot water at F$42 for up to three persons, plus several F$9 pp dormitories in the annex with two to four beds. You can pitch your own tent here at F$6 pp and still use the dorm's communal kitchen. A small discount is offered if you show a youth hostel, VIP, or Nomads card, and there's 10% off on weekly stays. It's a fine place to hang out. The Nadi travel agents don't promote this place because the owners won't pay them commissions, which makes it all the cheaper and less crowded for you. Fishermen on the beach sell fresh fish every morning, and cruising yachts often anchor off Saweni Beach. It's quiet and the so-so beach only comes alive on weekends when local picnickers arrive. A local company called **First Divers** (fax 651-571) offers scuba diving and snorkeling trips from Saweni. A bus runs right to the hotel from Lautoka five times a day. Otherwise any of the local Nadi buses will drop you off a 10-minute walk away (taxi from Lautoka F$6).

Inexpensive

Lautoka's top hotel is the **Waterfront Hotel** (Box 4653, Lautoka; tel. 664-777, fax 665-870), a two-story building erected in 1987 on Marine Drive. The 43 waterbed-equipped a/c rooms are F$111 single or double, F$135 triple (children under 16 are free if no extra bed is required). Weekly events include the Indian curry buffet on Friday night and the Sunday evening poolside barbecue (each F$16.50). There's a swimming pool, and members of tour groups departing Lautoka booked on Blue Lagoon cruises often stay here.

For information on Beachcomber Island and Treasure Island resorts, both accessible from Lautoka, turn to **The Mamanuca Group.**

FOOD

Several inexpensive local restaurants are near the bus station. The **Pacific Restaurant** (tel. 661-836; Mon.-Sat. 0700-1830, Sunday 0800-1500), on Yasawa St. near the Sigatoka Bookshop, has some of the hottest (spiciest) food you'll find anywhere in the Pacific.

Jolly Good Fast Food (tel. 669-980), Vakabale and Naviti Streets opposite the market, is a great place to sit and read a newspaper over a Coke. Eating outside in their covered garden is fun, and their "made to order" menu at the counter puts McDonald's to shame. The only drawback is the lack of beer.

The Foodcourt at back of **Morris Hedstrom Supermarket** (tel. 662-999; Mon.-Fri. 0830-1800, Saturday 0830-1600), Vidilio and Tukani Streets, offers fish or chicken and chips, hot pies, ice cream, and breakfast specials. It's a clean and only a bit more expensive than the market places.

Eat Italian at the **Pizza Inn** (tel. 660-388) in the Lautoka Hotel, 2 Naviti Street. **The Last Call** (tel./fax 650-525; closed Sunday), a more upscale Italian restaurant at 21 Tui St. near the Waterfront Hotel, has an internet service for visitors costing 44 cents a minute (technical help free). The homemade ice cream and imported cappuccino are also good.

Indian

Naran Ghela & Sons Milk Bar (tel. 667-502; Mon.-Fri. 0800-1800, Saturday 0800-1630), 85 Vitogo Parade, is a good place for an Indian-style breakfast of spicy snacks, *samosas,* and sweets with coffee.

For the finest vegetarian food in Lautoka, head for **Gopal's** (tel. 662-990; weekdays 0830-1730, Saturday 0830-1630), on the corner of Naviti and Yasawa Streets near the market. This is the Lautoka equivalent of Suva's Hare Krishna Restaurant. It's best at lunch with an all-you-can-eat vegetarian *thali* plate for F$6.50 but the selection declines toward closing. Come anytime for ice cream and sweets.

The unpretentious **Hot Snax Shop** (tel. 661-306), 56 Naviti St., may be the number-one place in Fiji to sample South Indian dishes, such as *masala dosai,* a rice pancake with coconut chutney that makes a nice light lunch, or *samosas, iddili, puri,* and *palau.* The deep-fried *puri* are great for breakfast.

Chinese

Yangs Restaurant (tel. 661-446; Mon.-Thurs. 0800-1745, Friday 0800-1830, Saturday 0800-1700), 27 Naviti St., is an excellent breakfast or lunch place with inexpensive Chinese specialties.

Enjoy ample servings of Cantonese food at the a/c **Sea Coast Restaurant** (tel. 660-675; closed Sunday) on Naviti St. near the Lautoka Hotel.

ENTERTAINMENT

Four movie houses offer several showings daily except Sunday.

The disco scene in Lautoka centers on the **Hunter's Inn** at the Lautoka Hotel (tel. 660-388; open Friday and Saturday 2100-0100 only; F$5 cover). There's also **Coco's** (tel. 667-900) at 21 Naviti St., above the Great Wall of China Restaurant, but you won't be admitted if you're wearing a T-shirt or flip-flops.

The roughest place in town is **Lady Touch Disco** (tel. 666-677), above Gopal's in the city center. It's open Thurs.-Sat. 2000-0100, but nothing much happens before 2200. The cover charge is F$5 (ladies free), and flip-flop shoes aren't allowed. They also open for happy hour Saturday 1200-1430.

Lautoka's old colonial club is the **Northern Club** (tel. 662-469) on Tavewa Ave. opposite the Cathay Hotel. The sign outside says Members Only, but the club secretary is usually willing to sign in foreign visitors. Lunch and dinner are available here from Mon.-Sat.; there's tennis and a swimming pool.

The **Lautoka Club** (tel. 660-637), behind the Sea Breeze Hotel, is another good drinking place with a sea view. The **Sports and Social Club** (tel. 660-837), on Narara Parade near Churchill Park, is another good local drinking place.

Sunday *Puja*

The big event of the week is the Sunday *puja* (prayer) at the **Sri Krishna Kaliya Temple** (tel. 664-112) on Tavewa Ave. at 1230, followed by a vegetarian feast at 1300. Visitors may join in the singing and dancing, if they wish. Take off your shoes and sit on the white marble floor, men on one side, women on the other. Bells ring, drums are beaten, conch shells blown, and stories from the Vedas, Srimad Bhagavatam, and Ramayana are acted out as everyone chants, *"Hare Krsna, Hare Krsna, Krsna Krsna, Hare Hare, Hare Rama, Hare Rama, Rama, Rama, Hare, Hare."* It's a real celebration of joy and a most moving experience. At one point children will circulate with small trays covered with burning candles, on which it is customary to place a donation; you may also drop a dollar or two in the yellow box in the center of the temple. You'll be readily invited to join the vegetarian feast later, and no more money will be asked of you.

OTHER PRACTICALITIES

Services

The ANZ Bank, Bank of Hawaii, Merchant Bank, and Westpac Bank are all on Naviti Street near the market. There's also an ANZ Bank branch diagonally opposite the post office, and a Westpac Bank branch a little west on Vitogo Parade beyond the Shell station. The ANZ Bank closer to the market has an ATM machine.

The Immigration Department (tel. 661-706) is at the corner of Namoli and Drasa Avenues.

Public toilets are on the back side of the bus station facing the market.

Yachting Facilities

The Neisau Marina Complex (Box 3831, Lautoka; tel. 664-858, fax 663-807), at the end of Bouwalu St., provides complete haul-out facilities for yachts in need of repair. A berth begins at F$7 a day, while to anchor offshore and use the facilities (showers, etc.) is F$15 a week. There's also a laundromat (F$3 to wash, F$2 to dry). Spencer's Bar here opens at 1800 daily except Sunday with special happy hour prices until 2000 (no T-shirts or flip-flops).

Information

The Department of Lands and Survey (tel. 661-800; Mon.-Thurs. 0800-1300/1400-1530, Friday 0800-1300/1400-1500), behind the Commissioner Western Division office near the Cathay Hotel, sells excellent topographical maps of all of Fiji at F$5 a sheet.

The Book Exchange (tel. 665-625), 19 Yasawa St., trades and sells used books.

The Western Regional Library (tel. 660-091) on Tavewa Ave. is open weekdays 1000-1700, Saturday 0900-1200.

Sunflower Airlines (tel. 664-753) is at 27 Vidilio St., while Air Pacific (tel. 664-008) is at 159 Vitogo Parade diagonally opposite the post office. Rosie The Travel Service (tel. 660-311) is next to Air Pacific.

Health

The emergency room at the Lautoka Hospital (tel. 660-399), off Thomson Crescent south of the center, is open 24 hours a day.

The privately operated Vakabale Street Medical Center (tel. 661-961; weekdays 0830-1300/1400-1700, Saturday 0830-1300), near the corner of Vakabale and Naviti Streets not far from the market, includes a general medical practitioner and a dental surgeon on its roster.

Vaccinations for tetanus, diphtheria, polio, and rubella are available at the Health Office (tel. 660-815) on Naviti St. opposite the Lautoka Hotel.

Transportation

Patterson Brothers (tel. 661-173), at 15 Tukani St. opposite the bus station, runs a bus/ferry/bus

service between Lautoka, Ellington Wharf, Nabouwalu, and Labasa (F$43), departing Lautoka on Tuesday, Thursday, and Saturday around 0400.

Buses, carriers, taxis—everything leaves from the bus stand beside the market. **Pacific Transport** (tel. 660-499) has express buses to Suva daily at 0630, 0700, 1210, 1550, and 1730 (five hours, F$8.95) via Sigatoka (Queens Road). Five other "stage" buses also operate daily along this route (six hours). The daily **Sunset Express** (tel. 668-276) leaves for Suva via Sigatoka at 0930 and 1515 (four hours, F$9). **Sunbeam Transport** (tel. 662-822) has expresses to Suva at 0615, 0630, 0815, 1215, and 1630 (six hours, F$11.05) via Tavua (Kings Road), plus two local buses on the same route (nine hours). The northern route is more scenic than the southern. Local buses to Nadi (F$1.36) and Ba (F$1.48) depart every half hour or so.

Car rentals are available in Lautoka at **Budget** (tel. 666-166) on Walu St. and **Central** (tel. 664-511) at 73 Vitogo Parade.

Day cruises to Beachcomber Island (F$60 pp including lunch, reductions for children) depart Lautoka daily at 1000—a great way to spend a day. Any travel agency can book them.

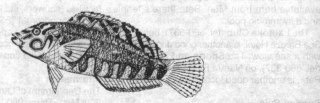

wrasse (Halichoeres nebulosus)

THE YASAWA ISLANDS

The Yasawas are a chain of 16 main volcanic islands and dozens of smaller ones, stretching 80 km in a north-northeast direction, roughly 35 km off the west coast of Viti Levu. In the lee of Viti Levu, the Yasawas are dry and sunny, with beautiful, isolated beaches, cliffs, bays, and reefs. The waters are crystal clear and almost totally shark-free. The group was romanticized in two movies about a pair of child castaways who eventually fall in love on a deserted isle. The original 1949 version of *The Blue Lagoon* starred Jean Simmons while the 1980 remake featured Brooke Shields. (A 1991 sequel *Return to the Blue Lagoon* with Milla Jovovich was filmed on Taveuni.) In 1999 *Castaway* with Tom Hanks was filmed in the Yasawas.

It was from the north end of the Yasawas that two canoe-loads of cannibals sallied forth in 1789 and gave chase to Capt. William Bligh and his 18 companions less than a week after the famous mutiny. Two centuries later, increasing numbers of mini-cruise ships ply the chain, but there are still almost no motorized land vehicles or roads. The backpackers' usual routine is to head for Tavewa or Wayasewa while the $1,000-a-day crowd is flown to Turtle Island. All access to the Yasawas is via Lautoka. In the local dialect called Vuda, *bula* is *cola* (hello) and *vinaka* is *vina du riki* (thank you).

Wayasewa Island

Dive Trek Nature Lodge (Box 6353, Lautoka; tel. 669-715, fax 724-363), also known as Wayalailai Eco-Haven, is on the south side of Wayasewa adjacent to Namara village. In 1972 most of the villagers moved to the northwest side of the island, and since 1994 the east side of the village has been developed into one of the largest backpacker camps in Fiji. The location is spectacular, opposite Kuata Island directly below Wayasewa's highest peak (349 meters), with Viti Levu clearly visible to the east behind Vomo Island. Photos don't do this place justice.

The resort is built on two terraces, one 10 meters above the beach and the other 10 meters above that. The lower terrace has the double, duplex, and dormitory *bures,* while the upper accommodates the former village schoolhouse, now partitioned into 14 tiny double rooms, and the restaurant/bar. Rooms with shared bath and open ceiling in the school building are F$35 pp, while the five individual *bures* with private bath and a small porch are F$50 pp. One duplex *bure* with four beds on each side serves as an eight-bed dormitory or *burebau* at F$30 pp. The camping space nearby is F$22 pp. If you pay seven nights the eighth is free. The minimum stay is three nights.

Three ample Fijian meals are included in all rates and the food is good with second helpings allowed (free tea and coffee throughout the day). Breakfast is served at 0700 to give you an early start. A barbecue and bonfire are held on Wednesday night, and Sunday afternoon a *lovo* is prepared. There's no shortage of water. The electric generator goes off at 2200 and disturbances in the double rooms or dorm (if any) are most likely to come in the early morning as people get up to see the sunrise or to do a pre-breakfast hike. Dive Trek appeals to all ages—even those who might normally opt for one of the more upmarket Mamanuca resorts will find the double *bures* quite acceptable. The extraordinary mix of guests is also due to the emphasis on scuba diving. Informal musical entertainment occurs nightly, and because this resort is owned by the village, the staff is like one big happy family.

There's lots to see and do at Dive Trek with hiking and scuba diving the main activities. The most popular hike is to the top of Vatuvula, the fantastic volcanic plug hanging directly over the resort. The well-trodden path circles the mountain and comes up the back, taking about 1.5 hours roundtrip excluding stops (a guide isn't really required). From the top of Vatuvula you get a sweeping view of the west side of Viti Levu, the Mamanucas, and the southern half of the Yasawa chain—one of the scenic highlights of the South Pacific. From Vatuvula you can trek northwest across the grassy uplands to another rock with a good view of Yalobi Bay (also known as Alacrity Bay).

The offshore reef features cabbage coral, whip coral, and giant fan corals in warm, clear waters teeming with fish, and scuba diving is well organized. Prices are F$65/100/135/157 for one/two/three/four tanks, equipment included, and Dive Trek's inexpensive PADI open-water certification course (F$330) makes this a great place to learn to dive. If you're new to the activity, try the "discover scuba" resort course at F$100. The resort's dive shop also caters to snorkelers with a snorkeling trip to Kuata Island at F$5 pp (minimum of five), or snorkeling on a reef halfway to Vomo at F$8 pp (minimum of six). With a buddy you could even snorkel over to Kuata, so long as you're aware of the currents (ask about this). There's a nice picnic beach on the side of Kuata facing Wayasewa, but the optimum snorkeling area is across the point on the southwest side. Look for the cave near the seagull rocks at the point itself.

Other activities include sunset fishing for F$5 pp (minimum of five), and on Tuesday and Saturday there's an organized visit to Naboro village for a kava ceremony and traditional *meke* entertainment (F$10 pp). Beach volleyball is every afternoon. No organized activities take place on Sunday.

Boat transfers from Lautoka depart Mon.-Sat. at 1300 (1.5 hours, F$40 pp one-way). The boat leaves Dive Trek to return to Lautoka Mon.-Sat. at 0900. In both directions the boat fare includes bus transfers to/from Nadi/Lautoka hotels. Dive Trek also offers speedboat transfers to most other resorts in this area upon request: to Yalobi village on Waya Island at F$10 pp, to Octopus Resort F$20 pp, to Mana Island F$35 pp (three-person minimum).

You can book Dive Trek through **Rabua's Travel Agency** (tel./fax 724-364), Office No. 23, upstairs from the international arrivals concourse at Nadi Airport (ask for "Rambo"), or just call the number listed above. Budget.

Waya Island

The high island clearly visible to the northwest of Lautoka is Waya, closest of the larger Yasawas to Viti Levu and just 60 km away. At 579 meters, it's also the highest island in the chain. Four Fijian villages are sprinkled around Waya: Nalauwaki, Natawa, Wayalevu, and Yalobi. The rocky mass of Batinareba (510 meters) towers over the west side of Yalobi Bay and in a morning or afternoon you can scramble up the mountain's rocky slope from the west end of the beach at Yalobi. Go through the forested saddle on the south side of the highest peak, and follow the grassy ridge on the far side all the way down to Loto Point. Many goats are seen along the way. An easier hike from Yalobi leads southeast from the school to the sandbar over to Wayasewa. At low tide you can walk across and there's good snorkeling anytime.

One of the most memorable walks in the South Pacific involves spending two hours on a well-used trail from Yalobi to Nalauwaki village. Octopus Resort is just over the ridge west of Nalauwaki, and from there it's possible to hike back to Yalobi down Waya's west coast and across Loto Point in another two or three hours. Due to rocky headlands lapped by the sea you can only go down the west coast at low tide, thus you must set out from Yalobi at high tide and from Octopus at low tide. It's a great way to fill a day.

Adi's Place (Adi Sayaba, Box 1163, Lautoka; tel. 113-226, 650-573, or 962-377), also called Backpackers Paradise, at Yalobi village on the south side of Waya, is a small family-operated resort in existence since 1981. Although primitive, it makes a good hiking base with prices designed to attract and hold bare-budgeteers. The accommodations consist of one eight-bunk dorm at F$30 pp, a solid European-style house with three double rooms at F$40 pp, and camping space at F$20 pp. Lighting is by kerosene lamp. The rates include three meals but the food is variable with great meals served when Adi herself is present and little more than cabbage and rice at other times. If you've got a portable camp stove and a tent you can skip the meals and prepare your own food while paying F$9 pp to camp. Bring your own alcohol. It's right on one of the Yasawas' finest beaches, and you can lie in a hammock and observe village life (church on Sunday, kids going back and forth to school, etc.). Every Monday a cruise ship calls at Yalobi and the villagers put on traditional dances that Adi's guests can watch for F$5 per head. Scuba diving is not available here and you should not leave valuables unattended. If you haven't been able to reserve one of the more structured Yasawa resorts such as Dive Trek or Coral View, you should have no problem getting in here, but it shouldn't be your first choice. Adi's boat, the *Bula Tale*, departs Lautoka's Fisheries Wharf or the Neisau Marina for Yalobi daily except Sunday, charging F$35 pp each way for the two-hour trip. The boat usually stays overnight at Lautoka and leaves for Waya in the morning, returning to Lautoka in the afternoon, but this varies. Inexpensive.

An even simpler place is **Lovoni Camping**, on a small rocky beach a 20-minute walk north of Natawa village on the east side of Waya. From Yalobi, it's a 30-minute hike across the ridge to Natawa. Lovoni is run by Adi's cousin Semi who had to rebuild everything after a hurricane in 1997. At last report there were two thatched *bures* at F$25 pp including meals and camping space. It's a place to hang out with some friend-ly people. Budget.

On a high white-sand beach in Likuliku Bay on northwestern Waya is **Octopus Resort Waya** (Box 1861, Lautoka; tel. 666-337, fax 666-210), run by Ingrid and Wolfgang Denk. Nalauwaki village is a 10-minute walk away over a low ridge. The four solidly constructed tin-roofed *bures* with private bath are F$68/88 single/dou-ble. Otherwise it's F$31 pp in a four-bed dorm, or F$22 pp to sleep in one of Octopus's set tents. If you bring your own tent it's also F$22 pp and there's an additional F$5 per tent fee to set it up (this unusual rate is part of a deliberate at-tempt to avoid overcrowding). Another two *bures* and a six-bed dorm may have gone up by the time you get there, but the Denks have no in-tention of expanding beyond that. Lunch and dinner are included in all rates. Drinks are served at their large restaurant/bar and a generator pro-vides electricity in the public area each evening. Yachties are welcome to anchor offshore and use the facilities (meals can be ordered at F$4/12 for breakfast/dinner). When there's enough in-terest the Denks organize a *meke* (F$15 pp). Fishing trips are F$25 pp including lunch, but there's no scuba diving. Octopus is in a quiet, se-cluded location with some of Fiji's finest snor-keling right offshore (spectacular coral). Reser-vations are essential as it's often full, and the most effective way to book is by fax as the phone connection doesn't always work. Allow ample time for this, and be persistent. Even then, read-ers have reported having their confirmed reser-vations canceled by Octopus at the last minute. Information may be available at the Cathay Hotel reception in Lautoka. Transfers depart Lautoka's

Neisau Marina Monday at 1400 and Thursday at 1000, departing Waya for the return Monday and Wednesday at 0900 (F$40 each way). In-expensive.

Naviti Island

Naviti, at 33 square km, is the largest of the Ya-sawas. Its king, one of the group's highest chiefs, resides at Soso, and the church there houses fine woodcarvings. On the hillside above Soso are two caves containing the bones of ances-tors. Yawesa, the secondary boarding school on Naviti, is a village in itself. There are no ac-commodations for visitors.

Tavewa Island

Tavewa is much smaller than Waya and twice as far from Lautoka, yet it's also strikingly beautiful with excellent bathing in the warm waters off a picture-postcard beach on the southeast side, and a good fringing reef with super snorkeling. Tall grass covers the hilly interior of this two-km-long island. Tavewa is in the middle of the Yasawas and from the summit you can behold the long chain of islands stretching out on each side with Viti Levu in the background. The sun-sets can be splendid from the hill.

There's no chief here, as this is freehold land. In the late 19th century an Irishman named William Doughty married a woman from Nacula who was given Tavewa as her dowry. A decade or two later a Scot named William Bruce married into the Doughty family, and some time thereafter beachcombers called Murray and Campbell ar-rived on the scene and did the same, with the re-sult that today some 50 Doughtys, Bruces, Mur-rays, and Campbells comprise the population of Tavewa. William Doughty himself died in 1926 at the ripe age of 77. Visit Auntie Lucy Doughty, the person who pioneered tourism to Tavewa back in the late 1970s, who lives next door to David Doughty's Place and sells books, maps, and postcards to visitors.

The islanders are friendly and welcoming; in fact, accommodating visitors is their main source of income. Most of their guests are backpackers who usually stay six nights, and most are sorry to leave. It's idyllic but bring along mosquito coils, toilet paper, candles, a flashlight (torch), bottled water, and a *sulu* to cover up. Be prepared for water shortages.

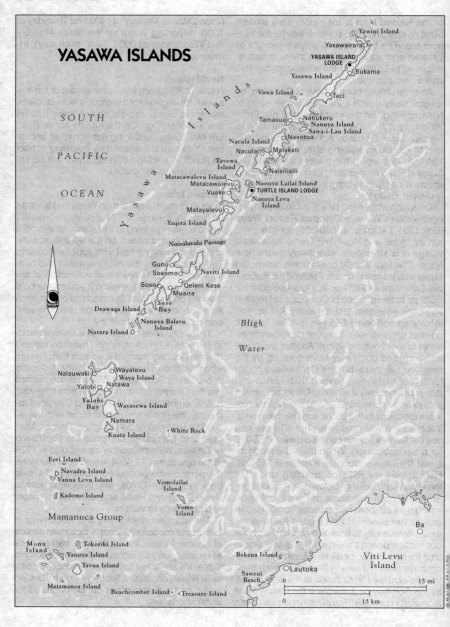

YASAWA ISLANDS

SOUTH

PACIFIC

OCEAN

Yasawa Islands

Yawini Island

Yasawairara

YASAWA ISLAND LODGE

Yasawa Island

Bukama

Vawa Island

Teci

Tamasua

Nabukeru

Nanuya Island

Sawa-i-Lau Island

Nacula Island

Navotua

Nacula

Malakati

Tavewa Island

Naisilisili

Matacawalevu Island

Matacawalevu

Nanuya Lailai Island

Vuake

TURTLE ISLAND LODGE

Matayalevu

Nanuya Levu Island

Yaqeta Island

Naivalavala Passage

Gunu

Sosomo

Naviti Island

Soso

Qeleni Kese

Muaira

Soso Bay

Drawaqa Island

Nanuya Balavu Island

Narara Island

Bligh

Water

Wayalevu

Nalauwaki

Waya Island

Yalobi

Natawa

Yalobi Bay

Wayasewa Island

Namara

White Rock

Kuata Island

Eori Island

Navadra Island

Vanua Levu Island

Vomolailai Island

Kadomo Island

Vomo Island

Mamanuca Group

Ba

Monu Island

Tokoriki Island

Yanuya Island

Bekena Island

Viti Levu Island

Tavua Island

Saweni Beach

Lautoka

Matamanoa Island

Beachcomber Island

Treasure Island

0   15 mi

0   15 km

In the budget-to-inexpensive category are three family-operated backpacker resorts on the east side of Tavewa. **Coral View Resort** (Box 9892, Nadi Airport; tel. 662-648) nestles in a cozy valley on a secluded beach with high hills on each side. It has six small thatched *bures* at F$66 double, four six-bunk dorm *bures* at F$30 pp, and mattresses in a large dormitory tent at F$25 pp. Camping with your own tent is F$22 pp. The new *bures* are F$80. There's no electricity in the *bures* but mosquito nets are supplied. You'll be lulled to sleep by the sound of the waves (unless you're in the two dorms near the noisy radio hut). Included are three generous meals (served promptly at 0800, 1200, and 1900) and one organized activity a day. Free boat trips are to Long Beach and Suntan Beach (both on Nacula Island), Honeymoon Island, and Blue Lagoon Beach. The excursion to Malakati village on Thursday morning or the boat trip to the Sawa-i-Lau caves requires a minimum of 10 people willing to pay F$20 to operate. Snorkeling gear is F$4 a day. In the evening a string band plays in the restaurant/bar and everyone sits around talking, drinking, or playing cards. Although there are lots of organized activities, Coral View is also a place where people come to relax and socialize, and most of the guests tend to be under 35. When the shuttle boat arrives from Lautoka all resort residents (including Snoopy the dog) line up on the beach to shake hands with new arrivals. Coral View tries to provide resort-style service (the staff wears matching uniforms), and Uncle Robert de Bruce keeps a close watch over everything from behind the scenes. Robert's son Don is captain of Coral View's 12-meter *Sabob III,* the fastest boat to Tavewa, which leaves Lautoka Wednesday at 1400 and on Tuesday and Saturday mornings, departing Tavewa for the return on Monday, Wednesday, and Friday mornings (2.5 hours, F$50 pp each way). Coral View bookings are handled at the reception of the Cathay Hotel in Lautoka, or at Coral View's Nadi Airport office (tel. 724-199, fax 724-780), upstairs in the commercial arcade at arrivals. The airport office will give you a 15% discount if you book directly through them and stay at least four nights (the bare minimum you'd want to stay in any case).

The other main accommodation is **David's Place** (David and Kara Doughty, Box 10520,

Nadi Airport; tel. 663-939, fax 724-244), in a coconut grove near the small church on the island's longest beach. There are eight *bures* at F$66 double and two 10-bed dorms at F$30 pp (no electricity). Camping is F$22 pp with your own tent. David's *bures* are larger and more comfortable than those at Coral View. Since they started cutting the grass the mosquito problem has declined, but the two communal toilets are sometimes inadequate. Three huge meals are included in the price with the Thursday *lovo* and Saturday barbecue part of the regular meal plan (opinions about the food vary). At David's you don't get the free trips provided at Coral View, but the optional tours are cheaper: F$12 for the cave trip and F$14 to visit Naisilisili village. David's solid new restaurant/bar with a concrete floor under the thatched roof serves as a hurricane shelter in time of need. David sells cold beer, soft drinks, and cigarettes here, and afternoon tea is available 1500-1630 to both guests and nonguests at 75 cents a piece for some of the richest banana or chocolate cake in Fiji, plus 50 cents for the tea. It's an island institution. In the evening people sit around playing backgammon and drinking kava, and often someone sings a couple of songs. In short, it's a good escape from civilization, and you'll be made most welcome. David's boats, the *Tai Maria* and the *Tai Dritolu,* leave Lautoka Tuesday, Thursday, and Saturday at 0830, returning from the island Monday, Wednesday, and Friday (F$40 pp each way). Bookings can be made through David's Travel Service (tel. 724-244, fax 721-820), upstairs in the arrivals concourse at Nadi Airport or at the reception of the Lautoka Hotel.

Your third choice is **Otto's Place** (Otto and Fanny Doughty, Box 7136, Lautoka; tel./fax 661-462), on spacious grounds near the south end of the island. They have two large double *bures* with kerosene fridge, toilet, shower, and sink at F$60 single or double, F$75 triple, plus F$25 pp for three good meals. The new *bure* is F$77/92 double/triple. The single eight-bed dormitory is F$30 pp, plus F$20 pp for meals. The generator is on 1800-2230 but the light is dim. The meals are optional and you can also cook for yourself. Yachties and people from the other hotels are welcome to order dinner here (F$10-15 pp depending on what you want), so long as ample notice is given. Afternoon tea is served

1500-1700 (tea and three cakes for F$2, or 50 cents for tea/coffee only). Otto's offers privacy and a bit more comfort for a slightly higher price, and they may have beds available when all the others are full. You can book through Westside Watersports in Lautoka, which also arranges boat transfers at F$50 pp each way.

Coral View caters more to the youth market while David's is fine for all ages. Pick Coral View if you want a lot of activities packed into a brief stay, David's if you want to relax. Be aware that bungalows on the island are in high demand and unless you have firm reservations you'll probably end up camping or staying in a dorm. If you definitely want a *bure* and nothing else, make this very clear when booking. Once on Tavewa, it may be difficult to extend your stay without taking somebody else's room. If you're still in Lautoka and hear that your prebooked room is no longer available because people already there decided to stay a few more days, insist that it is they who must move into the dormitory and not you. Unfortunately, these things happen far too often.

Westside Watersports has a dive shop on the beach between David's and Otto's where you pay F$50 for your first dive, F$40 for the second, and F$30 for the third and successive dives. After doing 10 dives you're awarded a souvenir T-shirt. Their two small dive boats go out at 0900 and 1400, and which side of the island you'll dive on depends on the wind. You can also rent a mask and snorkel at F$2.50 a day, plus F$2.50 for a set of fins.

Blue Lagoon Cruises has leased a stretch of beach at the south end of Tavewa where you see a group of picnic tables. You're not supposed to swim here when the tour groups are present, otherwise it's the finest beach on the island.

The resort boats leave from Lautoka's Fisheries Wharf near Fiji Meats Tuesday, Thursday, and Saturday mornings, returning to Lautoka on Monday, Wednesday, and Friday (F$40-50 one-way). Try to pay only a one-way fare on the boat up front, allowing yourself the chance to go elsewhere if you don't like the lodgings you're offered. The boat ride from Lautoka can take anywhere from three to six hours (or more) depending on weather conditions and the quality of the boat. Coral View and David's Place are very competitive, and David's guests are sometimes not allowed to use Coral View's better boat, the *Sabob III*. Don't expect luxuries such as toilets on these boats, so limit how much you drink before boarding. Also limit what you eat, or take seasickness pills if you're a poor sailor (a trip on one of the smaller boats can be frightful in rough weather). Be prepared to wade ashore at Tavewa.

Nanuya Levu Island

In 1972 an eccentric American millionaire named Richard Evanson bought 200-hectare Nanuya Levu Island in the middle of the Yasawa Group for US$300,000. He still lives there, and his **Turtle Island Lodge** (Box 9317, Nadi Airport; tel. 663-889 or 660-922, fax 665-220) has gained a reputation as one of the South Pacific's ultimate hideaways. Only 14 fan-cooled, two-room *bures* grace Turtle, and Evanson swears there'll never be more. He's turned down many offers to develop the island with hundreds more units or to sell out for a multimillion-dollar price.

Turtle is Tavewa at 20 times the price. The 28 guests (English-speaking mixed couples only, please) pay US$1,010 per couple per night plus 10% tax, but that includes all meals, drinks, and activities. Meals are served at remote and romantic dine-out locations, or taken at the community table; every evening Richard hosts a small dinner party. Ringo Starr is said to be a regular here. Aside from the per diem, it's another US$750 per couple for roundtrip seaplane transportation to the island from Nadi, and there's also a six-night minimum stay. (Turtle Island is off-limits to anyone other than hotel guests.) Luxury.

Blue Lagoon Beach on neighboring **Nanuya Lailai Island** is used by cruise-ship passengers and many yachts anchor just offshore. The snorkeling here is about the best in the area and boatloads of backpackers often arrive for a swim when the packaged tourists aren't around. You can tell the fish have been fed from the way they swim straight at you.

Sawa-i-Lau Island

On Sawa-i-Lau is a large limestone cave illuminated by a crevice at the top. There's a clear, deep pool in the cave where you can swim, and an underwater opening leads back into a smaller, darker cave (bring a light). A Fijian legend tells how a young chief once hid his love in this cave when her family wished to marry her off to another. Each day he brought her food until both could escape to safety on another island. Many cruise ships stop at this cave and the backpacker resorts on Tavewa also run tours. Yachties should present a *sevusevu* to the chief of Nabukeru village, just west of the cave, to visit. At last report Blue Lagoon Cruises wasn't visiting the cave anymore due to a dispute with the local chiefs over custom fees, while Captain Cook Cruises did visit—this could change.

Yasawa Island

The Tui Yasawa, highest chief of the group, resides at Yasawairara village at the north end of Yasawa, northernmost island of the Yasawa group.

Australian-owned **Yasawa Island Resort** (Box 10128, Nadi Airport; tel. 663-364, fax 665-044) opened in 1991 on a creamy white beach on Yasawa's upper west side. The 16 thatched a/c *bures* with private baths consist of four duplexes at F$795 double, 10 deluxes at F$890, a two-bedroom unit at F$1,025, and a honeymoon unit at F$1,200, plus tax. Prices are reduced slightly in February and March. All meals are included, but unlike at most other resorts in this category, alcoholic drinks are *not*. Scuba diving and game fishing also cost extra. Guests arrive on a chartered flight (F$175 pp each way), which lands on the resort's private airstrip. Children under 14 are only admitted during school holiday periods four times a year. To book only call during local business hours, otherwise you'll get their machine. Luxury.

KADAVU

This big, 50-by-13-km island 100 km south of Suva is the fourth largest in Fiji (411 square km). A mountainous, varied island with waterfalls plummeting from the rounded rainforested hilltops, Kadavu is outstanding for the quality of its vistas, beaches, and reefs. The three hilly sections of Kadavu are joined by two low isthmuses, with the sea biting so deeply into the island that on a map its shape resembles that of a wasp. Just northeast of the main island is smaller Ono Island and the fabulous Astrolabe Reef, stretching halfway to Suva. The birdlife is rich with species of honeyeaters, fantails, and velvet fruit doves found only here. The famous red-and-green Kadavu musk parrots may be seen and heard.

In the 1870s steamers bound for New Zealand and Australia would call at the onetime whaling station at Galoa Harbor to pick up passengers and goods, and Kadavu was considered as a possible site for a new capital of Fiji. Instead Suva was chosen and Kadavu was left to lead its sleepy village life; only today is the outside world making a comeback with the arrival of roads, planes, and a handful of visitors. Some 10,000 indigenous Fijians live in 60 remote villages scattered around the island.

SIGHTS

The airstrip and wharf are each a 10-minute walk, in different directions, from the post office and hospital in the tiny government station of **Vunisea,** the largest of Kadavu's villages and headquarters of Kadavu Province. Vunisea is strategically located on a narrow, hilly isthmus where Galoa Harbor and Namalata Bay almost cut Kadavu in two.

The longest sandy beach on the island is at **Drue,** an hour's walk north from Vunisea. Another good beach is at **Muani** village, eight km south of Vunisea by road. Just two km south of the airstrip by road and a 10-minute hike inland is **Waikana Falls.** Cool spring water flows over a 10-meter-high rocky cliff between two deep pools, the perfect place for a refreshing swim on a hot day. A second falls six km east of Vunisea is even better.

A road runs along the south coast from Vunisea to **Nabukelevuira** at the west end of Kadavu. There's good **surfing** at Cape Washington in this area but you'll need a boat and it's strongly suggested that you present a *sevusevu* to the village chief before engaging in the activity. Un-

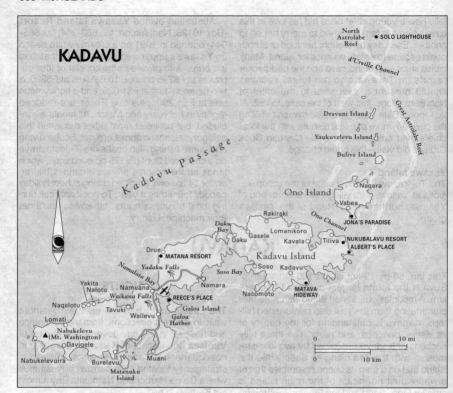

KADAVU

fortunately, the villagers have become rather hostile to surfers who turn up unannounced and pay no heed to local customs.

It's also possible to climb **Nabukelevu** (838 meters) from Nabukelevuira. There's no trail—you'll need a guide to help you hack a way. The abrupt extinct cone of Nabukelevu (Mt. Washington) dominates the west end of Kadavu, and petrels nest in holes on the north side of the mountain.

The Great Astrolabe Reef

The Great Astrolabe Reef stretches unbroken for 30 km along the east side of the small islands north of Kadavu. One km wide, the reef is unbelievably rich in coral and marinelife, and because it's so far from shore, it still hasn't been fished out. The reef surrounds a lagoon containing 10 islands, the largest of which is 30-square-km Ono. The reef was named by French explorer Dumont d'Urville, who almost lost his ship, the *Astrolabe,* here in 1827.

There are frequent openings on the west side of the reef, and the lagoon is never more than 10 fathoms deep, which makes it a favorite of scuba divers and yachties. The Astrolabe also features a vertical drop-off of 10 meters on the inside and 1,800 meters on the outside, with visibility up to 75 meters. The underwater caves and walls here must be seen to be believed. However, the reef is exposed to unbroken waves generated by the southeast trades and diving conditions are often dependent on the weather. Surfing is possible at Vesi Passage (boat required).

Many possibilities exist for ocean kayaking in the protected waters around Ono Channel and there are several inexpensive resorts at which to stay. Kayak rentals may not be available, thus one should bring along a folding kayak on the boat from Suva. Several companies mentioned in this book's main introduction offer kayaking tours in Kadavu.

PRACTICALITIES

Accommodations around Vunisea

Manueli and Tamalesi Vuruya runs **Biana Accommodation** (Box 13, Vunisea; tel. 336-010), on a hill overlooking Namalata Bay near the jetty at Vunisea. The six rooms are F$30/55 single/double including breakfast, plus F$5 each for a real Fijian lunch or dinner (or you can cook). They ask that you call ahead before coming. Budget.

Reece's Place (Bill and Serima Reece, Box 6, Vunisea, Kadavu; tel. 336-097), on tiny Galoa Island just off the northwest corner of Kadavu, was the first to accommodate visitors to Kadavu, and it's still the least expensive place to stay around Vunisea station. It's a 15-minute walk from the airstrip to the dock, then a short launch ride to Galoa itself (F$6 pp return). There are 18 beds in three Fijian *bures* and three two-room houses at F$15 pp, and a F$9 five-bed dormitory. Pitch your tent for F$6 pp. Unless you have a camp stove, cooking your own food is not possible, but Serima is an excellent cook and three ample meals can be had for F$17 pp. There could be minor water problems. They use an electric generator in the evening. The view of Galoa Harbor from Reece's Place is excellent, and there's a long beach nearby, but the snorkeling in the murky water is poor. For F$8 pp (minimum of four), you can ride to the Galoa Barrier Reef, where the snorkeling is vastly superior. Scuba diving (F$35/60 one/two tanks plus F$15 for equipment) and PADI certification courses (F$280) are offered. They'll also take you surfing on the Great Astrolabe. If you're there on Sunday, consider attending the service in the village church to hear the wonderful singing. Call ahead to check prices and availability. Shoestring.

A much more upscale operation is **Matana Beach Resort** (Box 8, Vunisea, Kadavu; tel. 311-780, fax 303-860) at Drue, six km north of

Vunisea. The two oceanview *bures* on the hillside are F$200/330 single/double, while the six larger beachfront units are F$220/370/495/580 single/double/triple/quad, three meals included (three-night minimum stay, children under 12 not accepted). Boat transfers from Vunisea airport are also part of the package. Sunsets over Mt. Washington from the bar's open terrace can be spectacular. Matana caters almost exclusively to scuba divers who've booked from abroad with **Dive Kadavu**. The morning two-tank boat dive is F$130, and if they have a minimum of four people they'll do a one-tank afternoon dive for F$75 (the same applies at night). Their PADI open-water certification course is F$495. This whole operation meets the highest international standards. Windsurfers, sea kayaks, and paddle-boards are free. The snorkeling off Matana's golden beach is good, and the fantastic Namalata Reef is straight out from the resort. To snorkel from the dive boat is F$30. Premium.

Accommodations on North Kadavu

Albert's Place (Albert and Ruth O'Connor, c/o P.O. Naleca, Kadavu; tel. 336-086), at Lagalevu at the east end of Kadavu, is similar to Reece's Place but more remote. Each of the 10 small *bures* has a double and a single bed, coconut mats on the floor, and a kerosene lamp for light at F$22 (share twin) or F$12 pp in a six-bed dorm. Camping is F$9 pp. The units share rustic flush toilets and cold showers with plenty of running water (except during droughts), and everything is kept fairly clean. Mosquito nets and coils are supplied.

Meals cost another F$30 pp for all three, and Ruth O'Connor and her daughter Ramona serve huge portions. Their meals are exceptional, consisting of fresh fish, lobster, chicken curry, or seafood soup, and they bake their own bread daily. If you wish to do your own cooking, ask about this when booking, and bring your own stove and food, as little is available in Michel and Jesse's small store on the premises. There are several lovely waterfalls nearby where you can swim, and in the evening everybody sits around the kava bowl and swaps stories. As there are never more than 20 guests here at a time, it gets very chummy. The snorkeling right off Albert's beach is excellent, and scuba with **Naiqoro Divers** (run by Ezra with the help of

Albert's sons Bruce and Julian) is F$50/70 for one/two tank boat dives, plus F$15 a day for equipment. Shore dives are F$10 a tank if you have your own gear. The equipment is new, the prices good, and these guys know their waters.

The easiest way to get there from Suva is by boat on the *Gurawa* or *Bulou-ni-Ceva*, which will bring you directly to Albert's Place or to Kavala Bay (a good hour west of Albert's on foot). Albert will pick you up at Vunisea Airport at F$55 for the first one or two plus F$25 for each additional person for the two-hour boat ride (these prices are fixed, so don't bother bargaining). Be sure to let him know you're coming. It's wise to allow plenty of time coming and going, so plan a stay at Albert's Place early on in your visit to Fiji so you don't have to be in a big rush to leave. People rave about this property—just don't expect luxuries like electricity at those prices! Budget.

The **Nukubalavu Adventure Resort** (Box 11522, Suva; tel. 520-089, fax 308-686) faces a two-km beach on the north side of Kadavu, between Albert's and Kavala Bay. Originally a backpacker camp, the resort has been upgraded and two-week dive vacationers are now the target market. With electricity, hot water, and private baths installed, rates for the five standard *bures* are F$50/75/105 single/double/triple, while the four deluxe units cost F$86/120/155. The 12-bed dorm is F$25 pp. The three-meal package is another F$60. Add 10% tax to all rates, plus another five percent if you pay by credit card. Scuba diving costs F$65/125/335 one/two/six tanks for boat dives or F$85 for night dives, plus F$25 for equipment rental, and a PADI certification course is offered at F$400. Snorkeling from the boat is F$25 including gear. The gorgeous Great Astrolabe Reef is only a five-minute boat ride away, and Nukubalavu claims to have purchased the exclusive right to dive on 50 different sites there! In any case, it's cheaper here than at the Matana Resort, though they don't have the same kind of boats available. The Nukubalavu launch can pick you up at Vunisea airport (F$35 pp each way with a two-person minimum), or come on by boat, which will drop you directly at the resort. (Incidentally, there's intense rivalry between Nukubalavu and Albert's Place, so take whatever you hear from one side or the other with a grain of salt.) Book-ings are handled by their Suva office (tel. 314-554) on the 2nd floor of Pacific House, Butt and MacArthur Streets. Inexpensive.

Not to be confused with the Matana Resort is a newer resort called **Matava, The Astrolabe Hideaway** (Mark O'Brien, Box 63, Vunisea; tel. 336-098, fax 336-099), a 30-minute walk east of Kadavu village and almost opposite tiny Waya Island. The beach in front of Matava is rather muddy and shallow but the snorkeling off Waya is fine. Organized snorkeling trips are F$12, plus $8 if you need a mask and snorkel. Three thatched *bures* with private bath cost F$68 single or double, four doubles with shared bath at F$35, and two quads at F$45. The quads are also used as five-bed dorms at F$17 pp, or you can camp at F$8 pp. A deluxe oceanview *bure* with private bath is F$90 double. The meal plan is F$30 pp. Add 10% tax to all rates at Matava. Scuba diving is available at F$40/75/350 for one/two/10 tanks, plus F$20 for equipment. Night dives are F$50. PADI open-water certification is F$350. Kayaks, canoes, and sailboards are for rent at F$10 a day. You can be picked up from Albert's Place at F$10 pp, or pay F$22 per each way for boat transfers from the airport. Budget to inexpensive.

Accommodations on Ono

Jona's Paradise Resort (Box 15447, Suva; tel. 315-889, fax 315-992), at Vabea at the southern tip of Ono Island, offers accommodation in five traditional beach *bures* at F$65/110/150 single/double/triple, or camping at F$30 pp (minimum stay three nights). Children under 12 are welcome at F$25 in the parents *bure* or F$15 in a tent. All prices include three tasty meals but you might bring a few snack foods with you. It's a small, family-style resort with a steep white-sand beach, great snorkeling (hundreds of clownfish in crystal-clear water). Dive Kadavu has recently opened a base at the resort (see the Matana Beach Resort listing above for scuba rates). Boat trips are F$65/100 per half/full day, and you can also go hiking in the hills. Husband Jona is the best fisherman around (expect fresh fish every day and mud crab occasionally), wife Ledua is a super cook, young son Veita is an expert guide, and grandfather Villame is a master builder. One reader called this place "the image of paradise." The ferries *Gurawa* and

Bulou-ni-Ceva drop passengers here once or twice a week, or you can arrange to be collected at Vunisea airport (F$50 pp each way). In Suva, book stays at Jona's at Global Air Services (tel. 315-889), 3 Ellery Street. Otherwise call Dive Kadavu. Budget.

A Canadian company plans to build a new 50-*bure* upmarket hotel called the **Yaukuve Vacation Resort** on Yaukuvelevu Island in the Astrolabe Lagoon north of Ono.

Other Practicalities

Vunisea has no restaurants, but a coffee shop at the airstrip opens mornings, and two general stores sell canned goods. A woman at the market serves tea and scones when the market is open, Tues.-Saturday. Buy *waka* at the coop store for formal presentations to village hosts.

No banks are to be found on Kadavu, so change enough money before coming (and don't leave it unattended in your room or tent). Occasional carriers ply the 78 km of roads on Kadavu, but no buses.

Getting There

Air Fiji arrives from Suva twice a day (F$92) and **Sunflower Airlines** has daily flights from Nadi (F$126). Be sure to reconfirm your return flight immediately upon arrival. Only Reece's Place meets all flights—boat pickups by the resorts on north Kadavu and Ono must be prearranged. The speedboats to north Kadavu are usually without safety equipment or roofs, and in rough weather everything could get wet. No road connects Vunisea to north Kadavu.

Boats arrive at Vunisea from Suva about twice a week, calling at villages along the north coast. The MV *Gurawa* of **Whippy's Shipping Co.** (tel. 311-507 or 340-015) leaves Suva for Ono and northern Kadavu Friday at 0600 (F$40 pp), returning to Suva on Saturday morning. Ask if lunch is included in the fare. The MV *Bulou-ni-Ceva* of the **Kadavu Shipping Co.** (tel. 311-766) also plies between Suva and Kadavu once or twice a week. Take seasickness precautions before boarding. For details turn to **Transportation** in the Suva section.

THE LOMAIVITI GROUP

The Lomaiviti (or central Fiji) Group lies in the Koro Sea near the heart of the archipelago, east of Viti Levu and south of Vanua Levu. Of its nine main volcanic islands, Gau, Koro, and Ovalau are among the largest in Fiji. Lomaiviti's climate is moderate, neither as wet and humid as Suva, nor as dry and hot as Nadi. The population is mostly Fijian, engaged in subsistence agriculture and copra making.

The old capital island, Ovalau, is by far the best-known and most-visited island of the group, and several small islands south of Ovalau on the way to Suva bear popular backpackers' resorts. Naigani also has a tourist resort of its own, but Koro and Gau are seldom visited, due to a lack of facilities for visitors. Ferries ply the Koro Sea to Ovalau, while onward ferries run to Vanua Levu a couple of times a week.

OVALAU ISLAND

Ovalau, a large volcanic island just east of Viti Levu, is the main island of the Lomaiviti Group. Almost encircled by high peaks, the Lovoni Valley in the center of Ovalau is actually the island's volcanic crater and about the only flat land. The crater's rim is pierced by the Bureta River, which escapes through a gap to the southeast. The highest peak is 626-meter Nadelaiovalau (meaning, the top of Ovalau), behind Levuka. Luckily Ovalau lacks the magnificent beaches found elsewhere in Fiji, which has kept the package-tour crowd away, and upmarket scuba divers have many better places to go, so it's still one of the most peaceful, pleasant, and picturesque historic places to visit in the South Pacific.

Levuka

The town of Levuka on Ovalau's east side was Fiji's capital until the shift to Suva in 1882. Founded as a whaling settlement in 1830, Levuka became the main center for European traders in Fiji, and a British consul was appointed in 1857. The cotton boom of the 1860s brought new settlers, and Levuka quickly grew into a boisterous town with more than 50 hotels and taverns along Beach Street. Escaped convicts and debtors fleeing creditors in Australia swelled the throng, until it was said that a ship could find the reef passage into Levuka by following the empty gin bottles floating out on the tide. The honest traders felt the need for a stable government, so in 1871 Levuka became capital of Cakobau's Kingdom of Fiji. The disorders continued, with extremist elements forming a "Ku Klux Klan," defiant of any form of Fijian authority.

On 10 October 1874, a semblance of decorum came as Fiji was annexed by Great Britain and a municipal council was formed in 1877. British rule soon put a damper on the wild side of the blackbirding. Ovalau's central location seemed ideal for trade, and sailing boats from Lau or Vanua Levu could easily enter the port on the southeast trades. Yet the lush green hills that rise behind the town were to be its downfall, as colonial planners saw that there was no room for the expansion of their capital, and in August 1882 Gov. Sir Arthur Gordon moved his staff to Suva. Hurricanes in 1888 and 1895 destroyed much of early Levuka, with the north end of town around the present Anglican church almost flattened, and many of Levuka's devastated buildings were not replaced.

Levuka remained the collection center for the copra trade right up until 1957, but the town seemed doomed when that industry, too, moved to a new mill in Suva. But with the establishment of a fishing industry in 1964 Levuka revived, and today it's is a minor educational center, the headquarters of Lomaiviti Province, and a low-impact tourist center. There's a public electricity supply.

The false-fronted buildings and covered sidewalks along Beach Street give this somnolent town of 4,000 mostly Fijian or part-Fijian inhabitants a 19th-century, Wild West feel. From the waterfront, let your eyes follow the horizon from right to left to view the islands of Gau, Batiki, Nairai, Wakaya, Koro, and Makogai, respectively. Levuka's a perfect base for excursions into the mountains, along the winding coast, or out to the barrier reef a kilometer offshore.

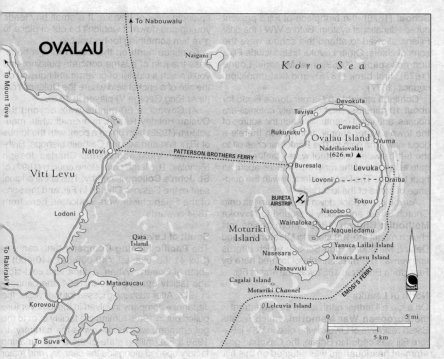

It's customary to say "Good morning," *"Bula,"* or simply "Hello" to people you meet while strolling around Levuka, especially on the back streets, and the locals have been rather put off by tourists who failed to do so. This is one of the little adverse effects of tourism, and a very unnecessary one at that.

Sights

Near Queen's Wharf is the old Morris Hedstrom store, erected by Percy Morris and Maynard Hedstrom in 1880s, great-granddaddy of today's Pacific-wide Morris Hedstrom chain. The store closed when the lease expired in 1979 and the building was turned over to the National Trust for Fiji. In 1981 the facility reopened as the **Levuka Community Center** (tel. 440-356; closed Sunday; admission F$2) with a museum and library, where cannibal forks vie with war clubs and clay pots for your attention. The many old photos of the town in the museum are fascinating, and a

side door leads into Patterson Gardens, a pleasant place to sit and take in the scene.

Stroll north along Levuka's sleepy waterfront to the **Church of the Sacred Heart,** erected by French Marist priests who arrived in 1858. The church's square clock tower was added in 1898 to commemorate the first priest, Father Breheret. The green neon cross on the stone tower lines up with another green light farther up the hill to guide mariners into port. Go through the gate behind the church to the formidable **Marist Convent School** (1892), originally a girls school operated by the sisters and still a primary school.

Totogo Lane leads north from the convent to a small bridge over Totogo Creek and the **Ovalau Club** (1904), adjoining the old **Town Hall** (1898), also known as Queen Victoria Memorial Hall, and the **Masonic Lodge** (1913), founded as "Little Polynesia" in 1875.

Recross the bridge and follow Garner Jones Road west up the creek to the **Levuka Public**

School (1879), the birthplace of Fiji's present public educational system. Before WW I the only Fijians allowed to attend this school were the sons of chiefs. Other Levuka firsts include Fiji's first newspaper (1869), first Masonic Lodge (1875), first bank (1876), and first municipal council (1877).

Continue straight up Garner Jones Road for about 10 minutes, past the lovely colonial-era houses, and you'll eventually reach the source of the town's water supply, from which there's a good view. The path to **The Peak** branches off to the left between the steel water tank and the gate at the end of the main trail. It takes about an hour to scale The Peak, preferably with the guidance of some of the local kids.

As you come back down the hill, turn left onto Church Street and follow it around to **Navoka Methodist Church** (1862). From beside this church mount the 199 steps to **Mission Hill** and Delana Methodist High School, which affords fine views. The mission school formed here by Rev. John Binner in 1852 was the first in Fiji.

North of Levuka

On a low hill farther north along the waterfront is the **European War Memorial,** which recalls British residents of Levuka who died in WW I. Before Fiji was ceded to Britain, the Cakobau government headquarters was situated on this hill. **Holy Redeemer Anglican Church** (1904), beyond, has period stained-glass windows.

Follow the coastal road north from Levuka to a second yellow bridge, where you'll see the **old Methodist church** (1869) on the left. Ratu Seru Cakobau worshipped here, and in the small cemetery behind the church is the grave of the first U.S. consul to Fiji, John Brown Williams (1810-1860). For the story of Williams's activities, see the chapter introduction. Across the bridge and beneath a large *dilo* tree is the tomb of an old king of Levuka. The large house in front of the tree is the residence of the present Tui Levuka.

Directly above is **Gun Rock,** which was used as a target in 1849 to show Cakobau the efficacy of a ship's cannon so he might be more considerate to resident Europeans. The early Fijians had a fort atop the Rock to defend themselves against the Lovoni hill tribes. Ask permission of the Tui Levuka (the "Roko") or a member of his household to climb Gun Rock for a splendid view of Levuka. If a small boy leads you up and down, it wouldn't be out of place to give him something for his trouble.

Continue north on the road, round a bend, pass the ruin of a large concrete building, and you'll reach a cluster of government housing on the site of a cricket field where the Duke of York (later King George V) played in 1878.

At Cawaci, a 30-minute walk beyond the Ovalau Holiday Resort, is a small white mausoleum (1922) high up on a point with the tombs of Fiji's first and second Catholic bishops, Bishop Julien Vidal and Bishop Charles Joseph Nicholas. The large coral stone church (1897) of **St. John's College** is nearby. This is the original seat of the Catholic Church in Fiji, and the sons of the Fijian chiefs were educated here from 1894 onwards.

South of Levuka

The **Pacific Fishing Company** tuna cannery (Box 41, Levuka; tel. 440-005, fax 440-400) is south of Queen's Wharf. A Japanese cold-storage facility opened here in 1964, the cannery in 1975. After sustaining losses for four years, the Japanese company involved in the joint venture pulled out in 1986, turning the facility over to the government, which now owns the cannery. In 1989 a F$2-million state-of-the-art can-making factory opened alongside the cannery, and major improvements to the wharf, freezer, storage, and other facilities were completed in 1992. The plant is supplied with albacore tuna caught in Kiribati and Solomons waters by Taiwanese longline fishing boats, and with skipjack and yellowfin by pole-and-line ships of the government-owned Ika Corporation. For both environmental and quality-control reasons, fish caught with nets are not accepted here. Most of the F$50 million worth of canned tuna produced each year is marketed in Britain by Sainsbury and John West, and in Canada by B.C. Packers. A thousand residents of Ovalau have jobs directly related to tuna canning, and the government has heavily subsidized the operation to keep it going.

A little farther along is the **Cession Monument,** where the Deed of Cession, which made Fiji a British colony, was signed by Chief Cakobau in 1874. The traditional *bure* on the other side of the road was used by Prince Charles during his 1970 visit to officiate at Fiji's independence. It's now the venue of provincial council meetings.

One of Fiji's most rewarding hikes begins at Draiba village, a kilometer south of the Cession Monument. A road to the right just after a small bridge and before four single-story apartment blocks marks the start of the 4.5-hour hike through enchanting forests and across clear streams to **Lovoni** village. Go straight back on this side road till you see an overgrown metal scrapyard on your right, near the end of the road. Walk through the middle of the scrapyard and around to the right of a decrepit tin-roofed building. The unmarked Lovoni trail begins at the foot of the hill, just beyond this building.

The Lovoni trail is no longer used by the locals and requires attentiveness to follow, so consider Epi's Midland Tour if you're not an experienced hiker. Be sure to reach Lovoni before 1500 to be able to catch the last bus back to Levuka. In 1855 the fierce Lovoni tribe, the Ovalau, burned Levuka, and they continued to threaten the town right up until 1871 when they were finally captured during a truce and sold to European planters as laborers. In 1875 the British government allowed the survivors to return to their valley, where their descendants live today.

If you forgo this hike and continue on the main road, you'll come to an old **cemetery** a little south of Draiba. A few kilometers farther is the **Devil's Thumb**, a dramatic volcanic plug towering above **Tokou** village, one of the scenic highlights of Fiji. Catholic missionaries set up a printing press at Tokou in 1889 to produce gospel lessons in Fijian. In the center of the village is a sculpture of a lion made by one of the early priests. It's five km back to Levuka.

Wainaloka village on the southwest side of Ovalau is inhabited by descendants of Solomon Islanders from the Lau Lagoon region who were blackbirded in Fiji more than a century ago.

Sports and Recreation
Ovalau Divers (Box 145, Levuka; tel. 440-095) operates out of Cafe Levuka. They offer diving on seven shipwrecks around Levuka at F$55/80 for one/two dives. **Ovalau Watersports**, run by Ovalau Tours and Transport, also offers diving.

Most of the hotels (including the Royal) will arrange boats for reef snorkeling at F$6 pp, or for

fishing at F$8 pp, upon prior notice. At high tide the river mouth near the Royal Hotel is an extremely popular swimming hole for the local kids (and some tourists). The rest of the day locals cool off by just sitting in the water fully dressed.

PRACTICALITIES

Accommodations
There's a good choice of budget places to stay around Levuka (and thankfully no luxury resorts). The **Colonial Inn** (Box 50, Levuka; tel. 440-057), on Convent Rd., has six double rooms above their restaurant at F$15/25 single/double, and dorm beds at F$10 pp, a cooked breakfast included. There's no hot water. Shoestring.

Another good bet is the **Old Capital Inn** (tel. 440-013) on Beach Street. The 15 fan-cooled rooms cost the same as rooms at Colonial Inn (where guests from both places take their breakfast). A separate cottage with cooking facilities is F$20/28/35 single/double/triple—good value. The quality of the beds in the dorm section here is poor, but a cool breeze blowing in from the east keeps the mosquitoes away. Budget.

Mavida Guesthouse (Box 4, Levuka; tel. 440-477) on Beach St., which has been functioning since 1869, is Fiji's oldest guesthouse. This old-fashioned English bed and breakfast owned by Patterson Brothers Shipping occupies a spacious colonial house on the waterfront near the Levuka Club. The 12 rooms are F$16/28 single/double, or F$9 in the dormitory (F$12 if you want a mosquito net), a cooked breakfast included. You can order an excellent dinner here. It's worth asking to see the room beforehand as all are different, and their nicest rooms go for F$30 double. Ask for a mosquito net. Unfortunately the Patterson Brothers bus that parks directly in front of the guesthouse every night cancels out some of the flavor. Budget.

For the full Somerset Maugham flavor, stay at the 15-room **Royal Hotel** (Box 47, Levuka; tel. 440-024, fax 440-174). Originally built in 1852 and rebuilt by Captain David Robbie in 1913 after a fire in the 1890s, this is Fiji's oldest regular hotel, run by the Ashley family since 1927. In the lounge, ceiling fans revolve above the rattan sofas and potted plants, and the fan-cooled

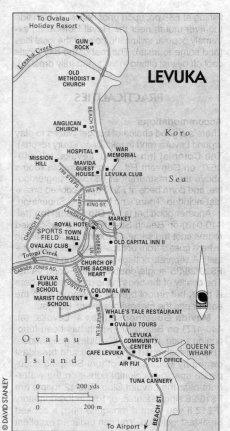

LEVUKA

To Ovalau
Holiday Resort

GUN
ROCK

Levuka Creek

OLD
METHODIST
CHURCH

ANGLICAN
CHURCH

Koro

HOSPITAL

WAR
MEMORIAL

MISSION
HILL

195 STEPS

MAVIDA
GUEST
HOUSE

LEVUKA CLUB

Sea

HILL RD.

CHAPEL ST.

KING ST.

LANGHAM

MARKET

BEACH ST.

CHURCH ST.

ROYAL HOTEL

SPORTS
FIELD

TOWN
HALL

NOBLES

OLD CAPITAL INN II

OVALAU CLUB

Totoga Creek

GABNER JONES RD.

CHURCH OF
THE SACRED
HEART

LEVUKA
PUBLIC
SCHOOL

CONVENT

TOTOGA

COLONIAL INN

MARIST CONVENT
SCHOOL

WHALE'S TALE RESTAURANT

OVALAU TOURS

BENTLEY'S LN.

O v a l a u

LEVUKA
COMMUNITY
CENTER

CAFE LEVUKA

AIR FIJI

POST OFFICE

QUEEN'S
WHARF

I s l a n d

MOON

TUNA CANNERY

0   200 yds

0   200 m

BEACH ST.

To Airport

© DAVID STANLEY

rooms upstairs with private bath and minifridge are pleasant, with much-needed mosquito nets provided. Each room is in a different style. It's F$18/28/33 single/double/triple in the main building. There are also three a/c rooms with shared cooking facilities in a garden building at F$55 double, plus one large family cottage capable of accommodating 11 persons in five rooms at F$77 for the unit. The most deluxe accommodations are the two new self-catering cottages facing Beach St., which go for F$77 double. The 11-bed dormitory near the bar is F$10 pp. Checkout time is 1000, but you can arrange to stay until 1500 by paying another 50% of the

daily rate (no credit cards accepted). Hotel staff will do your laundry for F$5. Everybody loves this place, but don't order dinner (F$8) as the food isn't highly rated. The bar, beer garden, snooker tables, dart boards, and videos are strictly for guests only. The colonial atmosphere and anachronistic prices make it about the best value in Fiji. Budget to inexpensive.

The **Sailor's Home** (Ovalau Tours and Transport, Box 149, Levuka; tel. 440-611, fax 440-405) is a restored 1870s house with two rooms at F$99 single or double (children under 12 free). There's a fully equipped kitchen and this old colonial house might just be the nicest place to stay in Fiji. Moderate.

Around the Island

A good choice for families is the **Ovalau Holiday Resort** (Stephen and Rosemary Diston, Box 113, Levuka; tel. 440-329, fax 440-019) on a rocky beach at Vuma, four km north of Levuka (taxi F$5). *Bures* are F$22/35/45 single/double/triple, or pay F$8 pp in the dorm. Camping is F$5 pp, with the use of the dorm facilities. Cooking facilities, fridge, and hot showers are provided, and there's the Bula Beach Bar in a converted whaler's cottage. Given sufficient advance notice the restaurant does some fine home cooking. Though often dry, the swimming pool is the only one on Ovalau, and the snorkeling around here is good. It's a nice place for an afternoon at the beach even if you prefer to stay in Levuka. Budget.

Ovalau Tours and Transport (Box 149, Levuka; tel. 440-611, fax 440-405) books accommodations at **Devokula village** at the north end of Ovalau, 11 km from Levuka. Guests sleep on mats under mosquito nets in one of seven authentic Fijian *bures* at F$99/155 single/double including all meals and activities. If you're willing to share the *bure* with other visitors it's F$55 pp. The only concession to the modern world here are the flush toilets and showers, otherwise it's the full Fijian experience. Transfers to Devokula are F$10 pp from Levuka or F$25 pp from the airport (minimum of two). Moderate to expensive.

Food

Few of the guesthouses in Levuka provide cooking facilities, but a half dozen small restaurants face Beach Street. All of these places are patronized mostly by foreigners, and prices are higher than what you may have paid in Suva or Lautoka, but with luck you'll enjoy some superior meals. In fact, many visitors seem to spend most of their time hopping from restaurant to restaurant.

Cafe Levuka (tel. 440-095), opposite the Community Center, has F$6 dinner specials daily until 2000. It's a good place to find out what's happening around town over coffee and cakes. Their fruit pancakes are great for breakfast.

Kim's Restaurant (tel. 440-059), also known as Pak Kum Loong, upstairs in a building near Court's Furniture Store, has a selection of Chinese dishes for less than F$5. It's a good place to come for lunch weekdays as several inexpensive dishes are kept in a glass warmer at the entrance (meals ordered from the menu are individually prepared). You can dine on their breezy front terrace with a view of the waterfront.

The **Whale's Tale Restaurant** (tel. 440-235) on Beach St. is a favorite for its real home cooking at medium prices. A cooked breakfast with coffee will be F$6.60, buttered pasta for lunch costs F$5.50, and the three-course dinner special with a choice from among five main plates is F$10. They're fully licensed so you can get a beer with your meal, and their specially percolated coffee is the best in town. They sell bags of kava, Fijian handicrafts, and lovely tapa greeting cards.

The **Sea Site Restaurant** (tel. 440-553), a bit north of Whale's Tale, is basic, overpriced, and not recommended.

The **Colonial Inn** (tel. 440-057), on Convent Rd., has an all-you-can-eat dinner Sunday at 1830 (F$7). There's a good selection of items in their buffet, and cold beer is available.

Entertainment

Despite the Members Only sign, you're welcome to enter the **Ovalau Club** (tel. 440-102), said to be the oldest membership club in the South Pacific. You'll meet genuine South Seas characters here, and the place is brimming with atmosphere. Ask the bartender to show you the framed letter from Count Felix von Luckner, the WW I German sea wolf. Von Luckner left the letter and some money at the unoccupied residence of a trader on Katafaga Island in the Lau Group, from which he took some provisions. In the letter, Count von Luckner identifies himself as Max Pemberton, an English writer on a sporting cruise through the Pacific.

A good place for sunsets is the **Levuka Club** (tel. 440-272) on Beach St., which has a nice back yard with picnic tables beside the water. It's less visited by tourists and a better choice than the Ovalau Club if you only want a quick beer.

Services

The Westpac Bank (tel. 440-346) and the National Bank (tel. 440-300) on Beach St. change traveler's checks.

Cafe Levuka will wash, dry, and fold your laundry within three hours for F$6.

The Ovalau Club at Levuka was once the reserve of British colonials. Although the sign by the door says Private—Members Only, the bartenders will sign you in.

Public toilets are available across the street from the National Bank.

Information

The Tourist Information Desk at the Levuka Community Center (tel. 440-356) should have information on the offshore island resorts and various land tours around Ovalau.

Lisa at the Whale's Tale Restaurant (tel. 440-235) will be happy to give you her frank opinion of the offshore resorts—invaluable when planning a trip. Cafe Levuka (tel. 440-095) maintains a "Tourist Information Book" containing current information about almost every aspect of travel around Ovalau. The restaurant staffs are probably the people most likely to give you a straight answer to any question you may have about Levuka. Cafe Levuka also runs a one-for-one book exchange.

Transportation

Air Fiji (tel. 440-139), across the street from the Levuka Community Center, has two or three flights a day between Bureta Airport and Suva (F$54). Sunflower Airlines has an office next to Ovalau Tours on Beach St., but no flights from Ovalau at present. The Ovalau Tours minibus from Levuka to the airstrip is F$3 pp (a taxi will run F$17).

Inquire at **Patterson Brothers** (tel. 440-125), beside the market on Beach St., about the direct ferry from Ovalau to Nabouwalu, Vanua Levu, via Natovi. The connecting bus departs Levuka Mon.-Sat. at about 0500. At Nabouwalu, there's an onward bus to Labasa, but bookings must be made in advance (F$51 straight through).

The bus/ferry/bus service between Suva and Levuka was discussed previously under **Transportation** in the Suva section. Two competing services are available, each taking just under five hours right through, and costing around F$24. The Patterson Brothers combination involves an express bus from Levuka to Buresala daily except Sunday at 0500, a 45-minute ferry ride from Buresala to Natovi, then the same bus on to Suva (change at Korovou for Lautoka). Bicycles are carried free on the ferry. The other choice is the *Emosi Express* leaving Queen's Wharf, Levuka, at 0900 on Monday, Wednesday, and Friday to Bau Landing, then a minibus to Suva (arriving at 1400). Southbound you can get off in Nausori and connect with the Sunbeam Transport bus to Lautoka at 1400. Inquire at the Old Capital Inn. From Levuka, Emosi's boat is more conveniently timed and there's a brief visit to Leleuvia Island, where free stopovers are possible. Advance bookings are required on the Patterson Brothers ferry/bus service, but not on Emosi's boat. Use a different service each way for a scenic circle trip from Suva.

Both taxis and carriers park across the street from the Church of the Sacred Heart in Levuka. Due to steep hills on the northwest side of Ovalau, there isn't a bus right around the island. Carriers leave Levuka for Rukuruku village weekdays at 0745, 1145, and 1700, Saturday at 1145 and 1430 (F$1.50) along a beautiful, hilly road. During the school holidays only the 1145 trip may operate. There are also occasional buses and carriers to Lovoni (F$1). There's no service on Sunday.

Tours

Epi's Midland Tour is a guided hike to Lovoni that departs Levuka Mon.-Sat. around 1000 (F$15 pp including lunch). You hike over and return by truck (or you can just go both ways by truck if you don't wish to walk). The route is steep and rugged footwear is essential. At Lovoni you can go for a swim in the river or meet the village chief. Epi is an enthusiastic young guy very knowledgeable about forest plants and there have been very good reports about his tour. His reservations books are at the Royal Hotel reception and at Cafe Levuka. Recommended.

Ovalau Tours and Transport (Box 149, Levuka; tel. 440-611, fax 440-405) operates a day tour to Devokula village. It's an intensive short course in Fijian culture with a kava presentation, handicraft demonstration, and many village activities explained. There's time to snorkel, and a traditional lunch is included in the F$25 pp price (minimum of six). The same company has a "tea and talanoa" program (F$25 for one or F$17.50 pp for two) which arranges for visitors to meet local residents in their own homes and gardens for tea and conversation. It's not at all "touristy" and you may end up revisiting your host as a friend outside the organized format. Ovalau Tours' historical town walking tour is F$15 for one or F$10 pp for two or more. They also have sea kayaking, trekking, and scuba diving tours.

If you wish to organize your own tour, you can hire a small carrier or taxi around the island for F$50.

ISLANDS OFF OVALAU

Yanuca Lailai Island

It was on tiny Yanuca Lailai Island, just off the south end of Ovalau, that the first 463 indentured Indian laborers to arrive in Fiji landed from the ship *Leonidas* on 14 May 1879. To avoid the introduction of cholera or smallpox into Fiji, the immigrants spent two months in quarantine on Yanuca Lailai. Later Nukulau Island off Suva became Fiji's main quarantine station.

It's possible to stay on Yanuca Lailai at **Lost Island Resort** (Box 131, Levuka). *Bure* accommodations cost F$26 double, camping F$12 pp, and three meals a day are another F$14 (F$7 for the *lovo* special). Reef tours from Lost Island are possible, and transfers from Levuka cost F$5 pp each way. It's also possible to visit on a day-trip from Levuka at F$20 pp, lunch included. For information contact Levi through the Tourist Information Desk at the Levuka Community Center (tel. 440-356). Budget.

Moturiki Island

Small outboards to Moturiki Island depart Naqueledamu Landing most afternoons. The finest beaches are on the east side of Moturiki. Camping is officially discouraged, but possible.

Caqalai Island

Caqalai (pronounced "Thanggalai") is owned by the Methodist Church of Fiji, which operates a small backpackers' resort on this palm-fringed island. The 12 *bures* are F$25 pp (triple occupancy), or camp for F$20 pp, three good meals included. You can use the communal fridge. It's primitive but adequate, and the island and people are great. Dress up for Sunday service in the village church. There's good snorkeling all around the island, and you can wade to Snake Island, where banded sea snakes congregate. Information should be available at Cafe Levuka (boat from Levuka Monday, Wednesday, and Friday mornings at F$10 pp each way). Those already staying on Caqalai can make shopping trips to Levuka at F$5 return. Budget.

Leleuvia Island

Emosi Yee Show of Levuka's Old Capitol Inn runs a small backpacker resort (Box 15212, Suva; tel. 301-584) on Leleuvia, a lovely isolated 17-hectare reef island with nothing but coconut trees, fine sandy beaches, and a ramshackle assortment of tourist huts scattered across the island. Accommodations run F$15 pp in the dorm, F$20/30 single/double in a thatched hut, F$30/45 in a wooden bungalow, or F$12 pp if you camp. Water is in short supply on Leleuvia, and bathing is with a bucket of brackish water. Food is extra and meals are served à la carte with the most expensive thing on the menu costing F$6. The small shop sells candy, cake, and drinks. The owners send as many people as they can to Leleuvia, and it can get crowded (pick Caqalai instead if you'd rather do your own thing).

Leleuvia is popular among backpackers who like to drink beer and party a lot (live Fijian music in the evening), so don't come expecting a rest. Actually, it sort of depends on who is on the island at the time. Sometimes it's great fun with lots of neat, congenial people, but other times the scene is dominated by "groupies," and newcomers are excluded. One reader called it "a Boy Scout holiday camp." Peace returns around 2230 when the generator switches off and everyone falls asleep. Emosi himself is a genuine character you'll enjoy meeting.

Plenty of activities are laid on, especially reef trips by boat (F$5 pp) and scuba diving (F$55/80 one/two tanks on the same day), and on Sunday they'll even take you to church! For a nominal amount they'll drop you off on one-tree "Honeymoon Island." Leleuvia is the only Lomaiviti resort offering scuba diving, and the resident instructors have taught diving to quite a few guests. This isn't surprising because at F$340, it's one of the least expensive PADI open-water certification courses available in Fiji (this price only applies if several people are taking lessons at the same time). Many backpackers learn to dive at Leleuvia before going to Taveuni where such courses are almost F$100 more expensive. If you just want a taste of diving, try their resort course. The snorkeling is also excellent though the sea is sometimes cold. Chances are, you'll love Leleuvia.

Getting there is easy on the *Emosi Express* from Levuka at 0900 Monday, Wednesday, and Friday. From Suva, you can catch the bus at 35

Gordon St. daily at 1200 and arrive via Bau Landing (F$35 roundtrip). Leleuvia is a free stopover on all of Emosi's regular trips between Levuka and Suva. Day-trips to Leleuvia from Levuka with lunch (F$22) are also offered. All bookings should be made through the Old Capital Inn in Levuka, or at Emosi Ferry Service (tel. 313-366), 35 Gordon St., Suva. Budget.

OTHER ISLANDS OF THE LOMAIVITI GROUP

Makogai

Makogai shares a figure-eight-shaped barrier reef with neighboring Wakaya. The anchorage is in Dalice Bay on the northwest side of the island. From 1911 to 1969 this was a leper colony staffed by Catholic nuns, and many of the old hospital buildings still stand. Some 4,500 patients sheltered here including many from various other Pacific island groups. Today Makogai is owned by the Department of Agriculture, which runs an experimental sheep farm here, with some 2,000 animals. A new breed obtained by crossing British and Caribbean sheep bears little wool and is intended as a source of mutton.

Wakaya

A high cliff on the west coast of Wakaya is known as Chieftain's Leap, for a young chief who threw himself over the edge to avoid capture by his foes. In those days a hill fort sat at Wakaya's highest point so local warriors could scan the horizon for unfriendly cannibals. Chief Cakobau sold Wakaya to Europeans in 1840, and it has since had many owners. In 1862 David Whippy set up Fiji's first sugar mill on Wakaya.

The German raider Count Felix von Luckner was captured on Wakaya during WW I. His ship, the *Seeadler,* had foundered on a reef at Maupihaa in the Society Islands on 2 August 1917. The 105 survivors (prisoners included) camped on Maupihaa, while on 23 August von Luckner and five men set out in an open boat to capture a schooner and continue the war. On 21 September 1917 they found a suitable ship at Wakaya. Their plan was to go aboard pretending to be passengers and capture it, but a British officer and four Indian soldiers happened upon the scene. Not wishing to go against the rules of

chivalry and fight in civilian clothes, the count gave himself up and was interned at Auckland as a prisoner of war. He later wrote a book, *The Sea Devil,* about his experiences.

In 1976 Canadian industrialist David Harrison Gilmour bought the island for US$3 million, and in 1990 he opened **The Wakaya Club** (Robert Miller, Box 15424, Suva; tel. 440-128, fax 440-406), with eight spacious cottages at US$1,275 double, all-inclusive (three-night minimum stay). Children under 16 are not accommodated. The snorkeling here is superb, and there's scuba diving, a nine-hole golf course, and an airstrip for charter flights (F$1,200 roundtrip per couple from Nadi). As you might expect at these prices (Fiji's highest!), it's all very tasteful and elegant—just ask Bill Gates, Pierce Brosnan, Carol Burnett, Michelle Pfeiffer, or Burt Reynolds. It's a hideaway for the rich and famous rather than a social scene. A third of Wakaya has been subdivided into 100 parcels, which are available as homesites at US$550,000 and up; red deer imported from New Caledonia run wild across the rest. Luxury.

Batiki

Batiki has a large interior lagoon of brackish water surrounded by mudflats. Four Fijian villages are on Batiki and you can walk around the island in four hours. Waisea Veremaibau of Yavu village on the north side of the island takes guests at F$15 pp a day. Fine baskets are made on Batiki. Due to hazardous reefs, there's no safe anchorage for ships.

Nairai

Seven Fijian villages are found on this 336-meter-high island between Koro and Gau. The inhabitants are known for their woven handicrafts. Hazardous reefs stretch out in three directions, and in 1808 the brigantine *Eliza* was wrecked here. Among the survivors was Charles Savage, who served as a mercenary for the chiefs of Bau for five years until falling into the clutches of Vanua Levu cannibals.

Koro

Koro is an eight-by-16-km island shaped like a shark's tooth. A ridge traverses the island from northeast to southwest, reaching 561 meters near the center. High jungle-clad hillsides drop sharply to the coast. The top beach is along the south coast between Mundu and the lighthouse at Muanivanua Point. Among Koro's 14 large Fijian villages is Nasau, the government center halfway up the east coast. Koro kava is Fiji's finest.

Koro has an unusual inclined airstrip on the east side of the island near Namacu village. You land uphill, take off downhill. Air Fiji can bring you here from Suva four times a week (F$104), and several carriers meet the flights. The twice weekly Consort Shipping Line ferry *Spirit of Free Enterprise* plying between Suva and Savusavu/Taveuni ties up to the wharf near Muanivanua Point. The *"Sofe"* calls northbound on early Wednesday and Sunday mornings; the southbound trips stop at Koro late Monday and Thursday nights. The fare to/from Suva is F$25/44 deck/cabin one-way.

There are no hotels on Koro or Gau, so you'll have to stay with locals or ask permission to camp. On both islands your best bet is to wait till you meet someone from there, then ask them to write you a letter of introduction to their relatives back home on the island. It's always better to know someone before you arrive. Make it clear you're willing to pay your own way, then don't neglect to do so.

Gau

Gau is the fifth-largest island in Fiji, with 16 villages and 13 settlements. There's a barrier reef on the west coast, but only a fringing reef on the east. A hot-spring swimming pool is close to the P.W.D. depot at **Waikama**. From Waikama, hike along the beach and over the hills to **Somosomo** village. If you lose the way, look for the creek at the head of the bay and work your way up it until you encounter the trail. There's a bathing pool in Somosomo with emerald green water.

A road runs from Somosomo to **Sawaieke** village, where the Takalaigau, high chief of Gau, resides. The remnants of one of the only surviving pagan temples *(bure kalou)* in Fiji are beside the road at the junction in Sawaieke. The high stone mound is still impressive.

The coop and government station (hospital, post office, etc.) are at **Qarani** at the north end of Gau. Two ships a week arrive here from Suva on an irregular schedule, but there is no wharf so

© DAVID STANLEY

they anchor offshore. The wharf at **Waikama** is used only for government boats. The airstrip is on Katudrau Beach at the south end of Gau. The five weekly flights to/from Suva on Air Fiji are F$76 each way.

The **Nukuyaweni Outpost** (Kevin Wunrow, Bay of Angels, Gau Island, Private Mail Bag, Suva; tel./fax 448-112) is a wilderness luxury lodge, on a point a couple of km southwest of Somosomo. It's rather different than other exclusive resorts around Fiji as it has been designed as a sort of artists' hideaway. There's a "creation station" with everything a Picasso might desire, and a state-of-the-art recording studio is to be added a kilometer up the beach so visiting musicians can combine business with pleasure. Nukuyaweni's eight beachfront cottages with private grotto showers cost F$1,300 double including meals, drinks, taxes, and all activities (minimum stay four nights). There are also two deluxe cottages with private pools at F$1,750 double (seven-night minimum). Children under 16 are not admitted to this "Sanctuary for the Romantic Soul." The resort bar and library is up in the trees. Great snorkeling is available off their beach, and there's extraordinary diving in Nigali Passage, just 10 minutes away by boat (large schools of big fish and manta rays). Check their website for current information.

VANUA LEVU

Though only half as big as Viti Levu, 5,556-square-km Vanua Levu ("Great Land") has much to offer. The transport is good, the scenery varied, the people warm and hospitable, and far fewer visitors reach this part of Fiji than heavily promoted Nadi/Sigatoka/Suva. Fijian villages are numerous all the way around the island—here you'll be able to experience real Fijian life, so it's well worth making the effort to visit Fiji's second-largest island.

The drier northwest side of Vanua Levu features sugarcane fields and pine forests, while on the damper southeast side copra plantations predominate, with a little cocoa around Natewa Bay (the biggest bay in the South Pacific). Toward the southeast the scenery is more a bucolic beauty of coconut groves dipping down toward the sea. Majestic bays cut into the island's south side, and one of the world's longest barrier reefs flanks the north coast. There are some superb locations here just waiting to be discovered, both above and below the waterline.

Fiji Indians live in the large market town of Labasa and the surrounding cane-growing area; most of the rest of Vanua Levu is Fijian. Together Vanua Levu, Taveuni, and adjacent islands form Fiji's Northern Division (often called simply "the north"), which is subdivided into three provinces: the west end of Vanua Levu is Bua Province; most of the north side of Vanua Levu is Macuata Province; and the southeast side of Vanua Levu and Taveuni make up Cakaudrove Province. You won't regret touring this area.

Nabouwalu

The ferry from Viti Levu ties up to the wharf at this friendly little government station (the headquarters of Bua Province), near the southern tip of Vanua Levu. The view from the wharf is picturesque, with Seseleka (421 meters) and, in good weather, Yadua Island visible to the northwest. Nabouwalu has a high-technology 24-hour electricity supply system based on windmills and solar panels installed in early 1998. Most of the 600 residents of this area are indigenous Fijians.

The large Patterson Brothers car ferry sails from Natovi on Viti Levu to Nabouwalu Tues.-Sat. around 0700 (four hours, F$33). The same boat departs Nabouwalu for Natovi Tues.-Sat. at 1130. At Natovi there are immediate ferry connections to/from Ovalau Island and buses to Suva. On Tuesday, Thursday, and Saturday at 1030 there's a direct Patterson Brothers ferry from Nabouwalu to Ellington Wharf near Rakiraki (F$33), where there are connections to Nananu-i-Ra Island and Lautoka. Patterson Brothers runs an express bus between Nabouwalu and Labasa for ferry passengers only (must be booked in conjunction with a ferry ticket). This bus takes only four hours to cover the 137 km to Labasa compared to the six hours required by the four regular buses, which make numerous detours and stops.

East of Nabouwalu

There's a 141-km road along the south coast of Vanua Levu from Nabouwalu to Savusavu, but eastbound buses only reach as far as Daria, westbound buses as far as Mount Kasi Gold Mine. The gap is covered by occasional carrier trucks. At Cogea, five km north of Daria, are some small hot springs the local people use for bathing.

The **Mount Kasi Gold Mine** near Dawara, in the hills above the west end of Savusavu Bay, 70 km from Savusavu, produced 60,000 ounces of gold between 1932 and 1946. Beginning in 1979 several companies did exploratory work in the area in hope of reviving the mine, and in 1996 it was recommissioned by Pacific Island Gold. In June 1998 the mine was forced to close and the 170 workers were laid off due to low gold prices on the world market. A few months later it was announced that the mine would reopen under new owners, Burdekin Resources. During the 1970s bauxite was mined in this area.

The only "official" place to stay along this coast is **Fiji's Hidden Paradise Eco Tourism Lodge** (Box 815, Young, NSW 2594, Australia; tel./fax 61-2/6382-4146), near Raviravi village, about 10 km south of Mt. Kasi. The three *bures* are about F$120 pp including meals. Lighting is by kerosene lamp. People come here to experience the people and land while retaining a bit of privacy. There's hiking, birdwatching, snorkeling, and cultural exchange with the villagers. Airport transfers from Savusavu are F$100 each way per car. In Savusavu, information should be available from Eco Divers or Sea Fiji Travel. Moderate.

The Road to Labasa
The twisting, tiring north coast bus ride from Nabouwalu to Labasa takes you past Fijian villages, rice paddies, and cane fields. The early sandalwood traders put in at **Bua Bay.** At Bua village on Bua Bay is a large suspension bridge and the dry open countryside west of Bua stretches out to Seseleka (421 meters).

Farther east the road passes a major rice-growing area and runs along the **Dreketi River,** Vanua Levu's largest. A rice mill at Dreketi and citrus project at Batiri are features of this area. The pavement begins near the junction with the road from Savusavu. In the Seaqaqa settlement area between Batiri and Labasa, about 60 square km of native land were cleared and planted with sugarcane and pine during the 1970s.

LABASA

Labasa is a busy Indian market town that services Vanua Levu's major cane-growing area. It's Fiji's fourth-largest town, with 25,000 inhabitants, four banks, and the Northern Division and Macuata Province headquarters. Vanua Levu's only sugar mill is here. Labasa was built on a delta where the shallow Labasa and Oawa rivers enter the sea; maritime transport is limited to small boats. Large ships must anchor off Malau, 11 km north, where Labasa's sugar harvest is loaded. Labasa's lack of an adequate port has hindered development.

Other than providing a good base from which to explore the surrounding countryside and an excellent choice of places to spend the night, Labasa has little to interest the average tourist. That's its main attraction: since few visitors come, there's adventure in the air, good food in the restaurants, and fun places to drink for males (a bit rowdy for females). It's not beautiful but it is real, and the bus ride that brings you here is great. This truly is the "friendly north."

If your time is very limited but you want to see a lot, catch a morning flight from Suva or Nadi to Labasa, then take an afternoon bus on to Savusavu, the nicest part of the trip. Otherwise stay in Savusavu and see Labasa as a long day-trip.

Sights
Labasa has an attractive riverside setting with one long main street lined with shops and restaurants. The park along the riverside near the Labasa Club is quite pleasant.

The **Labasa Sugar Mill,** beside the Oawa River two km east of town, opened in 1894. At the height of the crushing season May-Dec. there's usually a long line of trucks, tractors, and trains waiting to unload cane at the mill—a most picturesque sight. From the road here you get a view of **Three Sisters Hill** to the right.

Anyone with an interest in archaeology should take the two-km minibus ride to **Wasavula** on the southern outskirts of Labasa. Parallel stone platforms bearing one large monolith and several smaller ones are found among the coconut trees to the east of the road. This site (Fiji's first "national monument") is not well known, so just take the bus to Wasavula, get off, and ask. A small gift (F$2) should be given to anyone who shows you around. The Fijian villager who does so will assure you that the monoliths are growing in size!

Around Labasa
The **Snake Temple** (Naag Mandir) at Nagigi, 12 km northeast of Labasa, contains a large rock shaped like a cobra that—as at Wasavula—Hindu devotees swear is growing. Frequent buses pass Naag Mandir.

On the way back to Labasa from Nagigi ask to be dropped at Bulileka Road, just before the sugar mill. Here you can easily pick up a yellow-and-blue bus to the **hanging bridge,** a suspension footbridge at Bulileka, six km east of Labasa. Get off the Bulileka bus at Boca Urata where it turns around. The hanging bridge is 150 meters down the road from the place (ask). Cross the bridge and continue through the fields a few hundred meters to the paved road where you can catch another bus back to Labasa. The main reason for coming is to see this picturesque valley, so you may wish to walk part of the way back.

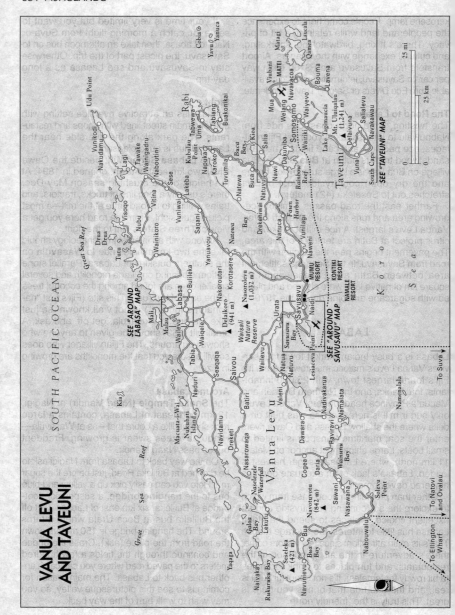

VANUA LEVU AND TAVEUNI

SOUTH PACIFIC OCEAN

Udu Point

Vunikodi
Nakudamu
Lagi
Tawake
Wainigadru
Naboutini
Sese
Vitina
Nubu
Visoqo
Tutu
Drua Drua
Drua Drua
Great Sea Reef

Rabi

Cobia
Yavu
Yanuca

Tabiang
Buakonikai
Uma
Tabwewa

Kioa
Salia

Kubulau Point
Karoko
Napuka
Tuvumila
Natewa

Buca Bay
Buca
Natuvu

Nawi
Dakuniba
Rainbow Reef

MATEI
Vuibani
Navakacoa
Waiyevo
Mua
Welagi
Somosomo
Waitik
Waiyevo

Taveuni

Lake Tagimaucia
Mt. Uluiqalau (1,241 m)

Bouma
Lavena

Salialevu
Navakawau

Delaivuna
Vuna
South Cape

SEE "TAVEUNI" MAP

Laucala
Qamea

Matagi

Yanuca

25 mi
25 km

Lakeba
Vuniwai
Saqani
Yanuavou
Nasorolevu (1,032 m)
Korotasere
Bay
Drekeniwai
Vunilagi
Naduri
Nanuca
Naweni

MUMU RESORT
KONTIKI RESORT
NAMALE RESORT

Urata
Savusavu
Naidi
Savusavu Bay
Lesiaceva Point

SEE "AROUND SAVUSAVU" MAP

SEE "AROUND LABASA" MAP

Mali
Malau
Wailevu
Waiqele
Labasa
Bulileka
Nakoroutari
Delaikoro (941 m)
Waisali Nature Reserve
Tabia
Seaqaqa
Saivou
Wailevu
Natua
Natuvu
Valeni

Tabiri
Batiri
Navidamu
Dreketi
Nasarowaqa

Macuata-i-Wai
Nukubati
Nukubati Island

Kia

Reef

Vanua Levu

Nadivakarua
Nemalata
Namenalala

Nadivarovo
Wainunu Bay
Cogea
Daria
Sawani
Nasawana

Koro Sea

Navutuvotu (842 m)
Sasaleka
Bua
Navuhevuyo
Sasaleka (421 m)
Bua Bay
Rukuruku Bay

Solevu Point

Galoa Bay
Lekutu

Naivaka

Nasetetete Waterfall

Nabouwalu

To Suva
To Natovi and Ovalau
To Ellington Wharf

Yaqaqa

Great Sea Reef

SOUTH PACIFIC OCEAN

The **Waiqele hot springs** are near a Hindi temple called Shiu Mandir about four km beyond Labasa airport, 14 km southwest of town (green-and-yellow Waiqele bus). Again, the only reason to come is to see a bit of the countryside.

You can get a view of much of Vanua Levu from the telecommunications tower atop **Delaikoro** (941 meters), 25 km south of Labasa, farther down the same road past the airport. Only a 4WD vehicle can make it to the top.

Farther afield is the **Floating Island** at Kurukuru, between Nakelikoso and Nubu, 44 km northeast of Labasa (accessible on the Dogotuki, Kurukuru, and Lagalaga buses).

At Udu Point, Vanua Levu's northeastern-most tip, a **Meridian Wall** has been built to mark the spot where the 180° meridian and international date line cut across the island. Both sunset and sunrise can be observed from the wall, and great crowds are expected to welcome the millennium here at midnight on 31 December 1999.

If you're a surfer, ask about hiring a boat out to the **Great Sea Reef** north of Kia Island, 40 km northwest of Labasa.

Sports and Recreation

The **Municipal Swimming Pool** (tel. 816-387), just before the hospital, is the place to cool off. Admission is F$1.10. A snack bar adjoins the pool and the Friendly North Inn's nice open bar is only a short walk away.

Budget Accommodations

The **Labasa Guest House** (Box 259, Labasa; tel. 812-155), on Nanuku St., has eight rooms at F$23/28 single/double. Some rooms have a toilet and shower, while others don't, but the price of all is the same (the two back rooms are the best). Ask to be given a fan. You can put your own padlock on your door. Communal cooking facilities are provided but the Hindu hosts don't allow guests to cook beef on the premises, and previous visitors seem to have walked off with all the cutlery. There's a laundry room in which to do hand washing.

The 10-room **Riverview Private Hotel** (Box 129, Labasa; tel. 811-367, fax 814-337) is in a quiet two-story concrete building on Namara St. beyond the police station. The four fan-cooled

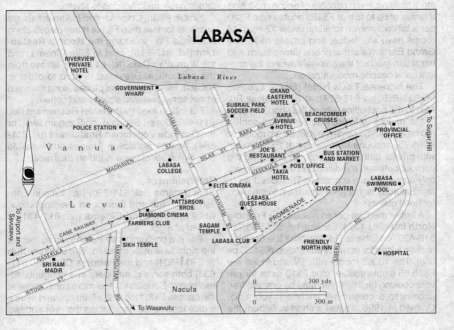

LABASA

rooms with shared bath are F$17/25 single/double, while another four with private bath are F$25/35. There are also two deluxe a/c rooms with TV, fridge, and hot plate at F$45/55/65 single/double/triple. The best deal is the breezy seven-bed dormitory with a terrace overlooking the river at F$12 pp (one of the nicest dorms in Fiji). Communal cooking and laundry facilities are available (F$5 a load), and bicycles are for rent at F$10 a day. Ask the manager Pardip Singh about canoe or kayak rentals. A very pleasant riverside bar is here.

Inexpensive

The splendid **Grand Eastern Hotel** (Box 641, Labasa; tel. 811-022, fax 814-011), on Gibson St. overlooking the river, just a few minutes' walk from the bus station, reopened in late 1997 after a complete renovation and is now one of Fiji's top hotels. The 10 standard rooms with terraces in the wing facing the river are F$95/115 double/triple, while the larger deluxe rooms facing the swimming pool are F$115/135. There are also four suites upstairs in the main two-story building, each capable of accommodating a family of up to five at F$155 double plus F$20 per additional person (children under 12 free). All rooms have a/c, fridge, and private bath. The Grand Eastern's atmospheric dining room and bar retain much of the colonial flavor of the original hotel despite modernization.

The high-rise **Takia Hotel** (Box 7, Labasa; tel. 811-655, fax 813-527), at 10 Nasekula Rd. next to the post office, above the shopping area in the middle of town, has seven fan-cooled rooms at F$45/55 single/double, 26 a/c rooms at F$65/75, and one family suite at F$80/90, all with private bath. The fan rooms are along the corridor between the disco and the bar and will only appeal to party animals on Thursday, Friday, and Saturday nights (free admission to the disco for hotel guests).

A better medium-priced place is the **Friendly North Inn** (Box 1324, Labasa; tel. 811-555, fax 816-429) on Siberia Rd. opposite the hospital, about a kilometer from the bus station (F$1.50 by taxi). The 10 a/c rooms with TV and fridge are F$55/65 single/double, plus F$10 extra for private cooking facilities (you may be granted free access to a communal kitchen if you ask). Opened in 1996, it's just a short walk from the municipal swimming pool, and the Inn's large open-air bar is a very pleasant place for a beer.

Offshore Resorts

The luxury-category **Nukubati Island Resort** (Jenny Leewai-Bourke, Box 1928, Labasa; tel. 813-901, fax 813-914) sits on tiny Nukubati Island, one km off the north shore of Vanua Levu, 40 km west of Labasa. The six spacious fan-cooled beach bungalows are F$1,100 double including meals (emphasis on seafood) and activities, with a five-night minimum stay. Children are not allowed, and alcoholic beverages are extra. It's F$550 a day to hire the resort's sport-fishing boat. Access is by speedboat or 4WD vehicle from Labasa (free for guests).

Food

Joe's Restaurant (tel. 811-766; Mon.-Sat. 0600-2200), upstairs in a building on Nasekula Rd., has an inexpensive fast-food area, and a more upmarket "wine and dine" section where you can order beer. Both are very popular, and the Chinese food served here puts Labasa's ubiquitous chow mein houses to shame.

Simple Fijian, Chinese, and Indian meals are available for less than F$3 at many places along Nasekula Rd., including the **Moon's Restaurant** (tel. 813-215), next to Elite Cinema, and the **Wun Wah Cafe** (tel. 811-653), across from the post office. Breakfast is hard to order in Labasa, although several places along the main street serve buttered scones and coffee.

For Indian food try the **Isalei Restaurant** (tel. 811-490; closed Sunday), on Sangam Ave., or the **Govinda Vegetarian Restaurant** (tel. 811-364), next to Sunflower Airlines on Nasekula Rd., which specializes in Indian *thali* meals.

Entertainment

Elite Cinema (tel. 811-260) has films in English and Hindi and there's an evening show, while the **Diamond Cinema** (tel. 811-471) is closed at night.

This is a predominantly Indian town so most of the nightlife is male oriented. The **Labasa Club** (tel. 811-304) and the **Farmers Club** (tel. 811-633) both serve cheap beer in a congenial atmosphere. Couples will feel more comfortable at the Labasa Club than at the Farmers, and there's a nice terrace out back facing the river and two large snooker tables. The bar upstairs at the Farmers Club is a bit more sedate (and perhaps less colorful) than the one downstairs (both open daily 1000-2200).

The pub upstairs in the **Takia Hotel** (tel. 811-655) is a safe, fun place to drink, even though the bartenders are enclosed in a cage! There's also a disco at the Takia open Thursday, Friday, and Saturday 2030-0100 (admission F$4).

Indian **firewalking** takes place once a year sometime between June and October at Agnimela Mandir, the Firewalkers Temple at Vunivau, five km northeast of Labasa.

Services and Information

The ANZ Bank is opposite the bus station, and the Westpac Bank is farther west on Nasekula Road.

There's a public library (tel. 812-617; weekdays 0900-1300/1400-1700, Saturday 0900-1200) in the Civic Center near Labasa Bus Station. Public toilets are adjacent to the library.

Health

The Northern District Hospital (tel. 811-444), northeast of the river, is available 24 hours a day in emergencies.

Less serious medical problems should be taken to a private doctor, such as Dr. Hermant Kumar of Kumar's Medical Center (tel. 814-155) on Jaduram St. near the Labasa Guest House. Nearby on Nanuku St. toward Nasekula Rd. is a private dentist, Dr. Ashwin Kumar Lal (tel. 814-077).

Transportation

Air Fiji (tel. 811-188) has service five or six times a day between Labasa and Suva (F$138). **Sunflower Airlines** (tel. 811-454), at the corner of Nasekula Rd. and Damanu St., flies direct to Nadi (F$180) four times a day, to Suva (F$148) twice daily, and to Taveuni (F$82) three times a week.

To get to the airport, 10 km southwest of Labasa, take a taxi (F$7) or the green-and-yellow Waiqele bus. Sunflower Airlines has a bus based at the airport that brings arriving passengers into town free of charge, but departing passengers must find their own way from Labasa to the airport. Air Fiji's bus takes passengers to/from the airport at 50 cents pp (when operating).

Patterson Brothers (tel. 812-444, fax 813-460) has an office near Sunflower Airlines on Nasekula Rd. where you can book your bus/ferry/bus ticket through to Suva via Nabouwalu and Natovi (10 hours, F$43). This bus leaves Labasa at 0600 daily except Sunday and Monday, and passengers arrive in Suva at 1715. There's also a direct bus/boat/bus connection from Labasa to Lautoka via Ellington Wharf (near Nananu-i-Ra Island) on Tuesday, Thursday, and Saturday, and another service straight through to Levuka. Ask about the through bus/boat service from Labasa to Taveuni via Natuvu, departing Labasa Monday, Wednesday, Friday, and Saturday at 0630 (six hours, F$16.20).

Beachcomber Cruises (tel. 811-492), in an office in the seafood warehouse next to the Grand Eastern Hotel, books passage on the car ferry MV *Adi Savusavu*. Their through bus/boat ticket to Suva via Savusavu is F$39/47 economy/first class (or F$5 less for the boat only).

Consort Shipping Line (tel. 811-144, fax 814-411) has an office at the Government Wharf at the north end of Damanu St. where you can book passage on the *Spirit of Free Enterprise* from Savusavu to Suva.

To be dropped off on Kia Island on the Great Sea Reef, negotiate with the fishing boats tied up near the Labasa Club. Village boats from Kia and Udu Point sometimes unload at the Government Wharf on the other side of town.

Four regular buses a day (at 0630, 1030, 1300, and 1430) go to Nabouwalu (210 km, F$7), a dusty, tiring six-hour trip. Another four buses a day (at 0700, 0900, 1200, and 1500) run from Labasa to Savusavu (94 km, three hours, F$4.35), a very beautiful ride on an excellent paved highway over the Waisali Saddle between the Korotini and Valili Mountains and along the palm-studded coast. Take the early bus before clouds obscure the views. Latchman Buses Ltd. (tel. 814-390) also has an express bus departing Labasa for Savusavu daily at 0700 (two hours, F$4.55).

Rental cars are available from **Budget Rent A Car** (tel. 811-999) at Niranjans Mazda dealership on Zoing Place up Ivi St. from opposite the Jame Mosque at Nasekula west of town. **Avis** (tel. 811-688) is at Asco Motors behind the Shell service station at Nasekula at the west entrance to

Labasa. Obtaining gasoline outside the two main towns is difficult, so tank up.

SAVUSAVU

Savusavu is a picturesque little town opposite Nawi Island on Savusavu Bay. The view from here across to the mountains of southwestern Vanua Levu and down the coast toward Nabou-walu is superlatively lovely. In the 1860s Europeans arrived to establish coconut plantations. They mixed with the Fijians, and even though business went bust in the 1930s, their descendants and the Fijian villagers still supply copra to a coconut oil mill, eight km west of Savusavu, giving this side of Vanua Levu a pleasant agricultural air. The urban population of 5,000 is almost evenly split between Fiji Indians and indigenous Fijians with many part-Fijians here too.

Savusavu is Vanua Levu's main port, and cruising yachts often rock at anchor offshore, sheltered from the open waters of Savusavu Bay by Nawi Island. The surrounding mountains and reefs also make Savusavu a well-protected hurricane refuge. The diving possibilities of this area were recognized by Jean-Michel Cousteau in 1990 when he started using Savusavu as the base for his Project Ocean Search. Access to good snorkeling is difficult, however, as the finest beaches are under the control of the top-end resorts and most other shore access is over extremely sharp karst. Although much smaller than Labasa, Savusavu is the administrative center of Cakaudrove Province and has three banks. In

the past few years tourism has taken off around Savusavu, with new resorts springing up all the time, though the town is far from being spoiled.

Sights

The one main street through Savusavu consists of a motley collection of Indian and Chinese shops, parked taxis, loitering locals, and the odd tourist. The **Copra Shed Marina** is like a small museum with map displays and historical photos, information boards, and most of Savusavu's tourist services. Color photos of all yachts that have visited recently are displayed in the office next to the notice board. In front of the marina is a stone dated 1880, which is said to be from Fiji's first copra mill.

Visit the small **hot springs** boiling out among fractured coral below the Hot Springs Hotel. Residents use the springs to cook native vegetables; bathing is not possible. These and smaller hot springs along the shore of Savusavu Bay remind one that the whole area was once a caldera.

For a good circle trip, take a taxi from Savusavu past the airport to **Nukubalavu** village (six km, F$5), at the end of road along the south side of the peninsula. From here you can walk west along the beach to the Cousteau Fiji Islands Resort on **Lesiaceva Point** in about an hour at low tide. Try to avoid cutting through the resort at the end of the hike as the Cousteau management disapproves. From Lesiaceva it's six km by road back to Savusavu.

For some mountain hiking ask one of the Labasa buses to drop you at the entry kiosk to the **Waisali Nature Reserve** established by the

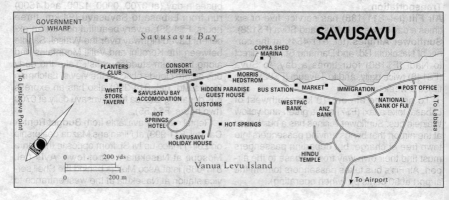

National Trust for Fiji in 1991, about 40 km northwest of Savusavu. This 116-hectare reserve protects one of Vanua Levu's last unexploited tropical rainforests with native species such as the *dakua, yaka,* and *kuasi* well represented. Viewpoints offer sweeping views and a nature trail leads to a waterfall where you can swim.

Sports and Recreation
Eco Divers (Box 264, Savusavu; tel. 850-122, fax 850-344) at the Copra Shed Marina offers scuba diving, snorkeling, dinghy hire, sailing, village visits, waterfall tours, and guided hiking. They charge F$94 for a two-tank boat dive, or F$380 for a PADI open-water certification course. Snorkeling from the boat is F$15 pp if four people go, F$25 pp for two people (two hours). Eco Divers and the Cousteau Fiji Islands Resort use 21 of the same buoyed dive sites off southern Vanua Levu. Ocean kayak rental is F$10/25 for one/three hours in a single-person kayak or F$15/35 in a double. They also rent mountain bikes at F$7/12 a half/full day and sailing catamarans at F$15 an hour. Eco Divers arranges 10-tank, seven-night diving/accommodation packages beginning at F$474 pp (double occupancy). Three-night guided kayak tours around northwestern Savusavu Bay are also offered.

Accommodations in Savusavu Town
We've arranged this accommodation section beginning at Savusavu Bus Station and working west through town to Lesiaceva Point, then east along the coast.

The **Copra Shed Marina** (Box 262, Savusavu; tel. 850-457, fax 850-344) has a self-catering apartment upstairs in the marina for rent at F$55 a night for up to three people (long term rates available). It's a great deal, but call ahead to reserve. Inexpensive.

Hari Chand's **Hidden Paradise Guest House** (Box 41, Savusavu; tel. 850-106), just beyond Morris Hedstrom, has six rather hot wooden rooms at F$15/23/32 single/double/triple with fan and shared bath, F$28 double in twin beds, including a hearty English breakfast. Cooking and washing facilities are provided, and it's clean and friendly—don't be put off by the plain exterior. You'll be well protected by iron grills, fences, and watch dogs. The Indian restaurant here is very inexpensive, but pork, beef, and booze are

banned. A member of the Chand family may offer to show you around the Hindu temple up on the hill, if you ask. Checkout time is 0900. Shoestring.

The **Hot Springs Hotel** (Box 208, Savusavu; tel. 850-195, fax 850-430), on the hillside overlooking Savusavu Bay, is named for the nearby thermal springs and steam vents. The 48 rooms, all with balconies offering splendid views, begin at F$120 single or double with fan, F$180 with a/c. There's no beach nearby, but the swimming pool terrace is pleasant. This former Travelodge is a convenient, medium-priced choice, and the hotel bar is open daily including Sunday. Catch the sunset here at happy hour (1700-1900) and ask about the buffet dinner laid out on Saturday nights. Just below the hotel they have a budget annex with a high sloping roof called the **Diver's Den** with four tiny single rooms, one room with two beds, and another with three beds. All beds can be converted into upper/lower bunks doubling the capacity. The Den is used mostly by Eco Divers scuba groups, which pay F$20 pp, and it's often fully booked. Budget to inexpensive.

David Manohar Lal's six-room **Savusavu Holiday House** (Box 65, Savusavu; tel. 850-149), also known as "David's Place," is just behind the Hot Springs Hotel. There are five rooms with shared bath at F$18/24/28 single/double/triple and one four-person family room at F$30. The seven-bed dorm is F$15 pp, while camping is F$9/15 single/double. Stay more than a week and you'll get 10% off and free laundry service. All rates include a good cooked breakfast and there's a well-equipped kitchen. David's a delightful character to meet and also a strict Seventh-Day Adventist, so no alcoholic beverages are allowed on the premises. A cacophony of dogs, roosters, and the neighbor's kids will bid you good morning. It's often full with people from Eco Divers—call ahead. Shoestring.

Savusavu Bay Accommodation (Box 154, Savusavu; tel. 850-100), above Sea Breeze Restaurant on the main street, has five standard rooms with bath at F$18/23 single/double, four a/c rooms at F$40 single or double, and one large four-person family room at F$50. Cooking facilities are provided, and on the roof of this two-story concrete building is a terrace where travelers can wash and dry their clothes or just sit and relax. Many of the rooms are rented on a long-term basis, and the atmosphere is not as nice as in the places previously mentioned (one reader called it "noisy and dirty"). Shoestring.

Accommodations around Savusavu

In 1994 a bankrupt hotel on Lesiaceva Point, six km southwest of Savusavu, was purchased by oceanographer Jean-Michel Cousteau, son of the famous Jacques Cousteau, and backers in California who redeveloped the property into the **Jean-Michel Cousteau Fiji Islands Resort** (Private Bag, Savusavu; tel. 850-188, fax 850-340). This stylish resort recreates a Fijian village with 18 authentic-looking thatched *bures*. Garden accommodations, transfers, and all meals begin at F$590/790/990 single/double/triple, plus 10% tax. The rooms have fans but no a/c, telephones, or cooking facilities. The restaurant is built like a towering pagan temple and nonguests wishing to dine there *must* reserve. Free activities include sailing, kayaking, and fishing. The snorkeling off their beach is pretty good (ask about "split rock"). In addition, Gary Alford's outstanding on-site dive operation, "L'Aventure Cousteau," offers scuba diving (F$77/139 for one/two tanks plus gear), PADI/TDI scuba instruction, underwater photography courses, and yacht charters with diving. The high-speed dive boat *Fiji Aggressor* is based here. There's good snorkeling off their beach, though the resort's large Private Property signs warn nonguests to keep out. A taxi from Savusavu will run F$5. Bring insect repellent. (The Fiji Islands Resort has no connection with the Cousteau Society in Paris and before his death in June 1997 Jacques Cousteau launched a legal action against his son to prevent the Cousteau name from being used as a trademark to promote private businesses of this kind.) Luxury.

The **Vatukaluvi Holiday House** (Box 262, Savusavu; tel. 850-457, fax 850-344), on the south side of the peninsula, one km west of Savusavu airport, accommodates four people at F$55 for the whole breezy house (or F$330 for two weeks). Cooking facilities and fridge are provided, and there's good snorkeling off the beach. Ask for Geoff Taylor, vice-commodore of the Savusavu Yacht Club. A taxi to Vatukaluvi will cost F$3 from the airport, F$5 from Savusavu. Inexpensive.

The most upmarket place around Savusavu is **Namale Resort** (Box 244, Savusavu; tel. 850-435, fax 850-400), a working copra plantation founded in 1874, on a white-sand beach nine km east of Savusavu. The superb food and homey atmosphere amid exotic landscapes and refreshing white beaches make this one of Fiji's most exclusive resorts. The 10 thatched *bures* are F$930/1,122 single/double per night including gourmet meals and drinks. The mosquito nets over the beds, ceiling fans, and louvered windows give the units a rustic charm. Airport transfers and all activities other than scuba diving are free (F$136 plus tax for a two-tank dive). Namale caters only to in-house guests—there's no provision for sightseers who'd like to stop in for lunch. Children under 12 are also banned. Luxury.

At last report, Kontiki Resort, 15 km east of Savusavu on the Hibiscus Highway, was closed due to legal complications, although it could eventually reopen under new management.

Vanua Levu's only real backpacker camp, **Mumu Resort** (Rosie Edris, Box 240, Savusavu; tel. 850-416), 18 km east of Savusavu, occupies the site of the spiritual home of Radini Mumu, a legendary queen of Fiji. The seven *bures* are F$45 single or double, the four bunkhouse rooms F$35 single or double, and the four-person "dream house" F$60. There's also a six-bed dorm at F$12 pp, and you can camp for F$4 pp. Communal cooking facilities are available, and Mumu's kitchen serves tasty Fijian and European dishes at budget prices. Mumu is surrounded by the Koro Sea on three sides, and two small uninhabited islands nearby are easily accessible. Although the scenery is good, the snorkeling is poor with a very long swim over a shallow flat before reaching a snorkelable area. Unfortunately Mumu has gone downhill in recent years and maintenance has been neglected. Beware of their dogs. A taxi here from Savusavu should be F$12, a bus around F$1, but call ahead unless you're planning to camp. Budget.

Ms. Collin McKenny from Seattle runs the **Lomalagi Resort** (Box 200, Savusavu; tel. 816-098, fax 816-099) in a coconut plantation a 15-minute walk from Nasinu village on Natewa Bay. It's up Salt Lake Rd. three km off the Hibiscus Highway, about 25 km from Savusavu airport. The six deluxe self-catering hillside villas are F$700-800 double including tax and transfers (children not admitted). The optional meal plan including a bottle of wine with dinner is another F$175 per couple. Two artificial waterfalls drop into the S-shaped saltwater swimming pool. Luxury.

Namenalala Island

Moody's Namenalala Island Resort (Private Mail Bag, Savusavu; tel. 813-764, fax 812-366), on a narrow high island southwest of Savusavu in the Koro Sea, is one of Fiji's top hideaways. In 1984 Tom and Joan Moody leased Namenalala from the Fiji government, which needed a caretaker to protect the uninhabited island from poachers. Their present resort occupies less than 10% of Namenalala's 45 hectares, leaving the rest as a nesting ground to great flocks of red-footed boobies, banded rails, and Polynesian starlings. Giant clams proliferate in the surrounding waters within the 24-km Namena Barrier Reef, and Nov.-March sea turtles haul themselves up onto the island's golden sands to lay their eggs. The corals along the nearby dropoffs are fabulous, and large pelagic fish glide in from the Koro Sea.

Each of the Moody's six bamboo and wood hexagonal-shaped *bures* are well tucked away in the lush vegetation to ensure maximum privacy. Illuminated by romantic gas lighting, each features a private hardwood terrace with 270-degree views. Alternative energy is used as much as possible to maintain the atmosphere (though there is a secret diesel generator used to do the laundry and recharge batteries).

The cost to stay here is F$484/610 single/double, including all meals. The food is excellent, thanks to Joan's firm hand in the kitchen and Tom's island-grown produce. The ice water on the tables and in the *bures* is a nice touch, but they don't sell liquor so bring your own.

This resort is perfect for birdwatching, fishing, and snorkeling, and scuba diving is available at F$60 per tank (certification card required). The soft corals at Namenalala are among the finest in the world. If you want a holiday that combines unsullied nature with interesting characters and a certain elegance, you won't go wrong here. A Turtle Airways seaplane from Nadi will run F$400 per couple if booked through the resort. Moody's closes from 1 March to 1 May every year. Luxury.

Food

The **Captain's Table** (tel. 850-511; open Mon.-Sat. 0830-2100, Sunday 1100-2100) at the Copra Shed Marina is a yachtie hangout claiming to offer "the best pizza on Vanua Levu," which isn't saying a lot when you think about it. Most of Savusavu's hip young locals show up here eventually, and in the evening the outdoor seating on the wharf is nice. Pick up a newspaper at the Bula Bookstore out front and enjoy a leisurely read while waiting for your order to arrive.

Several simple places around town offer basic meals of varying quality. The **New Ping Ho Cafe** (tel. 850-300), opposite the municipal market, accommodates vegetarians and everyone else with substantial portions of good food at decent prices. It's one of the few places open for dinner (1800-2100) and all the local expats eat here. (Ping Ho ran the bakery at the Mount Kasi Gold Mine during the 1930s and his descendants continue to operate the restaurant.)

The **A1 Restaurant** (tel. 850-153) near the bus station has Indian curries, but some of the cheapest curries in town are served at the **Sun Sang Cafe** (tel. 850-106) at Hidden Paradise Guest House. Also try the **Harbor Cafe** next to the Shell service station below the Hot Springs Hotel for Indian dishes.

The **Sea Breeze Restaurant** (tel. 850-100) below Savusavu Bay Accommodation serves mostly Chinese dishes, and the portions are large. It's open Sunday for lunch and dinner. It's slightly cheaper than the New Ping Ho Cafe, but not as pleasant.

The biggest market at Savusavu is early Saturday morning. Free public toilets are behind the market.

Entertainment

The **Light Ship Theater** next to A1 Restaurant shows action videos for F$1 admission.

Drinkers can repair to the **Planters Club** (tel. 850-233; Mon.-Thurs. 1000-2200, Friday and Saturday 1000-2300, Sunday 1000-1800) toward the wharf—the place is never out of Fiji Bitter. The weekend dances at the club are local events. Despite the Members Only sign outside, visitors are welcome. It's a vintage colonial club even without the colonists.

The **White Stork Tavern,** next to the Planters Club, is a rough public bar open Mon.-Sat. 1100-

2100. If there's a dance on Friday and Saturday they'll stay open until 0100.

Services and Information
The ANZ Bank, National Bank, and Westpac Bank all have branches at Savusavu.

The Bula Bookshop (Hans, Box 265, Savusavu; tel./fax 850-580), at the Copra Shed Marina, has Suva newspapers and tasty ice-cream sticks, plus postcards, T-shirts, and souvenirs. They sell Fijian nautical charts March-Oct. only. This is the local DHL Express agent.

Sea Fiji Travel (Box 264, Savusavu; tel. 850-345, fax 850-344), in the Copra Shed Marina, specializes in scuba diving and adventure travel.

Health
The District Hospital (tel. 850-437; open 0830-1600) is two km east of Savusavu on the road to Labasa (taxi F$2).

Dr. Joeli Tali's Savusavu Private Health Center (tel. 850-721; Mon.-Thurs. 0830-1600, Friday 0830-1400) is between the National Bank and the post office.

Yachting Facilities
The **Copra Shed Marina** (Box 262, Savusavu; tel. 850-457, fax 850-344) near the bus station allows visiting yachts to moor alongside at F$10 a day, or pay F$3 a day for an offshore hurricane mooring. Anchorage and use of the facilities by the whole crew is F$28 a week. You can have your laundry done for F$7 (wash and dry). The **Savusavu Yacht Club** (Box 3, Savusavu; tel. 850-561, fax 850-344) is based here.

Yachts can clear Fiji customs here. Arriving yachts should contact the Copra Shed Marina over VHF 16. The customs office (where yachties must report after the quarantine check) is next to the Shell service station below the Hot Springs Hotel. After clearing quarantine and customs controls, yachties can proceed to the Immigration Department, across the street from the Hot Bread Kitchen, a bit east of the market. If you check in after 1630 or on weekends or holidays there's an additional F$39 charge on top of the usual F$33 quarantine fee.

Transportation
Air Fiji (tel. 850-538), next to the post office, flies into Savusavu twice daily from Suva (F$118)

and Taveuni (F$82). **Sunflower Airlines** (tel. 850-141), in the Copra Shed Marina, has flights to Savusavu twice daily from Nadi (F$180) and Taveuni (F$82). The airstrip is beside the main highway, three km east of town. Local buses to Savusavu pass the airport about once an hour, or take a taxi for F$2.

The **Consort Shipping Line Ltd.** (tel. 850-443, fax 850-442), opposite the Shell service station below the Hot Springs Hotel, runs the large car ferry MV *Spirit of Free Enterprise* from Suva to Savusavu (12 hours, F$32 deck, F$55 cabin). The ferry leaves Suva northbound Tuesday and Saturday nights, and leaves Savusavu southbound Monday and Thursday nights. Northbound the Tuesday voyage continues to Taveuni, and between Savusavu and Suva the *"Sofe"* calls at Koro.

Beachcomber Cruises (tel. 850-266, fax 850-499), at the Copra Shed Marina, runs the 65-meter car ferry MV *Adi Savusavu* from Savusavu direct to Suva Wednesday and Sunday at 2000, and to Natovi with a bus connection to Suva Saturday at 0700 (F$34/42 economy/first class).

Patterson Brothers Shipping (tel. 850-161), at the Copra Shed Marina, operates the bus/boat connection to Taveuni via Natuvu, which should depart Savusavu Mon.-Sat. at 0900 (four hours, F$12.70).

Buses from Savusavu to Buca Bay and Napuka leave daily except Sunday at 1030, 1300, 1430, and 1600 (three hours, F$3.41).

Regular buses leave Savusavu for Labasa at 0730, 0930, 1300, and 1530, Sunday at 0930 and 1530 only (92 km, three hours, F$4.35). This ride is easily the most scenic in Fiji. The Latchman express bus to Labasa (two hours; F$4.55) departs Savusavu daily at 1430. There's also a bus that takes a roundabout route via Natewa Bay between Savusavu and Labasa, departing both ends at 0900 (F$8.45)—a scenic ride through an area seldom seen by tourists. Other Natewa Bay buses may finish their runs at Yanuavou or Wainigadru.

Buses leave Savusavu for Lesiaceva Point at 0715, 1200, and 1600 (54 cents). For more information on buses headed south or east of Savusavu, call Vishnu Holdings at tel. 850-276.

Numerous taxis congregate at Savusavu market; they're quite affordable for short trips in the vicinity.

Avis Rent A Car (tel. 850-911) has an office at the Hot Springs Hotel in Savusavu. **Budget Rent A Car** (tel. 850-700) is in the same office as Air Fiji next to the post office.

Eco Divers (tel. 850-122) at the Copra Shed Marina offers a variety of day tours, including a village tour (F$20), plantation tour (F$20), Labasa tour (F$90), and a Waisali Reserve tour (F$40). They only need two participants to run a tour.

BUCA BAY

Along the Hibiscus Highway

This lovely (if dusty) coastal highway runs 75 km east from Savusavu to Natuvu on Buca Bay, then up the east side of Vanua Levu to the Catholic mission station of **Napuka** at the end of the peninsula. Old frame mansions from the heyday of the 19th-century planters can be spotted among the palms, and offshore you'll see tiny flowerpot islands where the sea has undercut the coral rock. Buca Bay is a recognized "hurricane hole," where ships can find shelter during storms. Former Prime Minister Rabuka hails from **Drekeniwai** village on Natewa Bay, one of the largest bays in the South Pacific.

The **Buca Bay Resort** (Natuvu, Buca Bay; tel. 880-370), also known as Natuvu Plantation, next to the ferry wharf at Natuvu, is run by Jack and Pam Cobelens. They have two rooms with shared bath at F$55 double, one with private bath at F$66, a regular *bure* at F$55, a family *bure* at F$88, and a six-bed dorm at F$17 pp (campers F$10 per tent). The staff serves meals upon request and the dorm has cooking facilities and a fridge. A swimming pool and library are available. Yachties are welcome to anchor off the resort and use the facilities. Activities in this area include a hike to Tagici Peak, birdwatching (the rare orange flame dove inhabits the upper forest), and the scenic three-hour afternoon bus ride to Napuka and back (Mon.-Sat. at 1300). Budget.

Buses to Savusavu leave Buca Bay at 0530, 0800, and 1600 (75 km, three hours, F$3.41). The ferry *Grace* leaves Natuvu for Taveuni weekdays at 0800 (F$5) and to use it you must sleep at Buca Bay. The Patterson Brothers barge *Yaubula* departs Natuvu for Taveuni Mon.-Sat. at

1100 (F$7.70). It's a beautiful boat trip but it can be rough if the wind is up.

Vanaira Bay

In 1998 the **Vanaira Bay Backpackers** (Douglas Thompson, Box 77, Waiyevo, Taveuni; tel. 880-017, fax 880-033) opened on the bay of that name at the east end of Vanua Levu directly across Somosomo Strait from Taveuni. The only access is by boat from Taveuni at F$20 pp return (or F$30 pp to Buca Bay). Bure accommodations are F$50 double, dorm beds F$15 pp, or you can camp for F$8 pp. Meals are F$5 each. It's an electricity-free hideaway with snorkeling and hiking possibilities. Equipment rentals include kayaks at F$8 an hour, windsurfers F$10, and a Hobie cat at F$25. Libby Lesuma at Club Coco, next to the National Bank in Waiyevo on Taveuni, acts as their booking agent. A boat goes over from Waiyevo every Friday afternoon.

Anyone interested in more upscale accommodations should check out **Rainbow Reef Beach Estates** and its small self-catering villas, two bays southwest of Vanaira Bay. Libby at Club Coco on Taveuni will know all about it.

Kioa

The Taveuni ferry passes between Vanua Levu and Kioa, home of some 300 Polynesians from Vaitupu Island, Tuvalu (the former Ellice Islands). In 1853 Captain Owen of the ship *Packet* obtained Kioa from the Tui Cakau, and it has since operated as a coconut plantation. In 1946 it was purchased by the Ellice islanders, who were facing overpopulation on their home island.

The people live at **Salia** on the southeast side of Kioa. The women make baskets for sale to tourists, while the men go fishing alone in small outrigger canoes. If you visit, try the coconut toddy *(kaleve)* or more potent fermented toddy *(kamanging)*. The Patterson Brothers ferry *Yaubula* often stops briefly at Kioa on its way to Taveuni.

Rabi

In 1855, at the request of the Tui Cakau on Taveuni, a Tongan army conquered some Fijian rebels on Rabi. Upon the Tongans' departure a few years later, a local chief sold Rabi to Europeans to cover outstanding debts, and before WW II the Australian firm Lever Brothers ran a coconut plantation here. In 1940 the British government began searching for an island to purchase as a resettlement area for the Micronesian Banabans of Ocean Island (Banaba) in the Gilbert Islands (presently Kiribati), whose home island was being ravaged by phosphate mining. At first Wakaya Island in the Lomaiviti Group was considered, but the outbreak of war and the occupation of Ocean Island by the Japanese intervened. Back in Fiji, British officials decided Rabi Island would be a better homeland for the Banabans than Wakaya, and in March 1942 they purchased Rabi from Lever Brothers using £25,000 of phosphate royalties deposited in the Banaban Provident Fund.

Meanwhile the Japanese had deported the Banabans to Kusaie (Kosrae) in the Caroline Islands to serve as laborers, and it was not until December 1945 that the survivors could be brought to Rabi, where their 4,500 descendants live today. Contemporary Banabans are citizens of Fiji and live among Lever's former coconut plantations at the northwest corner of the island. The eight-member Rabi Island Council administers the island.

Rabi lives according to a different set of rules than the rest of Fiji; in fact, about all they have in common are their monetary, postal, and educational systems, kava drinking (a Fijian implant), and Methodism. The local language is Gilbertese and the social order is that of the Gilbert Islands. Most people live in hurricane-proof concrete-block houses devoid of furniture, with personal possessions kept in suitcases and trunks. The cooking is done outside in thatched huts.

Alcoholic beverages are not allowed on Rabi, so take something else as gifts. On Friday nights the local *maneaba* in Tabwewa village rocks to a disco beat and dancing alternates with sitting around the omnipresent kava bowl, but on Sunday virtually everything grinds to a halt. Another charming feature: adultery is a legally punishable offense on Rabi.

The island reaches a height of 472 meters and is well wooded. The former Lever headquarters is at Tabwewa, while the abandoned airstrip is near Tabiang at Rabi's southwest tip. Rabi's other two villages are Uma and Buakonikai. At Nuku between Uma and Tabwewa is a post office, Telecom office, clinic, handicraft shop, and general store. The hill behind

the Catholic mission at Nuku affords a fine view. Motorized transport on Rabi consists of two or three island council trucks plying the single 23-km road from Tabwewa to Buakonikai weekdays and Saturday mornings (60 cents each way). Enjoy another fine view from the Methodist church center at Buakonikai. The islanders fish with handlines from outrigger canoes.

Up on the hillside above the post office at Nuku is the four-room **Rabi Island Council Guest House.** This colonial-style structure is the former Lever Brothers manager's residence and is little changed since the 1940s except for the extension now housing the dining area and lounge. View superb sunsets from the porch. One of the rooms is reserved for island officials; the rest are used mostly by contract workers. Other guests pay F$55 pp a night, which includes three meals. The facilities are shared (no hot water) and the electric generator operates 1800-2200 only—just enough time to watch a video (the library next to the court house rents *Go tell it to the judge,* a documentary about the Banaban struggle for compensation). Inexpensive.

Considering the limited accommodations and the remoteness of Rabi, it's important to call the **Rabi Island Council** (tel. 811-666, extension 31, fax 813-750) for guesthouse bookings and other information before setting out. You could also ask at the office of the **Rabi Council of Leaders** (Box 329, Suva; tel. 303-653, fax 300-543), 1st floor, Banaba House, Pratt St. (above Hare Krishna Restaurant), Suva, but they'll probably only refer you to the island council. Foreign currency cannot be changed on Rabi and even Fijian bills larger than F$10 may be hard to break. Insect repellent is not sold locally.

To get there catch the daily Napuka bus at 1030 from Savusavu to Karoko. A chartered speedboat from Karoko to the wharf at Nuku on the northwest side of Rabi costs F$45 each way, less if people off the Napuka bus are going over anyway. The Patterson Brothers ferry *Yaubula* between Natuvu and Taveuni calls at Rabi about once a month depending on cargo, usually leaving Natuvu at 1100 on a Tuesday or a Thursday (any Patterson Brothers office should know). Two small trading vessels call at the jetty at Nuku on alternate Saturday mornings and they'll usually take you back to Karoko for F$5.

TAVEUNI

Long, green, coconut-covered Taveuni is Fiji's third-largest island. It's 42 km long, 15 km wide, and 470 km square in area. Only eight km across the Somosomo Strait from Vanua Levu's southeast tip, Taveuni is known as the Garden Island of Fiji because of the abundance of its flora. Around 60% of the land is under tropical rainforest and virtually all of Fiji's coffee is grown here. Its surrounding reefs and those off nearby Vanua Levu are some of the world's top dive sites. The strong tidal currents in the strait nurture the corals, but can make diving a tricky business for the unprepared. Because Taveuni is free of the mongoose, there are many wild chickens, *kula* lorikeets, parrots, honeyeaters, silktails, ferntails, and orange-breasted doves, making this a special place for birders.

The island's 16-km-long, 1,000-meter-high volcanic spine causes the prevailing trade winds to dump colossal amounts of rainfall on the island's southeast side, and considerable quantities on the northwest side. At 1,241 meters, Uluiqalau in southern Taveuni is the second-highest peak in Fiji, and Des Voeux Peak (1,195 meters) in central Taveuni is the highest point in the country accessible by road. The European discoverer of Fiji, Abel Tasman, sighted this ridge on the night of 5 February 1643. Scientists believe Taveuni has experienced 20 volcanic eruptions over the last 2,000 years, the most recent 340 years ago. The almost inaccessible southeast coast features plummeting waterfalls, soaring cliffs, and crashing surf. The 12,000 inhabitants live on the island's gently sloping northwest side. The bulk of the population is Fijian but Indians run most of the shops, hotels, buses, and taxis.

The deep, rich volcanic soil nurtures indigenous floral species such as *Medinilla spectabilis,* which hang in clusters like red sleigh bells, and the rare *tagimaucia (Medinilla waterousei),* a climbing plant with red-and-white flower clusters 30 cm long. *Tagimaucia* grows only around Taveuni's 900-meter-high crater lake and on Vanua Levu. It cannot be transplanted and blossoms only Oct.-December. The story goes that a young woman was fleeing from her father, who wanted to force her to marry a crotchety old man. As she lay crying beside the lake, her tears turned to flowers. Her father took pity on her when he heard this and allowed her to marry her young lover.

During the past decade Taveuni has become very popular as a destination for scuba divers and those in search of a more natural vacation area than the overcrowded Nadi/Coral Coast strips. Even the producers of the film *Return to the Blue Lagoon* chose Taveuni for their 1991 remake of the story of two adolescents on a desert isle. Despite all this attention, Taveuni is still about the most beautiful, scenic, and friendly island in Fiji. It's a great place to hang out, so be sure to allow yourself enough time there.

SIGHTS

Central Taveuni

Taveuni's post office, police station, hospital, government offices, and Country Club are on a hilltop at **Waiyevo,** above the Garden Island Resort. On the coast below is the island's bank and its biggest hotel.

To get to the **Waitavala Sliding Rocks,** walk north from the Garden Island Resort about four minutes on the main road, then turn right onto the signposted side road leading to Waitavala Estates. Take the first road to the right up the hill, and when you see a large metal building on top of a hill, turn left and go a short distance down a road through a coconut plantation to a clearing on the right. The trail up the river to the sliding rocks begins here. The water slide in the river is especially fast after heavy rains, yet the local kids go down standing up! Admission is free.

The **180th degree of longitude** passes through a point marked by a signboard one km south of Waiyevo. An 1879 ordinance placed all of Fiji west of the international date line, so you're no longer able to stand here with one foot in the past and the other in the present. In spite of this, it's still the most accessible place in the world crossed by the 180th meridian, and the perfect spot to welcome the new millennium at midnight on 31 December 1999 or 2000.

At **Wairiki,** a kilometer south again, are a few stores and the picturesque Catholic mission, with a large stone church containing interesting sculptures and stained glass. There are no pews: the congregation sits on the floor Fijian style. From Wairiki Secondary School you can hike up a tractor track to the large **concrete cross** on a hill behind the mission in 30 minutes each way. You'll be rewarded with a sweeping view of much of western Taveuni and across Somosomo Strait.

A jeep road from Wairiki climbs to the telecommunications station on **Des Voeux Peak.** This is an all-day trip on foot with a view of Lake Tagimaucia as a reward (clouds permitting). The lake itself is not accessible from here. The rare monkey-faced fruit bat *(Pteralopex acrodonta)* survives only in the mist forest around the summit. To hire a jeep to the viewpoint would cost F$60, otherwise allow four arduous hours to hike the six km up and another two to walk back down.

One of the only stretches of paved road on Taveuni is at Soqulu Plantation or "Taveuni Estates" (tel. 880-044), about eight km south of Waiyevo. This ill-fated condo development features an attractive golf course by the sea, tennis courts, and a bowling green, plus street signs pointing nowhere, empty roads, sewers, and 30 unfinished condominiums built by an undercapitalized real estate speculator who badly miscalculated Taveuni's potential for Hawaii-style residential development.

Southern Taveuni

Transportation to the south end of Taveuni is spotty with bus service from Somosomo Mon.-Sat. at 0800, 1200, and 1600 only. Since the 1600 bus spends the night at Vuna and doesn't return to Somosomo until the next morning, the only way to really see southern Taveuni is to also spend the night there. If this isn't possible, the roundtrip bus ride leaving Somosomo at 0800 and around noon is still well worth doing.

The bus from Somosomo runs south along the coast to Susie's Plantation, where it turns inland to Delaivuna. There it turns around and returns to the coast, which it follows southeast to Navakawau via South Cape. On the way back it cuts directly across some hills to Kanacea and continues up the coast without going to Delaivuna again. Southeast of Kanacea there is very little traffic.

A hike around southern Taveuni provides an interesting day out for anyone staying at Susie's Plantation or one of the other nearby resorts. From Susie's a road climbs east over the island to **Delaivuna,** where the bus turns around at a gate. The large Private Property sign here is mainly intended to ward off miscreants who create problems for the plantation owners by leaving open cattle gates. Visitors with sense enough to close the gates behind themselves may proceed.

You hike one hour down through the coconut plantation to a junction with two gates, just before a small bridge over a (usually) dry stream. If you continue walking 30 minutes down the road straight ahead across the bridge you'll reach **Salialevu,** site of the Bilyard Sugar Mill (1874-96), one of Fiji's first. In the 1860s European planters tried growing cotton on Taveuni, turning to sugar when the cotton market collapsed. Later, copra was found to be more profitable. A tall chimney, boilers, and other equipment remain below the school at Salialevu.

After a look around, return to the two gates at the bridge and follow the other dirt road southwest for an hour through the coconut plantation to **Navakawau** village at the southeast end of the island. Some of Fiji's only Australian magpies (large black-and-white birds) inhabit this plantation.

Just east of South Cape as you come from Navakawau is the **Matamaiqi Blowhole,** where trade wind-driven waves crash into the unprotected black volcanic rocks, sending geysers of sea spray soaring skyward, especially on a southern swell. The viewpoint is just off the main road.

At **Vuna,** the lava flows have formed pools beside the ocean, which fill up with fresh water at low tide and are used for washing and bathing. Tuesday around 1500 the local butcher dumps the week's offal into the sea near here and the sharks go into a feeding frenzy.

Northern Taveuni

Somosomo is the chiefly village of Cakaudrove and the seat of the Tui Cakau, Taveuni's "king"; the late Ratu Sir Penaia Ganilau, last governor general and first president of Fiji, hailed from here. The two distinct parts of the village are divided by a small stream where women wash their clothes. The southern portion is the island's commercial center with several large Indian

Necklaces of whale's teeth were a badge of chiefly authority. At night men would use wooden headrests to preserve their carefully coiffured hairdos.

stores and a couple of places to stay. Pacific Transport has its bus terminus here.

The northern part of Somosomo is the chiefly quarter with the personal residence of the Tui Cakau on the hill directly above the bridge (no entry). Beside the main road below is the large hall built for the 1986 meeting of the Great Council of Chiefs. Missionary William Cross, one of the creators of today's system of written Fijian, who died at Somosomo in 1843, is buried in the attractive new church next to the meeting hall. There's even electric street lighting in this part of town!

The challenging trail up to lovely **Lake Tagimaucia,** 823 meters high in the mountainous interior, begins behind the Mormon church at Somosomo. The first half is the hardest. You'll need a full day to do a roundtrip, and a guide (F$20) will be necessary as there are many trails to choose from. You must wade for half an hour through knee-deep mud in the crater to reach the lake's edge. Much of the lake's surface is covered with floating vegetation, and the water is only five meters deep.

Eastern Taveuni

There are three lovely waterfalls in **Tavoro Forest Park and Reserve** (admission F$5), just south of Bouma on the northeast side of Taveuni. From the information kiosk on the main road it's an easy 10-minute walk up a broad path along the river's right bank to the lower falls, which plunge 20 meters into a deep pool. You can swim here, and changing rooms, toilets, picnic tables, and a barbecue are provided. A well-constructed trail leads up to a second falls in about 30 minutes, passing a spectacular viewpoint overlooking Qamea Island and Taveuni's northeast coast. You must cross the river once, but a rope is provided for balance. Anyone in good physical shape can reach this second falls with ease, and there's also a pool for swimming. The muddy, slippery trail up to the third and highest falls involves two river crossings with nothing to hold onto, and it would be unpleasant in the rain. This trail does cut through the most beautiful portion of the rainforest, and these upper falls are perhaps the most impressive of the three, as the river plunges over a black basalt cliff, which you can climb and use as a diving platform into the deep pool. The water here is very sweet.

Tavoro Forest Park was developed with well-spent New Zealand aid money at the request of the villagers themselves, and all income goes to local community projects. In 1990 an agreement was signed putting the area in trust for 99 years and the forest park was established a year later.Eventually a trail will be cut from Tavoro right up to Lake Tagimaucia, but this awaits the creation of suitable overnight accommodations at Bouma and additional outside funding. For the time being visitors are allowed to sleep on mats in the park information kiosk (tel. 880-390) at F$5 per head; otherwise it might be possible to camp or stay with the locals.

Bouma is easily accessible by public bus daily except Sunday. If you depart Waiyevo or Somosomo on the 0800 bus, you'll have about 3.5 hours to see the falls and have a swim before catching the 1400 bus back to Waiyevo. This second bus does a roundtrip to Lavena, six km south (the 0800 bus finishes at Bouma), and it's worth jumping on for the ride even if you don't intend to get off at Lavena.

At Lavena the New Zealand government has financed the **Lavena Coastal Walk,** which opened in May 1993. The information kiosk where you pay the F$5 admission fee is right at the end of the road at Lavena and, when space is available, it's possible to sleep on one of the four mattresses on the floor upstairs in the kiosk at F$5 pp. There's no store here but the villagers will prepare meals for you at F$3 each. Otherwise, bring groceries and cook your own behind the kiosk—protect the food from mice. Lighting is by kerosene lamp, and mosquito coils are essential (the flies are a nuisance too). Additional accommodation may be available by the time you get there, and this is urgently required as it's not possible to visit Lavena as a day-trip by public bus (taxis charge F$50 roundtrip to bring you here). Buses depart Lavena for Somosomo Mon.-Sat. at 0600 and 1400, Sunday at 0800. The beach at Lavena is agreeable (be careful with the currents if you snorkel). The film *Return to the Blue Lagoon* was filmed here.

From the information kiosk at Lavena you can hike the five km down the Ravilevo Coast to **Wainibau Falls** in about an hour and a half, the last 30 minutes up the creek. Two falls here plunge into the same deep pool, and diving off either is excellent fun (allow four hours there and back from Lavena with plenty of stops). It's also possible to visit the falls by motorboat, which can be arranged at the kiosk. A boat to Wainibau Falls is F$50 for up to three persons or F$15 pp for groups of four to six. If you also want to see **Savulevu Yavonu Falls,** which plummet off a cliff directly into the sea, you must pay F$75 for up to three people or F$25 pp for up to six. Intrepid ocean kayakers sometimes paddle the 20 km down the back side of Taveuni, past countless cliffs and waterfalls. Be on the lookout for native birds.

Sports and Recreation

Taveuni and surrounding waters have become known as one of Fiji's top diving areas. The fabulous 32-km Rainbow Reef off the south coast of eastern Vanua Levu abounds in turtles, fish, overhangs, crevices, and soft corals, all in 5-10 meters of water. Favorite dive sites here include Annie's Bommie, Blue Ribbon Eel Reef, Cabbage Patch, Coral Garden, Jack's Place, Jerry's Jelly, Orgasm, Pot Luck, The Ledge, The Zoo, and White Sandy Gully. At the Great White Wall a tunnel in the reef leads past sea fans to a magnificent drop-off and a wall covered in awesome white soft coral. Beware of strong currents in the Somosomo Strait.

Way back in 1976, Ric and Do Cammick's **Dive Taveuni** (c/o Postal Agency, Matei; tel. 880-441, fax 880-466) pioneered scuba diving in this area, discovering and naming most of the sites now regularly visited by divers. They cater mostly to small groups that have prebooked from abroad.

Walk-in divers are welcome at **Aquaventure** (c/o Postal Agency, Matei; tel./fax 880-381), run by Tania de Hoon, which has its base on the beach beside Beverly Campground, walking distance from most of the places to stay on northern Taveuni. They charge F$99 for two tanks, plus F$17 for gear (F$429 for 10 dives). Night dives are F$66. When appropriate, snorkelers are taken along at F$33 pp including gear. Their five-day NAUI certification course costs F$479 including six dives (or F$110 for an introductory dive).

Rainbow Reef Divers (Glenn Dziwulski, Box 1, Waiyevo; tel. 880-286, fax 880-288) at the Garden Island Resort caters mostly to divers who've prebooked from the States. The daily two-tank dives are F$165 plus gear (no one-tank dives), night dives F$96, and PADI scuba certification costs F$660 (a one-tank "discover scuba course" is F$148). You'll find cheaper dive shops but Rainbow's facilities are first rate.

Budget-minded divers should check out **The Dive Center** (Box 69, Taveuni; tel./fax 880-125), run by Vuna Reef Divers at Susie's Plantation, which offers boat dives on the Rainbow Reef at F$50/85 for one/two tanks (plus F$15 extra for gear). The Center's four-day PADI scuba certification courses (F$370) usually begin on Monday and Susie's makes a perfect base for these activities.

Nok's Dive Center (Box 22, Taveuni; tel. 880-246, fax 880-072), at Kris Back Palace north of Susie's, offers diving at F$55/88/400 for one/two/10 dives, plus F$11 a day for gear. Night dives are F$66. Snorkelers can go along in the boat at F$10 pp although some dive sites are not really suitable for snorkeling (ask). The four-day

PADI certification course costs F$385, otherwise it's F$88 for a "baptism." Nok's dives the Great White Wall.

Offshore dive resorts such as Matangi Island and Qamea Beach Club receive mostly upscale divers who have booked from outside Fiji, and accommodations there are much more expensive than those on Taveuni.

Little Dolphin Sports (tel. 880-130), opposite Bhulabhai & Sons Supermarket, near the east end of the airstrip, rents paddle boats (F$15 a day), a three-person outrigger canoe (F$12/30 an hour/day), and snorkeling gear (F$8 a day). It's run by an Australian named Scott who is a mine of information. He'll ferry you out to a nice snorkeling spot on Honeymoon Island at F$10 pp roundtrip.

Adjacent to Aquaventure is **Ringgold Reek Kayaking** (tel. 880-083) with lots of two-person fiberglass kayaks for rent. It's run by Kenny Madden who lives up the hill.

The dive shop at the Garden Island Resort rents kayaks at F$5.50 an hour or F$22 a day.

ACCOMMODATIONS

Shoestring

Just north of Prince Charles Beach, a bit more than one km south of the airport, are two of Taveuni's two best-established campgrounds. **Beverly's Campground** (tel. 880-684), run by Bill Madden, is a peaceful, shady place, adjacent to the hallowed sands of Maravu Plantation's beach. It's F$6 pp in your own tent, or F$8 pp to sleep in a small set tent, F$9 pp in a large set tent. The toilet and shower block is nearby. Cooking facilities (one-time charge of F$2 for gas) are available, but bring groceries (Bill provides free fresh fruit daily). The kitchen shelter by the beach is a nice place to sit and swap traveler's tales with the other guests. The clean white beach is just seconds from your tent.

A few hundred meters south is **Lisi's Campground & Cottages** (c/o Postal Agency, Matei; tel. 880-194), in a small village across the road from a white-sand beach. It's F$6 pp to camp, or F$10 pp in two small *bures*. A cottage with fridge goes for F$15/25 single/double. An unlit shower/toilet block is reserved for guests. Primitive cooking facilities are available in a *bure*, and

your friendly hosts Mary and Lote Tuisago serve excellent Fijian meals at reasonable prices. Drawbacks include noise from the generator and throng of children running around, and the whole place is messy and dirty. Horseback riding can be arranged here.

A friendly Indian family runs **Kool's Accommodation** (tel. 880-395), just south of Kaba's Motel at Somosomo. The six rooms in two long blocks facing the eating area cost F$15/20 single/double, and cooking facilities are provided (but no fridge). As the price may suggest, it's basic but a good bet for those on the lowest of budgets.

Sunset Accommodation (Box 15, Taveuni; tel. 880-229), on a dusty corner near the wharf at Lovonivonu, has two basic rooms behind a small store at F$15/20 single/double. Again, this is mostly a low-budget place to crash.

Kris Back Palace (Box 22, Taveuni; tel. 880-246, fax 880-072), between Soqulu Plantation and Susie's Plantation in southern Taveuni, is on a beautiful stretch of rocky coastline with crystal-clear snorkeling waters. You can count on a good place to pitch your tent (F$7 for the first person in the tent and F$4 for the second). The two thatched two-bed *bures* are F$30 double, and there's also a five-bed dormitory *bure* at F$11 pp. The friendly managers will allow you to pick fruit at no cost in their plantation, and a three-meal deal is F$18 or you can cook your own. Scuba diving is available.

Budget

The Petersen family runs a backpackers hangout called the **Tovu Tovu Resort** (tel. 880-560, fax 880-722) at Matei just east of Bhulabhai & Sons Supermarket. It's across the road from a rocky beach with murky water, and guests often walk the two km to Prince Charles Beach to swim. The two front *bures* capable of sleeping three are self-catering at F$67/72 single/double. Just behind are another two *bures* with private bath but no cooking at F$56/62, and up the hill is a large dormitory *bure* with a communal kitchen at F$15 pp. A budget *bure* with shared bath costs F$25 double. You can also camp at F$6 per tent. The tin roofs are covered with thatch to keep them cool. The three-meal plan costs F$25 pp and the restaurant terrace is a nice place to sit and socialize. Bicycles rent for F$15 a day.

Niranjan's Budget Accommodation (c/o Postal Agency, Matei; tel. 880-406, fax 880-533) is just a five-minute walk east of the airport. The four rooms in the main building, each with two beds, fridge, fan, and cooking facilities, go for F$45/55/65 single/double/triple. Niranjan's also has an annex called **Airport Motel** two doors away, with four cheaper rooms with shared bath at F$44 double. The electric generator is on 1800-2200. The owner prepares one of the tastiest curry dinners in Fiji.

Brenda Petersen (tel. 880-171) who runs the airport snack bar can arrange rooms in the family house, the third driveway south of the airport on the inland side. Brenda's mother Margaret charges F$40 pp including all meals.

Bibi's Hideaway (Box 80, Waiyevo; tel. 880-443), about 500 meters south of the airport, has something of the gracious atmosphere of the neighboring properties without the sky-high prices. One room in a two-room cottage is F$30 single or double, while a larger family unit is F$70. The film crew from *Return to the Blue Lagoon* stayed here for three months, and with the extra income the owners built a deluxe *bure* with a picture window, which rents for F$50. All three units have access to cooking facilities and fridge, and you can pick fruit off their trees for free. Bibi's is located on lush, spacious grounds, and James, Victor, and Agnes Bibi will make you feel right at home. It's an excellent medium-priced choice if you don't mind being a bit away from the beach.

The original budget hotel on Taveuni was **Kaba's Motel & Guest House** (Box 4, Taveuni; tel. 880-233, fax 880-202) at Somosomo, which charges F$27/38/50 single/double/triple in one of four double rooms with shared facilities in the guesthouse. The cooking facilities are very good. The newer motel section is F$45/55/80 for one of the six larger units with kitchenette, fridge, fan, phone, and private bath. The water is solar-heated, so cold showers are de rigueur in overcast weather (ask for a discount in that case). Kaba's Supermarket is just up the street. No check-ins are accepted after 1800. Somosomo is a convenient place to stay for catching buses, but at night there's nothing much to do other than watch the BBC on TV.

Andrew's Place (Box 71, Waiyevo; tel./fax 880-241) is at Soqulu, a F$5 taxi ride south from

Waiyevo. The five rooms are in a 120-year-old plantation house at F$40/50 single/double (meals F$5/8/15 breakfast/lunch/dinner). The Soqulu Golf Course is only a four-minute walk away (greens fees F$20). Soqulu doesn't rent clubs but your Australian host Andrew Coghill will loan you a set, just bring your own balls. There's great snorkeling across the road, and Andrew can arrange hiking, birdwatching, and horse riding.

Susie's Plantation Resort (Box 69, Waiyevo; tel./fax 880-125), also known as Nomui Lala, just north of Vuna Point at the south end of Taveuni, offers peace and quiet amid picturesque rustic surroundings, at the right price. The 10 rooms in the plantation house are F$30/40 single/double with shared bath, or F$50/55 with private bath. Two simple seaside *bures* cost F$55 double, and a larger family *bure* costs F$60. A place in the six-bed dorm is F$15, and camping is F$10 pp (tolerated but not encouraged). Noisy late-night kava sessions often occur here, so choose your room accordingly. You can cook your own food (a well-stocked grocery store is at Vatuwiri Farm, a 10-minute walk south). Otherwise meals are available in the restaurant, housed in the oldest missionary building on the island (nonguests welcome). Electricity is available only during the dinner hours. This atmospheric resort right on the ocean has its own resident diving instructor, who leads daily trips to the Great White Wall and Rainbow Reef. The PADI scuba certification course offers a great opportunity to learn how to dive, but even if you're not a diver, you'll enjoy the superb snorkeling right off their rocky beach or at nearby Namoli Beach (better at low tide, as the current picks up appreciably when the tide comes in). Horseback riding can be arranged.

In 1998 **Vuna Lagoon Lodge** (Adi Salote Samanunu, Box 55, Waiyevo; tel./fax 880-627) opened on the Vuna Lagoon near Vuna village, a kilometer south of Vatuwiri Farm. Rooms here are F$30 double with shared bath or F$50 with private bath. Dorm beds cost F$15. Cooking facilities are provided or you can order meals. Wastes dumped by the local butcher into the sea nearby may have attracted sharks to this area and you should make inquiries before snorkeling. This place is run by the same people as Vakaviti Motel on the Coral Coast and information will be available there.

Inexpensive

Little Dolphin Sports (tel. 880-130), less than a kilometer east of the airport, has an airy, two-story bungalow with cooking facilities called the "treehouse." At F$75 a night it's good value.

Several expatriate residents of the airport area have built nice little bungalows next to their homes or fixed up rooms in their personal residences that they rent to tourists. For instance, Audrey of **Audrey's Cafe** (tel. 880-039), half a kilometer east of the airport, has a cottage at F$100 (children not admitted). An old steam tractor stands rusting under a coconut tree across the street. A few hundred meters west is **Coconut Grove Beachfront Cottages** (c/o Postal Agency, Matei; tel. 880-328), where Ronna Goldstein has three fan-cooled rooms with bath, one next to the restaurant at F$88/110 single/double and another below the beachfront terrace at F$110/132. The separate "Mango" bungalow with cooking facilities is F$132/154 (guests in the other two rooms must use the restaurant, which is no hardship as Ronna serves some of the best food in Taveuni). At both Audrey's and Ronna's, it's important to call ahead to check availability as the rooms are often full. Use the card phone at the airport for this purpose (Air Fiji sells phone cards).

Karin's Garden (tel. 880-511, fax 880-050), almost opposite Bibi's Hideaway 500 meters south of the airport, has two bungalows for F$75 that overlook the same coast as overpriced Dive Taveuni next door. You can cook and there's a restaurant on the premises.

The **Vatuwiri Farm Resort** (c/o Postal Agency, Vuna; tel./fax 880-316) at Vuna Point, a kilometer south of Susie's Plantation, offers the possibility of staying on an authentic working farm established in 1871 by James Valentine Tarte. The Tartes now produce beef, vanilla, and copra, and rent three small cottages to tourists for F$120 double a night. Three good meals are F$60 pp extra. The rocky coast here is fine for snorkeling, and horseback riding is available. The Tarte family is congenial and this is perhaps your best chance to stay on a real working farm in Fiji.

Moderate

The **Garden Island Resort** (Box 1, Waiyevo; tel. 880-286, fax 880-288) is by the sea at Waiyevo, three km south of Somosomo. Formerly known as the Castaway, this was Taveuni's premier (and only) hotel when it was built by the Travelodge chain in the 1960s. In 1996 the scuba operator Aqua Trek USA purchased the property and upgraded the facilities. The 30 a/c rooms in an attractive two-story building are F$138/168/198 single/double/triple, or F$30 pp in the two four-bed dorms. Air conditioning is F$15 extra but the ceiling fan should suffice. The buffet meal plan is F$75 pp, and eating by the pool is fun. There's no beach, but the Garden Island offers a restaurant, bar, evening entertainment, swimming pool, excursions, and water sports. Snorkeling trips are arranged twice a day to Korolevu Island and a large dive shop is on the premises. It's a nice place in which to hang out if you like large hotels. The Garden Island is also centrally located for touring Taveuni or catching interisland boats.

Luxury

About 600 meters south of the airport are two of Taveuni's most exclusive properties. **Maravu Plantation Resort** (Jochen Kiess, c/o Postal Agency, Matei; tel. 880-555, fax 880-600) is a village-style resort on a real 20-hectare copra-making plantation. It has 10 comfortable *bures* with ceiling fans from F$340/440/540 single/double/triple plus tax but including meals, transfers, horseback riding, bicycles, and some other activities. Up to two children under 14 can stay free, paying only for their meals (F$50-100 per day per child). A *meke* is held weekly. There's a bar and swimming pool on the landscaped grounds. Scuba diving and nature hikes are easily arranged. Airport transfers are F$6.

Almost across the street from Maravu Plantation is the deluxe **Dive Taveuni Resort** (Ric and Do Cammick, c/o Postal Agency, Matei; tel. 880-441, fax 880-466), formerly known as Ric's Place, patronized by an eclectic mix of scuba divers, fisherfolk, and honeymooners who arrive on prepaid packages. The five standard *bures* are F$360 pp, including meals, tax, and transfers. In addition, the clifftop honeymoon *bure* is F$1,180 double all inclusive, while the oceanfront suite is F$996 double. No alcohol is sold here, so bring your own. Dive Taveuni doesn't cater to people who stroll in unannounced. Stunning sunsets are observed from the open terrace dining area and the swimming pool

added in 1997 was designed to merge scenically with the sea on the horizon. They're closed
in February and March.

Taveuni still doesn't have a public electricity
supply but most of the places to stay have their
own generators, which typically run 1800-2100
only.

OTHER PRACTICALITIES

Food
Kumar's Restaurant (tel. 880-435; Mon.-Sat.
0700-2000), 200 meters south of the National
Bank in Waiyevo, is the cheapest regular restaurant on the island with surprisingly good curries
in the F$3 range. Recommended.

Several stalls in the fish market opposite the
Garden Island Resort serve cheap picnic-table
meals. The **Waci-Pokee Restaurant** (no phone;
open Mon.-Fri. 0800-2000, Saturday 0800-
1300/1700-2000, Sunday 1200-1430/1700-
2000), next to the National Bank in Waiyevo,
serves reasonable Chinese and local meals for
around F$5. The thatched **Cannibal Cafe** di-
rectly behind the Waci-Pokee dispenses alcoholic beverages, local authorities permitting. A
piece of chocolate cake is less than a dollar.
Their slogan is "we'd love to have you for dinner."
Enter through the restaurant or circle around
the adjacent store.

Several of the one-unit accommodation places
near the airport serve more upmarket meals, including Ronna Goldstein's **Coconut Grove Cafe**
(tel. 880-328). The setting is lovely with a terrace overlooking the sea and the food is first
rate, at prices to match. Ronna will be able to tell
you anything you want to know about Taveuni. A
similar scene revolves around **Audrey's Cafe**
(daily 1000-1800), run by an American woman at
Matei, a bit east of Ronna's. Audrey offers afternoon tea to guests who also enjoy the great
view from her terrace, and she has various
homemade goodies to take away. **Mrs. Lal's
Curry Place** (tel. 880-705), between Ronna's
and Audrey's, is cheaper with spicy Indian meals
at F$7.50 a serving. Watch for new places open-
ing in the same general area.

The **Vunibokoi Restaurant** (tel. 880-560),
at the Tovu Tovu Resort east of Bhulabhai &

Sons Supermarket at Matei, has a terrace where
nonguests can order medium-priced meals prepared by Mareta, formerly of the Coconut Grove
Cafe.

Groceries
Those staying on the northern part of the island
will appreciate the well-stocked **Bhulabhai &
Sons Supermarket** (tel. 880-462) at the Matei
Postal Agency between the airport and Nase-
lesele village. Their generous ice-cream cones
are almost worth a special trip. Bhulabhai &
Sons is closed on Sunday but a smaller Indian
store 100 meters east will sell to you through
the side window that day.

The variety of goods available at **Kaba's Supermarket** (tel. 880-088) in Somosomo is surprising, and a cluster of other small shops is adjacent. Small grocery stores also exist at Wairik
and Waiyevo. The only well-stocked grocery
store in southern Taveuni is at Vatuwiri Farm, a
kilometer south of Susie's Plantation.

Entertainment
The **180 Meridian Cinema** at Wairiki shows
mainly violence and horror films at 1930 or
weekends.

The **Taveuni Country Club** (tel. 880-133)
next to the police station up the hill at Waiyevo, is
a safe, local drinking place. It's open Thurs.-Sat
only.

There isn't any tourist-oriented nightlife on
Taveuni beyond what's offered at the **Garden Island Resort** (tel. 880-286), which stages a *meke*
and *lovo* Tuesday at 1830 (F$22 pp), but only
when enough paying guests are present.

Services
Traveler's checks can be changed at the Na
tional Bank (tel. 880-433; Mon.-Thurs. 0930
1500, Friday 0930-1600) near the Garden Is
land Resort at Waiyevo.

Club Coco (Box 75, Waiyevo; tel. 880-017
fax 880-033), next to the National Bank in Waiye
vo, sells a local clothing, handicrafts, books
maps, and souvenirs, and manager Libby
Lesuma can help with your travel and accommodations bookings.

A haircut from the barber next to Kaba's Mote
in Somosomo is F$2/3 for men/women.

Getting There

Matei Airstrip at the north tip of Taveuni is serviced twice daily by **Air Fiji** (tel. 880-062) from Suva (F$150) and Savusavu (F$82), and by **Sunflower Airlines** (tel. 880-461) from Nadi (three a day, F$222), Suva (daily, F$150), and Savusavu (twice daily, F$82). Sunflower also arrives from Labasa (F$82) three times a week. Flights to/from Taveuni are often heavily booked. You get superb views of Taveuni from the plane: sit on the right side going up, the left side coming back. Krishna Brothers (tel. 880-504) in Somosomo is the agent for Air Fiji. Sunflower doesn't have an agent on Taveuni and to book you must call Matei Airport at 880-461.

Consort Shipping operates the weekly *Spirit of Free Enterprise* service from Suva to Taveuni via Koro and Savusavu (23 hours, F$34/70 deck/cabin). This ferry departs Suva northbound Tuesday at 2100, and leaves Taveuni southbound Thursday at noon. The Consort agent, an Simpson (tel. 880-261), is at the fish market opposite the Garden Island Resort.

The **Beachcomber Cruises** car ferry *Adi Savusavu* departs Taveuni for Savusavu and Suva Wednesday at noon. It takes five hours to reach Savusavu, and after a three-hour stop continues to Suva, where it arrives at 0730 Thursday morning (F$38/44 economy/first class). The agent is Raj's Fruits and Vegetables (tel. 880-591), next to the Hot Bread Kitchen in Somosomo.

Patterson Brothers operates the barge *Yaubula* between Taveuni and Natuvu at Buca Bay on Vanua Levu, leaving Taveuni Mon.-Sat. at 0900 (two hours, F$7.70), leaving Natuvu at 1100. They also carry cars and vans for F$50. Through boat/bus tickets with a bus connection at Natuvu are available to Savusavu Mon.-Sat. (four hours, F$12.70) and to Labasa Monday, Wednesday, Friday and Saturday (six hours, F$16.20). The Patterson Brothers agent is Lesuma Holdings (tel. 880-036) in the back of the store next to the National Bank. Try to buy your combined boat/bus ticket at the Patterson Brothers office a day before, otherwise get one on the ferry itself as you board (arrive an hour before departure and be fast at holiday times as the 60-seater bus does fill up, unlike the 100-passenger ferry which always has space available). Coffee and snacks are sold on board the barge.

The small passenger boat *Grace* departs Taveuni for Natuvu Mon.-Fri. at 0545 (two hours, F$5), with regular bus connections to Savusavu (F$3). If you miss the bus connection, you'll have to wait around at Buca Bay all day for another bus to Savusavu (Public buses run from Natuvu to Savusavu only in the early morning and at 1600). If no bus is around, you should be able to find a carrier, but expect a rough trip. Information on the *Grace* is available from Mr. Latchman Prasad (tel. 880-134) who lives opposite Kaba's Supermarket in Somosomo.

If you arrive by boat at Taveuni, you could disembark at any one of three places. Some small boats from Vanua Levu transfer their passengers to the beach at Waiyevo by outboard. The large ferries from Suva tie up at a wharf a kilometer north of Waiyevo. There's another wharf called the "Korean Wharf" at Lovonivonu village, a kilometer north again, midway between Waiyevo and Somosomo, and this is usually used by the Vanua Levu ferries and other smaller cargo boats.

Getting Around

Pacific Transport (tel. 880-278) buses leave Waiyevo and Somosomo northbound to Bouma (F$2) Mon.-Sat. at 0800, 1200, and 1600; southbound to Vuna (F$2) they also leave at 0800, 1200, and 1600. The northbound 0800 bus turns around at Bouma, but the 1200 and 1600 buses carry on to Lavena (F$2). Both of the 1600 buses stop and spend the night at their turn-around points, Lavena and Navakawau, heading back to Somosomo the next morning at 0600 (at 0800 on Sunday). Sunday service is infrequent, although buses go to Bouma and Vuna at 1600. Check the current schedule carefully as soon as you arrive and beware of buses leaving a bit early. The buses begin their journeys at the Pacific Transport garage at Somosomo, but they all first head south to Waiyevo hospital to pick up passengers.

One of Taveuni's biggest drawbacks is the extremely dusty road up the northwest coast, which makes it very unpleasant to walk anywhere between Wairiki and the airport when there's a lot of fast traffic passing. This combined with rather expensive taxi fares and sporadic buses make getting around rather inconvenient. Taveuni's minibus taxis only operate on a charter basis and don't run along set routes picking up passengers at fixed rates. The taxi fare from the wharf to Somosomo is F$2; from the airport to Somosomo it will be F$10. In general, the taxi fare will be about 10 times the corresponding bus fare.

You could hire a minibus taxi and driver for the day. Write out a list of everything you want to see, then negotiate a price with a driver. Otherwise, save money by using the buses for long rides and taxis for shorter hops. Rental cars are not available (although Budget is reported to be opening a branch on the island).

OFFSHORE ISLANDS

Qamea Island

Qamea (pronounced "Nggamea") Island, just three km east of Taveuni, is the 12th-largest island in Fiji. It's 10 km long with lots of lovely bays, lush green hills, and secluded white-sand beaches. Land crabs (lairo) are gathered in abundance here during their migration to the sea at the beginning of the breeding season in late November or early December. The birdlife is also rich, due to the absence of the mongoose. Outboards from villages on Qamea land near Navakacoa village on the northeast side of Taveuni. The best time to try for a ride over is Thursday or Friday afternoons. Vatusogosogo, one of six villages on Qamea, is inhabited by descendants of blackbirded Solomon islanders. An upmarket resort is on the west side of Qamea.

Matangi Island

Matangi is a tiny horseshoe-shaped volcanic island just north of Qamea, its sunken crater forming a lovely palm-fringed bay. The island is privately owned by the Douglas family, which has been producing copra on Matangi for five generations and still does. In 1988 they diversified into the hotel business.

Matangi Island Resort (Noel Douglas, Box 83, Waiyevo; tel. 880-260, fax 880-274), 10 km northeast of Taveuni, makes no bones about serving as a base for scuba divers and some of the top dive sites in the world are close at hand. Guests are accommodated in 10 neat thatched bures well spaced among the coconut palms below Matangi's high jungly interior. It's F$368 pp including all meals and boat transfers from Taveuni, and most guests are on packages prebooked from abroad. Luxury.

Laucala Island

Laucala Island, which shares a barrier reef with Qamea, was depopulated and sold to Europeans in the mid-19th century by the chief of Taveuni, after the inhabitants sided with Tongan chief Enele Ma'afu in a local war. Today it's owned by Steven Forbes, son of the late multimillionaire businessman and New York publisher Malcolm Forbes, who is buried on the island. In 1972 Malcolm Forbes bought 12-square-km Laucala from the Australian company Morris Hedstrom for US$1 million. In 1984, six years prior to his death in 1990, Forbes opened his island to affluent tourists who now stay in seven bures, each with living room, bar, and kitchen. The price is F$475 pp per night (four-night minimum stay), including all meals, "a reasonable supply" of liquor, sports, scuba diving, and deep-sea fishing. The charter flight from Nadi to Laucala Island is F$198 pp each way. Luxury.

THE LAU GROUP

Lau is by far the most remote part of Fiji, its 57 islands scattered over a vast area of ocean between Viti Levu and Tonga. Roughly half of them are inhabited. Though all are relatively small, they vary from volcanic islands to uplifted atolls to some combination of the two. Tongan influence has always been strong in Lau, and due to Polynesian mixing the people have a somewhat lighter skin color than other Fijians. The westward migrations continue today: more than 40,000 Lauans live on Viti Levu and fewer than 13,000 on their home islands. Historically the chiefs of Lau have always had a political influence on Fiji far out of proportion to their economic or geographical importance.

Vanua Balavu (52 square km) and Lakeba (54 square km) are the largest and most important islands of the group. These are also the only islands with organized accommodations, and Vanua Balavu is the more rewarding of the two. Once accessible only after a long sea voyage on infrequent copra-collecting ships, four islands in Lau—Lakeba, Vanua Balavu, Moala, and Cicia—now have regular air service from Suva. Since the only places to stay are on Vanua Balavu, that's the logical island to head for. No banks are to be found in Lau and it's important to bring sufficient Fijian currency.

NORTHERN LAU

Vanua Balavu

The name means the "long land." The southern portion of this unusual, seahorse-shaped island is mostly volcanic, while the north is uplifted coral. This unspoiled environment of palm-ringed beaches backed by long grassy hillsides and sheer limestone cliffs is a wonderful area to explore. Varied vistas and scenic views are on all sides. To the east is a 130-km barrier reef enclosing a 37-by-16-km lagoon. The Bay of Islands at the northwest end of Vanua Balavu is a recognized hurricane shelter. The villages of Vanua Balavu are impeccably clean, the grass cut and manicured. Large mats are made on the island, and strips of pandanus can be seen drying before many of the houses.

In 1840 Commodore Wilkes of the U.S. Exploring Expedition named Vanua Balavu and its adjacent islands enclosed by the same barrier reef the Exploring Isles. In the days of sail, Lomaloma, the largest settlement, was an important Pacific port. The early trading company Hennings Brothers had its headquarters here. The great Tongan warlord Enele Ma'afu conquered northern Lau from the chiefs of Vanua Levu in 1855 and made Lomaloma the base for his bid to dominate Fiji. A small monument flanked by two cannons on the waterfront near the wharf recalls the event. Fiji's first public botanical garden was laid out here more than a century ago, but nothing remains of it. History has passed Lomaloma by. Today it's only a big sleepy village with a hospital and a couple of general stores. Some 400 Tongans live in Sawana, the south portion of Lomaloma village, and many of the houses have the round ends characteristic of

VANUA BALAVU

Bay of Islands
Nabavatu
Vutuna
Avea
Adavaci Island
Dakuirasia
Tota
Matavura
Mavana
Yanucaloa
Masomo Bay
Daliconi
Adavaci Passage
Malaka
Naruarua
Muamua
Mualevu
Boitace
Levukana
Uruone
Lomaloma
Yanuyanu
Dakuilomaloma
Narocivo
Nakama
Lagoon
Namalata
Ravi ravi Lagoon
Malata
Susui
SOUTH PACIFIC OCEAN
Susui
Munia
Urone

0   4 mi
0   4 km

© DAVID STANLEY

Lau. Fiji's current president, Ratu Sir Kamisese Mara, was born in Sawana.

Sights

Copra is the main export and there's a small coconut oil mill at **Lomaloma.** A road runs inland from Lomaloma, up and across the island to **Dakuilomaloma.** From the small communications station on a grassy hilltop midway there's an excellent view.

Follow the road south from Lomaloma three km to **Narocivo** village, then continue two km beyond to the narrow passage separating Vanua Balavu and Malata islands. At low tide you can easily wade across to **Namalata** village. Alternatively, work your way around to the west side of Vanua Balavu, where there are isolated tropical beaches. There's good snorkeling in this passage.

A guide can show you **hot springs** and **burial caves** among the high limestone outcrops between Narocivo and Namalata. This can be easily arranged at Nakama, the tiny collection of houses closest to the cliffs, upon payment of a nominal fee. Small bats inhabit some of the caves.

Rent a boat to take you over to the **Raviravi Lagoon** on Susui Island, the favorite picnic spot near Lomaloma for the locals. The beach and snorkeling are good, and there's even a cave you can explore if you're interested. **Munia Island** is a privately owned coconut plantation where paying guests are accommodated in two *bures*.

Accommodations

Mr. Poasa Delailomaloma (tel. 895-060) and his brother Laveti operate a charming traditional-style resthouse in the middle of Lomaloma village. A bed and all meals cost F$30 pp. Budget.

In Sawana village a short walk away from Poasa's is **Moana's Guesthouse** (Box 11, Lomaloma; tel. 895-006), run by Tevita and Carolyn Fotofili with the help of little daughter Moana. It's F$30 pp including all meals to share an oval-ended Tongan-style house with a three-bedded dorm and double room. Both places make perfect bases from which to explore the island, and you get a feel for village life while retaining a degree of privacy. The Fotofilis are planning to build some beach *bures* and a campground a kilometer from the village, so call and ask. Budget.

You can also stay at Joe and Hélène Tuwai's **Nawanawa Estate** (Box 20, Lomaloma), a kilometer from Daliconi village near the airport on the northwest side of the island. There's no phone but you can try announcing your arrival by writing them a letter as soon as you've booked your flight. They meet all flights and can accommodate 10 persons on the estate. In the unlikely event that they were full, something else could be arranged. The Tuwais charge F$40 pp including meals (children under 10 F$20). You'll share their attractive colonial-style home with solar electricity (no generator noise), and aside from hiking, snorkeling, and fishing, you can ask to be dropped on a deserted island for a small charge. Boat trips to the Bay of Islands are also possible. All three places above accept cash only. Budget.

In 1994 Ratu Sir Kamisese Mara, paramount chief of the Lau Group, opened the **Lomaloma Resort** (Box 55, Lomaloma; tel. 895-091, fax 895-092) on tadpole-sized Yanuyanu Island just off Lomaloma. The seven round-ended *bures* (or *fales*) furnished in the traditional style catered mostly to upmarket scuba divers and cost F$276/450 single/double including all meals. In 1998 the Lomaloma Resort was closed and it was still not known when/if they would reopen.

Getting There

Air Fiji flies to Vanua Balavu three times a week from Suva (F$150). The flights are heavily booked, so reserve your return journey before leaving Suva. A bus runs from the airstrip to Lomaloma. After checking in at the airstrip for departure you'll probably have time to scramble up the nearby hill for a good view of the island. Boat service from Suva is only every couple of weeks.

Several carriers a day run from Lomaloma north to Mualevu, and some carry on to Mavana.

Other Islands of Northern Lau

After setting himself up at Lomaloma on Vanua Balavu in 1855, Chief Ma'afu encouraged the establishment of European copra and cotton plantations, and several islands are freehold land to this day. **Kanacea,** to the west of Vanua Balavu, was sold to a European by the Tui Cakau in 1863, and the Kanacea people now reside on Taveuni. **Mago** (20 square km), a copra estate formerly owned by English planter Jim Barron, was purchased by the Tokyu Corporation of Japan in 1985 for F$6 million.

Naitauba is a circular island about 186 meters high with high cliffs on the north coast. Originally owned by Hennings Brothers, in 1983 it was purchased from TV star Raymond Burr by the California spiritual group Johannine Daist Communion for US$2.1 million. Johannine Daist holds 4- to 8-week meditation retreats on Naitauba for longtime members of the communion. The communion's founder and teacher, Baba Da Free John, the former Franklin Albert Jones, who attained enlightenment in Hollywood in 1970, resides on the island.

There's a single Fijian village and a gorgeous white-sand beach on **Yacata Island.** Right next to Yacata and sharing the same lagoon is 260-hectare **Kaimbu Island,** which was owned by the Rosa family from 1872 to 1969, when it was purchased by an American couple who opened a small luxury resort here in 1987. In 1998 Kaimbu was the target of a spectacular pirate raid by thieves who escaped with the contents of the resort safe, not the first time this has happened in Fiji. A year later the five units were rebuilt, and you can now expect to pay around F$2,000 per couple per day (minimum stay seven nights—children not accommodated), all inclusive. The chartered flight from Suva or Taveuni to Kaimbu's central airstrip is another F$1,000 pp return. Add 10% tax to all rates. Bookings are handled by Kaimbu Island Associates (Box 10392, Newport Beach, CA 92658, U.S.A.; tel. 800/473-0332, fax 949/644-5773; e-mail: kaimbu@earthlink.net). Luxury.

Vatu Vara to the south, with its soaring interior plateau, golden beaches, and azure lagoon, is privately owned and unoccupied much of the time. The circular, 314-meter-high central limestone terrace, which makes the island look like a hat when viewed from the sea, gives it its other name, Hat Island. There is reputed to be buried treasure on Vatu Vara.

Katafaga to the southeast of Vanua Balavu was at one time owned by Harold Gatty, the famous Australian aviator who founded Fiji Airways (later Air Pacific) in 1951.

Cicia, between Northern and Southern Lau, receives Air Fiji flights from Suva (F$138) twice a week. Five Fijian villages are found on Cicia,

and much of the 34-square-km island is covered by coconut plantations. Fiji's only black-and-white Australian magpies have been introduced to Cicia and Taveuni.

Wailagi Lala, northernmost of the Lau Group, is a coral atoll bearing a lighthouse, which beckons to ships entering Nanuku Passage, the northwest gateway to Fiji.

SOUTHERN LAU

Lakeba
Lakeba, the main island of southern Lau, is a rounded volcanic island reaching 215 meters. The fertile red soils of the rolling interior hills have been planted with pine, but the low coastal plain, with eight villages and all the people, is covered with coconuts. To the east is a wide lagoon enclosed by a barrier reef. In the olden days, the population lived on Delai Kedekede, an interior hilltop well suited for defense.

The original capital of Lakeba was Nasaqalau on the north coast, and the present inhabitants of Nasaqalau retain strong Tongan influence. When the Nayau clan conquered the island, their paramount chief, the Tui Nayau, became ruler of all of Southern Lau from his seat at Tubou. During the 1970s and 1980s Ratu Sir Kamisese Mara, the present Tui Nayau, served as prime minister of Fiji.

A 29-km road runs all the way around Lakeba and Air Fiji flies here from Suva. Tubou, on the south side of Lakeba, is an attractive village and one of the largest in Fiji, with a hospital, wharf, several stores, and the Lau provincial headquarters, but no hotels. Tubou was originally situated at Korovusa just inland, where the foundations of former houses can still be seen. Farther inland on the same road is the forestry station and a nursery.

The Tongan chief Enele Ma'afu (died 1881) is buried on a stepped platform behind the Provincial Office near Tubou's wharf. In 1847 Ma'afu arrived in Fiji with a small Tongan army ostensibly to advance the spread of Christianity, and by 1855 he dominated eastern Fiji from his base at Vanua Balavu. In 1869 Ma'afu united the group into the Lau Confederation and took the title Tui Lau. Two years later he accepted the supremacy of Cakobau's Kingdom of Fiji, and in 1874 he signed the cession to Britain. Alongside Ma'afu is the grave of Ratu Sir Lala Sukuna (1888-1958), an important figure in the development of indigenous Fijian self-government. David Cargill and William Cross, the first Methodist missionaries to arrive in Fiji, landed on the beach just opposite the burial place on 12 October 1835. Here they invented the present system of written Fijian.

Other Islands of Southern Lau
Unlike the islands of northern Lau, many of which are freehold and owned by outsiders, the isles of southern Lau are communally owned by the Fijian inhabitants. This is by far the most remote corner of Fiji. In a pool on **Vanua Vatu** are red prawns similar to those of Vatulele and Vanua Levu. Here the locals can summon the prawns with a certain chant.

Oneata is famous for its mosquitoes and tapa cloth. In 1830 two Tahitian teachers from the London Missionary Society arrived on Oneata and were adopted by a local chief who had previously visited Tonga and Tahiti. The men spent the rest of their lives on the island, and there's a monument to them at Dakuloa village.

Moce is known for its tapa cloth, which is also made on Namuka, Vatoa, and Ono-i-Lau. **Komo** is famous for its handsome women and dances *(meke)*, which are performed whenever a ship arrives. Moce, Komo, and Olorua are unique in that they are volcanic islands without uplifted limestone terraces.

The **Yagasa Cluster** is owned by the people of Moce, who visit it occasionally to make copra. Fiji's finest *tanoa* are carved from *vesi* (ironwood) at **Kabara,** the largest island in southern Lau. The surfing is also said to be good at Kabara, if you can get there.

Fulaga is known for its woodcarving; large outrigger canoes are still built on Fulaga, as well as on **Ogea.** More than 100 tiny islands in the Fulaga lagoon have been undercut into incredible mushroom shapes. The water around them is tinged with striking colors by the dissolved limestone, and there are numerous magnificent beaches. Yachts can enter this lagoon through a narrow pass.

Ono-i-Lau, far to the south, is closer to Tonga than to the main islands of Fiji. It consists of three small volcanic islands, remnants of a single crater, in an oval lagoon. A few tiny coral islets sit on the barrier reef. The people of Ono-i-Lau make the best *magi magi* (sennit rope) and *tabu kaisi* mats in the country. Only high chiefs may sit on these mats. Ono-i-Lau formerly had air service from Suva, but this has been suspended.

The Moala Group
Structurally, geographically, and historically, the high volcanic islands of Moala, Totoya, and Matuku have more to do with Viti Levu than with the rest of Lau. In the mid-19th century they were conquered by the Tongan warlord Enele Ma'afu, and today they're still administered as part of the Lau Group. All three islands have varied scenery, with dark green rainforests above grassy slopes, good anchorage, many villages, and abundant food. Their unexplored nature yet relative proximity to Suva by boat make them an ideal escape for adventurers. No tourist facilities of any kind exist in the Moala Group.

Triangular **Moala** is an intriguing 68-square-km island, the ninth-largest in Fiji. Two small crater lakes on the summit of Delai Moala (467 meters) are covered with matted sedges, which will support a person's weight. Though the main island is volcanic, an extensive system of reefs flanks the shores. Ships call at the small government station of Naroi, also the site of an airstrip that receives **Air Fiji** flights four times a week from Suva (F$136).

Totoya is a horseshoe-shaped high island enclosing a deep bay on the south. The bay, actually the island's sunken crater, can only be entered through a narrow channel known as the Gullet, and the southeast trades send high waves across the reefs at the mouth of the bay, making this a dangerous place. Better anchorage is found off the southwest arm of the island. Five Fijian villages are found on Totoya, while neighboring **Matuku** has seven. The anchorage in a submerged crater on the west side of Matuku is one of the finest in Fiji.

ROTUMA

This isolated six-by-14-km volcanic island, 600 km north of Viti Levu, is surrounded on all sides by more than 322 km of open sea. In the beginning Raho, the Samoan folk hero, dumped two basketfuls of earth here to create the twin islands, joined by the Motusa Isthmus, and installed Sauiftoga as king. Tongans from Niuafo'ou conquered Rotuma in the 17th century and ruled from Noa'tau until they were overthrown.

The first recorded European visit was by Captain Edwards of HMS *Pandora* in 1791, while he was searching for the *Bounty* mutineers. Christianity was introduced in 1842 by Tongan Wesleyan missionaries, followed in 1847 by Marist Roman Catholics. Their followers fought pitched battles in the religious wars of 1871 and 1878, with the Wesleyans emerging victorious. Escaped convicts and beachcombers also flooded in but mostly succeeded in killing each other off. Tiring of strife, the chiefs asked Britain to annex the island in 1881, and it has been part of Fiji ever since. European planters ran the copra trade from their settlement at Motusa until local cooperatives took over.

Rotuma is run like a colony of Fiji, with the administration in the hands of a district officer responsible to the district commissioner at Levuka. Decisions of the 15-member Rotuma island council are subject to veto by the national government. Some 2,800 Rotumans presently inhabit the island, and another 4,600 of their number live in Suva. The light-skinned Polynesian Rotumans are easily distinguished from Fijians. The women weave fine white mats. Fiji's juiciest oranges are grown here and Rotuma kava is noted for its strength. The climate is damp and hot.

Sights

Ships arrive at a wharf on the edge of the reef, connected to Oinafa Point by a 200-meter coral causeway, which acts as a breakwater. There's a lovely white beach at **Oinafa.** The airstrip is to the west, between Oinafa and Ahau, the government station. At **Noa'tau** southeast of Oinafa is a coop store; nearby, at **Sililo,** visit a hill with large stone slabs and old cannons scattered about, marking the burial place of the kings of yore. Look for the fine stained-glass windows in the Catholic church at **Sumi** on the south coast. Inland near the center of the island is Mt. Suelhof (256 meters), the highest peak; climb it for the view.

Maftoa across the Motusa Isthmus has a cave with a freshwater pool. In the graveyard at Maftoa are huge stones brought here long ago. It's said four men could go into a trance and carry the stones with their fingers. **Sororoa Bluff** (218 meters) above Maftoa should also be climbed for

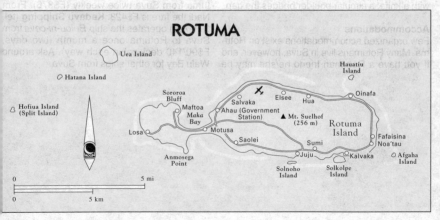

ROTUMA

CAPSULE HINDI VOCABULARY

aao—come
accha—good
bhaahut julum—very beautiful (slang)
chota—small (male)
choti—small (female)
dhanyabaad—thank you
ek aur—one more
haan—yes
hum jauo—I go (slang)
jalebi—an Indian sweet
jao—go
kab—when
kahaan—where
Kahaan jata hai?—Where are you going?
Kaise hai?—How are you?

khana—food
kitna?—how much?
kya—what
laao—bring
maaf kijye ga—excuse me
nahi—no
namaste—hello, goodbye
pani—water
rait—okay
ram ram—same as *namaste*
roti—a flat Indian bread
seedhe jauo—go straight
Theek bhai.—I'm fine.
Yeh kia hai?—What's this?
yihaan—here

the view. Deserted **Vovoe Beach** on the west side of Sororoa is one of the finest in the Pacific. A kilometer southwest of Sororoa is **Solmea Hill** (165 meters), with an inactive crater on its north slope. On the coast at the northwest corner of Rotuma is a natural **stone bridge** over the water.

Hatana, a tiny islet off the west end of Rotuma, is said to be the final resting place of Raho, the demigod who created Rotuma. A pair of volcanic rocks before a stone altar surrounded by a coral ring are said to be the King and Queen stones. Today Hatana is a refuge for seabirds. **Hofiua** or Split Island looks like it was cut in two with a knife; a circular boulder bridges the gap.

Accommodations

Few organized accommodations exist on Rotuma. Many Rotumans live in Suva, however, and if you have a Rotuman friend he/she may be willing to send word to his/her family to expect you. Ask your friend what you should take along as a gift. Although the National Bank of Fiji (tel. 891-023) has a small branch at Ahau on Rotuma, you should change enough money for all local expenditures before leaving Suva.

Rotuma Island Backpackers (Box 83, Rotuma; tel. 891-290) is operated by Vani Marseu of Motusa village who asks F$15 per couple to pitch a tent.

Getting There

Sunflower Airlines (tel. 891-084) flies to Rotuma from Suva twice weekly (F$376). From Nadi the fare is F$428. **Kadavu Shipping** (tel. 311-766) operates the ship *Bulou-ni-ceva* from Suva to Rotuma once a month (two days, F$90/140 deck/cabin each way). Ask around Walu Bay for other ships from Suva.

CAPSULE FIJIAN VOCABULARY

Although most people in Fiji speak English fluently, mother tongues include Fijian, Hindi, and other Pacific languages. Knowledge of a few words of Fijian, especially slang words, will make your stay more exciting and enriching. Fijian has no pure *b*, *c*, or *d* sounds as they are known in English. When the first missionaries arrived, they invented a system of spelling, with one letter for each Fijian sound. The reader should be aware that the sound "mb" is written *b*, "nd" is *d*, "ng" is *g*, "ngg" is *q*, and "th" is *c*.

Au lako mai Kenada.—I come from Canada
au la o—Vanua Levu version of *barewa*
au lili—affirmative response to *au la o* (also *la o mai*)
Au ni lako mai vei?—Where do you come from?
Au sa lako ki vei?—Where are you going?

barewa—a provocative greeting for the opposite sex
bula—a Fijian greeting

Daru lako!—Let's go!
dua—one
dua oo—said by males when they meet a chief or enter a Fijian *bure*
dua tale—once more

e rewa—a positive response to *barewa*

io—yes

kana—eat
kauta mai—bring
kauta tani—take away
kaivalagi—foreigner
koro—village
Kocei na yacamu?—What's your name?

lailai—small
lako mai—come
lako tani—go
levu—big, much
lima—five
Loloma yani.—Please pass along my regards.

maleka—delicious
magimagi—coconut rope fiber
magiti—feast
marama—madam
mataqali—a clan lineage
moce—goodbye

Na cava oqo?—What is this?
Nice bola.—You're looking good.
ni sa bula—Hello, how are you? (can also say *sa bula* or *bula vinaka*; the answer is *an sa bula vinaka*)
ni sa moce—good night
ni sa yadra—good morning

qara—cave

rewa sese—an affirmative response to *barewa*
rua—two

sa vinaka—it's okay
sega—no, none
sega na leqa—you're welcome
sota tale—see you again

talatala—reverend
tabu rewa—a negative response to *barewa*
tolu—three
tulou—excuse me
turaga—sir, Mr.

va—four
vaka lailai—a little, small
vaka levu—a lot, great
vaka malua—slowly
vaka totolo—fast
vale—house
vale lailai—toilet
vanua—land, custom, people
vinaka—thank you
vinaka vakalevu—thank you very much
vu—an ancestral spirit

wai—water

yalo vinaka—please
yadra—good morning
yaqona—kava, grog

NEW CALEDONIA
INTRODUCTION

New Caledonia—or Kanaky, as the indigenous Melanesian inhabitants call it—is unique. In Nouméa, the capital, the fine French restaurants, designer boutiques, and cosmopolitan crowds all proclaim that this is the Paris of the Pacific. Yet over on the east coast of the main island and on all of the outliers, the Kanaks (from *kanaka,* the Hawaiian word for "human") and *la Coutume* (native custom) have survived a century and a half of colonial repression.

During the 1980s, the clash of the irresistible force of Kanak nationalism against the immovable mass of entrenched French settlers catapulted the territory into world headlines more than once. Then in 1988, a 10-year truce was signed, consolidated in a 1998 referendum. A phased increase in local autonomy has been approved, and full independence could come after a 15 to 20-year transitional period. Peace has returned to the "Great Land" and its adjacent islands.

Though many tourists visit Nouméa, few cross the Chaîne Centrale to Grande Terre's exotic east coast, or travel by sea or air to the charming outer islands. Yet this is something you really must do to see the true New Caledonia. The possibilities are limitless, and it's often easier to visit New Caledonia than it is to tour Vanuatu or Solomon Islands, as there aren't a lot of custom fees to pay or permissions to seek, and public facilities are infinitely better. Wherever you go, you'll be received with warmth and interest, especially when people hear you speaking English. This big French colony just north of the tropic of Capricorn, midway between Fiji and Australia, is quite unlike any of its neighbors and will surprise you in every respect.

The Land
New Caledonia consists of a cigar-shaped mainland (Grande Terre), the Isle of Pines, the Loyalty Group, and the small uninhabited dependencies of Walpole Island (125 hectares), the d'Entrecasteaux Reefs (64 hectares), and the more distant Chesterfield Islands (101 hectares). The d'Entrecasteaux Reefs consist of two separate lagoons centered on tiny Huon and Surprise Is-

lands, with a deep strait 10 km wide between. The territory's 18,576 square km are divided into three provinces: North Province (9,583 square km), South Province (7,012 square km), and Loyalty Islands Province (1,981 square km).

Grande Terre is part of the great fold in the earth's surface that runs from the central highlands of Papua New Guinea to the northern peninsula of New Zealand. The geology is complex, with metamorphic, sedimentary, and volcanic rock present. Grande Terre is 400 km long and 50 km wide, the sixth-largest island in the

South Pacific (after New Guinea, the two islands of New Zealand, Tasmania, and New Britain). It's slowly sinking as the Indo-Australian Plate pushes under the Pacific Plate to the east; the winding, indented coastline is a result of this submergence. Ten km off both coasts is the second-longest barrier reef in the world, which marks how big the island once was.

Locals refer to Grande Terre as "Le Caillou" or "La Roche" (The Rock). The interior is made up of row upon row of craggy mountains throughout its length, such as Mt. Panie (1,639 meters) in

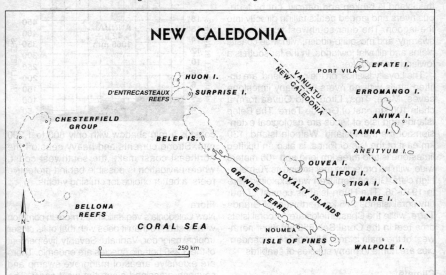

NEW CALEDONIA

NEW CALEDONIA AT A GLANCE

ISLAND	AREA (sq. km)	HIGHEST POINT (m)	POPULATION (1996)	PERCENT KANAK
Grande Terre	16,192	1,639	173,365	36.9
Isle of Pines	152	262	1,671	93.7
Mare	642	138	6,896	97.2
Lifou	1,196	90	10,007	96.7
Ouvea	132	39	3,974	97.8
Isles Belep	70	283	923	99.3
TOTAL	**18,576***		**196,836**	**44.1**

*includes other dependencies

the north and Mt. Humboldt (1,618 meters) in the south, and it contains 30% of the world's known reserves of nickel ore (enough to last another century at the present rate of extraction), as well as profitable deposits of other minerals such as tungsten, cobalt, copper, gold, manganese, iron, and chromium. The landscape, you'll notice, is wounded in many locales by huge open-pit mines—the Great Red Menace. Bulldozer tracks and drill holes leave ugly scars, and sediments unleashed by the mining turn the rivers thick red and kill the reefs. The verdant northeast coast of this island is broken and narrow, cut by tortuous rivers and jagged peaks falling directly into the lagoon. The drier southwest coast is low, swampy, and mosquito-ridden, with wide coastal plains and alluvial lowlands. In the far south is a lowland plain of lakes.

The Loyalty Islands, on the other hand, are uplifted atolls with no rivers but many limestone caves. Maré, Tiga, Lifou, and Ouvéa form a chain 100 km east of Grande Terre. The Belep Islands and Isle of Pines are geological extensions of the main island. Walpole Island, 130 km east of the Isle of Pines, is also an uplifted limestone island three km long and 400 meters wide, with no protective reef around its 70-meter-high cliffs. Guano (fertilizer) was exploited here in 1910-36. The Huon Islands consist of four tiny coral islands 275 km northwest of Grande Terre, while the Chesterfields are 11 coral islets on a reef in the Coral Sea 550 km west-northwest of the main island. All of these dependencies are home to many species of seabirds.

Climate

New Caledonia is farther south than most other South Pacific islands; this, combined with the refreshing southeast trade winds, accounts for its sunny, moderate climate, similar to that of the south of France. It can even be cool and windy from June to September, and campers will need sleeping bags. The ocean is warm enough for bathing year-round.

December to March is warm and rainy; it's also the cyclone season. The cyclonic depressions can bring heavy downpours and cause serious flooding. The windward northeast coast of Grande Terre catches the prevailing winds and experiences as much as 3,000 mm of precipitation a year, while the leeward southwest

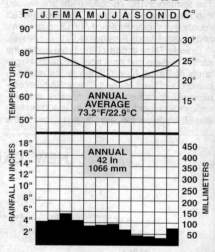

coast is a rain shadow with only 800 to 1,200 mm. Strong currents and heavy seas off the northeast coast make the southwest coast, where navigation is possible behind protective reefs, a better choice for cruising yachts.

Flora

New Caledonia's vegetation has more in common with Australia's than it does with that of its closer tropical neighbor, Vanuatu. Seventy-five percent of the 3,250 botanic species are endemic. There are extensive areas of mangrove swamp and savanna grassland along the west coast. The only sizable forests are in the mountains.

The territory's most distinctive tree is a pine known as the *Araucaria columnaris*, which towers 30-45 meters high, with branches only two meters long. It's common along the more forested east coast and in the south, standing on low hills along the rockier shorelines and on the offshore islands. Often confused with the better-known Norfolk pine or *Araucaria excelsa,* the *Araucaria columnaris* or "candelabra" pine has a cylindrical profile whereas the Norfolk pine is conical. They're the most prominent floral features of these neighboring islands when viewed from the sea, and European mariners from Captain Cook onwards have been suitably impressed.

The most characteristic tree of the savannas of the northern and western of Grande Terre is the *niaouli*, a relative of the eucalyptus. This tree has a white, almost completely fireproof bark, which peels off in papery layers and is used as an excellent medicinal oil, somewhat like eucalyptus oil. Through its ability to survive bush fires, the *niaouli* plays an important environmental role in this mountainous country by maintaining the continuity of the vegetation.

Fauna

The only native mammals are the flying fox, a bat, and the rat. The pig was unknown to the indigenous people prior to European contact. The deer that inhabit the savannas of Grande Terre are descended from two pairs introduced in 1862. Some of the butterflies possess a rare beauty. Eighty-eight species of birds are found in New Caledonia, 18 of them endemic. Only a few hundred specimens of the Ouvéa parakeet still exist. The purple swamp hen with its red beak and blue body is often seen running around west coast campgrounds.

The national bird is the flightless *cagou* (*Rhynochetos jubatus*), or kagu, about the size of a small rooster. This bird has lovely soft gray plumage, contrasted by striped brown-and-white wings. The *cagou's* crest rises when the bird is angered, and its cry is like the bark of a dog. It eats insects, worms, and snails. As it hatches only one egg a year and is slow on the ground, the *cagou* is threatened with extinction: dogs often outrun and kill it. Fewer than 1,000 survive in Rivière Bleue Provincial Park at the west end of Yaté Lake and elsewhere.

The extreme richness of life on the reefs compensates for the lack of variety on land. New Caledonia's 1,600 km of barrier reefs are home to 350 species of coral, 1,500 species of fish, and 20,000 species of invertebrates. The territory's protected lagoons total 23,000 square km, with an average depth of 20 meters—the largest lagoon complex in the world.

HISTORY

Prehistory

It's not certain when the Papuan peoples reached New Caledonia. Some 300 earth mounds dating from 6000 B.C. discovered on the Isle of Pines were once thought to prove habitation for at least 8,000 years, but the mounds are now accepted as having been constructed by extinct giant birds. What is known for sure is that Austronesian-speakers have been here for more than 3,000 years. *Lapita* sites have been found near Koné and on the Isle of Pines, the pottery carbon-dated at earlier than 1000 B.C. Prehistoric rock carvings are found throughout the territory. Back migrations of Polynesians reached the Loyalty Islands just a few hundred years before the Europeans.

The Kanak clans lived in small villages of 50 people and farmed their own land, using sophisticated irrigation systems and terraced taro gardens. Kanak culture has been called the "yam civilization," because of the importance of this

Masks such as these represented water spirits and were produced only in the north part of Grande Terre. The headdress and beard were made of human hair, and the lower portion of the costume shrouded the body of the dancer in a net of feathers.

FIELD MUSEUM OF NATURAL HISTORY, CHICAGO

tuber as a staple and in ceremonial exchanges. Land was owned collectively but controlled by the oldest son of the first clan to settle in the place.

The center of the village was the *grande case*, a large conical-roofed house where the chief lived and ceremonies were performed. Religion was animistic. Of the many spirits loose in the land, the most powerful were the clan ancestors. Society was based around a relationship between the living and their ancestors, both of whom the chief represented, in a sense.

A number of clans formed an autonomous tribe. Local tribes had little contact with each other, and thus many languages evolved; most people lived in the interior, and language groups extended across the main island, rather than down the coasts. When Captain Cook, the first European, arrived in September 1774, there were more than 70,000 Kanaks living in these islands.

Contact and Conquest

Cook landed at Balade, on the northeast coast of Grande Terre, and gave New Caledonia its name—the mountainous island reminded him of the Scottish Highlands (Caledonia was the Romans' name for Scotland). After more navigators (d'Entrecasteaux and Huon de Kermadec), traders arrived looking for sandalwood and bêche-de-mer. The first missionaries were Protestants from the London Missionary Society, who established themselves on Maré (1841) and Lifou (1842) islands. French Catholic missionaries arrived at Balade in 1843, but Kanak hostility and British protests caused them to withdraw four years later.

At this time France was watching enviously the establishment of successful British colonies in Australia and New Zealand. So in 1853, with the idea of creating a penal colony similar to that in New South Wales, Emperor Napoléon III ordered the annexation of New Caledonia. The Loyalties were claimed in 1866. Île Nou, an island in Nouméa Bay, never attained the notoriety of its contemporary, Devil's Island off South America, but between 1864 and 1897 some 20,000 French convicts sentenced to more than eight years hard labor were transported there, although no more than 8,000 were present at any one time. They were used for public works and construction projects in the early days.

Some 3,900 political prisoners from the Paris Commune were held at Ducos near Nouméa and on the Isle of Pines during 1871-79. Unlike the common criminals who had preceded them, many of the *communards* were cultured individuals. For example, Louise Michel, the "red virgin," taught Kanak children in Nouméa and took an active interest in the indigenous way of life. In her memoirs, Michel compared the freedom struggle of the Kanaks to that of Paris in 1871.

Colonialism and War

In 1864 Jules Garnier, a French mining engineer, discovered nickel on the banks of the Diahot River. Copper was found at Balade in 1872, cobalt in 1875. The Société le Nickel (SLN) was established in 1876, and mining began in earnest. This lead to an increase in the land seizures already underway, causing food shortages and the destruction of the Kanak way of life. In 1878 High Chief Atai of La Foa managed to unite many of the central tribes and launched a guerrilla war that cost 200 Frenchmen and 1,200 Kanaks their lives. Eventually Atai was betrayed by a rival tribe and assassinated.

The French government used the revolt as an excuse to establish a series of "indigenous reservations" for the confinement of the natives in areas the French miners and settlers didn't want, opening the rest of Grande Terre to mining and stock raising. Many clans were forced off their own lands onto that of other clans, leading to further rivalry and disruption. Most of the French political prisoners on the island, who had fought for their own freedom just a few years previously, assisted the colonial regime in repressing the "savages" (Louise Michel was an exception).

The French government assumed title to two-thirds of Grande Terre, another quarter was eventually given or sold to white settlers, and only 10% of the main island (in scattered, hilly areas) was left to the original inhabitants. Title to even these crowded holdings was uncertain. The *colons* (settlers) brought in cattle and sheep, and occupied the river valleys and coastal plains. Tribes were relocated in 150 villages under puppet chiefs and were easily controlled by French *gendarmes*. To obtain cheap labor, the French imposed a heavy poll tax on the Kanaks, effectively forcing them to work for the *colons* in order to obtain the money to pay. With their traditional way of life disrupted, the Kanak population declined from around 60,000 in 1878 to 42,500 in 1887, and 27,000 in 1926. Only during the 1930s did their numbers again increase.

In 1917, the forced recruitment of Kanaks into the French army led High Chief Noel to appeal to his people to fight the French at home as well as Kanak soldiers had fought the Germans abroad (1,000 Kanaks were killed in WW I). Although not as widespread as the 1878 revolt, the fighting lasted two months in north and northwest Grande Terre, and 11 Europeans and 200 Kanaks died. Further land alienations followed. The depression of the 1930s wiped out many small French farmers, and land was concentrated in the hands of a few, as it is today.

In June 1940, after the fall of France, the Conseil Général of New Caledonia voted unanimously to support the Free French government, and in September the pro-Vichy governor was forced to leave for Indochina. The territory became an important Allied base in March 1942, and the fleet that turned back the Japanese navy in the Battle of the Coral Sea (May 1942) was based at Nouméa. Hundreds of thousands of American troops and a lesser number of New Zealand troops passed this way; in the Pacific, only San Francisco handled more wartime cargo. Several Nouméa neighborhoods still bear names like "Receiving" and "Motor Pool" bestowed at this time. Kanaks employed by the Americans received much better treatment than they had come to expect from the French.

Political Development

After WW II, France had a fairly progressive colonial policy. Partly due to a shortage of labor in the nickel industry, the Kanaks were finally given French citizenship in 1946 and the repressive "indigenous regulations" that forbade them from leaving their reservations without police permission was repealed. In 1951, the French parliament gave the right to vote to a large number of indigenous people throughout the French Union, and Maurice Lenormand of the multiracial Union Calédonienne was elected to the French National Assembly. Lenormand's lobbying won an elected territorial assembly with the power to make laws, and in 1957, New Caledonia became an Overseas Territory and seemed on the road to independence.

Then came an armed uprising by French settlers on 18 June 1958, and the rise to power in France of Général de Gaulle, who dissolved the territorial assembly and appointed a repressive new governor. In 1963 Lenormand was jailed for a year, and deprived of his civil liberties by the French government for five years in a frame-up involving the bombing of the Territorial Assembly. The same year, the French National Assembly scrapped New Caledonia's limited autonomy and returned full control to the governor.

Lenormand's successor, Roch Pidjot, Kanak chief of the La Conception tribe near Nouméa, represented the Union Calédonienne in the French National Assembly for two decades until his retirement in 1986. His many proposals for self-government were never considered. A 1977 gerrymander created a second National Assembly seat for Nouméa and the west coast of Grande Terre, and this was taken a year later by businessman Jacques Lafleur, the wealthiest person in New Caledonia. In 1979 the Union Calédonienne united with four other pro-independence parties to form the Front Indépendantiste, which took 14 of the 36 seats in the Territorial Assembly.

On 19 September 1981, Pierre Declercq, secretary-general of the Union Calédonienne, was shot through a window of his Mont Dore home. No one has ever been brought to trial for this crime. Declercq's murder further united the independence movement, and in the 1982 elections, the Front Indépendantiste gained a majority in the territorial assembly. Jean-Marie Tjibaou (pronounced "chi-bow"), a former Catholic priest, became vice-president of the government council.

Crisis

Prior to the May 1981 election of François Mitterrand, the French left had assured the Kanaks that their right to self-determination would be respected. Once in power, the Socialists' promises proved empty. Thus disillusioned Kanak activists reorganized their movement into the Front de Libération Nationale Kanake et Socialiste (FLNKS), and decided to actively boycott the territorial assembly elections of 18 November 1984. Their demand was immediate independence.

Roadblocks were set up and ballot boxes destroyed. Though thousands of transient French cast ballots, voter turnout dropped from 75% in

MOUVEMENT UNION CALÉDONIENNE

Murdered activist Éloi Machoro remains a symbol of the independence struggle.

the 1979 elections to less than 50% in 1984. By default, the anti-independence Rassemblement pour la Calédonie dans la République (RPCR) won 34 of the 42 seats. On 1 December 1984 the FLNKS proclaimed a Provisional Government of Kanaky and tightened its roadblocks throughout the territory. President Mitterrand's personal envoy Edgard Pisani arrived on 3 December 1984 and declared that he would work out a plan for self-government within two months.

Two nights later, on 5 December 1984, a gang of French *colons* armed with automatic weapons, dynamite, dogs, and searchlights ambushed a group of 17 unarmed FLNKS militants as they drove home up a valley near Hienghène. Stopped by a felled tree and caught in a crossfire, the Kanaks tried to escape across a river. For half an hour the killers hunted them down like animals, finishing off the wounded until the river ran red with blood. In the end 10 Kanaks died, including two brothers of Jean-Marie Tjibaou, head of the provisional government. French *gendarmes* stationed five km away didn't bother to

visit the scene for 16 hours, although they were called shortly after the incident. A week later seven of the killers, including members of third- and fourth-generation settler families, gave themselves up and were jailed.

Appalled by this atrocity, Pisani sought a solution that would bring the two sides together in a semi-independent state freely associated with France. On 7 January 1985, Pisani announced a plan calling for a referendum on independence on 1 July 1985, and self-government in association with France from 1 January 1986. France would control defense and foreign affairs, and French citizens would have special status. Then on 12 January 1985, police sharpshooters shot and killed schoolteacher Éloi Machoro, minister of the interior in the provisional government, and Marcel Noraro, an aide, as they stood outside their rural headquarters near La Foa. (It's believed the same French secret service elements that later planned the *Rainbow Warrior* bombing at Auckland of July 1985 were responsible for this and other provocations in New Caledonia.) In retaliation, the giant French-owned Thio and Kouaoua nickel mines were blown up by the Kanaks as whites rioted against independence in Nouméa. The FLNKS rejected Pisani's "neocolonial" plan (which the RPCR also strongly opposed for daring to take seriously any notion of independence).

In March 1985 an undaunted Pisani submitted his plan to Mitterrand, and in April French Prime Minister Laurent Fabius announced a new decentralization program featuring greater autonomy, land reform, and a say for the Kanaks in the territory's affairs. The territorial assembly elected in November 1984 was to be abolished, and a 43-seat territorial congress created to represent four regions, northern and central Grande Terre, the Loyalty Islands, and Nouméa. Nouméa would have 18 seats elected by universal suffrage, the other three regions (with Kanak majorities), 25 seats. The congress was to decide on independence before the end of 1987.

After protests that the French population was not properly represented, the number of Nouméa seats was increased to 21 in a 46-seat body. In August 1985 President Mitterrand recalled the French National Assembly from holidays to enact the legislation. Territorial elections took place on 29 September 1985. The pro-independence

FLNKS won the three rural regions, while the anti-independence RPCR took Nouméa (more than 80% of Kanaks voted for the FLNKS). After this election, the political situation quietened down. Thirty-two people, Kanaks and French, died during the 1984-85 confrontations.

Reaction

In March 1986 conservatives under Prime Minister Jacques Chirac took over the French national assembly from the Socialists. Chirac immediately adopted a hard, anti-independence stance: the concessions granted under the Socialists were to be undone. Chirac's Minister of Overseas Territories, Bernard Pons, recentralized power in the high commissioner by transferring the funds intended for regional development away from the regional councils. The economic agency created to promote development in Kanak areas through soft loans and outright grants was abolished, and land purchased under the Socialists for redistribution to Kanak tribes was turned over to extremist French settlers. French elite troops were stationed at mobile camps next to Kanak villages, the same "nomadization" tactics the French army had used in Algeria and Chad to study and intimidate potential opponents.

These backward steps convinced the South Pacific Forum, meeting at Suva in August 1986, to vote unanimously to ask the United Nations to reinscribe New Caledonia on its list of non-self-governing territories (the territory had previously been on the list until 1947). On 2 December 1986 the U.N. General Assembly voted 89-24 to reinscribe New Caledonia on the decolonization list—a major diplomatic defeat for France. The situation in the territory was to be reviewed annually by the U.N. Committee of 24, focusing international attention on the situation.

Responding to international criticism, the French government held a referendum on independence in the territory on 13 September 1987. The Socialists had proposed a referendum giving voters the option of independence in association with France. Under Chirac the choice was simply complete independence or remaining part of France. The FLNKS insisted that only those with one parent born in the territory (be they Kanak or French settler) be allowed to vote. (Though Kanaks themselves couldn't vote at all

until 1953, the 25,000 immigrants who had entered the country between 1969 and 1974 were now to decide its fate.) Chirac insisted that everyone who had been there longer than three years must be allowed to vote. So, with the outnumbered Kanaks boycotting the vote, the result was 98% in favor of France.

In October 1987 Pons announced a plan that would redefine the council boundaries to ensure that Kanaks and settlers each controlled two regions, a net loss to the Kanaks of one. Henceforth the regional councils would only be responsible for municipal affairs, road maintenance, agriculture, and folklore. Authority was to be centralized in a 10-member executive council that would replace the territorial congress, overturning Fabius reforms granting the Kanaks limited autonomy in the regions outside Nouméa. Pons's plan denationalized the Kanaks by claiming that only French citizens existed in New Caledonia; the existing native reserves were to be considered freehold land available for sale to anyone. Kanak claims to land rights and independence were to be considered totally irrelevant. In January 1988 the right-wing French National Assembly voted 289-283 to adopt the Pons Statute. After this the Chirac regime simply refused to negotiate with the Kanaks.

The Ouvéa Massacre

In September 1986 a French examining magistrate named Semur ordered the release of the seven self-confessed killers of the 10 Kanaks murdered at Hienghène in December 1984 because they had acted in "self defense." This provoked an international furor, and on 20 November an appeal court ruled that the seven men had to stand trial. This took place in Nouméa in October 1987, and a jury of eight whites and one Indonesian deliberated over dinner for two hours before acquitting the defendants in a major travesty of justice.

From its founding in 1984 the FLNKS had preached nonviolence (although some of their supporters were not aloof from it). This policy seemed to have failed, so just prior to the 24 April 1988 elections for the four redistributed regions the FLNKS declared a "muscular mobilization" to accompany their election boycott. Throughout the territory, Kanaks erected roadblocks and fired on police who attempted to re-

move them. A general uprising was planned, but at dawn on 22 April a commando of 40 Kanaks acted prematurely and captured the *gendarmerie* at Fayaoué on Ouvéa in the Loyalty Islands, killing four police and capturing another 27. Sixteen of the prisoners were taken to a cave near the north end of the island and held hostage. Forewarned, every other *gendarmerie* in the territory went on alert.

On 4 May 1988, just three days prior to the French presidential elections, Chirac ordered an assault on the cave to garner right-wing support for his election campaign against Mitterrand. During "Operation Victor" at 0600 the next morning, 300 elite counterinsurgency troops attacked the cave, massacring 19 Kanaks and freeing the hostages unharmed, for a loss of two of the assaulting force. Kidnap leader, Alphonse Dianou, a former student priest, was beaten to death by the troops as he lay wounded on a stretcher, and six other Kanaks were executed by the French troops after they surrendered. There were no Kanak survivors—their bullet-ridden bodies were unrecognizable. Other Ouvéa residents were tortured by the French secret service agents, and 33 prisoners were deported to France. The soldiers who carried out these atrocities have never been brought to justice.

The Matignon Accords
The policies of Chirac and Pons had propelled New Caledonia to the brink of civil war, costing another 25 people their lives. Yet the Kanak

blood spilled at Ouvéa didn't rally sufficient support for Chirac to win the French presidency, and Mitterrand was reelected. A month later, parliamentary elections were held in France, and the Socialists returned to power. The renewed violence had chastened everyone, so on 26 June 1988 the FLNKS leader Jean-Marie Tjibaou and the RPCR chief Jacques Lafleur met in Paris under the auspices of Socialist Prime Minister Michel Rocard to work out a compromise. The settlers were worried the Socialists would be sympathetic to independence, while the Kanaks wanted back the economic powers they had enjoyed briefly under the Fabius plan.

Under the peace accords signed at the Matignon Palace in Paris by the French government, the RPCR, and the FLNKS on 20 August 1988, all sides agreed to direct rule from Paris for one year, followed by a federal system for nine. The Pons Statute was to be scrapped and the territory divided into three self-governing provinces, North Province, South Province, and Loyalty Islands Province, with provincial elections in June 1989. There was to be balanced economic development based on decentralization and new training programs for Kanaks. Tens of millions of dollars in development funds were to be channeled into the Kanak regions. A new referendum on independence was to take place in 1998, with voting restricted to those eligible to vote in 1988 and children of voting age. Amnesty was to be granted to 200 Kanak militants and to settlers charged with crimes against Kanaks. What the accords didn't do was significantly increase territorial autonomy, nor did they guarantee a more equal division of the territory's wealth, most of which remained concentrated in the settler-controlled South Province. The Kanak leaders who signed the accords failed to consult their followers to seek approval or to demand an inquiry into the Ouvéa Massacre.

On 6 November 1988 a referendum was held in France, and 80% of voters approved the plan. This meant that the agreement couldn't be altered by a simple act of parliament should the government in Paris change—a major Kanak demand. Yet FLNKS hardliners strongly opposed the accords as a sellout that didn't guarantee independence. They argued that the FLNKS should refuse to cooperate with continued colonial rule and mount a last-ditch, all-or-nothing independence struggle. The split deepened as several FLNKS factions refused to participate in the June 1989 elections. The Ouvéa people felt especially betrayed.

Then, on 4 May 1989, at a commemorative service on Ouvéa for the massacre victims, the final act: the moderate FLNKS leaders Jean-Marie Tjibaou, 53, and Yeiwéné Yeiwéné, 44, were shot and killed at point-blank range by Djoubelly Wea, whose father had died from electric shocks inflicted by French thugs a year before. Wea himself, who acted alone, was immediately slain by Tjibaou's bodyguard. As Jean Guiart, director of the Museum of Man in Paris, wrote in the French journal *Réalités du Pacifique:*

It was like a death in a Greek tragedy, the destiny of a man born from the blood of the dead of the 1917 insurrection, who dies for the blood spilled by other French soldiers in 1988.

The June 1998 issue of *Islands Business* magazine carries excerpts from Prof. Guiart's fascinating reconstruction of the above events, essential reading for anyone intrigued by the current French-fostered cult of Jean-Marie Tjibaou.

Recent Events

In June 1989, elections were held for the three provincial assemblies created under the Matignon Accords. The FLNKS gained majorities in North and Loyalty Islands provinces, while the settler-based RPCR won in South Province. The RPCR's large majority in Nouméa also gave it enough seats to control the Territorial Congress. The 1995 elections largely duplicated these results, although a new French centrist party called Une Nouvelle Calédonie pour Tous led by Didier Leroux took votes from the RPCR.

Between 1990 and 1997 the French government threw more than a billion U.S. dollars at New Caledonia in the form of schools, infrastructure, and administration buildings, all with the intent of tying the colony firmly to France by making it more economically dependent than ever. Yet despite job training programs, Kanak unemployment has remained high, and most of the new jobs created by the projects went to newly arrived migrants from France. Many young Kanaks are dissatisfied with an arrangement that has given their leaders luxurious lifestyles but themselves much less. France remains determined to hang onto New Caledonia for its mineral riches, both on land and undersea, and for the role it plays in projecting French influence around the world.

In May 1998, representatives of the FLNKS, RPCR, and the French government signed the Nouméa Accords, which call for a gradual devolution of authority to the territory over a period of 15 to 20 years. This "consensual solution" was approved by 72% of New Caledonia voters in a November 1998 referendum. A decade or two from now, persons who have lived in the territory for 20 years will vote in yet another referendum to decide whether they want full independence. In the meantime, France retains full control over justice, law and order, defense, and the currency.

GOVERNMENT

New Caledonia is a French associated territory with a high commissioner appointed by the president of France. In addition to the powers vested in France, the high commissioner has some control over international relations, foreign investment, mining, immigration, television broadcasting, navigation and air traffic, finance, research, and higher education.

Each of three provinces has a regional assembly in charge of planning, economic development, social welfare, housing, culture, and environmental protection within its area. The 32 members of the South Province Assembly, 15 members of the North Province Assembly, and seven members of the Loyalty Islands Province Assembly are elected by proportional representation every five years.

Together the members of the provincial assemblies make up the 54-member Territorial Congress, which controls public health, social services, primary education, employment, sports and culture, public transport, highways, electricity, communications, natural resources, foreign trade, taxation, and the territorial budget. The president and one of the two vice-presidents of the congress and each of the assemblies sit on the nine-member Consultative Committee with the high commissioner. A 16-member Customary Senate must be consulted on issues related to the Kanak identity.

Local government is organized into 33 communes, each with an elected mayor and municipal council. The communes are grouped into four administrative subdivisions, with headquarters at La Foa, Koné, Poindimié, and Wé (Lifou). Nouméa has a separate municipal government. In the French system, civil servants comprise an elite class not seen in English-speaking countries, and most government departments are headed by professionals seconded from France. The appointed bureaucrats running the subdivisions can override the decisions of the local councils and mayors.

Everyone born in New Caledonia is legally a French citizen and can vote in French presidential elections. Two deputies are elected to the French National Assembly, one from the east coast of Grande Terre and outer islands, one from the west coast and Nouméa. A senator, elected by the municipal and provincial councils, is also sent to Paris.

ECONOMY

New Caledonia provides France with raw materials while providing a market for finished French goods. France supplies 44% of the territory's imports and takes 32% of its exports. Japan is also a major customer for New Caledonia's mineral wealth. Yet despite exports averaging half a billion Australian dollars a year, imports exceed a billion dollars, and the territory has the second-largest trade deficit in the South Pacific (after Tahiti-Polynesia).

Economic power is centered in Greater Nouméa, with 70% of the retail trading space, all of the industry except mining, and most tourism and government services. Each year the French state transfers almost a billion U.S. dollars to New Caledonia, but much of it is used to pay the salaries of French civil servants and military personnel. Infrastructure expenditures profit mostly French corporations, which carry out most government contracts. Economic development plans have granted tax writeoffs to French businesses, and encouraged metropolitan French to purchase existing small companies. The subsidies have made the territory a consumer colony with a transfer economy, which explains why most non-Melanesians are so devoted to France.

The territory's taxation system is based on high indirect taxes on imports and exports (thereby inflating the cost of living), while direct company and income taxes (which would fall most heavily on Europeans) remain extremely low. The per capita gross domestic product is 10 times that of neighboring Vanuatu, but the income of the average Kanak family is only a third that of a Caledonian French family. A few powerful French families—Ballande, Barrau, Lafleur, Frogier, Daly, de Rouvray, and Pentecost—control the local economy and politics. They profit most from colonial rule and are firmly committed to continuing it.

Mining

New Caledonia ranks third in world nickel production (after Canada and Russia), and nickel accounts for 93% of territorial exports. Half of the nickel is exported as raw ore, the rest partly refined. The nickel ore is high grade, being free of arsenic, although the presence of asbestos has been linked to a high lung cancer rate among miners. Chrome and iron ore were formerly exported, but these operations have closed due to market conditions.

There are large nickel mines at Thio, Poro, and Népoui, and many of the deposits are on mountaintops. In 1990 Kanak-controlled North Province purchased Jacques Lafleur's Société Minière de Sud Pacifique for US$19 million. Since then the SMSP has increased its ore production ten-fold, and it now accounts for 70% of the territory's total. The other large mining company, Société le Nickel, which owns the smelter at Nouméa, belonged to the Rothschild conglomerate until its nationalization in 1982. Today it's part of the government-controlled Eramet consortium. Five smaller mining companies also operate.

To break the French monopoly over nickel processing and rebalance economic power in the territory, the SMSP has negotiated an agreement with the Canadian mining corporation Falconbridge to build a second nickel refinery in North Province, an arrangement long opposed by Eramet. In 1997 the FLNKS suspended all political negotiations with the French government until the issue was resolved, and in early 1998 Eramet finally agreed to transfer unused nickel reserves at Koniambo near Koné to the SMSP, thereby making the project feasible. World nickel prices permitting, Falconbridge may invest US$1 billion in the smelter, with construction to begin as early as 2002, and if built, the facility will dramatically shift the balance of economic power in New Caledonia. Another Canadian mining giant, INCO, is to construct a US$50 million pilot smelter at Goro in the south.

Agriculture

Agriculture represents just 4.9% of the gross domestic product. Beef cattle raising has always been the most important monetary agricultural activity, consisting mostly of large herds kept by Europeans on the west coast. Yet due to high demand, meat still has to be imported. Pig and prawn farming are well developed, and there's scallop fishing in the north.

Among the Kanaks, yams are the main subsistence crop, followed by taro, manioc, and sweet potatoes. From 1865 to 1890, the cultivation of sugarcane was attempted; it failed due to labor costs and milling problems. Cotton was grown from 1860 right up until the 1930s, when drought, disease, and the world depression brought it to an end. Coffee, introduced in the first days of French colonization, is still grown today, mostly the *robusta* type.

Only four percent of Europeans work in agriculture, compared to 60% of the Kanaks, yet two-thirds of the arable land is controlled by 1,000 French settlers with large estates. Land remains a basic issue in New Caledonia, and a Melanesian land-*using* culture continues to find itself confronted by a European land-*owning* culture.

Tourism

After nickel, tourism is the most important industry, with France, Japan, Australia, and New Zealand providing the most visitors. New Caledonia is the only South Pacific country where Japan is a leading supplier of tourists—more than a quarter of the 105,137 arrivals in 1997 were Japanese, a result of nonstop flights from Tokyo. The number of French visitors has also grown steadily in recent years due to an abundance of charter flights and package tours from Paris.

During the 1990s the Kanak-controlled North Province moved into tourism in a big way with a new Club Med at Hienghène, a major resort between Koumac and Poum, and direct investments in existing Nouméa hotels such as the Ibis and Surf. In partnership with the French Accor hotel chain, North Province has tried to break the stranglehold on tourism previously held by Nouméa businessmen.

In the tribal areas, the Kanaks have resisted outside efforts to set up hotels. Instead, a system of Melanesian-owned *gîtes* provides accommodations in rural areas. Thus, as guests of Kanak people, visitors to remote areas are not viewed as intruders. The upscale Drehu and Nengone resorts on Lifou and Maré respectively are owned by Loyalty Islands Province.

THE PEOPLE

Of the 200,000 inhabitants of New Caledonia, 44% are Melanesian, 34% European, nine percent Wallisian, three percent Tahitian, three percent Indonesian, and two percent Vietnamese. Other Asians, ni-Vanuatu, West Indians, and Arabs make up the remaining four percent. About 60% of the Europeans were born in New Caledonia. Most of the other 40% are French civil servants and their families temporarily present in the territory, or refugees from the former French colonies in Algeria, Vietnam, and Vanuatu. The Vietnamese and Indonesians were brought in to work in the mines early this century; by 1921 some 4,000 of them were present.

Nearly 60% of the population lives in Nouméa and vicinity, including 80% of the Europeans, 85% of the Asians, and 90% of the Polynesians. The capital is growing fast as regional centers such as La Foa, Bourail, Koumac, and Poindimié stagnate, with populations stuck around the 1,000 mark. With 71% of the total population living in cities and towns, New Caledonia is the most heavily urbanized entity in the South Pacific.

During the nickel boom of 1969-73, the European population increased in size by a third, and the number of Polynesians doubled. An average of 2,800 French immigrants arrived every year from 1985 to 1998. These migrations were encouraged by the French government primarily to make the Kanaks a minority, thus ensuring continued French rule, a violation of United Nations resolutions on the norms of conduct for colonial powers in non-self-governing areas. The 1998 Nouméa Accords created a special New Caledonian French citizenship status that should discourage immigration from France by making it possible to restrict voting and employment rights.

Of the 21,630 convicts transported to New Caledonia 1864-97, just over a 1,000 stayed on as settlers *(colons)* on land granted them when they were freed. These and other early French arrivals are called *Caldoches,* while the present transients who come only to make money to take back to France are referred to as *métros* or *zoreilles* (the ears). French shopkeepers and small ranchers in the interior are known as *broussards,* while the 2,500 French who migrated to the territory from Algeria are the *pieds noir* (black feet). The *Caldoches* are very friendly, and it's mostly the *métros* who react arrogantly toward anyone unable to speak their language fluently.

The Kanaks are also known as Ti-Va-Ouere, the Brothers of the Earth. They own all of the smaller islands surrounding Grande Terre and their reservations on the main island. There's a striking contrast between the affluent French community around Nouméa and the poverty of Kanak villages on the northeast coast of Grande Terre and on the outer islands.

About 67% of the total population is Catholic, 21% Evangelical, and four percent Muslim, but religion is polarized, with 90% of French settlers Catholic, and Kanaks constituting 90% of the membership of the two branches of the Église Évangélique.

La Coutume

In essence, most of the conflicts in New Caledonia have been a clash of cultures. For more than a century, the Kanaks have been obliged to adopt a foreign way of life that styled itself as superior to their own. Despite the Kanaks' acceptance of a foreign language, religion, dress, and a monetary economy, indigenous custom *(la Coutume)* continues to maintain a surprising strength just beneath the surface. Today the Kanak people struggle not only to regain their lands but also to reassert their own culture over another, which they both embrace and reject.

Language

There are some 30 indigenous languages, all Austronesian, which can be broadly organized into eight related areas: five on Grande Terre and one on each of the Loyalties. The Kanak languages all developed from a single mother tongue, but are today mutually incomprehensible (thus it's incorrect and denigrating to call them "dialects"). Lifou is the language with the most speakers: about 8,000 on Lifou itself, plus a few thousand in Nouméa. French is the common language understood by most (although a sixth of the Kanak population cannot speak French). Very few people in New Caledonia understand English.

ON THE ROAD

Highlights

New Caledonia's greatest attractions are undoubtedly its capital, the northeast coast of the main island, and the neighbor islands. Nouméa combines the ambience of a French provincial town with the excitement of a Côte d'Azure resort. Hienghène on Grande Terre's east coast is a place of remarkable beauty, with high mountains dropping dramatically to the sea. The Isle of Pines's Kuto/Kanuméra area is postcard perfect with exquisite white beaches backed by towering pines. New Caledonia's finest beach runs right up one side of Ouvéa, also a scene of martyrdom in the Kanak people's struggle against the scourge of French colonialism.

Sports and Recreation

Organized sporting activities are most easily arranged at Nouméa and on the Isle of Pines. The **Yacht Charters** section under Nouméa lists several bareboat and crewed yacht charter opportunities, and the sheltered waters from Nouméa to Prony Bay and the Isle of Pines are a prime cruising area. Windsurfers ply the waters off Nouméa's Anse Vata and the Isle of Pines's Kuto Bay. The Isle of Pines is also ideal for sea kayaking, and both canoeing and kayaking are offered on the Nera River at Bourail.

Many companies offer scuba diving from Nouméa, but it's also possible to rent tanks and head off on your own. Other dive shops are on the Isle of Pines and Lifou, at Bourail and Poindimié, at the Hienghène Club Med, and at the Hôtel Malabou Beach north of Koumac. There's no recompression chamber in New Caledonia, and in emergencies, victims must be evacuated to Sydney, Australia. There are few places to snorkel on Grande Terre, where you really do need a boat to get out to the barrier reef. To see coral from shore, you must go to the Loyalty Islands or the Isle of Pines.

Horseback riding is the favorite terrestrial recreational activity among the local French, with several well established ranches near Koné. There are numerous hiking opportunities around these large islands. The best-known long-distance hike is across the mountains from the Hienghène valley to Voh. Nouméa has two 18-hole golf courses, and another 18-hole course is near Bouloupari.

Public Holidays and Festivals

Public holidays include New Year's Day (1 January), Easter Monday (March/April), Labor Day (1 May), 1945 Victory Day (8 May), Ascension Day (a Thursday in May), Pentecost (a Monday in May), Bastille Day (14 July), Assumption Day (15 August), New Caledonia Day (24 September), All Saints' Day (1 November), Armistice Day (11 November), and Christmas Day (25 December). The school holidays run from 15 December till the end of February.

Bastille Day (14 July) features a military parade and aerial show at Anse Vata in Nouméa. Lots of free performances are staged during the August jazz festival in Nouméa. The parade on New Caledonia Day (24 September) recalls the day in 1853 when Admiral Despointes took possession of New Caledonia for France. The Agricultural Fair at Bourail in mid-August features rodeos and other colorful activities. Don't miss it. Koné's rodeo is in April.

There's a triathlon the third Sunday in May, the Dumbéa open golf tournament in July, an international marathon the third Sunday in July, and a bicycle race around Grande Terre in August or September.

The eighth Festival of Pacific Arts, scheduled for New Caledonia in October 2000, promises to be a stunning cultural event.

Accommodations

Prices at the hotels are manageable for two, but high for one. A small French country hotel is called a *relais,* while an *auberge de jeunesse* is a youth hostel.

New Caledonia's well-developed system of *gîtes* is unique in the Pacific. Basically a *gîte* offers simple Melanesian-style accommodations in thatched cottages, usually near a beach. Toilet facilities may be private or shared, and electricity may or may not be installed. Since the *gîtes* are operated by the Kanaks themselves, you'll be readily accepted in the community if you're staying there. Though some are poorly run, the best *gîtes* are good value. The main flaw in the system is that Air Calédonie and the tour operators require the *gîte* owners to charge exorbitant prices to allow for the high commissions paid to travel agents for their bookings. Bargaining isn't possible as the package tourism people have set strict rules to prevent any undercutting of their prices, and about the only way for independent travelers to get around the absurdly high package tour tariffs is to ask to camp on the premises, which in most cases the Kanak owners will happily allow you to do for a reasonable fee. For food, the *gîtes* are also required to charge prices similar to those at Nouméa restaurants (CFP 1,500-3,500 per meal), so check what other people are having before ordering as the price may not correspond to what you get. Best of all, ask for a place with shared cooking facilities which will allow you to sidestep this situation, at least. The *gîtes* are concentrated on the Loyalty Islands and Isle of Pines, but many are also found around Grande Terre. To reserve a bungalow at any of the *gîtes,* go to **Air Calédonie** (B.P. 212, 98845 Nouméa; tel. 28-78-88, fax 28-13-40), 39 rue de Verdun, Nouméa. If you only want to camp at a *gîte,* you can just show up.

Women should keep in mind that while monokini sunbathing is okay in Nouméa, it could lead to serious problems anywhere else in the territory. *Never* swim topless or naked in front of a Kanak village. There are lots of isolated beaches where you can do it, and if you want to be seen, there's always Nouméa.

Camping

New Caledonia is one of the few places in the South Pacific where camping is widely understood, practiced, and accepted. French soldiers on leave from Nouméa do it all the time, and bourgeois French locals consider it a legitimate way to spend a weekend. There are many organized campgrounds on Grande Terre (but none in Nouméa). On the west coast, the campgrounds are usually far off the main highway and not accessible by public transport, while those on the east coast are often right on bus lines. Most municipal campgrounds are free. On the outer islands camp at a *gîte.*

Almost anyone you ask will readily give you permission to pitch your tent, but do ask. Other-

wise you might be violating custom and could cause yourself a needless problem. Take care with your gear around Poindimié, where ripoffs have occurred. Otherwise it's hassle-free.

Food

New Caledonian's restaurants are good but very expensive. The easiest way to keep your bill down is to stick to one main plate *(plat de résistance)* and eschew appetizers, salads, alcohol, coffee, and dessert. The bread and water on the table are free and tipping is unnecessary. Also watch for the *plat du jour,* a reasonably priced businessperson's lunch of two courses, bread, and dessert. Outside Nouméa most hotel restaurants offer a *prix fixe* dinner, though it's usually cheaper to order one plate à la carte if you can.

A *bougna* is a Kanak food parcel consisting of sliced root vegetables such as taro, manioc, and yams soaked in coconut milk, wrapped in banana leaves with pork, chicken, or seafood, and cooked over hot stones in an earthen oven for a couple of hours. If you attend a Kanak feast you'll see dozens of *bougna* packages consumed by countless relatives. At some *gîtes* you can order a *bougna* capable of feeding four persons for about CFP 3,500.

Since New Caledonia is associated with the European Union, the foods available in the supermarkets are totally different from those offered in most other South Pacific countries. Buy long crusty baguettes and flaky croissants to complement the pâté, wine, and cheese. To-

stocking up with baguettes at a Nouméa bakery

gether these are the makings of a memorable picnic. The Oro fruit juice sold in one-liter plastic bottles is a great buy at CFP 140, and the Tarumba fruit juice in a cardboard container is even better value at CFP 110. Note that grocery stores are not allowed to sell beer or wine from Saturday at 1200 to Monday at 0600.

Unfortunately, fruit and vegetables sold at roadside stalls and urban markets is often absurdly expensive compared to what you'd pay in the other Pacific countries, or even in relation to supermarket groceries purchased locally. The vendors often seem to have little understanding of the value of money. Virtually all towns on the west coast are well-equipped with stores, while shopping facilities on the east coast are sometimes poor.

Visas and Officialdom

Citizens of the European Union, Canada, the U.S., Japan, Australia, and New Zealand do not require a visa. Others should check with their airline a few weeks ahead. Visitors from the U.S., Japan, Switzerland, and most Commonwealth countries are allowed to stay one month. Citizens of European Union and Australia countries get three months, and French are admitted for an unlimited stay. Everyone (French included) must have an onward ticket. This requirement is strictly enforced and there's no chance of slipping through without one.

Nouméa is the only port of entry for cruising yachts. Arriving yachts should contact the Capitainerie Port Moselle (tel. 27-80-95, fax 27-71-29), who will send customs and immigration to meet them at a dock opposite the charter boats on Moselle Bay. Customs is at VHF channel 67, otherwise call Nouméa Radio at channel 16. The formalities are simpler than those in Tahiti-Polynesia and no bond is required. The Cercle Nautique Caledonien (B.P. 235, 98845 Nouméa; tel. 26-27-27, fax 26-28-38) at Baie des Pêcheurs has a haul-out facility.

Money

The currency is the French Pacific franc or CFP (pronounced "say eff pay"). There are banknotes of 500, 1,000, 5,000, and 10,000 and coins of one, two, five, 10, 20, 50, and 100. The CFP is linked to the French franc: CFP 100 equals 5.5 French francs. One Euro is worth CFP 119.25 but the European currency will not be adopted here. You can determine the current value of the CFP by finding out how many French francs you receive for your dollar/pound, then multiplying by 18.18. As an approximate rule of thumb, US$1 = CFP 100.

New Caledonia's banks are among the biggest ripoffs in the South Pacific, charging one percent commission with a CFP 500-750 minimum for each foreign currency transaction, whether buying or selling. Thus it's important to plan ahead and not have to change too often. They usually give the same rate for cash or traveler's checks. The banks are generally open weekdays 0730-1530, and it's difficult or impossible to change foreign currency in rural areas—do it before you leave Nouméa. The American Express representative in Nouméa, Center Voyages, changes traveler's checks without commission (see the Nouméa chapter for details).

French francs in cash (but not traveler's checks) are converted back and forth at a fixed rate without commission, so that's the best type of money to bring by far, if you have it. Otherwise, it's highly unlikely you'll gain anything by buying French francs in your home country. When you're leaving, you can change surplus CFP into French francs without paying commission or losing anything on the exchange, but many banks will refuse to do it for persons without an account at their branch, even if you originally changed with them. New Caledonia and Tahiti-Polynesia use exactly the same currency, so just hang onto any leftover Pacific francs if you'll be continuing to Papeete. Credit cards are only useful in Nouméa or at upscale resorts.

New Caledonia's form of taxation—high import and export duties—and the elevated salaries paid to local French officials make this the South Pacific's most expensive country by far. You'll be hard pressed to find a cup of coffee for less than CFP 150, or the simplest *plat du jour* meal for even CFP 900. Paradoxically, that can also make visiting New Caledonia cheap since you'll be forced to limit your purchases to the bare essentials if you're on a budget. Backpackers can easily survive because the hitchhiking is easy, camping is accepted, and the supermarkets sell excellent picnic fare, but the cost of living will wallop you if you want to travel in relative comfort. Camera film is also much less expensive in Fiji, Vanuatu, and Australia, so bring a good supply. On the positive side, tipping isn't usually done in New Caledonia and is sometimes even considered offensive. Notice how the locals never tip in restaurants. Inflation is less than two percent a year, so the prices in this book should be fairly accurate.

Post and Telecommunications
Faxes *(télécopies)* can be sent from any post office, but it's expensive. Postage is also exorbitant here, so save your postcard writing for the next country of your trip. Most businesses receive their mail through their post office box or *boîte postale* (B.P.) at any of the territory's 49 post offices.

The easiest way to make telephone calls is with telephone card *(télécarte)*, available at any post office in denominations of CFP 1,000 (25 units), CFP 3,000 (80 units), and CFP 5,000 (140 units). Not only do international calls placed with telephone cards have no three-minute minimum, but they're charged at a rate 25% lower than if the call were placed manually through an operator. Using a card, it's CFP 150 a minute to Australia or New Zealand, CFP 300 a minute to North America, CFP 360 a minute to Britain or Germany. A one-third reduction is available to the Pacific and North America 2200-0600 daily. To place an international call with a card, dial the international access code 00, the country code, the area code, and the number. To place the call through an international operator, dial 3650 (three-minute minimum charge and higher rates). International calls placed from hotel rooms are charged double.

Telephone cards can also be used for local calls. Calls within the same province cost CFP 30 for nine minutes 2100-0600, CFP 30 for six minutes 0600-0800/1100-1400/1600-2100. At other times you get three or 4.5 minutes. Interprovincial calls within New Caledonia are CFP 30 for 2.4 minutes 2100-0600, CFP 30 for 1.6 minutes 0600-0800/1100-1400/1600-2100, and around CFP 30 a minute at other times. Obviously, it's smart to try to limit your calling to numbers within the same province. There's a CFP 120 charge to call information (tel. 12), so first look in the telephone book *(annuaire)*.

New Caledonia's telephone code is 687.

The two internet service providers here are Offratel (www.offratel.nc) and Cipac (www.canl.nc). A current directory of New Caledonia e-mail addresses can be accessed at www.canl.nc/noumea.com/neacom/annuaire.htm.

Business Hours and Time
Business hours are weekdays 0730-1100 and 1400-1800, and Saturday 0730-1100, though large supermarkets in Nouméa remain open Mon.-Sat. 0730-1900, and Sunday 0730-1130 and 1500-1900. Banking hours are weekdays 0730-1530. Main post offices are open weekdays 0745-1115 and 1215-1500, Saturday 0730-1100. Smaller branch post offices are sometimes closed on Saturday.

New Caledonia follows the same hour as Vanuatu, an hour before Sydney and an hour behind Auckland and Fiji. In summer (Dec.-Feb.) the sun comes up at 0430 and sets at 1900, while in winter (June-Aug.) daylight hours are something like 0630-1730. Thus it pays to be an early riser.

Media
The daily newspaper, *Les Nouvelles Calédoniennes* (B.P. 179, 98845 Nouméa; tel. 27-25-84 fax 27-94-43), is owned by French press baron Robert Hersant, proprietor of the Paris daily *Le Figaro.* Several weekly papers are published, including *Les Nouvelles Hebdo* (B.P. 3577, 98846 Nouméa; tel. 27-44-00, fax 27-44-45).

The largest broadcaster is the government-owned Radiodiffusion Television Française pour l'Outre-Mer (B.P. G3, 98848 Nouméa; tel. 27-43-27, fax 28-12-52, www.rfo.fr). Ninety percent of RFO's TV programming originates in France and the rest is mostly sports. A private television station, Canal Calédonie (B.P. 1797, 98845 Nouméa; tel. 26-53-30), operates on a subscription basis with an encrypted signal.

From Nouméa RFO-Radio broadcasts over 666 kHz AM, and two FM frequencies, 89.9 MHz (FM1) and 99.3 MHz (FM2). There's also a private commercial FM station called Radio Rythme Bleu (B.P. 578, 98845 Nouméa; tel. 25-46-46, fax 28-49-28) at 100.4 MHz. Both RFO and RRB also broadcast over numerous other frequencies around the territory. The pro-independence station, Radio Djiido (tel. 25-35-15, fax 27-21-87), also broadcasts over various FM frequencies: Boulouparis 96 MHz, Houaïlou 103 MHz, Koumac 103 MHz, Lifou 98.5 MHz, Maré 97.5 MHz, Nouméa 97.4 MHz, Ouvéa 96.5 MHz, Pouébo 97 MHz, Poya 97 MHz, Touho 96 MHz, and Voh 102 MHz. Radio Djiido tends to play the more international music (English, Spanish, Italian) and not just songs in French. In Nouméa there's also a 24-hour, youth-oriented music station called Nouméa Radio Joker (B.P. 3260, 98846 Nouméa; tel. 26-34-34, fax 28-16-27) at FM 93.5 MHz, which doesn't present news. The other three FM stations (RFO, RRB, and Djiido) do broadcast news reports, but in French only. There's no English broadcasting in New Caledonia.

Health

A yellow fever vaccination is required, but only if you've been in an infected area (South America or Africa) within the previous six days. Recommended vaccinations include poliomyelitis, immune globulin or Havriz, and typhoid fever, though only for backpackers traveling outside Nouméa. New Caledonia has one of the highest per capita incidences of HIV infections in the South Pacific, though still very low by U.S. standards. New Caledonia's tap water contains high levels of heavy metals resulting from mining, but it's unlikely to cause problems on a short visit. On the bright side, there's no malaria. Public hospitals exist in Nouméa, Poindimié, and Koumac, but it's cheaper and easier to see a private doctor.

TRANSPORTATION

Getting There

Aircalin (B.P. 3736, 98846 Nouméa; tel. 26-55-00, fax 26-55-61, www.aircalin.nc), previously known as Air Calédonie International, a local carrier 55% owned by the territorial government, links New Caledonia to Auckland, Brisbane, Melbourne, Nadi, Papeete, Port Vila, Sydney, and Wallis Island. The most direct access to New Caledonia from North America is via Aircalin's twice weekly flight to/from Nadi, Fiji, although connections through Australia are much more frequent.

Air France (tel. 25-88-00) is the main international carrier connecting New Caledonia to Europe and Japan with direct flights to Nouméa four times a week from Paris (Charles de Gaulle) via Tokyo. **Continental Airlines** (tel. 1-800/231-0856) operates between Guam and Nouméa three times a week, with connections to/from numerous points in Asia and Micronesia.

AOM French Airlines (tel. 24-12-12, fax 24-12-13) flies from Paris (Orly) to Nouméa three times a week via Colombo and Sydney. **Corsair** (tel. 28-27-27) has weekly flights from Bangkok and Paris (Orly), and like AOM, their tickets are several hundred dollars cheaper than comparable fares than Air France. For more information on AOM and Corsair, see **Getting There** in this book's main introduction.

The national airlines of several neighboring countries also fly straight to Nouméa: **Air New Zealand** (tel. 28-66-77) from Auckland weekly; **Air Vanuatu** from Port Vila daily; **Solomon Airlines** from Honiara weekly; and **Qantas** (tel. 28-65-46) from Brisbane, Melbourne, and Sydney. All of the above flights operate out of La Tontouta Airport (NOU).

Air New Zealand's seven-day advance purchase fare from Los Angeles to Nouméa is US$1,457/1,633 low/high season with a two-month maximum stay and 35% cancellation fee. Nouméa also fits into the **Visit South Pacific Pass** described in this book's introduction.

By Ship

Somacal (B.P. 2099, 98846 Nouméa; tel. 27-38-98, fax 25-93-15), 5 rue d'Austerlitz (rear courtyard), represents the **Compagnie Moana de Navigation,** whose ship, the MS *Moana III,* makes the Nouméa-Futuna-Wallis-Nouméa trip monthly. Occasionally it calls at Suva, Fiji. A single or double cabin for the five-day journey to Suva or Wallis is CFP 37,000 pp, meals included. There's also a six-bed dorm called the "bungalow," which costs CFP 30,000 pp including meals. Between Futuna and Wallis, it's CFP 6,000/8,700 bungalow/cabin.

The only other regular shipping service accepting passengers is the monthly round-the-world **Bank Line** service that calls at Nouméa between Auckland and Suva. The local agent is **Agence Maritime Ballande** (B.P. 97, 98845 Nouméa; tel. 28-33-84, fax 28-73-88), in the port area between downtown and Île Nou. You could catch it here for a leisurely two-month cruise back to Belgium via the Suez Canal, if you can afford a fare several times higher than the plane.

Joining a yacht as crew is a more practical way of leaving than either of the above. August-Oct., plenty of boats will be leaving for Australia, and you can also hitch rides to Vanuatu and Solomon Islands. Skippers often post notices at the youth hostel.

Getting Around by Air
Air Calédonie (B.P. 212, 98845 Nouméa; tel. 28-78-88, fax 25-03-26, www.air-caledonie.nc), the domestic commuter airline, uses Magenta Airport (GEA) near Nouméa. Several times a day their 46-passenger ATR 42s and 19-passenger Dornier 228s fly to the Loyalty Islands (Maré, Lifou, and Ouvéa), CFP 9,000 one-way. The interisland link between the three larger Loyalties and Tiga costs CFP 3,955 to CFP 6,055 per sector. There are two or more flights a day to the Isle of Pines, CFP 6,060 one-way. Twice a week you can fly from Koumac to remote Belep off the northwest coast of Grande Terre, CFP 6,270 one-way.

Ask Air Calédonie about special package tickets that allow a visit to the Loyalty Islands from Nouméa for one price with accommodations and airport transfers included. Their **Air Pass,** only available to nonresidents, allows any four flights for CFP 24,000 (additional flights CFP 5,000 each). The pass is valid two months, and a special 20-kilogram baggage allowance is included. Reservation changes cost CFP 1,000.

Otherwise, the baggage allowance is 10 kilograms, with overweight costing CFP 100-165 a kilo. There's a CFP 1,000 penalty if you change or cancel a reservation less than 48 hours in advance. Reconfirm your return reservation immediately upon arrival at an outer island. It's usually easy to get a seat to the Loyalty Islands,

but the flights to the Isle of Pines are often fully booked by Japanese day-trippers, so inquire well ahead. If you're told the plane is full, take the ferry to the Isle of Pines and fly back.

Getting Around by Other Means
Buses link most Grande Terre towns at least once a day, and the fares are reasonable (turn to the **Nouméa** section for information). All around the island *beware of buses leaving 15 minutes early!* Hitchhiking is a snap (when there's traffic) and you'll have some very interesting conversations, if you speak French. Payment is never expected. Renting a car is an easy way to go, and it allows you to save money by car camping and eating picnic fare.

For information on the high-speed vessel *Marie-Hélène,* turn to **Transportation** in the Nouméa section. It can zip you to the Isle of Pine or the Loyalties in less than five hours and costs significantly less than the plane, but check the current schedule well ahead.

AIRPORTS

International Airport
La Tontouta Airport (NOU) is 53 km northwest of Nouméa and 112 km southeast of Bourail. As your plane is taxiing up to the terminal, glance across the runway at the French air force hangars to see if their counterinsurgency helicopters or Neptune bombers are in.

The S.C.E.A. airport bus charges a stiff CFP 2,000 for the ride to Nouméa; private minibuses charge about the same. You can also wait for the blue interurban bus (CFP 400), to the left as you leave the terminal. They run hourly on the hour Mon.-Sat., but only until 1800 (every other hour on Saturday afternoon). On Sunday the blue bus runs every two hours. The blue bus follows the old road through picturesque towns and carries colorful local passengers, while the tourist bus zips along the toll road nonstop. Airport-bound, don't plan a tight connection if you travel this way. A taxi to Nouméa will be CFP 7,500. If hitching is your thing, just walk one km out to the main highway—you'll have a ride to Nouméa in no time. The car rental companies with counters at La Tontouta Airport are Avis (tel. 35-11-74), Best (tel. 35-12-88, fax 35-40-

98), Budget (tel. 35-10-88), Europcar (tel. 35-14-20), Hertz (tel. 35-12-77), JMJ Rent a Car (tel. 35-10-44, tel./fax 35-12-43), and Pacific Car (tel. 35-10-88).

The airport bank is open for most arrivals, but not all departures. They charge CFP 500 commission, and give a slightly lower rate than the banks in town. If it's closed, try the bank on the main highway near the airport. Due to security considerations, it's not possible to store excess luggage at the airport. The airport post office opens at flight times only, and the duty free shop is expensive. The CFP 1,160 airport tax is included in the ticket price.

Domestic Airport
Magenta Airport (GEA) is five km northeast of downtown Nouméa. City bus no. 7 will drop you right at the door (every 15 minutes 0515-1815, CFP 120). A taxi from the Place des Cocotiers costs about CFP 800. There are no coin lockers, so leave excess baggage elsewhere.

NOUMÉA

Nouméa was founded in 1854 by Tardy de Montravel, who called it Port-de-France, and in 1860 the French moved their capital here from Balade. A French governor arrived two years later and convicts condemned to the penal colony on Île Nou followed in 1864. In 1866 the town was renamed Nouméa. Robert Louis Stevenson, who visited in 1890, remarked that Nouméa was "built from vermouth cases." Like Rome, Nouméa stands on seven hills. The town remained a backwater until 1942, when American military forces arrived to transform this landlocked port into a bastion for the war against Japan. Admiral "Bull" Halsey directed the Solomon Islands campaign from his headquarters on Anse Vata.

Today this thriving maritime center near the south end of the New Caledonian mainland is a busy, crowded, cosmopolitan city made rich mostly by nickel. More than half the population of the territory resides here: 120,000 people if residents of nearby Mont-Dore, Dumbéa, and Païta are included. The city is predominantly French with an ambience reminiscent of Marseille, the only South Pacific town with a white majority (less than a quarter of the city's population is Kanak). Kanak women in their Mother Hubbard dresses add color to the market area, and bathing beauties bask at Nouméa's swank Anse Vata beach, where most of the luxury hotels are found. Windsurfers and sailboaters hover offshore, and it's clear that this is a moneyed tourist's paradise.

Since it's only a couple of hours by jet from Australia or New Zealand, most tourists limit their visit to Nouméa, but New Caledonia has more to offer than just its capital city. Leave Nouméa and you're back in Melanesia, among the island's original Kanak inhabitants, for whom land and custom are worth more than money. From European consumers to third-world tribes, it's quite a contrast, and you can't claim to have seen the territory until you get across to the northeast coast or out to one of the islands.

When planning your day, remember that on weekdays nearly everything in Nouméa closes for the 1100-1400 siesta—a three-hour break! Afternoon hours can be variable, so it's best to attend to important business first thing in the morning.

SIGHTS

Historic Nouméa
The **Place des Cocotiers,** with its statues, fountains, *pétanque* players, and tourist information office is the ideal place to begin your tour. November-Jan. the poincianas (flame trees) set this wonderful central park alight in hues of red and orange. Points of interest include the vintage bandstand, at the east end of the square, the Celeste Fountain (1892), point zero for all highway mileages on the mainland, in the middle, and the statue of Admiral Olry, governor 1878-1880, at the west end. The old town hall (1880), facing the north side of the square, is now the **Musée de la Ville** (tel. 26-28-05; Mon.-Sat. 0900-1645, Wednesday until 1900) with changing exhibitions. Admission is free; the attendant may try to sell you a French brochure, but you don't have to accept it.

Walk north on rue du Général Mangin past trendy rue de l'Alma to the **old military hospi-**

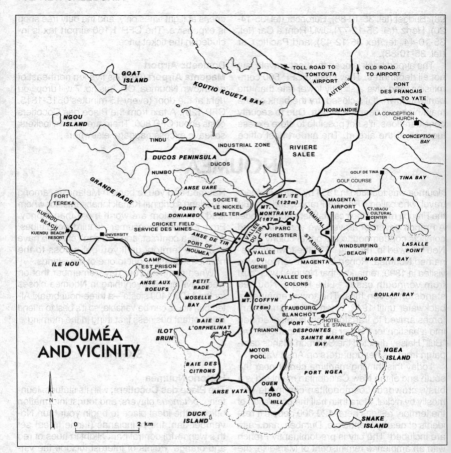

NOUMÉA AND VICINITY

0   2 km

---

tal, built by convict laborers in the 1880s, and still Nouméa's main medical facility. Only in 1982 did the territory take the hospital over from the army. Turn right on avenue Paul Doumer and you'll come to **Government House,** the residence of the French High Commissioner. Go right, then left up rue de la République two blocks, to the **Territorial Congress** on your right. A small collection of local rocks and shells is showcased just upstairs from the reception.

Go up the ramp off boulevard Vauban to the **Protestant Church** (1893) at the head of rue de

l'Alma, then continue south on Vauban to **St. Joseph's Catholic Cathedral** (1894), which was built by convict labor. Enter this fine old building overlooking the city through the side doors to see the stained-glass windows, timber roof, and wooden pulpit. Continue east from the cathedral along rue Frédéric Surleau to the **French army barracks** (caserne) on Place Bir Hakeim. The barracks have changed very little since their construction in 1869. The full names of the European servicemen from New Caledonia who died in WW I are listed on three sides of the war memorial in front of the barracks, but only the places of origin of the 372 Kanaks who died are given. The guns flanking the memorial once guarded the entrance to Nouméa harbor.

Return west along avenue de la Victoire to 41 avenue du Maréchal Foch and the **Bernheim Library** (tel. 27-23-43, fax 27-65-88; capriciously open Tuesday, Thursday, and Friday 1300-1730, Wednesday 0900-1730, Saturday 0900-1600). In 1901 Lucien Bernheim, a miner who made his fortune in the territory, donated the money for its first library (the only time a local mining mogul has ever given away anything). What had been the New Caledonian pavilion at the Paris Universal Exposition of 1900 was used to house the collection, and the original building still stands alongside the present reading room. To this day it's the only real public library in the territory.

New Caledonia Museum

This outstanding museum (B.P. 2393, 98846 Nouméa; tel. 27-23-42), 45 avenue du Maréchal Foch, two blocks south of the Bernheim Library, was founded in 1971. Kanak cultural objects are displayed downstairs, including elements from *cases* (traditional houses), masks, wooden statues, fishing, hunting, and farming implements, traditional currency, canoes, war clubs, ceremonial axes, bamboo carvings, baskets, and pottery. Upstairs are artifacts from Vanuatu, Solomon Islands, Papua New Guinea, and Irian Jaya. A *case* from Lifou is mounted inside the building, a botanical collection graces the courtyard, and in the rear garden behind the museum is a traditional full-sized *grande case* in the Canala style. The historic photos are good, and you can watch videos narrated in French. The museum's main shortcoming is that all of the labels are in French only. It's open daily except Tuesday and holidays 0900-1130/1215-1630; admission is CFP 200—don't miss it.

If you'd like to clear your head after the museum, climb **Mont Coffyn** for the sweeping view; there's an old ceramic map at the top for orientation. To get there, go south on avenue du Maréchal Foch to the American War Memorial, then left on rue Duquesne at the Maison du Sport and two blocks up to rue Guynemer, where you turn right, then left, and up the hill. Use the map in this book. As you stand beside the immense two-armed Cross of Lorraine, you'll be able to pick out Amédée Lighthouse.

Nearby Beaches

Baie des Citrons and Anse Vata, Nouméa's finest beaches, are near the southern end of the city's scalloped peninsula. Very attractive and easily accessible by bus, they're also cluttered with hotels and tend to be crowded; elsewhere in New Caledonia you can usually have a beach all to yourself. Topless sunbathing is fine for men and women at Anse Vata and Baie des Citrons.

The **Nouméa Aquarium** (B.P. 395, 98845 Nouméa; tel. 26-27-31; open Tues.-Sun. 1000-1645, admission CFP 630, students CFP 210, children CFP 115), located between Baie des Citrons and Anse Vata, has a good collection of reef fish, sponges, cuttlefish, nautilus, sea snakes, sea slugs, and fluorescent corals. It tends to be a little overrated, however, and the small size and jewelrylike displays are drawbacks. Go early on a fine afternoon, as the lighting is poor.

On Anse Vata east of the Aquarium is the new headquarters of the **Secretariat of the Pacific Community** (tel. 26-20-00, www.spc.org.nc), formerly known as the South Pacific Commission, which opened in 1995. A description of this regional organization is provided in this book's main introduction under the heading **Government**. The roof of the main conference building and library (to the left as you enter) is shaped like an inverted canoe. The library (open weekdays 0730-1600) is worth visiting to see the showcased artifacts and publications, or just to relax and browse the newspapers and magazines. Temporary exhibitions are often mounted in the conference center beyond, and the coral pathways across the gardens symbolize Micronesian navigational charts. Next door is ORSTOM, a major French scientific research agency.

A road to the left just beyond the municipal swimming pool leads up to **Ouen Toro Hill** and a fine panorama (a 15-minute walk). Two six-inch cannons were set up here in 1940 by the Australian army to cover the reef passage in the vicinity of Amédée Lighthouse, visible to the south. Promenade Pierre Vernier along Baie Sainte Marie east of Ouen Toro is an attractive place to stroll between the rows of palms, and there's a training track complete with pull-up bars, balance logs, etc.

Île Nou

This former island, jutting west of Nouméa, has been connected to the city by a land-reclamation project that used waste from the nickel smelter. English seaman James Paddon had a trading post here as early as 1845. After 1864, Île Nou became notorious when the French converted it into a penal colony called Nouville housing more than 3,000 prisoners at a time. **Camp Est Prison** on Île Nou is still a major prison.

Bus no. 13 will take you directly to the chapel, workshops, and buildings of the original 19th-century Nouville prison, until recently occupied by a mental health facility, and now part of the Université Française du Pacifique. A school teaching French as a foreign language occupies the former prison chapel (1882). There are quiet beaches to the west of the university, and you can walk the dirt road right around the end of Île Nou in about an hour.

An evocative sight is **Fort Tereka** (1878), perched on a hilltop at the far west end of Île Nou. This location offers one of the finest scenic viewpoints in the South Pacific, with the entire central chain of Grande Terre in full view. Four big 138-mm cannon mounted on wheels were set up here in 1894-96 to defend the harbor. Two more cannons were placed opposite, to create a crossfire, and are now in front of the war memorial on Place Bir Hakeim. From the university, it's a 20-minute walk west to the Kuendu Beach Resort, with the fort access road on the right, just before the descent to the resort. There are shortcuts to come back, and a swim at **Kuendu Beach** would certainly be in order. This is where Nouméa's European residents come on weekends to get away from the tourists at Anse Vata.

Société Le Nickel

The northern section of Nouméa is not as attractive as the southern; here, on Pointe Doniambo, is the giant metallurgical factory, Société le Nickel. Established in 1910 and expanded to its present size in 1958 and 1992, the smelter has about 1,700 employees (only 17% of them Kanaks). It processes much of New Caledonia's nickel ore, and the rest is exported to Japan in its natural state.

Toxic discharges of sulfur dioxide and nickel compounds have caused serious health problems among Kanaks living in the Cité Pierre Lenquette low-cost housing area directly east of the smelter (company regulations prohibit emissions when the wind is blowing south toward central Nouméa and Anse Vata). New Caledonia has the world's highest incidence of asthma-related deaths due to nickel dust thrown up by the mining and smelting.

If you're really interested, the Service des Mines (tel. 27-39-44), on rue Édouard Unger between the smelter and downtown, has a collection of rocks on display weekdays 0730-1115 and 1215-1530 (free).

Parc Forestier

Visit this botanical garden and zoo five km northeast of downtown to see the flightless and rapidly disappearing *cagou (Rhynochetos jubatus)*, New Caledonia's official territorial bird. The excellent ornithological collection also includes the rare Ouvéa parakeet. There are a few mammals, of which the flying foxes stand out. Allow two hours to see the birds and animals, and another two to study the plants, many of which are labeled. The garden (tel. 27-89-51) is open Tues.-Sun. 1015-1700, admission CFP 300 (children 12 and under CFP 100).

You can get to the Parc Forestier by taking bus no. 12 to the Cité Pierre Lenquette low-cost housing complex at Montravel, then walking 1.5 km uphill. Otherwise it's a 35-minute walk from the Nouméa Youth Hostel. Follow the ridge road north, turn up the signposted road beside the Notre Dame du Pacifique statue, and go past the three towers of the Centre Récepteur Radioelectrique. Keep heading toward the huge light blue tower with two circular terraces on top.

There are many excellent scenic views along the way, especially from the light blue telecommunications tower on **Montravel** (167 meters), accessible up a steep road just before you reach the Parc. Amédée Lighthouse is visible on the horizon south of the summit, just to the left of Ouen Toro. To the northeast the twin peaks of Mt. Koghi (1,061 meters) dominate the horizon, while due east the oval profile of Mont-Dore (772 meters) stands alone. Closer in, just on the far side of Magenta Airport, is the new Cultural Center. Two orientation tables indicate points of interest. You also get a good view of the apartment blocks of Cité Pierre Lenquette where thou-

Only a few hundred specimens of the Ouvea parakeet (Eunymphicus cornutus uveansis) *still exist in the world.*

sands of Kanaks live directly downwind of toxic emissions from the nickel smelter.

Jean-Marie Tjibaou Cultural Center

This extravagant cultural cocktail sits on the Tina Peninsula near the exclusive Golf de Tina, 12 km northeast of town. It opened on 4 May 1998, 10th anniversary of the assassination of Jean-Marie Tjibaou, the Kanak leader idolized by the French authorities as a symbol of the Matignon Accords. Designed by Italian architect Renzo Piano and built by big-budget French contractors, the center presents a sanitized version of Kanak culture. You won't learn much here about the Hienghène or Ouvéa massacres, the murder of Éloi Machoro, the 19th century land seizures, the muscle flexing and maneuvering that has prevented independence, etc.

Ten huge huts are clustered in three villages joined by a central avenue, and encircled by a Path of Legends leading through a cultural garden. Features include several theaters, a contemporary art gallery, temporary and permanent exhibitions of Kanak and other Pacific art, a library, and a sales room with books, magazines, videos, and music cassettes on Kanak culture. It's operated by the French-financed Agency for the Development of Kanak Culture (B.P. 378, 98845 Nouméa; tel. 41-45-45, fax 41-45-56) and is open daily 0900-1700, Thursday until 2000. The exhibitions are closed on Monday, and the library is closed Sunday and Monday. Admission is CFP 1,000, or CFP 500 for persons under 18 or over 65, and for students. Admission to per-

formances at the center is CFP 2,000-3,000. Bus no. 8 will drop you within two km of the Tjibaou Center.

The Barrier Reef

Amédée Lighthouse, on a tiny island 18 km south of Nouméa, was prefabricated in Paris and set up here in 1865 to guide ships through Grande Terre's barrier reef. At 56 meters high, it's still the tallest metal lighthouse in the world, and you can mount the 247 steps. Several companies offer day-trips to Amédée at around CFP 8,500 pp including Polynesian music and a buffet lunch. Among the boats doing this trip is the 30-meter cruiser *Mary D Princess* (B.P. 233, 98845 Nouméa; tel. 26-31-31, fax 26-39-79) with an office on the waterfront near the Parkroyal Nouméa. It leaves from pontoon K1 at Baie de la Moselle daily at 0745, and from the Club Med wharf daily around 0815, returning by 1600. These trips are grossly overpriced because most of the passengers are packaged Japanese tourists.

A cheaper way to get to Amédée Lighthouse is on the Amédée Diving Club's catamaran *Spanish Dancer* (see below). This departs the Club Med wharf daily except Tuesday at 0745, and costs only CFP 4,000 pp without lunch. The Club serves a good lunch on Amédée for CFP 1,970 extra, otherwise take along your own food and drink. The capacity is limited, so book a day or two ahead (scuba divers get priority and it's easiest to get aboard during the week).

Sports and Recreation

The **Amédée Diving Club** (Bernard Andreani, B.P. 2675, 98846 Nouméa; tel. 26-40-29, fax 28-57-55) is based at Marine Corail, 26 rue du Général Mangin in central Nouméa. They offer morning and afternoon dives on a choice of 11 sites around Amédée Lighthouse. Two-tank dives are CFP 10,800, plus CFP 2,000 for equipment (if required). When space is available snorkelers can go along at CFP 4,000 (mask and snorkel rental not included). Marine Corail (B.P. 848, 98845 Nouméa; tel. 27-58-48, fax 27-68-43) will also rent equipment alone for shore diving.

Nouméa Diving (B.P. 384, 98845 Nouméa Cedex; tel. 25-16-88, fax 24-09-70), 75 rue de Sébastopol behind the museum, is a large dive shop with trips every day at 0745 (CFP

6,000/11,400 for one/two tanks, plus equipment rental). This company also operates a taxi boat to Île aux Canards (CFP 500 pp) and Îlot Maître (CFP 2,000 pp), leaving the Club Med wharf at 0800, 0930, and 1100.

Less expensive scuba diving is offered by **Plongée Passion** (B.P. 14036, 98803 Nouméa; tel./fax 27-71-32), 20 rue Auguste Brun in the Latin Quarter. They charge CFP 7,000 for a two-tank boat dive, plus CFP 2,300 for equipment. They also do scuba certification courses (CFP 31,000 for PADI open-water).

Also try **Scubaventure Centre de Plongée** (tel./fax 28-58-18), facing Baie des Citrons. Beach diving starts at CFP 3,500 per tank.

Le Grand Bleu Plongée Scuba Diving (tel. 26-45-95) in the Galerie Palm Beach, Anse Vata, does hotel pickups every morning at 0730 (CFP 9,000 for two dives, gear extra). Their clientele is almost exclusively Japanese.

Sub-Austral (tel. 26-51-03, fax 27-60-68), on the beach at Hôtel Le Méridien, offers scuba diving at CFP 5,000/9,500/18,000/40,000 for one/two/four/10 dives, plus CFP 500 for equipment if you only go once or twice. They'll also do scuba certification courses at CFP 28,000. The watersports people at Hôtel Le Méridien will ferry you over to Île aux Canards anytime at CFP 1,500 for up to three people each way.

Nouméa's top scuba locales are near the Passe de Dumbéa where there's good shark action. Turtles are often seen near Îlot Maître, and the reef near Amédée Lighthouse is also visited.

In 1995, the 5,603-meter **Golf de Tina** (B.P. 14379, 98803 Nouméa; tel. 43-82-83, fax 43-82-84) opened on Tina Bay, four km beyond Magenta Airport and 11 km northeast of downtown Nouméa. It's very posh, with lovely ocean and mountain views. Greens fees for nine/18 holes are CFP 3,000/4,500 weekdays or CFP 4,000/6,000 weekends. Club hire CFP 2,000 is for nine or 18 holes, chariot hire CFP 1,000. Proper dress is mandatory: T-shirts, jeans, bathing suits, and tennis outfits are not permitted. Another rule states that you must finish nine holes in 2.25 hours, 18 holes in 4.5 hours. Bus no. 8 will drop you two km from the course (or call to request a CFP 1,500 return hotel transfer).

The attractive **municipal swimming pool** (tel. 26-18-43), just beyond Club Med at the far end of Anse Vata, is open Mon.-Sat. until 1700, Sunday until 1600, admission CFP 180. The adjacent **municipal tennis courts** are lighted at night.

Have a workout at the **Squash Club** (tel. 26-22-18; Mon.-Sat. 0800-2200, Sunday 1600-2000), 21 rue Jules Garnier opposite the Port Plaisance Mall on Baie de l'Orphelinat. A half hour costs CFP 300 before 1600 Mon.- Saturday, or CFP 600 after 1600 and on Sunday. Rackets are available and there's an inexpensive bar on the premises (a hangout for English-speaking yachties).

Most afternoons you'll see men playing *pétanque* in Place des Cocotiers and next to the beach at Anse Vata. Metal balls the size of baseballs are thrown, not rolled, at the other balls in this French bowling game.

Melanesian women playing cricket

There's horse racing at the **Hippodrome** at Anse Vata on weekends in June, July, and August.

ACCOMMODATIONS

Youth Hostel

The budget traveler's best headquarters is the Nouméa Youth Hostel (B.P. 767, 98845 Nouméa; tel. 27-58-79, fax 25-48-17), or *auberge de jeunesse,* on Colline de Semaphore just east of downtown (fantastic sunsets from here). The four-story accommodations wing built in 1990 contains 10 double rooms, 14 four-bed dorms, and three six-bed dorms. It's CFP 1,200 pp in a dorm, or CFP 2,900 double in a twin room. If you don't have a valid youth hostel card there will be a CFP 200 pp per day surcharge, otherwise you can buy a one-year card valid around the world at CFP 1,400 pp. Pillows and sheets are supplied. The office hours for checking in, reserving, or paying are 0800-1000 and 1800-1930 only. If you want a double room, it's wise to reserve by calling ahead, but dorm beds are usually available. Always call ahead if you know you'll be arriving after the office closes at 1930. If you happen to get there during the day, put your pack in the attic above the Ping-Pong tables and come back at 1800 to check in.

In each of the spacious dorms you have a secure personal locker in which to store your gear (lock provided), and all guests receive keys to individual kitchen and refrigerator lockers. One of the hostel's biggest advantages is the excellent cooking facilities, which allow you to save a lot of money on food. Cups, plates, cutlery, and cooking pots are provided, and alcohol is allowed in moderation. Token-operated washing machines are available at CFP 300 to wash (soap included), plus another CFP 300 to dry (or use the adjacent drying lines). Unlike some hostels, there's no age limit, you can stay as many nights as you like, and the premises remain open throughout the day (though the kitchen is closed for cleaning 1400-1600). The staff do their utmost to keep the place clean, and you'll be reminded of the need to cooperate if they see you leaving dirty dishes in the sink, etc.

Not only is this 94-person capacity hostel an inexpensive place to stay, but it's a center for exchanging information with other travelers. Young French immigrants often stay here when they first arrive in the territory, and ads or offers of employment, apartments, and vehicles are often posted on the walls. (The *métros* staying here stick together in their own superficially intimate cliques and don't mix much with anyone else.) The hostel will store excess luggage for you, and they also rent tents for trips around the island at CFP 1,000 a week. There's ample free parking on the street in front of the hostel, or in the parking area at the top of the adjacent hill. The hostel is accessible on foot up the stairway at the east end of rue Jean Jaures. Even if you don't usually stay at youth hostels, this one is so pleasant and convenient, it's well worth considering by virtually anyone on a budget. Wardens Jacky Sorin and Andrea Schaefer run a tight little ship—the finest and only *real* youth hostel in the South Pacific.

Inexpensive

The five-story **Hôtel Caledonia** (B.P. 2168, 98846 Nouméa; tel. 27-38-21, fax 27-81-45), 10 rue Auguste Brun, is on a busy corner in the Latin Quarter behind the museum. The 11 rooms with shared bath are CFP 4,500 single or double, the 10 rooms with private bath CFP 5,000, and six studios with kitchen CFP 5,500. A 10% discount is offered if you pay by the week, 30% by the month. The French owners are cheerful and it's good value.

The **Hôtel Lutetia** (B.P. 392, 98845 Nouméa; tel. 26-97-99), 10 rue du Docteur Lescour, a four-story hotel in the Latin Quarter, has 24 rooms at CFP 4,600 single or double, CFP 5,600 triple with TV. Otherwise it's CFP 20,000 a week, and monthlies are also available. An Algerian restaurant is downstairs. It's in a nice area without some of the traffic noise of the Hôtel Caledonia.

The raunchy, four-story **Hôtel San Francisco** (B.P. 4804, 98847 Nouméa; tel. 28-26-25), 59 rue de Sébastopol, is CFP 4,000 single or double, CFP 4,600 triple a night, or CFP 27,000 single or double, CFP 32,000 triple a week for a basic room with bath and cooking facilities. The hotel bar looks like something out of a Clint Eastwood flick.

The **Hôtel Lelapérouse** (B.P. 189, 98845 Nouméa; tel. 27-22-51, fax 27-11-87), 33 rue

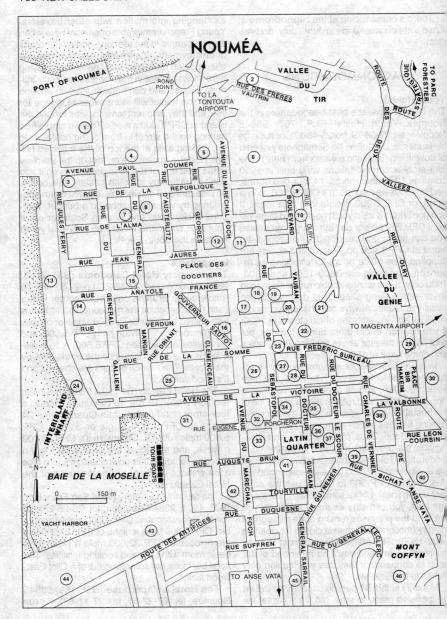

NOUMÉA

NOUMÉA

1. Service de l'Environment
2. Italian Consulate
3. Bingo Hall
4. General Hospital "Gaston Bourret"
5. Immigration Office
6. Government House
7. Centre des Colis Postaux
8. Champion Supermarket
9. Territorial Congress
10. Protestant Church
11. Australian Consulate
12. Musée de la Ville
13. Maritime Passenger Terminal
14. Casino Supermarket
15. City Hall
16. Restaurant Hameau II
17. American Express
18. Brasserie Le St. Hubert
19. Hôtel Le Lapérouse
20. Air Calédonie
21. Nouméa Youth Hostel
22. St. Joseph's Cathedral
23. Café de Paris/Hôtel Le Paris
24. Gare Maritime des Îles
25. Bus Terminal
26. Bernheim Library
27. Hôtel San Francisco
28. Rex Cinema
29. Restaurant La Case
30. Army Barracks
31. Market
32. Post Office
33. New Caledonia Museum
34. Plaza Cinema
35. Restaurant Quán Nhó
36. Relais de la Poste/La Chaumière
37. Hôtel Lutetia
38. Chez Camille
39. Restaurant El Cordobés
40. Palais de Justice
41. Hôtel Caledonia
42. American War Memorial
43. South Province Headquarters
44. Nouméa Yacht Charters
45. British Consulate
46. Mont Coffyn Viewpoint

de Sébastopol, is a decent five-story hotel opposite Le St. Hubert just off Place des Cocotiers. The 29 rooms are CFP 4,100/4,600 single/double with shared bath, CFP 5,200/5,650 with private bath. There are no cooking facilities.

The 62-room **Paradise Park Motel** (B.P. 9, 98845 Nouméa; tel. 27-25-41, fax 27-61-31) is at 34 rue du P.R. Roman, a 15-minute walk east of Place Bir Hakeim. An a/c studio with bath, kitchen, and TV is CFP 5,500 single or double a night, or CFP 37,500 a week. Studios without a/c are between CFP 21,000 and 24,500 a week, depending on the location, but these tend always to be taken. Further reductions are available for stays of two, three, or four weeks. The Paradise Park is inhabited mostly by French contract workers, as the four *pétanque* courts next to the swimming pool indicate. It's the only budget place with a resort atmosphere within walking distance of town. Bus No 2 (Vallée des Colons) passes nearby.

The **Mocambo Hôtel** (B.P. 678, 98845 Nouméa; tel. 26-27-01, fax 26-38-77), 49 rue Jules Garnier, a four-story building just off Baie des Citrons, has 40 rooms with TV, fan, and fridge beginning at CFP 5,000 single or double, CFP 6,000 triple—good value.

Two reasonably priced motels are in Val Plaisance near Anse Vata Beach, but both are often full. The three-story, 22-unit **Motel Anse Vata** (B.P. 4453, 98847 Nouméa; tel. 26-26-12, fax 25-90-60), 19 rue Gabriel Laroque, is only a five-minute walk from Anse Vata beach: CFP 5,500/6,000 single/double, plus CFP 500 to use the a/c (if required). On a monthly basis, it's CFP 100,000 double. The rooms are attractive and the French managers friendly. The two-story, 16-unit **Motel Le Bambou** (tel. 26-12-90, fax 26-30-58) is at 44 rue Spahr, a 10-minute walk farther inland: CFP 5,500/6,000 single/double with fan. The rooms at both motels have balcony, private bath, fridge, and cooking facilities, and monthly rates are available.

Moderate
The flashy **Hôtel Le Paris** (B.P. 2226, 98846 Nouméa; tel. 28-17-00, fax 27-60-80), just below the Catholic cathedral at 45 rue de Sébastopol, has 50 a/c rooms at CFP 5,650/6,200/7,200 single/double/triple (or CFP 29,000/32,000/40,000 a week) with TV, bath, and coffee making facili-

ties. This might be your place if you're interested in the local French social scene, though noise from the cafe downstairs is a drawback on the lower floors.

Just around the corner from the Mocambo Hôtel at Baie des Citrons is the **Marina Beach Hôtel** (B.P. 4622, 98847 Nouméa; tel. 28-76-33, fax 26-28-81), 4 rue Auguste Page. The 20 self-catering studio apartments begin at CFP 8,000 single or double (or CFP 35,000 a week).

The four-story **Lantana Beach Hôtel** (B.P. 4075, 98846 Nouméa; tel. 26-22-12, fax 26-16-12), 113 promenade Roger Laroque, faces Anse Vata (ask for a top floor room with a balcony overlooking the sea). The 37 a/c rooms are CFP 7,200/8,200/9,200 single/double/triple. A small shopping arcade is downstairs, and on weekends you have to be prepared for disco noise on the lower floors. Stay here if you want to sleep in the belly of the tourist strip.

Expensive

The lively **Hôtel Ibis Nouméa** (B.P. 819, 98845 Nouméa; tel. 26-20-55, fax 26-20-44), 8 promenade Roger Laroque, is opposite Baie des Citrons. The 60 a/c rooms with fridge and TV in this neat four-story building begin at CFP 8,800 single or double, CFP 9,800 triple (CFP 1,000 extra if you want a view of the sea). It's part of a well-known French "budget" hotel chain, and you're likely to encounter Japanese tour groups if you stay here. Nathalie's Bar below the Ibis is popular with a mix of yachties and off-duty French military personnel, especially at happy hour.

Le Surf Novotel (B.P. 4230, 98847 Nouméa; tel. 28-66-88, fax 28-52-23), on the point separating Anse Vata from Baie des Citrons, has 235 a/c rooms with TV, bath, and fridge in several connected high-rise buildings beginning at CFP 10,000 single or double garden view, CFP

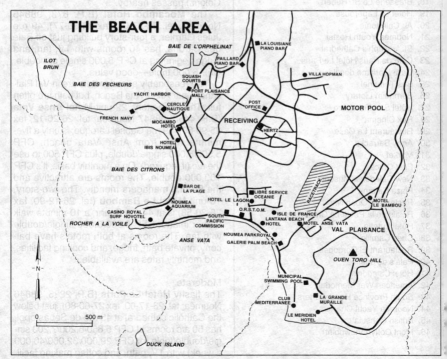

THE BEACH AREA

12,000 sea view. Rows of slot machines and the Casino Royal gambling hall are right on the premises. A swimming pool, fitness center, and Discotheque Atlantis are on the premises. It's only of interest as part of a cheap package tour.

Le Lagon Nouméa (B.P. 440, 98845 Nouméa; tel. 26-12-55, fax 26-12-44), 143 route de l'Anse Vata, is a six-story high-rise just in-land from the beach. Le Lagon has four single rooms at CFP 9,000, 41 studios at CFP 10,000 double, 13 one-bedrooms at CFP 13,000, and one two-bedroom at CFP 16,000. Most of the 59 tastefully decorated units have a kitchenette, fridge, and TV. Specify whether you want a double or twin beds.

Luxury

The **Parkroyal Nouméa** (B.P. 137, 98845 Nouméa; tel. 26-22-00, fax 26-16-77), 123 promenade Roger Laroque, is just across the road from the beach at Anse Vata. The 39 a/c garden view rooms in the four-story main building are CFP 18,000 single or double, while the 32 ocean view rooms are CFP 22,000. Third persons pay CFP 5,000. Behind the hotel are 16 rooms in four four-room villas at CFP 16,500. The two suites are CFP 46,000. The Parkroyal Nouméa caters mostly to Japanese groups. In 1999 a new 120-room wing complete with a 900-seat conference center opened behind the main building.

Nouméa's **Club Méditerranée** (B.P. 515, 98845 Nouméa; tel. 26-12-00, fax 26-20-71) is directly below Ouen Toro at the southeast end of Anse Vata. It's a glorified holiday camp for young adults, with lots of free social and sporting activities. The 280 simple a/c rooms are CFP 13,000 pp double occupancy a day with a 30% single supplement, plus the Club Med membership fee. Most of the rooms have twin beds, with meals and activities included in the tariff. Club Med caters almost exclusively to people on cheap package tours from Japan or Australia—you can't just walk in and ask for a room. In fact, you don't walk in at all: there are guards at the gate. Bookings must be made through a travel agency beforehand. This seven-story building (formerly the Hôtel Château Royale) is one of the only Anse Vata hotels without a road between it and the beach. Unlike the hotel, Club Med's beach and wharf are open to the public (enter down the stairs on the Anse Vata side).

Next door to Club Med is Nouméa's top hotel, the 253-room **Le Méridien** (B.P. 1915, 98846 Nouméa; tel. 26-50-00, fax 26-51-00), owned by local politician Jacques Lafleur. Rooms begin at CFP 26,000 single or double deluxe. For a suite you'll pay almost double or triple this, but most guests are here on package tours and pay much less. Two of the hotel's three curving high-rise wings built in 1995 enclose a large swimming pool, and Le Méridien also has direct access to the beach. A range of sporting facilities are available, including scuba diving with Sub-Austral. Nouméa's second gambling casino, a 400-seat ballroom, and five restaurants are here.

Hotels around Nouméa

The **Kuendu Beach Resort** (B.P. 404, 98845 Nouméa; tel. 27-89-89, fax 27-60-33) is on Kuendu Beach, near the west end of the Île Nou peninsula, six km from town. The 21 thatched bungalows with cooking and laundry facilities, each capable of accommodating up to five persons, are CFP 12,000/14,000 garden/beach single or double daily, or CFP 75,000/88,000 weekly. Extra persons beyond two are CFP 1,000 pp. The five overwater bungalows are CFP 29,000 double a night, or CFP 182,000 a week. (Upgrading work could have increased these prices.) On Sunday there's a buffet lunch (CFP 3,600) with folksy entertainment. Kayaks, pedal boats, snorkeling gear, and a swimming pool are provided free of charge, there's scuba diving with Sub-Austral (free initiation dive if you stay a week), and horseback riding is arranged. It's good if you're looking for more natural surroundings than are found in the city. Bus no. 13 comes this far every half hour, and the resort also offers a shuttle. Premium.

Hôtel Le Stanley (B.P. 1617, 98845 Nouméa; tel. 26-32-77, fax 25-26-56), 33 rue la Riviéra, is on a breezy hillside overlooking Sainte Marie Bay at Ouémo, beyond Magenta Airport. The 58 a/c studios and suites with kitchenette, balcony, TV, and fridge begin at CFP 12,000 single or double. On a weekly basis, it's excellent value at CFP 34,650 double. The accommodations are clean and new, with a view of Mont-Dore. Le Stanley's swimming pool is wedged between the main four-story building and a rocky shore. No shops are nearby, but bus no. 7 goes right there. Premium.

FOOD

Budget

Nouméa's ubiquitous snack bars will prepare a filling sandwich *(le sandwich)* for CFP 200 and up. This consists of a generous length of baguette-style bread with your favorite filling, plus lettuce and tomatoes. It's a meal in itself. One place serving this is the Vietnamese-run **Snack le Vilbar** (tel. 28-48-48), 55 rue de Sébastopol at Hôtel San Francisco.

The **Alimentation Générale** at 14 rue de Sébastopol (next to Brasserie Le St. Hubert) has excellent sandwiches and takeaway meals at the best prices in town, and the picnic-perfect benches in the Place des Cocotiers are just around the corner.

Chez Camille (tel. 28-59-86), 1 rue Charles de Vernheil in the Latin Quarter, is a Vietnamese takeaway with baguette sandwiches from CFP 200, Asian takeaways from CFP 400, and whole barbecued chickens from CFP 680. They've got everything you need for a picnic in nearby Place Bir Hakeim.

The Vietnamese-operated **Restaurant Le Hameau II** (tel. 28-48-32; weekdays 0600-1800, Saturday 0600-1330), 32 rue de Verdun, offers filling Asian dishes at reasonable prices. Inexpensive beer is available with the meals.

Better Restaurants

Nouméa has more than 130 restaurants serving dishes like *coq au vin* (chicken in wine sauce) and *champignons provençales* (mushrooms seasoned with garlic and parsley). The cuisine is *très bon;* indeed, given the prices, it has to be! The restaurants start serving lunch around 1100, and by 1200 the *plats du jour* could be gone, so arrive early. The more expensive dishes on the regular menu will be available till around 1330. Most establishments catering mainly to locals stop serving lunch at 1300 and dinner at 1900 (the top restaurants stay open until 2200). Many upscale places have a special tourist menu for a set three-course meal, varying anywhere from CFP 1,500 to CFP 2,500. It's often better value to order just one main plate à la carte.

Places offering a *plat du jour* lunch for less than CFP 1,000 weekdays include **Café Le Flore**

(tel. 28-12-47), 39 rue de Sébastopol, and **Café Moustache** (tel. 28-42-21; closed Sunday), 37 rue de Verdun. These are closed in the evening. The *plat de jour* at **Brasserie Le Lapérouse** (tel. 28-73-39), below Hôtel Lelapérouse, is advertised on a blackboard on the sidewalk outside.

Brasserie Le St. Hubert (tel. 27-21-42), 44 rue Anatole France on Place des Cocotiers, is popular among the local *pieds noir.* This is *the* place for reasonable pizza, draft beer, and local atmosphere—just don't voice any pro-Kanak sympathies, if you know what's good for you.

Restaurant La Case (tel. 25-42-28; Mon.-Sat. 1200-1330/1930-2200), or "Chez Mado and Manou," at 2 rue Jenner on the north side of Place Bir Hakeim, specializes in Melanesian chicken and pork plates, and Polynesian fish dishes. Their *plat du jour* is CFP 900.

Sample Vietnamese cooking at **Restaurant Vietnamien Quán Nhó** (tel. 28-56-72; open 1100-1330/1800-2200), 5 rue du Docteur Guégan. The chicken, duck, pork, beef, shrimp, and noodle dishes are not overpriced, and the menu is posted outside.

Restaurant La Chaumière (tel. 27-24-62; weekdays 1100-1330/1900-2130, Saturday 1900-2130), 9 rue du Docteur Lescour, next to the Relais de la Poste in the Latin Quarter, is one of Nouméa's finest French restaurants. They offer a three-course meal with a choice of anything on their menu at CFP 1,350/1,750 for lunch/dinner. It's a good choice for a splurge.

El Cordobès (tel. 27-47-68; closed Sunday), 1 rue Bichat in the Latin Quarter, is another top French restaurant despite the Spanish name. Their three-course lunch is CFP 2,500.

Baie des Citrons

Among the row of terrace restaurants facing the southern part of Baie des Citrons is **Bar de la Plage** (tel. 25-99-99) with a selection of sandwiches, hamburgers, and draft beer. It's great to have sundowners on their terrace, but be aware that drink prices go up after 2100 inside.

La Fiesta Chez Alban (tel. 26-21-33), 7 promenade Roger Laroque next to the Hôtel Ibis at Baie des Citrons, is run by Basques—good food at average prices. There's often live music on Thursday and holidays.

Anse Vata

Bambino (tel. 26-11-77) and **Jullius** (tel. 26-13-38), both between the Parkroyal Nouméa and Lantana Beach hotels, have things like hamburgers, *croques monsieurs* (grilled ham-and-cheese sandwiches), and French waffles at fair prices. **Snack Ulysse** (tel. 28-69-28), next to Libre Service Oceania, around the corner on route de l'Anse Vata, is a bit cheaper but doesn't have a terrace overlooking the sea.

Pizzeria San Rémo (tel. 26-18-02), 119 promenade Roger Laroque, next to the Lantana Beach Hôtel, has some of the tastiest pizza in the Southern Hemisphere (CFP 900 and up for one person).

Liberty Station (tel. 24-96-17; daily from 1100), at Résidence Isle de France, rue Louis Blériot, specializes in Tex-Mex dishes served American-style.

The Cantonese food at **La Grande Muraille** (tel. 26-13-28; closed Sunday night and all day Monday), near Hôtel Le Méridien, is expensive but still good value. Try the Imperial duck.

Surprisingly, the cheapest place to eat at Anse Vata is the bar in the slots area of the **Grand Casino de Nouméa** (tel. 24-20-20) at Hôtel Le Méridien. To hold their gambling clientele they serve draft beer at only CFP 200/800 a glass/pitcher, and huge baguette sandwiches are CFP 230.

Groceries

The **public market** (open daily 0430-1130), beside Baie de la Moselle, is the place to buy fish, fresh fruit, vegetables, and pastries. (Some of Nouméa's only free public toilets are here too.) Daily 1700-2300 a row of food vans parked along rue Georges Clémenceau, between the market and the New Caledonia Museum, dish out inexpensive takeaway curries in a colorful night market.

Nouméa has more than a half dozen large supermarkets and department stores. **Casino** (tel. 27-20-81; Mon.-Sat. 0730-1930, Sunday 0730-1230), opposite the Maritime Passenger Terminal two blocks west of Place des Cocotiers, is about the cheapest. There's another Casino open identical hours in the Port Plaisance Mall at Baie de l'Orphelinat. **Champion** (Mon.-Sat. 0730-1900), off rue du Général Mangin between

rue de l'Alma and rue de la République, is another of the few places open through lunchtime. **Oceania** (tel. 26-14-88), 145 route de l'Anse Vata near Hôtel Le Lagon, is open weekdays 0600-1930, weekends 0600-1230/1500-1930. Enjoy a memorable picnic in the Place des Cocotiers or on Anse Vata Beach with a baguette, Camembert cheese, and French table wine from any of these.

ENTERTAINMENT

Nouméa cinemas include the **Hickson City** (tel. 28-30-82), 6 rue Frédéric Surleau (behind Café de Paris), the **Rex** (tel. 27-24-83), on avenue de la Victoire, the **Plaza Twin** (tel. 28-87-87), 65 rue de Sébastopol, and the **Liberty** (tel. 28-30-35), 20 rue de la Somme. At least one of the films showing at the Plaza Twin may have some artistic merit. All foreign movies are dubbed into French, with no subtitles (screenings at 1400, 1700, and 2000, admission CFP 750). Admission fees are reduced to CFP 500 on Monday at the Hickson City, on Tuesday at the Plaza Twin, and on Wednesday at the Rex.

Night Club Le Tunnel (tel. 27-21-42), below Brasserie Le St. Hubert, 12 rue de Sébastopol, features live rock concerts on Saturday nights. If Le Tunnel fails to please, try **Club Discoteque Le Deep 501** (tel. 28-18-38), 46 rue Anatole France, which opens daily at 2130. At last report, admission was free!

Metropolis Club Discotheque (tel. 27-17-77), 1 rue Frédéric Surleau, behind Air France up facing the Catholic cathedral, was formerly known as Le Joker.

An older crowd waltzes to the music of a Tahitian kaina band every Friday and Saturday night from 2100 at **New Orléans** (tel. 27-80-05), 12 rue Général Mangin. Admission is free, a pitcher of beer CFP 1,500.

If you enjoy French chanson singing, seek out **Paillard Piano Bar** (tel. 26-28-80), 5 rue Jules Garnier, Baie de l'Orphelinat (hidden between Mr. Boeuf and Restaurant Flamboyant). It's brimming with atmosphere, and Friday and Saturday nights from 2100, you'll enjoy listening to Jean-Pierre's piano playing as Marie-Jo sings. Arrive early if you want a table, or try to reserve.

If you can't get into Paillard, there's also **La Louisiane Piano Bar** (tel. 26-11-16), just around the corner opposite the large anchor on Baie de l'Orphelinat, 5 route du Vélodrome. It often has live jazz Wed.-Sat. at 2200 (call to check).

Bars

The crowd at the **Relais de la Poste** (tel. 28-37-87), corner of Eugène Porcheron and Docteur Guégan in the Latin Quarter, is pleasantly bohemian, and you'll even see Kanaks in there. Ask about the Wednesday night rock concerts here. In past, a cyber café here has provided internet access 0900-1100 daily, but this service may have ended.

The manager at **Café de Paris** (tel. 28-20-00), 47 rue de Sébastopol, speaks English and is a bit of a character, but their café au lait is lousy. It's fun to sit and watch the off-duty French soldiers posing. You can often hear live music here on Sunday nights.

The **Hôtel San Francisco** (tel. 28-26-25), 55 rue de Sébastopol, has the only real American bar in Nouméa, and represents your best chance of meeting English speakers in Nouméa. This and the bar at the Squash Club on Baie de l'Orphelinat are good choices for happy hour.

Anse Vata

Broadway Night Club (tel. 28-60-22), below the Lantana Beach Hôtel, operates as a disco Friday and Saturday from 2130 (no cover charge). **Club 64 Discotheque** (tel. 25-28-15) in the Galerie Palm Beach opens daily except Tuesday at 2200 with music from the 1970s and 1980s. A CFP 2,500 cover charge (including a CFP 2,000 bar credit) is collected to attend the evening show and disco at **Club Med** (tel. 26-12-00). For an extra CFP 1,500 you can include the Friday night buffet.

Fun and Games

High rollers frequent the **Casino Royal** (tel. 26-16-90) at Le Surf Novotel on Anse Vata. The female casino staff wear evening gowns, the male croupiers black tie, and punters are also required to dress smartly to enter the gaming salon (no shorts, jeans, thongs, or running shoes). You must show your passport at the door—locals and persons under 21 aren't admitted. Dress requirements and admission restrictions don't

apply at the casino's slot machine section. The slots are operating from 1100 daily, the gambling salon from 2000.

The newer **Grand Casino de Nouméa** (tel. 24-20-20), at Hôtel Le Méridien, also has slot machines and a games room, open identical hours.

Less risky than the casinos are the **bingo games** held daily from 1400 onwards at 7 rue Jules Ferry (tel. 28-11-10; CFP 100 a card). Of course, you'll need to know French (or find a helper).

Two atmospheric local **pool rooms** are on rue Général Galliéni, between Anatole France and rue de Verdun: Billard Teva and Billard Le Tivoli.

Sitcoms

One of the top free shows in town is the proceedings at the **Palais de Justice** (tel. 27-93-50) on rue Bichat, just off route de l'Anse Vata downtown. Cases begin being heard in the Salle du Tribunal downstairs weekdays around 0800, and continue until the docket of that day has been cleared. Upstairs the Cour d'Appel evaluates more complicated appeals, also from 0800 onwards. The seats are comfortable, the air conditioning a relief, the situations often intriguing, and the opportunity to learn some French unexcelled.

Cultural Shows for Visitors

Polynesian dancing may be seen at the **Parkroyal Nouméa** (tel. 26-22-00) during the Friday night *Soirée Merveilleuse* and the Saturday *Soirée des Îles*. If you're not up to having the buffet (seafood Friday, island foods Saturday), just enter the bar and order a drink to enjoy it and the attempts of Japanese tourists to join in. On Sunday afternoons Polynesian dancing comes with the seafood buffet (CFP 3,100) at the **Kuen-du Beach Resort** (tel. 27-89-89).

No regular programs featureg Kanak dances or culture.

SHOPPING

Rue de l'Alma, with its numerous boutiques and specialty shops, is Nouméa's most exclusive shopping street. Watch for the *soldes* sign, which indicates a sale. One of the most popular places selling cheap souvenirs is **Curios du Pacifique** (tel. 26-97-52), 23 rue Jean Jaurès. Artifacts from the other Melanesian countries are shown at **Galerie Galéria** (tel. 27-19-85), 7 rue de la République.

One of Nouméa's better private art galleries is **Galerie Australe** (tel. 25-92-20), 13 rue de Sébastopol. **Galerie Aquatinte** (tel. 25-16-25), 8 rue de la Somme, has paintings by artists based in Polynesia, such as Ravello and Bobby Holcombe. Also visit **Arte Bello Galerie d'Art** (tel. 25-31-00), 30 rue Auguste Brun in the Latin Quarter. In fact, while rue de l'Alma may be Nouméa's trendiest shopping street, the Latin Quarter is a lot more fun to wander around and make little discoveries for yourself.

Nouméa has several smart shopping malls with many visitor-oriented shops, restaurants and activities offices. The largest of these are the **Galerie Palm Beach,** 127 promenade Roger Laroque next to the Parkroyal Nouméa on Anse Vata, and the **Port Plaisance Mall,** 10 rue James Garnier, Baie des Pècheurs (bus no. 6).

ceremonial jade mace, a symbol of chieftanship

Colorful stamps and first-day covers are available at the **Philatelic Bureau** (tel. 26-84-66; weekdays 0745-1145 and 1230-1430) in the main post office. They also sell the stamps of Tahiti-Polynesia and Wallis and Futuna.

Buy camping and snorkeling gear at **R. Deschamps** (tel. 27-39-61), 34 rue de la Somme. **Messageries Calédoniennes** (tel. 27-36-03), 46/48 rue Georges Clémenceau, sells inexpensive tents (from CFP 5,000).

For snorkeling and surfing gear, check **ABC** (tel. 27-90-06), 24 rue de Verdun. Better quality snorkeling and diving gear is available from **Marine Corail** (tel. 27-58-48), 26 rue du Général Mangin.

SERVICES AND INFORMATION

Money
Numerous banks along avenue de la Victoire toward Place Bir Hakeim will change money for CFP 500-750 commission (no commission on French francs in cash). The rates do vary slightly, and they're worth comparing if you're changing a lot of money. Avoid the Société Général, which deducts CFP 600/750 commission on cash/traveler's checks. The Banque Caledonienne, rue Anatole France and rue du Général Mangin, is open Saturday 0800-1200. Many banks have ATMs that give cash advances.

You can change American Express traveler's checks without paying a commission at Center Voyages (B.P. 50, 98845 Nouméa; tel. 28-40-40, fax 27-26-36; weekdays 0730-1730), 27 bis, avenue du Maréchal Foch. Their rate is slightly worse than the banks, so for amounts more than US$200 it's smart to find out what you a bank will give you, minus their commission, then choose. Center Voyages holds mail for American Express clients.

Post
The main post office (tel. 26-84-00), 7 rue Eugène Porcheron in the Latin Quarter, is open weekdays 0745-1530, Saturday 0730-1100. Poste restante at the main post office holds mail one month before returning to sender, but you can pay a CFP 2,400 fee to have them forward mail. There's a CFP 65 fee per letter to pick up mail.

It's possible to receive faxes addressed to fax 28-78-78 at this office, but it costs CFP 500 for the first page, plus CFP 100 for additional pages. To send a one-page fax here costs CFP 600 to Oceania, CFP 1,000 to France, CFP 1,100 to North America, or CFP 1,500 to other areas. Don't expect anyone at this post office to understand English; do expect to have to wait in line 30 minutes to buy *timbres* for your letters.

To mail a parcel, go to the Centre des Colis Postaux (tel. 26-86-00; weekdays 0745-1500), 17 rue de l'Alma. They don't sell mailing boxes or provide tape, but you can buy a box at the main post office.

Internet access is available at CFP 300 for 15 minutes at the Cybercom Cyber Cafe (tel. 27-25-45, www.cybercom.nc, weekdays 0800-2000, Saturday 0800-1200), 24 rue Dame Lechanteur, near Baie de l'Orphelinat.

Immigration Office

For an extension of stay, go to the Haut Commissariat de la République (tel. 26-65-18; weekdays 0745-1100/1200-1400), corner of Paul Doumer and Georges Clémenceau, and enter the office marked "Étrangers." Extensions are free, but bring along your plane ticket. You must apply at least a week before your current permit expires.

Consulates

The Australian Consulate General (tel. 27-24-14; open Mon.-Fri. 0800-1200), 7th floor, 19 avenue du Maréchal Foch, opposite the Musée de la Ville, issues tourist visas. They also represent Canadians, and everyone is welcome to come to read the Australian newspapers in the lounge (they get a new lot every Monday).

Other countries with diplomatic offices in Nouméa are Belgium (tel. 28-46-46), Nouméa Center Mall, 20 rue Anatole France; Indonesia (tel. 28-25-74), 2 rue Lamartine (Baie de l'Orphelinat); Germany (tel./fax 26-16-81), 19 rue Gazelle, Magenta (behind the university); Italy (tel. 26-32-23), 1 rue des Frères Vautrin, Vallée du Tir; Japan (tel. 25-37-29), 45 rue de 5 mai, Magenta; Netherlands (tel. 27-43-18), Hôtel Lelapérouse, 33 rue de Sébastopol; New Zealand (tel. 27-25-43), 4 boulevard Vauban; Switzerland (tel. 26-11-59), 18 rue Jim Daly, Val Plaisance (near Motel Le Bambou); United Kingdom (tel. 28-21-53), 14 rue du Général Sarrail, Mont Coffyn; and Vanuatu (tel. 27-76-21), 10 route du Vélodrome (Baie de l'Orphelinat). There's no U.S. diplomatic representation in New Caledonia.

Laundromats

Pat Pressing (tel. 27-11-81; weekdays 0700-1800, Saturday 0730-1230), 14 rue du Docteur Guégan, charges CFP 1,100 to wash and dry five kilos of laundry.

Lav Service (tel. 28-68-86; weekdays 0700-1830, Saturday 0700-1200, 47 rue Jeane Jaures, is cheaper at CFP 900 to wash and dry five kilos.

New Wash (tel. 26-24-74; Mon.-Sat. 0700-1900), in the Port Plaisance Mall, charges CFP 1,100 to wash and dry five kilos.

Information

The Office du Tourisme (B.P. 2828, 98846 Nouméa; tel. 28-75-80, fax 28-75-85), in the center of the Place des Cocotiers and with a branch office at Anse Vata, doles out free brochures on Nouméa and South Province, and can answer questions (preferably in French). Ask for their *Nouméascope* which details entertainment and events.

North Province has an information office (tel. 27-78-05, fax 27-48-87) next to Air Calédonie at 39 rue de Verdun. Air Calédonie itself is a good source of information on the three Loyalty Islands, as is Destination Îles Loyauté (B.P. 343, 98845 Nouméa; tel. 28-93-60, fax 28-91-21), 2nd floor, Immeuble Central, 27 rue de Sébastopol, and at 113 avenue Roger Laroque (in front of the Lantana Beach Hôtel).

The Institut Territorial de la Statistique (B.P. 823, 98845 Nouméa; tel. 28-31-56, fax 28-81-48), 2nd floor, 5 rue Galliéni, has specialized statistical publications.

Marine Corail (tel. 27-58-48), 26 rue du Général Mangin, handles nautical charts.

The Service de l'Environnement, Gestion des Parcs et Réserves (B.P. 2386, 98846 Nouméa; tel. 27-26-74; weekdays 0730-1130/1215-1600), 4 rue Galliéni, has maps of Rivière Bleue and other territorial parks and reserves.

Librairie Montaigne (tel. 27-34-88, fax 28-45-30), 23 rue de Sébastopol, has an excellent selection of books in French on New Caledonia and Tahiti. Librairie Pentecost (tel. 25-72-50, fax 28-54-24), 34 rue de l'Alma, is better for maps. Both bookstores have the colored IGN topographical maps of New Caledonia, including the excellent 1:500,000 "Carte Touristique" of New Caledonia. Pentecost also carries the four 1:200,000 "Carte Routière" highway maps (CFP 1,450 each), plus the 41 detailed 1:50,000 "Serie Orange" topographical maps (CFP 1,300). Pentecost sells nautical charts at CFP 3,500 each.

Photo Vata Image Center (tel. 26-24-07), next to the Parkroyal Nouméa at Anse Vata, also sells IGN topographical maps.

Airline Offices

Reconfirm your international flight reservations at Aircalin (tel. 26-55-00), 8 rue Frédéric Surleau opposite St. Joseph's Cathedral, Air France (tel. 25-88-00), 41 rue de Sébastopol, Air New Zealand (tel. 28-66-77), 14 rue de Verdun (Axxess Travel), AOM French Airlines (tel. 24-12-12), 1 rue d'Ypres, Air Vanuatu (tel. 28-66-77), 14 rue de Verdun (Axxess Travel), Corsair (tel. 28-

27-27), 39 rue de Verdun (Nouvelles Frontières), or Qantas (tel. 28-65-46), 36 rue de Verdun.

Health

The Hôpital "Gaston Bourret" (tel. 25-66-35), avenue Paul Doumer, accepts emergency cases 24 hours a day. A simple consultation here will cost CFP 7,200. The STD clinic at the hospital gives free AIDS (SIDA) tests (the AIDS information line is tel. 28-22-28). To call a doctor in emergencies, dial 15.

Dr. Jacques Gourand (tel. 27-53-00), 20 rue Austerlitz (upstairs from beside the Pharmacie in the Nouméa Center Mall) charges CFP 2,800 for a general consultation. He speaks English, and is on duty mornings from 0730 Mon.-Saturday.

Dr. Louis Lagarde (tel. 27-20-63; office open 0830-1130/1400-1800, Saturday 0830-1130), 30 rue de Verdun (upstairs), also charges CFP 2,800 for consultations.

Dr. Denis Renard (tel. 27-57-13; weekdays 0800-1200/1500-1900, closed Wednesday morning, Saturday 0800-1200), is at room 10, 17 rue Anatole France.

TRANSPORTATION

For information on domestic flights from Nouméa to other parts of New Caledonia, see **Transportation** in the chapter introduction.

Interisland Ferry

The **Compagnie Maritime des Îles** (B.P. 12241, 98802 Magenta; tel. 25-45-05, fax 26-95-11), at the Gare Maritime des Îles, 3 rue Jules Ferry, operates the high-speed 322-passenger ferry *Marie-Hélène* to the islands. Fares from Nouméa are CFP 4,900 to the Loyalty Islands, or CFP 3,200 to the Isle of Pines. Interisland fares between Lifou and Maré are CFP 2,400 (children half price). This sleek, 42-meter catamaran cruises at 30 knots, reaching the Isle of Pines in 2.5 hours, Maré in four hours, and Lifou in five hours. The ferry lands right in the towns, so you're spared airport transfer charges. During holiday periods the ferry is fully booked, and advance reservations are recommended at all times. The published schedule is unreliable, but refunds are no problem. Bring along your own food and drink.

Interurban Buses

Most long-distance buses leave from the Gare Routière (tel. 27-82-32), on rue d'Austerlitz opposite the market. The times quoted below could change, and there will only be one or two buses a day to the place you want to go, so always check the posted schedules a day ahead. Friday is a bad day to set out on a long trip as many buses are timed to take office workers home for the weekend, leaving Nouméa around 1730 and arriving at outlying towns very late. The buses do fill up, so arrive at the station early. The ticket office is open weekdays 0730-1200/1330-1600, Saturday 0730-1200; at other times, simply pay the driver.

The bus to La Tontouta Airport (one hour, CFP 400) departs from the bus station hourly 0530-1730 Mon.-Sat., every two hours on Sunday. You always pay the driver on this one. There's also the S.C.E.A. airport bus (tel. 43-31-41; CFP 2,000), which will pick you up right at your hotel.

The bus to Yaté (two hours, CFP 600) leaves at 1130 daily except Sunday. To Thio (two hours, CFP 900) the bus leaves at 1130 Mon.-Sat., at 1800 Sunday. Buses to Canala and Kouaoua via La Foa run daily.

The west coast is well served, with buses to Bourail (three hours, CFP 1,000) at 1230 Mon.-Thurs., at 1730 Friday, and at 1145 Saturday; to Koné (four hours, CFP 1,200) at 0930 Mon.-Sat., and at 1500 Sunday; to Koumac (5.5 hours, CFP 1,550) at 1130 Mon.-Sat., and at 1000 Sunday; and to Pouébo (seven hours, CFP 1,750) via Koumac at 0800 Wednesday and at 1730 Friday.

To the east coast, buses go to Houaïlou (four hours, CFP 1,150) at 1200 daily; to Poindimié (five hours, CFP 1,350) at 1030 Mon.-Fri., and at 1130 Saturday and Sunday; and to Hienghène (six hours, CFP 1,550) via Houaïlou at 0800 Mon.-Thurs. and Saturday, and at 1730 on Friday.

City Buses

Nouméa's city bus system *(transport en commun)* is excellent. There are 12 different routes, serving such places as Anse Vata (nos. 3 and 6), Baie des Citrons (no. 6), Magenta Airport (no. 7), and Île Nou (no. 13). The buses (or "baby-cars" as they're known locally) run every 10-30 minutes 0530-1815 daily. Catch them at the bus terminal downtown, or at marked bus stops along the routes. You must flag the bus down, but drivers won't stop if every seat is full (otherwise, they're very helpful). A flat fare of CFP 120 is charged (CFP 140 Saturday afternoon and Sunday), children under 10 CFP 80, and you always pay the driver.

Tourist Train

The **Palm Beach Express** (tel./fax 28-98-78), a miniature tourist train, shuttles between Anse Vata and most of the tourist sites around Nouméa, including the youth hostel and the Parc Forestier. A board in front of the Galerie Palm Beach at Anse Vata outlines the route. In theory, there are four trips a day from Palm Beach Station (at 0915, 1045, 1330, and 1515), and the day ticket (CFP 500/800 child/adult) allows you to stop off somewhere and catch a later service onward. In practice, the train is often booked by school groups, and the only day when all four departures usually operate normally is Sunday. This is convenient as other transportation is limited on Sunday. The funny little blue *cagou* signs you see around town are Petit Train stops.

Taxis and Hitching

The main Nouméa taxi stand is in the Place des Cocotiers. All taxis have meters (CFP 260 flag fall, plus CFP 97 per km 0600-1800, or CFP 129 per km 1800-0600 weekdays and anytime weekends). Trips outside Nouméa are CFP 150 a kilometer. Expect to pay CFP 800 to Anse Vata, CFP 1,200 to the Parc Forestier, CFP 1,600 to the Golf de Tina or Tjibaou Cultural Center, or CFP 7,500 to La Tontouta Airport for four persons maximum. If you speak French you can call a radio taxi 24 hours a day by dialing 28-35-12. An extra CFP 120 is charged in this case.

To hitch, take city bus no. 8 (Pont des Français) to Normandie at the junction of RT 1 to Bourail and RT 2 to Yaté. For the toll road north, take bus no. 9 to Rivière-Salée. Unless saving a few hundred francs is crucial, it's better to take the La Tontouta bus to the airport to get well out on the road to Bourail, or the Robinson, St. Louis, or Plum buses for the road to Yaté. Hitching up the southwest coast is easy, but it's slow elsewhere due to a lack of traffic. Also, very few drivers speak English.

Vehicle Rentals

Car rental rates begin around CFP 3,000 a day, plus CFP 30 a kilometer. Those kilometers can add up, so you're better off getting an unlimited kilometer rate (often with a two-day minimum rental). Many of the smaller car rental agencies not associated with the international chains will give you a large discount on their published rates if you take the car for a week or more. Bargaining may be possible, but hang onto all the paperwork as cases of credit card fraud have occurred here. Most companies will allow you to drop the car off at La Tontouta Airport at no additional charge.

Full collision insurance is CFP 1,300 a day and up, although the unlimited km rates usually include it. When checking the car rental insurance, ask how much the "franchise" is, as that's the deductible amount you will have to pay if you're found to be at fault, insurance or no insurance. It varies from CFP 50,000 with AB to CFP 100,000 at Europcar/Visa and Hertz. Any driver's license will do, but Avis, Hertz, Mencar, Euro Car, Tropic, and some of the others will only rent to those 25 and older (age 21 or older at AB and Europcar/Visa). Expect to pay CFP 100 a liter (or US$4 per American gallon) for gasoline, and in remote areas tank up every chance you get. Gasoline is the same price everywhere on Grande Terre.

Some companies don't want their cars taken out of South Province, and a clause in the rental contract may stipulate that the insurance will be void and the renter responsible for full damages and towing charges if the car is taken beyond Bourail. Riviére Bleue Provincial Park, roads south of Yaté, and all unpaved roads may also be banned. Chances are, the agency won't mention any of this to you, but it will be printed in the contract. Thus it's wise to read the contracts carefully when deciding who to rent from, and make sure North Province is included in the insurance coverage if you intend to go there.

Compared to the other Pacific islands, the roads of New Caledonia are excellent and a joy to drive. Surprisingly, however, the signposting is often poor, and there's a general absence of picnic or rest areas along the highways and benches in the town parks (except occasionally in Nouméa). Driving is on the right, and the use of seat belts is compulsory. The speed limit is 50 kph in town, and up to 110 kph on the open road. If two cars meet at an unmarked town intersection, the car on the right has priority. In case of an accident, report to the nearest *gendarmerie*.

Euro Car (tel. 25-20-20), corner of Maréchal Foch and avenue de la Victoire, offers a good price on unlimited kilometer weekly rentals (CFP 35,000 including insurance). **Europcar/Visa** (tel. 26-24-44, fax 28-61-17), 8 rue Auguste Brun, offers exactly the same thing, plus the security of dealing with a large chain.

AB Location de Voitures (B.P. 3417, 98846 Nouméa; tel. 28-12-12, fax 27-71-55), 36 avenue du Maréchal Foch, offers competitive unlimited-kilometer rates for two weeks (from CFP 62,900 all inclusive).

Mencar (B.P. 286, 98845 Nouméa; tel. 27-61-25, fax 28-17-59), 8 rue Jean Jaurès, rents Peugeot cars at CFP 36,000 a week, unlimited kilometers and insurance included.

Avis (B.P. 155, 98845 Nouméa; tel. 27-54-84, fax 28-62-90), 2 rue Georges Clémenceau (at the Toyota dealer behind the Total service station), offers cars with unlimited mileage and insurance included starting at CFP 40,500 a week.

Pacific Car (tel. 27-60-60, fax 28-45-40) and **Budget** (tel. 26-20-09, fax 27-82-65) have adjacent offices at 9 rue de Soissons, Faubourg Blanchot, a few blocks east of the Latin Quarter. Prices at the two are about the same (from CFP 40,000 a week including insurance and kilometers). At Anse Vata, Budget is represented by Amac Tours (tel. 26-38-38) at the Galerie Palm Beach.

Also at Anse Vata, try **Tropic Rent a Car** (tel./fax 27-26-99), 137 route de l'Anse Vata, two blocks inland from Libre Service Oceania. **Hertz** (B.P. 335, 98845 Nouméa; tel. 26-18-22, fax 26-12-19), 113 route de l'Anse Vata, has 4WD jeeps at CFP 10,500 a day including insurance and unlimited mileage (minimum two days). Hertz has the advantage of branch offices in Koumac (tel. 35-65-81), Koné (tel. 35-52-61), and Touho (tel. 42-88-38).

Take care when parking in the center of Nouméa as you must obtain a ticket from an automatic machine on the corner, and this must be placed face up on the dash inside the car for inspection. The fee is CFP 50 every 30 minutes, payable weekdays 0800-1100/1300-1600, Saturday 0800-1000. At last report, parking at Anse Vata was still free. There's plenty of free downtown parking in the lot on the west side of Baie de la Moselle, between the market and the American War Memorial. Elsewhere in the territory, you'll have no trouble finding free parking (except at Mont-Dore on the weekend).

Bicycle and Scooter Rentals

Reviens Bike Hire (tel. 27-88-65, fax 43-45-10; weekdays 0800-1700), in the Maritime Passenger Terminal downtown, rents mountain bikes at CFP 1,200/4,500 a day/week, scooters at CFP 2,950/14,900, 250-cc motorcycles at CFP 4,800/24,700, insurance, kilometers, and helmet included.

Nouméa Car (tel./fax 27-56-36), 9 rue Bichat, offers larger motorcycles at CFP 6,000 daily, plus CFP 30 a kilometer, or CFP 50,000 a week unlimited. A motorcycle license is required (also for the scooters).

Délices du Pacifique (tel. 27-14-41), the café in front of the Lantana Beach Hôtel, rents mountain bikes at CFP 500/900/1,000/1,400 for one/two/four/eight hours.

Tours

Amac Tours (B.P. A3, 98848 Nouméa Cédex; tel. 26-38-38, fax 26-16-62), at the Galerie Palm Beach, can handle most upmarket travel arrangements around New Caledonia. Amac's organized sightseeing tours from Nouméa include half-day trips to Mt. Koghi (CFP 4,900), and full-day trips to Rivière Bleue Provincial Park (CFP 6,400 pp), Yaté (CFP 7,000), Bourail (CFP 8,500), and Thio (CFP 9,000 pp). A minimum of six participants are required before any tour will depart, so it's wise to ask early which tour has the best chance of actually taking place. Don't book a one-day package to Ouvéa or the Isle of Pines, however, as these are rushed, overpriced (CFP 16,020), and superficial, and will only appeal to those who enjoy being herded by a Japanese-speaking guide.

Globetrotters (tel./fax 28-32-22), 153 route de l'Anse Vata next to Hôtel Le Lagon, offers seaplane excursions to the Isle of Pines and Casy Island, 4WD trips to Rivière Bleue, and dive tours to Amédée Lighthouse.

New Caledonia's most established adventure tour operator is **Terra Incognita** (B.P. 18, 98830 Dumbéa; tel./fax 41-61-19). They offer weekend canoeing and kayaking trips to wild rivers, tranquil lakes, and scenic bays throughout the territory. This is a great way to see some of New

Caledonia's beauty spots at their best while enjoying an exhilarating sport with the local pros. They also rent canoes and kayaks. **Aventure Pulsion** (B.P. 9131, 98807 Nouméa; tel. 26-27-48, fax 25-35-11), 12 avenue du Maréchal Foch, which also sells an excellent hiking guide (in French) to the entire territory.

On weekends a couple of times a year, three-day package tours to Norfolk Island are offered by the domestic airline **Air Calédonie** (tel. 28-78-88, fax 28-13-40), 39 rue de Verdun. For information about Norfolk, turn to this book's **Pitcairn Islands** chapter. If you happen to coincide, you'll find it a most interesting trip.

Yacht Charters

Nouméa Yacht Charter (B.P. 1068, 98845 Nouméa; tel. 28-66-66; fax 28-74-82), 1 route

des Artifices, Baie de la Moselle, offers bareboat or skippered charters out of Nouméa. The usual trip is to sail to the Isle of Pines and back in five to seven days. Luxurious six-berth, 11-meter Beneteau yachts are used. The yacht charter companies listed in the **Getting There** section of this book's introduction handle advance bookings. **Pacific Charter** (B.P. 1493, 98845 Nouméa; tel./fax 26-10-55), in the same building as Nouméa Yacht Charter, is similar.

Many crewed charter boats work out of Nouméa, including the catamaran sailboat *Nirvana* (tel./fax 25-94-61), the *Alcyon* (tel. 46-10-00), and the *Viking* (tel./fax 26-14-93). The actual fleet changes all the time as boats come and go, so check with the tourist office for current information. The optimum sailing months are April-November.

GRANDE TERRE

Grande Terre is by far the largest island covered in this book, and also the most varied. It's so big, the southern part of the island is noticeably cooler than the north. A mountain chain averaging 1,000 meters high runs right up the middle of the island for most of its 400-km length, crossed at intervals by six main highways linking the brown southwest coast to the green northeast. The island is divided into two provinces by a line cutting across Grande Terre to the north of Thio, La Foa, and Bourail. Although North Province is a third larger in land area, South Province has three times as many inhabitants.

It's very easy to hitch up the west coast and you can thumb your way almost anywhere if you have the time, but the only comfortable way to travel around Grande Terre and discover the hidden beauty is by rental car. You'll save money on accommodations by being able to drive to out-of-the-way campsites, and by picnicking along the way. Buses do exist, but their timetables are designed to serve the needs of local commuters and don't always coincide with those of travelers. As a supplement to hitching, they're fine, but you'll find them of limited use in touring the island extensively.

Strangely, once you leave Nouméa, you probably won't meet any English-speaking tourists at all anywhere on Grande Terre. Virtually all of the travel facilities around the island cater almost exclusively to the French visitors, especially local French who often go on weekend trips. This is a tremendous advantage to those of us in the know, as you'll find everything fresh and unspoiled by package tourism. A knowledge of French is an important asset, but everyone is so friendly and helpful even monoglots will get by. A great adventure awaits you.

YATÉ AND THE SOUTH

East of Nouméa

La Conception Church (1874), south of the highway just a few kilometers outside Nouméa, contains many plaques left to thank the Virgin Mary for favors and miracles. In the graveyard beside the road to the church is the tomb of the former secretary-general of the Union Calédonienne, Pierre Declercq, murdered on 19 September 1981 by persons unknown. His tombstone reads: *assassiné dans le combat pour la libération de peuple Kanak.* Roch Pidjot (1907-1990), co-founder of the Union Calédonienne, is also buried here.

To reach the **Shangri-La hiking area** in the hills behind Nouméa, take a Robinson or St. Louis bus to the Complex Sportif de Boulari, four km east of La Conception Church. Rue Jean Gabin, directly opposite the sporting complex entrance, leads two km through Lotissment Shangri-La to rue des Mandiniers and the trailhead. In a couple of hours, you can hike up to the cross atop the hill, with forests and fine views along the way.

Seven km east of La Conception Church is picturesque **St. Louis Mission,** founded in 1859, with New Caledonia's oldest church set in lovely grounds. A footbridge below the east side of the church leads to the Tribu de St. Louis and the impressive **Grande Chefferie de St. Louis** (no entry). High chief Roch Wamytam is also the leader of New Caledonia's FLNKS independence movement. Bus service from Nouméa to St. Louis (CFP 220) is about hourly weekdays, every two hours Saturday, and three times on Sunday.

Yaté

Excellent views of Grande Terre's grandiose, empty interior are obtained from **Col de Mouirange** (260 meters), eight km down the Yaté road from the Plum turnoff. The access road to **Parc Provincial de la Riviére Bleue** (tel. 27-26-74) is just before Yaté Lake, another 13 km northeast of the pass. This 9,045-hectare reserve harbors many endemic plant and animal species, including the endangered *cagou.* The park entry kiosk is 2.5 km off the main road, and admission is CFP 500 per car, plus CFP 100 pp. Camping is CFP 100 pp. Riviére Bleue is closed on Monday, but directly opposite the turnoff to the park, a *piste rouge* (red dirt track) leads southeast into the **Bois du Sud,** which is always open (free admission and free camping).

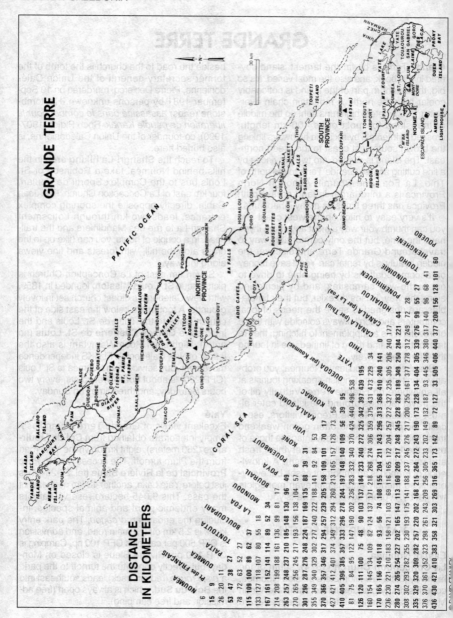

GRANDE TERRE

DISTANCE IN KILOMETERS

The road to Yaté winds 30 km along the south shore of Yaté Lake, with the deep blue waters of this 48-square-km reservoir juxtaposed against Grande Terre's bright red soil. A *piste rouge* to the **Chutes de la Madeleine** is 17 km east of the provincial park access road. A sign at the beginning of the *piste* reads *"accès restreint aux vehicles tout terrain"* (4WD vehicles only). The falls are 11 km south of the lake, and beyond them is the **Plaine des Lacs,** with its fascinating variety of drought-resistant, flowering shrubs.

On the left, six km east of the Chutes de la Madeleine road, is a two-km side road road to the giant **hydroelectric dam** that holds back Yaté Lake. Erected in 1959, the **Barrage de Yaté** is 61 meters high and 641 meters long, and produces about 270 million kilowatt-hours a year (a quarter of the territorial requirements). An old road accessible only on foot continues past the dam and seven km down to the **Yaté Generating Station** in Yaté village, passing a beautiful, high waterfall on the way.

Back on the main highway, you climb over the final pass and descend to the northeast coast, where everything becomes green again. At the bottom of the pass is Yaté Bridge and a three-way junction. The road to the left leads two km to the Unia Bridge, then another two km straight ahead to Yaté village. A supermarket near the Yaté powerhouse is open weekdays 0700-1200/1430-1800, Saturday 0730-1200.

Across Yaté Bridge, the paved road continues south to Goro, with a three-km stretch of dusty *piste* four km before Wadiana Falls. The Yaté area, 81 km east of Nouméa, is a popular weekend resort for Nouméa people, and several Kanak *gîtes* accommodate visitors. The bus route from Nouméa ends at **Touaourou Mission,** founded in 1888, 6.5 km southeast of Yaté Bridge. If you're traveling by public transport, you'll have to spend the night somewhere, as the bus back to Nouméa leaves Touaourou Mission Mon.-Sat. at 0600 (two hours, CFP 700). Getting there is easier, with departures from Nouméa Mon.-Sat. at 1145. It's possible to camp free on the beach at Touaourou Mission, otherwise hitching is easiest on the weekend.

The coastal plain is narrow here, and the alternate views of inlets, mountains, and sea are fine. At the southern tip of Grande Terre, about 22 km from Yaté Bridge, is Goro village. **Wadiana Falls** is visible from the road a kilometer beyond Goro. You can swim in a clear pool at base of falls, 20 meters from road, and climb to the top of the falls for the view across to the Isle of Pines and all the intermediate reefs (beware of loose rocks). The pavement ends at Gîte Wadiana nearby. In the 1930s Indonesian laborers built an iron and chrome mine on the plateau above Goro. A pair of giant rusting **cantilever loaders,** which once fed ore from conveyors directly into waiting ships, are beside the main road less than two km beyond the falls. The scenery is superb.

Accommodations at Yaté

A kilometer and a half north of Touaourou Mission is **Gîte Iya** (Paul Vouti, tel. 46-42-32), on landscaped grounds overlooking a lovely little cove with clear water and a fine beach. The three pleasant thatched bungalows are CFP 5,000 for up to three people, while camping is CFP 1,500 per tent. A grocery store is nearby. This is the only Yaté *gîte* directly accessible from

Visitors to Yaté are accommodated in these thatched cottages at Gîte San Gabriel.

Nouméa by bus (it's only 600 meters off the road). The large restaurant and everything else is very crowded on weekends, and you're much better off coming during the week. Inexpensive.

Gîte Saint Gabriel (Mr. Abel Atti, tel. 46-42-77) is set in a coconut grove right on the coast, four km south of Touaourou Mission. The three older thatched bungalows with bath are CFP 4,500, while the two newer tin-roofed bungalows with hot water are CFP 5,500. All are capable of accommodating up to four persons. Camping is CFP 1,000 per tent. If you just stop for a picnic here, it's CFP 500 per car. Meals are available. At low tide, explore the pools and crevices in the raised reef a kilometer northwest of Saint Gabriel along the beach. One deep pool full of eels appears to extend back into a submerged cave. The snorkeling is only so-so. On weekends, the conspicuous consumption and heavy drinking here are best avoided. Inexpensive.

The **Gîte Wadiana** (Mr. Charles Attiti, B.P. 34, 98834 Yaté; tel. 46-41-90), beyond Goro, 17 km south of Touaourou Mission and 100 km from Nouméa, is CFP 2,000 double with shared facilities, or CFP 3,000 with private bath. Camping is CFP 1,000 per tent. The camping area here is better isolated from intrusive tourists and local villagers than those at Saint Gabriel. The owner may be reluctant to give you a bungalow for some reason, but camping is always possible. The restaurant is popular among Nouméa residents, who often spend Sunday afternoon here. There's a relaxing sitting room and a beach (murky water). Gîte Wadiana is only 600 meters from the falls of the same name, which makes it a good base for hiking up into the hills behind Goro. Budget.

Gîte Kanua (B.P. 34, 98834 Yaté) opened in 1998 at Port Boisé, 16 km southeast of Gîte Wadiana on a good road. If you have a 4WD vehicle, you can return to Nouméa via Chutes de la Madeleine and La Capture, rejoining the main Yaté highway after 41 km of *piste rouge*. The four deluxe bungalows in traditional style are CFP 6,000/7,000 double/triple with bath, and there's a small camping area at CFP 1,500 per tent the first night, CFP 1,000 subsequent nights. In the attractive thatched restaurant you can get an excellent seafood meal for CFP 4,000, a mini-*bougna* at CFP 2,000 pp, or a regular meal at CFP 1,600. Gîte Kanua is run by Robert Attiti, son of the owner of Gîte Wadiana. It's on a white beach with clear water, and is surrounded by high forest—a very special retreat. Moderate.

THE CENTER

North of Nouméa

The 17-km toll road *(péage)* between Nouméa and La Tontouta Airport costs CFP 150 and saves time, but the old road through Dumbéa and Païta is more picturesque. The **Auberge du Mont Koghi** (B.P. K087, 98830 Dumbéa; tel. 41-29-29, fax 41-96-22), 20 km northeast of Nouméa, is at 500 meters elevation, five km off the old road to Dumbéa. A dozen well marked hiking trails wind through the majestic rainforest, and there's a splendid walk to the viewpoint on Malaoui Peak (636 meters). One tree in the park is estimated to be more than 2,000 years old. Admission is free. The local French come to the Auberge for the *fondue savoyarde* (CFP 2,600 pp, minimum of two) in the restaurant, and nearby are two wooden chalets with kitchen and private bath at CFP 7,500 for the first night, CFP 6,000 subsequent nights, for up to four people. In the forest, a 10-minute walk from the restaurant is a three-person treehouse at CFP 6,000 the first night, CFP 4,500 subsequent nights. There are also two refuges in the forest accommodating three or four persons at CFP 4,500 first night, CFP 3,000 additional nights. Sleeping bags and sheets are CFP 750 pp extra (optional). You may only occupy rooms after 1600 on arrival day, but may stay until 1400 on departure day. Inexpensive to moderate.

The 18-hole **Golf Municipal de Dumbéa** (tel. 41-80-00) is 26 km north of Nouméa, in the a river valley surrounded by green hills. It's a kilometer inland from the old highway, but easily accessible on the Dumbéa, Païta, and La Tontouta buses. Greens fees are CFP 2,500/3,800 for nine/18 holes weekdays, CFP 3,800/5,000 weekends. Club rentals are CFP 2,000 a half set, a chariot CFP 500. The New Caledonia International Golf Open takes place here in July.

A favorite day hike from Nouméa is to the summit of **Mont Mou** (1,220 meters). The route begins at the Col de la Pirogue between Païta and La Tontouta, easily accessible on the blue bus to the airport. Follow the paved side road

2.5 km east from the pass, and look for the trailhead just before a wooden bridge, 400 meters short of a sanatorium. It takes two hours to reach Mont Mou, 20 minutes beyond which is the wreck of an American wartime bomber. The vegetation and views along the way are superb, and you could even camp up there (take water). You'll easily be able to hitch back to Nouméa on the main highway, or wait for the blue bus (add about 25 minutes to the departure times mentioned in our La Tontouta Airport listing).

The nearest regular campsite to Nouméa is on **Plage d'Onghoué,** 19 kilometers off the main highway from Païta on an unpaved road via Tiare (transportation required). It's quiet and nicely isolated with lots of camping space along the beach, but no toilets or showers are provided, and water is only available from a hose at the caretakers office (CFP 200 per tent).

The small settlement on the main highway at the turnoff to **La Tontouta Airport** includes a large supermarket called Michel Ange (tel. 35-11-49; Mon.-Sat. 0630-1200/1430-1900, Sunday 0600-1200), next to the bank, less than a kilometer from the terminal. A smaller Alimentation Générale nearby keeps slightly longer hours and opens Sunday afternoon.

If you're bumped from a flight due to overbooking, the airline may put you up at the dreary **Tontoutel** (B.P. 8, 98840 Tontouta; tel. 35-11-11, fax 35-13-48), also called the "Ecotel," two km from the airport terminal and 52 km from Nouméa. It's run by a hotel school and costs about double what it should at CFP 6,500/8,000/9,000 single/double/triple. The 43 a/c motel rooms are in long single-story blocks. Hopefully the swimming pool, bar, and TV will keep you entertained. Moderate.

A well-known hiking trail right across Grande Terre begins 400 meters after the bridge over the Tontouta River, six km northwest of the airport. An unpaved mining road runs 17 km up the river valley to the ruins of the Gallieni Mine. Several hours beyond is the Refuge de Vulcain (970 meters), where most hikers spend the first night. The second night is spent at the Refuge du Humboldt (1,380 meters), an hour short of the summit of **Mont Humboldt** (1,618 meters), second-highest peak in New Caledonia. After visiting the peak in the early morning, one can either return to La Tontouta in a day, or continue east to the Kanak village of Petit Borindi on the east coast. Experienced hikers can complete this memorable trek on their own in three days, using detailed maps and trail guides obtained in Nouméa.

Bouloupari

About 24 km northwest of La Tontouta Airport is **Les Paillottes de la Ouenghi** (B.P. 56, 98845 Nouméa; tel. 35-17-35, fax 35-17-44), an attractive resort near the Ouenghi River, up against the mountains three km off the main highway. The 15 thatched bungalows are CFP 7,000 single or double, CFP 8,200 triple. There's an acclaimed restaurant/bar, swimming pool, tennis court, 18-hole golf course (greens fees CFP 2,500/3,500 weekdays/weekends plus CFP 2,000 for clubs and chariot), kayaking (CFP 700 an hour), and horseback riding (CFP 2,500 for two hours). Moderate.

Nine km beyond the Ouenghi River is Bouloupari, a French village at the foot of Mt. Ouitchambo, 78 km northwest of Nouméa. Here a paved road forks 47 km northeast to Thio over the Col de Nassirah (349 meters). Free camping is available in the small park at **Plage de Bouraké,** on Baie de St. Vincent opposite Leprédour Island, 15 km southwest of Bouloupari. It's easily accessible on a good paved road (signposted) through a French farming area. One of the best equipped campsites in New Caledonia, there are concrete picnic tables, toilets, showers, and water taps, all of it seldom used.

Thio

Since 1880, Thio has been the most important mining center in New Caledonia, with one of the world's largest nickel deposits in the surrounding hills. Thio leapt into international prominence in late 1984, when 200 FLNKS militants under Éloi Machoro overwhelmed the *gendarmerie* and captured the town, holding it for almost two months in a standoff against the French army. Seven roadblocks were set up, but when the FLNKS began house-to-house searches for arms and ammunition, the French sent in snipers to eliminate Machoro. Unfortunately, the police helicopter landed in the wrong place, and the marksmen were captured by the Kanaks. In January 1985 the French decided to take no chances and sent 300 *gendarmes* to surround an isolated farmhouse near La Foa where Machoro and some others were meeting. Soon after, another French death squad arrived and murdered Machoro and a second man in cold blood as they stood outside the building. In retaliation, Kanaks blew up the French mines at Thio, causing US$3 million in damages.

On arriving from Bouloupari, turn right to **Thio Mission,** Bota Méré Hill, and the beach. The Marist mission church dates from 1868. From the beach you can see the nickel workings on the plateau to the northwest and the port to the southeast. The ore is brought down by truck and loaded into ships bound for Nouméa and Japan for processing. Southeast of Thio Mission, a paved road leads to Borindi with a ferry crossing a few km before the village. Moara Beach, 10 km southeast of Thio Mission, offers white sands and lots of shady picnic or camping space. It's worth driving another four km beyond Moara for the view of Baie de Port-Bouquet.

Thio village is beside the Thio River at the foot of the plateau, two and a half km northwest of Thio Mission. It's a colonial-style town, with a post office, bank, *gendarmerie,* and clinic. The **Musée de la Mine SLN** mining museum (tel. 44-51-77; Monday, Tuesday, and Thursday 0730-1130/1300-1600, Saturday and Sunday 0900-1200), a block from the bridge, is CFP 100 to visit. The bus to Nouméa departs Thio Mon.-Sat. at 0500, and Sunday at 1515 (CFP 900).

The **Gîte d'Ouroué** (tel. 44-50-85), on Ouroué Beach, six km north of Thio, is in a beautiful location two km off the road to Canala. The four neat thatched bungalows with electricity are CFP 3,000 double, and there's lots of camping space (CFP 500 per tent) in a coconut grove along the beach. All guests share a common kitchen, with toilets and bathing facilities behind the dining hall. Meals can be ordered at CFP 300 for breakfast, CFP 1,200 for an ordinary meal, or CFP 2,500 for a seafood meal. The long brown beach here drops off sharply and should be used with caution. Budget.

A one-way dirt road to Canala begins nine km north of Thio, with a timetable *(horaire)* for traveling in each direction. You can travel northbound at 0500, 0700, 0900, 1100, 1300, 1500, and 1700, and anytime during the night. Southbound you can begin on the even hours. It takes

about 40 minutes to cover the 14-km one-way portion over the Col de Petchécara.

Independence martyr Éloi Machoro is buried next to the church in **Nakéty** village, at the northwest end of this road. Machoro's tomb is in the form of a small Kanak *case* next to the old church. The paved road begins again at Nakéty, and continues 10 km to Canala. There's no bus from Thio to Nakéty, and buses from Nakéty to Nouméa via Canala and La Foa leave before dawn. If you don't have a car you'll almost certainly have to hitch.

Around Canala

Canala Bay is the finest hurricane refuge for shipping on the northeast coast, and during the days of sail in the late 19th century this feature and mining activity made Canala an important center. Today it's Kanak country. The turnoff for **Ciu Falls** is two km southeast of Canala, then it's another four km in to the falls themselves. There's great swimming at the top of the falls (free), and a sweeping view of Canala Bay. Buses leave Canala for Nouméa before dawn (CFP 1,100).

Chez Jeannette (B.P. 7, 98813 Canala; tel. 42-30-13 or 42-31-03), near a small monument with a cross at the west entrance to Canala (no sign), offers nine basic rooms in a run-down colonial house at CFP 2,500/2,800/3,000 double/triple/quad. Otherwise it's CFP 800 pp in an eight-bed dorm. Camping is free on the understanding that you'll take the evening meal at CFP 1,250 pp. It's okay for singles hitching or traveling by bus, but couples with a car will do much better elsewhere. Budget.

At La Crouen, 11 km west of Canala, are **thermal hot springs,** where you can bathe in a 42° C sulfur pool. It's especially good for anyone suffering from arthritis, asthma, or rheumatism. Turn inland at a large bridge and follow the paved road one km to the Établissement Thermal. At last report, the main bath house was closed, but a small pool of thermal water beside the building was accessible anytime. A nice picnic spot overlooks the river. Farther west is the turnoff to the mining center of Kouaoua, 45 km northwest of Canala. From this junction, the main highway cuts south across the mountains to La Foa, passing tons of cascading water from several fantastic waterfalls along the way.

Around Sarraméa

Sarraméa, about 15 km before La Foa, is in a lovely valley. There's a large Kanak *case* in Petit Couli village, a few hundred meters north of the turnoff to Sarraméa. If you'd like to camp beside the river below the sports field at Sarraméa, ask permission at the nearby *mairie* (town hall) weekdays during business hours.

Caldoche-operated **Évasion 130** (B.P. 56, 98880 La Foa; tel./fax 42-32-35) is four km off the Canala road. The 14 bungalows with private bath are CFP 4,000/4,800/5,600 single/double/triple, and a picturesque swimming pool and restaurant are on the premises. Inexpensive. Évasion 130 is surrounded by verdant hills abounding in swimmable streams, and it makes an excellent base for hikers. An old mule track that once connected La Foa to Canala winds five km through the forest to the top of the **Dogny Plateau** from the hotel parking lot. It's a wonderful day hike, also possible on horseback. If you're not staying or eating at the hotel, you should park your car at the *mairie*, 700 meters away. If you're well prepared, you could camp at 950 meters elevation up on the plateau.

La Foa

La Foa, 65 km northwest of La Tontouta Airport, is an alternative place to spend the night before catching a flight. It's an orderly *Caldoche* town surrounded by lush fields, acacia trees, and stately *Araucaria columnaris* pines. People from nearby farms and villages come to shop at La Foa's supermarkets, and there are two banks. Fairly frequent buses up the west coast stop in front of the post office. The regular Nouméa bus begins its run here at 0600 daily except Sunday. At the south entrance to La Foa is a small metal bridge erected in 1909 by two students of Gustave Eiffel.

To visit the abandoned farmhouse where independence activists **Éloi Machoro** and Marcel Noraro were murdered by French police snipers in 1985, take the road inland from Restaurant L'Ermitage in La Foa. The pavement ends after 2.5 km at a complex marked "Distribution d'eau de La Foa." Keep left here and straight ahead another 11.5 km on a dirt road along the La Foa River, until you see a building with a red tin roof to the right of the road. Lengths of cloth hang from trees in front of the house in memory of Machoro and Noraro.

Hôtel Banu (B.P. 57, 98880 La Foa; tel. 44-31-19, fax 44-35-50), opposite the post office in the center of town, occupies an historic colonial-style building with a quaint bar where you should avoid making any pro-Kanak comments. The 12 rooms in a two-story building behind the restaurant are CFP 3,200/4,000 single/double without bath, CFP 4,200/5,000 with bath. In the back yard are four a/c bungalows with bath at CFP 6,000/6,800/6,800 single/double/triple. The Banu's miniature swimming pool is usually empty. The restaurant (closed Sunday night) at the hotel has a reasonable *plat du jour* lunch, but the seafood dinner is expensive. Inexpensive to moderate.

If you have a car you can camp free in the beach park at **Plage de Ouano,** 24 km south of La Foa (the last 10 km of it on a washboard gravel road off the west coast highway). It's a large open area near a local boat launching ramp. Picnic tables, barbecues, toilets, and deteriorating showers are provided, plus plenty of mosquitoes after dark.

The turnoff to **Fort Teremba** is 14 km west of La Foa, then it's another three km south on a paved road to the fort. Built by convict labor in 1874, Fort Teremba's round tower affords a good view of Teremba Bay and the surrounding area. Beyond Fort Teremba, a dirt road leads 5.5 km to **Plage de Tanguy** where you can camp free on the beach, though it's rather swampy and mosquito infested. No services are provided. On the way there you pass the territory's largest prawn farm.

Bourail

Although this town of 5,000 inhabitants, 167 km northwest of Nouméa, is the second largest in the territory, it's a disappointing little place after Nouméa. Along the one main street are the church (1877), post office, banks, supermarkets, gas stations, *gendarmerie*, town hall, and school, eight essential facilities you'll find in most New Caledonian towns. Use Bourail as a stopover on a trip around the island, or as a base for visiting the surrounding area. In mid-August a major agricultural fair is held here—the best time to meet *les broussards* (country people).

There's not a lot to see in Bourail, although a small market is held at the northwest end of town on Tuesday and Saturday mornings. Worth a visit is the **Bourail Museum** (tel. 44-10-80), on the highway just south of the center, in a storehouse remaining from the penitentiary set up here in 1867. The museum displays the history of the region, in particular the life of early French settlers, Kanak artifacts, seashells, and photos from WW II. A Kanak *case* and petroglyphs are in the museum yard. It's open Wednesday, Friday, Saturday, and Sunday 0800-1100 and 1300-1700; admission CFP 200.

Plenty of buses pass through Bourail, but the drivers will only let you on if there's an empty seat. This can be a problem on Sunday and with buses headed for the east coast, which arrive full from Nouméa. Thus it's smart to visit Bourail on your way back to Nouméa rather than getting out here on your way north. A bus to Nouméa begins its run in Bourail Mon.-Thurs. and Saturday at 0630, and Friday at 1230. Strangely, hitchhiking out of Bourail can be unpredictable with waits of more than three hours not uncommon.

Vicinity of Bourail

About nine km southeast of Bourail is a **New Zealand military cemetery,** to the right of the main highway from Nouméa. Bourail was an important New Zealand training base during WW II, and the peaceful cemetery has a striking location overlooking a valley. An account of the campaigns in which the servicemen died is posted. These days, the French army has two companies of infantry stationed at Camp Nandai, eight km north of Bourail.

One recommended trip from Bourail takes in **Pierced Rock** (Roche Percée), on a side road six km west of the Néra Bridge. A natural tunnel cuts through an eroded quartz cliff here, and at low tide you can get through to the other side. An anthropomorphic rock formation here has been called "le Bonhomme." Nearby is a good beach for swimming and snorkeling.

One km farther along the main road is a track up to **Belvédère Viewpoint,** with a fine view of Néra River, the coast, and Turtle Bay. **Turtle Bay** (Baie des Tortues), backed by towering *Araucaria columnaris* trees, is just up the coast from Pierced Rock, accessible by car from the road to the viewpoint. Be there early in the morning between November and March to see nesting turtles (extremely rare). Freelance camping is possible here.

Ten km past Pierced Rock along the same road is **Poé Beach,** the longest beach on Grande Terre. A camping ground and a small resort share 18 km of unbroken sands. This is one of the few coastlines around Grande Terre not protected by an offshore barrier reef.

Randonnées a Cheval (Mr. Velayoudon, tel. 44-14-90) offers horseback riding from Ranch de la Courie off the main west coast highway, four km northwest of Bourail. Riding is CFP 8,000 pp a day including lunch, setting out at 0800. Accommodations and all meals are provided if you wish to stay two or three days at CFP 8,000 a day. A one-hour ride is CFP 1,500. The five-hour ride to the summit of Néwatuu (598 meters) and back is superb.

Accommodations at Bourail

No hotels exist right in town. **Hôtel La Néra** (tel. 44-16-44, fax 44-18-31) overlooks the Néra River Bridge, two km southeast of central Bourail. The six a/c rooms with bath in a long block facing the swimming pool are CFP 4,800/5,600/6,400 single/double/triple, while the honeymoon suite is CFP 7,200/8,000 single/double. It's an attractive location for a highway hotel. Inexpensive.

Hôtel El Kantara (B.P. 244, 98870 Bourail; tel. 44-13-22, fax 44-20-33) is beside the Néra River, a couple of km southeast of the Pierced Rock and 10 km southwest of downtown Bourail. The *pied noir* owner has endowed his hotel with an Algerian air. The 20 rooms with bath in parallel zigzag blocks are CFP 4,800 single or double, CFP 5,400 triple. There's a swimming pool and tennis court, it's a good base for sports such as kayaking on the river (kayak and canoe rentals are nearby). Scuba diving is available with **Bourail Sub-Loisirs** (B.P. 98, 98870 Bourail; tel. 44-20-65, fax 44-14-87) at the mouth of the Nera River, two km south of the hotel. Inexpensive.

At the beginning of Poé Beach, 18 km southwest of Bourail, is an attractive **campsite** (tel. 44-22-90) offering plenty of sand, banyan trees, songbirds, fresh water, showers, toilets, and excellent surfing (CFP 800 per tent). If you don't wish to pay, you can camp free farther down the beach.

Beside the main west coast highway five km northwest of town is **Hôtel Le Club** (B.P. 358, 98870 Bourail; tel./fax 44-13-77) with five a/c rooms with bath in a long block at CFP 4,200 single or double. The Club's restaurant is patronized by soldiers from a French military base a few km farther out beyond the turnoff to Houaïlou. Information about Le Club will be available at Ch'ti Bar (tel. 44-13-94), opposite the bank in Bourail. Inexpensive.

THE NORTHEAST COAST

Vicinity of Houaïlou

The winding road from Bourail follows sparkling rivers and crosses the **Col de Roussettes** (381 meters), a pass named for the big red fruit bats of the region. The border between north and south provinces runs along this ridge. There are good views along the way, especially of the abandoned Kanak taro terraces.

At the Coula River, 35 km north on the road to Houaïlou from the junction of the west coast highway, there's a road upstream to a viewpoint over a large waterfall (keep right). Thirty km farther east is a bridge over the Houaïlou River, with the road to Poindimié across the bridge to the left and Houaïlou town one km to the right.

The riverside town of Houaïlou, four hours from Nouméa by bus, was the base of the famous Huguenot missionary Maurice Leenhardt from 1902 to 1920. Today it's a Kanak stronghold. No regular accommodations exist in Houaïlou, but you could camp free on the wild, deserted beach adjacent to abandoned Houaïlou airstrip *(aerodrome)*. The paved access road is two km north of the bridge, then it's another two km to the beach (go around the south end of the airstrip). There's plenty of driftwood for campfires here, but this site is very exposed to the wind and sea.

Up the Coast

As you continue up the coast, your first stop will be **Bâ Falls,** 14 km northwest of Houaïlou bridge and on the mountain side, only 1.5 km upstream from the highway. There's a large swimming area at the base of the falls. After a swim, climb to the top for the view. (There have been reports of break-ins to the parked cars of visitors to the falls.)

Ponérihouen, 44 km northwest of Houaïlou, is a picturesque little town by the river of the same name. Coffee is the main cash crop in this area, and there's an experimental station in the town.

The long one-way steel bridge two km west of Ponérihouen dates from WW II. Mr. Michel Blanchet (tel. 42-85-14) operates **Camping Amenagé de Tiakan** on a brown beach opposite his store, 11 km north of Ponérihouen. Many small thatched picnic shelters among the coconut trees provide shelter in case of rain. Toilets, barbecue pits, and showers are also provided. To camp is CFP 1,000 per group if you arrive by car, motorcycle, bicycle, or on foot, or CFP 1,800 per bus load. Picnicking is only CFP 300 per car.

Poindimié

This small town, 308 km from Nouméa, was founded during WW II, as several Quonset huts attest, and today it's the administrative center of the northeast coast. Stock up at the supermarkets or change money at one of the banks. Buses to Hienghène leave Mon.-Sat. at 1130, Tues.-Fri. and Sunday at 1300, and on Sunday at 1510. Most buses to Nouméa (CFP 1,350) leave Poindimié in the early morning Mon.-Sat. and around noon on Sunday. If you're driving, be sure to tank up at Poindimié as there's no gasoline at Hienghène, and unleaded fuel may not be available again until Koumac.

Koyaboa Hill offers a fine overlook from its 390-meter summit. Take the first paved road up the hill after the Quonset huts west of Hôtel Le Tapoundari. This soon becomes a grassy track, and you must walk to reach the radio towers on top. The **public swimming pool** at the east entrance to town features a 1951 mosaic by Victor Vasarely, the famous Hungarian creator of op-art. A traditional Kanak *case* is between the traffic circle at the west end of town and the beach.

Tieti Diving (B.P. 248, 98822 Poindimié; tel. 42-64-00, fax 42-64-01), based at the Monitel, offers scuba diving at CFP 4,500/5,500 without/with equipment. They do scuba instruction in the hotel pool (CFP 39,000 for PADI open-water certification). The scuba diving in this area is good because there isn't any mine-produced erosion killing the reefs with sediment.

At the Tiwaka River, 13 km north of Poindimié, a new road cuts across the island to Koné.

Accommodations at Poindimié

The lack of reliable budget accommodations makes it a risky business to plan a stop here if you're traveling by bus or hitching. **Hôtel Le Ta-**

poundari (B.P. 10, 98822 Poindimié; tel. 42-71-11, fax 42-76-11), opposite Poindimié's bridge, has 12 a/c rooms with private bath. The six rooms in a block next to the restaurant go for CFP 5,500/6,000 single/double, while the six older units in a row at the back are CFP 4,500/5,000. They're overpriced and often booked out by French contract workers. Inexpensive.

The **Hôtel de la Plage** (B.P. 97, 98822 Poindimié; tel. 42-71-28, fax 42-71-28) is an aging two-story concrete building next to a supermarket across the highway from Tiéti Beach at the west edge of Poindimié. The 15 fan-cooled rooms are CFP 5,500 single or double, while the three a/c apartments with kitchens go for CFP 6,500 for up to four persons. The hotel restaurant serves a good buffet breakfast, including an ample pot of local coffee (CFP 850). Inexpensive to moderate.

Poindimié's most upmarket place to stay is the **Monitel de Tiéti** (B.P. 154, 98822 Poindimié; tel. 42-72-73, fax 42-72-24), right on Tiéti Beach, with four rectangular beach bungalows, six a/c rooms in a long block, and two houses with four rooms each, all costing CFP 7,500/8,500 single/double. There's a swimming pool. Despite the hotel's category, the surrounding area is rather shabby. Moderate.

There's also a free municipal camping area at **Tiéti Beach.** It's a nice, grassy spot, with lots of camping space below the coconut palms behind the light brown beach, and toilets and showers are provided. It's a bit of a local hangout, and there's a longstanding problem of theft, so once your tent is up, you won't be able to go off and leave it.

Gîte Napoémien (B.P. 67, 98822 Poindimié; tel. 42-74-77, fax 42-71-77), in the verdant Napoémien Valley five km inland from Poindimié, has two bungalows with cooking facilities at CFP 1,500 pp. Camping is CFP 1,000 per tent (toilets and showers provided). There's no sign at the *gîte,* and the whole operation is poorly managed. The owner lives a kilometer back toward Poindimié (next to the bridge with a welcoming sign), and it's best to stop there for information. Better yet, call ahead for reservations, as this place is often closed. Budget.

Touho

This small settlement on a bay, 27 km northwest of Poindimié, is a good destination if you're traveling by bus as there are several inexpensive places to stay. A few local fishing boats are based here, and Touho is a pleasant place to hang out for a few days. Mandarin orchards, coffee plantations, and tall pines are hallmarks of this area. **Touho Mission** with its evocative old church (1889) is two km west of Camping Lévéque and one km off the main road (ocean side). For a splendid view of the entire area, hike up to the cross on the hill above the mission. The track leads off the main road from the top of the hill, 500 meters north of the mission turnoff. Go between the house and the water tank, and it's less than 10 minutes to the top. Touho's airport is three km southeast of Camping Lévéque, out on the road to Poindimié.

Camping Aménagé Lévéque (B.P. 3, 98831 Touho; tel. 42-88-19), behind the grocery store in Touho, charges campers CFP 350 per tent. There are also five small bungalows, each with two beds, a table, two chairs, and shelves, at CFP 1,500 single or double. No bedding is provided, so roll out your sleeping bag. There's electricity but the toilets and shower are outside. This is one of the few places in New Caledonia where you can still get a cheap room, but mosquito coils are essential and a net would be much better. It's right on a sheltered beach with clear water ideal for swimming, and next to the road to/from the small boat harbor if you've arrived by yacht. Shoestring.

Relais Alison (Madam Pisniak, B.P. 52, 98831 Touho; tel. 42-88-12), opposite Camping Lévéque, offers five a/c rooms with private bath in a long block behind the Total service station at CFP 4,500/5,000 single/double. Meals are pricey here. Inexpensive.

The **Mairie de Touho** (B.P. 4, 98831 Touho; tel. 42-88-07, fax 42-87-51), next to Relais Alison, rents five a/c bungalows with private bath on the beach opposite Centre Commercial Gastaldi, 500 meters west of Camping Lévéque. They're CFP 4,500 for up to three people, but you have to arrive during business hours to get in. Inexpensive.

Camping Gastaldi (tel. 42-88-14) is five km from Camping Lévéque. Take the Hienghène road over the hill to a turnoff to the right, then it's a kilometer farther in toward the beach. This free camping ground rates among the nicest and most peaceful on the island. Since it's at he mouth of a small river, the beach isn't as good as the one at Camping Lévéque, but there's a lot more privacy, and toilets and showers are provided. A grocery store is nearby.

Gîte de Mangalia (tel. 42-87-60), across the road from a pebble beach, 16 km northwest of Touho, has eight thatched duplex bungalows at CFP 4,000 single or double. Cooking facilities are not provided and breakfast is CFP 600 pp. Inexpensive.

HIENGHÈNE AND THE NORTH

The scenery around the small town of Hienghène (pronounced "yang-GAIN"), 376 km from Nouméa, is unquestionably the finest in New Caledonia. Hienghène is also a symbol of the Kanak struggle against foreign domination. A hundred years ago Kanaks under Bouarate fought French colonialism here; in December 1984, 10 unarmed Kanaks on their way home from a political meeting were ambushed and murdered just up the river by French settlers.

Araucaria columnaris *pines before Hienghène's Towers of Notre Dame*

At Tiouandé, 30 km northwest of Touho on the way to Hienghène, is a rocky crag known as **Napoleon's hat** next to the road. The entrance to Club Med is 5.5 km farther along, and beyond that you see high **limestone cliffs** on the right with a salt lake at their base. Five km beyond Club Med is a narrow one-km coral road leading to the huge **Lindéralique Cave** *(grotte),* on the far side of the cliffs (CFP 200 admission to the cave).

A kilometer closer to Hienghène at the top of the pass is a turnoff to the viewpoint *(point de vue)*—one of the most beautiful spots on the island. From here, you'll see huge isolated rocks named **Sphinx** (150 meters high) and **Brooding Hen** (60 meters high) guarding the mouth of Hienghène Bay. The town itself is on a rocky spur at the mouth of the river. Across the bay are nestled the tiny white buildings of **Ouaré Mission,** with the high coastal mountains behind. Four fine coral islets are seen offshore. From town the Brooding Hen looks more like the **Towers of Notre Dame,** its other name.

As you come into Hienghène, between the viewpoint and the bridge is the **Centre Culturel Goa Ma Bwarhat** (B.P. 72, 98815 Hienghène; tel. 42-81-50), which should be visited for its mixture of modern and traditional architecture. The exhibition room (open weekdays 0800-1200/1300-1600; admission CFP 100) displays traditional door jambs, war clubs, spears, tools, pottery, baskets, and indigenous currency. Authentic handicrafts are sold here, and the center also contains a library. Outside are two large *cases* with an open-air theater between.

For a sweeping view, hike up to the TV tower on **Pwihâ Duét** (499 meters). Take the Wérap road upriver from the bridge. After 1.5 km, the jeep track to the summit cuts straight up the hill to the left from a bend of the river.

Buses to Nouméa leave Hienghène at 1000 daily (CFP 1,550). A bus leaves Hienghène for Pouébo Monday, Tuesday, and Thursday at 1400, Friday at 1800. Hitchhikers will find that very little traffic comes this way (10-hour waits in the hot sun are not unusual).

Tiendanite

Tiendanite, the home village of former FLNKS leader Jean-Marie Tjibaou, has a special place in the history of New Caledonia. Fourteen Kanaks from this village were killed in a 1914 uprising against the French. During the 1917 uprising, the village was burnt to the ground, the men sent to prison in Nouméa, the women to work as servants for the *colons*. Later, Tjibaou's grandfather assembled some people to rebuild the village. In 1984, 10 men from this village of 120 people were brutally murdered by French *colons*, who were eventually set free by a French jury.

Eight km up the river from Hienghène on a rough gravel road are the rusting wrecks of two small trucks flanked by a flagpole and strips of cloth marking the spot where 10 men from Tiendanite were killed by French settlers on 5 December 1984 in the Wan'yaat ambush. A black marble stone bears their epitaph and names. The road continues along the Hienghène River another five km, to a turning to the left and a bridge across the river. A side road runs up a small stream four km to Tiendanite village, deep in the mountains. The 10 victims of the Wan'yaat ambush are buried in a row next to the Catholic church in the village. The grave of Jean-Marie Tjibaou (1936-89) is on the opposite hill facing the church.

Accommodations around Hienghène

Unfortunately, budget accommodations around Hienghène are scarce. The **Base de Plein Air Pai-Kaleon** (tel. 88-27-37), on the beach below the football field, allows camping in their yard at CFP 250 per tent, plus CFP 150 pp to use the toilet and shower. They also rent canoes at CFP 2,000/4,000 a half/full day, and bicycles at CFP 2,500/5,000.

There's a campsite with running water on the beach 600 meters down the side road to Lindéralique Cave, four km from Hienghène (CFP 750 per tent).

In 1992 the **Koulnoué Village Club Méditerranée** (B.P. 63, 98815 Hienghène; tel. 42-81-66, fax 42-81-75) opened on attractively landscaped grounds behind a long brown beach, 10 km south of Hienghène and 1.5 km off the main road. The local Kanak villagers received a 10% interest in the resort, plus 40 hotel jobs in exchange for providing the land. The 50 neat tin-roofed duplex bungalows with a/c are CFP 9,600 for up to four persons (CFP 1,000 higher on holiday weekends). Unlike most Club Meds, this one isn't a closely guarded camp, and they'll

gladly rent you a room if they have one. Meals are extra at CFP 1,300/1,800/2,500 for buffet breakfast/lunch/dinner. Activities include the swimming pool, tennis, horseback riding (CFP 2,500 pp an hour), and other standard Club Med features. Scuba diving costs CFP 5,000, plus CFP 1,000 for equipment, with reductions for two or six dives. Bicycles are CFP 500 an hour. The Lindéralique rock formations are just a 15-minute walk away (have your bathing suit on under your shorts if you wish to wade across to the caves—they're only 700 meters down the road on the other side of a small lagoon). The Hienghène Club Med has a lot more style than the one in Nouméa, and caters to a more up-scale crowd. When you consider what you get, it's actually good value compared to many other hotels around the island. Expensive.

Northwest from Hienghène

The coastline northwest from Hienghène features towering mountains with slopes falling right to the sea, empty beaches with fine coral just offshore, numerous high waterfalls clearly visible from the road, and deep green-blue rivers full of small fish such as you've never seen before. This is also the most traditional area on Grande Terre, with the greatest number of *cases*.

On the main road just north of Hienghène, stop for the excellent view from the **Col de Tanghene.** The church of the **Mission de Ouaré,** 3.5 km north of Hienghène, has colorful stained glass windows. The pavement ends at Tiluny, six km north of Hienghène.

The Ouenpouès tribe, between Ouaré and Ouaïème, about eight km northwest of Hienghène, runs the **Gîte Wéouth** (B.P. 62, 98815 Hienghène; tel. 42-81-19) in a small village near a beach. The eight rooms in four bungalows are CFP 1,600 pp. Camping is CFP 800 per tent. Budget.

You can also camp at **Chez Theo and Maria** at Ouenguip, a couple of km northwest of Ouenpouès (CFP 800 per tent). They'll ferry you out to one of the small coral islands offshore for CFP 1,500 pp (minimum of two), and one can scale the Ton-Non (988 meters) overlooking Ouaïème from here (CFP 2,500 pp, minimum of four).

There's a free ferry operating 24 hours a day at Ouaïème, 17 km northwest of Hienghène. A local legend explains that a bridge can never be built here because of a giant who lives up the river. The giant is part shark, and such a structure would block its route to the sea. What's known for sure is that the river is shark-infested, and it's unlikely you'll see any locals swimming here.

The **Camping de Panié,** 3.5 km north of the Ouaïème ferry, has a grassy camping area in a coconut grove right on an attractive gray beach relatively free of mosquitoes. A long thatched shelter provides refuge in case of rain. It's CFP 300 per tent, plus CFP 200 pp—a nice place to stop for the night. A grocery truck passes daily (ask the times). The turnoff to **Panié Falls** is 2.5 km northwest of the campground (CFP 600 per car to bathe in the pool).

Tao Falls is 10 km northwest of the Ouaïème ferry. The falls are clearly visible from the bridge, but to go to the base of the falls on foot is CFP 200 pp.

It's possible to climb to the top of **Mt. Panié** (1,639 meters), New Caledonia's highest peak, from near Tao Falls, and there are several shelters on the mountain for hikers. To climb Mt. Panié in one day would involve leaving at 0400 and only returning at dusk, so it might be better to spend a night on the mountain. A guide will cost CFP 6,000 per group.

Gîte de Galarino (Léon Foord, tel. 35-64-38), 20 km northwest of the Ouaïème ferry, has three thatched bungalows with private bath and cooking facilities at CFP 3,000/3,500 single/double, and a beachside camping area at CFP 1,000 per tent. It's an idyllic, end-of-the-world type of place. Go for a swim at Colnett Falls, only two km northwest. Budget.

The pavement recommences 28 km northwest of the Ouaïème ferry, and the first grocery store on this road is at **Yambé,** 50 km northwest of Hienghène. Also at Yambé is the home of Pierre "Ehna" Teimouec (tel. 88-14-45), who offers horseback riding at CFP 2,000/3,000 for one/two hours. A weekend trip with camping in the bush is CFP 8,000 pp. Ask for Ehna 400 meters southeast of the store. From Yambé it's only 11 km to Pouébo.

Pouébo

The first Catholic missionaries arrived at Pouébo in 1847, but were soon driven off by the Kanak inhabitants. The unrelenting fathers returned in 1852 for a more successful second try at establishing a mission. A gold rush here in the 1860s led to much French land grabbing and a Kanak revolt. **Pouébo Mission Church** dates from 1874, and it's worth visiting for its stained glass. At the entrance is a relic of Hippolyte Bonou, the first local chief to covert to Catholicism, who died on the Isle of Pines in 1867. The tomb of the colony's first Catholic priest, Guillaume Douarre, who died at Ballade in 1853, is inside the church.

A free municipal campground is on **St. Mathieu Beach,** 1.5 km north of Pouébo Church on the main road, then another 1.5 km northeast to the beach. Toilets, showers, and picnic tables are provided, and you get nice views of the mountains, but it's not the greatest beach for swimming (and the mosquitoes are a pain in the proverbial).

Buses leave Pouébo for Koumac Monday and Thursday at 1600, and Wednesday and Friday at 0825; for Nouméa (CFP 1,750) via Koumac Mon.-Thurs. at 0600 and Sunday at 1015; for Hienghène Tuesday at 1130 and Thursday at 0900; and for Poindimié via Hienghène Monday at 0340 and Friday at 0800. This haphazard schedule calls for careful planning unless you have a car or are prepared to hitch.

Balade to Ouégoa

Balade, 16 km northwest of Pouébo, also has a notable place in New Caledonian history, as this is where Captain Cook landed in 1774. Later, Rear Admiral Fébvrier-Despointes annexed New Caledonia for France at a ceremony near Balade on 24 September 1853, as an iron obelisk (erected in 1913) on a hill above the highway proclaims.

Just before the monument is the short access road to lovely **Mahamate Beach,** where Cook's men observed an eclipse of the sun on 6 September 1774. The first Catholic mass was celebrated here on Christmas Day, 1843. A traditional double-hulled canoe that sailed here from the Isle of Pines in 1993 for the 150th anniversary can be seen behind a plaque here. Lots of nice little secluded spots to camp freelance can be found along this beach, and there's even a water tap just before the canoe.

For CFP 1,000 per tent you can camp at **Camping Col d'Amos** (Léon Dubois) at Amos, on the way to Ouégoa, down a road to the right just before the beginning of the climb up the Col d'Amos Pass, eight km northwest of the obelisk.

The Diahot River, draining the far north of Grande Terre into Harcourt Bay, is navigable for 32 km. **Ouégoa** is a *Caldoche* farming community that attends church in a Quonset hut behind the *mairie*. **Le Normandon** (tel. 35-68-28), near the Diahot River Bridge, two km from the center of Ouégoa, has four basic rooms in a block called Le Caillou next to the restaurant. The two rooms with a/c and private bath are CFP 3,500/4,500 single/double, the one with private bath but no a/c is CFP 3,000/4,000, and two rooms with shared bath are also CFP 3,000/4,000. Camping is free if you take the CFP 2,000 dinner at the restaurant. It's not very good value, and often full with contract workers. Inexpensive. After the bridge, traffic along the road to Koumac increases.

THE NORTHWEST COAST

Koumac

This town, 370 km northwest of Nouméa, has a **Catholic church** (1950) on the roundabout that was originally an aircraft hangar! Inside is a striking modern stained glass window, and a number of outstanding Melanesian-style woodcarvings. The *cagou* lectern is by Léonce Weiss, while the altar formed from an outrigger canoe, tabernacle shaped like a Kanak *case,* and holy water bearer in the form of a man are by Léonce's father, Charles Weiss. The Christ figure is by his grandfather, Victor Weiss. **Léonce Weiss** (B.P. 547, 98850 Koumac; tel./fax 35-65-32; www. noumea.com/neacom/weiss.htm) currently has a studio three km out on the road to Nouméa (turn in at a white block marked "Sous-Station Koumac"). At CFP 4,000, his miniature *flèches faîtières* make excellent souvenirs. More woodcarvings and other souvenirs are available at **Curios de Koumac** (tel. 47-54-71), in the commercial center behind Snack la Panthère Rose.

The road inland beside the Catholic church leads eight km to some rather intriguing **limestone caves** (admission free, bring a flashlight). The first cave is back to the right and up some rocks, and the longest stretches three km underground. You could camp free at the entrance to the caves and there are picnic tables, but no water in the vicinity. The **Club Hippique La Crinière** (B.P. 319, 98850 Koumac; tel. 35-66-51; closed Monday), 4.5 km east of Koumac off the road to the caves, offers horseback riding.

Koumac's small boat harbor is three km southwest of the traffic circle (turn left on the first road after the *gendarmerie* and keep straight). Several charter yachts operate out of here, and it's a nice picnic spot with tables overlooking the beach. A large army base is at the southeastern entrance to the city.

Accommodations and Food

Camping de Pandop (Monsieur Robert Frouin, tel. 35-62-46) is windy but nicely situated by the sea, only two km from Koumac (take the road opposite the church at the traffic circle and keep left after the *gendarmerie*). Camping is CFP 500 pp. Toilets and showers and provided, and shelters with picnic tables. A security fence surrounds the property.

Hôtel Le Grand Cerf (B.P. 141, 98850 Koumac; tel. 35-61-31, fax 35-60-16), on the traffic circle in the center of Koumac, has nine wooden a/c bungalows with private facilities from CFP 5,400/6,000/6,600 single/double/triple. The restaurant is good and there's a swimming pool. Moderate.

Cheaper, but not as nice, is **Hôtel Le Passiflore** (tel. 35-62-10), 800 meters up the road to the caves. The six rooms with shared bath are CFP 3,500 single or double; the five with private bath cost CFP 4,500. Inexpensive. **Snack la Panthère Rose** (tel. 35-63-47) near Le Passiflore is a good place for lunch or a beer. **Libre-Service Chez Nino** (tel. 35-67-82) next door has barbecued chickens (CFP 890) on the weekend (you have to arrive around 1000 or 1600 to get one), and takeaway pizza is available upstairs at **Pizza Pedro** (tel. 47-55-55; closed Wednesday).

Koumac's most upmarket place is **Monitel de Koumac** (B.P. 75, 98850 Koumac; tel. 35-66-66, fax 35-62-85), a kilometer down the road to Nouméa, with 16 a/c rooms in a long block, and six duplex bungalows (another 12 rooms), all costing CFP 6,500/7,000/7,500 single/double/triple. The Monitel has a pleasant swimming pool, and an attractive restaurant/bar with a good value weekday *plat du jour* lunch at CFP 1,650. They have rental cars. Moderate.

Transportation

Koumac's airport is four km northwest of the traffic circle. Air Calédonie has flights from Koumac to the Belep Islands twice a week (CFP 6,270 one-way), and to Nouméa three times a week (CFP 8,640). The Air Calédonie agent (tel. 47-53-90) is at Hôtel Le Grand Cerf in the center of town.

Buses to Nouméa leave Koumac daily at 0430 and 1145, Monday and Thursday at 0745, Friday at 1600, and Sunday at 1530 (5.5 hours, CFP 1,550). Buses to Poum leave Koumac Monday 0345, Wednesday at 1315, and Friday at 1615. To Pouébo you can leave Monday and Thursday at 1315, and Wednesday and Friday at 0530. Koumac's bus station *(gare routière)* is just 500 meters southeast of the traffic circle in town.

Drivers must be aware that the gas stations in Ouégoa and Pouébo don't sell unleaded gas, and no gas at all is available at Hienghène. Thus it's important to tank up at Koumac if you're headed east.

North of Koumac

The paved coastal highway runs 56 km northwest of Koumac to the small town of Poum on Banaré Bay, with good views along the way. About 18.5 km north of Koumac is the entrance road to the old **Dôme de Tiébaghi** mining area. Entry is forbidden, but the abandoned mining town high up on the side of the 587-meter-high plateau is visible from the main road.

Facing the white sands of Néhoué Bay, 45 km northwest of Koumac and 15 km southeast of Poum, is the **Malabou Beach Resort** (B.P. 4, 98826 Poum; tel. 35-60-60, fax 35-60-70), part of the Accor/Novotel hotel chain. Opened in 1991, the hotel has 37 spacious a/c bungalows at CFP 10,600 for up to five persons, plus three suites at CFP 18,000 for up to six. Meals are CFP 1,300/2,800/2,800 for breakfast/lunch/dinner (no cooking facilities). Tennis courts, freshwater swimming pool, and full sporting facilities are offered, but car rentals are not available. The Malabou Beach is in a picturesque but isolated and desolate location, and the water off their beach is rather murky (though teaming with fish). To see coral you must engage the services of **Pacific Plongée** on the resort wharf, which charges CFP 6,000/9,000 for a one/two tank dive including all equipment. An 850-meter airstrip has been built adjacent to the property. This resort doesn't quite match the standards of the Club Med Koulnoué Village at Hienghène, and there's much less to see and do in the vicinity. Expensive.

Just past the Malabou Beach Resort is the turnoff to **Camping Amenagé Golone** (B.P. 14, 98826 Poum), on Tanle Bay, a recognized hurricane shelter for shipping. It's accessible on a rough, steep five-km dirt track that winds around the resort airstrip. The campground is on a better beach than the Malabou, and is very peaceful once you're there. It's CFP 600 pp with toilets and showers provided. There's a lovely view from the hill just before the final descent to the campground.

There's isn't much to see in **Poum village**, but you can climb barren Mt. Poum (413 meters) in about an hour. You can camp freelance on the beach off the road to Poum wharf, opposite a small white church, but it's not a very attractive spot. Don't go off and leave your gear unattended here. There's no water tap but the swimming is good. **Chez Madame Frouin Restaurant** (tel. 35-64-70), near the wharf at Poum, has two self-catering rooms in a block right by the shore, one double with a kitchen and bath, and one four-bed room with bath but no kitchen, both CFP 3,000. Outstanding seafood meals can be ordered here (CFP 2,500-3,000 depending on the plate). Budget. The bus back to Koumac leaves Poum Monday at 0535, Wednesday at 1500, and Friday at 1800.

Some 31 km north of Poum (26 km of it on a gravel road), near Boat-Pass, the northernmost tip of Grande Terre, is the **Gîte de Poingam** (Henry Fairbank, tel. 88-24-20), with seven thatched bungalows accommodating up to four persons at CFP 5,000/5,600/6,200 single/double/triple. Camping is CFP 600 pp. The seafood served in the restaurant is excellent. You'll need your own transport to get here. Inexpensive.

Voh

You can hike across the mountains from Voh to the Hienghène valley along the "Chemin des Arabes" in a couple of days. The trail begins at Pouépaï, with access from Voh on a rough road. **Ranch Chez de Gaulle** (tel. 35-57-76), 1.5 km east down the road from the war memorial in Voh, can provide horses and guides for trips along the Chemin des Arabes across the island to the Hienghène Valley (two days each way). Otherwise, horseback riding is CFP 1,000 an hour or CFP 6,000 a day. It's also possible to stay on the ranch at CFP 1,000 pp, plus CFP 1,200 pp for breakfast and dinner.

Camp free at **Plage de Gatope,** five km west of the war memorial in Voh (keep left where the roads divide). Toilets, showers, and picnic shelters are provided, and the palm-fringed beach is pretty. On weekends it can get crowded with local picnickers.

Koné

The 100-km road southeast from Koumac to Koné offers only occasional gum trees to break the monotony—this is cattle country. Koné is the capital of the North Province and a growing administrative center; several banks are here. Koné market is Saturday mornings (just down the road to Baco). Although Koné has some appeal, the main reasons for stopping are the horseback expeditions organized by two local companies. Both offer weeklong excursions across the mountains from Koné to Hienghène and back, or shorter three-day rides into the Pamalé Valley.

Koné Rodeo (Patrick Ardimanni, tel. 35-51-51), near Hôtel Koniambo, 400 meters down the road beginning at the east end of the airstrip, does a seven-day Hienghène ride and three-day mountain rides (CFP 22,000 pp). The price is all-inclusive (typical French Caledonian food, lodging, evening campfires, horses, etc.). A minimum of eight persons is required to do a trip, but they do as many as 30 a year, and individuals can join them, so call ahead. Patrick has 40 horses and speaks good English.

The **Centre Equestre ACNO** (B.P. 285, 98860 Koné; tel. 35-55-71), near Koné Rodeo, only does half-day rides for around CFP 3,600 pp.

The other horseback company is **Randonnées Equestres** (Eric Tikarso, tel. 35-53-68), based in the Kanak village of Atéou. Eric lives in Kone, 500 meters from the market out on the road to Baco (ask). Randonnées requires five participants, and you'll need to know a little French. Overnight riding trips must be booked in advance either by phoning, or through a travel agent in Nouméa. A five-day trip to Tipindjé in the Hienghène Valley is CFP 35,000 pp. A day ride

around Atéou is CFP 8,000 pp including lunch. A three-day ride to Atéou and Paoué is CFP 22,000 pp. If you're looking to join a group, weekends are best. This is a great opportunity if you can spare the cash.

Southbound buses to Nouméa leave Koné daily at 1310, Mon.-Sat. at 0805, and Sunday at 1215 (CFP 1,200). Northbound, you can catch a bus to Koumac Mon.-Sat. at 1540, and Friday and Sunday at 1410.

Accommodations at Koné

Budget travelers usually stay at **L'Escale de Koné** (B.P. 354, 98860 Koné; tel. 35-51-09), near the post office and right at the bus stop in Koné. The eight rooms with bath and TV in a two-story block behind the restaurant are CFP 4,000 single or double. To get a room, you must arrive when the restaurant is open (weekdays 0600-1400/ 1700-2200, Saturday 0900-1400/1700-2200), and on Sunday you'll have difficulty getting in. Good, inexpensive Chinese dishes are served in the restaurant. Inexpensive.

A block south of L'Escale de Koné is **Hôtel Restaurant Le Joker** (B.P. 12, 98860 Koné; tel. 47-37-07, fax 47-35-09), just up from the war memorial in the center of town. The four a/c rooms with bath in a neat block behind the restaurant are CFP 4,750/5,750 single/double, and once again, you can only check in when the restaurant is open (0900-1400/1900-2200). They serve a good *plat du jour* lunch at CFP 850. Inexpensive.

The 20-room **Monitel l'Hibiscus** (B.P. 45, 98860 Koné; tel. 35-52-61, fax 35-55-35), 100 meters down the road to Nouméa from the war memorial in the center of town, is CFP 5,000/ 5,500 single/double and up for an a/c room in a two-story building. A restaurant and bar face the swimming pool just beyond the reception. It's the flashiest place in town. The Hertz agent is here. Inexpensive to moderate.

The **Hôtel Koniambo** (Yannick Girard, B.P. 35, 98860 Koné; tel. 35-51-86, fax 35-53-03), directly opposite the airstrip three km west of Koné, has 13 self-catering rooms with bath and 12 a/c bungalows without cooking facilities, all CFP 5,500/6,000 single/double (plus CFP 500 if you use the a/c). Ask about their special weekend rate. The Koniambo allows camping in the garden free of charge for those taking dinner

(CFP 1,650 set menu) at their restaurant. They have a swimming pool, and car rentals are arranged. Inexpensive.

There's free camping in the park at **Foué Beach,** seven km southwest of the bridge at the south end of Kone. The toilets and showers are good, and tables and chairs are along the beach, but there can be some radio noise at night from the adjacent fishing village. Turn left to the beach just before you reach the ocean.

South of Koné
The new headquarters of North Province, the **Hôtel de Province Nord,** is four km south of Koné on the road to Nouméa. A traditional *case* stands in front of the provincial assembly building. As part of the development of this area, a new road has been built across the island from this complex to Poindimié.

Four km farther south is Pouembout and the **Hôtel Le Bougainville** (B.P. 78, 98825 Pouembout; tel. 35-50-60, fax 35-59-84) with six thatched bungalows at CFP 5,800 single or double, CFP 6,800 triple, and five a/c rooms in a long wooden block facing the valley at CFP 5,500. The hotel's restaurant and reception area share a mock Kanak *grande case.* A barbecue is held by the pool the first Sunday of each month (CFP 1,500 pp)), while their set dinner menu is CFP 1,650. Inexpensive.

Just before the Rouge River, 18 km south of Pouembout, is the short access road to a **war memorial** with a splendid view of the Plaine des Gaïacs, where there was a large airfield during WW II.

Free camping with a water tap and picnic shelter provided is at **Plage de Pindaï,** 11 km off the main road 35 km south of Pouembout. It's a lovely isolated spot backed by mangroves with a white beach and clear water for swimming. The turnoff is four km west of the Népoui access road.

Between Pouembout and Poya is the old nickel port of Népoui, now being redeveloped as an alternative port to Nouméa for North Province. Large open-cut nickel mines are here. **Restaurant Le Passage** (Mr. and Mrs. Sinem, tel. 47-12-28) at Népoui, six km off the main highway, rents rooms at CFP 3,500 single or double, CFP 4,000 triple. Meals are CFP 500/1,500 for breakfast/dinner. Inexpensive. Scuba diving is available here with Marceau Martel (B.P. 267, 98827 Poya; tel. 47-13-02, fax 47-13-06) at CFP 6,000 for two boat dives (plus CFP 1,500 for equipment).

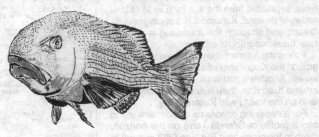

red snapper

ISLE OF PINES

Across a strait of shoals and coral banks, 70 km southeast of Grande Terre, is the stunningly beautiful Île des Pines, famous for the cocaine-white beaches of Kanuméra/Kuto. In 1774 Captain Cook named the 18-by-14-km island for its extraordinary 60-meter-high *columnaris,* but the Kanak name is Kwenyii (Kunié). Centuries before, the chiefs of this enticing isle had arrived from Aneityum in present Vanuatu, and the Kwenyii people were always great traders, sailing far and wide in their big outrigger canoes.

British Protestant missionaries landed in 1841, but were killed a year later when they became involved in a dispute between sandalwood traders and the Kwenyii islanders. Subsequently, the island served as a French penal colony. Today this southernmost island of Melanesia remains largely untouched—a tropical paradise of the first order. During the **Festival of the Yams,** which coincides with the yam harvest in March or April, you'll see *pilou* dancing and formal presentations of yams.

SIGHTS

Kanuméra/Kuto

Kanuméra/Kuto is one of the gems of the Pacific: Kuto with its long rolling surf, Kanuméra with its gentle turquoise waters. The talcum-soft beaches curve around a narrow neck of sand, which joins the **Kuto Peninsula** to the rest of the island. Towering pines contrast with curving palms, casuarinas, gum trees, ferns, wild orchids, and other flowers to create an environment of exotic richness, separated from the sea by a wide strip of snowy white sand. Kanuméra is a photographer's dream, and although the snorkeling is second-rate, the windsurfing is excellent.

Follow the footpath from the main wharf right around the Kuto Peninsula for a series of scenic views. Another good walk is to the northwest around Kuto Bay, then across the rocky headland on the trail to wild **Kutema Bay.**

For a sweeping panorama of the entire island and a profile of Grande Terre on the horizon, climb to the cross atop **Pic Nga** (262 meters) in

an hour (easy). The trailhead is midway on the Kanuméra/Kuto cutoff, but it's poorly marked; look carefully to the southeast of the house with several pine trees in the front yard. You'll know you're going the right way when you start seeing red paint splashed on the trees.

Farther Afield

During 1871-79, around 3,900 political prisoners from the Paris Commune were held on the Isle of Pines. After an amnesty in 1880 the *communards* were allowed to return to France but the island continued as a regular prison colony until 1912. Pigs now forage in the old prison yard and the narrow, cheerless brick cells—snuffling scavengers in the gloomy and forbidding atmosphere. Some of the ruins are visible behind the bakery at Ouro. One building can be reached via the track inland on the other side of the highway.

ISLE OF PINES

To get to the **Deportees' Cemetery,** continue one km north on the airport road and take the first turn on the right. The cemetery where some 260 deportees are buried is to the left, about 500 meters inland. To the right is a track right across the island.

The administrative center and largest village on the island is **Vao,** seven km east of Kanuméra. French Catholic missionaries arrived at Vao in 1848, and the present church dates from 1860. Climb up to the chapel above the church for the view. The chief's house *(chefferie)* at Vao is surrounded by a driftwood palisade.

Two km due east of the church is **St. Joseph Beach,** with as fine a collection of large dugout sailing canoes *(pirogues)* as you'll find anywhere in the Pacific. Oupi Bay is dotted with their sails and tiny mushroom-shaped islands. Daily at 0930 and 1330, the glass-bottom boat *Douétiko-rail* (tel. 46-10-10) does 90-minute scenic cruises around Oupi Bay from St. Joseph.

Scuba Diving

Scuba diving is offered by the **Kunié Scuba Center** (B.P. 18, 98832 Vao, Île des Pines; tel. 46-11-22, fax 46-12-27), based at the Relais de Kodjeue. A 12-dive package is CFP 42,000, but there's a surcharge if fewer than four divers are present. The top reef diving is at **Gadji Pass** off the north end of the island, especially the **Gie Island Drop-off** and fantastic **Oupere Grotto.** The strong tidal flow means abundant marinelife and spectacular coral and sponge coloration, which can be appreciated through rents in the reef. The Scuba Center also offers freshwater diving into **Paradise Cave,** with its huge stalactites and stalagmites—truly a unique experience.

PRACTICALITIES

Inexpensive Accommodations

Gîte Ouré (Christine Kouathe, B.P. 28, 98832 Vao, Île des Pines; tel. 46-11-20), at the east end of beautiful Kanuméra Bay, is a perfect place to camp (CFP 1,000 double). For those without a tent, there are eight small beach bungalows in a gardenlike setting. The charge is CFP 1,500/2,000 single/double in bungalows with shared facilities, and CFP 3,000/3,700 single/double in bungalows with private facilities capable of accommodating up to three or four (beware of mice in all units).

Gîte Nataïwatch (Guillaume et Eulalie Kouathe, B.P. 26, 98832 Vao, Île des Pines; tel. 46-11-13, fax 46-12-29) is in the same area as Gîte Ouré, but farther inland away from the beach. The four older thatched bungalows with a fridge, cooking facilities, and shared bath, and the eight newer units with private bath but no kitchens, are all CFP 4,900/5,500/6,100 single/double/triple. Camping is in a separate area near the beach with a shelter and amenities block (CFP 1,000/1,300 single/double). The restaurant (closed Sunday) at the Nataïwatch is pleasant (CFP 1,000/1,800 for breakfast/dinner). Rental cars are available (CFP 9,000).

Just inland from Kuto Bay and behind the restaurant of the same name is **Relais Kuberka** (Caroline Vendegou, B.P. 4, 98832 Vao, Île des Pines; tel. 46-11-18, fax 46-11-58), with two bungalows and eight rooms at CFP 4,800/5,400/6,000 single/double/triple, all with private bath, TV, and fridge (no cooking facilities). Camping is CFP 800/1,000 single/double. Rental cars are available here at CFP 5,000, plus CFP 30 a kilometer.

Gîte Manamaky (Nazaire Vakoume, B.P. 24, 98832 Vao, Île des Pines; tel. 46-11-11) is on lovely St. Joseph Beach, two km east of Vao. The one thatched bungalow is CFP 4,200/5,200 double/triple, while the four bungalows with TV and fridge are CFP 5,500/6,500 (no cooking facilities). If you'd like to tour the island by *pirogue,* ask here (CFP 2,000 pp, minimum of three).

Scuba divers often stay at the **Relais de Kodjeue** (Jojo et Agnès Lepers, B.P. 75, 98832 Vao, Île des Pines; tel. 46-11-42, fax 46-10-61) on an excellent beach at Ouaméo Bay. The 15 bungalows with private bath (six of them also with cooking facilities) are CFP 6,700 single or double. Six newer beach bungalows without kitchens are CFP 13,000. A six-unit block without cooking facilities costs CFP 4,800 per room. The Relais de Kodjeue has a swimming pool, tennis court, and sailboats for rent. You can rent a car (CFP 8,000 a day) or motor scooter, but check them carefully before you ride off. The food in the restaurant is excellent, and you can even buy groceries here if you want to cook.

Luxury

The **Hôtel Kou-Bugny** (Gustave Petersen, B.P. 1, 98832 Vao, Île des Pines; tel. 46-12-23, fax 46-13-23) is across the road from Kuto Bay. The 12 a/c bungalows are overpriced at CFP 15,000 for a triple unit, CFP 18,000 for a five-person family unit. The hotel restaurant caters mostly to Japanese day-trippers who have lunch here (CFP 2,000). Car rentals begin at CFP 8,000 a day.

In late 1998 a **Le Méridien Resort** (B.P. 175, 98832 Vao, Île des Pines; tel. 46-15-15, fax 46-15-16) opened at Oro Bay on the northeast side of the island. Environmentalists and a group of local residents had fought a long legal battle to try to prevent hotel development in this exceptional but fragile location. There are 10 a/c rooms at CFP 33,000 single or double, five freestanding bungalows at CFP 41,000, and 12 duplex bungalows at CFP 46,000, buffet breakfast included. Third persons pay CFP 7,000. A swimming pool is provided. Nearby are a natural rock pool and stunning white beaches.

Food

All of the *gîtes* serve meals, but eating at them twice a day quickly becomes expensive. Luckily there are four small grocery stores at Vao, open Mon.-Sat. 0700-1200 and 1500-1900, Sunday 1000-1200. The bakery at Ouro opens Mon.-Sat. 0630-1000 and 1630-1800 only. Early Saturday morning a small market materializes at Vao; another at Kuto is open Wednesday and Saturday mornings 0645-0800. If you're a drinker, bring your own supply from Nouméa.

Restaurant Kuberka (tel. 46-11-18), just inland from Kuto, specializes in upscale seafoods,

like small sweet lobster, marinated squid, and fried fish, served at trestle tables beneath a thatched roof. You must order ahead. Nearby is a French military vacation camp (tel. 46-11-07) with a well-stocked bar, but you're not welcome.

Services

The post office and clinic are in Vao, while the *gendarmerie* is at Kuto. There's no bank on the island, so change enough money before leaving Nouméa.

Transportation

Air Calédonie flies to the Isle of Pines from Nouméa between two and six times a day (CFP 6,060). Japanese day-trippers often pack the planes, so book well ahead. The isle's wartime airport sits on an 81-meter-high plateau at the center of the island, nine km from Kanuméra. All of the *gîtes* provide airport transfers for those who have reserved a room, with the price varying from CFP 1,200 to CFP 1,600 pp roundtrip. Air Calédonie has an office (tel. 46-11-08) at Kuto open weekdays 0730-0800, 0930-1115, and 1400-1600. At other times, read the blackboard outside.

The interisland ferry *Marie-Hélène* ties up to the wharf on Kuto Bay, charging CFP 3,200 each way for the 2.5-hour trip. The schedule is different every week, with Saturday and Sunday the most likely days for a trip. The ferry leaves Nouméa at 0700 and Kuto at 1700, allowing 7.5 hours on the island if you want to make a day-trip of it. Book ahead.

The *gîtes* can arrange car rentals. Traffic is thin around the island, but most people will give you a lift, and if you don't mind doing some walking, you should be able to complete the 40-km loop around the island in one day.

THE LOYALTY ISLANDS

Loyalty Islands Province accounts for just over 10% of New Caledonia's land area and population. This coralline group, 100 km east of Grande Terre, consists of the low-lying islands of Ouvéa, Lifou, Tiga, and Maré, each about 50 km apart, plus several islets. Though Captain Cook never saw them, the Loyalties are visible from the tops of New Caledonia's mountains. The people are mostly Kanak, although Ouvéa was colonized by Polynesians from Wallis Island hundreds of years ago. In 1899, the French government declared the Loyalties an indigenous reserve, thus they were spared the worst features of colonialism, and almost 99% of the population is Kanak.

The Protestant missionaries who arrived on Maré in 1841 and Lifou in 1842 had already converted most of the inhabitants by the time the French colony was declared in 1853. French Catholics arrived at Maré in 1866, and a period of religious strife ensued. After a battle on Maré in 1871, some 900 Catholicized islanders were exiled with their French missionaries to the Isle of Pines. Be aware that almost nobody in the Loyalties speaks English.

OUVÉA

Ouvéa (Iaai) is everything you'd expect in a South Pacific island. Twenty-five km of unbroken white sands border the lagoon on the west side of the island and extend far out from shore, giving the water a turquoise hue. The wide western lagoon, protected by a necklace of coral islands and a barrier reef, is unique in the Loyalties. Croissant-shaped Ouvéa is tilted, with rocky cliffs pounded by surf on the eastern ocean side of the island, but fine beaches may be found even here. At one point on this narrow atoll, only 45 meters separates the two coasts.

Traditional circular houses with pointed thatched roofs are still common in the villages, and the compound of each village chief on Ouvéa is surrounded by a high palisade of driftwood logs. Two of the finest of these are at St. Joseph. Due to a Polynesian invasion in the 18th century, the inhabitants of the far ends of the island (St. Joseph, Lékine, Mouli) speak the Wallisian language (Ua), while those in the center speak Iaai, the original Kanak tongue. All 4,000 Ouvéa islanders speak French as well. Until the political troubles of the 1980s, Ouvéa produced 80% of the territory's copra.

On 4 May 1988, this enchanted island was the scene of the Ouvéa Massacre when 300 French police stormed a cave near Gossana to rescue 16 *gendarmes* held hostage after being captured on 22 April by Kanak freedom fighters. Nineteen Kanaks died in the assault, including several who suffered extrajudicial execution at the hands of the French police after being wounded and taken prisoner. None of the hostages had been harmed. Thus Ouvéa is a symbol of martyrdom and the heroic resistance of the Kanak people to the savagery of French colonialism.

Northern Ouvéa
A paved highway extends south from St. Joseph to Fayaoué (23 km), the administrative center, then on to Mouli (another 19 km). St. Joseph is a friendly village strung along the lagoon, with several general stores and a large Catholic mission (1912). Near the mission is the low stockade of the local chief's *case*. This chief also runs the adjoining store, and he may give you permission to camp on the beach. The beach curves northwest away from St. Joseph.

At Wadrilla, visit the graves of the 19 Kanaks murdered by French troops in 1988. During a commemorative ceremony here for these men exactly one year after the event, FLNKS leaders Jean-Marie Tjibaou and Yeiwéné Yeiwéné were assassinated by a Kanak activist named Djoubelli Wea who felt they had sold out the independence cause by making a deal with the French government. Ironically, the death of the two leaders froze that agreement into a sort of holy writ, which no one has dared to tamper with since.

Southern Ouvéa
Beyond the east end of the airstrip, near the center of the island, is a road leading straight to a high limestone cliff thick with stalactites and

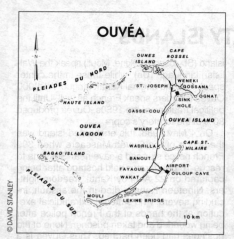

OUVÉA

© DAVID STANLEY

0   10 km

stalagmites. The entrance to **Ouloup Cave** is just opposite, a small opening at the back of the pit. Bones from old burials may be seen. The guide to the caves lives in the house at the end of the airstrip, and if he's around, ask his permission before proceeding. Midway between the house and the cliff is a banyan tree on the right; a deep hole under the tree contains water. It's thought that the roots of this banyan and those of another at Canala on Grande Terre connect through this "way of the spirits." Notice a waterfilled cave farther along on the right.

At Fayaoué, strung along the lagoon near the middle of the atoll, are the post office, clinic, and two small stores. Farther south, many tropical fish are visible from the bridge connecting Mouli to the rest of Ouvéa, and the swimming here is good (but beware of currents). The famous cliffs of Lékine are also clearly visible from this bridge. Approach them by following the beach around. Long ago, before the island was uplifted, wave action undercut these towering walls of limestone. Massive stalactites tell of the great caverns for which this area is noted. On this island of superb beaches, the nicest is at Mouli.

Accommodations and Food
Gîte Beaupré (Suzanne Oine, B.P. 52, 98814 Fayaoué, Ouvéa; tel. 45-71-32, fax 45-70-94) is opposite the beach at Banout, just north of the junction of the airport and lagoonside roads.

The three rooms with shared bath are CFP 3,500/4,000 single/double, while the three thatched bungalows with private bath are CFP 5,500 single or double. Good food is served here (dinner CFP 1,800), and they rent bicycles (CFP 1,500 a day). Inexpensive.

Several inhabitants of Ouassadieu between Banout and Wadrilla rent rooms with shared bath at CFP 3,000/3,500 single/double, and allow camping at CFP 500 pp. Both Benoît Kalepe (tel. 45-72-20) and Jöel Henere (tel. 45-70-56) offer this, and serve meals at CFP 350/850 for breakfast/dinner. Bicycles are CFP 1,000 a day.

The **Camping de Lékine** (Pierre Tooulou, tel. 45-70-07), opposite the Lékine cliffs, is CFP 1,000 per tent, plus CFP 200 to use the communal kitchen. To rent a tent is CFP 500 extra.

Restaurant Le Cocotier (Samuel Gogny, tel. 45-70-40) at Mouli has a traditional *case* where up to 10 people can stay at CFP 3,000 pp including breakfast and dinner. Camping is CFP 1,000, a bicycle CFP 500 for half a day.

Inexpensive meals are served at the **Snack du Centre Medical de Ouloup** (tel. 45-71-95) near the airport. Ouvéa has a water shortage, so use it sparingly.

Transportation
Air Calédonie (tel. 45-71-42) lands at Ouloup Airstrip, six km from Fayaoué. There are several flights a day from Nouméa (CFP 9,000), and three a week from Lifou (CFP 3,955). A bus meets most of the flights from Nouméa (except on Sunday) for the ride to Fayaoué post office (CFP 400), or all the way to St. Joseph, where the driver lives.

The interisland catamaran *Marie-Hélène* ties to a wharf on the lagoon side between Fayaoué and St. Joseph. The schedule is rather irregular, although the ferry often arrives from Nouméa (CFP 4,900) or Lifou (CFP 2,400) on Monday night, departing for Lifou on Tuesday morning. You can check the date by calling 25-45-05.

LIFOU

Lifou (Drehu), the largest and most populous of the Loyalties, is a bigger island than Tahiti or Samoa's Upolu. Like Maré, Lifou is a raised atoll, and the cliffs and terraces of the various periods of geologic emergence are clearly visible from the air.

Some 10,000 people live on Lifou, and Drehu, the local language, is the most widely spoken of the Kanak languages. Wé, the main town, is the administrative center of the Loyalty Islands, but the three grand chiefs of Lifou reside at Nathalo, Dueulu, and Mou. British Protestant missionaries arrived at Mou in 1842 and converted the local chief. When the Catholics landed after the French takeover in 1853, a rival chief in northern Lifou welcomed them, and a period of religious strife began that was finally settled when a French military expedition conquered Lifou in 1864.

Traditional round houses resembling beehives with conical roofs are still common on Lifou. During the cool season, the locals light a fire in the stone hearth of their *case* and sleep there on woven mats. The rest of the year people move back into their houses and the *cases* are vacant. You may be invited to occupy one.

Around Lifou

Wé is situated on Châteaubriand Bay at the south end of a truly magnificent white beach.

LIFOU

LIFOU ISLAND

0   5   10 km

Wé's Catholic church with its round towers looks like it was transported here from Mexico. Nearby is the grave of Fao, a Polynesian Protestant missionary who arrived in 1842 to found a mission. Just a five-minute walk from Gîte Luécilla near Wé is a cave with a clear freshwater pool where you can swim. To get there, take the Nathalo road and look for a path on the left.

The good modern highway from Wé to Mou and Xodé follows the coast beside a cliff thick with stalagmites and passes a superb protected beach with talcum sand at **Luengöni.** A large cave with an underground pool is found between Mou and Xodé, along with another fine beach on the coast here.

The *case* of the grand chief of **Nathalo,** near the airport, is the largest of its kind in New Caledonia. A low palisade surrounds this imposing structure held aloft by great tree trunks set in a circle. Ask permission to go inside. Even more massive is Nathalo Church (1883), a monument to the zeal of early French Catholicism. The interior retains the original decoration.

About 15 km northwest of Nathalo is **Doking** village, the houses of which are perched above the coastal cliffs. There's a chance to see whales in September and October, and the snorkeling here is good.

There's another cave and underground pool near the highway on the east side of Chépénéhe—in fact, you'll find these everywhere on Lifou if you ask. One of the most picturesque spots on the island is the **Chapel of Our Lady of Lourdes** (1898), perched atop a peninsula above Sandalwood Bay, five km east of Chépénéhe. To get there, take a bus or hitch five km west to Eacho, then follow a poorly marked track after the last house (ask). The view from the chapel is breathtaking, and there's a fair beach nearby (on any other island it would be considered excellent).

Sports and Recreation

Lifou Fun Dive (B.P. 515, 98820 Wé; tel./fax 45-02-75), next to the Hôtel Drehu Village at Wé, charges CFP 6,000/10,000 for one/two-tank dives.

Deep-sea fishing is organized by **Loyalty Fishing Charter** (Rénato Antoniazza, B.P. 55, 98820 Wé; tel./fax 45-19-98) at CFP 50,000/65,000 a half/full day for up to four anglers.

Accommodations

Gîte Le Servigny (Jean-Marie Albert, B.P. 401, 98820 Wé; tel./fax 45-12-44) at Kumo is the closest accommodations to the airport. *Case* accommodations are CFP 2,000 pp, a/c rooms CFP 5,000/6,000 single/double. A swimming pool and fancy French restaurant are on the premises. Moderate.

If the ferry drops you at Chépénéhé instead of Wé, you can pitch your tent at **Chez Benoit Bonua** (tel. 45-19-81) at Eacho for CFP 1,000. The three bungalows with shared bath are CFP 1,500 pp—good value for Lifou. A light breakfast will be another CFP 250. Fishing trips are arranged. Budget.

Faré Falaise (Georges Kahlemu, tel. 45-02-01), near a 40-meter cliff at Doking, 12 km northwest of the airport. *Case* accommodations are CFP 1,500 pp, and there's one bungalow at CFP 4,000 for up to three people. Camping is CFP 1,500. Meals cost CFP 500/1,000 for breakfast/dinner, airport transfers CFP 500 pp each way. Inexpensive.

The **Relais des Cocotiers** (Pierre Pilgrim, B.P. 75, 98820 Wé; tel. 45-11-36) is near the stadium at Wé, 15 km south of the airport. It's only a short walk from the administrative center but far from the beach. The six thatched bungalows with private bath are CFP 4,000/4,500/5,000 single/double/triple. The Relais has a popular restaurant/bar that's worth seeking out, even if you're not staying here. Inexpensive.

Lifou's most upscale place is the **Hôtel Drehu Village** (Pierre Zéoula, B.P. 265, 98820 Wé; tel. 45-02-70, fax 45-02-71), also at Wé and right on Châteaubriand Bay. It opened in 1996 with 20 a/c beachfront bungalows with bath and TV at CFP 8,500 single or double, CFP 10,500 triple. No cooking facilities are provided, and breakfast costs CFP 1,200 pp, lunch or dinner CFP 2,500 each. The Drehu Village has a swimming pool, and snorkeling gear and bicycles are loaned free. Airport transfers are CFP 1,500 return. Expensive.

The village you see across Châteaubriand Bay from the wharf at Wé is Luécilla. On the fine white beach near the village is **Motel Chez Rachel** (Rachel Peteisi, B.P. 95, 98820 Wé; tel. 45-12-43, fax 45-00-78), also known as the Gîte de Luécilla. The eight thatched bungalows with private bath and TV are CFP 6,500/7,000/7,500 single/double/triple, while the three rooms are CFP 6,000/6,500/7,000. Cooking facilities are provided in all of these. Otherwise you can camp at CFP 1,000/1,500 single/double. Bicycles are CFP 1,000 a day. Moderate.

The **Motel Le Grand Banian** (Franck Anastasio, B.P. 538, 98820 Wé; tel. 88-20-03), also at Luécilla but away from the beach, has three rooms at CFP 5,000/5,500/6,000 single/double/triple (CFP 30,000 a week). The meals are pricey. Inexpensive.

Marcel Wajoka (tel. 45-15-69), at Traput just southeast of Wé, offers *case* accommodations at CFP 3,000 pp including all meals. Camping is CFP 500 pp, and bicycles CFP 1,000. Airport transfers are CFP 1,000 pp return. Inexpensive.

Gîte Neibash (B.P. 308, 98820 Wé; tel. 45-15-68), at Luengöni in southeastern Lifou, has three bungalows at CFP 6,000/6,500 single/double, and one traditional *case* at CFP 2,500/3,000. Camping is CFP 1,500 per tent. Car rentals are CFP 7,500, plus CFP 52 a kilometer, and bicycles CFP 1,500. Moderate.

Noöl Pia (tel. 45-03-09) at Luengöni accommodates visitors in a *case* at CFP 1,000 pp, campers at CFP 500 pp. Noöl's meals are reasonable at CFP 350/600 for breakfast/dinner. His three-hour forest walk with a visit to a cave is CFP 1,500 pp. Budget.

Jeanne Forrest (tel. 45-16-56) at Luengöni charges CPF 2,000 pp in a *case* bungalow, CFP 1,500 pp in a traditional *case*, or CFP 1,000 pp to camp. Meals are CFP 350/750 for breakfast/dinner. Inexpensive accommodations of this kind also exist in Mou, Wédoumel, and Dueulu.

Other Practicalities

All clustered together at Wé you'll find the post office, two banks, town hall, clinic (tel. 45-12-12), Air Calédonie office (tel. 45-11-11), and *gendarmerie* (tel. 45-12-17). A grocery store is also at Wé.

Saturday morning there's a market in the hall in front of Wanaham Airport, two km from Nathalo village, and near the airport terminal is a small store where you can get hot tea and coffee.

Transportation

Air Calédonie flies to Lifou from Nouméa (CFF 9,000) between three and eight times a day from Maré (CFP 6,055) and Ouvéa (CFP 3,955, three times a week. The *gîtes* will pick up guests with reservations at the airport for CFP 1,900 roundtrip. Buses from Wé, Eacho, and other parts of the island connect with the afternoon flight to/from Nouméa, which makes this the best time to arrive.

The interisland ferry *Marie-Hélène* usually uses the wharf at Wé, but under certain weather conditions it could use another wharf at Chépénéhé, so ask. The service to Nouméa (CFP 4,900) is several times a week, to Ouvéa and Maré (CFP 2,400) once or twice a week. It's different every week, so check.

Lifou is so big that to really see the island you'll have to rent a car, and as with so much else here, it's costly. **Garage Avenod** (tel. 45-11-42, fax 45-15-21), at Luécilla near Wé, rents Peugeot cars at about CFP 7,500 a day, but make sure there's adequate fuel; Lifou often experiences shortages. The hitching on Lifou is much better than on Maré or Ouvéa, as there are many more cars and almost everyone stops.

MARÉ

Maré (Nengone) is an uplifted atoll, its elevated plateau flanked by dramatic cliffs and punctuated with caves. The island's 7,000 inhabitants speak a language known as Nengone, and there are divisions between Protestants and Catholics. Oranges were once common on Maré (harvested in May and June), but the orchards have not been replanted. It's a friendly, welcoming island.

Around Maré

Maré Airport is only two km from a large Catholic mission at La Roche. Massive stone walls enclose the mission compounds, and a tall, white Gothic church towers above the settlement, itself dominated by a high limestone cliff topped by a cross. You'll need sturdy shoes to climb up to the cross on a path departing from the north side of the church; there's a sweeping view of the pine-studded island. In time of war, the Maré people have always sought refuge on this cliff, and it's called "La Roche qui Pleure" (the rock that weeps). Religious fighting took place here in 1869, 1880, and 1890. A road leads north from La Roche Mission 1.5 km to the picturesque cliffs

on the coast (no beach). The **Yeiwéné Yeiwéné Cultural Center** (tel. 45-44-79) at La Roche contains an exhibition of paintings and frescoes.

Just beyond Wakoné, seven km east of La Roche, is a deep abyss in the coastal cliffs, five meters across, that ancient warriors would leap over to prove their bravery, giving the place its name, **Le Saut du Guerrier** (Warrior's Leap). The scenery around here is superb.

The island's administrative center is at **Tadine,** where the ferry from Nouméa calls. A monument at the wharf recalls the 126 persons who perished in the disappearance of the interisland trader *Monique* in 1953. No trace of the ship was ever found. The assassinated Kanak leader Yeiwéné Yeiwéné is buried in this, his hometown. South of Tadine is the so-called "natural aquarium," a blue hole connected to the sea.

At Nétché, eight km north of Tadine, is the residence of Nidoish Naisseline, grand chief of Maré and a leader of Liberation Kanak Socialiste (LKS). In 1995 he was elected president of Loyalty Islands Province. Several monuments near Chief Naisseline's house across from the adjacent church commemorate early Protestant missionaries.

Ceigeïté Beach, eight km south of Tadine, is Maré's finest, its palm-fringed white sands and clear waters inviting the swimmer and snorkeler. At Medu village, southeast of Wabao, is a deep karst cave. The 138-meter-high coastal cliffs south of Medu are the highest point on the Loyalty Islands.

Practicalities
The **Hnala Village** (Ernest Paala, B.P. 40, 98828 Tadine; tel. 45-43-96, fax 45-43-87), next to Tadine post office, has five rooms in a long block at CFP 5,000/6,000 single/double. A restaurant and car rental service (CFP 7,000 a day) are available. Inexpensive.

Maré's three main resorts are on Ceigeïté Beach just west of Wabao, 20 km southwest of the airport. **Gîte Si-Hmed** (Mr. Noël Wadrobert, B.P. 150, 98828 Tadine; tel./fax 45-41-51) has seven thatched bungalows with private bath at CFP 4,000/4,500/5,000 single/double/triple. This is the place to come if you wish to camp (CFP 1,200 per tent). Si-Hmed serves ample meals (seafood or local dishes), but you must order a few hours before. Bicycles are CFP 1,200 a day, airport transfers CFP 2,400 pp roundtrip. Inexpensive.

Nearby is **Gîte Yedjélé Beach** (Martine Wadrobert, B.P. 150, 98828 Tadine; tel. 45-40-47) with four self-catering bungalows with fridge and TV at CFP 6,500/7,000 single/double. The cooking facilities are an advantage. Bicycle rentals are CFP 1,000 a day. Airport transfers run CFP 2,400 pp return. Moderate.

Maré's top accommodations is the **Nengone Village Hôtel** (Mr. Whagué "Zaza" Lakoredine, B.P. 154, 98828 Tadine; tel. 45-45-00, fax 45-44-64), which opened in 1996. It's also at Cengeïté,

in a coconut grove facing a white beach on the south side of the island. The 15 a/c bungalows with bath and TV (but without kitchens) are CFP 8,500 single or double, CFP 10,500 triple. Add CFP 1,200 pp for breakfast, plus CFP 2,500 each for lunch or dinner. There's a beachfront swimming pool, and bicycles are loaned free. Airport transfers are CFP 2,000 pp. Expensive.

Beyond Medu south of Wabao, **Léon Duhnara** (tel. 45-43-70) at Eni offers *case* accommodations at CFP 1,500 pp. Airport transfers are CFP 1,500 pp return.

There's a post office, bank, *gendarmerie,* and clinic at Tadine. A market functions in the hall adjoining La Roche Airport on Wednesday and Saturday mornings. A co-op store with a limited selection is at Tadine.

Transportation
Air Calédonie has twice daily flights from Nouméa (CFP 9,000), and three flights a week from Lifou (CFP 6,055). Public transport doesn't exist on Maré, but the *gîte* owners pick up guests at the airport if they've been forewarned. The *gîtes* rent cars at CFP 7,500 a day, but if you rent one, make sure the fuel tank is full; Maré has been known to run out of gasoline. Renting a bicycle at a *gîte* is a much cheaper, better option on flat Maré, and hitching is also possible, so long as you're prepared to walk when no cars pass.

The interisland ferry *Marie-Hélène* calls at Tadine on its way to Lifou or Nouméa. Check the times well in advance, as it's always different.

kauri pine cone

CAPSULE FRENCH VOCABULARY

bonjour—good day
bonsoir—good evening
salut—hello
Je vais à . . .—I am going to . . .
Où allez-vous?—Where are you going?
Jusqu'où allez-vous?—How far are you going?
Où se trouve . . .?—Where is . . .?
C'est loin d'ici?—Is it far from here?
Je fais de l'autostop.—I am hitchhiking.
À quelle heure?—At what time?
horaire—timetable
hier—yesterday
aujourd'hui—today
demain—tomorrow
Je désire, je voudrais . . .—I want . . .
J'aime . . .—I like . . .
Je ne comprends pas.—I don't understand.
une chambre—a room
Vous êtes très gentil.—You are very kind.
Où habitez-vous?—Where do you live?
Il fait mauvais temps.—It's bad weather.
gendarmerie—police station
Quel travail faites-vous?—What work do you do?
la chômage, les chômeurs—unemployment, the unemployed
Je t'aime.—I love you.
une boutique, un magasin—a store
le pain—bread
le lait—milk
le vin—wine
casse-croûte—snack
conserves—canned foods
fruits de mer—seafood
café très chaud—hot coffee
l'eau—water
plat du jour—set meal
Combien ça fait?—How much does it cost?
  Combien ça coûte?
  Combien? Quel prix?
auberge de jeunesse—youth hostel
la clef—the key
la route, la piste—the road
la plage—the beach
la falaise—the cliff
cascade—waterfall
grottes—caves
Est-ce que je peux camper ici?—May I camp here?

Je voudrais camper.—I wish to camp.
le terrain de camping—campsite
Devrais-je demander la permission?—Should I ask permission?
s'il vous plaît—please
oui—yes
merci—thank you
cher—expensive
bon marché—cheap

NUMBERS

un—1
deux—2
trois—3
quatre—4
cinq—5
six—6
sept—7
huit—8
neuf—9
dix—10
onze—11
douze—12
treize—13
quatorze—14
quinze—15
seize—16
dix-sept—17
dix-huit—18
dix-neuf—19
vingt—20
vingt et un—21
vingt-deux—22
vingt-trois—23
trente—30
quarante—40
cinquante—50
soixante—60
soixante-dix—70
quatre-vingts—80
quatre-vingt-dix—90
cent—100
mille—1,000
dix mille—10,000
million—1,000,000

VANUATU
INTRODUCTION

In 1980, this string of lush green islands, 2,445 km northeast of Sydney and 800 km west of Fiji, was transformed from the ponderous Anglo-French New Hebrides Condominium into the Ripablik Blong Vanuatu. Since then, the country has expressed its independence by developing a new national identity based on Melanesian *kastom*. It's a colorful land of many cultures, full of fascinating surprises. Make discoveries for yourself by asking any ni-Vanuatu (indigenous inhabitant) for the nearest cave, waterfall, swimming hole, hot spring, blowhole, or cliff. The general beauty and relaxed way of life are its biggest attractions.

No other South Pacific country harbors as many local variations. The glamorous duty-free shops, casinos, and gourmet restaurants of the cosmopolitan capital, Port Vila, contrast sharply with unchanging, traditional villages just over the horizon. You'll be moved and touched by the friendliness, warmth, and sincerity of the ni-Vanuatu, certainly Vanuatu's biggest attraction. Away from the packaged day tours and com-mercial resorts, this unpolished jewel of the South Pacific is still a land of adventure.

The Land
The 83 islands of Vanuatu (the name means "Land Eternal") stretch north-south 1,300 km, from the Torres Islands near Santa Cruz in the Solomons to minuscule Matthew and Hunter Islands (also claimed by France) east of New Caledonia. This neat geographical unit is divided into three groups: the Torres and Banks Islands in the north, the Y-shaped central group from Espiritu Santo and Maewo to Efate, and the Tafea islands (Tanna, Aniwa, Futuna, Erromango, and Aneityum) in the south. Together they total 12,189 square km, of which the 12 largest islands account for 93%. Espiritu Santo and Malekula alone comprise nearly half of Vanuatu's land area.

Vanuatu is composed of ash and coral: volcanic extrusion first built the islands, then limestone plateaus were added through tectonic uplift. Vanuatu has more active volcanoes than any other South Pacific country, and these islands form part of a long chain of volcanic activity stretching from New Zealand up through Vanuatu and the Solomons to the islands off New Guinea. Besides Yasur Volcano on Tanna, there are active volcanoes on Lopevi, Ambrym, and Gaua, plus a submarine volcano near Tongoa.

Vanuatu sits on the west edge of the Pacific Plate next to the 8,000-meter-deep New Hebrides Trench. This marks the point where the Indo-Australian Plate slips under the Pacific Plate in a classic demonstration of plate tectonics. Its islands are pushed laterally 10 centimeters a year in a northwest direction, accompanied by earthquakes and volcanic eruptions. In the past three million years Vanuatu has also been uplifted 700 meters, or approximately two millimeters a year. Although Vanuatu is relatively young geologically, this uplifting has created the series of stepped limestone plateaus you'll see on many islands.

Climate
Vanuatu has a hot, rainy climate—tropical in the north and subtropical in the south. The rainy season is Nov.-April, but sudden tropical showers can occur anytime. May-July are the optimum months for hiking—cooler and drier, and June-Sept., evenings on the southern islands can even be brisk. The southeast trade winds blow steadily year-round, though they're stronger and more reliable April-October. During the wet season, winds from the north or west occur under the influence of hurricanes and tropical lows.

Vanuatu is the most hurricane-prone country in the South Pacific. Between 1970 and 1985 no fewer than 29 hurricanes struck Vanuatu; on average, any given locality can expect to be hit by a hurricane every other year (usually between January and April). As in other parts of the South Pacific, hurricanes have become more frequent and stronger in recent years (this may be related to the greenhouse effect). The southernmost islands are less vulnerable to hurricanes, and get less rain than the hotter islands north of Efate.

For weather information dial 22932.

Flora and Fauna
The eastern, or windward, sides of the islands are equatorial, with thick rainforests. The leeward sides, which get less rain, are often open tropical woodlands or savanna, especially in the south. Higher up on the mountains is a humid zone of shrub forest. About 75% of the natural forest cover remains, although pressure from logging and agricultural clearing is increasing.

A principal botanical curiosity of Vanuatu is giant banyan trees *(nabangas),* which often dominate village meeting or dancing places *(nasaras),* especially on Tanna. The multirooted banyan begins by growing around another tree, which it eventually strangles out of existence. These massive twisting mazes of trunks and vines are among the earth's largest living organisms. Also unique is a prehistoric giant tree fern called *namwele,* which has great cultural significance and is used in many of the large carvings sold in Port Vila.

The indigenous fauna includes flying foxes, lizards, spiders, and butterflies. Four of the 12 species of bats are fruit bats (flying foxes), Vanuatu's only indigenous land mammals. Unfortunately their survival is threatened in part by Port Vila restaurateurs, who are not above having this endangered species on their menus. Since the bats live in large colonies in caves or banyan trees, they are easily killed.

Of Vanuatu's two snakes, the Pacific boa and flowerpot snake, only the latter is poisonous,

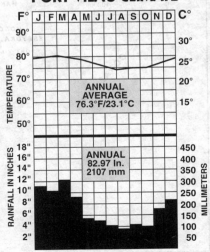

PORT VILA'S CLIMATE

ANNUAL AVERAGE 76.3°F/23.1°C

ANNUAL 82.97 In. 2107 mm

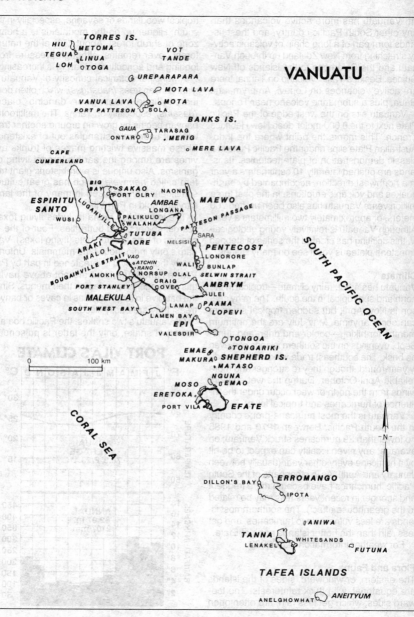

TORRES IS.
HIU
METOMA
TEGUA
LINUA
LOH
TOGA

VOT
TANDE

VANUATU

UREPARAPARA

MOTA LAVA

VANUA LAVA
PORT PATTESON
SOLA
MOTA

BANKS IS.

GAUA
TARASAG
ONTAR
MERIG

MERE LAVA

CAPE
CUMBERLAND

BIG
BAY
SAKAO
PORT OLRY
NAONE

ESPIRITU
SANTO
LUGANVILLE
AMBAE
LONGANA
MAEWO

WUSI
PALIKULO
WALAHA
PATTESON PASSAGE

TUTUBA
SARA

ARAKI
AORE
MELSISI

MALO I.
PENTECOST
LONORORE

BOUGAINVILLE STRAIT
VAO
ATCHIN
RANO
NORSUP
AMOKH
OLAL
WALI
BUNLAP

SELWIN STRAIT

PORT STANLEY
CRAIG
COVE
AMBRYM
ULEI

MALEKULA
SOUTH WEST BAY
LAMAP
PAAMA
LOPEVI

LAMEN BAY
EPI

VALESDIR

TONGOA
EMAE
TONGARIKI
MAKURA
SHEPHERD IS.
MATASO

MOSO
NGUNA
EMAO

ERETOKA
PORT VILA
EFATE

SOUTH PACIFIC OCEAN

CORAL SEA

N

DILLON'S BAY
ERROMANGO
IPOTA

ANIWA

TANNA
WHITESANDS
LENAKEL
FUTUNA

TAFEA ISLANDS

ANELGHOWHAT
ANEITYUM

0   100 km

© DAVID STANLEY

VANUATU AT A GLANCE

ISLAND	AREA (sq. km)	HIGHEST POINT (m)	POPULATION (1998 est.)	POPULATION DENSITY (persons per sq. km)
Espiritu Santo	4,010	1,879	32,416	8.1
Malekula	2,024	863	23,752	11.7
Efate	887	647	45,047	50.8
Erromango	887	886	1,651	1.9
Ambrym	666	1,270	8,202	12.3
Tanna	561	1,084	24,855	44.3
Pentecost	499	946	13,384	26.8
Epi	444	833	4,832	10.9
Ambae	399	1,496	9,434	23.6
Vanua Lava	343	946	1,580	4.6
Gaua	315	797	1,512	4.8
Maewo	300	811	2,966	9.9

though innocuous and rare. Three species of banded sea snakes are found in Vanuatu (of 52 species worldwide). The snakes crawl up on shore and hide among the rocks at night. Although poisonous, they're timid and no threat to snorkelers or scuba divers (though it would be foolish to try to handle them). Occasionally people wading through murky water will step on one, and they sometimes get caught in fishing nets, but even then, the bites are seldom fatal, as the snakes inject only a small amount of poison.

Vanuatu's colorful reefs hold its greatest store of life, including potentially dangerous tiger sharks in some areas (especially the corridor between Ambrym and eastern Malekula). In Vanuatu sharks are associated with a particular type of magic that involves certain individuals who can either become sharks or control sharks.

Though introduced by man, the pig is now considered indigenous. Ni-Vanuatu in the central and northern islands knock out the male animal's upper canine teeth so its lower tusks have nothing to grind against, and in six or seven years the tusks grow into a full circle. The pigs are highly valued by their owners, and the meat and tusks are prized at initiation rites and feasts. Culturally even more valuable than tusker pigs are the rare hermaphrodite pigs (naravé), usually found on northern islands such as Espiritu Santo, Malo, Ambae, Maewo, and northern Pentecost, where the world's highest ratio of intersexual

pigs per generation is found. In 1993 Florida reader James K. McIntyre identified a large number of hermaphrodite pigs at Avunatari village on Malo. Nowhere else in the world are pigs of this type found in such numbers.

Birdlife is rich; 54 native species include honeyeaters, fantails, finches, goshawks, kingfishers, parrots, peregrine falcons, pigeons, robins, swiftlets, thrushes, trillers, and warblers. Espiritu Santo has the greatest variety of birds, from great flocks of tiny red cardinals by the roadside to the chestnut-bellied kingfisher and the rare Santo mountain starling unique to the island's highest peaks. Large numbers of brown boobies nest on Monument Rock near Mataso Island in the Shepherd Islands.

HISTORY AND GOVERNMENT

Taem Blong Bifoa

Vanuatu may have been populated since before 3000 B.C., though little is known for certain as the early habitation sites are probably now below sea level. Lapita pottery found on Malo near Espiritu Santo dates 1300-1100 B.C., on Efate from 350 B.C. Around 700 B.C., new arrivals from the Solomons brought a second type of pottery called Mangaasi, with incised and applied relief designs, which they carried on to Fiji and New Caledonia. Fresh immigrants under the legendary Chief Roy

Mata occupied the central islands circa A.D. 1200. Excavations conducted by French archaeologist Jose Garanger on Eretoka Island off western Efate in 1967 uncovered a burial involving the sacrifice of 40 members of this chief's entourage, dating to 1265—a remarkable confirmation of oral tradition by modern science.

As today, the first inhabitants probably lived in small villages, and had a greater variety of languages and customs than the whole of Europe. Each clan was autonomous; relations between groups were often based on ceremonial gift-giving, while families bonded through arranged marriages. Wives, considered property, were exchanged between villages to create links. Spirits were controlled by magic. To work one's way up through the graded societies and become a "big man," an individual had to amass sufficient wealth in the form of pigs to purchase his rank. This *nimanke* system was more widespread in the north than in the center and south, where descent was usually hereditary. The borrowing and loaning of pigs between men created a complex system of bonds and obligations, which strengthened the group and relationships between groups (still a common practice). Only the most able men could rise in this system. Clans raided one another and the victim's bodies were eaten to capture the power of their spirits; these cannibal raids being reciprocal, and one never wandered far from his home village. One was relatively free from the danger of attack along traditional trade routes and within the area of traditional ritual links.

European Contact

The first European to arrive was the Hispanic explorer Pedro Fernandez de Quirós, who pulled into Espiritu Santo's Big Bay on 29 April 1606, believing he had found the "lost" southern continent. When he and his men landed, pious, God-fearing Quirós knelt and kissed the sand, naming the island Terra Austrialis del Espiritu Santo, after the Holy Ghost. He claimed possession of it and everything to the south as far as the South Pole in the name of the king of Spain and the Catholic Church. Quirós planned to build a model Christian settlement on the site, but his treatment of the inhabitants soon led to open hostility which, together with sickness and dissent among his own men, drove this visionary mystic away after only three weeks.

White men did not return for 162 years, when Bougainville sailed between Espiritu Santo and Malekula in 1768, disproving Quirós's hypothesis that they were part of a southern continent. Bougainville named the northern islands the Great Cyclades. In 1774, Captain Cook became the first European to really explore and chart the entire group, naming it New Hebrides, after the Scottish islands. The notorious Captain Bligh first sighted and named the Banks Islands in 1789.

Christianity and Depopulation

The sandalwood traders operated in the islands from 1825 to 1865. Their methods created deep resentment among the islanders, so when the first white members of the London Missionary Society landed on Erromango (Martyr Island) in

view of Tanna Island

M.G.L. DOMENY DE RIENZI

1839, they were clubbed and eaten. Samoan missionaries were sent next, but many were also killed or died from malaria. Worse still, they introduced diseases such as measles, influenza, and dysentery, which devastated whole populations. Well-wishers in Australia and elsewhere sent secondhand garments to clothe the naked savages. Regrettably, these were also impregnated with disease, and some sandalwood traders deliberately distributed clothes they knew to be infected with smallpox to wipe out the inhabitants of the areas they wished to exploit.

Since converts—who had the closest contact with missionaries—were the most affected by these epidemics, the newcomers were thought to be evil sorcerers, and the ni-Vanuatu resisted any way they could. From a precontact population of about half a million, the number of ni-Vanuatu dropped to 40,000 in 1920. Islands like Erromango remain relatively unpopulated today, and only after 1920 did Vanuatu's population begin to rise. Some ni-Vanuatu still refuse to accept Christianity and regard all white men with suspicion. Although a majority had been "converted" by 1900, their understanding of doctrine was shallow, and mass defections from the church have occurred since WW II, especially on Tanna. About 16% of the population continues to follow *kastom*.

The Melanesian Mission (Anglican) and the Presbyterians divided the group into spheres of influence, with the Anglicans in the northeast and the Presbyterians in the center and south. Rather than risk establishing a mission in the islands, Anglican Bishop George Selwyn took young ni-Vanuatu to New Zealand and Norfolk Island for training. Catholicism became established in the central islands after 1887, but little headway was made on Malekula and Espiritu Santo until recently. The missionaries managed to stop village warfare and cannibalism, facilitating the entry of the next two groups—the labor recruiters and European settlers.

The Blackbirders

From 1863 to 1904 some 40,000 ni-Vanuatu were recruited to work in the canefields of Queensland, Australia, and another 10,000 went to Fiji and New Caledonia. As much as half the adult male population of some islands went abroad. Though many young men welcomed the chance for adventure and escape from the restrictions

of village life, conditions were hard. The blackbirders sometimes resorted to kidnapping the islanders, or herding them together by brute force. Outriggers were sunk and the survivors "rescued"; others were bought outright from chiefs for beads, tobacco, mirrors, and muskets. Returnees often brought with them diseases and alcohol, which decimated the home population.

In the end, most of the laborers were deported from Australia in 1906 when the White Australia Policy took effect, but a large percentage died abroad. Some of the returnees to Tanna were so irate about being evicted from Australia that they drove all whites off the island. An enduring legacy of the labor trade was the evolution of a pidgin tongue called Bislama, the national language.

Planters and Land

The first impetus for establishing European plantations in Vanuatu was the high price of cotton during the American Civil War. When cotton collapsed, the planters switched to bananas, cacao, coffee, and copra. The first plantations were on Tanna and Efate, followed later by Espiritu Santo. Though British subjects from Australia arrived first, in 1882 the Compagnie Calédonienne des Nouvelles Hébrides began acquiring large tracts of native land. The Australian-based trading company Burns Philp followed in 1895, but by 1900 French colonists outnumbered British two to one.

Though the first traders and missionaries had been mostly English, the French recognized the agricultural potential of the islands and wanted another colony to strengthen their position in New Caledonia. This alarmed the Australians, who thought one French colony on their doorstep was enough. In 1878 the British and French governments agreed not to annex Vanuatu without consulting one another. To protect the planters' interests and regulate the labor trade, the two nations established a Joint Naval Commission in 1887 with jurisdiction over the islands. It could only intervene in the event of war; during the hurricane season, when the Naval Commission vessels had to be withdrawn, there was no law other than the musket.

During this period, 12% of Vanuatu's land, including the choicest tracts, was permanently alienated, 10% by French companies and two percent by Australian. Traditionally, land could

CARGO CULTS

The Tannese were declared converted to Presbyterianism in the early years of this century, yet just prior to WW II a movement to reestablish traditional values emerged in southern Tanna when a spirit began appearing at Green Point around sunset. In 1942, 1,000 men from Tanna were recruited by the Americans to work at military bases on Efate, and the sight of huge quantities of war materiel and black soldiers gave this movement a new meaning.

A sort of cultural hero emerged who would come from across the sea bringing wealth in abundance: Jon "from" America. As the symbol of their newfound religion, the Tannese took the red cross seen on wartime ambulances on Efate, and today the villages north of Yasur Volcano and elsewhere are dotted with little red crosses neatly surrounded by picket fences, bearing witness to this extraordinary chain of events.

The priests and prophets of these cargo cults are called "messengers," and they foretell the return of the ships laden with cargo for Man Tanna, escorted by Jon Frum, the reincarnation of an ancient deity. Towers with tin cans strung from wires, imitating radio stations, were erected so Jon Frum could speak to his people. The movement declares that money must be thrown away, pigs killed, and gardens left uncared for, since all material wealth will be provided in the end by Jon Frum.

Formerly it was felt that missionaries and government administrators had interfered with this Second Coming; thus the movement sometimes manifested itself in noncooperation with them. Beginning in 1940 the British authorities arrested cult leaders and held them without trial in Port Vila, but new devotees sprang up to take their places. There's also a Prince Philip cult among the custom people at Yaohnanen dating back to the prince's visit to what was then New Hebrides in 1974. Followers believe the prince originally came from Tanna in another form and will eventually return to rule over them.

not be sold in Vanuatu, only the use of the land temporarily assigned. Many sales were instigated by a few individuals and not agreed upon by consensus as custom required. The ni-Vanuatu had little understanding of the alienation taking place; when they tried to resist, British and French warships were sent to bombard coastal villages.

The Colonial Period

In 1902 the Germans began to show an interest in these "unclaimed" islands, so the British and French quickly appointed resident commissioners. In 1906, three years after an auspicious visit to Paris by the francophile English King Edward VII, the Anglo-French New Hebrides Condominium was established. The arrangement was formalized in the Protocol of 1914, then proclaimed in 1923.

The Condominium system of government resulted in an expensive duplication of services and administration, as each colonial power implemented its own judiciary, police force, hospitals, schools, etc. Each power had jurisdiction over its own citizens and the natives, but the ni-Vanuatu were not permitted to claim either British or French nationality, and in effect became state-

less. A Joint Court was set up, and land titles registered before 1896 could not be challenged. This institutionalized the large European plantations. In addition, the ni-Vanuatu didn't have the right of appeal from native courts to the Joint Court. Actually, this combination of administrations had little impact on the ni-Vanuatu, other than freezing an unjust social structure, and they could simply ignore the Condominium pandemonium if they wished. Education remained in the hands of the missionaries right into the 1960s. Although a teachers' college opened in 1960, there wasn't a British secondary school (Malapoa College) until 1966, a French secondary school (the lycée) until 1968.

Despite the fact that the budget of the French Residency was twice that of the British, the latter were more effective, due to a long-standing policy of localization and advanced training for Melanesians. France wasted much of its money on a large staff of expatriates, failing to train a French-speaking native elite capable of assuming power. In the early 1970s the French began a crash program to build a French-speaking majority, but it was too late.

On 20 July 1940, New Hebrides became the first French colony to recognize the Free French forces of General de Gaulle, two months before New Caledonia did so. During WW II, major American bases on Espiritu Santo and Efate were used as staging areas for the Solomons campaign. These islands didn't suffer as the Solomons and New Guinea did. The Japanese bombed Espiritu Santo once, but only managed to kill a cow. On Tanna the apparent wealth of the U.S. soldiers gave fresh impetus to the Jon Frum cargo cult, which already existed before the war. In turn, the romance of these islands inspired novelist James A. Michener to write *Tales of the South Pacific,* his first book, with Ambae starring as "Bali Hai."

The Road to Independence

The independence of Vanuatu was not generously granted, as it had been elsewhere in the South Pacific, but had to be won through a long, bitter struggle against bungling colonial administrators, entrenched settlers, and opportunists. In 1971, the New Hebrides Cultural Association emerged to resist large land purchases and subdivisions by an American businessman, one Eugene Peacock. Three months later, the Association became the New Hebrides National Party, headed by Father Walter Lini of Pentecost (an Anglican priest). The party soon won grassroots support throughout the islands, mostly among English-speaking Protestants, by calling for a return of all alienated land to its customary owners. Several French-oriented parties (the "moderates") were also created; they favored prolonged collabora-

tion with the British and French governments.

These factions forced the ruling powers to establish a Representative Assembly in 1975, but it was dissolved in 1977 following a boycott by the Vanua'aku Party (formerly the National Party), which demanded the elimination of appointed members, as well as immediate independence. The crisis was resolved in 1978, with the creation of a Government of National Unity temporarily uniting the two factions. A constitution was signed in October 1979, and in elections a month later the Vanua'aku Party won a two-thirds majority. Understandably, little of this was popular with the French! Most of the plantations were owned by French nationals, who outnumbered British subjects three to one, and their influence was especially strong on Espiritu Santo. The French administration adopted a disruptive policy of encouraging local divisions and disturbances as a means of wringing concessions from the pro-independence side. The British, who just wanted to get out as soon as possible, were unable to interfere with their partner because all Condominium decisions had to be bilateral and the French just stonewalled.

The Republic of Vemarana

The key figure in the independence disruptions was Jimmy Stevens, a charismatic Tongan/Scottish half-caste with a large following on Espiritu Santo and some of the central islands. Basically he was a nonconformist, suspicious of the Vanua'aku Party leadership, which was composed

Flashback to 1980: From left to right are Jimmy Stevens, the rebel leader; General Ted Diro, P.N.G. Defense Force commander at the time; Sir Julius Chan, former prime minister of P.N.G.; and Father Walter Lini, former prime minister of Vanuatu.

mainly of ni-Vanuatu British civil servants and Protestant clergy. They in turn regarded Jimmy as a dangerous cargo cultist. His Nagriamel Party began as an agricultural reform movement centered at Fanafo village in the bush 22 km north of Luganville. Nagriamel represented a turning away from European influence and a return to native ways. In 1971 Nagriamel petitioned the United Nations to halt further sales of land on Espiritu Santo to American interests for development as hotel and investment properties.

Ironically, by May 1980 Stevens had come full circle, after accepting US$250,000 in aid, arms, and radio transmitting equipment from the Phoenix Foundation, an American far right organization run by millionaire businessman Michael Oliver. In 1972, Oliver and associates had attempted to declare a tax-free Republic of Minerva on Tonga's Minerva Reef, until the king gave them the boot. Later Phoenix attempted to engineer the secession of Abaco Island in the Bahamas. When this failed, Oliver turned his attention to Espiritu Santo, which was to become a capitalist's paradise, free of government controls. Already four areas on the island had been subdivided into 5,000 lots, of which 2,000 had been sold to individual Americans. Aore Island, off Espiritu Santo, was to have a health resort and casino. Stevens, who now styled himself "President Moli Stevens," declared Espiritu Santo the independent "Republic of Vemarana," and Vanua'aku Party supporters were driven off the island. The Coconut War had begun.

Escalation

During it all, French police stood by and took no action. Stevens had visited Paris and received encouragement from French President Giscard d'Estaing prior to the rebellion. The French apparently intended to have Espiritu Santo continue as a separate French colony, as had occurred with Mayotte when Comoros in the Indian Ocean achieved independence from France in 1975. Chief Minister Walter Lini responded by imposing an economic boycott on Espiritu Santo, but he was unable to prod the British and French authorities into putting down the revolt, as no unilateral action was permitted under Condominium laws. A simultaneous disorder on Tanna dwindled when Alexis Yolou, its "moderate" leader, was shot dead.

There was talk of delaying the independence scheduled for 30 July 1980, but Lini announced that he would declare Vanuatu's independence unilaterally if Britain and France reneged on their promises. Additionally, neighboring countries such as Australia, New Zealand, and Papua New Guinea indicated that they would recognize such independence (Samoa was the first to actually do so). Thus, the colonial powers were forced to adhere to their original timetable, and Vanuatu became an independent republic on the scheduled day. To prevent bloodshed, the British and French sent military forces to Espiritu Santo to disarm Stevens's followers just a week before independence. Forced to leave afterward, the French ripped out telephones, air-conditioners, and anything else they could move from their offices to make things as difficult as possible for the new government. Had the British not been involved, the French might never have agreed to independence.

The Outcome

In August 1980, Papua New Guinea troops replaced the British/French forces on Espiritu Santo and arrested Jimmy Stevens, who was sent to Port Vila for trial. Stevens's son Eddie was killed by a grenade when he tried to run a roadblock. This was the first military intervention by the forces of one Pacific country in the territory of another since the 19th century, and it fostered a wave of Melanesian solidarity that led to the creation of the Melanesian Spearhead regional grouping in 1988.

Jimmy Stevens was sentenced to 14.5 years imprisonment for his part in the rebellion, during which Luganville was looted and burned. Most of the 70 ni-Vanuatu arrested along with Stevens were released within a year, but over the next two months 260 French residents who had sided with the rebellion were rounded up and deported to New Caledonia. Documents captured at the rebel headquarters at Fanafo implicated aides to French Resident Commissioner Jean-Jacques Robert (who himself had come to New Hebrides from Comoros) as direct accomplices in the secession.

After Independence

The first years of independence were uneventful, with the Vanua'aku Party government employing anticolonial, antinuclear rhetoric to forge a regional identity while quietly pursuing the capitalistic domestic policies established during the Condominium. The tax haven created in 1971 was left in place, and confiscated land could be leased back for up to 75 years at low rates. In short, little changed, and fears of "Melanesian socialism" proved unfounded. Development and power became centralized in Port Vila with an indigenous political elite working in tandem with expatriate business interests.

In 1982, Vanuatu closed its ports to American warships that refused to confirm or deny whether they were carrying nuclear weapons—the first Pacific country to do so. In 1983, legislation was passed that made Vanuatu the first totally nuclear-free nation in the Pacific: nuclear weapons, ships, power plants, and waste-dumping were all prohibited. Vanuatu was the first South Pacific country to acquire full membership in the Non-Aligned Movement. These positions proved useful in playing different groups of foreigners off against one another, and Vanuatu has been able to garner support from both right-wing libertarians and left-wing internationalists as a result.

Recent Events

By 1991 Lini's declining health and increasingly erratic, nonconsultative style of leadership had brought government business almost to a standstill, with mass sackings of government ministers and public servants suspected of "disloyalty." At the Vanua'aku Party congress in April 1991, Lini managed to have the election of a new party leadership postponed, but he suffered a mild heart attack soon after. In August, the party held a special leadership congress at Mele village and elected ex-foreign minister Donald Kalpokas to replace Lini (who boycotted the congress) as party president. Despite a vote of no confidence by the congress, Lini refused to resign as prime minister, but in September he was defeated in a parliamentary vote of no confidence and replaced by Donald Kalpokas as prime minister.

To mark the 20th anniversary of the founding of the Vanua'aku Party in August 1991, Jimmy Stevens was finally freed, after serving 11 years of his sentence at Port Vila's jail. His followers throughout the archipelago assembled 20 pigs with fully circled tusks to present to the government as an act of atonement (the pigs

were later returned to their owners). Stevens had been under hospital treatment for high blood pressure for some time, and his release, just weeks before Lini himself was voted out of office, culminated an era in the country's history. In 1994, Jimmy Stevens died at Fanafo.

After losing his post, Lini rallied his supporters and formed the National United Party (NUP) to contest the elections scheduled for December 1991. With the Vanua'aku Party thus divided, Maxime Carlot Korman's Union of Moderate Parties (UMP) won 19 of the 46 seats. Carlot Korman formed a coalition with the NUP, which had obtained 10 seats; a reversal of Vanuatu's former anti-French foreign policy soon followed. The election of 1995 resulted in a new coalition between the UMP and the NUP, with Serge Vohor as prime minister. During 1996 intense political maneuvering led to Vohor and Carlot Korman alternating in the top post three times.

In August 1996, the minister of finance, Barak Sope, was sacked after the ombudsman, Marie-Noelle Patterson, disclosed details of a US$100 million bank guarantee scam that could have bankrupted Vanuatu. Sope told parliament the ombudsman had violated a Melanesian custom that holds that women must not criticize men. A month later, the government changed and Sope was back as deputy prime minister. In October 1996, the paramilitary Mobile Force staged a mini-coup, holding the president hostage until a wage arrears claim was settled.

In late 1997, after the Office of the Ombudsman initiated court action against Vohor, Carlot Korman, and several cabinet ministers for accepting unlawful kickbacks, these same leaders pushed a bill through parliament repealing the Ombudsman Act itself. President Jean-Marie Leye refused to sign the bill, referring it to the Supreme Court. In January 1998, there was serious rioting in Port Vila after the ombudsman revealed that senior politicians and their cronies had been using overgenerous loans from Vanuatu's National Provident Fund, a compulsory pension plan, to illegally purchase government housing. A four-week state of emergency followed.

To restore stability, fresh elections were called for March 1998, and just a month prior to the vote, yet another ombudsman report alleged that Vohor had received tens of thousands of dollars from Asian businessmen in exchange for Vanuatu passports and honorary diplomatic posts. Despite all of this, most of the politicians named in the corruption reports were reelected thanks to entrenched party organizations and patronage. Donald Kalpokas, one of the few local leaders untainted by scandal, put together a coalition government with Walter Lini. In June 1998 a Leadership Code was enacted to reduce future opportunities for abuses of power, although the investigative powers of the ombudsman were also diminished. The political turmoil resumed in October as the Union of Moderate Parties replaced the National United Party in the ruling coalition. Another landmark event for Vanuatu was the February 1999 death of Walter Lini.

Government

Vanuatu has a parliamentary system of government with a prime minister who is the leader of the majority party in Parliament. Parliament's 52 members are elected for four-year terms, and the prime minister appoints his cabinet from among those members. A National Council of Chiefs (Malvatumauri) advises on matters relating to custom. Parliament and the heads of the provincial governments elect a president, who serves a five-year term as ceremonial head of state.

In 1994 the 11 local government councils were replaced by six provinces: Torba (Torres and Banks), Sanma (Santo and Malo), Penama (Pentecost, Ambae, and Maewo), Malampa (Malekula, Ambrym, and Paama), Shefa (Shepherds, Epi, and Efate), and Tafea (Tanna, Anatom, Futuna, Erromango, and Aniwa).

Vanuatu's cultural, political, and economic diversity is mirrored in the nation's politics. Close political allies can become foes overnight, and former bitter adversaries have no compunctions about forming alliances. Call it democracy or simply the Melanesian tradition of shifting alliances, much time and effort that should be going into solving the country's social and economic problems is devoted to politicking for personal gain. The six political parties represented in parliament are the Vanua'aku Pati, the Union of Moderate Parties, the National United Party, the Melanesian Progressive Party, the Jon Frum Movement, and the Vanuatu Republikan Party.

ECONOMY

Agriculture and Land

Roughly 75% of the population lives by subsistence agriculture. Root crops such as yams, taro, manioc, and sweet potatoes are grown, with copra produced for cash sale. Copra production declined from 42,000 tonnes in 1986 to 28,000 tonnes in 1993 due to hurricane damage and low world prices. The Commodity Marketing Board has subsidized copra prices with European Union aid money, to ensure a regular income for the village producers who account for 80% of Vanuatu's copra. By 1996, however, mismanagement and bad investments had put the Board millions of dollars in debt.

The constitution specifies that land can only be owned by indigenous ni-Vanuatu. At independence, all alienated land was returned to its customary owners; former landlords were given five years to go into partnership, lease the land, or otherwise dispose of it. Leases of up to 75 years are available. Land disputes are routine in Vanuatu, as many ni-Vanuatu claim the same areas.

Although about 40% of the land is arable, only 17% is presently utilized, mostly in coastal areas. Cattle bred from light-colored French Charolais and Limousin stock roam under the coconuts to provide beef for canning and export.

Trade

Vanuatu imports three times as much as it exports, and has a large imbalance with its largest trading partner, Australia, which sells Vanuatu 47 times more than it buys. New Zealand buys almost nothing from Vanuatu but is its second-largest supplier. Copra is the largest export, accounting for more than a third of total exports by value, shipped mostly from Luganville to Holland. Exports such as chilled beef (sold to Japan), sawn timber (sold to Australia and New Caledonia), cacao (sold to France, Holland, and Germany), and pumpkins (sold to Japan) are also significant. The export of unprocessed logs was halted in 1994, after it became clear that logging already underway would have stripped the country bare in five years. A flourishing sawmill industry at Luganville is the result.

Frozen fish was eliminated as an export item in 1986, when the U.S. stopped such imports (to Hawaii and Puerto Rico) from Vanuatu. As a result, the Japanese company that had operated the freezer plant at Palikulo on Espiritu Santo for 19 years decided to close the facility. Some 400 ni-Vanuatu serve as crew on Taiwanese fishing boats, on which they are reportedly overworked and otherwise exploited.

The import economy is dominated by large European and Chinese trading companies. In rural areas, cooperatives once collected agricultural exports and handled marketing, but individually owned stores are now becoming more common. In 1990 the Swedish brewer Pripps launched Vanuatu Brewing Ltd. as a 50-50 joint venture with the government to produce Tusker beer and Pripps Lager. An industrial park has been created on Espiritu Santo.

Taxation and Evasion

Although Vanuatu has periodically pursued a confrontational left/center foreign policy, its domestic policies (inherited from the Condominium) are ultra-right. There are no company taxes, personal income taxes, estate duties, capital gains taxes, or exchange controls. Instead, government revenue is obtained from customs duties, export taxes, company registration fees, licensing fees, property taxes (Port Vila and Espiritu Santo only), various tourist taxes, and fishing licenses.

In past, import duties accounted for more than half of government income, and were the major cause of the high cost of living. The American-dominated Asian Development Bank lobbied again this trade barrier, and in August 1998, the tariffs were replaced by a 12.5% value-added tax (VAT) on goods and services. About the same time, interest rates were hiked five percent to protect the local currency, and there have been rumors of an income tax. These moves damaged local businesses by encouraging imports while increasing the cost of borrowing. Vanuatu receives one of the highest per capita levels of outside aid in the region, with contributions nicely diversified between Australia, France, the European Union, Japan, New Zealand, the Asian Development Bank, and Britain.

Vanuatu has the South Pacific's oldest, largest, and best established "finance center," which offers excellent facilities to foreigners wishing to evade their own country's public auditing and tax laws. In 1971, the British Companies Regulation was enacted, giving tax-free status to companies registered in what was then New Hebrides. Today some 2,500 foreign companies, 10 trusts, and 80 dummy banks participate in the tax-haven scheme, providing about 350 jobs, paying US$5 million a year in government fees, and bringing in additional millions in flow-on benefits. Several dozen accounting, banking, legal, and investment services help Asian corporations avoid taxation. In 1991 the Australian and New Zealand governments passed legislation greatly restricting the use of tax havens by their citizens after televised revelations that some large corporations were paying only one percent tax by channeling their profits through these facilities. Vanuatu claims to run a clean operation, with money laundering from illegal sources strictly taboo (for more information, click on www.msvanuatu.com.vu or www.mooresrowland.com).

In 1981, Vanuatu also established a shipping registry or flag-of-convenience law modeled on Liberia's, which allows foreign shipping companies to duck taxation, safety regulations, union labor, and government controls. With the political chaos in Vanuatu's main competitors, Liberia and Panama, the annual number of ships registered has jumped from 76 in 1985 to about 500 in recent years with the main users American, Japanese, and Hong Kong ship owners. The New York company that administers the registry retains a 30% cut, and the rest goes to the Vanuatu government.

Tourism

From 1981 to 1987, tourism was controlled by Ansett Airlines, which provided the country's air link to Australia. Then Ansett pulled out after the government imposed a royalty fee for the right to fly the country's colors and refused to contribute to marketing costs. This forced the government to form Air Vanuatu and begin spending its own money on promotion. In 1989, the government also took over Australian-owned Air Melanesiae, which had run the domestic air service for a quarter of a century, and set up Vanair, which promptly increased its fares.

Tourism still focuses on the resorts of Port Vila, with Tanna serving as a day-trip destination. During the 1980s Espiritu Santo was played down as a tourist destination due to political fallout from the independence disturbances, and only since 1991 has tourism to Santo been actively promoted. Luganville's Pekoa Airport has been expanded, and in 1998 Tanna also got a new international airport. Direct flights from Nouméa have been announced for both, yet these have still to materialize.

Cruise ships call frequently at Port Vila, "Mystery Island" (Aneityum), and Champagne Beach (Santo), unloading about 70,000 one-day visitors a year. Thanks to its proximity to Australia, Vanuatu receives more cruise ship passengers than any other South Pacific country. More than half of the 50,000 airborne tourists are from Australia, with New Zealand and New Caledonia providing another eighth each. Vanuatu's tourism infrastructure (airports, guesthouses, roads, shops, and telecommunications) is much better developed than that of Solomon Islands, and prices are noticeably higher. Vanuatu gets more than three times as many visitors as the Solomons.

THE PEOPLE

Sixty-eight of Vanuatu's 83 islands are populated, but most of the country's 180,000 people live on 16 main islands. At 15 persons per square km, the population density is low. Yet after a century of depopulation due to warfare, blackbirding, and introduced diseases, Vanuatu now has one of the highest birthrates in the Pacific, and 45% of the population is under the age of 15. It also has one of the highest infant mortality rates in the South Pacific with 45 deaths per 1,000.

Ni-Vanuatu continue to migrate to Port Vila from rural areas in search of jobs, excitement, and better services. One in six now lives in the capital, with people from the same outer islands congregating in their own suburban communities. Although 4,000 young people enter the job market each year, formal employment opportunities exist only for 400 of them. Almost half of ni-Vanuatu children aged 5-19 don't attend school, and the illiteracy rate is near 50%.

Just over a third of the population is Presbyterian, with Anglicans, Roman Catholics, and followers of the Jon Frum Cargo Cult making up a sixth each. Smaller groups include the Seventh-Day Adventists, Church of Christ, and As-

An Ambrym man poses beside an image he carved.

semblies of God. About 10,000 people still follow traditional Pacific religions. Jon Frummers account for more than a quarter of the population of Tanna.

Although 98% of the population is Melanesian (ni-Vanuatu), there are also Europeans, Chinese, and Vietnamese. Thousands of indentured Vietnamese laborers were imported earlier this century to work on the French plantations, but most were repatriated by 1963. The number of non-ni-Vanuatu has declined from 6,880 in 1979 to 3,469 in 1989, more than half of them in Port Vila.

Although the Melanesians arrived in Vanuatu from the northwest thousands of years ago, a back migration of Polynesians from the east occurred less than 1,000 years ago. Polynesian languages are still spoken on Futuna, Emae, and Ambae islands, and in Ifira and Mele villages on Efate. A Polynesian hierarchy of chiefs is still evident in much of central and southern

Vanuatu. In physical appearance the Polynesians have been almost totally assimilated by the surrounding Melanesian peoples, largely due to a custom requiring a young man to take his bride from a neighboring clan.

Language
With 105 indigenous languages, most having several dialects, Vanuatu boasts the world's highest density of languages per capita. All of these tongues (none with more than 5,000 speakers) belong to the Austronesian family of languages spoken from Madagascar to Easter Island. Bislama is the national language understood by 90% of the population, although English and French are also official languages. About 40% of the population knows English and 20% speak French. Many ni-Vanuatu are fluent in five or six languages: a few in local languages, Bislama, English, and French.

Bislama developed as a traders' tongue in the 19th century and took hold among the indentured native laborers in Queensland. The name derives from bêche-de-mer, an edible sea slug sought by early traders. This dialect of Pidgin English is now spoken by around 60% of ni-Vanuatu and is the main communication medium between persons from different language groups, though they speak their mother tongues at home. Most parliamentary debates are conducted in Bislama, but education is still conducted in either English or French.

Bislama verbs have no tenses: finished and unfinished actions are defined by adverbs. Nouns are often descriptions of use. *Blong* indicates possession, while *long* takes the place of

WOMEN IN VANUATU

Women are more equal to men in the northern matrilineal islands; on islands like Ambrym, Malekula, south Pentecost, and Tanna, where descent is patrilineal, males dominate society. In times past, women on the central and northern islands belonged to secret societies, but always of lower grade than those of the men. Though men and women work together in the villages, the women are responsible for chores considered less prestigious, such as cooking and caring for gardens and pigs. The burdens of a subsistence economy usually fall more heavily on the women. Too often, the men in Port Vila spend much of their time drinking kava and gossiping with friends, while the women keep the families going.

A woman cannot become a "big man" by accumulating wealth—in fact, she herself is considered part of her husband's wealth. The payment of brideprice is still common throughout Vanuatu, and some young girls have even been called "Toyotas," an indication of their market value as potential wives. To control inflation, the Malvatumauri, Vanuatu's National Council of Chiefs, has placed a Vt300,000 ceiling on bride-prices (a Toyota costs more than Vt1.5 million). Being viewed as tradable objects is a heavy burden for ni-Vanuatu women; girls are often deprived of educational opportunities by their own families, which consider them primarily child-bearers for the clan of their future husband. Some educated women refuse to marry, as it would mean forfeiting all rights to the family's property.

Most women treated for injuries at hospitals are victims of domestic violence, and the police only take action in the most extreme cases. Desertion of families by men is also a big problem. Interestingly enough, maltreatment of women is often more common in missionized communities and the towns than in traditional areas where customary law prevails. A husband in a "kastom area" will try to avoid beating his wife ("without cause") as she might run away ("with just cause"), back to her original family, and the husband would thus lose the bride-price he paid.

Since independence, things have begun to change. There are now 50:50 quotas for both sexes in forms one to four, to give girls an equal chance to attend secondary school. In 1987, Hilda Lini (Walter Lini's younger sister) became the first ni-Vanuatu woman elected to parliament and, in 1991, Ms. Lini was appointed Minister of Health in the UMP/NUP coalition government. The **National Council of Women** (Box 975, Port Vila; tel. 23108, fax 27210) has 13 island councils and 107 smaller area councils around the country.

More ni-Vanuatu women wear Mother Hubbard dresses than women in any other Pacific country—they're common even in Port Vila. It's another manifestation of the enduring strength of Melanesian *kastom*, something you'll encounter often as you travel around this country.

most other prepositions. Vowels are pronounced as in Spanish. English speakers usually can't distinguish between b and p, d and t, f and v, and g and k. The letter b is preceded by an "m" sound, d by an "n" sound.

Bislama can sound deceptively simple to the untrained ear, but the meaning is not always what one would expect from a literal translation into English. Over the years it has developed into a complex language by adopting indigenous linguistic structures. Bislama is a lot further from English than Solomon Islands pidgin, and you'll only understand fragments without study (there are several dictionaries). The University of the South Pacific has a university-level Bislama course.

ON THE ROAD

Highlights
The overwhelming majority of tourists visit only Efate, Espiritu Santo, and Tanna, and indeed these three islands contain Vanuatu's best-known sights, including the country's only towns, Port Vila and Luganville. Tanna is acclaimed for Yasur Volcano and the Jon Frum Cargo Cult, Efate has an interesting road around its coast, and Espiritu Santo boasts one of the South Pacific's finest beaches. Ambrym is less known but outstanding for its active volcanoes. Virtually all of the islands are worth visiting by those willing to slow down and enjoy the unspoiled local environment and friendly people. It's easy to get lost and found in Vanuatu.

Sports and Recreation
Scuba diving is well developed with several active dive shops in Port Vila and a couple more at Santo. Diving is also possible from charter vessels off the north side of Efate. Game fishing is available at Port Vila. Other active sports to pursue are windsurfing in Vila's Erakor Lagoon, horseback riding at one of the two ranches on opposite sides of Port Vila, and yachting on a charter vessel based at Port Vila.

Golf is big here, with two major 18-hole golf courses on Efate and smaller resort courses at two Port Vila hotels. There's also a golf course at Santo.

All of the above is the domain of tourists, expatriates, and affluent locals; hiking is the sport most commonly practiced by the vast majority of the general population, although they'd hardly think of it as such. Well-used trails exist on all of the outer islands, with Tanna being especially accessible in this regard. It's quite possible to hike right across islands like Tanna, Malekula, and Erromango. Hiking around Espiritu Santo is a much bigger undertaking with local guides required.

Mountain climbers should consider the active volcanoes of Ambrym: Benbow and Marum in the south and Vetlam in the north. All are quite accessible to those willing to hire local guides and pay custom fees to the local chiefs. Ambae also has a central peak worth a climb. There are many other possibilities.

If surfing is Polynesia's finest gift to the world of sport, Melanesia's greatest contribution is perhaps bungee jumping, which A.J. Hackett saw on Pentecost Island in 1979 and later introduced to New Zealand. Hackett replaced the islanders' vines with expandable rubber lines, and today thousands of people a year prove something to themselves and others by taking the jump, just as the Pentecost men have been doing for hundreds of years.

Public Holidays and Festivals
Public holidays include New Year's Day (1 January), Custom Chiefs Day (5 March), Good Friday, Easter Monday (March/April), Ascension Day (April/May), Labor Day (1 May), Independence Day (30 July), Assumption Day (15 August), Constitution Day (5 October), All Saints' Day (1 November), National Unity Day (29 November), Christmas Day (25 December), and Family Day (26 December). The Monday or Friday before Independence Day is Children's Day, also a public holiday.

Important annual events include the Jon Frum Festival at Sulphur Bay, Tanna, on 15 February, and the Pentecost Land Dive weekly in April and May. Independence Day sees a parade, food and kava stalls, sporting events, and custom dancing in Port Vila. Expect all of the events to begin an hour late.

ACCOMMODATIONS AND FOOD

Accommodations

The 12.5% value-added tax is not included in some of the prices listed in this book. Hotels often quote the basic price and add the tax to your bill later. Meals at licensed restaurants serving alcohol are also taxed 12.5%, but unlicensed snack bars and small outer-island resorts are tax-free.

The only commercial tourist accommodations are on Efate, Tanna, and Espiritu Santo. Most of the outer islands served by Vanair have basic guesthouses operated by the churches, provincial administrations, women's groups, village chiefs, or others. Thatched resthouses run by local villagers exist on nearly all of the islands, and those mentioned in this book are only the most established. Such places seldom have electricity, and the water supply may be poor, but there's often some means of cooking your own food. These places almost never have telephones, but it's usually possible to announce your arrival by calling the local government or provincial office and asking them to convey the message. Bookings are not essential, however, and it's almost always possible to arrange something upon arrival with the help of the Vanair agent or otherwise.

Outer island guesthouses belonging to the Vanuatu Island Bungalow Association are used for packages organized by **Island Safaris** (Box 189, Port Vila; tel./fax 23288). These are excellent if you want to get to some really remote areas on a short trip and aren't too worried about the price. To protect their commissions, Island Safaris requires all guesthouses working with them to price their accommodations, meals, and activities at Australian levels, and persons not on their tours must pay the same inflated prices. Thus before heading for any place listed in the Island Safaris brochure, it's important to check the rates carefully, in order to avoid getting a severe shock. See their internet website, www.islandsvanuatu.com, for details.

Camping is possible and safe elsewhere, but always get permission from the landowner or chief. Often people will invite you into their own homes if they think you're in a jam, and in such cases it doesn't hurt to offer payment (gifts or money). Always give back as much as you receive, be considerate and polite, and make sure you don't overstay your welcome.

Food

Lap lap is the national dish. Bananas and root vegetables such as yams, taro, and manioc are grated, then kneaded to a paste, to which coconut cream and aromatic leaves are added. Pork or seafood can be included. The mixture is then wrapped in the leaves of a plant resembling the banana tree and cooked using hot stones in an earth oven. The best *lap lap* is made in remote villages, though it's also sold at the Port Vila market. In the northern islands breadfruit is pounded in a wooden bowl to make a food called *nalot.*

Other local specialties include mangrove oysters (served cold) and freshwater prawns (steamed with young bamboo stalks and mayonnaise). If you see "poulet" on a restaurant menu, don't assume it's chicken, as the local deep-water red snapper also goes by that name. Sadly, coconut crab is featured on the menus of several Port Vila restaurants, with the result that the slow-growing creatures are rapidly becoming an endangered species.

Kava

Kava is consumed in many Pacific countries, but that of Vanuatu is the strongest, bearing little resemblance to weak Fijian kava. It's especially potent because the roots are not dried as they are in Fiji, but are diced while still green, then mashed and mixed with water (not strained as in Fiji). Prior to independence, kava drinking in the towns was discouraged by missionaries and government officials, but today it's become a cultural icon, the indigenous alternative to Western alcohol. Traditionally, kava is a ritual *kastom* drink, but in Port Vila it's now entirely social, with the many kava saloons called kava bars or *nakamals* doing brisk business from 1800 onward.

Genetic and chemical analysis has demonstrated that kava has been cultivated in northern Vanuatu for at least 3,000 years, and from here its use may have spread to other areas. Some 72 varieties of kava exist here—more than anywhere else in the Pacific—with Tanna and northern Pentecost especially famous for their kava.

Its medicinal use as a natural tranquilizer is well recognized by the European pharmacological industry.

Kava is narcotic, rather than alcoholic. One coconut shell of it is enough; after several shells you won't be able to lift your arms or walk, and your mouth will feel as if the dentist had just given you novocaine. Don't eat anything before drinking kava or mix alcohol with it. Although it looks and tastes like dishwater, kava is pure relaxation, leaves no hangover, and never prompts aggression (unlike beer). The mind remains clear, and there are no hallucinations. It's not exactly hygienic though, because in central and southern Vanuatu, children chew the roots (at least on the outer islands). Most urban *nakamals* now use meat grinders to crush the roots.

SERVICES AND INFORMATION

Visas and Officialdom

Most nationalities don't require a visa for a stay of one month or less, although onward tickets are required. The immigration officer may ask at which hotel you intend to stay, but just name any of those listed in this book. Three extensions, one month at a time, are possible. The only immigration offices are in Port Vila and Luganville. Elsewhere, take your passport to a police station; they'll send it to Port Vila for the extension. Visa extensions are free. It's possible to obtain a residence permit by investing more than US$50,000 in a local business. Ten years residency is required for naturalization.

Both Port Vila and Luganville are ports of entry for cruising yachts. There are heavy fines for calling at outer islands before checking in (especially Tanna), and special permission is required to call at an outer island after checking out. At Port Vila the protected anchorage behind Iririki Island is good but deep.

Doing research of any sort in Vanuatu involves getting clearance from the Vanuatu Cultural Center (Box 184, Port Vila; tel. 22129, fax 26590). One should take care not to appear to be conducting research in the social sciences, as this requires prior approval. Cinematographers and others doing documentaries also require advance approval from the Cultural Center.

Money

The vatu is the unit of currency in Vanuatu; US$1 = Vt124 approximately (the word *vatu* means "stone"). There are notes of 500, 1,000, and 5,000, coins of one, two, five, 10, 20, 50, and 100. Though linked to special drawing rights (SDR) in the International Monetary Fund, the vatu is not well known abroad and can be hard to get rid of, so change your excess into the currency of the next country on your itinerary. Inflation is low, but remember the 12.5% value-added tax, which is often added at the cash register or checkout counter.

The main banks serving Vanuatu are the ANZ Bank, the Bank of Hawaii, and the Westpac Bank, with main branches at Port Vila and Luganville. The National Bank of Vanuatu also has branches at Lakatoro (Malekula), Craig Cove (Ambrym), and Lenakel (Tanna), and although these do change traveler's checks, it's a good idea to make sure you have enough vatu to see you through before leaving for an outer island. Rates of exchange differ slightly from bank to bank, so check around before changing large amounts. At last report there was no American Express representative in Vanuatu, although the Westpac Bank gives cash advances on American Express, MasterCard, and Visa credit cards. The Bankcard popular in Australia and New Zealand cannot be used in Vanuatu. Some merchants add a four percent surcharge if you pay by credit card.

Vanuatu is an expensive country by South Pacific standards, with a cost of living noticeably higher than neighboring Fiji or Solomon Islands but about the same as New Caledonia. There aren't many ways to spend money out in the bush, but most of the facilities associated with modern life come dear. Custom fees are often collected to visit cultural sites in rural areas, like old burial places, dancing grounds, etc. The local chiefs often have little understanding of the value of money, and will often ask ridiculous sums, such as Vt1,000 pp to see a heap of stones or a few rotting *tamtams* (drums). Tanna is notorious for this. As in most of the Pacific, there's no tipping in Vanuatu.

Telecommunications

Main post offices sell telephone cards in denominations of 30 units (Vt560), 60 units (Vt1,120), 120 units (Vt2,240), and 150 units (Vt3,000). Card phones have been installed on many islands, and by using them for international calls you avoid three-minute minimum charges. To call abroad, dial the international code 00, the country code, the area code (if any), and the number. To get the local operator dial 90, directory assistance 91.

At last report there were 15 public card phones around Port Vila, and elsewhere on Efate there were public phones at Erakor, Eratap, Ifira, Mele, and Takara villages and on Emao Island. In Luganville there are eight card phones. Outer islands with card phones include Ambae (Nduindui, Walaha), Ambrym (Craig Cove), Maewo (Betarara, Marino), Malekula (Atchin, Lakatoro, Lamap, Maskelynes, Metenessel, Norsup, Unmet, Vao, and Walarano), Mere Lava, Mota Lava, Pentecost (Baravet, Lonorore, Pangi), Sola, and Tanna (Lenakel).

Although Telecom Vanuatu has managed to install these phones, they're incompetent when it comes to keeping their sales outlets supplied with cards. It can be almost impossible to buy telephone cards on the outer islands (even in places that have card telephones), and you can't even count on being able to pick up a card at Port Vila Airport. Thus it's important to be sure you always have a card with sufficient units to cover all potential calls for the next few days. Don't wait until the card is empty before trying to buy a new one or you could be caught out.

Domestic calls within Vanuatu are much cheaper weekdays 2000-0600, and all day on weekends and holidays. At this time you can call anywhere in the country at a rate of one unit (Vt19) for six minutes. For international calls, a slightly reduced rate is available on calls to Australia, Fiji, New Caledonia, New Zealand, and Solomon Islands only Mon.-Sat. 2000-0600, and all day Sunday and holidays. Calls to North America are Vt523 a minute at all times (Vt413 a minute to Europe). In general, Vanuatu's international telephone rates are the highest in the South Pacific, and you're better off waiting to call from Fiji or Solomon Islands.

Vanuatu's telephone code is 678.

Business Hours and Electricity

Business hours are weekdays 0730-1130 and 1400-1700, Saturday 0730-1130. Post offices are usually open 0730-1630. Banking hours are generally weekdays 0800-1500. Most bureaucratic offices (including post offices) are closed for lunch 1130-1330, although shops, banks, and travel agencies remain open all day. Large supermarkets stay open until 1900 weekdays, the Chinese stores until 2000 or later.

The electric voltage is 220-240 volts, 50 cycles, with two- or three-pronged plugs.

Media

For intriguing insights into the local scene be sure to pick up a copy of the *Trading Post* (Box 1292, Port Vila; tel. 23111, fax 24111, e-mail: tpost@vanuatu.com.vu), published on Wednesday and Saturday. You'll get a good mix of local, regional, and international news for your Vt100. Publisher Marc Neil-Jones isn't shy about reporting on official corruption, and the paper's vicissitudes are a weathervane of Vanuatu democracy. The same company also brings out the outstanding tourist magazine, *Hapi Tumas Long Vanuatu,* and the monthly Bislama newspaper, *Wantok.* All three are great fun to read.

The *Vanuatu Weekly* (Private Mail Bag 049, Port Vila; tel. 22999, fax 22026, e-mail: vbtcnews@vanuatu.com.vu) is published in Bislama, French, and English every Saturday by the government's Department of Media Services. Both the *Weekly* and Radio Vanuatu have long been subject to government interference as the party in power seeks to deny a platform to its opponents.

Television broadcasting began in 1991 with 50-50 programming in English and French. **Television Blong Vanuatu** (TBV) is on the air daily 1700-2200 (from 1345 on Saturday). The news is at 1900 weekdays.

Radio Vanuatu (Private Mail Bag 049, Port Vila; tel. 22999, fax 22026) broadcasts from Port Vila over 1125 kHz AM, and from Luganville over 1179 kHz AM. You can pick up the programs on shortwave anywhere in the country over 3945 MHz 0600-1000 and 1730-2115, and over 4960 MHz 1000-1730.

Radio Vanuatu rebroadcasts the Radio Australia news at 0700 daily, the Radio France International news at 0800 daily, the BBC news at 0900 weekdays, and the local news in English at 1215 and 1800 weekdays.

On Espiritu Santo and elsewhere in the north, you can also pick up Radio Happy Isles over shortwave 5020 MHz, and Radio Australia at 7240 and 11880 MHz.

Health

Vanuatu is in the Melanesian malaria belt, which continues up through the Solomon Islands into Papua New Guinea; there's none in New Caledonia or Fiji. In 1995 there were 8,332 reported cases of malaria in Vanuatu, a 47% increase over 1994. Although malaria is mostly a problem on the islands north of Port Vila during summer (Nov.-May), prophylactic pills should always be taken, as the disease has been reported everywhere year-round. Begin taking pills a week before you arrive and continue for four weeks after you leave.

Officially you're supposed to have a prescription to buy malaria pills in Vanuatu, but the pharmacies in Port Vila usually sell the pills to tourists without bothering about prescriptions. Chloroquine-resistant *Plasmodium falciparum* malaria accounts for 73% of infections here, so turn to **Health** in the Solomon Islands chapter introduction and follow that advice. The malarial mosquito here is the female *Anopheles farauti,* which feeds at night or on overcast days and rests outdoors. The use of an insecticide-impregnated mosquito net greatly reduces the chance of getting bitten.

Dengue fever and hepatitis B are also present in Vanuatu, so read about them in the main introduction. Recommended (but not compulsory) vaccinations are immune globulin or the Havrix vaccine (for viral hepatitis A), and the one against typhoid fever. All minor cuts should be treated seriously: a little iodine at the right time can save you a lot of trouble later. The tap water in Port Vila and Luganville is safe to drink, but elsewhere one should take precautions. Public hospitals exist at Port Vila (Efate), Lenakel (Tanna), Norsup (Malekula), Luganville (Espiritu Santo), Lolowai (Ambae), and Nduindui (Ambae).

TRANSPORTATION

Getting There

The country's flag carrier, **Air Vanuatu** (Box 148, Port Vila; tel. 23848, fax 26591), flies to Port Vila from Nouméa daily, from Sydney five times a week, from Nadi and Brisbane three times a week, from Auckland twice a week, and from Honiara weekly. One of the Sydney flights is extended to Melbourne. Qantas code shares with Air Vanuatu's Brisbane, Melbourne, and Sydney flights, allowing a variety of connections throughout Australia. In the U.S. you can obtain information about Air Vanuatu by calling 1-800/677-4277. All Air Vanuatu flights are nonsmoking.

The New Caledonian carrier **Aircalin** (tel. 22739) has a service from Nouméa twice a week. **Solomon Airlines** (tel. 23848) flies between Honiara and Port Vila once a week. **Air Pacific** (tel. 22836) also flies from Nadi to Port Vila twice a week, with connections to/from Tokyo. The most direct route from North America is on Air Pacific's nonstop Los Angeles-Nadi service, connecting in Fiji for Vanuatu.

Air New Zealand has a three-month Coral Experience fare from Los Angeles to Port Vila at US$1,108/1,398/1,648 low/shoulder/high season (US$200 cheaper from Honolulu). This applies if you depart on a Monday, Tuesday, or Wednesday, and pay 14 days in advance. For the low season fare, you must begin your journey between mid-April and August. You get a free stopover in Fiji, but there are penalties for reservation changes or cancellations.

Vanuatu is included in Air Pacific's 30-day Pacific Air Pass (US$462), providing easy access from Fiji, and in the Visit South Pacific Pass, which allows a variety of routings. Air Vanuatu's Paradise Pass is similar. These passes are described in the main introduction to this book, under **Getting Around.**

Getting Around

Government-owned **Vanair** (Private Mail Bag 069, Port Vila; tel. 22753, fax 23910) offers more than 150 weekly services to 29 airstrips on 18 islands, with four 20-passenger Twin Otters based at Port Vila and Espiritu Santo. You can fly from Port Vila to Espiritu Santo (Vt9,800) four times a day, once or twice daily via Norsup. Flights from Port Vila to Tanna (Vt8,700) run three times a day, via Ipota or Dillon's Bay once or twice weekly. Vanair also operates reduced Sunday service to Espiritu Santo, Norsup, and Tanna. Details of Vanair's many local services appear throughout this chapter.

In recent years, fares on Vanair (which has a monopoly on internal air service) have remained high, making getting around Vanuatu an expensive proposition. No stopovers are allowed—the fare from Port Vila to Espiritu Santo is Vt9,800 direct, or Vt11,600 with a stopover at Norsup on the way. A routing Vila-Walaha-Santo-Norsup-Craig Cove-Vila will be Vt26,700 in total. Roundtrip fares are double the one-way fare. A tax of Vt250 is added to each leg of your ticket (included in the ticket price). The 25% student discount is worth asking about. Because airfares are so high, the planes are seldom fully booked (except when a group of politicians decides to travel).

A **Discover Vanuatu Pass** is available in North America through Air Promotion Systems (tel. 1-800/677-4277, www.pacificislands.com). For US$249, the pass would cover a routing Port Vila-Espiritu Santo-Port Vila-Tanna-Port Vila, which only represents a 10% savings over regular airfare.

Reservation changes must be made one day in advance, and "no shows" forfeit the full value of their ticket. Reconfirm your onward reservations immediately *upon arrival* at an outer island. Sometimes a plane will be diverted to make an unscheduled stop at an airstrip along the way if there are passengers to pick up or drop off. This can also work in reverse: they may forget to pick you up even though you've booked. On some flights you may be allowed to sit up front with the pilot if you ask nicely, and perhaps even fly a more scenic route (such as over Ambrym's

volcano). You'll get some excellent views from these planes.

Although the baggage limit is 10 kilograms, they probably won't say anything if you're only a bit overweight. Just carry heavy items in your hand luggage. Excess luggage is around Vt100 a kilo. Folding kayaks up to four meters long can be carried on the Twin Otters.

Interisland boat travel is far less common and more difficult in Vanuatu than it is in Fiji or Solomon Islands. Taking a boat from Port Vila to Luganville isn't really for the transportation, as it's not that much cheaper than the plane and the journey takes three or four days on deck (no cabins available). It's only worth considering for the experience of the voyage itself, and you do get to see the coastlines of many remote islands at stops along the way. Some of the local trading boats are described under **Port Vila,** following. There are no set schedules and conditions are basic.

Fishing boats and outboards can be hired to take you between nearby islands north of Efate, but it's only cheaper than flying if there are two or three of you. To be really independent, take along a small folding sea kayak and see delightful islands, bays, lagoons, beaches, and reefs on your own. The west coasts are better sheltered from the southeast trades, but avoid the hurricane season. Between the islands are big rollers and strong currents, so don't risk going interisland this way.

Rental cars and taxis are only available on Efate and Espiritu Santo. These two and northeast Malekula also have minibus services with set fares. Elsewhere you can hitch rides in trucks, but traffic is sparse and you're expected to pay the driver.

Airport

Port Vila International Airport (VLI) is six km north of Port Vila. This wartime airstrip is popularly known as Bauerfield, for Lt. Col. Harold M. Bauer, USMC, who was shot down over Guadalcanal in 1942. Bauer himself supervised construction of the airstrip in just 30 days in May 1942. There are separate terminals for domestic and international flights. The new international terminal was built with Japanese aid money in 1991; the old international terminal is now the domestic terminal.

The airport bus costs Vt400 pp. Otherwise walk 100 meters to the exit where the main road leaves the airport parking lot and wait for a regular public bus, which will take you into town for Vt100. These buses aren't allowed to compete by picking up passengers right in front of the terminal, but there's no problem using them once you get past the taxis. Taxis cost anywhere from Vt1,000-1,500 for the trip into town, depending on the destination.

Avis, Budget, Discount, and Hertz all have rental car dropoff desks near the international check-in counters, but these are unstaffed unless prior arrangements have been made. The head office of Avis (tel. 22570) is right next to the international terminal and they're open 0730-1700 daily. Federal Express adjoins Avis.

The tourist information counter at the airport can give you a list of every hotel in Vanuatu with current prices, then you can use the pay telephone near the departure check-in counters to call them up to verify availability and rates. The National Bank has a window (tel. 22189) also near the check-in counters, which opens for all international flights. They change traveler's checks without commission at a good rate. There's a duty-free shop, but the goods are overpriced and the selection is poor. You'll find that the snack bar in the adjacent domestic terminal is much cheaper than the one opposite the international check-in counters.

A departure tax of Vt2,500 in local currency is payable on international flights, the highest airport tax in the South Pacific (wasn't this supposed to be a tax haven?). Children aged 11 and under are exempt from the airport tax, as are transit passengers who continue on a connecting flight within 24 hours (roundtrips to/from a single city excluded). On domestic flights the tax is Vt250 but you pay it when you buy your ticket.

EFATE

The South Pacific's most beautiful capital city, Port Vila, sits on the southwest side of 42-by-23-km Efate (Vate) Island, in the lower middle of the Vanuatu chain. Havannah Harbor, on the northwest side of the island, was the original European settlement, but in the late 1870s, drought and malaria forced the settlers to shift 31 km to the site of Port Vila. Plantations were created, and a few traders set up shop, but only after establishment of the Condominium in 1906 did a town form. Commercial activities occupied the waterfront; the colonial administration settled into the hills above. The town expanded quickly during WW II, and again during the New Caledonian nickel boom of the early 1970s as the French reinvested their profits. Today it's one of the fast growing cities in the South Pacific.

You can ride right around Efate on a variable, 132-km highway, passing lonely coastlines, little villages, war relics, and countless coconut trees. Vast plantations with herds of grazing Charolais cattle characterize much of Efate's coastal plain, while the interior of this 887-square-km island is impenetrable rainforest. Vanair flights depart Efate's Bauerfield for all parts of Vanuatu.

PORT VILA

Port Vila (pop. 35,000) is the commercial, administrative, touristic, and strategic heart of Vanuatu, the crossroads of the islands to the north and south. Aside from being the national capital, Port Vila is the headquarters of Shefa Province. A cosmopolitan, attractive town, with many yachts anchored in the harbor, Port Vila snuggles around a picturesque bay, well protected from the southeast trades by a jutting peninsula. A narrow neck of land separates the harbor from the plush resorts on L-shaped Erakor Lagoon.

This compact, modern city features excellent facilities, scenic beauty, and a relaxed atmosphere. Add the French *joie de vivre* that pervades the town to the varied shopping, easy transport, sophisticated inhabitants, and many things to see and do, and you'll have one of the most exciting cities in the Pacific. Settle in for a week till you get your bearings, just don't spend all your time here, as Tanna, Espiritu Santo, Ambrym, and the other islands also have much to offer.

Be aware too that Port Vila is small enough for a cruise-ship-load of tourists to have an overwhelming impact. Thus it's best to drop into South Pacific Shipping (tel. 22387) opposite the Waterfront Bar and Grill early in your stay to ascertain the dates of impending cruise ship dockings, then make a point of avoiding the Australian carnival hordes by being elsewhere those days. The National Tourism Office should also know when the next "love boat" is due in. Even if you don't mind crowds, it's still important to be forewarned of their arrival as all organized tour and sporting activities will be monopolized by boat passengers that day.

On the brighter side, visitors arriving from the South Pacific Bible Belt will be relieved to hear that the restaurants and shops of Port Vila are open on Sunday. Just keep in mind the peculiar hours kept by the local bureaucracy, who usually start work around 0730, then knock off for a long siesta 1130-1400. Attend to any official business first thing in the morning. To date, it has been quite safe to wander around Port Vila at night.

SIGHTS

The exhibition hall at the **French Embassy,** on Kumul Highway in the center of town, often presents informative temporary displays on local themes, and admission is free.

Across the side street from the embassy is **Pilioko House,** adorned with colorful reliefs by Aloi Pilioko, one of Vanuatu's best-known contemporary artists. Aloi is a Wallisian, and his Russian associate, Nicolai Michoutouchkine, has an exquisite dress shop (tel. 23367) in the building. Have a look upstairs at Nicolai's brilliant line of hand-printed clothing created in the Oceanic tradition of usable art. You'll often find him at work in his shop, and this could be your chance to obtain a garment custom designed by a world-renowned artist in the astrological

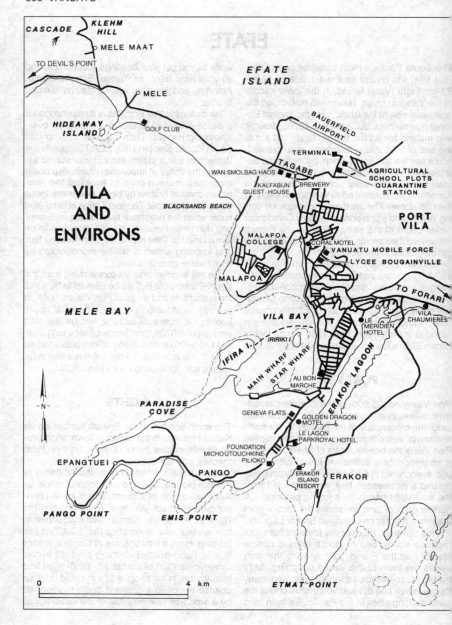

EFATE

CASCADE
KLEHM HILL
MELE MAAT
TO DEVIL'S POINT

EFATE ISLAND

MELE

HIDEAWAY ISLAND
GOLF CLUB

BAUERFIELD AIRPORT

TERMINAL

TAGABE

AGRICULTURAL SCHOOL PLOTS
QUARANTINE STATION

WAN SMOLBAG HAOS
KALFABUN GUEST HOUSE
BREWERY

VILA AND ENVIRONS

BLACKSANDS BEACH

PORT VILA

MALAPOA COLLEGE

CORAL MOTEL
VANUATU MOBILE FORCE
LYCEE BOUGAINVILLE

MALAPOA

MELE BAY

VILA BAY

TO FORARI

VILA CHAUMIERES

LE MERIDIEN HOTEL

IFIRA I.

IRIRIKI I.

MAIN WHARF
STAR WHARF

ERAKOR LAGOON

PARADISE COVE

AU BON MARCHE

GENEVA FLATS

GOLDEN DRAGON MOTEL
LE LAGON PARKROYAL HOTEL

FOUNDATION MICHOUTOUCHKINE-PILIOKO

EPANGTUEI

PANGO

ERAKOR ISLAND RESORT

ERAKOR

PANGO POINT

EMIS POINT

0   4 km

ETMAT POINT

colors of your star sign. High up on the wall outside, above the shop's corner door, is a bronze plaque announcing that "on this spot was proclaimed the Anglo-French convention of October 20th, 1906."

The road beside Pilioko House leads up to the **French war memorial** (1914-1918), from which you'll get an excellent view of Port Vila and Vila Bay. The island you see nearest town is Iririki, once the British commissioner's residence and now a major resort. Farther out is Ifira Island, where the customary landowners of much of the Port Vila townsite live (the name Vila is a European corruption of Ifira). The **prime minister's office,** the large building with the Vanuatu flag on the same hill as the war memorial, is the former French Residency (no entry).

Up the hill from here is the colonial-style **Supreme Court,** called the Joint Court in the Condominium days. During WW II the building served as a U.S. military headquarters. Between the prime minister's office and the Supreme Court a road leads south and winds around to the right to the ruins of the onetime **palace of the French resident commissioner.** After independence the building served as the domicile of the president, until it was destroyed by Hurricane Uma in 1987. The view from the terrace is even better than the one from the war memorial.

Continue south on a rough track, and find your way around to the right and down to **Independence Park,** the former British Paddock. Overlooking the park is the **Ministry of Home Affairs,** the old British Residency. Under the Condominium, the British community lived in this vicinity, while the more numerous French were on the plateau behind the French Residency, and in a quarter northeast of the Catholic cathedral.

Back down on the main street are two more colorful murals by Aloi Pilioko, one on the front of the **post office,** the other facing the ANZ Bank on the wall of the building across the street. In 1994 a new covered **market** opened at the south end of the pleasant Sea Front Promenade. People from Erakor village sell their produce here on Monday and Tuesday, whereas villagers from north Efate dominate the market Wed.-Saturday. The small pavilion across the street from the market is the former House of Parliament with an attractive mural (1980) by students of the French *lycée.* Behind this is the **Constitution Building,** once the headquarters of the Condominium bureaucracy and still government offices.

A free ferry shuttles frequently from near the BP Wharf to **Iririki Island,** site of one of Port Vila's top tourist resorts. There's a footpath right around the island, and good snorkeling at Snorkeler's Cove on the opposite side of Iririki from town (bring reef shoes if you have them). Where else can you go snorkeling in the main harbor of a country's capital? Many lovely trees grow on Iririki, and it's definitely worth a visit.

South of Town

From both the Iririki and Ifira boats, you can see the large, red-roofed **Parliament building,** erected with Chinese aid in 1992, overlooking the harbor to the south. There's an interesting socialist-style monument in front of the main entrance to Parliament.

Across the field opposite the monument is the **National Cultural Center Museum** (Box 184, Port Vila; tel. 22129, fax 26590), which opened in 1995. The previous museum in the city center was destroyed by a hurricane in 1993, and the roof of this splendid new building is securely attached! This is one of the finest museums in the South Pacific, with a rich collection of archaeological and ethnographic artifacts, musical instruments, weapons, seashells, and flora and fauna specimens. Of particular interest are the ritual objects from Malekula, and the slit gongs and fern carvings of Ambrym, which you can study here at your leisure. It's not to be missed. The museum is also an excellent place to pick up quality T-shirts, posters, books, cassettes, compact discs, and video cassettes. It's open weekdays 0900-1630, Saturday 0900-1200, admission Vt500.

Right next to the museum is the **Chief's National Nakamal,** a traditional-style building where traditional marriages are celebrated and meetings held. An impressive totem-pole slit gong from Ambrym, bearing five faces, stands before the building.

The beauty spot of Port Vila is undoubtedly the Erakor Lagoon. Take any southbound bus to the Erakor Island landing next to Le Lagon Hotel, then catch the free ferry (24-hour service) across to **Erakor Island,** a good place for an afternoon of lounging, sunbathing, swimming, and snorkeling on their white-sand beach. You're not al-

ALOI PILIOKO

lowed to bring your own food or drinks for a picnic, but lunch at the resort is reasonable (Vt850 and up). Until a cyclone in 1959, Erakor village (now on the lagoon's east side) was on this island. Samoan teachers from the London Missionary Society arrived here as early as 1845, and after 1872, Presbyterian missionaries Rev. and Mrs. J.W. Mackenzie were based on Erakor. The tombstones of Mrs. Mackenzie, three of her children, and some early Polynesian missionaries can still be seen on the island.

When you return to the mainland, wait at the landing for a city minibus to arrive, then ask the driver to take you to the **Foundation Nicolai Michoutouchkine et Aloi Pilioko** (Box 224, Port Vila; tel. 23053, fax 24224), just under two km southwest of here. This trip should cost no more than Vt100 pp. These well-known artists, whose work we saw in the city center earlier, have studios on the grounds, and the foundation's art gallery (open daily 0900-1700, admission free) contains many tastefully arrayed South Pacific artifacts and works of art. Don't miss this.

University Complex
The Emalus Campus of the **University of the South Pacific** (Box 12, Port Vila; tel. 22748, fax 22633), east of downtown at the beginning of the Forari highway, was erected with New Zealand aid in 1989 to house the USP's Pacific Languages Unit and Law Department. The Pacific Languages Unit was established in 1984 to elevate the status of the Pacific vernaculars and protect them from foreign influence. In 1996, the Emalus Campus Library (weekdays 0800-1130 and 1330-1700) opened at the rear of a central courtyard adorned with slit gongs from Ambrym and other artworks. Outstanding, inexpensive books on the Pacific written by the island people themselves are sold in the university bookshop (weekdays 0730-1130 and 1330-1630). If you're academically inclined, the campus is worth a visit, and any city minibus will bring you directly here for Vt100.

SPORTS AND RECREATION

Port Vila's most experienced scuba operator is **Nautilus Scuba** (Box 78, Port Vila; tel. 22398, fax 25255), next to the Waterfront Bar and Grill. They offer morning and afternoon scuba trips at Vt3,500 without gear (reductions on six- and 10-dive packages available). Snorkelers are welcome to go along for Vt1,000 (bring your own mask and snorkel). This professional diving center offers complete PADI open-water certification courses for Vt25,000 including all equipment. Scuba gear can be purchased here.

Pro Dive Vila (Box 230, Port Vila; tel. 23388, fax 23880), at the Iririki Island Resort, offers scuba diving at Vt3,500 a dive, plus Vt1,000 for gear hire. A 10-dive package will bring the per dive cost down to Vt2,500. Their PADI certification course is Vt30,000, or do an introductory resort dive for Vt5,000 (no experience necessary). Sailboats, jet skis, and other nautical gear can be hired, and even parasailing is offered. Look for them at the water sports hut, to the left along the beach as you get off the Iririki Island ferry. A late report indicates that Pro Dive Vila has changed hands, so some of the information above may also have changed.

The **Hideaway Island Dive Shop** (tel. 26660) charges Vt3,500 for one dive, plus Vt1,000 for equipment. PADI certification courses are Vt25,000.

Game fishing charters are offered on several powerboats based at the Waterfront Bar and Grill

These operators know their waters, and the catches are impressive (retained by the captain).

The **Club Hippique** (Box 1206, Port Vila; tel. 23347), seven km east of Port Vila, offers horseback riding at 0900 and 1500 daily expect Monday morning (Vt5,000 for 2.5 hours). The Adventure Center (tel. 22743), at the Hotel Olympic, runs half-day riding tours at Vt3,500 pp.

The 18-hole championship golf course at the **White Sands Country Club** (Box 906, Port Vila; tel./fax 22090), 18 km east of Port Vila, is the venue of the Vanuatu Golf Open in July or August. Greens fees are Vt2,500/5,000 for nine/18 holes, plus Vt700 for a half set of clubs. Call them up for information on their shuttle bus, which leaves Port Vila's post office daily at 0900, 1130, and 1530 (call to check the times).

The 18-hole **Port Vila Golf and Country Club** (Box 358, Port Vila; tel. 22564) at Mele is less expensive at Vt1,750 greens fees, plus Vt700 for clubs and a buggy. It's open daily. Both Le Méridien Resort and Le Lagon Hotel have smaller golf courses for guests.

See soccer from the bleachers at the municipal stadium every Saturday afternoon. Cricket is played in Independence Park on Saturday.

ACCOMMODATIONS

Shoestring
Ai Melmelo Guesthouse (Box 1622, Port Vila; tel. 27038) is about the cheapest place in town, with three rooms at Vt1,500 for singles or couples. There's a shared kitchen, and it's in a friendly local neighborhood. The trouble is actually finding the place: from the Mazda dealership next to Club Imperial, go north on the secondary paved road, then left on a coral road and start asking.

Budget
The longtime favorite of backpackers and budget travelers is **Kalfabun Guest House and Bungalows** (Box 494, Port Vila; tel./fax 24484), on the main road into town, two km from the airport. Bob Kalfabun and family have two dormitory rooms with four bunks each at Vt1,000 pp. The two three-room houses and four individual bungalows are Vt1,500/2,500 single/double (Vt200 surcharge if you stay only one night). You must pay cash in advance and keep your account paid up, but if you pay seven consecutive nights in advance, the eighth is free. Camping is half price, but they only allow it when all of the rooms are occupied. Facilities include a communal kitchen and fridge, TV lounge, and luggage storage room. Au Bon Marché Supermarket is just a five-minute walk away. Bob offers guests a tour around the island at Vt2,000 pp, and a Melanesian feast at Vt1,500. There's a lot of traffic noise, but it's still by far the most popular place in town.

Also good is the **VNCW Guest House** (Box 975, Port Vila; tel. 26964, fax 27210), up the hill from the Harbor View Chinese Restaurant, a 15-minute walk north of town. The seven rooms with shared bath and cooking facilities are Vt1,500/2,000 single/double. Otherwise you can also camp in their large yard at Vt500 pp (own tent), but in that case you're not supposed to use the guesthouse kitchen and lounge. Several kava *nakamals* are nearby. It's a friendly, safe place to stay, and all income goes to support the activities of the Vanuatu National Council of Women.

The **Emman and Imalo Motel** (Box 736, Port Vila; tel. 23927, fax 27345) overlooks the Municipal Stadium just north of town. A room in one of the three three- or four-room apartments with lounge and cooking costs Vt2,000 double. It's a chance to get to know the locals. Downstairs are two self-catering studios suitable for up to three people at Vt4,500/35,000 a day/month (you must buy your own cooking gas). Information is available at the house across the street.

Controversial political player Barak Sope owns the three-story **Talimoru Hotel** (Box 110, Port Vila; tel. 23740, fax 25369), on Cornwell St., Seaside. The 42 small, fan-cooled rooms (18 singles and 24 doubles) are Vt2,585/3,685 single/double without balcony, Vt2,750/3,850 with balcony. The toilet and shower are down the hall, but they're kept very clean, with hibiscus flowers decorating the washbasins. Aside from the restaurant and bar, the Talimoru has Port Vila's only hotel *nakamal* (kava bar) right on the premises, and poker machines are off the lobby.

Several of the missions in Port Vila provide accommodations. **Sutherland House,** on Gloucester St. opposite Vila East Primary School near the hospital, offers six rooms (and cooking facilities) at Vt2,000/3,800 single/double. Check in at the

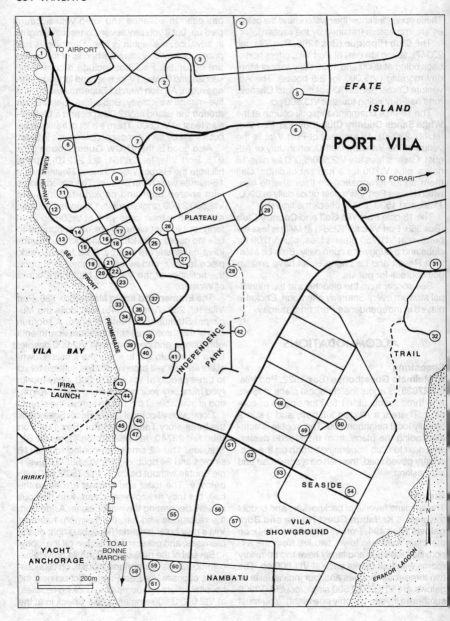

PORT VILA

1. Connie's Art Blong Yumi
2. Municipal Stadium
3. Emman and Imalo Motel
4. Vietnamese Cemetery
5. Ai Melmelo Guest House
6. Club Imperial
7. Georges Pompidou Building/Survey Dept.
8. Shefa Guest House
9. Tafea Guest House
10. Catholic Cathedral
11. Radio Vanuatu
12. The Office Pub
13. Rossi Restaurant
14. Hotel Olympic
15. Cultural Center Library
16. Natapoa Takeaway/Le Safari Club
17. British/Australian high commissions
18. Chinatown
19. Stop Press/New Zealand High Commission
20. Immigration Office/Bank of Hawaii
21. French Embassy
22. Pilioko House
23. Center Point Supermarket
24. Police Station
25. Town Hall
26. French War Memorial
27. Prime Oinister's office
28. ex-French Resident Commissioner's Residence
29. Supreme Court
30. University of the South Pacific
31. Holiday Motel
32. Le Meridien Hotel
33. Le Flamingo Night Club
34. ANZ Bank/Westpac Bank
35. Lolam House/Vanair
36. Post Office
37. Club Vanuatu
38. Frank King Tours
39. Market
40. Constitution Building
41. Presbyterian Church Office
42. Ministry of Home Affairs
43. BP Wharf
44. Iririki Ferry Wharf
45. Waterfront Bar and Grill/Nautilus Scuba
46. South Pacific Shipping
47. Marina Motel
48. Sutherland House
49. Sarabetu Transit House
50. Central Hospital
51. BP Service Station (taxi stand)
52. Ah Tong Motel
53. Talimoru Hotel
54. Red Laet Nakamal
55. Parliament
56. National Cultural Center Museum
57. Chiefs National Nakamal
58. The Galley Bar/Bistro
59. Cine Hickson
60. Melanesian Hotel
61. Kaiviti Village Motel

Presbyterian Church office (Box 150, Port Vila; tel. 22722) on Independence Park, weekdays 0800-1130 and 1330-1600. At other times go directly to the house.

The two-room Church of Christ **Sarabetu Transit House** (Box 638, Port Vila; tel. 22469), closer to the hospital, is Vt1,500 per person, and communal cooking facilities are provided.

For long-term rentals of houses and apartments, check the notices in the windows at Au Bon Marché and Center Point, and the classified ads in *The Trading Post*. Also inquire at **Alliance Reality** (tel. 26600, fax 24683) in Pilioko House. A furnished one-bedroom apartment could run Vt50,000 a month.

Inexpensive

The three-story **Coral Motel & Holiday Units** (Box 1054, Port Vila; tel./fax 23569) is at the head of Vila Bay on the main road between the airport and Port Vila. The 10 modern studios with cooking facilities and TV are Vt6,500/7,000 single/double, plus Vt500 extra for a third person, plus tax. Weekly and monthly rates are available, and bus service to town is good.

Pacific Adventures Guest House (Box 816, Port Vila; tel. 24601, fax 22577), above the Trading Post office on Kumul Highway just north of town, has four rooms with shared cooking and bathing facilities at Vt4,600 single or double.

Just south of downtown Port Vila opposite Nautilus Scuba is the **Marina Motel** (Box 681, Port Vila; tel./fax 22566). The 10 a/c apartments in the main two-story building are Vt5,000/5,500/6,000 single/double/triple with fan (Vt1,000 extra to use the a/c). Fridge and cooking facilities are in each room, and there's a swimming pool (usually empty). It's all a bit rundown.

The **Golden Dragon Motel** (Box 299, Port Vila; tel. 23933, fax 23932), in an L-shaped block on the hill just above Le Lagon Hotel, has 10 self-catering a/c rooms for up to three persons at

Vt5,000 a night or Vt20,000 a week. A large grocery store and Chinese restaurant on the premises. It's reasonable value, but they're often full.

The **Holiday Motel** (Box 277, Port Vila; tel./fax 23088), across the street from Le Méridien Resort, has 12 new self-catering apartments in three blocks. The three studios are Vt5,500, the six one-bedrooms Vt6,500, and the three two-bedrooms Vt7,500. You can get a 10% discount if you pay by the week.

Moderate

The three-story **Hotel Olympic** (Box 230, Port Vila; tel. 22464, fax 22953), also known as Iririki Centre Ville, is the only hotel in downtown Port Vila. The 21 a/c rooms with fridge are Vt7,920 single or double, while self-contained apartments are Vt11,000. The Olympic caters to business-people by providing direct-dial telephones, telex, and secretarial services.

The three-story **Kaiviti Village Motel** (Box 152, Port Vila; tel. 24684, fax 24685), next to the Melanesian Hotel, has nine two-bedroom apartments and 28 studio apartments with cooking facilities at Vt7,950 single or double, Vt11,500 for four people, Vt12,500 for five, Vt13,500 for six. Only the downstairs units have a/c, but those upstairs have balconies, and all have kitchens. Avoid the top floor as the rooms aren't as well maintained as those on the middle floor. This easy going motel also features a swimming pool, bar, and laundry facilities, and Au Bon Marché Supermarket is conveniently nearby.

Pacific Lagoon Apartments (Box 920, Port Vila; tel. 23425, fax 24377) faces the Erakor Lagoon, a few hundred meters southwest of Le Lagon Hotel toward Pango. The 10 two-bedroom units with fan and a fully equipped kitchen vary in price from Vt9,500-12,500 for up to four persons, depending on the location of the apartment.

Hideaway Island Resort (Box 1110, Port Vila; tel. 22963, fax 23867), on Mele Island, nine km northwest of Port Vila, is promoted as a scuba camp for packaged-tour Australians. The five bungalows are Vt7,900/11,000 single/double, the six double rooms with shared bath in a two-story building near the dive shop on the beach are Vt4,900/6,200, while a dormitory with six four-bunk rooms behind the restaurant is Vt2,000 pp (couples aren't allowed to stay in the dorm).

Hot water is available in the common shower block. The five bungalows are nicely secluded at the far end of the island, but a bit too close to the generator. Cooking facilities are not provided in any of the accommodations, so you must use their efficient restaurant. Airport transfers are Vt800 pp return. This tiny coral island can get crowded on weekends, and on cruise ship days it's literally flooded with day-trippers.

Expensive

The three-story **Melanesian Hotel** (Box 810, Port Vila; tel. 22150, fax 22678), formerly called the Windsor International, combines a resort atmosphere (swimming pool) with businesslike convenience to Port Vila. The 20 studios are Vt11,000 single or double, while the 11 one-bedroom suites are Vt12,600 single or double. There are also two two-bedroom apartments with washing machines at Vt16,600. All of the older fan-cooled rooms in the two-story blocks have kitchens, but the 54 a/c "orchid suites" in the new three-story blocks (Vt13,700 single or double) lack cooking facilities. All units have fridge, fan, and private bath. These prices are based on a minimum two-night stay (Vt1,650 surcharge for one-night stays), and the rates include a continental breakfast. Custom dancing and kava tasting by the swimming pool are Wednesday and Sunday at 1800.

Erakor Island Resort (Box 24, Port Vila; tel. 26983, fax 22983) has a better beach than Le Lagon Hotel just across the water, and is less expensive and more relaxed. The nine well-appointed, fan-cooled bungalows on a long sandy lagoon island are Vt12,000 single or double, Vt13,000 triple. In addition, there are four two-story bungalows accommodating up to five persons for a flat Vt15,400. No cooking facilities are provided, so you must eat at their restaurant. The bungalows are well away from the public beach in front of the restaurant, so resort guests aren't bothered by day-trippers. Access to Port Vila is quick and easy via their free ferry and public buses.

Luxury

Iririki Island Resort (Box 230, Port Vila; tel. 23388, fax 23880), on an island in Vila Bay directly opposite downtown Port Vila, opened in 1986. The 70 a/c bungalows are priced according to whether they face the garden (Vt16,800 single or double), or are right down on the water (Vt32,800). Rooms facing the harbor from above are Vt23,600, plus tax, buffet breakfast included. Each has one queen-size and one single bed, fridge, video, and furnished balcony. Included in the complex are an open-plan restaurant with an elevated terrace overlooking the pool and harbor. There's a one-for-one paperback exchange in the lobby. Nonmotorized water sports are free, but the beach isn't as good as those on the Erakor Lagoon. The snorkeling, on the other hand, is better. A convenient free ferry to town operates round-the-clock.

Le Lagon Parkroyal Hotel (Box 86, Port Vila; tel. 22313, fax 23817) is near the mouth of the Erakor Lagoon, three km from Port Vila. Aside from 109 a/c hotel rooms (from Vt17,650 single or double, plus tax) in seven two-story buildings, Le Lagon has 27 bungalows (from Vt24,850). All rooms are fridge-equipped, and a few have a jacuzzi (ask). As usual, a lagoon view costs more than a garden view. Le Lagon has a swimming pool, tennis courts, a 12-hole golf course, and nautical activities. Rebuilt in concrete after a hurricane in 1987, Japanese-run Le Lagon lacks some of the character of its competitors.

High-rise **Le Méridien Resort** (Box 215, Port Vila; tel. 22040, fax 23340), at the north end of the Erakor Lagoon, is a former Radisson Resort, and before that an Intercontinental Hotel, originally built in the 1960s. The waters here aren't as clear as those at Le Lagon, and Iririki Island is more convenient to town, but backed by rainforest, surrounded by gardens, and facing a bright, sandy beach, Le Méridien is still a pleasant place to stay. The 150 a/c rooms (most with balcony) begin at Vt21,250 single or double, plus tax; the 10 overwater bungalows on an island accessible from the main resort by suspension bridge are Vt46,750 (not worth it). Most guests are on package tours and pay prices much lower than these. Vanuatu's only genuine gambling casino is at this hotel, and there's a nine-hole golf course. Nonmotorized sporting activities such as windsurfing, snorkeling, surf skiing, catamaran boating, row boating, outrigger canoeing, golf, and tennis are free to guests, but nautical gear must stay within sight of the hotel. Nicolai Michoutouchkine stages a fashion show at Le Méridien every Wednesday at 1900.

FOOD

Budget Places to Eat

The 12.5% value-added tax only applies to licensed restaurants serving alcoholic beverages, so you'll save money twice over by dining at one of the gastronomical tax havens mentioned below. For example, **Olympic Takeaway** (tel. 27355), between Goodies and the Olympic Hotel, has inexpensive hamburgers and fish and chips (El Gecko Restaurant in the courtyard behind is much more upscale).

Better is **Natapoa Takeaway and Snack** (tel. 26377) on rue de Paris in Chinatown, inland a block from Goodies. A heaping plate of curry chicken and rice is Vt300, with free cold water to wash it down. Most of the dishes are based on chicken or beef, but a surprising variety of vegetables comes with the meals. It's open for lunch and dinner daily except Sunday.

The **Gone Bananas Cafe,** at the back of the Center Point parking lot, has meat and rice dishes for Vt300. **Jill's Cafe** (tel. 25125), opposite Air Vanuatu, serves American-style country breakfasts, burgers, hot dogs, sandwiches, chili, and ice cream. Also try **Cheng's Chinese Snacks** (tel. 24374), across the street and up the hill by the post office. The meals in the glass-covered warmers behind the counter to your left are less than Vt300, and you can eat on their outdoor terrace.

Another place to get an inexpensive breakfast or lunch is the self-service cafeteria in **Au Bon Marché Supermarket** (tel. 22945; daily 0630-1930), on the main road just south of town. Away from meal times, it's a cool, relaxed spot to sit and write postcards over a Vt70 cup of coffee.

Nearly all of the Chinese restaurants around Port Vila also have takeaways—a good way of saving money if you can get the food back to your room or to a picnic spot before it gets cold. The **Man Wah Restaurant** (tel. 23091), behind the Melanesian Hotel is the best of these. They're open for lunch Tues.-Sat. 1030-1330, daily from 1930 for dinner. Takeaways are also sold at the **Golden Dragon Restaurant** (tel. 23933), just above Le Lagon Hotel.

Upmarket Restaurants

The classy **Rossi Restaurant** (tel. 22528), in the center of town, has a garden terrace overlooking the harbor, great for a leisurely lunch. If you come for dinner, don't arrive too late and miss the sunset. It's also a fine place to stop for a morning or afternoon coffee, and a selection of newspapers is available for free reading. The cakes and pies are impressive.

Ma Barker's (tel. 22399) in the center of town is very touristy, but okay if you're dying for an Aussie-style steak. The thatched **Waterfront Bar and Grill** (tel. 23490; closed Sunday), south of the center, serves better steaks (local beef) and seafood, and has a salad bar and coconut pie (lunch specials Vt650). The bar here is a yachtie hangout.

Going upmarket, try **The Galley Bar & Bistro** (tel. 23045; weekdays from 1600 until late, weekends from 1100), opposite Cine Hickson. They offer Mexican dishes like burritos, enchiladas, fajitas, nachos, and tacos in the Vt950-1,550 range, steaks from Vt1,500 to 1,900, and a wide range of seafoods from grilled fish (Vt1,400) to lobster (Vt2,800) and mud crab (Vt3,000). The sunset views over the yacht anchorage and Iririki Island are superb.

L'Houstalet (tel. 22303; daily 1100-1300/1800-2230), just past Au Bon Marché Supermarket and on the opposite side of the road, offers 16 varieties of crisp oven-baked pizza, which are also available takeaway. The mindset of the French owner (and some of his customers) is indicated by the list of endangered species on L'Houstalet's regular menu.

Chez Gilles et Brigitte (tel. 26000; closed at lunch on Saturday and all day Sunday), next to beach at the Foundation Michoutouchkine-Pilioko on the way to Pango, features fine French cuisine with a choice of sauces and salads. To have lunch or dinner is this unique artistic environment next to the sea is something special, but call ahead.

Vila Chaumières (tel. 22866; Mon.-Sat. 1130-1400 and 1800-2300), east of town, serves a variety of seafoods on a terrace overlooking the lagoon. At lunchtime the city buses will drop you here, but for dinner you'll probably have to call a taxi to get home (unless you have a car).

Several of the large hotels have Sunday specials. The poolside barbecue buffet at **Iririki Island Resort** (tel. 23388), Sunday at 1300, is good value at Vt1,200, plus tax. Sunday brunch (1130-1400) at La Verandah Restaurant at **Le Méridien Resort** (tel. 22040) includes bottomless Champagne for Vt2,000, plus tax.

Cafes

La Terrasse (tel. 22428), across the street from the French Embassy in the center of town, is Port Vila's classic French cafe. Saturday nights there's a special party with tango and rumba dancing.

Le Café du Village (tel. 27789), a bit south of BP Wharf, has a smart harborfront location opposite Iririki Island. They feature an upscale seafood menu and keg beer.

Groceries

Port Vila's picturesque **market** operates Mon.-Sat. (including all night Friday in anticipation of the large Saturday market). In addition to fresh fruit and vegetables, a few handicrafts are sold. No one will hassle you to buy anything, so look around as you please, just don't bargain—the prices are low enough to begin with. The **Fis Market** (tel. 23344; Mon.-Thurs. 1000-2200, Friday 1000-2300, Saturday 0900-2000), on the south side of the vegetable market, sells very good takeaway packets of fish and rice at the right price.

For other groceries try the large supermarkets, Center Point and Au Bon Marché. **Center Point** (tel. 22631; daily 0700-1930) is especially well stocked, and has a good grocery section with fresh croissants and *pain au chocolat*. Tasty ice cream is dispensed from a cart in front of Center Point. The stores in Chinatown sometimes have cheaper canned goods.

Ah Pow Bakery (tel. 22215), on Dauphine St. just behind Houstalet Restaurant near Au Bon Marché, sells croissants and other pastries (this bakery delivers bread all around Efate every night). French baguettes are a great buy at Vt45.

Be aware that the supermarkets are not allowed to sell beer or alcohol after 1130 on Saturday and all day Sunday.

ENTERTAINMENT

Cine Hickson (tel. 22431) shows Hollywood films dubbed into French nightly except Thursday at 2000 (admission Vt400).

Cinema Studio 7 (tel. 27532), at Club Vanuatu, screens films in English at 1130, 1330, 1900, and 2100 Tuesday to Sunday (admission Vt300).

Le Flamingo Night Club (tel. 25788), opposite Center Point Market Place near the post office, is a video disco open Tues.-Sat. 2100-0500. Foreign visitors can sometimes escape the Vt500 cover charge by showing their hotel's business card or room key. Every Saturday afternoon 1400-1630 Le Flamingo has a "blue light" disco for kids under 18 (no smoking or alcohol, but unlimited soft drinks for the Vt600 admission). Dress regulations apply.

The sign outside **Cabaret Le Safari Club** (tel. 26664; Mon.-Sat. 2000-0300), on rue de Paris in Chinatown, says Strictly Members Only, but properly dressed tourists are quickly admitted. The Vt1,000 admission includes one drink.

Trader Vic's (tel. 27704), on Kumul Highway at the north end of town, is a onetime Italian restaurant that now functions as a disco open nightly except Sunday (admission Vt300).

Club Imperial (tel. 26541), next to the Mazda dealership up toward the university, is more of a local place, and on Friday and Saturday nights it really gets lively.

L'Houstalet Restaurant (tel. 22303), previously mentioned, functions as a nightclub Wed.-Sat. after 2230, and on Friday and Saturday nights it's packed. There's a Vt400 cover charge, but you only have to pay it on weekends. It's a good place to mix with francophone locals.

The **Palms Casino** (Box 1111, Port Vila; tel. 24308, fax 22394) at Le Méridien Resort features blackjack, baccarat, roulette, and slots. It's open daily from 1200 until the last customer leaves (admission free). Unfortunately many ni-Vanuatu are addicted to the gambling machines, both here and at Club Vanuatu and the Talimoru and Melanesian Hotels, and entire weekly pay packets are often swallowed by the monsters, leading to real hardship for local families. Several important members of parliament are casino shareholders, which is why this dirty business is allowed.

Bars

Club Vanuatu (tel. 22615), next to the Unelco electric generating plant on the back street behind the post office, is a private club but tourists are welcome (persons without shoes or a shirt are not admitted). The bistro facing the bar serves reasonably priced hot meals catered by the Rossi Restaurant, and the club's other facilities include a movie room, lending library, snooker, billiards, darts, bingo, slot machines, and a bar with Tusker on tap at Vt200 a glass. Watch CNN on a huge screen. They're open Mon.-Thurs. 1100-2200, Friday and Saturday 1100-0200, Sunday 1100-2100. Reynolds Herena's hot local reggae band Vatdoro often plays at the Club's Friday and Saturday night dances (Vt300 cover).

The Office Pub (tel. 24808; daily 1000 to late), on Kumul Highway just north of the center, is an unpretentious Australian-style place. The food menu is medium-priced, Tusker is on tap, and the Sunday roast at 1800 features a choice of meats from Vt1,000.

Tusker beer also on tap at the **Sunset Bar** (tel. 22150) at Club 21 Gaming Lounge, next to Cine Hickson.

Kava *Nakamals*

Around sunset the local expat community gathers for happy hour at the **Red Laet** (tel. 27048), near the Talimoru Hotel, one of around a hundred *nakamals* or kava bars in Port Vila serving that strong Vanuatu kava at Vt50-100 a shell. Another place to try kava any evening is the Chiefs National Nakamal. Most of the *nakamals* have a regular clientele from a particular outer island, and they function as social clubs. You'll be welcome if you enter with respect, keep your voice down, and don't make any abrupt movements (you might disturb someone "listening" to the kava). In the villages, local women aren't allowed to frequent the *nakamals,* but in Port Vila it's usually no problem. Kava drinkers are generally pretty mellow, but these are predominantly male enclaves. Locations change, so just ask for a kava bar near your hotel.

Cultural Shows for Visitors

If you're at all interested in live theater, you won't want to miss a performance by the **Wan Smolbag Theater,** a local troupe that brings contemporary social issues to the stage with unexpected professionalism and talent. Founded in 1989 by an English couple, Peter Walker and Jo Dorras, Wan Smolbag's success has sparked an interest in didactic theater throughout the Pacific. It's a mix of historical skits, storytelling, custom dancing, kava sampling, etc. You're allowed to take photos of the performances freely, and during the intermission *lap lap* is served in the foyer for a nominal fee. The kava after the show is on the house. At last report performances were Thursday at 1900 in Wan Smolbag Haos, around the corner from Vanuatu Brewing at Tagabe, 50 meters up the road to Mele. Check posters around town for the current venue, or ask at the Adventure Center (tel. 22743) at the Olympic Hotel. The Adventure Center sells tickets (Vt800-1,000 pp), or you can buy one at the door. (If you're very lucky, you may encounter Wan Smolbag in some remote village staging a performance in Bislama with a theme such as "building your own toilet," "family planning," or "violence against women," courtesy of some overseas aid donor.)

Foot-stompin' **custom dancing** accompanies the weekly barbecues and feasts at the major hotels, usually on Tuesday at Iririki Island Resort (tel. 23388), on Thursday at Le Méridien Resort (tel. 22040), and on Wednesday and Saturday at Le Lagon Hotel (tel. 22313). Le Lagon also presents Tahitian dancing on Tuesday night, and Shepherd Islands dancing on Friday night. If you're not that hungry, a drink at the bar should get you in to any of these. Call ahead to verify the show times.

Village feasts are held at Mele, Pango, and Erakor villages several nights a week with string band music, custom dancing, kava drinking, and island food served buffet style. Admission including transportation is usually Vt2,500 for adults or Vt1,250 for children. **Solo's Feast** at Mele village is every Thursday night 1900-2200, and Frank King Tours (tel. 22808) takes bookings. Unlike the tourist shows mentioned above, attending one of these is sort of like being invited to a private village party.

SHOPPING

You can buy one of those colorful Mother Hubbard dresses at the Chinese stores on the street running inland from Ma Barker's. The **Center Point Market Place,** across the parking lot from Center Point Supermarket, also has authentic Mother Hubbards. These dresses are highly recommended for women thinking of visiting remote areas, and they make great party attire at home.

In quite another category are the designer clothes available at many smart boutiques around Port Vila, just beware of fake products bearing counterfeit brand names. Better yet, stick to the autographed apparel available at **Michoutouchkine Creations** (tel. 23367), in Pilioko House, previously mentioned.

Vila Duty Free Gifts (tel. 23443) opposite the post office has cheap postcards, film, T-shirts, and souvenirs. The **Philatelic Bureau** (tel. 22000), on the left inside the post office, has some very colorful stamps.

Port Vila is called a duty-free port because there's no tax on watches, radios, cameras, and jewelry sold in the country. The duty-free shop at the airport has no advantage over the stores in central Port Vila, and the selection is much poorer. There *is* duty on camera film, however.

Avoid buying anything on a cruise ship day, as some prices are jacked up 15%.

Handicrafts

A good place to pick up authentic crafts is the **Handikraf Blong Vanuatu** shop (Box 962, Port Vila; tel. 23228), a nonprofit outlet that opened in 1982 adjacent to Cultural Center Library in the center of town. They sell stone- and woodcarvings, fern figures, slit gongs both large and small, bowls, war clubs, pig killing clubs, spears, bows and arrows, fish traps, model canoes, canoe prows, masks, rattles, panpipes, combs, shell necklaces, grass skirts, shoulder bags, mats, native pottery, and curved boar tusks. The finest articles come from Ambrym. Also notice the Pentecost money mats with batik designs. The large iron anchor embedded in cement in the courtyard was recovered in 1958 from the *Astrolabe,* one of the ships of French explorer La Pérouse, lost at Vanikolo in the Solomons in 1788.

Goodies Treasure Chest (Box 932, Port Vila; tel. 23445), across the street from Handikraf Blong Vanuatu, also has an excellent selection of handicrafts, including items from the other Melanesian countries. It's a good place to shop for postcards and other souvenirs.

L'Atelier (tel. 23654), across the street from Le Flamingo Night Club, has some very authentic-looking Malekula helmet masks for sale to serious collectors.

Connie's Art Blong Yumi (Box 880, Port Vila; tel. 27830), at the entrance to town from the airport, has a large selection of woodcarvings. The bamboo flutes are a good buy here. Connie is a talented artist and does portraits on request.

Before buying, check all wooden artifacts for cleanliness and freedom from borer pests. The Department of Agriculture's Quarantine Station (tel. 23130; weekdays 0730-1130/1315-1630) near the airport fumigates plants and plant products (fern carvings, grass skirts, etc.), and issues a phytosanitary certificate (Vt400-800) for their export.

SERVICES

Money
The Westpac Bank and the ANZ Bank opposite Air Vanuatu, and the Bank of Hawaii nearby, change traveler's checks without commission. All banks close at 1500 weekdays and exchange rates vary—check around.

You can also change money or get cash advances at Goodies (tel. 23445; open Mon.-Sat. 0730-1700, Sunday 0830-1600), opposite the Cultural Center Library, and their rates are often better than the banks! The National Bank has an exchange office inside Handicraft Blong Vanuatu near Goodies, which is open weekdays 0800-1130/1330-1700.

Post and Telecommunications
The post office opens weekdays 0730-1130/1330-1630. Poste restante mail is held two months. Parcel postage in Vanuatu is very expensive, and it's much cheaper to wait and mail things from Fiji or Solomon Islands, if you're headed that way.

Place long-distance telephone calls and send faxes at Telecom Vanuatu (tel. 22185; weekdays 0700-1800, Saturday 0700-1200), adjacent to the main post office. At Vt200 per page, you can receive faxes addressed to the public fax 678-22910 at this office. Long distance calls can be made from any of the card telephones around town.

Immigration Office
The Immigration office (tel. 22354; fax 25492; weekdays 0730-1130/1330-1630), above the French Pharmacy in central Port Vila, gives free visa extensions (return air ticket required).

Consulates
The French Embassy (tel. 22353) is on Kumul Highway in the center of town. The New Zealand High Commission (tel. 22933) is in BDO House, across the street from the French Embassy. If you need a P.N.G. visa (Vt1,600), go to the honorary consul of Papua New Guinea (tel. 22439), upstairs in Bougainville House opposite Le Kiosque Bookstore.

The European Union office (tel. 22501) is in Moore Stephens House at the north end of town. The Chinese Embassy (tel. 23598) is south of town, up the street from Au Bon Marché Supermarket. Other countries with diplomatic missions in Port Vila include Australia (tel. 22777), Britain (tel. 23100), and Sweden (tel. 22944). Canada is represented by Australia, but the U.S. has no representation in Vanuatu.

Laundromats and Public Toilets
Pacific Wash and Dry (tel. 26416; Mon.-Sat. 0700-1800, Sunday 0730-1230), in the Ballande Center near BP Wharf, is a genuine coin-operated laundromat costing Vt300 to wash or dry.

EZY Wash (tel. 24386), below the Olympic Hotel, is another self-service laundromat open Mon.-Sat. 0730-1800, Sunday 0730-1300 (also Vt300 to wash or dry).

Public toilets are at the south end of the waterfront between the market and the ships tied up at BP Wharf. They're overpriced at Vt40 a squirt. Another Vt40 public toilet is toward The Office Pub, on the north side of town. Free public toilets are found in Anchor House, a bit south of town, diagonally opposite the Shell service station.

Yachting Facilities
Yachting World (tel. 23273, VHF channel 60), next to the Waterfront Bar and Grill, charges visiting yachts Vt5,000 a week for sea wall tie up with power and water, or Vt3,800 a week for the 10 harbor moorings. For duty-free fuel, request the white form from customs. When arriving, beware of overhead power lines to Iririki Island, which sag to 17 meters at high tide.

The Vanuatu Cruising Yacht Club (Box 525, Port Vila; tel. 24634, VHF channel 60), below South Pacific Travel next to the Waterfront Bar and Grill, offers a book swap, mail forwarding, local information, and cruising guides to Vanuatu. Visiting yachts that use the facilities are charged Vt1,000 per yacht for annual membership. They may also know about yacht charters out of Port Vila, but the club is only staffed during the yachting season (October is a good month to get on a yacht here as crew, since many boats will be leaving).

S.E.L.B. Pacific (Box 34, Port Vila; tel. 22810, fax 23433) has a 20-ton mobile crane, the only haul-out facility here. Slipways are available at Luganville.

Health

The Central Hospital (tel. 22100) accepts outpatient consultations weekdays 0700-1000 (Vt3,000 for tourists). On weekends and holidays only emergency cases are accepted. You can fill prescriptions at the hospital dispensary.

Actually, it's cheaper, faster, and more efficient to see a private doctor, such as Dr. Jean-Luc Bador (tel. 23065) opposite Le Kiosque Bookstore (consultations Vt2,800). Dr. Bador speaks good English and he's very helpful to travelers. His specialty is acupuncture.

Dr. Hervé Collard (tel. 22306) has a well-equipped private dental surgery practice upstairs in the Oceania Building on rue de Paris. There's also ESU Dental Surgery (tel. 26958; weekdays 0800-1130/1330-1630), in the Ballande Center.

The Drug Store (tel. 22789), opposite the Westpac Bank, opens weekdays 0730-1800, Saturday 0730-1200, Sunday 0830-1200. Malaria pills are cheaper in Solomon Islands.

INFORMATION

The friendly National Tourism Office (Box 209, Port Vila; tel. 22685, fax 23889, e-mail: tourism@vanuatu.com.vu; weekdays 0730-1130 and 1330-1630, Saturday 0800-1100), in the alley across the street from Club Vanuatu, supplies useful maps and information sheets. Ask for free copies of *Hapi Tumas Long Vanuatu* and *Destination Vanuatu.*

Also visit Frank King's Visitors Club (Box 635, Port Vila; tel. 22808, fax 22885), across from the market, to pick up their yellow-colored *Holiday Planner,* which provides information not found in the Tourism Office publications.

The Statistics Office (Private Mail Bag 019,

Port Vila; tel. 22110, fax 24583), behind the prime minister's office, sells informative reports on the economy. Ask for a copy of their free publication *Vanuatu Facts and Figures.*

The Lands Survey Department (Private Mail Bag 024, Port Vila; tel. 22427, fax 25973; weekdays 0730-1100 and 1315-1600), upstairs in the Georges Pompidou Building, sells excellent topographical maps of all the islands of Vanuatu at Vt600 each. The black-and-white maps were published in 1979 and don't show more recent roads, although new colored sheets exist for some islands. Local navigational charts are also sold here (Vt4,200).

Cultural Center Library (Box 184, Port Vila; tel. 22721, fax 26590; weekdays 0900-1800, Saturday 0800-1130), in the center of town, offers cards at Vt500, plus a refundable Vt1,000 deposit. You're allowed to take out three books at a time. The library building once housed Vanuatu's first parliament.

The **Alliance Française** (Box 219, Port Vila; tel. 22947, fax 26700), just behind the French Embassy but in the same compound, has a library (weekdays 0900-1130/1400-1800, Saturday 0900-1130) with the latest French newspapers and magazines. The Alliance offers French language courses with two two-hour classes a week, and organizes interesting activities, such as video nights (Thursday at 1930), concerts, exhibitions, dancing classes, and even group hikes.

Bookstores

Port Vila has several good bookstores. Stop Press (Box 557, Port Vila; tel. 22232, fax 26776), opposite the French Embassy, carries a variety of topographical maps of Vanuatu and a few books on the Pacific. Le Kiosque (Box 814, Port Vila; tel. 22044), on Bougainville St., sells a handy French-Bislama phrasebook called *Apprenons le Bichlamar* (Vt350). Chew Store (Box 89, Port Vila; tel. 22989, fax 24298), across the street from Le Kiosque, sells current Australian newspapers. Snoopy's Stationery (Box 357, Port Vila; tel. 22328, fax 24604), opposite the market, is also worth checking.

Airline Offices

Air Vanuatu (tel. 23848), next to the post office, also represents Qantas and Solomon Airlines. Aircalin (tel. 22895) is opposite Hotel Olympic.

Vanuatu Travel Service Ltd. (tel. 22836), in Anchor House just before the Waterfront Bar & Grill, south of the center, represents Air Pacific and Air Niugini. Surata Tamaso Travel (tel. 22666), in La Casa d'Andrea e Luciano on the north side of town, represents Air New Zealand, British Airways, and Cathay Pacific.

TRANSPORTATION

By Air

Vanair (tel. 22753) has southbound flights from Port Vila to Tanna (Vt8,700) three times a day, to Tanna via Dillon's Bay twice weekly, and to Tanna via Ipota and Aniwa weekly. Twice a week the Tanna flights continue to Aneityum and Futuna. Northbound there are four flights a day to Espiritu Santo (Vt9,800), at least one a day to Espiritu Santo via Norsup, and a few also via Lamap or Southwest Bay. Three times a week the Port Vila-Espiritu Santo service goes via Lonorore, Sara, Longana, and Walaha. Other routes from Port Vila are to Emae (Vt3,700), Tongoa (Vt4,800), Craig Cove (Vt6,700), and Ulei (Vt6,300), all two or three times a week. For more information on internal flights, see **Transportation** in the Vanuatu chapter introduction.

Ships to Other Countries

There are no regular passenger-carrying freighter services to any adjacent country. **South Pacific Shipping** (tel. 22836) has lists of all large cargo boats coming in and where they're going. To arrange passage, you must deal directly with the captain of the ship concerned. The Bank Line has a monthly trip to Luganville, Honiara, Papua New Guinea, Singapore, and Europe, and South Pacific Shipping will know the dates (the fare will be higher than a plane ticket).

Local Shipping

Passenger-carrying cargo boats depart Port Vila for Luganville once or twice a week, with stops at Malekula, Epi, Paama, Ambrym, Pentecost, Maewo, and Ambae. The through trip takes two to four days, depending on ports of call, and the deck fare sometimes includes meals. Cabins are not available. Take along food, as the journey's length varies according to cargo and the weather. Some boats with Sev-

enth-Day Adventist crews stop running on Saturday (ask). Don't expect any luxuries on these ships—they're extremely basic and fares are high for what you get.

Ifira Shipping (Box 68, Port Vila; tel. 24445, fax 25934), with offices at B.P. Wharf and Star Wharf, runs the barge MV *Saraika* north to Epi, Paama, Ambrym, Pentecost, Ambae, and Espiritu Santo (Vt6,400 one-way), and south to Erromango, Tanna (Vt5,200 one-way), Aneityum, Futuna, and Aniwa on a regular basis. The *Saraika* has a closed room with benches for passengers, and two rear decks on which to sleep, but no cabins.

Pacific Transit (tel. 22031), in the Oceania Building a block back from Goodies, handles the MV *Kawale* to Luganville (Vt5,800 deck including meals) every two weeks.

Toara Coastal Shipping (Box 437, Port Vila; tel. 22370, fax 24807), at Cook Corner, Nambatu (next to Discount Rentals near Au Bon Marché), operates the MV *Marata* (20 passengers) and the larger MV *Aloara* (106 passengers) to Emae, Tongoa, Epi, Paama, Ambrym, Pentecost, and Santo. The *Marata* serves the Shepherds and Epi ports, while the *Aloara* goes as far as Luganville with all the stops. A dorm bed costs Vt4,000 to South Ambrym, Vt4,800 to Pentecost, and Vt6,000 to Santo, meals included.

Dinh Shipping (tel. 22865), on Kumul Highway almost opposite the *Trading Post* office north of town, handles the barge *Roena* to Tanna and Luganville.

If you're really serious about going by ship, continue asking around the wharves. Smaller boats like Jimmy Mole's *El Shaddai* (tel. 26408) also do the three-day Vila-Santo run (Vt5,000 one-way, food included). Other interisland boats are often found at the Star Wharf, which is the second wharf to check. The Harbormaster at the main wharf may have information on government boats (Marine Department). Shipping news is given on Radio Vanuatu in Bislama at 1030 and 1930.

Be aware that it's really rough to take a boat from Port Vila to Santo, and something only for hardened backpackers. A better idea for a taste of boat travel might be to fly to Espiritu Santo with a stop or two somewhere, then look for a boat back to Malekula, a journey of only half a day. Luganville—not Port Vila—is the shipping capital of Vanuatu. From there you might even find an interisland trading ship setting out on a two-week cruise to places few tourists ever see.

By Bus and Taxi

Although no regular public buses travel right around Efate, bus service is frequent within Port Vila itself. The minibuses are all privately owned by the drivers, and there aren't any set routes. You just flag down a bus headed in the right direction and tell the driver where you want to go. If it harmonizes with the previously requested destinations of the other passengers, he'll take you anywhere in the town area between Pango village, Le Lagon Hotel, Korman Stadium, and the airport for a flat fare of Vt100, not always by the most direct route. To Erakor village is Vt150, to Mele Hideaway Vt150, and to the Mele Maat cascades Vt200. The public buses are mostly the smaller 11-seat minibuses; the bigger 22-seat (usually white) buses are for package tours. Taxi drivers prevent the buses from picking up right at the airport door; so if you're there, walk down the road a short distance and flag down a bus. Service is frequent, but the last bus to Tagabe leaves at 2100.

Taxis have a red letter T in the license number, while public buses have a red letter B. Most taxis have meters that begin at Vt100 for the first km, then Vt10 for every 71 meters. At night, the Vt100 only covers the first 76 meters, then it's Vt10 per 71 meters again. Strangely, some meters are cheaper than others. It's always possible to ask the fare before setting out and get a fixed rate, without using the meter. If you call for a taxi (tel. 25135), you must pay for the driver's journey from the depot at the BP service station near Parliament, in addition to your trip. From the airport it's Vt1,000 to the center of town or Vt1,500 to Le Lagon Hotel. Considering how the local bus service operates, it should almost never be necessary to take a taxi.

You may be able to arrange a ride to North Efate in the back of a truck by asking the women at the market if they know of any vehicles headed that way. These usually leave after 1500 Wed.-Sat., and cost Vt500 pp. Any truck headed for Emua wharf could drop you at Nagar Bungalows, where camping is possible.

Car Rentals

Foreign driver's licenses are accepted, but most of the companies won't rent to persons under 25 years of age. Most rentals come with unlimited kilometers, and there are discounts for rentals of more than two days. All companies take Vt1,300-1,500 a day for compulsory insurance, but even with insurance you're still responsible for the first Vt100,000 in nonwaiverable damage to the car. Add 12.5% tax to all charges. On cruise ship days all vehicles will be taken, another reason to find out when the next love boat is due in so you can beat the fun-loving masses to the booking office and be gone when they arrive.

Gasoline is hard to come by outside Port Vila, so fill up before you set out around the island. The only gas station on the north side of Efate is next to the store at Emua. Driving is on the right. Speed limits are 40 kph in town, 60 kph elsewhere; in roundabouts, the vehicle entering from the right has the right of way. Cattle grids and speed bumps across the road are a real hazard for those driving around Efate and they must be crossed slowly. Check the spare tire as you take delivery of the car—you never know.

Discount Rentals (Box 537, Port Vila; tel. 23242, fax 23898), in the Adventure Center at the Olympic Hotel and opposite Au Bon Marché Supermarket south of town, rents cars with 200

WHY DRIVING IS ON THE RIGHT

While driving is on the left in many Pacific countries such as Australia, Fiji, New Zealand, and Solomon Islands, in Vanuatu it's on the right due to an unusual chain of events. Prior to 1919 there was occasional chaos as British residents drove their carts on the left-hand side of the road while French residents drove on the right. To resolve the problem, the British and French resident commissioners promulgated a decree that year stipulating that the origin of the next vehicle imported into the colony would decide which side everyone would henceforth be required to drive on. Shortly thereafter a buggy ordered by a Catholic priest arrived from Nouméa and the matter was resolved. The historic coach is now on display at the National Cultural Center Museum in Port Vila.

km free mileage from Vt3,800 a day, plus Vt1,300 insurance, plus 12.5% tax. If you rent for two days you get a free night at the Beachcomber Resort on the north coast. On three-day rentals the fourth day is free.

Budget Rent a Car (Box 349, Port Vila; tel. 23170, fax 23132), next to Au Bon Marché Supermarket south of town, charges Vt5,040 a day, but with unlimited kilometers (it's unlikely you'd do more than 200 km anyway). Insurance is Vt1,400. Budget often tries to unload old wrecks on unsuspecting tourists, so protest if they try to give you what appears to be Uncle Eddie's second car. If they tell you that's all there is left, insist on a discount.

Thrifty Car Hire (Box 128, Port Vila; tel. 22244, fax 23685) is Vt5,700 a day including 200 km (extra km Vt25). Insurance is Vt1,300. Book their cars at Handikraf Blong Vanuatu next to the Cultural Center, at Le Lagon Hotel, or at their head office next to Vanuatu Brewing in Tagabe.

Avis (Box 1297, Port Vila; tel. 24816, fax 24968) has a car rental desk at Le Méridien Resort. They also have an office at the airport (tel. 22570), but it's well hidden in a building outside the international terminal (look around the corner to the left as you come out). Their rates are Vt5,610 a day, plus Vt1,400 insurance, plus tax.

Hertz (Box 341, Port Vila: tel. 25700, fax 25511), at the Mazda dealership next to Club Imperial near the Emalus Campus, is the most expensive at Vt6,700 and up, plus Vt1,500 insurance.

Scooter Rentals

Scooters are for hire at **Nautilus Scuba** (tel. 22398) at Vt2,500/3,800 for a half/full day. Any driving license will be accepted, and the mandatory helmets are provided. The scooters aren't very effective on rough roads or steep slopes.

Local Tours

A growing number of tour operators offer sightseeing and activities packages around Vila. Before booking anything, check the blackboard outside **Frank King Tours** (Box 635, Port Vila; tel. 22808, fax 22885), across the main road from the market. Frank offers a wide variety of trips, including full-day around-the-island bus tours (Vt4,000), half-day 4WD treks up Mt. Erskine (Vt3,500), boat trips, horseback riding, scuba diving, fishing, guided hikes, and even

overnight trips to Tanna. He's very competitive, and usually undercuts the prices of everyone else without sacrificing quality.

The **Adventure Center** (tel. 22743), at the Olympic Hotel, acts as a booking office for most sporting and sightseeing activities available around Port Vila, and what's available is described on a large board on their wall with prices.

Island Safaris (Box 189, Port Vila; tel./fax 23288), in the Govan Building next to the Cultural Center Library, books two-night package tours to Ambrym, Epi, Erromango, Malekula, Tanna, and other islands at around Vt35,000 pp double occupancy, including airfare, accommodations, meals, and some sightseeing.

Aliat Wi Tours (Box 1462, Port Vila; tel. 25225, fax 26096), in La Casa d'Andrea e Luciano on Kumul Highway, offers circle-island tours Tuesday, Thursday, and Saturday (Vt4,600 including lunch).

Helicopters Vanuatu (Box 366, Port Vila; tel. 24424, fax 24693), opposite the Ballande Center, offers joy rides around southern Efate for Vt8,500 pp, or they'll drop you for the day on a deserted island or beach, or by a jungle river, for Vt12,500 pp (minimum of four persons).

Day Cruises

The "Shipwreck Cruise" on the glass-bottom boat *L'Espadon 2* offered by **Frank King Tours** (tel. 22808) is one of the best of its kind in Port Vila. There are several opportunities to snorkel (gear provided), and the commentary on coral and marinelife is interesting. The price varies, so check the blackboard outside their office opposite the market. Also inquire about snorkeling trips on the glass-bottom boat *Neptune,* which ties up on the Port Vila waterfront.

Several companies run day cruises along the north side of Efate from Havannah Harbor. For example, the classic 23-meter sailing ketch *Coongoola* (Box 991, Port Vila; tel. 25020, fax 22979), built at Brisbane in 1949, operates daily except Monday. The Vt6,800 pp price includes bus transfers from Port Vila, snorkeling gear, and a barbecue lunch. Scuba diving is available at Vt2,600 extra, gear included. Coongoola Cruises has an office on Kumul Highway next to The Beer Essentials, which also books scuba diving from Havannah Harbor with Tranquility Dive.

The 13-meter trimaran *Golden Wing* of **Sailaway Cruises** (Box 611, Port Vila; tel. 25155, fax 24452) does both north and south Efate snorkeling cruises (Vt7,500). Those prone to seasickness will be happy to know that the seven-meter-wide *Golden Dragon* doesn't lean over when it's sailing. Book through the Adventure Center at the Olympic Hotel. If you can spare the cash, the Havannah Harbor trips are a great day out, and a perfect way to see the other side of the island at its best.

AROUND EFATE

The American servicemen who built the 132-km road around Efate during WW II dubbed it U.S. Route No. 1. Today the road is steep and rough from Mele Maat to Emua, then much flatter and smoother from Emua all the way back to Port Vila. There's no bus service beyond Port Vila and vicinity, but you could try hitching around the island (difficult), take a circle-island bus tour (Vt3,800-5,000), or rent a car. If there are a few of you, consider chartering one of the Port Vila city buses for a full-day ride around the island at Vt8,000-10,000. A taxi around the island will run Vt10,000 for the car. Be aware that the far side of Efate is much less developed than the Port Vila side, so take enough to eat and drink, as shops may be few and far between. You may be asked to pay custom fees to use village beaches.

The highway climbs steeply from Mele Maat to the top of **Klehm Hill,** which provides an excel-

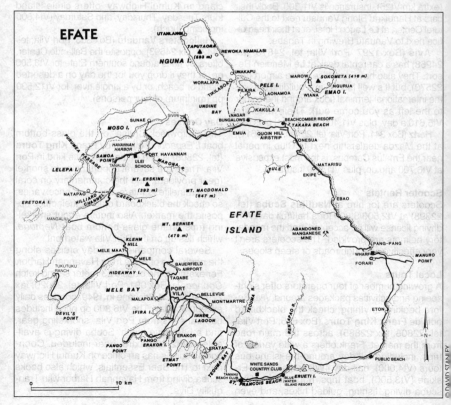

EFATE

© DAVID STANLEY

lent view. The road then crosses a plateau and descends to the beach at **Creek Ai,** 24 km from Port Vila. If you want to go across to Lelepa Island ring the gong and they'll come to pick you up. On Lelepa, there's a large cave beyond the village. Near the landing on the main island is the Naguswai Mooring Base where tourist boats such as *Coongoola* pick up day passengers for cruises around Havannah Harbor and beyond.

During WW II the U.S. Navy had a field hospital and base for the repair of damaged ships at **Havannah Harbor,** and several vestiges from this period remain. Five hundred meters east of Tanaliu village is Ulei School, and next to the road just beyond, a freshwater reservoir that once supplied the 10,000 American troops stationed here with drinking water. At the next bridge east of the pool is an American half track under a huge banyan tree, also next to the road. Close by to the east is one of the oldest colonial buildings in Vanuatu, a remnant of the days before Port Vila became capital. The edifice served as an officers' club during the war, and in the bush behind is an overgrown American airstrip.

At the entrance to **Siviri** village, a couple of kilometers off the main road, is a cave (Vt100 admission) used locally as a source of drinking water. Villagers commute to the large islands of Nguna and Pele from the wartime wharf at **Emua** on the north coast of Efate, 44 km from Port Vila. Village outboards to Emao Island leave from **Takara Beach,** 10 km farther east. The U.S.-built Quoin Hill fighter airstrip near here is kept usable. A couple of small resorts in this area offer bungalow accommodations and restaurants (see below). The large traditional building next to the road at **Ekipe** is used for cultural presentations to tourists on circle-island bus tours.

The broad, gravel road down the east side of Efate passes white sandy beaches and green lagoons bordered by coconut and pandanus palms, yellow acacia bushes, and huge banyan trees. At **Forari,** 25 km south of Takara, are remains from a French **manganese mine** that operated from 1962 until 1978, when reduced deposits and falling prices forced its closure. The ruins of a large cantilever loader and metal warehouses can still be seen next to an old wharf beside the road. The road opposite the Forari village access road leads four km east to **Manuro Point,** where an abandoned resort overlooks a fine white beach

in very attractive surroundings. From Forari it's 50 km back to Port Vila.

Eton Beach, seven km south of Forari, is great for a swim and snorkel (Vt500 admission per car), but beware of the five poorly marked speed bumps at Eton village just beyond Eton Beach. From Eton, you continue 25 km west past a few public beaches and through cattle country to the **White Sands Country Club,** Vanuatu's top golf course. When you reach the Erakor Lagoon, you're almost full circle back to Port Vila.

Hotels around Efate

Nagar Beach Bungalows (Box 939, Port Vila; tel. 23221, fax 27289) is at Paonangisu on the north side of Efate, 50 km from Port Vila clockwise on a rough, steep road, or 82 km counterclockwise on a wide, flat road. It's one of the only resorts on the island owned and operated by ni-Vanuatu. Fanny and Henry Cyrel have two two-bedroom bungalows accommodating up to six persons at Vt7,000, and four older double bungalows with shared bath at Vt1,500 pp plus tax. Camping on the grounds costs Vt500 pp. The units are attractive, each with a veranda and chairs. There are no cooking facilities, but a bowl of tropical fruit and a flask of hot water are provided free. The Cyrels' restaurant is open daily—try the steak sandwich (Vt550). Their beach is poor, but for Vt2,300 return per group they'll drop you on the white sands of Kakula (Rabbit) Island. Nagar is an ideal place to break a trip around the island but be prepared for the large groups on circle-island bus tours that often take lunch here. Budget to inexpensive.

The **Beachcomber Resort** (Box 947, Port Vila; tel. 23576, fax 26458), formerly called Takara Resort, three km east of Nagar, is another convenient stop on your way around the island. It's slightly more upmarket than Nagar, but it has the advantage of a unique circular thermal hot-spring pool for the exclusive use of house guests and restaurant patrons. The eight self-contained duplex units cost Vt6,500 for up to four persons, tax additional. Three rooms with shared bath are Vt1,500 pp. There's hot water in the showers, but no fridge or coffee-making facilities in the rooms. Meals in the restaurant are pricey. Some car rental agencies in Port Vila offer a free night at Beachcomber for those taking a car for two days, so ask around. Inexpensive.

You can camp at the **Teouma Tropical Gardens** on the east side of Teouma Bay at CFP 1,300 pp. Toilets and showers are provided, and the caretaker might let you ride one of his horses. Information is available at the Adventure Center in Port Vila.

TANNA

INTRODUCTION

Vanuatu's second-most visited island (after Efate), Tanna is renowned for its active volcano, potent kava, coffee plantations, custom villages, cargo cultists, exciting festivals, strong traditions, magnificent wild horses, long black beaches, gigantic banyan trees, two-meter-long yams, and day-tripping packaged tourists. Due to its southerly location it's cooler than Efate, and there's no problem with malaria. The alternating black and white beaches, often separated only by a narrow headland, are unusual. The island is Vanuatu's most heavily populated, and well-used trails crisscross the landscape. Leave the roads and you'll enter a wonderland of charming, innocent people living as close to nature as their ancestors did before them. Here the real Tanna remains, almost untouched by a century and a half of traders, missionaries, officials, and other visitors.

Kava

Every village has its *nasara,* an open area surrounded by gigantic banyan trees, where the men gather nightly to drink kava at the *nakamal* (men's house). Tanna kava is strong and sudden. One cup will stone you; two cups will knock you out. The green roots of a pepper shrub *(Piper methysticum)* are first chewed into a pulp, spit out on a leaf, then mixed with a little water and squeezed through a coconut frond into a cup to be drunk all at once.

If a man touches any part of the campfire during the ceremony, it's thought that his house will burn down. After finishing the kava, speaking above a whisper is extremely bad manners. Women in the villages are still forbidden to take part in this gathering or even to see it. If they're caught trying, they have to pay a fine of one good kava root. Way back when, they would have been put to death.

Events

Custom dances are held on the occasion of marriages, circumcisions (many in July), and other events. Ask around to find out where the next one will be held. The most important event of the year is the Nekowiar Festival, with its famous Toka Dance. This ritual may be held in August or around the end of the year. The Toka celebrates the circumcision of young boys and is accompanied by pig killing, feasting, and dancers with painted faces and grass skirts—the works.

It can take six or seven years to prepare for these massive ceremonial gift-giving sessions, which cement alliances between villages and clans. The festival lasts three to five days and on the eve of the last day, thousands of men from every village on the island participate in a wild dance, which continues through the night. The next morning, more than 100 pigs may be slaughtered. There's usually a Nekowiar on Tanna every year, and tourists pay a mere Vt5,000 admission to attend this stirring event.

Jon Frum festivals are held Friday nights at Sulpher Bay with music, singing, and dancing. On Saturday, a similar Jon Frum ceremony takes place at **Imanaka,** near White Grass on the other side of the island. The Jon Frum Cult is also active at **Middle Bush,** although custom people are in the majority. On 15 February the Jon Frum Festival is held at Sulphur Bay.

SIGHTS

Yasur Volcano

Yasur Volcano (361 meters high and 1.5 km wide at its base), the chief attraction of Tanna, is 30 km from Lenakel Airstrip in the eastern part of the island. It's one of the most accessible volcanoes of its kind in the world, and for the convenience of tour groups, a road goes almost to the summit on the mountain's south side. It's also possible to climb the path up the north slope, to the left between the vegetation and the ash field (40 minutes). Either way, you'll pay an exorbitant Vt2,000 pp "Volcano Landing Fee" to the "Volcano Committee" for each visit (only one of many such custom fees charged on Tanna).

At 940° C, Yasur hisses, rumbles, and spits, constantly erupting in minor explosions, which emit small filaments of volcanic glass called Pele's Hair. Cargo cultists believe that Jon Frum lives beneath the fires of Yasur, where he commands an army of 5,000 souls. The slopes are scattered with boulders considered sacred by the Tannese, and black dust from the crater cov-

ers everything for kilometers. Some days are better for viewing than others, depending on smoke, wind, etc. At night it's an unforgettable fireworks display.

The prime time to climb Yasur is around 1700, to see it and the surroundings in daylight, then stay for the sunset and to see the crater at night—the most spectacular time by far as molten lava shoots up into the sky every few minutes. Views down into the crater are quite spectacular—steam and masses of black ash seethe furiously, discharging cinders and rocks, while gas burns your throat. The sulfur fumes

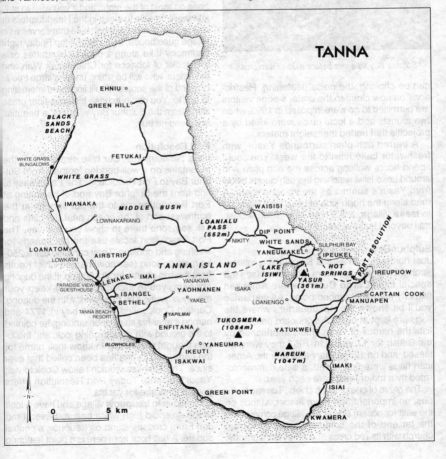

Sulphur Bay villagers before a Jon Frum cross

can be choking, the noise deafening. Restrictions on how close to the crater's edge visitors are permitted to go were imposed in 1995, when two tourists and a local guide were killed by a projectile that hurled them eight meters.

A barren ash plain surrounds Yasur, with freshwater Lake Isiwi to the west. You could spend hours walking across the ash plain and around Lake Isiwi watching the ash clouds billow from Yasur's summit as the volcano roars. A road along the north side of Lake Isiwi leads up to **Isaka** village; a 2.5-hour hike along a bush trail beyond Isaka is Vecel Falls.

Sulphur Bay

Just northeast of Yasur is Sulphur Bay village, stronghold of the Jon Frum movement (see the special topic **Cargo Cults**), where American flags fly from tall bamboo poles. As you arrive you'll be shown the Headquarters where the flags are kept at night. A signboard on the wall lists the names of three chiefs imprisoned by the British for 17 years. In 1957 they were released, and on 15 February that year the American flags were first raised, a date commemorated by a major feast here each year.

The grave of one of these chiefs, Tommy Nampus, an important Jon Frum leader, stands on the east (or ocean) side of the village common. At the far end of the common is the Jon Frum church with its red cross and other iconography.

Ask to speak to prophet Elizabeth, a daughter of Nampus, who lives just behind the church. To the right of Sulphur Bay's beautiful black beach, steam from Yasur Volcano curls among the cliffs flanking the bay. A fee of Vt200 to Vt1,000 pp may be charged to enter the village, depending on who you are and how you arrive.

On Friday nights Jon Frum supporters from most of East Tanna converge on Sulphur Bay for a ceremony, which begins around 2000 (admission Vt300 pp). Various "teams" take turns singing and playing music while villagers in grass skirts dance outside the shelter. The ceremony goes on most of the night, and if you wish to stay late you'll be able to sleep in the Headquarters or on the floor of a hut just opposite that serves as a village guesthouse. If you attend the Friday night ceremony take along a pack of cigarettes or a few sticks of tobacco for Chief Isaak Wan and the others, who will be sitting under a large tree at one end of the square. You'll find them interesting to talk to. You can purchase hibiscus-fiber grass skirts from the Sulphur Bay villagers, a beautiful and genuine buy.

Port Resolution

It's a pleasant 2.5-hour hike straight over the mountains on a well-trodden footpath from Sulphur Bay to Port Resolution. The trail is easy to find from the Sulphur Bay end. If beginning at Port Resolution, go to the hot springs at the northwest end of the beach near the cliffs and ask someone there to show you the way. The Port Resolution locals use the hot springs for washing and cooking. They can also call a 250-kg male dugong (sea cow) named Chief Kaufis from the sea nearby for Vt1,000 pp. If the dugong appears, you're lucky; if not they keep your money anyway. You may swim with the dugong. Captain Cook sailed into this bay in 1774 and named it after his ship. Upon landing, he pointed to the ground with a questioning look, and the locals thought we wanted to know their name for the earth, and Tanna has been called that ever since. The Tannese wouldn't allow Cook to visit Yasur Volcano. Today Port Resolution offers good anchorage for yachts.

Continue to **Ireupuow** village and have a look at the splendid high white beach. Several red Jon Frum crosses stand on Ireupuow's central square. A half hour from here is a point featuring a rock pyramid called **Captain Cook,** where the famous navigator made observations. A beautiful golden beach is next to the point. The main road goes back to Sulphur Bay or White Sands between Lake Isiwi and Yasur. Immense banyan trees line the way.

Across the Island

Tanna's largest village and administrative center is **Lenakel** on the west coast. The market and a cluster of general stores are near a large concrete wharf built by the Japanese in 1988. Most government offices are at Isangel, the headquarters of Tafea Province, on a hill about two km southeast. Coffee grown in northern Tanna is roasted in a factory at Lowkatai just north of Lenakel.

Village footpaths cross the island. One trail begins near the hospital, another next to the driveway into the Agriculture Station at Isangel (the "Melbourne" trail). A truck can drive six km up the latter route to Yanakwa, then it's another 10 km on foot through dense forest to Lake Isiwi. The path follows a ridge and from Isangel it's an easy uphill walk for about four hours, the first half through villages and the second through the jungle. The last two hours or so of the hike is downhill and across the ash plain to either White Sands or Sulphur Bay. These trails are well known, regularly used, and easy to learn about and follow. A good hiker could make it across in a day.

There are many more such hikes in both south and north Tanna, and the 1:50,000 topographical map (obtainable at the Survey Office in Port Vila) is the only guide you need. Hiking on Tanna is safe and easy as there are no thorns on the trees, no dangerous lizards on the ground, and even the local dogs are mellow. You'll pass through some of the 92 villages where people still live in the traditional way (no Christians or Jon Frummers).

The Custom Villages

The road to the custom villages begins at the top of the incline a few hundred meters south of the Tanna Beach Resort. **Yapilmai Falls** are about midway between the main road and Yaohnanen, down the hill to the right. **Yaohnanen** is the center of the custom area where the men wear penis sheaths or *nambas,* and the women wear colorful grass skirts. They attended church until the 1940s, when they returned to their traditional religion. Only in the 1970s did they shed Western clothing. Packaged tourists are often brought to Yaohnanen to see custom dances, buy grass skirts, and tour the "primitive" village.

Chief Jack Naiva of Yaohnanen is very friendly to visitors who respect his customs, and he may allow you to stay in the village if he likes you (a pack of cigarettes helps). If you're willing to put on a *namba* or a grass skirt and perhaps do some gardening you'll be very welcome. They'll feed you on rats and cicadas—actually, rat tastes quite good, sort of like chicken. Chief Jack's son Jack Malia can arrange dancing at **Yakel** village, about 500 meters up the road past the Kustom Skul. Here you'll probably see a few men and boys with long hair bound in the traditional style.

Consider making a full day out of Yaohnanen and Yakel, walking there and back. When you enter the village *nasara,* sit down and wait for somebody. A custom fee of Vt1,100 pp is charged to look around and to visit the Prince Philip house. After the evening kava, you could walk back to the main road and try to catch a lift.

PRACTICALITIES

Accommodations in West Tanna

Paradise View Guest House (Box 9, Tanna; tel. 68695, fax 68624) is a European-style frame house directly behind the Tafea Cooperative Store at Lenakel, one km from the airstrip. The six rooms with shared bath are Vt2,500/3,000 single/double, which makes it expensive for singles but fine for couples. Three of the rooms are only separated from the rest of the house by thin partitions, so peace and quiet will depend on who your neighbors are. You'll probably be allowed to camp next to the guesthouse when all of the rooms are full. Good communal cooking facilities are provided. This is the former personal residence of island traders Bob and Russell Paul, who decided to return to Australia after independence. A nice common lounge faces the garden, and the guesthouse is in a pleasant location overlooking the coast. (A female reader traveling alone complained of nocturnal prowlers outside the guesthouse.) Budget.

The **Tafea Council Guest House** (Box 28, Tanna; tel. 68638, fax 68687), behind the post office in Isangel, has five rooms at Vt2,000 pp. Check in at the local government offices during business hours. Although cooking facilities are provided and a store is nearby, it's overpriced, run-down, and not a very pleasant place to stay. Budget.

Also on the west coast are two clusters of overpriced tourist bungalows. The 11-unit **Tanna Beach Resort** (Box 27, Tanna; tel. 68626, fax 68610), on a narrow black-sand beach near Lenakel, five km south of the airstrip, has dingy rooms in a long hut facing the restaurant at Vt8,000 pp, and thatched bungalows facing the beach at Vt12,000 pp. There's a swimming pool. Not only are you wildly overcharged for your room, but they really sock you with meal prices of Vt1,100 for a sandwich or Vt4,200 for a three-course dinner (without drinks). There are no coffee-making or cooking facilities in the rooms. Their organized sightseeing tours also cost the earth—carefully check all prices before heading down this way. If you stay here you won't be able to see any of the fabulous sights of East Tanna unless you fork over additional big bucks for the tours. This is a place to be avoided. Premium.

White Grass Bungalows (Box 5, Tanna; tel./fax 68688) is in wild-horse country, 12 km north of Lenakel and far from everything except the new airport. The five thatched bungalows with solar energy and leaky roofs are Vt6,200/7,200/7,700 single/double/triple, including breakfast. Airport transfers are a rip-off at Vt2,000 pp return. Almost all of their guests arrive on prebooked Tanna tours. Moderate.

Accommodations at White Sands

Rather than putting up around Lenakel you're better off staying in East Tanna, close to the attractions you'll want to visit. **David and Alice Iou** (Box 16, Tanna; no phone), behind the Presbyterian church down the hill from the cooperative store at White Sands, rent two basic rooms in a ramshackle European-style house at Vt1,500/2,000 single/double. You can camp here at Vt700 pp, just be prepared to get some ash on your tent if the wind starts blowing this way. Local meals are available. Ask for "Pastor David." Budget.

In July 1997, Stephane and Murielle Orreindy opened **Friendly Bungalows,** on the beach near the French school at Lownasunen, just before White Sands. The large thatched house with three budget rooms and one porch is Vt1,200 pp with shared bath. The two separate thatched bungalows with private bath cost Vt5,000/6,000 double/triple, plus tax. Children under 12 are free. Mosquito nets are provided, and an electric generator runs at night. Good three-course meals are Vt1,000 each (breakfast Vt500). Canoes, horseback riding, hiking trips, and custom dancing are arranged. It's quiet and attractive, well worth a three-night stay. You can hear the roar of the volcano from your bed. **Nengau Entani** (Box 853, Lenakel; tel./fax 68676) handles bookings and airport transfers (Vt1,700 pp each way). Budget to inexpensive.

Nengau Entani also books the **Yasur Guesthouse** in Loanengo Village, near the access road up Yasur. The four basic rooms with shared bath in a thatched building are Vt3,550/4,300 single/double including breakfast, other meals Vt1,000 each. The full range of minibus tours is offered, and most guests arrive on prebooked packages.

Accommodations at Port Resolution

Adjacent to Ireupuow village near the eastern tip of Tanna is the **Port Resolution Nipikinamu Yacht Club** (Box 788, Tanna; tel. 68676) with seven thatched bungalows with shared bath at Vt4,150/6,300 single/double, including breakfast and dinner (lunch available at Vt1,000 extra). You may pay less than this if you find your way here on your own, although the tour operators try to enforce their high prices. Lighting is by kerosene lamp. Kava is served at the club *nakamal.* The location is splendid, atop a cliff overlooking Port Resolution, with several good beaches nearby. You'll see flying foxes in the evening. A full day sightseeing tour is Vt8,000 per group, plus any custom fees. Guests may snorkel with the local dugong at no additional charge, and the friendly staff takes guests out on interesting bush hikes to local hot springs, beaches, the Captain Cook rock, and gardens. They have their own taxi for island visits, and tours to Yasur Volcano are offered at fixed prices far lower than those charged by the Lenakel tourist bungalows. Airport transfers are Vt2,000 pp each way to a maximum of Vt6,000 per group. Yachts may anchor off the resort at no charge, and yachties are welcome at the Nipikinamu clubhouse and on the organized tours. Inexpensive.

The **Shark Bay Guest House** at Manuapen village, about six km southwest of Port Resolution, has one unit at Vt2,500 pp. Budget.

Food and Drink

A cluster of general stores is near the airstrip at Lenakel. The village women spread out their produce on the ground at various locations weekdays. The biggest market takes place beside the Tafea Cooperative Store in Lenakel on Monday and Friday. At Vt20 a bunch for almost anything, it's the best buy on the island. Bread is baked locally but it's often sold out by noon. Take all your own food with you if you go walkabout on the east coast.

Just south of the wharf at Lenakel is the friendly **Silae Restaurant,** where you can get a filling local meal of meat and rice, and everyone pays the same here! Nearby is John Louhman's **Uma Restaurant,** where similar fare is available at higher prices (be sure to ask first).

The **Rolling Sea Kava Bar** and several similar establishments are at the junction of the Isangel and circuminsular roads. These are male domains, although accompanied white women are allowed in. They're great places to socialize.

Services

The National Bank (tel. 68615), next to the Tafea Cooperative Store at Lenakel, changes traveler's checks weekdays 0800-1100 and 1330-1500. Bring plenty of cash with you to Tanna as anything associated with package tourism costs heaps of money. There's a card telephone at the co-op. The post office (tel. 68673) is at Isangel.

Transportation

Vanair (tel. 68667) has flights from Port Vila to Tanna (Vt8,700 one-way) three times a day, twice weekly via Erromango. From Tanna's old airport it's a pleasant 15-minute downhill walk to Lenakel. (In 1998 a new "international" airport to allow direct flights from Nouméa was built at White Grass, 10 km north of Lenakel. Check which one you'll be using.)

You can also come from Port Vila by ship. Lenakel receives a boat from Port Vila about twice a month, often the barges *Roena* and *Saraika.*

A couple of trucks and minibuses offer unscheduled service between Lenakel and White Sands (Vt300 pp) every weekday—be prepared to wait. It's essential to fix the price with the taxi-truck drivers before setting out, and even then they may ask Vt3,000 when you arrive. Be polite with them, but firm. There's quite a bit of traffic between Lenakel and White Sands, so if you suspect a ripoff, just wait for the next one. The drivers are quite accustomed to collecting large sums for transportation from tourists on pre-arranged packages, so be prepared.

Both of the west coast tourist bungalows offer overpriced sightseeing tours, such as the full-day trip to the custom village and Yasur by 4WD jeep (Vt14,150 pp, plus Vt2,500 extra to see the Port Resolution dugong). A morning trip to Yaohnanen to see people wearing *nambas* is Vt3,300 pp (kava included), while horseback riding costs Vt3,000 pp. The above prices are valid assuming at least two people are going; if you're alone it's 50% extra.

OTHER TAFEA ISLANDS

Erromango

Although rugged and untouristed, Erromango is a possible stopover between Port Vila and Tanna as Vanair flights between Port Vila and Tanna call at Dillon's Bay twice a week, at Ipota weekly. A truck sometimes meets the flights at Dillon's Bay airstrip and carries passengers the eight km to Unpongkor village for about Vt600. The road drops sharply into the Williams River Valley to the village, beautifully situated at the river mouth.

Meteson's Guest House (William Mete, Unpongkor Postal Agency, Dillon's Bay; tel. 68677) in the center of Unpongkor offers three beds with shared facilities at Vt4,500/6,000 single/double including two meals. It may be possible to pay less if you're not on a package tour, but don't count on it. There's a small co-op store nearby. You could also camp on the grass beside the river, or just set out hiking and camp up on the plateau.

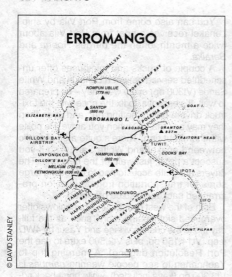

ERROMANGO

In 1825, Irish trader Peter Dillon discovered vast stands of sandalwood here. Dillon managed to obtain very little of the precious wood, and ships that followed soon clashed with the inhabitants. Plaques in the church at Unpongkor commemorate the martyrdom of John Williams and James Harris (1839), George and Ellen Gordon (1861), and George's brother, James Gordon (1872). On the other side of the river in the village cemetery are monuments to these well-meaning missionaries, killed by the Erromangans as a consequence of the methods used by the traders and the diseases introduced by the messengers of God themselves.

Later, many Erromangans were carried off to labor in the Australian cane fields, and those few who returned brought back further disease and discord. From 20,000 in the early 1800s, Erromango's population plummeted to 400 by 1930. There are only 1,650 inhabitants today. Old burial caves dot the cliffs along the west and south coasts.

Aniwa and Futuna

These two small islands east of Tanna, each with a population of around 400, are quite dif-ferent. Aniwa (eight square km) is a low island covered with orange trees, the fruit of which is very sweet and juicy. The villages are near the airstrip and the people very friendly. A magnificent snorkeling spot is north of the airstrip, and there's good anchorage.

The people of 11-square-km Futuna are Polynesian. You could stay at one of the villages near the airstrip but there's not much to do other than climb the 643-meter extinct volcano. Getting around is difficult, as the tracks go over ladders of bamboo, and in some cases you'll find yourself clinging to rocks 30 meters directly above the sea along the forbidding coast. Vanair flies to Futuna from Port Vila (Vt9,500), Tanna (Vt4,500), and Aneityum (Vt4,700) weekly.

Aneityum

Aneityum (Anatom), southernmost inhabited island in Vanuatu, is somewhat cooler and drier than the rest of the country. Its 160 square km rise to 852 meters, but ample flat areas are available for cultivation. Totemic petroglyphs and kauri stands are found on Aneityum, and 80 species of orchid flourish here. In the 1840s whalers from far and wide were based at Inyeug, a sandy islet just off the southwest side of Aneityum where the airstrip is today.

The Rev. John Geddie, first Presbyterian missionary to establish himself in Vanuatu, arrived in 1848 and built a 1,000-seat stone church, the ruins of which can still be seen. His efforts were in vain, however, as introduced diseases such as measles and dysentery ravaged the population, which eventually fell from 3,500 to 800, only 350 of whom were Geddie's converts. Today, about 550 people live in two villages on the south coast. Every two weeks a cruise ship drops as many as a 1,000 tourists at a time on this "Mystery Island."

Vanair flies into Aneityum from Port Vila (Vt11,300), Tanna (Vt4,500), and Futuna (Vt4,700) weekly. The launch transfer from Inyeug, the airstrip island, to Analgawat village on the main island is Vt200. The three-room **Mystery Island Guest House** on Inyeug accommodates visitors in a single thatched building at Vt1,000 pp. There's a communal kitchen but the toilet is outside.

MALEKULA

Shaped like a sitting dog, Malekula (Mallicollo) is a big 2,053-square-km island of 24,000 inhabitants speaking 30 different languages. The rugged interior of southern Malekula is inhabited by some of the most traditional clans on earth, while the island's east coast features the gentle beauty of continuous coconut plantations. Together with Ambrym and Paama, Malekula forms part of Malampa Province.

It's easy to visit Malekula on your way from Port Vila to Luganville. Vanair offers stopovers at Norsup for Vt1,800 extra airfare, or come by ship from Luganville. Although there are a few basic resthouses, Malekula is more for the adventuresome traveler who requires few amenities. The traditional areas of southern Malekula are still riddled with taboos, and visitors must tread very carefully. Offshore sharks can be a

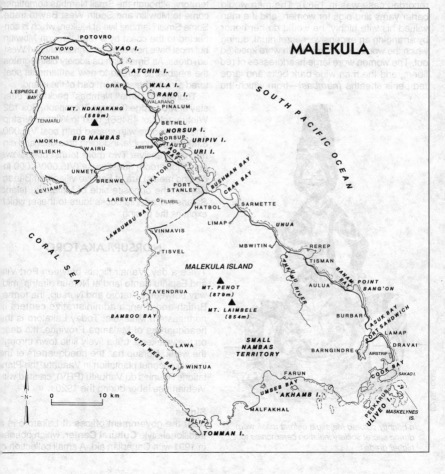

MALEKULA

MALEKULA ISLAND

SOUTH PACIFIC OCEAN

CORAL SEA

POTOVRO
VOVO
VAO I.
TONTAR
ATCHIN I.
L'ESPIEGLE BAY
ORAP
WALA I.
RANO I.
WALARANO
PINALUM
MT. NDANARANG
(589m)
TENMARU
BETHEL
NORSUP
AMOKH
BIG NAMBAS
WAIRU
NORSUP
TAUTU
URIPIV I.
URI I.
WILIEKH
AIRSTRIP
UNMET
BRENWE
LAKATORO
PORT STANLEY
LEVIAMP
LAREVET
FILMBIL
BUSHMAN BAY
CRAB BAY
SARMETTE
HATBOL
LAMBUMBU BAY
VINMAVIS
LIMAP
UNUA
TISVEL
MBWITIN
REREP
TISMAN
MALEKULA ISLAND
MT. PENOT
(879m)
AULUA
POINT
BANG'ON
TAVENDRUA
MT. LAIMBELE
(854m)
BURBAR
BAMBOO BAY
SMALL
NAMBAS
TERRITORY
LAMAP
DRAVAI
BARNGINDRE
AIRSTRIP
LAWA
FARUN
SAKAO I.
WINTUA
UMBEB BAY
AKHAM I.
COOK BAY
MELIP
MALFAKHAL
TOMMAN I.
ULIVEO I.
MASKELYNES IS.
SOUTH WEST BAY
BANAM BAY
LAKHU RIVER
ASUK BAY
PORT SANDWICH
PESKARUS I.

0   10 km

—N—

problem, so get local advice before swimming anywhere off Malekula.

The Big Nambas

The once-feared Big Nambas formerly lived on the plateau at Amokh in the northwest of the island, but since the death of Chief Virhambat in 1988, they've all moved down to the coast, and the fortified village at Amokh is now deserted. Up until the 1930s, internecine tribal fighting was conducted almost constantly among the 2,000 clansmen, and cannibalism was frequently practiced by the powerful hereditary chiefs (the last recorded case was in 1969). The men would barter yams and pigs for women, and if a man valued his wife highly, he would do her honor by arranging an expensive, secret ritual, during which the woman's two front teeth were knocked out. The women wore large headdresses of red fibers, and the men wide bark belts and large red penis sheaths *(nambas)*—from which the

LOUISE FOOTE

a brightly colored Malekula helmet mask worn during secret society initiation ceremonies to a higher grade

tribe derived its name. For better or worse, all of this is now a thing of the past.

The Small Nambas

The jungles of the interior of south Malekula are home to the Small Nambas. Because no missionaries penetrated here, the 400-500 clanspeople living in many scattered villages retained their traditional customs long after most other ni-Vanuatu had adopted white ways. The men wear small *nambas* made of banana leaves, and are famous for their gaudy face masks and body paint worn during funeral rites. No roads penetrate their territory, although the Small Nambas sometimes come to Mbwitin and South West Bay to trade. Some Small Nambas live at Melken, which is connected to the coast by a road through Mbwitin, but most have now adopted Christianity and western dress. As Small Namba society disintegrates, the inhabitants spread to new settlements scattered around the southern part of the island.

Tourists on "Small Nambas" packages often stay at **Alo Lodge** (George Thompson, Box 132, Wintua; tel./fax 48466), next to Wintua Airstrip. The four rooms with shared bath cost Vt6,000/8,000 single/double, including breakfast and dinner. Inexpensive. Two more tourist bungalows and a four-room guesthouse (Vt5,000/7,000 including meals) are at Fartavo village on Banam Bay, on the opposite side of Malakula. Island Safaris in Port Vila books tours to these, which explains the pricing.

NORSUP/LAKATORO

Twice a day, Vanair flights between Port Vila and Espiritu Santo land at Norsup airstrip, midway between Lakatoro and Norsup, the former British and French administrative centers in northeastern Malekula. Today Lakatoro is the headquarters of Malampa Province. It's dead on the weekend, but a lively little town through the week. Norsup has the headquarters of the largest coconut plantation in Vanuatu, the Plantations Reunies du Vanuatu (PRV), created with Vietnamese labor during the 1920s.

Sights

Near the government offices at Lakatoro is a traditional-style **Cultural Center,** which opened in 1991 with Canadian aid. A small collection of helmet masks and other artifacts is inside, but the museum is usually closed.

For a sweeping view of the whole northeastern side of Malekula, take the road opposite SK Wholesale Store, at the north end of Lakatoro, up to a red-and-white **radio repeater tower,** which you can easily climb.

From Norsup, it's possible to walk along the shore to **Tautu** village near the airport. The site of the old village, abandoned in 1918, is on a hill inland from the point where there are two large rocks on the beach before you reach the present village. You can still see the posts of the chief's house, an amphitheater of broken stone slabs for tribal meetings, a stone "bed" where the bodies of dead enemies were displayed before being consumed at dinner, stone boxes for holding skulls, and standing stones erected by men who had passed grading ceremonies. The place is now overgrown and ravaged by pigs. Beyond Tautu and right at the end of the airstrip is beautiful white Aop Beach.

A good day hike from Lakatoro begins by following the road inland along the south side of the PWD compound fence. You'll soon reach a small stream that you follow up the hill, and eventually you should find an overgrown trail on the north side of the stream. If you pay attention, this will take you all the way up to the top of the verdant hills behind Lakatoro. Some gigantic banyan trees are to be seen up there, and it really is an enchanting forest. From the ridge, keep right and go down the other side to a small stream, which you'd follow west for an hour or so. When another stream joins in and the river turns north, you'll reach a coconut plantation with a bush road heading out to the east coast. There's no continuous trail after the first ridge, and you'll have to bushwack through the rainforest. In the rainy season when the streams are full of water, this hike will be difficult and even dangerous. With a compass, you can do it in five or six hours. Just take ample food and water, and go alone only if you're an experienced hiker.

Budget Accommodations

The rustic **Lakatoro Resthouse** is on spacious grounds near the Cultural Center in the hilltop administrative compound, seven km south of Norsup. It has three rooms with six bunks each, and one double room for married couples. There's a communal fridge and cooking facilities, plus a video room. The white prefabricated **Norsup Resthouse** is in a residential area on the plateau, up the hill from the Norsup Co-op. The four rooms have bunk beds, and share the bathrooms, kitchen, fridge, and a tiny video player. The Lakatoro Resthouse is larger and more convenient, but the Norsup Resthouse is in better condition and more private.

At both resthouses, the charge is Vt1,500 pp, and to be admitted you must first contact the Malampa Provincial Office (Box 22, Norsup; tel. 48453 or 48491, fax 48442) in Lakatoro. Call ahead from Port Vila or Luganville to find out what's available. Both are used to accommodate delegates to provincial council meetings, and will be unavailable at those times. The officials may be reluctant to open the Norsup Resthouse, which is far from their office.

A better place to stay at Lakatoro is Sato Kilman's **SK Resthouse** (tel. 48401), next to the primary school just below the Lakatoro Resthouse. The four small one-bedroom apartments with private bath and cooking facilities are Vt2,500/3,500 single/double, but it's important to call ahead to check availability as some of the units are rented out for long periods. Upon arrival stop at the SK Wholesale Store at the north end of Lakatoro to pick up the keys, as there's no resident caretaker. The electricity only comes on in the evening, the mattresses are thin, and there's no fridge or fan, but it will see you through. (Sato Kilman himself has served as a cabinet minister in several Vanuatu governments, and is an interesting person to meet.)

Food

The **Lakatoro Consumer Co-op Restaurant** (weekdays 0630-1730), next to the Co-op and National Bank. serves unpretentious meals of meat and rice (Vt250) and coffee (Vt50).

Maxi Restaurant (tel. 48554; hours variable), next to Malekula Distributors Center supermarket on the main road at the south end of Lakatoro, has a few more ambitious meals on the menu, and you can order a beer.

On weekdays there's a market next to the well-stocked Lakatoro Co-op Store. At Norsup, the market is on Wednesday and Saturday only, in the large shelter between the Co-op Store and the sea.

Practicalities

The National Bank (tel. 48400) at Lakatoro changes traveler's checks. A public card phone is on the wall outside the National Bank, and there's another card phone at Norsup Airport. The hospital (tel. 48410) and post office (tel. 48452) are at Norsup.

Transportation

A pickup truck from Norsup Airstrip to either settlement will be Vt300. A bus would cost Vt100 (weekdays only). Grab any form of transport you see, or be prepared to walk the four km south to Lakatoro.

The Vanair office (tel. 48495) is between the Shell service station and Malekula Distributors Center at Lakatoro. The interisland ships tie up to a wharf at Litslits, a couple of km south of Lakatoro.

On weekdays minibuses circulate every hour or so between Lakatoro and Vao (from Lakatoro it's Vt100 to Norsup, Vt150 to Wala, Vt200 to Atchin, and Vt250 to Vao).

NORTH OF NORSUP

Many French-speaking villages are strung along the coast north of Norsup and on the small offshore islands. These islands are famous for their megalithic culture, especially the stone-lined dancing grounds *(nasara)* and drums *(tamtam)*. Only the people of Vao and Wala actually continue to use their dancing grounds for traditional ceremonies such as circumcisions. Those on Atchin, Rano, and Uripiv are more or less abandoned. The peoples of Vao, Atchin, Wala, and Rano speak different languages, and can only communicate among themselves in Bislama, English, or French. Ships between Norsup and Luganville call at these islands several times a week, and minibuses run periodically from Norsup to Atchin and Vao (Vt200-300).

Take a minibus all the way north to the landing opposite **Vao,** where a motorboat across to the island will cost Vt500 each way. You'll probably be able to find someone to paddle you over in a dugout canoe for Vt500 roundtrip, with an hour or so waiting time. Upon arrival, walk past the Catholic church with its two well-carved *tamtam* drums, and when you reach a store, turn left toward the middle of the island. This will eventually bring you to a large *nasara* with slit gongs, stone seats, banyan trees, a *nakamal* (kava drinking venue)—the works. Turn right here, and walk south toward a couple more of the seven *nasara* on Vao. If you're friendly, someone will offer to guide you around, and there's no charge to visit the *nasara,* although you might have to pay custom fees to take photos. The woodcarvers of Vao produce both raw or "ethnic" masks and canoe prows they're reluctant to sell, and polished airport art. Some very fine bowls go for Vt5,000. There's a long white beach near the Catholic mission where you'll first arrive, and the tidy island houses are wonderfully picturesque with stone walls or fences made of empty bottles. Vao has an almost magical air, and it's said that magic also controls the sharks and makes it safe to swim anywhere around the island. As yet, Vao is almost untouched by tourism.

Return to the mainland and walk south to **Atchin** in an hour. After sleepy Vao, the contrast of Atchin—mecca of ni-Vanuatu capitalism and a big SDA village—is startling. A long black-sand beach faces Atchin. Mr. Maxim Metsan has built a few small bungalows for tourists reside the road at Wormet, between Atchin and Wala.

On Wala between Norsup and Vao is the **Wala Island Resort** (Peter Fidelio, Box 55, Norsup, Northeast Malekula; tel./fax 48488) with six thatched bungalows at Vt5,350/7,700 single/double including breakfast. You may be able to get a local booking rate of Vt3,000/3,500 without breakfast, although the tour operators try to discourage any undercutting of their rates. All have a veranda overlooking a white-sand beach, but the toilets and showers are communal and there's no running water or electricity. It's on the site of a traditional dancing ground where wooden *tamtams* stand. Some old burials and magical stones around the resort may be taboo, so ask about that and the safety of swimming in these waters.

Alick Nawinmal on nearby **Rano Island** also takes guests. Both Wala and Rano offer a unique village experience, and tours to the mainland are arranged. Cruising yachts are welcome to anchor offshore.

ESPIRITU SANTO

With 4,010 square km, Espiritu Santo is Vanuatu's largest island. Mt. Tabwemasana (1,879 meters), highest peak in the country, has never known a recorded climb, and it's believed that still-uncontacted "pygmy" tribes reside in the impassable interior jungles. Espiritu Santo has played a central role in the history of the country, from Quirós's 1606 settlement on Big Bay, to the giant support base set up by the Americans during WW II, and the Coconut Rebellion of 1980. In 1994, Espiritu Santo and Malo were united as Sanma, the largest of Vanuatu's six provinces.

LUGANVILLE

Apart from Port Vila, Luganville is the only incorporated community in Vanuatu and the headquarters of Sanma Province. It lies at the island's southeast corner on the Segond Channel, a 13-km-long waterway that offers anchorages sheltered enough for a ship to ride out a hurricane. Luganville is called Canal by the locals because of this strait; to people in Port Vila, it's simply Santo.

Luganville is a mixture of French, Chinese, Vietnamese, and American influences, with a

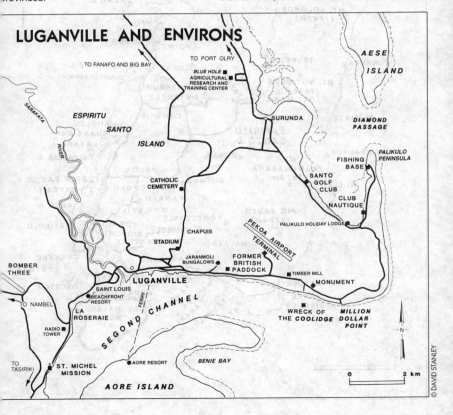

LUGANVILLE AND ENVIRONS

ESPIRITU SANTO

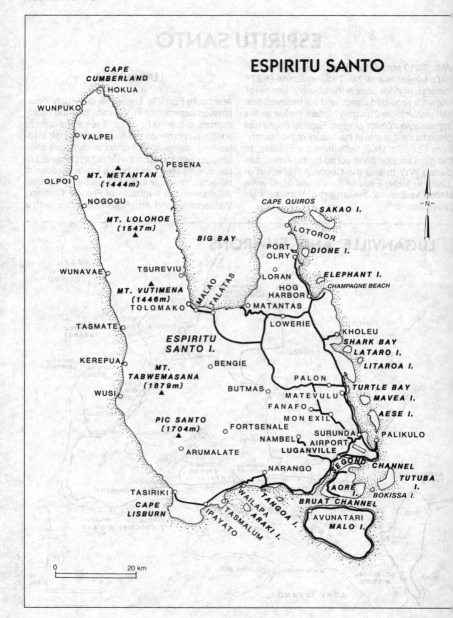

certain Wild West air. In May 1942, more than 100,000 American servicemen arrived on Espiritu Santo to construct an instant city, complete with telephones, radio station, movie houses, hospitals, crushed-coral roads, bridges, airfields, and wharves, so by the end of the war a whole infrastructure had been installed. Three bomber airfields and two fighter strips were here, and a major dry dock functioned at Palikulo. Even today, many of the buildings in Luganville are vintage Quonset huts.

With a population of 10,000, the town is an important economic center. Ninety percent of Vanuatu's copra, two-thirds of its frozen meat, most of its cut timber, and all its cacao pass through Luganville's main wharf. The town doesn't get nearly as many tourists as Port Vila, yet it has all the facilities and there's a large choice of places to stay. It also lacks some of the flair of the capital (and one reader called it shabby).

SIGHTS

Unity Park along Segond Channel near the mouth of the Sarakata River is the site of the PT-boat facility where John F. Kennedy and his *PT-109* were based until being transferred to the Solomons in 1943. Adjoining it are the town hall, market, and a traditional-style chiefs' *nakamal.* The **Women's Handicraft Center** (weekdays 0800-1130/1400-1630, Saturday 0800-1130) in Unity Park sells woodcarvings, baskets, mats, and other such items.

The Sarakata is one of Vanuatu's largest rivers, and Luganville originally occupied its west bank; the east bank, site of the present downtown, was a marsh until reclaimed by the Americans in 1942. Across the bridge over the river is the French high school at **Saint Louis,** site of the original prewar French settlement. Farther southwest, the road inland just before a high radio tower leads two km steeply up to **Bomber Three,** an abandoned WW II airfield. Picturesque **St. Michel Mission** (1912) is five km from town.

Palikulo Peninsula

The area east of Luganville as far as the Palikulo Peninsula is usually done as a day-trip. A large Malaysian-run lumber mill called Santo Veneer is a kilometer past the airport. About two km beyond the airport turnoff, just before the white monument on the left to Captain Elwood J. Euart of the 103rd Field Artillery Battalion (1942), is a road to the shore of Segond Channel. The wreck of the USAT *President Coolidge,* a 22,000-ton prewar luxury liner converted into a troop ship, lies completely submerged here on an angle at the edge of the reef, the bow 18 meters underwater. The *Coolidge* sank on 26 October 1942, when it hit two mines in its haste to get into

Abandon ship! Troops are taken off the USAT President Coolidge, which hit a mine off Santo on 25 October 1942. The wreck is now a favorite of scuba divers.

port without a pilot. Though 5,150 marines were on board at the time, it took two hours for the ship to sink, and most had time to get off. There were only two casualties, a fireman killed in the initial explosion, and Captain Euart, who became trapped in the galley after courageously helping a group of soldiers escape. Today the 210-meter *Coolidge* is famous among the scuba set as the largest diveable wreck in the world. The spot is marked by three floating anchor buoys 100 meters out from the beach.

One km farther along the coastal road is **Million Dollar Point,** where the U.S. forces dumped immense quantities of war materiel before their departure from Espiritu Santo. The local planters refused an American offer to sell them the equipment at a giveaway rate, thinking they'd get it all for free. But a ramp was built out into the water and all rolling stock driven off the end (anthropologist Kirk Huffman calls it "the greatest pig kill of all time"). Today, rusting metal litters the coast near the navigational light here. Million Dollar Point and the *Coolidge* were declared historical reserves in 1983, and it's illegal to take any souvenirs from this area.

After another four km on the coastal road, take the turnoff to the right, which leads north a short distance to the **Club Nautique.** There's a beach, picnic area, toilet, and shower here, and since Palikulo Bay is better protected from the southeast trades than Segond Channel, cruising yachts often anchor off the Club and use the facilities. At the end of the road, two km north of the club, is the **South Pacific Fishing Company** (Box 237, Luganville; tel. 36319), a formerly Japanese-operated cannery that exported fish to the U.S. from 1957 to 1986. The government now uses the facility to freeze and transship tuna from Taiwanese longline boats. Local fishing boats are repaired on the slipways here.

Sports and Recreation

Allan Power Dive Tours (Box 233, Luganville; tel./fax 36822), across the street from Hotel Santo, offers scuba diving on the *President Coolidge,* or at Million Dollar Point. Diving is Vt2,500/3,500 without/with equipment, or Vt2,000/3,000 each dive if you book six or more dives. He'll rent tanks, weights, and belt alone if you can show certification cards—but not for use in diving on the *Coolidge,* please! Allan has

done 20,000 *Coolidge* dives since 1969, and he knows every nook and cranny. Ask Allan to introduce you to Boris, a grouper as big as a seal, which also frequents the wreck. Unlike some dive shops that specialize in large groups from Australia, Allan caters mostly to individuals, and all of his dives are shore dives.

Kevin and Mayumi Green's **Aquamarine Dive Shop** (Box 395, Luganville; tel./fax 36196), at the Santo Sports Club, offers boat diving at Vt4,000/3,600/3,200 per dive for one/six/10 dives, hotel pickups included. Night dives from their boats are Vt500 extra. You can rent equipment such as buoyancy compensators, regulators, wetsuits, snorkeling gear, and torch at Vt1,700 for one dive or Vt2,500 a day. Aquamarine does introductory one-dive resort courses at Vt7,500 for one person, Vt6,300 pp for two or more, and an open-water certification course costs Vt42,000 for one, Vt32,000 pp for two or more (medical certificate required). While you're better off sticking with Allan for the *Coolidge,* Aquamarine's two dive boats can reach offshore wrecks and reefs he doesn't visit. Shark feeding is a specialty.

Pro Dive Espiritu Santo (Dave Cross, Box 323, Luganville; tel. 36911, fax 36912) is based at Aore Island Resort. They charge certified divers Vt4,000 a dive, plus Vt1,500 for equipment (if required). An introductory resort dive is Vt6,000, while PADI certification costs Vt30,000. Boat snorkeling safaris are Vt1,500 pp (minimum of two). This company strongly supports eco-friendly diving.

The nine-hole **Santo Golf Club** (no phone) is at Palikulo. Greens fees are Vt500 and club rental Vt400. You're unlikely to encounter other golfers during the week, and the bar is only open on Saturday. Cows bathe in the lagoon near the clubhouse where a spring provides fresh water, but the crocodiles that once frequented the seventh tee are long gone. The manager of the Westpac Bank in Luganville may have more information on the course.

ACCOMMODATIONS

Shoestring

The single-story **Riviere Motel** (Box 119, Luganville; tel. 36782, fax 36042), between the market and the Sarakata River bridge, has nine rooms with shared bath and communal cooking at Vt1,200/1,800 single/double, or Vt2,200 double with twin beds. It's run by the Catholic mission.

The **Church of Christ Transit House** (Box 36, Luganville; tel. 36633) has two houses near Simonsen Wharf, east of town. There's a two-room guesthouse near Vunamele Church, and a newer eight-room Conference Transit House adjacent. Rooms are Vt1,000/1,800 single/double, and good shared cooking facilities are available. For information, ask Adam Bani at South Pacific Shipping opposite Vanair during business hours, or go directly there after hours. Once you have a room it's fine, but it may take a bit of searching to find the person with the keys. Alcohol is not allowed.

Budget

Eight-room **Asia Motel** (Box 78, Luganville; tel. 36323, fax 36888), opposite the Westpac Bank, is good value at Vt1,500/2,000 single/double with private bath and fan. Room no. 9 at the back of the complex gets a nice sea breeze and is quieter than those in front. Communal cooking facilities are available.

The **New Look Hotel** (Box 228, Luganville; tel. 36440, fax 36095) nearby has nine clean fan-cooled rooms with private bath at Vt2,750/3,850/4,950 single/double/triple. The two rooms with a/c are Vt550 extra. Cooking facilities are provided. Look for the manager in the store below the motel.

The two-story **Unity Park Motel** (Box 85, Luganville; tel. 36052, fax 36025) overlooks Unity Park in the center of town. The 13 clean rooms with communal cooking and bathing facilities are Vt1,320/1,980/2,310/3,080 single/double/triple/quad downstairs, or Vt2,200/2,750 triple for a back/front room upstairs. You can use the washing machine for Vt400.

Jaranmoli Bungalows (Box 239, Luganville; tel. 36712, tel./fax 36857) is beyond Simonsen Wharf, up on the plateau next to a large coconut plantation, two km east of town on the way to the airport. It's owned by Sanma Province. You stay in one of nine thatched bungalows with three beds, fan, toilet, and shower at Vt1,260/2,625 single/double (discounts available for long stays). Cooking is possible in a kitchen shared by all guests. It's a pleasant spot, though a bit out of the way. Call to make sure they're open before going there.

Inexpensive

The **Natapoa Motel** (Box 107, Luganville; tel. 36643), two blocks back behind Hotel Santo, has seven units with cooking facilities, fridge, and private bath at Vt3,600/4,500 single/double, with weekly rates available.

Deco Stop Lodge (Russell and Margaret Donovan, Box 249, Luganville; tel. 36175, fax 36101), near the hospital high up on the hillside above Luganville, caters mostly to "decompression stop" scuba divers. There's a great

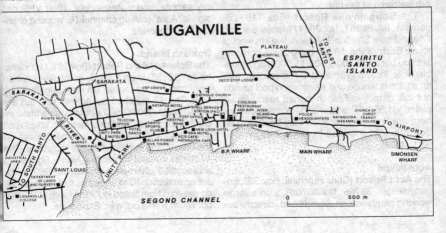

LUGANVILLE

view from the terrace. The five rooms with fan, fridge, and private bath are Vt4,950/6,600 single/double, while a four-bed bunkroom is Vt2,750 pp. If you stay four nights, the fifth is free, if you stay five nights, the sixth and seventh are free. No cooking facilities are provided but meals can be ordered (Margaret's toasted sandwiches are famous).

Moderate

Hotel Santo (Box 178, Luganville; tel. 36250, fax 36749) is a stylish two-story establishment in the middle of town. Its 22 a/c rooms with bath upstairs in the main building are Vt9,980/11,530/12,780 single/double/triple. The regular rooms are overpriced, but Hotel Santo also caters to scuba divers who usually stay in eight rooms facing the swimming pool at Vt5,200/6,000 single/double with bath and fan.

The Beachfront Resort (Mike and Kay Windle, Box 398, Luganville; tel. 36881, fax 36882) is on the beach at "Red Corner," two km west of town. The three a/c bungalows with bath facing the beach are Vt8,500 double, while a long block near the road has two fan-cooled rooms at Vt6,500 and a larger family room at Vt10,000. Cooking facilities are not provided, but there's a restaurant. The motel's spacious front lawn catches a nice breeze off Segond Channel, and an old American wharf and wrecked Taiwanese fishing boat are nearby. Cruising yachts often anchor just off the motel's beach, and yachties are welcome at the bar.

The **Bougainville Resort** (Box 116, Luganville; tel. 36257, fax 36647) faces Segond Channel near St. Michel Mission, five km west of town. Each of the 18 a/c bungalows here will set you back Vt8,500/9,500/11,500 single/double/triple, including breakfast. A restaurant with an attractive terrace and a swimming pool rounds out this attractive French-owned resort (main plates Vt1,650). The food and accommodations here are fine, and it's often fully booked. The beach across the road from the Bougainville isn't usable.

Aore Island

The **Aore Resort** (Chris Hutchins, Box 306, Luganville; tel. 36705, fax 36708) is on a large working plantation on Aore Island, directly opposite Luganville. The 10 thatched bungalows with bath, fan, and fridge are Vt9,570/10,600 single/double including breakfast. Eight of these have decks overlooking the beach, while two are set back in the garden. Try to get one of the beach units at the end farthest away from the restaurant and noisy generator. Another eight two-bedroom family bungalows on a hill above the wharf are Vt18,000 for up to four people. No cooking facilities are provided, but a medium-priced restaurant/bar faces the wharf.

You can snorkel right off their beach (not much to see) or swim in the pool (when it contains any water). Scuba diving is easily arranged with the dive shops in Luganville, and it's a relaxing place to stay while still convenient to town. The large coconut plantation behind the resort is interesting to explore. If you take the road directly inland you'll reach a ramp diagonally up the hill, which passes a large American ammunition bunker now populated by swallows. A dozen more such bunkers are scattered among the huge banyan trees on top of the plateau, and you'll see herds of beef cattle and cacao plantations.

The resort operates a boat shuttle to Luganville four times a day, which costs Vt100/250 each way for guests/nonguests (Vt100 each way for nonguests who order lunch). Airport transfers are Vt2,000 pp return. Cruising yachts are welcome to use the protected anchorage here, and there's mail holding, rubbish disposal, laundry service, and water supply. Their VHF call sign is "Aore" (call-up channel 16, working channel 68). Moderate.

Bokissa Island

The **Bokissa Island Resort** (Box 261, Luganville; tel./fax 36855) is on a sandy coral cay between Aore and Tutuba, seven km from Luganville by boat. The 12 thatched bungalows with fan are Vt14,100/21,000/29,500 single/double/triple including transfers and three meals. It takes a bit more than an hour to walk around Bokissa on the beach, and the reef diving is incredible. The 47-meter coastal trader MV *Henry Bonneaud* was scuttled 200 meters offshore in 1989 to create an attraction. Call ahead as they sometimes do day-trips from Santo including lunch at Vt3,000 pp, which works out well. Expensive.

OTHER PRACTICALITIES

Food

Local meals are served in a double row of hatched huts in Unity Park, and from counters along one side of the market itself. A large plate of beef, chicken, or fish and rice will be around Vt250.

KC's Cafe and Snack Bar (tel. 36675; weekdays 0630-1630, Saturday 0630-1300), opposite Vanair, is a good place for breakfast, lunch, or just a cup of coffee on their pleasant breezy terrace with picnic tables.

Leslie Tonklin's **Natangora Café** (tel. 36623; closed Sunday), on the main street, has a cozy atmosphere, and aside from the tasty cakes, pies, burgers, and omelettes, they have Luganville's top ice-cream cones. The coffee comes with one free refill. The kitchen closes at 1630 weekdays and at noon on Saturday.

The **Santo Sports Club** (tel. 36373; Mon.-Thurs. 0900-midnight, Friday and Saturday 0900-0100, Sunday 0900-2300), serves a good chicken and rice lunch for Vt300, or try the poulet fish at Vt750. The cozy little bar upstairs through the casino offers satellite TV and cheap beer, and you can eat on a balcony overlooking the main street. All this is fine, but it's sad to see the way the locals are exploited by the noisy slot machines in the adjacent gaming room.

The Coolidge Restaurant and Bar (tel. 36096; open 1700-2300 only), near the Shell service station, serves pizza with discounts on Tuesday, Wednesday, and Thursday nights.

Groceries

Since Burns Philp closed there has been no real supermarket in Luganville. However, the many Chinese stores stay open till sundown, even on weekends and holidays.

The selection of vegetables at **Luganville Market** is poor, mainly cabbage, tomatoes, peppers, and string onions.

The **French Bakery** (no sign) is in a white two-story building almost opposite Hardware Santo at the east end of town. They have buns and croissants as well as baguettes, but sell out by early afternoon.

Entertainment

The bar at the Santo Sports Club pretty well sums up Luganville's social scene. Kava is what people drink here, and a good choice is **Natangura Nakamal,** just around the corner from K. Paty's General Store, east of town a bit before the Simonsen Wharf. They open at 1800 daily, and kava is Vt50-100 a cup. Many other *nakamals* are in the Chapuis area beyond the stadium north of town.

Services

The Westpac Bank and National Bank are opposite Motel New Look, while the Bank of Hawaii and ANZ Bank are near the post office a block east. All are open weekdays 0800-1500. Evenings and weekends, you may be able to change money at the Sports Club.

The post office (tel. 36211; weekdays 0730-1130/1315-1630) contains a philatelic bureau. Card telephones are available at the Telecom office, a block back from Unity Park.

The Immigration office (tel. 36724) is at the east end of town.

The public toilets in Unity Park cost Vt30.

Yachting Facilities

Cruisers might like to know that one of the only slips in Vanuatu offering haul-out facilities for yachts is at the Seventh-Day Adventist Church-operated Aore Adventist College (tel. 36414), in Port Lautour on the south side of Aore Island. It can handle up to 40 tons (Vt20,000, plus a per diem), and a well-equipped workshop adjoins. Only boats drawing less than 1.9 meters can enter the lagoon here at high tide. The slipway at Palikulo can haul out ships up to 100 tons.

Information

The Department of Lands and Surveys (tel. 36330; weekdays 0730-1130/1330-1630), across the river in St. Louis, sells topographical maps of Vanuatu at Vt600 a sheet.

The USP Center Library (tel. 36438), inland four blocks on the road from the Santo Sports Club, opens Tues.-Thurs. 0800-1700, Friday 0830-1630, Saturday 0830-1030. The adjacent business office sells a variety of textbooks on the Pacific.

Health

The Northern District Hospital (tel. 36345) is on the hill above Luganville.

A better bet is Dr. Timothy Robert Vocor's Luganville Medical Center (tel./fax 36835; after hours tel. 36141; open weekdays 0900-1300/1400-1730), behind the Westpac Bank.

TRANSPORTATION

By Air

Vanair (tel. 36421), with an office near the Westpac Bank, flies from Espiritu Santo to Port Vila (Vt9,800) four times a day, twice daily via Norsup. Another route from Espiritu Santo to Port Vila goes via Walaha, Longana, Sara, and Lonorore three times a week, making stopovers on Ambae and Pentecost possible to/from Port Vila. Even if you don't plan to stop anywhere between Port Vila and Santo, ask to be booked on a flight that makes a few stops for some free aerial sightseeing. Aircraft based at Espiritu Santo also fly to Maewo (Vt4,800) three times a week, to Gaua (Vt6,000), Sola (Vt6,900), Mota Lava (Vt6,900), and Torres (Vt8,100) twice a week, and to Craig Cove (Vt6,100) and Ulei (Vt5,900) weekly. Many offbeat interisland flights operate between remote outer islands, so study the Vanair timetable.

By Ship

Many of the shipping companies operating the Luganville-Port Vila passenger services don't maintain offices here, so you have to go down to the wharf and start asking. There are several departures a week, with the ships stopping at many smaller islands along the way. The Saraika often ties up at BP Wharf near the center of town. Ask about the barge Roena at Dinh Shipping (tel. 36750) at Melcoffee Sawmill, west of town. You might also find a Chinese trading ship doing two-week trips out of Espiritu Santo collecting copra.

Inter-Island Shipping (Box 5, Luganville; tel. 36180, fax 36465), with an office between the main wharf and town, runs the MV Kawale from Luganville to Pentecost (Vt2,900), Ambrym (Vt3,400), and Port Vila (Vt5,800) every two weeks. Monthly there's a trip to Malekula (Vt2,200). No cabins are available, but the deck fare includes basic meals. It's four days to Port Vila, so this form of transportation is more of an option to Pentecost and Malekula, which onl takes one night.

Smaller copra boats shuttle between Lu ganville and Malekula. For instance, the M Tamata from Atchin Island departs Luganvill every Sunday for Vao, Atchin, Wala, and Rano charging Vt1,000 one-way. The MV Tali als does this run, which takes less than a day. Loo for other such boats at the Simonsen Whar east of Luganville, or at Melcoffee Sawmill, thre km west of town.

The ferry to Aore Island leaves the BP Wha four times daily (Vt250 pp each way).

By Road

Half a dozen minibuses run up and down th east coast between Hog Harbor and Luganvill leaving Hog Harbor in the morning and Luganvill around 1600 in the afternoon. This timing make it impossible to use them for a day-trip, but fine t get to Lonnoc Bungalows. The locals catch ther at Luganville market, but another good place t wait is the benches in front of the Shell servic station (Fung Kwan Chee, tel. 36352) in the cer ter of town. Most buses and trucks gas up her before leaving. Tuesday is market day for th South Santo people, so you can be sure of ride to Tangoa Island (Vt300) that afternoon. Th East Santo people come in on Thursday, so tha day you'll have a choice of rides to Big Bay, Ho Harbor (Vt300), and Port Olry (Vt400). On Sa urday, both groups arrive simultaneously, so yo might get a ride almost anywhere.

"Service" minibuses around town charge Vt7 pp anywhere between the hospital, Chapuis former British Paddock, Melcoffee Sawmill, an St. Michel Mission. To the airport is Vt150 pp, t Palikulo or Surunda Vt200 pp, to Turtle Ba Vt300 pp, to Hog Harbor Vt400 pp. A taxi to th airport is Vt400, to Palikulo Vt800.

Espiritu Santo is a large island and gettin around is difficult unless you hire a minibus o rent a car. Car rentals are available from Hote Santo (Box 178, Luganville; tel. 36250, fa 36749) at Vt3,400 a day, plus Vt34 a kilomete plus Vt1,200 insurance. Unlimited km renta are not available from them.

The Hertz agent is Surata Tamaso Trave (Pascal, Box 26, Luganville; tel. 36537, fa 36116), at the Mobil service station near th post office in town. They charge Vt6,700, plu

Vt1,500 insurance for the cheapest car, tax included. Only a few cars are available, so it's important to reserve.

Tours

Glen Russell of **Butterfly Tours** (Box 79, Luganville; tel. 36257, fax 36647) operates a sightseeing tour that takes in the plantation where James Michener stayed during WW II, the blue holes, and Champagne Beach. Glen charges Vt3,500 pp for two people, with reductions for larger groups (Vt2,000 pp for eight or more). Contact him through Hotel Santo, where he has a reservation book, and also ask about tours at KC's Cafe.

The Donovans at Deco Stop Lodge operate **Man Bush Eco Tours** (tel. 36175) with tours to the center of the island. Their Man Bush Day Tour visits underwater caves and a leaf village at Vt3,000 pp (minimum of four people).

It's also possible to hire one of the Luganville "service" minibuses and organize your own sightseeing tour at Vt4,000/8,000 a half/full day with an 11-seater vehicle, gas, and driver included. Write out a complete list of everything you might wish to see, then negotiate.

Airport

Pekoa Airport (SON), between Luganville and Palikulo, is five km east of town. Pekoa is a reconditioned WW II airstrip, one of five remaining in the area. Taxis (Vt400 for the car) and occasional minibuses (Vt150 pp) connect the airport to town.

EAST SANTO

The pavement on the east coast road ends five km north of Luganville, then it's a potholed coral road all the way to Port Olry. Two km north of Surunda (nine km northeast of Luganville), at the back of the Agricultural Research and Training Center, is a deep, spring-fed pool known as the **Surunda Blue Hole,** with transparent water. Turn in near the research center where you see a public telephone beside the road.

A 50-km ride up the coastal highway from Luganville, through coconut plantations crowded with cattle, brings you to friendly **Hog Harbor,** Espiritu Santo's second-largest village. An English-speaking village, Hog Harbor has a large *nakamal* where you can while away the hours

getting to know the inhabitants. The Co-op Store nearby sells cold drinks. In front of the Presbyterian church overlooking the village is a monument to Dr. John Bowie who introduced Christianity here in 1898. An American base was at Hog Harbor during WW II, and in the early 1970s, American land developer Eugene Peacock attempted to subdivide and sell choice beachfront property near his Lokalee Beach Resort to American Vietnam war veterans. Peacock's land grab set in motion the movement toward independence.

Champagne Beach, one of the finest in the Pacific, is three km off the main road near Hog Harbor (Vt500 admission fee per carload, or Vt200 pp for pedestrians). The talcum white sands curve around a turquoise lagoon, with a coconut plantation and high, jungle-clad slopes behind, and picturesque Elephant Island offshore. Look for a freshwater spring on the east side of the beach at low tide. Cows often stop there for a sunset drink.

Four km north of Hog Harbor on the road to Port Olry is the signposted **Blue Lagoon,** an arm of clear brackish water cut off from the sea by high cliffs. A fee is charged to visit or swim.

At the end of the road 13 km north of Hog Harbor is the French-speaking community of **Port Olry,** with its large Catholic mission. The site is idyllic, and two lakes are on nearby Dione Island, accessible on foot at low tide. Swim in a transparent, spring-fed pool, inland before the second gate on the track north from the village. Visit **Rennet Wharf** for the view, or climb the bush track west of Port Olry for a panorama of the entire area.

Accommodations in East Santo

The landing for **Oyster Island Resort** (Gaétan and Christian Giovanni, Box 183, Luganville; tel./fax 36283) is 300 meters north of the Matevulu College access road, then 500 meters off the main highway, 20 km north of Luganville. It lies on a small island about 200 meters offshore, and visitors are picked up at a dock near the mouth of the river that originates at the Matevulu Blue Hole. The eight fan-cooled bungalows with bath are Vt4,500/5,700/6,500 single/double/triple, breakfast included. Their Melanesian-style restaurant right on the beach serves dishes like poulet fish (Vt1,900), fresh oysters (Vt1,000), and pepper steak (Vt1,300). Dugout canoes for paddling around the lagoon are provided, and scuba diving can be arranged with Aquamarine. A taxi to the resort landing will cost about Vt1,500, or pay Vt200 pp on one of the afternoon minibuses. Yachties are welcome to drop in for a sundowner or a meal (good holding in 6-10 meters of heavy sand). Inexpensive.

One km west of Champagne Beach, 55 km north of Luganville and a bit more than a kilometer off the main road near Hog Harbor, is Kalmer Vocor's **Lonnoc Beach Resort** (Box 190, Luganville; tel./fax 36141). It has by far the most attractive setting of any of Espiritu Santo's resorts, on an idyllic beach with superb views. Nine units cost Vt2,420/3,875/5,325 single/double/triple, including breakfast and tax. The "honeymoon unit" is Vt5,000 double with private bath. Camping is also possible. Meals are Vt500-1,000 each, or you can ask permission to use the restaurant kitchen to cook your own food. This may be allowed when they're not busy, in which case it's wise to inquire when booking and to bring groceries from Luganville. The kerosene lighting and communal bucket showers add a romantic touch. It's set slightly back from the beach and is meticulously maintained. You can't beat the swimming, and there are neighboring villages to visit. Guides for short/long tours are Vt200/500. A day tour to Matantas is Vt5,000 for the whole truck. Other tours are possible to caves, gardens, and a blue hole. Outrigger canoes are Vt500/1,000 a half/full day. You could have the whole place to yourself, but call first to check that they're open. The Hog Harbor minibuses will bring you here most afternoons for Vt400 pp. Budget.

INTO THE INTERIOR

Matantas

Some 46 km north of Luganville, a road runs west through Sara to the **Vatthe Conservation Area** (Box 239, Luganville) at Matantas on Big Bay. The turnoff is a few km south of Hog Harbor. Ten km west of the coastal highway, you'll pass the junction with the rough jeep track south toward Fanafo (which connects with the road to

the western side of Big Bay). Keep straight and another seven km west toward Matantas you'll reach a spectacular viewpoint over Big Bay and the Vatthe reserve. From here the road drops sharply, reaching Matantas after another seven km (or 70 km total from Luganville).

It was here on Big Bay that the Spanish conquistador Quirós established his "New Jerusalem" in 1606. A wall eight meters long with two gun openings, near the point where the Jordan River empties into the bay, is reputed to date from this time. In 1995, most of this area were set aside as a nature reserve run by Chief Solomon and his clan. This ecotourism project is intended to protect 4,470 hectares of rainforest from logging, and it's a terrific place to visit if you don't mind spending a bit of money to support a worthy cause. All visitors pay a Vt500 pp conservation fee upon arrival.

Guests stay in an attractive thatched guesthouse at Vt2,750/3,500 single/double, breakfast included. Other meals cost Vt400-1,400 each. Activities include guided bushwalks (Vt1,000 pp for four hours), horseback riding (Vt500 an hour or Vt2,000 a day), fishing (Vt1,150 pp), canoeing (Vt300), and bow and arrow making. In Luganville, book through the Santo Environment Unit (tel./fax 36153); in Port Vila, Island Safaris (tel./fax 26779) arranges packages. Otherwise information should be available from Russell Donovan at Deco Stop Lodge (tel. 36175), or Surata Tamaso Travel (tel. 36537), at the Mobil service station near Luganville Post Office. Day tours from Luganville are Vt5,000 pp, including transportation, lunch, and a two-hour bushwalk. Budget.

Fanafo

Fanafo (also known as Tanafo or Vanafo), 22 km north of Luganville, was the center of the 1980 Santo Rebellion and Jimmy Stevens' Nagriamel Custom Movement (see **History** in the Vanuatu introduction). A taxi from Luganville should run Vt2,500 return. Until early 1992 Fanafo didn't officially exist. Officials weren't allowed to visit, and no taxes were paid. Today it's quieter, and tourists are even bused in to see traditional dances and similar activities. The villagers cling to custom as a political statement, although most have adopted Western dress.

Several large WW II ammunition storage bunkers and a number of dwarf coconut trees are beside the road from Luganville. The place where Eddie Stevens was killed, at Mon Exil before Fanafo, is now marked by flowers. A sign at the entrance to Fanafo itself announces a Vt500 pp village admission fee, collected daily 0800-1130/1330-1730. Ask for a guide to show you around. Near the information hut and a huge banyan tree is the spot where the pre-1980 cargo cult met in one of Vanuatu's most striking *nakamals,* narrow and very long. This was demolished in 1989, and your entry fee goes toward a new traditional-style *nakamal,* shorter than the old one, slowly being erected here.

In the center of the village is the concrete Nagriamel Upper Council office where Jimmy Stevens was captured as he sat outside with his family, drinking kava. Jimmy had 15 natural sons, 12 daughters, and 28 adopted children, and you may be introduced to Frankie Stevens, a former member of parliament and current Nagriamel leader. Adjoining the office is a flagpole, and nearby the tin-roofed Ten Head Committee building. In 1980 Nagriamel radio broadcast from the small green hut here. Facing the flagpole is the unfinished Federation Bank, construction of which was halted in 1980.

Not far from this area is the Stevens family compound where Jimmy was laid to rest in a circular thatched hut in 1994, after spending 11 years in jail. To enter the compound, your guide must sound a gong at the gate, and you may have to pay an additional fee to Yanki Stevens if you want to see Jimmy's tomb. Jimmy's house is the long thatched building behind the grave. A footpath beside the Stevens compound leads down to the Sarakata River, where you can swim.

You'll probably also be taken to meet Chief Tari Puluk (Terry Bullock) who lives at the end of a road, past peanut and kava plantations. Near an old *nakanal* halfway there is the tomb of Chief Paul Puluk, founder of Nagriamel, who died in 1982. Paul was imprisoned three times for his political activities, and a Bislama history of the movement is posted. Chief Tari Puluk runs a guesthouse next to his home called the **Fomif Bungalow,** where it's possible to stay at Vt500 pp. Activities might include a walk to the large

waterfall nearby, or a three-hour hike to the interior village of Butmas. Shoestring.

North of Fanafo
From Fanafo a steep, rough coral road leads 37 km north to the Jordan River, and on to Talatas, Maiao, and Tolomako on **Big Bay.** It's necessary to ford the Jordan on a concrete ramp, which is only possible in dry weather. Some 12 km before the Jordan, an overgrown bush track continues north to Matantas and Hog Harbor, but this should only be attempted in a 4WD vehicle. A much easier route to Hog Harbor is to the right, nine km north of Fanafo, just where the main road toward the Jordan turns sharp left. This shortcut goes via Palon village, straight to Turtle Bay.

If one is *very* keen (and a bit crazy), it's possible to walk from Big Bay to Wailapa in South Santo in six hard days. It's damp and slippery, and you'll have to cross fast rivers up to your neck, but you'll see some of the most remote people in the Pacific. Just don't go during the rainy season (Jan.-April) if you're not into drowning. You can buy food from villagers along the way, but you'll need a strong stomach. Take plenty of stick tobacco to give them. A guide, of course, would be required. Ask for Chief Robert at **Talatas.** Longer, but less rigorous, is the walk along the coast to Cape Cumberland. In fact, it's possible to hike right around Espiritu Santo this way, if you're experienced and well equipped. A new airstrip has recently opened on the west coast of Espiritu Santo with direct Vanair flights to Luganville (Vt4,800).

SOUTH SANTO

To see a bit of the island and experience village life, go to Santo market on Tuesday or Saturday before 1500, and look for a truck west on the road along Segond Channel through endless coconut plantations to **Tangoa Island.** In 1895, a Presbyterian Bible College intended to spread the Gospel to northern Vanuatu was established on Tangoa by Canadian missionary Joseph Annand, who spent 18 years on the island. At Tangoa, ask for local fisherman John Pama Vari and he'll put you up in his house. The people in the fish market by the river behind

Luganville Market know John well, and can help put you in touch. You may borrow his outrigger canoe to paddle up and down the strait between Tangoa and the mainland (excellent anchorage for yachts here), but don't swim—too

many sharks. Hike up to **Narango** for the view. This is an easy, rewarding trip. (The above appeared in previous editions of this book, and John has since written in asking us to send him *more* visitors!)

THE EASTERN CHAIN

Although the most visited parts of Vanuatu have already been described, there's still a long eastern chain of islands awaiting adventurers who wish to tread where few previous visitors have trod. Epi and Paama, just north of Efate, are the closest outer islands to Port Vila, and relatively inexpensive to fly to, yet few tourists arrive. Ambrym occasionally attracts those interested in its volcanoes or traditional culture. Pentecost is best known for its land diving, and very few foreigners arrive at other times, although North Pentecost offers sundry natural beauties. Ambae is a natural stepping stone for Santo-bound travelers interested in a taste of outer island life. The remote Banks and Torres islands are the least visited of all, lonely outposts of Pacific life beyond the horizons of tourism. Vanair flies to all these islands and each has a special character of its own.

PAAMA AND LOPEVI

Lush little Paama (32 square km) sits between two of Vanuatu's most spectacular volcanoes. Tavie Airport is at Paama's north end, almost opposite Ulei Airport on Ambrym. The administrative center and main wharf are at Liro, a few km southeast of Tavie via a roller-coaster road. Two small resthouses are available at Liro: a one-room guesthouse operated by the Presbyterian Church, and the privately operated **Tavira Guest House** with three rooms. Both charge around Vt1,000 pp, and have cooking facilities. Information should be available from the Malampa Provincial Office (tel. 48506 or 48411) in Liro. A road runs right across the center of Paama. Vanair fares to Paama are Vt6,100 from Port Vila, or Vt2,100 from Ulei. The local Vanair agent is quite strict about overweight baggage.

Paama's eastern neighbor **Lopevi** has a classic symmetrical cone 1,413 meters high, with a five-km base. It's one of the three most active volcanoes in Vanuatu, and when it last erupted in the early 1970s, Lopevi's population was permanently relocated to Epi.

AMBRYM

Ambrym, like Tanna, is famous for its traditional culture and active volcanoes, yet it's less impacted by tourism. Periodic eruptions have left an ash plain near the center of the island, lava valleys, and a rocky, broken coastline. Black sandy beaches run right along the south coast, and Ambrym's dark volcanic soil contrasts sharply with the deep green vegetation.

The island's 12-km-wide caldera probably formed during a cataclysmic eruption 2,000 years ago. It's the most active volcano in Vanuatu, and the only real reason to visit. The lava from Marum (1,270 meters) drains out onto the caldera floor, while Benbow (1,159 meters) drains through fissures into the western part of the island. During the last 200 years there have been at least eight large eruptions with lava flowing from the caldera. The most recent was in 1929.

The 8,000 inhabitants live in the three corners of this triangular island, and their only links are by foot or sea. Two of these communities, Craig Cove in the west and Ulei in the east, have airstrips, with Vanair flights from Port Vila (Vt6,700) two or three times a week, from Espiritu Santo (Vt5,100) and Lamap (Vt2,500) weekly. North Ambrym is accessible only from the sea.

Traditional Culture
The Ambrym islanders produce high-quality woodcarvings and tree fern figures in large quan-

AMBRYM

tities. As in most of northern Vanuatu, a powerful system of traditional copyright applies, and only those with the traditional rights to make certain types of objects are allowed to do so.

Vanuatu's most famous handicrafts come from North Ambrym, especially the tall slit drums called *tamtams* in Bislama. Craftsmen slot and hollow two-meter breadfruit logs, then carve faces on them, and these are used as signal drums. Also characteristic are the black tree ferns carved for the *mhehe* graded rituals, and bamboo flutes up to a meter long with burnt-in geometric designs. Painted masks with hair of bleached banana fiber are worn in rites to increase the yield of yams. Masks worn by participants in Rom dances during the Ole ceremony in July and August represent certain spiritual aspects of power associated with yams.

Storytellers on Ambrym use intricate sand drawings to illustrate their tales. Up to 180 stylized patterns that the artist draws without removing his finger from the sand can convey a variety of messages. Ambrym sorcerers are fa-

mous throughout Vanuatu for their magic, often associated with the destructive power of the island's volcanoes.

Southwest Ambrym

A dramatic black cliff blocks the north end of **Craig Cove,** where a high black beach curves around to the Catholic mission at Fali. Cruising yachts, interisland boats, and local speedboats anchor off this beach, and buy supplies at the adjacent co-op. Craig Cove airstrip is a 10-minute walk away.

Have a look at the fern carvings in front of the Craig Cove Co-op and the slit gong behind Fali's Catholic church. You can hike up to the radio tower on **Menei Hill** (375 meters) in about an hour. The road begins near Fali village, and follows the ridge of Merak Crater all the way. From atop the tower you'll have a sweeping view of western Ambrym, with Malekula and Pentecost also visible in the distance. At the final turn of the road up to the tower, a trail drops sharply to **Lake Fanteng** (visible from the tower) and the black beach beyond.

Halfway back to Craig Cove from the tower, another road runs east down into a coconut plantation. It's an interesting area to explore, and if you take the turn to the right each time the road divides, you should eventually return to the south coastal road. A number of "custom villages" are up this way (including Lele, Pelipetakeuer, and Emlotungan), but you could be asked to pay as much as Vt1,000 pp to visit their dancing grounds *(nasara)* and assorted *tamtam.* Several totempole-like *tamtam* at Lele village have five heads (you can see the same thing in Port Vila for free). Near the Catholic mission at **Sesivi** is a swimmable hot spring in the sea.

The corrugated-metal **Co-op Resthouse** (Box 74, Craig Cove; tel. 48499), facing the anchorage at Craig Cove and sometimes referred to as the "Commercial Center Resthouse," has three rooms at Vt500/800 pp when there isn't/is water. Cooking is possible, but there's no electricity. Shoestring.

The **Presbyterian Resthouse** (public phone at tel. 48507), next to the church and school in Wuro village, a five-minute walk from Craig Cove airstrip or the co-op, has two basic rooms at Vt400 pp with mats on the floor in place of furniture. There's a gas stove and outhouse toilet, but the only place to bathe is the beach. It's primitive, but you'll have the opportunity to observe typical village life here. Shoestring.

At Lonmuek village, just east of Craig Cove, Sam Baleng runs a thatched three-room resthouse. All these are primitive and not convenient as bases for climbing the volcano.

No market exists at Craig Cove, but the Co-op may have tomatoes and onions, and the local baker produces bread when he's in the mood. Small bags of peanuts are Vt20 at the co-op.

The National Bank office next to the co-op can change traveler's checks. The Craig Cove Post Office is a kilometer east of the Craig Cove Co-op on the road to Sanesup.

The Volcano

Anyone interested in climbing the volcano in a reasonable length of time will stay at **Milee Bungalows** (tel. 48555), at Sanesup, about 12 km from Craig Cove airstrip. The five traditional-style bungalows are Vt2,800 pp, including all meals. The pickup truck ride from Craig Cove airstrip to Sanesup is Vt2,000 per group each way (ask), but you may be able to go for less if you're alone and the resthouse owner, Enos Falau, happens to be there anyway. The volcano trip costs Vt4,000 pp, including guide, transport, and the "volcano fee." A cultural show with dancing and traditional magic is Vt7,000 per group. Ask Enos about the art of sand drawing. Island Safaris in Port Vila books packages to Milee. Inexpensive.

The route up to the vast ash plain in the center of the island begins near Lalinda, and you follow a creek bed. If your climb hasn't been prearranged, you'll have to pay the Vt1,000 pp volcano fee to the village chief, who will be able to supply a guide for another Vt1,000. Allow three hours' hard climbing to the Gate (750 meters). From here you can look across the vast ash plain to Benbow and Marum. Clouds can roll in and cover you quite suddenly, and your guide may claim he doesn't know the way to Marum and refuse to take you to Benbow. It's strictly business for the locals, and you only get what you pay for.

Southeast Ambrym

No specific tourist sites exist on southeast Ambrym. The airstrip at **Ulei** ends at a cliff, and few facilities such as resthouses or stores are available. You might be able to stay in the guesthouse of Rakonven Rural Training Center at Toak, a little more than a kilometer west of Ulei Airstrip. There are two rooms, and you can cook. Ask for the manager, Tias James. A road runs along part of the south coast, and it's possible to hike along the beach between the ends of the roads at Eas and Maranata in about five hours. This will put you near the route up the volcano.

North Ambrym

North Ambrym is one of the most traditional areas in Vanuatu. Paramount Chief Tofor resides at Fanla, less than an hour's walk from the SDA mission at Linbul. He'll show you an adze made from iron allegedly given to his ancestors by Captain Cook. Otherwise all there is to see at Fanla is a few slit drums on the dance platform and some statues. To take photos (and maybe just look around), stick tobacco and Vt1,000 must be presented. There's a Catholic mission at Olal. The northernmost villages are mostly French-speaking.

From Linbul it's a three-hour hike through gardens and bush to the top of Mt. Vetlam (1,175 meters), with good views in clear weather.

A thatched four-bed guesthouse is next to **Henyal Orkon Store** (Isiah Bong, tel. 48524) at Ranvetlam. It's Vt2,000 pp including all meals. A guide to Marum costs Vt1,000 a day, plus Vt500 a night, plus tent hire at Vt1,000 pp, plus the Vt1,000 volcano fee (this route is longer than the one from Lalinda). Budget.

Solomon Douglas Guest House (tel. 48405, fax 48467), a 15-minute walk from the co-op in Ranon, has two small bungalows and three rooms in a main house with cooking facilities at Vt2,000/3,500 single/double without meals, or Vt4,000/6,000 including meals. Budget. Clarify prices beforehand as the tour operators have tried to impose overseas rates here. A full-day hike to Marum Volcano is Vt3,800 pp. There's also the Women's Club House (ask for Sarah), a five-minute walk from Ranon co-op, and the **Good Samaritan Resthouse,** right near the Co-op itself (Vt1,000 pp). Budget.

Titus Bato operates **Temar Resthouse** (tel. 48460) at Nopul. The two rooms each have three beds at Vt500 pp, and you can cook. Shoestring.

There's no airport on North Ambrym. You can hike southeast along the coast to Ulei in two days, but not southwest to Craig Cove, as the way is blocked by lava flows. A motorboat from Ranon to Craig Cove will cost around Vt8,000-10,000 (2-3 hours), which can be shared among other passengers. Whenever flights arrive at Craig Cove airstrip, an outboard boat will probably set out for North Ambrym the same afternoon.

PENTECOST

Land Diving

South Pentecost is renowned for its land diving *(Nangol),* a thrilling spectacle on this thickly forested island. Men tie liana vines to their ankles, then jump head-first from atop 30-meter man-made towers, jerking to a halt just centimeters from the ground. Slack in the lifeline vine eases the shock as it stretches to its limit, and the platforms are designed to sway, so the jumpers are rarely injured. During the two weeks it takes to build a tower, women are banned from the area,

A Pentecost land diver leaps from a tower, liana vines tied to his ankles.

and guards are posted each night to protect it from the "poison man."

The story goes that the custom originated when a woman trying to escape an angry husband lured him into a trap by climbing a banyan tree. As the fellow climbed after her, she tied previously prepared liana vines to her ankles and jumped, followed by the man—he fell to his death while she was saved by the vines.

Today this daring feat is part of festival of yams, and there's no stigma attached to any diver who "chickens out." Before jumping, a participant can make a speech refuting allegations against him, or he can criticize anyone he likes, including the chief, on the assumption that if he lies, the spirit of the tower will let him die. The jumping is optional and done for fun—many men and boys do so at every opportunity. Even eight-year-olds prove their courage by hurling themselves from these giddy heights. Only speakers of the Sa language may perform the ritual.

When the plunging diver is about to smash to the ground, the vines stretch out fully. This slows—and finally stops—his fall just as his head brushes the spaded soil, symbolically refertilizing the earth for the next crop of yams. The diving takes place every Saturday in April and May, soon after the yam harvest. Today the diving has assumed on a second function: paying spectators have become the main cash crop for these villagers. It's a rare opportunity to witness an event that has unexpectedly become a part of modern life in the form of bungee jumping.

The tour operators in Port Vila run day-trips from Efate to see the land diving on Pentecost, every Saturday in April and May for Vt40,000 pp. Included in the package are a flight over Ambrym's crater to peek at the bubbling lava inside, and lunch (unless someone forgot to bring it along). In 1999 photography fees were sharply increased to Vt25,000 for a still camera, Vt40,000 for a video camera, or one million *vatu* for a TV camera.

The jumps were originally held at Bunlap village, on the southeast side of Pentecost, but in recent years they've been held at Wali near Lonorore airstrip to spare tourists an exhausting four-hour hike across the island. A new road runs across the south end of Pentecost from Bay Homo to Ranwas near Bunlap, so don't worry if you hear that the diving is at Bunlap again.

Although the tour companies will deny it, it's possible to stay with the locals and pay a custom fee of about Vt5,000-7,500 pp to see the jump. Any visitors who make it across to Bunlap are accommodated for Vt2,000 pp including meals. Bunlap is picturesque, built in the traditional style on a slope. This is a strong custom area, so inquire about taboo days, especially pertaining to women.

North Pentecost

Land diving aside, the north is the most scenically lovely part of Pentecost. High cliffs mark the northern tip of this verdant island, falling away to white beaches with colorful reefs offshore. It's an interesting area to explore without the tourism hype of the south.

Several small local resthouses (around Vt1,000 pp) are available on north Pentecost; for information call the Penama Provincial Offices at Abwatuntora (tel. 38304) or Loltong (tel. 38394). Camping is possible at Philip Varean's **Tiare Resort** is just southwest of Loltong, 12 km south of Sara airstrip. Philip's restaurant is popular among cruising yachties. Alfred Loli runs the three-room **Loli Guest House** at Angoro village, just a few km north of Sara. You can cook.

Sara receives direct Vanair flights from Port Vila (Vt9,300), Longana (Vt2,500), Walaha (Vt3,200), and Espiritu Santo (Vt4,800). Sara airstrip is short and rough, with a cliff at each end. It's subject to closure after rains. Unfortunately there's no connection to Craig Cove and Ulei on Ambrym. The flights between Port Vila and Pentecost pass right over Ambrym's volcanoes, and on a flight to Pentecost or Ambae, you should sit on the right-hand side for a view of central Efate, Epi, Lopevi, Paama, and Ambrym.

AMBAE

When early European explorers visited Ambae, they asked a local chief for the name of the island. He didn't quite understand them, but at that very moment a bird called an aoba flew past, and the chief assumed that was what they wanted to know. Thus, throughout the colonial period, Ambae was known as Aoba. During WW II, a U.S. serviceman named James Michener was stationed at Espiritu Santo, and the sight of Ambae on the horizon fascinated him so much that he called it "Bali Hai"—much better than the name "Leper Island," which Bougainville gave it in 1768 (there were no lepers on Ambae). Only after independence in 1980 did Ambae revert to its original name.

Ambae resembles a capsized canoe, with Maewo and Pentecost the broken outriggers. The people's skin color is lighter than that of other ni-Vanuatu, possibly due to some Polynesian mixing. During the colonial period, women from Ambae were considered good potential wives by local planters, though no European plantations were ever set up on Ambae itself. Today Ambae forms part of Penama Province, along with Pentecost and Maewo.

Ambae is noted for its massive volcanic peak, which rises 1,496 meters above sea level, or 3,900 meters from the sea floor. Lombenden Volcano is one of the world's few active volcanoes with warm-water sulfurous crater lakes. The summit has two large calderas containing three lakes. Manaro Ngoru is a dry lake, while Manaro Lakua is a dammed lake on the edge of the caldera. Lake Vui is two km in diameter. The lakes are thought to be the eyes of the mountain. The god Tagaro took the fire from these craters and threw it across to neighboring Ambrym. There are seven islands in the lakes, and a fumarole beside one. As you swim around, test the echo against the walls of the crater rim.

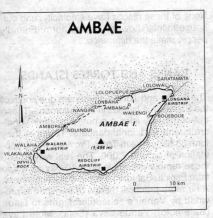

Serious eruptions may have occurred in 1575, 1670, and 1870, and over the past few hundred years there has been a number of devastating mudflows on both sides of the mountain, caused by heavy rains eroding ash deposits. In 1991 Lake Vui boiled, and the vegetation was burned as much as 120 meters above the waterline. This phenomenon was reported by a Vanair pilot; it had been unnoticed by local residents. The presence of the lakes makes Ambae the most dangerous volcano in Vanuatu, as a strong explosion could send mountains of ash and water crashing down to the coast. In December 1994 a sharp increase in volcanic activity was noted, and the volcano came close to erupting on 5 March 1995. Tremors were felt, and the volcano began emitting thick black clouds of ash and smoke. Scientists now consider a major eruption only a matter of time, and emergency evacuation plans have been prepared. During the 1994-1995 activity, Lake Vui's level dropped six meters.

The mountain can be climbed from **Ambanga** in four hours each way, but it's often socked in by fog. It's better to climb to the lakes from West Ambae, however, and a guide will be required in any case. Unless you plan to camp on top, it will take a full day, so set out before 0700. It's a difficult (but fantastic) hike, with bush knives chopping all the way.

A variety of Vanair flights service Ambae's three airstrips. Walaha receives flights from Espiritu Santo (Vt3,100) six times a week; Lonorore (Vt3,900), Sara (Vt3,200), and Port Vila (Vt9,700)

three times a week; and Maewo (Vt3,500) twice a week. Longana is served from Espiritu Santo (Vt4,200) six times a week; and from Lonorore (Vt3,700), Maewo (Vt2,700), Port Vila (Vt11,300), and Sara (Vt2,500) three times a week. Redcliff gets flights from Espiritu Santo (Vt3,600), Lonorore (Vt3,500), and Port Vila (Vt9,300) three times a week. With careful planning you could fly into one airstrip and out from another.

East Ambae

Saratamata, at the east end of Ambae, is the headquarters of Penama Province. **Longana** airstrip, three km from Saratamata, is on a slope, forcing the plane to land uphill and take off downhill. The Church of Melanesia mission, hospital, and post office (tel. 38347) are six km north at Lolowai, where Lake Wai Memea occupies a volcanic crater. The pretty village of Lolopuepue on the north coast is the former French headquarters, attested to by its Catholic church and stone buildings. The interisland ship ties up to a wharf here.

Due to high cliffs near the center of the island, no road runs right along the north coast, although the footpath between ends of the road is commonly used. A good plan would be to hike the 35 km from Longana to Walaha airstrip, with the strong possibility of a ride at least part of the way. A new road along the south coast connects Longana to Walaha via Redcliffe.

Tausala Guest House is the green-colored European-style guest house just across the airstrip from Longana's small terminal. It's run by Gladis Bani who works at the Penama Provincial Office (tel. 38348) at Saratamata. The one room with a double bed and two rooms with four bunks are around Vt1,500 pp, and cooking facilities are provided. Try to reserve as it's booked by contract workers. Budget.

There's also a **Provincial Resthouse** near the Penama Provincial Office at Saratamata, about three km from Longana Airport. The six rooms are Vt1,000 pp, and several stores and the beach are close at hand, which makes it a very convenient place to stay. Call ahead for reservations. Budget.

The hospital (tel. 38302) at Lolowai has one guest room available, as does Vureas High School (tel. 38378), two km northwest. Inquire about these locally.

West Ambae

If you're arriving from Longana, the road will have ended at Loloaru. A well-used footpath leads four km west to Lolombaeko, then there's a steep and winding road another four km to the Catholic mission at Loone Lakua, just above a small black-sand beach. **Nduindui,** the administrative and commercial center of West Ambae, is five km west of there. Nduindui has a small National Bank agency, open Monday, Wednesday, and Friday. **Walaha** airstrip is seven km southwest.

You can climb to Lake Vui from several points along the north coast, including Lovutialao and Lokwainavoaha above Loone Lakua. Allow at least four hours each way, plus the time you wish to spend on top. Expect the mountain to be cloud-covered.

If you have a bit of time to kill before your flight out of Walaha, walk southeast about 15 minutes up the road from Halelulu Guest House to Redcliffe. At the top of a grade, look for a track up through the bush to the tall **radio repeater tower** on Vuti Ngoro Ngoro. It's possible to climb the tower for the view.

A good base for climbing up to Lake Vui is **Chief Charlie Bani's Guest House** at Nanako, seven km northeast of Walaha airstrip. The house is just above the road, 500 meters east of Nduindui Hospital and the two rooms go for Vt1,000 pp with shared cooking. Several small stores and fruit markets are nearby. Information can be obtained by calling the hospital at tel. 38345. Budget. If Charlie's place happened to be full, you could also try the more basic **Sunshine Inn,** another 500 meters east at Navitora village. The two rooms are Vt1,000 single or double, and you can also cook. Shoestring.

Halalulu Community Guest House is in a large community center building, about a 15-minute walk up the road toward Redcliffe from Walaha airstrip. The two adequate rooms with cooking facilities are Vt1,000 pp. There's always a lot of activity around the community center and adjacent Apostolic church, so you get to meet people at the expense of some of your privacy. To send word that you're coming, call the airport snack bar (tel. 38362) and leave a message. Budget.

If Halalulu happened to be occupied, try the church-run guesthouse near another Apostolic church in Walaha village down on the coast.

None of these places have electricity, and outhouse toilets/showers are the norm. Friendly people make the difference.

BANKS AND TORRES ISLANDS

The Banks and Torres islands are due south of the Santa Cruz Islands in the Solomons. These out-of-the-way isles are noted for their handicrafts and traditional dancers. Together they form 882-square-km Torba Province with a population of around 7,000. The real way to see these remote islands is on a 10-day roundtrip from Espiritu Santo on a copra-collecting vessel. A far more practical means of transport is provided by Vanair's scheduled flights to Gaua (Saramolo), Vanua Lava (Sola), Mota Lava (Ablow), and Loh (Linua). Very few travelers make it this far.

Banks Islands

Gaua (Santa Maria) is a circular green island with many stone house foundations that recall the large prehistoric population ravaged by blackbirding and disease. Gaua is interesting for its fumaroles and sulfur springs, and especially the deep crater lake drained by a waterfall on smoking Mt. Garet (797 meters). The mountain can be climbed from Namasari village on the northeast side of Gaua. The **Charles Bice Wongrass Guest House** (tel. 38519) is a three-minute walk from Saramolo airstrip, not far from Namasari. The two rooms in one leaf house are Vt2,000/3,500 single/double. Meals are served, or you can cook for yourself. Gaua receives Vanair flights from Espiritu Santo (Vt6,000), Sola (Vt2,900), and Mota Lava (Vt3,500) twice a week. Budget.

Mere Lava is a circular volcanic island, four km in diameter, with a beautiful symmetrical cone 1,028 meters high. The volcano erupted in 1606 and 1906, yet terraced villages stand on its steep slopes.

Vanua Lava, located 22 km north of Gaua, is the largest and most heavily populated of the Banks Islands. The main airstrip for the Banks is four km northwest of Sola, headquarters of Torba Province. Vanair services from Espiritu Santo (Vt6,900), Gaua (Vt2,900), Mota Lava (Vt2,400), and Loh (Vt8,100) arrive at Sola, once or twice a week. Sola is on the south side of Port Patteson, a natural harbor with safe anchorage year-round. Jets of steam rise from the hot springs on the slopes of Mt. Sere'ama (921 meters), an active volcano that erupted in 1965.

The Torba Provincial Office (Box 12, Sola; tel. 38550) at Sola operates the **Sola Guest House** with three two-room houses at Vt2,000/3,500 single/double. Reservations are recommended as it's often occupied for extended periods by provincial employees. Budget. Nearby, Father Luke Dini operates **Leumerus Guest House** at Vt1,000 pp. It's easy to call him up for reservations at tel. 38553, and you'll be made most welcome. Budget.

Ureparapara Island is a sunken volcano with a drowned crater that large ships can sail into. Some 300 people live there.

Torres Islands

Surfers should consider the Torres Islands, an outlying corner of the Pacific not explored until the mid-1800s. Linua airstrip at the north end of **Loh** has a weekly Vanair service from Espiritu Santo (Vt10,300) and Sola (Vt8,100). The **Torres Guest House** at Lungharigi on Loh is operated by the community. It's a 15-minute walk from the airstrip, across the reef at low tide. The four rooms are Vt1,500/2,500 single/double, and you can cook. Budget.

CAPSULE BISLAMA VOCABULARY

bilong baim—for sale

Em ia haumas?—How much is it?
Em i hat smol smol.—It's warm.
Em i lait nau—It's late

go insait nating—admission fee
gut moning—good morning
gut naet—good night

i gut nomo—just fine

karim olsem yu laik—help yourself

Lukim yu.—See you later.

Me les lilbit—I feel a little tired.

Mi mus paiim long hau mas?—How much should I pay?

Mi no harim?—Beg your pardon?
Mi no save.—I don't understand/know.
Mi tekem emia.—I'll take this one.

Nam bilong mi . . .—My name is . . .

Olgeta samting bilong mi hia.—These are my things.
ol men—men's
ol woman—women's

plis—please
pusim—push
puspus—intercourse

taim i ren—rainy season
tata—goodbye

tenk yu tumas—thank you very much
tumora—tomorrow

Wanem nem bilong yu?—What's your name?
Wanem taim?—What time is it?
wan pikinini blong rot nomo—an illegitimate child

yo no toktok—silence
Yu orait?—How are you?
Yu save?—Do you understand/know?
Yumi mit wea?—Where can we meet?

SOLOMON ISLANDS
INTRODUCTION

One of the last corners of the world to fall under European religious and political control, the Solomon Islands today remain the best-kept secret in the South Pacific. It's all here: shark-callers, war wreckage, gold, and malaria; every Pacific race is present, from blue-black Papuans to chocolate-colored, blond Melanesians, bronze-skinned Micronesians, and fair-complexioned Polynesians. The variety of cultures and customs is striking, and the traditional ways are remarkably alive.

Like neighboring Vanuatu, it's a land of contrasts and adventure, with jungle-clad peaks, mighty volcanoes, uplifted atolls, crashing waterfalls, mist-enshrouded rainforests, dark lagoons, scattered islands, and brilliant coral reefs. No other island group in the Pacific has a greater diversity of landforms. Once you figure out where the Solomon Islands are and actually get there, you won't want to leave.

Unless you're on a tour, you'll find travel outside the capital, Honiara, an unstructured, make-your-own-arrangements affair. The number of visitors is negligible, and most of those who do come stay only for a few days, mainly in the capital or scuba diving at Gizo. This gives slightly intrepid travelers an unparalleled opportunity to get well off the beaten track and have a genuine South Sea paradise all to themselves. So you're in for something totally original! Indeed, these are the Happy Isles.

The Land

With its 27,556-square-km area, the Solomons is the second-largest insular nation of the South Pacific (after Papua New Guinea). This mountainous, thickly forested country, 1,860 km northeast of Australia, is made up of six large islands in a double chain (Choiseul, Isabel, Malaita, and New Georgia, Guadalcanal, Makira), about 20 medium-size ones, and many smaller islets and reefs—922 islands in all, 347 of them inhabited. The group stretches more than 1,800 km from the Shortlands in the west to Tikopia and Anuta in the east, and nearly 900 km from Ontong Java in the north to Rennell Island in the south. (Rennell is the world's largest uplifted atoll, while Ontong Java is the South Pacific's largest true atoll.)

The Solomons are on the edge of the Indo-Australian and Pacific plates, which accounts for volcanic activity, past and present. Tinakula,

Savo, Simbo, and Vella Lavella are active parts of the circum-Pacific Ring of Fire, and there's a submarine volcano called Kavachi just south of the New Georgia Group. The New Britain Trench, southwest of the chain, marks the point where the Indo-Australian Plate is shoved under the Pacific Plate. This causes frequent earthquakes and uplifting; consequently, many of the

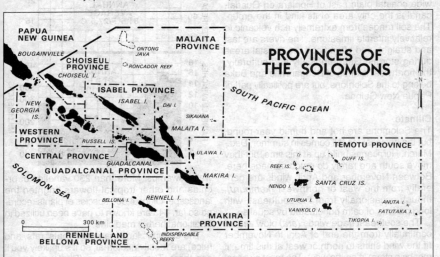

THE SOLOMONS AT A GLANCE

PROVINCE	MAIN TOWN	POPULATION (1997 est.)	AREA (sq. km)	HIGHEST POINT (meters)
Guadalcanal	Honiara	78,396	5,336	2,447
Malaita	Auki	96,951	4,243	1,303
Rennell and Bellona	Tingoa	2,729	276	220
Central	Tulagi	22,497	1,000	510
Western	Gizo	53,110	5,279	1,661
Choiseul	Taro	25,689	3,294	1,060
Isabel	Buala	19,770	4,014	1,392
Makira	Kirakira	30,599	3,188	1,250
Temotu	Lata	19,181	926	923
SOLOMON ISLANDS	**Honiara**	**348,922**	**27,556**	**2,447**

Polynesian outliers are elevated atolls. Rennell is one of the finest examples of a raised limestone atoll in Oceania.

The other islands are mostly high and volcanic, with luxuriant rainforest shrouding the rugged terrain. Under these conditions road-building is difficult; only Malaita, Makira, and Guadalcanal have fairly extensive networks. The wide coastal plain east of Honiara on Guadalcanal is the only area of its kind in the group. The soil ranges from extremely rich volcanic to relatively infertile limestone. The rivers are fast and straight, and often flood the coastal areas during storms. Geographically and culturally, the northwest islands of Bougainville and Buka belong to the Solomons, but are politically part of Papua New Guinea.

Climate

The Solomons are hot and humid year-round, but the heaviest rainfall comes in summer, Dec.-March. Hurricanes build up at this time, but they move south and rarely do much damage here. Between November and April, winds are generally from the west or northwest *(komburu)*, though occasionally from the southeast, with long periods of calm punctuated by squalls.

The southeast trade winds *(ara)* blow almost continually from the end of April to November (if the wind shifts to north or west at this time, it means a storm is on the way). The most pleasant time to visit is winter, July-Sept., when rainfall, humidity, and temperatures are at their lowest. On the high islands the southeast coasts, which face the winds, are far wetter than the more sheltered north coasts. Yet the cooling sea breezes temper the heat and humidity along all coasts year-round.

Flora and Fauna

Mangroves and coconut groves shelter the coastal strips, while the interiors of the high islands are swallowed by dense rainforest. The forest climbs through 24 belts, from towering lowland hardwoods to the mosses atop Guadalcanal's 2,300-meter peaks. Where the forests have been destroyed by slash-and-burn agriculture or logging, grasslands have taken hold. Crocodiles lurk in brackish mangrove swamps in the river deltas, while sago palms grow in fresh-

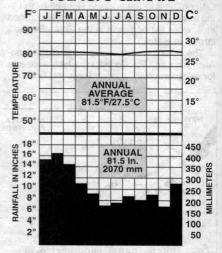

TULAGI'S CLIMATE

ANNUAL AVERAGE 81.5°F/27.5°C

ANNUAL 81.5 In. 2070 mm

water swamps. More than 230 varieties of orchids and other tropical flowers brighten the landscape. Of the 4,500 species of plants recorded so far, 143 are known to have been utilized in traditional herbal medicine.

The endemic land mammals (bats, rats, and mice) are mostly nocturnal, so it's unlikely you'll see them. The gray cuscus *(Phalanger orientalis)* is the only marsupial found in the Solomon Islands. Birdlife, on the other hand, is rich and varied, with about 223 species including 16 species of white-eyes, fantails, rails, thrushes, and honeyeaters that occur only here. The most unusual is the megapode or incubator, a bird that lays large eggs in the warm volcanic sands of the thermal areas. After about 40 days, the newly hatched megapodes dig themselves out and are able to fly short distances as soon as their wings dry. There are many species of colorful parrots and 130 species of butterflies, including several species of birdwings.

The 70 species of reptiles include crocodiles, frogs, lizards, skinks, snakes, toads, and marine turtles. The five species of sea turtles nest from November to February. Several of the 20 species of snake are poisonous, but fortunately they're not common and are no threat. Centipedes and scorpions are two other potentially dangerous but seldom-encountered jungle creatures. The isolated Santa Cruz Group has fewer indigenous species than the main island chain. Each year thousands of rare birds, reptiles, amphibians, and butterflies are exported from the Solomons to be sold in Asia, North America, and Europe.

HISTORY AND GOVERNMENT

Prehistory

The first inhabitants were Papuan-speaking hunters and gatherers, who may have arrived as early as 30,000 years ago. Some 4,000 years ago, Austronesian-speaking agriculturists joined their predecessors. The earliest date of known human habitation, provided by the radiocarbon dating of remains from Vatuluma Posovi Cave (excavated by David Roe) near the Poha River, Guadalcanal, is 1300-1000 B.C. Stone tools found here date from 4000 B.C. Due to the nature of the objects discovered and the absence of pottery (the 19th-century inhabitants of the island still had no pottery), it's believed that the occupants of this quite sizable cave were the direct ancestors of the present-day people of Guadalcanal. On the other hand, the many different languages currently spoken by the Melanesians illustrate a long period of mixed settlement.

Lapita pottery has been found in the Santa Cruz Islands, and New Britain obsidian was carried through the Solomons to Santa Cruz and New Caledonia some 3,000 years ago, probably by the first Polynesians. Today's Polynesian enclaves in the Solomons bear no relation to these original eastward migrations, however. Their forebears arrived in a back-migration within the last 1,500 years to Anuta, Tikopia, Bellona, and Rennell from Wallis and Futuna, and to Taumako (Duff Islands), Pileni (Reef Islands), Sikaiana, and Ontong Java from Tuvalu.

The Spanish Episode

There were three Spanish expeditions to Melanesia in the late 16th and early 17th centuries: two by Álvaro de Mendaña (in 1568 and 1595) to the Solomon Islands, and one in 1606 by Mendaña's pilot Pedro Fernandez de Quirós to Van-

uatu. Incan legends told of a rich land 600 leagues west of Peru, so the eager conquistadors prepared an expedition to find the elusive El Dorado.

Mendaña set out from Peru in November 1567 and arrived on 7 February 1568 at Estrella Bay, Isabel Island, to become the first European to "discover" the Solomons. Mendaña established a base on Isabel, where his men built a small, five-ton, undecked vessel to explore reefs that would have destroyed a bigger, clumsier ship. At the beginning of March, a fleet of war canoes paddled near the Spanish ship, presenting Mendaña with a quarter of baked boy, nicely garnished with taro roots. Mendaña sailed his brigantine among the islands, giving them the Spanish names still used today.

In retaliation for violence and treachery initiated earlier on Guadalcanal by a subordinate commander, the islanders massacred nine members of a watering party sent out by Mendaña. The Spaniards then burned every village within reach, and when they departed, Guadalcanal was left in ashes and death. Mendaña left Makira for Peru on the morning of 17 August 1568.

He returned in 1595, stopping en route to discover and name the Marquesas Islands in Polynesia. This time Mendaña landed on Nendo, in the Santa Cruz Group, where he hoped to found a Spanish colony. For this reason a number of women accompanied the expedition, including Mendaña's ambitious wife, Doña Isabel Barreto, who hoped to be queen of the wealthy Solomon Islands. Yet Mendaña himself and many others soon died of malaria. The three surviving Spanish ships left for the Philippines, though one became separated and probably sank off San Cristobal (Makira). In 1606 Mendaña's pilot, Pedro Fernandez de Quirós, made another attempt at colonization on Espiritu Santo in Vanuatu before the Spanish gave up on the area.

Mendaña found no gold in the Solomons, but he gave the islands their exotic name, implying to his royal patrons that they were as rich as, or even the source of, King Solomon's treasure—an early example of a real-estate salesman's trickery. The name soon appeared on maps and in formal reports, and was eventually adopted as official. Mendaña placed the Solomons far to the east of their actual location, and for the next 200 years they were lost to European explorers.

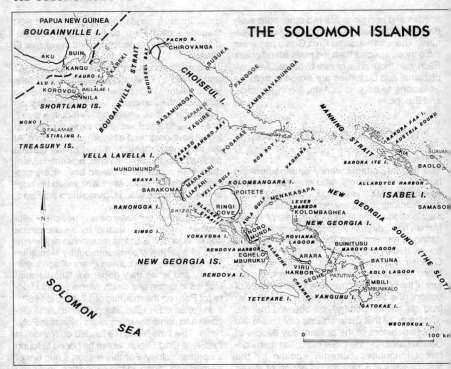

THE SOLOMON ISLANDS

Recontact and Exploitation

In 1767, Captain Philip Carteret rediscovered Santa Cruz and Malaita; he was followed a year later by Bougainville, who visited and named Choiseul and other islands to the north. Captain John Shortland sailed past Guadalcanal and San Cristobal in 1788, the same year the La Pérouse expedition was lost at Vanikolo. These explorations opened the door to traders, missionaries, and labor recruiters. Beginning in the 1830s, traders passed through regularly, purchasing bêche-de-mer, mother-of-pearl, turtle shell, and sandalwood. By 1860, stone tools had been replaced almost everywhere with iron. Some traders cheated the islanders and spread disease in their wake.

Copra became important in the 1870s, and labor recruitment for the cane fields of Queensland and Fiji also began about this time. The treacherous methods of the blackbirders, who often kidnapped workers, sparked a wave of intense anti-European feeling, which resulted in the murder of many honest traders and missionaries. Some recruiters even dressed in priests' gowns to ensure a peaceful reception on an island. Between 1870 and 1910, some 30,000 people were removed from the islands; 10,000 never returned. In retaliation, the natives killed Monseigneur Epalle, their first real Catholic bishop, on Isabel in 1845; Anglican Bishop John Coleridge Patteson on Nukapu, Reef Islands, in 1871; and Commodore Goodenough on Nendo, Santa Cruz, in 1875. The recruiting became more voluntary in the later 19th century, but it still amounted to economic slavery. This system died out in Queensland in 1904, when most blacks were expelled from Australia, and in Fiji in 1910.

The Missionaries

The earliest attempts to implant Christianity in the Solomons were by Catholics: first Mendaña in the 16th century, then the Society of Mary in the

1840s. Mendaña failed, and the Marists withdrew in 1848. A decade later, the Anglicans of New Zealand began to take an interest in the Solomons. Rather than sending white missionaries directly into the area, they used the more cautious technique of taking Solomon Islanders to a facility on Norfolk Island (between New Caledonia and New Zealand) for training. The Melanesian Mission of those days, covering both northern Vanuatu and the Solomons, has grown into today's Church of Melanesia (Anglican).

The Catholics returned at the end of the 19th century and established missions on Guadalcanal and Malaita. Around 1904, Solomon Islands laborers returning to Malaita from the cotton and sugar plantations of Queensland brought back the South Seas Evangelical Mission. Some who had worked in Fiji returned as Methodists;

as a result, the United Church (created by a merger of Methodists and Congregationalists in 1968) is active in the Western Solomons. The Seventh-Day Adventist (SDA) Church here dates from 1914 with the largest number of followers around the Marovo Lagoon and on Malaita.

Although the missionaries effaced many old traditions, they also pioneered education, health care, and communications, transforming the country from one of the most dangerous areas on earth to one of the most peaceful. Their influence remains strong today. Of the 97% of the population that now professes Christianity, 34% belongs to the Church of Melanesia, 19% is Catholic, 18% South Seas Evangelical, 11% United, and 10% SDA. Around 5,500 Solomon Islanders still follow traditional religions, although this number is declining.

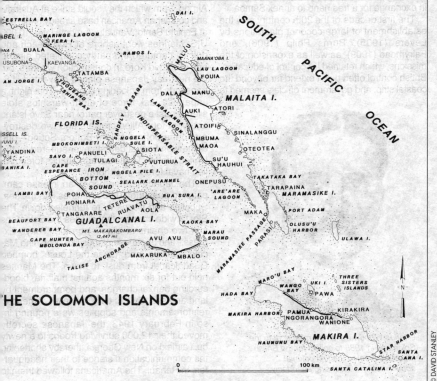

THE SOLOMON ISLANDS

© DAVID STANLEY

The Colonial Period

In 1884 Britain declared a protectorate over Papua in response to Australian alarm at German expansion into New Guinea. By the 1890s the Germans had established interests in the North Solomons (Bougainville and Buka), so in 1893 the British also declared a protectorate over New Georgia, Guadalcanal, Makira, and Malaita to limit German advances, protect resident Europeans, and in response to pleas from missionaries, to control the labor trade.

In 1896 C.M. Woodford, the first resident commissioner, set up headquarters at Tulagi in the Florida Group, with orders to raise sufficient local revenue to cover his own expenses. The Santa Cruz Group, Rennell, and Bellona became part of the British Solomon Islands Protectorate in 1898 and 1899. In 1900 Germany ceded to Britain the Shortlands, Choiseul, Isabel, and Ontong Java in exchange for a free hand to annex Samoa.

The first decade of the 20th century saw the establishment of large coconut plantations by Levers (1905), Burns Philp (1906), and Fairymead (1909), as well as expansion of the missions, which retained full control of education. British control often didn't extend far beyond the coastal strip, and government officials seemed to

Charles Woodward, a naturalist sent to the Solomans in 1885 to collect for the British Museum, created the first colonial administration almost singlehandedly.

appear in villages only to collect taxes and punish people. Life led a sleepy course until the Japanese seized the Solomons in 1942.

The Pacific War

After Singapore fell in February 1942, the South Pacific was fully exposed to attack. Stung by the Doolittle raid on Tokyo in April, the Japanese moved south and occupied Tulagi, Florida Group, in May 1942. A Japanese invasion fleet sailed toward Port Moresby in Papua, but was turned back in the Battle of the Coral Sea. On 4 June another invasion fleet was stopped at the Battle of Midway, in which Japan lost four aircraft carriers.

In the Solomons, however, the war was just beginning, as the Japanese landed on Guadalcanal on 7 July. They quickly began constructing an air base on the site of today's Henderson Airport, from which they could strike at Australia and counter an American base already underway at Espiritu Santo, Vanuatu. A month later, 10,000 U.S. Marines went ashore at Red Beach and quickly captured the partly completed airstrip and unarmed Korean construction workers, but the next day Japanese planes prevented U.S. transports from unloading supplies. That night, a Japanese task force of eight warships stole silently past a destroyer patrol near Savo Island and sent four Allied cruisers and two destroyers to the bottom of Iron Bottom Sound—one of the worst naval defeats ever suffered by the United States. These savage attacks forced Allied naval forces to withdraw.

The Japanese then began an intense campaign to push the 10,000 Marines into the sea. Supplies and troops were funneled down The Slot (a wide channel that divides the Solomons into two chains of islands) on the "Tokyo Express," and Japanese planes like "Washing Machine Charlie" and "Louie the Louse" bombed Guadalcanal from dusk to dawn. The Marines held out for six months against malaria, bloodcurdling banzai charges, and bombardment by land and sea. By this time, however, American reinforcements and supplies were pouring in, so in February 1943, the Japanese secretly moved their 12,000 surviving troops to a newly built airfield on New Georgia, thereby shortening the communication distance to their headquarters in Rabaul. The Americans followed them to

A B-17 bomber over the Solomons on 5 October 1942; in the background, smoke is rising from Gizo town.

New Georgia in July, with major actions at Rendova and Munda, but a few die-hard Japanese detachments held out on Choiseul and in the Shortlands until 1945. Guadalcanal is significant because it was the first U.S. victory against land-based Japanese forces during WW II.

Some 25,000 Japanese and 5,000 American soldiers were killed or wounded on Guadalcanal itself, plus many more in the surrounding sea and air. Official histories do not mention how many Solomon Islanders were killed. A Solomon Islands Defense Force was established in 1939, but at the time of the Japanese invasion it consisted of only seven Europeans, two Chinese, and 178 local police who were hurriedly evacuated from Tulagi.

In December 1942 a Service Battalion was formed, with a base on Malaita where Solomon Islanders were trained to act as scouts for the U.S. Marines. The Americans called the battalion the "International Brigade," due to its mix of British, New Zealand, Fijian, and Solomons personnel, who only numbered a couple of hundred. The battalion was disbanded after the liberation of Guadalcanal in 1943.

Also highly active was the coastwatching organization, which used radio transmitters to report on Japanese movements from behind enemy lines. Many of these coastwatchers were members of the British administration who knew the area well, but they were aided by militant churchmen, nuns, planters, mission nurses, and hundreds of loyal islanders. Throughout the conflict villagers risked their lives to rescue downed airmen and seamen, and many American lives were saved, including that of President John F. Kennedy.

The Aftermath

World War II left deep scars on the Solomons. The former capital, Tulagi, was devastated when the Americans recaptured it, so the returning British administration chose to establish a new capital at Honiara to take advantage of the infrastructure installed by the Americans during the war. A high percentage of the Solomons' roads and airstrips date from the war. Military dumps and scattered wreckage can still be found in the bush east of Henderson Airport, although time and souvenir-hunters are beginning to take their toll.

Perhaps the most unexpected outcome of the campaign was the rise of the Ma'asina Ruru movement (the Brotherhood), dubbed "Marching Rule" by local expatriates. Thousands of islanders who'd been forced into the bush to avoid the fighting returned and found great American armies possessed of seemingly limitless wealth and power. This spectacle, coupled with dissatisfaction in a colonial system that treated natives like naughty children, gave birth to a widespread cargo cult on Malaita. Ma'asina Ruru attempted to reorganize society on the basis of "custom," but in 1948 the British administration decided that things were moving in an undesirable direction and used police to crush the movement. By 1949, some 2,000 islanders had been imprisoned for refusing to cooperate with the government.

This adversity united the Malaita people for the first time, and the British were forced to respond. The Malaita Council, formed as a compromise in 1953, was the beginning of the system of local government followed in the Solomons today. Unlike cargo cults in Vanuatu and New Guinea, little remains of the original "Marching Rule," although individual Americans are still popular. By 1964 the local government councils were handling all regional affairs. A nominated Legislative Council was created in 1960; some elected members were added in 1964. In 1974 this became an almost entirely elected Legislative Assembly. Internal self-government followed in 1976, and full independence on 7 July 1978. A 1977 ordinance converted all alienated land owned by foreigners into 75-year, fixed-term estates on lease from the government, a system that continues today.

In 1988 Solomon Islands joined Papua New Guinea and Vanuatu to form the Melanesian Spearhead Group to support the independence struggle in New Caledonia. In 1992, however, relations with P.N.G. worsened abruptly after incursions into the Shortlands by the P.N.G. Defense Force in pursuit of rebels from Bougainville Island. In 1993 Solomon Islands sent additional field police to the area after two boatloads of P.N.G. troops landed on Mono Island and exchanged fire with Solomons police. In response to the crisis, Solomon Islands created a new paramilitary field force independent of its police.

After the 1997 election, Bartholomew Ulufa'alu assumed the post of prime minister with a promise to end the corruption, uncontrolled borrowing and spending, and general mismanagement that had characterized the administration of his predecessor, Solomon "Solo" Mamaloni. In early 1998 it was revealed that Mamaloni had ordered US$4 million in arms and ammunition, two light aircraft, and a helicopter gunship from American sources with the assistance of U.S. diplomats, allegedly for the defense of the country's northern border. Ulufa'alu tried to cancel the order, asserting that in Solo's hands the weapons could have led to a war with P.N.G., and it was rumored that at least part of the weaponry was destined for the Bougainville rebels. Australia strongly condemned

this American-sponsored destabilization of the southwestern Pacific.

Government

The head of state is an appointed governor-general who represents the British Crown. The 50-member National Parliament elects a prime minister from its ranks, while the 16-minister cabinet is chosen by the prime minister from among those members of parliament who supported him; opposition members routinely cross the floor after being tempted with ministerial appointments or paid bribes by special interests. Most members of parliament belong to one of several political parties based on personalities rather than issues; others are nominally independent and sell their votes to the highest bidder. There's a high turnover of members.

In 1981 seven provinces were created, each with an elected premier and provincial assembly. In 1991 Choiseul Province was separated from Western Province, and in 1993 Rennell and Bellona Province was created out of Central Province. Honiara is administered separately from Guadalcanal Province by the Honiara Town Council. Although many powers have been transferred from the national to the provincial governments, the latter are largely dependent on the former for financing. The provincial governments are supported by the head tax called "basic rate", a colonial levy originally intended to force the islanders to sell part of their produce or to work for planters. Within each province are various area councils—each with a president—that deal with local or village matters.

ECONOMY

The monetary economy is largely based on the exploitation of the country's rich natural resources by foreign corporations; expatriates control most business. Exports are reasonably diversified. Timber is the main export, followed by fish. Palm oil, copra, and cacao are a distant third, fourth, and fifth. The opening of a large mine on Guadalcanal in 1998 will add gold to the list of top exports. Imports are primarily manufactured goods, fuels, and processed food. Australia profits greatly from trade with the Solomons, selling it much more than it buys.

The government owns a huge chunk of the economy through the Investment Corporation of Solomon Islands (ICSI), a statutory authority under the Ministry of Finance. The ICSI holds equity in the Development Bank of the Solomon Islands (100%), Kolombangara Forest Products Ltd. (49%), National Shipping Services (100%), Sasape Marina Ltd. (100%), Solomon Airlines (100%), Solomon Islands Plantations Ltd. (30%), Solomon Taiyo Ltd. (51%), Solomon Islands Printers Ltd. (100%), and Solomon Telekom Ltd. (58%). Contrary to a stated official aim of privatization, several of the foreign partners in these enterprises, such as Taiyo, have tried to sell their shares to the government. In 1995 the government's Commodities Export Marketing Authority was forced to take over Levers Solomons Ltd., which had announced it was technically bankrupt, and CEMA now operates the company as Russell Islands Plantations Limited.

Solomon Islands has the weakest currency in the South Pacific, largely because the government prints money to cover budget deficits. Between 1992 and 1996, the retail price index increased from 100 to 145.5, far higher than anywhere else in the region. In 1996 inflation was 14.5%, and in December 1997 the Solomon Islands dollar was devalued 20%. For these reasons, visitors should be prepared to pay higher prices than those quoted in this book. Solomon Islands is indebted to the tune of SI$850 million, or SI$2,450 per person, a huge sum for most Solomon Islanders.

Solomon Islands receives about SI$200 million a year in foreign aid from Australia, Japan, the Asian Development Bank, the European Union, and New Zealand. Most Japanese aid money is spent on infrastructure, such as bridges, airports, harbors, and roads to support Japanese business activities. The U.S. has spent large sums on the construction of grandiose buildings, such as the National Parliament, and mammoth memorials to their WW II victories. Australia and New Zealand have tried to channel their aid in projects more directly beneficial to the people.

Tourism plays only a small role in the economy, though airport improvements now allow the largest jets to land at Honiara. In 1990 the government founded Solomon Airlines, which has operated a Boeing 737-400 on east-west routes.

In 1997 Solomon Islands received only 15,894 arrivals (5,599 of them on business), a third the number that visited Vanuatu and only four percent as many as Fiji. Just over a third of the tourists come from Australia, with New Zealand, Japan, and the U.S. each supplying another 10%, and the United Kingdom around six percent. A declining percentage of the Americans and Japanese are WW II veterans, whereas many of the Australians and New Zealanders are scuba divers. Very little is done to promote tourism in Solomon Islands, and there is local opposition to foreign hotel development outside Honiara. In 1987 the Australian-owned Anuha Island Resort off the north side of Nggela Sule was burned down over a land dispute, and few new resorts have appeared since then.

Logging

Throughout the Solomons, some of the Pacific's last untouched rainforests are falling to the chainsaw in a hit and run operation by Asian timber companies that export raw logs to Japan (only 10% of the exported wood is sawn timber, the rest is logs). Logging for export began only in 1961, but already about half the accessible lowland rainforest has been logged. Until recently, logging was going ahead at a rate of 750,000 cubic meters of logs a year, nearly three times the sustainable rate of 270,000 cubic meters a year.

During the 1990s the comparatively small South Pacific forests attracted the attention of Malaysian corporations due to sharply increased prices for tropical hardwood on world markets caused by the phasing out of log exports from Malaysia and Indonesia. Government ministers, provincial premiers, civil servants, local officials, and village chiefs have routinely pocketed bribes from the Asian logging companies to facilitate concessions and avoid taxation. One of the beneficial side effects of the Asian economic crisis of 1997 was that it eliminated much of the market for Solomons timber, giving the forests a respite.

Local villagers have had to fight ongoing battles against these companies and their own government for control of their lands. If a tree brings in SI$500, SI$405 of it goes to the overseas company, SI$85 to the government, and only SI$10 to the landowner. A sustainable alternative to this "robber economy" does exist in the form of portable or walkabout sawmills. Portable chainsaw milling by local people brings villagers 100 times the return of large-scale logging by foreign companies, and does far less harm to the environment. But with big royalties coming in, most government officials and international agencies are uninterested in options that bring in no royalties and few taxes.

The government is supposed to use almost half its share for reforestation, but it only replants its own land, not customary land. Reforestation takes 30-40 years in areas that have been carefully logged, or 45-200 years where environmental controls are disregarded (as has usually been the case). Less than a tenth of the areas presently being logged are replanted, and the lack of reforestation has caused rapid erosion—fouling water supplies and leaving the land infertile. The largest reforestation projects are on Choiseul and Kolombangara, with mostly fast-growing exotic species planted. As the giant slow-growing native trees disappear, many rare endemic species of birds and butterflies face extinction due to the destruction of their habitat.

Fishing
Commercial fishing is the Solomons' second-largest industry, with more than SI$100 million worth of fish exported each year. In 1972, the Japanese firm Taiyo Fisheries and the government set up a jointly run cannery at Tulagi, and in 1991 this facility was moved to Noro, near Munda. Thanks to transfer pricing, Taiyo has only reported a profit twice since 1972, allowing it to pay little or nothing in taxes. Taiyo freezes two-thirds of its tuna catch at Noro, and ships it to Japan, Thailand, and Fiji for processing. Canned fish is exported to the European Union, where it is exempt from the 24% duty paid by Asian canneries.

In 1990 the government sold the country's second fishing fleet, National Fisheries Developments Ltd., to the Canadian company B.C. Packers, after NFD accumulated large debts. The Canadians invested millions expanding the Tulagi-based operation, but in 1998, a U.S. company, TriContinental, bought them out. National Fisheries has a 37,000-tonne tuna quota caught using six pole-and-line fishing boats and three purse seiners. The fish are frozen and sent to Japan.

Solomons waters are among the richest tuna fishing grounds in the Western Pacific, and the Forum Fisheries Agency (FFA) is headquartered on a hill just east of Honiara. This body carries on the wartime tradition of coastwatching by attempting to police the 200-nautical-mile Exclusive Economic Zones of the 16 South Pacific Forum member states, and by negotiating licensing fees with overseas fishing interests. In 1998 the University of the South Pacific announced that its School of Marine Studies would be located at Honiara.

Mining
Since 1936, Solomon Islanders have collected alluvial gold by hand panning and sluicing along the Chovohio River at Guadalcanal's Gold Ridge. About 200 locals hold alluvial gold mining permits, selling around 30,000 grams of unrefined gold a year to 10 licensed traders. It's rumored that large quantities of gold are smuggled out of the country, creating a drain on the balance of payments and robbing customary landholders.

The gold ore site at Gold Ridge is estimated to harbor reserves of 1.3 million metric tonnes, and in 1998 the Australian company, Ross Mining, commenced open pit operations that it expects to produce 100,000 ounces of gold a year for 13 years. There are undeveloped bauxite deposits on Rennell and Vaghena, phosphates on Bellona, and nickel on San Jorge.

FRESH PACK

Solomon Blue BRAND

PACKED BY
SOLOMON TAIYO LTD.

Solomon Islands
Net Weight : 180gm
INGREDIENTS : skipjack tuna Flake
vegetable oil / salt added.

SKIPJACK BONITO WETEM OEL TAEM IU OPENEM TIN FINIS

Plantations

The government operates vast coconut plantations in the Russell Islands on tracts formerly leased to Lever Brothers, and the Solomons' first coconut oil mill opened at Yandina in 1989. Village copra production still accounts for 75% of the country's total, and the government subsidizes this industry heavily to provide an income for rural inhabitants.

The palm oil plantations and modern oil mill on Guadalcanal are joint efforts of the government which owns 40%), landowners (four percent), and the Commonwealth Development Corporation (56%). Most of the palm oil is exported to the European Union under preferential tariffs. In 1986 the rice industry on the plains of northern Guadalcanal was destroyed by Hurricane Namu, but after the area was rehabilitated, the Solomons began exporting rice again in 1990.

Alternative Development Agendas

The most active nongovernment organization bringing villagers into the mainstream of the development process is the **Solomon Islands Development Trust** (SIDT). Since 1984, the SIDT's outreach program has sent mobile units to hundreds of remote village groups to conduct workshops on natural resources, forestry, minerals, water supplies, health, and bait fish. Team members teach the villagers how to understand and prepare for disasters, both natural and man-made, while also covering themes such as balanced cash cropping, sanitation, and family planning.

SIDT teams have stymied rainforest destruction on some islands, while assisting with the reforestation of customary land on others. The SIDT theater group SEI! enhances villagers' awareness by acting out environmental and nutrition skits for village audiences. A women's section stresses issues of particular interest to their village sisters. The programs center on improving village life as a way of beginning and sustaining grassroots development.

Most of the SIDT's funding comes from church or development groups abroad, plus the governments of Australia, Canada, New Zealand, and the U.K. The SIDT's quarterly magazine, *link,* carries fascinating articles on subjects like gold mining, tourism, education, and youth, all seen from an authentic indigenous point of view. For an airmail subscription, send US$15 in cash to Solomon Islands Development Trust, Box 147, Honiara (tel. 21130, fax 21131, e-mail: sidt@welkam.solomon.com.sb). In Honiara, pick up a copy at their office in New Chinatown (see the Honiara map).

THE PEOPLE

Solomon Islanders are a shy, gentle people who are extremely friendly and helpful to visitors. If you make an effort, you'll find them among the most approachable and charming in the Pacific. About 93% of the country's 350,000 people are Melanesians. These islanders have an astounding variety of complexions—ranging from light tan to blue-black. Generally, the darker groups live in the west and north, the lighter in the southeast. Their features can be prognathous and heavy, or delicate and fine-boned. Bushy blond hair is often seen with chocolate-colored skin, especially on Malaita.

Another four percent of the population consists of Polynesians living on Rennell, Bellona, Sikaiana, Ontong Java, the Reef Islands, Anuta, and Tikopia—the so-called "Polynesian Fringe." To add to the variety, between 1955 and 1971 thousands of Micronesian Gilbertese were resettled near Honiara and Gizo, where small European and Chinese communities are also found.

Village Life

Eight out of 10 Solomon Islanders live on shifting, subsistence agriculture in small rural villages, operating much as they did before the white man arrived. Most villages are near the shore, so fresh fish plays an important role in the diet, supplemented by wild pigs hunted with dogs and spears, plus the occasional chicken. On Malaita many people live in the interior and keep small herds of cattle for food. Everywhere native vegetables, including taro, yams, sweet potato, and cassava, are grown in small individual plots and provide the bulk of the diet.

The basic social unit is the extended family or clan, which may consist of about 200 "wantoks." Some clan members can recite a genealogy of ancestors going back 10 generations. Villagers work collectively on community projects, and there's much sharing among clans, yet individuals keep their own gardens and can readily tell you

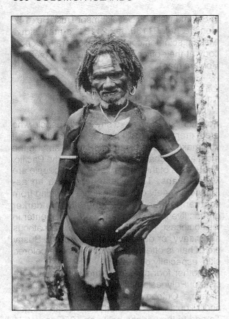

Australian photographer J.W. Beattie took this photo of a man of the Florida Islands in 1913.

what land they own. Land may be passed on by the mother or father, depending on local custom. Customary land accounts for 87% of the Solomons, another nine percent is owned by the government, and the rest by individual Solomon Islanders. About two percent is leased to foreigners, though only people born in the Solomons may own land. Disputes over land and boundaries are common. *Solomons Magazine* quoted Catholic aid worker Dr. John Roughan thus:

When I first got there, I thought the people were poor. In cash terms, they probably were. But when I asked "who owns that mountain over there?" they answered, "Mifela." "And who owns that one way over there?" "Oh, mifela, too." That broadened my horizons on the concept of wealth.

The achievements of individuals are evaluated by their value to the community as a whole, and a villager who shows too much initiative o ability in his own affairs is more likely to inspire jealousy and resentment rather than admiration Social status among the Melanesians is based on land ownership, but an individual can also increase his standing in the community by displaying his wealth at a ritual feast. A successful feast-giver becomes a "big man" in this way—descent is less important. (In Polynesia chiefs are hereditary.) Throughout the Solomons, custom or *kastom,* is used to justify any number of differing traditional social orders.

Social Issues

Some 82% of the population relies on subsistence agriculture. In 1997 only 26,000 people were in paid employment, and of this group (less than 10% of the total population), only one in five was a woman. Another 12,000 people work part-time. A third of all jobs are in the public sector, and almost 60% of all paid employment is found in and around Honiara.

There's strong opposition to family planning and the birthrate is 3.4%. Each Solomon Island woman has an average of 5.8 children, the highest fertility rate in the South Pacific. Some 47% of the inhabitants are under the age of 15 (the highest such proportion in the region), and the population doubles every 20 years. The life expectancy is also the South Pacific's lowest at 60 for men and 61 for women.

Education is neither compulsory nor free, and nearly half the population has no formal education whatever. Around 70% of Solomon Islanders are illiterate. Some 65% of children between the ages of five and 19 are not attending school (only Papua New Guinea's figure of 72% is worse).

Some 7,500 young people leave school each year, but only 15% find work, and the gap between the haves and have-nots is increasing Many young men hang on in Honiara for years as *liu,* a word that means "wanderer" but that we would translate as "unemployed." Thousands of *masta liu* from Malaita live in Honiara, and the influx of village people has strained the traditional custom of providing hospitality to visiting relatives. Squatter settlements have sprung up on the ridges behind Honiara, and some of the suburbs (including the area between the market and Chinatown) are potentially dangerous after dark. Alcoholism and crime, though sti modest compared to Papua New Guinea, are growing problems, and one need only look at the "rascal" situation in Port Moresby to appreciate the threat.

Language

Approximately 87 indigenous languages are presently in use in the Solomons, the most widely spoken of which are Kwara'ae (25,000 speakers on Malaita), Lau (10,000 speakers on Malaita), Roviana (9,000 speakers around New Georgia), and Cheke Holo (8,000 speakers on Isabel). Most of these derive from the same parent tongue, Austronesian, and all of the Polynesian languages are also Austronesian. Smaller groups speaking 11 Papuan languages are scattered throughout the Solomons and are perhaps remnants of an earlier population largely replaced or absorbed by the Austronesians. The most-used Papuan language is Bilua (6,000 speakers on Vella Lavella).

Today, most Solomon Islanders understand Pijin, and it has become the everyday tongue of tens of thousands of outer islanders living in the Honiara melting pot. Pijin takes its vocabulary largely from English, though the grammar is Melanesian. Pijin was introduced by sandalwood traders in the early 19th century ("pijin" is the Chinese pronunciation of "business"). It has always been used as a contact language between different groups.

Although the vocabulary may be limited, there's a richness and freshness to the grammatical constructions that always delights newcomers. Pijin has only two prepositions, *bilong*, which shows possession, and *long*, which covers all other prepositions. Solomon Islands Pijin varies considerably from the pidgins of New Guinea or Vanuatu. Trying to communicate in Pijin will add enjoyment to your visit as only about 20% of the population speaks English.

CONDUCT AND CUSTOMS

Conduct

Though it's okay to walk through a village along a road, ask permission of whoever's there before leaving the road. All lagoon waters are considered village property, and permission must be obtained before fishing or sometimes even snorkeling. Some Solomon Islanders resent being "exploited" by tourists who earn big money selling their snapshots to magazines, so ask before you shoot.

Keep your body well covered if you want to be treated with respect. Women should take care when visiting isolated areas or hiking alone in the Solomons, as cases of physical and sexual abuse by aggressive local males have been reported. Local women are subject to myriad taboos, and foreign women visiting remote villages should always ask if it's allowed to do certain things, such as sitting in a place reserved for men.

Custom Fees

From time to time you'll encounter a situation whereby people ask you to pay money to visit an archaeological or historic site, to see natural phenomena such as a hot spring or cave, or to enter a traditional village. Some people even claim to be the customary owners of Japanese and American war wreckage! Often local villagers will paddle out to a yacht as soon as the anchor goes down and demand a fee to use their reef, even a reef far offshore. The way the villagers look at it, these things belong to them, so how can wealthy outsiders expect to be able to use them for nothing?

They may start off by asking a ridiculously high amount (SI$20 pp), but will usually (though not always) come down after negotiations. The operators of the live-aboard dive boats pay SI$3 pp to dive on village reefs, and SI$80 per group to visit the villages themselves. All custom fees we know about are mentioned in this book. Have small bills with you, and try to avoid paying more than SI$10 pp. Please help out by sending us precise details of other custom fees you encounter, so we can mention them herein, giving future visitors the opportunity to decide in advance whether it's still worth the trouble and expense to go to a certain place.

Actually, the custom fees are not only aimed at tourists: villagers short of cash regularly demand "compensation" from each other for offenses such as speaking to a girl, walking under a clothesline, etc. Anyone unfortunate enough to have such a claim made against them should tread very lightly indeed. (In 1996 the Japanese TV company NHK canceled plans to film a tourism special in Solomon Islands after local officials demanded fees of US$5,000 per camera.)

ON THE ROAD

Highlights

Solomon Islands has many highlights, the most accessible of which are the war remains around Henderson Airport, the snorkeling or scuba diving on the two Bonegi wrecks northwest of Honiara, and the panpipe players who perform regularly at Honiara hotels. Another great experience is the boat trip from Honiara to Gizo, passing many romantic outer islands. Gizo itself is a delightful little town with adequate facilities, and the *Toa Maru,* which the American scuba newsletter *Undercurrent* calls "one of the top five wreck dives in the world." Once you've "done" these sights, you'll be ready for some real exploring.

Sports and Recreation

Solomon Islands offers some of the finest scuba diving in the South Pacific, with two professional dive shops in Honiara, two more in Gizo, and yet another in Munda. One of the Honiara shops has a branch at the Tambea Holiday Beach Resort; in Western Province, the Uepi Island Resort on the Marovo Lagoon caters almost exclusively to scuba divers. The Solomon's top diving facilities, however, are the live-aboard dive boats described in the **Transportation** section that follows. When diving, keep in mind that the nearest recompression chamber is in Townsville, Australia, and emergency air evacuation will cost A$30,000.

Golfers have at their disposal a flat nine-hole course outside Honiara. It's a friendly, inexpensive course worth trying if you happen to be there, but at last report no club rentals were available.

There are unlimited possibilities for hikers in the Solomons. Good day hikes are from Honiara to Mataniko Falls, Auki to Riba Cave, and Gizo to Titiana. Several strenuous long-distance hikes exist on Guadalcanal, including the three-day trek across the island via Gold Ridge. A guide is required on these. The really adventurous hiker will find many hiking areas where a white face is seldom seen on outer islands such as Malaita, Isabel, and Makira. The Marovo Lagoon area is being developed for sea kayaking.

Anglers are well catered for at the Zipolo Habu Resort on Lola Island near Munda. The resort boat is available for trolling in the lagoon or open sea, with rods, reels, and lures provided. Some of the Pacific's most productive fishing is in and around the Vonavona Lagoon, and manager Joe Entrikin is one of the Solomon's top fishermen. Game fishing is also offered at Gizo.

The most popular spectator sports here are rugby and soccer, with baseball and volleyball also seen.

Music

The traditional music of the Solomons varies greatly between the different cultural regions. One of the most interesting instruments is the bundle panpipe, a bundle of about a dozen tubes of different sizes open at both ends or closed at the lower end. The open-ended panpipes sound an octave higher than the closed variety, thus the closed pipes are longer. The player moves his head to blow the different tubes—the bundle itself remains stationary. The panpipe players stand or sit in two rows facing one another while whistles or bamboo trumpets produce a continuous background drone. The songs often imitate sounds of nature, such as the calls of birds, and are related to the spirit world. The panpipe ensembles play at funeral cycles, which can last up to eight years, or at important public events. The most famous contemporary panpipe bands are from Malaita.

A distant relative of these is the characteristic bamboo bands of the Western Solomons, invented here in the 1920s. Some 15 to 24 horizontal pieces of bamboo of varying length are struck on their open ends with rubber thongs, to the accompaniment of guitar and ukulele. As yet little known to the world of music, bamboo rhythms will win you at once.

Vocal choirs often sing while sitting in two rows, each person shaking a hand-held rattle-stick. Men's narrative songs may be accompanied by clapping sticks. Both the instrumental and vocal music of the Solomons is polyphonic (made up of several independent but harmonious melodic parts).

Public Holidays and Events

National holidays include New Year's Day (1 January), Good Friday, Easter Monday (March/April), Whitmonday (May/June), Queen's Birthday (the Friday closest to 14 June), Independence Day (7 July), and Christmas Days (25 and 26 December).

In addition, there's a provincial holiday called "Second Appointed Day": Choiseul (25 February), Temotu (8 June), Central (29 June), Isabel (8 July), Rennell and Bellona (20 July), Guadalcanal (1 August), Makira (2 August), Malaita (15 August), and Western (7 December). These dates can vary a day or two either way. The Church of Melanesia prohibits all custom dancing during the 40 days before Easter (March/April).

Gizo's Festival of the Sea in early December features canoe races, fishing and diving competitions, and traditional events. In April or May there's a yacht race from Brisbane to Honiara or Gizo. Contact the Queensland Yacht Club for details.

Arts and Crafts

All traditional handicrafts are either ceremonial or functional. The woodcrafts generally range from small domestic items such as combs and bowls, through a variety of figures and heads to objects as large as whole canoes, complete with decorated hulls and figureheads. Nontraditional carvings of fish, birds, or humans, although often good, are made solely to sell to visitors. Some traditional items, such as war clubs, masks, and *nguzunguzu,* are made in miniature to increase their desirability to tourists.

The fantastic cultural diversity of this country is reflected in its artwork. The most distinctive local carving is the *nguzunguzu* (pronounced "noozoo noozoo") of Western Province, depicted herein. The carved sharks and dolphins of the same area are made to European taste but are of exceptional workmanship. The shark is a popular figure because it's believed that the soul of a successful fisherman is reincarnated in a shark. Carving in the west is done in brown-streaked kerosene wood *(Corsia subcordata)* or black ebony, both hardwoods, which may be inlaid with nautilus shell or mother-of-pearl.

Another excellent purchase is the shell money of Malaita, made into beautiful necklaces. Handicrafts from Malaita are often useful items like combs, bamboo lime containers (for use with betelnut), rattles, flutes, panpipes, and fiber carrying bags. Watch too for traditional jewelry, such as headbands, earrings, nose and ear plugs, pendants, breastplates, and armbands, mostly made from shell. Bone and shell fishhooks make authentic souvenirs.

NGUZUNGUZU

Figureheads such as the one pictured here were once attached to the prow of war canoes, just above the waterline, as they set out from the Western Solomons on headhunting expeditions. Depending on the type of expedition, the doglike spirit would have beneath its chin either two clenched fists (war) a head (headhunting), or a dove (peace). The mother-of-pearl shell inlay work is characteristic. A *nguzunguzu,* such as those sold at craft outlets in Honiara, makes an excellent souvenir.

FIELD MUSEUM OF NATURAL HISTORY, CHICAGO

Guadalcanal people excel in weaving strong, sturdy bags, baskets, and trays from the *asa* vine (*Lygodium circinnatum*). These items are known collectively as Bukaware. The Polynesians of the Solomons make fine miniature canoes. The small woven pandanus bags of Bellona are commonly used by the people. Santa Ana and Santa Catalina in Makira Province are other sources of quality handicrafts, especially the striking black ceremonial pudding bowls inlaid with shell.

Solomon Islands handicrafts are of high quality. Bargaining is not practiced, but if you feel the cost is too high, hesitate a few moments, then ask the seller if he has a second price. Consider, however, the amount of time that went into making the object. Outside Honiara you can often trade cassettes, radios, watches, women's clothing, jeans, and sunglasses for handicrafts. The superb Melanesian-style decoration in some of the churches (especially Catholic) is worth noting. Remember that any handicrafts incorporating the body parts of sea turtles or marine mammals (e.g., dolphin or whale teeth) cannot be taken into the U.S., Australia, and many other countries.

ACCOMMODATIONS AND FOOD

The only large hotels are in Honiara and Gizo. There are tourist lodges at Auki, Malu'u, and Munda, cottages at Marau Sound and on Pigeon Island (Reef Islands), and beach resorts at Tambea, Vulelua (both near Honiara), Munda, and Uepi Island (Marovo Lagoon). Provincial resthouses (SI$15-20 pp) are found at Buala, Gizo, Kirakira, Lata, Taro, Tulagi, and elsewhere, and these always have cooking facilities. A 10% hotel tax is charged, and most room prices quoted in this book are without tax. Only the main hotels in Honiara and Gizo accept credit cards—everywhere else you must pay cash. Some hotels and dive shops in the Solomons quote rates in Australian dollars to make them look lower. In general, however, the Solomons offers some of the least expensive places to stay in the South Pacific in all categories.

Solomons Village Stay arranges accommodation in 15 remote villages all around the Solomons at A$50 pp a night, including all meals and activities within the village. Airport transfers and motorized boat tours are extra. This possibility is worth looking into if you have limited time, yet wish to experience the real Solomons. Be prepared for pit toilets and a lack of running water, and make reservations well in advance. For more information contact the Solomon Islands Visitors Bureau, click on www.angelfire.com/biz/solomonsvillagestay or write to soft adventure specialist Phil Feldman at **Above/Below/Beyond** (119 Logan Rd., P.O. Box 8161, Woolloongabba, Brisbane 4102, Australia; tel. 61-7/3843-1204, fax 61-7/3324-9017, e-mail: abb@one.net.au).

SERVICES AND INFORMATION

Visas and Officialdom

Everyone needs a passport and an onward ticket. Commonwealth citizens, Americans, and most Western European nationals are given a passport stamp upon arrival allowing a 30-day stay, or until the flight date on their plane ticket. Almost everyone with a confirmed onward reservation within seven days is eligible for a transit visa upon arrival.

Extensions of stay (SI$30) to a total of six months maximum in any 12-month period, can be had at the Immigration Office (fax 22964) in Honiara. You must bring along your air ticket with a confirmed reservation; the extension will be to the date of your flight out. Don't bother claiming that you're doing some sort of research as a way of getting more time; this requires prior clearance and will only raise questions.

Permanent immigration to the Solomons is very difficult. If you marry a Solomon Islander you must apply for a permit to stay two years, after which it may be possible to obtain permanent residence. Citizenship is possible after 10 years, and you must renounce your former citizenship. To obtain a work permit, you must apply from outside the country, enclosing a letter from your prospective employer. All immigration regulations are strictly enforced, and a cooperative attitude on your part is essential.

There are regular immigration offices at Gizo, Honiara, Korovou, Lata (Graciosa Bay), and Munda. It's possible to check out from any of these ports. All visiting yachts must pay a SI$100 lighthouse fee (despite this fee, many navigational lights are out of order—beware). If your boat will be entering through an obscure port, try to bring some Solomon Islands currency with you, or be prepared for customs officials and locals who insist that American, Australian, and Solomon Islands dollars are all worth the same!

Money

The Solomon Islands dollar (SI$) is linked to a trade-related basket of currencies, and the rate is adjusted daily. Before independence in 1978 the Australian dollar was the currency used in Solomon Islands and the SI$ was originally introduced at a rate of one to one. Since then it has depreciated to about A$1 = SI$3.12, or US$1 = SI$4.78. There are banknotes of two, five, 10, 20, and 50 dollars, and coins of one, two, five, 10, 20, and 50 cents, plus a seven-sided SI$1 coin depicting a *nguzunguzu,* which makes an excellent souvenir.

Banking hours in Honiara are weekdays 0900-1500. Otherwise you can change money at the Mendaña Hotel at a 10% lower rate. The National Bank, Westpac Bank, or ANZ Bank have branches where traveler's checks may be changed in Auki, Gizo, Kirakira, Lata, Munda, and Noro. Elsewhere, you must have enough local currency to tide you over as the minor National Bank agencies don't handle foreign currency. Only the Westpac Bank charges commission to change traveler's checks and the ANZ Bank generally gives a better rate than the National Bank (which is 51% owned by the Bank of Hawaii).

If you don't like carrying a lot of cash around with you, consider opening a SI$ passbook account at the National Bank, which will allow you to withdraw money at any of their 40 outer-island agencies, usually at post offices.

Before leaving, be sure to change all your leftover Solomon Islands dollars into the currency of the next country on your itinerary, as SI$ are hard to convert outside the country. It's prohibited to export more than SI$250 in Solomon Islands banknotes in cash.

Credit cards are accepted only in Honiara and Gizo, and the use of them can be expensive since the amount will first be converted into Australian dollars, then into your own currency. Obtaining cash advances is also expensive for the same reason, plus you'll have to pay interest. American Express is not represented. The sales tax rate is 10% on restaurant meals, hotel rooms, car rentals, and professional services. There's no tipping.

Telecommunications

Operator-assisted calls are not available in Honiara, so to make a long-distance call you must purchase a telephone card, sold in denominations of SI$10, SI$20, and SI$50. The cards are good for both domestic and international calls, and can be used at card phones all around the Solomons. Be aware that not all card telephones in the Solomons seem to charge the same rates: some phones will quickly devour your card, while others allow almost endless calls (the card phones at Honiara airport are voracious).

The cost of calls per minute (using a card) is officially SI$1.70 to Auki or Gizo, SI$4.83 to Australia, SI$5.06 to Fiji or New Zealand, SI$6.13 to Vanuatu and most other South Pacific countries, and SI$9.65 to North America and Europe. International calls are charged in segments of one minute. Domestic direct-dial calls are much cheaper weekdays 1800-0800 and all day weekends and holidays. Internationally, cheaper rates are in effect after 1800 Saturday and all day Sunday.

The international access code for overseas calls is 00. To get the operator, dial 100/102 domestic/overseas. The information number is 101.

For emergencies, it's 999. The Telecom New Zealand Direct number is tel. 08-64. The AT&T USA Direct number is tel. 08-11.

You can send or receive faxes via the "public fax" at Solomon Telekom offices throughout the country. These offices will also deliver faxes to post office boxes or individuals within their local areas, so it's a good way to make contact if the numbers provided herein prove inadequate: Auki (fax 40220), Buala (fax 35056), Gizo (fax 60128), Honiara (fax 23110), Kirakira (fax 50145), Lata (fax 53036), Munda (fax 61150), Noro (fax 61075), Tulagi (fax 32180). All of these places except Noro also have post offices.

Solomon Islands' telephone code is 677.

Print Media

Among the local newspapers are the *Solomon Star* (Box 255, Honiara; tel. 22062, fax 21572), which appears on Tuesday, Wednesday, and Friday; the *Solomons Voice* (Box 1235, Honiara; tel. 22275, fax 20090), published every Wednesday; and the Government Department of Information's *Solomon Nius* (Box 718, Honiara; tel. 21300, fax 20401), published monthly. The *Solomon Star* is very independent and presents a readable selection of news.

The Solomon Islands Development Trust's magazine *Link* (Box 147, Honiara; tel. 21130, fax 21131, e-mail: sidt@welkam.solomon.com.sb) is published quarterly.

Solomon Airlines has an interesting in-flight magazine called *Solomons*, which you can pick up at their Honiara office.

Radio

The Solomon Islands Broadcasting Corporation (Box 654, Honiara; tel. 20051, fax 23159), or "Radio Happy Isles," transmits from Honiara on AM 1035 kHz, 0600-2230 daily. In Lata, Temotu Province, look for them at 1386 kHz (at last report the Gizo SIBC frequency, 945 kHz AM, or "Radio Happy Lagoon," was off the air). If you have a shortwave receiver, you'll be able to listen to the SIBC over 5020 MHz, a strong signal also heard in Vanuatu and parts of Fiji.

The SIBC news in English is at 0700, 1800, and 2100 daily, and at 1200 on weekdays only. In addition, they rebroadcast the Radio New Zealand International news at 0800 weekdays, the Radio Australia news Mon.-Sat. at 0900, on

Sunday at 1000, and daily at 1300, and the BBC's *News Desk* weekdays and Sunday at 1700, and again daily at 2200. You hear the *World Business Report* from London in some pretty remote locations!

In Honiara, privately operated Island FM (Box 1234, Honiara; tel. 20101, fax 20707) broadcasts over 99.5 MHz 24 hours a day.

Information

The **Solomon Islands Visitors Bureau** (Box 321, Honiara; tel. 22442, fax 23986) puts out a number of useful brochures on the country.

BJS Agencies (Box 439, Honiara; tel. 22393, e-mail: bjs@welkam.solomon.com.sb) puts out an annual *Solomon Islands Trade Directory*, which provides considerable information on business conditions and regulations. Copies can be ordered by mailing them US$5 in cash, or visit their Mendaña Avenue office.

Solomon Airlines offices and agents on the outer islands are good sources of information about accommodations, transport, diving, etc., in their area.

HEALTH

A yellow fever vaccination is required if you've been exploring the jungles of Africa or South America within the previous six days, otherwise there are no requirements. Suggested (but not obligatory) vaccinations include the hepatitis A vaccine or immune globulin, typhoid fever, tetanus, and cholera.

All tap water should be boiled before drinking. Take along insect repellent, sunscreen, and something to treat cuts. Even the smallest coral scratch can turn septic in no time at all if left untreated. Sexually transmitted diseases are rampant in Honiara (one reader recommended steering clear of any person wearing makeup).

Malaria

Solomon Islands has the highest rate of malaria in the world with more than a third of the population infected each year. Half of all cases of malaria are on Guadalcanal, with Malaita and Central Province also heavily affected. It's found almost everywhere in the country below 400 meters altitude, including Honiara, and the rainy season is the worst time. A full-scale eradication program began in 1970, with DDT house spraying, case detection, and treatment, and by 1975 malaria seemed to be on the way out. As a result, funding was cut, and from 1977 to 1983, the number of cases treated in the Solomons increased from 10,496 to 84,527 (a third of the population). In 1990 there were 86,820 cases, a third more than were reported in 1989 (in part due to better record keeping).

Today health officials no longer talk of eradication, only control, primarily by encouraging villagers to sleep under mosquito nets, cleaning up stagnant waters where mosquitoes breed, and introducing fish that eat the eggs. In this way, it's hoped that the present rate of 350 cases per 1,000 inhabitants will eventually be reduced to 30 per 1,000. Unbelievably, spraying is no longer considered effective because studies have shown that the mosquitoes learned not to land on sprayed areas! In any case, the subsidized distribution of mosquito nets is much cheaper than spraying and does no damage to the environment. Mosquito nets treated with icon permethrine kill insects, but the chemical is harmless to birds and mammals.

Malaria is a blood disease involving a parasite called Plasmodium that destroys red blood cells. A mosquito sucks in blood from a person or animal with malaria, then injects it into the next individual it bites. This is the only way malaria can be transmitted. The parasites multiply in the liver and only cause symptoms when they are periodically released back into the bloodstream, which is why bouts of malaria come and go. Symptoms begin 10 days to one year after the bite.

Avoid being bitten by wearing long pants and a long-sleeved shirt from dusk to dawn, using a good insect repellent, burning a mosquito coil at night, and sleeping under a mosquito net (check for gaps—mosquitoes are attracted by the carbon dioxide you exhale and will search for hours for an opening). Dark clothing, perfume, and aftershave lotion attract mosquitoes.

The two nocturnal malarial mosquitoes found in the Solomons, Anopheles farauti and Anopheles punctulatus, both rest outdoors, so by sleeping in screened quarters you're partly protected. The first feeds in- and outdoors at night or during overcast days, while the second feeds only outdoors. The prime biting time is 1800-1900, and 90% of bites are on the ankles. The buzzing of the malaria mosquito can be heard, and their sting feels like a prick by a tiny hypodermic needle.

Since 1980, Chloroquine-resistant Plasmodium falciparum malaria has established itself in the Solomons and now accounts for 66% of cases. Fansidar is effective against this, though many doctors hesitate to prescribe it—there have been severe skin reactions and even fatalities following multiple doses of Fansidar in combination with Chloroquine. Fansidar must not be taken by pregnant women or anyone allergic to sulpha drugs. If you're traveling to remote areas, it may be useful to carry a presumptive three-tablet treatment dose of Fansidar to be taken at the first signs of malaria (general malaise, headache, chills, and fever).

The Australian Army antimalarial unit recommends that its personnel visiting Melanesia take a 100-mg Doxycycline tablet once a day, beginning a day before they arrive and continuing for four weeks after they leave. This is a fairly strong dose that should not be continued longer than six weeks in any case. For trips of more than two weeks, they prescribe 50 mg of Doxycycline a day, beginning a day before and continuing four weeks after, plus a 250-mg Chloroquine tablet taken once a week for the same period. Doxycycline is not advisable for women in pregnancy and children under eight.

Lariam (also known as Mefloquine) is also very effective against Plasmodium falciparum malaria. Start taking the drug (after a meal) a week before you arrive, and more importantly, continue four weeks after you leave (one 250-mg tablet each week). The Pharmacy in central Honiara sells Lariam over the counter without prescription at about US$5 per pill (far more expensive than most other drugs mentioned here). Lariam is not recommended for persons with a history of depression, heart disease, seizures, or epilepsy. Scuba divers may experience malaria-like symptoms underwater if they take Lariam and are probably better off using Doxycycline. However, 85% of those taking Lariam have no problems, and most of the rest suffer only minor headaches and dizziness. If you experience no adverse side effects during the first few weeks, it means you can probably continue taking Lariam as long as you like.

Though Chloroquine (sold under various brand names, including Nivaquine and Avloclor) may not prevent a *falciparum* malaria breakthrough, it will lessen the severity of an infection and prevent fatal malaria. Maloprim and Paludrine are also no longer 100% effective. A new antimalarial drug called Malarone is still in the testing stages (although already sold in Europe). Whichever drug you choose, read the instructions on the package carefully and/or consult your doctor (the tips provided above are purely anecdotal and we accept no responsibility for them).

If you develop a fever, get a blood smear as soon as possible (any doctor or clinic in the Solomons can arrange it). Later, if you become sick in another country (even *months* later), don't forget to tell the doctor you've been in the Solomons, because doctors often misdiagnose the symptoms as flu. Always assume it's malaria until the blood test proves otherwise. See **Health** in the main introduction to this book for more information. Don't let this situation prevent you from visiting the Solomons, but do take the precautions.

TRANSPORTATION

Getting There

The government-owned carrier, **Solomon Airlines** (Box 23, Honiara; tel. 20031, fax 23992, www.solomonairlines.com.au) flies its Boeing 737 to Honiara three times a week from Brisbane, twice a week from Port Moresby and Nadi, and weekly from Auckland, Port Vila, and Nouméa. To avoid duplication, most of these flights are joint services with Air Pacific, Air Niugini, and Qantas. In Brisbane, there are immediate connections to/from Melbourne and Sydney. From North America, the easiest way to get there is via Fiji. From Europe, you have a choice of Fiji or Australia.

Air Pacific's nonstop Los Angeles-Nadi flight connects in Fiji for Honiara (two-night layover). **Air New Zealand** offers Los Angeles-Nadi-Honiara-Los Angeles for US$1,248/1,498/1,748 low/shoulder/high season provided you begin on a Monday, Tuesday, or Wednesday (other days US$60 more). From Honolulu it's US$200 cheaper. The low season is April-August. You must purchase the ticket 14 days in advance,

pay US$75 to change flight dates, and pay a 35% cancellation penalty. Ask for the "Three-Month Coral Experience," which allows a free stop in Nadi. Air New Zealand's "No Stop Apex" is US$1,098/1,348/1,598 Los Angeles-Honiara with a one-month maximum stay.

About the cheapest way to get there is with a Visit South Pacific Pass, which costs US$440 for Nadi-Honiara-Nadi or Brisbane-Honiara-Brisbane. Similarly, **Air Pacific** has a 60-day Fiji/Vanuatu/Solomons Triangle Fare at US$617 (call 1-800/227-4446 in North America). Both of the above can only be purchased in North America or Europe, and full details are provided in this book's main introduction.

Getting Around by Air

Solomon Airlines (Box 23, Honiara; tel. 20031, fax 23992) offers convenient, punctual domestic air service, with almost 800 scheduled flights a month linking 25 airstrips in the Solomons. Their 18-passenger Twin Otters and nine-passenger Britten-Norman Islanders are fun to fly in. Island-hopping routes such as Honiara-Seghe-Munda-Gizo, Gizo-Ballalae-Choiseul-Gizo, Honiara-Bellona-Rennell-Honiara, and Honiara-Kirakira-Santa Cruz allow you see a number of islands without backtracking. They don't allow stopovers on through tickets, however, so you'll have to pay for each sector separately. The baggage allowance is 16 kilos on domestic flights, 20 kilos on international.

From Honiara there are flights to Auki (SI$105), Avu Avu (SI$75), Ballalae (SI$375), Bellona (SI$170), Choiseul Bay (SI$375), Fera/Buala (SI$135), Gizo (SI$280), Kirakira (SI$180), Marau (SI$95), Mbambanakira (SI$60), Mono (SI$380), Munda (SI$245), Parasi (SI$135), Rennell (SI$185), Ringi Cove (SI$260), Santa Ana (SI$230), Santa Cruz (SI$455), Seghe (SI$200), and Yandina (SI$95). These are the one-way fares, and a regular roundtrip is double.

There's a 10% discount on domestic flights if you have an international ticket on Solomon Airlines. All domestic flights are heavily booked—reserve as far in advance as possible. Because airfares are relatively low, flights from Honiara to Munda and Gizo are often full, and it can be hard to organize a visit if you're staying two weeks or less in the Solomons. Thus you might consider booking from abroad in conjunction with your international ticket. No shows who miss their flights forfeit their tickets.

North Americans and Europeans can purchase a **Discover Solomons Air Pass,** which allows four domestic flights within any 30-day period for US$249. This must be purchased prior to arrival, through Air Promotion Systems in Los Angeles (tel. 1-310/670-7302 or 1-800/677-4277, fax 1-310/338-0708, www.pacificislands.com). Additional flights can be added to a Discover Solomons Air Pass after arrival in the Solomons at US$50 each.

Solomon Airlines is fairly reliable and the flights are only canceled if a major hurricane is blowing. The advantage of plane travel is that the planes have a set schedule and you can pack a number of farflung destinations into a relatively short trip. On a brief visit, boat travel is really only practical to a few main centers like Auki, Buala, Tulagi, and Gizo.

Western Pacific Airline (Box 411, Honiara; tel. 36533, fax 36476), at Henderson Airport, flies to many small airstrips Solomon Airlines doesn't reach. This Seventh-Day Adventist Church-operated airline has scheduled flights to Malaita and Western Province, and it's always worth comparing schedules (no service on weekends). Prices are the same on both airlines.

Getting Around by Boat

Interisland travel by ship is more colorful and economical than air travel. Boat service from Honiara to Auki and Gizo is frequent and fairly regular, and virtually every other island in the country is accessible by boat. **National Shipping Services** (Box 1766, Honiara; tel. 25939, fax 26039) is the most reliable operator to the outer islands, while **Wings Shipping** (Box 4, Honiara; tel. 21259, fax 23644) and the **Malaita Shipping Company** (Box 584, Honiara; tel. 23502, fax 23503) are the largest private lines. Some of the oldest ships in the Pacific spend their last years in the Solomons, often ending up as scrap metal on the Honiara or Gizo waterfront. A few hours checking around the shipping offices in Honiara will give you an idea what's still going.

Fares are reasonable, with cabins costing only double the deck fare, so do try to get one if you'll be aboard more than one or two nights. You'll be expected to bring your own bedding.

Buy food before boarding, as you may not have another chance to shop until the next day; on a long trip, take enough food to see you through (including a good supply of navy biscuits). Hot water is supplied, but you'll need your own cooking and eating utensils. Purchase a grass mat to use for sleeping on deck or bring newspapers. Below deck, it may be hot and crowded. One of the main drawbacks on all the ships is the loud videos, which play well into the night and come back on before dawn. The schedule is often up to the captain, so ask him when he's leaving before you go ashore at some remote port of call. See **Transportation** under Honiara for details.

Scuba Tours

Ask any knowledgeable diver about Solomon Islands and they'll probably mention the two liveaboard dive boats operated by **Bilikiki Cruises Ltd.** (Jane and Rick Belmare, Box 876, Honiara; tel. 20412, fax 23897, http://bilikiki.com). Their Honiara office is upstairs in a well-marked building near the Point Cruz Yacht Club. The original vessel was the 38-meter, 10-stateroom MV *Bilikiki,* based here since 1989. In 1992 a sister ship, the 13-cabin MV *Spirit of the Solomons,* joined the fleet. Groups on cruises of seven, 10, or 14 nights anchor right at the remote wrecks and reefs of the Florida, Russell, and New Georgia islands, most of them accessible only in this way. The ships have been specially adapted for scuba diving, with low platforms for easy entries and exits, and dive tenders are used. Trips arranged at their Honiara office are US$296 pp per night all inclusive with a seven-night minimum (US$225 for a shared cabin with shared bath on the *Spirit of the Solomons*).

In 1994 a new dive vessel, the 25-meter, five-cabin MV *Solomon Sea* appeared on the Solomons live-aboard horizon. It's operated by **Blue Lagoon Cruises Ltd.** (Fred and Corina Douglas, Box 1022, Honiara; tel. 25300, fax 39377, www.solomonsea.com). The US$298 pp per day price includes double-occupancy accommodations with all meals, airport transfers, tax, and unlimited diving (seven-night minimum).

In 1999 a new live-aboard began operating out of Gizo, the **Solomon Islands Aggressor** (Live/Dive Pacific Inc., 74-5588 Pawai Pl., Building F, Kailua-Kona, HI 96740, U.S.A.; tel. 1-800/344-5662 or 1-808/329-8182, fax 1-808/329-

2628, http://pac-aggressor.com, e-mail: livedive@compuserve.com). From July to December this 33-meter vessel carries 14 passengers on seven-day cruises from Gizo to spectacular dive sites in the northwestern Solomons (US$2,695 pp double occupancy, excluding airfare, taxes, and tips).

Signing onto any of these ships locally would be pure luck, so buy an all-inclusive package through one of the scuba wholesalers mentioned in the main introduction to this book.

Airport

Henderson Airport (HIR) is 13 km east of Honiara. In 1942 this historic airfield was begun by the Japanese and finished by the Americans, and in early 1998 a new international terminal building was added with Japanese aid money. Outside the old domestic airport terminal are a couple of American war memorials and a Japanese AA gun. The original WW II control tower, a solitary steel-frame structure, overlooks Henderson's runway.

Public minibuses marked "CDC 123" pass fairly frequently on the highway in front of the airport and charge only SI$2 to town. Airport

bound, if you have an early departure and don't wish to risk waiting for the CDC minibus, take any bus to KG6. When you arrive there, offer the driver an extra SI$10 to continue on to the airport. Solomon Sights and Sounds (tel. 22230), at the King Solomon Hotel, does airport transfers at SI$20 pp each way—only a good deal if you're alone. The taxi fare to/from town is SI$30. Avis, Budget, and Hertz have counters at the airport.

There is no tourist information desk. The currency exchange counter opens for international flights but gives a poor rate (SI$5 commission when changing back upon departure). A bar and duty-free shop are inside the departure lounge. If you decide to buy anything at one of the "duty-free" outlets in town, allow one week for goods to be delivered here.

The customs checks are very thorough, in search of guns and video nasties on arrival, contraband gold, artifacts, and WW II munitions on departure. You'll probably have to open your bags (arrive a bit early to allow time for this). The departure tax is SI$40 on international flights only.

Queen Victoria's birdwing (Onithoptera victoriae) *is found only in the Solomon Islands. As specimens are among the most highly prized of all butterflies, their export is government controlled.*

GUADALCANAL

Totaling 5,302 square km, Guadalcanal is the largest island in the Solomons. The northern coastal plain contrasts with the Weather Coast in the south, where precipitous cliffs plunge into the sea. The interior is extremely rugged, rising to Mt. Makarakomburu (2,447 meters), the highest peak in the South Pacific islands (excluding P.N.G.).

The nation's capital, Honiara, on Guadalcanal's north side, began as an army camp during WW II. After the war the British administration decided to utilize the abandoned American facilities here rather than return to their former headquarters, Tulagi, which had been devastated during the fighting. Protected from rains by high mountains to the south, Honiara is also drier than Tulagi, and it's well placed to serve the North Guadalcanal plain. There are few safe anchorages on Guadalcanal, and Honiara's harbor is also poor—safe for yachts only from April to October. Still, it's the major port of the group, and interisland ships bustle along the waterfront.

Things to see and places to stay are abundant around Honiara. Most of the WW II battlefields east of Honiara can be seen on day-trips from the capital. The Marau Sound area is well worth a couple of days, and the adventuresome could continue west along the south coast. Many small hamlets in the interior, accessible only on foot, are reserved for the true explorer. Guadalcanal is *the* gateway to the Happy Isles.

HONIARA AND ENVIRONS

The name Honiara derives from the indigenous name for Point Cruz, *naho-ni-ara,* meaning "facing the east and southeast trade winds." Here in 1568, Mendaña, the European discoverer of the Solomons, raised a cross and claimed the island for Spain. Almost 400 years later in September 1942, the town area was the scene of heavy fighting, and the Mataniko River, which runs through the city, was the Japanese/American front line for several months. Quonset huts remain on the back streets from the U.S. base established after the Japanese withdrawal.

Today Honiara is a dusty minimetropolis of 40,000. Businesses and government offices crowd the narrow coastal strip behind Point Cruz, and residential areas cover the adjacent hillsides. Chinatown stretches along the right bank of the Mataniko River, while light industry and many schools are concentrated at Ranadi, a suburb farther east. A steady stream of traffic crawls up and down Mendaña Avenue all day. Many residents, even officials and business people, walk barefoot.

Between 1986 and 1996 the city's population doubled, and 11% of the country's population now lives here, about 60% of them males. Young men continue to be drawn to the bright lights, especially from Malaita and Western Province, and people with jobs are outnumbered by *masta liu,* the unemployed. There always seem to be a lot of people hanging around, watching and waiting for something to happen. Thanks to the role of the various churches in maintaining social control, this is still a safe city to wander around by day; after dark you might wish to invest in a taxi, particularly if you have to pass the market area. Yet compared to Port Moresby, Honiara is a breeze, and this city is a lot less touristy that Port Vila.

SIGHTS

A good place to start is the **Solomon Islands National Museum** (Box 313, Honiara; tel. 22309; open Tues.-Fri. 0900-1600, Saturday 0900-1400, Sunday 1400-1600; admission SI$2), opposite the Visitors Bureau. The museum presents a good introduction to the life, crafts, and natural environment of the country, with displays on customary currency, archaeology, weapons, languages, body ornaments, fishing activities, gardening and tools, weaving, and traditional music and dance. Some booklets and handicrafts are available. The museum **Cultural Center** within the same compound has a collection of traditional buildings from eight of the Solomon's nine provinces constructed in 1991. The first Melanesian Arts and Culture Festival was held in Honiara in July 1998, and there's often custom

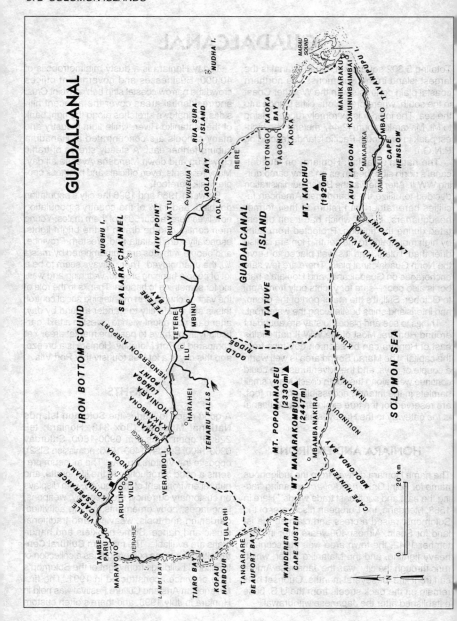

GUADALCANAL

dancing on the festival stage opposite the museum when a cruise ship is in.

Between the museum and the police station is "Pistol Pete," a 155-mm Japanese howitzer that caused havoc by shelling Henderson Field during the Guadalcanal campaign. Inside the **Central Bank** on the other side of the police station are Rennellese woodcarvings, paintings, and a good collection of traditional currency. Across the street is the **National Art Gallery and Cultural Center** (Box G20, Honiara; tel. 24593, fax 24594; weekdays 0900-1600; admission SI$5) in Government House, former residence of the governor-general. The center's waterfront gardens (free) are lovely. Farther west, beyond the post office, is the **High Court Building** (1963-64).

Continue west past the Town Ground. Opposite the Iron Bottom Sound Hotel, take the road inland past Radio Happy Isles and the prison checkpoint to the **Botanical Gardens** (tel. 22370, admission free), where the grounds are always open. There's an herbarium and lily pond, plus many attractive paths through the rainforest adjoining the gardens. Upstream but still within the confines of the gardens is **Watapamu village** (named for the nearby water pump), fairly typical of rural villages in the Solomons and well worth visiting for those who will not be journeying outside Honiara.

Return to Mendaña Avenue from the gardens and walk west about 500 meters to **Rove Market,** where you can buy a fresh coconut to drink. Next to Police Headquarters across the street is

the **Sergeant Major Jacob Vouza War Memorial** (1992) in memory of the country's most-decorated WW II hero. Captured and tortured by the Japanese, Vouza escaped to tell his story.

Back in the center of town, scramble up the hill behind the Mobil service station to visit the huge, conical **Parliament Building** (1993), which the United States government bankrolled to the tune of US$5 million in memory of the 450 U.S. soldiers and 1,200 marines who died on Guadalcanal. Ironically, the building was erected by a Japanese construction company. Enter the 600-seat public gallery if it's open. Parliament meets for three- to four-week sessions three times a year (March/April, July/August, and November/December), and at these times you can watch debates from the public gallery weekdays 0930-1200/1400-1600.

Chinatown and Around

Take any bus east to the pedestrian overpass near **Central Hospital.** Locally known as Nambanaen, this American-built wartime hospital began life as the "Ninth Station." In 1993 the Taiwanese Government erected the modern extension on the west side of the hospital. Go through the hospital parking lot to the beach just east of the mouth of the **Mataniko River** (watch where you step as some locals use the beach as a toilet, converting it into a minefield). In shallow water just off this beach is the wreck of a Japanese tank disabled by American artillery and small-arms fire on 23 October 1942. The area behind the beach is

These big leaf houses in Watapamu village at the upper end of Honiara's Botanical Gardens are typical of many in the Solomons.

Lord Howe Settlement, a large community of Polynesian people from Ontong Java.

Across the overpass is **Chinatown,** an Asian Wild West of photogenic high-porched wooden buildings adjacent to the riverside. Chinatown and the area around the old Mataniko bridge are among the prettiest parts of Honiara.

Walk through Chinatown, cross the old Mataniko River bridge, and proceed up **Skyline Drive** from the Catholic cathedral (notice the row of WW II-era Quonset huts across the road from the cathedral). Keep left and go up the ridge right to the top, a steep 15-minute climb. If it's a hot day, seriously consider catching a taxi from the Catholic cathedral to the U.S. War Memorial. It will only cost around SI$5 and you can easily walk back down.

You'll end up directly above a large squatter village of Malaita people. Notice the sago palms they use to roof their houses. It's also well worth coming up for the knockout view of Chinatown, the Mataniko Valley, the grassy hills behind Honiara, and the WW II battle sites. The main point of interest up this way, however, is the **U.S. War Memorial,** dedicated on 7 August 1992 to mark the 50th anniversary of the Red Beach landings. A stimulating account of the campaign from the American standpoint is inscribed on red marble tablets inside the monument compound. Skyline Drive, a WW II jeep track, meanders back into the boonies from here.

Mount Austin

Walk, drive, or take a taxi up the paved highway to the summit of Mt. Austin (410 meters) for a sweeping aerial view of the north coastal plains and across to Savo and the Florida Islands. Most of the historic battlefields are visible from here. For five months in the latter part of 1942, Japanese troops held Mt. Austin and used it to direct artillery fire on the American marines around Henderson Field below. Even after the main mountain fell, surrounded Japanese held out another month on ridges such as Gifu, Sea Horse, and Galloping Horse, until starvation, suicide, or banzai assaults finally cut them down.

The easy way to get there is to ride the Naha minibus to the end of its line, then stroll 15 minutes to the large white **Solomon Peace Memorial Park,** erected on the hillside in 1981 by Japanese veterans to commemorate all who perished in the Guadalcanal campaign. Facing the memorial is a bronze sculpture, *Sound of the Tide* by Eikichi Takahashi, a Japanese soldier killed in battle here. This stark memorial contrasts sharply with the grandiose U.S. War Memorial on Skyline Ridge that proclaims American military prowess.

An ordinary car driven with care can easily reach the summit of Mt. Austin, and a taxi from the memorial should cost around SI$10, if you can find one. On foot, allow about an hour. The Forestry Department plots, which you see along the way, have scientific names posted on some of the trees (notice the stand of kauri). The river you see below from the mountaintop is the Lungga. In October 1942, a Japanese army under General Maruyama plodded around behind Mt. Austin from White River in an abortive attempt to take Henderson from the rear. It's rumored that at least six big artillery pieces and much war materiel are strewn along the Lungga River north of the mountain.

The potholed paved road continues down to the jungle-clad Lungga Canyon itself, but don't try driving it unless you've got a jeep or pickup truck. On foot, the river is only 30 minutes from the summit. The last stretch of road is badly eroded, but if you walk a bit, you will reach a lovely pool and sandy beach at a bend of the river. In the rainy season the current can be too strong for safe swimming, but it's a good picnic spot anytime. The British built this road as part of a hydroelectric project that was stopped by land disputes and the discovery of limestone in the bedrock, which would have led to heavy leakage. The trail up the river from the end of the road passes two large tunnels constructed as part of the scheme.

There's no permanent habitation along the Mt. Austin road and no custom fees to pay. Go early, pack a lunch, and make a day of it. If it's not too late you can hike back down to Honiara via Mbarana village, over some of the old wartime battlefields. The dirt road westbound just before the Forestry Department plots leads to Mbarana, then it becomes a footpath called the **Tuvaruhu Trail,** which winds along grassy ridges with good views on all sides. Keep straight ahead on the path and generally to the left and you'll come out at Vara, near Chinatown. This may be the best part of the trip.

Mataniko Falls

One of the most amazing waterfalls in the South Pacific is only a two-hour walk south of Honiara up the Mataniko River. Follow the road from Chinatown up the riverside to its end at Tuvaruhu. Galloping Horse Ridge, a major WW II battlefield, towers over Tuvaruhu to the west. Cross the river and follow a trail up over the grassy hillsides and down toward a forest. You pass to the left of a small coconut grove and Harahei village. The final descent to the falls is down a steep, slippery, forested incline.

There are many large pools for cooling off after this exhausting hike, but the main sight is a gigantic, swallow-infested, stalagmite-covered cave, with an arm of the river roaring right through. The river itself pours out of a crack in a limestone cliff just above and tumbles down into the cave through a crevice totally surrounded by white water.

This jungle-girdled complex of cascades alone justifies a visit, but the intrepid should swim/hike down the Mataniko through the gorge back to Tuvaruhu in a couple of hours. You'll be floating with the current through deep water in places, so don't bring anything that can't get wet. Take along an inner tube if you can, and be careful, as people have drowned here. After a storm the river can flood. Caves on the slopes high above the river still contain the bones of the Japanese soldiers who died there.

The traditional landowner charges a SI$10 pp custom fee to visit Mataniko Falls (have exact change). For a bit more, someone might be willing to accompany you down the river—a good idea, but get the price straight beforehand. Travel agencies in Honiara also organize hikes to the falls at about SI$70 pp, but a local guide would be quite happy with considerably less than that. You'll never forget this excursion.

Sports and Recreation

Honiara's original dive shop is **Island Dive Services** (John and Ingrid Carr, Box 414, Honiara; tel. 22103, fax 21493), operating since 1982. They offer two scuba/snorkeling trips daily at 0900 and 1400 from their base at the Kitano Mendaña Hotel (open daily 0800-1700). Snorkeling is SI$75, scuba diving SI$185 for one tank, gear included. If you have your own equipment the prices come down to SI$42 for snorkeling, SI$115 for scuba diving (a second dive

the same day is always SI$115). Island Dive Services offers night dives on the two Bonegi wrecks to see the rare "flashlight fish," and they have a seven-meter boat for dives on offshore sites (although most of the dives are shore dives). Their PADI scuba certification course is SI$1,130 plus SI$150 for registration if you're alone, SI$1,000 pp for two, SI$870 pp for three, SI$750 pp for four. Certified divers can also rent tanks, backpacks, and weight belts here and organize their own shore diving from a rental car.

The new kid on the block is **Let's Go Diving** (Box 1620, Honiara; tel. 20567, fax 20577), at the King Solomon Hotel. They offer scuba diving at SI$120/175 without/with your own equipment, and snorkeling at SI$44/63. A resort course is SI$244, and certification courses are also offered. All types of equipment is for hire.

The main sites visited are two wrecked Japanese transport ships at Bonegi northwest of Honiara (good for snorkeling and diving), a sunken trading boat full of tame moray eels (scuba only), and Tasafaronga Reef. There's also a beach dive to a B-17 Flying Fortress bomber encrusted in soft corals 15 meters down off Ndoma. The Honiara dive shops offer mostly shore dives but some boat diving is also available.

The **Honiara Golf Club** (Box 195, Honiara; tel. 30181), across the road from King George VI High School between Honiara and the airport, charges greens fees of SI$25 for the nine holes. Caddy fees about SI$6 per nine holes (the caddies will tell you it's more, but that's the normal charge). Buy the caddy a soft drink if he's been helpful. Unfortunately no clubs are for hire, but there's a good bar here. The course is laid out on the old Kukum "Fighter Two" airstrip so it's dead flat, though the club's pleasant colonial atmosphere is fun. Visitors are welcome.

The **Squash Club** (tel. 24221) in Chinatown has two courts open weekdays 1500-1900, Saturday 0800-1000/1500-1800 (SI$10 to play).

The **Honiara Hash House Harriers** do a recreational run every Monday at 1730. For the location, look for the map in the window of Acor Bookstore Monday after noon.

On Saturday afternoon catch a game of rugby (Jan.-April) or soccer (April-Sept.) at the **Lawson Tama Stadium** opposite Central Hospital. The action starts about 1600, and the entrance fee is cheap.

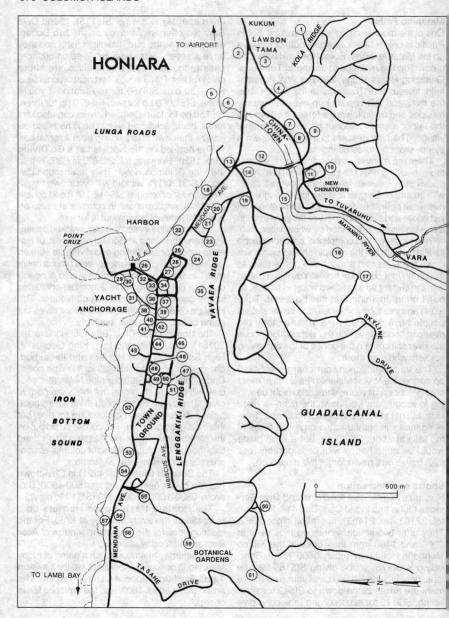

HONIARA

TO AIRPORT

KUKUM
LAWSON
TAMA

KOLA RIDGE

LUNGA ROADS

CHINA TOWN

NEW CHINATOWN

TO TUVARUHU

MENDANA AVE.

HARBOR

VAVAEA RIDGE

MATANIKO RIVER

VARA

POINT CRUZ

YACHT ANCHORAGE

SKYLINE DRIVE

IRON BOTTOM SOUND

TOWN GROUND

HIBISCUS AVE.

LENGGAKIKI RIDGE

GUADALCANAL ISLAND

0   500 m

MENDANA AVE.

TA SAHE DRIVE

BOTANICAL GARDENS

TO LAMBI BAY

N

HONIARA

1. Forum Fisheries Agency
2. Central Hospital
3. USP Center
4. Squash Courts
5. submerged Japanese tank
6. Lord Howe Settlement
7. Super Motel
8. Chan Wing Supermarket
9. Honiara Hotel
10. Solomon Islands Development Trust/DSE Building
11. Credit Union Resthouse
12. Public Library
13. Quonset Huts
14. Catholic Cathedral
15. Travelers Motel
16. Malaita village
17. U.S. War Memorial
18. Central Market
19. Solomon City Motel
20. Quality Motel
21. Island Lodge

22. Guadalcanal Provincial Offices
23. United Church Rest House
24. Chester House
25. Air Niugini
26. Hot Bread Kitchen
27. Westpac Bank
28. National Shipping Service
29. Pasofi Snack Bar
30. CEMA Warehouse
31. Canoes to Savo
32. Malaita Shipping Co./Quarantine Office
33. ANZ Bank
34. Lena Cinema
35. Parliament Building
36. Solomon Airlines
37. Kingsley's Fastfood Center
38. Point Cruz Yacht Club
39. NPF Plaza
40. Visitors Bureau
41. Kitano Mendaña Hotel

42. Solomon Islands National Museum
43. National Art Gallery
44. Police Station
45. King Solomon Hotel
46. Solomon Telekom
47. Motel Tropics
48. Post Office
49. High Court Building
50. Survey and Cartography Division
51. Hydrographic Office
52. Guadalcanal Club
53. Honimed Clinic/Dental Center
54. Iron Bottom Sound Hotel
55. Radio Happy Isles (SIBC)
56. Rove Police Headquarters
57. Rove Market
58. Police Club
59. Herbarium
60. Taiwanese Embassy
61. Watapamu village

ACCOMMODATIONS

Shoestring

Just under a dozen resthouses and hostels around Honiara offer reasonable shared bath accommodations, usually with communal cooking facilities. A few charge *per bed* and singles can often get the per person rate if they're willing to bargain a little. Houses available for long-term rentals are listed on notice boards outside The Pharmacy and Friendship Supermarket.

The Melanesian Brotherhood operates **Chester House** (Box 1479, Honiara; tel. 23372, fax 21098), the gray and blue two-story building with the crosses on the walls standing on the hillside off Hibiscus Ave., directly back from the Hot Bread Kitchen. This spacious new guesthouse has nine rooms upstairs and another seven downstairs at SI$35 pp. Communal toilets/showers/cooking facilities are provided, and the terrace has a great view of Iron Bottom Sound.

A dirt road east from Chester House leads to the 10-room **United Church Resthouse** (Michael Gavi, Box 18, Honiara; tel. 20028, fax 20453). From town, follow Cluck Street up from Mendaña Avenue and turn right at the top of the hill. The cost is SI$33 pp, and singles will be expected to share. Many travelers hang out here because of the great location, good facilities, and moderate rates, and it can be rather noisy due to foreigners chatting away on the front porch late at night and locals up preparing breakfast in the early morning. Keep your room door firmly locked at all times (even if you're only out on the porch) as there have been thefts. No alcohol is allowed in the resthouse. This place will be full if there's any sort of church meeting taking place.

The **Travelers Motel** (Box 56, Honiara; tel. 25721, fax 25735) has a good location in the "Fijian Quarters" just up the road inland on the west side of the Mataniko Bridge near Chinatown. The 17 rooms in this two-story building include three fan-cooled rooms with shared bath at SI$66 single or double, seven downstairs rooms with private bath at SI$77, and another seven upstairs rooms with private bath at SI$88. There are good communal cooking facilities.

The screened windows are not very soundproof, so you hear everything around you.

The **Solomon Islands Credit Union League** (Box 368, Honiara; tel. 20112, fax 20131) has a seven-room hostel behind their business office opposite the Red Cross in New Chinatown. Each room has a sink and two bunk beds, and communal cooking and bathing facilities are provided. It's primarily intended for Credit Union staff attending training seminars, but empty rooms are available to the public.

Budget

Motel Tropics (Box 1296, Honiara; tel. 25048) is a bit hard to find on Lenggakiki Ridge, directly up a concrete stairway behind the Hydrographic Office on Hibiscus Avenue. The seven rooms with bath and good views are SI$77 single or double. A common kitchen is available.

Also rather hidden is **Island Lodge** (Box 737, Honiara; tel. 23-139), near the United Church Resthouse on the west side of Quality Motel and down the hill. Look for the long wooden building with the public telephone on the outside wall (no sign). It has 16 rooms with shared bath: 13 of them are singles at SI$80 and three are doubles at SI$100. Ventilation screens above the doors tend to let in noise, but it's clean and central with communal cooking facilities provided.

The **Solomon City Motel** (Box 279, Honiara; tel. 25078, fax 26264) is conveniently located just up the hill from the Catholic cathedral. The 12 rooms are in two buildings: a large house with a spacious sitting room/kitchen downstairs and seven rooms upstairs, and a second building up the hill with another five rooms. Either way, it's SI$40 pp in a shared room or SI$90 for a family room.

Inexpensive

The 56-room **Honiara Hotel** (Box 4, Honiara; tel. 21737, fax 20376), near Chinatown, is a pleasant hotel with reasonable facilities. In the old wing are 13 non-a/c "budget" rooms with twin beds and shared bath at SI$94/104 single/double, plus 26 "standard" a/c rooms with private bath and fridge at SI$145/195/225 single/double/triple (one single and one double bed). Two standard rooms with a connecting door cost SI$305. On an upper terrace in the new wing are 12 "deluxe" rooms at SI$280 single or double, and five "exe-

cutive" rooms at SI$300. An offbeat funicular elevator carries you up to these. There's a swimming pool, and the hotel bar and adjacent French restaurant are good.

Since 1967 Honiara's premier hotel has been the 96-room **Kitano Mendaña** (Box 384, Honiara; tel. 20071, fax 23942), which the Japanese construction company Kitano purchased from the government in 1990. The standard a/c rooms with fridge and private bath are SI$180/200 single/double, deluxe rooms SI$300/320, plus 10% tax. A standard room at the three-story Mendaña is only twice the price of a noisy room at one of the cheapies listed above, and by international standards, it's good value. There's a freshwater swimming pool and the hotel's seaside terrace bar has pitchers of draught beer at SI$20. The Sunday night barbecue (SI$60) with Gilbertese dancing (free) and the continental buffet breakfast (SI$38) are good. Change money here only in emergencies as they give a rate 10% lower than the banks.

In 1995 the **Iron Bottom Sound Hotel** (Box 1892, Honiara; tel. 25833, fax 24123) opened near the access road to the Botanical Gardens. The 36 a/c rooms in six long six-room blocks next to the sea are SI$220/235 single/double, plus 10% tax. All rooms cost the same, so ask for a unit in one of the three front blocks, preferably the center one (rooms 201-206) which gets some shade. There's no beach, but you could snorkel here. The restaurant serves Cantonese food.

Moderate

Centrally located, the **King Solomon Hotel** (Box 268, Honiara; tel. 21205, fax 21771, www.islandshotels.com.au), on Hibiscus Ave., was taken over by Island Hotels Ltd. of Papua New Guinea in 1995. The six shabby rooms in the old wing down by the parking lot are SI$178/231 single/double, but the better part of the hotel is up on the hillside accessible via a funicular elevator copied from the one at the Honiara Hotel. The 40 deluxe hillview rooms are SI$286/341 single/double, while the 16 seaview rooms are SI$308/369. There are also 10 self-catering units at SI$473/517. Extra persons in the room are SI$40, but children under 12 may stay with their parents free. With its upper level swimming pool and "leaf haus" restaurant/bar, the King Solomon is a strong competitor to the more established Mendaña Hotel, although it lacks the harborside location.

Near the Mobil service station two km west of Rove Market is the **Lelei Resort** (Jeff Olson, Box 235, Honiara; tel. 20720, fax 22970), a two-story building on a rocky shore with a pleasant view of Savo Island. Although no beach is here, snorkeling should be possible. These nicely appointed international-standard accommodations consist of six a/c rooms with private bath and fridge at SI$275/319 single/double. A model Western Province war canoe stands in the Lelei's Tomoko Restaurant. Get there on the frequent White River minibus.

FOOD

Budget

Lots of basic snack bars around town serve curry beef with rice for SI$10. Many close at night, so if you have cooking facilities, plan on preparing your own dinner and having lunch on the run. Several places at the Central Market serve rice or noodle lunches. **Siwba Foodbar** (closed Sunday), facing the water on the east side of the market, has a variety of fish dishes, plus chicken, spaghetti, and steak.

The back counter at **Amy's Snack Bar** (tel. 25552; weekdays 0615-2200, weekends 0730-2200), next to the Westpac Bank, serves a good choice of dishes, such as sweet and sour pork, fried chicken, noodles, fish and chips, spring rolls, *rotis*, hot dogs, sausages, and meat pies, and there are plenty of plastic picnic tables at which to sit. Most dishes are less than SI$10, and the cold coconuts are a real treat at SI$1.20 to SI$1.50 depending on the size.

In the center of town, **Kingsley's Fastfood Center** (tel. 22936; weekdays 0720-1930, Saturday 0800-1730, Sunday 0900-1730), on the street running inland from The Pharmacy, specializes in barbecued chicken, rice dishes, hamburgers, and noodle soup.

Inexpensive meals can be obtained at the food court of the NPF Plaza opposite the National Museum. One place sells Thai food and better than average fish and chips. Also watch for the SI$3 *rotis.*

The coffee shop in the **National Art Gallery and Cultural Center,** opposite the Central Bank, serves fresh fruit, salads, and sandwiches at lunchtime, but the main attraction here is the pleasant garden. Bring some takeaway food and have a picnic at one of the tables in the garden.

Ozzy's Kitchen (weekdays 1200-1400), on Hibiscus Ave. in the compound of the Girl Guides Association directly behind the National Museum, serves a good cooked lunch on their pleasant outdoor terrace. You'll like the large portions of excellent local-style food (around SI$12), but arrive early to get a table.

Smats Cafe (tel. 25275; weekdays 0700-1600, Saturday 0800-1230), on Hibiscus Ave. directly behind the Westpac Bank, is good for breakfast, lunch, or a cup of coffee. There's no smoking here.

A Thai-Chinese lady runs **Pasofi Snack Bar** (tel. 21295), on Point Cruz, with fried noodles, sweet-and-sour fish, and beef curries. There are seats outside, and it's open till 1600 daily except Sunday—excellent.

Better Restaurants

Other than the good-value meals available at the Point Cruz Yacht Club, and the Wednesday and Sunday night barbecues at the Kitano Mendaña Hotel (SI$60), the options for fine dining in Honiara are dismal. There are lots of pricey Chinese restaurants around town, none of them worth singling out. Unlike American or European Chinese restaurants where everyone orders an individual meal such as chop suey or chow mein, at the Honiara Chinese restaurants all of the dishes are meant to be consumed collectively by everyone at the table. In the true Chinese fashion, they're served one at a time, and the process tends to be long and drawn out in the hope of selling you more drinks (not listed on the menu and expensive). Thus the success of your meal is closely related to your ordering ability and previous experience doesn't count. If you're still interested, you'll find them open only for lunch 1200-1400 and dinner 1900-2200. Expect prices to be higher at dinner and count on spending a minimum of SI$50 pp (double what a comparable meal would cost in Fiji). Expect 10% tax to be added to all of the prices on the menu.

Of the hotel restaurants, the Capitana Restaurant at the Kitano Mendaña has Japanese food, while the Honiara Hotel restaurant features French dishes. The restaurant at the

King Solomon Hotel serves pizza, steaks, and chicken. The buffet dinners at the Mendaña are much more popular than those at the Honiara Hotel.

Groceries

It pays to shop around, as grocery prices vary considerably in Honiara. The best stocked supermarket is **Chan Wing Ltd.** (tel. 22414; weekdays 0800-1200/1330-1800, Saturday 0800-1300), near Super Motel in Chinatown.

Wings Supermarket (tel. 20108), at the back of NPF Plaza, is the biggest in the center of town.

ELO 24 Retail Shop, on Cluck St. below the South Sea Restaurant, sells basic groceries 24 hours a day seven days a week.

ENTERTAINMENT

See four trashy action films daily at **Lena Cinema** (tel. 22255) in the center of town. No movies begin after 1700. Several other small cinemas around Honiara show video films. What you see depends on what caught the projectionist's eye at the video rental shop the day before, and karate is the favorite.

Weekdays after work, Honiara's expatriate community congregates at the **Point Cruz Yacht Club** (Box 203, Honiara; tel. 22500, fax 22073), and Friday afternoon the place is packed. Sit at a beachside table and enjoy the view of ships in the harbor and of Savo Island on the horizon. Cruising yachts anchor opposite the naval vessels, straight out from the yacht club beach, and the club has the usual notice board if you're looking for a yacht/crew. The club's food counter is open daily 1200-1400 and 1830-2100, and the Lelei Resort does the catering so the food is good with lots of seafood. To find out what's cooking, check the blackboard menu as you come in. The Yacht Club is open Mon.-Thurs. 1030-1400 and 1530-2230, Friday 1030-1400 and 1530-midnight, Saturday 0900-2230, Sunday 0900-2200. Have the doorman sign you in.

There's a dance at the **Police Club,** across the soccer field from Rove Police Headquarters, on Friday and Saturday nights (SI$10 admission).

Club Freeway (tel. 23332), on Hibiscus Ave.

next to the Shell station, a block back from the Westpac Bank, is the city's most popular disco. It's open Thursday, Friday, and Saturday 2100-0200, admission SI$10/15 for ladies/gents.

After dark, you've got a fair chance of being mugged if you're caught wandering anywhere between Chinatown and the market, so take a taxi.

Cultural Shows for Visitors

The top events of the week are the **panpipe performances.** The top panpipe band is Narasirato from Are'are in South Malaita (internationally renowned since their tours to England, Canada, and Australia). Narasirato T-shirts and cassettes are sold at the performances. The Mao Dancers from Kwara'ae and the Wasi Ka Nanara Pan Pipers from Waimarau, both on Malaita, are also very good, and if you have the chance, attend any performance by the Betikama Adventist bamboo band, St. Joseph's Tenaru panpipe group, or the boys of St. Martin's School who play panpipes and perform custom dances. Some of the panpipe groups incorporate bamboo band music into their performances.

The panpipe musicians often appear with **Gilbertese dancing,** but unfortunately most of the Gilbertese groups now perform Tahitian *tamure* dances. These can be rather boring due to the absence of the Polynesian drummers able to execute sudden changes in rhythm. Tahitian dancing to recorded music or singing just isn't the same, and it's a pity these people stopped doing their own authentic Gilbertese dances. Nevertheless, if you like the show, it's customary to show your appreciation by contributing a banknote or two to the dancer who pleases you most *during* the dance. Watch how the locals do it. Be careful if a dancer comes up and places a garland of flowers on your head. Next thing you know she'll have you dancing with her up on the stage!

The programs tend to vary, but Narasirato often performs at the Kitano Mendaña Hotel on Saturday night. On Wednesday night, other Areare panpipers perform, perhaps with Gilbertese dancing as a warmup. Sunday night there's a Gilbertese dance group from White River doing *tamure* dances. The Mendaña shows start between 1900 and 2000 (check beforehand).

Sunday at 1930, panpipers and *tamure*

dancers alternate at the King Solomon Hotel. More *tamure* dancing takes place on the large shell stage at the Honiara Hotel, Wednesday at 1930 and Friday at 2030. You can watch for the price of a drink.

SHOPPING

The **Central Market** (open all day but best before 1030) is the place to buy fruit, vegetables, and shell money. Prices vary considerably from one stall to another, so shop around. Don't bargain, just keep looking. Notice how there are more stores around Honiara selling used clothes than shops with new clothing.

The **Philatelic Bureau** (Box G31, Honiara; tel. 21821, fax 21472) beside the post office sells beautiful stamps and first-day covers, which make excellent souvenirs. The **Central Bank** (tel. 21791) nearby sells commemorative coins, many of which are on display in the lobby.

Afga Film (tel. 20943), Room 39, NPF Plaza, sells hard-to-find black-and-white and color slide films, and does developing.

overmodeled human skull

Crafts

Without question, Honiara's top buys are traditional handicrafts. Carvers peddle their wares outside the Kitano Mendaña Hotel, and dozens of people sell handicrafts in the compound behind the National Museum whenever a cruise ship docks. The handicraft shop in the museum itself is good (Tues.-Fri. 1100-1200/1500-1600), and in Room no. 40 in the NPF Plaza across the street you can buy items made by local women.

The **King Solomon Arts and Crafts Center,** opposite Solomon Airlines, has been recommended by readers as the least expensive place to buy handicrafts. **Melanesian Handicrafts** (tel. 22189), also on Mendaña Ave., sells a variety of handicrafts.

DJ Graphics Ltd. Island Souvenirs (tel. 22011), a few shops west of Solomon Airlines, sells cassettes and compact discs of Solomons music including panpipe bands. They also have numerous woodcarvings and T-shirts.

The Quarantine Office (tel. 21976), next to Mamara Estates Ltd., across the street from National Shipping Services, will fumigate handicrafts made of grass, leaves, or other natural materials and issue a certificate required to import the items into other countries. At least one working day is required and there's a SI$20 fee.

SERVICES

Money

The Westpac Bank, the ANZ Bank, and the National Bank are all near one another in the center of town (weekdays 0900-1500). The Westpac Bank charges SI$25 commission to change traveler's checks. The ANZ Bank deducts no commission and gives a slightly better rate. The National Bank also has no commission but their rate is less favorable. All this could change.

When the banks are closed, the cashier at the Kitano Mendaña Hotel will change money for about 10% less. American Express is not represented.

Post and Telecommunications

The main post office (tel. 21821) is open weekdays 0800-1630, Saturday 0800-1200. Honiara's post office is uncrowded, the staff are friendly and cooperative, and postal rates in the Solomons are low. Send all your parcels, postcards, and aerograms from here. Always use airmail, even for parcels, as sea mail to Europe or North America can take six months. Poste restante at the post office is usually reliable and they hold letters two months.

The parcel section at the rear of the main post office opens Monday, Wednesday, and Friday 0800-1600, Tuesday and Thursday 0800-1500, and Saturday 0800-1100. The convenient Post Shop inside the post office sells all sorts of envelopes. Unlike postage, postcards are very expensive in Honiara, costing around SI$2.50 each. Aerograms, on the other hand, are cheap.

The **DHL Courier Service** office is at BJS Agencies/Melanesian Handicrafts (tel. 22393; weekdays 0800-1700, Saturday 0900-1200), on Mendaña Avenue.

Solomon Telekom (tel. 21164, fax 24220; weekdays 0800-1630, weekends 0800-1200), next to the post office, has four private booths for making calls with telephone cards. Operator-assisted calls are not available. If you want to receive a fax at this office, have it sent to fax 23110 (SI$3 a page to receive). Many other public card phones are found around town.

Immigration

The Immigration office (tel. 21440, fax 22964), in the Ministry of Commerce across Mendaña Ave. from the post office, is open weekdays 0900-1100 and 1300-1500.

Consulates

Get Australian visas in 24 hours at the **Australian High Commission** (tel. 21561; weekdays 0800-1200), across the street from the King Solomon Hotel. You may have to pay a fee for a visa you could have obtained free at home. The Australian mission also represents Canadians.

The British High Commission (tel. 21705) is in Telekom House next to the post office. The New Zealand High Commission (tel. 21502) and European Union representation (tel. 22765) are on the second floor of the Y. Sato Building (above Guadalcanal Travel Service). Tradco Shipping Ltd. (tel. 22588), next to Guadalcanal Travel Service, is the German Honorary Consulate. The Japanese Embassy (tel. 22953) is on the third floor of the NPF Building behind the Westpac Bank. The Papua New Guinea High Commission (tel. 20561) is on second floor of the Anthony Saru Building, behind NPF Plaza next to the Solomon Islands National Museum. BJS Agencies/Melanesian Handicrafts (tel. 22393, e-mail: bjs@welkam.solomon.com.sb), on Mendaña Ave., is a semiofficial representative of the U.S. Embassy in Suva, Fiji.

Public Toilets

Public toilets are available in the Kitano Mendaña Hotel, the Honiara Hotel, and at the Point Cruz Yacht Club. At last report, there were no laundromats in Honiara.

INFORMATION

The helpful Visitors Bureau (tel. 22442, fax 23986; weekdays 0800-1200/ 1330-1600), across from the museum, can supply a complete accommodations list with current prices, plus many useful brochures. This is one of the few tourist offices in the South Pacific which is only too happy to advise on ways of getting off the beaten track, staying with local people, arranging rides in outboard canoes, etc. If you're looking for real adventure, they'll have plenty of suggestions.

The Survey and Cartography Division Map Sales Office (tel. 21511; weekdays 0800-1130/1300-1600), Hibiscus Ave. and Koti Lane, has detailed topographical maps of the whole country at SI$20 a sheet.

The Hydrographic Office, opposite the Survey and Cartography Division, sells locally produced charts and tide tables at SI$45 per chart.

Bookstores and Libraries

Australian newspapers are sold at News Power Newsagent (tel. 22069) in the Anthony Saru Building behind the NPF Plaza.

Riley's Pocket Bookstore (tel. 21737; weekdays 1000-1300/1400-1800, Saturday 0900-1300), in the lobby of the Honiara Hotel, is the only commercial bookstore in Honiara. They carry several intriguing books by local authors, such as *The Confession* by Julian Maka'a and *The Alternative* by John Saunana.

The University of the South Pacific Center

(Box 460, Honiara; tel. 21307, fax 21287), behind the National Gymnasium east of Chinatown, also carries books by Solomon Islanders. The library here is open Monday and Tuesday 0800-1630, Wednesday and Thursday 0800-1800, Friday 0800-1600, and Saturday 0900-1200.

The Public Library (tel. 23227), on Belama Ave. between the market and Chinatown, is open Monday, Tuesday, Thursday, Friday 1000-1730, Saturday 0900-1200, Sunday 1400-1700.

The National Library (Box 165, Honiara; tel. 21601; weekdays 0800-1200 and 1300-1630) is in the building directly behind the Public Library.

Nongovernment Organizations

The Solomon Islands Development Trust (Box 147, Honiara; tel. 21130, fax 21131), in an office marked Mi Minim Nao Haos in New Chinatown, publishes a fascinating quarterly magazine called *Link* on local social and environmental issues.

The Development Services Exchange (Box 556, Honiara; tel. 23760, fax 21339), also in New Chinatown, is an umbrella organization founded in 1991 that represents 50 NGOs active in Solomon Islands.

Airline Offices

Solomon Airlines (tel. 20031) is on Mendaña Ave. in the center of town. Travel Industry Service (tel. 20336), across the street from Solomon Airlines, represents Air Pacific and Qantas. Guadalcanal Travel Services (tel. 22586) next door is the Air Nauru agent (although that airline has no scheduled flights to Honiara). The Air Niugini> office (tel. 22895) is in Church House near the Hot Bread Kitchen.

HEALTH

The Central Hospital (tel. 23600) is overcrowded, so if you need medical attention, consider visiting a private doctor rather than spending a long time waiting there. Any of the clinics mentioned below should be able to do a malaria slide check quickly and inexpensively.

Dr. Pimbo Ogatuti of the Island Medical Center (tel. 23139; weekdays 0800-1200/1300-1600, Saturday 0800-1200), is on Cluck St. on the way up to the United Church Resthouse.

Dr. H. Posala's Honimed Clinic (tel. 22029;

Monday, Tuesday, and Thursday 0800-1200 and 1330-1600, Wednesday 0800-1200, Friday 0800-1200 and 1330-1500, Sunday 0900-1200), is next to the Iron Bottom South Hotel, just down from the Guadalcanal Club. It's SI$30 for a consultation or SI$5 for a prescription.

The Honiara Dental Center (tel. 22029; Mon.-Thurs. 0800-1200 and 1330-1630, Friday 0800-1200) is next to the Honimed Clinic. There's also a Dental Clinic (tel. 23600) at Central Hospital.

City Cruz Laboratory (Box 709, Honiara; tel. 20649; weekdays 0800-1200/1300-1600, weekends 0800-1200), upstairs in the building opposite Provincial Press, accessed down the lane behind Air Niugini, can do a malaria parasite survey (MPS) in 10 minutes for SI$8.

For malaria prevention, The Pharmacy (tel. 22911), opposite Solomon Airlines, suggests Maloprim at SI$70 for 10 tablets (one a week) or Paludrine at SI$16 for 30 tablets (one a day). The Dispensary (tel. 23587) in NPF Plaza sells Paludrine at 50 cents a pill, plus a SI$5 fee, and they have Chloroquine at SI$2.50 for 10 pills. At last report, Lariam was SI$160 for eight tablets at The Pharmacy, or SI$228 for a set of eight at The Dispensary. See **Health** in the chapter introduction for a discussion of these drugs.

TRANSPORTATION

For domestic air services from Honiara, see **Transportation** in the chapter Introduction.

Travel around the Solomons by boat is fairly easy, and it's one of the main attractions of the country. There are many services, and fares are reasonable—plan on doing much of your interisland travel this way. You'll make numerous friends on board and really get to see the Solomons.

Orient yourself by looking over the ships in Honiara harbor; most of the shipping companies have offices nearby. Some ships won't accept passengers for safety reasons, and you should pick the larger vessels if your ability as a sailor is in doubt. Cabin fares (when available) are about double one-way deck fares, and meals aren't usually included. If you want a cabin, try to book a few days in advance. Forget attempting to catch a boat just before Christmas when schedules and routes change at a moment's notice and everything's full.

Ships to Western Province

The boat trip from Honiara to Gizo is one of the finest scenic cruises in the South Pacific. It's less rough westbound from Honiara to Gizo than eastbound from Gizo to Honiara because you go with the prevailing winds. Thus if you were planning to fly one way, it's a good plan to go out by boat and return to Honiara by plane. However, you only get to see the Marovo Lagoon by day on the way back to Honiara.

Every Sunday at 1000 **Wings Shipping** (Box 4, Honiara; tel. 21259, fax 20463), on Hibiscus Ave. behind the Hot Bread Kitchen, sends the *Iuminao* to Patutiva (SI$59 deck), Munda (SI$71 deck), and Gizo (26 hours; SI$79 deck). First class costs a third to a half more, a cabin about double. The ship arrives in Gizo on Monday afternoon and starts back toward Honiara a few hours later, calling at the New Georgia and Marovo Lagoon pickup points on Tuesday and arriving in Honiara early Wednesday morning.

The *Iuminao* lies lower in the water than many of the other ships and is more stable. The accommodation is good with lots of wooden benches in economy. First class consists of individual reclining seats (recommended on crowded trips), although noisy videos can be a problem. On the way to Gizo, there will be markets of cooked food at some of the ports of call, but you have to be quick or you'll miss out. It's best to take your own food along.

Olifasia Shipping Services (Box 686, Honiara), in the aluminum warehouse behind National Shipping Services, runs the MV *Liofai* to Western Province whenever there's sufficient cargo.

Ships to Malaita

The **Malaita Shipping Co.** (Box 584, Honiara; tel. 23502, fax 23503), just down toward the harbor from the ANZ Bank, runs the MV *Ramos I* from Honiara to Auki Tuesday and Friday at 1800 (arriving 2330). Fares are SI$30 economy, SI$46 first class, and SI$64 cabin. On alternate Sundays, the *Ramos I* sails overnight from Honiara to northeast or south Malaita. On an overnight trip, first class or a cabin might be worth considering, although there's a large protected room downstairs for economy passengers. The *Ramos I* tosses a lot in rough weather and the lower in the ship you can get the better.

When it's not crowded, first class on the **Ramos I** is good, with long padded benches on which to stretch out. Unfortunately, noisy nocturnal videos will disturb your sleep in both the downstairs room and the first class lounge.

The high-speed, 136-passenger *Ocean Express* departs Honiara for Auki Thursday at 0700 and Sunday at 1200 (3.5 hours, SI$35). Tickets are available from Ocean Navigation Ltd. (Box 966, Honiara; tel. 24281; weekdays 0800-1200 and 1300-1630, Saturday 0800-1130), upstairs in the M.P. Kwan Building opposite the Guadalcanal provincial offices on Mendaña Avenue.

Ships to Isabel

The high-speed vessel **Ocean Express** (tel. 24281) zips from Honiara to Buala Tuesday at 0800 (6.5 hours, SI$55). There's a stop at Tatamba en route.

The **Isabel Development Co.** (Box 92, Honiara; tel. 22126, fax 22009), in the aluminum warehouse directly behind the National Shipping Services office, runs the *Ligomo* to Buala (SI$44 deck) once a week. Twice a month it continues up the west coast of Isabel as far as Kia.

Ship to Choiseul and Makira

Wings Shipping (Box 4, Honiara; tel. 21259, fax 20463), on Hibiscus Ave. behind the Hot Bread Kitchen, runs the MV *King Solomon* to Choiseul once a month. They call at all ports between Wagina and Taro, following the north or south coasts on alternative trips. Fares from Honiara are SI$82 to Wagina or SI$87 to Taro. The *King Solomon* travels to Makira monthly, visiting all ports as far east as Santa Ana. Fares from Honiara are SI$60 to Kirakira and SI$68 to Santa Ana.

Ships to Tulagi

The **National Fisheries Developments Ltd.** (Box 717, Honiara; tel. 21506, fax 21459), on Hibiscus Ave. opposite Wings Shipping, runs the *Moaika* from Honiara to Tulagi on Friday afternoon (two hours; SI$25). There often are additional departures during the week, so it's worth checking.

The high-speed **Ocean Express** (tel. 24281) departs Honiara for Savo (Reko), Tulagi, Taroniara, and Siota Friday at 0800, returning the same day in the afternoon (SI$25 one-way).

Florida Shipping Co. (tel. 20210), upstairs in the National Shipping Services building, occasionally runs its boat, the *Florida II,* to Tulagi on Wednesday or Friday (SI$20 each way). The copra run around Nggela is every other Monday. There are four bunks on the back deck of this small boat where you could sleep.

Sasape Marina Ltd. (Box 226, Honiara; tel. 22111, fax 32163), next to Florida Shipping upstairs in the National Shipping Services Building, has a boat to Tulagi on Monday, Wednesday, and Friday departing at 1400 at the earliest (later if there is additional cargo to load). It's SI$18 each way. This boat is often out of service due to special charters.

Ships around Guadalcanal

Once a week the **Guadalcanal Provincial Government** (tel. 20041, extension 29 or 30) has a ship right around Guadalcanal, traveling clockwise or counterclockwise on alternate weeks, a four-day trip. It's usually either the MV *Wango* or the MV *Kangava,* departing Honiara Tuesday at 0800. You could stop off at Marau Sound and fly back. Inquire at the Provincial Office on Mendaña Avenue.

To the Outer Islands

National Shipping Services (Box 1766, Honiara; tel. 25941 or 25939, fax 26039), formerly the Marine Division but now semiprivatized, operates nine ships to Makira, Malaita, Choiseul, and Temotu provinces. They only go at the request of the provincial governments and regular schedules don't exist, but information may be available on the blackboard at their harborfront office, where you also buy your ticket. For advance information from abroad, call or fax the operations manager in Honiara.

Three National Shipping Services vessels, the *Butai, Belama,* and *Baruku,* serve the eastern outer islands. Each ship has three double cabins and the monthly 25-day roundtrip voyage to Makira, Santa Cruz, Utupua, Duff, Vanikolo, Anuta, and Tikopia would cost SI$464. Otherwise it's about SI$116 deck one-way to the last stop, with bunks about twice the deck fare. No meals are included and passengers must bring all their own food, but reasonable cooking facilities are available for cabin passengers. The ship makes an extra circle around the Santa Cruz Islands

before calling at Vanikolo for the second time; thus, you could stop off for about four days on this remote island before reboarding the same ship to return to Honiara. Other stopovers are possible. Add to your journey by getting off at Kirakira (Makira) on the way back and visit Star Harbor and Santa Ana from there.

National Shipping Services has a ship to Sikaiana and Ontong Java every three weeks, and a monthly trip to Rennell and Bellona. These voyages average five days return.

The **Commodities Export Marketing Authority** or CEMA (Box 1087, Honiara; tel. 22528, fax 21262) runs cargo boats such as the *Marthalina, Mawo,* and *Regina* to islands as far afield as Santa Cruz, picking up copra and delivering petrol. About once a month they have a ship from Honiara to Santa Cruz, and deck fares for the three-day voyage from Honiara are SI$105 to Lata or SI$110 to the Reef Islands. It's possible to get a bunk in a large 20-bed covered room for about SI$10 for the trip. In Honiara ask at the CEMA office near the wharf (down the road from the ANZ Bank) or check at their warehouse on Point Cruz.

Other Ships

Less well-known are the old Chinese trading boats, full of South Seas flavor, that run between Honiara and Gizo fortnightly. There are also mission ships to many points; ask the crews along the waterfront.

The **Church of Melanesia Shipping Office** (Box 19, Honiara; tel. 21892, fax 21098), diagonally opposite the Hot Bread Kitchen, operates three well-maintained mission ships. The *Charles Fox* does the mail run to Taro in Choiseul Province, departing Honiara on Monday, Wednesday, and Friday (SI$20 deck, no cabins). The *Southern Cross* and the *Kopuria* serve Malaita, Isabel, Makira, and Temotu on an irregular basis. This pair is well worth checking as each has three or four double cabins, costing only double per bunk compared to going deck (SI$100/200 deck/cabin Honiara-Lata). All three are quite small, so only go if you're sure of your sailing and social abilities.

By Canoe

To reach Savo Island, ask if any canoes are going back from the landing beside the Point

Cruz Yacht Club. Unless you insist on the "hitching" rate of SI$20 pp, you'll be expected to pay SI$150-200 for a special trip. Try to do the canoe journey in the early morning before the wind wakes up the sea, and be prepared to get soaked even on an apparently calm day. You'll pass through schools of dolphins and flying fish.

Canoes to Koela and Kaoqele villages on Savo also leave from Tamale village, just south of Cape Esperance, 36 km west of Honiara. They usually depart on their regular trip in the early morning, returning to Guadalcanal around midday. Passengers on the regular trips pay SI$15 pp, while a special charter from Tamale will be SI$120 each way for two people at any time during the day.

A good plan is to go to Savo from Point Cruz and return via Cape Esperance.

By Bus
Scores of private minibuses cruise up and down the main road from White River to KG6 (King George VI High School), passing every five minutes or so. Some buses go as far west as White River. Eastbound they reach CDC123 out beyond Tetere about every 15 minutes throughout the day. Buses marked Naha turn inland at Kukum before reaching KG6. Buses within the town area operate until 2100 daily. All buses have destination boards in the front window, and fares are SI$1 anywhere between White River and KG6, SI$2 to the airport, SI$2.50 to Foxwood Timbers, SI$4 to CDC2, and SI$5 to CDC3. Baggage is free and the conductors are fairly honest, but it's wise to have small bills.

By Truck
Passenger trucks depart Honiara market for Lambi Bay (SI$15) and Aola (SI$15), at opposite ends of the north coast highway, daily except Sunday at about 1500. Other trucks make more frequent, shorter trips. Vehicles bearing white license plates with black lettering are public vehicles that charge fares.

Taxis
Taxi drivers are also honest, but always ask the price beforehand, as they don't have meters, and expect prices to increase at night. Estimate how much you might be willing to pay, then offer that amount to the driver before getting in. It's

usually SI$3-4 a kilometer and SI$30 maximum to the airport (don't tip the driver). Single passengers sit in front.

If you're in a small group, you could hire a taxi for the day to tour the battlefields around the airport for about the same money it would cost to rent a car. Make a list of the places you want to see, then get a flat rate, including waiting time, gas, and mileage.

Car Rentals
Driving is on the left. This may be one of the few countries of the world to enter the 21st century without any traffic signs, and while driving around Honiara you must be prepared for a confusing system of unmarked one-way side streets. Watch out for minibuses stopping suddenly, and at night be on the lookout for people walking along the edge of the road and drunken drivers everywhere. Expect rough roads and narrow bridges, and don't leave valuables unattended in a parked car.

Honiara is the only place in the Solomon Islands where rental cars are available, but there's a shortage of vehicles, so book as far in advance as possible, especially on weekends. On the positive side, car rental prices are not exorbitant and gasoline is very cheap at SI$1.57 a liter (in the South Pacific, only Samoa has cheaper gas). Other than going by taxi or on a tour, it's the only easy way to visit areas beyond the minibus routes.

Budget/Solomon Motors (Box 20, Honiara; tel. 23205, fax 23593; weekdays 0800-1200/1330-1630, Saturday 0800-1200, Sunday 0800-0930) is next to the Mobil Garage near the Mendaña. Their airport office only opens if there are bookings. An unlimited-mileage Suzuki costs SI$130/780 daily/weekly, plus SI$30/180 mandatory collision insurance (SI$2,500 deductible), plus 10% tax. Ask about their reduced half-day rate (valid 0900-1500). Drivers under 21 or over 65 are not accepted.

More expensive is **Avis/Pacific Car Rentals** (Box 87, Honiara; tel. 24180, fax 24181), with locations at the airport, next to Super Club in Chinatown, and inside the Kitano Mendaña Hotel (weekdays 0800-1200/1330-1630, Saturday 0800-1200, Sunday 0900-1200). Their cheapest Daihatsu is SI$150 a day with unlimited km, plus SI$30 compulsory collision insurance, plus 10% tax. If you rent for seven days, you get one day free.

Tours

If time is short, several companies offer guided sightseeing tours of Honiara and the WW II sites. **Guadalcanal Travel Service** (Box 114, Honiara; tel. 22586, fax 26184), across the street from Solomon Airlines, offers the three-hour "eastern battlefields" tour (SI$80) three times a week. The five-hour "western battlefields" trip (SI$150) includes lunch at Tambea Resort, but it's long and dusty.

Solomon Sights and Sounds (Box 1227, Honiara; tel. 22230, fax 22231), at the King Solomon Hotel, offers a variety of excursions around Honiara and north Guadalcanal, costing SI$65 for a half-day city tour or SI$150-175 for a full day tour east or west with lunch.

WEST OF HONIARA

At **Bonegi Private Beach,** 14 km west of Poha, are the wrecks of two Japanese freighters sunk offshore in November 1942. One is partly above water, the other only three meters down, and it's easy to swim from shore and snorkel over both. Bonegi is labeled Koilo Point on topographical maps. It's a nice picnic spot and the scuba companies often bring their clients here. No fishing is allowed. Admission to the beach is SI$5/20 per car/minibus and it's all clearly signposted. To visit an old U.S. tank called *Jezebel* on the other side of the hill from Bonegi costs SI$10 extra per group. A taxi from Honiara will be SI$50 for the car.

West of Bonegi you pass coastal plantations where cattle graze below orange tinted coconut trees. The pavement ends at Ndoma, 23 km west of Honiara. Drive slowly on the gravel road west of here as it's easy to start sliding.

About 24 km west of Honiara is the **Vilu War Museum** (daily 0800-1800; admission SI$10 pp, video cameras SI$220) at Vilu village, 650 meters off the main road. The open air collection includes four large Japanese field guns from Camp Express near Visale, two Douglas dive bombers, a Corsair with W-shaped wings and body, a B-38 Lightning aircraft raised from the sea at Ranadi, four wings of F46 hellcats, a carrier-based Grumman Wildcat with one wing still capable of being folded back, the wing of a B17 bomber, part of a Japanese Betty bomber, an an-

tiaircraft gun, several smaller field guns, and a piece of a Japanese tank. A number of small war memorials have been set up here and the site is of interest to WW II buffs.

Just less than a kilometer west of the turnoff to the War Museum is the **Coastal Aquaculture Center,** an experimental giant clam farm established in 1988 by the International Center for Living Aquatic Resources Management. Sponsored by Australia and the European Union, this facility breeds six of the world's eight Tridacna species. The clams are kept in circular tanks at ICLARM for six months, then held in cages in the sea by local farmers another six months, after which they are exported to Germany and the U.S. to serve the aquarium trade. Through farming, the largest of all clams, the *Tridacna gigas,* may be saved from extinction. Sea cucumbers are also bred here, eventually to be exported to Japan for food. Visitors are also shown some pearl oysters. The facility is open to the public weekdays 0900-1600, Saturday 1000-1600, Sunday 1030-1630 (admission SI$5, children under 16 SI$2).

In the early morning outboard canoes cross to Savo Island from a village near **Cape Esperance Lighthouse,** 36 km west of Honiara. To go costs SI$12 pp. Visale village, with its large Catholic mission, is about two km west of the cape. Japanese submarine *I-123* is on the reef just offshore from Veuru, 1.5 km west of Visale. It's only a few hundred meters offshore in two meters of water. You must pay a SI$20 pp custom fee to snorkel over the wreck.

The **Tambea Holiday Beach Resort** (see below) is 2.5 km beyond Veuru (and 42 km west of Honiara). It was from this area that many Japanese troops made their final escape from Guadalcanal in February 1943. A large white bus with a Tambea destination sign runs from Honiara Central Market to Tambea at 1100 and 1600, returning from Tambea toward Honiara at 0600 and 1200 (SI$7 pp).

Selwyn College, at Maravovo, 47 km west of Honiara, opened in 1991. This large modern complex run by the Church of Melanesia accommodates 500 students in forms seven to 12. Opposite the college is a long gray public beach, but better white sandy beaches are to the southwest. Beyond these are four or five small rivers all vehicles must ford, and Verahui village, 57 km west of Honiara.

The end of the drivable road for most cars is just beyond Nuku Plantation, eight km short of Lambi Bay, where a larger river with no bridge and a quickly deteriorating road bring most trips to an end. The north coast highway terminates at **Lambi Bay,** 69 km west of Honiara. Village trucks leave Lambi Bay for Honiara nearly every morning.

A more adventurous way to get there is to take a boat to **Tangarare,** then walk back to Lambi Bay in a day or more. There are two chest-deep crocodile creeks to cross. A good surfing spot (right-handers) is near the river mouth at Tangarare, and there's good diving along this beautiful coastline. A footpath travels the entire south coast from village to village.

Accommodations

If you'd like a holiday away from it all by a sheltered black beach, consider visiting **Tambea Holiday Beach Resort** (Box 4, Honiara; tel. 29639, fax 29082), 42 km west of Honiara. The 24 bungalows, each with fan, fridge, toilet, and shower are SI$234/306/356 single/double/triple, plus tax. Cooking facilities are not provided, but meals are served in the restaurant (dinner SI$39). It's a good place to spend the weekend because there's a special feast and custom dancing on Saturday night when enough guests are present (call ahead to ask), plus a barbecue at noon on Sunday (SI$39). A Japanese war memorial stands between the swimming pool and the beach, and you get a nice view of Savo from the resort's curving gray-black shore.

There's no coral here so beach snorkeling is not an option, but many nonmotorized nautical activities are offered free to guests. Dive Tambea at the resort offers scuba diving on nearby reefs, caves, and perhaps Japanese submarine *I-123* at SI$90/140 for one dive with/without your own equipment. Six, 10, and 15-dive packages available at reduced rates, and scuba certification courses are available. The resort also offers horseback riding at SI$20 and there's sportfishing from motorized fiberglass canoes. A lending library is at the bar. The Honiara Hotel (which, like Tambea, is owned by Honiara businessman Tommy Chan) organizes transfers to Tambea at 0830 daily, leaving Tambea to return to Honiara at 1500 (SI$20 pp each way). Moderate.

EAST OF HONIARA

The Coastal Plain

Catch a KG6 minibus east along the Kukum Highway (known as "Highway 50" to American troops) past King George VI School. The bus route ends a kilometer east of the school at the access road to **Betikama Carvings** (Box 516, Honiara; tel. 30223, fax 30174), on the grounds of Adventist High School, 1.5 km off the main road. There's a good display of woodcarvings made at SDA villages in the Marovo Lagoon area, a deteriorating collection of WW II relics including several plane parts, a small war muse-

A single gun guards Red Beach near Foxwood Timbers where the U.S. Marines landed on 7 August 1942.

NORTH GUADALCANAL

1. Kakambona
2. Lelei Resort
3. Tasahe Drive
4. Kukum
5. Vara
6. Galloping Horse Ridge
7. Harahei
8. Mataniko Falls
9. Tuvaruhu
10. Sea Horse Ridge
11. Mbarana
12. Solomon Peace Memorial
13. Mt. Austin
14. Tenaru Falls
15. Honiara Golf Club
16. King George VI School
17. Betikama Carvings
18. underground hospital
19. Bloody Ridge
20. Henderson Airport
21. Airport Motel
22. Alligator Creek
23. Foxwood Sawmill/Red Beach
24. site of Koni Airfield
25. abandoned landing vehicles
26. Albatross Monument
27. Palm Oil Mill

um, and a crocodile. Some of the crafts sold here are excellent quality. It's open Mon.-Thurs. 0800-1200 and 1300-1700, and Friday and Sunday 0800-1200 (free).

Return to the Kukum Highway and cross the Lungga River bridge, from which two tunnels are visible slightly to the right. The first was General Vandegrift's command post and later a communications center. The tunnel has many rooms on each side and goes under the hillock to the other side. An **underground wartime hospital** is farther to the right at a higher elevation and goes under the nearby hill with a house on top. Both tunnels are accessible with a flashlight, though prominent signs warn that it could be dangerous to enter.

Bloody Ridge, perhaps the most meaningful WW II site in the Solomons, was the turning point of the ground war in the Pacific. If you'd like to visit, follow the dirt road around the west end of the airstrip and turn right at the T-junction. A white triangular memorial crowns Bloody Ridge, also known as "Edson's Ridge" for the American field commander. This is a hot 40-minute walk each way (no shade), but the views from the ridge are rewarding. A **Japanese War Memorial** is a kilometer farther along in the same direction. Over the past decade, several villages have appeared around Bloody Ridge.

Henderson Field was the center of fighting during the first part of the Solomon Islands campaign. The initial Japanese counterattack came from the east on 21 August 1942, at Alligator Creek. This thrust was turned back, and on 8 September Edson's Raiders, who had arrived fresh from the capture of Tulagi, drove inland the Japanese positioned east of Henderson. On the nights of 13 and 14 September, these Japanese troops attacked the U.S. forces on Bloody Ridge, three km south of the airstrip. They were broken up, but five weeks later another Japanese army struggled along the Maruyama Trail from White River, passing behind Mt. Austin. On the nights of 23 and 24 October, they struck once more at Bloody Ridge but were again defeated, after suffering more than 2,000 casualties.

Return to the main road and catch another minibus to the Foxwood Sawmill, which adjoins **Red Beach.** The first U.S. Marine Division landed here on 7 August 1942 to begin its costly six-month offensive to capture Guadalcanal. One cannon still points out to sea, a silent, rusted sentinel.

Beyond the sawmill, you'll pass some copra/cacao estates and huge palm-oil plantations. Get off the bus at CDC2 market, within sight of the huge palm oil mill. Solomon Islands Plantations Ltd., in conjunction with the Commonwealth Development Corporation (CDC), has made Guadalcanal a major exporter of palm oil. (A hectare of oil palms produces three times more oil than a hectare of coconuts.) Rice was also once grown in this area.

Walk 2.5 km straight down the road that passes the palm oil mill to **Tetere Beach.** Follow the beach a few hundred meters to the right till you see the monument to five Austrian explorers from the *Albatross* expedition, murdered in 1896 by natives who wanted to prevent them from climbing sacred Mt. Tatuba (Tatuve) near Gold Ridge. Come back and follow the road along the beach to the west and turn inland on a track to see a large number of abandoned WW II **amphibious alligators** (LVT) lined up in hoary rustiness. As many as 27 of these are visible, and more are hidden from view in the bush (admission SI$10 pp).

The main road east from Honiara ends at **Aola** (60 km), the capital of Guadalcanal before WW II. Trucks leave Honiara market for Aola around 1500. Charles Woodward, the British naturalist who became resident commissioner in 1896, lived on Mbara Island just off Aola in 1885 and 1886.

Accommodations

If you'll be renting a car to explore the battlefields east of Honiara, the **Airport Motel** (Box 251, Honiara; tel. 36255, fax 36411), makes a good base. The 13 a/c rooms with bath begin at SI$132/165 single/double. The motel also has a beachfront section called the "Guadalcanal Beach Resort" a kilometer from the motel with six units at SI$165/198 single/double. Unfortunately cooking facilities are not provided in either section, although there's a restaurant and bar. The main motel is only about 500 meters east of the domestic airport terminal, so it's worth considering if you have to catch a very early flight. Inexpensive.

Vulelua Island Resort (Brendan O'Shea, Box 96, Honiara; tel./fax 29684) is on a tiny island surrounded by a white beach a kilometer off the north shore of Guadalcanal, 68 km southeast of Honiara. The six thatched seaside bungalows with private bath are SI$148 pp midweek, SI$158 pp on weekends. These prices include all meals, taxes, activities, and nautical gear (masks, snorkels, and canoes). On Sunday a seafood buffet is served, and coffee and tea in the restaurant are free all day. Only alcohol is excluded, but drink prices on the island are fair. Reductions are possible if you book locally (call from Honiara for reservations). Credit cards are not accepted, but traveler's checks are okay. The snorkeling is good (much better than at Tambea), and there's a tennis court. If you want to scuba dive, make arrangements with Island Dive at the Mendaña Hotel, as they'll gladly pick up divers at Vulelua. Trolling for fish is also possible. It's a great place to relax, but gets crowded when local expats arrive for the weekend. Yachties are welcome here. Guadalcanal Travel Service offers transfers from Honiara at SI$75 pp each way (two-person minimum), otherwise look for a truck at Kukum or Central markets, which will be only SI$14 pp. The CDC3 minibus might be willing to extend its journey this far for a flat SI$30 on top of the regular fare. If you arrive at the landing at Ande-Ande on your own, flash your headlights or a mirror to call the free motorized shuttle canoe. An enthusiastic welcome awaits you. Inexpensive.

SOUTHEAST GUADALCANAL

It's possible to hike right across the island from CDC1, east of Honiara, to Kuma on the south coast via **Gold Ridge.** This is a major undertaking, requiring a local guide and three days of hard slugging. Villages like Old Case and Tinomeat date from the 1936 gold rush, and the locals still earn pocket money from gold won from the streams. In 1998 Gold Ridge Mining Ltd. (tel. 25807) opened an open cut mine at a site 45 km from Honiara, which is expected to produce 100,000 ounces of gold a year for 10 years. Wastes from the mine are threatening to pollute local streams.

There are provincial resthouses on the Weather Coast, near the airstrips at Avu Avu, Marau Sound, and Mbambanakira (with Solomon Airlines flights three times a week). The flight from Honiara to Avu Avu (61 km, SI$75) takes you across at low altitude, with wonderful views of the valleys. A cheaper way to get to Marau Sound is to ask about motorized canoes at Honiara's Point Cruz, which charge SI$50 pp each way and will drop you at Tavanipupu or wherever else you want to go. They often leave on Friday afternoon, and you can easily arrange to come back to Honiara Monday morning.

A road—built in 1978 and not maintained since—links Avu Avu to Marau Sound (50 km), but the only vehicles on it are tractors, which pass every couple of weeks. It's a slightly boring two-day walk. The south coast is the rainiest part of the country, and during rainy season (July-Sept.) the short, shallow rivers become impassable after big storms.

Marau Sound

Marau Sound at the east tip of Guadalcanal has an extensive system of barrier reefs, offshore islands, and secure anchorages for yachts. Giant clams are found in this area. Direct Solomon Airlines flights to Marau Sound (RUS) are available three times a week from Honiara (103 km, SI$95). Ask if the high speed vessel Ocean Express (tel. 24281) is serving Marau Sound again.

Most people come to stay in one of the six tall thatched vales at the Tavanipupu Island Resort (Box 236, Honiara; tel./fax 29043), set on the emerald lagoon flanked by fine white beaches. Three large traditional-style buildings serve as

a lounge, dining room, and reception. Originally purchased by Norwegian trader Oscar Svensen in 1890 for five rifles, the present owners, Dennis Bellote and Keith Peske, bought the place from the Humphrey family in 1986 and have created this exotic hideaway since then. The price for rooms is SI$275 pp plus 10% tax, including three meals. Book at the Guadalcanal Travel Service in Honiara. Inexpensive. Another option is one of the three rooms at the rundown Manikaraku Resthouse, on the mainland a 15-minute walk from the airstrip (SI$20 pp). Shoestring.

The Moro Cult

In 1953 a cargo cult led by visionary Chief Moro was founded at Makaruka, a village three km up the Alualu River between Avu Avu and Marau Sound. In 1957 Moro called for a return to the kabilato and grass skirts after a visit by a spirit who instructed him to lead his people in a return to the old ways. He taught people how to live in harmony with each other and nature. Today the Moro movement, known as the Gaenalu Association, has 5,000 followers scattered around Guadalcanal. Of the four associated villages, today only Komuvaolu is totally traditional, and the custom house "bank" brimming with shell money and tambu objects is still well guarded there.

To visit the Moro community, you must first ask permission, then may be required to adopt traditional dress, which means a small bark loincloth for men and grass skirts for women (to visit the custom house you'll definitely have to wear these costumes). Ask for the Principal Administration Officer at the Guadalcanal Provincial Office (tel. 20041) in Honiara. He will contact Chief Moro to make sure he doesn't mind seeing you. Otherwise, ask for the cultural officer, Victor Totu, in an unmarked office near Seoul Cafeteria behind the provincial offices (everybody knows Victor). He'll put you on the right track. To get there you must either fly to Avu Avu and charter an outboard canoe for the 20-km trip east, try using the weekly provincial boat around Guadalcanal, or hike several days across the island from the end of the road below Gold Ridge.

MALAITA PROVINCE

This hot, humid, thickly forested island is the second-largest and most densely populated of the Solomons: its 95,000 inhabitants comprise almost a third of the country's population. Malaita is one of the country's few islands where people reside in the jungle-clad interior. The bush people live in isolated hamlets of two or three houses, and as many as 10,000 still believe in ancestral spirits (though tenacious missionaries are working to change this).

Many Malaitans have tried to escape their island's limited economic opportunities by emigrating to other islands; there's a large community of them in Honiara. In blackbirding times, nearly 10,000 Malaitans labored in the cane fields of Queensland, Australia. Today, they work on plantations throughout the Solomons and are likely to be your fellow passengers on interisland ships. Copra production is one of the few ways most Malaitans have of making cash money, although there have been attempts to introduce cattle and cacao.

Malaita has the most extensive road network in the Solomons, but most are in bad repair and can be closed by rains. The main town is Auki. There's little difficulty going inland, provided you have a guide. Malaita is wet, and the forest floor is permanently damp. The walking is slow, and good boots are essential. This may be the best place in the Solomons to experience culture tourism.

History

The Malaitans have a historic reputation of cantankerousness, and during the 19th century, shipwrecked sailors were regularly cooked and eaten. The tribes conducted headhunting raids against the Isabel islanders and each other, forcing their people to live in fortified villages. When blackbirders kidnapped villagers, the Malaitans took revenge by attacking visiting European ships. Punitive raids followed the murder of missionaries, leading to new retaliatory attacks, and the traditional conflict between the peoples of the coast and interior intensified with the introduction of firearms by returning workers.

In 1927 the British district officer and a police party were massacred during a campaign to collect head taxes and all outstanding rifles. The British responded by sending an Australian cruiser to shell coastal villages, turning native police from rival tribes loose on those responsible, poisoning Kwaio taro gardens, and arresting 200 Kwaio tribesmen (of whom 30 died in captivity, six of them hanged).

Even before WW II, Malaitan plantation workers were refusing to obey overseers who kept them in line with whips and dogs. When war came, many Malaitan men went to work for the Americans on Guadalcanal. The fair, generous treatment they received and the sight of black Americans dressed like whites and enjoying equal, though separate, rights had an impact. In the hope of trading American rule for British, the Marching Rule cargo cult emerged in 1944. Villages were reorganized under new chiefs and surrounded by stockades with watchtowers, and huts were prepared to store the cargo soon to arrive from the United States.

By 1949 the British decided things were getting out of hand and suppressed the movement by arresting 2,000 of its followers. Though things calmed down in 1952, when local councils were established to represent the people, many Malaitans still distrust outsiders, and large numbers in the interior resist all forms of Western influence. They in turn are often resented by other Solomon Islanders, who see them forming communities on other islands and playing a disproportionately active role in today's cash economy.

AUKI

Auki (population 4,000), at the northern end of the Langa Langa Lagoon, has been the administrative center since 1909. It's a lazy, laid-back little town with frequent ferry service from Honiara (106 km). The setting is picturesque, and there are many interesting places to visit in the vicinity. A trip to Kwai Island off East Malaita is possible when the road to Atori is open, but the excursion to Malu'u is much easier. Auki is closer to the bush than Honiara, more colorful and relaxed, so it's a fast, easy escape from the dusty capital. For most visitors, Auki is Malaita's port of entry.

Lilisiana

For 18 generations the saltwater people of the Langa Langa Lagoon have lived on tiny artificial-reef islands, which offered protection from raids by the bush people of the interior and were free of mosquitoes. A perimeter was made in the lagoon from blocks of coral, filled with more coral and covered with earth to form an island. The inhabitants remained dependent on their mainland gardens and fresh water, but a unique culture evolved.

One such artificial island is Auki Island, within view of Auki wharf. The two families on this island still maintain a few traditional sites, but most inhabitants moved away after a hurricane devastated their homes. It's now possible to walk (20 minutes) to Lilisiana, the new village on the mainland—to the right as you look out to sea from Auki. Here you can observe shell money being manufactured in authentic surroundings. If you show an interest people will bring out shell money necklaces for sale. There are isolated

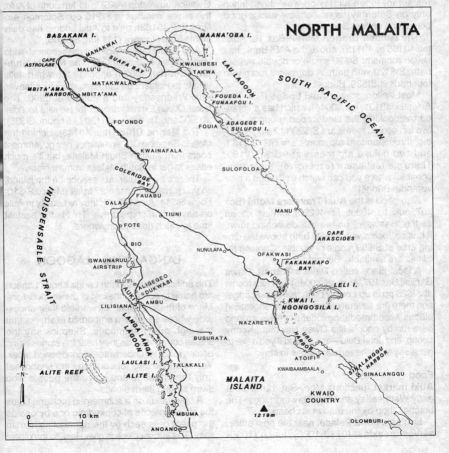

stretches of sandy beach along the track to the right just before you reach Lilisiana.

Accommodations

The spotless **South Seas Evangelical Church Transit House** (Box 14, Auki; tel. 40173, fax 40220), behind Auki Bookshop, has three rooms (eight beds) at SI$30 pp. There are cooking facilities and a sitting room. It's a clean, quiet place to stay (no smoking allowed). Shoestring.

The **Auki Motel** (Box 153, Auki; tel. 40014, fax 40298), above a store on the road to Malu'u, is SI$39 per bed in five three-bed rooms. Their restaurant (open all day on weekdays, lunch only on Saturday) is reasonable and a good place for a coffee. Budget.

The **Golden Dragon Motel** (Box 16, Auki; tel. 40166 or 40113), above the ANZ Bank, has seven rooms at SI$90 single or double without bath, SI$120 with bath. A dormitory room with four beds is SI$39. Budget.

Most visitors stay at **Auki Lodge** (Box 171, Auki; tel. 40131, fax 40044), which has a veranda overlooking the landscaped grounds. The two fan-cooled rooms are SI$90/112 single/double, three standard a/c rooms are SI$130/163, and two deluxe a/c rooms are SI$150/180. There's a restaurant (expensive), a bar (reasonable) where you can watch CNN, and a nice veranda. Budget.

Also good is the **Auki Travelers Motel** (Box 207, Auki; tel. 40395, fax 40220), formerly known as the "Seaview," on the hillside behind town. It has six rooms with private bath above the dining area at SI$99 single or double. Cooking facilities are available. Budget.

A local place called **Dave's Transit** (David Ganifiri, Box 197, Auki; tel. 40045) with four rooms at SI$25 pp is up Lokafu Lane from Auki Lodge, and there are several other unmarked shoestring places accommodating local travelers around here run by people like Owen Newman, Kenny Leong, and John Bulu—ask around if you'd like to get away from the regular places to stay.

Food

Auki market functions Mon.-Sat. but is best early Wednesday and Saturday mornings. The butcher shop by the market is cheap.

Louisa's Food Palace, near the post office, serves breakfast (0730-1000), lunch (1030-

1500), and dinner (1900-2130) daily, but on Sunday it's only dinner. The food is surprisingly good for such an unpretentious place.

Services

The ANZ, National, and Westpac banks have branches in Auki that will change foreign currency and traveler's checks. The post office is open weekdays 0800-1200 and 1300-1530, Saturday 0900-1100. Kilu'ufi Hospital (tel. 40272) is three km north of Auki.

Transportation

Gwaunaruu airstrip (AKS) is 11 km north of Auki; the airline minibus is SI$10 pp. Solomon Airlines (tel. 40163), next to Auki Lodge, has daily flights from Honiara (111 km, SI$105).

Auki is also well serviced by passenger ships to Honiara (six hours, SI$30). The **Malaita Shipping Co.** (tel. 40076) opposite the wharf sells tickets to Honiara on the *Ramos I*, which leaves Auki Wednesday and Saturday at 0900. The faster *Ocean Express* departs for Honiara Monday at 0900 and Thursday at 1130 (3.5 hours, SI$35).

The **Marine Office** (tel. 40143), behind the Malaita Shipping Co., sometimes has government boats from Auki to South Malaita, but it's much easier to get to South Malaita from Honiara.

There's no regular bus service on the island, so you travel by passenger truck (Malu'u SI$10, Fouia SI$14, Atori SI$12); they're usually in Auki on days when ships arrive. This is the easiest time to catch rides to anywhere.

LANGA LANGA LAGOON

The artificial islands in the Langa Langa Lagoon are home to some of the last of the shark callers. Many of these people still worship their ancestors, whose spirits are embodied in sharks that the high priest summons. Skeptics say the sharks come because they hear the stones being beaten together underwater, a conditioned reflex. Yet no one knows for sure why the sharks eat only the offerings and leave the people who swim among them alone.

A boy stands on a submerged rock and feeds the sharks pieces of cooked pig one by one as the priest calls each by the name of its human spirit. The largest piece is given last, to the oldest

TRADITIONAL CURRENCY IN THE SOLOMONS

The shell money of the Langa Langa Lagoon, on the northwest side of Malaita, is made by breaking shells into small pieces, boring them with a drill, and stringing them together. Patient rubbing of the shell pieces between two grooved stones gives them their circular shape. Thousands of minute discs go into a *tafuliae*, or string, which contains 10 strands of shells two to three meters long and bears a fixed rate of exchange to the official currency. This auxiliary form of currency is used for quasi-ceremonial transactions, such as buying wives (10 strings), pigs, canoes, or land, and as settlement or compensation for injuries.

Shells vary in value according to the color and size of the shell parts used: pink is the most expensive, then orange, white, and lastly black. Generally, the smaller the size of the shell piece, the more expensive it is. Pink-lipped *spondylus* ("pink money") is made only from the lip of the shell and is the most valuable, worth four or five times as much as white.

Dolphin teeth are also used as custom money on Malaita (1,000 teeth for a wife, at 40 cents a tooth), and dolphin drives to obtain teeth are conducted at Mbita'ama Harbor (northwest Malaita), Port Adam (Maramasike Island), and Sulufou (Lau Lagoon). A sorcerer in a canoe taps magical stones together underwater to attract the dolphins, which are then led ashore by other villagers in canoes, butchered, and the meat divided. Flying-fox teeth and pigs are also exchanged on Malaita.

In the Western Solomons, ceremonial currency is in the form of large heavy rings, four centimeters thick and 24 centimeters in diameter, cut out of the shell of the giant clam. A ring with a small patch of yellow on the edge is worth more than a plain white one. In Santa Cruz, great rolls of red-feather money are used as bride price. The men who have the customary rights to make the coils pluck a few feathers from captured scarlet honeyeaters before releasing the birds.

---

shark. Should a fisherman be capsized in the deep sea, he can summon a shark, using a special language the shark understands. After the shark has carried him ashore, the fisherman must offer a sacrificial pig, otherwise he will be eaten on his next fishing trip. (Note, however, that shark calling is not included in regular artificial island tours.)

Laulasi

On this small island, 13 km south of Auki, are large spirit houses with high pitched roofs, the names of famous priests inscribed on the gables. The three highest priests live in individual tree houses. When a priest dies, his body is taken to neighboring Alite to rot. Later the skull is retrieved and placed in the House of Skulls. A large snake will appear on Alite if offered the head of goat. At these times believers can ask favors of the animal and enlist its help in punishing enemies.

Offerings are also presented at shark-calling ceremonies in the gap between the two islands. The pigs used for these offerings are held by the shore in pens big enough for a man—the offering in times past, before pigs were substituted. Shark feeding usually takes place around Christmas, and visitors must present one pig

(worth around SI$250) to witness the ceremony. Traditional dress must also be worn.

Women and children are forbidden to enter the custom houses, and no one dressed in red or black will be permitted to land on the island. Tourists are shown how to make shell money using manual stone drills; after they're gone, the metal-headed drill bits come back out. The village on Alite is similar.

Getting There

Colin Bauwane, a teacher at Auki Primary School (tel. 40284), and others organize outboard tours to Laulasi or Alite islands (five hours). The SI$250 per group price includes custom dancing, a demonstration of shell money making, a tour of the custom places, and lunch. Book 24 hours in advance, and find out what kind of custom fees you'll have to pay upon arrival.

Sometimes you can hire a motorized canoe to Laulasi from near Auki Market for SI$150, then pay the islanders a variable custom fee for the right to look around (no dances or lunch). Unfortunately, the Laulasi islanders are a little greedy, and may demand outlandish custom fees to land, then extra fees to see certain things, so ask about this before going.

The road south from Auki reaches beyond Su'u Bay, and passenger trucks go as far as Hauhui. There's more frequent service to Talakali (14 km, SI$5), on the mainland opposite Laulasi. There you can bargain for an outboard to take you over, or hire a dugout and paddle yourself the two km across). You'll still be charged the usual fees to look around, and similar fees are collected at Alite. Talakali's population, incidentally, is Seventh-Day Adventist, so don't bother going on a Saturday.

MALU'U

This pleasant little government station at the island's northern tip, halfway between Auki and Fouia, makes an excellent base from which to visit heavily populated North Malaita. The villagers are very friendly and warmly welcome visitors, and traffic to and from Auki is fairly frequent.

Sights

On the beach at Malu'u is a monument to the first missionary to land on Malaita (in 1894). From the market, walk east along the beach until you meet the main road again. There's a bathing beach here, and the reef protects you from most sharks. Go snorkeling on Diula, opposite the tiny offshore island. Out across the lagoon, good surf breaks at the west end of the reef. This lefthander works best at high tide in a 1.5-meter swell (Nov.-March only). Where the swells come from two directions the shifting peaks cause

a clamshell ornament from Malaita incised with frigate bird designs

havoc. There's also good diving along the inside edge of the lagoon.

At **A'ama** village on the hilltop just above Malu'u, visit the *biu* (young men's house). At **Manakwai** village, a few kilometers west of Malu'u on the main road, is a small cascade, a minihydro station, and a good place to swim in the river. Ask the person in the electric generating station if you can follow the trail up the large water pipe.

To get to **Basakana Island,** take a truck to the beach opposite and light a smoky fire. Someone will come across from the village to fetch you. There's a cave to visit on Basakana, plus many fine beaches.

Accommodations and Tours

Bartholomew Wanefalea's **Malu'u Lodge** (no phone), above Tang's store facing the waterfront, has seven clean, functional double rooms with shared bath at SI$44/66 single/double. Communal cooking facilities are available, and there's a large sitting room. A two-hour snorkeling trip to the reef and to see the submerged Japanese plane costs SI$100 for the boat (up to seven people can go for that price). To rent the boat for a full day of surfing or sightseeing costs SI$200. Guided visits to local villages (SI$200 a day) and panpipe concerts are also possible. Shoestring.

The **Baptist Church** at Keru village on the hill behind Malu'u has a two-room guesthouse with cooking facilities at rates much lower than those charged at Malu'u Lodge. Ask for Henrik Rilalo or his father Rubin Rilalo. They can supply guides for bush walks into the surrounding hills. It's a good choice if you want to stay in a village environment.

Groceries may be purchased at the three stores down by the harbor or from the market (open Monday, Wednesday, Thursday, and Saturday 0600-0900).

LAU LAGOON

More than 60 artificial islands are found in the 36-km-long Lau Lagoon on the northeast side of Malaita. These are inhabited by the so-called island builders, who bring coral blocks, sand, and earth on log rafts to convert lagoon shallows into solid land. With the constant cool breezes, the air is incredibly fresh out on these man-made islands. On the mainland they grow taro, yams, potatoes, papaya, leafy vegetables, bananas, and sugarcane. The women travel back and forth from their island homes to the gardens, and the men fish most of the time. The large canoes for dolphin-hunting are made by sewing together long planks of wood and caulking the seams with a putty made from the nut of the tita tree *(Parinari glaberrima)*.

Though Christianity is increasing, some people on islands such as Foueda, Funaafou, and Adagege still practice the same custom religion as the people of Laulasi/Alite. Here you'll find a *beu* (men's house) where chiefs are buried in their canoes, plus heathen places of worship, with a sacrificial altar, cemetery, House of Skulls, etc. Entry to the *beu* is prohibited, but you can often see in from outside. There is no *beu* at Sulufou, which is now thoroughly Christianized. After childbirth women are sent to a *bisi* (women's house) for 30 days. Shark calling is also practiced here on special occasions, announced by the pagan priests.

Takwa

Takwa is only 12 km from the end of the road at Fouia. The final passage to Takwa wharf by boat passes many artificial islands, a fitting introduction to the Lau Lagoon. A market near the Catholic mission at Takwa sets up every Saturday with shell money and porpoise teeth circulating alongside Solomon Islands currency. Swim in the river at the landing where the dugout canoes of the saltwater people arrive. Kwailibesi airstrip is near Takwa.

Sulione

People from the traditional islands of Foueda and Funaafou come to the market at Sulione on the main road near Fouia every Monday and Thursday, and it might be possible to go back with them. In 1935, the Seventh-Day Adventist converts on Foueda were banished to nearby Ropa, now linked to Foueda by a wooden footbridge. Foueda is mostly Christian today. On Funaafou is a Cultural Center housing old artifacts and many *tambu* places.

Sulufou

The road and truck route from Auki ends at **Fouia** wharf (120 km), on the mainland opposite

the artificial islands of Sulufou and Adagege. For a few dollars someone will paddle you the 500 meters over to Sulufou, largest and oldest of the artificial islands. The picturesque village is partly built on stilts over the lagoon. In front of the big Anglican church is a stone where fugitives from northern Malaita sat to obtain sanctuary and protection. You could be requested to contribute something to this church for the visit.

Unfortunately, there's no organized place to stay at Fouia or Sulufou, so you either have to make it a day-trip from Malu'u or go native. You can sometimes catch a ship or outboard down the coast to Atori or Kwai.

SOUTHEAST MALAITA

East Malaita

Take a truck from Auki via Dala to **Atori**, provided the road hasn't been closed by rains. Midway at Nunulafa is a bridge over the Auluta Gorge. Some good **surfing beaches** are north of Atori. Fakanakafo Bay is the closest, accessible by canoe from Atori, but press on to Manu village for the good left-handers. A coastal trail runs north from Fakanakafo Bay to Fouia.

Kwai is a beautiful island with kind, friendly people. Village houses are densely packed here and on neighboring Ngongosila Island. There's a native resthouse with cooking facilities at the edge of the island, where you can stay (ask for Paul Alafa or David Loke, the village baker). It's only three km from Atori to Kwai Island, but the outboard boys charge exorbitant fares, so try to hitch a ride with someone off your truck. Outboard canoe rentals are totally unreasonable throughout this area.

In 1927, British District Officer William Bell, his cadet K.C. Lillies, and 13 native policemen were speared by Kwaio tribesmen at Kwaiambe (Gwee'abe) on Sinalanggu Harbor. Later, British officials looked the other way when north Malaita police murdered about 70 Kwaio prisoners, including women and children, in cold blood to avenge their slain comrades, and the Kwaio have never received compensation for the 200 tribespeople who died during the affair. The book *Lightning Meets the West Wind,* by Roger Keesing and Peter Corris (Melbourne: Oxford University Press, 1980), tells the story. To visit the graves of Bell and Lillies, wade across the sandbar from Kwai to Ngongosila at low tide.

A road is underway from Atori to Atoifi, presently as far as Nazareth. Atoifi on Uru Harbor is a center for those Kwaio who have accepted Christianity and a large Seventh-Day Adventist hospital and School of Nursing are here. There's an airstrip with Western Pacific Airline flights from Honiara (SI$120) Mon.-Fri., some of which also call at Auki or Kwailabesi. The pagan population lives in small, scattered hamlets on the upland plateaus. Kwaibaambaala, in the foothills between Atoifi and Sinalanggu, is one traditional village sometimes visited.

Trips deeper into the **Kwaio Country** above Sinalanggu to visit the remote "Hidden People" can be arranged, but be prepared for high charges for transport and guides. Even today, the Kwaios in the hills follow the traditions and taboos of their ancestors, and visitors are rare.

In 1965 a missionary from New Zealand was killed here. The Solomon Island government collects taxes from these people but provides no services, and even the Seventh-Day Adventist Church links desperately needed medical aid to conversions.

South Malaita

No road connects South Malaita to Auki, so either fly to Parasi (SI$98 one-way from Auki) or take a truck south to Hauhui, then a motorized canoe on south. The Wairaha River, south of Hauhui, is Solomon Island's largest.

Apio is at the southwest entrance to Maramasike Passage. Just 3.7 meters deep near the center, this passage is only open to vessels of light draft. A bush road now runs from Apio, opposite Maka on Malaita, to Olusu'u, near the southeast end of Maramasike, or Small Malaita. Few tourists come here.

RENNELL AND BELLONA PROVINCE

Two hundred km south of Guadalcanal are two Polynesian islands, Rennell and Bellona, about 25 km apart. This is the westernmost land colonized by Polynesians. Due to the murder of three Melanesian Seventh-Day Adventist missionaries in 1910, Rennell was closed to Europeans until 1934. Conversion to SDA Christianity took place in 1938, when a picture of Christ was seen to speak. Overnight the people gave up their traditional ways, such as tattooing, and adopted Western dress. In 1993 Rennell and Bellona (or "Renbel") separated from Central Province to form a province of their own. There's no malaria on Rennell or Bellona, but the mosquitoes are of a type that bite all night (not just at dusk), so bring plenty of repellent. Although regular flights exist from Honiara and both islands have their attractions, they're still well off the tourist track.

RENNELL

Rennell (Mungava), an 86-by-15-km raised atoll surrounded by sheer 100-meter cliffs, is much larger than Bellona. In fact, at 692 square km it's the largest, and perhaps the finest, elevated atoll on earth. **Lake Te Nggano** (155 square

km), on the southeast side of Rennell, is the largest lake in the South Pacific. It's the former lagoon of this uplifted island, and about 200 small islands are dotted around its edge. The saline water in the lake is at sea level but it's surrounded by high cliffs. In 1998 East Rennell was added to UNESCO's World Heritage List, only the third

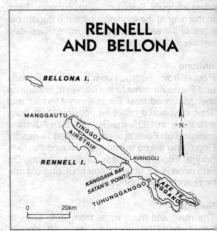

RENNELL AND BELLONA

BELLONA I.

MANGGAUTU

TINGGOA AIRSTRIP

RENNELL I.

LAVANGGU

KANGGAVA BAY
SATAN'S POINT

TUHUNGGANGGOO

LAKE TE NGGANO

-N-

0   20km

South Pacific site to achieve this status (Henderson and Easter islands are also honored).

Eighty percent of Rennell is forested and the island has more endemic bird species than any other in Oceania, excluding much larger places like New Caledonia. Of the 50 species of birds on Rennell, 21 are endemic. The docile Rennell Island krait *(Laticausa crockeri)*—or Tugihono as the Rennellese call it—a unique sea snake, lives only in Lake Te Nggano.

Other than a few tiny stores, no business of any kind exists on Rennell, and all 2,500 villagers live from their gardens. The local stores have little more than canned fish, corned beef, and stick tobacco, so bring food. Among the many handicrafts made on Rennell are walking sticks, hardwood crocodile carvings, miniature weapons, woven bags, and mats. At custom feasts the Rennellese practice *hetakai,* a form of traditional wrestling in which the object is to knock the opponent down. Bauxite deposits exist here, and in 1977 the Japanese mining company Mitsui did exploratory work, pulling out when bauxite prices fell.

Accommodations

In 1989 Paul Tauniu opened the **Tahamatangi Guesthouse** (no phone), an airy European-style building on the shores of Lake Te Nggano. Up to five persons are accommodated in the one main building at SI$35 pp. Paul organizes bushwalking and lake tours to see the unique wildlife of the area. Locally produced meals of crab, fish, chicken, pineapple, papaya, banana, and taro are served (additional charge). The Tourist Authority in Honiara will have information. Shoestring.

Transportation

Solomon Airlines flies into Tinggoa airstrip (RNL), at Rennell's west end, three times a week from Honiara (SI$185) and Bellona (SI$60). A road leads through lush rainforest to the small port, Lavanggu, where the monthly ship from Honiara calls. The ship also stops at Tuhungganggo. A canoe from Lavanggu to Tuhungganggo is SI$10 pp or SI$120 for a special trip (one hour), possible in good weather only. From Tuhungganggo a steep stairway known as "ten story" climbs over sharp limestone cliffs, then it's a four-km stroll to Te Nggano village, one of four on the lake.

Getting around Rennell is a problem, as the tractor that's supposed to meet the boats and planes often breaks down, and the distances are large. To walk from Tinggoa to Lavanggu will take six hours if you go straight or eight with stops. Theoretically a tractor-trailer (50 cents pp) leaves the airstrip end of Rennell around 0630 and takes two hours to get to Lavanggu along a coral road, returning shortly after arrival at Lavanggu. To hire a tractor from the airstrip to Lavanggu is SI$20 an hour. You'll get soaked if it rains. Take heart: the beach at Lavanggu is great, and there's a splendid view of it from the village above.

Fortunately, things are getting better. A new European Union-financed road runs from Lavanggu to Tebaitahe village right on Lake Te Nggano. Since the east is by far the most magical part of Rennell, plans are underway to build a new airstrip near the lake for the convenience of tourists. For yachts, there's good anchorage on the south shore of Kanggava Bay with excellent snorkeling.

BELLONA

Like Rennell, Bellona (Mungiki) is a cliff-girdled uplifted atoll. Rich phosphate deposits exist here, but the islanders rightly fear that mining would devastate their homeland. Since it's smaller (12 by three km), Bellona is much easier to visit than Rennell. The handsome, intelligent people are a fun-loving bunch descended from the same stock as the Rennellese. Most live in the fertile interior. If you have an underwater flashlight, ask someone to take you crayfishing at night.

The Polynesians first migrated to this island 25 generations ago and upon arrival wiped out the Hiti, Melanesian cave dwellers who previously inhabited the island. The Hiti caves still dot the cliffs and are fascinating to explore, though they're very cramped. Solomon Airlines has flights to Bellona from Honiara (SI$170) and Rennell (SI$60) three times a week.

Accommodations

John and Nita Tay run '**Aotaha Cave Lodge** near Matangi village, about five km east of the airstrip by road. The accommodations are in a natural cave below high cliffs at the eastern end of the island. Crushed white coral covers the floor, the air is cool, and mosquito nets are provided. The three double and three single beds are SI$36 pp, otherwise two thatched bungalows above the cave are SI$25 pp. It's possible to cook your own food in the cave kitchen, and there's a small trade store on the site. Otherwise fresh local meals can be ordered at SI$10 each. You can see across to Rennell from the cave sitting room and the rock pools below are

good for swimming. The Visitors Bureau in Honiara may be able to help you contact 'Aotaha by radio telephone. For the trip from the airstrip, the area council tractor and trailer can be hired at SI$20 for the vehicle. Shoestring.

Suani Resthouse (Box 592, Honiara; tel. 23846), in Bellona's lush interior several km west of the airstrip, offers accommodations in the main five-bed building are SI$30 pp. Shoestring.

CENTRAL PROVINCE

Central Province comprises an odd assortment of islands, including the Florida Islands, Savo, and the Russell Islands, which are linked to Honiara but not to each other or to the provincial headquarters on Tulagi. Other than two guesthouses at Tulagi and a basic ecotourism resort on Savo, there are no hotels on any of these islands. With a bit of planning, one can easily spend a couple of days at Tulagi, and Savo is worth the effort for its volcanic wonders. The Florida Islands are there for adventurers in search of the "real" Solomon Islands, while the Russells are one big coconut plantation.

Tulagi

Tulagi (population 1,750), a small island about five km in circumference in the Florida Group, was the island capital of the Solomons 1896-1942. Burns Philp had its head station on Makambo Island, nearby. The Japanese entered unopposed on 3 May 1942 after a hasty British evacuation, and Tulagi was badly damaged during the American invasion three months later. The Americans built a seaplane base on nearby Ghavutu Island, and a good concrete wharf from that time remains. Their PT-boat squadrons were also based at Tulagi. Another remnant of the old days on Tulagi is the marine base, where shipbuilding and repairs are still carried out.

The deep strait between Tulagi and Nggela Sule forms a good harbor, well sheltered from the southeast trade winds. In 1973, the Japanese Taiyo Corporation took advantage of this by establishing a fish-freezing and canning plant here, but in 1990 this facility was shifted to Noro in Western Province. Today the Singapore-owned National Fisheries Development Ltd. fishing fleet

is based here. There's a striking hand-hewn passage cut by prewar prisoners between the wharf and the resthouse. The British resident commissioners lived at Nambawan Haos, on the hill above the cut. Follow a footpath (three hours) clockwise around the island for great views.

The **Central Province Resthouse** has six double rooms with shared cooking facilities at SI$30 pp. Shoestring. Check in at the Provincial Office (tel. 32100). Also try **Vanita Accommodation** (Annette Dennis, Box 26, Tulagi; tel. 32186), near the wharf, with two rooms at SI$50 pp. Shoestring. There are no cooking facilities for guests; instead meals are served in their restaurant/bar and they also have a bakery. Tulagi has a market and two Chinese stores. Buy frozen skipjack at the NFD cold storage.

The Florida Islands

There are two large islands here, Nggela Sule and Nggela Pile, separated by narrow Utaha Passage. Tulagi is off the south coast of Nggela Sule. To get away for a week, take a walk around Nggela Pile for its scenic views, golden beaches and village life. Catch the *Ocean Express* from Honiara to **Siota** on a Friday (SI$25). A century ago the Melanesian Mission set up its first college at Siota to train local clergy, and from here Henry Welchman spread the Gospel to Isabel. From Siota, walk a couple of days along the coast to Vuturua village and have someone paddle you across to Peula. Three stalactite caves are along the way, but you'll need a guide to find them. Continue on the coast to Ndende and across to Dadala village on Utaha Passage. Finish your expedition with a canoe ride to **Taroniana Shipyard**, where you should be able to find a canoe to Tulagi or a ship back to Honiara. The

Ocean Express also calls here on Friday. (Attention yachties: this Church of Melanesia-operated shipyard can handle major repairs! Contact them at tel. 29021 or fax 29486.)

Savo

Savo is a cone-shaped island on Iron Bottom Sound, named for the number of warships sunk in the vicinity during WW II. Savo's volcano last erupted in 1840, but it's still considered potentially dangerous. Near the center of the island are two craters, one inside the other. A trip up to the steaming, 485-meter-high crater is worth trying—if you can find a guide and you're fit. Two boiling hot springs are on the crater's edge, and more on the volcano's sides are used for cooking. The chief of Kaonggele collects a custom fee to use the village path to the crater.

Savo is also famous for its megapode bird *(Megapodius freycinet)* or *skrab dak*. This small dark bush turkey lays billiard-ball-sized eggs underground, then leaves them to hatch by heat from either the sun or the island's warm volcanic sands. After two months the fledglings dig themselves out and can run at birth. Unfortunately, the number of megapodes is declining fast due to unrestrained harvesting of the eggs. See them in the early morning near Panueli.

A tractor track runs right around 31-square-km Savo's shark-infested shores, passing 14 villages. The inhabitants all speak a Papuan language, Savosavo, one of the few non-Austronesian languages of the Solomons. Traditionally Savo people fish by suspending a hook from a kite behind the canoe. There's a fissure just a short distance inland from Siata village where the locals cook their food. All drinking and washing water on Savo comes from wells, and the water in them is also often warm; boil it before drinking. A rural water supply project is gradually improving this situation but there's still no electricity.

The only regular place to stay is the **Legalau Nature Side Village** (Ben Duva, Box 922, Honiara), on the northwest side of Savo, with two three-bed cottages at SI$30 pp. Local meals are served and guides are provided for hikes to the megapode field or the volcano. Ask at the Solomon Islands Tourist Authority about this place. A boat to Legalau often leaves from the Point Cruz Yacht Club at 1300 (SI$20 pp). Shoestring.

It's also possible to stay with local villagers, such as John Tome at Kakalaka village. This is probably only worth pursuing if Legalau happens to be full on the day you arrive.

Although most outboards (SI$20 pp) go to Honiara or Visale on Guadalcanal, it's sometimes possible to find a ship from Savo to Tulagi and vice versa. On Friday the *Ocean Express* calls at Reko on Savo between Honiara and Tulagi in both directions.

The Russell Islands

The Russell Islands consist of two adjacent larger islands, Mbanika and Pavuvu, plus many smaller islets. Huge coconut plantations cover the islands, and the Solomon's first coconut-oil mill opened here in 1989. In 1995 the government's Commodities Export Marketing Authority was forced to take over the operation from the Australian company Lever Brothers Ltd. after Levers declared technical bankruptcy. CEMA now runs the operation under the name Russell Islands Plantations Limited.

The U.S. took the Russells unopposed in February 1943 and built a pair of airstrips from which to launch attacks on New Georgia. The American Quonset huts facing Yandina wharf are now used for copra storage. Local children can show you a WW II military dump near Renard Airfield, featuring what's left of a U.S. fighter plane.

Some 2,000 head of CEMA cattle range across the islands, and wild water buffalo dwell in the swamps of Mbanika, descendants of escaped domestic stock. Wild donkeys are also seen in and around Yandina at night. In 1995 the Mamaloni government deployed its paramilitary police to protect loggers sent by the Malaysian company Maving Brothers to clearcut the pristine rainforests of Pavuvu, over the heated objections of local residents. Anti-logging activist Martin Apa was brutally murdered by persons unknown in October 1995, yet the police refused to investigate.

Tourism isn't promoted in the Russell Islands, though the plantation management is friendly once they know you. The only regular place to stay is the **Yandina Resthouse** (tel. 21779, fax 21785), behind the administration offices, 500 meters to the left from the wharf. Unexpected arrivals are not appreciated, so call the financial controller at Yandina for advance bookings and information. The resthouse itself has cooking facilities and a lovely seaside view. If you stay there, you'll be able to use the facilities of the nearby Mbanika Club, including swimming pool, tennis courts, library, and bar (the only place to get a beer).

Groceries are sold at two stores, a block to the right of the post office and main wharf as you arrive. The butcher shop near the post office sells cheap beef, but there's a four-kilogram-per-day limit on purchases. Yachties often share their quota among others and stock up here. Ask the butcher when they'll be dumping the offal at Shark Point, as sharks appear from nowhere whenever

this happens and go into a feeding frenzy, which is fun to watch from the cliff. Bring adequate mosquito repellent to the Russells.

Getting there is easy, as most ships between Honiara and Gizo call at Yandina on the east side of Mbanika (SI$36 deck from Honiara, SI$69 deck to Gizo one-way). The ship ties up at a wharf right in town, a little more than a kilometer from the airport terminal. Solomon Airlines flies to Renard Airfield (XYA) from Honiara (95 km, SI$95 one-way) twice a week. The Solomon Airlines bus into nearby Yandina is free. To get back to the airport, check with the Solomon Airlines office (tel. 29779) in the administration building.

WESTERN PROVINCE

Western Province with the New Georgia Group at its core is easily the most attractive and varied area in the country. High vegetation-shrouded volcanoes buttress the enticing lagoons of Marovo and Roviana, respectively off the eastern and southern coasts of New Georgia. These vast stretches of dazzling water are dotted with hundreds of little green islets, either covered in dense jungle or planted with coconuts. To the north, the remote Shortland and Treasury groups form Western's outback. Sadly, commercial logging is gradually decimating the great rainforests of New Georgia, Rendova, and Kolombangara.

The inhabitants have the darkest skins in the Solomons. More than a dozen different languages are spoken, but people in this province have long had contact with missionaries, and you'll find very eloquent, well-informed individuals in the most unlikely places. Here the women own the land, which is passed down through the oldest daughter. Headhunting once forced the inhabitants to build their homes on inaccessible interior ridges (where many custom places are now found), but with the demise of interisland raiding the people soon moved down to cooler coastal sites. In the 1950s and '60s thousands of Micronesian Gilbertese were resettled at Gizo, Shortland, and Vaghena, adding to the diversity.

Travel among the many islands of the New Georgia Group is almost totally by sea, which makes getting around easy, yet there are also feeder roads from the main centers of Munda, Noro, Ringi Cove, and Gizo, which help the hiker and hitcher. There are many villages, and the people are helpful and hospitable. In recent years, scuba diving on the many wrecks and reefs has become a big attraction here, and good facilities are available at Munda and Gizo. Sportfishing is being developed. The scheduled weekly passenger ship from Honiara to Gizo via Patutiva, Viru Harbor, Mburuku, Munda, and Ringi Cove offers an excellent introduction to the New Georgia Islands.

The Marovo Lagoon

On the ship from Honiara, you travel first through the huge Marovo Lagoon, the largest lagoon in the world with a double barrier reef system. James A. Michener called it "one of the seven natural wonders of the world." A thin string of islands shelters this semicircular lagoon as it swings around Vangunu Island from Gatokae to New Georgia. West of Njae Passage it's known as the Nono Lagoon. The greater part of Marovo is less than 25 meters deep, whereas the Nono Lagoon is as deep as 50 to 60 meters.

Marovo is 35 km long and 8-50 km wide, and its hundred tiny islands are a mix of sandy cays, mangrove islets, raised reefs, and small volcanic islands. The nicest beaches are on the ocean-side coral islands; mangrove swamps are more common along the volcanic shorelines within. The reef dropoffs are characterized by gorgonian fan forests, black coral gardens, giant clams, sea turtles, manta rays, eels, barracuda, gray whaler sharks, and cruising shoals of pelagic fish. The Marovo Lagoon is one of two sites in the Solomons presently under consideration for UNESCO World Heritage Site status.

A cruise through the lagoon makes for great scenic viewing, though some of the ships from Honiara pass at night. The southern gateway is through Mbili Passage at the north end of Gatokae Island. For years Marovo has been a favorite of scuba divers, and recently kayak tours have been developed from Uepi Island. You can also launch your own folding kayak from the ferry landing at Patutiva and hop your way around the lagoon between the growing number of eco-lodges.

You won't see any dancing anywhere around the Marovo Lagoon, as the Seventh-Day Adventist Church has banned it (rumor indicates that dancing causes pregnancy). The SDA devotees frown on all "heathen" customs, but will carve and market many a *nguzunguzu* for profit. The SDA sabbath runs from sundown on Friday to sundown on Saturday—a bad time to arrive.

Northeast Vangunu

There's a large Seventh-Day Adventist mission at **Batuna** on Vangunu Island, with a post office, hospital, sawmill, agricultural school, shop, and Thursday market. High quality handicrafts can be purchased at Batuna Vocational School.

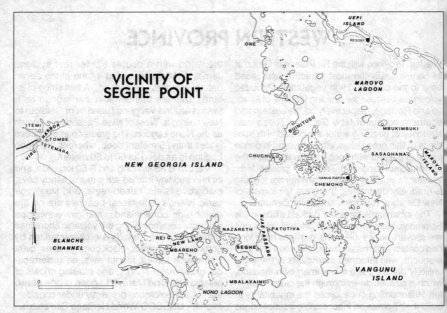

Ask for Philemon Pulekele, a teacher at the school, who can usually arrange paying-guest accommodation. Western Pacific Airline flies directly here from Honiara (SI$215) and Munda (SI$105) two or three times a week.

Backpackers often stay at Mr. Muven Kuve's **Hideaway Lagoon** near Cheke village, about eight km northwest of Batuna by boat. You'll pay about SI$30 pp a day, including all the tropical fruit you care to eat, for a bed in a four-room leaf hut near his lumber yard. Camping is half price and cooking is possible (three meals available at SI$10 pp a day). Muven has an outboard canoe you can hire to get around the lagoon and up jungle rivers. Fish barbecues and custom feasts are arranged if three or four people are present. He'll also loan you a dugout to paddle yourself, or provide a guide for bush hikes to the waterfall or wherever. Custom fishing using poisonous buna leaves and sand is demonstrated upon request. Over the years Muven has hosted dozens of readers of this book, and he remains as engaging and hospitable as ever. To get there, take the *luminao* to Gassini or Chea, where you'll have to charter a speedboat. Shoestring.

West of Cheke opposite Telina village is **Kajoro Sunset Lodge** (no phone), run by John Wayne, one of Marovo's most famous woodcarvers. There are presently only two rooms (four beds), but additional thatched beach huts on stilts are planned. The Lodge is set in a garden with pathways and a large communal open-air leaf hut overlooking the sea. Rooms are SI$25/45/60 single/double/triple (or by the week SI$165/305/390). Prepared meals are available or you can choose to cook your own food. Good snorkeling is accessible right offshore, and boat trips are organized at around SI$60 regardless of how many people go. Woodcarving classes are around SI$100 for six days (you'll learn about the various types of woods used, the basic techniques of carving, styles, etc.). John is a charming host, and if you just want somewhere to hang out and snorkel, this might be the place. If you book through the Visitors Bureau in Honiara, John will pick you up at Gasini, Batuna, or Seghe for about SI$30 pp each way. Shoestring.

In the same general area is **Lagoon Lodge,** a guesthouse right on the lagoon. Unfortunately the restaurant is fully enclosed, so you don't get any views.

Uepi Island

The only international tourist resort on the lagoon is Uepi Island (Roco Ltd., Box 920, Honiara; tel./fax 26076—ask for Jeffrey Simbe), 12 km northeast of Patutiva, on a white coral beach midway down the chain of islands forming Marovo's western barrier. The six bungalows with private bath and fridge go for SI$237/330 single/double. There are also two rooms with bath but no fridge and a three-room lodge with fridge but shared bath at SI$155/246. Although there's no hot water, the accommodations are adequate for such a remote location and a generator provides electricity. The compulsory meal add-on is SI$172 pp per day. They'll give you a picnic-basket lunch, and the three-course buffet dinner is served at two long communal tables, so you soon get to know everyone. The food is good (ample seafood and fresh fruit), but drinks at the bar are expensive. Guests are flown into Seghe, then taken by canoe to Uepi (pronounced "you-pee"). Transfers from Seghe to the island are SI$122 pp roundtrip. Add 10% tax to everything.

At those prices Uepi caters mostly to packaged Australians on scuba or kayaking tours. You're charged extra for everything you do here, except playing volleyball with the staff or paddling a dugout canoe. Paid activities include the custom village tour, the river tour, and lagoon fishing. Scuba diving is SI$116 per dive (night dives more expensive). Bring your own snorkeling gear with you or be prepared to shell out more money. There's good snorkeling right off their dock on Charapoana Channel at the east end of Uepi—lots of fish. Yachties are not welcome at Uepi Island. Uepi Island bookings must be confirmed by Tropical Paradise Ltd., Box 84 HP, Hermit Park, Queensland 4812, Australia (tel./fax 61-7/4775-1323). In Honiara book through Guadalcanal Travel Service (and be aware that it's often full). Inexpensive to moderate.

Vanua Rapita

In 1995 a new ecotourism resort was established on a tiny island near Michi village just off northern Vanguna. Vanua Rapita (Stanley Vaka, c/o Seghe Postal Agency, Marovo Lagoon) consists of an attractive tin roofed central building with an open terrace right over the lagoon, plus two leaf huts, one with two double rooms and another with three double rooms. The "honeymoon" bungalow has one room. It's SI$44 pp to stay, plus SI$50 pp for three meals. The accommodations are clean and supplied with mosquito nets, and you can use the fridge (bring own alcohol, if necessary). Snorkeling is possible and two dugout canoes are supplied. A complete activities package is offered at SI$75 a day. Transfers from Seghe/Patutiva are SI$30 pp each way (25 minutes). Information is available from the Worldwide Fund for Nature (Box 21, Gizo; tel. 60191, fax 60294), on the hill above Gizo. Budget.

Seghe Point

Seghe, on New Georgia Island at the southwest end of the lagoon, is the communications hub of Marovo. Solomon Airlines has almost daily flights from Munda (71 km, SI$80), Gizo (122 km, SI$115), and Honiara (256 km, SI$200) to a wartime airstrip (EGM) the Americans built in only 10 days. There's a sunken P38 Lightning fighter in the water off the passage end of the airstrip. During WW II, coastwatcher Donald Kennedy and a small force of Solomon Islanders carried out many daring guerrilla raids against the Japanese near Seghe and supplied vital information on their movements. Author James Michener called Seghe Point, "my favorite spot in the South Pacific."

The passenger ships all stop at **Patutiva** wharf on Vangunu Island, just across scenic Njae Passage from Seghe. A good, cheap market materializes at Patutiva whenever the Honiara ship arrives—jump off and back on quickly to buy oranges and bananas. Dugout canoes propelled by outboard, paddle, or sail carry people around the lagoon from Patutiva, and hitching a ride isn't too hard. However, even low-budget backpackers look rich to some, so agree on a price beforehand.

Nono Lagoon

Mr. Gillis Palmer of **Mbareho Island** in the Nono Lagoon has written us inviting yachties and other travelers to visit his island. According to Gillis, the attractions of Mbareho include taboo places, coral reefs, carvings, war wreckage, good anchorage, and friendly people. He offers to provide a welcome and arrange accommodations.

Two SDA brothers, Renter and Eddie Tivuru, operate **Horena Hideaway** on a tiny coconut-covered island near Mbareho. Accommodations in two leaf houses are SI$40/60 single/double. Meals are served at SI$25 pp a day in a separate building with a large veranda. Snorkeling and canoe trips through the mangroves are attractions here. The canoe transfer to Horena from Seghe is SI$60 per group. Shoestring.

Farther south is Benjamin and Jilly Kaniotoku's **Matikuri Lodge** on eight-hectare Matikuri Island just off Vanganu's attractive mangrove-fringed coast. The large thatched house on stilts over the lagoon, and three small cottages by the shore accommodate travelers at SI$45 pp, plus tax (children under 16 half price). There's no electricity, but cooking facilities and a kerosene fridge are provided. Take basic staples with you as there's only a market at nearby Patutiva twice a week when the boat from Honiara calls. Activities include canoeing, snorkeling, fishing, boat trips up the Nema River or to Hele Bar, rainforest hikes, and village visits. Transport from Seghe/Patutiva to Matikuri is SI$20 pp each way, and motorized canoes are for rent at SI$50 a day plus gasoline. The "Lagoon Eco-Tour" is SI$75 pp including a night on Gatokae Island. Benjamin also has a cottage at Seghe that costs SI$35 pp. Information about Matikuri is available from Noel Wagapu at the Labor Division (tel. 21849) in the Ministry of Commerce and Primary Industries opposite Honiara Post Office. You can also contact Matikura by radio telephone from any Telecom office (they listen 0800-0830, 1200-1300, and 1600-1700). Budget.

Rendova

The Honiara-Gizo ship ties up at Mburuku (Ughele) on the high volcanic island of Rendova, another major WW II battlefield. You'll have about 10 minutes to get off and buy food at the impromptu market on the wharf. Grab a pineapple, some bananas, and a green coconut before they're gone. The native pudding is also good. If you make prior arrangements, you can be picked up here by the Lubaria Island Resort boat (see **Munda and Vicinity,** below).

Rendova's neighboring island, Tetepare, is one of the largest uninhabited islands in the South Pacific. The original population left more than 200 years ago due to disease, and descendants are now scattered throughout Western Province. Tetepare's lowland forest is one of the last totally undisturbed rainforests of its kind in the Pacific, yet logging companies are busy lobbying to harvest it.

MUNDA AND VICINITY

Munda, the metropolis of New Georgia, is little more than a string of villages centered on Lambete beside the Roviana Lagoon; the name "Munda" describes the whole area. The government wharf, administration offices, air terminal (MUA), and resthouses are all at **Lambete,** while the United Church maintains its Solomon Islands headquarters and runs Helena Goldie Hospital at **Kokenggolo** near an old wharf, two km west of Lambete. The United Church also operates **Goldie College** near the Diamond Narrows. A vast wartime airstrip stretching from Lambete to Kokenggolo still dominates Munda, a huge plain of crushed coral. The Americans built the fine coral roads here by dredging up limestone, crushing it with a steamroller, then pumping saltwater over the road to harden it like cement.

The dark-skinned people of the Roviana Lagoon were once much-feared cannibals who raided far and wide in their long canoes. In 1892 a punitive raid by a British warship broke the power of the headhunters, and a few years later Methodist missionaries converted the survivors. Though the change from those days is striking, much remains the same around this lagoon. You might see old men netting fish, outriggers bringing in live turtles, and fish leaping through the sea.

Sights

Have a swim in the spring-fed freshwater pool near the canoe house at Lambete wharf. Next, follow the coastal road east from Lambete a kilometer to **Kia** village. In the bush just behind the houses of Kia is a large U.S. military dump with huge landing craft deliberately cut in half, amphibious tanks, trucks, aircraft engines, guns, and even a small Japanese tank, all piled up where the Americans left them when they pulled out after the war. Many beautiful pink and blue orchids bloom in the bush beyond. Ask for Mr. Rennelmamu, the village chief, who will be happy to show

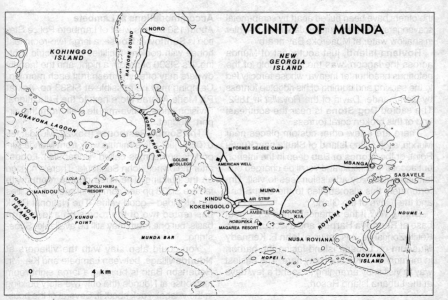

VICINITY OF MUNDA

you around for a SI$10 pp custom fee. Much more war materiel is sunken or dumped in the lagoon off Kia, and small copra driers along the waterfront still utilize wartime 44-gallon petrol drums.

Now head for **Kokenggolo.** The Japanese secretly built the gigantic airstrip that dominates this area. They camouflaged their work by suspending the tops of coconut trees on cables above the runway—surely one of the more remarkable accomplishments of the war. The Americans captured Munda on 5 August 1943 after heavy fighting. Avid snorkelers should visit the sunken aircraft in the lagoon just off the beach near Kokenggolo hospital: a single-engine Corsair fighter is beside a pole near shore, while a larger two-engine Nelly bomber in good condition is farther out in about seven meters of water. If there are a few of you, try hiring a motorized canoe at Lambete wharf as these planes can be hard to find on your own.

Follow the coastal road northwest from Kokenggolo to **Kindu** village. Women are often seen washing clothes in a large spring-fed pool at the end of the village, right beside the road. Swim here or continue one km to a clear freshwater stream.

Midway between pool and stream is a road leading inland toward Noro. About a kilometer up this road, on the left just before a slight rise, is an old American well and water supply system. Continue along the road till it meets the new highway to Noro. Cross the highway and go straight ahead on a bush trail five minutes to two large **Japanese AA guns** flanking a flagpole foundation, all that's left of the big U.S. Seabee Camp that once covered this area. Hitch back to Munda along the highway for a circle trip.

Vicinity of Munda

A copra-exporting facility is near the Japanese fish freezer at **Noro,** 16 km northwest of Munda by road or by boat through the Diamond Narrows. The Solomon Taiyo Ltd. cannery established at Noro in 1991 cans 20,000 tons of tuna a year, including the dark-meat Solomons Blue *tin pis* (canned fish). There are three wharfs at Noro: the government wharf where the Honiara-Gizo ship ties up, the Fisheries wharf, and the Taiyo wharf next to the cannery.

At **Enoghae Point,** east of Noro, four 140-mm Japanese coastal defense guns still lurk in the bush. Only one of the guns is still in good shape;

the others have been pulled apart by scrap-metal scavengers. There's a sunken Japanese freighter in shallow water at Mbaeroko Bay nearby.

Roviana Island, just southeast of Munda across the lagoon, was the stronghold of the notorious headhunter Ingava, whose ferocity led to the sacking and burning of his ridgetop fortress by Commander David of the *Royalist* in 1892. The sacred **Dog Stone** is near the southeast end of this broken coral fortress.

There are a few other custom places near Munda, such as the **Island of Skulls** near Kundu Point, or the **Stones of Bau** deep in the interior, but access is difficult, and you'll be charged outlandish customary admission fees to visit. Unfortunately this also applies to the Dog Stone and the "Cave of the Giant."

During WW II the Americans had a PT-boat base at **Rendova Harbor,** and a local man, Mr. Kettily Zongahite, has set up a **John F. Kennedy Museum** on Lubaria Island facing the harbor, in memory of JFK's brief stay here. The easiest way to visit is by arranging to spend a few days at the Lubaria Island Resort.

Sports and Recreation

Dave and Mariana Cooke's **Solomon Sea Divers** (Box 145, Munda; tel. 61224, fax 61225), at Agnes Lodge in Lambete, offers scuba diving at SI$170 without gear, SI$280 with gear. Snorkeling is SI$90 with or without gear. They'll give you a resort course for SI$280, or full PADI open-water certification for SI$1,325. The Roviana Lagoon waters offer limited visibility but Solomon Sea Divers visits many sites beyond the reef.

THE CRAWL

In 1898 a 12-year-old Roviana islander named Alick Wickham introduced the world to the traditional swimming technique we now know as the crawl. Alick had gone to Sydney two years earlier with his Australian father, and when he easily beat all the Aussie kids at a local swimming carnival, an Australian coach noticed. The technique was perfected and became a sensation at the 1900 Olympics. Alick later worked as a stuntman in a circus, served with the coastwatchers during WW II, and died in Honiara in 1967 at the ripe age of 81.

Accommodations at Lambete

About 150 meters west of Lambete Police Station is **Sunflower House,** a large two-room leaf house with cooking facilities and electric lighting. It's SI$90 per room a night, and the friendly owners may offer you fresh fruit each morning. Camping may be possible at SI$33 pp. Ask at PX Merle Aqorau store next to the Educational Division office, a five-minute walk from the airport. Budget.

The **Somba Resthouse** (Box 22, Munda; tel. 61083), just a five-minute walk from Munda Airport, is sometimes called "Sogabule's Lodge" after the owner, John Sogabule. There's no sign on the building. The three double rooms with fan are SI$33 pp and communal cooking facilities are provided—good value. The National Bank has rented two of the rooms on a long term basis, but one room may still be available. Shoestring.

You could also stay with the villagers at **Ndunde** village, between Lambete and Kia. Mr. Robertson Bato is building a large eight-room resthouse at Ndunde (the only two-story building in the village)—ask about it. Several of the houses nearby are owned by Mrs. Vera Lilo, who rents them out for long stays. Don't expect any electricity at Ndunde.

Just a stone's throw from the air terminal and government wharf is 22-room **Agnes Lodge** (David Kera, Box 9, Munda; tel. 61133, fax 61225), formerly the Munda Resthouse. It's SI$220 for up to three persons in a room with shared bath in the old wing, SI$300 in a double room with bath in the new wing. A deluxe room is SI$345 for up to four persons. There's also a "backpackers' rate" of SI$50 per bed in shared rooms in the old wing. Add 10% tax to all rates, plus another 20% commission if you book through a travel agent in Australia. A meal and accommodation package is SI$280 pp (double occupancy). During the off season (Nov.-April) you can stay five nights for the price of three (backpacker accommodation excluded). No cooking facilities are provided, so you must patronize their restaurant. Sandwiches are available, but a sign at the bar advises patrons that nonguests must order full meals after 1800. This is the only place in Munda to get a beer (check your change). The staff will pressure you to sign up for their half-day lagoon trips which are artificial and rather expensive. Budget to moderate.

Under the same ownership is **Noro Lodge** (Box 9, Munda; tel. 61238), about a five-minute walk from the government wharf at Noro. The four rooms without bath are SI$156 for one to four persons, while another four rooms with bath are SI$235 single or double. Budget to inexpensive.

Island Resorts

The **Maqarea Resort** (Box 66, Munda; tel./fax 61164), pronounced "Mangaraya," on tiny Hobupeka Island just offshore from Lambete, has four thatched bungalows with private bath at SI$125 pp, plus tax. No cooking facilities are available, no choice of food is possible at meal times, and there's not a lot to do other than relax. Inexpensive.

If you want to have an island to yourself, Agnes Lodge rents out a lovely part-leaf cottage on nearby **Hopei Island**, just offshore from Munda, complete with fridge, oven, and toilet. It's SI$250 a night for three persons, plus SI$15 for transfers. You can bring your own food, otherwise full provisions can be ordered. It may seem remote, but be aware of theft. Inexpensive.

Mr. Kettily Zongahite's **Lubaria Island Resort** (Box 27, Munda; tel. 61149) is on a small island facing Rendova Harbor, 10 km southwest of Munda. The three double rooms in the European-style guesthouse with shared cooking facilities are SI$30/50/80 single/double/triple, while a room in the three-room thatched family cottage is SI$100. Lighting is by gas lamp. You must bring all your own food with you, as there are no stores here, although fresh fruit, fish, and vegetables can occasionally be purchased from local villagers. If the guesthouse is full, you could camp on Lubaria. When enough guests are present, a cultural-exchange concert evening is arranged. Motorized canoe transfers are SI$70 from Munda or SI$90 from Mburuko roundtrip per group. A number of canoe tours around the area are offered, and they're rather expensive due to the high customary entry fees built into the price. Add 10% tax to all costs. To assure an easy arrival at Lubaria, write to Kettily a week or two in advance, or ask for Kettily's sister, Rosie Zongahite, who works at Hellena Goldie Hospital (tel. 61121) at Kokenggolo. Budget.

One of the nicest little hideaways in these parts is Joe and Lisa Entrikin's **Zipolo Habu Resort** (Box 164, Munda; tel./fax 61178) on Lola Island at the east entrance to the Vonavona Lagoon. Lola's a medium-size island with a white sandy beach from which one gets a lovely lagoon view. Set in a coconut grove, all buildings on the premises are built from local materials. The three two-bedroom cottages with fridge, gas stove, kerosene lamp, and mosquito nets are SI$66/88/110 single/double/triple. Camping is possible. Guests are encouraged to bring food and do their own cooking. A small shop at the resort sells basic groceries and rents snorkeling gear. It's a perfect place to get away from it all and relax. As you lie in bed the jungle sounds lull you to sleep. Thirty minutes from Munda by boat, this resort is a real favorite among anglers, and the resort canoe is available for fishing or surfing trips, sightseeing, and shopping excursions at fixed rates. Credit cards are not accepted here. Transfers cost SI$60 per cottage from Munda or Noro return (free if you stay five nights or longer). Budget.

Food and Entertainment

There are four general stores at Lambete. The **Hot Bread Kitchen** near the police station by the airport bakes bread daily (arrive early on Sunday). Sporadic markets happen near Lambete wharf and Kokenggolo hospital.

There's custom dancing at Munda on 23 May, anniversary of the arrival of the first missionaries (in 1902), 7 July (Independence Day), Christmas, and New Year's Day. The singing and dancing show the influence of Tongan missionaries. Ask if any bamboo bands will be playing while you're there.

Services

The National Bank has a branch next to the airport terminal at Lambete and another at Noro; both change traveler's checks.

Getting There

Solomon Airlines (tel. 61152) has daily flights to Gizo (SI$65), Seghe (71 km, SI$115), and Honiara (327 km, SI$245), several times a week to Ringi Cove (SI$55), Ballalae (211 km, SI$190), Choiseul Bay (217 km, SI$180), and Mono (SI$170).

Solomon Airlines office, the customs office, and the immigration office are all inside the airport terminal. The small coffee counter in the terminal opens at flight times. Western Pacific Airline has an office at Mae General Trading store near the air terminal.

The *Iuminao* calls here Monday morning bound for Gizo, Monday afternoon for Honiara. Boat fares from Munda are SI$71 deck to Honiara, SI$36 deck to Gizo.

A barge called the *L.C. Swift,* based at Munda and owned by the United Church, carries lumber between Gizo, Munda, and the Marovo Lagoon on a regular basis. It's not really a passenger boat, but the captain might agree to take you.

Due to the lack of a main wharf at Munda, the ships from Honiara cannot tie up here and you must negotiate with a private canoe owner to take you to/from the small wharf next to Agnes Lodge at Lambete. The Munda-Honiara boat stops some distance offshore, and canoe operators will want SI$10 pp to take you there. One way to avoid this is by disembarking at Noro, where there is a wharf, and hitching down to Munda (16 km). If arriving from Honiara during daylight you'll get the added bonus of seeing the Diamond Narrows (which are just after Munda).

Since the airfare from Munda to Gizo is relatively low, consider taking the boat from Honiara direct to Noro, hitching a ride down to Munda in the back of a truck, flying from Munda to Gizo, then either taking the boat or flying from Gizo back to Honiara. Try to book the Munda-Gizo leg before leaving Honiara.

Getting Around

Good roads connect Munda to Mbanga landing (near Sasavele) and Noro. The Port Authority truck (marked "SIPA") carries passengers from Noro to Munda sporadically at SI$2 pp. Otherwise you could simply hitch, although there isn't a lot of traffic. It's easier to go from Lambete to Noro. Weekdays just before 0800, you can usually get a ride from Lambete to Noro in the truck that brings children to school at Lambete. Ask around the night before.

KOLOMBANGARA

Kolombangara is a classic cone-shaped volcano 30 km across and almost circular in shape that soars to 1,770 meters. The native name of this island-volcano is Nduke. You can climb it from Iriri or Vanga villages, accessible by canoe from Gizo market, where the locals sell their products and shop. To go up and down in one day would be exhausting, so camp partway and reach the top early the next morning; by midday the summit is shrouded in clouds and you'd miss the view. But in the mist, the stunted, moss-covered forest on top will haunt you. The extinct crater is four km across and as much as 1,000 meters deep, with the Vila River, which passes Ringi, draining it on the southeast side.

A coastal road runs around the island's 678 square km, with old logging roads up most of the ridges. Ringi, two km from the wharf (where the Honiara ships stop), is the former headquarters of Levers Pacific Timbers, which pulled out of Kolombangara in 1986 after 20 years of logging. At the moment, Kolombangara Forest Products (which is 51% owned by the Commonwealth Development Corporation) has a 18,000-hectare reforestation project on Kolombangara, intended to provide a sustainable alternative to uncontrolled logging of old growth forests. Since 1995 the project has been self-supporting, and eco-friendly timber from the island supplies a niche market in Europe.

Ringi Cove and Vicinity

The wharf and airport are on opposite sides of Ringi Cove station, both a 15-minute walk away. There's a small market in Ringi. Vilu Plantation, on Blackett Strait just south of the cove airstrip, was an important Japanese base during WW II. Rusted Japanese guns molder in the bush near the airstrip. There are weekly Solomon Airlines flights from Ringi Cove to Munda (29 km, SI$55), Gizo (31 km, SI$55), and Honiara (356 km, SI$260). Find outboard canoes to Noro or Munda near the canoe shed at the Ringi Cove wharf.

The very comfortable **KFPL Resthouse** (tel. 60230, fax 60020) is up toward the Forestry Department nursery, three km from the wharf or a 15-minute walk from the airstrip. It's the former private residence of the general manager of the logging company. There are five rooms, four with two double beds at SI$20 pp (shared bath) and one self-contained double room at SI$80 for the room. Meals are SI$15/15/30 for breakfast/lunch/dinner, or you can cook for yourself. There's 24-hour electricity. Call ahead for reservations. Budget.

GIZO

The administrative center of the Western Solomons since 1899, Gizo (4,500 inhabitants) is a pleasant little town, the second largest in the Solomons. It's quite a "modern" place, with electric street lights, a hospital, banks, and many Chinese stores. Downtown Gizo is like a second version of Honiara's Chinatown. The name recalls a legendary warrior, Izo, and although the town is called Gizo, the island name is spelled Ghizo, yet both are pronounced the same.

An important shipping and shopping center for the Western Solomons, Gizo lies 383 km northwest of Honiara. A large Gilbertese community has been resettled here since 1955. Gizo has a lovely setting with several small islands sitting just offshore. Logha Island directly opposite Gizo is owned by the Catholic Church, which operates a seminary there. Nusaburaku village, on Ghizo Island to the left, is populated by Gilbertese people from Wagina Island, while farther out is a fishing village of Malaita people. The dramatic view of Kolombangara looming across Blackett Strait to the right is particularly picturesque.

After their PT boat was cut in half by a Japanese destroyer on 1 August 1943, John F. Kennedy and his 10 shipmates took shelter on Kasolo, or Plum Pudding Island, between Ghizo and Kolombanga, from which he was rescued by a Solomon Islander. The ship from Honiara passes right beside Plum Pudding (anyone aboard could point it out).

Although you'll probably like the leisurely lifestyle and variety of things to see and do, Gizo is becoming rather commercialized as it caters more and more to packaged scuba divers from Australia. Shore diving or snorkeling isn't possible here, and the expense of always going out by boat to dive adds up. You have to spend money to do almost anything at Gizo.

Sights

Near Gizo's police station is a memorial to Captain Alexander McKenzie Ferguson, master of the *Ripple*—"Killed by natives at Bougainville Island." Another monument in front of the station remembers Captain Thomas Woodhouse, "The Old Commodore," who died at Gizo in 1906. From here a road climbs the hill behind town, and it's worth the effort for the great view of the harbor and surrounding islands. During WW II the Japanese had a major barge-repair base in the bay you see below.

A good half-day trip from town involves taking a truck from Gizo market to the end of the line at the Gilbertese village of **Titiana,** then returning to town along the beach in a couple of hours. You may have to use the road from Titiana to New Manra village to avoid mangroves, and the section from New Manra to Gizo jail is best done at low tide, but all in all, it's an easy scenic walk. If you can't find a truck to Titiana at the market, do the walk in reverse, following the road east out of town past the hospital and jail, and along the beautiful beach, then return to Gizo by road directly from New Manra village.

Sports and Recreation

Danny and Kerrie Kennedy's **Adventure Sports** (Box 21, Gizo; tel. 60253, fax 60297), or "Dive Gizo," opposite Koburutavia Divers Lodge, offers scuba diving at SI$140 including tank, belt, and weights, SI$200 with all equipment (two dives SI$330). Snorkeling is SI$47/78 for a half/full day without equipment. Unlike those at Honiara, these are boat dives. If you've never done scuba before, you can take their "resort course" for SI$265 or a full PADI/NAUI scuba certification course for SI$1,250 all-inclusive. You won't find a more relaxed place than Gizo in which to learn how to dive. Danny himself is something of a

GHIZO ISLAND

South Seas beachcomber who has been here since 1985. You'll find his easy-going enthusiasm and good humor contagious. Adventure Sports also sells handicrafts.

Scuba diving is also offered by **Dive Solomons** (Box 30, Gizo; tel. 60199, fax 60137), at the Gizo Hotel. Scuba diving is SI$156 without gear, SI$188 with gear; snorkeling SI$88 with gear. They offer a resort course for SI$293 and open-water scuba certification for SI$1,200. In addition, they have trolling or bottom fishing trips at SI$215/425 for three/six hours (up to four passengers). Dive Solomons works mostly with packaged dive groups from Australia, and it's rather commercialized; Danny Kennedy is

a better bet if you're on your own. These companies do compete and it's sometimes worth comparing prices.

Be sure to dive on the 140-meter Japanese transport ship *Toa Maru*, if nothing else. This enormous wreck 18 meters below in Kololuka Bay is still intact in 8-35 meters of water, with sake bottles in the galley and two-man tanks in the hold. Grand Central Station, a sloping dropoff off the north end of Ghizo, is the ultimate fish and coral dive. Other dive spots include the shallow reef at Nusatupe Island, Naru Wall, the Hellcat fighter near Q-Island in the Vonavona Lagoon, and a Zero aircraft in five meters of water just off Gizo's market—ideal to finish off a tank.

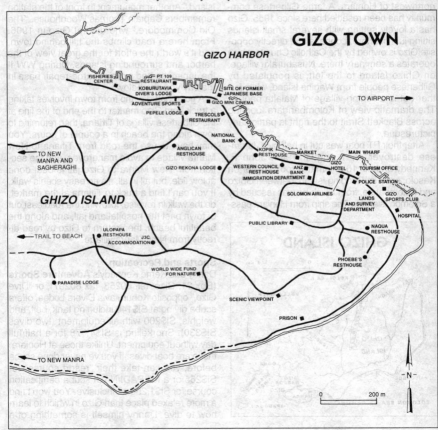

According to Danny Kennedy, there have never been any problems with sharks in the waters he frequents off Ghizo.

Dirk and Kathy Sieling of **Sports Fishing Solomon Islands** (tel./fax 60321), at the Gizo Hotel, offer deep sea fishing on the MV *Amanda Jane*, a 10-meter game rigged powerboat. This costs SI$1,120 for four hours, but they also have an open seven-meter fiberglass fishing boat available at SI$112 an hour for two anglers, plus SI$17 an hour for additional persons. The fish caught belong to the boat and most billfish are released, but anglers are allowed to keep a few smaller fish for personal consumption. The Sielings put together food and accommodation packages at island resorts between Ghizo and Munda for SI$240 pp (cost of fishing additional).

Shoestring Accommodations

The recent opening of several new guesthouses has relieved the pressure on the Gizo accommodations scene. One of the best buys is the four-room **Naqua Resthouse** (Box 127, Gizo; tel. 60274 or 60012), also known as the "KML Resthouse," run by Meshach Ngodoro and family on the hill just above the wharf. There are great views of Kolombangara from the breezy balcony, and the communal cooking facilities and fridge are excellent, all at SI$35 pp. Alcohol is not allowed. Information is available at KML Hardware next to the National Bank.

On a breezy slope a bit farther up the same way past Naqua is **Phoebe's Resthouse** (Box 61, Gizo; tel. 60336, fax 60128) with four double rooms with shared bath at SI$35 pp including tax. There's a comfortably furnished lounge, cooking facilities, and a veranda with one of the most panoramic views in the South Seas. You're treated like one of the family.

Gizo Rekona Lodge (Box 91, Gizo; tel. 60368, fax 60120), just up from the National Bank, has five fan-cooled rooms with shared bath at SI$35 pp. There's a fridge and communal cooking facilities, and good views from the upstairs balcony. It's very popular and often full.

Nelson Tokotoko runs **Pepele Lodge** (Box 116, Gizo), the building with large paintings on the outside walls just behind Adventure Sports (Pepele means "butterfly"). The four rooms with shared bath and cooking facilities are SU$30 pp, and there's a breezy elevated terrace.

The **Anglican Resthouse** (Box 93, Gizo; tel. 60159), a bit inland from Adventure Sports, has seven rooms with shared bath at SI$25 pp. There are communal cooking facilities in this European-style building, but it's a bit hot here.

Budget Accommodations

Also up on top of the hill behind town is **Paradise Lodge** (Box 56, Gizo; tel. 60024, fax 60200). The "backpackers" section downstairs includes three five-bedded rooms and two doubles with shared bath at SI$62 pp, plus tax. Upstairs are four rooms with private bath at SI$265 single or double. Communal cooking and a fridge are provided downstairs; upstairs are a bar, restaurant, and veranda with great views. For upmarket accommodations, it's better value than the Gizo Hotel if you don't mind being away from the action. Paradise Lodge is run by May Sogabule who will pick you up at the wharf if you call ahead. Otherwise it's a long walk.

Koburutavia Divers Lodge (Box 50, Gizo; tel. 60257, fax 60297) has a seven-room waterfront lodge opposite Adventure Sports which is often crowded with Australian scuba divers on short packaged holidays. The cost is SI$62 pp plus tax with shared bath. Cooking facilities are provided. The kind owners, Lawry and Regina Wickham, also operate a restaurant/bar behind the lodge that has a great view of Gizo harbor.

Moderate Accommodations

The **Gizo Hotel** (Box 30, Gizo; tel. 60199, fax 60137, www.islandshotels.com.au), in the center of town, has 45 rooms, all with private bath, fridge, and tea- and coffee-making facilities. The seven hot and dumpy "budget" rooms above the reception are SI$157/199 single/double, while the eight "old wing" rooms at the rear of the hotel are SI$198/248/292 single/double/triple. These rooms are fan cooled. For a/c you must upgrade to the 14 "poolside" rooms in an L-shaped two-story block angled around the shallow figure-eight-shaped swimming pool at SI$286/341 single/double. The 16 "seaview" rooms along the main street are SI$308/369. Two children under 12 can stay free with their parents in the old wing only. The meal plan is SI$145 pp. In 1995 a Papua New Guinea company bought the Gizo Hotel and most guests are on pre-booked packages from Australia.

Food

The **Gizo Women's Snack Bar** (weekdays 1030-1630), at the west end of the market, serves local meals at SI$10 a plate.

Iden's Kitchen, on the waterfront between the Chinese stores, also has good plates of rice and meat for SI$10.

Barbara Unusu's **Trescols Restaurant** (tel. 60090) serves more upscale meals Mon.-Sat. 0600-2130. Lunch prices run SI$8-22.

The **Fast Food Snack Bar** (weekdays 0900-1700), almost opposite Trescols, has cheap snacks you eat standing up.

Perhaps the top place in town is the **PT 109 Restaurant** (tel. 60257), overlooking the lagoon behind Koburutavia Divers Lodge. You can order a three-course meal here with tea or coffee for less than SI$40, but dinner must be reserved before 1600. It's better value than the restaurant at the Gizo Hotel.

There's a market along the waterfront Mon.-Saturday. The Western Fishermen's Coop (tel. 60040) and Indian Pacific Seafood, both on the waterfront west of town, sell fresh fish in the morning (only frozen fish in the afternoon).

Gizo tap water is not fit for drinking.

Entertainment

The **Gizo Hotel** (tel. 60199) presents a bamboo band on Wednesday and Gilbertese *tamure* dancing on Friday. The spectacles are accessible to both diners at the hotel restaurant and to those who only buy a drink at the hotel bar. The action begins around 1930, but it's all canceled when the hotel is short of guests.

The **Gizo Sports Club** (tel. 60163), just east of the main wharf, has an attractive terrace overlooking the harbor. However, complaints from the pastor of the adjacent United Church about the rowdy behavior of some of the patrons may lead to the club being relocated in the near future (or permanently closed down). A tourism-oriented group is trying to take the place over and convert it into a Gizo Yacht Club, styled after the Honiara Yacht Club. Check it out to see which side won, the Bible or the bottle.

The **Gizo Mini Cinema,** next to KHY Store, screens tacky videos at 1130, 1400, and 1730.

Services and Information

The ANZ Bank (tel. 60262) and the National Bank (tel. 60134) at Gizo change traveler's checks. ANZ gives cash advances against Visa and MasterCard credit cards (SI$10 telex fee).

The post office is in a temporary building at the market. The Telecom office (tel. 60127, fax 60128), opposite the market, has public phone booths just inside.

Extensions of stay can be arranged at the Immigration Department (tel. 60214), up the street opposite Gizo market.

The Culture Tourism Environment Office (tel. 60251), near the main wharf and opposite the police station, can answer most questions and has interesting displays on the walls. The noted Pacific poet Jully Makini works in this office.

The Lands and Surveys Department (tel. 60162), between the police station and the hospital, has a few topographical maps for sale, but the selection is much better in Honiara.

Adventure Sports (tel. 60253) runs a mini-travel agency and can book you into outer island resorts all around Western Province (including Vanua Rapita). They also arrange bushwalks with Wilson Hivu at SI$30 pp.

Transportation

Solomon Airlines (tel. 60173), across the street from the police station, has daily service from Gizo to Munda (51 km, SI$65), Seghe (122 km, SI$115), and Honiara (377 km, SI$280), three flights a week to Choiseul Bay (166 km, SI$140) and Ballalae (159 km, SI$140), and weekly to Ringi Cove (31 km, SI$55) and Mono (SI$140). Don't forget to reconfirm your onward bookings. The airstrip (GZO) is on Nusatupe Island, a quick boat ride (SI$10 pp) from the wharf in front of the Gizo Hotel. The transfer is free for Gizo Hotel guests.

Between Gizo and Honiara the plane follows an easterly flight path, while northbound it flies more to the west. For optimum views, one should sit on the right side of the aircraft in both directions. While taking off or landing on Nusatupe, notice the aquatic resources station on the island, where research into creating a cultured pearl industry is underway.

The Wings Shipping ship *luminao* departs Gizo for Honiara Monday at 1500. On the journey from Gizo to Honiara, the *luminao* sleeps anchored off Noro, calls at the New Georgia and Marovo Lagoon ports on Tuesday, and arrives in Honiara Wednesday at 0500. Deck fares from Gizo are: Ringi Cove SI$26, Noro SI$36, Munda

SI$39, Ughele SI$42, Viru Harbor SI$50, Patutiva SI$50, Chea SI$50, Gasini SI$52, Yandina SI$72, and Honiara SI$84. To Honiara, it's SI$105 first class or SI$143 in a cabin. Tickets can be purchased at the Gizo Hotel reception.

The Shipping Officer in the Provincial Office (tel. 60183) opposite the police station may know about boats from Gizo to the Shortland Islands and elsewhere. Two small trading vessels based at Gizo are the *Parama,* which serves the Shortland Islands, and the *Ozama Twomey,* which sails to Choiseul.

Outboard canoes leave Gizo market for Vella Lavella (SI$10 pp), Kolombangara, Ranongga, and Simbo. Ask along the waterfront. You can hire an outboard canoe to go right around Gizo or elsewhere at SI$150 for a full day, petrol included. Ten people can go for that price.

A white truck provides passenger service between Gizo market and Titiana about five times a day (SI$2). The blue truck between the market and Pailongge is SI$3 pp.

Dive Solomons (tel. 60199), at the Gizo Hotel, is a full activities center offering scuba diving, snorkeling, sightseeing tours, and equipment rentals. They even have Kolombangara overnight volcano treks (SI$500 pp) and a tour of the Simbo Island megapode hatchery (SI$350). Mountain bikes are for hire at SI$28 for the first two hours, SI$14 additional hours, SI$85 a day—about the most expensive bicycle rentals in the South Pacific. Still, it's about the only place in Solomon Islands where you can rent a bicycle. The same folks rent single/double kayaks at SI$42/56 for the first two hours, SI$14/20 each additional hour, or SI$100/125 a day. Their Saeraghi tour is SI$90 for two people, SI$70 pp for three or more. Fishing trips in an aluminum boat are SI$215/425 for three/six hours.

THE SHORTLAND ISLANDS

The Shortland Islands are one of most isolated outposts in the Pacific. Together with the adjacent Treasury Islands, the group is traditionally known as Famoa for Fauro, Mono, and Alu, the three largest islands. This intriguing area receives no more than a dozen individual visitors a year, so you'll be in for something totally original!

Though officially part of Solomon Islands' Western Province, the Shortlands are much closer geographically, culturally, and linguistically to North Solomons Province in Papua New Guinea. The modern partition of the area dates from 1899, when the Germans ceded the Shortlands to Britain but held onto Bougainville itself. During WW II the Japanese fortified the islands to shield their large bases in southern Bougainville. Though the New Zealanders took the Treasury Islands just to the southwest in October 1943, the Japanese entrenched in the Shortlands themselves were bombed and bypassed by the Allies.

In early 1992 fighting between the secessionist Bougainville Revolutionary Army and the Papua New Guinea Defense Force spilled over into the Shortlands when P.N.G. patrol boats and troops made incursions into Solomon Island territory in pursuit of BRA fighters and persons supplying contraband gasoline to the Bougainville rebels. As a result of the 1992 border incidents, Solomon Islands set up a paramilitary field force that presently has bases at Kamaleai at Alu's northernmost tip, at Lofang near Korovou, and at Kareki on Fauro Island.

Ballalae

The airstrip (BAS) serving the Shortlands is on uninhabited Ballalae Island, with access to and from Korovou by motorized canoe (30 minutes, SI$20 pp). Be prepared to get wet. There are Solomon Airlines flights from Ballalae to Gizo (159 km, SI$140) and Honiara (536 km, SI$375) four times a week, to Choiseul Bay (66 km, SI$80) three times a week, and to Munda (211 km, SI$170) twice a week.

During WW II the Japanese forced several hundred British civilian prisoners brought from Singapore to build the airstrip on Ballalae and none left the island alive. Sadly, no memorial has been erected to those who suffered and died here, and the victims have been forgotten. What can be seen are numerous vestiges of Japanese military might. Japanese propellers flank the small airport terminal, and on the short trail from the terminal to the beach you pass a half dozen Japanese trucks in various stages of decay and one wrecked plane. Three small steamrollers used to build the airport are in the bush west of the terminal and another is behind the beach.

A Japanese AA gun is between the southwest end of the airstrip and the point, but the real attraction is the large number of wrecked Japanese planes including fighters and twin-engined "Betty" bombers. They're in the bush on both sides of the airstrip: turn right at the terminal and walk northeast about halfway down the airstrip. There, cut in on either side and search (the planes are easy to find and no guide is required). The planes are surrounded by large circular craters left by the bombs that destroyed them, and if you look long enough you might see the crumpled aluminum fuselages of several dozen aircraft, a few still in fair condition despite the years.

Flights between Ballalae and Gizo often depart in the afternoon, and if you can find someone to take you over in the morning, you'll have ample time to look around before the flight. Bring insect repellent and be prepared for black stinging ants.

Alu

Alu, the largest island of the group, is off the southern tip of Bougainville. The tiny government station of **Korovou** is in Alu's southeast corner, and cruising yachts can clear the Solomons here. The boat to Gizo usually ties up at one of two wharfs near the copra shed at Korovou, directly opposite Faisi Island. Near the shore just west of Korovou are a Japanese bomber and a Zero aircraft, clearly visible from the surface.

The Solomon Airlines agent runs BBE Store on tiny Teulu Island near Maleai village. It's well stocked with beer and other essentials. One small trading boat does the 11-hour trip between the wharf at Teulu Island and Gizo every week or two (SI$40 each way). The Catholic mission station of Nila on Poporang Island is just across the water from Korovou. On the northwest side of Alu Island are the Gilbertese resettlement villages of Kamaleai and Harapa.

Oba Store at the west end of Kulitana Bay near Korovou is the best-stocked store in this area. It's run by a Gilbertese man whose brother and sister were killed at Kamaleai by P.N.G. troops during a brief incursion into Solomon Islands territory to cut off sources of fuel and supplies to the Bougainville rebels. A large stockpile of petrol drums can be seen here, and the mouth of the bay is protected by police posts on both sides. The Faisi Island Guest House offers a picture-window view of it all.

An interesting half-day motorized canoe trip is to **Nankai Point** at the south tip of Alu, where the Japanese set up three large coastal defense guns pointing at Allied-occupied Mono Island. To get there you travel along the back of Magusaisai Island, reaching the open sea just beyond Nuhu village. West of here is a large coconut plantation at Haleta, where one can land on the beach and follow it around to the guns, which are right by the shore just west of tiny Manualai Island. About 50 meters east of the first gun is a short trail up the hill to a stockpile of ammunition with live Japanese shells still piled high.

Faisi

The only regular place to stay in this area is at the southwest end of Faisi Island, directly opposite Korovou and 10 km south of Ballalae airport. The two-room **Faisi Island Guest House** (no phone), run by a woman named Silvester Gali, is the former personal residence of ex-governor general Sir George Lepping, and it's a great budget place to rest. A covered porch faces a lovely white beach, and some nice coral and lots of fish are right offshore. Silvester asks SI$60 pp for a room with communal cooking and bathing facilities, but this price may be negotiable, especially for long stays. She may throw in a dugout canoe to use for snorkeling, sightseeing, and shopping trips. Assume that the guesthouse generator will be out of service during your stay. Silvester lives a few hundred meters away on the southeast side of Faisi, so you'll have the whole house to yourself unless there are other guests. To give advance warning of your arrival, radio the Administration Officer at Korovou.

Bring some food with you for the first day or two (protect your food from mice and ants). Women paddling past in canoes may stop to sell you fruit or vegetables, and you can order fresh coconuts from any of the island men. Also bring adequate toilet paper and mosquito coils.

Silvester can help with the necessary canoe hires, but make sure the price is well understood. Expect to pay SI$60 a day plus gasoline, or SI$40 each way for a special trip to Ballalae Airstrip. For example, Dennis Tanutanu offers canoe trips to Nankai Point and elsewhere at reasonable rates. It's not hard to hitch rides on passing canoes to Nila or elsewhere from the end of the stone wharf near the guesthouse. Almost anyone at Ballalae airport will bring you directly to Faisi for SI$20 pp.

Faisi is a pleasant little island inhabited by three families who earn a living cutting copra and by running the guesthouse. Two cows, one dog, and many pigs are also on the island. Red and green parrots and white cockatoos screech and clatter between the coconut trees that circle the island, and frigate birds glide by. The wreck of a small plane is beside the trail at the north end of Faisi, and a more complete plane, its tail wedged between a rock and a tree, its engine on the ground in front, is on the east side of the island. Blue glass from broken Japanese sake bottles is seen on the ground near the wharf and copra driers not far from the guesthouse.

Poporang

The highlight of any visit to the Shortlands is a tour of Poporang Hill where the Japanese had their main base during WW II. Upon arrival on Poporang Island it's customary to pay a courtesy call on the Catholic priest at Nila, who may be able to suggest someone willing to act as a guide (ask for Billy). An overgrown Japanese road, complete with a truck stalled halfway down, winds around the hill from the mission cattle ranch. On top of Poporang are two intact Japanese radar trailers, and just beyond that, at least four anti-aircraft batteries, one with two metal shell boxes alongside. Your guide will then show you a huge searchlight, a few of the seven 140-mm coastal defense guns remaining on the hill (several others

have been removed), an underground metal ammunition bunker the size of a container, and a Japanese motorcycle with its sidecar still attached. You'll pass numerous trenches cut into the coral rock, and go down another wartime road directly to Sapusapuai village.

Also ask to see the six Japanese seaplanes by the shore next to Kopokopana village, a few minutes walk southwest of Nila. Two more planes are in shallow water a stone's throw from the others. Other sunken seaplanes are at the bottom of the bay between Alu and Poporang Islands with one nearly intact Japanese bomber in eight meters of snorkeling water just east of Nila. All of the abovewater relics can be seen in a couple of hours with the help of a guide who will have earned his gratuity. Wednesday is a good day to come as there will be a small market at Nila. (Heavy fines are imposed on anyone attempting to remove war relics from these islands.)

Treasury Islands

The Treasury Islands are the westernmost islands included in this handbook. All of the people live on larger Mono Island, but the airstrip and a lot of war wreckage are on adjacent Stirling. No vehicles or roads are found on these remote islands, and all travel is by foot or canoe. Although few visitors get this far, there are weekly Solomon Airlines flights from Gizo (SI$140), Munda (SI$170), and Honiara (SI$380). Mr. R. Adrian has set up **Eco-Tourist Lodge** (Mono Postal Agency, Treasury Islands, Western Province) here, and information may be available from Adventure Sports in Gizo.

CHOISEUL PROVINCE

Choiseul (pronounced Choysle), which separated from Western Province in 1991, is linked far more closely to the Shortlands and Gizo than to distant Honiara. At 2,538 square km, Choiseul is the sixth-largest island in the Solomons. In 1768 French explorer Louis-Antoine de Bougainville named Choiseul after a French minister, but traditionally the island is known as Lauru. Lots of footpaths cross central Choiseul, for instance Sasamungga to Susuka, but a guide would be essential. The new provincial capital, **Taro,** is on the tiny airport island in **Choiseul Bay,** near the northwest end of the island. Choiseul Bay is an interesting little place, well worth a two-day visit.

The airstrip cuts across Taro from north to south, and all of the offices, shops, houses, and the wharf are on the east side of the island facing the mainland. A small group of refugees from Bougainville live at the north end of Taro. In wet weather there are many mosquitoes, in dry weather water shortages. Taro's shoreline con-

Massive clamshell plaques bearing dancing figures of this kind were once used on Choiseul to close the opening of a container bearing the skull of a dead chief.

sists of mangroves alternating with white sandy beaches. Watch the sun set over the Shortland Islands and Bougainville from the small beach near the south end of the airstrip. Dogs are not allowed on Taro.

The paramilitary police have a post on the northern point of Sipuzae Island, which can be reached from Taro by wading across the lagoon at low tide from the north end of the airstrip. At high tide you can easily snorkel between Taro and Sipuzae.

Only one tractor/trailer and one pickup truck are found on Taro, but numerous fiberglass outboard canoes zip around the bay. Just across Choiseul Bay from Taro is **Tarekukure** where some 300 students board at Choiseul Bay Secondary School. During WW II, Japanese troops excavated tunnels in the coral rock below the school, and they also built a wharf still used to load and unload the copra kept in a warehouse near the school. In recent years Eagon Resources has built a network of logging roads inland from the wharf, and round logs awaiting export can be seen piled up nearby.

The locals often take their motorized canoes a couple of km up the winding Sui River directly east of Taro to a high cascade where they collect fresh water, do their washing, and have a swim. If you offer to supply five liters of petrol, it shouldn't be that hard to convince someone to go. It's a scenic 30-minute trip up the river between the mangroves, and at low tide you might even spot the odd crocodile on a sandbank. These animals are thought to embody the spirits of ancestors, and are thus protected from hunters. In return, no crocodile attack has ever been recorded here.

A logging road runs across Choiseul from Tarekukure wharf to **Chirovanga,** connecting halfway with a road south to a big logging camp opposite Mole Island. Chirovanga, on the northeast side of Choiseul, is a Catholic mission station with a church on a hill overlooking the sea. About 10 villages lie inland from the mission, and traditional pottery is still made in this area. You'll find a waterfall on the Tarapa River near Mamarana village.

Accommodations and Food

The **Provincial Resthouse** (Box 34, Taro, Choiseul Bay), the long yellow building overlooking the soccer field, 200 meters from Taro's airport terminal, is SI$20 per bed in the seven double rooms (SI$40 if you want a room to yourself). A shared kitchen is available in this new one-story building. Shoestring.

Billy's Resthouse (Billy Savevai, Box 29, Taro, Choiseul Bay) is a comfortable resthouse above the National Bank, near the air terminal. The four airy rooms with shared bath are SI$25 pp, and a kitchen is downstairs. It's clean and has a generator in case the public electrical supply goes out. Billy is one of the chiefs of this area, and his outboard motorboat is available for trips. Shoestring.

Near Taro wharf are four or five small grocery stores with rice, noodles, tinned fish, and biscuits. A bakery is next to Billy's Resthouse.

On Tuesday and Friday mornings a market forms near the wharf at Taro. On Saturday mornings, there's a small market near Choiseul Bay Secondary School at Tarekukure, just across the bay. If your luggage isn't overweight, bring food from Gizo or Honiara.

Getting There

Solomon Airlines flies direct to Choiseul Bay (CHY) from Gizo (166 km, SI$140) and Honiara (SI$375) five times a week, from Ballalae (66 km, SI$80) three times a week, and from Munda (SI$175) twice a week.

The real way to "do" Choiseul, however, is to take a weeklong trip around the island on the fortnightly National Shipping Services supply ship. You might visit up to 45 villages this way, some only for a few minutes to drop off passengers, some others for a few hours. As almost all the villages are on the coast, you get good value for your money. Smaller boats arrive at Choiseul Bay from Gizo.

Vaghena

Since 1963, a large Gilbertese community has been resettled on Vaghena (Wagina) Island off the southeast end of Choiseul. The original Melanesian inhabitants of Vaghena were wiped out by headhunters from Choiseul. Vaghena's 78 square km of uplifted coral contain significant bauxite deposits considered not economically viable to mine. The Choiseul boat stops at Vaghena both north- and southbound, and there are also flights.

Solomon Airlines flies to Vaghena (KGE) twice a week from Honiara (SI$275) and weekly from Munda (SI$110) and Gizo (SI$115). A German cattle rancher named Eric lives on the small airport island Kagau and serves as the local Solomon Airlines agent. You can contact him by radio telephone, and it might be possible to arrange a place to stay. Kagau has lovely white sandy beaches but the three villages on Vaghena are a 45-minute canoe ride southeast of Kagau.

ISABEL PROVINCE

Named for Álvaro de Mendaña's wife, Isabel's 240-km-long northwest-southeast landmass is the longest in the Solomons, and at 4,588 square km, it's the second-largest island in the country. The indigenous name for Isabel is Bughotu. The jungly interior is thick with towering vine-clad trunks and umbrella ferns, forming a habitat for monitor lizards and an array of birds. On small islands such as Leghahana near Sisiga Point off the northeast coast are flightless megapode birds.

Headhunters from Simbo and the Roviana Lagoon depopulated much of northern Isabel during the early 1800s, and today most of the inhabitants live in the southeast corner of the island, the point farthest away from New Georgia. As in Santa Cruz, most extended families on Isabel are matrilineal; descent and land pass through the mother. Some villages like Kia have quite an assortment of husbands from all around the Solomons! Almost the entire population of Isabel belongs to the Church of Melanesia. One of the Pacific's rarest varieties of tapa originates on Isabel: stained pale blue with a leaf dye.

Southeast Isabel

The administrative center is at **Buala** (population 2,000) on the Maringe Lagoon in southeast Isabel. The seven-room **Mothers' Union Rest-**

house (tel. 35035) in Buala provides accommodations with cooking facilities at around SI$33 pp. This Church of Melanesia-operated place is super friendly, provided you don't drink. The six-room **Provincial Government Resthouse** (tel. 35031) is SI$15 pp. The **Diocesan Resthouse** (tel. 35011) has nine rooms at SI$38 pp, and you can cook. A video center of sorts, post office, police station, and a good hospital (tel. 35016) complete the amenities of Buala.

An hour's walk southeast of Buala is **Tholana Falls,** where the Sana River falls straight into the sea. The river dries up during the dry season. Another hour or two inland from the falls is Hirotonga village, with a sweeping view of the entire Maringe Lagoon and even Malaita. You can also climb Mt. Kubonitu (1,392 meters), just southwest of Buala and the highest peak on Isabel.

Transportation

Solomon Airlines has flights from Honiara (156 km, SI$130) three times a week to the airstrip (FRE) on Fera, a four-km-long offshore island from which motorized canoes cross to Buala (SI$5 pp).

Ships ply between Honiara and Buala about weekly, while government boats cover this route about once a month. The high-speed vessel *Ocean Express* leaves Buala for Honiara Wednesday at 0800 (SI$55). The National Shipping ships *Leili* or *Butai* go right around Isabel in four or five days every two weeks with stops at about 15 villages. One especially attractive stop is Furona Island halfway down the west coast. Only Buala, Kia, and Keavanga have wharves. Whenever possible, the government boat spends the weekend at Buala.

MAKIRA/ULAWA PROVINCE

Makira (San Cristobal) has some level land in the north, but the south coast falls precipitously to the sea. **Makira Harbor,** on the southwest coast, is the most secure anchorage in the Solomons, and **Star Harbor,** at the east end of the island, is also good. In 1595 the *Santa Isabel,* one of the four ships of Mendaña's ill-fated second expedition, became separated from the others at Santa Cruz. It sailed on to Makira, where passengers and crew camped on a hilltop at Pamua on the north coast, west of Kirakira (near the site of the present St. Stephen's Anglican Secondary School). Their eventual fate is unknown.

Remote caves in Makira's inaccessible interior are rumored to be inhabited by the **Kakamora,** a race of midgets a meter tall who have been called "the leprechauns of the Pacific." They go naked, have very small teeth, and their long straight hair comes down to their knees. Most are harmless, but some Kakamora have been known to attack other men. It's said that one Kakamora is as strong as three or four men. Unfortunately, however, the Kakamora are probably more myth than fact.

Local craft items include carved figures, black inlaid ceremonial food bowls from Santa Ana, and talking drums.

KIRAKIRA AND AROUND

Ships and planes between Honiara and Santa Cruz call at Kirakira (population 3,000), the administrative center of the province, on the middle north coast of Makira. This verdant little town with huge trees shading its sleepy streets and inaccessible slopes rising behind is untouched by tourism. There are few specific attractions around Kirakira, just the chance to observe the quiet life of a small provincial settlement and enjoy some pleasant walks in the area. The National Bank opposite the post office will change traveler's checks.

Sights

A Santa Ana-style custom house stands next to the soccer field in the center of Kirakira. Nearby, fiberglass canoes are pulled up on the shore by the concrete breakwater. A bit south is the mouth of Puepue Creek with the market alongside, and from here a long brown beach stretches west almost to the airstrip, a 20-minute walk away. At low tide it's worth going out on the reef beyond the airstrip to watch the waves surging through the deep rock crevices here.

The road behind the resthouse leads north to a large coconut plantation with a small white beach halfway to Honighoro Point, another nice walk.

Roads run along Makira's north coast in both directions from Kirakira, 18 km east to the Warihito River and about 100 km west to Maro'u Bay. The road west is well maintained as far as St. Stephens High School at Pamua, but west of Pamua it deteriorates and there are many rivers to ford (no bridges). Two-thirds of the way along, another road cuts south to Omaanihioro on the south coast. A settlement of Tikopian people is at Nukukaisi, 34 km west of Kirakira. Solomon Mamaloni's Malaysian-backed logging company, Soma Ltd., is busy cutting down western Makira.

Taratarau village is a pleasant 20-minute walk east of Kirakira, past some huge betel nut trees. It's typical of rural leaf villages all around the island, and there's a small brown beach a bit beyond. The walking beyond Taratarau is not productive as you can't see a lot from the unshaded road. The Ravo River, eight km east of Kirakira, must be forded, and from here a high brown beach stretches along Wanione Bay, east from Arohane. The heavy surf stirs up the sand and makes it unsuitable for swimming.

Several footpaths cross the island from the vicinity of Kirakira, including one via the Maghoha River to Marunga Harbor, and another up the Maepua River to Apurahe Bay. On both it's necessary to spend one night in the bush halfway up and a guide would be required.

Uki and the Three Sisters are flat islands, yet still visible on the horizon from Kirakira. Crocodiles inhabit a pool on Malaupaina Island, largest of the Three Sisters. There's a lovely white sandy beach and coral lagoon at Pio Island, northwest of Uki. To hire a canoe from Kirakira to Pio would cost SI$50 for the canoe, plus SI$110 for fuel. Ask at the provincial fisheries office near the landing in Kirakira.

Accommodations and Food

The nine-room **Kirakira Provincial Resthouse** (tel. 50076) provides Spartan fan-cooled accommodations with shared bathing and cooking facilities at SI$20 pp. To book, call the accounts clerk at the provincial office. The resthouse has water problems. Shoestring.

The market down by the river only has a good selection of foods in the morning. However, you can get betelnuts and coconuts all day, plus fish and chips, and often pineapples.

A schoolteacher named John Wyhiro runs the **Hauta Ecotourism Camp** in the Bauro Highlands up the Ravo River, inland from Arohane. You must cross the river numerous times on the half day hike from Kirakira, and the climb into the highlands is strenuous. At 700 meters elevation, Hauta and nearby Hunama are cool and free of mosquitoes, and there are nice places to swim in the river. John can be contacted by radio between 0800 and 0830 from the Telecom office in Kirakira, and information may also be available through the Solomon Islands Development Trust office in Honiara. People come here on prearranged ecotours from Australia (www.caa.org.au/travel), and this one of the best places in the country to observe butterflies and birds.

Transportation

Solomon Airlines (tel. 50198) flies to Kirakira from Honiara (237 km, SI$180) four times a week, and from Santa Cruz (429 km, SI$305) twice weekly. For good views, sit on the right side of the aircraft on the way from Honiara to Kirakira. Ngorangora Airstrip (IRA) is three km west of Kirakira by road, and you can easily hitch a ride into town.

The ship *Bulawa,* owned by the Makira/Ulawa provincial government, is based at Kirakira, and travels to Honiara every two weeks (tickets sold on board). In Honiara, inquire at National Shipping Services. The ship also does trips right around Makira, or to Ugi, Ulawa, and the Three Sisters. In past, the MV *Ocean Express* has traveled Honiara-Marau Sound-Kirakira on Friday, and it's always worth checking. Also ask about ships to Star Harbor, Santa Ana, and Santa Catalina, the most beautiful areas in the province. No wharf is available at Kirakira, and passengers and cargo must go ashore by canoe or aluminum longboat.

There are no regular passenger trucks with set fares around Kirakira, and the big trucks you see with loads of passengers in back are either privately owned or have been hired by someone. It's possible to hitch rides in these, and the favorite places to wait are in front of the store next to the Catholic church if you're headed east, or at the store between the hospital and public works garage if westbound.

TEMOTU PROVINCE

Temotu Province, 665 km east of Honiara, is by far the most remote of the major island groupings. It's closer to the northernmost islands of Vanuatu than it is to the rest of Solomon Islands. Included are 43-by-24-km Santa Cruz, the Reef Islands, the Duff Islands, and the high islands of Utupua and Vanikolo. Tinakula, just north of Santa Cruz, is a surpassingly graceful, almost symmetrical, active volcano. The Reef Islands are composed of low coral terraces and sandy cays, while the others are mostly volcanic, with steep jungle slopes. Hundreds of kilometers southeast are tiny Tikopia and Anuta.

The Melanesians settled on the larger islands, the Polynesians on the smaller, more isolated outliers. *Lapita* pottery has been found on both Santa Cruz and the Reef Islands. A dozen languages are spoken in Temotu Province, and intriguingly, all of the non-Polynesian languages are Papuan.

The first European to arrive was the Spaniard Mendaña, who attempted to establish a colony at the south end of Graciosa Bay on Santa Cruz in 1595. Days later, when mutiny set in, Mendaña went ashore and executed his camp commander. After Mendaña himself died here on 18 October 1595, the settlement was abandoned. The crew, sick and dying, called Santa Cruz "a corner of hell in the claws on the devil." Of Mendaña's 378 men, death claimed 47 within a

month. The next to arrive was Carteret, on 12 August 1767. As he anchored off Santa Cruz, he observed a "wild country and black, naked, woolly-haired natives."

The province is famous for its feather money, and a single roll can bear the red feathers of 3,000 scarlet honeyeaters stuck onto a coiled band as much as 10 meters long. The honeyeater is a very territorial bird, and to capture it the islanders would use a decoy to lure the bird to a branch where its feet would become stuck with a type of glue. After some feathers were taken, the bird would be released. Feathers from the gray Pacific pigeon were used as a backing. Feather money was traded for women and canoes from Santa Cruz to the Reefs and Taumako. Ten belts was the traditional price of a bride (widows half price).

SANTA CRUZ

Santa Cruz (Nendo) is by far the largest island of Temotu Province, its densely wooded hills rising to a height of 517 meters. The island has considerable reserves of bauxite. The mangrove-fringed south and east coasts contrast with the rocky northern shores, where fine beaches are often found. The usual rule here is "sun in the

Uninhabited 800-meter-high Tinakula Island in Temotu Province is the most active volcano in the Solomons. In 1595 one of Mendaña's ships sank near Tinakula, which was erupting at the time. This photo shows the island during the brief 1971 eruption.

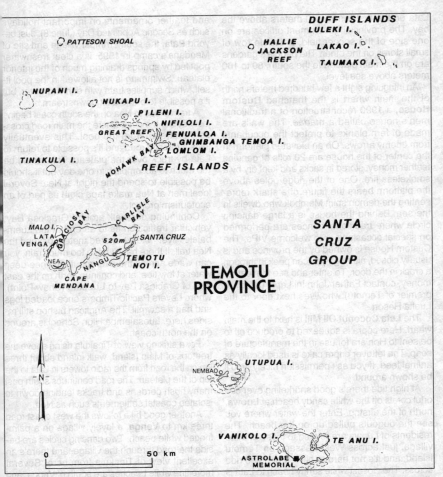

morning means rain in the afternoon, while rain in the morning means rain all day," but recently these islands have suffered prolonged droughts.

The administrative center of Temotu Province is at **Lata** (population 1,500), at the northwest corner of Santa Cruz on the west side of Graciosa Bay. Malo (Temotu) Island partly closes this bay to the north. The airstrip and wharf are both within minutes of Lata.

At Venga, on the sandy west shore of Santa Cruz, people perform custom dances unchanged

since time immemorial. Dancers at Banua village wear traditional shell and feather ornaments as they dance and sing around a betel tree all night. August and September are the best months to see custom dancing on Santa Cruz, but no dancing at all takes place in Temotu Province during Lent (the 40 days before Easter).

Sights

The heavily populated area west of Graciosa Bay consists of a series of coral terraces, with the

Lata on the first terrace 40 meters above the bay. The provincial government offices are on one side of the soccer field, a double row of small stores on the other. The people's gardens are on the main plateau to the south, 80 to 160 meters above sea level.

An intriguing sight a few hundred meters north of the main wharf is the thatched **Custom House**, a 1990 reconstruction of a traditional men's house called a *madae*. The walls are made of fern planks to protect the occupants from enemy arrows. On an elevated platform in the center of the house are 20 rolls of genuine feather money, stored in sacks and kept dry by a smokeless fire. One of the ridge poles above the platform bears the figure of a shark representing the demon spirit Membok who dwells in the sea. Behind the house is a large dancing circle where traditional dances are performed on special occasions or to welcome VIPs. The Custom House is owned by the province and is usually closed, although you can peek in through a crack in the door. To enter and see the feather money, contact Father John Ini Lapai (a former premier of Temotu) who lives next door to the Luelta Resort.

The **Lata Coconut Oil Mill** is next to the main wharf. Here copra is squeezed to produce oil to be sent to Honiara for use in the manufacture of soap. The leftover copra cake is used locally as animal feed. If you ask permission nicely, you'll be shown around.

At high tide there's good snorkeling over colorful corals off the white sandy beach at **Luowa**, north of the airstrip. Enter the water where you see the dugouts pulled up on the beach. The residents of Luowa are related to those of Malo village, just across West Passage on Temotu Island, and it's not hard to hitch a paddled ride across. The closest white sandy beach to Lata is at **Nela**, a small collection of houses just south of the west end of the airstrip.

The seven-km road south along the west side of Graciosa Bay passes 14 beautifully situated villages. Each day the villagers scale the forested cliffs behind the coastal strip to plant taro, sweet potatoes, bananas, pineapples, green peppers, pumpkins, manioc, and cabbage to feed their families or to sell at Lata market. Most of the villages have a dancing circle visible from the main road, where dancers adorn themselves with shell

and feather ornaments on important holidays such as Second Appointed Day (June 8). Just beyond **Pala,** the southernmost village and site of Mendaña's camp in 1595, is a clear freshwater pool fed by springs draining much of the interior plateau. Swimming is not allowed in the pool itself, which supplies Lata with drinking water, but it's possible to bathe a bit downstream.

A trail across to **Nea** on the south coast begins just beyond the point where the main road crosses the stream from the pool. This eventually joins a forestry road and it's possible to return to Lata by truck over the plateau. This would be too much to accomplish in one day but it should be possible to spend the night at Nea. Several local men at Nea make tapa cloth as part of an ecotourism project.

Continuing our walk around Graciosa Bay, vehicular traffic comes to an end at the Luembalele River, a few hundred meters beyond the Nea trail. If there hasn't been too much rain, you can wade across the river mouth in knee deep water at low tide, and continue north up the east side of Graciosa Bay to **Luesalo** (Shaw Point), where Levers Pacific Timbers once loaded logs and had a sawmill. The Anglican bishop still resides here. Luesalemba High School is around on the north coast.

For a striking view of Tinakula rising above the treetops of Malo Island, walk inland about three km on the road from the radio towers in Lata to the top of the plateau. The road continues south past many bush gardens and tracks leading down to isolated coastal settlements such as Nea.

Another good hike follows the west coast road three km to **Venga**, a lovely village on a palm-fringed white beach. Two dancing circles are beside the road through the village, and there's an excellent view of Tinakula from here. Several more fine white beaches are south of Venga, and lush rainforests on the steep side of the plateau.

An anchor allegedly from one of Mendaña's ships lies on the south side of **Nemba** village, on the coast eight km southwest of Venga. Of course, it's of much more recent origin, yet the villagers still demand custom fees as high as SI$200 just to set eyes on it. Thus it's prudent to show no interest at all if you happen to pass through Nemba. An excited crowd will gather if you approach the anchor, or even stop to look at it from the main road, and you'll probably end up having to pay something, so take care.

The coastal road ends at **Banyo** and only a coastal footpath goes on to Nea. A footpath climbs up onto the plateau from Banyo, allowing a return to Lata by the plateau road for a full-day circle trip. It's also possible to climb up onto the plateau from Nemba and this would be much shorter than going via Banyo, if you can avoid getting ensnared in the anchor scam.

At the entrance to Carlisle Bay on the north shore of Santa Cruz is an overgrown memorial to Commodore Goodenough, killed here in 1875. The scenic white beach and good yacht anchorage are Carlisle Bay's other attractions.

Canoe your way to Nangu on the south coast, where there's a damaged wharf, store, radio operator, etc. Temotu Noi Island, just 15 minutes from Nangu by outboard, has a crocodile-infested freshwater lake.

Accommodations
The Temotu Development Authority operates the **Lata Resthouse** (Box 49, Lata, Santa Cruz; tel./fax 53145), at the end of the road to the left of the SIBC Santa Cruz studio. The five rooms with shared bath, cooking facilities, and fridge are SI$20 pp. There are chronic water problems here, and some of the rooms have awful sagging beds. No fans are provided. Otherwise it's in a nice hilltop location and is fine. You could have difficulty finding the caretaker to get a room unless you booked ahead. Shoestring.

The best place to stay is the new **Diocese of Temotu Transit House** (Box 50, Lata, Nendo; tel. 53120, fax 53092), a 24-room conference center operated by the Church of Melanesia at Luowa, a 20-minute walk from the airport terminal toward the beach. In addition to the double rooms, there are four large 20-bed dormitories, and cooking facilities are provided. Information is available at the church bookstore next to the National Bank in Lata.

Lata's only real hotel is **Luelta Resort** (Box 42, Lata; tel. 53144, fax 53115), 100 meters south of the main wharf, run by the Solomon Airlines agent, Simon Barclay. The 12 small rooms in this two-story building are SI$30 pp. Each has a fan, but the toilets and showers are in a separate block. Cooking facilities are not provided but dinner can be ordered for SI$15. On weekends the Luelta's bar is the favorite local drinking

place, and to avoid loud music or video noise, you should ask for an upstairs room on the side facing away from the restaurant. If you find the atmosphere in the bar insalubrious, you can sit and drink on the upstairs balcony, still enjoying a good view of everything. Shoestring.

Brown Teai, nicknamed "Paul," runs a rest-house at Freshwater Point, 50 meters north of the wharf via a footpath along the shore. There's a small beach just below the rocks and a cooling sea breeze, but the facilities are basic (SI$20 pp). Gas cooking and electric lighting may or may not be available. Still, it's friendly, and the location is the nicest of any of Lata's places to stay. Shoestring.

Food
George Pea's **PLGP Snack Shop** (tel. 53095), among the row of small grocery shops facing the soccer field, theoretically opens Mon.-Sat. 0600-2200.

Some fruit and vegetables are also sold under the large mango tree across the street from the National Bank up on the plateau (check again in the afternoon when people return from their gardens). More of the same is also sold every Wednesday and Saturday morning, when a small produce market forms under the trees near the wharf. The Fisheries Department by the wharf sells fresh fish.

Services and Information
The National Bank has an agency at Lata that changes foreign currency. The Immigration office (tel. 53061), between the hospital and the Telecom dish up on the plateau, will give visa extensions, and yachts can check in and out here. If they're closed, ask at the police station on the next corner.

Transportation
Solomon Airlines (tel. 53157) arrives at Santa Cruz (SCZ) twice a week from Honiara (647 km, SI$455) and Kirakira (428 km, SI$305). The flights are often full between Honiara and Kirakira, but seats are usually available between Kirakira and Santa Cruz. Overweight luggage is SI$6.50 a kilo. Solomon Airlines has an office (usually closed) 150 meters east of the airport terminal.

Ships tie up to the wharf on the west side of Graciosa Bay just below Lata. The Commodities Export Marketing Authority (tel. 53062), behind the coconut mill near the wharf, should have information on their monthly chartered ship to Honiara (SI$105) and the Reef Islands (SI$50). A National Shipping boat, the MV *Butai,* makes roundtrips Lata-Mohawk Bay-Nangu-Utupua-Vanikolo-Lata about once a month (SI$84 deck one-way). National Shipping Services doesn't have an office at Lata, and for information on the arrival date of their ship you must call Honiara.

Ask around the wharf for outboards to Nangu or the Reef Islands and contribute for gas. Fisheries near the wharf rents out their large motorized canoe with driver at SI$65 a day plus petrol.

OTHER ISLANDS

The Reef Islands

These low coral islands, 70 km northeast of Graciosa Bay, have long sandy beaches and no malaria. The inhabitants are mostly Melanesians, excepting the Polynesians on tiny Nifiloli and Pileni, as well as Nupani Island to the northwest. Nalogo, a tiny islet near Nupani, is home to tens of thousands of sea birds. Gnimbanga or Temoa Island has a series of caverns containing freshwater pools. Anglican bishop J.C. Patteson was murdered on Nukapu in 1871 after a blackbirding ship spread ill will throughout the area.

One of the remotest outer island resorts in the South Pacific is the **Ngarando Faraway Resort** on Pigeon Island, Mohawk Bay. The accommodations on offer are Ngarando House, a European-style bungalow with two bedrooms at SI$134/215 single/double; and Nanivo Cottage, a leaf house costing slightly less. Both units have shower, toilet, and cooking facilities. Meals with the host family cost SI$22/32/54 for breakfast/lunch/dinner (add 10% tax to all charges). Cash payment only will be accepted. Videos are shown for SI$5, and the resort's satellite dish picks up TV stations from around the world. Snorkeling gear, canoes, and outboards are provided free (you pay only for the gas). There's excellent snorkeling, and scuba-diving gear is for rent (certification card required). You can contact Ngarando by radio telephone from the Telecom office in Lata for SI$3. Inexpensive.

Ngarando is run by the Hepworth clan, including twin brothers Bressin and Ross and their mother Diana, a colorful bunch of genuine South Seas characters who've been here longer than anyone can remember. In 1997 Ross Hepworth was elected president of Temotu Province. The Hepworth's general store sells local vegetables, fresh fruit and fish, canned groceries, and other trade goods as if this were still the 19th century. The wild parrots add to Pigeon Island's veritable Robinson Crusoe air.

Transfers from Graciosa Bay to Pigeon Island are by motorized canoe, a three-hour, 100-km trip, costing SI$270/350/400 for two/three/four persons. Construction of an airstrip on adjacent Lomlom Island has been pending for years. Check with National Shipping Services in Honiara for a government ship direct to Mohawk Bay.

The Duff Islands

The Duff Islands, 88 km northeast of the Reef Islands, consist of nine small volcanic islands in a line 27 km long. Taumako Island, the largest, is 366 meters high. The inhabitants are Polynesian.

Vanikolo

This Melanesian volcanic island (also called Vanikoro) was stripped of its kauri trees by an Australian firm earlier this century. Both ships of the La Pérouse expedition, the *Boussole* and the *Astrolabe,* were wrecked on the reef at Vanikolo during a terrible storm in 1788. Despite a search for La Pérouse by d'Entrecasteaux four years later, his fate was unknown to the world for four decades until Irish sea captain Peter Dillon happened upon the remains in 1826 and solved the mystery (Dillon was knighted by the French government and given a pension for his efforts). Two years later, Dumont d'Urville visited Vanikolo, recovered some cannon and anchors, and set up a memorial to La Pérouse on the south side of the island.

The two wrecked French frigates are about 500 meters apart on the northwest side of the island. From the wreckage, archaeologists have theorized that the *Boussole* dropped its anchors as it was driven toward the reef; the ship swung round and had its stern ripped apart. Evidently, the *Astrolabe* tried to go through a false pass nearby in an attempt to rescue the crew of the first ship from behind, but was also wrecked. The Vanikolo people told Peter Dillon how the French survivors had built a small ship from the wreckage

the monument to French explorer La Pérouse on Vanikolo Island, Solomon Islands

and sailed away. Their eventual fate has never been learned, but even today expeditions continue to visit Vanikolo in search of more relics of this dramatic episode in Pacific history.

TIKOPIA AND ANUTA

Tikopia

This three-by-five-km dot in the ocean, 120 km southwest of the nearest other dot (Anuta), is an ancient volcano with a crater lake, Te Roto, rising to 366 meters. Pandanus trees surround the brackish lake waters, which are home to ducks and fish. The inhabitants of both Tikopia and Anuta are Polynesians who arrived in planned expeditions from Wallis Island some 14 generations ago. Wallis itself was colonized from Tonga, thus this is an outpost of the old Tongan culture. Anthropologist Raymond Firth did fieldwork here in 1928-29, and his book *We, The Tikopia* is still the classic on the island. Firth returned in 1952 and wrote *Social Change in Tikopia*.

Tikopia and Anuta are the southern and eastern limits of betel chewing in the Pacific. Kava was last made on Tikopia in the 1950s in connection with the traditional religion. Now if someone arrives from Fiji with powdered kava, people will mix and drink it mainly out of curiosity. Kava plants are said to still grow on Tikopia, but nobody bothers to harvest them, probably because the church is against it and also out of respect for sacred sites and paraphernalia.

Shops, government offices, and police don't exist on Tikopia, though there is a well-equipped clinic at Faea and a two-way radio. Visitors can usually stay at the nurse's house near the clinic for a small fee. The reef is the only toilet. Take care with the amiable chief of Faea District and his family, as they're out to get what they can—be it in the nicest way—and will give a distorted view of the place. Spend more time in Ravenga and Namo districts; the three chiefs of Ravenga are all very welcoming.

Very few people speak English; Pidgin or a Polynesian language are more useful. It's forbidden to purchase old artifacts from the people; if you do, the chiefs will confiscate the goodies. Bring mosquito repellent.

Anuta

Anuta is the easternmost inhabited island of the Solomons. It's less than a kilometer across and 65 meters high. The people speak a language related to Samoan, and it's ruled by two traditional chiefs whose genealogies go back to the 16th century. Radiocarbon dating reveals that the first habitation was around 900 BC. Anuta was abandoned around 500 AD, only to be resettled a few centuries later. Like Tikopia, the influence of the Solomon Islands government is minimal here, and many people still dress in tapa, though some of the young now wear Western garb. Advance permission is required to stay on the island. Fatutaka Island (Mitre), 42 km southeast of Anuta, is uninhabited.

CAPSULE SOLOMON ISLANDS PIJIN VOCABULARY

aesboks—refrigerator
arakwao—white man
bagarap—broken down
bele ran—diarrhea
belo—noon
bia blong Solomon—betel nut
basta yu man!—damn you!
bulumakao—cattle

daedae—to be in love with

garem—to have
gudfala—nice

haomas?—how much?
hem i stap wea?—where is he (it)?

iu go baek!—go away!

kabilato—loincloth
kabis—edible greens
kago—luggage, goods
kaikai—food
kalabus—jail
kaliko—clothes

kasem—to reach
kastom kaliko—traditional dress
kastom mani—traditional currency
katkat wani—hey good lookin!
koko—penis
kokorako—chicken
klosap—near, close
kros—angry

liu—jobless
longwe—far
luksave—to recognize

mere—woman
mifala—us
mi no save—I don't understand
moabetta—better

naes bola!—hey good lookin!
nambaten—the worst
nambawan—the best
nating—no

pikinini—child

raosem—to clear out

saedgo—that side
saedkam—this side
samting nating—it doesn't matter
sapos—if
save—to know
save tumas—wise
smol rod—footpath
staka—plenty
susu—milk, breast

taem bifoa—the past
tanggio tumas—thank you very much

wanem—what did you say?
wantok—kinsperson
waswas—shower, swim
waswe—why
wetim—with

yumi—we

mole cowries (Cypraea talpa)

RESOURCES
INFORMATION OFFICES

REGIONAL

Tourism Council of the South Pacific, Box 13119, Suva, Fiji Islands, tel. 679/304-177, fax 679/301-995, www.tcsp.com; e-mail: spice@is.com.fj

Tourism Council of the South Pacific, Box 7440, Tahoe City, CA 96145, U.S.A. tel.1-530/583-0152, fax 1-530/583-0154, e-mail: HPascal@compuserve.com

Tourism Council of the South Pacific, 203 Sheen Lane, East Sheen, London SW14 8LE, United Kingdom, tel. 44-181/878-9876, fax 44-181/878-9955, e-mail: ajbalfour@aol.com

Tourism Council of the South Pacific, Petersburger Strasse 94, D-10247 Berlin, Germany, tel. 49-304/225-6027, fax 49-304/225-6287, e-mail: tcsp.de@interface-tourism.com

Pacific Asia Travel Association, One Montgomery St., Telesis Tower, Suite 1000, San Francisco, CA 94104-4539, U.S.A., tel. 1-415/986-4646, fax 1-415/986-3458, www.pata.org, e-mail: patahq@pata.org

Pata Pacific Division, Box 645, Kings Cross, NSW 2001, Australia, tel. 61-2/9332-3599, fax 61-2/9331-6592, e-mail: pata@world.net

TAHITI-POLYNESIA

Tahiti Tourisme, B.P. 65, Papeete, 98713 Tahiti, Polynésie Française, tel. 689/50-57-00, fax 689/43-66-19, www.tahiti-tourisme.com, e-mail: tahiti-tourisme@mail.pf

Tahiti Tourisme, 300 North Continental Blvd., Suite 160, El Segundo, CA 90245, U.S.A., tel. 1-310/414-8484, fax 1-310/414-8490, e-mail: tahitilax@earthlink.net

Tahiti Tourisme, 36 Douglas St., Ponsonby, Auckland, New Zealand, tel. 64-9/360-8880, fax 64-9/360-8891, e-mail: renae@tahiti-tourisme.co.nz

Tahiti Tourisme, 620 St. Kilda Rd., Suite 301, Melbourne 3004, Victoria, Australia, tel. 61-3/9521-3877, fax 61-3/9521-3867, www.ozemail.com.au/~tahiti, e-mail: tahiti@ozemail.com.au

Pacific Leisure Group, 8th floor, Maneeya Center Building, 518/5 Ploenchit Rd., Bangkok 10330, Thailand, tel. 66-2/652-0507, fax 66-2/652-0509, e-mail: eckard@plgroup.com

Tahiti Tourisme, Sankyo Building (No. 20) Room 802, 3-11-5 Ildabashi, Chiyoda-Ku, Tokyo 102, Japan, tel. 81-3/3265-0468, fax 81-3/3265-0581

Oficina de Turismo de Tahiti, Casilla 16057, Santiago 9, Chile, tel. 56-2/251-2826, fax 56-2/251-2725, e-mail: tahiti@cmet.net

Office du Tourisme de Tahiti, 28 Boulevard Saint-Germain, 75005 Paris, France, tel. 33-1/5542-6121, fax 33-1/5542-6120, e-mail: tahitipar@calva.net

Fremdenverkehrsbüro von Tahiti, Bockenheimer Landstrasse 45, D-60325 Frankfurt/Main, Germany, tel. 49-69/971-484, fax 49-69/729-275

Tahiti Tourisme, Piazza Castello 11, 20121 Milano, Italy, tel. 39-2/7202-2329, fax 39-2/7202-2306, e-mail: staff@aigo.com

EASTER ISLAND

Servicio Nacional de Turismo, Avenida Providencia 1550, Santiago de Chile, Chile, tel. 56-2/236-1420, fax 56-2/236-1417, www.segegob.cl/sernatur/inicio.html, e-mail: sernatur@ctc-mundo.net

COOK ISLANDS

Cook Islands Tourism Corporation, Box 14, Rarotonga, Cook Islands, tel. 682/29-435, fax 682/21-435, www.cook-islands.com, e-mail: tourism@cookislands.gov.ck

Cook Islands Tourism Corporation, 5757 West Century Blvd., Suite 660, Los Angeles, CA 90045-6407, U.S.A., tel. 1-310/641-5621, fax 1-310/338-0708, e-mail: cooks@itr-aps.com

Cook Islands Tourism Corporation, 1/127 Symonds St., Box 37391, Parnell, Auckland, New Zealand, tel. 64-9/366-1100, fax 64-9/309-1876

Cook Islands Tourism Corporation, Box H95, Hurlstone Park, NSW 2193, Australia, tel. 61-2/9955-0446, fax 61-2/9955-0447, e-mail: cookislands@speednet.com.au

Pacific Leisure, Tung Ming Building, 40 Des Voeux Rd., Central, Box 2382, Hong Kong, China, tel. 852/2525-1365, fax 852/2525-3290

NIUE

Niue Tourism Office, Box 42, Alofi, Niue, tel. 683/4224, fax 683/4225, www.niueisland.com, e-mail: niuetourism@mail.gov.nu

Niue Tourism Office, Box 68-541, Newton, Auckland, New Zealand, tel. 64-9/366-0716, fax 64-9/308-9720, e-mail: niuetourism@clear.net.nz

KINGDOM OF TONGA

Tonga Visitors Bureau, Box 37, Nuku'alofa, Kingdom of Tonga, tel. 676/21-733, fax 676/23-507, www.vacations.tvb.gov.to, e-mail: tvb@kalianet.to

Tonga Visitors Bureau, Box 18, Neiafu, Vava'u, Kingdom of Tonga, tel. 676/70-115, fax 676/70-630, e-mail: tvbvv@kalianet.to

Tonga Visitors Bureau, 4605 Driftwood Court, El Sobrante, CA 94803-1805, U.S.A., tel. 1-510/223-1381, fax 1-510/758-6227, e-mail: tonga@value.net

Tongan Consulate, 360 Post St., Suite 604, San Francisco, CA 94108, U.S.A., tel. 1-415/781-0365, fax 1-415/781-3964, e-mail: tania@sfconsulate.gov.to

Tonga Visitors Bureau, 642 King St., Newtown, Sydney, NSW 2042, Australia, tel. 61-2/9519-9700, fax 61-2/9519-9419

Tonga Visitors Bureau, Box 24-054, Royal Oak, Auckland 1003, New Zealand, tel. 64-9/634-1519, fax 64-9/636-8973

Tongan High Commission, 36 Molyneux St., London W1H 6AB, United Kingdom, tel. 44-71/724-5828, fax 44-171/723-9074

AMERICAN SAMOA

Office of Tourism, Box 1147, Pago Pago, American Samoa 96799, U.S.A., tel. 684/633-1091, fax 684/633-1094, www.samoanet.com/americansamoa,e-mail: samoa@samoatelco.com

SAMOA

Samoa Visitors Bureau, Box 2272, Apia, Samoa, tel. 685/26-500, fax 685/20-886, www.samoa.co.nz, e-mail: samoa@samoa.net

Samoa Visitors Bureau, 1800 112th Ave. N.E., Suite 220E, Bellevue, WA 98004-2939, U.S.A., tel. 1-425/688-8513, fax 1-425/688-8514, e-mail: SDSI@compuserve.com

Samoa Visitors Bureau, Box 361, Minto Mall, Minto, NSW 2566, Australia, tel. 61-2/9824-5050, fax 61-2/9824-5678, e-mail: samoa@ozemail.com.au

Samoa Visitors Bureau, Level 1, Samoa House, 283 Karangahape Rd., Box 68-423, Newton, Auckland, New Zealand, tel. 64-9/379-6138, fax 64-9/379-8154, e-mail: samoa@samoa.co.nz

TOKELAU

Office for Tokelau Affairs, Box 865, Apia, Samoa, tel. 685/20-822, fax 685/21-761

TUVALU

Ministry of Tourism, Trade, and Commerce, Private Mail Bag, Vaiaku, Funafuti, Tuvalu, tel. 688/20184, fax 688/20829

Tuvalu Embassy, Box 14449, Suva, Fiji Islands, tel. 679/301-355, fax 679/301-023

FIJI ISLANDS

Fiji Visitors Bureau, Box 92, Suva, Fiji Islands, tel. 679/302-433, fax 679/300-970; www.fijifvb.gov.fj or www.bulafiji.com; e-mail: infodesk@fijifvb.gov.fj

Fiji Visitors Bureau, Box 9217, Nadi Airport, Fiji Islands, tel. 679/722-433, fax 679/720-141, e-mail: fvbnadi@is.com.fj

Fiji Visitors Bureau, Suite 220,
5777 West Century Blvd., Los
Angeles, CA 90045, U.S.A., tel.
1-310/568-1616 or 1-800/932-
3454, fax 1-310/670-2318,
e-mail: fiji@primenet.com

Fiji Visitors Bureau, Level 12, St.
Martin's Tower, 31 Market St.,
Sydney, NSW 2000, Australia,
tel. 61-2/9264-3399, fax 61-
2/9264-3060, e-mail:
fijiau@ozemail.com.au

Fiji Visitors Bureau, Box 1179,
Auckland, New Zealand, tel.
64-9/373-2133, fax 64-9/309-
4720, www.bulafiji.co.nz,
e-mail: info@bulafiji.co.nz

Fiji Visitors Bureau, 14th floor,
NOA Bldg., 3-5, 2-Chome,
Azabudai, Minato-ku, Tokyo
106, Japan, tel. 81-3/3587-
2038, fax 81-3/3587-2563,
e-mail: fijijp@red.an.egg.or.jp

Fiji Embassy, 34 Hyde Park Gate,
London SW7 5DN, United
Kingdom, tel. 44-171/584-3661,
fax 44-171/584-2838

NEW CALEDONIA

Nouvelle-Calédonie Tourisme,
B.P. 688, 98845 Nouméa, New
Caledonia, tel. 687/24-20-80,
fax 687/24-20-70,
www.newcaledonia.org;
e-mail: tourisme@offratel.nc

New Caledonia Tourism, 2nd
floor, 30 Clarence St., Sydney,
NSW 2000, Australia,
tel. 61-2/9299-2573,
fax 61-2/9290-2242, e-mail:
newcal@nctourism.com.au

New Caledonia Tourism, 3rd floor,
57 Fort St., Box 4300,
Auckland, New Zealand,
tel. 64-9/307-5257,
fax 64-9/379-2874,
e-mail: newcal@xtra.co.nz

Maison de la France, Landic No.
2, Akasaka Park Building, 2-10-
9 Akasaka, Minato-ku, Tokyo
107, Japan, tel. 81-3/3583-
3280, fax 81-3/3505-2873,
e-mail: newcal@mb.infoweb.or.jp

Nouvelle-Calédonie Tourisme,
370 rue Saint-Honoré, 75001
Paris, France, tel. 33-1/4703-
6323, fax 33-1/4703-6327

VANUATU

National Tourism Office of
Vanuatu, Box 209, Port Vila,
Vanuatu, tel. 678/22685, fax
678/23889,
www.vanuatutourism.com;
e-mail: tourism@vanuatu.com.vu

SOLOMON ISLANDS

Solomon Islands Visitors Bureau,
Box 321, Honiara, Solomon
Islands, tel. 677/22442,
fax 677/23986,
www.commerce.gov.sb, e-mail:
commerce@commerce.gov.sb

Government Information Service,
Box G1, Honiara, Solomon
Islands, tel. 677/21300,
fax 677/20401

BIBLIOGRAPHY

DESCRIPTION AND TRAVEL

Bell, Gavin. *In Search of Tusitala*. London: Picador, 1994. A young Scottish journalists' experiences in the Marquesas, Tahiti, Hawaii, Kiribati, and Samoa in the footsteps of Robert Louis Stevenson.

Birkett, Dea. *Serpent in Paradise*. London: Picador, 1997. The candid tale of a British woman who spent several months on Pitcairn secretly preparing a memoir. In the end she became involved in an affair and was forced to flee on a passing tanker, leaving her book rather tarnished by negativity. Despite this, Birkett allows us a fascinating glimpse of Pitcairn as it is.

Frisbie, Robert Dean. *The Book of Pukapuka, A Lone Trader on a South Sea Atoll*. Honolulu: Mutual Publishing. A delightful depiction of daily life on one of the Northern Cook Islands in the interwar period.

Gravelle, Kim. *Romancing the Islands*. Suva: Graphics Pacific, 1995. In these 42 stories ex-American Fiji resident Kim Gravelle shares a quarter century of adventures in the region. A delightfully sympathetic look at the islands and its characters. Copies can be ordered from the author at Box 12975, Suva, Fiji Islands (US$25 postpaid).

Lewis, David. *We, the Navigators*. Honolulu: University of Hawaii Press, 1994. A second edition of the 1972 classic on the ancient art of land-finding in the Pacific. Lewis' 1964 journey from Tahiti to New Zealand was the first in modern times on which only traditional navigational means were used.

McCall, Grant. *Rapanui: Tradition and Survival on Easter Island.* Honolulu: University of Hawaii Press, 1994. A comprehensive summary of what is known about the island and its current inhabitants.

Phelan, Nancy. *Pieces of Heaven.* St. Lucia, Australia: University of Queensland Press, 1995. After four decades away, a former aid worker returns to revisit Cook Islands, Samoa, and Kiribati, and the Pacific of the 1950s and 1990s combine in a fascinating portrait of the region.

Stevenson, Robert Louis. *In the South Seas.* New York: Scribner's, 1901. The author's account of his travels through the Marquesas, Tuamotus, and Gilberts by yacht in the years 1888-90.

Theroux, Paul. *The Happy Isles of Oceania.* London, Hamish Hamilton, 1992. The author of classic accounts of railway journeys sets out with kayak and tent to tour the Pacific.

GUIDEBOOKS

Hammick, Anne. *Ocean Cruising on a Budget.* Camden, Maine: International Marine Publishing, 1991. Hammick shows how to sail your own yacht safely and enjoyably over the seas while cutting costs. Study it beforehand if you're thinking of working as crew on a yacht. Also from International Marine is Beth A. Leonard's *The Voyager's Handbook: The Essential Guide to Blue Water Cruising.*

Hinz, Earl R. *Landfalls of Paradise: Cruising Guide to the Pacific Islands.* Honolulu: University of Hawaii Press, 1999. With 97 maps and 144 illustrations, this is the only cruising guide to Oceania's 75 ports of entry and many lesser harbors and anchorages.

Levy, Neil. *Micronesia Handbook.* Chico: Moon Travel Handbooks. Covers the North Pacific countries of Nauru, Kiribati, the Marshall Islands, the Federated States of Micronesia, the Republic of Palau, Guam, and the Northern Marianas.

Pacific Travel Fact File. A reliable annual guide to upmarket accommodations all across the Pacific with exact prices listed. Travel agents will find it invaluable. Copies can be ordered from Box 622, Runaway Bay, Queensland 4216, Australia, fax 61-7/5537-9330.

Parkinson, Susan, Peggy Stacy, and Adrian Mattinson. *Taste of the Pacific.* Honolulu: University of Hawaii Press, 1995. More than 200 recipes of South Pacific dishes.

Ryan, Paddy. *The Snorkeler's Guide to the Coral Reef.* Honolulu: University of Hawaii Press, 1994. An introduction to the wonders of the Indo-Pacific reefs. The author spent 10 years in Fiji and knows the region well.

Seward, Robert. *Radio Happy Isles: Media and Politics at Play in the Pacific.* Honolulu: University of Hawaii Press, 1998. An insightful and unexpected look at radio stations all across the Pacific.

Stanley, David. *Fiji Handbook.* Chico: Moon Travel Handbooks. There's also a *Tahiti Handbook,* which also includes Easter Island and the Cooks, and a *Tonga-Samoa Handbook* with a chapter on Niue. These country guides are more focused than *South Pacific Handbook,* with detailed reviews of virtually every accommodation possibility, in-depth coverage of special topics such as scuba diving or music, and additional maps.

GEOGRAPHY

Crocombe, Ron. *The South Pacific: An Introduction.* Suva: Institute of Pacific Studies, 1989. A collection of lecture notes covering a wide range of topics from one of the region's leading academics.

Oliver, Douglas L. *The Pacific Islands*. Honolulu: University of Hawaii Press, 1989. A third edition of the classic 1961 study of the history and anthropology of the entire Pacific area.

Ridgell, Reilly. *Pacific Nations and Territories*. A high school geography text that provides an overview of the region and also focuses on the individual islands. *Pacific Neighbors* is an elementary school version of the same book, written in collaboration with Betty Dunford. Both are published by Bess Press, 3565 Harding Ave., Honolulu, HI 96816, U.S.A., tel. 1-800/910-2377 or 1-808/734-7159, fax 1-808/732-3627, www.besspress.com.

NATURAL SCIENCE

Bahn, Paul, and John Flenley. *Easter Island, Easter Island*. London: Thames and Hudson, 1992. A well-illustrated study of man's impact on an isolated island environment, and how that led to his degradation. A message from our past for the future of our planet.

Lebot, Vincent, Lamont Lindstrom, and Mark Marlin. *Kava—the Pacific Drug*. Yale University Press, 1993. A thorough examination of kava and its many uses.

MacLeod, Roy M., and Philip F. Rehbock. *Darwin's Laboratory*. Honolulu: University of Hawaii Press, 1994. Evolutionary theory and natural history in the Pacific.

Mitchell, Andrew W. *A Fragile Paradise: Man and Nature in the Pacific*. London: Fontana, 1990. Published in the U.S. by the University of Texas Press under the title *The Fragile South Pacific: An Ecological Odyssey*.

Pratt, Douglas. *A Field Guide to the Birds of Hawaii and the Tropical Pacific*. Princeton, N.J.: Princeton University Press, 1986. The best in a poorly covered field.

Randall, John E., Gerald Robert Allen, and Roger C. Steene. *Fishes of the Great Barrier Reef and Coral Sea*. Honolulu: University of Hawaii Press, 1997. An identification guide for amateur diver and specialist alike.

Veron, J.E.N. *Corals of Australia and the Indo-Pacific*. Honolulu: University of Hawaii Press, 1993. An authoritative, illustrated work.

Watling, Dick. *Mai Veikau: Tales of Fijian Wildlife*. Suva: Fiji Times, 1986. A wealth of easily digested information on Fiji's flora and fauna. Copies are available in Fiji bookstores.

Whistler, W. Arthur. *Flowers of the Pacific Island Seashore*. Honolulu: University of Hawaii Press, 1993. A guide to the littoral plants of Hawaii, Tahiti, Samoa, Tonga, Cook Islands, Fiji, and Micronesia.

Whistler, W. Arthur. *Wayside Plants of the Islands*. Honolulu: University of Hawaii Press, 1995. A guide to the lowland flora of the Pacific islands.

HISTORY

Bellwood, Peter. *The Polynesians: Prehistory of an Island People*. London: Thames and Hudson, 1987. A succinct account of the archaeology of Polynesian expansion.

Bonnemaison, Joël. *The Tree and the Canoe: History and Ethnogeography of Tanna*. Honolulu: University of Hawaii Press, 1994. The story of how the Tannese revived their original creation myths as a defense against outside influences.

Crocombe, Ron. *The Pacific Islands and the USA*. Suva: Institute of Pacific Studies, 1995. A comprehensive study of almost every aspect of the relationship from the 18th century to the present day. Crocombe's account of the self-serving manipulations practiced by a succession of U.S. officials over the years should chasten any Americans still unwilling to come to terms with their country as just another imperialistic colonial power.

Denoon, Donald, et al. *The Cambridge History of the Pacific Islanders*. Australia: Cambridge

University Press, 1997. A team of scholars examines the history of the inhabitants of Oceania from first colonization to the nuclear era. While acknowledging the great diversity of Pacific peoples, cultures, and experiences, the book looks for common patterns and related themes, presenting them in an insightful and innovative way.

Dunmore, John. *Who's Who in Pacific Navigation.* Honolulu: University of Hawaii Press, 1991. An encyclopedia-style catalog of famous and obscure Pacific explorers.

Field, Michael J. *Mau: Samoa's Struggle for Freedom.* Auckland: Pasifika Press, 1991. The story of a nonviolent freedom movement.

Hough, Richard. *Captain James Cook.* W.W. Norton, 1997. A readable new biography of Captain Cook that asserts that Cook's abrupt manner on his third journey may have been due to an intestinal infection that affected his judgment and indirectly led to his death at the hands of Hawaiian islanders.

Howe, K.R., Robert C. Kiste, and Brij V. Lal, eds. *Tides of History.* Honolulu: University of Hawaii Press, 1994. A collection of essays on the Pacific islands in the 20th century.

Moorehead, Alan. *The Fatal Impact.* Honolulu: Mutual Publishing. European impact on the South Pacific from 1767 to 1840, as illustrated in the cases of Tahiti, Australia, and Antarctica. Much information is provided on Captain Cook's three voyages.

Samson, Jane. *Imperial Benevolence: Making British Authority in the Pacific Islands.* Honolulu: University of Hawaii Press, 1998. An insightful analysis of the impulses behind British imperialism.

Van Trease, Howard, ed. *Melanesian Politics: Stael Blong Vanuatu.* Suva: Institute of Pacific Studies, 1995. In the appendix is a rather damning confidential French document left behind during the hurried French withdrawal from Vanuatu in 1980.

PACIFIC ISSUES

Danielsson, Bengt, and Marie-Thérèse Danielsson. *Poisoned Reign: French Nuclear Colonialism in the Pacific.* Penguin Books, 1986. An updated version of *Moruroa Mon Amour,* first published in 1977. A wealth of background on the former French nuclear testing program in Polynesia.

Dé Ishtar, Zohl, ed. *Daughters of the Pacific.* Melbourne: Spinifex Press, 1994. A stirring collection of stories of survival, strength, determination, and compassion told by indigenous women of the Pacific. The stories relate their experiences, and the impact on them by nuclear testing, uranium mining, neo-colonialism, and nuclear waste dumping.

Emberson-Bain, 'Atu, ed. *Sustainable Development or Malignant Growth? Perspectives of Pacific Island Women.* Suva: Marama Publications, 1994. Contains valuable background information of the regional environment.

Faleomavaega, Eni F.H., *Navigating the Future: A Samoan Perspective on U.S.-Pacific Relations.* Suva: Institute of Pacific Studies, 1995. American Samoa's congressman in Washington lays out the issues of the day.

Jalal, Patricia Imrana. *Law for Pacific Women: A Legal Rights Handbook.* This 700-page book is essential reading for anyone planning an extended stay in Cook Islands, Fiji, Samoa, Solomon Islands, Tuvalu, or Vanuatu. Order from the Fiji Women's Rights Movement, Box 14194, Suva, tel. 679/313-156, fax 679/313-466.

Maclellan, Nic, and Jean Chesneaux. *After Moruroa: France in the South Pacific.* This timely examination of French colonialism from the French Revolution to the Matignon Accords and the end of nuclear testing also speculates on France's future in the region in light of the political changes in Europe. Available from Ocean Press, GPO Box 3279, Melbourne 3001, Australia, tel. 61-3/9372-2683, fax 61-3/9372-1765, e-mail: ocean_press@msn.com.au.

Robie, David, ed. *Tu Galala: Social Change in the Pacific.* Wellington: Bridget Williams Books, 1992. In this book, Robie has collected a series of essays examining the conflicting influences of tradition, democracy, and Westernization, with special attention to environmental issues and human rights.

SOCIAL SCIENCE

Foerstel, Lenora, and Angela Gilliam, eds. *Confronting the Margaret Mead Legacy: Scholarship, Empire, and the South Pacific.* Philadelphia: Temple University Press, 1992. Mead's impact on western anthropology and her views of colonialism, imperialism, and business interests in the South Pacific.

Freeman, Derek. *Margaret Mead and Samoa: The Making and Unmaking of an Anthropological Myth.* Cambridge, Mass.: Harvard University Press, 1983. An Australian academic refutes Margaret Mead's theory of Samoan promiscuity and lack of aggression.

Huntsman, Judith, and Antony Hooper. *Tokelau, A Historical Ethnography.* Honolulu: University of Hawaii Press, 1997. This readable ethnographical study provides a wealth of background information on this little-known island group.

Kwa'ioloa, Michael. *Living Tradition: A Changing Life in Solomon Islands.* London: British Museum Press, 1997. The story of a Kwara'ae man who spent his childhood in the forests of Malaita before moving to Honiara, as told to Ben Burt. Distributed in North America by the University of Hawaii Press.

Levy, Robert. *Tahitians: Mind and Experience in the Society Islands.* Chicago: University of Chicago Press, 1973. Levy's study, based on several years of field work on Tahiti and Huahine, includes an intriguing examination of the *mahu* (transvestite) phenomenon.

Lynch, John. *Pacific Languages: An Introduction.* Honolulu: University of Hawaii Press, 1998. The grammatical features of the Oceanic, Papuan, and Australian languages.

Mead, Margaret. *Letters from the Field.* Edited by Ruth Nanda. New York: Harper & Row, 1977. Describes Mead's experiences in American Samoa, Manus, the Sepik, and Bali. See also Mead's *Coming of Age in Samoa.*

Oliver, Douglas L. *Native Cultures of the Pacific Islands.* Honolulu: University of Hawaii Press, 1989. Intended primarily for college-level courses on precontact anthropology, history, economy, and politics of the entire region.

Pollock, Nancy J. *These Roots Remain.* Honolulu: University of Hawaii Press, 1992. Food habits of the central and western Pacific since European contact.

Welsch, Robert L., ed. *An American Anthropologist in Melanesia.* Honolulu: University of Hawaii Press, 1998. The story of Albert Buell Lewis' 1909-1913 expedition, which laid the basis for the outstanding Melanesian collection at Chicago's Field Museum of Natural History.

LITERATURE

Bermann, Richard A. *Home from the Sea.* Honolulu: Mutual Publishing. A reprint of the 1939 narrative of Robert Louis Stevenson's final years in Samoa.

Day, A. Grove, and Carl Stroven, eds. *Best South Sea Stories.* Honolulu: Mutual Publishing. Fifteen extracts from the writings of famous European authors.

Figiel, Sia. *Where We Once Belonged.* Auckland: Pasifika Press, 1996. The acclaimed first novel by a female storyteller, which recounts the experience of growing up in a Samoan village. Sex, violence, and the struggle for a personal identity appear in an island setting. Available in North America through the University of Hawaii Press. Figiel's second novel, *The Girl in the Moon Circle,* about Samoan life as seen through the eyes of a

10-year-old girl, is published by the Institute of Pacific Studies.

Hall, James Norman. *The Forgotten One and Other True Tales of the South Seas.* Honolulu: Mutual Publishing. A book about expatriate writers and intellectuals who sought refuge on the out-of-the-world islands of the Pacific.

Hau'ofa, Epeli. *Tales of the Tikongs.* Auckland: Longman Paul Ltd., 1983. Reprinted by Beake House (Fiji) in 1993 and the University of Hawaii Press in 1994. An amusingly ironic view of Tongan life: "Our people work so hard on Sunday it takes a six-day rest to recover." The development aid business, exotic religious sects, self-perpetuating bureaucracy, and similar themes provide a milieu for the tales of the Tikongs: in Tiko nothing is as it seems. The University of Hawaii Press has also reprinted Hau'ofa's *Kisses in the Nederends,* a satire of life in a small Pacific community.

London, Jack. *South Sea Tales.* Honolulu: Mutual Publishing. Stories based on London's visit to Tahiti, Samoa, Fiji, and the Solomons in the early 20th century.

Maka'a, Julian. *The Confession and Other Stories.* Suva: Institute of Pacific Studies, 1985. A collection of nine short stories about young Solomon Islanders attaining manhood. Though unpolished, the stories contrast the alienation of city life with social control of the village.

Maugham, W. Somerset. *The Trembling of a Leaf.* Honolulu: Mutual Publishing. The responses of a varied mix of white males—colonial administrator, trader, sea captain, bank manager, and missionary—to the peoples and environment of the South Pacific. Maugham is a masterful storyteller, and his journey to Samoa and Tahiti in 1916-1917 supplied him with poignant material.

Melville, Herman. *Typee, A Peep at Polynesian Life.* In 1842 Melville deserted from an American whaler at Nuku Hiva, Marquesas Islands. This semifictional account of Melville's four months among the Typee people was followed by *Omoo* in which Melville gives his impressions of Tahiti at the time of the French takeover.

Michener, James A. *Return to Paradise.* New York: Random House, 1951. Essays and short stories. Michener's *Tales of the South Pacific,* the first of more than 30 books, opened on Broadway in 1949 as the long-running musical *South Pacific.* This writer's ability to gloss over the complexities of life explains his tremendous popularity, and the predictable stereotypes in his one-dimensional South Seas tales perpetuate the illusory myth of the island paradise.

Saunana, John. *The Alternative.* Honiara: University of the South Pacific, 1980. The struggle of a young Solomon Islander to find his place in a world still dominated by the declining absurdities of colonial rule—a well-written vignette of the time.

Wendt, Albert. *Flying Fox in a Freedom Tree.* Auckland: Longman Paul Ltd., 1974. A collection of short stories in which the men cannot show fear or emotion, while the women appear only as sex objects.

Wendt, Albert. *Leaves of the Banyan Tree.* Honolulu: University of Hawaii Press, 1994. A reprint of the 1980 Wendt classic. Wendt was the first South Pacific novelist of international stature and his semiautobiographical writings are full of interest.

Wendt, Albert, ed. *Nuanua: Pacific Writing in English Since 1980.* Honolulu, University of Hawaii Press, 1995. This worthwhile anthology of contemporary Pacific literature illustrates the reluctance of many indigenous writers to divulge the underlying power structures of island societies. The selections by Alistair Campbell are among the few with any deeper psychological content, and most of the rest are rather superficial descriptions of reality with little exploration of the motives and relationships below the surface. One feels Wendt's writers would have been more comfortable expressing themselves in their native tongues to an audience of their peers.

Wendt, Albert. *Pouliuli*. Auckland: Longman Paul Ltd., 1977. This is probably Wendt's finest novel, masterfully depicting the complex values and manipulative nature of Samoan society. No other book explains more about Samoa today.

Wendt, Albert. *Sons for the Return Home*. Auckland: Longman Paul Ltd., 1973. The story of a Samoan youth brought up amid discrimination in New Zealand, yet unable to readjust to the cultural values of his own country. The University of Hawaii Press distributes reprints of Wendt's early works, plus his 1995 novels *Ola* and *Black Rainbow*.

THE ARTS

Bonnemaison, Joël, Kirk Huffman, Christian Kaufmann, and Darrell Tryon. *Arts of Vanuatu*. Honolulu: University of Hawaii Press, 1997. This book goes far beyond the visual arts reflected in the title to present a complete anthropological picture of the country. Some 383 illustrations accompany the text.

Holcombe, Bobby. *Bobby: Polynesian Visions*. Pacific Bridge, 56 Park Ave., Avalon, NSW 2107, Australia, tel. 61-7/5499-9440, e-mail: bob.e@bigpond.com. Color reproductions of the paintings of this Hawaiian artist who was so influential in the art and music of French Polynesia.

Kaeppler, Adrienne L. *Polynesian Dance*. Honolulu: Bishop Museum Press, 1983. Describes the traditional dances of Hawaii, Tahiti, the Cook Islands, Tonga, and Niue.

Kaeppler, Adrienne, C. Kaufmann, and Douglas Newton. *Oceanic Art*. Abrahams, 1997. The first major survey of the arts of Polynesia, Melanesia, and Micronesia in more than three decades, this admirable volume brings the reader up to date on recent scholarship in the field. Of the 900 illustrations, more than a third are new.

Lee, Georgia. *The Rock Art of Easter Island: Symbols of Power, Prayers to the Gods*. Mon-
umenta Arqueologica 17. A readable 1992 examination of a fascinating subject. Also recommended are Alan Drake's *The Ceremonial Center of Orongo* and Dr. William Liller's *The Ancient Solar Observatories of Rapa Nui*. These and many other excellent publications on Easter Island are available from the Easter Island Foundation, Box 6774, Los Osos, CA 93412-6774, U.S.A., fax 1-805/534-9301, e-mail: rapanui@compuserve.com.

Linkels, Ad. *Fa'a-Samoa: The Samoan Way*. Published in 1995 by Mundo Étnico, Sibeliusstraat 707, 5011 JR Tilburg, The Netherlands, this book is a complete survey of Samoan music from conch shell to disco. Also see *Sounds of Change in Tonga* by Ad Linkels, available from the Friendly Islands Bookshop in Nuku'alofa.

St Cartmail, Keith. *The Art of Tonga*. Honolulu: University of Hawaii Press, 1997. The first book solely devoted to this powerfully fresh art style.

Thomas, Nicholas. *Oceanic Art*. London: Thames and Hudson, 1995. Almost 200 illustrations grace the pages of this readable survey.

REFERENCE BOOKS

Connell, John, et al. *Encyclopedia of the Pacific Islands*. Canberra: Australian National University, 1999. Published to mark the 50th anniversary of the Pacific Community, this important book combines the writings of 200 acknowledged experts on the physical environment, peoples, history, politics, economics, society, and culture of the South Pacific.

Craig, Robert D. *Historical Dictionary of Polynesia*. Metuchen, NJ: Scarecrow Press, 1994. This handy volume contains alphabetical listings of individuals (past and present), places, and organizations, plus historical chronologies and bibliographies by island group. A similar work on Melanesia is in preparation.

Douglas, Ngaire and Norman Douglas, eds. *Pacific Islands Yearbook*. Suva: Fiji Times Ltd.

Despite the title, a new edition of this authoritative sourcebook has come out about every four years since 1932. Although a rather dry read, it's still the one indispensable reference work for students of the Pacific islands.

Fry, Gerald W., and Rufino Mauricio. *Pacific Basin and Oceania.* Oxford: Clio Press, 1987. A selective, indexed Pacific bibliography, which actually describes the contents of the books, instead of merely listing them.

Jackson, Miles M., ed. *Pacific Island Studies: A Survey of the Literature.* Westport: Greenwood Press, 1986. In addition to comprehensive listings, there are extensive essays that put the most important works in perspective.

Motteler, Lee S. *Pacific Island Names.* Honolulu: Bishop Museum Press, 1986. A comprehensive gazetteer listing officially accepted island names, cross-referenced to all known variant names and spellings.

BOOKSELLERS AND PUBLISHERS

Many important books about the Pacific are out of print and not available in regular bookstores or from www.amazon.com. Major libraries will have some, otherwise write to the specialized antiquarian booksellers or regional publishers listed below for their printed lists of hard-to-find books on the Pacific. Sources of detailed topographical maps or navigational charts are provided in the following section.

Antipodean Books, Box 189, Cold Spring, NY 10516, U.S.A., tel. 1-914/424-3867, fax 1-914/424-3617, www.antipodean.com, e-mail: antipbooks@highlands.com. They have a complete catalog of out-of-print and rare items.

Bibliophile, 24A Glenmore Rd., Paddington, Sydney, NSW 2021, Australia, tel. 61-2/9331-1411, fax 61-2/9361-3371, www.ozemail.com. au/~susant, e-mail: susant@anzaab.com.au. An antiquarian bookstore specializing in books about Oceania. View their extensive catalog on line.

Bishop Museum Press, 1525 Bernice St., Honolulu, HI 96817-0916, U.S.A., tel. 1-808/848-4135, fax 1-808/848-4132, www.bishop.hawaii.org/bishop/press. They have an indexed list of books on the Pacific; a separate list of "The Occasional Papers" lists specialized works.

Book Bin, 228 S.W. 3rd St., Corvallis, OR 97333, U.S.A., tel. 1-541/752-0045, fax 1-541/754-4115, e-mail: pacific@bookbin.com. Their indexed mail-order catalog, *Hawaii and Pacific Islands,* lists thousands of rare books, plus current research, art books, and atlases, and they also carry all the titles of the Institute of Pacific Studies in Suva. If there's a particular book about the Pacific you can't find anywhere, this is a place to try.

Books of Yesteryear, Box 257, Newport, NSW 2106, Australia, tel./fax 61-2/9918-0545, e-mail: patbooks@ozemail.com.au. Another source of old, fine, and rare books on the Pacific.

Books Pasifika, Box 68-446, Newtown, Auckland 1, New Zealand, tel. 64-9/303-2349, fax 64-9/377-9528, www.ak.planet.gen.nz/pasifika, e-mail: books@pasifika.co.nz. Besides being a major publisher, Pasifika Press is one of New Zealand's best sources of mail order books on Oceania, including those of the Institute of Pacific Studies.

Bushbooks, Box 1370, Gosford, NSW 2250, Australia, tel. 61-2/4323-3274, fax 61-2/9212-2468, e-mail: bushbook@ozemail.com.au. An Australian source of the publications of the Institute of Pacific Studies in Suva.

Cellar Book Shop, 18090 Wyoming Ave., Detroit, MI 48221, U.S.A., tel./fax 1-313/861-1776, http://members.aol.com/cellarbook, e-mail: cellarbook@aol.com. Their catalog, *The 'Nesias' & Down Under: Some Recent Books,* includes a wide range of books on the Pacific.

Empire Books, Colin Hinchcliffe, 12 Queens Staith Mews, York, YO1 6HH, United Kingdom, tel. 44-1904/610679, fax 44-1904/641664, e-mail: colin@empires. demon.co.uk.

An excellent source of antiquarian or out-of-print books, maps, and engravings.

Institute of Pacific Studies, University of the South Pacific, Box 1168, Suva, Fiji Islands, tel. 679/313-900, fax 679/301-594, e-mail: ips@usp.ac.fj. Their catalog, *Books from the Pacific Islands,* lists numerous books about the islands written by the Pacific islanders themselves. Some are rather dry academic publications of interest only to specialists, so order carefully. USP centers all across the region sell many of these books over the counter. For internet access to the catalog, see the University Book Centre listing below.

International Marine Publishing Co., Box 548, Blacklick, OH 43004, U.S.A., tel. 1-800/262-4729, fax 1-614/759-3641, www.pbg.mcgraw-hill.com/im. Their catalog, *Boating Books,* includes all the books you'll ever need to teach yourself how to sail. They also have books on sea kayaking.

Jean-Louis Boglio, Box 72, Currumbin, Queensland 4223, Australia, tel. 61-7/5534-9349, fax 61-7/5534-9949, www.maritimebooks.com. An excellent source of new and used books on the French territories in the Pacific.

Michael Graves-Johnston, Bookseller, Box 532, London SW9 0DR, United Kingdom, tel. 44-171/274-2069, fax 44-171/738-3747. Sells antiquarian books only.

Mutual Publishing Company, 1215 Center St., Suite 210, Honolulu, HI 96816, U.S.A., tel. 1-808/732-1709, fax 1-808/734-4094, www.pete.com/mutual, e-mail: mutual@lava.net. The classics of expatriate Pacific literature, available in cheap paperback editions.

Pan Pacifica, 4662 Sierra Dr., Honolulu, HI 96816, U.S.A., fax 1-808/739-2326, www.Pan-Pacifica.com, e-mail: panpac@lava.net. A source of recent official publications and research-level documents from museums and universities. Their primary clients are large research libraries.

Peter Moore, Box 66, Cambridge, CB1 3PD, United Kingdom, tel. 44-1223/411177, fax 44-1223/240559. The European distributor of books from the Institute of Pacific Studies of the University of the South Pacific, Fiji. Moore's catalog also lists antiquarian and secondhand books.

Serendipity Books, Box 340, Nedlands, WA 6009, Australia, tel. 61-8/9382-2246, fax 61-8/9388-2728, www.merriweb.com.au/serendip. The largest stock of antiquarian, secondhand, and out-of-print books on the Pacific in Western Australia. Free catalogs are issued on a regular basis.

South Pacific Regional Environment Program, Box 240, Apia, Samoa, tel. 685/21-929, fax 685/20-231, www.sprep.org.ws. They have a list of specialized technical publications on environmental concerns.

University Book Centre, University of the South Pacific, Box 1168, Suva, Fiji Islands, tel. 679/313-900, fax 679/303-265. An excellent source of books written and produced in the South Pacific itself. Check out their site.

University of Hawaii Press, 2840 Kolowalu St., Honolulu, HI 96822-1888, U.S.A., tel. 1-888/847-7377 or 1-808/956-8255, fax 1-808/988-6052, www2.hawaii.edu/uhpress. Their annual *Hawaii and the Pacific* catalog is well worth requesting if you're trying to build a Pacific library.

MAP PUBLISHERS

Defense Mapping Agency, Nautical Charts and Publications, Public Sale: Region 8, Oceania. NOAA Distribution Division N/ACC3, National Ocean Service, Riverdale, MD 20737-1199, U.S.A., tel. 1-800/638-8972 or 1-301/436-8301, fax 1-301/436-6829, www.noaa.gov. A complete index and order form for nautical charts of the Pacific.

International Maps. Hema Maps Pty. Ltd., Box 2660, Logan City, Queensland 4114, Australia, tel. 61-7/3290-0322, fax 61-7/3290-0478, www.hemamaps.com.au. Maps of the Pacific, Fiji, Solomon Islands, Vanuatu, and Samoa.

Pacific Islands, Catalog of topographic and other published maps. Information Services, U.S. Geological Survey, Box 25286, Denver Federal Center, Denver, CO 80225-9916, U.S.A., tel. 1-303/202-4700, fax 1-303/202-4693. A description and order form for the two color maps of American Samoa available from the USGS.

Reference Map of Oceania. Honolulu: University of Hawaii Press, 1995. A most useful double-sided map of the Pacific by James A. Bier, who also produced the worthwhile *Islands of Samoa* map (1990).

PERIODICALS

Center for South Pacific Studies Newsletter. Centre for South Pacific Studies, University of New South Wales, Kensington, NSW 2052, Australia, tel. 61-2/9385-3386, fax 61-2/9313-6337, www.arts.unsw.edu.au/Centres/SouthPacific/homepage.html, e-mail: J.Lodewijks@unsw.EDU.AU). A useful publication that catalogs scholarly conferences, events, activities, news, employment opportunities, courses, scholarships, and publications across the region.

Commodores' Bulletin. Seven Seas Cruising Assn., 1525 South Andrews Ave., Suite 217, Fort Lauderdale, FL 33316, U.S.A., tel. 1-954/463/2431, fax 1-954/463-7183, www.ssca.org, e-mail: SSCA1@ibm.net; US$53 a year worldwide by airmail. This monthly bulletin is chock-full of useful information for anyone wishing to tour the Pacific by sailing boat. All Pacific yachties and friends should be Seven Seas members!

The Contemporary Pacific. University of Hawaii Press, 2840 Kolowalu St., Honolulu, HI 96822, U.S.A., tel. 1-808/956-8833, fax 1-808/988-6052, www2.hawaii.edu/uhpress, e-mail: uhpjourn@hawaii.edu, published twice a year, US$35 a year. Publishes a good mix of articles

of interest to both scholars and general readers; the country-by-country "Political Review" in each number is a concise summary of events during the preceding year. The "Dialogue" section offers informed comment on the more controversial issues in the region, while recent publications on the islands are examined through book reviews. Those interested in current topics in Pacific island affairs should check recent volumes for background information.

Environment Newsletter. The quarterly newsletter of the South Pacific Regional Environment Program, Box 240, Apia, Samoa, tel. 685/21-929, fax 685/20-231, www.sprep.org.ws. Back issues can be viewed on their website.

Europe-Pacific Solidarity Bulletin. Published monthly by the European Center for Studies Information and Education on Pacific Issues, Box 151, 3700 AD Zeist, The Netherlands, tel. 31-30/692-7827, fax 31-30/692-5614, www.antenna.nl/ecsiep, e-mail: ecsiep@antenna.nl.

German Pacific Society Bulletin. Dr. Freidrich Steinbauer, Feichtmayr Strasse 25, D-80992 München, Germany, tel. 49-89/151158, fax 49-89/151833. At DM 90 a year, Society membership is a good way for German speakers to keep in touch. News bulletins in English and German are published four to six times a year, and study tours to various Pacific destinations are organized annually.

Islands Business. Box 12718, Suva, Fiji Islands, tel. 679/303-108, fax 679/301-423, e-mail: subs@ibi.com.fj; annual airmailed subscription A$35 to Australia, NZ$55 to New Zealand, US$45 to North America, US$55 to Europe. A monthly newsmagazine with in-depth coverage of political and economic trends in the Pacific. It's more opinionated than *Pacific Islands Monthly* and even has a gossip section that is an essential weather vane for anyone doing business in the region. In the December 1995 issue "Whispers" accurately forecast the devaluation of the Fiji dollar two years later. Travel and aviation news gets some prominence, and subscribers also receive the informative quarterly magazine *South Pacific Tourism*.

Journal of Pacific History. Division of Pacific and Asian History, RSPAS, Australian National University, Canberra, ACT 0200, Australia, tel. 61-2/6249-3140, fax 61-2/6249-5525, http://coombs.anu.edu.au/Depts/RSPAS/PAH/index.html or http://sunsite.anu.edu.au/spin/RSRC/HISTORY/jphsite.htm. Since 1966 this publication has provided reliable scholarly information on the Pacific. Outstanding.

Journal of Pacific Studies. School of Social and Economic Development, University of the South Pacific, Box 1168, Suva, Fiji Islands, tel. 679/314-900, fax 679/301-487. Focuses on regional developments from a social sciences perspective.

Journal of the Polynesian Society. Department of Maori Studies, University of Auckland, Private Bag 92019, Auckland, New Zealand, tel. 64-9/373-7999, extension 7463, fax 64-9/373-7409, www2.waikato.ac.nz/ling/PS/journal.html. Established in 1892, this quarterly journal contains a wealth of material on Pacific cultures past and present written by scholars of Pacific anthropology, archaeology, language, and history.

Pacific Islands Monthly. Box 1167, Suva, Fiji Islands, tel. 679/304-111, fax 679/303-809, www.pim.com.fj, e-mail: fijitimes@is.com.fj; annual subscription A$40 to Australia, A$45 to New Zealand, US$40 to North America, and A$60 to Europe. Founded in Sydney by R.W. Robson in 1930, *PIM* is the granddaddy of regional magazines. In June 1989 the magazine's editorial office moved from Sydney to Suva and it's now part of the same operation which puts out *The Fiji Times*. PIM's yachting feature is by Sally Andrew.

Pacific Magazine. Box 25488, Honolulu, HI 96825, U.S.A., tel. 1-808/377-5335, fax 1-808/373-3953, www.pacificmagazine.com; every other month; US$15 a year surface mail, US$27 airmail to the U.S., US$39 airmail elsewhere). This business-oriented news-magazine, published in Hawaii since 1976, will keep you up-to-date on what's happening in the South Pacific and Micronesia. The format is built around pithy little news bites on people and events rather than the longer background articles one finds in the other regional magazines.

Pacific News Bulletin. Pacific Concerns Resource Center, 83 Amy St., Toorak, Private Mail Bag, Suva, Fiji Islands (fax 679/304-755, e-mail: pcrc@is.com.fj; A$15 a year in Australia, A$30 a year elsewhere. A 16-page monthly newsletter with up-to-date information on nuclear, independence, environmental, and political questions.

Pacific Studies. Box 1979, BYU-HC, Laie, HI 96762-1294, U.S.A., tel. 1-808/293-3665, fax 1-808/ 293-3664, websider.byuh.edu/departments/ips, e-mail: robertsd@byuh.edu, quarterly, US$30 a year. Funded by the Polynesian Cultural Center and published by Hawaii's Brigham Young University.

Pacifica. Quarterly journal of the Pacific Islands Study Circle (John Ray, 24 Woodvale Ave., London SE25 4AE, United Kingdom, http://dspace.dial.pipex.com/jray/pisc.html, e-mail: jray@dial.pipex.com. This philatelic journal is exclusively concerned with stamps and the postal history of the islands.

Rapa Nui Journal. Box 6774, Los Osos, CA 93412-6774, U.S.A. (fax 1-805/534-9301, e-mail: rapanui@compuserve.com; quarterly, US$30 a year in North America, US$40 elsewhere. An interesting mix of scholarly reports and local news of interest to Rapanuiphiles. The June 1998 issue includes a fascinating study of Palmerston Island in the Cooks.

South Sea Digest. Box 4245, Sydney, NSW 2001, Australia, tel. 61-2/9288-1708, fax 61-2/9288-3322, A$150 a year in Australia, A$175 overseas. A private newsletter on political and economic matters, published every other week. It's a good way of keeping abreast of developments in commerce and industry.

Surf Report. Box 1028, Dana Point, CA 92629, U.S.A., tel. 1-949/496-5922, fax 1-949/496-7849, www.surfermag.com; US$35 a year. Each month this newsletter provides a detailed analysis of surfing conditions at a different destination. Back issues on specific countries are available, including a 14-issue "South Pacific Collection" at US$50. This is your best source of surfing information by far, and the same people also put out the glossy *Surfer Magazine* (US$25 a year).

Tahiti Pacifique. Alex Duprell, B.P. 368, 98728 Moorea, tel. 689/56-28-94, fax 689/56-30-07, www.tahitiweb.com/f/info, e-mail: tahitipm@mail.pf. For those who read French, this monthly magazine offers a style of informed and critical commentary quite unlike that seen in the daily press of the French territories.

Tok Blong Pasifik. South Pacific Peoples Foundation of Canada, 1921 Fernwood Rd., Victoria, BC V8T 2Y6, Canada, tel. 250/381-

4131, fax 250/388-5258, www.sppf.org, e-mail: sppf@sppf.org; C$25 a year in Canada, US$25 elsewhere. This lively quarterly of news and views focuses on regional environmental, development, human rights, and disarmament issues.

Undercurrent. Box 1658, Sausalito, CA 94966, U.S.A., www.undercurrent.org. A monthly consumer protection-oriented newsletter for serious scuba divers. Unlike virtually every other diving publication, *Undercurrent* accepts no advertising or free trips, which allows them to tell it as it is.

Washington Pacific Report. Fred Radewagen, Box 26142, Alexandria, VA 22313, U.S.A., tel. 1-703/519-7757, fax 1-703/548-0633, e-mail: piwowpr@erols.com; published twice a month, US$164 a year domestic, US$189 outside U.S. postal zones. An insider's newletter highlighting U.S. interests in the insular Pacific.

DISCOGRAPHY

In compiling this selection of Pacific music we've tried to list noncommercial recordings that are faithful to the traditional music of the islands as it exists today. Island music based on Western pop has been avoided. Most of the CDs below can be ordered through specialized music shops; otherwise write directly to the publishers.

Bagès, Gérard, ed. *Chants de L'Ile de Pâques* (92553-2). Buda Musique, 188 boulevard Voltaire, 75011 Paris, France, tel. 33-1/4024-0103. Sixteen traditional songs from Easter Island, in the collection "Musique du Monde" (recording date not provided).

Coco's Temaeva (S 65808). Manuiti Productions, B.P. 755, 98713 Papeete, Tahiti, fax 689/43-27-24. Founded by Coco Hotahota in 1962, Temaeva has won more prizes at the annual Heiva i Tahiti festivals than any other professional dance troupe.

Cook Islands National Arts Theater (CD MANU 1447). The drums, songs, and chants of the

Cook Islands produced by Ode Record Company, Auckland (recording date not provided).

Crowe, Peter, ed. *Vanuatu: Singsing-Danis Kastom* (VDE-796). Disques VDE-Gallo, Ale 31, 1000 Lausanne 9, Switzerland, tel. 41-21/312-1154, fax 41-21/312-1134. Recordings made on Ambae and Maewo in 1972-77. Extensive notes come with this unique collection.

Fanshawe, David, ed. *Exotic Voices and Rhythms of the South Seas* (EUCD/MC 1254). Cook Islands drum dancing, a Fijian *tralala meke,* a Samoan *fiafia,* a Vanuatu string band, and Solomon Islands panpipes selected from the 1,200 hours of tapes in the Fanshawe Pacific Collection. Order from ARC Music Inc., Box 2453, Clearwater, FL 33757-2453, U.S.A., tel. 1-727/447-3755, fax 1-727/447-3820, www.arcmusic.co.uk, e-mail: arcamerica@ij.net, or Fanshawe One World Music, Box 574, Marlborough, Wilts, SN8 2SP, United Kingdom, tel. 44-1672/520211, fax 44-1672/ 521151, www.fanshawe.com, e-mail: fanshaweuk@cwcom.net.

Fanshawe, David, ed. *Heiva i Tahiti: Festival of Life* (EUCD/MC 1238). Fanshawe has captured the excitement of Tahiti's biggest festival in these pieces recorded live in Papeete in 1982 and 1986. Famous groups led by Coco Hotahota, Yves Roche, Irma Prince, and others are represented.

Fanshawe, David, ed. *Spirit of Polynesia* (CD-SDL 403). Saydisc Records, Chipping Manor, The Chipping, Wotton-U-Edge, Glos. GL12 7AD, United Kingdom, tel. 44-1453/845-036, fax 44-1453/521-056, www.qualiton.com, e-mail: Saydisc@aol.com. An anthology of the music of 12 Pacific countries recorded between 1978 and 1988. More than half the pieces are from Tahiti-Polynesia and Cook Islands. There's also a *Spirit of Micronesia* (CD-SDL 414) and a *Spirit of Melanesia* (CD-SDL 418) in the "Spirit of the Pacific" series.

Holcomb, Bobby. *Bobby* (OCN CD 15). Océane Production, B.P. 3247, 98713 Papeete, Tahiti, tel. 689/42-69-00, fax 689/43-30-24). A collection of songs recorded on Tahiti by the late Hawaiian artist/musician Bobby Holcomb. A happy combination of traditional music and pop.

Linkels, Ad, and Lucia Linkels, eds. *Fiafia* (PAN 150CD). PAN Records, Box 155, 2300 AD Leiden, The Netherlands, tel. 31-71/521-9479, fax 31-71/522-6869, e-mail: paradox@dataweb.nl. The traditional dances of 11 Pacific countries recorded during six field trips between 1979 and 1992. This and many other PAN Records compact discs by the Linkels of Tongan, Samoan, Cook Islands, Tuvalu, and Easter Island music form part of the series "Anthology of Pacific Music" and extensive booklets explaining the music come with the records. Music stores can order PAN compact discs through Arhoolie, 10341 San Pablo Ave., El Cerrito, CA 94530, U.S.A., tel. 1-510/525-7471, fax 1-510/525-1204.

Linkels, Ad, and Lucia Linkels, eds. *Hula, Haka, Hoko!* (PAN 162CD). A selection of traditional Polynesian dance music recorded on Easter Island, Cook Islands, Tuvalu, Rotuma, Tonga, and Samoa between 1982 and 1996.

Music of Marginal Polynesia (VICG 5276). In the series "World Sounds" produced by Victor Entertainment, Inc., Tokyo, Japan, and distributed in the U.S. by JVC Music, Inc., 3800 Barham Blvd., Suite 305, Los Angeles, CA 90068, U.S.A., tel. 1-213/878-0101, fax 1-213/878-0202. The music of Fiji, Wallis and Futuna, and Tuvalu, recorded 1977-85.

Music of Polynesia in the series "World Sounds" available from JVC Music. This four-record series includes Vol. I (VICG 5271), with the music of Tahiti and the other Society Islands, Vol. II (VICG 5272), music of the Tuamotu and Austral islands, Vol. III (VICG 5273), music of Easter Island and the Marquesas Islands, and Vol. IV (VICG 5274), music of Samoa and Tonga.

Nabet-Meyer, Pascal, ed. *The Tahitian Choir, Vol. I* (Triloka Records 7192-2). Triloka Records, 2415 Princeton Dr. NE, Suite L, Albuquerque, NM 87107, U.S.A., tel. 1-800/578-44419, www.triloka.com. Recorded at Rapa Iti in 1991.

South Pacific Drums (PS 65066). Manuiti Productions, B.P. 755, 98713 Papeete, Tahiti, fax 689/43-27-24. A compilation of 39 of the best percussion recordings in Manuiti's archives—an excellent introduction to the traditional music of Polynesia.

Te Vaka, The Canoe (EUCD 1401). ARC Music Inc., Box 2453, Clearwater, FL 33757-2453, U.S.A., tel. 1-727/447-3755, fax 1-727/447-3820, www.arcmusic.co.uk, e-mail: arcamerica@ij.net. Te Vaka's dynamic interpretations of Tokalauan music and dance created a sensation during the 10-member band's 1997 European tour. A few New Age elements are entwined with the Pacific sounds in this delightful recording.

Tumuenua Dance Group, *Cook Island Drums, Chants, and Songs* (CD VOY 1335). A 1991 release by Ode Record Company, Auckland, New Zealand. An outstanding selection of traditional Cook Island music. Distributed through the PAN network previously mentioned.

Wasi Ka Nanara Pan Pipers (MGV CD 630). Mangrove Productions, B.P. 12777, 98803 Nouméa Cedex, New Caledonia, tel./fax 687/28-56-85. Twenty tracks of pan flute music by West Are Are pipers from Malaita (recording date not provided).

Zemp, Hugo, ed. *Musics & Musicians of the World: Solomon Islands* (D 8027). Paris: Unesco Collection Auvidis, 1990. A compact disc of Fata-

leka and Baegu music from Malaita, recorded in 1969 and 1970. Zemp also edited the CD *Polyphonies of the Solomon Islands (Guadalcanal and Savo)* (LDX 274 663) in the series "Le Chant du Monde" released by the Musée de l'Homme, Paris (recorded 1974). Both discs display the virtuosity of Solomon Island pan-pipe players. Also in the series is *Kanak Songs: Feasts and Lullabies* (LDX 274 909), recorded in New Caledonia during 1984-87.

THE INTERNET

USEFUL WEBSITES

Asia Pacific Network
www.asiapac.org.fj
David Robie's lively journalism site with links to most South Pacific print and broadcast news media.

CDC Travel Information
www.cdc.gov/travel/index.html
All the travel health advice you could ever want from the Centers for Disease Control in Atlanta, with general descriptions linked to specific information.

David Stanley's South Pacific
www3.sympatico.ca/davidstanley
The site of this handbook's author provides links to all regional tourist offices and airlines.

Olsen Currency Converter
www.oanda.com
Quick quotes on most international currencies, including those of the South Pacific.

Pacific Area Travel Association
www.pata.org
Useful links to most regional airlines, tourist offices, and travel media.

Pacific Islands Internet Resources
www2.hawaii.edu/~ogden/piir/index.html
Michael R. Ogden's vast catalog of South Pacific links.

Pacific Islands Monthly
www.pim.com.fj
A salutary source of news and comment summarizing about eight feature articles a month.

Pacific Islands Report
http://pidp.ewc.hawaii.edu/pireport
A joint project of several educational institutions in Hawaii, it's your best source of recent political and economic news from the islands. Around 15 stories are posted daily and you can browse through recent issues. Outstanding.

South Pacific for Less
www.southpacific4less.com
This unique site lists budget accommodations all across the Pacific with exact prices and contact info provided.

South Pacific On-Line
www.tcsp.com
Rather unreliable tourist information displayed in tiny frames by the Tourism Council of the South Pacific (www.pi-travel.co.nz is similar).

The Weather Underground
www.wunderground.com
Weather Underground's "Islands" section provided detailed two-day weather reports on points all around the Pacific, plus worldwide hurricane tracking.

WEBSITE DIRECTORY

General Interest
Bank of Hawaii
www.boh.com/econ
City Seahorse, Dallas, Texas
www.SeaHorseTales.com
European Center
for Pacific Issues
www.antenna.nl/ecsiep
Foghorn Outdoors
www.foghorn.com
Forum Fisheries Agency, Honiara
www.ffa.int
Forum Secretariat, Suva
www.forumsec.org.fj
Moon Travel Handbooks
www.moon.com
Pacific Explore, Nouméa
www.pacific-center.com

Pacific Internet Sites
www.nla.gov.au/oz/pacsites.html
Pacific Islands Investment, Hawaii
www.pacislands.com
Pacific Media Watch
www.pactok.net.au/docs/pmw
Polynesian Voyaging Society
http://leahi.kcc.hawaii.edu/org/pvs
Press Foundation of Asia
www.pressasia.org/PFA
Regional Environment
Program, Apia
www.sprep.org.ws
Secretariat of the Pacific
Community
www.spc.org.nc
South Pacific for Less
www.southpacific4less.com
South Pacific Peoples
Foundation, Canada
www.sppf.org
United Nations Development
Program
www.undp.org
Weather Reports
www.accuweather.com

Tahiti-Polynesia
Aranui Cruises, California
www.aranui.com
Archipels Croisieres, Moorea
www.archipels.com
Bali Hai Hotels, Moorea
www.balihaihotels.com
Bora Bora Lagoon Resort
www.orient-expresshotels.com
Chris Davis' Polynesia
www.cd-enterprises.com/french_polynesia
Club Méditerranée
www.clubmed.com
Dolphin Quest, Moorea
www.dolphinquest.org
Government of France
www.outre-mer.gouv.fr/domtom
Hôtel Bora Bora
www.amanresorts.com
Iaora Tahiti Ecotours
www.iaora.com

La Dépêche de Tahiti
  www.la-depeche-de-tahiti.com
Le Méridien Hotels, Tahiti
  www.lemeridien-tahiti.com
Mana Internet Provider, Papeete
  www.mana.pf
Marquesas Home Page
  www.alptuna.com
Office des Postes, Papeete
  www.opt.pf
Outrigger Hotels of Hawaii
  www.outrigger.com/pacific
Parkroyal Hotels
  www.tahiti-resorts.com
Perles de Tahiti, Papeete
  www.tahiti-blackpearls.com
Philatelic Bureau, Papeete
  www.tahiti-postoffice.com
Radisson Seven Seas Cruises
  www.rssc.com
Renaissance Cruises
  www.renaissancecruises.com
Tahiti Communications Inc., Tahiti
  www.tahiti.com
Tahiti Explorer, Los Angeles
  www.tahiti-explorer.com
Tahiti Friendship Society,
California
  www.tahitinet.com
Tahiti Invest
  www.tahiti-invest.com
Tahiti Nui Travel, Papeete
  www.tahiti-nui.com
Tahiti's Internet Guide
  www.tahitiweb.com
Tahiti-Pacifique
Magazine, Moorea
  www.tahitiweb.com/f/info
Tahiti Tekura Travel, Papeete
  www.tahiti-tekuratravel.com
Tahiti Tourisme, Papeete
  www.tahiti-tourisme.com
Tahiti Vacations, California
  www.tahitivacation.com
The Moorings, Florida
  www.moorings.com
Vahine I. Resort, Taha'a
  www.ila-chateau.com/vahine/
  index.htm

Pitcairn Islands
Pitcairn Island Government
  http://users.iconz.co.nz/pitcairn
Pitcairn Island Website
  www.visi.com/~pjlareau/pisg.html

Easter Island
Easter Island Foundation
  http://sites.netscape.net/
  kumoyama/rapanui/eif.html
Easter Island Home Page
  www.netaxs.com/~trance/
  rapanui.html
Kon Tiki Museum, Oslo
  www.media.uio.no/Kon-Tiki
Mysterious Places
  www.mysteriousplaces.com/
  Easter_ Island/index.html
Secrets of Easter Island
  www.pbs.org/wgbh/nova/easter
Servicio Nacional de Turismo
  www.segegob.cl/sernatur/
  inicio.html
Te Rapa Nui
  www.rapanui.co.cl

Cook Islands
Ara Moana Bungalows, Mangaia
  www.aramoana.com
Ara Moana Bungalows, Mangaia
  www.ck/aramoana/aramoana.htm
Are Manuiri Guest House, Atiu
  www.adc.co.ck
Casinos of the South Pacific
  www.cosp.com
Cook Islands Business and
Tourism
  http://cookpages.com
Cook Islands Connection
  www.maui.net/~jbonline/
  index.html
Cook Islands News, Rarotonga
  www.cinews.co.ck
Cook Islands Tourism
Corporation, Rarotonga
  www.cook-islands.com
Crown Beach Resort, Rarotonga
  www.crownbeach.com
Edgewater Resort, Rarotonga
  www.edgewater.co.ck
Kiikii Motel, Rarotonga
  www.kiikiimotel.co.ck
Maui Pearls
  www.mauipearls.com/mauipearls
Pacific Divers, Rarotonga
  www.pacificdivers.co.ck
Rarotongan Resort Hotel,
Rarotonga
  www.rarotongan.co.ck
Shangri-La Beach Cottages,

Rarotonga
  www.shangri-la.co.ck
Stars Travel, Rarotonga
  www.stars.co.ck
Telecom Cook Islands, Rarotonga
  www.oyster.net.ck
Telecom Cook Islands, Rarotonga
  www.yellowpages.co.ck
Vara's Beach House & Lodge,
Rarotonga
  www.varas.co.ck
Welcome to Paradise
  www.ck

Niue
Niue Dive, Alofi
  www.dive.nu
Niue Telecom
  www.niuenet.com
Niue Tourism Office, Alofi
  www.niueisland.com
Niue Tourism Office, Alofi
  www.visit.nu
This is Something Really .Nu!
  http://something.really.nu

Tonga
'Atenisi Institute
  http://kalianet.candw.to/atenisi
ANZ Bank, Nuku'alofa
  www.candw.to/banks
Cable & Wireless Kalianet,
Nuku'alofa
  www.candw.to
Fafa Island Resort, Nuku'alofa
  http://kalianet.candw.to/fafa
Friendly Islander, Nuku'alofa
  http://kalianet.candw.to/papiloa
Friendly Islands Kayak Company
  www.fikco.com/kayaktonga
Heilala Holiday Lodge, Nuku'alofa
  http://kalianet.candw.to/quick
Hotel Nuku'alofa, Nuku'alofa
  http://kalianet.candw.to/sanft
Kiwi Magic, Vava'u
  http://kalianet.candw.to/kiwifish
Matangi Tonga
  www.netstorage.com/kami/
  tonga/matangi
Millennium Site
  www.allabout2000.com/
  millennium/tn.html
Our Kingdom of Tonga
  www.tongatapu.net.to

Paradise Adventures
www.paradiseadventures.com.
au/tonga.htm
Paradise Hotel, Neiafu
http://kalianet.candw.to/paradise
Paradise Shores Resort
http://kalianet.candw.to/parashor
Royal Beer Co., Nuku'alofa
www.royalbeer.to
Royal Sunset Island Resort
http://kalianet.candw.to/royalsun
Royal Tongan Airlines, Nuku'alofa
www.candw.to/rta
Sailing Safaris, Vava'u
www.tongaonline.com/
sailingsafaris
Sunsail Yacht Charters, Auckland
www.sunsail.co.nz
Teta Tours, Nuku'alofa
http://kalianet.candw.to/tetatour
The Moorings, Florida
www.moorings.com
Tonga Chronicle, Nuku'alofa
www.netstorage.com/kami/
tonga/news
Tonga Game Fish Association
http://kalianet.candw.to/TIGFA
Tonga On Line
www.tongaonline.com
Tonga Study Circle
http://hometown.aol.com/
TongaJan/ttcmsc.html
Tonga Times, Nuku'alofa
www.tongatimes.com
Tonga Visitors Bureau, Nuku'alofa
www.vacations.tvb.gov.to
Tongan Beach Resort, Vava'u
www.thetongan.com
Tongan Wildlife Center
http://kalianet.candw.to/birdpark
Tonic Domain Name Registry,
Nuku'alofa
www.tonic.to

American Samoa

Asnic Domain Registry
www.nic.as
Congressman Faleomavaega,
Washington
www.house.gov/faleomavaega
Fagatele Bay Sanctuary
http://wave.nos.noaa.gov/nmsp/
FBNMS
KSBS-FM, Pago Pago
www.samoanet.com/ksbsfm

National Park of American Samoa
www.nps.gov/npsa/index.htm
Office of Tourism, Pago Pago
www.samoanet.com/
americansamoa
Pagopago, Inc.
www.pagopago.com
Planet Samoa
http://planet-samoa.com
Samoa Chat
www.samoa.as
Samoanet, Internet
Gateway to Samoa
www.samoanet.com
Samoa News, Pago Pago
www.iPacific.com
Telecommunications Authority
www.samoatelco.com

Samoa

Aggie Grey's, Apia
www.samoa.net/local/aggies.html
Books Pasifika
www.ak.planet.gen.nz/pasifika
Chamber of Commerce, Samoa
www.samoa.net/coc
Coconuts Beach Club, Upolu
www.coconutsbeachclubsamoa.
com
Dept. of Trade,
Commerce & Industry
www.samoa.net/invest
Eco-Tour Samoa Ltd., Upolu
www.ecotoursamoa.com
Hotel Insel Fehmarn, Apia
www.samoa.net/local/insel.html
Pasefika Inn, Apia
www.samoa.net/local/pinn.html
Pasefika Publications
www.samoa.net/local/pp.html
Polynesian Airlines, Apia
www.polynesianairlines.co.nz
Sails Restaurant, Apia
www.samoa.net/local/sails.html
Samoa Internet Service Provider
www.samoa.net
Samoa Realty &
Investments, Apia
www.samoa.net/samoarealty
Samoan Sensation
www.samoa.co.uk
Samoa Visitors Bureau, Apia
www.samoa.co.nz
Samoa Visitors Bureau, Apia
www.interwebinc.com/samoa

Seacology Foundation, Utah
www.seacology.org
Seipepa Samoan
Travel Home, Apia
www.d90.se/seipepa
Sinalei Reef Resort, Upolu
www.samoa.net/local/sinalei.html
Waterways Travel, U.S.A.
www.waterwaystravel.com

Wallis and Futuna

Uvéa Sharp Center, Wallis Island
www.wallis.co.nc/usc
Wallis & Futuna, Bienvenue
http://wallis-islands.com/index2.htm

Tuvalu

The .TV Corporation
www.internet.tv
Tuvalu Online
http://members.xoom.com/
tuvaluonline

Fiji

Air Fiji, Suva
www.airfiji.net
Air New Zealand
www.airnz.co.nz
Air Pacific, Nadi
www.airpacific.com
Air Promotion Systems,
Los Angeles
www.pacificislands.com
Applied Geoscience
Commission, Suva
www.sopac.org.fj
Aquaventure, Taveuni
www.aquaventure.org
Aqua-Trek, Nadi
www.aquatrek.com
Astral Travel, California
www.island.to/astral.htm
Avis Rent a Car, Nadi
www.avis.com.fj
Banaban Society, Australia
www.ion.com.au/~banaban
Beqa Divers, Pacific Harbor
www.beqadivers.com
Canada 3000 Airlines
www.canada3000.com
Captain Cook Cruises, Nadi
www.captcookcrus.com.au
Centra Suva Hotel
www.parkroyal.com.au

Communications Fiji Ltd., Suva
www.fijivillage.com
Cousteau Fiji Islands Resort,
Savusavu
www.fijiresort.com
Crystal Divers, Nananu-i-Ra
www.crystaldivers.com
Dive Taveuni, Taveuni
www.divetaveuni.com
Dominion International Hotel
www.dominion-
international.com
Fiji Aggressor, Hawaii
www.pac-aggressor.com
Fiji For Less, Suva
www.fiji4less.com
Fiji Government Official Site
http://fiji.gov.fj
Fijilive Network
www.fijilive.com
Fiji Reservations & Travel, Hawaii
www.fiji-islands.com
Fiji Television Ltd., Suva
www.fijitv.com.fj
Fiji Travel, Los Angeles
www.fijitravel.com
Fiji Visitors Bureau, Suva
www.bulafiji.com
Fiji Visitors Bureau, Suva
www.fijifvb.gov.fj
Fiji Visitors Bureau, Suva
www.FijiIslands.org
Fiji Web Center
www.ivanetdesign.com/fijiweb
Fish-Eye Bicycle Tours
www.cyclefiji.com
Forum Secretariat, Suva
www.forumsec.org.fj
Garden Island Resort, Taveuni
www.aquatrek.com
Hidden Paradise Eco Lodge,
Savusavu
www.eco-fiji.com/fiji/hiddenfiji/
index.html
Hot Springs Hotel, Savusavu
www.HotSpringsHotel.com
Integral Multimedia &
Communications, Suva
www.ifiji.com
International
Telecommunications, Suva
www.fintel.com.fj
Internet Fiji, Suva
www.internetfiji.com

Internet Services, Suva
www.fiji-online.com.fj
Island Hoppers, Nadi
www.helicopters.com.fj
Jacks Handicrafts, Nadi
www.jacks.handicrafts.com.fj
Lomalagi Resort, Savusavu
www.lomalagi.com
Maravu Plantation Resort,
Taveuni
www.maravu.com
Marlin Bay Resort, Beqa
www.marlinbay.com
Matangi Island Resort, Taveuni
www.matangiisland.com
Matangi Princess II
www.Tropicalinspirations.com
Matava Astrolabe Hideaway,
Kadavu
www.matava.com.au
Ministry of Mineral
Resources, Suva
www.mrd.gov.fj
Mocambo Hotel, Nadi
www.shangri-la.com
Mollie Dean Cruises, Lami
www.sere.com.fj
Nai'a Cruises, Lami
www.naia.com.fj
Navini Island Resort, Mamanucas
www.navinifiji.com.fj
Nukubati Island Resort, Labasa
www.nukubati.com
Nukuyaweni Outpost, Gau
www.bayofangels.com
Outrigger Hotels, Fiji
www.outrigger.com/pacific
Ovalau Tours and Transport
www.ecotoursfiji.com
Ovalau Watersports, Levuka
www.owlfiji.com
Pacific Magazine, Honolulu
www.pacificmagazine.com
Philatelic Bureau, Suva
www.stampsfiji.com
Ra Divers, Nananu-i-Ra
www.radivers.com
Rainbow Reef Beach Estates,
Vanua Levu
www.rainbowreeffiji.com
Rob Kay's Fiji Guide
www.fijiguide.com
Rolle Realty Ltd., Suva
www.fiji-online.com/rolle

Sheraton Resorts, Nadi
www.sheraton.com
Sea Fiji Travel, Savusavu
www.sni.net/dive
Sea for Yourself
www.snorkeltours.com
Sea Sports Ltd., Sigatoka
www.ida.net/users/davefx/
Seasport.htm
Seven Seas Cruising Association,
U.S.A.
www.ssca.org
Shangri-La's Fijian Resort, Nadi
www.shangri-la.com
Significantly Original Holidays
www.soholidays.com
Sonaisali Island Resort, Nadi
www.sonaisali.com.fj
South Seas Private Hotel, Suva
www.fiji4less.com
Subsurface Fiji, Lautoka
www.fijidiving.com
Sunflower Airlines, Nadi
www.fiji.to
Taveuni Development Co., Suva
www.fijirealestate.com
Telecom Fiji, Suva
www.is.com.fj
The Last Call Cyber Cafe
www.ivanetdesign.com/
thelastcall
Toberua Island Resort, Suva
www.toberua.com
Tourist Information Center, Nadi
www.fijiadventures.com.fj
Treasure Island Resort,
Mamanucas
www.treasure.com.fj
Turtle Island Lodge, Yasawas
www.turtlefiji.com
University of the South
Pacific, Suva
www.usp.ac.fj
Vatulele Island Resort, Nadi
www.vatulele.com
Victory Inland Safaris, Nadi
www.victory.com.fj
Yasawa Island Resort, Yasawas
www.yasawaislandresort.com

New Caledonia
Agence de Développement de la
Culture Kanak
www.adck.nc

Agence de Développement
Economique
  www.adecal.nc
Air Calédonie, Nouméa
  www.air-caledonie.nc
Aircalin, Nouméa
  www.aircalin.nc
Bank of Hawaii, Nouméa
  www.boh.com
Caledonet, Nouméa
  www.caledonet.nc
Club Méditerranée
  www.clubmed.com
Cybercom Cyber Café, Nouméa
  www.cybercom.nc
Escapade Island Resort, Nouméa
  www.parkroyal.com.au
ISP Cipac, Nouméa
  www.canl.nc
ISP Offratel, Nouméa
  www.offratel.nc
Kanaky Online
  www.altern.org/kanaky
Le Méridien, Nouméa
  www.forte-hotels.com
Le Vallon Dore, Mont-Dore
  www.vallondore.com
New Caledonia Informations,
Nouméa
  www.noumea.com
New Caledonia Tourism
  www.newcaledonia.org
New Caledonia Tourism
  www.nouvelle-caledonie-
tourisme.nc
Nouméa Diving
  www.newcaledonia-diving.com
Nouméa Diving
  www.noumea-diving.nc
Nouméa Parkroyal, Nouméa
  www.parkroyal.com.au
Nouvelles Frontières
  www.nouvelles-frontieres.nc
Office des Postes et
Telecommunications
  www.opt.nc
Orstom, Nouméa
  www.orstom.nc
Province Sud, Nouméa
  www.province-sud.nc
Radio NRJ, Nouméa
  www.caledonet.nc/nrj
Services Administratifs
  www.territoire.nc

South Pacific On Line
  www.sponline.nc
Welcome to New Caledonia
  www.new-caledonia.com
Yahoue Sites Index, Nouméa
  www.yahoue.com

Vanuatu
Adventure Center, Port Vila
  www.adventurevanuatu.com
Aquamarine Dive Shop,
Luganville
  www.aquamarine-santo.com
Alliance Reality, Port Vila
  www.vol.com.vu/realestate.html
Iririki Island Resort, Port Vila
  www.iririki.com
Islands Safaris, Port Vila
  www.islandsvanuatu.com
Jon Frum Home Page
  http://203.23.131.2/cargocult/
jonfrum
Le Lagon Parkroyal Hotel,
Port Vila
  www.parkroyal.com.au
Le Méridien Resort, Port Vila
  www.meridien.com.vu
Moores Rowland Chartered
Accountants
  www.mooresrowland.com
Moore Stephens Vanuatu
  www.msvanuatu.com.vu
National Cultural Center
  http://artalpha.anu.edu.au/
web/arc/ vks/vks.htm
National Tourism Office, Port Vila
  www.vanuatutourism.com
Telecom Vanuatu Ltd., Port Vila
  www.vanuatu.com.vu
Transpacific Property Consultants
  www.transpacificproperty.com
USP School of Law, Port Vila
  www.vanuatu.usp.ac.fj
Vanuatu, a Perspective
  www.members.home.net/
scombs/vanuatu.html
Vanuatu Online
  www.vanuatu.net.vu
Vanuatu Online
  www.vol.com.vu
Vanuatu Weekly, Port Vila
  www.vol.com.vu/vanuatuweekly.
html

Web Blong Yumi
  www.chez.com/webyumi/index.html

Solomon Islands
Bilikiki Cruises, Honiara
  www.bilikiki.com
Blue Lagoon Cruises, Honiara
  www.solomonsea.com
Dive Gizo, Gizo
  www.divegizo.com
High Commission of the Solomon
Islands
  www.solomon.emb.gov.au
Island Dive Services, Honiara
  www.ids.com.sb
Islands Hotels Ltd.
  www.islandshotels.com.au
Kayak Solomons, Marovo
  www.kayaksolomons.com
Kolombangara Forest Products
Limited
  www.kfpl.com.sb
Let's Go Diving, Honiara
  www.letsgo.com.sb
Pacific Traditions Society
  http://planet-hawaii.com/vaka
Solomon Airlines
  www.solomonairlines.com.au
Solomon Islands Aggressor
  http://pac-aggressor.com
Solomon Islands Visitors Bureau
  www.commerce.gov.sb
Solomon Telekom
  www.solomon.com.sb
Solomons Village Stay
  www.angelfire.com/biz/
solomonsvillagestay
Travel Health Information
  http://travelhealth.com/malaria.htm
Uepi Island Resort, Marovo
  www.uepi.com

E-MAIL DIRECTORY

Tahiti-Polynesia
Air Tahiti, Papeete
  rtahitim@mail.pf
Air Tahiti Nui, Papeete
  fly@airtahitinui.pf
Aranui Cruises
  cptm@aranui.com
Archipels Croisieres
  archimoo@mail.pf

Bathy's Club, Moorea
bathys@mail.pf
Bora Bora Beach Club
trhppt@mail.pf
Bora Bora Lagoon Resort
BBLR@mail.pf
Bora Pearl Cruises
haumana@mail.pf
Dolphin Quest, Moorea
dqfp@mail.pf
Dolphin Watch, Moorea
criobe@mail.pf
Institut Territorial de la Statistique
itstat@mail.pf
Iaora Tahiti Ecotours
ecotours@mail.pf
Kia Ora Village, Rangiroa
gecco@gte.net
Kuriri Village, Maupiti
Teiva@tahiti.com
Le Maitai Polynesia, Bora Bora
maitaibo@mail.pf
Le Méridien Hotels
sales@lemeridien-tahiti.com
Moana Beach Parkroyal, Bora
Bora
borabora@parkroyal.pf
Moorea Beach Club
trhppt@mail.pf
Moorea Beachcomber Parkroyal
moorea@parkroyal.pf
Moorea Fun Dive
fundive@mail.pf
Nemo World Diving, Bora Bora
divebora@mail.pf
Ono-Ono, Papeete
onoono@mail.pf
Outrigger Hotels of Hawaii
reservations@outrigger.com
Résidence Linareva, Moorea
linareva@mail.pf
Royal Tahitien Hôtel, Tahiti
royalres@mail.pf
Tahiti Beachcomber Parkroyal
tahiti@parkroyal.pf
Tahiti Country Club, Tahiti
trhppt@mail.pf
Tahiti Nui Travel, Papeete
sales@tahitinuitravel.pf
Tahiti Tourisme, Papeete
tahiti-tourisme@mail.pf
Tahiti Yacht Charter, Papeete
tyc@mail.pf

Tahiti-Pacifique Magazine,
Moorea
tahitipm@mail.pf
Tekura Tahiti Travel, Papeete
go@tahiti-tekuratravel.com
Te Tiare Beach Resort, Huahine
tetiarebeach@mail.pf
The Moorings Ltd., Raiatea
moorings@mail.pf
Tiki Village Theater, Moorea
tikivillage@mail.pf
Vahine Island Resort, Taha'a
vahine.island@usa.net

Cook Islands
Air Rarotonga, Penrhyn
penrhyn@airraro.co.ck
Air Rarotonga, Rarotonga
bookings@airraro.co.ck
Ara Moana Bungalows, Mangaia
jan@gatepoly.co.ck
Are Manuiri Guest House, Atiu
adc@adc.co.ck
Ariana Bungalows Motel,
Rarotonga
bob@gatepoly.co.ck
Atiu Motel, Atiu
atiu@gatepoly.co.ck
Ati's Beach Bungalows,
Rarotonga
atis@atisbeach.co.ck
Backpackers International,
Rarotonga
annabill@oyster.net.ck
Budget/Polynesian Rentals,
Rarotonga
rentals@budget.co.ck
Carolyn Short & Associates,
Rarotonga
carolyn@gatepoly.co.ck
Central Motel, Rarotonga
stopover@central.co.ck
Club Raro, Rarotonga
holiday@clubraro.co.ck
Cook Island Divers, Rarotonga
divecook@oyster.net.ck
Cook Island Divers, Rarotonga
gwilson@ci-divers.co.ck
Cook Islands News, Rarotonga
editor@cinews.co.ck
Cook Islands Press, Rarotonga
cipress@gatepoly.co.ck
Cook Islands Tourism Corporation
tourism@cookislands.gov.ck

Cook Islands Tours, Rarotonga
raroinfo@citours.co.ck
Crown Beach Resort, Rarotonga
crownltd@oyster.net.ck
Daydreamer Accommodation,
Rarotonga
byoung@daydreamer.co.ck
Edgewater Resort, Rarotonga
stay@edgewater.co.ck
Hugh Henry & Associates,
Rarotonga
hhenry@gatepoly.co.ck
Island Hopper Vacations,
Rarotonga
travel@islandhopper.co.ck
Island Tours, Aitutaki
islands@gatepoly.co.ck
Kiikii Motel, Rarotonga
relax@kiikiimotel.co.ck
Lagoon Lodges, Rarotonga
des@lagoon.co.ck
Little Polynesian Motel,
Rarotonga
lit-poly@gatepoly.co.ck
Matareka Hostel, Rarotonga
backpack@rarotonga.co.ck
Mauke Cove Lodge, Mauke
aguinea@gatepoly.co.ck
Moana Sands Resort, Rarotonga
beach@moanasands.co.ck
Muri Beachcomber Motel,
Rarotonga
muri@beachcomber.co.ck
Oasis Village, Rarotonga
oasis@gatepoly.co.ck
Pacific Divers, Rarotonga
dive@pacificdivers.co.ck
Pacific Resort, Rarotonga
thomas@pacificresort.co.ck
Palm Grove Lodges, Rarotonga
beach@palmgrove.co.ck
Paradise Inn, Rarotonga
paradise@gatepoly.co.ck
Polyaccess, Rarotonga
republic@banana.co.ck
Puaikura Reef Lodges, Rarotonga
paul@puaikura.co.ck
Raina Beach Apartments,
Rarotonga
raina@gatepoly.co.ck
Rarotongan Resort Hotel,
Rarotonga
sales@rarotongan.co.ck

Rarotongan Sunset Motel, Rarotonga
welcome@rarosunset.co.ck
Shangri-La Beach Cottages, Rarotonga
relax@shangri-la.co.ck
Stars Travel, Rarotonga
holidays@starstravel.co.ck
Takitumu Conservation Area, Rarotonga
kakerori@tca.co.ck
Telecom Cook Islands, Rarotonga
info@oyster.net.ck
Tiare Village Dive Hostel, Rarotonga
tiarevil@gatepoly.co.ck
Tipani Tours, Rarotonga
tours@tipani.co.ck
Vara's Beach House, Rarotonga
backpack@varasbeach.co.ck
Wild Palms, Rarotonga
drink@ronnies.co.ck

Niue

Alofi Rentals, Alofi
alofirentals@sin.net.nu
Coral Gardens Motel, Niue
sguest@cas.nu
Matavai Resort, Niue
matavai@mail.gov.nu
Niue Dive, Alofi
niuedive@dive.nu
Niue Hotel, Alofi
niuehotel@sin.net.nu
Niue Island Yacht Club, Niue
yachtclub@sin.net.nu
Niue Rentals, Alofi
niuerentals@sin.net.nu
Niue Tourism Office, Auckland
niuetourism@clear.net.nz
Niue Tourism Office, Niue
niuetourism@mail.gov.nu
Peleni's Guest House, Alofi
peleni@mail.gov.nu
Wahoo Fishing Charters, Alofi
wahoo@sin.net.nu

Tonga

Beluga Diving, Neiafu
beluga@kalianet.to
Deep Blue Diving, Nuku'alofa
deepblue@kalianet.to
Fafa Island Resort, Nuku'alofa
fafa@kalianet.to

Friendly Islander Hotel, Nuku'alofa
papiloa@kalianet.to
Friendly Islands Bookshop, Nuku'alofa
fibs@kalianet.to
Friendly Islands Kayak Company, Vava'u
kayaktonga@kalianet.to
German Clinic and Pharmacy, Nuku'alofa
medical@kalianet.to
Heilala Holiday Lodge, Nuku'alofa
quick@kalianet.to
Hook-Up Vava'u, Neiafu
hookup@kalianet.to
Hotel Nuku'alofa, Nuku'alofa
sanft@kalianet.to
International Dateline Hotel, Nuku'alofa
idh@kalianet.to
Kalia Cafe, Nuku'alofa
kaliacafe@invited.to
Kiwi Magic, Neiafu
kiwifish@kalianet.to
Langafonua, Nuku'alofa
lgafonua@kalianet.to
Matangi Tonga Magazine
vapress@kalianet.to
Moore Electronics, Nuku'alofa
moore@tongatapu.net.to
Mounu Island Resort, Vava'u
mounu@kalianet.to
New Millennium Radio A3V
vearw@alaska.net
Pacific Island Seaplanes, Nuku'alofa
pacisair@kalianet.to
Pacific Royale Hotel, Nuku'alofa
royale@kalianet.to
Paradise Hotel, Neiafu
paradise@kalianet.to
Paradise Shores Resort, Tongatapu
paradise_shores@kalianet.to
Polynesian Airlines, Nuku'alofa
polyair@kalianet.to
Popao Village Eco Resort, Vava'u
Popao@hotmail.com
Royal Sunset Island Resort, Nuku'alofa
royalsun@kalianet.to
Royal Tongan Airlines, Nuku'alofa
rtamktng@kalianet.to

Sailing Safaris, Neiafu
sailingsafaris@kalianet.to
Samoa Air, Neiafu
tfpel-vv@kalianet.to
Sandy Beach Resort, Foa
sandybch@tongatapu.net.to
Sea for Yourself
info@snorkeltours.com
Sisifa Rental Cars, Nuku'alofa
kiwitonga@kalianet.to
Sunsail, Auckland
res.v@sunsail.co.nz
Target One, Neiafu
fishtarget@kalianet.to
Teta Tours, Nuku'alofa
tetatour@kalianet.to
The Moorings, Neiafu
moorings.tonga@kalianet.to
Times of Tonga, Nuku'alofa
times@kalianet.to
Tonga Chronicle, Nuku'alofa
chroni@kalianet.to
Tonga Telecommunications Commission
ttc@kalianet.to
Tonga Visitors Bureau, Lifuka
tvbhp@kalianet.to
Tonga Visitors Bureau, Neiafu
tvbvv@kalianet.to
Tonga Visitors Bureau, Nuku'alofa
tvb@kalianet.to
Tonga Visitors Bureau, U.S.A.
tonga@value.net
Tongan Beach Resort, Neiafu
tonganbeach@kalianet.to
Tongan Consulate, San Francisco
tania@sfconsulate.gov.to
Tongan Wildlife Center, Tongatapu
birdpark@kalianet.to
Winnies Guesthouse, Nuku'alofa
winnies@kalianet.to

American Samoa

KSBS-FM, Pago Pago
ksbsfm@samoanet.com
National Park
NPSA_Administration@ccmail.itd.nps.gov
Office of Tourism, Pago Pago
samoa@samoatelco.com
Samoa Air, Pago Pago
samoaair@samoatelco.com

Samoa News, Pago Pago
samoanews@samoatelco.com
Ta'alolo Lodge, Ili'ili
taalolo@samoatelco.com
Tutuila Dive Shop, Vaitogi
tutuiladiveshop@samoatelco.com

Samoa
Aggie Grey's Hotel, Apia
aggiegreys@samoa.net
Apia Rentals, Apia
apiarentals@samoa.net
Coconuts Beach Club, Upolu
cbcsamoa@aol.com
Coconuts Beach Club, Upolu
cbc@samoa.net
Computer Services Limited, Apia
cafe@samoa.net
Eco-Tour Samoa Ltd., Upolu
enquiries@ecotoursamoa.com
Island Hopper Vacations, Apia
islandhopper@samoa.net
Kitano Tusitala Hotel, Apia
kitano@samoa.net
Magik 98 FM, Apia
magic98fm@samoa.net
Pacific Quest Divers, Upolu
pqdivers@samoa.net
Polynesian Airlines
enquiries@polynesianairlines.co.nz
Regional Environment Program
sprep@sprep.org.ws
Salani Surf Resort, Upolu
salanisurf@samoa.net
Samoa Marine, Apia
pmeredith@samoa.net
Samoa Visitors Bureau, Apia
samoa@samoa.net
Samoa Visitors Bureau, Australia
samoa@ozemail.com.au
Samoa Visitors Bureau,
New Zealand
samoa@samoa.co.nz
Samoa Visitors Bureau, U.S.A.
SDSI@compuserve.com
Samoan Outrigger Hotel, Apia
outrigger@samoa.net
Seipepa Samoan Travel Home,
Apia
seipepa@samoa.net
Sinalei Reef Resort, Upolu
sinalei@samoa.net

Fiji
Air Fiji, Suva
airfiji@is.com.fj
Air Pacific, Nadi
airpacific@is.com.fj
Air Promotion Systems, Los
Angeles
jpfm@itr-aps.com
Adventure Fiji, Nadi
rosiefiji@is.com.fj
American Express/Tapa
International, Suva
tapa@is.com.fj
Anchorage Beach Resort,
Lautoka
tanoahotels@is.com.fj
Aquaventure, Taveuni
aquaventure@is.com.fj
Aqua-Trek, Nadi
aquatrek@is.com.fj
Avis, Nadi
aviscarsfj@is.com.fj
Beachcomber Island, Lautoka
beachcomber@is.com.fj
Bedarra House, Sigatoka
bedarrahouse@is.com.fj
Beqa Divers, Pacific Harbor
divefiji@is.com.fj
Blue Lagoon Cruises, Lautoka
blc@is.com.fj
Captain Cook Cruises, Nadi
captcookcrus@is.com.fj
Cathay Hotel, Lautoka
cathay@fiji4less.com
Centra Resort Pacific Harbor
centrapacharb@is.com.fj
Centra Suva Hotel, Suva
centrasuva@is.com.fj
Coconut Grove Cottages, Taveuni
coconutgrove@is.com.fj
Communications Fiji, Suva
fv@fm96.com.fj
Consort Shipping Line, Suva
consortship@is.com.fj
Copra Shed Marina, Savusavu
coprashed@is.com.fj
Cousteau Fiji Islands Resort,
Savusavu
fiji4fun@is.com.fj
Crystal Divers, Nananu-i-Ra
crystaldivers@is.com.fj
Daily Post, Suva
postman@is.com.fj

Daku Garden Resort, Savusavu
daku@is.com.fj
Department of Information, Suva
info@fiji.gov.fj
Dive Kadavu, Kadavu
divekadavu@is.com.fjDive
Taveuni, Taveuni
divetaveuni@is.com.fj
Dominion International Hotel,
Nadi
dominionint@is.com.fj
Eco Divers, Savusavu
ecodivers@is.com.fj
Fiji Aggressor
fijiaggressor@is.com.fj
Fiji Dive Operators Assn.,
Savusavu
diveoperators@is.com.fj
Fiji For Less
info@fiji4less.com
Fiji Museum, Suva
fijimuseum@is.com.fj
Fiji Recompression Chamber
Facility
recompression@is.com.fj
Fiji Reservations and Travel,
Hawaii
fiji@maui.net
Fiji Times, Suva
fijitimes@is.com.fj
Fiji Trade & Investment Board,
Suva
ftibinfo@ftib.org.fj
Fiji Travel, Los Angeles
pacmkt@fijitravel.com
Fiji Visitors Bureau, Nadi
fvbnadi@is.com.fj
Fiji Visitors Bureau, Suva
infodesk@fijifvb.gov.fj
First Landing Resort, Lautoka
firstland@is.com.fj
Forum Secretariat, Suva
info@forumsec.org.fj
Garden Island Resort, Taveuni
aquatrek@is.com.fj
Grand Eastern Hotel, Labasa
grest@is.com.fj
Greenpeace Pacific Campaign,
Suva
greenpeace@is.com.fj
Hidden Paradise Eco Lodge,
Savusavu
mal@geko.net.au

Hideaway Resort, Korolevu
hideaway@is.com.fj

Hot Springs Hotel, Savusavu
hotspringshotel@is.com.fj

Islands Business Magazine, Suva
subs@ibi.com.fj

Jacks Handicrafts Ltd.
jacks@is.com.fj

Jona's Paradise Resort, Ono
divekadavu@is.com.fj

Kaba's Motel, Taveuni
kaba@is.com.fj

Kaimbu Island Associates,
California
kaimbu@earthlink.net

Kaimbu Island Resort, Northern
Lau
kaimbu@is.com.fj

Khan's Rental Cars, Nadi
rehnuma@is.com.fj

Lomalagi Resort, Savusavu
lomalagi@is.com.fj

Mamanucas
matamanoa@is.com.fj

Mana Island Resort, Mamanucas
mana@is.com.fj

Maravu Plantation Resort,
Taveuni
maravu@is.com.fj

Marlin Bay Resort, Beqa
marlinbay@is.com.fj

Matamanoa Island Resort,

Matana Beach Resort, Kadavu
divekadavu@is.com.fj

Matangi Island Resort, Matangi
info@matangiisland.com

Matava Astrolabe Hideaway,
Kadavu
matava@suva.is.com.fj

Mocambo Hotel, Nadi
mocambo@is.com.fj

Mollie Dean Cruises, Lami
sere@is.com.fj

Musket Cove, Mamanucas
musketcovefiji@is.com.fj

Nadi Bay Motel, Nadi
nadibay@is.com.fj

Naigani Island Resort, Lomaiviti
naigani@is.com.fj

Nai'a Cruises, Lami
naia@is.com.fj

Namale Resort, Savusavu
namale@is.com.fj

Namotu Island Resort, Nadi
namotu@is.com.fj

Navini Island Resort, Mamanucas
naviniisland@is.com.fj

Naviti Resort, Korolevu
naviti@is.com.fj

Nukubati Island Resort, Labasa
nukubati@is.com.fj

Nukuyaweni Outpost, Gau
outpost@bayofangels.com

Otto's Place, Tavewa
westside@is.com.fj

Outrigger Reef Resort, Korotogo
reefresort@is.com.fj

Ovalau Tours and Transport,
Levuka
otttours@is.com.fj

Pacific Concerns Resource
Center, Suva
pcrc@is.com.fj

Pacific Islands Monthly, Suva
fijitimes@is.com.fj

Pacific Islands News Association
pina@is.com.fjPacNews, Suva
pacnews@is.com.fj

Plantation Island Resort,
Mamanucas
plantation@is.com.fj

Qamea Beach Club Resort,
Qamea
qamea@is.com.fj

Ra Divers, Nananu-i-Ra
radivers@is.com.fj

Raffles Gateway Hotel, Nadi
rafflesresv@is.com.fj

Rainbow Reef Beach Estates,
Vanua Levu
rainbowreef@is.com.fj

Rainbow Reef Divers, Taveuni
aquatrek@is.com.fj

Rakiraki Hotel, Rakiraki
tanoahotels@is.com.fj

Review Magazine, Suva
review@is.com.fj

Rivers Fiji, Pacific Harbor
riversfiji@is.com.fj

Rosie The Travel Service, Nadi
rosiefiji@is.com.fj

Rosie's Deluxe Apartments, Nadi
rosiefiji@is.com.fj

Sandalwood Inn, Nadi
sandalwood@is.com.fj

Saweni Beach Apartments,
Lautoka
saweni@fiji4less.com

Scubahire, Suva
divefiji@is.com.fj

Sea Fiji Travel, Savusavu
seafijidive@is.com.fj

Sea for Yourself
info@snorkeltours.com

Seashell Cove Resort, Nadi
seashell@is.com.fj

Sea Sports Ltd., Sigatoka
seasports@is.com.fj

Seven Seas Cruising Association,
U.S.A.
SSCA1@ibm.net

Shangri-La's Fijian Resort
fijianresort@is.com.fj

Sheraton Fiji Resort, Nadi
kmutton@is.com.fj

Sheraton Vomo Island Resort
sheratonvomo@is.com.fj

Shotover Jet, Nadi
shotoverjet@is.com.fj

Skylodge Hotel, Nadi
tanoahotels@is.com.fj

Sonaisali Island Resort, Nadi
sonaisali@is.com.fj

South Sea Cruises, Nadi
southseaturtle@is.com.fj

South Seas Private Hotel, Suva
southseas@fiji4less.com

Subsurface Fiji, Lautoka
subsurface@is.com.fj

Sunflower Airlines, Nadi
sunair@is.com.fj

Suva Apartments, Suva
fasanoc@is.com.fj

Tanoa Apartments, Nadi
tanoahotels@is.com.fj

Tanoa International Hotel, Nadi
tanoahotels@is.com.fj

Tavarua Island Resort, Nadi
tavarua@is.com.fj

The Beachouse, Korolevu
beachouse@is.com.fj

The Last Call Restaurant, Lautoka
thelastcall@is.com.fj

Thrifty Rent a Car, Nadi
rosiefiji@is.com.fj

Toberua Island Resort, Suva
toberua@is.com.fj

Tokatoka Resort Hotel, Nadi
tokatokaresort@is.com.fj

Tokoriki Sunset Resort,
Mamanucas
tokoriki@is.com.fj

Tourism Council of the South
Pacific, Suva
  spice@is.com.fj

Tourist Information Center, Nadi
  hostelsfiji@is.com.fj

Tradewinds Hotel, Suva
  tradewindsresv@is.com.fj

Travel Inn, Suva
  travelinn@fiji4less.com

Travelers Beach Resort, Nadi
  beachvilla@is.com.fj

Tubakula Beach Resort, Korotogo
  tubakula@fiji4less.com

Turtle Airways, Nadi
  southseaturtle@is.com.fj

Turtle Island Lodge, Yasawas
  turtle@is.com.fj

University of the South Pacific
  webmaster@usp.ac.fj

Vatukaluvi Holiday House,
Savusavu
  coprashed@is.com.fj

Vatulele Island Resort
  vatulele@is.com.fj

Vatulele Island Resort
  vatu@magna.com.au

Victory Inland Safaris, Nadi
  touristinfofj@is.com.fj

Wakaya Club, Lomaiviti
  wakaya@is.com.fj

Warwick Hotel, Korolevu
  warwick@is.com.fj

Waterfront Hotel, Lautoka
  tanoahotels@is.com.fj

Westside Watersports, Lautoka
  westside@is.com.fj

West's Motor Inn, Nadi
  westsmotorinn@mail.is.com.fj

Yasawa Island Resort, Yasawas
  yasawaisland@is.com.fj

New Caledonia
Agency for the Development of
Kanak Culture
  adck@canl.nc

Air Calédonie, Nouméa
  aircal@canl.nc

Aircalin, Nouméa
  acinou@canl.nc

AOM French Airlines, Nouméa
  comedia@cipac.nc

Budget Rent-a-Car, Nouméa
  car@offratel.nc

Corsair, Nouméa
  nfnc@canl.nc

Destination Îles Loyauté
  destil@canl.nc

Europcar/Visa Location, Nouméa
  nta@offratel.nc

Globetrotters Tours, Nouméa
  globtrot@canl.nc

Hertz Rent-a-Car, Nouméa
  hertz@canl.nc

Hôtel Kou-Bugny, Isle of Pines
  koubugny@canl.nc

Hôtel Le Stanley, Nouméa
  stanotel@canl.nc

Kuendu Beach Resort, Nouméa
  com.we@offratel.nc

Le Lagon Nouméa, Nouméa
  lelagon@offratel.nc

Le Méridien Hotel, Nouméa
  meridien@meridien.nc

Les Nouvelles Caledoniennes
  lnc@canl.nc

Librairie Montaigne, Nouméa
  montaigne@canl.nc

Mangrove Records, Nouméa
  mangrove@canl.nc

Mencar Rent-a-Car, Nouméa
  mencar@canl.nc

Nouméa Diving, Nouméa
  diving@noumea-diving.nc

Nouvelle-Calédonie Tourisme
  tourisme@offratel.nc

Nouvelles Frontières
  nfcorsair@canl.nc

Office des Postes et
Telecommunications
  opt@opt.nc

Secretariat of the Pacific
Community
  spc@spc.org.nc

Vanuatu
Adventure Center, Port Vila
  info@adventurevanuatu.com

Alliance Française, Port Vila
  alliafra@vanuatu.com.vu

Alliance Reality, Port Vila
  realestate@vanuatu.com.vu

Aore Resort, Luganville
  aore@vanuatu.com.vu

Aquamarine Dive Shop,
Luganville
  aquamrne@vanuatu.com.vu

Avis, Port Vila
  avis@vanuatu.com.vu

BDO International, Port Vila
  bdo@vanuatu.com.vu

Bokissa Island Resort, Luganville
  bokissa@vanuatu.com.vu

Coongoola Cruises, Port Vila
  drewco@vanuatu.com.vu

Discount Rentals, Port Vila
  teppdmtl@vanuatu.com.vu

Erakor Island Resort, Efate
  erakor@vanuatu.com.vu

Hideaway Island Resort, Efate
  hideaway@vanuatu.com.vu

Iririki Island Resort, Port Vila
  reservation@iririki.com

Islands Safaris, Port Vila
  islands@vanuatu.com.vu

Kava Kompani, Port Vila
  kava@vanuatu.com.vu

La Violante Charters, Port Vila
  violante@vanuatu.com.vu

Le Lagon Parkroyal Hotel, Port
Vila
  lelagon@vanuatu.com.vu

Le Méridien Resort, Port Vila
  hotelsales@meridien.com.vu

Moores Rowland Chartered
Accountants
  offshore@mooresrowland.com

National Cultural Center
  vks@vanuatu.pactok.net

National Tourism Office
  Port Vila
  tourism@vanuatu.com.vu

New Look Hotel, Luganville
  newlook@vanuatu.com.vu

Oceanic Expeditions, Port Vila
  herman@vanuatu.com.vu

Palms Casino, Port Vila
  palmscas@vanuatu.com.vu

Pro Dive Espiritu Santo, Luganville
  pdsanto@vanuatu.com.vu

Pro Dive Vila, Port Vila
  prodive@vanuatu.com.vu

Sailaway Cruises, Port Vila
  sailaway@vanuatu.com.vu

Snoopy's Stationery, Port Vila
  snoopy@vanuatu.com.vu

Telecom Vanuatu Ltd., Port Vila
  info@tvl.net.vu

Trading Post, Port Vila
  tpost@vanuatu.com.vu

Transpacific Property
  consultant@transpacificproperty.com

Vanuatu Finance Center Assn.,
Port Vila
  fincen@vanuatu.com.vu
Vanuatu Online, Port Vila
  vol@vanuatu.com.vu
Vanuatu Weekly, Port Vila
  vbtcnews@vanuatu.com.vu

Solomon Islands
Adventure Sports, Gizo
  DiveGizo@welkam.solomon.com.sb
Avis/Pacific Car Rentals, Honiara
  dquan@welkam.solomon.com.sb

Bilikiki Cruises Ltd.
  bilikiki@horizon.bc.ca
Bilikiki Cruises Ltd.
  bilikiki@welkam.solomon.com.sb
BJS Agencies, Honiara
  bjs@welkam.solomon.com.sb

Blue Lagoon Cruises, Honiara
  solsea@welkam.solomon.com.sb
Commodities Export Marketing
Auth.
  cema@welkam.solomon.com.sb
Forum Fisheries Agency, Honiara
  ffa@ffa.int
Gizo Hotel, Gizo
  gizohtl@welkam.solomon.com.sb
Guadalcanal Travel Service,
Honiara
  gts@welkam.solomon.com.sb
Island Dive Services, Honiara
  johncarr@welkam.solomon.com.sb
Island Dive Services, Honiara
  ssd@ids.com.sb
Islands Hotels Ltd.
  ihres@islandshotels.com.au
KFPL Resthouse, Kolombangara
  office@kfpl.com.sb

King Solomon Hotel, Honiara
  kingsol@welkam.solomon.com.sb
Let's Go Diving, Honiara
  letsgo@welkam.solomon.com.sb
Solomon Airlines, Honiara
  solair@welkam.solomon.com.sb
Solomon Airlines
  solomonair@solomonairlines.com.au
Solomon Islands Aggressor
  livedive@compuserve.com
Solomon Islands Development
Trust
  sidt@welkam.solomon.com.sb
Solomon Islands Visitors Bureau
  commerce@commerce.gov.sb
Solomon Telekom
  sales@cw.com.sb
Solomon Telekom
  telekom@welkam.solomon.com.sb
Uepi Island Resort, Marovo
  uepi@ultra.net.au

INTERNATIONAL AIRPORT CODES

AKL—Auckland
APW—Apia/Faleolo
BNE—Brisbane
CHC—Christchurch
CNS—Cairns
DPS—Denpasar/Bali
FGI—Apia/Fagalii
FUN—Funafuti
GEA—Nouméa/Magenta
GUM—Guam
HIR—Honiara
HNL—Honolulu
INU—Nauru

IPC—Easter Island
IUE—Niue
LAX—Los Angeles
MEL—Melbourne
MNL—Manila NAN—Nadi
NOU—Nouméa/La Tontouta
OSA—Osaka
POM—Port Moresby
PPG—Pago Pago
PPT—Papeete
RAR—Rarotonga
SCL—Santiago
SEA—Seattle

SFO—San Francisco
SIN—Singapore
SUV—Suva
SYD—Sydney
TBU—Tongatapu
TRW—Tarawa
TYO—Tokyo
VLI—Port Vila
WLG—Wellington
WLS—Wallis
YVR—Vancouver
YYZ—Toronto

ALTERNATIVE PLACE NAMES

Alu—Shortland
Ambae—Aoba
Anatom—Aneityum
Aneityum—Anatom
Aoba—Ambae
Bass Islands—Marotiri Islands
Bellingshausen—Motu One
Bughotu—Isabel
Choiseul—Lauru
Danger—Pukapuka
Drehu—Lifou
Easter Island—Isla de Pascua
Easter Island—Rapa Nui
Ellice Islands—Tuvalu
Efate—Vate
Espiritu Santo—Santo
Falcon—Fonuafo'ou
Fonuafo'ou—Falcon
French Polynesia—Tahiti-
Polynesia
Futuna—Hoorn
Gaua—Santa Maria
Gilbert Islands—Kiribati
Grande Terre—New Caledonia
Hervey—Manuae
Hoorn—Futuna
Hull—Maria
Iaai—Ouvéa
Isabel—Bughotu
Isabel—Santa Isabel
Isla de Pascua—Easter Island
Isle of Pines—Kwenyii
Kanaky—New Caledonia
Kiribati—Gilbert Islands
Kolombangara—Nduke

Kwenyii—Isle of Pines
Lauru—Choiseul
Lifou—Drehu
Lord Howe—Ontong Java
Luangiua—Ontong Java
Luganville—Santo
Maiao—Tapuaemanu
Makira—San Cristobal
Malekula—Mallicollo
Mallicollo—Malekula
Manuae—Hervey
Manuae—Scilly
Maré—Nengone
Maria—Hull
Marotiri Islands—Bass Islands
Maupihaa—Mopelia
Maupiti—Maurau
Maurau—Maupiti
Mbilua—Vella Lavella
Mohotani—Motane
Mopelia—Maupihaa
Moruroa—Mururoa
Motane—Mohotani
Motu Iti—Tupai
Motu One—Bellingshausen
Mururoa—Moruroa
Nduke—Kolombangara
Nendo—Santa Cruz
Nengone—Maré
New Caledonia—Grande Terre
New Caledonia—Kanaky
New Hebrides—Vanuatu
Niue—Savage
Olohega—Swains
Ontong Java—Lord Howe

Ontong Java—Luangiua
Ouvéa—Iaai
Penrhyn—Tongareva
Port Vila—Vila
Pukapuka—Danger
Rapa Nui—Easter Island
San Cristobal—Makira
Santa Cruz—Nendo
Santa Isabel—Isabel
Santa Maria—Gaua
Santo—Espiritu Santo
Santo—Luganville
Savage—Niue
Scilly—Manuae
Shortland—Alu
Sikaiana—Stewart Island
Stewart Island—Sikaiana
Swains—Olohega
Taha'a—Uporu
Tahiti-Polynesia—French
Polynesia
Tapuaemanu—Maiao
Tokelau—Union Group
Tongareva—Penrhyn
Tupai—Motu Iti
Tuvalu—Ellice Islands
Union Group—Tokelau
Uporu—Taha'a
Uvéa—Wallis
Vanikolo—Vanikoro
Vanikoro—Vanikolo
Vanuatu—New Hebrides
Vate—Efate
Vella Lavella—Mbilua
Western Samoa—Samoa

GLOSSARY

aa **lava**—*see* pahoehoe

ahimaa—*see* umu

ahu—a Polynesian stone temple platform

anse—cove (French)

aparima—a Tahitian hand dance

archipelago—a group of islands

ariki—a Polynesian high chief; the traditional head of a clan or tribe; in Tahitian, *ari'i*

Arioi—a pre-European religious society that traveled among the Society Islands presenting ceremonies and entertainments

atoll—a low-lying, ring-shaped coral reef enclosing a lagoon

balolo—in Fijian, a reef worm *(Eunice viridis),* called *palolo* in Samoa

bareboat charter—chartering a yacht without crew or provisions

bark cloth—*see* tapa

barrier reef—a coral reef separated from the adjacent shore by a lagoon

bêche-de-mer—sea cucumber; an edible sea slug; in Tahitian, *rori;* in French, *trépang; see* also pidgin

betel nut—the seed of the fruit of the betel palm *(Areca catechu),* chewed in Melanesia with a little lime and leaves from the pepper plant

blackbirder—A 19th-century European recruiter of island labor, mostly ni-Vanuatu and Solomon Islanders taken to work on plantations in Queensland and Fiji.

breadfruit—a large, round fruit with starchy flesh grown on an *uru* tree *(Artocarpus altilis)*

BYO—Bring Your Own (an Australian term used to refer to restaurants that allow you to bring your own alcoholic beverages)

caldera—a wide crater formed through the collapse or explosion of a volcano

Caldoche—Early French settlers in New Caledonia, some of whom had originally been convicts. Now used to distinguish long-time residents of French origin from more recent arrivals.

cargo cult—Melanesian religious movement or movements promising salvation through the return of ancestors who will bring European-introduced goods (cargo) to their descendants

cassava—manioc; the starchy edible root of the tapioca plant

CFP—*Cour de Franc Pacifique;* the currency in the three French Pacific territories

chain—an archaic unit of length equivalent to 20 meters

ciguatera—a form of fish poisoning caused by microscopic algae

CMAS—Confédération Mondiale des Activités Subaquatiques; the French counterpart of PADI

coastwatchers—Allied intelligence agents who operated behind Japanese lines during WW II

coir—coconut husk sennit used to make rope, etc.

confirmation—A confirmed reservation exists when a supplier acknowledges, either orally or in writing, that a booking has been accepted.

copra—dried coconut meat used in the manufacture of coconut oil, cosmetics, soap, and margarine

coral—a hard, calcareous substance of various shapes, composed of the skeletons of tiny marine animals called polyps

coral bank—a coral formation more than 150 meters long

coral head—a coral formation a few meters across

coral patch—a coral formation up to 150 meters long

CUSO—Canadian University Students Overseas, the Canadian equivalent of the Peace Corps

custom owner—traditional tribal or customary owner based on usage

cyclone—Also known as a hurricane (in the Caribbean) or typhoon (in Japan). A tropical storm that rotates around a center of low atmospheric pressure; it becomes a cyclone when its winds reach force 12 or 64 knots. At sea the air will be filled with foam and driving spray, the water surface completely white with 14-meter-high waves. In the Northern Hemisphere, cyclones spin counterclockwise, while south of the equator they move clockwise. The winds of cyclonic storms are deflected toward a low-pressure area at the center, although the "eye" of the cyclone may be calm.

dalo—see taro

deck—Australian English for a terrace or porch

desiccated coconut—the shredded meat of dehydrated fresh coconut

direct flight—a through flight with one or more stops but no change of aircraft, as opposed to a nonstop flight

dugong—a large plant-eating marine mammal; called a manatee in the Caribbean

EEZ—Exclusive Economic Zone; a 200-nautical-mile offshore belt of an island nation or seacoast state that controls the mineral exploitation and fishing rights

endemic—native to a particular area and existing only there

ESCAP—Economic and Social Commission for Asia and the Pacific

expatriate—a person residing in a country other than his/her own; in the South Pacific such persons are also called "Europeans" if their skin is white, or simply "expats."

fa'afafine—the Samoan term for men who act and dress like women; called mahu in Tahiti-Polynesia, fakaleiti in Tonga

FAD—fish aggregation device

fafa—a "spinach" of cooked taro leaves

fale—Samoan house; in Tahitian fare

farani—French; français

fautau—the highest formal representative of the Samoan people

filaria—parasitic worms transmitted by biting insects to the blood or tissues of mammals. The obstruction of the lymphatic glands by the worms can cause an enlargement of the legs or other parts, a disease known as elephantiasis.

fissure—a narrow crack or chasm of some length and depth

FIT—foreign independent travel; a custom-designed, prepaid tour composed of many individualized arrangements

fringing reef—a reef along the shore of an island

gendarme—a French policeman on duty only in rural areas in France and French overseas territories

GPS—Global Positioning System, the space age successor of the sextant

guano—manure of seabirds, used as a fertilizer

guyot—a submerged atoll, the coral of which couldn't keep up with rising water levels

Havaiki—legendary homeland of the Polynesians

hurricane—see cyclone

jug—a cross between a ceramic kettle and a pitcher used to heat water for tea or coffee in Australian-style hotels

kanaka—a human being in both Polynesia and Melanesia; formerly used in the pejorative sense for "native"

kava—a Polynesian word for the drink known in the Fijian language as yaqona and in English slang as "grog." This traditional beverage is made by squeezing a mixture of the grated root of the pepper shrub (Piper methysticum) and cold water through a strainer of hibiscus-bark fiber.

knot—about three kilometers per hour

kumara—sweet potato (Ipomoea batatas)

lagoon—an expanse of water bounded by a reef

langi—a megalithic tomb for early Tonga kings, in the form of a stepped limestone pyramid

Lapita pottery—pottery made by the ancient Polynesians from 1600 to 500 B.C.

laplap—see pareu

lavalava—see pareu

lava tube—a conduit formed as molten rock continues to flow below a cooled surface during the growth of a lava field. When the eruption ends, a tunnel is left with a flat floor where the last lava hardened.

LDS—Latter-day Saints; the Mormons

leeward—downwind; the shore (or side) sheltered from the wind; as opposed to windward

lei—a garland, often of fresh flowers, but sometimes of paper, shells, etc., hung about the neck of a person being welcomed or feted

le truck—a truck with seats in back, used for public transportation on Tahiti

live-aboard—a tour boat with cabin accommodation for scuba divers

LMS—London Missionary Society; a Protestant group that spread Christianity from Tahiti (1797) across the Pacific

maa Tahiti—Tahitian food

mahimahi—dorado, Pacific dolphinfish (no relation to the mammal)

mahu—a male Tahitian transvestite, sometimes also homosexual; in Tongan the term is *fakaleiti*, in Samoan *fa'afafine*

mairie—town hall (French)

makatea—an uplifted reef around the coast of an elevated atoll

mama ruau—actually "grandmother," but also used for the Mother Hubbard long dress introduced to Tahiti by missionaries

mana—authority, prestige, virtue, "face," psychic power, a positive force

manahune—a commoner or member of the lower class in pre-Christian Tahitian society

mangrove—a tropical shrub with branches that send down roots forming dense thickets along tidal shores

manioc—cassava, tapioca, a starchy root crop

maohi—a native of Tahiti-Polynesia

Maori—the Polynesians of New Zealand and the Cook Islands

marae—a Tahitian temple or open-air cult place, called *me'ae* in the Marquesas; a Samoan village green *(malae);* a Maori meeting place. The Fijian word is *rara*.

masi—see *tapa*

matrilineal—a system of tracing descent through the mother's familial line

Melanesia—the high island groups of the western Pacific (Fiji, New Caledonia, Vanuatu, Solomon Islands, Papua New Guinea); from *melas* (black)

Micronesia—chains of high and low islands mostly north of the Equator (Carolines, Gilberts, Marianas, Marshalls); from *micro* (small)

moai—an Easter Island statue

monoï—perfumed coconut oil

motu—a flat reef islet

nakamal—in the villages of Vanuatu, an open area surrounded by gigantic banyan trees, where men gather nightly to drink kava

namba—a penis wrapper or sheath worn by the Big and Small Namba tribes of interior Malekula, Vanuatu

NAUI—National Association of Underwater Instructors

NGO—Nongovernment organization

ni-Vanuatu—an indigenous inhabitant of Vanuatu

Oro—the Polynesian god of war

ORSTOM—Office de la Recherche Scientifique et Technique d'Outre-Mer

ote'a—a Tahitian ceremonial dance performed by men and women in two columns

overbooking—the practice of confirming more seats, cabins, or rooms than are actually available to ensure against no-shows

pa—ancient Polynesian stone fortress

Pacific rim—the continental landmasses and large countries around the fringe of the Pacific

PADI—Professional Association of Dive Instructors

pahoehoe lava—A smooth lava formation with wavy, ropelike ripples created when very hot, fluid lava continues to flow beneath a cooling surface. *Aa* lava, on the other hand, is slow-moving, thick, and turbulent, creating a rough, chunky surface.

palagi—a Polynesian word used throughout the region to refer to Europeans; also *papalagi, palangi;* in Tahitian *papa'a*

palolo—see *balolo*

palusami—a Samoan specialty of coconut cream wrapped in taro leaves and baked

pandanus—screw pine with slender stem and prop roots. The sword-shaped leaves are used for plaiting mats and hats. In Tahitian, *fara*.

parasailing—a sport in which participants are carried aloft by a parachute pulled behind a speedboat

pareu—a Tahitian saronglike wraparound skirt or loincloth; *lavalava* in Samoan, *sulu* in Fijian, *laplap* in Melanesia, *sarong* in Indonesian

pass—a channel through a barrier reef, usually with an outward flow of water

passage—an inside passage between an island and a barrier reef

patrilineal—a system of tracing descent through the fathers familial line

pawpaw—papaya

pelagic—relating to the open sea, away from land

peretane—Britain, British in Tahitian

pidgin—a form of speech with a limited vocabulary and simplified grammar used for communication between groups speaking different languages; also known as *bêche-de-mer, Bislama,* and Neo-Melanesian.

pirogue—outrigger canoe (French), in Tahitian *vaa*

PK—*pointe kilométrique,* a system of marking kilometers along highways in the French territories

poe—a sticky pudding made from bananas, papaya, pumpkin, or taro mixed with starch, baked in an oven, and served with coconut milk

poisson cru—raw fish marinated in lime (French), in Tahitian *ia ota;* in Fijian *kokoda;* in Japanese *sashimi*

Polynesia—divided into Western Polynesia (Tonga and Samoa) and Eastern Polynesia (Tahiti-Polynesia, Cook Islands, Hawaii, Easter Island, and New Zealand); from *poly* (many)

punt—a flat-bottomed boat

pupu—traditional Tahitian dance group

Quonset hut—a prefabricated, semicircular, metal shelter popular during WW II; also called a Nissan hut

raatira—Tahitian chief, dance leader

rain shadow—the dry side of a mountain, sheltered from the windward side

Ratu—a title for Fijian chiefs, prefixed to their names

reef—a coral ridge near the ocean surface

sailing—the fine art of getting wet and becoming ill while slowly going nowhere at great expense

scuba—self-contained underwater breathing apparatus

SDA—Seventh-Day Adventist

self-contained—a room with private facilities (a toilet and shower not shared with other guests); the brochure term "en-suite" means the same thing; as opposed to a "self-catering" unit with cooking facilities

sennit—braided coconut-fiber rope

shareboat charter—a yacht tour for individuals or couples who join a small group on a fixed itinerary

shifting cultivation—a method of farming involving the rotation of fields instead of crops

shoal—a shallow sandbar or mud bank

shoulder season—a travel period between high/peak and low/off-peak seasons

siapo—see tapa

SPARTECA—South Pacific Regional Trade and Economic Cooperation Agreement; an agreement that allows certain manufactured goods from Pacific countries duty-free entry to Australia and New Zealand

SPREP—South Pacific Regional Environment Program

subduction—the action of one tectonic plate wedging under another

subsidence—geological sinking or settling

sulu—see pareu

symbiosis—a mutually advantageous relationship between unlike organisms

tabu—also *tapu, kapu;* taboo, sacred, set apart, forbidden, a negative force

tahua—in the old days a skilled Tahitian artisan or priest; today a sorcerer or healer

tamaaraa—a Tahitian feast

Tamaha—daughter of the *Tu'i Tonga Fefine* (queen of Tonga)

tamure—a new name for Ori Tahiti, a very fast erotic dance

tanoa—a special wide wooden bowl in which *yaqona* (kava) is mixed; used in ceremonies in Fiji, Tonga, and Samoa

ta'ovala—a mat worn in Tonga by both sexes over a kilt or skirt

tapa—a cloth made from the pounded bark of the paper mulberry tree *(Broussonetia papyrifera).* It's soaked and beaten with a mallet to flatten and intertwine the fibers, then painted with geometric designs; called *siapo* in Samoan, *ngatu* in Tongan, *masi* in Fijian.

tapu—see tabu

taro—a starchy elephant-eared tuber *(Colocasia esculenta),* a staple food of the Pacific islanders; called *dalo* in Fijian

tatau—the Tahitian original of the adopted English word tattoo

tavana—the elected mayor of a Tahitian commune (from the English "governor") *tifaifai*—a Tahitian patchwork quilt based on either European or Polynesian motifs

tiki—a humanlike sculpture used in the old days for religious rites and sorcery

timeshare—part ownership of a residential unit with the right to occupy the premises for a certain period each year in exchange for payment of an annual maintenance fee

tinito—Tahitian for Chinese

TNC—transnational corporation (also referred to as a multinational corporation)

toddy—The spathe of a coconut tree is bent to a horizontal position and tightly bound before it begins to flower. The end of the spathe is then split, and the sap drips down a twig or leaf into a bottle. Fresh or fermented, toddy *(tuba)* makes an excellent drink.

to'ere—a hollow wooden drum hit with a stick

trade wind—a steady wind blowing toward the equator from either northeast or southeast

trench—the section at the bottom of the ocean where one tectonic plate wedges under another

tridacna clam—eaten everywhere in the Pacific, its size varies between 10 centimeters and one meter

tropical storm—a cyclonic storm with winds of 35 to 64 knots

tsunami—a fast-moving wave caused by an undersea earthquake

tu'i (Polynesian)—king, ruler

umara—see *kumara*

umu—an underground, earthen oven; called *ahimaa* in Tahitian, *lovo* in Fijian. After A.D. 500, the Polynesians had lost the art of making pottery, so they were compelled to bake their food, rather than boil it.

vigia—a mark on a nautical chart indicating a dangerous rock or shoal

volcanic bomb—lumps of lava blown out of a volcano, which take a bomblike shape as they cool in the air

VSA—Volunteer Service Abroad, the New Zealand equivalent of the Peace Corps

VSO—Voluntary Service Overseas, the British equivalent of the Peace Corps

VTT—*vélo à tout terrain;* mountain bike

wantok—a pidgin English term for a member of the same clan or tribe

windward—the point or side from which the wind blows, as opposed to leeward

yam—the starchy, tuberous root of a climbing plant

yaqona—see *kava*

zories—rubber shower sandals, thongs, flip-flops

INDEX

Italicized page numbers indicate information in captions, charts, illustrations, maps, or special topics.

A

A'ama: 896
Abaca: 655-657
acclimatizing: 117
accommodations: 79-82; Cook Islands 313; Easter Island 297-300; Fiji 575-578; New Caledonia 725-726; Pitcairn Island 284; Samoa 469-470; Solomon Islands 864; Tahiti-Polynesia 148-149; Tokelau 515; Tonga 380; Tuvalu 534; Vanuatu 793; *see also specific place*
Adams, John: *282,* 286
Adamstown: 286
Afareaitu: 200
Afu Aau Falls: 502-503
Afulilo Reservoir: 494
Agakauitai: 266
Agricultural Fair: 147
Ahe: 258
Ahu Akahanga: 296
Ahu Akivi: 295
Ahu Ature Huki: 296
Ahuii Waterfall: 270
Ahu Naunau: 296
Ahu Tahai: 295, *298*
Ahu Te Pito Kura: 296
Ahu Tepeu: 295
Ahu Tongariki: 296
Ahu Vaihu: 296
Ahu Vinapu: 295
AIDS: 119-120
airports: 955; Bora Bora (Tahiti-Polynesia) 244; Faa'a International (Tahiti-Polynesia) 165; Fagali'i (Samoa) 474; Faleolo International (Samoa) 474; Fua'amotu International (Tonga); Hanan International (Niue) 366; Henderson (Solomon Islands) 870; La Tontouta International (New Caledonia) 730-731; Mataveri (Easter Island) 303; Maupiti (Tahiti-Polynesia) 247; Moorea

Temae (Tahiti-Polynesia) 210; Nadi International (Fiji) 588-589; Nausori (Fiji) 589; Nuku Ataha (Tahiti-Polynesia) 272-273; Pago Pago International (American Samoa) 441; Port Vila International (Vanuatu) 797-798; Raiatea (Tahiti-Polynesia) 228; Rarotonga International (Cook Islands); Tubuai (Tahiti-Polynesia) 251
air transportation: 84-95, 104-105; *see also specific place*
Aitutaki: 337-343, *337*
Aitutaki Golf Club: 339
Akamaru: 265
Alao: 444
Alava, Mt.: 446
Albert Park: 627
Aleipata: 494, 495-497
All Saints' Day: 147
All Souls Day: 313
Alofaaga Blowholes: 503
Alofi (Niue): 360-366, *364*
Alofi (Wallis and Futuna): 528
Alu: 916
Amédée Lighthouse: 735-736
Ambae: 844-846, *845*
Ambrym: 840-843, *841*
American Samoa: 430-456, *431, 432,* 930, 947, 952; climate 431; economy 434-435; fauna 431-432; government 433-434; history 432-433; holidays and festivals 437-438; land 430-431; people 435-436; services and information 438-439; transportation 439-441
Anaho: 271
Anahoa Beach: 273
Ana Kai Tangata: 295
Anakena Beach: 296
Anaraura: 349
Anau: 235
Aneityum: 824
animals: *see* fauna
Aniwa: 824

Ano, Lake: 424
Anokula: 407
Anuta: 927
Aoba: *see* Ambae
Aola: 890
Aorai, Mt.: 172-173
Aore Island: 834
Apia: 475-500, *478; accommodations 481-484; climate* 458; entertainment 486-487; food 484-486; services and information 488-490; shopping 488; sights 475-480; sports and recreation 480-481; transportation 490-493
Apia Observatory: 476
Apia Park: 481
Apia Samoa Temple: 479
Aquarium de Moorea: 198
Arahoho Blowhole: 187
Ara Metua: 322, 323
Araura Marine Research Station: 339
archaeology: 211, 291-292
Arches of Talava: 361
area: *50;* American Samoa *432;* Cook Islands *306;* Easter Island 289; Fiji *549;* New Caledonia *713;* Niue 356; Pitcairn 280; Samoa *432;* Solomon Islands *849;* Tahiti-Polynesia *131;* Tonga *369;* Tuvalu *530;* Vanuatu: *781;* Wallis and Futuna 519
Are-Karioi-Nui National Auditorium: 322
Arorangi: 322-323, 330
arts and crafts: 78-79; Cook Islands 333; Fiji 574; Samoa 469; Solomon Islands 863-864, 881; Tokelau 515; Tonga 379-380
Arue: 171
Arutanga: 337-343, *340*
Asau: 504
Assemblies of God: 67
Atafu: 517, *517*

Atata Island: 404-405
Atauloma Girls School: 445
Atchin: 828
'Atenisi Institute: 395
Atiraa Falls: 200
Atiu: 344-348
ATMs: 111
atolls: 25-29, 27
Atori: 897
Atuona: 132, 275-278
Atwater, Dorence: 191
Auberge du Mont Koghi: 754
Aukena: 265
Auki: 892-894
Aunu'u Island: 444-445
Austin, Mt.: 874
Austral Islands: 248-252
Austronesians: 39-40
automated teller machines: 111
Avaiki Sea Cave: 361
Avana Valley: 323
Avarua: 318-322, 319, 325-337
Avatoru: 253-254

B

Ba: 651
Bâ Falls: 759
baggage: 95, 123
Baha'i House of Worship: 480
Bain du Vaima: 189
Bain Loti: 169
Baker, Shirley: 411
Balade: 763
Balboa, Vasco Núñez de: 41, 43
Ballalae: 915-916
balolo: 569
Banks Islands: 846-847
banyan trees: 779
Banyo: 925
Barrage de Yaté: 753
Basakana Island: 896
Basilica of St. Anthony of Padua: 387
Bastille Day: 147, 725
Batiki: 680
Batuna: 903-905
Bau Island: 644-645
Beachcomber Island: 608-609
Bellingshausen: see Motu One
Bellona: 899-900
Beqa Island: 623-624
Bernheim Library: 733
betel chewing: 84
beverages: 83-84

bibliography: 931-944
bicycling: 100, 108-109; see also
    specific place
birds/birdwatching: 35, 132, 305-
    306, 431-432, 459, 781, 850
Bislama: 847
blackbirders: 783
black pearls: see pearls
Black Rock: 322
Bligh, William: 133, 281, 409, 552-
    553
Bloody Ridge: 889
Blue Lagoon (Tahiti-Polynesia):
    255
Blue Lagoon (Vanuatu): 837
blue-ring octopus: 37
Blunt's Point: 441
boat transportation: 95-96, 105-
    108, 109; see also freighters;
    yachting; specific place
Bois du Sud: 751
Bokissa Island: 834
Bomb Day: 534
Bonegi Private Beach: 887
booksellers: 938-939
Bora Bora: 233-244, 234;
    accommodations 236-240;
    entertainment and events 241-
    242; food 240-241; history 233-
    234; services and information
    242; shopping 242; sights 234-
    236; transportation 242-244
Bougainville, Antoine de: 133, 169
Bounty, HMS: 281-282, 282, 552-
    553
Bourail: 757-758
Bourail Museum: 757-758
Breakers Point: 444
Brooke, Rupert: 68
Bua Bay: 683
Buala: 919-920
Buca Bay: 693-694
Bughotu: see Isabel Province
bungee jumping: 843-844
buses: 108; see also specific
    place; Fiji 584-585; New
    Caledonia 748; Samoa 491-
    492; Solomon Islands 886;
    Tonga 398; Vanuatu 814
Byron, John: 43, 43

C

Cakobau, Ratu Seru: 553-55
cameras: 125-126

camping: 82, 123; Fiji 576; New
    Caledonia 726; Tahiti-Polynesia
    149, 201-202; Vanuatu 793
Canala Bay: 756
candelabra pines: 714
canoeing: 109
Cape Esperance Lighthouse: 887
Cape Mulinu'u: 503-504
Cape Taputapu: 445-446
Caqala Island: 679
cargo cults: 784, 820, 891
car rentals: 108; American Samoa
    453-454; Cook Islands 336; Fiji
    586-587; New Caledonia 748-
    749; Samoa 492-493; Solomon
    Islands 886-887; Tahiti-
    Polynesia 164, 184-185; Tonga
    398; Vanuatu 814-815; see
    also specific place
Carnival: 147
casinos: 744
cassava: 34
Castaway Island: 606
Ceigeïté Beach: 775
Centenary Church: 386-387
centipedes: 38
Central Province: 900-902
Centre Culturel Goa Ma Bwarhat:
    761
Cession Monument: 674
Champagne Beach: 837
Chapel of Our Lady of Lourdes:
    773
Chief's National Nakamal: 801
children: 73, 100
Chinatown (Honiara): 873-874
Chinese New Year: 147
Chirovanga: 918
Choiseul Province: 918-919
cholera: 121
Christian, Fletcher: 281-282
chronology: 46
Church of Jesus Christ of the
    Latter-day Saints: see
    Mormons
Church of Saint-Etienne: 273
Church of the Sacred Heart: 673
Chutes de la Madeleine: 753
Cicia: 707
ciguatera: 120-121
Ciu Falls: 756
climate: 33-34; American Samoa
    431; Cook Islands 305, 306;
    Easter Island 290; Fiji 550, 551;

New Caledonia 714; Niue 356-357; Pitcairn Island 280; Samoa 458; Solomon Islands 850; Tahiti Polynesia 131-132, *132;* Tokelau 511; Tonga 368; Tuvalu 530; Vanuatu 779; Wallis and Futuna 519-520
clothing: 71-72, 123-125
Coastal Aquaculture Center: 887
Coffyn, Mont: 733
Col de Mouirange: 751
Col de Roussettes: 759
Col de Tanghene: 762
Colo-i-Suva Forest Park: 629-630, *629*
colonialism: 45-47
colonization: 40-41
commercial fishing: 58-59
conduct: 71-73; Fiji 569-570; Samoa 465-467; Solomon Islands 861; Tahiti-Polynesia 143-144; Tokelau 514-515; Tonga 376-377; Tuvalu 533
cone shells: 37
Constitution Celebration (Cook Islands): 312
Constitution Celebrations (Niue): 359
consulates: 110; New Caledonia 746; Samoa 489; Solomon Islands 882; Fiji 638-639; Tahiti 181-182; Tonga 396; Vanuatu 811
cooking: 84
Cook Islands: 304-355, *305,* 306, 929-930, 946, 950-951; accommodations 313; climate 305, *306;* economy 308-310; fauna 305-306; food 314; history and government 306-308; holidays and festivals 312-313; land 304-305; people 310-311; music and dance 312; services and information 314-316; sports and recreation 312; transportation 316-318; *see also* Aitutaki; Atui; Manguia; Mauke; Rarotonga
Cook Islands Center: 322
Cook Islands Christian Church: 322
Cook, James: 43-44, *43,* 133, 197, 211, 222, 306-307, 370
copra production: 561

Copra Shed Marina: 688
coral/coral reefs: 29-33, *30, 31,* 668-669
country codes: 113
crafts: *see* arts and crafts; *specific craft*
Craig Cove: 841-842
credit cards: 111
cricket: 481, *515*
cruises: 162-163, 587-588
Cultural Center (Fiji): 619
Cultural Village (Cook Islands): 323
Cumming Street: 625-627
currency: *see* money
custom fees: 861
Custom House: 924
customs: 62, 71-73; Fiji 567-569; Samoa 465-467; Solomon Islands 861; Tahiti-Polynesia 143-144; Tokelau 514-515; Tonga 376-377; Tuvalu 533
customs regulations: 110

D
Dakuilomaloma: 706
Dampier, William: 43, *43*
dance: 77; Cook Islands 312; Fiji 573; Samoa 469; Tahiti-Polynesia 146; Tuvalu 534

Danger: *see* Pukapuka
David's Drill: 538
decolonization: 47-48
Denarau Golf & Racquet Club: 592
dengue fever: 121, 311, 796
Des Voeux Peak: 696
diarrhea: 118
discography: 942-944
Distillerie de Moorea: 198-199
doctors: *see* medical care
Dogny Plateau: 757
Doking: 773
dolphins: 36, 209-210
Dôme de Tiébaghi: 765
Drehu: *see* Lifou
Drekeniwai: 693
dress: 71-72
driving: 108; *see also* car rentals; *specific place*
Ducie: 286
Duff Islands: 926

E
Easter Island: 289-303, *290, 291,* 929, 946; government 293; history 290-293; land 289-290; people 294; practicalities 297-303; sights 295-297
Eastern Chain: 840-847
economy: 54-60, *54;* American Samoa 434-435; Cook Islands 308-310; Fiji 561-563; New Caledonia 722-723; Niue 358-359; Samoa 461-463; Solomon Islands 856-859; Tahiti-Polynesia 137-140; Tokelau 513-514; Tonga 372-374; Tuvalu 531-533; Vanuatu 788-790; Wallis and Futuna 521
ecotourism: *80*
eels: 37-38
EEZ: 50, *57*
Efate: 799-818, *800, 804-805, 816;* accommodations 803-807, 817-818; entertainment 808-810; food 807-808; services and information 811-813; shopping 810-811; sights 799-802, 816-817; sports and recreation 802-803; transportation 813-816
Église de la Sainte Famille: 200
Eiao: 278

DIVING

general discussion: 74-75, 97-99, 869-870
American Samoa: 446-447
Cook Islands: 324, 339
Easter Island: 296
Fiji: 572-573, 588, 590-592, 610, 620, 630, 648, 657, 675, 689, 698-699
New Caledonia: 735-736, 769
Niue: 362
Samoa: 480
Solomon Islands: 875, 911-913
Tahiti-Polynesia: 171-172, 236, 214, 271, 201, 223, 254-255, 257-258
Tonga: 387-388, 411, 417
Vanuatu: 802, 832

Ekipe: 817
electrical current: 114-115; Cook Islands 315; Samoa 471; Tonga 382; Vanuatu 795
Ellice Islands: *see* Tuvalu
e-mail: 113, 950-955
embassies: 110, 489
Emperor Gold Mine: 650-651
Emua: 817
Enoghae Point: 907-908
entertainment: 76-77; *see also specific place*
environmental issues: coral reef conservation 32-33; greenhouse effect *29;* nuclear testing 48-49, 135-136, 260-263; rainforest destruction 35, 857-858
Erakor Island: 801-802
Erromango: 823-824
'Esi Makafaakinanga: 403
Espiritu Santo: 829-840, *830;* accommodations 832-834, 837-839; food and entertainment 835; services 835-836; sights 831-832, 837-840; transportation 836-837
Eton Beach: 817
'Eua Island: 406-408, *407*
European exploration: 41-45, *43*
European War Memorial: 674
exchange rates: *21*
exclusive economic zones: 50, *57*
exploration, European: 41-45, *43*

F

Faanui Bay: 235-236
Faaroa Bay: 228
Fafa Island: 403-405
Faga: 505
Fagalele Boys School: 445
Fagali'i Airport: 474
Fagaloa Bay: 494
Fagamalo Cove: 455
Fagatogo: 443-444
Fagatogo Public Market: 444
Faie: 219
Faie Glaces: 219
Faioa Island: 524
Faisi: 916-917
Fakaofo: 518, *518*
Fakarava: 258-259
Falealili: 498
Falelupo: 503-504

Falefa Falls: 479
Faleloa: 414
Faleolo International Airport: 474
Fanafo: 838-839
Fanteng, Lake: 841
Fare: 213-218, *213*
Fare Pote'e Eco-Museum: 218
fares: 86, 89-94
Fatu Hiva: 277-278
fauna: 35-38, *38;* American Samoa 431-432; Cook Islands 305-306; Fiji 551-552; New Caledonia 714-715; Niue 357-358; Samoa 458-459; Solomon Islands 850-851; Tahiti-Polynesia 132; Vanuatu 779-781; Wallis and Futuna 520
Fautaua Falls: 171
Fautaua Valley: 169-170
Feleti Barstow Library: 443
Feletoa: 425
Festival of Pacific Arts: 77, 725
Festival of the Yams: 768
festivals: 77-78; American Samoa 437-438; Cook Islands 312-313; Easter Island 294; Fiji 573-574; New Caledonia 725; Niue 359; Samoa 468-469; Solomon Islands 863; Tahiti-Polynesia 146-147; Tonga 378-379; Tuvalu 534; Vanuatu 792; Wallis and Futuna 521
Fêtes de Juillet: 241-242
Fetuna: 229
Fiji Golf Club: 630
Fiji Indian Cultural Center: 636
Fiji Islands: 547-711, *548, 549, 550,* 930-931, 947, 952-954; accommodations 575-578; arts and crafts 574; climate *550,* 551; economy 561-563; entertainment 573; flora and fauna 551-552; food 578-579; history and government 552-560; holidays and festivals 573-574; land 549-551; language *710, 711;* people 564-570; services and information 579-582; shopping 574-575; sports and recreation 571-573; transportation 582-590; *see also* Kadavu; Lau Group; Lautoka; Lomaiviti Group; Mamanucas; Nadi; Rotuma;

Suva; Taveuni; Vanua Levu; Viti Levu; Yasawa Islands
Fiji Museum: 627
film: 125-126
firewalking: 567-568, 573
first aid kit: 124-125
fish: 36
fishing, commercial: 58-59, 561, 858
fishing, sport: 76; American Samoa 447; Cook Islands 325, 339; Niue 362; Samoa 480-481; Solomon Islands 913; Tahiti-Polynesia 214, 236; Tonga 417; Vanuatu 802-803
Flag Day (American Samoa): 437
FLNKS: 717-721
flora: 34-35, *34;* Fiji 551-552; New Caledonia 714-715; Niue 357-358; Samoa 458-459; Solomon Islands 850-851; Tahiti-Polynesia 132; Vanuatu 779-781
Florida Islands: 900-901
flying fox: 399, 432, 551
Flying Fox Sanctuary: 399
Foa: 414
food: 83-84; Cook Islands 314; Fiji 578-579; New Caledonia 726-727; Samoa 470; Tahiti-Polynesia 149-150; Tokelau 515-516; Tuvalu 534-535; Vanuatu 793-794
Forari: 817
foreign aid: 54-55
Fort Tereka: 734
Fort Teremba: 757
Forum Fisheries Agency: 52
Forum Secretariat: 52
Foué Beach: 767
Foundation Nicolai Michoutouchkine et Aloi Pilioko: 802
Frangi Road Race: 325
freighters: 95-96; *see also specific place*
French colonialism: 48
French nuclear tests: 260-263
French Polynesia: *see* Tahiti-Polynesia
French University of the Pacific: 52, 192
Frigate Passage: 623-624
Front de Libération Nationale Kanake et Socialiste: 717-721

Fua'amotu International Airport: 385
Fuipisia Falls: 494
Fulaga: 708
Funafuti: 537-542, *538, 539*
Fungatave Beach: 407
Futuna (Vanuatu): 824
Futuna (Wallis and Futuna): 527-528, *527*

G
Galerie Aad Van der Heyde: 198
Galerie Api: 199-200
Galerie Baie de Cook: 198
Gambier Islands: 264-266, *264*
garment industry: 561-562
Gau: 681, *681*
Gaua: 846
Gauguin Museum: 188-189
Gauguin, Paul: *166* 188-189, 275
Gauguin's Pearl: 253-254
geckos: 38
Gerbault, Alain: 234-235
Gizo: 911-915, *911, 912*
glossary: 957-961
gods: 63-64
Goldie College: 906
Gold Ridge: 890-891
golf: 76; Cook Islands 339; Fiji 572, 592, 630, 657; New Caledonia 736, 754; Samoa 481; Solomon Islands 875; Tahiti-Polynesia 145, 147, 190; Tonga 388; Vanuatu 803, 832
Golf de Tina: 736
Golf Municipal de Dumbéa: 754
Gospel Day: 313
government: 51-53; American Samoa 433-434; Cook Islands 307-308; Easter Island 293; Fiji 560; New Caledonia 721-722; Niue 358; Pitcairn 282-283; Samoa 461; Solomon Islands 856; Tahiti-Polynesia 136-137; Tokelau 512-513; Tonga 371-372; Tuvalu 531; Vanuatu 788; Wallis and Futuna 520-521
Governor's Mansion (American Samoa): 443
Grande Terre: 751-767, *752*
Grand Pacific Hotel: 627
Grave of 99 Stones: 500
Great Astrolabe Reef: 668-669

greenhouse effect: *29*
Guadalcanal: 871-891, *872;* accommodations 877-879, 888, 890; entertainment 880-881; food 879-880; services and information 881-883; shopping 881; sights 871-876, 887-891; transportation 883-887
Gun Rock: 674

H
Ha'aluma Beach: 406
Ha'amonga 'a Maui: 403
Ha'ano Island: 414
Haaotupa Bay: 270
Ha'apai Festival: 378
Ha'apai Group: 409-415, *409;* Foa 414; Kao 410; Lifuka 410-414; Tofua 410; 'Uiha 414-415; Uoleva 414
Haapu: 221
Ha'atafu Beach: 399-400
Hafu Pool: 407
Hakamoui Bay: 273
Hall, James Norman: *68-69*
Hanan International Airport: 366
Hanga Roa: 295
Hao: 259
Harrison, John: 44
Hash House Harriers: 325, 875
Hatana: 710
Hatiheu: 271
Hatutu: 278
Hau'ofa, Epeli: *69*
Havannah Harbor: 817
Hawaiki Nui Va'a: 147
health: 116-122; *see also* medical care
Heilala Festival: 378
Heiva i Tahiti: 146-147
Henderson: 286-287
Henderson Airport: 870
Henderson Field: 889-890
hepatitis: 121, 122, 472, 796
hermit crab: *53*
Hervey: *see* Manuae
Hibiscus Festival: 636
Hienghène: 761-762
hiking: 75, 100; American Samoa 446; Fiji 571, 653, 697; New Caledonia 751; Solomon Islands 890-891; Tahiti-Polynesia 145, 229

Hindi: *710*
history: 39-51, *46;* American Samoa 432-433; Cook Islands 306-308; Easter Island 290-293; Fiji 552-560; New Caledonia 715-721; Niue 358; Pitcairn Island 281-282; Samoa 459-461; Solomon Islands 851-856; Tahiti-Polynesia 132-136; Tokelau 511-512; Tonga 369-372; Tuvalu 530-531; Vanuatu 781-788; Wallis and Futuna 520
Hitiaa: 187
Hiva Oa: 275-277, *275*
Hofiua: 710
Hog Harbor: 837
holidays: 77-78; *see also* festivals
homestays: 81
Honiara: 871-891, *876-877;* accommodations 877-879; entertainment 880-881; food 879-880; services and information 881-883; shopping 881; sights 871-876; transportation 883-887
Honiara Golf Club: 875
Hoorn: *see* Futuna
horseback riding: Cook Islands 325; Easter Island 297; New Caledonia 766; Tahiti-Polynesia 145, 201, 214, 223, 236, 271
hospitals: *see* medical care
hotels: 79-81; *see also specific place*
Houaïlou: 759
Houme Chasm: 361
House of Parliament (Tonga): 386
House of Rocks: 503
Huahine: 211-221, *212;* history 211-213; sights 214, 218-219, 221; accommodations 214-216, 219-221; entertainment 216; food 216; services and information 217; transportation 217-218
Huahine-iti: 221
Huanaki Museum and Cultural Center: 360
Hufangalupe: 401
Hunganga Island: 427
hunting: 76
Huvalu Forest: 361

I

Iaai: *see* Ouvéa
Ieoneroa: 349
iguanas: 551
Île aux Récifs: 255
Île Nou: 734
illnesses: 116-122; *see also*
    health; medical care
Imanaka: 818
immunizations: 121-122
Independence Days (Samoa):
    468-469
Independence Memorial: 476
Indians: 564-565
information: 115-116, 929-931;
    American Samoa 439; Cook
    Islands 316; Easter Island 301-
    302; Fiji 582; New Caledonia
    726-727; Niue 365; Pitcairn
    284; Solomon Islands 868;
    Tahiti-Polynesia 154-155;
    Tokelau 516; Tonga 383;
    Tuvalu 541; Vanuatu 812-813
insects: 38, 118
Institute of Pacific Studies: 628
insurance: 116-117
interline tickets: 87
International Bula Marathon: 574
international date line: 113-114,
    382, 685, 695
International Golf Course Olivier
    Breaud: 190
internet: 945-955
intestinal parasites: 118
Ireupuow: 820-821
Iririki Island: 801
Isabel Province: 919-920
Isla de Pascua: *see* Easter Island
Island of Skulls: 908
islands: 27-28, 27
Isle of Pines: 768-770

J

Jame Mosque: 654
Japanese War Memorial: 889
Jardin Kellum Stop: 199
Jardin Public Vaipahi: 189
Jean-Marie Tjibaou Cultural
    Center: 735
Jean P. Haydon Museum: 443
Jehovah's Witnesses: 67
jellyfish: 37
John F. Kennedy Museum: 908
John Williams Memorial: 475
Jon Frum cults: *784*, 820
Joyita: 513

K

Kabara: 708
Kadavu: 667-671, *668*
kagu: 715
Kahana Spring: 407
Kaimbu Island: 707
Kakamora: 920
Kanacea: 706
Kanaky: *see* New Caledonia
Kanokupolu: 399
Kanti Chinese Temple: 171
Kanuméra: 768
Kao: 410
Katafaga: 707
kava ceremonies: 62, 84; Fiji 568-
    569; Samoa 464; Vanuatu 793-
    794, 809, 818
kayaking: 75, 101, 109; Cook
    Islands 324; Fiji 572, 699;
    Tonga 417
Kia: 906-907
Kioa: 693
Kirakira: 920-921
Klehm Hill: 814-815
Kokenggolo: 906, 907
Kolombangara: 910
Komo: 708
Komuvaolu: 891
Koné: 766-767
Kopu Pooki: 349
Koro: 680-681
Korolevu: 617-618
Korolevu: 653
Koromiri Island: 323
Korotogo: 616-617
Korovou (Fiji): 646
Korovou (Solomon Islands): 916
Koroyanitu National Heritage
    Park: 655-657
Koumac: 764-765
Koyaboa Hill: 759
Kuendu Beach: 734
Kula Eco Park: 616
Kulukulu: 615-616
Kuto: 768
Kwai: 897-898
Kwaio Country: 898
Kwenyii: *see* Isle of Pines

L

Labasa: 683-688, *685*
Labasa Sugar Mill: 683
La Conception Church (Grande
    Terre): 751
La Foa: 757
Lagoonarium: 192

Lakatoro: 826-828
Lakeba: 707-708
Lakufa'anga: 406
Lalolalo, Lake: 522
Lalomanu: 497
Lambete: 906, 908-909
land: 25-34; American Samoa
    430-431; Cook Islands 304-
    305; Easter Island 289-290; Fiji
    549-551; New Caledonia 712-
    714; Niue 356; Pitcairn Island
    280; Samoa 458; Solomon
    Islands 848-850; Tahiti-
    Polynesia 129-132; Tokelau
    511; Tonga 367-368; Tuvalu
    529-530; Vanuatu 778-779;
    Wallis and Futuna 519
land diving: 843-844
Langa Langa Lagoon: 894-896
language: 67-70, 957-961;
    Bislama 791-792, *847*; Fijian
    549, 567, *711;* French 142-143,
    777; Hindi *710;* Pijin 861, *927;*
    Samoan *510;* Tahitian 143,
    279; Tongan *429;* Tuvaluan
    544
Lano: 505
Lanoto'o, Lake: 479-480
Lanutavake, Lake: 522
Lapaha: 402
Lata: 923
Lata Coconut Oil Mill: 924
La Tontouta International Airport:
    730-731
Laucala Island: 704
Laufuti Falls: 456
Lau Group: 705-708
Lau Lagoon: 896-897
Laulasi: 895
Lauru: *see* Choiseul Province
Lautoka: 654-660, *656*
Lautoka Golf Club: 657
Lautoka Sugar Mill: 655
Laval, Honoré: 265
Lavena Coastal Walk: 698
lawn bowling: 325
Law of the Sea: *57*
Leala Sliding Rock: 445
Le Diadème: 192
Lee Auditorium: 443
Leeward Islands: 247-248; *see
    also* Bora Bora; Huahine;
    Maupiti; Raiatea; Taha'a
Leleuvia Island: 679-670

Lenakel: 821
Leone: 445
Leone Falls: 445
leper colony: 187
Le Saut du Guerrier: 775
Lesiaceva Point: 688
Letolo Plantation: 502-503
le truck: 164, 184
Levuka: 672-679, 676
Levuka Community Center: 673
Levuka Public School 673-674
Li'angahuo'a Maui: 406-407
Library and Museum of the Cook
    Islands: 322
lice: 118, 472
Lifou: 772-775, 773
Lifuka: 410-414, 410
Lilisiana: 893-894
Limu Reef: 361
Lindéralique Cave: 761
logging: 35, 857-858
Lomaiviti Group: 672-681
Lomalagi, Mt.: 652
Lomaloma: 706
London, Jack: 68
Lopevi: 840
Loti, Pierre: 68, 169, 230
Lovers' Leap: 503
Lovoni: 675
Loyalty Islands: 771-776
Luengöni: 773
Luesalo: 924
Luganville: 829-837, 829, 833;
    accommodations 832-834; food
    and entertainment 835;
    services 835-836; sights 831-
    832; transportation 836-837
luggage: 95, 123
Lulu Fakahega, Mt.: 522
Luowa: 924
Lycée Professionnel Agricole: 199

M
Ma'ama'a Cove: 445
Machoro, Éloi: 718, 718, 757
Maeva: 218-221
Mafa Pass: 494
Maftoa: 709
magazines: 115, 940-942
Magellan, Ferdinand: 41, 43
Mago: 706-707
Mahaena: 187
Mahamate Beach: 763
Mahana Park: 191

Maiao: 194
mail: see postal services
Mairie de Arue: 171
Mairie de Faa'a: 192
Makaha'a Island: 403-405
Makalea Cave: 361
Makaroa: 265
Makaruka: 891
Makatea: 259
Makira/Ulawa Province: 920-921
Makogai: 680
Malaita Province: 892-898, 893
malaria: 118-119, 796, 866-868
Malekula: 825-828, 825
Mallicollo: see Malekula
Malolo Island: 605-606
Malololailai Island: 603-605
Malu'u: 896
Mamanuca Group: 603-609, 604
Mana Island: 607-608
Manakwai: 896
Mangaia: 350-351, 350
Mangareva Islands: see Gambier
    Islands
mangroves: 34
Manihi: 257-258
Manihiki: 354, 354
Manono Island 500-501
Manuae (Cook Islands): 352
Manuae (Tahiti-Polynesia): 248
Manu'a Group: 454-456
Manureva, Mt.: 249
Manuro Point: 817
maps: 939-940
Maputeoa, Grégoire: 265
Maraa Fern Grotto: 191
Marau, Mt.: 173
Marau Sound: 891-892
Maré: 775-776, 775
Mare Vaiorie: 245
Marina Apooiti: 229
marine mammals: 36
Mariner's Cave: 425
Marist Convent School: 673
Marketplace of Fiji: 619
Marotetini: 236
Marovo Lagoon: 903
Marquesas Islands: 266-278, 267;
    Fatu Hiva 277-278; Hiva Oa
    275-277; Nuku Hiva 269-273;
    Tahuata 277; Ua Huka 274-
    275; Ua Pou 273-274
Marquesas Islands Festival: 77-
    78, 268

Marsters, William: 352
Massacre Bay: 446
Matafao, Mt.: 446
Matai Landing: 345
Matalanga 'a Maui: 406
Matamaiqi Blowhole: 696
Matangi Island: 704
Mataniko Falls: 875
Matantas: 838
Mataoa Gardens: 191
Matapa Chasm: 361
Mata Utu Cathedral: 522
Matava'a o te Henua Enata: 268
Matavai Pool: 504
Matavanu, Mt.: 504
Matavera: 323
Matega i Si'uvao Beach: 503
Matignon Accords: 720-721

MARAE (TAHITIAN TEMPLES)

Aehautai: 235
Afareaito: 199
Ahu o Mahine: 199
Anini: 221
Arahurahu: 191
Arai-te-tonga: 323
Arangirea: 338
Farehape: 189-190
Fare Miro: 219
Fare Opu: 236
Mahaiatea: 190-191
Manunu: 219
Matairea Rahi: 219
Nuurua: 200
Nu'utere: 188
Orongo: 346
Paepae Ofata: 219
Rauhuru: 219
Taianapa: 236
Tainuu: 229
Taputapuatea: 228
Taputaputea: 322
Te Ana: 219
Teapiripiri: 345
Te Ava: 219
Tefano: 219
Te Poaki O Rae: 338
Titiroa: 199
Vaiahu: 245
Vairakaia: 345

Matira: 241
Matira Beach Park: 235
Matuku: 708
mat weaving: 469
Maugham, W. Somerset: *68*
Mauia Paepae: 270
Mauke: 348-350, *348*
Maunga Orito: 295
Maungapu, Mt.: 338
Maupihaa: 247-248
Maupiti: 245-247, *246*
Maurau: *see* Maupiti
Mbareho Island: 905
media: 115
medical care: Apia 490; Bora
    Bora 242; Honiara 883;
    Huahine 217; Labasa 687;
    Lautoka 660; Luganville 836;
    Moorea 207-208; Nadi 600;
    Neiafu 421; Nouméa 747;
    Nuku'alofa 397; Port Vila 812;
    Raiatea 227; Rarotonga 335;
    Suva 640; Taha'a 231; Tahiti
    183; Tahiti-Polynesia 155;
    Tutuila 453; Tuvalu 535; *see
    also* health
medical kit: 124-125
megapodes: 850
Mehetia: 194
Melanesia: *see* Fiji Islands; New
    Caledonia; Solomon Islands;
    Vanuatu
Melanesian Arts and Cultural
    Festival: 77
Melanesians: 64-66
Melville, Herman: *68,* 197, 270-
    271
Mendaña, Álvaro de: 41, *43,* 267,
    851
Menei Hill: 841-842
Mere Lava: 846
Meridian Wall: 685
metric system: 114
Michener, James A.: *69,* 233-234
Middle Bush: 818
Million Dollar Point: 832
minerals: 57-58
mining: 561, 722-723, 756, 858
missionaries: 45, 66, 134, 211-
    213, 307, 459, 782-783, 852-
    853
Mission Hill: 674
Mitiaro: 352
Moala Group: 708

Moce: 708
Moerai: 249
Mohotani: *see* Motane
Momi Bay: 602
Monasavu Hydroelectric Project:
    652-653
money: *21,* 110-111, 125;
    American Samoa 438; Cook
    Islands 314-315; Easter Island
    301; Fiji 579-580; New
    Caledonia 727-728; Niue 365;
    Pitcairn Island 284; Samoa
    470-471; Solomon Islands 865;
    Tahiti-Polynesia 151-152;
    Tokelau 516; Tonga 381;
    Tuvalu 535; Vanuatu 794-795;
    Wallis and Futuna 525
mongoose: 551-552
Mont Coffyn: 733
Mont Humboldt: 755
Mont Mou: 754-755
Montravel: 734-7455
Moorea: 196-210, *196;*
    accommodations 201-205;
    entertainment 206-207; food
    205-206; sights 197-201;
    services and information 207-
    208; sports and recreation 201;
    transportation 208-210
Moorea Blue Marathon: 147
Moorea Temae Airport: 210
Mopelia: *see* Maupihaa
Mormons: 67, 376
Moro cult: 891
Moruroa: 261-262
Moso'oi Tourism Festival: 437
Moso's Footprint: 503
Motane: 278
Moto Iti: *see* Tupai
Moto Nui: 296
Motu Oa: 273
Motu One: 248
Motu Paio: 255
Motu Reef: 361
Moturiki Island: 679
Mount Kasi Gold Mine: 682
mountain climbing: 172-173
Muake: 270
Muani: 667
Mulinu'u Peninsula: 476
Munda: 906-910, *907*
Munia Island: 706
Mu Pagoa Waterfall: 503
Muri Lagoon: 323

Mururoa: *see* Moruroa
Musée Communal: 274
Musée de la Mer: 229
Musée de la Mine SLN: 756
Musée de la Ville: 731
Musée de Marine: 235
Musée Ségelin-Gauguin: 275
Museo Antropológico: 295
Museum of Tahiti and the Islands:
    191-192

MUSEUMS

general discussion: *65*
Bourail Museum: 757-758
Fare Pote'e Eco-Museum:
    218
Fiji Museum: 627
Galerie Aad Van der Heyde:
    198
Galerie Api: 199-200
Galerie Baie de Cook: 198
Gauguin Museum: 188-189
Huanaki Museum and
    Cultural Center: 360
Jean P. Haydon Museum:
    443
John F. Kennedy Museum:
    908
Library and Museum of the
    Cook Islands: 322
Musée Communal: 274
Musée de la Mer: 229
Musée de la Mine: SLN 756
Musée de la Ville: 731
Musée de Marine: 235
Musée Ségelin-Gauguin:
    275
Museo Antropológico: 295
Museum of Tahiti and the
    Islands: 191-192
National Cultural Center
    Museum: 801
National Museum (Cook
    Islands): 322
New Caledonia Museum:
    733
Robert Louis Stevenson
    Museum: 477
Solomon Islands National
    Museum: 871-873
Vilu War Museum: 887

music: 77, 942-944; Cook Islands 312; Solomon Islands 862; Tahiti-Polynesia 146
Mutalau: 361
mynah birds: 35
mythology: 63-64

N
Nabouwalu: 682
Nabukelevu: 668
Nabukelevuira: 667
Nadarivatu: 652
Nadi: 590-601, *591, 594;* accommodations 592-597; climate *550;* entertainment 598-599; food 597-598; services and information 599-600; sights 590; sports and recreation 590-592; transportation 600-602
Nadi Airport Golf Club: 592
Nadi International Airport: 588-589
Naililili: 644
Nairai: 680
Naiserelagi: 646
Naitauba: 707
Nakéty: 756
Nakauvadra Range: 647
Nambas: 826
Namenalala Island: 691
Namoala: 402
Namotu Island: 606
Nananu-i-Ra Island: 647-650
Nankai Point: 916
Nanukuloa: 646
Nanumaga: 542
Nanumea: 542
Nanuya Lailai Island: 666
Nanuya Levu Island: 666
Napuka: 693
Nassau: 354
Natadola Beach: 610-611
Nathalo: 773
National Art Gallery and Cultural Center (Solomon Islands): 873
National Cultural Center (Cook Islands): 322
National Cultural Center Museum (Vanuatu): 801
National Library (Cook Islands): 322
National Museum (Cook Islands): 322
National Park of American

Samoa: 437, 446
National Trust for Fiji: 571
nature tours: 99
Nausori Airport: 589
Nausori Highlands: 651-652
Nausori: 643-644
nautilus shell: *210*
Navakawau: 696
Navala: 651-652
Navatu Rock: 647
Navini Island: 606-607
Naviti Island: 663
Navoka Methodist Church: 674
Navua: 621-622
Nduke: *see* Kolombangara
Nea: 924
Neiafu: 415-423, *418;* accommodations 418-419; entertainment 420-421; food 419-420; services and information 421; sights 416-417; transportation 421-423
Nekowiar Festival: 818
Nela: 924
Nemba: 924-925
Nendo: *see* Santa Cruz
Nengone: *see* Maré
neolithic society: 41
New Caledonia: 712-777, *713, 714,* 931, 949, 954; accommodations 725-726; climate 714; economy 722-723; flora and fauna 714-715; food 726-727; government 721-722; history 715-721; holidays and festivals 725; land 712-714; language *777;* people 723-724; services 727-729; transportation 729-731; *see also* Grande Terre; Isle of Pines; Loyalty Islands; Nouméa
New Caledonia Day: 725
New Caledonia Museum: 733
New Hebrides: *see* Vanuatu
New Jerusalem: 338
newspapers: 115; American Samoa 438; Cook Islands 315; Fiji 581; New Caledonia 728; Pitcairn Island 284; Samoa 472; Solomon Islands 866; Tahiti-Polynesia 154; Tonga 382-383; Tuvalu 535; Vanuatu 795
New Year's Eve: 147

New Zealand military cemetery: 758
Ngatangiia Harbor: 323
Nga'unoho: 423-424
nguzunguzu: 863
Niuafo'ou: 428-429, *428*
Niuas: 427-429
Niuatoputapu: 427, *427*
Niue: 356-366, *357,* 930, 946, 951; climate 356-357; flora and fauna 357-358; government and economy 358-359; history 358; holidays and festivals 359; land 356; people 359
Niulakita: 542-543
Niutao: 543
Niutoua Beach: 427
Noa'tau: 709
Nono Lagoon: 905-906
Nordhoff, Charles: *68*
Norfolk Island: 287-288
Noro: 907
Norsup: 826-828
Notre Dame Catholic Cathedral: 169
Notre-Dame Cathedral: 270
Nouméa: 731-750, *732, 738-739, 740;* accommodations 737-741; climate *714;* entertainment 743-744; food 742-743; services and information 745-747; shopping 744-745; sights 731-735; sports and recreation 735-737; transportation 747-750
Nouméa Aquarium: 733
Nubutautau: 653
Nuclear-Free and Independent Pacific: 52
nuclear testing: 48-49, 135-136, 260-263
Nui: 543
Nuku'alofa: 385-399, *390;* accommodations 388-393; entertainment 394-395; food 393-394; services and information 396-397; shopping 395-396; sights 385-388; sports and recreation 387-388; transportation 397-399
Nukufetau: 543
Nuku Hiva: 269-273, *269*
Nuku Island: 425
Nukulaelae: 543
Nukunamo Island: 414

Nunonu: 517, *517*
Nu'utele Island: 494

O
ocean kayaking: 75
O'Connor, James: 233
Oeno: 286, *287*
Ofu: 454-455, *455*
Ogea: 708
Oinafa: 709
O Le Pupu-Pu'e National Park: 495
Olohega: *see* Swains
Olosega: 454-455, *455*
Olotele, Mt.: 446
Omai: 44, *44*
Oneata: 708
180th meridian: 695
Oneroa: 350-351
Oneroa Beach: 345
Ono-i-Lau: 708
onward tickets: 89
Oopa, Pouvanaa a: 136, 169
Opaahi Reef: 360
Opunohu Valley: 199
Orongo: 295-296
Orovaru Beach: 346
Ouaré Mission: 761, 762
Ouégoa: 764
Ouen Toro Hill: 733
Ouloup Cave: 772
Ouvéa: 771-772, *772*
Ouvéa Massacre: 719-720, 771
Ovalau Island: 672-679, *673, 676*
overbooking: 94-95

P
Paama: 840
Pacific Concerns Resource Center: 52-53
Pacific Conference of Churches: 66
Pacific Fishing Company: 674
Pacific Harbor: 618-621, *619*
Pacific Islands National Wildlife Refuges: 456
packing: 123-125
Paepae A: 349
Paepae 'o Tele'a: 402
Pago Pago: *431*, 444
Pago Pago International Airport: 441
Paia: 504
Paikea's Grave: 349

Pala: 924
Palaha Reef: 361
Palikulo Peninsula: 831-832
Palmerston: 352-353
Palolo Deep Marine Reserve: 480
Pangai: 410-414, *412*
Pangaimotu Island: 403-405
Panié Falls: 763
Panié, Mt.: 763
Papapapai-tai Falls: 495
Papara: 191
Papase'ea Sliding Rocks: 479
Papeete: 168-169, *170*, 171, *174*, 174-186; accommodations 173-177; climate *132;* entertainment 179-180; food 177-179; health 183; services and information 181-183; sights 168-169; shopping 180-181; sports and recreation 171-172; transportation 184-186
Papenoo River: 187
Papetoai: 199
Papua Waterfall: 324
Para O Tane Palace: 322
Parc Forestier: 734-735
Parc naturel Te Faaiti: 190
Parc Provincial de la Rivière Bleue: 751
Parea: 221
Parliament Building (Solomon Islands): 873
Parliament of Fiji: 628
Parliament of Samoa: 476
Parliament of the Cook Islands: 322
Parque Nacional Rapa Nui: 289-290
passports: 109, 125, 374; *see also* visas
Patutiva: 905
Peapea Cave (Upolu, Samoa): 495
Peapea Cave (Savai'i, Samoa): 504
pearls/pearl farming: 138-139, 169, 253-254, 310, 333
Penrhyn: 355
Pentecost: 843-844
people: 61-70; American Samoans: 435-436; Cook Islanders 310-311; Fijiians 564-567; Indians 564-565; New

Caledonians 723-724; ni Vanuatu 790-792; Niueans 359; Pitcairners 283-284; Polynesians 140-143; Rapanui (Easter Island) 294; Samoans 463-465; Solomon Islanders 859-861; Tokelauans 514; Tongans 374-376; Tuvaluans 533; Wallisians and Futunans 521
periodicals: *see* magazines
photography: 125-126
Pic Nga: 768
pidgin: 70
Pierced Rock: 758
pigs: 781
Pijin: 861, *927*
Pilioko House: 799-801
Pitcairn Islands: 280-288, *281*, 946; climate 280; history 281-282; land 280; people 283-284; practicalities 284-285
Piula Cave Pool: 479
Place des Cocotiers: 731
Plage de Bouraké: 755
Plage de Ouano: 757
Plage de Pindaï: 767
Plage de Tanguy: 757
Plage d'Onghoué: 755
Plaine des Lacs: 753
plane tickets: 86-94
plants: *see* flora
plate tectonics: 25-29, *27*
Poé Beach: 758
Pofai Bay: 235, 240-241
Poi: 528
Poike Peninsula: 296
Poindimié: 759-760
Point Venus: 171
Polynesians: 62-64, 70, 140-143
Pomare Vahine IV, Queen: 134-135
Ponérihouen: 759
Poporang: 917
population: *50*, 61; American Samoa *432;* Cook Islands *306;* Easter Island 294; Fiji *549;* New Caledonia *713;* Niue 359; Pitcairn Island 283; Samoa *432;* Solomon Islands *849;* Tahiti-Polynesia *131;* Tokelau 514; Tonga *369;* Tuvalu *530;* Vanuatu *781*
porpoises: 36

Port Olry: 837
Port Resolution: 820-821
Port Vila: 799-816, *800, 804-805;* accommodations 803-807; climate *779;* entertainment 808-810; food 807-808; services and information 811-813; shopping 810-811; sights 799-802; sports and recreation 802-803; transportation 813-816
Port Vila Golf and Country Club: 803
Port Vila International Airport: 797-798
postal services: 111-112, *112;* American Samoa 438; Easter Island 301; Fiji 580; New Caledonia 728; Samoa 471; Tahiti-Polynesia 152-153; Tonga 381
pottery: 614
Pouébo: 763
Poum: 765
prehistory: 39
Presidential Palace (Fiji): 628
prickly heat: 118
Puama'u: 275-276
publishers: 938-939
Pukapuka: 354
Puke, Mt.: 528
Pulemelei stone pyramid: 502
Punapau: 295
Pwihã Duét: 761

Q
Qamea Island: 704
Qarani: 681
Quirós, Pedro Fernandez de: 41, *43,* 782

R
Rabi: 693-694
radio: 115; American Samoa 439; Cook Islands 315-316; Fiji 581-582; New Caledonia 729; Samoa 472; Solomon Islands 866; Tahiti-Polynesia 154; Tonga 383; Vanuatu 796
Raemaru, Mt.: 323
rafting: 572, 622; *see also* kayaking
Raiatea: 222-229, *224*
rain: *see* climate
Rain Forest Canopy Walkway: 503

rainforest destruction: 35
Raivavae: 251
Rakahanga: 354-355
Rakiraki: 646-647
Rangiroa: 253-257, *254*
Rano Island: 828
Rano Kau: 295-296
Rano Raraku: 296
Rapa: 251-252
Rapa Nui: *see* Easter Island
Rarotonga: 318-337, *319, 320-321;* accommodations 325-319; climate *306;* entertainment and events 331-332; food 329-331; services and information 333-335; shopping 332-333; sights 318-324; sports and recreation 324-325; transportation 335-337
Rarotonga International Airport: 317
Raviravi Lagoon: 706
recreation: 74-76; *see also specific recreation*
Red Beach: 890
Red Lake: 444-445
Reef Islands: 926
reefs: *see* coral/coral reefs
religion: 45, 63-64, 66-67; Fiji 567; Samoa 464-465; Tahiti-Polynesia 142; Tonga 375-376
Rendovo: 906
Rennell: 898-899
Rennell and Bellona Province: 898-900, *898*
reptiles: 38
reservations: 81
restaurants: 83-84
Return to Paradise Beach: 495
Rewa Delta: 644
rice cultivation: 561
Rimatara: 251
Ring of Fire: 25
Ringi Cove: 910
Robert Louis Stevenson Museum: 477
Roggeveen, Jacob: 43, *43,* 292
Rose Atoll: 456
Rotuma: 709-710, *709*
Round Raro Run: 312-313
Roviana Island: 908
Royal Palace (Tonga): 386
Royal Samoa Country Club: 481
Royal Suva Yacht Club: 629
Royal Tombs (Tonga): 387

rugby: 875
Rurutu: 248-250
Russell Islands: 901-902

S
Sa'anapu: 499
Sa'anapu-Sataoa Mangrove Forest: 495
Sables Roses: 255
safety: 37-38; Cook Islands 311; Fiji 570; Samoa 466
Safotu: 504
sailing: 145
Saleapaga: 497-498
Salelologa: 505
Saletele: 494
Salialevu: 696
Samoa: 457-510, *458,* 930, 947, 952; accommodations 469-470; area *432;* arts and crafts 469; climate 458; conduct and customs 465-467; economy 461-463; dance 469; flora and fauna 458-459; food 470; history and government 459-461; holidays and festivals 468-469; land 458; language *510;* people 463-465; population *432;* services and information 470-472; transportation 472-474
Samoa Packing Plant: 444
San Cristobal: *see* Makira Ulawa Province
Santa Cruz: 922-926
Santa Isabel: *see* Isabel
Santa Maria: *see* Gaua
Santo: *see* Espiritu Santo
Santo Golf Club: 832
Saoluafata Beach: 479
Sapapali'i: 505
Sarraméa: 757
Sauago: 494
Savage: *see* Niue
Savai'i: 501-509, *501*
Savo: 901
Savulevu Yavonu Falls: 698
Savusavu: 688-693, *688*
Sawaieke: 681
Sawa-i-Lau Island: 666-667
Scilly: *see* Manuae
scuba diving: *see* diving
sea cucumbers: *47*
sea turtles: 38

sea urchins: 37
Secretariat of the Pacific Community: 51, 733-734
Seghe Point: *904*, 905
Selwyn College: 887
seniors, tours for: 99-100
Sergeant Major Jacob Vouza War Memorial: 873
services: American Samoa 438-439; Cook Islands 314-316; Easter Island 301; Fiji 579-582; New Caledonia 727-729; Niue 364-365; Pitcairn Island 284; Samoa 470-472; Solomon Islands 864-868; Tahiti-Polynesia 150-155; Tokelau 516; Tonga 380-383; Tuvalu 535-536; Vanuatu 794-796; Wallis and Futuna 525
Seven-in-One Coconut Tree: 318
Seventh-Day Adventist Chruch: 67
Shangri-La hiking area: 751
shark calling: 894-895
sharks: 36-37, 894-895
shells: *895*
ships: *see* boat transportation; yachting
shopping: American Samoa 451; Bora Bora 242; Cook Islands 332-333; Easter Island 300; Fiji 574-575, 637-638; New Caledonia 744-745; Niue 364; Samoa 488; Solomon Islands 881; Tahiti-Polynesia 147-148, 180; Tonga 395-396; Vanuatu 810-811
Shortland Islands: 915-917
Sia Ko Kafoa: 424
Sigatoka River Trek: 653, *653*
Sigatoka Sand Dunes: 611
Sikh Temple: 654
Sililo: 709
Silisili, Mt.: 504
Singatoka: 611-615, *614*
Siota: 900
Siviri: 817
skinks: 38
Snake Temple: 683
snakes: 38, 432, 551, 779-781
snorkeling: 75; *see also* diving
Société Le Nickel: 734
Solmea Hill: 710
Solomon Islands: 848-928, *849*,

850, *852-853*, 931, 950, 955; accommodations 864; arts and crafts 863-864; climate 850; economy 856-859; flora and fauna 850-851; history and government 851-856; holidays and festivals 863; land 848-850; music 862; people 859-861; services and information 864-868; transportation 868-871; *see also* Central Province; Choiseul Province; Guadalcanal; Isabel Province; Makira/Ulawa Province; Malaita Province; Rennell and Bellona Province; Temotu Province; Western Province
Solomon Islands Development Trust: 859
Solomon Islands National Museum: 871-873
Solomon Peace Memorial Park: 874
Somosomo (Gau, Fiji): 681
Somosomo (Taveuni, Fiji): 696-697
Sopo'aga Falls: 494
Sororoa Bluff: 709-710
South Pacific Applied Geoscience Commission: 57-58
South Pacific Commission: *see* Secretariat of the Pacific Community
South Pacific Distilleries: 655
South Pacific Forum: 51-52
South Pacific Games: 78
South Pacific Regional Environment Program: 52
South Pacific Regional Trade and Economic Cooperative Agreement: 56
SPARTECA: 56
sportfishing: *see* fishing, sport
sports: 74-76; *see also specific sport*
squash: 325, 481, 736, 875
Sri Krishna Kaliya Temple: 654, 659
Sri Siva Subrahmaniya Swami Temple: 590
St. John's College: 674
St. Joseph Beach: 769
St. Louis Mission: 751
St. Mathieu Beach: 763

stamps/stamp collecting: 112, 283; *see also* postal services
Stevens, Jimmy: 785-786, 839
Stevenson, Robert Louis: *68-69*, 476-479
stonefish: 37
Stones of Bau: 908
stoning: 466
sugarcane: 34-35, 561
Sukuna Park: 627
Sulione: 897
Sulphur Bay: 820
Sulufou: 897
Sumi: 709
sunburn: 117-118
surfing: 75-76, 100-101; Easter Island 296-297; Fiji 571-572, 623-624; Tahiti-Polynesia 145, 172, 201
Surunda Blue Hole: 837
Suva: 625-643, *626*, *631*; accommodations 630-634; climate *550*; entertainment and events 636-637; food 634-636; services and information 638-640; shopping 637-638; sights 625-630; sports and recreation 630; transportation 640-643
Suva Cemetery: 629
Suva Prison: 629
Suwarrow: 353
Swains Island: 456
Swallows Cave: 425
swimming: *908*

T
Ta'aoa: 275
tabua: 569
Tadine: 775
Tafahi Island: 427-428
Tafua: 502
Tagimaucia, Lake: 697
Taha'a: *224*, 230-232
Tahauta: 277
Tahiti: 166-195, *167*; accommodations 173-177, 192-194; entertainment and events 179-180; food 177-179; health 183; land 166-168; services and information 181-183; sights 168-171, 186-192; shopping 180-181; sports and recreation 171-173; transportation 184-186

Tahiti-iti: 187
Tahiti Open: 147
Tahiti Perles Center: 169
Tahiti-Polynesia: 129-279, *130,*
929, 945-946, 950;
accommodations 148-149;
climate 131-132; conduct and
customs; 143-144; economy
137-140; entertainment 145-
146; food 149-150; government
136-137; history 132-136;
holidays and festivals 146-147;
land 129-132; music and dance
146; people 140-143;
shopping147-148; services and
information 150-155; sports and
recreation 145, 147;
transportation 155-165; *see
also* Austral Islands; Bora Bora;
Gambier Islands; Huahine;
Leeward Islands; Marquesas
Islands; Maupiti; Moorea;
Raiatea; Taha'a; Tahiti;
Tuamotu Islands
Taiohae: 270
Taipivai: 270-271
Takamoa Mission House: 318
Takamoa Theological College:
318
Takara Beach: 817
Takitaki Cave: 346-347
Takitumu: 323
Takitumu Day: 313
Takutea: 352
Takwa: 897
Talau, Mt.: 417
Tamarua: 351
Tangoa Island: 839-840840
Tanna: 818-823, *819*
Tao Falls: 763
tapa cloth: 78-79; Fiji 574; Samoa
469; Tonga 379
Tapati Rapa Nui: 294
Tapioi Hill: 223
Tapuaemanu: *see* Maiao
Taravai: 265-266
Tarekukure: 918
Taro: 918
Tasman, Abel: 43, *43,* 369-370
Ta'u: 455-456, *455*
Taunganui Harbor: 346
Taungaroro: 346
Tautira: 188
Tautu: 827

Tavarua Island: 606
Taveuni: *684,* 695-704;
accommodations 699-702; food
and entertainment 702;
services and information 702;
sights 695-698; sports and
recreation 698-699;
transportation 703-704
Tavewa Island: 663-666
Tavoro Forest Park and Reserve:
697-698
Tavua: 650
Tavuni Hill Fort: 615
taxes: 89
taxis: Fiji 585-586; New Caledonia
748; Samoa 491; Solomon
Islands 886; Tahiti-Polynesia
164-165, 184; Tonga 398;
Vanuatu 814
Teahupoo: 188
Te Aito: 147
tectonic plates: 25-29, *27*
Tefa'aurumai Waterfalls: 187
telephone services: 112-113;
American Samoa 438; Cook
Islands 315; Easter Island 301;
Fiji 580-581; New Caledonia
728; Niue 365; Pitcairn Island
284; Samoa 471; Solomon
Islands 865-866; Tahiti-
Polynesia 153-154; Tokelau
516; Tonga 381-382; Tuvalu
541; Vanuatu 795; Wallis and
Futuna 525
television: American Samoa 438-
439, 443; Fiji 581; New
Caledonia 728-729; Tahiti-
Polynesia 154; Vanuatu 796
Temae: 198
Te Marae O Rongo: 348
Temehani, Mt.: 229
Temehea Tohua: 270
Temotu Province: 922-927, *923*
temperatures: *see* climate
Te Nggano, Lake: 899
tennis: 325, 481
Terei'a Beach: 245
terra australis incognita: 41-43
Te Rua Manga: 323-324
Teruarere Cave: 351
Tetere Beach: 890
Tetiaroa: 194-195, *194*
Teulia Tourism Festival: 469
Thio: 755-756

Thio Mission: 756
Tholana Falls: 920
Thurston Botanical Gardens: 627
Tiare Festival Week: 313
Tiendanite: 761-762
Tikehau: 259-260
Tikopia: 927
timber industry: 561
time zones: 113-114, *114;*
American Samoa 471; Cook
Islands 315; Fiji 581; New
Caledonia 728; Samoa 471;
Tonga 382
Tinomana Palace: 323
Tiputa: 253-254
Tiriara, Lake: 351
Tirotto, Lake: 346
Titiana: 911
Titikaveka: 323, 330
Toafa Church Farm: 424-425
Toataratara Point: 249
Toberua Island: 645
Tofua: 410
Togitogiga FAlls: 495
toiletries: 124-125
Tokelau: 511-518, 930;
accommodations 515; arts and
crafts 515; climate 511; conduct
and customs 514-515;
economy 513-514; food 515-
516; government 512-513;
history 511-512; people 514;
services and information 516;
transportation 516-517
Tokou: 675
Tonga Golf Club: 388
Tonga, Kingdom of: 367-429, *368,
369,* 930, 946-947, 951-952;
accommodations and food 380;
arts and crafts 379-380; climate
368; conduct and customs 376-
377; economy 372-374; history
and government 369-372;
holidays and festivals 378-379;
land 367-368; language *429;*
people 374-376; services and
information 380-383; sports and
recreation 378; transportation
383-385
Tonga National Center: 387
Tongan Wildlife Center: 401
Tongareva: *see* Penrhyn
Tongatapu: 385-405, *386;*
accommodations 388-393, 400-

402; entertainment 394-395; food 393-394; services and information 396-397; shopping 395-396; sights 385-388, 399-400-403; sports and recreation 387-388; transportation 397-399

Tongo Chasm: 361

Toouo Beach: 188

Toovii Plateau: 270

Torres Islands: 846-847

Totoya: 708

Touaourou Mission: 753

Touho: 760

Touho Mission: 760

Toula: 417

Touri Cave: 351

tourism: 59-60, 60; Cook Islands 309-310; Fiji 563; New Caledonia 723; Tahiti-Polynesia 139-140; Tonga 374; Vanuatu 789-790

tours: 96-103; bicycle 100; for children 100; diving 97-99; hiking 100; kayak 101; nature 99; for seniors; 99-100; surfing 100-101; for veterans 100; yacht 101-103; *see also specific place*

toxic fish: 120-121

trade: 54-56, 54

transportation: 84-109; American Samoa 439-441; Cook Islands 316-317; Easter Island 302-303; Fiji 582-590; New Caledonia 729-731; Niue 365-366; Pitcairn Island 285; Samoa 472-474; Solomon Islands 868-871; Tahiti-Polynesia 155-165; Tokelau 516-517; Tonga 383-385; Tuvalu 536-537; Vanuatu 796-798; Wallis and Futuna 525-526

Trapaku Landing: 345

travel agents: 86-87

traveler's checks: 110-111, 125

travel seasons: 33-34, 87

Treasure Island: 609

Treasury Islands: 917

Triangle, The: 627

Tuamotu Islands: 252-263; Ahe 258; Fakarava 258-259; Hao 259; Makatea 259; Manihi 257-

258; Moruroa 261-262; nuclear test zone 260-263; Rangiroa 253-257, 254; Tikehau 259-260

Tuatini Cave: 351

Tubuai: 248, 250-251, 250

Tufuvai: 407

Tu'i Tongas: 369

Tula: 444

Tulagi: 850, 900

Tuloa Rainforest Reserve: 402

Tumu Mountain: 454

tuna fishing: 58-59

Tupai: 247

Tupou College: 402

Tupou I, George: 370

Tupou III, Salote: 371

Tupou IV, Taufa'ahau: 371

Turangi Valley: 323

Turtle Bay: 758

turtles: 38

Tutuila: 441-454, 442; accommodations 447-449; entertainment 450-451; food 449-450; language 544; services and information 451-453; shopping 451; sights 441-446; sports and recreation 446-447; transportation 453-454

Tuvalu: 529-544, 530, 930, 947; accommodations 534; climate 530; conduct and customs 533; economy 531-533; food 534-535; government 531; history 530-531; holidays and festivals 534; land 529-530; people 533; services 535-536; transportation 536-537

Tuvalu Maritime Training School: 538

Tuvaruhu Trail: 874

Typee Memorial: 270

U

Ua Huka: 274-275

Uafato: 494

Ua Pou: 273-274, 273

Uepi Island: 905

Ufilei Beach: 407

'Uiha: 414-415

Ulei: 842

Union Group: *see* Tokelau

United States: 53, 432-433

Unity Park: 831

Université française du Pacifique: 52, 192

University of the South Pacific: 52, 479, 628-629, 802

Uoleva: 414

Upolu: 475-500, 496; accommodations 481-484; entertainment 486-487; food 484-486; services and information 488-490; shopping 488; sights 475-480, 494-495; sports and recreation 480-481; transportation 490-493

Uporu: *see* Taha'a

Uranie Cemetery: 192

U.S. War Memorial: 874

'Utula'aina Point: 425

Utulei: 441-443

Uturoa: 222-228

Uvéa: *see* Wallis

V

vaccinations: 121-122

Vaea, Mt.: 478-479

Vaghena: 919

Vaiaau: 229

Vaiare Wharf: 197

Vaihakea Cave: 362

Vaiharuru Falls: 187

Vaihiria, Lake: 189-190

Vaikona Chasm: 361

Vai Lahi: 428

Vaileka: 646-647

Vailima: 476-478

Vai Ma'u: 349

Vai Moiniri: 345

Vai Moraro: 349

Vai Nauri: 352

Vai Ou: 349

Vaipoiri Grotto: 188

Vaitafe Spring: 361

Vaitape: 234-244

Vai Tongo Cave: 349

Vai Tunamea: 349

Vaitupu: 543-544

Vaiufaufa Viewpoint: 188

Vaka Village: 323

Vanaira Bay: 693

van Diemen, Anthony: 41

Vanikolo: 926-927

Vanikoro: *see* Vanikolo

Vanua Balavu: 705-706, 705

Vanua Lava: 846-847

Vanua Levu: 682-694, 684

Vanua Rapita: 905

Vanuatu: 778-847, *779, 780, 781,*
931, 949, 954-955;
accommodations 793; climate
779; economy 788-790; flora
and fauna 779-781; food 793-
794; history and government
781-788; holidays and festivals
792; land 778-779; people 790-
792; services and information
794-796; transportation 796-
798; *see also* Eastern Chain;
Efate; Espiritu Santo; Malekula;
Tanna
Vanua Vatu: 708
Vao (New Caledonia): 769
Vao (Vanuatu): 828
Vate: *see* Efate
Vatia: 444
Vatthe Conservation Area: 838
Vatu Vara: 707
Vatukoula: 650
Vatulele Island: 622-623
Vava'u Festival: 378, 420
Vava'u Group: 415-426, *416*
Vava'u Island: 415-425, *418;*
accommodations 418-419;
climate *368;* entertainment 420-
421; food 419-420; services
and information 421; sights
416-417, 423-425;
transportation 421-423
Venga: 924
veterans, tours for: 100
Victoria, Mt.: 652
videos: 115
Vila: *see* Port Vila
Vilu War Museum: 887
Virgin's Grave: 504-505
visas: 109; American Samoa 438;
Cook Islands 314; Easter Island
301; Fiji 579; New Caledonia
727; Pitcairn Island; Samoa
470; Solomon Islands 864-865;
Tahiti-Polynesia 150-151;
Tonga 380-381; Tuvalu 535;
Vanuatu 794; Wallis and
Futuna 522
Viseisei: 655

Viti Levu: 590-660, *612-613; see
also* Lautoka; Nadi; Suva
Viwa Island: 645
vocabulary: 957-961; Bislama
847; French *777;* Pijin *927;*
Tahitian *279;* Tongan *429;*
Tuvaluan *544*
vocubulary: Samoan *510*
Voh: 765-766
Vovoe Beach: 710
Vuna: 696
Vuna Wharf: 385-386
Vunisea: 667

W
Wadiana Falls: 753
Wadrilla: 771
Waikama: 681
Waikana Falls: 667
Wailagi Lala: 707
Wainaloka: 675
Wainibau Falls: 698
Waiqele hot springs: 685
Wairiki: 696
Waisali Nature Reserve: 688-689
Waitavala Sliding Rocks: 695
Waiyevo: 695
Wakaya: 680
Wallis: 522-526, *523, 524; see
also* Wallis and Futuna
Wallis and Futuna: 519-528, *520,*
947; climate 519-520; economy
521; fauna 520; government
520-521; history 520; holidays
and festivals 521; land 519;
people 521; transportation 525-
526
Wallis, Samuel: 43, *43,* 133
Wasavula: 683
Watapamu: 873
water-skiing: 172
Waya Island: 662-663
Wayasewa Island: 661-662
Wé: 773
weather: *see* climate
weaving: 78, 379
websites: 945-950
weights and measures: 114-115

Wendt, Albert: *69*
Western Province: 903-917
Western Samoa: *see* Samoa
whales/whalewatching 36, 306,
423, 432
White Sands Country Club: 803,
817
Williams, John: 222, 307, 445,
459, 475, 505
Williams, John Brown: 554
windsurfing: 75-76; American
Samoa 447; Fiji 572
Windward Islands: 194-195; *see
also* Moorea; Tahiti
women: 61-62, 72-73, *791*
woodcarving: 79, 379, 469, 574
World Environment Day: 147
World War I: 47
World War II: 47, 233, 854-855,
889-890

Y
Yacata Island: 707
yachting: 75, 101-103, 105-108;
American Samoa 452; Cook
Islands 334; Easter Island 301;
Fiji 588, 639, 659, 692; New
Caledonia 750; Niue 365;
Tahiti-Polynesia 151, 163, 182;
Tonga 397, 422; Tuvalu 541;
Vanuatu 811-812, 835
Yagasa Cluster: 708
Yakel: 821
Yambé: 763
Yanuca Island: 611, 623
Yanuca Lailai Island: 679
Yaohnanen: 821
Yapilmai Falls: 821
yaqona ceremonies: 568-569
Yasawa Island: 667
Yasawa Islands: 661-667, *664*
Yasur Volcano: 818-820
Yaté: 751-754
Yeiwéné Yeiwéné Cultural
Center: 775
yellow fever: 122, 866

Z
Zion Church: 445

ABOUT THE AUTHOR

THREE DECADES AGO, David Stanley's right thumb carried him out of Toronto, Canada, onto a journey that has so far wound through 171 countries, including a three-year trip from Tokyo to Kabul. His travel guidebooks opened the South Pacific, Micronesia, Alaska, Eastern Europe, and Cuba to budget travelers for the first time.

During the late 1960s, David got involved in Mexican culture by spending a year in several small towns near Guanajuato. Later he studied at the universities of Barcelona and Florence, before settling down to get an honors degree (with distinction) in Spanish literature from the University of Guelph, Canada.

In 1978 Stanley linked up with future publisher Bill Dalton, and together they wrote the first edition of *South Pacific Handbook.* Since then, Stanley has gone on to write additional definitive guides for Moon Travel Handbooks, including *Fiji Handbook, Tonga-Samoa Handbook,* and *Tahiti Handbook,* and early editions of *Alaska-Yukon Handbook* and *Micronesia Handbook.* He wrote the first three editions of Lonely Planet's *Eastern Europe on a Shoestring* as well as their guide to *Cuba.* His books have informed a generation of budget travelers.

Stanley makes frequent research trips to the areas covered in his guides, jammed between journeys to the 73 countries and territories worldwide he still hasn't visited. In travel writing David Stanley has found a perfect outlet for his restless wanderlust.

www.moon.com

Enjoy our travel information center on the World Wide Web (WWW), loaded with interactive exhibits designed especially for the Internet.

ATTRACTIONS ON MOON'S WEB SITE INCLUDE:

ATLAS
Our award-winning, comprehensive travel guides cover destinations throughout North America and Hawaii, Latin America and the Caribbean, and Asia and the Pacific.

PRACTICAL NOMAD
Extensive excerpts, a unique set of travel links coordinated with the book, and a regular Q & A column by author and Internet travel consultant Edward Hasbrouck.

TRAVEL MATTERS
Our on-line travel 'zine, featuring articles; author correspondence; a travel library including health information, reading lists, and cultural cues.

ROAD TRIP USA
Our best-selling book, ever; don't miss this award-winning Webguide to off-the-interstate itineraries.

Come visit us at: **www.moon.com**

MOON TRAVEL HANDBOOKS

LOSE YOURSELF IN THE EXPERIENCE, NOT THE CROWD

For more than 25 years, Moon Travel Handbooks have been the guidebooks of choice for adventurous travelers. Our award-winning Handbook series provides focused, comprehensive coverage of distinct destinations all over the world. Each Handbook is like an entire bookcase of cultural insight and introductory information in one portable volume. Our goal at Moon is to give travelers all the background and practical information they'll need for an extraordinary travel experience.

The following pages include a complete list of Handbooks, covering North America and Hawaii, Mexico, Latin America and the Caribbean, and Asia and the Pacific. To purchase Moon Travel Handbooks, check your local bookstore or check our Web site at **www.moon.com** for current prices and editions.

"An in-depth dunk into the land, the people and their history, arts, and politics."
—*Student Travels*

"I consider these books to be superior to Lonely Planet. When Moon produces a book it is more humorous, incisive, and off-beat."
—*Toronto Sun*

"Outdoor enthusiasts gravitate to the well-written Moon Travel Handbooks. In addition to politically correct historic and cultural features, the series focuses on flora, fauna and outdoor recreation. Maps and meticulous directions also are a trademark of Moon guides."
—*Houston Chronicle*

"Moon [Travel Handbooks] . . . bring a healthy respect to the places they investigate. Best of all, they provide a host of odd nuggets that give a place texture and prod the wary traveler from the beaten path. The finest are written with such care and insight they deserve listing as literature."
—*American Geographical Society*

"Moon Travel Handbooks offer in-depth historical essays and useful maps, enhanced by a sense of humor and a neat, compact format."
—*Swing*

"Perfect for the more adventurous, these are long on history, sightseeing and nitty-gritty information and very price-specific."
—*Columbus Dispatch*

"Moon guides manage to be comprehensive and countercultural at the same time . . . Handbooks are packed with maps, photographs, drawings, and sidebars that constitute a college-level introduction to each country's history, culture, people, and crafts."
—*National Geographic Traveler*

"Few travel guides do a better job helping travelers create their own itineraries than the Moon Travel Handbook series. The authors have a knack for homing in on the essentials."
—*Colorado Springs Gazette Telegraph*

MEXICO

"These books will delight the armchair traveler, aid the undecided person in selecting a destination, and guide the seasoned road warrior looking for lesser-known hideaways."
—*Mexican Meanderings* Newsletter

"From tourist traps to off-the-beaten track hideaways, these guides offer consistent, accurate details without pretension."
—*Foreign Service Journal*

Archaeological Mexico	**$19.95**
Andrew Coe	420 pages, 27 maps
Baja Handbook	**$16.95**
Joe Cummings	540 pages, 46 maps
Cabo Handbook	**$14.95**
Joe Cummings	270 pages, 17 maps
Cancún Handbook	**$14.95**
Chicki Mallan	240 pages, 25 maps
Colonial Mexico	**$18.95**
Chicki Mallan	400 pages, 38 maps
Mexico Handbook	**$21.95**
Joe Cummings and Chicki Mallan	1,200 pages, 201 maps
Northern Mexico Handbook	**$17.95**
Joe Cummings	610 pages, 69 maps
Pacific Mexico Handbook	**$17.95**
Bruce Whipperman	580 pages, 68 maps
Puerto Vallarta Handbook	**$14.95**
Bruce Whipperman	330 pages, 36 maps
Yucatán Handbook	**$16.95**
Chicki Mallan	400 pages, 52 maps

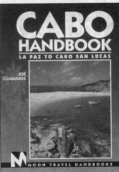

"Beyond question, the most comprehensive Mexican resources available for those who prefer deep travel to shallow tourism. But don't worry, the fiesta-fun stuff's all here too."
—*New York Daily News*

LATIN AMERICA AND THE CARIBBEAN

"Solidly packed with practical information and full of significant cultural asides that will enlighten you on the whys and wherefores of things you might easily see but not easily grasp."

—*Boston Globe*

Belize Handbook	**$15.95**
Chicki Mallan and Patti Lange	390 pages, 45 maps
Caribbean Vacations	**$18.95**
Karl Luntta	910 pages, 64 maps
Costa Rica Handbook	**$19.95**
Christopher P. Baker	780 pages, 73 maps
Cuba Handbook	**$19.95**
Christopher P. Baker	740 pages, 70 maps
Dominican Republic Handbook	**$15.95**
Gaylord Dold	420 pages, 24 maps
Ecuador Handbook	**$16.95**
Julian Smith	450 pages, 43 maps
Honduras Handbook	**$15.95**
Chris Humphrey	330 pages, 40 maps
Jamaica Handbook	**$15.95**
Karl Luntta	330 pages, 17 maps
Virgin Islands Handbook	**$13.95**
Karl Luntta	220 pages, 19 maps

NORTH AMERICA AND HAWAII

"These domestic guides convey the same sense of exoticism that their foreign counterparts do, making home-country travel seem like far-flung adventure."

—*Sierra Magazine*

Alaska-Yukon Handbook	**$17.95**
Deke Castleman and Don Pitcher	530 pages, 92 maps
Alberta and the Northwest Territories Handbook	**$18.95**
Andrew Hempstead	520 pages, 79 maps
Arizona Handbook	**$18.95**
Bill Weir	600 pages, 36 maps
Atlantic Canada Handbook	**$18.95**
Mark Morris	490 pages, 60 maps
Big Island of Hawaii Handbook	**$15.95**
J.D. Bisignani	390 pages, 25 maps
Boston Handbook	**$13.95**
Jeff Perk	200 pages, 20 maps
British Columbia Handbook	**$16.95**
Jane King and Andrew Hempstead	430 pages, 69 maps

Canadian Rockies Handbook	**$14.95**
Andrew Hempstead	220 pages, 22 maps
Colorado Handbook	**$17.95**
Stephen Metzger	480 pages, 46 maps
Georgia Handbook	**$17.95**
Kap Stann	380 pages, 44 maps
Grand Canyon Handbook	**$14.95**
Bill Weir	220 pages, 10 maps
Hawaii Handbook	**$19.95**
J.D. Bisignani	1,030 pages, 88 maps
Honolulu-Waikiki Handbook	**$14.95**
J.D. Bisignani	360 pages, 20 maps
Idaho Handbook	**$18.95**
Don Root	610 pages, 42 maps
Kauai Handbook	**$15.95**
J.D. Bisignani	320 pages, 23 maps
Los Angeles Handbook	**$16.95**
Kim Weir	370 pages, 15 maps
Maine Handbook	**$18.95**
Kathleen M. Brandes	660 pages, 27 maps
Massachusetts Handbook	**$18.95**
Jeff Perk	600 pages, 23 maps
Maui Handbook	**$15.95**
J.D. Bisignani	450 pages, 37 maps
Michigan Handbook	**$15.95**
Tina Lassen	360 pages, 32 maps
Montana Handbook	**$17.95**
Judy Jewell and W.C. McRae	490 pages, 52 maps
Nevada Handbook	**$18.95**
Deke Castleman	530 pages, 40 maps
New Hampshire Handbook	**$18.95**
Steve Lantos	500 pages, 18 maps
New Mexico Handbook	**$15.95**
Stephen Metzger	360 pages, 47 maps
New York Handbook	**$19.95**
Christiane Bird	780 pages, 95 maps
New York City Handbook	**$13.95**
Christiane Bird	300 pages, 20 maps
North Carolina Handbook	**$14.95**
Rob Hirtz and Jenny Daughtry Hirtz	320 pages, 27 maps
Northern California Handbook	**$19.95**
Kim Weir	800 pages, 50 maps
Ohio Handbook	**$15.95**
David K. Wright	340 pages, 18 maps
Oregon Handbook	**$17.95**
Stuart Warren and Ted Long Ishikawa	590 pages, 34 maps

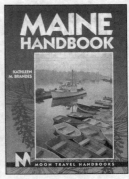

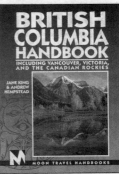

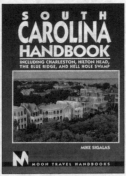

Pennsylvania Handbook	$18.95
Joanne Miller	448 pages, 40 maps
Road Trip USA	$24.00
Jamie Jensen	940 pages, 175 maps
Road Trip USA Getaways: Chicago	$9.95
	60 pages, 1 map
Road Trip USA Getaways: Seattle	$9.95
	60 pages, 1 map
Santa Fe-Taos Handbook	$13.95
Stephen Metzger	160 pages, 13 maps
South Carolina Handbook	$16.95
Mike Sigalas	400 pages, 20 maps
Southern California Handbook	$19.95
Kim Weir	720 pages, 26 maps
Tennessee Handbook	$17.95
Jeff Bradley	530 pages, 42 maps
Texas Handbook	$18.95
Joe Cummings	690 pages, 70 maps
Utah Handbook	$17.95
Bill Weir and W.C. McRae	490 pages, 40 maps
Virginia Handbook	$15.95
Julian Smith	410 pages, 37 maps
Washington Handbook	$19.95
Don Pitcher	840 pages, 111 maps
Wisconsin Handbook	$18.95
Thomas Huhti	590 pages, 69 maps
Wyoming Handbook	$17.95
Don Pitcher	610 pages, 80 maps

ASIA AND THE PACIFIC

"Scores of maps, detailed practical info down to business hours of small-town libraries. You can't beat the Asian titles for sheer heft. (The) series is sort of an American Lonely Planet, with better writing but fewer titles. (The) individual voice of researchers comes through."

—*Travel & Leisure*

Australia Handbook	$21.95
Marael Johnson, Andrew Hempstead,	
and Nadina Purdon	940 pages, 141 maps
Bali Handbook	$19.95
Bill Dalton	750 pages, 54 maps
Fiji Islands Handbook	$14.95
David Stanley	350 pages, 42 maps
Hong Kong Handbook	$16.95
Kerry Moran	378 pages, 49 maps

Indonesia Handbook	$25.00
Bill Dalton	1,380 pages, 249 maps
Micronesia Handbook	$16.95
Neil M. Levy	340 pages, 70 maps
Nepal Handbook	$18.95
Kerry Moran	490 pages, 51 maps
New Zealand Handbook	$19.95
Jane King	620 pages, 81 maps
Outback Australia Handbook	$18.95
Marael Johnson	450 pages, 57 maps
Philippines Handbook	$17.95
Peter Harper and Laurie Fullerton	670 pages, 116 maps
Singapore Handbook	$15.95
Carl Parkes	350 pages, 29 maps
South Korea Handbook	$19.95
Robert Nilsen	820 pages, 141 maps
South Pacific Handbook	$24.00
David Stanley	920 pages, 147 maps
Southeast Asia Handbook	$21.95
Carl Parkes	1,080 pages, 204 maps
Tahiti Handbook	$15.95
David Stanley	450 pages, 51 maps
Thailand Handbook	$19.95
Carl Parkes	860 pages, 142 maps
Vietnam, Cambodia & Laos Handbook	$18.95
Michael Buckley	760 pages, 116 maps

OTHER GREAT TITLES FROM MOON

"For hardy wanderers, few guides come more highly recommended than the Handbooks. They include good maps, steer clear of fluff and flackery, and offer plenty of money-saving tips. They also give you the kind of information that visitors to strange lands—on any budget—need to survive."

—*US News & World Report*

Moon Handbook	$10.00
Carl Koppeschaar	150 pages, 8 maps
The Practical Nomad: How to Travel Around the World	$17.95
Edward Hasbrouck	580 pages
Staying Healthy in Asia, Africa, and Latin America	$11.95
Dirk Schroeder	230 pages, 4 maps

Cross-Country Adventures on America's Two-Lane Highways

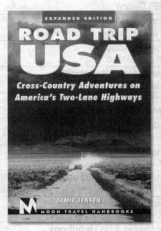

EXPANDED EDITION

ROAD TRIP USA

Cross-Country Adventures on America's Two-Lane Highways

JAMIE JENSEN

MOON TRAVEL HANDBOOKS

Exit the interstates and create your own driving adventures on America's two-lane scenic highways. This second edition of *Road Trip USA* offers expanded coverage of 35,000 miles of classic blacktop, combining a versatile format with an effervescent style.

"A book so full of the pleasures of the American road, you can smell the upholstery."
—**BBC Radio**

$24.00   940 pages

"An immensely sophisticated masterwork. For those who feel an adrenaline rush every time they hear the words "road trip," and who understand that getting there is at least half the fun, this is quite simply the best book of its type ever published."
—**Condé Nast *Epicurious***

"Tired of traveling cross-country on boring, endless Interstates? Take the next exit and get yourself onto a two-lane highway. You will have an unforgettable experience. A stylish retro experience. An American experience. And the book to guide you down these soulful and charismatic routes is *Road Trip USA*."
—***Roadside***

"A fantastic guide, easily the best book of its type. The lively text celebrates the pleasures of the open road without ever getting too preachy about it, and vintage WPA photography provides a gorgeous finishing touch."
—***Money***

"Graphically handsome, the book adroitly weaves together sightseeing advice with history and restaurant and lodging recommendations. For budding myth collectors, I can't think of a better textbook."
—***Los Angeles Times***

THE PRACTICAL NOMAD

✈ TAKE THE PLUNGE

"The greatest barriers to long-term travel by Americans are the disempowered feelings that leave them afraid to ask for the time off. Just do it."

✈ TAKE NOTHING FOR GRANTED

"Even 'What time is it?' is a highly politicized question in some areas, and the answer may depend on your informant's ethnicity and political allegiance as well as the proximity of the secret police."

✈ TAKE THIS BOOK

$17.95   580 pages

With experience helping thousands of his globetrotting clients plan their trips around the world, travel industry insider Edward Hasbrouck provides the secrets that can save readers money and valuable travel time. An indispensable complement to destination-specific travel guides, *The Practical Nomad* includes:

airfare strategies

ticket discounts

long-term travel considerations

travel documents

border crossings

entry requirements

government offices

travel publications

Internet information resources

"One of the best travel advice books ever published. . . .
A fantastic resource."
—Big World

U.S.~METRIC CONVERSION

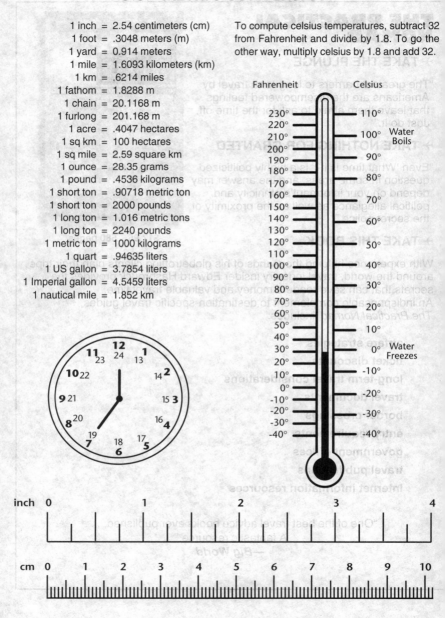

1 inch	= 2.54 centimeters (cm)
1 foot	= .3048 meters (m)
1 yard	= 0.914 meters
1 mile	= 1.6093 kilometers (km)
1 km	= .6214 miles
1 fathom	= 1.8288 m
1 chain	= 20.1168 m
1 furlong	= 201.168 m
1 acre	= .4047 hectares
1 sq km	= 100 hectares
1 sq mile	= 2.59 square km
1 ounce	= 28.35 grams
1 pound	= .4536 kilograms
1 short ton	= .90718 metric ton
1 short ton	= 2000 pounds
1 long ton	= 1.016 metric tons
1 long ton	= 2240 pounds
1 metric ton	= 1000 kilograms
1 quart	= .94635 liters
1 US gallon	= 3.7854 liters
1 Imperial gallon	= 4.5459 liters
1 nautical mile	= 1.852 km

To compute celsius temperatures, subtract 32 from Fahrenheit and divide by 1.8. To go the other way, multiply celsius by 1.8 and add 32.

Get the real story on
"Paradise"

Readers in over 40 countries rely on *Tok Blong Pasifik* magazine to keep informed about social justice, environment, human rights and development issues in the Pacific Islands. Published quarterly by the South Pacific Peoples Foundation. To subscribe and/or learn about other SPPF programs, contact:

South Pacific Peoples Foundation
1921 Fernwood Road
Victoria, BC, V8T 2Y6, CANADA
Tel: 250-381-4131
Fax: 250-388-5258
Email: sppf@sppf.org
Website: http://www.sppf.org

❏ **I want to subscribe to *Tok Blong Pasifik* magazine**
❏ **Individual ($25.00)**
❏ **Student ($15.00)**
❏ **Organization ($40.00)**

Enclose payment (cheque in Canada or US; bank draft in US$ for other countries).

Please print

Name _____

Address _____

_____

Postal Code _____ Country _____

Tel: _____

Email: _____

THE EASTER ISLAND FOUNDATION

Organized in 1989 to help preserve and promote the archaeological and historical heritage of Easter Island, the Foundation directs its efforts toward conserving and protecting the fragile heritage of the island.

The non-profit Foundation also provides books and scholarships, and supports research libraries on Easter Island and in Viña del Mar, Chile.

Publications include a series of books about Easter Island as well as the quarterly *Rapa Nui Journal*, featuring anthropological and archaeological reports, news of the island, and reviews of new books.

Subscriptions are $30 (US and Canada); $40 for overseas.

Easter Island is unique in the world. Increased tourism and development plans threaten the existence of many priceless sites. Please join us in helping to preserve this special island in the Center of the World by becoming a member of the Easter Island Foundation

Visit our Easter Island Web Site
<http://www.netaxs.com/~trance/rapanui.html>
Our books can be seen on line at
<http://www.fortunecity.com/victorian/stanmer/326/eifpublications.html>

For book lists, subscriptions, and other information, contact us at:
<rapanui@compuserve.com>

PO Box 6774, Los Osos, CA 93412   Fax: (805) 528-6279